# THE CAMBRIDGE GUIDE TO
# ENGLISH LITERATURE

# THE CAMBRIDGE GUIDE TO ENGLISH LITERATURE

## Michael Stapleton

Consultant Editor
Nicolas Barker

## CAMBRIDGE UNIVERSITY PRESS

## NEWNES BOOKS

Published by

The Press Syndicate of the University of Cambridge
The Pitt Building, Trumpington Street, Cambridge CB2 1RP
32 East 57th Street, New York, NY 10022, USA
296 Beaconsfield Parade, Middle Park, Melbourne 3206, Australia

and:

Newnes Books,
a division of The Hamlyn Publishing Group Limited,
84–88 The Centre, Feltham, Middlesex, England TW13 4BH
and distributed for them by The Hamlyn Publishing Group Limited,
Rushden, Northants, England

British Library Cataloguing in Publication Data
The Cambridge Guide to English Literature
   1. English Literature—History and criticism
   I. Stapleton, Michael
   820.9    PR83

Library of Congress Cataloging in Publication Data
Main entry under title:
The Cambridge Guide to English Literature
   1. English Literature—Dictionaries
   2. English Literature—Bio-Bibliography
   3. American Literature—Dictionaries
   4. American Literature—Bio-Bibliography
   5. English Literature—Commonwealth of Nations Authors—Dictionaries
   6. English Literature—Commonwealth of Nations Authors—Bio-Bibliography
I. Stapleton, Michael
PR85.D28   1983   820'.9 [B]   83–1967

ISBN 0 521 25647 X Cambridge University Press
ISBN 0 600 33173 3 Newnes Books

Filmset in Bembo by Filmtype Services Limited,
Scarborough, North Yorkshire, England
Printed in Great Britain by Butler & Tanner Limited, Frome, Somerset, England

Designed by Grahame Dudley and Bryan Dunn
Illustrations Research by Sheila Corr

TO
MY BROTHER, DICK, AND TO PEGGY

NOTE

To make the Guide easy to use
cross-references are plainly stated without
the use of symbols. In the main entries for authors,
the use of bold italics indicates a separate
entry for the work named.

# PREFACE

The purpose of this book is to provide a guide to the literature of the English-speaking world in a single volume. It covers more than a thousand years and includes the literature of Great Britain, the United States, Australia, Canada and New Zealand; the English writing from Ireland and South Africa, and the new and exciting contributions from the West Indies and Nigeria since the Second World War. With such an enormous subject the chief problem was how to give the greatest help to readers and yet avoid a closely packed, small-printed and unwieldy volume which offered facts and nothing else. The publishers decided that the book would stick to its subject: it is solely concerned with literature. A guide to a great literature is a guide to great ideas, often expressed in poetry, fiction and drama with such force that the masterpieces of literature transcend the forms chosen by their creators. The written word takes us back in time and preserves the expression of man's hopes and aspirations, his ideas of justice and order, his protests against oppression and his ideas of God. Without it the thoughts of Socrates, the Buddha and Jesus would never have been preserved; the riches of the Bible, of Homer, of the Mahabharata might have been lost.

This book offers the reader more than facts. A guide who never makes a comment makes a dull companion, and since enthusiasm and an abiding love of the subject were essential to the writing of this book the author is hopeful of transmitting these to the reader and encouraging the further exploration of a priceless legacy which belongs to us all. However, facts are essential: the entries begin with these and all-important dates will also be found. The lives of many writers are intrinsically interesting as well as significant to their work, and in cases where the details are known

they are given at some length. Major works of poetry, fiction, drama, satire, history, philosophy and religion are described; so are the outstanding characters created by our major writers. A host of subjects and terms merit entries of their own – metrical romances, metaphysical poetry, the Marprelate controversy, the closure of the playhouses: picaresque, latitudinarianism and transcendentalism are some of them. Two major ones, *The English Language* and *The Bible in English*, were specially commissioned from Barbara M.H. Strang and C.H. Sisson respectively.

The most difficult part of the guide, designed to cover English literature from earliest times to 1970, was the selection of living writers and here the author can do no more than apologize for those whose omission seems unwarranted. (The author will no doubt also be required to apologize for some of those he has not omitted. It is an argument which can only be left to time.)

A list of the scholars and scholarly works to which the author is indebted would need a separate bibliography. The reader who wants to explore farther into literary history cannot do better than ask for advice at the excellent public libraries with which we are blessed. However, the author must record the names of Nicolas Barker of the British Library and Jon Stallworthy of Cornell University, because their scholarship and perception have been at his disposal from the beginning and have helped immeasurably, and of Janet Liebster, for her unfailing encouragement and reassurance during the four long years it took to write this book. The publishers have been very generous in their support and Carole Hampton, The Hamlyn Publishing Group librarian, has been both patient and tireless.

M.S. 1983

# PREFACE

# FOREWORD

It is an amazing reflection that, of all the people who will use this book, the vast majority will be natives of some other country than that which gave birth to the English language. Not since the Romans left the imprint of Latin on Europe, fifteen hundred years ago, has any foreign language so influenced the culture of more than its immediate neighbours. But if Latin words and their structure are still an integral part of expression and thought from Bucharest to Lisbon, Latin literature had lost its immediacy long before the language ceased to be the *lingua franca* of Europe. How different it is with English, itself an amalgam of words drawn from a wide variety of ethnic and linguistic sources. The fluidity and flexibility that came with these disparate beginnings now ensure the survival of the language over a wider area than the old British 'sphere of influence'. Its ability to penetrate far beyond the places where English was once the language of government is due to this power to accept words and idioms (and, indeed, literature) from new and different societies without strain.

Even more striking is the interest thus evinced not just in English as a convenient common means of expression, but in the literature of which it is the vehicle. *Sir Gawain and the Green Knight* in Japan, Shakespeare in India, T.S. Eliot in Brazil, all have an appeal, a meaning in an entirely different society and environment, which the classical authors enjoyed only after Greek and Latin had ceased to be living languages. Shakespeare's plays are thus not just the object of academic study all over the world: they are still adding new meaning to the language thousands of miles from the London where they were first acted.

Even more important than the many countries where English is still, however useful, a 'second language' are those where English is the first or only language. The greatest of these is the United States of America, possessor for almost two centuries of a complete sharing of language and literature with the mother country, co-heir to the earlier tradition, and, beginning in the seventeenth century and growing still in vitality and volume, the joint creator of what 'English Literature' means today. Australia and New Zealand, South Africa, Canada, India, and, most

recently, the newer nations of the West Indies and Africa have added their share to what is incomparably the greatest and most various literature in the world.

To compile a guide to something so vast and polymorphous, so old and yet still constantly changing, is a task at once daunting and enormously stimulating.

Watching, as I have, the growth of the work since its inception has been a fascinating experience. Michael Stapleton came to the task with a wide knowledge and deep love of literature in English of all periods and places, both unbiased (so far as I could judge) by dogmatic preconceptions. This experience had, however, to be measured and weighed against the needs and demands of contemporary readership, not only in this country and in those where English is, in some sense, native, but in all the many others where English is studied, either as a second language or as a foreign language. The opinions and influence of modern critics had to be weighed, as well as the works themselves, and a point of view established, receptive to current opinions and needs, yet independent and, above all, consistent with itself.

This task was both eased and complicated by the existence of comparable and celebrated works, whose objective is rather different. Such other works have dealt with a whole range of extraneous material, from natural history to the books of the Bible, with which the reader of English literature might wish to be acquainted. The definition of English literature itself, by contrast, has tended to be less catholic: American literature has tended to be treated as a separate entity; Irish writers have been apt to get short measure, and those in other parts of the world where English is the main or sole language have been even more neglected. But, for a work designed to meet the needs of the last quarter of the 20th century, a different approach seemed to be needed, and a different goal set. Now, it seemed more important not only to widen the geographical scope to include all countries in which literature in English is written, but to provide for them a more comprehensive coverage of authors and works. It is, in short, nothing less than a guide to the literature of the English speaking world. General subjects and forms, such as metaphysical poetry, deism, picaresque, or the details of the stage presentation, have been introduced with the specific purposes of illustrating the history of literature as such. What is represented, then, is intended as a comprehensive source of reference for English literature, not just the 'Eng. Lit' of the school and university syllabus (though that need has always been in the forefront of the compiler's mind), but a subject-matter very much more closely defined, both by academic study and a wider range of appreciation, than it was a generation ago.

The compilation of a reference book is at once a piece of servitude and an exercise of power. The compiler is the slave of his subject matter, more closely circumscribed than the author of a critical or historical work; he is also the master, with absolute command by inclusion or exclusion, length or brevity, and by the judgement which informs these decisions, as well as the text. The irony with which Dr Johnson defined a lexicographer as 'a harmless drudge' shows how clearly he understood this dual role. Every good reference book is meant to be read, not simply referred to. Indeed, a good reference book will lead the reader on, so that, half an hour after he meant to spend five minutes refreshing his memory of the plot of *Measure for Measure*, he emerges, reflecting on the staying power of Sydney Smith's wit. Judged by this standard, I believe Michael Stapleton's work to be first rate. I may not always agree with him, but I seldom turn to his text without taking at least twice as long as I really need to look up what I first wanted.

I have learned much about early American writers, Anne Bradstreet, Joel Barlow, Royall Tyler. I have been fascinated by the unexpected and yet evocative accidents of alphabetic juxtaposition: try, for example, *Absalom, Absalom* with *Absalom and Achitophel*, or *Daggoo* and *The Daisy Chain*, or (two admirable articles) *North and South* and *Northanger Abbey*. Note the sympathetic assessment of, at one end of the time scale, Caedmon, and, at the other, John Dos Passos. Admire the skill that has gone into the concise summaries of the complex plots of *Morte Darthur*, the *Mabinogion* and *The Idylls of the King*; *The Fairie Queene* is a masterpiece of this genre – remember Macaulay's famous dictum 'Very few and very weary are those who are in at the death of the Blatant Beast.' Most of all, admire the dispassionate but deeply felt summaries of the greatest writers and their works, especially those, like Shaw, for example, who are currently out of fashion.

I do not always agree. I would take a more sympathetic view of Peacock's lesser novels; would have said more of Edwin Arlington Robinson, Ralph Hodgson or Isaac Rosenberg. But then I did not have the responsibility of balancing the books, so to speak, of measuring them against the great mass of other writers and works. But I am lost in wonder at the skill with which Michael Stapleton has penetrated the maze, passing from known to unknown clues with equal address. The implicit equation of Dr Wortle and Trollope, the neat comparison of George Washington Cable and Joel Chandler Harris, the generous appreciation of Herman Melville's works: all these are admirable. So is the perception that can sum up the late Henry James in the deft quotation of his response to Edith Wharton's complaint that he had stripped the characters of *The Golden Bowl* of their 'human fringes' – 'My dear, I didn't know I had', or note that Blake was writing simple verse when Wordsworth was a schoolboy.

Often the judgements contain observations of real originality: for example, that '*Macbeth* and his lady used to be played by formidable middle-aged actors with booming voices, but the parts are, more and more, entrusted to younger players, and the tragedy of this grim and lowering play comes into clearer focus.' The recent revival of Kate Chopin's short stories is given proper credit, and, after all the brouhaha, the summary of *Lady Chatterley's Lover* and Lawrence himself is crisp but sympathetic, engaged yet balanced.

But it is time to let other readers in on their share of the enjoyment that this book will provide. English literature is a vast field, and one that is different to everyone who approaches it. Wide as it is, it is still growing, and time will alter every judgement. But for those who need a view of the subject as it stands today, in plain yet vivid words, concise yet comprehensive, treating small subjects and minor writers with the same respect as the greatest, illustrated wherever a pictorial image seems to convey what words cannot, *The Cambridge Guide to English Literature* will provide what they want. The real test of any reference book is that of time; use and revision fit it still better to readers' needs; those needs adapt themselves to the form in which information is available. Here, then, is the foundation of a new source of reference for literature in the English language as it stands today. What the future will build on it, only time can tell: I for one am content to abide the judgement of time.

Nicolas Barker
The British Library. October 1982.

# PUBLISHER'S NOTE

*The Cambridge Guide to English Literature* in its first edition marks the begining of a relationship between the co-publishers. It provides in a single handy volume a reference work which covers the whole of literature in English: not just the original tradition of the United Kingdom and Ireland, but the newer literatures of the USA, Canada, Australia, South Africa, the Caribbean and Black Africa. To attempt to cover all these literatures in English and to follow them as far as the present day is a new enterprise, and this Guide is a pioneer in this respect.

The principal entries are given to the authors themselves. The emphasis here is factual and biographical, since it is facts such as dates and titles which the reader will need first of all. There are also entries for individual works of literature, and for the main characters in novels and plays. The other categories of entry include relevant historical events and the main technical literary terms.

A very wide readership is envisaged: users may range in age from students still at school who want to look up *ottava rima* to the retired crossword-puzzle solver who needs to know whether Fabian is a character in *Twelfth Night*, through the serious reader (who may or may not be a formal student of English and whose native language may not be English) who wants a good article on 'Eliot, George', or 'Eliot, Thomas Stearns' as background to present and future reading. But there are all sorts of occasions when all sorts of people say 'who wrote . . .?' or 'how do you define . . .?' If this *Guide* is on their bookshelf, they will find it helpful over the whole range, but particularly helpful on literatures in English which extend and supplement the old island tradition, and on modern literature.

Further editions are planned, and corrections and suggestions are invited.

# THE CAMBRIDGE GUIDE TO
# ENGLISH LITERATURE

# A

**Aaron** The Moor of Shakespeare's *Titus Andronicus*, brought captive to Rome in the train of the defeated Tamora. Aaron, Tamora's lover, abets her in her revenge on the family of Andronicus: he incites Tamora's sons to the rape and mutilation of Lavinia, arranges the murder of Bassianus and the conviction of Titus' sons for the deed, and cuts off Titus' hand after leading him to believe the sacrifice will free his sons. Tamora bears Aaron a son and he extracts a promise, at the end of the play, from the victorious Lucius Andronicus to spare the child, though he knows his own life is forfeit.

**Abbey Theatre** See **Yeats, William Butler.**

***Abbot, The*** A novel by Sir Walter Scott, first published in 1820, and intended as a sequel to *The Monastery*. The abbot of this novel is the Edward Glendinning who became a monk in the closing pages of *The Monastery*.

Roland Graeme, a page in the service of the Lady of Avenel, is sent by the regent, Murray, to serve as page to Mary, Queen of Scots, imprisoned in Lochleven Castle. He is instructed to keep watch on the queen; but he is the victim of stronger influences – he falls in love with Mary's lady-in-waiting, Catherine Seyton, and is exhorted by his fanatical grandmother, Magdalen Graeme, to serve the queen. His own chivalrous nature, too, works against his instructions and he helps in Mary's flight. Mary rallies her supporters but they are defeated by Murray's army at Langside; she flees to England, hoping for the support of Elizabeth. Roland is pardoned by Murray and marries Catherine Seyton.

**Abercrombie, Lascelles** 1881–1938. Abercrombie was the son of a stockbroker and was born at Ashton-on-Mersey, Cheshire. He was educated at Malvern College and Victoria University, Manchester, and after some years as a journalist and critic became a lecturer in poetry at the University of Liverpool (1919). Later he became Professor of English Literature at Leeds University (1922) and Goldsmith's Reader in English at Oxford (1935).

As poet and critic Abercrombie is a Georgian of the period before the poetic revolution brought about by the work of Eliot and Pound. A collected volume, *The Poems of Lascelles Abercrombie* (1930), was supplemented by the posthumous *Lyrics and Unfinished Poems* (1940). Among his critical works were *Thomas Hardy* (1912), *The Idea of Great Poetry* (1925), and *Principles of Literary Criticism* (1931).

**Abessa** In Spenser's *The Faerie Queene*, Book I, the personification of superstition.

**Abrahams, Peter (Henry)** 1919– . Abrahams was born in Vrededorp, a slum district of Johannesburg, and like many coloured South Africans found that educational qualifications – he was a scholarship boy – were of no help in his working life. He published a volume of poems, *A Black Man Speaks of Freedom*, in 1940, and then got to England by joining the crew of a merchant ship. *Dark Testament* (1942) was a book of short stories, and then Abrahams made a reputation as a novelist with *Mine Boy* (1946), *Wild Conquest* (1951), and *A Wreath for Udomo* (1956). He visited Jamaica in 1955 and later went to live there. He is Chairman of Radio Jamaica and Editor of *The West Indian Economist*. Other books by Peter Abrahams are *Song of the City* (1945), *Path of Thunder* (1948), *Return to Goli* (travel report, 1953), *Tell Freedom: Men of Africa* (1954), *Jamaica* (1957), *A Night of Their Own* (1965), and *This Island Now* (1966). He edited, with Nadine Gordimer, *South African Writing Today* (1967).

***Absalom, Absalom!*** A novel by William Faulkner, first published in 1936. The story is related by Quentin Compson to Shreve McCannon, his friend at Harvard (see **Sound and the Fury, The**). The period is the early 19th century.

The Sutpen family live in the Virginia lowlands and the father does odd jobs on a plantation. One day he sends his son, Thomas, to the big house with a message, and the boy is turned away from the door by a Black man in livery. The incident fires Thomas with an ambition to own a plantation and slaves, and 12 years later he has acquired, by dubious means, a hundred square miles of land near the frontier town of Jefferson. Only General Compson, Quentin's grandfather, knows that he has acquired his 20 slaves in Haiti, where he married a planter's daughter, discovered that she had Negro blood, and put her away – keeping 20 slaves as an indemnity. In Mississippi he builds his mansion, Sutpen's Hundred, from timber and bricks made from clay on his own land.

In Jefferson he marries again, the daughter of a pious family, and becomes the father of Henry and Judith as well as the biggest cotton planter in Yoknapatawpha county. But later, when Henry comes home from university he brings a friend with him, the older and worldlier Charles le Bon, who becomes engaged to Judith. Then Sutpen learns that Charles is his son by his first marriage; he orders him from the house and Henry, refusing to believe that Charles is his half-brother, renounces his birthright and follows Charles to New Orleans. After the Civil War Charles is determined to marry Judith; he would have renounced her if Sutpen had recognized him as his son. Henry, who now knows that Charles is his half-brother, murders him to prevent him from pursuing his intention. Henry is not disturbed that Charles is Judith's half-brother – he is outraged that Charles should have such intentions; Charles has Negro blood in him.

Thomas (now Colonel) Sutpen sets out to rebuild his fortunes. His plantation is in ruins, his son has disappeared, his wife is dead, his slaves dispersed, and most of his land is seized for debt. He opens a crossroads store, and makes a proposal to his wife's sister, Rosa, to the effect that they try and produce a child – if it proves to be a son he will marry her. Rosa won't play, understandably, and then Sutpen seduces Milly Jones. She bears him a daughter, whereupon he repudiates her; her father, who had been one of the colonel's admirers, kills him. Judith dies of yellow fever, and the great house has just one inhabitant, Clytie, a mulatto, Sutpen's daughter by one of his slaves. She grows old there, and Henry comes home to die. When the townspeople, hearing that Henry is ill, send an ambulance for him Clytie believes he is going to be arrested for the murder of Charles. She fires the house and they both die in it.

The story is a Gothic tragedy which symbolizes the inevitable doom of Southern culture. Sutpen's character itself, based on the arrogance that only belongs to a man who owns other human beings and uses and rejects them as he sees fit, and cannot possibly be deterred from rape and theft. But nemesis is only a few paces behind him, and self-destruction is complete.

**Absalom and Achitophel**  A satirical poem by John Dryden, written in heroic couplets and first published in 1681.

The subject of the poem, an allegory, is the efforts of Lord Shaftesbury and his party to have the Duke of York excluded from the succession in favour of Charles II's bastard son, the Duke of Monmouth. James, Duke of York, the king's brother, was the rightful heir and became James II; the hopes of Shaftesbury turned on the contemporary dislike of Catholics. The 'Popish Plot' fabricated by Titus Oates (1678) was fresh in the memory but the dislike remained and James was a declared Catholic. Dryden's celebrated satire examined the motives and characters of Shaftesbury and Monmouth and helped tilt the balance against them.

Absalom is Monmouth; Achitophel, his evil counsellor, is Shaftesbury; Zimri (*2 Kings* ix. 31) is the Duke of Buckingham, and David is Charles II. Dryden, probably to give his story the correct emphasis, makes Achitophel (Ahitophel in the Authorized Version) the prompter of Absalom's rebellion against his father whereas in the Bible Absalom needs no prompting from anyone. Other characters satirized by Dryden are Edward Seymour, Speaker of the House of Commons (Amiel, Chief of the Sanhedrin), Titus Oates (Corah), and Bethel, Sheriff of London (Shimei).

A second part (1682) was written chiefly by Nahum Tate and revised by Dryden, who contributed 200 lines containing savage satire on two of his rivals, Thomas Shadwell (Og) and Elkanah Settle (Doeg).

**Absentee, The**  A novel by Maria Edgeworth, first published in 1812. As in *Castle Rackrent*, Maria Edgeworth sets her story on one of the large land holdings in Ireland. Many of the landlords were only interested in the money the estates could yield, which they spent in London or other fashionable places, and had no interest whatever in the land. Such a man is Lord Clonbrony, the absentee landlord of the title, who is being forced into debt in London by the social ambitions of his silly wife: she tries to buy acceptance by extravagant spending. His son visits the estates in Ireland and is shocked by their condition. The novel tells how he persuades his father (by paying his debts for him) to return to his responsibilities, in spite of the opposition of his mother.

**Achebe, Chinua** 1930–  .  The son of a mission teacher, Achebe was born in Ogidi in the Eastern Region of Nigeria and educated at the University College of Ibadan. In 1954 he joined the Nigerian Broadcasting Corporation and after serving as Talks Producer and Controller at Enugu became Director of External Broadcasting in 1961. His first novel, *Things Fall Apart* (1958), gave the

African view of the White man's intrusion into tribal life and values and attracted considerable attention. In addition to a distinguished career as a writer, principally as a novelist, Chinua Achebe has taught at the universities of Massachusetts and Connecticut and is now a professor at the University of Nigeria at Nsukka. He has been editor of *Okike: Nigerian Journal of New Writing* since 1971. Since *Things Fall Apart* Achebe has published *No Longer at Ease* (1960), *The Sacrificial Egg and Other Stories* (1962), *Arrow of God* (1964), *A Man of the People* and *Chike and the River* (1966), *Beware, Soul Brother and Other Poems* (1971), *Girls at War* and *How the Leopard got his Claws* (1972), *Morning Yet on Creation Day* (essays, 1975), *The Flute* (1977), and *Don't Let him Die* (1978).

**Acrasia** In Book II of Spenser's *The Faerie Queene*, she symbolizes intemperance. Sir Guyon destroys her Bower of Bliss.

*Actions and Reactions* See **Kipling, Rudyard.**

*Adam Bede* George Eliot's first novel, it was published in 1859. She told her publisher that it was going to be a country story – and indeed it is one of the best in English fiction – but the impulse for the plot was the account her aunt, Elizabeth Evans, a Methodist preacher, gave her of the night she spent in the condemned cell of Nottingham Jail with a girl who was hanged on the following morning for the murder of her child.

Adam Bede, a rather hard and high-principled carpenter of a Midlands village, is in love with Hetty Sorrel, the pretty and light-hearted niece of the amiable farmer, Martin Poyser. The young squire, Arthur Donnithorne, is very attracted to Hetty, and she is vain enough to consider the possibility of becoming the squire's lady. Arthur's light-hearted flirtation with Hetty is observed with growing anxiety by Adam, who tries to intervene with both of them. But Arthur, his way made easy by his attraction for her, seduces Hetty – and then drops her.

Adam, devoted to Hetty in his stern, unyielding way, earns the reward of his loyalty; Hetty, heartbroken at Arthur's desertion, consents to marry him. But then she finds herself pregnant and flies from her home in a desperate search for Arthur. Adam's grief is to some extent mitigated by the affection of his gentle brother, Seth, and by the warm sympathy of Dinah Morris, a young Methodist preacher for whom Seth bears a hopeless love. Seth, however, sees clearly the growing attraction between Adam and Dinah. The unfortunate Hetty, meanwhile, has not been able to find Arthur Donnithorne. She is arrested,

Hetty Sorrel and Arthur Donnithorne in the dairy. An incident from *Adam Bede* depicted by the Victorian artist, Edward Henry Corbould. The Royal Library, Windsor Castle.

charged with the murder of her child, and convicted. Dinah now spends all her time at the hapless girl's side.

The close of the novel is a harrowing account of how Hetty, with Dinah, faces her final ordeal. But she is reprieved at the last moment and her sentence changed to one of transportation. Seth resigns himself to his brother's love for Dinah, and they are united with his blessing.

*Adam Bede*, by any standards, and in spite of any faults, is a novel of fine quality; in its day it must have been astonishing. The author's character delineation had grown in confidence, and her evocation of authentic rural England presented the reader with something new – in place of dainty shepherdesses and merry peasants her country people are real, hard-working men and women. Noteworthy, too, are the transgressors, Hetty and Arthur; they are two attractive young people, thoughtless perhaps, and both more than a little vain. It is this vanity which, in the setting of mid-Victorian England, makes the ensuing tragedy inevitable. A memorable character, apart from the principals, is Mrs Poyser, Hetty's aunt, a shrewd, cool country-woman who brings the very breath of rural wisdom on to the page. Memorable, too, are the scenes of Dinah's vigil with the condemned girl. These could have been dreadful, depicted by a lesser artist; George Eliot handles them with unfaltering skill.

**Adams, Andy** 1859–1935. Adams was born in Indiana but spent much of his working life in the Texas cattle country and, later, in the booming mining centres of Colorado. His stories of cowboy life and the westward expansion of the railways, along with the sharp practice that attended much of it, are notable for their lack of sentimentality in a period when the fiction of frontier life suffered greatly from its intrusion. Adams' most notable book is *The Log of a Cowboy* (1903); others were *The Outlet* (1905), *Cattle Brands* (1906) – short stories of frontier life, and *Reed Anthony, Cowman* (1907).

**Adams, Brooks** 1848–1927. Brooks Adams was the younger brother of Henry Brooks Adams and was born in Quincy, Massachusetts. His first book, *The Emancipation of Massachusetts* (1887), expresses with considerable force his view that the early colonists were the victims of a repressive theocracy and traces their efforts to move beyond its confines. *The Law of Civilization and Decay* (1895), regarded as his most distinguished work, presents his theory of history, which shows the endlessly recurring cycle of the centralized state. This apparently established order always contains the elements of its own decline, since it will, sooner or later, be overcome by economic forces that lead to the establishment of another order, which will also run its course.

In 1919 he evoked his distinguished family's tradition in a long preface to his brother's *A Letter to American Teachers of History* and published the whole as *The Degradation of the Democratic Dogma*. See also **Adams, Henry Brooks.**

**Adams, Henry Brooks** 1838–1918. The grandson of John Quincy Adams, the 6th president of the USA, Henry Brooks Adams was born in Boston, Massachusetts. He continued his education in Germany after graduating from Harvard and became his father's secretary when Charles Francis Adams became the US minister to England during the Civil War. His first published work was an essay on Captain John Smith, published in 1867, and he continued to write articles and reviews when he returned to the USA in 1868.

Henry Brooks Adams was out of sympathy with reconstruction politics. This was reflected in his writings and it also decided him to abandon a political career. He taught history at Harvard for seven years (1870–77). He also edited *The North American Review* during this period and married Marian Hooper in 1872.

After Harvard, Adams went to Washington; he intended to write history and observe the political scene at first hand. In 1871, with his brother Charles Francis Adams, he published *Chapters of Erie and Other Essays* and while at Harvard he edited *Essays on Anglo-Saxon Law* (1876) and *Documents Relating to New England Federalism 1800–1815* (1877). In Washington he wrote *The Life of Albert Gallatin* and *The Writings of Albert Gallatin* (both published in 1879), in which he examined the career of the émigré Swiss who became a controversial politician, Jefferson's secretary of the treasury, and the author of a pioneering study of the North American Indian. In the following year Adams published, anonymously, a novel about political life in Washington, called *Democracy,* and he also wrote in 1880 a biography, *John Randolph.* In 1884 he wrote a novel called *Esther* under the pseudonym of Frances Snow Compton. The heroine of the novel was modelled on Adams's wife, Marian, whose suicide in 1885 apparently brought to a head the discontentment that Adams had been feeling for some time with life in America. In the same year he began his travels; he was to become, like Henry James, a distinguished expatriate.

His first journey was to the Orient, with the artist John La Farge; then he travelled in the Sierras with the geologist Clarence King. He returned to Washington to complete the nine-volume *History of the United States during the Administrations of Jefferson and Madison* (1889–91) and then resumed his travels. *Memoirs of Marau Taaroa, Last Queen of Tahiti* (1893) was the result of the time he spent in the Pacific and the famous *Mont-Saint-Michel and Chartres* (1904) recorded his reflections after some years in France. At the Chicago and Paris expositions he observed the great dynamos, the instruments of power, proudly exhibited and pondered the implications of them in the future of mankind. *A Letter to American Teachers of History* (1910) presents his theory of history and this was reprinted in *The Degradation of the Democratic Dogma* (1919) by his brother, Brooks Adams.

His most famous work is *The Education of Henry Adams* (1907), in which he examines the failure of education in terms of himself – Henry Adams is, in the long term, a failure because nothing he was taught was a true preparation for living in the 'multiverse'. 20th-century man was moving beyond the universe as understood by those who taught. Adams died in Washington in 1918.

**Adams, Parson** The curate of the church near the Boobys' country seat in *Joseph Andrews* by Henry Fielding. He becomes Joseph's companion on the journey home from London. A guileless and courageous man, he is a true Christian as well as a warm and affectionate friend.

**Addison, Joseph** 1672–1719. The son of the Dean of Lichfield, Addison was educated at Charterhouse School and Magdalen College, Oxford. One of his schoolfellows at Charterhouse was Richard Steele, born in the same year as Addison and whose friend and collaborator he later became. Addison was a notable classical scholar – his Latin verse was praised by Dryden and he became a fellow of Magdalen. In 1699 he was able to travel in Europe through the good offices of influential friends, who secured him an annual pension; these travels were, ostensibly, training for the diplomatic service. Addison returned to England in 1703 upon the death of King William III and his friends secured him the post of Commissioner of Excise in 1705. The fact that Addison had written a poem in heroic couplets to celebrate the victory at Blenheim – *The Campaign* (1704) – no doubt pleased his sponsors; posterity's verdict is rather different and Addison has no stature as a poet. He entered Parliament in 1708 and went to Ireland as chief secretary to Wharton, the Lord Lieutenant. When the Whig government lost power in 1710 he returned to England, remaining a Member of Parliament for the rest of his life though he lost his government appointment.

Addison became a member of the Kit-Cat Club, where he renewed the friendship with his schoolfellow Richard Steele and made a new one with Swift. He contributed to **The Tatler** and founded **The Spectator** with Steele in 1711; it continued until December 1712 and between then and 1714, when the paper was revived, Addison wrote a blank-verse tragedy, **Cato** (1713). This was produced at Drury Lane and enjoyed considerable success. Addison was, meanwhile, also contributing to Steele's *The Guardian*. A prose comedy, *The Drummer* (1715), was a failure.

The Whigs returned to power in 1715 and Addison was soon restored to office as chief secretary for Ireland. He became a Lord Commissioner of Trade in 1716 and married the Countess of Warwick in the same year. He was Secretary of State (1717–18) and retired with a generous pension. *The Freeholder* (1715–16) was a political newspaper to which he contributed but by this time Addison was beginning to repeat himself. He had not been successful as Secretary of State and the essays in *The Freeholder* echo his political prejudices that in the *Old Whig*, his last journalistic venture, estranged him from his friend Steele. He died at the age of 47 and was buried in Westminster Abbey.

Addison was perhaps fortunate that his friend Steele was an inventive journalist. Addison was not an innovator of any kind and his work in the fashionable forms – verse, translations from the Latin, travel writing – have not left a mark on English letters. He was too careful a man for the bold adventurous ideas that led to *The Tatler* and *The Spectator* but when he entered the field his quality as a writer realized itself; he became an astute popularizer of remarkable skill and added a note of gravity to the comparatively breezy tone of Steele. The emerging middle classes were very responsive to a journalist who could bring Isaac Newton and John Locke within reach, making them subjects for lively conversation. Addison

An early 18th-century coffee-house. Coffee-houses were the preferred meeting-places of this period for those who sought conversation and an exchange of views, and who provided a public for the writings of Joseph Addison, Richard Steele, and their contemporaries. Frontispiece to *Vulgus Britannicus*, Part IV, 1710.

was a moralist, like Steele; but in Addison's work there is a peculiar smugness which raises a suspicion that his comments on conduct and manners are merely what he knew would please – but many generations of successful journalists have been guilty of that.

**Adonais,** *An Elegy on the Death of John Keats.* Shelley's most famous poem, written in Spenserian stanzas, was first published in 1821. Keats died in February of that year and Shelley heard the news in May. He and Keats had not been close friends but Shelley admired Keats unreservedly and, like Byron, felt furious indignation at the way Keats was treated by the critics. In his elegy he depicts the mourning at the poet's bier; but the lament gives way to a declaration of immortality, in the triumph of the poet's art: 'The soul of Adonais, like a star, Beacons from the abode where the Eternal are.'

**Adriana** The lady of Ephesus married to Antipholus, one of a pair of twin brothers. When the other twin turns up in Ephesus her confusion contributes much to *The Comedy of Errors* by William Shakespeare.

**Advancement of Learning, The** (*The Twoo Bookes of Francis Bacon: Of the Proficience and Advancement of Learning, Divine and Humane*). A philosophical treatise by Francis Bacon, first published in 1605. It was extended in the Latin version, *De augmentis scientiarum* (1620), and forms in that version the first part of *Instauratio magna*. See also **Bacon, Francis.**

Bacon propounds the value of education in the opening to his book and, in the context of his time, enumerates the advantages of learning and disposes of objections to it. He goes on to examine the various methods of advancing knowledge and shows their defects and demonstrates that learning would be immeasurably advanced if the student worked from experiment and observation rather than from pre-stated theory. The author then examines the principal parts of knowledge; history, poetry, and philosophy. Bacon insisted that, by applying the correct methods, man had the power to control nature.

**AE** (*or* **A.E.**) See **Russell, George William.**

**Aegeon** The merchant from Syracuse in Shakespeare's *The Comedy of Errors*. In searching for his twin sons and their twin slaves he has come to Ephesus, an enemy city, where his life is forfeit unless he can pay a huge fine.

**Aelfric** *c.*955–*c.*1020. Aelfric 'Grammaticus', 'the Grammarian', became a Benedictine monk at Winchester when Aethelwold was abbot. He followed the ideals of Dunstan's monastic reform and became the greatest scholar of the Benedictine revival in England. From Winchester Aelfric went to the newly founded abbey at Cerne Abbas, where he composed two sets of homilies in English, one series on the liturgical year and another on historical and doctrinal subjects. A third series dealt with *The Lives of the Saints*.

Aelfric became the first Abbot of Eynsham in Oxfordshire. He also wrote a life of Aethelwold in Latin, an English version of Bede's *De Temporibus*, a Latin grammar, a Latin–English vocabulary, and a dialogue, or *Colloquy*, in Latin. The *Colloquy* is between a novice, his teacher, and men (herdsman, shepherd, ploughman, hunter, and merchant) who tell of their work. It was intended for the novices of Winchester in order to instruct them in Latin usage and gives a remarkably clear picture of Aelfric's times. He also prepared a paraphrase in English of the first seven books of the Bible, which was of enormous value to those who preached to the unlettered.

God's Covenant with Abraham. An illustration from Aelfric's English paraphrase of the first seven books of the Bible, 1025–50. God descends a ladder from Heaven to address Abraham. *MS Cott. Claudius B. IV, f.29r.* British Library.

Aelfric is regarded as the finest prose writer in Old English. He was also a man who held strong convictions: he denied the Immaculate Conception and disputed the doctrine of Transubstantiation.

Aelfric's first set of homilies was published by the Early English Text Society in an edition by B. Thorpe: *The Homilies of the Anglo-Saxon Church* (1844–46). The third set, *The Lives of the Saints*, was translated and edited for the society by W. W. Skeat (1881–1900). Aelfric's *Colloquy* was edited by G. N. Garmonsway (1939).

**Aelred of Rievaulx**  See **Rievaulx, Aelred of.**

*Aeneid*  Virgil's *Aeneid*, translated by Gavin Douglas, was the first complete translation into English of a major classical poem. It was begun about 1511 and completed in 1513, apparently a few days before the Battle of Flodden. See **Douglas, Gavin**.

**Aethelwold** (*or* **Ethelwold**), **St** *c.*908–84. Aethelwold was born at Winchester and became a monk at Glastonbury when St Dunstan was abbot. He established a monastery at Abingdon where he introduced the Benedictine Rule. When Edgar became king he made Dunstan Archbishop of Canterbury and appointed Aethelwold Bishop of Winchester. His importance to English literature lies in the stimulus to learning which, under the enlightened rule of King Edgar, owed so much to the efforts of Dunstan, Oswald, and Aethelwold. The king entrusted Aethelwold with the task of translating the Benedictine Rule into English for the benefit of novices and postulants, who could not be expected to understand Latin. He founded a school at Winchester, which became a centre of learning.

*Afternoon Men*  See **Powell, Anthony (Dymoke).**

**Agassiz, (Jean) Louis (Rodolphe)** 1807–73. Louis Agassiz was born in Switzerland. By the time he went to the USA in 1846 he was a distinguished naturalist; Agassiz was a pioneer in the classification of fossil fishes and of glacial deposits and movement. He became Professor of Natural History in the Lawrence Scientific School at Harvard in 1848 and was the founder of what became the Harvard Museum of Comparative Zoology. His influence on the study of natural history in the USA was great; William James and Sir Charles Lyell were among his pupils. His most considerable published work in America was the four-volume *Contributions to the Natural History of the United States* (1857–63).

*Age of Innocence, The*  A novel by Edith Wharton, first published in 1920. It was dramatized by Margaret Ayer Barnes in 1928. The story is set in New York during the 1870s.

Ellen Olenska, née Welland, is the wife of a Polish count; she has left him because of his dissolute character but she cannot divorce him. As it is, society treats her coldly as a separated woman but Newland Archer, a lawyer engaged to Ellen's cousin May, and his mother are sympathetic. Their friendship is both a help and reassurance; and even Ellen's starchy old grandmother begins to show her a degree of tolerance.

Newland is intelligent and cultured while May is simply a reflection of her strict environment. But May is woman enough to perceive that Ellen and Newland have a great deal in common; and they do fall in love. May, however, uses her wits and contrives to keep them apart. The wedding proceeds and Ellen goes to live in Washington.

Mrs Manson Mingott, Ellen's grandmother, is in need of care and Ellen returns to New York to look after her. May discovers that Newland has yielded to his feelings; he and Ellen have resumed their relationship. She goes to Ellen and discloses that she is pregnant. Ellen, finding the constraints of society and the strength of her feelings are making life intolerable, departs from her cousin's life to live in Paris.

Many years later Newland, now a widower, visits Paris with his son, Dallas. He knows now that May was aware of his love for Ellen. He is about to take his son to visit his Aunt Ellen but at the last moment he decides that Dallas shall go alone. Newland prefers to forgo present reality and keep a past ideal.

Edith Wharton's evocation of the New York of her girlhood, with its rigid conventions and adherence to form, is brilliantly drawn and it is here that she comes closest to the work of her friend Henry James. The narrative is clear and the prose impeccable. The characters are acutely observed and, while the author's sympathies are inevitably on the side of Ellen, she succeeds in being objective about May, who for all her limitations is a sympathetic character.

*Age of Reason, The*  Thomas Paine's essay on deism – natural religion as opposed to revealed religion – was written in Paris. He completed the first part in 1793 while a member of the Convention; the fall of the Girondists, the party he supported, in that year resulted in Paine's imprisonment, during which he wrote the second part (1794). The two parts were published in 1794 and 1795; the full title is *The Age of Reason: being an Investigation of True and Fabulous Theology.*

The first part of the book declares the author's belief in the existence of God (Paine came from a

Quaker family) and presents his supporting arguments. But the knowledge of God has been obscured; slavish adherence to the Bible and obedience to established churches have prevented humanity from perceiving the true God in creation and external nature. Organized religion is a means 'to terrify and enslave mankind, and monopolize power and profit.' In the second part of the book Paine attacks the Bible, the flaws and fallibility of scripture as a whole, pointing out the cruelty and stupidity of many of the principal characters and the improbability of the account of Jesus's birth.

Paine's book was one of the reasons he suffered rejection from those who had been his friends; he was ostracized when he returned to America in 1802. The reaction to the excesses of the French Revolution had set in, and the Cult of Reason had been part of those excesses.

**Agnes Grey** A novel by Anne Brontë, first published in 1847. The autobiographical element is strong, based on Anne's experiences as a governess in much the same way as her sister Charlotte's were reflected in the writing of *Villette*. Agnes Grey is a rector's daughter who takes a post as a governess with the Murray family. She is badly treated and painfully lonely, enjoying only the kindness of the curate, Weston, with whom she eventually finds happiness. It is a simple story, with no element of the greatness achieved in the work of her sisters, and perfectly fulfils the author's modest aspirations.

**Aguecheek, Sir Andrew** Olivia's silly suitor in Shakespeare's *Twelfth Night*. He is soundly thrashed by Sebastian, whom he mistakes for Cesario (Viola) who has aroused his jealousy by being favoured by Olivia.

**Ahab, Captain** The obsessed commander of the whaling ship *Pequod* in Herman Melville's *Moby-Dick*. He has lost a leg, bitten off in a former encounter with the whale; now he wears a leg made of whalebone and is determined to conquer the great white whale at all costs.

**Aiken, Conrad (Potter)** 1889–1973. Born in Savannah, Georgia, Conrad Aiken's early life was shadowed by tragedy when his father killed his mother and then committed suicide. He was brought up by relatives in Massachusetts and educated at Harvard, where his contemporaries included T. S. Eliot, Robert Benchley, and Walter Lippmann. His first collection of verse, *Earth Triumphant* (1914), showed his talent for subtle rhythm and his preoccupation with subjective self-analysis. His collections in this vein continued to appear at rapid intervals: *Turns and*

*Intervals* and *The Jig of Forslin* (both 1917), *Nocturne of Remembered Spring* (1917), *The Charnel Rose* (1918), and *The House of Dust* (1920). *Punch: The Immortal Liar* (1921), *Priapus and the Pool* (1922), and *The Pilgrimage of Festus* (1923) mark his use of direct psychology in his subject matter.

Aiken published a volume of criticism, *Scepticisms* (1919), which examined the work of his contemporaries; two collections of short stories, *Bring! Bring!* (1925) and *Costumes by Eros* (1928); and the novels *Blue Voyage* (1927), *Great Circle* (1933), *Conversation* (1940), and *King Coffin* (1935). All his writing, verse and prose, demonstrates his interest in psychological enquiry. His *Selected Poems* (1929) won him a Pulitzer Prize. He published a further nine collections. Aiken also published a psychological autobiography, *Ushant* (1952), and a volume of critical essays, *Reviewer's ABC* (1958).

**Ainsworth, William Harrison** 1805–82. The son of a solicitor, Ainsworth was born in Manchester and educated at the grammar school. He was more interested in writing than in the law and, though early miscellaneous works were published in Manchester, moved himself to London fairly soon. He married the daughter of a publisher and went on writing, scoring his first success with *Rookwood*, in 1834. He became editor of *Bentley's Miscellany* in 1840; he was also editor, at different periods, of *Ainsworth's Magazine* and *The New Monthly Magazine*, but he

The rescue of Lady Rookwood. An illustration by George Cruikshank for the 1836 edition of Ainsworth's *Rookwood*.

continued to exploit the successful vein of historical romance he had first tapped with *Rookwood*. He wrote 39 novels in all but real success eluded him, since he had not the gifts of his great exemplar, Scott, and never really succeeded in creating memorable characters. His writing is lively and vigorous, however, and he took care with his settings and period detail. His best-remembered books, apart from *Rookwood*, are *Jack Sheppard* (1839), which also features a notorious criminal (in *Rookwood* it is Dick Turpin); *The Tower of London* (1840), which makes a set piece of the short reign and death of Lady Jane Grey; *Old St Paul's* (1841), which uses the Plague and the Great Fire of London; and *The Lancashire Witches* (1849), which is set in Pendle Forest and is unequivocal about the women of the title being real witches. Cruikshank and Phiz were notable illustrators of Ainsworth's novels.

**Akenside, Mark** 1721–70. Akenside was a butcher's son and was born at Newcastle upon Tyne. Originally intended for the ministry, he went to Edinburgh University; but while there he turned to medicine and after Edinburgh went on to Leyden to complete his studies. He had a successful practice in London, where he became physician to St Thomas's and Christ's Hospitals in 1759. Akenside wrote poetry, none of it of much interest except to scholars, and books on medical matters. *The Pleasures of Imagination* (1744), revised as *The Pleasures of the Imagination* (1757), anticipates Wordsworth in places, and is interesting as a poem inspired by political, ethical, and social – but not poetical – matters.

**Alastor,** *or The Spirit of Solitude.* A poem by Percy Bysshe Shelley, regarded as his first important work and first published in 1816. It reflects his personal condition at that stage of his life; the poet-idealist is contented in his vision of beauty and with his lofty thoughts. In the real world he seeks the counterpart of his ideals but disappointment and frustration result; he dies of despair. The poem is both a lament for the condition of man and a criticism of self-centred idealism.

**Albany, Duke of** Goneril's husband in Shakespeare's *King Lear*. He grows progressively colder towards her in the play; the blinding of Gloucester appals him but he leads the British army against Cordelia since she is the invader. He becomes ruler with Kent and Edgar after the death of Lear.

**Albee, Edward (Franklin)** 1928– . Albee was born in Washington DC, and educated at Columbia University. He achieved his first success as a dramatist with the one-act *The Zoo Story*, first produced in Berlin in 1959. *The Death of Bessie Smith*, another one-act play, was also first produced in Berlin, in the following year, and the two plays are frequently performed together. *The Sandbox* (1959), *Fam and Yam* (1960), and *The American Dream* (1961, with James Hinton) were also one-acters: Albee's first full-length play, *Who's Afraid of Virginia Woolf?* (1962), was an immediate success and made him internationally famous. *Tiny Alice* (1964) and *A Delicate Balance* (1966, Pulitzer Prize) were equally successful. Albee has dramatized Carson McCullers' *The Ballad of the Sad Cafe* (1963) and Truman Capote's *Breakfast at Tiffany's* (1966), and adapted the English playwright Giles Cooper's *Everything in the Garden* for the American stage (1967). Other works are *Box and Quotations from Mao Tse-Tung* (1968), *All Over* (1971), *Seascape* (1975, Pulitzer Prize), *Listening* (1976), *Counting the Ways* (1977), and *The Lady from Dubuque* (1978).

**Albino and Bellama, the Pleasant Historie of** A verse romance by Nathaniel Whiting (*c.*1612–*c.*1662) published in 1637. See **seventeenth-century verse romances**.

**Alchemist, The** A comedy by Ben Jonson, first produced in 1610 and published in 1612.

During an outbreak of the plague in London, Lovewit leaves the city and the care of his house to his servant, Face. Face is a confidence trickster and with his henchman, Subtle, uses Lovewit's house as a centre for his frauds. Subtle poses as an alchemist with possession of the philosopher's stone and therefore the ability to confer knowledge of secret processes for increasing wealth, restoring youth, and generally realizing the dreams of the gullible. Taking part in their operations is Subtle's woman, Doll Common. Their victims represent the foolish and greedy from different walks of life: Sir Epicure Mammon, a knight, is a greedy voluptuary; Abel Drugger a tobacconist; Dapper a lawyer's clerk; Ananias and Tribulation Wholesome are two hypocritical Puritans; young Kastril is newly rich and quarrelsome, looking for a suitable match for Dame Pliant, his sister. The villains come close to exposure when Surly, a gambler, sees through their imposture; and they are finally confounded when Lovewit returns to his house without notice. Subtle and Doll take to their heels and Face is left to face his master. Lovewit finds the booty from the frauds in his house and decides to keep it. Face cleverly puts Dame Pliant, who is comely as well as rich, in Lovewit's way. Lovewit marries her and Face is at peace with his master.

**Alcibiades** The historical Alcibiades appears as a character in Shakespeare's *Timon of Athens*. Banished by Athens, he has something in common with Timon, who has exiled himself. Timon gives Alcibiades gold from his newly found treasure to organize a force for an attack on the city.

**Alcott, (Amos) Bronson** *c*.1799–1888. Born on a Connecticut farm, the pioneer of new educational methods in America had little formal schooling and earned his living as best he could. It was while he was a pedlar in the southern states that he became aware of the existence of a way of life different from that of New England. He became a teacher in 1823 and at once put new ideas, opposed to Calvinist disciplines, into practice. In 1830 he married Abigail May; one of his daughters was Louisa M. Alcott, the writer.

In 1834 Alcott opened the Temple School in Boston. The basis of his teaching philosophy was that all should be directed toward the full development of the individual child – personal education. He was a Transcendentalist and when his assistant at the Temple School, Elizabeth Peabody, assisted him in committing his ideas to paper he gained the support of the younger William Ellery Channing, James Freeman Clarke and Emerson. In England he won the good opinion of Thomas Carlyle and in New England of Thoreau, who did not, however, agree with Alcott's faith in cooperative communities. In fact, none of Alcott's ventures in that field achieved any real success. Until he became school superintendent in Concord in 1859 he depended largely on his daughter Louisa's success for support.

From his work in Concord grew the Concord School of Philosophy (1879–88) which was run by his disciple, William T. Harris, and had a lasting influence on education in America. Alcott's educational views can be found in *Observations on the Principles and Methods of Infant Instruction* (1830), *Record of a School, Exemplifying the General Principles of Spiritual Culture* (1835), and *The Doctrine and Discipline of Human Culture* (1836). *Sonnets and Canzonets* (1882) was written in memory of his wife.

**Alcott, Louisa May** 1832–88. The author of *Little Women* was born in Pennsylvania at the time when her father, Bronson Alcott, was teaching at Germanstown. She was educated at home and no doubt benefited from the guidance of her father's friends, among whom were Emerson and Thoreau. Louisa and her mother, and her three sisters, took any work they could find, supporting the household while Bronson Alcott disseminated his educational theories in various ways. But Louisa wanted to write and had actually completed a book by the time she was 16; this was *Flower Fables*, which was not published until 1855. She also wrote poems, plays (she would have liked to become an actress), and short stories – good enough to be published in the *Atlantic Monthly*.

Louisa May Alcott became a nurse during the Civil War and served in a hospital until her health failed. She made good use of the experience in *Hospital Sketches* (1863), a book that brought her recognition. A novel, *Moods*, was published in 1865 and she visited Europe in the same year. She became editor of *Merry's Museum*, a juvenile magazine, in 1867. The first part of *Little Women* was published in 1868, the second in 1869; Louisa became famous and, for the first time, the Alcott family knew security. Louisa's mother and sisters were the models for the characters.

The books that followed *Little Women* were in much the same vein and the encouraging response continued. Louisa's public expanded and, while her later books were eagerly bought, they have not achieved the classic status of her first great success, which is never out of circulation and which has been translated into several languages. Louisa was interested in reform and women's suffrage, as can be discerned in her work, which also presents an accurate picture of the New England of her time. She also described, with detachment and humour, her father's attempt to establish a cooperative community at Fruitlands in 'Transcendental Wild Oats' in her *Silver Pitchers* (1876).

Meanwhile, she published *An Old-Fashioned Girl* (1870); *Little Men* (1871), which is about her nephews; and *Work* (1873). She paid another visit to Europe in 1871. *Eight Cousins* (1875) and *Rose in Bloom* (1876) successfully maintained the tone and style of *Little Women*. Her later work included volumes of short pieces and the novels *Jack and Jill* (1880) and *Jo's Boys* (1886). She died in Boston, on the day of her long-lived father's funeral.

**Alcuin (*or* Ealhwine)** *c*.735–804. Alcuin was born in York and educated at Archbishop Egbert's school, where he became a master in 766. After visiting Rome he met Charlemagne at Parma on the homeward journey, and the emperor persuaded him to stay in his dominions to advise him on religion and education. Alcuin was the moving spirit in the revival of learning often called the Carolingian Renaissance, which kept the flame of knowledge alive when, in Alcuin's own country, it was being virtually extinguished by the Norse raiders. He became Abbot of Tours and established a royal library. His system of teaching was largely based on the dialogue method and it is as an educator that he is most important. Though he wrote a great deal, his written work made virtually no contribution to the development of literature in Latin or in English: it consists of letters, poems, educational manuals, disputations, liturgical works, and a revision of the text of the Latin Bible (the Vulgate). Alcuin acknowledged his great debt to the library and teachers of York; it was this tradition of scholarship and thought which was kept alive by Alcuin and which contributed so much to European culture.

**Aldhelm, St** d. 709. Aldhelm was the first Bishop of Sherborne; what is known of his life comes from two 12th-century writers, William of Malmesbury and Faricius of Abingdon. Aldhelm was a kinsman of Ine, King of Wessex, and the author of a number of works in Latin which show him to have been familiar with classical writers. He wrote some poetry in English and was apparently an accomplished minstrel, but none of his vernacular poetry survives. His Latin works, which have survived, consist of a prose treatise in praise of virginity and a versification of the same; another prose treatise on numbers; occasional poems in Latin; and a number of letters.

Aldhelm has no high place in literature but two of his letters have considerable historic importance. One, addressed to Geraint, King of Wales, criticizes the behaviour of the king's clergy in incisive terms, without adornment. The other is written to Eahfrid (probably a friend), after Aldhelm's visit to Ireland. He insists that England is the equal of Ireland in learning and parades his own learning in a remarkably self-conscious display.

Aldhelm's *Opera* was edited by J. A. Giles (1844).

**Aldrich, Thomas Bailey** 1836–1907. The New England novelist, poet, and short-story writer was born in Portsmouth, New Hampshire. He hoped to go to Harvard but was obliged to find work at the age of 16 when his father died. His first literary efforts were poems; these were accepted by magazines and his first collection, *The Bells*, was published in 1855. Aldrich became a successful journalist and was editor of the *Illustrated News* during the Civil War. His following appointment as editor of *Every Saturday* (1866–74) realized his hopes of living in Boston and mingling with the New England writers he admired. Later he became editor of the *Atlantic Monthly* (1881–90).

Aldrich published a novel based on his childhood in Portsmouth, *The Story of a Bad Boy* (1870), which remains his best-known work. He was the author of a number of volumes of verse and essays, books of short stories, and novels. Apart from his *The Story of a Bad Boy*, however, not much of his work is still read. *Marjorie Daw and Other People* (1873) is a book of short stories, the title piece of which is well regarded, and *The Stillwater Tragedy* (1880) is a good example of the early American mystery story.

**Alexander, Sir William, Earl of Stirling** *c.*1580–1640. Alexander was born at Menstrie and was descended from an ancient Highland family. After his education at Glasgow and Leyden he became tutor to the Earl of Argyle and travelled with him in Europe. He came to London with King James, who awarded him a mining patent and a knighthood when Alexander was attached to the retinue of Prince Henry. In 1626 he became Secretary of State for Scotland and in 1633 Earl of Stirling. He was also much honoured by Charles I and held exalted office; but he was a very unpopular figure – his ideas for land investment in Canada lost money for those who participated because the French occupation rendered the scheme worthless – and he died in poverty.

Alexander's best-known work is the book of songs and sonnets called *Aurora*, which was published in 1604 but may have been written while he was studying at Glasgow University. Other works were *The Monarchick Tragedies* (1603–07), four plays on the theme of destructive ambition; and a long poem, *Doomsday* (1614). These are described by Maurice Lindsay as 'unactable plays [and] an unreadable poem'.

**Alexander of Hales** *c.*1170–1245. Known by his birthplace – Hales in Gloucestershire – Alexander was educated in Paris and later taught there. In 1236 he joined the Franciscan order but he retained his position as a teacher (customarily scholars renounced academic posts when they became friars). A *Summa Theologiae* commissioned by Pope Innocent IV was attributed to Alexander (and rejected with contempt by Roger Bacon) but is now known to contain only some work by him, being a compilation by a group of Franciscans in Paris. Nevertheless it earned Alexander the description Doctor Irrefragabilis. He collaborated with other Franciscans on *Expositio in Regulam S. Francisci* (1242) and, before he became a friar, a series of glosses on the *Sententiae* of Peter Lombard.

***Alexander Selkirk, Verses Supposed to be Written by*** A poem by William Cowper, first published in his *Poems* (1782). The lines attributed to the original of Robinson Crusoe are among the most famous Cowper ever wrote: 'I am monarch of all I survey' and 'Oh, solitude! where are the charms That sages have seen in thy face? Better dwell in the midst of alarms, Than reign in this horrible place.'

**Alfred (***or* **Aelfred), King** 849–901.  Alfred the Great, King of the West Saxons, has an important place in the literature of England. It was largely through his efforts that learning was restored after being virtually destroyed by the Norse raiders: on his accession to the throne of the little kingdom of Wessex in 870 there was not a scholar to be found who could read a Latin service book. Moreover, the *Anglo-Saxon Chronicle* would have earned a lasting place in letters for its inspirer no matter who he had been; that Alfred should have been a king who also achieved historical greatness is proof of his remarkable mind.

Alfred's first book was a *Handbook*, now lost, of extracts from scripture and the early Christian fathers translated into the West Saxon language. The next was probably his translation of Gregory the Great's primer of instruction to the clergy, the *Cura Pastoralis*. Alfred gave the translation a preface in which he tells of the lack of learning in his troubled times and states his resolve to effect a restoration. This is probably the earliest work by King Alfred that we possess, though the precise sequence of his works is uncertain. The next was probably the *Historia adversus Pagonos* by the 5th-century Spanish priest and historian Paulus Orosius, a friend of St Augustine. The *Historia* is a controversial work but Alfred translated the parts he found of value (chiefly the history and geography), adding accounts of the travels of Wulfstan and Ohthere, who had voyaged to the Baltic and the White Sea and who gave direct narratives to Alfred.

Alfred's version of *De Consolatione Philosophiae* is not a translation in the true sense, but was of great importance in bringing to England the reflections, written in prison, of an early Christian martyr. As an expression of Stoic philosophy this was for centuries a much-loved book of moral guidance. Alfred's famous version contains much that is his own and its interest is thereby increased. A shortened version of Bede's great *History* has been attributed to Alfred but this is now questioned by some scholars. His translation of St Augustine, *Soliloquies*, has also been questioned; but it is believed to be by Alfred

since it displays the sort of intellect that gave England his version of Boethius. To the *Soliloquia* Alfred adds portions from other works by Augustine, Gregory the Great, and St Jerome. The Preface is an exquisite short piece by the king, who advises his subjects to look with care for their materials when they build, as he did; a fair house is made of fair beams, and perhaps they will live in the peace which was denied to him.

The *Soliloquies* is believed to have been Alfred's last work. As his reign progressed, scribes in the monasteries were diligently copying manuscripts and keeping records, though no original work emerged. But the records of events seem to have arrested the king's attention, and he encouraged the systematic revision of these; at the same time there began, in 890, a wide survey of the history of the West Saxons. The evidence suggests that Alfred directly supervised the part which extends to the year 892. But the work continued after his death in 901 and the ***Anglo-Saxon Chronicle*** extends to the middle of the 12th century. England's debt to Alfred is immense: he kept literature alive in England when it could have perished and inspired what has been called 'the first great book in English prose'.

**Alger, Horatio** 1834–99.  The son of strict Puritan parents, Horatio Alger was born in Revere, Massachusetts. He was educated at Harvard and Harvard Divinity School; after graduating in 1852 he rebelled against his background and went to live in Paris. After a period of bohemian living and a serious illness he returned to Massachusetts and became a Unitarian minister in 1864. In 1866 he went to New York and became chaplain to the Newsboys' Lodging House in Manhattan; he spent the rest of his life working on behalf of the cause. Alger had literary ambitions but his work was to be reflected chiefly in his stories of boys who made good in spite of poverty and deprivation. These stories proved to be enormously popular; the *Ragged Dick, Luck and Pluck*, and *Tattered Tom* series were part of an output of over 120 books that sold over 20 million copies. Alger also wrote biographies of famous men for young readers; these were intended to stress the lessons of his fiction and his famous men were those who succeeded by their own efforts.

***Algerine Captive, The; or, The Life and Adventures of Dr Updike Underhill.***  A novel by Royall Tyler, first published in 1797, it is told in the form of an autobiography and provides a satirical commentary on US life. Dr Underhill tells of the useless education he receives at a New England college and the dubious quality of medical practice he discovers when he becomes a doctor. In the southern states he sees slavery in practice and has experience of life on board a slave ship; his comments are unsparing of those concerned in the trade and in the use of slaves. Later he is lost in Africa and spends seven years as a slave in Algeria. He narrowly escapes being forcibly converted to Islam and succeeds in writing his account of his experiences.

**Algren, Nelson** 1909– . Algren was born in Detroit but his work is associated with Chicago, the city where he lives and works. He graduated from the University of Illinois School of Journalism in 1931 and spent much of the Depression as a migratory worker in the south-western states. In 1935 he returned to Chicago to a WPA Writers' Project and published his first novel, *Somebody in Boots*, in the same year. He became coeditor of *The New Anvil Magazine* in 1939, and worked as a controller on the Venereal Disease programme for the Chicago Board of Health from 1941 to 1942, when his second novel, *Never Come Morning*, was published. Nelson Algren is best known as a reporter of life at its worst in urban America – a scene he knows extremely well and which provided the material for his award-winning novel of narcotic addiction, *The Man with the Golden Arm* (1949, National Book Award). Other books are *The Neon Wilderness* (1946, short stories), *Chicago: City on the Make* (1951), *A Walk on the Wild Side* (1955), *Who Lost an American?* (1962, travel), *Notes from a Sea Diary: Hemingway all the Way* (1965), and *The Last Carousel* (1973, short stories).

**Alice's Adventures in Wonderland** See **Carroll, Lewis.**

**Allegro, L'** One of two famous poems written by John Milton in 1632 during his vacations from Cambridge whilst staying at his father's house at Horton. It is a sunny celebration by the 22-year-old poet of the cheerful side of life, whether lived among delightful rustic scenes or among the busy pleasures of the city. (See also **Penseroso, Il**, which in contrast celebrates the quality of meditative withdrawal.)

**Allen, James Lane** *c.*1849–1925. Allen was born and bred in Kentucky, where he spent his working life until 1880 as a schoolteacher. His first attempts at writing were short pieces – stories, descriptive articles, and critical essays, mostly contributions to *Harper's Magazine*. The first collection was *Flute and Violin* (1891), which was warmly received; it was praised for its craftsmanship and polished style. The principal theme was man's relationship to the natural world. *The Blue-Grass Region of Kentucky* (1892) was a collection of short pieces which Allen contributed to *Harper's,* and he returned to his principal theme in his first novel, **A Kentucky Cardinal** (1894), and its sequel, *Aftermath* (1896). **The Choir Invisible** was published in 1897.

Allen was a successful novelist and short story writer until he died in 1925, the year his last collection of short stories, *The Landmark*, was published. His work is notable for its quality of sober realism (Mark Twain was the great exemplar), which was the essential corrective to the over-romantic literature produced by the South.

**Allen, Walter (Ernest)** 1911– . Walter Allen was born in Birmingham and educated at King Edward's Grammar School, Aston, and Birmingham University. He worked as a teacher and university lecturer in England, and spent some time in the USA as a visiting lecturer and Professor of English at American universities. He was also a journalist and later a broadcaster, and published his first novel, *Innocence is Drowned*, in 1938. This and the two which followed, *Blind Man's Ditch* (1939) and *Living Space* (1940), are notable pictures of working-class life in England on the eve of World War II and deserve to be better known. *The Black Country* (1946) is a topographical study of the crowded industrial Midlands of which his native Birmingham is the centre.

After World War II Allen increased the range and maintained the quality of his fiction with *Rogue Elephant* (1946), *Dead Man Over All* (1950, *The Square Peg* in the USA), and probably his best novel *All in a Lifetime* (1959, *Threescore and Ten* in the USA). In this book an elderly radical looks back over an honourable career of success and failure and reflects on the changes in English working-class life and how they were brought about. The characters represent a wide social spectrum and the narrator's tone is shrewd and unsentimental.

Allen's critical work was well known through his contributions to *The Times Literary Supplement*, *The New Statesman*, *New Writing*, and *Encounter* before he published his study *Arnold Bennett* in 1948. In the same year came *Writers on Writing* (*The Writer on His Art* in the USA). This was followed by *Reading a Novel* (1949), *Joyce Cary* (1953), *The English Novel: A Short Critical History* (1954), *The Novel Today* (1955), *Six Great Novelists* – biographical studies of Defoe, Fielding, Scott, Dickens, Stevenson, and Conrad (1955), *George Eliot* (1964), and *Tradition and Dream* (*The Modern Novel in Britain and the United States* in the USA). Walter Allen, as the titles listed indicate, offers an excellent guide to fiction in English. He has also published a book of stories for children, *The Festive Baked-Potato Cart* (1948).

***All for Love,*** *or The World Well Lost.* A tragedy in blank verse by John Dryden, first produced in December 1677, and first published in 1678. The historical events in Dryden's play are concentrated in the last days of Antony and Cleopatra at Alexandria, after the Battle of Actium. In his preface, Dryden states that he was mistaken in introducing Octavia and her children into the play because it drew attention from Antony and Cleopatra, whose story this is. They could not command the same sympathy as the wronged Octavia, and thus he weakened his play. Dryden notes, however, that none of his critics raised the point. He also pays tribute to 'the divine Shakespeare' who 'as Ben Jonson tells us, without learning, should by the force of his own genius perform so much, that in a manner he has left no praise for any who come after him'.

In *All for Love* Cleopatra struggles for possession of Antony with his general Ventidius, his friend Dolabella, and his wife Octavia. The latter nearly succeeds; Caesar (Octavian) is prepared to come to terms with Antony but requires him to separate from Cleopatra and return to his wife (Octavian's sister). The plan founders when Antony grows jealous of Dolabella, thinking the younger man may supplant him in Cleopatra's affections. His suspicions are skilfully fed by Octavia but, with the desertion of the Egyptian fleet and the report that Cleopatra is dead, the play returns to historical fact and the tragedy runs its course.

This is Dryden's finest tragedy but unfortunately it is overshadowed by Shakespeare's untidy, if magnificent, *Antony and Cleopatra*. In comparison, *All for Love* is compact and fast-moving; it is an excellent play on the page but has not been revived since 1922, when Edith Evans played Dryden's heroine. There are memorable scenes for Antony and Ventidius, and a fine unhistorical encounter between Octavia and her glamorous rival. ('Dost thou not blush to own those black endearments, That make sin so pleasing?' 'You may blush, who want them.')

**Allingham, William** 1824–89. Allingham, the son of a baker, was an Englishman born at Ballyshannon in Donegal, Ireland. He became a customs officer, wrote for Leigh Hunt's *London Journal*, and was a member of the Pre-Raphaelite circle. He also wrote a great deal of unmemorable verse; his *Collected Poems* (six volumes, 1888–93) was popular for a time. His main importance was his use of Irish themes combined with a lyric gift; this provided encouragement for better poets, including Yeats, who followed him.

***All Passion Spent*** See **Sackville-West, V(ictoria Mary)**.

***All's Well that Ends Well*** A comedy by William Shakespeare. The date of the play remains undecided, some scholars making it an early play (*c.*1595) but others placing it as late as 1604. It was first published in the First Folio of 1623. The source of the play is a story in Boccaccio's *Decameron*, which appears in an English version in William Painter's *The Palace of Pleasure* in 1566. If *All's Well that Ends Well* belongs to the 1604 period it is an extraordinary work to come from the poet who had written *Hamlet* and was to go on to greater things still. If it is an early work there is a possibility that it is the *Love's Labour's Wonne* mentioned by Francis Meres but no evidence exists that could take the argument further. As a later work it is supported by incidental virtues but, Shakespeare being Shakespeare, there are incidental virtues in everything he touched.

Helena is the daughter of a great physician, Gerard de Narbon, and a ward of the Countess of Rousillon. She loves Bertram, the countess's son and Count of Rousillon. Bertram is summoned to court in Paris, where the King of France suffers from an incurable disease. Helena follows Bertram and succeeds in curing the king with one of her father's remedies. The king grants her the reward of the hand of one of his nobles. She chooses Bertram who is unwilling but is obliged to obey the king and they are married. Bertram swears that, married or not, he will not take Helena to his bed. He leaves for the Tuscan wars with all the haste he can muster, aided and abetted by his friend Parolles, a mendacious braggart. He leaves a letter for Helena telling her that until she can get the ring from his finger and conceive a child by him she cannot regard him as her husband.

Helena trails after Bertram and turns up in Florence dressed as a pilgrim. At her lodging she discovers that her hostess's daughter, Diana, is being courted by none other than Bertram. She tells the women that she is Bertram's wife, arranges to take Diana's place in Bertram's bed, and sends false news to Bertram that Helena is dead. After the night Bertram returns to Rousillon, where the king is visited by the countess. The king sees on Bertram's finger a ring he gave to Helena and demands to know how Bertram came by it. (Helena had given it to him on that night, in exchange for the one on his hand.) Bertram tries to excuse his possession of it but the king forces him to tell the truth. Helena appears, alive and well, and displays Bertram's ring; he must now accept her as his wife as she has shared his bed. Bertram accepts her.

And heaven help him thereafter, one might reflect. Nothing on earth can stop Helena getting what she wants and she can call it love if she likes. Bertram could be pitied if he were a pleasant character; he isn't, he is shallow and spoiled and too much under the influence of Parolles, who has most of the good lines. Love's labours are mightily exerted by Helena, so they could be said to be 'wonne', but the play loses because her kind of love is frightening.

**All the King's Men** See **Warren, Robert Penn**.

**Allworthy, Mr** The country gentleman in *Tom Jones* by Henry Fielding who finds an abandoned baby in his bed and becomes his guardian. The baby is the hero of the story, Tom Jones.

**Almanzor and Almahide** See **Conquest of Granada, The**.

**Alton Locke,** *Tailor and Poet.* A novel by Charles Kingsley, first published in 1850.

Alton Locke is the son of a small shopkeeper, brought up and taught by his widowed mother, a narrow and unsympathetic woman. He is apprenticed to a tailor and comes into contact with the squalid conditions of sweated labour. A talent for poetry develops with his consciousness of the sore need for reform and he takes easily to the Chartist cause. His poetry leads to the acquaintance of Eleanor Staunton, her cousin Lillian, and Saunders Mackaye, a bookseller. At the urging of Lillian and her well-to-do father, Alton allows his revolutionary verse to be made innocuous before publication; this earns him the contempt of his Chartist comrades. Their taunts lead him to undertake a mission that provokes a riot and Alton is sentenced to three years in prison. Lillian, with whom he has fallen in love, marries someone else during his imprisonment, and it is Eleanor who stands by him when he falls ill with typhus. She nurses him back to health and conveys to him her views of reform and the role of Christianity. Alton, disillusioned by demagogy and violence, becomes a Christian Socialist, and at the close of the story dies on his way to the USA.

*Alton Locke,* regarded as work of literature, is imperfect in almost every respect, but the parts that matter are forceful and convincing and Kingsley succeeded in his aim of drawing attention not only to the wretchedness of many people's lives, but also to what he believed was the wrong way of achieving reform.

**Amazing Marriage, The** A novel by George Meredith, first published in 1895.

Carinthia Jane Kirby is the daughter of a sea captain and a runaway countess. She is the charge of her uncle, the miserly Lord Levellier, who resents it very much. Lord Fleetwood, immensely rich and spoiled, meets Carinthia at a ball and is so charmed that he proposes to her during a quadrille. The artless inexperienced girl accepts him.

Fleetwood, realizing his own irresponsibility, hopes Carinthia will realize it too. But she doesn't, and Lord Levellier is determined to hold Fleetwood to the engagement so he can be rid of her. Fleetwood goes through with the marriage – and treats her abominably in a sustained rage at being forced into it, eventually abandoning her and their child.

Carinthia makes her way to Whitechapel to the house of Gower Woodseer, whom she met in Europe. Woodseer's father is a minister among the poor and Carinthia is given shelter there. Gower, also a friend of Fleetwood, tries to effect a reconciliation, but when he succeeds with Fleetwood it is already too late – Carinthia will not have him. She is going as an army nurse to Spain with her brother Chillon. Fleetwood ends his days as a Roman Catholic monk.

**Ambassadors, The** A novel by Henry James, first published in serial form in the *North American Review*, from January to June 1903. It appeared in volume form in 1903 with two chapters, 28 and 35, which did not appear in the serialized version.

Chadwick (Chad) Newsome has been in Paris for far too long in the opinion of his mother, a rich widow from Woollett, Massachusetts. She wants him to come home and enter the family business; he does not write and she feels sure that he is involved in some undesirable liaison. Mrs Newsome has an admirer, the editor of a cultural review that she finances. This is Lambert Strether, a widower of 55, and Mrs Newsome asks him to go to Paris and persuade Chad to return to Woollett, Massachusetts. His success as her ambassador will ensure him the hand of Mrs Newsome.

In England, on the way to Paris, Strether meets the expatriate Maria Gostrey, a poised and mature woman who becomes a sympathetic commentator on the events that follow and with whom he always feels comfortable. She also goes to Paris, a city in which Strether feels remarkably content – the atmosphere and way of life seem far more attractive that anything he has so far experienced. One evening at the theatre Strether, his friend Waymarsh, and Maria Gostrey are joined by Chad.

Strether finds Chad to be a polished and elegant young man and he is in no doubt that Paris – and whatever liaison he is involved in – are responsible for his assurance and sophistication. Chad displays no eagerness to return to Woollett, Massachusetts, and Maria Gostrey supplies the information that Chad's particular attachment is to Jeanne de Vionnet and her mother; the Countess de Vionnet and Maria had been at school together. Strether is charmed by Jeanne when he meets her; when he calls on Madame de Vionnet he is more than charmed – she is accomplished and beautiful, a woman of exquisite grace and sensibility. There is no doubt now which lady has been the refining influence on Chad's life. Strether completely loses sight of the principal reason for his embassy.

Strether's letters to Mrs Newsome persuade her to send more ambassadors, in the persons of her daughter Sarah, Sarah's husband Jim Pocock, and Jim's sister Mamie, who had hopes of marrying Chad. But the Pococks' appeal to Chad is useless and they find Strether no help whatever. They retire in angry frustration and Mrs Newsome becomes estranged from Strether, whose sympathies are now on the side of Chad and the Vionnets. But Chad is beginning to show signs of readiness to go back to Woollett, Massachusetts.

Strether goes to Lambinet in the country for a day, only to encounter Chad and Madame de Vionnet. They dine at a village inn – and a chance remark reveals to Strether that Chad and Madame de Vionnet are lovers. The picture is at last clear; Strether had believed that, while Marie de Vionnet's influence had transformed the young American, the 'liaison' had existed between Chad and Jeanne. Strether exhorts Chad to remain with the woman to whom he owes so much; then he takes leave of Maria Gostrey and returns to America.

Strether, in spite of his regard for Marie de Vionnet and his conviction that her liaison with Chad was fundamentally something good and valuable, is a prig who returns from Europe with nothing (even Maria is primly put aside) and therefore a clear conscience. Chad will, the reader feels, leave Marie de Vionnet and their association has, in any case, been tarnished by the necessity for lies and subterfuge – to no avail – when Strether encounters them at Lambinet. The episode is drawing to a close and Lambert Strether will return to being a widower in Massachusetts.

*The Ambassadors*, like the other two novels of the author's last phase, is suffocating at times and as many readers will dislike it as will admire it. The 'performance' is evident in this novel and, once more, the question arises as to whether all this performing actually leads to a satisfactory result. The reader who likes the book has as strong a case as the person who detests it. The latter may well object to such an elaborate fuss (performance) over nothing very much: but nothing less than a remarkable performance could have unfolded with such precision the awakening of the mind of Lambert Strether to the realities of a world in which, whatever its immediate attractions, he is clearly out of his depth.

*Amelia* A novel by Henry Fielding (his last), first published in 1751.

Amelia and William Booth have married against the wishes of Amelia's mother. William is an army officer, attractive, brave, and not much else, and the couple are soon in difficulties in London. William is imprisoned in Newgate on a false charge and Amelia's beauty exposes her to unwelcome attentions from, among others, Captain James, supposedly William's friend. William, in Newgate, encounters Miss Matthews, an adventuress wise in the ways of corruption who knows exactly how far a bribe can go: her cell is in fact a boudoir. She listens to William's account of army life and his pursuit of Amelia; then she seduces him. Amelia, meanwhile, had successfully fended off her suitors and when William is released he is conscience-stricken about his affair. The couple's situation grows desperate, though when Amelia learns of William's infidelity she forgives him. William is weak enough to believe that gambling will solve their financial problems and is soon in a debtors' prison. Amelia's desperate situation is relieved when her mother's will is discovered to have been forged; she, and not her sister who holds the property, is the true heiress. William is rescued from prison and the couple retire to the country – to a peaceful life, one hopes. But William's character, so well drawn by the author, places a question mark over this apparently happy ending.

*Amelia*, unlike Fielding's other fiction, is a domestic novel set in one place. London comes under Fielding's scrutiny in the way that England had in *Joseph Andrews* and *Tom Jones*. His examination is more unsparing in this novel and the social scene plays a more important part. The picture of London which emerges is a grim one and the characters who affect the couple's progress are drawn with darker and sharper lines. The honest clergyman, Dr Harrison, is a long way from Parson Adams of *Joseph Andrews* and Miss Matthews is a merciless portrait of a predatory female devoid of moral sense. Amelia is believable, a good woman who loves a weak and foolish man and whose resolution is never shaken. But William is, perhaps, overdrawn; a good woman's love cannot redeem the wretched creature, and the reader's patience is severely tried by Amelia's devotion to him.

*Amelia* can be read in a modern edition by George Saintsbury, published in Everyman's Library (1930).

**American, The** A novel by Henry James, first published as a serial in the *Atlantic Monthly*, from June 1876 to May 1877, and in volume form in 1877. It was published in England in 1879. The author dramatized the novel and it was produced in 1891. A version of the play was privately printed in the same year.

Christopher Newman is a wealthy American visiting Paris. There he meets Madame Claire de Cintre, a widow and daughter of a noble family. (Newman has become tired of business and wants to enjoy life and an American friend, Mrs Tristram, is privately amused by his 'business-like' way of looking for a wife.) Newman also meets, in the Louvre, Noémie Nioche, who copies great paintings for a living; her father becomes Newman's teacher in French. When Newman pursues his acquaintance with Claire her brother, the Marquis de Bellegarde, snubs him. However, the younger de Bellegarde, Valentin, becomes Newman's friend and encourages him to court his sister. Claire accepts Newman; he believes that de Bellegarde and the Dowager Marquise, an Englishwoman, are beginning to accept him, albeit grudgingly, and he meets some of their friends. He is, after all, very rich.

To provide her with a dowry, Newman generously orders a number of paintings from Noémie; he also introduces her to Valentin, whom he finds an attractive and amusing companion who has a lighthearted acceptance of all the advantages of privilege. But Valentin is no fool and he perceives that Noémie is tough and self-seeking; however, it suits him to go on seeing her. The Marquis, meanwhile, and the Dowager Marquise have persuaded Claire to break off her engagement. Then Valentin becomes involved in a duel because of Noémie and is fatally wounded. On his deathbed he is disgusted to hear of his family's behaviour and tells Newman that the Dowager's maid, Mrs

Bread, knows something about them; Newman could force them to yield if he wanted to.

Mrs Bread, after Valentin's funeral, tells Newman that the Dowager killed her husband. He goes to the family and confronts them with the evidence but they will not budge. Newman sets out to expose them – but then he is overcome with a weary revulsion. He destroys the evidence and turns his back on the de Bellegarde family, which is exactly what they thought he would do – they knew him better than he knew himself. Having decided finally that he was unsuitable in spite of his wealth, they rejected him; Claire's feelings were of no account.

*The American* does not succeed completely. The reasons for the murder of the old Marquis are quite unbelievable. Claire is not interesting enough – Valentin and Newman are far closer than Newman and Claire. But as a presentation of a 'new world' man confronted with the arrogance bred by centuries of privilege the book is very rewarding.

**American Notes** Charles Dickens's account of his first visit to the USA, which took place in 1842 and lasted for six months. He sailed with his wife, Catherine and her maid, Anne Brown, on the first Cunard steamship, the *Britannia*, in January and endured a dreadful crossing in an overcrowded vessel.

Dickens enjoyed a warm welcome in Boston, where they landed, and it seemed a wonderful place after their winter crossing. But the first sour notes came when he referred to the question of copyright – his novels sold in millions in America but not a penny ever reached the author. His hosts reacted with wounded dignity, since they had gone to a lot of trouble helping to arrange Dickens's trip and had spent money themselves to entertain him. In New York he was infuriated by the behaviour of people who followed him in the street and felt entitled to knock on his door whenever it occurred to them. He detested the overheated rooms.

His and Catherine's disenchantment grew with every journey they made and every institution they visited. Dickens records it all, ending with an attack on slavery which may not impress us now but which was seen as blisteringly strong at the time.

The Americans did not like what Dickens wrote about them but after the cold reception of *Martin Chuzzlewit* they were reading his novels as eagerly as ever.

**American Senator, The** A novel by Anthony Trollope, first published in *Temple Bar* (May 1876 to July 1877).

The Senator is Mr Gotobed, who comes to England at the invitation of John Morton, whom he meets in Washington. He is going to study English institutions, which have such an attraction for Americans – who persist, nonetheless, in regarding England as decayed and worn out. He stays in the town of Dillborough and visits Bragton Hall. His comments are outspoken and diverting but some critics thought the novel spoiled by the addition of two love affairs, which pad the story out to the obligatory Victorian three volumes. Others found the Senator boring, rude, and hardly credible in the social climate of the time.

**American Tragedy, An**  A novel by Theodore Dreiser, first published in 1925. It was dramatized successfully by Patrick Kearney in 1926. For the framework of his plot, Dreiser used an actual murder case of 1906, in which a man named Chester Gilette was convicted of the murder of Grace Brown.

Clyde Griffiths is the son of a drab and pious family of evangelists in Kansas City – and wants to escape the dreary life as quickly as he can. He goes to work as a bellboy in a luxury hotel; soon he is sharing and enjoying the lively existence of his more sophisticated workmates. But this comes to an end when he is involved in a car accident and is legally culpable. He is lucky in a chance meeting with Samuel Griffiths, his uncle, who has become a successful manufacturer in New York State. Samuel Griffiths is charmed by his nephew's personality and gives him a job in his factory. In the small town nearby lives Sondra Finchley, a rich girl who represents the elegance and culture to which Clyde has always aspired. Meanwhile, he seduces one of the factory girls, Roberta.

Clyde falls in love with Sondra and finds his attentions are not unwelcome. But Roberta becomes pregnant and demands that Clyde marry her. Clyde, who sees his hopes on the verge of being fulfilled with marriage to Sondra within his grasp, decides to dispose of the unfortunate Roberta, a simple girl who had hopes of a simple marriage. He takes her to a lake resort, deserted at that time of year, where he plans to murder her. He lacks the resolution to carry out his plan but when the boat overturns accidentally he swims away and leaves Roberta to drown.

Clyde is accused of the girl's murder and the rest of the novel traces the investigation, indictment, trial, and conviction. The relentless detail of the process demonstrates the inexorable closing in of fate on a young man whose character is basically weak and follows him to his execution for a murder that he did not commit – though he is totally responsible for the girl's death. The tragedy of the title is that Clyde will do anything to achieve success, which Dreiser saw as the degeneration, by the 1920s, of what had been the American dream. Clyde Griffiths has no other goal in life and he is not strong enough to realize it.

**Amerigo, Prince**  The impoverished Italian nobleman who marries Maggie Verver in *The Golden Bowl*, by Henry James. He had once been in love with Charlotte Stant, who becomes the wife of Maggie's father, Adam Verver. He embarks on an affair with Charlotte in the course of the story.

**Ames, William** 1576–1633.  A Calvinist theologian, Ames was one of the younger school who grew restive under the uncompromising nature of his creed and could no longer accept a God who required eternal prostration. Ames, in his *Medulla Sacrae Theologiae* of 1623 (translated into English in 1642), seeks to bring reason and intellect into the practice of a true religion. The book had considerable influence, notably on John Milton and his ideas of Christianity.

**Amis and Amiloun**  A Middle English verse romance of the 13th century, adapted from *Amis et Amile*, a 12th-century French romance. (See **metrical romances**.) Amis and Amiloun are foster-brothers of noble birth. Amis is subjected to trial by combat after seducing his overlord's daughter; his accuser is the steward. Guilty, he cannot defend himself, so Amiloun impersonates him in the combat and succeeds in killing the steward. For this he is stricken with leprosy and reduced to beggary. When Amis succeeds in finding his foster-brother he obeys the bidding of an archangel to cure Amiloun with his own children's blood. But the gods acknowledge his sacrifice without accepting it; Amiloun is cured and the dead children are restored to Amis and his wife Belisante. William Morris translated the original story, well known in western Europe, as *Of the Friendship of Amis and Amile* (1894). The text of the English romance was edited by Mace Leach for the Early English Text Society (1937). A modern version by B. B. Broughton was published in *Richard the Lion-hearted and other Medieval Romances* (New York, 1966).

**Amis, Kingsley (William)** 1922–  .  Amis was born in London and educated at the City of London School and St John's College, Oxford. After serving in the army (1942–45) he taught English at University College, Swansea (1949–61) and Peterhouse College, Cambridge

(1961–63). His first published work was poetry, *Bright November* (1947) and *A Frame of Mind* (1953), but he became famous with his first novel, *Lucky Jim* (1954), a satire on social and academic pretensions which earned him the Somerset Maugham Award. Other works of fiction by him are *That Uncertain Feeling* (1955), *I Like it Here* (1958), *Take a Girl Like You* (1960), *My Enemy's Enemy* (1962, short stories), *One Fat Englishman* (1963), *The Egyptologists* (1965, with Robert Conquest), *The Anti-Death League* (1966), *I Want it Now* (1968), *Colonel Sun* (1968, as Robert Markham), *The Green Man* (1969), *Girl 20* (1971), *The Riverside Villa Murder* (1973), *Ending Up* (1974), *The Alteration* (1974), and *Jake's Thing* (1978). Further collections of poems are *A Case of Samples: Poems 1946–56* (1956), *A Look Around the Estate: Poems 1957–67* (1967), and *Collected Poems* (1979). A prolific journalist, Amis has also published *Socialism and the Intellectuals* (1957), *New Maps of Hell: A Survey of Science Fiction* (1960), *Spectrum* (1961 – science-fiction anthology with Robert Conquest), *The James Bond Dossier* (1965), *Lucky Jim's Politics* (1968), *What Became of Jane Austen?* (1970), and *Rudyard Kipling and His World* (1975). He is the editor of *Selected Short Stories of G. K. Chesterton* (1972) and *The New Oxford Book of Light Verse* (1978).

**Amoret** In Books III and IV of Spenser's *The Faerie Queene*, she is the twin sister of Belphoebe. She is married to Scudamour, abducted by Busirane, and unrequitedly loved by Timias.

**Amoretti** A sonnet sequence by Edmund Spenser that was published with his *Epithalamion* in 1595. It contains 88 sonnets and is believed to reflect the course of his love and courtship of Elizabeth Boyle, his second wife. The most famous, perhaps, is LXXV, beginning with the lines 'One day I wrote her name upon the strand'.

**Amory, Blanche** In Thackeray's *Pendennis*, the woman Major Pendennis hopes his nephew Arthur will marry for the sake of social advancement. She is pretty and amusing but she has a sharp eye for the main chance.

**Amory, Thomas** *c.*1691–1788. Amory was born in Ireland and educated at Trinity College, Dublin. He studied medicine for a time but was able to afford a life of leisure, which he spent in Dublin and London. He was acquainted with Swift and is known as the author of *Memoirs of Several Ladies of Great Britain* (1755) and *The Life and Opinions of John Buncle, Esquire* (1756 and 1766). Amory said that he was for a long time engaged on a great work, 'The Ancient and Present State of Great Britain', and he travelled extensively in the British Isles on its account. The manuscript was destroyed by fire – and he used the material in fiction.

*Memoirs of Several Ladies of Great Britain* was the story of just one, in the event. Mrs Marinda Benlow is a bluestocking and the story wanders off into a curious tour of the Hebrides, where Amory places a Green Island of exotic flora, on which stands a ladies' academy. *The Life and Opinions of John Buncle, Esquire* was published in two volumes with an interval of 10 years between them. It purports to be an autobiography: the narrator, like the author, is a Unitarian, amorous but virtuous – seven wives of remarkable beauty and intelligence obligingly die within a few years of marriage to him, so he can eat his cake and have it too. Buncle's matrimonial ventures take him to remote and beautiful places, well depicted, where surprisingly desirable women seem to live. The novel demonstrates sentimentality and sensibility in 18th-century style but is only of interest to scholars.

**Amos Barton, The Sad Fortunes of the Revd** See **Scenes of Clerical Life**.

**Amphitryon: or The Two Socias**. A comedy by John Dryden, first produced in October 1690 and published in the same year. The songs in the play were set to music composed by Henry Purcell. The subject of Jupiter in the guise of Alcmena's husband had been used by Molière and, in the classical theatre, by Plautus. In the original Greek myth Zeus and Alcmena became the parents of Heracles as a result of their dalliance.

Amphitryon, returning from the war, sends his slave Socia ahead to prepare his wife Alcmena for his homecoming. Jupiter finds Alcmena beautiful and, assuming the form of Amphitryon, orders Mercury to take the form of Socia in order to keep out the real one. The result is a comedy of errors with two Amphitryons, two Socias, and a bewildered and intrigued Alcmena. The resolution comes with the inevitable confrontation of the false Amphitryon with the true one.

**Analogy of Religion, The** See **Butler, Joseph**.

**Anarchical Fallacies** Jeremy Bentham's riposte to the arguments contained in the Declaration of the Rights of Man decreed in the French Constituent Assembly of 1791 was written in the same year and was published in the collected edition of his works (1838–43). The theory that equality and freedom were 'natural rights' of which man had been deprived by governments was put forward by Rousseau, and in England by Richard Price, and had become popular. In his essay Bentham points out that all 'rights' are the creation of law: 'natural rights is simple nonsense'. Bentham was not out of sympathy with the Revolution but with woolly sentimental thinking. He was in fact made a citizen of France in 1792.

**Anastasius,** *or Memoirs of a Modern Greek*. A picaresque novel first published in 1819 – and once believed to be the work of Byron – is the single work by which the author Thomas Hope (1770–1831) is known. A rich much-travelled man, he made extensive use of his knowledge of the Near East. His novel is in the form of an autobiography of an unscrupulous Greek of Chios in the 18th century. The book is very long and the author's adventures – in Albania fighting rebels, in Turkey evading an amorous lady, in Egypt achieving eminence with the Mamelukes, in Smyrna, in Arabia, etc. – have a smug monotony. It is chiefly interesting for its description of oriental places and customs.

**Anatomie of Abuses, The**  See **Stubbes, Philip.**

**Anatomy of Melancholy, The**  See **Burton, Robert.**

**Ancient Mariner, The Rime of the**  A poem by Samuel Taylor Coleridge, first published in *Lyrical Ballads*, by Wordsworth and Coleridge, in 1798. The elaborate prose gloss that accompanies the poem in most modern editions was added by Coleridge when he included the poem in his collection *Sybilline Leaves* (1817). The poem tells of the 'ancient mariner' who meets three gallants on the way to a marriage feast; he detains one who listens spellbound to the mariner's story in spite of the sounds of 'bridal music'. He hears of a voyage during which the ship was driven south by a storm into the ice of the South Pole. An albatross appears and proves to be a bird of good omen; the ship escapes from the ice and a south wind arises. The great bird follows the ship until the mariner, in an act of mindless violence, shoots it down. His shipmates upbraid him at first but are willing to condone the crime when they seem to have a clear passage, which they attribute to the killing of the albatross; they are therefore accomplices, and all are punished. The ship is carried north into the Pacific, into tropic seas where it is becalmed; the water runs out and the crew blame the mariner; they hang the corpse of the albatross around his neck. After the passing of a ghost ship the crew begin to die. The mariner's pardon begins with a vision of the creatures of God and the beauty of His world, seen by moonlight. When he is at last able to pray the dead bird falls from his neck and into the sea,

A detail from one of Gustave Doré's engravings for Coleridge's *The Rime of the Ancient Mariner*. The engraving, published in 1876, is for Part I: the ship is driven towards the South Pole by a storm.

and Mary, the mother of God, sends a life-giving rain. The mariner is eventually rescued and confesses to a Hermit, who shrives him; but he knows his penance will continue throughout his life. He must go on relating his dreadful story and make it a lesson of love for all God's creatures. *The Ancient Mariner* is the only one of Coleridge's major poems that is complete. It is a powerful Romantic work in ballad form; the surface itself is brilliant, the narrative compelling – using the most direct and simple language the poet expresses a wide range of feeling and emotion.

**Ancrene Riwle, The (**or ***The Ancrene Wisse*)**  A devotional manual in Middle English prose dating from about the beginning of the 13th century. The author is unknown and may have been a woman; it is in any case notable as a book written especially for women. The title means 'The Anchoresses' Rule'; an anchoress was a devout woman who, after a term of training in a nunnery, dedicated herself to a secluded life outside. It is highly praised by scholars, not only for its charm and tenderness but as a definite landmark in vernacular prose style. Versions in Latin and French also exist.

The best-known modern edition of *The Ancrene Riwle* is by J. R. R. Tolkien for the Early English Text Society (1962).

**Anderson, Maxwell** 1888–1959. The son of a Baptist minister, Anderson was born in Atlantic, Pennsylvania, and brought up in North Dakota, where he completed his education at the state university in 1911. After further study at Stanford University, California, he took his MA in 1914 and for a time was a teacher. He abandoned that for journalism and eventually went to live in New York. His first play, *White Desert* (1923), attracted no particular attention; his second, *What Price Glory* (1924) with Laurence Stallings, was an immensely successful war play. The partnership continued with *First Flight* (1925) and *The Buccaneer* (also 1925) and Anderson established his position in the theatre with the sole authorship of *Saturday's Children* (1927), a marital comedy. His first verse play was *Elizabeth the Queen* (1930), about Elizabeth and Essex, and it gave him a leading position among US playwrights. Anderson also used blank verse for *Night over Taos* (1932), but returned to prose for *Both Your Houses* (1933, Pulitzer Prize), a political satire. *Mary of Scotland* (also 1933) is in blank verse. Anderson's next play, *Valley Forge* (1934), makes use of an American historical theme, and *Winterset* (1935) of a modern one. The author had used the Sacco and Vanzetti case in an earlier play, the unsuccessful *Gods of the Lightning* (1928, with Harold Hickerson); in the second attempt he used blank verse and achieved a remarkable success.

Anderson continued to be a prolific and successful playwright almost to the end of his life. After *Winterset* came *Wingless Victory* and *The Masque of Kings* (1936), *High Tor* and *The Star Wagon* (1937), *Key Largo* (1939), *Journey to Jerusalem* (1940), *The Eve of St Mark* (1942), *Storm Operation* (1944), *Joan of Lorraine* (1947), *Anne of the Thousand Days* (1948), and *Barefoot in Athens* (1951). Anderson collaborated with the composer Kurt Weill on *Knickerbocker Holiday* (1938) and *Lost in the Stars* (1948), which was based on Alan Paton's *Cry the Beloved Country*.

**Anderson, Sherwood** 1874–1941. Sherwood Anderson was born in Camden, Ohio, and had completed his education by the time he was 14. He drifted from job to job and then served in the Spanish-American War (1898). After that he tried to settle down in Ohio; he married and managed a paint factory in Elyria. Then, appar-

ently – the truth of the story has been questioned – he left family and job and went to Chicago to pursue a literary career. In Chicago he wrote advertising copy and met Carl Sandburg and others who encouraged him. His first book was *Windy McPherson's Son* (1916), which displayed the strain of autobiography that is part of all his fiction. *Marching Men* (1917), is set among the coal miners of Pennsylvania, and then Anderson published a book of verse, *Mid-American Chants* (1918). He attracted considerable attention with *Winesburg, Ohio* (1919), a collection of stories of small-town life, rendered in the most idiomatic unliterary prose brought to American fiction since Mark Twain.

*Winesburg, Ohio* is given a sort of unity by the character George Willard, a reporter on the town newspaper who has literary ambitions, and to whom all the characters gravitate in the course of the book. The setting is realistic and rendered in detail but all the characters are seen at the dark moments, suddenly illuminated in a way that stresses their alienation and their desperate efforts to communicate. The method throws the everyday world into relief, and small town life is thereby vividly realized. *Poor White* (1920) tells how successful technology changes the lives of everyone in Bidwell, Ohio, and particularly the life of the inventor Hugh McVey, who at the beginning of the novel is the shy inhibited poor White of the title.

Anderson's fiction continued to exploit the two themes – the stultifying effect of the machine age and the possibility of liberation through sexual honesty, implicit in *Winesburg, Ohio* and *Poor White* – for the rest of his career but without decreasing his success. His later work included the collections of short stories *The Triumph of the Egg* (1921), *Horses and Men* (1923), and *Death in the Woods* (1933) and the novels *Many Marriages* (1923), *Dark Laughter* (1925), *Tar, A Midwest Childhood* (1926) and *Beyond Desire* (1932).

Sherwood Anderson's influence on American fiction was considerable and he acknowledged his own debt to Gertrude Stein. He introduced the young Hemingway to Gertrude Stein with letters when Hemingway went to Paris and he also encouraged William Faulkner in the early stages of his career. He is important in American letters as perhaps the first essentially American novelist of the Middle West, one who, in Edmund Wilson's words 'grew up, like the native grass, without any foreign fertilizer.' His autobiography, *A Story Teller's Story* (1924), contains the story of his suddenly turning his back on family and job to go out and become a writer.

*Andrea del Sarto*  A poem by Robert Browning, first published in 1855 in the volume *Men and Women*. The inspiration for the poem was the account of the painter's life in Vasari's *The Lives of the Painters*. Andrea del Sarto (1486–1531) was a contemporary of Michelangelo and Raphael and inevitably overshadowed by them; but Browning's subtitle, 'The Faultless Painter', echoes the description the painter earned during his lifetime. Vasari wrote that Andrea del Sarto was less committed to his art than to his love for his wife, the beautiful Lucrezia, and Browning's poem is a dramatic monologue addressed to her by Andrea del Sarto. He is patient and resigned, aware of his deficiencies. He accepts Lucrezia, unfaithful and greedy though she is, because his love for her is the strongest force in his life.

*Andreas*  A poem in Old English, preserved in *The Vercelli Book*. It has been attributed to Cynewulf by some scholars but this is disputed by others. The subject of the poem is the apostle St Andrew; he is commanded by God to go to the aid of St Matthew, who is in danger of death in the land of the savage Mermedonians in Ethiopia. Andrew sets forth in a boat manned by God and two angels, and after a stormy voyage reaches his destination. But he too is captured and tortured, until he saves himself and Matthew by a miracle and converts the Mermedonians. The poem is famous for its vivid description of Andrew's stormy voyage. A translation by C. W. Kennedy is included in his *Early English Christian Poetry* (1952).

**Andrewes, Lancelot** 1555–1626.  The name of the first scholar on the roll of those chosen to make the authorized version of the English Bible was Lancelot Andrewes, then Dean of Westminster. He was born in the parish of All Hallows, Barking, and educated at the Merchant Taylors' School. Later he went to Pembroke Hall, Cambridge, and became a fellow in 1576. In 1589 he became both Master of his college and vicar of St Giles, Cripplegate. Cripplegate was attached to a prebend of St Paul's and it was there that his quality as a preacher brought him to the attention of Queen Elizabeth. She offered him two bishoprics, Salisbury or Ely; Andrewes declined, unhappy at the conditions concerning the revenues, but became Dean of Westminster in 1601.

King James was no less impressed with Andrewes than Elizabeth had been. Andrewes was a distinguished scholar and master of 15 languages and at the Hampton Court Conference of 1604 he played an important part; his contribution to the English Bible was the Penta-teuch and the historical books. King James made him Bishop of Chichester (1605), then of Ely (1609), and of Winchester (1619).

Andrewes recoiled from the rigid extremes of the Puritans and was one of the shaping influences in Anglican theology. His friends were Richard Hooker and George Herbert and the European scholars Hugo Grotius, Pierre du Moulin, and Isaac Casaubon. His sermons are classics of Anglican homiletic but their appeal must have been limited to a small circle since understanding of them requires some acquaintance with Greek and Latin and a willingness to listen to an exhaustive analysis of the texts. *Ninety-six Sermons* was published in 1629, *Preces Privatae* (Private Devotions) in 1648, and *A Pattern of Catechistical Doctrine* in 1630. The complete works were published in 11 volumes (1841–54) edited by J. P. Wilson and J. Bliss.

**Andrews, Pamela**  The heroine of *Pamela, or Virtue Rewarded* by Samuel Richardson. A maidservant, she is left without protection when her mistress dies. The lady's son, Mr B., hopes to take advantage of her, but her virtue proves unassailable. She wins Mr B.'s hand eventually, and succeeds in being accepted by his disapproving family.

*Angel in the House, The*  A poem in four parts by Coventry Patmore, celebrating conjugal love. The four parts were published as *The Betrothal* (1854), *The Espousals* (1856), *Faithful for Ever* (1860), and *The Victories of Love* (1862). The poems follow the courtship and marriage of Felix and Honoria, a dean's daughter, and the progress of their marriage; the poems unfold against a background of everyday life.

**Angelo**  In Shakespeare's *Measure for Measure*, the cold-blooded deputy to whom the Duke of Vienna consigns full authority during his absence. Angelo immediately enforces the long-lapsed strictures on moral behaviour and this leads to Claudio being sentenced to death. Claudio's sister Isabella intercedes with Angelo and she arouses his lust. He demands Isabella's chastity in return for her brother's life.

*Anglo-Saxon Chronicle*  The *Chronicle* is the product of monks who worked at various centres to compile a chronicle of events in England from the arrival of Christianity until the middle of the 12th century (the wretched reign of King Stephen). This chronicle was initially written, and continued, in the vernacular, even though English had disappeared as a scholar's language by the time the chronicle ceased. By then the language of the *Chronicle* had developed from

Old to Middle English. It was begun at Winchester under the inspiration of King Alfred; later contributions came from scribes at Peterborough, Abingdon, Worcester, and Canterbury. The versions inevitably vary in content and quality according to the place of writing; the long account contains some dry passages but lack of embellishment is part of its virtue, whilst the passages telling of the struggles with the Danes, the story of Cynewulf and Cyneheard, and the dark years of Stephen's reign are justly celebrated. Over all, its value is incalculable, both as a fundamental authority for events in pre-Conquest England and as the first history of a western European country in its own language.

The history of the progress of the *Anglo-Saxon Chronicle* is complicated and has presented scholars of Old English literature with years of exacting work. Six complete versions exist in manuscript, plus two fragments. Version A, *The Parker Chronicle*, is in the library of Corpus Christi College, Cambridge; Version E, *The Laud-Peterborough Chronicle*, is in the Bodleian Library, Oxford. The rest, including the fragments, are in the British Library: Versions B and C, *The Abingdon Chronicles*; D, *The Worcester Chronicle*; and F, the bilingual *Canterbury Epitome*. Version E takes the *Chronicle* to the latest known date (1154).

A highly regarded edition is that by C. Plummer, using Versions A and E, first published at Oxford (1892–99) using the edition of J. Earle (1865). A translation of the *Anglo-Saxon Chronicle* into modern English, by G. N. Garmonsway, was published in Everyman's Library (1953).

**Animal Farm** See **Orwell, George**.

**Annabel Lee** A lyrical ballad by Edgar Allan Poe, first published in 1849 in the New York *Tribune* just after the poet's death. It has since become his most famous poem. The theme is the loss of a beloved; the form is six stanzas of alternate four- and three-stress lines.

**Annales Cambriae** The earliest extant manuscript of the ancient annals of Wales dates from the second half of the 10th century and was written in Latin. After the work of Nennius (*Historia Britonum*) and of Gildas, who refers obliquely to the Battle of Mount Badon (*De Excedio et Conquestu Britanniae*), the *Annales* contain the first reference to King Arthur's deeds. It gives dates for the Battle of Mount Badon (518), when Arthur carried the cross on his shoulders and won a great victory, and for the fatal encounter with

Medraut (Mordred) at the Battle of Camlan (539).

The text of *Annales Cambriae* was edited by E. Phillimore (1888).

**Annals of the Parish, The** A novel by John Galt, first published in 1821.

The parish is Dalmailing, in Ayrshire, and the annals are related by the Rev Micah Balwhidder. The period covered is from 1760 to 1810, and Mr Balwhidder's relation of events is amusingly subjective. Galt's success in the unfolding of events as told by the minister has made this the most popular of his books. The life of the people of Dalmailing, the social changes of the momentous years, and the character of the minister himself are part of a remarkably successful picture of life in the Lowlands during the reign of George III.

**Anna of the Five Towns** See **Bennett, (Enoch) Arnold**.

**Anne of Geierstein** A novel by Sir Walter Scott, first published in 1829. The setting is England during the reign of Edward IV, Switzerland, and Burgundy.

Arthur de Vere and his father, the Earl of Oxford, pursue Lancastrian intrigues in Europe after their side's defeat at Tewkesbury. During a storm in the Alps they are given refuge by Arnold Biederman of Unterwalden and his niece, the Countess Anne of Geierstein. The de Veres' assumed name is Philipson and their business is with Charles the Bold, Duke of Burgundy. The Swiss are sending a delegation to protest to the duke about his treatment of their citizens, and the Philipsons travel with it. They hope to gain assistance for the Lancastrian cause from him in exchange for Provence.

The Philipsons have a narrow escape from death when they fall into the hands of the vicious Archibald of Hagenbach. They are saved when the townspeople rise against Archibald and hand him over to be tried by the Vehmgericht, of which Anne's father, Count Albert, is the head. Hagenbach is executed; but the Philipsons' hopes come to nothing when the duke is defeated by the Swiss at Granson and Morat and killed while besieging Nancy. They return to Unterwalden, and Arthur marries the Countess Anne.

**Anne of Green Gables** See **Montgomery, L(ucy) M(aud)**.

**Annus Mirabilis, The Year of Wonders, 1666** A poem by John Dryden, first published in 1667 and written at Charlton in Wiltshire, where the Drydens had gone to escape the plague raging in London. It is composed in 300 quatrains, the first

200 quatrains dealing with the war at sea against the Dutch and concluding with the victory at the North Foreland in July 1666. The remaining 100 quatrains tell of the Great Fire of London.

**Anson, George, Baron** 1697–1762. Anson was born at Colwich in Staffordshire, entered the Navy, and became a commodore and eventually First Lord of the Admiralty. As Commodore Anson he sailed with a squadron of seven ships from Spithead in 1740. The voyage was planned for Panama, by way of Cape Horn, and to the South Seas. The storms at the Cape were so severe that only three ships staggered into shelter at Juan Fernández, where two ships refitted and continued the voyage. In the Pacific a Spanish galleon was captured and her treasure, a million and a half dollars in silver, taken. Only one ship of the squadron, loaded with loot, returned to England. Anson's journals were edited by his chaplain, Richard Walter, and published as *Voyage Round the World* (1748). A junior officer, a survivor of the wreck of the *Wager* on the coast of Chile, was John Byron, the poet's grandfather, who published an account of his experiences, *The Coasts of Patagonia and the Loss of the Wager* (1768).

**Anstey, Christopher** 1724–1805. Anstey was born at Brinkley, Cambridgeshire, and educated at Eton and King's College, Cambridge. He was the author of a popular series of verse letters concerning a family called Blunderhead and their adventures in Bath. *The New Bath Guide*, as it was called, was first published in 1766.

**Anstey, F.** 1856–1934. The pseudonym of Thomas Anstey Guthrie, the son of a military tailor in London. He was educated at King's College School and Trinity Hall, Cambridge, where he read law. Two years after being called to the Bar he published *Vice Versa: or a Lesson to Fathers* (1882). In this story a father and a son exchange ages and personalities and both of them learn a great deal from the experience. The farcical tone is sustained throughout with complete success and the novel has become a classic of its kind, though much more of a favourite with boys than with their fathers.

Anstey devoted himself to writing and forsook the law completely. He became a regular contributor to *Punch* and joined the magazine in 1887. His output was fairly large, but humour is ephemeral and much of his work is forgotten, with the exception of *The Brass Bottle*, a successful comedy about an inefficient Jinn, which was published in 1900.

**Antigonus** Paulina's husband in Shakespeare's *The Winter's Tale*. He is ordered to abandon Leontes' baby daughter but he is killed by a bear while carrying out a deed he loathes ('my heart bleeds; and most accurst am I').

**Anti-Jacobin, The** A weekly journal founded by George Canning, which was published from 20 November 1797 to 7 July 1798. Its platform is described by its title and it was successful in combating the radical politics and philosophy which the revolution in France encouraged. Among its contributors were George Canning, George Ellis (a former Whig), and John Hookham Frere, and the editor was William Gifford. *The Anti-Jacobin* published news and notable satirical verse: famous examples were the parody of Southey, 'The Needy Knife-grinder', the parody of Erasmus Darwin's *The Botanical Garden* called 'The Loves of the Triangles', and the burlesque of German drama, 'The Rovers'. The most notable of all was George Canning's anti-French 'The New Morality'.

Charles Edmonds's edition of *The Poetry of the Anti-Jacobin* (1852) identified the authors of each contribution. A later edition (1924) was edited by L. Rice-Oxley.

**Antipholus** In Shakespeare's *The Comedy of Errors*, the name given to the identical twin sons of Aegeon of Syracuse.

**Antiquary, The** A novel by Sir Walter Scott – his own favourite – first published in 1816. While in many ways it follows the pattern of its predecessor, *Guy Mannering*, it is altogether a sunnier book and one of Scott's best.

Major Neville, calling himself William Lovel, follows Isabella Wardour to Scotland. She has rejected him in deference to her father, Sir Arthur, who believes Neville to be illegitimate. On the way to Scotland, Lovel (Neville) falls in with the Wardours' neighbour, Jonathan Oldbuck, the antiquary of the title, and with him meets the king's bedesman, Edie Ochiltree. Sir Arthur has fallen under the influence of Dousterswivel, a plausible German scoundrel. Oldbuck has a quarrelsome nephew, Hector M'Intyre. Ochiltree saves Sir Arthur and Isabella from drowning, and the favour in their eyes which this earns him is important to the plot. He also helps Lovel to expose Dousterswivel and save the Wardours from ruin. Lovel proves to be the Heir of Glenallan and all ends happily.

**Antonio** The merchant in Shakespeare's *The Merchant of Venice*. On behalf of his friend Bassanio he borrows 3000 ducats from Shylock. When he can't meet the debt Shylock invokes the clause that gives him the right to a pound of Antonio's flesh. Shylock hates him because his generosity keeps down the rate of usury and because Antonio frankly despises Jews. As observed by their friends Salerio and Solanio, Antonio loves Bassanio unreservedly.

**Antonio and Mellida** and **Antonio's Revenge, The History of** A play and a tragic sequel by John Marston, first produced about 1600 and first published in 1602.

In the first part Antonio is in love with Mellida. Antonio's father is Andrugio, Duke of Genoa, and Mellida's father is Piero, Duke of Venice; the two states are at war. Piero sets a price on the heads of Andrugio and his son; nevertheless Antonio goes to Venice disguised as an Amazon and persuades Mellida to run away with him. They are captured and Andrugio offers himself to his enemy for his son's life. Piero, to the Genoans' surprise, relents and gives his consent to the marriage of Antonio and Mellida.

In the second part it is revealed that Piero has been biding his time. He kills Andrugio and in order to prevent the coming marriage brings about his own daughter's dishonour. He plots the destruction of Antonio and, meanwhile, succeeds in winning the hand of Andrugio's widow. Mellida dies of grief. Antonio is visited by the ghost of his father, the murdered Duke; he disguises himself as a fool and succeeds in gaining access to Piero, whom he kills.

The play has distinct echoes of Kyd's *The Spanish Tragedy*, produced some eight years before, and strong elements are to be found in *Hamlet*, which came two or three years later.

**Antony, Mark** In Shakespeare's *Julius Caesar*, the unswerving ally of Caesar. He treads warily among the conspirators after Caesar's murder and then turns the tables on them with a magnificent speech to the people over Caesar's body. He effectively turns the people into a vengeful mob and the assassins are forced to flee. Antony forms the triumvirate with Octavius and Lepidus and defeats Brutus and Cassius at Philippi. See also *Antony and Cleopatra*.

**Antony and Cleopatra** A tragedy by William Shakespeare, first produced *c*.1607, and published in the First Folio of 1623. The source of the play is Plutarch's *Lives*, which had been published in Sir Thomas North's English version in 1579.

Mark Antony, the Roman triumvir, is besotted with love for Cleopatra, the Queen of Egypt. In her younger days Cleopatra had also captivated Julius Caesar and borne him a son; it was largely to Caesar that she owed her undisputed possession of the throne. Caesar's nephew Octavius is Antony's fellow triumvir in Rome and his impatience with Antony's dalliance is growing. A large part of the action of the play is set in Alexandria in the palace of the Ptolemies, where in the first scene two of Antony's friends comment on his behaviour.

Antony's wife Fulvia, in the unsettled conditions following the murder of Caesar, had raised a force against Octavius. She had been defeated and died immediately after; Antony is obliged to drag himself away from Cleopatra and report to Rome. The threatened breach with Octavius and Lepidus is halted – but one of the gestures required of Antony is marriage to Octavius' sister, Octavia; the idea comes from Agrippa, who hopes to cement the reconciliation. The news is brought to Cleopatra and her rage is unbounded – she attacks the unfortunate messenger with her own hands. But Antony soon falls out with Octavius again over their dealings with Sextus Pompeius, and he returns to Cleopatra.

Hostilities soon break out between Rome (Octavius) and Egypt (Antony and Cleopatra). Cleopatra insists on accompanying Antony on campaign and at Actium she is criticized for this by Enobarbus; she is too much of a distraction for the successful prosecution of the war. His uneasiness about her is borne out when, at the Battle of Actium, her ships withdraw and turn for Egypt. Antony deserts his fleet and follows her. Octavius follows them to Alexandria, certain of victory, and demands that Cleopatra surrenders Antony to him. Antony, his army intact, resumes the war on land but after an initial success he is defeated. Cleopatra withdraws with her maids Charmian and Iras to take refuge in one of her monuments and, to test Antony's temper with regard to her now he is defeated, sends her eunuch, Mardian, to tell him she has killed herself.

The news in fact destroys Antony: Cleopatra gone ('Since the torch is out, lie down, and stray no farther') and the prospect looming now of being displayed in Octavius' triumph. He commands Eros, his friend and sword bearer, to kill him; Eros kills himself rather than do it and Antony finds strength in that example ('Thrice nobler than myself! Thou teachest me, O valiant Eros'). Diomedes, sent by Cleopatra, finds Antony dying and carries him to Cleopatra's refuge for their last moments together. Cleopatra knows very well what her fate will be if she becomes Octavius' prisoner but she will never submit to it ('Our lamp is spent, it's out. Good sirs, take heart. We'll bury him; and then, what's brave, what's noble, let's do it after the high Roman fashion, and make death proud to take us.').

The Romans take the monument and one of them, Dolabella, confirms that Cleopatra is meant to grace a Roman triumph. Charmian and Iras dress her in her royal robes and insignia and a basket of figs is delivered to the queen. The hour has come ('I have immortal longings in me') and Cleopatra dies from the poisonous serpent hidden among the figs. Her women die with her, Charmian the last, pronouncing her mistress's elegy: 'Now boast thee, death, in thy possession lies a lass unparallel'd.'

History tells us that Antony was 41 years old when he met Cleopatra; at the end, in 30 BC, he was 51 and Cleopatra was 37 and she had borne him three children. The love that resulted in the extinction of the Macedonian dynasty (which had ruled Egypt for nearly 300 years) and led to Octavius becoming the first Emperor of Rome lasted for ten years. And Shakespeare was in his 40s when he wrote this wonderful play.

*Antony and Cleopatra* is the devil to stage, as a glance at the text will show. It is even more of a devil to cast – the two principals must be able to suggest physical magnificence as well as be able to speak the verse, sustained on the highest level of Shakespeare's tragedies and surpassing all of them in the great music of the closing scenes. This is a play unparalleled; it is not only wrought in the finest poetry, it is also intensely dramatic and the lovers are fascinating – and not only in their love. Antony was great – every reference made by his friends, and later by himself, reinforces the past tense. But the look of greatness has not left him yet. Cleopatra has to match the awesome quality of Enobarbus' famous apostrophe in Act II and incredibly she does. There is no explaining a woman of such 'infinite variety'; the challenge is to present her and yet convince the audience that such a woman loves her Antony absolutely. Shakespeare could meet the challenge; he had the language at his command.

**Apemantus** In *Timon of Athens*, the sour-tempered philosopher who warns Timon of impending ruin in Shakespeare's play. He visits Timon in his cave but it is a meeting of two misanthropes; the visit ends with Timon throwing stones at Apemantus to drive him away.

**Apologia pro Vita Sua** A spiritual autobiography by John Henry Newman, first published in seven parts with an appendix (21 April–2 June 1864). The full title was *Apologia pro Vita Sua: Being a Reply to a Pamphlet entitled 'What, then, does Dr Newman mean?'* The pamphlet was by Charles Kingsley (1864): in a review of Froude's *History of England* (volumes 7 and 8), contributed to *Macmillan's Magazine* in January 1864, he wrote 'Truth for its own sake has never been a virtue of the Roman clergy. Father Newman informs us that it need not and on the whole ought not to be.' Newman published *Mr Kingsley and Dr Newman* in February 1864; this was the correspondence with Kingsley and his publishers over the offending passage, and Kingsley's pamphlet followed. Newman's *Apologia* was written in answer to Kingsley. The first two parts and the appendix, which were unsparing of his opponent, were omitted from the volume edition published in 1865.

Newman's book is a primary historical source for the Oxford Movement; but more importantly it is, as a later subtitle explained, a history of the author's religious opinions. A powerful justification of his actions, the book convinces by its sincerity and its appeal transcends sectarian sympathies.

Modern editions of *Apologia pro Vita Sua* have been edited by A. C. Pegis for The Modern Literary (New York, 1950), S. Leslie for Everyman's Library (1955), P. Hughes (1956), A. D. Culler (1956), Basil Willey for The World's Classics (1964), and by M. J. Svaglic for the Oxford English Texts (1967).

**Apologie for Poetrie, The (or The Defence of Poesie)** Sir Philip Sidney's essay was first published in 1595. One printer, Ponsonbie, called it *The Defence of Poesie*; the other, Olney, called it *The Apologie for Poetrie*, by which title it is slightly more familiar. It was written about 1580 during Sidney's sojourn at his sister's house while out of favour at court.

Sidney's contemporary, Stephen Gosson, was a playwright (his works have not survived) who became converted to Puritanism and who wrote in 1579 *The Schoole of Abuse*, an invective against poets and players. He dedicated this to Sidney without his permission. Thomas Lodge published a reply in 1580, and Sidney's essay was probably written in the same year. It is a careful examination of the art of poetry and a critical discussion of English poetry in Sidney's day and is particularly valued for its elegant prose style and the author's careful presentation. It marked an advance in literary criticism but it is very much of Sidney's time; for instance, in his reservations about popular drama, which – within a few years of his death – had entered upon a golden age.

**Apperley, Charles James** 1779–1843. A Shropshire squire, Apperley spent his schooldays at Rugby. He became a journalist to counteract diminishing returns from his land, contributing articles on sport to *The Quarterly Review* and *The Sporting Magazine* and becoming a staff editor on *The Sporting Review*. His first book was *Memoirs of the Life of John Mytton* (1837). Mytton was Apperley's neighbour in Shropshire and they shared enthusiasms and experience; both were obliged, at one stage, to leave for Calais in a hurry to escape their creditors. *The Life of a Sportsman* (1842) is valued for its picture of country life and for the level of the writing, which was higher than was usual on the subjects of hunting and country pursuits. Apperley wrote under the pseudonym 'Nimrod' and his books were illustrated by Henry Alken.

*Araygnement of Paris, The*: *A Pastorall*. A pastoral play in verse by George Peele, written to be played before Elizabeth I in her honour and first published in 1584.

Paris is to be found in the company of his wife Oenone, tending his flocks on Mount Ida. The three goddesses Juno, Venus, and Pallas bring the Golden Apple and ask him to decide to which of them it shall be awarded. Paris decides for Venus, who promptly carries him off, leaving poor Oenone deserted. Juno and Pallas accuse Paris of partiality in his judgment and arraign him before the assembled gods. The judgment of who is most deserving of the Golden Apple is referred to Diana, who evades the tricky choice by awarding it to the nymph Eliza, 'our Zabeta fair'. The play has no worth as a stage piece but is notable for its lyrics, particularly the song of Paris and Oenone, 'Fair and fair, and twice so fair'.

**Arbuthnot, John** 1667–1735. Arbuthnot was born at the manse of Arbuthnot in Kincardineshire, educated at Marischal College in Aberdeen and abroad, and entered University College, Oxford, in 1692 to study medicine. He took his MD at the University of St Andrews and pursued a distinguished career. Arbuthnot became a Fellow of the Royal Society in 1704 and physician to Queen Anne in 1705; he became a Fellow of the College of Physicians in 1710. He supported the union of England and Scotland and set out his reasons in *A Sermon Preached to the People at Mercat Cross, Edinburgh* (1706); this brought him in touch with the peace party at court.

A man of considerable learning and diverse talents, Dr Arbuthnot became the friend of Alexander Pope and Jonathan Swift and their friends, who formed the Scriblerus Club. He was a valued friend to all of them and seems to have possessed a warm and generous disposition as well as wit and humour. Inevitably, in that company, he became a writer: his best known work is a group of five pamphlets published in 1712, *The History of John Bull*, an effective political satire advocating an end to Marlborough's military campaigns and a return to peace. The best parts of the *Memoirs of Martinus Scriblerus*, first published in Pope's *Works* of 1741, are also attributed to him. As a physician Arbuthnot is admired as being generally in advance of his time; he published *An Essay concerning the Nature of Ailments* (1731), which stressed the value of a suitable diet in the treatment of illness. He brought medicine and common sense together (a rare marriage in the medicine of his time) in *An Essay concerning the Effects of Air on Human Bodies* (1733). Other works by Dr Arbuthnot are *An Essay on the Usefulness of Mathematical Learning* (1701) and a poem, *Know Thyself* (1734).

*Arcadia* Sir Philip Sidney's prose romance, or prose epic as described by some scholars, was begun in 1580 at Wilton, his sister's house, where the poet had gone after quarrelling with the Earl of Oxford at court. It was published after his death, in 1590.

The setting is Arcadia, a never-never pastoral world, in a golden age, and the story is difficult to follow; but it must be remembered that Sidney did not sit down to compose a prose epic. 'This idle work of mine, this child which I am loth to father' as he called it once was to some degree an indulgence in fancy, an agreeable exercise that he shared with his sister Mary, Countess of Pembroke. But his poetic imagination was stirred during its composition and *The Old Arcadia*, as the first version is called (finished in 1580), was taken up for revision two years later. He completed the new version of two books, most of a third – and then left it. The published version, called *The Countess of Pembroke's Arcadia*, contained the revised portions and was made complete with three books from the first version.

Pyrocles, son of the King of Macedon, and Musidorus, his cousin, have been wrecked on the shore of Laconia. King Basilius of Arcadia, in obedience to an oracle, has retired to the forest with his wife Gynecia and his daughters, Pamela and Philoclea. Musidorus is brought to Arcadia by shepherds; Pyrocles makes his own way there disguised as a woman, Zelmane – he has fallen in love with Philoclea after seeing her in the forest. Basilius falls in love with 'Zelmane'; so do Gynecia and Philoclea – but they have spotted that he is a man.

Musidorus falls in love with Pamela and discovers Pyrocles in Arcadia. He becomes servant to Pamela's guardian and makes love to Mopsa to cover his true feelings for Pamela. The story of the true Zelmane is told; she had loved Pyrocles, had disguised herself as a page to be near him, sickened, and died. Now Cecropia, heiress to Arcadia until Basilius married and had children, abducts Pamela, Philoclea, and Zelmane-Pyrocles. She tries to force one of them to marry her son, Amphialus. The valour of Zelmane-Pyrocles saves them and they return to the forest.

Musidorus and Pamela run away together. Zelmane-Pyrocles endures persistent advances from both Gynecia and her husband Basilius. He makes an assignation with both, to confront them with each other, and Gynecia prepares a love potion for Pyrocles. But Basilius drinks it by mistake and falls, apparently dead. Gynecia confesses that she prepared the potion; Pyrocles is discovered in Philoclea's chamber and arrested; Musidorus is captured.

Philoclea is to be sent to a nunnery; Gynecia will be buried alive; Pyrocles and Musidorus are sentenced to death. Enter a stranger, who reveals that Pyrocles is heir to Macedonia and Musidorus is heir to Thessaly. Basilius comes to life again – the love potion was only a sleeping draught, after all. General pardons and explanations ensue.

The early impulse to prose fiction that can be seen in the Elizabethans followed the interest in European models, particularly from Italy. Sidney's *Arcadia* was based on the *Arcadia* of Jacopo Sannazaro, and Sidney followed him in the setting of a golden age, with poems (pastoral ecologues) to conclude each book. As an early essay in English prose fiction it is without successors and was written for no public. But this extravagant fancy uses the English language to express, not merely an extravagant style, but Sidney's thoughts on a multitude of subjects, representative of a fine mind in a remarkable age. The poems include the famous 'My true love hath my heart and I have his', which comes at the end of the third book.

**Archer, Isabel**   The heroine of *The Portrait of a Lady*, by Henry James. She has a great need to fulfil herself completely and is aided in this by the generosity of her admirer, Ralph Touchett. But her unsophisticated enthusiasm leads her into a disastrous marriage to the conceited and mean-spirited Gilbert Osmond.

**Archimago**   In Spenser's *The Faerie Queene*, the enchanter who deceives Una in Book I in the guise of the Red Cross Knight. He symbolizes

The frontispiece to the third edition of *Arden of Feversham*, 1633. The murderers attack Arden as he plays backgammon with Mosbie, his wife's lover.

hypocrisy. After being exposed and imprisoned in a dungeon he escapes in Book II to make Sir Guyon suffer for what he has endured.

***Arden of Feversham, The Tragedy of Mr***   A play first published in 1592 and once attributed to Shakespeare by Swinburne among others. The authorship is unknown but the play is of considerable interest as a domestic tragedy in the lives of ordinary people – a field that the Elizabethan and Jacobean playwrights largely ignored. It was based on a murder of 1550 that was mentioned in the chronicles of Raphael Holinshed. Mistress Arden does not love the husband she was obliged to take and has fallen in love with Mosbie. They hire two villains, Black Will and Shakbag, to murder Arden. The murder is discovered and Mosbie and Mistress Arden are executed for the crime. Performances of the play are rare and the critical assessment is, generally, that the really convincing scenes are those after the murder has been committed, when the play is three-quarters done.

***Areopagitica: a Speech of Mr John Milton for the Liberty of Unlicensed Printing to the Parliament of England.***   The title of John Milton's celebrated plea for a free press and free discussion (1644) takes its title from the Greek *Areopagus*, the hill of Ares in Athens where the highest judicial tribunal of the city used to meet. Milton had earned the displeasure of the Parliamentary party with his four pamphlets on divorce, which were remarkably liberal for the times. The Parliamentarians used their own censorship of 1643 (having abolished the Star Chamber in 1641) and it was clear to Milton that an old restraint on personal liberty was being reimposed. He pointed out that Parliament was using the very weapon it had found objectionable in other hands; moreover the use of it would be a grave discouragement and affront to learning. Above all liberties Milton demanded the 'liberty to know, to utter, and to argue freely, according to conscience.'

*Argument against Abolishing Christianity, An*
A satirical pamphlet by Jonathan Swift, first
published in 1711. Swift proceeded on an
assumption – made for the purposes of his argument – that there was a popular movement in
favour of abolishing Christianity; the writer is
protesting mildly that such a step would be 'attended with some Inconveniences'. Swift, in this
pamphlet, was attacking the attitude to religion
among the powerful; he wanted Christianity to
be taken seriously, not merely used. Other satirical pamphlets in the same vein reinforced his
arguments: *The Sentiments of a Church of England
Man* (1711) had been a clear warning to adherents
of, and place seekers in, both the Whig and Tory
parties; and *A Letter Concerning the Sacramental
Test* (1709) turned a bright light on the Tory
practice of making do with the Dissenters as long
as the latter paid lip service to Church of England
requirements – what Swift called Occasional
Conformity. His *Project for the Advancement of
Religion* (1709) offers a solution, based on his
own unambiguous views, to the contemporary
problem of the Church's position in the State.

**Ariel**  Prospero's 'brave spirit' in *The Tempest* by
William Shakespeare. Ariel had been confined in
a cloven pine tree by the witch Sycorax, when
she ruled the island, for refusing to obey her.
Prospero released him by his magic art and uses
him in the execution of his plans. When they are
complete Prospero releases Ariel from his service.

**Armado, Don Adriano de**  In Shakespeare's
*Love's Labour's Lost*, the 'fantastical' Spaniard.
He is rich in words and illusions, if little else, and
falls in love with the dairymaid, Jaquenetta.

**Armin, Robert**  *c.*1580–1612.  One of the actors
in Shakespeare's company, The Lord Chamberlain's Men, Armin became the principal
comedian after Will Kemp's departure. He
contributed a considerable portion to a play that
gave him a fine part, *The History of the two Maids
of More-clacke* (published 1609). He was also the
author of the satirical prose tract *Foole upon Foole,
or, Six Sortes of Sottes* (1605), which he later enlarged as *A Nest of Ninnies* (1608), and a verse
translation of an Italian tale, *The Italian Taylor
and his Boy* (1609).

**Armstrong, John**  *c.*1709–79.  Armstrong was
the son of a minister of Roxburghshire. He
studied medicine at Edinburgh University and
practised it in London, where his fellow Scot,
James Thomson, was one of his friends; Armstrong contributed four stanzas to *The Castle of
Indolence*. He also wrote some medical works

and, in 1736, published *The Oeconomy of Love*, a
blank-verse sex manual for the instruction of the
newly married. *The Art of Preserving Health*
(1744) is a competent didactic work, quite
pleasantly done in the manner of Thomson.

*Arnalte and Lucinda*  A verse romance by Leonard Lawrence, published in 1639. See
**seventeenth-century verse romances**.

**Arnold, Sir Edwin**  1823–1904.  Arnold was
born at Gravesend in Kent and educated at King's
College, London, and University College, Oxford. He won the Newdigate Prize in 1852 with
his poem 'Belshazzar's Feast'. In 1856 he went to
India to become Principal of Deccan College,
Poona, and in 1861 joined the staff of *The Daily
Telegraph*. Arnold studied Eastern languages and
made a considerable reputation, publishing his
first translation, from Sanskrit, in 1861:
*Hitopadésa*, 'The Book of Good Counsels'. His
luxurious blank-verse epic on the life and teachings of the Buddha, *The Light of Asia* (1879), was
once enormously popular but is largely unknown
today. He did not repeat his success with his later
*The Light of the World* (1891).

**Arnold, Matthew**  1822–88.  The son of
Thomas Arnold, the headmaster of Rugby
School, Matthew Arnold was born at Laleham in
Middlesex. He was educated at Rugby and at
Oxford, where he went as a Balliol Scholar in
1841. In 1843 he won the Newdigate Prize for
poetry with 'Cromwell' and became a fellow of
Oriel College in 1845. He continued to write
poetry and, when he left Oxford, considered the
possibility of a diplomatic career and became
private secretary to Lord Lansdowne in 1847. He
accepted an appointment as Inspector of Schools
with no particular enthusiasm in 1851; he said
later that he had done so because it provided the
money for his marriage to Frances Lucy Wight-
man. But he became engrossed in his work and
earned considerable distinction. His recom-
mendations were far-sighted and his work in the
field of education helped to form his views as the
most distinguished social and political critic of
Victorian England. His position as a literary
critic is equally distinguished and developed
from his work as a poet.

Arnold's first volume of poems, *The Strayed
Reveller, and Other Poems* (1849), contained the
famous **The Forsaken Merman**. It attracted little
attention and he withdrew it from circulation
after a few weeks. He had no better success with
**Empedocles on Etna,** and Other Poems (1852),
which contained **Tristram and Iseult**, and he
withdrew that also. He was convinced that the

title poem was the reason for the book's failure and 15 years passed before Browning persuaded him to republish it. In 1853 he published a volume containing new and revised work, *Poems: A New Edition. The Scholar-Gipsy* and **Sohrab and Rustum** are among the new poems but it is of equal importance that Arnold, in his preface, made his first mark as a critic and a writer of fine lucid prose. He also made, with this volume, a reputation as a poet. *Poems: Second Series* (1855) contained 'Balder Dead' and 'Separation' and some fragments from the withdrawn 'Empedocles on Etna'. Arnold was appointed Professor of Poetry at Oxford in 1857 and with the exception of *Merope, A Tragedy* (1858) did not publish another volume for nine years. *New Poems* (1867) contained **Dover Beach**, *Thyrsis* (the elegy on the death of his friend Arthur Hugh Clough), and the republished 'Empedocles on Etna'.

Through these years Arnold continued his interest in education and in 1859, as Foreign Assistant Commissioner on Education, he went on a tour of European countries to study the organization of their primary schools. *The Popular Education of France, with Notices of that of Holland and Switzerland* (1861) followed the tour. *A French Eton* (1864) was an examination of a lycée in Toulouse. A further mission to Europe in 1865 resulted in *Schools and Universities on the Continent* (1868). A posthumous volume, *Reports on Elementary Schools 1852–1882*, was edited by Sir Francis Sandford (1889).

Arnold's third career, as a critic, continued with the three published lectures *On Translating Homer* (1861) and was fully established with the collection *Essays in Criticism* (first series, 1865). Arnold offered a wide range of subject and a tone and style influenced by Sainte-Beuve and Ernest Renan. He departed from the heaviness of the English critical writing of his time and made his points with deceptive ease. *The Study of Celtic Literature* (1867), *Culture and Anarchy* (1869), *St Paul and Protestantism* (1870), *Friendship's Garland* (1871), *Literature and Dogma* (1873), *God and the Bible* (1875), *Last Essays on Church and Religion* (1877), *Mixed Essays* (1879), and the posthumous *Essays in Criticism* (second series, 1889) examine every aspect of English culture and civilization in Arnold's time and question its accepted values. Arnold was disturbed by the vulgarity and complacence of the great Victorian public and by the hardness and self-seeking of the middle classes. He found his fellow men fond of advocating personal liberty but reluctant to assume the responsibilities to others that liberty brings.

Matthew Arnold's poetry was nearly all written by the time he was 45. Its most persistent theme is the isolation and alienation of man in the modern world, though the poet uses various settings for his statement. He seems to have abandoned poetry after making this statement and to have moved to a different medium to offer constructive criticism.

The recommended modern edition of Arnold's poetry is by Kenneth Allott (Longman's Annotated English Poets, 1965). Other editions are by C. B. Tinker and H. F. Lowry (Oxford Standard Authors, 1950) and by Kenneth Allott (Everyman's Library, 1965). Selections have been prepared by Lionel Trilling in *The Portable Arnold* (New York, 1949) and J. Bryson in *Poetry and Prose* (the Reynard Library, 1954). *The Complete Prose Works* of Matthew Arnold are edited by R. H. Super in 11 volumes (Vol. 1, 1960, Ann Arbor, Michigan) of which 6 have so far appeared, including *Culture and Anarchy* (Vol. 5, 1965). *Essays on English Literature* was edited by F. W. Bateson (1965).

**Arnold, Thomas** 1795–1842. The son of a customs collector, Arnold was born in the Isle of Wight and educated at Winchester School and Corpus Christi College, Oxford. He became a fellow of Oriel College in 1815 and was known as an exceptional classical scholar. In 1828 he was appointed headmaster of Rugby School, then at a low stage in its reputation. With his carefully prepared system of education, based upon religious training, he made it the first choice of middle-class parents who at that time were seeking 'public' (that is, private) schools for their offspring. His purpose was to educate the boys to a sense of duty and to realize the importance of character; he succeeded to a remarkable degree and Rugby became the model for English public schools. He was later caricatured by Lytton Strachey in *Eminent Victorians* (1918). Arnold was appointed Regius Professor of Modern History at Oxford in 1841. He published an edition of Thucydides (1830–35) and left unfinished his *History of Rome* (1838–42).

**Artegall, Sir** The knight of justice in Book V of Spenser's *The Faerie Queene*. He is loved by Britomart and kills the Soudan with the help of Prince Arthur. The Soudan represents Philip II of Spain.

**Artful Dodger, the** In Dickens's *Oliver Twist*, the sharp-witted juvenile criminal of Fagin's thieves' kitchen. He spots Oliver on the road to London and sees the hungry destitute boy as ideal material for Fagin's tuition. The Dodger is caught picking pockets and is facing transportation when he leaves the story in Chapter 43. His real name is Jack Dawkins.

**Arthur, King** That there was a historical Arthur is now generally accepted. He is named in the ancient annals of Wales, *Annales Cambriae*, in which the Battle of Mount Badon is named and dated (AD 518) as well as the Battle of Camlan (539), in which Arthur was killed. Nennius, believed to be the author of *Historia Britonum*, names him as a war leader who fought no less than 12 battles, including Mount Badon, against the Saxons. Geoffrey of Monmouth, in his early 12th-century *Historia Regum Britanniae*, turns Arthur into a romantic king aided by the magic of Merlin; he introduces into the story of an ancient king or leader the pre-Christian mythical elements of the ancient Welsh romances in which Arthur appears.

Wace of Jersey, a Norman writer who followed soon after Geoffrey of Monmouth, used the latter's work as a basis for his *Roman de Brut* or *Geste des Bretons* (*c.*1154) and introduced the Round Table into the story of Arthur. In the English language, Arthur did not appear until about 1200, when Layamon wrote his *Brut* (or *History of Britain*) in which magic is a strong feature. (*Brut* refers to a Trojan, Brutus, who, like Aeneas, sails away after the fall of Troy and founds another realm – Britain, in this case.)

Meanwhile the Arthurian story had been developed in France; the version in French by Wace may have prompted writers like Chrétien

---

Sir Bedivere, after the last battle, returns Excalibur to the lake at King Arthur's bidding. Arthur, mortally wounded, waits to hear of the sword's reception. From a medieval French manuscript, *MS 10294 f.94*, now in the British Library.

de Troyes, Thomas, and Robert de Boron to make use of the *matière de Bretagne* for their work. (For the French writers the Bretagne world was the Breton one – Brittany, Wales, Ireland, and Cornwall.) The Grail story and the story of Tristram, Launcelot, and others became intertwined with that of Arthur, and it is a feature of Malory's great work that Arthur occupies the chief place only at the beginning and at the end.

The Arthur of romance is begotten by Uther Pendragon on Igraine, wife of Gorlois of Cornwall, with the help of the magician Merlin. Arthur removes the sword from the stone, becomes King, and conquers as far as Iceland and the Orkneys. Guenever is the noble lady whom he marries, and his court is at Caerleon. He refuses to pay tribute to the Emperor and goes to war with Rome, leaving Guenever and the kingdom to his nephew Modred. He is about to taste victory when he is urged to return: Modred has seized his kingdom and Guenever. Arthur hurries back with Gawain, whom Modred kills when he lands. Arthur drives Modred back but in Cornwall, where Modred suffers defeat and death, Arthur is mortally wounded. He is taken to Avalon to be healed of his wounds and Guenever takes the veil. The Norman version by Wace leaves the story with the expectation that one day Arthur, healed of his wounds, will return and resume his kingdom. But in other versions Arthur dies of his wounds, and the Round Table comes to an end.

Malory, in his *Le Morte Darthur*, took the framework supplied by the existing Celtic, Breton, French, and English versions (some of which were versions of versions) and fashioned a book which includes the greater part of Arthurian legend, with the pre-Christian element largely intact. A curious mixture of mythological elements occurs in Malory in the defeat of Modred (whom he calls Mordred). Mordred is actually Arthur's son by his incestuous union with Morgause, his half-sister and the wife of King Lot of Orkney.

See also **Gildas, St**; *Black Book of Carmarthen, The*; *Taliesin, The Book of*; *Kulhwch and Olwen*; *Mabinogion, The*; *Dream of Rhonabwy, The*; *Lady of the Fountain, The*; *Peredur, Son of Evrawg*; *Gereint and Enid*; *Launfal, Sir*; *Golagros and Gawain*; *Awntyrs of Arthure at the Terne Wathelyne, The*; *Ywain and Gawain*; *Morte Darthur, Le*; *Morte Arthure*; and *Gawain and the Green Knight, Sir*.

**Arthur, Prince** In Spenser's *The Faerie Queene*, the symbol of 'magnificence' – that is, in the perfection of all virtue. He takes part in the knights' adventures and helps bring them to a successful conclusion.

**Arthur, Prince, Duke of Britaine** King John's nephew in Shakespeare's play *King John*. He was the son of John's elder brother, Geoffrey, and Constance of Brittany. His claim to the throne (Arthur was born after Geoffrey's death) was strong; he was acknowledged as heir by Richard I. In *King John* he dies accidentally trying to gain his freedom but it is very likely, if never proved, that John had him murdered. The historical Arthur was 17 at the time of his death.

**Arviragus** The younger son of the king in Shakespeare's *Cymbeline*, stolen by Belarius and given the name Cadwal. He finds Fidele (Imogen) apparently dead and speaks the famous 'Fear no more the heat o' the sun' with his brother Guiderius when they lay her to rest.

*Ascension, The* A poem in Old English by Cynewulf, preserved in *The Exeter Book*. It forms the second part of the three-part poem *Christ*, which was once believed to be entirely by Cynewulf; but scholars now attribute positive authorship to *The Ascension* only. The poem deals with Christ's ascension and reception into heaven. A translation by C. W. Kennedy is included in his *Early English Christian Poetry* (1952).

**Ascham, Roger** 1515–68. Educated at St John's College, Cambridge, Ascham distinguished himself in classics and became Reader in Greek at Cambridge in 1538. He wrote his letters in Latin, as well as some poems, and wrote Greek more easily than he did English – though he was to write his major works in his own language and make a contribution to English prose. He was tutor to Princess Elizabeth and became Latin secretary to Edward VI. Though a Protestant he continued to serve Queen Mary in the same capacity and in 1558 became Queen Elizabeth's private tutor.

Ascham's *Toxophilus: The Schole of Shootinge Conteyned in Two Bookes* (1545) is a treatise on archery in dialogue form and it stresses the importance of physical training as part of education. It was dedicated to Henry VIII and insists on the superiority of the longbow over the crossbow. More famous is *The Schoolmaster* (*The Scholemaster: Or Plaine and Perfite Way of Teachyng Children the Latin Tong*), published in 1570 (two years after Ascham's death). In it he criticizes the disciplines prevailing in the education of his time; his own treatise is both practical and humane, and warns against the idleness and indulgence that often followed the time of learning.

Ascham lived and died a poor man because – according to Camden – he loved cock fighting (acknowledged in *The Schoolmaster*) and gambling (condemned in *Toxophilus*). His contribution to English prose was his unadorned style, much admired by Gabriel Harvey. Ascham kept to English and rejected the anglicizing of foreign words that was so much practised at the time.

An interesting note in *The Schoolmaster* is Ascham's denunciation of *Le Morte Darthur*, the pleasure of which, he declared, lay in its preoccupation with 'mans slaughter, and bold bawdrye'.

**Ashbery, John (Lawrence)** 1927– . Ashbery was born in Rochester, New York, and grew up on his father's farm at Sodus in New York State. He was educated at Deerfield (Mass.) Academy and the universities of Harvard, Columbia, and New York. He worked in publishing until 1955, when a Fulbright Scholarship enabled him to study in France. He became art critic for the European edition of the *New York Herald Tribune* and was actively involved in the publication of journals of aesthetics, returning to America in 1965. Ashbery published his first volume of poetry in 1953, *Turandot and Other Poems*. Other volumes are *Some Trees* (1956), *The Poems* (1960), *The Tennis Court Oath* (1962, Harriet Monroe Memorial Prize), *Rivers and Mountains* (1966), *Sunrise in Suburbia* and *Three Madrigals* (1968), *Fragment* (1969), *The Double Dreams of Spring* and *The New Spirit* (1970), *Three Poems* (1972, Shelley Memorial Award), *The Vermont Journal* (1975), *Self-Portrait in a Convex Mirror* (1977), *Houseboat Days* (1978), and *As We Know* (1979). Commenting on his poetry, Ashbery says: 'There are no themes or subjects in the usual sense, except the very broad one of an individual consciousness confronting or confronted by a world of external phenomena.' (*Contemporary Poets*, 1975). He has published three plays, *The Heroes* and *The Compromise* (1960) and *The Philosopher* (1964), and is the joint author of a novel, *A Nest of Ninnies* (1969, with James Schuyler).

*As I Lay Dying* A novel by William Faulkner, first published in 1930. It is Addie Bundren who lies dying, and her husband and children prepare to carry out her last wish to be buried in Jefferson, Mississippi, not on the remote hill farm where her marriage has brought her. The novel is an account of the family's transport of the coffin across country to Jefferson, an incredible journey beset by the vagaries of nature, a simpleminded father Anse, and an idiot son Darl. The daughter, Dewey Dell, is pregnant and looks forward to acquiring the 'medicine' to 'cure' her condition when they get to Jefferson; Anse looks forward to a new set of false teeth. It is a macabre comedy but has an extraordinary feeling of truth, and the author shirks no unpleasant detail.

**Asloan Manuscript, The**   See **Scottish anthologies and collections.**

**Aspern Papers, The**   A story by Henry James, first published in the *Atlantic Monthly*, from March to May 1888, and as the title story of a volume in the same year.

Jeffrey Aspern was a romantic poet of the early 19th century, who wrote a number of letters to a mistress, 'Juliana'. Juliana is the now aged Miss Bordereau, who lives in a crumbling palazzo in Venice with her niece, Miss Tina. An American editor (the narrator) takes lodgings in the palazzo under an assumed name; he wants the Aspern papers but he finds that Miss Bordereau is a shrewd old woman who has only let him rooms so that she can put some money by for Tina, an unattractive spinster.

The editor cultivates Tina and she is more than responsive; she is virtually confined to the house, where her aunt's principal activity seems to lie in introspection in darkened rooms – no one has ever been able to persuade her to yield up the Aspern papers or reveal their contents. The narrator's approaches are fielded with haughty skill and he confides his mission to Tina. Then Miss Bordereau falls ill and he foolishly attempts to rifle her desk while the household is preoccupied. But the old woman surprises him in the attempt; he is foiled and Miss Bordereau suffers a relapse.

Returning to Venice a fortnight later, he discovers that Miss Bordereau has died. Miss Tina receives him with warmth and he realizes that out of her inexperience she now has expectations of him. The Aspern papers? She could only give them to 'a relative' of the family. The veiled proposal is plain and the editor baulks at its implications. He leaves and when they next meet she dismisses him with dignity. The Aspern papers? She has burned them.

*The Aspern Papers* is justly famous, a short story of the highest quality from an author whose country is celebrated for its contributions to the form. Michael Redgrave made an excellent dramatization of the story, which enjoyed great success when it was presented in London in 1959. There was an unforgettable performance from Flora Robson as Miss Tina.

**Assembly of Ladies, The**   A poem of unknown authorship once attributed to Chaucer and probably a work of the mid- to late 15th century. The 'voice' in the poem is that of a woman but it is doubtful that the poem was a woman's work. The form is the familiar dream-vision allegory and the content concerns four ladies and their petitions to Lady Loyalty, who dwells in the house called Pleasant Regard. See also *Flower and the Leaf, The.*

**Asser**   d. 909.   The biographer of King Alfred was a Welsh monk of St David's, whose reputation as a scholar led to an invitation to the king's court at Winchester. He was the king's companion and helper from this time (*c*.885) until Alfred died. Asser received from the king the monasteries of Amesbury and Banwell and a grant of Exeter; later he became Bishop of Sherborne. He wrote his life of Alfred (up to 893) in Latin, and was also the author of a brief history (849–87).

Asser's brief life of Alfred has been the subject of scholarly disputes and his authorship has been denied by some. In 1731 the manuscript was lost in a fire that destroyed part of Sir Robert Bruce Cotton's collection; existing early printed editions are known to contain interpolations and also show evidence of editorial interference. But opinion, supported by the scholarship of W. H. Stevenson (*Asser's Life of Alfred, together with the Annals of St Neots erroneously ascribed to Asser,* Oxford 1904), favours Asser's book as an authentic memoir of the king by one who knew him well.

**Assingham, Fanny**   In *The Golden Bowl*, by Henry James, an American married to a retired English colonel, to whom she frequently relates the course of events. An inexhaustible interferer in her friends' lives, Fanny is the agent of Maggie Verver's marriage to Amerigo and later deservedly feels guilty about her concealment of Amerigo's earlier involvement with Charlotte Stant when the two become lovers.

**Astrophel and Stella**   A sonnet sequence by Sir Philip Sidney, probably begun in 1581 and circulated in manuscript in the following year. It was first published in 1591 with an epistle by Thomas Nashe, who was probably the editor; two further editions appeared in the same year. The inspiration for the sequence was the poet's love for Penelope Devereux, who was married against her will to Lord Rich. She was never in love with Sidney – she wanted Charles Blount, Earl of Devonshire, and he married her after her divorce from Rich. Astrophel (Greek *astrophil*) means star lover and Stella is Latin for star.

*Astrophel and Stella* was the first English sonnet sequence. Sidney's grace, ease, and command of the language was hard to equal, though there were many imitators; Spenser's *Amoretti* (1595) was the first to claim anything like the same attention. The most famous poem in Sidney's sequence is probably Sonnet XXXIX, beginning 'Come, Sleep! O Sleep, the certain knot of peace'.

**As You Like It** A comedy by William Shakespeare first produced *c*.1599 and published in the First Folio of 1623. The source of the play was Thomas Lodge's romance *Rosalynde*, published in 1590. The part of Touchstone was probably created by Robert Armin, since the clowns in Shakespeare's comedies become more complex at this stage in his career. Will Kemp, the creator of Dogberry and probably Bottom, left the company in 1600 and Armin, a more disciplined actor, replaced him. See **Kemp, Will** and *Henry IV*.

Rosalind and Celia are cousins; Celia's father is Duke Frederick, now in power, having usurped the ducal throne of his older brother, who is Rosalind's father. Orlando and Oliver are the sons of Sir Rowland de Boys: Oliver is the older brother and their father's will has given him charge of the estate; his cruelty has driven Orlando from home. Orlando takes part in a wrestling match at the court and defeats a powerful opponent. Rosalind and Celia watch the bout and Rosalind falls in love with Orlando. Duke Frederick is angered by this; Sir Rowland was a friend of the exiled duke. Rosalind is banished from the court.

Rosalind dresses as a country boy and calls herself Ganymede. She lives in the Forest of Arden with the clown Touchstone and Celia, who has accompanied her cousin. Celia calls herself Aliena and passes as Ganymede's sister. They meet Orlando there; he has joined the exiled duke, who also lives in the forest. Ganymede encourages Orlando to talk of Rosalind and leads him to confess his love for her. Oliver comes to the forest at the bidding of Duke Frederick, to kill Orlando and bring Celia back to the court. But he is attacked by a lioness and it is Orlando who saves him: Oliver emerges a changed man. He falls in love with Aliena and, happy in his reconciliation with the forgiving Orlando, arranges to marry her the following day. Ganymede promises Orlando that his Rosalind will be found for the next day also. The exiled duke presides over the nuptials: Rosalind and Celia are out of disguise now. The wicked Duke Frederick, they learn, had been preparing to attack and destroy his exiled brother and followers but has been dissuaded from his course by 'an old religious man'. He has relinquished the usurped throne and will become a monk.

The improbabilities – the disguises that no one can see through, the change in disposition undergone by Oliver and Duke Frederick – are lightly borne in this utterly charming play, the sunniest of all Shakespeare's comedies. As in *Much Ado About Nothing*, *The Merchant of Venice*, and *Twelfth Night*, there is a remarkable heroine: Rosalind takes her place with Beatrice, Portia, and Viola as a woman rarely found. She sparkles with wit and amorous teasing but the audience is never in any doubt that she loves. The play also has a memorable character in the melancholy Jaques, a wry observer of the human comedy, and there is a singularly happy invention in the puzzle of Silvius, the shepherd who loves Phebe, who loves Ganymede, who must be, since 'he' is Rosalind, 'for no woman'. Touchstone finds his Audrey and, being of rougher stuff than Rosalind, is rough in his disposal of Audrey's other suitor, William.

**Atalanta in Calydon** A verse drama by Algernon Charles Swinburne, first published in 1865. His intention was 'to do something original in English which might in some degree reproduce for English readers the likeness of a Greek tragedy with something of the true poetic life and charm'. The publication of *Atalanta in Calydon* made Swinburne famous. The subject is the myth of Meleager and the hunt for the Calydonian boar, a monster sent by the goddess Artemis to punish King Oeneus for neglecting to honour her. His queen, Althaea, is the mother of Meleager; at his birth the Fates promised him strength and good fortune but his life would last no longer than the stick burning in the hearth fire. When they had departed Althaea snatched the stick from the fire, put out the flames, and hid it. When a great hunt was organized to kill the boar one of the participants was the virgin huntress Atalanta, daughter of Iasius of Arcadia and a favourite of Artemis; Meleager fell in love with her. The boar was successfully killed but a quarrel arose over the distribution of the spoil (the hide and tusks); when the besotted Meleager gave everything to Atalanta his uncles, Toxeus and Plexippus (Althaea's brothers), objected. Meleager killed them, and Althaea, in revenge, brought out the stick that measured her son's life. She burned it and destroyed him.

The poem, dedicated to the memory of Walter Savage Landor, opens with the Chief Huntsman's address to Artemis and Apollo: 'Maiden, and mistress of the months and stars'. This is followed by the famous choric hymn to the goddess: 'When the hounds of spring are on winter's traces'. Equally famous is the comment of the chorus when Althaea goes to prepare her son for the hunt: 'Before the beginning of years There came to the making of man Time, with a gift of tears; Grief, with a glass that ran'.

***Athelston*** A short verse romance in Middle English of the mid-14th century. (See **metrical romances**.) The story, from an Old English source, tells of four men who meet in a forest and swear brotherhood. One of them, Athelston, gains the throne of England and is able to confer honours on the other three, who become Archbishop of Canterbury, Earl of Dover, and Earl of Stane; Stane marries Athelston's sister. Dover, out of jealousy, whispers to Athelston that Stane and his wife are plotting against the throne. Athelston imprisons them; his queen intercedes for them, and the angry king assaults her: a kick kills her unborn child. Canterbury now intercedes; Athelston orders him to resign his office but the archbishop retorts with excommunication. The threat of a popular rising makes Athelston give way. Stane undergoes trial by ordeal and is proved innocent; in the same test Dover is proved guilty and executed. The son of the Earl and Countess of Stane is made Athelston's heir and reigns as Edmund; the poem makes a romantic connection with history by identifying him with St Edmund. *Athelston* was edited by A. McIntosh Trounce for the Early English Text Society (1951).

***Atlantic Monthly, The*** This literary and contemporary affairs journal was founded in Boston in 1857 by Oliver Wendell Holmes and James Russell Lowell, who both wrote for it. Other contributors were Emerson, Longfellow, Whittier, and Harriet Beecher Stowe. At first it was principally a magazine of literature and art though its anti-slavery attitude was plain. Current affairs were more prominently featured when J. T. Fields became editor (1861–71) but less so when William Dean Howells took over (1871–81). Howells extended the range of the magazine; it had often been called the voice of New England 'Brahminism' but now drew its contributors from farther afield, including reviews and features on science and education. The magazine has maintained its high place among American journals.

***Atterbury, Francis*** 1662–1732. Atterbury was born at Milton Keynes in Buckinghamshire and educated at Westminster School and Christ Church, Oxford. After ordination, his progress in the church was rapid, in spite of his opposition to the crown and the bishops on behalf of the lower clergy. He became Bishop of Rochester and Dean of Westminster in 1713. In 1720 he was imprisoned for alleged complicity in a plot to restore the Stuarts; he was deprived of his offices and banished in 1723, to die in exile. He was a notable contributor to the Phalaris controversy (see **Temple, Sir William** and **Swift, Jonathan**). His principal published works were concerned with church dogma but his *Sermons and Discourses on Several Subjects and Occasions* (1723–34) are named by some scholars as the best of their time.

***At the Back of the North Wind*** See **MacDonald, George**.

***Aubrey, John*** 1626–97. Aubrey was born at Kingston in Wiltshire and educated at Trinity College, Oxford. His father left him a considerable estate, but unfortunately the estate brought Aubrey a good deal of litigation, which devoured his inheritance by the time he had reached his forties.

Aubrey became an antiquarian while still an undergraduate; but while he was very industrious in making collections of material on Surrey and Wiltshire he published none of it during his lifetime. He wrote a life of his friend Thomas Hobbes, which he gave to Anthony à Wood, with a mass of other autobiographical writings, for his *Athenae Oxoniensis*. This material was *Brief Lives*, which was first published in 1813 as Volume II of *Letters Written by Eminent Persons*. He left a manuscript, *A*

John Aubrey. A drawing by Faithorne in black-lead and India ink in the Ashmolean Museum, Oxford.

*Perambulation of Surrey*, which was published in Richard Rawlinson's edition as *The Natural History and Antiquities of the County of Surrey* in 1719. In fact the only work that Aubrey published in his lifetime was his *Miscellanies* (1696), a book about dreams, omens, and occult phenomena.

The *Brief Lives*, Aubrey's chief claim to fame, reflect the magpie mind that was no doubt the chief obstacle to his successful completion of any projects of his own. He was interested in everything he heard and, as the son of a gentleman of means, most doors were open to him. He put everything down and left Wood to sort it out; a note of Aubrey's on the Earl of Clarendon in fact led Wood to make the judgment that brought down the wrath of the 2nd Earl. But Aubrey's apparent lack of discipline in collecting facts about famous men put posterity in his debt. Much of what he recorded about Shakespeare, Ben Jonson, Sir Walter Raleigh, John Milton, and others was at several removes from first hand but it has a ring of delicious gossip containing a kernel of truth.

The standard edition of *Brief Lives* is the one by A. Clark (1895); a selection from Aubrey's works, by Anthony Powell, was published as *Brief Lives and Other Selected Writings* (1949). Aubrey's collection of material on Wiltshire was published in editions by J. Britton (*The Natural History of Wiltshire*, 1867) and J. E. Jackson (*Wiltshire, The Topographical Collections of John Aubrey*, 1862).

**Auden, W(ystan) H(ugh)** 1907–73. W. H. Auden was born in York but his childhood was spent in Birmingham, to where his family moved when he was a year old. He was educated at Gresham's School, Norfolk, and at Oxford University, where he was twice editor of the anthology *Oxford Poetry*, and became one of the left-wing English poets of the period. His first collection, *Poems* (1928), was privately printed by his friend and fellow poet Stephen Spender; his reputation as a sharp-edged and witty poet and critic of society was made with *The Orators* (1932) and grew while he earned his living as a teacher and continued to write. But during World War II his socialist preoccupations gave way to a growing interest in Protestant Christianity, marked by his *New Year Letter* (1941, called *The Double Man* in the USA). *For the Time Being* (1944), *The Age of Anxiety* (1947), *Nones* (1951), *The Shield of Achilles* (1955), and *Homage to Clio* (1960) are among the later collections. *The Age of Anxiety* was awarded the Pulitzer Prize.

Auden collaborated with his friends and contemporaries in *Letters from Iceland*, a book of verse

Left to right: W. H. Auden, Christopher Isherwood, and Stephen Spender. Detail from a photograph by Howard Coster, 1936.

and prose, with Louis MacNeice (1937); *Journey to a War*, commentary and verse after visiting China, with Christopher Isherwood (1939); plays with Christopher Isherwood – *The Dog Beneath the Skin* (1935), *The Ascent of F6* (1936), and *On the Frontier* (1938); and the opera libretti with Chester Kallman, *The Rake's Progress* (1951), *Elegy for Young Lovers* (1961), and *The Bassarids* (1966).

In 1938 Auden married Erika Mann, the daughter of Thomas Mann; he emigrated to the USA in 1939 and became an American citizen in 1945. In 1956 he became Professor of Poetry at the University of Oxford. His critical essays are published in *The Enchafed Flood* (1950) and *The Dyer's Hand* (1962).

**Audrey** In Shakespeare's *As You Like It*, the country girl with whom Touchstone, the self-exiled jester, consoles himself. From him she gets the dubious tribute that she is 'an ill-favoured thing sir, but mine own'.

**Audubon, John James** 1785–1851. The American painter and naturalist was of French parentage and was born in Haiti. He was educated in France, where one of his teachers was Jacques-Louis David. He returned to the New World in 1804 and lived on his father's estate in

Pennsylvania, travelling from there to Louisiana, Kentucky, and other parts of the USA. He opened a general store in Louisville after his father went bankrupt; but his partners in the business allowed him freedom to travel, observe, and record. *The Birds of North America*, his most famous work, was published over a period of nine years (1831–39) as *Ornithological Biography*. *Viviparous Quadrupeds of North America* was a collaboration with the naturalist John Bachman; this was published as two volumes of plates (1824–25) and three volumes of text (1846–54).

Audubon's journals contain material of great interest and extracts were published in 1926 (*Delineations of American Scenery and Character*), 1929 (*Journal of John James Audubon, Made during his Trip to New Orleans in 1820–1821*), and 1940 (*Audubon's America*). Audubon was an industrious portrait painter, but his fame rests on his fine work as an artist–naturalist.

**Aufidius, Tullus** The Volscian general of Shakespeare's *Coriolanus*. He was defeated in battle by Coriolanus, who later turns to him as an ally to revenge himself on Rome. Aufidius has an admiration for Coriolanus but he is deeply jealous of him. His feelings turn to hatred when Coriolanus withdraws the Volscian army from Rome and he doesn't hesitate to destroy him.

*Auguries of Innocence* See **Blake, William**.

**Augustan age** In English literature the Augustan age usually refers to the reign of Queen Anne, or the age of Joseph Addison and Alexander Pope and their contemporaries; or English literature from Dryden to the beginning of the Georgian period. The term is rather a silly one; an Augustan age is more correctly an age of literary eminence, such as the reign of the Emperor Augustus and the great period of the Latin poets – Virgil, Ovid, Tibullus, Horace, and others – and it could be reasonably argued that there were greater periods of eminence in English literature than the one termed Augustan. Stylistically, it can be used to represent the post-Restoration period and the movement away from coarseness and licence. On the whole, however, it would be better if the term were not used at all.

*Auld Lang Syne* See **Ayton, Sir Robert** and **Burns, Robert**.

*Aureng-Zebe* A tragedy by John Dryden, first produced in November 1675, and first published in 1676. It was the last of his plays to be written in rhymed couplets. The story, set in Mogul India, concerns the love story of Aureng-Zebe and his betrothed Indamora, a captive queen, and the struggle for power in the reign of Shah Jehan. The play has only a sketchy relation to history but is regarded as one of Dryden's most successful works for the theatre.

Aureng-Zebe's antagonist is Morat, son of Shah Jehan's second wife Nourmahal; both Morat and the emperor lust after Indamora, and Aureng-Zebe's life is further complicated by the advances of Nourmahal. In spite of himself, Aureng-Zebe becomes jealous when he realizes that his father and stepbrother covet Indamora. The plot reaches a climax in the struggle for the throne, in which Aureng-Zebe remains loyal to Shah Jehan and Morat is killed. Nourmahal takes poison after her son's death, and Shah Jehan, reconciled with his son, withdraws his attentions from Indamora.

Dryden's tragedies are very rarely revived and their theatrical quality is difficult to assess; however, *Aureng-Zebe* is often praised for its fine characterization, particularly of the ambitious Morat, his fiery and passionate mother Nourmahal, and the calm and courageous Indamora.

*Aurora Leigh* A romance in blank verse by Elizabeth Barrett Browning, first published in 1857. The poet's views on a number of subjects are expressed during the course of the narrative. She was, at this stage of her career, principally interested in writing about the position of women and the plight of the poor. She had been happily married to Robert Browning since 1846, and the political and social questions which had always interested her now received her full attention. She was also actively interested in the cause of Italian freedom from the Austrian yoke. The subject of *Aurora Leigh* is the life and development of a woman who wants to make writing her career; Aurora herself is the narrator.

Aurora Leigh is the daughter of an English father and an Italian mother; her mother has died and her father has brought her up in Italy. When her father dies Aurora is 13; she is sent to England to the care of her father's sister, a maiden aunt who wants to make Aurora into a young lady and educates her with this in mind. But Aurora finds her father's library more rewarding and becomes interested in poetry. Her cousin, Romney Leigh, is heir to the family fortune and interested in philanthropy and social reform. He proposes to Aurora when she is 20; but it is clear that he wants her to give up her literary ambitions and support his work. Aurora declines, to her aunt's intense annoyance; she had never taken Aurora's published verse seriously and saw Romney as the perfect match.

Six months later the aunt dies and Aurora inherits an income of £300 a year. She could also have £30,000 from Romney but refuses his generous gift and departs for London, hoping for a career. Romney pursues his social programme of schools, hospitals, and almshouses and succours a poor girl, Marian Erle, who has fled from her drunken parents and wretched existence. He sets her up in London as a seamstress. Aurora has been in London for three years, earning money by journalism while striving to improve her poetry, and has earned a small reputation. One day she is visited by the coarse and confident Lady Waldemar, who wants to marry Romney Leigh. But Aurora's cousin intends to marry Marian Erle and must be dissuaded from such a foolish course. Aurora visits Marian, hears her story, and refuses to interfere. She tells no one of Lady Waldemar's visit.

Marian jilts Romney and disappears, leaving him a letter declaring that she could not be happy as his wife. Aurora goes on with her career and concentrates on a major work about contemporary life. She is lonely and depressed to learn that Romney is to marry Lady Waldemar. He has turned Leigh Hall into a home for working women. Aurora decides to go back to Italy after completing her poem, and at her first stop in Paris she meets Marian, who now has an illegitimate son. She explains to Aurora that Lady Waldemar had visited her several times and convinced her that Romney's proposal was prompted by his social conscience in spite of his true love for her, Lady Waldemar. Marian, who had accepted Romney out of gratitude, agreed to Lady Waldemar's plan for her emigration. But she was tricked, abandoned when the ship reached France, and raped. She now supports herself and her son by gruelling labour as a seamstress. Aurora takes Marian and her baby with her to Florence, where the two women enjoy relative happiness. But a letter from England makes Aurora realize that she had indeed loved Romney.

Romney arrives in Florence and Aurora believes him married to Lady Waldemar. But he is not; now that he knows Marian's whereabouts he wants to marry her. Marian refuses him; her child is her whole life and she will not prejudice his future by marriage to a man she does not love and with whom she would have legitimate children. Aurora realizes that Romney is blind. Lady Waldemar has deserted him, bored by his philanthropy, and Leigh Hall has been destroyed in a fire started by its unruly inhabitants. Romney lost his sight trying to save a Van Dyke painting. Aurora and Romney declare their love and Romney asks that Aurora's poetry become a voice for both of them.

The book enjoyed a great success when it was published but a reading of it now is an exercise in patience. The echoes of Elizabeth Gaskell, Charlotte Brontë, and Eugène Sue (*Les Mystères de Paris*) are distractingly loud. Mrs Browning's knowledge of ordinary domestic economics was obviously slight: Aurora's income of £300 a year would have enabled her to live comfortably in London in the 1850s without any lonely struggle in modest lodgings, doing hack work to pay the household bills. The heroine narrator of *Aurora Leigh* now seems unconvincing and the poem as a whole overlong.

**Austen, Jane** 1775–1817.   Jane Austen was born at Steventon in Hampshire where her father, who was also her tutor, was the rector. She lived at Steventon until her father retired in 1801, when they moved to Bath. When her father died she lived at Southampton for a while, then at Chawton Cottage near Alton in her home county. She died at Winchester at the age of 41 and she is buried there.

That the life of one of England's best-loved novelists can be related so simply will surprise many of those who have read and loved her books. She was a person of warm affections; she

Jane Austen. A detail from an unfinished sketch by her sister Cassandra, 1810. This is the only authentic likeness of the author. National Portrait Gallery, London.

had five brothers and was happy with them – happiest perhaps in the company of her sister Cassandra. She was apparently frivolous in her girlhood and there is little evidence of an attachment of any moment to any young man: there is no evidence whatever that this caused her any unhappiness. She progressed gracefully toward being a chaperone and, one feels certain, observed her world with absorbed interest. She enjoyed reading – Mrs Radcliffe, Samuel Richardson, and Fanny Burney – and her formidable intelligence probably rejected all contrivance even in the authors whom she liked. This intelligence, and her wit, showed itself early: Jane was 15 when she wrote *Love and Friendship*, a delightful burlesque of Richardson.

The work of the great 18th-century novelists departed from the neoclassicism of the early decades of the century and gave us English life and social customs in fiction; the comedy of manners continued while the apparently flourishing gothic romances did not. The work of Richardson, Fielding, and Smollett was followed by that of Fanny Burney and Maria Edgeworth, smaller in scale and subtler in tone, admitting the reader to an easier identification with characters and situations. The author of *Pride and Prejudice, Mansfield Park, Persuasion,* and the rest brought the comedy of manners to a level of excellence that transcended her times. It is difficult to think of Fielding's characters, or Richardson's, or Smollett's – or for that matter of Scott's or Dickens's – outside the pages of their novels but Jane's are met in every walk of life. Custom and manners make demands on character and impose the moral boundaries. Jane Austen's exploration of relationship and motive is not confined by those boundaries; she doesn't attempt the task of defining them but she demonstrates how life is met and measured within them. She is moral, certainly, but never prim; a prim woman could never have written *Mansfield Park*.

Jane Austen's novels are an object lesson to aspiring writers, though it must necessarily be borne in mind that neither her wit nor her intelligence can be emulated. But her precision and economy, her knowledge of the world she wrote about, and her wisdom in using that world alone for her subject – all these factors help to account for her success. She worked hard, too; the sextet of famous works contains only one that was written with confident speed – *Emma* – and the author had four successful novels behind her by then. That Jane Austen's world is a limited one is acknowledged, and she has been criticized for that. But the criticism has no validity: it is

hardly more than a criticism of her for succeeding. Because she does succeed; her character drawing is faultless and the consistency of her characters complete. The way they change as the comedy progresses is entirely a matter of that character – Elizabeth Bennet, Anne Elliot, Emma Woodhouse – responding to events, but no one could say, for instance, that Emma is a different woman at the end of the novel. She is nicer and we like her better – she has learned that her vaunted values are a personal conceit – but she is still Emma. Jane Austen, it should never be forgotten, was the first novelist to portray a middle-class society, the one she knew; she did it with remarkable subtlety and she makes it a reflection of infinitely more.

The first of her published novels was **Sense and Sensibility** in 1811. The next was **Pride and Prejudice** (1813), then **Mansfield Park** (1814) and **Emma** (1816). **Northanger Abbey** was first sold to a publisher in 1803 but he did not issue it and she retrieved the manuscript in 1816. **Persuasion** was completed in 1816, the year before she died, and it was published posthumously, with *Northanger Abbey*, in 1818. We also have a tantalizing fragment of a novel, **Sanditon**, which Jane was working on during the year she died.

**Autobiography of a Super-Tramp** See **Davies, W(illiam) H(enry)**.

**Autocrat of the Breakfast Table, The** Essays, poems, and occasional pieces in the form of table talk in a Boston boarding house by the elder Oliver Wendell Holmes. The papers first appeared in *The Atlantic Monthly* and were first published in 1858. Among those present at the 'breakfast table' are a schoolmistress, the landlady and her daughter, a divinity student, a poor relation, and an old gentleman. The autocrat is the author and Holmes's view of life and the character of New England is conveyed with wit and warmth.

See also **Holmes, Oliver Wendell (i)**.

**Autolycus** In Shakespeare's *The Winter's Tale* he is 'a rogue' (and a shameless one), who fleeces the rustics during the pastoral merrymaking in Act IV.

**Ave Atque Vale** A poem by Algernon Charles Swinburne, first published in *The Fortnightly Review* in January 1868. Swinburne read of the death of Charles Baudelaire in a French newspaper in April 1867; the poem is an elegy on the passing of the French master whom Swinburne so much admired. Baudelaire, though seriously ill, did not die and the report was premature. Swinburne completed the poem and put it away;

but the French poet did die in August of that year. The poem was included in *Poems and Ballads* (second series, 1878).

**Awake and Sing!**  See **Odets, Clifford**.

**Awakening, The**  A novel by Kate Chopin, first published in 1899.

Edna Pontellier, from Kentucky, is the wife of Leonce Pontellier, a successful Creole speculator. They are spending the summer at Mme Lebrun's holiday establishment at Grand Isle and Edna is very struck by the freedom of expression among her Creole friends, particularly the beautiful Adèle Ratignolle, who is devoted to Edna and to whom she seems the personification of womanly grace. Robert Lebrun, her hostess's eldest son, is assiduous in his attentions towards Edna; this is accepted with equanimity by her husband but Adèle is disturbed by the effect this is having on Edna – a woman whose upbringing has left her unprepared. Adèle speaks to Robert in terms which they both understand and soon after that Robert, attendant on Edna throughout a whole day, behaves like a perfect gentleman. Edna, however, has begun to respond to Robert's presence and is stunned when he departs abruptly for Mexico – Robert realizes the only real conclusion that their association can have. Edna has never looked to the future; but now she is appalled at being left. In a conversation with Adèle she tries to explain that, notwithstanding the externals of her life and what she owes her husband and children, she is just beginning to comprehend her own physical identity – this identity she will surrender to nothing.

The Pontelliers return to New Orleans and it is soon obvious to her husband and to Adèle that Edna's grasp of the outward essentials of life is slipping – her unpredictable flouting of convention causes them uneasiness. She seeks out Mademoiselle Reisz, the cynical old musician with whom Robert had been impressed at Grand Isle, and starts to mix with a rather raffish set, among whom is the persistent amorist Arobin. Edna is stunned to discover that, while she has heard nothing from him, Robert writes regularly to Mademoiselle Reisz. Then her husband goes to New York on business and her children go to their grandmother at Iberville. Edna, alone for the first time, is aware of overwhelming relief. She accepts Arobin, calmly and without love. She loves Robert – but Robert has gone. His younger brother, Victor, makes it plain that he has hopes but Edna, believing herself in command of her life now, keeps him at arm's length. Adèle, expecting a baby, asks Edna if she will come to her when delivery is due; Edna promises

her that she will but simply sidesteps Adèle's delicately offered advice. Then Robert returns.

The author traces, with great subtlety, Edna's progress towards a discovery that she is not, as wife and mother, a free woman in her own world – and cannot be. Men order the boundaries of a woman's life after nature has already ordered its place. But Edna has become more self-aware and will not accept life in those terms. She comprehends that even Robert's love, which he has now declared, will impose conditions on her; that she could become *his* after having belonged to Leonce. It is clear that Robert wants her for himself and Edna cannot endure the thought of belonging to anyone. She takes her life.

A paperback edition of *The Awakening* was published in February 1978 by Virago Ltd.

**Awkward Age, The**  A novel by Henry James, first published in *Harper's Weekly*, from October to December 1898, and in volume form (with revisions) in 1899.

Nanda Brookenham's awkward age is the period of transition from her entry into her mother's London salon and the marriage market to her decision to be in charge of her own life. The story relates Nanda's attachment to two men: Vanderbank and Mitchett. Her mother, Mrs Brookenham, is also in love with Vanderbank, while Mitchett is sought by the Duchess as a husband for her niece, Aggie. The Duchess, to gain her purpose, will use her knowledge of Mrs Brookenham and Vanderbank; but Mrs Brookenham knows of the Duchess's affair with Lord Petherton – so the ladies are evenly matched. But Nanda, observing all this, has also learned more than the senior ladies might think; her friend Tishy Grendon is unhappily married and her confidences give Nanda some knowledge of the world.

Nanda attracts the attention of Mr Longdon, who is returning to London society after a long self-imposed absence. He once loved Nanda's grandmother and is touched by the girl's resemblance to her. They become friends and he sympathizes with her point of view. When he realizes that she would be happy to marry Vanderbank he gives her a large dowry; Vanderbank is ambitious and Longdon hopes this will attract him. Mitchett, who has been hopeful of marrying Nanda, leaves the field and marries Aggie; but still Vanderbank does not propose. He is finally alienated when Mrs Brookenham, seeing Nanda as a loser in the market, orders her daughter to leave Mr Longdon's house and return to London – where Vanderbank is a regular visitor to her salon.

Mrs Brookenham has made the wrong move. Vanderbank, it is now clear, does not want to marry. Nanda will not consent to being a property – which is how her mother, knowingly or not, has been regarding her. She establishes herself in a separate suite and later goes to live at Longdon's country house. They understand each other and Nanda has emerged from the awkward age.

The novel is written almost entirely in dialogue – dialogue that is, as R. C. Churchill puts it, 'of a kind that has seldom been heard outside the imagination of the author'. True – and also true of the dialogue in many fine comedies. In *The Awkward Age* the dialogue dazzles, like the glitter of the salons that Nanda eventually rejects when she understands that they are, for girls like herself and Aggie and Tishy, the setting for a marriage market. For a man like Vanderbank they are preferable to the responsibilities of marriage and the reader may well speculate on the future of Vanderbank in the setting he has chosen. One cannot help feeling that the future of Nanda promises rather more.

**Awntyrs of Arthure at the Terne Wathelyne, The** A Middle English romance in alliterative verse of the 14th century. (See **metrical romances**.) There are two *awntyrs* (adventures) but strictly speaking neither is Arthur's. The Terne Wathelyne is Wadling Tarn near Hesket in Cumberland; Arthur and his court are at Carlisle and they are enjoying a day's hunting. A storm comes up and Dame Gaynoure (Guinevere), escorted by Gawain, is confronted with a fearful figure which emerges from the waters of the tarn. Gawain addresses the spectre, which in turn replies that she is come 'To speke with youre Qwene'. It is the tormented spirit of Gaynoure's mother who warns Gaynoure that she is paying the price for her paramours and passions. When addressed by Gawain she prophesies the end of the Round Table, Arthur's last battle, and Gawain's death. The spectre fades away like mist, and a horn call from the hunting party brings Gaynoure and Gawain back to the concerns of the present. The second adventure tells of the combat between Galleron of Galway and Gawain: Arthur had taken Galleron's lands and given them to Gawain. Peace is restored when Arthur returns Galleron's lands, and makes Gawain lord of Wales in recompense. The text of *The Awntyrs* was edited by J. Pinkerton (1792), by D. Laing in *Ancient Popular Poetry of Scotland* (1822), by J. Robson in *Three Early English Metrical Romances* (1842), by F. J. Amours for the Scottish Text Society (1897), and by R. J. Gates (Philadelphia, 1969).

**Ayala's Angel** A novel by Anthony Trollope, first published in 1881.

Egbert Dormer's death leaves his two daughters, Ayala and Lucy, penniless and orphaned. Dormer, an artist, had been extravagant and life had been comfortable: at his death there were only debts. Ayala is taken in by Aunt Emmeline, wife of Sir Thomas Tringle; she is vulgar and smug in her affluence – Sir Thomas is a millionaire. Lucy goes to her uncle, Reginald Dosett, a civil servant of modest means, with a depressingly conscientious wife, in a dull little house in Notting Hill.

Ayala proves to lack the deference to her relations and cousins expected by her aunt. Lucy is miserable and rebellious in her uncle's drab little home. The two households effect an exchange, but both girls continue to disappoint. Lucy falls in love with a penniless artist, Isadore Hamel, while Ayala refuses three promising suitors, among them Tom Tringle, her cousin. The others are Captain Batsby and Colonel Stubbs. Colonel Stubbs persists and in spite of his unpromising looks wins Ayala in the end – he is the Angel her romantic nature had sought. He is also generous and provides for Lucy and Isadore.

The novel is a social comedy, handled with considerable success. The Tringle ménage, tiresome in its affluence, and the Dosett, tiresome in its rectitude, are both repugnant in their different ways to the Dormer girls, after their father's relaxed and unpretentious household.

**Aylwin** See **Watts-Dunton, Walter Theodore**.

**Ayrshire Legatees, The** A novel by John Galt, first published in 1820.

Dr Zachariah Pringle and his family go to London to take possession of a legacy. The year is 1820 and an eventful one; George III dies, and the new reign is immediately plunged into the scandal of George IV's relationship with Queen Caroline. These and other matters, and the impact of the capital, are the subjects of Dr Pringle and his family's correspondence with their friends in Scotland and provide the shape of the book.

**Ayton** (*or* **Aytoun**), **Sir Robert** 1570–1638. Educated at St Andrews, Ayton became secretary to Anne of Denmark, James I's queen, and held the same appointment to the next queen, Henrietta Maria. His family were wealthy landowners in Fifeshire descended from an illegitimate scion of the Stuart house.

Ayton was the friend of Ben Jonson and Thomas Hobbes and he wrote with ease in

French, Greek, and Latin. A minor figure in English literature, he was probably the first Scot to write in the English of the south as opposed to the Scottish of his contemporaries. His verses are elegant and spare; they are memorable and popular with anthologists: 'The Exercise of Affection', 'To an Inconstant Mistress', and 'Inconstancy Reproved' are well known. Best known of all is the song beginning 'Should old acquaintance be forgot', which was credited to Ayton by James Watson in 1711. The melody to which Burns' more celebrated version is sung is an old Scots air called 'Old lang syne' and would have been known to Ayton. However, Ayton's song is more directly romantic in tone than Burns'. Ayton's English and Latin poems were published in 1963 in an edition prepared by C. B. Gullans for the Scottish Texts Society. A selection of his English songs and poems by H. M. Shire was published in 1961.

**Aytoun, William Edmonstoune** 1813–65. Aytoun, the son of an Edinburgh lawyer, was educated at the Academy of Edinburgh. He went on to the university and became both lawyer and man of letters. A firm Scots Tory, he was awarded a sheriffdom in Orkney in 1853 for services to the party. The appointment was a sinecure; Aytoun was already Professor of Rhetoric and Belles Lettres at Edinburgh. Through his father-in-law, John Wilson, Aytoun began to write for *Blackwood's Magazine*. He is not remembered as an original poet but his *Lays of the Scottish Cavaliers* (1849) and *The Ballads of Scotland* (1858) once enjoyed considerable popularity. Aytoun invented the term 'spasmodic' to describe the work of Sydney Dobell, Philip James Bailey, and Alexander Smith; he published **Firmilian, or The Student of Badajoz: A Spasmodic Tragedy** (1854), which satirized them brilliantly. He exercised his gift for parody again in *The Bon Gaultier Ballads* (1855) with Theodore Martin; in this the poetry of both Tennyson and Elizabeth Barrett Browning was satirized.

*Azarias* A poem of 75 lines in Old English, preserved in *The Exeter Book*. It tells the story, taken from the Book of Daniel, of the children in the fiery furnace.

# B

**B., Mr** The heroine's would-be seducer in *Pamela, or Virtue Rewarded* by Samuel Richardson. A squire and a Justice of the Peace, he finds the maidservant Pamela alone when his mother dies and does not hesitate to plan her seduction. Pamela's helplessness causes no particular concern in the circles in which Mr B. moves.

*Back to Methuselah* A play in five parts by George Bernard Shaw, subtitled 'A Metabiological Pentateuch'. It was published in 1921 and first produced at the Garrick Theatre, New York, in February 1922. The first production in England was by Barry Jackson at the Birmingham Repertory Theatre in October 1923. In his postscript, which appeared as late as 1944 when Shaw was 89, he wrote of the modern world's dilemma: '...civilization means stabilization; and creative evolution means change. As the two must operate together we must carefully define their spheres, and co-ordinate them instead of quarrelling and persecuting as we do at present. We must not stay as we are, doing always what was done last time, or we shall stick in the mud. Yet neither must we undertake a new world as catastrophic Utopians, and wreck our civilization in our hurry to mend it.' Shaw wrote his postscript before the first nuclear bomb was used but his point remains valid. The creative evolution that is so important a feature of *Back to Methuselah* is a positive idea, in opposition to the resignation and confusion that followed the eclipse of religion and the impact of Darwin: 'The will to do anything can and does, at a certain pitch of intensity set up by conviction of its necessity, create and organize new tissue to do it with.' The five parts of the play have separate titles.

*In the Beginning*. The setting is the Garden of Eden, with Adam and Eve contemplating death for the first time; a fawn has tripped and broken its neck and the mystery of existence and continuity confronts them. From the Serpent Eve learns of conception and birth and imagination, and this does something to dissipate the fear and uncertainty brought to her mind and Adam's when they found the dead fawn. The Serpent tells how Lilith, who came before Adam and Eve, saw the necessity of renewal, and out of herself by sheer will-power had created two, male and female, the burden of renewal being too much for one to bear.

'A few centuries later' in Mesopotamia, Adam delves and Eve spins, and Cain, the first murderer, scorns his endlessly toiling parents. He killed Abel – but Abel killed his creatures and offered them in fire, as the Voice had bidden him. Cain had made offering of the results of his toil, and had been rejected: killing was right, obviously. Eve, repelled by her son's delight in destruction as a way of life, is also disgusted by Adam's dogged labour. There must be something more;

she is certain of that, though she does not know what it is.

*The Gospel of the Brothers Barnabas*. The place is Hampstead and the time is the 1920s. In this part of the play the author introduces the idea of Creative Evolution. Franklyn Barnabas was once in the church and has been involved in politics; he is now a philosopher and he has written a book on longevity. Conrad Barnabas is a biologist. Burge, ex-prime minister, and Lubin, a rival politician, call on Franklyn to enlist his aid in a coming election. Franklyn replies that if asked to speak he will proclaim the Gospel of the Brothers Barnabas: the need to live at least 300 years, since man only attains the beginning of wisdom as his life draws to a close. Among those present are a young rector, Haslam, and a parlour maid.

*The Thing Happens*. The scene is 'The official parlour of the President of the British Islands', and the time is AD 2170. Burge-Lubin, a composite of the politicians in the second part, is President. The play turns on the consternation aroused by the discovery that the Archbishop of York, a middle-aged-looking man, has been active in various careers for an inexplicable length of time. Summoned by the president, he looks very like the young rector of the second part. He declares, under threat of being called a fraud and a swindler, that he is 283 years old. The Domestic Minister, Mrs Lutestring, arrives to deliver her quarterly report, and recognizes him. She was a parlour maid in the second part; now she is 274 years old, and the significance of meeting another long-liver prompts both the archbishop and Mrs Lutestring to seize the moment, especially as each reveals the existence of others who have lived for centuries. They decide to marry.

*The Tragedy of an Elderly Gentleman*. The scene is Galway and the time is AD 3000. The centre of the British Empire has moved east, and the capital is Baghdad. An elderly gentleman has made a pilgrimage to the islands of his ancestors, Bolge and Bluebin, accompanying his son-in-law, an English envoy, and a warlike emperor, travelling incognito, who have come to consult the Oracle of the ancient land. The elderly gentleman is baffled by the inhabitants, who look young enough to be his children but who are as old, or older, than he is. The vestiges of his dignity, which he protects by pompous and oblique utterance, fall away in conversation with the youthful long-livers, who have a language shorn of metaphor and symbol. The warlike emperor foolishly tries to intimidate the Oracle, who makes short work of him. The envoy's question is one concerning party politics and a coming election, and the Oracle replies, 'Go home, poor fool.' When the envoy makes it clear to the elderly gentleman that he will take back a mendacious report of the Oracle's answer the old man despairs – his whole world has begun to disgust him. He pleads with the Oracle to allow him to stay, and in pity she sends him to a quiet death at her feet.

*As Far as Thought Can Reach*. The time is AD 21920, and a group of young people are disclosed in a sunlit glade before a Temple. They are all born from eggs, fully grown – a girl is delivered from her egg by a She Ancient and joins them. Pygmalion has made two artificial people, one male and one female. The male announces himself as Ozymandias and speaks in the language of Shelley's poem; the female emulates him, announcing herself as Cleopatra Semiramis. She is quarrelsome and jealous and when Pygmalion intervenes she bites his hand. From this he dies and the She Ancient and He Ancient are obliged to take charge. They warn the young people of the dangerous folly of making living toys; let them play with dolls, which are not dangerous. In the discussion that follows the Ancients talk of what has gone before and what their ultimate destiny will be: immortality, the escape from matter into intelligence, into a vortex of pure thought – thought will be life eternal.

When night falls and Ancients and young people disperse, the spirits of Adam, Eve, Cain, and the Serpent appear and comment on what has become of the race whose beginnings they witnessed. More important than any of them is Lilith, who delivers a fine monologue which brings the play to an end. 'I can wait . . . I have waited always to see what they will do tomorrow. Let them feed that appetite well for me. I say, let them dread, of all things, stagnation; for from that moment I, Lilith, lose hope and faith in them, they are doomed.'

**Bacon, Francis** 1561–1626. Francis, eighth and youngest son of Sir Nicholas Bacon, Lord Keeper of the Seal to Elizabeth I, was born at York House in the Strand in London. He entered Trinity College, Cambridge, in 1573 and Gray's Inn in 1576. Ambitious for a public career, he entered the service of the English ambassador in Paris to study diplomacy. He was obliged to return to London upon the death of his father in 1579 and found it necessary to engage in a profession – his father had left him without means. He tried to find an official post but neither his parentage nor his connections (his mother was related to the powerful Cecils) availed him anything and he turned to the law. Bacon's gifts

Francis Bacon. A detail from the portrait by J. Vanderbank in the National Portrait Gallery, London.

in this field were soon apparent and the queen sometimes asked his counsel; the Earl of Essex became his patron and he entered parliament in 1584. He opposed the queen's tax programme with remarkable efficiency and his quality as a parliamentarian was as obvious as his quality as a lawyer. He did not rise: Elizabeth was not a woman to oppose and she never liked him, though she used his talents in preparing the case against Essex. Bacon prosecuted his erstwhile friend and benefactor with cold-blooded skill.

His rise began in the next reign; James I was impressed with Bacon's performance in parliament and made him Solicitor-General in 1607. The next year Bacon became Clerk of the Star Chamber; he became Attorney-General in 1613, Lord Keeper of the Seal in 1617, and Lord Chancellor in 1618. In 1618 he was also made Baron Verulam; in 1621 he became Viscount St Albans. He married Alice Bernham in 1606.

Bacon's chief rival in his field was Edward Coke, who from his position as Chief Justice of the King's Bench had quarrelled ceaselessly with the Court of Chancery until the king dismissed him in 1616. In 1620, when a commission was authorized by parliament to examine abuses in the courts of justice, Coke instigated a charge of bribery and corruption against the Lord Chancellor. Bacon admitted that he had received bribes from suitors in his court but he later wrote to the king and protested that, while he had accepted gifts, he had never sought to prevent the course of justice and it is true that almost none of his judicial decisions were ever reversed. But Coke and the rest of Bacon's enemies (there were many – hardly anyone seems to have liked him) succeeded in bringing him down. He was disgraced and retired into private life in 1621.

But the man whom nobody liked became, in a field that was closer to his apparently stony heart than the law in which he shone so brightly, the philosopher and writer whom generations have admired. While at Cambridge Bacon had perceived that Aristotle had served his purpose; a new system of philosophical instruction was needed. His first writing was political; the *Temporis partus masculus* (1584) outlined a policy of tolerance and moderation – but a *Letter of Advice to Queen Elizabeth* a few years later advocated stern measures against the Catholics: he may have thought it would please the queen. However, his **Essays** were published in 1597 in a book of ten; the last edition, in 1625, contained 58 and they are a demonstration of his range as a writer of English prose. He wrote **The Advancement of Learning** (1605) in English also, but turned to Latin for **De Sapienta Veterum** (1609), later translated as *The Wisedome of the Ancients* (1619). Latin was also chosen for the celebrated **Novum Organum** (1620) and for the enlargement of the *Advancement of Learning*, called *De augmentis scientiarum* (1623). Bacon's mastery of Latin was as complete as his mastery of English, to which he returned in **The Historie of the Raigne of King Henry the Seventh** (1622), *Apophthegms New and Old* (1624), and **The New Atlantis** (1626). Among his professional works as a lawyer were *A Collection of Some Principall Rules and Maximes of the Common Lawes* and *A Reading on the Statute of Uses*. He left complete, besides much unpublished miscellaneous writing, *Sylva Sylvarum; or A Natural History*, which was published in 1627. He was studying the preservative properties of snow at his estate of Gorhambury during the winter of 1626 when he caught a chill from which he died.

*The Advancement of Learning* (*De augmentis scientiarum* in the Latin, extended version), *Novum Organum*, and *Sylva Sylvarum* are the three parts of Bacon's *Instauratio magna*, the great renewal of learning and, more important, of how to learn; it is in this that Bacon's true greatness lies. His quality as a master of English and Latin prose is indisputable and inevitably, the methods he advanced were overtaken by time and increasing scientific knowledge. It is also true that he was a scientific amateur. But he possessed scientific imagination in abundance, a quality shared by one of those who admired him in a later day, the great Darwin. Bacon disposed of assumptions, superstitions, primordial images in the mind of man which he called 'idols'. It was not apparent to his contemporaries but the era of modern scientific enquiry had begun.

Bacon's essays are so full of wit and wisdom they are more quoted than read, which is a pity. They are cool, certainly; that was the nature of the man. But the wisdom is there, and politicians, among others, could avail themselves of it to some profit. The same quality brings considerable rewards in the observation of the minds of the ruling class of Bacon's day and in his unquenchable curiosity about the nature of the world and the behaviour of his fellow men.

The collected works of Francis Bacon were edited by James Spedding, R. L. Ellis, and D. D. Heath and published in 14 volumes (1857–90).

**Bacon, Roger** *c*.1214–92. Roger Bacon's birthplace was either at Ilchester in Somerset or at Bisley in Gloucester; there is a little evidence to support either statement. He studied at Oxford and by 1236 had made his way to Paris, where he was one of the first teachers on the works of Aristotle. In Paris also he became interested in experimentation and about 1247 decided to devote himself to science. He returned to England about 1251 and entered the Franciscan order. He was back in Paris by 1256 and at this stage in his life suffered a long period of ill-health; he had to abandon his studies for something like ten years.

By the time Bacon was in his early 50s word had reached Rome of the English scholar and Pope Clement IV asked him for an account of his doctrines in confidence; *Opus Majus, Opus Minus,* and a work on alchemy, *De Multiplicatione Speciarum,* were sent to Rome about 1268. But Pope Clement died in that year and the commendation Bacon hoped for did not materialize. He returned to Oxford, where he wrote Greek and Hebrew grammars, completed his *Opus Tertium,* and wrote a sharp attack on the clergy and the monastic orders, criticizing the ignorance and vice of which they were guilty, in *Compendium Studii Philosophiae* (*c*.1272). In the same work he attacked scholastic pedantry also.

Roger Bacon, known as Doctor Mirabilis, wrote in Latin but his scholarship and enquiring restless mind made its own contribution to literature. The three *Opera* comprised an all-embracing treatise, dealing with mathematics, physiology, geography, the relation between philosophy and theology, and experimental science. He challenged most of the assumptions current in his time and tells of his conflicts with his superiors in *Opus Tertium.* He insisted on the need for a knowledge of Hebrew and Greek (he read Aristotle in the original Greek and held in contempt those teachers who relied on Latin versions) to arrive at a true understanding of the scriptures.

**Badman, The Life and Death of Mr** An allegory in the form of a dialogue by John Bunyan, published in 1680. The story is related by Mr Wiseman to Mr Attentive, who makes comments and asks questions. While *The Pilgrim's Progress* is an allegory of man's journey to salvation, *Mr Badman* might be described as an allegory of man's way to damnation. Bunyan's central character has no redeeming features but the author has conceived him entirely in human terms. His mendacity and lack of care for anything but his own needs and desires; his dishonest courtship of a good woman and his total lack of real solicitude for her thereafter; his physical degeneration and the death of his wife; his second marriage to a bawdy companion – all these end in his death, which is, ironically, as peaceful and calm as that of a child in sleep.

Mr Wiseman's narrative is uncompromisingly realistic and the reader is given a vivid picture of life in a 17th-century market town. Bunyan knew well the types that went into his portrait of a man with no redeeming features and he succeeds completely in making Mr Badman credible.

With this book Bunyan made a major contribution to the development of the novel, a remarkable achievement in the light of his nonconformist piety and preoccupation with salvation. But his honesty and realism are what matter and these were new: *Mr Badman* is the forerunner of the novels of Daniel Defoe.

**Bagehot, Walter** 1826–77. The son of a successful banking and shipping magnate, Bagehot was born at Langport in Somerset. He was educated at Bristol and at University College, London, then studied law and was called to the Bar in 1852. Bagehot's interests included literature, economics, history, and philosophy. He contributed to periodicals during his twenties and became joint editor, with R. H. Hutton, of *The National Review* (1855). He became editor of *The Economist* in 1860 and stayed with it until his death.

Bagehot's best known work is *The English Constitution* (1867), an appraisal of acute speculative insight that has not been superseded. *Lombard Street* (1873) examines the money market with the same sharp eye and gift for exposition. Other books by Bagehot are *Physics and Politics: or Thoughts on the Application of The Principles of 'Natural Selection' and 'Inheritance' to Political Society* (1872) and *Literary Studies* edited by R. H. Hutton (1879).

*The English Constitution*, with an introduction by Lord Balfour, is published in The World's Classics (1928). R. H. S. Crossman's edition (1964) contains a bibliography on government and politics.

**Bailey, Philip James** 1816–1902.  Bailey was born in Nottingham and studied at Glasgow University with the intention of becoming a Presbyterian minister. He changed his mind and became a barrister. Bailey was prompted by his admiration of Goethe's *Faust* to attempt a great poem in the same vein and published *Festus* in 1839. In its final form (1889) the enormous poem contained 52 scenes and ran to 40,000 lines. The first edition was given serious attention and Tennyson found good things in it. This was during the period between the Romantics and the great Victorians; by the time of Bailey's enlarged second version (1845) new voices were being heard and Bailey was evidently not likely to prove their equal. Apparently he failed to realize this and went on writing poetry with less and less success: *The Angel World* (1850), *The Mystic and The Spiritual Legend* (1855), *The Age* (1858), and *Universal Hymn* (1867). Bailey was one of those whom William Aytoun dubbed a member of the 'Spasmodic School' of poets.

**Baillie, Joanna** 1762–1851.  Joanna Baillie was born in Hamilton, Lanarkshire, and enjoyed a reputation as a poet and playwright. Her *Plays on the Passions* were published in three volumes in 1798, 1802, and 1812. The first volume contains the drama *De Montfort*, in which Sarah Siddons enjoyed a great success in 1800. *The Family Legend* was produced in 1810. Her verses were published in *Fugitive Verses* (1790) and *Metrical Legends* (1821) and were admired for their neatness and humour. A further volume of plays, *Miscellaneous Plays*, was published in 1836. A friend and contemporary was Sir Walter Scott, who admired Joanna Baillie's plays.

**Baker, Father Augustine** 1571–1641.  The author of more than 40 treatises, 'Or Directions for the Prayer of Contemplation, etc.', Baker was a Catholic mystic whose work was edited by Father R. F. S. Cressy. It was published posthumously (1657) as the *Sancta Sophia*, a kind of Catholic parallel to Traherne's *Centuries of Meditation*.

**Balderstone, Caleb**  Ravenswood's faithful retainer in Scott's *The Bride of Lammermoor*, who goes to absurd lengths to conceal his master's impoverished condition from the rest of the world.

**Baldwin, James (Arthur)** 1924–  .  The son of a preacher, James Baldwin was born in Harlem, New York City. He left home at the age of 17 and eventually made his way to Paris, where he lived for some years and where he began to write. His first novel, *Go Tell It On The Mountain* (1953), was based on his experience of Harlem and he was welcomed as a Black writer of unusual promise. The promise was born out in further novels, plays, short stories, and essays which have also shown him to be a fine spokesman for his people and a powerful, articulate enemy of racial discrimination. After *Giovanni's Room* (1956), which is set in Paris, Baldwin returned to Black America for his fiction: *Another Country* (1962), *Going to Meet the Man* (1965, short stories), *Tell Me How Long the Train's Been Gone* (1968), *If Beale Street Could Talk* (1974), and *Just Above my Head* (1979). His essays – his best work in the opinion of some critics – are published in *Notes of a Native Son* (1955), *Nobody Knows My Name* (1961), *The Fire Next Time* (1963), *No Name in the Street* (1971), and *The Devil Finds Work* (1976). James Baldwin is the author of three plays, *The Amen Corner* (1955), *Blues for Mr Charlie* (1964), and *One Day, When I Was Lost* (1972).

**Bale, John** 1495–1563.  The son of poor parents from Suffolk, Bale entered the Carmelite monastery in Norwich at the age of 12. He completed his education at Jesus College, Cambridge, where he met Thomas Cranmer. He took the degree of BD in 1528 or 1529 and travelled in Europe before taking his DD about 1533. Soon after that he abandoned his monastic vows and became a priest.

Bale was an early and vigorous supporter of the Reformation in England. He rejected celibacy and married, and was imprisoned in 1536. He was the author of Protestant polemics and attracted the attention of Thomas Cromwell, who secured his release but could not prevent his ejection from his living at Thorndon in 1537. When Cromwell fell in 1540, Bale fled to Germany and did not return to England until the accession of Edward VI. He was made rector of Bishopstoke in Hampshire (1547), vicar of Swaffham in Norfolk (1551), and was appointed Bishop of Ossory in Ireland in 1553. His fervent Protestantism made him very unpopular and with the accession of Mary he was obliged to take to his heels again. He returned to England upon the accession of Elizabeth in 1559 and did not go back to his see. He settled at Canterbury where he was a canon and prebendary until he died.

Bale was a man of considerable learning but his writing was so bitter and coarse that Thomas Fuller called him 'Bilious Bale'. He wrote, apart from his anti-Catholic polemics, a number of plays which range from the morality form to the historical *King John*. The plays themselves are anti-Catholic in feeling (even King John opposes the pope), and under Cromwell's sponsorship Bale and his troupe of itinerant players performed them in various parts of England. All but five of the plays are lost and four of them are moralities in the old style: *God's Promises, John the Baptist*, and *The Temptation of Our Lord* form a trilogy; *The Three Laws* is concerned with Nature, Moses, and Christ. The fifth play to survive, *King John* (*c.*1558), marks a departure and looks forward to the Elizabethan historical plays; it may have existed in an early draft as early as 1539. But it must be said that it looks forward from an immense distance; Bale cannot forbear to make one of the meanest villains to wear the English crown into an idealized Christian hero – because King John opposed the pope. It was, nevertheless, a comparatively sophisticated play for a professional company and made a contribution to the progress of English drama.

In his later years Bale devoted himself to the compilation of a catalogue of English, Scottish, and Welsh authors and their works with biographical information. In spite of bias and inaccuracies the *Illustrium majoris Britanniae scriptorum, hoe est, Angliae Cambriae ac Scotiae Summarium* is an indispensable source of information.

**Balfour, Arthur James, 1st Earl of** 1848–1930. Balfour was born at Whittingeame in East Lothian and educated at Eton College and Trinity College, Cambridge. Before he entered politics and became prime minister (1902–05), Balfour had a reputation as a philosopher. *A Defence of Philosophic Doubt* (1879) was an expression of the conviction that science and all forms of human knowledge left residual problems which defied intellectual solution; the ultimate convictions of mankind rest on religious faith, which is nonrational ground. He developed this position in *Foundations of Belief* (1895), which because of Balfour's prominence in political life attracted wide attention, and in two series of Gifford Lectures, *Theism and Humanism* (1915) and *Theism and Thought* (1923).

**Balfour, David** The hero of *Kidnapped*, by Robert Louis Stevenson. He survives his Uncle Ebenezer's attempt to kill him and after many adventures gets control of his inheritance. In *Catriona*, because he witnessed the crime, he risks his own life on behalf of an innocent man accused of murder.

**Balibari, Chevalier de** In Thackeray's *Barry Lyndon*, Barry's raffish old uncle who lives on his wits. Barry has no more than his wits, either, and quickly learns all the chevalier can teach him.

***Balin and Balan*** See *Idylls of the King, The*.

***Ballad of Good Counsel*** A popular Scottish poem once attributed to King James I of Scotland. See **Scottish anthologies and collections**.

***Ballad of Kynd Kittok*** A poem by William Dunbar, of uncertain date. It relates in comic vein the story of an alewife's arrival in heaven, and how, in need of a fresh drink, she wanders off – out of heaven and back to her alehouse.

***Ballad of Reading Gaol, The*** A poem in six-line stanzas by Oscar Wilde, first published in 1898 over the pseudonym 'C.3.3.', the poet's number as a convict. The ballad, one of Wilde's best-known works, was written at Berneval-sur-Mer near Dieppe, soon after his release from prison. The centre of the ballad is the execution of a fellow prisoner whom Wilde and the others saw daily in the exercise yard while preparations were being made to hang him. (He was a young soldier, Trooper C. T. Wooldridge, who had been convicted of murdering his wife in a fit of jealousy.) The mounting tension is powerfully evoked and the whole poem, a masterpiece of horror and compassion, is unrivalled in prison literature.

***Ballad of the Sad Café, The*** See **McCullers, Carson**.

**Ballantyne, R(obert) M(ichael)** 1825–94. A writer of adventure stories for young people who followed the lead of (and was commercially more successful than) Frederick Marryat. As a boy of 16 Ballantyne went to Canada, where for six years he worked for the Hudson's Bay Company and saw the North at its wildest. He had been back in Scotland for eight years, working in a publisher's office, when he published *The Young Fur Traders* (1855), which was successful enough to launch him on a full-time writing career. *Ungava* (1857) was also set in the wild North but after that he broadened his canvas and started to write about parts of the world which he did not know. *The Coral Island* (1858), which tells of the survival of three boys wrecked on a coral island, is his most famous and popular book and probably benefited from the author's habit of carefully researching subjects and places of which he had no first-hand knowledge. *Martin Rattler* (1858), *The Lifeboat* (1864), *The Lighthouse* (1865), and *The Iron Horse* (1871) all did well, but students of children's books usually agree that there is a certainty of touch about his stories of the Canadian wilderness that is lacking in the other books. He returned to that scene for *The Dog Crusoe* (1861) and *The Wild Man of the West* (1863).

Ballantyne was also the author of charming little books in verse that he illustrated himself, notably *Three Little Kittens* (1856) and *The Robber Kitten* (1860).

**Bancroft, George** *c*.1800–91.  The US historian was born in Worcester, Massachusetts. He graduated from Harvard at the age of 17 and continued his studies in Greek and the natural sciences in Berlin and Göttingen, where he absorbed the German research methods which were to prove so influential in American historical writing. While in Europe he also met Goethe, Hegel, Mazzini, and men of similar stature. When he returned to New England he taught for some years, using progressive methods, and was then appointed Collector of the port of Boston. President Polk made him Secretary of the Navy in 1845 and Bancroft was instrumental in the establishment of the US Naval Academy at Annapolis. He served as acting Secretary of War, as minister to England, and as minister to Germany.

Bancroft's reputation as a historian was earned by his massive *A History of the United States* (to 1789), the first volume of which appeared in 1834 and was accorded high praise. The ten volumes were completed in 1874; the book was widely translated and, remarkably, was a bestseller for the rest of the century. It has hardly survived into the 20th century: the influence of German historiography brought forward the objective pragmatic approach and Bancroft's nationalistic and rhetorical style, plus the use of philosophical concepts, soon fell out of favour. He was, nonetheless, the father of American history.

The ten-volume *History* was published in a revised edition of six volumes in 1876. A further edition of 1883–85 included Bancroft's *History of the Formation of the Constitution*, which was first published in 1882. An abridgment of the *History*, edited by R. B. Nye, was published in 1967.

**Banim, John** 1798–1842.  An. Irish author whose best work lies in the volume of short stories which he wrote with his brother Michael, *Tales by the O'Hara Family* (1825). He was also

the author of a tragedy, *Damon and Pythias*, which enjoyed a successful production at Covent Garden and was published in 1821. His essays, *Revelations of the Dead Alive* (1824), satirical comments on his times, were a popular success.

**Banim, Michael** 1796–1874.  The older brother of John Banim, whom he outlived by more than 30 years. He wrote, with his brother, *Tales by the O'Hara Family* (see **Banim, John**). He was the author of several novels, including *The Croppy* (1828), *Father Connell* (1842), and *The Town of the Cascades* (1864).

**Bannatyne, George** 1545–*c*.1608.  Bannatyne was born at Newtyle, Forfarshire, and became a wealthy merchant of Edinburgh. During an outbreak of the plague in the capital Bannatyne retreated to Newtyle, where to pass the time he copied out works of the Scottish poets he admired. Nothing is known of the texts in his possession but his manuscript anthology is the only source for the work of many 15th- and 16th-century Scottish poets. Poems by Dunbar, Henryson, Lindsay, and Alexander Scott among others are preserved for us by George Bannatyne. Allan Ramsay used the Bannatyne manuscript for most of the material for his *The Ever Green* (1724), which helped to revive interest in the older Scots poets. Sir Walter Scott founded the Bannatyne Club in 1823 for the editing and publishing of Scottish literature and history. He also wrote a memoir of Bannatyne.

*The Bannatyne Manuscript* (the original is over 800 pages long) was published by the Scottish Texts Society (1928–34), edited by W. T. Ritche.

**Bannatyne Manuscript, The**  See **Scottish anthologies and collections**.

**Banquo**  One of King Duncan's successful generals in Shakespeare's *Macbeth*. He is returning from the war with Macbeth when the witches appear and make their first prophecy. Macbeth has him murdered because the witches tell Banquo that he is the ancestor of kings. His ghost appears at Macbeth's feast.

**Barbauld, Anna Laetitia** 1743–1825.  Anna Laetitia Aikin was born at Kibworth, Leicestershire, and was educated by her father, a schoolmaster. She published a collection of verse, *Poems*, in 1773, the year before her marriage to a French Protestant teacher. From that time her work was educational and devotional in character – an aid to her husband's teaching. *Hymns in Prose for Children* (1781) was very popular and continued to be reprinted well into the 19th century. Her *Lessons for Children* (1778) was equally popular and was also translated into French. Mrs Barbauld's 'Ode to Life' was once a regular anthology piece.

**Barbour, John** *c.*1320–96. Nothing is known of John Barbour's early life. He is heard of first in 1357, in an application to Edward III for a safe-conduct for himself and three scholars, to enable the latter to go to Oxford to study. At that time Barbour was archdeacon of Aberdeen and no university had as yet been established in Scotland. The safe-conduct for Barbour himself was for a more important purpose: he was to act on the commission for the ransom of King David of Scotland, then a prisoner of the king of England. Barbour's life was much concerned with the affairs of his country and with his king's household, but he did succeed in spending two terms of study in France and in writing the first considerable work in Scottish literature, **The Bruce, or the Metrical History of Robert I King of Scots.**

After *The Bruce* was completed the king of Scotland, Robert II, awarded him ten pounds from the revenues of Aberdeen, and in 1378 an annual pension. The pension was raised tenfold in 1388, and Barbour, honoured by his king and respected by his countrymen, died in 1396.

Other works of the time have been attributed to Barbour, most plausibly a translation from two French books as *The Buik of Alexander.*

**Barchester Towers** The second novel of Anthony Trollope's Barsetshire series. It was first published in 1857.

There is a new bishop in Barchester, Dr Proudie, who has a masterful and bullying wife and an intriguing chaplain, Obadiah Slope, who is her rival for the control of the diocese. Their principal opposition is over the vacant wardenship of Hiram's Hospital, for which there are two candidates – the former warden Septimus Harding and Mr Quiverful, incumbent of a small parish and the father of 14 children.

Slope seeks the hand of Eleanor Bold, Harding's widowed daughter; but he is infatuated with the daughter of Canon Stanhope. That lady, Signora Vesey-Neroni, is in a difficult position since her married status is equivocal. Slope is undeterred and also seeks the deanery of Barchester. Harding, despite the strong support of Archdeacon Grantly, is defeated in his hopes of regaining the wardenship. But Slope's satisfaction in this little victory over Mrs Proudie is short-lived since Harding is then offered the deanery. Worse follows when Eleanor Bold rejects him – his proposal to her prompts his exposure by Signora Vesey-Neroni. Slope loses his chaplaincy and disappears from Barchester.

Eleanor marries Francis Arabin, a protégé of Archdeacon Grantly. The author returns to the scene of Barsetshire in *Doctor Thorne.*

**Barclay, Alexander** *c.*1475–1552. Alexander Barclay is believed to have been a Scot but little is known of his early life. He was a monk, and while priest to the College of St Mary at Ottery in Devon he translated Sebastian Brant's *Das Narrenschiff* (1494) into English as *The Shyp of Folys of the Worlde* (*The Ship of Fools,* 1509). Later, while at the Benedictine house of Ely (1515–21), he wrote his *Egloges* (Eclogues). Barclay survived the Dissolution and became vicar of Much Baddow in Essex. His translation of Sallust's *Bellum Iugurthinum* of the first century BC into English prose (*c.*1520) is usually regarded as his best work; his *Introductory to Wryte and Pronounce French* (1521) anticipates the decorated prose style of the later 16th century.

*The Ship of Fools* used the well-tried device of a collection of diverse types of person in a particular place or in particular circumstances and gives a satirical picture of contemporary manners. Barclay's version is very free, in rhyme royal, and three times as long as Brant's original; it was made from Latin and French versions. The *Egloges* are an early attempt at pastoral poetry in English but were more directly influenced by the work of the contemporary Italian Mantuanus (Johannes Baptista Spagnuoli) than by the original classical form and are not read now.

A modern version of *The Ship of Fools* was published by T. H. Jamieson in 1874.

**Barclay, John** 1582–1621. The son of a Scottish jurist, Barclay was born at Pont-à-Mousson in Lorraine and was connected with the court of

The frontispiece to Alexander Barclay's *The Ship of Fools.* Barclay's translation of Sebastian Brandt's *Narrenschiff* (1494) was first published in 1509.

James I. He wrote in Latin and was much admired in Europe. *Euphormionis Satyricon*, written and extended 1603–07 and with no real conclusion, is a series of episodes of adventure, satire, and discourse, with an obvious model in Petronius. *Icon Animorum* (1614), translated by Thomas May as *The Mirror of Minds* (1631), is a book of essays on types, national and temperamental. *Argenis* (1621), translated by, among others, Ben Jonson in 1623 (but his version was lost in a fire), was an allegorical romance with a contemporary setting. It was printed over 40 times in the original Latin but none of the numerous English translations secured a lasting place. The last one, by Clara Reeve, was a revision of Kingsmill Long's translation of 1625, and was published as *The Phoenix* (1772).

**Barclay, Robert** 1648–90. The son of David Barclay, a notable Scottish soldier, Robert Barclay was born at Gordonstown in Elginshire and educated at the Scottish Catholic College in Paris. He followed his father in the Quaker movement in 1667. Barclay's wide learning and formidable intellect made him the leading Quaker theologian and his first published work was his *Catechism and Confession of Faith* (1673). In 1676 he published in Latin an apologia supporting the Quaker theses he had circulated in English, Dutch, French, and Latin, and defended at Aberdeen. The English version was called *Apology for the True Christian Religion, as the same is set forth and preached by the People called in Scorn, 'Quakers'* (1678). It is the main exposition of Quaker principles and also contains a powerful attack on Calvinism.

Barclay was held in favour by James II and assisted William Penn in the founding of Pennsylvania; he was himself appointed governor of East New Jersey in 1683. Other works by Robert Barclay are *The Anarchy of Ranters* (1676) and *The Possibility and Necessity of an Inward and Immediate Revelation* (1686).

**Bardell, Mrs** Mr Pickwick's landlady in Dickens's *The Pickwick Papers*. She mistakes his enquiries about the possibility of keeping someone (he is contemplating the engagement of Sam Weller as his servant) as a tentative proposal. Her misapprehension leads to the famous breach-of-promise trial.

**Barham, Richard Harris** 1788–1845. Barham was born in Canterbury and educated at St Paul's School (he was school captain for two years) and Brasenose College, Oxford. While at Oxford a severe illness turned his thoughts from his original purpose of going into law and he entered the church instead. He became a minister in Kent, where he wrote a novel, *Baldwin, or A Miser's Heir* (1820), while recovering from a broken leg; the novel sank without trace. Barham became a minor canon at St Paul's in 1821 and used his newly-found facility with a pen to supplement his income, contributing light verse and occasional reviews to *Blackwood's Magazine*, *The Globe*, and *John Bull*. He was appointed a chaplain in the royal household in 1824. He became a regular contributor to *Bentley's Miscellany* and *The New Monthly Magazine* where his deft versifying and ability to tell a good tale made the stories and ballads of 'Thomas Ingoldsby, Esq' enormously popular. Collections were published as *The Ingoldsby Legends* (1840–47) with illustrations by Leech, Cruikshank, and Tenniel. Some of his material was original but most was gathered from old tales, anecdotes related by friends, and his own experiences. Though Barham is largely forgotten now *The Ingoldsby Legends* is well worth revival, and the young Thackeray owed much to the style of the amiable clergyman who was in his fifties before he became a celebrity.

**Barlaam and Josaphat** A Middle English verse romance of the 14th century. (See **metrical romances**.) The origin of the story is in an 8th-century Greek work by John of Damascus, and three French poems on the theme predate the English version. Josaphat is the son of the Indian King Abenner, who persecutes the Christians. It is prophesied of Josaphat that he will become a Christian and will have a glorious reign in a higher kingdom. King Abenner, disturbed by the prophecy, keeps his son in seclusion but eventually yields to the boy's entreaties and allows him to go out into the world. A holy man, Barlaam, converts Josaphat to Christianity; Josaphat converts his father just before the king dies. Josaphat hands his kingdom over to his friend Barachias and then goes in search of Barlaam. He ends his days as a holy hermit, in prayer and meditation – a Christian plagiarism of the story of the Buddha.

**Barlow, Joel** *c*.1754–1812. The son of a Connecticut farmer, Barlow was educated at Dartmouth College and Yale. He was an army chaplain during the War for Independence but with the return of peace was admitted to the bar (1786). He resumed his association with the literary group known as the Connecticut or Hartford Wits whom he had known at Yale, wrote a new version of the Psalms, opened a bookshop in Hartford, and edited the *American Mercury*.

Barlow is remembered as a poet – but more for

USA and that it should be concerned with research into and instruction in the sciences and the arts.

In 1811 Madison sent Barlow to Europe to negotiate a commercial treaty with Bonaparte but on his way to meet the emperor in Poland Barlow was taken ill and died in Cracow.

**Barnaby Rudge** A novel by Charles Dickens, first published as a weekly serial in *Master Humphrey's Clock* (February to November 1841). It was first published in volume form in 1841. It was planned in 1836 but the huge success of *Pickwick* gave Dickens a new valuation of his worth as a novelist; after disagreements with Macrone and Bentley, it finally appeared under the imprint of Chapman & Hall.

The novel is in two parts, the second part beginning with Chapter XXXIII, and draws into the background of the Gordon Riots of 1780 the characters the reader has met in the first part. A five-year gap separates the two. Sir John Chester, a callous and selfish gentleman, has a son, Edward, who loves Emma Haredale. Emma's father, Geoffrey Haredale, is a Roman Catholic and the enemy of Sir John Chester. Geoffrey Haredale's brother Reuben has been murdered but the mystery of his death has not been solved. His steward, Rudge, is believed to have been murdered at the same time but there are strange reports of his 'ghost' having been seen. He has left a widow and a harmless half-witted son, Barnaby, who carries a pet raven, Grip, everywhere with him in a basket. Barnaby is entrusted with the carrying of messages, and some of these go back and forth between Gabriel Varden, the locksmith at Clerkenwell, and the Maypole Inn, at Chigwell, on the edge of Epping Forest.

At the Maypole, the host is obstinate prejudiced John Willett; his son is Joe, who is in love with Gabriel Varden's daughter, Dolly. Apprenticed to Gabriel Varden is Simon Tappertit, a bantam-sized fellow of extravagant vanity with an eye on Dolly and dreams of apprentices organizing themselves into a formidable force. Back at the Maypole is Hugh, the ostler, a wild-looking misanthropic young man whose mother was hanged for passing bad notes to keep them from starvation.

The second part introduces the figure of Lord George Gordon, the unbalanced pious Protestant, who sees danger for all in the Act of 1778 which lightened the repression suffered by Roman Catholics. Gordon being a Protestant fanatic, he sees anyone opposed to him as a Catholic fanatic. He becomes the focus for every

Joel Barlow, the Connecticut poet. Detail from A. B. Durand's engraving of the painting by Robert Fulton.

his charming three-canto celebration of an American dish, *Hasty Pudding*, than for the epic **The Columbiad**, which he believed to be his great work. He went to Europe in 1788 as agent for an Ohio land deal and spent 17 years there. He found friends in Joseph Priestley, William Godwin, and Thomas Paine and his conservative New England convictions underwent a change: Barlow became a democrat. The French awarded him citizenship for his *A Letter to the National Convention of France*.

Barlow arranged the publication of his friend Thomas Paine's *The Age of Reason*, when the author was imprisoned in France (1794 to 1795). Paine had inspired Barlow's *Advice to the Privileged Orders* (1792), in which Barlow argued that the state was the agent of all society, not of any particular class. It was while living in France that he wrote *Hasty Pudding* (1796).

In 1795 Barlow was appointed US consul to Algiers. He secured the release of US prisoners and negotiated treaties with the North African states. He was one of the first to encourage Robert Fulton's ideas for the use of steam to drive ships. Upon his return to America in 1805 he was honoured with the confidence of Jefferson and James Madison, though he lived a quiet life as a scholar for the next six years. He published *A Prospectus of a National Institution* (1805) proposing that such an institution be established in the malcontent in London – from Simon Tappertit to Sir John Chester, who has purposes of his own – busily recruited by his evil lieutenant, Gashford. Poor Barnaby is seduced into joining them for the innocent pleasure of wearing a bow and carrying a flag. Dennis, the hangman of Newgate Prison, is very contented – he has fifty legal reasons for hanging people and he wants no changes, either.

The Gordon Riots are the matter of the second part (two-thirds) of the book and Dickens handles the material of fact, mixed with his own fiction, with complete success; his characters become part of the historical events and develop against the background with total consistency. Many critics have said that the author fails with the characterization of Barnaby, that he is not really convincing. It may be true that he is not – but neither is he the book. *Barnaby Rudge* is a fine novel of compelling power and irresistible momentum, full of memorable characters. The behaviour of a mob has never been so vividly described.

**Barnacle, Clarence**  In Dickens's *Little Dorrit*, Clarence Barnacle, together with Lord Decimus, Ferdinand, and Mr Tite, are the personification of comfortably entrenched and incompetent officials. The Circumlocution Office has become, for them, almost a family business.

**Barnes, Barnabe**  *c.*1569–1609.  A minor Elizabethan poet, Barnes was the son of the Bishop of Durham and educated at Brasenose College, Oxford. He published the sonnet sequence *Parthenophil and Parthenophe* (1593) and a series of religious sonnets called *A Divine Century of Spiritual Sonnets* (1595). He wrote two plays: one, *The Battle of Hexham*, is lost; the other, *The Devil's Charter*, is an anti-Catholic play with Alexander Borgia as the central character.

**Barnes, William**  1801–86.  Barnes was born at Blackmoor Vale near Rushey in Dorset and was a farmer's son. He worked as a solicitor's clerk and did some teaching until 1838, when he went to St John's College, Cambridge, and took holy orders. He is notable as the regional poet of Dorset; his first efforts were published in local papers and were issued in book form as *Poems of Rural Life in the Dorset Dialect* (1844), *Hwomely Rhymes* (1859), another *Poems of Rural Life in the Dorset Dialect* (1862), and *Poems of Rural Life in Common English* (1868). He became rector of Came in Dorset in 1862 and published his *Collected Poems* in 1879. He was a regular contributor to *Macmillan's Magazine* and *Fraser's Magazine* and

published works on the dialect of Dorset and the antiquities of the county. Barnes brought the work of a genuine folklorist to his talent as a poet; his verses – love poems, natural scenes, and poems of regional life – look forward to the work of another Dorset man, Thomas Hardy, who published a selection of Barnes's poetry with a preface and a glossary (1908).

**Barrack-Room Ballads**  See **Kipling, Rudyard.**

**Barren Ground**  A novel by Ellen Glasgow, first published in 1925. The barren ground is the poor land of her father's farm, which Dorinda Oakley hopes to help restore by earning money. She goes to work at Nathan Pedlar's store where she falls in love with a doctor's son, Jason Greylock. Dorinda's hopes for her father's farm are temporarily forgotten and her own hopes of happiness dissolve when Jason is forced to acknowledge his commitment to another woman. She goes to New York and, after a street accident, finds work looking after her doctor's children. Another doctor wants to marry her but, to Dorinda, marriage is no longer the sole meaning of a woman's life so she refuses him. She spends her spare time studying advances in agriculture and returns to Virginia when her father dies. Unaided – her mother is helpless, her brother idle and selfish – Dorinda brings fertility back to the barren ground and creates a prosperous dairy farm. She does marry, when her mother dies, the same Nathan for whom she first worked; he is a widower and Dorinda can keep a home going for his children. After Nathan's death she gives shelter to the wretched and drunken Jason Greylock – but she does not love him any more; she is simply being kind to a man who is dying. She will not marry again; she tells enquirers that she is thankful 'to have finished with all that'. See also *Virginia* and *Vein of Iron.*

**Barrie, Sir J(ames) M(atthew)**  1860–1937. J. M. Barrie was the ninth child of ten born to a handloom weaver of Kirriemuir in Forfarshire, Scotland. His early education he owed to his mother, who taught him to read and encouraged him to write stories even before he went to school. After local schools Barrie continued his education at Dumfries Academy and Edinburgh University. While at university Barrie wrote dramatic and literary criticism for Edinburgh papers, and after graduating (1882) joined the staff of the *Nottingham Journal*, where he worked until 1884. During those two years he had sold some pieces to London papers, and in 1885 he went to live there and earn what he could as a freelance journalist. A play, *Caught Napping*, was never produced but was privately printed in 1883 at the author's expense. The same thing happened with a satirical novel, *Better Dead* (1887). But he meanwhile contributed sketches of Scottish life to the *St James's Gazette* and *Home Chimes*, and had his first success when these were published in book form as *Auld Licht Idylls* (1888). He exploited this vein with continued success in *An Edinburgh Eleven: Pencil Portraits from College Life* (1889), collected from contributions to *The British Weekly*, and *A Window in Thrums* (1889). Thrums was his fictional name for his birthplace, Kirriemuir. Among a number of novels, collections of short stories, and plays either not produced or indifferently received about this period was *The Little Minister* (1891), a sentimental novel which he later dramatized and which became a resounding success on the stage. Meanwhile Barrie enjoyed increasing success with *Margaret Ogilvy*, his book about his mother, and a novel, *Sentimental Tommy: The Story of His Boyhood* (both 1896). A sequel to the novel, *Tommy and Grizel* (1900), moves from a sentimental view of his characters to a tragic one, but on the whole it was Barrie's particular brand of sentimentality which gave his works their strongest appeal.

Barrie achieved his first success on the stage with a dramatization of *The Little Minister* (Haymarket Theatre, 1897) and sealed his reputation

Captain Hook and Peter Pan. An illustration for *The Peter Pan Picture Book* (1907) by Alice B. Woodward.

with *Quality Street* (Vaudeville Theatre, 1902), a beautifully wrought comedy about Phoebe Throssel; she impersonates an imaginary niece to recapture the heart of Valentine Brown, who has been away in the army for ten years. Also in 1902 Barrie published the story *The Little White Bird*, in which he included a character who featured in the stories he told to children. He made the boy the subject of a play and *Peter Pan: or The Boy Who Would Not Grow Up* was produced at the Duke of York's Theatre in December 1904. The success of this play alone would have made Barrie rich but he would have done quite well without it. It has a powerful and lasting appeal for children; a narrative version, *Peter and Wendy*, was fashioned by Barrie and published in 1911.

Barrie's success in the theatre continued. Among his best-known plays are *What Every Woman Knows* (Duke of York's Theatre, 1908), *The Admirable Crichton* (Duke of York's Theatre, 1914), *A Kiss for Cinderella* (Wyndham's Theatre, 1916), *Dear Brutus* (Wyndham's Theatre, 1917), and *Mary Rose* (Haymarket, 1920). He seemed to gather honours without effort: Rector of St Andrews University (1919), Chancellor of Edinburgh University (1930), and the Order of Merit (1922), not to mention the baronetcy conferred on him in 1913. The death of Michael Davies, one of his adopted sons, in 1921 was a heavy blow and no major work appeared for some time. *The Boy David* (His Majesty's Theatre, 1936) was written for the German actress Elisabeth Bergner; it failed on the stage but some writers believe it one of his best plays. It awaits revival, so that it can be properly judged in terms of the stage.

**Barrow, Isaac** 1630–77. A 17th-century divine who enjoyed in his later years the personal patronage of Charles II, Barrow was the son of a linen merchant. He entered Trinity College, Cambridge in 1647, during the Civil War, and in spite of his Royalist sympathies became a fellow of Trinity in 1649 (the Royalist cause had been lost by then). He travelled in Europe and the Near East from 1655 to 1659 and was ordained in the Church of England upon his return. A fine scholar, Barrow became Professor of Greek at Cambridge in 1660, Professor of Geometry at Gresham College, London, in the same year, and was the first Lucasian Professor of Mathematics at Cambridge in 1663. He resigned the Lucasian Professorship in 1669 to his pupil Isaac Newton, preferring to concentrate on theological studies. Charles II made him a royal chaplain, a DD by royal mandate (1670) and Master of Trinity College (1673). Barrow published little during his lifetime, but his sermons, though extremely long, were famous and he was notable in his time for his reasonable views, after the 'enthusiasm' of both Puritan and Anglican had reduced religious controversy to the level of pious recrimination. *Exposition of the Creed, Decalogue and Sacraments* (1669) and two works on geometry were published during his lifetime. His theological works were collected and edited by Archbishop John Tillotson (four volumes, 1683–87) and include his *A Treatise of the Pope's Supremacy*. Barrow's prose style was extravagantly praised by Coleridge in his *Anima Poetae*.

***Barry Lyndon, The Luck of,*** A Romance of the *Last Century, by Fitz-Boodle.* Subsequently titled *The Memoirs of Barry Lyndon, Esq. by Himself,* the novel by W. M. Thackeray first appeared in *Fraser's Magazine* in 1844 in 12 instalments. It is in the form of an autobiography in an 18th-century setting.

Redmond Barry, believing he has killed a man in a duel, flees from Ireland at the age of 15. Robbed of the little money he carries and impressed into the army, he serves both England and Prussia as a soldier of fortune and becomes aware that if he does not use the world the world will certainly use him. In Europe he meets his uncle, the Chevalier de Balibari, a likable old scoundrel who finds in Barry a man after his own heart. Barry deserts from the Prussian army and becomes a gamester and man of fashion, living on his wits at first.

Apparently successful and well-to-do, Barry comes to England and meets the wealthy Countess of Lyndon, a vain and selfish widow. He decides to marry her and by sheer persistence – bullying, almost – he succeeds. He adopts the name of Lyndon and cares nothing for his wife and her son. However, he loves and spoils his own son and dissipates his wife's fortune. He humiliates Lady Lyndon more and more until, at last, she is rescued from him by her family. He loses his son, a bitter blow to him, and faces ruin, bested by Lady Lyndon and her family. He ends his days in the Fleet Prison.

*Barry Lyndon* was Thackeray's first success in fiction and his picaresque novel presents a man giving his own account of himself. His resource as an adventurer is admirable but he reveals himself to be a cruel and mean-spirited man when he succeeds in persuading the countess to marry him and is convinced that he has achieved worldly success. Recalling his adventures and his ultimate downfall, Barry has no apologies to offer. It is a measure of Thackeray's success that the later conduct of his character is so believable.

**Bart, Lily** The tragic heroine of *The House of Mirth*, by Edith Wharton. Lily is born into the upper reaches of New York society but her father's financial ruin leaves her in a precarious position after her parents' death. She cannot envisage any other life for herself and is quite prepared to endure a loveless marriage to make her position in society secure. But in the end she is defeated because she is too insecure, as well as too honest, to survive in the jungle that New York society really is.

**Barth, John (Simmons)** 1930– . Barth was born in Cambridge, Maryland, and educated at Johns Hopkins University, where he has been Alumni Centennial Professor of English since 1973. After publishing short stories in various periodicals he attracted considerable critical atttention with a novel, *The Floating Opera* (1956), in which a nihilist, contemplating suicide, reviews the events of his life and decides not to kill himself after all. Other novels are *The End of the Road* (1958), *The Sot-Weed Factor* (1960), *Giles Goat Boy: or The Revised New Syllabus* (1966), *Chimera* (1974), which won him the National Book Award, and *Sabbatical* (1982). *Lost in the Funhouse* (1968) is a volume of short stories.

**Bartholomaeus Anglicus** fl. 1230. Possibly Bartholomew de Glanville, though this is not certain. 'Bartholomew the Englishman' was a minorite friar and a professor of theology at the University of Paris. He was sent to Saxony in 1231 to organize the Franciscans and it may have been during his sojourn here that he wrote his *De Proprietatibus Rerum*, an encyclopedia of the world of nature. It was translated by John Trevisa (1398).

***Bartholomew Fayre*** A farce by Ben Jonson, first produced in 1614 and published in 1631. The actual fair of the title was held annually at Smithfield on St Bartholomew's Day, 24 August. Jonson brings a number of assorted characters to the fair and relates their adventures. Adam Overdo, a justice, comes to the fair in disguise to spy out its iniquities. The country squire, Bartholomew Cokes, comes with his servant Waspe, and his unwillingly betrothed, Grace Wellborn. They are followed by rival suitors for Grace's hand, Winwife and Quarlus. A group of Puritans is headed by Zeal-of-the-Land Busy, a scripture-quoting hypocrite. A notable character of the fair is Ursula the pig-woman, whose stall with its roast pork is a gathering point for all the rogues and con men who attend the fair. Bartholomew Cokes is a simpleton and is robbed of everything, including his future wife; Waspe overreaches himself and ends up in the stocks for brawling. Both Zeal-of-the-Land Busy and Adam Overdo end up in the stocks too. The play is rarely revived but is commended by scholars for its vivid representation of a London carnival in the early 17th century.

**Bartleby, the Scrivener** See **Piazza Tales, The**.

**Barton, Bernard** 1784–1849. Barton was born at Carlisle in Cumberland of a Quaker family of manufacturers. He was educated at a Quaker school in Ipswich and apprenticed to a shop-keeper at the age of 14; he married his employer's daughter in 1806. After teaching in Liverpool for a year he went to work in a bank at Woodbridge in Suffolk, where he spent the rest of his life. He began to correspond with Southey in 1812, the year he published his first poems (*Metrical Effusions*). He published a great deal more in-ferior verse and became a great success. In 1822 he took Lamb to task for his remarks about Quakers and the two became lifelong friends. In 1845 he dedicated *Household Verses* to Queen Victoria, and Sir Robert Peel secured him a Civil List pension. His daughter married Edward Fitzgerald. The work of Bernard Barton is now forgotten.

**Barton, John** The heroine's father in Elizabeth Gaskell's *Mary Barton* and the most striking character in the book. He is an upright man turned into a bitter one by the hopeless struggle for existence in the industrial climate of the time; he has seen his wife die of want and his fears for his daughter's future drive him to desperation. The author knew such men and threw the full weight of her sympathy on their side. (Her original title for the novel was 'John Barton', and this was only changed at the insistence of her publisher.)

**Bartram, John and William** John Bartram (1699–1777) was a Quaker and the first native American botanist of distinction. Largely self-taught, he was appointed botanist for the American colonies to King George III and recorded his work in his journals, the best known being *Observations made by John Bartram in his travels from Pensilvania to Lake Ontario* (1751). He introduced many plants to America and won the admiration of no less a man than Linnaeus (Carl von Linne). The botanical garden he established in his native Philadelphia became internationally famous. The man and his work are celebrated by Crèvecoeur in *Letters from an American Farmer*.

John Bartram's son, William (1739–1823), worked for a time as a planter and a merchant but was soon as absorbed in botany as his father and accompanied him on some of his journeys. William Bartram was able to travel farther afield during his own career and proved to be a writer of considerable powers. His *Travels through North and South Carolina, Georgia, East and West Florida, the Cherokee Country,* . . . (1791), earned high praise from Coleridge and, in its remarkable descriptions of a world still unknown, proved to have a strong appeal for creative writers of the time. William Bartram was also a pioneer orni-thologist and listed 215 native American species.

**Basilius** The King of Arcadia, living in the forest at the bidding of an oracle, in Sir Philip Sidney's *Arcadia*. He falls in love with Zelmane, not knowing 'she' is Pyrocles in female disguise.

**Bassanio** In Shakespeare's *The Merchant of Venice* he is Antonio's friend, for whom Antonio makes the bond with Shylock that nearly costs him his life. Bassanio wants the money to make him present a suitable figure for his wooing of Portia. He finds to his dismay that all the wealth he has married cannot deflect Shylock from in-voking his bond.

**Bassianus** Saturninus' brother and rival for the imperial throne in Shakespeare's *Titus Androni-cus*. He abducts Lavinia, Titus' daughter, when he fails to get the throne. He is murdered by Tamora's sons.

**Bates, John** One of the three soldiers who meets the king, incognito, on the eve of Agin-court in Shakespeare's *Henry V*. In a remarkable exchange in prose dialogue the king learns of the ordinary soldiers' feelings.

**Bathurst, Mrs** See **Traffics and Discoveries**.

**Battel of Alcazar, The** A play in verse by George Peele, first published in 1594 but prob-ably written about 1589. It is patriotic and anti-Spanish in tone.

Muly Mahamat, a usurper, has been defeated and expelled from Morocco by the rightful king, Abdelmelec. He goes to Sebastian, King of Portugal, and offers to become his tributary if he succeeds in conquering Morocco; his motive is revenge against Abdelmelec. Sebastian is per-suaded and invades Morocco but is killed at the Battle of Alcazar. Abdelmelec falls too, and Muly Mahamat is drowned when he tries to flee from the scene of the defeat.

A real-life character in the play is the English adventurer Thomas Stukely, who was killed at the historical battle which took place in 1578. Stukely was said to have been a natural son of Henry VIII.

**Battle Hymn of the Republic, The**   The famous patriotic song was written by Julia Ward Howe at the suggestion of James Freeman Clarke while visiting Washington during the Civil War in December 1861. He pointed out that 'John Brown's Body' was popular with the soldiers and Mrs Howe wrote new words to the old tune. (She awoke one morning with the words in her head and promptly wrote them down.) The song was published in the *Atlantic Monthly* and given its name by James T. Fields in February 1862.

**Battle of Brunanburh, The**   A poem in Old English, which appears in four of the manuscripts of the *Anglo-Saxon Chronicle* (Versions A, B, C, and D).

The battle took place in 937 but the site of Brunanburh is not known. King Athelstan and his brother Edmund meet the Danish army under Anlaf; the Danes have an ally in the treacherous Scots King Constantinus, who had once sworn allegiance to Athelstan but had changed sides. Athelstan and Edmund win a great victory.

A notable version of the poem in modern verse was made by Tennyson, based on a prose translation published by his son, Hallam, in the same year (1876). It is also included in C. W. Kennedy's *An Anthology of Old English Poetry* (1960).

**Battle of Life, The**   See **Christmas Books**.

**Battle of Maldon, The**   A poem in Old English, probably composed at the end of the 10th century; the manuscript was lost in the fire which destroyed part of the collection of Sir Robert Bruce Cotton in 1731. Fortunately a transcript had been made by J. Elphinston, though the beginning and end of the poem are lost; this transcript was printed by T. Hearne at Oxford in 1726. The battle is described in the *Anglo-Saxon Chronicle*.

In the year 991 the Danish leader Anlaf harried the towns of Kent and East Anglia, and drew up to land at Maldon in Essex on the bank of the River Blackwater. The Danes are faced by Ealdorman (*or* Earl) Byrhtnoth – Aelfric's friend – and his men. The Danes' herald announces that the raiders will withdraw in return for payment (an example of *danegeld*). Byrhtnoth rejects the approach with contempt, but the inevitable battle has to wait because of the rising tide. When the tide ebbs Byrhtnoth even allows the enemy to cross the river (probably on stepping stones) before battle is joined. The English scatter and re-form after the valiant earl is killed by a poisoned spear. But after all the English leaders have fallen – Godric is the last – the poem ends; however, the outcome must have been a tragic defeat, for soon afterwards (this occurs during the reign of Ethelred) *danegeld* became an annual tribute.

Translations into modern verse of *The Battle of Maldon* are included in C. W. Kennedy's *An Anthology of Old English Poetry* (1960) and Michael Alexander's *The Earliest English Poems* (Penguin Classics, 1966).

**Battle of the Books, The**   A prose satire by Jonathan Swift, written in 1697 and first published in 1704. Swift was staying at Moor Park, the home of his erstwhile employer Sir William Temple, when his host wrote an essay, *Ancient and Modern Learning*. Temple had given uncritical praise to the spurious Epistles of Phalaris and became the target for the censure of Richard Bentley and William Wotton. Swift treats the question with satirical humour and finds many targets of his own.

The ancients occupy the highest peak of Parnassus; the moderns request them to leave their eminence, where they have been hitherto unchallenged. A bee has become entangled in the web of a spider in a library and Aesop intervenes. The bee, he claims, is like the ancients in that it goes to nature for its honey; the spider is like the moderns, who spin scholastic lore out of their entrails. Aesop's comment infuriates the moderns, who open hostilities. The ancients are led by Homer under the patronage of the goddess Pallas; the moderns' deity is Criticism. The advantage, at the close of the essay, seems to be with the ancients, but a parley ensues and there is no real decision. A notable incident is Virgil's encounter with Dryden, his translator, whose helmet is nine times too big for him. Swift had not forgiven his cousin Dryden for the comment made by him on one of Swift's Pindaric odes.

**Battle-Pieces and Aspects of the War**   The Civil War poems of Herman Melville, first collected and published in 1866. Among them are 'The Portent', on the hanging of John Brown; 'Misgivings', on the brutal contradiction of freedom that slavery represents in a new country so recently freed by the efforts of her people ('. . . the world's fairest hope linked with man's foulest crime'); and the beautiful 'Shiloh. A Requiem'.

**Baxter, Richard**   1615–91. A Presbyterian divine, ordained in 1633 and a military chaplain during the Civil War, Baxter was a prolific writer of devotional literature. Baxter disliked the growth of sectarianism in the Commonwealth and contributed to the change of feeling that led to the Restoration. He accepted the position of royal chaplain and refused a bishopric but the uncompromising conscience that had led him into Presbyterianism and then to criticism of it now brought him trouble. As a Nonconformist he endured petty persecution; this became severe under James II – he was sentenced to imprisonment in 1685 and vilified by Judge Jeffreys. He enjoyed some peaceful years under the rule of William and Mary.

Baxter's best-known works are *The Saint's Everlasting Rest* (1651), *A Call to the Unconverted* (1658), and his moving and intimate tribute to his beloved wife who died in 1681, *A Breviate of the Life of Margaret Baxter* (1681). His own account of his turbulent life, *Reliquiae Baxterianae*, was published in 1696.

**Bayou Folk** A collection of stories and anecdotes of Louisiana in the 19th century by Kate Chopin, first published in 1894. Among them should be mentioned *La Belle Zoraide*, the story of a quadroon slave of great beauty who falls in love with a handsome Negro and has his child. Her owners forbid a marriage between them and take the child away; she loses her mind and her sad unbalanced affections become focused on a doll. She refuses to part with the doll, even clinging to it and turning away from her child when it is brought to her.

*A No-Account Creole* is the tale of Placide Santien, vain and self-centred, who is looking forward to his marriage to a girl of considerable wealth. On the day before the wedding he learns that she loves another man and is wretchedly unhappy. Santien redeems his faults by releasing her from her engagement.

*Désirée's Baby* is generally regarded as the best in the book – a classic in a form in which American literature is particularly rich. Armand, a Louisiana 'aristocrat', marries a beautiful orphan girl, Désirée. When their first baby is born the child shows definite signs of Black ancestry and Armand is beside himself. He turns Désirée and their baby son out of the house and they disappear. Alone, Armand finds among some papers a letter of his mother's – and discovers that the Black strain is in his own family.

**Bay Psalm Book, The** Published at Cambridge, Massachusetts, in 1640 by Stephen Daye, this was the first book to be printed in the American colonies. The full title was *The Whole Booke of Psalmes Faithfully Translated into English Metre*. The editors, Richard Mather, John Eliot, and Thomas Welde, stated their intention of seeking accuracy above all else and the translators were '30 pious and learned ministers'. The revision of 1651 was in use for over a hundred years and was popular in Scotland.

**Beat Generation** The term 'beat' was explained by those who proclaimed themselves part of it in two ways: as exhausted – by all aspects of the conventional world; and as beatific – their disaffiliation from that crass and corrupt conventional world would bring, with help from drugs and drink, blissful illumination. The movement made itself heard in the 1950s with the publication of Allen Ginsberg's *Howl and Other Poems* (1956) and Jack Kerouac's *On The Road* (1957). The term was first used by Kerouac and an article in the *New York Times* in 1952 by John Clellon Holmes, who described the movement in his novel *Go* (1952), made 'beat' into Beat – a fashionable label eagerly worn for a few years by followers who had found something new – beatniks, as they were called. Among other writers whose names became associated with the Beat Generation are William Burroughs, Gregory Corso, Lawrence Ferlinghetti, Peter Orlovsky, and Gary Snyder.

**Beatrice** The witty bantering heroine of Shakespeare's *Much Ado About Nothing*. She is Leonato's niece and Hero's cousin and she fascinates Benedick, who is exasperated by her refusal to take him seriously. But she does respond when she is convinced that he truly loves her.

**Beattie, James** 1735–1803. A farmer's son, Beattie was born at Laurencekirk, Kincardineshire, and became a teacher. He rose steadily in the academic world and became Professor of Moral Philosophy and Logic at Marischal College, Aberdeen, in 1760. He began to publish verse in 1765 (*The Judgment of Paris*) and in 1770 attracted a great deal of attention with *An Essay on the Nature and Immutability of Truth*, an attack on David Hume which was widely welcomed by the philosopher's critics. Beattie's rewards included a pension from George III and an honorary doctorate of civil law from the University of Oxford. In the aftermath of this celebrity Beattie published the first book of *The Minstrel* (1771), a poem in Spenserian stanzas on the development of an imaginary poet of olden days. The second book was published in 1774, and Beattie was an 'honoured poet' in his lifetime, praised by Samuel Johnson. *The Minstrel*, like the rest of Beattie's poems, is largely forgotten, though it has what Maurice Lindsay describes as 'a thin-coloured talent for nature-painting', which allows the poem 'to retain a certain watery charm'.

**Beauchamp's Career** A novel by George Meredith, first published in serial form in the *Fortnightly Review* (August 1874 to December 1875).

Nevil Beauchamp does well in the navy and earns the approval of his rich uncle, the Hon Everard Romfrey. Beauchamp is inclined to be radical in his political views, while Romfrey's are those of a medieval nobleman. Beauchamp enters political life after the Crimean War and, unsuccessfully, stands for parliament. He makes a close friend of Dr Shrapnel, whose politics are far more revolutionary than Nevil's and who earns the hatred of Romfrey and his friends. When Romfrey attacks Shrapnel with a horsewhip Beauchamp is determined, as a point of honour, that his uncle shall apologize to his victim.

Beauchamp's determination becomes an obsession and at the same time his emotional life goes awry. His early love, Renée, has married an elderly Frenchman and is now desperately unhappy. Cecilia, his present love, is under pressure from his family to marry his dull – but in their eyes worthier – cousin. Renée runs away from her husband and comes to England; her presence is a severe temptation that Beauchamp succeeds in resisting but he succumbs to brain fever from the emotional pressures that beset him. Shrapnel takes Beauchamp to his house, where his ward, Jenny Denham, helps him to nurse him back to health. Romfrey visits Beauchamp there and to the latter's great joy at last apologizes to Dr Shrapnel.

Beauchamp marries Jenny Denham and they enjoy a brief spell of happiness before he is drowned while trying to save a child from the sea. His career is cut short and it is tragically plain to both the reactionary Romfrey and the revolutionary Shrapnel what a loss that is.

**Beaumont, Francis** 1584–1616. (For the dramatic works written by Beaumont in collaboration with John Fletcher see **Beaumont and Fletcher**.) Francis Beaumont was the son of a judge and was born at Grace-Dieu in Leicestershire. He was educated at Broadgates Hall, Oxford, and entered the Middle Temple in 1600. In London Beaumont became friends with Ben Jonson and his circle and became a critical sounding board for the plots of Jonson's plays. About 1607 he began his collaboration with Fletcher, which lasted until about 1613, when Beaumont married an heiress and retired from the theatre. He died soon after at the age of 32.

The plays that can be attributed to Francis Beaumont's authorship number only two (this is the opinion of E. K. Chambers, the great scholar of the Elizabethan theatre): *The Woman Hater* (1606) and *The Knight of the Burning Pestle* (almost entirely Beaumont's work and published in 1607).

**Beaumont and Fletcher** (See also **Beaumont, Francis** and **Fletcher, John**.) The plays that resulted from their collaboration are usually regarded as the best work of both men, with the possible exception of Beaumont's *The Knight of the Burning Pestle* and Fletcher's *The Faithful Shepheardess*. Their collaboration was a short one of six or seven years but two collections published in the 17th century propagated the idea that a great number of works represented their joint efforts. In 1647 an enterprising publisher issued a folio containing 34 plays and a masque, declaring it to contain the hitherto unpublished works of Beaumont and Fletcher. Some writers protested but in the absence of copyright laws there was no way of asserting that a lot of the work was Fletcher's alone and that a fair part was Massinger's. In 1679 a volume appeared called *Fifty Comedies and Tragedies. Written by Francis Beaumont and John Fletcher, Gentlemen*, which added another 18 plays to the first 34 (making the total more than 50). However, after a great deal of textual scholarship it is now believed that seven plays, no more, can be attributed to Beaumont and Fletcher. These are *Four Plays in One* (produced *c*.1608), *Cupid's Revenge* (published 1615), *The Scornful Ladie* (published 1616), *The Maid's Tragedy* and *A King and No King* (both published 1619), *Philaster* (published 1620), and *The Coxcombe* (published 1647).

*Four Plays in One* is four short pieces, two of them based on stories of Boccaccio, one on a story of Bandello's, and the fourth an original by the playwrights; the themes are Honour, Love, Death, and Time. *The Scornful Ladie* is a comedy in which the title character is rendered more agreeable. *The Coxcombe* is a romantic comedy in which two separate stories are brought together to produce an unconvincing plot. *Cupid's Revenge* is based on material from Sidney's *Arcadia* and, like the three works mentioned here, is regarded as one of the less enduring products of Beaumont and Fletcher.

The importance of Beaumont and Fletcher in an age when playwrights of high quality seem to have been thick upon the ground lies in their collaboration, which brought out the best attributes of both. Beaumont's writing was the stronger, in formal and dramatic terms, while Fletcher, a better poet, was more deft and inventive; work flowed from his pen with ease. Fletcher's dialogue moves toward colloquial speech even when he uses the blank verse that was the usual form for playwrights; metaphor and allusion became less acceptable in a play. Every playwright of the era stands in the shadow of the great Shakespeare and little is seen, now, of the works of Beaumont and Fletcher. But they made a positive contribution to the development of English drama.

***Beaux' Stratagem, The*** A comedy by George Farquhar, first produced in March 1707, and published in the same year. The part of Archer was played by Robert Wilks, the playwright's friend; Anne Oldfield, who had succeeded Anne Bracegirdle as London's leading actress, played Mrs Sullen. The play has held the stage; a London production in 1949 ran for over a year, and it was also given by the National Theatre in the 1970s.

Bonniface keeps an inn in Lichfield with the help of his daughter Cherry. To the inn come Archer and Aimwell, two young gentlemen in search of better prospects. Archer poses as Aimwell's valet; Aimwell poses as Lord Aimwell (his brother). The two are the focus of some interest and Bonniface decides they must be highwaymen. Dorinda, the unmarried daughter of the manor house, falls in love with Aimwell when she sees him in church.

Dorinda's brother Sullen is an oafish drunk; Mrs Sullen is bored with her husband and her life. Aimwell gains admittance to the manor house by feigning illness; he is ministered to by Lady Bountiful, Dorinda's mother, and Mrs Sullen and Archer feel a mutual attraction. (Mrs Sullen, out of boredom, had planned a harmless rendezvous with Count Bellair, a French officer who is held as a prisoner in Lichfield.) When the manor house is attacked by Gibbet, a highwayman, Archer and Aimwell rescue the ladies and decide to make the most of their opportunity. However, Aimwell decides he must tell Dorinda the truth.

The frontispiece of an 18th-century edition of Farquhar's *The Beaux' Stratagem*. The second scene of Act V: the servant, Scrub, raises the alarm and interrupts Archer and Mrs Sullen at their dalliance. Victoria & Albert Theatre Museum, London.

Sir Charles Freeman, Mrs Sullen's brother, has come to take his sister away from her dreadful husband. He also brings news that Lord Aimwell is dead; his brother inherits the title but Dorinda has already decided that she wants him. Sir Charles gets Sullen to agree to a divorce and the way is clear for Archer to ask for Mrs Sullen's hand.

**Beckett, Samuel (Barclay)** 1906– . Samuel Beckett was born in Dublin. His family's circumstances were comfortable and Beckett was educated at Portora Royal School and Trinity College, Dublin. He went to Paris as a lecturer in English in 1928 and, apart from two years as Lecturer in French at Trinity College (1930–32), has made France his home. He worked for a time as James Joyce's secretary, and published some poetry in Paris before World War II. His first novel, *Murphy*, was published in England in 1938. Beckett translates his own works from French into English and from English into French. During the war he worked with the French Resistance, collating intelligence: when his group was betrayed he fled to Vichy France with his wife and worked as an agricultural labourer. He was awarded the Nobel Prize for Literature in 1969.

Beckett's best-known novels (the dates given are of the first English publication) are *Molloy* (1951), *Watt* (1953), *Malone Dies* (1956), *The Unnamable* (1958), and *How it is* (1964). His plays are usually included in any comment on the 'Theatre of the Absurd' – the proposition that life is basically both meaningless and incoherent, and that a play which aims to give a true reflection of life must do so by exploring the full range of absurdity. *All that Fall* (1957), *Endgame* (1958), *Krapp's Last Tape* (1959), and *Happy Days* (1962) are performed all over Europe and the USA but they are overshadowed by *Waiting for Godot* (1956), his first play and the work that made him world famous.

'A Tragicomedy in Two Acts', *Waiting for Godot* presents two tramps waiting by a tree in a country road. Gogo (Estragon) and Didi (Vladimir) are waiting for Godot; he has been to the tree before. Through their cross-talk comedy – the humour is Irish – seriousness intrudes from time to time, and Didi introduces the story of the two thieves who were crucified with Jesus. The Christian symbolism permeates the play, with the Cross, the Tree, and the character of Jesus. Two characters come along and the tramps think that Godot has arrived – they do not, in fact, know Godot and could not identify him. But the formidable one is Pozzo; his slave, whom he

The first production in English of *Waiting for Godot* took place at the Arts Theatre, London, on 3 August 1955. Peter Woodthorpe as Estragon (left), and Paul Daneman as Vladimir.

keeps tethered on a rope, is Lucky. Pozzo ill-treats his slave and makes him dance. Then he makes him think, and Lucky complies in a long, allusive, and incoherent tirade (which presents a formidable task for the actor playing him). Master and slave depart; a boy arrives to tell Gogo and Didi that Mr Godot will not be there that evening 'but surely tomorrow'. Master and slave return on the next day; Pozzo is now blind and Lucky is dumb. After they pass the boy comes in with the same message he had brought the day before; even though they are tramps the boy addresses them as 'Sir'. Gogo and Didi contemplate hanging themselves on the Tree if Godot does not come on the next day: 'We are not saints, but we have kept our appointment. How many people can boast as much?' The playwright declared that he did not know who Godot was; if he had known he would have said so. The play is a remarkable reflection of the mood of the time and aroused very positive reactions: it was profound, or it was nonsense, according to how spectators and readers responded to it. It was first produced in England at the Arts Theatre on 3 August 1955.

**Beckford, William** 1759–1844. The son of an immensely wealthy merchant of the same name, who was also a politician and became Lord Mayor of London, Beckford was born at the family mansion of Fonthill in Wiltshire. He inherited a huge fortune from his father and his unstable temperament apparently rendered him incapable of any sustained effort in the arts which interested him so much. He studied architecture with Sir William Chambers and painting with Alexander Cozens, who accompanied him to Italy in 1782. Beckford published a notable travel book, *Dreams, Waking Thoughts and Incidents*, in 1783 (reprinted as *Italy, with Sketches of Spain and Portugal*, 1834), and his romance, **Vathek, An Arabian Tale**, in 1786.

He was a compulsive – and haphazard – collector and possessed a fine library, which included that of Edward Gibbon, purchased by Beckford. He commissioned James Wyatt to build him a Gothic extravagance and meanwhile wrote two burlesques, *Modern Novel Writing: or The Elegant Enthusiast* (1796) and *Azemia* (1797). Fonthill Abbey was completed in 1807, and Beckford, one assumes, enjoyed his monstrous mansion, which had an entrance hall so large that it could hold more people than could ever have lived in the house. He published a satire on art criticism called *Biographical Memoirs of Extraordinary Painters* (1824) and another notable travel book, about Portugal, in 1835: *Recollections of the Monasteries of Alcobaca and Batalha*.

Beckford dutifully served as an MP on two occasions, for Wells and Hindon, though he had little interest in politics, and lived in seclusion in his Gothic extravagance from 1796, probably observing it take shape around him. His great fortune was dissipated by the time he died, and Fonthill Abbey fell into ruins. The travel books are generally praised by scholars but are largely unknown to most readers. Beckford is remembered in English literature for *Vathek*, a fantasy which had no literary ancestors, and no descendants, either, until the time of Aubrey Beardsley and, later, Ronald Firbank.

**Beddoes, Thomas Lovell** 1803–49. The son of a doctor who was a friend of Coleridge and Southey and a nephew of Maria Edgeworth, Beddoes was born at Clifton in Somerset. He was educated at Charterhouse School and Pembroke College, Oxford, and while in his first year at university published *The Improvisatore, in Three Fyttes, with Other Poems* (1821), three tales in verse. This was followed by *The Bride's Tragedy* (1822), a sombre play of murder, reflecting his interest in Elizabethan and Jacobean drama. **Death's Jest-Book: or The Fool's Tragedy** was begun about 1825 and continually altered in successive years.

Beddoes went to Zurich in 1825 to study medicine and spent most of the rest of his short life living abroad. He was of unstable temperament and this became alarmingly manifest in the last years of his life, when he made several attempts, eventually successful, at suicide. *Death's Jest-Book* was published in 1850, and a collection of his works, edited by T. F. Kelsall, in 1851. Beddoes touched greatness in his poetry, especially in sections of *Death's Jest-Book*; but his work is too much in tune with his own morbid preoccupations to reach a large public and he believed that he had no great talent for rhyme or lyric poetry. His fine blank verse was admired by Tennyson and Browning.

The standard edition of Beddoes is *Plays and Poems*, edited by H. W. Donner (1950), who also published a biography, *Thomas Lovell Beddoes: The Making of a Poet* (1935).

**Bede** (*or* **Baeda**), **St** *c.*673–735. The 'Venerable' Bede, called the 'father of English history', was born at Monkton, in the present county of Durham, and at the age of seven was sent to the monastery at Monkwearmouth. The following year he went to Jarrow, then newly founded, and, like Monkwearmouth, under the rule of St Benedict Biscop. He was ordained deacon at the age of 19 and became a full priest when he was 30 (*c.*703). As far as can be ascertained, Bede never went farther from Jarrow than visits to York and Lindisfarne.

The study of scripture, writing, and teaching occupied Bede's life and his interests were wide; theology was dominant but his works reveal a lively interest also in grammar and poetry, history, and natural sciences; he knew Greek and Hebrew as well as Latin. Among his works are the *Life of St Cuthbert*, composed in Latin verse (*c.*704) and later rendered in a prose version (*c.* 720); *De Temporibus* (705) on time and the calendar, with a very brief glance at world history; *De Natura Rerum* (720–25), a sort of compendium of the 'science' of his age, owing much to Isidore of Seville, Pliny, and Suetonius. *De Temporum Ratione* (725) extended the work of *De Temporibus* and was of great importance for its influence on subsequent chroniclers; Bede himself attached due importance to dates, the first chronicler to do so. His greatest work, *Historia Ecclesiastica Gentis Anglorum*, was completed in 731. Bede was also the author of numerous biblical commentaries, homilies, hymns, a martyrology, and a letter to Egbert, Bishop of York, which survives to provide a valuable glimpse into the religious life of the time.

Bede's *Historia* (*A History of the English Church and People* or, more exactly, **Ecclesiastical History of the English Race**) is, in its straightforward unaffected style and narrative power, a classic of history. For all his immense learning Bede was, on the evidence of his history, a man without

An illustration for a 12th-century manuscript of Bede's *Life of St Cuthbert* (c.704), executed at Durham and now in University College, Oxford.

pretension and of warm humanity; this informs his great work and lifts it to the level of a masterpiece.

Only one of Bede's English (Old English) works, his Death Song, survives: this is preserved in a letter written by his pupil Cuthbert to a friend, Cuthwin. The great man died at Jarrow at about the age of 63, serene in his passing and hopeful 'to behold my King Christ in His beauty'.

**Beerbohm, Sir Max** 1872–1956. Max (Henry Maximilian) Beerbohm was the son of a corn merchant from Memel in Lithuania who settled in London and founded a group of trade papers. He was born in Kensington, London, and educated at Charterhouse School and Merton College, Oxford. In school and university publications he demonstrated his talent for satire and caricature; the latter appeared in a series in the *Strand Magazine* (1892) and marked his professional debut. His first essays were published in *The Yellow Book* (1894), then in *The Savoy*, and a collection was published with the impudent title of *The Works of Max Beerbohm* (1896). *The Happy Hypocrite: A Fairy Tale for Tired Men* (1897) followed, and in 1898 Beerbohm succeeded George Bernard Shaw as dramatic critic of *The Saturday Review*. He stayed until 1910; his pieces were collected and published as *Around Theatres* (1924), *More Theatres* (1969), and *Last Theatres* (1970). Meanwhile his impeccable prose style and gift for caricature were displayed in *Caricatures of Twenty-Five Gentlemen* (1896), *More* (1899, essays), *Yet Again* (1909, essays), *The Poet's Corner* (1904, caricatures), and *The Book of Caricatures* (1907). He published a satirical novel, *Zuleika Dobson: or An Oxford Love Story*, in 1911. *Fifty Caricatures* (1913) and *A Christmas Garland* (1912) completed the list of his books published before World War I. *The Garland* parodies to brilliant effect, in a series of discourses on Christmas themes, the styles of Kipling, Wells, Chesterton, Hardy, Bennett, Galsworthy, Conrad, Belloc, Shaw, Meredith, George Moore, and five other contemporaries. In 1910 Beerbohm married Florence Kahn and went to live in Rapallo, near Genoa.

In 1919 Beerbohm published *Seven Men*, which contains 'Enoch Soames' and 'Savonarola Brown'; a new volume of caricatures, *A Survey*, appeared in 1921. His career as the first gentleman of elegant irony continued for the rest of his life. He displayed a remarkable skill as a broadcaster with his first appearance in the medium in 1935; *Mainly on the Air* (1946) is a selection of his broadcast talks. He was knighted in 1939.

A scene from Act III of *The Beggar's Opera*. Macheath in prison; Polly and Lucy plead with the Turnkey for his release. The painting by William Hogarth (1729) was commissioned by Sir Archibald Grant and is now in the Tate Gallery, London.

***Beggar's Bush, The***  A romantic drama by John Fletcher and, probably, Philip Massinger, first produced about 1622. It was first published in 1661 as the work of Beaumont and Fletcher and is an interesting early example of the use of thieves' and vagabonds' cant in dramatic dialogue.

Florez is a successful merchant from Bruges and is in love with Bertha of the burgomaster's household. Florez does not know that he is, in fact, heir to the county of Flanders. Gerrard, the king of a gang of beggars near Bruges, is his father and is the true Count of Flanders: he was driven out by the usurper, Wolfort. In his assumed role, however, Gerrard watches over his son. Bertha does not know that she is the heiress of Brabant, stolen in infancy; Wolfort knows, however, and intends to marry her, thereby becoming master of Flanders and Brabant.

Wolfort sends Hubert, a nobleman, to negotiate the marriage. But Hubert is in love with Jacqueline, Gerrard's daughter, and he joins the beggars. Between them Hubert and Gerrard succeed in overthrowing Wolfort so that Gerrard regains his county. Bertha and Florez learn their true identities and they are happily married; and Hubert is accepted by Gerrard as his son-in-law.

***Beggar's Opera, The***  This musical play, or ballad opera, by John Gay was written after Swift had suggested the idea of a 'Newgate pastoral'. Gay's lyrics were to be sung to the tunes of familiar airs and ballads. The play was refused by

Colley Cibber but accepted by John Rich, who presented it at Lincoln's Inn Fields on 29 January 1728. It proved to be the most popular play ever presented hitherto. The songs were arranged and scored by John Christopher Pepusch, who also composed an overture. *The Beggar's Opera* was successfully revived in a rather dainty version in London in 1920 and 1925; the score has also been set by Benjamin Britten and, for an unsuccessful film, by Arthur Bliss. The play was adapted by Bertolt Brecht for a German setting in the 1920s, with a new score by Kurt Weill (*Die Dreigroschenoper*, 1928).

Peachum, a receiver of stolen goods, does most of his unlawful trade with the highwayman Macheath. Polly, his daughter, falls in love with Macheath and they marry secretly. Peachum, who is also an informer, is furious because he can no longer use Polly in his business and decides to dispose of Macheath. He informs against him and pockets the money; Macheath is apprehended and sent to Newgate, where he will certainly be hanged – Polly will then be a widow and have to return to her father. The warder of Newgate, Lockit, has a pretty daughter, Lucy, who also falls in love with Macheath and a spirited rivalry is born between the two girls. Lucy, in spite of her jealousy of Polly, helps Macheath escape from Newgate. However, he is recaptured through the unwitting indiscretion of Mrs Trapes, a bawd. At the end of the play Macheath is in the condemned cell but the Beggar intervenes just then, advised by the Player that his opera must end happily to accord with the taste of the town. Macheath is reprieved.

The play is full of vivid characters in the smaller parts; in addition to Mrs Trapes mention should be made of Jenny Diver, who decoys Macheath, and Jemmy Twitcher of Macheath's gang. Gay's satire encompasses most aspects of early 18th-century society, including Italian operatic style, fashionable life, marriage, and politics – Robert Walpole's displeasure with Gay was soon to be demonstrated.

See also *Polly*.

**Behn, Aphra** (*or* **Aphara**) 1640–89. The daughter of John and Amy Amis, Aphra Amis is known to have spent some time in Surinam, to which her father was bound, it is believed, to take up his appointment as lieutenant governor. Amis died during the journey and his daughter eventually returned to London about 1658 but there is no reliable source for these details and not even the place of her birth is known for sure. In 1666 Aphra Behn (she had married a city merchant of Dutch extraction) was in Antwerp as an English agent of Charles II during the wars with the Dutch. *The Life and Memoirs of Mrs Behn, Written by One of the Fair Sex* was published in Charles Gildon's edition of *Histories and Novels of the Late Ingenious Mrs Behn* (1696). This is her own account of her adventures and some scholars believe it to be fictional (see also *Oroonoko*).

Mrs Behn was in London and writing plays by 1670: her first, *The Forced Marriage* (1670) was staged by Thomas Killigrew. Between that date and 1696 she wrote no fewer than 18 plays, none of which have held the stage; indeed they are barely readable and give the impression of a dramatist who, knowing what the theatre-going public of her day would enjoy, industriously gave it to them. Though her plays had not enough quality to appeal to succeeding generations Aphra Behn enjoyed a successful career and numbered Southerne, Dryden, and Thomas Otway among her friends. Among her major successes were *The Rover* (in two parts, 1677 and 1681), *The Feigned Courtizans* (dedicated to Nell

Anne Bracegirdle, a celebrated actress of the Restoration, as the Indian Queen in Aphra Behn's *The Widow Ranter* (1689). Mrs Behn was the author of no less than eighteen plays, successful in their day; most of them are forgotten now. From a mezzotint in the Victoria & Albert Theatre Museum, London.

Gwynne, 1678), *The Round-Heads* (1681), and *The False Count* (1681). Her last play *The Younger Brother* (1696) was based on one of her novels.

Prose romances occupied the later part of Aphra Behn's career. *Three Histories* (1688) contained **Oroonoko, or The Royal Slave**, *The Fair Jilt*, and *The Lucky Mistake* and there were a number of others. *Oroonoko* holds an honoured place in English fiction as an early prose romance with an authentic background in the West Indies, skilfully evoked and as the first expression of sympathy in English literature for the appalling existence endured by the slaves. Aphra Behn also wrote a number of occasional poems. She was buried in Westminster Abbey.

The most complete edition of her work is *The Plays, Histories and Novels of the ingenious Mrs Aphra Behn*, edited by R. H. Shepherd (six volumes, 1871).

**Bek of Castleford, Thomas** fl. 1350. The author of a Middle English verse chronicle which exists in a single manuscript in the library of the University of Göttingen. The chronicle is written in the northern dialect of medieval England (of Castleford in Yorkshire) and closes at the accession of Edward III (1327). The manuscript has not been edited for publication.

**Belarius** In Shakespeare's *Cymbeline*, the wrongfully banished lord who steals the king's two sons and brings them up in the forest in Wales. He lives under the name of Morgan and extends hospitality to the disguised Imogen.

**Belch, Sir Toby** Olivia's uncle in Shakespeare's *Twelfth Night*. Relaxed and jovial, he is admired by the silly Andrew Aguecheek while Malvolio thoroughly disapproves of him. He gets his own back on Malvolio but is the first to see when the joke has gone far enough. He marries Maria, Olivia's maid.

**Belford, John** Lovelace's principal correspondent in *Clarissa* by Samuel Richardson. As cynical and immoral as his friend, he is reformed by the results of Lovelace's obsession with Clarissa.

**Belford Regis** See **Mitford, Mary Russell**.

**Bellamy, Edward** *c*.1850–98. Bellamy was born in Massachusetts and became a lawyer in 1871, having spent a year travelling in Europe. He abandoned the law and became a journalist, first in Springfield as editor of the *Union* and then as a writer for the New York *Evening Post*. He published his first novel in 1878 and three more before 1888, when **Looking Backward: 2000–**

*1887* attracted great attention. Nothing else of Bellamy's writing is remembered; his remarkable book is a conception of a new social order expressed in fictional form.

Edward Bellamy's ideas were to a large degree embodied in the programme offered by the Populist party in the presidential election of 1892. Bellamy, meanwhile, had founded two journals, the *Nationalist* (1889–91) and the *New Nation* (1891–94), and was lecturing to large audiences. With his early death (he was 48) the movement towards social reform lost momentum; but he had raised questions about state capitalism and the idea of a cooperative commonwealth which are still being discussed.

**Bellaston, Lady** The rich woman who keeps the hero, when he becomes her lover, in *Tom Jones* by Henry Fielding. She tries to procure Sophia Western for her dissolute friend Lord Fellamar.

**Belle Dame sans Merci, La** (i) A ballad (his own description) by John Keats, written in 1819 but not published until 1848 when it was included in *Life, Letters, and Literary Remains of John Keats*, edited by Richard Monckton Milnes. The poem is deceptively simple but remarkably powerful: it tells of a knight who meets 'a lady in the meads', she seduces him with her faery beauty and the promise 'I love thee true'. He falls into an ecstatic sleep but wakens to find himself alone, deserted 'On the cold hill side'. That is why he is 'Alone and palely loitering, Though the sedge has wither'd from the lake, And no birds sing'.

**Belle Dame sans Merci, La** (ii) A love poem translated from the French of Alain Chartier by Sir Richard Ros about 1450. Though the original was written in 1424 after Chaucer's death, the translation was for some time attributed to Chaucer.

**Belloc, (Joseph) Hilaire (Pierre René)** 1870–1953. Hilaire Belloc was the son of a French barrister and an English mother and was born at La Celle St Cloud near Paris. His family went to England when Paris was under siege during the Franco-Prussian War, and settled in England when Belloc *père* died in 1872. He was educated at the Oratory School, Birmingham, and at Balliol College, Oxford; he gained first-class honours in history but failed to obtain a fellowship at All Souls College. He became a British citizen in 1902.

Belloc wrote a great number of essays, poetry, fiction, travel, and history – some 150 books in all, beginning with *Verses and Sonnets* and *The*

*Bad Child's Book of Beasts* (1896). His interest in the French Revolution was marked by the publication of *Danton: A Study* (1899); his first travel book was *Paris* (1900); his first novel, *Emmanuel Burden, Merchant*, and his first book of essays, *Avril*, on the poetry of the French renaissance, were published in 1904. Belloc became Liberal MP for South Salford in 1906 but he saw the party system as a sham and left politics in 1910. *The Party System* (1911, with Cecil Chesterton) and *The Servile State* (1912) suggest that Parliament lost a promising member in an era of mediocrities. The latter foreshadowed the coming of the Welfare State and considers how much freedom the citizen might have to yield in exchange for security.

Belloc met G. K. Chesterton in 1900 and the two became close friends; Chesterton illustrated most of Belloc's novels. Both were Catholics, a fact which some critics of the day regarded as a built-in fault colouring all their writing. Belloc's work, in fact, only suffered from its sheer quantity, not from his religion; some of it is highly regarded and his verse is much anthologized. Among his best-known works are the collections of essays *Hills and the Sea* (1906), *First and Last* (1911), *Short Talks With the Dead* (1926), and *The Silence of the Sea* (1940); the travel books *The Path to Rome* (1902), *The Pyrenees* (1909), *The Cruise of the Nona* (1925), and *Return to the Baltic* (1938); and the historical studies *Robespierre* (1901), *Marie Antoinette* (1909), *The French Revolution* (1911), and *Richelieu* (1929). His *Collected Verse* was published in 1958.

**Bellow, Saul** 1915–   . The son of emigrant Russian parents, Bellow was born in Quebec. The family moved to Chicago in 1924 and Bellow was educated at the University of Chicago and at Northwestern University in Evanston, Illinois. He has followed an academic career since 1938. His first novels were *Dangling Man* (1944) and *The Victim* (1947); a picaresque novel, *The Adventures of Augie March* (1953), won him his first National Book Award. *Seize the Day* (1956), *Henderson the Rain King* (1959), *Herzog* (1964), *Mr Sammler's Planet* (1970, National Book Award), *Humboldt's Gift* (1975), and *The Dean's December* (1982) contributed to the steadily increasing esteem he enjoyed as the interpreter of the struggle of modern urban man to retain his identity. He was awarded the Nobel Prize for Literature in 1977. Among Saul Bellow's other books are *Recent American Fiction* (1963), *The Future of the Moon* (1970), *Technology and the Frontiers of Knowledge* (1974), and *To Jerusalem and Back* (1976). He edited *Great Jewish Short Stories* (1963) and is the author of three plays, *The Wrecker* (1954), *The Last Analysis* (1964), and *A Wen* (1965).

**Bells and Pomegranates**  See **Browning, Robert**.

**Belman of London, The,** *Bringing to Light the Most Notorious Villanies That Are Now Practised in the Kingdome*.  A pamphlet by Thomas Dekker, first published in 1608 and depicting the low life of London among the unfortunate as well as the vicious. It demonstrates how circumstance is responsible for the condition of both levels, the most deprived and the most brutalized. The bellman (night-watchman) is the reporter.

**Below the Mill Dam**  See *Traffics and Discoveries*.

**Belphoebe**  The chaste huntress of Spenser's *The Faerie Queene*. She is the daughter of the nymph Chrysogone and twin sister of Amoret. She appears in Books II, III, and IV and represents Elizabeth I.

**Belton Estate, The**  A novel by Anthony Trollope, first published in the *Fortnightly Review* (May 1865 to January 1866). The author had little regard for this novel and Henry James, reviewing it, called it 'stupid, and a success. . . . It is utterly incompetent to the primary functions of a book, of whatever nature, namely – to suggest thought.' But a modern critic, Michael Sadleir, ranked it among the best of Trollope's novels.

The Belton estate is the property of Mr Amedroz and is in Somerset. The owner has, in default of a son of his own, entailed it on a cousin, Will Belton. In fact Amedroz has a son, Charles, but he commits suicide; this puts his sister Clara's future in jeopardy – when her father dies she will have nothing. However, the death of Charles brings cousin Will Belton onto the scene. He is confident and capable, offers help to Amedroz, and puts the affairs of the estate in order.

Clara Amedroz is in love with Captain Aylmer, who has promised his aunt, on her deathbed, that he will marry Clara (she is related to him). Aylmer proposes to Clara and she accepts him though she has no real idea of his character. Will Belton has also proposed to her, and because of Aylmer, been rejected. As the story develops Clara's disillusionment is completed: Aylmer's mother and sister are detestable, and his own nature is revealed to be cold and mean-spirited. Will Belton wins her in the end, after she breaks her engagement to Aylmer.

**Benedick**  A young lord of Padua in the service of the Prince of Arragon in Shakespeare's *Much Ado About Nothing*. During the prince's visit to

Messina he falls in love with Beatrice, the governor's niece, whose consistent teasing makes him swear to remain unmarried. But his friends and Beatrice's contrive successfully to bring them together.

**Ben-Hur, *a Tale of the Christ*.**  A novel by Lew Wallace, first published in 1880. It was successfully dramatized by William Young in 1899 and has been filmed twice (in 1926 and 1959). The period of the story is indicated by the title.

Judah Ben-Hur and Messala the Roman are apparently close and devoted friends but Messala, in search of advancement, accuses Ben-Hur of an attempt on the life of the Roman governor. Ben-Hur is sent to the galleys for life, his mother and sister imprisoned. In the slave train to the coast Ben-Hur is given water by a stranger outside a carpenter's workshop. Years later he returns to Judaea as a free man and a Roman officer; he challenges Messala in the chariot races in Caesarea. His mother and sister, meanwhile, have contracted leprosy and, turned out of the prison by the fearful authorities, barely survive. Ben-Hur wins the chariot race and Messala, who has staked everything on the victory, is ruined. He is seriously injured and his wife, Isas, kills him when his evil nature is revealed. Ben-Hur rescues his mother and sister and they return to Jerusalem – on the day of the Crucifixion. The stranger who once succoured Ben-Hur when he was a slave dies on the cross but his passing cures the lepers. Ben-Hur and his family embrace the new faith.

**Benito Cereno**  See *Piazza Tales, The*.

**Benlowes, Edward** 1602–76.  The heir of a rich Catholic family who changed his faith at the age of 25, Benlowes travelled for two years before settling down as a patron of the arts on his estate in Essex. His benevolence towards other writers, combined with the depredations of the Civil War (he was a staunch Royalist), reduced him to poverty, and his last years were spent in reading and writing quietly at Oxford.

Benlowes' long religious poem, *Theophila or Love's Sacrifice*, was published in 1652. Perhaps the best that can be said of it is that it contains some fine lines: he wanted to express the soul's (Theophila's) quest for grace but lacked a poet's ability and, more seriously, a true poet's discipline. He deserves to be remembered for his generosity toward others.

**Bennet, Elizabeth**  The heroine of Jane Austen's *Pride and Prejudice*. High-spirited and intelligent, her integrity is absolute and Darcy's initially unwilling love for her flourishes through this. In spite of her prejudice towards him she falls in love with him and they are married at the end of the book.

**Bennett, (Enoch) Arnold** 1867–1931.  Arnold Bennett was born at Hanley, Staffordshire, in the area known as the Potteries, which featured in his work. His father was a solicitor and Bennett went to work for him at the age of 18; later he was articled to a firm of solicitors in London. His family were Methodists; they were also cultured, musical, and well read, and Bennett's subsequent career owed something to both circumstances. Before going to London he wrote a weekly article for the local newspaper, and in London was soon contributing popular articles on legal matters to a magazine. A short story, 'A Letter Home', was accepted by *The Yellow Book* in July 1895 and Bennett, encouraged by this acknowledgement from the most fashionable magazine of the day, embarked on a novel. His law studies had been put aside, meanwhile; he had become an assistant editor on *Woman* in 1893, and editor in 1896, writing everything from social chit-chat to cookery recipes and literary and theatrical reviews. His novel, *The Man from the North*, was published in 1898 and made him little money; but he was an excellent journalist and much in

Arnold Bennett, 1911. Photograph by E. O. Hoppé.

demand, writing for such austere organs as *The Academy* as well as for the popular press.

Bennett went to live in Paris in 1902 and stayed there for ten years. He had written serial novels for magazines and these appeared as novels: *The Grand Babylon Hotel* (1902), *Anna of the Five Towns* (1902), and *The Gates of Wrath* (1903). The Five Towns of the Potteries area – Hanley, Turnstall, Burslem, Stoke-upon-Trent, and Longton – had been used as his fictional background, largely due to the influence of George Moore, and this was to be an important ingredient in his future success. Among the 14 volumes of successful fiction that Bennett published during the next five years were *Tales of the Five Towns* (1905) and *The Grim Smile of the Five Towns* (1907). A successful and prolific writer, he became a celebrated one with *The Old Wives' Tale* (1908). This novel of the sisters Constance and Sophia Baines, who begin life in a draper's shop in one of the Five Towns, is Bennett's best known and was for long his chief claim to remembrance in English literature. However, revaluation of his work has focused attention on the early *Anna of the Five Towns*, in which he created a striking heroine. The sisters in the other novel are finely drawn characters in a vividly realized background but Anna is something more, a woman of honesty and compassion who refuses to conform in a Methodist society. In dealing with the Methodist background Bennett is scrupulously fair and this gives remarkable weight to the events of Anna's life.

Bennett published another 15 novels, the *Clayhanger* trilogy, and 4 volumes of short stories; he wrote 14 plays, most of which were produced, 2 volumes of one-act plays, and some 40 volumes of essays and miscellaneous pieces. Among his novels were *The Card* (1911) set in the Five Towns, *Mr Prohack* (1922), *Riceyman Steps* (1923), and *Imperial Palace* (1930); but pride of place is always given to the *Clayhanger* trilogy: *Clayhanger* (1910), *Hilda Lessways* (1911), and *These Twain* (1915). Edwin Clayhanger's life occupies the first novel, and his almost hopeless love for Hilda Lessways, whom he is on the point of attaining at the end after many vicissitudes; Hilda's life and character occupy the second novel; their life together is closely observed in the third, with the progress of George, Hilda's son before her marriage to Edwin, who has a deep affection for the boy. The *Clayhanger* trilogy was Bennett's last work about the Five Towns. He was offered a knighthood in 1918, which he declined.

Of Arnold Bennett's plays the only lasting successes were *Milestones*, written in collaboration with Edward Knoblock and first produced at the Royalty Theatre in March 1912, and *The Great Adventure*, based on his novel *Buried Alive* (1908) and first produced at the Kingsway Theatre in March 1913. *The Journals of Arnold Bennett 1896–1928*, a fascinating account of his life and times, were edited by Newman Flower and published in three volumes (1932–33).

**Benson, Thurston** The compassionate Nonconformist minister of Elizabeth Gaskell's *Ruth*. He saves Ruth from suicide and, with his sister, Faith, gives her a home. The harmless lie told by Faith Benson recoils on their heads when Thurston's pharisaical parishioners learn the truth about Ruth and her son. The character of Benson was based on the Rev William Turner of Newcastle (the Eccleston of the novel is Newcastle), whom the author knew and honoured for his total selflessness in helping the less fortunate.

**Bentham, Jeremy** 1748–1832. The son of a successful lawyer, Bentham was born in London and attended Westminster School. He completed his education at Queen's College, Oxford, which he detested, studied law at Lincoln's Inn, and was called to the Bar. He was a brilliant child and mastered French, Latin, and Greek with remarkable speed; he took his BA at 16 and his father was immensely proud of his abilities. He expected him, as a lawyer, to reach the Lord Chancellorship. But his son was more interested in the theory of law and never practised; his father bore his disappointment and supported Bentham while the latter pursued further studies. He published, anonymously, at the age of 28, *A Fragment on Government: Being an Examination of what is delivered in William Blackstone's Commentaries*. The work contained the outline of Bentham's theory of government and made enough of an impression to be attributed to Edmund Burke by many readers. *A View of the Hard Labour Bill* followed in 1778, and by then the *Fragment* had made him well known; he moved in political, legal, and intellectual circles.

Bentham's only journey outside England was made in 1785, when he visited his younger brother, Samuel, who was in the service of the Tsar of Russia at Kritchev, promoting industry. Bentham spent some time travelling in eastern Europe as well as studying his brother's work, particularly Samuel Bentham's method of work inspection. From his observations Bentham developed his *panopticon* plan for prison management, which he hoped would dispense with the practice of transportation. He failed to convince the government of its worth after 25 years' intermittent labour on the details. Meanwhile, in

Jeremy Bentham. A detail from the portrait by H. W. Pickersgill, 1829. National Portrait Gallery, London.

Russia, he completed *Defence of Usury* (1787), and returned to England in 1788.

Bentham's **Introduction to the Principles of Morals and Legislation** (1789) had been privately printed in 1780, for personal circulation. His friends pressed him to publish it and eventually he agreed, leaving much of the editorial work to them. Most of it was carried out by Etienne Dumont, the Swiss scholar, who at that time was tutor to the son of Lord Shelburne, at whose house Bentham met the foremost statesmen and political thinkers of the period. Dumont prepared Bentham's manuscript for publication – chiefly in French. A great deal of Bentham's work reached English readers in translation.

Bentham's ideas on prison management were first aired in public in *The Panopticon: or Inspection House* (1791), and thereafter his thoughts on important issues – the poor law, education, the administration of justice, the freedom of the press, parliamentary reform, and jurisprudence – were not only published but had an influence far beyond England. A constant helper was James Mill, an unbending democrat whose experience and uncompromising approach to reform influenced Bentham in the direction of philosophical radicalism, later called utilitarianism. *The Westminster Review* was founded by

Bentham in 1824 as an organ for the party which became known as the Philosophic Radicals. They stressed the need for constitutional reform – no improvement could be achieved without it.

When Bentham died his fame was international (a word he invented) and the constitutional changes that had been his party's goal had been carried out. The Reform Bill was given the royal assent on 7 June 1832, the day after Bentham's death.

John Stuart Mill, James Mill's son who edited Bentham's *The Rationale of Evidence*, wrote that Bentham 'has swept away the accumulated cobwebs of centuries – he has untied knots which the efforts of the ablest thinkers . . . had only drawn tighter'. A Jeremy Bentham would be a blessing in the 20th century: the increase in the pace and stress of life since his day seems to have encouraged the spinning of cobwebs in corners – law, government, religion – over which 'he was the first to shed the light of reason'. He was concerned chiefly with the practical aspects of human existence and when he rejected a principle always tried to propose a better-considered alternative.

The complete *Works* of Jeremy Bentham were collected by Sir John Bowring, the first editor of *The Westminster Review*, and published in 11 volumes (1838–43). The last two volumes contain a life of Bentham and an index to his works. The great mass of Bentham's manuscripts are being scrutinized for a new complete edition in preparation at University College, London. In addition to the titles already mentioned the following were some of those published during Bentham's lifetime: **Anarchical Fallacies** (1791, in criticism of the Declaration of the Rights of Man), *A Protest Against Law Taxes* (1795), *Poor Laws and Pauper Management* (September 1797, in *Annals of Agriculture*), *The Panopticon versus New South Wales* (1802), *A Plea for the Constitution* (1803), *Scotch Reform, with A Summary View of a Plan for a Judicatory* (1808), *A Table of the Springs of Action* (1815; edited by James Mill, 1817), *Chrestomathia* (1816; papers on education), *Swear not at all* (1817), *A Catechism of Parliamentary Reform* (January 1817, in *The Pamphleteer*), *Papers on Codification and Public Instruction* (1817), *Church of Englandism and its Catechism Examined* (1818), *A Radical Reform Bill, with Explanations* (December 1819, in *The Pamphleteer*), *Elements of the Art of Packing as Applied to Special Juries* (1821), *On the Liberty of the Press* (1821), *The Rationale of Evidence* (1827), and **A Constitutional Code for the Use of all Nations** (1830).

**Bentley, Richard** 1662–1742. The celebrated scholar was born at Oulton, in Yorkshire. Of humble stock, he entered St John's College, Cambridge, at the age of 14 and after university was headmaster of Spalding Grammar School for a year. He then became tutor to the son of Edward Stillingfleet, Dean of St Paul's and Bishop of Worcester; he was also ordained about this time.

In 1692 Bentley became the first Boyle lecturer with *Evidences of Natural and Revealed Religion*; this and *Remarks upon a Late Discourse of Freethinking* (1713) showed him a skilled defender of orthodox Christianity but he had already attracted attention as a classical scholar in 1691. The New Testament scholar, John Mills, prepared an edition of the *Chronicle* of the Byzantine John Malalas (late 6th century AD) and Bentley contributed an appendix on the Greek dramatists, *Epistola ad Millium*, which demonstrated the range of his textual knowledge.

Bentley became Keeper of the Royal Library in 1694 and Master of Trinity College, Cambridge, in 1700. He had, meanwhile, become involved in the controversy over the 'Phalaris' letters (see also **Temple, Sir William**; **Swift, Jonathan**; and **Phalaris**), which Temple had cited as an example of classical excellence. Bentley's *Dissertation upon the Epistles of Phalaris* (1699) nailed the *Epistles* as spurious, confounded his critics, and won him a European reputation.

Bentley's career as Master of Trinity was despotic and stormy – but it lasted for 40 years since his fellows could never get the better of him in manoeuvres to have him removed. His editions of Horace, Terence, and Manilius are celebrated. Bentley's edition of Milton's *Paradise Lost* (1732) is a curiosity of English literature, an arbitrary re-editing, in terms of the classical 'higher criticism', of one of the masterpieces of English poetry.

**Beowulf** A narrative poem of 3183 lines in Old English, preserved in a single manuscript. The manuscript, which probably dates from the late 10th century, formed part of the collection of Sir Robert Bruce Cotton (1571–1631). It is now in the British Library. The origin of the poem can be traced, from historical references, to the 6th century. The manuscript is in the West Saxon dialect and contains Christian as well as pre-Christian references; the indications are that while the manuscript is the work of a Christian scholar the matter of the poem is essentially that of a pre-Christian legend, set in the Norse lands. England is no part of the epic: Beowulf, the hero, belongs to a tribe called the Geats, who lived in the south of Sweden.

The beginning of the poem celebrates the deeds of Scyld Scefing, King of the Danes, and describes his ship-burial. The king's successors are briefly described, then his great-grandson, Hrothgar, ascends the throne. Hrothgar builds a great hall in which to entertain his court and calls it Heorot, and his reign seems to be set fair. But one night a giant in human form, descended from Cain, enters the hall and carries off 30 of the king's thanes. The monster is Grendel; he and his equally monstrous mother live in a cave in a dark mere and eat human flesh.

For 12 years the court of Hrothgar lives in fear of Grendel, who raids with impunity. Then the nephew of Hygelac, King of the Geats, decides to go to the help of the Danes: he is Beowulf, a young man of great strength. He goes to Hrothgar's court with 14 companions; the king welcomes him, and tells him of his friendship with Beowulf's father. That night the king and queen and the court withdraw from the hall while Beowulf and his companions occupy it. Grendel breaks in and devours one of the companions; Beowulf attacks him without sword or armour and in the struggle succeeds in tearing off one of the monster's arms. Grendel flees from the hall, mortally wounded.

Celebrations follow, and minstrels sing the story of Finn and the lady Hildeburh; the king showers gifts on Beowulf and the queen hangs a necklace of great value round his neck. (The necklace was afterwards worn by Beowulf's uncle, Hygelac, but fell into the hands of the Franks after his death.) That night, after Hrothgar and his queen and Beowulf have retired, a number of thanes stay in the hall – and Grendel's mother comes to avenge her son. She carries off Aeschere, the king's counsellor and friend. Hrothgar summons Beowulf; he tells him of the dark mere where the monsters are believed to dwell. Beowulf promises to battle with the giant hag and sets off to find the mere. He wears woven armour and a sword given him by Hunferth, a Dane with whom he was on unfriendly terms but who now acknowledges Beowulf's valour.

Beowulf dives into the mere and finds the cave. He fights with the giant hag but his own sword cannot harm her; only his woven armour (and God's assistance, according to the manuscript) save him from destruction. In the cave he finds a giant's sword with which he decapitates the monster; he finds the body of Grendel in the cave also. The monster's blood dissolves the sword, so with the hilt and Grendel's head Beowulf returns in triumph to Hrothgar's court. He is given further rewards and accorded lavish praise, though Hrothgar comments on the dangers of pride. Beowulf and his companions return home, where Beowulf presents all his gifts from Hrothgar to King Hygelac, who in turn rewards him with a great sum of money, a sword, and a share of the kingdom.

Many years later Beowulf succeeds to the throne; Hygelac and his son Heardred have fallen in battle. Beowulf reigns for 50 years, until his old age is disturbed by the ravages of a dragon. The dragon had been set to guard the treasure of men long since dead; but after 300 years a runaway slave succeeded in stealing the treasure, and now the dragon is raging through the land of the Geats spreading death and destruction. Beowulf decides to go and fight it himself. (There is a digression at this point in the poem, when Beowulf dwells on his adventures and on events in the kingdom that led to his ascent of the throne.) He sets out with 11 companions for the dragon's lair; when they reach it Beowulf tells the men to wait for him and he enters the lair alone. When he engages the dragon Beowulf finds that his sword is powerless against the dragon's skin. Wiglaf calls the rest of the companions to help their king but the other ten flee in terror; Wiglaf and Beowulf kill the dragon together but Beowulf is mortally wounded.

The dying Beowulf asks Wiglaf to bring forth the treasure so that he may see it. Then he gives his armour and ornaments to Wiglaf and dies. The companions return in shame; they are bitterly reproached by Wiglaf, who sends news of Beowulf's death back to the court. A great funeral pyre consumes the hero's body, the treasure, and Beowulf's armour. A spokesman warns the people that the future is bleak, now that their hero-king is gone.

There are a number of versions of Beowulf in modern English, including C. W. Kennedy's *Beowulf: the Oldest English Epic* (1940), G. Bone's *Beowulf in Modern Verse* (1945), David Wright's version in prose in the Penguin Classics (1957), and Michael Alexander's in verse also in the Penguin Classics (1973).

*Beppo: A Venetian Story.* A poem by Lord Byron, first published in 1818. Byron had studied Italian literature and was intensely interested to discover through John Hookham Frere's *Whistlecraft* (1817) the possibilities of using the *ottava rima* in English verse. He later translated part of the *Morgante Maggiore* of Luigi Pulci (1432–84), an exercise that Frere had also attempted. (Byron's English version of the first canto was published in the last issue of *The Liberal* in July 1823.) In mock-heroic style, the poem satirizes both English and Italian life, telling of the return during carnival of a long-lost soldier, Beppo (Giuseppe). Beppo, disguised as a Turkish merchant, finds his wife has consoled herself with another (a *cavaliere servente*). All seems set for a violent confrontation but this was not Byron's intention. He was writing in the tradition of the Italian *novella* of the Renaissance and the atmosphere is one of gentle irony and amused tolerance: the dilemma is resolved over a cup of coffee.

**Berkeley, George** 1685–1753. The son of an English family settled in Ireland, George Berkeley was born at Dysert Castle, near Kilkenny, and attended the same school as Congreve and Swift. Like them he went on to Trinity College, Dublin, where he was ordained and where he became a junior fellow in 1707. His first published works were tracts on mathematics – written in Latin – and the mental order and method of thought required by such exercises were to prove a valuable discipline in his subsequent career. He earned a considerable reputation as a mathematician and was always abreast of the scientific thought of his lifetime. His most notable work in mathematics was *The Analyst* (1734), written late in his career, in which he asserted that the assumptions of mathematicians were much harder to understand than Christian dogma. Mathematicians became very heated about this and Berkeley answered their criticisms in *A Defence of Free-thinking in Mathematics* (1735).

But Berkeley's fame was earned as a philosopher and he is one of the great names among English thinkers. His first book, *An Essay Towards a New Theory of Vision* (1709), propounded a psychological theory of perception based on two propositions: the objects and ideas of sight have nothing in common with the objects and ideas of touch; the connection between them comes only from experience and there is no abstract element common to both. Berkeley detested abstractions; he wrote his treatise in English prose that has commanded admiration ever since for its lucidity. He was 24 years old.

The first part of *The Treatise concerning the Principles of Human Knowledge* followed in 1710. The second part, concerning morals, existed in a first draft but this was lost while Berkeley was travelling in Italy and he never found the inclination to 'do so disagreeable a thing as writing twice on the same subject.' The treatise, in essence, insists that it is the mind that is the creative force: ideas are not merely the representations of reality, they are reality. The theory received a further polish in *Three Dialogues between Hylas and Philonous* (1713), a book admired by English scholars as a model of its kind. Amateurs of philosophy have to place Berkeley in the correct historical context and remember that he was a churchman. Otherwise Bertrand Russell's famous summing-up in *A History of Western Philosophy* will come as something of a surprise: 'Material objects only exist through being perceived ... owing to God's perceptions (they) have an existence as continuous as common sense supposes. This is, in (Berkeley's) opinion, a weighty argument for the existence of God.' In his century Berkeley's arguments were stimulating and provocative and his method of presenting them skilful and persuasive.

In 1713 Berkeley was in England and soon became the friend of Addison, Pope, Swift, and Steele. He travelled for some years and when he returned to England he found the country in the grip of the depression that followed the collapse of the South Sea Company (1720). His *Essay towards Preventing the Ruin of Great Britain* (published anonymously in 1721) gave the decay of religion and irresponsible conduct in public affairs as the reason for the disaster. His appointment as Dean of Derry came in 1724, the year after the death of Esther Vanhomrigh (Swift's 'Vanessa'), who left him half her property. His appointment was a rich one and with such affluence at his command Berkeley launched a scheme for the foundation of a missionary college in Bermuda that would be of great benefit to Americans, both native and immigrant. His plan is described in his *Proposal for the better supplying of Churches in our Foreign Plantations* (1725); he sailed for America in 1729 with high hopes and the promise of an essential grant from Robert Walpole. But three years went by, which Berkeley spent in Newport, Rhode Island, waiting for the grant that never materialized. But he did not waste his time; he formed a Literary and Philosophical Society and wrote the dialogue *Alciphron, or the Minute Philosopher* (1732), which sees the application of his philosophical principles in the defence of religion. His model for a college was put to excellent use in the founding of King's College in New York City – it later became Columbia University. Berkeley Divinity School in New Haven, Connecticut, was named after him; so was the city in California where the state university was founded in 1868. After returning to England Berkeley published his *Theory of Vision, or Visual Language Vindicated and Explained* (1733).

In 1734 Berkeley was given the bishopric of Cloyne, a remote diocese in the county of Cork in Ireland – perhaps as a consolation for the failure of his hopes in America. He remained in Ireland until 1752, his mind occupied with questions of social reform and religious speculation. *The Querist* (1735) shows the reformer asking penetrating questions about the matter of Ireland. *Siris: a Chain of Philosophical Reflexions* (1744) examines both physical and metaphysical questions. Berkeley retired to Oxford, where he died; he is commemorated by a marble tablet in Christ Church. Berkeley's notes, *The Commonplace Book*, were first published in A. C. Fraser's edition of *The Works of George Berkeley* (1871, revised edition 1901).

**Berners, John Bourchier, 2nd Baron** 1467–1533. Berners was probably born at Oxford and eventually succeeded to the baronage of his grandfather, gaining a knighthood of his own on the way. His sympathies lay with the Lancastrian faction and he was involved in an unsuccessful attempt to place the Earl of Richmond on the throne. He fled to Brittany, and when Richmond eventually won the throne at Bosworth in 1485 Berners was in favour with the new dynasty. He served both Henry VII and Henry VIII (he was Chancellor of the Exchequer in Henry VIII's reign and attended him at the Field of the Cloth of Gold).

As Captain Deputy of Calais from 1520, Lord Berners occupied his idle hours with translation, achieving results of such excellence that his place in English letters is assured. His principal work is his English version of Froissart's *Chroniques* (1523–22); also notable is **Huon of Bordeaux** (1535). Other translations include his graceful version of the unremarkable Breton *Arthur of Little Britain* (1555); *The Castell of Love* (1540); and an English version of a French translation (taken from the Spanish of Antonio de Guevara, purporting to be, but in fact not, from a Latin original), *The Golden Boke of Marcus Aurelius* (1535), which proved remarkably popular. Unfortunately this dubious book called for an ornate prose style, which was well within Berners' range, but the book's popularity opened the way for imitators and a great deal of affected rhetorical prose resulted.

**Berowne** In Shakespeare's *Love's Labour's Lost*, one of the lords attendant on the King of Navarre and who goes along, with reservations, with the withdrawal from the world. He falls in love with Rosaline, a lady attendant on the Princess of France, and she charges him to put his wit to better use.

**Berryman, John** 1914–72. Berryman was born in McAlester, Oklahoma. He was educated at South Kent School, Connecticut, Columbia University, and Clare College, Cambridge. He taught at the universities of Princeton, Washington, and Cincinnati and joined the faculty of the University of Minnesota in 1955. He taught there until his death. John Berryman's poems appeared in small magazines and reviews during the 1930s and he was one of *Five American Poets* (1940); his first volume was *Poems* (1942). His career continued with *The Dispossessed* (1948) and recognition came with *Homage to Mistress Bradstreet* (1956), a dialogue in verse between Berryman and the spirit of the 17th-century colonial poet (see **Bradstreet, Anne**). *77 Dream Songs* (1964, Pulitzer Prize) was the first part of a poetic sequence, almost a verse novel in which the central character, a middle-aged teacher, holds hard to permanent values in a shallow society which seems to recognize none. The sequence was completed with *History, His Dream, His Rest* (1968). In 1967 Berryman published the 115 love poems composed during the 1940s, *Berryman's Sonnets. Love and Fame* (1970) was the last volume published during his lifetime – he committed suicide in 1972. A posthumous volume, *Delusions* (1972), shows the poet looking towards the end of his life, the subject also of a novel, *Recovery* (1973). John Berryman was the author of a notable biography, *Stephen Crane* (1950).

**Bertram**  The young Count of Rousillon in Shakespeare's *All's Well that Ends Well.* The King of France gives him, against his will, to Helena, his mother's ward, as husband. He goes to war to get away from her, but the play ends in a questionable reconciliation.

*Bertrams, The*  A novel by Anthony Trollope, first published in 1859.

George Bertram, after distinguishing himself at Oxford, decides to travel for two years before a career at the Bar. He has expectations from his old uncle: he also has the love of Caroline Waddington who, while she confesses she could not be happy with a poor man, is nevertheless distressed when George Bertram goes abroad. A school-fellow of George's, Sir Henry Harcourt, who moves in influential circles, takes advantage of George's absence. Caroline has received no communications from George and decides to accept Harcourt.

Harcourt proves to be a time-serving shallow character, who was only anxious to marry Caroline because of her family's wealth. When George Bertram returns to England, Harcourt makes a point of parading his beautiful wife – who might have been George's. But to his fury Caroline falls in love with George all over again. They behave honourably, but Harcourt's jealousy leads to violent scenes and Caroline leaves him. The wretched Harcourt commits suicide.

A parallel story tells of Adela and Arthur; Adela has no expectations, nor has Arthur, but Adela marries him just because she loves him.

The novel has not been regarded with much favour and had a mixed reception. The other Bertrams, apart from George, are his shiftless amusing father, Sir Lionel, and his miserly uncle who possesses most of the family's wealth.

*Beryn, The Tale of*  An anonymous verse tale of unknown authorship which, until the work of W. W. Skeat, was attributed to Chaucer. Its date is uncertain but later than 1400; it exists in a single manuscript, the Northumberland Manuscript. A Prologue tells of the Pilgrims' arrival at Canterbury and the adventures of the Pardoner with a barmaid; a story, *The Second Merchant's Tale*, starts the homeward journey.

**Besant, Sir Walter** 1836–1901.  Walter Besant was born in Portsmouth, educated at King's College, London, and Christ's College, Cambridge, and was for a time a teacher in Mauritius. His health obliged him to leave the islands and he became secretary to the Palestine Exploration Fund from 1868 to 1886. His first published work was *Early French Poetry* (1868). This was followed by *Jerusalem* (with E. H. Palmer) in 1871 and *The French Humourists* in 1873. He was a contributor to *Once a Week* and through this made the acquaintance of James Rice (1844–82), a journalist, with whom he was to enjoy a successful collaboration in fiction. Their cooperative efforts produced several novels which achieved financial success though they are forgotten now. Among them were *Ready-Money Mortiboy* (1871), *The Golden Butterfly* (1876), *By Celia's Arbour* (1878), and *The Chaplain of the Fleet* (1881).

On his own, Besant wrote novels for a time which relied on a historical background; then, in 1882, he published *The Revolt of Man*, a romance which satirized the claims of women to political power. Thereafter his fiction expressed his thoughts on social conditions – to considerable effect in *All Sorts and Conditions of Men* (1882), and *Children of Gibeon* (1886), in which he drew attention to the appalling conditions which existed in the East End of London. He devoted a considerable amount of time and effort to establishing the People's Palace in Mile End

Road in the heart of east London as a many-faceted recreation centre for the people of the area. He helped to found the Society of Authors in 1884 and edited *The Author* (1890). He did much to clarify the author's financial position in *The Pen and the Book* (1889).

Historical works include *Rabelais* (1879), *Captain Cook* (1889), and (with W. J. Brodribb) *Constantinople* (1879). He began an ambitious *Survey of London* but did not live to complete it. The three volumes published were *London* (1892), *Westminster* (1895), and *South London* (1889). A posthumous *Autobiography* was published in 1902.

**Best, George** fl. 1578. Best was a friend of the explorer Martin Frobisher, who made three attempts to find a Northwest Passage in 1576, 1577, and 1578. Best wrote an account of Frobisher's first two voyages: *A True Discourse of the Late Voyages of Discoverie, for the Finding of a Passage to Cathaya by the Northweast, under the Conduct of Martin Frobisher Generall* (1578).

**Bestiary, The** An allegory of the late 12th or early 13th century, using a form long popular in western Europe for satirical observations on human character and probably originating in the

---

A drawing from a 12th-century English bestiary. A huge legendary fish, the Aspidochelone, deceives mariners into believing that its back is an island; then it submerges and drowns them all. *MS Ii.4.26, f.54v.* Cambridge University Library.

fables of Aesop. The name was also applied to popular studies in natural history. Bestiaries were known as early as the 5th century, and in later times were often illustrated. The Middle English poem so named is based on the Latin *Physiologus* of Thetbaldus and is chiefly of interest to scholars as an example of English verse in the making. Editions of the *Bestiary* are by T. Wright and J. O. Halliwell (1841) and by R. Morris for the Early English Text Society (1872). A modern edition is by J. A. W. Bennett and G. V. Smithers in *Early Middle English Verse and Prose, 1155–1300* (1968).

**Betjeman, Sir John** 1906–84. John Betjeman, the son of a business family of Dutch ancestry, was born in London. He was educated at Marlborough School and Magdalen College, Oxford, and turned to writing instead of entering the family business. He was a successful journalist and broadcaster, and an early advocate of the worth of Victorian architecture, long out of favour and in danger of being obliterated. He became general editor of the *Shell Guides* in 1934 and has published some 20 books of topographical and architectural interest. His verse, for which his name is most celebrated, was first published in 1931: *Mount Zion: or In Touch with the Infinite*. Succeeding collections were *Continual Dew: A Little Book of Bourgeois Verse* (1937), *Old Lights for New Chancels* (1940), *New Bats in Old Belfries* (1945). W. H. Auden made a selection of his work, published as *Slick: But not Streamlined* (New York, 1947) and a further selection was chosen and prefaced by John Sparrow (1948). *A Few Late Chrysanthemums* and *Poems in the Porch* (1954) were followed by *Collected Poems* (1958) and John Betjeman found himself in the enviable and rare position of being a best-selling poet. *Summoned by Bells* (1960), an ambitious autobiographical poem, succeeded equally well with the public. The author was knighted in 1969 and succeeded Cecil Day-Lewis as poet laureate in 1972.

**Betrothed, The** A novel by Sir Walter Scott, one of the two *Tales of the Crusades*, though in this novel the story takes place on the Welsh Marches during the reign of Henry II. It was first published in 1825.

The betrothed are Eveline Berenger and Hugo de Lacey, Constable of Chester. Hugo, just before departing for the Crusades, saves Eveline's life when her father is killed during an attack by the Welsh prince, Gwenwyn. A gallant and distinguished man, Hugo is much older than Eveline; her response is influenced by gratitude and respect.

Hugo leaves for the Crusades and Eveline is entrusted to the care of Hugo's nephew, Damian. The years of Hugo's absence are painful and difficult; Randel, a de Lacey kinsman, covets the estate, and there is malicious gossip about Eveline and Damian. Eveline does love Damian, but she intends to honour her pledge to Hugo. Randel succeeds in concocting a false charge of treason implicating Eveline and Damian, inevitably adding to it an accusation of their dishonourable love in Hugo's absence. But Hugo returns from the Holy Land and disposes of the false charge; he also releases Eveline from her pledge and bestows her on Damian.

**Betty** In Elizabeth Gaskell's *Cousin Phillis*, the shrewd forthright servant in the Holman household who sees, more clearly than anyone else, the reason for Phillis's decline and whose sharp wisdom puts her on the road to final recovery.

*Bevis: The Story of a Boy* A novel by Richard Jefferies, first published in 1882. It found its real audience when it was edited by E. V. Lucas and republished in 1904, as a book for young people. It was probably the first book in a vein which was later to be tapped with enormous success by writers like Arthur Ransome – holiday adventures recounted by children, in which they are the chief and sometimes the only characters. Bevis and Mark enjoy their adventures near their home, with 'the New Sea' and the surrounding country as their playground, and the attention to nature and the rural life form a large part of the book's appeal. The reservoir at Coate, where Jefferies was born, becomes 'the New Sea' of the story.

*Bevis of Hampton (or Beves of Hamtoun).* A Middle English verse romance of the early 14th century. (See **metrical romances**.) The story of Bevis is also told in Michael Drayton's *Polyolbion* and contains elements of Old English storytelling. Bevis is the son of Guy, Earl of Southampton; Guy is murdered at his wife's instigation by Mordure, son of the emperor of Germany. Guy's mother then marries Mordure and sells Bevis as a slave. At the court of the Saracen king, Ermyn, the handsome slave gains great favour and is offered the hand of Princess Josian. As a Christian he refuses, though he saves her from Brademond, an unwelcome suitor. He accepts Josian when she promises to change her faith; but the king refuses to countenance his daughter's apostasy, and sends Bevis to Brademond with a sealed letter. The letter contains orders that Bevis be imprisoned and he is held in a vile dungeon for seven years. Josian is given in marriage first to Yvor of Mombrant, who repudiates her when the marriage is not consummated, and then to Earl Miles, whom she murders on the wedding night. Bevis escapes, and she flees to England with him after he rescues her from the stake. He kills Mordure and regains his inheritance, marries Josian, and is welcomed as a worthy knight by King Edgar. *Bevis of Hampton* was edited by W. B. Turnbull for the Maitland Club (1838), and by F. Kolbing for the Early English Text Society (1885–94). Modern versions are by L. A. Hibbard (1911) and A. Sampson (1963).

**Bianca** (i) Katharina's younger sister in Shakespeare's *The Taming of the Shrew*. She is prettier than her sister, is her father's favourite, and has many suitors – but she must wait until Katharina has a husband before she can marry.

**Bianca** (ii) Cassio's mistress in Shakespeare's *Othello*. Cassio gives her the handkerchief that Iago had concealed among his belongings; he does not know it belongs to Desdemona but Bianca sees at once that it is a woman's handkerchief. The scene between them is deliberately misinterpreted to Othello by Iago; Othello believes that Cassio's words of love refer to Desdemona.

*Bible, The Great* See **Coverdale, Miles**.

**Bible in English, The** The history of the Bible in English goes back to Anglo-Saxon times. No complete translation was made then, but there were partial translations, including one of the first fifty psalms which may have been the work of Alfred the Great himself, and if not was certainly part of the literary movement which took place with his encouragement and under his protection. With the West Saxon gospels, which belong to a date round AD 1000, there is already a foreshadowing of language which has echoed down the centuries to our own day: 'Faeder ure þu þe eart on heofonum, si in nama gehalgod': 'Our Father, which art in heaven, hallowed be thy name'. There were metrical and prose versions of some parts of the Bible in Middle English, but the next major development was the translation done under the influence of John Wycliffe (1329–84) and partly by his own hand. The outlines we know appear, here and there, a little more clearly: 'Oure fadir that art in hevenes halowid be thi name'. Wycliffe was a reformer, critical of papal pretensions and holding that the Bible was the true test of Christian belief and behaviour; guilty, in his numerous works, of not less than 267 errors – or so the Council of Constance (1415) said, and thought there was nothing for it but to burn his books and dig up his bones. The Wycliffite versions of the Bible, however, continued in circulation, with the help of the Lollards and others of like mind.

These early versions were made from the Latin Vulgate. With Tyndale (?1494–1536) the Greek New Testament and the Hebrew Old Testament became sources. Like Wycliffe, Tyndale was a reformer. He found it impossible to do his work in this country, because of the disfavour, to put it no more strongly, of the ecclesiastical authorities. He was strangled and burnt at Vilvorde, near Brussels, but his edition of the New Testament in English (1526) and his translations from the Old Testament made their way. Much more than Wycliffe, Tyndale contributed to the style and rhythms of the Authorized Version of King James I's reign. He wrote simply and directly, with the very tone of common conversation where that was required. He also had a grasp of the parallelism of Hebrew poetry, a feature which the Authorized Version reproduces. Tyndale's work was attacked by, among others, More (now St Thomas More), who certainly did not always have the best of the argument; the saint's primary concern was the maintenance of the authority of Rome. The next version after Tyndale's was that of Miles Coverdale (1488–1568), whose best-known work is the Psalms, which remained in use in the Book of Common Prayer after the completion of the Authorized Version. Coverdale used a diversity of sources, including contemporary vernacular versions and in particular the German. His version has indeed been described (by A. C. Partridge, *English Biblical Translation*, 1973) as 'an eclectic Bible, "a translation of translations", in which attention was confined to a faithful, elegant and readable text.' Other versions about this time were the Great Bible (1539), the Geneva Bible (1560) started by and for Protestant exiles in Mary's reign, the Bishop's Bible (1568), and the Roman Catholic Douai-Reims version (1582–1609).

In the light of this history, one can understand why the translators of the Authorized Version (1611), in their address to the Reader, eirenically explained that they 'never thought from the beginning' that they would 'need to make a new translation, nor yet make of a bad one a good one . . . but to make a good one better, or out of many good ones, one principal good one, not justly to be excepted against.' The work was initiated by King James I in 1604. There was a panel of 54 translators divided into six groups, two centred in Westminster, two in Oxford, and two in Cambridge. The work of these groups was revised by a smaller group comprising two translators from each centre; the revisers apparently heard each verse read aloud to them, so that the final judgment was on the spoken word – which must partly account for the consistently high aural quality of the work. Tyndale's, Coverdale's, and the Geneva Bible were the main 'good ones' out of which this 'principal good one' was made, though traces of other versions, including Wycliffe's, are to be found. The translators were themselves learned in Greek and Hebrew, and at the head of the first Westminster group was no less a person than Lancelot Andrewes.

It is this Authorized Version, the culmination of so many and so long labours, which became *the* Bible in English and effectively ousted all others. With the Book of Common Prayer (1549, revised 1552, 1559, and 1662), it became the central literary work of which all Englishmen knew something, of which all knew something by heart; those who could not read hearing the books read Sunday by Sunday in their parish churches, or at the least at christenings, marriages, and funerals. The frivolity of thinking of these books as 'designed to be read as literature' was left to the 20th century; they were read as a source of truth and for a pattern of conduct, and *used* as much as read. Their importance in the history of English literature is far from being thereby diminished. Jonathan Swift, in *A Proposal for Correcting the English Tongue* (1712), was 'persuaded that the translators of the Bible were masters of an English stile much fitter for the work, than any we see in our present writings' and spoke of 'the simplicity which runs through the whole'. The Prayer Book he thought has as much 'true sublime eloquence' as was 'any where to be found in the language'. More remarkably, he observed that 'if it were not for the Bible and the Common Prayer Book in the vulgar tongue, we should hardly be able to understand anything written among us an hundred years ago: for those books being perpetually read in churches, have proved a kind of standard for the language, especially for the common people.' Swift was aware, as any literate person must be, of the importance of not losing touch with the past. But what have the relatively illiterate lost? 'Yea, though I walk through the valley of the shadow of death . . . .' – such sentences, known to everybody, have for centuries echoed in the common language in times of stress; the psalms are full of such matter. The short prayers called 'collects' are likewise full of phrases which are only now slipping from ordinary usage, to our great loss ('read mark, learn and inwardly digest';

'out of the mouths of babes and sucklings'), and which once provided a familiar model of language homely, succinct, and judicious.

The language of the Authorized Version and the Book of Common Prayer, having entered into common speech, provided a point of reference open to all and facilitating communication between people of all kinds by providing a common fund of allusions, conscious and unconscious. If these books have provided a fund of homely phrases in ordinary conversation, down to our own time, they have also been woven into the texture of our general literature, to an extent now unsuspected by the ordinary reader – so much so that pretending to a knowledge of English literature, without knowledge of the Authorized Version, is almost as bad as pretending to a knowledge of Greek literature without a knowledge of Homer. It is not merely such books as Herbert's *The Temple* that require such understanding; more profane literature, and in particular novels, are full of it. Thomas Hardy, who certainly did not regard himself as a Christian, is full of allusions, as a glance at any annotated edition of, say, *Jude the Obscure* will illustrate. Developments in technology, the internationalizing of the English language, and the abuse of technical terminologies by people whose understanding of them is slight have increasingly threatened the central coherence of the language, and give a new force to Coleridge's remark about the English Bible, that 'without this holdfast, our vitiated imaginations would refine away language to mere abstractions'.

Revisers and translators of the Bible since and including the Revised Version (1881–95) have been increasingly reckless. The Revised Version counts as extremely conservative, but it had the seeds of destruction in it in the care the translators took always to translate the same word in the original by the same word in English – a mechanical principle which the authors of the Authorized Version had expressly avoided. There have been a number of new versions since then, none of them of any literary value. That they should so largely have displaced the Authorized Version for use in churches, as the Alternative Service book (1980) has largely replaced the Book of Common Prayer, must be taken as a mark of an inability to draw on the resources of the past. This means, in effect, an impoverishment of the intelligence, in the world at large as well as in the Church. One of the keys to a thousand years of English thought and literature is being thrown away.

C. H. SISSON

***Bible in Spain, The*** An account of travels in Spain by George Borrow.

Borrow was a colporteur (distributor) for the British and Foreign Bible Society in Spain for five years, between 1835 and 1840, a time of unrest due to the Carlist claims to the throne. At that time Spain was as exotic as Persia and Borrow's book was a great success in England. It is regarded as a classic among English travel books, giving a vivid and truthful picture of life in Spain.

**Bickerstaff, Isaac** See **Swift, Jonathan**.

**Bickerstaffe, Isaac** *c*.1735–1812. An Irishman, Bickerstaffe was, according to the *Dictionary of National Biography*, dismissed from the Marines 'under discreditable circumstances' and became a successful writer of lyric comedy in London. His first, *Thomas and Sally: or The Sailor's Return* (Covent Garden, November 1760), included songs and led the way to his next success, the ballad opera *Love in a Village* (Covent Garden, December 1762). He was the author of six more, the best of which had the advantage of original songs by Charles Dibdin: *The Maid of the Mill* (Covent Garden, January 1765) and *Lionel and Clarissa* (Covent Garden, February 1768). Other works were *The Hypocrite* (Drury Lane, November 1768), which was an adaptation of Molière's *Tartuffe*, and a number of comedies now forgotten. Bickerstaffe, who numbered David Garrick, Samuel Johnson, and Oliver Goldsmith among his friends, was suspected of 'a capital crime' in 1772, again according to the *Dictionary of National Biography*. A spiteful contemporary pamphlet, aimed at Garrick, suggests that the 'capital crime' was a homosexual offence. Bickerstaffe fled to the continent and spent the rest of his life in exile. He died in poverty.

**Bierce, Ambrose Gwinnet** 1842–*c*.1914. Ambrose Bierce was born in Horse Cave Creek, Ohio. His father was a farmer and sternly religious; Bierce received the most basic education and later in life was embarrassed by his origins. The Civil War gave him the chance of escaping from his environment and he reached the rank of major. But the war disgusted him and he saw his part as a soldier as little more than that of a paid assassin. This bitterness was later to give great force to his Civil War stories.

After hostilities ceased Bierce went West, to California, and lived as best he could until he found himself as a journalist with contributions to the celebrated *Overland Monthly*, which Bret Harte had helped to establish. Later he published his own newsletter and with Harte, Mark Twain, and Joaquin Miller constituted a Western literary circle. This became a virtual literary establishment, and with the departure of Mark Twain and Harte for the East, one where Bierce's position was unchallenged. He began to publish his stories about this time and was already famous as a critic. His marriage to the daughter of a successful Nevada silver miner enabled the Bierces to spend some time in Europe (1872–76).

In England Bierce was a busy contributor to periodicals and published three collections of sketches; but he was not quite such a success as he had been in San Francisco and he returned there to write for Hearst's *Examiner*. His years in England had sharpened his style. His column 'The Prattler', which offered gossip, stories, and epigrams, was widely read and he was something of a literary dictator in the West. He published *Tales of Soldiers and Civilians* in 1891 (called *In the Midst of Life* in England and in the 1898 edition), and *Can Such Things Be?* in 1893.

Bierce went to Washington in 1897 as the capital correspondent for the Hearst papers. He contributed to *Cosmopolitan* and in 1906 published *The Devil's Dictionary*, a volume of ironic definitions. He also published verse and essays and in 1909 produced the first volume of his *Collected Works*, which reached 12 volumes in 1912.

The author's personal life did not remain happy; he was divorced in 1904 when he was 62 and after that severed all connection with his family. He went to Mexico, where civil war was raging, in 1913 – and disappeared. No one knows exactly when or how he died.

**Biglow Papers, The** These satirical verses by James Russell Lowell were aimed at particular targets. The first series, written in 1848, opposed the Mexican War and the second (1867) the policy of the Confederate states in the Civil War. The papers are written in Yankee dialect.

In the first series Hosea Biglow is a young farmer in New England. Three of the 'papers' are letters to him in verse from his friend Birdofredom Sawin, who is now a private soldier. Birdofredom at first accepts the call of destiny but is later totally disillusioned when he is required to murder for ninepence a day (he earned more money slaughtering animals) folks who 'ain't much diff'rent from wut we be'. The other six papers are Hosea's comments on politicians, recruiting officers, declarations of 'principles', etc.

In the second series Birdofredom is now living in the South and is convinced by Confederate propaganda: two of the 'papers' are letters from him. The rest are Hosea Biglow's comments on the struggle (Jefferson Davis is mercilessly burlesqued), Southern attitudes and England's selfish involvement because of the cotton trade, 'conciliation', the approaching peace, and reconstruction.

**Big Money, The** The third novel of the trilogy *U.S.A.* See **Dos Passos, John (Roderigo)**.

**Billings, Josh** 1818–85. The pseudonym of Henry Wheeler Shaw, who was born in Massachusetts. He worked in a variety of occupations and spent some time in the West. Like Artemus Ward, Petroleum V. Nasby, and Mark Twain, he began his career as a humorist with contributions to local newspapers (he was 45 by this time). Artemus Ward liked the pieces by 'Josh Billings' and helped him publish his first collection, *Josh Billings, His Sayings*, in 1865. Thereafter he became a favourite exponent of agrarian folk wisdom and reached an immense public with his comments on government, fashionable pretension, and political corruption. He lectured in his Josh Billings persona to huge audiences and his collections were eagerly bought: *Josh Billings on Ice, and Other Things* (1868), *Everybody's Friend* (1874), *Josh Billings' Trump Kards* (1877), and others. From 1869 to 1880 he published a parody annual called *Farmer's Allminax*.

**Billy Budd, Foretopman** A short novel by Herman Melville, more than one draft of which was found among his papers after his death. It was not published until 1924 but has since become as famous as *Moby-Dick*. The book is dedicated to 'Jack Chase, Englishman. Wherever that great heart may now be'. Jack Chase was the captain of the maintop on the *United States* when Melville served on her (see *White-Jacket*) and Billy Budd, the Handsome Sailor, is in part modelled on him. The action of the novel is set in 1797 during the French Revolutionary Wars, on board a British man-of-war. During that year there was mutiny in the British Navy.

*HMS Indomitable* impresses a seaman from a merchant ship. Lt Ratcliffe, upon sight of Billy Budd, takes him to serve on the *Indomitable*, without sparing a glance for the rest of the crew. The captain tells him he is depriving him of his best man and launches into a hymn of praise: 'the jewel of 'em'. Billy is a man who brings peace with him, yet is as strong as he is beautiful. The ship's bully 'now really loves Billy . . . but they all love him. Some of 'em do his washing, darn his old trousers for him.' Ratcliffe takes his prize, '. . . where's my beauty? Ah, here he comes . . . Apollo with his portmanteau!'

On board the *Indomitable* Billy is discovered to be a foundling; he has no knowledge of his parentage. He is illiterate but he can sing; the only flaw he seems to possess is a stammer which afflicts him in times of stress, making it almost impossible for him to utter a word. His commander on the man-of-war is Captain Vere, cultured and inclined to be withdrawn, but a fine seaman and a good captain to serve under. The master-at-arms is John Claggart, a mysterious character of whom it is rumoured that he was obliged to go to sea because of something discreditable in his past. But nothing factual is known, only that he is of a different stamp. Claggart is tall and has strong fine features. He is an excellent master-at-arms but is not popular with the crew.

Claggart's attitude to Billy Budd, now becoming the love of the *Indomitable*, is equivocal. He calls him 'a sweet and pleasant lad' and yet seems harsh with him. An old hand, Dansker, warns Billy that Claggart is down on him. Billy is incredulous; he is naive and cannot see why the master-at-arms should bear him ill will. But after the unsuccessful pursuit of an enemy ship Claggart reports to Vere that there is discontent among the crew; Billy Budd is at the root of it.

Billy, struck dumb by the monstrous accusation in front of the captain, strikes Claggart a violent blow and kills him. Vere, whatever his feelings may be, is in command of a ship in HM Navy and Billy Budd has killed the master-at-arms. Vere knows that Claggart was lying and he is aware that Billy suffers from a paralysing stammer in moments of great mental stress. He summons a drumhead court and, with a great many words to demonstrate his awareness of the factors which humanity insists must be considered, yet holds the court to the basic fact of murder and to the recent mutinies in the navy. In effect he tells them what their verdict must be and then tells Billy that he will be hanged.

Billy's body is sewn into his hammock and consigned to the deep. The ship's surgeon confides to the purser that the execution puzzled him. Billy had called a blessing on Captain Vere; after that the hanging had proceeded but there were none of the usual horrors, no frenzied threshing and violent spasms. It was as if Billy had willed himself dead before the execution was carried out. A year later Vere, dying in action, murmurs Billy's name. But not in remorse.

The novel presents three archetypes in a closed setting. Billy represents serene innocence and he is a believable character, in spite of the merchant captain's eulogy at the opening. His stammer is the weakness inflicted by nature that saves him from impossible perfection. Claggart is his antithesis; both handsome and capable, he is also pale, withdrawn, and charmless. Billy, without knowing it, exerts a powerful attraction for him and Claggart is tortured by the boy's presence, which diminishes him in his own eyes. He would give anything for Billy's regard yet what leads him to destruction is the terrible knowledge that he would never be equal to it. Vere is contemptible: a man who can find time to read and think but to whom life can only be lived within the certain confines of a duty for him to perform.

The book closes with the poem 'Billy in the Darbies'. The title means that Billy is in irons, waiting for his last hour, and thinking of how it will be. The poem is one of Melville's best, a moving epilogue to a remarkable novel.

After decades of obscurity, *Billy Budd* is now as famous as *Moby-Dick*. Considerable credit for the renewal of interest in Melville's work in England must be given to John Lehmann, who published the lesser-known books in attractive formats after World War II. Benjamin Britten's opera from *Billy Budd* also helped draw attention to an unjustly neglected book, but E. M. Forster's libretto does peculiar things to Melville. Claggart is a cypher and Vere is presented as the sort of captain any sailor could have told Forster has never existed, even if he provides the chorus (the crew) with a reason for singing things like 'Long live our Captain, Starry Vere!'

**Bingham, Joseph** 1668–1723. A native of Yorkshire, Bingham was born at Wakefield and attended Wakefield Grammar School. He completed his education at University College, Oxford, where he became a fellow in 1689. In literature he is remembered for his exhaustive *Origines Ecclesiasticae: or The Antiquities of the Christian Church*, a 20-year labour that was published in ten volumes (1708–22) and has never been superseded.

**Binyon, (Robert) Laurence** 1869–1943. Laurence Binyon was born in Lancaster and educated at St Paul's School and Trinity College, Oxford. His poem 'Persephone' won him the Newdigate Prize and he continued to write poetry while becoming a distinguished art historian. He joined the Department of Printed Books in the British Museum in 1893, and later became Keeper of the Department of Oriental Prints and Drawings, where he stayed until 1933. Binyon published a fair amount of poetry but is known to most readers as the author of two war poems: 'For the Fallen' (1914) and 'The Burning of the Leaves' (1942). His verse translation of Dante's *Divina Commedia* was published in three parts – *The Inferno* (1933), *The Purgatorio* (1938), and *The Paradiso* (1943) – and was well received. Among his books on the fine arts were *Dutch Etchers of the Seventeenth Century* (1895), *Paintings in the Far East* (1908), and *Landscape in English Art and Poetry* (1931). Binyon published a volume of *Collected Poems* in 1931.

**Biographia Literaria** A 'literary autobiography' by Samuel Taylor Coleridge, first published in 1817. The autobiographical thread which is in fact very slight, is found in the early part of the book. The middle section is now regarded as unimportant, being a presentation of philosophical matter taken directly from, but not acknowledged to, the German philosopher Friedrich von Schelling. The last part is the most prized, being regarded as the finest philosophical poetic criticism in the English language up to that time.

**Birch, Thomas** See **seventeenth-century historical collections**.

**Birney, (Alfred) Earle** 1904–  . Earle Birney was born in Calgary, Alberta, and grew up in the mountains of Alberta and British Columbia. He was educated at the University of British Columbia and also studied at the universities of California and London. He became Professor of English at British Columbia in 1946, and Writer in Residence at the University of Toronto in 1965. Birney became literary editor of *The Canadian Forum* in 1936 and began to make a reputation as a poet with the publication of *David and Other Poems* (1942). Among his other books of verse are *Now is Time* (1945), *The Strait of Anian* (1952), *Ice Cod Bell or Stone* (1962), and *Near False Creek Mouth* (1964). *Trial of a City* (1952) is a poetic drama; *Turvey* (1949) and *Down the Long Table* (1955) are novels. *The Creative Writer* is a book of literary essays.

**Birrell, Augustine** 1850–1933. The son of a Baptist minister of Liverpool, Birrell became a barrister in 1875 and entered Parliament in 1889. He became President of the Board of Education (1905) and Chief Secretary for Ireland, a post he resigned after the storm in Parliament following the Easter Rising in 1916. Birrell's collections of literary essays, *Obiter Dicta* (1884, 1887, and 1924), were popular; his other writings include *The Life of Charlotte Brontë* (1887) and also *William Hazlitt* (1902) and *Andrew Marvell* (1905), both contributions to the English Men of Letters series.

**Bishop orders his Tomb at St Praxed's Church, The** A poem by Robert Browning, first published in *Dramatic Romances and Lyrics*, one of the *Bells and Pomegranates* series, in 1845. The poem is a dramatic monologue delivered by a bishop on his deathbed, his 'nephews' (illegitimate sons) gathered round him. He wants to be buried in far better style than his rival and predecessor Gandolf, who envied him his mistress but who seized the best site for his tomb. The poem is a study in character, a subtle and concentrated picture of a Renaissance prince of the Church, sensual and worldly, highly placed in a world where the Church often wielded more power than kings. The bishop sees nothing untoward in the thought of interceding with St Praxed so that his sons will have healthy mistresses and fine horses, though the saint (Santa Prassede, whose church is in Rome, on the Esquiline) was a holy virgin who gave all she possessed to the poor.

**Bishop's Bible, The** A version of the Bible that was in effect a revision, under the direction of Archbishop Matthew Parker, of *The Great Bible* of Miles Coverdale. It followed the verse divisions of *The Geneva Bible* and gave the initials of each editor at the end of his part of the work. It was published in 1568 and was the official English Bible until the Authorized Version of 1611.

**Bishops' Wars, The** The precursors of the Civil War in England, 'The Bishops' Wars' (1639, 1640) were the result of the Scots' resistance to Charles I and to the Book of Common Prayer, which he decided would be beneficial to them and which they detested. It not only bore the scent of popery but it came from England and discontent, which had hitherto smouldered chiefly among the upper classes on account of the Act of Revocation of 1625, now spread to the ordinary Scottish people. The first Bishops' War in 1639 never actually happened because Charles I was unable to raise an effective army. The Treaty of Berwick (18 June 1639) ended with the king giving assurance that ecclesiastical matters would be determined by a general assembly. The Scots promptly swept away Anglican episcopacy (which they regarded as the next thing to popery) and set about overturning the Act of Revocation. Charles I saw his authority in Scotland reduced to nothing and the 'war' was resumed in 1640. The king's army was a scratch force and when his troops were faced by the Scots at Newburn on the Tyne they simply threw down their arms and ran away. The sequel was the calling of Parliament – the Long Parliament – which was eventually to prove fatal for Charles I.

**Black, William** 1841–98. A Scots novelist who enjoyed considerable popularity during his lifetime. His principal theme was the character produced by the Highland and Hebridean environment, who seeks his fortune in alien places. *A Daughter of Heth* (1871), *A Princess of Thule* (1874), and *Macleod of Dare* (1878) were highly regarded – the last had illustrations by no less than 12 different artists. *The Strange Adventures of a Phaethon* (1872) was a blend of guidebook and novel, notable for Black's gift as a word painter. William Black was war correspondent for the *Morning Star* during the Franco-Prussian War and subsequently subeditor of the *Daily News*.

**Black Arrow, The**   A story for young people by Robert Louis Stevenson, first published in *Young Folks* (June to October 1883) as *The Black Arrow: A Tale of Tunstall Forest*, by Captain George North. It did not appear in volume form until 1888.

After *Treasure Island* Stevenson was asked for another serial for the magazine. He was fond of browsing in the Paston Letters and he wrote a story of the times of the Wars of the Roses. In the event, it proved much more popular with young people than *Treasure Island*, though the earlier novel far outstripped it in quality, and remains a perennial favourite while *The Black Arrow* is now hardly known.

**Black Beauty**   See **Sewell, Anna**.

**Black Book of Carmarthen, The**   A Welsh manuscript of the 12th century containing a collection of ancient Welsh poetry, *The Black Book of Carmarthen* is the oldest known manuscript of the work of the Welsh bards of the 6th and 7th centuries. Of particular interest is 'Stanzas of the Graves', which refers to Arthur and the mystery surrounding his grave and implies the existence of a belief that Arthur will return. Ancient songs containing that belief were known to William of Malmesbury, and the tradition was strong in Wales, Cornwall, and Brittany. The Battle of Camlan is mentioned, and Arthur's principal knights, Bedwyr (Bedivere) and Kai (Kay). Gereint (Geraint) appears as one of Arthur's warriors in one poem, whilst another takes the form of a dialogue between Arthur and his gatekeeper, Glewlwyd of the Mighty Grasp. Questioned by Glewlwyd, Arthur describes his court and his followers – a foreshadowing of the tradition of the Round Table. *The Black Book of Carmarthen* was edited by J. G. Evans (1907).

**Black Dwarf, The**   The first of Sir Walter Scott's *Tales of My Landlord*, published in 1816.

Elshie of the Mucklestanes (Elshender the Recluse) is a dwarf of great strength and ugliness who has built himself a retreat of heavy stones in wild country; he has a reputation for harshness with regard to his fellow men. The period is the early 18th century. The dwarf, in spite of his reputation, seems to have remarkable and mysterious influence in the surrounding countryside and in the end is revealed to be the rich Sir Edward Manley who, embittered by a hopeless love and his own deformity, prefers to live away from his fellow men.

**Black Lamb and Grey Falcon**   See **West, Dame Rebecca**.

**Blackmore, R(ichard) D(oddridge)**   1825–1900.   Blackmore was born at Longworth in Berkshire and educated at Blundell's School and Exeter College, Oxford. He began his writing career as a poet but turned to fiction in 1864 with *Clara Vaughan* and *Cradock Nowell* (1866). His third novel, **Lorna Doone** (1869), was a major success, a bestseller in its day and a favourite ever since.

Blackmore, a popular novelist from that time on, went on to write more romances with a historical background: *The Maid of Sker* (1872), *Alice Lorraine: a Tale of the South Downs* (1875), *Cripps the Carrier* (1877), *Christowell: a Dartmoor Tale* (1881), *Springhaven: a Tale of the Great War* (1887), and many more. He was also the author of two works of historical investigation, *Fotheringay and Mary Queen of Scots* (1886) and *The Betrothal Ring of Mary Queen of Scots* (1887). But, like Charles Reade, he is one of those authors who has secured a place in English fiction with one novel that surpasses in quality the rest of his work.

**Blackstone, Sir William**   See *Commentaries on the Laws of England*.

**Blackwood's Magazine**   William Blackwood, the Edinburgh publisher, was encouraged to found his monthly magazine by the success of Constable with *The Edinburgh Review* and Murray with *The Quarterly Review*. He held Tory sympathies and hoped to offer more effective opposition to *The Edinburgh Review* than did the more literary *Quarterly*. The magazine started badly in July 1817, and after the first three numbers Blackwood decided on sensationalism, turning to John Gibson Lockhart, James Hogg, and John Wilson. Their joint effort produced the *Chaldee MS*, which satirized Edinburgh worthies in scriptural language, making *Blackwood's* notorious and widely bought. The same fourth issue included Wilson's attack on Coleridge and *Biographia Literaria* and Lockhart's on Leigh Hunt, editor of the radical *The Examiner*, and his 'adherents', among them Shelley and Keats. Lockhart's vicious attack on Keats was published in the issue of August 1818. William Maginn, an Irishman who joined Wilson and Lockhart, probably invented the *Noctes Ambrosianae*, which were a popular feature of *Blackwood's* from 1822 to 1835. A notable contributor in the early years of the magazine (the *Maga*, as its fans called it) was Thomas De Quincey.

**Blair, Robert** 1699–1746. Blair was born in Edinburgh, the son of a clergyman, and became a clergyman himself. While minister at Athelstaneford in East Lothian, he wrote a blank-verse poem called *The Grave* (1743), which owed much to Edward Young's *Night Thoughts*. A curious example of morbid meditation in the 'graveyard' mode, it was popular with middle-class dissenters for a number of years and one edition (1808) was illustrated by William Blake, no less.

**Blake, Nicholas** See **Day-Lewis, C(ecil)**.

**Blake, William** 1757–1827. William Blake was the son of James Blake, originally O'Neill, an Irishman who kept a successful hosier's shop in London, near Golden Square. James Blake was a Dissenter and had been attracted to the doctrines of Emanuel Swedenborg; nevertheless his son William was baptized at St James's Church in Piccadilly. He never went to school; he was an obstinate boy and his education was chiefly imparted by his mother. The home was apparently a warm and happy one; Blake remembered his parents with affection and his free spirit was nourished by the lack of conventional restraints, though he came close to being soundly thrashed for declaring that he saw, among other visions, a tree filled with angels at Peckham Rye. He read anything that came his way, including Shakespeare, Milton, Ben Jonson, and the Bible, and somehow picked up a knowledge of French, Italian, Latin, Greek, and Hebrew.

At the age of 14 Blake was apprenticed to the engraver James Basire at Great Queen Street. Basire was the second choice of master to the boy who displayed a talent for drawing as soon as he could hold a pencil; the first, William Ryland, was rejected by Blake after a visit to his studio with his father. The reason he gave was that Ryland had the mark of the gallows on him; 12 years later Ryland was hanged for forgery.

Basire sent his pupil to make drawings of Westminster Abbey and other old churches and buildings. The influence of gothic art on Blake began at this time, as did his fascination with the nude, through a study of Henry Fuseli's translation of Johann Joseph Winckelmann's *Reflec-*

William Blake. A detail from the portrait by T. Phillips, 1807. National Portrait Gallery, London.

*tions on the Painting and Sculpture of the Greeks.* Blake stayed with Basire until he was 21, when he was accepted at the recently founded Royal Academy at Somerset House. He wanted to be more than a journeyman engraver, though his skill in that field would have assured him a fair living. He married Catherine Boucher in 1782, and the Blakes had their first home in Leicester Fields. Among their neighbours were Joshua Reynolds, the pioneer surgeon and anatomist John Hunter, and Jane Hogarth, the artist's widow.

In 1783 two of Blake's friends, the artist John Flaxman and a blue-stocking named Mrs Mathew, decided to print a collection of his poems. One of them actually dated from his 12th year and most were written before he was 21; Blake himself regarded them as no more than attempts at writing poetry but his friends took a different view and they were right. *Poetical Sketches* contains such poems as 'To the Muses' and 'My silks and fine array'. At the Royal Academy meanwhile, Blake the artist was beginning to feel restless; an institution which honoured tradition was not the place for him though he benefited greatly from its facilities, particularly in the study of anatomy and its life classes.

If Blake was restless at the Royal Academy he

was uncomfortable in society. Flaxman and other influential friends introduced him, and about 1783 or 1784 Blake attempted a satire on it. *An Island in the Moon* was not completed and was unknown until the 20th century. Not a success, it is chiefly notable for the first drafts of three poems that appeared later in the little coloured book known as *Songs of Innocence* (1789), published in the same year as *The Book of Thel*. A work written during those years, the rhythmical chant *Tiriel*, was not published until 1874; it is heavily symbolic, but the mystic strain evident in its lines found more lasting expression in *Songs of Innocence* and *The Book of Thel*.

In 1794 Blake added *Songs of Experience* to an edition of *Songs of Innocence*; the complete title of the collection was **Songs of Innocence and of Experience** *shewing the Two Contrary States of the Human Soul* (no separate edition of *Songs of Experience* is known). These short rich poems enshrine Blake's humanity and his questioning of the condition of his world; more important still they are the expression of his attitude, and are unique in English poetry. Between the publication of *Innocence* (1789) and *Experience* (1794) Blake's friendships with William Godwin and Thomas Paine developed and the poet's revolutionary spirit with them. He published two sets of prose aphorisms, *There is no Natural Religion*, and a third, *All Religions are One* (both *c.*1788) as well as *The French Revolution, A Poem in Seven Books* (*c.*1791). Only one book of *The French Revolution* exists; this survived in a printer's proof and was not published until 1913. It is not known whether Blake completed more than the first book, or if he destroyed the manuscript of the completed poem. The latter is possible for the speed of events in the Revolution overtook many writers. But events could have no influence on Blake the revolutionary philosopher: 1790 was the year in which he engraved **The Marriage of Heaven and Hell**, his principal prose work. The Blakes moved south of the Thames to Lambeth in 1793.

In his new home Blake executed some of his most famous engravings, including those for *The Book of Job* and for Edward Young's *Night Thoughts*. He wrote *The Visions of the Daughters of Albion* (1793) and introduced the figures of his personal mythology – Urizen, the grim symbol of restrictive morality, and Orc, the arch-rebel. Urizen appears in all his depressing characteristics in *America: a Prophecy* (1793). The following year saw the publication of *Songs of Experience*, almost the last of the direct heartfelt utterances that gave Blake his place among the major English poets. His mind seems to have been so full

that a means of expressing any coherent philosophy eluded him. Flashes of beauty frequently occur and are treasured; but the mystical poems are little read. Lovers of Blake's songs retire baffled after trying to follow the direction of Blake's thoughts, unsure, even with a new mythology as a guide, of what he is trying to say.

The ideas expressed in *The Marriage of Heaven and Hell* (1790) and the personified principles encountered in *The Visions of the Daughters of Albion* are developed in *Europe* and *The Book of Urizen* (1794), *The Book of Ahania*, *The Book of Los*, and *The Song of Los* (1795), in which Blake pursues his exposure of the errors of the moral code. Urizen, giver of restrictive morality, has been expelled from the abode of the immortals and has taken possession of man; his agent, or archangel, is Enitharmon. Los is apparently the champion of Light and the lord of Time, but is held in bondage. Orc is the symbol of anarchy, opposed to Urizen. The whole sequence is a curious inversion of Milton's *Paradise Lost*; Blake denounced Milton for trying to justify the evil committed by God, but his admiration for the poet was unlimited. Blake's criticism of Christianity is strongest in *Europe* and *The Song of Los*. *Vala* was probably begun in 1795 but remained in manuscript until first published in the 20th century. The altered version was called *The Four Zoas, The Torments of Love and Jealousy in the Death and Judgement of Albion the Ancient Man* (1797). This is usually cited as the most difficult of Blake's works; the original title continued with the words 'or The Death and Judgement of the Ancient Man, A Dream of Nine Nights'. The nine nights of the poem and the deeds of the four Zoas – Urizen (reason), Urthonah (spirit), Luvah (passion), and Tharmas (the body) – are traced in a great cloud of symbols; Urizen and Orc are opposed to each other; the oppressive moral code is condemned; Orc and liberty are triumphant, and the figure of Jesus as Redeemer is introduced.

In 1800 Blake was taken up by a wealthy dilettante, William Hayley, who had a brief reputation as a poet, and the Blakes went to live in Hayley's house at Felpham in Sussex. They stayed for three years but the association was not a success and they returned to London in 1803. At Felpham Blake began work on *Milton, A Poem in Two Books, To Justify the Ways of God to Men*; it was completed and engraved between 1803 and 1808. The best-known part of this poem, in which Milton returns to Earth and in the person of the living poet corrects the spiritual error glorified in *Paradise Lost*, is the conclusion of the preface – the lines beginning 'And did those feet in ancient time'. *Jerusalem: The Emanation of the Giant Albion*, composed between 1804 and 1820, is a difficult poem expounding Blake's theory of imagination. Albion (Man) is continually torn between the forces of imagination and the forces of natural religion. The poem contains statements which, once read, lodge in the mind: 'He who would do good to another must do it in Minute Particulars'; 'General Good is the plea of the scoundrel, hypocrite and flatterer'; 'For Art and Science cannot exist but in minutely organized Particulars'. But the most familiar lines from Jerusalem are those beginning 'England! awake!'. *The Ghost of Abel* (1822) came the year after Byron's *Cain* and challenges the younger poet's viewpoint in a poetic drama of no more than 70 lines. The shadow of Cain is seen as Satan's work, not Jehovah's, and the atonement is made on Calvary. Other notable poems by Blake are difficult to place in the chronology of his career. His work was not published in the usual meaning of that word; much of it only appeared as part of an elaborate artistic production, while some poems were simply not known until his papers were examined after his death. The famous engraved productions never reached more than a small circle of readers and Coleridge and Wordsworth were hardly aware of his existence. *Auguries of Innocence* probably dates from 1802 or perhaps earlier; *The Everlasting Gospel* probably from 1810.

The years between Blake's return to London and his death were difficult, and he never enjoyed even modest affluence. The publisher Robert Hartley Cromek cheated him in the commission of 'The Canterbury Pilgrims'; later, in 1809, an exhibition of his work, while it made him a subject for discussion, did not make him prosperous. However, the *Descriptive Catalogue* is a prized addition to his works. When he died he had virtually nothing but he left no debts. Catherine, the gardener's daughter who could not even write her name when he married her, believed in him completely and loved him unquestioningly. She outlived him by four years and died in the contented expectation of rejoining her William. The great man was buried in the public cemetery at Bunhill Fields in an unmarked grave.

Blake questioned every accepted value of his age, in poetry, art, religion, and philosophy. His lyric poetry anticipates the great change that was coming, the total departure from the formalism and conceits of the 18th century, from the work of men who, in Blake's words, 'knew enough of artifice, but little of art'. Wordsworth was still a schoolboy when Blake was writing lines of apt and simple beauty. It has already been noted that

the difficult mystical poems have few readers; here his thought seems beyond his means of expression, and the volumes of commentary and explanation are hardly the concern of those who love poetry for its own sake. But in *Poetical Sketches*, *Songs of Innocence and of Experience*, *Auguries of Innocence*, *The Everlasting Gospel*, and all the shorter poems Blake's mind is open to everyone; volumes of meaning are expressed in apparently simple musical lines.

*The Complete Writings of William Blake* was edited by Geoffrey Keynes (1925). This has been added to and enlarged in successive editions, the latest of which was published in Oxford Standard Authors (1966). G. E. Bentley produced a critical edition, complete with expensive reproductions (Oxford English Texts, 1978). The recommended biography is *The Life of William Blake* by Mona Wilson (1926); a new edition was prepared by Geoffrey Keynes (1971).

**Blatant Beast** In Book VI of Spenser's *The Faerie Queene*, the monster overcome by Sir Calidore. Begotten of Envy and Detraction, the Beast represents the voice of calumny.

*Bleak House* A novel by Charles Dickens, first published in 20 monthly parts (March 1852 to September 1853).

The cousins Richard Carstone and Ada Clare, wards of the court in the case of Jarndyce and Jarndyce, are taken to live with the elderly John Jarndyce. Ada is accompanied by Esther Summerson, an orphan, who is part-narrator of the story. John Jarndyce grows to love Esther, who is many years his junior. One of the claimants in the Jarndyce case is Lady Dedlock, the beautiful young wife of Sir Leicester Dedlock, baronet, an honourable and unimaginative old man.

One day Lady Dedlock, in the presence of the lawyer Tulkinghorn, is startled by the sight of some handwriting on a legal document, copied by a nameless scrivener. Tulkinghorn, legal advisor to Sir Leicester, scents a mystery and his enquiries lead him to a ragged half-starved orphan, Jo, who scratches an existence as a crossing-sweeper. Jo remembers a poor penniless scrivener who was kind to him while he lived. Lady Dedlock, meanwhile, has been pursuing her own enquiries about the handwriting on the document and they lead her to Jo also.

Richard Carstone and Ada Clare, meanwhile, have fallen in love and have married secretly. The Jarndyce case in which they are concerned has been in the Court of Chancery for so long, at the mercy of the law's delays, that it is a cruel joke in the legal profession and a source of steady income to scores of its members. Richard, with the

'Mr Chadband "Improving" a tough subject.' An illustration by Phiz for *Bleak House*. The tough subject is poor Jo, the crossing-sweeper, subjected to the preaching of the smug, greasy Rev. Mr Chadband.

prospect of a fortune that should come to him, becomes idle and shiftless. Esther encounters Jo, who unknowingly carries with him the germs of the manifold diseases that rage in the dreadful hovels of Tom-all-Alone's, the crumbling unclaimed slum near Lincoln's Inn. Jo, frightened by the enquiries that all seem to lead to the 'berryin ground', runs away.

Tulkinghorn uncovers Lady Dedlock's secret. She had once loved a Captain Rawdon and borne him a child. She believed that Rawdon was dead, and her child, too, when she married Dedlock. But Rawdon was the nameless scrivener who had been kind to poor starving Jo; the daughter of the love affair is Esther Summerson. Tulkinghorn confronts Lady Dedlock with the facts; he is murdered before he can reveal them but Dedlock knows the story all too soon and Lady Dedlock flees into the night. She is found dead at the gate of the burial ground, and the killer of Tulkinghorn proves to have been Hortense, Lady Dedlock's maid. Hortense detested her mistress and was pleased to help the lawyer uncover the mystery. Tulkinghorn, however, makes the mistake of treating Hortense with contempt after his schemes have succeeded. Esther contracts smallpox from her encounter with Jo, who dies in want and exhaustion, hiding in Tom-all-Alone's. Richard Carstone descends to ruin, the mirage of the Jarndyce fortune before his eyes. And the Jarndyce case *is* settled – but the fortune is gone, devoured by the endless legal costs.

*Bleak House* has a fair claim to being not only Dickens's best book but one of the finest novels in the language. Never as popular as *David Copperfield*, it is more ambitious, and the author attacks with deadly skill the society of his time and its rotten institutions. The Court of Chancery in his day was a perfect target and there are uncomfortable parallels to be found with some areas of the law in contemporary England. Mrs Jellaby and her concern for the natives of a distant continent, to the neglect of her own family, is a permanent feature of our society – it is always easier to be interested in distant events than in the lonely pensioner a few houses away, dying of cold. And the book is full of unforgettable characters: poor Miss Flite, the half-crazy little woman haunting the Court of Chancery; the Smallweeds, models of dingy meanness; Skimpole, selfish and irresponsible, relying on charm, and Jo the crossing-sweeper, who has nothing, not even an understanding of why he is alive. One other 'character' is the London of the day; Dickens knew its dreadful corners very well, and the evocation of a huge, sprawling city burning millions of tons of smog-producing coal conveys the acrid smell to the reader's nostrils.

***Blessed Damozel, The*** A poem by Dante Gabriel Rossetti. The first version was published in *The Germ* in 1850 and a revised version appeared in *The Oxford and Cambridge Magazine* in 1856. The maiden of the poem has been in heaven for ten years but 'Herseemed she scarce had been a day One of God's choristers'. She leans out 'From the gold bar of Heaven' and looks on the world. She sees the souls mounting up to 'God's house' and the reunion of those separated by death. She prays to be united to her own love, whose hopes are also expressed. *The Blessed Damozel* is Rossetti's most famous poem and shows clearly the influence of Keats.

***Blickling Homilies, The*** The late 10th century was a period of religious zeal in England; the revival of learning initiated by Alfred had inevitably depended much on the monasteries and the churchmen, and much of the writing of the time was religious. A popular form, in a period when the millennium was approaching and most people believed that the end of the world was at hand, was the homily or sermon. A notable collection is that of the 19 *Blickling Homilies* (*c.* 970) preserved in a manuscript at Blickling Hall in Norfolk. The Early English Text Society published *The Blickling Homilies* in an edition prepared by R. Morris (1874–80).

**Blifil, Mr** Mr Allworthy's nephew in *Tom Jones* by Henry Fielding. The foundling boy, Tom, is brought up with Blifil, who resents him and eventually succeeds in turning Mr Allworthy against him. He also conceals the truth of Tom's parentage.

***Blithedale Romance, The*** A novel by Nathaniel Hawthorne, first published in 1852. The Blithedale Farm of the book was based on the Brook Farm experiment of Hawthorne's Transcendentalist friends in Concord. The story is told by Miles Coverdale – Hawthorne himself in fictional guise.

Miles Coverdale is a visitor to Blithedale Farm, a socialized community which seeks a better way of life. Among those involved are the farmer Silas Forster and his wife, the passionate and regal Zenobia, the former blacksmith Hollingsworth who is as subtle as a sledgehammer and the strongest character in the community, and Priscilla, a delicate girl from the city. Zenobia and Priscilla both fall in love with Hollingsworth – but he is too concerned with mankind in general to consider the feelings of individuals.

Later, after his return to Boston, Coverdale meets some of the community again. Zenobia is a wealthy and fashionable woman; she is being wooed by Hollingsworth, who has left Blithedale Farm in the care of the Forsters during his absence. Priscilla, who is actually Zenobia's half-sister, has fallen under the influence of a mesmerist. The forceful Hollingsworth extricates her and takes her back to Blithedale, where he returns her love and decides to marry her. Zenobia, having lost Hollingsworth, drowns herself; Coverdale learns that Hollingsworth had wooed her to obtain more money for his work.

Hollingsworth does marry Priscilla but Zenobia's suicide has robbed him of his resolution. The sceptical Coverdale notes that the formerly delicate and apparently weak-willed Priscilla is now supporting the erstwhile strong man and continues to ponder the worth of such urges to live a Utopian life.

***Bloody Brother, The:*** *or The Tragedy of Rollo, Duke of Normandy.* A play by John Fletcher, Ben Jonson, and others, probably Philip Massinger and George Chapman. It was first produced about 1616 and first published in 1639.

The brothers Rollo and Otto have inherited Normandy jointly upon the death of their father, the late duke. Rollo, the elder, wants to be sole ruler; he kills his brother and orders a proscription of all those who withhold their support for his cause. One of these is his old tutor, Baldwin, whose daughter Edith comes to Rollo to plead for her father's life. Her beauty charms him and he gives the order to stay the execution. But he is too late and Edith swears to avenge her father. Rollo visits her but his obvious repentance weakens her resolution. Rollo falls to the sword of the brother of another of his victims.

**Bloomfield, Robert** 1766–1823. The son of an agricultural labourer of Honington in Suffolk, Bloomfield would have been a labourer himself but for his diminutive stature; he was sent to London at the age of 15 to work for his brother George, a shoemaker. His life was hard and extremely poor but he had been taught to read and write by his mother and succeeded, in 1802, in gaining a modest post in the Office of Seals. This was after the publication of *The Farmer's Boy: A Rural Poem* (1800), which enjoyed popular success. *Rural Tales* (1802) was followed by a steady stream of verse but he is remembered only for *The Farmer's Boy*. His success was certainly deserved but his talent was not an original one and his mode of expression, if not his subjects, was in the manner of the fashionable versifiers of his time. *A Selection of Poems by Robert Bloomfield* was edited by R. Gant (1947).

**Bloudy Tenent of Persecution, The**  A tract by Roger Williams attacking the Puritan theocracy of New England in the person of John Cotton (1584–1652). It was published in London in 1644. It takes the form of a dialogue between Peace and Truth, who are unable to find a home in a world where conscience is persecuted. The persecutors (Cotton and his colleagues) are squarely accused of 'bloudy and slaughterous conclusions'. Cotton replied in *The Bloudy Tenent Washed and Made White in the Bloud of the Lamb* (1647). The indefatigable Williams dealt with that in his tract of 1652 – *The Bloudy Tenent Yet More Bloudy by Mr Cotton's Endeavour to Wash it White in the Bloud of the Lamb.*

**Blount, Charles**  See **deism**.

**Blue Hotel, The**  See *Monster, The*.

**bluestocking**  A term to describe a woman with intellectual tastes – or one who affects to have them. In the 1750s the main diversion was card playing, and Elizabeth Montagu, Elizabeth Vesey, Hester Chapone, and other rich women introduced a much-needed alternative in imitation of the French women's salons. The male guests were not required to wear full dress and the familiar black silk hose of that period began to be replaced by other colours – Stillingfleet, a poet of the time, wore blue worsted habitually, and this led to Admiral Boscawen's description of the salons as the Blue Stocking Society. The term is also found in Boswell's *Life of Johnson*.

**Blunden, Edmund (Charles)**  1896–1974. Edmund Blunden was born at Yalding in Kent and educated at Christ's Hospital. He won a classics scholarship to Oxford but the outbreak of World War I interrupted his studies; he served in France, during which time he was awarded the Military Cross, and was unable to return to university until 1919. However, he found it impossible to become a student after his experience of the war, and he became assistant editor of *The Athenaeum* until 1922, when he took a sea voyage to South America for his health's sake. Before World War II he was appointed Professor of English Literature at the University of Tokyo, and then became fellow and tutor of Merton College, Oxford. After World War II he became head of the English department at the University of Hong Kong, and Professor of Poetry at the University of Oxford in 1966. Ill health prevented him from serving the latter term for the full five years and he retired in 1968.

Edmund Blunden published his first poetry in 1914 and his work was included in *Georgian Poetry* in 1916. His collected poems appeared in 1957 in the volume entitled *Poems of Many Years* and several small volumes have been published since then. His early work was that of a country and nature poet; after the war years his reputation as such grew steadily with *The Waggoner and Other Poems* (1920), *The Shepherd, and Other Poems of Peace and War* (1922), and *English Poems* (1925). *Undertones of War* (1928) was completely different; in prose and verse he wrote one of the classics of World War I describing his experiences as a subaltern in the infantry.

As a critic and essayist Blunden attracted a new audience to a number of writers. Among his editions are *Poems Chiefly from Manuscript by John Clare* (1920), *Madrigals and Chronicles: Being Newly Found Poems by John Clare* (1924), *A Song to David, with Other Poems by Christopher Smart* (1924), *Leigh Hunt's Examiner Examined* (1928), *The Poems of William Collins* (1929), and *The Poems of Wilfred Owen* (1931). Among prose works are *The Bonaventure: A Random Journal of an Atlantic Holiday* (1922), *Leigh Hunt: A Biography* (1930), *Thomas Hardy* (1941, for the English Men of Letters Series), and *Cricket Country* (1944).

**Blunt, Wilfrid Scawen**  1840–1922. Blunt, the son of a family of Catholic landowners in Sussex, entered the diplomatic service at the age of 18. He served as an attaché in Athens, Constantinople, Frankfurt, Madrid, and Paris, where he met the woman he refers to as Skittles. She was the inspiration for the love poetry generally regarded as his best work – *Sonnets and Songs of Proteus* (1875, 1881, 1892) and *Esther* (1892). Blunt left the diplomatic service in 1869, when he married Lady Anne Noel.

Blunt became a traveller in 1875, when he paid his first visit to Egypt with his wife. Two years later she accompanied him to Arabia, where they travelled widely and where Blunt probably began to react against imperialism. This reaction coloured the rest of his life's activities. He championed nationalism in Arabia, Egypt, and India and was imprisoned in 1887 after a speech at a meeting in support of Irish nationalism. Blunt's translation *The Seven Golden Odes of Pagan Arabia* was published in 1903, *My Diaries 1888–1914* in 1922.

**Bly**  The remote country house that is the setting for Henry James's celebrated ghost story, *The Turn of the Screw*.

**Boece (*or* Boyce), Hector**  1465–1536. Boece was born in Dundee and studied philosophy in Paris. He taught there also and his lifelong friendship with Erasmus began there in the last decade of the 15th century. About 1500 Boece returned to Scotland and became canon of Aberdeen Cathedral and principal of the newly founded university. He wrote in Latin and is remembered for his *Historia Scotorum* (1527), which is full of interesting stories but not highly regarded for accuracy. The story of Macbeth was derived from Boece by Holinshed and thus transmitted to Shakespeare. The *Historia* was translated into vernacular Scots by John Bellenden in 1540 at the request of James V.

Bellenden's *The Chronicles of Scotland of Hector Boece* was edited by R. W. Chambers, E. C. Batho, and H. W. Husbands for the Scottish Texts Society (1938–41).

**Boffin, Mr and Mrs Nicodemus** The 'Golden Dustman' and his wife of Dickens's *Our Mutual Friend*. The older Harmon's fortune goes to Boffin, his foreman and friend, when John Harmon disappears. They are an estimable warm-hearted couple.

**Bois-Guilbert, Sir Brian de** The fiery passionate Templar of Scott's *Ivanhoe*, whose own nature and fierce love for Rebecca (who loves Ivanhoe) make him the villain of the story.

**Bold, Dr John** In Anthony Trollope's *The Warden*, the young doctor whose allegations of malpractice cause such distress to Mr Harding, the warden of Hiram's Hospital.

**Boldrewood, Rolf** 1826–1915. The pseudonym of Thomas Alexander Browne. Born in London, Browne and his family emigrated to Australia in 1830 and he was educated in Sydney. He found his pseudonym in the work of Scott but he did not begin to write until he was in his forties. For some years Browne was a squatter in Victoria, living the sort of life he later described in his fiction. Later he became a commissioner in the goldfields and a magistrate. His best-known novel, *Robbery Under Arms*, was published as a serial in *The Sydney Mail* before appearing in volume form in 1888. This story of a bushranger gang, led by the immigrant Englishman Captain Starlight, is narrated by an ex-bushranger. *A Colonial Reformer* and *A Squatter's Dream* (both 1890) are generally regarded as the best fictional pictures of the squatter's life. *The Miner's Right* (also 1890) is a novel about the goldfields, and *Nevermore* (1892) a story of prison life. *A Sydney-side Saxon* (1891) and *A Modern Buccaneer* complete the list. Boldrewood's novels are notable for their vigorous narratives, unambiguous character drawing, and for their picture of life recorded by a keen observer.

**Bolingbroke, Henry, Earl of Derby and Duke of Hereford** Son of John of Gaunt, Duke of Lancaster, and afterwards King Henry IV. Richard II made him Duke of Hereford in 1397 and in the following year occurred the quarrel with Mowbray, Duke of Norfolk, which opens Shakespeare's *Richard II*. In the play Henry is not only referred to by his titles but is also called Bolingbroke – the name refers to his birthplace, his father's castle of Bolingbroke in Lincolnshire.

**Bolingbroke, Henry St John, 1st Viscount** 1678–1751. Henry St John was born at Battersea, the son of Sir Henry (later Lord) St John. He was educated at Eton and (probably) Christ Church, Oxford, and then made the fashionable tour of Europe. He entered Parliament in 1701, supporting Harley and the Tories. St John was a fine speaker and soon became an important figure: he was Secretary-at-War from 1704 to 1708 and Secretary of State in 1710; in 1712 he was created first Viscount Bolingbroke. When Harley's ministry collapsed in 1714 Bolingbroke formed a ministry – he was opposed to the Hanoverian succession and wanted the crown to remain with the Stuarts. But the day after Bolingbroke formed his ministry Queen Anne died and his political fortunes foundered. With the accession of George I and the new Whig ascendancy Bolingbroke, the supporter of the rejected dynasty, found himself impeached. He fled to France and made the extraordinary political mistake of becoming Secretary of State to the Stuart claimant, Prince James (the Old Pretender), though that did not last long. Prince James dismissed him and from 1716 Bolingbroke lived the life of a scholar in France, studying and writing. He severed his connection with the Stuarts completely and this no doubt helped the efforts of his friends in England to secure his pardon. This was granted in 1723 and he returned to England; his property was restored but he was banned from holding office. He settled in his villa at Dawley, near Oxford.

In literature Bolingbroke is distinguished as a historian and political writer. Most of his work dates from his return from exile but during his political ascendancy he was the friend and patron of writers; he founded the Brothers Club in 1711 at the prompting of Swift. A centre for conversation and companionship among literary men, the club also assisted deserving writers. Swift, Arbuthnot, Orrery, and Matthew Prior, as well as adherents of the Tory party, were among the members. Alexander Pope and Daniel Defoe were also friends of Bolingbroke.

While in exile Bolingbroke wrote *A Letter to*

*Sir William Wyndham* (1717, published in 1753), his apologia for the years 1710–15, incorporating his current views on the Jacobite question; he had forsworn his former loyalty to the Stuarts and the *Letter* is not completely honest in its presentation of fact. But it is persuasively written and full of interest to historians for Bolingbroke's comments on his former colleagues – particularly Harley – and for the description of the Old Pretender's court. *Reflections in Exile* was written the year before, in 1716. After he returned to England Bolingbroke was soon in active opposition to the Whigs, now securely in power with Robert Walpole at their head. Nicholas Amherst founded a periodical called *The Craftsman* in 1726 and Bolingbroke was an anonymous and regular contributor. These pieces are printed in *Remarks upon the History of England* (1743) and *A Dissertation upon Parties* (1735). The latter reprints an attack upon Walpole written in 1733; the article did not harm Walpole, however, and Bolingbroke retreated to France once more, to live in his French wife's home at Chanteloup, in Touraine.

*Letters on the Study and Use of History* (published in 1752) were written in 1735 and addressed to Lord Cornbury (Clarendon's great-grandson). In these Bolingbroke put forward the thesis that history teaches by example, therefore England should follow the example of her European neighbours and produce written histories. (Bolingbroke intended to write a history of his own times.) *Letters on the Study and Use of History* was widely read, and not only in England – Voltaire acknowledged its influence. *A Letter on the True Use of Retirement and Study* and *A Letter on the Spirit of Patriotism* were both written in 1736. The latter (published in 1749) looks hopefully to the coming men and a Tory party inspired by, first and foremost, patriotism. It was to influence a great Tory of later days, Disraeli. *The Idea of a Patriot King* (written in 1738 and published in 1749) takes the idea a little farther. *Some Reflections on the Present State of the Nation* (1749) examines the question of the public debt.

Bolingbroke's writings were collected and published by David Mallet in 1754. Included in the edition were *Philosophical Works*, the occasional writings that influenced Pope in his *Essay on Man*. Bolingbroke was an impressive conversationalist and a fine orator, but unfortunately his writings can seem over-rhetorical to the modern reader.

**Booby, Lady**   One of the amorous predators in *Joseph Andrews* by Henry Fielding. She tries to seduce her footman, Joseph; he leaves her house in a hurry. Lady Booby is the sister of Mr B. in

Samuel Richardson's *Pamela*; Fielding had already named her in his burlesque of that novel, *An Apology for the Life of Mrs Shamela Andrews*.

**Book for a Rainy Day, A**, *or Recollections of the Events of the Years 1766–1833*.   See **Smith, John Thomas**.

**Book of Ahania, The**   See **Blake, William**.

**Book of Common Prayer, The**   See **Cranmer, Thomas**.

**Book of Los, The**   See **Blake, William**.

**Book of St Albans, The**   The third printing press in England was established in 1479 and published eight books, of which *The Book of St Albans* was the last (1486). It is a volume containing treatises on hawking, hunting, and heraldry and seems to be a compilation, with a possible attribution of the hunting treatise to Juliana Berners, Prioress of Sopwell. A later edition, printed by Wynkyn de Worde in 1496, carries an additional treatise, on fishing.

**Book of the Duchess, The**   A poem of 1300 lines by Geoffrey Chaucer on the death of Blanche, Duchess of Lancaster and the first wife of John of Gaunt. The duchess died in September 1369 and Chaucer's allegorical lament, the first work of the poet that can be dated with reasonable certainty, was probably composed in the same year.

The poet relates a dream in which, as a member of the emperor's hunting party, he comes upon a knight in black seated against an oak tree in a glade, composing a lament. The poet's questions elicit the tale of his love, of her beauty and perfection. When the poet asks where is the lady now he learns that she is dead. The sound is heard of the hunt returning and the poet wakes. The bell is tolling for the noon hour, and in his hand is the book telling the story of Ceyx and Halcyone (from classical mythology), which he had been reading.

**Book of the Governor, The**   See **Elyot, Sir Thomas**.

**Book of Urizen, The**   See **Blake, William**.

**Booth, Amelia**   The heroine of *Amelia* by Henry Fielding. She is steadfast in her devotion to a worthless husband, and achieves a doubtful happiness in the end.

**Booth, William**   The heroine's spineless husband in *Amelia* by Henry Fielding. He falls an easy prey to the adventuress Miss Matthews, his fellow prisoner in Newgate.

**Borde** (*or* **Boorde**), **Andrew** *c*.1490–1549. Borde was a traveller and a physician who wrote about the kingdoms and peoples of Europe in *The Fyrst Boke of the Introduction of Knowledge, the Whyche dothe Teache a Man to Know the Usage and Fashion of all Maner of Countreys* (1548). Other works were medical advice for the layman: *The Boke for to Lerne a Man to be Wyse in Buylding of his House for the Helth of Body* (*c*.1540), *A Compendyous Regyment or a Dyetary of Helth made in Monntpyllior* (1542), and *A Breviary of Helth* (1547). His travels are the matter of *The Peregrination of Doctor Boarde* (*c*.1542) and he is believed to have been the compiler of **Merie Tales of the Mad Men of Gotham** (*c*.1565).

A *Compendyous Regyment* and *The Fyrst Boke of the Introduction of Knowledge* were edited by F. J. Furnivall and published by the Early English Text Society in 1870.

**Borough, The** A poem by George Crabbe, first published in 1810, in 24 'Letters' that describe the life of a town of moderate size. The town is Aldeburgh, where Crabbe was born and which he knew very well, though he was never happy during any of the periods he lived there. The picture he draws is not a cheerful one but the poet's insistence on realism is informed by sympathy. He is at his best in the portrayal of character, whether in individual studies or in the context of the institutions – church, almshouses, prisons – in which they are encountered. One character, Peter Grimes, became famous in a different medium when Benjamin Britten used him as the subject of his first international success in opera. Another, Ellen Orford, was made part of the libretto but she is not the Ellen of the poem. Another notable character is Clelia, a good-time girl who ends in the almshouse. Most vivid of all is the condemned man in the 23rd Letter, 'Prisons', which Crabbe based on a visit to Newgate while trying to earn his living in London.

**Borrow, George** 1803–81. The son of a recruiting officer, George Borrow was born at East Dereham in Norfolk. He was articled to a solicitor after completing his education but turned to languages and writing and contributed to the six volumes of *Celebrated Trials, New Newgate Calendar* of 1825. *Romantic Ballads*, translated from the Danish, was published in 1826. After that he took to the open road, first tramping around England and then farther afield in Europe, where his aptitude for languages was a great boon. He became an agent for the British and Foreign Bible Society and this took him as far as Russia – and to Spain, the latter providing material for his first real success. He was also correspondent for the *Morning Herald*.

Borrow married Mary Clarke in 1840 and settled down at Oulton Broad in Suffolk. His books are a peculiar mixture of autobiography and, later, picaresque romance. *The Zincali, or an account of the Gypsies in Spain* (1841), gave notice of what was to be the main theme of his best-remembered work. **The Bible in Spain** (1843) is a travel book which proved to be very popular. **Lavengro** (1851) and *The Romany Rye* (1857), its sequel, are called novels but the autobiographical element is strong. **Wild Wales** (1862) is an open road book. His interest in Gypsies brought them into English literature, though his accounts and observations of them could never be called systematic. But, more importantly, he wrote about them better than any of his scholarly contemporaries.

George Borrow's readership during his lifetime was one that thirsted for accounts of faraway places and strange customs. The Gypsies and the Spaniards were very exotic to mid-Victorians and Borrow also conveys a feeling of contact with adventurous and lawless life – of a freedom his readers could yearn for but could never attain. That quality survives, thanks to the force of Borrow's personality, and his books are still read. *Romany Lavo-Lil*, his word book of the English-Gypsy language, was published in 1874.

**Bors de Ganis** One of the knights of the Round Table, so named in Malory's *Le Morte Darthur* (Bohort in the French versions). He is Sir Launcelot's nephew and the first to set eyes on the baby son of Launcelot and Elaine, who becomes Sir Galahad. He is one of the three knights who achieve sight of the Grail, and bears the news of the deaths of Galahad and Percival back to the court. He is Launcelot's true friend throughout.

**Bostonians, The** A novel by Henry James, first published in serial form in the *Century Magazine*, from February 1885 to February 1886, and in volume form in 1886.

A young lawyer from the South, Basil Ransom, comes to Boston to practise, and meets his cousins, Olive Chancellor and her sister, the widow Mrs Luna. Olive is rich, highly strung, and neurotic while Mrs Luna is plainly taken with Basil and sets her cap at him – in contrast to Olive, who has better things to do with her life than become involved with men. She takes Basil to a suffragette meeting, where he meets Miss Birdseye, a philanthropist. Miss Birdseye's causes are universal; she is gentle and generous, enthusiastic about doing good always – a perfect cloud of good intentions. At the meeting an excellent address is delivered by a beautiful girl, Verena Tarrant, and both Olive and Basil are immediately interested in her.

With little persuasion, Verena yields to Olive's suggestion that she share Olive's luxurious home. Verena's mother is a compulsive adherent to good causes; after all, her father was Abraham Greenstreet, an abolitionist. But Mrs Tarrant's philanthropy is unconsciously mingled with a desire for a social life and Verena is only too happy to leave her home (her father, Selah Tarrant, claims to be a mesmeric healer and used to be a pedlar). Olive sets out to make Verena a leader in feminist causes and pleads with her to forswear the very thought of marriage. Basil Ransom, however, is interested in Verena for reasons that have nothing to do with causes; besides, Mrs Luna's attentions are becoming a nuisance. It is not long before Olive and Basil are regarding each other with hostility.

Olive prepares Verena in her own image. An active feminist, for the first time Olive has someone in whom she can both invest her reformist convictions and centre her emotions. Mrs Luna believes that she has chosen wrongly; Olive, knowing Verena's background and parentage, looks forward to a lifetime of content and aspiration with her protégée. Verena is groomed to deliver a course of lectures; she is, meanwhile, in Olive's eyes, irresponsibly pleased by Basil's attentions.

Miss Birdseye dies and Verena loses confidence in her purpose. She is about to begin her lectures when Basil's appearance in the hall unnerves her; the climax comes when she has to choose between Basil and Olive. She chooses Basil. Olive, no matter what her efforts, cannot offer Verena what the girl really wants – Mrs Luna is proved to have been right.

*The Bostonians* is a brilliantly sustained comedy and in the opinion of many critics only surpassed in the work of Henry James by *The Portrait of a Lady*. In the words of J. I. M. Stewart, 'The novel has a background in delusion and affords a mordant and amusing panorama of the near-lunatic fringe of an earnest, intellectual and culturally unfurnished society.' In the same paragraph: 'He (James) is appalled by a society apparently unable to cultivate privacy, a society in which the people have rights but the person has none.' The latter quotation explains much about Henry James's decision to live in England; but his acute observation of the Bostonians is paralleled by his observation of European society in novel after novel. He makes it plain that while each society has much to offer the other they are a very long way from finding common ground and enriching each other. Olive Chancellor is a tragic figure, by no means as unsympathetic as an outline of the story would suggest. Verena is grateful for her attention and her generosity – her upbringing would make her warm to anyone who looked like a rescuer; but, the opportunity being there, her real nature will draw her to the sort of life that is closed to Olive. Basil Ransom, an outsider who regards the activities of the Boston ladies with a bemused eye, swings her emotions to their true focus like a compass needle. And the book is full of delights in its portraits of the lesser characters – Selah Tarrant, his wife who clings to society as part of a reforming movement, and Matthias Pardon the reporter. Best of all, perhaps, are the contrasting women – Mrs Farrinder, whose very presence heralds achievement (where she is achievement *cannot* be far behind), and the successful physician who commands even Basil's respect, Dr Prance, who has really achieved something, 'having as many rights as she had time for.'

**Boswell, Sir Alexander** 1775–1822. The eldest son of James Boswell, born at Auchinleck. Alexander Boswell inherited his father's interest in literature: he had a particular interest in his fellow Ayrshireman Robert Burns and initiated the movement for a monument to Burns on the banks of the River Doon. Like many of his contemporaries in Scottish literature he was a collector of songs; he also wrote occasional verse and political squibs. One of his political verses, 'The New Whig Song', was published in *The Glasgow Sentinel* and offended James Stuart of Dunearn. Stuart and Boswell fought a duel on 26 March 1822 and Boswell died of his wounds. Boswell's *Poetical Works* were collected and edited by S. H. Smith and published in 1871.

**Boswell, James** 1740–95. The son of Alexander Boswell, who as a judge of the Court of Session of Scotland became Lord Auchinleck, James Boswell was born in Edinburgh. After his education at Edinburgh High School, Boswell studied law at Edinburgh University. Further study at Glasgow followed and while there Boswell published his first work, *A View of the Edinburgh Theatre*. In 1760 he ran away to London and his father wisely encouraged his influential friends there to entertain his son. Boswell, a randy young man, had been afflicted with guilt about this by his pious mother's Calvinistic training; he was encouraged to sow his wild oats in London. He decided on a career in the army and asked his father to buy him a commission. Lord Auchinleck, an estimable man in spite of his inability to understand his son, came to London and arranged a meeting with the Duke of Argyll. Nothing came of it, and he persuaded Boswell to return home with him. Boswell returned to the study of law and spent his spare time playgoing and whoring, but he passed his civil law examination in 1762. Then he renewed his pleas to be allowed to try and obtain a commission and his father agreed to his going to London again. His published work so far amounted to some verse and correspondence of little account.

From November 1762 until August 1763 Boswell was in London. He did not succeed in gaining a commission but he certainly did not waste his time; his friends included Thomas Sheridan and Garrick, and on 16 May 1763 came the most important meeting of his life: he met Johnson in Thomas Davies's bookshop (see **Johnson, Samuel**). Otherwise he lived a fairly squalid life, obsessed with pursuit of sexual experience for its own sake. Lord Auchinleck, well informed of his son's behaviour, ordered him to settle for a career in law or politics – or take a commission in a foot regiment, if he really wanted an army career. Johnson, meanwhile (to whom, about this time, Boswell proposed the famous journey to Scotland), had taken to the young Scot and encouraged him to go on keeping a journal. His

James Boswell. Portrait by G. Dance, 1793. National Portrait Gallery, London.

sojourn in London is recorded in fascinating detail in *Boswell's London Journal*, the first volume of the Yale Edition of the Private Papers of Boswell, published in 1950.

On 5 August 1763 Johnson accompanied Boswell to Harwich, where he embarked for Holland. Boswell completed his law studies in Utrecht and became involved with Elisabeth van Tuyll, a Dutch bluestocking to whom he eventually proposed marriage. In June 1764 Boswell set out on his European travels. The particular gifts that were to find their greatest expression in his biography of Johnson began to show themselves about this time. With a mixture of charm and unabashed persistence he secured several meetings with Jean-Jacques Rousseau and the great Voltaire. In Italy, where there were numerous Scots exiles, he met John Wilkes, whose sceptical amoral approach to the opposite sex filled him with delight and envy – the accounts of his expenses demonstrate how Boswell himself sought physical relief.

Boswell went to Corsica in October 1765, prompted by Rousseau's description of a rugged people who had preserved their independence of feeling in spite of being ruled by others for centuries. Rousseau and Count Rivarda had given him letters of introduction to the formidable Pasquale Paoli. He made a deep impression on Boswell, who regarded him as one of the greatest men in Europe. In Genoa, where he arrived in November, he received a letter from his father, who had been seriously ill, which asked him to come home. Boswell returned by way of France and learned in Paris of his mother's death. It was in Paris, also, that he wrote to Elisabeth van Tuyll proposing marriage. Nothing came of that and Boswell arrived back in London in February 1766. His first call was on Samuel Johnson; he recorded his 'admiration of his extraordinary mind'. His stay in London was brief but he spent much of it campaigning for Paoli and the Corsicans, even securing an interview with the elder Pitt. The details of this part of Boswell's life are recorded in his private papers: *Boswell in Holland, 1763–1764* (1952) and the two volumes of *Boswell on the Grand Tour* (1953 and 1955).

Boswell was admitted to the Scottish Bar in July 1766 and for the next 17 years he practised as an advocate in Edinburgh. Lord Auchinleck was probably relieved and satisfied; but not Boswell, who hankered after a literary or political career. The celebrated Douglas inheritance case prompted him to write a short romance called *Dorando* (1767) in which the protagonists were placed in a Spanish setting. Forgotten now, the story was a success at the time, and when Archibald Douglas won his case Boswell published a review of the affair, *The Essence of the Douglas Cause* (1767). He returned to his earlier interest with *An Account of Corsica, the Journal of a Tour to That Island; and Memoirs of Pascal Paoli* (1768) and *British Essays in Favour of the Brave Corsicans* (1769) and visited London as often as he could. Samuel Johnson had advised him to 'Mind your own affairs, and leave the Corsicans to others', and England, in the event, did nothing to help the Corsicans, though Paoli became a guest of the government when he was exiled. Boswell, after several false starts, achieved marriage in 1769; the lady was his cousin Margaret Montgomerie. This part of his life, as recorded in his journals, is published in *Boswell in Search of a Wife, 1766–1769* (1956).

Boswell's London circle was growing and now included Joshua Reynolds, Goldsmith, Burke – the members of The Club – and he was a frequent guest at the Thrales' house. He succeeded in persuading Johnson to undertake the long-discussed visit to Scotland in 1773; he observed his distinguished friend closely and recorded every word, to the delight of posterity. He became a proprietor of *The London Magazine* in 1777, and began writing the series of essays by 'Hypochondriack' which continued until 1783 and which were published as *Boswell's Column*, edited by Margaret Bailey (1928 and 1951). His career as an advocate, as recorded in his journals, is published in *Boswell for the Defence, 1769–1774* (1959). He succeeded to the estate of Auchinleck upon his father's death in 1782 and entered politics, where his career was undistinguished.

In May and June of 1784 Boswell was in London; he dined with Johnson at Reynolds's house and accompanied him to his door afterwards. It was the last time he saw him; Johnson died in December of that year.

Charles Dilly, the London bookseller and Boswell's friend, asked Boswell for a 400-page volume of Johnson's utterances by February of the following year – that is, in less than seven weeks. Boswell declined; instead he prepared to write Johnson's life. He published **The Journal of a Tour to the Hebrides with Samuel Johnson** in 1785 and moved his legal practice to London in the following year. The move was not a wise one and Boswell found his talents as an advocate largely unwanted. But it gave him time to forge ahead with preparations for the biography, which represented enormous labour. His wife had returned to Auchinleck for her health's sake and she died there in 1789. By the following year Boswell had abandoned his hopes of a political career and with the help and encouragement of the scholar Edmund Malone completed what is generally regarded as the finest biography in the English language. **The Life of Samuel Johnson LL D** was published on 16 May 1791.

Boswell's last years were spent in London; he hoped for some sort of political responsibility, not understanding that the true Boswell had realized himself in his great biography. He was restless and debauched – and popular; Boswell was excellent company and that was one reason he had always been able to find his way to the side of men who interested him. He revered Johnson, who out of a genuine affection for the bright and wayward young Scot had advised him, supported him, and, almost, taught him to respect himself. He died on 19 May 1795 after a short illness, in London.

In addition to the titles already mentioned of the Yale Edition of the Private Papers of Boswell are *Portraits by Sir Joshua Reynolds* (1952), *Boswell's Journal of a Tour to the Hebrides with Samuel Johnson 1773* (1961), *Boswell: The Ominous Years 1774–1776* (1963), *Boswell in Extremes 1776–1778* (1971). The editors are F. W. Hilles, H. W. Liebert, E. C. Aswell, Edward Kuhn, F. E. Taylor, and Frederick A. Pottle, who is also the chairman of the edition. The series is still in progress. A limited edition of *The Private Papers of James Boswell from Malahide Castle*, edited by Geoffrey Scott and Frederick A. Pottle, was published between 1928 and 1934 (in 18 volumes), with an index volume appearing in 1937.

**Bottom, Nick**   A weaver of Athens in Shakespeare's *A Midsummer Night's Dream*. He plays the part of Pyramus in the Interlude for the duke's wedding and is given an ass's head by Puck in the enchanted wood. Titania is magicked into falling in love with him. Oberon gives him his own head back before morning and Bottom is bemused by his 'dream, past the wit of man to say what dream it was'. Bottom is a simple man of remarkable integrity, in no way out of countenance in court or fairyland.

**Bottomley, Gordon** 1874–1948.   A Yorkshireman, Bottomley was intended for a banking career but was obliged to live quietly through ill health. He wrote poetry and poetic dramas, but had not sufficient stagecraft to give him the success in the theatre that he really wanted. He conducted a long and mutually encouraging correspondence with the painter Paul Nash, which was published as *Poet and Painter* in 1955.

Bottomley's poetry is romantic with a Celtic tone. The first collection was *The Mickle Drede and Other Verses* (1896). Among his plays were

*King Lear's Wife* (1916) and one about Lady Macbeth called *Gruach* (1921). Gordon Bottomley was the coeditor, with D. W. Harding, of *The Collected Works of Isaac Rosenberg* (1937).

**Boucicault, Dion(ysus Lardner)** 1822–90. Dion Boucicault (originally Boursiquot) was born in Dublin and educated at London University. He became an actor and was only 21 when his first play, *London Assurance*, achieved great success (Covent Garden, 1841). His success continued; he had an infallible certainty for what would 'work' on the stage, an eye for detail, and was a deft hand with plot and dialogue. *London Assurance* was successfully revived by the Royal Shakespeare Company and played in London for several months in the 1970s. Among his most successful plays were *The Queen of Spades* (Drury Lane, 1851); *The Corsican Brothers* (Princess Theatre, 1852); *The Octoroon*, the first play to treat Black people with sympathy and featuring an explosion on a Mississippi steamboat (New York, 1859); *The Colleen Bawn* (New York, 1860); *Arragh-na-Pogue: or The Wicklow Wedding* (Theatre Royal, Dublin); and *The Shaughraun* (New York, 1874). His adaptation of *Rip van Winkle* (1865) was for decades a favourite in the USA. *The Shaughraun* was successfully revived at The Abbey Theatre, Dublin, and in London during the 1960s.

**Bourchier, Sir John** See **Berners, John Bourchier, 2nd Baron.**

**Bourne, George** 1863–1927. George Bourne, whose real surname was Sturt, was born and educated at Farnham in Surrey. He became a teacher but gave it up when his father died (1884) and he inherited his wheelwright's business. His first published work was *A Year's Exile* (1898), a novel of country life and the first of a notable series of books about life among working people in Surrey in the 19th century. These include *The Bettesworth Book: Talks with a Surrey Peasant* (1901), *Memoirs of a Surrey Labourer* (1907), *The Ascending Effort* (1910), *Change in the Village* (1912), *Lucy Bettesworth* (1913), *William Smith, Potter and Farmer 1790–1858* (1920), *A Farmer's Life, with a Memoir of the Farmer's Sister* (1922), and *A Small Boy in the Sixties* (1927). Bourne's best book is acknowledged to be *The Wheelwright's Shop* (1923), which tells the story of the shop at Farnham and describes the craft of the wheelwright.

**Bowen, Elizabeth (Dorothea Cole)** 1899–1973. The daughter of a wealthy Irish barrister, Elizabeth Bowen was born in Dublin and educated at Downe House School in Kent. She settled in England after her marriage to Alan Charles Cameron in 1923, the year which also saw the publication of *Encounters*, a collection of short stories. Her first novel, *The Hotel*, was published in 1927 and established her as a scrupulous craftswoman who used fiction to explore personal isolation and the subtle factors which jeopardize human relationships. To her distinguished reputation as a novelist and short-story writer can be added one as a critic and essayist – *English Novelists* (1942) and *Collected Impressions* (1950). Elizabeth Bowen's novels and short-story collections are *Ann Lee's* (1926, short stories), *The Last September* (1929), *Joining Charles* (1929, short stories), *Friends and Relations* (1931), *To the North* (1932), *The Cat Jumps* (1934, short stories), *The House in Paris* (1935), *The Death of the Heart* (1938), *Look at All Those Roses* (1941, short stories), *The Demon Lover* (1945, short stories), *The Heat of the Day* (1949), *A World of Love* (1955), *The Little Girls* (1964), *A Day in the Dark* (1965), and *Eva Trout* (1969).

**Bowles, Paul** 1910– . Bowles was born in New York and attended the University of Virginia before going to Paris, where his first work – poetry – was published in *transitions* during the 1920s. He studied musical composition with Virgil Thompson and Aaron Copland and first visited Morocco in 1931 at the suggestion of Gertrude Stein. After some years as a composer and music critic he turned to writing and his first novel, *The Sheltering Sky* (1949), found him back in Morocco. The theme of spiritually weary Westerners retreating to a different environment with mistaken hopes only to find themselves displaced and afraid was explored further in Bowles's work, notably in *The Delicate Prey* (1950, called *A Little Stone* in England), *Let it Come Down* (1952), and *The Spider's House* (1955). Resident in Tangier since 1952, the author has presented original accounts of indigenous life by means of tape-recorded narratives; these he has transcribed and translated as *A Life Full of Holes* (by Driss ben Hamad Charhadi, 1964), *Love with a Few Hairs*, *M'Hashish* and *The Lemon*, *The Boy Who Set the Fire*, *Look and Move On*, and *Harmless Poisons, Blameless Sins*, *The Big Mirror* and *The Beach Cafe*, and *The Voice* (1967, 1969, 1974, 1976, 1977, and 1980 – all by Mohammad Mrabet), and *For Bread Alone* (by Mohammad Choukri, 1973). Among other books by Paul Bowles are *Pages from Cold Point and Other Stories* (1968), *Their Heads are Green and Their Hands are Blue* (1963, travel sketches) and *Scenes* (1968, poems).

**Bowles, William Lisle** 1762–1850. Bowles was the son of the vicar of King's Sutton in Northamptonshire, where he was born. He was educated at Winchester School and at Trinity College, Oxford, and in 1804 became vicar of Bremhill in Wiltshire and prebendary of Salisbury Cathedral. Later he became a canon and was made chaplain to the Prince Regent in 1818. In 1789 Bowles published, anonymously, *Fourteen Sonnets, Elegiac and Descriptive, Written During a Tour*. These were the first poems of distinction in the sonnet form for a great many years and were to have considerable influence on the work of Coleridge and Southey. Bowles wrote a fair amount of poetry but was surpassed by his younger contemporaries and is no longer read. His edition of Alexander Pope (1806) brought him into conflict with Campbell, to whom he replied in *The Invariable Principles of Poetry* (1819). Byron joined Campbell, but Bowles effectively defended his views. His original sonnets were widely read; eight editions were published by 1805.

**Bowling, Tom** The hero's benevolent uncle in *Roderick Random* by Tobias Smollett. A lieutenant in the navy, he is one of the first well-portrayed seamen in English fiction, drawn from Smollett's own experiences.

**Boyd, Martin (A'Beckett)** 1893–1969. An Australian, Martin Boyd was born in Lucerne and brought up in Melbourne but divided his time between his home country and Europe. He was studying architecture when World War I broke out; he enlisted in the British Army and later transferred to the RFC. In a period of post-war indecision he tried life as a journalist and spent some time in a Franciscan community before becoming a novelist. His first novels were published under the name of Martin Mills, notably *The Montforts* (1928), a dense but elegant and ironic family chronicle of Anglo-Australian life. This has been the theme of his best novels: *Lucinda Brayford* (1946), *The Cardboard Crown* (1952), *A Difficult Young Man* (1955), *Outbreak of Love* (1957), and *When Blackbirds Sing* (1962). Of his other novels the most notable is *Such Pleasure* (1949). Martin Boyd published two volumes of autobiography, *A Single Flame* (1939) and *Day of My Delight* (1965).

**Boyer, Abel** 1667–1729. A French Huguenot, Boyer was educated in the Netherlands and came to England in 1689. He was tutor to Allen Bathurst (afterwards 1st Earl Bathurst) and taught French to the Duke of Gloucester. In 1703 he began to publish an annual calendar of events and continued this until 1713. He made his mark as a historian with *The History of King William III* (1702) and *The History of the Life and Reign of Queen Anne* (1722). His translation of the *Mémoires de la Vie du Comte de Gramont* (1714) contained a number of errors; this was revised and annotated by Sir Walter Scott and republished in 1811.

**Brabantio** A senator of Venice, and Desdemona's father in Shakespeare's *Othello*. Furious that his daughter has married the Moor in secret, he believes that she was 'abused, stolen from me, and corrupted' and has Othello brought before the duke. He never accepts the marriage completely.

*Bracebridge Hall; or, The Humorists: A Medley*. This book was in effect Washington Irving's second 'Sketch Book' and like the first was published under the pseudonym of Geoffrey Crayon, Gent. It contains 49 tales and sketches and was published in 1822. It was as successful as the first but is not as famous today, having no characters as memorable as Rip Van Winkle and Ichabod Crane. The stories *Dolph Heyliger*, about a boy who dares to visit a haunted house, and *The Storm Ship*, variations on the Flying Dutchman theme, are usually accorded praise as the book's best pieces.

**Brackenridge, Hugh Henry** *c.*1748–1816. Brackenridge was born in Scotland, of Calvinist parents; his family emigrated to Pennsylvania when he was five years old. A schoolfellow of Philip Freneau at Princeton, he collaborated with him on the graduation poem *The Rising Glory of America* (1772) and taught with him in Maryland after they finished college. Brackenridge studied theology and took his master's degree in 1774, the year he wrote *A Poem on Divine Revelation*. He served as chaplain during the War for Independence and during that time wrote two patriotic plays, *The Battle of Bunkers-Hill* (1776) and *The Death of General Montgomery* (1777), for amateur production. Neither survived the occasion which prompted them. His sermons in support of the patriotic cause were published in *Six Political Discourses* (1778) and he edited the *United States Magazine*.

In 1781 Brackenridge left the church, finding he could no longer accept strict dogma. He took up law and settled in what was then the frontier village of Pittsburgh. He also took part in politics but his position lay somewhere between the Federalists and the Democrats and he was not happy with either. But he was Democratic mediator during the Whisky Rebellion provoked by Alexander Hamilton's excise tax on liquor. He published *Incidents of the Insurrection in the Western Part of Pennsylvania* in 1795 and was appointed to the Pennsylvania Supreme Court in 1799.

Brackenridge's literary reputation rests on the massive novel **Modern Chivalry**, which was published in instalments (1792–1815). It was an exposition of his views and proved a notable contribution to the development of the American novel.

**Bracton, Henry of** d. 1268. It seems uncertain how Henry's name should be given; he is sometimes Henry of Bratton, sometimes Henry de Bretton. He was a cleric appointed to high judicial office under Henry III and became Archdeacon of Barnstaple later in life. He attempted the first complete treatise on the laws and customs of England, *De Legibus et Consuetudinibus Angliae*, on which he was still working when he died. It has proved of enormous value to historians of medieval England and English law. Henry's *Notebook*, illustrated by his own comments and describing some 2000 cases from the plea-rolls, is equally valuable.

*De Legibus et Consuetudinibus Angliae* was edited by Travers Twiss (Rolls Series, 1878–83) and by G. E. Woodbine (1915). Henry's *Notebook* was edited by F. W. Maitland (1887).

**Bradbury, Ray (Douglas)** 1920– . Bradbury was born in Waukegan, Illinois, and contributed short stories to periodicals regularly before publishing a collection of them as *Dark Carnival* (1947). He became famous with *The Martian Chronicles* (1950, called *The Silver Locusts* in England), stories of arresting quality with the colonization of Mars as the theme. The success of the book labelled Bradbury as a science-fiction writer but his range has always been broader than that; his particular vein of poetic fantasy simply extends to science-fiction when he requires it to. He is equally effective in gothic tales, many of which have been inspired by his childhood in the Middle West. His output is considerable and he is poet, playwright, and successful writer of screenplays, including *Moby Dick* (1954). Among his collections of stories are *The Illustrated Man* (1951), *The Golden Apples of the Sun* (1953), *The October Country* (1955), *A Medicine for Melancholy* (1959, called *The Day it Rained Forever* in England), *Something Wicked This Way Comes* (1962), *The Machineries of Joy* (1964), and *I Sing the Body Electric!* (1969). Ray Bradbury's novel *Fahrenheit 451* (1953), a tale of the future when the written word is forbidden, was badly mangled by François Truffaut in an attempt to film it.

**Braddon, Mary Elizabeth** 1837–1915. Best known as the author of the Victorian thriller, **Lady Audley's Secret** (1862). She was a prolific writer, the author of some 80 novels, a regular contributor to *Punch* and *The World*, and editor at different times of *Temple Bar* and *Belgravia*. Some work was published under the pen name of Babington White.

**Bradford, William** *c.*1590–1657. The New England historian was probably born in Nottinghamshire. He was a member of the dissenting church of Scrooby in that county, which fled to the Netherlands in 1609. He was one of those who sailed in the *Mayflower* when the Leyden community decided to emigrate to the New World. The *Mayflower* reached land to the north of the emigrants' intended destination and they founded a new colony; they called it Plymouth after the port in England from which their ship had set sail in 1620.

The colony's first governor was John Carver; he died in 1621 and Bradford succeeded him. He held the post 30 times between 1621 and 1656, sometimes declining the office to have a rest from the demands that leadership imposed. He began to write his **History of Plimmoth Plantation** in 1630 and was occupied with it until 1651. Miscellaneous writings by Bradford include poems and dialogues that have been published by the Massachusetts Historical Society, but his true claim to a place in American letters lies in his history of the Pilgrim Fathers and the fortunes of the Plymouth colony.

**Bradley, A(ndrew) C(ecil)** 1851–1935. A. C. Bradley was the brother of the philosopher Francis Herbert Bradley and was born at Cheltenham. He was educated at Cheltenham College and Balliol College, Oxford, and became a fellow of his college in 1874. He lectured at Balliol in English and philosophy from 1876 to 1881 and became Professor of Literature and History at Liverpool University (1882), Professor of English Language and Literature at Glasgow University (1890), and Professor of Poetry at Oxford (1901).

Bradley's *Shakespearean Tragedy* (1904), a group of published lectures on *Hamlet, Othello, King Lear,* and *Macbeth*, has maintained an honoured position in the field of Shakespeare studies. Bradley, while giving due attention to the text, approaches the plays through the characters and their independent lives as implied in the text. Equally distinguished, though less well known, are *A Commentary on 'In Memoriam'* (1901) and *Oxford Lectures on Poetry* (1909).

**Bradley, Francis Herbert** 1846–1924. Francis Bradley, brother of the Shakespearean scholar A. C. Bradley, was born at Clapham in London. He was educated at Marlborough School and University College, Oxford, and became a fellow of Merton College in 1870. His first contribution to philosophy was his essay *The Presuppositions of Critical History* (1874), in which he examined the foundations of historical credibility; the Gospels, which presented facts with no parallel in authentically recorded experience, he rejected as historical documents. In his published work, *Ethical Studies* (1876), *The Principles of Logic* (1883), *Appearance and Reality* (1893), and *Essays on Truth and Reality* (1914), Bradley presented both a carefully reasoned criticism of current metaphysical thought and his own philosophy, which owed something to the growing interest in Hegel. In *Appearance and Reality* Bradley argued that contradictions so plainly exist in all fields – ethics, religion, natural science – that it is not possible to accept them as reality. Similarly, our ideas of self and personality are unreal; therefore the theories of a transcendent and personal god (Theism), and of personal immortality, have to be rejected.

**Bradstreet, Anne** *c*.1612–72. The first woman of America to achieve distinction as a poet, Anne Bradstreet was the daughter of Thomas Dudley, who had been steward to the Earl of Lincoln. She married Simon Bradstreet at 16 and, still in her teens, sailed for America with her husband and her father in 1630. Both her husband and her father became governors of Massachusetts, and the Bradstreets' home was first in Ipswich and then in North Andover. She became the mother of eight children.

Her first work, a collection entitled *The Tenth Muse Lately Sprung Up in America*, was issued without her knowledge in London in 1650. An admiring brother-in-law had taken the manuscript to a London publisher. Her corrections and additions were prepared for a second edition, which was published in Boston in 1678, six years after her death. This edition, *Several Poems Compiled with a Great Variety of Wit and Learning*, was published in a scholarly edition with further additions in 1867.

Anne Bradstreet was admired for her long poems in her lifetime but, apart from the erudition they display, they seem rather dull now. Her models were the Elizabethans – *Contemplations* is in the manner of Spenser – as she acknowledged and there is an imitation of Guillaume du Bartas on the four aspects of life based on Joshua Sylvester's translation of the

Gascon poet; *The Four Monarchies* is a versification of Raleigh's *History of the World*. She is valued now for the later poems, which spring from her own emotions and her observation of her New England world. In these she finds a voice of her own and depends less on poetic conventions. Her world was a masculine one, often harsh, essentially practical; Anne Bradstreet's poetry is a unique expression of the woman's place in it.

A modern American poet, John Berryman, has used Anne Bradstreet as the foundation for a long work on New England thought and feeling – *Homage to Mistress Bradstreet* (1956).

**Braggadochio** The braggart of Spenser's *The Faerie Queene*. He appears in Books II, III, and V.

**Brakelond, Jocelin de** fl. 1200. A monk of St Edmundsbury (Bury St Edmunds in Suffolk), Jocelin was the author of a chronicle (1173–1203) principally concerned with his monastery, its internal life and economics, and its immediate connection with the world outside. The work is a valuable document of social life as well as of monastic institutions at the turn of the 13th century.

Jocelin's *Chronica* was used by Thomas Carlyle in his *Past and Present* and thus became fairly well known. It was edited for the Camden Society by J. G. Rokewode (1840) and by Thomas Arnold as *Memorials of St Edmund's Abbey* (Rolls Series, 1890–96). Translations are by T. E. Tomlins (*Monastic and Social Life in the Twelfth Century*, 1844), Sir Edward Clarke (1903), and H. E. Butler (1949).

**Bramble, Matthew** The Welsh squire touring through England and Scotland in *Humphry Clinker* by Tobias Smollett. He relates his adventures and encounters in letters.

**Bramble, Tabitha** Matthew Bramble's disagreeable sister and travelling companion in *Humphry Clinker* by Tobias Smollett. She is on the watch for a husband and eventually succeeds in marrying Lismahago.

**Breck, Alan** In Robert Louis Stevenson's *Kidnapped* and *Catriona*, the homesick Jacobite whose fortunes become entwined with those of David Balfour.

**Breeches Bible, The** See **Geneva Bible, The.**

**Breton, Nicholas** *c*.1545–1626. Born in London, the son of a merchant, Breton was educated at Oxford and became an industrious poet, prose writer, and pamphleteer; he wrote nearly 60 works of various kinds. His first poems appeared in *A Smale Handfull of Fragrant Flowers* (1575) and the best work of a large output is reckoned to be 'The Passionate Shepheard' and the lyrics that appear in *Englands Helicon*, the anthology of 1600. Breton was equally prolific in prose: *Wits Trenchmour* (1597) is a fishing idyll that influenced Isaak Walton; *The Strange Fortune of Two Excellent Princes* (1600) is a prose romance; *A Mad World, My Masters* (1603) is a 'merrie dialogue betwixt the taker and the mistaker'; *Fantasticks* (1626) is a collection of observations on men and things according to the progress of the calendar.

**Bricks Without Straw** See **Tourgée, Albion W(inegar)**.

**Bride Comes to Yellow Sky, The** See **Open Boat, The**.

**Bridehead, Sue** In Thomas Hardy's *Jude the Obscure*, the neurotic and sexually ambivalent cousin of Jude Fawley. She runs to him, with disastrous results, after her ill-starred marriage to the schoolmaster, Phillotson.

**Bride of Lammermoor, The** A novel by Sir Walter Scott, in the third series of *Tales of My Landlord*, first published in 1819.

The Master of Ravenswood, a sombre impoverished nobleman, saves the life of Lucy Ashton and her father Sir William and Lucy falls in love with him. Sir William is the author of Ravenswood's misfortunes, having helped to dispossess his father, Lord Ravenswood, of land and title after the Civil War of 1679. Political changes (a new king, amongst other things) bring better prospects for Ravenswood, and his father's enemy decides to win his friendship. Ravenswood, in love with Lucy, is compliant and becomes secretly betrothed to her.

But Lucy's domineering mother wants a marriage with the Laird of Bucklaw; she dismisses Ravenswood and proceeds to bully her daughter into submission. Ravenswood, about to depart on a mission abroad, renews the pledge with Lucy: but Lady Ashton is relentless and Lucy apparently submits – only asking that a letter from her shall be sent to Ravenswood asking for his release from their pledge. Lady Ashton intercepts the letter and Lucy, hearing nothing from Ravenswood, consents to the wedding arrangements. Ravenswood arrives just after the ceremony and the hapless Lucy's mind is unbalanced by the resulting revelations and the uproar which follows. That night Lucy murders the husband who was forced on her and dies shortly after.

Ravenswood, at dawn the next day, is going to meet Bucklaw and Ashton, Lucy's brother, and fight a duel with them, but in accordance with an ancient prophecy loses his life in the quicksands on the shore where the encounter was to take place.

**Brideshead Revisited** See **Waugh, Evelyn (Arthur St John)**.

**Bridge of San Luis Rey, The** See **Wilder, Thornton (Niven)**.

**Bridges, Robert** 1844–1930. Bridges was born at Walmer, in Kent, and educated at Eton College and Corpus Christi College, Oxford. He became a doctor (1874) and served as a physician at St Bartholomew's Hospital in London until indifferent health forced him to abandon medicine. After travelling in Europe and the Middle East, he settled at Yattendon in Berkshire, his home from 1882 to 1904. At Oxford he met Gerard Manley Hopkins, whose close friend and eventual literary executor he became. Like Hopkins, Bridges was absorbed in metrical experiment and he shared his friend's fastidious taste in poetry. He published *Poems* (1873) privately and followed this with a considerable body of work: four more volumes of *Shorter Poems* (1879, 1880, 1890, and 1893), *The Growth of Love* and *Carmen Elegiacum* (1876), and *Eros and Psyche* (1885). He wrote eight dramas in verse: *Nero* (part I, 1885) and *Palicio*, *The Return of Ulysses*, *The Christian Captives*, *Achilles in Scyros*, *Nero* (complete version), *The Humours of the Court*, and *The Feast of Bacchus* (all 1890). *Prometheus the Firegiver* (1883) and *Demeter* (1904) are masques.

Bridges was known only to a small circle until 1912, when Oxford University Press published his *Poetical Works* (excluding the eight dramas) and introduced him to a wider public. But he was still not really well known by 1913, when he was appointed poet laureate; the appointment was severely criticized by some journalists. However, the passage of time and the level and considered tone of his technically excellent verse made him a highly respected figure, if not a venerated one. *The Spirit of Man* (1916) was a carefully selected anthology of verse and prose having special bearing on the spiritual needs of a country at war. *New Poems* (1925) was well received and *The Testament of Beauty* (1929), a philosophical poem of 4000 lines published when Bridges was 85, at last made him a popular success; it went through 14 impressions during the first year.

As a prose writer Bridges also earned respect though now his work in this field is hardly known: it includes *Milton's Prosody* (1893), *John Keats: A Critical Essay* (1895), and *The Necessity* of *Poetry* (1918). Bridges also delivered one of the first broadcast lectures, *Poetry* (1929). He contributed to *The Yattendon Hymnal* (1895–99) and published *A Practical Discourse on Hymn-Singing* (1901). His executorship of the works of his friend, Gerard Manley Hopkins, is well known. Bridges spent his last years at Boar's Hill in Oxford. His reputation is not high at present but he will probably always enjoy respect for his integrity and conscientious craftsmanship. 'London Snow', 'Awake, my heart', 'The Storm is Over', and 'Nightingales' are to be found in most anthologies. *The Poetical Works of Robert Bridges* includes *The Testament of Beauty* (Oxford Standard Authors, 1953). John Sparrow's edition, *Poetry and Prose*, was published in 1955.

**Brighton Rock**  See **Greene, (Henry) Graham**.

**Brinkelow, Henry**  d. 1546. Nothing is known of the life of Henry Brinkelow apart from the mention of him by the Tudor bibliographer John Bale, who says that he had been ('somtyme') a grey friar. He was the author of *The Lamentacion of a Christian Against the Citie of London, by R. Mors* (*c*.1542) and *The Com-playnt of Roderyck Mors for the Redresse of Certen Wicked Lawes unto the Parliament Howse of England* (*c*.1548). The *Lamentacion* is moral and theological but the *Com-playnt* is of historic importance. Many of the clergy who had looked forward to reform were bitterly disillusioned and Brinkelow, a Lutheran, was one of these. He approved of the dissolution of the monasteries but after it had taken place he found the new landlords were far worse than those they supplanted – their motive was profit and wealth, and a pursuit of material gain had become the main force abroad in the land. The prose is clear and eloquent and Brinkelow's book deserves to be better known. Both the *Lamentacion* and the *Com-playnt* were edited by J. M. Cowper and published by the Early English Text Society in 1874.

**British Prison-Ship, The**  Philip Freneau's poem, on his experiences as a captive of the British during the War for Independence, was first published in 1781 in four cantos. Freneau recast it later in three cantos: the first one relates how he was captured; the second describes the prison ship *Scorpion*, where he suffered acutely from the bad water, the rotten food, and the absence of fresh air (the prisoners were also cruelly handled); and the last canto tells how he was transferred to the hospital ship *Hunter*, where the treatment was equally inhumane. See also **Freneau, Philip (Morin)**.

**Britomart**  The warrior maiden of Books III and V of Spenser's *The Faerie Queene*. She symbolizes chastity and falls in love with Artegall after seeing his face in a magic mirror.

**Broken Heart, The**  A tragedy by John Ford. The play was first produced about 1629 and published in 1633.

The setting of the play is Laconia, where Penthea is married to a brutal and jealous nobleman, Bassanes. Penthea was in love with Orgilus; they intended to marry but Penthea's brother Ithocles had forced her to marry Bassanes. She cannot bring herself to return Orgilus' love, feeling herself prostituted in her marriage. Ithocles, meanwhile, has been successful in war; he returns from the conquest of Messene and is greatly favoured by the king, who gives him the princess Calantha as a bride. Orgilus, whose life has been wrecked, watches Penthea die of self-starvation and is determined to have revenge on Ithocles. At a feast, Calantha hears of the death of Penthea and, soon after, news is brought of the death of her father, the king. A third blow is news of the murder of Ithocles and the apprehension of Orgilus. She continues at the feast, her feelings under control, and waits until the feast is over before ordering the execution of Orgilus. Then she dies of a broken heart.

**Brome, Richard**  *c*.1590–1652. Brome is first identified in the preface to Ben Jonson's *Bartholomew Fayre*; he seems to have been Jonson's servant and apprentice and his first play, *A Fault in Friendship*, was written with Jonson's son in 1623. His work was good enough to be performed regularly by The King's Men, the leading company of London to which Shakespeare belonged. Of Brome's plays 15 have survived and the influence of Jonson is clear, though Brome was more concerned than Jonson to present a credible plot. Brome's work displayed steady improvement and he might have achieved real distinction if the Puritans had not closed the theatres in 1642, thus blasting his career. He died in poverty.

*The Dramatic Works of Richard Brome* was edited by R. H. Shepherd and published in three volumes in 1873. The most highly regarded of his plays are **The Northern Lasse** (published 1632), **The City Witt** (published 1653), and **A Joviall Crew,** or *The Merry Beggars* (published 1652), the last play to be acted in London before the theatres were closed.

**Brontë, The Life of Charlotte**  See **Gaskell, Elizabeth Cleghorn**.

**Brontë sisters** (**Charlotte** 1816–55; **Emily** 1818–48; **Anne** 1820–49). The Brontë sisters so famous in English literature were the surviving daughters of Patrick Brontë, an Irish clergyman, and Maria Branwell, a Cornish girl of gentle birth. (Two older sisters died as a result of their time at Carus Wilson's school at Cowan Bridge.) In their home – the bleak parsonage at Haworth, which overlooked a grim and over-used graveyard – the sisters and their brother Branwell turned in upon themselves and created imaginary worlds that they recorded in tiny notebooks, which have since been written about exhaustively. The girls' lives were a continual struggle against ill health and defeated aspirations, and their ventures beyond Haworth were never attended by success. Emily taught for a while, as did Anne; Charlotte taught in Brussels, at Constantine Heger's school, and unhappily fell in love with her employer. Eventually they all went back to the parsonage, where the care of their ageing father, and their anxiety over Branwell, who was sinking into incurable alcoholism, had the effect of concentrating their attention on what they wrote, something for which they had had, so far, no particular ambitions.

In 1845 Charlotte came upon a book of verse in Emily's handwriting. Emily, the most private of women, was wrathful that her poems had been read. Then Anne produced some poems which she had written, and Charlotte persuaded her sisters to allow her to submit their selected poems for publication – Charlotte wrote poems, too. The selection was published in 1846 as poems by 'Currer, Ellis, and Acton Bell', and earned some praise. A month later, exactly two copies had been bought. But the publication of their poems was what decided each of the sisters to embark on a novel.

Haworth Parsonage. The frontispiece illustration for The World's Classics edition of Elizabeth Gaskell's *The Life of Charlotte Brontë*, 1929. By W. J. Linton.

Charlotte was the one who 'pushed', sending the three novels to publisher after publisher. Eventually, in 1842, *Wuthering Heights* by Ellis Bell and *Agnes Grey* by Acton Bell were published; *The Professor* by Currer Bell was rejected. However, the rejection letter Charlotte received from another publisher, Smith, Elder & Co. contained encouragement; 'he [Currer Bell] could produce a book which would command success'. She had been working on another novel; she finished it with all possible speed and in October 1847 *Jane Eyre. An Autobiography Edited by Currer Bell* was published. *Wuthering Heights* and *Agnes Grey* appeared in December of the same year under the imprint of another publisher.

*Jane Eyre* was a resounding success. Thackeray read it at a sitting and 'lost a whole day' doing so; he recognized at once that the author was a woman. *Jane Eyre* was not only a highly praised book, it was also a celebrated one, outstripping its companions completely. Its second edition was dedicated to Thackeray; he called it 'The greatest compliment I have ever received in my life.' *Wuthering Heights* aroused intense interest and, for the most part, intense dislike; Emily's powerful imagination had produced a novel of a kind that was completely new. *Agnes Grey*, the work of the gentle, retiring Anne was received with a warm appreciation that has continued to be felt by all her readers; it could have been overpowered by Charlotte's and Emily's books but it has not been and has succeeded on its own terms.

It would be pleasant to record that literary success transformed the sisters' lives, but Haworth and its demands exacted a dreadful toll. Branwell's debts were paid off by Charlotte and her father, but his slavery to alcohol and drugs was complete, and nursing him made terrible demands on three young women who were constantly debilitated by ill health. Branwell died in September 1848 but already Emily was succumbing to consumption and died in December of the same year. To Charlotte's grief was added the shock that Anne was ill, too. The medical treatment in those days was inefficacious, and though Anne's second novel, *The Tenant of Wildfell Hall*, was completed and published by Smith, Elder in 1848, the youngest of the sisters died at Scarborough in May 1849. Charlotte and her father were alone; it is astonishing that Charlotte had the strength and resolution to go on. She was now 33.

*Shirley*, her second published novel, appeared in 1849. Charlotte was now a literary celebrity and sometimes went to London as the guest of her publisher. A strange, mousy little figure, to

Charlotte Brontë. Portrait by George Richmond, 1850. National Portrait Gallery, London.

many she appeared dull; Thackeray, to his eternal credit, championed the 'tiny, delicate, serious little lady' and discerned the 'independent, indomitable spirit' who 'spied out arrogance and affectation with extraordinary keenness of vision'. But the visits to London exhausted her and she suffered appalling headaches. Meanwhile, she met and became friends with Harriet Martineau, Sir James and Lady Shuttleworth, and most important of all, Elizabeth Gaskell (see the entry for her).

*Villette* was published in 1853, and the following year Charlotte accepted the proposal of Arthur Bell Nicholls, her father's curate. She enjoyed a brief happiness; but the Fates who attended the members of this hapless family were not done with them yet. Charlotte, pregnant, contracted a chill after being caught in a rainstorm while walking on the moors. She died, like her sisters, of consumption, in March 1855. *The Professor*, her first written novel, was published posthumously, in 1857, and a fragment, called *Emma*, in the *Cornhill Magazine* in 1860.

The Brontë sisters were of Haworth, and it is hard not to speculate on the possible course of their careers if they had not been obliged to spend their lives there. The village lay on the Yorkshire moors, at the centre of the wool trade, in a period of the Industrial Revolution when living conditions were absolutely appalling. Forty per cent of Haworth children died before reaching the age of six; there was no drainage system; and illustrations of the village and the parsonage at the Brontës' time suggest a bleak and inhospitable place. But Haworth, the sisters and their brief lives, are inextricable in readers' minds, now, from the remarkable flowering that made 1847 such an important year in the history of the novel.

Of the poems only Emily's have lived. They are few enough but their strength is remarkable and rereading them makes one aware, as one critic put it, that they have a haunting ability to make one wonder about the 'silences' in them. They could only have been written by the author of *Wuthering Heights*.

**Brooke, Dorothea**  In George Eliot's *Middlemarch*, the aspiring ardent girl who marries a dull elderly would-be scholar, Casaubon. She believes that his work is as important as his behaviour implies and discovers too late what a mistake her marriage is.

**Brooke, Henry** 1703–83.  Brooke was a native of County Cavan in Ireland and was educated privately before entering Trinity College, Dublin. Later he went to London, where he spent some ten years. He began to write when he returned to Ireland to live in Dublin: he was fortunate in enjoying a comfortable private income. Brooke was a strong advocate for the relaxation of the laws against the Catholics.

*Design and Beauty: an Epistle* (1734) was followed by a far more ambitious poem called *Universal Beauty* written in six parts (1734–36), on the perfection of design in the universe. This is admired for Brooke's skill in handling a difficult subject on a large scale but is no longer read. His translation of Tasso's *Gerusalemme liberata* Books I and II followed in 1738 and a tragedy, *Gustavus Vasa*, appeared in 1739. The play was banned, however, because Walpole fancied there was a likeness to himself in the villain of the piece. But it was produced in Dublin as *The Patriot* in 1744. Another play, *The Earl of Essex*, was produced in Dublin in 1750 and published in 1761. Brooke wrote two novels: *Juliet Grenville* (1774), the second, was soon forgotten but **The Fool of Quality** (five volumes, 1766–72) attracted considerable attention and was much admired by John Wesley and Charles Kingsley.

**Brooke, Rupert (Chawner)** 1887–1915. Rupert Brooke was born at Rugby, Warwickshire, and was the son of a teacher at Rugby

School where he was educated. Later he went to King's College, Cambridge, and graduated in 1909. He travelled in Europe, and while in England made his home at the Old Vicarage, Grantchester. During 1913–14 he travelled in America and the South Pacific, and at the outbreak of World War I took a commission in the Royal Naval Division. He went to the Dardanelles in 1915 but did not live to take part in the campaign. He died of blood poisoning and was buried on the island of Scyros.

Rupert Brooke began to write poetry while still at Rugby, and his first collection, *Poems*, was published in 1911. *1914 and Other Poems* was published in the year of his death. A collected edition of his poems, with a memoir, was published by Edward Marsh (1918); *Poems* (1952), edited by Geoffrey Keynes, is the most complete. *The Prose of Rupert Brooke* (1956), containing a selection from books, articles, and unpublished manuscripts, was edited by Christopher Hassall, who wrote the standard biography (1964). Brooke's articles to *The Westminster Gazette*, written from the United States, were published as *Letters from America* (1916) with a preface by Henry James.

A remarkably beautiful young man, Brooke was cast as the young hero of war by an admiring public before the war became too awful. He was overpraised for a time; then he was devalued in the years of disillusion. His real stature began to emerge after World War II, when he was recognized as a young poet of real quality who did not live to fulfil his great promise.

**Brooke, Stopford Augustus** 1832–1916. Brooke was born at Glendowan, near Letterkenny in Donegal. He completed his education at Trinity College, Dublin, and was ordained in 1857. He became known as an effective preacher at St Mary Abbots in Kensington and accompanied the Princess Royal to Berlin as her chaplain in 1863. He became Chaplain-in-Ordinary to Queen Victoria in 1867 but left the Church of England in 1880, finding it impossible to reconcile his Broad Church views with continued ministry. Brooke published books on theology and church matters but is chiefly remembered for *The History of Early English Literature* (1892) and *English Literature from the Beginning to The Norman Conquest* (1898).

**Brookenham, Nanda**  The heroine of *The Awkward Age*, by Henry James. Nanda objects to her position as a property in the marriage market and is enabled to escape from it by the elderly and sympathetic Mr Longdon, who once loved her

grandmother. He provides her with a dowry, thus giving her the freedom to choose.

***Brook Kerith, The***: *A Syrian Story*.  A novel by George Moore, first published in 1916. Moore was born into a Catholic family and was educated at a Catholic college. Later he became a Protestant, and, eventually, an agnostic. The brook referred to in the title of the novel is that by which Elijah, in *The First Book of the Kings*, dwelt at the Lord's command: 'Get thee hence, and turn thee eastward, and hide thyself by the brook Cherith, that is before Jordan.'

The novel describes how Joseph of Arimathea, a child full of dreams of the prophets, persuades his father to have him taught Hebrew and Greek. When he grows up he enters his father's business, but in Jerusalem at the Passover he listens to the Pharisees and Sadducees disputing the meaning of the scriptures. He turns away from that and seeks out the Essenes in their retreat above the Jordan. He teaches Hebrew and Greek to the converts but generally finds the life, with its preoccupation with philosophical discussion, unrewarding. He is given leave to seek out the new prophet, John the Baptist, and through him comes his realization that Jesus, whom he had seen as a shepherd among the Essenes, is the man he must follow. The narrative continues on the lines of the story in the gospels. After Joseph gains permission to take Jesus's body down from the cross, he is alone in the tomb when he discovers that Jesus is not dead. He carries him off to his house, where he restores him to health. Then Jesus again becomes a shepherd of the Essenes, on the hills above the brook Kerith.

Thirty years pass, and the Essenes give refuge to Paul, who learns the identity of the shepherd. But Jesus has rejected his former belief in himself and is horrified to learn of the teaching that Paul believes and preaches. He insists on going to Jerusalem to reveal the truth and Paul travels with him. On the journey Paul manages to convince Jesus that his revelation would never be believed. So they part at Caesarea, Jesus to join a group of travellers from India, whose ideas interest him, Paul to set forth for the Gentile world, with his story of a risen Messiah.

**Brougham, Henry Peter** 1778–1868. Brougham was born in Edinburgh and educated at Edinburgh High School and Edinburgh University, where he studied law. He joined the group of lawyers interested in reform, and with one of these, Francis Jeffrey, and Sydney Smith, Brougham founded ***The Edinburgh Review*** in 1802. Brougham went to London, was called to the Bar, and entered Parliament in 1810. He fought tirelessly for the abolition of slavery and was a powerful advocate of popular education and sound commercial practice; he played a leading part in the establishment of London University in 1829.

Henry Brougham was chosen by Queen Caroline as her Attorney General and he successfully defended her in 1820. He became Lord Chancellor in 1830 and Baron Brougham and Vaux. He supported the Reform Bill and his speech at the second reading is famous in parliamentary annals. He lost office with the fall of Melbourne's government; but he sat in the supreme Court of Appeal and on the Judicial Committee of the Privy Council, helping bring about some badly needed reforms in the Court of Chancery. A man of remarkable energy, Brougham was often the target of Tory wits (Thomas Love Peacock satirized him in *Crotchet Castle*) but in fact no Tory could equal him.

Brougham was distrusted by his colleagues on *The Edinburgh Review* for trying to use the magazine to express his own views. He published political discourses, historical works, and two novels: *Albert Lunel: or The Château of Languedoc* (1844) and *Masters and Workmen* (1851). His most notable works were *Practical Observations upon The Education of the People* (1825), *Historical Sketches of Statesmen who Flourished in The Time of George III* (1839), *The British Constitution* (1844), and *The Life and Times of Lord Brougham* (published posthumously, 1872).

**Broughton, Rhoda** 1840–1920. A novelist contemporary with Mary Elizabeth Braddon and Mrs Henry Wood. Unlike them, she is remembered for no particular work, though in her time she enjoyed similar success, notably with *Cometh up as a Flower* (1867).

**Brown, Charles Brockden** 1771–1810. The son of a prosperous Quaker family of Philadelphia, Brown was trained for the law and practised for a time – but he detested it, abandoning it as soon as he could. After a visit to his friend Elihu Smith – one of the 'Connecticut Wits' – he decided to make writing a career. He had contributed some romantic essays to the *Columbia Magazine* in his youth. His first book, *Alcuin: A Dialogue* (1798), was directly influenced by William Godwin; it is a treatise on the rights of women. Godwin's *Caleb Williams* influenced him when he began to write fiction and in two feverishly busy years he published four novels: *Wieland* (1798), and *Arthur Mervyn, Ormond,* and *Edgar Huntly* (all 1799).

From 1799 Brown was editor of *The Monthly Magazine and American Review*, an activity which provided him with a living; his works were well received but paid him little. A legacy then allowed him to return to writing fiction and he published *Clara Howard* and *Jane Talbot* in 1801. These were more conventional romances and, apart from the unfinished *Memoirs of Carwin* (1803), he wrote no more fiction. He invested in an importing business and edited a new magazine, *The Literary Magazine and American Register,* and married in 1804. The importing business failed in 1806 but the new magazine was a success. Brown died of consumption at the age of 39. He always blamed his poor health on his family, who had insisted on rigorous study to prepare him for the lawyer's practice that he loathed.

Charles Brockden Brown was the first American to make a profession of writing and the first novelist to use America as the setting for his stories. He was an American gothic novelist who had not quite digested the different influences of William Godwin, Ann Radcliffe, Horace Walpole, and Samuel Richardson. His own influence, however, can be seen in Hawthorne, Poe, and later writers; he also earned the respect of Keats and Scott. His work is unreadable now, almost a caricature, with his extravagant gothic horrors (the mad son Wieland, of the mad father Wieland, who explodes in spontaneous combustion; Philadelphia in the grip of the plague; the somnambulist Edgar, to whom everything can happen; Ormond the wealthy rapist; etc.) and his unabashed use of coincidence. But a country's fiction has to begin somewhere and Brown, whatever his failings, deserves serious consideration on that score.

**Brown, John** 1800–59. The celebrated Abolitionist leader was the son of an active Abolitionist and underground railway agent, Owen Brown. He was born in Torrington, Connecticut, and was a restless and unsuccessful jack-of-all-trades in his adult life though he married and had numerous children. At the age of 55 he joined his sons in the Ossawatomie settlement in Kansas; the year before had seen the passing of the Kansas-Nebraska Bill which, like the Missouri Compromise, allowed the settlers themselves to determine whether slavery should be permitted or not. Like most compromises it provoked strife – Kansas was bordered, on the east and south, by slave states. John Brown's Abolitionism erupted; he decided that God intended him to destroy proslavery settlers so, with four of his sons and another sympathizer, Brown murdered five men on 24 May 1856. Retaliation soon followed –

Brown and the Ossawatomie settlement were dispersed and their dwellings burned. Brown gathered arms and money from leading Abolitionists and on 16 October 1859, with 21 men, staged an attack on the US armoury at Harper's Ferry, in Virginia. His intention was to establish a base from which he could begin to free the slaves by using arms. He captured the armoury but he and his group were defeated by a force of marines under Robert E. Lee; Brown himself was wounded and taken prisoner.

During his trial Brown's steadfast dignity and sincerity made a remarkable impression and his declaration that his purpose was to free men from slavery would not be forgotten. He was hanged at Charlestown on 2 December 1859 – and became a martyr of the Abolitionist cause. He is celebrated in literature by Thoreau (*The Last Days of John Brown*), Carl Sandburg (*Ossawatomie*), Whittier (*John Brown of Ossawatomie*), Stephen Vincent Benet (*John Brown's Body*), and by many others. The Civil War song 'John Brown's Body' was sung to the same tune as 'The Battle Hymn of the Republic', a composition of uncertain origin but usually ascribed to William Steffe of South Carolina.

**Brown, Thomas** 1663–1704. A native of Shropshire, Brown went to Christ Church, Oxford, where Dr John Fell was dean. Dr Fell threatened to expel Brown for some misdemeanour and Brown coined the jingle 'I do not love you, Dr Fell, But why I cannot tell; But this I know full well, I do not love you, Dr Fell', based on one of Martial's *Epigrams*. Otherwise Brown was a translator, one of the team who wrote an English version of Paul Scarron's *Le Roman Comique* and, also with others, translated works by Petronius and Lucian. Brown wrote sketches of London life that were published as *Amusements Serious and Comical* (1700). His collected works were published in four volumes (1707–11).

**Browne, Charles Farrar** See **Ward, Artemus**.

**Browne, Sir Thomas** 1605–82. Thomas Browne was born in London and educated at Winchester and Oxford. Later he studied at Montpellier, Padua, and Leyden, where he completed his education in medicine and took his degree. He practised at Oxford for about four years and took his MD there. About this time (1634–37) he is believed to have written the first draft of **Religio Medici**, which he completed at Shibden Hall in Halifax. He settled at Norwich in 1637 and married in 1641.

During the Civil War Browne, anti-Puritan and a convinced Royalist, went on quietly with his work as a doctor and became the father of at least 10 children (there may have been as many as 12), meanwhile writing the occasional tracts that have given his name a place in English literature. The first, *Religio Medici*, was circulated in manuscript form for some time until a printer published it without Browne's permission (1642). It is an examination of his faith – a clarification to himself, through examination, of his religious belief. The next book was **Pseudodoxia Epidemica**, more usually called *Vulgar Errors* (1646), which contains not only a diverting examination of popular beliefs but reflections on the nature of evidence and on the human credulity that relates this to truth.

During the rest of the Civil War and for some years afterwards Browne published nothing. His next works, **Urn Burial** and *The Garden of Cyrus*, appeared together (1658). The first was a reflection on burial ceremonies and immortality; the second a treatise on the various applications of the *quincunx* figure, from its use in architecture to the belief in the mysterious properties of the number 5. This was the last work to appear during the author's lifetime; posthumous publications were *Certain Miscellany Tracts* (1684), *A Letter to a Friend, Upon occasion of the Death of his Intimate Friend* (1690), and *Christian Morals* (1716). Browne enjoyed an extensive correspondence with such distinguished contemporaries as Aubrey, John Evelyn, and Elias Ashmole, and wrote to his sons affectionate letters that are a charming mixture of paternal solicitude and lightly worn erudition. The letters were first published in S. Wilkin's edition of Browne's works (1835–36).

Browne was knighted by Charles II in 1671 during a royal visit to Norwich. He was an illustrious and honoured figure in the city and the mayor yielded precedence to him. Browne's enquiring mind was not scientific in the pure sense, though the science of the day would have learned much from his splendid common sense. He was interested in everything, as well as being a religious man, as *Religio Medici* demonstrates. But his interests were subjected to the profound reflection of an intensely poetic mind, which found expression in the finest prose the English language had so far known.

**Browne, Thomas Alexander** See **Boldrewood, Rolf**.

**Browne, William** *c*.1591–*c*.1643. Browne was born in Tavistock, Devon, and educated at Exeter College, Oxford, and the Middle Temple. He admired Spenser above all other poets and numbered Chapman, Drayton, and Ben Jonson among his friends. He was a scholar of English as well as of classical learning and had hopes, which were not realized, of publishing an edition of Thomas Occleve.

Browne's principal work is the long poem in three books called *Britannia's Pastorals* (the first book published in 1613, the second in 1616, and the third not until 1852). He collaborated on a book of pastorals, *The Shepherd's Pipe* (1614), with his friends Davies of Hereford, George Wither, and Christopher Brooke and inserted a poem by Thomas Occleve into the book, hoping to draw attention to the 14th-century writer. (The lack of interest shown discouraged him from further efforts in that direction.)

William Browne is a poet very much in the tradition of Spenser and Sidney. His feeling for his own West Country shines through the loves and tears of his stock pastoral figures and gives his verse an enduring freshness. He was admired by Milton and Keats. Browne was the author of the famous epitaph, once attributed to Jonson, on the Countess of Pembroke beginning 'Underneath this sable hearse'. William Hazlitt's collected edition of Browne's works, published 1868–69, includes the *Inner Temple Masque*, performed in January 1615.

**Browning, Elizabeth Barrett** 1806–61. Elizabeth Barrett was the eldest of 12 children born to Edward Moulton Barrett and his wife Mary. Her birthplace was Coxhoe Hall, about 16 miles south of Durham, and both her parents were wealthy. The family moved to Hope End in Herefordshire while she was still an infant and the young Elizabeth, though a slight girl, was healthy and vigorous until she began to suffer at about the age of 15 from a tubercular complaint. It is not certain that she had a diseased spine, and in her letters there is no confirmation to be found of the once-held belief that she was crippled for years from a fall while riding. But she was seriously ill and suffered acute pain, and her father insisted on her being treated as an invalid from that time on. She used laudanum and morphine to the end of her life; relief from pain probably resulted in a dependence that never left her, though she made a valiant effort to reduce it when she met Robert Browning.

She was precociously intelligent and insisted upon having the same lessons her brother was given by his tutor, studying French, Latin, Greek, and Italian. She read widely and wrote verses from childhood, publishing (anonymously) *The Battle of Marathon* (1820) when she was 14. The consolation in her physical frailty was the enjoyment of the pleasures which her formidable intelligence put within her reach. The family moved from Hope End to Sidmouth in Devonshire and eventually settled in the house at 50 Wimpole Street in 1837. By then Elizabeth had published more poems: *Essay on Mind, with Other Poems* (1826) and a volume containing her version of Aeschylus, *Prometheus Bound: and Miscellaneous Poems* (1833). She had made an important friend in a distant cousin, John Kenyon, to whose unfailing kindness she was to owe a great deal. He introduced her to Mary Russell Mitford and several friends in literary London, fostered her romance with Browning, helped them after their marriage when they were short of money, and left them part of his fortune when he died. He encouraged Elizabeth when she was despondent, and the unfortunate woman had good reason for that. According to the limited medical knowledge of the day, she was to stay in her room (which was up three flights of stairs) and not be touched by fresh air; the windows were sealed, there were double doors, and her sister Arabel occupied the same room each night. Elizabeth spent five years there and her father, who slept in the next room, prayed over his afflicted child nightly before retiring. Elizabeth Barrett became nervous of visitors and the thought of ever leaving her room terrified her.

*The Seraphim and Other Poems* (1838) was widely reviewed and made her a name as a promising poet; from then her work began to appear regularly in the literary magazines. A personal tragedy, the loss of her favourite brother Bro (Edward) in a sailing accident, nearly extinguished her writing career, but her tenacious spirit somehow pulled her through. She became a regular contributor to *The Athenaeum*, was read by Dickens and Thackeray, and found the work of two young poets, Alfred Tennyson and Robert Browning, of particular interest. Her *Poems* (1844) included the famous 'The Cry of the Children', her appeal to the social conscience of England, and established her reputation in England and the USA. At this time also she collaborated with Richard Hengist Horne and Robert Bell in *A New Spirit of the Age*, a review of the literature of the day. But her *Poems* was more important. Browning wrote to her, full of admiration: she was six years older than he and had made a reputation. He had none as yet but she admired his work and was eventually persuaded to see him by John Kenyon on 20 May 1845. Her father, who epitomized Victorian domestic tyranny, had forbidden his children to marry. He never forgave his favourite, Elizabeth, for falling in love with Robert Browning and marrying him.

There is no doubt that love literally put Elizabeth back on her feet. The apparently hopeless invalid learned to move about her room, to negotiate the stairs to the ground floor, and to go for walks. The Brownings made their home in Florence, at the Casa Guidi, and Elizabeth became the mother of a son at the age of 43. While at Florence she published *Poems* (1850), the volume that contained the **Sonnets from the Portuguese**, written during the months of Browning's courtship and regarded as her most enduring and successful poems. In the same year *The Athenaeum* recommended that she be made poet laureate to follow Wordsworth: 'There is no living poet of either sex who can prefer a higher claim than Mrs Elizabeth Barrett Browning.' But the new laureate was Tennyson.

*Casa Guidi Windows* (1851) was a poem about Italian independence, a cause which Elizabeth embraced fervently. She was at work also on something more ambitious, in spite of her uncertain health. Her recovery had been a miracle but she never really enjoyed good health. *Aurora Leigh* was completed while staying with John Kenyon when the Brownings visited England in 1855. The poem, dedicated to Kenyon, was published in 1857 to mixed reviews. High praise came from Ruskin, the Rossettis, Swinburne, and Landor but they were already admirers;

more important was the public response to this verse novel, which is longer than *Paradise Lost*. It was reprinted three times in the first year and reached a 17th edition by 1882. It is not well known now, but in the 1850s Elizabeth Barrett Browning was speaking for women; some were shocked by it but many women were deeply impressed, among them Queen Victoria.

Elizabeth's sympathy for the Italian cause continued and was expressed in *Poems before Congress* (1860). Her health collapsed soon after and she died at Casa Guidi in 1861. *Last Poems* was published in the following year. Her reputation lessened as the years went by and she does not now command the high esteem she knew during her lifetime, when she was far more celebrated than her husband. She had no real ability for drama or narrative and her technique was uncertain; her best work, *Sonnets from the Portuguese*, benefited greatly from the form, which imposed its own discipline. There have been few modern editions of the work of Elizabeth Barrett Browning; there is a single-volume *Complete Poems* in the Oxford Standard Authors (1904). F. E. Ratchford and D. Fulton produced an annotated edition of *Sonnets from the Portuguese* (1950). *Aurora Leigh and Other Poems* is edited by Cora Kaplan (1978).

**Browning, Robert** 1812–89. The son of a clerk at the Bank of England, Browning was born at Camberwell. Now a part of London, Camberwell in the early years of the 19th century lay amid green fields. Browning's father had literary and artistic enthusiasms; his mother was a Nonconformist of simple and endearing piety. The home at Camberwell was a happy place where Browning, the indulged and only son, gained his education, was encouraged in his passion for poetry, and was contented enough to stay until he was 25. The young Browning's appreciation of the arts also extended to music, which he learned at home, and his talent for drawing was admired by Rossetti.

As a boy Browning was, he said himself, an almost compulsive rhymer, and by the time he was 12 or 13 he had written enough poems for a small volume. His father was impressed and tried to have them published. *Incondita* was sent to Benjamin Flower of the *Cambridge Intelligencer*; the collection was not published and Browning destroyed the poems, which had been copied by Eliza Flower, soon after. But her sister Sarah had also made a copy and two poems survive: 'The First-Born of Egypt' and 'The Dance of Death'. The poet's destruction of his own work is believed to have been prompted by his reading of

Elizabeth Barrett Browning. A daguerrotype of the late 1850s.

Shelley for the first time, at the age of 14. Browning chanced upon a copy of *Queen Mab* on a bookstall; he read more of Shelley and became an atheist and a vegetarian. He read *Adonais* and sought the poems of Keats; he also responded to Byron wholeheartedly and the two poems of his boyhood display the influence clearly.

Browning's atheist and vegetarian period lasted for about two years, and he looked back on it with dislike in later life. He ate bread and potatoes; this weakened his eyesight and he was persuaded to go back to a normal diet. His atheism was disruptive and it says much for his parents that his behaviour left no bitterness behind. He went to London University at 16 but stayed only two terms; his father forfeited £100. Browning's biographer, Maisie Ward, suggests that he was probably bored – his education at home had been rich and varied, far in advance of that of his fellow students – and that his tutors could well have been teaching him things he had already learned.

The poet was 20 when he wrote *Pauline: A Fragment of a Confession*, which was published anonymously in 1833, when he was 21. It won two favourable notices, in *The Athenaeum* and *The Monthly Repository*, but attracted no other attention. In the following year Browning, who was thinking of a diplomatic career and wondering if he could afford it (many of the junior posts were unpaid in those days), was invited by the Russian consul-general, George de Benkhausen, to visit St Petersburg. It is not known how Browning became friends with the Russian diplomat (he destroyed his early letters to his family) but there can be no doubt that the journey through northern Europe by coach to the Russian capital, the spectacle of the ice breaking on the Neva to herald the coming of spring, the pleasure and convenience of official life, must have had a strong appeal to a romantic young man uncertain what to do with his life. On his return to England Browning applied for a post on a mission to Persia.

Meanwhile another friend, Count Amédée de Ripert-Monoler, suggested to Browning that Paracelsus, the Swiss alchemist, physician, and philosopher, was an excellent subject for a poem. (The count knew Browning through a relation in Rothschild's bank in Paris; Browning's correspondence with him is still under seal.) But another subject had taken hold of Browning's imagination, the 12th-century Mantuan poet, Sordello. This was to occupy him intermittently for seven years and he completed other poems in the meantime; several, including 'Porphyria's Lover', appeared in *The Monthly Repository*, and

in 1835 he published ***Paracelsus***. It did not make him rich or famous but John Forster gave it high praise in *The New Monthly Magazine*, and men like Wordsworth, Walter Savage Landor, Dickens, the actor William Macready, and Carlyle sought his acquaintance. The friendship with Carlyle was a particularly warm and lasting one. Browning's application for a diplomatic post was turned down.

Browning's next work was in part the result of his friendships with Forster and Macready. Forster had written about the Earl of Strafford and the period of the Civil War; Macready, who had no new play to perform in England but did not want to go to America, asked Browning to write him one. The result was *Strafford*, which Macready's great experience told him was not stageworthy. He went ahead with it, however; his company performed it at Covent Garden in May 1837 and it lasted five performances only. But Longmans published the text, the first work of Browning's not to be published at his own expense.

***Sordello*** was published in 1840 and such small favour as Browning had so far earned almost disappeared. He had visited Italy in 1838 and had fallen in love with it. The poem was a fine evocation of the Italian cities but the period, with the destructive hatred of Guelph for Ghibelline, and the reasons for the Italian city-states' allegiances, are incomprehensible to the uninformed. There were numerous parentheses and an absence of connecting information. Whatever its considerable virtues as poetry the whole poem mystified his readers, of whom Browning had clearly expected too much. At this time Henry Moxon, who was to become Tennyson's publisher also (through Browning; the great contemporaries were excellent friends), suggested a plan for publishing Browning's poems as they were written, in inexpensive pamphlets to popularize them. The pamphlets were called *Bells and Pomegranates*, and the first one to appear, ***Pippa Passes*** (1841), is the story of a girl who ponders on her world in a small Italian town. It is not a complete success as a dramatic poem but has considerable charm. There were seven more of the *Bells and Pomegranates* series: *King Victor and King Charles* (1842), a tragedy; *Dramatic Lyrics* (1842); *The Return of the Druses* (1843), a tragedy; *A Blot in the 'Scutcheon* (1843), a tragedy; *Colombe's Birthday* (1844), a play; *Dramatic Romances and Lyrics* (1845); and *Luria and A Soul's Tragedy* (1846).

*A Blot in the 'Scutcheon* was written for William Macready, who after tiresome prevarication produced it – very badly, Browning believed – in

1843 at Drury Lane, where it failed. In 1844 Charles Kean wanted to produce *Colombe's Birthday* but asked Browning to hold publication until the play was produced. Browning by now was wary of actors and managers with their incomprehensible uncertainty of purpose, and he refused. The play was eventually staged in 1853 at the Haymarket, produced by Samuel Phelps, and lasted for two weeks. But by then the poet had ceased to write for the theatre and had simply been hoping that the production would prove financially rewarding. The poems in *Bells and Pomegranates* were a very different matter, revealing Browning's rich and varied talents. **My Last Duchess**, **Soliloquy of the Spanish Cloister**, 'In a gondola', and **The Pied Piper of Hamelin** are among the poems in *Dramatic Lyrics*; 'The Lost Leader', 'Home thoughts from Abroad', 'Meeting at Night', 'The Glove', **The Bishop orders his Tomb at St Praxed's Church**, and 'Saul' are among those in *Dramatic Romances and Lyrics*.

Browning visited Italy again in 1844 and upon his return to England read the newly published *Poems* by Elizabeth Barrett who had, in a series of articles on English poets in *The Athenaeum*, praised Browning's work very highly. A mutual friend, John Kenyon, encouraged the poets to correspond and Browning's generous praises were thrilling to the gifted woman, six years his senior and apparently confined forever by her disability to a room in Wimpole Street. He was in love with her already by the time they met, on 20 May 1845, and he did not waste time in telling her so. They became engaged in September and were married in September of 1846. A week later they were on their way to the Casa Guidi in Florence, which became their home. Theirs is one of the great romances of literary history.

Browning published nothing for four years. His life was full enough, certainly; he admired his wife's talents extravagantly and their son, their only child, was born in March 1849. His reputation as a poet was at this period much lower than his wife's. *Christmas Eve and Easter Day* (1850) is a poem about religion and what it meant to Robert Browning. The poem was coldly received and did not sell; such praise as it earned appeared in *La Revue des Deux Mondes* and the writer, Joseph Milsand, was to become a close friend of the Brownings. They visited England in 1851 and stayed in lodgings, though Tennyson and another friend, Joseph Arnold, had offered them their houses. But they were warmly welcomed and entertained by Tennyson, Carlyle, John Forster, Fanny Kemble, Ruskin, Landor, Coventry Patmore, Rossetti, Kingsley, and their dearly loved friend John Kenyon. Carlyle, who

Robert Browning. A detail from the portrait by M. Gordigiani, 1858. National Portrait Gallery, London.

never threw compliments directly at anyone, said of Browning to a friend that the poet was '. . . one of the bravest and most gifted of English souls now living'. The circle of friends continued to grow when the Brownings fled the English winter and returned to the Continent, where they knew George Sand, Dumas, Thackeray, Lockhart, Aubrey de Vere, and the painter Frederic Leighton.

*Men and Women* (1855) was not a success with anyone except the Brownings' growing circle of personal admirers. The publisher, Henry Chapman, infuriated Browning by never replying to his enquiries about the book's progress, and the reviews were unfavourable. The book contains such poems as 'Love among the Ruins', 'Up at a Villa – Down in the City', **Fra Lippo Lippi**, **A Toccata of Galuppi's**, 'Any Wife to any Husband', **Childe Roland to the Dark Tower Came**, 'Bishop Blougram's Apology', **Andrea del Sarto**, 'The Heretic's Tragedy', and 'One Word More'. His wife's career, in contrast, was flourishing; *Aurora Leigh* (1851) was a great success. Mrs Browning became immersed in the cause of Italian unity, which Robert understood, and in spiritualism, which he did not and which infuriated him. But he loved Elizabeth absolutely and her uncertain health was his first concern. He could not bear to live in Florence after she died in June 1861; he went to England with his son Robert ('Pen') and settled in a house in west London, at Warwick Crescent. It was 17 years before he went to Italy again.

During the later years in Florence Browning began work on a poem about a murder which took place in Rome at the end of the 17th century. It occupied him for many years but he completed other work meanwhile, working in France during the summer. *Dramatis Personae* (1864) seemed at first to fare no better than Browning's earlier volumes, even though it contained such poems as 'A Death in the Desert', 'Rabbi Ben Ezra', **Caliban Upon Setebos**, 'Confessions', and 'Mr Sludge "the Medium"'. But things were changing in England; *Essays and Reviews* had been published (Jowett became a friend of Browning's) and Christian dogma was being questioned as never before. The poet who had hardly been read now became interesting, especially to the younger university men, and for the first time in Browning's career (he was 52) one of his books reached a second edition, within a year of publication. Early in 1867 he was made an honorary fellow of Balliol College, and the way was ready paved for a major success. The murder in Rome, which had engaged Browning's attention when he happened on the details in an old book, had become the subject of his most ambitious poem.

**The Ring and the Book** was published in four volumes (1868–69) and was rapturously received; *The Athenaeum* called it 'the most precious and profound spiritual treasure that England has produced since the days of Shakespeare'. Posterity's verdict is different (as it is about most contemporary reviews of Browning's work) and the parts are acknowledged to be greater than the whole. It has, as Henry James said, the elements of a fine novel, as well as being a searching examination of the ways of man and the necessity of judgment in the maintenance of social order. The sustained poetic effort commands admiration.

Browning was now one of the most famous and sought-after men in England. In the autumn of 1869 he may have proposed to Lady Ashburton while staying with her in Scotland. But it is quite likely, as Maisie Ward observed in her biography of Browning, that he did *not* propose and that might have offended the lady even more. At any rate the friendship came to an end. His career moved on smoothly: he was still criticized in spite of his fame but he wrote what he pleased: *Balaustion's Adventure* and *Prince*

*Hohenstiel-Schwangau* (both 1871), *Fifine at the Fair* (1872), *Red Cotton Night-Cap Country* (1873), *Aristophanes' Apology* (1875), and *The Agamemnon* of Aeschylus (1877). Browning had included transcripts from another Greek poet, Euripides, in *Balaustion* and *Aristophanes* but while his knowledge of and love for Greek tragedy are evident he was not, in the opinion of most critics, the right poet to render them in English.

*The Inn Album* (1875) is a tragic novel in verse; *Pacchiarotto and Other Poems* contains the fine wistful 'St Martin's Summer' and 'Numpholeptos'; and *La Saisiaz and The Two Poets of Croisic* (1878) followed the sudden death of a close friend, Anne Egerton Smith. In the autumn of 1878 Browning went back to Italy for the first time since Elizabeth's death. He went on writing, his poetic vitality undiminished and his visits to Italy an annual feature of his life. His work of this period includes *Dramatic Idyls*, first series (1879); *Dramatic Idyls*, second series (1880); *Jocoseria* (1883), containing 'Ixion', 'Never the time and place', and 'Adam, Lilith and Eve'; *Ferishtah's Fancies* (1884), the allegories and parables of a Persian sage who is recognizably Robert Browning; and *Parleyings with Certain People of Importance* (1887), a series of verse conversations with Bernard de Mandeville, Christopher Smart, Gerard de Lairesse, and others. In 1887 Browning's son Robert (the nickname 'Pen' came from his childish inability to pronounce his middle name, Wiedemann, Browning's mother's maiden name, which always emerged as 'Penini') married and bought a palazzo in Venice. Browning spent two summers there. He completed *Asolando* (published posthumously, 1890) at Asolo, the little town of *Pippa Passes*, and died in Venice on 12 December 1889.

Browning's reputation suffered as much from the reaction against the Victorians as did that of his contemporary Tennyson; but the later counterreaction has not favoured Browning to the same degree. Yet Browning offers a wide range of events and characters, a gift for dramatic situation, and a rich variety of forms and rhythms. It is not easy now to credit Browning with originality but it is one of his most arresting characteristics, the reason why he wrote for 30 years without success. Browning and Tennyson might be said to have erased whatever influence remained of 18th-century forms and preoccupations and to have become in turn influences themselves. Browning is more influential than Tennyson, a wonderful poet to hear, as Geoffrey Tillotson pointed out: 'His early attraction to the stage and persistent liking for dramatic form strike deep; it is as if he continued to write parts for actors ...'. His skill in the use of dramatic monologue – the form that is forever associated with his name – indicated a method of expression that has been seized upon by many 20th-century poets. Most important of all, perhaps, is the quality upon which Henry James commented in his 'Browning in Westminster Abbey. 1890' (*English Hours*, 1905): 'If Browning had spoken for us in no other way, he ought to have been made sure of, tamed and drained as a classic, on account of the extraordinary beauty of his treatment of the special relation between man and woman.'

The Florentine Edition of Browning's *Complete Works* was edited by C. Porter and H. A. Clarke (14 volumes, 1898). The Centenary Edition was edited by F. G. Kenyon (10 volumes, 1912). Single-volume editions are by F. G. Kenyon and Augustine Birrell (1915), by S. Commins (Modern Library, 1934), and by Ian Jack (Oxford Standard Authors, 1970). There are numerous separate editions of *Men and Women* and *The Ring and the Book*, and selections of Browning's poetry abound. *Letters of Browning and Elizabeth Barrett Browning* was edited by R. B. Browning (1899); further letters were published in 1935 in *Twenty-two unpublished letters of Robert and Elizabeth Barrett Browning*, edited by William Rose Benét.

**Bruce, James** 1730–94. After some years in the Near East and Egypt the traveller James Bruce reached Abyssinia (now Ethiopia) in 1769. He spent two years in Abyssinia, then unknown to western travellers, and published *Travels to Discover the Source of the Nile* (1790). (Bruce had followed the Blue Nile to its source in the high mountains of Ethiopia.) His account was very romantic and disbelieved for a number of years, but its veracity was supported by the diplomat Henry Salt, who visited the country 40 years later and found that Bruce had made a lasting impression on the people.

**Bruce, Michael** 1746–67. Bruce was the son of a weaver of Kinnesswood in Kincardineshire. He struggled through Edinburgh University and became the friend of John Logan. He started teaching at Alloa when he was 19 and died of consumption at the age of 21. His family entrusted his papers to Logan, who published *Poems on Several Occasions by Michael Bruce* (1770). This included Bruce's premonition of his early death in the 'Elegy for Spring' and the 'Ode to the Cuckoo'. In 1781 Logan published *Poems*, which included another version of the 'Ode' and some metrical paraphrases which had appeared in the

Bruce volume. Which man wrote what has been keeping controversialists busy for some time. The metrical paraphrases have been adopted by the Church of Scotland, and Logan's 'The Braes of Yarrow' is declared the equal of anything written by Bruce.

John Logan (1748–88) was ordained and became a minister in Leith. His tragedy *Runnamede* was presented in Edinburgh in 1783 and accepted for Covent Garden. But it was considered too advanced, politically, by the church and Logan was deprived of his living. He spent the rest of his life in London, earning a living as a pamphleteer and political commentator.

***Bruce, The,*** *or The Metrical History of Robert I King of Scots*. An epic poem by John Barbour in 7000 octosyllabic couplets, completed about 1375.

The poem relates the story of Robert the Bruce and James Douglas, his gallant comrade, in the struggle with England. The tone is romantic with a strong feeling for medieval chivalry, but apart from the initial – and inexplicable – confusion of Robert the Bruce with his grandfather of the same name (the rival of John Balliol for the crown of Scotland), the history is substantially accurate. It is embroidered with traditional anecdotes and episodes from French romances and the hero Bruce is the finest and bravest of all men. The best passages are those in praise of freedom and in the account of Bannockburn, which certainly benefited from the fact that Barbour must often have talked to men who fought in the great victory.

W. W. Skeat's edition, *Barbour's Bruce*, was first published by the Early English Text Society (1870–89, reprinted 1968).

**Brute (*or* Brutus)** The legendary founder of the British race, according to Geoffrey of Monmouth, who said that he found the account in an ancient book given him by Walter, Archdeacon of Oxford. Brutus, great-grandson of Aeneas, was guilty of the death of his father Sylvius, and sailed away with the last remaining Trojans to found a new land. He made landfall at Totnes and found an island sparsely inhabited by giants. Brutus founded New Troy (London) and established a royal line. Among the kings of this line were Gorboduc, Lud, Cymbeline, Coel (Cole), Vortigern, and Arthur. Michael Drayton relates the story in *Poly-Olbion* and John Selden, in his *Illustrations* to the same work, examines the legend.

**Brutus, Marcus** In Shakespeare's *Julius Caesar*, the conscience-torn assassin of Caesar, whom he loves and admires but whom he fears will accept a crown and destroy the republic. He is pushed towards the murder by Cassius but is no match for Mark Antony, who turns the city against the conspirators. He kills himself when defeated at the Battle of Philippi.

**Bryant, William Cullen** *c.*1794–1878. The US poet was born at Cummington, Massachusetts, and completed his education at Williams College. He wrote poetry from the age of 14 (*The Embargo*, satires against Jefferson's government, was actually written at that age) but studied law and followed a legal career until he was 31.

Bryant was still a young lawyer when the first version of *Thanatopsis*, which he had written when he was 16, was published in *The North American Review* in 1817 and made him famous. He published his first collection, *Poems*, in 1821 (the year he married) and read his 'The Ages' at Harvard. During 1824 and 1825 he contributed regularly to the *United States Literary Gazette*. The poems of this period established him as America's foremost poet.

In 1825 Bryant became an editor of the *New York Review and Athenaeum Magazine* and in 1829 chief editor of the New York *Evening Post*. He kept the editorship for nearly 50 years and during that time moved from his position as a solid democrat; he was a vigorous opponent of slavery and this drew him to the new Republican party. His career as a poet continued: his second collection, the *Poems*, published in 1832, is regarded as the essential Bryant, though additions and occasional poems continued to appear. In his old age Bryant translated the *Iliad* (1870) and the *Odyssey* (1871), blank verse versions of notable simplicity and dignity.

Perhaps dignity and simplicity are the best qualities of Bryant's poetry. It is approachable and easy to appreciate and his lines linger in the mind. His emotional range was not great and he never strayed beyond the themes of man and nature; but he stayed within his range and was consistently successful. The strongest influence in his work was that of Wordsworth; in Bryant's poetry nature is the visible manifestation of God and thus nature influences man – if he will perceive – to his ultimate good. The poet conveys the transience of worldly things; death is a certainty to which all life progresses – but never a Puritan's gateway to an awful judgment.

Bryant was intensely concerned with the future of his country, aware of its unique position and painfully aware of the evils it seemed to have inherited with so little concern. Humanitarian and liberal as an editor, his opposition to slavery was fundamental and took him through the

The Prairie Hunter. An illustration for William Cullen Bryant's poem, 'The Prairies'.

course of his life from federalism to democracy and, ultimately, to the new Republican party. He lived to see slavery abolished in the USA by the 13th amendment in 1865. An editor of exceptional quality, Bryant encouraged young Americans to look for poetic inspiration in their own country. His own poetry is not particularly American but it is quite likely that Bryant knew this perfectly well and was showing the way for the future.

**Bryce, James, 1st Viscount** 1838–1922. Bryce was born in Belfast, where he attended the High School before proceeding to the University of Glasgow. Later he studied at Trinity College, Oxford, and the University of Heidelberg. He became a barrister in 1867 and was appointed Regius Professor of Civil Law at Oxford (1870–93). Bryce entered politics in 1880 and was chief secretary for Ireland (1905–06) and ambassador to the USA (1907–13). As a historian, Bryce is remembered for his *The Holy Roman Empire* (1864), for many years a standard work, which grew out of a prize essay written at Oxford. Among other books, *The American Commonwealth* (1888, revised 1920) and *Studies in History and Jurisprudence* (1901) maintained his high reputation; *Impressions of South Africa* (1897) was a sharply observed picture of the country on the eve of the Boer War.

**Buchanan, George** 1506–82. Buchanan was born at Killearn in Stirlingshire and educated at St Andrews and in Paris. He is regarded as the most distinguished of the Scottish Latinists, the one who demonstrates the greatest command of Latin style. Buchanan taught in Paris for ten years and returned to Scotland in 1536 as tutor to one of the bastard sons of James V; but was soon back in Europe again, having aroused the wrath of the Church with his attacks on the Franciscans. He taught in various places including Bordeaux (where one of his pupils was Montaigne), and prepared a Latin verse paraphrase of the Psalms that became a standard text in Scottish schools.

Buchanan became a Protestant and returned to Scotland in 1561. He attended Mary of Scotland as a court poet (he had been her tutor for a short time) and composed an epithalamium for her marriage to Darnley. But he contrived, while accepting the queen's patronage and pension, to support Knox in church and educational matters. He deserted the queen after the murder of Darnley and later became principal of St Leonard's College, St Andrews. He was tutor to the infant James VI.

His mastery of Latin served Buchanan well in his tragedies, including *Baptistes* and *Jephtha*, both written about 1541. His 20-volume history of Scotland was completed at the end of his life (*Rerum Scoticarum Historia*, 1582). His personal reputation is low: his conviction that Mary was guilty of Darnley's death was shared by many; but the document *Detectio Maria Reginae* (written in 1564), which he carried to London to lay at the feet of Elizabeth I, is an indictment in his skilful Latin of the woman whose patronage he was once pleased to enjoy. And it has been shown by historians to be untruthful in places where Buchanan, an intimate of Moray's, would have known perfectly well what the real truth was.

**Buck**   The central character of Jack London's *The Call of the Wild*, Buck is the dog who responds to the atavistic urges of his wild ancestry when circumstance places him in the wilderness and his savage cousins, the timber wolves, arouse feelings unknown in his life as a domestic pet. Buck is a cross between a shepherd dog and a St Bernard.

**Bucket, Inspector**   The investigating policeman of Dickens's *Bleak House*, who takes charge of the case when Mr Tulkinghorn is murdered.

**Buckle, Henry Thomas** 1821–62.   The son of a wealthy shipowner, Buckle was born at Lee in Kent. He was privately educated and enjoyed the means to study and travel as he pleased. He learned the principal European languages and planned to write *A History of Civilization in England*. He adopted a more scientific basis for his history, criticizing his predecessors for taking no account of physical conditions, including climate and soil, as factors in the development of a nation. Buckle had considerable influence as a historian.

The first two volumes of Buckle's *History* (1857 and 1861) explained his principles, applying them to Spain from the 5th to the 19th centuries and to Scotland in the 18th. The author died prematurely at Damascus at the age of 41, leaving his work incomplete.

**Buck, Pearl** 1892–1973.   Pearl Sydenstricker was the daughter of missionaries and was born in Hillsboro, West Virginia. She spent her childhood in China and returned to Virginia to complete her education, graduating from the Randolph-Macon Women's College in 1914. She returned to China as a missionary and teacher herself in 1921 and spent some years in Nanking, where she married John Lossing Buck, also a missionary. She was a successful writer of short stories before publishing the first of her moving and compassionate novels of Chinese life, *East Wind, West Wind*, in 1930. The author of some 85 books, Pearl Buck became celebrated with her trilogy, *The House of Earth*: *The Good Earth* (1931), *Sons* (1932), and *A House Divided* (1935). *The Good Earth* was awarded the Pulitzer Prize, and in 1938 the author became the first American woman to win the Nobel Prize for Literature. In 1949 she founded Welcome House, to care for the children of Asian women and American servicemen; the Pearl Buck Foundation of Philadelphia, which helps in the adoption of Eurasian children, is largely maintained by royalties from her books. Among her other novels about China are *The Mother* (1934), *This Proud Heart* (1938), *Dragon Seed* (1941), and *Kinfolk* (1949). *The Exile* and *Fighting Angel* (1936) are biographies of her parents; her autobiography, *My Several Worlds*, was published in 1954.

**bucolic**   See **eclogue**.

*Buke of the Howlat, The*   See **Holland, Sir Richard.**

**Bullein, William** d. 1576.   Bullein was an Elizabethan physician and writer whose best-known written work was *A Dialogue both Pleasaunte and Pietifull Wherein is a Goodly Regiment against the Fever Pestilence with a Consolacion and Comfort against Death* (1564), which gives a vivid picture of town and country life and presents a rich array of characters. He also wrote *Bullein's Bulwarke of Defence againste all Sicknes, Sornes, and Woundes* (1562). The *Dialogue* was edited by M. and A. H. Bullen and published by the Early English Text Society in 1888.

**Bulwer-Lytton, Edward, 1st Baron Lytton** 1803–73.   The son of General Bulwer and the wealthy Elizabeth Lytton, Edward Bulwer led a carefree man-about-town existence until his first marriage, which alienated his mother and resulted in his income being drastically reduced. At the age of 22 he was therefore obliged to earn money and writing was the obvious means – he had published a volume of poetry at the age of 17. He became an indefatigable and successful novelist, playwright, and story writer and went on writing until the year he died. He also enjoyed a successful political career: he was MP for St Ives and Lincoln and became Secretary for the Colonies. When he inherited Knebworth from his mother he also took her name, hence Bulwer-Lytton. He became a peer in 1866 as Baron Lytton of Knebworth.

Bulwer-Lytton deserved his contemporary success; he worked hard, wrote well, and was never averse to attempting new subjects. Of his considerable output (a collected edition, published from 1859 to 1863, 10 years before he died, ran to 43 volumes), some of his novels are still read, notably *Eugene Aram* (1832), *The Last Days of Pompeii* (1834), *Rienzi* (1835), *The Last of the Barons* (1843), *Harold* (1848), *The Coming Race* (1871), and *Kenelm Chillingly* (1873). Two of his stories, *The Haunted and the Haunters* and *A Strange Story*, are favourite anthology choices, and his immensely successful plays, *The Lady of Lyons*, *Money*, and *Richelieu*, were produced everywhere in the English-speaking world.

**Bumble, Mr** The parish beadle of Dickens's *Oliver Twist*, an example of the petty fascist in a small world. In reply to Mr Brownlow's observation that the law supposes that Mrs Bumble acts under her husband's direction, he utters the classic, 'If the law supposes that, the law is a ass – a idiot.'

**Bumppo, Natty** The hero of James Fenimore Cooper's *Leather-Stocking Tales*, through which the reader can follow him from youth in *The Deerslayer* to his peaceful death in *The Prairie*. He is a perfect outdoors hero who dislikes a settled life and whose integrity is as indestructible as his knowledge of the forest and the prairie is unrivalled. Courageous and resourceful, he enjoys the friendship of the 'Red' men no less than that of the advancing Europeans. He is a fine creation, the hero of every boy's dreams. See also *Leather-Stocking Tales*.

**Bungay, Thomas de** A 13th-century Franciscan friar of Bungay in Suffolk, Thomas became head of the order's foundation at Cambridge. He lectured at Oxford and could certainly have known Roger Bacon, a fellow Franciscan. See also *Friar Bacon and Friar Bungay*.

John Bunyan. Portrait by T. Sadler, 1684. National Portrait Gallery, London.

**Bunyan, John** 1628–88. The son of a tinker (tinsmith), Bunyan was born in the village of Elstow near Bedford. He learned to read and write at the village school and followed his father's trade. At the age of 16 he was conscripted into the Parliamentary army where he served for two years. He married in 1646, and among his wife's few possessions were two Puritan devotional books, Arthur Dent's *The Plain Man's Pathway to Heaven* (1601) and Lewis Bayly's *The Practice of Piety* (1612). Such books were widely read in an age when no-one could escape from the climate of religious contention. Bunyan was certainly influenced by such books and also began to study the Bible.

Bunyan's wife died in 1656, by which time he had become an itinerant preacher for a Nonconformist group, travelling from place to place in Bedfordshire. His preaching was attacked by the followers of Fox and the Quakers, and his first writing was in answer to the Quakers: *Some Gospel Truths Opened* (1656), *A Vindication* (1657), and *A Few Sighs from Hell* (1658). He married again in 1659.

At the Restoration in 1660 Bunyan was arrested for preaching without a bishop's licence. He refused absolutely to submit to the discipline of the Church of England and spent the next 12 years in prison. He was convinced that he had been called by God and that he had been granted 'gifts of edification'; he also claimed the right to preach where he would and to worship anywhere. He was not set free until 1672 when, in the Declaration of Indulgence, Charles II suspended the penal laws in ecclesiastical matters. But the king was opposed by Parliament, and the following year it decided that only Parliament could decree such matters: the representatives of the people decided, in fact, that the people should have no freedom in matters of religion. Bunyan went to prison again in 1675 but this time he spent only six months in Bedford Gaol.

While in prison Bunyan was able to read and write, and to help support his family by making metal lace tags. He wrote eight devotional works, which are of no importance to English literature apart from having served to develop his gifts; but his ninth was *Grace Abounding to the Chief of Sinners* (1666). During his last imprisonment he completed the first part of **The Pilgrim's Progress,** *from this World to that which is to come.* In all he wrote no less than 60 works of various kinds, four of which have made him immortal: the two already mentioned, **The Life and Death of Mr Badman** (1680), and **The Holy War,** *made by Shaddai upon Diabolus* (1682).

After his release from prison in 1675 Bunyan seems to have been spared further molestation. He continued his preaching and was in London when he died. He was buried in Bunhill Fields.

The Civil War was a point of departure for English literature. The dominance of the scholarly writer, read chiefly by his peers in learning, was not to fade for some time but a new sort of voice was also being heard. Bunyan himself, in the preface to *Grace Abounding*, says that he could have 'stepped into a style much higher than this' but that rather than 'play' (with words and adorned language) he would be '. . . plain and simple, and lay down the thing as it was.' His mind and his audience were remote from the Church of England divines whose pronouncements had become cluttered with all manner of conceits and parades of learning. But the Civil War lost them their audience and the nonconformist spirit was growing; people outside court and scholarly circles also wanted to hear and they had to be addressed in plain English. Bunyan's English is remarkably plain; those who know him only as the author of *The Pilgrim's Progress* should go on to read *Mr Badman*, from where the way to Defoe and the English novel is clear.

Bunyan himself was probably a difficult man, convinced as he was that through him God's word would be transmitted to the minds of his fellow men. However, in his time such a belief was possible and his direct earthiness and eloquence commanded attention from those to whom he spoke. In our time attitudes are very different: now, as James Sutherland has pointed out, '. . . even to most Christians the absolute necessity of conversion, the existence of a clear dividing line between the elect and the damned, is unacceptable doctrine . . . What Bunyan is hammering at so insistently in book after book is something that means little to many readers, and is indignantly rejected by others.' He was, nevertheless, an original in English literature and his contribution to its development should not be underestimated.

**Burgess, Anthony** 1917– . The pen name of John Burgess Wilson, who was born in Manchester and educated at Xavierian College and Manchester University. Burgess served in the army from 1940 to 1946 and then became a teacher, chiefly of English literature. From 1954 to 1959 he was an education officer in Malaya and Borneo, and during that period published his first novels, *Time for a Tiger* (1956), *The Enemy in the Blanket* (1958), and *Beds in the East* (1959), a trilogy set in Malaya. A prolific writer – he publishes also as Joseph Kell and under his real name – Burgess has written some 20 novels and a dozen books of essays on literature, television scripts, and two novels for children. He is best known for his mordant satires of contemporary life, one of which, *A Clockwork Orange* (1962), became a controversial and celebrated film. Among his other novels are *Nothing Like the Sun* (about Shakespeare's sex life, 1964), *Earthly Powers* (a best-seller, 1980), and *The End of the World News* (1982). *Here Comes Everybody* (1965) is an introduction to the work of James Joyce. *The Novel Now: A Student's Guide to Contemporary Fiction* was published in 1967.

**Burgoyne, John** 1722–92. The unsuccessful English general in the War for American Independence was also a minor Georgian playwright. He was born at Sutton Park in Bedfordshire and after returning to England returned to the drama – his *The Maid of the Oaks* had been produced by David Garrick in 1775. He had a major success with **The Heiress** (1786), which combined the fashionable comedy of manners with an authentic note of pathos in the character of Miss Alton, otherwise a long-lost heiress, loved by Lord Gayville, the hero. *Richard Coeur de Lion* (1786) was a historical drama adapted from the French.

**Burke, Edmund** 1729–97. The second son of an Irish lawyer, Burke was born in Dublin. His father was a Protestant, his mother was a Catholic, and young Edmund was sent to a Quaker school in Balitore. His education there, under Abraham Shackleton, had a lasting influence and he revered his teacher's memory until the end of his life. He completed his education at Trinity College, Dublin, and went to London to study law at the Middle Temple in 1750; however, he was never called to the Bar. Burke was later to criticize the system of legal training in England but meanwhile he frequented the society of writers, and his first two published works appeared in 1756: *A Vindication of Natural Society* and *A Philosophical Enquiry into the Origin of Our Ideas of the Sublime and the Beautiful.* He married Jane Nugent in the same year and the need for a steady income was answered when he and Robert Dodsley founded *The Annual Register* in 1758 and Burke became its first editor. He remained in charge for ten years, and became the friend of Samuel Johnson, Joshua Reynolds, and the original members of The Club.

Burke entered public life in 1759, when he became secretary to William Gerard Hamilton, Chief Secretary for Ireland. Later he became secretary to Lord Rockingham, Prime Minister for a brief period, who took Burke into Parliament as member for Wendover in 1765. Rockingham became Burke's patron; the latter was often in need of money and Rockingham supplied it – and in his will ordered that all such debts be cancelled. His protégé delivered his maiden speech in 1760 and was to become the mainstay of the Whig opposition. The Tory administration of Lord North was industriously making a mess of things in America and there was an attempt to reassert the royal prerogative: combat on these issues brought Edmund Burke to the fore.

The stupidity of George III's ministers eventually succeeded in alienating the English in America and a new nation was born as a result. Similar attitudes towards Ireland looked like producing another eruption and Burke turned his attention to that issue. It was not a popular cause in England and his efforts were, to the grief of future generations, unavailing. He lost his seat in the Commons in 1780; he was member for Bristol at that period and the people of a thriving seaport had no sympathy with any cause, on behalf of the American colonists, the Irish, slaves, or anyone else, which might interfere with their prosperity. He re-entered Parliament in 1781 as member for Malton, and continued his campaign for the Irish in his writings.

Meanwhile, events in India were drawing the attention of the English government to the affairs

Gillray's cartoon showing Warren Hastings assaulted by Edmund Burke (left), and Lord North and Charles James Fox (right).

of the East India Company, a profit-making trading company which had been obliged to fill the vacuum left by the collapse of the Moghul Empire. Burke was one of those against the welfare of the people of India being left in the hands of the company, and pressed for the transference of its power to the government. He took enormous trouble to become well informed about a country he had never seen and led the prosecution against Warren Hastings when the former Governor General's trial opened in 1788. The appalling affair dragged on for seven years; Burke's summing-up went on for *nine days.* Hastings was acquitted; the interminable prosecution engaged, as well as those of Burke, the energies of Fox, Sheridan, and Francis – a declared enemy of Hastings, who emerged as the victim of persecution, not the accused in a trial.

Burke actively supported William Wilberforce in his campaign against the slave trade, from 1788 to 1789. The Revolution in France began in 1789, and Edmund Burke, the champion of the oppressed, opposed it with all his eloquence. He was alarmed by the hurricane force of the new ideas; he could work for what he believed to be right in the world he knew but could not conceive of that world being turned upside-down. The conflict produced his most famous work, *Reflections on the Revolution in France* (1790). Thomas Paine's reply, *The Rights of Man* (1791), is more rewarding to read; Burke's celebrated *Reflections* contains an argument by a master of oratory who could not, apparently, accept that the way of the world was going to change completely. Many of the values he strove to preserve have always been in danger from the doctrinarians, those arrogant enough to believe that they know what is best for everyone else.

Most people would agree with Burke that reform is always preferable to revolution; however, when reform is too long deferred, revolution is usually the result. *A Letter to a Member of the National Assembly* and *An Appeal from the New to the Old Whigs* appeared in 1791; in the latter he defends himself against the charge of inconsistency in his attitudes to two revolutions, the American and the French. The French Revolution and the revolutionary wars were the subject of *Thoughts on French Affairs* (1791), *Remarks on the Policy of the Allies* (1793), and *Letters on a Regicide Peace* (1795–97).

Burke retired from parliament in 1794 and was awarded a pension (he was Paymaster of the Forces). The Duke of Bedford, the Earl of Lauderdale, and others criticized him for accepting it and his retort, *A Letter to a Noble Lord* (1796), is a fine performance as well as an apologia. Burke's writings and published speeches were collected by F. Lawrence and W. King and published in eight quarto volumes, between 1792 and 1827. The last edition of the collection was published in Boston in 12 volumes, between 1865 and 1867. Among works on particular issues may be mentioned *Thoughts on the Cause of the Present Discontents* (1770), in which Burke states his constitutional creed and objects to the growing control of parliament by the king's friends; *Observations on 'The Present State of the Nation'* (1769), *On American Taxation* (1774), and *On Conciliation with the Colonies* (1775) are criticisms of the government's conduct in America; *A Plan of Public Economy* (1780) sought the reform of established institutions in public affairs; *At the Guildhall in Bristol* (1780), *To a Peer of Ireland on the Penal Laws* (1782), and *To Sir Hercules Langrishe* (1792) were concerned with Ireland.

The complete works of Edmund Burke were published in The World's Classics in six volumes, edited by W. Willis and F. W. Raffety (1906–07). A modern edition of *Reflections on the Revolution in France*, edited by Conor Cruse O'Brien, was published in the Penguin Classics (1969).

**Burnet, Gilbert** 1643–1715. Of an Aberdeenshire family, Burnet was born in Edinburgh, but returned to Aberdeen for his education at Marischal College. He became Professor of Divinity at Glasgow University in 1669, and came to England in 1675 as chaplain to the Rolls Chapel, a position he held until 1684. Burnet was on familiar terms with Charles II and James, Duke of York, and was a well-known preacher. However, he offended Charles by remonstrating

with him about his conduct and was dismissed in 1684; he went abroad in the following year. Abroad, Burnet enjoyed the confidence of William of Orange and Mary, and sailed for England in 1688, persuading the usurping William at the last moment to land at Torbay instead of at Exmouth. William took the throne of England unopposed, and Burnet was rewarded with the bishopric of Salisbury (1689).

Burnet's chief works are his *The History of the Reformation of the Church of England*, published in three parts (Vol. 1 1679, Vol. 2 1681, and Vol. 3 1714) and his *The History of My Own Times* (published posthumously, 1724–34). His *Reformation* was begun during the years of the 'Popish Plot', when English Catholics endured a reign of terror; Burnet's history, written by a moderate, helped to reduce the temperature of the times. *The History of My Own Times* is the work of a good storyteller but Burnet did not have Clarendon's gift of presenting character. His tone is lighter than Clarendon's, his style more conversational; the *History* is a work of great value and essential reading for any student of the period.

Burnet's contributions to English literature began in history and biography with *The Memoires of the Lives and Actions of James and William Dukes of Hamilton and Castleherald* (1677), constructed from documents and, in the French manner, held together by Burnet's narrative links. The result of his exercise pleased a number of readers, including Charles II, and showed Burnet where his talents lay. His *Reformation* began to appear in 1679 and the results of his conversations with the dying Earl of Rochester, *Some Passages in the Life and Death of the right honourable John Earl of Rochester*, in 1680. *The Life and Death of Sir Matthew Hale* (1682) is a highly regarded short biography of the distinguished jurist. Burnet's admired translation of More's *Utopia* was published in 1684.

As a 17th-century divine Burnet was a notable moderate and always aware of the feelings of laymen – a quality rare in theologians of any age. His *Exposition of the Thirty-Nine Articles* (1699) became a standard work in English divinity studies.

**Burnett, Frances Eliza Hodgson** *c.*1849–1924. Frances Hodgson Burnett's family went to the USA from Manchester when she was 16 and settled in Knoxville, Tennessee. She married Dr Swan Burnett in 1873. With her first novel, *That Lass o'Lowrie's* (1877), Frances Hodgson Burnett achieved enough success to set her career as a novelist on a firm foundation, though there was no particular distinction so far in her adult romances or in her novels for children. But in 1886 she published **Little Lord Fauntleroy**, which made her famous. A stage adaptation was a great success and the book has been filmed and adapted for television. Cedric, the little lord of the title, has every quality of a boy angel except the ability to fly; but his character is nevertheless consistent and well drawn. Unfortunately the description of his appearance – supported by the illustrator – with his long curly hair and the lace collars and his habit of always calling his mother Dearest make the little lord a fairly stomach-turning proposition today. The suspicion that Frances Hodgson Burnett made a successful novel out of her own fantasizing is hard to shift; certainly her success lay with the thousands of doting mothers who bought her book.

**The Little Princess** (1905) is better, a shade less glutinous, but the woeful snobbery of the author is again apparent; little Sara behaves as nobly as little Cedric – a true little princess. So she should; she is a rich and favoured little girl and Cedric is the heir of Dorincourt. **The Secret Garden** (1910) is by far the best thing Mrs Burnett ever wrote; the characters of the children have depth and complexity and the development of Mary, the chief character, is realized with a sure touch.

Frances Hodgson Burnett achieved considerable wealth and fame and wrote a number of other books for adults and children, most of which are forgotten now. She ended her days in a beautiful house on Long Island. Whatever one may think of Cedric or Sara now the fact remains that they were a huge success in their time; and *The Secret Garden*, at least, has lasting quality and continues to be read.

**Burney, Fanny** 1752–1840. The daughter of Dr Charles Burney, the musician, Frances Burney was born in London and seems to have largely educated herself. Her father was part of Samuel Johnson's circle and she assumed a place in it by right. She published her first novel with no help from anyone. **Evelina, or The History of a Young Lady's Entrance into the World** (1778) is in the epistolary form and in many ways uses the best of Richardson and Fielding. The sentiment is from Richardson and the social comedy from Fielding – the English novel was taken a stage farther, and Fanny Burney was famous.

Her next work was a play; she wrote eight plays in all but only one, *Edwy and Elgiva*, was ever produced (1795). Her next novel, **Cecilia, or Memoirs of an Heiress** (1782), was also a success; but in 1786 Fanny Burney became Second Keeper of the Robes to Queen Charlotte. The position

Fanny Burney. Portrait by E. F. Burney, c.1785. National Portrait Gallery, London.

tried her severely, as will be plain to anyone who reads her *Diary*. She asked permission to retire; this was granted, and in 1791, with a pension of £100 a year, she left the court and set about regaining her health.

Fanny Burney married a French refugee officer, General Alexandre Gabriel Jean-Baptiste d'Arblay, in 1793, and in 1796 published her third novel, **Camilla, or A Picture of Youth**, which restored her position in contemporary letters but has been found wanting in interest by posterity. D'Arblay, who had been adjutant general to Lafayette, returned to France with his English wife in 1802 and Fanny lived there for ten years, returning to England for the publication of her last novel, *The Wanderer* (1814), which was not a success. She spent the rest of her life in England, and her last published work was her edition of her father's memoirs (*The Memoirs of Dr Burney*, 1832).

From the progress of her career one can draw the inference that Fanny Burney became less of a novelist when she achieved happiness in her marriage. It might be so but her gifts were not large; her great distinction lies in the skilful use she made of them. The born storyteller in Fanny was using the material of every day and making it absorbing; in doing this she was giving the novel a direction which had been suggested by Richardson in parts of *Sir Charles Grandison*. She was to be followed by Jane Austen, who paid generous tribute to her.

The best qualities of Fanny Burney are also to be found in her *Diary*, which is fascinating in its details and one of the best sources for first-hand portraits of late-18th-century characters. She was a shy girl, in spite of her assured position in London, but her broad streak of common sense balanced that and she had plenty of spirit. She kept her authorship of *Evelina* a secret from her family but she danced an ecstatic jig around a mulberry tree at hearing it praised by Samuel Johnson. The famous incident at Kew when, as a servant of the court, she found herself pursued by King George III demonstrates her strength of character. Frightened out of her wits, she could still understand Dr Willis's imploring 'You must [stop] Ma'am. It hurts the King to run', and remain still while her pursuer caught up with her. Fanny was not to know that the benevolent, not quite sane old man would not have hurt a hair of her head: he had espied a familiar face and was baffled when she ran away from him. Her bondage at court brought Horace Walpole, James Boswell, Edmund Burke, and Joshua Reynolds out in her support: they harried her father until he supported her too – Dr Burney had a great love of royal patronage and wanted his daughter to stay.

It is as the author of *Evelina* and for her *Diary* that Fanny Burney is remembered best. She wrote very successful (in her day) novels in *Cecilia* and *Camilla* but they were in many ways the mixture as before; *The Wanderer* was regarded as a failure by her admirers, Macaulay among them. Her strength lay in social comedy and the comedy of domestic life, and her quality reached its highest level in *Evelina*. 'To read Miss Burney,' wrote Walter Allen, 'is rather like having a mouse's view of the world of cats: the cats are very terrifying, but the mouse's sense of the ridiculous could not be keener.'

A modern edition of *Evelina* was edited by Edward H. Bloom (1968) and issued in Oxford Paperbacks (1970); *Camilla* was edited by Edward H. and William D. Bloom for the Oxford English Novels series (1972). *The Journals and Letters of Fanny Burney*, edited by Joyce Hemlow, commenced publication in 1972; eight volumes have been issued so far.

**Burning Babe, The** A short poem (32 lines) on a Christmas vision of the infant Jesus. It is the best-known work of the Catholic martyr and poet Robert Southwell.

**Burns, Robert** 1759–96. Robert Burns was the first of seven children born to William and Agnes Burnes – the poet was the first to adopt the more familiar spelling. William Burnes had a small market garden at Alloway, near Ayr, and Robert was born in a two-roomed thatched cottage. His father was an intelligent man and as well read as his circumstances allowed. His mother had a fund of old tales her children loved to listen to and a fine musical ear; Burns heard traditional songs from his earliest years. His growing up was coloured by his restless opposition to his father's stern Calvinism; but he owed his education to him, one which was better than the struggling man could really afford.

William Burnes became a farmer in 1766, at Mount Oliphant nearby, but did not succeed in making it profitable. He was forced then to earn his living as an agricultural labourer at Lochlea, and Robert worked in the fields with him – exhausting labour with which he was only too familiar: 'This kind of life, the cheerless gloom of a hermit and the unceasing toil of a galley slave, brought me to my sixteenth year.' However, he found relief in a debating society at nearby Tarbolton and learned to dance there, too, to his father's disapproval. He read everything he could find and became deeply interested in the culture and traditions of Scotland. He escaped from the toil of a farm-labourer's life in 1781 when he became a flax dresser at Irvine; it was also an escape from his father's eye and his physical appetites found free rein. He was 22.

William Burnes died in 1784 and Robert, with his brother Gilbert, resumed farming at Mossgiel. It was there that Burns fell in love with Jean Armour, the daughter of a mason of nearby Mauchline. This attachment possibly induced emotional turmoil in the passionate young man and may have had much to do with the apparently compulsive womanizing that followed. Alternatively, Burns may have acquired the habit of promiscuity before he met Jean Armour, the only woman who played a lasting part in his life. Burns's ardent poetic temperament was crabbed and confined by the gruelling round of work on a small farm: frustration is not always sexual in character and sex can become as compulsive an antidote to frustration as alcohol. In the crowded farmhouse he shared a bothy with a labourer and at night worked away at the verses which occupied his mind during the day. In July 1786 the Kirk, which frowned over the lives of the people of Ayrshire, had its revenge on Robert Burns, who had circulated verse satires on its members. Jean Armour was pregnant; the Kirk exacted public penance from Jean and Robert.

Jean's parents forced her to repudiate him and then removed her to Paisley, though the two may well have been married by 'declaration', a form acceptable under Scottish law until 1939.

Deprived of his Jean, Burns embarked on an affair with Mary Campbell (Highland Mary) and had hopes of persuading her to start a new life with him, free from Calvinistic gloom. He had been promised a job on a plantation in Jamaica and to raise the money for their passage Burns assembled a collection of poems and published them in Kilmarnock. Mary died in the October of 1786 but the Kilmarnock poems made Robert Burns famous. *Poems Chiefly in the Scottish Dialect* (1786) contained social satire, nature poems, mock elegies, verse epistles, and the famous celebration of domestic life 'The Cotter's Saturday Night'. The church satires were omitted from this volume.

Burns went to Edinburgh towards the end of 1786. He was lionized by the intelligentsia and a new subscription edition of his poems was arranged. It was published in 1787 by William Creech and earned Burns enough money to lease a farm eventually at Ellisland in Dumfriesshire. He was a tremendous success in the social life of the capital; canny, unaffected, and forthright, he possessed natural grace in abundance. But

---

Robert Burns. A detail from the portrait by Alexander Nasmyth, 1787. National Portrait Gallery, London.

society's appetite for novelty is a poor substitute for genuine appreciation and a ploughman who wrote rustic verse was the identity Burns was expected to maintain. The city defeated him; he was simply not a clever enough operator, in modern terms, to extract a comfortable material future from the swarm of wealthy and influential contacts he made. James Johnson enlisted his services for his repository of Scots folk songs, *The Scots Musical Museum* (1787–1803), to which Burns was to contribute some 200 new or adapted songs. Some of his loveliest lyrics appear in the five volumes and in the later *A Select Collection of Original Scottish Airs* (1793–1811), initiated by George Thomson, to which Burns contributed over 100 lyrics. But for the stimulus of these, it is hard to see where the poet would have turned. A retreat from Edinburgh was inevitable; Burns settled down at Ellisland with Jean Armour, now his acknowledged wife, and struggled with the farm. He and Jean had four children and Burns became an excise man to supplement his income. For the £50 a year it paid him Burns was required to be abroad in all weathers; it did at least stave off bankruptcy. He relinquished the farm in 1792 and moved to Dumfries, where in the excise office he was able to earn, at most, £90 a year. Further promotion was not forthcoming; his support of the revolutions in America and France put him out of favour with his superiors. Apart from his contributions to the song books (which earned him nothing – they were a labour of love) and some election pieces in the style of old ballads, Burns's last works were **Tam O'Shanter** and 'Captain Matthew Henderson'. In 1795 he was stricken with rheumatic fever and a year later he was dead; the harrowing toil of his youth produced a form of endocarditis and he had not the strength left to struggle. He was 37 years old.

The poetry of Robert Burns is the work of a young Scot who used the material and language which suited him best and it places him on a very high level among British poets. His education, so hardly won, proved to be of great value; he was in reality a ploughman poet but the idea of him being an unlettered rustic is preposterous. He was well read in English poetry (he read French, too) and could use English forms when it suited him; the stanzas of 'The Cotter's Saturday Night' are Spenserian – Spenser had enough imitators to make the form familiar to Burns even if Spenser was not part of his reading. But his finest work springs from his own soil, from his compassionate and generous nature, and from the Scots poetic tradition transmitted through Allan Ramsay and Burns's tragic near-contemporary, Robert Fergusson. His *Epistle to John Rankine*, a verse rather than prose letter, recounting his first collision with the Kirk, was probably the first demonstration of his unique gifts. He employed the Scottish vernacular with more skill and in a greater range than either Ramsay or Fergusson; he was in direct contact with its source and the themes of Scots rural life provided an inexhaustible field for poetic expression.

The Kilmarnock poems display his quality best, showing his success in several forms, but some fine pieces written at the same period were not published until later, among them the church satires 'The Ordination' and 'Address to the Unco Guid', and the remarkable cantata **The Jolly Beggars**. Burns had forgotten he had written it and it was not published until 1799, after his death. Thomas Carlyle and Matthew Arnold praised it highly. The period at Mossgiel was altogether astonishingly productive; it gave us the famous 'Address to the Deil', 'The Holy Fair', 'To a Mouse', 'Man was Made to Mourn', 'To a Louse', 'The Twa Dogs', **Holy Willie's Prayer**, 'Death and Dr Hornbook', 'Corn Rig', 'Highland Mary', 'For a' that and a' that', and many more. The song books of Johnson and Thomson demonstrate his lyric gifts – so much so that for many Burns is a songwriter first and foremost; 'Tam O'Shanter' is a late narrative poem of bouncing energy.

The standard modern edition, *The Poems and Songs of Robert Burns*, edited by James Kinsley, is published in the Oxford English Texts series (1968). Kinsley is also the editor of the single-volume edition, with a useful glossary, in Oxford Standard Authors (1969) and Oxford Paperbacks (1971). Penguin have published a selection in their English Poets series (1946), edited by W. Beattie and H. W. Meikle. The standard edition of Burns's *Letters* is that by J. De Lancey Ferguson (1931).

**Burton, Sir Richard Francis** 1821–90. The son of an army officer, Burton was born in Torquay, Devon, and went to Trinity College, Oxford. He left without graduating in 1842 to join the Indian Army and served under Sir Charles Napier. He wrote an account of his experiences in *Scinde, or The Unhappy Valley* (1851). Burton had a genius for languages – he was master of more than 30 – and a thirst for adventure. He also had a remarkable talent for presenting a romantic and somewhat dubious persona to the English public, which wondered about his character while reading with great eagerness accounts of his adventures. In 1853 his command of Arabic enabled him to visit the Arabs' holy city of Mecca and live to tell the tale

(he would have been killed if he had been discovered) in *A Personal Narrative of a Pilgrimage to El-Medinah and Mecca* (1856). His travels in Africa are related in *First Footsteps in East Africa* (1856), *The Lake Regions of Central Africa* (1859) and *Abeokuta and the Cameroons, Wanderings in West Africa*, and *Mission to Gelele, King of Dahomey* (all 1863). Other faraway places are the subject of *Exploration of the Highlands of Brazil* (1869), *Letters from the Battlefields of Paraguay* (1870), *Ultima Thule; a Summer in Iceland* (1875), *Two Trips to Gorillaland and the Cataracts of the Congo* (1876), *The Gold Mines of Midian and Ruined Midianite Cities* (1878), and *The Land of Midian Revisited* (1879).

Burton is also distinguished as the translator of *The Thousand Nights and a Night* (1885–88), the first unexpurgated English version. His translation of *The Lusiads* (1880) of the Portuguese poet Luis de Camoens is not, however, highly regarded. Burton served as British consul in Damascus and later in Trieste, where he died. He was knighted in 1885.

After his death Burton's widow, Lady Isabel Burton, destroyed his papers, which apparently contained volumes of information on the erotic and esoteric customs of Eastern cultures. By deciding to 'protect' his reputation in this way Lady Burton deprived posterity of the full range of her remarkable husband's knowledge.

**Burton, Robert** 1577–1640. Burton was a native of Leicestershire and a product of Oxford. He entered Brasenose College in 1593 and was elected a student of Christ Church in 1599; he lived in Christ Church for the rest of his life and never travelled, making the most of the college library and the newly founded Bodleian. He became vicar of St Thomas's, Oxford, in 1616, held a Lincolnshire living from 1624 to 1631, and a Leicestershire one in 1632 from his patron, Lord Berkeley.

Burton wrote Latin verses and a Latin comedy, *Philosophaster* (1606), but is remembered for his treatise, *The Anatomy of Melancholy*, which he published in 1621. Burton intended a medical work; the complete title (and Burton's pseudonym) reads as follows: *The Anatomy of Melancholy, What it Is; With all the Kindes, Causes, Symptomes, Prognostickes, and Severall Cures of it; in Three Maine Partitions with their Severall Sections, Members and Subsections, Philosophically, Medicinally, Historically, Opened and Cut up, by Democritus Junior*. Burton was only a physician 'by inclination' and what he wrote in fact was a psychology of melancholy – that is, of the states of mind that were called melancholy in Jacobean times. After an introduction in which he declares all men are subject to melancholy, 'an inbred malady', he sets out, in the first part, to reach a definition, examine causes, and identify symptoms. In the second part he reaches for a cure and in the third part examines the melancholy of love and the melancholy of religion.

Burton's scholarship, his extraordinary range of reading, and the blessed leisure to indulge them that he enjoyed led to the expansion of his theme to cover the complete range of life, physical and mental wellbeing, the social and political forces, and the contemporary advances in astronomy with their possible bearing on his thesis. Every conceivable source and opinion is examined – the Bible, the Greek and Latin classics, the early Christian fathers, and European scholarship. The whole is written with humour, pathos, and tolerance and conveys a mind brimming with commonsense. The book is a remarkable storehouse of erudition and a record of the state of knowledge in the Jacobean age. It was treasured by Johnson, Sterne, Lamb, Coleridge, Southey, Keats, Byron, and many others. Burton revised his book five times, adding new material for each edition.

An edition of *The Anatomy of Melancholy* was prepared for Everyman's Library by H. Jackson and published in three volumes in 1932.

**Bury, John Bagnell** 1861–1927. Bury was born at Monaghan in the county of Monaghan in Ireland. He was educated at Foyle College in Londonderry and Trinity College, Dublin. He was elected a fellow of Trinity in 1885 and acknowledged as a classical scholar of exceptional quality. He became Professor of Modern History at Trinity College in 1893 and Regius Professor of Modern History at Cambridge in 1903.

Bury is perhaps best known to the general reader for his edition of Gibbon's *The History of the Decline and Fall of the Roman Empire* (1896–1900) but his histories of the ancient world are notable for their scope and for Bury's firsthand knowledge of eastern sources. *A History of the Later Roman Empire from Arcadius to Irene, 395–800 AD* (1889), *The Students' Roman Empire 27 BC–180 AD* (1893), *A History of Greece to the Death of Alexander the Great* (1900), *The Ancient Greek Historians* (1909), *A History of the Eastern Roman Empire from the Fall of Irene to the Accession of Basil I* (1912), and *A History of the Later Roman Empire from the Death of Theodosius I to the Death of Justinian* (1923) are some of the titles in which he made a contribution to the published knowledge of Greek and Byzantine history.

Bury was a prolific contributor to journals; he also contributed *The Ottoman Conquest* (1902) and *Russia 1462–1682* (1908) to the *Cambridge Modern History* and in his younger days published editions of Pindar – *The Nemean Odes* (1890) and *The Isthmian Odes* (1892). *The Cambridge Medieval History* (1911–36) was planned and the scheme of each of its eight volumes was worked out by him.

**Bury, Richard de** 1281–1345. Of Bury St Edmunds in Suffolk, Richard was the son of Sir Richard Aungerville and educated at Oxford. His scholarship – he shone in philosophy and theology – brought him to the attention of the court and he was appointed tutor to Edward Prince of Wales, later Edward III. Richard was envoy to the papal court at Avignon, where he met Petrarch, in 1330 and 1333; he became Dean of Wells and eventually Bishop of Durham. He founded a library at Durham College, Oxford, and bequeathed to it his own painstakingly collected volumes and manuscripts. The library still stands but the collection is lost; the college, a Benedictine house, was dissolved during the Reformation, to be replaced eventually by Trinity College. A patron of learning and a great lover of books, Richard was the author of *Philobiblon*, an autobiographical sketch which celebrates his preoccupation. A contemporary of Boccaccio and Petrarch, he knew little Greek but shared the preoccupation with the classics that was to lead to the Renaissance.

Richard of Bury's *Philobiblon* was edited and translated by E. C. Thomas (1903).

**Busirane** The abductor of Amoret in Book III of Spenser's *The Faerie Queene*. He symbolizes unlawful love and is defeated by Britomart.

***Bussy D'Ambois*** A tragedy by George Chapman, based on the career of Louis de Clermont Bussy-d'Amboise, favourite of the Duc d'Alençon, brother of Henri III. It was first published in 1607.

Bussy D'Ambois was introduced to the court as the protégé of Monsieur (Alençon), brother of the king, Henri III. He is courageous but insolent and in a quarrel is forced to defend himself against three courtiers, whom he kills. He also quarrels with the Duc de Guise. Monsieur is in love with the Countess of Montsurry (Monsoreau) but the lady favours Bussy D'Ambois. Monsieur, giving way to jealousy, reveals to Montsurry that his wife has dishonoured him, and the count forces his wife, by torture, to send a letter summoning her lover. He is overpowered and murdered upon his arrival.

The story was also used by Dumas *père* (*La Dame de Monsoreau*) in 1846. Both he and Chapman make the same alteration to history: it was the king, who loathed Bussy-d'Amboise, who betrayed him to Monsoreau.

***Bussy D'Ambois, The Revenge of*** A tragedy by George Chapman, first published in 1613. It is a sequel to *Bussy D'Ambois*.

Clermont D'Ambois, close friend of the Duc de Guise, is a gentleman of honour and courage. The ghost of his murdered brother, Bussy, urges him to avenge the crime; Clermont will do so – but only by the honourable method of a formal duel. He sends a challenge to his brother's murderer, Montsurry, who proves to be a coward and evades it. The ghost of Bussy renews the urging, so Clermont goes to Montsurry's house and forces him to fight. He kills him – and then learns that his friend, the Duc de Guise, has been assassinated. In despair at the vicious time in which he lives, he kills himself.

**Butler, Joseph** 1692–1752. Butler was born at Wantage in Berkshire. The son of Presbyterian parents, he attended the Dissenting Academy at Tewkesbury. While still in his teens Butler entered upon a correspondence with Samuel Clarke on his Boyle Lectures of 1704 and 1705 (see **Clarke, Samuel**); this gives an indication of his intellectual powers. He abandoned Presbyterianism and entered Oriel College, Oxford, in 1714; he was ordained at Salisbury in 1718 and was appointed Clerk of the Closet to Queen Caroline in 1736. He became Bishop of Bristol in 1738 and of Durham in 1750.

Butler published *Fifteen Sermons* in 1726. These were delivered while he was preacher at the Rolls Chapel (1718–26) and gained him a considerable reputation as an exponent of natural theology and ethics. Butler's most famous work is *The Analogy of Religion, Natural and Revealed, to the Constitution and Course of Nature* (1736), a defence of Christianity which demonstrated that the 'natural' religion of the deists posed as many unanswerable questions as 'revealed' religion. Butler makes no direct reference to the deists, but the quality of his argument discredited their movement more effectively than the contemporary direct attacks on them.

**Butler, Samuel** (i) 1612–80. Butler, a farmer's son, was born at Strensham in Worcestershire. He was educated at King's School, Worcester, and then served in the household of Elizabeth, Countess of Kent, where he made the acquaintance of John Selden. Details of Butler's life are scarce but he seems to have earned his living as a secretary to various country gentlemen; Sir Samuel Luke, the Puritan colonel and John Bunyan's commander, was one of these. It is

known that in 1660 he became the Earl of Carbury's steward at Ludlow Castle (Carbury was Lord President of Wales). The first part of **Hudibras** was published in 1663 and the second in 1664, and Butler became famous. His mock-heroic poem found a great admirer in King Charles II, and Butler became secretary to the Duke of Buckingham from 1670 to 1674. He accompanied Buckingham on a diplomatic mission to France in 1670, and helped him, it is believed, in the composition of *The Rehearsal*. The third part of *Hudibras* was published in 1678. Butler was awarded a pension and several grants of money by King Charles but in spite of that seems to have died in penury. He lies buried in Westminster Abbey.

Butler's other works were mostly published after his death. There are some verses, a number of prose 'characters', and 'Miscellaneous Thoughts' in epigrammatic form. Much of these appeared in *The Genuine Remains in Verse and Prose of Mr Samuel Butler* (1759, edited by Robert Thyer). The two volumes contained 120 'characters'; the complete edition of Butler's works edited by A. R. Waller (three volumes, 1905–28) contains 68 more as well as a number of 'Observations and Reflexions'. Butler's satire on Sir Paule Neale of the Royal Society was written twice and published in the 1759 edition. *The Elephant in the Moon* has for its subject a mouse which has found its way into a telescope. Butler first treated it in octosyllabic couplets, the metre he used for *Hudibras*; he then tried decasyllabic couplets in the manner of Dryden, as if undecided which metre suited him best.

**Butler, Samuel** (ii) 1835–1902. Butler, the grandson of a Bishop of Lichfield and the son of a Canon of Lincoln, was born at Langar in Nottinghamshire. He was intended for the Church and educated at Shrewsbury and St John's College, Cambridge.

Butler chafed against the authority of his overbearing father and eventually rejected the Church as a career. Financially dependent on his father, Butler was forced into open rebellion and emigrated to New Zealand. He spent five years there, became a successful sheep-farmer, and returned to England with a modest fortune. (His father felt enough pride to publish his son's letters home, as *A First Year in Canterbury Settlement*, in 1863.) Butler had, while in New Zealand, published essays in the Christchurch *Press*. In London he made a home at Clifford's Inn and dabbled in both painting and music.

***Erewhon*** was published in 1872 and in the following year, *The Fair Haven*, a spoof defence of what Christians saw as evidence of the material foundation of their faith. This continued the vein of satire that had begun in 1865 in a pamphlet entitled *The Evidence for the Resurrection of Jesus Christ*, and which was followed in *Erewhon*. Butler was intensely interested in Darwin's theories and much of his work contributed to the controversy: *Life and Habit* (1877), *Evolution Old and New* (1879), *God the Known and God the Unknown* (1879), *Unconscious Memory* (1880), *Luck or Cunning* (1887), and the *Deadlock in Darwinism* (1890). His principal contribution was his insistence that will and memory be taken into account in evolution, that chance alone is not sufficient. He had, as long ago as 1872, begun work on a book called **The Way of all Flesh**. He put it aside in 1885 and went on with other work. He published two travel books, *Alps and Sanctuaries of Piedmont and the Ticino* (1881) and *Ex Voto* (1888). Another satirical work, *The Psalm of Montreal*, was published in 1884, and *The Life and Letters of Samuel Butler* (his grandfather) in 1896.

His increasing interest in Homer arose from his consideration of material for a libretto for an oratorio – Butler, the amateur musician, was a great admirer of Handel. *The Authoress of the Odyssey* appeared in 1897 and translations of the *Iliad* and the *Odyssey* in 1898 and 1900. An interesting contribution to the apparently insoluble identity of 'Mr. W. H.' was published in his *Shakespeare's Sonnets, Reconsidered and in part Rearranged* (1899). **Erewhon Revisited** was published in 1901 and his most famous book, *The Way of all Flesh*, was published in 1903, the year after he died, edited by R. A. Streatfield. A selection from his manuscripts by Henry Festing Jones was published in 1912 as *The Notebooks of Samuel Butler*.

A geat deal of what Butler, the satirist, attacked is gone now but he must be credited with the will, as well as the skill, to open fire on the stagnation of late Victorian England. His critics, since then, have tended to reduce his stature and it is true that his doggedness, at its worst, seems only a degree removed from crankiness. His criticism of the society he knew is best expressed in *The Way of all Flesh*. From this distance it is imperfect both as fiction and as a prosecution document; nevertheless, its effect at the time was startling, and it provided English novelists with a new direction.

**Buzfuz, Serjeant** In Dickens's *The Pickwick Papers*, the counsel for the plaintiff in Mrs Bardell's breach-of-promise suit against Mr Pickwick.

**Byrd, William** *c.*1674–1744. A Virginian landed aristocrat, Byrd was educated in England at the Middle Temple and enjoyed the friendship of Congreve and Wycherley. He became master of his family's estates (26,000 acres) at Westover in 1704 and was a tireless and successful manager who increased his family's land holdings to 180,000 acres. He served on the Royal Council of Virginia for 37 years.

In literature Byrd is noted for his *History of the Dividing Line betwixt Virginia and North Carolina*, which was a journal of his commission to survey the boundary line between the two states in 1729. Not published until 1841, it contains an outline of the history of Virginia and some acid comments on the people of North Carolina; it is full of incidental information about the period and Byrd's writing is witty and vivacious. Included in the volume was his *A Journey to the Land of Eden* – 'Eden' being the land he owned in what became the state of North Carolina.

Byrd, who passessed the largest library in the British colonies (4000 volumes), kept a diary in shorthand, was a member of the Royal Society, and spent two periods as Colonial Agent in England (1697–1705 and 1715–26). None of his writings – the Westover Manuscripts – were intended for publication but two portions of his diary have been deciphered and published: *The Secret Diary of William Byrd of Westover, 1709–1712* (1941) and *Another Secret Diary 1739–1741* (1942). His work is of great historical interest and has the added virtue of being lively and readable.

**Byrom, John** 1692–1763. A native of Cheshire, Byrom received his early schooling at Chester and later went to the Merchant Taylors' School. At Cambridge he became a fellow of Trinity College, though he lived chiefly in Manchester. Byrom is perhaps remembered best for the epigram of Handel and Buononcini that introduced Tweedledum and Tweedledee into the language, for the hymn 'Christians Awake', and for the epigram on King and Pretender ('But who Pretender is, or who is King, God bless us all – that's quite another thing.') that reflected his Jacobite sympathies. Byrom studied medicine in Montpellier but never practised. He taught shorthand in Manchester and wrote a quantity of religious verse that is now forgotten with the exception of the occasionally anthologized piece 'My Spirit Longeth for Thee'.

Byrom was an admirer of William Law; *The Private Journal and Literary Remains of John Byrom*, first published 1854–57 (re-edited in 1950 by Henri Talon), is an important source of information on Law.

**Byron, George Gordon, Lord** 1788–1824. Byron was born in London, the son of Catherine

Gordon of Gight, a Scottish heiress descended from James I of Scotland, and Captain 'Mad Jack' Byron, a profligate who wasted his wife's money as well as his own. Soon after his son's birth Captain Byron withdrew to France to hide from his creditors, and Catherine took her son to her home in Aberdeenshire, where they lived in somewhat straitened circumstances. Byron's father died when he was three and the boy was educated at home and later at Aberdeen Grammar School. His mother sometimes petted and sometimes abused him; but mother and son had a real affection for each other. The boy roamed free when he could, though unfortunately lame from a malformation of his right foot. The stirring scenery of Deeside, Lochnagar, and the Grampian mountains made an impression that stayed with Byron all his life.

In 1798 Byron's great-uncle William, 5th Baron Byron, died at the Byron estate of Newstead in Nottinghamshire and the barony passed to the ten-year-old boy. He went to Harrow School in 1801 and there enjoyed learning for the pleasure it gave him, not from any desire to shine as a scholar. His first poems were written while a schoolboy at Harrow. Byron proceeded to Trinity College, Cambridge, in 1805 and in January 1807 published a small volume of verse, *Fugitive Pieces*. A friend at Cambridge advised him that some of the contents were rather too sensual and Byron destroyed most of the printing; only four copies have survived. The revised volume was published in the same year; 'miraculously chaste' was how the poet described his *Poems on Various Occasions* (1807), which contained 12 new pieces. With remarkable speed (in March of that year) Byron published *Hours of Idleness*, a collection of lyrics more distinguished than any of his previous work. But in January 1808 a notice of *Hours of Idleness* appeared in *The Edinburgh Review*, savaging his work and scorning his pretensions. On the title page Byron had mentioned his minority, and the reviewer, Henry Brougham, was at pains to point out that this was no excuse for a volume of bad verse.

Byron's bitterness was intense and lasting, but he wasted no time in returning the blow. He had written a satire called *British Bards*, which he rewrote and extended, publishing the new work as *English Bards and Scotch Reviewers* (1809). The satire went through four editions and made Byron famous, and he acknowledged later that it was the work of a very angry young man. He attacked Southey, Coleridge, Wordsworth, and Scott; he later realized that his youthful judgments were hasty and was generous enough to say so, but he does make some telling satirical

Byron in Albanian costume. A detail from the portrait by T. Phillips, 1813. National Portrait Gallery, London.

points about the poetry esteemed in his day. Soon after the publication of *English Bards* Byron attained his majority and took his seat in the House of Lords; then he left for a tour of the Mediterranean in June 1809 with a friend from Cambridge, John Cam Hobhouse, whose expenses he bore. Byron was an unstintingly generous man.

Byron's letters from Spain, Portugal, and the eastern Mediterranean, written during the years he was away, are remarkably vivid documents and important in their own right. But the poet's mind responded to the myriad sensations of his experiences, later producing some of the most celebrated romantic verse ever written. Meanwhile he composed *Hints from Horace* (1811) and, after visiting the tyrant of Ioannina, Ali Pasha, began work on another poem; at the same time he encouraged Hobhouse, who was writing his *Journey through Albania*.

After returning to England Byron completed the first two cantos of the poem begun in Albania. **Childe Harold's Pilgrimage:** *A Romaunt* (1812) made Byron a celebrity, and he became the most sought-after figure in English society. Between then and the uproar of 1816 he published *The Curse of Minerva* (1812), *The Giaour* and *The Bride of Abydos* (1813), **The Corsair**, *Lara*, and *Jacqueline* (1814), *Hebrew Melodies* (1815), and *The Siege of Corinth* and *Parisina* (1816).

In 1815 Byron married Annabella (Anne Isabella) Milbanke. Perhaps the worst mistake of his life, the marriage may have been a reaction to the hysterical and destructive passion of Lady Caroline Lamb, or Byron may have wanted some order imposed on his existence. The cold and unimaginative Annabella was at the opposite pole from Byron's nature: she could not accept him for himself and their marriage lasted little more than a year. After the birth of their daughter in December 1815 she left him and obtained a separation. London was soon humming with speculation about the reasons, including, possibly, Byron's attachment to his half-sister, Augusta Leigh, and his bisexuality, about which Lady Caroline Lamb was eager to speak. The English public was now seized with 'one of its periodical fits of morality', as Macaulay put it, rightly adding that there was 'no spectacle so ridiculous'. Without knowledge of the facts, the public supported Lady Byron and subjected a great English poet to insult. The bewildered, then deeply wounded, Byron left England on 25 April 1816 and never returned.

After sailing up the Rhine to Switzerland Byron joined the Shelleys at Sécheron on Lac Léman. The two poets enjoyed each other's companionship and stayed together long enough to justify leasing two properties; during this period Mary Shelley, then 18 years old, wrote her immortal *Frankenstein*. Byron seems to have accepted the fact of English hypocrisy (he was in a position to know of the corruption that lay below the surface of Regency society) and put his bitterness aside to return to poetry. The third canto of *Childe Harold* was written in Switzerland in 1816, as was *The Prisoner of Chillon*. In January 1817 Shelley's sister-in-law, Claire Clairmont, who was staying in the Shelleys' villa, bore a daughter who was named Allegra. It was Claire who had first urged Byron to visit the Shelleys when he was planning to leave England, and she had made herself available to him, though she had been Shelley's mistress and regarded him as responsible for her. The liaison had continued throughout 1816 but Byron did not pretend any real attachment to her. He agreed to be responsible for Claire's and Allegra's support, and when the Shelley household returned to England in 1817 Byron went to Venice.

Venice was notorious for its loose morals and Byron made the most of his sojourn there. But the historic past, so splendidly present all around him, soon fired the poet's imagination. To this period belongs *The Lament of Tasso* (1817), the fourth canto of *Childe Harold* (1818), **Manfred** (1817), **Beppo** (1818), **Mazeppa** (1819), and the first cantos of **Don Juan**. His connection with Teresa, Countess Guiccioli, whose home was in Ravenna, began in Venice in April 1819 and proved a lasting one. Her husband, a man in his sixties, accepted the liaison placidly and Byron moved to Ravenna in December of the same year. He was, meanwhile, in close touch with England in spite of his exile; letters to and from his friends – John Murray, Scott, Thomas Moore, Hobhouse, and others – were important to him and he was an avid reader of English literary reviews. Friends also visited him in Venice, including Shelley, Hobhouse, and Moore, who wrote a vivid account of Byron's domestic life at this period. Teresa, Shelley was glad to see, was a good influence on Byron; she inspired *The Prophecy of Dante*, chiefly by interesting him in the cause of Italian freedom. At Ravenna Byron wrote another dramatic poem (*Manfred* was the first), this time on a Venetian subject, **Marino Faliero** (1821). *The Prophecy of Dante* was published in the same volume. Two more dramatic poems appeared in the same year, **Sardanapalus** and **The Two Foscari**, in a single volume which also included **Cain**; he also wrote more of *Don Juan* and *Heaven and Earth* (1821). His reputation had by now spread beyond the bounds of England and Byron was famous throughout Europe; Goethe, after reading *Manfred*, entered upon a correspondence with the younger poet. *Sardanapalus* is dedicated to Goethe and Byron was honoured by him in the second part of the German master's *Faust*, where he appears as Euphorion, the child of Faust and Helen.

Teresa Guiccioli obtained a separation from her husband and moved to the house of her brother Pietro, Count Gamba. She and Byron, now 15 miles from Ravenna, became more closely involved with the Carbonari, the Italian freedom movement, of which Count Gamba was a leader. Byron was a ready adherent and supported it as much as possible with money and influence. However, the movement foundered and the Gamba property was confiscated; they fled to Pisa and set up house in the Palazzo Lanfranchi in the autumn of 1821. Byron was pleased to find Shelley living in the same city and also made the acquaintance of Trelawny.

In 1822 the literary quarrel with Southey, which had begun with a hostile article contributed by Southey to *Blackwood's Magazine* (August 1819), was resolved. Byron had replied in *Some Observations* (1820), in which he quite plainly accused the poet laureate of slander and apostasy. In the following year Southey published **A Vision of Judgement**, and prefixed it with an ill-considered, almost hysterical, attack on *Don Juan* and its author – the founder of 'the Satanic school'. Byron's answer was to satirize Southey's laureate encomium on the passing of George III with a poem, *The Vision of Judgement*, published in Leigh Hunt's magazine *The Liberal* in 1822. He demolished Southey with brilliant ease; but the government in London was less than pleased and brought a charge against the publisher of 'calumniating the late King and wounding the feelings of his present Majesty'. The same year brought Byron news of the death of his daughter Allegra and the departure of the Shelleys and Trelawny, after a street brawl, for Spezia in May. Byron and the Gambas went to Leghorn, and two months later Shelley was drowned in the Gulf of Spezia. After moving on to Genoa, Byron resumed work on *Don Juan*, which was completed in March 1823. The domestic tragedy *Werner*, the verse tale *The Island*, and the satirical poem *The Age of Bronze* were also published in 1823. *The Deformed Transformed*, Byron's unfinished drama, followed in 1824.

The end of the Carbonari and of Italian aspirations to independence from their Austrian overlords in 1821 saw Byron embracing another cause – one perhaps closer to his heart and dating back to his travels in the eastern Mediterranean (1810–11). His interest was expressed in *Childe Harold* and *Don Juan*, and the new cause took on reality in 1821. Greek liberation from centuries of Turkish oppression found a sympathetic response in England and a committee was formed to organize aid. The committee asked Byron, probably the most famous Englishman in Europe, to help; without hesitation, he turned all his energies to aiding the Greeks. He armed a brig, the *Hercules*, and set sail from Leghorn with Trelawny and Gamba on 24 July 1823. He reached Cephalonia ten days later and soon proved to be a born leader. The factional quarrels which had plagued the Greek rebels dissolved as they rallied to their great English lord and some even hinted that he could become king of a free Greece. Byron worked ceaselessly and in January 1824 joined Alexander Mavrocordato (to whom Shelley dedicated his *Hellas*) at Missolonghi on the north shore of the Gulf of Patras. The Greek leader had brought a fleet of ships, and Byron's plan was to attack the Turkish stronghold at Lepanto. But in April he caught a severe chill after being soaked to the skin in an open boat. Rheumatic fever set in, and Byron died on 19 April 1824. The Greeks were stunned by his death and wanted to bury him in Athens, but only his heart stayed in Greece. His body was brought back to England, but was refused burial in Westminster Abbey on account of his reputation. He was buried in the family vault in the village church of Hucknall Torkard, near Newstead Abbey in Nottinghamshire. Tennyson, a boy of 14 when he heard the news of Byron's death, said 'the whole world seemed darkened to me'; on a rock at his home in Somersby he inscribed the words 'Byron is dead'.

Byron's career and character will continue to be examined and discussed. Possibly no English poet ever caught the imagination of Europe as he did: books about his life, his work, and his enormous influence are written in every European language. He was a child of his time, of that strange period when poetry, philosophy, and politics were fired by revolution and embraced its coming – only to see it dishonoured. Many believed the revolutionary ideal to be defeated, but this was not so – events in France had seen only a beginning and were to bear fruit; for the time being, however, reaction seemed to have triumphed. The Romantic era in the arts rose out of a profound disillusion, and the work of both Byron and Shelley contains scathing references to the status quo. The poetry of Byron – for many the arch-Romantic – is surprisingly 'classical' in form, particularly in his celebrated satires *English Bards and Scotch Reviewers*, *The Vision of Judgement*, and *Don Juan* (regarded as his best). Essentially Romantic in spirit, Byron was not prepared, as were his younger contemporaries, to turn his back completely on classical disciplines and he was an unfailing champion of the work of Alexander Pope. The Romantic poetry of *Childe Harold* was Byron's response to a romantic world – a world he saw with his own eyes but which others, like Scott, had to conjure from their reading. Byron painted from life and the public was dazzled by the glittering world he portrayed. Moreover, despite his denials, the public insisted on identifying the poet with the hero: after the first two cantos, and public reaction to the failure of his marriage, Byron became Harold, a heartsick exile who sought distraction in wandering and pleasure. The Byronic hero was born, and Byron may have felt some wry amusement at the way Harold's world was examined by scores of avid readers in the succeeding cantos. In truth there was little of the Romantic hero about Lord Byron himself: 'Mad, bad, and dangerous to know' was Lady Caroline Lamb's description, in her journal, of the most glamorous man in London, at whose head she threw herself and whose response did not satisfy her. His own letters reveal a man who was witty, practical, impatient of humbug, and averse to emotional displays.

The standard edition of Byron's poems is included in the 13-volume edition of the poetry, letters, and journals (1898–1904). Volumes 1–7 contain the poetry, edited by E. H. Coleridge; the remaining volumes are edited by R. E. Prothero. There is also Frederick Page's single-volume edition, corrected by John Jump (Oxford Standard Authors, 1945 and 1974), and G. Pocock's three-volume edition (Everyman's Library, 1949). The recommended biography is by L. A. Marchand, *Byron: A Biography* (1957). The recommended edition of Byron's letters is also by L. A. Marchand (begun 1973 and continuing).

# C

**Cabell, James Branch** 1879–1958. Cabell was born in Richmond, Virginia, and educated at William and Mary College, Williamsburg. He published his first novel, *The Eagle's Shadow*, in 1904 and four more books of fiction before his first use of an imaginary medieval domain, Poictesme, in *The Soul of Melicent* (1913). Poictesme was the setting for *Jurgen* (1919), which made him famous when it was described as obscene and attempts were made to suppress it. Jurgen is a medieval pawnbroker with a garrulous wife, Lisa; he arranges with the Devil to have her vanish and then, prodded by conscience and gossip, sets out to try and find her. Wearing the shirt of Nessus, he is transported to a timeless world where he enjoys all sorts of amatory adventures, including one with the love of his youth, Dorothy. At the end of the tale he asks for a return of things as they were, Lisa is restored, and they resume their humdrum comfortable life. But conventional morality has been well examined in the course of the story.

Cabell wrote another dozen or so books set in his invented medieval world, including collections of short stories and verse, and had a large public following in the 1920s. The fiction is pointedly antirealistic but Cabell's attempts at moral allegory were submerged in his too-careful adherence to the style of his invented setting, and his novels are now largely unread.

**Cable, George Washington** *c.*1844–1925. Cable's father was a Virginian but Cable himself was born in New Orleans. He served in the Confederate cavalry during the Civil War and afterwards studied engineering, working as a warehouse clerk until illness turned him to writing. His humorous sketches were published by the New Orleans *Picayune*, under the pseudonym of Drop Shot, and he joined the paper for a while as a reporter. He became a contributor to *Scribner's Magazine* and to *Appleton's Journal* (1873–79) and, increasingly, used the history and background of New Orleans for his material. His first collection, **Old Creole Days**, was published in 1879 and was very well received.

His next book was a novel of Louisiana, *The Grandissimes* (1880), concerning the fortunes of a Creole family. **Madame Delphine** (1881) was the story of a quadroon woman's dilemma. Cable continued to write fiction, much of it based on the collision of Northern and Southern manners and morals (*Dr Sevier*, 1885; *Bonaventure*, 1888; *John March, Southerner*, 1894; and *Bylow Hill*, 1902). In 1884 he published *The Creoles of Louisiana* and offended the Creoles with this history; they were beginning to be rather touchy about Cable and the opinions he expressed.

Cable's father had kept slaves and Cable detested the institution. Though the Civil War was over and the abolition of slavery a fact there was still an unshakable slave-owning mentality in existence; Cable wanted reform and a real effort made to improve the lives of the Black people. In 1885 he published *The Silent South*, a collection of essays expressing his views – and found it wise, in the light of the furious reaction to it, to leave the South. He settled in Massachusetts, where he published *Strange True Stories of Louisiana* (1889), *The Negro Question* (1890), and *The Southern Struggle for Pure Government* (1890).

George Washington Cable's contribution to American literature was as notable as his outspoken humanitarianism. His fiction and sketches brought the authentic Creole background on to the literary scene with the accuracy of an acute observer and, as in the case of Joel Chandler Harris, a faultless ear. (He also earned the praise of Mark Twain, incidentally.) With the advent of Harris and Cable literature in the South began to be literature *of* the South.

See also **Harris, Joel Chandler.**

*Cadenus and Vanessa* A poem by Jonathan Swift, written in 1713. 'Vanessa' was Esther Vanhomrigh ('Stella' was Esther Johnson) and Cadenus (an anagram of *decanus* or dean) was Swift. Vanessa fell in love with Swift but he did not return her passion, though he treated her with respect and honoured her with his esteem. The poem, in mock-classical form, was written for Vanessa and gives an account of their relationship. Esther Vanhomrigh preserved the poem and it was published in 1726. See **Swift, Jonathan.**

**Caedmon** fl. 670–80. Nothing more is known of Caedmon or his work than is related by Bede in his *Historia Ecclesiastica*, Book IV, Chapter 24. Bede tells of a herdsman who, being ignorant of poetry and unable to sing, always retired after a feast for fear he would be asked to sing, like the rest of the company. One night having done this he slept in the stables, and a man came to him in a dream and asked him to sing. He replied that he could not but the man persisted. Then Caedmon asked of what, then, should he sing? The answer was of the beginning of things, so Caedmon sang in praise of God the Creator. After he awoke he remembered his song, and could sing it, and soon he was adding to his song. Caedmon was, according to Bede, a man of mature years when he had this dream; he then became a monk at Streoneshalh (Whitby) during the rule of the abbess, St Hilda (614–80). He was taught more of the Bible by learned men, and turned the scriptures into songs of such beauty that scholars wrote them down. But the single hymn of the Creation, nine short lines, is the only poem that can be attributed with any certainty to Caedmon. The poems contained in the *Junius Manuscript*, which were once believed to be the work of Caedmon, are now known to be of later date.

17 manuscripts of *Caedmon's Hymn* are known to exist, from the Latin of Bede's transcription,

The Creation of Light, from the so-called Caedmon Manuscript in the Bodleian Library, Oxford. (*MS Junius XI, f.81*). The manuscript, c.1000 AD, consists of verse paraphrases from Old Testament stories, once believed to be the work of Caedmon.

and Old English translations of Bede, to West Saxon and Northumbrian dialect versions. Caedmon is believed to be the first English poet.

**Caelia** The Lady of the House of Holiness in Book I of Spenser's *The Faerie Queene*. Her daughters are Fidelia (faith), Speranza (hope), and Charissa (charity).

*Café des Exiles* See *Old Creole Days.*

*Cain: A Mystery.* A tragedy by Lord Byron, first published in 1821, when it produced a storm of abuse; many found it blasphemous, ignoring the argument it presented. Blake's writings in the same vein were not known until after he died in 1827.

Cain rebels against his life of unremitting toil; it is no choice of his own, and he suffers through the fault of his father, Adam. His observation of the world is irreconcilable with what he has been taught of the omnipotent God, and he turns to Lucifer to find the answer to the problems of existence. Cain's revolt against the life he is forced to lead is further incited by Lucifer; his brother Abel's devotion to Jehovah enrages him and Cain kills him. Remorse follows the murder, then the inevitable punishment, and Cain goes forth into exile.

**Caine, Sir (Thomas Henry) Hall** 1853–1931. A novelist who earned a fortune with his books and was forgotten soon after his death. George Sampson's verdict is unequivocal: in the *Concise Cambridge History of English Literature* (1941) he says, briefly, 'The numerous novelistic melodramas of T. H. Hall Caine must be dismissed unnamed.' Hall Caine was half Manx and was close to D. G. Rossetti during the last two years of the poet's life. He published *Recollections of D. G. Rossetti* in 1882, and *King Edward: a Prince and a Great Man* in 1910. Among his novels were *The Bondman: a New Saga* (1890), *The Eternal City* (1901), and *The Woman thou Gavest Me* (1913).

**Caird, Edward** 1835–1908. Caird was born in Greenock and educated at Greenock Academy, the universities of Glasgow and St Andrews, and Balliol College, Oxford, where his tutor was Benjamin Jowett. He enjoyed a brilliant academic career, becoming fellow and tutor of Merton College and Professor of Moral Philosophy at Glasgow University in 1866. He succeeded Jowett as Master of Balliol in 1893. *A Critical Account of the Philosophy of Kant* (1877) and *The Critical Philosophy of Immanuel Kant* (1889) are highly regarded works of philosophical exposition and criticism. *Hegel* (1883) is equally valued; *The Evolution of Religion* (1893) is the text of his Gifford Lectures.

**Caird, John** 1820–98. The elder brother of Edward Caird. He became a minister of the Church of Scotland in 1845 and Professor of Divinity at Glasgow University in 1862. He became Principal of the university in 1873. Like his brother Edward he was influenced by Hegel but his own teachings were close to Christian orthodoxy. He published *An Introduction to the Philosophy of Religion* (1880); the text of his Gifford Lectures, *The Fundamental Ideas of Christianity* (published posthumously, 1899), contained a memoir by his brother.

*Cakes and Ale* See **Maugham, W(illiam) Somerset**.

*Calamus* A sequence of 45 poems by Walt Whitman, first published in the third edition of *Leaves of Grass* (1860). The calamus plant is the sweet flag; the aromatic root represents continuing life, the close-clinging fascicles represent love and friendship, and the leaves symbolize mortality. The theme is the spiritual love of man for man – in Whitman's words 'beautiful and sane affection of man for man'. One explicit love lyric, 'Long I thought that knowledge alone would suffice me', appeared only in the 1860 edition. This has led to conclusions about Whitman's psychology and aroused some heated arguments. The poems are remarkable in any context and should be read for their intrinsic quality.

**Calderwood, David** 1575–1650. An adherent of the kirk, Calderwood was the author of a number of Presbyterian anti-episcopal tracts; he recorded the strife between the two in Scotland in *The Historie of the Kirk of Scotland, beginning at Patrik Hamilton and ending at the death of James the Sixt*, published posthumously (1678).

*Caleb Williams, Things as they are: or the Adventures of.* A novel by William Godwin, first published in 1794, the year after his celebrated *Political Justice*. His novel demonstrates the evils of the prevailing system, which rendered the humble man powerless in the face of injustice and the wrongdoer, if privileged and powerful enough, completely immune.

The vicious squire, Tyrrel, ruins his tenant Hawkins who goes against his wishes; he is also guilty of the death of his own niece, whom he bullies remorselessly to marry one of his oafish friends. Later Tyrrel quarrels with a neighbouring landowner, Falkland, and assaults him in public. Then Tyrrel is found murdered and suspicion falls on Falkland, who succeeds in implicating the hapless Hawkins and his son: both men are tried and hanged for the murder of Tyrrel.

In the second part of the novel, Falkland takes as his secretary the self-educated son of humble parents, Caleb Williams. After a time Caleb, who is devoted to his employer, becomes convinced of Falkland's guilt but refuses to betray him. Falkland becomes aware of Caleb's conviction, however, and persecutes his servant, eventually accusing him of a theft and securing his imprisonment. The innocent Caleb escapes from prison and goes into hiding: Falkland employs agents to find him and Caleb is hunted from place to place. Eventually, in desperation, Caleb confronts Falkland and accuses him of his crimes, although he has no proof to offer. But the strength of Caleb's confrontation breaks down Falkland and in the end he does confess.

Godwin's novel, in spite of its faults of clumsiness and contrivance, is original and he brought to it a passionate personal commitment that ensures its place in the history of English fiction.

**Calef, Robert** *c*.1648–1719. A merchant of Boston, Robert Calef was the author of *More Wonders of the Invisible World*, published in 1700. This was a bitter attack, well documented and carefully argued, on those responsible for the Salem witchcraft trials of 1692. His principal target was Cotton Mather. It was effective enough to provoke Increase Mather, then Rector of Harvard, to order it to be burned in the college yard.

**Caliban** In Shakespeare's *The Tempest*, the sole inhabitant of the island on which Prospero and his infant daughter were cast. The son of the witch Sycorax, he is savage and deformed. Prospero made him his servant and taught him to speak but stopped treating him kindly when Caliban tried to force his attentions on Miranda. In the play he is a sullen slave to Prospero, who leaves him on his island at the end of the tale.

*Caliban Upon Setebos* A poem by Robert Browning, first published in 1864 in the volume *Dramatis Personae*. The title refers to Caliban's reflections upon the nature of his god, Setebos, and his purpose in creating the world. Caliban is lying in his cave, out of Prospero's way, and his reflections cautiously refer to himself in the third person ('he') lest his god ('He' or 'Him') detect a mere creature's impudent questioning and resentment. Setebos himself is subordinate to a higher power, The Quiet. Caliban's conclusions are that Setebos is a creature much like himself and the world exists for his amusement. Caliban lets his reflections carry him to the point of fury and the hope that Setebos will be overcome by The Quiet; but he incautiously utters the personal pronoun and a raven, hearing him, flies off to Setebos, who unlooses a thunderstorm to frighten Caliban into his usual subjection. Browning's poem is an examination of man's relationship to God and his fellow men. The character taken from Shakespeare is not quite human, and this serves to throw into sharp relief the point of the continuing mistake made by man in his anthropomorphic idea of God. The poem's epigraph is from Psalm 50: 'Thou thoughtest that I was altogether such an one as thyself.'

**Calidore, Sir** In Book VI of Spenser's *The Faerie Queene* the knight of courtesy. He is loved by Pastorella and subdues the Blatant Beast.

*Calisto and Melibea, A new commodye in englyshe in manner of an enterlude.* This early play was adapted from the Spanish by an unknown author and first printed in 1530, by John Rastell. The original was the *Celestina* of Fernando de Rojas, which was to be translated with great success by James Mabbe in 1631. *Celestina* is written entirely in dialogue form and lent itself particularly well to dramatization.

Calisto is a high-born young man who loves Melibea from the moment of first meeting her; but the violence of his passion turns her away from him. He enlists the aid of Celestina, a bawd, who succeeds in bringing Melibea to Calisto's arms; soon Melibea is as violently in love as Calisto and Celestina is rewarded. But Calisto's servants Parmeno and Sempronio murder the bawd for a share of the reward and they are put to death for the crime. Meanwhile Calisto and Melibea continue with their guilty love, until Calisto, keeping a tryst in a tower, falls off a ladder and is killed. In consequence Melibea leaps to her own death.

The play version is spoiled by the introduction of a different ending, in which Melibea, weakening enough to desert the path of virtue, is dissuaded by her father, Danio, who brings her to repentance by relating the details of what may befall in a terrible vision he has been vouchsafed.

**Callaghan, Morley Edward** 1903– . Morley Callaghan was of Irish descent and was born in Toronto. He was educated at Toronto University and later studied law. He was called to the Bar in 1928 but by that time he was a reporter on the Toronto *Daily Star*. One of his colleagues on the paper was Ernest Hemingway, who encouraged him to write, and Callaghan published his first novel, *Strange Fugitive*, in 1928. He spent the next year in Paris, where he met James Joyce, Scott Fitzgerald, and Gertrude Stein, but he was back in Toronto, to stay, in 1929. *That Summer in Paris* (1963) is a memoir of the time he spent in France.

Callaghan is an urban novelist and his examination of moral values takes place in the context of modern city life. His work has been highly praised by such critics as Edmund Wilson and Wyndham Lewis. Among his novels, *Strange Fugitive* is the story of a bootlegger; *It's Never Over* (1930) is a harrowing novel about the effect of the crime on the family and friends of a murderer; *They Shall Inherit the Earth* (1935) tells of an ordinary family struggling through the depression; and *More Joy in Heaven* (1937) of a reformed prisoner who discovers that the world will not let him lead a new life. Others are *Such is My Beloved* (1934); a novel with the two cultures of Canada as its theme, *The Loved and the Lost* (1951); and *The Many Colored Coat* (1960).

Morley Callaghan's collections of short stories – *A Native Argosy* (1929), *No Man's Meat* (1931), and *Now that April's Here* (1936) – are as highly regarded as his novels.

**Call of the Wild, The** A novel by Jack London, first published in 1903.

A cross between a St Bernard and a shepherd dog, Buck is a much-loved pet in the Miller home in California. He is stolen, beaten into subjection, and then sold as a pack dog in the Klondike. He is forced to fight for his life with the leader of the sledge team, Spitz. He wins the fight and becomes the team leader but his existence is chiefly one of brutal subjection as he passes from one owner to another. Eventually he turns on one owner and is nearly beaten to death; he is saved by John Thornton, a gold prospector, who treats him with gentle kindness. Buck is devoted to Thornton and saves him from drowning; he also wins money for him by drawing a monstrously loaded sledge in a wager. Meanwhile, he responds more and more to the wilderness and mingles briefly with the wolves he hears in the forest.

Thornton's camp is attacked by Indians and Buck fights savagely for his master. He succeeds in driving them off – only to find his master has been killed. Buck will not leave the camp and fights against the wolves that move in. But the call of the wild is complete and Buck soon abandons his connection with mankind. He joins the wolf pack.

*The Call of the Wild* is Jack London's most famous book and the author creates a dog's world which is completely convincing. He also presents a vivid picture of the North and the climate of the gold rush, which he knew at first hand. See also **White Fang**.

**Calphurnia**  Caesar's wife (his third, in fact) in Shakespeare's *Julius Caesar*. Haunted by strange dreams, she tries to persuade Caesar to stay away from the Capitol on the Ides of March.

**Calverley, Charles Stuart** 1831–84.  The son of a clergyman, Calverley was born at Martley in Worcestershire and educated at Marlborough, Harrow, and Balliol College, Oxford. He was sent down from Balliol and completed his university education at Christ's College, Cambridge, where he became a fellow. He became a barrister in 1865 but a severe accident sustained while skating disabled him for the rest of his life. He made a reputation as a skilful parodist and as a translator from Greek and Latin. He published *Verses and Translations* (1862), *Translations into English and Latin* (1866), *Theocritus translated into English Verse* (1869), and *Fly Leaves* (1872). *Literary Remains* was edited by W. J. Sendall (1885), who contributed a memoir; Calverley's *The Eclogues of Virgil, translated into English Verse* was edited by M. Hadas (1960). Calverley signed his parodies with his initials C. S. C.

**Cambel**  In Book IV of Spenser's *The Faerie Queene* Cambel fights Triamond, the knight of friendship, who proves the most redoubtable suitor for the hand of Cambel's sister, Canace. Cambel marries Cambina, Triamond's sister. The characters of Cambel (Cambal) and Canace were taken by Spenser from Chaucer's unfinished *Squire's Tale*.

***Cambises, King of Percia***  See **Preston, Thomas**.

**Cambridge Platonists**  At the University of Cambridge, between 1633 and 1688, there evolved from a group of divines a philosophical approach to religion that marked a path between High Anglicanism and Puritanism. The chief contemporary influence was the philosophy of René Descartes, though they could not accept his materialistic view of the inanimate world. The Cambridge Platonists advocated tolerance and insisted on the need for comprehension, seeing reason as the arbiter of both natural and revealed religion: morality itself is based on reason, and reason and religion are essentially in harmony.

**Camden, William** 1551–1623.  The son of a painter from Lichfield, William Camden was born in the Old Bailey and educated at Christ's Hospital, St Paul's School, and Magdalen and Christ Church colleges, Oxford. He became headmaster of Westminster School in 1593 and one of his pupils was Ben Jonson, who had a warm admiration for him. An accomplished classical scholar – he wrote in Latin and his Greek grammar of 1595 was in use for many years after his death – Camden was also an antiquary and a historian. He published the results of his extensive journeys of enquiry, begun in 1582, as *Britannia sive florentissimorum regnorum Angliae, Scotiae, Hiberniae Chorographica descriptio* (1586). It became a source book for poets who delved into England's legends and was very popular both in Philemon Holland's translation of 1610 and it its original Latin, six editions of which had appeared by 1607.

Camden's great work was his history of England and Ireland in the reign of Elizabeth, *Rerum Anglicarum et Hibernicarum Annales, regnante Elizabetha*. This was first published in Leyden, the first part in 1615 and the second in 1625. The first part was published in England – in a French translation – in 1642. Then both parts were published in French in Paris in 1627. Abraham Darcie translated the first part into English – from the French – in 1625; Thomas Browne translated the second part in 1629. A modern translation of Camden, unfortunately, does not exist.

Camden founded a chair of history at Oxford University and he is regarded as the finest of the Elizabethan antiquaries and historians. In the latter task he enjoyed the confidence of Burghley, who placed a huge mass of state papers at his disposal. In the former: 'I have neglected nothing', he wrote, 'that could give considerable light towards the discovery of truth in matters of antiquity'. His *Remaines of a Greater Worke Concerning Britaine* was published in 1605. Camden's 'greater worke' was a history of England that he never completed.

***Camilla, or A Picture of Youth***.  A novel by Fanny Burney, first published in 1796. The length of the story rather overpowers the substance, which concerns the efforts of a group of young people to achieve, by various means, some kind of adult security. Camilla Tyrold and her sisters hope for marriage; their brother Lionel has no scruples and provides an amiable and shiftless character in contrast. The Tyrold family is also shown in the grip of the recurring crises of middle-class life in the 18th century: the expenditure believed to be essential for correct social behaviour leading to a mounting pile of debts. Camilla Tyrold eventually finds happiness with Edgar Mandlebert.

Macaulay was convinced that *Camilla* suffered a great deal from the fact that Fanny Burney could no longer rely on the advice of her admirer, Samuel Johnson, who had died in 1784, two years after the publication of *Cecilia*.

**Camillo**  In Shakespeare's *The Winter's Tale*, a lord of Sicily ordered by King Leontes to murder

Roy Campbell. A photograph taken in 1946.

Polixenes. Instead, he warns Polixenes of the king's jealous rage and escapes with him to Bohemia. At the end of the play he seems likely to marry Paulina.

**Campbell, Roy Dunnachie** 1901–57. Roy Campbell was born in Durban in South Africa, of Scots and Irish ancestry. He attended Durban High School but much of his childhood and early youth was free and easy and he roamed at will on the veld and in the bush. At the age of 17 he visited England and France and decided not to enter Oxford University. After returning to Durban he wrote *The Flaming Terrapin* (1924), a long symbolic poem which was well received in England, and founded the literary journal, *Voorslag* (Whiplash), with William Plomer. The journal was outspoken and far too advanced for South Africa and only survived for a year (1926–27). Campbell's critical attitude towards the country's leaders was expressed in the angrily satirical *The Wayzgoose* (1928); he returned to Europe in the same year.

Campbell settled in Provence and in 1930 published *Adamastor*, a lively and romantic collection of lyrics which contains some of his most highly regarded work. *The Georgiad: A Satirical Fantasy in Verse* (1931) is in heroic couplets and at the expense of the Georgian literary world; *Pomegranates* (1932) and *Flowering Reeds* (1933) followed, then he became a Roman Catholic and settled in Toledo in Spain. During the Spanish Civil War Campbell worked for Franco's side as a reporter and propagandist; but he always rejected the charge that he was a fascist: his feeling was that there should be as few politics as possible, and he was himself a strong traditionalist as well as a fervent Roman Catholic.

*Mithraic Emblems* (1936) and *Flowering Rifle* (1939) preceded his enlistment in the army for World War II, during which he served in East Africa. He was injured and invalided out, returning to England with a pension; he worked for some years at the BBC. *Talking Bronco* (1946) was his last collection of original verse but his versions from the Spanish, *The Poems of St John of the Cross* (1951), received high praise. He bought a farm in Portugal in 1952 and went to live there, and was killed in a car accident in 1957.

As a translator Roy Campbell earned high praise, particularly for his versions of Iberian classics. As well as his version of *St John of the Cross* there were two novels by the Portuguese Eça de Queiroz, *Cousin Bazilio* (1953) and *The City and the Mountains* (1955); Tirso de Molina's *Trickster of Seville* and Calderón's *Life is a Dream* in *The Classic Theatre* (edited by Eric Bentley 1959); and *Nostalgia: Poems by J. Paço d'Arcos* and Calderón's *The Surgeon of his Honour* (both published posthumously, 1960). His autobiography, *Light on a Dark Horse* (1951), tells of his life up to 1935.

Campbell was a poet who used traditional forms and a traditional vocabulary expanded by colloquialisms and army slang. A romantic poet in the modern age, he was a vigorous man of action who tended to heartlessness. At its best his work is very rewarding but the tempo can become tiring unless taken in careful measures. 'The Serf', 'Horses on the Camargue', and 'The Zulu Girl' are usually found in anthologies of modern verse.

**Campbell, Thomas** 1777–1814. The son of a prosperous merchant, Campbell was born in Glasgow and educated at Glasgow University. He was the author of a number of poems written before he was 30, some of which have remained popular, especially in school anthologies. His first success was *The Pleasures of Hope* (1799), which has ensured his inclusion in dictionaries of quotations ('Tis distance lends enchantment to the view'). He was skilful and might have achieved more had his inclination to poetry been stronger. He is remembered best for such poems as 'The Battle of Hohenlinden', 'Lord Ullin's Daughter', and 'Ye Mariners of England'.

**Campion, Thomas** 1567–1620.  Thomas Campion was orphaned while still a child; fortunately his parents were people of means and his education was assured. He entered Cambridge in 1581 as a gentleman pensioner to Peterhouse College. He left in 1584, without taking a degree, and was admitted to Gray's Inn in 1586 but was never called to the bar. He is believed to have served with Essex's volunteer expedition in aid of Henri IV in 1591.

Campion seems to have forsaken law in 1595, when he left Gray's Inn and published his Latin *Poemata*. This was not his first work; five songs of his had appeared in an edition of Sidney's *Astrophel and Stella* ('other sonnets of divers gentlemen') published in 1591. His first collection of songs appeared in a joint volume with his friend Philip Rosseter, *A Booke of Ayres to be Sung to the Lute, Orpherian and Base Violl* (1601). Campion both composed charming 'ayres' and wrote fine lyrics to be sung to them.

During this period (1595–1602) Campion had begun the study of medicine and became a doctor some time after 1602. In 1602 also Campion wrote his *Observations in the Art of English Poesie*, an arbitrary statement in favour of classical forms in opposition to the use of rhyme. Despite his eloquence he was refuted by Samuel Daniel (see **Daniel, Samuel**), who – without intensive historical knowledge – argued more persuasively from a background of sense and sensibility. Campion, having delivered his *Observations*, seems to have forgotten them in his own work; he used rhyme in his songs continually.

His first masque was published in 1607 in *The Discription of a Maske at White-Hall in Honour of the Lord Hayes and his Bride; other Small Poemes*. His next song book was *Two Bookes of Ayres* (1613); the same year brought *Songs of Mourning Bewailing the Death of Prince Henry* and two further masques: *A Relation of . . . the Lords Maske on the Marriage Night of the Count Palatine and the Ladie Elizabeth* and *The Description of a Maske at the Mariage of the Earle of Somerset* (1614). Campion's *The Third and Fourth Booke of Ayres* was published in 1617; his musical treatise, *New Way of Making Fowre Parts in Counterpoint*, is believed to belong to that year also. *Ayres that were Sung and Played at Brougham Castle* (the occasion was the Earl of Cumberland's entertainment of James I) was published in 1618.

Campion's lyrics, at their best, exist independently of the airs for which they were composed and hardly improve when sung. His gifts were unique; he was a 'lyric' poet in a special sense and a master of the art of setting words to music. His complete works were edited by A. B. Grosart (1879), A. H. Bullen (1889 and 1903), and S. P. Vivian (1909).

**Canon's Yeoman's Tale, The**  See *Canterbury Tales, The*.

**Can Such Things Be?**  A book of 24 stories by Ambrose Bierce, first published in 1893. The author includes stories of the Civil War and episodes of life in California, but the book is more famous for its sardonic and chilling tales of crime and retribution.

*One Kind of Officer* is an exceptional war story. Bierce's war was the Civil War but the theme transcends the particular and will give any thoughtful reader pause. Captain Ransome obeys his general's orders – which result in firing on his own troops. The general whose mistake led to the tragedy is killed in battle, so Ransome is left with the responsibility for what happened – and the penalty. *My Favorite Murder* is black humour, in which the narrator concludes that his own killing of Uncle William has never been excelled. *The Famous Gilson Bequest* is a masterpiece in a vein similar to that exploited years later by Mark Twain in *The Man that Corrupted Hadleyburg*. Gilson is a California horse thief who is apprehended and hanged. He leaves a will, bequeathing his considerable wealth to the man who convicted him – but only if no one can prove that he was robbed by Gilson. Anyone who can will have first claim on the money and the legatee will have to surrender it. The bequest sets in motion a tempest of litigation, brings to the surface an appalling array of moral dubiety, and eventually ruins the legatee.

**Canterbury Tales, The**  The greatest work of Geoffrey Chaucer, who began its composition about 1386. The poet was then living in Kent and there is no word left by him to tell us how the idea of a party of pilgrims, setting out for Canterbury, occurred to him. We only know that it did occur to him and provided a perfect framework for one of the masterpieces of English literature. The 29 pilgrims travel at a leisurely pace along their road; they represent a cross-section of the people of 14th-century England, shrewdly but generously observed by the poet as the various groups come together and converse, separate, then regroup and separate again, revealing their characters in the process.

The order of the Tales – that is, the order the poet intended – has never been resolved. Chaucer did not complete his great work and its unfinished state presents contradictions of detail and unanswerable questions about the possible whole: the Squire does not resume his tale, whilst seven of the pilgrims tell no story at all; the Man of Law, in the poet's introduction, announces that he will speak in prose, but his tale is in seven-line stanzas; and so on. The editors of Chaucer have used what links can be found in the progression of the narrative but sometimes these dissolve; the first group, for instance, comes to a stop with *The Cook's Tale*, which is incomplete. The work of F. J. Furnivall for The Chaucer Society (1868) and of W. W. Skeat (1894) gave the order of the Tales that is generally accepted now. Most of *The Canterbury Tales* is written is heroic couplets, with departures into rhyme-royal and seven- and eight-line stanzas.

*The Prologue.* The poet joins a party of 30 pilgrims (though the text states the number as 29) at the Tabard Inn in Southwark. Their objective is the shrine of Thomas à Becket at Canterbury, and when supper is over the Host of the Inn, Harry Bailly, suggests that each pilgrim should tell two stories on the journey to lighten the hours of travelling they face. They could do the same thing on the way back; the Host will accompany the party as their guide and will judge the stories – the teller of the best will have a free supper upon their return. (Chaucer's original plan – assuming that this is what the Prologue gives us – was not completed, and ten of the pilgrims described here do not deliver their story. They are the Yeoman, three priests, the Haberdasher, the Carpenter, the Weaver, the Dyer, the Tapicer (tapestry maker), and the Ploughman. A Canon's Yeoman who joins the

A woodcut from Caxton's second edition of *The Canterbury Tales*, c.1484. The scene is from the Prologue, and shows the Pilgrims at supper at the Tabard Inn. The same woodcuts were used in the 1498 edition of Wynkyn de Worde.

party on the road does tell a story, and the poet also, plus one which is interrupted – the Tale of Sir Thopas. So there are 23 tales.) The time is April, the party sets off at daybreak, and at St Thomas's fountain the lot falls to the Knight to tell the first tale.

*The Knight's Tale.* Palamon and Arcite, royal cousins of Thebes, are prisoners of Theseus, Duke of Athens. They are both in love with Emilia, whose sister is Hippolyta, the duke's wife and queen of the Amazons. Arcite is released but banished from Athens; he returns in the guise of a servant. Palamon escapes from prison but stays in Athens, as determined as Arcite to win Emilia. The cousins meet by accident and agree to fight on the next day for the right to their lady. The fight is interrupted by Theseus, who orders the cousins to return to Athens one year hence, with a hundred knights each, to fight a tourney. At the tourney Palamon is defeated: Arcite is the favourite of Mars, while Palamon has prayed to Venus, goddess of love. But Venus invokes the help of Saturn, and Arcite is thrown and mortally injured at his moment of triumph. He yields Emilia to Palamon as he dies. The story originated in Boccaccio's *Teseide*.

After *The Knight's Tale* the Host turns to the Monk for the next story – but the Miller, who is drunk, insists on being heard first.

*The Miller's Tale.* The old carpenter, John, has a young wife, Alison. She has her eye on Nicholas, a scholar lodging in their house, but looks coldly on Absolon the parish clerk, who fancies her. Nicholas convinces John that a second flood is coming and persuades him to hang three tubs in the attic so that all three can float to safety. Old John falls asleep in his tub and Alison creeps downstairs with Nicholas to make love. But Absolon is outside yearning for a kiss; Alison puts her arse (Chaucer's word) through the window and he kisses her passionately before he realizes what he is doing. He retreats, outraged, with the lovers' mirth ringing in his ears. But later in the night the lovers hear him outside again, offering a gold ring for another kiss. This time it is Nicholas who puts his arse through the window – but instead of a kiss he receives a red-hot iron which Absolon has borrowed from the smith. The screams of Nicholas and Alison rouse Old John, who, believing the second flood has come, promptly severs the ropes holding the tubs and crashes to the ground to the mirth of the whole village.

The pilgrims have reached Deptford by the time *The Miller's Tale* is told and the company is convulsed with laughter – all, that is, except the

Reeve (steward), who is also a carpenter. His tale is a riposte to that of the Miller.

*The Reeve's Tale*. Two scholars, John and Alan, believe that the miller Simkins is cheating their college. When they first set watch he makes their horse bolt and helps himself to even more of the college's grain. When they return he scornfully offers them a lodging for the night. They accept – and turn the tables on him: Alan steals into the miller's daughter's bed, whilst John by rearranging the furniture misleads the miller's wife into his bed in the dark. The miller's daughter tells Alan where the stolen grain is hidden and he goes to waken John, who is in the other bed. However, the one he wakes is the miller, and in the ensuing uproar the miller's wife knocks her husband out by mistake. The scholars retrieve their grain – plus some extra – and get away safely.

The Cook is delighted with *The Reeve's Tale* and offers to tell another bawdy story.

*The Cook's Tale*. Perkin or Peterkin, an apprentice cook, is too fond of gambling and girls, so his master gives him the sack. Perkin moves himself to the house of a friend, whose wife keeps a shop as a front – she earns a living as a prostitute . . . And that is all we have. Chaucer wrote no more of *The Cook's Tale*.

The first group (A) ends with *The Cook's Tale* and the next one begins with the Host persuading the Man of Law to tell his tale.

*The Man of Law's Tale*. The Sultan of Syria wants to marry Constance, daughter of the Emperor of Rome, and becomes a Christian in order to do so. Constance goes to Syria, but meanwhile the Sultan's mother, outraged by her son's action, plots the girl's destruction. She succeeds in getting her cast away in a rudderless boat. The boat drifts ashore in Northumberland, where Constance is succoured by the Constable and his wife Hermengilda. A young knight conceives a passion for Constance, who rejects him. The knight then murders Hermengilda and contrives to throw the blame on Constance. But a miracle enables Constance to prove her innocence to the king, Alla, who makes her his queen. However this ruler also has a murderous mother, Donegild, who wants the kingdom to return to the old pagan gods. While the king is absent, Constance's son Maurice is born; Donegild puts Constance and her son in another boat and off she goes again. This time she drifts to Rome, where a Senator gives them shelter. King Alla eventually turns up in Rome; the grief and remorse he suffers after killing his evil mother weigh heavily on him, so he has made a pilgrimage. He is reunited with Constance and the family returns to Northumberland. After the king dies Constance returns to Rome where Maurice, in the fullness of time, becomes Emperor. This silly story was familiar in the medieval world (see also **Emarê**) and was used by John Gower in *Confessio Amantis* as an exposition of the qualities of fortitude and resignation, embodied in the figure of Constance.

The Host, after *The Man of Law's Tale*, turns to the Parson. But the Parson's response suggests that he might be preparing to deliver a sermon. The Shipman stops him and tells a tale of his own.

*The Shipman's Tale*. A merchant of St Denys has a pretty wife, and a friend who is both virile and handsome – and a monk. The merchant invites his friend to visit him, as he will soon have to leave for Bruges on business. One morning, while the merchant is in his counting house, his wife confides to the monk how her husband's meanness has resulted in her debt, for clothes, of one hundred francs. The monk then asks the merchant for a loan on behalf of the Abbey of one hundred francs, which the merchant grants without quibbling. The monk returns to the Abbey, the merchant goes off to Bruges, and the money is promptly given to the wife – who is delighted to take the handsome monk to bed. When the merchant returns he calls on the monk to collect his debt; the monk tells him that he has already repaid the loan – to the merchant's wife. At home, the merchant enjoys his marital rights as a possessive and dominant husband, then taxes his wife with the matter of the hundred francs. She immediately declares she believed it to be a gift to her, so that she could present herself in dress befitting the wife of a successful merchant. And her husband, after all, is well paid for any favours he grants her. *The Shipman's Tale* was based on a popular *fabliau* of the time and there is a version in Boccaccio's *Decameron*.

The next pilgrim called upon by the Host is the Prioress, who begins the prologue to her tale with a line from the eighth Psalm.

*The Prioress's Tale*. A widow's child, a boy of seven, learns a hymn in honour of Mary and sings it on the way to school every day. His way takes him past the Ghetto and Satan inspires the Jews who live there to have him murdered. Their assassin cuts his throat then throws his body into a privy drain. Jesus and Mary cause the dead child to sing again and so his body is found. His murderers are hanged, whilst the boy is buried as a Christian martyr. This unpleasant tale was based on a legend well known – and probably believed – at that time; the lines separating ignorance, superstition, and religion then had little definition. Two versions of the legend (the stories of Hugh of Lincoln and William of Norwich) are separated by a century though they differ only in detail.

The Host now turns his attention to Chaucer and asks him to relate a merry tale to follow the one told by the Prioress.

*The Tale of Sir Thopas* (or *Topaz*). Chaucer begins to tell a parody of a knightly romance in which Sir Thopas, an exemplary knight, rides forth. Following a dream, he is determined to have an elf queen for his love, and he is in quest of one. He encounters a giant, Sir Olifaunt (Elephant), who threatens to destroy him because he trespasses on the land of the Queen of Faerie. Sir Olifaunt throws a hail of stones at him but Sir Thopas gets away. He will return the next day to challenge the giant; now he prepares his knightly accoutrements.

The Host interrupts Chaucer and puts a stop to his burlesque, asking him for something sensible to listen to. Chaucer agrees and tells the prose tale of Melibeus (*or Melibee*).

*The Tale of Melibeus.* Chaucer's tale is in fact a moral debate on the ethics of vengeance – whether Melibeus would be right or not to punish with violence the three thieves who, when attempting to rob his house, assaulted his daughter, Sophia. The chief speaker is Dame Prudence, the wife of Melibeus. Among those quoted are the early Christian fathers, Latin philosophers, St Paul, Job and Solomon. The conclusion asserts the virtue of magnanimity – that is on the part of Melibeus, persuaded by Dame Prudence. The unfortunate Sophia is not given the opportunity to speak.

One theory concerning *The Canterbury Tales* suggests that *The Tale of Melibeus* was originally intended for the Man of Law, whose tale is in verse but who states his intention to speak in prose. *Melibeus* contains a great deal of legal language.

The Host makes several comments on his own married life – and says his wife should have heard about Dame Prudence and her philosophy. The party is in sight of Rochester when the Host turns to the Monk, a well-fed and personable character whose clothes and horse are of the best, and asks him to tell the tale which the Miller had so rudely set aside. He announces that he will relate a series of tragedies.

*The Monk's Tale.* The Monk sees 'tragedy' as the story of one who falls from glory; he relates the stories of Lucifer, Adam, Samson, Hercules, Nebuchadnezzar, Belshazzar, Zenobia, King Peter (Pedro) of Spain who was killed by his brother Enrique, King Peter of Cyprus (Pierre de Lusignan), Bernabo Visconti of Milan, Count Ugolino of Pisa, Nero, Holofernes, King Antiochus the Illustrious (Antiochus Epiphanes), Alexander, Julius Caesar, and Croesus. Although Chaucer takes his characters from a wider range the model for this sort of story existed in Boccaccio.

The Host and the Knight have both found the Monk's story a dampening one so they ask him to discourse on something pleasanter – the hunt perhaps? The Monk declines, and the Host turns to the Nun's Priest, who promises to tell a tale in lighter vein.

*The Nun's Priest's Tale.* Chanticleer, a splendid cock, belongs to a widow and has charge of seven hens, of which the most beautiful is Pertelote, his favourite. One night Chanticleer wakes from a nightmare, in which he is nearly caught by a fox. He tells Pertelote, who offers no sympathy whatever. Indeed she is scornful, blames his dream on indigestion, and tells him to eat some laxative herbs. She quotes to him the words of Cato, who had said one should take no account of dreams. He in turn recites to her a number of instances proving the importance of dreams, citing St Kenelm, Daniel, Pharaoh, Croesus, and Andromache. Peace is eventually restored between them but meanwhile Sir Russel the fox is lurking near the yard making plans. One day he waylays Chanticleer and asks him if he can sing as well as his father used to. Chanticleer rises on his toes, opens his wings, and lifts his head – eyes closed – to sing. Russel promptly seizes him and bolts. The widow hears the uproar made by Pertelote and the other hens, and at once a party of men and dogs sets off in pursuit. Chanticleer is carried off towards the woods; he dares Russel Fox to stop and taunt his pursuers. Russel falls for the ruse – and is outwitted in his turn; the moment he opens his jaws to call out insults Chanticleer is free. He promptly flies into a tree and is safe. The story told by the Nun's Priest had its origin in the French *Roman de Renart*. It ends the second group (B).

The Host enjoys the story of Chanticleer and comments on the Priest's fine physique and bright eyes. He could, ventures the Host, do some lively treading among females, if he had a mind to, like his hero. Then he turns to the Physician and asks him for a tale.

*The Physician's Tale.* After some didactic lines on the upbringing of children, the Physician relates the story of Virginia, the Roman maiden who has to choose between shame at the hands of the lecherous judge Appius Claudius, or an honourable death at the hands of her father Virginius. She accepts the latter – whereupon

Appius Claudius charges him with murder. But the people of Rome overthrow Appius Claudius, who kills himself in prison. The story originated in Livy, the source Chaucer puts into the mouth of his Physician, but it was retold by Petrarch and is to be found in *Le Roman de la Rose*.

The Host finds this story pitiful and reflects that beauty can be a fatal gift. He asks the Pardoner to tell him something funny; he agrees – but they must stop at a tavern first because he wants a drink. Some of the pilgrims object to the Pardoner telling a funny story because it's bound to be a dirty one. He agrees to tell them a moral tale instead, and his Prologue reveals him as a cynical judge of his fellow men and their weaknesses. (A Pardoner was commissioned by the Pope to sell indulgences to those who believed they could save souls from Purgatory. Indulgences were supposed to be gained through prayer but the corrupt popes put them on sale, to the wrath of men like John Wycliffe; they were on sale again at the time when Martin Luther succeeded in bringing about the Reformation.) Chaucer's Pardoner lectures readily against anything that could be called a vice – that is how he earns his living; how he himself lives, he says, is quite another matter.

*The Pardoner's Tale.* During a plague three young louts see one of their friends carried off in a coffin. Death is abroad and has claimed hundreds of others; the three declare that they will halt Death's progress – if they can but meet him. They go forth and rudely enquire of a venerable old man why he is still alive. He replies that Death will not take him. They ask him where, then, is Death to be found? He tells them the way to a grove; they will find Death under an oak tree. They reach the oak tree – but what they find is a huge heap of gold coins. They decide that they must guard their treasure until night, when they can safely carry it away. But meanwhile they will need food, so draw lots to decide which one will go to the town to buy it. The youngest draws it and hurries away; while he is gone the other two agree to murder him when he comes back. There will be more treasure for two. The youngest, meanwhile, has decided that one, not three, shall have the treasure. He buys bread and wine, and a deadly poison to put in the wine. When he returns to the grove the others fall on him and stab him to death. Then they refresh themselves with wine before digging a hole in which to bury him. They die in agony – the three had indeed found Death where the old man had said they would. The origin of the story is believed to be in an Italian book of ancient tales, *Cento Novelle Antiche*; *The Pardoner's Tale* ends the third group (C).

The Pardoner, having told his tale of avarice and gained an attentive audience, shamelessly offers to sell them pardons for their sins; he turns first to the Host. Harry Bailly insults him so violently that the Knight has to restore peace; the pilgrims then continue on their way and the next tale begins at once, with no preamble between the Host and the storyteller, the comfortable and worldly Wife of Bath.

In the Prologue to her tale the Wife of Bath discourses on the evils of celibacy. She has had five husbands and while she has no quarrel with chastity, male or female, if that is the preferred condition, it is not for her. And why, she asks the company, were men and women created as they are – if they were not meant to enjoy the results? She delivers some womanly wisdom on the management of husbands provoking amused comment from the Friar on the length of the good Wife's preamble. The Friar is then subjected to gratuitous rudeness from the Summoner who, it is clear, does not like friars. The Friar promises a story about a Summoner that will amuse the company; the Summoner replies angrily that he has several tales he can tell about friars and the company will hear them before

The Wife of Bath. One of the illustrations in the Ellesmere MS of *The Canterbury Tales*, now in the Henry E. Huntington Library and Art Gallery, San Marino, California.

they reach Sittingbourne. The Host intervenes and calls them to order, and the next tale begins.

*The Wife of Bath's Tale.* At King Arthur's court a lusty knight is found guilty of raping a maiden, and condemned to be beheaded. Pleas for his life reach the queen, and he is given a year and a day in which to find the answer to the question 'What is it that women most desire?' If he does not find the answer he will lose his head. He sets forth without much hope, and all his questions bring answers that disagree with each other. Then one day at the edge of a wood he comes upon a group of ladies dancing; he decides to put the question to them. But as he approaches they disappear and all he finds is a hideous old woman. She comes to him and asks what he seeks: she offers to give him the answer in return for his promise to grant her a request when his life is safe. He agrees and they go to court, where the queen and her ladies assemble to hear him. The correct answer is that women most desire sovereignty over their husbands, and the queen acknowledges that the knight has saved his head. The old hag now comes forward to claim the promise the knight made to her: he must make her his wife. Under the eyes of the queen the knight can do nothing but honour his word, so the ill-assorted pair are duly married. When they retire the hag tells the knight that she can stay ugly and he will be guaranteed faithfulness or she can become beautiful – and he must risk what the attentions of other men may provoke. He chooses beauty, and kisses her, whereupon she is immediately transformed into a beautiful young woman. She promises to be faithful, too. The story is similar to the tale of Florent in Gower's *Confessio Amantis* but with a different setting.

The Friar, in the Prologue to the next tale, commends the Wife of Bath, saying that he will tell a story about a summoner, one of those wretches everyone detests. The Host calls him to order once more but the Summoner says that the Friar can tell what tale he likes – he knows enough about friars to strike this one dumb, as he will discover. The Friar begins his story.

*The Friar's Tale.* A summoner serves a harsh archdeacon who administers the church law without compassion. The summoner is the lowest kind of corrupt betrayer, who even pays bawds to name the men who come to them. (At this point the Friar says he will tell the truth about summoners – who have no jurisdiction over friars. The Summoner rushes to the attack and the Host is obliged to intervene once more.) This summoner, the Friar continues, has made himself rich through bribes from people who fear his word to the archdeacon may bring them disaster, and by blackmail of wealthy men who enjoy wenching. One day the summoner, on his way to extort some money from a poor widow, meets the Devil disguised as a bailiff. The summoner says that he's a bailiff too: but the Devil reveals himself, they swear friendship, and discuss their different methods of extortion. They pass a carter whose horse and load of hay are stuck in the mud; the carter is loudly consigning both horse and load to the Devil. The summoner's instincts prompt him: he tells the Devil to take what is now his due. But the Devil replies that the carter does not mean what he says; and the carter's next words, commending his horse to Jesus for his great strength in hauling the load out of the mud, bear him out. Then they reach the widow's hut where the summoner tries to extort 12 pence from her. The widow wrathfully consigns him to the blackest devil in hell. She really means what she says, so the Devil gleefully seizes the summoner and carries him off.

Next the Summoner, shaking with rage, tells in his Prologue the tale of the friar who in a vision was taken down to hell. He saw multitudes of sinners there, paying the penalty for their misdeeds, and asked if any friars were ever sent to hell. He is taken to Satan, who lifts up his tail to show him the 20,000 friars who shelter in his arse. And that, says the Summoner, is all the Prologue his tale requires. (A summoner was one, as the Friar's tale implies, who was paid to summon sinners to appear before the ecclesiastical courts. The office was obviously a desirable one for any man without scruples, or open to corruption. Chaucer, in his Prologue to *The Canterbury Tales*, presents a summoner of revolting aspect and of a character similar to the kind the Friar describes.)

*The Summoner's Tale.* Inevitably this tale concerns a friar, whom the Summoner presents as mendacious and greedy. He calls on a house where the master, Thomas, is lying ill – and irritable, as his wife complains to the friar. The friar endlessly exhorts him to put away his anger – an evil thing – and make his confession to him. Thomas tells him he has confessed already that day. The friar then returns to his request for money, already implicit in his homilies about anger. Thomas's irritability has now turned to wrath: when he promises the friar something rare. He makes him swear to share it equally with his fellows. The friar agrees, of course, and Thomas tells him it is concealed in the bed, under his buttocks. The friar stretches his arm into the bed to search for it, and when he reaches the obvious place Thomas farts explosively into his hand. The friar complains to the lord of the manor, but only meets with a ridiculous mock-serious discussion about the best way to share his rare reward. *The Summoner's Tale* closes the fourth group (D).

The Host addresses the Clerk, a lean and solemn man who loves his books and has been content to listen attentively. What of him, he surely has a tale to tell? The Clerk agrees, and in his Prologue tells the company that he got his tale from the great Italian poet Petrarch.

*The Clerk's Tale.* The Marquis of Saluces, Walter, is beloved of his subjects as a just and generous lord. But Walter enjoys his life to the full and has never stopped to consider marriage. His subjects are worried; they want him to have an heir, feeling this will ensure their continued wellbeing. They approach him and explain their uneasiness, and he promises to choose a bride. This proves to be Griselda, daughter of the poorest man in a nearby village. She is beautiful, and proves a perfect wife and a capable consort. But Walter decides to test her devotion: he has their first-born child taken away, telling her that his heirs must not share her low ancestry. Four years later he deprives her of their son in the same way. Griselda, borne down with grief, submits to her husband's will. Later still he divorces her, and she returns to her father in a smock – a smock being all she owned when the marquis took her to be his wife. The preparations for a new wife must be made: Walter sends for Griselda and orders her to make his house ready. The 'new bride' proves to be Griselda's daughter; she is restored to her mother, and so is her son: Griselda's patient devotion and humility are rewarded. With father, husband, and children she settles down in contentment. Chaucer based *The Clerk's Tale* on Petrarch's Latin version of a tale by Boccaccio, later used by Thomas Dekker as the basis of a play. It can have little meaning for modern readers but in its day was a popular allegorical moral tale about the constancy that all should show in the face of adversity. Chaucer, in his own person, delivers an *Envoy to The Clerk's Tale*, which is celebrated for its poetic dexterity.

The Merchant, after hearing *The Clerk's Tale*, observes sourly that few women resemble Griselda. The Merchant has been married only two months and he is regretting it already. The Host promptly asks him for a story, the tone of his request implying that the Merchant is sure to have something interesting to say.

*The Merchant's Tale.* January, an aging knight of Pavia, decides it is time, now his lusty days are over, to take a wife. He ignores advice to the contrary and marries the youthful May. His squire, Damian, falls in love with her at the mar-

riage feast – so passionately that he becomes ill. May cures him by sending him a letter promising to requite his passion and he gets well at once. January has a walled garden where he loves to walk and to which only he has a key. Unseen by him, Pluto and Proserpine enjoy his garden too. January becomes blind and very jealous, whilst May has stolen the key of the garden and had a copy made, which she has given to Damian. Damian lets himself into the garden and climbs into a pear tree, where May will join him. Pluto, observing this, gives January back his sight so that he can see he is betrayed: Proserpine (on behalf of her sex) retorts that she will frustrate his plan. January's sight returns and he sees May and Damian coupling energetically in the pear tree, into which January had helped his wife when May had said she wanted some of the fruit. He is raging round the tree when May tells him that she had to struggle with a man in a tree in order to restore his sight. January retorts that she was not struggling – far from it. But she persuades him that the returning light has dazzled him, and he has only thought he saw . . . what he saw. May and Proserpine have outwitted January and Pluto.

The Host exclaims over the duplicity of women. He has a wife, too – but he will say little of her faults because such words have a way of being overheard and carried back to their subject. *The Merchant's Tale* ends the fifth group (E); the next pilgrim to be asked for a story is the Knight's son, the Squire.

*The Squire's Tale.* Cambuscan, King of Tartary, has reigned for 20 years and is holding a birthday feast. A knight from the King of India and Araby attends the feast bringing four gifts: a brass horse, a mirror, a ring, and a sword. The brass horse will fly, the mirror will show the truth and what is to befall, the sword will cut through armour but will also heal, and the wearer of the ring will understand the speech of birds and know the healing power of every plant that grows. The king's daughter Canace wears the ring and her first experience of its magic gives her the ability to understand the sad story told by a lovelorn falcon.

That is where *The Squire's Tale* virtually ends. A few more lines promise the stories of the king's reign and the adventures of his sons Cambalo and Algarsyf. But after the first couplet of the third part the Squire is interrupted by the Franklin – and nowhere in *The Canterbury Tales* is the Squire's story resumed. (Edmund Spenser continues the story of Cambalo, as Cambell, and Canace and the magic ring in Book 4 of *The Faerie Queene*.)

The Franklin. One of the illustrations in the Ellesmere MS of *The Canterbury Tales*, now in the Henry E. Huntington Library and Art Gallery, San Marino, California.

The Franklin commends the Squire for his 'gentlemanly' tale, and goes on to say that he could wish his own son as worthy – but he is wilful and spendthrift. The Host punctures the Franklin's fawning words with a reminder that a tale is expected of him, too. The Franklin agrees to tell one as long as no-one expects fancy measures or colours of rhetoric. (A franklin was a freeholder, often a landowner of considerable wealth, but not a nobleman. Chaucer's Franklin is obviously a man with aspirations.)

*The Franklin's Tale.* Arveragus, a Breton knight, leaves his wife Dorigen to go to Britain in quest of knightly adventures. Dorigen loves her husband and accepts him as her lord. In the absence of Arveragus, Dorigen is wooed by Aurelius, a squire who has loved her for a long time; but she simply longs for her husband's return. She deals lightheartedly with Aurelius, telling him his love will be requited when the rocks which mar the Breton coast and make it dangerous are moved away. Arveragus returns; but Aurelius enlists the help of a magician, who for a thousand pounds agrees to create the illusion that the rocks have disappeared. This achieved, he reminds Dorigen of her words. She tells her husband of her lightly given vow; he

says that she must then honour it, however it was given. This display of honour shames Aurelius into withdrawing, and Dorigen and Arveragus are secure in their happiness once more. The magician, too, is honourable, waiving his fee from Aurelius since his illusion did not achieve its purpose. The Prologue to *The Franklin's Tale* suggests that it is based on a Breton lay but none exists that bears this out; the theme does occur in the stories of Boccaccio. The sixth group (F) ends with *The Franklin's Tale*: there is no interpolation between this and the next one given, *The Second Nun's Tale.* This was the *Life of St Cecily*, a version of a medieval Latin account of the martyrdom of St Cecilia and believed to be a work of Chaucer's 'second period' which he interpolated with a brief Prologue, an Invocation to Mary, and some verses on the name of Cecilia.

*The Second Nun's Tale.* Cecilia, of a noble Roman family, is betrothed to Valerian. She is a Christian and tells him at their marriage that she is guarded by an angel: if her husband touches her the angel will strike him dead. Valerian goes at her bidding to Urban (St Urban, a martyred pope of the 3rd century) to be baptised. This gives him enough grace to see the angel, who crowns them with flowers and instructs them to live pure lives. Tiburtius, Valerian's brother, is also converted, and the three come to the notice of the Prefect Almachius. He orders them to sacrifice to Jupiter or suffer death. The officer, Maximus, and the torturers arrive, but they are converted too. The two brothers are beheaded by Almachius' orders and Maximus is flogged to death. But Cecilia defies the Prefect, who orders her to be roasted in a bath-house. She remains unscathed, so the headsman strikes three times. But she lives for three days, surrounded by a grieving band of the faithful. Urban buries her body in Rome, in what is now Trastevere.

Chaucer's pilgrims are nearing Boughton-under-Blean when they are joined by a secular Canon and his Yeoman. They are welcomed by the Host, who in the Prologue to the next tale asks the Yeoman if his master has a story or two to tell. He learns that the Canon is an alchemist and a fraud, and that the Yeoman's discoloured skin results from his labours over fires and chemicals. The Canon overhears the Yeoman discussing him with the Host and orders him to be silent. But the Yeoman, encouraged by the Host, defies him, declaring that he will leave his service. The Canon, realizing that none of his secrets are safe now, rides off and leaves the pilgrims; the Yeoman curses him and the whole craft of alchemy before embarking on his tale.

*The Canon's Yeoman's Tale.* The Yeoman tells

of a secular canon who gulls a priest into helping him 'convert' quicksilver and copper into silver. Then he sells the priest the method for forty pounds – and disappears.

Chaucer's alchemical details are accurate and reliable; his obvious detestation for fraudulent characters and his knowledge of their practices comes from the years he spent as a Justice of the Peace in Kent. *The Canon's Yeoman's Tale* ends the seventh group (G); the narrative goes straight on to the Prologue to *The Manciple's Tale*.

The Host is in a merry mood and teases the Cook for being drunk. The Manciple does so too; the Cook swings a blow at him – but only succeeds in losing his seat and falling off his horse. The Host and the Manciple get him back into the saddle, and the Manciple gives him a good draught of wine. Then he tells his story. (A manciple was a man in charge of provisioning for such places as colleges and inns of court – Chaucer's Manciple is from the Inner Temple.)

*The Manciple's Tale*. The Manciple relates the story of Phoebus and his white bird who sings sweetly and has the gift of human speech. But one day the bird brings evil tidings: Phoebus' wife is adulterous. Phoebus kills his wife and also turns his wrath on the bird. He tears out the white feathers and deprives it of its sweet voice. Now it is only a crow. The story's origins are to be found in the Greek myth of Apollo and Coronis, well known to medieval Europe in the Latin version of Ovid. *The Manciple's Tale* is the single story of the eighth group (H).

The Manciple's story complete, the Host observes that the day is drawing to a close. He asks the Parson for a story, but is told quite firmly that he will get a discourse, if people want one – fables and romances are no part of a parson's life. The pilgrims ask the Host to persuade the Parson to proceed with a discourse at the close of day and the Parson agrees.

*The Parson's Tale*. The last of *The Canterbury Tales* is a prose sermon on penitence, the nature of the Seven Deadly Sins, and the best way of dealing with temptation. It has been suggested that the Parson's sermon represents the preparation for a Tale which Chaucer did not write. *The Canterbury Tales* closes (Group I) with the author's *Retractions*, in which he expresses the hope that, if many of the stories are found sinful and frivolous, he will be forgiven in the light of his authorship of many moral works.

**Canute, The Song of** (*or* **Canute Song**) A relic of verse from the Middle English period consisting of four lines said to have been sung by the king as he rowed past Ely. It was written down by a monk of Ely about 1167 and is an example of the first attempts to give rhythm and form in the native tongue.

**Can you Forgive Her?** The first of Anthony Trollope's 'Palliser', or political, novels, it was first published in 20 monthly parts, from January 1864 to August 1865. The fully formed characters of Plantagenet Palliser and Lady Glencora are here presented for the first time.

The novel is concerned with the stories of Alice Vavasor, Lady Glencora, and, to a lesser degree, Mrs Greenow. Mrs Greenow's would-be comic adventure with her two suitors has no real bearing on the events of the novel, and Sir Edward Marsh advised readers 'to skip it ruthlessly'.

Alice Vavasor had been half-engaged to her cousin, George, but had drawn back from full commitment because of his false and faithless nature. She has since accepted John Grey – but now finds herself uneasy with John's character; he is everything that George Vavasor is not, and Alice wonders if she can really aspire to the hand of a man like that. She agrees to go to Switzerland with Kate, George's sister, even though George is going to be their escort.

Alice's friend Lady Glencora McCluskie has fallen in love with Burgo Fitzgerald, and his family are eager promoters of the marriage – Glencora is an heiress. Her family have different ideas, however, and bully her into marrying the politically promising but personally insipid Plantagenet Palliser. Glencora and Alice commiserate: Alice has George back in her life, while Glencora is unhappy in the marriage into which she was coerced.

Alice's story is prominent, and a remarkable illustration of Trollope's art. Her indecision is really the book; it provokes George Vavasor to attempt murder, with John Grey as his victim. She marries John in the end, while Glencora is making the best of her loveless marriage. Burgo Fitzgerald and George Vavasor, their part done, now bow out of the story.

**Capgrave, John** 1393–1464. A native of King's Lynn in Norfolk, John Capgrave was ordained a priest in 1418: he was already an Augustinian friar and it is believed that he entered the order at an early age. Capgrave became Provincial of the Augustinian Friars in England in 1456. He wrote mostly in Latin – theological works, Bible commentaries, and a hagiography, *Nova Legenda Angliae*. There is also the life of his patron, *Vita Humfredi Ducis Glocestriae*, and a peculiar collection of lives of 'famous Henrys', *Liber De Illustribus Henricis* (he lived through the reigns of three of them).

John Capgrave's contribution to English literature was small but significant. Of little importance are the lives of St Katharine in verse, and St Gilbert of Sempringham in prose, and a guide for pilgrims to Rome; but he also wrote in English *The Chronicle of England*, which he presented to King Edward IV. *The Chronicle* is written in a straightforward unadorned style. It is a valuable authority on the reign of Henry IV but, perhaps more important, it is also one of the few 15th-century historical sources in English prose.

**Capote, Truman** 1924–84. Capote was born in New Orleans and lived there until 1942. *Other Voices, Other Rooms* (1948), his first novel, was a successful essay in an original surrealistic style on the theme of youthful innocence in a decadent world. *A Tree of Night and Other Stories* (1949) and *The Grass Harp* (1951) are set in the same Southern world but his next fiction, *Breakfast at Tiffany's* (1958), is a deft comedy of life in New York, where Capote had been living since leaving the South. *A Christmas Memory* (1966), a collection of short stories, was overshadowed in the same year by *In Cold Blood*. This was an exhaustive investigation of the murder of a Kansas family by two rootless young criminals. Capote wrote it in the form of a novel and included his conversations with the killers before their executions. The book was heavily promoted and became a best-seller. Truman Capote is also a very successful journalist and has published collections of his pieces as *Local Color* (1950), *Selected Writings* (1963), *The Dogs Bark* (1973), and *Music for Chameleons* (1981). *The Muses are Heard* (1956) is a diverting account of an officially sponsored tour of Russia by an American company playing Gershwin's *Porgy and Bess*.

**Captain Craig** A collection of poems by Edwin Arlington Robinson, first published in 1902. The title poem is a blank verse narrative about an old man whose company is prized by the young men of Tilbury Town because he has wit and courage and has lived a rich and varied life. He tells of himself in letters, sonnets, and ballads written to one of his young friends who has left Tilbury. Also in blank verse is the tale of 'Isaac and Archibald', two old farmers recalled from the poet's childhood, whose love and concern for each other is plain; it tells how they gave generously of their hard-earned wisdom.

**Captains Courageous** See **Kipling, Rudyard**.

**Captain Singleton, The Life, Adventures and Piracies of the Famous** A novel by Daniel Defoe, first published in 1720, it is a narrative of romantic adventure, told in the first person.

Singleton is kidnapped as a child and then sent to sea. Off Madagascar he and some of the other sailors mutiny, but their venture fails and they are put ashore. From there he reaches Africa, which he succeeds in crossing and where he obtains enough gold to live a comfortable life when he returns to England. He foolishly dissipates his wealth, however, and is obliged to return to sea; he becomes a pirate in the West Indies. Successful, Singleton ranges as far as the China Seas and once more acquires a considerable fortune. At the end of the novel he is home in England, his adventures over, and married to his shipmate's sister.

Defoe is at pains to present his hero as a man without 'sense of virtue or religion' because of his upbringing. Virtue is represented by his shipmate and friend William Walters, who is nevertheless a character of considerable charm. In the end it is William who is the saviour of Singleton, both morally and physically. The adventures are based on incidents culled from Defoe's wide reading and are superbly told; they include escapes, rescues, and bizarre encounters in the heart of Africa.

**Capulet** The Veronese family in Shakespeare's *Romeo and Juliet*, enemies of the Montagues. Juliet is a Capulet.

***Cardinall, The*** A tragedy by James Shirley, first produced in 1641 and first published in 1652.

The cardinal, ambitious for his family, obtains the King of Navarre's support for his plan to marry his nephew, Columbo, to the widowed duchess Rosaura. The duchess is the king's daughter-in-law; Columbo is the king's general. Rosaura is formally betrothed to Columbo but she loves Count Alvarez and takes advantage of Columbo's absence in the field to plead her case with the king. She succeeds but on her wedding night Columbo, back from the wars, murders Alvarez.

The vengeful duchess finds an ally in Hernando, a colonel whom Columbo has affronted in the field. Hernando contrives a duel with Columbo and kills him; the hand of Rosaura is to be his reward. The cardinal becomes the avenger now; he suspects Rosaura of complicity in his nephew's death so he attempts to violate her and then kill her. Hernando surprises the cardinal in his attempt but he is too late to save Rosaura, whom the cardinal has succeeded in poisoning by a trick. Hernando kills the cardinal and then takes his own life.

The date of the play makes it the last in a long line of English Renaissance tragedies and many scholars regard it as Shirley's best play. But its limitations are enough to keep it from being placed in the first rank. An outline of the plot indicates its derivative nature, an imitation of much that had gone before. Its best feature is the character of the cardinal, a shadow over the play's events until he occupies the centre of the stage to excellent effect in the last act.

**Carew, Thomas** 1594/5–1640. Carew was a Cavalier poet, of the company of Suckling and Lovelace, and one of the many poets of his time to show the influence of Ben Jonson and John Donne.

He was the son of Sir Matthew Carew, a Master in Chancery, and enjoyed the opportunities that his father's position made available; he graduated from Merton College in 1611 and entered the Inner Temple to study law in 1612. His father's fortunes, however, took a bad turn, and about 1613 Thomas Carew became secretary to Sir Dudley Carleton, ambassador to Venice and later to the Netherlands. He lost his post in 1616 for slandering his employer and Lady Carleton, and spent the next three years in idleness in London. His next employment was with Sir Edward Herbert (later Baron Herbert of Cherbury) during his time as ambassador to France. The five years with Herbert seem to have been well spent; his reputation as a poet and wit was sufficient, by the time he was 30, to ensure his acceptance at court and eventually a place in the royal household.

Carew's poems were not collected and published during his lifetime; a volume issued in the year of his death (1640) is incomplete. His early love poetry, particularly 'The Rapture', is generally regarded as his best, and while he does not rank as a major poet he is, like many of his contemporaries, deservedly remembered in anthologies. He was the author of a masque, *Coelum Britannicum*, performed for Charles I in 1634.

**Carey, Henry** *c.*1687–1743. Carey is remembered best for his song 'Sally in our Alley'. He was a Yorkshireman, who received his education and learned the rudiments of music at his mother's school; he earned his living as a music teacher. He published *Poems on Several Occasions* (1713) but acknowledged that poetry was a pastime for him, not a profession. He was also the author of a burlesque tragedy, *Chrononhotontho-logos*, produced in 1734 ('the Most Tragical Tragedy that ever was tragediz'd'). He invented the term 'Namby-Pamby' when he was being rude about Ambrose Philips.

**Carey, The Memoirs of Robert** Sir Robert Carey (*c.*1560–1639) became the 1st Earl of Monmouth

under James I. He rode posthaste from the deathbed of Elizabeth I, his cousin, and was the first Englishman to salute James as his king. His memoir is short but has some value for its account of Elizabeth's last days. It was completed about 1627 and published in 1759.

**Carleton, William** 1794–1869. William Carleton was the youngest of 14 children of a peasant of Prillisk, in Tyrone. His mother and father were a great repository of traditions, stories, and ballads which his mother sang to him. His parents wanted him to be a priest but they were too poor to afford him the necessary education, and after various employments he made his way to Dublin, where he was given a job on *The Christian Examiner* by Caesar Otway. Carleton contributed 30 sketches of Irish life to the periodical, and these were collected and published in 1832. *Traits and Stories of the Irish Peasantry* was an immediate success: a second series was published in 1833 and *Tales of Ireland* in 1834. He also wrote a number of novels, of which **Fardorougha, the Miser** (1839) earned the most praise, but they are too full of comment on action and motive to be readable today.

**Carlyle, Jane Welsh** 1801–66. Jane Baillie Welsh was born at Haddington, East Lothian, the only daughter of a doctor. She was a precocious child and could read Virgil in the original Latin at the age of nine. She inherited her father's estate at Craigenputtock in Dumfriesshire at the age of 18, and was introduced to Thomas Carlyle by her tutor and admirer Edward Irving. She married Carlyle in October 1826, and they lived at Craigenputtock for 15 years. The isolation and her husband's difficult and withdrawn character reduced her normally high spirits and provoked the ill health from which she suffered for the rest of her life. Nevertheless her marriage was a remarkable success inasmuch as, in her own words, 'I married for ambition'. Her husband became one of the most famous men in London and every person of distinction was a visitor to their house at Cheyne Row in Chelsea; she became the close friend of many and corresponded with them. After her death Carlyle missed her sorely; as a tribute he edited her correspondence and handed the completed work to his friend James Anthony Froude, the historian, leaving him to decide upon publication. Froude had no doubts and *The Letters and Memorials of Jane Welsh Carlyle* was published in 1883. Further collections have been edited by L. Huxley, *Jane Welsh Carlyle: Letters to Her Family 1839–1863* (1924), and by T. Scudder, *Letters of Jane Welsh Carlyle to Joseph*

*Neuberg 1848–1862* (1931). A selection by T. Bliss, *Jane Welsh Carlyle: A New Selection of Her Letters*, was published in 1950.

**Carlyle, Thomas** 1795–1881. The son of a stonemason of Ecclefechan in Dumfriesshire, Carlyle was the child of strictly Presbyterian parents. He attended the village school and Annan Grammar School and went to Edinburgh University at the age of 15. He was destined for the church; but after completing an arts course and beginning his studies for the ministry he suffered a spiritual crisis. He abandoned his studies and began to teach, first at Annan and later at Kirkcaldy, where he became friends with Edward Irving. But teaching did not suit Carlyle and he gave it up in 1818 in some despair; he was 23 and had already experienced two false directions. He returned to the university and tackled law, which he gave up in 1822. He earned a living as a private tutor and also began to write.

In 1817 Carlyle read Madame de Staël's *De l'Allemagne* and was arrested by the revelation of German art and letters. This enthusiasm served him well; he had been fortunate in being given the commission for several articles for Sir David Brewster's *Edinburgh Encyclopaedia*, and though hack work it was paid for and enabled Carlyle to use his leisure in the study of German literature and its great figures. His first considerable essay, on Goethe's *Faust*, was published in *The New Edinburgh Review* (April 1822). In the same year, through his friend Edward Irving, Carlyle gained an appointment as tutor which gave him a chance to see London and Paris and move in a new world. Meanwhile (1821) he had met Jane Welsh through Irving.

Carlyle's ambitious *Schiller's Life and Writings* (he was not in a position to undertake original research) was accepted by *The London Magazine* and the first instalment appeared in October 1823. By the time it was published in volume form (*The Life of Schiller*, 1825) Carlyle had earned a reputation; the study of Schiller was highly praised. Meanwhile he had turned his attention to something even more challenging, a translation of Goethe's *Wilhelm Meister*. *Wilhelm Meister's Apprenticeship A Novel from the German of Goethe* (1824) earned Carlyle the esteem of the ageing German master and the acquaintance of Coleridge, Hazlitt, and Thomas Campbell. *German Romance: Specimens of its Chief Authors with Biographical and Critical Notices* (1827) was four volumes containing work by Musaeus, La Motte Fouqué, Tieck, Hoffmann, and Richter and the latter part of Goethe's *Wilhelm Meister* (*Wilhelm Meister's Travels*).

*German Romance* did not reach a wide public but Carlyle was now contributing regularly to *The Edinburgh Review*, *Foreign Review*, and *Foreign Quarterly Review*; his fine essays on German literature formed the greater part of the collection *Critical and Miscellaneous Essays* (1838).

In 1826 Carlyle married Jane Welsh. She was a doctor's daughter of Haddington in East Lothian and owned a farm at Craigenputtock, in the moorlands of Dumfriesshire. After a brief period in Edinburgh the Carlyles moved to the farm, where they lived for six years. The marriage has been the subject of a great deal of speculation: that Jane was frigid; that Carlyle was intimidated by his sharp-witted and forthright spouse; that the wedding night was a disaster from which their intimate relationship never recovered; that Carlyle – and we only have Frank Harris's word for it – was impotent. It is known that Carlyle was a victim of chronic dyspepsia, but suffered from it long before he married Jane. Whatever the truth, the marriage endured in spite of its incompatibilities, and Carlyle mourned Jane for 15 years after her death in 1866.

At Craigenputtock he was occupied by the essays commissioned by Francis Jeffrey for *The Edinburgh Review*. Among these were 'The Signs of the Times' (1829) and 'Characteristics' (1831), which mark his progress as a social philosopher. He began a philosophical-autobiographical novel, *Wotton Reinfred*, which he never completed. He received an American visitor, Ralph Waldo Emerson, who became a lifelong friend and regarded Carlyle as his mentor. Another attempt at a philosophical work was successfully carried out and published in *Fraser's Magazine*, to which Carlyle had been contributing for some years. **Sartor Resartus** appeared in instalments from November 1833 to August 1834 and attracted almost no attention. Then it was published in volume form in the USA with a preface by Emerson in 1836, and in England in 1838. One reviewer, when the book appeared in *Fraser's*, had called it 'clotted nonsense' and the proprietors only agreed to publish it if Carlyle would accept less than his usual fee. It is unlikely that *Sartor Resartus* was or will ever be widely read. Its principal interest lies in what it shows of Carlyle's development as a writer and a social critic; the force of his moral indignation against the conditions of his age is unmistakable.

But by 1838 the situation changed: anything Carlyle had written attracted attention. In May 1834 Thomas and Jane had gone to London – the best place, he realized, for a writer to be. With what little capital they could muster they settled into the house at Cheyne Row in Chelsea that was to be their home for the rest of their lives. With occasional contributions to periodicals (there was no other income) Carlyle turned his back on the German romantics and settled down to write a history. *The French Revolution* is described by most critics as a romantic history; but whatever its historical faults it is a fascinating book with powerful narrative and vivid portraits and it brought success to Thomas Carlyle soon after it was published in 1837. Meanwhile, the great book behind him, he accepted a series of lectures to bolster the family exchequer and resumed periodical journalism, chiefly in *Fraser's Magazine* and *The Westminster Review*. He was the principal force that led to the founding of the London Library in 1840, and in the same year delivered the group of lectures **On Heroes, Hero-worship and the Heroic in History**. Meanwhile, his political convictions were given a positive statement in his essay *Chartism* (1839) and repeated at greater length in **Past and Present** (1843), a political essay written in the short space of seven weeks. Carlyle's advocacy of the strong man and leader, rather than the democratic process, as the best remedy for society's ills is expressed here for the first time.

Oliver Cromwell's Letters and Speeches, with Elucidations (1845) was in some ways a byproduct of Carlyle's uncertainty about another history, which might have taken the form of an account of the Civil War or of the Commonwealth. But the byproduct became the product: Carlyle felt there was nothing he could add to his portrait of the life and times of the Protector. Carlyle presented the man in a clear light and earned extravagant praise from his friend, biographer, and fellow historian James Anthony Froude. *Latter-Day Pamphlets* (1850) show Carlyle as political critic and social philosopher once more. His views were essentially those expressed in earlier writings but the *Pamphlets* were so splenetic that friends were alienated and admirers fell away. John Stuart Mill was completely estranged. The effect was worsened by Carlyle's inability to suggest what his fellow men should do while the better world remained so far in the distance. *The Life of John Sterling* (1851) is a biography of a friend whose promising career was cut short by consumption. Sterling was also the friend of Tennyson, John Stuart Mill, and Palgrave but left no mark on literature. The biography is chiefly interesting for what it tells us about Carlyle himself and for the portrait of Coleridge it contains.

Carlyle's most ambitious work had been in preparation for some years; the first volume of *The History of Friedrich II of Prussia, called Frederick the Great* was published in 1858, the sixth and last volume seven years later. The labour was immense and Carlyle visited the background of Frederick's life and reign with tireless industry. As factual history and vivid portraiture the book is difficult to fault and little new has since been written about the Prussian king. But he failed in his attempt to present a hardheaded practical realist as a heroic idealist. The book was published in Germany in the same year.

In 1865 Carlyle was invited by the students of Edinburgh University to become their Lord Rector and he delivered his inaugural speech on 2 April 1866. The honour meant a great deal to him, coming from his own country and the university where he had struggled so hard to find his true direction. But tragedy overshadowed it; Jane had slipped out of life while driving in her carriage in Kensington Gardens, and the news reached Carlyle while he was still in Scotland. He published one more book, *The Early Kings of Norway* (1875), but it is not a notable one. For the most part his writing was confined to letters to *The Times*; one of these, on behalf of Germany in her war against France, impressed Bismarck so much that the Order of Merit of Prussia was conferred on the author. Carlyle refused Disraeli's offer to secure him an honour in England. During his last few years Carlyle completely ceased writing, having lost the use of his right hand; he died on 4 February 1881. His friends wanted a burial at Westminster Abbey, but his wishes were honoured and his grave is in Ecclefechan.

Carlyle made his mark in English literature at a time when much that had seemed immutable was beginning to be questioned. Religion had received a severe hammering throughout the Western world, the natural sciences were developing, and the established church was in disarray; the condition of the poor represented a volcano that a few people realized could lead to bloody revolution in England. In New England the Transcendentalists were preparing a grave for Calvinism, which no longer had the answer to people's needs. In England Carlyle introduced a note of moral certainty that had nothing to do with politics, art, or intellectual aspiration and depended upon an ideal of virtue, service, and abnegation. His own character was full of contradiction and it is doubtful that he was ever happy, being tormented by what he saw as necessary of attainment by man for man, and the hopelessness of achieving such an end. He did not know how it could be achieved; the best he could do was to insist upon the necessity and thereby concentrate men's minds on what could be done as a beginning. The worst he could do (as he did in *Latter-Day Pamphlets*) was to confuse them; his views were so shifting and uncertain that they were probably of as little value, in the end, to his own times as they are to posterity. But he wrote well enough to make people feel and think, and if they learned to think beyond their own lives through reading his work, his was no small achievement.

The Centenary Edition of *The Collected Works of Thomas Carlyle* was edited by H. D. Traill (30 volumes, New York, 1896–1901; reprinted in London, 1968). Froude's biography was first published in 1882–84.

**Carpet-Bag** A shortlived (1851–53) humorous weekly published in Boston by B. P. Shillaber, who was the contributor of many of the popular 'Mrs Partington' sketches. (Mrs Partington was a New England version of Mrs Malaprop.) The magazine achieved a wide circulation and among those who appeared in print for the first time in its pages were Mark Twain, Artemus Ward, and G. H. Derby.

**Carroll, Lewis** 1832–98. The pseudonym by which Charles Lutwidge Dodgson is famous the world over. He was born at Daresbury in Cheshire, one of the rector's 11 children. As a child he lived in remote country places – after Daresbury his next home was Croft in Yorkshire – and depended very much on the company of his brothers and sisters. He displayed an early talent for 'nonsense' in writing and composed a series of rules for railway travellers (trains were as exotic then as spaceships are now) at the age of eight. Throughout his schooldays (he hated his three years at Rugby) and his first term at Oxford, he spent much spare time on the family 'magazine', contributing both text and pictures.

He was a successful scholar, took a distinguished degree in mathematics at Christ Church, and became senior student and lecturer in 1855. He contributed humorous poems and parodies to periodicals and for one of these, *The Train*, he used the pseudonym Carolus Ludovicus (Charles Lutwidge or Ludwig). Later he reversed it and retranslated it as Lewis Carroll.

As a mathematician Charles Dodgson published a formidable body of work but, a very shy man with a stammer, he always responded to children. He was immediately at ease with them and in their company his stammer left him. Among the children who became his friends were those of George MacDonald and the Dean of Christ Church, Henry George Liddell. The second Liddell child was a girl named Alice, three

years old. Six years later he told the Liddell children, after a boating party, the story of 'Alice's adventures underground', and undertook to write it out for Alice. This was completed and illustrated by 1863 and one day Henry Kingsley, calling on the Liddells, saw the book in the drawing room. He picked it up – and didn't put it down again until he'd finished it, enchanted. He told Alice's mother that it should be published and she told the author what Kingsley had said.

Dodgson took some convincing, but after revising the text, he sent it to Macmillan. *Alice's Adventures in Wonderland*, with illustrations by Sir John Tenniel, was published in 1865, three years after the boating party. It was a success from the beginning. *Through the Looking Glass* was begun in 1868, after an encounter in Onslow Square with a distant cousin, a little girl whose name, fortuitously, proved to be Alice Raikes. The book was published for Christmas in 1871 and was a greater success even than the original *Alice*. Two classics, for children of every age and for all adults who retain a particle of wonder in their character, had entered the language. The understanding and love of children had been combined with the precision of a mathematician to produce two wonderful books that, as the author himself said, 'do not teach anything at all.'

He was never to reach that level again, though he worked hard on *Rhyme? and Reason?* (1883)

Alice and the Queen of Hearts. One of Sir John Tenniel's illustrations for *Alice's Adventures in Wonderland*.

and *Sylvie and Bruno* (1889). The latter was developed from a fairy tale, *Bruno's Revenge*, which he contributed to *Aunt Judy's Magazine* in 1867. Both books, however, contain some charming things. A complete success, on the other hand, was *The Hunting of the Snark* (1876), a long nonsense poem, which is both funny and subtle, about the elusive Snark who proves to be a Boojum. Mention should be made, perhaps, of Dodgson's most highly regarded mathematical treatise, *Euclid and his Modern Rivals*, published in 1879.

**Carton, Sydney** In Dickens's novel *A Tale of Two Cities*, the cynical and dissolute barrister who loves Lucie Manette and gives his life to ensure her happiness.

**Cartwright, William** 1611–43. Cartwright enjoyed a considerable success among his contemporaries but posterity has been less kind and his work is only known to students of 17th-century literature. He was educated at Westminster School and went up to Christ Church, Oxford, in 1628; he spent the rest of his short life there. He wrote four plays, intended for academic performance: *The Ordinary or The City Cozener* (1634) shows clearly the influence of Ben Jonson; *The Lady Errant*, *The Royall Slave*, and *The Siedge or Love's Convert* were published in 1651. *The Royall Slave*, with designs by Inigo Jones and music by Henry Lawes, was acted for King Charles I and Henrietta Maria at Oxford in 1636 and proved a great success. Cartwright took holy orders in 1638 and wrote no more plays but he became a celebrated preacher; in 1642 he became reader in metaphysics to the university. A Royalist, Cartwright preached at Oxford before the king after the Battle of Edgehill. The edition of his works published in 1651 contained 51 commendatory verses by writers of the day, including Izaak Walton and Henry Vaughan. *The Plays and Poems of William Cartwright* were collected and edited by G. Blakemore Evans and published in 1951.

**Cary, Henry Francis** 1772–1844. The first notable translator of Dante into English, Cary was born in Gibraltar, where his father was an army officer. After grammar school he completed his education at Christ Church, Oxford, and was ordained in 1796. He became vicar of Abbot's Bromley in Staffordshire and an assistant librarian at the British Museum (1826–37). His translation of the *Divina Commedia* interested no one in England, apparently, so he was obliged to publish himself the *Inferno* (1805–06) and the *Purgatorio* and *Paradiso* (1814). Cary published his translation with the Italian text on the opposite page, plus copious notes and a life of the poet. It was the first time that the Italian text had been published in England. The translation was praised by Coleridge and this led Taylor and Hessey, publishers of Keats and John Clare, to publish a superior edition (1819) which made Cary famous. Other works by Cary were translations of Pindar and *The Birds* of Aristophanes, a series of articles on early French poetry for *The London Magazine*, and editions of Milton, Pope, Thomson, Young, and Cowper.

**Cary, (Arthur) Joyce (Lunel)** 1888–1957. Joyce Cary was born in Londonderry, Northern Ireland, and educated at Tunbridge Wells and Clifton College. He went on to Trinity College, Oxford, after studying art in Edinburgh and Paris (1904–09). In 1912 he went to Montenegro to serve with a British Red Cross unit in the Balkan Wars; then he went to Nigeria as a district magistrate and administrative officer, and was wounded while serving with the Nigerian Regiment in the Cameroons during World War I.

Cary resigned from the colonial service in 1920 and settled down in Oxford, where he applied himself to learning the novelist's art: his only published work so far had been a small volume, *Verse* (1908), signed by Arthur Cary. He adopted his mother's surname when he published his first novel in 1932, *Aissa Saved*, at the age of 44. The novel of the African girl and the missionaries was the first of four novels set in West Africa; the others were *An American Visitor* (1933), *The African Witch* (1936), and *Mister Johnson* (1939), the most highly regarded of them. Johnson is an African clerk from a mission school who identifies himself with the White man's way of life: the resident magistrate, Rudbeck, has a passion for cutting roads through the bush. Johnson attaches himself to Rudbeck and helps him further his schemes; but his methods are dubious and Rudbeck is eventually obliged to fire him. In the end he is his executioner, to save him from the gallows. Rudbeck's benevolence towards the mission-school boy begins a tragedy which arises from each man's acceptance of the other's presentation of himself. The consequence of this unconscious effort on the part of a human being 'to create a universe which suits his feelings' was a stated theme of Cary's; he later demonstrated his ability to use it for comedy. Also written at this time was the period piece *Castle Corner* (1938), which the author regarded as a failure.

After his African novels Cary wrote two about children, *Charley is My Darling* (1940), about an evacuee in wartime England, and *The House of*

*Children* (1941), which describes life among the children of a wealthy house in Northern Ireland during the 1890s. *Herself Surprised* (1941), *To Be a Pilgrim* (1942), and *The Horse's Mouth* (1944) form a trilogy and are Cary's strongest claim to a permanent place in English letters. Two further novels, *The Moonlight* (1946) and *A Fearful Joy* (1949), were followed by a second trilogy, *Prisoner of Grace* (1952), *Except the Lord* (1953), and *Not Honour More* (1955), about a politician, Chester Nimmo, following the pattern of the first trilogy with rather less success. *The Captive and the Free* (published posthumously, 1959) was edited by Winifred Davin from an unfinished manuscript and is a novel about a faith healer.

*Herself Surprised* is the story of Sara, a servant in a rich house who marries Matthew Monday, one of the sons. Matt is very jealous of Sara, who – though blameless – is powerfully aware of Gulley Jimson, a gifted painter and amoral scrounger to whom Matt has given studio space in the house. Sara becomes Jimson's mistress after her husband dies, but leaves him when he becomes violent; he has scrounged on her too, and she is in debt. She goes to work for Wilcher, an elderly solicitor with an urge for young girls. Sara is about to marry Wilcher when she is arrested for theft: she has been stealing small articles from Wilcher's house and his daughter has discovered this; she has also been in trouble through Jimson, passing bad cheques to keep going. Sara writes her story from prison: she is warm, womanly, and too generous for her own good, but the author makes her credible. *To Be a Pilgrim* is Wilcher's story. After Sara has been sent to prison he is in the care of his niece Ann at Tolbrook Manor in Devon. He looks back over his life, and the author creates a brilliant picture of a cranky old man whose emotional life has been repressed and would like nothing better than to join Sara, who never denied him warmth and sympathy. The comedy is sustained on a high level, much of it arising from Wilcher's brothers and sisters, all of them stronger characters than he. *The Horse's Mouth* is Gulley Jimson's story and here Cary's knowledge of art supports the novel superbly. Jimson has just emerged from prison; he is as he was in *Herself Surprised* but older and dirtier and with no scruples about anything but the pursuit of his art. This picaresque novel succeeds brilliantly while the reader's sympathy for Jimson is held, and becomes wearisome when it is not; for many the third novel is the finest of the trilogy.

Cary wrote two books about Africa, *The Case for African Freedom* (1941) and *Britain and West Africa* (1946), and two books of verse, *Marching Soldier* (1945) and *The Drunken Sailor: A Ballad-Epic* (1947). *Spring Song* (published posthumously, 1960) is a book of five short stories.

**Casaubon, Rev Edward** In George Eliot's *Middlemarch*, the elderly pedant who marries Dorothea Brooke. He is totally selfish and finally spiteful and mean when he realizes that Dorothea has warm feelings for his cousin, Will Ladislaw.

**Casby, Christopher** In Dickens's *Little Dorrit*, the rapacious landlord of Bleeding Heart Yard, the squalid tenement where he likes to appear as a benevolent patriarch, while Mr Pancks has the task of extracting the rents from the hard-pressed tenants.

**Cassio, Michael** The freshly promoted lieutenant to the Moor in Shakespeare's *Othello*. The appointment provokes the sour and envious Iago (who has been passed over) to set in motion the chain of events that lead to Othello's destruction. He survives Roderigo's attempt on his life – planned by Iago – and confirms Iago's guilt.

**Cassius** In Shakespeare's *Julius Caesar*, the leading spirit in the conspiracy to murder Caesar. A republican, he is alarmed by Caesar's power and persuades Brutus that Caesar's ambitions will lead him to assume a crown. He takes his own life when defeated at the Battle of Philippi. Cassius is in many ways the most interesting character in the play, as John Gielgud demonstrated in a memorable performance. His republican sentiments are tinged with jealousy and the scene between him and Brutus at Sardis (Act IV) reveals him to have an 'itching palm'. A more experienced soldier than Brutus, he advises against the encounter at Philippi.

***Castle Dangerous*** The last novel by Sir Walter Scott, in the fourth series of *Tales of My Landlord*. It is an uninteresting example of Scott's work, a tale of the defence of Douglas Castle against Robert the Bruce and the Black Douglas in 1306. It was published in 1832, the year of Sir Walter's death.

***Castle of Indolence, The*** A romantic allegory by James Thomson, written in Spenserian stanzas, in two cantos, first published in 1748. The poet had begun its composition 15 years before, in 1733, and it is acknowledged his most consistent and polished poem. The first canto tells of the wizard, Indolence, and the castle into which he lures world-weary pilgrims. There they surrender to idleness in an atmosphere of delicious ease until their degeneration leads to their rejection; they are thrown into dungeons and abandoned. The second canto tells of the Knight of Arts and

Industry, his overthrowing of the wizard Indolence, and his destruction of the castle. Thomson introduces himself ('A bard here dwelt, more fat than bard beseems') and a number of his friends into the action of the first canto.

**Castle of Otranto, The,** *A Gothic Story*. A novel by Horace Walpole, first published in 1765. In the first edition the novel was offered as a translation 'From the Original Italian of Onuphrio Muralto, Canon of the Church of St Nicholas at Otranto' and the translator named as 'William Marshall, Gent.'. Walpole acknowledged his authorship in the second edition, published in the same year. The story is set in the 13th century.

Manfred, Prince of Otranto, is the grandson of a usurper and has no lawful claim to the realm; his grandfather had poisoned the rightful prince, Alfonso. A strange prophecy proclaimed that the usurpers would remain in power as long as they had male issue to continue their line and while the castle remained large enough to hold the lawful ruler. Manfred has arranged the marriage of his son, Conrad, to the beautiful Isabella, daughter of the Marquis of Vicenzo; but on the night before the wedding Conrad meets with a mysterious – and fatal – accident. Manfred knows that a gigantic figure haunts the castle and, now suddenly bereft of an heir, he determines to marry Isabella himself and beget another. He sets in motion plans to divorce his wife but Isabella, who is terrified of Manfred, escapes from the castle of Otranto with the help of a young peasant, Theodore, who is under suspicion of being connected in some way with Conrad's death. Manfred's daughter, Matilda, loves the handsome peasant, and when he is arrested and imprisoned she releases him. Manfred is convinced that Isabella and Theodore are in love; he learns that Theodore is keeping a tryst by Alfonso's tomb. He goes there, stabs the lady – and discovers that he has murdered his daughter Matilda. The ghost of Alfonso, now grown too enormous to be contained by the castle, throws it down and rises from the ruins. Manfred confesses the usurpation by his family, and the ghost proclaims Theodore the lawful prince. Theodore and Isabella are married at the end of the tale.

Walpole wrote his novel during the summer of 1764 at his mock-Gothic home in Twickenham and produced the first novel of terror in English fiction. In spite of impressive moments it has little, now, to recommend it. But every form in art has to begin somewhere and it is remarkable that a bad novel should have started so much; fiction was given a direction which was to be explored to far better effect by others. The author acknowledged that he wrote it in reaction to Samuel Richardson's lengthy exploration of domestic sentiment and, while the execution was bungled on the whole, there was nothing wrong with the idea. The book was translated into French and Italian and became popular in Germany.

*The Castle of Otranto* is published in modern editions in Everyman's Library, in the Penguin English Library *Three Gothic Novels*, and in the Oxford English Novels series, edited by W. S. Lewis (1964).

**Castle Rackrent**   A novel by Maria Edgeworth, first published in 1801. It tells the story of the Rackrent family on the way to ruin; the storyteller is Thady Quirk, the steward of the property, who begins with the first Rackrent he knew, the hard-drinking Sir Patrick. The story comes to an end with the last, Sir Condy, who runs through the remnants of the family property and loses it to Thady Quirk's son, a sharp-minded unscrupulous attorney. The novel is a remarkable picture of the profligate landlord in Ireland in the 18th century.

**Castle Richmond**   A novel by Anthony Trollope, first published in 1860. It is set in Ireland, which Trollope knew well and used as the setting for his early fiction. More important, perhaps, was the author's first-hand knowledge of Ireland during the catastrophic famine. Anthony Trollope was English, a civil servant, and an acute observer. A contemporary review in the *Athenaeum* says that his remarks 'are, on the whole, true and judicious': the *Spectator* comments on his 'judicious reticence'. But the *Dublin Review*, 12 years later, praised the book for its truthful reporting in forthright terms.

The story concerns the Fitzgeralds, Owen and Herbert; the former is sober and virtuous, the latter a scamp who is loved by both Clara – a weak heroine – and her mother, the Countess of Desmond, a powerful villainess.

Trollope's own comment on *Castle Richmond* in his *Autobiography* runs: 'The scene is laid in Ireland, during the famine; and I am well aware now (twenty-three years later) that English readers no longer like Irish stories.' The sentence is fascinating for what it implies about the attitudes of Victorian England toward Ireland: the book did not receive bad notices – quite the contrary; but the public registered it hardly at all.

**Castlewood, Beatrix**   In Thackeray's *Henry Esmond*, the beautiful and selfish cousin of the hero – whom she scorns, believing him illegitimate. She also features, a generation later, in *The Virginians* as Baroness Bernstein.

**Castlewood, Rachel, Lady**  In Thackeray's *Henry Esmond*, the wife of the 4th Viscount (Henry Esmond is supposedly the illegitimate son of the 3rd Viscount). She falls in love with Henry, but she is older than he and keeps silent when he becomes infatuated with her daughter, Beatrix.

**Cathedral, The**  A poem by James Russell Lowell, first published in 1869. In blank verse, the poet describes a day at Chartres and, in the shadow of the great cathedral, ponders the 19th-century dilemma of science in apparent opposition to religion. The poet reconciles the two in his own terms, accepting science as evidence of progress, while the deity is a depersonalized God whose presence is manifest in every example of sweetness and nobility.

**Cather, Willa (Sibert)**  1873–1947.  Willa Cather was born in Virginia but grew up in Nebraska, where her family had emigrated when she was nine years old. She was educated at the University of Nebraska and graduated in 1895. She taught for a short time before finding herself as a writer, mainly through journalism. Her first published work was a book of poems, *April Twilights* (1903); a book of short stories, *The Troll Garden*, followed in 1905. She joined the staff of *McClure's Magazine* in New York in 1906 and stayed for six years, leaving when her first novel, *Alexander's Bridge*, was published in 1912. Sarah Orne Jewett, whom she admired, advised her to use her own background and in 1913 Willa Cather published *O Pioneers!*, the first of her notable novels about frontier and immigrant life. She was to explore various aspects of the subject and its people, particularly the women, to excellent purpose in a distinguished career.

*The Song of the Lark* (1915) and *My Antonia* (1918) are built around the lives of women but in *One of Ours* (1922) the central character is a man who longs to escape from the life of the Midwest farms. The book was well received and won her the Pulitzer Prize but is not now seen as one of her better novels. In *A Lost Lady* (1923), *The Professor's House* (1925), and *My Mortal Enemy* (1926) Willa Cather can be seen to have acknowledged the change in life in what was, in her youth, virtually pioneer country; her characterization becomes subtler and her characters' lives more complex. An interest in religion, discernible in *The Professor's House*, led to her famous **Death Comes for the Archbishop** (1927), a novel about the work of the Catholic Church in

New Mexico, and to *Shadows on the Rock* (1931), set in Quebec in the 17th century. *Lucy Gayheart* (1935) and **Sapphira and the Slave Girl** (1940) completed her novels; *Youth and the Bright Medusa* (1920) is a book of short stories and *Obscure Destinies* (1932) comprises three short novels of life in small communities in the Midwest. In *Not Under Forty* (1936) Willa Cather presents her ideas of fiction and acknowledges the writers who influenced her work, among them Flaubert, Henry James, and Sarah Orne Jewett.

Willa Cather, like her distinguished contemporary Ellen Glasgow, was a regional novelist only inasmuch as her richest expression was prompted by a thorough knowledge of the country in which she found her characters; it is the characters who stay in the mind, though the vividly depicted background is an added reward for the reader. There is an unmistakable note of regret in her novels, too; the feeling that unspoiled values give way to modern life too swiftly, so that a traditional life with solid standards has no chance to develop and establish itself. In this respect she presents a fascinating contrast to Ellen Glasgow, who found traditional life based on dubious values – and subjected it to a searching examination.

**Catherine,** *a Story, by Ikey Solomons, Esq., junior.* A novel by W. M. Thackeray, first published in *Fraser's Magazine* (May 1839 to February 1840).

A tale of criminal life, based on the career of Catherine Hayes, who was executed in 1726, found guilty of murdering her husband. Thackeray's story was written in reaction to the sentimentalizing of criminals in the fiction of his time.

**Cathleen ni Houlihan**  See **Yeats, William Butler**.

**Catiline his Conspiracy**  A tragedy by Ben Jonson, first produced in 1611 and published in the same year. The play, rarely revived, follows the events of Roman history in the days of the republic, specifically the conspiracy of 63 BC. Catiline (Lucius Sergius Catilina) was a patrician who had been Praetor and Governor of Africa but whose dissolute life ruined him financially. He was defeated when he stood for the consulship in 64 BC, the votes going to Cicero and Antonius. Catiline renewed his candidature in the following year but was again rejected. Jonson's play begins at this point; the impoverished and desperate Catiline, with the secret encouragement of Caesar and Crassus, is preparing to overthrow the government. But Cicero is warned by Fulvia of the intention to assassinate him as the first part of the conspiracy; he summons the Senate and accuses Catiline, who immediately leaves the city for Faesulae, where his supporters have raised an army. Proof is delivered to Cicero by the ambassadors of the Allobroges (a Gallic tribe), who had been approached by Catiline for aid. The evidence is submitted to the Senate; Catiline and the other conspirators are sentenced to death. However, Catiline is defeated and killed in battle by the government general, Petreius.

**Catnach, James** 1792–1841. Catnach, a printer's son, was born at Alnwick in Northumberland. He went to London and in 1813 became a printer himself at Seven Dials, specializing in popular literature, an original and important enterprise for that period. His broadsheets and street ballads are an important source of information on the life of working people in the early 19th century and contained some vivid crime reporting – the confession of Corder, in the Red Barn case, sold over a million copies. Catnach published a burlesque of *Pierce Egan's Life in London* in 1820.

**Cato** A tragedy in blank verse by Joseph Addison, first produced in 1713 and first published in the same year. It enjoyed considerable success in the climate of the time; Queen Anne was dying and the succession was a question that divided the country into two opposing parties. The play has not been revived and is now better known for quotations such as 'Tis not in mortals to command success, But we'll do more, Sempronius; we'll deserve it.' The play is based on the last weeks of the life of Cato (Marcus Porcius Cato, the republican), besieged in Utica by Caesar in 46 BC. Cato has been betrayed by Sempronius, a senator, and the Numidian general, Syphax. Faithful to him is Juba, Prince of Numidia. Addison introduces romantic interest in the character of Marcia, Cato's daughter, who is loved by Juba, and in the rivalry of Cato's two sons for the hand of Lucia.

**Cave, Edward** See *Gentleman's Magazine, The*.

**Cavendish, George** 1500–c.1561. A gentleman-usher of Cardinal Wolsey's household, Cavendish is accorded the honour of being the first true biographer in English literature. His brother was William Cavendish, who grew rich in the despoiling of the Catholic Church, married Bess of Hardwick, and founded the ducal houses of Devonshire and Newcastle.

George Cavendish entered the cardinal's service some time in the early 1520s, after the Field of the Cloth of Gold, and stayed with him until he died at Leicester Abbey. Cavendish then retired from public life and towards the end of 1554, during the reign of Mary (Cavendish never abandoned his Catholic faith), began his life of Wolsey. He completed it in 1558, three years before he died and before Catholic England passed away forever. *Thomas Wolsey late Cardinal his Life and Death* was not published until 1641 (in a garbled version) but was widely read in manuscript – Shakespeare obviously knew it well, so did John Stow. A. F. Pollard, the modern historian of the Tudor period, described Cavendish's biography as 'history as it appears to a gentleman-usher' and as a work of history the description is fairly earned. There was much that a gentleman-usher was not privy to; but there were many occasions, crucial ones, when Cavendish was with his master and his writing is equal to it. Some of his descriptions are tedious but his picture of the cardinal at the summit of his power and in his descent into disgrace is arresting and vivid.

R. S. Sylvester edited Cavendish's biography for the Early English Text Society in 1959. Roger Lockyer's edition was published in 1962.

**Caxton, William** c.1421–91. England's first printer was born in the Weald of Kent and apprenticed to Robert Large, a London cloth merchant of considerable wealth and influence, in 1438. Robert Large died in 1441, and Caxton seems to have gone to Bruges, in the Low Countries – information about this part of his life is scanty. But it seems certain that he prospered: he was governor of the English merchants in Flanders by 1463 and in 1469 entered the service of Margaret Duchess of Burgundy, sister of Edward IV. He first saw a printing press at Cologne in 1471, the most important event of his life, and he helped in the work as a means of learning the craft. He had in fact begun to write before he went to Cologne, working from 1469 on a translation of the French romance *Le Recueil des Histoires de Troie*. Back in Bruges he set about establishing a press of his own in collaboration with the Flemish illuminator Colard Mansion.

The first book printed by Caxton at Bruges was his own translation, *Recuyell of the Histories of Troy* (1474). He returned to England in 1476 and set up his press in a house in the precincts of Westminster Abbey. His enterprise won the favour of Edward IV and royal approval continued under the Tudors. Caxton's press published 80 different books, including many translations from the French by himself and others. There were works by Lydgate; Chaucer (including two editions of *The Canterbury Tales*,

The earliest representation of a printing press appears in this illustration from *La Grat Danse Macabre*, Lyons 1499.

the second with a prologue by Caxton himself, explaining how a reader had secured for him a manuscript of the book from which he prepared his new uncorrupt edition); Gower; *The Golden Legend* in his own translation; and, perhaps of the greatest importance, Malory's *Le Morte Darthur*: Caxton's was the definitive text for nearly three centuries since until 1934 no manuscript of the work was known to exist.

Caxton was very much a man of letters and what he printed displayed his own tastes – he had no one to dissuade him. The number of printed books that entered circulation on account of his European background and his knowledge of French and Latin must have had a considerable influence on the literature of his day. He admired Chaucer unreservedly and placed a memorial tablet to him in Westminster Abbey.

Following Caxton, printing presses were established at Oxford (1478) and St Albans (1479); the first in London was established by John Lettou (1480) under the patronage of William Wilcock.

***Cecilia**, or Memoirs of an Heiress.* A novel by Fanny Burney, first published in 1782.

The heroine, Cecilia Beverley, inherits a large fortune, on condition that the man she marries take her surname and that, until she comes of age, she live in the care of one of her guardians. There are three of these: Harrel, Briggs, and the Hon Compton Delvile. Harrel is a gambler, who attempts to exploit Cecilia to support his way of life (later, to save himself from ruin). After an embarrassing scene at Vauxhall Gardens Harrel shoots himself in the presence of his wife and Cecilia. Briggs proves to be impossibly vulgar and greedy (Fanny Burney dissects his character

with elegant relish and a sharp eye) and Cecilia goes to live in the house of the third. Compton Delvile is arrogant, insufferably proud, and treats Cecilia with contempt; he is furious when his son, Mortimer, falls in love with her and outraged at the idea that his son should forswear his name.

Cecilia resolves to give up her inheritance in order to marry Mortimer and the young couple plan their wedding. But their plans are wrecked by Monckton, whom Cecilia had believed her friend. The fact is Monckton has had his own eye on the fortune that would come with Cecilia's hand; he is married to an older woman and plans on keeping Cecilia unmarried until the way is clear for him. Fortunately, Monckton's plans are revealed and the objections of old Delvile are eventually overcome.

***Celebrated Jumping Frog of Calaveras County, The*** A sketch by Mark Twain, first published in the New York *Saturday Press* in 1865. It was reprinted as the title piece in the collection of sketches that made up Twain's first published book (1867). The story was an old tale related in California: how the champion jumping frog, Dan'l Webster, was defeated by one owned by a stranger. His owner, Jim Smiley, discovers after the race that the stranger had managed to fill Dan'l Webster's gullet with quail shot.

**Celestial City, the** The goal of Christian's pilgrimage, i.e. Heaven, in John Bunyan's *The Pilgrim's Progress*.

**Celia** Rosalind's cousin in Shakespeare's *As You Like It*. When her father, the usurping duke, banishes Rosalind she goes with her to the Forest of Arden, assuming the character of Aliena, sister to Ganymede. Oliver, the elder brother of Orlando, falls in love with her.

***Cenci, The*** A tragedy in five acts by Percy Bysshe Shelley, first published in 1819. It was given its first stage production by the Shelley Society in 1886 but is generally regarded as a poem to be read, not as a successful stage drama. Shelley sent it to the manager of Covent Garden, where a great tragic actress, Eliza O'Neill, might have played the part of Beatrice Cenci. However, the play was refused.

The Cenci were a noble Roman family and the events upon which the play is based took place in the late 16th century. Count Francesco Cenci was a vicious and debauched man who tyrannized his children. Beatrice later insisted at her trial that her father had attempted to rape her and had virtually imprisoned her and her stepmother Lucrezia in an isolated castle. Cenci was murdered by hired assassins, one of whom revealed the details of a plot by Lucrezia and Beatrice and her brothers, and the whole family were brought to trial. Giovanni, Beatrice, and Lucrezia were condemned to death and the younger brother, Bernardo, to the galleys for life. The pope, Clement VIII, refused to pardon them in spite of Cenci's reputation; it was said that the wealth of the Cenci would pass into papal hands by the destruction of the family, hence his upholding of the sentence. The executions took place on 11 September 1599. Shelley makes Beatrice, whose portrait by Guido Reni he had seen in the Colonna palace in Rome, the central figure of his tragedy.

**Centlivre, Susannah** *c.*1667–1723. Susannah Freeman was probably born at Holbeach, Lincolnshire, and was first married at the age of 16 and twice widowed before her marriage to Joseph Centlivre in 1706. She became an actress, achieved no great distinction – she was happiest in the men's parts, which suited her figure – and began writing for the stage under her second married name, Susannah Carroll. She saw 7 of her plays produced before her marriage to Centlivre (he was Queen Anne's cook at Windsor) and another 11 after it.

Mrs Centlivre had a sense of the stage and practically nothing else; her work was popular in her time and provided useful vehicles for actors but it is never revived. Among her 18 plays may be mentioned *The Gamester* (January 1705, at Lincoln's Inn Fields), adapted from *Le Joueur* by Jean-François Regnard; *The Wonder: A Woman Keeps a Secret* (April 1714, Drury Lane); and *A Bold Stroke for a Wife* (February 1718, Lincoln's Inn Fields). The last two provided successful parts for David Garrick and Anne Oldfield.

**Cerimon** In Shakespeare's *Pericles, Prince of Tyre*, the Ephesian physician who revives the apparently dead Thaisa.

**Chaffanbrass, Mr** The lawyer created by Anthony Trollope, who first appears in *The Three Clerks*, and reappears in *Orley Farm*. He is perhaps at his most vivid in *Phineas Redux*; he defends Phineas Finn when the latter is charged with the murder of Bonteen.

**Chainbearer, The** A novel by James Fenimore Cooper, first published in 1845. It was the second novel of the trilogy called the *Littlepage Manuscripts*.

Cornelius and Anneke Littlepage, of the Mooseridge and Ravensnest frontier estates, live at Satanstoe in Westchester county. The period is the close of the War of Independence and their son, Mordaunt, has been educated at Princeton and has served as an ensign. His comrade in arms was Andries Coejemans, a surveyor, who is employed by Mordaunt's father on his frontier estates. Andries' nickname is Chainbearer.

Mordaunt joins Chainbearer on the frontier and falls in love with his friend's niece, Dus Malbone. He also becomes friends with the Onondaga scout, Susquesus, who had guided Mordaunt's father to safety during the war with the French. A greedy squatter, Aaron Thousandacres, is suspected of plundering the timber at Ravensnest and Mordaunt and Susquesus go to spy on him to gain proof. But Thousandacres is too wily and succeeds in capturing them.

Susquesus escapes from Thousandacres and takes the news to Chainbearer, who goes to try and deal with the squatter – against whom there is no real proof. Thousandacres' demand that Dus shall marry his son outrages Chainbearer: he refuses to consider it and an altercation follows which becomes violent and the squatter kills Chainbearer.

Mordaunt is rescued and a posse comes to bring Thousandacres to justice. He resists and is killed. The story closes with the betrothal of Dus and Mordaunt; it continues in *The Redskins*.

**Chamberlayne, William** 1619–89. A minor Caroline poet, Chamberlayne was a physician at Shaftesbury in Dorset. He was the author of *Pharonnida* (1659), a historical romance in couplets – the poetic fashion of his day – which runs to 14,000 lines. His play *Love's Victory* was published in 1658. See also **seventeenth-century verse romances**.

*Chance: A Tale in Two Parts*. A novel by Joseph Conrad, first published in *The New York Herald* (21 January–30 June 1912) and in volume form in 1913. It was Conrad's first commercial success, and a bestseller in the USA and England. Conrad employs his narrator, Marlow, in this novel, which tells the story of Flora de Barral, daughter of an over-ambitious financier who goes to prison for fraud. Flora is motherless and has been placed in the care of a governess, who has been using her wealthy charge as bait to ensnare a man of her own. When de Barral is ruined, the governess abuses the girl and then deserts her. Flora, completely demoralized, is befriended by Mr and Mrs Fyne, and pulled out of her depression by Captain Anthony, Mrs Fyne's brother, who persuades Flora to elope with him. They marry and collect de Barral upon his release from prison; then all three live on board Anthony's ship *Ferndale*. But Anthony's love and best intentions do not prevail: the Fynes are resentful of Flora's elopement, and convince him that Flora is only marrying him as a refuge.

De Barral, unbalanced by his experiences, regards his daughter's marriage as a betrayal. Anthony's behaviour toward Flora is that of a perfect knight and the marriage is not consummated; but de Barral attempts to poison him. He is detected by Powell, the second mate, and takes the poison himself, and after that Flora and Anthony come together. Some years later the *Ferndale* collides with another ship; Powell and Flora are among the survivors but Anthony goes down with his ship. At the end of the novel the sympathetic Powell is wooing Flora and there is a prospect of happiness.

**Chances, The** A comedy by John Fletcher. The date of the first production is unknown; the first published version of 1647 contains a prologue and an epilogue written by another hand. The play is based on a novel by Cervantes; the 'chances' are the coincidences and complications that beset Constantia and the Duke of Ferrara when they decide to elope. Others concerned are Vecchio, a wizard, Dame Gillian, the hostess, and two Spanish gallants, Don John and Don Frederick. The play contains what is regarded as Fletcher's best dialogue.

**Chandler, Raymond (Thornton)** 1888–1959. Raymond Chandler was born in Chicago. At the age of eight he was taken to England and was educated at Dulwich College. He worked briefly as a journalist in London but decided to return to the USA when he was 24; after serving with the Canadian forces in World War I he worked in the offices of various oil companies in California. Chandler was 45 before he began to write; his crime stories were accepted by *Black Mask*, the leading magazine in crime fiction, and he contributed to it steadily until 1939. *The Big Sleep* (1939) introduced his detective, Philip Marlowe, and offered a distinctive literary style as the framework for tough incisive thrillers. Unlike Dashiell Hammett, his distinguished predecessor, he developed character and situation, instead of using the larger part of the story as resolution of the plot. Chandler's novels became more mannered as his career progressed but, in terms of a large following, his success continued and his works are rarely out of print. His novels, in order of publication, are *Farewell, my Lovely* (1940), *The High Window* (1942), *The Lady in the Lake* (1943), *The Little Sister* (1949), *The Long Goodbye* (1953), and *Playback* (1958). Stories are collected in *Trouble is my Business* (1950), *Killer in the Rain* (1964), and *The Sweat of Fear* (1965). Chandler discusses his methods in *The Simple Art of Murder* (1950) and *Raymond Chandler Speaking* (1962).

**Changeling, The** A tragedy by Thomas Middleton and William Rowley, first produced about 1623 and published in 1653. The word 'changeling' in the title refers to both the main and subplots but is not used in the sense of a substituted child. In the subplot the changeling is Antonio, who pretends to be an idiot – or changeling – to further his designs on Isabella; while the chief character in the main plot, Beatrice, is a changeling – inconstant – by nature. The subplot has no bearing on the main one and is believed to be Rowley's contribution.

Beatrice Joanna is the daughter of the Governor of Alicant, who arranges her marriage to Alonzo de Piracquo. But Beatrice has fallen in love with a Venetian, Alsemero; however, she succeeds in having the wedding postponed and, to escape it, enlists the help of De Flores, a servant of her father's. De Flores has a passion for Beatrice but he is repulsive to her; however, he murders Alonzo for her. She gives him the ring she had once given Alonzo; then she offers him gold. But it is soon plain to Beatrice that he has a different reward in mind; and he takes her. Beatrice is both revolted and fascinated; but soon she is totally dependent upon him both for the control of the consequences of their crime – and for the satisfaction of her physical appetites, though she marries Alsemero and nearly succeeds in deceiving him that she is chaste. This makes her maid, Diaphanta, a dangerous witness, so De Flores kills her. But Alsemero has been growing suspicious and it is he who unmasks Beatrice and her lover. They kill themselves when their crimes become known.

The subplot concerns the efforts of Antonio and his friend to seduce Isabella, the wife of an old and jealous doctor who runs a lunatic asylum. They are admitted to the asylum, pretending to be mad. The servant, Lollio, is convinced that his mistress, Isabella, is going to become Antonio's lover – and tries to blackmail her in the same terms as De Flores blackmails Beatrice. But Isabella does not want Antonio; she stops Lollio in his tracks by promising to murder him if he persists.

The subplot has been argued over by scholars; many reject it as an excrescence on an otherwise excellent play and certainly the quality of the writing is on a much lower level. Other scholars accept it as a mirror of the main plot: Isabella, in the centre of chaos, is not tempted and so remains in control of her life; Beatrice is tempted and descends into chaos. The main plot is what the great moments in the play rest on and the characters of Beatrice and De Flores are finely drawn: the one developing from a capricious and selfish girl into a murderess whose every action is henceforth dictated by fear of discovery and sexual servitude; the other complete, almost, from his first utterance. De Flores knows that he repels Beatrice; but he will have her and she will respond to him, he is certain. Their whole relationship is a series of confrontations, brilliantly portrayed in Middleton's taut, pointed dialogue.

**Channing, William Ellery** c.1780–1842. Born in Newport, Rhode Island, Channing was a graduate of Harvard Divinity School and was ordained in 1803 as a Congregational minister. In American literature he is notable principally for his influence on the movement away from Calvinism: his *Baltimore Sermon* (1819) and *The Moral Argument against Calvinism* (1820) stated plainly his opposition to dogma and coercion and his rejection of the basic tenet that man is essentially depraved. Thus the warmer and more humane ideas of the Unitarians and the Transcendentalists were to be found expressed in the work of the important New England writers such as Emerson and Thoreau.

Channing's ideas on pacifism, prison reform, child labour, and education were forcibly expressed in pamphlets and sermons and he was fiercely opposed to slavery. In his time his influence was considerable and his views widely discussed. His writings were collected and published in six volumes (1841–43).

**Chapman, George** c.1559–c.1634. Chapman was born near Hitchin in Hertfordshire; it is believed that he served as a soldier in the Netherlands but little is known of his early life. His later years, also, are obscure, and it is not known where or how he acquired his considerable learning though it is conjectured that he was educated at Oxford. In his 30s he arrived on the Elizabethan literary scene as a poet with *The Shadow of Night* (1594), *Ovid's Banquet of Sence* (1598), and a continuation of Marlowe's *Hero and Leander* (1598). Also in 1598 came the publication of his first play, the popular comedy *The Blind Beggar of Alexandria*, which Philip Henslowe had produced in 1595. Chapman had begun to publish his translation of Homer by this time.

An industrious playwright, Chapman was the friend of Marlowe, Jonson, Raleigh, Matthew Roydon the mathematician, and the astronomer Thomas Harriot. His patrons were Prince Henry and Robert Carr, Earl of Somerset. Not all of his plays have survived; those which have are *An Humorous Day's Mirth* (1599), *All Fools* (1605),

*Eastward Hoe* with Ben Jonson and John Marston (1605), *The Gentleman Usher* (1606), *Monsieur D'Olive* (1606), *Sir Giles Goosecap, Knight* – now attributed to Chapman – (1606), **Bussy D'Ambois** (1607), *The Conspiracy and Tragedy of Charles, Duke of Byron* (Biron) *Marshall of France* (1608), *May-Day* (1611), *The Widow's Tears* (1612), **The Revenge of Bussy D'Ambois** (1613), *Caesar and Pompey* (1631), and *The Tragedy of Chabot, Admiral of France* (1639). The comedy *Eastward Hoe* contained allusions to the Scots, which offended the court, and all three authors served a prison term.

In addition to his contribution to the theatre Chapman made another claim to distinction as a translator and a poet. Besides the poetry already noted mention should be made of *Euthymiae Raptus: Or the Teares of Peace* (1609) and *An Epicede or Funerall Song on the Death of Henry Prince of Wales* (1612). Chapman was the author of a masque designed by Inigo Jones, *The Masque of the Middle Temple and Lyncolnes Inn*, to celebrate the marriage of Princess Elizabeth to the Elector Palatine (1613). His translations were from Petrarch, the *Seven Penitential Psalms*, which were published with other 'philosophicall poems' and a hymn to Christ on the Cross (1612); the poems of the 6th-century Greek poet Musaeus (1616); Hesiod, *Works and Days*, which Chapman called *Georgicks* (1618); and the fifth satire of Juvenal (1629).

Through all this activity Chapman also worked on his translation of Homer – the Homer that inspired John Keats and is regarded as one of the masterpieces of translation. The first instalment was *Seven Books of the Iliad of Homer, Prince of Poets* (1598). The second came in the same year, *Achilles' Shield*, which was the 18th book of the *Iliad*. Books III to VI and Book XII were added to the first seven and the volume published as *Homer, Prince of Poets . . . in Twelve Books of the Iliad* (1609), and the whole work was published complete as *The Iliad of Homer* in 1611. Chapman used a rhyming 14-syllable line, but he changed to heroic couplets of ten syllables for his version of the *Odyssey*. His first instalment, *Homer's Odyssey, Books 1–12*, was published in 1614 and the whole work in the following year. Chapman completed his Homer, 'The work that I was born to do', with the hymns, epigrams, and smaller pieces in a volume he called *The Crown of all Homer's Works* in 1624.

Chapman's plays, nowadays, are known from the published texts – they are rarely, if ever, staged now. Swinburne and others have praised them. Chapman could be the 'rival poet' of Shakespeare's sonnets in the view of some critics, but then – in the view of other critics so could a number of others.

**characters** The original writer of 'characters' was Theophrastus, in 3rd-century BC Athens. He presented 30 short pictures of typical characters of his time, e.g. the garrulous man, the stingy man, the vain man, etc. Theophrastus was translated into English by Isaac Casaubon (1592) and by John Healey (1616). The form was first used in English by Joseph Hall in *Characters of Virtues and Vices* (1608), mostly dealing with ethical types in the manner of Theophrastus. Later writers extended the range and related their characters more closely to their own life and times. See also **Cleveland, John; Earle, John;** and **Fuller, Thomas.**

*Characters of Shakespeare's Plays* See **Hazlitt, William.**

*Charge of the Light Brigade, The* See **Tennyson, Alfred.**

*Charles Grandison, The History of Sir* A novel by Samuel Richardson first published in 1754.

Harriet Byron arrives in London and is soon the centre of admiration. Sir Hargrave Pollexfen, arrogant and wealthy, used to having his own way, proposes to her. Harriet declines the honour; Pollexfen persists, growing angrier with each refusal. Then he has her abducted from a masked ball and tries to bully her into a secret marriage. Failing in this, he bundles her into a carriage to take her off to his country house. Pollexfen's carriage, however, encounters that of Sir Charles Grandison, a man of perfect grace, exalted birth, and the highest integrity; he is also very wealthy. Harriet is rescued by Sir Charles and they fall in love.

But Sir Charles, while in Italy, had become attached to Clementina della Porretta, daughter of a noble family. The house of Porretta was indebted to him and Clementina had fallen in love with him; they had not married because the obstacle of their different religions had not yet been overcome. Clementina's noble parents share the suffering which this dilemma has brought upon their daughter, who suffers a mental breakdown. Sir Charles Grandison answers the Porretta family's summons to Italy, of course, where he learns that they will accept him on any condition for the sake of Clementina. His presence restores her to health; but, recovered, she sees where her duty lies. She asks Sir Charles's forgiveness for preferring to embrace the faith of her fathers to embracing him. Harriet Byron perceives how noble a character is Clementina della Porretta. Sir Charles Grandi-

son is absolved from considering the unthinkable – changing his faith – and, his noble character unsoiled, lives happily ever after with Harriet Byron, who, by the way, is beautiful and accomplished.

*Sir Charles Grandison* carries the heavy burden of three characters whom Richardson launches from an impossibly high level of virtue. His partiality to virtuous women was well known but, he declared in a letter to a friend in 1751: 'I am teazed by a dozen ladies of note and of virtue, to give them a good man.' In portraying a virtuous man Richardson enlisted the advice of his many female friends and admirers and, inevitably, produced a cardboard character. He could hardly be otherwise. John Butt stated the case perfectly when he said 'It would scarcely be an exaggeration to say that *Sir Charles Grandison* was written in committee.' In addition, though the principals are placed in high society their quality is essentially middle class. This is particularly true of Harriet Byron; Sir Charles Grandison belongs nowhere outside a sentimental imagination and Clementina della Porretta is an exotic, a foreign lady, noble though she is. But the book cannot be dismissed, because Richardson moved English fiction one step nearer to the novel of manners. The book is more loosely constructed than either *Pamela* or *Clarissa* and the author revealed a talent for domestic observation which made it a favourite with Jane Austen. Charlotte Grandison, the lighthearted and witty sister of the eponymous paragon and Harriet's chief correspondent, is particularly well drawn; so is her admirer, Captain Anderson. Again, the skill with which Richardson allowed his characters to portray themselves in their letters is admirable and it never fails him in the course of this immensely long novel.

**Charles the Bold** 1433–77. Duke of Burgundy (1467–77). He owned considerable land in the Netherlands in addition to Burgundy and coveted Alsace–Lorraine. He became allied to England in 1468 when he married Margaret, sister of Edward IV. He was killed at the siege of Nancy. He features in two of Scott's novels, *Quentin Durward* and *Anne of Geierstein*.

**Charmian** One of the queen's attendants in Shakespeare's *Antony and Cleopatra*. It is her idea that Cleopatra retire to her monument and send word to Antony that she is dead (Act IV Scene 13). She poisons herself with the same serpent that kills her mistress but lives long enough to deliver the famous epitaph, 'It is well done, and fitting for a Princess descended of so many royal kings.'

***Chaste and Lost Lovers, The*** A verse romance by William Bosworth (1607–*c*.1650) written in the author's youth but not published until 1651. See **seventeenth-century verse romances**.

***Chast Mayd in Cheape-side, A*** A comedy by Thomas Middleton, first published in 1630.

Yellowhammer, a wealthy goldsmith, intends his daughter Moll for the dissolute Sir Walter Whorehound, whose principal recommendation is that he is heir to the riches of the childless Sir Oliver Kix. However, Moll is in love with Touchwood Junior, who is without means. Whorehound has a discarded mistress whom he presents as his niece (the 'chaste maid' of the title) and the Yellowhammers have decided that the niece of Sir Walter Whorehound is a fit wife for Moll's brother, Tim, a bird-brained youth just down from Cambridge. The marriage of Tim Yellowhammer and the 'chaste maid' eventually takes place.

Touchwood Junior appeals for support to his brother Touchwood Senior, who – in contrast to Sir Oliver Kix – is so potent that he has to live apart from his wife – he simply cannot support more children. Another character who takes a poor view of Whorehound's marital intentions is Allwit, who lives in perfect comfort as a 'mari complaisant'. Mrs Allwit fills Whorehound's bed and Whorehound fills Allwit's purse. The arrangement suits the Allwits perfectly.

Touchwood Senior persuades Sir Oliver Kix to drink a harmless medicine, telling him it will make him potent if he exercises while digesting it. Sir Oliver is kept jumping about in the house and then sent on long rides lasting hours while Lady Kix is rendered fertile by the potent Touchwood Senior. The comedy's climax is approached in a scuffle between Touchwood Junior and Whorehound in which the latter is wounded. Feeling sorry for himself, he reproaches the Allwits for encouraging him in his sinful life, when news arrives that Touchwood Junior has died after the scuffle. This has brought Moll to her deathbed also and, worse, Lady Kix is with child – so Whorehound has no expectations and mounting debts. He appeals to the Allwits but they refuse him shelter or help of any kind, justifying their conduct in an attitude of bland and insolent hypocrisy.

Sir Oliver Kix is convinced that Touchwood Senior has made him potent and assures his future. Moll and Touchwood Junior are of course alive and well; and ready for the marriage that has now no impediments. The Allwits open a bawdy house in the Strand and Whorehound is arrested for debt.

An outline of the play can only give an idea of its tone. In performance it would probably prove uproarious (it has not been produced in the modern theatre) but the laughter might well be uneasy. It is a very black comedy indeed.

**Chatterton, Thomas** 1752–70. The poet commemorated by Wordsworth as 'the marvellous boy ... that perished in his pride' and to whose memory Keats dedicated *Endymion* was born in Bristol, the posthumous son of a schoolmaster. He was educated at a charity school, Colston's Hospital, and apprenticed to an attorney when he was 14. His family was associated with the church of St Mary Redcliffe and Chatterton, who could fabricate pedigrees and coats of arms from supposed originals, became interested in the archives of the parish. From this preoccupation he fabricated a 15th-century Bristol as the setting for the poems of 'Thomas Rowley, a Secular Priest of St John's'. An identification with the past was a current literary fashion – in the work of Macpherson, Percy, and Walpole, for instance – and Chatterton created a past of his own, though his first poem had been published in a local journal when he was 11 years old. His principal source was the documents relating to a

A pen and wash drawing by John Flaxman entitled 'Despair offering a bowl of poison to Chatterton.' The drawing, now in the British Museum Print Room, was executed a few years after Thomas Chatterton's death in 1770.

15th-century merchant and mayor of Bristol, William Canynges; he became the imaginary patron of the imaginary Rowley.

Chatterton's master released him in April 1770 and he went to London. A practised writer – he had been contributing to London journals since the year before – he might have succeeded in earning a living with topical verse and as a literary journeyman. But the poems which he offered to Dodsley and the document he offered to Horace Walpole were refused, and only one of the Rowley poems, 'Elinoure and Juga', was published in Chatterton's lifetime (in *The Town and Country Magazine* in 1769). In a fit of depression (presumably – there is nothing of the poet's state of mind to be discerned in his work) Chatterton took arsenic and died in a room in Holborn on 24 August 1770. He was not yet 18.

The controversy began a few years later. A single poem, 'Bristowe Tragedie: or, The Dethe of Syr Charles Bawdin', was published in 1772; the remainder of the Rowley poems were collected and edited by the Chaucer scholar Thomas Tyrwhitt and published in 1777. Tyrwhitt and many others were persuaded that the poems were discoveries; but three other Thomases were doubters – Gray, Percy, and Warton recognized the poems as fabrications and eventually convinced Tyrwhitt. The 1778 edition of *Poems, supposed to have been written at Bristol, by Thomas Rowley, and others, in the Fifteenth Century* contained *An Appendix tending to prove that they were written by Chatterton*. The poems' style is Spenserian; the vocabulary is mostly Chaucerian. The quality of the poems, belatedly recognized by the critics, is Chatterton's. The obstacle to recognition was the difficulty in believing that they could be the work of a boy – the earliest of them dates from 1764, when Chatterton was 12. The tale of six Thomases nearly obscured the fact that a poet of remarkable quality, who was to become a favourite of the English romantics, had come and gone, his genius concealed by his strange insistence on writing from an imaginary world. He is unlikely to become a popular poet – his choice of vocabulary keeps the general reader stumbling along behind him, trying to recognize the words – but 'An Excelente Balade of Charitie' and the minstrel's song from *Alla*, 'O! synge untoe mie roundelaie' are well known.

*The Complete Works of Thomas Chatterton* was edited for the Oxford English Texts series by Donald S. Taylor and Benjamin B. Hoover and published in 1971.

**Chaucer, Geoffrey** *c.*1340–1400. Chaucer's father was a prosperous wine merchant of London. John Chaucer and his wife Agnes lived in Thames Street, up river from London Bridge on the north bank, and Geoffrey Chaucer was probably born there. He was most likely educated nearby – at least three schools were available to him – but it is not known where; he entered the household of Prince Lionel, later Duke of Clarence, some time in his teens (1357). Chaucer was possibly a page to Elizabeth, Prince Lionel's wife, an appointment that would have dramatically widened the young Chaucer's horizons.

In October 1359 Prince Lionel was part of the army that his father Edward III took to France; Chaucer was with the prince's forces, but he was not to know military distinction. At the end of the year, or at the beginning of 1360, Chaucer was taken prisoner while on a foraging expedition near Arateau-Porcien in the Ardennes. He was ransomed on 1 March 1360 and returned to England in May of the same year after the Treaty of Brétigny.

Chaucer may have studied law in the Inner Temple and may have visited Spain on a mission for John of Gaunt; this period of his life is obscure. He married Philippa Roet, one of Queen Philippa's ladies, in 1366 (Philippa was sister to Katherine Swynford, who was later, after many years as his mistress, to become the wife of John of Gaunt) and from 1367 was an esquire of the royal household with a regular pension. He was with the king's army in France again in 1369 and later in Italy (1372–73), where he may have met Petrarch and Boccaccio. His services to the crown brought positive rewards and in 1374 he was able to lease the gatehouse of Aldgate from the city of London. Diplomatic missions to Flanders and France followed in 1377 and to Milan in 1378, the year after the king's death.

Chaucer's progress in the realm's affairs seems to have found no impediment – he sat in Parliament as knight of the shire for Kent in 1386 – until 1387, when John of Gaunt's position in command of affairs during the minority of Richard II was dislodged by the Duke of Gloucester. Chaucer's wife Philippa died in the same year. Gaunt retrieved his ascendancy but Chaucer did not regain the prosperity he had enjoyed hitherto. He gave up the Aldgate house, but his place of residence until 1399, when he leased a house in the garden of St Mary's, Westminster, is not known. He held various appointments under Richard II, who granted him a pension of £20 a year, a large sum by their standards; but the evidence of records suggests that Chaucer was being very careful about his money. In 1399 John of Gaunt's son, the same Henry of Lancaster to whom Gower gave his allegiance, supplanted Richard II, and Chaucer's pension was doubled. He died on 25 October 1400, and was buried in the chapel of St Benedict in Westminster Abbey. The resting place marked the beginning of the Poets' Corner.

The broad experience of life reflected in Chaucer's work would have begun in his childhood – his father's house would have seen constant comings and goings of men from France and Spain who dealt in wine or who carried it to England. Chaucer would certainly have known the French and Latin languages from an early age, as most educated Englishmen did in his times, and his appointment in the household of Prince Lionel would have sharpened his response to the courtly tradition in French poetry. Of immense importance, too, was his place at court, where he met every man of distinction in the kingdom. The earliest work to which a date can be given is **The Book of the Duchess**, an elegy written for Blanche, Duchess of Lancaster and John of Gaunt's first wife, who died in 1369. The poet would then have been about 30 and a translation of *Le Roman de la Rose*, a French verse romance, is also believed to have occupied some of his earlier years.

The decade after *The Book of the Duchess* gave Chaucer his experience of the wider world. His debt to Italian literature is acknowledged, though it is not known when he learned the language. He may possibly have learned it in London, where many Italian merchants could be found, and it may be that a knowledge of the language was the reason for his being sent to Italy in 1372. Chaucer's work cannot be dated with any certainty and it is remarkable that a busy servant of his country succeeded in writing so much. He was in a less favoured position after 1387, when John of Gaunt's position seemed likely to suffer an eclipse, and he may have had more personal freedom then; but it is known that Chaucer worked hard during all his adult life.

There are three 'periods' accorded to the poet's work by scholars, reflecting the influences of his early work and the progress towards his achievement as the first poetic genius of the English language. The first, the period of French influence, includes *The Book of the Duchess* and **The Romaunt of the Rose**, his incomplete translation of *Le Roman de La Rose*. The second is the 'Italian' period, influenced by Petrarch and Boccaccio and the work of Dante. The period lasted roughly from 1372 until 1386, during which years Chaucer probably wrote **The Parlement of Foules**, **The Hous of Fame**, **Troilus and Criseyde**, and **The Legende of Good Women**. Some of the early Tales – notably *The Knight's Tale* – are also attributed to this period of his life. The last period, 1386 until the poet's death in 1400, is that of **The Canterbury Tales**.

The chronological placing of Chaucer's less celebrated work has exercised the talents of scholars as much as has the establishment of a Chaucer canon. It is generally agreed that the *Ballades* ('To Rosamounde', 'The Former Age', 'Truth', 'The Lack of Steadfastness', and 'Gentilesse'), the *Complaints* ('unto Pity', 'of Mars', 'to his Lady', and 'of Venus'), and the *ABC* (a set of verses to Our Lady, each verse beginning with a different letter of the alphabet) belong to his first period. *Anelida and Arcite*, the prose translation from the Latin of Boethius' *De Consolatione Philosophiae*, the *Envoy to Bukton*, and the *Envoy to Scogan*, are probably the work of his second period. To his last – that of *The Canterbury Tales* – can be added the unfinished prose *Treatise on the Astrolabe*, which was written for the poet's ten-year-old son Lewis, and the *Complaint of Chaucer to his Empty Purse*.

Geoffrey Chaucer – learned, well travelled, and an omnivorous reader – was a man who saw kings at close quarters, whose friends included John of Gaunt, Gower, Ralph Strode, the architect Henry Yevele, Eustace Deschamps and, probably, Wycliffe himself; he was also a man of sympathy and humour and a shrewd observer of his fellow men. His tireless practice of his craft and his close study of, and experimentation with, the forms of poetry in other languages enabled his genius to find expression in his own; he is traditionally called the father of English literature. He is also the epitome of England in the 14th century; *The Canterbury Tales* are told by pilgrims who are vividly presented in the Prologue in an extraordinary range of character, whilst the tales convey, as no other work of literature does, the mind of western European man at that time. But *The Canterbury Tales* represents the flowering of his genius; *The Book of the Duchess*, written nearly 20 years before, was the work of a man of 30 and a gifted poet: between the two came a body of work that cannot be praised too highly either for its own achievement or for the summit to which it led.

A portrait of Chaucer by his disciple Thomas Occleve exists in the margin of one of his manuscripts. But for centuries after his death Chaucer's canon was known much less certainly than his appearance. *The Canterbury Tales* was printed by Caxton (*c*.1478 and *c*.1484) and a 'collected works' was issued by W. Thynne in 1532. However, much that was Chaucerian but not by Chaucer was eliminated from the editions of Thynne and others by Thomas Tyrwhitt, who

Geoffrey Chaucer. This is the earliest-known portrait, painted for Thomas Occleve's *De Regimine Principum*, in which the later poet pays tribute to Chaucer. The unknown artist worked from memory; Chaucer died in 1400 and Occleve's work was published in 1412. *MS Harley 4866, f.88.* British Library.

in his edition of *The Canterbury Tales* (1775–78) identified the master's dialect and metre. F. J. Furnivall, for The Chaucer Society, worked out the order of *The Canterbury Tales* (1868); later W. W. Skeat published his edition of the *Complete Works of Geoffrey Chaucer* in six volumes (1894). An additional volume, *Chaucerian and Other Pieces*, followed (1897). Skeat's work is regarded as definitive by most scholars. J. M. Manly's and Edith Rickert's eight-volume *The Text of The Canterbury Tales* (USA, 1940) contains the critical text made from a close examination of all the surviving manuscripts. The most famous of these is the Ellesmere Manuscript, which is illustrated throughout. It is in the Huntington Library, San Marino, California.

For readers who have no knowledge of the language in which Chaucer wrote there are versions of *The Canterbury Tales* in modern English. The most accessible introduction is Nevill Coghill's version of *The Canterbury Tales* (1951).

**Cheeryble, Charles and Edwin** The almost impossibly benevolent brothers – businessmen – of Dickens's *Nicholas Nickleby*. They arrive like two good fairies in Chapter XXXV and start putting the world to rights for the Nickleby family.

**Cheever, John** 1912–82. Cheever was born in Quincy, Massachusetts, and studied at Thayer Academy in Braintree until he was expelled at the age of 17. His expulsion was the subject of his first story, which was accepted by *The New Republic* and marked the beginning of a successful career. His stories of life in rural New England were a familiar feature of *The New Yorker* and other magazines and the first collection was published as *The Way Some People Live* (1943). Further collections – *The Enormous Radio* (1953), *The Housebreaker of Shady Hill* (1958), *Some People, Places and Things That Will Not Appear in My Next Novel* (1961), *The Brigadier and the Gold Widow* (1964), and *The World of Apples* (1973) – give a clear picture of the changing world and the author's dislike of the new America is reflected in the increasingly satirical tone. His first novel, *The Wapshot Chronicle* (1957), is the story of a New England family and won him the National Book Award. *The Wapshot Scandal* (1964) is a sequel, and his other novels are *Bullet Park* (1969), *Falconer* (1977), and *Oh What a Paradise It Seems* (1982).

***Chepman and Myllar's Prints*** See **Scottish anthologies and collections**.

***Cherrie and the Slaye, The*** See **Montgomerie, Alexander**.

**Chester cycle of mystery plays** See **miracle plays**.

**Chesterfield, Philip Dormer Stanhope, 4th Earl of** 1694–1773. Lord Chesterfield was born in St James's Square, Westminster. He was taught at home until he was ready to go to Cambridge, where he completed his education at Trinity College. After the customary grand tour for the sons of gentlemen he entered parliament (1716) and became England's ambassador at The Hague from 1728 to 1732. But he was never on good terms with Sir Robert Walpole and he held no further office in the latter's government. After Walpole's government fell Lord Chesterfield (he succeeded to the title in 1726) entered Newcastle's cabinet as Secretary of State (1744), and became Lord Lieutenant of Ireland from 1745 to 1746. In that difficult post, at a dangerous time, he acquitted himself with honour, earning the gratitude of the people for his tolerance and for leaving the country in a peaceful and stable condition.

However, Chesterfield found Newcastle as

difficult a colleague as Walpole, though he was Secretary of State again from 1746 until 1748, when he retired. He declined the offer of a dukedom. Chesterfield had a number of valued friends whom he kept until death separated them, ranging from the Earl of Scarborough to a Dublin bookseller, and from Lady Suffolk to his protégé Chenevix, who later became Bishop of Killaloe in Clare. The letters to his friends are among the most pleasant in the language – spontaneous, witty, and full of natural kindness. One of the recipients earned a certain immortality; the diplomat Solomon Dayrolles was Chesterfield's godson, and visited the earl on his deathbed. Chesterfield's impeccable manners never deserted him: 'Give Dayrolles a chair' were his last words.

But Chesterfield's most famous letters were written to his son and to another godson who was a member of his family and was to become the fifth earl. The son was illegitimate, born in 1732; Chesterfield gave him his name (Philip Stanhope) and, when the boy was five, began the letters of advice that were intended for no one else's eyes. The godson, also Philip Stanhope, was born when the son was 25; he began to receive letters when he was four, and these also were intended for the recipient only. The letters to both were written in English, French, and Latin and all of them contain the affectionate interest and honourable wisdom of a remarkable man; he had made grave mistakes during his own life and hoped to save the young men the same pain; he did his best to show them how to live. How well he succeeded is open to question. His son married in secret and had two sons and Chesterfield only became aware of the fact when his son died at the age of 36. He wrote to the widow, Eugenia Stanhope, in the kindest terms and assumed responsibility for his grandsons' upbringing. When he died, Chesterfield's legacy to them did not please Eugenia Stanhope and she realized that his letters to her late husband were a valuable property. The first public appearance of the famous letters was in 1774: *Letters to his Son, Philip Stanhope, together with several other Pieces on various Subjects*. Some of those to his heir and godson appeared in *The Art of Pleasing: in a Series of Letters to Master Stanhope* and were published in two numbers of *The Edinburgh Magazine* in the same year, and after that more and more of the Chesterfield letters were published. The most complete edition of them is contained in the six-volume *Letters* edited by Bonamy Dobrée and published in 1932, which also contains an admirable account of Chesterfield's life and work. Additional letters were published by S. L. Gulick

(1937) and C. Price (1948). (See also **Johnson, Samuel**.)

**Chesterton, G(ilbert) K(eith)** 1874–1936. G. K. Chesterton was born at Campden Hill, London, and was educated at St Paul's School and the Slade School of Art. His talent as an illustrator can be seen in his contribution to the novels of his friend, Hilaire Belloc, but he made a more definite mark as a prolific journalist, essayist, novelist, poet and playwright. His first published work appeared in periodicals – *The Bookman* and *The Illustrated London News* (the latter every week for 25 years) – and various newspapers. His first book was a collection of verse and sketches, *Greybeards at Play - Literature and Art for Old Gentlemen* (1900). This was followed by *The Wild Knight and Other Poems* in the same year and a book of essays, *The Defendant* (1901). A second collection of essays, *Twelve Types* (1902), was followed by a series of essays and studies, some in collaboration, on various writers: *Thomas Carlyle* (1902), *Robert Louis Stevenson* (1902), *Leo Tolstoy* (1903), *Charles Dickens* (1903), *Robert Browning* (1903, for the English Men of Letters series), *Thackeray* (1903), and *G. F. Watts* (1904). His first novel, *The Napoleon of Notting Hill*, was published in 1904.

In addition to a vast amount of journalism Chesterton published over 100 more books of fiction, verse, and assorted essays. After 1922, when he became a Roman Catholic, he added the role of Catholic apologist to his other fields of activity. An accomplished versifier, Chesterton is encountered in anthologies, and his excellent prose ensures his inclusion in collections of essays. Most readers know something of his fiction, especially the Father Brown stories and *The Man Who was Thursday* (1908). But for all the respect he earned in different fields Chesterton did not write a single undisputed masterpiece. He was extraordinarily able and versatile and is estimated now only as highly as during his lifetime.

Among Chesterton's best-known works are the novels *The Club of Queer Trades* (1905) and *The Flying Inn* (1914); the detective stories in the collections *The Innocence of Father Brown* (1911), *The Wisdom of Father Brown* (1914), *The Incredulity of Father Brown* (1926), *The Secret of Father Brown* (1927), and *The Scandal of Father Brown* (1935); his literary studies *George Bernard Shaw* (1910), *William Blake* (1910), and *Chaucer* (1932); books on religious subjects, *St Francis of Assisi* (1923) and *St Thomas Aquinas* (1933); and the collections *All Things Considered* (1908), *A Miscellany of Men* (1912), *The Uses of Diversity*

(1920), and *As I Was Saying* (1936). He published his *Autobiography* in 1936. Most of his verse can be found in *Collected Poems* (1933).

**Chettle, Henry** *c.*1560–*c.*1607. Chettle was a Londoner, the son of a dyer, who was apprenticed to a printer in 1577. He later (1591) became a partner in a printing house; he prepared Greene's *A Groatsworth of Wit* for publication after that writer's death. The printing house failed and Chettle became a writer, first with a pamphlet in the fashion of the time called *Kind Harts Dreame* (1593), in the preface of which he expresses regret for allowing Greene's jealous attack on Shakespeare to be printed without trying to moderate it. *Piers Plainnes Seaven Yeres Prentiship* (1595) is a picaresque romance that C. S. Lewis praised in glowing terms and regarded as a better work than anything in the same vein by Lyly, Greene, or Lodge.

From 1598 Chettle became a working playwright, chiefly for Philip Henslowe's theatre, the Rose in Bankside. He wrote 13 plays and was part-author of 35 more; only five plays of his own survive. Chettle seems to have enjoyed little success – he was imprisoned for debt – and his work for the stage is not well regarded. He is remembered for the preface to *Kind Harts Dreame*, which contains an arresting comment on Shakespeare, and for *Piers Plainnes*. The surviving plays are *The Downfall of Robert, Earle of Huntington* (1601), *The Death of Robert, Earle of Huntington* (1601), *The Pleasant Comodie of Patient Grissil* (1603), *The Tragedy of Hoffman or a Revenge for a Father* (1631), and *The Blind-beggar of Bednal-Green* (1659). *Englande's Mourning Garment* (1603) is an elegy on the death of Elizabeth I.

**Chicago Poems** The first collection of poems by Carl Sandburg, first published in 1916. The famous 'Chicago' appears in this volume (although it had been published two years before in Harriet Monroe's *Poetry* magazine) and 'I am the People, the Mob', with its remarkable 'Sometimes I growl, shake myself and spatter a few red drops for history to remember. Then – I forget.'

**Chickamauga** See *In the Midst of Life*.

**Childe Harold's Pilgrimage** A poem in four cantos of Spenserian stanzas by Lord Byron. The first two cantos were published in 1812, the third in 1816, and the fourth in 1818. The poem was begun in Albania in 1809 during Byron's visit to the eastern Mediterranean with John Cam Hobhouse. The publication of the first two cantos made Byron famous.

The poem described the wanderings of a

An illustration for an edition of Byron's *Childe Harold's Pilgrimage* published in 1841. The scene is from Canto III (1816); Brussels on the eve of Waterloo.

young man who, disillusioned with his empty pleasure-seeking existence, looks for distraction in far-away places. (The term 'Childe' is used in the sense of a young man of privileged birth.) The first two cantos follow him to Portugal and Spain, the eastern Mediterranean (the Ionian islands and Albania), and Greece, whose 'haunted, holy ground', under Turkish domination, had made an indelible impression on the poet's mind. The third canto finds the pilgrim in Belgium on the eve of Waterloo ('There was a sound of revelry by night'), on the Rhine, and in the Alps and the Jura, evoking the historical associations of each place. In the fourth canto Byron speaks with his own voice and Childe Harold is abandoned; the poet describes a fascinating tour of Italy, her great cities, and her great men, from Venice to Rome.

**Childe Roland to the Dark Tower Came** A poem by Robert Browning, first published in 1855 in the volume *Men and Women*. Browning wrote this sombre and enigmatic poem in two days and said that it came to him as a kind of dream. A great deal has been written about its meaning but it is as simple or as mysterious as the reader's response makes it. A simple meaning is that Childe Roland has an appointment with destiny; a mysterious one is the nature of his destiny, in search of which he must travel through a landscape wasted by some nameless evil. As he advances farther, Roland finds he has fewer and fewer spiritual resources that might support his resolution; when he arrives at the Dark Tower he is spiritually naked. The poem ends with Roland's announcement of his arrival. The strange other-world mood is sustained throughout a haunting poem which, once read, is difficult to forget.

'Children of the Chappell' followed by 'Gentlemen of the Chappell'. The Children of the Chapel Royal Choir and the Children of St Paul's attended the choir schools and were often called upon to entertain at court. In the early years of the 17th century they appeared in works by Jonson, Marston, and Chapman in the theatre at Blackfriars. The children's companies came to an end when the parents objected to their children's exploitation. *Add. MS 35324, f.31v.* British Library.

---

***Child of the Jago, A*** See **Morrison, Arthur.**

***Children of Adam*** A sequence of 16 poems by Walt Whitman, first published as *Enfans d'Adam* in the third edition of *Leaves of Grass* (1860). The present title dates from 1867. The sequence is a celebration of physical love, of the sexual impulse as the dynamic of the universe. ***I Sing the Body Electric*** and ***Once I Pass'd Through a Populous City*** are part of this sequence as is 'Spontaneous Me', a catalogue of sensuous evocations demonstrating the author's amorous hypersensitivity.

***Children of the New Forest, The*** A novel for young people by Frederick Marryat, first published in 1847. The setting is the time of the Civil War, and the story concerns the Beverley children. They are rescued from the Roundheads by the courageous old retainer, Jacob Armitage, and brought up in his cottage in the New Forest. There they learn self-sufficiency and grow to understand that virtue isn't confined to their own side; the integrity of Heatherstone, their Cromwellian neighbour, is an important part of the story. Edward Beverley's growing love for Patience Heatherstone, after adventures and vicissitudes for the Beverleys, results in a happy marriage at the end of the book.

Probably Marryat's best-loved book, *The Children of the New Forest* is, paradoxically, neither a story of the sea – in which Marryat was unrivalled – nor of his own times. It succeeds nevertheless on every level and can be enjoyed by adults as well as by its intended audience.

***Children of the Night, The*** A collection of poems by Edwin Arlington Robinson, first published in 1897. Among the poems in this volume are 'Credo', an affirmation of faith, the poet's tributes to Whitman and Crabbe, and 'John Evereldown', a song about a compulsive womanizer in Tilbury Town.

**children's companies of actors** Strictly speaking these were companies of boy actors, particularly attached to choir schools. The Children of Paul's (St Paul's) and The Children of the Chapel (the Chapel Royal Choir) had entertained at court and given performances in public at the Blackfriars Theatre in the old priory (1576) before Shakespeare came to London but they had been gradually replaced by adult professionals as drama became more sophisticated. The Blackfriars house was leased by Burbage, who built a new theatre on the site – a theatre he was prevented from using by the resentful citizens who had endured the uproar of the theatre's construction. This theatre was rented from Burbage in 1600 by Nathaniel Giles and Henry Evans who put on performances by The Children of the Chapel.

Their success was immediate and soon The Children of Paul's were also in favour with Londoners. The children's companies were called to perform at court for the Christmas Revels. They were rivals to the professional companies – Shakespeare's was across the river, at Bankside – and performed works by John Marston, Ben Jonson, and George Chapman. Eventually the children's companies came to an end; they were exploited too much, being profitable, and parents objected to their sons, who were trained to sing in choirs, being used as actors, though one of them, Nathan Field, became a celebrated actor in Shakespeare's company. The children's companies had ceased to be a part of the London theatre scene by the end of the first decade of the 17th century.

**Children's Hour, The**  See **Hellman, Lillian**.

**Child's History of England, A**  This book by Charles Dickens was first published in parts, at irregular intervals, in *Household Words*, and then in three volumes, between 1852 and 1854. It has been severely criticized – George Saintsbury called it 'deplorable'. Dickens did no research and his view of history is black and white. But Derek Hudson reminds us that 'it is a boy's book, founded on a strong sense of social justice', and it is certainly no more biased than the history taught in most of our junior schools.

**Chillingworth, William**  1602–44.  A godson of Archbishop Laud, and inevitably a Protestant, Chillingworth fell among Jesuits after leaving Oxford and became a Catholic in 1630. He was persuaded by his godfather and others that this was a mistake and he returned to the Protestant fold, accepting preferment at Salisbury in 1638. In 1637 he published *The Religion of Protestants a Safe Way to Salvation*, which argued that disagreements among Protestants were not a hazard to their salvation and that honest seeking after truth could not be condemned. This brought down on his head the wrath of first the Catholics and then the Puritans, since both sects held an absolute conviction that the way to God was known only to them. A Royalist, he fought at the siege of Gloucester; he was captured at Arundel Castle, where he lay ill in 1644, and died in the same year.

**Chimes, The**  See *Christmas Books*.

**Chinese Nightingale and Other Poems, The**  A collection of poems by Vachel Lindsay, first published in 1917. The title poem evokes China's ancient culture while the poet sits visiting his friend Chang, a laundryman of San Francisco. 'The Ghost of the Buffaloes' is a dream vision of the Great Plains before the coming of the White man. 'In Praise of Johnny Appleseed' celebrates the man, John Chapman of Massachusetts, who extended the cultivation of orchards to the frontier regions of America in the early 19th century.

**Choir Invisible, The**  A novel by James Lane Allen, first published under the title *John Gray* in 1893. It was revised by the author and published under its new title in 1897. The period of the story is the late 18th century.

John Gray is a Kentucky schoolmaster with inflexible moral convictions. He is determined to find a wife whose outlook will parallel his own but falls in love with the silly Amy Falconer. Committed to marriage, he realizes what a dreadful mistake he has made when he meets Amy's aunt, Jessica. Jessica is the perfect woman for him but she is already married. Gray goes to Philadelphia to work, trying to make the best of his marriage.

When his son is grown-up Gray takes the young man to live with Jessica, convinced that her example will be of great benefit. It is only then that he confesses that he loved her – and learns that she responded to his love but could not honourably declare her feelings any more than he could.

**Chopin, Kate** 1851–1904.  Kate O'Flaherty was born in St Louis, of an Irish father and a French mother, and went to live in New Orleans when she married Oscar Chopin. Chopin took over a Louisiana cotton plantation but he died of swamp fever when Kate was 31. She found the management of the plantation too demanding and after two years returned to St Louis with her son, Jean, and turned to writing. She wrote occasional pieces, stories for children, and a play; she published a novel, *At Fault* (1890), which was not a success but which demonstrated her skill at evoking the Creole and Cajun backgrounds of her life in Louisiana.

Mrs Chopin was a short-story writer of enormous promise; her small output has been compared to the work of Guy de Maupassant, whom she admired above all others. But her career was blasted by the storm of criticism directed at her for *The Awakening* (1899), a novel about a well-to-do wife and mother and her growing awareness of her physical self. The tensions of sexual relations within a marriage had been part of her first novel nine years before; but now her touch was sure and her delicate restraint produced a novel – decades ahead of its time – which deserves to be far better known. It is difficult to understand, even in the context of her times, why Mrs Chopin's book should have raised such a storm. Her writing was approved by all but the moral tone condemned by all; the effect upon a remarkable writer was to prove disastrous. Her short stories were published regularly by *Vogue*, *Atlantic Monthly*, and *Century*, and the first collection, **Bayou Folk**, was published to considerable praise in 1894. Most of the notices praised her as an exponent of 'local colour' but *Atlantic Monthly* discerned a 'characteristic of power awaiting opportunity'. At this stage editors began to find a note in her stories that was disturbing; a number were turned down. Nevertheless her second collection, **A Night in Acadie**, was published in 1897. Her writing was praised again but critics, too, were beginning to find some of her work disturbing. Mrs Chopin, meanwhile, had completed *The Awakening* and it had been accepted; she had reason to feel confident about her literary future. The hostile reception stunned her; the book was taken out of circulation by the libraries of St Louis and she was denied membership of the St Louis Fine Arts Club. She submitted a third collection of stories in the same year (1899) but it was rejected. She wrote and published almost nothing after that and died in 1904.

Kate Chopin's work remained lost to the general reader (it still is, largely, as scholarly editions are simply not within the general reader's range) until a young Norwegian, Per Seyersted, who was studying in the USA, became interested in her. *The Complete Works of Kate Chopin*, which he collected with scrupulous care, was published in two volumes in 1969 by the Louisiana State University Press. Amongst other works, it contains **The Storm**, a short story unpublished during the author's lifetime.

**Christabel**   A poem by Samuel Taylor Coleridge, first published in 1816. The first part was written at Nether Stowey in 1797, just after the completion of *The Ancient Mariner* (see **Coleridge, Samuel Taylor** and **Wordsworth, William**). Work was resumed at Keswick in Cumberland in 1800; the poet had gone to live there after returning from Germany. 'Christabel' is unfinished; Coleridge said he feared he 'could not carry on with equal success the execution of the idea, an extremely subtle and difficult one'. He demonstrates his mastery in the use of the rhyming four-stressed line, conveying with great beauty and subtlety an atmosphere in which supernatural forces are ever present. Christabel, the daughter of the baron Sir Leoline, goes 'A furlong from the castle gate' at midnight,

seeking solitude in a wood to pray for her betrothed. At the foot of a great oak where she kneels she hears a moan of distress and finds a damsel of great beauty dressed in white. The damsel says that she has been abducted by five warriors; they have left her by the oak tree and will return for her. Her name is Geraldine, and Christabel takes her to her father's house; Geraldine cannot cross the threshold unaided and her passage provokes a grumble from the mastiff at the gate. Geraldine is hospitably received by Sir Leoline and she tells him she is the daughter of Lord Roland de Vaux of Tryermaine, who had been Sir Leoline's good friend until a quarrel separated them. But Christabel realizes that Geraldine is false; the damsel is an enchantress bent on evil and has assumed the shape of Geraldine. A spell forces silence on Christabel, while Sir Leoline prepares to send his bard, Bracy, to Lord Roland to take news of his daughter and looks forward to a reconciliation. There the poem ends.

Coleridge's plan for the rest of the narrative was as follows, according to his friend Dr Gillman: The bard and his companion find that Lord Roland's castle no longer exists and hurry back to tell Sir Leoline. Geraldine, aware of this, is obliged to change her appearance to that of Christabel's betrothed, and Christabel feels an unaccountable revulsion towards her erstwhile love, to the puzzlement of Sir Leoline. She yields to her father and goes to the altar with the false knight; but the true knight appears in time to claim her. Geraldine disappears.

**Christian**   The hero of John Bunyan's *The Pilgrim's Progress*, who sets out for the Celestial City carrying his burden of sin.

**Christian Year, The**   See **Keble, John**.

**Christis Kirk on the Grene**   A popular Scottish poem once attributed to King James I of Scotland. See **Scottish anthologies and collections**.

**Christmas Books**   Charles Dickens began to write his Christmas books in 1843. When they were first collected he wrote in the preface that he saw them as 'a whimsical kind of masque intended to awaken loving and forbearing thoughts'. The appeal of Christmas to Dickens was very strong and this, combined with the period taste for the supernatural, resulted in some excellent short works which increased his popularity. The stories contained in the volume called *Christmas Books* first appeared in successive years – with a gap in 1847, when he was working on *Dombey and Son* – and are *A Christmas Carol*, *The Chimes*, *The Cricket on the Hearth*, *The Battle* *of Life*, and *The Haunted Man*. Thereafter, short tales in a similar vein appeared at Christmas in *Household Words* and *All the Year Round*.

*A Christmas Carol*. Miserly old Scrooge receives a visit, on Christmas Eve, from the ghost of Marley, his late business partner. Marley shows him visions of Christmas past, Christmas present – including Scrooge's responsibility for a great deal of unhappiness – and Christmas future. The future holds his own death and Marley shows him what that will be like for him. On Christmas Day Scrooge is a changed man. For the first time he is kind to his ill-paid and much-bullied clerk, Bob Cratchit, and generally behaves like the kind old fellow people are happy to encounter. The story is a great favourite.

*The Chimes*. Toby Vick is a porter and has a nightmare. He sees his daughter Trotty suffer a succession of misfortunes, and encounters different manifestations of the social ills which were always in the forefront of Dickens's mind. Alderman Chute and Sir Joseph Bowley are examples of those who, with relatively good intentions, perpetuate social evils. All Toby's nightmare visions are happily dissipated at the end.

*The Cricket on the Hearth*. The cricket on the hearth is the fairy influence that prevents John Peerybingle from thinking his girl-wife, Dot, is insincere – a suspicion planted by the spiteful old Tackleton. Tackleton is on the point of marrying a young wife, too – May Fielding; May's lover is believed to be dead. John sees an old man, who has lodged with them, remove his wig and become a young man in intimate conversation with Dot. He proves to be May's lover, returned in time to prevent her marriage to Tackleton.

*The Battle of Life*. Marion and Grace are both in love with Alfred, the young man brought up in their home almost as a brother by their father, Dr Jeddler. Alfred feels an equal affection for both sisters. It is 'understood' that Alfred will marry Marion, the younger, and when he goes abroad to study he leaves her in the care of Grace. Marion knows that Grace loves him, too, and when Alfred returns she pretends to elope with another man to leave the field clear for Grace. Six years later, Alfred and Grace, married and with a child called Marion, are overjoyed by Marion's return. Alfred settles down contentedly with both girls – though one has to assume that his relationship with one of them is chaste.

One feels compelled to agree with Thackeray that the story is 'a wretched affair'. But it has a remarkable biographical interest, pointed out by Christopher Hibbert. Dickens loved Mary Hogarth, married her sister Catherine, and was happy to have his household run by their sister Georgina. He seems to have convinced himself that he could have been happy with Mary or Georgina; no wonder Catherine was unhappy.

*The Haunted Man and the Ghost's Bargain*. Redlaw is visited by his Evil Genius. Though a successful chemist, Redlaw is a prey to morbid introspection, and his Evil Genius convinces him that his memories are a curse. He offers to remove the memories, if Redlaw will himself communicate the power of obliterating unhappy memories to those around him. He agrees, and discovers too late that all goodness is blotted out, too. Redlaw's good angel, Milly Swidger, puts things right at the end.

**Christmas Carol, A** See **Christmas Books**.

**Christmas Garland, A** See **Beerbohm, Sir Max**.

**Christmas Stories** Not to be confused with the **Christmas Books** of Charles Dickens, which are a group of long short stories, totalling five in all. Dickens also wrote a great number of stories, much shorter, after the last of the *Christmas Books* (*The Haunted Man*) and they appeared regularly in the Christmas numbers of *Household Words* and *All the Year Round*. A volume containing them is usually included in standard editions of the author's works.

**Chronicles of the Canongate** The inclusive title given by Sir Walter Scott to three of his stories, which he presents as the recollections of Mrs Bethune, Baliol of the Canongate in Edinburgh. These are written down by her friend, Mr Croftangry, who tells his own story as an introduction. The first series was published in 1827, the second (*The Fair Maid of Perth*) in 1828.

*The Highland Widow*. A grim story of the widow of MacTavish Mhor, one of the last of the Highland fighting men of the '45, who is obsessed with the idea of her son being raised to be like his father. When the son grows up the world has changed and he wants a different life; he decides to enlist and go to America. His mother first drugs him to make him outstay his leave and then taunts him into resisting arrest when a sergeant arrives from his regiment. The boy kills the sergeant. The widow dies alone in the mountains in an agony of guilt and grief when her son is shot as a deserter and murderer.

*The Two Drovers*. Robin Oig M'Combich, a Highland drover, and Harry Wakefield, a Yorkshire drover, set out for England with Robin's cattle. When they reach Cumberland they have cross words over the halt for the cattle: Harry takes it badly. At an inn he provokes a quarrel with Robin, the Highlander, and soon the whole company is on his side against the stranger.

Robin will not, as a Highland gentleman, fight with his fists and Harry knocks him down. Robin, jeered at by all, recovers his dirk from a comrade 12 miles away. Then he trudges back to the inn to confront Harry and kills him. He gives himself up to justice.

*The Surgeon's Daughter.* Janet Gray is the surgeon's daughter in the village of Middlemass. Brought up with her is an orphan boy, Richard Middlemass, who falls in love with her. When Richard comes of age, however, he goes to India to make his fortune and comes under the influence of Mme Montreville, an adventuress. She is acting as a procuress and Richard falls in with her plans to lure Janet out to India, where she will be handed over to Tippoo Sahib. The presence in India of Adam Hartley, Richard's one-time fellow-pupil who also loves Janet, saves her. Adam secures the intervention of Hyder Ali, who orders Janet's release and Richard's arrest. Hyder Ali orders that Richard be crushed to death by an elephant for his crime.

*The Fair Maid of Perth, or Valentine's Day.* A story of Scotland in the 14th century, in the reign of Robert III. The fair maid of Perth is Catharine Glover. The worthless Duke of Rothsay, the king's son, and his evil friend, Sir John Ramorny, try to kidnap Catharine but are driven off by Henry Smith, the armourer, who loves her; Henry strikes off Ramorny's hand during the fight. Ramorny is determined on vengeance: first on Henry, and also on Rothsay whom he blames as the author of his misfortune. He lures Rothsay to Falkland Tower, with the promise of Catharine, and has him murdered. The gentle Catharine, meanwhile, in spite of her father's urging, refuses Henry; his great strength and love of combat are not for her. Henry's rival, Conachar, is also his enemy since their two clans are at feud, and in an arranged battle Conachar is finally confronted by Henry. Conachar's courage deserts him and Henry wins the day when Conachar runs from the field. But Henry is sickened by the carnage and, when he learns that Conachar has killed himself in shame at his cowardice, he resolves to hang up his broadsword forever. Catharine accepts him in the light of this vow.

**Chrysal,** *or The Adventures of a Guinea.* See **Johnstone, Charles.**

**Chrysaor** The sword of Sir Artegall in Book V of Spenser's *The Faerie Queene.*

**Churchill, Charles** 1731–64. Churchill was the son of a curate of St John's, Westminster, who later became rector of Rainham in Essex. Born in Westminster, Churchill attended Westminster School. An exceptional scholar, he went on to St John's College, Cambridge, but he blighted his academic prospects by a clandestine marriage at the age of 17 to Martha Scott. Churchill was fortunate in his father, who gave the young couple a home and had his son trained for the only career he could now look to, the church. Young Churchill was ordained and in 1758 succeeded his father as incumbent of St John's at Westminster; he taught in a girls' school to supplement his income. He was not really suited to the church and Martha was extravagant; two children had to be supported and Churchill turned to writing. Two poems, 'The Bard' and 'The Conclave', failed to find publishers; Churchill published *The Rosciad* with his own money – and became an overnight success. Estranged from his wife by now, he was able to make her an allowance, and began to live a most unchurchman-like life as a man about town.

Churchill's success as a verse satirist (*The Rosciad* was a satire, in praise of Garrick and in criticism of some other actors – Churchill had been at school with George Colman the Elder) led to his friendship with John Wilkes, whose rakish example he lost no time in following. **The North Briton**, Wilkes's political weekly, owed a great deal of its success to Churchill, who wrote at least half of it. *The Prophecy of Famine* (1763) was a satirical blast at Bute; but Wilkes made sure that his friend escaped prosecution in the uproar which followed publication of no. 45 of *The North Briton*, asserting that Churchill had not written it.

After Wilkes's departure for exile, Churchill continued his social and political satires: *The Apology* and *Night* (1761) and *Ghosts* (1762) preceded the suppression of *The North Briton*; and *The Conference, The Author, An Epistle to William Hogarth* (1763), *The Duellist, The Candidate, Gotham, Independence, The Times,* and *The Farewell* (1764) followed it. In November 1764 Churchill sailed for France to visit his friend Wilkes. He died at Boulogne, soon after landing. *The Journey*, a fragment, and some satirical verses directed at Bishop Warburton, were published in 1765.

Churchill's short life may have prevented a fine craftsman from realizing himself. His skill in the use of the heroic couplet in polemic places him close to Pope; but the immediacy which is an essential part of successful contemporary satire confines interest in his work to interest in his times. He does not command attention otherwise, for all his quality.

A modern edition of Churchill's poems is by

Douglas Grant (1956), which contains extensive, and necessary, notes.

**Churchill, Frank** In Jane Austen's *Emma*, Mr Weston's lively and handsome son, seen by Emma as a desirable match for Harriet, her protégée. He is, however, far too strong a character to be manipulated by Emma.

**Churchill, Winston** 1871–1947. The American novelist (no relation to the British statesman) was born in St Louis, graduated from the Naval Academy at Annapolis in 1894, and published his first novel, *The Celebrity: An Episode*, in 1898. His next was a best seller, *Richard Carvel* (1899), and Churchill continued to enjoy great success as a novelist until *The Dwelling-Place of Light* (1917), his last book.

*The Celebrity* was a satire on a larger-than-life journalist and *Richard Carvel* was a romance set during the American Revolution; *The Crisis* (1901) was another set in St Louis during the Civil War. *The Crossing* (1904) concerns the settlement of Kentucky and the frontier as a factor during the revolution; it is regarded as his best work. *Coniston* (1906) has also received high praise and contains Churchill's best piece of character drawing, that of the politician Jethro Bass; the story is set in New England in the mid-19th century. *Mr Crewe's Career* (1908) concerns a railway monopoly; *A Modern Chronicle* (1910), the problems of divorce; *The Inside of the Cup* (1913), the role of religion in modern life; and *A Far Country* (1915) is set in the Middle West and tells of the conflict between private interests and public-spirited idealism. Churchill was also the author of a play, *Dr Jonathan* (1919), and *The Uncharted Way* (1940), an expression of his personal religious beliefs.

Winston Churchill spent most of his life in New Hampshire and served in the state legislature. He was a very successful and popular novelist of the best intentions, conscientiously setting his novels against backgrounds and issues of significance in American life and history. However, he lacked the art of character drawing and his plots were arbitrary and unconvincing.

**Churchyard, Thomas** *c.*1520–1604. At one time page to the Earl of Surrey, Churchyard was a minor writer, a hopeful soldier (hopeful of fortune), and a member of the court fringe. He published broadsides and small books of verse of a narrative and topical nature. Described by Spenser in *Colin Clout* as Old Palaemon, he 'sung so long untill quite hoarse he grew', Churchyard could perhaps be commended for industry if for nothing else. His best work is his contribution to

*A Mirror for Magistrates*, the narrative called *Shore's Wife*.

**Chuzzlewit, Jonas** Old Martin's nephew in Dickens's novel. He hurried his father into the grave – and is fearful of the fact becoming known. He marries Pecksniff's daughter, Mercy (Merry), treats her abominably, and enters into the crooked schemes of Montague Tigg. Cold-hearted and cruel, he murders Tigg when his secret is found out, but is terrified of retribution and poisons himself when he is caught.

**Cibber, Colley** 1671–1757. The son of a Danish sculptor who had settled in England, Colley Cibber became an actor at Drury Lane in 1690, when the theatre was under the management of Thomas Betterton. Lacking good looks or commanding physique, Cibber became a skilful comedian; he enjoyed a major success as Lord Foppington in Vanbrugh's *The Relapse*. Cibber turned to writing plays to augment his income when he married, and his first play, *Love's Last Shift* (1696), was a success. He wrote more than 20 plays and all were produced; he was a good workman and knew what would please, but his plays have not held the stage. His most celebrated work was his adaptation of Shakespeare's *Richard III* (1700); his acting text, with interpolations and alterations, was the standard one for over 150 years. Another success was his adaptation of Molière's *Tartuffe* as *The Non-Juror* (1717).

Cibber became manager of Drury Lane in 1710 and was successful though cordially disliked by most of the actors and playwrights who worked with him. He was careless of other people's feelings but he cultivated men with great names and high positions and gained the poet laureateship in 1730. The appointment aroused the scorn of Alexander Pope and Henry Fielding. The best work left by Colley Cibber is *Apology for the Life of Mr Colley Cibber, Comedian* (1740) an autobiography containing the most complete picture of the contemporary theatre and invaluable descriptions of the art of Anne Bracegirdle, Thomas Betterton, James Nokes, Anne Oldfield and others.

*Citizen of the World, The* A collection of letters by Oliver Goldsmith, purporting to be the correspondence of a philosophic Chinese gentleman, Lien Chi Altangi, living in London. They were written for John Newbery's *The Public Ledger* (1760–61) and published under the present title in 1762. The letters offer a satirical comment on contemporary English life and manners, mental and moral characteristics, and literary matters. Two notable characters appear, Beau Tibbs and The Man in Black.

**City Madam, The**  A comedy by Philip Massinger, first produced in 1632 and first published in 1659.

Sir John Frugal is a successful merchant; his wife and daughters have grown in affectation and vanity as his wealth has increased. Living in his household is his younger brother, Luke, a ruined prodigal Sir John has succoured and whose manner is one of humble gratitude. Sir John, exasperated by his family, pretends to retire to a monastery and hands the management of the household over to his brother. Luke shows his true colours at once, appropriating his brother's fortune and displaying a remarkable rapacity in calling in debts. He ridicules Lady Frugal and her daughters – and is prepared to sell them to three 'Indians' who want three women for human sacrifice. The Indians, however, are in fact Sir John and two young men who unsuccessfully wooed his daughters; and Luke is unmasked. Unrepentant ('I care not where I go . . . what's done, with words cannot be undone'), Luke is driven from the house and the relieved and repentant ladies promise to behave better in future.

The play gives a realistic picture of London society at various levels in the Caroline period, ranging from the integrity of Sir John, the honest merchant, and his family to the stews where Shavem and Secret, prostitutes, are ready to fight with knives against fashionable ruffians who would make victims of them. The pretensions of aristocracy are given utterance by one suitor, Sir Maurice Lacy, and vigorously challenged by the other, Master Plenty, a yeoman farmer's son whose wealth and station came from hard work. The play was successfully revived in 1964 in a production by John Harrison at the Birmingham Repertory Theatre.

**City of Dreadful Night, The**  A poem by James Thomson, first published in *The National Reformer* in 1874. The city, in Thomson's poem, symbolizes the isolation of man. Thomson had become an atheist through the influence of Charles Bradlaugh and the poem is a sombre and powerful expression of a man's attempts to come to terms with the pain of life and the inevitability of death without the support of faith. The theme and imagery of Thomson's poem have found strong echoes in the work of a number of 20th-century poets.

See also **Thomson, James** (*or* **B.V.**).

**City Witt, The,** *or The Woman Wears the Breeches.* A comedy by Richard Brome, first produced about 1628 and published in 1653. The amiable young Crasy, generous to a fault, finds himself ruined and constantly nagged by his mother-in-law, Mrs Pyannet Sneakup. When he goes to his friends for help they ignore him, while his wife is quite willing for him to leave her so that she can play the strumpet. Crasy is determined to teach them all a lesson and enlists the help of Jeremy, his manservant. Jeremy disguises himself as a woman and is presented as the rich widow Tryman. Between them, Crasy and Jeremy confound all those who offered him meanness in return for his generosity, regaining all his money by playing on their vices. They also thrash his wife's would-be lovers and expose his mother-in-law to ridicule.

**Civil Disobedience, On the Duty of**  An essay by Henry David Thoreau, developed from a lecture and first published in 1849 in *Aesthetic Papers*. It was prompted by the author's imprisonment for refusing to pay a poll tax to help finance the Mexican War. His essay asserts that the true lover of the law is the man who observes it – even when the government has ceased to do so. When the actions of governments are questionable man must look to his own conscience, rather than condone a government's ill doing.

**Claggart, John**  The master-at-arms in Herman Melville's *Billy Budd*. His love-hatred for Billy tempts him to accuse him falsely of fomenting mutiny. Billy kills him in the presence of Captain Vere.

**Clandestine Marriage, The**  A comedy by George Colman the Elder and David Garrick, first produced at Drury Lane in February 1766 and first published in the same year. The idea for the play came from Hogarth's *Marriage-à-la-Mode*.

Mr Sterling is a wealthy and socially aspiring London merchant with two daughters, anxious for an alliance with a noble family. He has contrived a marriage between his elder daughter and Sir John Melvil, nephew of Lord Ogleby; they are financially embarrassed and Melvil is resigned to marrying Miss Sterling – but at the last moment he reveals his passion for the younger daughter, Fanny.

Fanny, however, has married, without her father's knowledge or consent, his clerk, Lovewell, and dare not reveal the fact. Melvil induces Sterling to allow the marriage arrangements to be transferred to the younger daughter but at this point Mr Sterling's sister, the wealthy Mrs Heidelberg, orders Fanny to be sent packing; Mrs Heidelberg is furious at the way her family is being treated. Fanny in despair appeals to Lord Ogleby, but the vain old man imagines that she is courting him, and decides he will marry her himself. The young people's dilemma is not resolved until a lover is found in Fanny's bedroom; the whole family waits to witness his exposure, and it turns out to be Lovewell.

The young couple are saved from Sterling's wrath by the intervention of Lord Ogleby, no less, who is touched by their plight. He takes Lovewell under his own protection and the clandestine marriage has at last some hope of success. For a modern edition of the play, see **Colman the Elder, George**.

**Clare, John** 1793–1864. Clare, the son of an agricultural labourer of Northamptonshire, was born at Helpstone, a village between Stamford and Crowland. Clare's father was on parish relief when he was born; he was a literate man and enjoyed popular penny sheets, but the poet's mother was completely unlettered. Clare had little more than the basic schooling that gave him the ability to read and write. He was a weakly child but a precocious one and was soon reading anything he could lay his hands on: the Bible, chapbooks, popular ballads, *Robinson Crusoe*. He was obliged to help with farm work by the time he was seven years old and was apprenticed to a gardener at 17. After discovering poetry through reading a copy of Thomson's *The Seasons* when he was 13 he began to scribble verses on scraps of paper.

Clare served in the Northamptonshire militia for two years (1812–14); he then returned to gardening and went on writing poetry. The first attempt to get his work into print, *Proposals for Publishing a Collection of Trifles in Verse* (1817), was paid for by himself, at nearby Market Deeping. But Taylor & Hessey, Keats's publishers, were interested in the poems he sent them (the 'proposals' had not, alas, elicited any subscriptions) and his hopes were realized with *Poems Descriptive of Rural Life and Scenery* (1820). The author was described on the title page as 'John Clare a Northampton Peasant', at the instigation of the publishers. The volume sold very well but the novelty of a peasant poet was not likely to last. However, the success of his poems, of which three editions were quickly sold out, enabled Clare to marry Martha ('Patty') Turner, and his new volume, *The Village Minstrel and Other Poems*, was ready for publication in 1821. The 'peasant poet' label was no longer a novelty and this collection had less success; but the contents were rewarding even if his publishers, and others such as Charles Lamb, seemed unaware

that Clare, like Burns, was a true poet and needed no labels.

In London Clare met William Hazlitt, Coleridge, and Thomas De Quincey, as well as Lamb. He tried to please his publishers by extending his range and his next collection was not ready for some years. He had a wife and several children and was obliged to take on labouring to provide them with food. Some people helped him, and a cottage at Northborough was given him in 1823. *The Shepherd's Calendar* was published in 1827 and the full title (*with Village Stories and Other Poems*) shows how hard he tried to write what was expected of him. The book, as published, was a failure; no more than 400 copies were sold in two years. The best pieces of the collection were the pictures of the rural scene in all its variety, which came to him naturally. *The Rural Muse* (1835) was his last published work; his mind gave way under the strain of his circumstances and his attempt to be the kind of poet who wrote in the accepted fashion of the day. His publishers added to the strain by their insistence upon editing, even censoring, everything he wrote.

Clare first became unstable in 1823, when the evidence of delusions became apparent. In 1837 he was taken to Dr Allen's asylum at High Beech near Epping Forest in Essex, and for four years seemed to enjoy some peace. Dr Allen was humane and intelligent and Clare spent much of his time working, sometimes wandering, contentedly out of doors. Then he absconded; but he was left at his home for five months in the hope that all would be well. At the end of 1841, unhappily, he had to be confined again, this time in the General Lunatic Asylum at Northampton. He spent the remaining 23 years of his life there and was treated kindly, continuing to write poetry during his lucid intervals.

John Clare's poetry reveals a wonderful eye for the country world as it really was, and he had little patience with Keats's 'never-never land' where no wood was without its fauns and no stream without a naiad. Clare knew the rural world of the early 19th century at its most harsh, but it was *his* world and no poet saw it more clearly or described it so truthfully. There are also other aspects to Clare, as the poems 'I am', 'A Vision', 'The Dream', 'Song's Eternity', 'Dying Child', and his amatory verses demonstrate. His work, as he originally wrote it, was hardly known until many years after his death. *The Shepherd's Calendar* was reduced by Taylor from 3382 lines to 1761, and he demanded a new version of 'July'. Valuable work was done by Edmund Blunden and A. Porter in *John Clare:*

*Poems Chiefly from Manuscript* (1920). *Madrigals and Chronicles*, edited by Edmund Blunden (1924), *Poems of John Clare's Madness*, edited by Geoffrey Grigson (1949), and the original version of *The Shepherd's Calendar*, edited by Eric Robinson and Geoffrey Summerfield (1964), have made proper use of John Clare's manuscripts and presented some of his work in its true form. Much remains to be done; Clare contributed a large number of poems to periodicals and a definitive collected edition has not yet appeared. *Sketches in the Life of John Clare Written by Himself*, edited by Edmund Blunden (1931), and *The Prose* and *The Letters of John Clare*, edited by J. W. and Anne Tibble (1951), provide absorbing information about the poet's life.

*Clarel: A Poem and Pilgrimage in the Holy Land.* A poem by Herman Melville of 7000 lines, first published in two volumes in 1876. The work is an expression of the author's reflections on his visit to the Holy Land, 20 years before. The printing of the first edition was sponsored by Melville's uncle, Peter Gansevoort.

The poem is an enquiry into and a search for faith. The characters are diverse: many of them express to some degree a doubt which arises from their background of religion, experience, or philosophy; while others are comfortably certain of their faith. The author, the student Clarel, finds no-one among them whose point of view can assist him.

The poem is not a success; written in octosyllabic couplets, the work is too long to be successfully sustained in them. Melville's observation of a large number of characters is too sober: 'The spirit of Matthew Arnold, not Chaucer, presides over this pilgrimage', as Lewis Mumford commented in his biography of Melville. However, it is not without interest and extracts from it are frequently anthologized.

**Clarendon, Edward Hyde, 1st Earl of** 1609–74. The first great historian in the English language, Clarendon was the son of a country gentleman of Wiltshire. He was educated at Magdalen Hall, Oxford, and also studied law. He entered Parliament in 1640 and sat in the Commons throughout the Short and the Long Parliaments, first for Wootton Bassett and then for Saltash. His politics were at first in accord with the popular party who opposed the king's policies, but he was soon out of sympathy with the tenor of the opposition and with the Presbyterians. In 1640 he was one of the king's best advisers, giving him through his writings the image of a lawful king unlawfully warred against.

Edward Hyde, 1st Earl of Clarendon. Detail from the portrait, after A. Hanneman, c.1650. National Portrait Gallery, London.

When Charles I gave the Prince of Wales a council and court of his own in the West Country during the Civil War (1645) Hyde was appointed to this and he followed the prince into exile. While with him in the Scilly Isles (1646) Hyde began to write his *History*.

At the Restoration he became Lord Chancellor and at Charles II's coronation was created Earl of Clarendon; he was Charles II's chief minister until 1667. The mismanagement of the war with the Dutch (which Clarendon had opposed) gave his political enemies an opportunity to bring about his downfall. Because they feared his possible return to the political stage (his daughter Anne was married to James, Duke of York and heir-presumptive) Lord Arlington and the others moved his impeachment. Charles II did not lift a finger on behalf of the man who had served him so faithfully, and Clarendon went into exile, never to return. He lived for a time at Montpellier, and at Rouen, where he died. During these years he completed *The True Historical Narrative of the Rebellion and Civil Wars in England* and his autobiography, much of which he later incorporated into the *History*. **The History of the Irish Rebellion and Civil Wars in Ireland** was first published separately but appeared later as part of the main work.

Clarendon's speeches, political tracts, and essays were collected and published as *A Collection of Several Tracts* (1727). His criticism of Hobbes, in *Leviathan, A Brief View and Survey*, was published two years after his death. From the Restoration until his flight from England Clarendon was Chancellor of the University of Oxford, which inherited his manuscripts. The profits from the publication of his work provided the funds for the building of the Clarendon Press.

**Clarendon, The Life of Edward, Earl of** The autobiography of the Earl of Clarendon was written during his exile in France after his fall from power in Charles II's government. Some of the material in his memoirs paralleled events in his great *History*, into which he fitted his personal story with great skill. The manuscript was part of the Clarendon papers presented to the University of Oxford by his heirs, and was published separately (1759).

**Clarendon State Papers** See **seventeenth-century historical collections**.

**Clarissa,** *or, the History of a Young Lady*. A novel by Samuel Richardson first published in seven volumes, between 1747 and 1748. Richardson's second novel, it follows the epistolary form first employed in *Pamela*. It is the longest novel in the English language, running to over a million words. The letters are written by the principal characters: Clarissa Harlowe's to her friend Miss Howe, and Robert Lovelace's to his friend John Belford.

Clarissa Harlowe is being pressed by her parents to marry Mr Solmes, a man she detests. She is drawn to the attractive Lovelace, who is also paying court to her, but her parents reject him because of his dubious reputation. Clarissa, a dutiful girl, resists Lovelace's advances but her refusal to marry Solmes provokes her family to imprison her in her room. Pressure is increased to make her conform but Clarissa gains a sympathetic response from Lovelace, with whom she is secretly corresponding about her plight. When it looks as if her family's pressures will succeed, Clarissa throws herself on Lovelace's protection and runs away with him. She soon discovers that she has placed herself in his power and that his intentions are dishonourable.

Clarissa has fallen in love with the man she thought her deliverer. He installs her in the care of Mrs Sinclair, a procuress, and does his best to seduce her, at first with subtlety and later, when her virtue proves unassailable, with a scarcely suppressed rage that turns his importunities into threats. Clarissa also has to endure the abuse of

An illustration for an edition of Richardson's *Clarissa* published in 1768. This is the frontispiece to Vol. III and shows Clarissa and Lovelace at breakfast with Mrs Sinclair and her nieces.

her family; but her resolution holds. Eventually Lovelace drugs her, rapes her, and then proposes marriage. Clarissa, now, is beyond any appeal of this kind. Lovelace's family, and his friends, plead with her; Clarissa rejects Lovelace totally and withdraws to live in solitude. But not for long. She dies in grief and shame, and Lovelace is challenged, and killed, by her cousin Colonel Morden. John Belford, Lovelace's libertine friend and correspondent, is horrified by the outcome of Lovelace's obsession and turns his back on his former life. He becomes Clarissa's executor and edits her correspondence.

The novel encompasses less than a year in its span of action and its length seems excessive for the incidents outlined above. But an outline cannot give an idea of the intense examination of the characters and the inexorable march of events that overtake Clarissa Harlowe. In outline, too, Clarissa sounds too good to be true; yet it is one of the features of this remarkable novel that she is believable. So is Lovelace, her despoiler – indeed, many critics see him as the triumph of Richardson's art. The characterization is brilliant throughout: Belford, Mrs Sinclair the bawd, and Anna Howe, the prudent and sensible friend who does not succeed in saving Clarissa, whose 'only crime is her merit'.

**Clark, William** 1770–1838.   The co-commander of the Lewis and Clark expedition was born in Caroline County, Virginia. His maps and drawings of the expedition were of enormous value to subsequent enterprises. He was appointed Superintendent of Indian Affairs at St Louis in 1807 and later became governor of Missouri Territory in 1813.

See also **Lewis, Meriwether.**

**Clarke, Austin** 1896–1974.   Clarke was born in Dublin and educated at Belvedere College, a Jesuit school, and at University College, Dublin. He was lecturer in English at the university for a time and then went to live in England, where he earned his living as a journalist. In 1937 Clarke returned to Ireland, where he founded the Dublin Verse Speaking Society and the Lyric Theatre Company for the production of plays in verse. His poems are largely based on themes from Celtic mythology and the first to appear was *The Vengeance of Fionn* (1917). Others were *The Fires of Baal* and *The Sword of the West* (both 1921) and *The Cattledrive in Connaught and Other Poems* (1925). Clarke's first verse play was *The Son of Learning*, produced at Cambridge in 1927. He wrote a score of verse plays which were produced at the Abbey, Gate, and Peacock Theatres in Dublin as well as being broadcast.

Clarke continued to write poetry and several volumes followed the *Collected Poems of 1936*. He was also the author of novels and volumes of reminiscences, including *First Visit to England* (1945), *Twice Round the Black Church* (1962), and *The Celtic Twilight and the Nineties* (1969).

**Clarke, Marcus Andrew Hislop** 1846–81. Marcus Clarke was born in London; he emigrated to Victoria, Australia, in 1863 and became a journalist. He wrote a weekly column in *The Australasian* (1867–70) and started *The Colonial Monthly* in 1868. His first novel, *Long Odds*, was serialized in the *Monthly*, and his second, *For the Term of His Natural Life*, in the *Australian Journal* (1870–72). A third, *Felix and Felicitas*, was left unfinished when he died at the age of 35. Clarke was harassed by debt after the failure of *The Colonial Monthly* and *Humbug*, a comic weekly that he had founded in 1869. *For the Term of His Natural Life* arose from a commission to research the penal record of Tasmania.

His best-known work, it is a classic picture of a penal settlement and a vivid evocation of Tasmania at the time.

**Clarke, Samuel** 1675–1729.   Clarke was born in Norwich and educated at Caius College, Cambridge. He was appointed chaplain to the Bishop of Norwich in 1698. In 1704 and 1705 he delivered the Boyle Lectures that were known in their published form (1716) as *A Discourse concerning the Being and Attributes of God, the Obligations of Natural Religion, and the Truth and Certainty of the Christian Revelation*, a carefully reasoned defence of rational theology against the empiricism of John Locke. Clarke was a critic of deism but he was in sympathy with some of the philosophy's ideas.

**Claudio** (i)   In Shakespeare's *Measure for Measure*, the victim of Angelo's rigid exercise of the long-lapsed morality laws. His appeal to his sister Isabella brings about her encounter with Angelo.

**Claudio** (ii)   A young lord of Florence in the service of the Prince of Arragon in Shakespeare's *Much Ado About Nothing*. When the prince visits Messina Claudio falls in love with the governor's daughter, Hero. But he is convinced by Don John's plot to discredit her and jilts her at the altar. Benedick, who was his friend, challenges him at the behest of Beatrice, Hero's cousin.

**Claudius**   The guilty king in Shakespeare's *Hamlet*. He is the dead king's brother and Hamlet's uncle; he assumed the crown after seducing the queen and murdering the king. He tries to dispose of Hamlet as soon as it is clear that his nephew knows all. Hamlet kills him at the end of the play.

**Clavering, Lady**   In Thackeray's *Pendennis*, the 'Begum'. She is the mother of Blanche Amory by a former marriage. Amiable and vulgar, she is now married to the despicable Sir Francis Clavering – who is himself being blackmailed by Blanche's father.

***Claverings, The***   A novel by Anthony Trollope, first published in the *Cornhill Magazine* (February 1866 to May 1867).

Julia Brabazon, with too many expensive tastes and heavy debts, marries the worn-out, old, debauched – but wealthy – Lord Ongar. She has forsaken her lover Harry Clavering to do so. Harry becomes engaged to Florence Burton, an engineer's daughter; Harry had lived in her father's house while he was a pupil. Florence is completely different from the glamorous Julia Brabazon.

Julia has a dreadful life as Lady Ongar, and the

spiteful old man contrives, at the last, to leave a stain on her honour. When he dies, Julia returns to London, but Ongar has succeeded too well and she is now a social outcast. Her attraction for Harry is strong, however, and he becomes entangled with her again; he is soon causing grief to Florence and earning the contempt of her brother – whom Harry had looked down on. He does marry Florence in the end.

Trollope seems to have put a male Alice Vavasor (see *Can you Forgive Her?*) in the lead in this novel, and it might be asked of Julia Brabazon and Florence Burton whether they could forgive him. It was not the author's intention to make Clavering the centre of his book (his *Autobiography* makes it plain that Julia Brabazon is that) but he occupies far too much of it. The chastened Julia and the modest adoring Florence are exceedingly well done, and the author shows that the spineless Harry Claverings will always evoke some kind of response from women. That they do is well known; this presentation fails because what the reader feels most is exasperation, not a continuing interest.

**Clayhanger** See **Bennett, (Enoch) Arnold**.

**Cleanness** An alliterative poem of the later half of the 14th century, *Cleanness* (or *Purity*) is the second poem in the manuscript Cotton Nero Ax. (See also *Pearl*.) The lesson of purity is expounded through three subjects taken from the Old Testament: the Flood, Sodom and Gomorrah, and the Vision of Belshazzar. The prologue's discussion of the virtue of cleanness takes for its texts the sixth beatitude, 'Blessed are the pure in heart . . .' and the parable of the king's wedding feast (Matt. xxii. 1–14). The most highly regarded passages are the denunciation of Sodom and the destruction of Babylon.

*Cleanness* was edited by R. Morris for the Early English Text Society (1864), by R. J. Menner (Yale, 1920), and by I. Gollancz (see *Pearl*). A. C. Cawley and J. J. Anderson's edition contains the four poems of the Cotton manuscript (Everyman's Library). Brian Stone's translation is included in *The Owl and the Nightingale, Cleanness and St Erkenwald* (Penguin Classics, 1971).

**Cleges, Sir** A Middle English verse romance of the late 13th century. (See **metrical romances**.) Sir Cleges is a knight whose reckless generosity reduces him to poverty. When his prospects are at their worst it is Yuletide and the ground is covered with snow – but a cherry tree in his garden is richly laden with fruit. Cleges gathers the fruit to take to Cardiff, where King Uther and his court are residing; he hopes the gift of fruit in winter will help restore his fortunes. But court officials bar his way until he promises to share his reward with them; then they allow him access to the king. Uther is delighted with Cleges' gift, and asks the knight to name his reward. Cleges asks for 12 strokes, which are immediately delivered to the greedy officials. The king learns of Cleges' reputation for generosity and restores his fortunes. *Sir Cleges* was edited by H. Morley in *Shorter English Poems* (1876), and by G. H. McKnight in *Middle English Humorous Tales in Verse* (Boston, 1913). There is a modern version by Jessie L. Weston (1902).

**Cleland, John** 1709–89. A Londoner, Cleland was educated at Westminster School and held minor government posts in Smyrna and Bombay before becoming a professional writer in London. He is best known for *Memoirs of a Woman of Pleasure* (1748–49), usually called *Fanny Hill*. *Memoirs of a Coxcomb; or The History of Sir William Delamere* (1751) and *The Surprises of Love* (1764) are his other novels. Cleland also wrote dramatic pieces and philological studies.

*Fanny Hill* was for long a book that literary historians simply did not mention, though it was one of the most popular novels of the 18th century. Cleland's principal skill lies in his description of several kinds of sexual intercourse. He avoids breathless generalities, offering physiological exactitude in its place. A modern edition of *Fanny Hill*, edited by Peter Quennell, was published in 1963.

A detail from one of the illustrations to *Cleanness* in the *Cotton Nero Ax. MS, f.60.* The little craft is Noah's Ark. British Library.

**Clemens, Samuel Langhorne**  See **Twain, Mark.**

**Clennam, Arthur and Mrs**  In Dickens's *Little Dorrit*, Arthur Clennam is the middle-aged, returned-from-abroad son who does his best to help the Dorrits and grows to love Amy (Little) Dorrit. Mrs Clennam, who is not his real mother, professes strict principles but in fact has seriously harmed the Dorrits by suppressing a codicil in a will. She lives in a single room, paralysed; but her paralysis is hysterical, caused by guilt.

**Cleopatra**  A tragedy in blank verse by Samuel Daniel, first published in 1594. It deals with the events that followed the death of Antony. Octavius tries to persuade Cleopatra to leave the monument in which she has taken refuge; he wants to parade her in triumph in Rome. But after a last celebration of great magnificence she takes her life by the application of a venomous serpent. At the same time her son by Julius Caesar, Caesarion, is murdered by Octavius and the line of Ptolemy is extinguished.

**Clerk of Pennecuik, Sir John** 1676–1755. Clerk was one of the circle of friends who grouped around Allan Ramsay in the reviving literary life of Edinburgh in the early 18th century. Ramsay was a regular guest at Clerk's country house. Clerk was a pupil of Corelli and in 1698 composed a set of five cantatas for solo voice; he also wrote a number of songs. He gave up his artistic pursuits when he inherited the baronetcy but his *Memoirs* give an illuminating picture of his times; they were published by The Roxburghe Club in 1895. Clerk was also the author of *Observations on the Present State of Scotland* (1730).

**Clerk's Tale, The**  See *Canterbury Tales, The.*

**Cleveland, John** 1613–58.  As a poet Cleveland enjoyed great fame in his lifetime but nowadays his work is hardly known. Opinions differ as to the quality of his poetry, some believing it due for revival and others finding it too much of its own time to bear close scrutiny and representation in ours. His case bears some resemblance to that of his contemporary Abraham Cowley.

Cleveland was the son of a Yorkshire clergyman who moved to the living of Hinckley, Leicestershire, in 1621. He was educated at Christ's College, Cambridge, and was made a fellow of St John's in 1634. He was a contemporary of Milton at Christ's College, and contributed a poem to the volume of elegies on the death of Edward King. He opposed the election of Cromwell as MP for Cambridge in 1640 and was, like Cowley and Crashaw, ejected from his fellowship in 1645; but like them he had already (1643) left Cambridge. After two years at Oxford he joined the Royalist garrison at Newark and served as judge-advocate until the surrender of the town in 1646.

Now destitute, Cleveland made his way to London, existing on the kindness of friends, and sometimes contributing to Royalist journals. He never compromised his loyalties, not even when arrested and imprisoned (1655–56) on the vague charge of being a dissident Royalist. Indeed, in a personal appeal to Cromwell, he proclaimed his service to his king as a reason for his vindication. His appeal succeeded, and upon his release Cleveland returned to London where he spent his last two years at Gray's Inn.

Cleveland's first published work appeared in *The Character of a London-Diurnall; with Severall Select Poems* (1644). The same title appeared in 1647, when the volume was entirely Cleveland's. Editions of his work followed steadily, an enlarged one of 1651 continuing to be issued and read for ten years or more. He was the author of amatory verse, of 'characters' that depicted a type of contemporary man in order to reflect his times, and, perhaps most notably, of satires, particularly on Presbyterians. The most admired are 'The Rebel Scot' and 'The King's Disguise'.

**Cliff-Dwellers, The**  See **Fuller, Henry Blake.**

**Clive, Mrs Archer**  See *Paul Ferroll.*

**Clock Without Hands**  See **McCullers, Carson.**

**Cloister and the Hearth, The:** *A Tale of the Middle Ages.*  A novel by Charles Reade, first published in 1861. The book is unanimously regarded as the author's finest work. It was a development of the theme and characters of an earlier story called *The Good Fight* (1859).

The time is the 15th century and the place is Tergou, in Holland. Gerard is a mercer's son, and intended for the Church. But he falls in love with Margaret, the daughter of a poor scholar, Peter Brandt, who is suspected of sorcery. He finds not only his parents opposed to the marriage but also his two brothers and the burgomaster: their motives differ, but Gerard is helpless against them and his determination results in his being imprisoned. He escapes and joins Margaret, his betrothed, but he is being hunted and is obliged to flee the country.

Gerard wanders through Burgundy, Germany, and Italy and the author gives a vivid picture of the life of the times in taverns, stews, monasteries, and the homes of the nobility.

Gerard is in Italy when he receives news that Margaret is dead. He surrenders to debauchery for a time and then becomes a Dominican monk and a preacher. He does not know that the news sent him was false; Margaret is alive and has borne him a son, Erasmus.

Gerard returns to Holland as a preacher and finds Margaret again, and his son, but he is unable to marry her now because of his vows. However, he accepts a living at Gouda to be near them and achieves a measure of content before Margaret succumbs during an outbreak of the plague. Gerard, heartbroken, dies soon after, but his son lives on to become the great Erasmus of history.

Reade's background study for his novel was in the work of Froissart, Luther, and inevitably Erasmus himself, and his practice of careful documentation served him well. He moves his chief character, Gerard, without haste through a broad landscape and through a western Europe that was searching for a new direction. He also created two memorable lovers who, however much experience causes them to develop, remain in love with each other. Reade's historical characters – Villon, Gringoire, Deschamps, and the rest – also blend perfectly with invented ones such as Denys, Gerard's companion on the road, and the master-beggar, Cul de Jatte.

**closure of the playhouses** The Protestants who followed Calvin left their sense of proportion behind. Perhaps they had none to begin with; no one who could consider nailing the conduct of everyday life to the altar of scriptures of a Middle Eastern culture dating back (in its latest expression) 12 or 14 centuries could be said to have had much wit. There was no sanction in the Bible for drama – that was part of the heathen culture of the doubly damned Greek and Roman civilizations. That an expression of humanity could exist in such works was not considered; but then, humanity was never a preoccupation of Calvin's. The manifestation of Calvin's attitudes in England, in the form of Puritanism, was the enemy of the theatre from the beginning.

The miracle plays and moralities were condemned as impious; the mixture of religion and folk tradition was offensive to the Puritan mentality and, besides, it dated back to popery, like the Mass. The complainers, as always, shouted loudest; William Alley, who was Bishop of Exeter, William Crashaw, and John Northbrooke all denounced plays and other forms of light-mindedness, particularly things that might divert people on the Sabbath. In 1579 Stephen Gosson, who had been a player and a playwright,

published *The Schoole of Abuse*, a pamphlet 'against Poets, Pipers, Players, Jesters, and such like'; it was, in fact, a smart exercise by one who had enjoyed little success in the world he was attacking. But the piece attracted considerable attention: Thomas Lodge's reply, *Honest Excuses* (1579), was suppressed. Philip Stubbe's *The Anatomie of Abuses* (1583) catalogues all his complaints against popular amusements.

However, the drama was developing fast and might have seemed too healthy to be worried by the snapping of those who disapproved. It flourished under the patronage of great noblemen, provided poets with a new field for their efforts, and, with the accession of the Stuarts, was given royal approval. And it was royal patronage that, in the end, exposed it to Puritan wrath.

It would be unfair to equate Puritanism in England with Calvinism in Geneva; it was never quite as ugly. But it suffered to some degree from the strange madness that saw pleasure as dangerous and, by association, things pleasant – such as stained glass, paintings, statues, pretty churches, and priceless manuscripts treasured in monasteries. Puritanism recoiled like a humourless virgin from the high spirits displayed by its own supporters during the Marprelate controversy; and never smiled again. The opponents of the king during the Civil War were not essentially Puritans, as a reading of history will show, but the fanatics among them, as usual, made more noise than the humane and fairminded men who saw much farther than mere forms of worship or how to spend free time on Sundays. One of the noisiest was William Prynne (1600–69), whose *Histrio-Mastix: the players' scourge or actors' tragedy* (1633) contains over a thousand pages of abuse of the playhouses and players.

The ascendancy of the Parliamentarians inevitably favoured the Puritans; they had a common enemy. By 1641 London was an unhappy place, with an atmosphere of gloom and apprehension; a tract called *The Stage Player's Complaint*, published in that year, gives a remarkable picture of the prevailing mood. The Parliamentarians had some way to go before achieving complete victory but in the following year they disposed of Laud and Strafford and released Prynne from life imprisonment. He was without his ears, which had been cut off in the pillory – martyrs, like ghosts, are easily raised; the difficulty is in laying them. In the same year (1642) the playhouses, those centres of Royalist support that provided excellent opportunities, it was said, for subversive demonstrations, were closed by parliamentary ordinance. Public performances were banned; and further ordinances of 1647 and 1648 instituted whipping for players and fines for audiences. The decision of 1642 was probably made from a mixture of motives – plays could be given privately; and Cromwell approved of the performance of plays in schools. But the fanatics could make a triumph of it and strengthen their convictions thereby. They were able to congratulate themselves for 18 years; the great age of English drama was over.

See also '**Marprelate, Martin**'; **Stubbes, Philip**; and **Prynne, William**.

**Cloten** In Shakespeare's *Cymbeline*, the king's stepson and Imogen's unwanted suitor. A bully and an oaf, he follows Imogen to Milford Haven wearing her banished husband's clothes but is killed in the encounter with Guiderius, who cuts off his head. Imogen believes the decapitated corpse to be her husband's.

***Cloud of Unknowing, The*** A mystical treatise of unknown authorship, written in English in the 14th century. The 'cloud of unknowing' is the great gulf between God and man: the gulf can only be crossed (the 'cloud' pierced) by love – not by reason. The prologue explains that the work is meant for those called to the contemplative life, not for those just beginning a spiritual life. The probable date of the work is somewhere between the time of Richard Rolle (d. 1349) and Walter Hilton (d. 1396). It can be read in several modern English versions.

**Clough, Arthur Hugh** 1819–61. Clough was the son of a cotton merchant and was born in Liverpool. He was taken to the USA at the age of four, when his father emigrated, but was sent back to England to be educated; he entered Rugby School in 1829. Clough became a favourite pupil of Thomas Arnold and eventually (he was four years older) a close friend of Matthew Arnold. Clough became a Balliol Scholar and went to Oxford in 1837; he became a fellow of Oriel College in 1842. But his religious doubts produced a crisis: feeling unable to subscribe to the Thirty-Nine Articles he resigned his fellowship and in the following year accepted the headship of nonsectarian University Hall in London.

Clough's poetry reflects his inward struggles. He arrived at Oxford in the period of the Tractarians and the new biblical criticism. He was influenced by German philosophy also and there seems to have been no lightening of his preoccupations until after his marriage to Blanche Smith in 1854. His wife's first cousin was Florence Nightingale and he became very interested in her work. His later poems show less interest in himself and this development was promising. He died in Florence in 1861 at the age of 42.

Clough's first published poem was *The Bothie of Toper-na-Fuosich* (1848), a narrative poem in classical hexameters which he described as a 'Long-Vacation Pastoral'. It tells of the love of an Oxford scholar for the daughter of a Highland farmer and was his best-liked poem for many years. The short poems which he had already written were collected in *Ambarvalia* (1849). During a visit to Rome in 1849 he composed *Amours de Voyage*, and in Venice in 1850 he began work on *Dipsychus*; these and the rest of his poems from 1849 were not collected and published until after his death. *Amours de Voyage*, also written in hexameters, is an account of a romance in the form of letters; the hero's lack of committal leads to an unhappy ending. *Dipsychus* is a dialogue between the poet and a Mephistophelean figure and, in Clough's words, represents the 'conflict between a tender conscience and the world'.

Some of Clough's shorter poems – 'Say Not the Struggle Nought Availeth', 'The Last Decalogue', 'There is No God', and 'How pleasant it is to have money' – have become popular anthology pieces. The first collection of his poems was published with a memoir by F. T. Palgrave (1862). The definitive modern edition was edited by F. L. Mulhauser (Oxford English Texts, 1974).

**Cobbett, William** 1762–1835. The son of a small farmer and innkeeper, Cobbett was born at Farnham in Surrey. He enlisted in 1784 and educated himself while serving in the army, reaching the rank of sergeant major. He proved very useful – because he was lettered – as a sort of general clerk to the regiment. He served in Nova Scotia and New Brunswick and then bought his discharge when he was 29; he was convinced that several of his officers were guilty of corruption and laid charges accordingly. But he was not given the facilities to press his case and was not even called to the court martial. He retreated to France and stayed long enough to learn the language; then he emigrated to America and settled in Philadelphia in 1792.

Cobbett opened a bookshop and published a paper called *Porcupine's Gazette* (1797–99). He called himself Peter Porcupine, wrote a number of pro-British and anti-French pamphlets, and was constantly treading on thin ice in his disregard of libel laws. *The Life and Adventures of*

*Peter Porcupine* (1796) describes this period of his life. Eventually, he went too far: he libelled Dr Benjamin Rush, Washington's physician, and was convicted – then he libelled the judge. He returned to England in haste in 1800 and his pro-British pamphlets stood him in good stead. His first venture, *The Porcupine*, did not succeed; but he gained the public ear with *Cobbett's Political Register*, a weekly which he launched in 1802. From being a Tory he graduated to political independence and eventually became a convinced and active radical. He was the true spokesman of the small trader and farmer.

A man of remarkable energy, Cobbett also published *Parliamentary Debates* (later undertaken by Hansard) and *State Trials*; and he was an enthusiastic model farmer. In 1809 he wrote an article against the practice of flogging in the army and was sentenced to two years' imprisonment. The *Register* continued but Cobbett's farm was ruined in his absence and he was heavily in debt. He reduced the price of his paper to twopence in 1816 – and the circulation rose to 40,000; but he was still in debt and retreated to the United States for two years (1817–19). He farmed in Long Island, disputed with Morris Birkbeck on the subject of colonization in the west, and wrote a *Grammar of the English Language* (1818) for working-class students. *The Journal of a Year's Residence in the United States* (1818) incorporated the *Journal* of the English radical Thomas Hulme. Hulme, living in America, protested against conditions arising in England because of the Industrial Revolution. Cobbett was to return to that subject at a later date.

Upon returning to England, Cobbett resumed the direction of his *Register* and found his following as strong as ever; in fact his influence began to increase. He wrote on everything (his published output was enormous) from farming to politics, from correct conduct to be taught to young people to the particulars of justice. Cobbett is almost notorious for his particularizing and dismissal, or ignoring, of the general view. The celebrated **Rural Rides** (1830) is to be enjoyed as a picture of a vanishing world; the economic and political observations are questionable.

The first Reform Bill enabled Cobbett to enter parliament, and he was the member for Oldham from 1832 until he died. A remarkably opinionated man, he was a fine political journalist; his writing is vigorous and direct and his observation impressive, particularly in matters of agriculture and the use of the land. In Hazlitt's words, he used 'plain, broad, downright English'.

A recommended selection from Cobbett's *Political Register* (1802–35) is G. D. H. and Margaret Cole's *The Opinions of Cobbett* (1944). *The Progress of a Ploughboy*, edited by W. Reitzel (1933), constructs an autobiography from William Cobbett's notes. It was reissued in 1947 as *The Autobiography of William Cobbett*.

**Cockaygne, The Land of** A Middle English poem in octosyllabic couplets depicting a utopian land where it is always feeding time. The intention was a coarse satire at the expense of monks and friars and symptomatic of the growing revolt against clerical influence. The walls of the monastery are made of pastry, flesh, fish, and rich meat; there are pinnacles of fat puddings. Entry to this gluttons' paradise could only be gained by wading through swine's dung up to the chin. The text appears in G. Sampson's *The Cambridge Book of Prose and Verse* (1924); J. A. W. Bennett and G. V. Smithers' *Early Middle English Prose and Verse* (1968); and K. and C. Sisam's *The Oxford Book of Medieval English Verse* (1970).

**Cocke Lorelle's Bote** An anonymous verse satire of the first decade of the 16th century, of which only a fragment survives. Cocke Lorelle, the master of the boat, is a tinker and was possibly a real character. The passengers tell their tales but, while there is promise of good things, the satire never amounts to anything of real value and the verse is indifferent. It was published in 1817 by the Roxburghe Club in an edition by H. Drury.

**Coke (*or* Cook), Sir Edward** 1552–1634. The great champion of the common law in England was born in Norfolk and completed his education at Trinity College, Cambridge. He became a barrister of the Inner Temple and his future was assured when he attracted the attention of Lord Burghley, who gave him the post of attorney general. His rival for the office was Francis Bacon, whose opponent in law he remained. Coke became Chief Justice of the Court of Common Pleas in 1606, and waged a steady war against the courts of privilege; one of his triumphs was the acceptance of the principle that the king could not change the common law by proclamation. King James, and all the adherents of the idea of government by *rex*, were determined to overcome the champion of *lex* and James 'promoted' him to Chief Justice of the King's Bench. Coke and the other judges were involved in a direct challenge with the king in 1616, when they decided that he could not command the common-law courts to desist from hearing cases pending, even if the royal interest was involved. When summoned before the king's council Coke was the only judge who stood his ground, and the king dismissed him. This was one of the grave mistakes of the early Stuarts in the matter of *rex v. lex*: King Charles' attempt to arrest the five members of parliament in 1642 was the climax of this ill-judged course of conduct.

Coke's place as a writer on English law is a proud one. His *Reports* (13 volumes, 1600–15) and *Institutes* (four volumes, 1628–44) contain a superb exposition of the rules of English common law.

**Colenso, John William** 1814–83. Colenso was born at St Austell in Cornwall. By hard work and with help from local people who recognized his ability he overcame his humble beginnings and entered St John's College, Cambridge, as a sizar; he was elected a fellow in 1837. After some years as a mathematics teacher at Harrow and a tutor at his own college Colenso became vicar of Forncett St Mary in Norfolk. He was appointed bishop of the new diocese of Natal in 1853; there his deeply committed interest in his African flock and his broadminded approach to tribal customs in marriage earned him the displeasure of the establishment. *A Commentary on the Epistle to the Romans* (1861) was very much a product of the new liberal theology and the establishment's disapproval increased; the storm broke over *The Pentateuch and Book of Joshua Critically Examined* (1862–79), which challenged the historical accuracy of those books and concluded that they were written during the post-Exile period. The Bishop of Cape Town, Robert Gray, deposed Colenso, who in turn challenged Gray's jurisdiction. Colenso was confirmed as holder of the see by the law courts in 1866 and he continued in the affection of his diocese until he died.

**Coleridge, Hartley** 1796–1849. The eldest son of Samuel Taylor Coleridge, Hartley Coleridge was born at Clevedon in Somerset. He attended Ambleside School, where his education was supervised by Robert Southey, and went on to Merton College, Oxford. He became a probationer fellow of Oriel College but was dismissed for 'intemperance' – with the puzzling circumstance that he was also paid £300 in compensation. The result was that he was obliged to earn a living outside university life, and he was no better fitted for this than his father would have been; he did some teaching and worked as a journalist. Hartley Coleridge is regarded as a poet of considerable promise which was never fulfilled. The small number of poems he left behind are of fine quality, particularly the sonnets, but they are not well known. His brother Derwent Coleridge edited his *Complete Poems*, with a memoir (1851)

and *Essays and Marginalia* in the same year. Hartley Coleridge published *Biographia Borealis, or The Lives of Northern Worthies* (1833), a *Life of Marvell* (1835), and an edition of *The Dramatic Works of Massinger and Ford* (1840).

**Coleridge, Mary Elizabeth** 1861–1907. Mary Coleridge was born in London and was a member of the same family as Samuel Taylor Coleridge. During her lifetime she gained a reputation as a novelist, earning praise from Robert Louis Stevenson for *The Seven Sleepers of Ephesus* (1893). Her poems were not published until after her death: her *Poems Old and New* (1907) and *Gathered Leaves* (1910) were for a time widely read. She is said to have refrained from publishing them out of deference to her great predecessor. The tone of her verse is mainly one of gloom and suffering; in spite of their acknowledged quality her poems did not stay in favour for very long. *The Collected Poems of Mary Coleridge* was edited by T. Whistler (1954).

**Coleridge, Samuel Taylor** 1772–1834. The son of John Coleridge, clergyman and schoolmaster of Ottery St Mary in Devonshire, Samuel Taylor Coleridge was the youngest of ten children by his father's second marriage and was intended for the Church. The child of John Coleridge's old age, he was his father's favourite, and this was not to his advantage in a house full of children. Bullied by his eldest brother, and by the family nurse who believed him to be overindulged, he withdrew into books and acquired a dislike for physical activity. The centre of his world, his father, died when Coleridge was nine years old. His mother sent him off to boarding-school, to Christ's Hospital near Clerkenwell in north London. It was a cheerless place, and once there he saw little of his mother or any member of his family, except for his brother George, who had become a teacher at nearby Hackney and was kind to him. At school, however, he was soon discovered to be uncommonly bright and he found a substitute family at the home of his friend Tom Evans. Coleridge developed an attachment for Mary Evans, Tom's sister.

While at Christ's Hospital Coleridge read the sonnets of William Lisle Bowles; his interest in poetry was sharply stimulated and also pointed away from the restrictive formalism of the 18th century. He went on to Jesus College, Cambridge, in 1791 with a modest exhibition to maintain him for seven years; it was expected that he would take holy orders and proceed to a fellowship. But at Cambridge his inability to manage his modest affairs resulted in a situation which, in spite of any financial help his brother

George could give him, seemed to get progressively worse. In 1773, at home in Ottery St Mary, his brothers found the money to pay his debts; on the way back to Cambridge he indulged in a 'tempest of pleasure' in London. At Cambridge he discovered that there was another suitor for Mary Evans's hand; being without means to compete for her 'though I knew she loved me', his way out of the impasse was to do something romantic. He joined the army under the name of Silas Comberbache. It seems plain however that, having made his gesture, Coleridge would have been horrified had he been taken seriously and left to make a military career. His brothers rescued him, returned him to Cambridge, and again paid his debts. But the university had no more to offer Coleridge and he left without taking a degree.

In June 1794 Coleridge set out on a walking tour with a college friend. Their destination was Wales, with a stop at Oxford on the way. The other university was quite different from Cambridge, where new ideas, predominantly those of the Revolution in France, were small change among the students. Oxford had remained undisturbed for the most part; but inevitably it seems, one of its few radical spirits, Robert Southey, was introduced to Coleridge at Balliol College. Southey was a monument of self-discipline compared to Coleridge, who was immediately attracted to the tall handsome classical scholar, at that period no less romantic than Coleridge himself. They discussed the founding of a community in America; Coleridge called it a Pantisocracy, but the idea got no farther than words. It was, however, important since it provoked Coleridge to eloquence, and a poet emerged from his unformed idealism. In 1795 he married Sara Fricker, a friend of Southey, after the Pantisocracy idea had died and Southey had turned, to Coleridge's disappointment, to a career in law. Sara's sister Edith became Southey's wife.

Coleridge's career as a poet began in 1793 with verses published in the *Morning Chronicle*; these contributions continued to 1795. In 1796 he founded a newspaper, *The Watchman*, but it lasted for only ten issues. His only other published work at this time was the first act of an historic drama, *The Fall of Robespierre*; Acts 2 and 3 were by Southey. In 1796 Joseph Cottle, publisher of the first edition of **Lyrical Ballads**, published Coleridge's first collection, *Poems on Various Subjects. Poems by S. T. Coleridge* (the second edition, 1797) also contained verses by Charles Lloyd, and by Charles Lamb, who had been at Christ's Hospital with Coleridge and was a friend and

Samuel Taylor Coleridge. The portrait by R. Hancock, 1796. National Portrait Gallery, London.

regular correspondent. *Fears in Solitude* (1798) contains 'France: an Ode' and 'Frost at Midnight'.

The Coleridges went to live at Nether Stowey in Somerset in January 1797, and in June of the same year visited William Wordsworth and his sister Dorothy, who were living at Racedown, 64 kilometres (40 miles) away. Wordsworth had met Coleridge first in Bristol two years before and greatly admired his talents. He visited him at Nether Stowey in March 1797, when he lifted Coleridge's spirits considerably, for Coleridge, chronically insolvent, had been deeply depressed. Wordsworth, though equally poor, lived in better order; his character was quite different from that of Coleridge, and Dorothy was fortunately at his side. Later the Wordsworths moved to Alfoxden, where the poets were in daily contact, which led to the publication of *Lyrical Ballads* in 1798. (See **Wordsworth, William** and *Lyrical Ballads*.) Early in the same year Coleridge met William Hazlitt, who was to be greatly influenced by the course of Coleridge's life.

Coleridge's contributions to *Lyrical Ballads* were 'The Foster-Mother's Tale', 'The Dungeon', 'The Nightingale', and **The Rime of the Ancient Mariner**. In the same period (1797–98) he wrote the first part of **Christabel** and **Kubla Khan**. This was one of his most productive and settled periods: the influence of Wordsworth, whom he admired unreservedly, was paramount;

at Nether Stowey he also enjoyed the friendship of Thomas Poole, a radical and scholarly bachelor who made a rich living in tanning and was unfailingly generous to the improvident Coleridge. Then the philanthropic and wealthy Wedgwood brothers provided him with a small annuity.

At the end of 1798 Coleridge went to Germany, where he felt his education would be completed. He considered that to possess talent was not enough while he was 'without the materials of Knowledge or systematic Information'. His wife Sara had just given birth to their second child and Thomas Poole and other friends disapproved of his action. But Coleridge thought 'the scheme of high importance to my intellectual utility; and of course to my moral happiness'. He travelled with the Wordsworths and John Chester, a neighbour at Nether Stowey. The child, Berkeley Coleridge, died in February 1799 and the news was sent to Coleridge by Thomas Poole.

When he returned from Germany in August of that year Coleridge had acquired another language, and some knowledge of physiology, anatomy, and natural history; he also brought back a box of books on metaphysics. A visit from the Southeys, on a walking tour in the West Country, helped re-establish a friendship which had definitely cooled. He then visited the Wordsworths in Grasmere but did not bother to inform his wife, who believed him to be in Bristol; whilst away he fell in love with Sara Hutchinson whose sister Mary married Wordsworth. Coleridge now accepted a job on *The Morning Post*, to which he was a regular contributor from 1798 to 1802. But in spite of his need of money, his considerable quality as a journalist, and an offer of the enormous salary of £2000 a year from the proprietor, Daniel Steward, to take a share in the running of *The Morning Post*, Coleridge had no liking for Grub Street. As a way of earning money to get himself away, he accepted an offer from Longmans to translate Schiller's *Piccolomini* and *Wallenstein's Death* as *Wallenstein* (1800).

Coleridge went to live near Keswick in Cumberland in July 1800, principally to be near Wordsworth. He had ambitions to write a biography of Gotthold Ephraim Lessing, and also to finish 'Christabel'. He wrote the second part of 'Christabel' and 'Hymn before Sunrise', saw a great deal of the Wordsworths, and walked in the spectacular Lake District; but his financial position seemed to worsen daily. He had been using opium since 1797 and was by now addicted to it; but it had not yet wreaked havoc with his life. 'Dejection: an Ode' dates from this period,

and in 1803 a third edition of *Poems* was published, selected and arranged by Charles Lamb. In the summer of the same year Coleridge went on a tour of Scotland with the Wordsworths but he returned home alone. They were travelling in an open carriage and the weather was continually bad; so too was Coleridge's health, but the Wordsworths allowed him to go alone, perhaps because his opium habit made him a difficult companion. Whatever the reason for their separation the friendship endured, and in April 1804 Wordsworth somehow found £100 to enable Coleridge to travel to Malta to take a post as secretary to the governor. It was hoped that the Mediterranean would improve his health, but Coleridge returned to England in August 1806 a physical wreck. He was completely dependent on opium; he was fat and drinking heavily; he could put his mind to nothing apart from the separation from the sorely tried Sara, to whom he granted the Wedgwood annuity to live on.

Coleridge stayed with the Wordsworths and somehow rallied his remaining mental powers. His gifts as a critic were demonstrated in lectures on the English poets delivered at the Royal Society (1808); then he began to plan a weekly, to be called *The Friend*. Wordsworth immediately appealed to influential friends, Scott and Lord Lonsdale among them, to subscribe; they did so but Wordsworth suffered some embarrassment when, after some months, the weekly had not appeared. However, helped by Sara Hutchinson, Coleridge published the first issue of *The Friend* in June 1809, and with the help of his friends kept it going through 28 issues, which were published in book form in 1818. In 1810 came the estrangement from his best friend (see also **Wordsworth, William**). In London Coleridge was fortunate enough to inspire the kindness of more friends, whilst a modest success in the theatre came to him with the production of *Remorse*, a tragedy, at Drury Lane in 1813. This was formerly called *Osorio* and written as early as 1797; two excerpts, 'The Dungeon' and 'The Foster-Mother's Tale', were part of Coleridge's contribution to *Lyrical Ballads*.

In spite of his ruined health, his addiction to opium, and the sad lack of application resulting in so few poems, Coleridge's mental powers could still rise to remarkable levels. His collection of critical essays, ***Biographia Literaria***, was written between 1808 and 1815, when he almost succeeded in dragging himself out of the pit. The work reveals his formidable intellect more clearly than any other: it has set a standard in English letters for such exercises.

In 1816 Coleridge settled in the house of Dr and Mrs James Gillman in Highgate; here he was well cared for and his opium addiction was kept under control. His work now was chiefly philosophical essays; the poet was irretrievably gone, but the critic was to be discovered when his unpublished writings came to light after he died in 1834. The idea of a work on spiritual philosophy was much in his mind during this last period but it remained unwritten, like the biography of Lessing. He published literary and political essays; a play, *Zapolya* (1817); *Sibylline Leaves* (1817), a collection of poems that did not include 'Christabel', 'Kubla Khan', and 'The Pains of Sleep', which were published together in 1816; *Aids to Reflection* (1825), and a satirical poem written in collaboration with Southey, *The Devil's Thoughts* (1827). *Anima Poetae*, edited from his notebooks by E. H. Coleridge (1895) contains some 'table-talk' and some philosophical writing that shows clearly the influence of the German transcendentalists.

Coleridge is a unique figure in English poetry and what little he produced contains great, yet unfinished, pieces. He was fortunate indeed in his friends: he seems to have had no sense of commitment to anyone and, had he not possessed considerable personal magnetism, he might – despite his brilliance – have been left to fend for himself early in his career. Posterity is concerned with Coleridge's genius, which contributed something lasting, rather than with his character. His addiction to opium should not be judged too harshly; laudanum (tincture of opium) was then the only known painkiller and for an unstable temperament the step from laudanum to opium was tragically easy. Coleridge was born in time to be excited by the changes happening in Europe, and then to react against them: but the Revolution in France was paralleled by another, in the arts, and Coleridge, more than any writer of the period, moved English literature out of the 18th century into new ways of thought and expression. Imagination was restored as the ruling creative force; emotion, pathos, and the finer shades of feeling became once more the concern of the poet.

The standard edition is *The Complete Poetical Works* edited by Ernest Hartley Coleridge (Oxford English Texts, 1912); the same text is in the single volume in Oxford Standard Authors (1912) and Oxford Paperbacks (1969). W. J. B. Owen's edition of *Lyrical Ballads* was published in 1969; J. Shawcross's edition of *Biographia Literaria* includes 'Aesthetical Essays' (1907). *The Collected Letters* were edited by Earl Leslie Griggs (six volumes, 1956–71).

**Colet, John** *c.*1467–1519. John Colet was born at Sheen in Surrey. He was the son of Sir Henry Colet, who was twice Lord Mayor of London. He studied at Oxford, in Paris, and in Italy (where he learned classical Greek). After returning to England Colet gave a series of lectures at Oxford (1496–1504) on the Epistles of St Paul. These were notable for their examination and exposition of Paul's words in the context of their time, rejecting the suffocating mass of metaphysical speculation that was the favourite occupation of generations of theologians. Erasmus attended Colet's lectures.

Colet was a vigorous critic of the condition of the church, though he never challenged religious dogma. He became Dean of St Paul's in 1505, and upon his father's death used a large part of his inherited fortune in the founding of St Paul's School. With the first headmaster of his school, William Lily, Colet wrote a Latin grammar, which Erasmus revised and which remained a standard textbook for 200 years. In 1758, after further emendations, it became the *Eton Latin Grammar*.

Colet's influence on learning and literature was profound. A great English scholar and a representative of the Renaissance, he was centuries ahead of his time in interpreting scripture. His friends Erasmus and Thomas More were also his students. He refused to allow any church interference in the running of his school, rejected the belief in relics and pilgrimages, and refused any money in his will for the saying of masses for the good of his soul.

***Colin Clouts Come Home Againe*** A pastoral poem by Edmund Spenser, first published in 1595. It was written in 1591, after the poet's visit to London for the publication of the first three books of *The Faerie Queene*, and dedicated to Raleigh. The poet speaks through Colin, a shepherd, who tells his friends about his journey over the sea and his visit to the court of Cynthia (Elizabeth). The queen is pleased with Colin's piping (poetry) and is generous to him; the arts are honoured at her court and a number of poets attend there. However, the court is also a place where ambition is ruthlessly pursued and Colin comes home again. He tells his friends that love cannot exist in such an atmosphere, and goes on 'Of loves perfection perfectly to speake'. Spenser describes love in the Platonic sense, as a force for universal good, and recalls his own love for Rosalind, the lady also spoken of in *The Shepheardes Calender*. Other figures who appear in the poem are Gabriel Harvey, who is called Hobbinol, and Raleigh, who is the Shepherd of the Ocean.

*Colkelbie's Sow, The Tale of*  A Scottish poem of the 15th century, telling how Colkelbie (the laird of Colkelbie in Stewarton, Ayrshire) sells a sow for three pence. The tale itself is really about the three pennies (the price of the sow) and what became of them and Colkelbie's subsequent fortunes.

The author of the poem is unknown. It is referred to by Gavin Douglas in his *Palice of Honour* (*c*.1501) and there is a manuscript of 1568. It was printed in David Laing's *Select Remains of the Ancient Popular Poetry of Scotland* (1822).

**Collier, Arthur** 1680–1732. A native of Wiltshire, Collier was educated at Pembroke and Balliol colleges, Oxford, and held the living of Langford Magna until his death. As a churchman Collier incurred suspicion because of his leaning toward Arianism and his interest in the teachings of Apollinarius the Younger (AD *c*.310–*c*.390). His *Clavis Universalis – or a Demonstration of the Non-Existence and Impossibility of the External World* (1713) is interesting because it demonstrated that Collier had arrived, independently, at the same conclusions as Berkeley had in *The Principles of Human Knowledge*. See **Berkeley, George**.

**Collier, Jeremy** 1650–1726. A nonjuring clergyman (one who, having taken the oath to James II, withheld it from William and Mary) and later a nonjuring bishop, Collier was educated at Ipswich School and Caius College, Cambridge. He was rector of Ampton, Suffolk (1679), and lecturer at Gray's Inn (1685). He remained loyal to King James and was imprisoned in 1689 and 1692; in 1696 he incurred further wrath by giving absolution, on the scaffold, to two men charged with attempting to assassinate King William. Collier was outlawed and fled the country; but he returned in 1697 and was not molested.

A man of unwavering courage, Collier was the author of *Essays upon Several Moral Subjects* (three parts, 1698–1705), *The Great Historical, Geographical, Genealogical and Poetical Dictionary* (1701); a translation, praised by Matthew Arnold, of the *Meditations of Marcus Aurelius* (1701) and *The Ecclesiastical History of Great Britain* (two volumes, 1708 and 1714). He is best known for his attack, *A Short View of the Immorality and Profaneness of the English Stage* (1698). (See **Congreve, William** and **Vanbrugh, Sir John**; both replied to Collier's attack. See also **Dennis, John** and **D'Urfey, Thomas**.) Collier went on relentlessly with further attacks (1699, 1700, 1703, and 1708) but fortunately did not prevail; had he done so he would have closed the theatres as firmly as did the Puritans in 1642.

**Collins, Anthony** 1676–1729. Collins was born in Heston, Middlesex, and educated at Eton and King's College, Cambridge. He became Deputy-Lieutenant of Essex in 1715.

An admirer of John Locke, he became his close friend and a freethinker and deist of considerable influence. His *Essay Concerning the Use of Reason* (1707) denied the accepted separation between those things that are beyond human reason and those that are not. *Priestcraft in Perfection* (1709) was an attack on the authority the church had assumed in the Thirty-Nine Articles (Article 20) to decree rites and ceremonies. *A Discourse of Freethinking, occasioned by the Rise and Growth of a Sect call'd Freethinkers* (1713) is a sharp attack on ministers of all denominations; it argues that free enquiry is the only way to the truth and, moreover, is the way commanded in scripture. The book was, inevitably, attacked by many churchmen, including Richard Bentley and Jonathan Swift. Collins's *A Philosophical Inquiry concerning Human Liberty and Necessity* (1715) is regarded as an able and clearly written statement of determinism.

**Collins, (William) Wilkie** 1824–89. The son of the painter William Collins, the author was born in London and always wanted to be a writer. But his father placed him in business until he was 22, when he was entered at Lincoln's Inn to read for the Bar. He was actually called to the Bar when he was 27 but by then he was writing and had published a memoir of his father (1848) and a historical novel, *Antonina: or the Fall of Rome* (1850). He was acquainted with Dickens and the two men became firm friends: they travelled together in Europe, acted in plays, and collaborated in writing. Collins was the author of two melodramas that Dickens produced and acted in, *The Lighthouse* (1855) and *The Frozen Deep* (1857), a number of short stories, in a sinister vein, most of them published in Dickens's periodical, *Household Words*, and three further novels, before he achieved a major success with **The Woman in White**, which began to appear in *All the Year Round* in November 1859. This and **The Moonstone** (1868) are his best work and have effectively pushed the rest of his novels, good as they are, into the background of Victorian fiction. Length requirements for serial publication, combined with the deliberate painstaking style of writing then in vogue, have to be transcended by something like genius to make books lastingly popular and it is a measure of the quality of these two that they are still read and enjoyed. Collins knew his law, and he took the trouble to be properly informed about medicine, drugs, chemistry, and hypnotism. He brought all his knowledge to bear in his other crime stories, of which the most notable are *No Name* (1862), *Armadale* (1866), and *Heart and Science* (1883). He went on writing novels, short stories, crime novels, and dramatic versions of his books and his output was large; but his claim to lasting fame lies in *The Woman in White* and *The Moonstone*.

**Collins, William** 1721–59. The son of a hatter, Collins was born in Chichester. He was educated at Winchester College and then at Magdalen College, Oxford – which he left upon taking his degree, having a dislike of academic pedantry. After a period of aimless dissipation and a refusal to take holy orders (his guardian saw the church as the only place where he could hope for some security), he went to London (1744) with almost no money, determined on a literary career.

Collins began to write poetry as a schoolboy and completed the *Persian Eclogues* (published in 1742) when he was 17. He spoke of them with contempt later; they were republished as *Oriental Eclogues* (1757). In London he published *Odes on Several Descriptive and Allegoric Subjects* (1746) but did not gain recognition immediately; he accepted an advance from a London bookseller for a translation of Aristotle's *Poetics* and retired to Chichester. Then he inherited £2,000 and promptly repaid the advance; he also abandoned the translation of Aristotle, but his plans for future work halted when his mental and physical health began to fail. He broke down completely after a journey in France (1750) and died insane at the age of 38, at his sister's house in Chichester.

Although small in quantity, the best of Collins's poetry suggests that his achievement might have been great. His temperament was unstable and he was always 'doubtful of his dinner or trembling at a creditor'. As Samuel Johnson went on to say, such a man 'is not much disposed to abstract meditations or remote inquiries'. His inheritance came too late to save him and his powerful imagination was not permitted the exercise that might have perfected its utterance. However, the poetry he left – less than 1500 lines – shows an original artist struggling to escape from the poetic conventions of his time and frequently succeeding. *Ode to Simplicity*, *Dirge in Cymbeline*, *Ode to Evening*, *How Sleep the Brave* (*Ode, Written in the Beginning of the Year 1746*), and the posthumous *Ode on the Popular Superstitions of the Highlands* have an honoured place in English poetry.

Collins's *Complete Works* were edited for the Oxford English Texts series by Richard Wendorf and Charles Ryskamp (1978). The standard modern edition is by Roger Lonsdale (1977) in *Gray and Collins: Poetical Works* in the Oxford Standard Authors and Oxford Paperbacks series.

**Collins, William** The silly, obsequious clergyman of Jane Austen's *Pride and Prejudice*. In a brilliantly written scene he proposes to Elizabeth Bennet, who rejects him decisively. But his self-satisfaction and his 'connections' will not allow him to take her refusal seriously.

*Collyn Clout* See **Skelton, John.**

**Colman the Elder, George** 1732–94. Colman was born in Florence, where his father was the English ambassador. He attended Westminster School, later went to Christ Church, Oxford, and was intended for a legal career. He was called to the Bar in 1757 but his friendship with David Garrick turned his attention to the theatre. A farce from his pen, *Polly Honeycombe*, was presented as Garrick's work at Drury Lane in 1760 and acknowledged as Colman's work after the success of his *The Jealous Wife*, based on episodes in Fielding's *Tom Jones* (Drury Lane, February 1761). The success of the latter play owed something to the expert advice Garrick gave his friend. *The Musical Lady* and *The Deuce is in Him*, two more farces, were produced at Drury Lane (March 1762 and November 1763) and Colman made adaptations of Beaumont and Fletcher's *Philaster* and Shakespeare's *A Midsummer Night's Dream*, but his next major success did not come until he collaborated with Garrick on **The Clandestine Marriage** (Drury Lane, February 1766). Unfortunately, the production caused a breach between them because Garrick did not want the part of Ogleby, which was written for him. In the event the part was played by Tom King; he and the play scored a great success but Colman moved away from Drury Lane and took over the management of Covent Garden, which he held until 1774. During his management Spranger Barry became famous as an actor and the plays of Goldsmith were presented. A number of Colman's own plays, of no importance now, were also presented there.

Colman took over the Haymarket from Samuel Foote in 1777 and managed it until 1789. Some of the plays he produced in his later career were by his son, George Colman the Younger, and he also published an edition of the works of Beaumont and Fletcher in ten volumes (1778). Colman translated the comedies of Terence (1765 and 1766) and *De Arte Poetica* of Horace (1783).

As a playwright Colman seemed to fare best when Garrick was at his side. *The Clandestine Marriage*, particularly, holds the stage and was very popular in translation in France and Germany. A modern edition of the play is published in The Modern Library *Twelve Famous Plays of the Restoration and Eighteenth Century*, edited by Cecil A. Moore (1933).

**Colman the Younger, George** 1762–1836. The younger Colman was educated, like his father, at Westminster School and Christ Church, Oxford. He also attended Aberdeen University before becoming fully involved in the theatrical activities of his father, who staged his son's first plays. The third one, called *Inkle and Yarico*, was a comic opera (Haymarket, August 1787) and enjoyed a real success. In 1789 Colman took over the management of the Haymarket from his father and in 1824 he became Examiner of Plays. As an administrator of censorship he earned considerable resentment, exercising a prudery in judgment at odds with his own work. His plays were successful; he wrote no less than 20, including *The Iron Chest* (Drury Lane, March 1796), based on Godwin's novel *Caleb Williams*, which later became a fine vehicle for Edmund Kean; *The Heir at Law* (Haymarket, July 1797); and *John Bull: or The Englishman's Fireside* (Covent Garden, March 1803).

*The Iron Chest* is published in a modern edition in The World's Classics *Eighteenth-Century Tragedy*, edited by Michael R. Booth (1965).

*Colonel Jack* (*The History and Remarkable Life of the Truly Honourable Colonel Jacque, commonly call'd Colonel Jack*). A novel by Daniel Defoe, first published in 1722. Like the earlier *Captain Singleton*, the novel is a romantic adventure narrated in the first person.

The narrator tells how he was abandoned by his parents while a small child. He falls among bad company, becomes a pickpocket, and reaches early manhood living on his wits. 'Colonel Jack' is the nickname given to the hero when he is a homeless waif living in the London stews. When his way of life becomes inimical to him he enlists as a soldier – but promptly deserts when faced with the prospect of fighting in Flanders. Next he is abducted and shipped to Virginia, where he is sold as a slave to a planter and where he begins at last to make his way in the world: he is promoted to overseer and eventually freed. He becomes a planter and is so successful that he is able to return to England a rich man. He experiences some vicissitudes in his married life but by the end of the tale he is prosperous and mellow. The early chapters are among the finest in Defoe's fiction.

**Colum, Padraic** 1881–1972. Patrick Colm was the son of the warden of the workhouse of Longford in Ireland. He went to school in Longford and then went to work as a railway clerk in Dublin. There his interest in literature took him to the circle of Yeats, Synge, AE, and Lady Gregory and to his first play, *Broken Soil* (1903). His enthusiasm for the Irish revival led him to adopt the Gaelic spelling of his name and he became Padraic Colum. In Ireland he made an impression as a playwright with further plays: *The Land* (1905), a play on the tragic flight, through poverty, of the Irish from their country; *The Miracle of the Corn* (1907), a one-act miracle play; and *Thomas Muskerry* (1910), a grim play about a workhouse warden. He began to publish poetry in 1907, with *Wild Earth*, and in 1916 founded *The Irish Review* with Thomas MacDonagh.

Colum went to the USA first in 1914 and eventually settled there in 1939. He is best known as a lyric poet and his work is frequently encountered in anthologies; 'She moved through the fair' is deservedly famous. *Collected Poems* (1932) was enlarged in 1953; *The Poet's Circuit: Collected Poems of Ireland* was published in 1960. *Our Friend James Joyce* (1958, with Mary Colum) is a book of reminiscences; *Ulysses in Nightgown* (1959, with M. Barkentin) presents dramatized episodes from Joyce's novel.

*Columbiad, The* A poem in heroic couplets by Joel Barlow, published in 1807. Barlow's aim was to write an American epic and the composition of this work occupied him on and off through the first part of his creative life. The first version, *The Vision of Columbus*, was published in 1787; Barlow believed that the final version was his masterpiece.

The poem tells of a vision revealed to the dying Columbus by an angel in which he sees the coming glory of America. Posterity has not been kind to the poem on which Barlow spent so much time and care; the model was Milton but Barlow only succeeded in producing an inflated and boring work.

**Combe, William** See *Syntax in Search of the Picturesque, Dr*.

*Comedy of Errors, The* A comedy by William Shakespeare and probably his first. It may have been produced as early as 1592 but there is a confirmed date of performance in 1594 and it was first published in the First Folio of 1623. The source of the comedy is the *Menaechmi* of Plautus: E. K. Chambers pointed out that while Shakespeare may well have had 'small Latin', in the words of Ben Jonson, the plays of Plautus and

Terence were fashionable in Elizabethan England and it would have been likely that Shakespeare was familiar with translations of them. *The Comedy of Errors* is an adaptation and for many years earned low opinions from the critics. But a production by the Royal Shakespeare Theatre in the early 1960s was a major success and demonstrated that Shakespeare, so early in his career, possessed remarkable stagecraft.

A merchant of Syracuse, Aegeon, has been arrested in Ephesus, an enemy city. He is required to pay a thousand marks – or his life is forfeit. Aegeon does not possess the sum but he explains to the Duke of Ephesus why he is in the enemy city. He is looking for his son, Antipholus – who is looking for his brother, also Antipholus: they are identical twins. When the boys were born, Aegeon and his wife Aemilia bought two slaves, also identical twins, and called them Dromio; those two boys became the sons' attendants. The family suffered a shipwreck and Aemilia and the first-born Antipholus with his Dromio became separated from Aegeon: he had never seen them since. On reaching manhood Antipholus of Syracuse and his Dromio had gone in search of them – and disappeared. Aegeon had searched for them for five years and come at last to Ephesus. The duke is moved enough by the story to grant the old man a stay of execution; he would spare him if the law allowed. Aegeon is given the rest of the day to find the ransom.

Antipholus the first-born has made his life in Ephesus after the shipwreck; he has married Adriana and his Dromio, who also survived, attends him. Antipholus of Syracuse and his Dromio have arrived in Ephesus on the day of Aegeon's arrest – and the comedy of errors begins. Dromio of Ephesus summons Antipholus of Syracuse home to dinner – and is claimed by Adriana as her husband. Antipholus of Ephesus is denied entrance to his own house and his understandable rage leads to his confinement as a lunatic. Adriana is infuriated by the behaviour of Antipholus of Syracuse, whom she thinks is her husband – he takes refuge in a convent to get away from her. The two Dromios are helplessly caught in the crossfire. The resolution comes at the end of the day when Aegeon's execution is due. The duke is confronted by Antipholus of Ephesus and the abbess – accompanied by an identical Antipholus of Syracuse. The knot is untied, the abbess proves to be Aemilia the long-lost mother, and all ends happily.

**Comical Revenge, The,** or *Love in a Tub*. A comedy by George Etherege, first produced in March 1664 and published in the same year. The play shows the influence of Molière's early style and is set in the last months of the Commonwealth.

The very slight comic plot concerns Sir Frederick Frolick's wooing by a rich widow, the impudence of the valet, Dufoy, who is wedged into a tub by his irritated fellow servants, and the cheating of the country knight, Sir Nicholas Cully. His cheaters are Palmer and Wheadle, and he is married off to Sir Frederick's former mistress, Lucy. Sir Frederick decides to marry the rich widow. The serious plot, in rhymed couplets, is almost a satire on the 'heroick' play: Aurelia loves Colonel Bruce, who loves Aurelia's sister Graciana, who loves Lord Beaufort. Bruce and Beaufort quarrel over Graciana and fight a duel; Beaufort wins, and Bruce tries to kill himself in despair. Beaufort takes Graciana; Bruce recovers from wounds both physical and mental, and is comforted by Aurelia.

**Coming of Arthur, The** See *Idylls of the King, The*.

**Coming Race, The** A romance by Bulwer-Lytton, first published in 1871. In the bowels of the earth there lives a race which in past ages took refuge there from floods. The narrator describes his visit to them and their discovery of Vril, an energy form embodying all the natural forces. Their society is utopian and despises those who need 'government'. It is also matriarchal and the narrator's life is endangered when he is considered a desirable choice as a mate. However, the sentimental ending brings the love of a good woman to help him escape and return to his own world.

**Commentaries on the Laws of England** An examination of statute and common law in England by Sir William Blackstone (1723–80), who was appointed first Vinerian Professor of Law at Oxford University in 1758 and became a judge in 1770. Blackstone endeavoured to present English law as an organic structure and his book, published in four volumes (1765–69), was praised for its clarity, dignity, and eloquence. However, it slips too easily into a hymn of praise and this provided Jeremy Bentham, who had heard Blackstone lecture at Oxford, with the material for his first published work, *A Fragment on Government* in 1776.

**Com-playnt of Roderyck Mors, The** See **Brinkelow, Henry**.

**Compleat Angler, The,** or the *Contemplative Man's Recreation*. Izaak Walton's classic discourse on fishing is in the form of a dialogue. A fisherman (Piscator), a huntsman (Venator), and a fowler (Auceps) each commend their own form of recreation; then Venator is tutored in angling by Piscator, and the two of them fish along the River Lea. (The River Lea runs into the Thames just below Blackwall Tunnel; in the 17th century its course, from its source in Hertfordshire, would have run through unspoiled country.) Piscator (Izaak Walton) gives instruction on every aspect of freshwater fishing, and a great deal of country lore and description find their way into the book as well as some instruction on the preparation of fish for the table.

The fifth edition of *The Compleat Angler* (1676) contains a continuation wherein the dialogue is between Piscator and a traveller, Viator, who is the Venator of the original. The continuation is the work of Charles Cotton, a Staffordshire gentleman and writer who takes his pupil fishing along the River Dove. His knowledge of fly-fishing supplies the instruction in which Walton, in the greater part of the book, proved deficient.

Walton's countryside is remarkably cheerful and sunlit – almost idyllic – and one should remember that he did not live in it. He was a successful townsman who used the country for recreation and this gives his picture its somewhat rosy colour. But his main achievement lies in keeping the reader's interest and in communicating a remarkable feeling of content.

**Compton–Burnett, Ivy** 1892–1969. Ivy Compton-Burnett was born in London and educated privately before proceeding to Royal Holloway College, University of London. She published a novel, *Dolores*, in 1911 but it was not until 1925 that with her second one, *Pastors and Masters*, that she found the setting and formula which suited her perfectly. She confined her characters to an Edwardian family setting and realized her plots through conversation – her novels are chiefly composed in dialogue. 'Appearances are not held to be a clue to the truth,' says one of her characters, 'but we seem to have no other.' Thus the author presents her characters and plots, without comment and with considerable wit. Ivy Compton-Burnett's experience was limited but within her chosen framework her observation, objective and unsentimental, covers a remarkable range of behaviour from the pettiest emotion to blackmail and murder. Her other novels are *Brothers and Sisters* (1929), *Men and Wives* (1931), *More Women than Men* (1933), *A House and its Head* (1935), *Daughters and Sons* (1937), *A Family and a Fortune* (1939), *Parents and Children* (1941), *Elders and Betters* (1944), *Manservant and Maidservant* (1947), *Two Worlds and Their Ways* (1949), *Darkness and Day* (1951), *The Present and the Past* (1953), *Mother and Son* (1955, James Tait Black Memorial Prize), *A Father and his Fate* (1957), *A Heritage and its History* (1959), *The Mighty and Their Fall* (1961), *A God and his Gifts* (1963), and *The Last and the First* (1971).

**Comus** (*A Maske Presented At Ludlow Castle 1634: On Michaelmasse night, before the Right Honorable, John Earle of Bridgewater, Vicount Brackly Lord President of Wales. . .*). A pastoral entertainment by John Milton, written at the request of his friend Henry Lawes to celebrate the Earl of Bridgewater's appointment to Wales and the Marches in 1634. The title 'A Maske' was used in the first three editions but it is not a masque in the court sense, in which singing and spectacle were more important than words. It was published anonymously in 1637. At the first performance the parts of the lady and her brothers were taken by the Earl of Bridgewater's children.

Three travellers, a lady and her two brothers, are stranded in a forest by nightfall. The brothers go in search of a spring and, attracted by sounds of revelry, the lady's wandering brings her to a shepherd, who offers her shelter in his cottage. He is Comus, son of Circe and Bacchus, and he has dismissed his rout at sight of the lady, his passion having been aroused by her beauty. When the brothers return they are told of what has happened by the benign Attendant Spirit, who has taken the form of a shepherd, Thyrsis. He warns them that Comus is an evil sorcerer who lies in wait for travellers and, in the guise of hospitality, gives them a potion that changes their faces into those of wild beasts and they then become part of his rout. The Attendant Spirit gives the brothers the root of the Haemony plant, of use against all enchantments, and shows them the way to the palace of Comus.

Comus has placed the lady in a chair that holds her fast by magic. His rout is enjoying a feast and the sorcerer presses a glass, containing the potion, on the lady. She refuses it and struggles to rise but he tells her that only his wand can release her. The brothers burst in with drawn swords; they subdue the rout but Comus escapes, taking the wand with him. However, the Attendant Spirit invokes Sabrina, goddess of the nearby River Severn, who releases the lady with pure drops of water from her own spring. After a song of thanks to Sabrina the lady and her brothers, guided by the Spirit, complete their journey to Ludlow Castle.

*Comus* was conceived by Henry Lawes (who

Ludlow Castle, where *The Masque of Comus* was first performed. A detail from an illustration in the edition of 1637.

apart from composing the music played the part of the Attendant Spirit) as a family entertainment. It is in fact neither a masque nor a play, and it continues to be read for the quality of its poetry.

**Confederacy, The** A comedy by John Vanbrugh, adapted from *Les Bourgeoises à la Mode* (1692) by Florent Dancourt. It was first produced in October 1705, and published in the same year.

Gripe and Moneytrap are both mean moneylenders, grown rich by charging high interest. Gripe falls in love with Mrs Moneytrap; Moneytrap falls in love with Mrs Gripe. The ladies confide in each other: both are going to exploit their husbands' weaknesses. Mrs Gripe, to pay her debts, has pawned her necklace to Mrs Amlet, a seller of cosmetics, whose unprincipled son Dick poses as a colonel and pursues Corinna, Mrs Gripe's daughter.

Dick has enlisted the help of Mrs Gripe's maid, Flippanta; his friend Brass acts as his footman. Mrs Gripe and Mrs Moneytrap use the maid and the footman as go-betweens, and each succeeds in extracting money from the other's spouse. Dick Amlet, meanwhile, has stolen Mrs Gripe's necklace from his mother and sends Brass out to sell it. But the goldsmith recognizes it as the one reported lost and takes it to Gripe. His wife, Moneytrap, and Mrs Moneytrap are present when the exposure takes place; the wives close ranks and challenge their husbands about the money, freely given though one wife has been forced to pawn her necklace. Dick Amlet's true character being exposed also, his prospects look bleak; but Corinna loves him and his mother makes him a generous cash settlement.

**Confessio Amantis** John Gower's major English poem was completed about 1390 and dedicated to King Richard II. Gower revised it about three years later, with a new dedication to 'his most valorous lord Henry of Lancaster', who usurped the throne and became Henry IV. The poem consists of 34,000 lines in couplets.

After a prologue in which he reviews the condition of the human race and announces that he will now write of love, a subject of universal

The poet makes confession to Genius, the priest of Venus. A scene from Book I of Gower's *Confessio Amantis. MS Egerton 1991, f.7v.* British Library.

interest, the poet (here the didactic Gower) adds that he will treat the subject in such a way as to instruct and entertain – for it is one in which men need guidance.

The Lover (the author) is one who feels that he has been too long in the service of love without reward. He wanders into a wood in the month of May and wishes for death. The god and goddess of love appear in the wood; the god will have none of him but Venus, appealed to, tells him to confess to her priest, Genius. If Genius is satisfied he will absolve him; then Venus will consider his case. The Lover complies and the priest instructs him on the Seven Deadly Sins, using stories to illuminate his lessons. Eventually Venus re-appears and shows the Lover his grey hair in a mirror: he is too old for love and so she dismisses him.

The poem's central interest lay in the collection of tales taken from classical and medieval sources. For the rest there is a great deal of moralizing though there is not an original thought to be found anywhere in the thousands of lines. In this respect Gower reflects his age better, perhaps, than does the genius of Chaucer; but the interest of his times is not alone a good enough reason for reading his work. He is most rewarding in short stretches when his skill and fluency are best appreciated.

Gower appears as Chorus in Shakespeare's *Pericles*, which is based on one of the stories in *Confessio Amantis*.

**Confessions of a Justified Sinner, The Private Memoirs and** A novel by James Hogg, first published in 1824.

George Colwan, the amiable and decent Laird of Dalcastle, marries Robina Orde. His wife shares his bed on the wedding night and conceives a child. Robina, however, is a religious fanatic, completely under the influence of her adviser, the Rev Robert Wringhim; she withdraws from her marriage bed into prayer and meditation. After a son is born to her, Robina becomes pregnant again and bears another son, whom the laird rejects, suspecting (rightly, the author implies) that the father is Robert Wringhim. While the laird allows the second son to grow up in his house, Robina enforces the separation of the two boys. Her conviction of the Calvinist doctrine of predestination is absolute; her lawful son is the offspring of earthly wickedness while the other, Robert, is the child of virtue. The brothers grow to manhood, usually apart and always at odds when they meet. The lawful son is murdered in a dark street in Edinburgh; the laird dies of a broken heart and the

minister's son inherits everything. Dissolute and vicious, Robert Wringhim goes on his evil way, until the late laird's housekeeper is able to confirm her suspicion that he is guilty of fratricide. But when the law officers go to arrest him he has vanished – though the servants had declared him to be in the house.

The second part of the novel is Robert Wringhim's story. Assured by his father that he is one of God's elect, he acknowledges no moral restraints whatever. The dreadful influence of his parents is reinforced by his friend Gil-Martin, a mysterious young man with whom, at their first meeting, he feels a powerful sympathy. Gil-Martin assures him that the opposition of others, if non-elect, is sinful; Robert is easily persuaded to persecute his half-brother and, eventually, to murder him. One of Robert's servants, attempting to warn him, tells him the story of Auchtermuchty, the village where all the people were deceived by a brilliant preacher – who was the devil in disguise. Wringhim has been growing uncertain about Gil-Martin's intentions towards him; now he finds himself at the young man's mercy.

The third part of the book is a brief conclusion. The narrator of the first part relates how he came into possession of Wringhim's story in manuscript and how the justified sinner died. Drawn to destruction as inexorably as Faust, though without realizing – he cannot conceive it – who Gil-Martin represents, he comes to his end. A drover sees two figures circling a hayrick in a strange way; he goes to see, but can find only one – a man who has hanged himself, Robert Wringhim.

*The Confessions of a Justified Sinner* should be far better known than it is. Walter Allen called it 'a psychological document compared with which Stevenson's *Dr Jekyll and Mr Hyde* is a crude morality.' André Gide introduced the edition published in 1947. John Wain, writing in 1980, unequivocally called it a major novel and makes the historical context a factor in his appreciation: 'The early nineteenth century, a period haunted by dreams and visions, when Western man felt himself to have passed through a cataclysm that had ended the old order and was not yet able to foresee the new.'

Modern editions of *The Confessions of a Justified Sinner* are by André Gide (already mentioned) and John Carey in the Oxford Paperbacks series (1970).

**Confessions of an English Opium Eater** An autobiographical account by Thomas De Quincey, which first appeared in two parts in *The London Magazine* in September and October

1821. It was first published in book form in 1822 with a medical appendix added. In 1856 De Quincey enlarged the book as Volume V of the *Selections Grave and Gay* published in Edinburgh (1853–60). In the 1856 edition De Quincey greatly extended the autobiographical material and filled out the short book with digressions: the 1822 version is preferred.

De Quincey tells how he first used opium (as laudanum) to give him relief from toothache, then a stomach disorder, and later to calm his nerves. Later he discovered the pleasures it could bring when he surrendered to its influence. His addiction began while De Quincey was at Oxford and at its strongest (*c.*1813) amounted to no less than 8000 drops each day. About 1816 De Quincey became alarmed at his condition and began to fight his dependence; the narrative ends with his account of how he conquered it. By the time of his marriage to Margaret Simpson (1817) he had, by a great effort of will involving severe distress, effected a gradual withdrawal. The book contains a vivid account of the extraordinary dreams he experienced; 'The Pleasures of Opium' is balanced by 'The Pains of Opium'.

*Confessions of an English Opium Eater* has been edited by Malcolm Elwin (both versions, with *Suspiria de Profundis*, 1956) and by J. E. Jordan (Everyman's Library, 1960).

**Confidence-Man, The:** *His Masquerade.* An unfinished novel by Herman Melville, first published in 1857. This satire was Melville's last work of fiction to be published during his lifetime.

A deaf mute boards the *Fidele*, a Mississippi steamboat, at St Louis; she is bound for New Orleans. He carries a slate on which he inscribes 'Charity thinketh no evil; suffereth long, and is kind; endureth all things; believeth all things; and never faileth.' This leads the other passengers to regard him as unbalanced, though the steamboat's barber's notice of no credit is seen as sane and proper. Confidence and lack of confidence – suspicion – are then personified in a series of characters who occupy various episodes.

*The Confidence-Man* is a puzzling book which remains low in Melville's canon for most of his admirers. Biographers and thesis writers pick their way through it, looking for revelations of his character at this stage of his life.

**Congo and Other Poems, The** A collection of poems by Vachel Lindsay, first published in 1914. The title poem is a celebration of Black Americans, using alliteration, rhyme, and syncopated rhythms, and including directions on how the poem should be read. More famous,

perhaps, is 'Abraham Lincoln Walks at Midnight'. Lindsay was born in Springfield, the town with which Lincoln's name was so closely associated. In the poem Lincoln walks once more in Springfield, his shade unable to rest because Europe is on the brink of war and pain and terror will soon be abroad in the world.

**Congreve, William** 1670–1729. Congreve was born at Bardsey in Yorkshire. His father commanded a garrison in Ireland, and Congreve received his education at Kilkenny School and Trinity College, Dublin, where Jonathan Swift was a fellow student. Congreve entered the Middle Temple to study law in 1690 but there is no evidence that he ever practised. His first work was a novel, *Incognita* (1692); his next a comedy, **The Old Bachelor**, which he showed to Dryden. The master was so impressed that he and Thomas Southerne generously helped the young Congreve polish it for the stage. It was produced in 1693 and made the author famous.

*The Double Dealer* (1694) and *Love for Love* (1695) were followed by his only tragedy, at the time successful, *The Mourning Bride* (1697). During the following year Jeremy Collier published his *Short View of the Immorality and Profaneness of the English Stage*, concentrating his attack on Congreve and Vanbrugh; Congreve published a reply, *Amendments of Mr Collier's false and imperfect citations* (1698). His last play, **The Way of the World** (1700), was not a success, and so, it is said, Congreve gave up writing for the stage.

Financially, Congreve was secure, having obtained three lucrative sinecures through the influence of his patron, Charles Montague (later Lord Halifax). Alexander Pope, Swift and Richard Steele were among his friends, and he was visited by Voltaire when the great French writer came to England in 1726; but the visit disappointed Voltaire. Congreve enjoyed the continuing friendship of Anne Bracegirdle, the celebrated actress who was the star of his comedies, and of Sarah Churchill.

Other works by Congreve were a pastoral elegy on the death of Queen Mary, *The Mourning Muse of Alexas* (1695); *A Pindarique Ode* (1695) on one of King William's victories; a poem, *The Birth of the Muse* (1698); a masque, *The Judgement of Paris* (1701); *A Hymn to Harmony* (1703); a pastoral, *The Tears of Amaryllis* (1703); and *A Pindarique Ode* (1706) on the victories of Queen Anne's armies. *Semele* was published in 1710 and a tale, *An Impossible Thing*, in 1720. *Semele*, described as 'an unacted opera', was used with additions by Alexander Pope, for the libretto of

Handel's secular oratorio and was first sung in 1744. The most considerable work of Congreve's 28 years since *The Way of the World* was his edition of *The Dramatic Works of John Dryden* (1717). Pope dedicated his version of *The Iliad* to Congreve in 1715.

Congreve's later years were troubled by gout and blindness but he enjoyed the company and esteem of both the literary world, in which he no longer competed, and society. According to Macaulay, Congreve had always aspired to worldly success and had found his way into the most exclusive society through his plays. In his affluent later life it bored him, apparently, to hear his comedies praised and this infuriated Voltaire. Congreve dismissed his stage successes as the product of an idle hour and preferred to be regarded as a gentleman. 'If you had been merely a gentleman, I should not have come to see you,' was Voltaire's reply. Congreve never married, and in his later years spent much time with the Duchess of Marlborough, daughter of John Churchill. Sarah was by then the Dowager Duchess and he left her, though she had no need of it, the bulk of his estate when he died. He suffered a fall when his carriage overturned during a visit to Bath in the summer of 1728, and died in January 1729. He lies buried in Westminster Abbey.

Congreve's first work for the stage came 33 years after the Restoration but he is always classified as a Restoration dramatist, as are Vanbrugh and Farquhar. With Congreve the comedy of manners reached a level of achievement shared with little else in English drama; perhaps only *The School for Scandal* and *The Importance of Being Earnest* can be considered in the same breath as *Love for Love* and the best scenes of *The Way of the World*. Congreve is the finest of the Restoration playwrights because his wit is subtler and his observation keener than that of his contemporaries; he is more poised and detached, with more of that indefinable quality – style. He was not good at plots; its feeble plot spoils *The Way of the World* and gives pride of place to *Love for Love*, a less brilliant comedy. It is regrettable that Congreve, after the infinite promise of his two best plays, wrote no more for the theatre.

The complete plays of Congreve were edited by H. J. Davis (1967). Bonamy Dobrée's two-volume edition also contains poems and miscellanies (The World's Classics, 1925–28).

**Coningsby**, or *The New Generation*. A novel by Benjamin Disraeli, first published in 1844.

Harry Coningsby is the orphan grandson of the Marquess of Monmouth. Upon his parents'

death (they had married without the Marquess's approval), Harry is favoured by his grandfather and sent to Eton. His friend there is Oswald, son of the wealthy manufacturer, Millbank, who is Lord Monmouth's bitterest enemy. It falls to Harry to save Oswald's life.

Harry completes his education at Cambridge and develops political views opposed to his grandfather's. He also falls in love with Edith Millbank, Oswald's sister. Lord Monmouth, growing more estranged by his grandson's leanings and resenting his love for Edith Millbank, dies and disinherits Harry, who becomes a barrister. Now Millbank, who had opposed the marriage as strongly as Lord Monmouth, has a change of heart, impressed by Harry's resolution. All ends well with Harry Coningsby married to Edith, and elected to parliament for Millbank's constituency.

The political background of *Coningsby* is the period between the Reform Bill of 1832 and the fall of Melbourne's government in 1841. Disraeli's political enemy was Sir Robert Peel and he blamed him, rightly or wrongly, for most of what was wrong with the Conservative approach. Disraeli and the Young England faction of the Conservatives saw that change was urgently needed and wanted to be the initiators of that change, thereby having it on their terms while holding on to power.

**Conington, John** 1825–69. Conington was born at Warwick and educated at Rugby School and Magdalen College, Oxford. He became a fellow of University College and was appointed the first Professor of Latin at the University of Oxford in 1854. Conington published editions of the first two parts of the *Oresteia* of Aeschylus (1848 and 1857), Virgil (1858–71), Persius (1872), and Horace (1863). He also published translations of Virgil, Persius, and Horace and completed P. S. Worsley's translation of *The Iliad* (1868).

**Connecticut Wits** An American literary group of the late 18th century, also called the Hartford Wits, because the members were centred at Hartford (though most of them came from Yale), where there was a development of interest in literature at this period. Though they copied English models, particularly the Augustans, their aim was to further American literary independence. However, they clung to orthodox Calvinism and opposed egalitarianism; the verse satires *The Anarchiad* (1786–87), *The Echo* (1791–1805), and *The Political Greenhouse* (1799) were expressions of their views. Among the 'wits' were Joel Barlow, Timothy Dwight, and John Trumbull.

*Connecticut Yankee in King Arthur's Court, A*
A satirical fantasy by Mark Twain, first published in 1889.

Hank Morgan, a mechanic, is knocked out during a fight; when he comes round he finds himself at Camelot in the year 528. Sir Kay the Seneschal is put in charge of him and promptly imprisons him. Paraded before the Knights of the Round Table, Hank is condemned to death; but he poses as a magician and successfully predicts an eclipse. Arthur is so impressed that he makes Hank one of his ministers and the Yankee strengthens his position at court by using his knowledge of 19th-century technology. However, the court, the church, Merlin, and Morgan-le-Fay close ranks against him when he tries to use his knowledge to improve the lives of the peasantry. He accompanies Arthur when the king, in disguise, goes among his people to see how they live. A plot to capture Arthur is foiled when Hank's specially trained troop of knights arrives on bicycles to rescue them.

Hank falls in love with Alisande, whom he calls Sandy, and they marry. When their daughter falls ill he takes his little family to France. While they are away, however, Arthur's enemies undo his work and kill the king – soon England is in the grip of civil war. Hank hurries back; with a group of friends he proclaims a republic and with modern weapons defeats an attack. He is wounded, however, and accepts Merlin's offer of his healing arts. But Merlin puts him into a deep 400-year sleep and history returns to its normal course.

If *A Connecticut Yankee* is not a complete success it is because Mark Twain, the humorist, is sometimes defeated by his own gifts. The book is very funny in places but in others, where subtlety is essential, he tumbles into excess and weakens his satire. The book is notably poignant; Hank's realization that he is back in the 19th century brings him the pain of knowing that his Sandy and their baby are lost to him forever. And there is a persistent ache for the green fields and clear streams of man's childhood; technology is marvellous, but is the sunlight as clear now?

**Connell, Evan (Shelby), Jr** 1924– . Connell was born in Kansas City and educated at Dartmouth and the universities of Kansas, Stanford, and Columbia. He served in the US Navy during World War II. A steadily successful writer of short stories, he published his first collection in 1957 as *The Anatomy Lesson and Other Stories. Mrs Bridge* (1958) used the life of a suburban woman, depicted in a series of sketches embracing her successful husband and her children; Mrs Bridge is an unfailingly kind but not very bright woman and the author achieved a remarkable range of humour and pathos. Among other works by Evan Connell are *Mr Bridge* (1969), an unsuccessful attempt to provide a parallel story to *Mrs Bridge*; the novels *The Patriot* (1960), *The Diary of a Rapist* (1966), and *The Connoisseur* (1974); *At the Crossroads* (1965, short stories); a philosophic poem, *Notes from a Bottle Found on a Beach at Carmel* (1963); and a volume of verse, *Points From a Compass Rose* (1973).

*Conquest of Granada, The; or Almanzor and Almahide.* A heroic tragedy in two parts by John Dryden, first published in 1672 and written in rhymed couplets. The first part was produced in December 1670, the second in January 1671. John Evelyn attended a performance on 6 February 1671 but the entry in his diary confines praise to 'very glorious scenes & perspectives, the worke of Mr Streeter'. He may well have found the story difficult to follow, with three love stories of varying importance going on at once. The main plot concerns the last days of Granada, before the city falls to Ferdinand and Isabella. The Moorish ruler Boabdelin is harried by the rivalry of the principal families, the Abencerrages and the Zegrys. Almanzor, a noble stranger, arrives in the city and fights for the Moors. Almahide, betrothed to Boabdelin, falls in love with the stranger but repulses his advances. Boabdelin is jealous of Almanzor but needs his prowess. When the Spaniards capture the city Boabdelin is killed and it transpires that Almanzor is of noble Spanish birth. Almahide and Almanzor are married at the end of the play.

*Conquest of Granada, A Chronicle of the*
Washington Irving's history of the defeat of the Moors in Spain was first published in 1829. A revised edition was issued in 1850. In spite of Irving's decision to present the chronicle in a fictional frame (it purports to be based on a work by a fanatical monk, Antonio Agapida) the book was praised by W. H. Prescott for its careful documentation. Irving's sympathies are with the Moors; the Spaniards are displayed as coarse and barbarous in comparison.

**Conrad, Joseph** 1857–1924. Jozef Teodor Konrad Nalecz Korzeniowski was born near Berdichev in the Polish Ukraine. The area is now held by the USSR; in Conrad's childhood it was held by Tsarist Russia and Conrad's father, Apollo Korzeniowski, became involved in revolutionary politics. He also wrote plays and poetry and translated Victor Hugo and Shakespeare, but his interest in politics attracted more

Joseph Conrad, 1904.

attention and in 1862 he was sent, with his family, to the harsh climate of Vologda in Russia. The hardships of exile led to his wife's death three years later, when his son was seven years old. For the next four years Apollo Korzeniowski struggled to bring up his son and educate him: the boy Jozef found in reading some refuge from a life that was both harsh and dull, and he was attracted to the romances of Captain Marryat and Fenimore Cooper. His father taught him French and he spoke and read the language with ease as an adult.

In 1869 Korzeniowski was allowed to travel. His health was breaking down and he was issued with a passport that would have allowed him to travel as far as Madeira. But he had no money and he returned to Poland with his son, first to Lwow and then to Cracow, where the boy went to a day school. Korzeniowski died of tuberculosis in May 1869, and Jozef's guardianship was undertaken by his maternal uncle, Tadeusz Bobrowski, who for 25 years gave unstinting help, affection, and advice to a boy whose turbulent childhood had made him a moody and difficult charge. Jozef, the son of a landlocked country, had only seen the sea once, when his uncle took him to Odessa, but he wanted to be a sailor and his reading, no doubt, had something to do with his am-

bition. His uncle tried to dissuade him but, as the son of a political convict, Jozef was liable for service in the Russian army – long years to be served in the ranks. Tadeusz yielded, and Jozef went to Marseilles; in 1874 he made his first voyage, to Martinique, as an apprentice.

Kind Uncle Tadeusz was summoned to Marseilles in 1878: Jozef had lost borrowed money gambling at Monte Carlo and had shot himself. He had had many other adventures and fortunately the self-inflicted wound did not prove fatal. Recovered, he joined an English ship bound for Constantinople and went to Lowestoft on the homeward voyage. His first visit to England, this found him with only a few words of the language (June 1878). In October of that year he sailed from London to Australia on a wool clipper; in 1880 he qualified as Second Mate, in 1884 as First Mate. He became a British citizen in 1886 and took his Master's certificate in the Merchant Service in the same year. His first experience of a steamship was as Mate on the *Vidar* in 1887; the voyage up the Congo, which damaged his health and provided the background for **Heart of Darkness**, took place in 1890. The backgrounds of all his novels are authentic and can be traced in the story of his life.

Korzeniowski began to write in his London lodgings. His command of the written language is astonishing and his emergence as an original prose stylist may be explained by his use of English as a literary language. He never learned to speak it well and indeed had never heard it spoken until he was 21. His first novel took five years to write: *Almayer's Folly* was completed in the same year that Tadeusz Bobrowski died (1895). It was read by Edward Garnett at T. Fisher Unwin, of Paternoster Row in the shadow of St Paul's, and published in 1895 under the name of Joseph Conrad. He was 37; he had begun another book meanwhile, *An Outcast of the Islands* (1896), and he married Jessie George in 1896.

Recognition by the public came slowly but the literary world took a lively interest in Joseph Conrad from the beginning. **The Nigger of the Narcissus** (1897), *Tales of Unrest* (1898), **Lord Jim** (1900), *Youth* (1902), *Typhoon* (1903), **Nostromo** (1904), **The Secret Agent** (1907), *A Set of Six* (1908), **Under Western Eyes** (1911), and *Twixt Land and Sea* (1912) give some idea of his unflagging industry. He also collaborated on two novels with Ford Madox Ford, *The Inheritors* (1901) and *Romance* (1903), and published two books of autobiography, *The Mirror of the Sea* (1906) and *A Personal Record* (1912). He achieved financial success with **Chance** (1914), which became a best-seller, and followed it with another, *Victory* (1915). *Within the Tides* (1915), *The Shadow-Line* (1917), *The Arrow of Gold* (1919), *The Rover* (1923), *Suspense* (1925), and *Tales of Hearsay* (1925) were part of a larger body of work that included essays, journalism, and three dramatizations from his fiction: *One Day More*, produced in 1905, from 'Tomorrow' in *Typhoon*; *The Secret Agent*, produced in 1922, from the novel of the same name; and *Laughing Anne*, not produced, but published in 1924, from 'Because of the Dollars' in *Within the Tides*.

Joseph Conrad is acknowledged by most critics as the most distinguished novelist, with Henry James, of the late 19th and early 20th centuries. He is a moralist, an examiner of the springs of action and the nature of modern man – living in an age of anxiety when the strength of his defences against betrayal, corruption, and evil depends on his keeping faith with himself – and of the consequences when those defences are breached. Conrad often employs a narrator, an observer who speaks for him and through whom all aspects are scrutinized. The device works to fine effect in some works, notably *Lord Jim* and *Heart of Darkness*, but is seen to be overused by 1913, when Conrad wrote *Chance*. *Nostromo*, considered by many to be his finest novel, dispenses with a narrator and presents a gallery of finely observed characters.

Conrad suffered from ill health during his later years but he went on writing and, as one of the most famous of living authors, had a triumphant but exhausting reception in the USA in 1923. In his last year he was offered a knighthood which he declined. He died at Oswalds, his home near Canterbury, on 3 August 1924.

**Conscious Lovers, The** A comedy by Richard Steele, first produced at Drury Lane in 1722 and first published in 1723. The plot is based on the *Andria* of Terence and reflects the author's attitudes to the fashionable behaviour of the time. The hero is Bevil, who is contracted to marry Lucinda, the daughter of rich Mr Sealand. But Bevil loves his ward, Indiana, whom he found as a destitute orphan and has supported ever since; Indiana returns his love. Bevil's friend Myrtle loves Lucinda, while Lucinda herself is pestered by another suitor, Cimberton, whose motive is her wealth. Bevil makes an honest statement to Lucinda; the marriage was his father's wish but he loves Indiana. Myrtle is offended by Bevil's candour, feeling it offensive to Lucinda, and challenges Bevil to a duel. Bevil declines and the author takes the opportunity in the scene to ridicule the convention of duelling. The resolution of the play comes with the revelation that Indiana is Sealand's lost child, a daughter from his first marriage. Lucinda's dowry is halved for the benefit of Indiana and the two girls are happily provided for. The greedy Cimberton withdraws when he learns that Lucinda's wealth will be only half what he had hoped for. *The Conscious Lovers* was a popular success; it held the stage for a number of years but has not been revived in the modern theatre.

**Conspiracy of Pontiac, History of the** See **Parkman, Francis** and *France and England in North America*.

**Constable, Henry** 1562–1613. Constable is remembered for his contribution to the sonnet-eering that became fashionable in the late 16th century. He was educated at St John's College, Cambridge, and lived in Paris after becoming a Roman Catholic. In 1599 Constable went to Scotland as papal envoy and was later awarded a pension by Henri IV of France. He returned to England in 1603 but was imprisoned in the Tower for a brief period in 1604 and left England once more after his release. He died in Liège. Constable's work owes much to the French of Philippe Desportes. His book of 23 sonnets, *Diana, the Praises of his Mistres*, was first published in 1592 and reissued in 1594 with additional poems by Constable and others.

**Constitutional Code for the Use of all Nations, A** A system of democratic government by Jeremy Bentham, first published in 1830. The author had extensive knowledge of the extent to which the vested interests ('sinister interests' in his words) of rank, profession, and trade are inimical to the public interest and he recommends a system which will keep their promotion under control. The full title of Bentham's book continues 'and all governments professing liberal opinions'.

**Contarini Fleming:** *A Psychological Romance*. A novel by Benjamin Disraeli, first published in 1832.

Contarini Fleming, wretched at school with his imaginative and romantic disposition, runs away, and is introduced to the social and political circles of his father, a Saxon nobleman. His father encourages him to realize his wish to be a writer. He visits the home of his mother, a Venetian woman of ancient family, and while in Venice falls in love with and marries his cousin, Alceste Contarini. The marriage fails within a year and Alceste leaves him. After travels in the Levant and Spain, Contarini settles down in Rome and opens his house as a centre for the study and creation of 'the beautiful'.

**Contention of Ajax and Ulisses for the Armor of Achilles, The**   See **Shirley, James.**

**Contrast, The**   The first US comedy, *The Contrast* was written by Royall Tyler in three weeks after attending a performance of *The School for Scandal* in New York. It was produced in the same year (1787) and published in 1790.

Maria van Rough is to marry Bill Dimple; the match has been arranged by Maria's father. Dimple is intensely anglophile and a disciple of Lord Chesterfield, which he believes sanctions his silly flirtations with the wealthy Letitia and with Charlotte Manly. Charlotte's brother, Colonel Manly, is in love with Maria. Dimple gambles away his fortune and decides that he should marry Letitia; Maria's father discovers his baseness and gives his blessing to Colonel Manly's suit. Dimple finally comes to grief when Letitia learns of his flirtation with Charlotte Manly.

A subplot concerns Manly's servant, Jonathan, and Dimple's, the devious and conceited Jessamy. They both court Jenny, a maid, and Jessamy offers Jonathan what appears to be good advice but which is calculated to make him appear foolish. However, Jenny rejects both of them when she learns what has been going on.

**Cook, Captain James** 1728–79.   The great navigator left records of his three principal voyages and also published his *Sailing Directions* (1766–68). The journal of his first voyage (1768–71) was edited by Captain W. J. L. Whar-

ton and published as *Journal During his First Voyage* (1893). *A Voyage towards the South Pole and Round the World in 1772–1775*, the second voyage, was published in 1777. The last, *A Voyage to the Pacific Ocean in 1776–1780*, was published in three volumes (1784): the first two volumes are by Cook, who was killed in Hawaii, and the third, which includes the voyage home, by Captain T. King.

**Cooke, John Esten** *c.*1830–86.   Cooke was a Virginian; and almost all his work is concerned with life in colonial Virginia and the Old South. His novels could be dismissed as sentimental evocations of a past which never really existed; but his purpose was to entertain and he must have succeeded as his work was very popular in his lifetime. Set in Virginia were *Leather Stocking and Silk* (1854) and, more notably, **The Virginia Comedians** (1854) and its sequel *Henry St John, Gentleman* (1859).

Cooke served in the Confederate army throughout the Civil War but managed nonetheless to complete his *Life of Stonewall Jackson* (1863). The war over, he published a biography, *Robert E. Lee* (1871), then went on to write military essays and a series of historical romances of which the most interesting was **My Lady Pokahontas** (1885).

**Cook's Tale, The**   See **Canterbury Tales, The.**

**Coolbrith, Ina Donna** 1842–1928.   The work of Ina Coolbrith has not survived the judgment of posterity. The first poet of California, her importance now is as part of regional development in Western literature. Her poetry is simple lyric verse and was published in *A Perfect Day* (1881), *The Singer of the Sea* (1894), and *Songs from the Golden Gate* (1895). Ina Coolbrith was associated with Bret Harte in the editorship of the *Overland Monthly*.

**Cooper, James Fenimore** 1789–1851.   The son of William Cooper, an enterprising and wealthy land agent who founded Cooperstown in upstate New York, James Fenimore Cooper was born in Burlington, New Jersey. He was educated at Albany (his father had established an estate at Cooperstown) and later received a first-class classical training at Yale. He also found his social level, among the sons of the 'first families' – the young democracy was remarkably class-conscious – but was expelled in 1805 for a prank.

Cooper spent the next five years at sea, first on merchantmen and then as a midshipman in the US Navy. He left the sea in 1811 to marry the daughter of one of the first families; he was 21 years old and materially secure.

A scene from Royall Tyler's comedy *The Contrast*, first published in 1790. Jonathan goes to the defence of his master, Colonel Manly.

'Going down the rapids.' An illustration for James Fenimore Cooper's *Leather-Stocking Tales*.

The Coopers were living at Searsdale when Cooper's wife, Susan (née Delancey), heard him grumbling about an English novel he was reading. She challenged him to do better and he wrote a novel of manners in English society, *Precaution* (1820), which could be described as Jane Austen on the frontier. Cooper was 30 years old and a convinced republican living in comfortable circumstances; but he fulfilled himself as a novelist, and there is no doubt that his experiences as a sailor were invaluable – he could write with first-hand knowledge of a wider world than the one his contemporaries knew. He achieved success with his second novel, **The Spy** (1821), and in 1823 published a novel of the sea, *The Pilot*, and the first of the **Leather-Stocking Tales – The Pioneers**. The Coopers moved to New York City; he became established as a leading American author and founded the Bread and Cheese Club as an informal meeting place for American writers.

Cooper planned a series of novels to celebrate each of the 13 original states of America and published *Lionel Lincoln* (1825), a story of Boston during the Revolution. But the success of *The Pioneers*, and Cooper's preoccupation with the meeting of civilization with wilderness – the frontiers were moving ever westward – led to **The Last of the Mohicans** (1826) and **The Prairie** (1827) in which he extended the life and adventures of his frontiersman, Natty Bumppo. The books made him world-famous, offering a theme new to the world of letters, with representations of the North American Indian that had enormous appeal for a romantic age. To his fellow Americans his novels seemed a celebration of the frontier spirit that, to the east-coast Americans in the 1820s, was already a matter of romantic nostalgia.

Cooper took his family to Europe in 1826 and stayed there for about seven years. He became a nominal US consul (at Lyons) and travelled a great deal, but he continued to write. A story of the sea, *The Red Rover*, was published in 1827, a novel of early American frontier life, *The Wept of Wish-ton-Wish*, in 1829, and another sea story, *The Water Witch,* in 1830. An ambitious historical trilogy, *The Bravo* (1831), *The Heidenmauer* (1832), and *The Headsman* (1833), completed a remarkable period of activity in fiction. He became friends with Scott while in Europe and – perhaps more significantly – with Lafayette. He wrote political essays and was on the way to forming the convictions that, when expressed in his writing, later earned him unpopularity in America. He returned there in 1832.

Cooper believed that a democratic republic could not survive if it insisted too firmly on egalitarianism. He was depressed by the America he had returned to, and saw the original conception of liberty upon which his country was founded being manipulated by those who used money as power as effectively as privilege and position were used in the Europe he had left. Cooper was a very famous American and commanded attention; he expressed his views with considerable energy in a satire, *The Monikins* (1835), and in the four volumes of *Gleanings in Europe* (1837–38) he presented a sharp-edged report on the Old World. *The American Democrat* (1838) encapsulates his political beliefs; the novels *Homeward Bound* and *Home as Found* of the same year present them in fictional form. He was, inevitably, attacked in the press but he brought libel actions against the more vicious newspapers and won every case.

The last decade of the author's life was prolific – he wrote no less than 21 books. The most notable are **The Pathfinder** (1840) and **The Deerslayer** (1841), which completed the *Leather-Stocking Tales*; two novels of the sea, *Afloat and Ashore* and *Miles Wallingford* (1844), which drew on his own experiences; and a trilogy of contemporary life in New York State called the **Littlepage Manuscripts: Satanstoe**, **The Chainbearer** (both 1845), and **The Redskins** (1846). This last group is considered to be his finest work by many scholars.

James Fenimore Cooper's young life resembles

something imagined by a Hollywood script-writer. He was the son of a land agent who achieved material success and personal distinction (he became a judge) by hard work, enterprise, and imagination. His father's knowledge of frontier life and of the wilderness so recently conquered had a continuing fascination for the young Cooper and he knew the territory extremely well. At the same time he was a rich man's son, with the confidence and assurance that such security bestowed on him. But he was spirited and adventurous enough to face years at sea when a sailor's life offered a great deal of hardship and danger. He was, obviously, a fortunate young man inasmuch as he could leave the sea when he wanted to. Nevertheless his convictions did grow out of a wide-ranging experience of life and he always had the courage to state them, never yielding because of the resulting unpopularity, and counterattacking, with notable success, a press which was under no restraint in what it chose to say about him.

Cooper's great fame was deserved and his best work deserves its classic status; this in spite of its considerable faults in structure and character drawing. When he was not dealing with frontiersmen or Indians or seamen he failed to give life to his characters and he did not begin to overcome this fault until the last trilogy. But his readers were fascinated by the redskins and palefaces and the romance of frontier life; that was what mattered and the reason why, probably, he has remained a favourite with younger readers, to whom conventional adults are always made of wood in any case. But as a celebration of the westward move of America the five novels of the *Leather-Stocking Tales* have no rival and Cooper's sea stories earned the praise of Herman Melville. The last trilogy, the first family chronicle in the American novel, deserves to be better known.

**Coral Island, The**  See **Ballantyne, R(obert) M(ichael)**.

**Corbett** (*or* **Corbet**), **Richard** 1582–1635. The son of a London gentleman, Corbett managed his advancement deftly enough to secure the patronage of the Duke of Buckingham, becoming chaplain to James I, Dean of Christ Church, and Bishop of Oxford and of Norwich in succession. He also wrote some verse, published after his death: *Certaine Elegant Poems. Written by Dr Corbet, Bishop of Norwich* (1647) and *Poëtica Stromata* (1648). From the former comes his best-known poem, **Farewell, Rewards & Fairies**.

**Cordelia**  The youngest of the three princesses in Shakespeare's *King Lear*. She answers her father honestly – a grave mistake, since he is looking for flattery and extravagant avowals of undying affection. The King of France marries her after she is dispossessed and banished by her father. Her part in the play is quite small – she is turned out in the first scene and is off-stage until Act IV Scene 4, when she brings an army to England to avenge the wrongs done to the father who had dealt with her so harshly. She is murdered on the orders of Edmund.

**Corelli, Marie** 1854–1924. The pseudonym of the novelist Mary MacKay. She was trained as a musician, but after a psychical experience turned to literature and became a bestselling author with her first novel, *A Romance of Two Worlds* (1886). In this she wrote about her own experiences and, she said, about 'spirit power and universal love'. In another 25 novels and some volumes of short stories she held and increased her public, with titles like *Ardath: the Story of a Dead Self* (1889), *Barabbas: a Dream of the World's Tragedy* (1893), *The Sorrows of Satan* (1895), *Zisha: the Problem of a Wicked Soul* (1897), and *The Young Diana: an Experience of the Future* (1918). She was very serious and her readers took her seriously, comfortable in the certainty that no matter how far she outstripped them in wisdom and knowledge she was, like them, perfectly clear as to what was good and what was evil. Marie Corelli could perhaps be described as a female Victorian Dennis Wheatley.

**Corflambo**  In Book IV of Spenser's *The Faerie Queene*, the huge man who carries off Amoret. He symbolizes lust.

**Coriolanus**  A tragedy by William Shakespeare of the days of republican Rome. It was first produced *c*.1608 and published in the First Folio of 1623. The play is based on the life of Caius Marcius, called Coriolanus, by Plutarch. An English version of Plutarch's *Lives* had been made by Sir Thomas North in 1579.

Caius Marcius is a great soldier but a proud and arrogant man who treats the citizens with contempt. He wins a great victory for Rome against the Volscians and captures their city, Corioli. Henceforth he is honoured by the name of Coriolanus and is urged by his friends Cominius and Menenius Agrippa to seek the consulship. The Senate supports him but he is opposed by the tribunes Sicinius and Brutus. He must also have the people's support.

Coriolanus finds it hard to seek the favour of the masses. Then Sicinius and Brutus succeed in arousing the people against him and the scorn and loathing Coriolanus feels for them is plainly manifest. The tribunes demand his banishment but Coriolanus banishes himself ('I would not buy their mercy at the price of one fair word'). He goes to Antium and puts his sword at the disposal of Tullus Aufidius, the Volscians' general.

The Volscian army, led by Coriolanus, advances to the walls of Rome. Menenius goes as an emissary to Coriolanus and pleads with him to spare the city. He fails, and then Coriolanus' mother Volumnia, his wife Virgilia, and his son Marcius come to the Volscian camp in mourning to plead with him. Volumnia succeeds where Menenius failed but Coriolanus knows what it will mean for him ('O! You have won a happy victory to Rome. But, for your son, believe it, O! believe it, most dangerously you have with him prevail'd, If not most mortal to him.').

Coriolanus makes a favourable treaty for the Volscians and returns his army to Antium. Tullus Aufidius accuses him of betraying them in the interests of Rome and excites the Volscians against him. Coriolanus is cut to pieces by the mob.

*Coriolanus* is the play of Shakespeare's in most danger of being 'explained' instead of being produced for what it is. It almost became one of the ruins knocked about by Bertolt Brecht and ironically it was two producers from Brecht's own company who produced the play at the National Theatre in London in 1971 – they had apparently discovered that Shakespeare's original had some merit in it.

*Coriolanus* is not quite like any other play of Shakespeare's and was probably the last of the great tragedies. It is rapid, forceful, and unsubtle – a statement of a flawed man's fall played against a political background. The honour of Coriolanus lies in his courage, his patrician breeding, and his commitment to Rome. His flaw is his arrogant conceit, which Shakespeare exposes so pitilessly. He has performed heroic deeds but he is no hero and his proud patrician mother brings him down by evoking one of the factors, his commitment to Rome, that made him what he is.

**Cornelius** Physician to the court in Shakespeare's *Cymbeline*. Suspicious of the queen's motives, he supplies a harmless sleeping potion in place of the poison she asks him for.

*Cornhuskers* The second collection of poems by Carl Sandburg. First published in 1918, it was awarded a special Pulitzer prize in the following year. Probably the most celebrated poem in the collection is the contemplation of mortality, 'Cool Tombs'. The book also contains his celebration of the Great Plains, 'Prairie'. See **Sandburg, Carl**.

**Cornwall, Barry** See **Procter, Bryan Waller**.

**Cornwall, Duke of** Regan's husband in Shakespeare's *King Lear*. Every bit as cruel as his wife, he performs the blinding of Gloucester and dies of his wounds when one of his own servants, shocked, attacks him with a sword.

*Corsair, The* A poem by Lord Byron, first published in 1814. The story, narrated in heroic couplets, concerns Conrad, a pirate of the Aegean. Seyd, the Turkish pacha, is preparing to attack the pirate's island stronghold but Conrad is warned and plans to outwit him. He takes leave of Medora, his beloved, and goes to the pacha as a dervish who claims to have escaped from the pirates. Conrad's men launch their attack on the pacha's ships – but too soon, and Conrad's plan is spoiled. The pirate is wounded and taken; during the fighting he has saved the life of Gulnare, the favourite of the pacha's harem, and she falls in love with him. The pacha condemns Conrad to death; Gulnare succeeds in having the execution postponed, then brings Conrad a dagger and plans the opportunity for him to murder Seyd while he sleeps. Conrad's single virtue, chivalry, is revolted by this, and Gulnare kills the pacha herself; when Conrad escapes she goes with him but he is now completely repelled by her. Arriving at his island, Conrad finds Medora dead from grief, having believed him killed in his unsuccessful attack on the pacha's fleet. Conrad leaves the island and disappears.

**Cory, William Johnson** 1823–92. William Johnson was born in Torrington, Devonshire, and changed his name to Cory in 1872. He was educated at Eton College and King's College, Cambridge, and was an assistant master at Eton for a time. Most of his published work was concerned with education and his *Letters and Journals* (1897), edited by F. Warre-Corwish, were once greatly valued. His most famous work, however, was the book of poems called *Ionica* (1858), which contains his translation of the epigram by Callimachus on his friend Heraclitus of Halicarnassus, beginning 'They told me, Heraclitus, they told me you were dead'.

**Coryate, Thomas** *c.*1577–1617. The son of a rector of Odcombe in Somerset, Thomas Coryate was educated at Gloucester Hall, Oxford, and was for a time a member of the household of Henry, Prince of Wales. In 1608 he set off on his travels in Europe, mainly on foot, moving from France to Italy; after a sojourn in Venice he returned by way of Switzerland, Germany, and Holland. He published a lively account, *Coryats Crudities, Hastily Gobbled up in Five*

*Moneths Travells* (1611), notable for its vitality and his inexhaustible curiosity. He was off again in 1612, and this time travelled by way of Greece, Turkey, Egypt, Mesopotamia, and Persia to the court of the Mogul emperor. His notes on this journey were preserved in letters and in *Thomas Coriate Traveller for the English Wits: Greeting from the Court of the Great Mogul* (1611). Coryate had mastered Greek at Oxford and he learned a number of oriental languages. He was able to address the Mogul in Persian and hold his own in Hindustani with shopkeepers and traders. He died in Surat on the way home, still a young man but exhausted by his exertions.

**Costard**   The clown of Shakespeare's *Love's Labour's Lost*. He is Don Armado's rival for the favours of Jaquenetta and he rebukes the lords and ladies who laugh at Nathaniel in Act V.

**Costigan, Captain**   In Thackeray's *Pendennis*, the father of the actress Miss Fotheringay (Emily Costigan), with whom Arthur Pendennis becomes entangled at the age of 16. Costigan believes Arthur to be the heir to a great estate and for that reason accepts him, repudiating him when he learns the truth from Major Pendennis.

**Cotton, Charles** 1630–87. Cotton, the son of a wealthy landowner, was born in Beresford Hall in Staffordshire. As a young man he travelled in France and Italy, and in England became a friend of Donne, Herrick, Jonson, Izaak Walton and, later, Dryden. He is remembered for his translation of Montaigne's *Essays* (1685), which was a marked improvement on John Florio's of 1603. A competent minor poet, his *Poems on Severall Occasions* (published posthumously 1689) did not make a great impression, though his burlesques of Virgil (1664) and Lucian (1675) were popular during his lifetime. Cotton is the author of the dialogue in the second part of the fifth edition of Walton's **The Compleat Angler** (1676) between Piscator and Viator.

**Cotton, Sir Robert Bruce** 1571–1631.  As a writer Sir Robert Bruce Cotton remained a minor figure but as an antiquary and particularly as a collector of manuscripts he has earned the gratitude of all scholars of English literature. He was educated at Westminster School and Jesus College, Cambridge, and he gave free access to his fine library to scholars, among whom were Bacon, Raleigh, Camden, Ussher, and Selden. Cotton also made a gift of manuscripts to the newly founded Bodleian Library in 1602. Cotton's own library was largely composed of manuscripts from the dissolved monasteries; this precious material might otherwise have been destroyed or lost. The Cottonian Library was left to the nation by Sir Robert's grandson, Sir John Cotton, and housed first in Essex House and then in Ashburnham House, where a disastrous fire in 1731 destroyed some of it. What was saved was eventually housed in the British Museum in 1753. Among the treasures of the Cottonian Library that survive are the single manuscript of *Beowulf*, the manuscripts of *Gawaine and the Green Knight* and *Pearl*, several biblical manuscripts, and the Lindisfarne Gospels.

Cotton's writing was mostly concerned with political tracts – he became a Parliamentarian during the reign of James I.

***Countess Kathleen, The***   See **Yeats, William Butler.**

***Count Frontenac and New France under Louis XIV***   See **Parkman, Francis** and *France and England in North America*.

***Count Robert of Paris***   A novel by Sir Walter Scott, in the fourth series of *Tales of My Landlord*, first published in 1832, the year before he died. The setting is Constantinople at the time of the first Crusade. The story deals with the adventures of an oafish French count and his wife and an impossibly chivalrous English member of the emperor's Varangian guard. The book contains an excellent portrait of Anna Comnena, the emperor's daughter and chronicler of the time in Byzantium; otherwise it is hardly worthy of mention, a sad reflection of Sir Walter's waning powers and exhausted spirit.

***Country of the Pointed Firs, The***   A book of sketches of life in a seaport town in Maine by Sarah Orne Jewett, first published in 1896.

The narrator spends her summers at Dunnet and stays as a boarder with Mrs Almiry Todd. Through conversations with Almiry the narrator comes to know about the people who live in and around Dunnet. She meets a number of them and her sketches reveal them to the reader, together with a world that is passing, unable to keep pace with the explosion of modern America. Among the characters are Almiry's poor cousin, Miss Joanna Todd, who, after being jilted, lives alone on Shell-Heap Island; Almiry's mother, a charming old lady on Green Island; Almiry's brother William, a shy fisherman who has loved the same woman – and waited for her – for 40 years; Esther Hight, William's love, a shepherdess who cannot forsake an invalid mother; Abby Martin, proud of being born in the same hour as Queen Victoria; Captain Littlepage, who met an insane old Scot in Hudson's Bay claiming to have discovered Purgatory in the Arctic; and perhaps most memorable of all Almiry herself, who is warm, witty, and shrewd. The book ends with the death of old Mrs Hight and the happy marriage of Esther and William.

Sarah Orne Jewett's book achieves perfection within its strictly defined limits, evoking the life of a small community with delicate precision.

**Country Wife, The** A comedy by William Wycherley, first produced in January 1675 and published in the same year. One of the greatest of Restoration comedies, the play raised some eyebrows even in its own day, and was toned down by David Garrick when he presented it as *The Country Girl* in 1766. The play in its new guise was successful enough and Mrs Jordan, a great favourite with London playgoers, enjoyed a triumph when she played Garrick's version in 1785. But Wycherley's original was not seen again until the Phoenix Society of London revived it in 1924. In the 1930s it was produced by the Old Vic and proved a popular success. Though enjoyed by modern audiences as a bawdy piece, the play is also uproariously amusing, constructed by a master of comedy. An outline of the action does no justice to its effect in the theatre.

Pinchwife and his wife, Margery, go to London for the marriage of Pinchwife's sister Alithea, to Sparkish. Pinchwife is paying his sister's dowry, the real reason for Sparkish wanting to marry her. He is a foolish character who bores his acquaintance, among them Horner, a cynical libertine who has put it about that he suffers from impotence; jealous and suspicious husbands are content to trust their wives to Horner's company, believing him harmless. Pinchwife has married a country girl much younger than himself, and Margery is agog with excitement at being in London. Sparkish takes Alithea for granted and eventually loses her. The fashionable ladies soon discover that Horner is far from impotent but keep their apparent secret to themselves. Horner finds Margery irresistible; she is driven into his arms by the jealousy of Pinchwife. In a brilliant closing scene the wives discover to their wrath that they all share the same secret, but they have to close ranks and swear to Horner's impotence in order to protect themselves from their husbands' rage. The curtain comes down to a dance of cuckolds. *The Country Wife*, like the earlier *Love in a Wood*, has a still centre, in this case Harcourt, who wins Alithea from the worthless Sparkish.

**Court, Alexander** One of the three soldiers who meets the king, incognito, on the eve of Agincourt in Shakespeare's *Henry V*.

**Courtier, The** (*Il Cortegiano*). A prose dialogue by Baldassare Castiglione (1478–1529). It takes place at the court of Urbino, is presided over by the duchess, and discusses the qualifications of the ideal courtier. It was translated into English by Sir Thomas Hoby in 1561 but was well known in England in the original Italian. Its influence can be found in the work of Surrey, Wyatt, Spenser, and Sidney.

**Court of Love, The** A poem of unknown date and authorship usually assigned, on the evidence of a single existing manuscript, to the early 16th century. Regarded as the last example of English poetry to bear the hallmark of medieval tradition, it demonstrates – in spite of its undeniable quality – that the tradition's contribution to poetry had run its course.

The subject is a court of love where the central character, Philogenet, gives his allegiance and wins a lady.

**Courtship of Miles Standish, The** A narrative poem by Longfellow, first published in 1858. Miles Standish, captain of the Plymouth colony, asks his friend, the better-educated John Alden, to woo Priscilla for him. But Alden loves her too. Nevertheless he stammers out his friend's suit – only to be asked why he does not speak for himself. Standish, blaming Alden for the failure of his hopes, goes off to fight the Indians. He is believed to have been killed and Alden and Priscilla plan their marriage. Standish returns safely and is reconciled to his friend after asking his pardon for his anger.

**Cousin Phillis** A story by Elizabeth Gaskell, first published in four parts in the *Cornhill Magazine* (November 1863 to February 1864).

The narrator is Paul Manning who, having been found a good position in a burgeoning railway enterprise, is lodging in Eltham. At his mother's suggestion, since he is among strangers, he visits his relatives at Hope Farm – minister Holman, his wife and their daughter, Phillis. Holman is a farmer as well as a Nonconformist minister – a handsome generous man who is interested in everything. Phillis makes a deep impression on Paul with her self-contained contentment which also intimidates him. But they soon become friends.

Paul's superior, Holdsworth, a young man of considerable charm and much admired by Paul, is introduced to Hope Farm and is liked by everyone: Phillis and her mother are charmed and Holman enjoys his meeting with a lively enquiring mind. When Holdsworth falls ill they take him in so that he can rest and convalesce in the peace of the farm.

Holdsworth, soon after, is appointed to an important post in Canada where the railway industry is booming. He has to go without seeing the Holmans, and tells Paul he regrets that he is unable to see Phillis again. Paul is kept busy by the man who replaces Holdsworth, and when he contrives to visit Hope Farm again, is shocked by the change in Phillis, who is visibly declining. Ill-advisedly, though he is right in his assumption of the cause of her low spirits, he tells her that Holdsworth had spoken lovingly of her and hoped to come back to her. Phillis blooms anew and for a time all is well. Then Holdsworth writes from Canada to announce his engagement to a French-Canadian girl. Phillis sustains the shock of the news with apparent stoicism and keeps her own counsel, as she has always done, about Holdsworth. The Holmans, with their busy ordered lives, suspect nothing. Only Betty, their shrewd servant, has fully realized how serious things are – she had been impervious to Holdsworth's charm and she regards Paul as little more than a 'big child'. She is unhappy, too, at the Holmans' lack of awareness that their child is a young woman now.

The crisis comes when a formal announcement of Holdsworth's marriage reaches the Holmans and Phillis collapses completely. After a long struggle and devoted care by her parents, Phillis begins to struggle back to health – but it is Betty's sharp and wise words that finally set her on the road to real recovery.

*Cousin Phillis* is one of the most successful stories in Victorian fiction, a perfectly conceived and finished work in the *nouvelle* form.

**Coventry, Francis** d. 1759? Francis Coventry was educated at Magdalene College, Cambridge, and became vicar of Edgware near London. He was acquainted with the poet Thomas Gray. That is almost all that is known about him, apart from his authorship of *The History of Pompey the Little* (1751). The novel is a satire, with a lap-dog's observation of life while he is passed from one owner to another with bewildering speed, and experiences a wide range of welfare, depending on who owns him. A modern edition is published in the Oxford English Novels series, edited by Robert A. Day (1974).

**Coventry cycle of mystery plays** See **miracle plays.**

**Coverdale, Miles** 1488–1568. Coverdale, who produced the first complete Bible in English, was born in Yorkshire and educated at Cambridge, becoming a priest in 1514. He entered the house of the Augustinian friars at Cambridge and during his 12 years there became an enthusiast for church reform. The prior, Robert Barnes, was probably a strong influence and in 1526 was actually defended by Coverdale when charged with heresy. Coverdale himself was an active preacher against certain Church practices and in the same year thought it wise to retreat to the continent. He probably met Tyndale in Antwerp and soon became a member of the group of Cambridge reformist scholars in Germany. He became a translator, too, and was encouraged by Thomas Cromwell.

Coverdale did not possess the scholarship of Tyndale and he could not work from the Greek and Hebrew sources. He used Tyndale's New Testament, Pentateuch, and Jonah; the rest came from the Vulgate (Latin) and from Luther's and other Germans' translations. He had a complete Bible in English printed in Zurich in 1535 – the first. His claims for his work were modest but the result was remarkable; Coverdale wrote English prose of enduring strength and beauty. His Bible may with some justice be called a version of the work done by other hands – the point is that his version is memorable and the King James version owes much to it.

Meanwhile another Englishman, John Rogers, had also met Tyndale in Antwerp and had been his pupil. He began assembling an English Bible from existing material; he used the unpublished portions of Tyndale (Joshua to the Second Book of Chronicles), a revised version of Tyndale's New Testament, and parts of Coverdale's Old Testament. This was printed in Antwerp in 1537 and dedicated to Henry VIII, who licensed it for general reading. This 'authorized' version gave the editor's name as Thomas Matthew (who was John Rogers) and the book became known as *Matthew's Bible.*

However, Coverdale began a revision of his work under the auspices of Thomas Cromwell (1539) and after Cromwell's fall under those of Cranmer (1540). This came to be known as *The Great Bible* and Cranmer contributed a Prologue. Coverdale returned to England and became Bishop of Exeter in the reign of Edward VI. He fled to the continent again upon the accession of Mary and stayed away until her sister Elizabeth had succeeded her. He returned to England in 1559 and became a DD of Cambridge in 1563. In the same year he was made rector of St Magnus at London Bridge but he was tending towards Puritanism and gave up the post, preaching privately until his death.

**Coverley, Sir Roger de** One of the characters invented by Joseph Addison in *The Spectator* as a member of the Spectator Club, to represent the country gentleman, being a baronet of Worcestershire. The Coverley papers – contributions, usually in the form of letters – are often regarded as the most successful feature of *The Spectator*, offering engaging vignettes of early 18th-century life in England.

**Coward, Noël (Pierce)** 1899–1973. Noël Coward was born at Teddington in Middlesex. He attended a day school and was trained for the stage at the Italia Conti Academy in London. He first appeared on the stage at the age of 11, and had his first play, *I'll Leave it to You*, produced in London in 1920. A comedy, it was followed by another, *The Young Idea* (1922), and he enjoyed his first great success with *The Vortex* (Everyman Theatre, 1924), a play about shallow society in which he also played the male lead. In the previous year he had been conspicuously successful as both writer and player in a revue, *London Calling* (Duke of York's Theatre, 1923), the first of many which made him famous in England and the USA. *The Vortex* also enjoyed a success in New York and for a time it seemed that Noël Coward could not put a foot wrong. *Fallen Angels* (Globe Theatre, 1925) and the revue *On With the Dance* (London Pavilion, 1925) ran concurrently, and his next comedy, *Hay Fever* (Ambassadors Theatre, also 1925), offered as neat and skilful a piece of stagecraft as anything seen in the 20th century. Its sole plot is that a retired actress and her husband and two children have all invited a guest for the weekend without telling each other. The weekend becomes a pandemonium of bickering and on the second morning the guests creep away, unnoticed by the family who are busily arguing at breakfast. The wit is unflagging and the play, though extremely difficult to produce – it depends on perfect timing – is frequently revived.

Coward's success continued with *Easy Virtue* (Duke of York's Theatre) and *The Queen was in the Parlour* (St Martin's Theatre), both produced in 1926, and *The Marquise* (Criterion Theatre, 1927); a falling-off came with *Home Chat* (Duke of York's Theatre, 1927), and failure with *Sirocco* (Daly's Theatre, later in the same year). But contemporary accounts suggest that there were many in London eager to confer a failure on Coward. In the following year he wrote the book for the revue *This Year of Grace* (1928), and followed it with the book, lyrics, and music for *Bitter Sweet* (His Majesty's Theatre, 1929), proving that he could succeed in another field. He was already a sought-after actor, a successful playwright, and a master of the difficult art of

A scene from Act II of Coward's *Private Lives* at the Phoenix Theatre, London, in 1930. Noël Coward as Elyot, Gertrude Lawrence as Amanda. Victoria & Albert Theatre Museum, London.

revue. He appeared in his next comedy, *Private Lives* (Phoenix Theatre, 1930); actor and playwright had never shone so brightly and the play has become a 20th-century classic. The plot, again, is almost nonexistent: Elyot and Amanda, divorced, meet again on the occasion of their honeymoons at Deauville after marriage to new partners. Their attraction for each other is still too powerful to resist and they desert their new spouses. They know their behaviour is crazy ('We're going to be sorry for this. I can feel it in my bones,' says Amanda) but they run off to Paris, where all the reasons for their original separation become plain in a finely paced and witty scene. Their deserted spouses catch up with them just when their squabbling begins to take physical form. On the following morning they come together again and tiptoe away when the other pair start squabbling: whatever Elyot and Amanda may do to each other, they plainly cannot live without each other. Two years later Coward gave another, and surprising, proof of his versatility with a spectacle at Drury Lane Theatre, *Cavalcade*, which combined a patriotic pageant with a very English upper-class family chronicle.

Coward wrote two more revues, five more musical comedies, fifteen more plays, and three sets of one-act plays. Among the most successful plays were *Design for Living* (New York, 1933), *Blithe Spirit* (Piccadilly Theatre, 1941), and *Present Laughter* (Haymarket Theatre, 1943). He published two volumes of autobiography, *Present Indicative* (1937) and *Future Indefinite* (1954), and five collections of short stories. His stage sense was unerring and his ear for spoken dialogue flawless. His plays are published in the seven volumes called *Play Parade* (1934–62), with introductions by Coward himself. He was knighted in 1969.

**Cowley, Abraham** 1618–67. One of the most celebrated poets of his day, and one whose reputation scarcely outlasted his lifetime, Cowley was the posthumous son of a wealthy London stationer. He was educated at Westminster School and Trinity College, Cambridge, where he took his BA in 1639, was made a fellow in 1640, and became MA in 1643. Like Richard Crashaw he was deprived of his fellowship by the Parliamentary party during the Civil War but, also like Crashaw, had already left Cambridge when this happened. He joined the king at Oxford, and departed for France with the queen, Henrietta Maria, in 1644 as a secretary. Ten years later he came back to England and was immediately imprisoned; upon his release he appears to have submitted to the Cromwellian regime but some doubt exists about his true motives and his submission may have been a cloak for Royalist activities. During this time he studied medicine at Oxford and became MD in 1657.

At the Restoration Cowley's fellowship was restored and he was granted land by Henrietta Maria. Thereafter he lived a retired life at Chertsey, devoting his time to botany and to the writing of the essays which were the only part of his work that continued to be read.

Cowley was writing at the age of 10 and had published two romantic epics by the time he was 15; a pastoral drama appeared when he was 20 and he wrote a Latin comedy in the same year. His first collection of verse was *The Mistress: or Several Copies of Love Verses* (1647). In 1656 a multiple collection was published in which *The Mistress* was included; it contained also *Miscellanies, Pindarique Odes*, and four books of an epic on an Old Testament subject, *Davideis*. Cowley wrote an 'Ode Upon the Blessed Restoration' in 1660 and *A Discourse by way of Vision concerning the government of Oliver Cromwell* in 1661. In the same year he published his *Proposition for the Advancement of Experimental Philosophy*. A folio edition of his works published in 1668, the year after his death, contained *Several Discourses by way of Essays, in Verse and Prose*: these were the essays that kept his name alive.

The poet's reputation earned him a splendid funeral and burial in Westminster Abbey beside Chaucer and Spenser. It is essential to try and assess him in the terms of his time. He was deeply interested in the scientific advances of his age and was nominated for the Royal Society (he did not accept). Thomas Hobbes was his intimate friend and he enjoyed the patronage of the highest in the land. Cowley was not the only poet to seem a master in his time and something much less than that thereafter. His failing lay in what Helen Gardner calls a 'misconception of the nature of his talents'. The models he followed, notably Donne and Pindar, were beyond his own range and the results are unacceptable now. He is the first subject of Samuel Johnson's *The Lives of the Poets*.

**Cowley, Hannah** 1743–1809. Hannah Cowley, a minor Georgian playwright, was born Hannah Parkhouse at Tiverton in Devon and married Captain Cowley of the East India Company in 1768. Her best work was in the comedy of manners and her plays include *The Runaway* (1776), *Which is the Man?* (1782), *A Bold Stroke for a Husband* (1783), and *The Town Before You* (1794). Her most successful comedy was *The Belle's Stratagem* (1780), one of the earliest to be played in America (1794). It was played by the Kembles, by Ellen Terry and Henry Irving, and was revived as late as 1913 in London.

**Cowper, William** 1731–1800. Cowper was the son of the rector of Great Berkhampstead, in Hertfordshire. He was born in the rectory and as a child attended a private school, going on to Westminster School later, where his contemporaries included Warren Hastings, Charles Churchill, and George Colman the Elder. He studied law at the Inner Temple and was called to the Bar in 1754.

Cowper lost his mother when he was six years old, and suffered from bullying at his first school. While studying law he fell in love with his cousin, Theodora Cowper, and hoped to marry her; his happiness was blasted by his father, who forbade the marriage on the ground of consanguinity. After being called to the Bar Cowper made no attempt to practise; he wrote verse and various articles and lived the life of a man about town. He suffered periods of depression but he was 32 before his mental instability was manifest. An uncle nominated him for the Clerkship of the Journals of the House of Lords, a sinecure. The appointment required a purely formal examination but the prospect of it drove him from depression into mania and he tried to kill himself. The care of Dr Nathaniel Cotton at St Albans cured him and his brother and some friends set him up in comfortable lodgings in the country, at Huntingdon, with a small income. There he came under the influence of Morley Unwin and his wife, Mary, and became close friends with the family; he went to live in their home. Unwin was a retired Evangelical clergyman who did a certain amount of teaching. He died in 1767 from a fall from his horse, and Mrs Unwin and her children moved to Olney in Buckinghamshire. Cowper went with them and came under the influence of John Newton, an Evangelical pastor with a strong leaning to Calvinism. A more unfortunate influence for the timid and sensitive Cowper, with his precarious mental balance, would be hard to imagine; Newton was a bulldozer of enthusiasm and Olney was a poor and wretched place. Cowper slipped back into melancholy, unable to meet the demands being made upon him. His talent for verse was harnessed to the production of a hymn book Newton was planning. *Olney Hymns* was published in 1779 and contains a number by Cowper, identified by the single initial, C; but they were written more than six years before.

In 1773 the hapless Cowper acquired a conviction that he was damned and that God required his life as a sacrifice. Mary Unwin nursed him and her devoted care brought him back to the world; by 1776 he was corresponding with his friends. In 1779 Newton was made rector of St Mary Woolnoth in London and departed, no doubt full of enthusiasm for making a large number of Londoners feel wretched. Cowper entered upon a simple contented country life; his disposition was cheerful and he began to write verse again. In reply to his cousin, Martin Madan, who had written a book in favour of polygamy, he wrote *Anti-Thelyphthora; a Tale in Verse* (1781), and at Mary Unwin's suggestion embarked on a series of satires, beginning with one on the progress of error. *Poems* (1782) contains the satires, not highly regarded by poetry scholars, and some short poems. The weakness of the satires lies in the fact that Cowper simply did not know enough of the world; their virtue is their precision and his skilful use of the couplet. The last of the set, 'Retirement', is acknowledged to be the best. Among the shorter poems are 'The Shrubbery', 'Invitation into the Country', 'Boadicea: an Ode', and *Verses Supposed to be Written by Alexander Selkirk*.

A new neighbour, Lady Austen, had mean-while become the poet's friend. She was intellectual and worldly and her friendship stimulated Cowper. A suggestion from her led to the composition of *The Task* – starting with an object in his room; 'The Sofa' is the first of the six books of *The Task*. She also told him the story of John Gilpin. *The Diverting History of John Gilpin* was first published in *The Public Advertiser* (1782), *The Task* in 1785; the volume included *John Gilpin* in its pages and also Cowper's attack on the public schools, *Tirocinium*.

William Cowper and Mary Unwin never married – his breakdown in 1773 made it impossible – but they remained devoted companions, and in 1786 they moved to a pleasanter house and neighbourhood in Weston, Northamptonshire. The poet's cousin, Harriet, now Lady Hesketh, enlarged their circle of friends and Cowper wrote a number of short poems which were published after his death. Among them are 'The Poplar Field', 'On the Loss of the Royal George', 'To Mary', and the sonnet 'To Mrs Unwin'. In 1785 he hit on the idea of translating Homer, starting with a blank-verse translation of the *Iliad*. The project was announced and Cowper's letters to Lady Hesketh on the subject suggest that he was

William Cowper. A detail from the portrait by L. F. Abbott, 1792. National Portrait Gallery, London.

well fitted for the task; he knew Pope's version very well and compared it line by line with the Greek original. Cowper's Homer was well subscribed and was published in 1791; it is now unread, except by Cowper specialists. He was a great admirer of Milton and Homer reads like Milton in Cowper's version.

Mary Unwin fell ill and died in 1794. Cowper attended his beloved and steadfast friend until the end and the strain was too much for him. He retreated into physical and mental invalidism: he was successful; his friends cared deeply for him; he was awarded a royal pension in 1794 – none of these mattered any more. His last sad years gave us the powerful despairing poem 'The Castaway', and he died on 25 April 1800.

Cowper's Homer was not his only translation. He contributed to a volume of Horace in English verse (1757–59), to a translation of Voltaire's *The Henriade* with Smollett and others (1762, Cantos 5–8), H. R. van Lier's Latin *The Power of Grace* (1792), and the poems of the French Quietist Jeanne-Marie Bouvier de la Motte-Guyon (published posthumously, 1801). Also published posthumously was *The Latin and Italian Poems of Milton translated into English verse, and a Fragment of a Commentary on Paradise Lost*, edited by William Hayley (1808).

Of great importance in a consideration of William Cowper are his letters. He wrote for no one but himself and his correspondent – unlike Gray, Walpole, and Pope. They reveal a man who was often sorely tried but who was, while in good mental health, cheerful and sympathetic, interested in the simplest things and interesting about them; they are, in his own words, 'talking letters'. Not for him the art of letter writing; to have indulged in that 'would have made me as disgusting a letter-writer as Pope'.

William Cowper was not dedicated to poetry; he wrote verse as a young man and his talent for it proved to be an antidote to despair, as Mary Unwin was quick to perceive. Cowper did not have a lofty approach to his art; he did not look for great themes or seek to demonstrate his intellectual powers. He moved poetry back to simplicity because ordinary human nature and the countryside were the subjects which interested him, not because he intended to give poetry a new direction. But, unwittingly, that is what he did; English poetry departed from the brilliant cleverness of Pope and his imitators and the way was open for a great poetic revival.

The complete poems of William Cowper are being edited by John D. Baird and Charles Ryskamp for the Oxford English Texts series. The first volume will cover the years 1748 to 1782.

Recommended selections are by Hugh l'Anson Fausset in Everyman's Library (1931) and Bernard Spiller in The Reynard Library (1968). *The Letters and Prose Writings of William Cowper*, edited by James King and Charles Ryskamp, is in preparation.

**Crabbe, George** 1754–1832. George Crabbe was born at Aldeburgh on the coast of Suffolk on Christmas Eve. His father, also George Crabbe, was a collector of salt duties and had a liking for poetry, which he used to read to his family. The young George was apprenticed to a doctor at Wickhambrook, near Bury St Edmunds, and then to another at Woodbridge, where he met Sarah Elmy whom he later married. In 1772 he is believed to have published his first poems in a ladies' magazine under a pseudonym; but his first work as George Crabbe appeared in 1775. This was a poem in three parts called *Inebriety*, which he published himself at Ipswich. It was very much in the 18th-century mode dictated by Alexander Pope and is regarded as an apprentice work that displayed considerable power. He completed his medical apprenticeship in the same year and returned to Aldeburgh; but he was unhappy in his father's house and had little interest in being a parish doctor. He stayed until 1779 and practised his poetic craft during those years, producing several religious verses, a poem addressed to 'Mira' (Sarah Elmy) and a blank verse piece entitled 'Midnight'. He became more interested in botany and entomology than in medicine and also turned to religion; but at the end of 1779 he could endure his life at Aldeburgh no longer. He left for London in April of the following year and hoped to make a living as a writer.

In London Crabbe had a very bleak time and was nearly destitute when, in March 1781, he left some poetry and a letter at the house of Edmund Burke. Burke was favourably impressed; he was also generous, and gave the young man enough money to cover his needs. Crabbe now had a patron who selected *The Library* as the best poem for publication, and oversaw the revision which it needed. It was published anonymously in July 1781 and became quite popular though it is not one of his better works. Crabbe was now living in Burke's house at Beaconsfield; his patron introduced him to the Bishop of Norwich, who ordained him, and in 1782 Crabbe found security as chaplain to the Duke of Rutland at Belvoir.

*The Village* (1783) was in progress when Crabbe left his work at Burke's house; the completed poem was an immediate success. It was a new kind of poetry, which told the truth about

Aldeburgh, in a 19th-century coloured drawing in the Moot Hall. George Crabbe was born in Aldeburgh in 1754 and it is the setting for his best-known poetry.

the harshness of country life and forcefully rejected the idealization projected during nearly two centuries of English verse. He married Sarah Elmy in 1783 but published little poetry of any worth for some time; *The Newspaper* (1785) was a satire, believed to have been a reworking of an early piece.

*Poems* (1807) contained new works, including 'The Parish Register', which developed the theme of *The Village* and revealed Crabbe's increasing power as a realist in narrative poetry. In the same volume is the striking 'Sir Eustace Grey', a poem about madness, probably influenced by the fact that Crabbe, by this time, was in the habit of taking opium. Like many of his contemporaries the poet used it originally as a painkiller, but he was fortunate that the drug never got the better of him, as it did Coleridge. *The Borough* (1810) is in 24 parts, or 'Letters', describing the life and people of Aldeburgh. Uneven, and simply dull in places, it yet contains some of Crabbe's finest poetry. *Tales* (1812) is a collection of 21 stories in verse and introduces a vein of sharp-edged humour into his work. *Tales of the Hall* (1819), his last published volume during his lifetime, continues in the same vein but is marred by carelessness; Crabbe was now famous and apparently less inclined to take trouble about polishing his work.

In 1814 Crabbe was appointed to the living of Trowbridge, in Wiltshire, where his circumstances were comfortable and from where he visited his distinguished friends, among them Wordsworth, Southey, Scott, and Samuel Rogers. He left a considerable amount of unpublished work at his death in 1832; much of this was included in the collection edited by his son, George, who in the same edition published a notable biography of his father (1834).

Crabbe, in his poetry, wrote about something new, a change that was badly needed. But his method was old: by the time he died poetry in England had changed completely with the writings of Coleridge, Wordsworth, Byron, Shelley, and Keats, whilst Crabbe went on writing in the 18th-century manner left behind with the publication of *Lyrical Ballads* in 1798. But within the limits of his chosen form Crabbe achieved much, earning the praise of the 'new' poets: Byron, Wordsworth, Scott, and Tennyson greatly admired him and his work should be better known.

The standard edition of Crabbe's collected work is *Poems*, edited by A. W. Ward (1905–07). There is a single-volume edition by A. J. and R. M. Carlyle (Oxford Standard Authors, 1914). *The Life of George Crabbe* by his son included an introduction by E. M. Forster (The World's Classics, 1932).

**Craik, Mrs** See **Mulock, Dinah Maria.**

**Crane, (Harold) Hart** 1899–1932. Hart Crane was born in Garretsville, Ohio, and was brought up in his grandmother's house when his mother (his parents had separated) was obliged to spend a long period in a sanatorium. A bleak childhood was briefly enlivened by a visit to his grandfather's fruit plantation when he was 17, and this provided additional images for the poetry that he had begun to write at the age of 13. His parents' divorce alienated him from his family and he went to New York, working at anything and continuing to practise poetry in his spare time. His first publications came in little reviews. His first collection, *White Buildings* (1926), and the long single poem, *The Bridge* (1930), were all that he ever published; some unpublished poems were added to the *Collected Poems* (1933), which was edited by Waldo Frank. Crane never succeeded in coming to terms with life. He went from a disastrous home life in the small-town philistine Middle West to the climate of Greenwich Village, then in its most arty and pretentious period. He was homosexual but felt the need to try to establish a physical relationship with a woman; he also drank too much. The lack of stability eventually eroded his faith in his work and he drowned himself on a voyage back from Mexico. The small body of work that he left is highly valued for its rich imagery, verbal ingenuity, and careful craftsmanship.

**Crane, Ichabod** See **Sketch Book, The** by Washington Irving.

**Crane, Stephen** 1871–1900. The youngest son of a Methodist minister, Stephen Crane was born in Newark, New Jersey. His father wrote religious tracts and his mother was for a time editor of the *Christian Advocate*. Crane's education was erratic and in advanced terms amounted to no more than single courses at Lafayette College and Syracuse University. He went to New York to become a journalist and had a fairly lean time; intermittent reporting for the *Tribune* and the *Herald* kept him going and, meanwhile, he began work on a novel about the harsher side of New York life, which he had come to know very well. The novel was consistently rejected by New York publishers and Crane eventually published it with money borrowed from his brother.

*Maggie: A Girl of the Streets* (1895) was neither bought by the public nor noticed by the critics but William Dean Howells and Hamlin Garland both read it and their personal praise gave the author some badly needed encouragement. *The Red Badge of Courage* (1895) was in some degree inspired by his reading of Tolstoy and furnished with further reading about the Civil War: Crane had no experience of war but he wrote one of the classic novels about a man's encounter with it. The novel was so successful that *Maggie* was reissued (as well as read and reviewed) and Crane's reputation was established. *The Red Badge of Courage* was greatly admired in England and brought high praise from Joseph Conrad and Henry James. The two

Stephen Crane.

novels demonstrate the successful exercise of a powerful imagination projecting scenes outside the author's experience.

Stephen Crane's next publication was a book of verse. Howells had introduced him to the work of Emily Dickinson and *Black Riders* (1895) demonstrates her influence. The Civil War was again the subject of *The Little Regiment* (1896), a book of short stories; squalid urban life in New York features in *George's Mother* (1896). The *Third Violet* (1897) is a romance about a young artist.

This remarkable burst of activity was followed by commissions as a journalist – he was very much in demand now. He spent time in the Southwest and Mexico and on a journey to Cuba at the end of 1896 was shipwrecked, spending nearly three days in an open boat. The experience was used in a fine short story **The Open Boat** (1898); in it Crane returned to the high level of his first two novels. He met and married Cora Taylor in Florida in 1897 and she joined him when he went to Greece as a war correspondent. But ill health forced him to return and they went to England: his marriage had led to a certain degree of ostracism in the USA because Cora had run a sporting house in Florida before her marriage. The novel *Active Service* (1899) arose from his experience of the Greco-Turkish war.

Crane went to Cuba to report the Spanish-American War for the New York papers the *World* and the *Journal* but his health broke down completely so he returned to England. Joseph Conrad had become his friend and the Cranes were to receive generous evidence of Conrad's regard in the home they established in Surrey. Henry James, living in Rye, was a regular visitor. But Crane's condition was deteriorating rapidly and he was taken to a health centre in the Black Forest. He died there, of tuberculosis, at the tragically early age of 29.

No other book of Stephen Crane's reached the level of *The Red Badge of Courage* and the tragedy of his death leaves his admirers with no clues to his possible development. But at least four of the stories in *The Open Boat* and **The Monster** (1899) can be accorded classic status. Also published during the author's lifetime were *Wounds in the Rain* (1900), sketches and stories from his life as a correspondent; *War is Kind* (1899), a book of verse; and *Whilomville Stories* (1900), about childhood in a small town in New York State. Stephen Crane's *Collected Works* were published in 12 volumes (1925–26).

*Cranford* Elizabeth Gaskell's most celebrated novel was first published in *Household Words* (December 1851 to May 1853) and in volume

An illustration by Hugh Thomson for an edition of *Cranford* published in 1898. Miss Matty is apprehensive about being carried in a sedan chair.

form in 1853. The first numbers that she sent to Dickens, the editor of *Household Words*, had him in a fever of impatience for more, and his friend and biographer Forster predicted a great success. The book *was* well received, but it was not the great success Forster had foreseen until after the author's death, since when there has hardly been a year when *Cranford* has not been in print in some edition or other. It is often waved at schoolchildren but it is, as Peter Keating writes in his introduction to the Penguin edition, 'emphatically a book for adults, not schoolchildren' and 'many adult readers ... find *Cranford* an extraordinarily sensitive and at times painfully moving work'. It is certainly those things, and much more than the 'prose idyll' it is frequently dubbed.

The village of Cranford has its prototype in Knutsford, where Elizabeth Gaskell spent some very happy years. Her portraits of village life – it is hardly just to describe them as sketches – are painted by a woman obviously younger by some years than the chief characters, one who has some connection with industrial urban living. Called Mary Smith, she displays a keen observation and gentle wit. The time is the 1830s and 1840s, the world is changing round the lives of Cranford, and the simplicity of the values by which it lives are seen by Mary Smith as something of real worth, easily lost. The principal characters are the two daughters of the former rector, Matilda and Debōrah (who will have it so pronounced)

Jenkyns; Captain Brown, genial and kind, whom the ladies take to their hearts; his two daughters, Miss Brown and Miss Jessie Brown; Lady Glenmire; and Mr Hoggins, the surgeon. Their lives are shown to us and the incidents leave an indelible impression – perhaps most of all the life of Matilda Jenkyns (Miss Matty), with her unhappy little love affair, her ruin with the failure of the bank, the efforts of her friends to help her, and the joyful return to Cranford of her long-lost brother, Peter.

**Cranmer, Thomas** 1489–1556. Cranmer was born at Aslacton in Nottinghamshire and educated at Jesus College, Cambridge, to which he was elected a fellow in 1511. He would have been at Cambridge when Erasmus was there and Cranmer's intensive study of scripture and the early Christian fathers began during his years at Cambridge. He married, thereby losing his fellowship; but after his wife died he was able to regain it. He was ordained a priest in 1523. Cranmer's rise can be dated from 1529, when Henry VIII's proceedings for a divorce seemed to be grinding to a halt. Cranmer suggested to two of the king's advisers that the theologians of the universities of Europe be consulted; a favourable opinion could certainly be obtained if the universities were carefully selected and if they lay outside the domains of the emperor, who was Katherine of Aragon's nephew. Henry got his favourable opinion and was delighted with clever Master Cranmer and took him into his service.

On an embassy to the emperor in 1532 Cranmer met Margaret Osiander, daughter of a Lutheran reformer. They were secretly married in the same year, an eventful one for Cranmer; Archbishop Warham died, and Cranmer was appointed to the see of Canterbury. Warham was no supporter of the Reformation, and while he was not exactly a formidable opponent his primacy was an irritation to Henry; but Thomas Cranmer was the king's man. He annulled the king's marriage in 1533; in 1536 he annulled the king's marriage again – this time the one to Anne Boleyn, which Cranmer had performed himself. He married the king to Anne of Cleves, and he annulled that too. Meanwhile, when he was not doing what he was told by Henry, Cranmer helped prepare the Ten Articles of 1536 – the first articles of faith of the Reformed Church. However, he did oppose the Six Articles, which the king – wanting to keep the Reformation in England under his own control – ordered to be published in 1539. These contained no contribution of Cranmer's and indeed, since they enforced clerical celibacy, they separated Cranmer from his wife.

After Henry's death Cranmer was able to further the aims of the Reformation, a cause he fervently supported. During the reign of Edward VI he swept away the remnants of Catholic worship from religious practice and authorized the destruction of relics and images. In 1549 and 1552 he made a contribution to English literature for which he is justly honoured; *The Book of Common Prayer*, as the old Litany became, is chiefly attributable to Cranmer. After numerous squabbles it took its final form in 1662 and has remained unchanged ever since. Unhappily it now looks like being laid aside in favour of a 'popular' version in the same way as the matchless Bible of the King James version. Cranmer also published the first book of *Homilies* (sermons) of the Reformed Church in 1547.

The weakness in Cranmer's character allowed him to recognize, albeit reluctantly, Lady Jane Grey as the lawful successor on the death of Edward VI, though he was no friend of Northumberland's. But in those unsettled years, with the new church barely established, the accession of Mary, a fervent Catholic, was dreaded. In the event Mary did acceed, and Cranmer was sent to the Tower. He could expect nothing from Mary, whose mother he had degraded, whose faith he rejected, and whose lawful title to the crown he had joined in setting aside. He was found guilty of treason, but Mary spared his life while preparing his next ordeal, the charge of heresy. He was excommunicated in November 1555, deprived of his archbishopric in December, and on 14 February, 1556, confirmed as a heretic. The queen signed his death warrant ten days later. However, a month went by while Cranmer was confined in comfortable circumstances at Christ Church, Oxford; the Catholic Church in England hoped that their chief prize would recant and he did, no less than seven times. But in the end he found the courage to repudiate his recantation, and was burned at the stake at Oxford, on 21 March, 1556.

Like many figures of the Reformation, Cranmer would seem to belong to history rather than literature. But his influence was considerable and the majestic language of *The Book of Common Prayer* is also an object lesson in precision and economy. He was largely responsible for the order that the Bible in the English language should be available in every church for the edification of all.

**Crashaw, Richard** 1612–49. Richard Crashaw was the only son of William Crashaw, a Puritan preacher at the Temple whose wrathful sermons contributed much to the hostility of the Puritans to the theatre. Richard spent his short adult life in increasing reaction to the intolerance and austerity of his father's religion. He entered Pembroke College, Cambridge, graduated in 1634, and was awarded a fellowship of Peterhouse in the following year: both colleges were markedly High Church. The defeat of the Royalists in the Civil War inevitably had serious consequences for Crashaw; he was deprived of his fellowship in 1644 but had already left Cambridge the previous year. He had been a popular preacher at Little St Mary's Church adjoining Peterhouse but there is some doubt that he ever took orders. He probably witnessed the stripping of the chapel of Peterhouse and the destruction of devotional decorations in his church by the Parliamentary Commission in 1643. After two years, mostly in exile, he became a Roman Catholic, and ended his days in a minor office at the Cathedral of Loreto.

Crashaw is best remembered as a religious poet. He sometimes achieves a memorable sequence of lines but the matter of his poetry is, as D. J. Enright says, 'lovingly handled, but sometimes too lovingly fondled'. This is clearly seen in his only original secular lyric (his others are versions from other languages) 'Wishes: to his (supposed) Mistress', in which a charming idea is fondled to death. But there are fine lines to be found in Crashaw, especially when the poet's intensity of feeling imposes its own discipline on his baroque extravagance. His first collection, *Steps to the Temple. Sacred Poems with other Delights of the Muses*, was published in 1646; a revised and enlarged edition followed two years later. In 1652 Crashaw's friend Miles Pinkney published a more complete collection, the posthumous volume *Carmen Deo Nostro*.

Cranmer denounced as a heretic by the friars of St Mary's. An illustration from the 1610 edition of Foxe's *Book of Martyrs*.

**Cratchit, Bob** In Dickens's *A Christmas Carol*, the overworked and bullied clerk to Ebenezer Scrooge. He and his family benefit greatly from Scrooge's transformation.

**Crawford, Francis Marion** 1854–1909. The son of the sculptor, Thomas Crawford, whose work can be seen in the bronze figure of Freedom which embellishes the Capitol in Washington, Francis Marion Crawford was born in Italy. He was educated in the USA and at Cambridge and travelled extensively. He was also an accomplished liguist.

Crawford was 28 when his first novel *Mr Isaacs, A Tale of Modern India* (1882) was published. It was a popular success and he went on to write nearly 50 more; he enjoyed a large following until he died and his books continued to be popular for many years. He stated his own views on the novel in *The Novel – What It Is* (1893); he saw its true purpose as entertainment, not as a vehicle for moralizing or a framework for the realism that was becoming fashionable at the time. Crawford could certainly entertain, as the sales of his romances, historical novels, and tales of cosmopolitan life demonstrated.

Among his novels are *Via Crucis* (1898), *The Prima Donna* (1908), and *The White Sister* (1909). Many of his novels were successfully adapted for the stage and he wrote *Francesca da Rimini* (1902) for Sarah Bernhardt. His tales of the supernatural, *Wandering Ghosts*, were published in 1911 after his death.

**Crawford, Mary** In Jane Austen's *Mansfield Park* Mary Crawford is the beautiful and shallow neighbour who captures the affections of Edmund Bertram. She rejects him when he proposes to her and freely criticizes Fanny, who has turned down her brother, the handsome and immoral Henry. She implies that Fanny's acceptance of Henry would have conferred respectability on his philandering.

**Crawley, Grace** In Anthony Trollope's *The Last Chronicle of Barset*, the daughter of the accused Josiah Crawley. She loves Archdeacon Grantly's son – but has to win over the archdeacon too, not wishing to marry against his wishes. The archdeacon capitulates after one meeting with her and her story ends happily.

**Crawley, Rawdon** In Thackeray's *Vanity Fair*, the second son of Sir Pitt Crawley by his first marriage. The wealthy Miss Crawley's favourite nephew, he forfeits her good will and his likely inheritance when he allows Becky Sharp to inveigle him into a secret marriage.

**Crawley, Rev Josiah** In Anthony Trollope's *The Last Chronicle of Barset*, the honourable but cross-grained perpetual curate of Hogglestock who is charged with theft. Harassed by poverty, he cannot explain why he suddenly has enough money to pay his debts. A remarkable creation, Crawley is invested by the author with an integrity and a sort of harsh nobility that sustains him during his trials.

**Creevey, Miss La** 'A mincing young lady of fifty', Miss La Creevy is the Nicklebys' landlady when they come to London after their father dies in Dickens's *Nicholas Nickleby*. She paints miniatures, is a warm-hearted soul, and takes an immediate dislike to Ralph Nickleby. She marries Tim Linkinwater, the Cheeryble brothers' clerk.

**Creevey, Thomas** 1768–1838. Creevey was born in Liverpool and was a Whig MP, first for Thetford in Norfolk and later for Appleby in Westmoreland. He held office as Treasurer of Ordnance and Treasurer of Greenwich Hospital. Charles Greville, in his *Memoirs*, refers to Creevey's amiable and sociable character; *The Creevey Papers: a Selection from the Correspondence and Diaries of the Late Thomas Creevey* was edited by Sir Henry Maxwell (1903). As a politician Creevey was, to put it mildly, adaptable; the papers are gossipy and irreverent and interesting for the light they shed on the principal figures of the later Georgian period.

**Creighton, Mandell** 1843–1901. Creighton, who became Bishop of London in 1897, was born in Carlisle and educated at Merton College, Oxford, of which he later became a fellow. He was appointed Professor of Ecclesiastical History at Cambridge (1884) and made a reputation as a historian with his *A History of the Papacy during the Period of the Reformation* (1882–94), which was praised for its detachment and erudition. He became the first editor of *The English Historical Review* (1886), which he directed until he was made Bishop of Peterborough (1891). Other works by Bishop Creighton include *A History of Rome* (1875), *The Tudors and the Reformation* (1876), *Cardinal Wolsey* (1888), *Queen Elizabeth* (1896), *A History of the Papacy from the Great Schism to the Sack of Rome* (1897), and *The Life of Simon de Montfort* (published posthumously, 1905).

**Cresseid, The Testament of** A poem by Robert Henryson, written as a continuation of Troilus and Criseyde ('Writtin be worthie Chaucer glorious'). It was first printed in William Thynne's edition of Chaucer (1532).

Diomeid has wearied of Cresseid and cast her off. She takes refuge with her father Calchas, and blasphemes against Venus and Cupid, reproaching them for what has befallen her. The gods punish her: Saturn deprives her of her beauty and she is afflicted with leprosy. As a beggar by the wayside outside the city she is given alms by Troilus. They do not recognize one another but she learns his identity, and comes to realize that she has betrayed him: when she is dying she sends him the ring he had once given her.

Henryson picks up the story in the episode of Cresseid's surrender to Diomeid; however, in Chaucer's version Troilus is killed by Achilles at the end of the poem.

**Cressida** In Shakespeare's *Troilus and Cressida* the daughter of the priest Calchas, who leaves her in Troy when he deserts to the Greeks. Troilus falls in love with her but she responds to the advances of Diomedes when her father succeeds in having her claimed by the Greeks in exchange for the Trojan prisoner Antenor.

**Crèvecoeur, J. Hector St John de** *c.*1735–1813. Crèvecoeur was born in Normandy and christened Michel-Guillaume Jean de Crèvecoeur. He received part of his education in England and was a lieutenant in Montcalm's army in Quebec. After the city fell to the British in 1759 he explored the Great Lakes area and the Ohio river valley and travelled in New York and Pennsylvania. In 1769 he settled in Orange County, New York, where he bought a farm and married a girl from Yonkers who bore him two children. His travels are partly described in *Voyage dans la Haute Pennsylvanie et dans l'état de New York* (1801).

The 11 years in New York were the happiest of Crèvecoeur's life. During this time he wrote his famous **Letters from an American Farmer** (1782) and another collection of essays (not published until 1925), which was to be called *Sketches of Eighteenth-Century America*. Included in the volume is a play, *Landscapes*, which describes the hypocrisy, mendacity, and abuse of power that underlay much of the movement towards revolution. The Revolution, when it came, was a disaster for Crèvecoeur; he agreed with Franklin's ideals but was a loyalist at heart. When a mob of 'patriots' attacked his farm in 1780 he had to fly for his life, first to New York and then to France.

Three years passed before he could return to America. His wife was dead and his home was burned; his children had vanished but he succeeded in finding them safe and well in the care of a Boston merchant. He stayed in New York, where he became French consul, until 1790, when he returned to France to end his days. His *Letters* are essential reading for anyone interested in rural life in early America.

***Cricket on the Hearth, The*** See ***Christmas Books***.

***Critic, The,*** *or a Tragedy Rehearsed*. A comedy by Richard Brinsley Sheridan, first produced at Drury Lane in October 1779 and published in 1781. Sheridan, in this burlesque, satirized both the sentimental drama of his day and malignant criticism of it. The critics are Dangle and Sneer; Sir Fretful Plagiary is the paltry and pretentious poet, and Puff is what would nowadays be called a theatrical hustler. Puff, however, has written a tragedy called *The Spanish Armada* and invites Dangle and Sneer to his rehearsal. His tragedy is a ridiculously funny affair about Tilbury Fort on the eve of the Armada, with the governor's daughter, Tilburina, going mad for love of Whiskerandos, a Spanish prisoner. The whole is accompanied by brilliant dialogue, whether in Sneer and Dangle's reptilian destruction of Sir Fretful's pretensions or in Sneer, Dangle, and Puff's discussion of the tragedy being rehearsed.

**Crockett, Davy** 1786–1836. Davy Crockett was born in Tennessee and led a free contented frontier boyhood and youth with little more than basic schooling. He served with General Andrew Jackson during the rebellion of the Creek Indians in 1814 and then entered the state legislature. To his surprise he was elected to Congress and served from 1827 to 1831 and again from 1833 to 1835. He disagreed with Jackson's politics and Jackson's opponents made capital of Crockett's backwoods 'wisdom'. Crockett, a frontier hero of inexhaustible gumption blessed with the pioneer spirit, cooperated in propagating his own mythology. However, his departure from his original principles alienated his supporters and he lost his seat in Congress. He left Tennessee to fight in the war for Texas and died in the defence of the Alamo. *A Narrative of the Life of David Crockett* (1834) is apparently his autobiography but this has been disputed. A number of books attributed to him from 1833 to 1836 are, in any case, believed to be the work of busy political journalists and it is not possible to say with any certainty what is 'by' Davy Crockett.

***Crock of Gold, The*** A fantasy by James Stephens, first published in 1912.

Two Philosophers, who enjoy listening to each other's thoughts, marry The Grey Woman of Dun Gortin and The Thin Woman of Inis

Magrath. The two wives give birth on the same day, in the same hour; the children are a boy called Seumas Beg and a girl called Brigid Beg. Neither woman likes her own child, so they swap – each loves the other child better. (It is never stated which woman gave birth to which child.) When the children are ten one Philosopher decides he is quite old and wise enough and whirls himself to death. His wife, The Grey Woman, decides he is right and she whirls herself to death too. The Thin Woman of Inis Magrath buries them under the hearthstone.

Meehawl (Mícheál) MacMurrachu, a farmer, consults the surviving Philosopher about his wife's washboard, which has been stolen. The Philosopher tells him to look under a certain tree; but under the tree Meehawl finds, not the washboard, but a crock of gold belonging to the leprechauns. In revenge for the taking of their gold the leprechauns kidnap Seumas and Brigid. Then Meehawl's daughter, Caitlin, meets Pan. He is naked and unashamed so she follows him and disappears. The leprechauns decide to let the children go, and the Philosopher sends them to help Meehawl find his daughter: but Caitlin refuses to be parted from Pan. The leprechauns, still angry about their stolen gold, denounce the Philosopher to the police, who find two bodies under the hearthstone and march the Philosopher away to prison. Seumas and Brigid, having watched the police, play at digging in the forest – and come upon the leprechauns' gold, buried there by Meehawl. They restore it to its rightful owners, and then accompany the Philosopher's wife to appeal to their god, Angus Og. It transpires that Caitlin has become the god's wife, and the god is soon persuaded to come to earth and secure the Philosopher's freedom.

The author weaves the world of faery and folk wisdom into the fabric of everyday life with great skill, and there is true poignancy in the stories the Philosopher hears from the other prisoners.

**Croker, John Wilson** 1780–1857. Croker was the son of a surveyor general of customs and excise. He was born in Galway and educated at Trinity College, Dublin. A prominent Tory MP, he held various offices and was Secretary of State for the Navy for 20 years. He was a regular contributor to the Tory periodical *The Quarterly Review* and wrote the notorious attack on Keats' *Endymion*. His *Essays on the Early Period of the French Revolution* (1857) was a collection of *Quarterly* contributions, enlarged. *The Croker Papers* (1884) were published long after his death and provide useful information about the politics of the early 19th century. Croker edited *Royal Memoirs of the French Revolution* (1823); his edition of Boswell's *The Life of Samuel Johnson* (1831 and 1848) contains useful notes.

**Croly, George** 1780–1860. George Croly wrote novels of horror describing earthly nastiness in historical settings. Educated at Trinity College, Dublin, Croly became rector of St Stephen's, Walbrook, and was also the author of a tragedy, *Catiline* (1822), and a number of romantic and narrative poems. His heroes might be called Byronic but the description would not have flattered Byron, who refers to him as 'Revd. Rowley Powley' in his *Don Juan*.

*Salathiel* (1829) uses the Wandering Jew theme, and Croly indulges in descriptions of the horrors of life in Rome under Nero and during the destruction of Jerusalem by Titus. *Marston* (1846) is set in the days of the French Revolution and the Napoleonic Wars.

**Crosbie, Adolphus** In Anthony Trollope's *The Small House at Allington*, the shallow and ambitious civil servant who jilts Lily Dale after a visit to an aristocratic household. He achieves an ambitious marriage but it turns out badly.

*Crossing the Bar* A poem by Tennyson written in 20 minutes on an old envelope while he was crossing the Solent from Lymington. He had been seriously ill, had made an excellent recovery, and had been pondering a suggestion from Nurse Durham, who had attended him, that he write some lines in thanksgiving. It was first published in *Demeter and Other Poems* (1889).

*Crossing the Brooklyn Ferry* Originally called 'Sun-Down Poem', it appeared in Walt Whitman's second edition of *Leaves of Grass* (1856) and was given its present title in the third edition (1860). It is a rhapsody of the daily crowds and the city of New York as Whitman often saw them (and now sees himself as among them) from his home in Brooklyn.

*Crotchet Castle* Thomas Love Peacock's penultimate novel, first published in 1831. It follows the style of his other fictional works, the plot being little more than the framework upon which Peacock can construct his satire. It is less directly personal than the others, however: the first Reform Bill was not far away and the pressures of increasing industrialism were being felt – welcomed by many and deplored by many. Interesting in expression are the views, both learned and gastronomical, of the traditional clergyman, Dr Folliott, who is against the 'march of mind' – a direct slam at Henry

Brougham, one of the pioneers of popular education. There is also a picture of an increasingly familiar figure of the times, Sir Simon Steeltrap, Lord of the United Manors of Spring-Gun and Treadmill.

**Crowe, Catherine** 1800–76. A novelist and short story writer of the 19th century, whose tales of terror and the supernatural enjoyed considerable popularity. *Adventures of Susan Hopley; or Circumstantial Evidence* (1841) and *The Story of Lilly Dawson* (1847) are straightforward novels of terror; but in her later book of short stories, *The Night Side of Nature*, she tried to find rational explanations for the ghostly incidents she related.

**Crowne, John** *c*.1640–*c*.1703. A minor Restoration dramatist, Crowne was popular with his audiences and with Charles II but his work has never been revived. Details of his origins and life are nonexistent but it is believed that some of his early years were spent in Nova Scotia, where his father had emigrated. His first published work was a prose romance, *Pandion and Amphigenia* (1665), and his first play *Juliana: or The Princess of Poland* (1671). Crowne was the author of 11 tragedies, and some comedies which scholars regard as his best work. The most notable is *Sir Courtly Nice: or It Cannot Be* (1685). Although held in high esteem by the king, and invited, through the Earl of Rochester, to write the court masque *Calisto: or The Chaste Nimph* (1675), Crowne seems to have had an aversion to court life. His plays are regarded now as skilful syntheses of elements that would succeed in the Restoration theatre. Most of his plays were edited by J. Maidment and W. H. Logan (four volumes, 1873–77). The edition does not include *Andromache* (1674), *The Misery of Civil War* (1680) and *Henry the Sixth* (1681).

**Croy, Kate** In *The Wings of the Dove*, by Henry James, the penniless niece of the wealthy Mrs Lowder, whose guest is the rich and ailing American girl, Milly Theale. Kate Croy loves Merton Densher but he has no fortune. When she realizes that Milly is attracted to Merton, she plans a marriage for them, certain that it will be shortlived and that Merton will emerge from it a wealthy man.

**Crummles, Vincent** In Dickens's *Nicholas Nickleby*, the head of a company of strolling players who provides Nicholas and Smike with employment after their flight from Dotheboys Hall. Dickens had a warm appreciation of strolling players and his pages describing the progress of Crummles and his company are some of the best in the novel.

**Cry, the Beloved Country** See **Paton, Alan**.

**Cuckoo and the Nightingale, The,** *or The boke of Cupid god of love*. First published as the work of Chaucer but now identified as the work of a Hereford gentleman, Sir Thomas Clanvowe. The date of writing is close to Chaucer (between 1390 and 1403) and it is composed in the dream-vision form popular at the time. The poet tells of the cuckoo who laughs at love, and of the nightingale's praise of it.

**Cudworth, Ralph** 1617–88. One of the more prominent of the Cambridge Platonists, Cudworth was born at Aller in Somerset, where his father was rector. His academic career was remarkably distinguished: fellow of Emmanuel College, Cambridge, in 1639, he was appointed Master of Clare Hall by the Parliamentary commission in 1645; he became Regius Professor of Hebrew in the same year and Master of Christ's College in 1654. He rejected the Hobbesian type of atheism and was a steadfast opponent of religious dogmatism. His chief work (left unfinished) was *The True Intellectual System of the Universe* (1678); it argues that the Christian religion is the only real source of knowledge. His *Treatise concerning Eternal and Immutable Morality* was published posthumously (1731).

**Culverwel, Nathaniel** *c*.1618–*c*.1651. Culverwel was one of the group of platonists who flourished at Cambridge University in the middle of the 17th century. He was a fellow of Emmanuel College, and spent the few years of his adult life as a teacher and preacher; his *Discourse of the Light of Nature* was published after his death. In this book, generally believed to have been part of a greater design, he asserts that Reason is only subordinate to God and revelation; but he also states that it would be blasphemous to say that God would ever oppose Right Reason. The book is chiefly interesting as an example of the confusion of thought in religion and philosophy that Thomas Hobbes did much to disperse.

**Cumberland, Richard** 1732–1811. Cumberland, a clergyman's son, was the grandson of the scholar Richard Bentley. He was born in the Master's lodge at Trinity College, Cambridge, and attended Westminster School. He went to Cambridge, was later made a fellow of his college, Trinity, and then held a number of government posts, including that of Secretary to the Board of Trade. His career as a playwright began from a need to make money and got off to an inauspicious start. *The Banishment of Cicero* (1761), a tragedy, was never performed; *The*

*Summer's Tale* (1765), a comic opera, was, but was not a success with the public. Cumberland did better with *The Brothers*, a comedy (Covent Garden, December 1769), and enjoyed a success with another comedy, *The West Indian* (Drury Lane, January 1771). Cumberland was a prolific playwright, the author of nearly 40 works for the stage, and two of them were very popular: *The Fashionable Lover* (Drury Lane, January 1772) and *The Jew* (Drury Lane, May 1794), both comedies. Cumberland was so sensitive to criticism that Sheridan found in him the model for Sir Fretful Plagiary in *The Critic*. He was also the author of two novels, *Arundel* (1789) and *Henry* (1795), and a translation of *The Clouds* of Aristophanes. His dramatic works contributed nothing to the development of the form and they have not been revived.

**cummings, e(dward) e(stlin)** 1894–1962. e. e. cummings always wrote his name without capital letters. He was the son of a teacher and minister and was born in Cambridge, Massachusetts. He graduated from Harvard in 1916, and became an ambulance driver in France during World War I. In 1917 he was mistakenly charged with treasonable correspondence and confined in a French detention camp for several months. After the war he remained in Paris for some time, painting and writing poetry. His first published work was a novel, *The Enormous Room* (1922), an autobiographical fiction about his experience in the prison camp. The narrative is set in the form of a pilgrimage and cummings uses the contemporary vernacular with powerful effect. He also used it in his poetry; his first collection was a group of neo-Romantic verses called *Tulips and Chimneys* (1923) and he continued in that vein in *XLI Poems* (1925). His highly individual voice began to be heard in *&* and *is 5* (both 1925); he published a further six collections but insisted on typographical tricks in their presentation, discouraging many readers who might otherwise have found his poetry rewarding. It is ironic, funny, powerful, and at times of simple beauty: 'plato told', 'it is at moments after i have dreamed', 'come, gaze with me upon this dome', 'my father moved through dooms of love', and 'the way to hump a cow' give a fair idea of his quality. *The Complete Poems* was published in 1918.

Among other works by e. e. cummings are *him* (1927), a play in verse and prose; *Eimi* (1933), a travel diary that is also an attack on the treatment of individuals in Soviet Russia; *Santa Claus* (1946), a morality play; and *i* (1953), a collection of six 'non-lectures' delivered at Harvard.

**Cunningham, Allan** 1784–1842. Cunningham was born at Dalswintin in Dumfriesshire. He became a stonemason but he kept a vivid memory, from the age of six, of Robert Burns reading 'Tam O'Shanter' in his parents' home, and later collected material for Robert Cromek's *Remains of Nithsdale and Galloway Song* (1810). He made the acquaintance of James Hogg and Sir Walter Scott and went to London a few years later, at Cromek's invitation. He became a parliamentary reporter and secretary to the sculptor Sir Francis Chantrey, and wrote the standard autobiography of the painter Sir David Wilkie in 1843. Cunningham was the author of a play, *Sir Marmaduke Maxwell* (1820), which was praised by Scott but was never performed, some forgotten novels, *The Songs of Scotland, Ancient and Modern* (1825), and *Lives of Eminent British Painters, Sculptors and Architects* (1829–33).

**Cunninghame Graham, R(obert) B(ontine)** 1852–1936. Cunninghame Graham was born in London and educated at Harrow School. His father belonged to an old Scots family and his mother was of Spanish descent. He first visited South America at the age of 17; there he rode with the gauchos and became such an expert on horses that he was commissioned to buy them for the British government during World War I. A traveller and explorer, he is remembered for *Mogreb-el-Aksa* (1898), an account of a dangerous journey to the, at that time, unknown interior of Morocco. He also published a number of stories and essays and *A Vanished Arcadia* (1901), which tells the story of the Jesuit settlements in Paraguay.

***Cunning Murrell***  See **Morrison, Arthur.**

***Cursor Mundi*** A Middle English poem of the early 14th century, in rhyming couplets, of 24,000 lines. 'The Course of the World' was written, the unknown author declares in a prologue, to the Virgin Mary. The poem follows the scripture story from the Creation to the Acts of the Apostles and has a section on Doomsday; it closes with a homily on the fleeting nature of earthly pleasures and a prayer to Mary. The poem includes a mass of Christian legend, including material from the Apocrypha. The poem was widely read and a number of manuscripts survive; it is notable for its warm humanity and the author's skill in handling verse narrative. The author was a cleric, probably a monk, and is believed to have written at the end of the 13th or the beginning of the 14th century. *Cursor Mundi* was edited by R. Morris for the Early English Text Society (1874–93). Selections from the text appear in G. Sampson's *The Cambridge Book of Prose and Verse* (1924) and in J. A. W. Bennett and G. V. Smithers' *Early Middle English Verse and Prose* (1968).

**Custome of the Countrey, The** A play by John Fletcher and Philip Massinger, first produced about 1620 and first published in 1647. The plot is based on Cervantes' *Persiles y Sigismunda*.

The custom of the country is *le droit de seigneur*, which Count Clodio intends to exercise in the case of Zenocia, who has spurned his attentions and is going to marry Arnoldo. Arnoldo has no intention of allowing Clodio access to Zenocia's bridal bed and his older brother Rutilio helps him organize the escape of all three from the country. The three have various adventures while the fates of the young newlyweds form the main plot of the play. Zenocia is captured by a Portuguese captain and taken to Lisbon, where she is made servant to Hippolita. Arnoldo arrives, looking for her, and Hippolita falls in love with him; she is also the witness of a scene that shows Zenocia to be her rival. Clodio, meanwhile, repenting of his behaviour, arrives in Lisbon and just in time – Hippolita has given orders for her rival to be strangled. Clodio secures Zenocia's release and she is restored to Arnoldo. The furious Hippolita now enlists the aid of Sulpitia, a witch, and Zenocia begins to waste away. But when Arnoldo begins to waste away, too, in sympathy, Hippolita is overcome with remorse. She orders Sulpitia to break the evil spell and resigns herself to losing him. All ends happily for Zenocia and Arnoldo; and for Rutilio, who has been having adventures of his own.

**Cymbeline** A play by William Shakespeare that was listed among the tragedies by the editors of the First Folio in 1623, in which it was first published. It was first produced *c.*1610 – perhaps 1611, the same year as *The Tempest*. The source of the play is in the chronicles of Raphael Holinshed, who probably drew it from Geoffrey of Monmouth's *Historia*. Cymbeline, or Cunobelin, was King of Britain in the first decades of the Christian era and the father of Caractacus, but there is nothing historical in *Cymbeline*. The story of the wager on virtue is from Boccaccio's *Decameron*.

Cymbeline has brought up at his court Posthumus Leonatus, with whom his daughter Imogen has fallen in love. The queen, Imogen's stepmother, has an unattractive son Cloten and wants Imogen for his wife. But Imogen has secretly married Posthumus and the queen betrays her to her father. Cymbeline banishes Posthumus, who makes his way to Rome. His servant Pisanio promises Imogen he will keep sharp watch for any word from him.

In Rome, Posthumus' belief in Imogen's virtue is challenged by Iachimo, an Italian gentleman. Posthumus offers Iachimo the diamond ring he wears if he can prove Imogen false; the ring was Imogen's gift. Iachimo goes to Britain carrying letters for Imogen from her husband. He loses no time in trying to charm Imogen but she turns him down even when he suggests that Posthumus is something less than virtuous. Imogen simply refuses to believe him and he changes tack – he was, he implies, looking for the great virtue Posthumus praised, and has found it. He then persuades Imogen to take charge of a chest, in which he and some friends have stored some gifts for the emperor. While Imogen sleeps he emerges from the chest and notes the details of her chamber; then he slips the bracelet from her wrist.

Posthumus, confronted with what seems to be proof of Imogen's infidelity, writes to Pisanio and directs him to kill Imogen, who is meanwhile being pursued by Cloten. She receives a letter from Posthumus, telling her that he has arrived in Wales (Cambria) and she prevails upon Pisanio to hurry there with her. But near the end of the journey Pisanio gives her the letter accusing her of having 'play'd the strumpet'. But he cannot possibly bring himself to kill her; he gives her boy's clothes and directs her to Milford Haven, where she can watch Posthumus while safely disguised. Then he leaves her and she encounters Morgan and his two sons, Cadwal and Polydore. They are in fact Belarius, unjustly banished by Cymbeline years before, and Guiderius and Arviragus, two sons of Cymbeline whom Belarius stole when he was banished. Imogen tells them her name is Fidele. The brothers take to their new friend with great affection but she does not accompany them on a hunt, feeling bowed down with care. She takes a cordial given her by Pisanio and falls into a death-like sleep. The cordial was a trick of the queen's, who hoped to poison Imogen. Believing her dead, her hosts lay her in a glade and cover her with leaves and flowers. They speak a dirge and depart sorrowfully. They had, unknown to Imogen, encountered Cloten, who had followed her and fought with Guiderius. Cloten lost the fight and his head. They dump the body in the glade where they have laid Imogen, who sees it upon awakening. She is prostrated at discovering that the headless body wears her husband's clothes – it was a conceit of Cloten's to take Imogen for himself in the clothes of Posthumus, whom he hated for having supplanted him.

Romans invade Britain under Lucius, who finds 'Fidele' in the forest and makes him a page. Cymbeline's army is reinforced by Posthumus and by Belarius and his foster-sons. Lucius is defeated and taken prisoner with his page. Posthumus had hoped for death in battle; now he surrenders to Cymbeline, knowing his life is forfeit while he is under sentence of banishment. In the final assembly are all the chief characters, including Iachimo, who was an officer in the Roman army. Lucius asks Cymbeline to spare the life of his page, 'a Briton born'. Cymbeline is favourably impressed and Imogen seizes the moment to demand that Iachimo explain how he came by the diamond ring he is wearing. . . .

This strange – but beautiful in the utterance – play goes on from this confrontation to a welter of explanations, recognitions, forgivings, and general happy-ever-afters. The audience should be given a detailed *dramatis personae*, printed in large letters, to study before the curtain rises; then they will know who everyone is and they can simply enjoy the play – and feel indulgent about the complicated sortings-out at the end. Does Shakespeare, of all poets, require our indulgence? Yes, he does, and we should give it ungrudgingly, remembering that he was a very hard-working man indeed; no less than 37 plays came from his pen in 20 years. This is one of the last plays and indulgence has its rewards because there are wonderful things to be found in this play. One of them is Imogen, a heroine who can stand beside Rosalind and Viola; another is the pair of contrasting villains, the bored and destructive Iachimo and the greedy, stupid Cloten. It is sometimes hard to remember that it is at Cloten's behest that the aubade to Imogen, 'Hark, hark! the lark at heaven's gate sings', is sung. The dirge from *Cymbeline* would by itself keep the play's name alive forever: 'Fear no more the heat o' the sun' is spoken, rightly. What could music add to this achingly beautiful poem? Perhaps indulgence is not required, after all. The better one knows this play the more it seems like a garden on a late summer's evening.

**Cymochles** In Book II of Spenser's *The Faerie Queene*, the profligate husband of Acrasia. He seeks revenge on Sir Guyon for the death of Pyrochles, his brother.

**Cynewulf** A poet of the late 8th and early 9th centuries. Cynewulf's identity is known to us from his own inscription, in Runic characters, of his name in the epilogues of the four poems preserved in *The Exeter Book* and *The Vercelli Book*. He is believed to have been a Mercian who spent much of his life in Northumbria (the sea is a vivid element in his poetry). However, his work appears in the West Saxon dialect in the surviving manuscripts. He was evidently a man of learning: his work is based on Latin originals and his poetry displays a Latin discipline rarely found in Old English.

The poems identified as the work of Cynewulf are: *The Ascension*, the second part of the three-part *Christ* in *The Exeter Book*; *Juliana*, which concerns the virgin martyr, also in *The Exeter Book*; *Elene*, the story of St Helena, which is in *The Vercelli Book*; and *The Fates of the Apostles*, in the same collection. The poems were translated by C. W. Kennedy (1910 and 1949).

*Cynthia's Revells, or The Fountaine of selfe-love* A comedy by Ben Jonson, first produced in 1600 and published in 1601. The satire in this play is aimed at figures of the court who are given pseudoclassical names: Queen Elizabeth is represented by Cynthia and the Earl of Essex by Actaeon. The play has almost no plot and the satire is meaningless out of its own period; but the beautiful lyric hymn to Diana given to Hesperus in Act V, 'Queene, and Huntress, chaste and faire', has become a favourite poem with anthologists.

# D

**Daggoo** The Black harpooner of the *Pequod* in Herman Melville's *Moby-Dick*. The author likens him to a king '. . . with a lion-like tread', who moves about the decks with all the pomp of his great height (6ft 5in).

*Daisy Chain, The* A novel for young people by Charlotte M. Yonge, first published in 1856. It is concerned with Ethel May, a short-sighted clumsy girl, thin and sallow-faced. But she is clever, unselfish, loves going to church, and is always thinking up noble plans for the betterment of others. The book enjoyed enormous popularity and Ethel May was a favourite with Victorian schoolgirls.

*Daisy Miller* A novel by Henry James, first published in the *Cornhill Magazine* (June to July 1878) and in volume form in the same year. A dramatized version by the author was published in the *Atlantic Monthly* in 1883 and again in volume form in the same year.

Mrs Miller, newly rich and implacably commonplace, is from Schenectady and is visiting Switzerland with her daughter Daisy and her small son Randolph. The Millers' sojourn in

Vevey is observed by Frederick Winterbourne, an American expatriate who is astonished by their ignorance of, and unconcern for, social convention in Europe. He encounters the family again in Rome and finds that Daisy has taken up with Giovanelli, a young Italian of no social position; and as a result the American colony in the city looks askance at her. All this is lost on Daisy; she is quite uncultivated and her mother simply does not realize that manners in Europe differ from those in New York state. The American community in Rome, on the other hand, self-consciously conforming, is soon ostracizing Daisy.

Daisy blithely proceeds in her friendship with Giovanelli. Winterbourne, who has been charmed by her innocence, is suddenly disturbed to meet the pair one night, viewing the Colosseum by moonlight. He believes that she must have lost all moral sense to engage in such an excursion and he is less than kind. The girl is shocked and at once returns to her hotel. She becomes ill with malaria and dies after a week. At her graveside Giovanelli comments: 'She was the most beautiful young lady I ever saw, and the most amiable . . . and she was the most innocent.'

The author places Daisy in the centre of the stage but his disposal of her is ambiguous; the reader has to decide whether she succumbs to social disapproval as voiced by Winterbourne – or to fever. But James's observation of her compatriots is excellent, an acute and witty comment on Americans abroad who have so hurriedly embraced the 'other' culture that they can no longer recognize the virtues of their own. Daisy's innocence offends them because they have forgotten that it can exist.

**Dale, Lily** In Anthony Trollope's *The Small House at Allington*, the younger daughter at the Small House. She is loved by Johnny Eames, but falls in love with the weak and selfish Adolphus Crosbie. When Crosbie jilts her, Johnny Eames gives him a thorough thrashing.

**Dalgetty, Dugald** The self-seeking soldier of fortune in Scott's *The Legend of Montrose*. Loquacious and a pedant, he is perfectly willing to serve either side, depending upon the pay and prospects offered.

**Dampier, William** 1652–1715. The voyager, discoverer, and privateer was born in the West country, near Yeovil. His career took him to the West Indies, South America, the Pacific, Australia, and the East Indies. During one of Dampier's early voyages (1703–04) a Scottish seaman named Alexander Selkirk asked to be put ashore on the Pacific island of Juan Fernández after a quarrel with his captain. (See also **Rogers, Woodes** and ***Robinson Crusoe***.) Dampier's accounts of his travels and adventures are vivid and entertaining and are of considerable historical interest: *A New Voyage Round the World* (1697), *Voyages and Descriptions* (1699), and *A Voyage to New Holland* (1703–09).

**Dana, Richard Henry** 1815–82. The son of a minor poet and journalist of the same name, Dana was born in Cambridge, Massachusetts. He went to Harvard, but at the end of his second year (1834) withdrew because of eye trouble. For the sake of his health he signed on as a seaman for a voyage to California around Cape Horn. He worked on the Pacific coast for a year, collecting and curing hides, and then returned to Boston by sea to complete his education at Harvard Law School.

Dana's first published work resulted from a deeply felt anger at what he had seen on his voyages. In the *American Jurist* in 1839 his article 'Cruelty to Seamen' appeared and in 1840, the year he was admitted to the Bar, he published ***Two Years Before the Mast***, the book which made him famous and which described the life of the ordinary seaman as it was lived, day by day. The following year saw the publication of *The Seaman's Friend*, which among other things explained to sailors exactly what their rights – as well as their duties – were. It was published in England as *The Seaman's Manual*.

Another aspect of Dana's championship of the underprivileged was his opposition, in word and deed, to slavery. He freely gave his assistance to fugitive slaves and antagonized the Boston mill-owners in doing so because cheap raw materials from the South boosted their profits. Dana wanted a political career but his edition of Wheaton's *Elements of International Law* involved him in accusations of plagiarism (1866) and a hoped-for appointment as ambassador to Britain was withdrawn by the Senate (1876). Convinced that his life had been a failure, he withdrew to Europe in 1878, where he died four years later. He published another account of a voyage in *To Cuba and Back* (1859) but it did not enjoy anything like the success of *Two Years Before the Mast*, which Dana insisted was 'a boy's work'. It is much more than that, whatever the author's opinion, and opened the way for writing about the sea that led to the work of Melville and Conrad.

***Dance of the Sevin Deidlie Synnis, The*** A poem by William Dunbar written between 1503 and 1508. It is a poetic *danse macabre*, in which those guilty of the Sins are seen, in the poet's vision, called by the fiend Mahoun, and enduring the punishments to be their penalty when they die.

***Dance to the Music of Time, A***   See **Powell, Anthony (Dymoke).**

***Dangerous Corner***   See **Priestley, J(ohn) B(oynton).**

***Daniel***   A poem in Old English preserved in the *Junius Manuscript* in the Bodleian Library, Oxford, and wrongly attributed to Caedmon by Francis Junius. The poem contains an introduction and parts of the Book of Daniel in verse. The selection was probably made to enable the poet to deliver his own homilies on religious virtue.

**Daniel, Samuel** 1562–1619.   The son of a music master of Somerset, Daniel entered Magdalen Hall, Oxford, in 1579 and stayed at the university for three years without taking a degree. After visiting Italy he became tutor to William Herbert, third Earl of Pembroke, in 1592 and enjoyed the patronage of the Countess of Pembroke, who was Philip Sidney's sister and a friend of Edmund Spenser. In the same year Daniel published *Delia*, a collection of sonnets modelled on Desportes and Tasso, and *The Complaynt of Rosamond*, a poem in rhyme royal on the sorrows of Rosamund Clifford in her love affair with Henry II. Spenser refers to Daniel in **Colin Clouts Come Home Againe** as 'a new shepheard late up sprong, The which doth all afore him far surpasse'. Daniel depended upon patronage and in this he was fortunate. After the Countess of Pembroke he was favoured by Lord Mountjoy and Fulke Greville (Lord Brooke) and from 1604 achieved a place at the court of King James. The Earl of Hertford (1605) and, again, the Countess of Pembroke (1609) were both benefactors of Samuel Daniel, a poet of considerable grace and style – but without the outstanding quality to give him a major place in a period of unparallelled richness in poetry. He retired to a farm at Beckington, in Somerset, after a successful career as a professional poet.

Daniel wrote a Senecan tragedy, **Cleopatra** (1594); *Musophilus; Containing a Generall Defence of Learning* (1599), an affirmation in verse of his belief in literature as a civilizing and refining element; *A Defence of Rhyme* (1603), which replies to Thomas Campion's *Observations in the Art of English Poesie* and the tendency to fit English poetry into classical models (Daniel proved an accomplished advocate for English rhymed verse); and a masque, *Twelve Goddesses*, which was played at court in 1604. **The Tragedy of Philotas** (1605), another Senecan tragedy, was regarded as seditious by some because of certain likenesses to

the real-life tragedy of Essex, but Daniel defended himself successfully and continued to serve at court. Among his court entertainments were the pastorals *The Queen's Arcadia* (1605), *Tethys Festival* (1610), and *Hymen's Triumph* (1615). In 1609 Daniel published a new edition of his long historical poem *The Civile Warres betweene the Howses of Lancaster and Yorke*, which had first appeared in 1595. This recounts, in eight books, the history of England from the Conquest to the accession of Henry VII.

Daniel was admired by Spenser, Drummond of Hawthornden, and Sir John Harington (but not by Ben Jonson) and was praised by Coleridge. *The Complete Works* of Samuel Daniel was edited by A. B. Grosart and published in five volumes (1885–96).

***Daniel Deronda***   George Eliot's last novel, first published in 1876.

Gwendolen Harleth is beautiful, confident, and selfish. She is also near to destitution, and to avoid this condition for herself and her mother, marries Henleigh Grandcourt. Grandcourt has wealth and position; he is arrogant and selfish and Gwendolen is well aware of the wretchedness of his mistress's position – there are illegitimate children, and the unhappy woman extracts a promise from Gwendolen not to accept his proposal. But Gwendolen does, and finds herself married to a brute.

In her unhappiness she turns more and more to Daniel Deronda, the man whom she first met at the gaming tables in Europe: he had watched her and the other gamblers with puzzled compassion. Daniel's origins are obscure but his wisdom and kindness are what Gwendolen clings to in the ruins of her life. Daniel saves the girl Mirah from suicide, and finds that Mirah's brother Mordecai is a man of noble character to whom he is increasingly drawn. It is through them that he learns of his origins and that, like Mirah and Mordecai, he is Jewish.

Grandcourt drowns while boating off Genoa: he had bullied Gwendolen into accompanying him and she feels guilt for his death – prompter action from her might have saved him, she believes. She turns to Daniel, but the course of his life is already decided: he is going to marry Mirah, then with Modecai they will go to Palestine and work for the Jewish cause. Gwendolen takes leave of Daniel; he had been her best hope and she resigns herself to the loss. Her last word to Daniel is a short letter on his wedding, expressing the hope that she will realize the better person that Daniel, alone, had seen in her.

*Daniel Deronda* was a success with the reading

public, and considerable attention was paid to the way George Eliot treated her Jewish characters with sympathy and understanding. In a letter to Harriet Beecher Stowe she said that she 'felt that the usual attitude of Christians towards Jews is – I hardly know whether to say more impious or more stupid, when viewed in the light of their professed principles. . .' The young A. T. Balfour, then at Cambridge, praised the book highly – 40 years later he established the Palestine Mandate.

As a novel *Daniel Deronda* is not on the level of *Middlemarch* but it is going too far, as many critics have done, to call it a failure. The political ideas can be argued about but the author's genius is manifest in every character. Gwendolen Harleth is a triumph, a superb portrait of a selfish idle girl who depends on her wits and her considerable charm to get what she wants. Grandcourt, who nearly breaks her, and Klesmer, the dedicated musician who makes it plain to her that charm and looks will avail her nothing in her pretensions to a career, are nearly as good. Daniel, Mordecai and Mirah, in contrast, represent a world where Gwendolen has no real place and her growing awareness of how far from her it is helps her understand how much she must depend on herself in dealing with life. Daniel is, perhaps, too good to be true, and he is the failure: but he is not the whole novel, and so much of it succeeds that it can never be overlooked.

**Darcy, FitzWilliam** The leading man of Jane Austen's *Pride and Prejudice* (it would be unsuitable to call him a hero). His pride is his stumbling block until he meets Elizabeth Bennet and learns humility through his love for her.

***Darkness at Noon*** See **Koestler, Arthur**.

**Darley, George** 1795–1846. Darley was born in Dublin and educated there at Trinity College. After failing to gain a fellowship he went to London to earn a living as a writer and became a contributor to *The London Magazine*. *The Errors of Ecstacie: A Dramatic Poem, and Other Pieces* (1822); *The Labours of Idleness: or Seven Nights Entertainments* (1826, prose sketches as Guy Penseval); *Sylvia, or The May Queen: A Lyrical Drama* (1827) and *Nepenthe* (1835) were his principal works. He also published *Thomas à Becket: A Dramatic Chronicle* (1840); *Ethelstan, or The Battle of Brunanburh: A Dramatic Chronicle* (1841) and an edition of *The Dramatic Works of Beaumont and Fletcher* (1840). He was an accomplished mathematician, the author of four textbooks on the subject. His principal contributions to *The London Magazine* and later to *The Athenaeum*, were essays in dramatic criticism.

Darley is chiefly remembered for a single poem, 'The Loveliness of Love'. This was included by Palgrave in his *Golden Treasury* in 1861; Palgrave believed he had stumbled on a lyric by an unknown Cavalier poet and the incident points both to Darley's success in the poetic idiom of another time and his failure to recognize the challenge of his own. But his best poems – 'Winds of the West, arise!', 'O blest unfabled Incense Tree', 'Wherefore, unlaurelled Boy', 'Serenade of a Loyal Martyr', and *Nepenthe* demonstrate that his lyric poetry was of high quality.

**Darnay, Charles (St Evremonde)** The heir to the cruel and arrogant Evremonde family in Dickens's *A Tale of Two Cities*. Trying to save his old tutor, Gabelle, he is arrested and nearly dies on the guillotine.

**Dartle, Rosa** In Dickens's *David Copperfield*, Mrs Steerforth's companion. A twisted and malicious woman who, in Steerforth's words, 'brings everything to a grindstone and sharpens it. . . She has worn herself away by constant sharpening. She is all edge.'

**Darwin, Charles Robert** 1809–82. The grandson of Erasmus Darwin, Charles Darwin was born at Shrewsbury in Shropshire. He was educated at Shrewsbury School, Edinburgh University, and Christ's College, Cambridge, and was 22 when he sailed as naturalist on HMS *Beagle*, bound for South America on a scientific expedition. The voyage lasted until 1836, and Darwin began the publication of his own and the expedition's observations in 1838, with *The Zoology of the Voyage of HMS Beagle*. In five parts, edited and superintended by Darwin, it was completed in 1843, the year after he settled at Down House near Downe, in Kent.

Darwin published more than a score of works during his lifetime. But it was not until 1859 that his *On the Origin of Species by Natural Selection* formulated the theory which had been in his mind for some time; he had written it down and confided it to close friends as early as 1842. In 1858 Dr Alfred Russel Wallace, recovering from illness at Ternate in the East Indies, reflected on the theories of Thomas Robert Malthus and arrived at the theory of natural selection; he set it down in writing and sent it to Darwin without delay. Darwin had also studied Malthus; he published his theory, giving Wallace generous acknowledgement of the inspiration. Darwin said later that the completion of his theory came while in his carriage, and he could identify the spot on the road where 'natural selection by

Charles Darwin. A detail from the portrait by J. Collier, 1881. National Portrait Gallery, London.

means of the survival of the fittest' occurred to him. Dr Wallace's letter, 16 years later, encouraged him to publish the theory, which led to a storm of controversy; Darwin's supporters included Thomas Henry Huxley, Sir Joseph Hooker the botanist, and the geologist Sir Charles Lyell. *The Descent of Man, and Selection in Relation to Sex* was published in 1871.

Darwin, a modest man and no controversialist, had no doubt whatever that there was much more to be considered about the origin of species and natural selection: he later modified his own statement to take into account the influence of environment. But the history of thought shows a sharp change of direction after the publication of his famous book in 1859.

**Darwin, Erasmus** 1731–1802. The grandfather of the celebrated naturalist, Erasmus Darwin was born at Elston in Lincolnshire and educated at St John's College, Cambridge. He became a physician and practised for most of his life at Lichfield, where he also pursued his interest in poetry and botany. He established a botanical garden at Lichfield and wrote a poem called *The Botanic Garden*, which embodied Linnaeus' system (Part 2, *The Loves of the Plants*, was published first, in 1789; Part 1, *The Economy of Vegetation*,

in 1791). The poem is in heroic couplets, with the goddess of Botany's exposition occupying the first four cantos; it was ridiculed by John Hookham Frere and George Canning in *The Loves of the Triangles*, published in *The Anti-Jacobin*. Erasmus Darwin published his theory of the laws of organic life on the evolutionary principle in *Zoonomia* (1794–96) and *Phytologia* (1799).

**Dashwood, Elinor and Marianne** The sisters of Jane Austen's *Sense and Sensibility*, embodying the qualities of the novel's title.

*Daughters of the Vicar* A story by D. H. Lawrence, first published in 1914 in the volume entitled *The Prussian Officer, and Other Stories*. The vicar is Mr Lindley, in a colliery parish; his disappointed wife has retreated into invalidism; his daughter Mary has married Mr Massy as part of her family duty; his daughter Louisa feels a desire to put Mr Massy 'out of existence'. Louisa, opposed by her father and mother, marries Alfred Durant; he had been a collier, had gone to sea, and now has a farm. Their wooing gains poignancy from the loss of Alfred's mother; Louisa has observed that the Durants' relationship held particular warmth for mother and son. Whatever her future life, and whatever the objections of her snobbish family – snobbish from custom and class, not from conviction of anyone else's worth or otherwise – Louisa knows she is coming down on the side of life. Her dreadful bloodless family have no prospects, apart from the grave.

**D'Avenant, Sir William** 1606–68. The son of the keeper of the Crown Inn in the Cornmarket in Oxford, D'Avenant was at the centre of a rumour (which he took pains to encourage) that his true father was no less than William Shakespeare. He was in fact the great man's godson – Shakespeare and the innkeeper were friends.

D'Avenant was educated at grammar school in Oxford, then became page to the Duchess of Richmond and subsequently to Fulke Greville, who was his patron for a time and encouraged his interest in the theatre. His *The Tragedy of Albovine* was published in 1629 and *The Cruel Brothers* was staged in the same year. He led a wild life in the fashionable society of the time – and paid for it by nearly dying of syphilis (his nose was disfigured by the disease and he endured jokes about it for the rest of his life) – but nevertheless wrote three masques, two plays, and a volume of poems. From 1635, following the pleasure occasioned at court by his masque *The Temple of Love*, he was given charge, including authorship, of all such entertainments during

Strolling players performing at a banquet in a rich man's house. From Moyses Waler's *Album Amicorum*, c.1610. During the Puritan interregnum the closure of the playhouses obliged the actors to live any way they could. But a ban on private 'entertainment' was impossible to enforce and D'Avenant had little trouble assembling a company of skilled players at the Restoration. *Add. MS 18991, f.11*. British Library.

the king's reign; he enjoyed the favour of Henrietta Maria to such a degree that she created a precedent by attending a performance of his work at a public playhouse. *Madagascar, with Other Poems* was published in 1638 and D'Avenant was made poet laureate (Ben Jonson having died in 1637).

The first wars of King Charles I's reign (the Bishops' Wars) saw D'Avenant fighting for his sovereign; he continued to serve him in the Civil War and was knighted at the siege of Gloucester in 1643. With Cowley, Waller, and Thomas Hobbes he was one of the group of exiles in Paris with Henrietta Maria from 1646 until his appointment as Governor of Maryland in 1649. He was captured at sea by Cromwell's forces and imprisoned in the Tower, where he continued

work on his verse epic *Gondibert*. His pardon, which came in 1654, was probably the result of John Milton's intervention on his behalf.

Free once more and with his love for the theatre unimpaired by vicissitude, D'Avenant organized clandestine theatrical performances. Cromwell's personal rule had only two years to run and the Puritan attitude to the theatre seems to have relaxed: at any rate D'Avenant secured authority for the presentation of an entertainment which, while given at a private house, could be attended by anyone who paid for admission. So in 1656, at Rutland House, *The Siege of Rhodes* was performed and drama began to return to life in England after being suppressed for 14 years.

At the Restoration D'Avenant received one of the king's patents to form a company of players (the other went to Thomas Killigrew); he set about recruiting the best of the younger men and introducing new ideas of presentation such as the proscenium, elaborate scenery, and the use of machinery. He produced adaptations of Shakespeare that infuriated many but did serve to bring Shakespeare back to the stage and to nourish the reawakened English theatre. D'Avenant will, and should, always be remembered for the part he played in that reawakening, though his own contributions to English drama have not held the stage. He is buried in Westminster Abbey.

**Davenport, Robert** fl. 1623–40. Davenport was a minor Jacobean playwright of whose life no details are known. One tragedy and two comedies by him survive. *King John and Matilda* (date unknown) uses material already exploited by Henry Chettle and Anthony Munday. *The City-Night-Cap* (1624) and *A New Tricke to Cheat the Divell* (*c.*1639) are comedies that have not held the stage. Davenport's works were collected by A. H. Bullen and published in 1890.

***David and Faire Bethsabe, The Love of King*** A play in verse by George Peele, first published in 1599, on the subject of the title and containing some of Peele's best poetry. Bethsabe's song 'Hot sunne, coole fire, temperd with sweet aire' is the most famous piece but the level throughout is exceptional.

***David Copperfield*** A novel by Charles Dickens, first published in 20 monthly parts (May 1849 to November 1850). It was the author's favourite of his works, and there is much of Dickens himself in the experiences of David.

Miss Betsey Trotwood is present at the birth of David Copperfield. She is intensely annoyed when the baby turns out to be a boy; she wanted a great-niece, not a great-nephew, and immediately renounces any interest in the child. David nonetheless has a happy infancy with his gentle mother, his nurse Peggotty, and her family at Yarmouth, which includes Little Em'ly, Mr Peggotty's niece and David's first love. But David's mother marries again and the once happy home is now dominated by Murdstone and his sister, cold and cruel. David's mother dies; his stepfather sends him to a grim school run by Creakle and there David first meets Traddles and Steerforth. From there he goes to employment in Murdstone & Grinby's warehouse and is lodged with the impecunious Micawbers, who at least are kind to him. When the Micawbers are obliged to leave London David runs away and arrives penniless and starving at Betsey Trotwood's house at Dover.

Miss Trotwood adopts David, deals firmly with the Murdstones, and sends David to school at Canterbury where he lodges with Miss Trotwood's lawyer, Wickfield, and his daughter Agnes. David takes an immediate dislike to Uriah Heep, Wickfield's fawning clerk, but is happy in the companionship of the lovely Agnes, who falls in love with David.

After his schooling David is articled to Mr

David Copperfield's future is decided. The illustration by Phiz depicting the momentous interview in which Betsy Trotwood confronts the Murdstones. Also present are David (left) and Mr Dick (centre).

Spenlow and becomes a lawyer. He meets Steerforth again and, mistaking his friend's true nature, introduces him to the Peggottys. Steerforth runs off with Emily; her uncle sets out to find her, following the trail through country after country. He recovers her when Steerforth, bored with his adventure, casts her off. David, meanwhile, has married the pretty but silly Dora, daughter of Spenlow, and finds success as a writer. Dora dies after a few years of marriage and Steerforth is drowned in a shipwreck.

David finds that all is far from well with Agnes and her father. The mask of fawning humility worn by Uriah Heep covers a cunning villain; he has gained complete control over Wickfield, who appears to be on the edge of ruin. Heep even aspires to the hand of Agnes. Traddles, now a barrister, with the help of Mr Micawber uncovers Heep's villainy and exposes him as a forger and a thief.

At the conclusion David finds happiness with Agnes, the Peggottys and Micawbers emigrate to Australia, and Heep pays the penalty for his crimes in prison.

*David Copperfield* has a stature which no other novel of Dickens enjoys. *Oliver Twist* is as famous – perhaps more so – but *Copperfield* has always been more highly regarded. It is a remarkably comfortable book and will disturb no one who reads it; at the same time it is a masterpiece of narrative – none of Dickens's books is so well told as this first-person account of an eventful life, beginning with 'I am born'. And the characterization is at Dickens's highest level.

***David Simple, The Adventures of:*** *containing an Account of his Travels through the Cities of London and Westminster in the Search of a Real Friend.* A moral romance by Sarah Fielding, first published in 1744.

David Simple discovers that his younger brother, to whom he is devoted, has tried to rob him of his inheritance, using a forged will and bribing two servants to help him. Disillusioned, David sets out on a journey to try and rediscover honest friendship. His experiences, and encounters with Mr Orgueil and his insolent wife, Mr Spatter, who is the chief critic of Orgueil, and Mr Varnish, the chief critic of Spatter, nearly drive him to despair. Then he meets Cynthia, excluded from her father's will and ill-treated by her employer; and Camilla and Valentine, brother and sister who have become the victims of their stepmother's perfidy.

David helps them, and the four become friends. They walk around London and discuss what they see of life in the city. David and Camilla, and Valentine and Cynthia, arrive at love by the most delicately shaded development of emotions and are betrothed. Camilla and Valentine are reconciled to their father, and the two couples settle down in a happy community established by David's generosity. The novel gives an excellent picture of the London scene and Sarah Fielding's moralizing is skilfully controlled. The book was very popular in France.

There is a modern edition of *David Simple* in the Oxford English Novels series, edited by Malcolm Kelsall (1969).

**Davidson, John** 1857–1909. Davidson was the son of an Evangelical minister of Barrhead in Renfrewshire. Soon after his birth Davidson's family moved to Greenock; he was educated at Greenock Highlanders' Academy and went on to Edinburgh University. Davidson was a teacher for 11 years at Glasgow, Paisley, Greenock, and Crieff and published *Diabolus Amans: A Dramatic Poem* (1885), the novel *The North Wall* (1885), the verse play *Bruce* (1886), and *Smith: A Tragedy* (1888). He went to London in 1889 to make a living as a writer and was an occasional visitor to the Rhymers' Club; he also gained the friendship of Yeats, Edmund Gosse, Max Beerbohm, and the artist William Rothenstein.

However, in spite of the goodwill and active help of distinguished people (he was secured a Civil List pension in 1906 and Shaw made him a gift of money in 1908 to enable him to concentrate his energies on poetry) Davidson never fulfilled his promise and success eluded him. He did not succeed in earning enough to supplement his pension and live in even modest comfort. He used Shaw's gift to support himself while he wrote a historical melodrama, a form for which he was quite unfitted and which was never accepted. Believing he was suffering from cancer, he posted the manuscript of *Fleet Street and Other Poems* (1909) to his publisher and drowned himself off Penzance.

Davidson was rather different from the other members of the Rhymers' Club. (Only one of them, Yeats, achieved lasting greatness.) In his view they lacked 'blood and guts' and he introduced a harsh note into what was otherwise a rather precious world. The others might have been the better for it but Davidson was misguided in many ways and only succeeded in being disruptive. His best work, according to his fellow Scot Maurice Lindsay, is to be found in the two parts of the uncompleted trilogy *God and Mammon* (1907), which also reveals his character to some extent. 'In these he shows himself to have been an inverted Calvinist, although influenced not by Schopenhauer but by Nietzsche'; his best-known poem, 'Thirty Bob a Week', carries distinct echoes of that. In addition to his plays and poems Davidson published essays, short stories, novels, and translations from the French. *The Poems of John Davidson* were collected and edited by Andrew Turnbull (1974). *John Davidson: A Selection of His Poems* by Maurice Lindsay (1961) contains a preface by T. S. Eliot and an essay by Hugh McDiarmid.

**Davies, John** *c.*1565–1618. Usually called John Davies of Hereford (his birthplace) to distinguish him from his contemporary, Sir John Davies. Davies of Hereford was a minor poet who wrote a philosophical poem, *Mirum in Modum, A Glimpse of God's Glory and the Soul's Shape* (1602); the physiological and psychological *Microcosmos* (1603); and *Humours Heav'n on Earth* (1605), a description of the plague of 1603. *The Scourge of Folly* (*c.*1610) is a book of complimentary epigrams addressed to distinguished figures of his time, including John Donne, Shakespeare, Ben Jonson, and Samuel Daniel.

**Davies, Sir John** 1569–1626. A native of Wiltshire, Davies was educated at Winchester School and Queen's College, Oxford, before becoming a barrister at the Middle Temple in 1595. He was active in public life, MP for various English and Irish constituencies, and attorney-general for Ireland (1606–19). He was appointed chief justice in the King's Bench by Charles I in 1626 but he died before taking up office. In literature Davies is a minor poet with an accomplished technique and a feeling for contemporary conceits and the current philosophy. *Orchestra, or a Poeme of Dauncing* (1596) is in seven-line stanzas presenting natural phenomena in the ordered motion of a dance. *Nosce Teipsum!* (1599) is a long poem in quatrains on the nature of man and the immortality of the soul; Coleridge expressed admiration for it. *Hymnes of Astraea* (1599) is a group of 26 'acrosticke' poems to Elizabeth I, the Astraea of the title. Davies wrote his own view of the Irish question in *A Discoverie of the True Causes why Ireland was never Entirely Subdued until the Beginning of His Majestie's happie Raigne* (1612), which is no more, and no less misguided than most utterances on the subject at the time.

**Davies, W(illiam) H(enry)** 1871–1940. The son of a publican, W. H. Davies was born at Newport, Monmouthshire, and received some elementary schooling before drifting into casual labour and, eventually, taking to the road. He made his way to New York, and decided to head for the Klondike after years of casual labour, working on cattle boats, and begging. Jumping a train in Canada he fell and injured a leg so badly that it had to be amputated. He returned to England, where his family had contrived to save up a small allowance for him, and lived in dosshouses for sixpence a night. He was in his thirties by now, and he spent his days writing poems, which he collected and published at his own expense. He sent *The Soul's Destroyer* (1905) to well-known people and asked them to send him the price of the book. George Bernard Shaw was one of those who did.

*New Poems* (1907) and *Nature Poems and Others* (1908) followed; Shaw wrote a preface to *The Autobiography of a Super-Tramp* (1908) and gave Davies a push that took him to celebrity. He was a prolific poet (600 poems appeared in his *Collected Poems* of 1943) of brief and affecting nature lyrics, which became famous, and of some grim and unadorned poems which hold up a mirror to a side of life most people never see: 'Pease-Pudding Toe', 'The Inquest', 'The Bird of Paradise', and 'Body and Spirit' are in striking contrast to 'The Happy Child', 'The Kingfisher', and 'The Cat'.

Davies was the author of two novels, *A Weak Woman* (1911) and *Dancing Mad* (1927), and further autobiography in *Beggars* (1909), *The*
*True Traveller* (1912), *A Poet's Pilgrimage* (1918), and *Later Days* (1925).

**Davis, Henry Edwards** See **Gibbon, Edward**.

**Davys (or Davis), Sir John** *c*.1550–1605. Davys, one of the most remarkable explorers of the Elizabethan period, was born in Devon and may well have known Ralegh and Gilbert. He made three voyages to the Arctic and extended considerably the knowledge first brought back by Frobisher: he was unusual in his age for making an effort to stay on friendly terms with the native peoples he encountered. His first two voyages, in 1585 and 1586, were a direct commission to find the Northwest Passage. Continuing interest in the idea also led to his third voyage in 1586. Davys revealed more of the Arctic than was known to anyone in Europe and his careful maps and charts proved invaluable to those who followed him.

Davys' later voyages were in the southern oceans and he was killed by Japanese pirates off Sumatra. He wrote a treatise on navigation, *The Seamans Secrets* (1594), and *The Worldes Hydrographical Discription, whereby appeares that from England there is a Short and Speedie Passage into the South Seas* (1595).

**Day, John** *c*.1574–1640. A minor Elizabethan–Jacobean playwright, Day was one of the journeyman playwrights employed by Philip Henslowe. He collaborated in play cobbling as required; the most distinguished of his colleagues was Thomas Dekker. His best work was done for The Children of the Revels (see **children's companies of actors**) and includes three comedies: *Law-Trickes, or Who would have thought it* and *Humour out of Breath* (both published 1608), and *The Ile of Guls* (published 1606). These are commended by scholars for their precise and economic dialogue. *The Parliament of Bees* (published 1641), regarded as his best work, is not a play in the real sense but 12 short dialogues in verse, some of them taken directly from the plays of Thomas Dekker.

Day's works were collected by A. H. Bullen, whose edition was published in 1881.

**Day-Lewis, C(ecil)** 1904–72. Day-Lewis was born in Ballintogher, Sligo, in Ireland and educated at Sherborne School and Wadham College, Oxford. He signed his books 'C. Day Lewis', and published his first poems in 1925: *Beechen Vigil and Other Poems*. He made a reputation as a lyric poet with *Transitional Poem* (1929), and in the 1930s became one of a group of poets with left-wing sympathies though he was a more individual poet than his contemporaries, a lyricist in the classical tradition. He became Professor of

Poetry in the University of Oxford in 1951, and succeeded John Masefield as poet laureate in 1968. *Collected Poems* (1954) was followed by *Pegasus and Other Poems* (1957), *The Gate and Other Poems* (1962), *The Room and Other Poems* (1965), and *The Abbey that Refused to Die* (1967).

A respected critic, Day-Lewis was the author of *A Hope for Poetry* (1934), *Poetry for You* (1944), *The Poetic Image* (Clark Lectures, 1947) and *The Lyric Impulse* (1965). Translations were *The Georgics of Virgil* (1940), Valery's *Cimetière Marin* (*The Graveyard by the Sea*, 1946), *The Aeneid of Virgil* (1952), and *The Eclogues of Virgil* (1963). He was the author of three novels, two novels for children and, under the pseudonym of Nicholas Blake, of 20 detective novels.

**Dayspring Mishandled** A story by Rudyard Kipling, included in the collection entitled *Limits and Renewals* (1932). Castorley and Manallace are hack writers employed by the same syndicate. Castorley comes into money, having meanwhile dishonoured a good woman's name and earned the undying hatred of Manallace; now he will stop being a hack and turn to serious literature. He becomes a critic and a Chaucer scholar; Manallace, too, makes steady progress as a writer and devises a way of ruining Castorley's reputation. A fragment of a hitherto unknown Canterbury Tale turns up in the USA, and Castorley pronounces it authentic. In fact Manallace has forged it and is waiting for the best moment to expose his enemy. Castorley has been awarded a knighthood and the moment seems ripe but Manallace cannot bring himself to do it; having exhausted his hatred, he feels no more than compassion – and he learns that Castorley is dying of cancer. Manallace then devotes his energies to preventing Castorley's wife from revealing the secret: she loathes her husband and disclosure would finish him, leaving her free to marry his surgeon. Manallace wants his old enemy to die in peace.

**Day's Work, The** See **Kipling, Rudyard**.

**Deans, Jeanie** The heroine of Scott's *The Heart of Midlothian*, Jeanie Deans is one of the great characters of English fiction. Her honesty and resolution (which help her in the scene with Queen Caroline) are conveyed with complete success. She has no glamour: 'She was short, and rather too stoutly made for her size, had grey eyes, light-coloured hair, a round good-humoured face, much tanned with the sun, and her only peculiar charm was an air of inexpressible severity. . .'.

**Death Comes for the Archbishop** A novel by Willa Cather, first published in 1927. The nar-

rative is based on the careers of two French missionaries, Jean-Baptiste Lamy and Joseph Machebeuf, who worked in the New Mexico territory in the middle of the 19th century.

Bishop Jean Latour and his vicar, Father Joseph Vaillant, organize a new diocese in the territory of New Mexico and establish pioneer missions in remote areas. Latour and Vaillant are lifelong friends and, while they share a wistful regret for their own country, are completely dedicated to their life's work. Latour is an aristocrat and an intellectual, a man of endless charity but at the same time a private person. Vaillant is practical, vigorous, and cheerful. The novel follows their struggles: the Navajo and Hopi Indians are not to be drawn; the Spanish clergy already in the territory oppose them, while the harsh climate and unrewarding land tax them to the uttermost. But the missionaries are totally committed and help comes – chiefly from their devoted guide, Jacinto, and the frontiersman Kit Carson. Their success is completed by the establishment and consecration of the cathedral at Santa Fe. The two friends are separated when Father Joseph is made a bishop and sent to Colorado; but death is near and they die within a short time of each other, their work done.

**Death's Jest-Book: or The Fool's Tragedy**. A play by Thomas Lovell Beddoes, begun in 1825 and revised continually during the author's lifetime. It was posthumously published in 1850 and no less than three versions exist in manuscript. It has not been staged but contains some fine blank verse, the song 'Dream Pedlary' and the dirges for Sibilla and Wolfram. The play concerns the brothers Wolfram and Isbrand who enter the service of Duke Melveric, Wolfram as a knight and Isbrand as a court fool. They seek vengeance on the duke for the death of their father and the dishonour of their sister. Wolfram is obliged to rescue the duke and Sibilla, another captive, whom he loves, from the Moors. He succeeds in his knightly mission but discovers that the duke is in love with Sibilla and looks upon Wolfram as his rival. The duke kills Wolfram before returning to his own country but he is haunted by his victim's ghost. From that point the play's action becomes very confused and a supernatural element is introduced into a Jacobean welter of horrors. The duke, at least, gets his just deserts at the end.

**Debits and Credits** See **Kipling, Rudyard**.

**de Bourgh, Lady Catherine** Darcy's aunt and Mr Collins' patroness in Jane Austen's *Pride and Prejudice*. She considers Elizabeth Bennet an unsuitable match for Darcy and her arrogant pride persuades her to try and separate them.

***Decline and Fall of the Roman Empire, The History of the*** Edward Gibbon's history was published in three instalments: Volume I in 1776, Volumes II and III in 1781, and Volumes IV, V, and VI in 1788. The instalments form three divisions: from Trajan and the age of the Antonines to the reign of Constantine; from the foundation of Constantinople to the western empire of Charlemagne; from the establishment of the western (Holy Roman) empire to the long history of the eastern empire (Byzantium) and the taking of Constantinople by the Turks in 1453.

Gibbon traces the history of more than 13 centuries and treats of the great events as well as the inevitable historical progression. The establishment of Christianity is dealt with in detail and Gibbon's detached approach brought him a great deal of criticism ('The scanty and suspicious materials of ecclesiastical history seldom enable us to dispel the dark cloud that hangs over the first age of the church'). Gibbon examines the movement and encroachment of the Teutonic tribes who eventually held the western empire in fee; the rise of Islam, and the Crusades. He looks backward in history to illuminate the period of his work and forward from it to show what has been its legacy.

*The Decline and Fall* is a model of clarity and completeness and is as accurate as the condition of historical research in Gibbon's day allowed. He is scrupulous about acknowledging his sources and only in respect of available knowledge has he been superseded. The history is finely organized, the narrative power unflagging, the historian's arguments irresistibly persuasive. If the work lacks anything it is charm; Gibbon makes no concessions to human sympathies and remains detached. His comment on the reign of Antoninus Pius illuminates his suspicion of enthusiasts of any kind: 'His reign is marked by the rare advantage of furnishing very few materials for history; which is, indeed, little more than the register of the crimes, follies and misfortunes of mankind.' But every other quality of superb history and literary excellence is present in this, the greatest historical work in the English language.

The best edition of *The Decline and Fall* is acknowledged to be that of J. B. Bury, whose scholarly notes provide the reader with an additional pleasure (seven volumes, 1896–1900). The Everyman's Library edition by Oliphant Smeaton (seven volumes, 1926–29) has additions 'to Gibbon's notes with a view to bringing the information up to the level of modern historical scholarship'.

**Dedlock, Lady Honoria** In Dickens's *Bleak House*, the beautiful wife of the upright and hidebound baronet, Sir Leicester. Her secret is the mainspring of the plot.

***Deephaven*** A collection of fictional sketches of life in a decaying seaport in Maine, by Sarah Orne Jewett, first published in 1877. The life of Deephaven (based on the York of Miss Jewett's girlhood) is observed by Helen Dennis on a summer visit with her friend Kate Lancaster. Deephaven has declined since the days of sail and whaling; it seems to be populated by people left behind in some way, such as the captains who exchange anecdotes about their days at sea and Miss Chauncy, the dotty old relic of better days. In a town where reminiscence seems to occupy most people the liveliest characters are the busy housewives and Sarah Orne Jewett presents memorable portraits of Mrs Bonny, Widow Jim, and Mrs Kew, the lighthouse keeper's wife.

***Deerslayer, The*** A novel by James Fenimore Cooper, first published in 1841. In order of events it is the first novel of the *Leather-Stocking Tales* but the last one to be written. The period is the time of the French and Indian wars of the late 17th century.

Thomas Hutter, a trapper, with his daughters, Judith and Hetty, lives on the shore of Lake Otsego in what is now upstate New York. Hetty is feeble-minded. Hutter's log fort is attacked by Iroquois Indians but he gains help from the frontiersmen Hurry Harry and Natty Bumppo, who is called Deerslayer by the Delaware Indians. Harry and Hutter are captured and carried off to the Iroquois camp. Deerslayer is joined by his Mohican friend, Chingachgook, and they attempt to ransom Harry and Thomas Hutter. Chingachgook is personally concerned because the Iroquois are holding his bride, Hist. Hetty, on her own initiative, slips off to the Iroquois camp, where, because of the Indian veneration for the unbalanced, she roams without interference. She returns with the information that her father, Harry, and Hist are there. The ransom of the two men is successfully concluded.

Deerslayer and Hutter then help Chingachgook to rescue Hist – but Hutter is killed and Deerslayer is captured. The Iroquois release Deerslayer on a sworn parole so that he can visit his friends for the last time. Judith tells him that she and Hetty are not Hutter's children; she has discovered that their origins are noble. She also

An illustration for the *Seaside Library* edition (1878) of James Fenimore Cooper's *The Deerslayer*, first published in 1841. Deerslayer (Natty Bumppo) is seen with Judith Hutter.

tells him that she loves him and implores him not to honour his word to the Iroquois. But Deerslayer knows how the 'White man' will be judged if he breaks his oath; he returns to the Iroquois and waits for his ceremonial torture and death. The day comes but Judith appears in the camp and delays the proceedings for long enough to save Deerslayer's life; Chingachgook arrives with a troop of English soldiers. Hetty is killed in the ensuing fight and Judith disappears from Deerslayer's life. He later learns that she has married an English officer and treasures a romantic memory of her.

**Defarge, Thérèse**   The fiery, vindictive revolutionary of Dickens's *A Tale of Two Cities*. She overturns the verdict in favour of Charles Darnay by producing the damning document from Dr Manette's incarceration in the Bastille. Later she is killed by Miss Pross to save Lucie and her family from the Terror.

**Defence of Guenevere, The**   A poem by William Morris, first published in 1858. The poem is written in *terza rima* and Morris found his material in Malory's *Le Morte Darthur*. Guenevere defends herself to King Arthur on the charge of adultery with Launcelot, brought against her by Gauwaine, who has become Launcelot's enemy. The queen's defence of her honour is eloquent but her true feelings for Launcelot become clear as she speaks.

**Defence of Poetry, A**   An essay by Percy Bysshe Shelley, written in the early part of 1821 but posthumously published in *Essays, Letters from Abroad, Translations and Fragments*, edited by Mary Shelley (1840). Shelley's essay was an angry retort to his friend Thomas Love Peacock's *The Four Ages of Poetry*, which appeared in Charles Ollier's *Literary Miscellany* (1820). Peacock had called the revival of imagination in romantic poetry a futile reversion to the habits of the past. Shelley's *Defence* concerns the essential place of poetry and its importance to the well-being of mankind. Poetry is not possible without love and imagination, which are the secret of creation, discovery, and goodness: 'Poets are the unacknowledged legislators of the world.'

**Defoe, Daniel** 1660–1731.   Daniel Defoe was born in the year of the Restoration, the son of James Foe of Stoke Newington, then just north of London. James Foe was either a tallow chandler or a butcher and there was no 'de' in his name; his son started calling himself Defoe about 1703. Daniel was intended for the ministry and

The end of William Morris's poem 'The Defence of Guenevere'. An illustration by Jessie M. King for the 1900 edition.

BUT·STOOD·TURN'D·SIDEWAYS·LISTENING,

educated at the Stoke Newington Academy, a Dissenters' school; but he rejected the intention of his parents and, until his marriage to Mary Tuffley in 1683, travelled in Europe in various jobs to do with trade. At the time of his marriage he was a hosiery merchant in Cornhill. Defoe took part in Monmouth's rebellion in 1685 but seems not to have suffered for it; he became a committed supporter of William of Orange (William III) and joined his army in 1688.

Defoe's mercantile experience led to his first writings, on economics – *Essay upon Projects* (1697); he also wrote pamphlets on the subject for William III. His first success was *The True Born Englishman* (1701), a verse satire supporting William against those who said that a Dutch king was wrong for England. Defoe had no claims to be a poet but he was a clever versifier and verse was the preferred medium for satire. In Defoe's satire his proposition was that no such thing as a true-born Englishman existed: 'We have been Europe's sink, the jakes where she Voids all her offal outcast progeny.' The vigorous bouncing verses were a great success; but his next satire was in the form of a tract, a blast at High-Church fanatics from a Dissenter, called *The Shortest Way with the Dissenters* (1702). In this the author played the character of a High-Church Tory and the ironic conclusion was that the shortest – and best – way was extermination. Unfortunately his timing was wrong; Whigs and Tories were engaged on the question of the succession (none of Queen Anne's children had survived) and Defoe brought down the wrath of both parties on his head. The Tories were in power and Defoe was fined, imprisoned, and exposed in the pillory. He became a popular hero, however, and was released through the intervention of the moderate Earl of Oxford, Robert Harley, who became his employer. While in prison Defoe wrote his *Hymn to the Pillory* (1703).

But the experience left Defoe badly scarred and he blamed the failure of his business career on his term in prison; thereafter his loyalty to any party or person became a doubtful matter. Meanwhile Harley sponsored the establishment of **The Review**, first published in February 1704. It was a newspaper of notable moderation, with considerable interest for merchants and traders. Defoe had published a volume of collected pieces before his imprisonment in 1703 and he published another in 1705. He was a prolific – perhaps compulsive – writer and published over 500 works during his lifetime; it is remarkable how much of his output is worth remembering.

*The Review* owed a great deal to Harley, who perceived how important the press could be; but

Daniel Defoe. Portrait by M. van der Gucht after J. Taverner, 1706. National Portrait Gallery, London.

of course its success as a paper was due to Defoe, who was a journalist of genius. He made his first attempt at fiction with *A True Relation of the Apparition of one Mrs Veal* (1706), a clever handling of a contemporary ghost story. Though he wrote the copy for the thrice-weekly *The Review* Defoe somehow contrived to act also as Harley's agent in Scotland; Harley was committed to the Union of 1707 and Defoe's underground activities helped bring it about. But the Tories, including the moderate Harley, were ousted by the Whigs; Defoe transferred his allegiance to the party newly in power and resumed his activities. His *History of the Union* (1708) is a valuable and detailed account.

By 1712 the governing party's leadership had changed and, while Defoe's allegiance to either side was questionable, political leaders of the time were not of the kind to command devotion. Defoe was loyal to his own conviction that the Jacobites were a bad proposition and supported the Hanoverian succession. His satirical *Reasons against the Succession of the House of Hanover* (1712) was as ill judged as his *Dissenters* tract of 1702; the irony misfired and once more Defoe was imprisoned, this time for publishing treasonable matter. *The Review* ceased publication and upon his release Defoe edited a trade journal called

*Mercator*, supporting Viscount Bolingbroke's treaty of commerce, until 1714. Defoe's pamphlets, called *A General History of Trade*, were published in 1714; these presented a powerful case for free trade.

The Hanoverian succession took place with the death of Queen Anne in 1714. Defoe was charged with libelling Lord Annesley in 1715 but he escaped prosecution by offering his services as an agent to Lord Townshend, the Whig Secretary of State. He also worked for the 'other side', for the Jacobite publisher Nathaniel Mist – *An Appeal to Honour and Justice* (1715) is regarded by some scholars as a sort of preliminary apologia. Defoe's double role continued until 1720; by that time he had ceased to write as a political controversialist. *The Family Instructor* (Volume I, 1715; Volume II, 1718) was a conduct book, and in 1715 Defoe also published *The History of the Wars of His Present Majesty Charles XII King of Sweden*. This was followed by *Memoirs of the Church of Scotland* and *The Life and Death of Count Paktul* (both 1717) and *Memoirs of the Duke of Shrewsbury* and *Memoirs of Daniel Williams* (both 1718).

In April 1719 Daniel Defoe was nearly 60 and his industry did not flag for another ten years. But that month saw the first work of his great period, during which the real treasures, the manifestation of his genius, shone out from the continued flood of talent. **Robinson Crusoe** was followed in a few weeks by *The Farther Adventures of Robinson Crusoe*. *The History of the Life and Adventures of Mr Duncan Campbell*, **Memoirs of a Cavalier**, and **The Life, Adventures and Piracies of the Famous Captain Singleton** were all published in 1720; **The Fortunes and Misfortunes of the Famous Moll Flanders**, **A Journal of the Plague Year**, and **Colonel Jack** followed in 1722; and **Roxana,** or *The Fortunate Mistress* was published in 1724. These eight books would themselves have conferred immortality on Defoe, but there was much more. *The Great Law of Subordination Considered* (1724) was a close examination of the treatment of servants; *A Tour Thro the Whole Island of Great Britain* (three volumes, 1724–27) was a guide book of the period as well as of the country; *The Complete English Tradesman* (1726) marks the entry of the merchant class into 'honourable' society; *Plan of the English Commerce* (1728) reinforces Defoe's claims to attention as a writer on trade; and *Augusta Triumphans, or the Way to make London the Most Flourishing City in the Universe* was a hopeful Utopian plan full of fascinating ideas.

Defoe, the founder of English journalism and the father of the English novel, was a new sort of man in the English literary scene. His education began and ended in a school for the children of Dissenters but he displayed remarkable learning in his work and could read in seven languages. Art and literary styles meant nothing to him; Defoe, in Bonamy Dobrée's words, 'dealt entirely with fact' but what matters to us is 'what he did with fact'. Professor Dobrée put his finger neatly on the point; again and again in Defoe the reader is confronted with apparently casual additions to a scene that leave it indelibly printed on the mind. He is in the mind of Moll Flanders and Roxana as completely as he is in the mind of Crusoe and somehow he achieves truth, not verisimilitude; his novels reach us, as Walter Allen wrote, as 'transcripts of actual experience'.

Daniel Defoe died on 26 April 1731 in his lodgings in Ropemakers Alley in Moorfields. Alexander Pope and Jonathan Swift had looked down their noses at this man of the lower classes, with his energy, unquenchable curiosity, and explosive energy, rather in the way the University Wits had looked down on Shakespeare: Swift's 'the Fellow that was Pilloryed, I have forgot his name' (1709) sounds like studied rudeness of the most contemptible kind. But judgment, as always, lies with posterity and Defoe can be seen as an original genius which Swift, for all his brilliance, was not.

**Degradation of the Democratic Dogma, The** Henry Brooks Adams's *A Letter to American Teachers of History* is contained in this volume, with a lengthy preface by his brother, Brooks Adams. The *Letter* first appeared in 1910 and this volume in 1919. In the *Letter* Henry Brooks Adams elaborates his dynamic theory of history, already presented in *The Education of Henry Adams*, which was privately printed in 1907. He questions the premise that technological advances reflect progress in the human condition.

**Deirdre** See **Yeats, William Butler.**

**Deirdre of the Sorrows** See **Synge, John Millington** and **Yeats, William Butler.**

**deism** This viewpoint in theological thought accepted the Supreme Being as the source of finite existence but rejected the supernatural element in Christianity, as well as Christian revelation as the only way to true salvation. Lord Herbert of Cherbury was the first English philosopher to propound the ideas and John Locke's *The Reasonableness of Christianity* (1695) gave support in his contention that man and his use of reason is evidence enough of the existence of God, who must have given man the capacity. But Locke's further contention that the Gospels were of far more moral value to most men than all the philosophical speculations in history gave the opponents of deism a powerful argument against it. Deism offered reason as an alternative to the practice of formal religion; consequently it had no lasting adherents. Reason provides cold comfort, while the conviction of the God who must be served, in a particular form, offered the hope of a better life in the hereafter and a means of consolation in the present. And Joseph Butler, Bishop of Durham, argued in his *Analogy of Religion* (1736) that it was no more difficult to accept 'revealed' religion than it was to grapple with the idea of 'natural' religion as put forward by the deists, which stated the case perfectly for the feeling of the age. But the ideas of the deists had intrinsic strength and were to influence Voltaire, Jean-Jacques Rousseau, and Denis Diderot in France; Matthew Tindal's *Christianity as Old as Creation* (1730) was translated into German and deism became popular in Germany during the reign of Frederick the Great. Charles Blount, meanwhile, had published *Anima Mundi* (1679), in which he emphasized the merits of other faiths and offered a form of 'natural' religion. He also voiced his scepticism of the belief in immortality. His *Great is Diana of the Ephesians* and *The Two First Books of Philostratus, concerning the Life of Appolonius Tyaneus* (1680) were hostile to 'priestcraft' and attacked the fundamentals of Christianity.

See also **Toland, John**; **Clarke, Samuel**; **Butler, Joseph**; **Collins, Anthony**; and **Tindal, Matthew**.

**Dekker, Thomas** *c*.1570–*c*.1632. It is generally agreed that Thomas Dekker was a Londoner though nothing is known of his parentage or his early life. Famous as a playwright, he is also the finest reporter of London life at the beginning of the 17th century. His pamphlets are the most vivid first-hand accounts written before Defoe, demonstrating a remarkable knowledge of the city in which his own existence was apt to be precariously balanced between wellbeing and destitution. Dekker spent many years in prison for debt but there is nothing in his work to suggest that bitterness ever entered his character; in fact he has the sunny disposition frequently encountered in a London street market and much of the same kind spirit. He detested the cruelty of the bear gardens and the popular sport of bull baiting.

Dekker is first identified as one of the working playwrights employed by Philip Henslowe, working with Drayton, Jonson, and others. The first play of his own was **Old Fortunatus**, followed by **The Shoemaker's Holiday** (both

1600). He was involved in the 'war of the theatres' (see **Jonson, Ben**) and contributed his part in **Satiromastix** with John Marston (1602). **The Honest Whore** was published in two parts; the first part was written with Thomas Middleton and published in 1604; the second and finer part is entirely by Dekker but was not published until 1630. The plays that are recognized as solely by Dekker after 1604 do not bear out his original promise. *The Whore of Babylon* (1607), *If it be not good, the Devil is in it* (1612), *Match me in London* (1631), and *The Wonder of a Kingdome* (1636) are undistinguished pieces but Dekker's talents had not disappeared as completely as this might suggest. Apart from his contributions to some notable plays in collaboration with others he had also been engaged on the famous pamphlets that tell of life in the London of his time, on the satirical **The Gul's Hornebooke** (1609) and, remarkably, on a prose work of devotion called **Fowre Birds of Noahs Arke** (also 1609). Dekker was in prison for debt from 1613 to 1619 – he was probably too generous to keep what he earned.

The plays in which Thomas Dekker collaborated are **The Roaring Girle** (1611) with Middleton; **Northward Hoe** and **Westward Hoe** (1607) and **The Famous History of Sir Thomas Wyat** (1607), all with Webster; **The Virgin-Martir** (1622) with Philip Massinger; and **The Witch of Edmonton** (1623) with John Ford and William Rowley. Henry Chettle and William Haughton contributed to **Patient Grissil** (1603), which is best remembered for Dekker's charming lyric 'Art thou poore yet hast thou golden Slumbers? O sweet content!'. It should be remembered that Charles Lamb said of him: 'As for Dekker, why, he had poetry enough for anything.'

The plague depicted on the title page of Thomas Dekker's pamphlet *A Rod For Run-awayes* (1625).

The best of Dekker's pamphlets are *The Wonderfull Yeare* (1603), *The Seven Deadly Sinnes of London* (1606), *The Belman of London* (1608), *Lanthorne and Candle-Light* (1608), *Worke for Armorours* (1609), and *A Rod for Run-awayes* (1625). He was also the author of masques and Lord Mayors' entertainments.

The dramatic works of Thomas Dekker were edited by F. T. Bowers and published in four volumes (1964–66), with two volumes of commentary by C. Hoy (1974). The nondramatic works were edited by A. B. Grosart and published in five volumes (1884–86).

**De la Mare, Walter** 1873–1956. Of Huguenot descent, Walter De la Mare was born at Charlton, Kent, and educated at St Paul's Choir School. In 1890 he went to work for the Standard Oil Company, and became a writer in his spare time. His stories, contributed to periodicals, were published under the pseudonym of Walter Ramal. He used the same name for his early poetry, written for children, and for the first published collection, *Songs of Childhood* (1902). *Henry Brocken* (1904), a prose fantasy, demonstrated his talents for a different form, and *Poems* (1906) confirmed his claim to serious attention. De la Mare was awarded a small Civil List pension in 1908 and he was able to give all his time to writing. He continued to write until he was in his eighties, a poet, storyteller, novelist, and writer for children, who defied categorization and was honoured throughout the English-speaking world. He was made a Companion of Honour in 1948 and awarded the Order of Merit in 1953.

Among 20th-century writers De la Mare is unique for his sense of the numinous, the feeling of wonder at and communication with the world outside this one. It is perhaps this quality that gives his work for children the peculiar toughness and lack of sentimentality that connects so well with the child's mind: De la Mare saw no need to look down at children protectively, since their sense of wonder is unimpaired. A lyric poet who combined a feeling for natural beauty with a remarkable talent for suggesting the inexpressible, he also raised the anthology to a distinct kind of literature: *Come Hither* (1933), *Desert Islands* (1930), *Love* (1943), *Behold this Dreamer* (1939), and *Early one Morning* (1935) were much more than collections; they demonstrate a carefully considered approach, which leads the reader into fascinating places where the strangeness of familiar things, and vice versa, is a continual enchantment.

Walter De la Mare published 27 books of poems, 21 books of poems and stories for children, 5 novels, and 7 books of short stories. *The Complete Poems* (1969) is definitive; E. Wagenknecht's edition of *The Collected Tales of Walter De la Mare* (1950) contains all the short stories published before 1955. *Collected Rhymes and Verses* (1944) contains De la Mare's poetry for children; *Collected Stories for Children* (1947) is complete. A recommended selection is by W. H. Auden, *A Choice of De la Mare's Verse* (1963).

**Delectable Mountains** In John Bunyan's *The Pilgrim's Progress*, Christian and Hopeful reach the mountains after escaping from Giant Despair and there they are counselled by the shepherds Knowledge, Experience, Watchful, and Sincere.

**Deloney, Thomas** *c.*1543–*c.*1600. Deloney was a London silk-weaver who wrote ballads in a popular style and pamphlets on subjects of the day; he wrote three, for instance, on the defeat of the Spanish Armada. He is remembered for his prose fiction, written for a public of tradesmen and small merchants, who are almost always idealized as characters and who probably read his stories eagerly. They are in episodes, drawn together to make a continuous narrative of sorts, sometimes with a historical background. The tone is coarse and sometimes cruel – probably reflecting the day-to-day quality of Elizabethan London – and displays a good ear for common speech. The best-known is *The Gentle Craft: A Discourse Containing many Matters of Delight* (1597 and 1633, two parts), which tells 'What Famous Men have been Shoemakers'. From this came the story of Simon Eyre, which Dekker made into *The Shoemaker's Holiday*. *The Pleasant Historie of John Winchcomb called Jack of Newberry* (Jack of Newbury) was first printed in 1619; *Thomas of Reading, or the Six Worthy Yeomen of the West* in 1612.

**Demetrius** In Shakespeare's *A Midsummer Night's Dream*, the young Athenian who loves Hermia and is chosen for her by her father. Demetrius is harsh towards Helena, who loves him.

*Democracy in America* (*La Démocratie en Amérique*). Comte Alexis de Tocqueville's celebrated report on America was written in two parts, in 1835 and 1840, and was the result of his official mission to the USA to study the penal system, an appointment authorized by the judicature at Versailles.

He was impressed by the success of the principles of liberty and equality, which had evolved in the Old World and were rapidly developing in the new country. He saw the trend of history as being toward equality and the future of France –

indeed the future of the western world – being dependent on the acceptance of democratic principles. These were, he believed, the true defences against tyranny. Comte de Tocqueville's report was the first impartial and systematic study of the USA. Volume II contains a penetrating analysis of American literature at the time of his visit and a shrewd assessment of the course it was likely to follow.

**Democratic Vistas** A prose pamphlet by Walt Whitman, first published in 1871. It was later included in *Two Rivulets* (1876), the second volume of the sixth edition of *Leaves of Grass*.

Whitman was an ardent democrat and a passionate individualist. He asserts his belief in the compatibility of the two points of view and sees this as the basis for a cultural order for the United States. Cultural independence was of the utmost importance, he believed, and essential to this was an indigenous American literature. In this statement Whitman also condemns the gross and often corrupt materialism of the USA after the Civil War.

**Denham, Sir John** 1615–69. Contemporary with Edmund Waller and, like him, a poet who used the couplet to great advantage, Denham was born in Dublin and educated at Trinity College, Oxford. His youth was apparently one of lively dissipation but he studied law at Lincoln's Inn and was called to the Bar in 1639. He was a staunch Royalist and his fortunes rose and fell with the king's. The Restoration saw him rewarded with a knighthood and the appointment of Surveyor of the Royal Works, and he also served as MP for Sarum for a time. He has the distinction of having paid the first public tribute to Milton's *Paradise Lost*, which he did in the House of Commons immediately it was published.

Denham was 26 when his play *The Sophy*, a blank-verse tragedy, was published and brought him fame. In the same year he published the long poem *Cooper's Hill*, set in the country near his home at Egham in Surrey. His verse is stronger and more concise than Waller's, relying less on the use of the couplet, but his use of the form strengthened the case for its adoption in the interest of discipline and rhythm. It is known that Denham worked also on translations of Homer and Virgil, but it is as the author of *Cooper's Hill* that he earned his place in English letters.

**Denis Duval** An unfinished novel by W. M. Thackeray. The completed parts were published in the *Cornhill* (April to June 1864). The author had died in December 1863.

The setting is Rye in the late 18th century. Denis Duval tells of his involvement with the smugglers of the area; of his love for Agnes de Saverne and the story of her victimized mother, and of the villainous de la Motte.

Thackeray left sketches for the completed book, which took him back to the sort of full-scale historical novel he had been so successful with in *Esmond*. The fragment of the novel we have promised a considerable work, with the author in command of the powers that seemed to have deserted him in *Philip*.

**Dennis, John** 1657–1734. The son of a prosperous saddler, Dennis was born in London and attended Harrow School. At Cambridge, he was expelled from Caius College for stabbing a fellow student, but finished his education at Trinity Hall. After university he travelled in France and Italy and became a member of Dryden's circle when he returned to England. An unsuccessful dramatist (he wrote eight plays), Dennis had more success as a critic, though he became cantankerous in later life and was ridiculed by Alexander Pope in *The Dunciad*. His principal essays are *The Impartial Critick* (1693), an attack on Thomas Rymer; *The Advancement and Reformation of Modern Poetry* (1701), *The Grounds of Criticism in Poetry* (1704) and *Three Letters on the Genius and Writings of Shakespeare* (1711). Dennis's *Original Letters, Familiar, Moral and Critical* (1721) is a valuable source of information on the literary world of his time.

**Dennis, the Hangman** In Dickens's *Barnaby Rudge*, the hangman of Newgate Prison, who is drawn to the side of Lord Gordon and becomes a leading figure in the narrative of the Gordon Riots. He is a chilling figure, a successful essay in evil. He is so much the brutalized instrument of society that his responses are entirely in terms of his calling. He ends, to his stupefaction, on the gallows himself.

**Deor** Also called *The Complaint of Deor* and *Deor's Lament*, a short poem of 42 lines in Old English, preserved in *The Exeter Book*. Deor is a minstrel, and three-quarters of the poem refers to the misfortunes of others while the last part tells of the minstrel's own misfortune: he has fallen out of favour and has been supplanted as the bard of the Heodenings by the minstrel named Heorrenda. Translations of the poem were made by C. K. Scott-Moncrieff in *Widsith, Beowulf, Finnsburgh, Waldere, Deor* (1921) and C. W. Kennedy in *An Anthology of Old English Poetry* (1960).

**De Profundis** Oscar Wilde's last prose work, an extended letter to Lord Alfred Douglas written during the author's imprisonment in Reading Gaol. The title was given by Robert Ross, Wilde's friend and literary executor, who published an abridged version (1905). This first appeared in German in a translation by Max Meyerfield; an English edition followed soon after. A fuller version, edited by Wilde's son Vyvyan Holland (1949), was described as 'the first complete and accurate version of *Epistola: in Carcere et Vinculis*'. But the definitive text from the manuscript was not in fact published until it was included in *The Letters of Oscar Wilde* edited by Rupert Hart-Davis (1962). A document of remarkable power, it records the author's relationship with Douglas, his bitterness at the other's selfishness and extravagance, and his conviction that Douglas was the principal agent in his destruction. The tone gradually changes from bitterness and hatred to humility and resignation, acknowledging Wilde's own responsibility and hoping for a calmer friendship in the future. Though the letter is brutal to Douglas, Wilde does not spare himself but conducts a merciless inquest on their affair.

**De Quincey, Thomas** 1785–1859. The son of a prosperous merchant, Thomas De Quincey was born in Manchester. He was a child of seven when his father died and he was sent to Manchester Grammar School when he was 15. He ran away after 18 months and wandered about in Wales before making his way to London. In the metropolis De Quincey lived as a 19th-century 'dropout'; his attachment to Ann, a prostitute, makes a vivid episode in the **Confessions of an English Opium Eater**. He was eventually sent to Oxford by his guardians, and at Worcester College De Quincey withdrew into himself and became absorbed in learning. Here, too, he first began to take opium for minor illnesses and, more importantly, as a tranquillizer. His fears were not imaginary: he left the college in 1808 in a nervous panic before completing his examinations and did not take a degree.

De Quincey became interested in German literature and was an early admirer of Wordsworth and Coleridge; indeed he had much in common with Coleridge, who was also interested in German literature and addicted to drugs. In 1809 De Quincey moved to the Lake District, where the poets he admired had their homes, determined to follow the literary career that had been in his mind since the age of 17. He became absorbed in reading, studying the classics (he was a brilliant Greek scholar), and cultivating Coleridge and the Wordsworths. His first published work, apart from a prize translation

from Horace (1800), was an appendix to Wordsworth's *The Convention of Cintra, Concerning the Relations of Great Britain, Spain and Portugal* in 1809. De Quincey's contribution to the literary circle of the Lake District is difficult to discern, and during those years he was sometimes in financial trouble. His friendship with the Wordsworths did not prosper; he had an affair with a local girl named Margaret Simpson and married her in 1817, by which time he and the Wordsworths were no longer friends. He edited *The Westmoreland Gazette* (1818–19) and the De Quinceys moved to London in 1821.

With the help of Charles Lamb, with whom he was already acquainted, De Quincey became a contributor to *The London Magazine*. In September and October of 1821 the two parts of *Confessions of an English Opium Eater* were published in the magazine, bringing the author fame. The remarkable intimacy of the *Confessions* and the rich sensuous prose make the book a striking contribution to English Romantic literature. Not even this success, however, could bring order and design into De Quincey's life. He was abnormally sensitive, having experienced bewildered grief as a child when his father and his sister died. The behaviour of a callous nurse at that time left a lasting scar and De Quincey was always afraid of the world. He became the father of a large family but never had a settled home; he lived as a scholarly recluse and rarely entertained,

Thomas De Quincey. A detail from the portrait by J. Watson-Gordon, 1845. National Portrait Gallery, London.

but the dreamy brilliant eccentric was courteous and generous to his friends.

Contributions to periodicals formed the greatest part of De Quincey's output. He lived in rooms in London and Bath and in 1828 drifted up to Edinburgh, where he lived in various lodgings until he died, when masses of his papers were discovered at different addresses. He wrote much for *Blackwood's Magazine*, *Knight's Quarterly Magazine*, the *Edinburgh Saturday Post*, *Tait's Magazine*, and the *Encyclopaedia Britannica*; his contributions to the last-named were essays on Shakespeare, Pope, Goethe, and Schiller. De Quincey also published an English version of *Walladmor* (1825), an oddity from the German which the author, G. W. H. Haering, claimed was a translation of a novel by Sir Walter Scott; a novel, *Klosterheim* (1832); and *The Logic of Political Economy* (1844).

Meanwhile interest in De Quincey had grown in the USA. The Boston publishers Ticknor & Fields, with the author's consent, began to issue *De Quincey's Writings* in 1851. In the following year James Hogg (the Edinburgh publisher, not the writer) persuaded the author to make his own collection. J. T. Fields's edition in America was reprinted directly from magazines and was completed in 24 volumes in 1859. Publication of the Edinburgh edition, *Selections Grave and Gay, from Writings Published and Unpublished of De Quincey, Revised and Arranged by Himself*, began in 1853 and was completed in 1860, the year after he died. The 14th and last volume was prepared by the author. The extended version of the *Confessions* was published in Volume V (1856) of that edition. Of the collected editions produced since, *The Collected Writings* edited by David Masson (14 volumes, 1889–90) is described by scholars as the most important though not completely satisfactory. *Uncollected Writings* was edited by James Hogg (1890); *Posthumous Writings* by A. H. Japp (1891–93); and De Quincey's contributions to the *Edinburgh Saturday Post* and the *Edinburgh Evening Post* as *New Essays* by S. M. Tave (1966).

Thomas De Quincey's mass of written work is of uneven quality, and occasionally his writing is impossible to relate to the author of the *Confessions* and the finer essays. Even allowing that he often wrote to order as a journalist his inferior work is longwinded and tiresomely waggish. Nevertheless, De Quincey earned a secure place in English literature with the *Confessions*, **Recollections of the Lake Poets**, **On Murder Considered as One of the Fine Arts**, and **On the Knocking at the Gate in Macbeth**.

**Desdemona**  See **Othello, The Moor of Venice**.

**Deserted Village, The**  A poem by Oliver Goldsmith, first published in 1770. The couplets in which it is composed are relaxed and genial and do not draw attention to the skill with which they are fashioned – they serve to express the natural feeling that Goldsmith complained had gone from poetry in his *An Enquiry into the Present State of Polite Learning* (1759). The theme is the enforced departure from the land brought about by the Enclosure Acts and the drift into the cities – the Industrial Revolution had just begun. The poem describes the past and present condition of an English village, Auburn, which is, inevitably, idealized. The truth of rural life was infinitely harsher and Goldsmith had no real knowledge of its demands; but it was fair to question the value of the change in English life caused by the revolution. As a pastoral elegy the poem succeeds completely.

**Désirée's Baby**  See **Bayou Folk**.

**Desperate Remedies**  Thomas Hardy's first novel, published in 1871.

Cytherea Graye is obliged by poverty to accept a post as lady's maid to Miss Aldclyffe. The latter is a woman whom Cytherea's father once loved but had been unable to marry. Under the pressure of Miss Aldclyffe's urging and the need to provide for her sick brother, Cytherea accepts Miss Aldclyffe's illegitimate son, Aeneas Mauston. Cytherea is in fact in love with Edward Springrove – but Edward is engaged.

Aeneas Mauston is a dubious character, whose first wife is believed to have died in a fire. The wedding proceeds and Cytherea learns that Edward has broken off his engagement. She also discovers that there is reason to believe that Mauston's first wife is still alive and this gives her the opportunity to escape from him. The rest of the story relates how the two lovers collect the evidence against Mauston, who had in fact murdered his first wife to gain Cytherea. Mauston hangs himself in his prison cell.

**Destiny**  A novel by Susan Ferrier, first published in 1831.

The third of Susan Ferrier's novels of Scottish life is the least satisfactory. A chronicle of the Malcolms, a Highland family, and their vicissitudes, it begins with Glenroy Malcolm's desertion by his second wife, Lady Elizabeth, when she finds life in her husband's home intolerable. It ends with the marriage of the altruistic Ronald to Edith, who has been jilted by her cousin Reginald. Edith is the daughter of Glenroy Malcolm by his first wife.

**Deuceace, Hon Algernon Percy** Youngest son of the Earl of Crabs. See *Yellowplush Correspondence, The*.

**De Vere, Aubrey Thomas** 1814–1902. De Vere was born at Adare in Limerick, Ireland. He was educated at Trinity College, Dublin, and as a young poet was influenced by Wordsworth and Coleridge. Though he spent much of his time in England, where he became a friend of Tennyson and Browning, his sympathies were strongly drawn to Ireland and he became a Roman Catholic in 1851. He published verse, literary and political essays, and *Inisfail, A Lyrical Chronicle of Ireland* (1862) and *The Legends of St Patrick* (1872).

*Devil is an Ass, The* A comedy by Ben Jonson, first produced in 1616 and published in 1631. The play exposes the activities of 'projectors' (in modern terms, fixers and confidence tricksters), witchfinders, and healers of demoniacs (supposed victims of satanic possession). The plot concerns Meercraft, a projector, who proposes a scheme for reclaiming land. His victim is Fitzdottrel, who parts with his estate on the promise of being made Duke of Drowndland. Fitzdottrel, in turn, deceives the law by pretending to be bewitched. Another character in the plot is Pug, a minor devil allowed out by Satan for one day to practise his wickedness on earth. But the wickedness he encounters on earth is worse than his own; he is completely outwitted by human knaves and ends up in Newgate gaol.

**Devizes, Richard of** fl. 1191. Richard of Devizes was a Winchester monk who made a contribution to the chronicles of Anglo-Norman England with his *De Rebus Gestis Ricardi Primi*, a contemporary record of the first three years of the reign of Richard I.

Richard of Devizes' chronicle was edited by R. Howlett in *Chronicles of the Reigns of Stephen, Henry II and Richard I* (Rolls Series, 1886). John T. Appleby's translation, *The Chronicle of Richard of Devizes*, was published in 1973.

*Dial, The* See **Transcendentalism**.

*Dialoge of Comfort against Tribulacion, A* See **More, Thomas**. It was first published in 1553, and a modern edition by P. E. Hallett can be found in the Everyman's Library volume that also contains *Utopia* (1910 and 1951).

*Dialogues Concerning Natural Religion* A treatise in dialogue form on natural theology by David Hume, first published in 1779, three years after his death. The narrator is Pamphilus, and the interlocutors are the philosopher Cleanthes, the sceptic Philo, and the orthodox Christian Demea. The subject is the nature of God (the existence of God is not in question) and the dialogues examine further the questions raised in the essays *On Miracles* and *The Natural History of Religion*. The dialogues give a remarkable impression of a recorded discussion, with their varying pace and rhythm, sharp exchanges and interruptions, and, at times, the irresistible flow of words when a speaker is holding forth with total conviction.

*Diamond Lens, The* See **O'Brien, Fitz-James**.

**Diana** The Florentine woman whom Bertram tries to seduce in Shakespeare's *All's Well that Ends Well*. It is with Diana's help that Helena, his wife, gains Bertram's bed.

*Diana of the Crossways* A novel by George Meredith, first published in 1885. It was begun as a story in the *Fortnightly Review* and, like *The Tragic Comedians*, developed as a full-length novel.

Diana Warwick (née Merion) is far more intelligent than her husband, a government official. He stupidly misinterprets her actions and, believing her faithless, he brings an action for divorce against her. He loses the case but the Warwicks, inevitably, separate. Diana is supported in her trials by her friend Lady Dunstane and by her admirers, among whom are Percy Dacier and Thomas Redworth.

The most ardent is Dacier and when Warwick persecutes Diana, she is strongly tempted to become Dacier's mistress to gain his protection. Lady Dunstane falls ill, however, and Diana becomes more concerned with that than with Dacier's attentions. He remains her ardent admirer and after a time Diana is once more nearly persuaded that her best course would be to accept his protection. Then Dacier discovers that a political confidence that he made to her has been given to the press; pecuniary embarrassment had played a large part in Diana'a action but Dacier cannot forgive her. The break between them is final.

Thomas Redworth, who has quietly loved and appreciated Diana for years, remains her faithful champion and she marries him when her husband dies.

**Diceto, Ralph (or Raoul) de** d. 1202. Ralph de Diceto was Archdeacon of Middlesex and became Dean of St Paul's in 1180. 'Diceto' probably refers to his birthplace but its whereabouts are unknown. His *Imagines Historiarum* chronicles the years 1148 to 1202 and is valued particularly for the period from 1172 onwards. The earlier period had already been chronicled by the

Norman Robert de Monte (Robert of Torigni) in his *Chronica*, but Ralph's original memoranda began in 1172 and he had access to important contemporary documents.

The *Imagines Historiarum* was edited by William Stubbs (Rolls Series, 1876).

**Dickens, Charles** 1812–70. Charles Dickens was the second child of a clerk in the Navy Pay Office at Portsmouth, John Dickens, who was an affectionate man but hopelessly improvident. Charles's childhood left him with bitter memories of loneliness and want – and of the debtors' prison, the Marshalsea.

The family moved to London in 1823 and lived in Camden Town. They had already gone from Portsmouth to Chatham before that, and the young Charles had, at best, an intermittent education. His father's affairs, in London, went from bad to worse – though he still had his post – and Mrs Dickens hoped to start a small school. Charles, at 12, was sent to work in a blacking factory near Charing Cross owned by James Lamert, an acquaintance of his father. The boy was better paid than the others and Lamert, trying to be kind, offered to give him lessons during the lunch hour. Meanwhile, Mrs Dickens's vague plans for her school came to naught, and John Dickens was committed to the Marshalsea prison on a debt of £40. The Navy Pay Office had not stopped his wages, however, so the whole Dickens family moved into the Marshalsea when everything they possessed had been sold. Charles was found lodgings, first in Camden Town, and then in Southwark with a family who were kind to him. He worked 12 hours a day at the blacking factory; he was lonely and deeply unhappy and felt his family's misfortunes were shameful. Every day he trudged through the London streets, from Camden Town to Charing Cross, from there to the Marshalsea in Southwark and, for a time, all the way from Southwark to Camden Town. Those few weeks, from February to April 1824, made an indelible impression on him.

John Dickens was released when his mother died and left him a little money. The family found a seedy house near Camden Town, and John Dickens immediately quarrelled with James Lamert, who had prospered and had better premises where Charles worked in better conditions, by a window facing the street. Passers-by would often pause and watch the boys at work and John Dickens objected to his son being on display. Lamert, who had been a godsend to the family, was understandably angry and discharged the boy, who was happy to go. But Mrs Dickens was more realistic and smoothed

matters – Charles could go on working at the blacking factory. John Dickens would not agree; the boy should be educated. Charles Dickens never forgot that his mother wanted to send him back to a life he hated, and his novels teem with feckless, unloving, or inadequate parents.

Thereafter Charles Dickens attended private schools and was articled to a solicitor's clerk in 1827. The following year he became a freelance reporter, mastered shorthand, and reported the parliamentary debates on the Reform Bill for the *Morning Chronicle*. He began to move about a great deal, read much in the British Museum and, in 1833, slipped a manuscript into the editor's box of *The Monthly Magazine*; it was a sketch, 'A dinner at Poplar Walk'. The magazine did not pay for contributions and Dickens had to buy the next issue for half-a-crown to find out if his had been accepted. It had – and the editor wrote and asked him for another contribution, and then more. The first ones had been unsigned but now the author's pen-name appeared: it was the nickname of his young brother Augustus, originally Moses; then Boses, as pronounced through the nose – then Boz. The sketches attracted attention; Boz was published in the *Morning Chronicle*, then in the *Evening Chronicle*. And one day Harrison Ainsworth, visiting the *Chronicle* offices, invited Boz to dinner, where Dickens met Disraeli, Cruikshank, Daniel Maclise, and others; most important of all he met Ainsworth's publisher, John Macrone, who wanted to publish the sketches in book form.

*Sketches by Boz*, with illustrations by George Cruikshank, was published in two series in 1836. Dickens was 24, and he was at work on a proposal from Chapman & Hall for a serial, in 20 monthly instalments of 12,000 words each. He had secured favourable terms (enabling him to marry Catherine Hogarth) and the first number appeared in April 1836. After the fourth issue it became extraordinarily successful: the new work by Boz was **The Pickwick Papers**, and the author achieved immense popular success and financial security. He had, meanwhile, also become editor of *Bentley's Miscellany*, and in that magazine he had another serial running by February 1837. The new one appeared under the familiar pen-name, though all England knew by this time that Boz was Charles Dickens, and it was called **Oliver Twist:** *or, The Parish Boy's Progress*. Dickens's genius as a storyteller was manifest; so was his demonic energy. For the rest of his life work simply poured from his pen.

***Nicholas Nickleby*** came next, in 20 parts, completed in November 1839. Dickens persuaded Chapman & Hall, who were well aware of his value to them, to publish a weekly magazine for him – *Master Humphrey's Clock* – and into this went, amongst a mass of miscellaneous writing, **The Old Curiosity Shop**, from April 1840 to February 1841, and **Barnaby Rudge**, from February to November 1841.

In 1842 the author visited the USA, where he rightly attacked the practice of pirating books published in England. **American Notes** was published in 1842, and the Americans didn't like it very much. **Martin Chuzzlewit** (20 parts, from January 1843 to July 1844) they liked even less: but it was not a great success in England, either, compared to *The Old Curiosity Shop*. One must remember, however, that Dickens was enjoying considerable fame by now: that *Chuzzlewit* was not a success compared to *The Old Curiosity Shop* only meant that the latter was selling 70,000 copies an instalment while *Chuzzlewit* never exceeded 23,000. With all this, Dickens was writing his **Christmas Books**, too, beginning with *A Christmas Carol* in 1843. They appeared annually: *The Chimes, The Cricket on the Hearth, The Battle of Life,* and *The Haunted Man.*

**Pictures from Italy** resulted from a tour of that country in 1844 and were first published in *The Daily News.* **Dombey and Son** was started in 1846 during a visit to Lausanne and appeared in 20 parts, from October 1846 to April 1848. **David Copperfield** came next, also in 20 parts, from May 1849 to November 1850, and the tireless Dickens had meanwhile launched the weekly *Household Words* in March 1849. (This periodical continued until 1859, when it was succeeded by *All the Year Round* which continued until he died.)

**Bleak House** began to appear in the spring of 1852 (20 parts, from March 1852 to September 1853), and **Hard Times** appeared in *Household Words*, from April to August 1854. **A Child's History of England** had been appearing intermittently in the same weekly, between 1852 and 1854.

Dickens was apparently slowing down; the first instalment of his next novel, **Little Dorrit**, did not appear until December 1857. But this is only in terms of his major works of fiction; he was still writing ceaselessly as well as editing. During the following year he and his wife separated, and to his literary labours Dickens added the public readings from his work that were immensely profitable and that added to the strain, which even his demonic energy could not carry indefinitely. **A Tale of Two Cities**, his shortest novel, began to appear in *All the Year Round* in December 1857; so did the first of the fine occasional pieces which were published in

Charles Dickens. A detail from the portrait by A. Scheffer, 1855. National Portrait Gallery, London.

book form in 1861 and 1866 as **The Uncommercial Traveller**.

**Great Expectations** appeared in *All the Year Round*, from December 1860 to August 1861, and then Dickens, occupied with his public readings, wrote only short pieces until **Our Mutual Friend**, which appeared in 20 parts, from May 1864 to November 1865. He was seriously ill in 1865, the year in which he was also involved in the great rail disaster at Staplehurst. Against advice, he went on a reading tour to the USA in 1868 and earned something like £20,000. But the strain was appalling and Charles Dickens died of a stroke in 1870. He left **The Mystery of Edwin Drood** unfinished.

Volume upon volume has been published examining the life, works, and times of Charles Dickens. Rightly so – there is no one like him, and we shall be fortunate indeed if we ever find his like again. There are volumes of adverse criticism, too, and volumes which sift out layers and periods, comparing one with another and finding reasons for a thesis in everything he wrote. In the last analysis, the mountains of published comment are a tribute to the genius of Charles Dickens, a genius rooted in English common life. He has a wonderful ear for dialogue, his prose embraces a great range of effects, and his unerring touch of fantasy gives life, in a vivid and memorable way, to characters who are some-times a considerable distance from reality. His sentimentality can be quite repellent; but one must remember that Dickens was writing at a time when bathos was not easily recognized as pathos out of control. He went awry, some-times, in his exposure of the social inhumanities of his time: but he saw those inhumanities clearly and, at his best, wrote about them to devastating effect. His touch was not infallible, and he had his failures, but his vitality and inventiveness were staggering and he died with them undiminished – *Our Mutual Friend* is one of his best novels and the unfinished *Edwin Drood* showed every sign of becoming a remarkable one. Thackeray declared that '. . . if he [lives] to be ninety, Dickens will still be creating new characters. In his art that man is marvellous.'

His brilliant, many-faceted personality has been commented upon by all his contemporaries. He learned very quickly what his work was worth and could drive a hard bargain. He was sentimental, disastrously so, in his relations with women, and took the wrong sort of wife – though it is hard to imagine the woman who would have been the right sort. The domestic state soon bored and irritated him; he was always imploring his friends to come and stay. He was sentimentally fond of children but his own were a responsibility and he seems to have had little understanding of them; he was bitterly hurt when his behaviour alienated them. He bore with the importunities of his dreadful father, a pathological borrower who would have tried the patience of a saint: but the unhappy Catherine, his wife, had only to stumble to induce com-plaints about her clumsiness. Whatever love he imagined he had for her soon passed and in his letters there is a note of resentment about her recurrent pregnancies, as if she were in some way to blame. Catherine left him after 22 years of marriage. (It is fascinating to reflect upon Dickens's admission to his friends that he had put much of himself into the character of Quilp in *The Old Curiosity Shop* – Quilp, among other things, is a marital bully.)

The conventions of his time – and the ethics of his lower-middle-class background – placed constraints on Dickens which were unendurable but indissoluble. The man who was Charles Dickens was a victim of the times in which Charles Dickens lived. But it was those times that provided the setting in which he shone so brightly, and which he recorded for us so vivid-ly. He will be discussed and argued about for as long as there is literature and he will never cease to be read.

**Dickey, James (Lafayette)** 1923– . Dickey was born in Atlanta, Georgia, and educated at Vanderbilt University in Nashville, Tennessee. He published his first collection of poems in 1960, *Into the Stone and Other Poems*. Other collections are *Drowning with Others* (1962), *Helmets* and *Two Poems of the Air* (1964), *Buckdancer's Choice* (1965), and *The Eye-Beaters, Blood, Victory, Madness, Buckhead and Mercy* (1970). *Poems 1957–1967* was published in 1968. James Dickey has also published English versions of the poems of Yevgeny Yevtushenko, *Stolen Apples* (1971), and one novel, *Deliverance* (1970).

**Dickinson, Emily** 1830–86. America's greatest woman poet was born in Amherst, Massachusetts, and spent all her life there apart from a year at Mount Holyoke Female Seminary. Her father was a lawyer and Emily Dickinson led what was apparently a life without incident; she never married but managed her father's house.

Her friends were the important influences in Emily's life, from her first association with a student in her father's law office, Benjamin Newton, for whom she may have cherished a secret love. Newton was important in her development because he advised her what to read and encouraged her to work at her poetry. His early death in 1853 was enough of a loss to per-suade her to seek religious guidance and she turned to Charles Wadsworth of Philadelphia, a clergyman she met in 1854. Wadsworth was married but Emily was happy to call him her dearest earthly friend; her work of this period (though it is not possible to be quite certain of the dates of any of her poems) contains the image of a lover, identified as Charles Wadsworth, whom she was only to know in her imagination. In 1862 Wadsworth was sent to San Francisco and from this time Emily withdrew from her own society in Amherst, becoming more and more con-cerned with her work. But she began a literary correspondence with T. W. Higginson, the writer and Unitarian minister whose papers she had read in the *Atlantic Monthly*.

Higginson, though he tended to 'correct' her poems, gave Emily real encouragement and his friendship meant much to her. She kept her work to herself except for the occasional glimpse of odd poems vouchsafed to Helen Hunt Jackson, Samuel Bowles, and one or two others; her family never saw it and she always wrote in secret. She lived an enclosed puritan life in a small New England town until she died at the age of 56. Incredibly, she left behind over 1700 poems, only two of which were published during her lifetime – and those without her consent.

Emily Dickinson's poetry is, in Edith Sitwell's phrase, 'technically insufficient'. The comment is just and is one made in different form by a number of critics and poets, who nonetheless acknowledge the quality of Emily Dickinson's work and her importance in American poetry. Her poems are all short and she favoured the four-line stanza; she was never concerned with publication and had no need to please anyone with her poems, so her technical imperfections persist throughout her work. The effect is a bit like encountering a piece of grit in a small ripe fruit; but it is the texture and taste of the fruit that really matter in the end and these are unique. The importance of Emily Dickinson lies much more in poetic utterance than in prosody. Hers was a small enclosed world but in it she could find the significance of the universe, articulate her questioning of accepted faith, and speculate on love and death.

In the disordered mass of work that Emily Dickinson left behind were poems in every stage of composition, from half-formed ideas jotted down on scraps of paper to poems completed after careful revision. The first volume to be published was *Poems* (1890), followed by *Poems: Second Series* (1891). These were edited by her Amherst friend, Mabel L. Todd, and T. W. Higginson. *Poems: Third Series* (1896) was edited by Mabel L. Todd, and the next volume, called *The Single Hound* (1914), was edited by the poet's niece, Martha Dickinson Bianchi. *Further Poems* (1929) and *Unpublished Poems* (1936) were edited by Martha Dickinson Bianchi and Alfred Leete Hampson. There was also a *Poems: Centenary Edition* in 1930. These collections were not well produced; there was no effective order and often the texts were inaccurately printed. But *Bolts of Melody* was carefully edited by Mabel L. Todd and Millicent Bingham in 1945 and gave the public a number of poems by Emily Dickinson that had been suppressed because of family conflict. The edition prepared by Thomas H. Johnson for the Harvard University Press and published in three volumes in 1955 is the definitive one and was much needed (*The Poems of Emily Dickinson*). Thomas H. Johnson also edited the Harvard edition of the *Letters* (1958).

**Dictionary of the English Language, A** Samuel Johnson's great work was first published in 1755. It had been in his mind for some time and he issued *The Plan of a Dictionary of the English Language* in 1747. At the prompting of Robert Dodsley, the London bookseller, Johnson, rather against his will, *Addressed* [the project] *to the Right Honourable Philip Dormer, Earl of Chesterfield, one* of *His Majesty's Principal Secretaries of State*. Johnson's uneasiness about patronage was to have an unhappy sequel – see **Johnson, Samuel**. His *Dictionary* represented eight years' labour and the work was executed while the author was engaged in several concurrent projects, driven as he was by the need to earn as much money as possible. One of these was *The Rambler*, and he concluded that series of essays with a declaration that he had striven to refine the language to grammatical purity 'and to clear it from colloquial barbarisms, licentious idioms, and irregular combinations' (1752). The *Dictionary's* complete title, upon its publication in 1755, indicated the range of Johnson's aspirations: *A Dictionary of the English Language: In Which the Words are Deduced from their Originals, and Illustrated in their Different Significations by Examples from the Best Writers. To Which are Prefixed A History of the Language, and an English Grammar.*

Johnson's earliest authorities were Sidney and Spenser – he held firmly that the golden age of the English language began with the Elizabethans; he also honoured, as fully as the knowledge of the time permitted, provincialisms and dialect. He set himself to reject all the 'Gallick structure and phraseology' which had found its way into the language since the Restoration and was in danger of reducing 'us to babble a dialect of France'. In the 18th century there was scant etymological knowledge to help Johnson but he brought to his task his monumental commonsense and a devotion to his subject. The highest praise for his great pioneering work has always come from his successors.

An abridgment of the *Dictionary* was published in 1756. Five editions of the original two-volume folio were printed during Johnson's lifetime. The last, with his revisions, appeared in 1773.

**Dido Queene of Carthage, The Tragedie of** See **Marlowe, Christopher**.

**Digby, Sir Kenelm** 1603–65. Digby's father was one of the men executed for complicity in the Gunpowder Plot of 1606. However, the son remained a Catholic and was educated at Gloucester Hall (now Worcester College), Oxford. A successful naval commander, Digby was interested in science and became a founder member of the Royal Society in 1660. His first work, not published until 1827, was his *Private Memoirs*, written in 1628 to refute gossip about his wife, Venetia Stanley. In 1638 he published a reaffirmation of his Catholic faith, *Conference with a Lady about Choice of Religion*, after flirting with Protestantism, and a criticism of Browne's *Religio Medici* (*Observations upon Religio Medici*) in

1643. A Royalist, he pleaded the cause of King Charles in Rome, and was banished in 1649, the year of the king's execution. He lived in Paris, where he became a friend of Descartes, until the Restoration, when he returned to England as Chancellor to Queen Henrietta Maria. Other works were *Of the Immortality of Man's Soul* (1644), *On the Cure of Wounds* (1658) and *A Discourse Concerning the Vegetation of Plants* (1660), an address to the Royal Society on the necessity of oxygen to plant life.

**Dillon, Wentworth, 4th Earl of Roscommon** *c.*1633–85. The nephew and godson of Thomas Wentworth, Earl of Strafford, Dillon was born in Ireland and educated at the University of Caen. He returned to England at the Restoration after spending some years in Europe, and became a friend of John Dryden. Dillon was interested in founding a British Academy on the lines of the Académie Française to 'refine and fix the standard of our language'. He was the author of an *Essay on Translated Verse* (1684) and a blank verse translation of Horace's *The Art of Poetry* (1680). He was among the first to recognize the greatness of John Milton.

**Dinmont, Dandy** The Lowland farmer who becomes Harry Bertram's friend in Scott's *Guy Mannering*, and who breeds a special kind of terrier. He helps Meg Merrilies frustrate the plans of the villain, Glossin. An attractive character, he was apparently an original invention, though after the novel had made the name famous, it became attached to Mr James Davidson of Hindlee, who had successfully bred a new sort of terrier.

***Discoverie of the True Causes why Ireland was Never Entirely Subdued . . .*** *until the beginning of his Majestie's happie Raigne.* A history by Sir John Davies, which has been praised as a lucid presentation of the defects of England's policy in Ireland until the 'happie Raigne' of James I, under whom Davies was concerned in the plantation of Ulster. The book was published in 1612: Ireland remained 'entirely subdued' for most of the next 20 years.

**Disraeli, Benjamin, 1st Earl of Beaconsfield** 1804–81. A Conservative Prime Minister and novelist, Disraeli was born in London, the son of an antiquarian and occasional writer, Isaac D'Israeli. He was educated entirely at home. In 1821 he was articled to a firm of solicitors and entered Lincoln's Inn in 1824. He later withdrew from the law, having started to write. His first novel, ***Vivian Grey***, appeared in three volumes, from 1826 to 1827, and enjoyed considerable success. It is a political novel which the years have rendered

Benjamin Disraeli. A detail from the portrait by C. Bone, 1828. National Portrait Gallery, London.

increasingly obscure. In the same vein were *The Voyage of Captain Popanilla* (1828) and *The Young Duke* (1831).

The author had contrived to make the grand tour, in spite of financial difficulties and his next novel, ***Contarini Fleming:*** *A Psychological Autobiography* (1832) is set in the Levant. Foreign settings were used to give colour to much of his fiction at this period (1833) – *The Wondrous Tale of Alroy*, *The Rise of Iskander*, and *Ixion in Heaven*. *The Infernal Marriage* was published in 1834, and an unsuccessful attempt at a love story, ***Henrietta Temple***, in 1837. *Venetia*, the same year, uses elements – then little known – of the lives of Byron and Shelley.

Disraeli entered parliament in the same year and embarked on a political career which completely eclipsed his one as a novelist. However, it was slow at first and his novelist's career resumed with ***Coningsby,*** *or The New Generation* in 1844; ***Sybil,*** *or The Two Nations* followed in 1845, and ***Tancred,*** *or The New Crusade* in 1847. The next few years saw the increasing success of the politician, and the next novel, ***Lothair***, did not appear until 1870. ***Endymion***, his last, was published in 1880. A volume, *Tales and Sketches*, was posthumously published in 1891, edited by J. L. Robertson.

The amount of other writing – verse, biography, political comment – by Disraeli was considerable. Notable are his *A Vindication of the English Constitution* (1835) and *Lord George Bentinck: A Political Biography* (1852).

Disraeli has never been a popular novelist but he continues to find readers. The later novels, from 1844, are those which express political ideas; they also give a vivid picture of the circles in which he moved. Characterization is not his strength – his people are almost all attractive and witty, and sometimes they are exhaustingly so, a quality which deprives the novels of much of the force inherent in their themes. Disraeli's knowledge and observation were sound but his effect, through his fiction at any rate, is debatable.

**Diversity of Creatures, A** See **Kipling, Rudyard.**

**Dixon, Richard Watson** 1833–1900. Dixon was born in Islington and educated at King Edward's School, Birmingham, and Pembroke College, Oxford. He became part of a distinguished group of friends, which included William Morris, Edward Burne-Jones, Gerard Manley Hopkins, and Robert Bridges. He entered the Church and was canon of Carlisle for many years. Dixon was the author of *The History of the Church of England from the Abolition of Roman Jurisdiction* (six volumes, 1878–1902) and several volumes of poetry. His best poems are generally acknowledged to be those found in *Poems: A Selection, with a Memoir*, edited by Robert Bridges (1909).

**Dobell, Sydney Thompson** 1824–74. The son of a wealthy wine merchant, Dobell was born at Cranbrook in Kent and educated privately. His first published work, *The Romans: A Dramatic Poem* (1850), was a reflection of popular feeling in favour of the oppressed Italians and was very successful. *Balder* (*Part the First*, 1854), no more of which was written, contains some good lines but is a strange work and earned the author inclusion among Aytoun's 'Spasmodic School'. It tells of a poet who believes he has been chosen to discover the secret of the universe and spends most of his time in mystic meditation in his gloomy tower. His neglected young wife bears a child, which sickens and dies, whereupon the poor girl goes mad. Balder eventually kills her, unable to bear her sufferings. Aytoun satirized Dobell in his mock tragedy *Firmilian* (1854). Other works by Dobell were *Sonnets on the War* (1855) with Alexander Smith (the war was the Crimean), *England in Time of War* (1856), and *Love, to A Little Girl* (1863).

**Dobson, Henry Austin** 1840–1921. The son of an engineer, Dobson was born in Plymouth. He worked at the Board of Trade for most of his adult life but he also enjoyed a career as a writer of light verse and a literary essayist, specializing in the 18th century. Among his published works were *Hogarth* (1879), *Fielding* (1883, for the English Men of Letters series), *Thomas Bewick and his Pupils* (1884), *The Life of Oliver Goldsmith* (1888), and *Horace Walpole* (1890). His *Eighteenth-Century Vignettes* were published in three series (1892, 1894, and 1896). *The Complete Poetical Works of Henry Austin Dobson* was edited by A. T. A. Dobson (1923).

**Doctor, The** A miscellany by Robert Southey published anonymously (five volumes, 1834–38); two more volumes were published by J. W. Warter, the poet's son-in-law (1847). The collection of stories and articles is provided with a slender continuity in the person of a Dr Daniel Dove of Doncaster and his horse Nobs. It contains fine descriptions of the Yorkshire dales, the history of the cats who lived at Greta Hall, the poet's home in Keswick, and 'The Story of the Three Bears'.

**Doctor Faustus, The Tragicall History of** A tragedy in blank verse and prose, first produced *c*.1589 but not published until 1604. The medieval legend of the bargain with the devil first found its way into printed form at Frankfurt in 1587, when the chief character was identified with a Doctor Georg Faust, a necromancer of the late 15th and early 16th centuries in Germany. In the Frankfurt *Volksbuch* he is called Johann Faust and Marlowe uses the same name (John) in his (the first)

The title page illustration of Christopher Marlowe's *The Tragicall History of the Life and Death of Doctor Faustus*, 1620 edition.

dramatization of the story. The play was acted by the same company who produced *Tamburlaine*, The Admiral's Men, who were now called The Earl of Nottingham's Men – in recognition of their patron's new eminence. Edward Alleyn played Doctor Faustus.

Faustus is weary of his studies and the sciences and turns to magic. He invokes the aid of the devil, who sends his agent Mephistophilis in the form of an ugly beast. Faustus commands him to change his shape to that of a friar – which Mephistophilis meekly does. This gives Faustus confidence and he makes his bargain; Lucifer will give him 24 years of life, Mephistophilis to do his bidding: at the end of that time Faustus will be taken, body and soul, by Lucifer.

The contract executed gives Faustus everything he asks for, except for certain questions Mephistophilis will not answer ('Now tell me, who made the world?'), declaring the answers to be his master's interest. Faustus' guardian angel goes on trying to redeem him, while a Bad Angel goes on persuading him he is damned. Lucifer himself comes to Faustus and shows him the pleasures in the Seven Deadly Sins. After a confrontation with the pope and cardinals in Rome, Faustus invokes the ghost of Helen of Troy. An Old Man pleads with Faustus to step back from the brink – there is still hope of redemption. Faustus makes his choice: he invokes the spirit of Helen again and embraces her ('Her lips suck forth my soul'). The climax of the play is Faustus' monologue anticipating the terrors that await him in his last hour of mortal life ('See, see, where Christ's blood streams in the firmament! One drop would save my soul, half a drop. Ah, my Christ!'). It is a magnificent poem, a great theme expressed in language that is equal to it.

*Doctor Faustus* shows an advance in stagecraft on Marlowe's part after the almost-solo play *Tamburlaine*. The comic scenes, it is generally agreed, were added to the text during the preparation for the stage and were probably by other hands. The most widely accepted text of the play is the one prepared by W. W. Greg, published in 1950.

**Doctor Thorne** The third of Anthony Trollope's Barsetshire novels. It was first published in 1858.

Roger Scatcherd, a stonemason, killed Henry Thorne when the latter seduced Roger's sister. She emigrated after the trial and married; Roger served a prison sentence. The girl Mary Thorne, brought up by Henry's brother – the Dr Thorne of the title – is Henry's child but this is not generally known in Greshamsbury, the town where the story is set.

Roger Scatcherd, after his release, succeeds in life and becomes wealthy. One of his debtors is the squire, Gresham; Gresham's improvidence is largely due to his aristocratic wife, a de Courcy, and his property is mortgaged to Scatcherd. Gresham's son, Frank, falls in love with Mary Thorne; but his family, thinking of their straits, do their best to persuade him to marry an heiress, Miss Dunstable, instead of an obscure and penniless girl. The dilemma is resolved when Mary is made his heiress by Roger Scatcherd. The fourth of Trollope's Barsetshire novels is *Framley Parsonage*.

**Dodgson, Charles Lutwidge** See **Carroll, Lewis.**

**Dodsley, Robert** 1703–64. Robert Dodsley was born near Mansfield, Nottinghamshire, and was educated at the free school where his father was headmaster. Apprenticed to a stocking maker, who ill-treated him, the young Dodsley ran away and found work as a servant, eventually becoming footman to the Hon. Mrs Lowther. He was fortunate in his employer; she helped him publish his poem *Servitude* (1729) and called attention to her footman's gifts. She also persuaded her friends to subscribe to a second book. (*Servitude, a Poem* was later reissued as *The Footman's Friendly Advice to his Brethren of the Livery*.) Literary London became interested in Dodsley, and the friendship of Pope and Swift eventually brought him to the notice of John Rich.

Dodsley's play *The Toyshop, a dramatic Satire* (written about 1732) was successfully produced by Rich at Covent Garden in 1735 and Dodsley used his modest success to open a bookshop at Tully's Head in Pall Mall. Alexander Pope invested £100 and Horace Walpole, Lord Lyttelton, and Joseph Spence helped him select poetry when he became a publisher. Dodsley seems to have had a gift for attracting friends.

In addition to the works of Pope, Dodsley published those of Thomas Gray, Mark Akenside, William Collins, Edward Young, and William Shenstone; he also published work by Samuel Johnson and Oliver Goldsmith. His great service to the poets of his time was the publication of their work in permanent volumes called *A Collection of Poems by Various Hands*, the first of which was published in 1748; six volumes appeared in ten years. Dodsley's *Collections* are of great value to students of English poetry; his collection of *Old Plays* (12 volumes, 1744) is, similarly, of great value to students of English drama. His place of honour in English publishing was further enhanced by the founding, with Edmund Burke, of *The Annual Register* in 1758.

Dodsley was also successful in the theatre; his work has not been revived but of five plays produced during his life the most notable was a tragedy, *Cleone*, first acted in 1758. Using the same theme as Shakespeare in *Othello*, Dodsley has a white hero and focuses the dramatic interest on the wronged wife, Cleone.

**Dodsworth**  See **Lewis, (Harry) Sinclair**.

**Dogberry**  The constable of Shakespeare's *Much Ado About Nothing*. In charge of the watch, he stumbles over the truth of Don John's malicious plot to discredit Hero and helps bring the villains to justice. A great comic creation with his bumbling but persistent good intentions and his imperfect grasp of words ('O villain! thou wilt be condemn'd into everlasting redemption for this!'), he can be hilarious in performance, as George Rose demonstrated in Sir John Gielgud's famous production of 1951.

**Dolores**  A poem by Algernon Charles Swinburne, first published in *Poems and Ballads* (first series, 1866). It was probably the most censured poem of that severely criticized volume, being a powerful and remarkably sensual litany to cruel love and plainly masochistic in tone: 'O splendid and sterile Dolores, Our Lady of Pain'.

**Dombey and Son,** *Dealings with the Firm of.* A novel by Charles Dickens. It was first published in 20 monthly parts (October 1847 to April 1848).

Mr Paul Dombey is a successful businessman, head of a shipping company. He is wealthy, arrogant, and cold and has little affection for his daughter Florence. When the story opens he has become the proud father of an heir but his wife dies in childbirth. Dombey's hopes and ambitions are centred on the boy, Paul, who is delicate and dreamy; Florence he neglects more and more. A man of little imagination and no real love, Dombey sends his son to Dr Blimber's school, where the strenuous discipline proves too much for him. After he dies Florence's estrangement from her father is increased.

Florence is attracted to Walter Gay, a warm-hearted charming young man in her father's employ. Dombey disapproves and sends Walter to the West Indies on a business trip. He is shipwrecked on the way and believed to have been drowned. Dombey also sets about contracting a new marriage, with the proud and penniless Edith Granger: he uses his manager, Carker, to arrange the contract, having no more wit than to see it as anything else. Carker is a moral thug and Edith recognizes him for one. At the same time she knows that she is being bought: she despises

herself for it but finds that Dombey is a man deserving of no respect or warmth. Only Florence touches her and she feels that her affection for the girl will only taint her. Edith deserts Dombey and elopes with Carker – then she rejects Carker, effectively ruining him. Dombey, his pride shattered, rejects his daughter completely, and then learns that his business has failed. For Florence all ends happily. Walter returns, saved from the shipwreck, and, in the way of Dickens's heroines, she forgives her unspeakable father, who has been reduced to living in straitened solitude.

The note of caricature in *Dombey and Son* is more subdued than in the novels which preceded it. Dickens's touch is more certain through the range of characters and both upper and lower classes are confidently described. What emerges is a clear picture of society in his time and this represents a certain point of departure in his work. But the novel as a whole suffers from unnecessary complications in its plot – one wonders if it would not have been better if the author had not been committed to keeping his readers interested month after month. Dickens's faults, and his genius, are clearly seen in the character of Dombey: the arrogant loveless man is a superb creation; the reformed old duck of the ending, oozing affection and humility from every pore, is ridiculous. Again, the amiable and generous Toots is a success, while Captain Cuttle, intended to be even more lovable becomes, in Chapter XLIX, sentimental to a fault.

**Domes Daege, Be**  A poem of the late Old English (pre-Conquest) period, freely translated from the Latin. The original, *De Die Judicii*, has been ascribed by some scholars to Bede and by others to Alcuin. This consists of 157 lines; the Old English version expands the subject (Doomsday, or Day of Judgment) to 304 lines, which are regarded as finer poetry than the original. The dream vision of the Second Coming and the Day of Judgment looks forward to the form which became so popular in the Middle Ages. The poem is preserved in a manuscript in the library of Corpus Christi College, Cambridge. The text was edited by J. R. Lumby (Early English Text Society, 1876).

**Domestic Manners of the Americans**  An account of life in the USA by Frances Trollope, published in 1832. Mrs Trollope acknowledged that the material level was higher for most Americans than it was for most Europeans but she saw the preoccupation with democracy as a curb to intellectual progress. She disliked the affected airs assumed by American women and sharply criticized the interminable boasting – and the tendency to sharp practice – of American men in business. She detested slavery, and some of the best pages contain her attack on that deplorable institution.

**Domett, Alfred** 1811–77. Domett was born at Camberwell Grove, Surrey, and became a barrister of the Middle Temple after leaving St John's College, Cambridge. He emigrated to New Zealand, where he became prime minister; he published two books of poetry reflecting his experiences there after his return to England. However, neither *Ranolf and Amohia* (1872) nor *Flotsam and Jetsam* (1877) are known to modern readers. 'A Christmas Hymn', which was once a familiar anthology piece, was one of the occasional poems published by *Blackwood's Magazine* before Domett went to New Zealand. A friend of Robert Browning, Domett is the 'Waring' of Browning's well-known poem (1842).

*Don Juan* An 'Epic Satire' by Lord Byron, in 16 cantos. The first two cantos were published in 1819; cantos III, IV, and V in 1821; VI–XIV in 1823; and cantos XV and XVI in 1824. Byron used the *ottava rima* in which he had written *Beppo* in 1818, turning the legendary Great Lover into an ingenuous young man to whom adventures happen. In a letter to his friend Thomas Moore (19 September 1818) he wrote 'It is dedicated to Southey in good, simple, savage verse, upon the Laureate's politics, and the way he got them.' Byron is also rude to Wordsworth, Coleridge, Lord Castlereagh, Wellington, and Lord Londonderry. *Don Juan* could be described as a social comedy on an epic scale: some of Byron's finest poetry is to be found in this great work, upon which he was intermittently engaged for the last five years of his short life.

Donna Inez of Seville sends her son Juan abroad to stop his affair with Donna Julia: Juan is 16 years old. On the way from Cadiz to Leghorn the ship is wrecked in a storm and passengers and crew are forced to take to the longboat. They suffer from the elements and are threatened with starvation; Juan's spaniel is eaten, then his tutor Pedrillo. Juan is eventually cast away on a Greek island. (The famous lyric 'The Isles of Greece!' is in Canto III.) Juan is found, apparently lifeless, by the beautiful Haidée, daughter of a Greek pirate believed to be dead. She restores Juan and the two fall in love; but Haidée's father comes back and, finding them together, has Juan put in chains aboard the pirate ship. Griefstricken, Haidée loses her mind and dies. Juan is taken to Constantinople to be sold as a slave; a sultana falls

Don Juan fighting with the Sultan. An illustration from an edition of Byron's *Don Juan* published in 1850. The incident occurs in Canto VIII.

in love with him and buys him, but she plagues him with her jealousy. She has the power of life and death over him and Juan escapes as soon as he can to the Russian army, which is besieging the town of Ismail. He acquits himself with credit in the attack and the capture of the town and is sent to St Petersburg with despatches. The Empress Catherine shows him favour and later sends him to England on a diplomatic mission.

There would have been more of *Don Juan* had Byron lived longer. The later parts of the poem tell of Juan's love affairs and, more importantly, of the impact England makes upon him; this is satire of the highest order. There is a modern edition by T. G. Steffan (Penguin English Poets, 1977).

***Don Juan in Hell*** See ***Man and Superman***.

**Donne** (*or* **Dunne**), **John** 1572–1631. John Donne was the son of John Donne, a prosperous London ironmonger, and a daughter of John Heywood, the dramatist. Jasper Heywood, his uncle, was a Jesuit, while his brother Henry died in Newgate in 1593 after being arrested for harbouring a priest. On his mother's side, Donne was the great-grandson of Thomas More's sister Elizabeth, so a more firmly Catholic background could hardly be imagined. He was educated at both Oxford and Cambridge but as a Catholic he could not take a degree. About 1590 he travelled abroad; in 1591 he resumed his studies at the Inns of Court, working for six hours each day on language, law, and theology and spending the rest of his waking hours enjoying the theatre and all the pleasures available to a personable young man in London at that time.

Donne travelled again in Europe between 1594 and 1596 and then, through his Oxford friend Sir Henry Wotton, met the Earl of Essex. He took

John Donne. Collection of the Marquess of Lothian.

part in Essex's expeditions to Cadiz (1596) and the Azores (1597) and on the latter became friendly with Thomas Egerton. Egerton's father was Sir Thomas, Lord Keeper of the Great Seal and a powerful man in public life. Donne became his secretary in 1598 and entered parliament in 1601; his father had died in 1576 and he was making his own way in the world – not without success, it seemed. He must, by this time, have abandoned the faith of his fathers; he could not venture into public office as a Catholic. But disaster came from another direction; he fell in love with Anne, daughter of Sir George More and niece of Lady Egerton, and unwisely married her in secret without the blessing of her father. Egerton dismissed him and More procured his imprisonment. Donne's hopes of a public career were at an end and, though he only spent a few days in prison, his prospects were bleak. More allowed the marriage to proceed after a few months and the lovers were reunited; but Donne's private means were exhausted, and his family began to increase.

From 1602 to 1606 the poet and his family lived in the house of Donne's friend Sir Francis Woolley at Pyrford, where Donne, in the hope of resuming his career, studied canon and civil law. He went to the continent for a year as travelling companion to Sir Walter Chute and returned to the vicinity of London in 1606, taking a small house at Mitcham. He enjoyed the patronage of the countesses of Bedford and Huntingdon and Sir Robert Drury but they could do nothing to advance his public career. Fortunately Sir George More relented sufficiently to pay his daughter's dowry in 1608 and the household enjoyed a little ease. Donne accompanied Sir Robert Drury abroad in 1611 and on his return was able to move his household back to London. He wrote for his patrons and assisted his friend Thomas Morton, Dean of Gloucester, in his controversies with the Catholics, and it was Morton who perceived that the best way forward for Donne would be for him to enter the Church. But Donne had not given up hope of advancement in public life – that was what he really wanted. Yet the secular world apparently had no use for him, whereas his religious writings, *Pseudo-Martyr* and *Ignatius his Conclave*, impressed King James. Meanwhile Donne was lucky in the patronage of the king's favourite, Robert Carr, Viscount Rochester, of Lord Hay, and of Lord Ellesmere (Egerton, now elevated and in a forgiving mood) and with their support he approached the king. The king made it clear that he wanted Donne in the Church and the poet submitted, taking holy orders in 1615.

Ironically, Donne now found himself at the centre of affairs. He was made a royal chaplain and reader in divinity at Lincoln's Inn and sent on a diplomatic mission to Germany with Viscount Doncaster. His sermons made him famous and attracted large crowds, and King James made him Dean of St Paul's in 1621. Sadly, his Anne enjoyed only two years of Donne's eminence; she died in 1617, having borne 12 children, 7 of whom survived.

Donne suffered a severe illness in 1623 and during his recovery began to write his *Devotions*, which was an acknowledgement of mortality, but he returned to his work in 1624 as vicar of St Dunstan's-in-the-West, where one of his admiring parishioners was Izaak Walton. Donne was beginning to run down; his health was precarious by 1630 and on the first Friday of Lent 1631 he preached his last sermon, *Death's Duell*, in the presence of King Charles I; he knew that he was dying. The end came on 31 March 1631.

The poetry of John Donne is, for most readers, of two kinds – the superb love poetry and the religious poetry – and it is easily assumed that the latter resulted from the conversion of a man who, after many trials, rejected the nature of his younger self – the high-spirited young man of the Inns of Court and the naval expeditions who found exquisite delight in sex and gave us some of the finest love poems in the English language. We have no explicit statements from the poet himself but the outline of his life shows that there was no change or rejection – rather a progression. His love for Anne More, for whom he sacrificed everything, must have been profound and lasting, and in its first impact overwhelming, to have made him behave so foolishly. His love poems were written before his marriage; so was *The Progresse of the Soule*, and the famous third *Satyre*, which found him anxiously pondering the question of faith and criticizing in the harshest terms the religious follies of the times. Donne has to be recognized as a man for whom such matters were of paramount importance; his Catholic birth and training implanted a preoccupation with the metaphysical, while his passionate nature ensured that all such questions would be subjected to searching examination. By the time he reached his 30s he had found the old religion wanting, and the practice of it – particularly in its Jesuitical teachings – inimical. By this time, like the passionate young man he was, he had experience of physical love, and he was 26 years old when he first met Anne More.

Important factors in the subsequent development of his career were his own ambitions and the nature of the Church in those times. Donne was very keen to get on in the world and his circle of friends was a mixture of noblemen, poets, and intellectuals; he needed a 'place' in that world and he was miserable out of it, as a man of his learning would be. It is pleasant to remember, in passing, how well supported he was in the bad times, by his friends and patrons. The Church itself has always been a legitimate field for advancement; it is now, but the range was far wider then, and churchmen could play a much larger part in affairs. Donne's friend Morton saw it as the place for him; not the Catholic Church, which he had left, but the reformed one, where Donne could take his obvious gifts – and his wife and children. But seven or eight years were to pass before Donne took the step and entered the final stage of his literary career also.

Very little of Donne's work was published during his lifetime, though much of his poetry was circulating in manuscript. The first stanza of 'The Expiration' was published in 1609 with a musical setting in a book of *Ayres* by A. Ferrabosco; 'Upon Mr Thomas Coryats Crudities' is one of the panegyrics in *Coryats Crudities* (1611). *An Anatomie of the World (The First Anniversary)* was published in 1611 and again in the following year, with *An Anatomie of the World. The Progresse of the Soule (The Second Anniversary)*, and the two poems appeared together in further editions in 1621 and 1625. The first stanza of

'Breake of day' was published with a musical setting in *The Second Booke of Ayres* by W. Corkine (1612); 'Elegie upon the untimely death of the incomparable Prince Henry' was published with other elegies in Joshua Sylvester's *Lachrimae lachrimarum* (1613). Donne's prose appears in several sermons, singly or in small groups of two or three: *Pseudo-Martyr* (1610), *Ignatius his Conclave* (1611), and *Devotions upon Emergent Occasions* (1624).

The exact dates of the composition of the majority of his poems cannot be ascertained. *The Progresse of the Soule* is actually dated, 16 August 1601, and both 'Anniversaries' must belong to the period of Sir Robert Drury's patronage since they commemorate his daughter Elizabeth. Of this period also are *Biathanatos* (an essay on suicide) and *Essays in Divinity*. For the most part the order of the poems in the first published collection of 1633 is accepted for the want of any more positive chronology. The collection was enlarged in 1635 and 1650.

*Songs and Sonets* belong to Donne's early manhood 'ere he was twenty-five years old' according to his friend, Ben Jonson. It is a group of poems so full of famous lines as to defy quotation; there can be no lover of English poetry who does not know 'The Good-Morrow', the song beginning 'Goe, and catche a falling starre', 'Lovers Infinitenesse', 'The Prohibition', and the rest. *Epigrams* belongs to the same period, in Sir Herbert Grierson's opinion. Sixteen of them were published in the 1633 collection, and three more were found in manuscripts. *Elegies* and *Heroicall Epistle* (the last-named is grouped with the *Elegies* by Grierson) are believed to belong to the last decade of the 16th century and to Donne's meeting with his Anne. Donne's love poetry reaches new heights in the *Elegies*; Donne is at his greatest in these poems and his lines convey, as perhaps no other poetry does, the importance of the flesh in the union of souls.

*The Progresse of the Soule. Infinitati Sacrum. 16 Augusti 1601. Metempsychosis. Poema Satyricon* is, fortunately, dated. Donne wrote 51 stanzas of ten lines each; the 52nd seems to be a later, hurried 'full-stop' to what was intended to be a longer poem but one he knew that he would not complete. The work is ambitious: the passage of the soul from vegetable origins (the apple in the Garden of Eden), through animal metamorphoses, to its final form contained in man. It is also a very peculiar conception and various theories have been advanced about the poet's intentions: Ben Jonson declared that he was tracing the progress of the heretic soul, from Cain to Calvin. But Donne was, by this time, a long distance from his Catholic background and the final stanza suggests that he had intended to examine the nature of good and evil in relative terms. An opening prose epistle refers to the doctrine of metempsychosis ('the Pithagorian') and extends Pythagoras to include the vegetable world. In the same year as he began, and put down, this poem, Donne resolved his emotional problems by marrying Anne More in secret; the poem's conception and partial execution may reflect the crisis in his life.

*Epithalamions* consists of four poems: a marriage song for Princess Elizabeth's marriage (February 1613); an 'Ecclogue' and marriage song for the Earl of Somerset's marriage (December 1613); and 'Epithalamion made at Lincolnes Inne', which is attributed to his student days there. The first three *Satyres* are dated 1593 in the Harleian Manuscript; the other two are placed 1597–1600 by Sir Herbert Grierson. The deliberately harsh and lumpy style serves the poet's purpose but makes them a torment for the modern reader, whose distance from the subjects cancels the purpose anyway. The third *Satyre*, already mentioned, is different from the others in the combination of self-examination with criticism. *Letters to Severall Personages* are verse epistles to various friends and patrons, most of them written between the time of Donne's disgrace and his entry into the Church. They are the least read of Donne's poems and are chiefly of interest as a reflection of his condition in those years. The subject of the two *Anniversaries* was Elizabeth Drury, daughter of Donne's patron, who died at the age of 15 in 1610. The poet commemorated her in 'A Funerall Elegie', and in 1611 on the anniversary of her death wrote *An Anatomie of the World: The First Anniversary*. He wrote the next in 1612, *An Anatomie of the World: The Progresse of the Soule* while travelling with Sir Robert Drury in Europe. The poems are, inevitably, much more about John Donne than about Elizabeth Drury, whom the poet never met; they are his reflections on death and contain memorable lines, but they are not easy to understand. Of less interest are the *Epicedes and Obsequies* of the same period: the subtitle, 'Upon the deaths of sundry Personages', explains the occasions for them. Donne's genius was not always present; it is difficult to imagine a poet less fitted to write to order.

In the *Divine Poems* Donne returns to the high level of the *Elegies*. His Catholic background serves him in the idea of meditation, in the method of Ignatius Loyola, on such great Christian issues as the Crucifixion, the Last Judgment, and death. Most of 'The Holy Sonnets' were written before he entered the Church in 1615 but three, found only in the Westmoreland Manuscript and not included in the collection of 1633, were written after the loss of his wife in 1617. 'A Hymne to Christ', 'The Lamentations of Jeremy' (Jeremiah), 'A Hymne to God my God, in my Sicknesse', and 'A Hymne to God the Father' were written after his ordination.

Donne's prose is clearly separated into secular and sacred by the circumstances of his life. *Juvenilia: Or Paradoxes and Problems* was his essay as a young man into a form fashionable at that time, one that exercised the wit and erudition of the writer. The casuistical essay on suicide, *Biathanatos*, was written about 1608; *Pseudo-Martyr* (published 1610) declared that Catholics should take an oath of allegiance to their king, even if he was a Protestant; *Ignatius his Conclave* (published 1611) is a satire on Loyola and the Jesuits and displays Donne's awareness of the new scientific learning. *Essays in Divinity* was a two-part series of reflections on the Creator and the Deliverance and was probably written about 1614. The famous *Devotions upon Emergent Occasions* was written during the winter of 1623, after Donne had been seriously ill and close to death. His thoughts and feelings during his journey through the valley of the shadow of death were expressed in a triple exercise: 'Meditations upon our humane condition', 'Expostulations, and debatements with God', and 'Prayers, upon the severall occasions, to Him'. Meditation XVII, beginning 'Perchance hee for whom this bell tolls', is one of the most famous pieces of prose in the English language; number XII – 'What will not kill a man if a vapor will?' – is almost as well known. *The Sermons*, upon which Donne's greatest fame as a prose writer rests, were written either before they were delivered or just after; he had no use for extempore preaching and knew exactly what he was going to say. The 160 sermons were nearly all published a few years after his death – in 1640, 1649, and 1660. The first 80 to be published appeared with Izaak Walton's life of Donne (1640). Famous as they are, however, the *Sermons* are not likely to warm or please a modern reader unless his psychology matches Donne's. At this distance, for all they reveal of a brilliant mind, they seem rigid and harsh, too preoccupied with sin and death, corruption and resurrection, the devil's instrument that was Rome, and the Anglican Church that was God's. Donne was a man of his time, certainly; but other men of his time possessed more charity and sweetness and displayed more independent minds.

Donne's poetry went out of fashion about the time of the Restoration, but he had effectively taken English verse out of the too-settled form of fluency and ease to which the Elizabethan fashion seemed to have directed it. His poetry is sharper and more concentrated and hardly seems to belong to the period at all. At his best he is remarkable, but his best was not consistent and readers coming to him for the first time may well be irritated by the self-conscious intellectual display – conceits – which are present in his poetry no less than in his prose and seem to be his resort when he is writing at less than his highest level. But his highest level gives him, indisputably, the rank of a major poet.

Despite his eclipse in the 17th century Donne was not forgotten by the literary world, and the poems were being read again towards the end of the 18th century. But a real revival did not come until the end of the 19th, when James Russell Lowell in America (1895) and E. K. Chambers in England (1896) published complete editions. The standard edition for many years has been Sir Herbert Grierson's of 1912, and a new one by Helen Gardner and W. Milgate is in progress. Single volumes of the poems are the Oxford Standard Authors edition based on Grierson and first published in 1929 and John Hayward's edition for the Nonesuch Press (1929), which contains a selection of Donne's prose.

**Donnithorne, Arthur**  In George Eliot's *Adam Bede*, the young squire whose light-hearted affair with Hetty Sorrel leads to tragedy.

**Dooley, Mr**  See **Dunne, Finley Peter.**

**Doolittle, Hilda** 1886–1961. Hilda Doolittle, who used the pseudonym, H.D., was born in Bethlehem, Pennsylvania. She was educated at Bryn Mawr, where a fellow student was Marianne Moore. She went to live in Europe in 1911, and in London renewed her acquaintance with Ezra Pound, whom she had known in her college days when he was a student at Pennsylvania University. She was already writing Imagist poetry, and Pound was to be her first publisher in his *Des Imagistes* (1914). She married the English novelist Richard Aldington in 1913 and divided her time between England and Switzerland; her first collection of verse, *Sea Garden* (1916), was published in London. Her fondness for classical images reflected her love of Greek and was allied to a fine visual sense: in her later work she moved beyond the Imagists with whom for many years her name was associated. *Hymen* (1921) is a masque with Greek figures; further collections are *Heliodora and Other Poems* (1924) and *Red Roses for Bronze* (1929). *Hippolytus Temporizes* (1927) is a drama in classical form and anticipated her translation of the *Ion* of Euripides, published in 1937.

Hilda Doolittle also wrote novels – *Palimpsest* (1926), *Hedylus* (1928), and *The Hedgehog* (1936) – and in 1944 published the first part of a poetic trilogy, *The Walls do not Fall*, followed by *Tribute to Angels* (1945) and *Flowering of the Rod* (1946). *By Avon River* (1949) is a prose and verse tribute to Shakespeare and the Elizabethans, *Tribute to Freud* (1956) is a prose love poem, and *Bid Me to Live* (1960), a novel, was the last work published during her lifetime. *Helen in Egypt* (published posthumously, 1961), a long lyrical poem, is regarded as her finest work by many critics. Three poems that give a sample of her style and quality are the frequently anthologized 'Orchard', 'Fragment XXXVI – I know not what to do', and 'Number XXXVI – Ah (you say), this is Holy Wisdom'.

**Dorrit, Amy**  The heroine of Dickens's *Little Dorrit*, Amy – Little Dorrit – is the diminutive youngest child of William Dorrit and was born in the Marshalsea Prison. Steadfast and true-hearted, she is the only one of the family who doesn't change when the Dorrits escape from the prison into affluence. She loves Arthur Clennam and at the end of the book they are married in the Marshalsea.

**Dorrit, William**  The prisoner in the Marshalsea in Dickens's *Little Dorrit*. He is called the Father of the Marshalsea because he has been there for 23 years.

**Dos Passos, John (Roderigo)** 1896–1970. John Dos Passos was the grandson of a Portuguese immigrant and was born in Chicago. He graduated from Harvard in 1916 and went to Spain to study architecture; the USA entered World War I in the following year and Dos Passos served in the US medical corps. His first fiction was based on his war experiences but he became prominent with *Manhattan Transfer* (1925), a searching look at the remarkable diversity of New York life. Dos Passos's method of portraiture was to build it up from hundreds of fictional episodes and he developed it to the limit a few years later. His next book, *Orient Express* (1927), was a travel diary and demonstrated the author's growing interest in social problems. This was emphasized in his three plays: *The Garbage Man* (1926) concerns a representative New York couple grappling with life; *Airways Inc.* (1926) has as its background a builders' strike; and *Fortune Heights* (1933) concerns a real estate development in boom and depression.

The first part of Dos Passos's trilogy *U.S.A.* was *The 42nd Parallel* (1930), followed by *1919* (1932) and *The Big Money* (1936). The whole was published in 1938. *U.S.A.* relates the history of the United States in the first 30 years of the 20th century. Beginning in the first novel with the adventures of Fainy McCreary, the idealistic young socialist, the trilogy's canvas broadens more and more and a host of fictional characters are introduced, whose lives are a reflection of history. The contemporary atmosphere of each fictional episode is invoked and stream-of-consciousness passages identify the characters' reactions to events like the Spanish–American War, the hopes for socialism in the years before World War I, the war itself, the boom years, and the appalling outcome of the Sacco and Vanzetti case. The most successful and contented character is Richard Ellsworth Savage, son of a poor but respectable New Jersey family who is a go-getter through and through. The final episode concerns an unnamed vagrant, on the road through the USA; he subscribed to the same beliefs as Richard Ellsworth Savage – but he didn't make it. Exhausted and hungry, he is mocked by the American promise.

The author's social conscience informs his considerable output of fiction, travel reporting, and comment on current affairs, but he ceased to believe in the politics of the Left as the answer to his country's problems. He moved to the democratic conservatism expressed in *The Head and Heart of Thomas Jefferson* (1954) and a number of books, notably a second trilogy called *District of Columbia*, trace his increasing rejection of too much power in any quarter, Left or Right, socialist or capitalist. The trilogy's parts are *The Adventures of a Young Man* (1939), *Number One* (1943), and *The Grand Design* (1949). Among other books by John Dos Passos are the antiwar, anti-army novel *Three Soldiers* (1921); *In All Countries* (1934), in which he reports on Russia, Mexican agrarian socialism, and examines the Sacco and Vanzetti case; and a satirical novel about the idealistic trends of the interwar years, *Most Likely to Succeed* (1954).

**Double Dealer, The** A comedy by William Congreve, first produced in October 1693 and first published in 1694. The play, which was commended by Dryden, is a more direct attempt at satire than Congreve's other work and was not as well received as his first play, *The Old Bachelor*. Neither is revived in the modern theatre.

Lady Touchwood is in love with Mellefont, Lord Touchwood's nephew and heir. Mellefont has rejected her advances and is to marry Cynthia, daughter of Sir Paul Plyant; the furious Lady Touchwood is determined to ruin him. A former lover, Maskwell, is enlisted to help her (he is the double dealer of the title). Maskwell poses as Mellefont's friend; at the same time he makes Plyant suspect that Mellefont is conducting an intrigue with Lady Plyant. He also hopes that if Mellefont loses Cynthia he will get her for himself. His next step is to convince Touchwood that Mellefont is deceiving him with Lady Touchwood; he contrives that Touchwood shall discover Mellefont in his wife's chamber. The furious Touchwood disinherits Mellefont, and Plyant refuses to allow the marriage to Cynthia to proceed. Cynthia is affianced to Maskwell but this makes the plot go awry because now Lady Touchwood becomes jealous of Maskwell. She upbraids him furiously and is overheard by her husband, so Maskwell's treachery is disclosed. Maskwell makes an attempt to carry off Cynthia, but this too is frustrated by Lord Touchwood.

**Doughty, Charles Montagu** 1843–1926. Doughty was the son of a clergyman and was born at Theberton Hall in Suffolk. He was intended for the navy, but failing to reach the physical standard he went to Caius College, Cambridge, where he studied geology. This was pushed aside by his increasing interest in poetry and philology, which was later to find remarkable expression. Doughty began his travels in the Arab world in 1870, visiting North Africa, Syria, and Arabia. He studied Arabic from 1875 to 1876 and for the following two years travelled with the Bedouin; he made the pilgrimage to Mecca.

The account of his adventures, *Travels in Arabia Deserta* (1888), is highly valued but difficult to read, with its mixture of archaism and philological virtuosity. Doughty's determination to reproduce the sounds, much less the equivalent, of the words he heard makes for a stilted unreality in every utterance he quotes. But with that reservation the book enjoys high status even today, and became essential reading for every subsequent traveller in Arabia.

Doughty himself considered his poetry his best work. This includes *The Dawn in Britain* (six volumes, 1906); *Adam Cast Forth* (1908), *The Cliffs*, a verse play (1909), *The Clouds* (1912), *The Titans* (1916), and *Mansoul: or The Riddle of the World* (1920). The response to these works was not enthusiastic. An abridgment of *Arabia Deserta* was edited by Edward Garnett and published as *Wanderings in Arabia* (1908).

*Douglas* A romantic tragedy in blank verse by John Home, first produced in Edinburgh in 1756 and at Covent Garden in 1757; it was published in 1757. The author brought the wrath of the elders of the Church of Scotland down on his head – the Church was anti-theatre and prosecuted its ministers if they attended it; they were outraged that a minister should have *written* a play. It was a great success and, after being rejected by Garrick for production in London, was accepted by John Rich and produced at Covent Garden with Peg Woffington as Lady Randolph and Spranger Barry as Young Norval. It was a great success in London, too, and was regularly revived; Lady Randolph provided a fine part for Sarah Siddons. The piece is occasionally revived at drama festivals.

The plot is based on an old Scots ballad and concerns the son of Douglas and a lady who is afterwards married off to Lord Randolph. The lady's father, Sir Malcolm, orders the infant to be exposed; it is found by Norval, a shepherd, who brings him up as his son. Young Norval, as he is called, saves Lord Randolph's life and is offered a commission in the army. He accepts, but Randolph's favour to the young man is bitterly resented by Glenalvon, Randolph's heir-presumptive, who does his best to calumniate Young Norval. Glenalvon waylays Young Norval; he is killed by his intended victim – who in turn is killed by Randolph. Young Norval's true identity emerges and Lady Randolph commits suicide.

**Douglas, Lord Alfred** 1870–1945. Douglas, son of the Marquess of Queensberry, was born at Ham Hill, near Worcester. He was educated at Winchester School and Magdalen College, Oxford, and was introduced to Oscar Wilde in 1891 by Lionel Johnson. (See also **Wilde, Oscar**.)

Douglas published a good deal of verse, two books about his relationship with Wilde that are not regarded as reliable (*Oscar Wilde and Myself*, 1914, and *Oscar Wilde: A Summing Up*, 1940), and *The Autobiography of Douglas* (1929). He translated Wilde's *Salome* from the French (1894) and edited *The Academy* (1907–10). Douglas made no lasting impression with his poetry, the best of which is acknowledged to be *Sonnets – in Excelsis* (1924) and *Sonnets and Lyrics* (1935).

**Douglas, Gavin** *c*.1474–1522. The third son of the Earl of Angus, Gavin Douglas was educated for the church and became Provost of St Giles cathedral in Edinburgh. After James IV fell at Flodden the country was seething with intrigue and dynastic feuds – never far from the surface in Scotland – and the poet, very much a Douglas, was soon in the thick of them. He gained the bishopric of Dunkeld in 1515 but he had many enemies who succeeded in preventing him from taking possession. When the Douglases were brought down in 1521 Gavin Douglas fled to England, a proscribed traitor. He died in 1522 in London, of the plague.

Whatever his politics, Douglas has an undisputed place in literature. His translation of Virgil's *Aeneid* (1513) was the first complete translation of a major classical work into English – that is, 'into the Scots', as Douglas called it: this 'language' was by then so rich and flexible that it could do justice to an epic poem from another language. In his own language Douglas's chief works are the conventional allegory *The Palice of Honour* (*c*.1501), concerned with statecraft and the suitable way of life for an honourable courtier, and *King Hart* – but the attribution to Douglas of the last named is not absolutely certain. It was printed in 1786 from a manuscript, and published in John Pinkerton's *Ancient Scotish Poems*. The works of Gavin Douglas were collected and edited by John Small (1874).

Douglas's translation of the 12 books of Virgil's *Aeneid* contains a prologue to Book I which makes plain his respect for the original and his intentions in his undertaking clear: he wants to convey to the reader as closely as possible the meaning of Virgil's Latin in the language of his readers. The result is a rhymed-couplet version honoured both for its poetry and its immediacy (Ezra Pound praised it unstintingly) but which emerges as a medieval verse romance. Douglas used images familiar to his readers: the fall of Troy and the adventures of Aeneas take place in a medieval world. Douglas also composed prologues in verse to each Book, and in these his quality as an original poet emerges with remarkable force. The Scottish Text Society published a four-volume critical edition by D. F. C. Coldwell: *Virgil's Aeneid translated into Scottish verse by Gavin Douglas* (1957–64).

**Douglas, George** 1869–1902. The pen name used by George Douglas Brown, the illegitimate son of an Ayrshire farmer. He won a scholarship to Glasgow University, where he gained a first in classics. At Glasgow he was befriended by Gilbert Murray; he went on to Balliol College, Oxford, as an exhibitioner and seemed set for a distinguished career. But his mother was dying and Douglas, instead of concentrating on his finals, nursed her devotedly. This wrecked his prospects; with a third-class degree he settled in London and earned a living writing stories for boys and contributing to fiction magazines. Success came with his novel *The House with the Green Shutters* (1901). But the promise was never borne out; Douglas died in the following year, of pneumonia, at the age of 33.

**Douglas, Keith**  See **poets of World War II.**

**Douglas, (George) Norman** 1868–1952. Norman Douglas was born in Falkenhorst in Austria; his father was a Scot and his mother was Scottish-German. He was educated at Uppingham School and at Karlsruhe and then joined the Foreign Office, serving in St Petersburg (1894–96) before settling down to live in Italy on the island of Capri. His first published fiction was *Unprofessional Tales* (1901), written in collaboration with his wife Elsa (née Fitzgibbon). His next books were charming discursive volumes, basically travel books but containing information and reflections about everything: *Siren Land* (1911), *Fountains in the Sand* (1912), and *Old Calabria* (1915). *South Wind* (1917), his first novel, gave him his only popular success. The south wind's enervating influence on moral standards coincides with the visit of Thomas Heard, Bishop of Bambopo, to the island of Nepenthe (obviously Capri). The meeting of the bishop with a host of characters of various moral and sexual persuasions makes for an erudite and Rabelaisian series of conversation pieces. The novel was considered shocking in 1917.

Douglas wrote of an Italy which had not yet developed its modern tourist industry but had for some considerable time been a retreat for Englishmen who could afford to live there. He wrote two more novels, *They Went* (1920) and *In the Beginning* (1927), and further books of travel and essays.

***Dover Beach***  A poem by Matthew Arnold, first published in 1867 in *New Poems*. A short poem (39 lines), it is probably the best known of all his works, and expresses his belief that in the modern world, where so much uncertainty reigns, the affections of the heart are the strongest support.

**Dowden, Edward** 1843–1913. Dowden, the son of a wealthy merchant and landowner, was born in Cork. He was educated at Queen's College in Cork and at Trinity College, Dublin, where he became Professor of English Studies in 1867. He was the author of *Shakespeare: His Mind and Art* (1875) and *A Shakespeare Primer* (1877), and he published editions of 12 of Shakespeare's plays. He is remembered principally as a Shakespearean scholar but his *The Life of Percy Bysshe Shelley* (1886) is highly regarded. Among Dowden's other works were *Southey* for the English Men of Letters series (1879), *Robert Browning* (1904), and *Michel de Montaigne* (1905).

**Dowson, Ernest Christopher** 1867–1900. Ernest Dowson was born in Kent and received part of his education in France. He became part of the group known as the Rhymers' Club and contributed to *The Books of the Rhymers' Club* (1892 and 1894) and to the periodical *The Savoy*. From 1894 Dowson spent what little was left of his life in Paris and Dieppe; he died of pulmonary tuberculosis. He published *Verses* (1896), *Decorations in Verse and Prose* (1899), and translations of Voltaire, Zola, Balzac, and E. de Goncourt. Among the 12 poems he contributed to *The Books of the Rhymers' Club* was the haunting *Non sum qualis eram bonae sub regno Cynarae*, with its many memorable lines. This poem and *Vitae summa brevis spem nos vetat incohare longam* ('They are not long, the weeping and the laughter') are virtually the only work by Dowson known to most readers. His poems are collected in *The Poetical Works* edited by Desmond Flower (1934), which includes 40 poems hitherto unpublished.

**Doyle, Sir Arthur Conan** 1859–1930. Born in Edinburgh, Doyle was the son of a civil servant. He studied medicine at Edinburgh University, took his MD in 1885, and was a doctor at Southsea for eight years (1882–90) with some intervals as a ship's doctor. To supplement his income he wrote short stories, published anonymously in a variety of magazines, and a novel, *A Study in Scarlet* (1887), which was accepted by Ward Lock for £25 and published in *Beeton's Christmas Annual*. The central character was Sherlock Holmes, based on one of Doyle's teachers, Dr Joseph Bell. The story aroused no particular interest in England but the editor of the American *Lippincott's Magazine* found it more promising and his representative in London commissioned more work. The result was *The Sign of the Four*, which appeared in *Lippincott's* in February 1890. In the same year it was published in London as *The Sign of Four*. The two novels are not among Doyle's best work but his character, Sherlock Holmes, caught the imagination of the public and Newnes asked for Sherlock Holmes stories for his *Strand Magazine*. The first one appeared in July 1891.

Doyle, meanwhile, had been at work in the form he preferred, the historical romance, and *Micah Clarke* was published by Longmans (Andrew Lang spotted it) in 1889. The Sherlock Holmes stories continued to appear in the *Strand* and Doyle's *The White Company* – his favourite among his novels – was published in 1891. His two careers ran side by side with great success but Doyle was bored with Sherlock Holmes and tried to kill him off in *The Final Problem* (1893), sending both Holmes and Moriarty to their deaths over the Reichenbach Falls in Switzerland. The public, however, could not have enough and

Sir Arthur Conan Doyle the slave of his creation, Sherlock Holmes. Cartoon by Bernard Partridge, 1926. National Portrait Gallery, London.

Doyle was obliged to bring Sherlock Holmes back eight years later in the best of all his adventures, **The Hound of the Baskervilles** (1902), and keep him going for another 35 stories.

The historical romances and short stories continued: *The Great Shadow* (1892), *The Exploits of Brigadier Gerard* (1896), *Rodney Stone* (1896), and *Sir Nigel* (1906) are among the best known. He was also immensely successful with the tales of terror in which Professor Challenger appears: *The Lost World* (1912), *The Poison Belt* (1913), and *The Land of Mist* (1926). Doyle was a master at this form; the nastiness lurking outside is what makes *The Hound of the Baskervilles* such a marvellous story, not the omniscience of Sherlock Holmes. The detective himself has become a cult figure.

Doyle was an honest imperialist: his defence of British policy in South Africa won him a knighthood. However, he signed a petition for the reprieve of Sir Roger Casement even after he had been presented with proof of what was, in those days, regarded as shocking – that Casement was homosexual. The loss of his son in World War I was a blow from which Doyle never really recovered and it turned his mind more and more to spiritualism. One of his last books was a *History of Spiritualism* (1926).

The Sherlock Holmes stories are collected in *The Adventures of Sherlock Holmes* (1892), *The Memoirs of Sherlock Holmes* (1894), *The Return of Sherlock Holmes* (1905), and *The Case Book of Sherlock Holmes* (1927).

**Doyle, Sir Francis Hastings Charles** 1810–88. Doyle, the second baronet, was born at Nunappleton, Yorkshire, and educated at Eton College and Christ Church, Oxford. He became a fellow of All Souls and Professor of Poetry at Oxford. He was popular as a writer of military and patriotic verse (including 'The Red Thread of Honour', 'A Private of the Buffs', 'The Loss of the Birkenhead', and 'The Unobtrusive Christian') during the high noon of the British Empire.

**Drabble, Margaret** 1939– . Born in Sheffield, Margaret Drabble was educated at York University and Newnham College, Cambridge. Her first novel was *A Summer Birdcage* (1963), and she enjoyed a considerable success with her second, *The Garrick Year* (1964). Other novels are *The Millstone* (1965), *Jerusalem the Golden* (1967), *The Waterfall* (1969), *The Needle's Eye* (1972), *The Realms of Gold* (1975), *The Ice Age* (1977), and *The Middle Ground* (1980). Margaret Drabble is also the author of a play, *Bird of Paradise* (1969), and of *Wordsworth* (1966), *Arnold Bennett* (1974), *A Writer's Britain* (1979), and a children's book, *For Queen and Country* (1978).

**Drake, Joseph Rodman** *c.*1795–1820. Born in New York City, Drake studied medicine and, after a visit to Europe, earned his living running a drugstore. His early death was due to consumption.

He was the author, with Fitz-Greene Halleck, of satirical verses called *The Croaker Papers*. These featured current topics and appeared in the New York *Evening Post* and the *National Advertiser* in 1819; they were the only writings by Drake published during his lifetime. He asked his wife to destroy the manuscripts of his 'trifles in verse' but they were preserved and a selection was published in 1836 as *The Culprit Fay and Other Poems*. His poems were collected in 1935.

Drake was a member of the 'Knickerbocker Group', which included Washington Irving and William Cullen Bryant and was to be a target for Edgar Allan Poe's sharp-edged criticism.

**Drapier's Letters, The**  A group of seven pamphlets written by Jonathan Swift, five of which were published in 1724 (March to December); the other two were not published until 1735.

They became known as *The Drapier's Letters* from Swift's adoption of the character of a Dublin draper (M. B. Drapier) as their author.

There was a need for 'small money', halfpence and farthings, in Ireland and King George I had given his greedy ageing mistress, the Duchess of Kendal, a patent to supply it. (The Duchess of Kendal was Ehrengard Melusina von der Schulenberg.) She sold the patent to William Wood for what was, at the time, the enormous sum of £10,000. The Irish Parliament was not consulted but in 1722 the English government acknowledged Wood's possession of the patent. When the English Parliament protested to the king in 1723 he promised an enquiry, which opened in April 1724. By then the first of Swift's pamphlets had appeared and everyone in Ireland was aware that Wood's patent could make him an enormous fortune (£100,000) if he were allowed to supply copper and brass coins to Ireland – base metals, in fact. Swift carried the campaign to success; it was part of his fight against the arrogant and thoughtless treatment of Ireland by the English. Wood, a mine owner and dealer in iron, is the 'obscure Ironmonger' of the pamphlets.

**Drayton, Michael** 1563–1631. Drayton was born in Hartshill, Warwickshire, and probably educated at a grammar school in Coventry. He became a page in the service of Sir Henry Goodere of Polesworth, in Warwickshire, where he may have received further education, and his young life was bound up with that of the Goodere family. He also served in the household of Thomas Goodere and fell in love with Anne, Sir Henry's youngest daughter. Anne eventually married Sir Henry Rainsford and Michael Drayton remained a bachelor all his life.

Drayton wanted to be a poet, he tells us, from the age of ten. But he was obliged, like Samuel Daniel, to rely on patronage and, like Daniel, he was fortunate. When Sir Henry Goodere died in 1595, he had arranged for Drayton to enter the household of the Countess of Bedford. That lasted for seven years; Sir Walter Aston became his patron in 1602 and Drayton lost the favour of the countess, which was unfortunate, because he had otherwise no way into court circles when James I became king in 1603. He wrote *To the Majestie of King James: a Gratulatorie Poem* – but many other poets wrote similar pieces. Fortunately there were other patrons, including Sir Walter and the Earl of Dorset, and Drayton continued to write poetry and live, one presumes, in some comfort to the age of 68.

His first published work was *The Harmonie of the Church: Spirituall Songes and Holy Hymnes* (1591), which C. S. Lewis described as 'drab scriptural paraphrases'. He turned to a completely different subject and style in *Idea: The Shepheardes Garland in Nine Eglogs* (1593) with considerable success. His poetic master was Edmund Spenser and he wisely eschewed the 'olde rusticke language' that only Spenser could use with success. Anne Goodere has been named as the inspiration for the poems.

Drayton's next work was the first of his 'historical legends' in verse, *Peirs Gaveston* (1593). The sonnet sequence *Ideas Mirrour: Amours in quaterzains* followed in 1594 and again Anne Goodere has been named as the inspiration. Whether she was or not the sequence is a good example of the poet's work – and of his diligence in polishing and revising; the edition of 1619 followed eight others and is highly regarded by scholars of English literature. The famous 'Since there's no help, come let us kiss and part' appeared first in the 1619 edition. A historical legend, *Matilda, the Daughter of Lord Fitzwater*, was also published in 1594. In 1595 came *Endimion and Phoebe: Ideas Latmus*, a classical legend in rhymed decasyllabic couplets that may owe something to Shakespeare's exercise in the same vein, *Venus and Adonis*. Drayton rewrote it but *The Man in the Moon* (the 1606 title) is not regarded as an improvement.

History was the subject of Drayton's next three works. *Mortimeriados: The Civell Warres of Edward the Second and the Barrons* (1596) was in seven-line stanzas; he published a new version, *The Barrons Wars* (1603) in eight-line stanzas. *Englands Heroicall Epistles* (1597) was enlarged in 1598; the epistles are verse exchanges between historical characters such as Rosamond Clifford and Henry II, Jane Shore and Edward IV, and Guildford Dudley and Lady Jane Grey. Most critics name the *Epistles* as Drayton's best historical verse. Of his ventures into drama for Henslowe's company only *The First Part of the Historie of Sir John Oldcastle* (1600), a collaboration with Anthony Munday, Robert Wilson, and Richard Hathway, survives. Drayton contributed five poems to the 1600 edition of *Englands Helicon*.

Drayton's *Poemes Lyrick and Pastorall* (1606) contains his most successful work – from the standpoint of fame; 'Fair stood the wind for France', 'To the Virginian voyage', and 'The heart'. He had meanwhile, written a biblical poem, *Moyses in a Map of his Miracles*, a satire called *The Owle*, and *A Paean Triumphall for the Societie of Goldsmiths Congratulating his Highnes Entring the Citie* (all 1604). His last historical legend in verse, *The Legend of Great Cromwell*, was published in 1607 (revised 1609). The historical legends all contain good work; Drayton was a skilful (although not an inspired) versifier.

In 1613 Drayton published the first part of the extensive poem on which he had been working for some time, **Poly-Olbion**, described as 'a chorographicall description of this renowned Isle of Great Britaine' in the second printing of 1613. The second part did not appear until 1622. Probably the longest single poem in English, *Poly-Olbion* is an extended rhapsody: a description both historical and topographical (much of the information came from the *Britannia* of William Camden) of the physical beauty and glorious past of his country.

Drayton's last poems include an epic, *The Battaile of Agincourt* (1627), which has much less to recommend it than the ballad of 1606. The charming *Epistle to Henery Reynolds* or *First Steps up Parnassus*, the faerie poem *Nymphidia*, and the pastorals in Elizabethan manner, *The Quest of Cynthia* and *The Shepheards Sirena*, all belong to a collection of 1627. The beautiful lines of 'Soe well I love thee' were said to have been written by Drayton 'the night before hee dyed'.

Drayton wanted to be a poet more than anything else and certainly he worked hard at it. He admired Spenser and Marlowe extravagantly and possessed enormous skill and variety. His best work entitles him to rank as a major poet – Saintsbury placed his sonnets below only Shakespeare's. He would have shone more brightly in a less illustrious age, and he wrote too much – the hazard of being a professional poet who depended upon patronage. But when he is good Drayton is very good indeed.

An excellent selection of Drayton's poetry is by J. Buxton, published in two volumes in 1953. The complete works were edited by J. W. Hebel, B. H. Newdigate, and K. Tillotson and published in five volumes (1931–41).

**Dream of Gerontius, The** A poem by John Henry Newman, first published in two parts in *The Month* (April and May 1865) and in book form in 1866. The poem is the dramatic monologue of a just soul on the point of death. Edward Elgar's oratorio setting of the poem was composed in 1900.

**Dream of Rhonabwy, The** A Welsh tale of the late 12th century. It appears in *The Red Book of Hergest* and was translated by Lady Charlotte Guest in her *The Mabinogion*.

Rhonabwy is in the service of Madawg, Lord of Powys, who is determined to subdue his jealous and unruly brother Iorwerth. Rhonabwy and his companions seek shelter from Heilyn the Red; the house is stinking and filthy but a storm rages outside, and during the night Rhonabwy, to escape the fleas, goes to sleep on a yellow ox skin on a platform, where he dreams. In the dream Rhonabwy and his men are making for the ford on the River Havren. They are overtaken by a young man dressed in green, wearing a mantle of yellow brocade and riding a yellow horse. They fear him and flee, but he rides them down. He assures them he means no harm: he is Iddawg, the Churn of Britain, whose eagerness for battle led him to provoke the Battle of Camlan between Arthur and Medrawt. He repented and did penance for seven years at the Grey Stone (Y Llech Las) in Scotland. Another rider, beardless and dressed in red, comes up: he is Rhuvawn the Radiant, who joins Iddawg; the two move on. Rhonabwy reaches the ford; on an islet below it is Arthur whilst on the bank is a great host. There follows a confrontation between Arthur and Owein over a chesslike board game, *gwyddbwyll*, and a recall of the atmosphere of the great battle. The satirical note is strong and the unknown storyteller displays a talent for allegory. In addition to Arthur and Owein (Uwaine), Gawain (Gwalchmei), Perceval (Peredur), Tristan (Drystan), and Kay (Kei) are among the Arthurian figures named in the story. Rhonabwy sleeps for three days and nights on the yellow ox skin, experiencing a dream of exhausting detail.

**Dream of the Rood, The** A poem of 150 lines in Old English, preserved in *The Vercelli Book*. It has been attributed to both Caedmon and Cynewulf but there is not sufficient evidence for a positive identification of the poet. Regarded as one of the finest of Old English Christian poems, *The Dream of the Rood* appears in the West Saxon dialect in the Vercelli manuscript.

In a dream the poet stands before the Holy Rood (the Holy Cross); it is decorated with jewels and shines with glory; angels guard it. The poet is afraid because he knows himself to be a sinner. The Rood changes and becomes plain wood; blood flows from it – and then it speaks. It tells of the Crucifixion, the descent of Jesus, and the Resurrection. The poet reflects on what he has heard; henceforward the Cross will guide him.

There are a number of translations of *The Dream of the Rood*, notably by G. Bone in *Anglo-Saxon Poetry* (1943) and C. W. Kennedy in *Early English Christian Poetry* (1952).

**Dred,** *a Tale of the Great Dismal Swamp*. A novel by Harriet Beecher Stowe, first published in 1856. Like *Uncle Tom's Cabin*, it was successfully adapted for the stage.

The Gordon estate in North Carolina passes to Nina Gordon upon her father's death. She places the management of it in the hands of her half-brother, Harry, rather than in those of her brother Tom. Harry is a mulatto.

Nina dies of cholera and then Tom comes into possession; Harry immediately becomes the focus of his spite and to escape Tom's cruelty he runs away. He makes for the swamp, where he is protected by Dred, a Black religious fanatic who has also found refuge there. Tom hunts his half-brother through the swamp, where other refugees are the children of the trader John Cripps. Cripps' treatment of them had driven Old Triff, his slave, to run with the children to the only place where he believes they will be safe. Edward Clayton, who was Nina Gordon's fiancé, enters the story as Tom's opponent and it is he, after Tom's hunters have killed Dred, who gets Harry, Triff, and the Cripps children away to safety in Canada.

**Dreiser, Theodore (Herman Albert)** 1871–1945. Theodore Dreiser was the ninth child of a poor godfearing family of Terre Haute, Indiana. His father's harsh bigotry made his background something to escape from as soon as he could, leaving him with a distaste for organized religion. Dreiser managed a year at the University of Indiana and then obtained a job on the Chicago *Globe* as a reporter. He also worked in St Louis and Pittsburgh and arrived in New York in 1894. His reading had meanwhile extended to Huxley, Herbert Spencer, Hardy, and the naturalist John Tyndall.

Dreiser had worked in New York for some years as a journalist by the time he completed his first novel, *Sister Carrie* (1900). It was accepted by Frank Norris for the publishers Doubleday; Norris was very impressed but the publisher's wife, shrinking from the book's realism, interfered with the publication and only a token edition was printed. Dreiser managed to survive the blow with the help of his brother Paul and returned to journalism. He managed to earn a fairly comfortable living as an editor for a company, Butterick, specializing in women's magazines and later became head of the company. Ten years passed before he wrote another novel; this was *Jennie Gerhardt* (1911) and, while the new novel provoked discussion and was attacked for its realism, it was not a popular success. The book was a variation on the theme of his first novel, *Sister Carrie*, which was reissued in 1912; the author's objective presentation of American life had begun but it was a long time before he received recognition.

*The Financier* (1912) and *The Titan* (1914) were the first two novels of a trilogy about a big business magnate (the trilogy remained incomplete until the posthumous publication of *The Stoic* in 1947) and *The 'Genius'* (1915) was a novel examining the artistic temperament. Dreiser achieved real success with **An American Tragedy** (1925), for which he used a murder case of 1906 as the focus for an examination of the USA in the 1920s. One other novel, *The Bulwark*, was published the year after he died, in 1946.

Apart from his novels Theodore Dreiser wrote an account of a visit to the Soviet Union, *Dreiser Looks at Russia* (1928), and gave further expression to his growing hopes for socialism in *Tragic America* (1931) and *America is Worth Saving* (1941). *Plays of the Natural and Supernatural* (1916), the tragedy *The Hand of the Potter* (1918), which anticipated *An American Tragedy*, and books of verse, short stories, essays, and autobiography were also published. *Twelve Men* (1919) contains an affectionate portrait of his brother, Paul, who spelt his name Paul Dresser and became famous as a song writer.

As a literary artist Theodore Dreiser seems to divide the critics. Reading his work can be a great labour; it is clumsy and graceless and there are passages in his early novels that would not dishonour a sloppy women's magazine of the 19th century. But his attention to detail is unremitting – the reader is given a vivid picture of the world into which Sister Carrie goes forth and of the background of the events that doom Clyde Griffiths in *An American Tragedy*. It seems laughable, now, that he was attacked for being raw or obscene; but it should be remembered that he was born in 1871 and was much more a man of the 19th century than the 20th when he wrote *Sister Carrie*. For all that may be wrong with his work, Dreiser's best novels have force and honesty and, more than any novelist in America before him, he demonstrated that human nature simply does not fit into an imagined moral or social framework. He never hectors his readers, though he may bore them for long stretches; he does persuade them, in the end, to listen to him. For some years already writers in different parts of the United States had been looking hard at various aspects of the life around them and not liking what they saw. Theodore Dreiser seemed to be looking at the United States as a whole and finding that prosperity – or even survival – depended on being able to grab first: that there was little satisfaction in any other aspect of life for most ordinary Americans, anyway. That was the American tragedy that his novels described – what had happened to the American dream. He was 54 when his best novel, *An American Tragedy*, was published; he had come a long way from poverty in a small town in Indiana and he knew what he was talking about.

**Dr Jekyll and Mr Hyde, The Strange Case of** A novel by Robert Louis Stevenson, first published in 1886. A first draft was written in three days as a result of a bad dream – and destroyed when the author's wife criticized it. The second draft, which pleased both of them, was also completed in three days.

A philanthropic and well-liked physician, Dr Jekyll, becomes interested in the problems of good and evil and ponders on the mixture in the nature of man. The question preoccupies him and he wonders if the two natures could be separated. Experiments yield a drug, and when he takes it the evil side of his nature takes charge of him. There is an antidote which restores him to his better self.

The evil creature which emerges he calls Mr Hyde – but he finds that, once realized, it becomes more and more difficult to restrain, and eventually he is guilty of an atrocious murder. Jekyll now finds Mr Hyde impossible to control; the antidote is becoming less and less effective. Finally, with discovery imminent and one of the ingredients of the antidote impossible to procure, he commits suicide.

**Dromio** In Shakespeare's *The Comedy of Errors*, the name given to the identical twin slaves who serve the twin brothers named Antipholus.

**Drummond, William Henry** 1854–1907. Drummond was born at Currawn in the country of Leitrim in Ireland. His family emigrated to Canada when he was 11 years old and his father died not long afterwards. The boy studied telegraphy and found his first job at Bord-à-Plouffe on the Rivière des Prairies, about 16 miles south of Montreal, in 1869. In this region, not far from the American border, Drummond was fascinated by the stories told by the travellers, backwoodsmen, and the French-Canadian dwellers in the small town. He saved enough money to resume his education by 1876 and he graduated in medicine at Bishop's College, Montreal, in 1884. He practised as a doctor for some years and lectured in medical jurisprudence at his old college; in 1905 he became rich through a successful venture, with his brother, in a silver mine at Cobalt in Ontario. But he died of a cerebral haemorrhage in 1907.

Drummond succeeded in capturing the patois of the French-Canadian people in the New World, who much of the time expressed themselves in a language not native to them. He made poetry of it, without a hint of caricature. His four volumes of verse were *The Habitant* (1897), *Johnny Courteau* (1901), *The Voyageur* (1905), and *The Great Fight* (published posthumously, 1908). A collected volume, *The Poetical Works*, was published in 1912.

**Drummond of Hawthornden, William** 1585–1649. The son of a distinguished Scots family, Drummond was born at the manor of Hawthornden near Edinburgh. He was educated at Edinburgh University and studied law in France. He lived at Hawthornden from 1610 and was to have married Mary Cunningham of Barns in 1615. Mary died on the eve of the wedding and much of Drummond's work was to reflect the tragedy in his life.

Drummond was a royalist and anti-presbyterian and wrote many pamphlets in support of his views. He was a correspondent of Michael Drayton's and was visited at Hawthornden by Ben Jonson in 1618; he read widely in Italian and French literature and amassed a considerable library of books in those languages. His first published poem was a lament on the death of Prince Henry in 1613, *Tears on the Death of Moeliades*. The year after the death of Mary Cunningham he published *Poems, Amorous, Funereall, Divine, Pastorall, in Sonnets, Songs, Sextains, Madrigals* (1616), and in 1617 contributed to the verses written to celebrate the visit of James I to Edinburgh ('Forth Feasting', published in *The Muses Welcome*, 1618). Ben Jonson's visit prompted Drummond to keep notes of the occasion and these were printed in 1832.

A collection of religious verse, *Flowres of Sion* (1623), contains the religious sonnets 'Saint John Baptist' and 'For the Magdalene', which are among his best-known works. The volume also contains the prose essay on death, *A Cypresse Grove*, which was written in 1630. This is the only prose work of Drummond's to hold a place in English letters, though he was the author of a number of royalist pamphlets and a *History of Scotland 1423–1524* (1655, posthumously), which occupied him for many years.

Drummond married Elizabeth Logan in 1632 and provided the lines for the entertainment staged for the Scottish coronation of Charles I in 1633. He died in 1649, the year of the king's execution. His poetry is frequently called derivative, but if that means he learned much from his wide reading he learned very well; his poems are elegant and musical and he used various forms with equal ease. A critical edition of Drummond was prepared for the Scottish Texts Society by L. E. Kastner and published in 1913 (*Poetical Works, with A Cypresse Grove*).

***Drum Taps*** and ***Sequel to Drum Taps*** The Civil War poems of Walt Whitman, containing the two laments for Lincoln ('When Lilacs Last in the Dooryard Bloom'd' and 'Oh Captain! My Captain!) and 'Pioneers! O Pioneers!', were first published in these groups (1865–66). They were both incorporated into the fourth edition of *Leaves of Grass* (1867).

Whitman saw the face of war at its worst, outside the heat of battle and the urge to glory: he was confronted hour by hour with the broken and bleeding bodies of the aftermath. His poems are powerful and uncompromising, from the reflective 'By the Bivouac's Fitful Flame', to his memory of passing along the rows of dead where among them he sees the face of one young man ('... I think I know you – I think this face is the face of the Christ himself, Dead and divine and brother of all, and here again he lies', from 'A Sight in Camp in the Daybreak'), and to the images of suffering in 'The Wound Dresser'.

***Dr Wortle's School*** A novel by Anthony Trollope, first published in *Blackwood's Magazine* (May to December 1880).

This comparatively short novel tells of a successful private school which numbers several noble families among its patrons. The proprietor is Dr Wortle, a forthright and independent man whose character is resented by some, who are nonetheless prepared to acknowledge his success. For his school, Dr Wortle engages Mr Peacocke, a man in orders with a distinguished academic record, who has been in America for five years. The Peacockes are a success; he is a good teacher and she is a sympathetic matron whom the boys warm to.

Then the five-year absence of Peacocke in America becomes a subject for gossip among Dr Wortle's enemies, and leads to questions from his bishop, who resents Dr Wortle's easy-going attitude to authority. The spiteful Mrs Stantiloup questions not only Peacocke's past but his present, too – his marriage, and Mrs Peacocke.

Dr Wortle asks his new teacher for the truth, and learns that Mrs Peacocke's first husband was a brutal man, often the worse for drink. They had presumed him dead; but he had reappeared, and their marriage was unlawful. In spite of the increasing scandal, Dr Wortle's sympathies are with the Peacockes, and the rest of the novel concerns his fight for his school and his principles, until the death of the evil husband results in his success.

There is also a love affair, between Lord Carstairs and Dr Wortle's daughter, Mary. The progress of this has a direct bearing on the final resolution of the novel.

**Dryden, John** 1631–1700. Dryden's family were landed gentry of Northamptonshire who leant towards Puritanism and supported the Parliamentary cause during the Civil War. The poet was born at Aldwincle, in the rectory of All Saints; a tablet in the church, placed by one of his descendants in 1959, commemorates his baptism. The rector was his maternal grandfather and his father was the son of a baronet. Both Dryden's grandfather and his uncle, Sir John Pickering, suffered prison sentences for refusing to obey the tax laws of Charles I. The Drydens and the Pickerings were neither anti-Royalist nor fanatical Puritans: rather, they objected to the government of a bad ruler, and in those days a great deal of dissent was allowable within the Church of England.

Dryden was sent to Westminster School about 1646, and was in his last year there when King Charles was executed. As a boy he read Spenser and Joshua Sylvester's translation of Guillaume du Bartas' *La Semaine*; his fondness for reading history stayed with him all his life. His headmaster at Westminster was Richard Busby, who used the birch freely but seems to have been a great teacher; Dryden sent his own sons to be taught by him in later years, and both John Locke and Christopher Wren were his pupils. Dryden began to write poetry while still at Westminster and published his elegy *Upon the Death of the Lord Hastings* in 1649. He went to Trinity College, Cambridge, in 1650 and took his BA in 1654; he then disappeared from the records until 1659, when he published his poem on Cromwell. Sir John Pickering was Cromwell's Lord Chamberlain, and Dryden may have worked for Cromwell's administration during those years. The Restoration of 1660 found him writing poetry professionally – if the term could be applied in those times – with an income from his family's holdings to support him. His works were produced to celebrate occasions and dedicated with an eye to returns from the most influential persons involved. Dryden's calculated self-seeking was to earn him the wrath of Samuel Johnson: 'he no longer retains shame in himself, nor supposes it in his patron.' Johnson was the more incensed because Dryden 'had all the forms of excellence ... combined in his mind, with endless variation'.

Dryden's poem on Cromwell (1659) was followed by one celebrating the return of the monarchy, *Astraea Redux* (1660), 'on the Happy Restoration and Return of his Sacred Majesty'. Next came *To His Sacred Majesty, A Panegyrick on his Coronation* (1661) followed by *To My Lord Chancellor* (1662); the Lord Chancellor was

Clarendon. *Annus Mirabilis, The Year of Wonders, 1666* was published in 1667; Sir William Davenant died in April 1668, and Dryden succeeded him as Poet Laureate in the same month. He had travelled carefully and arrived safely, but Johnson's acknowledgment of his quality must be remembered: Dryden's gifts as a poet, whether shown in the smooth precision of the couplets of the earlier poems or in the quatrains of *Annus Mirabilis*, cannot be gainsaid.

The theatre, meanwhile, had provided another outlet for his talents. *The Wild Gallant*, a comedy, was performed in 1663 without much success though it was revived in 1669 in revised form; *The Rival Ladies* (performed 1664) did better, Dryden having moved into a more serious vein. The drama in England had by now left behind its great Elizabethan origins and was displaying the influence of foreign fashions, particularly those of France, since many who returned to England with the Restoration came from exile in Paris in the suite of Henrietta Maria. Dryden moved from the prose of his first effort to verse and rhyme in *The Rival Ladies*, finding a successful formula in a mixture of verse and prose. Apart from *Verses to Her Royal Highness the Duchess of York* (1665) Dryden was to be occupied with drama and criticism from 1668 to 1681. He was made Historiographer Royal in 1670.

After *The Rival Ladies* Dryden collaborated with his brother-in-law, Sir Robert Howard, in *The Indian Queen* (1664); this 'heroic' play led to *The Indian Emperor* (1665), of which Dryden was sole author and which established his reputation as a dramatist in the heroic style. From this time his comedy too displayed a new confidence and both styles were practised with considerable success. *An Evening's Love, Tyrannick Love, Sir Martin Mar-All*, and *Secret Love* (1667), *The Conquest of Granada*, or *Almanzor and Almahide* (1668), *The Assignation* and *Marriage à la Mode* (1672), and *Amboyna* (a piece against the Dutch in the East Indies, also 1672) were followed by a strange essay of homage to John Milton. *The State of Innocence and Fall of Man* (1674) was a dramatization of *Paradise Lost*. Dryden returned to his own heroic style in *Aureng-Zebe* (1676) and *All for Love* (1678) but then decided to adapt 'old-fashioned' plays of Shakespeare. *The Tempest, or The Enchanted Island* (1667) was written with D'Avenant and, predictably, merits no more than mention. *Limberham, or the Kind Keeper* (1678) saw his return to comedy, and in the same year Dryden collaborated with Nathaniel Lee on *Oedipus*. In 1679 came *Troilus and Cressida, or Truth Found too Late*; Dryden's efforts to adapt Shakespeare's astringent masterpiece to the mood of a different age are best forgotten.

In 1681 Dryden appeared as a satirist. Acutely responsive to contemporary events, he sets as targets Lord Shaftesbury and the Duke of Monmouth, who were attempting, with considerable support, to change the succession. James, Duke of York, the king's brother, was the legitimate but Catholic heir and Shaftesbury led the opposition to him: Monmouth, the king's son by Lucy Walter, was illegitimate, though acknowledged and generously treated by his father. Dryden placed his characters in an Old Testament context and *Absalom and Achitophel* was immensely popular: it turned the tide of feeling against Monmouth (Absalom) and his evil counsellor Shaftesbury (Achitophel). *The Medall. A Satyre against Sedition* was published in 1682 (the supporters of Shaftesbury had had a medal struck in his honour when he was arrested for sedition) and provoked a reply from Thomas Shadwell in *The Medall of John Bayes*. Dryden answered back with *Mac Flecknoe*, and the round was completed with *The Second Part of Absalom and Achitophel* (also in 1682); this was mostly written by Nahum Tate but contains 200 brilliant lines by Dryden satirizing Shadwell and Elkanah Settle. *Absalom and Achitophel* is generally acknowledged as the finest political satire in the English language. Dryden himself had also been the target of satire. His continuing success and use of a new heroic style led to a burlesque, *The Rehearsal* (1671), concocted by several wits including the Duke of Buckingham and possibly Samuel Butler.

The year 1682, a busy one for Dryden, also saw publication of *Religio Laici, or a Layman's Faith*, a poem expressing the feelings of many in a period disturbed by Shaftesbury's manoeuvres and by the infamous Titus Oates: most people desired freedom from squabbling theologians in order to find their own peace with God. Dryden eventually found his in the Roman Catholic Church, a conversion that his detractors were quick to declare was contrived to keep him in favour with a Catholic king when Charles II died. But had James II indeed favoured Dryden he might have listened to his advice and kept his kingdom: Dryden's moderation would have worked far better than James's determination to advance his religion by rule, which alienated many of his Catholic supporters. James II came to the throne in 1685. Dryden wrote an ode on the death of Charles II, *Threnodia Augustalis* (1685), and another on the birth of an heir (the old Pretender), *Britannia Rediviva* (1688); neither is a good example of his work. He wrote an indifferent libretto for a forgotten opera by Louis Grabu, *Albion and Albanius* (1685); but in the following year came his ode *To The Pious Memory of the Accomplisht Young Lady, Mrs Anne Killigrew*, regarded as the best of his lyrics – Samuel Johnson declared it the finest ode in the language. (Anne Killigrew, the painter, was drowned in the Thames.) This period saw the first of Dryden's translations from the classics, Plutarch's *Lives*. Although 'by several hands' it is usually referred to as 'Dryden's Plutarch'; he contributed a life of Plutarch also, and the work was complete in 1686.

**The Hind and the Panther.** *A Poem. In Three Parts* (1687) was prompted by criticism of Dryden's religion from Edward Stillingfleet, later Bishop of Worcester. In the form of a long allegorical fable, the poem expresses Dryden's faith and his attitudes to religious questions; but far from bringing him favour from either side, it earned sour looks from both, and gave the lie to those who had seen his conversion as a matter of expediency. The Revolution of 1688, in any case, made it clear that the poet's conscience could not be seduced. He refused to take the oath to William and Mary and was deprived of his laureateship as a consequence; he also lost the position in the Customs House which he had held since 1683.

Dryden was now in his middle fifties. He had married Elizabeth Howard, daughter of the Earl of Berkshire, in 1663 and was the father of three sons. *Don Sebastian*, a romantic play, was produced in 1690, and he contributed a libretto to Henry Purcell's opera *King Arthur* (1691). A tragedy, *Cleomenes, the Spartan Hero* followed (1692); **Amphitryon**, a comedy, was produced in 1690, though written some years before; *Love Triumphant* (1694) was an unsuccessful tragicomedy and *The Secular Masque* (1700) was his last work for the stage. But work of more enduring value had appeared in the meantime, including the *Song for St Cecilia's Day* (1687). Translations of Juvenal and Persius, made with the help of his sons Charles and John, were published in 1693. He translated some Homer, Ovid, Horace, Theocritus, and Lucretius; his *The Works of Vergil* was published in 1693 as was the second ode for St Cecilia's day, *Alexander's Feast. Fables, Ancient and Modern* (1700) contains translations of Ovid and Boccaccio, and of Chaucer; it could be said to have kept alive interest in the English master but Dryden 'adapted' him as he had attempted to adapt Shakespeare. More important for posterity was the Preface, one of Dryden's most highly regarded prose pieces.

Modern English prose begins with Dryden. His critical essays, the prefaces to his plays, the

John Dryden. A detail from the portrait after Sir Godfrey Kneller, 1698. National Portrait Gallery, London.

*Life of Plutarch*, **Essay of Dramatick Poesie** (1668) and *Essay of Heroick Plays* (1672) are but a few examples of the lucidity and directness which this master of language, an astute independent observer, brought to any subject. Dryden was attacked and badly beaten in Covent Garden on 18 December 1679; for some time the Earl of Rochester was believed responsible, having taken exception to some lines attributed to Dryden. The earl has been exonerated but the mystery remains of who paid three thugs to waylay the finest critic of the age. (See **Sheffield, John**.)

The poet died on 1 May 1700 and was buried in the same grave as Chaucer in Westminster Abbey. Younger writers of quality, particularly Congreve, had received generous praise from him and his own activity had never slackened. The major literary figure of his time, Dryden was one of the most skilful and accomplished artists in English letters, a professional in the modern sense of the word. However, it is unlikely that he is now read much by anyone apart from scholars: like Milton, whom he so much admired, Dryden is accorded every honour except popularity. But he deserves every English reader's gratitude for the high standards set by his own excellence. Lyric, didactic and satirical poetry, in rhyming couplets and in blank verse; a generous contribution to the newly flourishing drama; critical essays of lasting value and prose of great elegance and clarity: Dryden could rise to the challenge of all these. But if he possessed the ability to move his reader, he chose not to exercise it. For one so celebrated in his own lifetime, he seems to have been a rather private person.

Editions of Dryden's works are available in a number of different forms. The standard collected edition was that of Sir Walter Scott in 18 volumes (1808–21), revised by George Saintsbury (1882–92); this is being superseded by the 'California' Dryden, edited by E. N. Hooker and H. T. Swedenberg, now in progress (volume 1, 1956). Dryden's poems are available in two fine editions, that of G. R. Noyes from Harvard (1909, revised 1950), and that of J. Kinsley from Oxford (four volumes, 1958). There is also a single volume edition of Kinsley (Oxford Standard Authors, 1962). Dryden's plays first appeared in a collected edition in six volumes (1717) edited by William Congreve and containing a memoir. A modern collection is that of M. Summers (six volumes, 1931–32). Dryden's prose is collected in E. Malone's four-volume *The Critical and Miscellaneous Prose Works of John Dryden* (1800), for many years the only source of details of the poet's life. *Dramatic Essays* was edited by W. H. Hudson (Everyman's Library, 1912) and *Of Dramatick Poesie and other Critical Essays* by G. Watson in two volumes (Everyman's Library, 1962).

*Dubliners* A book of short stories by James Joyce, first published in 1914. Joyce began writing them nine years before, when he had returned to Dublin from Paris. Some of them were first published in the periodical *Irish Homestead*, and the style predates the author's experiments in prose. The stories reflect Joyce's angry resentment of the condition of life endured by most people in the Dublin he knew, dominated by the pub and the church, and culturally paralysed. Of the 15 stores in the volume the most celebrated is 'The Dead,' which tells of a young couple's almost obligatory attendance at the annual party given by the young man's aunts. Because he is a schoolteacher he is deferred to and he is obliged to make a speech. He is painfully aware that he is falling back on clichés and easy sentiment but he succeeds in pleasing. After the party he finds his wife unresponsive, and discovers that a song sung during the evening has reminded her of a boy who once loved her, and indeed died because of her. The experience conveys to him a depth of feeling he had never comprehended before.

**Dubois, William Edward Burghardt** *c.*1868–1963. The distinguished Black sociologist and writer was born in Great Barrington, Massachusetts. He was educated at Fisk University, Tennessee, and at Harvard, where he received his PhD in 1895. His doctoral thesis on the suppression of the African slave trade was the first volume in the Harvard Historical series.

Dubois taught economics and history at Atlanta University, Georgia, from 1896 to 1910 and soon became famous for his studies of the status of Black people in the USA: *John Brown* (1909), *The Negro* (1915), *The Gift of Black Folk* (1924), and *Black Reconstruction* (1935). Sketches and verses about the life of Black people are the matter of *The Souls of Black Folk* (1903) and *Darkwater* (1920). *Color and Democracy: Colonies and Peace* (1945) argues powerfully for the rights of small nations and rejects all aspects of imperialism, whether political, economic, or any other. Dubois was the author of a single novel, *The Dark Princess* (1928), and coeditor with Guy Benton Johnson of the *Encyclopedia of the Negro* (publication was begun in 1945). The autobiographical *Dusk of Dawn* (1940) was, he declared, 'the autobiography of a concept of race'. For 24 years he edited *The Crisis*, a magazine devoted to improving the lot of his race.

Politics inevitably played a large part in Dubois' life. He was a radical leader in the first decade of the century, in sharp disagreement with the policy of Booker T. Washington, who advocated gradual development and careful training – Dubois demanded full rights for his race at once. His writings, passionate and eloquent, proved to be of great interest at a much later date and were eagerly read. Dubois left Atlanta University to become one of the founders of the National Association for the Advancement of Colored People but he later became impatient with the Association's studied moderation. He became director of the Peace Information Center in New York in 1949 and joined the Communist Party in 1961 at the age of 93.

Dubois died in Ghana where, as editor of *Encyclopaedia Africana*, he had gone to live in 1961. He became a citizen of that country in the year of his death.

*Duchess of Malfi, The* A tragedy by John Webster. It was first published in 1623; the date of the first production is not known but is believed to have been before 1614. The plot is based on a story by Matteo Bandello.

The Duchess of Malfi is a widow. One of her brothers is a cardinal; another, the elder, is Ferdinand, Duke of Calabria; both brothers are inordinately jealous of their high birth and warn their sister that she must not remarry. Another consideration is her duchy, which they want to inherit. But the duchess has fallen in love with her steward, Antonio, and secretly marries him. The suspicious brothers introduce a spy into her household in the person of Bosola, an escaped galley slave.

Bosola, suspicious of his mistress's condition, provokes confirmation in the famous scene with the fresh 'apricocks' and her secret is out; she is pregnant as well as married. She and Antonio are forced to separate and become fugitives from the vindictive brothers. The duchess is captured and confined to her house, where Ferdinand indulges in a frenzy of spiteful cruelty, carried out by Bosola, until she and her children are murdered.

After the murder of the duchess (it occurs in Act IV – the rest of the play is Bosola's) Ferdinand and the cardinal decide they must remove Bosola, who – already shaken by his victim's courage and nobility – regards his masters with loathing. When he realizes that they are in a hurry to be rid of him he determines on revenge. He kills the man he believes is the cardinal, finding to his horror that it is in fact Antonio, whom he had now determined to save; despair is added to remorse. The unbalanced Ferdinand now descends into total insanity. Bosola succeeds in murdering the cardinal but is himself killed by the mad Ferdinand; his single consolation is to see the madman killed by Antonio's friends.

Bosola is Webster's most considerable character, a man with a knowledge of evil – evil that he has witnessed and understands better than his loathsome masters, who commission evil but shrink from seeing it performed; they are worse by far and will flick him from their sight without conscience. In modern terms, Ferdinand is a psychopath; he could never explain convincingly why he acts and feels as he does. Both these characters and the cardinal are remarkable studies, against which the character of the duchess, with her unfailing courage and dignity, shines like 'a good deed in a naughty world', to quote another playwright.

**Duenna, The** A comic opera with text by Richard Brinsley Sheridan and music by Thomas Linley. It was first produced at Covent Garden in November 1775, and published in the same year. The plot concerns Don Jerome and his desire for a match between his daughter Louisa and Isaac. But Louisa is in love with Antonio and she enlists the help of her duenna as intermediary with him. Don Jerome finds out; he locks up Louisa and dismisses her duenna. Louisa escapes from the

house disguised as the duenna, who takes her place. Isaac is deceived into marrying the duenna and into bringing about the marriage of Louisa to her Antonio.

**Duessa** In Book I of Spenser's *The Faerie Queene*, the daughter of Deceit and Shame – falsehood generally, and the Roman Church in particular. In Book V she is tried at the court of Mercilla, the maiden queen, and plainly represents Mary of Scotland. Mary's son, James VI of Scotland, was greatly offended by this passage.

**Dugdale, Sir William** 1605–86. Sir William Dugdale was born at Shustoke, near Coleshill in Warwickshire, and became a pursuivant extraordinary in the reign of Charles I through the influence of Sir Henry Spelman and Lord Hatton. He published his *The Antiquities of Warwickshire* (1656) during the Commonwealth; the book is regarded as the fullest and most accurate of its kind until that date, one that set a new standard of quality. His *Monasticon Anglicanum*, an account of English monastic foundations, was published in three volumes in 1655, 1661, and 1673; and the valuable record of old St Paul's before it was destroyed by fire, *The History of St Paul's Cathedral*, appeared in 1658. *The History of Imbanking and Drayning of Divers Fenns and Marshes* (1662) goes far beyond the brief suggested by the title and contains historical matter of great interest, including an account of Hereward the Wake's last stand against the Normans. His other works were *Origines Juridicales* (1666), a history of the administration of law in England; *The Baronage of England* (1675–76); and *A Short View of the Late Troubles in England* (1681), an expression of his Royalist principles. Dugdale has a high place among English antiquarians for his careful scholarship and clear attractive style. He became Garter King of Arms to King Charles II and was knighted in 1677.

**Duke's Children, The** A novel by Anthony Trollope, the final volume of the 'Palliser' series. It was first published in *All the Year Round* (October 1879 to July 1880).

Lady Glencora, Duchess of Omnium, is dead and Plantagenet Palliser, the duke, is no longer prime minister. He is finding little pleasure in his children, two sons and a daughter, now grown up: while he is a member of the old order, they are looking forward to the new one. He is conscious of his noble birth and ancient lineage – so conscious that he is unable, in spite of his humane and gentle character, to see that the changes in his children's outlook will not necessarily render irreparable harm to all he holds sacred.

His eldest son, Lord Silverbridge, has failed at Oxford; the next is Lord Gerald, and the youngest is Lady Mary. Their vicissitudes try their father's patience but he loves them in his way, and a fair amount of happiness is promised at the end of the story. Lord Silverbridge marries an American heiress, Isabel Boncassen, and Lady Mary marries Frank Tregear; neither marriage is unopposed but the duke has to give way. Silverbridge, after opposing his father in politics, comes round to his views in the end, and the duke returns to office in the cabinet of the new government.

The story ends on a bright note, with Palliser evincing positive pleasure in the way things have turned out, and the duke's children displaying some of the qualities which made their mother, Lady Glencora, a continuing pleasure to readers throughout the series.

**Dumain**  In Shakespeare's *Love's Labour's Lost*, one of the lords attendant upon the King of Navarre. He accepts the withdrawal from the world with enthusiasm, only to fall in love with Katharine, a lady attendant on the Princess of France.

**Dunbar, Paul Laurence**  1872–1906.  The Black poet was born in Dayton, Ohio. His parents had been slaves and Dunbar received his education at the public schools in Dayton, where he was usually the only Black pupil in his class. He had an ambition to be a lawyer but this was quite beyond his family's means and he was obliged to earn his living as an elevator boy. He started to write poetry about this time and had a small collection, *Oak and Ivy*, privately printed in 1893. His next, *Majors and Minors* (1895), was published with the help of a lawyer and a doctor from Toledo, who had been impressed by the first collection, which had meanwhile come to the attention of William Dean Howells. *Lyrics of a Lowly Life* (1896) was published by Dodd, Mead and Co. and recognition quickly followed. Dunbar was the first Black poet to command an audience in the USA since Phyllis Wheatley, in the 18th century. Lecture tours followed – audiences wanted to hear Dunbar read his own work, with its skilful use of dialect and its folk quality, but the strain was hard on the poet's constitution. He did, however, enjoy a visit to England – an experience he was to treasure for the rest of his short life. Through the influence of Colonel Robert G. Ingersoll he obtained a post in the Library of Congress.

Dunbar died of tuberculosis at the age of 34. He was the author of four novels that are not read now and his poetry today is largely rejected by Black Americans for its sentimental and sub-missive tone. Other collections were *Lyrics of the Hearthside* (1899), *Lyrics of Love and Laughter* (1903), and *Lyrics of Sunshine and Shadow* (1905). Dunbar's *Complete Poems* was published in 1913.

**Dunbar, William**  *c*.1460–*c*.1513.  William Dunbar's career was that of a court poet, but details of his life are extremely scarce and, as in the case of his fellow Scot Robert Henryson, there is no certainty about the dates of his birth and death. What little is known stems from the fact that he was at the court of King James IV of Scotland, and from historical events to which some of his poems refer. It is known that he was educated at St Andrews (MA 1479), spent some years in France from 1491, and was certainly in England in 1501. He was a friar during the years between university and his return from France (by 1500) when he became a priest at court and a minor official. The years in Paris evidently made a deep impression on him and there is a distinct French influence in his work.

William Dunbar was a member of the Scottish embassy to the court of Henry VII during negotiations for the marriage of Margaret Tudor to the Scottish king, and he had probably begun to write poetry by then. His first considerable poem, *The Thrissill and the Rois* (1503), takes the royal marriage for its theme; it is an elaborate allegory executed with remarkable skill, using the dream-vision method that looked back to Chaucer. Dunbar is often described as one of the Scottish 'Chaucerians' but some modern critics, while acknowledging the debt of all poets of the time to Chaucer, place Dunbar very highly in his own right – as a Scottish poet who challenges Burns; as a master of several styles his gifts would have made him outstanding in any age.

Dunbar's principal poems are the allegorical *The Thrissill and the Rois* (The Thistle and the Rose) and *The Goldyn Targe* (*c*.1508); the three-part conversation piece *Tretis of the Twa Mariit Wemen and the Wedo* (*c*.1508); *The Dance of the Sevin Deidlie Synnis* (1503–08), a vision describing a *danse macabre*; the narrative *The Freirs of Berwik*; *Tidings from the Session*, a sharp satire on the Edinburgh law courts, and *Satire on Edinburgh* in which he attacks the condition of that city, one of the filthiest in Europe; the *Ballad of Kynd Kittok*, about a thirsty alewife; *The Flyting of Dunbar and Kennedie*, a savage attack on his rival Walter Kennedy; and *The Lament for the Makaris*, a poem on the passing of human endeavour. (Much of Dunbar's poetry cannot be dated, even approximately.)

William Dunbar's name vanishes from the records after the death of King James IV at

Flodden (1513), and it is possible that the poet fell there also. But this is challenged by some scholars who assign a late poem, *Orisone*, to 1517 or later.

Dunbar's works were collected by David Laing, the Scottish antiquary and bibliographer, in 1834.

**Duncan, King**  King of Scotland in Shakespeare's *Macbeth*. He is murdered by his host when he stays in Macbeth's castle.

**Dunciad, The**  A satirical poem by Alexander Pope, first published anonymously in 1728; authorship was not acknowledged until 1735. The first *Dunciad* consisted of three books; a fourth, *The New Dunciad*, was published in 1742 and the complete work in 1743.

The subject of the satire is dullness, but the object was Pope's desire to hit back at Lewis Theobald, who had severely – and accurately – criticized Pope's edition of Shakespeare in 1726. Pope made him the hero of *The Dunciad* but moved Colley Cibber into that position in the poem's final form. Cibber had alluded to the failed play, *Three Hours after Marriage*, to which Pope had contributed, in his production of *The Rehearsal*. Pope abused Cibber for this; but Cibber refused to emend the text and published *A Letter from Cibber to Pope* (1717). Colley Cibber was a lively and experienced writer; his *Letter* was cool – but there was enough truth in it to enrage his attacker and Pope acquired a new target for his *Dunciad*. The body of the satire is full of ridicule for those writers who had earned the poet's displeasure or disapproval but it is a brilliantly wrought attack on literary vices also.

The four books describe the triumph of dullness. In Book I the character Bayes (Colley Cibber) is trying to decide where his talents will best be deployed. The poet laureate, Laurence Eusden, has died and Bayes' decision is made for him; the goddess anoints him king in place of Eusden, who now 'sleeps among the dull of ancient days'. Book II describes the celebrations following the enthronement of Bayes as King of the Dunces; his domain is the empire of Emptiness and Dullness. The celebrations as described are a burlesque of the funeral games for Anchises in the *Aeneid*. Everyone falls asleep while poetry is being read. In Book III Bayes, sleeping in the goddess's lap, sees in his dreams the past and future triumphs of the empire of Dullness extended to all arts and sciences, the theatre, and the court. Bayes' guide in his dream is Elkanah Settle, who had been one of Dryden's literary opponents. Book IV sees the dream realized; the goddess gives her messengers instructions to discover silly pursuits that will be encouraged. Thought is discouraged and dullness triumphs.

**Dunne, Finley Peter** 1867–1936.  The journalist who created the character of Mr Dooley, the barman, was born in Chicago. The Chicago-Irish barman, Mr Dooley, first appeared in 1898 in *Mr Dooley in Peace and in War* and had become nationally famous by the early years of the century. His comments on the events of the day, sceptical and witty, were often in the form of asides to his colleague, Malachi Hennessey, and close attention was paid to these utterances. Dunne invested him with considerable homespun wisdom. The last of several collections was *Mr Dooley on Making a Will* (1919).

**Dunsany, Edward John Moreton Drax Plunkett, 18th Baron** 1878–1957.  Dunsany was born in London and educated at Eton College and the Royal Military College, Sandhurst; after World War I he became Professor of English Literature in Athens. He was a prolific writer of short stories with a vein of fantasy woven in and these enjoyed a certain popularity during his own lifetime. His first fictions, *The Gods of Pegana* (1905), *Time and the Gods* (1906), and *The Sword of Welleran* (1908), were based on a mythology of his own devising. Dunsany was persuaded by Yeats to write for the Abbey Theatre, Dublin, and his first play, *The Glittering Gate* (1909), was predictably a dramatic fantasy, about two burglars hoping to enter heaven. He wrote a number of plays, many of them little more than dramatic anecdotes, which have not held the stage. His autobiography, *Patches of Sunlight*, was published in 1938.

**Duns Scotus, John** *c*.1264–1308.  Details of the life of the medieval philosopher do not go beyond a few facts. He was born at Maxton in Roxburgh and he joined the Franciscan order; he studied theology at Oxford (where he probably became a friar) and went to Paris about 1302. About five years later he went to Cologne and had not been there long when he died.

Duns Scotus, known as Doctor Subtilis and Doctor Marianus, was one of the first to challenge the doctrine of Thomas Aquinas; Duns Scotus rejected the harmony of faith and reason, asserting that there could be no connection between reason and revelation. He also accepted the theory of universal matter propounded by the Arab thinker Ibn Gebirol. Duns Scotus is frequently described as a realist in philosophy but the historical context must be borne in mind; he was arguing within defined limits. Thus, he was able to defend the doctrine of the Immaculate

Conception with great vigour. The disparagers of Duns Scotus described his followers, the Scotists, as Dunsmen or Dunses, and the description has survived in the word 'dunce'.

Duns Scotus wrote in Latin. *De Modis Significandi sive Grammatica Speculativa* was printed in 1499; a book of logical *Quaestiones* appeared in edited form about 1474; *De Rerum Principio* (about 1497) is a work on metaphysics, and *Opus Oxoniense* (printed 1481) is a commentary on the *Sententiae* of Peter Lombard.

**Dunstan, St** 924–88. The son of a noble family, Dunstan was born at Glastonbury and received his education from Irish scholars who had settled there. He was persuaded by Aelheah (*or* Elphege), Bishop of Winchester, to take monastic vows while under expulsion from the court of King Aethelstan on suspicion of being a wizard. He became Abbot of Glastonbury during the reign of Edmund, but had to take refuge in Flanders to escape the wrath of the later king, Edwig, whom he had boldly rebuked for his vicious life. He was recalled by King Edgar, who made him Archbishop of Canterbury in 960. Dunstan was

St Dunstan kneeling at the feet of Christ. Dunstan drew his own kneeling figure, and wrote the inscription above it. From an edition of Eutychis, *Treatise on Grammar*, c.950. *MŚ. Auct. F.4. 32, f.1r.* Bodleian Library, Oxford.

a major influence in the revival of learning which took place under the enlightened rule of Edgar; Glastonbury became a famous school under his guidance.

**D'Urbeyfield, Tess** The 'pure woman faithfully presented' in Thomas Hardy's *Tess of the D'Urbervilles*. She is a victim both of circumstances and of men: she is, like everyone, helpless in the grip of the former; with the latter she is helpless because she is young and poor. In a novel with no hero she has the stature of a tragic heroine.

**D'Urfey, Thomas** 1653–1723. D'Urfey (or Tom Durfey as he was often called) was of Huguenot descent and a prolific but minor Restoration dramatist and song-writer who wrote at least thirty plays. He enjoyed great popularity, if no reputation in literary circles, and was well acquainted with both Charles II and James II. Most of his songs made use of old tunes, in new settings by composers of the day. His collection of songs and ballads, *Wit and Mirth, or Pills to Purge Melancholy*, was published in six volumes (1719–20). In the preface to one of his plays, *The Campaigners* (1698) D'Urfey wrote an effective reply to Jeremy Collier's attacks on the London stage.

**Durham, Simeon of** fl. 1096–1129. A Northumbrian chronicler of whose life very little is known, Simeon was precentor of the monastery of Durham and his work is a principal source for Anglo-Norman history. The work of Bede gave Simeon the first part of his chronicle; for the period from the end of Bede's *Historia* (the early 8th century) to the beginning of the 9th century his source was a Northumbrian chronicle now lost; from the 9th century to 1121 the source is Florence of Worcester's *Chronicon ex Chronicis*; from 1121 to 1129 a brief contribution, probably by Simeon himself, brings the history to a close. There is no means of ascertaining whether Simeon was more than a compiler or editor but the value of his work is indisputable. (See also **Hexham, Richard and John of.**)

Simeon of Durham's *Historia Regum* in *Opera Omnia*, was edited by T. Arnold (Rolls Series, 1882–85). A translation was made by J. Stevenson for *The Church Historians of England* (1853–56).

**Durrell, Lawrence (George)** 1912– . Durrell was born in India. He attended the College of St Joseph in Darjeeling and completed his education at St Edmund's School, Canterbury. He and his family lived on the island of Corfu before the war, then he became a government press officer and attaché in Greece, Egypt, and Yugoslavia. A prolific and various writer, his first published work was poetry: *Quaint Fragment. Poems Written Between the Ages of Sixteen and Nineteen* (1931). His first novel, *Panic Spring* (1935), was published under the pseudonym of Charles Norden but for the second, *Pied Piper of Lovers* (also 1935), he used his own name. After World War II Durrell published his first book about Greece, *Prospero's Cell* (1945). He worked for the British Council in Greece and Argentina and later published his lectures as *A Key to Modern Poetry* (1952, called *A Key to Modern British Poetry* in the USA). Further volumes of poetry are *The Ikons* (1966) and *Vega and Other Poems* (1973); *Collected Poems* was published in 1960 (new edition, 1968). *Sappho* (1950), *An Irish Faustus* (1963), and *Acte* (1961) are verse plays. As a novelist Durrell first reached a wide public with *Justine* (1957), the opening novel of *The Alexandria Quartet*, continued in *Balthazar* (1958), *Mountolive* (1958), and *Clea* (1960). Two further novel-sequences have followed: *Tunq* (1968) and *Nunquam* (1970); and *Monsieur* (1974), *Livia* (1978), and *Constance* (1982). The books about Greece continued with *Reflections on a Marine Venus* (1953) and *Bitter Lemons* (1957, Duff Cooper Memorial Prize). Lawrence Durrell was elected a Fellow of the Royal Society of Literature in 1954.

**Dutch Courtesan, The**  A comedy by John Marston, first published in 1605. It was first produced at least two years before that, in the reign of Elizabeth I; the title page states that it was played 'by the children of her Majesties revels'.

The Dutch courtesan of the title is Franceschina. Her protector is Freevill, who falls in love with Beatrice, the daughter of Sir Hubert Subboys, and decides that he must terminate the liaison with Franceschina. Meanwhile he takes his stiff-necked friend Malheureux with him on a visit to Franceschina; he intends to amuse himself at his friend's uneasiness – but Malheureux conceives a violent passion for her. When Franceschina discovers Freevill's plans to marry she uses Malheureux's passion for her; she will respond if he will kill Freevill and bring her proof by taking from his hand a ring given him by Beatrice.

Malheureux recoils from the proposal and reveals it to Freevill, who arranges a mock fight, gives his friend the ring, and goes into hiding. But when Malheureux takes the ring to Franceschina she denounces him as a murderer to Sir Hubert and Freevill's father. Malheureux finds himself charged with Freevill's death and sentenced to the gallows. Freevill reappears in time to rescue him. Franceschina is punished for her wickedness.

Freevill, who comments on the motives and emotions of the others and manipulates them some of the time, is one of the most unpleasant characters in Jacobean drama. Late in the action he declares himself enchanted with the prospect of marriage to Beatrice, while looking forward to the confounding of Franceschina: 'Providence all wicked art o'er tops.' If that were true he could expect to find himself brought down very hard some time in the future. But there is no such moral framework in *The Dutch Courtesan*: expedience is all in Marston's play.

**Dutch Republic, The Rise of the**  See **Motley, John Lothrop**.

**Dwight, Timothy** *c*.1752–1817. A grandson of Jonathan Edwards, Dwight was born in Massachusetts. He attended Yale at the remarkably early age of 13, and one of his fellow students was John Trumbull. Dwight became a tutor at the age of 19 but he worked and studied with such fervour that he had a nervous breakdown at 25. To aid his recuperation he undertook extensive walking and horseback journeys, which provided the material for his *Travels in New England and New York*, published in four volumes (1821–22).

His health restored, Dwight, with his friend Trumbull, worked for the study of contemporary English literature at Yale – the genesis probably of the group which became known as the Connecticut Wits. Dwight served as an army chaplain during the War for Independence and in 1783 became pastor of the Congregational church at Greenfield Hill, Connecticut. He stayed until 1795 and became a leader in the community. A Calvinist and a federalist, Dwight's poetic talents were expended in support of his views: *The Conquest of Canaan* (1785), *Greenfield Hill* (1794), and *The Triumph of Infidelity* (1788).

Of more importance was Dwight's presidency of Yale, to which he was appointed in 1795. In spite of his rigidly held opinions Dwight proved to be an admirable college head, greatly enlarging the curriculum and sanctioning the engagement of distinguished scholars. He published a number of statements of his political views, and his sermons were published in five volumes after his death. His most highly regarded prose work, however, is his *Travels*, which is also a valuable source of information.

**Dyer, John** 1700–58. A native of Carmarthenshire, Dyer was born at Aberglasney and educated at Westminster School. He studied painting with Jonathan Richardson but was an unsuccessful artist. He was ordained in 1741, after returning from Italy, where he contracted malaria, and was the incumbent of Coningsby and Kirkby in Lincolnshire when he died. Dyer is remembered in English literature for his poem *Grongar Hill* (1727), written during the time when he was an itinerant painter in South Wales. The poem celebrates the valley of the River Towy in Carmarthenshire, and is a romantic poem written before the time of romantic poetry. Dyer used the octosyllabic couplet of Milton's *L'Allegro* and *Il Penseroso* and brought a remarkable freshness of observation to the countryside. Later, more ambitious poems by Dyer, *The Ruins of Rome* (1740) and *The Fleece* (1757), are regarded as failures by most scholars. *Grongar Hill* is published in a modern edition in Everyman's Library *Minor Poets of the Eighteenth Century*, edited by Hugh l'Anson Fausset (1930).

**Dynasts, The,** *An Epic-Drama of the War with Napoleon, in three Parts, nineteen Acts and one hundred and thirty Scenes.* Thomas Hardy's ambitious poetic sequence was published in three parts, in 1904, 1906, and 1908. It is written mainly in blank verse, with interpolations in other forms and descriptive connecting sequences and stage directions. The cast ranges from monarchs to foot soldiers and includes a chorus, formed of 'intelligences'. The action opens in 1805, with England under threat of invasion, and ends with Bonaparte's final defeat. Parallel with the great scenes are vignettes of ordinary life, episodes showing how ordinary people are affected by great events.

Hardy's 'intelligences' are Spirits – of the Years, of the Pities, of Rumour; Spirits Sinister and Ironic. Also taking part are the Shade of the Earth and the Recording Angel, and above them all presides the Immanent Will that orders the universe. All of these, from their detached eminences, comment on the significance of events. To his epic poem, as to his novels, Hardy brings a fatalist's view of men and events; neither the great nor the humble have any real control over their fates. The figure of Bonaparte stands at the centre: Emperor for one year, he is at the height of his brief but brilliant career when Part I opens. The wars have brought the great victory at Austerlitz as well as the defeat at Trafalgar. The events of Part II include the Battle of Jena, the defeats of the Peninsular War, and Bonaparte's divorce of Josephine to marry a Habsburg princess and found a dynasty. Part III tells of the downward path of his fortunes; the disastrous invasion of Russia, his abdication, the Hundred Days, and the end at Waterloo in 1815.

# E

**Eadmer** *c.*1055–*c.*1124. Eadmer was brought up at the monastery of Christ Church, Canterbury, and became preceptor. He was a writer on religious subjects, including lives of St Dunstan and St Wilfrid, but his most valued works are his life of his friend St Anselm, *Vita Anselmi*, and his *Historia Novorum in Anglia*, both important sources for the history of the times. The *Vita Anselmi* deals with the years 1033 to 1109; the *Historia* covers the period 1066 to 1120 and is a narrative of contemporary events. Eadmer wrote in his preface of the importance of a faithful record of events as they occurred: his *Historia* is an invaluable first-hand account of the reigns of William II and Henry I, turning on the relationship of the crown with the see of Canterbury.

Eadmer's *Historia* was edited by M. Rule (Rolls Series, 1884); G. Bosanquet's translation, *History of Recent Events in England*, was published in 1964. *Vita Anselmi* was edited by R. W. Southern (Oxford Medieval Texts, 1962).

**Earle, John** *c.*1601–55. A member of Lord Falkland's circle at Great Tew, Earle was a fellow of Merton College, Oxford, at the age of 18 and became famous with the publication of his *Microcosmographie, or a Peece of the World Discovered in Essays and Characters* (1628). It was published anonymously but the identity of the author was well known. It was a collection of 'characters', a form much in fashion at that time. Earle's book is reckoned to be the best of its kind. The author was a humane and deeply learned man and his characters are presented with insight; they are also recognizable in the day-to-day life he knew, and unlike some of his contemporaries he avoided the temptation to be smart.

Earle became tutor to Prince Charles, remaining loyal to him as king and throughout the Civil War. He translated *Eikon Basilike* into Latin during his 16 years' exile as a Royalist. At the Restoration he was made Dean of Westminster and later became Bishop of Salisbury. *Microcosmographie* ran into four editions in 1628; further editions were enlarged (1629 and 1633).

**Earnshaw, Catherine** The heroine of Emily Brontë's *Wuthering Heights*. She responds to the passionate devouring love of her foster brother, Heathcliff, but is still attracted to the graces of the world, represented by the elegant Lintons. Her marriage to Edgar Linton provokes the vindictive revenge of Heathcliff: she dies in childbirth, but he loves her even in death and, ultimately, only longs to join her.

**Earthly Paradise, The** A poem by William Morris, first published in three volumes (1868–70). The poem is written in Chaucerian metres and is Chaucerian in style, with a prologue and linking narratives between the 24 tales related in the poem.

A company of Norsemen flee from the pestilence (the Black Death) ravaging Europe in the 14th century. They set sail from Scandinavia and search for the Earthly Paradise across the western sea where none grow old. After long and fruitless journeyings they arrive, old and tired, at 'a nameless city in a distant sea', where Greek culture and civilization have been preserved and where the gods of the Greeks are still worshipped. They are made welcome and spend their remaining years there. Twice a month they meet their hosts at a feast and each side relates a story. One of the Norsemen tells a tale of their past and one of their hosts tells a classical legend. Lyric poems connect the months and describe the landscape in the changing year. The acknowledged triumph of the poem is Morris's version of the *Laxdaela Saga*, 'The Lovers of Gudrun'.

*The Earthly Paradise* has a dreamlike atmosphere and the prologue offers the reader an escape ('Forget six counties overhung with smoke, Forget the snorting steam and piston stroke') from the conditions that Morris abhorred and worked unceasingly to improve. He wrote most of the poem on train journeys between London and Oxford during the summer of 1857. It was a great favourite with the Victorian public and established Morris as the leading poet of the day. The lyric interludes between the tales are much admired.

**Easter 1916** See **Yeats, William Butler.**

**East Lynne** A novel by Mrs Henry Wood, first published in 1861, and later dramatized with enormous success. Her most celebrated if not her best work, it concerns the transgression and repentance of Lady Isabel Vane, who leaves her husband and runs off with another man. Vane divorces her and remarries. Later Lady Isabel returns to the household disguised as a nurse: she is alone now and wants to be near her children. After many vicissitudes, and domestic tragedy, the Vanes are reconciled.

**Eastward Hoe** A comedy by George Chapman, Ben Jonson, and John Marston, first performed at Blackfriars by the Children of the Revels and published in 1605.

The plot tells of Touchstone, a goldsmith, his two daughters, Mildred and Gertrude, and his two apprentices, Golding and Quicksilver. Gertrude, who wants to be fashionable and ride in her own coach, marries Sir Petronel Flash, who turns out to be a penniless adventurer. The industrious apprentice, Golding, has eyes for her sister, the unpretentious Mildred, who is happy to marry him and proud to see him become deputy-alderman. Sir Petronel filches Gertrude's dowry and sends her off on a coach – to an imaginary castle. As soon as she is gone he sets off for Virginia in company with the idle apprentice, Quicksilver, who has robbed his master.

Sir Petronel and Quicksilver are apprehended when their ship is wrecked on the Isle of Dogs and brought up before Golding, the deputy-alderman. A term in prison brings about repentance and they are eventually released through Golding's good offices.

The play is interesting for its setting; like Dekker's *The Shoemaker's Holiday* of 1600 it dealt with tradesmen and their lives. A passage in Act III was considered to be insulting to the Scots and gave offence at the Stuart court. The three authors were punished with imprisonment.

**Ecce Homo** A life of Christ by John Robert Seeley, first published anonymously in 1865. The title of the book (*Behold the Man!*) suggests the author's purpose in presenting something other than a study of 'the metaphysical Christ of the Creeds' and Seeley's success in presenting the historical Jesus was considerable. It was bought in great numbers; the readable portrayal of a great teacher and reformer was very comforting to many people, though John Henry Newman, Dean Stanley, and Gladstone challenged the orthodoxy of the author. Seeley published *Natural Religion*, an attempt to reconcile the claims of Christianity to those of natural science, in 1882.

**Ecclesiastical History of the English Race** (*Historia Ecclesiastica Gentis Anglorum*). A history of the English people and the coming of Christianity to England, in five books, by Bede. The history was composed in Latin; it begins with the invasion by Julius Caesar and closes in 731. Bede uses numerous sources and is scrupulous in his acknowledgments; he is also careful to tell his reader when he is giving an account on hearsay evidence.

The first book gives a description of England then recounts its history from Julius Caesar's invasion up to 603. It includes the arrival of Augustine in Kent, sent by Pope Gregory to refound the Church in England. The second book covers 30 years (to 633) and contains the famous scene in the brightly lit hall at Goodmanham in 627 when Edwin, King of Northumbria, is debating with his nobles the acceptance or rejection of the Gospel as taught by Paulinus, Bishop of York. A sparrow flies into the hall, and then out again into the darkness: one of the noblemen, who is not named, likens the bird's flight to the life of man – a brief sojourn in the light. The second book ends with the death of Edwin in battle with the heathen Cadwallon. The third book, up to 664, relates how Aidan came from Iona at the request of Oswald, King of Northumbria, to continue the work of Paulinus. Lindisfarne is established and Oswald is killed in battle by Penda, the pagan King of Mercia. The work of Wilfrid of York is described. The fourth book, up to 698, includes the story of Deusdedit, the first Anglo-Saxon Archbishop of Canterbury; the arrival in England of Theodore of Tarsus and the events of his archbishopric; and all we know of Caedmon. The fifth and last book includes an account of St John of Beverley (to whom Henry V ascribed his victory at Agincourt), an account of the condition of England in 731, and a short chronological summary.

The oldest manuscript of Bede's *History* is preserved in the University Library of Cambridge. It is dated to within two years of the death of Bede. The first translation, by Thomas Stapleton, was published at Antwerp (1565). Stapleton hoped to influence Elizabeth I in favour of the English Catholic Church. C. Plummer's edition (Oxford 1896) is regarded as definitive. The *History* has been translated into modern English as *A History of the English Church and People* by Leo Sherley Price (Penguin Classics, 1954).

***Ecclesiastical Politie, Of the Laws of*** See **Hooker, Richard.**

**eclogue** A dialogue in verse in a pastoral setting. The speakers are usually shepherds, or shepherds and their lovers, but the setting and the speakers are a device for comment on all manner of things, not just the care of flocks. Another name for the form is *bucolic*; Virgil's celebrated sequence of ten are sophisticated allegories and that form was much used in England after the Renaissance.

**Eden, Richard** *c.*1521–76. The pioneer of the literature of voyaging in English. Eden's purpose was to make known in England the work of the Portuguese and Spanish explorers. He translated the Latin of Sebastian Munster as *A Treatyse of the Newe India, with other Newe Founde Landes and Ilands, as well Eastwarde as Westward*, in 1553.

Also from the Latin of Peter Martyr Anglerius, was *The Decades of the Newe Worlde or West India* (1555), which was enlarged by Richard Willes and reprinted as *The History of Travayle in the West and East Indies* in 1577. Of considerable value was his translation of the Spanish manual by Martin Cortes, *The Arte of Navigation*, in 1561.

***Eden Bower*** A poem by Dante Gabriel Rossetti, first published in 1870 in *Poems by D. G. Rossetti*. Adam's first wife, according to rabbinical literature, was Lilith; she was supplanted by Eve. In Rossetti's poem Lilith persuades Satan to let her become the instrument of Eve's temptation and thus gains her revenge.

**Edgar** The son of Gloucester in Shakespeare's *King Lear*. His half-brother Edmund succeeds in discrediting him and Gloucester disowns him. He takes on the guise of a beggar (Tom O'Bedlam, Poor Tom) and shares his hovel with Lear and the Fool. Later he succours his blinded father and prevents him from committing suicide. Edgar reveals Goneril's adultery to Albany and kills Edmund in single combat.

**Edgeworth, Maria** 1767–1849. Maria Edgeworth's father, Richard Edgeworth, was MP for Edgeworthstown in Longford, much married, and the father of various sets of children to whom Maria, a dutiful daughter, acted as governess. She also acted as her father's housekeeper and general manager and as an assistant in his writings. Richard Edgeworth was an amateur philosopher and it was to illustrate his book on new methods of education that Maria wrote her early fiction, *The Parent's Assistant*, a collection of tales published in six volumes in 1796. Others were *Early Lessons* (1801, 1814) and *Moral Tales for Young People* (1801). All these were heavily influenced by her father, who succeeded in obtruding a purposeful and didactic note that Maria was never quite to eradicate from her writing. Fortunately her better work transcends this limitation but her novels of life in Ireland retain the observing, superior tone of the Anglo-Irish Edgeworths and they cannot be regarded as novels of Irish life: Maria Edgeworth managed her father's estates and never identified with the people who worked on them. Within her limitations, however, she was a novelist with a high level of achievement, and a sharp ear enabled her to reproduce the sound and rhythm of Irish country speech. She also wrote novels of fashionable life, and these have the virtues of wry observation and humour (her father's house received all manner of people, from amateurs of philosophy and social progress to the merely fashionable and privileged) and the limitations – implanted by her father's influence – of too often seeming to make a point at the expense of the narrative. While she often failed, and was to be surpassed at her best, she helped to establish the social novel. In the tales written to illustrate her father's educational theories, she creates recognizable children and she was almost the first English novelist who succeeded in doing that.

Her best work began with a novel of life in Ireland, *Castle Rackrent* (1801), which was followed by *The Absentee* (1809) and *Ormond* (1817). Other novels are *Belinda* (1801), which could be said to have extended the range of the novel by demonstrating that several themes could be handled simultaneously, *Patronage* (1814), *Harrington* (1817), and *Helen* (1834).

**Edinburgh Review, The**   The Edinburgh Review was founded by Francis Jeffrey, a Scottish lawyer, together with Sydney Smith, then an Edinburgh tutor, and Henry Brougham, who had been recently called to the Bar and later became Lord Chancellor. The *Review* was published by Constable in Edinburgh and by Longman in London, the first issue appearing on 10 October 1802 as *The Edinburgh Review and Critical Journal*. A quarterly, *The Edinburgh Review* offered a new standard of criticism: the regular circulation had risen to 14,000 by 1818. It was esteemed so highly that various issues were reprinted as often as ten times. A notable contributor in its early years was Scott, who withdrew because his Tory principles conflicted with those of the *Review*'s Whig founders. Brougham contributed the article on Byron's *Hours of Idleness* that provoked the poet to write *English Bards and Scotch Reviewers*. Macaulay first attracted wide attention with his essay on Milton in *The Edinburgh Review* in August 1825. *The Edinburgh Review* ceased publication in 1929.

**Edmund**   The bastard son of Gloucester in Shakespeare's *King Lear*. Jealous of Edgar, his half-brother, he discredits him with his father and sees him turned out. Later he betrays his father to Goneril and Regan, which results in the blinding of Gloucester by Cornwall. He juggles with the desires of both sisters – quite happy to wait and see which one comes out on top. It is upon his orders that Cordelia is hanged. Edgar kills him in single combat. In a play that bristles with villains Edmund is the most successful because he is the one who cares only for himself.

**Education of Henry Adams, The**   Basically an autobiography of Henry Brooks Adams, this book is subtitled *A Study of Twentieth-Century Multiplicity* and complements his earlier *Mont-Saint-Michel and Chartres*. It was privately printed in 1907 and published in 1918. The subtitle is an indication of Adams's theory of accelerating forces in history, which lead to metaphysics and science of a bewildering multiplicity: the universe has become a multiverse. The extensive education of Henry Brooks Adams simply does not prepare him for the world in which he lives. The purely autobiographical pages are among Adams's best work and describe his experience as both student and teacher at Harvard, his impressions of England during the American Civil War years, and the impact of Charles Darwin's theories. He contrasts the dynamo, the symbol of modern life, with the Virgin, the unifying symbol of the 12th century (the subject of the earlier book), and perceives (he was one of the first Americans who did so) that 20th-century man will, somehow, have to find a way of establishing an ordered life in the modern multiverse.

**Edward III, The Raigne of**   A chronicle play first published in 1596. The authorship is unknown but some scholars claim to have found traces of Shakespeare's hand in it. Apart from the historical content, dealing with Edward III and the Hundred Years War, the play is concerned with the king's attentions to the Countess of Salisbury, which are quite unwelcome and nearly drive the poor lady to suicide.

**Edwards, Jonathan** *c.*1703–58.   A remarkably precocious boy with an interest in natural science, Edwards emerged as a religious philosopher in his adult life, and it is as a religious philosopher that he keeps a place in American letters. He was born in Connecticut, into a family of Puritan ministers, and entered Yale University when he was 12 years old. While there he read Locke's *On the Human Understanding*, with imperfect understanding but with enormous enthusiasm and interest. He graduated at the age of 16, but embarked on a further two years of study in theology. The enthusiasm fired by his study of Locke, and his interest in Newton's physics, combined with his background to produce a remarkable harmony of outlook that was based on his conviction of God's benevolence. (He describes his arrival at this frame of mind in his diary and in *70 Resolutions* and *Personal Narrative* – the last two written about 1740 and not intended for publication.)

In 1726 Edwards became colleague to his grandfather, who was minister of the church of Northampton, Massachusetts; later he became sole minister, and his energies became focused on an effort to stem the drift away from the 'Great Awakening' of about 1734, the religious revival his writing and preaching had brought about. But the mass of the people lacked the will and intellect of men like Edwards, and the Great Awakening saw a wave of emotionalism and morbid piety sweeping New England. Edwards, who inevitably defended the revival, also deplored its excesses (*A Faithful Narrative of the Surprising Works of God*, 1737). Edwards was guilty of his own excess, too – he wanted to exclude all the 'unconverted' (i.e. those who did not accept his presentation of doctrine absolutely) from the Communion. He was dismissed, or obliged to resign, from Northampton in 1749.

Edwards moved to Stockbridge, to a frontier missionary church where the work was with the Housatonic and Mohawk Indians. During his years there he expounded his religious philosophy in four books, of which the most important was *A Careful and Strict Enquiry into the Modern Prevailing Notions respecting that Freedom of Will which is supposed to be essential to Moral Agency* (1754). He was awarded the presidency of the College of New Jersey, which later became Princeton University, in 1757, but died from a smallpox inoculation after three months in office.

Edwards rejected the proposition that man's will is free – God chose and rejected; therefore man could not choose goodness. His ideas have some interest for students of American 18th-century thought in religious matters; but at the heart of his expositions lies Edwards' compulsion to defend the Calvinistic doctrine of 'election' and predestination, which to most people, nowadays, is unacceptable. Other works by Edwards include *An Humble Enquiry into the Rules of the Word of God* (1749), *The Great Christian Doctrine of Original Sin Defended* (1758), and *Two Dissertations* (1765).

**Edwards, Richard** See *Paradyse of Daynty Devises, The.*

**Edward the First, The Famous Chronicle of King** A historical play by George Peele, which loosely follows the reign of Edward I. It was written for Philip Henslowe's company, The Admiral's Men (their patron was Lord Howard of Effingham), and probably played at the Rose, Henslowe's theatre in Southwark. It was first published in 1593.

**Edward the Second, King of England: The Troublesome Raigne and Lamentable Death of** A historical tragedy in blank verse by Christopher Marlowe, first produced by the Earl of Pembroke's Men *c.*1592 and published in 1594.

Shakespeare had been very successful with *Henry VI* in 1592 and the English history play had become a successful medium for dramatists.

The play begins with Edward's recall of his favourite Gaveston upon his accession to the throne (Gaveston had been banished by Edward's father, King Edward I), and follows the grim events that succeed. These include the growing hatred of the queen, Isabella of France (the She-Wolf), and the revolt of the barons that culminates in their capture and killing of Gaveston; the rise of Hugh le Despenser in Edward's affections until he wields as much influence as Gaveston had; the queen's alliance with her lover Mortimer and the successful rebellion; the execution of Despenser and his father; and the confinement of the king in Berkeley Castle and his degradation and murder.

As drama, *Edward II* is the best constructed of all Marlowe's works, though its detractors complain that it lacks the grandeur and lofty language of the others. It is more personal than historical, though the history is well handled and the march of events perfectly clear: this results in due weight being given to the characters of Isabella and Mortimer, so that *Edward II* is less a play for a single character than the other three.

**Edwin Drood, The Mystery of** Charles Dickens's unfinished novel. It was planned to appear in monthly parts, like so many of his books, beginning in April 1870. Only six parts were published (to the end of Chapter XXII); the author died on 8 June of that year.

John Jasper, precentor of Cloisterham cathedral, teaches music to Rosa Bud, an orphan girl betrothed from childhood to his nephew, Edwin Drood. The formal betrothal has prevented any real love from ripening between them and Edwin treats Rosa in a casual fashion. He is devoted to his uncle, John Jasper, but that man nurses a passion for Rosa, who finds Jasper repulsive. Neville and Helena Landless arrive in Cloisterham and Neville, attracted to Rosa, takes a strong dislike to Edwin for his careless behaviour toward her. Jasper foments their dislike and there is a violent quarrel between the two young men.

Edwin visits Rosa and they agree they have nothing really to marry for; they dissolve their engagement, but Edwin puts off telling Jasper of his decision. That night Edwin disappears: the circumstances suggest foul play and suspicion falls on Neville; John Jasper strongly fosters the suspicion. Then Mr Grewgious, Rosa's guardian, breaks the news to Jasper that his ward had broken off her engagement. Jasper gives a cry of horror and collapses in a faint.

Neville is arrested, but the body of Edwin is not found, so Neville is not brought to trial. Released, he finds himself ostracized and goes to London, where he is not known. Jasper, meanwhile, continues to work against Neville; he also pursues Rosa, who goes to London in the care of Mr Grewgious to escape his attentions. Mr Grewgious now prepares to deal with Jasper and his allies assemble: Mr Crisparkle, canon of Cloisterham, and Mr Tartar, a retired naval officer. The last character of importance to appear is the mysterious Mr Datchery, who is enquiring into Jasper's movements... and that is all we have.

As far as it goes, the book is absorbing enough and enormous regret is felt by Dickens's countless admirers that the story remains unfinished. Numerous 'endings' have been contrived by other hands, but somehow none of them convinces. It seems unlikely that Dickens set out to write no more than a mystery story and we can only guess at the range and extent of his new invention. As Angus Wilson has written, 'Dickens was the sort of artist whose parts (whatever the contrary appearance) are so interrelated that only the whole gives the key to the whole.'

**Egan, Pierce** 1772–1849. Egan, a London journalist, achieved success with **Life in London; or The Day and Night Scenes of Jerry Hawthorn and his Elegant Friend Corinthian Tom**, which was published in 20 parts (1820) and later in volume form (1821). The book was illustrated by the Cruikshank brothers. Egan launched the weekly *Pierce Egan's Life in London* in 1824; it was later called *Bell's Life in London* and was incorporated into *Sporting Life* in 1859. He also published *Boxiana; or Sketches of Antient and Modern Pugilism* (1812–13, enlarged 1815–29).

**Egerton, 'George'** See **'New Women' novelists.**

**Egeus** Hermia's father in Shakespeare's *A Midsummer Night's Dream*. He orders his daughter to marry Demetrius, whom she does not love.

**Eggleston, Edward** 1837–1902. The son of a strict Methodist family of the Indiana countryside, Edward Eggleston and his brother George were educated in back-country schools; the two influences shaped their later careers. Edward Eggleston had a busy career as a Bible agent and became a Methodist minister on circuit; he also wrote and edited juvenile magazines as an extension of Sunday-school teaching. He was 37 when he abandoned Methodism and went to New York, where he founded a Church of Christian Endeavour in Brooklyn. He was its pastor for

Edward Eggleston.

five years but in 1879 he retired to devote himself to writing, in which he had already achieved some distinction.

*The Hoosier Schoolmaster* (1871) contained a realistic presentation of rural life in Indiana and made excellent use of Indiana dialect. It was a success in spite of its pious tone. Later novels, of which the most highly regarded is **Roxy** (1878), included *The End of the World* (1872), which made use of frontier religious excesses as the background of a love story. *The Circuit Rider* (1874) exploits this theme at greater length (it is set in the early part of the 19th century in Ohio) and gives a picture also of frontier life. In *The Mystery of Metropolisville* (1873) Eggleston uses the land boom in Minnesota as a background. His novels are, in short, a picture of life in the Middle West during the expansion of the USA. Unfortunately, he believed he could write to better purpose if he concentrated on didactic historical works and he was the author of historical texts and biographies that are almost forgotten. However, two volumes of his uncompleted *History of Life in the United States*, published posthumously in 1904, have some merit as social history.

Eggleston wrote three more novels. **The Hoosier Schoolboy** (1883) is a boy's view of the life described in his first novel; *The Graysons* (1888) is a romance based on Abraham Lincoln's days as a lawyer in Springfield, Illinois, when he successfully defended a man accused of murder; and *The Faith Doctor* (1891) is a satirical view of the wealthy devotees of the then new Christian Science teaching.

**Eggleston, George Cary** 1839–1911. The younger brother of Edward Eggleston, George became a teacher in back-country Indiana at the age of 16. His experiences provided his brother with the material for two of his novels. George Eggleston served in the Confederate army during the Civil War and practised law for a time before becoming a journalist. He was literary editor of the New York *Evening Post* and worked for Joseph Pulitzer on the New York *World* for 11 years. He was also the author of a number of novels and books for boys.

**Eglinton, John** See **Magee, William Kirkpatrick**.

**Eglintoun, Sir Hew of** *c*.1321–*c*.1376. See **Huchoun of the Awle Ryale**.

**Egoist, The** A novel by George Meredith, first published in 1879.

The central character of Meredith's comedy is Sir Willoughby Patterne, rich and handsome, selfish, fatuous, and conceited, too. He is loved by Laetitia Dale and does nothing to discourage her; but he has proposed to Constantia Durham, who has accepted him. Constantia, however, learns in time what sort of man he is and elopes with an officer of Hussars.

Patterne recovers from the humiliation and now decides that the ideal woman to be his wife is Clara Middleton, a professor's daughter. Clara is subjected to a whirlwind courtship, and won, but she knows about Constantia and is equivocal about marriage. Her father, an epicurean, is enlisted on his side by Patterne, who can lavish hospitality on him. Others involved are Vernon Whitford, a handsome scholar, and the boy Crossjay, a poor relation of Patterne. Patterne had once been arrogantly rude to Crossjay's father and the boy gleefully avenges the insult when he overhears Patterne proposing to Laetitia Dale – he is becoming worried by Clara's prevarication and wants to hedge his bets.

Crossjay tells Clara, who has in any case fallen in love with Vernon. Patterne turns to Laetitia who, with pride intact, refuses him. In the end, Patterne, stripped of his pretensions, persuades Laetitia to marry him and she becomes the lady of Patterne Hall. She does love him, in spite of everything.

Mrs Mountstuart Janekinson, with her witty observations on Patterne's manoeuvres, is amusing. Dr Middleton, Clara's father, is based on Thomas Love Peacock, Meredith's father-in-law.

**Eikon Basilike:** *the Pourtraicture of His Sacred Majestie in His Solitudes and Sufferings*. A book by John Gauden, Bishop of Worcester, which he presented as the prayers and meditations of Charles I during his imprisonment. It was published on the day of the king's burial, 9 February 1649, and became enormously popular – 40 editions were printed before the Restoration in 1660. Gauden probably compiled his book from the notes and memoranda of Charles I and succeeded remarkably well in presenting the late king as a royal martyr. See also **Milton, John**.

**Elegy Written in a Country Churchyard** A poem in quatrains (four-line stanzas) of ten-syllabled lines by Thomas Gray, first published in 1750. Gray had worked on the poem since 1742, and the churchyard is believed to be that of Stoke Poges in Buckinghamshire, where Gray lies buried beside his mother. The poem is a reflection on life and death and the hopes attendant on human endeavour. Samuel Johnson's words on it explain its universal appeal: it ' . . . abounds with images which find a mirror in every mind, and with sentiments to which every bosom returns an echo'.

**Elene** A poem in Old English by Cynewulf, preserved in *The Vercelli Book* and regarded as the poet's masterpiece. The poet relates in 14 cantos how Helena, mother of Emperor Constantine, was inspired in her old age to search for the True Cross (following her son's victory at the Milvian Bridge and his vision of the cross) and how she discovered it in the Holy Land. A 15th canto contains a fascinating personal note: the poet tells how he enjoyed this world's pleasures but lived in sin, until he was granted grace by God. Now he is old and ready to depart this life; he is at peace because he has a true understanding of the significance of the Cross. A translation of the poem by C. W. Kennedy is included in his *Early English Christian Poetry* (1952).

**Elia, The Essays of** The miscellaneous essays that Charles Lamb contributed to *The London Magazine* from August 1820 to December 1823, beginning with *Recollections of the South-Sea House*. (For the origin of the pseudonym 'Elia' (pronounced Ell-ya) see **Lamb, Charles**.) The essays contain general comment and criticism but are chiefly prized for the personal recollections of childhood, descriptions of characters from Lamb's wide range of acquaintances, his own experiences as a man, and his reflections on being a wage earner. But the personal essays should not be regarded as autobiographical; Lamb used personal experience as a starting point and then let his imagination take over. Also included are the purely fanciful or melancholy exercises that have become celebrated, such as *Dream Children*, *A Dissertation upon Roast Pig*, and *A Chapter on Ears*. Others include *Poor Relations*, *Old China*, *Christ's Hospital*, *The Superannuated Man*, and *Blakesmoor in H----shire*, which recalled his childhood days at Blakesware.

The first collection of *The Essays of Elia* was published in 1823; the remainder appeared with other essays in *The Last Essays of Elia* (1833). The first complete volume, *Elia*, was published in 1835.

**Eliot, George** 1819–80. The pseudonym of Mary Ann (*or* Marian) Evans, daughter of a Warwickshire farm manager, Robert Evans. She was born at Arbury Farm in the parish of Astley. Her childhood and education were strongly influenced by pious teaching but this was, fortunately, mitigated by her meeting with Charles Bray when she was 22. Her reading, which ranged from devotional literature and theology, through French and German writers, to the Romantics, had probably prepared her for the encounter. Charles Bray, who was still only 30, was a controversial figure with advanced views on education and religion, a sceptical philosopher who was looked at askance by Mary Ann's parents. She, however, responded to Bray's views, and though for a while she was persuaded for her family's sake to be more conformist, was reaching out to the independence of mind and spirit which was to discomfit so many of her contemporaries. Mary Ann's entry to the world of letters was as a translator of D. F. Strauss's *Das Leben Jesu*, though her name did not appear in the published volume.

After her father's death, Mary Ann travelled on the continent with Charles and Caroline Bray. Upon her return to England she renewed her acquaintance with the publisher, John Chapman, and at his behest became assistant editor when he acquired the *Westminster Review*. At Chapman's house she met many of the literary figures of the time, European and American as well as English: one of them was George Henry Lewes, two years her junior, a versatile writer who had published a successful and popular history of philosophy. This period of her life, from 1850 to 1853, while it gave her experience of writing and a close view of the literary world, contained no hint of her future career.

Her liaison with George Henry Lewes is believed to have begun in the autumn of 1853. He was married to, and was separated from, Agnes Jervis; the affair with Marian Evans (as she was calling herself now) might easily have been that, and no more, but they stayed together until he died in 1878, and his influence was of enormous importance to her and, it can be argued, to the English novel. They could not marry; Lewes had condoned his wife's infidelity (the least he could do – he was a well-known amorist himself) and could not sue for divorce. Marian allowed herself to be called Mrs Lewes whenever she and George Henry ventured abroad together.

Lewes encouraged Marian to write fiction (she had translated L. Feuerbach's *Wesen des Christentums* in 1854) and became her literary agent when she completed *The Sad Fortunes of the Revd Amos Barton*, sending it to his own publisher for *Blackwood's Magazine*, as one of a series to be called **Scenes of Clerical Life**. It was accepted and published in 1857. Next came *Mr Gilfil's Love Story*, but meanwhile John Blackwood wanted the author's name. Marian decided on George Eliot, because George was Lewes's name and Eliot an easy one to pronounce and remember. *Scenes* was completed by *Janet's Repentance* and the whole was published in book form in January

George Eliot. Photograph by Mayall, 1858.

1858. It was well received – and Dickens spotted at once that the author was a woman. In Warwickshire, her home county, the author caused a rumpus; events and characters were so truthfully presented that it was clear who the originals were. 'George Eliot' and John Blackwood were kept busy for some time replying to letters but Marian had in the meantime begun to write **Adam Bede**. Blackwood was taken into Marian's and Lewes's confidence and the identity of George Eliot was disclosed. He agreed to share the secret.

*Adam Bede* was not serialized in *Blackwood's Magazine*, but published by Blackwood in volume form in February 1859. It was a success of the first order, called by *The Times* 'a first-rate novel', and three editions were printed in the first year. Its success enabled Marian and Lewes to take a house in Wandsworth, which gave them elbow room – they were both writing – and facilities for guests. Callers included the admiring Dickens, Bulwer Lytton, Wilkie Collins and Samuel Laurence. A story, 'The Lifted Veil', was published in Blackwood's in 1859 and the next novel was **The Mill on the Floss**, published in the following year. The novelist's advance was obvious: *Adam Bede* is a notable novel by any standards, with its remarkable use of the pastoral background; *The Mill on the Floss* adds an examination of character and motive in the lives of Maggie Tulliver and her brother Tom which has rarely been bettered. **Silas Marner**, published in 1861, is a short novel and a simple one, but it is flawlessly fashioned. Once more, the pastoral background is evoked with unfailing skill.

The drawing room at The Priory, Regent's Park, which became the home of George Eliot and George Henry Lewes in 1863, and thereafter a meeting place for London's intelligentsia. An illustration for *George Eliot's Life* by J. W. Cross (1885).

Marian and Lewes went abroad before publication of *Silas Marner*, and in Florence Marian was soon hard at work researching the background for what Blackwood had referred to as 'the Italian story' in 1858. This was to be **Romola**, which she completed in 1862. However, Blackwood had been outbid and the new novel was bought by Smith, Elder for the stupendous price of £10,000 – in 1862 that sum was a fortune. Lewes has been blamed, as her literary agent, for the shabby treatment of Blackwood, a publisher – as Marghanita Laski puts it – 'such as writers dream of'; certainly Blackwood himself believed Lewes was the rapacious one. If this is true it is rather sad that Marian, if she was blameless, should have had her first failure. Compliments came, indeed, but the book was not a success, either critically or financially. The author had stepped out of rural England into the Florence of Savonarola. *Romola* was a good story, in a carefully researched setting; but the public had no desire to plough through the historical background of a long novel, which never came to life in the way her previous books had.

To recover from the effort of writing *Romola*, Marian wrote little for the next three years. Another story, 'Brother Jacob', was published in the *Cornhill* in 1864. A house was bought near Regent's Park, where Lewes instituted Sunday afternoon receptions. Marian began, and left unfinished, a blank-verse drama, *Savello*, and in March of 1865, in bad health, she began **Felix Holt**. It was finished after 14 months – and turned down by Smith, Elder. Lewes then sent it to Blackwood, without a word about Smith, Elder's refusal, and Blackwood was glad to have 'George Eliot' back. This political novel was politely received, in 1866, but was not a real success; Blackwood lost money on it. On the whole, though, there was a feeling that the author was back on native ground and that was a good thing. The next year she visited Spain, and 1868 saw the publication of an excursion into verse, *The Spanish Gypsy*. Her theme in this poem is the conflict between happiness and duty, and while it has fine passages, inevitably, its didacticism makes it unreadable now.

The following year, 1867, she began work on **Middlemarch**. It was a bad year, with Lewes's son Thornton in the grip of a fatal illness. Henry James, then 26, met George Eliot, now 50, in May. The new novel had to be laid aside while Marian gave her attention to the dying boy, though she did write the poem, *The Legend of Jubal*, the 'Brother and Sister' sonnets and others, published by Blackwood in 1874.

*Middlemarch* was published by Blackwood in

instalments, from 1871 to 1872. Its success was immediate, with readers and critics alike, and it is interesting that the *Spectator* put forward a claim for it to be regarded as one of the great books of the world. Such praise is rarely supported by posterity but *Middlemarch* goes on being acknowledged as one of the masterpieces of fiction.

Marian and Lewes were now an almost respectable couple, though Queen Victoria, who admired the novels of George Eliot very much did not receive them. They were also comfortably off and the house near Regent's Park saw a perfect parade of visitors at Lewes's Sundays: T. H. Huxley, Walter Bagehot, Browning, Burne-Jones; Herbert Spencer was an old friend, George du Maurier a new one.

In 1872, during a visit to the spa at Homburg, Marian observed the gaming tables and players, and recorded her disgust at the addiction gambling could become. This was the beginning of her next book, **Daniel Deronda**, which began to appear in instalments in 1876. An imperfect novel, it received the enormous critical attention due to the author of *Middlemarch* and was to be her last work of any consequence. Lewes died in November 1878, and Marian struggled back to life in the following year. She worked on one of his uncompleted manuscripts and published, with the encouragement of the unfailingly generous John Blackwood, the book of essays called *Impressions of Theophrastus Such*. The book made little impression; but Blackwood was no doubt right in coaxing her back to writing. That excellent man died in 1879 – but Marian, at the age of 60, was in love again, with John Walter Cross, more than 20 years her junior. She enjoyed a year of (legitimate) married life before she died in 1880.

The literary reputation of George Eliot slumped soon after her death, probably helped by Cross's biography, published in 1882. This was an idolatrous piece of whitewashing which the literary world, who knew Marian Evans and George Henry Lewes very well, rejected completely. George Eliot, one of the great English novelists, remained in the critical shadows until after World War II: Virginia Woolf had championed *Middlemarch* in 1919 (*The Common Reader*), and reassessment began with F. R. Leavis (*The Great Tradition*, 1948) and Joan Bennett (*George Eliot: The Critical Heritage*, 1948). But, as usual, the public decided for itself, ignoring the critics' pronouncements. A glance at any list of English classics in popular editions will show that the works of George Eliot have continued to be read.

**Eliot, T(homas) S(tearns)** 1888–1965. T. S. Eliot was the son of a Unitarian family whose roots lay in Massachusetts but he was born and brought up in St Louis, Missouri. His parents were wealthy and he was given a training in the classics before going to university. Eliot's mother encouraged his talent for verse, and he arrived at Harvard in 1906 eager to absorb what that great seat of learning had to offer. George Santayana and Irving Babbitt were among his teachers and the latter, particularly, influenced him to use the past to measure the present and gave him the leaning towards an antiromantic approach which coloured his work. His chief poetic interests were the works of Dante and Jules Laforgue but his studies were in philosophy.

Eliot obtained his BA and MA degrees and then embarked on a study of the English philosopher F. H. Bradley. He went to Europe in 1914, and after study in Germany, Paris, and Merton College, Oxford, settled in London. He taught at Highgate School for a time, reviewed books for *The Times Literary Supplement* and other reviews, and worked at Lloyds Bank from 1919 to 1922. He served a short term as assistant editor of *The Egoist*, and then in 1923 became editor of a newly founded quarterly review called *The Criterion*, sponsored by Lady Rothermere and published by the house of Faber & Gwyer. Faber & Gwyer became Faber & Faber and Eliot became a director; he edited *The Criterion* until it ceased publication in 1939. In 1927 Eliot was confirmed in the Church of England and became a British citizen.

The first poetry of T. S. Eliot was published in Harriet Monroe's *Poetry: A Magazine of Verse*, founded in Chicago in 1912. Conrad Aiken advised Eliot, in September 1914, to visit their compatriot Ezra Pound in London. Pound sent a copy of Eliot's 'The Love Song of J. Alfred Prufrock' to Harriet Monroe, and thereafter kept a big-brotherly eye on T. S. Eliot who was three years his junior. (The poem was written in 1911, when Eliot was 23.) *Prufrock and Other Observations* (1917) was followed by *Ara vos prec* (1920), which contained 'Gerontion'. **The Waste Land**, on which Ezra Pound had given him extensive editorial help, was published in the first number of *The Criterion* in 1922 and is dedicated to Pound. *Poems 1909–1925* (1925) collected his published poems and included 'The Hollow Men'. The next collected volume, *Collected Poems 1909–1935* (1936), contained 'Ash Wednesday', his contributions to the attractive single-poem series, the Ariel Poems, among them 'Journey of the Magi' and 'A Song for Simeon', fragments of 'Sweeney Agonistes', and 'Burnt Norton'. *Old Possum's Book of Practical Cats*

(1939) was written for children and the poems had been in private circulation for several years. 'Old Possum' was Pound's nickname for Eliot as a critic and referred to his soft-footed circuitous approach. It has enjoyed an unbroken run of success with adults and children alike and in 1981 reached a vastly wider public through the success of Andrew Lloyd Webber's musical, *Cats*.

'Sweeney Agonistes' (about 1926) was the precursor of Eliot's essays in verse drama, which culminated in a degree of popular success in the 1950s. *The Rock* (1934) was a pageant play in aid of London churches, and was first performed at Sadlers Wells. **Murder in the Cathedral** (1935) was written for the annual festival of Canterbury Cathedral; it was filmed in 1951. Eliot went to Aeschylus (*Eumenides*) for the basis of *The Family Reunion* (1939), and after the war scored a commercial as well as an artistic success with *The Cocktail Party* (1950). He went to Euripides (*Ion*) for the starting point, but no more, of *The Confidential Clerk* (1954), and to Sophocles (*Oedipus at Colonus*) for that of *The Elder Statesman* (1959). *Murder in the Cathedral* is the most successful verse play of the 20th century and is frequently revived.

Eliot's first collection of critical essays was *The Sacred Wood* (1920), from contributions to *The Egoist*, *The Athenaeum*, and *The Times Literary Supplement*. *Homage to John Dryden* (1924) contained his essays on Marvell and the Metaphysical Poets; his next volume, *For Lancelot Andrewes: Essays on Style and Order* (1928), reflects his Anglo-Catholic interests: *Dante* (1929) is regarded by many scholars as his finest critical essay. *Selected Essays* (1932, enlarged 1934 and 1951) presents his criticism and literary views of the period from 1917 to 1932, before they underwent a change. In his Harvard lectures *The Use of Poetry and the Use of Criticism* (1933) Eliot wrote: 'From time to time . . . it is desirable that some critic shall appear to review the part of our literature, and set the poets and the poems in a new order. This task is not one of revolution but of readjustment . . .' Eliot, by the 1940s and 1950s, was adjusting his own readjustments, most notably in his lecture to the British Academy on *Milton* (1947). Among other critical essays were *After Strange Gods* (1934), *Notes Towards the Definition of Culture* (1948), and *On Poetry and Poets* (1957), which contains the lecture on Milton.

T. S. Eliot's poetry also reflected his Anglo-Catholic preoccupations. 'Burnt Norton' had appeared in the 1909–35 collection; with 'East Coker' (1940), 'The Dry Salvages' (1941), and 'Little Gidding' (1942), it was published as the first poem of the celebrated sequence called *The Four Quartets* (1943). This was Eliot's last major poetic achievement, a long distance from 'The Love Song of J. Alfred Prufrock' but recognizably the work of the same poet. He was a much-honoured figure at the time of his death; the Nobel Prize for literature and the Order of Merit were both awarded him in the same year, 1948.

**Elliot, Anne** The heroine of Jane Austen's *Persuasion*, whose 'bloom had vanished early'. She re-encounters, at 27, the man she was persuaded to reject eight years before.

**Ellison, Ralph (Waldo)** 1914– . Ellison was born in Oklahoma City and studied music at Tuskegee Institute from 1933 to 1936. A meeting with fellow Black American Richard Wright in New York in 1936 led him to take up writing and he published short stories, articles and criticism in reviews and journals from 1939. He served in the merchant marine during World War II. His first and, so far only, novel was *Invisible Man* (1952), which was acclaimed on both sides of the Atlantic as one of the most impressive novels from America since World War II. The narrator is a Black American like the author; unlike the author he does not succeed in establishing an identity and at the end has acknowledged that he

T. S. Eliot, 1960.

never will. He goes to live underground, resigned to invisibility. His road to resignation is a vivid and memorable account of the modern Black American experience. The novel won the National Book Award. *Shadow and Act* (1964) is a collection of essays on Black life and culture in the USA. Ralph Ellison has enjoyed a distinguished academic career and has been Albert Schweitzer Professor in the Humanities at New York University since 1970.

**Ellwood, Thomas** 1639–1713. Ellwood was the son of an Oxfordshire squire who, according to his memoirs, suffered from a tyrannical father. Peaceable and devout, Ellwood inevitably gravitated to the society of like men and became the friend of William Penn. He became a Quaker, and was for some years reader to the blind Milton. It was Ellwood who suggested to Milton the theme of *Paradise Regained*. Ellwood was the author of *Davideis: the Life of David King of Israel* (1712), a sacred poem, *A Collection of Poems on various Subjects* (1710) and *The History of the Life of Thomas Ellwood*, published the year after his death. The last has additional value as a historical document; his account of prison life (he suffered in prison, like all the first Quakers) in the 17th century is vivid and detailed. Ellwood prepared Fox's *Journal* for publication.

**Elsie Venner:** *A Romance of Destiny*. A novel by Oliver Wendell Holmes (1), published in 1861, after first appearing in serial form as *The Professor's Story*. Holmes, a scientific humanist, detested the Calvinism of his forebears and stated his intention to 'test the doctrine of original sin and human responsibility'.

The professor's story concerns a New England girl, Elsie Venner, whose serpentine nature he traces to an incident during her mother's pregnancy when she suffered a snakebite. Elsie loves one of the professor's students, Bernard Langdon, but he does not return her love, though she saves his life when he encounters a rattlesnake. She also exercises a peculiar fascination for a schoolteacher, Helen Darley. Elsie, rejected by Bernard, falls ill and as she weakens her strange quality begins to fade. When it leaves her completely she dies.

**Elyot, Sir Thomas** *c.*1490–1546. Elyot was probably born in Wiltshire, and he was Clerk of Assize to the Justices on the Western Circuit. His father was a jurist and Elyot learned Latin and Greek at home. He completed his training in law at the Middle Temple and his education at Oxford. As a young man he enjoyed the friendship of Linacre and More and was advanced by Wolsey to

Clerk of the Privy Council in 1523. Elyot lost his position when Wolsey fell from favour in 1529 but he and Thomas Cromwell had become friends and it was through Cromwell's influence that Elyot returned to public life. Meanwhile, living in the country, Elyot wrote and published *The boke named the governour* in 1531, which he dedicated to Henry VIII. In the same year he was appointed ambassador to the court of the emperor, Charles V. *The Castel of Helth* (1539) followed some dialogues and translations from the classics and the early Christian fathers and the first version (1538) of his Latin-English dictionary, in which work he was encouraged by the king, to whom it is dedicated.

*The boke named the governour*, better known as *The Book of the Governor*, follows the impulse shown by the other humanists of his time to instruct those in power in the discharge of their office: Castiglione, Machiavelli, Erasmus, and Patricius can be named, among others less famous. Elyot's book is full of good sense, based on classical precedents, and written in clear and careful prose. Seven editions were printed in 50 years and a critical edition, edited by H. S. Croft, was published in 1880.

*The Castel of Helth* is a medical handbook, notable inasmuch as it was written in English and by a layman. It contained prescriptions and remedies culled from Galen onwards with plentiful anecdotes. Inevitably Elyot was attacked by the doctors; he was also attacked by his own class, who thought that a gentleman should have better work to do. He delivered a spirited retort to both in the second edition.

*The Dictionary of Syr T. Elyot Knyght* appeared in a revised edition (1545) as *Bibliotheca Eliotae*. It proved to be of great value in England at a time when the classics were being rediscovered and revalued. Elyot wrote in his own language for his countrymen and helped them to an appreciation of the civilizing influence of the classical writers.

*Emarè* A verse romance of 1035 lines in 12-line stanzas, dating from the late 14th century. The story of the constant Constance was well known to the medieval world and Gower used it in *Confessio Amantis*. See also **Canterbury Tales, The** for *The Man of Law's Tale*.

**Emerson, Ralph Waldo** *c.*1803–82. The son of William Emerson, minister of the First Unitarian Church of his native Boston, Emerson himself became a pastor in 1829 after he completed his education at Harvard. His course in life seemed set to follow that of his father and grandfather. But the orthodoxy of Unitarianism, so far removed from the original Calvinism of New

Ralph Waldo Emerson.

England, was something Emerson could not accept. He saw orthodox behaviour as an obstacle to personal integrity. His wife, Ellen Tucker, whom he had married in 1829, died in 1831 and in the following year he was involved in a controversy with his congregation over a sermon on the Lord's Supper. He resigned his ministry and sailed for Europe in 1832, his mind disturbed by personal grief and religious confusion. He had begun to keep a journal in 1820 while still at Harvard and the habit continued through the rest of his life.

Emerson was in Europe for a year and met Thomas Carlyle, Coleridge, and Wordsworth. His interest and wide reading in religion and philosophy received a stimulus from his contact with European thinking and back in Boston he drifted away from preaching and into the broader field of lecturing. He drew his material from the journals to which he committed his reflections. The restraints of the pulpit removed, he found that he could command attention from huge audiences who came to hear him expound his natural philosophy. He was much sought after and was one of the first and most successful exponents of the art so popular with Americans – that of the lecturer in cultural subjects. In 1834 he married Lydia Jackson and in the following year the Emersons settled in Concord, Massachusetts, where his ancestors had first settled in the New World and where Transcendentalism took form. He became part of the circle which included Hawthorne, Bronson Alcott, Thoreau, and Margaret Fuller.

In 1836 Emerson's first book, **Nature**, was published. *The American Scholar*, an oration in which he applied Transcendentalist views to national and cultural questions, was published in 1837. In the following year Emerson gave the Divinity School Address at Harvard. His statement of his belief that the intuitive spiritual experience of the individual was of more importance than any formal church ensured his exclusion from Harvard for almost 30 years.

The tendency of the Concord group toward communal experiment was not favoured by Emerson but he was interested in reform and his ideas extended the range of his lectures. In 1840 he became involved in the publication of the Transcendentalist quarterly magazine, *The Dial*, and was its editor from 1842. More important was the publication of his first book of *Essays* (1841): another volume was published in 1844. Emerson's reputation, already considerable in the USA, was now established in Europe also. In 1847 he earned further distinction as a poet. His first collection, *Poems*, displayed his intellectual discipline and his ability to express his thoughts in verse. A further collection, *May-Day and Other Pieces*, was published in 1867. Emerson wrote the first American poetry to show a movement away from its English base and it is worth noting that he was among the first to praise the work of Walt Whitman.

Emerson went to England in 1847 and lectured in Oxford and London. He renewed his friendship with Carlyle and met English intellectuals. At home again in Concord he published his English lectures, **Representative Men**, in 1850. *English Traits* (1856) is a critical but amiable examination of his erstwhile hosts. During this period, as the journals demonstrate, he became deeply interested in the issue of slavery and saw its abolition as a matter of paramount importance. Two further volumes of his lectures were published – *The Conduct of Life* (1860) and *Society and Solitude* (1870). He was listened to with such attention that he was in demand as far west as the Mississippi but he gave up his strenuous lecture tours in 1866 – the year in which Harvard, no less, conferred on him the degree of Doctor of Law. Thereafter Emerson's power began to wane though he lectured at Harvard in 1870 and travelled to California (1871) and Europe (1872). He lived for another ten years, cared for with devotion by his wife and four children while his mind simply faded away.

Ralph Waldo Emerson is justly celebrated as a philosopher and a poet whose work is a major contribution to the development of life and letters in America. Times change and his essays and printed lectures cannot escape the historical perspective. This does not reduce his importance but his philosophy has less significance for us than it had for his contemporaries. His poetry maintains its position; among the first American poets his place is an honoured one. As a liberal idealist with a gift for communication he was unrivalled. He had no philosophical system; that was part of his strength. He believed that individualism, a refusal to conform, self-reliance, the acknowledgment of instincts, and the value of optimism were far easier to understand than any system.

Edward Waldo Emerson edited his father's *Complete Works* (1903–04) and his *Journals* (ten volumes, 1909–14). The *Journals* are regarded by many scholars as Emerson's best works, a remarkable record of the tensions, doubts, and flights of happiness of his life. Emerson's *Letters* were edited by R. L. Rusk and published in six volumes in 1939.

**Emigrants, The**  A novel by Gilbert Imlay, first published in 1793. It is the first novel to use the frontier area between Pennsylvania and the Mississippi as a setting but has little else to recommend it. It is told in epistolary form and champions social reform, the rights of women, and liberal divorce laws. But it offers the USA as the promised land at the expense of the 'old world', and Imlay's presentation is too biased and sentimental to be of any lasting value.

**Emilia**  See *Othello, The Moor of Venice*.

**Eminent Victorians**  See **Strachey, (Giles) Lytton**.

**Emma**  Jane Austen's novel was begun in January 1814 and completed in March of the following year. It was first published in 1816.

For many of her admirers this is Jane Austen's best novel. She was uncertain of its chances of success – it followed *Mansfield Park*, a work which she believed contained 'good sense', and she thought that Emma Woodhouse was a heroine that no one but herself would much like. Jane was right in both cases, if perhaps only half-right in the latter. Emma Woodhouse is liked by many people while others, like the present writer, ponder on the future life of Mr Knightley and wonder how much Emma has really changed. It is a mark of Jane Austen's genius that Emma, like her or not, is a creation that can provoke a lively argument. About the merits of the novel there can hardly be argument; it is one of the finest prose comedies in the English language.

Anne (Miss Taylor), governess and companion to Emma Woodhouse and her father (an amiable hypochondriac), has left the household to marry Mr Weston, a neighbour. Emma, bereft of her companionship, makes a protégée of pretty Harriet Smith, the 17-year-old boarder at Mrs Goddard's school, a girl with no future since she is illegitimate. Emma, self-satisfied and self-important, sets about arranging Harriet's life.

George Knightley of Donwell Abbey is a friend of the Woodhouses, and his younger brother John is married to Emma's sister Isabella. He laughs at Emma's smug assumption that Anne Taylor's marriage is largely due to her skill as a matchmaker but he dislikes her attempts to manipulate Harriet into what she decides is a good marriage. One of his tenants, a young farmer named Robert Martin, proposes to Harriet; Emma sees to it that Harriet turns him down. She tries to effect a match for Harriet with Elton, a young vicar, in spite of Knightley's warning: Elton despises Harriet and has set his sights higher – he wants Emma, a rich girl with a comfortable home. Emma, for her part, half fancies herself in love with Mr Weston's son by his first marriage, Frank Churchill, who has now appeared on the scene. Harriet, meanwhile, has become more interested in George Knightley and his unaffected warmth and intelligence. Emma, reassuring Harriet after the departure of Elton, is now considering Frank Churchill for her: she has always, without giving the thought expression, regarded Knightley as hers. The realization of this, with the discovery that Frank Churchill is engaged to Jane Fairfax and that Harriet might supplant her in Knightley's affections, delivers the shock to Emma that forces her to examine her own conduct and resolve to behave better. Knightley proposes to her while Harriet, left to decide for herself, happily marries the young farmer, Robert Martin.

**Empedocles on Etna**  A poem by Matthew Arnold, first published in 1852. The philosopher Empedocles (*c.*450 BC) has fallen on bad times; once a powerful figure whose voice was listened to, he is now a lonely exile from his city, Agrigentum, and his philosophy no longer supports him. He goes to Etna with Pausanias, a physician who hopes to cure his depression. They are joined by the poet Callicles. The philosopher's despair does not yield to the wisdom of the physician or the strength of poetry and at the end he kills himself in the crater of Etna. The songs of the poet Callicles were published separately by Arnold in 1855 in *Poems: Second Series* before he republished the whole poem in 1867. See also **Arnold, Matthew.**

**Empson, William** 1906–   . A native of Yorkshire, Empson was educated at Winchester School and went on to study mathematics and literature at Cambridge. His university dissertation became his first critical work, *Seven Types of Ambiguity* (1930), in which he illustrated, by copious quotation, how many arresting effects in poetry arise from double meanings, conscious or not, which reflect echoes and tensions in the poet's mind. Empson's use of ambiguity in *Poems* (1935) is deliberate, and too clever for most readers, needing notes to explain the poems.

During the 1930s Empson was Professor of English Literature in Tokyo and Peking; he was occupied in broadcasting to the Far East during World War II, and returned to Peking to teach after the war. In 1953 he was appointed Professor of English Literature at the University of Sheffield. His best-known volume of verse, *The Gathering Storm*, was published in 1940; it drew on his experience in the Far East and also made clear his attitude to the forces that were dragging the world into war. His complete poetical output is in *Collected Poems* (1955). Further volumes of criticism are *Some Versions of Pastoral* (1935), *The Structure of Complex Words* (1951), and *Milton's God* (1961), a study of *Paradise Lost*.

**Encantadas, The,** *or Enchanted Isles.* See **Piazza Tales, The**.

**Endymion**   Benjamin Disraeli's last novel, published in 1880. It details the rise to positions of eminence and influence of Endymion and Myra Pitt Ferrars, twin children of a rising politician who dies penniless. Myra rises in the world because she is beautiful and captivating; Endymion benefits from this – his brother-in-law is Lord Roehampton, the Foreign Secretary. The novel gives a picture of politics and society in the 1830s, with Palmerston represented as Lord Roehampton.

**Endymion:** *A Poetic Romance.* A poem in four books by John Keats, first published in 1818. Keats inscribed the poem to the memory of Thomas Chatterton. The basis of the poem is the Greek legend of Endymion, variously a prince of Elis or a beautiful young shepherd, who falls asleep on the slopes of Mount Latmos. The moon goddess Selene (Cynthia in Keats's version) falls in love with him and causes him to sleep eternally so that she may always enjoy his beauty. In Keats's poem Cynthia takes him away to eternal life with her, but into this fabric are woven the stories of Venus and Adonis, Glaucus and Scylla, and Arethusa, as well as an ambitious, if not completely successful, allegory of the quest for perfection and the distraction of human beauty. The celebrated 'Hymn to Pan' is in Book I; the roundelay 'O Sorrow', leading into the lovely song of the Indian maid, 'Beneath my palm trees, by the river side', is in Book IV. The poem is full of music and colour and sustains an enchanted atmosphere throughout.

**England's Helicon**   A miscellany of poems first published in 1600 and generally acknowledged as the best of the Elizabethan anthologies. The compiler's name is not known. Among minor poets represented are Nicholas Breton, Richard Barnfield, and Anthony Munday (as 'Shepheard Tonie', it is believed). Some of the pieces signed 'Ignoto' may be the work of Ralegh, and there are contributions from Spenser, Drayton, Sidney, Marlowe, Robert Greene, and Thomas Lodge. A notable feature is the inclusion of songs of the musicians of the period, among them Byrd, Dowland, and Morley. The first modern edition of the collection was by A. H. Bullen, in 1887; a later one, by H. Macdonald, was published in 1950.

**England's Parnassus**   A collection of 'elegant extracts' (selected quotations) from Elizabethan poets, first published in 1600. The compiler is believed to have been one Robert Allott. There is a modern edition by C. Crawford (1913).

**English Constitution, The**   See **Bagehot, Walter**.

**English Humourists of the Eighteenth Century, The**   A group of lectures which W. M. Thackeray delivered in England and the USA in 1852–53. The series was a great success and the lectures were published in 1853.

**English Language, The**   To every human being his mother tongue is of unique importance. Objectively, however, we can claim that English is unique among the languages of the world. It has at present the widest use of any language in history, both in numbers of users (amongst whom native speakers are probably in a minority) and in range of uses. The corollary of this is that it has an extraordinary diversity of forms. Only mankind's exceptional capacity for abstraction enables us to conceive of such a thing as *the* English language underlying the hugely different realizations we are liable to encounter. But the right-hand man of this capacity for abstraction is the written form of the language. This prevails worldwide, with only trivial divergences, and of course has long been the vehicle of literature.

Even where writers attempt to portray dialect their portrayal has for centuries been mediated by the conventions of standard orthography.

What is true of the current range of English is almost matched by the duration and diversity of the historical record. At fourteen hundred years this is by no means the longest in the world, but it is among those of high duration, and it incorporates changes, sometimes obvious, sometimes covert, of immense extent and profundity.

*External History*. The language came to England in the mouths of Germanic settlers who arrived in substantial numbers from the mid-5th century, though some had certainly come earlier. They were of various tribes, including Angles and Saxons, from a long stretch of the northern European littoral. Their dialects, which were closely related but not uniform, belonged to the wider Germanic (Gmc) family, itself a subgroup of Indo-European (IE), whose membership includes the Celtic (the antecedent language family in Britain), the Italic-Romance (including Latin and all its modern descendants), the Hellenic, the Balto-Slavonic, the Indo-Iranian, and many others. As always happens, the new societies in what is now England developed their own linguistic norms; their members converged in usage, and in doing so diverged from that of the Germanic communities they left behind. Extension of settlements throughout the country was a protracted business. Once settlements were made the village would constitute, for most people, their effective circle of communication. Under such conditions distinct dialects develop in two or three generations, and it is natural to suppose that this happened from village to village in pre-Conquest England. Customarily four large dialect areas are recognized, not because speech in these areas can have been internally uniform, but because this is as much as we can detect from the surviving written records: these are the South-Eastern, South-Western, Mercian (Midland), and Northumbrian. The language from the settlement to the Norman Conquest is called Old English (OE), and in late OE West Saxon had national currency as a standard for written prose.

The first settlers were only minimally literate. A tiny minority of them were masters of the runic method of inscription in angular symbols designed for carving, developed in the Gmc world probably about AD 200. Literacy in the normal sense was a by-product of the conversion to Christianity, beginning in the south with the Roman mission of Augustine in 597, and almost simultaneously with Celtic missions in the north. The alphabet developed for OE was basically Roman, omitting *j*, *q*, *v*, and usually *k* and *x*, and adding one Celtic and two runic symbols. The first written English words in it date from 597, but continuous documents in English are considerably later, though some incorporate 6th-century material which at first had been transmitted orally. Literacy remained rare, the province of two minority groups, the clergy and a handful of well-born laymen. Surviving pre-Conquest manuscripts are a small fraction of what must have existed, but even if all had survived their representation of the language would have been selective. Manuscript production was costly in materials and skilled labour and would have been authorized only for purposes which seemed convincing to ecclesiastical authorities or landowners. The surviving records are also unevenly distributed over a period of five centuries and a wide geographical area.

From the close of the 8th century, Viking raids and eventual settlement over most of northern and eastern England brought into contact two languages closely related in origin and mutually comprehensible. In 1066 came a shock as profound but wholly different in kind. The Normans (themselves originally Vikings – Northmen) were, by comparison with 11th-century Englishmen, barbarians whose strength lay in military and administrative success, the bringer of wealth. Once again the great religious houses were as much a target as the great secular estates – now not for plunder but for takeover. In most parts of the country control of the leading scriptoria soon passed into Norman hands; documents not written in Latin were for the most part written in French, and original English texts are rare from 1066 to *c*.1200. We have least documentation for the century that seems to have witnessed the deepest and swiftest changes ever to have affected the language. Norman influence was not, like Scandinavian influence, variable by locality, but variable by class, affecting most those who had most to do with centres of wealth and power, where Norman-French was current. In 1204 new legislation prevented the holding of estates in both England and France. Thenceforth those who stayed were committed to England. Their families grew up English-speaking and English began to extend into public and governmental functions. During the same period English took its first small step overseas, to Ireland, with the settlement of an English landowning cadre in 1210.

In the following centuries two developments proceeded hand in hand – a vast increase in the number and types of English documents and an extension of the uses of English for all public purposes. Generally the forms of writing show marked discontinuities from those current in OE, mainly under French influence; what is more, the national currency of one standard form has been lost. Most scribes clearly wrote within a tradition they had learnt, but these traditions were local, and so diverse that a recent survey has identified over 1100 of them in a single century. However, the increased public role of English created a need for standardization. From 1330 to 1430 four successive and competing standards have been identified. Type III is familiar today as Chaucer's English, and Type IV is the ancestor of the modern standard. When printing was introduced in 1476 the existence of identical multiple copies made standardization even more important. Neither 15th-century nor 16th-century printed English is standard in the modern sense of being virtually self-consistent and uniform, but it is broadly true that, punctuation apart, Caxton established the range of options within which the modern system would be selected. In large measure the spellings we now use are those favoured by Johnson in his *Dictionary* (1755), but he correctly claimed that most of his preferences were determined by tradition.

English from about the Norman Conquest to the emergence of Type IV is known as Middle English (ME), and from the mid-15th century to the present as Modern English (ModE), within which Present-day English (PE) is distinguished. There are long periods of overlap and transition, and change takes place at different rates from dialect to dialect; the dates are not meant to be precise.

The 16th century saw the inception of two main developments which were to continue to the present day. Externally these involved the first planting of the language outside Europe, through exploration, trade, settlement, and colonization, in Africa, America, and the Far East. In most of these distant places the English were preceded by and interacted with other Europeans – Portuguese, Spanish, Italian, French, Dutch. They encountered new flora, fauna, topographical and climatic features, commodities, processes, social organizations, and languages, not only the languages of Africa, Asia, and America; there was greater linguistic influence from other Europeans than there had ever been in Europe, except from the French. They developed new institutions and established new kinds of official. Everything had to be named. The linguistic effect was overwhelmingly on the repertoire of nouns.

Among the commodities were human cargo, slaves from many African tribes transported in conditions where inevitably their African linguistic heritage was blended with the language of the owners to create new languages whose Englishness is hotly disputed.

In the late 18th century Australia and New Zealand were settled, and in the 19th century southern and eastern Africa.

Meanwhile, the War for Independence in America was rapidly followed by Webster's declaration that 'our honor requires us to have a system of our own, in language as well as government' (1789). He encoded this, the source of the differences in written standard English between America and Britain to this day.

English was therefore in an unprecedented position when the 19th–20th-century explosion of scholarship, scientific discovery, and technical development took place. So many of the early advances were made by English speakers and published in English that researchers everywhere had to know English, and its scholarly use snowballed. When a language of worldwide currency was required for international air traffic it had to be English. In many countries where English has no native speakers it is the only practicable medium of higher education. Its worldwide role has increased, not shrunk, with the decline of the Empire.

Reverting to the 16th century, the second main development is preoccupation with the identification and fostering of a spoken standard on a par with the written one. Commentators agree in giving it a socio-geographical basis: it is the speech of courtly (not ordinary) Londoners, but it can also be heard from a thinly scattered population of gentry in every county. Though there were to be many modifications, we recognize for the first time a distinctively modern variety-structure typical of England – not of Britain, and certainly not of English worldwide.

*Internal structure.* A systematic account of a language needs to describe two interdependent systems – systems of transmission and of meaning. The primary means of transmission is speech; secondary, less widely distributed but not necessarily derivative, is writing. The meanings and distinctions which can or must be transmitted are organized in two ways: they may be realized by open-class items, infinitely extensible rapidly changing repertoires, the vocabulary of a language, notably nouns, verbs, adjectives, and adverbs; or closed-system items, each set few in number, rarely added to or lost, its members interdependent. These constitute the grammar and may be realized by abstract contrasts, such as tense, or by wordlike items, such as prepositions, conjunctions, and personal pronouns.

Only the briefest characterization of the English sound system is possible, and some characteristics of orthography have already been mentioned. Writing in English centres on letters, and it may be for this reason that we tend to think of strings of distinctive segments (phonemes) as the essential constituents of speech. They do indeed have an important function; changing the initial segment enables us to distinguish *bin* from *din*, *kin*, *gin*, etc., the middle one *bin* from *ban*, *bun*, *bean*, etc., and the final one *bin* from *bid*, *bit*, *big*, etc. Most varieties of English have at all times had rather more than 40 of these distinctive sounds, and though their lexical distribution has changed through time the overall shape of the system has been remarkably constant. But in many ways the suprasegmentals, which writing largely ignores, are more primary in English than the segmental sounds. These involve syllables, what shapes they can take, how stress contrasts are distributed over them, and temporal patterning (rhythm) and pitch movement (intonation). An example of the dominance of suprasegmentals can be seen in the vowel system: stressed syllables are the domain of a system of some 20 different vowels; unstressed syllables of only two. With minor variations this has been true for a thousand years.

In what we do know of OE vocabulary over half the words (normally the commonest) are of IE origin, about one sixth Gmc, one sixth borrowed from Latin (usually the rarest), and the rest from minor or unknown sources. Vocabulary then, as at all times, responded to new demands to a large extent by word formation (WF) (chiefly compounding, as in modern *blackbird*, or derivation, as in *blacking*). In late OE clearly Scandinavian influence must have been great in the north and east, but few loanwords appear in the record till ME; those that have stayed in the language include basic words of every grammatical class, e.g. *law* (replacing OE *ae*), *egg* (replacing OE *aeg*), *ill*, *take*, *till*, *they*, *their*, *them*; hundreds have been lost. The influence of French, mainly after the Norman Conquest, was also slow to appear in the record. However, by the late 14th century Chaucer alone uses some 4000 French loans, which represent almost all semantic fields. In subsequent centuries loans flooded into English from over 100 other languages, but at all times French and classical loans have been most numerous.

Since the Norman Conquest additional methods of formation have come into prominence: zero–derivation, in which a word is established in a new grammatical class without change of form (cf. *look*, *walk*, *love*, sbs. and vs.);

back–derivation, as when *peddle*, *burgle* are formed from *pedlar*, *burglar*, various sorts of sound-motivation, such as vowel gradation in *flim-flam*, *shilly-shally*, or of graphic motivation, as in the acronyms *radar*, *NATO*; there are also invented and blended words (e.g. *blatant*, *brunch*). In the present century about 30 words a day, on average, have been added to the repertoire. Naturally there are losses as well as gains – of the recorded OE stock about seven items have been lost for every four preserved. Survivals may not be obvious – they can undergo radical change of shape (OE *nafo-gar*, PE *auger*) or meaning (OE *thing*, 'meeting').

It is in grammatical structure that English has undergone the most sweeping changes. Three are of central importance. First the structure of the noun phrase (NP), which in OE was more like its Latin than its PE counterpart in its range of declensions, genders, cases, and rules of concord. By early ME the present simplified system was complete in essentials, but a new contrast – definite (using articles *the*, *a*) had grown up. What have remained constant are rules of order (*the duke's large well-built timber-framed hunting-lodge*, for instance).

In the verb phrase (VP) Gmc had diverged sharply from IE. An older system of rich inflectional contrasts gave way to an oversimplified tense system inherited by OE. The past tense was marked either by internal change or, following a Gmc innovation, by adding a suffix; thus OE *he rad* (corresponding to PE *he rode*, *was riding*, *has ridden*, *had ridden*) or *he lufode* (*he loved*, etc.). In contrast with the past was the non-past tense, corresponding to everything else (*he rideþ*, PE *he rides*, *is riding*, *will/shall ride*). This drastically reduced system was already being re-expanded in Gmc and the process has continued ever since, using not inflection but preverbal particles, auxiliaries, forming at any one time a closed system. The perfective (forms in *has/have/had* plus past participle) is pre-English, and so is a new passive (in OE with *weorþan*, 'become', later with *be*, plus past participle). Within OE clearly modal uses begin (those now involving *will*, *would*, *shall*, *should*, *can*, *could*, *may*, *might*, *must*) but the modals did not emerge as a system till early ModE nor take their full present functions till *c*.1700. The aspect contrast (*he is riding* carved out of the former territory of *he rides*) did not come into its own till the 17th century (though scattered examples are frequent before that) and is still evolving. The semantico-syntactic categories have been refined; referential distinctions (number and person) have declined. Except in *be* (*was*, *were*, a pure number contrast) only the non-past is affected, distinguishing third person singular from the rest – singular or plural – by addition of -s. However, the largely syntactic contrast of subjunctive with indicative has also been almost completely lost.

Verbs are central to the functioning of negation, and here too change has been profound. OE negated by putting *ne* before the verb, a pattern that goes back to IE. This changed steadily and *c*.1600 began to take on its present shape, which has two essential features – the first the use of *not*, *n't* after the finite verb; second, the requirement that *not*, *n't* be attached only to auxiliaries, so that if no auxiliary is present the dummy *do/does/did* must be inserted (*he isn't riding* but *he doesn't ride*). The interrogative was made in OE by simple inversion of subject and verb; now this too must have an auxiliary as its domain and calls on *do/does/did* in the absence of any other (*he's riding, isn't he?* but *he rides, doesn't he?*).

The third major area of change is clause structure. In OE, as in Latin for the same reason, the subject did not always need to be expressed. The nucleus of the clause, the prime domain of rules of order, was therefore the verb and whatever nominal structure was needed to complete it. With the reduction of verb inflections expression of the subject became indispensable; it was given initial position, and if it had no semantically required realization a dummy was inserted (*It's raining*; *There isn't enough*). From the 15th century the nucleus of the sentence has been subject–verb, in that order (except for interrogation or special effect). Rules of order were also much affected in OE, as in modern German, by the nature of the clause and its type of onset. All these special patterns were abandoned in favour of the nuclear type.

It is no wonder that a language which has been the vehicle of much of the experience of so much of humanity should also be the vehicle of the world's richest literature, not only English literature but that of English-speaking communities in every continent and of an unparalleled number of great writers whose mother tongue was not English. Yet, as we have seen, 'English' subsumes many Englishes. Each has in its repertoire many 'false friends', words and structures that look familiar but have quite different functions in the text from those the reader expects. Constant vigilance is needed to save the inexhaustible well from turning into a snake-pit.

BARBARA M. H. STRANG

***English Traveller, The*** A tragedy by Thomas Heywood, first published in 1633. The date of its first performance is not known but it may have been many years before. *A Woman Killed with Kindness* was published in 1607 and first acted four years before that; but that play succeeds in the handling of a domestic tragedy, which *The English Traveller* approaches with much less certainty – and supports with a complicated subplot based on the *Mostellaria* of Plautus. *The English Traveller* was probably written earlier.

The main plot concerns the return of the traveller, Geraldine, to find that the woman he loves has married. Her husband is an old and worthy gentleman named Wincot, to whom Geraldine is beholden. Geraldine and Mistress Wincot make a promise to each other; she will marry him when Wincot dies and, until then, he will remain unmarried. But Geraldine's friend Delavil seduces Wincot's wife and the knowledge of this prompts the heartbroken Geraldine to set out on further travels. Wincot gives a feast to honour his departure; his wife reproaches Geraldine for deserting her. The sorely tried Geraldine is thereby provoked to a denunciation of her as an adulteress and thus the happiness of all three is destroyed.

**Enobarbus, Domitius** In Shakespeare's *Antony and Cleopatra*, Antony's friend and a commentator on the situation of his friend. Enobarbus acknowledges the fascination of Cleopatra and delivers the famous apostrophe of Act II Scene 2, but he is uneasy about Antony's complete surrender to her. He deserts Antony at the end and dies heartbroken.

***Enoch Arden*** A poem by Alfred Tennyson, written between 1861 and 1862 and first published in 1864. The poem was based on a prose sketch written for Tennyson by his friend Thomas Woolner, the painter. A similar theme occurs in Elizabeth Gaskell's novel *Sylvia's Lovers* (1863) and in Adelaide Anne Procter's poem 'Homeward Bound' (1858). The chief characters in Tennyson's poem are Enoch Arden, a sailor's orphan son, Philip Ray, a miller's son, and Annie Lee whom they both love, the prettiest girl in the little seaport town. Enoch works very hard and succeeds in buying his own boat and becoming a successful fisherman. He wins Annie and Philip accepts the fact that she loves him best. Enoch and Annie enjoy seven years of married life until Enoch is badly injured in a fall. They and their children endure considerable privation when a rival fisherman takes advantage of Enoch's accident to usurp his trade. For his family's sake Enoch sails on a merchantman; before he leaves he sells his boat and with the money opens a store for Annie to live on until he returns with a seaman's pay. The store does not succeed and now Philip comes to Annie's aid, caring for her and her children until Enoch returns. But the ship is wrecked and Enoch believed lost, and Annie eventually marries Philip. Enoch has survived, however, and after being rescued from a lonely island, returns. He observes the happiness of Annie and Philip and the children, and quietly resolves to leave them be. No one recognizes him; but he confides his secret to Miriam, the tavern keeper, when he knows he is dying. It is Miriam who tells of Enoch's death; she conveys his last blessing to his wife and children, and to Philip.

**Enquiry Concerning Human Understanding, An** See *Treatise of Human Nature, A.*

**Enquiry Concerning the Principles of Morals, An** See *Treatise of Human Nature, A.*

**Enquiry into the Present State of Polite Learning in Europe, An** An examination by Oliver Goldsmith, first published in 1759; it was his first published book. The author traces the course of polite learning from classical times to his own and examines its condition in western Europe. He finds it in decay in England and seeks the reasons; he concludes that university education is unsatisfactory, that poetry is being stifled by pedantry and is too far removed from a natural concern with natural matters, and that dramatic writers are obliged to follow the rules of current taste if they want to be heard. The book is regarded as too short to contain Goldsmith's ambitious statement but interesting as a declaration of his artistic beliefs.

**Entail, The** A novel by John Galt, first published in 1823.

The obsession of Claud Walkinshaw, a packman, is to recover the estates which formerly belonged to his family. He can only bring this about by disinheriting his eldest son in favour of his second, an idiot, and he goes to those lengths. The story follows the disastrous recoil on the Walkinshaw children and grandchildren. The novel is powerful in many scenes but is not a complete success, chiefly because of the shift of interest, after Claud Walkinshaw's death, to his widow.

**Eothen** See **Kinglake, Alexander William**.

**Epicoene,** *or The Silent Woman*. A comedy by Ben Jonson, first produced in 1609 and first published in 1616.

The plot concerns the deception of Morose, a self-centred bachelor with a detestation of noise. Suspecting that his nephew, Sir Dauphine Eugenie, finds him ridiculous, Morose proposes to remove him from his will; he also intends to marry if he can find a woman who is quiet enough. He is told of such a lady by his barber, Cutbeard, who brings him Epicoene, soft-spoken and of few words. Morose marries her but immediately after the ceremony Epicoene is transformed; she becomes loquacious and quarrelsome. Then the house is invaded by noisy well-wishers; among them are Sir Jack Daw and Sir Amorous LaFoole, who both claim to have enjoyed Epicoene's favours in the past, and a group called the Ladies Collegiate – 17th-century exponents of women's liberation – to advise Epicoene on how to manage a husband. In the end the distraught Morose is forced to accept his nephew's help in getting rid of Epicoene – but he must give Sir Dauphine a generous allowance and restore his inheritance. Morose agrees: his nephew thereupon removes Epicoene's wig and reveals that 'she' is a youth who has been trained for the plot. Morose is obliged to accept the bargain – and Daw and LaFoole to cover their embarrassment as best they can.

**Epicurean, The** A romance by Thomas Moore, first published in 1827. The story tells how Alciphron, an Epicurean philosopher, visits Egypt in the 3rd century AD to search for the secret of eternal life. Assisting a priestess, Alethe, in her duties, he discovers that she is a secret Christian, and he helps her to escape from the temple. Through her he is converted to Christianity, and when she suffers martyrdom he is condemned to the mines, where he dies.

**epigram** Originally, in ancient Greece, an epigram was an inscription, usually on a tomb. However, the term came to be applied to any short, condensed, and pointed poem; it could be not only elegiac but also amorous, anecdotal, contemplative, or satiric. Often an epigram ends with a witty or surprising turn of thought. The Latin poet Martial provided the model for the sharp satiric epigram. The form was favoured by early 17th-century English poets – notably Donne, Herrick, and Ben Jonson, who acknowledged the classical poets as their masters.

**Epigrams** Ben Jonson's poems called *Epigrams* were published in the 1616 edition of his works. The satirical epigrams reflect the poet's sharp view of contemporary manners and they have little appeal for the modern reader. Better known are the sweeter-toned addresses, compliments, and epitaphs – among the last named are poems on the poet's son ('On my first sonne') and on a child actor ('On Salomon Pavy, a Child of Queen Elizabeth's Chapel').

***Epithalamion*** The title of Edmund Spenser's poem comes from Greek and refers to the marriage chamber. The poem was published in 1595 with the sonnet sequence *Amoretti* and is almost certainly a celebration of Spenser's marriage to Elizabeth Boyle in 1594. The events of the wedding day are followed, from the joyous morning to the fulfilment of the wedding night. Spenser's imagery is rich and the music of this celebrated hymn is remarkably well sustained – his finest work in the opinion of some scholars.

**Erasmus, Desiderius** *c.*1466–1536. Erasmus was probably illegitimate and was born in Rotterdam. His father's name was Gerrit or Gerard; Erasmus is believed to have been a Greek equivalent of Gerard: Desiderius is the Latin form of Erasmus and the great Dutch humanist combined the two to give himself a public name in adult life. The meaning is 'the one desired'. He received his education in the cloisters and yielded to the family pressure to become a monk at the Augustinian abbey of Steyn, near Gouda, in 1486. He was ordained a priest in 1492, but was fortunate in the patronage of Henry of Bergen, Bishop of Cambrai, who gave him permission to leave the monastery. After four years of study in Paris he gained a pupil in William Blount, Baron Mountjoy, whom he accompanied to England in 1499. His pupil was to become his patron, and Erasmus enjoyed six very rewarding months in the company of the foremost English scholars – Colet, More, Grocyn, Linacre, and Fisher. John Colet, who shared Erasmus' dislike of scholasticism, encouraged his study of the New Testament. John Fisher persuaded him, later, to lecture on Greek at Cambridge and gave him the newly created chair of Greek and theology (1511–14).

Erasmus had been glad to return to England at Mountjoy's suggestion on the accession of Henry VIII; he had been disappointed in the intellectual climate of Italy, where he had gone in 1506. He was Thomas More's guest, writing *The Praise of Folly* (*Moriae Encomium*) in More's house at More's suggestion (1509), and was honoured by the universities of Oxford and Cambridge. During this period in England Erasmus completed his translation into Latin of the New Testament and received the benefice of Aldington from Warham, Archbishop of Canterbury.

In 1516 Erasmus was invited to Brussels by the future Charles V and became a royal councillor for a brief period. In 1517 the pope freed him from his monastic obligations and Erasmus resumed his travels, coming to rest in Basle in 1521. He made his home there in the house of the printer John Froben. He was obliged to flee the city during the Reformation and lived in Freiburg-im-Breisgau for six years but in 1535 was able to return to Basle, where he died.

Erasmus was one of the moving spirits of the Reformation. He was acutely aware of the corruption of the clergy and his writings satirized them mercilessly. His Latin translation of the New Testament (*Novum Instrumentum*, 1516) was accompanied by a blistering commentary on the condition of the church. *The Praise of Folly* is a satire directed against monasticism, highly placed churchmen, and theologians. Erasmus was averse to the metaphysical speculation of his day and an early work, his *Enchiridion Militis Christiani* (1504), indicates that his own Christian faith was a straightforward matter. This book, translated into English by William Tyndale in 1533 as *The Manuell of the Christen Knyght*, is a manual of simple piety based on the teachings of Jesus. The Reformation, in the form in which it eventually arrived, disturbed him by its violence and he refused to become a declared Protestant. But his criticism of the Catholic Church remained and he refused to speak for either side at the Diet of Worms in 1521. His early sympathy for Luther had gone by then, and in 1524 he entered the controversy with *De Libero Arbitrio*, taking issue with Luther's views on human free will. Luther replied with *De Servo Arbitrio* (1525) and Erasmus returned to the attack with *Hyperaspistes* in 1526.

Inevitably, Erasmus became suspect to both sides, and the University of Paris censured his teachings in 1527. The first Counter-Reformation pope, Paul IV, banned his work in 1559; the ban was repeated by Sixtus V in 1590.

***Erewhon*** A satirical novel by Samuel Butler, first published in 1872. Erewhon (nowhere) is discovered by the narrator on the far side of a chain of unexplored mountains in a remote colony. His description represents Butler's attack on the mental and moral stagnation and hypocrisy he found in England, and on his society's attitudes to crime, religion, and the rearing of children. The narrator (Higgs) escapes from Erewhon in a balloon he constructed himself, accompanied by a girl he has fallen in love with.

***Erewhon Revisited*** A satirical novel by Samuel Butler, first published in 1901. It is a sequel to *Erewhon*, published nearly 30 years before.

Higgs has a strong desire, 20 years after escaping from Erewhon in a balloon, to revisit the place. When he arrives he discovers that his ascent into the sky has called a religion into being

– Sunchildism; a great temple to him is about to be dedicated. Higgs is horrified at the way people's credulity is being exploited by Professors Hanky and Panky and Butler extends into this setting the satire of the original book.

**Eric, or Little by Little**   See **Farrar, Frederick William**.

**Erigena, John Scotus** *c*.810–877. Erigena was an Irish scholar and philosopher who found favour at the court of the Carolingian king Charles II. He took part in theological disputes on predestination and the Eucharist and it is possible that he came to England in later life at the invitation of Alfred the Great. Erigena's philosophy attempted to reconcile the Neo-Platonist idea of emanation with the Christian idea of creation. *De Divisione Naturae* is a consideration of God and the natural world; *De Predestinatione* argued that evil and its punishment is no part of God's laws – sin bears the punishment in itself. Erigena translated the writings of Dionysius the Areopagite, St Maximus the Confessor, and St Gregory of Nyssa into Latin. His *De Divisione Naturae* was condemned by Pope Honorius III in 1225.

**Eros** Antony's friend and servant in Shakespeare's *Antony and Cleopatra*. He refuses Antony's command to kill him after his defeat and kills himself instead.

**Ervine, St John Greer** 1883–1971. Ervine was born in Belfast and became manager of the Abbey Theatre in Dublin in 1915. He was by then an established playwright, author of *Mixed Marriage* (1912), *The Magnanimous Lover* (1912), *Jane Clegg* (1914), and *John Ferguson* (1915) – plays in the naturalistic vein. Ervine became dramatic critic of *The Observer* after World War I and settled in England, writing for the paper until 1936. His later plays enjoyed success in England and the USA and provided excellent vehicles for actresses of the quality of Sybil Thorndike and Edith Evans. Among them were *The Ship* (1922), *The Lady of Belmont* (1923), *Mary, Mary, Quite Contrary* (1923), *Anthony and Anna* (1925), *The First Mrs Fraser* (1929), *People of Our Class* (1936), *Boyd's Shop* (1936), and *Robert's Wife* (1938). The dates given are those of publication. Among other works by St John Ervine were the novels *Mrs Martin's Man* (1914) and *The Wayward Man* (1927) and the biographies *Parnell* (1925), *God's Soldier* (1934, the life of General Booth) and *Bernard Shaw: His Life, Work and Friends* (1956).

Ervine was appointed dramatic critic to the BBC in 1932 and was awarded honorary doctorates of literature by the universities of St Andrews (1934) and Belfast (1945).

***Essay concerning Human Understanding*** A philosophical treatise by John Locke, first published in 1690. Further editions, with revisions by the author, were published in 1694, 1700 and 1706. A modern edition of the *Essay*, by J. W. Yolton, was published in the Everyman's Library in 1961. For the genesis of the *Essay*, see **Locke, John**. *Some Thoughts on the Conduct of the Understanding in the Search of Truth*, originally designed as a chapter of the *Essay*, was published posthumously in 1762.

Locke rejected the doctrine of inborn ideas or knowledge, maintaining that the source of knowledge is experience. His intention in his *Essay* was to enquire into the origin and extent of man's knowledge; he also examined the nature and limits of knowledge – of what man can hope to know and what he cannot. Locke was an innovator; much of what he rejected is agreed to be worthless now, but he was writing and thinking in the later part of the 17th century. In the course of his *Essay* Locke threw new light on the working of the human mind and the association of ideas, and thereby influenced generations of poets and novelists. His philosophy is conveyed in lucid and unadorned prose.

***Essay of Dramatick Poesie*** A critical symposium by John Dryden, written while he lived in Charlton, Wiltshire, to escape the plague in London. It was first published in 1668. Those taking part are Charles Sackville, Earl of Dorset (Eugenius), Sir Robert Howard (Crites), Sir Charles Sedley (Lisideius) and Dryden (Neander). The four friends are boating on the Thames. After discussing the fighting between the Dutch and English fleets in the Thames estuary (June 1665) they go on to discuss the English drama of earlier days, and in their own time, comparing English drama with French. There is a lively discussion of the use of rhyme in drama and a fine appreciation of the art of Shakespeare. The *Essay* is notable both for Dryden's lucid prose and for its observations on English dramatic writing.

***Essay on Criticism, An*** A poem in heroic couplets written by Alexander Pope when the poet was 21 and first published in 1711. Didactic in purpose, it contains a description of the rules of taste and the principles by which a critic should be guided; a demonstration follows showing departures from these principles by certain critics. The inspiration for the poem was Horace's *Ars Poetica* and, while original thought is not to be found in it, the skill with which Pope used the form and the concentration of witty utterance it contained made him famous. Some of the lines have the status of proverbs: 'A little learning is a dangerous thing' and 'Some praise at morning what they blame at night; But always think the last opinion right.'

**Essay on Man** A poem by Alexander Pope, in four epistles, addressed to his friend Henry St John, Lord Bolingbroke. The poem was partly inspired by Bolingbroke's occasional philosophical writings. The first three epistles were published anonymously in 1733, the poet feeling uncertain of their reception. The fourth was published in 1734 under Pope's name. The original plan was for a poem upon the nature of man on a more ambitious scale but Pope did not continue with it. The first epistle is concerned with the nature of man and his place in the universe; the second with man as an individual; the third with man in society; and the fourth with man and the pursuit of happiness. The overall purpose of the poem was to demonstrate the essential rightness of the world as ordered by God; man's inability to realize this is the fault of his limited perception. The poem itself displays Pope's remarkable skill and gift for witty aphorism – but as philosophy it has no standing whatever. It bristles with lines that have found their way into every dictionary of quotations: 'Hope springs eternal in the human breast', 'The proper study of mankind is man', 'Whate'er is best administered is best', and 'An honest man's the noblest work of God' come immediately to mind.

**Essay on the History of Civil Society** An examination of the principal features of societies in various stages of progress and decline by Adam Ferguson, first published in 1767. Ferguson published it against the advice of David Hume and it has been called plausible and superficial; nevertheless, it was well received and translated into French and German. Some of Ferguson's conclusions strike an uncomfortably familiar chord in modern readers: he saw the process of decline as beginning with the failure of citizens to play their due part in public affairs; the division of labour tends to focus citizens' attention on their own concerns, to the exclusion of the commonwealth; good order in society will follow when men are placed where they are best qualified to serve, and 'Involved in the resolutions of our company, we move with the crowd before we have determined the rule by which its will is collected. We follow a leader, before we have settled the ground of his pretensions . . .'

**Essays, The** or *Counsels, Civill and Morall*. Francis Bacon's essays were first published in a book of ten in 1597; the second book of 1612 contained 38, and the third in 1625 contained 58. For the most part the essays are reflections and observations fashioned into counsels for the conduct of a successful life. But they also contain less serious matter and display Bacon's pleasure in the world of nature and reflections on love and friendship, truth, and marriage. Douglas Bush's amusing comment that 'While Montaigne's chief concern is in man sitting upon his "owne taile" Bacon's is on man sitting in an office chair' is a just one and a fair indication of the nature of Francis Bacon. Nevertheless, much wisdom is to be found in his essays; it is jolting to read, in an age of ineffectual government and management, that nearly 400 years ago Bacon observed that 'He that plots to be the only figure among ciphers, is the decay of the whole age' (*Of Ambition*). Modern architects and 'planners' should read *Of Building*, with particular attention to 'Houses are built to live in and not to look on; therefore let use be preferred before uniformity, except where both may be had'. One could go on, and almost make an encyclopedia of quotations from the essays of Francis Bacon. 'Virtue is like a rich stone, best plain set'; 'If the hill will not come to Mahomet, Mahomet will go to the hill'; 'A wise man will make more opportunities than he finds'; 'Money is like muck, not good except it be spread' – and many, many more. The celebrated essay *Atheism* was first published in the second edition of 1612.

**Essays and Reviews** A book of essays by seven authors on the necessity of free enquiry into religious matters, published in 1860. Among the contributors were Benjamin Jowett of Balliol College, Oxford, Mark Pattison of Lincoln College, Oxford, and Frederick Temple, who was at that time headmaster of Rugby School. The liberalism of the book aroused the wrath of Bishop Samuel Wilberforce, who tirelessly sought its condemnation and succeeded in 1864.

**Estella** In Dickens's *Great Expectations*, an orphan child adopted by Miss Havisham and schooled by her to be cool and unresponsive to men. Pip loves her, but she marries Bentley Drummle.

**Esther Waters** A novel by George Moore, first published in 1894. The author was strongly influenced by his years in France and had written several novels in a realistic vein before this one but *Esther Waters*, with its sympathetic treatment of the characters and faithful portrayal of all levels of society, departed from Victorian conventions and gave Moore his first great success.

Esther Waters is a religious girl, a member of the Plymouth Brethren, who leaves home to escape from a drunken stepfather. She goes into service at Woodview, the home of the Barfield family whose main interest is their racing stables; the exception is Mrs Barfield, who – like Esther – belongs to the Plymouth sect. Esther, aged only 17, is easily seduced by the footman, William Latch, who then deserts her. Esther is dismissed, and only Mrs Barfield tries to be kind. She bears a son and endures a bitter and humiliating struggle to rear him. Esther is admired by a respectable man, a Salvationist, who wants to marry her; but William Latch comes back into her life and for their son's sake she marries him. William makes a good husband and father; but he is a publican in Dean Street in Soho as well as a bookmaker, and his constant attendance at races ruins his health. Further misfortune comes when he is suspected of using the pub as an unlicensed betting centre and the house is closed. William dies, leaving his family penniless; but Esther's son is soon able to fend for himself and at the close of the novel Esther returns to Woodview. Mrs Barfield, now an impoverished widow, lives alone in a corner of the old house, and there at last Esther finds peace.

**Ethan Frome**   A short novel by Edith Wharton, first published in 1911. It was dramatized by Owen and Donald Davis in 1936.

On a poor farm in western Massachusetts Ethan Frome struggles to wrest a living from the soil. His wife Zeena (Zenobia) is a whining hypochondriac as well as a slattern and spends much of Ethan's hard-earned money on quack remedies. Her cousin, Mattie Silver, is left destitute when her parents die and the farm is the only place she can go. Ethan and Mattie are attracted to each other and Zeena's jealousy is aroused, though Mattie works diligently on the endless labours of the farm. After a year Zeena drives Mattie off the farm to make way for a hired woman and Ethan takes her to the railroad station through the winter snow. On the journey Ethan and Mattie acknowledge that they cannot bear to part; they are travelling on a sledge and when they reach a familiar slope Ethan sends it crashing at great speed into an elm. But the hoped-for death is denied them and they are carried back, crippled, to the farm. Zeena becomes nurse to them and they live out their days under her care. Ethan is resigned, while Mattie turns into a complaining invalid. The three are imprisoned in a world whose small horizons and inflexible conventions are all they know.

**Etherege, George** c.1634–91.  Details of the life of this Restoration playwright are scarce; the production of his first comedy was in 1664, but almost nothing before that date is known. He is believed to have been the son of a modest Oxfordshire family; but it is possible that his father had been a planter in Bermuda. He may have been brought up in France; his father died there in 1649 and certainly Etherege had a considerable knowledge of French literature and manners. After his first comedy, **The Comical Revenge,** or *Love in a Tub* (1664) Etherege became part of the rakish London society of the Restoration and a friend of the Earl of Rochester.

He went to Constantinople as secretary to Sir Daniel Harvey, the English ambassador, in 1668, the year of his second play, **She Wou'd if She Cou'd**. He returned to England in 1671 and resumed his boisterous existence, getting involved in tavern brawls and generally behaving outrageously. **The Man of Mode,** or *Sir Fopling Flutter*, his masterpiece, was produced in 1676, and Etherege was knighted in 1680. He married a wealthy widow in the same year.

Upon the death of Charles II Etherege was given a diplomatic appointment in Ratisbon, where he remained until James II fled from England. He died in Paris, where he had gone after the accession of William and Mary. His letters to various friends – Dryden, the Earl of Middlesex, Sir William Trumbull – from Ratisbon, where he was very bored, are among the best of the period. *The Letterbooks of Sir George Etherege* were edited by Sybil Rosenfeld (two volumes, 1928 and 1952). The standard edition of Etherege's plays is that of H. F. B. Brett-Smith (two volumes, 1927). A third volume, to include the poems and letters, was not completed but the poems were published in an edition prepared by J. Thorpe (1963).

Etherege's plays are comedies of manners, and the attitude to life expressed in them is acceptable as representative of its time. There is indeed hardly a more representative Restoration man than Etherege, and while he took his pleasure where he found it, such behaviour came naturally in his society. An interesting feature of his work is the character of his heroines, witty and emancipated young women whose presence gives a particular 'glow' to Restoration comedy. Etherege set the pattern for the comedy of manners that was to reach such a high level in the work of Congreve, Vanbrugh and Farquhar.

**Eugene Aram**   A novel by Bulwer-Lytton, first published in 1832. It was based on a murder case:

the real Eugene Aram was a schoolmaster of Knaresborough, apparently an accomplished and gentle man, who murdered a shoemaker. In Bulwer-Lytton's novel Aram is a young and romantic character who, in the grip of poverty, agrees to the murder of Daniel Clarke, the shoemaker, with an accomplice, Houseman, who actually does the killing. Aram, tormented by guilt, settles in a distant village and falls in love with Madeline Lester. Retribution follows when Houseman betrays him: he is taken on his wedding day. Madelinc, who is related to Clarke, succumbs to the shock of the crime revealed and Aram's subsequent condemnation.

Thomas Hood's poem, 'The Dream of Eugene Aram', is based on the same story.

**Euphues** A prose romance by John Lyly. The first part, *Euphues: the Anatomy of Wit*, was published in 1578; the second, *Euphues and his England*, in 1580. Lyly based his book on *Diall of Princes*, Sir Thomas North's translation of Antonio de Guevara's *El Relox de Principes*, written in 1529. It is chiefly a moral treatise, written to please Lord Burleigh, on youthful folly and the pursuit of wit for its own sake.

In the first part a young Athenian, Euphues, is in Naples, where he becomes friends with an Italian, Philautus. Euphues, friendship notwithstanding, woos Lucilla, loved by Philautus; he succeeds in winning her – but in turn is replaced by a third suitor, Curio. Euphues and Philautus, after quarrelling with each other, blame Lucilla for what has happened. They are friends again when Euphues returns to Athens, leaving a pamphlet of advice to lovers for Philautus. The second part finds the two friends in England, where Philautus, advised by Euphues, embarks on a number of love affairs. Euphues returns to Athens, where he composes an address to the ladies of Italy, 'Euphues' glass for Europe', a description of English manners, institutions, women, men, and of England's queen. The book ends with a general letter of advice to Philautus.

The story, which amounts to nothing, was simply a device for a series of discourses. More important than story or content is Lyly's prose style, which in its use of antithesis, alliteration, and allusion gave rise to a host of imitations and came to be called 'euphuism'. It did little for the English novel, but Lyly's use of it required a discipline that did much for English prose, bringing to it an economy and design that had not been present hitherto.

**euphuism** See **Lyly, John** and *Euphues*.

**Europe** See **Blake, William**.

**Europeans, The** A novel by Henry James, first published as a serial in the *Atlantic Monthly*, from July to October 1878, and in volume form in a slightly revised text in 1878.

Felix Young and his sister Eugenia come to Massachusetts to visit their relatives, the Wentworths, whom they have never seen before. Felix, an artist, is lighthearted and charming; he is soon engaged on flattering portraits of wealthy Bostonians. Eugenia is the morganatic wife of a German nobleman, who is about to renounce her for reasons of state; she is looking for a rich husband. Mr Wentworth establishes the pair in a house nearby and soon his son and two daughters are their intimate friends. Gertrude, who has an 'understanding' with the Unitarian pastor, Mr Brand, falls in love with Felix. Charlotte, who has feelings of her own about Mr Brand, presses Gertrude to take her 'understanding' to a logical conclusion. Clifford Wentworth becomes infatuated with Eugenia, who has also attracted Robert Acton; but the latter is more experienced in worldly matters than the Wentworths. Nevertheless, Eugenia's charms are considerable and he is by no means unattentive.

The comedy plays itself out. Gertrude and Felix grow closer; Mr Brand goes on regarding Gertrude with longing, while Charlotte does some longing of her own; Eugenia cannot resist the idea that young Clifford should be her captive, while Acton's young sister Lizzie has hopes of him too; and Lizzie's brother's attentions to Eugenia are positive – but there is a cool rcscrve in them which Eugenia cannot seem to penetrate.

At the end of the tale Robert Acton has the measure of Eugenia, and Clifford's common sense enables him to stay out of her reach. Mr Wentworth gives his consent to Felix's engagement to Gertrude and Mr Brand begins to discover Charlotte's virtues. Clifford becomes engaged to Lizzie Acton. Eugenia, having overplayed her hand, returns to Europe, defeated.

**Eustace, Lady Lizzie** The central character of Anthony Trollope's *The Eustace Diamonds*. She is a pretty woman who can usually enlist men's sympathies – for a time; then they discover that she is both greedy and untruthful. She also appears in *Phineas Redux*.

**Eustace Diamonds, The** A novel by Anthony Trollope, first published in the *Fortnightly Review* (July 1871 to February 1873). This is the third of the 'Palliser' novels; Plantagenet Palliser and Lady Glencora are on stage again, as well as the glamorous Marie Goesler, Lady Midlothian, and many others.

Admiral Greystock's daughter Lizzie is beautiful; she is also greedy and an unscrupulous liar. She becomes Lady Eustace when she marries the ailing and very rich Sir Florian Eustace, to whom she bears a son and who soon leaves her a widow. She has not been liked by Sir Florian's family, who saw her more clearly than he did.

Sir Florian presented Lizzie with the Eustace diamonds, a necklace valued at £10,000 (in 1870). The Eustace family insist that the necklace has been in the family for generations: it is an heirloom. Lizzie is determined to keep it and the Eustace family's lawyer sets out to retrieve it. Lizzie is also determined to marry Lord Fawn – but he, a worthy little man of no great spirit or wealth, wants her to let the diamonds go. A further complication arises when it transpires that the Eustace family's lawyer, Camperdown, is Lord Fawn's lawyer, too. Lizzie, when she learns that her title to the necklace is a matter for legal dispute, takes the diamonds and bolts to her castle in Ayrshire.

The adventures of Lady Eustace are dictated by her greed and her inexhaustible contrivances to hang on to the diamond necklace. She succeeds in alienating everyone whose aid her wits have managed to enlist, including Lord Fawn and her cousin, Frank Greystock. She is left without the diamonds, and with a husband, Joseph Emilius, whose single status is in some doubt.

Trollope succeeds in holding the reader's interest in the appalling Lady Eustace, and nowhere does he soften her with a redeeming feature. The book has the added attraction of glimpses into the lives of the Pallisers and the Duke of Omnium.

**Eva, Little**   In *Uncle Tom's Cabin*, the St Clare child who is saved by Uncle Tom during the voyage down the Mississippi. Her father buys Uncle Tom and Eva becomes devoted to him. Eva's death leads to Tom being sold to Simon Legree by Mrs St Clare.

*Evangeline, A Tale of Acadia.*   A narrative poem by Longfellow, first published in 1847. Acadia was the province of Canada roughly corresponding to present-day Nova Scotia. It was claimed by the English but the settlers in the area were mostly French. The story concerns Evangeline Bellefontaine of Grand Pré, who is to marry Gabriel Lajeunesse, the blacksmith's son. The French and Indian Wars prompt the English to send the French residents to safer areas and the two families are separated. Gabriel and his father make their way to Louisiana. Evangeline continues to seek them; she eventually finds the father, Basil, but he has become separated from Gabriel. Fruitlessly they search together for many years. Prematurely aged, Evangeline becomes a Sister of Mercy in Philadelphia. During a pestilence there she recognises a dying old man as her lover. She dies of grief and they are buried together in the Catholic cemetery.

The poem is in unrhymed hexameters. The Louisiana of the poem is not the present state of Louisiana but the enormous territory which lay to the west and extended from the Caribbean to the Great Lakes.

*Evan Harrington*   A novel by George Meredith, first published in 1861.

Evan Harrington and his three sisters are the children of Melchizedek Harrington, a successful tailor with a grand manner, nicknamed 'the Marquis' and 'the great Mel'. The sisters have made good marriages and they would like to sever their connection with trade and find a grand marriage for their brother. One sister, the Countess de Saldar, is Evan's hostess in Lisbon where he is working for the British envoy. He has fallen in love with Rose, the envoy's niece.

Evan's father dies, leaving heavy debts. The countess now tries to launch her brother into high life, while his mother, in Lymport, wants her son to come back and take care of the business. The rest of the comedy tells of the countess's determination to launch her brother; of the truth of Evan's background emerging and Rose's acceptance of him nevertheless; and of the countess's damage to her brother's character while doing her best to discredit his rival, Ferdinand Laxley. All ends well, helped by the intervention of Rose's cousin Juliana and Evan's uncle Tom Cogglesby.

*Evelina, or The History of a Young Lady's Entrance into the World.*   A novel by Fanny Burney, first published in 1778; it is written in epistolary form.

Evelina Belmont and her mother have been abandoned by her father. Sir John Belmont expected to receive a large fortune upon marriage and departed when it did not materialize. Evelina is brought up by Mr Villars, a clergyman who was a friend of her grandfather, and leads a quiet life with her guardian until she first goes to London to visit her friend Lady Howard. She is introduced to London society and is jarred to encounter her grandmother, Madame Duval, whose vulgarity is indestructible, and her equally vulgar relatives, the Branghtons. She is tirelessly pursued by an unwanted suitor, Sir Clement Willoughby, and mortified by her relatives' exploitation of Lord Orville, the handsome and graceful man with whom she has fallen in love. Evelina's life is further complicated by the fact that she is apparently without parents, and pressure is brought to bear on Sir John Belmont to acknowledge her as his daughter. But Belmont protests that his daughter is in his care – not merely acknowledged; Lady Belmont's nurse had brought him the child after his wife's last illness. The puzzle is solved; the nurse had passed off her own child as Sir John's. Evelina is acknowledged as Sir John's heir and is happily married to Lord Orville.

Fanny Burney extracts the maximum humour from Evelina's continuing dilemma; she is acutely responsive because she is, like her creator, very shy. Fanny Burney also casts a very cold eye on the manners of her time.

**Evelyn, John** 1620–1706. The second son of Richard Evelyn, a gentleman of Surrey, John Evelyn was educated at Balliol College, Oxford. After university he travelled in Europe a great deal, though he was in England in 1642 to render service as a Royalist volunteer. His sympathies remained with the Royalist cause but he detested the Civil War and left England in 1649, the year of the execution of Charles I. He published his first work in that year, a translation from the French of one of F. de la Mothe le Vayer's essays which he called *Of Liberty and Servitude*. During

---

John Evelyn. Portrait by R. Nanteuil, 1650. National Portrait Gallery, London.

his self-exile Evelyn held a correspondence with Charles II and he maintained this when he decided to return to England in 1652, resigned to living in a republic.

At the Restoration the Royal Society was founded and Evelyn became one of the first Fellows. Samuel Pepys was elected four years later and, remarkably, two good friends became the most famous diarists in the English language. In 1661 Evelyn, distressed by the increasing smoke and grime of London's air, proposed carefully considered remedies in *Fumifugium*. The government expressed great interest, then sank back exhausted after making such an effort, and in fact nothing was done. *Tyrannus, or the Mode*, an objection to foreign fashions in dress, was also published in 1661, and *Sculptura*, a book on engraving, followed in 1662. At this time there was an acute need for ships for the navy, and a shortage of timber would have been perilous. The Royal Society, alerted by the Navy Office, gave the problem to Evelyn, who wrote *Sylva: or a Discourse of Forest Trees* (1664), a manual of practical arboriculture which was responsible for a movement of tree-planting and conservation.

Evelyn, like Samuel Pepys, stayed at his post during the Plague and the Fire, helping to organize relief. His plan for the rebuilding of London after the Fire suggested improvements which bear comparison with those of Christopher Wren and Robert Hooke. Evelyn published his treatise on *Navigation and Commerce* in 1674, but left unpublished a memoir of his friend Mrs Godolphin. He translated a number of works from the French, and wrote essays on vineyards, medals, and salads. His garden at Sayes Court, Deptford, became a showplace and was visited by the royal family.

The diary for which John Evelyn is most famous began as a supplemented account of his life: he was always jotting down memoranda in the blank pages of almanacs and began to put them into intelligible order about 1660 (when Samuel Pepys also began his diary) in a volume called *Kalendarium*, which opens with his announcement of his birth 'about 20 minuts past two in the morning' on 31 October 1620. The book begins to be something like a true diary about 1684 but Evelyn often draws his entries from the contemporary press and pamphlets. He left a priceless history of his times but, unlike Pepys, little of himself. His intelligence and integrity are never in doubt but he remains somewhat distant from his readers.

John Evelyn's diary remained in his family, unseen, until the early 19th century, when Lady

Evelyn employed the antiquary William Upcott (1779–1845) to inspect the manuscript at Wotton House, near Dorking in Surrey: it is said that Upcott found two large volumes in a clothes-basket. Upcott realized the importance of the volumes, wherever he found them, and Lady Evelyn agreed to publication. The editor was William Bray (1736–1832) and the first publication was as *The Memoirs of John Evelyn* (two volumes, 1818). An improved text, also by Bray, was published in the following year. After various editions, the first with detailed notes by Austin Dobson was published (three volumes, 1906). The definitive edition is that of Esmond S. de Beer, the complete text with useful footnotes (six volumes, 1955). From this an excellent one-volume edition was made (Oxford Standard Authors, 1959). Evelyn's *The Life of Mrs Godolphin* was edited by Bishop Wilberforce (1847).

**Eve of St Agnes, The**   A poem in Spenserian stanzas by John Keats, written during 1819 and first published in 1820. The subject of this poem, and also of *Isabella* and *Lamia* (which appeared in the same volume), is love. Upon the medieval superstition that a virgin, on the eve of St Agnes, is vouchsafed a vision of her love, Keats imposed a French story called *Pierre de Provence et La Belle Maguelone*. His poem tells of Madeline, who is told the legend of St Agnes' Eve. Her lover is Porphyro, whose family is the enemy of hers. During a feast Porphyro succeeds in entering the castle, helped by Madeline's nurse Angela, who leads him to Madeline's chamber. Madeline wakes from a dream of Porphyro to find him at her side. They elope in the stormy night, stealing past a drunken porter and a bloodhound that stays quiet when it recognizes Madeline. There is an interesting reference to another of Keats's poems in stanza XXXIII, when Porphyro gently rouses his Madeline with ' . . . an ancient ditty, long since mute, In Provence call'd, "La belle dame sans mercy"'.

**Everdene, Bathsheba**   The heroine of Thomas Hardy's *Far from the Madding Crowd*. A thoughtless joke makes her the object of Boldwood's affections, but she is dazzled by Sergeant Troy and marries him. Another suitor is Gabriel Oak, whose love is constant and rewarded in the end.

**Ever Green, The**   See **Bannatyne, George**.

**Everlasting Gospel, The**   An unfinished poem by William Blake, probably written about 1810. It could be described as a mature expression of his religious beliefs, stated in the introduction. He rejects the God of the Old Testament, whose laws Jesus overturned. Jesus came to announce one Gospel – the forgiveness of sins – and does not share the icy detached purity of God the Creator. The theme of forgiveness is given remarkable expression in the finest lines of the poem, the dialogue between Jesus and Mary Magdalene, who is here the woman taken in adultery.

**Everlasting Mercy, The**   See **Masefield, John**.

**Everyman**   The most celebrated of all morality plays was Dutch in origin and first given in an English version between 1495 and 1500.

Everyman is summoned by Death, and he looks hopefully for a companion on his last journey. He finds that of those he valued – Fellowship, Worldly Goods, Beauty, Kindred – none is willing to go with him. The only one to remain true to him is Good Deeds; but he is weak from neglect by Everyman, and Knowledge and Confession have to be called to renew his strength. Then Everyman and his Good Deeds go together to the grave.

**Every Man in his Humour**   A comedy by Ben Jonson, first produced in 1598 at the Curtain Theatre in Shoreditch by The Lord Chamberlain's Men. Shakespeare was a member of the company and created the part of Edward Knowell. The play was originally set in Italy; but in the revised version, published in 1616, Jonson changed the setting to London. The first publication was in 1601. In Ben Jonson's work a

A woodcut from an edition of *Everyman* published in 1530.

'humour' is the predominant characteristic or the predominant emotion manifest in a character in a critical situation.

The merchant, Kitely, has a younger brother who brings his boisterous friends to the house. Dame Kitely is young and pretty and her husband is jealous of her, thinking that his brother's friends have designs on her. One of the young men, Edward Knowell, suffers from his father's excessive concern for his son's moral welfare; he woos Kitely's pretty sister, Bridget. A 'hanger on' of the group of young men is Captain Bobadill, an old soldier who is both vain and cowardly, forever boasting of his valour. Knowell's servant, Brainworm, maliciously plays on Kitely's jealousy and Dame Kitely's credulity brings about a confrontation between them in a house where each believes the other present for an immoral purpose. Captain Bobadill's pretensions are exposed and he is beaten. Misunderstandings are resolved at the end by Justice Clement, a shrewd observer of human folly, and Knowell wins the hand of Bridget.

**Every Man out of his Humour** A comedy by Ben Jonson, first performed in 1599 and published in 1600. It followed *Every Man in his Humour*; like its predecessor the play was concerned with 'humours' and how their possessors are confounded by them. It is not highly regarded by scholars now, being too much the same mixture as before. Among the characters ridiculed are Fungoso, a student pursuing fashion, whose aim is to be a courtier; his uncle Sogliardo, who wants to be accounted a man of quality; and Sir Fastidious Brisk, the courtier who can never stop being a courtier.

**Ewing, Juliana Horatia** 1841–85. The daughter of Margaret Gatty, she married a Major Alexander Ewing. Like her mother, Juliana was a successful writer for children and she took over the running of *Aunt Judy's Magazine* when her mother died. She increased the entertainment, reduced the educational pages, and could name among her contributors Lewis Carroll, Mrs Molesworth, and F. Anstey. Her output as a writer was considerable and some of her more successful books were *Mrs Overtheway's Remembrances* (1866), *A Flat Iron for a Farthing* (1870), *The Brownies* (1871), *Jan of the Windmill* (1872), and *Daddy Darwin's Dovecot* (1881). She is regarded as a better writer than her mother in every way, and the moralistic tone is largely absent; but Mrs Ewing's work is hardly known nowadays.

**Excursion, The** A poem in nine books by William Wordsworth, first published in 1814. Wordsworth had planned, as early as 1798, what he describes in his preface as a 'philosophical poem, containing views of man, nature, and society, and to be entitled *The Recluse*, as having for its principal subject the sensations and opinions of a poet living in retirement'. *The Excursion* was the only part of the project that Wordsworth completed, but is in fact his longest work. Though the poem was not well received at the time of publication (Coleridge, who knew more than anyone about Wordsworth's poetry believed the unpublished *The Prelude* to be a far finer work) it was a measure of the poet's reputation that *The Excursion* did claim so much attention. The general opinion is that whatever its shortcomings, it contains great passages, one of which is 'The Ruined Cottage' or 'The Story of Margaret', the fine pastoral composed in 1797.

The poet travels with a Wanderer; through him he meets the Solitary, a recent enthusiast for the French Revolution and now dispirited by the outcome. The Solitary is reproved for his lack of faith and loss of confidence in man. The Solitary's arguments are ineffectual (one of the weaknesses of the poem), and a Pastor enters the scene. He offers the consolations of virtue and faith, illustrating his sermon with accounts of the lives of those buried in his churchyard. At the Pastor's house the Wanderer offers his conclusions, philosophical and political, from the debate which has gone before. The last two books present Wordsworth's thoughts on the Industrial Revolution and the havoc it played with the lives of the poor. He makes a strong plea for the education of children.

**Exeter Book, The** A collection of manuscripts of Old English poetry given to Exeter Cathedral by Bishop Leofric in the 11th century and preserved in the cathedral library. The manuscripts, which include many fragments, were executed some time during the latter half of the 10th century but the poems themselves are much older, some possibly as old as the 6th century and originating in minstrelsy. The inscription describes the collection as 'A large English book, on all sorts of things, wrought in verse'. *The Exeter Book* was first published in 1842, under the editorship of B. Thorpe.

See *Azarias*; *Widsith*; *Deor*; *Ascension, The*; *Wanderer, The*; *Juliana*; *Seafarer, The*; *Guthlac*; *Wife's Complaint, The*; *Husband's Message, The*; and *Ruin, The*.

*Exodus* A poem in Old English preserved in the *Junius Manuscript* in the Bodleian Library, Oxford. It was wrongly attributed to Caedmon by Francis Junius. The poem does not follow in detail the Exodus of the Old Testament but describes the passage of the Red Sea and destruction of the pursuing Egyptians.

# F

*Fable for Critics, A* A satire in verse by James Russell Lowell, first published (anonymously) in 1848.

At a gathering on Olympus a critic, who worships Apollo, tries to find a literary lily at the god's request. The critic examines the work of a number of authors but the best he can produce is a thistle. The authors who come under review are Holmes, Emerson, Bronson Alcott, Longfellow, William Cullen Bryant, Margaret Fuller, Washington Irving, Whittier, Poe, Hawthorne, James Fenimore Cooper, and Lowell himself. The verse is careless but the criticism is shrewd and Lowell makes the point that American literature is now rich enough to be considered in such terms.

**fabliau** A short tale, usually of everyday life and in a comic vein. It came to England from France, where it was an important feature of poetry in the 12th and 13th centuries. In medieval England there was no prose form and *fabliaux* were related in octosyllabic rhyming couplets.

*Façade* A suite of 37 poems by Edith Sitwell, first published in 1922. In the Notes to her *Collected Poems* (1954) the poet wrote: 'The Poems in *Façade* are abstract poems – that is, they are patterns in sound. They are, too, in many cases, virtuoso exercises in technique of an extreme difficulty, in the same sense as that in which certain studies by Liszt are studies in transcendental technique in music.' In 1923 the first public performance of 21 of the poems, with a musical accompaniment by William Walton, was given in London and aroused considerable critical hostility; but the poems, the concert version, and Frederick Ashton's witty ballet are now accepted as 20th-century classics and regularly performed. Some of the poems are in a vein of captivating very English nonsense ('Trio for Two Cats and a Trombone', 'Four in the Morning', 'Fox Trot', 'Jodelling Song', 'Popular Song', 'Scotch Rhapsody'); others have deeper implications and stay in the mind, such as 'Clowns' Houses', 'Said King Pompey', 'Mariner Man', and 'The Cat'.

*Facey Romford's Hounds, Mr* See **Surtees, R(obert) S(mith)**.

*Faerie Queene, The* The most celebrated work of Edmund Spenser was never completed. It was planned in 12 books and Spenser was occupied with it from about 1580, when he was 28, until the end of his life. When the first three books were ready the poet came to London with his friend Raleigh, to whom he addressed the prefatory letter 'expounding his whole intention in the course of this worke: which for that it giveth light to the Reader, for the better understanding is hereunto annexed'. The first three books were published in 1590 and gained the poet a pension of £50 a year from Elizabeth I; and it was successful enough to prompt the publication of a volume of Spenser's shorter works by the printer Ponsonbie. *The Faerie Queene* represents, in the poet's design, 'glory in my generall intention, but in my particular I conceive the most excellent and glorious person of our soveraine the Queene'. Elizabeth bears different names in the poem – Belphoebe, Mercilla, Astraea, and – most famous of all – Gloriana. The poem combines two forms, the medieval allegory and the epic romance of the Italians Ariosto and Tasso. Spenser's Faerie Land is a place in which every deed, adventure, and emotion is experienced and expressed, and each of the books that he completed contains an allegorical theme. The basis of the poem is that 12 knights, examples of different virtues, each undertakes an adventure on 12 succeeding days of the Queene's festival. All virtues are combined in Prince Arthur, who has a vision of the Faerie Queene and, determined to seek her out, becomes involved – usually as a rescuer – in the adventures of other knights. But the part intended for Arthur in the resolution of the story is not contained in what we have; Spenser began his poem with the adventures of the knights and did not live to complete it.

The first three books were revised and published with the last three in 1596. In 1598 the rebellious Irish attacked and burned Spenser's castle in Cork and it is presumed that some of the rest of the poem was lost. What survives is the fragment known as *The Cantos of Mutabilitie*. The sequence of the six books runs as follows:

*Book I*. The adventure of the Red Cross Knight of Holinesse (holiness in this case being the Anglican Church). The knight is the guardian of Una, a virgin representing truth. Their adversaries are Archimago (hypocrisy) and Deussa (falsehood – the Roman Church in this book) and these are overcome.

*Book II*. The adventures of Sir Guyon, the

A woodcut from the first edition of the first three books of Spenser's *The Faerie Queene*, 1590.

Knight of Temperaunce, who is helped by a Palmer (pilgrim) and opposed by, among others, Archimago, who has escaped from the dungeon into which he was thrust by the Red Cross Knight in Book I, Duessa again, and the enchantress Acrasia (incontinence). Guyon defeats Mammon, which leads to the successful overcoming of Acrasia and her Bower of Bliss.

*Book III.* The knight in this book is a female one, the warrior maiden Britomart – Chastitie. She engages in combat with Sir Guyon and wins because chastity is a greater virtue than temperance. She also defeats the champions of Malecasta (unchaste), the lady of Castle Joyeous. Other characters are Florimell (womanly virtue and chastity), who is pursued by the lustful knight Marinell. Belphoebe (symbolizing Elizabeth I) finds herbs to heal the wounded Timias, Arthur's squire (representing the poet's friend Raleigh), and her twin sister Amoret, married to Sir Scudamour, is carried off by Busirane (unlawful love). She is eventually rescued by Britomart.

*Book IV.* The principal character of this book is taken from the unfinished *Squire's Tale* of Chaucer, whose genius Spenser acknowledged. The theme of the book is friendship, and Chaucer's Cambalo is here called Cambel. His sister Canace is present also, her hand contested for by three brothers in combat with Cambel. Triamond wins her with the help of his sister Cambina, who marries Cambel. Cambel and Triamond exemplify friendship, and other illustrations of Spenser's theme appear in the stories of Scudamour and Amoret, Britomart and Artegall (justice), Timias and Belphoebe, and Florimell and Marinell.

*Book V.* The theme is justice, personified by the knight Artegall. Elizabeth I is symbolized in the goddess of justice, Astraea, who departed from the world at the end of the Golden Age, and represented in the person of Mercilla at the trial of Duessa, who in this book represents Mary of Scotland. Artegall's quest is to destroy Grantorto (grievous wrong) and release Irena (peace, Ireland) from him. Sir Sangliere (Tyrone) is a knight forced by Artegall to carry his victim's head before him in shame. In one of Artegall's adventures he is seduced by Radigund and unmanned; Britomart rescues him. This symbolizes the commonly held view of the time that women should not rule – except Elizabeth I, of course, who was raised by Heaven, no less, to 'lawfull soveraintie'. This book contains much allegorical reference to contemporary events, including the war in the Netherlands, the Armada and, inevitably, the Irish, who obstinately refused the benefits that would ensue when their country became an English colony.

*Book VI.* The theme is 'Courtesie', personified by the knight Calidore (in Spenser's terms courtesy is *noblesse oblige*). Calidore's knightly course is interrupted when he pauses to enjoy the delights of Meliboee's pastoral retreat but adventures in courtesy continue in the deeds of Arthur, Timias, and Serena. Meliboee's daughter, Pastorella, falls in love with Calidore, and Colin Clout (Spenser) makes the music to which the Graces dance.

*Two Cantos of Mutabilitie.* These two cantos are the surviving fragment of a book that would have dealt with the virtue of 'Constancie'. Mutabilitie, a daughter of the Titans, is charged with changing the divine order of things and comes to make her case, in the court of Nature, against Jupiter's strictures. She wins her case, demonstrating that the glory of the physical world is a consequence of mutability.

Spenser put so many things into the six books and fragment of *The Faerie Queene* that any reader might be pardoned for wondering, from time to time, whether he is in romance, moral allegory, historical allegory, or poetic philosophy. In fact the reader is in all those things; any one of them can lead into any of the others during the poem's course. *The Faerie Queene* can be criticized for never quite being the thing that various aspects of it suggest it is going to be, and many of the allusions are significant only for Spenser's time. But judged by any standards the great passages alone give the poet his claim to immortality; the design may be faulty but the music is matchless. (The House of Holiness, Canto x, Book I; Guyon in the Cave of Mammon, Canto vii, Book II; the Garden of Adonis, Canto vi, Book III; the Temple of Venus, Canto x, Book IV; the Temple of Isis and Osiris (or the Temple of Justice), Canto vii, Book V; and the Dance of the Graces, Canto x, Book VI.) It should be read in short extracts, perhaps one canto at a time – the stately measure becomes monotonous – but incidental pleasures abound in the numerous stories of the adventures, and Spenser's imagery has what C. S. Lewis called 'the violent clarity and precision which we find in actual dreams'.

**Fagin** In Dickens's *Oliver Twist*, the evil head of a thieves' kitchen where boys are taught to steal. Oliver is taken to him by the Artful Dodger. Fagin is also a receiver, and Monks's willing servant in his attempt to destroy Oliver. He is apprehended and hanged at the end of the story. Dickens's narrative of his trial and last hours – a demented villain without a trace of hope – is memorable.

**Faire Quarrell, A**  A comedy by Thomas Middleton and William Rowley, first published in 1617.

Captain Ager challenges a fellow officer to a duel; he regards a comment made by the other as an insult to his mother's virtue. Before the duel takes place Ager visits his mother and recounts the incident to her, wanting to be certain that his fight will be justified. His mother is indignant at first but when she realizes that a duel will follow she wants to avert the danger to her son; she acknowledges that the accusation is true.

Ager calls off the duel – and his opponent brands him as a coward. He now has real grounds for a fight and renews his challenge. He fights and wounds his opponent, who withdraws the charge of cowardice; the two are finally reconciled. The main story is supported by a bawdy subplot (probably the work of Rowley) but the principal interest of the drama lies in Ager's moral dilemma.

An illustration from the title page of Middleton and Rowley's comedy, *A Faire Quarrell*, 1617.

**Fairfax, Thomas, 3rd Baron** 1612–71.  The victor of Naseby. In spite of his birth Fairfax was a steadfast opponent of Charles I's policies; he became one of the most distinguished and humane of the Parliamentary generals. He opposed the execution of Charles I and in the following year retired from the army, of which he was commander-in-chief. In his house at Nun Appleton in Yorkshire he tended his gardens, employed Andrew Marvell as tutor to his daughter Mary, and himself wrote verse of no distinction. After Cromwell's death Fairfax, like many of the nobility who had opposed Charles I, favoured the restoration of the monarchy. His *Memorials of the Civil War* was edited by R. Bell (1849).

See also **seventeenth-century historical collections**.

**Fair Maid of Perth, The**  See *Chronicles of the Canongate*.

**Fair Maid of the West, The,** or *A Girle Worth Gold*.  A romantic comedy by Thomas Heywood, first published in 1631.

The Earl of Essex's expedition is about to leave Plymouth for the Azores in 1597. Besse Bridges, 'the flower of Plymouth', is saved from molestation by Spencer; but he has the misfortune to kill the man while protecting Besse and has to flee the country. To provide for Besse he makes her the proprietress of the Windmill Tavern in Fowey. Spencer sails for the Azores, where his compulsive gallantry leads him to try and stop a quarrel; he is wounded and, apparently dying, sends a farewell to Besse, leaving all his property to her.

Besse fits out a ship to go to the Azores and bring Spencer's body back to England for burial. She finds him alive but a prisoner of the

Spaniards. After many adventures, however, she rescues her gallant Spencer and they sail home to happiness.

**Fair Penitent, The** See *Fatal Dowry, The*.

**Faithful Shepheardess, The** A pastoral comedy by John Fletcher, first produced about 1608 and first published about 1610. The play did not succeed on the stage and it is generally regarded as too undramatic for revival; but it is acknowledged as a poetic masterpiece and Fletcher's finest work in this vein. One of the reasons for its failure on the stage is the length of the play and the fact that it carries a formal theme (it is too thin to be called a plot).

The faithful shepherdess of the title is Clorin, who has vowed fidelity to her dead lover and lives by his grave. She is skilled in the use of herbs, which she gathers for the good of others. Thenot loves her, he thinks; but really he loves her devotion to love. Amarillis loves Perigot, who loves Amoret. Repulsed by Perigot, Amarillis tries to seduce him by assuming the form of Amoret. Cloe, the wanton shepherdess, thinks she wants Daphnis; he proves too coy for her, so she turns to Alexis. The Sullen Shepherd is always ready to connive at the furtherance of lechery. Misunderstandings abound, virtue and chastity are sorely tried, and the pursuers of lust are rejected.

**Faith Healer, The** See **Moody, William Vaughn**.

**Falconer, William** 1732–69. Falconer was born in Edinburgh, where his father was a barber. He went to sea as a boy and one of his youthful experiences was a shipwreck off the mainland of Greece. He became a ship's purser and published his narrative poem in rhyming couplets, *The Shipwreck*, in 1762. This proved immensely popular and was revised and republished twice, in 1764 and 1769. Falconer moved from the merchant service to the Royal Navy and published *An Universal Dictionary of the Marine* in 1769, the year he was drowned at sea when the frigate *Aurora* sank during a gale. He was also the author of a few occasional poems and naval articles but his work is largely forgotten now. *The Shipwreck* includes a love story, narrated by one character to another before the storm breaks, and was admired by Robert Burns.

**Falkland, Lucius Cary, 2nd Viscount** 1610–43. A cultured and thoughtful nobleman, Lord Falkland was a friend of many poets and philosophers of his day: his house at Great Tew, Oxfordshire, became a centre for discussion and the exchange of ideas. Falkland himself epitomized the Christian humanism of his small circle, whose members included Ben Jonson, Thomas Carew, Edmund Waller, William Chillingworth, John Earle, and John Hales, and he detested the spiteful squabbling over petty matters that characterized religious division. He left Great Tew for the first Bishops' War in 1639, and entered Parliament in the following year. There he bent all his efforts, as a moderate Anglican, towards the preservation of the reformed church, the ideal of a constitutional monarchy, and the prevention of strife. He became secretary of state in 1642, the same year in which the Civil War broke out.

Falkland is the subject of one of Clarendon's character portraits; Clarendon suggests that the apparent futility of all his efforts broke Falkland's spirit. He was killed at the Battle of Newbury, aged 33.

Falkland's works are not remembered. He wrote poems and *Of the Infallibilitie of the Church of Rome* (1613) in which, like his friend Chillingworth, he pleads the importance of fundamental Christianity and deplores sectarian squabbling.

**Falstaff, Sir John** The fat, dishonest, and disreputable knight of Shakespeare's *Henry IV* and *The Merry Wives of Windsor*. Falstaff had an historical original in Sir John Oldcastle, a Lollard leader of the reign of Henry V, but the character who has become so famous was Shakespeare's invention. His death is reported by Mistress Quickly in *Henry V*, Act II; the young king's rejection of him had 'kill'd his heart'.

**Famous Gilson Bequest, The** See *Can Such Things Be?*

**Famous History of Sir Thomas Wyat, The** A historical drama by Thomas Dekker and John Webster, first published in 1607 and probably produced a few years before. The Wyat of the title was the son of the poet Sir Thomas Wyatt. He was a rather hot-headed and not very intelligent man who opposed the marriage of Mary Tudor to Philip of Spain and the return of a Catholic to the English throne. He raised a rebellion in 1554 that was suppressed: he was executed and his rebellion resulted in the removal of other persons who might become the focus for further revolt. The life of Princess Elizabeth was in grave danger for a time; the 16-year-old Lady Jane Grey was beheaded in the Tower.

**Fanny Hill** (*Memoirs of a Woman of Pleasure*). See **Cleland, John**.

**Fanshawe, Lady Anne** 1625–80. The widow of Sir Richard Fanshawe, a devoted Royalist who suffered considerably for his convictions, Anne Fanshawe wrote her memoirs for her son. Sir Richard Fanshawe was the translator of Giambattista Guarini's *Il Pastor Fido*, and after the Restoration became ambassador to Portugal and later, to Spain. His adventurous life as a Royalist, and his later distinction, make an interesting account though its objective approach prevents the work from being anything more. *The Memoirs of Lady Fanshawe* was not published in full until 1829.

**Farange, Maisie** The child through whose eyes and sensibilities Henry James relates the events of *What Maisie Knew*. After her parents' divorce Maisie becomes an awkward obligation but she learns how to deal with the situations in which she finds herself.

**Far Away and Long Ago:** *A History of my Early Life.* An autobiography of his childhood and youth by W. H. Hudson, first published in 1918.

Hudson was born on a farm near Buenos Aires in Argentina and he was educated at home by a succession of eccentric and sometimes effective tutors. He and his brothers enjoyed remarkable freedom to roam the pampas and to meet a number of characters whom Hudson describes vividly: the gauchos with their strenuous and often brutal lives; the descendants of the 16th-century Spanish settlers; and the Hermit, a strange old beggar in grotesque clothes, who eventually dies alone on the pampas. Hudson's account of the wild life of the pampas is equally vivid, and the book closes with a description of the memorable old gaucho whose friendship is so important to Hudson during a long illness.

**Fardorougha, the Miser** A novel by William Carleton, first published in the *Dublin University Magazine* (1837–38).

Fardorougha, a farmer, has married late in life and has one son, Conor, whom he worships. He also has a passion for money and is a notorious usurer. One of his victims is Flanagan, who, after his ruin, enters his service and plans revenge. He succeeds in framing Conor for a crime of his own; Fardorougha is heartbroken when his son is transported. Flanagan is basically evil and, with Conor out of the way, he decides to carry off Conor's sweetheart. He persuades the Ribbonmen (the Catholic secret society) to help him but he goes too far and in the end is unmasked. Condemned to the gallows, he confesses his crime against Conor, who is pardoned.

**Farewell, Rewards & Fairies** First published in 1647, this is the poem by which its author, Richard Corbett, is remembered. It is a lament for the England that passed with the coming of Puritanism.

**Farewell To Arms, A** See **Hemingway, Ernest (Miller)**.

**Far from the Madding Crowd** A novel by Thomas Hardy, first published in the *Cornhill Magazine* (January to December 1874).

Bathsheba Everdene inherits her father's farm and becomes an independent farmer in her own right. Gabriel Oak has lost his independence as a shepherd and now works for Bathsheba, who has no idea that the regard of her neighbour, Boldwood, is a passionate love for her. Gabriel was her first suitor and he still loves her. Bathsheba herself falls in love with a soldier, the handsome and unprincipled Sergeant Troy, who has deserted Fanny Robin, the mother of his child.

Bathsheba marries Troy, and soon discovers her mistake. He is faithless and, eventually, to suit himself, disappears and allows it to be believed that he has drowned. Bathsheba, apparently a widow, is now sought by Boldwood and she accepts him – but Troy reappears and claims his wife. Boldwood shoots him dead and loses his reason; he ends his days confined as criminally insane. The story ends with Bathsheba marrying Gabriel.

Apart from the rather breathless climax, the novel was better than anything Hardy had written so far (it was his fourth book) and his career was launched. The basically simple story of Bathsheba's lovers is set against a rural background in which the rhythms of the seasons and the disciplines of farming life seem to move the narrative as much as the characters themselves.

---

Troy at the coffin of Fanny Robin and her baby; Bathsheba looking on. An illustration by Helen Allingham for Hardy's *Far from the Madding Crowd*, serialized in *The Cornhill Magazine* in 1874.

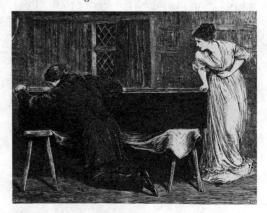

**Farquhar, George** 1678–1707. The work of
George Farquhar marks a point of departure
from the cynical licentiousness which had
become characteristic of Restoration comedy.
Farquhar brought warmth and humour to a
medium notable for wit and a lack of sympathy
in its view of mankind; Farquhar certainly
possessed wit but with him a sunnier disposition
came to the drama.

An Irishman, the son of a clergyman, Farquhar
was a sizar at Trinity College, Cambridge, at the
age of 17, but after a year and a half left without
taking a degree and may have been expelled. He
became an actor but gave up after wounding a
fellow player by accident during the last act of
Dryden's *The Indian Emperor*. In Dublin he met
Robert Wilks, the English actor, and the two
men remained close friends for the rest of
Farquhar's short life. Wilks helped Farquhar to
come to London in 1697; he brought with him a
play, *Love and a Bottle*, which was successfully
produced at Drury Lane in December 1698. *The
Constant Couple* (1699) consolidated his reputation and was followed by a sequel, *Sir Harry
Wildair* (1701) and *The Inconstant* (1702).

In 1702 Farquhar also published *Love and Business in a collection of Occasionary Verse and Epistolary Prose*, and produced a revision of one of
Fletcher's comedies. A melodrama, *The Twin
Rivals*, belongs to the same year but Farquhar had
not written anything of major quality since *The
Constant Couple*. The feverish activity of 1702
was probably due to his marriage; his wife was
penniless and he had two children to provide for.
He left London with a lieutenant's commission
and went to recruit a company in Lichfield and
Shrewsbury. His experiences gave him the background for **The Recruiting Officer**, an immediate success upon its production in April
1706. Farquhar's circumstances at this period are
not known, but in spite of his success he was, by
the end of 1706, in real difficulties, in mean lodgings and in failing health. His friend Robert
Wilks supported him, and Farquhar wrote his
finest play, **The Beaux' Stratagem**, in six weeks.
It was produced in March 1707, and has held the
stage ever since. Farquhar, only 29 years old,
died two months later.

Farquhar's tragically early death probably
deprived English drama of the one playwright
who could have left us with a real sense of the life
of his times – which are only partially presented
by Wycherley, Congreve, Vanbrugh and other
dramatists. For *The Recruiting Officer* and *The
Beaux' Stratagem*, he moved away from fashionable London into areas of feeling long ignored by
successful playwrights. He is warm as well as
witty and has an Irishman's detached view of
English social pretensions.

*The Complete Works* of George Farquhar were
collected and edited by Charles Stonehill (two
volumes, 1930).

**Farrar, Frederick William** 1831–1905. Farrar
was born in Bombay and educated at London
University and Trinity Hall, Cambridge. He
became headmaster of Marlborough School
(1871–76) and was one of those much influenced
by Thomas Arnold. Eventually he became Dean
of Canterbury. He published a mass of sermons
and theological writings, *The Life of Christ*
(1874), and three stories about schooldays of
which the most famous was *Eric, or Little by Little*
(1858), a glutinous version of the world of *Tom
Brown's Schooldays*, emphasizing virtue and vice
and sentimentally pious. Farrar had legions of
readers, nonetheless, probably because he was an
able storyteller.

**Farrell, James T(homas)** 1904–79. James T.
Farrell was born on Chicago's South Side, and
the city provides the background for his realistic
and bitter novels of life in a stifling urban environment. Farrell worked at a number of jobs
after leaving school, and managed to attend some
classes at the University of Chicago. *Young
Lonigan* (1932) was followed by *Gas-House
McGinty* (1933); Farrell returned to the adventures of his first hero in *The Young Manhood of
Studs Lonigan* (1934) and completed his trilogy,
*Studs Lonigan*, with *Judgment Day* (1935). The
first novel relates how William (Studs) Lonigan,
the son of a Catholic family, grows up in
Chicago's South Side, and how, whatever his
natural feelings and impulses may be, he is
shaped and coloured by his environment. He
reaches manhood in the second novel, which includes the years of World War I, and continues
from the age of 27 in the third, *Judgment Day*. He
discovers that he has a weak heart and, apprehensive about the future, tries to bring some order
into his life. But he invests his savings badly and
loses them, and dies at the age of 29 during the
Depression. Farrell's evocation of the background is brilliant; it is also unsparing, and salutary, and the author's criticisms are unhappily
true after another world war and the passage of
four decades. The 20th-century megalopolis
offers Studs Lonigan no more ideals or moral
values than it offers his equivalent in the 1980s.

One of the marginal characters of *Studs
Lonigan*, Danny O'Neill, became the hero of a
later sequence: *A World I Never Made* (1936), *No
Star is Lost* (1938), *Father and Son* (1940), *My Days
of Anger* (1943), and *The Face of Time* (1953).

Danny, who grows up in the same environment as Studs Lonigan, rises above it and leaves the prison of Irish-Catholic Chicago, about which Farrell is completely uncompromising, and succeeds as a writer. In *Tradition and Dream* (1964) Walter Allen poses the question that Farrell's work does not answer: 'The circumstances in which Studs and Danny grow up are much the same: one is damned by them, the other triumphs over them and escapes; but why one and not the other?'

Among other novels by James T. Farrell are *Tommy Gallagher's Crusade* (1937), *Ellen Rogers* (1941), and *This Man and This Woman* (1951). He also published eight collections of short stories and several books of literary criticism.

**Fatal Curiosity, The**   A tragedy by George Lillo, first produced at the Haymarket in May 1736 and published in the same year. Lillo set his play in Jacobean England and it was based on an old story of murder in Cornwall. The same theme was the basis of a modern French play by Albert Camus, *Le Malentendu* (1945). Lillo's characters are humble people, as in his other better-known tragedy, *The London Merchant*, but he uses blank verse in this play rather than the stilted prose of the other. The plot concerns an old couple reduced to poverty and their only son, believed to be lost at sea. A stranger deposits a casket with them and the old man, Wilmot, murders the stranger at the prompting of his wife. The murdered man proves to be their son. Lillo's play was also the inspiration for the German dramatist Friedrich Werner in his *Die Vierundzwanzigste Februar* (1810).

There is a modern edition of *The Fatal Curiosity*, edited by W. H. McBurney (Nebraska, 1966).

**Fatal Dowry, The**   A tragedy by Philip Massinger and Nathan Field. It was first published in 1632 and only a corrupt text exists. The exact date of the first performance is not known.

Charalois' father, an old soldier distinguished for his service as marshal to the Duke of Burgundy, fell on hard times and died in a debtors' prison. Charalois cannot claim his father's body for burial until the debts are settled; but the creditors accept his offer to enter prison as succeeding debtor and release the old soldier's body for an honourable funeral. Charalois goes to prison with his friend, the soldier Romont. Charalois' loyalty to his father's memory and Romont's loyalty to his friend move Rochfort, former president of the parliament, to help them; he procures their release and gives Charalois his daughter's hand in marriage.

The daughter, Beaumelle, is still attracted to a former suitor; one day Romont comes upon her and Novall enjoying an amorous embrace. Charalois is loath to believe his friend; but he surprises the lovers together, kills Novall in a duel, then calls on Rochfort to judge his daughter. Beaumelle is found guilty by her father whereupon Charalois kills her. Rochfort, shocked by Charalois' lack of mercy, hands him over to justice as a double murderer. However, Charalois is acquitted, but is killed in revenge by a friend of Novall.

Nicholas Rowe took this play and refashioned it as *The Fair Penitent*; it was produced in May 1703 and first published in the same year. The characters have different names and the emphasis lies with the dilemma of Calista (Beaumelle), given to Altamont (Charalois) by her father Sciolto (Rochfort); she is unable to end her liaison with Lothario (Novall) and is observed by Horatio (Romont) in her guilt. The character of Lothario is completely different; he is still a libertine but Novall was no more than a meanspirited dandy in the earlier play. Calista is the fair penitent of the title and the end of the play finds her both sorry and reconciled. David Garrick played Lothario with great success and Calista was one of Sarah Siddons' famous roles. Samuel Johnson much admired Rowe's play, which held the stage for over a century.

**Fatal Marriage, The:** *or The Innocent Adultery*.   A tragedy by Thomas Southerne, first produced in February 1694 and published in the same year. It was based on a novel by Aphra Behn, *The Nun, or The Perjur'd Beauty* (?1688). The part of Isabella provided Elizabeth Barry with a great opportunity and the play was revived, somewhat altered, by David Garrick as *Isabella, or The Fatal Marriage*.

Isabella and Biron have married against the wishes of Biron's father, who sends his son to the wars. Biron is reported killed at the siege of Candy, and the widowed Isabella is repudiated by her father-in-law. However, she has a devoted admirer in Villeroy though she does not accept him as a husband. But after seven years of unselfish devotion her resolve weakens, and Biron's younger brother Carlos urges her to accept. Isabella marries Villeroy.

Biron returns; he has been a prisoner-of-war. It emerges that Carlos had known his brother was alive but had kept the truth to himself, hoping to supplant Biron as the heir. He had urged Isabella to marry Villeroy so as to widen the rift between her and Biron's father and discredit her son. Isabella, shattered to find her husband still living, is driven to despair at the revelation of Carlos' perfidy. Carlos, his carefully-laid plans in danger of foundering, waylays his brother and murders him. His villainy is exposed after Isabella commits suicide.

**Fata Morgana** A mirage that sometimes appears on the Calabrian coast near the Straits of Messina. In Italian literature (*Orlando Furioso* and *Orlando Innamorato*) Morgana is an enchantress, identified with Morgan le Fay of Arthurian legend.

***Fates of the Apostles, The*** A poem in Old English by Cynewulf, preserved in *The Vercelli Book*. The subject is the deeds of the 12 apostles and their deaths.

***Father and Son*** See **Gosse, Sir Edmund William**.

**Faulconbridge, Philip (the Bastard)** In Shakespeare's *King John* the son of King Richard I and Lady Faulconbridge and so acknowledged by John. In the play he is a commentator on the action and a patriotic Englishman whose loyalty to his country is unwavering. He swears fealty to the boy king Henry III at the end of the play and delivers the celebrated closing lines. The only known mention of Faulconbridge outside Shakespeare's play is a brief one in Holinshed; the character is essentially a creation of the playwright's.

**Faulkner, William (Harrison)** 1897–1962. William Faulkner (originally Falkner) was born in New Albany, Mississippi, and brought up in Oxford County, the seat of the state university. After a desultory education he joined the Royal Flying Corps in Canada but World War I ended before he was commissioned and he returned to the USA. He attended some courses at the University of Mississippi and worked at various jobs while learning to write: he published a collection of verse, *The Marble Faun*, in 1924 without attracting much attention. He went to work for a newspaper in New Orleans, where he met Sherwood Anderson and was helped and encouraged by the older writer. His first novel, *Soldiers' Pay*, was published in 1926, and told of the return to the South of a dying soldier, from World War I. It is a harrowing story but it launched Faulkner as a novelist and he followed its publication with a brief visit to Europe. *Mosquitos* (1927) is a satirical novel about artistic life in New Orleans, and *Sartoris* (1929) is the first of his novels to be set in Yoknapatawpha County, a fictional area in the northern part of Mississippi state, with the town of Jefferson as its centre. ***The Sound and the Fury*** (also 1929) is about the

Compson family and was the novel that brought William Faulkner to the attention of the critics. His reputation grew with ***As I Lay Dying*** (1930) but suffered a sharp reversal with *Sanctuary* (1931), which made him a great deal of money – the reason, the author said, for writing it. A sadistic horror story, it is the most read of all Faulkner's novels in spite of its critical reception.

Faulkner returned to his fictional county for ***Light in August*** (1932); ***Absalom, Absalom!*** (1936) takes place there in the early 19th century. A minor novel about aviators, *Pylon* (1935), came in between and *The Wild Palms* (1939), a novel about the Mississippi in flood, came after. *The Hamlet* (1940) begins the story of the Snopes family in Yoknapatawpha, and *Go Down, Moses* (1942) is a volume of short stories in the same setting. *Intruder in the Dust* (1948) is more relaxed and directly compassionate and is an excellent introduction to the work of William Faulkner and his view of the South. The accused negro, a hostage to generations of racial prejudice, is contrasted with the 14-year-old boy, whose moral awareness has time to take root before adulthood in his environment pitches him into the same straightjacket of attitudes which diminishes his elders and 'betters'. *Requiem for a Nun* (1951) is a sequel to *Sanctuary* and deals with the redemption of Temple Drake, the central

William Faulkner, 1950.

character of the first novel. *A Fable* (1954) won the Pulitzer Prize for the author but divided his admirers; it is an allegory of Jesus and the gospel story related in terms of World War I. Faulkner returned to the Snopes family in *The Town* (1957), *The Mansion* (1959), and *The Reivers* (1962), his last novel. He was awarded the Nobel Prize in 1950.

Yoknapatawpha county is William Faulkner's microcosm of the South and in his novels about it he wrote about life without offering judgments of his own. He presents his world with complete conviction and presents it whole; his novels should be read by anyone who wants to understand that grim and complex area of American life. The reading is not easy to begin with – the author's style can be very discouraging, especially in the openings of his novels – but the rewards are considerable. The South is the principal theme of Faulkner's short stories – many characters from his novels appear in them – published in *These Thirteen* (1931), *Idyll in the Desert* (1931), *Miss Zilphia Gant* (1932), *Dr Martino* (1934), *The Unvanquished* (1938), *Go Down, Moses* (1942), and *Knight's Gambit* (1949).

**Fawley, Jude** The central character of Thomas Hardy's *Jude the Obscure*. He is an orphan boy with a passion for learning he can never realize. He is attractive to the opposite sex but has no talent for handling his attachments. His second one, to Sue Bridehead, results in tragedy.

**Federalist, The** A collection of essays in support of a constitution for the USA, which was originally in the form of letters addressed to the New York press under the pseudonym Publius. They were written mainly by Alexander Hamilton with contributions by John Jay and James Madison. The letters appeared from 1787 to 1788; they were revised by Hamilton and the collected edition published in two volumes in 1788. Critical editions are numerous; the latest was by B. J. Wright in 1961.

The purpose of the letters was to influence New York voters in favour of the federal constitution and the arguments are of such quality as to be honoured in the present day, even influencing Supreme Court decisions. There are 85 essays in all and Hamilton is credited with the authorship of 51 of them.

**Felix Holt**, *the Radical*. A novel by George Eliot, first published in 1866. Often described as a political novel, it does not go further into politics than the novels of Kingsley and Elizabeth Gaskell had already taken the English reader, and in many ways its conclusions are the same as theirs

– that the mass of working people must learn to think and act for themselves.

Felix Holt has taken work as an artisan in the hope that he can imbue his fellow-workers with enthusiasm for an independent and enquiring attitude to politics. In contrast to him is Harold Transome, rich and charming and a political opportunist of the worst kind. Both men love Esther Lyon, an Independent minister's daughter. During an election riot Felix accidentally kills a man, and his trial makes Esther realize that he is the one she loves. Running through the story are the threads of a mystery surrounding the heroine's birth, and the tangled history of her claim to the Transome estates.

*Felix Holt* is probably no one's favourite George Eliot novel. The opening chapters are finely done and, inevitably, there are pleasures to be gained from reading a minor work by a major writer. She had, as for *Romola*, done her homework on industrial relations and litigation – with such care, indeed, as to stupefy the reader with the knots of the Transome case. A greater fault, perhaps, lies in the character of Felix Holt, who is too good to be true.

*Female Quixote, The* See **Lennox, Charlotte.**

**Fenton** The suitor who wins Anne Page in Shakespeare's *The Merry Wives of Windsor*. He confesses that it was her father's wealth that first provoked his attentions (Act III) but now 'I found thee of more value than stamps in gold.'

**Fenton, Sir Geoffrey** *c*.1539–1608. An Elizabethan translator, Fenton published *Tragicall Discourses* (1567), 13 stories by Matteo Bandello. Other translations are *Golden Epistles* (1575), from the Spanish of Antonio de Guevara with other pieces from Latin, French, and Italian; a version of Etienne Pasquier's *Monophile* (1572); and a translation of Francesco Guicciardini's *Storia d'Italia*.

**Ferdinand** The shipwrecked Prince of Naples in Shakespeare's *The Tempest*. He believes himself the only survivor on the strange island, where he falls in love with Miranda, Prospero's daughter.

**Ferdinand, King of Navarre** In Shakespeare's *Love's Labour's Lost*, he turns his court into a retreat for study and contemplation for three years. The arrival of the Princess of France makes hay of his resolution and soon he is writing love poems to her.

*Ferdinand Count Fathom, The Adventures of* A novel by Tobias Smollett, first published in 1753.

His third novel, it is Smollett's first move away from the picaresque and into romantic fiction.

Ferdinand is the child of a camp-follower to Marlborough's army and he is depicted as a completely self-seeking and amoral villain in what Smollett intended to be a cautionary tale. Ferdinand assumes the title of Count Fathom, and a benevolent German nobleman, Count de Melville, receives him and brings him up with his own family. Ferdinand hopes to secure the count's daughter as his wife but his attempt to woo her fails. He then turns to plundering the count's house with the help of the daughter's maid. He cheats Renaldo, the count's son, and tries to seduce Monimia, Renaldo's betrothed; Monimia escapes his attentions by feigning death. Eventually Ferdinand's wickedness is revealed and Monimia is restored to Renaldo. Ferdinand is saved from the punishment he deserves when Renaldo relents towards him; as a result Ferdinand reforms.

The book is a failure on the whole; the author's invention deserted him and the conclusion is feeble. Smollett's powerful talent is present nevertheless and he anticipates some of the gothic horrors of later writers. There is a modern edition of *Ferdinand Count Fathom* in the Oxford English Novels series, edited by Damian Grant (1978).

**Ferguson, Adam** 1723–1816. Ferguson was born at Logierait in Perthshire and was educated for the ministry at the universities of St Andrews and Edinburgh. He served in the Black Watch regiment, and succeeded David Hume in the library of the Faculty of Advocates. At Edinburgh University he was successively Professor of Natural Philosophy, of Moral Philosophy, and of Mathematics.

Ferguson was the author of one tract, one pamphlet, three books of philosophical enquiry, and one history. His **Essay on the History of Civil Society** (1767) attracted favourable notice, and **The History of the Progress and Termination of the Roman Republic** (1783) provided a carefully designed introduction to Gibbon's great work on the Roman Empire.

**Ferguson, Sir Samuel** 1810–86. The son of a Scots-Irish family, Ferguson was born in Belfast and educated at Trinity College, Dublin. Later he studied law and was called to the Bar; he became a Queen's Counsellor in 1859. A scholar and antiquary, Ferguson became Deputy Keeper of the Irish Records in 1867; he had published his first poems in 1861 and more were to be published by his widow after his death. He was knighted in 1878.

Ferguson's contribution to literature was his part in the restoration, from the original Irish, of the ancient literature which had been lost to generations brought up and taught in another language; he was not himself a poet of great distinction. *Lays of the Western Gael* (1864) contained 'The Tain-Quest', his version of the *Táin Bó Cúailgne* (The Cattle Raid of Cooley), and brought back to poetic circulation the myth of Cuchulain and the redoubtable Queen, Maev of Connaught. Other poems concerned Fergus, Conor, Deirdra, and Dermid (in Ferguson's spelling). *Congal* (1872) is a poem on the last heroic stand of Celtic paganism against triumphant Christianity. Among other works by Ferguson were *Deirdra* (1880), *The Forging of the Anchor* (1883), and *Ogham Inscriptions in Ireland, Wales and Scotland* (1887). A collection of his prose tales was edited by Lady Ferguson and published as *Hibernian Nights' Entertainment* (1887).

**Fergusson, Robert** 1750–74. Fergusson was born in Edinburgh and spent part of his childhood in Aberdeenshire before his parents returned to the city. He attended Edinburgh High School for three years and followed this with two years at Dundee Grammar School on a bursary. He went to St Andrews University as a divinity student but had to leave after four years because of his father's money troubles. He worked for an uncle in Aberdeenshire, John Forbes, but the two were hopelessly incompatible and Fergusson was obliged to walk back to Edinburgh after a quarrel. He succeeded in getting work as a copier in the Commissary Clerk's office, where he stayed for the rest of his short life.

Fergusson's first poems were lyrics to Scots airs but they were in imitation of English styles; he did not find his true voice until he began to write in the vernacular he heard spoken all round him. Walter Ruddiman, the proprietor of *The Weekly Magazine, or Edinburgh Amusement*, published Fergusson's *The Daft Days* in January 1772 and became the young poet's patron, giving his work regular publication and helping him establish a reputation. Fergusson had an ability to make friends, he was witty, and possessed a sweet singing voice; he was popular and sought-after and then inexplicably, early in 1774, he became afflicted with religious mania. He died insane in October of that year at the age of 24. He was the most notable Scots poet before Burns in the 18th-century emergence and might have surpassed him, in the opinion of some scholars, if he had lived long enough. As it is, Burns' debt to his hapless predecessor is clear. Fergusson was the poet of Edinburgh, the smoky city to which he gave a nickname in his most famous poem, *Auld Reekie*, which traces the progress of an Edinburgh day.

*The Poetical Works* of Robert Fergusson were first published in a critical edition by D. Irving (1800). A modern edition was published by The Scottish Text Society in two volumes (1954 and 1956), edited by M. P. McDiarmid.

**Ferrar, Nicholas** 1592–1637. Born in London, Ferrar entered Clare Hall, Cambridge, in 1605 and became a fellow in 1610. A brilliant scholar, he travelled on the continent for five years before embarking on what seemed to be a promising career at home. He entered Parliament in 1624, but his weak health, his uneasiness in the political climate, and his religious aspirations led him to retire to Little Gidding, an estate in Huntingdonshire that was the property of his mother.

Ferrar was joined at Little Gidding by his brother and brother-in-law and their families, and they established a kind of community life based on Church of England principles. In 1626 he was ordained a deacon by Bishop Laud, and the community of some 30 people lived an ordered life of work and prayer. Charles I visited Little Gidding in 1633 and declared himself greatly impressed with the way of life. Ferrar did much more than establish a community of introverted piety. The members were active in good works in the neighbourhood and helped to teach the children. There was a study circle, a craftsmen's establishment specializing in bookbinding, and a particular interest in the care of the sick.

The community was not, however, to survive the Puritans, who denounced it as an attempt to reintroduce Catholic practices into England. A Parliamentary raid in 1646 ended Little Gidding; Ferrar's manuscripts were destroyed, so his only surviving writings are his published translations of Valdez's *Divine Considerations* (with notes by his friend George Herbert) and of Lessius' treatise *On Temperance*.

See also **Inglesant, John** and **Eliot, T(homas) S(tearns)**.

**Ferrier, Susan (Edmundstone)** 1782–1854. The daughter of an Edinburgh official, who was a colleague of Sir Walter Scott, Susan Ferrier led a quiet life, managing her father's household after her mother died. She was acquainted with literary society through her father's friends and was warmly esteemed by Sir Walter Scott. The author of three novels of Scottish life, she has something in common with Jane Austen though, unlike her great contemporary, she is quite ex-

plicit in her comment. *Marriage* was published in 1818, and *The Inheritance* in 1824. Her last novel was *Destiny*, published in 1831.

**Ferumbras, Sir** A Middle English verse romance, based on an Old French source. (See **metrical romances**.) The story tells how the Saracens captured Rome and how Charlemagne came to the relief of the city; how Olivier, Charlemagne's champion, fought Ferumbras, son of the Sultan of Babylon, and overcame him; how Ferumbras became a Christian; how his sister Floripas, in love with the French knight Sir Guy, assisted the Christians and married her knight; and how the couple were rewarded. *Sir Ferumbras* was edited for the Early English Text Society (1879 and 1966).

**Feste** Olivia's jester in Shakespeare's *Twelfth Night*. He has the three memorable songs: 'O mistress mine', 'Come away, come away, death', and 'When that I was and a little tiny boy'. For the last one he leaves the play, which is over, and addresses the audience. Feste has the function of a commentator on the quirks of the principals. Malvolio despises him (Act I Scene 5), and Feste's joining the plot to discredit the steward brings him into the action of the play.

**Field, Nathan** c.1587–c.1633. One of the actors in Shakespeare's company, Field was also a minor Jacobean playwright. He wrote *A Woman is a Weather-Cocke* (published 1612); *Amends for Ladies* (published 1618); *The Fatal Dowry* (with Philip Massinger, published 1632); *Four Plays* (with John Fletcher, published 1647); and *The Honest Man's Fortune*, *The Knight of Malta*, and *The Queen of Corinth* (with Fletcher and Massinger, all published 1647).

**Fielding, Henry** 1707–54. The son of a general, and descended from the Earls of Desmond, Henry Fielding was born at Sharpham Park, near Glastonbury in Somerset. He was educated at Eton and lived in London after leaving school. Fielding spent a few years as a very young man about town and became interested in the theatre. His comedy in the Restoration manner, *Love in Several Masques*, was his second work (the first was a poem of no distinction called *The Masquerade*); it was given at Drury Lane in February 1728 and published in the same year. On the stage it only ran for four performances and Fielding, discouraged, went to Leyden to study law. However, he was back in London within a year, determined on a career as a playwright.

Fielding wrote 25 plays during the next eight years. His talent was for satire and the

Henry Fielding, by an unknown artist. National Portrait Gallery, London.

contemporary scene provided him with plenty of material. He would introduce Robert Walpole, George II, and Queen Caroline into his work in the boldest manner, thinly disguised. The establishment could not let him get away with it indefinitely and in June 1737 he was effectively silenced by the Theatrical Licensing Act, which enforced censorship and left only Covent Garden and Drury Lane open. Fielding's plays are rarely revived, being too closely concerned with contemporary manners, literary fashions, and politics to be of much interest to the general reader or playgoer. His most successful production was his version of Molière's *L'avare*, produced at Drury Lane in February 1733 as *The Miser. Tom Thumb: a Tragedy* is usually described as his best play. It was produced at the Haymarket in April 1730 and revived in the following year as *The Tragedy of Tragedies: or The Life and Death of Tom Thumb the Great*. It was a boisterous parody of the heroic drama associated with Dryden and Nathaniel Lee, set in the court of an unheroic King Arthur. His most highly regarded dramatic satires are *Pasquin* (Haymarket, March 1736) and *The His-*

*torical Register for the Year 1736* (Haymarket, March 1737). *Rape upon Rape*, an earlier farce (Haymarket, June 1730), was revived in London with some success during the 1950s.

Deprived of his medium, Fielding returned to the law (November 1737) and was called to the Bar in June 1740. Meanwhile, he became a successful journalist, the editor of the anti-Walpole *The Champion, or British Mercury*, published three times a week (between November 1739 and June 1741); after Walpole's fall, of *True Patriot, and History of Our Own Time* (between November 1745 and June 1746); and the burlesque *Jacobite's Journal* (between December 1747 and November 1748), which reflected his progovernment, antiJacobite views.

Fielding married Charlotte Cradock in 1734 and was to model the heroine of his most famous novel on her. The publication of Richardson's *Pamela* in 1740 provoked him to blast the work and its author with a travesty entitled *An Apology for the Life of Mrs Shamela Andrews*, published under the pseudonym of 'Mr Conny Keyber'. Fielding, like many readers then and now, could not accept the valuation placed by Richardson on his heroine or on her conduct. Pamela, though she is ready to burble 'about my Vartue' for an hour and a half, or of 'honourable Designs' all day, is depicted as a calculating and shameless hussy. Mr B., to whom Pamela did not surrender until she was properly married, is given an appropriate surname – Booby.

Out of this came Henry Fielding's first novel. After sending up Richardson in a travesty he decided to write a sort of counter-novel, with Pamela's brother, Joseph, at the mercy of Lady Booby. But the novel, once begun, took hold of the author, as novels often do, and became something else. *The History of the Adventures of Joseph Andrews* (1742) struck as new a note in English fiction as *Pamela* had. A picaresque novel of two innocents, Joseph Andrews and Parson Adams, it narrates a journey where the only true kindnesses encountered are at the hands of the apparently low characters, while respectable folk behave only with perfect circumspection. But, as Fielding is at pains to show, behaving is not the same thing as being; the Pharisees are always with us.

His next novel, *The Life of Jonathan Wild the Great*, was contained in the three volumes of *Miscellanies* which Fielding published in 1743. His brilliance as a contemporary satirist reaches its peak in this masterpiece of irony retailing the 'greatness' of an executed criminal (Wild was hanged in 1725). His chief character succeeds completely in his chosen field, hence he is great:

he is not good; but that, in the values of his society, Fielding implies, is neither here nor there. Another work contained in the *Miscellanies* is a narrative in the manner of Lucian, *A Journey from this World to the Next*, a satirical fragment on the progress of the soul.

Charlotte Fielding died in 1744 and the author was deeply involved with journalism for the next few years, particularly of an antiJacobite nature. He married Mary Daniel, who had been his wife's maid, in 1747, and in 1748, through the influence of Lord Lyttelton, became Justice of the Peace for both Westminster and Middlesex. Henry Fielding was a dedicated magistrate and one of considerable influence in the cause of order and justice. His essays demonstrate his grasp of the social conditions which lay at the root of the revolting squalor and brutality of the capital: *A Charge Delivered to the Grand Jury* (1749); *An Enquiry into the Causes of the Late Increase of Robbers etc. with Some Proposals for Remedying the Growing Evil* (1751 – Fielding's proposals were in fact the kernel of the modern police force); *Examples of the Interposition of Providence in the Detection and Punishment of Murder* (1752); and *A Proposal for Making an Effectual Provision for the Poor* (1753). His astuteness is shown in *A True State of the Case of Bosavern Peulez* (1749) and *A Clear State of the Case of Elizabeth Canning* (1753).

Before he became Justice of the Peace Fielding was at work on a third novel. **The History of Tom Jones, a Foundling** was published in 1749, reprinted almost at once, and published again in a revised edition in the same year. Fielding's masterpiece, it is faultlessly plotted and characterized; it has a warm and spirited heroine and a huge cast drawn with diamond sharpness. It has a new kind of hero, too: an unheroic one. Tom has a generous heart and, for all his faults and weaknesses, is the sort of person we would all welcome as a friend.

Fielding turned from an unheroic hero to a notably positive heroine in his next novel, **Amelia** (1751). Amelia has something, scholars believe, of Charlotte Fielding in her, as Sophia Western has; but the setting in which the new heroine exists is much more confined. The novel divides Fielding's admirers but the context of the author's life should be taken into account when considering it. He was overworked and his health was failing – though he was not yet in his 45th year. The novel displays weaknesses, certainly: Fielding's active social conscience intrudes, probably because his experiences of crime and punishment haunted him; the clumsy construction, too, is a disappointment, coming from the author of *Tom Jones*. No work by Henry

Fielding deserves less than the closest attention, however, and there are considerable rewards in compensation.

Unfortunately, it was his last novel. Had Fielding turned to fiction earlier we might well have an even richer legacy. But the tired and ailing man turned back to journalism and began *The Covent Garden Journal* in January 1752, under the pseudonym of 'Sir Alexander Drawcansir'. Some fine essays appeared in the *Journal* and also his literary quarrel with Smollett (see the entry for that novelist). By the middle of 1753 Fielding was a very sick man; medical science then could not combat asthma and dropsy and the only palliative was a stay in a more sympathetic climate. He set out for Lisbon on 26 June 1754 with his wife and daughter and wrote an account of the journey. He died in Lisbon on 8 October 1754 and lies buried in the English cemetery there. *The Journal of a Voyage to Lisbon* was published in 1755 and shows that his powers were undiminished; the shrewdness and the sharp observation are as strong as ever and to them was added his own zestful humanity. It makes a memorable travel diary.

During his comparatively short life Henry Fielding had ranged from gentle middle-class beginnings to being a writer who had to work like the devil in the theatre to keep himself, to being a lawyer and journalist, to becoming a novelist almost by accident, to being an administrator of the law who saw life at its worst. The 18th century is represented by Fielding as vividly as by Hogarth, his friend (Hogarth's *Gin Lane* was probably inspired by Fielding's pamphlet *An Enquiry into the Causes of the Late Increase of Robbers*). He was perhaps an overgenerous man, both with his money and his health, and he was deeply concerned with the worst aspect of Georgian society – the helplessness of the individual in the face of arbitrary power. His deep and varied experience of life, allied with his literary genius, gave us three remarkable novels and one indisputably great one. His fiction contains not only the social and historical background of his time but his sharp and considered criticism of them, too.

The most complete collected edition of Fielding's works is the 16-volume one by W. E. Henley, first published in 1903 and reissued in New York in 1967. The comedy *The Tragedy of Tragedies: or The Life and Death of Tom Thumb the Great* is included in *Eighteenth-Century Comedy*, edited by Simon Trussler. Numerous standard editions of the individual novels are available and there are two collected editions: Sir Walter Scott's of 1821 and the 10-volume Shakespeare

William Hogarth's engraving, 'Gin Lane'. Hogarth's friend Henry Fielding was a dedicated and far-seeing magistrate who saw the need for a properly organized force to maintain law and order. His pamphlet, *An Enquiry into the Causes of the Late Increase of Robbers* (1751) is believed to have inspired Hogarth's engraving. Victoria & Albert Museum, London.

Head Press one of 1926. The Wesleyan Edition of the *Works* of Henry Fielding began publication in 1967.

**Fielding, Sarah** 1710–68. Henry Fielding's sister was his junior by three years and was born in East Stour in Dorset. She went to live in Hammersmith, near to London in the 18th century, and became the friend of Samuel Richardson. She published **The Adventures of David Simple** in 1744 and achieved considerable celebrity; Richardson, no admirer of Sarah's brother, was generous with his praise for her. *Familiar Letters between the Principal Characters in David Simple* was published in 1747, and a second edition of *The Adventures* in the same year; Henry Fielding contributed prefaces. *The Governess, or, The Little Female Academy* (1749) preceded a continuation of *David Simple, Volume the Last* (1753). Other works were: *The Cry: a New Dramatic Fable* (1754, with Jane Collier), *The Lives of Cleopatra and Octavia* (1757), *The History of the Countess of Dellwyn* (1759), and *The History of Ophelia* (1760). Sarah Fielding published a translation of Xenophon's *Memorabilia* and *Apologia* in 1762. Her reputation rests on *David Simple*.

**Fiennes, Celia** 1662–1741. Celia (christened Cecilia) Fiennes was born at the manor of Newton Toney near Salisbury. Her father was Colonel Nathaniel Fiennes, second son of the 1st Viscount Saye and Sele; her mother was the daughter of another Roundhead colonel, Richard Whitehead. She began to travel in England about 1685, 'to regain my health by variety and change of aire and exercise ... whatever promoted that was pursued.' She wrote accounts of her journeys because, among other reasons, she felt 'that if all persons, both Ladies, much more Gentlemen, would spend some of their tyme in Journeys to visit their native Land ... It would form such an Idea of England, add much to its Glory and Esteem in our minds and cure the evil itch of overvalueing foreign parts.' She observed tartly that many 'Gentlemen in general service of their country ... are ignorant of anything but the name of the place for which they serve in parliament.'

The account of her journeys was intended by Celia Fiennes for the members of her large family and remained in manuscript. A copy of the first draft came into the hands of the poet Robert Southey, who quoted from it in *Omniana or Horae Otiosiores* (1812); the fuller, later manuscript was acquired by the 16th Baron Saye and Sele about 1885. Emily Griffiths, the baron's daughter, transcribed most of it and published it as *Through England on a Side Saddle in the Time of William and Mary* (1888). In spite of careless editing the book interested historians, particularly G. M. Trevelyan, who acknowledged this account in his *English Social History*. But no scholarly edition appeared until 1947, when Christopher Morris's highly praised one was published in The Cresset Library series.

Christopher Morris's edition divides *The Journeys of Celia Fiennes* into four parts: The Early Journeys in the South (*c.*1685–96), The Northern Journey and the Tour of Kent (1697), 'My Great Journey to Newcastle and to Cornwall' (1698), and London and the Later Journeys (*c.*1701–03). G. M. Trevelyan reaffirmed his enthusiasm for Celia Fiennes when Morris's edition appeared and gave it unqualified praise. The book, which unfortunately remains little known, gives a valuable picture of life in England in the late 17th century and is prized as a source of economic and social history; Trevelyan placed it on the same high level as Defoe's *A Tour thro' the whole Island of Great Britain*.

**Finching, Flora** In Dickens's *Little Dorrit*, a former love of Arthur Clennam's. The daughter of the mean old Casby, she has married during

Arthur's years abroad and is a widow when Arthur returns. She is fluffy, romantic, and endearingly silly; she is also warm-hearted and kind.

**Finlay, George** 1799–1875. Finlay was one of the enthusiasts for Greek freedom who had been with Byron in Missolonghi. He was born at Faversham in Kent and studied law at Glasgow University and at Göttingen. He went to Greece in 1823 and after the struggle for independence had succeeded he decided to settle there. He bought an estate in Attica and eventually died in Athens. He began his histories of Greece while living there; he eventually covered the centuries that followed the subjugation by the Romans to its hard-wrested freedom from the Turks. *Greece under the Romans* (1844), *The History of Greece from its Conquest by the Crusaders to its Conquest by the Turks, and of the Empire of Trebizond* (1851), *The History of the Byzantine and Greek Empires 716–1453* (1853), *The History of Greece under Othman and Venetian Domination* (1856), and *A History of the Greek Revolution* (1861) supplemented the histories of Grote and Thirlwall and are pioneer works in their treatment of a continuous theme. Many of Finlay's letters from the new-born country were published in *The Times* (1864–70). They are historically valuable but so far have not been collected. Finlay's histories were published collectively as *A History of Greece from its Conquest by the Romans to the Present Time: 146 BC to AD 1864* (1877).

***Finnegans Wake*** See **Joyce, James (Augustine Aloysius).**

***Finnsburh*** The name given to a fragment of 50 lines of Old English poetry discovered, in the cover of another manuscript, in the library of Lambeth Palace in the early 18th century by George Hickes. Hickes made a copy, which according to H. M. Chadwick is 'extremely corrupt'; this is the only surviving trace of the poem – the original manuscript is lost. The subject of the poem was evidently popular since it occupies a part of Beowulf, being sung by the king's minstrel after the defeat of Grendel. Finn is King of the Frisians, and Hildeburh is his queen; Hnaef is the queen's brother. There is fighting between Finn and Hnaef in Finn's country (exactly why is not made clear) and Hnaef is killed. Later Hnaef's men attack Finn and the Frisians (whom they have sworn to serve after their leader's fall); they kill Finn, then carry off the queen and Finn's treasure. The *Finnsburh* fragment describes the defence of the hall in which Hnaef and his men are under attack. There are translations of the fragment in C. K. Scott-Moncrieff's *Widsith, Beowulf, Finnsburgh, Waldere, Deor* (1921), and C. W. Kennedy's *An Anthology of Old English Poetry* (1960).

**Firbank, (Arthur Annesley) Ronald** 1886–1926. Ronald Firbank was the son of a wealthy company director and was born in London. He was educated at Uppingham School and went on to Cambridge, but left in 1909 without graduating and travelled in the Mediterranean. He became a Roman Catholic while at Cambridge, attracted by the ritual. Delicate in health and thoroughly eccentric, Firbank, whose character is described by his friend Osbert Sitwell in *Noble Essences*, had wealth enough to indulge his own way of life. He engaged a gardener to come and water the palm tree in his apartment twice a day, and wrote his novels on deep blue postcards. He grew up in the 1890s and died in the 1920s, publishing his first book of stories, *Odette d'Antrevernes* and *A Study in Temperament*, in 1905. The series of novels for which his name is famous began with *Vainglory* (1915) and continued with *Inclinations* (1916), *Caprice* (1917), *Valmouth: A Romantic Novel* (1919), *Santal* – a short story (1921), *The Flower Beneath the Foot* (1923), *Prancing Nigger* (1924), and *Concerning the Eccentricities of Cardinal Pirelli* (1926). *The Princess Zoubaroff: A Comedy* (1920) was not produced during his lifetime, and several more short poems were published posthumously.

Firbank's novels almost defy description and his wit exists only in their context. There is a strange dreamlike atmosphere about them: completely artificial, they carry what A. Alvarez described as 'a sense of ominous unease' like some of the drawings of Aubrey Beardsley; certainly his work has the stamp of another time upon it.

***Firmilian, or The Student of Badajoz.*** A parody by William Edmonstoune Aytoun of the poetry of the poets he dubbed the 'Spasmodic School': Sydney Dobell, Philip James Bailey, and Alexander Smith. It was first published in 1854. Firmilian is writing a poetic tragedy on the subject of Cain. Feeling he must, to do his subject justice, acquire some insight into the 'mental spasms of the tortured Cain', Firmilian goes out and starts committing crimes, with ludicrous consequences.

**Fisher, John** 1459–1535. John Fisher was born in Beverley in Yorkshire. He was educated at the cathedral school of Rochester and Michaelhouse College, Cambridge. A brilliant scholar, Fisher became master of his college in 1497 and confessor to the Queen Mother, Margaret Beaufort.

Elected chancellor of the university in 1504, he was re-elected regularly and finally became chancellor for life. He became Bishop of Rochester in 1504. Fisher worked hard to improve the standard of Cambridge University and it was under his aegis that Erasmus taught there; Fisher himself undertook the study of Greek at this stage of his life.

Fisher was just as aware as Colet that the condition of the church deserved severe criticism, but unlike Colet he felt the full force of the Reformation in England. In his writings he upheld the doctrines of the Roman Catholic church and asserted its right to reform itself, without state interference; his faith was coming under attack as Protestant tendencies grew in the universities. He was Catherine of Aragon's confessor and protested strongly against Henry VIII's plans to divorce her, speaking against it in the legate's court in 1529. His unwavering opposition to Henry doomed him; he refused to take the Oath of Supremacy acknowledging the king as head of the Church. He was imprisoned in the Tower, his property confiscated and his health failing. Cromwell entreated him to yield and in May 1535 the pope made him a cardinal in recognition of his merits. But this only enraged the king and Fisher was beheaded on Tower Hill a month later. He was canonized by the Catholic Church in 1936.

Fisher belongs to history rather than literature and his contribution to written literature in English is no larger than the rest (excepting More) of the group of Renaissance Englishmen to which he belongs. His real contribution lies in his influence as one of the greatest teachers and scholars of his day and he assembled one of the finest libraries in Europe. A 16th-century life of Fisher, preserved in the Harleian Manuscripts in the British Library, was edited by R. Bayne and published by the Early English Text Society in 1921.

See also **Erasmus, Desiderius**; **Grocyn, William**; **Colet, John**; and **Linacre, Thomas**.

**Fitz-Boodle, George Savage** One of Thackeray's pen-names. *The Fitz-Boodle Papers* appeared in *Fraser's Magazine*, from June 1842 to February 1843.

**Fitzgerald, Edward** 1809–83. Fitzgerald was born Purcell; when his maternal grandfather died in 1818 the family adopted his name and arms. Fitzgerald's father was John Purcell, a country gentleman of Bredfield Hall near Woodbridge in Suffolk, where Edward was born. He was educated at King Edward VI School in Bury St Edmunds and at Trinity College, Cambridge.

He became a close friend of Thackeray at Cambridge and later of Tennyson and Carlisle. After leaving Cambridge in 1830 Fitzgerald spent a short time in Paris; then he returned to Suffolk and made his home there. He married in 1849 the daughter of Bernard Barton and helped her with the publication of a selection from her father's works. But the marriage was not a success and they soon separated. Fitzgerald's first publication was *The Meadows of Spring*, verses which appeared in *Hone's Year Book* in 1831. *Euphranor: A Dialogue on Youth* (1851) was a comment on English education; *Polonius: A Collection of Wise Saws and Modern Instances* (1852) was a book of quotations.

He had meanwhile become interested in Spanish literature and studied the language with his friend Edward Cowell, a linguist, and published *Six Dramas of Calderón* in 1853. These were versions in blank verse and prose, not translations, and the volume was disliked by the critics. But readers encouraged Fitzgerald and he published two more plays by Calderón in 1865: *Such Stuff as Dreams are Made of* and *The Mighty Magician* (*La Vida es Sueño* and *El Mágico Prodigioso*). His studies with Cowell led him to an interest in Persian poetry and in 1855 he began to work on a version of the *Salámán and Absál* of Jámí, an allegory, published in 1856. In 1859 he published **Rubáiyát of 'Omar Khayyám,** *the Astronomer-Poet of Persia, translated into English Verse*. The first edition contained 75 *rubáiyát* (quatrains); a second revised edition contained 110; the total was reduced to 101 in 1872 and further revised; the fourth edition of 1879 is the one familiar to modern readers.

This is the work for which Fitzgerald is remembered. He continued to work on English versions but produced nothing else which so caught his readers' fancy. Other works are *Agamemnon: A Tragedy taken from Aeschylus* (1869), *The Downfall and Death of King Oedipus* (1881), from the two plays by Sophocles, and *A Bird's-eye View of Faríd-Uddín Attar's Bird-Parliament* (published posthumously, 1889). Fitzgerald knew many distinguished Victorian writers and was an excellent letter writer; his *Letters and Literary Remains* were edited by W. A. Wright (1889).

**Fitzgerald, F(rancis) Scott (Key)** 1896–1940. F. Scott Fitzgerald was born in St Paul, Minnesota, and attended Newman School, New Jersey, before going on to Princeton, where one of his contemporaries was Edmund Wilson. Wilson remained a steadfast admirer of Fitzgerald throughout the vicissitudes of the latter's career.

Fitzgerald served in the US army during World War I but was not posted to Europe. He used the time spent in army camps to work on a novel and to woo Zelda Sayre, whom he married. *This Side of Paradise* (1920) made Fitzgerald famous, and a collection of short stories, *Flappers and Philosophers*, was published in the same year. *The Beautiful and Damned* (1922) was not so favourably received, with its satirical picture of the American boom, the neurotic round of parties, and the preoccupation with money. Fitzgerald had arrived among the rich through his success and he was a merciless observer of them; but the spirit of the time infected him also and the Fitzgeralds were soon living to the limit in Europe and the USA, the money coming from Fitzgerald's steady production of stories for expensive magazines. A second collection, *Tales of the Jazz Age* (1922), contained 'The Diamond as Big as the Ritz'; a third, *All the Sad Young Men* (1926), the story called 'The Rich Boy': both stories identify the particular malaise of the time, while the fine, flawed novel **Tender is the Night** (1934) demonstrated Fitzgerald's understanding of it. Meanwhile, in France, he met Ernest Hemingway, whose talent he had already spotted and to whom he was unstintingly helpful; here he wrote his best book, **The Great Gatsby** (1925), the key novel of the American Jazz Age.

Scott Fitzgerald and Zelda Sayre in 1919, at the Sayre home in Montgomery, Alabama. They were married in 1920.

Fitzgerald lived briefly in America in 1927 and 1928 and had an unrewarding time with Hollywood; the film industry and he were to come together later but he returned to Europe in 1928. Zelda Fitzgerald's mental instability was gaining on her and Fitzgerald himself was unable to deal with the pressures of the playboy life; he wrote for money, drank too much, tried to care for his wife, and somehow managed to write *Tender is the Night. Taps at Reveille* (1935) was his last collection of stories. He returned to America and his health broke down completely, a period of his life recorded with memorable precision in contributions to the journal *Esquire* in 1936 and included in *The Crack-Up* (1945), which was edited by Edmund Wilson. He was loaded with debts and struggling with alcoholism when he went to Hollywood again in 1937 to earn money. During this final period he worked on *The Last Tycoon*, a novel about a Hollywood producer which he did not complete, and wrote 17 short stories. He died in 1940 in Hollywood, of a heart attack. *The Last Tycoon* was published in 1941; the last stories were collected as *The Pat Hobby Stories* and published in 1962.

*The Letters of F. Scott Fitzgerald* (1963) was edited by Andrew Turnbull, who also wrote a biography, *Scott Fitzgerald* (1962).

**Flashman** The bully of Rugby School in *Tom Brown's Schooldays*. See **Hughes, Thomas.**

**Flatman, Thomas** 1637–88. A fellow of New College, Oxford, Flatman was much esteemed as a painter of miniatures. His *Poems and Songs* was published in 1674 and his verse occasionally appeared in anthologies. He was one of a host of minor poets in a period that produced several major ones and his work receives little attention now.

**Flecknoe, Richard** *c.*1600–*c.*1678. Flecknoe was a minor poet and playwright of whose youth little is known beyond what he reveals in a book of letters written to friends while on his travels, *Relation of Ten Years Travels in Europe, Asia, Affrique and America* (1654). He was probably Irish and may once have been a priest. He wrote five plays, of which only one, *Love's Dominion* (1654), was ever performed; *Enigmaticall Characters*, a collection of prose sketches (1658); and a book of verse, *Epigrams of All Sorts* (1670). His *Short Discourse on the English Stage* (1664) roused Marvell to lampoon him (*An English Priest at Rome*) and Dryden to satirize him (*Mac Flecknoe*).

**Fletcher, Giles (Senior)** 1546–1611. The son of a Kentish clergyman, Fletcher was educated at Eton and King's College, Cambridge. He became a fellow and a lecturer in Greek and held various appointments in the college, which he relinquished upon his marriage. Fletcher became a doctor of Civil Law in 1581 and entered public life in the following year as chancellor of the diocese of Sussex. He sat in parliament for Winchelsea (1584) and was appointed Remembrancer of the City of London (1585). Soon after that he served on diplomatic missions to Holland, Hamburg, and Scotland; in 1588 he became ambassador to Russia.

Fletcher secured a favourable trade agreement with Russia and in 1589 he presented Elizabeth I with a manuscript containing a description of his sojourn in Russia and his impressions of the country: *Of the Russe Common Wealth*. It was to have been published in 1591 but the Russia Company objected and a shortened version appeared in the first volume of Hakluyt's *Voyages* in 1598. Further editions were published in 1643, 1656, and 1657 and it was widely read – a firsthand account by an Englishman of the life of an exotic far-away people. The complete text appeared first in Bond's edition of 1856.

Other works by Giles Fletcher are *Licia: Poems of Love; the Rising to the Crowne of Richard the Third* (1593) and a book of Latin verse, *De literis antiquae Britanniae* (1633). *Licia* contains a sonnet sequence and some love poems; the *Rising* is a 'Fall of Princes' monologue, in the manner of *A Mirror for Magistrates*. Fletcher had ambitions to write a history of Queen Elizabeth's reign, in Latin, but was obliged to abandon it when he failed to secure Burghley's patronage.

**Fletcher, Giles (Junior)** 1585–1623. The younger son of the diplomat and poet Giles Fletcher, he was educated at Westminster School and at Trinity College, Cambridge, where he was a distinguished Greek scholar and became reader in the Greek language.

Fletcher left the university in 1619 and became a rector of Alderton in Suffolk, where he died at the age of 38. He is remembered for his long allegorical poem in eight-line stanzas, *Christs Victorie and Triumph in Heaven and Earth, Over and After Death* (1610). His poetic ancestor is Edmund Spenser and his poem was obviously read by Milton. It is an example of baroque religious poetry, executed with many flourishes and with great care in presentation, and was popular in its day.

**Fletcher, John** 1579–1625. (For the dramatic works written by Fletcher in collaboration with Francis Beaumont see **Beaumont and Fletcher**.) John Fletcher was the son of Richard Fletcher, who became Bishop of London, and was cousin

to Giles and Phineas Fletcher. He was born at Rye in Sussex and educated at Benet College, Cambridge.

Nothing is known of Fletcher's life from the time he entered Cambridge until his appearance in London about 1606 as a working playwright for the children's companies in collaboration, usually, with Francis Beaumont. From the children's companies Fletcher graduated to writing for The King's Men at the Globe Theatre – Shakespeare's company – and worked with Beaumont until the latter died in 1616. Facile and inventive, Fletcher collaborated successfully with other contemporaries and even claimed a contribution to his own efforts by another busy, if senior, playwright – William Shakespeare himself.

Fletcher's sole authorship is attributed to the following plays: *The Faithful Shepheardess* (produced 1610); *The Loyal Subject* (produced c.1618); *Valentinian* and *The Mad Lover* (produced before 1619); *The Humorous Lieutenant* (produced 1619); *The Island Princess* (produced 1621); *Rule a Wife and Have a Wife* and *A Wife for a Month* (produced 1624); *Monsieur Thomas* (published 1639); and *Women Pleased, The Pilgrim, The Woman's Prize, Bonduca*, and *The Chances* (all published 1647). Not more than half of these works are given more than mere acknowledgement by scholars and the same is true of the mass of work Fletcher wrote with Massinger, Rowley, Middleton, Shirley, and others.

Among the plays by Fletcher and Massinger are *Sir John van Olden Barnavelt* (produced 1619); *The Spanish Curate* (produced 1622); and *The Little French Lawyer* and *The Custome of the Countrey* (both published 1647). Also by Fletcher, probably with both Massinger and Beaumont, is *The Beggar's Bush* (produced 1622). *The Elder Brother* (published 1637) and *The Lovers' Progress* (published 1647) were by Fletcher and revised by Massinger. *The Bloody Brother* (produced 1616) is attributed to Fletcher, Massinger, Jonson, and Chapman. *The Two Noble Kinsmen* (published 1634) contains additions by Shakespeare and *Henry VIII* by Shakespeare has contributions by Fletcher.

Fletcher died at the age of 46, a victim of the severe outbreak of plague in London in 1625.

**Fletcher, Phineas** 1582–1650. The elder son of Giles Fletcher, the diplomat and poet, and brother of Giles Fletcher, Junior. He was born at Cranbrook, in Kent, and educated at Eton and King's College, Cambridge, which he entered in 1600. He stayed at the university for 11 years and during that time wrote a quantity of verse which, like that of his brother Giles, followed the manner of Spenser. However, he made no particular reputation with it and from 1612 to 1614 lived as guest of the Willoghby family at Hilgay in Norfolk. He wrote a play for the visit of King James to King's College in 1615 but the king left before the play was staged. After this disappointment Fletcher took holy orders, married, and became chaplain to Sir Henry Willoghby at Risley in Derbyshire. He became rector of Hilgay in 1621 and spent the rest of his life there.

Fletcher's poetry was published after 1621 and is of no particular interest other than as an example of the period. It is diffuse and repetitious, and the anti-Catholic strain contributes no virtue. *Locustae: vel pietas Jesuitica* and the longer English version *The Locusts or Apollyonists* (1627) is an anti-Catholic poem in which Satan launches the Counter-Reformation with the Jesuits as his generals. Fletcher's next work was published as *Brittain's Ida Written by that Renowned Poet Edmond Spencer* in 1628; it is an erotic narrative poem about Venus and Anchises and the deliberate attribution to another – and infinitely greater – poet may have been because Fletcher was by then a practising cleric. *Sicelides a Piscatory* (1631) was the play that King James did not stay to see in Cambridge; it is a pastoral with fishermen added. *The Purple Island* (1633) purports to explore the nature, psychology, and physical construction of man; the science available to Fletcher at that time was very limited but there was more than enough religion to make a very long poem, with the vices and virtues fighting for possession of the soul.

The poetical works of Giles and Phineas Fletcher were collected and published in two volumes (1908–09) edited by F. S. Boas.

**Flite, Miss** In Dickens's *Bleak House*, a pathetic old woman with a suit in chancery. She lives out her life in the shadow of the court, hoping for a judgment, and keeps birds in cages which she will release 'When my judgment should be given'.

**Florence of Worcester** See **Worcester, Florence of.**

*Flores and Blancheflour* A Middle English verse romance of the 13th century. (See **metrical romances**.) Blancheflour is the daughter of a French widow who, while on a pilgrimage, was captured by a Saracen king and carried off to Spain. The Saracen queen bears a son, Flores, on the same day and the two are brought up together. They fall in love, the king disapproves, and while Flores is absent Blancheflour is sold to a slave dealer; Flores is told that she is dead. When

he tries to kill himself his parents relent and try to help him recover her. He goes to the East in disguise and traces Blancheflour to the harem of the Emir of Babylon. He bribes his way into the harem but the reunited lovers are discovered and condemned to death. One of the courtiers suggests to the emir that it would be as well to discover how Flores managed to get into the harem, and he tells the emir his story. The emir is touched, forgives the lovers, and gives Blancheflour, whom he had intended to marry, to Flores. When Flores returns to Spain and succeeds to the kingdom he becomes a Christian. *Flores and Blancheflour* was edited by C. H. Hartshorne (1829), by D. Laing for the Abbotsford Club (1857), and by J. R. Lumby for the Early English Text Society (1866); it was revised by G. H. McKnight (1901) and by A. B. Taylor (1927). A modern version by B. B. Broughton was published in *Richard the Lion-hearted and other Medieval Romances* (New York, 1966).

**Florimell** The virtuous woman of Books III and IV of Spenser's *The Faerie Queene*. She loves the knight Marinell, who, after first disregarding her devotion, is eventually touched by her love.

**Florio, John** *c.*1553–1625. Florio was the son of an Italian Protestant refugee and his Christian name was originally Giovanni, though he was born in London. Florio was educated at Magdalen College, Oxford, which he did not enter until the age of 28 after spending much time abroad. He had been fortunate in the patronage of the Earl of Leicester and in 1578 dedicated his *First Fruits* to him. This was a youthful miscellany of translations, proverbs, and linguistic instruction, and Florio published his first full-scale translation, the *Voyages* of Jacques Cartier, in 1580. He was in the service of the French ambassador in London from 1583, following his years at Oxford, where he had taught French and Italian.

After another miscellany, *Second Fruits* (1591), Florio published his great Italian–English dictionary in 1598 and his talent for securing noble patronage is evident from the dedication, to the earls of Rutland and Southampton and the Countess of Bedford (the Earl of Leicester had died the previous year). His most famous work was his translation of the *Essais* of Michel Eyquem de Montaigne, the definitive edition of which had been published in Paris in 1595. Florio published his translation in 1603 and once more littered the dedication page with the names of aristocratic patrons. He became reader in Italian to Anne, James I's queen, in 1603, and a groom of the privy chamber in 1604. He was married to Rosa,

Samuel Daniel's sister, who was the Rosalind of Spenser's *The Shepheardes Calender*.

Florio succeeded in conveying the quality of Montaigne in spite of his tendency to extravagance and eccentricity of style and the influence of the *Essays* in late-Elizabethan and Jacobean England was strong. His *Dictionary* acquired an English–Italian supplement in 1657 by G. Terriano and was a standard work for a hundred years. Florio's last years are obscure but he may have lost his place at court; it is believed that he was living in poverty and died of the plague.

**Florizel** The son of Polixenes, King of Bohemia, in Shakespeare's *The Winter's Tale*. He falls in love with the pretty shepherdess, Perdita, but his father opposes the marriage to a low-born girl. With the help of Camillo, he elopes to Sicily with Perdita, not knowing that she is a lost princess of that country.

*Flower and the Leaf, The* A poem of unknown authorship of the latter half or end of the 15th century, believed by some scholars to be by the author of *The Assembly of Ladies*. The 'voice' in this poem also is a woman's; this lady observes the followers of the Leaf and the followers of the Flower. The allegory demonstrates the opposition of qualities – the Leaf for steadfastness and the Flower for transitory beauty – and concludes that each has much of worth to contribute.

The poem was one of those attributed to Geoffrey Chaucer until scholarship established a Chaucer canon. It is regarded as the best of the Chaucer 'apocrypha', and, when still believed to be the master's work, was used by William Hazlitt as an example of the exceptional merits of Chaucer the poet.

*Flush* See **Woolf, (Adeline) Virginia**.

**Fool** The court fool in Shakespeare's *King Lear*. He goes out into the stormy night with Lear and in all his scenes provides a commentary on the old king's behaviour. The commentary becomes more pointed as their situation becomes more serious. He disappears from the play at the end of Act III Scene 6 after his 'And I'll go to bed at noon.'

*Fool of Quality, The* A novel by Henry Brooke, published in five volumes (1766–72).

Henry, second son of the Earl of Moreland, is called a 'fool of quality' because he seems dull and unintelligent in comparison to his elder brother. Rejected by his parents, he is reared by his foster mother and educated by his uncle. He grows into a splendid young man of strength and beauty; he is also a man of virtue who spends his time in helping the unfortunate.

On this slender framework Brooke hangs a number of discourses on various subjects, chiefly the human condition and, in the latter part, on Christian mysticism. The book has no status as a novel and the device of discussion between the author and a friend on the issues raised is very cumbersome. But Henry Brooke does raise issues that were to be taken up in the near future by Jean-Jacques Rousseau, William Godwin, and Thomas Paine. John Wesley admired Brooke's ideas and made an edited version of the book for use by Methodists (1781), and Charles Kingsley wrote a preface to the 1859 edition giving the work high praise.

*Fool's Errand, A* See **Tourgée, Albion W(inegar)**.

**Foote, Samuel** 1720–77. Foote was born at Truro, in Cornwall, the son of wealthy parents, and was educated at Worcester College, Oxford. His extravagant way of life exhausted his fortune and he was obliged to earn his living and, having some experience as an amateur, decided to become an actor. His first ventures were not successful but he found his real forte in comedy. In 1747 he took over the management of the Haymarket, which did not have a patent as a playhouse; but Foote evaded the Licensing Act by 'inviting' an audience and serving refreshment to his ostensible guests. He enjoyed considerable success in his burlesques of public figures and fellow actors but he inherited another fortune in 1749, which he happily spent in Paris.

Foote was the author of two successful farces, *The Englishman in Paris* (1753) and *The Englishman Returned from Paris* (1756), and, his second fortune exhausted, he returned to the theatre to pursue his career in earnest. He took over the Haymarket again and in 1760 presented his most successful comedy, *The Minor*, a satire on George Whitefield and the Methodists. In 1766, as a guest of Lord Mexborough, Foote became the victim of a practical joke which was to have serious consequences. He was provided with a horse which proved to be unmanageable; the horse threw him and smashed one of his legs, which had to be amputated; Foote's career as an actor was at an end. The company, appalled by the turn of events, sought to make amends and the Duke of York, who was present, persuaded the king to grant a patent to Foote for his theatre, which became London's third Theatre Royal.

Foote's wit and mimicry were acknowledged to be brilliant – and cruel. Samuel Johnson admitted his gifts but he despised his use of them; David Garrick was often the target of Foote's malice and probably annoyed Foote by declining to acknowledge the fact. A figure of theatrical, rather than literary, history, Samuel Foote kept wit alive in the 18th-century theatre at a time when it might have suffocated from sentimentality.

**Ford** In Shakespeare's *The Merry Wives of Windsor* Frank Ford is unreasonably jealous of his wife, Alice, and is stung to fury when he hears that Falstaff is pursuing her. He masquerades as 'Master Brook' to find out more from the fat knight.

**Ford, Ford Madox** 1873–1939. The son of Franz Huffer, a German printer and newspaper proprietor who emigrated to England and anglicized his name, Ford Madox Hueffer was born in Merton, Surrey. His maternal grandfather was the painter Ford Madox Brown. Hueffer was educated at a private school in Folkestone and at University College School in London. His first published work was *The Brown Owl: A Fairy Story* (1891), followed by *The Feather* (1892), a novel *The Shifting of the Fire* (1892), and his first book of verse, *The Questions at the Well* (1893). Hueffer collaborated with Joseph Conrad on two novels, *The Inheritors* (1901) and *Romance* (1903), and continued to publish fiction, verse, criticism, travel books, and memoirs until the end of his life. He was the first editor of *The English Review*, founded in 1908, and the first publisher of work by D. H. Lawrence and Ezra Pound. Other writers to appear in the *Review* under his editorship were Hardy, Henry James, H. G. Wells, Arnold Bennett, and Galsworthy. During World War I he was invalided home, shell-shocked, and never regained normal health. He changed his name to Ford Madox Ford in 1919.

With a respectable reputation as a novelist, poet, editor, and critic Ford began to attract serious critical attention with *The Good Soldier* (1915), a fine ironic novel of 'civilized' life, and the four postwar novels with Christopher Tietjens as the central character: *Some Do Not* (1924), *No More Parades* (1925), *A Man Could Stand Up* (1926), and *The Last Post* (1928); the whole sequence is known as *Parade's End*. The most considerable of his prewar novels was *The Fifth Queen* trilogy, about Katherine Howard and Henry VIII: *The Fifth Queen and How She Came to Court* (1906), *Privy Seal: His Last Venture* (1907), and *The Fifth Queen Crowned* (1908). Among his critical writings were *Ford Madox Brown* (1896), *Rosetti* (1902) *The Pre-Raphaelite Brotherhood* (1907), *The Critical Attitude* (1911), *Women and Men* (1923), and *Portraits from Life* (1937).

*The Good Soldier* is related by John Dowell, an American in Germany with his wife Florence. They meet Captain Ashburnham and his wife Leonora; Ashburnham has a fine reputation as a soldier, magistrate, and landlord and has an estate in Hampshire. The progress of the friendship and the events of the following nine years are related in the order in which Dowell succeeds in fitting them together, not chronologically. Leonora Ashburnham, a Roman Catholic, proves to be a cold-hearted woman who has no sympathy with her husband's generous treatment of his tenants and workers. It puts a strain on his means and Leonora succeeds in gaining control of the Ashburnham finances. She restores prosperity but her treatment of their dependants drives Ashburnham away from her. He indulges in casual affairs; but Leonora offers the world an impeccable façade. Dowell, meanwhile, discovers Florence's adultery with a young American: she also becomes Ashburnham's mistress and, when this is discovered, she commits suicide. When Nancy, whose father is stationed in India, goes to live with Leonora and her husband she and Ashburnham fall in love. Ashburnham sends Nancy back to her father in India; Leonora has tried to persuade the girl to surrender to Ashburnham, not knowing that he has resolved not to touch Nancy. After she leaves he kills himself, and Leonora remarries and moves away. Dowell buys the estate, and provides a home for Nancy, and realizes that he has been hopelessly deceived by his assumptions about the lives of civilized people behaving in accordance with a code of conduct. The novel is finely organized and compulsively readable to the end, when the pattern is complete.

**Ford, John** *c*.1586–*c*.1639. Like Tourneur and Webster, Ford is one of the Jacobean–Caroline playwrights of whom we know very little apart from their work. He was born in Devonshire, may have been educated at Oxford (a John Ford registered at Exeter College in 1601), and entered the Middle Temple in 1602. He may have practised law in London and he probably died in Devonshire. His literary activities, which are better documented than his personal life, began with an elegy on the Earl of Devonshire, who died after some years of being out of favour at court: *Fame's Memoriall* (1606). In the same year Ford published a prose pamphlet, chivalric in tone, called *Honor Triumphant: or The Peere's Challenge*; to this was appended a poem, *The Monarches Meeting*. A tract on proper conduct, *A Line of Life*, was published in 1620. After these early literary works he became involved in drama.

Ford's first work for the theatre was in collaboration with Thomas Dekker and William

Rowley, *The Witch of Edmonton* (1623). *The Spanish Gipsie* (published 1653) was written in collaboration with Thomas Middleton and *The Late Murder of the Son upon the Mother* (now lost) was a hurried piece of play cobbling with Dekker, Rowley, and John Webster (1624). *The Sun's Darling* was a masque written with Dekker (1624). The plays that represent Ford's own work begin with *The Lover's Melancholy* (published 1629), a romantic piece about a melancholy prince. *The Broken Heart* (published 1633) is believed to have been his next play and shows a marked advance in stagecraft, though the characters are not really convincing. *Love's Sacrifice* (published 1633) is a further improvement but it is hardly actable out of its time, unrelieved piece of grief that it is. *'Tis Pity She's a Whore* (published 1633) is regarded as Ford's best play but it lacks the genius that went into *The Duchess of Malfi* and *The Changeling* to make the nastiness bearable; and Ford simply does not rise to those levels. *Perkin Warbeck* (published 1634) has more to recommend it; it is a chronicle play of considerable quality that has claims to revival. *The Fancies, Chast and Noble* and *The Ladies Triall* (both 1638) are insignificant comedies.

Ford's claims to attention lie in his subtle blank verse, which sustains the interest of his dialogue, and his attention to human sympathies. His works were collected and edited by W. Gifford and published in 1827. A revision by A. H. Bullen was published in 1895.

**Ford, Mistress** One of the merry wives of Windsor in Shakespeare's play of that name, Alice Ford contrives to punish Falstaff for his presumption and her husband for his jealousy at the same time. Her ally in these plans is her friend Meg (Mistress Page).

**Forrest, The** Ben Jonson gave this name to the collection of short poems he included in the edition of his works published in 1616. Some of his best-known pieces appear in the collection: 'That Women are but Men's Shaddowes', 'To Penshurst', 'Come, my Celia, let us prove', and the celebrated 'Song: to Celia' ('Drinke to me, onely, with thine eyes').

**Forsaken Merman, The** A poem by Matthew Arnold, first published in 1849 in *The Strayed Reveller and Other Poems*. A merman laments his wife, a girl from the land; she bore him children and then felt the call of her own world in the sound of the church bells at Easter. She leaves her sea king and never returns. The poet uses a variety of metres and achieves remarkable pathos in his telling of the merman's grief.

**Fors Clavigera: Letters to the Workmen and Labourers of Great Britain.** A series of monthly pamphlets by John Ruskin in the form of letters, begun in 1871 and continued, not quite regularly, until 1884. There are 96 letters in all. A great range of subjects is covered in the collection but the principal theme is the wretchedness of life for most people in England, its causes, and the means of changing it. Much of what Ruskin wrote in *Fors Clavigera* has been shown to have permanent value. He deplored the waste of acquired skill and experience occurring in a society devoted to finding ways of cheaper and quicker production with the consequent denial of skill and craft. On the other hand he valued the progressive use of machinery and urged better design. Ruskin himself explains his title: '*Fors Clavigera* is fortune bearing a club, a key, and a nail, symbolizing the deed of Hercules, the patience of Ulysses, and the law of Lycurgus.' (Lycurgus was the legislator of Sparta in ancient Greece.)

**Forster, E(dward) M(organ)** 1879–1970. E. M. Forster was born in London and educated at Tonbridge School and King's College, Cambridge. His father died when the boy was less than two years old and Forster's security was centred on his mother, but in spite of a spoiled unpromising childhood and a perfect hatred of Tonbridge School he had many friends at Cambridge and was happy there. In his last year he became a member of the Apostles society, which at the time included Bertrand Russell, Lytton Strachey, A. N. Whitehead, Leonard Woolf, and Desmond MacCarthy among its members. After he left Cambridge, Forster had no need to work, thanks to a legacy from his great aunt, Marianne Thornton, which had already paid for his education; he went with his mother on an extended tour of Italy, which lasted a year. He taught Latin at the Working Men's College for a brief period in 1902, and then went on a tour of Greece. His literary career began in the following year, with contributions to *The Independent Review*.

In 1905 Forster accepted an appointment in Germany, to tutor the children of the Countess von Arnim at Nassenheide for some months, and returned to England for the publication of his first novel, **Where Angels Fear to Tread**. He resumed his classes at the Working Men's College, and lectured on Italian art and history for the Cambridge Local Lectures Board. His second novel, **The Longest Journey** (1907), received some favourable reviews but was not liked by friends from his Cambridge days. *A Room With a View* (1908) was given a warmer

E. M. Forster, c.1910.

reception by both critics and friends, and *Howard's End* (1910) established him as one of England's leading novelists. *The Chicago Tribune*, oddly enough, believed the author to be a woman; Forster had no knowledge whatever of sex between men and women and Katherine Mansfield, writing in *New Age*, declared herself puzzled to know how Helen Schlegel ever got pregnant, whether 'by Leonard Bast or his fatal forgotten umbrella'.

Forster was 31, celebrated, and soon knew everyone in the literary establishment. A volume of short stories, *The Celestial Omnibus* (1911) was, however, his last book for some time. He made his first visit to India in 1912, travelling with R. C. Trevelyan, Goldsworthy Lowes Dickinson, and G. H. Luce. In India Forster became friends with the Maharajah of Dewas Senior and, having observed them at close quarters, learned to detest the British as they behaved in India.

Upon returning to England Forster began work on a novel, *Maurice*, which was not published during his lifetime. World War I broke out in the following year and 1915 found Forster in Alexandria working for the International Red Cross. He stayed until 1919, and during that period became friends with the Greek poet C. P. Cavafy. For a few months after his return to England in 1919 Forster was literary editor of the

*Daily Herald*, and contributed essays and reviews to a number of periodicals. In 1921 he returned to India as secretary and companion to the Maharajah of Dewas Senior, and resumed work on a novel about India which he had begun as a consequence of his first visit in 1912. His *Alexandria: A History and A Guide* was published in 1922, and meanwhile his Indian novel was not going well. He began again after he returned to England and it was published in 1924.

*A Passage to India* is Forster's most famous novel, and the last one he wrote. It was highly praised in England and the United States, though there was considerable criticism of his portraits of the English in India. Forster made a humane and liberal Englishman, Fielding, a rare exception and this was less than fair. But his diagnosis of the less than perfect relationship of the Indian to his Anglo-Saxon overlord as arising from insensitivity and arrogance on the one hand, and generations of endured rudeness and condescension on the other is accurate as a factor in politics, as many non-Englishmen can testify. Forster was frequently asked why he stopped writing novels: 'I have nothing more to say,' he replied.

Forster's literary career continued, however. He was a very active journalist and highly respected critic, and in 1927 his Clark Lectures at Cambridge were published as *Aspects of the Novel*. *The Eternal Moment* (1928) is a volume of short stories; *Goldsworthy Lowes Dickinson* (1934) is the biography of his friend – in the same year Forster became president of The National Council for Civil Liberties; *Abinger Harvest* (1936) is a collection of essays (the title refers to his home at that time, at Abinger Hammer in Surrey); his libretto, *Billy Budd*, from Herman Melville's novel, for Benjamin Britten was written in 1949 – he refused a knighthood in that year; *Two Cheers for Democracy* (1951) is a collection of essays, reviews, and broadcasts; *The Hill of Devi* (1953) recalls India 'being letters from Dewas State Senior' – Forster became a Companion of Honour in the same year; *Marianne Thornton* (1956) is a biography of his great aunt. The Order of Merit was awarded him in 1969, the year before he died. *Maurice* (1971) and *The Life to Come* (1972) were published posthumously.

**Forster, John** 1812–76. Forster was born in Newcastle and attended the grammar school there before entering University College, London. He studied law and was called to the Bar at the Inner Temple, but instead of practising law became a journalist. He became assistant editor of *The Examiner* and later editor (1847–55); he was also editor of *The Foreign Quarterly Review*

(1842–43) and of *The Daily News* (1846). He is remembered for his biographies, *Walter Savage Landor* (1869) and *The Life of Charles Dickens* (1872–74). He wrote only the first volume of *The Life of Jonathan Swift* (1875) before he died. Among other works were *The Life and Times of Goldsmith* (1848, enlarged 1854), *Daniel De Foe and Charles Churchill* (1855), and *The Arrest of the Five Members by Charles the First* (1860).

**Fortescue, Sir John** *c*.1394–*c*.1476. Little is known about Fortescue until his admission to Lincoln's Inn about 1420. By 1430 he was serjeant-at-law and by 1437 a Member of Parliament; his knighthood came with his appointment as Chief Justice in 1442. Fortescue took part in politics in an advisory capacity and inevitably became identified with the Lancastrian government; Yorkist successes led to his removal as Chief Justice and he threw in his lot with Henry VI and Queen Margaret, remaining faithful during the king's deposition and exile. At the Battle of Tewkesbury (1471), which destroyed the Lancastrian hopes, Fortescue was taken prisoner. But he was pardoned and actually became a member of the Council of his erstwhile foe, Edward IV. He is regarded as the earliest English constitutional lawyer.

Fortescue's importance lies in his use of the English language. Like his near-contemporary Pecock, who turned to his own language to express his religious beliefs, Fortescue wrote legal treatises in English as well as in Latin. *De Natura Legis Naturae* (1461–63) was rendered in English as *Monarchia or The Difference between an Absolute and a Limited Monarchy*. *De Laudibus Legum Angliae* (1468–70) was meant for the young Prince Edward, in whose education Fortescue seems to have played some part.

After Tewkesbury, Fortescue was the servant of the Yorkists, who preferred to use the vernacular; Fortescue's renunciation of his Lancastrian beliefs was written in English, *A Declaration upon Certain Wrytinges* (1471–73). His most important work, *The Governaunce of England* (*c*.1473), is a distillation of his political theory. His argument is presented in clear straightforward English, in contrast to the long complicated sentences of Pecock. Fortescue was read, understood, and freely quoted, and English prose benefited greatly.

Fortescue's works, both English and Latin, were collected and edited by Thomas Fortescue, Lord Clermont (1869).

*For the Term of his Natural Life* See **Clarke, Marcus**.

**Fortunes of Nigel, The** A novel by Sir Walter Scott, set in London in the reign of James I. It was first published in 1822.

Nigel Oliphaunt, Lord Glenarvon, is in desperate need of a large sum of money which his father advanced to the king during a crisis in his fortunes. Without the money Nigel will lose his estates, which are heavily mortgaged. He comes to London and is received by the king, who signs an order on his behalf on the treasury of Scotland. But Prince Charles and the Duke of Buckingham covet the Glenarvon estates, and they send their favourite, Lord Dalgarno, apparently to befriend Nigel but in fact to lead him into trouble and earn the king's displeasure. Margaret Ramsay, the London clockmaker's daughter, has taken a fancy to Nigel and is uneasy about his friendship with Dalgarno: that gentleman's wronged wife, Hermione, is Margaret's patroness. Then Nigel discovers Dalgarno's true design and strikes him, an offence which, at the court of King James, could cost him his right hand. Nigel escapes to the underworld of Alsatia, while Margaret enlists the help of Lady Hermione and Richard Moniplies, Nigel's servant, on his behalf.

Nigel is taken, and sent to the Tower. Margaret tries to rescue him and at last disguises herself as a page to gain the king's attention. She succeeds, and at the same time secures reparation for Lady Hermione. Nigel marries Margaret and returns to Scotland. Dalgarno pursues him but is killed by robbers on the way.

A successful historical romance, in spite of echoes from his more notable books (Margaret's appeal to the king is a very poor relation to Jeanie Deans' appeal to Queen Caroline in *The Heart of Midlothian*; and the end of Dalgarno is a tired device which disposes of a villain), *The Fortunes of Nigel* presents a vivid picture of both the court and the stews of the underworld and of post-Elizabethan London.

**Fortunes of Richard Mahony, The** A novel in three parts by Henry Handel Richardson. The parts were published as *Australia Felix* (1917), *The Way Home* (1925), and *Ultima Thule* (1929). The author drew heavily on the facts of her own father's madness for the closing chapters of the book.

Richard Townshend Mahony, a brilliant young doctor, is fascinated by the accounts of Australia and the gold rush which he reads in the English press. He gives up his practice and emigrates, arriving in Melbourne in the 1850s. Six months of prospecting at Ballarat finds him doing very badly and he uses his last resources to buy a barrow-load of sundries. With these he opens a 'Diggers Emporium'. A friend, Purdy Smith, who followed his example and emigrated to Australia, introduces him to the Beamish family in Melbourne; at their hotel he meets Mary Turnbull, a girl from England whom he marries. The emporium at Ballarat prospers until Mahony refuses to support the diggers in a militant action against the authorities. The diggers boycott him and he is forced to sell up.

Mary persuades Mahony to return to medicine, but in spite of his ability he lacks the essential sympathy for his patients. He also becomes morbidly sensitive to patronage, real or imagined, and alienates patients at all levels of society. He retreats into himself, preoccupied by books, and turns first to religion and then to spiritualism. When things seem at their lowest ebb some shares in a dubious mine soar in value and the Mahony fortunes are reversed. He and Mary return to Europe and he spends lavishly.

The crash comes when Richard's agent absconds. He returns to Australia and learns that he is ruined, but he hides the full truth from Mary, who has joined him with their children. The strain of trying to get his affairs back in order takes severe toll of Richard, who eventually suffers a mental and physical collapse. At the end of the tale Mary, resolute and uncomplaining, works as a postmistress in a remote settlement, nursing her husband in his last weeks of life. The novel is unhurried and covers a broad canvas of events and characters.

**42nd Parallel, The**  The first novel of the trilogy *U.S.A.* See **Dos Passos, John (Roderigo)**.

**Four Georges, The**  A group of lectures (his second) which W. M. Thackeray delivered in England and the USA in 1855–56. The series was published in the *Cornhill* (July to October 1860).

**Four Quartets**  A poem in four parts by T. S. Eliot, first published in complete form in 1943. The four parts were published in 1936 ('Burnt Norton'), 1940 ('East Coker'), 1941 ('The Dry Salvages'), and 1942 ('Little Gidding'). It is regarded by many critics as Eliot's greatest poem, and presents the poet's reflections on time, eternity, identity, and the poet's art in the modern world. The four poems are related to four different places: Burnt Norton is a house with a rose garden, East Coker is an English village from where the poet's ancestors emigrated to New England, the Dry Salvages is a group of rocks off Cape Ann in Massachusetts, and Little Gidding the site of Nicholas Ferrar's Anglican community in 17th-century Huntingdonshire. These philosophic and religious meditations have a musical structure, as implied by their collective title.

**Fowler, Katherine** 1632–64.  The daughter of a London merchant, Katherine Fowler was probably the first English woman poet to have her work published. She married a gentleman of substance from Cardigan, James Philips, and seems to have moved effortlessly into the literary circle adorned by Vaughan, Cowley, and Jeremy Taylor. She was known by her pseudonym 'Orinda' and the name appears on the collection of her *Letters* (1705), which give a useful picture of the early 17th-century literary world. Her translation of Corneille's *Pompée* was performed in Dublin (1663) and a collection of her verses was published posthumously (1667).

**Fowre Birds of Noahs Arke**  A book of devotions by Thomas Dekker, first published in 1609. The four birds are the dove, the eagle, the pelican, and the phoenix; Dekker uses them as symbols for his collection of prayers written in fine simple prose without a trace of affectation. The author's attractive character is generally acknowledged and the book is notable for its human sympathy and sincere religious feeling. It should be better known: the last edition was F. P. Wilson's, published in 1924.

**Fox, George** 1624–91.  The son of a Leicestershire weaver, George Fox was born at Fenny Drayton. Apprenticed to a shoemaker, he gave up all family and friendship ties at the age of 19 to search for enlightenment. After three years of wandering and inward searching he arrived at a way of life based on the belief that truth was to be found in the Inner Light of the living Christ – God speaking to the soul. He abandoned churchgoing and began to preach, and was frequently imprisoned; but his obvious integrity attracted an increasing number of followers and from these beginnings the Society of Friends, or Quakers, was born. Fox was an organizer of genius and he also made several missionary journeys to Ireland, Holland, America, and the West Indies. He married Margaret Fell in 1669.

In English literature Fox is remembered for his remarkable *Journal*, which was prepared for publication by a committee under Thomas Penn and was edited (for Fox dictated his journal) by Thomas Ellwood. The *Journal* is a record of spiritual searching, related with absolute simplicity and illustrated with vivid vignettes; the early Quakers were remorselessly persecuted by the Puritans but Fox's journal contains no complaints. *A Collection of Epistles* was published in 1698, and *Gospel Truth* in 1706. The original

*Journal*, from Fox's manuscript, was edited by N. Penney and T. E. Harvey (two volumes, 1911). The standard modern edition is that by J. L. Nickalls (1952).

**Foxe, John** 1517–87. The most famous English martyrologist was born in Boston, Lincolnshire. He was educated at Brasenose College, Oxford, and became a fellow of Magdalen. But he resigned his fellowship in 1545 when required to conform to the demands of the statutes on matters of religion; Foxe was a supporter of the Reformation. He worked as a tutor to various highly placed families and when Mary became Queen of England in 1553 Foxe left the country. He went first to Frankfurt, to the company of John Knox and other Protestants, and later to Strasbourg, where he published his first draft of the work from which his name is inseparable. The Latin text was called *Commentarii Rerum in Ecclesia Gestarum* and appeared in 1554; an enlargement was published in Basle in 1559 and an English version, further enlarged, in a huge folio in 1563 as *The Actes and Monuments of these Latter and Perilous Days . . .*, which is known as *The Book of Martyrs*, or *Foxe's Book of Martyrs*.

Foxe worked in Basle for the printer Herbst from 1555 to 1559. Herbst published the 1563 edition of Foxe's *Commentarii* and also his less well-known appeal, in 1557, for tolerance on the part of the English nobility, called *Christus*

An illustration from the 1610 edition of Foxe's *The Book of Martyrs*. Henry VIII tramples on Pope Clement and receives the English Bible from Cranmer. Cardinals Pole and Fisher go to the Pope's assistance.

*Triumphans*. He returned to England in 1560 and was ordained by Grindal, Bishop of London. The printer John Day published the English version of his *Actes and Monuments* in the same year as Foxe became a canon of Salisbury. His book was eagerly read and four editions were printed during his lifetime. Meanwhile Foxe, consistent in his Protestantism, objected to the use of the surplice and declined to contribute to the cost of repairs to the cathedral. Nevertheless, he was given a further benefice at Durham. He lived in London and preached a sermon at Paul's Cross in 1570, *On Christ Crucified*. He lies buried at St Giles, Cripplegate.

Foxe's first work, *De Non Plectendis Morte Adulteris* (1548), was a plea for mercy; his plea for tolerance, written in exile, has already been mentioned. But there is no attempt, in *The Book of Martyrs*, to attribute anything but evil and cruelty to 'the Romische Prelates' and he dwells with unhealthy relish on descriptions of torture. The book has great force, however, particularly in the accounts of eyewitnesses.

The standard edition of Foxe is the eight-volume one (1837–41), prepared by S. R. Cattley and G. Townsend.

***Fragmenta Regalia,*** or *Observations on the late Queen Elizabeth her Times and Favourites*. Sketches of life at the court of Elizabeth I, written by a courtier, Sir Robert Naunton, and interesting for its firsthand character portraits. It was written about 1630 and published in 1641.

***Fragment on Government, A*** The subtitle of Jeremy Bentham's work describes his purpose: *Being an Examination of what is delivered in William Blackstone's Commentaries*. It was first published, anonymously, in 1776 (see **Commentaries on the Laws of England**). Bentham's examination of Blackstone discredits the latter's book completely: he finds that there is no basis whatever for Blackstone's smug assumption that English law and constitutional government offered what Blackstone believed 'the true line of the liberty and happiness of the community'. Bentham declares his Utilitarianism in this work and acknowledges his debt to David Hume, Claude-Adrien Helvétius, and the Italian jurist Cesare Beccaria.

***Fra Lippo Lippi*** A poem by Robert Browning, first published in 1855 in the volume *Men and Women*. Filippo Lippi (*c.*1406–69) was a painter of the Florentine school and a Carmelite monk. An orphan from the age of two, he was placed in a monastery when eight years old because his aunt, who had the care of him, could not support him. Browning was inspired to write his dramatic monologue by a passage in Vasari's *Lives of the Painters* but he gives Fra Lippo Lippi a childhood that derives more from poetic licence than the few known facts. However, the poem opens on a fact recorded by Vasari: his patron, Cosimo de' Medici, used to lock him in at night to keep him off the streets and out of trouble (Vasari records that Lippi had the morals of a satyr). But Lippi got out through the window and thereafter Cosimo let him come and go in case he injured himself climbing down from the window. Fra Lippo Lippi tells us that poverty made him a monk, but that could not suppress the man. More importantly, it could not suppress the artist's pursuit of truth: 'For, don't you mark? We're made so that we love First when we see them painted, things we have passed Perhaps a hundred times nor cared to see; And so they are better, painted – better to us, which is the same thing. Art was given for that; God uses us to help each other so, Lending our minds out.'

**Framley Parsonage** The fourth of Anthony Trollope's Barsetshire novels. It was first published in the *Cornhill Magazine*, from January 1860 to April 1861.

The living of Framley is given to Mark Robarts by the widowed Lady Lufton; he is a close friend of her son, Lord Ludovic Lufton. Through Lord Lufton Mark meets Mr Sowerby and the Duke of Omnium, neither of them ideal companions for a young clergyman; Sowerby is a spendthrift and Omnium is disreputable. After agreeing to support bills for Sowerby, Mark gains a prebendary at Barchester through the influence of Sowerby and the duke and proceeds to conduct himself in a way that annoys his patroness, Lady Lufton.

Lord Lufton falls in love with Lucy Robarts, Mark's sister, but his mother opposes the match. Lucy will not marry Ludovic without Lady Lufton's complete acceptance of her and eventually her integrity and Ludovic's persistence carry the day. Mark, meanwhile, has been getting into deep water and is rescued by the generous Ludovic; he forswears the idle life which is really beyond his means. Sowerby himself is near ruin – his property is heavily mortgaged to the duke – and hopes to marry the rich Miss Dunstable; but she refuses him and marries Dr Thorne. The novel features familiar Barsetshire characters – the Grantlys and their daughter Griselda, who marries Lord Dumbello; Bishop and Mrs Proudie; and the Rev Josiah Crawley. The author's next Barsetshire novel was *The Small House at Allington*, though the story and characters lie outside the mainstream of life surrounding the cathedral at Barchester.

**France and England in North America** The collective name by which Francis Parkman's history of the Europeans in North America is now known. The author's original plan was a history of the war with the French in Canada but it grew to include the conflict between England and France in North America and the resistance of the Indians to both. The work covers eight books in all, not published in strict historical sequence, and holds pride of place in the histories of the American nation. No writer since Parkman has attempted to cover the same ground and that, perhaps, is the greatest tribute of all. The titles are as follows: *Pioneers of France in the New World* (1865), *The Jesuits in North America in the Seventeenth Century* (1867), *LaSalle and the Discovery of the Great West* (1869), *The Old Regime in Canada* (1874), *Count Frontenac and New France under Louis XIV* (1877), *History of the Conspiracy of Pontiac* (1851), *A Half-Century of Conflict* (1892), and *Montcalm and Wolfe* (1884).

**Francis, Sir Philip** 1740–1818. Francis was born in Dublin and educated at St Paul's School, where one of his fellow pupils was Henry Sampson Woodfall, who later became publisher of *The Public Advertiser*. After holding minor public offices Francis became a councillor to the Governor General of India in 1773. In India his disagreements with Warren Hastings earned him attention and led to the bitter enmity which provoked him to initiate the prosecution of Hastings after he returned to England in 1781. Francis did not achieve success as a prosecutor or a politician; he entered parliament in 1784 and gave up his seat in 1804. Warren Hastings was acquitted in 1795 of the charges of corruption and cruelty brought against him, after a long and exhausting trial. Francis owed his knighthood to his friendship with the Prince Regent.

There is evidence for identifying Francis as 'Junius' of the famous letters. However, this was denied by Woodfall, the publisher, and some of Francis's friends are harshly dealt with in the letters.

**Frankenstein,** *or The Modern Prometheus.* A novel by Mary Shelley, first published in 1818. It developed from a story which she wrote when she, her husband, and Byron, at the latter's suggestion, wrote ghost stories to pass the time during a dull wet summer in Switzerland in 1816. She took the idea from a discussion between Shelley and Byron of an experiment by Erasmus Darwin, in which he was supposed to have imparted the spark of life to inanimate matter.

Frankenstein, a student of natural philosophy in Geneva, constructs a creature in the semblance of a man and gives it life. The creature inspires only horror in those who see it and possesses unnatural strength. But the creature also has a basic goodness and is miserable and lonely. Frankenstein, his own life a misery, deserts his creation but is pursued, and at Chamonix, where the creature confronts him, he agrees to make a mate for him. However, a wave of remorse makes him destroy the female he has been constructing, and the creature swears revenge on his creator.

He kills Frankenstein's bride on the wedding night, Frankenstein's father dies of grief, and Frankenstein's mind gives way. Eventually he recovers and sets out to destroy the creature he has made. The creature, goading him, leads him an insane chase across the world. Confronted at last in the Arctic wastes, Frankenstein is brought to his death by the creature, who then laments his creator's passing and disappears into the frozen wilderness, hoping for his own annihilation.

Mary Shelley was 19 when she wrote *Frankenstein* and in spite of its faults (laboured dialogue and wild improbabilities – not all of them scientific) it is immortal. There had never been anything like it before and even now it can be discussed on several levels. There is no hint that Mary could have seen how far into the pit scientific advances could take mankind. But the creature Frankenstein made proved to be a force he could not control, and the parallel to 20th-century man is an uncomfortably close one.

**Franklin, Benjamin** *c*.1706–90. The son of a dealer in soap and tallow, Franklin was born in Boston and worked in his father's business at the age of ten. When he was 12 he was apprenticed to his half-brother, the Boston printer James Franklin, to whose *New England Courant* he was contributing while still an apprentice. These pieces, called the *Do-Good Papers*, were published anonymously and purported to have been written by a parson's widow. They were not ascribed to Franklin until James Parton published his biography in 1864.

Franklin's formal education was sketchy but he was a voracious reader and interested in everything. He quarrelled with James Franklin in 1723 and went to Philadelphia, where he found employment with another printer, Samuel Keimer. In Philadelphia Franklin attracted the attention of Keith, governor of Pennsylvania, who offered him his patronage and sent him to England to buy equipment for his own press. But Keith was rather irresponsible; having sent Franklin to

England he forgot all about him, so the young man (Franklin was not yet 20) was obliged to support himself in a strange country as best he could. He found work in a London printing house and stayed for two years. During that time Franklin wrote the tract *A Dissertation on Liberty and Necessity, Pleasure and Pain* (1725). He returned to America in 1726.

In Philadelphia Franklin set up his own press and in 1729 published the first issue under his own proprietorship of *The Pennsylvania Gazette*. He made Deborah Read his common-law wife in 1730 and became the father of two children. (He was also the father of two more outside that union.) Franklin contributed regularly to his own paper; as well as essays on current matters there were disputatious letters from 'Anthony Afterwit' and 'Alice Addertongue' and weather reports – something new in American journalism. The paper prospered and Franklin managed it until 1766. He is believed to have introduced the cartoon to American journalism when he drew one for his report on the Albany Congress in 1754.

The successful newspaper proprietor became a well-known figure when he founded the influential social and debating society called the Junto Club in 1727 and launched **Poor Richard's Almanack** in 1733. His prosperity gave him time and means to become involved in public affairs and he planned the lighting and maintenance of streets, a police force for Philadelphia, and a circulating library. He founded a city hospital and an Academy for the Education of Youth, which was the basis of Pennsylvania University. He continued to write and contributed to his own *The General Magazine*, which he launched in 1741. He was also becoming actively interested in science and published the results of his celebrated kite experiments in *Experiments and Observations on Electricity* (1751–54). He invented the Franklin stove and devised a new kind of clock; the first bifocal spectacles were Franklin's idea.

Franklin became Deputy Postmaster-General for the colonies in 1753 and was Pennsylvania's representative at the Albany Congress, when the colonies took their first tentative steps towards confederation. He presented a Plan of Union and in 1757 was the chosen emissary to England to seek better government from the home country. He was to remain abroad for most of the following years – until the eve of the War of Independence. He was well qualified to represent his countrymen's aspirations: he had begun to teach himself foreign languages in 1733 and became fluent in French; he had continued his scientific

'Americans throwing the cargoes of the Tea Ships into the River at Boston.' An 18th-century engraving depicting the celebrated act of resentment against the Townshend Acts, which Benjamin Franklin worked so hard to get repealed.

researches and had achieved sufficient distinction to be welcomed by his peers; and Oxford conferred on him the degree of Doctor of Civil Law in recognition of his role as a man of letters and a public servant.

In 1764, representing Georgia, New Jersey, and Massachusetts as well as Pennsylvania, he petitioned for the colonies to be made a royal province of England so that his fellow Americans might enjoy the same rights as British citizens. But his hopes suffered one blow after another and the passing of the Townshend Acts, virtually stating that the colonies had no rights whatever in deciding how their imports should be taxed (for they had no representation in the British Parliament), alienated the colonists. Franklin worked hard to get the Acts repealed, and to a large extent they were, but the British insisted on collecting duties on tea as a token of supreme authority and the Boston Tea Party in 1773 was not seen as a warning of things to come. Franklin went back to America in 1775, convinced that war was inevitable. He served in the Continental Congress and was a member of the committee that ordered the drafting of the Declaration of Independence. He was sent back to Europe again and secured the alliance with France; the French were more than ready to help undermine British authority but their response to Franklin's wis-

dom, charm, and erudition was a decisive factor and they recognized the new republic in 1778. His last action before departing from Europe for the last time (he was 77 years old) was to sign, with John Jay and John Adams, the Treaty of Paris (1783) which concluded the War for Independence. In 1787 he signed the Constitution; he was then over 80 and probably the most famous man alive, as celebrated in the old world as he was in the new. He died in Philadelphia and the inscription on his tomb reads 'Benjamin Franklin, Printer'.

Franklin used his skill with words in the service of America as adroitly as he did in his journalism and in his scientific expositions. Among his friends in England were Chatham, Burke, Adam Smith, and David Hume; he was honoured by three English universities. That his published observations while in London on the relations of Britain with her colonies in America did not influence the course taken by the British government suggests that nothing in the world could have done; Franklin's prestige was enormous, his pragmatic good sense irrefutable. The government of Lord North had supreme authority – but not the wit to understand that this authority was not enough. Franklin's two satires, *Edict by the King of Prussia* and **Rules by which a Great Empire may be reduced to a Small One** (both published in 1773, the former in Philadelphia, the latter in London), should have been studied more closely. A month before his death his ironic letter *On the Slave Trade* reinforced his memorial to Congress for the abolition of slavery.

Franklin's *Autobiography* was begun in 1771

but he never completed it, taking his life story only as far as 1757, with sketches of the following two years. It was published first in England (1795) in an imperfect text, then in France and Germany; America had to wait until 1818 for an edition, also imperfect. The complete text was eventually published in 1867.

Benjamin Franklin was more than a great American. He was unquestionably a great man, an example of 18th-century enlightenment with few to rival him. His endless curiosity benefited greatly from his connection with the world of work and his Junto Club was formed for the benefit of artisans. His background was Puritan but this in no way confined his humane and questing spirit, which enabled him to understand Voltaire and Rousseau as well as invent a better way of keeping warm during bitter winters and to devise his own vocabulary for the results of his experiments in the nature and use of electricity. His writing conveys his tolerance, his common sense, his refreshing Yankee approach to all aspects of life; it is clear, precise and tangy.

**Franklin's Tale, The**  See **Canterbury Tales, The**

**Fraser's Magazine**  In February 1830 Hugh Fraser published the first issue of this notable monthly with William Maginn, formerly of *Blackwood's Magazine*, as his editor. Among the early contributors were Thomas Carlyle, Lockhart, James Hogg, Coleridge, Harrison Ainsworth, Southey, and Thackeray and among the editors who followed Maginn were J. A. Froude and William Allingham. The magazine ceased publication in 1882; Longmans, who had taken over publication in December 1863, replaced it with *Longman's Magazine*, which continued until October 1905.

**Frazer, Sir James George**  1854–1941.  Frazer was born in Glasgow, and attended Helensburgh School before proceeding to Glasgow University and later to Cambridge; he became a fellow of Trinity College. Frazer was intended for the law but though he completed his training and was called to the Bar he never practised. Instead he turned to anthropology and the classical studies which later combined to produce his great works, *The Golden Bough* (1890–1915) and his translation and edition of *Pausanias; Description of Greece* (1898).

Frazer's first published work was his edition of Sallust's two histories as *Catalina et Jugurtha* (1884). This was followed by *Totemism* (1887) and by the first two volumes of *The Golden*

*Bough: A Study in Comparative Religion* (1890). Frazer was prompted by a desire to explain the meaning of the sinister ritual of succession in the priesthood of the goddess Diana *Nemorensis* in the sacred grove of oak trees on the north shore of Lake Nemi not far from Rome. But the two volumes proved the beginning of an exploration which embraced anthropology, myth, religion, folk-lore, and magic, reached back to the origins of man, and covered the whole world. Extending to 13 volumes, it influenced literature and psychology in the 20th century and, remarkably, proved an attractive and readable work as well as a masterpiece in its field. The 13 volumes are: *The Golden Bough* (vols. I and II, 1890); *The Magic Art and the Evolution of Kings, Taboo and the Perils of the Soul*, and *The Dying God* (vols. III–VI, all 1911); *Adonis, Attis and Osiris* (vols. VII and VIII, 1914); *Spirits of the Corn and the Wild* (vol. IX, 1912); *The Scapegoat* (Vols. X and XI, 1913); *Balder the Beautiful* (Vol. XII, 1913); and an extensive *Bibliography and General Index* (Vol. XIII, 1915). Sir James (he was knighted in 1914) published a valuable abridgment in one volume in 1922.

In addition to the considerable works already named (*Pausanias* ran to six volumes) Frazer published editions and translations of Apollodorus (1921) and Ovid (1929) for the Loeb Classical Library, *Folk-lore in the Old Testament* (1918), *Myths of the Origin of Fire* (1930), *The Fear of the Dead in Primitive Religion* (1933–36), and editions of *The Letters of William Cowper* (1912) and *The Essays of Joseph Addison* (1915).

**Freeman, Edward Augustus**  1823–92.  Freeman was born at Harborne in Staffordshire and was privately educated before going to Trinity College, Oxford, where he became a fellow. Freeman was a regular contributor to periodicals, including *The Saturday Review*, and later published his essays in book form as *Historical Essays* (four collections, 1871, 1873, 1879, and 1892). He published his lectures on *The History and Conquests of the Saracens* in 1856, *The History of Federal Government* in 1863, and his best-known work, *The History of the Norman Conquest of England; its Causes and its Results*, in 1867–79. Freeman was also the author of a number of essays on architecture but is chiefly remembered as a historian. Among his other works are *A History of Europe* (1876), *The Turks in Europe* (1877), *The Historical Geography of Europe* (1881), *The Reign of William Rufus and the Accession of Henry I* (1882), *William the Conqueror* (1888), and *The History of Sicily from the Earliest Times* (1891–94). Freeman died of smallpox while travelling in

Mary Wilkins Freeman.

Spain. His historical work is not highly regarded now. Freeman worked entirely from printed chronicles and many of his conclusions were shown to be invalid when manuscripts came to be more closely studied.

**Freeman, Mary Eleanor Wilkins** 1852–1930. A short-story writer and novelist from New England, Mrs Freeman was born in Randolph, Massachusetts. The background she chose for her writing was eastern Massachusetts and her best work is an observation of character in small repressed communities resentful of advancing thought and opinion. The author, by use of the community's dialects and skilful economy of presentation, earns her place among the American fiction writers who extended the range of literary forms in the USA. Her short stories are usually regarded as her best work: *A Humble Romance and Other Stories* (1887) and *A New England Nun and Other Stories* (1891). Other works are a play about the Salem witch trials, *Giles Corey, Yeoman* (1893); and the novels *Jane Field* (1893), *Pembroke* (1894), *The Heart's Highway* (1900), *The Portion of Labor* (1901), and *Jerome, A Poor Man* (1897), which is probably the best. She also wrote a volume of ghost stories, *The Wind in the Rose Bush* (1903). Her last book was a further collection of short stories called *Edgewater People* (1918).

**French Revolution, The.** *A History*. By Thomas Carlyle, first published in 1837. It was written in London, after the Carlyles had gone to live in Chelsea. Carlyle gave the manuscript of the first volume to his friend John Stuart Mill to read; Mill had helped assemble the great quantity of books that formed Carlyle's essential reading before beginning to write his magnum opus in 1834. Mill lent the manuscript to a friend, Mrs Taylor, who was very interested – and Mrs Taylor's housekeeper used the manuscript to light the fire. Mill was horrified and pressed Carlyle to accept a sum of money to keep going while he wrote the first volume again. Carlyle accepted half and rewrote the volume between July and September of 1844.

Carlyle's history begins with the death of Louis XV (1774) and closes with the suppression of the Vendémiaire (5 October 1795) by Bonaparte. The work is not a carefully documented scientific history but a 'personal' one by a passionate social critic, demonstrating that nemesis follows the continued abuse of power and the callous disregard of duty and responsibility. Carlyle's greatest work, it is a prose epic with one of the most momentous events of history as its subject. The historical portraits – Mirabeau, Danton, Robespierre, Lafayette – are magnificent, and the great moments – the taking of the Bastille, the flight of the royal family, the murder of Marat by Charlotte Corday, the Reign of Terror, the fall of Robespierre – are finely narrated.

**Freneau, Philip (Morin)** *c*.1752–1832. Of Huguenot ancestry, Philip Freneau was born in New York City and grew up in New Jersey. He was educated at the College of New Jersey (which became Princeton University), where Aaron Burr, Hugh Henry Brackenridge, and James Madison were among his schoolfellows. Freneau wrote poetry at college and collaborated with Brackenridge on *The Rising Glory of America*, which was read at their graduation (1771). The poem was published in the following year, by which time both men were teaching in Maryland and the first rumblings of the Revolution were being felt. Freneau devoted his energies to writing satirical poems in support of the American cause; but to earn a living he became secretary in 1776 to a prominent planter in the West Indies. The island of Santa Cruz inspired his first notable poetry: 'The Jamaica Funeral', 'The Beauties of Santa Cruz', and 'The House of Night' (which he published in an extended version in his *Poems*, 1786).

Freneau stayed in the West Indies for two years but on his voyage home was captured and briefly held by the British. At home he served in the militia and wrote patriotic verse but then, on the way back to the islands in 1780, was captured once more by the British. This time he was tried as a rebel and imprisoned aboard the hulk *Scorpion* in New York harbour. He was not held captive for long, being released in the same year in an exchange of prisoners; but he was treated brutally and starved and he wrote a deeply felt poem, **The British Prison-Ship**, about the experience (1781).

For three years Freneau was employed by the post office in Philadelphia. He went on writing satirical verse until 1784, when he became master of a brig trading in the Atlantic and the Caribbean. The new life gave added impulse to his talents and his first collection, *Poems*, was published in 1786. *Miscellaneous Works* followed in 1788. He married in 1790, abandoned the sea, and for a year was editor of the New York *Daily Advertiser*. He began the publication of the *National Gazette* in October 1791; he had for a short time worked for Jefferson in the state department and supported him wholeheartedly. Jefferson, for his part, was unstinting in his praise of Freneau while the federalists, particularly Washington and Hamilton, were unstinting in their abuse. Freneau's journalism continued until 1799 but the material rewards were small and he was obliged to serve as master of coasters from 1803 to 1807.

But the work of Philip Freneau the poet continued. *Poems Written between the Years 1768 and 1794* was published in 1795. He published a collection in 1809 and, prompted by the War of 1812, another that included all his patriotic and satirical verse. The occasional poems that had appeared in periodicals between 1815 and 1832 were collected and published in 1946 as *Last Poems*. A notable book of essays, *Letters on Various Interesting and Important Subjects*, was published in 1799.

Freneau's last years were tragic. His New Jersey home had suffered both from the war and from his struggle with poverty. The house was destroyed by fire in 1815 and Freneau began to drink. His death was due to exposure, after he was caught in a December snowstorm.

A great deal of Philip Freneau's energies were consumed by the exigencies of his troubled times. He is known as the poet of the American Revolution but he was unquestionably a poet of considerable quality – the first romantic poet of the new country, at his best in his celebration of nature and his use of American themes.

**Friar Bacon and Friar Bungay** (*The Honorable Historie of Frier Bacon and Frier Bungay*). A comedy in prose and verse by Robert Greene,

The title page illustration of the 1666 edition of Greene's *Friar Bacon and Friar Bungay*, first published in 1594.

first printed in 1594 but probably produced a few years before. Friar Bacon and Friar Bungay are based on the 13th-century Franciscans of Oxford, Roger Bacon and Thomas Bungay.

Bacon makes a brass head with the help of Bungay; then, with the help of the Devil, confers the power of speech on it. It will utter in the course of a month but they must be present to hear it speak or all their labours will go for nothing. After a three-week vigil, day and night, Bacon hands the watch over to Miles, his servant, and falls into an exhausted sleep. When the head speaks it utters but two words, 'Time is' – Miles thinks it of insufficient importance to wake his master. Next the head says, 'Time was'; then it says, later, 'Time is past' – and falls on the floor, breaking into pieces. Bacon awakes, and the unfortunate Miles receives the full fury of his wrath. A subplot tells of the love of Lord Lacy and the Prince of Wales for the pretty Margaret, the gamekeeper's daughter of Freshingfield. A notable scene has Bacon and Bungay and a German rival displaying their powers before the kings of England and Castile and the emperor of Germany.

**Friar Rush** An old folk tale of northern Europe relates the adventures of Bruder Rausch, who is the devil in disguise as a monk. His intention is to corrupt the brothers of the monastery in which he takes service and the story is a series of clever devices by Friar Rush (Bruder Rausch) that lead the monks into sin. An English version of the story was published by William Copeland in 1568.

**Friar's Tale, The**  See **Canterbury Tales, The**.

**Frobisher, Martin**. See **Best, George**.

**Froissart, Jean** *c.*1337–*c.*1410.  Best known to English readers for his *Chronicles*, Froissart was a poet as well as a historian. He was born at Valenciennes in Hainault and in 1361 came to England, where he was able to obtain the protection of Queen Philippa (also of Hainault). He travelled in England and Scotland and accompanied the Black Prince to Bordeaux and the Duke of Clarence to Milan: all his experience and travel augmented the material he was collecting for the chronicles he planned to write.

Philippa of Hainault died in 1369, and Froissart retired to Valenciennes to work on the first version of his first *Chronicle*, which dealt with events from 1325. He found a new patron in the Comte de Blois, who provided him with ecclesiastical sinecures that allowed him to travel in France and Flanders, and he revisited England (1394–95). He took his *Chronicles* up to the year 1400 and is believed to have died about 1410 (certainly after 1404).

Froissart's *Chronicles*, written in four books, provide a history of the Hundred Years' War with reference to affairs in other European countries affected by the war. He tells of the feats of arms, the exploits of the feudal chivalry of France and England, including pillage, massacre, rape, and repression as a matter of course: the victims are given no space, since they are usually common folk and rarely of interest to Froissart. He writes with impartial respect and admiration for both sides, French and English, and the result is a vivid impression of the course of this ridiculous war and the minds of the men conducting it. But the reader will look in vain for any account of the conditions that drove the people of the Île-de-France to the rebellion of the *Jacquerie* or the real reasons for the similar rebellion led by Wat Tyler in England. Froissart's *Chronicles* provide a record of the historical facts and are of high value in this respect: he was concerned with events rather than causes, and the *Chronicles* have to be approached with this in mind. The *Chronicles* were a new sort of history, fresh and lively and related with enthusiasm – a far cry from the dull heavy chronicles of earlier years. Lord Berners' translation, his greatest achievement, succeeded in making an English classic from a French one.

**Frost, Robert (Lee)** 1874–1963.  Robert Frost was born in San Francisco. After his father's death in 1884 his mother moved to Lawrence, Massachusetts, where Frost attended school before going to Dartmouth College. He left college after a year and went to work in a cotton mill, and married in 1894. After a two-year

course at Harvard Frost took up farming in New Hampshire but the venture failed and he migrated to England with his family in 1912.

Frost had been interested in poetry from his schooldays and it remained his first interest in spite of a restless life. His chosen subject was the rural life of New England, but it was not until he lived in the old country that his gifts began to flower. He met most of the young English poets and became the friend, to their mutual benefit, of Edward Thomas. His first books of verse were published in England: *A Boy's Will* (1913) and *North of Boston* (1914). The last-named gave him a reputation in the USA, to which he returned in 1915. He settled on a New Hampshire farm but most of his subsequent life was spent as a sought-after poet and lecturer; he was awarded no less than 44 honorary degrees. *Mountain Interval* (1916), *New Hampshire* (1923, Pulitzer Prize 1924), and *West-Running Brook* (1928) were followed by *Collected Poems* (1930, Pulitzer Prize 1931); *A Further Range* (1936) brought him a third Pulitzer Prize, and *A Witness Tree* (1942) a fourth. *A Masque of Reason* (1945) and *A Masque of Mercy* (1947) are two dramatic poems in blank verse in which biblical characters discuss ethics and man's relation to God in modern settings; *Steeple Bush* (1947) is a collection of lyrics. Frost wrote poetry to the end of his life and published a new collection, *In the Clearing* (1962), the year before he died.

The most accessible of modern poets, Frost is one of the best loved. His lyrics and narrative poems, from the first collection published in England, spring from the rural New England where he went to live at the age of ten. 'Mowing,' 'The Death of the Hired Man,' 'The Road not Taken,' 'Putting in the Seed,' 'The Onset,' and 'The Gift Outright' will be found in most collections of American verse.

**Froude, James Anthony** 1818–94.  The younger brother of the Tractarian Richard Hurrell Froude, James Anthony was born at Totnes in Devon. He was educated at Westminster School and Oriel College, Oxford, where like his brother he came under the influence of John Henry Newman. Newman's conversion to Rome weakened Froude's faith in Christianity; he wrote about this period of life in *Shadows in the Clouds* (1847) and *The Nemesis of Faith* (1848), two essays in semifictional autobiography. Two years later he met Thomas Carlyle and became his lifelong friend and disciple.

Like other 19th-century historians Froude wrote a great deal for journals, contributing essays, mainly historical, to *The Westminster*

*Review* and to *Fraser's Magazine*, which he edited (1860–74). A notably essay, *England's Forgotten Worthies* (1852), printed in *The Westminster Review*, attracted attention and gave some hint of his sympathies as a historian. The first two volumes of *A History of England from the Fall of Wolsey to the Death of Elizabeth* were published in 1858 and the work was completed in 12 volumes in 1870. Froude was severely criticized for his presentation of history: he followed Carlyle in the belief that only extraordinary men initiate and control great events, and his approach was too often polemical. In spite of that his history was highly successful, even while Macaulay's was still in progress. The reasons for its success were Froude's narrative gifts, his scrupulous research (he frequently paraphrases original documents and carefully identifies them), and his excellent prose style. He is as prejudiced as Macaulay and, unlike the older historian, sometimes ingenuous. His history is in fact a very good read; however, the attacks upon Froude, led mainly by *The Saturday Review*, persisted and eventually proved fatal to his reputation as a historian.

*The English in Ireland in the Eighteenth Century* (1872–74) grew out of a series of lectures which Froude delivered in the USA. This book also became the centre of controversy and W. E. H. Lecky dealt with it very firmly in his *The History of England in the Eighteenth Century* (1878–92); this contained five volumes on Ireland and demonstrated how guilty of mis-statement Froude was. In 1874 Froude went on a government mission to South Africa to investigate the possibilities of federation; he also travelled in Australia (1884) and the West Indies (1886) and published *Oceana: or England and her Colonies* (1886) and *The English in the West Indies: or The Bow of Ulysses* (1888), both readable and interesting for the contemporary view. As Thomas Carlyle's literary executor he was from 1881 engaged in the publication of the biographical remains of his friend and of Jane Welsh Carlyle: *Thomas Carlyle, Reminiscences* (1881) and *Letters and Memorials of Jane Welsh Carlyle* (1883). He performed the task with what now seems commendable frankness; contemporary critics were, however, indignant with him. Froude's memoirs of Carlyle are published in *Thomas Carlyle: a History of the First Forty Years of his Life* (1882), *Thomas Carlyle: A History of his life in London* (1884), and *My Relations with Carlyle* (1886).

Froude was appointed Regius Professor of Modern History at Oxford in 1892. Among his other works were the collections of his best essays, *Short Studies on Great Subjects* (four series,

1867, 1871, 1877, and 1883); *Bunyan* (1880), for the English Men of Letters series; *The Knights Templars* (1886); *Lord Beaconsfield* (Everyman's Library, 1890); and *The Divorce of Catherine of Aragon: being A Supplement to The History of England* (1891).

**Froude, Richard Hurrell** 1803–36. The elder brother of the historian James Anthony Froude, and one of the early leaders of the Oxford Movement, Froude was born near Totnes in Devonshire. He contributed to *Tracts for the Times* and was the intimate friend of John Henry Newman; after his early death Newman wrote a preface to his friend's *Remains*. These were edited by J. B. Mozley (1838 and 1839) and were chiefly extracts from his private diary. They caused a disturbance in the Movement by their hostility to the leaders of the Reformation.

**Fry, Christopher** 1907– . The name adopted by Christopher Harris, who was born in Bristol and educated at Bedford Modern School. He taught in preparatory schools, became an actor and producer in repertory companies in Bath, Tunbridge Wells, and Oxford, and began his writing career with revue sketches. His first play was a one-act retelling, in verse, of the legend of Cuthman, saint of Sussex: *The Boy with a Cart* was written for and produced at a village church festival at Colman's Hatch in Sussex in 1937. *A Phoenix too Frequent* (Mercury Theatre, 1946), a one-act verse comedy based on a story in Petronius, demonstrated his gift for words and his remarkable verbal dexterity but his next work was a full-length play with a biblical theme, *The Firstborn* (Edinburgh, 1948). Fry was on the staff of the Arts Theatre in London when he wrote *The Lady's not for Burning*, produced there in 1948. His gifts had found a perfect subject and the production at the Globe Theatre in the following year made him celebrated. *Thor, with Angels* (Canterbury, 1948) was another religious play; *Venus Observed* (St James's Theatre, 1950) was commissioned by Laurence Olivier; a religious allegory, *A Sleep of Prisoners* (University Church, Oxford, 1951) was highly praised, and *The Dark is Light Enough* (Aldwych Theatre, 1954) was graced by the presence of Dame Edith Evans in the leading role.

Fry was also brilliantly successful with his English versions of Anouilh: *Ring Round the Moon* (*L'invitation au Château*: Globe Theatre, 1950) and *The Lark* (*L'alouette*: Lyric Theatre, Hammersmith, 1955), and Giraudoux: *Tiger at the Gates* (*La guerre de Troie n'aura pas lieu*: Apollo Theatre, 1955), *Duel of Angels* (*Pour Lucrèce*: Apollo Theatre, 1958), and *Judith* (Her Majesty's

Theatre, 1962). After some years as a script writer in films he returned to the stage with *Curtmantle* (Aldwych, 1962), a play about Henry II. *A Yard of Sun* (1970) completes the 'seasonal' cycle of plays as the summer piece: spring is represented by *The Lady's not for Burning*, autumn by *Venus Observed*, and winter by *The Dark is Light Enough*.

**Fudge Family in Paris, The,** edited by *Thomas Brown the Younger*. Satirical verses by Thomas Moore in the form of letters, first published in 1818. The Fudges are a pompous but superficial family who take themselves very seriously. In this book and the later *The Fudges in England* (1835) Moore deftly satirizes the manners of the fashionable and the behaviour of the English abroad.

**Fugard, Athol (Harold)** 1932–  . Fugard was born in Middleburg, Cape Province, and completed his education at Cape Town University. He became an actor but was soon demonstrating his talents as a playwright concerned with the issue of personal and political survival in a country where the imposition of apartheid has bred bitterness and distrust in every level of society. His first plays (dates given are of publication), *Nongogo* (1956) and *No Good Friday* (1957), were first produced in Johannesburg in 1960. But he has reached audiences throughout the English-speaking world since the production of *The Blood Knot* in London in 1971. He has been director of the Serpent Players at Port Elizabeth since 1965 and was co-founder of the Space Experimental Theatre in Cape Town in 1972. He produces his own plays and sometimes appears in them. Athol Fugard is the author of one novel, *Tsotsi* (1980). His plays are published as *The Blood Knot* (1962), *People are Living There* and *Hello and Goodbye* (1973), *Boesman and Lena* (1973), *Three Port Elizabeth Plays: Sizwe Bansi is Dead, The Island, Statements After an Arrest Under the Immorality Act* (1974), and *A Lesson from Aloes* (1981).

**Fugitive Movement**  See **Ransom, John Crowe**.

**Fulgens and Lucrece** *(A Godely Interlude of Fulgens, Cenatoure of Rome, and Lucres his Daughter)*. A play by Henry Medwall, first acted *c.*1497 and first printed between 1512 and 1516. Medwall was chaplain to Cardinal Morton and was also the author of a morality, *Nature*, which traced the course of a man's life and showed the struggle waged by vice and virtue for possession of his soul. *Fulgens and Lucrece* was not known to exist until a copy was discovered in 1919 and it has proved to be the earliest purely secular play in English to survive complete.

The title page of Henry Medwall's *Fulgens and Lucrece*, which was first performed c.1497. The illustration comes from a rare copy of the first published text, between 1512 and 1516; it is believed to have been the first printed English play.

The play concerns a Roman senator, Fulgens, and his daughter Lucrece – the difficulty of choosing the right husband for her and the question of whether true nobility lies in birth or in proven worth. The suitors are Cornelius, wealthy, well-born, and profligate; and Gaius Flaminius, who has risen from low beginnings to high honour for services to the state. A subplot concerns the servants of Cornelius and Flaminius, both of whom woo Lucrece's maid. At the end of the play Lucrece chooses Flaminius.

**Fuller, Henry Blake** 1857–1929.  Fuller was born in Chicago, the city which provided the background for his best-remembered books. His work varies from the historical romances with which he began his career under the pseudonym of Stanton Page, to the realistic novels of his own city, books of verse, short stories set in Europe and America, and a satire on the film industry. He reviewed books for Chicago newspapers and his knowledge of European life (he was much-travelled) helped him introduce international writers to readers in the Midwest. He was also very active in the support and promotion of Harriet Monroe's *Poetry* magazine.

Fuller's most successful novel was *The Cliff-Dwellers* (1893), concerning the lives of those who live in a Chicago skyscraper, the Clifton Building, ranging from the rich owner of the building, Arthur Ingles, to the ambitious clerk,

George Ogden, who works in Erastus Brainard's bank. These, and the various women who contribute to their fortunes and misfortunes, are well drawn and the novel is a fine example of the 'Grand Hotel' theme.

*With the Procession* (1895) tells of a successful Chicago merchant who is wholly occupied with the success of his business. When his three younger children decide to take advantage of their father's wealth to enter the fashionable world he cannot keep pace 'with the procession' and dies, leaving his business in chaos. But his personal fortune is intact and his children continue on their way.

**Fuller, Margaret** *c.*1810–50. A leading figure in the Transcendentalist society of Concord, Massachusetts, Margaret Fuller was born in Cambridgeport. Her early life was dominated by her father, a possessive parent who undertook her education himself. After his death she became Bronson Alcott's assistant and a friend of Emerson's and head of a school in Providence. She was an early feminist and, as a member of the foremost group of intellectuals in New England, enjoyed the stimulus of views and discussions that formed the material of *Woman in the Nineteenth Century* (1845).

Margaret Fuller was editor of *The Dial* (1840–42) and published *Summer on the Lakes* in 1843 after a visit to Chicago, when she experienced her first encounter with the expanding West and the frontier. She became literary critic of Horace Greeley's New York *Tribune* and in 1846 was sent to Europe; her letters from 'abroad' were distinguished enough to appear on the *Tribune's* front page. In Europe she met Wordsworth, Mazzini, George Sand, Chopin, and Carlyle. She admired Mazzini and began to write a book on the events in Rome (1848–49). She also fell in love with and married the Marquis Angelo Ossoli. In 1850 they sailed for America with their infant son but their ship was wrecked in a storm off Fire Island. The whole family perished.

In addition to her own work Margaret Fuller left another impression of her dynamic personality; she was the inspiration for Zenobia in Hawthorne's *The Blithedale Romance* and for Holmes's *Elsie Venner*. She is also Miranda in Lowell's *A Fable for Critics*.

**Fuller, Roy (Broadbent)** 1912–    . Fuller was born in Failsworth, Lancashire, and went to school in Blackpool. He was articled to a solicitor at the age of 16 and his law career has been entirely concerned with building societies. He became solicitor to the Woolwich Equitable Building Society in 1958 after having been assistant solicitor for 20 years; he became Vice-President of the Building Societies Association in 1969. He published his first collection, *Poems*, in 1940 and served in the Royal Navy from 1941 to 1945. His next volumes, *The Middle of a War* (1942) and *A Lost Season* (1944), drew attention to his quality as a war poet while *Epitaphs and Occasions* (1949) and *Counterparts* (1954) showed him as a post-war one uneasy about modern English life. The tone becomes more reflective and analytical in *Brutus's Orchard* (1957). Roy Fuller published *Collected Poems 1936–1961* in 1962 and further volumes are *Buff* (1965), *New Poems* (1968), *Off Course* (1969), *To an Unknown Reader* (1970), *Song Cycle from a Record Sleeve* (1972), *Tiny Tears* (1973), *An Old War* (1974), and *An Ill-Governed Coast* (1976). He became Professor of Poetry at Oxford in 1968 and published his lectures as *Owls and Artificers* (1971) and *Professors and Gods* (1973). Among other works are several novels and some stories for children. Roy Fuller was awarded the Duff Cooper Memorial Prize in 1968.

**Fuller, Thomas** 1608–61. Fuller was born at Aldwincle St Peter's in Northamptonshire. He began his career as the youngest MA to come out of Cambridge University – he was 20 years old. After Cambridge he became a Bachelor of Divinity in 1635; he had by this time established himself as a preacher, and had been prebendary of Salisbury and rector of Broadwindsor. In 1641 he was appointed preacher to the Chapel Royal at the Savoy and during the Civil War was chaplain to the Royalist commander Sir Ralph Hopton. He married twice, in 1638 and 1652.

A Royalist and an Anglican, Fuller returned to London after the surrender of Exeter. He was allowed to preach but led an unsettled life until he secured the curacy of Waltham Abbey in 1649. He regained his old preferments at the Restoration but did not live long to enjoy them.

Fuller was a celebrated preacher in his lifetime and also a prolific writer; he wrote poems, histories, and a satire directed at Cromwell, *Andronicus or the Unfortunate Politician* (1646). His first book of note was about the Crusades, *The Historie of the Holy Warre* (1639–40). His *Good Thoughts in Bad Times* (1645), *Good Thoughts in Worse Times* (1647), and *The Cause and Cure of a Wounded Conscience* (1647) were tracts for his troubled times and have been praised by Coleridge but these were less popular than the earlier *The Holy State and The Profane State*, a book of 'characters' and essays on diverse subjects. Later works are *A Pisgah-Sight of Palestine*

(1650) and *The Church History of Britain: from the Birth of Christ till 1648* (1655). His most highly regarded book, *The History of the Worthies of England*, was never completed and was not published until the year after his death. It is rather more than the biographical encyclopedia suggested by the title: Fuller travelled a great deal around England verifying dates and checking sources and he included every item of interest he encountered. It is also a topographical survey of the England of his day, since Fuller carefully describes – with a light touch – each of the counties he visits. The last complete edition of *The Worthies* was edited by P. A. Nuttall (1840).

**Furnivall, Frederick James** 1825–1910. Furnivall was born at Egham, Surrey, and educated at University College, London, and Trinity Hall, Cambridge. He helped to found The Working Men's College in 1854 and was a member of the Philological Society from 1847. In 1861 Furnivall became editor of the society's English dictionary, which eventually became the *Oxford English Dictionary*. Furnivall was a dedicated scholar, and founder of the Early English Text Society, the Ballad Society, the Chaucer Society, the New Shakespeare Society, and the Wycliffe, Shelley, and Browning societies. He contributed no less than 65 editions and commentaries to those societies and a further five to the Roxburghe Club.

**Furphy, Joseph** 1843–1912. The son of Irish immigrant parents, Furphy was born near Melbourne, Victoria. After a sketchy education, and work on farms, roads, and goldfields, he became a teamster in the Riverina area of New South Wales. The failure of his business in 1884 obliged him to sell his bullock teams and find work in a foundry at Shepparton in north Victoria; it was at this time that he first began to write.

Furphy's first stories were published in *The Bulletin* in 1889 under the pseudonym of Tom Collins. In 1897 the literary editor of the paper, A. G. Stephens, was the recipient of a large unwieldy manuscript entitled *Such Is Life: Being Certain Extracts from the Life of Tom Collins*. He recognized a classic of its kind – a novel right out of the heart of Australia – and after essential revision and shortening it was published in 1903. From the rich material trimmed from *Such Is Life* two more books were published after Furphy's death: *Rigby's Romance* (1946) and *The Buln-Buln and the Brolga* (1948). He died at Claremont in Western Australia, where he and his wife had moved to join their sons.

There is no formal plot in *Such Is Life*, a picaresque novel of many digressions and reflections which one American critic, C. Hartley Grattan, described as 'a primary document for any student of Australian attitudes'. Furphy wrote of his work as 'Temper democratic; bias offensively Australian.'

# G

**Gahagan, Major** A character like Baron Munchausen, whose adventures were invented by Thackeray, told in the first person, and published in the *New Monthly Magazine* (1838–39).

**Galahad** In Malory's *Le Morte Darthur*, the son begotten by Launcelot on Elaine, daughter of King Pelles; she is given the likeness of Guenever, Launcelot's true love, to bring about the union. King Pelles has the keeping of the Grail, and later in the story becomes the Maimed King whose wound will not heal until the Grail is achieved by one who is wholly pure. This is his grandson Galahad, who is alone fit to occupy the Siege Perilous when he comes to the Round Table. After achieving the Grail, Galahad takes it to Sarras, where he asks for his own death a year later.

**Galsworthy, John** 1867–1933.  Born at Coombe, Surrey, and educated at Harrow School and New College, Oxford, Galsworthy

Galahad draws the sword from the stone in the river. The incident is related in Malory but the illustration is from a medieval French manuscript. *MS. Fr.110, f.405.* Bibliothèque Nationale.

studied law and was called to the Bar in 1890. He practised briefly, but he could afford to travel and made a voyage to the Far East; on another journey he met and encouraged Joseph Conrad and the two became lifelong friends. Galsworthy's first published fiction was a book of short stories, *From the Four Winds* (1897); he used the pseudonym of John Sinjohn. He did not use his own name until his fifth book, a novel called *The Island Pharisees* (1904).

Galsworthy enjoyed a double success in 1906 with the production of his play *The Silver Box* at the Royal Court Theatre and the publication of *The Man of Property*. His career continued in both spheres with enviable success for the rest of his life, and a resurgence of interest in him was recently brought about by television. After *The Man of Property* the author returned to the Forsyte family from time to time; following five collections of short stories, eight novels, and ten plays he wrote *In Chancery* (1920) and *To Let* (1921), and *The Forsyte Saga* was published in 1922. He returned to the Forsytes again in *The White Monkey* (1924), *The Silver Spoon* (1926), and *Swan Song* (1928) – the trilogy known as *A Modern Comedy* (1929). Many of the same characters, particularly Fleur and Michael, appear in *Maid in Waiting* (1931), *Flowering Wilderness* (1932), and *Over the River* (1933), a further trilogy published after his death as *End of the Chapter* (1934). The Forsytes also appear in the short stories collected in *Two Forsyte Interludes* (1927), *Four Forsyte Stories* (1929), and *On Forsyte Change* (1930). His other novels and short stories are virtually forgotten. The Forsyte novels and short stories provide an interesting guide to the lives of the English *haute bourgeoisie* from Edwardian times to the 1930s and Galsworthy was a very good storyteller. He fails, however, with Irene, the wronged wife of Soames in the first novel: her apparent magnetism is not convincingly realized and when, in *To Let*, she and Jolyon tell their son that he must not marry Fleur, Soames's daughter, because it would make his mother and father very unhappy, the author does not seem to understand what extraordinary selfishness they are displaying. Soames himself undergoes a metamorphosis from monster of possessiveness and archetypal man of property to universally respected senior.

As a playwright Galsworthy enjoyed a success which rivalled that of Shaw and Barrie; no fewer than 31 full-length plays and a number of one-acters were produced in London, some with great success. In his best plays he comments to considerable effect on social injustice and prejudice and one of them, *Justice* (Duke of

John Galsworthy, 1921. Photograph by E. O. Hoppé.

York's Theatre, 1910), led to reform of the practice of solitary confinement in prisons. *The Silver Box*, his first play, shows the difference in the treatment a rich man and a poor man can expect from the law. *Strife* (Duke of York's Theatre, 1909) remains one of the best English plays about the effect of a strike. *The Skin Game* (St Martin's Theatre, 1920) is a trenchant commentary on jealously guarded privilege and social snobbery. John Galsworthy was awarded the OM in 1929.

**Galt, John** 1779–1839. The son of a sea captain, Galt was born in Irvine, Ayrshire, and spent his early life in Greenock. He went to London in 1804 and set up as a merchant, writing in his spare time and publishing verse and occasional prose pieces. His business failed in 1808 and he set off on a commercial journey to the Continent, where he made the acquaintance of Byron. He continued in the poet's company to Greece and Turkey and subsequently published an account of his journeys in 1812 in *Voyages and Travels in the Years 1809, 1810 and 1811*. He also wrote a biography of the poet, *The Life of Lord Byron*, in 1830, but it was not well received. After 1813 he was back in London in various business posts and writing busily – to little purpose. He wrote a great deal; but it was not until his work was published in *Blackwood's Magazine* in 1820 that he achieved distinction. He dealt with the sort of people and places he really knew in *The Ayrshire Legatees* (1821) and produced a successful novel about contemporary Lowland Scots; his earlier work had been about historical and exotic people and places.

*The Annals of the Parish* (1821), *The Provost* (1822), and *The Entail* (1823) are in the same vein and these are the books by which John Galt is best remembered. In 1826 he went to Canada as secretary to a company for development in what is now Ontario. He stayed for three years and then lost his post when the company's affairs went through a bad period. He returned to England but, short of money, was soon in debt and spent some months in prison. His straits were relieved by a gift of £200 from King William IV, and he spent the remainder of his life in ill health, still writing but achieving nothing that measured up to his work in the early 1820s.

**Game at Chess, A** A comedy by Thomas Middleton, first published in 1625. It is a political allegory and unlike any other work of the playwright's. The public enjoyed it very much but King James and the Spanish ambassador were offended. Further performances were banned and proceedings were begun against the company, which was The King's Men (it was played at the Globe), and the author. It is possible, but not verifiable, that Middleton was imprisoned

for a time. The subject was the projected Spanish marriage and the rivalry between the White House (England) and the Black House (Spain). There was great popular resentment of the proposal that Prince Charles marry a Spanish princess and the play celebrated the frustration of the plan. Among the characters were the King of England, the King of Spain, the Prince of Wales (Charles), the Duke of Buckingham, and Gondomar, the Spanish ambassador.

**Gamelyn, The Tale of** A verse romance, usually dated about 1350, of 900 lines. It has been called *The Cook's Tale of Gamelyn* and attributed to Chaucer, but scholarship, while rejecting the attribution to Chaucer, suggests that he may well have intended to use the story for *The Canterbury Tales*. Thomas Lodge used some of the story in his *Rosalynde* (1590); this version formed the basis of Shakespeare's *As You Like It*.

Sir John de Boundys leaves his property in equal parts to his three sons, of whom Gamelyn is the youngest. The eldest proves to be evil and as soon as their father is dead robs Gamelyn of his share and generally maltreats him. Gamelyn appeals to the Church but the priests prefer to be on the stronger side, so Gamelyn resorts to force as soon as he is strong enough. He beats the fearsome wrestler sent against him and kills the castle porter. He finds an ally in Adam the steward, and together they trounce the priests whom they find at the feast given by the evil brother.

Pursued by the sheriff and his men Gamelyn and Adam take to the forest as outlaws. The eldest brother himself becomes sheriff and Gamelyn is taken – but the second brother, Ote, gives his bond for Gamelyn's release, the latter giving his word to appear for trial. When he does so he finds Ote in chains, a victim also of the evil brother's spite. The younger brothers and Adam succeed in overthrowing the evil one, who is hanged, and are eventually given high office by the king.

**Gamester, The** See **Moore, Edward**.

**Gamester, The** A comedy by James Shirley, first produced in 1633 and published in 1637. The plot is based on a story told in the *Heptameron* of Marguerite of Navarre. The title was also used for plays by Susannah Centlivre and Edward Moore.

Wilding is addicted to gambling; he is also in love with his wife's ward and kinswoman, Penelope. When he tells his wife of his passion for Penelope, Mrs Wilding accepts the disclosure with equanimity. Later she tells him that she has arranged an assignation for him with her ward. But by the appointed time Wilding has become

The title page illustration of Middleton's comedy, *A Game at Chess*, 1624.

involved in a gambling bout he cannot bear to leave; he sends his friend Hazard to take his place, certain that an encounter in darkness will conceal his friend's identity. On the next day Mrs Wilding confounds him by disclosing that it was she, not Penelope, who kept the tryst. Wilding, to avoid further embarrassment and humiliation, persuades the willing Hazard to marry Penelope. Then he is finally confounded upon discovering that the assignation never took place at all. Among the minor characters are Barnacle, whose ambition is to be a 'roaring boy', and the young lovers, Leonore and Violante.

**Gammer Gurton's Needle** A comedy that was possibly written in 1553 and vies with *Ralph Roister Doister* for the honour of being the first English comedy if the later date for Udall's work is accepted (see **Ralph Roister Doister**). Authorship has been attributed to at least three people but the favourite is William Stevenson, identified by Henry Bradley from the 'Mr S. Mr. of Art' on the title page of the printed edition of 1575, which also refers to the work as 'Played on Stage, not longe ago in Christes Colledge in Cambridge'. An earlier printed edition (*c*.1563) has not survived; but Stevenson fulfils the requirements of the evidence – he was styled Master (Mr) of Arts in 1553–54 at Christ's College, where he produced plays from 1550 to 1554. The play is notable for its total Englishness; there is no trace whatever of the influence of Terence or Plautus, hitherto inescapable. The play is written in rhymed doggerel.

The action of the play turns on the losing of Gammer Gurton's needle, with which she mends the clothes of Hodge, her servant; the resolution is the finding of the needle in the seat of Hodge's breeches. The play is rich in character and the inventiveness never flags. Among the characters are Diccon of Bedlam, who enjoys mischief-making; Gammer Gurton's enemy Dame Chat; Doctor Rat the curate; the servants Tib, Doll, and Spendthrift; and Gib the cat.

**Gamp, Mrs Sairey** In Dickens's *Martin Chuzzlewit*, the coarse midwife and professional nurse, 'dispoged' to gin and closely acquainted with life and death. Her fictional recollections of conversations with her nonexistent friend, Mrs Harris, are a marvellous blend of crooked wisdom, folklore, and the knowledge that all women share of life.

**Gardener, The** A story by Rudyard Kipling, included in the volume entitled *Debits and Credits* (1926). Helen Turrell has succeeded in bringing up, in a small English village, the illegitimate son of her brother George and retaining the respect of her neighbours as well. The boy, Michael, grows up – and is killed at Ypres during World War I; Helen goes to Flanders after the war to look for his grave. At the war cemetery she encounters another woman who confesses to her, in great distress, that she had to deny her son and bring him up as another's. Finding her way through the endless crosses Helen encounters a gardener who asks her who she is looking for: '"Lieutenant Michael Turrell—my nephew," said Helen slowly and word for word, as she had many thousands of times in her life.' The man regards her with 'infinite compassion': '"Come with me," he said, "and I will show you where your son lies"'. At the end of the story, leaving the cemetery, Helen sees the man working among the flowers; 'and she went away, supposing him to be the gardener.'

**Garden of Proserpine, The** A poem by Algernon Charles Swinburne, first published in *Poems and Ballads* (first series, 1866). One of Swinburne's most anthologized pieces ('Here, where the world is quiet'), it is completely pagan in spirit. The poet's note says that it was intended to capture 'that brief total pause of passion and of thought, when the spirit, without fear or hope of good things or evil, hungers and thirsts only after the perfect sleep.'

**Gardiner, Samuel Rawson** 1829–1902. Gardiner was born in Hampshire and became a student at Christ Church, Oxford, at the age of 19. After Oxford he became a teacher in London and devoted most of his spare time reading at the British Museum Library and the Public Record Office, preparing the material for his history of England in the early Stuart and Commonwealth periods. He published *Parliamentary Debates in 1610* (1862) and *A History of England from the Accession of James I to the Disgrace of Chief Justice Coke* (1863). The series continued with *Prince Charles and the Spanish Marriage* (1869), *A History of England under the Duke of Buckingham and Charles I* (1875), *The Personal Government of Charles I* (1877), and *The Fall of the Monarchy of Charles I* (1882). The entire work is known as *The History of England from the Accession of James I to the Outbreak of the Civil War*. Gardiner ended his great chronicle with *The History of the Great Civil War* (1886–91) and *The History of the Commonwealth and Protectorate* (1894–1901), which was completed by C. H. Firth with *The Last Years of the Protectorate* (1909).

Gardiner, who was descended from Henry Ireton and Bridget, daughter of Cromwell, is usually awarded the first place among 19th-century historians for accuracy and scrupulous impartiality. He became a lecturer in 1872 and later Professor of Modern History at King's College, London; he was offered but declined the Regius Professorship at Oxford and became Ford Lecturer in 1896. He was elected a fellow of All Souls (1884) and of Merton (1892). Among his other works were *The Thirty Years War* (1874), *A School Atlas of English History* (1892), and his Ford Lectures, *Cromwell's Place in History* (1897).

**Gareth and Lynette** See *Idylls of the King, The*.

**Gargery, Joe**  The warm-hearted blacksmith of Dickens's *Great Expectations*. Pip's mean-spirited rejection of him, when he becomes a young gentleman, does not shake Joe's affection and loyalty.

**Garland, (Hannibal) Hamlin**  1860–1940. Hamlin Garland was born in West Salem, Wisconsin. His background was farm life in Iowa and South Dakota until, at the age of 24, he went to Boston to study with hopes of becoming a writer. He studied economics and social science as well as literature and was influenced chiefly by Henry George and William Dean Howells. In 1887 he returned to the Midwest, where the condition of the small farmers made a deep impression on him. The promised land of former times seemed to him unbelievably drab and agrarian hardship the most crushing of all conditions. Such poverty of spirit was already known to him from his own boyhood and he had been impressed by E. W. Howe's *The Story of a Country Town*.

Garland's first book was a collection of short stories, **Main-Travelled Roads** (1891); *Prairie Folks* followed in 1893 and *Wayside Courtships* in 1897 but most of his stories were in fact written before 1890. He was active in the reform movement and published novels which broadcast the ideas of Henry George, *Jason Edwards: An Average Man* (1892), exposed political corruption, *A Spoil of Office* (1892), and attacked the power of the railroad interests, *A Member of the Third House* (1892).

His novels of agrarian life and the spoliation of the country include *A Little Norsk* (1892), **Rose of Dutcher's Coolly** (1895), *The Captain of the Gray-Horse Troop* (1902), and *Cavanagh, Forest Ranger* (1910). A book of essays, *Crumbling Idols* (1894), sets forth his theories on the use of realism in fiction. Garland moved back to the Midwest in 1893 and soon began to discover the far West. He travelled through the Rocky Mountains, reported a gold rush, and visited France and England in 1899. His best work, in the critics' view, was still to come. This was the pair of auto-biographical volumes, **A Son of the Middle Border** (1917) and *A Daughter of the Middle Border* (1921).

Garland continued to exploit this vein, with less success, until the end of his working life. But his reputation is secure in his stories of frontier life and the autobiographical volumes that recreate their background. He focused the attention of readers on aspects of American life new to American letters and his autobiographical volumes are a recommended source of information to anyone interested in the early Midwest. The essays in *Crumbling Idols* have not stood the test of time and even in their own time drew astringent comment from Kate Chopin in *St Louis Life* in 1894.

**Garrick, David**  1717–79. The great actor was of Huguenot descent, the son of an army officer, and was born in Hereford. He displayed an inclination for the theatre at an early age but had to complete his schooling first. The later part of that found him being taught by Samuel Johnson at the latter's unsuccessful school at Edial near Lichfield. When Johnson went to London for the production of his first tragedy Garrick went with him; he was to enter the wine trade but he soon abandoned that. His early career is obscure but at the age of 24 he was playing small parts under Giffard at Goodman's Fields Theatre, and it was there that he became the talk of London after his debut as Richard III on 19 October 1741.

Garrick's brilliant career belongs to the history of the theatre rather than to the history of literature, though he was a master of stagecraft and could turn out a well-tailored farce with the best of his contemporaries: *Miss in her Teens* (1747) and *Bon Ton; or High Life Above Stairs* (1775). His arbitrary way with Shakespeare's plays has been severely criticized but he did, nonetheless, deliver performances of the master's great parts which gave new generations an appreciation of Shakespeare's genius. Garrick, as an actor, drew his inspiration from life and his observation of it; he was hot-tempered, vain, and snobbish but his greatness was attested by everyone who saw him on the stage. When he died he was buried in Westminster Abbey and the carriages of the mourners stretched all the way back to the Strand.

**Garrison, William Lloyd**  1805–79. The leader of the New England Abolition movement was born in Newburyport, Massachusetts. For five years, in Baltimore, he edited *The Genius of Universal Emancipation* with Benjamin Lundy. He parted company with Lundy after being imprisoned for libel – Lundy found Garrison's approach too radical. Garrison launched *The Liberator* in Boston in 1831 and published it until the end of the Civil War saw the main part of his policy carried out. Before the Civil War Garrison was in favour of secession: the Constitution, as it was published, did not forbid slavery and Garrison regarded the South and its institutions as anathema. Slavery was actually abolished in the Thirteenth Amendment to the Constitution (1865).

**Garth, Mary** In George Eliot's *Middlemarch*, the daughter of Caleb Garth, the builder. She loves the worthless Fred Vincy, a young man with 'expectations' which come to nothing. The steadfast affection of Mary and her family are the making of Fred.

**Gascoigne, George** *c.*1539–77. Gascoigne was born at Cardington in Bedfordshire and educated at Trinity College, Cambridge. After Cambridge he entered Gray's Inn and became Member of Parliament for Bedford for two years in 1557. He married Elizabeth Breton, a widow and the mother of the poet Nicholas Breton, in 1561. He spent some time at court and knew Edmund Spenser, then served with the English forces in the Netherlands for two years (1572–74). Gascoigne led a dissipated life and never completed his training for the Bar; he spent some of that period in a debtors' prison. His early death occurred at Stamford, where he is buried.

Gascoigne did not achieve a major place in English literature but he contributed much to the climate in which succeeding greater figures flourished. In 1573, in *A Hundredth Sundrie Flowers Bounde up in One Small Poesie*, he introduced the sonnet sequence and he uses prose narrative in *The Adventures of Master F. J. The Posies of George Gascoigne Esquire* (1575) contains much that appeared in the first book; it also contains the first critical essay on poetry in English, *Certayne Notes of Instruction*; *Dan Bartholomew of Bathe*, a tale in verse; *Jocasta*, the first Greek tragedy translated into English (from *The Phoenician Women* of Euripides); and *The Supposes*, a prose comedy translated from Ariosto. Further works by Gascoigne include the prose *The Glasse of Government, a tragicall Comedie* (1575); a quasi-masque, *The Princely Pleasures at Kenelworth Castle* (1576); *The Steele Glas, A Satyre* written in blank verse (1576); and *The Spoil of Antwerp* (1577), an account of some of his experiences in the Netherlands. *The Complaynt of Philomene, An Elegy* (1576) is verse narrative in the style of Ovid – the form Shakespeare used in *Venus and Adonis* and *The Rape of Lucrece*.

Gascoigne is a transitional poet, a forerunner of the great Elizabethans for whom he left many models drawn from the Renaissance writers of Europe. His work has distinction and he wrote with ease in many forms, but his work is not memorable.

**Gaskell, Elizabeth Cleghorn** 1810–65. Elizabeth Gaskell was the daughter of William Stevenson, a civil servant who had once been a Unitarian minister. Her birthplace was Chelsea, but her mother died a month after she was born and Elizabeth was brought up at Knutsford in Cheshire by an aunt. She married William Gaskell, a Unitarian minister of Manchester, when she was 22. He collaborated with his wife in her earliest literary effort, a poem 'in the manner of Crabbe' called *Sketches among the Poor*, which appeared in *Blackwood's Magazine* in 1837.

Her husband's ministry was a very definite factor in the shaping of Elizabeth Gaskell as a novelist: she was always acutely aware of social conditions and shared her husband's concern for the poor. She began to write her first novel in 1845. When their only son died of scarlet fever in 1844, William had encouraged his wife to write as a distraction from her grief. The late 1830s and early 1840s had been a time of great unrest and when the book *Mary Barton* appeared in 1848

Elizabeth Gaskell. Portrait by George Richmond, 1851. National Portrait Gallery, London.

the first tentative efforts were being made to alleviate the horrors of the great industrial areas. Elizabeth Gaskell believed that workmen should be honoured as men and brethren and that there was little hope until this had been tried. The success of *Mary Barton* brought her the attention of her contemporaries, notably Dickens, who published her work regularly in *Household Words* and *All the Year Round*.

From 1850 there had been, meanwhile, a steady production of occasional pieces and some of these, after appearing in *Household Words*, were collected, enlarged, and published in 1853 as the immortal **Cranford**, the author's favourite among her books. The same year saw the publication of **Ruth** – and suddenly Elizabeth Gaskell found herself at the centre of an ethical controversy. Her novel knocked the self-righteous smirk off the face of the smug Victorian bourgeoisie which had long forgotten that kindness and compassion were an essential part of Christ's teaching.

**North and South** was published in 1855. The author was perfectly aware of the social progress which had been made since *Mary Barton*, but the problems were still there and *North and South* exposed them.

In 1855 her friend Charlotte Brontë died. A number of ill-considered reports in magazines and newspapers worried the dead author's friends and family and Ellen Nussey wrote to Charlotte's husband, Arthur Nicholls, suggesting that Elizabeth Gaskell be asked to write an article about Charlotte which represented her fairly. Patrick Brontë, who survived his daughter, wrote to Elizabeth – who had not even known of Charlotte's last illness – and requested her, formally, to undertake an authoritative account of Charlotte's life and work. She accepted, though she was later to realize that Arthur Nicholls was not in favour of the enterprise.

The *Life of Charlotte Brontë* was published in 1857, and almost at once the author faced trouble from Carus Wilson, who ran the dreadful school at Cowan Bridge, and from Mrs Robinson of Thorp Green, where Branwell Brontë had lodged – Elizabeth Gaskell implied that her conduct towards Branwell had been somewhat less than proper. But the book weathered these troubles and has become a classic of English literature, a biography which in spite of all the restraints of the age has a force and truthfulness which make it the point of departure for the legions of Brontë admirers. Elizabeth Gaskell, an accomplished and successful novelist, was also a woman of fine sympathies. George Eliot confessed to having wept over the book.

Shorter works occupied her for some time, most of them appearing in *Household Words* and *All the Year Round*. Particularly notable was *Lois the Witch* (1859), set in Salem during the hysterical witch-hunts of the 17th century, and detailing the circumstances which make an innocent girl die on the gallows. Her next book, **Sylvia's Lovers**, was published in 1863. It is a novel on a large scale, revealing the author's unerring skill with domestic drama, set against the maritime struggles of the previous century. **Cousin Phillis** came in 1864 and **Wives and Daughters** was almost complete when Elizabeth Gaskell died, at Holybourne in Hampshire, in 1865.

Everyone who knew her seems to have been fond of Elizabeth Gaskell, a comely woman of rare content and kindness who lived in perfect harmony with her William, was happy in her four daughters, and was devotedly served by her household staff. Generous in her appreciation of others, she was admired by Dickens, Thackeray, George Eliot, Thomas Carlyle, Ruskin, Henry James, and Frederick Maurice. George Sand, in a letter to Lord Houghton, wrote: 'Mrs Gaskell has done what neither I nor other female writers in France can accomplish; she has written novels which excite the deepest interest in men of the world, and yet which every girl will be the better for reading.' Mrs Gaskell gave the shy little Charlotte Brontë her only experience of spontaneous and sympathetic response, on a personal level, from another woman. Her great friend Susanna Winkworth said, 'When you were with her, you felt as if you had twice the life in you that you had at ordinary times.'

Acutely aware of her times and of the changing social scene, Elizabeth Gaskell made far more of an impact with *Mary Barton* than Disraeli ever did with his essays into the social-problem novel because she deals with people, not abstractions, and her touch is sure; the world she describes was there in Manchester and she saw much of it, as it was the scene of her husband's work.

'Mrs Gaskell exploited her femininity, for which we are grateful.' Thus Geoffrey Tillotson, and perhaps no one has expressed better the quality which informs all her work, and reaches such a level of excellence in *Cranford* and *Wives and Daughters*. But a stronger term than femininity is needed: she could tackle the challenging issues contained in *Mary Barton*, *Ruth* and *North and South* with a confident womanliness that carries integrity in every line.

**Gatty, Margaret** 1809–73. Born Margaret Scott, daughter of Nelson's chaplain on board the *Victory* at Trafalgar, she married the Rev

Alfred Gatty. Mrs Gatty founded *Aunt Judy's Magazine* in 1865 and edited and contributed to it from 1866 until she died. The magazine was enormously popular with children. Mrs Gatty was a writer for children, best known for her *Parables from Nature*, published in a series of five books (1855–71). Other titles that enjoyed great popularity were *The Fairy Godmothers* (1851), *Aunt Judy's Tales* (1859), and *Aunt Judy's Letters* (1862). It is unlikely that Margaret Gatty's essentially Victorian moral stories would be borne with any patience by children today, and she is no longer read.

**Gawain** Before the introduction of Launcelot into the Arthurian cycle (he came from the French or Breton writers) Gawain held pride of place as a knight of King Arthur, embodying all the virtues and named in the earliest versions of the stories. He is Arthur's nephew, son of Arthur's half-sister Morgause and King Lot of Orkney, and he is Arthur's ambassador to Rome. In Malory's *Le Morte Darthur* he becomes Launcelot's sworn enemy when Launcelot kills his brothers, and dies in combat with him. A curious hangover from pagan times accompanies Gawain into *Le Morte Darthur*: his strength increases with the sun and begins to decline after the meridian – a direct connection of Gawain with the ancient Welsh sun god, Gwalchmei.

See also *Gawain and the Green Knight, Sir.*

**Gawain and the Green Knight, Sir** An alliterative poem of the late 14th century, *Sir Gawain and the Green Knight* is the fourth poem in the Cotton Nero A.X manuscript. (See also *Pearl*.) Unlike the other three poems, which are purely didactic, *Sir Gawain* is a romance – perhaps a didactic romance. The author of this unique work, one of the greatest of the Middle Ages, remains unknown.

The poem is in four parts which correspond to the main stages of the story. The opening takes the reader to 'Camylot upon Krystmasse': it is New Year's Day at Arthur's court. A strange figure on horseback enters the hall; he has gigantic stature and is comely – and he is green. His dress, his horse, his hair and beard, are all green; in one hand he carries a branch of holly, in the other a great axe. Arthur offers him hospitality; the Green Knight replies that he has not come to stay, but to challenge. The challenger must swear that, after striking the first blow, he will seek the Green Knight one year hence and receive a blow in return. Gawain takes up the challenge and the Green Knight gives him the axe; Gawain strikes his head off. The body of the Green Knight comes forward and picks up the head, and holds

Sir Gawain beheads the Green Knight; Arthur and Guinevere look on. Late 14th or early 15th-century illustration from *MS. Cotton Nero A. x, f.90v*. British Library.

it while it gives voice: Gawain must go to the Green Chapel one year hence. Then the Green Knight, carrying his severed head, mounts his horse and departs.

In the second part the seasons' passing is noted; a year goes by quickly and Gawain is searching for the Green Chapel after Arthur and the other knights have taken a sad farewell. He travels through Logres (Britain) to Wales and on to Anglesey and the Wirral, all frozen in the grip of winter. He enters a deep forest and comes upon a castle. The lord, a big man with a red beard, makes him welcome and tells him that the Green Chapel is nearby. The chatelaine is young and lovely, but she is accompanied by an old and withered hag. Gawain spends Christmas at the castle, and for the three last days before his tryst his host bids him rest. The lord hunts each day and makes a bargain with his guest: each evening he and Gawain will exchange what each has won during the day.

The third part tells of the three days. The beautiful hostess gives Gawain a kiss which he gives to the lord when he returns. But the hostess had stolen into Gawain's chamber to kiss him and she is bolder on the second day: the lord is kissed twice by Gawain when he returns. On the third day Gawain kisses him three times but conceals a girdle of green lace which the lady had given him as a charm against evil. The third part closes with a feast on New Year's Eve.

In the last part Gawain sets forth with a guide and comes to the Green Chapel, a cave in the wilderness. The guide tries to dissuade Gawain from the fatal encounter; Gawain refuses and the guide leaves him. The Green Knight appears and Gawain kneels; as the axe descends Gawain flinches and the Green Knight mocks him. Gawain remains immobile when the axe is raised again; the Green Knight pauses. Then the axe falls on Gawain – but lightly, to give him no more than a graze. The compact is settled. The Green Knight reveals himself as the lord of the castle, Bercilak de Hautdesert. The test was contrived by Morgan le Fay, Arthur's half-sister, to test the knights and frighten Guinevere. Gawain had been true in all things but one: he had concealed the green lace and for that he was given a slight wound. Gawain returns to the court and tells the story and all agree to wear green lace in honour of the adventure. But Gawain feels no honour and wears the girdle of green lace as a badge of penitence.

The poem has several strands of myth running through it: the Green Man, the symbol of fertility; the waste land through which the hero wanders, determined to keep his compact; Gawain himself, a survival of Gwalchmei, the sun god who restores life to the land. But the author of *Sir Gawain and the Green Knight* was writing a poem and using available elements of magic – the stuff of poetry – not retelling a myth. The myths are simply part of the fabric of this magnificent poem.

*Sir Gawain and the Green Knight* was edited by R. Morris (1864, 1869, and 1897), by J. R. R. Tolkien and E. V. Gordon (1925), by I. Gollancz, M. Day, and M. S. Serjeantson for the Early English Text Society (1938), and by R. A. Waldron (1970). A. C. Cawley and J. J. Anderson's edition contains the four poems of the Cotton manuscript (Everyman's Library). Modern versions of the poem are by E. J. B. Kirtlan (1912), K. Hare (1918, revised 1948), S. O. Andrew (New York, 1929), M. R. Ridley (1944), Gwyn Jones (1953), J. L. Rosenberg (New York, 1959), J. Gardner (Chicago, 1965), and M. Borroff (1968). Brian Stone produced a modern version (Penguin Classics, 1959).

**Gay, John** 1685–1732. The son of a Nonconformist family in comfortable circumstances, Gay was born in Barnstaple, in Devon. He was educated at Barnstaple Grammar School and then apprenticed to a silk merchant in London; but he found the trade uncongenial, returned home, and began to write verse. He returned to London to renew acquaintance with his fellow townsman Aaron Hill, who published *The British Apollo*, and became friends with the contributors. His first work to be published appeared anonymously; this was a poem called *Wine* (1708), a piece in blank verse that postulated the impossibility of a water drinker succeeding as a writer. An article, *The Present State of Wit* (1711), brought him to the attention of Pope and his circle of friends. Looking for an assured income, Gay became secretary to the Duchess of Monmouth in 1712, the year of his essay on young upper-class thugs, *An Argument Proving that the Present Mohocks and Hawkubites are the Gog and Magog of Revelation*, and his play on the same theme, *The Mohocks*. Gay had a real feeling for the life of London and knew more about its shadows than any of his friends. It was his friends' influence, however, that secured him the post of secretary to Lord Clarendon on his mission to Hanover; but this promising appointment ended abruptly when Queen Anne died. However, he was fortunate in finding patrons in the Duke and Duchess of Queensberry.

Gay published *The Fan* (1713) in three books; this was an imitation of Pope's *The Rape of the Lock*. He also contributed *Rural Sports* to Steele's *Guardian* in the same year; dedicated to Pope, it also read like Pope. Gay did not achieve a success that was really his own until 1714, when he parodied the pastorals of Ambrose Philips in **The Shepherd's Week**. He had by now mastered the couplet form and wrote with ease. His next work was a satirical farce, *What d'ye Call it*, successfully produced in 1715, and his most successful poem, **Trivia**: *or The Art of Walking the Streets of London*, followed in 1716. The model was Swift and the execution impeccable; Gay was a successful poet. But his career in the theatre suffered a reverse with the failure of *Three Hours after Marriage* (1717), which was a collaboration with Pope and Arbuthnot.

The next ten years were occupied with miscellaneous verse and the *Fables*, 50 of which appeared in two volumes in 1728. These were didactic poems originally written for young Prince William and were the works by which Gay was best known as a poet for the next century. A further book of 16 poems was published in 1738. Meanwhile, after a remark by his friend Jonathan Swift that a Newgate pastoral 'might make an odd pretty sort of thing' (Swift had raised the point first in a letter to Pope in August

1716, '... what do you think of a Newgate pastoral, among the whores and thieves there?'), Gay embarked on his ballad opera, using the music of old songs and airs. **The Beggar's Opera** was produced by John Rich at Lincoln's Inn on 29 January 1728 and published in the same year. Gay wrote a sequel, **Polly** (1729), which was banned from the stage by Walpole; consequently the published version enjoyed a great success.

The lyrics from *The Beggar's Opera* and *Polly* are deservedly popular anthology pieces and his poem written on the completion of Alexander Pope's translation of the *Iliad*, *Mr Pope's Welcome from Greece*, is a deft and felicitous piece. Gay was also the author of *Acis and Galatea* and *Achilles*, operas produced at Covent Garden in 1732 and 1733 respectively. Handel composed the score of *Acis and Galatea*, in which words and music are happily matched – everyone knows 'O ruddier than the cherry'. Modern editions of Gay's works are *The Poetical Works* edited by Geoffrey Faber (1926), which includes selections from his dramatic works; *Selected Poems*, edited by A. Ross (1950); and *Letters*, edited by C. S. Burgess (1966). The Everyman's Library selection includes the text of *The Beggar's Opera*, which is also to be found in the Oxford Paperback collection entitled *Eighteenth Century Comedy*. The complete *Poetry and Prose* was edited by Vinton A. Dearing and Charles E. Bookwith and published in two volumes in 1974.

**General William Booth Enters into Heaven and Other Poems** The first collection of poems by Vachel Lindsay, published in 1913. The title poem was intended to be sung to the music of the popular hymn 'The Blood of the Lamb' and the text contains careful annotation recommending how it should be performed as well as the instruments for accompaniment. Also in the collection is 'The Eagle That is Forgotten', the poet's elegy on the death of the Liberal governor of Illinois, J. P. Altgeld.

**Genesis** A poem of nearly 3000 lines in Old English, preserved in the *Junius Manuscript* in the Bodleian Library, Oxford. It was wrongly attributed to Caedmon by Francis Junius. The poem follows scripture in relating the Creation and events up to the story of Isaac, and contains an interpolation (lines 235–851) that repeats some of the story in a different, darker tone. Edward Sievers, a German scholar, conjectured in 1875 that the interpolation came from an Old Saxon version of *Genesis*. Sievers was proved right when a manuscript containing fragments of the Old Saxon version was discovered in the Vatican Library in 1894. The interpolation, for which no explanation was offered, is usually called *Genesis B*, the rest of the poem *Genesis A*. A translation of the poem appears in C. W. Kennedy's *Early English Christian Poetry* (1952).

**Geneva Bible, The** William Whittingham (*c.* 1524–79), a fellow of All Souls, Oxford, expressed Calvinistic views during the reign of Mary. He was obliged to flee the country and joined the English congregation at Frankfurt that was led by John Knox. When Knox was expelled after a dispute Whittingham followed him to Geneva and succeeded Knox as a 'minister' though he had never been ordained. He returned to England in Elizabeth's reign and was made Dean of Durham in 1563. But he would not accept the Prayer Book and was generally so troublesome that the Archbishop of York started proceedings to deprive him of his office. The archbishop would probably have succeeded, since Whittingham had never been ordained, but Whittingham died before the proceedings were concluded.

During his years on the continent Whittingham translated the New Testament for the Protestant exile congregation. This was the first time it was divided into verses and printed in roman type and it was published in Geneva in 1557; the psalms followed in 1559. Whittingham completed the whole Bible with the help of Anthony Gilby and Thomas Sampson. *The Geneva Bible*, as it came to be called, was published in 1560 and dedicated to Queen Elizabeth. It was based on the existing translations of Tyndale and Coverdale and influenced by Knox, Theodore Beza, and other European Protestants. The marginal notes display an extreme Protestant viewpoint.

Though it did not have the Church and royal authority bestowed on *The Great Bible* of Miles Coverdale *The Geneva Bible* was very popular in England and the verse divisions were followed in every version that succeeded it. The size contributed to its popularity; it was printed on quarto, instead of on the huge unwieldy folios of its predecessors. It became known as the 'Breeches' Bible from the rendering of Genesis 3:7 of the passage 'they knew that they were naked... and made themselves aprons' (AV). In *The Geneva Bible* Adam and Eve make breeches, not aprons, out of fig leaves.

**Gentleman Dancing-Master, The** A comedy by William Wycherley, first produced in March 1672 and published in 1673. The play, which approaches deftly turned farce, had its source in the Spanish *El Maestro de Danzar* by Calderón.

Mr Formal, home from Spain, is more Spanish

than the Spaniards, affecting Spanish dress and manners. His daughter Hippolita has been in the care of her aunt, Mrs Caution, who has kept her confined. Formal, who calls himself Don Diego, has arranged Hippolita's marriage to her cousin, home from France. Hippolita knows no other man, thanks to her aunt, but she despises her silly cousin, who calls himself Monsieur de Paris and apes French fashion and language. She contrives that Gerrard, a friend of Monsieur de Paris, should visit the house and immediately falls in love with him. The attraction is mutual, and when Formal surprises them together Hippolita introduces Gerrard as her dancing-master. But Gerrard, required to go through his paces, is hopelessly incompetent and Mrs Caution sees through the deception at once. Formal, in his pompous Don Diego pose, will not believe he can be fooled; his squabble with Mrs Caution gives the young lovers a respite, though Gerrard is finally exposed. A parson who has arrived to marry Hippolita to her cousin is tricked by the lovers into marrying her to Gerrard instead.

**Gentleman's Magazine, The** A periodical founded by Edward Cave (1691–1754), the enterprising son of a cobbler in Rugby, who became a printer in London. Of all his enterprises he is best remembered for *The Gentleman's Magazine*, which he launched in 1731 under the pseudonym of Sylvanus Urban. It began as a review of news, essays, and comment from other journals but by January 1739 it was publishing original work and Samuel Johnson became a regular contributor. Johnson's suggestions to Cave influenced the character of the paper and it assumed a more serious tone, publishing parliamentary reports, maps, reviews of publications and music. Johnson became the author of the parliamentary reports after first being the editor. *The Gentleman's Magazine* continued to be published until 1914.

**Geoffrey Hamlyn, The Recollections of** A novel by Henry Kingsley, first published in 1859. The setting is Australia, where the author spent some years after leaving Oxford under a cloud. The story leads up to the many reasons why a group of settlers prepare to leave England and then follows their fortunes in the vast undeveloped continent. The author was an excellent reporter and presents a vivid picture of the landscape and the hazards faced by the emigrants. (It should be noted that the hero's recollections are recounted after he returns to England.) The book is loose and rambling but the author's style is pleasing and leaves an impression of a warm and sympathetic man.

**Geoffrey of Monmouth** See **Monmouth, Geoffrey of.**

**George, Henry** 1839–97. The son of middle-class Episcopalian parents, the political economist was born in Philadelphia. He left home at the age of 16 to go to sea and a voyage to India showed him the appalling extremes of wealth and poverty existing side by side, making an indelible impression on him. He went to San Francisco at 18 on the promise of work and, in the event, was to lead a varied life in a number of occupations, all of which were really a continual struggle to survive. He achieved his first success after 11 years with a contribution to the *Overland Monthly* in 1868, which expressed his doubts about the future of the new country of California: it was becoming clear that land speculators and railway barons were despoilers. He was right; the railways were to have no effect on poverty other than, in many cases, to promote it; but a small number of people would gain enormous wealth from them.

George published his *Our Land and Land Policy* in 1871. This pamphlet attacked the land grants to the railroad companies and put forward the idea of a single tax. He began *Progress and Poverty* (1879) during the depression and labour unrest of 1879; in it he put forward the theory that rent was the perpetuating factor in poverty. He suggested that a single tax on the ownership and yield of land (whatever the use to which it was put) would ensure a more just reward for labour and provide the means to remedy social ills. George held to this theory and developed it in further publications and in extensive lectures in Europe and the USA.

Henry George's ideas became less valid with the enormous growth of industrialism but in his time his perception was original and valuable; his influence was considerable. Echoes are to be found in Tolstoy, G. B. Shaw, and the American novelists Jack London, Frank Norris, Hamlin Garland, and William Dean Howells.

**George Barnwell** See **London Merchant, The.**

**George Silverman's Explanation** A short story by Charles Dickens, first published in the *Atlantic Monthly* (1868).

**Georgia Scenes** See **Longstreet, Augustus Baldwin.**

**Geraint and Enid** See **Idylls of the King, The.**

**Gerald of Barry** See **Giraldus Cambrensis.**

**Gerard, John** 1545–1612. Gerard was the superintendent of Lord Burghley's gardens. He listed all the plants of the gardens in his charge in 1596 and thus made the first catalogue of English garden flowers. His fame rests on the *Herball or General Historie of Plantes* (1597), which was largely based on the French version (by L'Ecluse) of the Dutch *Niewe Herball* of Rembert Dodoens which was published in 1578. Gerard's *Herball* became a celebrated book in England and a revised edition (by Thomas Johnson) was published in 1633. The book gives a description of each plant, where it may be found, the origin of its name, and the medicinal properties. Gerard also disposes of many old superstitions connected with plants. The *Herball* is illustrated with numerous woodcuts of fine quality.

**Gereint and Enid**  A Welsh tale which appears in the manuscripts of *The White Book of Rhydderch* (early 14th century) and *The Red Book of Hergest* (late 14th century) and was translated by Lady Charlotte Guest in her *The Mabinogion*. The subject was also used by Chrétien de Troyes (late 12th century) in *Erec*, and by Tennyson in *Geraint and Enid* (1859). Gereint is the son of Erbin of Cornwall and distinguishes himself at the court of Arthur; he also wins the hand of Enid. But he neglects all for love of her, his knightly duties and his obligations to his own lands. Enid grieves and Gereint begins to doubt her love for him. He sets out on chivalrous adventures and takes her with him, ordering her to keep silence on the way. But Enid cannot be silent when danger threatens him and she disobeys his orders. After a painful and near-fatal encounter with the doughty Little King, Gereint and Enid meet Arthur and his knights in a forest. Gereint fights with Kei (Kay) but is beaten by Gwalchmei (Gawain). Arthur summons his physician and Gereint is cured, whereupon he rides off again with Enid. Eventually Enid is threatened with dishonour and Gereint comes to his senses. He saves her, loves her again, and even brings himself to make friends with the Little King.

**Gereth, Mrs**  In *The Spoils of Poynton*, by Henry James, Mrs Gereth has assembled a fine collection of furniture and *objets d'art*. Her son Owen inherits Poynton and its contents but he has not inherited his mother's faultless taste; to her dismay he proposes to marry the vulgar Mona Brigstock. Mrs Gereth hopes to redirect his attentions to Fleda Vetch, who shares her appreciation of Poynton and its contents.

**Germ, The**  See **Pre-Raphaelite Brotherhood**.

**Gertrude**  Queen of Denmark in Shakespeare's *Hamlet*. Her son is outraged that she should marry Claudius and reign with him as queen within a month of the old king's death. It is not suggested in the play that she connived at the murder of her husband and in fact his ghost remains unseen by her in the closet scene, but there is a definite statement from the ghost that Claudius won her 'to his shameful lust'. She dies through drinking from the poisoned cup intended for Hamlet.

**Gesta Romanorum**  A collection of tales from various sources which took shape in Europe during the 14th century. They were written in Latin prose but the title is meaningless, since few of the stories are concerned with Rome and a number are eastern in origin. Each tale was designed to point a moral but in many cases the moral is transparently contrived; the collection was really popular as a storybook and was plundered for subjects by succeeding generations. It was first printed at Utrecht in 1472; the first English version was printed by Wynkyn de Worde in 1510. *The Early English Versions of the Gesta Romanorum* was edited by S. J. H. Herrtage for the Early English Text Society (1879).

**Gesta Stephani** (*The Acts of Stephen*).  A chronicle of the years 1135–47 by an anonymous historian of the reign of King Stephen. The chronicler may have been the king's confessor and the *Gesta* is valued for its accuracy and vividness. It was edited by R. C. Sewell (English Historical Society, 1846) and by R. Howlett (Rolls Series, 1886). T. Forester's translation of the less highly regarded *Historia Anglorum* of Henry of Huntingdon contains a translation of the *Gesta Stephani* (1853).

**Gest Hystoriale of the Destruction of Troy**  A Middle English verse romance of the 14th century. (See **metrical romances**.) Here the matter of classical antiquity is given medieval clothing and elements of magic are introduced. The romance includes the story of Troilus and Briseida, invented by Benoît de Sainte-Maure and told in his *Roman de Troie* (*c*.1160). As Troilus and Cressida the lovers have become, in English, as famous as Romeo and Juliet. *The Destruction of Troy* was edited by G. A. Panton and D. Donaldson for the Early English Text Society (1866–74).

**Ghost of Abel, The**  See **Blake, William**.

**Ghost of Hamlet's father**  The most famous (and articulate) ghost in literature. In Shakespeare's *Hamlet* he reveals the truth to his son about his death and the seduction of Gertrude. There is a chilling reference to his term as a soul in purgatory, 'I am ... doomed for a certain term to walk the night, and for the day confined to fast in fires.'

**Giant Despair** Of Doubting Castle, in John Bunyan's *The Pilgrim's Progress*. He captures and maltreats Christian and Hopeful.

**Gibbon, Edward** 1737–94. The son of a family of comfortable circumstances and distinguished connections, Edward Gibbon was born at Putney-on-Thames (now a part of Greater London). He was one of six brothers; the others died in infancy. Gibbon was educated at a preparatory school at Kingston-upon-Thames and at Westminster School, and entered Magdalen College, Oxford, as a gentleman-commoner just before his 15th birthday. But the remarkable boy was bitterly disappointed in Oxford, which he found smug, self-satisfied, and offering little more than the remnants of an outdated system of studies. He studied by himself and was received into the Catholic Church in June 1753. At 16 he turned his back on Oxford.

Gibbon's father, alarmed at the turn of events, sent him to Lausanne and a tutor in the form of a Calvinist minister, Pavillard. The result was fortunate; Gibbon was fond of religious disputation and argued the case for Rome with gusto. He grew very attached to Lausanne and to his tutor, a kind and tactful man who succeeded in detaching Gibbon from his youthful allegiance to a new religion. At Lausanne, too, Gibbon formed the only romantic attachment of his life, to Suzanne Curchod, who eventually married Jacques Necker; the attachment was broken off because Gibbon's father would not give his approval.

Gibbon returned home in 1758, and published his first work in 1761. This was *Essai sur l'Étude de la Littérature*; Gibbon had mastered French and written a defence of classical literature in that language. (The English version was published in 1764.) He served in the Hampshire militia for four years and reached the rank of colonel (1759–63). The experience of military matters and the history of campaigns was to prove very useful to him later on; meanwhile he pondered a subject on which to write. It was the age of the historian, as David Hume said, and Gibbon's reading had always tended to historical subjects.

After his service with the militia Gibbon visited Europe, spending some time in Paris and Lausanne, and proceeded to Rome intent on archaeological study. He reached the city in October 1764 and on the 15th of that month he found the historical subject he sought. 'It was at Rome . . . as I sat musing amidst the ruins of the Capitol, while barefoot friars were singing vespers in the Temple of Jupiter, that the idea of

Edward Gibbon. Portrait by H. Walton. c.1773. National Portrait Gallery, London.

writing the decline and fall of the city first started to my mind.' He had, meanwhile, been practising his craft. From a mass of miscellaneous reviews and exercises the *Observations on the Design of the VIth Book of the Aeneid* (1770) could perhaps be named as the most notable: Gibbon rejected Warburton's view of the sixth book as a symbolic representation of Roman religious mysticism with considerable skill, but the modern view tends to agree with Warburton. Gibbon's father died in the same year, leaving a chaotic mess for his son to clear up; Gibbon did, however, manage to salvage enough money to establish himself in London. He needed access to libraries, intellectual stimulus, and scholarly society.

Gibbon became a Member of Parliament in 1774. The House of Commons was 'a school of civil prudence, the first and most essential virtue of an historian', as he said in his memoirs. He was a steadfast supporter of Lord North's government and was rewarded with the post of Commissioner of Trade and Plantations in 1779. He held it until 1782, when it was abolished, and found the salary useful. His political career amounted to little but his literary career had begun: the first volume of **The History of the Decline and Fall of the Roman Empire** was published on 17 February 1776 and was greeted with a chorus of praise. Three editions were needed to supply the demand for it and it was gratifying that the Neckers were in London to offer personal congratulations. David Hume and William Robertson wrote him letters of generous and sincere admiration. Visiting Paris in the following year, he was honoured as an eminent man of letters in the style which was unique to France at that period. There was a certain amount of sniping from the religiously orthodox but Gibbon could afford to ignore much of it. Only when criticism or reservation was expressed by a thoughtful and stylish writer such as Richard Watson, Regius Professor of Divinity at Cambridge, did he acknowledge it. When the critic was plainly on the warpath and trying to discredit him, Gibbon retorted as he did to Henry Edwards Davis, who had accused him in his *Examination of the Fifteenth and Sixteenth Chapters of Mr Gibbon's History* of both plagiarism and misrepresentation of Latin authors. Gibbon's *A Vindication* (1779) demolished the mouse, Davis, and in doing so silenced others. The cause of all the contention in these two chapters was Gibbon's assertion that Christianity had spread naturally, not with the help of miraculous demonstrations; and that the treatment of Christians by their pagan rulers compared favourably with the cruelty and intolerance offered by Christians to those who did not share their sectarian convictions. Gibbon, like Voltaire, detested intolerance and bigotry. The attacks on Edward Gibbon continued throughout his lifetime.

The second and third volumes of the *History* were published in 1781 and at that time Gibbon resolved to extend it to cover the eastern Roman empire, Byzantium, as well. He was weary of London and moved to Lausanne in 1783 to share a house with his friend Georges Deyverdun. He completed his *History* there in 1787 and took the three volumes to London in 1788 for the publisher. Deyverdun died in 1789 and Gibbon decided to undertake no more major works. *The Antiquities of the House of Brunswick* was begun but Gibbon, who had no German, did not complete it. He left Lausanne in 1791 and returned to England, where his closest friend, John Baker Holroyd, now Earl of Sheffield, gave him unstinting and paternal hospitality at Sheffield Park in Sussex and in his London house. Lord Sheffield was to prepare his friend's *Memoirs* for publication (1796), as well as his (admirably edited) collections of *Miscellaneous Works*. Gibbon died in London on 16 January 1794 and lies buried in the Sheffield family tomb in Fletching church in Sussex.

Gibbon chose a tremendous theme for his history and he was equal to it. A distinguished historian of later days, J. B. Bury, held him to be the finest example of 'the union of the historian and the man of letters'. As a historian Gibbon owes something to classical writers, something to the French for the scientific method with which he selects material, and something to David Hume and William Robertson for his artistic use of scientific method. His detachment is remarkable and essential in tackling such an enormous subject. The book known as *Memoirs of My Life and Writings* was put together from autobiographical fragments of various dates by Lord Sheffield – who earns the gratitude of every student of literature for doing so.

**Gibson, Clare** Formerly Clare Fitzpatrick, Mr Gibson's second wife in Elizabeth Gaskell's *Wives and Daughters*. She is selfish, shallow, and stupid and has no idea that she proclaims her character every time she speaks.

**Gibson, Molly** The heroine of Elizabeth Gaskell's *Wives and Daughters*. She adores her father, the widowed doctor, and does her best to like his new wife. She loves the squire's son, Roger Hamley.

**Gibson, Wilfrid Wilson** 1878–1962. Gibson was born at Hexham in Northumberland and educated privately. He published his first collection of poems, *Urlyn the Harper and Other Songs*, in 1902, and thereafter his work appeared regularly in *New Numbers* and in Edward Marsh's *Georgian Poetry*. His output was considerable and genuinely compassionate, his chosen subject being the plight of the unfortunate, particularly the ordinary men and women at the mercy of industrial and political change. His quality was uneven and his poetry sometimes lacks urgency in spite of his good intentions. Gibson's *Collected Poems* (1926) was followed by another dozen collections before his death. *Within Four Walls* (1950) contains five verse plays.

**Gifford, William** 1756–1826. Gifford was born at Ashburton in Devonshire. A glazier's son, he was apprenticed to a shoemaker, but through the kindness of a surgeon, William Cookesley, was able to enter Exeter College, Oxford, where he took his degree in 1782. He first came to notice with two satires, *The Baviad* (1794) and *The Maeviad* (1795), directed against a contemporary school of poetry notorious for its pretensions, the Della Cruscan, and became editor of *The Anti-Jacobin* in 1797. Later (1809) he became editor of *The Quarterly Review*.

Gifford published *The Satires of Juvenal Translated* (1802) and *The Satires of Persius Translated*

(1812). A short autobiography was prefixed to his *Juvenal* and this was published separately in 1827, after his death. Gifford's criticism is characterized by a sourness which is attributed to his early struggles. He held to established forms and could discern little virtue in anything new. He was rebuked by William Hazlitt in *A Letter to Gifford* in 1819.

Gifford prepared notable editions of some Jacobean dramatists: *Philip Massinger* (1805) and *Ben Jonson* (1816); *John Ford* (1827 posth.) and *James Shirley* (completed by Alexander Dyce, 1833).

**Gilbert, Sir Humphrey** *c.*1539–83. Gilbert was half-brother to Sir Walter Ralegh and one of the famous company of Elizabethan explorers. His goal was to find a Northwest Passage and in 1576 he published *A Discourse of a Discoverie for a New Passage to Cataia*. See **Hakluyt, Richard**.

**Gilbert, William** 1540–1603. The Elizabethan scientist and royal physician studied medicine at Cambridge, gaining his MD in 1569, and was elected a fellow of St John's College. Later he practised in London and became president of the College of Physicians in 1599. The following year he was appointed physician to Elizabeth I and held the same position under James I.

Gilbert's fame however, rests on his investigations into physical science, which were published in *De magnete magneticisque corporibus* (1600). He arrived at his conclusions through experiment and his theory of magneticism remained unchallenged until the 19th century. Gilbert was the first to separate magnetism from another force, for which he found a name – *vis electrica*. Gilbert discerned the existence of gravitation and the relative thinness of the earth's atmosphere. He accepted the Copernican theory of the Sun as the centre around which the planets moved and wrote in support of it.

**Gilbert, Sir William Schwenk** 1836–1911. Gilbert was born in London and was trained for the law at the Inner Temple. He became a barrister in 1863, served as a magistrate in Middlesex, and was a captain in the militia. His literary career began with contributions to a periodical called *Fun* in 1861; these were comic verses and were published under the pseudonym of 'Bab'. The publication of a collection of these as *Bab Ballads* (1869) made him well known, but in the meantime he wrote a Christmas burlesque at the suggestion of his friend the playwright T. W. Robertson: *Dulcamara, or The Little Duck and The Great Quack* was successfully staged at the St James's Theatre (1866). Gilbert developed his talent for the stage over the next few years with comedies, comic-opera libretti, adaptations, and various extravaganzas and enjoyed his first real success with *The Palace of Truth* (Haymarket, 1870); in the cast were W. H. Kendal, Madge Robertson (who became his wife), and Gilbert himself. *Pygmalion and Galatea* (Haymarket, 1871) consolidated his reputation and was a favourite vehicle for star actresses until well into the next century.

Gilbert's first collaboration with Arthur Sullivan was in 1875, by which time he was the author of no less than 17 stage works. *Trial by Jury* (Royalty, 1875) was the first of the phenomenally successful series that made both men – and Richard D'Oyly Carte – rich and famous in two continents. It was followed by *The Sorcerer* (Opéra Comique, 1877), *HMS Pinafore* (Opéra Comique, 1878), *The Pirates of Penzance* (New York, 1879), and *Patience* (Opéra Comique, 1881). D'Oyley Carte opened his new theatre, the Savoy, in 1881 and transferred *Patience* there. The next production was *Iolanthe* (1882), followed by *Princess Ida* (1884), *The Mikado* (1885), *Ruddigore* (1887), *The Yeomen of the Guard* (1888), *The Gondoliers* (1889), *Utopia Limited* (1893), and *The Grand Duke* (1896), all at the Savoy.

But all these were only a part of Gilbert's untiring industry. He published *More Bab Ballads* (1873) and the lyrics from the Savoy operas as *Songs of a Savoyard* (1890) and wrote the libretti for works by Arthur Cellier, George Grossmith, Edward German, and others; more than ten plays by him were staged in London between 1870 and 1911. Gilbert was a difficult partner and the years of the great successes were by no means harmonious; the partnership eventually dissolved when Gilbert quarrelled with Sullivan and D'Oyley Carte over the cost of a carpet for the Savoy Theatre. He was knighted in 1907. The Garrick Theatre in London was built by Gilbert and opened in 1889. Gilbert's plays have not been revived in the modern theatre.

**Gildas, St** *c.*500–*c.*570. The first English historian, Gildas was born in Strathclyde and was obliged, probably owing to the strife of the times, to flee from his home. He went to Wales, where he married, and after his wife died became a monk. His history, *De Excidio et Conquestu Britanniae ac flebili Castigatione in Reges, Principes et Sacerdotes*, was probably written between 516 and 547 and is the only known history of the Celts. It covers the period between the coming of the Romans and Gildas' time. Its value as history is doubtful: Gildas is inclined to dwell too much on the evils of his times. Gildas does not mention Arthur, but does mention the Battle of Mount Badon, which tradition associates with him (see **Arthur, King**). The heroic figure named by Gildas is Ambrosius Aurelianus, who some modern writers identify as the original of the semi-legendary Arthur.

*Gilded Age, The: A Tale of Today*. A novel by Mark Twain and C. D. Warner, first published in 1873. It was successfully dramatized by Twain and G. S. Densmore in the following year.

Colonel Sellers is always full of ideas for making a lot of money. In the years following the Civil War he is in the undeveloped area of Missouri. Si ('Squire') Hawkins is persuaded to join him there from Tennessee. After ten years or so Hawkins' assets have gone and when he dies his family, who have lived in expectation of becoming very rich, move to Hawkeye, the current centre of Colonel Sellers' operations.

Through Sellers, Harry Brierly, a New York engineer, is involved in a railroad land speculation. Harry falls in love with Laura Van Brunt, Hawkins' adopted daughter; but Laura has been seduced by Colonel Selby and, infected by avarice, regards Harry as useful, no more. In contrast to Laura is Ruth Bolton, a Quaker girl, who is loved by Harry's friend Philip Sterling. Laura, meanwhile, has attracted the attention of Senator Dilworthy; at his invitation Sellers and Laura go to Washington and become involved in the senator's dubious financial deals.

Laura's seducer, Selby, turns up in Washington, and she resumes her liaison with him. He is quite ready to drop her again when it suits him – and Laura murders him. There is a spectacular trial and she is acquitted; then she capitalizes on the experience and accepts a lecture tour. However, she has overreached herself and proves to be a failure. She dies of a heart attack. Philip Sterling, meanwhile, has proved a success, exploiting the Bolton coalmining enterprise, and he marries Ruth.

The novel is a comment on the boom years following the Civil War and the era has been named after the book. Avarice seemed to have become the principal national characteristic and many good men found the climate of the times depressing. However, *The Gilded Age* does not wear well and while it would probably be true that in such an era there would be difficulty in separating the honest men from the not-quite-honest, the novel's lack of focus makes it unrewarding for modern readers.

*Gilfil's Love-Story, Mr* See *Scenes of Clerical Life*.

**Gilpin, William** 1724–1804. Gilpin was a clergyman and teacher from Boldre in Hampshire who enjoyed contemporary success (enough for him to be satirized by Combe and Rowlandson) as a traveller in search of the picturesque. Gilpin illustrated his travel books himself; they included *The Wye and South Wales* (1782), *The Lakes* (1789), *Forest Scenery* (1791), *The West of England and the Isle of Wight* (1798), and *The Highlands* (1800).

**Ginsberg, Allen** 1926– . Ginsberg was the son of a teacher and poet, Louis Ginsberg, and was born in Paterson, New Jersey. He completed his education at Columbia University and worked at various jobs, including reviewing books for *Newsweek*, before publishing his first work as *Howl and Other Poems* (1956). This identified him with the Beat Generation, and his subsequent work bears out both his continuing rejection of modern American materialism and his belief in finding new methods of expression. His poetic ancestors are William Blake and Walt Whitman. Widely travelled, Ginsberg has outlasted the Beat movement with which he was first identified and his later poetry reflects his commitment to anti-authoritarianism. Among his books of verse are *Empty Mirror: Early Poems* (1961), *Kaddish and Other Poems 1958–1960* (1961), *Reality Sandwiches 1953–1960* (1963), *Planet News 1961–1967* (1968), *The Moments Return* (1970), *The Fall of America: Poems of These United States* (1973), *Mind Breaths: Poems 1971–1976* (1978), and *Poems All Over the Place* (1978). Ginsberg's *Allen Verbatim: Lectures on Poetry, Politics, Consciousness* (1974) won him the National Book Award.

**Giraldus Cambrensis (***or* **Giraldus de Barri)** *c*.1146–*c*.1220. Gerald of Barry, the son of Angharad, a daughter of one of the Welsh royal houses, was born in Pembrokeshire. His uncle, David, became Bishop of Bangor and Gerald unsuccessfully sought the same preferment at St David's. He was Archdeacon of Brecon but twice (1176 and 1198) was denied his ambition, first by Henry II and then by Hubert Walter, Archbishop of Canterbury, because he was a Welshman. Gerald, a passionate upholder of his country's honour, first appealed to Rome and then sought to raise his countrymen in support. Henry outlawed him and he fled to France; but Henry forgave this turbulent priest and Gerald was reconciled to both king and archbishop, who regarded him as too rewarding a scholar and character to be dispensed with for very long.

In 1184 Henry II's favour resulted in his being sent to Ireland with Prince John. He studied at

Lincoln from 1192 until his second rejection in 1198. The experience of Prince John's behaviour is related without equivocation in *Topographia Hibernica*; Henry's campaign in Ireland is described in *Expugnatio Hibernica*; whilst the *Itinerarium Cambriae*, which describes a journey through Wales, is a valuable contemporary record as well as vivid and entertaining – the most highly regarded of his works. *De Rebus a se Gestis* is Gerald's autobiography; other works include lives of St Hugh of Lincoln, St Ethelbert, St David, and St Remigius the Apostle to the Franks. *Gemma Ecclesiastica* is a handbook of instruction to the Welsh clergy, illuminating the conditions of his time. *De Principis Instructione* contains a clear description of Henry II's appearance and sharp criticism of his character; it also tells the story of the finding of the coffins of Arthur and Guinevere at Glastonbury.

Gerald is usually given pride of place as the most entertaining and informative of 12th-century chroniclers. To his scholastic training in Paris he added a devouring curiosity and fondness for gossip, a refusal to be intimidated by kings or prelates, and a love of his native land. His complete works, *Opera*, were edited for the Rolls Series by J. S. Brewer, J. F. Dimock, and G. F. Warner. *De Principis Instructione* (*On the Instruction of a Prince*) was translated by J. Stevenson for *The Church Historians of England* (1853–56). *De Rebus a se Gestis* was translated by H. E. Butler (1937). *Historical Works* is a translation by T. Forester, R. C. Hoare, and T. Wright for Bohn's Antiquarian Library (1863). *Topographia Hibernica* was translated by J. J. O'Meara (1951).

**Gissing, George** 1857–1903. A pharmacist's son, George Gissing was born in Wakefield. He went to Owens College – now the University of Manchester – on a scholarship and was a brilliant classical scholar, but his academic career was cut short by his conviction for petty theft in 1876. He had stolen the money to help a prostitute, Marianne Harrison, and he served a short prison sentence. With the help of friends he went to America, where he had a hard struggle to earn enough to eat; eventually, in Chicago, he managed to sell some short stories to the *Tribune* and other papers.

He returned to England in 1877 and married Marianne Harrison. It was a mistake, one which Gissing was to repeat after her death when he married another girl of no education – and inevitably having no sympathy with his struggle to earn a living as a writer. The need to earn kept him turning out book after book (he published more than 20), and to make extra money he worked as a part-time teacher. None of his novels brought him much reward, though they gained the attention of Henry James and H. G. Wells.

Gissing contrived to scrape enough money together to visit Greece and Italy and he separated from his second wife in 1897. He met Gabrielle Fleury in Paris in 1898, but could not obtain a divorce, so he lived in France with Gabrielle from 1899. H. G. Wells became his friend and helped to care for him in his last days.

Gissing's first novel was *Workers in the Dawn* (1880) and the last to be published during his lifetime was **The Private Papers of Henry Ryecroft** (1903). Two novels, *Veranilda* and *Will Warburton*, appeared after his death, and two books of stories, *The House of Cobwebs* and *A Victim of Circumstances*. Of those published during the years between only **New Grub Street** (1891) is well known, and probably only **The Odd Women** (1893) is good enough for revival. His one travel book, *By the Ionian Sea: Notes of a Ramble in Southern Italy* (1901), has been praised and the writing is said to be Gissing's best by some critics. *Charles Dickens: A Critical Study* (1898) is an excellent book about a writer who influenced him greatly but could not, alas, impart to him by example a streak of humour.

Gissing's claim to attention lies in his power to write unflinchingly about the grim side of the struggle to live and in his ability to explore a state of mind. His failure to keep our attention for very long lies, in spite of his quality as a writer of prose, in being what Walter Allen described as 'the novelist of the special case – his own'. Whatever Gissing's qualities, the outlook for his work is not bright: appreciation of the writer depends too much on knowledge of the man.

**Glanvill, Joseph** 1636–80. The son of a Puritan family in Plymouth, Glanvill became interested in neoplatonism and science while at Oxford and later became an Anglican clergyman who ended his days with the living of the Abbey Church in Bath. Glanvill, like many young men of his time, was bored and restless with the university's way of teaching and was an advocate of scientific enquiry. He was 25 when he published *The Vanity of Dogmatizing* (1661), a remarkable pioneering work in the interests of the new approach to learning. He published a new edition as *Scepsis Scientifica* (1665), with some revisions and a dedicatory letter to the Royal Society, and a third as *Essays on Several Important Subjects* (1676), which shows Glanvill's final rejection of ornamented affected prose.

*The Vanity of Dogmatizing* contains the story of the Scholar Gipsy, which inspired Matthew Arnold's poem. Glanvill's *Plus Ultra* (1668) emphasizes further the value of experimental science and deplores the prestige of useless knowledge in academic circles. Among his other works there is the strange *Saducismus Triumphatus* (1681), an attempt to prove the existence of witchcraft. He was a minister of the Church and believed that to deny the existence of witches was to deny the existence of God. In James Sutherland's words, the book 'remains a curious reminder of the uncertainty all through this period of what are now called "climates" of opinion.'

**Glasgow, Ellen (Anderson Gholson)** 1874–1945. Ellen Glasgow was born in Richmond, Virginia. She was educated privately, being a delicate girl, and read extensively in her father's library. She never married and her home state, which she rarely left, provided the background for nearly all her 19 novels and numerous short stories. Her first published work was a novel of New York bohemian life (which she only knew at second hand) called *The Descendant* (1897). *The Voice of the People* (1900) traces the rise of a politician from humble beginnings on a farm and follows his career to his death during a riot. The background was the South and in succeeding novels it became plain that Ellen Glasgow's view of it was a long way from sentimental nostalgia, particularly in her portraits of Southern women. Her realistic novels of Southern life continued with *The Battleground* (1902) and *The Deliverance* (1904) and she became one of the most respected American novelists of the 20th century.

Ellen Glasgow's most celebrated novels are *Virginia* (1913), which made her famous, *Life and Gabriella* (1916), **Barren Ground** (1925), **Vein of Iron** (1935), and *In This Our Life* (1941), which was awarded the Pulitzer Prize. Three of her novels, *The Romantic Comedians* (1926), *They Stooped to Folly* (1929), and *The Sheltered Life* (1932), display a sharp vein of satire that reinforces her cool and carefully judged observations of Southern life and manners. A collection of short stories, *The Shadowy Third*, was published in 1923; *A Certain Measure* (1943) is a book of prefaces to her novels. Ellen Glasgow published a single book of verse, *The Freeman, and Other Poems* (1902), at the beginning of her career. Her autobiography, *The Woman Within*, was published posthumously in 1954.

**Gloriana** Elizabeth I in Spenser's *The Faerie Queene*. She is also represented by Mercilla, Belphoebe, and Astraea.

**Gloucester, Earl of** In Shakespeare's *King Lear*, the father of both Edgar and Edmund – the latter illegitimate and the more favourably regarded, to Gloucester's eventual cost. Edmund betrays his father to Regan and Cornwall when he shelters the old king; Cornwall blinds him, convinced that he is in league with France. Gloucester is succoured by Edgar, whom he had turned out, believing Edmund's lies about him. He dies of heartbreak when he realizes which of his sons he owes his life to.

**Gloucester, Robert of** fl. 1250–1300. The name 'Robert of Gloucester' (Robertus Glocestrencis) comes from the Tudor antiquarian John Stow, who identified Robert as the author of a Middle English verse chronicle which was certainly composed in the abbey of Gloucester about 1300. To a monk named Robert are attributed the last 3000 lines, which take the chronicle to the death of King Henry III (1272). It is reasonably certain also that the existing chronicle was revised by Robert, and the whole is usually called *The Metrical Chronicle of Robert of Gloucester*, a history of England from earliest times. It begins with the traditional assumption that English history began with the fall of Troy (see **Monmouth, Geoffrey of** and **Layamon**) but the authors also make use of such authentic historians as William of Malmesbury, Aelred of Rievaulx, and Henry of Huntingdon. The most valued portion of the *Chronicle* is the last part, a near-contemporary account of the reign of Henry III; this contains an account of the struggle for Gloucester between the king and the rebel barons, a description of the Battle of Evesham (1265) and the end of Simon de Montfort, and a vivid account of the town and gown riots in Oxford in 1263. *The Metrical Chronicle of Robert of Gloucester* was edited by W. A. Wright (Rolls Series, 1887).

**Glover, Richard** 1712–85. Glover was born in London, where his father was a successful merchant. He followed the same career and was Member of Parliament for Weymouth (1761–68) in opposition to the ruling party headed by Robert Walpole. Glover wrote a great deal of poetry in the style of the time and most of it is unread today. It included *Leonidas* (1737) in 9 books and *The Athenaid* (posth. 1787) in 30 books. He was the author of two tragedies, *Boadicea* (1753) and *Medea* (1767), both produced at Drury Lane, and one, *Jason* (posth. 1799), which was not produced. *Admiral Hosier's Ghost* (1740), a ballad on the misfortunes of Hosier and his fate in the West Indies, was very popular and was included in Thomas Percy's *Reliques of Ancient English Poetry*.

Laura at Goblin Market, buying with her golden hair. Dante Gabriel Rossetti's frontispiece illustration for the 1865 edition of the poem by his sister, Christina. *Goblin Market* was first published in 1862.

**Goblin Market**   A poem by Christina Rossetti, first published in 1862. Two sisters, Lizzie and Laura, watch the goblins in the glen. The goblins offer a gorgeous range of fruit and Laura is tempted; Lizzie resists. Laura has no money and offers in exchange a lock of her golden hair. The goblins' fruits bewitch her with their sweetness and she longs for more; but when the sisters return to the glen the goblins are silent and invisible to Laura. Obsessed by her longing for the forbidden fruit, she begins to pine. Lizzie goes to the glen to seek the goblins but she knows that she must not eat the fruit herself. The goblins invite her to their feast; she refuses and tells them she has only come to buy. They attack her and try to force her to eat but she resists all their efforts and, by defeating them, redeems her sister. The goblins leave the glen and never return.

**Godric, St**   d. ?1170   Godric was a former merchant, said to have sinned in various ways before becoming a saintly hermit. Carlisle and Durham are associated with him but very little is known about him apart from the attribution of three fragments of poetry written before 1170 and among the first examples of Middle English verse, *Cantus Beati Godrici*. The most distinguished piece is 'Sainte Maria Virgine', said to have been inspired by Mary while he knelt at the altar.

**Godwin, William**   1756–1836.   Godwin was the son of a Presbyterian minister of East Anglia. He was trained for the Church and actually practised for five years before he turned his back on religion completely and became an atheist. Thereafter he turned his attention to writing and to expressing his philosophy of rational individualism. He brought to the consideration of this the rigorous discipline of his upbringing and in 1793 he published the book that made him famous, *An Enquiry Concerning Political Justice*. Godwin's advocacy of anarchy, reliant upon reason, proposes a society that history suggests is completely unworkable. But in his time the prevailing system was both unjust and outworn – his book seemed to offer a pattern for the change so fervently sought by the younger generation. Of more importance, and more enduring, was the concern for the rights of all men that permeates Godwin's book. His philosophy is further illustrated in his novel *Caleb Williams*, published in the following year.

In 1797 Godwin regularized his alliance with Mary Wollstonecraft in the interests of their unborn child. Mary died giving birth to a daughter, another Mary, who became the wife of Shelley. In 1798 Godwin commemorated his wife in the biography *Memoirs of the Author of 'A Vindication of the Rights of Woman'*. He married again in 1801; his second wife was a Mrs Clairemont, whose daughter by her first marriage was the Claire Clairemont who became the mother of Byron's daughter Allegra.

Godwin wrote a great deal but only the works named have lasting value. His novel of the 16th century, *St Leon* (1799), is not of the same order as *Caleb Williams* but it contains a fine portrait of Mary Wollstonecraft.

**Goesler, Madame Max (***or* **Marie)**   In Anthony Trollope's 'Palliser' novels, the beautiful and wealthy widow who loves Phineas Finn. Her love, steadfast and unwavering, brings its reward when Phineas is acquitted of the charge of murdering Bonteen. Phineas proposes to her and they enjoy a happy marriage.

**Golagros and Gawain**   A Middle English romance of the 14th century in alliterative verse. (See **metrical romances**.) The poem follows the course of a pilgrimage to the Holy Land by Arthur and his knights, and a feature is the contrasting characters of Kay (rude and vulgar) and Gawain (the perfect gentle knight). Golagros is a bellicose lord with a castle on the River Rhône, and Arthur is determined to subdue him. Gawain defeats Golagros in single combat; Arthur behaves chivalrously towards the vanquished lord, who swears fealty to Arthur. *Golagros and Gawain* was edited by J. Pinkerton (1792) and by F. J. Amours for the Scottish Text Society (1897).

**Gold Bug, The** A story by Edgar Allan Poe, first published as a prize entry in a competition held by the Philadelphia *Dollar Magazine* in 1843. It is notable as an example of Poe's interest in, among other things, cryptography, which had a fascination for his acutely analytical mind. The story tells of Legrand, an impoverished Southern gentleman, and his only companion, the Negro Jupiter. One day they capture a rare golden scarab beetle and find a parchment which yields a cipher and a drawing of a death's-head. The scarab beetle is also marked with a death's-head. Legrand manages to decipher the parchment, which requires the use of the 'gold bug' before its promises can be realized. He is successful, discovers riches, and resumes his place in society.

**Golden Asse, The** A celebrated satirical novel by Lucius Apuleius, of the 2nd century AD, in which the storyteller, having been transformed into a donkey through an error on the part of a sorceress's servant, observes the follies and vices of his fellow men. It first appeared in English in 1566, translated from the Latin by one William Adlington, of whom nothing is known. A modern translation by Robert Graves was published in 1950.

**Golden Bowl, The** A novel by Henry James, first published in 1904.

Adam Verver is an American millionaire living in Europe and amassing an art collection. With him is his daughter, Maggie; father and daughter are very close. They are so close as to be perfectly content with each other – but Maggie Verver is of marriageable age and, with the help of her implacably interfering 'friend', Fanny Assingham, is found an Italian prince, Amerigo. To London comes the beautiful Charlotte Stant to stay with Fanny – and to bother Fanny's peace of mind, because Fanny knows that Amerigo and Charlotte had been in love. They could not marry; Amerigo, prince or not, is penniless and so is Charlotte. Fanny had introduced the prince to Maggie Verver when he broke with Charlotte.

Charlotte has no trouble persuading Amerigo to accompany her when she goes on shopping expeditions in search of a wedding present for Maggie. At an antique dealer's she wants to give Amerigo a present also, a gilded crystal bowl. The presence of a flaw in the bowl brings it within range of Charlotte's purse; Amerigo, however, is disturbed that the bowl is flawed and declines the gift. Fanny Assingham, meanwhile, is busy convincing herself that Charlotte is behaving nobly and should really have a worthwhile husband.

A year later, in the great country house called Fawns where the Ververs live, Amerigo and Maggie's son becomes a mutual focus for Adam and Maggie. Charlotte is asked to come and stay and Adam Verver proposes to her. He cannot have Maggie's exclusive attention any longer, since she has a husband and a child. Adam, though a grandfather, is not yet 50 and he is very wealthy. Charlotte marries him. A year or two later Adam cannot attend a state reception, being unwell, and Charlotte goes with Maggie and Amerigo. Maggie leaves the reception early to look after her father. Fanny Assingham is present and is a perfect mountain of disapproval over Maggie's behaviour: but while she makes it plain to Amerigo that he should have escorted Maggie and not stayed to escort Mrs Adam Verver she learns that Adam and his daughter seem to be closer than ever. In spite of separate households, it is clear that Charlotte cannot be a substitute for Maggie and Amerigo cannot be a substitute for Adam. And Charlotte, by now, has given up the hope of having any children by Adam Verver. While Adam and Maggie are cooing over the baby prince at Eaton Square, Charlotte visits Amerigo, alone at Portland Place. Excluded as they are by the Ververs they turn to each other and at a glamorous house party given by Lady Castledean at Matcham, attended also by the Assinghams, they contrive an opportunity for a daytime rendezvous. Fanny Assingham confides to her husband her knowledge of the true state of affairs in the Verver and Amerigo households and dwells on the characters of Adam and his daughter.

Maggie becomes aware of the liaison but says nothing to Amerigo. Adam is aware of it, too, but says nothing to Charlotte. Father and daughter do not speak of it, though it is her father's 'attitudes' that, more than anything else, alert Maggie to the truth. She is told by Fanny Assingham, to whom she relates her suspicions, that they are unfounded; Maggie knows this is untrue but she gives outward acceptance of Fanny's reassurance. For her father's birthday she goes shopping for something antique and comes back with a gilded crystal bowl for which she has paid a high price. She has not noticed that it is flawed but the dealer feels compelled to point it out and calls on her. He recognizes the photographs of Amerigo and Charlotte, so Maggie learns from him that the pair had visited his shop and rejected the bowl during the days of her engagement to Amerigo. She sends for Fanny and makes it clear that she knows the whole truth now: the golden bowl is the proof. Fanny Assingham is both outraged and guilty; she had never told Maggie of the earlier liaison between Charlotte and Amerigo before the marriage; neither had she murmured a word about their behaviour at Matcham. She smashes the golden bowl just as Amerigo enters the room. In the scene that follows, Maggie's confrontation of Amerigo leaves him helpless, because she implants a doubt, which he has no way of resolving, of how much *Adam* knows about Charlotte's faithlessness.

Neither Adam nor Maggie gives any outward sign, now, of what they know and they do not speak of it to each other. And when Maggie is certain that Amerigo has not told Charlotte of his wife's confrontation she can play the game out with all the best cards in her hand. Amerigo stops seeing Charlotte; Adam gives no hint to her that he knows; Maggie conducts herself with unruffled serenity. Charlotte, wondering at her lover's withdrawal, is left to exist in this perfect order, her nerves stretched to breaking point. She cannot provoke Maggie to any kind of exchange, since the other woman's armour is impenetrable. It is Adam who resolves the situation and to some extent repays Maggie's efforts to preserve his marriage and his peace of mind. His daughter loves her husband, so Adam decides to return to America with Charlotte. He would rather stay in Europe with the happiness that Maggie's presence unfailingly bestows on him but his departure opens the way for the complete reconciliation of Maggie and Amerigo.

The committed Jamesian would no doubt regard it as sacrilege if one were to suggest that *The Golden Bowl* would be a far better book if it had been written in the period of, say, *The Portrait of a Lady* and *The Spoils of Poynton*, and the question must also arise whether Henry Janes, at that point in his career, could have created the story and characters of *The Golden Bowl*. But it remains true that there are great faults in this book, one of the worst being the frequency with which the reader has to stop and think hard even to understand which location the story has moved to. The endless parentheses are maddening and all the characters speak in the same way – husband-and-wife dialogue is indistinguishable from father-and-daughter dialogue. The revelation of the bowl's significance by the antique dealer's concern for honesty is hard to swallow, unless antique dealers have changed greatly since 1904; and the convolutions of the prose, the great stumbling block for many new readers of Henry James, are as exhausting here as in the rest of the works of the novelist's last phase. For the reader who stays the course the reward is considerable. The story of Maggie Verver and her implacable determination that the centre will hold is an arresting one. The best scenes – the mutual surrender of Charlotte and Amerigo to their feelings, the observation of the house party at Matcham, the compulsively interfering and awful Fanny Assingham – are finely done. But it is a pity that so much labour is required of the reader, who has to run an obstacle race to reach the heart of the matter.

**Golden Legend, The**  In origin a manual, *Legenda Aurea*, compiled to foster piety and containing a history to the year 1250, the lives of the saints, and commentaries on Christian festivals. It was the work of Jacob of Voragine, Archbishop of Genoa (1230–98), and was also known as the *Lombardica Historia*. The chapters are arranged to follow the Church's year, and the text, full of anecdotes and strange etymologies, conveys an engaging warmth on the part of the archbishop. It became exceedingly popular and was soon being translated from the Latin. Versions in French and English appeared in profusion, with variations on the original and with additions. As a kind of 'morality' that was also entertaining, it had acquired classic status long before Caxton decided to publish an edition which he fashioned from the Latin, French, and English versions already in existence. This was completed in 1483 and published soon after, with the Earl of Arundel as patron of the investment required.

*The Golden Legend* is best known in England in this version by William Caxton and in its day was far more popular than Chaucer and Malory. The translation that Caxton made from the French printed version is slipshod and seems to contain attempts at translating literally words misprinted in the original. However, when Caxton writes in his own language he achieves a high standard of 15th-century English prose.

**Golden Treasury of Songs and Lyrics, The**  See **Palgrave, Francis Turner.**

**Golding, Arthur** *c.*1536–*c.*1605. Golding was the son of an Essex gentleman and was educated at Jesus College, Cambridge. In English literature he is remembered for his translations from Latin and French. Among these were Caesar's *Commentarii de bello Gallico* (1565), Seneca's *De Beneficiis* (1578), Justin's version of the *Historiae Philippicae* of Trogus Pompeius (1570), and religious commentaries by Calvin and Theodore Beza – Golding was Puritan in his sympathies. His most considerable work was his verse translation of Ovid's *Metamorphoses*, which was published in two parts: *The Fyrst Fower Bookes of P. Ouidius Nasos Worke, Translated into Englishe Meter* (1565) and *The XV Bookes of P. Ouidius Naso, Translated into Englishe Meter* (1567). Golding also completed Sir Philip Sidney's translation of Duplessis-Mornay's *Traite de la vérité de la religion chrestienne* as *A Worke Concerning the Trewnesse of the Christian Religion* (1587).

**Golding, William (Gerald)** 1911– . Golding was born at St Columb Minor in Cornwall. He was educated at Marlborough Grammar School and Brasenose College, Oxford, and became a teacher in 1939. He served in the Royal Navy during World War II and then returned to teaching. Golding's first published work was *Poems* (1934) but with his first novel, *Lord of the Flies* (1954), 20 years later he became famous. The author took the characters of Ballantyne's 19th-century romance, *Coral Island*, and showed them being 'turned' by their circumstances instead of rising above them as the God-fearing Victorian boys do. Golding's boys revert to savagery under the leadership of Jack Merridew, erstwhile leader of a choir-school group. The tendency towards evil in man is Golding's principal theme. He is the author of two radio plays, *Miss Pulkinhorn* (1960, adapted from one of his short stories) and *Break my Heart* (1962); a play, *The Brass Butterfly* (1958); *The Anglo-Saxon* (1962, short story); *The Hot Gates and Other Occasional Pieces* (1965); *The Scorpion God* (1971, three stories); and the novels *The Inheritors*

(1955), *Pincher Martin* (1956, called *The Two Deaths of Christopher Martin* in the USA), *Free Fall* (1960), *The Spire* (1965), *The Pyramid* (1967), *Darkness Visible* (1979), *Rites of Passage* (1980) and *The Paper Men* (1984). He was awarded the Nobel Prize for Literature in 1983.

**Goldsmith, Oliver** ?1728–74. The son of an Anglican clergyman in Ireland, Oliver Goldsmith was born at Pallasmore in the parish of Forgney in county Longford – or at Ardnagowan in Roscommon; the family Bible gives the former but his mother's family (Jones, of Ardnagowan near Elphin) said that Mrs Goldsmith was staying in her mother's house when Oliver, her fifth child, was born. The date remains in doubt because that page of the Bible is badly torn and it is missing. In 1730 Goldsmith's father succeeded his uncle as curate of Kilkenny West and the family lived at Lissoy in Westmeath, where Goldsmith received his first lessons from Thomas Byrne, the village schoolmaster. He suffered from smallpox when he was seven or eight years old and was badly scarred.

Goldsmith's education continued at Elphin, at Athlone, and at Edgeworthstown, where he found a sympathetic teacher, Patrick Hughes, who elicited the best response from the unattractive and sensitive boy. He was marked down for Trinity College, Dublin, but his father, a poor manager, could not send him there as anything but a sizar (a poor scholar who worked for his

Trinity College, Dublin, in the 18th century. Oliver Goldsmith graduated from Trinity College in 1749. National Gallery of Ireland.

keep). Oliver hated the prospect; his elder brother Henry had gone there as a pensioner and obtained a scholarship, but he yielded eventually and went to Trinity College in June 1744. He was unhappy and, inevitably, a bad student; he was too spirited a character to submit to an unsympathetic tutor and he was also wretchedly poor. He had a talent for the flute and wrote ballads, which he sold for five shillings (25p) each. His father was dead by the time he left college with a BA (1749), and there seemed little future for him apart from a career in the church. However, he spent the next two years in idleness and was rejected by the Bishop of Elphin when he presented himself for ordination. Eventually his despairing family, through the generosity of an uncle, sent him to Edinburgh to study medicine (1752). The record of his adventures so far, which is only known through Goldsmith's own words, is a dubious one; he was addicted to gambling and was probably an experienced liar as well. He went on needing the support of his already impoverished family and later alienated his mother completely.

After two years in Edinburgh he went to Leyden and then on a tour of Europe on foot, living on his wits and his flute playing. He wrote from Padua asking his family for money to get him home; it was sent, but he said it never reached him. After a year of wandering he reached Dover in February 1756, penniless. He was 27 years old. In London he became an apothecary's assistant; he was helped again, by a friend from his Edinburgh days, and was able to practise as a physician in Southwark (where he obtained his medical degree is anybody's guess). The only-to-be-expected failure of Goldsmith as a doctor led to his correcting proofs for Samuel Richardson and teaching at Dr Milner's school in Peckham. At Milner's table he met a bookseller, Ralph Griffiths, who was impressed by Goldsmith's learning and wanted some new talent for *The Monthly Review*. He engaged him, gave him bed and board, and made him work hard from nine until two. Goldsmith entered Grub Street and a literary career – a possible field for his talents that had apparently never occurred to him. He was well qualified; he was a fair classical scholar and had a wide knowledge of English poetry; his French was excellent and he had travelled, the hard way, in Europe. He worked for Griffith as a reviewer until his employer's relentless editing vexed him too much and from September 1757 he earned a living by writing occasional pieces for *The Literary Magazine* and other periodicals. He also embarked on his first sustained literary effort, a translation of J. Marteilhe de Bergerac's *The Memoirs of a Protestant, condemned to the Galleys of France, for his Religion*. This was published in 1758 but did nothing for Goldsmith's fortunes. He tried to find a post as a medical officer in an overseas station; then he applied at Surgeons' Hall, hoping to be taken on as a surgeon's mate. He was rejected as 'not qualified'.

Goldsmith had, meanwhile, embarked on *An Enquiry into the Present State of Polite Learning in Europe* (1759) and contributed to *The Critical Review*, edited by Tobias Smollett, *The Busy Body*, and other periodicals. Then the publisher John Wilkie asked him to edit a weekly, *The Bee*, and Goldsmith found himself. As an essayist and critic he made his mark in literary London and attracted the attention of Samuel Johnson. Smollett enlisted him for the new *The British Magazine* and John Newbery (the Jack Whirler of Johnson's *The Idler*) for *The Public Ledger*. A feature of his contributions to periodicals during this period was the growing quantity of Goldsmith's verse.

*The Bee* had been short-lived, but Goldsmith's contributions had been published in book form immediately afterwards. Those he penned for *The Public Ledger*, ostensibly written by a Chinese visitor to London, were finished in August 1761 and in May 1762 were published in book form as *The Citizen of the World*; they gave him his first substantial success. Financially, however, Goldsmith was still marking time (Johnson had to pull him out of trouble in 1762 by persuading Newbery to buy the manuscript of a novel by Goldsmith for £60 without reading it) and the hack work and 'book-making' continued at a fierce rate: editing *The Lady's Magazine*, four volumes of *Plutarch's Lives* (1762), *The Life of Richard Nash of Bath* (1762), prefaces and notes to sets of world history and natural history by other hands, and *An History of England in a Series of Letters from a Nobleman to His Son* (1764) were some of the subjects that kept him busy. In 1764 Goldsmith became a founder-member of Johnson's The Club and thereby moved into the society of the London intelligentsia. At the end of that year he published *The Traveller; or, a Prospect of Society*.

Goldsmith's famous poem had been in his mind as long ago as 1754; he had sent the outline of it to his brother Henry from Switzerland and the finished work, ten years later, was dedicated to him. It was a success and Johnson's praise was generous. Interest in other works by Goldsmith prompted the issue of a volume of *Essays by Mr Goldsmith* and more verse: *The Double Transformation* and *A New Simile* (all 1765). The unread manuscript of Goldsmith's novel was quickly read and published in 1766; it made no money for Goldsmith or Newbery but **The Vicar of Wakefield** has made generations of readers happy. Meanwhile, Goldsmith continued to labour with his pen in any way that would secure him a living and the possibility of success in the theatre was attractive. (*The Citizen of the World* contains some amusing comments about the London playhouses, where sentimentalism held sway.)

**The Good-Natur'd Man** was completed in the spring of 1767 and the author offered it to David Garrick. He kept the play for weeks and suggested alterations; but the fact was he simply did not want to produce it. He resented something Goldsmith had said about actor-managers in *The Bee* and his prevarication may have been malicious. Goldsmith lost patience with him and gave the play to George Colman; it was produced at Covent Garden on 29 January 1768 with a prologue written by Samuel Johnson. *The Good-Natur'd Man* was produced late in the season and its success was eclipsed by that of Hugh Kelly's *False Delicacy*, a sentimental comedy staged by Garrick at Drury Lane six days before. Nevertheless, it made money for the perennially hard-up Goldsmith and was published a month later, in which form it sold very well.

Goldsmith's brother Henry died in May 1768 and Oliver, at work on *The Roman History* (a commission, published in 1769), found time to work also on a poem to commemorate him. **The Deserted Village** (1770) is acknowledged as his finest poem and it went into five editions in its first year. *The Haunch of Venison* (1776), a poetical epistle to Lord Clare, was written about this time; a medley of recollection and experience, it shows Goldsmith in a lighter-hearted vein. Sentimental comedy, meanwhile, was doing well in London. Garrick's production of Cumberland's *The West Indian* was staged at Drury Lane in January 1771 and Goldsmith once more tried his hand at something better. His second play was offered to Colman, who accepted it – and then found reasons for not putting it on. Johnson prevented the despairing author from giving it to Garrick and bullied Colman into mounting a production. **She Stoops to Conquer** opened at Covent Garden in March 1773 and Goldsmith enjoyed an unqualified success.

It came rather late, however, and Goldsmith was exhausted by the constant pressure to earn. He was working on *Retaliations*, a book of epitaph-epigrams, when he was taken ill with nervous fever; he died in April 1774. Goldsmith lies buried in the grounds of the Temple church and a memorial was erected to him in Westminster Abbey two years later, with a Latin epitaph by Samuel Johnson. In addition to the works already mentioned he was the author of a great deal of journalism and commissioned work; little of it is remembered apart from the essays, which are regarded highly enough to be ranked next to Charles Lamb's. Goldsmith's character, influenced by his early poverty and his unfortunate appearance, seems to have been cantankerously self-defensive and led to Walpole's, Garrick's, and Boswell's comments at his expense. But he could number Johnson, Reynolds, Percy, and many others among his friends, and his complete inability to handle money, while it made him the despair of his family, certainly did not make him mean. His genius, maturing steadily over a short period (he did not start to write until he was 28), was individual and owed nothing to any writer who went before. His best work is small in quantity but the quality is of the highest.

A notable modern edition of Goldsmith's work is Arthur Friedman's *The Collected Works of Oliver Goldsmith* (1966). Friedman edited in addition *The Vicar of Wakefield* for the Oxford English Novels series (1974); it also appears in The World's Classics (1901), Everyman's Library (1906), and the Penguin English Library (1982). A recommended selection of Goldsmith's work is Richard Garnett's (1950), and the poetry is included with that of Gray and Collins in Roger Lonsdale's volume in the Oxford Standard Authors series (1969). *She Stoops to Conquer* is included in W. D. Taylor's *Eighteenth-Century Comedy* in Oxford Paperbacks, in the Penguin *Four English Comedies* (1969), and in the Modern Library *Famous Plays of the Restoration and Eighteenth Century* (1933).

**Goldyn Targe, The** An allegorical poem by William Dunbar written about 1508. Like his *The Thrissil and the Rois*, it is an example of Dunbar's skill in the medieval courtly romance – a form which, by his time, had become so formalized that it ceased to have much life. The May-morning dream-vision form is used for an allegory demonstrating the use of Reason as a defence against Love.

**Goneril** The eldest daughter of Lear in Shakespeare's *King Lear*, married to the Duke of Albany. By the third scene of the play she is out of patience with her father's demands and begins the process of cold rejection. It is her suggestion ('Pluck out his eyes', Act III Scene 7) that leads to Gloucester's blinding. She responds to Edmund and begins to despise Albany; her rivalry with her sister for Edmund's attentions leads her to poison Regan. Goneril stabs herself when Albany realizes the truth about her.

***Gone with the Wind***  The single novel written by Margaret Mitchell (1900–49), a journalist from Georgia in the USA, who spent nine years (1926–35) researching and writing it. It was published in 1936 and awarded the Pulitzer Prize in 1937. As well as being the most famous best-seller of the century (3,500,000 by 1941) and translated into 18 languages, it holds a strong position as the classic romance of the Civil War in the USA (1861–65).

The heroine, Scarlett O'Hara, is the daughter of Gerald O'Hara, who owns the plantation, Tara. She is in love with Ashley Wilkes, the son of a nearby plantation owner when the story opens; Ashley's engagement to another girl, the gentle and resolute Melanie Hamilton, coincides with the outbreak of the Civil War. Scarlett, out of pique, marries another man and is widowed quite early in the war. She also encounters Rhett Butler, a gentleman adventurer; his powerful attraction for Scarlett is something she will not admit to herself – she keeps hoping that some day she will have Ashley. The story moves to Atlanta, the state capital soon under siege, and to Scarlett's unwilling attendance on Melanie, who is expecting Ashley's child: there is a fine set-piece when Rhett Butler helps the girls escape from the burning city with Melanie's baby. Scarlett makes her way back to Tara, to find it a ruin of its former elegance, her mother dead, and Gerald's mind unbalanced. Scarlett is determined to keep Tara and win financial security and she bends her every energy to this end. She marries again, with this in view, but is haunted by the hope of Ashley, returned from the war and reunited with Melanie, whose health has been dangerously weakened by privation. After losing her second husband in a fight she accepts Rhett Butler; but in the end her selfishness and continuing infatuation with Ashley try Rhett beyond endurance. When Melanie dies and Ashley rejects Scarlett's eager sympathy, Rhett walks out on her – he does not any longer, he says 'give a damn.' The novel encompasses the war, the defeat, and the agony of reconstruction and the author relates them closely to the characters' lives.

***Good-Natur'd Man, The***  A comedy by Oliver Goldsmith, first produced at Covent Garden in January 1768 and published in the same year. (See **Goldsmith, Oliver**.)

Sir William Honeywood despairs of his nephew, who is both generous and improvident. Young Honeywood is in love with the wealthy Miss Richland, but he is too wanting in self-confidence to propose. Sir William has him arrested for debt – to let him see who his true friends are and to stop him wasting his generosity on importuners. Young Honeywood believes that Lofty, a government official, is responsible for his release; Lofty is pressing his suit with Miss Richland and Honeywood, mistakenly grateful, recommends him to the lady. In fact it was Miss Richland who secured his release. The exasperated heroine and uncle between them expose Lofty's imposture and secure the marriage of Honeywood and Miss Richland.

The subplot concerns Croaker, Miss Richland's guardian, who wants his son Leontine to marry the heroine. Leontine, sent to Lyons to bring his sister home from school, returns with Olivia, a girl he has fallen in love with. He passes off Olivia as his sister and, in an effort to strengthen the pretence, proposes to Miss Richland; but the heroine knows the truth and mischievously accepts him. In desperation Leontine and Olivia try to elope but their plan is frustrated by Sir William. However, he persuades Croaker to consent to their marriage. Miss Richland, the heroine, indicates the departure from the sentimental comedy fashionable at the time: she is the equal of most of the male characters and superior to some of them.

***Good Soldier, The***  See **Ford, Ford Madox**.

**Googe, Barnabe**  1504–94.  Googe was a long-lived kinsman of William Cecil, who employed him in Ireland for ten years. He was an industrious translator of Latin anti-Catholic pieces, and his Puritan nature is plainly discernible in his *Eglogs, Epytaphes, and Sonnetes* (1563), his principal claim to notice as a poet. The eclogues are among the earliest examples of pastoral poetry in English though, like those of his near-contemporary Alexander Barclay, they display little of the spirit of the classical originals.

***Gorboduc,*** *or The Tragedy of Ferrex and Porrex*.  A blank verse tragedy by Thomas Norton (Acts 1–3) and Thomas Sackville (Acts 4 and 5). The origin of the story is found in Geoffrey of Monmouth's *Historia Regum Britanniae*; Gorboduc is Gorbogud in Book II of Spenser's *The Faerie Queene*.

Gorboduc and Videna are king and queen in legendary Britain and their sons are Ferrex and Porrex. The sons quarrel over the division of the kingdom and Porrex murders his brother. In revenge Videna kills Porrex and the Duke of Albany tries to seize the kingdom. Civil war ensues, and the people turn on Gorboduc and

Videna and kill them. At the end of the play the royal line is extinguished (the line of Brute) and the country is in chaos.

The play adheres to the Senecan model and there is almost no action; it could be read as effectively as it could be played. But it departs from both the morality tradition – there are no personifications, only characters – and the Aristotelian unities of time and place and in doing so moves towards the flexibility of action of the great age of English drama.

**Gordimer, Nadine** 1923– . Nadine Gordimer was born at Springs, near Johannesburg. She studied at Witwatersrand University but left without taking a degree. With her first book of short stories, *Face to Face* (1949), Nadine Gordimer attracted attention as an acute observer of life in South Africa. Her focus is on the White community, a society which has welcomed a very high level of material comfort – and pays a heavy price for it with repressive legislation and social strictures. The result has been heightening tension as the individual struggles to hold on to moral values in a world where true feeling and expression are increasingly subdued. Her picture of a society backing itself into a blind alley is uncompromising and grows bleaker with the years. Other books by Nadine Gordimer are the novels *The Lying Days* (1953), *A World of Strangers* (1958), *Occasion for Loving* (1963), *The Late Bourgeois World* (1966), *A Guest of Honour* (1971), *The Conservationist* (1974), and *July's People* (1981); and the collections of short stories *The Soft Voice of the Serpent* (1952), *Six Feet of the Country* (1956), *Friday's Footprints* (1960), *Not for Publication* (1965), *Livingstone's Companions* (1972), and *A Soldier's Embrace* (1980).

**Gordon, Adam Lindsay** 1833–70. The son of a retired Indian Army officer, Gordon was born in the Azores and educated at Worcester Royal Grammar School. A classical education and the background of a cultured home encouraged an interest in poetry which stayed with him throughout his short but adventurous life. When he was 20 Gordon's father sent him to Australia; he was wild and reckless and the developing continent was an obvious place for one of his temperament. He arrived in Adelaide, South Australia, in 1853.

Most of Gordon's working life in Australia was spent with horses – as mounted trooper, horse breaker, livery-stable keeper, and more notably as a steeplechase rider, a field in which he became famous. His first published work, *The Feud*, appeared in 1864 and he contributed regularly to *Bell's Life in Victoria* and *The Australasian*. A collection was published as *Sea Spray and Smoke Drift* (1867). *Ashtaroth, A Dramatic Lyric*, an unsuccessful exercise on the Faust theme, was published in the same year. Further poems were published in Marcus Clarke's paper *The Colonial Monthly*, but things were going badly for Gordon otherwise. He made claim to a substantial family property in Scotland but failed to secure it; he was extravagant and always short of money. He retired from steeplechasing in 1870 and his volume of poems *Bush Ballads and Galloping Rhymes* (1870) earned him praise but little else. He returned to steeplechasing and suffered a serious fall from which he never really recovered. He shot himself in the same year, at the age of 37.

Gordon was short-sighted and his poetry, perhaps in consequence, contains little of the observation that is a feature of the work of his contemporary Henry C. Kendall. His work is concerned more with the spirit of his own way of life; 'sportsmanship' and adventure are a fair part of it. However, there is also a vein of melancholy, clearly heard in his autobiographical poem 'Whisperings in Wattle-Boughs', and in 'The Sick Stockrider'.

**Gore, Catherine Grace** 1799–1861. A prolific novelist of the early 19th century, Mrs Gore wrote 70 assorted works in under 40 years, including plays and occasional pieces. Forgotten today, she was very popular in her own time; her novels were successful and her plays were produced. She wrote novels of fashionable life but they had nothing that would find a readership in another age; and like fashionable female novelists in our own time she was caricatured – by Thackeray, no less, in *Punch* in 1847. *Mrs Armytage, or Female Domination*, is generally regarded as her best work.

**Gosse, Sir Edmund William** 1849–1928. Edmund Gosse was born in London. His father, Philip H. Gosse, was a zoologist of distinction and a rigid member of the Plymouth Brethren. Edmund Gosse was educated privately and became an assistant librarian at the British Museum (1867), a translator at the Board of Trade (1874), lecturer in English literature at Trinity College, Cambridge (1884), and librarian of the House of Lords (1904). He published poems and plays and his growing interest in Scandinavia led to *Studies in the Literature of Northern Europe* (1879). He knew everyone in the literary circles of London and was a friend of Swinburne, Robert Louis Stevenson, and Henry James.

After World War I Gosse became a contributor

to *The Sunday Times* with a regular and influential essay on current books. He was knighted in 1925. Gosse published a great deal, chiefly literary studies and poems, but his work is little read now. He deserves great credit for bringing the work of Henrik Ibsen to the attention of the English public; he was honoured for this by the Norwegians in 1901. He translated *Hedda Gabler* (1891) and *The Master Builder* (1893, with William Archer).

Gosse's best-known work is *Father and Son* (1907), a striking autobiography for which the author (it was published anonymously) was at first attacked for being unfilial. Gosse subtitled his book 'A Study of Two Temperaments'; with his liberal education in a post-Darwinian age he collided with his father's rigid adherence to the principles of the Plymouth Brethren sect – principles to which he was obliged to pay service until he could assert his own identity and separate himself from them. The book gives a remarkable picture of the Gosse household.

Among Gosse's other books were *Thomas Gray* (1882), *Jeremy Taylor* (1903), and *Sir Thomas Browne* (1905) for the English Men of Letters series; *The Life and Letters of John Donne* (1899), *Ibsen* (1907), *Two Visits to Denmark, 1872 and 1874* (1911), and *The Life of Algernon Charles Swinburne* (1917).

**Gotham (or Gotam), Merie Tales of the Mad Men of** The possible compiler of the 16th-century jest book relating the deeds of the men of Gotham was a physician, Andrew Borde. A printed text dated 1630 exists. The tradition that the men of Gotham, a village of Nottinghamshire, were wise dates from the reign of King John. The king passed that way on the road to Nottingham and was prevented from proceeding by the villagers – he would have to cross their meadows, which would have made thereafter a public road where the king had passed. When the king's commissioners arrived the men of Gotham, in fear of the royal displeasure, were found to be engaged in all sorts of stupid tasks, such as trying to hedge in a cuckoo and trying to drown an eel in a pool of water. The king's men left Gotham to the mad men who lived there. The 'mad' men of Gotham, for obvious reasons, became known as the wise men of Gotham. There is a reference to them in the Wakefield cycle of mystery plays.

**Gothic, On the Nature of** See **Stones of Venice, The.**

**Gower, John** *c.*1330–1408. The son of a Kentish family of considerable means, John Gower

may have been born in London; certainly this was where he lived from most of his life. He was known at court, acquainted with Richard II, and entered the service of the usurper Henry of Lancaster, who made himself Henry IV. Geoffrey Chaucer was his friend – some years his junior but whom he outlived. Gower spent the later years of his life in a lodging assigned to him by his patron, in the priory of St Mary Overes in Southwark. He was a generous benefactor of the priory and lies buried in the church (now St Saviour's). He was blind for the latter part of his life.

Gower was a master of both French and Latin and could use both languages for literary expression; but it is by his English **Confessio Amantis**, a late work, that he is best known. Gower's views on the events and the moral climate of his times were strongly held and these are given expression in his work. *Vox Clamantis* (*c.*1382) finds the boy King Richard blameless for the conditions that led to the Peasants' Revolt. *Confessio Amantis* (1390) was written at the king's request and dedicated to him, and the poet hopes that Richard, now 23, will reign successfully. But within three years he had revised his opinions, and some manuscripts bear a revision of the epilogue showing his hopes for Richard changed to hopes for England. About this time begins his allegiance to Henry of Lancaster. In a late Latin poem, *Cronica Tripertita*, his disillusion is complete and Henry IV, the new king, embodies his hopes for the future.

Gower's principal works are *Speculum Meditantis* or *Mirour de l'Omme*, written in French (1376–79); *Vox Clamantis*, written in Latin (see above); and *Confessio Amantis*. Minor poems in three languages have been collected by Thomas Wright, *Political Poems and Songs* (1859), and included in H. O. Coxe's edition of *Vox Clamantis* (1850).

*Speculum Meditantis* is a didactic poem, which in Gower's own words 'treating of vices and of virtues, as also of the various conditions of men in the world, endeavours rightly to teach the way by which the sinner who has trespassed ought to return to the knowledge of his Creator'. The poem is 30,000 lines long. The poet's descriptions of the various conditions of man build up a valuable picture of the life of his time (the work was originally called *Speculum Hominis* corresponding to the French title, *Mirour de l'Omme*). For centuries the poem was lost but was rediscovered in 1895 in the Cambridge University Library.

*Vox Clamantis* is much shorter; this Latin poem of 10,000 lines treats of the Peasants' Revolt of

1381. The first book gives an account of the revolt whilst the rest examines the corruption and misrule that led to it.

*Confessio Amantis* marks the poet's acknowledgment of his own language, to the use of which he brought his technical skill and an ease and fluency of expression. Chaucer's example of the plain English style was present and Gower's, in this poem, is substantially the same. Gower's influence on the use of the English language was considerable although he was didactic and inclined to be humourless. But while he has been outstripped in fame and regard by his contemporary, Chaucer, he was popular for many years and well known to the Elizabethans.

***Grace Abounding*** *to the Chief of Sinners*. John Bunyan's narrative of his personal and spiritual history. It was written during his long imprisonment and published in 1666. He tells of his birth and his misspent years, and his service in the Parliamentary army when death was very near. He relates how his awakening began with the reading of two devotional books, which his wife brought to him among her few possessions when he married in 1646, and his joining a Nonconformist group in Bedford.

The book is remarkable for its ruthless self-examination and for the author's agonized awareness that each step forward can lead him into the sin of pride. Bunyan was a countryman with no sophistication; his learning was remarkably limited compared to that of the many religious writers who were his contemporaries. His account is lean and honest, set in the Bedfordshire countryside of his birth, and the writing is fresh and direct.

**Grail, the** The legend of the Grail (*or* Graal – the Sangreal in Malory) has always remained fixed in secular literature and storytelling, never receiving recognition by ecclesiastical authority. As a talisman sought by a questing hero, the mysterious vessel is an ancient theme of Celtic myth. Coming from the Other World, it was something whose appearance only a true hero could encounter and survive. The story first appears in written form in the late 12th century in the *Perceval* or *Conte del Graal* of Chrétien de Troyes, which is unfinished. Robert de Boron, of the late 12th or early 13th century, developed the theme in a trilogy, *Joseph d'Arimathie*, *Merlin*, and *Perceval*, which linked the theme of the simple knight and the mysterious vessel to the Arthurian tradition. This Perceval's quest for a vessel and a lance (the part of the story that Chrétien did not complete), which had a mythological background thousands of years old, became a knightly Christian quest for the vessel used by Jesus at the Last Supper and brought from the Holy Land by Joseph of Arimathea; it contained some drops of the Redeemer's blood shed on the cross.

The earliest English poems on the subject are the 14th-century *Joseph of Arimathea* of unknown authorship and the *History of the Holy Grail* by Henry Lovelich, who wrote in the 15th century and took his story from a French original.

Joseph of Arimathea converts Evalak, King of Sarras, by telling him the story of Christ, whose

Perceval at the castle of The Grail. He receives a sword from the Maimed King (left). On the right The Grail is carried to a table. Illustration from a medieval French manuscript. *MS. Fr. 12577, f.18v.* Bibliothèque Nationale.

blood he preserves in the vessel he carries. He aids Evalak in his war against Babylon, praying to Christ on the king's behalf and giving him a white shield marked with a red cross. The king's brother-in-law is also converted and takes the name of Naciens. Joseph goes on a missionary journey and arrives in Britain. The Grail is given into the care of two guardians at the castle of Carbonek, but the castle's whereabouts are unknown. Malory, in *Le Morte Darthur*, continues the story with the adventure of Launcelot at the castle of King Pelles (where he lies with the king's daughter, Elaine, who is given the likeness of Guenever whom he loves) and the questions of the hermit about the identity of the knight who will occupy the empty chair at the Round Table (the Siege Perilous). The child of Launcelot and Elaine is brought to the Round Table one Pentecost by Naciens, now an old man. The boy is Galahad and the knights know him as the one destined to achieve the quest for the Grail. He takes the empty place and the Grail enters among them in a great burst of light and thunder – but none of them sees it. The knights are filled with zeal for the quest; but Naciens warns them that only one who is pure will achieve it. Nevertheless, led by Gawain, the knights set out. Galahad, without a shield, comes to the White Abbey and there is proved worthy to wear the one Joseph gave to Evalak, which lies behind the abbey's altar. There are several stories thereafter of various knights' adventures in the quest: Gawain withdraws, from weariness; Launcelot comes close, but each time is warned to withdraw because of his sins. Only three knights, Percival, Bors, and Galahad, are worthy of the quest and they succeed in making their way to the castle of Carbonek.

The three are vouchsafed a vision of the Redeemer and partake of His body. They receive the Grail and carry it back to Sarras, where Galahad becomes the king. He has asked that he may receive his death when he prays for it. He is king for one year and then his death is granted; Percival and Bors have taken their farewells of him and they witness the Grail being taken up by a divine hand to Heaven, never to be seen again.

**Gramont, Mémoires de la Vie du Comte de** Philibert, Comte de Gramont, was the dissolute son of an illustrious French family; he was banished from the court of Louis XIV because of his unwise attentions to a royal favourite. He came to England, was received at court by Charles II, and married Elizabeth Hamilton. The *Mémoires* were in part dictated to Anthony Hamilton (1646–1720), Gramont's brother-in-

law, and in part composed by Hamilton. The book was first published anonymously at Cologne in 1713; an English translation by Abel Boyer was published in 1714. The translation, full of errors, (Hamilton's French, incidentally, is much admired) was revised and annotated by Sir Walter Scott in 1811, and the book is now accepted as a distinct contribution to memoirs in English literature.

The first part deals with Gramont's life in France and Europe, the second with life at the English court. Despite the fact that Gramont cannot be trusted completely, the *Mémoires* presents a vivid picture of his times and is an important source of information. Gramont himself died in 1707 and never bothered to publish the book.

**Grand, Sarah** See 'New Women' novelists.

**Grandcourt, Henleigh** In George Eliot's *Daniel Deronda*, the wealthy and brutal suitor who wins Gwendolen Harleth and reduces her to wretchedness. He drowns in a boating accident off Genoa.

**Grandissimes, The:** *A Story of Creole Life.* A novel by George Washington Cable, first published in 1880. The setting is New Orleans and the period is the early 19th century.

There is a feud between the Grandissimes and the De Grapions, aristocratic families of Louisiana. Nancanou De Grapion is killed in a duel; his widow Aurora is the last survivor of the family and goes to live with her daughter Clothilde in New Orleans. Impoverished, they live in seclusion.

Honore Grandissime, a banker and now head of the family, becomes acquainted with Joseph Frowenfeld, a young apothecary, through old Dr Keene. Joseph is in love with Clothilde De Grapion and through Joseph Honore meets Aurora – and falls in love with her. But there is much in the way of marriage between Honore and Aurora, not least the Grandissime family's attitude to an impoverished widow who also represents a past which no one wants to recall. The situation comes to a head when Agricola, the arrogant and haughty member of the family who killed Aurora's husband, antagonizes Honore's quadroon half-brother and is stabbed by him. It is Honore's sister who, at the deathbed of Agricola, effects a reconciliation between the two families and the way is cleared for Honore and Aurora, and Clothilde and Joseph.

**Grand Question Debated, The** A poem by Jonathan Swift, first published in 1729. Hamilton's Bawn is a building belonging to Sir Arthur Acheson and the question is whether it shall be turned into a malthouse, to yield a steady income, or into a barracks, to please Lady Acheson – she would revel in the proximity of military men in handsome uniforms. The poem satirizes the general stupidity of the military mind – Swift detested the idea of war and the maintenance of an army.

**Granger, Edith** In Dickens's *Dombey and Son*, the beautiful and penniless widow who becomes Paul Dombey's second wife. She soon deserts him and elopes with his business manager, James Carker. Despising both men, it is her form of revenge. Once Carker is compromised, she abandons him.

**Grantly, Archdeacon** In Anthony Trollope's Barsetshire novels, the Archdeacon of Barchester Cathedral. Inclined to be overbearing and headstrong, he is nevertheless a warm and loyal man – his wife and children know him very well and humour him with affection when he seems to strike attitudes.

**Grantorto** The tyrannical spirit of unrest and rebellion in Book V of Spenser's *The Faerie Queene*, from whom Artegall rescues Irena (Ireland).

**Grapes of Wrath, The** A novel by John Steinbeck, first published in 1939. The main narrative concerns the Joad family and their progress; it is interspersed with panoramic essays which place their particular significance in the general one of migrant labour in the USA in the 1930s. The Joads have lost their land in the Oklahoma dust bowl (the erosion of the soil which followed intensive crop farming) and set out hopefully for California in a dilapidated truck. Grampa and Granma die on the journey but the rest make it to California, where they are hounded by unsympathetic sheriffs and labour contractors. On the verge of starvation, they find refuge for a time in a government camp. Casy, an ex-preacher and socialist who joined them en route, is encountered again when the family takes work at a labour-blacklisted orchard. Tom Joad, who before the trek began had been in prison for killing a man in a fight, finds Casy leading the strikers, and in a fight Casy is killed. Tom kills Casy's murderer, and the Joads flee from the orchard. The family hides Tom, and work at cotton-picking, but Ma Joad, uneasy and exhausted by her responsibilities as head of the family, sends him away for all their sakes. Tom determines to continue Casy's work as a labour organizer, and Ma Joad, with no resources with which to face the future, will continue; she can do no other, and there is no such thing as a Promised Land.

**Graves, Richard** 1715–1804. Graves was born at Mickleton in Gloucestershire and educated at Pembroke College, Oxford. He became a Fellow of All Souls and rector of Claverton, near Bath, in 1749. Graves was a poet of sorts, translated Marcus Aurelius, and became chaplain to the Countess of Chatham. He was a popular figure at Bath and enjoyed a correspondence with distinguished people; he was artlessly pleased to meet four duchesses in a single day. He was a friend of William Shenstone, Samuel Johnson's friend and a minor poet, of whom he published a *Recollection* in 1755 and who appears in two of Graves's novels.

*The Spiritual Quixote* (1733), *Columella, or the Distressed Anchoret* (1779), *Eugenius: or Anecdotes of the Golden Vale* (1785), and *Plexippus: or The Aspiring Plebeian* (1790) are his novels. They are interesting for their depiction of the social conditions of the time; but *The Spiritual Quixote* is the only one for which he is remembered. He was at Pembroke College with George Whitefield, the Methodist preacher who adopted Calvinist views in America. *The Spiritual Quixote* satirizes Whitefield and Methodism.

**Graves, Robert (von Ranke)** 1895– . Robert Graves was born in London and educated at Charterhouse. He served in World War I, going to the front while still in his teens, and was mistakenly reported as killed after a shell blast. As a result he read his own obituary before he was 21 and suffered from shell-shock for about ten years after the war. Immediately after the war he went to Oxford to study for a degree, and then taught in Egypt for a brief period before deciding to earn his living as a writer.

Graves published his first poetry in 1916, a collection called *Over the Brazier*. This was reissued in 1920 in a revised edition; Graves frequently revised his poems throughout his career and sometimes rejected his earlier efforts. The reader's best way to a definitive text is through the versions in *Collected Poems* (1938), *Collected Poems 1914–1947* (1948), *Collected Poems* (1955), *Collected Poems* (1959), and *Collected Poems* (1965), *Poems 1965–1968* (1968) and *Beyond Giving* (1969). His war experiences, his failed first marriage, his liaison with Laura Riding, the American poet, and his eventual and successful marriage to Nancy Nicholson all colour his poetry, which, while remaining in the English tradition and subscribing to no movement, is markedly individual and scrupulously crafted. He was Professor of Poetry at the University of Oxford from 1961 to 1966.

Graves published his autobiography, *Goodbye*

Robert Graves. Pastel portrait by Eric Kennington, official war artist from 1916 to 1919.

*White Goddess: A Historical Grammar of Poetic Myth* (1948), *The Nazarene Gospel Restored* (1953, with Joshua Podro), and an edition of *The Greek Myths* (1955) with a characteristic commentary and fascinating notes.

**Gray, Thomas** 1716–71. Thomas Gray was the fifth and only surviving child of Philip Gray, an exchange broker, and Mary Antrobus, a milliner. He was born in his father's house in Cornhill in the city of London and was fortunate in having his uncle Robert as a tutor. Robert Antrobus was a fellow of Peterhouse College, Cambridge, and had been an assistant master at Eton, where Gray entered as a pupil in 1727. He continued to be fortunate; his tutor there was Robert's younger brother, William, who secured permission for Gray, not a robust boy, to lodge with his Uncle Robert; he was thus spared the horrors of public school life. He made friends with Horace Walpole, Richard West, and Thomas Ashton, and in 1734 went to Pembroke College, Cambridge, pending his admission to Peterhouse. (His friend West went to Christ Church, Oxford, in the following year; the two young men hated university life, according to their letters.)

Gray's intentions were vague at this time but he was apparently considering a legal career. He spent some aimless years at Cambridge and in 1739 went travelling in Europe with Horace Walpole; he kept detailed notes of the journey and wrote numerous letters home to his mother and his friends, describing the theatre of Racine, art and architecture, his meeting with the Abbé Prévost, the impressions made on him by Alpine scenery. He quarrelled with Walpole in Reggio Emilia – and deserted him, though Walpole was seriously ill. Gray proceeded to Venice with other companions picked up in Florence, and then made his way home, arriving in London in September 1744. He went to stay at Pope's house at Hatfield in 1742, and his first English verse, a fragment of a tragedy, *Agrippina*, dates from this period. Richard West died on 1 June 1742 – just too late to receive Gray's *Ode on the Spring*, which the poet had despatched shortly before his friend's death. *The Sonnet on the Death of Richard West*, *Hymn to Adversity*, *Ode on a Distant Prospect of Eton College*, and *Hymn to Ignorance* were written at Stoke Poges, where his now widowed mother lived, before Gray returned to Cambridge to resume, in haphazard fashion, his pursuit of a law degree. He was reconciled to Walpole (1744) and wrote *Ode on the Death of a Favourite Cat*; the cat was Walpole's, 'Drowned in a Tub of Gold Fishes' (1747). Among his friends were William

*to All That*, one of the finest books about World War I, in 1929 and it was successful enough to enable him to make his home on the island of Majorca. His fiction, which began with some arresting short stories such as *My Head! My Head!* (1925) and *The Shout* (1929), brought him popular success with *I, Claudius* (1934). He exploited the historical vein with continued success in, among other novels, *Claudius the God* (1934), a novel about Justinian's general – *Count Belisarius* (1938), two novels about the American War of Independence – *Sergeant Lamb of the Ninth* (1940) and *Proceed, Sergeant Lamb* (1941), *Wife to Mr Milton* (1943), which makes that poet a domestic villain, *The Golden Fleece* (1944), a retelling of the story of Jason, and *King Jesus* (1946), which seeks to place Jesus in the context of the Jewish tradition from which he arose.

A very readable and provocative critic, Graves has published several collections of essays, among them *A Survey of Modernist Poetry* (1927, with Laura Riding), *The Reader Over Your Shoulder* (1943, with Alan Hodge), *The Common Asphodel* (1949), *The Crowning Privilege* (1955), and *The Crane Bag and Other Disputed Subjects* (1969). Other books in a rich and varied prose output are *Lawrence and the Arabs* (1927), *The*

Mason, Conyers Middleton, and Christopher Smart; he was leading an apparently aimless life and then, in June 1750 from Stoke, he sent Horace Walpole the manuscript of *Elegy Written in a Country Churchyard*, on which he had been working, on and off, for some time. The publication of it in 1751 made him the foremost poet of his day. *Designs by Mr R. Bentley for Six Poems by Mr T. Gray* (1753) was the first attempt to collect Gray's work, though the poet was only 37. The additions were *A Long Story* and *Hymn to Adversity*; of the *Stanzas to Richard Bentley* of 1752 only a mutilated copy survives. Gray did not publish anything more until 1759, when Horace Walpole brought out *The Progress of Poesy* and *The Bard*, two Pindaric odes. *The Fatal Sisters*, *The Descent of Odin*, and *The Triumphs of Owen* first appeared in *Poems by Mr Gray*, published in 1768.

The laureateship had been offered to Gray in 1757, upon the death of Colley Cibber. He rejected it and the rest of his life was not very productive (the Pindaric odes were, like most of Gray's poems, exhaustively revised and polished before they were published). He spent two years studying Old English manuscripts in the British Museum, with the idea of writing a history of English poetry; from 1762 until 1771 he made several tours in England and Scotland and wrote memorable letters to his friends about them. In 1768, meanwhile, he became Professor of Modern History at Cambridge; the appointment was a sinecure and its only product was the *Ode ... at the Installation of his Grace* [the] *Duke of Grafton, Chancellor of the University* (1769). Gray died at Cambridge on 30 July 1771 and was buried next to his mother at Stoke Poges. He never married.

An illustration from the 1769 edition of Thomas Gray's *Elegy Written in a Country Churchyard*. The poem was first published in 1750.

Gray wrote one Latin poem and two Latin fragments. Returning from Italy he visited the monastery of the Grande Chartreuse in the Dauphiné for the second time (he had been there on the outward journey) and inscribed an Alcaic ode in the visitors' album: *O tu severi Religio loci*, familiar in English in R. E. E. Warburton's translation. In Florence he began a Latin verse translation of Locke's *Essay concerning Human Understanding*, which he entitled *De Principiis Cogitandi*. He completed 200 lines and then abandoned it; upon the death of Richard West he composed a lament of about 30 lines (1742), *Liber Quartus*.

Gray's output is remarkably small for a major poet, a position to which his beautifully balanced and musical verses entitle him. By training he was both a classicist and an academic but he points the way to the English romantics more strongly, perhaps, than any other 18th-century poet. Emotionally responsive, introspective, and inclined to melancholy, he completely escapes the trap of sentimentality. His work is based on enormous knowledge of the craft of poetry, a craft he exercised with scrupulous care and discipline. His letters are among the finest in the language, revealing his remarkable erudition, his acute response to new experiences, his descriptive powers, and wit.

*The Complete Poems of Thomas Gray* is the standard edition, by H. W. Starr and J. R. Hendrickson (1966). *Gray and Collins: Poetical Works* edited by Roger Lonsdale (1977) is in the Oxford Standard Authors and Oxford Paperbacks series. *The Correspondence of Thomas Gray* was edited by Paget Toynbee and Leonard Whibley (1935).

**Gray Manuscript, The** See **Scottish anthologies and collections.**

**Great Divide, The** See **Moody, William Vaughn.**

**Great Expectations** A novel by Charles Dickens, first published in *All the Year Round* (December 1860 to August 1861). In book form it was first issued in three volumes in 1861.

The story is concerned with the growth and development of the village boy, Pip (Philip Pirrip). He is brought up in the Kent marshes by his unpleasant sister, who is married to the gentle and warm-hearted Joe Gargery, a blacksmith, and Pip's unfailing friend. One day in the churchyard where his own family lies buried Pip encounters an escaped convict, who terrifies him into providing him with food and a file. Pip steals some food from his sister's larder and a file from the smithy.

Later the convict is captured and transported

and Pip is sent off to the house of the strange Miss Havisham. The latter was deserted by her lover on their wedding day and she now lives in a grim house near Rochester, dressed in her mouldering wedding clothes, with the girl Estella, an orphan she is bringing up to despise all men. Pip is wary of Estella and her supercilious airs but he settles down in the grim house and is introduced to manners and grace: it is a shock to him to find that he has been indentured to Joe Gargery as an apprentice.

Four years later, when Pip is nursing an unrequited love for Estella and feels at the end of his tether – he hates the village and the forge – he is visited by Jaggers, a lawyer, who tells him that the means to provide Pip with an education and a new life are in his hands. Pip accepts this as coming from Miss Havisham, though his benefactor's identity is not disclosed. He goes to London after being fitted out with new clothes at Trabb's, the local tailor, where he is subjected to the amused and impudent gaze of Trabb's boy. Pip becomes a young gentleman and is soon looking down on Joe Gargery and his own humble beginnings. His conceit of himself is rudely disturbed when, back in the village, he is sent up by Trabb's boy who knew him in humbler days, and when Estella, now a beautiful young woman, responds to him not at all. She marries the mean-spirited Bentley Drummle – and soon regrets it.

Pip's education in life is brutally completed when his unknown benefactor proves to be the convict, Magwitch, whom he briefly befriended as a boy. Magwitch is in danger of his life for returning to England – and he is in fact recognized. Pip tries to help him get out of the country but his plans are thwarted and Magwitch is taken, injured, in the attempted escape. Pip is present when the old convict, with 31 other men and women, is sentenced to death. Magwitch dies before the gallows claim him, however, and Pip's 'expectations' die with him. The cold unkind Estella was Magwitch's child and Jaggers was Miss Havisham's lawyer.

Adversity reduces Pip in more ways than one: but Joe comes to London and nurses him back to health. He also pays Pip's outstanding debts and then goes back to the village to marry Biddy, the sweet girl who cares for him as a widower and who teaches him to write. Pip goes abroad and makes good, and the story ends with his meeting with the sadder and wiser Estella, now a widow. There is no promise in the encounter, just a note of hope.

*Great Expectations* is a fine novel, and it came after the author's short, vivid *A Tale of Two Cities*, which is so oddly dismissed by many critics as being 'un-Dickensian'. The conciseness of the earlier book is a feature of *Great Expectations* and has contributed a great deal to its popularity. If it has any fault it lies where it is most 'Dickensian' – in the character of Joe Gargery; the warm-hearted blacksmith is in grave danger of being spoiled by being given speech and mannerisms that almost turn him into a caricature.

***Great Gatsby, The***   A novel by F. Scott Fitzgerald, first published in 1925. The story is told in the first person by Nick Carraway, who lives next door to the luxurious mansion of Jay Gatsby on the wealthy Long Island shore. Across the harbour lives the rich and vulgar Tom Buchanan; his wife, Daisy, is Nick Carraway's cousin. Gatsby gives huge expensive parties which have become famous, and which are attended by many uninvited guests. Carraway becomes Gatsby's confidant; Gatsby tells him that he was a farm boy from Minnesota, whose life had changed when he became the protégé of a copper magnate who left him $25,000. In the army during World War I, he was a young officer in Louisville when he met Daisy, rich and privileged, and had a brief love affair. He went to the front in Europe, gained promotion and was decorated, and even went to Oxford for a time. But Daisy got tired of waiting for him and married Tom Buchanan, a Yale athlete and very rich. But Gatsby, who used to be Jimmy Gatz, has not given up. He has turned himself into a millionaire by bootlegging and he wants his girl. He persuades Nick Carraway to effect a reintroduction. Tom Buchanan is carrying on with Myrtle Wilson, the wife of a garage owner; but he is furious at the thought that Daisy, who has been overwhelmed by Gatsby's extravagant devotion and become his mistress, should leave him. In a violent scene he tries to discredit Gatsby and the source of his wealth but the lovers leave, Daisy driving Gatsby's car. Myrtle Wilson, who has been imprisoned by her jealous husband, breaks out of her room and, running into the street, is hit and killed by Daisy, who drives on. Gatsby tries to protect Daisy but she, unnerved, runs back to Tom Buchanan, who revenges himself on Gatsby by telling Wilson that it was Gatsby who killed her; Wilson murders Gatsby before committing suicide. Nick Carraway takes charge of Gatsby's funeral arrangements and Tom and Daisy, as cold and self-centred as one another, 'retreated back into their money or their vast carelessness, or whatever it was that kept them together'.

***Great God Brown, The***   See **O'Neill, Eugene (Gladstone).**

**Great-heart** Christiana's escort when she follows her husband's path in Part II of John Bunyan's *The Pilgrim's Progress*.

**Great Tew** See **Falkland, Lucius Cary, 2nd Viscount**.

**Green, Henry** 1905–73. The pseudonym of Henry Vincent Yorke, an engineer and later managing director of his family's engineering company in Birmingham. He was born in Tewkesbury, Gloucestershire, and educated at Eton College and at Oxford. While still at university he attracted critical attention, if not a large readership, with his first novel, *Blindness* (1926). He also began but did not complete a second, *Mood*. *Living* (1929) is set in the sort of engineering works he knew very well (he worked as a foundryman) and *Party Going* (1939) among an upper-class group who possess wealth and no sense of responsibility. Green's next book was a chapter of autobiography, *Pack my Bag: A Self Portrait* (1940); he resumed his career as a novelist with *Caught* (1943), a story of the Auxiliary Fire Service in World War II, and *Loving* (1945), which is of the same wartime period but set in a remote castle in Ireland. *Back* (1946), *Concluding* (1948), *Nothing* (1950), and *Doting* (1952) complete the list of his fiction.

Henry Green is distinguished as a novelist by his elegant impressionistic prose, his indirect and oblique dialogue, and his rapid cutting from scene to scene. His work is not yet well known to the wider public but it holds considerable rewards for new readers. Green's work displays a talent for observation, and a vein of poetry in evidence most strongly, perhaps, in *Living*. But he applies his gifts with equal success to different settings and in *Loving*, arguably his best novel, he delivers an excellent comedy about a group of English servants in an Irish castle. They are out of the war, and are both glad and ashamed of this. The story and eventual resolution stem from the housemaid Edith's discovery of Mrs Jack in bed with her lover. The plot unfolds through dialogue and external description: no attempt is made to enter the characters' minds but it is a measure of the author's skill that they come vividly to life.

**Green, John Richard** 1837–83. Green was born in Oxford and educated at Magdalen College School and Jesus College, Oxford. He was ordained and served as a curate in various parts of London until ill health forced him to give up his duties; he became librarian of Lambeth Palace in 1869. Green had always been interested in history and his post gave him an opportunity

for research; he became a frequent contributor to *The Saturday Review* and achieved a notable success with *A Short History of the English People* (1873). Green's narrative and descriptive powers are of a high order: they give life to his account of the literary and artistic, as well as political and economic, events which make up the history of a nation, and he demonstrates that the humble as well as the exalted contribute to a nation's progress. Green's work proved the most popular history since Macaulay's. *Stray Studies from England and Italy* (1876) is a collection of essays; in the following year Green began publication of an extended version of his 'short' history as *A History of the English People* (four volumes, 1877–80). With the help of his wife, Alice Stopford Green, he expanded certain themes in *The Making of England* (1881) and *The Conquest of England* (1883).

**Green, Matthew** 1696–1737. Green was born in the city of London and was a civil servant for most of his life. He is remembered in English literature for his poem *The Spleen* (1737). 'Spleen' was the 18th-century word for boredom and depression; Green's fluent and witty verse discusses the condition and offers suggestions for its prevention and cure. The poem may be found in a modern edition in Everyman's Library *Minor Poets of the Eighteenth Century*, edited by Hugh l'Anson Fausset (1930).

**Green, Thomas Hill** 1836–82. Green was the son of the rector of Birkin in Yorkshire; he was educated at Rugby School and Balliol College, Oxford, where he became White's Professor of Moral Philosophy in 1878. He made his first contribution to philosophy with two extended introductions to an edition (1874) of David Hume's *Treatise on Human Nature*; here he presented detailed criticisms of John Locke, George Berkeley, and Hume, arguing that neither John Stuart Mill nor Herbert Spencer had advanced beyond the ideas presented by Hume in 1739. He suggested that students of philosophy should study the work of Kant and Hegel rather than that of the English empiricists. Green's principal work was *Prolegomena to Ethics* (1883).

**Greene, (Henry) Graham** 1904– . Graham Greene, a schoolmaster's son, was born at Berkhamsted in Hertfordshire. He was educated at his father's school and at Balliol College, Oxford, and joined the staff of *The Times* in 1926. In 1927, upon his marriage, he became a Roman Catholic. Greene's first published work was a volume of verse, *Babbling April* (1925); but his first novel, *The Man Within* (1929), enjoyed a modest success and fixed the direction of his career. A tale of smuggling in the early 19th century, it is his only novel with a historical setting. *The Name of Action* (1930) and *Rumour at Nightfall* (1931) followed, and the first novel called 'An Entertainment', *Stamboul Train*, in 1932. This description was attached to a series of spare tough thrillers which present aspects of the human situation in contemporary settings. *Stamboul Train* places a representative group on the Orient Express; *A Gun for Sale* (1936; *This Gun for Hire* in the USA) has the pursuit of a political assassin as its theme; *The Confidential Agent* (1939) is about the Spanish Civil War; *The Ministry of Fear* (1943) takes place in London during the Blitz and *The Third Man* (1950) in war-wrecked Vienna under occupation. *Our Man in Havana* (1958) is set in Cuba before Castro's revolution.

Those novels of Graham Greene which are not called 'entertainments' continued with *It's a Battlefield* (1934) and *England Made Me* (1935); a journey in West Africa was described in *Journey Without Maps* (1936) and was followed by *Brighton Rock* (1938), which was called 'an entertainment' in the USA and 'a novel' in England. This was his first explicitly Catholic novel and why that or his other fiction should carry a label is not easy to understand. A second travel book, *The Lawless Roads* (1939), describes Mexico, which also provided the setting for *The Power and The Glory* (1940); here he continued his exploration of Catholic ideas of grace, and good and evil. *Brighton Rock*, set in the dingy underworld of the seaside resort, dramatizes the conflict between two completely different attitudes to life. One is personified in the vicious young Pinkie, a Catholic who chooses evil and has a horror of sex from witnessing his parents' regular copulations. Ida is middle-aged, warm-hearted, and promiscuous. She suspects Pinkie of being responsible for murder, and Ida knows the difference between Right and Wrong. She also believes that 'God doesn't mind a bit of human nature'. Her attitude to life makes her loathsome to Pinkie. His victim, the pathetic waitress Rose, revolts him too; he forces himself to marry her so that she cannot bear witness against him. He deals her a vicious blow when he goes to his own death. Ida's world is clearly marked and comfortable to live in; Pinkie's, because of his Catholic training, is a minefield of terrors and he is pathetic even in his nastiness. *The Power and the Glory* takes place in revolutionary Mexico, where the church is banned and priests are outlawed. A bad priest, guilty of drunkenness and lechery, is sustained by his original commitment when confronted with the ultimate challenge; the police lieutenant,

his opponent, represents the nonreligious humanist view and is a good and honourable man, as the priest acknowledges at the end. The two characters are finely realized, as are the atmosphere of the revolution and the simple faith of the very poor who have only a bad priest to turn to in their extremity. The bad priest emerges almost as a saint at the conclusion. The book established Greene's reputation as a novelist and was awarded the Hawthornden Prize.

Greene was literary editor of *The Spectator* until 1940 and was a regular contributor to *The London Mercury*, *The Fortnightly Review*, *The Observer*, *Time and Tide*, and other periodicals. He worked at the Foreign Office during World War II, and published *The Heart of the Matter*, one of his most discussed novels, in 1948. Scobie, the hero, goes to Hell (in terms of his own Catholic creed) because he is a victim of his own compassion for others. Many critics, among them George Orwell and Walter Allen, rejected the novelist's conception of Scobie as sentimental and the novel as unsatisfactory. If the novel depends on an understanding of the Catholic view of sin and guilt it must be said to fail since its implications are bound to be lost on a great many readers. But the author's command of narrative and his taut finely planed style reach a pitch of excellence that make his work compulsively readable. *The End of the Affair* (1951) is a tale told by a jealous lover, who is forced to acknowledge that he has been supplanted not by love for another man but by the love of God.

In 1955 Greene returned to the wider world of his 'entertainments' and the theme of betrayal. *The Quiet American*, which is not called an 'entertainment', is much more serious in purpose: the story of events in Vietnam and the quiet young American agent became bitter reading 12 years later, when the French had gone and the Americans were reaping a terrible harvest in a war they could not win. *A Burnt-Out Case* (1961) is set in a leper's hospital in the Congo just before the Belgian withdrawal; *The Comedians* (1966) in the Haiti of Duvalier and the Tontons Macoute; *The Honorary Consul* (1973) in Paraguay, and *The Human Factor* (1978) in London in the half-world of secret agents. These four novels deal with the committed and the uncommitted caught up in places and events in which the 'comedians' are those who will never feel the need for any kind of committal.

Greene also published two slight, light-hearted novels, *Loser Takes All* (1955) and *Travels with My Aunt* (1969). His short stories are collected in *The Basement Room and Other Stories* (1935), *Nineteen Stories* (1947), *Twenty-One Stories*

Graham Greene, 1964.

Greene was immensely popular and, remembering his way of life, remarkably prolific, completing 35 works in less than 12 years: pamphlets, romances, and five plays (which were not produced during his lifetime). The pamphlets include a continuation of Lyly, in the same style, called *Euphues, his Censure of Philautus* (1587). Greene's particular voice is clearly heard in 1591 in *A Notable Discovery of Coosnage* (cozenage), or *The Art of Conny-catching*, a racy picture of low life in London in Greene's day – direct, humorous, and unadorned. 'Conny-catching', in modern terms could be described as smart operating, the art of the confidence trickster. The vein was exploited further in three more 'conny-catcher' pamphlets in 1591 and 1592, but the pamphlet form was also used for autobiographical sketches and criticism of contemporary life. His best work as a prose writer, it is generally agreed, is to be found in these, the most notable being *A Quip for an Upstart Courtier: or, a Quaint Dispute Between Velvet Breeches and Cloth Breeches* (1592) and the posthumous *Greenes, Groats-worth of Witte, Bought with a Million of Repentance*. The latter is particularly famous for its direct reference to Shakespeare (Shakescene), the first in literature, and for its warning to other playwrights – university men like himself – that mere players (Shakespeare again) were presuming to write for the stage, having learned how to from the work of properly educated men.

Greene's romances began with *Arbasto: The Anatomie of Fortune* (1584) but are usually dismissed as worthless until *Pandosto: The Triumph of Time* (1588), when he found the style that

(1954), and *May We Borrow Your Husband? and Other Comedies of the Sexual Life* (1967). Four plays by Graham Greene were successfully produced: *The Living Room* (Wyndham's Theatre, April 1953), *The Potting Shed* (Bijou Theatre, New York, January 1957), *The Complaisant Lover* (Globe Theatre, June 1959), and *Carving a Statue* (Haymarket, September 1964). He has written a number of stories for children, a chapter of autobiography called *A Sort of Life* (1971), and *Lost Childhood, and Other Essays* (1951).

**Greene, Robert** *c.*1560–92. The Elizabethan bohemian and 'University Wit' was born in Norwich. He was educated at St John's College and Clare Hall, Cambridge, receiving his master's degree in 1583. He received another from Oxford, in 1588, and was always proud of his academic achievements. He travelled in France and Italy with Thomas Nashe and George Peele, two other University Wits, and married in 1585. He deserted his wife and went to live in London, where seven years of extravagant dissipation brought his life to an end in extreme poverty – a month after dining too well on pickled herrings and Rhine wine with Thomas Nashe.

The title page illustration for Robert Greene's pamphlet, *A Quip for An Upstart Courtier*, 1592.

suited him. The story contains some successful lyrics and gave Shakespeare the basis for *A Winter's Tale. Menaphon* (1589) showed improved ease in dialogue and contains the famous lyric, 'Weepe not, my wanton'. *Mourning Garment, Never too Late*, and *Francesco's Fortunes* all belong to 1590; the first is based on the parable of the prodigal son; the second and third are really two parts of the same story and much of Robert Greene is found in the character of Francesco. Among others were *Perimedes the Blacke-smith* (1588) and *Philomela: the Lady Fitzwaters Nightingale* (1592).

As a playwright Greene was part-author, it is believed, of the original text of the three parts of *King Henry VI*. His surviving plays are *The Comicall Historie of Alphonsus King of Aragon* (1599), *A Looking Glasse for London and England* (1594) with Thomas Lodge, *The Historie of Orlando Furioso* (1594), *The Honorable Historie of Frier Bacon and Frier Bongay* (1594), and *The Scottish Historie of James the Fourth* (1598). Of these the only one that is known to any but scholars is now called **Friar Bacon and Friar Bungay**, while *The Scottish Historie* introduced the figure of Oberon to English literature. But Greene made a very definite contribution to the golden age of drama, introducing qualities of verisimilitude and human feeling that were taken to greater heights by those who followed him.

*Green Mansions: A Romance of the Tropical Forest*. A novel by W. H. Hudson, first published in 1904. It is in the form of a first-person narrative to a friend by Abel Guevez de Argensola (Mr Able), who has returned to civilization after having been a political refugee in Venezuela. He fled to the wilderness of the upper reaches of the Orinoco River and lived among the Indian tribes. He explored a forest that the Indians were afraid to enter and there heard a beautiful voice that stayed near him; the owner remained unseen. The Indians warned him that it was the voice of the Didi's daughter (the Didi was an evil spirit). Abel discovered that in fact the voice belonged to a shy and beautiful girl who stopped him from killing a snake; she protected all living creatures. He followed the girl and suffered a serious fall; when he regained consciousness he was being tended by an old man, Nuflo, and he learned that the girl, Rima, believed herself the old man's granddaughter. Rima was a complete forest child, at one with all creatures; she wove her clothing from spider filaments.

From Nuflo Abel learned of Rima's mother, who had appeared to Nuflo and his companions on the mountain, Riolama. She spoke an unknown language and Abel supposed that she must have been a survivor from a remote community. Nuflo and his companions helped her down the mountain to a Christian village where her daughter was born and christened Riolama; she came to be called Rima.

Rima persuaded Abel and Nuflo to set out in search of Riolama, where she hoped they would find her mother's people; by then Abel and Rima were deeply in love. When Abel and Nuflo returned to the forest they found the hut had been destroyed by the Indians; Rima had taken refuge in a tree but they had set fire to it. Abel could only think of revenge and he attacked the Indians' village and killed the inhabitants.

Abel has returned to civilization and now lives apart with his memories and an urn containing the ashes of Rima.

**Gregory, Augusta, Lady** 1852–1932. Augusta Persse, the daughter of a wealthy family, was born at Roxborough House near Coole in Galway. Her father's lands were adjacent to those of the Gregorys at Coole Park and she married Sir William Gregory in 1880. Her husband died in 1892 and Lady Gregory developed her interest in Irish folklore and mythology. This was stimulated by her meeting with W. B. Yeats in 1896; she became his patron and Coole Park his refuge and retreat. In 1899 Lady Gregory, with

Lady Gregory. A detail from the portrait by Flora Lion, 1913. National Portrait Gallery, London.

Edward Martyn and Yeats, founded the Irish Literary Theatre; Yeats, Martyn, and George Moore were the directors. This later became the Irish National Theatre, with Yeats, Synge, and Lady Gregory as directors. It performed in two buildings adapted to form a playhouse, acquired through the generosity of Miss A. E. Horniman, in Abbey Street in Dublin. The Abbey Theatre benefited enormously from the two ladies; to Lady Gregory's tireless involvement as maid of all work and organizer were added a talent for portraying peasant life in the west of Ireland and a natural grasp of dramatic construction which she put at the service of the theatre. She was also successful in her dramatic essays into Irish folk tales, and in an adaptation of Molière to an Irish rural setting.

Among the best-known of Lady Gregory's works are *Spreading the News* and *The Rising of the Moon* (published 1906), *The Gaol Gate* and *The Workhouse Ward* (1909), *The Travelling Man* (1910), and *The Would-be Gentleman*, adapted from Molière (1928). Lady Gregory's *Journals 1916–1930* were edited for publication by Lennox Robinson (1946). Her son, Major Robert Gregory, was killed in action during World War I and is commemorated in W. B. Yeats's poem 'In Memory of Major Robert Gregory' (1917).

**Grenfell, Julian (Henry Francis)** 1888–1915. Like Rupert Brooke, Grenfell was one of the young poets who was lost during World War I. Unlike Brooke, he died of wounds sustained in action in May 1915; but both poets died at a time when going to war might still be thought of as gallant and romantic. Grenfell was the eldest son of Lord Desborough, educated at Eton and Balliol, and made the army his career. His poem 'Into Battle' was published in *The Times* on the day of his death and is the one by which he is best known. His poems are few in number and are usually to be found in anthologies, such as T. S. Moore's *Some Soldier Poets* (1919).

**Greville, Charles Cavendish Fulke** 1794–1865. Greville, who was born at Wilbury in Wiltshire, became Clerk to the Privy Council in 1821 and held office until 1859. His brother Algernon Sidney Greville was Wellington's private secretary and Greville became the intimate friend of both Wellington and Palmerston; he knew every statesman of any account in his lifetime. He published anonymously *The Past and Present Policy of England to Ireland* (1845), in which he advocated a more liberal policy for religious endowments. But more interesting are his memoirs, which are probably the most rewarding of their kind; with Greville's portraits of the principal figures of the period they are indispensible to students of English history from the accession of George IV to 1860. *The Greville Memoirs* appeared in three series: the first (1874) covers the reigns of George IV and William IV, the second (1885) the years 1837–52, and the third (1887) the years 1852–60. The second and third series were edited by Henry Reeve, who considered it advisable to suppress some of the contents. The complete text was eventually published in 1938.

**Greville, Fulke** 1554–1628. Greville's family were Warwickshire landowners and he was sent to Shrewsbury School in the same year as Philip Sidney, his exact contemporary and later his close friend. Greville went to court with Sidney, after completing his education at Jesus College, Cambridge, and became a member of the Areopagus club with Sidney, Spenser, and others. He represented Warwickshire in Parliament and enjoyed a long and distinguished public career under both Elizabeth I and James I. He was knighted in 1597, served as Treasurer of the Navy from 1589 to 1604, and as Chancellor of the Exchequer from 1614 to 1622. James I made him first Baron Brooke in 1621 and presented him with Knowle Park and Warwick Castle. Greville was murdered by his servant, Haywood, who believed that his master had left him out of his will. Greville was a gentleman of letters and, apart from Philip Sidney (whose pall-bearer he became in 1586), numbered among his friends Samuel Daniel, Francis Bacon, William Camden, and Edward Coke. He entertained Giordano Bruno during his visit to England in 1584.

Greville's own writings were never published during his lifetime. The most famous is *The Life of the Renowned, Sir Philip Sidney*, probably written between 1610 and 1614 and first published in 1652. The sequence of songs and sonnets called *Caelica* was begun with the guidance of Sidney himself and contains love poems and religious and philosophical verses; it first appeared in 1633 in the volume called *Certaine Learned and Elegant Workes Written in his Youth and Familiar Exercise with Sir Philip Sidney*. In the same volume were his two tragedies *Alaham* and *Mustapha*; these were not theatre pieces but Greville's expression of thoughts on political matters. A third one, on Antony- and Cleopatra, reflected his feelings about the fall of Essex, who had been his friend, but the author destroyed it. Greville also wrote *Treaties* (treatises) on *War, Religion, Monarchy, Fame and Honour*, and *Humane Learning*.

The standard modern edition of Greville is *Poems and Dramas of Fulke Greville First Lord Brooke* by G. Bullough (1939).

***Greyslaer:*** *A Romance of the Mohawk.* A novel by Charles Fenno Hoffman, first published in 1840 and successfully adapted for the stage in the same year. The setting is the Mohawk Valley and the period is at the outbreak of the War of Independence.

Max Greyslaer, a young lawyer, is imprisoned for revolutionary agitation. He escapes with the help of friends and goes to his guardian, Mr de Roos. The de Roos home is attacked by Joseph Brant and his loyalist Mohawks; de Roos and his daughter Tyntie are killed. Another daughter, Alida, is taken prisoner with the recaptured Greyslaer, who loves her.

Alida reveals to Greyslaer that she was, years before, forced into marriage with the ruffianly Bradshawe, whom she loathes. She and Greyslaer succeed in escaping and they discover that Alida's marriage was unlawful; but she will not marry him until her good name can be proclaimed.

Greyslaer goes to fight with the revolutionary army. So does Alida's brother, Derrick, who is killed and leaves an infant son in her care. The baby is a half-breed and rumours gather that the baby is in fact Alida's. In her depressed condition Alida breaks off her relationship with Greyslaer, who goes to Albany to find Bradshawe – whom Greyslaer sees as the source of all their troubles.

Greyslaer finds Bradshawe and, after a furious brawl, the latter disappears. Greyslaer is charged with murdering him but a hunter, Balt, testifies that he killed him. The story ends with the lovers united and with a providential document proving that the baby boy is Derrick's son.

**Grieve, Christopher Murray**   See **McDiarmid, Hugh**.

**Griffin, Gerald** 1803–40. An Irish novelist and poet. He was the author of *The Collegians* (1829), which was highly regarded; but Griffin's fame was eclipsed by Dion Boucicault, who turned the novel into *The Colleen Bawn* in 1860 and scored one of the great successes of the Victorian theatre. The novel underwent a third transformation as *The Lily of Killarney*, a once popular opera by Julius Benedict, in 1863.

***Griffith Gaunt,*** *or Jealousy.* A novel by Charles Reade, first published in *Argosy* (December 1865 to November 1866).

The story takes place in Cumberland in the 18th century. An impecunious gentleman, Griffith Gaunt, marries a Roman Catholic heiress, Kate Peyton. The marriage runs into trouble because of Kate's attention to her young spiritual adviser, Father Leonard. A mischief-making servant hints to Griffith that Father Leonard's attention to Kate is unnecessarily close and one day Griffith comes upon his wife and the priest in ambiguous circumstances. He leaves his wife after a violent quarrel.

Griffith, alone, is nursed through a bad illness by an innkeeper's daughter, Mercy Vint, who knows him as Thomas Leicester. Thomas Leicester is in fact Griffith's bastard half-brother, and Griffith marries Mercy under that name. One day he goes back to his former home to recover some money and accidentally meets his lawful wife, Kate. He is reconciled to her; now he has to tell the truth to Mercy and separate himself from her. But Kate discovers the truth; her rage leads her not only to a blistering verbal attack but to threats as well. As Griffith retreats from the house a pistol shot is heard and a cry of murder. Later a disfigured body is found floating in a neighbouring pond and Kate Gaunt is arrested and tried for the murder of her husband.

It is Mercy Vint who proves that the dead man is none other than the real Thomas Leicester and Kate is released. Griffith comes back and she is reconciled to him. Sir George Neville, long an admirer of Mercy's, proposes to her and is accepted.

This farrago of incredible events was once described (at the time of its publication) as immoral. W. T. Young, in 1916, called it a near masterpiece. That it could have been taken seriously as late as 1916 is a tribute to Reade's narrative skill, and even W. T. Young saw the bigamous marriage as its flaw. The modern reader will find the novel pitted with flaws, not the least of which are the character of Griffith Gaunt, composed of jelly, apparently, and the inexhaustible goodness of Mercy Vint.

**Grimald (** *or* **Grimvalde), Nicholas** *c.*1519–*c.*1562. Nicholas Grimald of Christ's College, Cambridge, was chaplain to Bishop Ridley and contributed 40 poems to *Tottel's Miscellany* (1567). He translated orations by Cicero and the same writer's *Three Books of Duties* (1553 and 1556) and published an edition of the *Georgics* of Virgil (1591). Grimald was the author of two Latin verse tragedies on religious subjects: *Christus redivivus* (1543) and *Archipropheta* (1548).

**Grip** Barnaby's pet raven in Dickens's *Barnaby Rudge.*

**Grocyn, William** *c.*1446–1519. Grocyn, who was largely responsible for the introduction of Greek studies at Oxford, was born at Colerne in Wiltshire. Educated at Winchester and New College, Oxford, he studied Latin and Greek in Italy, where Lorenzo de' Medici allowed him to attend the Greek classes of the Medici children. After his return to Oxford he taught Greek there (the first Englishman to do so) for five years and earned a great reputation as a scholar and teacher. He was the oldest of the group of humanist scholars who made such a deep impression on Erasmus ('who does not marvel at such a perfect round of learning?'), being nearly 60 at the time. A representative of the Renaissance, Grocyn's influence on Greek studies was such that after his time Englishmen could benefit from the riches of Greek learning without having to go abroad.

**Grosseteste, Robert** *c.*1175–1253. Grosseteste was the son of a poor family of Stradbroke in Suffolk; little is known of his early life or of the steps that made it possible for him to study at Oxford and, probably, Paris. However, he was teaching at Oxford in the early 13th century and earning a considerable reputation. He was to become the most celebrated teacher of his time and was offered many sinecures and benefices, among them the archdeaconry of Leicester. After a serious illness in 1232 he resigned all his

Robert Grosseteste depicted in the *Harleian MS. 3860, f.48r.* British Library.

positions apart from that of prebend in Lincoln. From 1224 to 1235 Grosseteste taught at the Franciscan college at Oxford; the standard set by Grosseteste was maintained by the Franciscans and the college's reputation in Europe was very high. He was elected Bishop of Lincoln in 1235 and earned praise as a great administrator who would not countenance any failing in their duties by the considerable numbers of priests, abbots, and priors in his enormous diocese. Grosseteste's firm hand was not pleasing to all but Pope Innocent IV arbitrated in the bishop's favour in his conflict with his dean and chapter. Grosseteste attended the Council of Lyons in 1245 and visited Rome in 1250, when he challenged corrupt and nepotic practices in his speech 'De Corruptelis Ecclesiae'.

At Oxford Grosseteste translated Aristotle's *Nicomachean Ethics* and prepared commentaries of his logic and physics. His *Compendium Scientiarum* classified all the departments of knowledge known in his day. *Château d'Amour*, an allegorical poem written in French in praise of the Virgin and Son, was translated into Latin and then into English. His interests were wide and included every branch of natural science; Roger Bacon's interest in the subject sprang from Grosseteste's teaching. He was the author of a great number of philosophical and theological works but is best remembered for his translation of Aristotle and for his emphasis on the importance of experiment in scientific enquiry.

**Grote, George** 1794–1871. The son of a banking family, Grote was born at Beckenham in Kent, and was educated at Charterhouse School. He was a follower of Bentham and James Mill and published pamphlets in support of reform. He entered the family business in 1830, and in 1832 became MP for the City of London. He had meanwhile, since 1823, worked intermittently on his *A History of Greece*, and after retiring from Parliament (1841) and banking (1843) he devoted himself to its completion. It was published in 12 volumes (1845–56) and surpassed the similar work (1835–44) by his friend from Charterhouse days, Connop Thirlwall. Grote wrote two works on Greek philosophy: *Plato and the other Companions of Sokrates* (1865) and *Aristotle* (posthumously published, 1872).

**Grundy, Mrs** See **Morton, Thomas**.

*Gryll Grange* Thomas Love Peacock's last novel, first published in 1860–61, and his best in the view of many critics. Peacock's setting is the familiar house party in Wales, but here the slender story is interwoven with more skill into the brilliant conversations that are the outstanding feature of his novels. The host, Mr Gryll, personifies the England of the immediate rosy past, which exists in the minds of those who dislike the present, and Dr Opimian is the amiable clergyman, comfortable and erudite; Mr Falconer is a Romantic but he has no delusions about reforming mankind, and Miss Ilex is an old maid of real charm. The book is mellower than its predecessors and its characters are not made to seem ridiculous: the result is that their views are much easier to attend to and the author makes his points without effort – the reader's patience is never tried.

**Gude and Godlie Ballatis, The**  James, John, and Robert Wedderburn of Dundee were three ministers who compiled 'Ane Compendious Book of Godlie Psalms and Spiritual Song collected out of sundrie partes of the Scriptures with sundrie other ballads changed out of prophane sangis for avoyding of sinne and harlotrie with the augmentation of sundrie gude and godle Ballats not contend in the first edition' (1567). The first edition (*c*.1546) does not survive. The book contained metrical versions of the Psalms in vernacular Scots, popular songs reworded to glorify the Kirk, and the aforementioned other ballads changed out of 'prophane' songs for the 'avoyding of sinne'. The book enjoyed a wide circulation, was loudly approved by the adherents of the Reformation, and effectively stifled poetry in Scotland for a hundred years.

**Guenever**  King Arthur's wife in the Arthurian legends, her name is spelled in many different ways (Guanhumara, Guinevere, Gwenhwyvar, Finnabair, etc). In Geoffrey of Monmouth's version she is seduced by Arthur's nephew Mordred, but Malory follows the French tradition and gives her an illicit and passionate love with Launcelot. In Malory she is seized by Mordred when that knight rebels in Arthur's absence, and after the battle in which Arthur is mortally wounded she renounces Launcelot and takes the veil at Almesbury. Her death is shown to Launcelot in a vision, and he buries her next to Arthur at Glastonbury.

**Guest, Stephen**  In George Eliot's *The Mill on the Floss*, Lucy Deane's betrothed. The attraction he feels for Maggie Tulliver (Lucy's cousin) is reciprocated; but it is Stephen's thoughtlessness that leads to Maggie's disgrace.

**Guiderius**  In Shakespeare's *Cymbeline*, the eldest of the king's sons, stolen in infancy by Belarius and given the name of Polydore. He kills Cloten and speaks the famous 'Fear no more the

heat o' the sun' with his brother Arviragus over the apparently dead Fidele (Imogen).

**Guinevere**  See *Idylls of the King, The*.

**Gulliver's Travels** (*Travels into Several Remote Nations of the World, in Four Parts, by Lemuel, Gulliver, first a Surgeon, and then a Captain of several Ships*).  Jonathan Swift's satire was first published in 1726, anonymously. The four parts of the book are concerned with Lilliput; Brobdingnag; Laputa, Balnibarbi, Luggnagg, Glubbdubrib, and Japan; and the country of the Houyhnhnms.

Lilliput, the island where Gulliver is shipwrecked, is inhabited by tiny people, in proportion one twelfth the size of ordinary people. The characteristics of the Lilliputians are examined; their virtues and failings are represented as reflections of people – Swift's fellow Englishmen particularly – at large. The tone of Utopian travel and adventure is perfectly maintained and, the satire notwithstanding, has made the first part a favourite story for young people since its publication. The second part is popular with young readers also and the first two parts are usually the portion of the book they are given to read.

In the second part Gulliver is accidentally marooned on the coast of Brobdingnag. In contrast to Lilliput, everyone here is as tall as a steeple. The inhabitants, giants though they are, emerge as sympathetic and practical, and Swift's sense of scale – after the opposite perspective in Lilliput – is unfailing. He delivers a remarkable attack on human pride and relates Gulliver's baffled reaction to the discovery that abstractions are unknown on Brobdingnag: 'Mathematicks' are applied only in terms of what is useful. The King of Brobdingnag cannot grasp the science of politics – but he is horrified at Gulliver's description of gunpowder. His summing-up of the character of Europe is a famous piece and led some later critics to accuse Swift of being cynical and misanthropic: 'By what I have gathered from your own Relation . . . I cannot but conclude the Bulk of your Natives, to be the most pernicious Race of little odious Vermin that Nature ever suffered to crawl upon the surface of the earth.' In this second part Swift the literary artist and satirist of human pretensions is really into his stride.

The third part of *Gulliver's Travels* finds him on the flying island of Laputa and the neighbouring continent and capital of Lagado. Swift had followed the *Transactions of the Royal Society* with close attention and his satire in the third part (it was written last) is directed at scientists,

Gulliver waiting to be hauled up to the flying island of Laputa. An illustration from the edition of 1731. *Gulliver's Travels* was first published in 1726.

philosophers, economists, and historians. The South Sea Bubble affair lent him some powerful ammunition. The wise men of Laputa have no knowledge of anything but their own chosen field and are perfect idiots outside it; in Lagado scientists are working to extract sunlight from cucumbers. In Glubbdubrib, the Island of Sorcerers, Gulliver is enabled to invoke the great men of the past – and discovers from them how much mankind is deceived by written history. Gulliver also encounters the Struldbrugs, a race endowed with immortality and thoroughly miserable with it.

The last part was written before the third.

Gulliver in the land of the Houyhnhnms was to provoke, in the 19th century, a wail of indignation. In the country of the Houyhnhnms the horses are endowed with reason, while the race of men, the Yahoos, are not. The Houyhnhnms are dignified and conduct their lives with a noble simplicity; the Yahoos are brutal and disgusting – really disgusting, that is. The 19th-century critics recoiled in distaste. Within the framework of his idea Swift's satire is deadly and poor Gulliver, seeking to offer some evidence of man's nobility, works himself deeper and deeper into expressing just how ignoble he actually is. Swift saw clearly that reason is man's priceless gift and that the ultimate appeal must always lie there.

*Gul's Hornebooke, The* A satirical book of manners by Thomas Dekker, first published in 1609. The gull is the archetypal young man of means – and pretensions – who comes to London wanting to cut a dash and be noticed. The means adopted by such insensitive and stupid young men was inevitably obnoxious and usually followed the course recommended by Dekker's attack on them. The London scene was Dekker's home ground and he follows his gull through the streets, into (St) Paul's Walk, taverns, ordinaries (eating houses), and the playhouse. The last scene, described by a hard-working playwright, gives the most detailed and vivid picture of a Jacobean theatre audience in English literature.

**Gunn, Ben** The marooned mariner of Robert Louis Stevenson's *Treasure Island*, who hopes that Jim Hawkins carries cheese about with him. He provides the solution to the whereabouts of the treasure.

**Gunn, Thom(son William)** 1929– . Thom Gunn is the son of a journalist and was born at Gravesend in Kent. He was educated at University College School, London, and Trinity College, Cambridge, and published his first verse, *Poems* (1953), while still an undergraduate. His second collection, *Fighting Terms* (1954, revised 1958), earned him the Levinson Prize. From 1954 to 1957 Gunn studied and taught at Stanford University in California; *The Sense of Movement* (1957) earned him the Somerset Maugham Award, which enabled him to live in Italy for a time. He now lives in San Francisco and teaches in the Department of English at the University of California. Other volumes of poetry by Thom Gunn are *My Sad Captains* (1961), *A Geography* (1966), *Positives* (with Ander Gunn) and *Touch* (1967), *The Garden of the Gods* (1968), *The Explorers*, *The Fair in the Woods*, *Sunlight* and *Poems 1950–1966: A Selection* (1969),

*Last Days at Teddington* and *Moly* (1971), *Mandrakes*, *Song Book*, and *To the Air* (1974), *Jack Straw's Castle* (1976), and *Games of Chance* (1979).

**Gutenberg, Johann** *c.*1398–1468.  The Renaissance gave rise to a thirst for books that the copyists alone could not satisfy; the rise of a new industry to provide books was to be one of the principal means by which the great European revolution known as the Reformation was brought about. To Johann Gutenberg of Mainz is usually given the credit for the invention of movable type, which revolutionized printing. (However, movable type was used also by Coster, Gutenberg's contemporary at Haarlem.)

Gutenberg's great printed Bible, the first, was the Latin Vulgate (1456) and by the end of the 15th century there were 97 editions of the Bible printed in Europe. England was not in the vanguard of printing – in fact she was the ninth country in Europe where a printing press was established and Westminster was the 71st city. The printer was William Caxton; the year 1476.

**Guthlac**  A poem of 1370 lines in Old English, preserved in *The Exeter Book*. Authorship has been attributed to Cynewulf but the question has not been resolved. The first part (up to line 818) is usually acknowledged as by another hand than Cynewulf's and was probably written during the life of St Guthlac. The second part, usually called *Guthlac B*, is based on a Latin original and is believed to be by Cynewulf.

St Guthlac travelling to Crowland in a fishing boat. From the 12th-century *Guthlac Roll*, now in the British Library.

St Guthlac (d. 714) was a young nobleman of Mercia who devoted his life to worship and severe asceticism on an island in the marshes near the site of Crowland Abbey in Lincolnshire. A life of St Guthlac was written in Latin during the 8th century by Felix of Crowland.

**Guy Livingstone**  A novel by George Alfred Lawrence, first published anonymously in 1857.

Guy Livingstone is wealthy, sporting, and unprincipled; he is also physically magnificent and an officer in the Life Guards. In contrast to Guy is Bruce, who finds no pleasure in hunting or shooting and is not regarded as a manly chap. Bruce is engaged to Isabel, Guy's cousin, and Guy is engaged to Constance Brandon. One day Constance comes upon Guy kissing Flora Bellasys. Guy's friend Forrester elopes with Isabel, and they live happily for the nonce, while Constance falls into a decline and dies. Bruce tracks down Isabel and kills Forrester. Then Guy tracks down Bruce and justice is done. Guy, a little mellowed by his experiences, dies from a fall while hunting.

**Guy Mannering**  A novel by Sir Walter Scott, first published in 1815. The title notwithstanding, it is the story of Harry Bertram, heir to Ellangowan, who was kidnapped when a child at the instigation of the lawyer Glossin, who hopes to gain the estate himself if there is no-one to inherit. Bertram grows up with the name of Brown, serves with the army in India, earns the good opinion of his colonel, Guy Mannering, and falls in love with Julia, the colonel's daughter. A misunderstanding leads Mannering to believe that Harry is paying attentions to his wife; a duel follows, and Harry is left for dead. But he recovers and returns to England. He finds that Julia is in Dumfries, in the neighbourhood of Ellangowan, and he makes his way there.

On his journey he helps a sturdy Lowland farmer, Dandy Dinmont, beat off a gang of thieves, and at Ellangowan – now in the hands of Glossin – he is recognized by the Gypsy woman, Meg Merrilies, who is devoted to the Bertrams. Glossin, learning of the reappearance of the heir, is determined to have him murdered before he can discover his true parentage. The plot is frustrated by Meg, with the help of Dandy, and the villain Glossin meets his death at the hands of his henchman, Hatteraick. The novel ends happily: Harry gains his inheritance and is restored to Guy Mannering's favour, so the way is clear for his marriage to Julia.

**Guy of Warwick**  A Middle English verse romance of the early 14th century containing distinct elements of Old English storytelling. (See **metrical romances**.) Guy of Warwick is also the subject of a poem by John Lydgate and appears in Michael Drayton's *Polyolbion*. Guy is the son of Siward, steward to the Earl of Warwick, and aspires to the hand of Felice, the earl's daughter. He acquits himself in various adventures abroad and is honourably received by the king, Aethelstan, upon his return. He wins the earl's daughter, and after his marriage has more adventures in the Holy Land. Upon returning to England he kills the dragon of Northumbria; then he goes off on more adventures, and returns again when Aethelstan is hard pressed by the Danes under Anlaf. By his defeat of Colbrand the Dane Guy becomes the saviour of England; then he returns to Warwick. He decides to end his days as a hermit, receiving his daily bread from the hands of Felice, who only knows that the hermit is her husband when, dying, he sends her his ring. Various texts of *Guy of Warwick* exist; the most complete edition is by J. Zupitza for the Early English Text Society (1966).

**Guyon, Sir** The knight of temperance in Book II of Spenser's *The Faerie Queene*. The visit to the Cave of Mammon and the destruction of Acrasia's Bower of Bliss are part of his adventures.

*Guy Rivers* A novel by William Gilmore Simms, first published in 1834. Guy Rivers is an outlaw in northern Georgia in the 1820s, when a gold rush contributed to an increase in crime and social disorder. Rivers had been a lawyer but, embittered by his lack of advancement and his rejection by Edith Colleton, he has changed his name and now leads a lawless gang. One of Rivers' victims is Ralph Colleton, a penniless cousin of Edith's. Ralph is rescued from the attack by Mark Forrester, a backwoodsman, and nursed by Lucy Munro. Lucy's father is a member of Rivers' gang. Ralph takes part in a battle between the militia and the gang and Rivers, already jealous because Edith Colleton loves Ralph, is determined to kill him. Rivers and Munro mistakenly kill Forrester in their attempt to kill Ralph but succeed in fixing the blame on Ralph.

The innocent man is saved when Munro, dying after an encounter with the sheriff, confesses all to Lucy. Rivers is taken and commits suicide; Ralph and Edith are united and make a home for the orphaned Lucy.

**Gynecia** The wife of Basilius, King of Arcadia, in Sir Philip Sidney's *Arcadia*. She falls in love with Pyrocles, having seen through his female disguise.

# H

**Habington, William** 1605–54. William Habington was the son of a Catholic gentleman of Worcester, Thomas Habington, who was very active in his church's cause and suffered imprisonment for his involvement in the Gunpowder Plot. William is remembered as a minor poet who avoided involvement in anything, apart from his courtship of and marriage to Lucy Herbert; he celebrated this in his book of verse, *Castara*, published anonymously in 1634. An edition of 1635 contains additional poems, elegies on a friend, whilst a third (1640) contains further work in the form of religious verse, regarded by some as his best. This edition identified Habington as the author. He also wrote (with his father, Thomas) *The Historie of Edward the Fourth* (1640), *Observations upon Historie* (1641), and a play, *The Queene of Arragon* (1640).

**Haggard, Sir H(enry) Rider** 1856–1925. Rider Haggard was born at Bradenham in Norfolk and educated at Ipswich in Suffolk. The son of a lawyer, he was intended for the law but at the age of 19 was taken as secretary by Sir Henry Bulwer, Governor of Natal. Haggard spent five years in South Africa, returning to England to study law; he was called to the Bar in 1884, at Lincoln's Inn.

Haggard had written *Cetewayo and His White Neighbours* (1882) and two novels, *Dawn* (1884) and *The Witch's Head* (1885), before becoming famous with *King Solomon's Mines* (1885). The success of that romance enabled Haggard to retire to a country house in his native Norfolk and write a succession of immensely popular romances, making excellent use in some of them of his knowledge of Africa. Among them were *She* (1887), *Allan Quatermain* (1887), *Eric Brighteyes* (1891) – with an Icelandic setting, *Nada the Lily* (1892), *Montezuma's Daughter* (1893), *The Pearl Maiden* (1903) – about the fall of Jerusalem, *Ayesha: The Return of She* (1905), *Queen Sheba's Ring* (1910) and *The Wanderer's Necklace* (1914).

Apart from his career as a novelist Haggard served on a number of Royal Commissions and government committees. He was particularly interested in agriculture and country affairs and expressed his views in *A Farmer's Year* (1899), *Rural England* (1902), *The Poor and the Land* (1905), and *Rural Denmark* (1911). Rider Haggard led a useful life (he was knighted in 1912) and an intensely busy one: he wrote 50 novels and 23 other books. He met Kipling in 1889 and the two became lifelong friends, sharing conservative and imperialist attitudes.

*Hail and Farewell* See **Moore, George Augustus.**

*Hairy Ape, The* See **O'Neill, Eugene (Gladstone).**

*Hajji Baba of Ispahan, The Adventures of* A novel by James Morier, first published in 1824. It is an account of the life and adventures of Hajji Baba, a barber's son who succeeds by his wits and reaches the position of Mirza Hajji Baba, the shah's deputy. He is in turn barber, doctor, and executioner's assistant; he is vain and none too scrupulous – he has a sharp eye for the main chance. He tells his own story, and his reflections reveal a man who is warm and sympathetic and who has learned a great deal from life. (His observations on the climate of cruelty are notable.)

How well Morier succeeded in capturing the life of Persia in his time is indicated by the protests of the Persian minister in London. The author printed these in the introduction to a sequel which brought his hero to London, where he observed the western world through unbelieving eyes. The Everyman's Library edition of *Hajji Baba* (1914) contained an appreciation by Sir Walter Scott.

**Hakluyt, Richard** *c.*1552–1616. The son of a Hereford family, Hakluyt was educated at Westminster School and Christ Church, Oxford. Apart from his crossing to France, as chaplain to the English ambassador, Sir Edward Stafford, he never undertook a voyage but as an undergraduate he read travellers' tales and accounts of exploration in several languages.

While in Paris, Hakluyt relates, he heard his countrymen scoffed at for their 'sluggish security' in matters of exploration and adventure; he also heard the maritime enterprises of other countries widely discussed. He resolved to collect and set down an account of all the great exploits of Englishmen, a task he undertook with tireless industry. His first volume was dedicated to Sir Philip Sidney and published in 1582: *Divers Voyages Touching the Discoverie of America and the Ilands Adjacent unto the Same, Made First of all by our Englishmen, and Afterward by the Frenchmen and Britons.*

This was a foretaste of what was to become a priceless compendium of information about travel and discovery: *The Principall Navigations, Voiages and Discoveries of the English Nation, Made by Sea or over Land, to the most Remote and Farthest Distant Quarters of the Earth at any Time Within the Compasse of these 1500 Yeares* (1589). The second edition, published in three volumes (1598, 1599, 1600), extended the period to 1600 'yeares'. Hak-

luyt used first-hand narratives wherever they were to be found and, while some of these are inevitably plain and factual, the volumes contain treasures in plenty. He included the accounts of Ralegh, which are highly prized; the narratives of the voyages of Drake and Hawkins, on the other hand, are very dull reading – but the narrative is first-hand and that fact makes them priceless. Sir Hugh Willoughby's fatal venture in search of a Northeast passage to China is recorded only because of Hakluyt's indefatigable researches.

The standard edition of Hakluyt was published by The Hakluyt Society in 12 volumes (1903–05). The preparation of a new edition was undertaken by the Society and the Peabody Museum of Salem, Massachusetts, in 1965.

**Halcombe, Marian** The real heroine of Wilkie Collins's *The Woman in White*. She saves Laura Fairlie, her half-sister and the 'love interest' of the novel, from the horrible fate intended for her by Sir Percival Glyde and Count Fosco.

**Haldane, Richard Burdon, 1st Viscount** 1856–1928. Haldane was born in Edinburgh and educated at the universities of Edinburgh and Göttingen. He was best known as a politician, becoming Secretary of State for War (1905–12) and Lord Chancellor (1912–15). He was also, however, a student of philosophy and published a translation of Schopenhauer's *The World as Will and Idea* (1883–86), *The Pathway to Reality* (1903), *The Reign of Relativity* (1921), *The Philosophy of Humanism* (1922), and *Human Experience* (1923).

**Hale, Margaret** The heroine of Elizabeth Gaskell's *North and South*. She is translated to the industrial north by her father's quixotry and regards the life she finds there with confident superiority. She has the same regard for John Thornton, who falls in love with her, and opposes him implacably in the matter of industrial relations. But her pride is brought low by circumstances out of her control and she discovers that Thornton's good opinion is of acute importance to her.

**Hale, Sir Matthew** 1609–76. This distinguished English jurist was a rare example of an incorruptible judge in an age when too many of his colleagues were the instruments of the ruling power. Hale became a judge in the Court of Common Pleas (1654), Baron of the Exchequer (1660), and Chief Justice of the King's Bench (1671). As a writer on law Hale is best known for his *History of the Common Law in England* (1713) published, like most of his work, after his death. He is the subject of a biography by Gilbert Burnet.

**Hales, Alexander of** See **Alexander of Hales**.

**Hales, John** 1584–1656. According to Clarendon 'one of the least men in the kingdom, and one of the greatest scholars in Europe', Hales was, like Chillingworth, one of those who in the early 17th century pleaded for individuals to be allowed 'the plain guidance of Scripture'. On the one hand he detested the tyranny of Rome, but he also came to detest Calvinism after attending the Synod of Dort. His sermons and tracts were partly collected by John Pearson and published in 1659 as *Golden Remains*. Fellow of Merton College and Regius Professor of Greek, Canon of Windsor, and fellow of Eton, he was deprived of all these positions during the Commonwealth and was obliged to sell his library in order to live.

*Half-Century of Conflict, A* See **Parkman, Francis** and *France and England in North America*.

**Haliburton, Thomas Chandler** 1796–1865. Probably the first original Canadian writer in English, Haliburton was born in Windsor, Nova Scotia, and educated there. After studying law he went on to a successful career and became a judge of the province's Supreme Court. He published *A Historical and Statistical Account of Nova Scotia* (1829), the source of Longfellow's *Evangeline*, and was persuaded by the publisher, Joseph Howe, to contribute to the latter's paper, *The Nova Scotian*, in 1835. Haliburton's contributions took the form of the 'Sam Slick' papers – observations by a shrewd itinerant clockmaker on life on the eastern shore of America, often at the expense of the affected and inert immigrants from the old country.

The sketches were first collected and published as *The Clockmaker* (1836) and were so successful that further ones followed (1837, 1838, and 1840). *The Attaché; or Sam Slick in England* (1843 and 1844) was equally successful and further papers appeared as *Sam Slick's Wise Saws and Modern Instances* (1853) and *Nature and Human Nature* (1855). Other books by Haliburton were *The Letter Bag of the Great Western; or, Life in a Steamer* (1839) and *The Old Judge; or, Life in a Colony* (1843).

Haliburton went to England in 1856. He represented Launceston in Parliament for six years and died in England. *The Season Ticket* (1860) tells of three contrasted characters travelling in British North America and is full of the shrewd comments and observation for which the Sam Slick papers had been famous. *Rule and Misrule of the English in Canada* was published in 1851. Artemus Ward, the American humorist, declared that American homespun philosophy and frontier humour stemmed directly from Haliburton; he was the literary progenitor of the form exploited by Mark Twain, Ward, Josh Billings, and others.

**Halifax, Marquess of** See **Savile, George, Marquess of Halifax**.

**Halkett, Lady Anne** 1622–99. *The Life of the Lady Halkett* was published in 1701 and is a fragmentary but interesting memoir by a woman whose personal life reads like fiction and whose associations are of historical interest. She enjoyed a love affair with the heir to Lord Howard of Escrick when she was 21, and was later successfully wooed by Colonel Joseph Bampfield, a Royalist agent with whom she helped contrive the escape of the young Duke of York. Unfortunately it transpired that Bampfield had a wife already; Anne loved him and was reluctant to face the truth about him. She married a Scottish widower, Sir James Halkett, when she was 35. The *Life* was edited by J. G. Nichols and last printed by the Camden Society (1875).

**Hall, Edward** 1498–1547. The Tudor historian was born in London and educated at Eton and King's College, Cambridge. He read law at Gray's Inn and held various political appointments; later he became a member of parliament and a judge. His chronicle, which covers the Wars of the Roses and the reigns of the first two Tudor kings, was first published in 1542. Hall uses nearly a hundred words to entitle his book but in so doing he states his intention of showing cause and effect and how the examples of history repay attention. His book, which is usually called *The Union of the Two Noble and Illustrate Famelies of Lancastre & Yorke*, was printed again in 1548 and 1550 by Richard Grafton. But it was strongly Protestant and Queen Mary ordered it to be burned. Hall owes much to the work of Polydore Vergil and Thomas More. His prose was criticized by Roger Ascham but too severely in the view of C. S. Lewis.

**Hall, John** 1627–56. A member of the group of friends that included Thomas Stanley and William Hammond, John Hall's short life and career were remarkably promising. His work, which earned praise from Herrick, Henry More, Hobbes, and (later) Saintsbury, included a book of lively essays, *Horae Vacivae* (1646), *Poems* (1647), and the first English translation of Longinus. His *An Humble Motion to The Parliament of England Concerning the Advancement of Learning: And Reformation of the Universities* was written when he was 22.

**Hall, Joseph** 1574–1656. A Caroline divine who began his career as a Low Churchman, Hall became a stout defender of episcopacy. He was born at Ashby-de-la-Zouch and educated at Emmanuel College, Cambridge. After taking orders he was appointed chaplain to Prince Henry (1608) and as Dean of Worcester was one of King James's representatives at the Synod of Dort. He became Bishop of Exeter (1627) and of Norwich (1641). A friend of John Donne and Sir Thomas Browne, he was a versatile writer of verse satires, devotional literature, and 'characters'. His *Episcopacy by Divine Right, Asserted by J. H.* brought him into conflict with Milton (1641) and he was one of the 13 bishops imprisoned by Parliament in 1642. In 1647 he was evicted from his palace and retired to a small farm. He was the 'Remonstrant' of Milton's *Animadversions* (1641).

His verse satires were published as *Virgidemiarum* (1597 and 1598). He also published a prose satire, *Mundus Alter et Idem* (1605), *Characters of Virtues and Vices* (1608), and *Heaven upon Earth* (1606). His best-remembered devotional work is *Meditations and Vows* (1605). The *Mundus Alter et Idem* was translated into English by J. Healey (1609).

**Hallam, Henry** 1777–1859. Henry Hallam was the father of Arthur Hallam, the friend of Tennyson, whose untimely death led to the writing of *In Memoriam*. Henry Hallam, son of the Dean of Wells, was born at Windsor. He was educated at Eton College and Christ Church, Oxford, and became a barrister at the Inner Temple. With a sinecure appointment (Commissioner of Stamps) he was able to devote himself to writing and was first published as a contributor to *The Edinburgh Review*. He was the author of *A View of the State of Europe during the Middle Ages* (1818), *The Constitutional History of England from the Accession of Henry VII to the Death of George II* (1827), and *An Introduction to the Literature of Europe in the 15th, 16th and 17th Centuries* (1837–39). *The Constitutional History*, regarded as his best work, deals with the conflict of the British principles of law with the claims of royal prerogative. Hallam published a memoir of his son in *Remains in Verse and Prose of A. H. Hallam* (1834).

**Halleck, Fitz-Greene** *c*.1790–1867. A member of the 'Knickerbocker Group', Halleck was born in Guilford, Connecticut. He worked in a bank and as personal secretary to John Jacob Astor before achieving fame as the coauthor of *The Croaker Papers* (1819) with Joseph Rodman Drake. *Fanny* (1819) was a satirical look at New York society, using Byron's *Beppo* as a model, and was very popular – he published another version in 1821 with 50 stanzas added. He visited Europe in 1822; *Alnwick Castle, with Other Poems* (1827) is very much influenced by Scott and, again, by Byron. Halleck published his collected *Works* in 1847.

**Hamilton, Elizabeth** 1755–1816. The author of the song 'My Ain Fireside' was born in Belfast, and died in Harrogate, but spent much of her life in Scotland as the ward of a farmer uncle of Stirlingshire. She also wrote *The Cottagers of Glenburnie* (1808), a novel about the harsh existence of the small tenant farmers, and several books of instruction for young people.

**Hamilton, Sir William** 1788–1856. Hamilton was born in Glasgow and completed his education at Balliol College, Oxford. He made a reputation as a philosopher in a series of contributions to *The Edinburgh Review* (1829–36). In 1836 he became Professor of Logic and Metaphysics at the University of Edinburgh.

Hamilton's collected articles were published in *Discussions of Philosophy and Literature, Education and University Reform* (1852). *Lectures on Metaphysics and Logic* were published posthumously (1859–60). He also prepared an edition of *The Works of Thomas Reid*, his fellow Scot, in 1846. Hamilton used to be more highly regarded as a philosopher than he is today and his views were attacked by John Stuart Mill. His contemporary importance lay in his introduction of continental philosophy into the mainstream of English thought, which was dominated by Locke, Berkeley, and Hume. Hamilton was a man of great erudition and through him the work of Spinoza, Leibniz, and Kant became well known in England. Hamilton's main contribution in logic was a modification of the traditional doctrine; known as 'The Quantification of the Predicate', his theory was elaborated by two contemporary mathematicians, Augustus De Morgan (1842) and George Boole (1854), and was given further exposition by Thomas Spencer Baynes (1850) and William Thomson (1852).

***Hamlet, Prince of Denmark*** A tragedy by William Shakespeare, first produced *c*.1602 and printed in a quarto of 1603. An improved quarto followed in 1604, and it was published in the First Folio of 1623 as *The Tragedy of Hamlet*. The Folio text contains some omissions. The source of the play was the *Gesta Danorum*, a 13th-century history of Denmark in Latin by Saxo Grammaticus. The name Hamlet was evolved from the original

Amleth, and the story was also known from the *Histoire Tragiques* (1559) of François de Belleforest. Scholars believe in the existence of another play on the subject known to Shakespeare but long lost. Hamlet is the classic example of the revenge play and owes something to Kyd's *The Spanish Tragedy*.

The night watch of the royal castle at Elsinore have seen an apparition of the late king and, dreading its reappearance, tell Horatio, Prince Hamlet's friend. He comes to see for himself. The ghost appears again but Horatio's attempts to commune with it go for nothing; when the cock crows the apparition vanishes.

Hamlet, the late king's son, has seen his father's brother Claudius marry his mother, the widowed Gertrude, and supplant Hamlet on the throne. The indecent haste of his mother's remarriage has shocked Hamlet and he will not respond to the blandishments of Gertrude and Claudius. Horatio brings him news of the ghost of his father and he goes with him to the battlements that night. They hear the sound of revelry in the castle, carried on the bitter wind. The ghost comes and beckons to Hamlet: his friends implore him not to go with the ghost but he does and learns of his father's murder: Claudius had seduced Gertrude and poured poison into his brother's ear while he slept in the orchard. Claudius must pay; as for Gertrude, 'leave her to heaven'. The ghost vanishes and Hamlet swears his friends to secrecy.

Hamlet's course is clear – but he is torn between his duty and his own nature, which is introspective and irresolute: under the weight of what he knows and what he should do, he is questioning every aspect of human relationships. The court believes him to be losing his reason, a belief he encourages to prevent Claudius from suspicion. Ophelia, daughter of the old counsellor Polonius, was once courted by Hamlet; now he treats her offensively and it is assumed that she is the cause of his behaviour. Claudius and Gertrude ask two courtiers, Rosencrantz and Guildenstern, to watch Hamlet's behaviour and keep them informed.

A troupe of players comes to Elsinore and Hamlet coaches them in a play to be acted before the court. 'The Murder of Gonzago' reproduces the murder of Hamlet's father and Claudius betrays himself. He determines to send Hamlet out of Denmark and commissions Rosencrantz and Guildenstern to escort him. Hamlet comes upon his uncle who, overcome with remorse, is on his knees at prayer. He could kill him easily but he convinces himself that it is not the time; he will wait until Claudius is again enjoying the consequences of his deeds, not repenting of them. He goes to confront his mother; but Polonius is there, recommending that Gertrude confront her son. The old man conceals himself behind the arras when Hamlet enters.

The scene that follows is one of the most famous in all drama. Hamlet's violent attack on his mother is preceded by her terror that Hamlet means to harm her. Her cry for help provokes a response from the hidden Polonius and Hamlet stabs him through the arras, believing it is Claudius concealed there. Then he turns on his mother and reduces her to tears. The ghost of his father appears – but it is only visible to Hamlet. Gertrude is certain her son is mad.

Claudius is resolved to kill Hamlet. He sends him on a mission to England, where the murder can be carried out; but Hamlet encounters a pirate ship and a letter to Horatio announces that he will soon be back in Denmark. Meanwhile, Hamlet's behaviour and the murder of Polonius have brought true madness to the hapless Ophelia. Claudius makes it plain to Laertes, Ophelia's brother, who is responsible. When Ophelia drowns in her crazy wanderings, Laertes swears revenge on Hamlet, who returns in time to witness the funeral. Claudius has an ally now, to help rid him of Hamlet.

A formal duel is arranged, with rich prizes, between Hamlet and Laertes. Laertes uses a poisoned sword and a poisoned cup is prepared to hand to Hamlet if he wants to drink. The duel commences and Laertes wounds Hamlet; then, in a scuffle, the rapiers fall and each picks up the other's weapon. Hamlet wounds Laertes. Gertrude, meanwhile, has taken the cup intended for Hamlet and, before Claudius can prevent her, has drunk from it. She falls, poisoned, and Laertes, knowing he is dying, tells Hamlet the truth. He warns him he, too, is dying from the poisoned blade. Hamlet's last act is to kill the king.

Hamlet is the most discussed play ever written and will probably go on providing material for theses and books of scholarly investigation for as long as English is read and the play is performed. The complexity of the play is indicated by this and as a dramatic exercise it is inexhaustible. The tragedy lies in Hamlet himself, a character conveyed in his examination of himself. He is not a hero, beyond his position as the chief character; he is simply not equal to the enormous charge laid upon him and his remorseless self-questioning results from that. If he were resolute he would have killed Claudius at the first opportunity but then he would have not been a subject for Shakespeare's extraordinary genius. He does not even excite our pity; that is reserved for the wretched, bewildered Ophelia and, against reason, for the guilty and unhappy Gertrude. Hamlet is a man of sensibility with an enquiring mind who, with the revelations from his father's ghost, is pitched into a situation in which everyone, except his dull and well-intentioned friend Horatio, is a stranger, because the whole world is now out of focus. And a man like Hamlet cannot but examine this out-of-focus world. He is not forced into action until he inadvertently kills Polonius and after that he is simply defending himself. He would have made a very bad king, one can't help feeling. The play can be seen a dozen times and still leave the spectator with the feeling that there is something more about it to be discovered.

**Hammett, (Samuel) Dashiell** 1894–1961. Dashiell Hammett was born in Maryland and educated at the Polytechnic Institute of Baltimore. He served in World War I and after various jobs went to work for the Pinkerton Agency in San Francisco as a private detective. His experiences served him well when he turned to writing detective stories, and he published his first novel, *Red Harvest*, in 1929. He introduced an unadorned realistic style that suited his material perfectly and he soon drew admiring comments from André Gide, Sinclair Lewis, and Robert Graves. He also drew a host of imitators, but not all of them realized how important intelligence and acute observation were to the credibility of Hammett's heroes; they were not merely tough: he produced *The Dain Curse* (1929), *The Maltese Falcon* (1930, probably his best work), *The Glass Key* (1931), and *The Thin Man* (1932). In addition to his regrettably small output of novels Hammett published a number of short stories in the magazine *Black Mask*. Collections of these have been published in *The Adventures of Sam Spade* (1944), *The Creeping Siamese and Other Stories* (1950), and *The Continental Op* (1976). His devoted friend, the playwright Lillian Hellman, contributed a memoir of Hammett to her selection of his stories called *The Big Knockover* (1966), which includes his unfinished autobiographical novel, *Tulip*. Hammett also served in World War II, in the Aleutian Islands. He was one of the victims of McCarthy's witch-hunt, and a period in prison did fatal damage to an already weakened constitution.

**Hammon, Jupiter** *c.*1720–1800. A slave in a Long Island household, Hammon was the first Black poet of America. *An Evening Thought* appeared in 1760 and amongst further work is a poem dedicated to Phyllis Wheatley; but his verse, like hers, is of debatable value (see also **Wheatley, Phyllis**). However, the two together did make a point of considerable importance.

A more notable work by Jupiter Hammon is his *An Address to the Negroes of the State of New York* (1787). He urged his fellow slaves to be patient, and at the same time urged those who owned slaves to free the children. His address had some point in the northern states at that time, when the antislavery movement was gathering momentum and had the support of Benjamin Franklin and other distinguished Americans.

**Hammond, Henry** 1605–60. An Anglican clergyman who is sometimes called the father of English biblical criticism, Hammond published his *Paraphrase and Annotations on the New Testament* in 1653. He also published a number of theological works and sermons, which are highly regarded for their clarity and their quality of Christian tolerance (1649, 1657, and 1660). His *Twenty-nine sermons preached on several occasions* was published posthumously (1664).

*Handlynge Synne* A translation into English verse by Robert Mannyng of Brunne (Bourne in Lincolnshire), who lived from 1288 to 1338, of the *Manuel des Pechiez* of William of Waddington, of whom little is known. The French original was probably written for Norman settlers in the north of England. Mannyng's version, in couplets, runs to some 24,000 lines and was written, according to the author, in plain English for the edification of simple men who knew no French. He sets forth the precepts and practice of morality, dealing with the Ten Commandments, the Seven Deadly Sins, sacrilege, the Sacraments, and finally the elements of confession. The poem is notable for the elaboration of the scheme with popular anecdote, legend, history, fable, and scripture, both canonical and apocryphal. Mannyng has earned high praise as a storyteller and his poem is valued as a picture of contemporary manners. *Handlynge Synne* was edited by F. J. Furnivall (1862, extended and revised 1903).

*Hand of Ethelberta, The* A novel by Thomas Hardy, first published in the *Cornhill Magazine* (July 1875 to May 1876). The author himself described the book as a somewhat frivolous narrative and a servant's-eye view.

Chickerel, a butler, has a number of children. The cleverest is his daughter, Ethelberta, who transforms her social position by marrying the son of the house where she is governess – only to find herself a fashionable widow at the age of 21. The story concerns her struggle to maintain her position, while at the same time using it to help her brothers and sisters, and somehow conceal her relationship to Chickerel. She has an admirer in Christopher Julian, a musician, but in the end she surrenders him to her sister, Picotee, and marries a wealthy old peer.

**Handy Andy: a Tale of Irish Life.** A Novel by Samuel Lover, first published in 1842. It tells of Andy Rooney, the hopelessly inefficient servant of Squire Egan, and Egan's rivalry with Squire O'Grady. At the end of a string of humorous incidents, Andy proves to be the heir of Lord Scatterbrain.

**Hanley, James** 1901– . Hanley was born in Dublin, and after an elementary education went to sea at the age of 13. Ten years as a seaman were to provide the material for some of his best fiction but meanwhile he worked where he could until he succeeded in becoming a journalist. His first novel was *Drift* (1930) and in the same year he published *A Passion Before Death. The Last Voyage, Men in Darkness: Five Stories*, and *Boy* all appeared in 1931 and established him as a novelist with a direct painstaking style who could make a powerful effect. The life of a seaman was his principal subject but with *The Furys* (1935) he found another, the lives of the deprived in the Dublin slums. The theme is continued in *The Secret Journey* (1936) and *Our Time is Gone* (1940) and the trilogy is considered his best work by many critics. Among many other books by James Hanley, a prolific writer, are *Ebb and Flow, Stoker Haslett*, and *Aria and Finale* (1932), *Captain Bottell* (1933), *Resurrexit Dominus* and *Quartermaster Clausen* (1934), *Stoker Bush* and *At Bay* (1935), *Half an Eye* (1937, short stories), *People are Curious* and *Hollow Sea* (1938), *Soldier's Wind* (1938, essays), *Between the Tides* (1939, essays), *The Ocean* (1941), *No Directions* and *Sailor's Song* (1943), *Crilley and Other Stories* (1945), *What Farrar Saw* (1946), *Emily* (1948), *A Walk in the Wilderness* (1950), *The Closed Harbour* (1952), *Don Quixote Drowned* (1953, essays), *Levine* (1956), *Say Nothing* (1962), *Another World* (1972), *A Woman in the Sky* (1973), and *A Kingdom* (1978). *Broken Water* (1937) is a volume of autobiography, and Hanley is the author of two plays, *The Inner Journey* (1967) and *A Stone Flower* (1968).

**Hannary, Patrick** ?–1629. Little is known of the life of Hannary, a minor Jacobean poet. In 1622 he published a long poem, *The Nightingale*, and provided a tune to which lines could be sung 'by those that please'. He also wrote a romance in verse called *Sheretine and Mariana*.

**Hard Cash** A novel by Charles Reade, first published in 1863. The author uses the characters he had created for his earlier novel, *Love me Little, Love me Long*, published in 1859.

The 'hard cash' of the title is the hard-earned money which David Dodd, sea-captain, is bringing home from India; the accumulated savings are intended for his family's support. Dodd has an eventful journey home with storms, shipwreck, encounters with pirates, etc. He entrusts his money to Richard Hardie, a banker; he does not know that Hardie is dishonest and bankrupt, too. Dodd's savings are lost (in fact misappropriated by Hardie) and he suffers a mental breakdown; he is confined to a private asylum.

Dodd's daughter, Julia, is engaged to Alfred, Richard Hardie's son, who is determined to expose his father. Hardie has his son committed to an asylum too, to prevent him from revealing the truth. The following chapters are used by the author to expose the horrifying conditions in lunatic asylums – to such effect that a storm of protest came from those quarters who knew themselves attacked. The story ends with Dodd's escape from the asylum and return to sea, the rescue of Alfred, and the exposure of Richard Hardie.

**Hardcastle, Kate** The heroine of Oliver Goldsmith's *She Stoops to Conquer*. Marlow mistakes her for a servant and surprises her with his intensity, when his reputation is for being bashful and tongue-tied. Kate knows exactly how to handle him and he falls in love with her.

**Hardcastle, Mr** In Oliver Goldsmith's *She Stoops to Conquer*, the heroine's father and a gentleman who has no time for fashion. He loves 'everything that's old'.

**Hardcastle, Mrs** In Oliver Goldsmith's *She Stoops to Conquer*, the mother of Tony Lumpkin, whom she indulges to a ridiculous degree (Hardcastle is her second husband). She is impatient with her husband's contentment and hankers after a trip to town 'to rub off the rust a little'.

**Harding, Rev Septimus** In Anthony Trollope's *The Warden*, the gentle and conscientious guardian of the charitable organization which cares for 12 old men – the warden of Hiram's Hospital.

**Hard Times, For these Times.** A novel by Charles Dickens. It was first published in *Household Words* (April to August 1854). The volume form came out in the same year, which also saw the publication of *A Child's History of England*. One of Dickens's shorter novels – running to 100,000 words nonetheless – it was written with remarkable speed. The author was apparently in a restless frame of mind at this period and the novel, concise and often sharp though it is, displays a confusion of thought about the social scene which defeats whatever case Dickens was making. Thus the 'self-made man' who has lost touch with his own humanity and everyone else's is such a despicable character that he invalidates everything the author has to say about the hardworking single-minded man who fights his way to the top. The workers in *Hard Times* are abominably treated – but they are given a strike-leader who is squalid and self-seeking, as if the author were protecting himself on both flanks. *Hard Times* has never been popular with readers and for a long time came in for little praise though Shaw, in 1912, wrote in its favour. Then F. R. Leavis, in an appendix to *The Great Tradition*, in 1948, bestowed his approval and since then the book has been overpraised. It is interesting, certainly, like all Dickens's work, and the depiction of Coketown is powerful; but it is not one of his better novels.

Thomas Gradgrind, a successful citizen of Coketown, which is a centre of heavy industry, has two children, Louisa and Tom. He represses their imaginations and brings them up always to acknowledge hard facts. Louisa is given in marriage to Josiah Bounderby, an oafish and boastful manufacturer 30 years her senior. She doesn't object to the marriage; she has no happiness in her father's house and, besides, her brother Tom is placed in Bounderby's bank. Tom is the only person in the world she cares for and she hopes to be able to help him.

But Tom is a mean-spirited character. He robs his employer and contrives to have the blame fixed on Stephen Blackpool, an honest mill hand burdened with an alcoholic wife. Louisa, for her part, finds her married life appalling and is then subjected to the attentions of Harthouse, an amoral politician who does his best to seduce her.

Gradgrind is faced with the consequences of his children's upbringing when Louisa flees Bounderby's roof and goes to her father for protection and when Tom is shown to be a thief. Bounderby, who always proclaimed loudly how he made himself from nothing, is shown to have an adoring mother and to have come from a comfortable little cottage home.

**Hardy, Thomas** 1840–1928. The son of a master mason, Thomas Hardy was born in Upper Bockhampton, Dorset. He was apprenticed to an architect in Dorchester when he was 16, and his mother encouraged him to go on studying. His career in letters notwithstanding, Hardy retained an interest in stonework and architecture all his life. It was his profession as an architect that took him to London in 1862, about the time when he first began to write. In this he received encouragement from his friend, Horace Moule, a university-trained scholar. The friendship was a valuable stimulus to the young Hardy; Moule was eight years his senior and had a classical background. (Moule committed suicide in 1873, believing himself a failure. His death affected Hardy deeply, and some of his characters – notably Jude – have more than a suggestion of his friend in them.)

Hardy stayed in London, about which he had definite reservations, until 1867, reading incessantly, attending performances of Shakespeare, and visiting the opera. He went back to Dorset to assist in church restoration, and at the same time began to write a novel containing some verse. This, called *The Poor Man and the Lady*, was never published; but comments from one reader, George Meredith for Chapman & Hall, contained good advice and Hardy's next novel, **Desperate Remedies**, was published in 1871. It was not well received but **Under the Greenwood Tree** (1872) was also accepted, and did better, being praised for the author's delicate evocation of Dorset life. **A Pair of Blue Eyes** followed, appearing as a serial in *Tinley's Magazine* and then in volume form in 1873. J. I. M. Stewart says it 'may be regarded as a last apprentice piece' and certainly his next book, **Far from the Madding Crowd** (1874), demonstrated Thomas Hardy's mastery of his form. He felt assured and successful enough to embark on marriage with Emma Gifford.

His confidence in himself was justified; he was now being asked for his work. **The Hand of Ethelberta** (1876), however, to some degree disappointed his admirers. This was because the early instalments of *Far from the Madding Crowd* had been likened to the work of George Eliot and Hardy was determined to write something completely different. **The Return of the Native** followed in 1878, written at the Hardys' first home at Sturminster Newton.

The Hardys returned to London in 1878. Hardy, as well as researching the background for **The Trumpet-Major** (1880), was also taking his place among well-known writers; he met Tennyson and Browning and began his life-long friendship with Edmund Gosse. He was taken ill in the autumn of 1880 but succeeded in completing *A Laodicean* (1881), mostly by dictation, and the Hardys went back to Dorset in the late spring of 1881.

The next novel was a romance, *Two on a Tower* (1882), while *The Mayor of Casterbridge* (1886) and *The Woodlanders* (1887) were already in his mind. In 1885 the Hardys moved into their house 'Max Gate', the building of which Hardy had superintended, and welcomed their first visitor, Robert Louis Stevenson. Hardy's next major work was *Tess of the D'Urbervilles* (1891) but meanwhile there were a number of short stories, including two notable collections, *Wessex Tales* (1888) and *A Group of Noble Dames* (1891).

Hardy was by now chafing more and more at the restraints that convention was placing on truth in his fiction. Publishing so much in serial form, he was often obliged to savage his work to make it 'acceptable'. He resented having to do it for *Tess*; when he was called on to do the same thing for *Jude the Obscure* (1896) his disillusion was nearly complete. Both *Tess* and *Jude*, in volume form, were the complete texts and, predictably, they were severely criticized. The marital scene, too, was becoming strained, and this was hardly helped by Emma Hardy's over-estimation of her own contribution, and by her opposition to *Jude*. Apart from the light *The Well-Beloved* (1897), *Jude the Obscure* was Thomas Hardy's last novel. What should be mentioned here, before turning to his poetry, is the series of fine short stories that are an important part of his fiction. Apart from the volumes already mentioned there was *Life's Little Ironies* (1894) and the collection called *A Changed Man, The Waiting Supper and Other Tales* which was published in 1913. A story for children, *Our Exploits at West Poley* (1892), was first published in an American magazine, *Household*, and did not appear in England until 1952.

Hardy had written poetry from the outset of his career, but his first published volume, *Wessex Poems and Other Verses*, with illustrations by Hardy himself, did not appear until 1898. It was indifferently received but he continued: *Poems of the Past and the Present* came out in 1902 and then, in 1904, the first part of *The Dynasts*, a verse drama of the time of the Napoleonic Wars. The completed work brought him immense acclaim. From then on he was an honoured man of letters, revered throughout England, an honorary D.Litt. four times over, received by the king, and awarded the Order of Merit and the RSL Gold Medal. Another volume of poems, *Time's Laughing-stocks*, was published in 1909.

Emma Hardy died in 1912, and the poems that followed, in *Satires of Circumstance* (1914), reflect his feeling of both loss and guilt – he deeply regretted the strained relations of the last years. By then he had married Florence Dugdale and World War I had begun. His next book of verse, *Moments of Vision* (1917), contained the patriotic verse which he and other English poets had felt called upon to write. *Late Lyrics and Earlier* was published in 1922; the Prince of Wales called on Thomas Hardy at 'Max Gate' in 1923, and *The Famous Tragedy of the Queen of Cornwall*, a verse drama about Tristan and Iseult, was published at the end of that year. *Human Shows* (1925) was the last book of poems published during his lifetime.

Thomas Hardy died on 10 January 1928, at the age of 87, and was honoured with a tomb in Westminster Abbey. His last volume of poems, *Winter Words*, was published in the October of that year.

Hardy's work seems to divide his admirers: some prefer the great storyteller, some the poet; others admire *The Dynasts* and nothing else. The greater number accept him complete and it is a tribute to him that he has so much to offer those who do not. Even those who are cool about his novels will admit to finding memorable things in his short stories. His greatest strength no doubt lies in the deeply rooted Wessex character which

Thomas Hardy, 1914. Photograph by E. O. Hoppé.

informs most of his work; Hardy was a country-man without sentimentality and a fatalist. He knew perfectly well that a way of life was disappearing but this was not, to him, something to deplore; life was in many ways going to be better, with wider horizons. But the tension of being between two worlds lends great poignancy to much of his work and is at the heart of some of his novels. What he truly deplored was the rigid code of behaviour which existed in his time and the inflexibility imposed by tradition and routine which was the enemy of truth.

His poetry had to wait for his feeling that he could say no more in fiction; poetry was his first love and now he felt ready to be heard. After a slow beginning, he was listened to with great attention and with increasing appreciation for his imaginative vision and his undeluded mind.

**Hariot, Thomas** 1560–1621. Hariot was a gifted astronomer and mathematician of the late Elizabethan and Jacobean period who sailed with Sir Richard Grenville on his second voyage to Virginia in 1586. He spent two years there and in 1588 wrote *A Briefe and True Report of the New Found Land of Virginia*, an account of considerable historical importance that was published by Hakluyt in 1590, with the celebrated drawings of his fellow colonist John White. Hariot was a member of the group of London intellectuals that included Marlowe and Ralegh and was a friend of Francis Drake. He gave Ralegh assistance in chronology and geography in the writing of *The History of the World*.

**Harland, Henry** 1861–1905. The son of a Connecticut family, Harland was born in New York. After a visit to Paris he entered Harvard Divinity School. He stayed there only a short time and embarked upon a literary career under the pseudonym of Sidney Luska. He wrote several novels about Jewish immigrants and even pretended to be a Jew. (Harland often pretended; he also led people to believe, at different times, that he was born in St Petersburg and that he was the son of English aristocrats.) He dropped his manufactured character in 1890 and went to England, where he became the first editor of *The Yellow Book*.

Harland settled down contentedly in his new character, that of an expatriate American aesthete. He was the author of a number of short stories and historical novels, among the most successful of which were *The Cardinal's Snuff Box* (1900) and *My Friend Prospero* (1904).

**Harleth, Gwendolen** In George Eliot's *Daniel Deronda*, the selfish and beautiful girl who mar-ries Henleigh Grandcourt for mercenary reasons and soon regrets it. She turns to Daniel Deronda and, while her hopes in him are never fully realized, gains a certain peace through his kindness and compassion.

**Harlowe, Clarissa** The tragic heroine of *Clarissa* by Samuel Richardson. She becomes the quarry of Lovelace, a handsome and accomplished rake. Her resistance to him turns his desire for her into an obsession, with tragic results.

**Harmon, John** In Dickens's *Our Mutual Friend*, the returning heir to a fortune who is believed to have been murdered when a body bearing his papers is recovered from the Thames. He was betrothed to Bella Wilfer, whom he had never seen.

*Harold, the Last of the Saxon Kings*. A historical romance by Bulwer-Lytton, first published in 1848. Into the events of the last years of Edward the Confessor and the brief reign of Harold, Bulwer-Lytton introduces Hilda, a Saxon prophetess, and his true love and mistress Edith, who emerges as a rather different character from the Edith Swan-Neck of whom the chroniclers tell. Edith's death beside Harold's corpse after the Battle of Hastings (Senlac) is unhistorical. The narrative, otherwise, follows the course of history very closely.

Tennyson's *Harold* is a historical drama, published in 1876, and presents in dramatic form the same events as Bulwer-Lytton's romance.

**Harpur, Charles** 1813–68. Charles Harpur, Australian-born and the son of convict parents, was the first distinctively Australian poet. His first poems, *Thoughts: A Series of Sonnets* (1845), show the influence of the poets he admired – Wordsworth, Shelley, Blake – and have no particular flavour of the great south land, although they are well turned and show that he understood his craft. However, Harpur spent much of his life in the bush and he came to turn more for inspiration to his own environment. He practised many forms of lyrical poetry but found his most suitable medium in blank verse narrative and description. His broad vision and simplicity of emotion fitted well with his style in *The Bushrangers, a Play; and Other Poems* (1853), *A Poet's Home* (1862), *The Tower of the Dream* (1865), and *Poems* (1883). *The Bushrangers* is not regarded as a success but 'Other Poems' of the volume and the volumes that followed are regarded as his best work. His sonnets and 'The Creek of the Four Graves' are found in most collections of Australian verse.

**Harrington, James** 1611–77. The author of *The Commonwealth of Oceana*, Harrington was an extensively travelled man who to some extent formed his political ideas from his observations of Holland and Venice. He was himself a Republican though he took no part in political affairs. His *Oceana* is a carefully considered idea of a commonwealth, presented in the manner of Thomas More's *Utopia*. In contrast to Thomas Hobbes (*Oceana* is often said to be a reply to *Leviathan*) Harrington is positive and constructive, and in political terms his book is a major contribution. It has never been popular as literature and indeed is a dull book to read but a remarkable number of Harrington's ideas – limitations on inherited property, limitations on income, the principle of rotation in office at regular intervals, the selection of representatives by the people themselves – are now the small change of popular democracy. His book was a powerful influence on the thinking of the settlers in America.

Harrington was imprisoned during the Restoration and the experience severely affected his health. Among his friends were John Aubrey, Andrew Marvell, and Samuel Pepys.

**Harris, Joel Chandler** *c.*1848–1908. The creator of Uncle Remus was born in Georgia, in a small town near Macon. He worked on plantations and in a printing shop before finding a position on a Macon newspaper. He had further experience working on papers in New Orleans and Savannah and then joined the staff of *The Atlanta Constitution* in 1876.

It was for the *Constitution* that Harris drew on his memories of Negro life and wrote 'Negro Folklore' (1879). 'The Story of Mr Rabbit and Mr Fox, as told by Uncle Remus' was the story which opened his first collection, **Uncle Remus: His Songs and His Sayings** (1881). This book was followed by *Nights with Uncle Remus* (1883), which introduced Daddy Jack, *Uncle Remus and His Friends* (1892), *Mr Rabbit at Home* (1895), *The Tar-Baby and Other Rhymes of Uncle Remus* (1904), and *Uncle Remus and Br'er Rabbit* (1906). The collections increasingly appealed to young readers as they appeared. This was inevitable for Harris drew upon his own youthful experience; he would have listened to many Uncle Remuses while working on plantations and he was, after all, a Georgian, who knew Black folks very well. His classic status is secure; there is ancient wisdom in the Uncle Remus stories which has its roots in the generations before Uncle Remus became, or was born, a slave. The simplicity (except for Daddy Jack's dialect, which is diffi-cult) is the mark of a born storyteller and Harris's ear is unfaltering; Mark Twain paid tribute to him as the only writer who could give a true rendering of Negro speech. That Harris was a White man makes his achievement the more striking; H. L. Mencken rightly said that Harris's work was the product of Black Georgia.

Harris was neither Southern aristocrat nor poor White trash. His respect went to those who earned it whether Black or White. The experience of the Civil War was followed, in the South, by the agonies of reconstruction and he watched the activities of the landgrabbers and the carpetbaggers with a cold eye. He became editor of *The Atlanta Constitution* and knew better than the legislators in Washington that reconciliation could never be achieved merely by the passing of laws.

The world of the South was explored further in **Mingo,** *and Other Sketches in Black and White* (1884) and *Tales of the Home Folks in Peace and War* (1898). *Sister Jane: Her Friends and Acquaintances* (1896) was a novel of postwar Georgia and another novel, *Gabriel Tolliver: A Story of Reconstruction*, was published in 1902. *On the Plantation* (1892) recalled his early years and *Free Joe, and Other Georgian Sketches* (1887) is notable for the title story, which examines the problems of a man who finds himself free, having spent his whole life as a slave.

See also **Cable, George Washington.**

**Harrison, William** 1534–93. Born in London and educated at Westminster School, Oxford, and Cambridge, Harrison became rector of Radwinter and canon of Windsor. He was contributor to Holinshed's *Chronicles* of the *Description of Scotland* (anglicized from the Scottish of John Bellenden's translation of Boece's Latin *Historia Scotorum*) and the highly regarded *Description of England*. This was Harrison's own work and presents a vivid picture of Shakespeare's England. He is sunny and brisk in style, gossipy and curious by nature.

An edition of Harrison's *Description*, based on the 1587 Holinshed and collated with F. J. Furnivall's edition (1877–1908), was prepared by G. Edelen and published by Cornell University in 1968.

**Harry** (*or* **Hary**), **Blind** *c.*1440–*c.*1492. The Scottish poet or bard Blind Harry, author of **Wallace,** was probably a wandering minstrel who earned a living by reciting his poem in the houses of the Scottish nobles. It is known that he was blind, though probably not from birth, and that is all. Nothing is known of his parentage or birthplace. The poem was written down by John

Ramsay (who made the two existing manuscripts of John Barbour's *The Bruce*) in 1448, possibly at Blind Harry's dictation, and the manuscript is now in the National Library of Scotland.

**Harry Richmond, The Adventures of** A novel by George Meredith, first published in 1871.

Richmond Roy is the son of a member of the royal family and an actress. Extravagant and charming, he teaches singing in the household of Beltham, a wealthy squire, and charms the daughters of the house. He runs off with one of them and she bears him a son but his unreliable character drives her to an early grave. Beltham, hating Roy, is determined to gain custody of his daughter's child, Harry Richmond. Roy, however, is obsessed with the idea of obtaining some exalted position for the boy.

Harry loves his charming irresponsible fool of a father, who eventually gets himself accepted at the courts of petty German princes. At one of these Harry and Princess Ottilia fall in love and Roy is determined to overcome all obstacles to the impossible marriage. Beltham, for his part, sees Harry's future in England, married to Janet Ilchester. Harry, through his father, is exposed to embarrassment and humiliation and Roy's silly scheme is brought to nought. Harry eventually marries Janet and the squire's plans are realized.

**Harte, (Francis) Bret** 1836–1902. Bret Harte was born in Albany, New York, and went to the West at the age of 18. In California he earned his living in a variety of ways: he was a prospector, teacher, and Wells Fargo expressman among other things, gradually finding his way to journalism and making friends with Mark Twain meanwhile. He contributed to the *Golden Era* and *The Californian*, and became editor of the latter. He commissioned weekly articles from Mark Twain.

Harte was appointed secretary of the US Mint in San Francisco in 1863 but he continued to write. His first book of poems, *The Lost Galleon*, was published in 1867 and *Condensed Novels and Other Papers*, with its clever parodies of distinguished authors, in the same year. In 1868 he helped establish **Overland Monthly** as an outlet for Western writers. He edited the *Monthly* for two years and some of his own best stories appeared in it.

In 1870 he published his comic ballad, *Plain Language from Truthful Jones*, and the collection of stories which made him famous, **The Luck of Roaring Camp and Other Sketches**. The book's success brought him an offer from *The Atlantic*

*Monthly* which persuaded him to drop an appointment to the new University of California and return to the East. The decision was to prove unwise; removed from the source of its inspiration Bret Harte's work became repetitious – it seemed that what had looked like a great talent had already reached its limits.

Nevertheless, Bret Harte continued to write and publish collections of stories and sketches; apparently his reputation was enough to enable him to live on his work at least until 1878, when he was appointed US consul in Germany. He was consul at Glasgow from 1880 to 1885 and spent the rest of his life in London. He also wrote some novels, now forgotten, and collaborated on a play, *Ah Sin*, with Mark Twain.

Bret Harte's best work is a true reflection of the authentic West, unspoiled by the gloss of Hollywood and the 'Wild West' industry, and it was that vein which occasionally reappeared in the later volumes. His best work is notable for its realism and earned the praise of Dickens.

**Hartley, David** 1705–57. Hartley was born at Luddenden, near Halifax in Yorkshire, and was educated at Bradford Grammar School and Jesus College, Cambridge. He became a physician, was a fellow of Jesus College, and is remembered for one of the earliest attempts at psychological enquiry in English. *Observations on Man: his Frame, his Duty and his Expectations* (1749) relates psychology to physiology, and was a contribution to the development of the 'association of ideas' theory.

**Hartley, L(eslie) P(oles)** 1895–1973. L. P. Hartley was born at Whittlesey in Cambridgeshire and educated at Harrow and Balliol College, Oxford. During World War I he served as a subaltern in the Norfolk Regiment. Hartley's first published fiction was a volume of short stories, *Night Fears* (1924); his first novel, *Simonetta Perkins*, followed in 1925. *The Killing Bottle* (1932, short stories) was followed by *The Shrimp and the Anemone* (1944), the first part of a trilogy which was completed by *The Sixth Heaven* (1946) and *Eustace and Hilda* (1947). The trilogy is acknowledged as Hartley's best work, a penetrating study of a brother–sister relationship from childhood to maturity which won him the James Tait Black Memorial Prize. Other novels are *The Boat* (1949), *My Fellow Devils* (1951), *The Go-Between* (1953, Heinemann Foundation Award), *A Perfect Woman* (1955), *The Hireling* (1957), *Facial Justice* (1960), *The Brickfield* (1964) and its sequel *The Betrayal* (1966), *Poor Clare* (1968), and *The Love Adept* (1969). Other collections of short stories are *The*

*Travelling Grave* (1951), *The White Wand* (1954), and *Two For the River* (1961). Hartley is also the author of a volume of critical essays, *The Novelist's Responsibility* (1968).

**Harvey, William** 1578–1657. William Harvey, Charles I's physician (Harvey was with the king at the Battle of Edgehill) and a pioneer of medical science, was born in Folkestone, Kent. After attending King's School, Canterbury, Harvey went on to Caius College, Cambridge, and then to the University of Padua where Galileo was a teacher and where he took his medical degree in 1602. In London he became a physician at St Bartholomew's Hospital and lecturer at the College of Physicians – where he expounded his theory of the circulation of the blood in 1616. He did not publish his treatise on the subject until 12 years later, in *Exercitatio Anatomica de Motu Cordis et Sanguinis in Animalibus* (On the Movement of the Heart and Blood in Animals, 1628). Harvey's theories, the result of observation and experiment carried out without the help of a microscope, were completely substantiated after 200 years of slow acceptance. Harvey also made considerable contributions to the knowledge of embryology and comparative anatomy.

**Hatton, The Correspondence of the Family of** The Hatton papers deal with the years 1601–1704 and are a useful source of information on the period, particularly for the later part of the century. They were edited by E. M. Thompson (1878).

**Haunted Man, The** See *Christmas Books*.

**Havelok the Dane, The Lay of** A Middle English verse romance of the early 14th century. (See **metrical romances**.) The name of the hero is believed to originate in the Welsh, Abloyc, itself a form of Olaf or Anlaf. Anlaf was defeated, as told in the Old English *The Battle of Brunanburh* (AD 937) with his ally Constantine of Scotland. In the Middle English verse romance, which is derived from an Old English source, Havelok is the son of Birkabeyne, King of Denmark. His guardian is Godard, who is ambitious. Godard orders a fisherman, Grim, to drown Havelok; but the fisherman is warned by a mystic light playing about the boy's head and knows him to be a royal child. Grim takes the boy and flees to England. He lands at Grimsby and Havelok becomes a scullion in Earl Godrich's household. Godrich is also guardian to a king's child – Goldburgh, daughter of Aethelwold, King of England, and he is as ambitious as Godard. Havelok's grace and strength make a favourable impression

and Godrich determines to marry him to Goldburgh for such a marriage would deprive her of her inheritance. But Goldburgh also sees the mystic light and realizes who her husband is. The steadfast Earl Ubbe, who is watching events in Denmark, persuades Havelok to return to his father's kingdom, and the wheel of fortune begins to turn. Havelok becomes king and retribution is visited upon Godard (the gallows) and Godrich (the stake). *The Lay of Havelok the Dane* was edited by F. Madden for the Roxburghe Club (1828) and by W. W. Skeat for the Early English Text Society (1902). Skeat's edition was revised by Kenneth Sisam (1915). Modern versions are by E. Hickey (1902), L. A. Hibbard (1911), and R. Montagu (1954).

**Havisham, Miss** The recluse of Satis House in Dickens's *Great Expectations*. Jilted on her wedding day, she keeps the trappings of the reception on display and continues to wear her wedding dress. She adopts an orphan girl, Estella, and tries to pass on to the girl her own detestation of men. Pip believes her to be his benefactor.

**Hawbuck Grange** See **Surtees, R(obert) S(mith)**.

**Hawes, Stephen** 1474–1523. A Suffolk man, the poet Stephen Hawes was educated at Oxford and became Groom of the Chamber to King Henry VII. His poetry belongs to an age of transition but more properly looks back to the Chaucerian tradition, though there are suggestions of the poetry that was to come with the age of Spenser. The dates of composition of Hawes's work are sometimes confused with the dates of the first editions: printing had come to England and Wynkyn de Worde issued most of Hawes's works. The chief of these are *The Temple of Glass* (printed 1505), *A Joyful Meditation of the Coronation of Henry VIII* (1509), *The Example of Virtue* (1504), and *The Passtyme of Pleasure* (1505).

*The Passtyme of Pleasure, or the Historie of Graunde Amoure and La Belle Pucel* is an allegory of the progress of life, related as a chivalric romance. The knight, Graunde Amoure, acquires the accomplishments needed to make a perfect knight and to be worthy of the love of La Belle Pucel.

**Hawker, Robert Stephen** 1803–75. A Cornishman, Hawker was educated at Pembroke College, Oxford, and became vicar of Morwenstow in Cornwall. He published a fair amount of poetry during his lifetime but little is remembered apart from a popular school anthology piece, 'The Song of the Western Men' with its refrain of 'And shall Trelawny die?'. A selection of Hawker's poetry was edited by John Drinkwater in 1925 but no modern edition exists.

**Hawkins, Jim** The narrator of Robert Louis Stevenson's *Treasure Island*. He sails on the *Hispaniola* as a cabin boy, and overhears his erstwhile friend, Long John Silver, plan to seize the ship and the treasure.

**Hawkins, Sir John** 1532–95. The Elizabethan sea captain and slave trader led three expeditions to West Africa and Spanish America in 1562, 1564, and 1567 and published his account of the third one in 1569, *A True Declaration of the Troublesome Voyadge of M. John Haukins to the Parties of Guynea and the West Indies, in the Yeares of Our Lord 1567 and 1568.* It is valued as a first-hand account and for its direct and forceful style.

**Hawkins, Sir Richard** 1562–1622. The son of Sir John Hawkins and like his father a naval commander. Like his father also he wrote a description of an expedition: *The Observations of Sir Richard Hawkins Knight, in his Voiage into the South Sea, Anno Domini 1593* (1622).

**Hawthorne, Nathaniel** *c.*1804–64. Nathaniel Hawthorne was the first of the distinguished New England group of writers who was solely a writer. He was born in Salem, Massachusetts; his family was almost as old as the Massachusetts colony. One of its members, William Hathorne

Nathaniel Hawthorne.

– as the name was formerly spelt – was a judge, 'a bitter persecutor' in Hawthorne's words, and his son, Colonel John Hathorne, was a magistrate. Hawthorne found the record of the part played by both men in the Salem witch trials so detestable that he became almost obsessed with it; Puritan manners and morals provide the background for some of his best work.

Hawthorne's father was a sea captain who died of yellow fever in Dutch Guiana in 1808. His mother withdrew into a secluded life, which was to have considerable influence on the boy's character, and moved to Maine when Nathaniel was 12. The boy spent a lot of time on his own until he was sent to Bowdoin College, where one of his classmates was Longfellow, graduating in 1825. Then he returned to Salem (he was 21) and, continuing his solitary life, struggled to become a writer. Using colonial New England as a background, he wrote historical sketches and short stories and published a novel, *Fanshawe* (1828), anonymously and at his own expense. The book enjoyed little success and Hawthorne burned the unsold copies; but it attracted the attention of Samuel Griswold of Goodrich, the publishing house. Goodrich published many of Hawthorne's short stories in his annual gift book, *The Token*, and collections appeared in 1837 and 1842 as *Twice-Told Tales*. One of these, *Endicott and the Red Cross*, contains an incident which was later developed for **The Scarlet Letter**. Most of the stories, in fact, deal with Puritan life and the surge of human feeling that remained active below the surface, producing a society riddled with guilt.

In 1836 Hawthorne went to work for Goodrich as an editor and journalist. He became a busy desk writer for the next six years, compiling books of knowledge and history for young people and collections of stories for children, many written by himself. After leaving Goodrich he worked in the Boston Customs House for two years.

Mistakenly, Hawthorne also took part in a communal living experiment at Brook Farm though no one was less fitted for such a venture than the solitary and sensitive Hawthorne. He was quick to perceive how short-lived such a Utopian idea, with its evasion of essential points of leadership, was bound to be. However, he did meet and marry Sophia Peabody, whose sister Elizabeth was an active member of the Transcendentalist circle. The Hawthornes moved to the Old Manse at Concord in 1842.

Transcendentalism left Hawthorne feeling calm. He continued writing, contributing sketches and stories to *The Democratic Review* of

Washington and writing more stories for children. His contributions to the *Review* were published in 1846 as *Mosses from an Old Manse*. He became Surveyor of the Port of Salem (1846–49) but lost the post during a change of administration. The following year he published *The Scarlet Letter* (1850). **The House of the Seven Gables** followed in 1851 and **The Blithedale Romance** in 1852. It was a remarkable period for Hawthorne: *The Snow Image and Other Twice-Told Tales* was also published in 1851, his retelling of Greek myths for children, *A Wonder-Book*, in 1852, and *Tanglewood Tales* in 1853. He moved to the Berkshire Hills and became friends with Melville, who admired his work. When his college friend, Franklin Pierce, ran for president, Hawthorne wrote his campaign biography; upon his election Pierce rewarded Hawthorne with the consulship at Liverpool (1853).

Hawthorne was now famous; *The Scarlet Letter* alone, a disturbing story written in impeccable prose with an acute feeling for the tone of another time and remarkable brevity, had set a new standard in American fiction. Hawthorne spent four years in England and the following two in Italy, returning to the USA in 1860 to settle in Concord. **The Marble Faun** (1860) is a novel set in Italy and *Our Old Home* (1863) is a book of essays on England which demonstrates how shrewd an observer he was. He contributed to **The Atlantic Monthly** but otherwise his creative gifts seemed to lack direction in the last two years of his life. He left behind fragments of four different novels. His notebooks were edited after his death by his wife: *Passages from the American Notebooks* (1868), *Passages from the English Notebooks* (1870), and *Passages from the French and Italian Notebooks* (1871).

Hawthorne's fiction, both short stories and novels, is like a signpost in American literature, showing the way for those who followed him. His work demonstrates the value of psychological enquiry into motive as a basis for action, rather than acceptance of deed and consequence at face value. His detested Puritan ancestors were made to serve him well in this respect (*The Scarlet Letter*, *The House of the Seven Gables*, and a number of his short stories) and he almost succeeded in burying the last remnants of the Puritan tradition. His experience as an American in Europe (*The Marble Faun*) instituted a theme which Henry James, who admired Hawthorne enormously, exploited with consummate skill.

**Hay, John Milton** 1838–1905. John Hay was born in Salem, Indiana, and grew up in Pike County, Illinois. After graduating from Brown University he entered a law office, next door to Abraham Lincoln's, in Springfield. The two men became friends, though Hay was much younger, and Hay became one of Lincoln's private secretaries (the other was John Nicolay) when Lincoln was elected president. Hay also served in the US legation in Paris but upon his return to the USA left the political scene to take up journalism. In 1871 he published *Castilian Days*, a travel book combined with historical comment, which was the fruit of his European experience, and a volume of dialect poems, **Pike County Ballads**.

Hay re-entered politics as assistant secretary of state when Rutherford Hayes became president and became friends with Henry Adams, in whose work he frequently appears. He published (anonymously) *The Bread-Winners* (1884), a novel, and in 1890 the exhaustive ten-volume biography, *Abraham Lincoln: A History*, which he and Nicolay, lifelong friends, had been preparing since 1865. An effective diplomat for the rest of his career, Hay was President McKinley's ambassador to Britain, secretary of state under both McKinley and Theodore Roosevelt, and responsible for the treaty which gave the USA control of the Panama Canal. A further collaboration with John Nicolay was the collection and editorship of the Abraham Lincoln papers (12 volumes, 1905).

**Haydon, Benjamin Robert** 1786–1846. The English Romantic painter and art critic was born in Plymouth and began his studies at the Royal Academy in 1807. He was the friend of Wordsworth, Keats, Hazlitt, and Lamb and published *Lectures on Painting and Design* (1844–46). His work was severely criticized by Ruskin in *Modern Painters* and his reputation has not worn well. He painted portraits of Wordsworth and Keats and Wordsworth addressed a sonnet to him. In literature he is remembered for *The Life of Haydon, from his Autobiography and Journals* (1853), which was selected from 27 volumes of his journal by the playwright Tom Taylor. Modern editions are by Edmund Blunden (The World's Classics, 1927) and Malcolm Elwin (1950).

**Hay Fever** See **Coward, Noël (Pierce)**.

**Hayward, Sir John** *c*.1564–1627. Hayward was a lawyer, educated at Pembroke College, Cambridge, who is remembered for his contribution to historical writing in English. His first book got him into trouble; this was the *First Part of the Life and Raigne of King Henrie the IIII* (1559). In it he dwelt too much on the deposition and death of Richard II for Queen Elizabeth's comfort and the dedication to Essex made matters worse. Hayward served a term of imprisonment.

He also wrote *The Lives of the III Normans, Kings of England* (1613), *The Life and Raigne of King Edward the Sixt* (1630), and *The Annales of the First Four Years of the Raigne of Queene Elizabeth* (1639). Hayward was one of the first English historians to offer a realistic interpretation of events and to examine the character and behaviour of those involved in them as a contribution to their course. Hayward was also the author of a devotional work, *The Sanctuary of a Troubled Soul*, written some time between 1601 and 1607.

**Hazard of New Fortunes, A**  A novel by William Dean Howells, first published in 1890. Dryfoos, a Pennsylvania German, discovers natural gas on his farm and becomes immensely rich. He moves to New York and, hoping to dissuade his son Conrad from entering the ministry, finances a magazine called *Every Other Week*. He leaves the management of the magazine to Fulkerson, who engages Basil March (a character who appears in other novels by Howells) as his editor. March takes an ageing German socialist, Lindau, on to his staff. Dryfoos, meanwhile, is busy trying to find an entry into society for his two daughters; he objects to the views of Lindau and resents his influence on Conrad. When he demands the dismissal of the old man both Fulkerson and March oppose him, to his wrath; but Lindau resigns. Later, during a strike of streetcar drivers and conductors, Lindau attempts to mediate and he is attacked; Conrad tries to help him but a stray bullet kills him, while Lindau dies from the beating he has suffered. Dryfoos pays for the old man's funeral, though he is prostrated by the loss of his son. However, he decides that his daughters' progress into society will be swifter in another country; so he sells the magazine to Fulkerson and March and departs for Europe.

**Hazlitt, William**  1778–1830. The son of William Hazlitt, a Unitarian minister, Hazlitt was born at Maidstone in Kent. Hazlitt senior was a man of considerable ability and independence of mind, who at one stage moved his family to America in the belief that his ideals of personal liberty could find true expression there. After three years he found America wanting and returned to become minister at Wem, in Shropshire. The young William, now ten years old, grew up in Wem and lived there for most of the next 12 years. Passionately fond of nature, he became a solitary walker, tramping into Wales and as far as Peterborough. When Hazlitt was 15 his father sent him to the Nonconformist seminary, Hackney College, just east of London; here he enjoyed metaphysical speculation but also discovered that the ministry was not for him. His brother John was working in Sir Joshua Reynolds' studio and William, a frequent visitor, was fascinated. After a year at school he returned home without any definite ideas for his future, but at the age of 18 he read Edmund Burke's *A Letter to a Noble Lord* and grew ambitious to be a writer.

In the same year (1796) Hazlitt met Coleridge, and through him Wordsworth. But his fascination with painting persisted, and after some weeks in London with his brother John he spent several months in Paris copying paintings. His liking for art and metaphysics stayed with him all his life: his perceptive eye and disciplined mind were of great value to him as a critic. Back in London he spent much time with Charles and Mary Lamb (a friendship that stemmed from his acquaintance with Coleridge and Southey) and in 1808 married Sarah Stoddart, Mary's friend. Sarah owned a cottage at Winterslow, near Salisbury, where the couple lived; but the marriage failed and after three years Hazlitt spent little time there. Meanwhile he had published *An Essay on the Principles of Human Action* (1805), *Free Thoughts on Public Affairs* (1806), and *A Reply to the Essay on Population by the Rev T. R. Malthus* (1807). Now he began to write for reviews, periodicals, and newspapers: *The Morning Chronicle*, *The Examiner*, *The Edinburgh Review*, *The Champion*, *The Times*, and *The London Magazine* were all, during his comparatively short life, graced by his work. He was a radical and though he admired the poetry of Coleridge and Wordsworth he despised their eventual conservatism. Hazlitt was ten years old at the time of the French Revolution and held all his life to the conviction that it was essentially the dawn of a new era, even when it fell short of expectations. His critical integrity, however, remained steadfast: few men were more conservative than Sir Walter Scott, whom Hazlitt honoured as the greatest and wisest novelist of his day.

In 1810 Hazlitt completed the unfinished *Memoirs of the Late Thomas Holcroft* (not published until 1816) and in 1817 he published two volumes of essays, *The Round Table* and *Characters of Shakespeare's Plays*. The essays on 'literature, men and manners' in *The Round Table* first appeared in John and Leigh Hunt's *The Examiner*; the collection reveals an individualist who commanded a clear and vigorous prose style. Hazlitt is lively and provocative, and, necessarily, subjective: 'I endeavour to recollect all I have ever observed or thought upon a subject, and to express it as nearly as I can.' It is Hazlitt's personal view that is so interesting.

*Characters of Shakespeare's Plays*, Hazlitt's first volume of literary criticism, is a collection of lectures. His dramatic criticism began in 1813 in *The Morning Chronicle* and his qualifications were of the best; to his ability as a descriptive and reflective writer he added a great love of the theatre. He loved Shakespeare and held none of the 18th century's reservations regarding Shakespeare and the 'rules' of drama. Hazlitt's infectious enthusiasm communicates more to the reader than can a dozen careful academic studies. His *A View of the English Stage* (1818) is a collection of dramatic criticism contributed to various papers and provides a vivid record of the theatre from 1813 to 1818; his writings about acting are totally original and to read him on Kean, Sarah Siddons, the Kembles, Macready, and Booth is to experience an arresting certainty of their capacity as players.

Shakespeare is further considered in *Lectures on the English Poets* (1818), completing Hazlitt's appreciation of the master. Pope, Swift, Collins, Gray, Thomson, and Chatterton are also discussed; Spenser is the sole Elizabethan apart from Shakespeare; he also writes about Rogers, Campbell, Moore, Byron, and Scott. Hazlitt deals fairly with Wordsworth in spite of his personal feelings and, having done so, comments on Coleridge and Southey. *Lectures on the English Comic Writers* (1819) is a wide-ranging study, covering the Elizabethans, the Restoration, and 18th-century essayists and novels: Hazlitt was the first major critic to discuss the work of Richardson, Fielding, Smollett, and Sterne.

Regular collections followed and Hazlitt's range and quality increased with *Political Essays, with Sketches of Public Characters* (1819), *The Dramatic Literature of the Age of Elizabeth* (1820), and *Table Talk: or Original Essays* (1821–22). *Liber Amoris: or The New Pygmalion* (1823) is an autobiographical record of his infatuation with Sarah Walker, his landlord's daughter. He was divorced from Sarah Stoddart in 1822; his newfound sentimental passion was not a good choice of subject and Hazlitt's account is a puzzling exercise that only wholehearted confession might have redeemed. After his involvement with Miss Walker Hazlitt married again (1824) but his second wife left him in 1827.

Essays on art formed the substance of *Sketches of the Principal Picture-Galleries in England* (1824), *Notes of a Journey through France and Italy* (1826), and *Conversations of James Northcote Esq. R.A.* (1830). Fine painting affected Hazlitt in the same way as did fine poetry and he brought the same

William Hazlitt. Portrait by W. Bewick, 1825. National Portrait Gallery, London.

individual honesty to his appraisal. He recognized the genius of Turner long before Ruskin did.

His famous work, *The Spirit of the Age: or Contemporary Portraits* (1825), is indeed a mirror of his times. He discusses his contemporaries in relation to their work, giving some remarkable physical descriptions, well observed by his trained eye. Criticism is laced with wit, at times to devastating effect. Posterity has found little room for disagreement with Hazlitt's reviews of his contemporaries: Charles Lamb, Jeremy Bentham, William Godwin, Coleridge, Wordsworth, Southey, Scott, William Gifford, and the rest.

*The Plain Speaker: Opinions on Books, Men and Things* (1826) and *The Life of Napoleon Buonaparte* (1828–30) were also published during Hazlitt's lifetime. His son William edited *Literary Remains of the Late William Hazlitt* (1836) and *Sketches and Essays, now first Collected by his Son* (1839); *Winterslow: Essays and Characters written there, Collected by his Son* (1850) contains the hitherto unpublished *My First Acquaintance with Poets*, probably Hazlitt's most famous single essay.

Written in 1823, it describes his meeting with Coleridge and Wordsworth in 1798 and the importance it was to have for him.

Hazlitt's principal interests were literature, painting, philosophy, and politics: much pleasure is afforded to the reader by his positive response, for he is never merely clever or destructive. He is sometimes angry, and his Nonconformist background provides a necessary independence of judgment, so that his writings continue to live and to please.

A complete collection of Hazlitt's works was nearly achieved by his son (12 volumes, 1838–51); seven volumes were edited by his grandson William Carew Hazlitt (1869–86). The first *Collected Works* was edited by A. R. Waller and A. Glover (1902–06); this was superseded by *The Complete Works*, edited by P. P. Howe (1930–34). Separate books in modern editions are *Characters of Shakespeare's Plays* (Everyman's Library and The World's Classics); *The Spirit of the Age* (The World's Classics) is also published together with *Lectures on the English Comic Poets* (Everyman's Library). *Table Talk* is in Everyman's Library, as is *The Round Table* (with *Characters of Shakespeare's Plays*). Recommended selections are by George Sampson (1917), Geoffrey L. Keynes (1930), C. M. Maclean (1949), and R. Vallance and J. Hampden (1964).

**Headlong Hall** The first novel of Thomas Love Peacock, published in 1816. The setting is Squire Headlong's house party at Christmas and the book is chiefly taken up by the conversation of the characters present. There is scarcely any plot, but telling a story was not the author's purpose: this novel is the first essay into satire, for which Peacock was to continue to use the vehicle of prose fiction. The character of Mr Foster, the 'perfectibilian', represents the youthful Shelley.

**Headstone, Bradley** In Dickens's *Our Mutual Friend*, the schoolmaster who takes up Charley Hexam as his special pupil and falls in love with Charley's sister, Lizzie. His jealousy of Wrayburn leads him to make a murderous attack on the latter.

**Hearn, Lafcadio** 1850–1904. Hearn, the son of an Irish surgeon serving in the British army and his Greek wife, was born on the Ionian island of Levkas (formerly Santa Maura). He was educated by the Jesuits at Ushaw College and emigrated to the USA at the age of 19. He lived on his wits for a time and eventually became a journalist, working in Cincinnati and New Orleans. Hearn moved to St Pierre in Martinique in 1887 and lived there for two years. The ex-

perience of life there is recorded in *Two Years in the French West Indies* and in a forgotten novel called *Youma* (both 1890).

In 1890 Hearn went to Japan, commissioned to write a series of articles for an American publisher. He stayed there for the rest of his life: he married the daughter of a Samurai family, took the name of Koizumi Yakumo, and became Professor of English at Tokyo University. The books Hearn wrote after 1890 interpreted Japan to the West and he proved adept at conveying the beliefs, customs, scenery, and atmosphere of his adopted country.

Hearn was handicapped by partial blindness but he succeeded in a varied and exotic career. Before going to Japan he published, in addition to the two books already mentioned, *One of Cleopatra's Nights* (stories translated from the French of Gautier, 1882), *Stray Leaves from Strange Literature* (1884), *Gombo Zhebes* (Creole proverbs, 1885), *Some Chinese Ghosts* (1885), *Chita: A Memory of Last Island* (1889), and *Karma* (fiction, 1890). From Japan came, among other books, *Out of the East* (1895), *Kokoro* (1896), *In Ghostly Japan* (1899), *Shadowings* (1900), *A Japanese Miscellany* (1901), and *Japan: An Attempt at Interpretation* (1904); the best-known and most highly regarded was *Glimpses of Unfamiliar Japan* (1894).

**Hearne, Thomas** 1678–1735. Hearne, who became the second Keeper of the Bodleian Library (1712), was born at Littlefield Green, in Berkshire, and educated at St Edmund Hall, Oxford. He was deprived of his office, as a Nonjuror, in 1716 and thereafter refused invitation to political office of any kind, adhering to his Jacobite convictions.

Hearne was the author of *Reliquiae Bodleianae, or Some Genuine Remains of Sir Thomas Bodley* (1703) and *Ductor Historicus, or a Short System of Universal History and an Introduction to the Study of it* (1704–05); he was the editor of a valuable series of texts by English chroniclers and published editions of John Leland and William Camden.

**Heartbreak House** A play in three acts by George Bernard Shaw, subtitled 'A Fantasia in the Russian Manner on English Themes'. The author began the play before World War I but it was not produced until November 1920, at the Garrick Theatre, New York. The first London performance was at the Court Theatre, October 1921. The play was published in 1919 and the action takes place, ostensibly, during the war since it closes during an air raid. But the war is not mentioned by any of the characters and the air raid has to be seen as a device to bring about a resolution. Shaw wrote that 'Heartbreak House ... is cultured, leisured Europe before the war'. He presents a series of extraordinary encounters and mistaken identities in a crazy house (part of which has been rebuilt as the after-deck of a sailing ship) owned by the eccentric retired Captain Shotover, aged 88, and presided over by one of his daughters, Mrs Hector Hushabye. She invites her friend, Ellie Dunn, to stay. Ellie Dunn is engaged to Boss Mangan, an oaf of a millionaire, for the sake of her father Mazzini Dunn who, though clever and an idealist, has been out-manoeuvred by financiers. Ellie confides to Mrs Hushabye that she has fallen in love with Marcus Darnley, whom she met at a concert; but he turns out to be Hector Hushabye, a pathological liar and philanderer. Captain Shotover wonders if Ellie's father can be the boatswain and ex-pirate he once employed; but that man, Billy Dunn, turns up to burgle the house and be killed in the air raid with Boss Mangan. Another visitor to the house is Lady Utterword, another of the captain's daughters, whose husband has been governor of all the Crown Colonies in succession. The play is rather long, for its farcical character, and the final curtain is not very certain. Its great virtue lies in the exploration of motive in a very uncertain world, mostly through the conversations between Captain Shotover and Ellie; she seems able to focus his sympathy and intelligence better than anyone and provokes his fascinating comments on the present, which he observes from the eminence of his great age.

**Heart is a Lonely Hunter, The** See **McCullers, Carson**.

**Heart of Darkness** A story by Joseph Conrad, written in 1899 and first published in 1902 in the volume called *Youth: A Narrative, and Two Other Stories*. In this story Conrad first used the narrator Marlow, who next appears in the novel *Lord Jim*.

Marlow is appointed by a European trading company to command one of their river steamers in Africa; the captain has been killed by natives. He arrives at the trading-station up river in the Congo; the company is building a railway in the face of crippling difficulties and the Africans, in forced labour, are dying like flies. He hears of Kurtz, an apparently remarkable person and a brilliantly successful ivory trader in charge of the farthest trading-post. The White traders hate him for his success and have isolated him in the hope that he will die in the merciless climate. Marlow is obliged to tramp 200 miles with carriers to find the Central Station and his ship, which he finds grounded in a backwater. Raising it and repairing it take months, during which time Marlow hears more about Kurtz from the man's only White associate.

When Marlow draws closer to the farthest station the steamer is attacked and a hail of arrows pours from the jungle. Gunfire from the ship has no effect but the attackers flee in panic at blasts from the steam whistle. By now Marlow has learned that Kurtz is a man depraved and perverted; he has made himself a godlike figure and the centre of unnameable rites. Now he is mortally ill and is brought to the steamer on a stretcher. He tries to get away, crawling back into the jungle on hands and knees, but he is taken down river, raving. Marlow hears the hollow, lofty statements with which Kurtz covers his total surrender to evil; but Kurtz cannot deceive himself and the horror overcomes him as he dies. Marlow, observing the rapacity and meanness of the traders who are his passengers, and who are there to plunder, feels more in tune with the evil grandeur of Kurtz than with the moral jackals around him, and it is their evil that he finds at work when he returns to Europe. But he recognizes that Kurtz – an oblique figure, Conrad gives him no real outlines – is a hollow man; where the heart's response should lie there is only darkness. Kurtz lived out his days in the heart of darkness, in the heart of a continent where the White man, without fear of observation or correction, could descend to the depths of greed and exploitation.

**Heart of Midlothian, The** A novel by Sir Walter Scott, which formed the second series of *Tales of My Landlord* and was published in 1818.

The heart of Midlothian is the Tolbooth prison, and the story opens with the Porteous Riots of 1736. Porteous, commander of the city guard, had opened fire without reasonable provocation at the hanging of a robber named Wilson. Porteous was acquitted at his trial but the mob, led by Robertson (an associate of Wilson), stormed the prison. Robertson loves Effie Deans, imprisoned within on a charge of child murder, and the attack on the prison thus has a double motive for him. The mob drags Porteous from the prison and lynches him; Effie refuses to escape, preferring to face trial, knowing herself innocent. But at her trial her sister Jeanie, having taken the oath, cannot bring herself to lie and thus ensure Effie's acquittal. Effie is convicted and sentenced to death.

Jeanie sets out to walk to London to gain audience with Queen Caroline and is fortunate in having the help of the Duke of Argyle. The ·queen is moved by Jeanie's honesty and believes her, and a pardon is secured for Effie. Jeanie is enabled to marry her suitor, Reuben Butler.

Robertson, who was in the forefront of the attack on the Tolbooth, is now revealed as George Staunton, a rather wild son of good family and the father of Effie's child. He persuades Effie to marry him and, as Lady Staunton, she receives intelligence that her son, whom she was accused of murdering, is alive. He had been stolen by the midwife's insane daughter, Madge Wildfire, and was eventually left with a band of robbers. Staunton is unwittingly killed by his own son when he tries to get him back from the robber band.

*The Heart of Midlothian* is Scott's finest novel and Jeanie Deans is the most perfectly realized of all his characters. The attack on the Tolbooth, at midnight, is magnificently done and the historical period perfectly caught. Memorable, too, are the trial of Effie and the agony of the sisters and their father.

**Heart of the Matter, The**   See **Greene, (Henry) Graham**.

**Heathcliff**   The central character of Emily Brontë's *Wuthering Heights*. He is brought home, a Gypsy waif, by Mr Earnshaw who finds him in the streets of Liverpool. His love for Catherine Earnshaw is the total motivation of his life: her marriage to Edgar Linton awakes in him a thirst for revenge that eventually exhausts his spirit.

**Heaven's My Destination**   See **Wilder, Thornton (Niven)**.

**Heber, Reginald** 1783–1826.   The son of the rector of Malpas in Cheshire, Heber was educated at Brasenose College, Oxford, and won the Newdigate Prize with his poem 'Palestine' in 1807. He was made a fellow of All Souls, was ordained in 1807, and became vicar of Hodnet in Shropshire. In 1823 Heber became Bishop of Calcutta and he died in Trichinopoly four years later. He was the author of a *Narrative of a Journey through the Upper Provinces of India 1824–1825*, a number of poems, and some hymns by which he is perhaps best remembered: 'Brightest and best of the sons of the morning!', 'From Greenland's icy mountains', 'The Son of God goes forth to war', 'Holy, Holy, Holy! Lord God Almighty!', and others. Heber published an edition of *The Whole Works of Jeremy Taylor* (1822).

**Heep, Uriah**   The fawning, crooked villain of Dickens's *David Copperfield*. He is Mr Wickfield's clerk, and under the guise of knowing his 'umble place cheats and robs his employer and aspires to the hand of his daughter Agnes. He is unmasked by Traddles and Micawber.

**Heiress, The**   A comedy by John Burgoyne, first produced at Drury Lane in January 1786, and published in the same year. It was a great success and was quickly translated and played in France and Germany. The plot concerns the wooing of Lady Emily Gayville by Clifford, her brother's close friend. Lord Gayville himself is expected to marry the vulgar Miss Alscrip, daughter of a newly rich family, because of her wealth. When Miss Alscrip is introduced to Emily, Gayville is made painfully aware of how silly and pretentious his fiancée is. Then he encounters a girl in the street, Miss Alton, and loses his heart to her. He follows her to her modest lodging and is so eager that he embarrasses her; to escape his attentions she goes into service – with Miss Alscrip. All ends well when she is discovered to be Clifford's long-lost sister, and the true heiress to the Alscrip fortune.

**Heir of Redclyffe, The**   A novel by Charlotte M. Yonge, first published in 1853.

Sir Guy Marville, heir of Redclyffe, pays the debts of a disreputable uncle and is accused of gambling by his malicious cousin, Philip. Guy is in love with Amy, his guardian's daughter, but the unexplained financial shortfall is looked on with extreme disfavour. Guy refuses to betray his uncle, and his guardian, believing the worst, banishes him from the house.

Guy's uncle intervenes when he hears what has happened, and Guy, meanwhile, has been able to save the lives of some shipwrecked sailors. Rehabilitated, Guy marries Amy and they go to Italy on their honeymoon. They find Guy's cousin there, dangerously ill with fever. Guy not only forgives him – he nurses him back to health too. Then, having caught the fever from Philip, he dies. Philip, transformed by Guy's generosity and goodness, becomes the heir of Redclyffe.

**Helena** (i)   Hermia's friend and in love with Demetrius – who spurns her – in Shakespeare's *A Midsummer Night's Dream*. She follows him when he goes in pursuit of Hermia and Lysander.

**Helena** (ii)   The iron-willed heroine of Shakespeare's *All's Well that Ends Well*. She cures the sick King of France and, when he offers to reward her, demands the hand of Bertram, son of her guardian, the Countess of Rousillon. Bertram doesn't want her and makes it plain, but Helena wants him and he cannot oppose the king. Bertram denies her his bed but she tricks herself into it – Bertram, in fact, hasn't a chance against a woman like Helena.

**Heller, Joseph** 1923– . Heller was born in Brooklyn and served as a bombardier in the US Air Force during World War II. After the war Heller studied literature at the universities of New York, Columbia, and Oxford and enjoyed a successful career as an advertising and promotions manager for leading American magazines. His first novel, *Catch-22* (1961), a bitter and compassionate satire of army life and personal greed, made use of his wartime experiences and made him world-famous: the title has entered the language as a catch phrase. Since then Heller has published two more novels, *Something Happened* (1974) and *Good as Gold* (1979). He is the author of two plays, *We Bombed in New Haven* (1967) and *Clevinger's Trial* (1974). Joseph Heller is now Instructor in English at Pennsylvania State University.

**Hellman, Lillian** 1905–84. Lillian Hellman was born in New Orleans and completed her education at the universities of New York State and Columbia. Her first play, *The Children's Hour* (1934), was a success and marked the arrival of a playwright of acute intelligence and careful workmanship. *The Children's Hour* tells of the havoc caused by a malicious schoolgirl's defamation of her teachers; the personal drama is heightened by Lillian Hellman's attention to the social attitudes which nourish the supposed case against the accused. Her next play, *Days to Come* (1936), concerned a strike and was a failure but *The Little Foxes* (1939), about a vulgar and predatory family of Southern industrialists, more than fulfilled the promise of her first play. *Watch on the Rhine* (1941) dramatized the struggle of an anti-Nazi leader, who faces betrayal on the neutral ground of America. The playwright succeeded remarkably well in producing a moving story as well as a warning that the USA was concerned in the danger to liberty which the Nazis represented. *The Searching Wind* (1944) is a play about the 1930s and the spineless appeasement which contributed to the rise of fascism. *Another Part of the Forest* (1946) concerns the predatory family of *The Little Foxes*; here they are in earlier days, sharpening their teeth on each other. Other plays by Lillian Hellman are *The Autumn Garden* (1951) and *Toys in the Attic* (1960). Autobiographical volumes are *An Unfinished Woman* (1969), *Pentimento* (1973), and *Scoundrel Time* (1978).

The playwright was a radical liberal in her politics and like many of her colleagues was ordered to appear before the Un-American Activities Committee in 1952. She refused to testify against friends and colleagues; the ugly episode is related in *Scoundrel Time*.

**Hemans, Felicia Dorothea** 1793–1835. Felicia Dorothea Browne was the daughter of a merchant of Liverpool, where her first works, *Poems* and *England and Spain*, were published in 1808. *The Domestic Affections, and Other Poems* (1812) appeared in the year of her marriage to Captain Alfred Hemans; the marriage was unhappy and ended in separation in 1818. Mrs Hemans went to live in Dublin in 1832 and became a well-known literary figure. She had continued writing and by then had published 16 further books of verse; she published three more and left a considerable number behind when she died. She was well liked and even admired to some degree by Wordsworth and Byron, and by Scott – who arranged the production of her play, *The Vespers of Palermo*, at Edinburgh in 1824. Mrs Hemans was a regular contributor to periodicals such as *Blackwood's Magazine* and *The Edinburgh Monthly Magazine*; she had a considerable following in America but is remembered now for a handful of poems, including 'Casabianca', 'The Better Land', and 'The Hour of Death'. A minor poet, she enjoyed considerable success during her lifetime but has since been read less and less.

**Hemingway, Ernest (Miller)** 1898–1961. Ernest Hemingway was born at Oak Park, Illinois, and his background was the American wilderness of the Great Lakes region. After school he worked as a reporter for a newspaper in Kansas City, and there volunteered for service in World War I. He served with an ambulance unit and was wounded near the Austro-Italian frontier in 1918. The experience, and his father's suicide, gave him a preoccupation with the vulnerability of man and man's efforts to confront it, which coloured all his writing. After the war he was a journalist in Chicago and Toronto, and married Hadley Richardson, seven years his senior, in 1921. Her income enabled them to live in Paris, visit Spain so that Hemingway could watch bullfights, and ski in the Austrian alps. He sent articles to the Toronto *Star* and was paid for the ones that were printed.

Hemingway made friends easily. He was completely dedicated to a literary career and among those who helped him realize it were Ezra Pound, Gertrude Stein, Sylvia Beach, and Ford Madox Ford. Scott Fitzgerald, before meeting him, recommended his work to his editor, Maxwell Perkins of Scribners. However, it was another publisher, Liveright, who issued Hemingway's first collection of stories, *In Our Time* (1925). The 15 tales relate the boyhood of Nick Adams in the Great Lakes region: his relationship to his doctor father, the Indians, and the guides. Between the tales are vignettes of World War I and the bull-ring, and Hemingway succeeds brilliantly in im-plying the continuity he does not state. The last story about a trout-fishing trip, 'Big Two-Hearted River', takes place after the war and it is Nick's return to the healing springs of his life. The volume demonstrates all of Hemingway's remarkable gifts as a writer of prose fiction: the spare style which eschews abstraction and goes straight to the task of rendering in words the life of the senses. He gave something new to fiction in the 20th century. *The Torrents of Spring* (1926), his first novel, satirizes Sherwood Anderson, whom Hemingway had once admired but whose latest novel, *Dark Laughter*, he regarded as a worthless mechanical imitation of what had gone before. Hemingway's next work was published by Scribners, since Liveright declined *The Torrents of Spring*. It was *The Sun Also Rises* (1926) and it made the author famous. It also launched him in the lucrative field of American short-story publishing, which had yielded such rewards to Scott Fitzgerald who, incidentally, had per-suaded Hemingway to change the opening of the book.

*The Sun Also Rises* is set among English and American expatriates who live in France. Two of them are wrecks: Jake Barnes has been emasculated during the war, and Lady Brett Ash-ley has lost the man she loved in it and turned to sex and liquor. They have an agonised, frustrated love for each other. They move in a crowd of people who do no work, drink too much, and sleep around, and it is only when real values intrude that Brett is put to the test: she renounces Pedro Romero, the young bullfighter she loves, because she knows she would ruin him. Jake is honest, and true to his own feelings: that is the best he can do but that is what makes him, in spite of everything, a real man. In contrast to them, and to Pedro, is the writer Robert Cohn, who is in love with Brett and viciously jealous of Pedro. Cohn has no validity as a man because he has nothing authentic about him: he is not true to his feelings, he is at the mercy of them. The centre of the novel is the fiesta at Pamplona, brilliantly described in Hemingway's terse, vivid style.

*Men Without Women* (1927) contains 14 short stories and among them are 3 of Hemingway's best. 'The Killers' tells of Anderson, whom two thugs have been hired to kill, and his surrender to the fact that his death is inescapable. 'The Un-defeated' tells of the pointless heroism of Garcia, an aging bullfighter, and his last fight. 'Fifty Grand' is a brutal and cynical tale of prizefighters and how Jack Brennan bets fifty grand on his own defeat. *A Farewell to Arms* (1929) is for many

readers the finest of all Hemingway's books, a short novel in which the familiar style served him perfectly and to which was added great poignancy. The simple story is related by Frederic Henry, an American lieutenant in the Italian ambulance ser-vice during World War I. He and Catherine Barkley, an English nurse, fall in love. When Henry is wounded and sent to a hospital in Milan, it is Catherine who nurses him and their love progresses while he recovers. Catherine becomes pregnant but she will not marry him, fearing that she will be sent back to England if she does. Henry returns to the front in 1917 and is involved in the horror and suffering of the disas-ter at Caporetto and the subsequent retreat. Henry deserts – he makes a separate peace – and goes to Stresa in civilian clothes; Catherine has been transferred there. He is suspected, and he and Catherine flee into neutral Switzerland across the lake at night. Catherine dies in child-birth, her baby dies too, and Henry is alone. The retreat from Caporetto is perhaps Hemingway's finest piece of descriptive writing and the dilem-ma of the young lovers is intensely moving. When they say their farewell to arms they can only do it by opting out of society, and their separate peace has no future.

*Winner Take Nothing* (1933) contains another 14 stories, of less consistent quality than *Men Without Women* but with definite rewards nonetheless: 'A Clean Well-Lighted Place', 'The Sea Change', and 'A Natural History of the Dead' are among them. But Hemingway the art-ist who gave a new direction to fictional style began to give way to The Hemingway Legend. *Death in the Afternoon* (1932) is a study of bull-fighting; *The Green Hills of Africa* (1935) is about safari and big-game hunting. *To Have and Have Not* (1937) is a short novel about smuggling in the Caribbean, cobbled from short stories. The manner that Max Eastman described as 'false hair on the chest' replaced the great original and only *The Fifth Column and The First Forty-Nine Stories* (1938) demonstrated the master's hand in two stories, 'The Snows of Kilimanjaro' and 'The Short Happy Life of Francis Macomber'. *The Fifth Column* is a play about espionage in the Spanish Civil War and was produced in New York and in wartime England. The Spanish Civil War, in which Hemingway was involved as a war reporter, provided the background for *For Whom the Bell Tolls* (1940), an ambitious novel with the theme, implied in the title, that the loss of freedom anywhere is a diminution of it everywhere. The author was at the height of his fame and every word he wrote fetched a high price; 270,000 copies were sold in the first year of publication. In spite of some fine things the novel is too long for Hemingway the artist to sustain and the dialogue is often painful, a laboured attempt to render Spanish speech forms in English.

During World War II Hemingway was a war correspondent in France, and in 1950 published his first novel for ten years, *Across the River and Into the Trees*. It was badly received, but with *The Old Man and The Sea* (1952) he produced a fine story about a Cuban fisherman and his struggle to bring home a great marlin he has caught, and the most celebrated American writer became a Nobel Prize winner in 1954. In the years left to him Hemingway struggled with failing powers, artistic and physical. He found it a torment that writing was increasingly difficult and the active outdoor life, which was so essentially a part of him, was being curbed more and more. *A Moveable Feast*, a memoir of his days in Paris, was complete and Hemingway was planning to revise it in the spring of 1961. He shot himself at his home in Ketchum, Idaho, on 2 July of the same year.

The memoir was published in 1964 and might have been better left among his papers. It is a book of recollections, written down 30 years

Ernest Hemingway, 1944.

later from the isolation and uncertainty of failing powers. The Hemingway legend remains intact but the characters of others are badly mauled. *Islands in the Stream* (1970), a novel, was also left unrevised, and does not affect the author's reputation one way or the other.

**Henchard, Michael** The central character of Thomas Hardy's *The Mayor of Casterbridge*. He becomes mayor of Casterbridge (Dorchester) through hard work and is a successful merchant until shadows emerge from his past.

**Henley, William Ernest** 1849–1903. Henley, the son of a bookseller, was born in Gloucester and educated at the Crypt Grammar School in that city. He suffered a severe tubercular illness when he was 12 years old and as a result he lost a foot; later he was threatened with a recurrence and was only saved from a further amputation after nearly two years in the Edinburgh Infirmary. It was while in Edinburgh that Henley met Stevenson, with whom he collaborated and later quarrelled. His hospital experiences found expression in *Hospital Verses*, first published in *The Cornhill* (1875) and later in volume form (1903), containing the famous 'Invictus' ('Out of the night that covers me').

Henley collaborated with Stevenson on the plays *Deacon Brodie* (1880), *Admiral Guinea* (1884), *Beau Austin* (1884), and *Macaire* (1885). A busy journalist with pronounced imperialist tendencies, he promoted *The National Observer* (it had been a modest Edinburgh journal called *Scots Observer*) to provide an outlet for his ideas and was an ardent champion of the young Kipling. Henley is not numbered among the major talents of the late 19th century, but as the author of 'Invictus' and 'England, my England' he is likely to be remembered. Among his other books of verse are *A Book of Verses* (1888), *The Song of the Sword* (1892), *London Voluntaries* (1893), *Hawthorn and Lavender* (1893), and *For England's Sake* (1900).

**Henrietta Temple** A novel by Benjamin Disraeli, first published in 1837.

Ferdinand Armine, son of poor but noble parents, enters the army and is soon in debt; but he has hopes of a legacy from his grandfather. When this does not materialize, he proposes to his cousin, Katherine Grandison, because she is wealthy. But he falls in love with the penniless Henrietta Temple – and becomes engaged to her, too. When Ferdinand's perfidy is exposed uproar follows, inevitably. Henrietta leaves for Italy after an illness; Ferdinand himself nearly succumbs to brain fever.

In Italy Henrietta meets Lord Montfort; he

falls in love with her and her father presses her to marry him. Katherine, meanwhile, has forgiven Ferdinand and released him; he is fortunate in the friendship of Katherine and Count Mirabel, who do their best for him. He meets Henrietta again and her love for him is reawakened; Lord Montfort is drawn to Katherine. Lord Montfort gives up Henrietta, who inherits a fortune and succours Ferdinand. Katherine marries Lord Montfort.

**Henry IV, King**   A historical play in two parts by William Shakespeare. It was first produced *c.* 1597 and was printed in quartos: Part I in 1598 and Part 2 in 1600. It was published in the First Folio of 1623. The source of the play is acknowledged to be the chronicles of Raphael Holinshed.

*Part 1.* King Henry IV (the usurper Bolingbroke, of *Richard II*) longs for peace in the kingdom and harbours a desire to go to the Holy Land to atone for the murder of his predecessor. Invading Scots are defeated by Hotspur (Henry Percy, son of the Earl of Northumberland), who has taken a number of prisoners. Hotspur refuses to yield his captives to the king until Henry ransoms his kinsman Mortimer, a prisoner of the Welsh rebel Owen Glendower. Henry refuses because Mortimer is making claims to the throne. Meanwhile the king's son Prince Hal disappoints his father by his riotous life in the taverns with Poins, Peto, Bardolph – and Sir John Falstaff. But Hal goes to his father's side when Hotspur joins the rebellion of Glendower and commands a force at Shrewsbury (1403). He saves his father's life and kills Hotspur; he also finds Falstaff apparently dead on the field. But as soon as the coast is clear Falstaff rises and sees the body of Hotspur. He claims to have killed him, but Prince Hal knows better.

*Part 2.* Hal returns to his riotous living with Falstaff and his friends. But in spite of the defeat at Shrewsbury civil war continues, with Northumberland, Mortimer, Hastings, and Archbishop Scroop now opposing the king. Falstaff is given the task of recruiting and in Gloucestershire falls in with Justice Shallow and Silence. Shallow tries to match Falstaff in his boasting about his lusty youth and Falstaff encourages him ('We have heard the chimes at midnight, Master Shallow') so that he can continue to enjoy his hospitality. The campaign against the rebels takes a turn for the better when Northumberland deserts them; Prince John of Lancaster tricks them into dispersing their forces at Gaultree Forest. The king, worn out in mind and body, lies dying at Westminster; his conscience will not let him rest ('O sleep, O gentle sleep, Nature's

soft nurse, how have I frighted thee?'). Prince Hal comes to watch by his father and in a remarkable scene tries on the crown while the king lies in troubled sleep; but father and son are reconciled before the king dies. Falstaff is delighted that his roistering companion is now King Henry V; he borrows a thousand pounds from Shallow, now having great expectations. But his last hours with his father have wrought a change in the young king's heart and Falstaff is repudiated ('I know thee not, old man').

The comedy scenes occupy a great deal of the play and succeed when a fine actor plays the fat knight. Falstaff is a splendid comic character but Shakespeare's great achievement is in not sentimentalizing him. He is an innovation in the historical play – a fiction who equals in importance the major historical figures. The part was first played by Will Kemp and in modern theatre will always be associated with the name of Ralph Richardson. Shakespeare's genius gives us a character in the round; he demonstrates that the old rogue is the best company in the world – but dangerous company, as Hal begins to realize. Men like Falstaff are often the centre of an uncritical group of admirers but he is a liar and a coward, dishonest as well as dissolute, and in the end pitiable.

**Henry V, The Life of**   A historical play by William Shakespeare, first produced *c.*1599 and printed in an imperfect draft in a quarto in 1600. It was published in the First Folio of 1623. At the end of *Henry IV* Part 2 the audience is promised that 'our humble author will continue the story, with Sir John in it'. But Falstaff does not appear in this play – in fact he is killed off. He dies in Act II Scene 3 and his passing is related by Mistress Quickly. The reason may have been that Will Kemp, who created the part, had left the company: but Shakespeare may have been obliged to exclude him because of pressure from the descendants of Sir John Oldcastle, on whom the figure of Falstaff was based.

Henry V is free of the doubts that tormented his father; to be a king is his rightful destiny and he will press his claims to France. The roistering companions of his youth are still together but Falstaff, whom the king rejected when he came to the throne, dies and the others – Nym, Bardolph, and Pistol – go with the army to France. Before embarking, King Henry deals with the plot of Scroop, Grey, and Cambridge, who are arrested for treason. The invasion of France and the siege and capture of Harfleur follow; the campaign reaches its climax at the Battle of Agincourt and a great victory (1415). Henry woos and marries Katharine, princess of France. The antics of Pistol and the rest provide a comic subplot.

The play succeeds because Shakespeare's genius makes it infinitely more than an exhibition of patriotic fervour. It is that, certainly, but it is full of poetry and, from a man who never went to war, of remarkable observation. The eve of Agincourt is profoundly moving and the part played by the ordinary soldier, with his apprehensions of the morrow, a major factor in its effect. A notable comic scene is Pistol's discomfiture at the hands of the doughty Welsh captain, Fluellen – 'if you can mock a leek, you can eat a leek'.

*Henry VI* A trilogy of historical plays by William Shakespeare, probably the first work of his to be performed. Scholars believe they have detected the work of Lodge, Nashe, Marlowe, Kyd, and others in the published text of the First Folio of 1623. The play was produced *c*.1592 and parts of it appeared in quartos without the author's name long before the First Folio: Part 2 in 1594 as *The First Part of the Contention Betwixt the Two Famous Houses of Yorke and Lancaster*; Part 3 in 1595 as *The True Tragedie of Richard, Duke of Yorke, and the Death of Good King Henrie the Sixt*. The most likely sources of the trilogy are the chronicles of Edward Hall and Raphael Holinshed.

*Part 1.* Henry V is dead and his infant son succeeds him. Henry VI's kingdom is administered by his uncles, John, Duke of Bedford, and Humphrey, Duke of Gloucester. The French have reopened the war and the hitherto victorious English are driven back by the resurgent French under Joan la Pucelle (Joan of Arc). The major figure of the English army is Talbot, Earl of Shrewsbury, who is killed at Bordeaux with his son. In England, meanwhile, Richard Plantagenet secures his claim to the title of Duke of York and quarrels with the Beauforts, a powerful family related to the young king. The incident in the Temple garden where the two factions select a white rose for York and a red rose for Lancaster (Act II, Scene 4) was invented by Shakespeare. To seal a truce in the war with France, a marriage is arranged between Henry VI and the daughter of the wealthy Count of Armagnac. But the Earl of Suffolk persuades Henry to take Margaret, daughter of the Duke of Anjou, instead.

*Part 2.* Suffolk, now raised to a dukedom, is Margaret's lover and between them they control the king. They plot to overthrow the Protector, Humphrey of Gloucester; first they discredit him through his wife's dabbling in witchcraft, then Suffolk plots with the Beauforts to have him murdered. The murder is done but Suffolk is known to be guilty and executed. The Duke of York convinces the earls of Salisbury and Warwick of his right to the throne: he is directly descended from Edward III, while Henry VI is merely the grandson of the usurper Bolingbroke. York encourages the rebellion of Jack Cade and leaves for Ireland to suppress a revolt. When he

An illustration from Holinshed's *Chronicles*, 1577. The Duke of Burgundy besieging Calais during the reign of Henry VI.

returns to England he opens the civil war and wins the first victory, defeating the king's army at St Albans (1455).

*Part 3.* Henry VI, defeated by York, asks to be allowed to keep the throne for his lifetime. York agrees, but it will mean that Margaret's son will be disinherited. The queen raises an army and defeats York at Wakefield (1460), in spite of the efforts of York's sons Edward and Richard. York's other son, Edmund of Rutland, is killed by the queen's forces. After her victory Margaret impales the head of York on that city's gate 'So York may overlook the town of York'. York's sons Edward and Richard avenge their family at Towton (1461) and Margaret, with Henry and the Prince of Wales, flees to Scotland. Edward mounts the throne as Edward IV and Henry is captured and imprisoned in the Tower when he returns to England. Edward and Warwick quarrel over Edward's marriage to Elizabeth Grey; but at the final reckoning (Tewkesbury, 1471) the house of York wins the day. The Prince of Wales is killed and Edward's brother Richard, now Duke of Gloucester, murders Henry VI in the Tower. Margaret is banished. In the closing scenes Gloucester is already identified as the dark villain of *Richard III*.

**Henry VIII, The Life of King** A historical play by William Shakespeare, with the help of a collaborator acknowledged to have been John Fletcher. It was first produced in 1613 and it was during a performance of *Henry VIII* that the Globe caught fire and burned down. It was first published in the First Folio of 1623.

After the Field of the Cloth of Gold the Duke of Buckingham is disturbed at the growing power of Cardinal Wolsey and wants to warn the king to beware of him. But Wolsey succeeds in bringing a charge of treason against Buckingham and the duke is executed. The play proceeds with Henry pressing for a divorce and Queen Katherine's immovable but dignified resistance to it; Wolsey's opposition to Henry's plans to marry Anne Bullen and his fall from power; the death of Wolsey, while under arrest for treason, and Cranmer's annulment of the king's marriage to Katherine; the marriage of the king to Anne Bullen and the attempt, which fails, of the jealous nobles to discredit Cranmer; and finally the death of Katherine and the birth of the Princess Elizabeth.

The play is unbalanced; the great weight of sympathy goes to Katherine, who has the most memorable scene in it and leaves the audience with little interest in, or sympathy with, anyone else but the cardinal, who, if he is not sympath-

etic, is certainly interesting. Henry, Anne Bullen, and Cranmer are very dull in contrast. *Henry VIII* came at the end of Shakespeare's career and it is tempting to see his contribution to it as a favour performed out of loyalty to his company.

**Henry Esmond, Esq., The History of** A novel by W. M. Thackeray, first published in 1852. It was the only one of his novels which was not first printed in serial parts. The story is set in the time of Queen Anne and told in the first person by Esmond himself.

Henry Esmond, illegitimate son of the 3rd Viscount Castlewood, killed at the Battle of the Boyne, enters the service of the 4th Viscount as a page. Lord and Lady Castlewood are kind to him and he becomes devoted to Lady Castlewood (Rachel). Henry is the unconscious agent of an outbreak of smallpox in the household to which Rachel falls victim. She loses some of her beauty and finds her husband apparently less devoted than formerly. Relations between the Castlewoods are strained to the point of bitterness, and the sinister Lord Mohun takes advantage of their estrangement to try and seduce Rachel. He is discovered by Lord Castlewood; Henry, distracted by the unhappiness in a family which has treated him so well, tries to take the quarrel on himself. But a duel follows and Lord Castlewood is mortally wounded.

On his deathbed Lord Castlewood reveals that the 3rd Viscount was married to Henry's mother – Henry is the rightful heir. Henry decides to keep the secret, for Rachel and her son Frank's sake, but Rachel, shattered by what has happened, reproaches him violently for letting the duel take place and turns him out of the house. Henry enlists as a soldier and fights under Marlborough, earning distinction in the duke's great victories.

Back in England, he hears that Rachel is going to marry her chaplain, Tusher. He hurries to see her and they meet again in Winchester Cathedral. The news is false: in fact Rachel loves Henry deeply but she is Henry's senior by eight years, and her children are now grown up. Her daughter Beatrix is exquisitely beautiful and Henry falls in love with her; Rachel keeps her feelings to herself and remains silent when Beatrix, selfish and ambitious, rejects him – an illegitimate son is beneath her. Henry's infatuation for her, however, is not dissolved until she wilfully interferes with Frank's (the new viscount) and Henry's plans for the proclamation of Prince James Edward Stuart (the son of James II) as the rightful heir to the throne after Queen Anne. Beatrix flirts with the prince and he follows her to Castlewood when his presence in London is essential: she has thus destroyed the Stuart cause out of selfish vanity.

Henry's disillusion is followed by the disclosure of who he really is: he marries Rachel, they leave England together, and their subsequent fortunes – and those of the younger Castlewoods – are related in *The Virginians*.

*Henry Esmond* should not be thought of as a historical romance. It is a novel in a historical setting and a fine one – Thackeray's best book apart from *Vanity Fair*. His cold eye demolishes historical fancy but his own characters are in the round, acutely observed, and they dovetail with the historical ones. The selfishness and vanity of Beatrix is as deadly as her beauty: the latter wreaks havoc with Henry, while the former provides the perfect instrument for showing the worthless Pretender in his true colours. Rachel's behaviour in the prolonged crisis of her life is not commendable but it is only too believable, and her meeting with Henry after the long separation is beautifully done. Notable, too, is Thackeray's confident handling of the other historical characters: Richard Steele and his wife, Marlborough and Sarah Churchill, Joseph Addison, and Jonathan Swift.

**Henry of Bracton**  See **Bracton, Henry of.**

**Henryson, Robert** *c.*1430–1506. Of the life of this Scottish poet almost nothing is known. Apart from the appearance of his name on manuscripts and printed books there is a single reference in the work of his fellow poet William Dunbar placing him in Dunfermline: a Robert Henryson was Master of the Grammar School of the Benedictine abbey of Dunfermline, and this may have been the poet. There is also a connection of the name with the incorporation of Glasgow University in 1462, and some notarized deeds in Dunfermline bearing his name. And that is all.

Henryson was one of the small group of 15th-century Scottish poets of remarkable quality usually described as Scottish 'Chaucerians', and his work, whatever it owes his great exemplar, is rooted in his Scottish world; his imagery is drawn from everyday life in his time and is notable both for its sharp observation and rich flavour. His best-known works are *The Testament of Cresseid* (continuing the story where Chaucer leaves off), *The Morall Fabillis of Esope the Phrygian, Orpheus and Eurydice*, and an early form of the pastoral, *Robene and Makyne*.

**Henry St John, Gentleman**  See *Virginia Comedians, The.*

**Henry the Minstrel**  See **Harry, Blind.**

**Henslowe, Philip** d. 1616. The Elizabethan theatre manager was born in Lindfield, Sussex, but the year of his birth is unknown. He was settled in Southwark by 1577 and married to the widow of a dyer. She was a wealthy woman and Henslowe was able to indulge his talent for dealing in property, becoming master of inns and various small businesses. He was also a moneylender and a pawnbroker. By 1585 he had opened a theatre at Newington Butts in Surrey, not far from London Bridge; two years later he built a theatre on Bankside, the Rose, which lay conveniently across the river and was close to bear gardens and brothels.

In 1592 Henslowe's stepdaughter Joan married the foremost actor of the age, Edward Alleyn, and it was inevitable that the two men's interests would come together. Alleyn was part-owner in Henslowe's theatrical ventures and after he retired from the stage as an actor became owner, with Henslowe, of the new theatre, the Hope, which Henslowe built on Bankside. More important, Alleyn was a man of considerable wealth when he left the stage; he founded The College and Hospital of God's Gift – more familiarly known as Dulwich College. Such a gesture would never have occurred to Henslowe, who was notoriously mean, even though he was probably richer than Alleyn. But upon Henslowe's death his papers passed to Alleyn; they are now housed in Dulwich College.

Henslowe's *Diary* is the most valuable source of information we have for the English theatre in its most important period. The first scholarly edition prepared for publication was by Walter Greg in two volumes (1904–08). A later edition, by R. A. Foakes and R. T. Rickert, was published in 1961.

**Henty, G(eorge) A(lfred)** 1832–1902. The author of more than 90 books, chiefly for boys, Henty was a much-travelled man who led an adventurous freebooting life before settling down to dictate something like 14,000,000 words. The tone of Henty – even in his titles – is exasperatingly jingoistic and steeped with the smug idealism of an empire upon which the sun was never going to set. His books are often to be found in secondhand bookshops and are sometimes bought by wistful elderly gentlemen. Representative titles are *With Clive in India* (1884), *With Roberts to Pretoria* (1902), *In Freedom's Cause* (1885), *The Bravest of the Brave*

(1887), *St George for England* (1885), and *True to the Old Flag* (1885).

**Hepburn, Philip**  In Elizabeth Gaskell's *Sylvia's Lovers*, the man whose love for Sylvia leads him into the dishonourable behaviour which ruins his life.

**Herbert, Edward, 1st Baron of Cherbury** 1583–1648.  The elder brother of George Herbert was a man of varied talents who combined an adventurous political and military career with aspirations as a writer. He was one of the large number of English gentlemen upon whom the new monarch, James I, bestowed knighthoods.

He was educated at Oxford, where he spent four years, and during this period married his cousin Mary. About 1606 he moved to London and was soon a frequenter of the court and the society of wits; but man of the world though he was (he travelled in Europe and knew the French court well) he never ceased to study. His most considerable work was *De Veritate*, a philosophical treatise in Latin on the principles of natural religion, written while he was King James's ambassador to France (1619–24). His poetry is regarded less highly; English verse was not the best medium of expression for a writer who achieved distinction in philosophy written in Latin.

Lord Herbert's public career was undistinguished apart from his best years as ambassador. King Charles I made him Baron Herbert of Cherbury in 1632 and appointed him to the Council of War. But he seems to have had no liking for military command and retired to Montgomery Castle in 1644 during the Civil War. The following year, in ill health, he submitted to Parliament and received a pension.

He wrote his autobiography when he was over 60 but the book ends in 1624, when his diplomatic career was over. It has been judged as an exercise in self-aggrandisement by a man whose earlier years held a promise that was never fulfilled. It has, nevertheless, considerable value as a picture of his times. His *The Life and Reign of Henry VIII* (1649) has been respected rather than highly praised.

**Herbert, George** 1593–1633.  One of three brothers who attained distinction during their lifetime, George Herbert was a member of the noble family that included the earldoms of Pembroke and Montgomery among their holdings. An elder brother, Edward, became Baron Herbert of Cherbury and another was Sir Henry Herbert, Master of Revels. The poet's mother Magdalen was friend and patroness to John Donne, who became the younger man's friend and whose career Herbert's resembled.

Herbert was a brilliant scholar and became a fellow of Trinity College, Cambridge, at the age of 22. He seems to have striven very hard for high public office; his fellowship required him to take holy orders within seven years but he became Public Orator at Cambridge and later (1624 and 1625), MP for Montgomery. When King James I died in 1625 the court circle changed, perhaps ending his hopes of advancement and his life changed course at this time. He became a deacon in 1626 and thus debarred himself from civil employment. His mother died in 1627, he resigned his Public Oratorship in 1628, and married Jane Danvers in 1629.

It was probably during this period that he began writing the poems that were to be published in a collection called *The Temple*. His health, never robust, grew worse, and possibly his spirit was troubled by the conflicting aspirations that had attracted him to religion, only to be forsaken in his pursuit of worldly advancement. His work suggests that to the end of his life he remained uncertain whether his final choice was dictated by his soul's true need or by his all too human frailty. He became a priest in 1630 and through the good offices of his kinsman the Earl

George Herbert. Engraving by Robert White, 1674, after the poet's death. British Museum Print Room.

of Pembroke obtained the living of Bemerton in Wiltshire.

He was a good rector, taking his work very seriously and gaining a reputation for unobtrusive kindness, but his health failed and by the early part of 1633 he knew that he was dying. It was at this time that he sent his poems to his friend, Nicholas Ferrar, asking him to print them or burn them, whichever course seemed right.

Herbert died on 1 March 1633. The collection of verses he had sent to Ferrar, *The Temple, Sacred Poems and Private Ejaculations*, was published in the same year, and by 1680 had gone through 13 editions. Izaak Walton wrote a life of the poet in 1670 (revised editions 1674 and 1675). A prose work, the short *A Priest to the Temple, or the Country Parson* (1652) contains guidance for the country priest. Almost all Herbert's English poetry (there is some in Latin) is to be found in *The Temple*; his reputation rests on this remarkable collection, which he described as the expression of both spiritual unrest and final peace.

His reputation began to fade towards the end of the 17th century though William Cowper and John Wesley admired his work and the latter published a small selection (1773). Then in 1799 a new edition of *The Temple* appeared; Coleridge wrote an appreciation of Herbert in his *Biographia Literaria* (1817) and 30 editions of *The Temple* were published in the 19th century.

Religious poets were numerous in the early 17th century and Herbert ranks among the finest. He took great pains with his work and the result can be seen in the precision with which he conveys poetic ideas of remarkable force in a diversity of forms and shapes. His scrupulous craftsmanship brought clarity to the expression of arresting thoughts and unusual images, often in very short poems.

**Herbert, (Alfred Francis) Xavier** 1901– . The son of a locomotive engineer, Herbert was born at Port Hedland in Forrest on the north coast of Western Australia. As a child his companions were Aborigine children and he learned to speak their language. Later he studied medicine at the universities of Western Australia and Melbourne but turned to writing for a career. He travelled extensively in the northern outback, working at anything that came his way. He visited England briefly and found it a totally alien country in spite of the common language. Herbert is best known for the sprawling chronicle of Aborigines and white men in the northern outback called *Capricornia* (1938), in which his sympathy for the native Australians is clear. The novel won the Commonwealth Sesqui-

Centenary Literary prize. The author served in the AIF during World War II. Other novels by him are *Seven Emus* (1958) and *Soldiers' Women* (1960). Herbert is also the author of *Larger than Life* (1963, short stories), *Disturbing Element* (1963, autobiography), and *Poor Fellow my Country* (1975), which won him the Miles Franklin Literature Award.

**Hereward the Wake** Charles Kingsley's last novel, published in 1866.

Hereward, in Kingsley's novel, is the son of Leofric of Mercia and Lady Godiva and a seasoned adventurer before ever William the Norman lands in England. He is outlawed for robbing a monastery and has a number of adventures in Flanders as well as in England. He marries the Lady Torfrida, but the possibility of a calmer existence is lost when William defeats Harold at Hastings and conquers England. Hereward and his friends fight their campaign against William from the Fen country, and the married life of Hereward and Torfrida is soon in ruins. Hereward is attracted to another woman and his lieutenant, Martin, falls in love with Torfrida. Martin is honourable – but Hereward is faithless. The book ends on a bleak note with Hereward's defeat by William at Ely.

**Hermia** In Shakespeare's *A Midsummer Night's Dream*, the daughter of Egeus, ordered by her father to marry Demetrius, whom she does not love. She confides to Helena her intention of running away with Lysander, her true love, and Helena tells Demetrius.

**Hermione** The ill-used wife of Shakespeare's *The Winter's Tale*, Hermione is Queen of Sicily. Her husband, Leontes, believes her unfaithful with his friend, Polixenes, and not only confines her to prison but disposes of her baby daughter. Hermione's friend, Paulina, tells Leontes that his wife is dead; but Hermione survives and forgives Leontes in the play's resolution.

**Hero** Daughter of Leonato, Governor of Messina, and cousin to Beatrice in Shakespeare's *Much Ado About Nothing*. She and Claudio fall in love but he jilts her at the altar, believing she has dishonoured him. The plot against her is discovered in time for a happy ending.

**Hero and Leander** An erotic 'epyllion', or brief epic, by Christopher Marlowe, based on a 5th-century version of the story by Musaeus of Alexandria. Marlowe completed only the first two sestiads (his name for the two parts – Sestos is the goal of Leander's nocturnal swim) before he was murdered in 1593. The text was first published in 1598 and in the same year reissued with George Chapman's completion, the third sestiad. Chapman, the translator of Homer and a successful playwright, introduces moral speculation – a quality quite absent in Marlowe's joyful celebration of physical desire. The subject is the classical myth of Leander of Abydos, who nightly swam the Hellespont to Sestos, where his Hero awaited him, guiding him with the light of a torch. In Marlowe's version Leander arouses the lust of the god Neptune to add to the hazards of his nightly swim. Chapman's third sestiad, its different tone notwithstanding, is highly regarded as poetry.

**Heroes, Hero-worship, and the Heroic in History, On**    The title of a group of six lectures delivered by Thomas Carlyle in May 1840 and first published in 1841. Carlyle's premise was that the heroic can be manifest in any field of human ability. In his first lecture he said 'The History of the World is but the Biography of great men ... Could we see *them*, we should get some glimpses into the very marrow of the world's history.' The illustration of his premise is elaborately carried out, and Carlyle's choice of figures looks distinctly odd in retrospect. He was addressing an audience of the 1840s, but the best parts of *On Heroes* have stood the test of time and it remains one of his most attractive works. The six lectures are: 'The Hero as Divinity. Odin. Paganism: Scandinavian Mythology', 'The Hero as Prophet. Mahomet: Islam', 'The Hero as Poet. Dante; Shakespeare', 'The Hero as Priest. Luther; Reformation: Knox; Puritanism', 'The Hero as Man of Letters. Johnson, Rousseau, Burns', and 'The Hero as King. Cromwell, Napoleon: Modern Revolutionism'.

**Heroes, The**    Charles Kingsley's retelling of the Greek myths of Perseus, Theseus, and Jason. Intended for his older children, they were further prompted by the appearance of Hawthorne's *Tanglewood Tales*, which reduced the timeless stories to nursery level. Kingsley's versions are excellent, with a true vein of poetry; they are a first-class introduction to a fascinating world. The book was first published in 1854.

**Herrick, Robert**    1591–1674. Herrick was the son of a London goldsmith, who died when Robert was in his infancy. The boy was apprenticed to his uncle, Sir William Herrick, also a goldsmith, at the age of 16, and little is known about the young Herrick's life at this time. But he seems to have given up his apprenticeship because after six years, at the late age of 22, he went up to Cambridge. He graduated from Trinity Hall in 1620 and returned to London, where he mixed with the writers and artists of the day, notably Ben Jonson and Henry Lawes, and enjoyed the patronage of Endymion Porter.

Herrick became known as a poet during this period though he published none of his works; at some time between 1623 and 1625 he took holy orders and was chaplain to Buckingham's expedition to the Île de Ré. In 1629 the king appointed him to the living of Dean Prior in the diocese of Exeter, and he settled down to the life of a parish priest. The best of Herrick's work was written during the calm existence of the next 18 years. Events in England, however, were to disrupt his life and upon his refusal to subscribe to the Solemn League and Covenant (for the further reform of the church on Presbyterian lines) he was ejected from his living. He returned to London and was probably supported by his relatives until 1662, when the restored king, Charles II, reinstated him. He spent the remainder of his life in his parish and died in 1674, a bachelor of 83.

Though a few of his poems were printed and circulated during his first period in Devon his principal collection was not published until 1648, a year after he was turned out of Dean Prior. The title, *Hesperides, or the Works, both Humane and Divine of Robert Herrick, Esq*, glances back to his home in the West Country, and the book contains his religious verse under a separate title page, *Noble Numbers*, dated 1647. It is on the *Hesperides* that his reputation rests: the religious verse displays a similar poetic discipline but without evidence of the searching intellect shown so keenly in the work of some of his contemporaries. In contrast, among his secular poems are charming lyrics inspired by rural life and given expression by a poet steeped in the classical tradition, and love poems that leave in the reader's mind images at once vivid and delicate. There is a wistful note in these songs – Herrick conveys exquisitely the look of the lips and limbs of the girls he celebrates but the total effect is remarkably chaste.

The poet's reputation during his lifetime was not great but in the 19th century interest in his poetry led to the publication of his complete works in T. Maitland's edition (1823). While Swinburne's praise, 'the greatest song-writer ever born of English race', may sound extravagant now, Herrick's place in English poetry is secure.

**Herrick, Robert**    1868–1938. One of the 'Chicago' novelists, Herrick was actually born in Cambridge, Massachusetts, and educated at Harvard. His experience of the Midwest began with his appointment to the Department of English at the University of Chicago in 1893; he taught there for 30 years. His first novel was *The Man Who Wins* (1897), about the conflict of professional and personal ideals in the life of a scientist. He pursued the theme further in *The Gospel of Freedom* (1898), *The Web of Life* (1900), *The Healer* (1911), *His Great Adventure* (1913), and other novels. Herrick also wrote several realistic novels about modern industrial life and the threat to personal integrity that the competition for material success so often brings: *The Common Lot* (1904), *The Memoirs of an American Citizen* (1905), *A Life for a Life* (1910), and *Clark's Field* (1914).

*Herself Surprised* See **Cary, (Arthur) Joyce (Lunel)**.

**Hervey, James** 1714–58. Hervey, a prominent member of early Methodist circles, was born at Hardingstone in Northamptonshire and completed his education at Lincoln College, Oxford. He became rector of Collingtree and Weston Favell in Northamptonshire, and was the author of *Meditations among the Tombs* (1746), *Reflections on a Flower Garden*, and *Contemplations on the Night* (both 1747), which were popular in their day.

**Hervey of Ickworth, John, Baron** 1694–1743. Lord Hervey, the son of the Earl of Bristol, was born at Ickworth in Suffolk. He was educated at Westminster School and Clare Hall, Cambridge, and went on the fashionable grand tour of Europe in 1716. In Hanover he met and became friends with Prince Frederick, son of George II (he later quarrelled with him), and in 1720 he married Molly Lepell, a noted London beauty and maid-of-honour to the Princess of Wales. In politics he supported Walpole, becoming Vice-Chamberlain to George II in 1730. From 1733 until 1742, when Walpole fell from power, Hervey was Lord Privy Seal. He enjoyed the confidence of the queen, Caroline of Ansbach, throughout his career.

Hervey was a friend of Lady Mary Wortley Montagu and, inevitably, the enemy of Pope, who is rude about him in his *Epistle to Dr Arbuthnot* and *The Dunciad*. Hervey's talents as a satirist were no match for Pope's but he earned a different sort of place in English literature when his memoirs were published in 1848 as *Memoirs of the Reign of George the Second*, edited by J. W. Croker. Hervey's memoirs were written during the last 15 years of his life but had remained in manuscript. They are detached and cynical but remarkably fair, mercilessly clear when describing political stupidity and searching out motive.

The author seems to like no one, apart from the queen, yet there is a feeling of truth in his record of events: one feels certain that the king, Walpole, and the rest spoke freely to him, and the memoirs present a vivid picture of the court of George II. The recommended edition is that of R. Sedgwick (1931, revised in 1952), which contains a biography. The recommended life is Robert Halsband's *Lord Hervey* (1973).

**Hewlett, Maurice** 1861–1923. Born in Weybridge, Maurice Hewlett was the son of a civil servant and trained for the law. He was called to the Bar in 1890 and succeeded his father at the Record Office in 1893.

His first novel was *The Forest Lovers* (1898), a medieval romance that was an immediate success, and he was able to devote himself to full-time writing. His popularity continued and he had a wide and appreciative public until he turned to poetry, in 1916, with *Song of the Plow*. He confined himself to verse and essays after that but he was always better known as a romantic novelist. He is not much read today, in spite of the former popularity of such novels as *Richard Yea-and-Nay* (1900) and *The Queen's Quair* (1904).

**Hexam, Charley** The heroine's young brother in Dickens's *Our Mutual Friend*, a selfish and cold-blooded boy who forsakes, with complete self-justification, both his sister and his mentor, Bradley Headstone, when it suits him.

**Hexam, Lizzie** The heroine of Dickens's *Our Mutual Friend*. The daughter of a coarse, predatory Thames waterman, who eventually dies in the river from which he has recovered many bodies, Lizzie is loved by both the barrister, Wrayburn, and Bradley Headstone, the schoolmaster.

**Hexham, Richard and John of** fl. 1129–54. Richard, Prior of Hexham, was a Northumbrian chronicler who continued the account of Anglo-Norman history from 1129, the date at which Simeon of Durham left off. Richard's son John, also Prior of Hexham, continued the work to the end of the reign of King Stephen (1154). Both Richard and John of Hexham are highly valued for the quantity of original information they offer about a turbulent period in English history.

Richard of Hexham's *Historia de Gestis Regis Stephani et de Bello de Standardo* (1135–39) was edited by R. Howlett in *Chronicles of the Reigns of Stephen, Henry II and Richard I* (Rolls Series, 1886). John of Hexham's *Historia* (1130–54) was edited by T. Arnold and included in his edition of Simeon of Durham's *Opera Omnia*, Vol. 2 (Rolls Series, 1885). See also **Rievaulx, Aelred of**.

**Heylyn, Peter** 1600–62. A religious controversialist, Heylyn was a supporter of Archbishop Laud. He was also the author of a description of the known countries of the world, published as *Microcosmus: a little Description of the Great World* (1621). This was enlarged and republished (1652) as *Cosmographie*. His principal work was *Ecclesia Restaurata, or The History of the Reformation of the Church of England* (1661). Two posthumously published works were *Cyprianus Anglicus, or The History of the Life and Death of Archbishop Laud* (1668), which was a defence of the dead archbishop against the vicious railing of William Prynne, and *Aerius Redivivus, or The History of Presbyterianism* (1670), which sees Calvinism as the destructive force leading to the strife in England.

**Heywood, John** *c*.1497–*c*.1580. Little is known about the early life of John Heywood beyond Anthony à Wood's statement that he was educated at Broadgates Hall, Oxford, but found it 'not suiting with his airy genie'. He married the daughter of John Rastell, the printer, whose wife was Thomas More's sister, Elizabeth. (Heywood's daughter was John Donne's mother.) The connection with More proved very valuable to Heywood, who became a singer and player of the virginals at the court of Henry VIII from 1519 to 1528. He became a court pensioner in 1528 and held office in the City of London, later becoming a freeman. He remained in favour at court until 1544, when, as a zealous Catholic, he became involved in a conspiracy directed against Thomas Cranmer. He was actually convicted of treason but he saved his life by recanting. Later he became a favourite of Queen Mary's, but upon the accession of Elizabeth and the end of Catholic hopes in England he went into exile. He was last heard of in Malines, in the Netherlands, in 1578.

Heywood published several collections of epigrams and proverbs and contributed to court masques during the reigns of Edward VI and Mary. But his importance to English literature lies in his contribution to the development of English drama. His short dramatic interludes marked a complete departure from allegory and instruction, being concerned with the human comedy in terms of his own world. Among them were *The Play of the Wether* (1533), *A Play of Love* (1534), and *A Dialogue Concerning Witty and Witless* (first printed 1846). He moved nearer to true stage comedy with *The Playe Called the Foure PP* (*c*.1544), in which Palmer, Pardoner, and 'Pothecary dispute the value of their respective occupations. They are joined by a pedlar, who offers a prize to the one who shows the greatest capacity for lying. The palmer wins by declaring that he had never known 'Any woman out of patience'. *A Mery Play Betwene the Pardoner and the Frere, the Curate, and Neybour Pratte* (1533) follows the course of a dispute between a pardoner and a friar that increases in animosity until they resort to physical violence and the neighbour Pratte and the curate have to separate them. *A Mery Play Betwene Johan the Husbande, Tyb his Wyfe, and Syr Jhann the Preest* (also 1533) was adapted from the French and concerns a deceived husband, a lecherous priest, and a complaisant wife. Heywood is plainly restoring the comedy of which Chaucer, in narrative if not in drama, had been a master.

John Heywood was perhaps the first true exponent of English stage comedy, though his own particular contribution was not developed and exists in a peculiar isolation – he lived almost until the time of the Armada but his interludes were written in the reign of Henry VIII. Elizabethan comedy, when it came, was of an entirely different form.

**Heywood, Thomas** *c*.1572–*c*.1650. Details of Thomas Heywood's birth and early life have not so far been discovered but it is believed that he was the son of a Lincolnshire clergyman and educated at Cambridge. It is possible that he became a fellow of Peterhouse; but it is also possible that he left Cambridge without taking a degree. He is known to have been in London by 1596, identified in Henslowe's diary, working with The Lord Admiral's Men and associated with the earls of Southampton and Worcester. He was an actor and a playwright – one of the most industrious in an age of busy dramatists and a surprisingly long-lived one for those times. He claimed to have been involved in the composition of no less than 220 plays and in his *An Apology for Actors* (1612) left a valuable document of his own profession.

From the mass of work attributed to Heywood not very much is worth remembering; he was the author of a large number of occasional works – seven pageants among them. His translation of Sallust was published in 1608. *The Life and Death of Hector*, published in 1614, was adapted from Lydgate's *Troy Book*. *The Hierarchie of the Blessed Angells. Their Names, Orders and Offices* (1635) was a poem with prose divisions. *Nine Bookes of Various History concerninge Women* was published in 1624. *Englands Elizabeth* (1631) was a patriotic effusion and *Pleasant Dialogues and Drammas* (1637) was a commonplace book containing translations from Lucian. *Exemplary Lives . . . of Nine the Most Worthy Women* was published in

1640. The *Lives of All the Poets* was begun about 1614 but never finished and the fragment is unfortunately lost.

Among Heywood's plays, in order of publication, are *King Edward the Fourth* (1599), though his authorship has been questioned; *If You Know Not Me, You Know No Bodie: or The Troubles of Queen Elizabeth* (Part 1 1605, Part II 1606); *A Woman Killed with Kindness* (1607); *The Fayre Mayde of the Exchange* (attributed to Heywood, 1607); and *The Rape of Lucrece* (1608). He wrote a Homeric series: *The Golden Age* (1611), *The Silver Age*, and *The Brazen Age* (1613), and *The Iron Age* some years later (*c.*1632). *The Four Prentises of London* was published in 1615; *The Fair Maid of the West, or A Girle Worth Gold* in 1631; *The English Traveller* in 1633; *The Royal King and the Loyall Subject* in 1637; and *The Wisewoman of Hogsdon* in 1638.

There are many more – but Heywood's reputation rests on a single play. *A Woman Killed with Kindness* is a domestic tragedy on a level attained by no other playwright of the Elizabethan–Jacobean age. Heywood's dramatic works were edited by R. H. Shepherd and published in six volumes (1874). *A Woman Killed with Kindness* is included in The World's Classics volume *Five Elizabethan Tragedies* (1938, edited by A. K. McIlwraith).

**Hiawatha, The Song of** A narrative poem by Longfellow, first published in 1855. The author had been deeply interested in the work of the ethnologist, Henry Rowe Schoolcraft, who had been among the first to translate Indian poetry. The historical Hiawatha (Haiohratha) was a Mohawk chief of the 16th century, who was credited with the formation of the eastern tribes into the Iroquois Confederacy. This was the beginning of the North American Indian nation, the hopes of which were destroyed by the coming of the White man. However, their unity made the eastern tribes a formidable military power which held England and France in check until the 18th century. Longfellow, following an error of Schoolcraft's, placed his Hiawatha among the forest tribes of the northern Midwest, on the shores of Lake Superior.

Nokomis of the Ojibway tribe, daughter of the Moon, brings up her grandson Hiawatha on the south shore of Lake Superior. He learns the wisdom of the wild and how to make moccasins which will give him mile-long strides. His magic mittens enable him to crush rocks. Reaching manhood, he seeks to avenge the wrong done to his mother Wenonah by his father the West Wind. The combat ends in reconciliation and Hiawatha becomes the leader of his people. He defeats the Corn Spirit, from whose body then springs the maize as a source of food, and defeats Pearl Feather, who commands disease. He marries Minnehaha of the once hostile Dakotahs and their wedding feast inaugurates a period of peace and advancement under the rule of Hiawatha and his friends Chibiabos the musician and Kwasind the strong man. The golden age comes to an end with the deaths of Chibiabos and Kwasind and the quarrel with Pau-Puk-Keewis, whom Hiawatha kills for an insult. Want and disease visit his people and Minnehaha dies. Hiawatha has foretold the coming of the White men; swarms of golden bees herald their approach. He counsels his people to give hearing to the religion they will bring – and departs for the Isles of the Blest.

The peculiarly hypnotic metre of the poem has been parodied almost from the day *Hiawatha* was published. Longfellow based it on the rhythms of the Finnish epic, *The Kalevala*.

**Higden, Betty** In Dickens's *Our Mutual Friend*, the sturdy self-reliant old woman who is terrified of falling victim to 'the workhouse'.

**Higden, Ranulf** d. 1364. A Benedictine monk of St Werburgh's, Chester, Ranulf Higden was the author of a universal history, *Polychronicon*, which he completed about 1350. It began with the Creation and ended in his own time, taking in not only the history that was known but also the accumulated legends. Written in Latin and translated by John Trevisa in 1387, it was a book of information and accepted as truthful in its time.

**Highland Widow, The** See *Chronicles of the Canongate*.

**Hilda Lessways** See **Bennett, (Enoch) Arnold**.

**Hill, Geoffrey (William)** 1932– . Hill was born in Bromsgrove, Worcestershire, and completed his education at Keble College, Oxford. He published his first work, *Poems* (1952), while still at Oxford; his second, *For the Unfallen, 1952–1958* (1959), brought him recognition and the Gregory Award. *Preghiere* (1964) was followed by *King Log* (1968), which confirmed his reputation and gained both the Hawthornden Prize and the Geoffrey Faber Memorial Award. *Mercian Hymns* (1971), a collection of prose poems, presents the 8th-century King Offa as a representative of the tyranny which is too easily exercised in every level of society when the moral imperative is ignored. *Mercian Hymns* won the Whitbread Award and the Alice Hunt Bartlett

Award. The latter prize went to Hill again for *Somewhere is Such a Kingdom: Poems 1952–1971* (1975). *Tenebrae* (1978) won the Duff Cooper Memorial Prize. Geoffrey Hill is Professor of English at the University of Leeds. His version of Ibsen's *Brand* was produced in London in 1978.

**Hillingdon Hall** See **Surtees, R(obert) S(mith).**

**Hilton (or Hylton), Walter** d. 1396. Nothing is known of Walter Hilton apart from the fact that he was an Augustinian canon and was for a time head of the Priory at Thurgarton in Nottinghamshire. His spiritual writings were popular in England in the 15th century – his progress towards grace is described in clear and vigorous English. His most famous book, *Scala Perfectionis* (*The Ladder of Perfection*), was first printed in 1494 but the date of its composition is unknown. It can be read in several modern English editions. Other works are *Epistle to a Devout Man in Temporal Estate* (printed 1506) and *The Song of the Angels* (printed 1521).

**Hind and the Panther, The** A poem by John Dryden, first published in 1687. The poet was converted to the Church of Rome in 1685, and the poem expresses his views. It is interesting to compare it with his first poetic expression of faith, *Religio Laici*, in which his argument against the Roman Catholic Church is the less convincing part. Dryden became a moderate Catholic, as he had been a moderate Anglican, and was uneasy with James II's efforts to create a Catholic England. The Protestants were nervous and easily stampeded as it was. James managed to alienate both Protestant and Catholic Englishmen in the end.

For John Dryden the confusions of the Church of England were both strident and inimical to peace of mind; he found the old faith free of confusion, contradiction, and compromise. The poem is divided into three parts. The first describes various religious sects, likening their characters to various beasts: the hind is the Catholic Church, 'immortal and unchanged', while the Church of England is the panther. The second part is an argument between the two churches. The third, a satirical discussion of political and temporal questions, contains the fable, told by the panther, of the swallows deluded by a martin who tells them there is no need for the flight across the sea. They enjoy a 'St Martin's summer' and are then destroyed by a harsh winter. It is a warning to Catholics not to be overoptimistic under the rule of James, and to Anglicans lest they become persecutors. The hind replies to the panther with the fable of the

pigeons, pampered birds who become jealous of the lowly domestic poultry. They invite the buzzard to become their leader; but at this point their owner intervenes to assure them that they have all their rights, except that of persecuting other birds. The pigeons are the Anglicans, the poultry the Catholics; the buzzard is both William of Orange and Bishop Burnet. The master is King James, and his assurances represent the Declaration of Indulgence of April 1687.

**Hippolyta** The Queen of the Amazons in Shakespeare's *A Midsummer Night's Dream*. She is betrothed to Duke Theseus of Athens, who has defeated her in battle.

***Historia Britonum*** Originally the *Historia Britonum* was a collection of historical tracts compiled in England about 679. Additions were made in following years and in about 800 a revised text of the whole was made by the historian known to us as Nennius. The complete revision by Nennius has not survived, though much of the text is quoted by other writers. The best version extant is the Irish version by Gilla Coemgin made in the 11th century.

The *Historia Britonum* contains notes on the history and geography of Anglo-Saxon England, a short life of St Patrick, and – of particular interest – mention of Arthur as a historical character who emerges after the death of Hengist as *dux bellorum* against the Saxons. The *Historia* was probably known to Bede and was certainly used by Geoffrey of Monmouth for his *Historia Regum Britanniae*.

The *Historia Britonum* was edited by J. Stevenson (1838). It was translated by A. W. Wade-Evans: *Nennius's History of the Britons* (1938).

***Historia Ecclesiastica Gentis Anglorum*** See ***Ecclesiastical History of the English Race.***

***Historie of the Raigne of King Henry the Seventh, The*** A historical biography by Francis Bacon, first published in 1622. Bacon had once planned a history of the Tudors and had thoroughly researched the background. To his careful documentation he added his legal and political experience and his own theory of history and the work benefits from his mastery of English prose. The *Historie* is highly regarded though Bacon's assessment of Henry VII makes him a more Machiavellian character than he actually was.

The book was the first product of Bacon's enforced leisure after his fall from grace.

***History of England from the Accession of James II, The*** Macaulay's history was published in five volumes: the first two in 1849, the next two in 1855, and the last, edited by his sister Hannah, Lady Trevelyan, posthumously in 1861. Macaulay intended to continue his history to the accession of the Hanoverians but had only reached the death of William III when he died in 1859. His history is immensely readable, researched with scrupulous care, and unarguably Macaulay's personal view: it was not for nothing that his contemporaries nicknamed him 'cocksure Tom', and he rarely changed his mind about anyone or anything. For Macaulay the world began to be a better place as soon as William III mounted the throne of England; events before and after that are interpreted to fit this view. He libels William Penn most outrageously and his comments on Marlborough were accepted as truth until Winston Churchill adjusted the balance in defence of his famous ancestor in 1936. But in narrative style, in the clarity of its political analyses, and for its exhaustive study of the reign of William III (hitherto ignored by historians), Macaulay's history is a major work of the 19th century.

**History of Great Britain**  David Hume's *History* was published in separate volumes in 1754, 1756, 1759, and 1762. The complete *History* was first published in 1763.

Hume begins with the reign of James VI of Scotland and I of England; the political divisions of the mid-18th century had their origin in the accession of a Scottish king to the throne of England, and the first volume closes with the reign of Charles I. The second volume continues with the Commonwealth, the Restoration, and the flight of James II. Thereafter, Hume worked backwards; the next two volumes concerned the reign of the Tudors, and the last two examined the history of Great Britain from the invasion of Julius Caesar to the accession of Henry VII.

The first two volumes are regarded as the finest part (in the complete *History* they become the closing volumes). The material available to historians since Hume's day has increased enormously and this means that his work has been superseded; some scholars' examination of his work suggests that Hume's research was confined to the books available to him in the library of the Faculty of Advocates in Edinburgh (see **Hume, David**). It is also true that the times before the Tudors held less interest for him and he wrote about them for the sake of completeness. He did not write a scientific history; his intention was to offer a provocative one, in a spirit of philosophic impartiality. His correspondence demonstrates how hard he strove to keep his history free of political bias. He succeeded in making his history attractive; it is acknowledged a masterpiece of composition, written in lucid and polished English, elegant and ironical. His style is admirably suited to his examination of past events to show how the conditions of his own day came about. The first volume he completed, concerning the early Stuarts, examines the steps by which the people of Great Britain first questioned the prerogative of the crown, then challenged it and, finally, rejected it with violence.

The *History* was, at first, coldly received, but interest grew with the publication of the second volume and the success of his work gave Hume financial independence. The book was much admired by Edward Gibbon, and by Hume's fellow historian William Robertson.

**History of Mr Polly, The**  See **Wells, H(erbert) G(eorge)**.

**History of New York, A**. *From the Beginning of the World to the End of the Dutch Dynasty, by Diedrich Knickerbocker*. Washington Irving's burlesque history was first published in 1809. In seven books it relates the discovery of America, early Dutch colonization, the founding of New Amsterdam, the hostilities with the neighbouring English colonists and so on, ending with the period of Peter Stuyvesant, the last Dutch governor of what was called the New Netherlands before the surrender to the English in 1664. Irving takes the opportunity to caricature figures like Thomas Jefferson (he was himself a diehard federalist) but, in spite of its tone, the book remains a permanent source of information on the early settlement of New York before it became an English possession.

**History of Pompey the Little, The**  See **Coventry, Francis**.

**History of the Irish Rebellion and Civil Wars in Ireland, The**  Clarendon's account was written as a separate book, as was his *Life*, but the Irish Rebellion was incorporated totally in the great *History* as being an integral part of the events recorded. It was published as a separate book in 1721.

**History of the Rebellion and Civil Wars in England, The**  The title usually given to Clarendon's history of his times. It was begun in 1646, when Edward Hyde (later the Earl of Clarendon) accompanied Prince Charles to the Scilly Isles. It was resumed in Jersey later in the same year, then laid aside until 1671 when Clarendon was an exile in France. He had been there since 1667 and had meanwhile written his autobiography, portions of which he incorporated into the *History*.

The *History* is the first great historical work in English literature and is a priceless source of information about the momentous years of perhaps England's greatest historical upheaval. His qualifications were unchallengeable; he wrote as a witness of the times and was, moreover, a lawyer who was never guilty of ill-considered judgments. To these he added a firsthand acquaintance with the principals and a remarkable gift for characterization. The *History* was first published at Oxford (1702–04). W. D. Macray's edition is generally accepted as definitive (six volumes, 1888).

**Histrio-Mastix** See **Prynne, William.**

**Hoadly, Benjamin** 1676–1761. Hoadly was Bishop of Bangor (1716), Hereford, Salisbury, and Winchester successively. He was born at Westerham in Kent, and a serious illness in his youth, possibly polio, left him so incapacitated that he usually preached on his knees. However, he completed his education at St Catherine Hall, Cambridge. A latitudinarian, Hoadly provoked an uproar with his sermon before the king (George I) on 31 March 1717 in which he insisted that the gospels afford no warrant for any visible church authority (the 'Bangorian controversy'). He was the author of a number of works concerned with the religious questions of his time and argued for toleration. *A Plain Account of the Nature and End of the Lord's Supper* (1735) maintained that the Last Supper was commemorative, no more; his reputation is principally that of a controversialist.

**Hoadly, Benjamin** 1706–57. The son of the Bishop of Bangor who later became Bishop of Winchester, Hoadly was a physician in the royal household and became the friend of David Garrick. Like many others he owed such success as he was to enjoy as a playwright to the great actor, who staged Hoadly's comedy, *The Suspicious Husband*, at Covent Garden in February 1747 and found an excellent part as Ranger, an audacious rake. Hoadly was the author of some medical textbooks; no other play of his was produced though he is believed to have written a total of three.

**Hobbes, John Oliver** 1867–1906. The pseudonym used by Mrs Reginald Craigie, the author of some novels (*The Serious Wooing*, 1901; *The School for Saints*, 1897; *Robert Orange*, 1902) and successful plays (*The Ambassador*, 1892; *A Repentance*, 1899). The theme of religious doubt, much in the air at the end of the century, occurs in some of her fiction.

**Hobbes, Thomas** 1588–1679. The son of a parson, Hobbes was born at Westport in Wiltshire. He graduated from Magdalen Hall, Oxford, in 1608 and became tutor to William Cavendish (later 1st Earl of Devonshire). He stayed with Cavendish as secretary and companion, spending much time at Welbeck Abbey and Chatsworth, where he made the acquaintance of Ben Jonson and Lord Herbert. The connection with the Cavendish family was longstanding and proved of inestimable value to Hobbes – he enjoyed opportunities to travel (during which he met Galileo, Descartes, and Père Mersenne), had access to fine libraries, and was able to spend five years (1621–26) working with Francis Bacon. He left England in 1640 with the first group of Royalist émigrés and lived in Paris for the next 11 years. He was appointed tutor to the Prince of Wales, later Charles II.

He had meanwhile discovered geometry and this, with the influence of Galileo, had helped to clarify his ideas of philosophy as something that could be demonstrated in positive terms: 'the rules and infallibility of reason.' He wrote *Elements of Law, Natural and Politic*, which was circulating in 1640, although it was not published until the 19th century. While in France he worked on a plan for an extensive treatise, beginning with matter as the first part, and going on to deal with human nature, society, and government.

However, events in England (the Civil War had begun in earnest in 1642) persuaded him to embark at once on the proposed third part, *Elementorum Philosophiae Sectio Tertia De Cive* (1642). The English text appeared in 1651 as *Philosophical Rudiments Concerning Government and Society*. The year 1651 also saw the publication in London of Hobbes's most famous work, ***Leviathan*** *Or the Matter, Form, and Power of a Commonwealth Ecclesiastical and Civil*. It offended everyone – Royalists, churchmen, and Parliamentarians alike. Charles, the Prince of Wales, dismissed him with some regret (he enjoyed his company) and Hobbes decided to return to England. He completed the first part of his projected treatise, *De Corpore*, in 1655 and published *Questions Concerning Liberty, Necessity and Chance* (1656). The second part of his treatise, *De Homine*, came in 1658.

Hobbes had returned to the Cavendish family in 1653 and spent the rest of his life with them. His enthusiasm for mathematics misled him, however, and his papers on the subject to the Royal Society were coldly received. But this remarkable man embarked in his old age on a translation of Homer, publishing his *Odyssey* at the age of 85 and his *Iliad* in the following year.

Thomas Hobbes. A detail from the portrait after J. M. Wright, 1670. National Portrait Gallery, London.

(He was not, incidentally, a stranger to that scholarly exercise, having translated Thucydides in 1629.) He died at the age of 92 and posthumous works include *Behemoth: the History of the Civil Wars of England* (1679 and 1681) and *A Dialogue between a Philosopher and a Student of the Common Laws of England* (1681).

The substance of *Leviathan* is Hobbes's theory of society and it is expounded in English that admits no ornament or flourish. He was both a formidable thinker and a writer on the highest level and it is pleasant to remember that Charles II, in possession of his kingdom, granted his old tutor an annual pension, though he could do nothing to stop the Commons' bill against blasphemous books, among which *Leviathan* was listed. Hobbes was forbidden to publish any political and religious books and his published works were publicly burned.

Hobbes was a materialist who argued from first principles: he refused to assume, because it was the habit of his time to proceed too easily from assumption, and he always questioned that first. His dismissal of Christian terminology in his religious comments not only provoked a storm of abuse but obliged his contemporaries to argue with him in print: consequently they widened the whole range of discussion to a remarkable degree and in so doing were forced to express themselves in something akin to the lucid, trenchant prose of the greatest name in 17th-century philosophy.

**Hoccleve, Thomas** See **Occleve, Thomas.**

**Hoffman, Charles Fenno** 1806–84. A New Yorker, Hoffman enjoyed a successful career as a writer and editor until, at the age of 43, he became insane. As an editor he held positions on *The Knickerbocker Magazine, The New York Mirror,* and the *American Monthly Magazine.* He made a journey on horseback in the West, through the scarcely settled regions of Illinois and Michigan, and wrote two valuable accounts of his experiences: *A Winter in the West* (1835) and *Wild Scenes in the Forest and Prairie* (1839).

*Greyslaer,* a novel, was published in 1840 and was a popular success. Three books of poems appeared between 1842 and 1847; many of the poems evoke the Hudson River setting of his New York home. A collection, *The Poems of Charles Fenno Hoffman,* was published in 1873.

**Hogg, James** 1770–1835. James Hogg was born on a Border farm near Ettrick Forest in Selkirkshire. His education was so sketchy that he could barely read or write and had no schooling beyond his seventh year. He became a herd boy at the age of eight and then a shepherd – he was to become known as the Ettrick Shepherd. He improved his rudimentary education by whatever means he could, and it was through the kindness of one of his employers, William Laidlaw of Blackhouse, that a number of books first became available to him, in 1796. He was 26 years old. Hogg first heard of Burns in the following year, when someone stopped to talk to the shepherd on the hill and recited 'Tam O'Shanter'. He later said that the encounter changed his life; he wept to hear that Robert Burns had died in 1796.

Hogg worked away on his own and some pieces were published in journals. Then Laidlaw introduced him to his friend Sir Walter Scott, who enlisted his help in the preparation of *The Minstrelsy of the Scottish Border.* Hogg visited Edinburgh briefly in 1801 for the publication of *Scottish Pastorals, Poems and Songs* (1801), and evidently felt perfectly at ease there; he was to return some years later to attempt to earn a living by his pen. *The Mountain Bard,* a collection of his early ballads, and a handbook which proved of value to several generations, *The Shepherd's Guide: being a practical treatise on the diseases of sheep,* were both published in 1807 and earned him enough money to buy a farm. The venture was

The frontispiece to Vol. II of *The Poetical Works of The Ettrick Shepherd* (1838–40) by James Hogg. The engraving is of the town of Jedburgh.

a failure and Hogg, at the age of 40, returned to Edinburgh, where with perfect confidence he entered the literary world. He founded a weekly, *The Spy*, which struggled on for a year, and a debating society, The Forum; he published **The Queen's Wake** in 1813 and enjoyed considerable success. He might have enjoyed security, too, but the publisher went out of business. Fortunately William Blackwood gave him a place on his *Edinburgh Magazine* and he met Wordsworth, Southey, Byron, and John Murray. An admirer, the Duke of Buccleuch, gave him a farm at Altrive in Yarrow, near his native Ettrick Forest, at a nominal rent, in 1816. Hogg made it his home for the rest of his life.

Hogg went on writing poetry but, apart from *The Queen's Wake*, none of it is highly regarded now. He wanted to be Burns's successor but what he lacked, simply, was the spark of genius. He also admired Scott, and his own work suffers from uncertainty about where his real gifts lay, whether in the vernacular or in the wider field where Scott was the master. It was in fiction that Hogg earned a lasting place in English letters; **The Private Memoirs and Confessions of a Justified Sinner** (1824) is both a remarkable novel and a powerful criticism of the glowering Calvinism which Robert Burns abhorred.

That Hogg could succeed in Edinburgh when Burns could not was probably due to the former's complete lack of modesty; he had no doubt whatever of his gifts in the early stages of his career. In the 'anonymous' memoir included in *The Mountain Bard* he relates how the books made available by William Laidlaw affected him: '... no sooner did I begin to read so as to understand them, than, rather prematurely I began to write.' Hogg is looking back 11 years, and speaking of his first attempts to write 'songs and ballads made up for the lassies to sing in chorus'. 'I had no more difficulty in composing them than I have at present, and I was equally well pleased with them.' The nickname 'the Ettrick Shepherd' was given him by John Wilson in one of the *Noctes Ambrosianae* papers in *Blackwood's Magazine*. The imaginary conversation between Christopher North (Wilson) and the Ettrick Shepherd (Hogg) gives an exaggerated but truthful impression of Hogg's brash, irrepressible character.

Other books of verse by James Hogg were *The Forest Minstrel* (1810), *The Pilgrims of the Sun* (1815), *Mador of the Moor* (1816), *Queen Hynde* (1826), and *The Jacobite Relics of Scotland* (1819 and 1821); other fiction, *Brownie of Bodsbeck* (1817), *The Three Perils of Man* (1822), and *The Three Perils of Women* (1823). He was also the author of *The Domestic Manner and Private Life of Sir Walter Scott* (1834), which caused great annoyance to Scott's son-in-law and biographer, J. G. Lockhart.

**Hoggarty Diamond, The Great** A story by W. M. Thackeray, first published in *Fraser's Magazine*

(September to December 1841). The Hoggarty Diamond is given to Samuel Titmarsh by his aunt and involves him with swindlers and shady dealings. Samuel's wife rescues him from trouble.

**Holcroft, Thomas** 1745–1809.  The son of a shoemaker, Holcroft was born in London and worked as a pedlar and a stable boy at Newmarket before becoming a strolling player. He reached London in 1778, playing at Drury Lane, and wrote a comedy, *Duplicity* (1781), on the evils of gambling. The comedy was a success and he gave up acting for writing. He wrote a great deal – fiction, essays, adaptations from the French – as well as some 20 plays. Entirely self-educated, Holcroft became the friend of Godwin, Thomas Paine, and Charles Lamb. He learned French well enough to memorize *Le Mariage de Figaro* while in Paris and staged it in London as *The Follies of a Day* (Covent Garden, December 1784). Holcroft edited the invaluable *Theatrical Recorder* from 1805 until he died. William Hazlitt edited Holcroft's *Memoirs* for posthumous publication in 1816. The best of Holcroft's plays is acknowledged to be *The Road to Ruin* (Covent Garden, February 1792), a sentimental comedy which was loved by actors for its fine parts of Goldfinch and Mr Sulky. It was last revived in London in 1937. Two of Holcroft's novels, *Hugh Trevor* (edited by Seamus Deane, 1973) and *Anna St Ives* (edited by Peter Faulkner, 1970), were published in modern editions in the Oxford English Novels series.

**Hole in the Wall, The**  See **Morrison, Arthur**.

**Holiday Romance**  A story for young people in four parts by Charles Dickens. It was first published in *Our Young Folks* (Boston, Mass.), between January and May 1868.

**Holinshed, Raphael** fl. 1577.  Almost nothing is known about Holinshed, not even the exact year of his death. He may have come from Cheshire or from Warwickshire; Anthony à Wood, the 17th-century antiquary, described him as a minister of religion. He was working in London during the early years of Elizabeth's reign as a translator for the printer Reginald Wolfe. Wolfe planned the 'histories of euery knowne nation' and Holinshed's contribution (the great project never materialized) was the preparation of the history and geography of England, Scotland, and Ireland, written by Holinshed and others. The first edition appeared in 1577; a revised and expanded one was published by John Stow in 1585.

*The Chronicles of England, Scotland and Irelande* actually begins in the time of Noah and draws from other historians in its presentation of events. It became a valuable source for Shakespeare in his historical plays and for the story of Macbeth (see also **Boece, Hector**). Holinshed's collaborators were William Harrison (*Description of England* and *Description of Scotland*), John Hooker (the translation of Giraldus Cambrensis on his native Wales), and Edmund Campion and Richard Stanyhurst (*Description of Ireland*). Harrison's contribution is particularly prized for its vivid description of life in Shakespeare's England but the whole work is notable for its clear, straightforward prose.

**Holland, Philemon** 1552–1637.  Philemon Holland, who has been called 'the Translator Generall in his Age', taught at Coventry for 20 years before taking a medical degree at Cambridge in 1597. He practised medicine for a time, then returned to Coventry and resumed teaching in 1608 as an usher at the Free School. He became the master of the Free School in 1628 and was honoured with the freedom of the city in 1632.

Holland's mastery of Greek and Latin enabled him to go directly to the original texts and he combined immense scholarship with a true feeling for antiquity. His first classical author was Livy; his translation, *Romane Historie*, was published in 1600. Pliny came next, in the form of *Plinie's Natural Historie of the Worlde* (1601). Plutarch was his first Greek author – the *Moralia* appeared in Holland's English as *The Philosophie, Commonly Called the Morals* (1603). He returned to Latin with Suetonius, *The Historie of the Twelve Caesars* (1606). The later history of Rome appeared in English when Holland translated Ammianus Marcellinus (1609). William Camden's *Britannia* followed in 1610. Xenophon's account of Persia, the *Cyropaedia*, he translated from the Greek in 1632.

Holland modestly referred to his 'meane and popular stile'. His contemporaries and posterity owe him a great deal for his style, his scholarship, and for his affinity with the classical world.

**Holland, Sir Richard** fl. *c*.1450.  A Scottish clergyman who wrote *The Buke of the Howlat* for Elizabeth Dunbar, Countess of Moray; her first husband was a member of the Douglas family who, like many of the Scottish barons, resisted the king's attempts to be masters of their realm. The Douglases were brought down by James II and became pensioners in exile at the English court. Holland seems to have accompanied his patrons to England and, apart from brief missions to Scotland, to have spent the rest of his life there.

*The Buke of the Howlat* is an alliterative poem about an owl – the 'howlat' – who feels that nature has been less than kind in the matter of his plumage. Eventually he is granted a feather from each of the assembled birds, under the chairmanship of the pope, to adjust his dull appearance. But this makes him so proud and insolent that Dame Nature orders him to be stripped of them once more.

The historical application of all this has never been clear. That the author intended one is plain from the celebration of the Douglases that his poem contains, included no doubt to please the Countess of Moray; but this has no interest apart from presenting an account of Sir James Douglas's journey with the heart of Bruce that is different from the version given by John Barbour. The celebration of his patrons by Holland spoils what is otherwise a deft and clever poetic essay on the theme of the bird in borrowed plumage.

**Holmes, Oliver Wendell** 1809–94. The son of Abiel Holmes, a Congregational clergyman who had compiled *The Annals of America*, Oliver Wendell Holmes was born in Cambridge, Massachusetts. He was educated at Harvard and graduated in 1829. He went on to study medicine and during that period (1831–32) published two pieces entitled 'The Autocrat of the Breakfast Table' in the *New England Magazine*. He took his MD at Harvard in 1836.

In the same year Holmes published his *Poems*, a collection of occasional and witty verses; but it was the last of his purely literary efforts for some time because he became Professor of Anatomy at Dartmouth. He did, however, publish two considerable medical works, on homeopathy (1842) and puerperal fever (1843). In 1847 he became Parkman Professor of Anatomy and Physiology at Harvard and held the chair until he retired in 1882. He was Dean of Harvard Medical School for six years.

While Holmes was at Harvard his father lost his parish in Cambridge through the active ill will of a Calvinist group and this transformed Holmes's dislike of Calvinism into a strong opposition which pervades much of his work. He was a notable success as a teacher; his lectures became famous beyond the bounds of Harvard and people flocked to hear him at public engagements. The establishment of **The Atlantic Monthly** gave him the opportunity to expand the papers he had written as a young man and **The Autocrat of the Breakfast Table** (1858) was a great success; it contains some effective slaps at Calvinism. He continued to exploit this outlet to excellent effect in *The Professor at the Breakfast Table* (1860), *The Poet at the Breakfast Table* (1872), and *Over the Teacups* (1891). He used his scientific training as the background for three novels based on abnormal psychology, of which the most successful was the first, **Elsie Venner** (1861). His other work includes volumes of essays, medical articles, and biographies of J. L. Motley and Emerson. He was a prolific writer of occasional verse and used this talent against Calvinism. Some of his poetry has lasted and 'The Last Leaf', 'The Chambered Nautilus', and 'Contentment' are found in many anthologies.

Holmes should be seen as a major influence, if not a major writer. A scientific rationalist who commanded a wide audience, a witty conversationalist whose company was sought by everyone, and an academic with a brilliant record, his lectures and essays were followed with close attention and his manifold talents enabled him to discredit Calvinism not only by laughing at it ('The Deacon's Masterpiece', a satirical poem of 1858) but also by showing how its rigid dogma

Oliver Wendell Holmes as seen by the cartoonist, Spy.

stifled people's lives. He was equally angry with medical bigotry, as his essay on puerperal fever (1843) demonstrated. Holmes was a humanist, even though he might not, in his day, have recognized the description.

**Holmes, Oliver Wendell** *c.*1841–1935. The son of Oliver Wendell Holmes the doctor, he fought in the American Civil War and achieved great distinction as a jurist. He taught at Harvard like his father (where he was Professor of Law) and became Chief Justice of the Massachusetts Supreme Court (1899–1902). He was appointed to the US Supreme Court by Theodore Roosevelt and for the length of his office (1902–32) was distinguished for his championship of human rights and free speech. His *The Common Law* (1881) is recognized as a classic treatise. His Civil War diary and letters were published in 1946 under the title of *Touched with Fire*.

**Holmes, Sherlock** Sir Arthur Conan Doyle's celebrated private detective who appears in over 60 short stories and novels, perhaps most notably in *The Hound of the Baskervilles*. The character was based in some respects on Dr Joseph Bell, an Edinburgh surgeon of some eminence under whom Doyle studied (he was an MD and practised medicine for some years before becoming famous as a writer). Sherlock Holmes is addicted to cocaine, has fits of depression, and is an accomplished violinist.

**Holofernes** The pedantic schoolmaster of Shakespeare's *Love's Labour's Lost*. His erudition is profound – but it has enveloped him: to him learning is all.

**Holy Grail, The** See *Idylls of the King, The*.

**Holy War, The**, made by Shaddai upon Diabolus. An allegory by John Bunyan and his last major work, published in 1682.

The City of Mansoul (man's soul) has been conquered by the wiles of Diabolus, and King Shaddai, who built the city, sends his captains to recover it. His son Emmanuel leads the besieging army. The city is regained and the king returns but the city gradually relapses into evil ways and Diabolus takes possession again. Emmanuel, however, holds the citadel and this Diabolus cannot take; eventually he is totally defeated.

Bunyan used a great deal of his own experience as a soldier in his account of the siege of Mansoul, and some parallels in contemporary history can be found in his description of the city's life as it falls into evil. In this book he moves from his usual field – the individual in life's progress – to

a broader and more objective examination of motives and deeds. *The Holy War* has never been popular; Bunyan was at his best in his feeling for individual character and that is lacking here. The author was tackling a more complex task and it cannot be said that he really succeeded.

**Holy Willie's Prayer** A satirical poem by Robert Burns, first published in *Poems Chiefly in the Scottish Dialect* in 1786. It takes the form of a dramatic monologue, the reflections of Holy Willie, a bigoted elder of the Kirk. With considerable eloquence and the conceit of the humourless, Willie exposes himself as a canting hypocrite – but not to himself. Burns detested the intrusion of the Kirk into every aspect of life and Holy Willie is based on William Fisher, an elder of the parish church of Mauchline. Fisher fell from grace in 1790, accused of drunkenness by the Kirk, and froze to death in a snow-filled ditch in 1809. He was also believed to have been guilty of pilfering from the alms-box and Burns refers to the charge in a later poem, 'The Kirk's Alarm' (1790).

**Homage to Catalonia** See **Orwell, George**.

**Home, John** 1722–1808. Home was born in Leith, where his father was town clerk. He was educated at Edinburgh University and became a Broad Church minister after graduating. Home fought on the side of the crown during the rebellion of 1745 and for a time was a prisoner in Jacobite hands at Doune Castle. In 1747 he became minister of Athelstaneford in East Lothian and a member of a group of friends which included James Macpherson, his kinsman David Hume, the historians Adam Ferguson and William Robertson, and Adam Smith. Home's literary career began with his tragedy **Douglas**, and his career in the church ended with it; it offended the church leaders, who initiated proceedings against Home and his friend Alexander Carlisle, another minister, who had attended the first performance in Edinburgh in December 1756. The play, in spite of its great success, was rejected by David Garrick, who had also rejected an earlier play, *Agis*, but it was staged at Covent Garden in March 1757 and Home's career in the theatre was successfully launched. Five more tragedies by him were successfully produced: *Agis* (Drury Lane, February 1758), *The Siege of Aquileia* (Drury Lane, February 1760), *The Fatal Discovery* (Drury Lane, February 1769), *Alonzo* (Drury Lane, February 1773), and *Alfred* (Covent Garden, January 1778).

The attitude of the Church led Home to resign his living and move to London, where he became secretary to Lord Bute. Later he became tutor to the Prince of Wales, who, as George III, granted Home a pension of £300 a year. Home's career as a London dramatist had been one of diminishing success over 21 years; he retired to Edinburgh and settled into the flourishing intellectual life of the northern capital. His *The History of the Rebellion in 1745* was published in 1802. *Douglas* is occasionally revived at drama festivals but Home's other tragedies are forgotten. His works were collected by Henry Mackenzie and published with Mackenzie's life of Home in 1822.

**Honest Whore, The** A play by Thomas Dekker in two parts, the first of which was published in 1604 and the second in 1630. Philip Henslowe's diary gives us the information that Middleton contributed to the first part. The setting is apparently Italy but the atmosphere is Dekker's own London.

In the first part Count Hippolito is in love with Infelice, a duke's daughter. The duke is not in favour of the marriage and packs his daughter off to a convent, giving out the news that she is dead. Hippolito's friends take him to the house of the beautiful Bellafront who is unabashed in her advances. But Hippolito discovers that she is a harlot; he not only repels her but attacks her for her way of life before withdrawing from her house. Then he is brought news that Infelice is alive and he hastens to the convent; he rescues her and marries her at once. The angry duke, arriving too late to prevent the marriage, is reconciled to it. Bellafront, meanwhile, has abandoned her old life – she had fallen in love with Hippolito and had nursed a hope that she could win him. Hippolito, however, had remained faithful to Infelice and his constancy had been rewarded. The duke arranges the marriage of Bellafront to Matheo, her first seducer. There is also a subplot concerning the linen draper, Candido, and his wife, Viola. Candido is a man of such patient kindness that he drives his wife into a frenzy of exasperation; she has him committed to an asylum, since he is obviously not right in the head. He is released at the end, deeply concerned for his wife's wellbeing.

In the second part Matheo, Bellafront's husband, is in prison. He is vicious and worthless but Bellafront is now a devoted wife; she goes to Hippolito to seek his help. Matheo is released – but Hippolito has now been married for some time and Bellafront's beauty arouses him. Matheo stops at nothing to find the means to support his pleasures and suggests that his wife resume her old way of life to supply him with money. But his servant, Orlando, is in fact Bellafront's father and he keeps a sharp eye on both Matheo and Hippolito, whose unwelcome attentions to Bellafront he helps to avert. It is Orlando who saves his daughter when she is falsely accused of being a prostitute and ordered to a house of correction – and proves her innocent when Matheo accuses her of betraying him with Hippolito. The saintly Candido, meanwhile, has acquired a second wife; but he is now better able to deal with her than he was with his first.

Dekker's play has not been revived for the modern theatre, which is a pity, because the irony lies as much in the dialogue as in the plot itself. Bellafront, the honest woman, is not angelic by any means; she would have been willing to abandon her trade if anyone had asked her to – she only asks that the man is reasonably attractive and reasonably well-to-do. But she is honest in her resolve and stands by it, while her former judge, now married to his heart's desire, is soon pawing the ground in the hope of seducing her. Candido, meanwhile, learns that virtue is not enough in a husband and he is well on the way to successfully handling a second wife who would also be a shrew if he let her.

**Hood, Robin** England's legendary outlaw is the centre of a cycle of ballads, the most notable being *Robin Hood and Guy of Gisborne*, which was published in Percy's *Reliques of Ancient English Poetry* in 1765. Verse narratives appeared in 1632 (*True Tale of Robin Hood*) and 1670 (*Robin Hood's Garland*) and a prose tale in 1678. Scott gives him the part of King Richard's ally in the siege of Torquilstone in *Ivanhoe*.

According to the antiquary John Stow there were many outlaws who lived in the forests in late 12th-century England; among them were Robin Hood and Little John, who robbed only the rich and never molested the poor. Robin is mentioned in the Pipe Rolls (exchequer records) of Yorkshire for 1230 as a fugitive and in *Piers the Plowman*; he is a definite historical figure in Andrew of Wyntoun's chronicle of Scotland (*c*.1420). A later antiquary, Joseph Ritson, collected all the songs and ballads about Robin in the 18th century and identified him as Robert Fitz-Ooth, born at Locksley in Nottinghamshire about the middle of the 12th century. A positive date for his death is given in the *True Tale of Robin Hood* – 18 November 1247; the legend tells that he was bled to death by a nun who wished him ill at Kirklees in Yorkshire, where he had gone to have his wounds tended.

Joseph Hunter, writing some years after Ritson, was another antiquary who found Robin Hood in medieval records but he places him in a later century. Hunter investigated the court rolls of Wakefield and stated that Robin Hood was a contemporary of Edward II and a supporter of Thomas of Lancaster. Robin Hood is the subject of song 26 in Michael Drayton's *Polyolbion* (1622).

**Hood, Thomas** 1799–1845. Hood was the son of a bookseller and was born in London. He started work as a clerk at the age of 13 but his health was causing his parents concern by the time he was 16 and he was sent to stay with relatives in Dundee. While in Scotland he began to write, contributing articles to local journals. Two years later he returned to London and worked as an engraver for a time before joining the staff of *The London Magazine* in 1821. He became friends with Thomas De Quincey, Charles Lamb, William Hazlitt, and John Hamilton Reynolds, whose sister Jane he married in 1825.

Hood had to work hard as a journalist all his life in spite of indifferent health. He was editor of *The Gem* and *The Comic Annual*. In 1834 financial difficulties obliged him to withdraw to the continent; he lived at Ostend and Coblenz and succeeded, through unremitting work, in paying all his debts. He returned to England in 1840 and edited *Hood's Magazine* and *The New Monthly Magazine* until Sir Robert Peel secured him a Civil List pension. His last years were materially comfortable but he died at the age of 46. The pension continued to be paid to Jane Hood after his death.

Hood is a poet of the second rank with a secure place in literature. His best poems – 'The Bridge of Sighs', 'The Elm Tree', 'The Haunted House', 'A Death-bed', 'The Plea of the Midsummer Fairies', and 'The Last Man' – are essential inclusions in anthologies. His famous and bitter protest against sweated labour, 'The Song of the Shirt', was published anonymously in *Punch* in 1843 and helped secure the success of that magazine. 'The Dream of Eugene Aram' was published in *The Gem* in 1829 and is a fine dramatic narrative poem. The most commercially successful of his works was *Odes and Addresses to Great People* (1825), satirical verse written in collaboration with Reynolds. Hood also published a novel, *Tylney Hall* (1834), and *Up the Rhine* (1840), satirical observations on the behaviour of the English abroad.

**Hook, Theodore Edward** 1788–1841. A fashionable novelist of the early 19th century, Hook catered successfully for those who were not members of the society he described. He was educated at Harrow, moved in fashionable circles, and was appointed Accountant General in Mauritius in 1813. He was dismissed after four years for a deficiency amounting to £12,000. In 1820 he became editor of the Tory *John Bull*, and published his first stories in 1824 in a volume called *Sayings and Doings*, the first of a series of four. Other books were *Maxwell* (1830), *Gilbert Gurney* (1836), and *Jack Brag* (1837). He was the model for Thackeray's Mr Wagg in *Pendennis*.

**Hooker, Richard** 1553–1600. The great advocate of Anglicanism was born at Heavitree, near Exeter. He was admitted to Corpus Christi, Oxford, through the influence of another notable advocate of the same cause, John Jewel, Bishop of Salisbury, and became a fellow in 1577. Upon his marriage in 1584 he resigned his fellowship and was appointed rector of Drayton Beauchamp in Buckinghamshire; the following year he became Master of the Temple.

The afternoon lecturer at the Temple was Walter Travers, a leading English Puritan, and soon the humane and learned Hooker was in the lists against him. No Puritan could ever admit to being wrong about anything, whereas the new Master of the Temple could proclaim his fallibility with a serene mind, and he held his own against Travers for six years. In 1591 he began work on the book that made him one of the foremost English theologians. This, too, was in

Richard Hooker. The portrait by Wenzel Hollar executed in 1657, many years after Hooker's death. British Museum Print Room.

answer to the Puritans, a group of whom had published, in 1572, a well-written and forceful address, *An Admonition to the Parliament*, the elements of which would have made all men good Puritans and imposed 'severity of discipline' on those who might think of being less. Hooker asked for a country living so that he could continue his work and was made rector of Boscombe in Wiltshire in 1591. In 1595 he moved to Bishopsbourne in Kent, where he died.

*Of the Lawes of Ecclesiastical Politie* was published in eight books. The first four appeared in 1594, the fifth in 1597. The posthumous volumes came in 1648 (the sixth), 1651 (the eighth), and 1662 (the seventh). Their total authenticity is in doubt, but the worth of the whole has never been in doubt; a more persuasive plea for moderation and humanity in the matter of worship could not be imagined. The doctrines of Rome had been rejected in England; the danger lay at the other pole, where it was claimed that the Scriptures were the only law appointed by God unto Man, therefore there must be an infallible form of worship that admitted no alteration.

Hooker never raises his voice. He is eloquent and calm, a man of great learning and deep humility in a period of passionate and violent advocacy who had the wisdom to perceive – and the courage to say – that no one form of church government is prescribed as an immutable pattern by Scriptures and that the Church is an organic institution whose rules and administration can change with time and circumstance. Hooker earned the admiration of the Catholics; Thomas Stapleton and Cardinal Allen brought his work to the attention of Pope Clement VIII, describing a style 'that expressed such a grave and so humble a majesty, with such clear demonstration of reason, that in all their readings they had not met with any that exceeded him'. Pope Clement agreed; after his first reading of Hooker's volumes he declared 'There is in them such seeds of eternity . . . they shall last till the last fire shall consume all learning.'

Richard Hooker is one of the subjects of Izaak Walton's *Lives* (1665).

**Hoosier Schoolboy, The**  A novel by Edward Eggleston, first published in 1883. The setting is that of Eggleston's earlier novel *The Hoosier Schoolmaster* and demonstrates the pupils' view of the conditions under which they were taught, which were inimical both to aspirations and to contentment.

See also **Eggleston, George Cary**.

**Hoosier Schoolmaster, The**  A novel by Edward Eggleston, first published in 1871. The word 'Hoosier' is the name given to Indiana – the Hoosier state – though there is no certain basis for the use of it. One theory claims that it is a corruption of Husher, or champion – one who can hush all challengers. Eggleston based his novel on the experiences of his brother, George Cary Eggleston, who was a teacher in Indiana.

Ralph Hartsook is a district teacher in rural Indiana. Jack Means has his eye on Ralph, regarding him as a suitable husband for his daughter, Mirandy. Ralph, however, is in love with Hannah Thompson, a bound servant girl of the Means household, a fact that excites the resentment of the family when they find out. In addition Ralph's position as teacher is made untenable when a false accusation of theft is made against him. His pupils take the cue for their behaviour from their elders, who persecute him. All ends happily: the charge is proved false when Ralph is brought to trial and a further disclosure proves that Hannah is of age. She cannot legally be a bound servant against her will, so she is free to marry Ralph.

**Hope, A(lec) D(erwent)**  1907–  . A. D. Hope was born in Coona, New South Wales. He studied at Sydney University and gained a scholarship to Oxford; upon returning to Australia he became a teacher, and then a lecturer in English first at Sydney Teacher's College and then at Melbourne University. He became Professor of English (1950–69) and was Library Fellow at Canberra University College from 1969 until he retired in 1972. Hope's first poems appeared in magazines after World War II; his first collection was *The Wandering Islands* (1955) and he was welcomed as a poet who made skilful use of traditional verse forms for shrewd comment on modern values. *Poems* (1960), *New Poems 1965–1969* (1969), *Dunciad Minor: An Heroick Poem* and *A Midsummer Eve's Dream: Variations on a Theme by William Dunbar* (both 1970), *A Late Picking: Poems 1965–1974* (1975), *A Book of Answers* (1978), and *The Drifting Continent* (1979) have given A. D. Hope a leading place in modern poetry and he has been awarded the Arts Council of Great Britain Poetry Award (1965), the Britannica Australia Award for Literature (1965), the Levinson Prize for Poetry (1968), the Ingram Merrill Award for Literature (1969), and the Robert Frost and Age Book Awards (1976). An influential critic, Hope has published his essays in *Australian Poetry* (1960), *Australian Literature 1950–1962* (1963), *The Cave and the Spring* (1965), *Native Companions* (1974), and *The New Cratylus* and *The Pack of Autolycus* (both 1969). His *Collected Poems 1930–1970* was published in 1972.

**Hope, Anthony (** *or* **Sir Anthony Hope Hawkins)** 1863–1933. The son of a clergyman of Clapton in east London, Anthony Hope Hawkins was an excellent scholar who completed his education with a scholarship to Balliol College, Oxford. He read for the Bar at the Middle Temple and became a successful lawyer, living in his father's house (his father was now Vicar of St Bride's, Fleet Street). He used his spare time to write and published a number of short stories; he also published a novel, *A Man of Mark* (1890), at his own expense, but without reward. His first success came with his sketches of the London season for *The Westminster Gazette* in 1893. These were published in book form in 1894 as *The Dolly Dialogues* and enjoyed considerable success but they have little meaning for readers today, in spite of their lightness of touch.

His famous *The Prisoner of Zenda* was written in a month (December 1893) and published the following April. Its success was sensational and it earned high praise from Robert Louis Stevenson and Andrew Lang; it was dramatized by Edward Rose for Sir George Alexander and enjoyed huge popularity on the stage. Hope gave up his career as a lawyer and devoted his whole time to writing, producing a sequel to *The Prisoner of Zenda* in 1898, *Rupert of Hentzau*, which was almost as successful. Thereafter Hope became a popular novelist and playwright without ever touching the same heights – inevitably, perhaps, since the brilliant idea of *The Prisoner of Zenda* could only be used once. Another notable feature of the two books about Ruritania (Hope added the word to the English language) was their brevity; at a time when most novels were too long his were notably taut.

The author was knighted for his services at the Ministry of Information during World War I. Hope's other books were *The Chronicles of Count Antonio* (1895), *Phroso* (1897), *Simon Dale* (1898), and *Sophy of Kravonia* (1906).

**Hope, Thomas** See *Anastasius.*

**Hopkins, Gerard Manley** 1844–89. Hopkins was the eldest of the eight children of Manley Hopkins, who ran a successful marine insurance business in London. Gerard was born at Stratford in Essex; the family moved to Hampstead in 1852 and he attended Highgate School before entering Balliol College, Oxford, in 1863. There he met his lifelong friend Robert Bridges and was the pupil of Benjamin Jowett and Walter Pater. The influence of the Oxford Movement was still powerful, and Hopkins soon followed the example of John Henry Newman in embracing the authority of the Church of Rome; he was received into it by Newman himself in 1866. After graduating Hopkins taught at Newman's Oratory School and in 1868 became a novice in the Society of Jesus. He was ordained priest (1877), taught at Stonyhurst School (1882–84), and was appointed Professor of Greek at University College, Dublin, a post he held until his death of typhoid fever at the age of 45.

Hopkins' friends, among them Robert Bridges, Coventry Patmore, and Richard Watson Dixon, knew that he was a poet of rare quality but the knowledge took some time to reach the general reading public. Two of his best-known poems, *The Wreck of the Deutschland* (1876) and 'The Loss of the *Eurydice*' (1878), were rejected by *The Month*, the Jesuit magazine. His literary executor, Bridges, waited until 1918 before publishing an edition of his friend's poems. A few years later he published Hopkins' correspondence, which gives a remarkably clear picture of the development of the poet's mind. Until then, Hopkins' work had appeared briefly in anthologies, though his fellow Jesuit Joseph Keating had wanted to publish a complete edition in 1909. Bridges refused, no doubt because his own edition was in preparation. Hopkins had in fact written poems since he was a schoolboy, but had burned most of them when he entered the Society of Jesus. Some years later he reconciled his religious calling with that as a poet and was prompted to write again when he learned of the wreck of the *Deutschland* in the Thames estuary (1875).

That Hopkins' poetry attracted enormous attention from the 1920s onward is evident from the volumes of comment which have continued to pour out, with contributions by every well-known poet and critic. His work proved enormously attractive to budding poets, who frequently made the mistake of believing that a remarkable poet's methods and style can be successfully imitated. A skilful innovator in rhythm, Hopkins sought new ways to give force to his meaning, using original word associations and the famous 'sprung and outriding rhythms'. These, in Hopkins' own words, were 'the nearest to . . . the native and natural rhythm of speech' as 'the governing principle of scansion'. However, George Sampson pointed out that 'Sprung rhythm is nothing more novel than the verse of *Piers Plowman* or of later poets who have sought the effect of two adjacent stresses. If a slightly varied rhythm is imposed upon the original pattern, the result is "Counterpoint Rhythm". Milton constantly used counterpoint rhythm.' Too much attention has been given to the matter of prosody in the poetry of Gerard Manley

Hopkins and, as R. C. Churchill puts it, 'When prosody comes in at the door, poetry is apt to fly out of the window.' To quote George Sampson again: 'His major contribution to poetry is the almost incandescent intensity of apprehension for which he sought to find a fitting expression, and for which his difficulties are worth surmounting. Hopkins is one of the few poets of ecstasy without excess. Hopkins can be a great influence for good upon any humble seeker after the spirit, and the worst of models for the self-confident in search of a manner.'

Hopkins is a difficult poet, but those approaching him for the first time will be rewarded and encouraged by a reading of 'Heaven – Haven: A Nun takes the Veil', 'The Habit of Perfection', 'The Wreck of the *Deutschland*', 'Felix Randal', 'I Wake and Feel the Fell of Dark', and 'To R.B.'. The first collection, *Poems* (1918), was edited by Robert Bridges; the second edition, with additional poems, by Charles Williams (1930); and the third, revised and enlarged, by W. H. Gardner (1948). The fourth edition, with a new biographical and critical introduction by W. H. Gardner and N. H. Mackenzie, appeared as *The Poems of Gerard Manley Hopkins* (1967). This edition was also published in Oxford Paperbacks (1970). *The Letters of Gerard Manley Hopkins to Robert Bridges, and the Correspondence of Gerard Manley Hopkins and Richard Watson Dixon* was edited by Claude Collier Abbott (1935). *A Selection of Poems and Prose* was edited by W. H. Gardner (Penguin Poets, 1966); other selections are by Graham Story (1967) and J. Reeves (1953). *A Hopkins Reader* was edited by J. Pick (1953).

**Horatio** Hamlet's friend and the one who tells him of the ghost in Shakespeare's *Hamlet*. He is convinced of Claudius' guilt after the play scene; later, he tries to dissuade Hamlet from accepting Laertes' challenge. Horatio is an essential rock of steadiness in Hamlet's disordered world but he is not a very interesting character in himself.

*Horestes* See **Puckering, Sir John**.

**Horne, Richard Henry** 1803–84. Horne was born in London and educated at Sandhurst. He led an adventurous life until his early thirties, fighting in the war for Mexican independence and searching for gold in Australia. Later he changed 'Henry' into the fanciful 'Hengist'. Horne wrote a number of poems and verse tragedies, as well as children's stories and critical essays – all of them forgotten. He was never highly regarded even during his lifetime and he published his epic poem, *Orion* (1843), at the price of one farthing as a mark of the public's obvious disregard for epic poetry. Much of this disregard was reserved for Horne's work, and he gave up poetry in 1850.

Horne went to Australia in 1852 as Commissioner for Crown Lands and stayed there until 1869. His *Australian Facts and Prospects* and *Australian Autobiography* (1859) give an excellent account of the continent at that time. Horne was a friend of Elizabeth Barrett's before her marriage to Robert Browning, and collaborated with her on a book of critical essays, *A New Spirit of the Age* (1844). He published *The Letters of Elizabeth Barrett Browning addressed to Horne* in 1877. Among Horne's other works were the tragedies *Cosmo de' Medici* (1837), *The Death of Marlowe* (1837), and *Gregory VII* (1840); *The History of Napoleon* (1841); and an edition of *The Complete Works of Shakespeare* (1857).

*Horseman in the Sky, A* See *In the Midst of Life*.

*Horse-Shoe Robinson: A Tale of the Tory Ascendancy*. A novel by John Pendleton Kennedy, first published in 1835. It was successfully adapted for the stage by Clifton W. Tayleure in 1856.

The time is towards the end of the War of Independence; the setting is Virginia and the Carolinas. Mildred Lindsay's Tory father wants her to marry Tyrrel, the English spy. But she loves Arthur Butler, the patriot, and is an ardent supporter of the revolution. She secretly marries Arthur; but he is captured and she depends very much during her subsequent adventures on the help and support of Horse-Shoe Robinson, the resourceful frontier blacksmith. At the end of the tale Tyrrel is caught and hanged and Mildred and Arthur are reunited.

*Horse's Mouth, The* See **Cary, (Arthur) Joyce (Lunel)**.

**Hotspur, Henry** The son of the Earl of Northumberland, Bolingbroke's supporter in Shakespeare's *Richard II*, in which play he is called Henry Percy. He is known by the more familiar name in *Henry IV* Part I, in which he rebels against the king. He is killed by Prince Hal at the Battle of Shrewsbury. The historical Hotspur was 23 years older than the prince.

*Hound of Heaven, The* See **Thompson, Francis**.

*Hound of the Baskervilles, The* A novel by Sir Arthur Conan Doyle, first published in *The Strand Magazine* (1901–02). It concerns the trials of the Baskerville family, in their great lonely house on the Devon moorland, and the mysterious hound of enormous size and weight, which they all fear. Sherlock Holmes (reintroduced in this novel after his apparent death eight years before) and Dr Watson are brought into the case by the heir of the Baskervilles to solve the mystery of the death of Sir Charles Baskerville, apparently caused by the monstrous dog. The book is the best of the Sherlock Holmes stories, with a well-sustained atmosphere of terror.

**House of Life, The** A series of sonnets by Dante Gabriel Rossetti. The first part was published in *Poems by D. G. Rossetti* (1870) and the second part in *Ballads and Sonnets* (1881). It is not a sonnet sequence inasmuch as there is no definite connection in theme; the poet described each sonnet as a 'moment's monument' and he drew on his knowledge of the Italian poets for his imagery. *The House of Life* is generally regarded as Rossetti's finest work. It is the expression of his emotional life and reflects his belief that the physical impulses of love are a symbol of the union of souls. The best-known sonnets are probably 'Lovesight', 'The Choice', 'A Superscription', and 'The One Hope'.

**House of Mirth, The** A novel by Edith Wharton, first published in 1905.

Lily Bart is almost penniless, though she is related to the prominent families of New York. Her aunt, Mrs Peniston, has given her a home and irregular allowances. Lily moves among the best people but she is now 29; a rich husband, who can ensure her rightful place in society, is becoming an urgent need. Simon Rosedale is rich but has not been accepted by society; Lawrence Selden has, but then he is just a lawyer and not rich. Lily takes tea with Lawrence at his bachelor apartment; upon leaving she encounters Simon and, flustered, tells him a clumsy lie.

At a house party she loses money to Gus Trenor and decides that prim, dull, but very wealthy Percy Gryce will be the answer to her problems. But the squalid and promiscuous Mrs Bertha Dorset has her eye on Lawrence Selden and Lily has an enemy. Percy Gryce leaves the house party suddenly and her hostess warns Lily to tread carefully. But Lily is never careful enough; she chooses Gus Trenor, who is a wealthy businessman, to confide her circumstances to and asks him to invest the little money she has. She is gratified when sums of money begin to arrive. She receives a horrible shock when Trenor tells her it is his own money and demands, not repayment for it, but payment for it. In a humiliating scene she learns that Simon Rosedale has talked of her appearance outside Selden's apartment. Trenor had been enjoying her companionship, no more than that; but it was a subject for New York gossip and had been

conveyed to Lily's aunt, Mrs Peniston. Lily does not know of this; she tells Trenor she will pay him back every penny and leaves. She is thankful to be invited on a yachting trip in the Mediterranean by George and Bertha Dorset, especially when she discovers that Simon Rosedale wants to marry her.

Bertha Dorset has a lover in the yachting party. She has asked Lily to join them so that George will be diverted. But at Monte Carlo Bertha is in grave danger of being found out and she ruthlessly turns the tables by making Lily, whose reputation is hardly secure, the target of a scandal – too many people are ready to believe that she is George's mistress. She is no longer accepted in society and after her aunt dies Lily finds that she has been disinherited in favour of a spiteful cousin. She has been left 10,000 dollars; she works for a milliner and has to wait out a year before she will receive the money.

Lily could expose Bertha but she will not, even if there is a strong possibility that she could have George as a result. She could accept Simon Rosedale, who admires her and would happily provide the means for bringing Bertha to justice in society; but while Lily appreciates his regard she is too dispirited, now, to face the idea of marrying him. Besides, she knows why Bertha wanted her on the yachting trip; but she had accepted the invitation because she was glad to go anywhere out of New York. She cannot hold down her job at the milliner's and regularly takes a sedative at night to keep her defeat by a futile and worthless society from haunting her. She had believed that its comforts and privileges were the only things worth having, but she was not clever enough (or was too honest) to comprehend fully the rules of the game it played. Selden, belatedly, wants to marry her but his past lack of resolution where Lily was concerned brings its own penalty. By this time Lily has received her aunt's bequest; she has paid back every penny to Gus Trenor and settled all her bills. She has a few dollars left in the world when she takes an overdose of sedative.

**House of the Seven Gables, The** A novel by Nathaniel Hawthorne, first published in 1851.

The Pyncheon home in Salem lies under a curse pronounced on it by 'Wizard' Maule generations earlier, when Colonel Pyncheon dispossessed him and took the property for himself. (One of Hawthorne's ancestors was a judge at the Salem witch trials and was cursed by one of his victims.) Now the time is the mid-19th-century and the owner is Judge Pyncheon, whose carefully measured benevolence wins him honour.

But he is a mean hypocrite who takes care not to live in the decaying house, which is now occupied by his poor cousin, Hepzibah. The Judge's benevolence does not extend to her and she runs a small shop to earn a living. Hepzibah's brother Clifford, ill and feeble-minded, has spent 30 years in prison, wrongfully convicted of the murder of a rich uncle and sentenced by Judge Pyncheon. Upon his release Clifford goes to Hepzibah and lives with her in the house of the seven gables. His presence is an added problem for Hepzibah but the gloom is somewhat lightened by the arrival of Phoebe, a fresh and pretty young cousin from the country, and of a young daguerrotypist called Holgrave, who takes lodgings in the house. Phoebe and Holgrave are immediately attracted to one another.

Judge Pyncheon now begins to persecute Clifford: he is trying to find the deeds to the murdered uncle's property and believes his cousin knows their whereabouts. Clifford knows nothing but the judge threatens to have him certified and confined as a lunatic though Hepzibah does her poor best to protect her brother. Then the judge dies suddenly and his considerable wealth is inherited by Hepzibah and Clifford. Holgrave, who intends to marry Phoebe, reveals that he is the last descendant of 'Wizard' Maule and that the rich uncle and the judge were victims of the same curse. He helps to locate the missing deeds and to rehabilitate poor Clifford. Holgrave's marriage to Phoebe removes the curse and Hepzibah and Clifford live a comfortable old age in the house of the seven gables.

***House with the Green Shutters, The*** A novel by George Douglas, first published in 1901.

John Gourlay is the most successful man in Barbie, a small Scottish town. He is, simply, more astute, harder working, and has a more powerful personality than the rest. Unfortunately, he is arrogant and contemptuous of the feelings of others. His wife has degenerated into a slovenly, dull-minded woman whose only feeling is for their son John; their daughter Janet becomes father's favourite. Gourlay's home, the House with the Green Shutters, preoccupies him as the symbol of his success and he lavishes money on it while evincing a dingy meanness in other things.

When James Wilson returns to Barbie to open a general store Gourlay is insufferably rude to him: Wilson's father was a mole catcher and Gourlay has set himself to be the arbiter in social matters. Wilson prospers and sends his son to high school: Gourlay sends John to the same school and on to university. John has a minor academic success and Gourlay sees him as a brilliant scholar. But John, fearful and insecure, takes to drink and is finally expelled. Gourlay's business, meanwhile, has been going downhill.

Back in Barbie, John becomes involved in a tavern brawl and arrives home seething with hatred and frustration at what his life has been. Gourlay has heard about the brawl and taunts his son; John kills him with a poker in the presence of his mother and sister. The family succeed in convincing the doctor that Gourlay met his death by accident; but they discover that he was by that time in debt to the bank and that The House with the Green Shutters is mortgaged. To a chorus of whispers from the townspeople Gourlay had treated with contempt, his family sinks in ruin.

Both Gourlay and his weak, rebellious son are strongly characterized and the atmosphere of the small town is beautifully conveyed. Douglas's early death was tragic because this, his only novel, promised so much.

**Housman, A(lfred) E(dward)** 1859–1936. A. E. Housman was born at Fockbury in Worcestershire. He had an undistinguished record at Oxford, failing to obtain a pass degree, and for the following ten years worked in London as a civil servant. In spite of that he became a meticulous and renowned classical scholar, and his contributions to academic journals led to his appointment as Professor of Latin at University College, London (1892–1911), and Professor of Latin at Cambridge from 1911. He published critical editions of Manilius (1903–1930), Juvenal (1905), and Lucan (1926).

Housman's fame in the wider world is as a poet, whose small output of meticulously crafted poems reached an enormous public. *A Shropshire Lad* (1896), *Last Poems* (1922), *More Poems* (posth. 1936, edited by his brother Laurence Housman), and *Additional Poems* (published posthumously 1937, in *A.E.H.: Some Poems, Some Letters and a Personal Memoir* by Laurence Housman) contain some haunting poems which express with remarkable force the regrets and frustrations that everyone has experienced at some time. The settings of many of his poems, in an idealized English countryside, add to their poignancy. Housman's poetic processes are indicated in his notable lecture, *The Name and Nature of Poetry* (1933). The first edition of *The Collected Poems* was published in 1939.

**Housman, Laurence** 1865–1959. Born in Bromsgrove, Worcestershire, the younger brother of A. E. Housman. A prolific writer of novels, poems, plays, and fantasies, he is remembered for his play sequences in the domestic life of Queen Victoria, *Victoria Regina* (1934) and *Happy and Glorious* (1945).

**Hous of Fame, The** An unfinished poem of 1080 lines by Geoffrey Chaucer. It belongs to the poet's 'second period' and scholars give 1380 as the probable year of its composition. It is another example of Chaucer's dream-vision method of storytelling.

In his dream the poet visits the Temple of Venus, where he finds inscribed the story of Aeneas – his flight from Troy, his reception by Dido at Carthage, and his betrayal of Dido. The poet is then taken to the House of Fame by an eagle, a garrulous and comic character.

The lady Fame presides in the House, where the poet observes and comments on a great range of aspirants. Success or failure is announced by Aeolus on the two trumpets Fame and Slander. But the poet seeks knowledge of love and happier things; a stranger takes him to the Laborintus, which keeps whirling round. The eagle picks up the poet then sets him down inside where he finds himself in the House of Rumour.

The poem ends here; there is no way of telling what the author's intentions were, though attempts have been made to explain the poem in terms of Chaucer's life or the affairs of England at that time.

**Hoveden (or Howden), Roger of** d. *c.*1201. Roger of Hoveden was a clerk at the court of Henry II and also served as a travelling judge. A late chronicler of the Northumbrian school, he wrote *Chronica* (1173–1203) and was probably also the author of *Gesti Henrici Secundi* and *Gesta Ricardi* (1170–92); the latter was ascribed by William Stubbs to Benedict of Peterborough, but Austen Lane Poole, writing in 1951, asserts that Stubbs is wrong and that the authorship is unknown.

Roger of Hoveden's *Chronica* was edited by William Stubbs (Rolls Series, 1868–71). *Gesti Henrici Secundi* and *Gesta Ricardi* were also edited by William Stubbs (1867).

**Hovey, Richard** 1864–1900. Richard Hovey published his first poems at the age of 16. He was born in Illinois and educated at Dartmouth, graduating in 1885. After following a variety of interests for six years he went to Europe and while in France came under the influence of the Symbolists; he translated Mallarmé and a number of Maeterlinck's plays. Back in the USA he embarked on a collaboration with the Canadian poet Bliss Carman; this resulted in the three volumes *Songs from Vagabondia* (1894), *More Songs from Vagabondia* (1896), and *Last Songs from*

*Vagabondia* (1901). These are remembered more for their tone than their quality: American poetry was scholarly but anaemic and the buoyant bohemianism of Hovey and Carman was a needed corrective. Fortunately, it did not become an end in itself.

*Along the Trail* (1898) was published in the year of the Spanish-American War and contains some embarrassing chauvinistic verse as well as the familiar 'Spring' with its refrain 'A Stein Song'. Hovey was also working on a cycle of poetic dramas with love as the theme, based on *Le Morte Darthur*, but he did not live to complete it; *The Holy Graal* (1907) contains the fragments. A posthumous collection of poems, *To the End of the Trail*, was published in 1908.

**Howe, E(dgar) W(atson)** 1853–1937. E. W. Howe was born in Indiana, brought up in Missouri and Nebraska, and became proprietor of a newspaper in the town of Atchison, Kansas. Howe edited the *Daily Globe* from 1877 to 1911, and was also editor of *E. W. Howe's Monthly* from 1911 to 1937. He published novels, collections of editorials and aphorisms – and one book that is regarded as a landmark of uncompromising realism in the American novel. This was *The Story of a Country Town* (1883) which was rejected by publishers over and over again, so was privately printed in the original edition. It was highly praised by Mark Twain and others and has been steadily reprinted ever since.

**Howe, Julia Ward** 1819–1910. A New Yorker, Julia Ward Howe is best remembered as the author of *The Battle Hymn of the Republic* but she was, as well as a poet who enjoyed some regard during her lifetime, a reformer and humanitarian who worked untiringly for female suffrage and the abolition of slavery. With her husband, Samuel G. Howe, she edited the abolition paper, *Commonwealth*, in Boston. She wrote a *Life of Margaret Fuller* (1883), *Sex and Education* (1874), and *Modern Society* (1881). Her poems were published in *Passion Flowers* (1854) and *Later Lyrics* (1866).

**Howe, Miss** The heroine's principal correspondent in *Clarissa* by Samuel Richardson. She does her best to advise her friend but Clarissa's virtue admits of no compromise.

**Howell, James** *c.*1594–1666. A minor diplomat in the reign of Charles I, Howell was, for his time, a much-travelled man and a fine linguist. He became an MP in 1627, and was imprisoned as a Royalist for eight years from 1642. At the Restoration he was appointed Historiographer Royal.

At the time of his arrest Howell was the author of two books, *Dodona's Grove* (1640), a political allegory, and *Instructions for Foreign Travel* (1642). He also wrote political pamphlets and his years in prison saw the beginning of the book by which he is remembered, *Epistolae Ho-Elianae: Familiar Letters*, written to imaginary correspondents about a multitude of subjects. The four books (1645, 1647, 1650, and 1655) are the most arresting source of detail about many contemporary events. Other books are his satirical *Perfect Description of the Country of Scotland* (1649) and *Londinopolis; an Historical Discourse or Perlustration of the City of London* (1657).

**Howells, William Dean** 1837–1920. The son of a printer, William Dean Howells was born in Martin's Ferry in Belmont county, Ohio. His father moved from place to place in Ohio and Howells had very little formal education. At the age of nine he was already setting type for his father as well as reading voraciously in the pressroom and among his father's books. By the time he was 15 he was contributing essays and poems to Ohio newspapers. He was also deep in the study of languages.

Howells' father settled in Columbus eventually and in 1856 Howells joined the staff of the *Ohio State Journal*, where he worked for five years, making friends with John James Platt. Their *Poems of Two Friends* was published in 1860, the same year in which Howells wrote a campaign biography of Abraham Lincoln and made a sort of literary pilgrimage to Boston. The *Atlantic Monthly* had published one of his poems. Howells was received by Oliver Wendell Holmes and James Russell Lowell; the 23-year-old Howells made an excellent impression on the older men and on J. J. Fields, the publisher of the *Atlantic*. This was to prove of great value to Howells in the near future. Meanwhile, he was rewarded for his Lincoln biography by an appointment as US consul in Venice (1861–65), a rich and rewarding period for Howells and a wonderful opportunity to perfect his Italian. He also wrote *Venetian Life* (1866) and *Italian Journeys* (1867).

After returning to the USA in 1865 Howells was briefly associated with *The Nation* and was then offered the subeditorship of the *Atlantic Monthly*; he became editor five years later and stayed in charge for ten years (1871–81), happy as an adopted New Englander but with his frontier egalitarianism intact. His first novel was *Their Wedding Journey* (1872); this, and *A Chance Acquaintance* (1873) and *A Foregone Conclusion* (1875), use his experience of travel and Italy. His next novels, including *The Lady of the Aroostook* (1879) and *A Fearful Responsibility* (1881), introduce the contrast between Americans and Europeans, and the factor of social position. *The Undiscovered Country* (1880) deals with spiritualism and the Shakers; *Dr Breen's Practice* (1881) is the story of a society woman who becomes a physician and proves to be an incompetent one.

Howells left the *Atlantic* in 1881; he was established and his novels were now serialized in the *Century Magazine*. His subject matter also was changing about this time, the comedy of manners giving way to searching character studies and the moral dilemmas of his time. *A Modern Instance* (1882) and *A Woman's Reason* (1883) were followed by his two best novels, **The Rise of Silas Lapham** (1885) and **Indian Summer** (1886). *The Minister's Charge* (1887) was published in the same year as Howells' scholarly *Modern Italian Poets*.

Howells' tireless industry continued with *April Hopes* (1888) and *Annie Kilburn* (1889), which is a sharp and critical comment upon the economic system of his time. Upon completion of *Annie Kilburn* in 1888 Howells moved to New York to join the editorial staff of *Harpers*; the effect was to broaden his appreciation of American life and American writing. New York was rougher than Boston, noisier, and much more free in expression. It was also a city of contrasts, of extreme wealth, and of desperate actions by the poor. Strikes, the questionable executions of those convicted for the Haymarket Riots, the brutal suppression of the Homestead Strike in Pennsylvania – all these events had an effect on Howells, a humane and honest man, and the climate of the times turned him towards socialism. The work of Tolstoy and the US economist Henry George influenced his thinking, and Zola influenced his approach to the novel.

**A Hazard of New Fortunes** (1890) described the decay of moral and ethical standards in a competitive society; *The Quality of Mercy* (1892) is the story of a crime resulting from economic circumstances; *An Imperative Duty* (1893) introduces a Black heroine; *The World of Chance* (1893), written in a lighter vein, tells of literary life in New York; and *The Coast of Bohemia* (1893) relates the fortunes of a girl studying art. But Howells' industry remained unflagging; he wrote over 40 novels and, inevitably, the standard varied. A utopian novel, *A Traveller from Altruria* (1894), and *The Son of Royal Langbirth* (1904) are worth mentioning, as well as two novels about his Ohio background, *New Leaf Mills* (1913) and *The Leatherwood God* (1916). Howells also wrote two volumes of short stories concerned with the supernatural, 31 plays, 11 travel books, some books of verse, and several volumes of reminiscences. Three books of criticism appeared: *Criticism and Fiction* (1891), *My Literary Passions* (1895), and *Literature and Life* (1902).

In later life Howells was the foremost man of letters in the USA. He was generous in his encouragement of new talent, as Hjalmar Boyesen, Hamlin Garland, Paul Lawrence Dunbar, Stephen Crane, Frank Norris, Robert Herrick, and others were to discover. His friendship embraced both Mark Twain and Henry James with equal warmth. He was totally opposed to the Spanish-American War and said so, without equivocation. Honours from abroad as well as from his own country came in steadily and repeated offers were made of academic posts.

While *The Rise of Silas Lapham* is accorded classic status the novels of William Dean Howells are hardly read today, though his works are being reprinted in the USA in carefully edited texts. The reason may well be what Marcus Cunliffe calls in *The Literature of the United States* 'his faintly old-maidish quality'. 'Never wholly at ease with literature that could not safely be read aloud within the family circle, he saw little need to justify himself for not emulating Zola: American life as well as American taste was more refined that that of Paris.' In a few lines Mr Cunliffe has described enormous limitations. Within them, the artist that Howells undeniably was produced one fine, and several good, novels but nothing less than genius can make art of the commonplace, as the example of George Eliot shows. It is a pity that, having become acutely aware of the harshness of the real world, Howells should have baulked at describing more of it in his skilful and economic prose.

**Howleglass** See *Till Eulenspiegel.*

**Hubert de Burgh** Given no rank or title in Shakespeare's *King John*, the historical Hubert was a baron who served the king. In the play he is Prince Arthur's custodian and disobeys the king's order to blind the boy. He tries to keep the prince safe but Arthur dies in trying to escape.

**Huchoun of the Awle Ryale** The identity of Huchoun has never been established but has been a question for scholars of early English literature since his name was given by Andrew of Wyntoun, in the early 15th century, as the author of a series of romances. Wyntoun, describing King Arthur's deeds, says that the matter had been treated by Huchoun of the Awle Ryale, in his *Gest Hystoriale* – meaning, very roughly, that

Huchoun, an office-holder of some kind, had written of the historical deeds of King Arthur. Wyntoun mentions *The Gret Gest of Arthure*, *The Anteris of Gawayne*, and *The Epistill als of Suete Susane* (Susanna and the Elders).

These works have been identified as follows: *The Gret Gest of Arthure* with the Thornton Manuscript at Lincoln of *Morte Arthure*; *The Antleris (Adventures) of Gawayne* as possibly *The Awntyrs off Arthure at the Terne Wathelyne* (The Adventures of Arthur at the Wadling Tarn, in Cumberland), or *Golagros and Gawayne*, or *Sir Gawayne and the Grene Knight*. *The Epistill als of Suete Susane* exists in several versions; it was a popular subject of the time and one of the versions is probably Huchoun's. Also attributed to Huchoun is the *Gest Hystoriale of the Destruction of Troy*.

It seems probably that there was a Scottish poet of the 14th century, an older contemporary of John Barbour, who served the Scottish kings David II and Robert II. He has been identified by some scholars as Sir Hew of Eglintoun.

**Huckleberry Finn, The Adventures of** A novel by Mark Twain, first published in 1884. Conceived as a sequel to *Tom Sawyer*, it was begun in 1876 and, while it makes use of some of the characters of the other book, soon departs from it in feeling. *Tom Sawyer* remains a perennial favourite among children's books and there is much, at first, that young people can take in their stride. The setting and period are the same in *Huckleberry Finn* but when the narrative really gets under way Twain goes deeper into regional character, the implications of slavery, and the experience of frontier life; the book becomes a novel which moves away from the juvenile public. Then, full circle, the closing chapters return to the feeling of *Tom Sawyer*. The narrator is Huckleberry Finn himself.

Huck, who was adopted by Widow Douglas at the close of *Tom Sawyer*, is now 14 and living with her and her sister, Miss Watson. Miss Watson owns a slave, Jim, and she is not very kind to him. Huck's blackguard father turns up, having heard of the money Huck and Tom recovered from the cave of Injun Joe; he demands the money as Huck's legal father. Huck places the money with Judge Thatcher; his father kidnaps him and imprisons him in an isolated cabin. Huck fakes his own murder and escapes to hide on Jackson's Island. There he meets Jim, Miss Watson's slave; he is hiding, too.

Jim had overheard Miss Watson's plans to sell him; Widow Douglas tried to dissuade her but Miss Watson replied that she found the price she

Huckleberry Finn and his father. A wood engraving by
E. W. Kemble for the first edition of *Huckleberry Finn*
by Mark Twain (1884).

had been offered irresistible. When Huck learns
that his own 'murder' has been blamed on Jim,
the runaway slave, the two take to the river on a
raft, going downstream and hoping to reach the
shore of Illinois. Huck's intention is to make for
the Ohio River and go upstream to the free states.
But a fog envelops the river and the raft floats
down past the junction with the Ohio – and into
the South. Then a steamboat hits the raft and Huck
and Jim, separated, have to swim for their lives.

Huck swims to the Kentucky bank where he is
given hospitality by the slave-owning Grangerford family. The Grangerfords are feuding with
the Shepherdson family; Buck Grangerford,
who is the same age as Huck and becomes his
friend during this episode, explains the feud to
him – only leaving out its origin. In fact Buck
does not even know the origin, though he is a
victim of the bloody gunfight that is the episode's
climax. Jim has, in the meantime, also reached
land near the Grangerford house and been hidden
and fed by the family's slaves. After the gun
battle he and Huck depart on their salvaged raft.
They give refuge to two crooks, the 'King' and
the 'Duke', and they soon regret it. At various
halts the swindlers engage in low-down cheating
and confidence tricks; on the raft their bullying
makes life a misery for Jim and Huck; Huck is
desperate to shake them off.

He almost succeeds when he frustrates their
plans to cheat the three Wilks girls of their inheritance – but they manage to extricate themselves and regain the raft. Then they sell Jim.

The raft has reached Arkansas, where Tom
Sawyer's Aunt Sally – Mrs Phelps – lives. With a
faked 'Wanted' notice offering $200 for a runaway
slave answering to Jim's description, they trade
him for $40 to the Phelps family and Jim is con-
fined on Phelps's Farm. Huck has to decide what
to do, knowing that to rescue Jim will outlaw him
forever from the only society he knows. He
decides to rescue Jim and damn the consequences.

Since he is supposed to be dead, he goes to
Phelps's Farm and is welcomed as Tom Sawyer,
who is expected. Then Tom himself turns up.
Nine chapters are spent on Tom Sawyer's
elaborate and ridiculous plans to help Huck
rescue Jim, during which some funny incidents
occur – but during which Jim is subjected to
physical suffering. The main part of the story is
referred to in the apprehension of the 'King' and
the 'Duke', who are tarred and feathered by the
mob. Tom's silly schemes result in Jim's confinement being made even more cruel. But in fact Jim
was really free all the time and Tom knew it –
Miss Watson had died and had freed him in her
will – she had felt ashamed of wanting to sell him
down the river because the price had tempted
her. Why did Tom do it? 'Why, I wanted the
*adventure* of it . . .' He does not know that Jim
could have got away in accordance with his 'adventure' but had stayed to help him when Tom
received a bullet in the leg. And while the line
between being a 'mischeevous' boy and being a
monstrous one is, obviously, a very thin one,
what makes the close of the book unacceptable is
that the author betrays the character of Huck in
making him, even half-heartedly, go along with
Tom Sawyer's silly schemes. Unacceptable
because Huck has rejected (Chapter 3) Tom
Sawyer's world which, in any case, is totally different from the reality of his own; Tom's is
'mischeevous' and Huck's is real – so real that the
smells come off the page. Even more unacceptable because Huck (Chapter 3) has looked at his
world and rejected it; mere mischief no longer
has a part in it. Huck is himself again in the last
chapter, when he rejects the idea of being adopted and 'sivilized' by Aunt Sally. Jim tells him
how his evil father died, so Huck has his money
safe, with no impediment to the use of it. He
decides to go out West.

In his Introduction to the Penguin English Library edition of the novel Peter Coveney writes
'. . . immediately Huck arrives at Phelps's Farm
. . . we are confronted with one of the most extraordinary changes in tone in the whole range of
the modern novel . . . the moral heart of the novel
leaks away'. Bernard De Voto's and Hemingway's comments are similar; those of Lionel

Trilling and T. S. Eliot are in disagreement. Leslie A. Fiedler gives an elaborate explanation of the minds of Huck and Jim in terms of their society in an attempt to make the nine chapters acceptable and goes on to say 'The burlesque tone of the finale manages to suggest such ideas' (one has to disagree – the ideas are Mr Fiedler's) 'but at the same time keeps them in the realm of slapstick, where they do not appear either problematical or horrifying.' This is to ignore all that has gone before, which is precisely what does make the ending what De Voto calls a 'chilling descent' – from what has been, hitherto, one of the finest novels to come from America. It is not quite a masterpiece but three-quarters of it is masterly.

**Hudibras** A satire in three parts by Samuel Butler. Each part consists of three cantos and the whole is composed in octosyllabic couplets: Part 1 was published in 1663, Part 2 in 1664 and Part 3 in 1678. The character of Hudibras (the name comes from *The Faerie Queene*) was based on Sir Samuel Luke, whom Butler served as secretary for a time. Luke was a colonel in Cromwell's army and a zealous Puritan surrounded by cronies who probably indulged in nostalgia for the past: they are the 'caterwauling brethren' of Butler's satire. The strongest influences on Butler were Cervantes and Rabelais.

In Part 1 we meet Hudibras, a Presbyterian who goes forth 'a-colonelling'. He rides a worn-out horse and carries rusty arms. His squire Ralpho is an Independent, and the two never cease from sectarian squabbling. They come upon a crowd preparing for a bear baiting, a sport condemned by Puritans; they attack the bear baiters and put their leader Crowdero in the stocks. The bear baiters rally and counterattack; they capture Hudibras and Ralpho and release their leader. Hudibras and Ralpho are put in the stocks, where they continue to squabble.

In Part 2 Hudibras is visited in the stocks by a widow whose property he covets. The widow exposes his mercenary motives, and requires him to undergo a whipping in order to regain her favour. Hudibras doesn't like this at all; then Ralpho suggests that the penance could be accepted by proxy. His master is delighted and promptly selects Ralpho as his substitute, to the latter's fury. After a furious quarrel they consult an astrologer, Sidrophel, to discover Hudibras' prospects with the widow. Hudibras learns that Sidrophel is a fraud; he beats him, robs him, and leaves him for dead. He makes himself scarce, leaving Ralpho behind to face any charges that will result. (Sidrophel is a satirical representation of Sir Paul Neale of the Royal Society.)

Hudibras and the rich widow, whose sympathy he is trying to arouse. Loud knocking at the door warns him that he is facing exposure as a fraud. An illustration from an edition of 1710 of Butler's *Hudibras*. The incident occurs in Part III, Canto 1.

In Part 3 Hudibras visits the widow and gives her a fictitious account of all he has endured for her sake. But Ralpho has forestalled him and he is exposed once more. A loud knocking strikes terror into him; he believes supernatural agents are pursuing him and he hides under a table. The astrologer's friends, in fiendish disguises, haul him out and thrash him, and make him confess his many sins. On the advice of a lawyer, Hudibras starts to woo the widow by letter.

At this point Butler seems to have found himself at a loss. Hudibras is forgotten and the last two cantos of Part 3 are concerned with the activities of the Republicans just before the Restoration. Butler gives a notable study of Anthony Ashley Cooper, who became the Earl of Shaftesbury – the Achitophel of Dryden's famous satire. Butler's intentions are not known, if indeed he had any in regard to *Hudibras*: Part 3 came 14 years after Part 2, and Butler was dead two years later.

*Hudibras* is so energetic as to leave the reader breathless. But readers are few now, since the energy is expended on targets which no longer exist. On the other hand, it has great value as a document, a remarkable expression of the Englishman's distaste for secular tyranny and for the unpleasant leaders every such tyranny produces. If John Bunyan showed us the fair side in Pilgrim, Butler shows us the foul, self-righteous one in Hudibras, and his invention and humour move at a high level to the end of the second canto of Part 3. That large numbers of Englishmen were delighted to have Butler speak for them is attested by his success: Part 1 went through nine printings in the year of publication. The standard modern edition of *Hudibras* is that of J. Wilders (Oxford, 1967).

**Hudson, W(illiam) H(enry)** 1841–1922. W. H. Hudson was the son of an American family who farmed in Argentina not far from Buenos Aires. He worked on his father's farm until he was 15, when his health gave way and he became unfitted for outdoor work. He was devoted to nature and spent much of his time observing the wild life of the pampas and the estuary of the Rio de la Plata. He emigrated to England in 1869 and lived as best he could, on what work he could find and the occasional contribution to periodicals. *The Purple Land that England Lost* (1885) was one of the romances set in South America that later became famous; some stories and two novels, *A Crystal Age* (1887) and *Fan* (1892), followed, but most of his writing during the 1890s was the work of a naturalist with an attractive, clear-cut style. He earned considerable respect in the literary world with *The Naturalist in La Plata* (1892), *Birds in a Village* and *Idle Days in Patagonia* (1893), *British Birds* (1895), *Birds in London* (1898), *Nature in Downland* (1900), and *Birds and Man* (1901).

In 1901 Hudson was awarded a Civil List pension, which made life easier for him and enabled him to travel through England. *El Ombu and Other Tales* (1902) and *Hampshire Days* (1903) were followed by a romance, **Green Mansions** (1904), and Hudson enjoyed his first real success. He published 12 more books, two of which – *A Shepherd's Life* (1910) and **Far Away and Long Ago** (1918) – have given his name a permanent place in English literature. Hudson's vivid interpretation of the English scene was no doubt helped by his observing it with the fresh unsentimental eye of one who came from an exotic distant land, one that emerges so powerfully from the pages of *Green Mansions* and the naturalist's books about Argentina. The Hudson Memorial in Hyde Park, London, was designed and sculpted by Jacob Epstein in 1925 and presents the figure of Rima, the heroine of *Green Mansions*.

Among other books by W. H. Hudson were *A Little Boy Lost* (1905), *Afoot in England* (1909), and *The Birds of La Plata* (1920). *Letters from W. H. Hudson to Edward Garnett* was published in 1923.

**Hueffer, Ford Madox**  See **Ford, Ford Madox**.

**Hugh**  The handsome, illiterate, half-savage ostler at the Maypole Inn in *Barnaby Rudge*. He has an affinity with animals, loves his dog, and feels a rough affection for the poor half-witted Barnaby. He saw his mother hanged at Tyburn and his complete anti-socialism leads him to a principal role in the Gordon Riots. He is the son of Sir John Chester, who cast off the girl who became Hugh's mother – but neither of them is aware of that.

**Hughes, Richard (Arthur Warren)** 1900–76. Of Welsh descent, Hughes was born in Weybridge, Surrey, and educated at Charterhouse School and Oriel College, Oxford. After graduating in 1922 he helped found the Portmadoc (Caernarvonshire) Players and directed the company until 1925; he was Vice President of the Welsh National Theatre from 1924 to 1936. His first work was for the theatre, a one-act play called *The Sister's Tragedy* (1922), which was produced in London. In the same year he published *Gypsy Night and Other Poems*. A volume of Hughes's plays was published in 1924 and more poetry in *Confessio Juvenis* (1925). The author travelled in Europe, North America, and the West Indies and in 1929 published his celebrated *A High Wind in Jamaica* (called *The Innocent Voyage* in the USA), a striking novel about children among pirates and the devastating effect of their unwanted presence. Richard Hughes's output was regrettably sparse; the drama did not keep his interest and another novel did not appear until 1938. *In Hazard: A Sea Story* tells of men at sea whose lives are first threatened by a hurricane – and then by fears of a mutiny. The suspected leader, Ao Ling, is finely drawn and realized with great sympathy: his character makes a good book into an excellent one. During World War II Hughes served at the Admiralty and later wrote, with J. D. Scott, one of the official war histories, *The Administration of War Production* (1956). He made a welcome return to fiction with a proposed series to be called *The Human Predicament*, of which two parts, *The Fox in the Attic* (1961) and *The Wooden Shepherdess* (1972), were published. His short stories were published in *A Moment of Time* (1926) and *The Spider's Palace and Other Stories* (1931).

**Hughes, Ted** 1930– . Edward James Hughes was born in Mytholmroyd in Yorkshire and completed his education at Pembroke College, Cambridge. His first volume of poetry, *The Hawk in the Rain* (1957), won him both the Guinness and New York Center First Publications awards; *Lupercal* (1960) confirmed his place as a leading modern English poet. A prolific writer, Hughes has published 14 books of stories and verse for children, plays, essays, reviews and other prose pieces, and translations of Seneca (*Oedipus*, 1969), Yehuda Amichai, and Janos Pilinsky. His poetry has not so far been published in a collected volume: in addition to the titles already mentioned, he has published *Recklings* (1966), *The Burning of the Brothel* (1966), *Wodwo* (1967, poems, short stories, and a play), *Crow: From the Life and Songs of the Crow* (1970), *A Few Crows* (1970), *A Crow Hymn* (1970), *Crow Wakes* (1971), *Eat Crow* (1971), *In the Little Girl's Angel Gaze* (1972), *Eclipse* (1976), *Gaudete* (1977), *Chiasmadon* (1977), *Orts* (1978), *Cave Birds, An Alchemical Cave Drama* (1978), *A Solstice* (1978), *Remains of Elmet, A Pennine Sequence* (1979), *Moortown* (1979), *Brooktrout* (1979), *In the Black Chapel* (1979), and *Wolverine* (1979). Ted Hughes won both the Somerset Maugham Award and the Hawthornden Literary Prize in 1960. He was married to the American poet, Sylvia Plath.

**Hughes, Thomas** 1822–96. The son of a country gentleman, Hughes was born at Uffington in Berkshire and educated at Rugby School and Oriel College, Oxford. He was called to the Bar in 1848. He was the author of *The Scouring of the White Horse, or the Long Vacation Ramble of a London Clerk* (1859), a patronizing account of rustic life in fictional form, combined with nostalgic pictures of his birthplace. He also published biographies of *Alfred the Great* (1869) and *David Livingstone* (1889), *A Layman's Faith* (1868), and *Memoir of a Brother* (1873) – about his brother, George Hughes, who wrote a popular poem on the subject of the boat race. None of his work is famous apart from **Tom Brown's Schooldays: by an Old Boy** (1857), his account of life at Rugby during the headship of Thomas Arnold. Hughes was an advocate of Arnold's muscular Christianity and the book was to be great propaganda – with parents, at any rate – for public-school, especially boarding-school, life. It was followed four years later by *Tom Brown at Oxford* (1861), which was less successful. Hughes contributed the introduction to Frederick Denison Maurice's *Christian Socialism* (1898).

**Hulme, T(homas) E(rnest)** 1883–1917. T. E. Hulme was born at Endon in Staffordshire and educated at Newcastle-under-Lyme High School and St John's College, Cambridge. He was sent down from Cambridge for brawling in 1904 and continued his studies in London. After visiting Canada, Hulme went to Brussels in 1907 to teach English while he learned French and German, and developed the interest in philosophy for which he is best known. After a visit to Italy he was readmitted to Cambridge through the good offices of Henri Bergson, but he now found the Cambridge atmosphere too academic and he left (1912). He published his translations of Bergson's *Introduction to Metaphysics* and Georges Sorel's *Reflections on Violence* in 1913, and became a regular contributor to *New Age*, continuing after joining the army when war broke out in August 1914. *The Complete Poetical Works of T. E. Hulme*, which consisted of five brief imagist pieces, appeared in *New Age* in January 1912. Hulme was killed in action near Nieuport in September 1917.

Hulme's unpublished manuscripts, uncollected pieces, and verse fragments were published after his death: *Fragments, from the Notebook of T. E. Hulme* (1921) was published in *New Age; Speculations: Essays on Humanism and the Philosophy of Art* (1924) was edited by Herbert Read, as was *Notes on Language and Style* (1929); *Further Speculations* (1955) was edited by Sam Hynes. Hulme's antiromantic philosophy was a powerful influence in modern poetry and criticism.

**Humble Romance and Other Stories, A** A collection of stories about New England life by Mary Wilkins Freeman, first published in 1887. The following stories are notable in this first collection.

*A Humble Romance.* Jake Russell is a pedlar in tin goods. His wife has eloped with another man and Jake believes himself free, many years later, to marry again. Then his first wife returns and blackmails him, with the threat of a charge of bigamy, into returning to her. But Jake's second wife stands by him and keeps his business going successfully until he is able to free himself and resume his happy life with her.

*The Bar Light-House* conveys vividly the stormy New England coast and tells of the lighthouse keeper's paralysed wife, who undergoes a religious conversion after a succession of seemingly miraculous incidents. The author reveals a notable vein of wit in this story.

*Cinnamon Roses* was a celebrated story for many years. Two unmarried sisters receive a great deal of attention from a very eligible bachelor in the village. He is the victim of continual frustration because the woman he wants to marry is convinced that he is pursuing her more attractive sister, who is of course delighted to encourage the man. It ends happily only after many years.

*Old Lady Pingree* is so called because of her inexhaustible kindness and charity towards others, though she is in fact impoverished. The villagers see to it that when she dies she is laid to rest in the family plot – the only thing she wanted for herself.

**Hume, David** 1711–76. David Hume was the second son of Joseph Hume, laird of Ninewells, a small estate in Berwickshire, and was born in Edinburgh. He was intended for the law and studied at Edinburgh University but left without taking a degree. The next three years he spent at his father's house, reading intensively and probably pondering the issues that provided the material for his works. In 1734 he went to France, where he spent three years, first at Rheims and then at La Flèche on the Loire, where, at the Jesuits' college, he was stimulated by the study of history then being pursued by French scholars. At La Flèche he began his *A Treatise of Human Nature*, publishing the first two volumes in 1739; the concluding volume appeared in 1740. The work was published anonymously and attracted little attention. The first notice appeared seven months after publication and it was plain that the critic had not comprehended the work. Hume then published an abstract of the *Treatise*, also anonymously.

He published his next work in the following year, the first of his *Essays Moral and Political* (1741). The second volume followed in 1742 and a book of three more came out in 1748. His writings began to attract attention and Hume applied for the chair of moral philosophy at Edinburgh University. He failed and accepted an engagement as tutor to the Marquis of Annandale (1745). This came to an end because the marquis neglected to pay him – Hume was obliged to go to law to secure what was owing to him. In 1747 he accompanied General St Clair as judge advocate on the disastrous expedition to Port L'Orient; he also went with the general on diplomatic missions to Vienna and Turin in 1748. In the same year he published *Philosophical Essays* (later called *An Enquiry*) *Concerning Human Understanding. An Enquiry Concerning the Principles of Morals* followed in 1751.

In 1752 Hume took the post of librarian to the Faculty of Advocates and stayed in it for five years. It was poorly paid but allowed him considerable time and facilities for research. *Political Discourses* (1752) was translated into French and aroused great interest; Hume became famous in Europe as a philosopher. *Essays and Treatises on Several Subjects* (1753–56) contained his published essays in four volumes, but he had, meanwhile, been at work on his **History of Great Britain**. Volume I 'containing the Reigns of James I and Charles I' was published in 1754; Volume II 'containing the Commonwealth, and the Reigns of Charles II and James II' in 1756. Hume travelled backwards; the *History of England under the House of Tudor* (1759) was followed by the *History of England from the Invasion of Julius Caesar* (1762): the complete history, which begins at Julius Caesar and ends at the flight of James II, was published in eight volumes in 1763. The first history of Great Britain was coolly received at first but acceptance did come and then celebrity. For many years it was regarded as the standard work, until further material which was not available to Hume could take the subject farther.

Hume had resigned from the library in 1757 and, in 1763, in comfortable circumstances from the sale of his works, he went to Paris with the Earl of Hertford, as secretary to the embassy. He was not a popular figure in England – his philosophy and his approach to history were too challenging – but the French welcomed him as an eminent man of letters. Voltaire, Diderot, and d'Alembert became his friends (Hume left d'Alembert £200 in his will); so did Rousseau – for as long as that morbidly suspicious man could be a friend of anyone. Disregarding the warnings of those who knew Rousseau better, Hume procured asylum for the stateless philosopher in England. He even found him a dog and a mistress and no doubt played a large part in procuring him an English government pension. But after a year and a half, Rousseau's persecution mania persuaded him that Hume, for some reason, intended his ridicule and a public quarrel ensued. Rousseau departed for France and Hume, in his own defence, published their correspondence. It proved to be a perfect vindication; Rousseau was more than a little mad.

Hume completed other works while the *History of Great Britain* was in progress. *Four Dissertations* (1757) contained **The Natural History of Religion**, *Of the Passions, Of Tragedy,* and *Of the Standard of Taste. Two Essays* (1777) contained *Of Suicide* and *Of the Immortality of the Soul*; these were originally intended as part of the volume of dissertations and were published anonymously after Hume's death. **Dialogues Concerning Natural Religion** (1779) was, in accordance with Hume's will, published posthumously, though it was written during the 1750s. An autobiographical sketch, *The Life of David Hume. Written by Himself.*, was published by Adam Smith in 1777.

David Hume. A detail from the portrait by Allan Ramsay, 1766. National Gallery of Scotland, Edinburgh.

From 1767 to 1769 Hume was in London as Under Secretary of State, and disliked the English capital. He built himself a house in Edinburgh and spent the remaining years of his life there. He died of cancer on 29 August 1776. Boswell, the incurable reporter, had visited him on 7 July, and contrived a discussion with the dying philosopher on the subject of immortality. Boswell's account makes it plain that the visit was prompted by rude curiosity; he wanted to know how a sceptical philosopher as distinguished as Hume faced annihilation. David Hume was true to himself and Boswell had the grace, in his account, to acknowledge that he retired from the visit discomfited.

The only person who seems to have quarrelled with David Hume was Rousseau, though many disagreed with him and wrote at length to express their disagreement. He was, according to his friend Adam Smith, as wise and virtuous a man as human frailty will admit. His later years were passed among his friends in comfort and content and he waited for death with a clear and tranquil mind.

Hume, the historian, has now been superseded; much more information became available to succeeding historians. But his was the first English history to achieve literary excellence, the first to which a philosopher's mind was brought. As a philosopher, Hume's influence has been profound. He was impatient with abstractions and philosophical systems: 'I found that everyone consulted his fancy in erecting schemes of virtue and of happiness, without regarding human nature, upon which every moral conclusion must depend.' *A Treatise of Human Nature* presented the basis of his philosophy; the essays that followed presented its arguments in more polished form and applied them to economics, politics, religion, and history. The philosopher and historian benefited each other greatly.

The edition by T. H. Green and T. H. Grose of Hume's *Philosophical Works* (1874–75) is generally acknowledged as the definitive one. Hume's *Letters* were edited by J. Y. T. Greig (1932).

**Humorous Lieutenant, The,** or *Generous Enemies*. A comedy by John Fletcher, first produced about 1620 and first published in 1697.

The play's title comes from the character of a lieutenant who suffers from a mysterious infirmity that makes him courageous in battle. When cured his courage deserts him; but it returns when he is convinced he is unwell again. The main plot concerns Celia who is held captive at the court of King Antigonus. Both the king and his son Demetrius fall in love with her and while Demetrius is at the wars Antigonus pursues his suit with Celia. She, however, loves Demetrius and resists him. Demetrius, returning victorious from the war, is greeted with the news that Celia is dead. Antigonus, leaving Demetrius to his despair, then tries to obtain a response from Celia with a love philtre. Unfortunately, the humorous lieutenant accidentally drinks the philtre and immediately falls in love with the king. Celia eventually persuades Antigonus, by her loyalty and virtue, to restore her to Demetrius.

**Humphry Clinker, The Expedition of** A novel by Tobias Smollett, first published in 1771. In this, his last novel, Smollett used the epistolary form, with five of the characters writing the letters, thus giving different views of incidents and encounters. The episodic, picaresque arrangement recalls the early novels but there is a strong echo of the author's *Travels through France and Italy*, published in 1766.

Matthew Bramble, a cranky but kind-hearted Welsh squire, travels through England and Scotland with his family: his unpleasant and domineering sister Tabitha, hungry for a husband; his amiable nephew Jerry, just down from

Oxford; his niece Lydia, Jerry's sister, a girl in her teens; accompanying them is Winifred Jenkins, Tabitha's maid. Humphry Clinker appears about a quarter of the way through the book: an ostler who becomes their postillion and proves a resourceful and devoted servant. The family's travels take them to Bath, London, Harrogate, and Durham, where they are joined by Lieutenant Obadiah Lismahago, an eccentric and impecunious Scots soldier whose pride remains intact despite his condition. The expedition is really Matthew Bramble's and his family's, so the name of the book is only explained by Smollett's fondness for that sort of title.

The adventures of the group offer a lively string of episodes and give the author an opportunity to comment on English life and manners in the 1760s, with various characters changing the perspective when required. Humphry, a Methodist, converts Tabitha; Tabitha succeeds in marrying Lismahago; Lydia falls in love with a handsome young actor who, fortunately, proves to be of good family; Humphry is arrested on a fake charge and imprisoned for a short while; Winifred Jenkins and Humphry fall in love; Humphry proves to be Matthew Bramble's son – which raises Winifred to a disconcertingly high status for a former servant but which she faces with blunt common sense. Matthew Bramble contributes the best part of the correspondence and is the principal character.

There is more humour in *Humphry Clinker* than in Smollett's earlier novels and less violence in the adventures. The panorama of English life, so obscured by stench and cruelty before, emerges in this book with remarkable clarity and Smollett's characterization is never better. *Humphry Clinker* is the best of his novels, with his virtues as a writer strikingly displayed. But Smollett is still Smollett, and there are aspects of life he apparently cannot forbear to dwell upon. Here is Bramble's comment on the atmosphere of Bath: 'Imagine to yourself a high exalted essence of mingled odours, arising from putrid gums, imposthumated lungs, sour flatulencies, rank armpits, sweating feet, running sores and issues ... besides a thousand frowzy streams, which I could not analyse.' His first description of Lismahago nearly demolishes the character altogether because he presents him as a sort of monstrous human insect.

Modern editions of *Humphry Clinker* are published in The World's Classics, Everyman's Library, the Penguin English Library, and in the Oxford English Novels series, edited by Lewis M. Knapp (1966).

**Hunt, (James Henry) Leigh** 1784–1859. Leigh Hunt was the son of a preacher and teacher, an immigrant from the USA born in Barbados. Isaac Hunt had supported loyalty to the crown and, though a successful pamphleteer in Pennsylvania, had no audience in England. His son, James Henry Leigh Hunt, was born at Southgate, Middlesex, and inherited his father's facility with words. He was educated at Christ's Hospital and a book of poems was published by his proud father when Hunt was 17 (*Juvenilia*, 1801).

In 1805 Hunt began to write dramatic criticism for his brother John, who was editor of *News*. Hunt's reviews were an advance in the craft, being better balanced than previous writing in that field and based on regular attendance at the London theatres. A collection, *Critical Essays on the Performers of the London Theatres*, was published in 1807. He continued to write theatre criticism in *The Reflector*, a quarterly, from 1810 to 1811. He had meanwhile joined his brother John on the weekly *The Examiner* (1808), where he continued until 1821. Both brothers were sent to prison for two years in 1813 for attacking the Prince Regent and the experience damaged his health. Hunt was not a political journalist as such but the general tone of *The Examiner* was unsympathetic to the Tories and evoked a considerable response. Visitors to the prison included Jeremy Bentham, Charles Lamb, Byron, and the young Charles Cowden Clarke, who later introduced Keats to him. It was at Hunt's house in Hampstead that Keats later met Shelley.

Hunt was a prolific and talented journalist and lived a chaotic domestic life; there was never quite enough money in his large household in spite of his manifold talents. An additional spark might have made Hunt a genius; as it was he never rose to the level of those around him, who, apart from the poets, included Lamb, Hazlitt, and Thomas De Quincey. He learned Italian while at Christ's Hospital and adapted Italian poetry, and as an experienced journalist and editor seemed just the man Shelley and Byron needed for their projected periodical, *The Liberal*. Hunt duly went to Italy with his six children but Shelley's death by drowning was unfortunate for him. His children were unruly and played havoc with the apartments Byron had acquired for them. Hunt was uncertain with the great Lord Byron and wavered between the attitude of a friend and that of one grateful for patronage. The light-hearted liberal who endured a prison sentence in 1813 had become the harassed family man of 1822. He was present with Byron at Shelley's cremation; but Byron, roused by the news from Greece, hurried off, to die there in

April 1824. He had made some arrangements for Hunt but was plainly no longer interested in *The Liberal*. Hunt and his family nearly starved and had, somehow, to get back to England. His *Lord Byron and Some of His Contemporaries* (1828) contains useful information as well as a fair amount of personal criticism.

Hunt is remembered as an excellent journalist and critic, as a minor poet, and for his recognition of Shelley and Keats. He lived long enough to welcome the arrival of Tennyson on the literary scene, and was famous enough to serve as the model, in some respects, for Skimpole in Dickens's *Bleak House*. He was awarded a Civil List pension in 1847. Among the more notable of his many published works are the poems *The Story of Rimini* (1816), *Hero and Leander, and Bacchus and Ariadne* (1819), *Amyntas: A Tale of the Woods* (1820, translated from the Italian of Tasso), and *Captain Sword and Captain Pen* (1835); the play *A Legend of Florence* (produced at Covent Garden, 1840); and *The Autobiography* (1850). *The Dramatic Works of Wycherley, Congreve, Vanbrugh and Farquhar* (1840) provoked Macaulay's attack on them in his essay *The Comic Dramatists of the Restoration*. A fine selection of his *Dramatic Essays* was edited by William Archer. Hunt's short poems 'Abou Ben Adhem' and 'Jenny kissed me' are favourite anthology pieces.

**Hunted Down** A crime story by Charles Dickens, written for and first published in the *New York Ledger* in 1859. The villain, Slinkton, was based on the poisoner and forger Thomas Griffiths Wainewright.

**Hunter, Mrs Leo** In Dickens's *The Pickwick Papers* she is encountered by Mr Pickwick at the Eatanswill election. She appears at the fancy-dress breakfast as Minerva, prepared to deliver her 'Ode to an expiring frog'.

**Huntingdon, Henry of** See *Gesta Stephani* and **Worcester, Florence of**.

**Hunting of the Snark, The** See **Carroll, Lewis**.

**Huon of Bordeaux** Lord Berners' translation of a French 13th-century *chanson de geste* of the Charlemagne cycle, *Huon de Bordeaux* is a late and degenerate example of the form. The story concerns the aged emperor and the knight Huon, who is attacked by a mysterious assailant. Huon kills his assailant and then discovers that he is none other than the treacherous Charlot, the emperor's son. Huon has to undergo ordeal by battle and he is successful; but the old monarch is implacable and the death sentence remains. Then Huon is of-

fered a reprieve if he will go to Babylon and kill Emir Gaudisse. He is to bring back four teeth and a handful of the emir's hair: he must also kill the emir's champion and kiss the emir's daughter, Esclarmonde. With the help of the fairy king Oberon (Auberon) Huon achieves his adventure.

The book was printed by Wynkyn de Worde in 1534, and it was this work that gave Shakespeare his fairy king for *A Midsummer Night's Dream*.

**Husband's Message, The** A poem in Old English, preserved in *The Exeter Book*. The message is to a woman of royal rank; the husband has been forced to flee because of a vendetta, and he sends her assurances of love, pleading with her to take ship for the south and join him in the spring. The message is apparently carved on a staff in runic letters. The poem suffers from a tear in the manuscript sheet, and while H. M. Chadwick believes it is connected with *The Wife's Complaint*, also in *The Exeter Book*, there is disagreement from other scholars. Translations were made by C. C. Abbot in *Three Old English Elegies* (1944) and C. W. Kennedy in *An Anthology of Old English Poetry* (1960).

**Hutchinson, Lucy** b. 1620. The wife of Colonel John Hutchinson, a Puritan soldier in the Civil War, Lucy Hutchinson wrote a partial autobiography and *The Memoirs of the Life of Colonel Hutchinson* for the interest of her descendants. The *Memoirs* were not published until 1806 (edited by J. Hutchinson and including the autobiography) and 1885 in Sir Charles Firth's edition (revised 1906).

Lucy Hutchinson's book is as much a memoir of herself as of her husband; it has a particular value both as a picture of the life of a Puritan family of some distinction and for its comments – frankly subjective – on those around her. The colonel emerges as a quiet man who found himself swept along by the tide of events and did his conscientious best. He was a soldier on the rebel side, an MP, and a signatory of Charles I's death warrant (1649). At the Restoration he would certainly have suffered an unpleasant death had his wife not sent an eloquent letter of penitence to the Speaker of the House of Commons. He was left in peace for two years but was then arrested for alleged complicity in plots against the restored monarch and he died in prison.

Lucy Hutchinson was also the author of *On the Principles of the Christian Religion*, edited by J. Hutchinson (1817).

**Huxley, Aldous (Leonard)** 1894–1963. Aldous Huxley was the son of the biologist Thomas

Henry Huxley and was born at Godalming in Surrey. He was educated at Eton College and Balliol College, Oxford, but his hopes of a career in the medical profession were blighted by a serious eye condition. He graduated in 1915 and became a journalist; he was on the staff of *The Athenaeum* briefly, wrote dramatic criticism for *The Westminster Gazette* (1920–21), and published a volume of short stories, *Limbo* (1920). His principal work is in fiction and essays but his first published works were collections of verse: *The Burning Wheel* (1916), *Jonah* (1917), *The Defeat of Youth and Other Poems* (1918), and *Leda* (1920). He published further collections in 1929 and 1931 but his reputation does not rest on his poetry. *Crome Yellow* (1921) was his first novel and set the pattern of witty cynical novels of ideas which continued through *Antic Hay* (1923), *Those Barren Leaves* (1925), and *Point Counter Point* (1928). With *Brave New World* (1932) he turned his formidable intellect to something which was in the air and which he feared and detested; his novel offers a nightmare vision of the lengths to which psychological conditioning can be taken. The decade was hardly over before his novel proved to be prophetic.

Huxley's novels thereafter are sombre and pessimistic: *Eyeless in Gaza* (1936), *After Many a Summer* (1939), *Time Must Have a Stop* (1944), *Ape and Essence* (1948), *The Genius and the Goddess* (1955), and *Island* (1962). However, in spite of

their brilliance, the novels lack essential character drawing and many readers find that, once read, they do not stay in the mind. This fault is not to be found in his excellent short stories; *Limbo* was followed by the collections *Mortal Coils* (1922), *The Little Mexican* (1924), *Two or Three Graces* (1926), and *Brief Candles* (1930).

In 1938 Huxley settled in the USA. After *Grey Eminence* (1941), a study of the career of Joseph le Clerc du Tremblay, Richelieu's *le Père Joseph*, and *The Art of Seeing* (1942), a description of the eye-training method of a New York doctor which helped to save the author's sight, Huxley published *The Perennial Philosophy* (1946). He had been pondering the artist's difficulty in reconciling reality, often disgusting, with art, which too often idealizes reality and becomes increasingly involved with mysticism. *The Perennial Philosophy* expressed his belief in the need for an extension of awareness. He continued to expound his ideas in *Themes and Variations* (1950) and *Adonis and Alphabet* (1956). *The Doors of Perception* (1954) created a sensation with its examination of the possibility of achieving this through the use of natural drugs known to certain races for thousands of years. *Heaven and Hell* (1956) takes his examination farther. *The Devils of Loudun* (1952) examined a celebrated case of supposed demonic possession among some nuns in France during the reign of Louis XIII. In addition to the unspeakable nature of the whole case, the physical and physiological details were revolting and Huxley conveyed them in remarkable detail.

Huxley's essays do not exist in a complete collection; the *Collected Essays* (1959) is a generous selection edited by the author. He was also the author of two lively travel books, *Jesting Pilate* (1926) and *Beyond the Mexique Bay* (1943). In 1932 he edited *The Letters of D. H. Lawrence*: his introduction is prized as one of the best essays on that writer.

**Huxley, Thomas Henry** 1825–95. The son of a schoolmaster, Huxley was born at Ealing. He was educated at his father's school and at London University, where he studied medicine. He continued his studies at Charing Cross Hospital and was particularly interested in comparative anatomy. In 1846 Huxley went to sea as assistant surgeon on HMS *Rattlesnake*, and became a Fellow of the Royal Society through his studies on marine organisms (1851). He left the navy in 1850 and earned his living as a teacher, soon proving to be an expositor of rare quality. His lectures, essays, and books cover natural science, philosophy, and religion; his approach to

Aldous Huxley, 1931.

religion is indicated by his invention of the word 'agnostic' to describe himself. He published *On the Educational Value of the Natural History Sciences* (1854), *On Races, Species and their Origin* (1860), *Evidence as to Man's Place in Nature* (1863), *On the Methods and Results of Ethnology* (1865), *The Evidence of the Miracle of Resurrection* (1876), *The Advance of Science in the Last Half-century* (1887), *Social Diseases and Worse Remedies* (1891), and *Evolution and Ethics* (1893). His essays and lectures were published as *Collected Essays* (nine volumes, 1893–94).

Huxley is remembered for his powerful support of Darwin, particularly in the famous debate at the meeting of the British Association at Oxford in 1860 in which he argued with Bishop Wilberforce on the subject of Darwin's evolutionary theory. He incurred Matthew Arnold's displeasure because he supported the view, shared by Herbert Spencer, that science was a far better basis of education than the humanities. He also insisted that certain knowledge of the teaching and convictions of Jesus was impossible. Huxley was a tireless champion of free investigation and free speech. He argued that man cannot know the nature of spirit or matter and that his principal duty in life is the relief of suffering and ignorance through the application of knowledge.

## Hyde, Douglas 1860–1949.

Hyde was born in Roscommon, Ireland, and was educated at Trinity College, Dublin. For a time he was Professor of Modern Languages at the University of New Brunswick, but his real interests lay in Ireland where, upon his return, he became President of the Gaelic League when it was founded in 1893. Hyde published a great deal of work during his lifetime but its intrinsic merit is debatable. Of more importance was his contribution to the Irish cultural revival; he drew attention to the literature and traditions of the Irish-speaking areas of Connaught and published his findings in *Beside the Fire* (1890), *The Love Songs of Connacht* (1893), *The Religious Songs of Connacht* (1906), and other books. *The Literary History of Ireland* (1897) gave the English their first information about native Irish literature. Hyde published the Irish text in his Connaught volumes, with an accompanying English version, and revealed a genuine idiom which J. M. Synge was later to use with consummate artistry. Hyde, with Lady Gregory, W. B. Yeats, and Edward Martyn, was one of the founders of the Irish Players and the Abbey Theatre and wrote the first play in Irish to be given professionally, *Casadh an tSúgáin* (*The Twisting of the Rope*, 1901). An active politician, Hyde became the first President of the Republic of Ireland (1938–45).

**Hyde Park** A comedy by James Shirley, first produced in 1632 to celebrate the opening of Hyde Park as a place of recreation to the public. The play, first published in 1637, has the slightest of plots and offers a comment on the fashionable life of Caroline London.

**Hymn to Proserpine** A poem by Algernon Charles Swinburne, first published in *Poems and Ballads* (first series, 1866). The subtitle of the poem reads *After the Proclamation in Rome of the Christian Faith* and the epigraph is *Vicisti, Galilaee* ('Thou hast conquered, Galilean') uttered by the emperor Julian the Apostate on his deathbed. Julian (AD 332–63) had tried, and failed, to restore the worship of the Greek gods. The poem's theme is that all things change in the movement of time; change is represented by the goddess Proserpine, who has seen the passing of the Olympians and will see Christianity run its course. The poem is frankly anti-Christian ('Thou hast conquered, O Pale Galilean; the world has grown grey from thy breath') but, surprisingly, did not come under as heavy fire as the supposedly immoral poems in the same volume.

**Hypatia,** *or New Foes with an Old Face.* A novel by Charles Kingsley, first published in *Fraser's Magazine* (January 1852 to April 1853), and in volume form in 1853.

The setting is Alexandria in the 5th century AD. The city is governed ineffectually by the pagan prefect, Orestes, and his legions, and the threat of the tribes advancing from the heart of Europe hangs over everything. The Christian Church is the strongest power in the city, guided by the patriarch, Cyril, and is opposed to the Neoplatonic philosophy expressed in the teachings of Hypatia, daughter of the mathematician, Theon.

Philammon, a young Christian monk, comes to Alexandria from the desert. He is repelled by the mindless fanaticism of his fellow-monks, and fascinated by the great city. He is drawn away from the arrogance of his fellow Christians, and towards the beautiful Hypatia and the moderation and humanity of her doctrines. At the same time he is discouraged by the weary scepticism of the intellectual, Raphael.

Violence explodes when the Christians are led to believe that Hypatia has set the prefect against them; Philammon witnesses a mob cut her to pieces outside the academy. He returns to the solitude of the desert, appalled by the atmosphere of the great city and convinced of the virtue of tolerance towards all men.

Kingsley stays close to the known facts about the historical Hypatia. The climate of uneasiness, and the fanatical Christianity at the end of the Roman era are skilfully evoked. His portrayal of the great intellectual centre on the eve of its fall and his descriptions of every facet of the city's life are memorable.

***Hyperion*** Two unfinished poems by John Keats. One version was published in 1820; the volume contained an Advertisement stating that it was included at the publishers' wish, not the poet's. 'The poem was intended to have been of equal length with *Endymion*, but the reception given to that work discouraged the author from proceeding.' The second version is called *The Fall of Hyperion, A Dream* and was published by Monckton Milnes in 1856; a note to the title reads: 'An attempt made at the end of 1819 to reconstruct the poem.' Keats's letters show that he could not accept Christian philosophy and turned to the mythology of ancient Greece, with which he was much more in sympathy. He stopped writing the poem, he declared in a letter of 21 September 1819, because 'there were too many Miltonic inversions in it' – a different statement from that printed in the Advertisement in the 1820 volume. *The Fall of Hyperion* is a dream related in the first person; it is a draft, not a finished poem.

In the first version, called 'A Fragment' by the poet, the story of Hyperion is narrated. Saturn and the other Titans are grieving over their fall (Saturn is the Latin counterpart of the Greek Cronus, who was overthrown by his son, Zeus). The Titans consider how they may recover their lost power, and place their hopes in the one of their number who remains undeposed, the sun god Hyperion (or Helios). But with the coming of Apollo, god of knowledge, poetry, and music, the Titans' rule is ended.

The second version is narrated by the poet, who in a dream is granted entry to a shrine because of his awareness of the misery in the world. Moneta, the Titans' priestess, relates the fall of Hyperion and the coming of Apollo. An old order has gone, yielding place to a new. Ian Jack, commenting on *The Fall of Hyperion* in *English Literature 1815–1832*, refers to the lines beginning 'The poet and the dreamer are distinct' and writes that Keats was 'returning to one of his deepest preoccupations, the difference between romance (poetry of delight and escape) and the greatest poetry, which helps us to interpret the significance of human life itself.'

# I

**Iachimo** In Shakespeare's *Cymbeline*, the mendacious and malicious villain who impugns Imogen's virtue for the sake of a wager. He gains access to Imogen's chamber by concealing himself in a chest.

**Iago** See ***Othello, The Moor of Venice***.

***Ideas of Good and Evil*** See **Yeats, William Butler**.

***Ides of March, The*** See **Wilder, Thornton (Niven)**.

***Idler, The*** A series of papers contributed by Samuel Johnson to *The Universal Chronicle or Weekly Gazette* from 15 April 1758 to 5 April 1760. The papers are similar in character to *The Rambler* but they are shorter in length and generally lighter in tone; representative characters are not given Latin names as in *The Rambler* but English names easily remembered – Tom Restless, Jack Whirler, Mr Sober, the author (Johnson), and the critic Dick Minim. A monthly journal running from 1892 to 1911, edited by Jerome K. Jerome and Robert Barr, was also called *The Idler*.

***Idylls of the King, The*** The poems of Alfred Tennyson's Arthurian sequence were composed at various stages in his career. When he was 24 he wanted to compose a 'whole great poem' on the theme and wrote 'Morte d'Arthur', which was not published until 1842. However, the reviews were discouraging and Tennyson did not work on the subject of Arthur again until 1859. 'Vivien', 'Enid', 'Elaine', and 'Guinevere' were the poems of the volume called *The Idylls of the King* (1859); 'The Coming of Arthur', 'The Holy Grail', 'Pelleas and Ettarre', and 'The Passing of Arthur' were published in *The Holy Grail and Other Poems* (1869); *Gareth and Lynette* (1872) contained the title poem and 'The Last Tournament'; and 'Balin and Balan' was published in *Tiresias and Other Poems* (1885). The final sequence runs as follows:

*The Coming of Arthur*. Arthur, the newly crowned king, sets out to restore order to the kingdom and subdue the unruly barons. He falls in love with Guinevere, daughter of Leodegran, King of Cameliard. Successful in his campaigns, he seeks her hand but Leodegran hesitates; Arthur's mysterious origins make him doubtful. He is persuaded by Bellicent, wife of King Lot of Orkney, who tells him the truth about Arthur's birth, upbringing, and coronation and of Merlin and Excalibur. Arthur and Guinevere are married. The source of the poem is Malory's *Le Morte Darthur*.

*Gareth and Lynette*. Arthur's court, not long established, is the goal of all aspiring young men, one of whom is Gareth, son of King Lot of Orkney and his queen, Bellicent. His mother, to discourage him, will only give him permission to leave if Gareth will serve the hard way first – as a scullion in the kitchens – for one year. Gareth accepts the condition and works his allotted term under Kay, the seneschal. Lynette, a noble lady, comes to Arthur and asks for Lancelot to save her sister Lyonors, who is besieged in her castle by four knights. Gareth, the year over but still a scullion, claims the adventure, so Arthur makes him a knight and grants his wish. Lynette is disgusted and treats Gareth with elaborate discourtesy, addressing him as Sir Kitchen-Knave. But he defeats the first three knights and then confronts the last, costumed as Death. Lancelot arrives and Lynette wants him to undertake the last combat. But Gareth fights and prevails, and finds the fourth knight is just a boy, brother of the other three, in hideous armour that strikes dread into the hearts of those who try to help Lyonors. The brothers had hoped to fight, and kill, both Arthur and Lancelot. The source of the poem is Malory's *Le Morte Darthur*, in which Gareth marries Liones, the lady he rescues. In Tennyson he marries either Lyonors or Lynette; an old tale says one, a later tale the other, according to the closing lines of the poem.

*The Marriage of Geraint* and *Geraint and Enid*. 'Enid' was one of the original poems in *The Idylls of the King* (1859) and was divided into two parts in 1873; they were given separate titles in 1886. The sources were the story of *Gereint and Enid* in *The Mabinogion* and the *Erec* of Chrétien de Troyes. Geraint, one of Arthur's knights, is married to Enid, daughter of Yniol. Uneasy about the character of the queen, Guinevere, he decides to withdraw from the court and remove Enid from her influence. A remark of Enid's is misunderstood by him and he believes her faithless. He keeps her with him during his knightly encounters but forbids her to speak to him. But her devotion to him in all sorts of dangers reassures him of her love.

*Balin and Balan*. This was the last poem of *The Idylls* to be written, and was intended to introduce the story of Merlin and Vivien. The source of the story is Malory's *Le Morte Darthur*. Balin (Balin le Savage in Malory) is a violent and irascible but brave knight who is devoted to Queen Guinevere. His brother Balan, leaving to pursue a dangerous half-human forest creature, warns Balin to curb both his temper and his devotion. Disturbed by the queen's friendship with Lancelot, Balin curses himself for a fool and leaves the court, then kills Sir Garlon, who dishonours the queen's name. Garlon's father, King Pellam, who is descended from Joseph of Arimathea, orders his knights to pursue Balin, who flees through Pellam's castle looking for a weapon. He finds a spear before an altar and uses it to vault through a casement to make his escape. Later he is found asleep in the forest by Vivien, the queen's favour hanging on a tree above him. From pure malice, Vivien confirms Balin's unease about the queen. Balin's temper gets the better of him and, howling with rage, he destroys the emblems of his devotion. His wild cries are heard by Balan, who believes he has found his quarry and rides to the attack. Balin takes Vivien's squire's horse and the spear and rides to meet the enemy. Balan does not know him, since he has thrown away his shield in his rage. The two brothers kill each other; Vivien rides away unconcerned after seeing them fall.

*Merlin and Vivien*. In Tennyson's version Vivien is the child of a king whom Arthur defeated; she now dwells at the court of King Mark of Cornwall and hears a minstrel sing of the purity of the knights and ladies of Arthur's court. She goes to Camelot with a distressed and pleading countenance and begs, as an orphan, protection from the queen. She tries to sow suspicion and to seduce the king but does not succeed for Arthur hardly notices her. She decides that Merlin, the master of all secret arts, will serve her purpose better. When Merlin, weary of his great knowledge, leaves the court for Broceliande Vivien follows him. She succeeds in extracting from him a charm which she uses to seal him up for ever in a giant oak tree. The character of Vivien in Tennyson is his own invention, but the story of Merlin's enchantment is in Malory's *Le Morte Darthur*.

*Lancelot and Elaine*. The story of Elaine, the lily maid of Astolat, and her hopeless love for Lancelot follows closely the events related in the French prose *Lancelot* and the English *Le Morte Arthur* (not to be confused with Malory's *Le Morte Darthur*) but does not continue to Agravain's betrayal of Lancelot and Guinevere. (See **Launcelot of the Lake**.)

*The Holy Grail*. The quest for the Holy Grail, in Tennyson's poem, is related by Sir Percivale, who has taken off his armour and left the court to become a monk, to his fellow monk, Ambrosius. The first vision of the Grail is conveyed to a holy nun, Percivale's sister, who tells her brother that 'all the world be healed' if a quest for the Grail succeeds. She recognizes in Galahad, the youngest of all the knights, the purity which is essential, and she makes him a sword-belt of her hair. Galahad occupies the Siege Perilous, the vision of the Grail is seen by the knights of the Round Table, and the quest begins. (See **Grail, the** for the story of Bors, Gawain, Lancelot, Percivale, and Galahad in the quest. Tennyson's version is chiefly based on the account in Malory's *Le Morte Darthur*.)

*Pelleas and Ettarre.* Pelleas, guileless and strong, sets out for Arthur's court to seek knighthood. On the way he meets the beautiful Ettarre and falls in love with her. He is welcomed by Arthur, many of his knights being absent on the quest for the Grail, gains his knighthood, and wins the prize at a tournament. He gives the prize to Ettarre, who had encouraged him solely because she wanted the prize. She then turns her back on him and returns to her own castle. Pelleas follows her and she will not admit him; she sends her knights to kill him but he defeats them one by one. Then all three attack and bind him; he is taken before Ettarre and though he recognizes her greed he still loves her. She has him thrown out, bound, but he is rescued by Gawain 'passing by.' Gawain undertakes to further Pelleas' suit but betrays him with Ettarre, and Pelleas, heartbroken, rides away. His feelings change from grief to bitterness after he encounters Percivale and learns from him that Lancelot and Guinevere, too, are false. When he meets Lancelot he attacks him furiously, telling him 'a scourge am I to lash the treasons of the Table Round'. Lancelot defeats him and the two return to Camelot. Pelleas rejects the queen's graciousness and leaves the court; Guinevere and Lancelot have a fearful sense of impending doom whilst Modred watches and waits. Tennyson's poem is based on the events related in Malory's *Le Morte Darthur*, but with changes to the characters to underline the decay of the ideals of the court of Arthur and the knights of the Round Table.

*The Last Tournament.* The tournament is held on a wintry day, and Arthur's court has become a bleak reflection of its former glory. The story opens with the rescue of a baby girl from an eagle's nest by Lancelot; the baby wears a ruby necklace. Lancelot takes the baby to Guinevere but in spite of her loving care the baby dies. The queen gives the necklace to Arthur to use as a prize in a tournament: 'Perchance – who knows? – the purest of thy knights May win them for the purest of my maids.' The Tournament of Dead Innocence is presided over by Lancelot. Arthur has gone with the younger knights to quell the

growing disorder in the kingdom; before leaving he tells Lancelot of his depressed state of mind – or does he simply imagine that his world has turned sour? Lancelot knows too well that Arthur's depression is soundly based; he presides over the tournament with a heavy heart. The ruby necklace is won by Tristram, who does not want it for his wife, Isolt the White of Brittany. His paramour is Isolt, the wife of King Mark, and he goes to her at Tintagel; King Mark surprises him with Isolt and kills him. Meanwhile Arthur's campaign has reinforced his depression. He encounters the hate-filled Pelleas as the Red Knight and returns to his castle to find that Guinevere has left him. He is greeted by his jester in tears: 'I am thy fool, And I shall never make thee smile again.' The events concerning Tristram are loosely based on Malory; the rest is Tennyson's own. The jester, Dagonet, is a notable creation.

*Guinevere.* Tennyson's poem is an original creation. The queen retires to Almesbury in Malory's *Le Morte Darthur* but only after she hears that Arthur has been killed. Arthur is away on campaign and Modred seeks the kingdom for himself. He has spied on the queen and has been discovered by Lancelot; but after that incident Guinevere is acutely aware of being watched and feels increasing guilt about her betrayal of Arthur. She implores Lancelot to leave the court; eventually he agrees and they arrange a last meeting. They are overheard by Vivien; she hurries to tell Modred, who with his band of followers surprises the lovers. Lancelot hurls Modred from the tower, and while he lies stunned Guinevere tells Lancelot that now they must part forever. She goes to the nuns at Almesbury and Lancelot returns to his lands. Among the novices she discovers that the names of Guinevere and Lancelot are notorious as faithless wife and false friend. Arthur comes to the nunnery; he has made war on Lancelot and Gawain and many knights have been killed. But he is forced to return: Modred and half the kingdom are in rebellion and Arthur has a presentiment that his death is not far off. He forgives Guinevere and leaves; she remains with the nuns, becoming their abbess, and dies after three years.

*The Passing of Arthur.* In 1842 the final poem of *The Idylls* was written around Tennyson's 'Morte d'Arthur', which occupies lines 170–440 of *The Passing of Arthur*. The last great battle in the west, between the armies of Arthur and Modred, is about to take place. Bedivere hears Arthur's despairing prayer in which he wonders how it is that only in the ways of men are the ways of God not to be found. The ghost of Gawain tells the king that he will pass away on

The dying Arthur. One of Dante Gabriel Rossetti's designs for Tennyson's *The Idylls of the King*. City of Birmingham Museum and Art Gallery.

the next day: 'Farewell! there is an isle of rest for thee.' After the battle Modred is dead but Arthur is dying; Bedivere is the only one of his knights left and Arthur bids him return the sword Excalibur to the water whence it came. Bedivere cannot bring himself to do that and hides it by the lake. But Arthur knows by Bedivere's words that the sword has not been returned. It is only on his third order that Bedivere obeys, though he grieves to part with the 'relic of my great lord'. He hurls the sword far out into the middle of the lake; 'But ere he dipt the surface, rose an arm Clothed in white samite, mystic, wonderful, And caught him by the hilt, and brandished him Three times, and drew him under in the mere.' Bedivere carries Arthur down to the water's edge to await the barge, with its three queens, which will bear the dying king to Avilion. He comforts Bedivere as best he can, in the famous lines beginning 'The old order changeth, yielding place to new, And God fulfils himself in many ways . . .' Bedivere watches the barge until it is out of sight. The source of the poem is Malory's *Le Morte Darthur*, with the difference that in Malory Sir Bedivere later sees Arthur's tomb, in a hermitage. The three queens originate in Malory and remain unexplained; they could represent the three Fates – there is a distinctly pagan and mythological air about them.

**Ignoramus** A farcical comedy by George Ruggle, produced at Cambridge University in 1615 during a visit by King James and Prince Charles. The king enjoyed the performance so much that he asked for the play to be performed again on a subsequent visit. The play is a satire on lawyers and the title refers to the Recorder of Cambridge, Francis Brackyn, who is burlesqued as the foolish victim of various adventures. (Brackyn was also a target in *The Parnassus Plays*.) Ruggle based his play on an Italian comedy by Giambattista della Porta (1538–1613) called *La Trappolaria*.

George Ruggle (1575–1622) was a fellow of Clare College who is believed to have written other plays, but *Ignoramus* is the only one to survive. It was first published in 1630.

**Igraine** The mother of King Arthur by Uther Pendragon, her name is variously spelled (Ygraine, Ygerne, Igerne). The wife of Gorlois, Duke of Cornwall (he is not named in Malory), she attracts King Uther's attention at court and her husband, enraged, takes her back to Cornwall and locks her up in Tintagel. Uther, with Merlin's help, assumes the guise of her husband and gains access to her after killing her husband. Igraine becomes his wife and he confesses to his guile in gaining her bed.

***Imaginary Conversations of Literary Men and Statesmen*** A series of dialogues by Walter Savage Landor. Volumes I and II were first published in 1824, III in 1828, and IV in 1829. *Pericles and Aspasia* (1836) and *Imaginary Conversations of Greeks and Romans* (1853) are in the same style. The dialogues range from classical times to Landor's day, some containing action and incident. They cover a wide field: dramatic, satirical, idyllic, social, political, and literary; the best are those that avoid the presentation of the author's own views. Among the best-known are 'Epicurus and Leantion and Ternissa', 'Leofric

Igraine and Uther Pendragon. The frontispiece illustration to the first book of Malory's *Le Morte Darthur* in Wynkyn de Worde's edition, 1529.

and Godiva', 'Dante and Beatrice', 'Leonora d'Este and Father Panigarola', 'Princess Mary and Princess Elizabeth', 'Lord Bacon and Richard Hooker', 'Calvin and Melancthon', and 'Aesop and Rhodope'.

*Pericles and Aspasia* began as one of the conversations but outgrew the form and became a series of letters. It covers the period from the first meeting at the theatre to the death of Pericles during the plague in Athens in 429 BC.

**Imlay, Gilbert** *c*.1754–*c*.1828. Imlay was born in New Jersey and fought in the War of Independence as a captain. He was the author of *A Topographical Description of the Western Territory of North America* (1792), which is written in the form of letters to a friend in England, and **The Emigrants** (1793), an epistolary novel. *The Emigrants* is a romance, the first ever written about the frontier area of Pennsylvania, from Pittsburg west to the Mississippi.

Imlay was obliged to leave the USA in 1783 after becoming involved in dubious land deals in Kentucky and turned up in London in the 1790s. He frequented the radical circles of his fellow Americans Joel Barlow and Tom Paine, and lived for a time with Mary Wollstonecraft, who bore him a son. He is buried in Jersey; the year of his death is uncertain.

**Imogen**   The heroine of Shakespeare's *Cymbeline*. The king's daughter, she married Posthumus secretly, to the wrath of the queen, her stepmother, who wanted her for her son, Cloten. A victim of Iachimo's malice, she is aided by her exiled husband's servant, Pisanio, and discovers her long-lost brothers (she does not know who they are) in the forest in Wales while disguised as a boy. She is one of Shakespeare's most attractive heroines and the principal reason why the play, for all its faults, continues to be produced.

**Importance of Being Earnest, The**   The comedy by Oscar Wilde, first produced in February 1895 at St James's Theatre. It was the author's last play and his finest work for the stage. The slender story concerns two young men, John and Algernon, and how they find happiness with Gwendolen and Cecily. More important than the plot is the characterization, especially of Gwendolen's mother, Lady Bracknell, and also of Miss Prism and Canon Chasuble. The play includes a deftly worked resolution, wonderfully funny encounters, and some of the wittiest dialogue ever written for the stage. It is uncompromisingly artificial and one of the finest comedies in the English language.

A scene from the first production of *The Importance of Being Earnest* at the St James's Theatre, London, on 14 February 1895. In Act II of Wilde's comedy are, left to right, Allan Aynesworth as Algernon, Evelyn Millard as Cecily, and George Alexander as John Worthing. Victoria & Albert Theatre Museum, London.

**Imposture, The**   A comedy by James Shirley, first produced in 1640 and first published in 1652. The imposture of the title is by Juliana, the cast-off mistress of Flaviano, the Duke of Mantua's favourite. The duke's daughter, Fioretta, is being wooed by the Prince of Ferrara; Flaviano was ambitious to marry her himself and Juliana has been in his way. Juliana masquerades as Fioretta; and in a 'change-partners' series of situations the characters sort themselves out happily.

**In a Glass Darkly**   A book of short stories by Sheridan Le Fanu, first published in 1872.

The stories in this volume are presented as a collection of cases investigated by an alienist, Dr Martin Hesselius, who explores much of the supernatural in terms of psychopathology. With such stories as 'Green Tea', 'The Watcher', 'The Room in the Dragon Volant', and 'Carmilla' the book has become a classic of mystery and occult suspense.

**Inchbald, Elizabeth**   1753–1821.   Elizabeth Simpson was born near Bury St Edmunds in Suffolk. She ran away from home at the age of 18 to join her brother George, who was an actor, and became an actress in spite of a speech impediment she never completely overcame. She married an actor named Joseph Inchbald in 1772 and made the acquaintance of distinguished players such as Sarah Siddons and Tate Wilkinson. She appeared at Covent Garden in 1789 but after that gave up acting to become a full-time writer, achieving considerable success in a series of sentimental and didactic comedies, among them *I'll Tell You What* (1785), *Everyone has his Fault* (1793), *The Wedding Day* (1794), and *Wives as They Were and Maids as They Are* (1797). Elizabeth Inchbald was the author of two novels, **A Simple Story** (1791) and *Nature and Art* (1796), neither of them a complete success but looking forward to the 19th century in the sure touch she brought to the characters' emotional make-up.

*Indian Summer* A novel by William Dean Howells, first published in 1886. In Florence on holiday, Theodore Colville meets a friend from his boyhood, Evalina Bowen. Colville, a publisher from Indiana, is middle-aged, but he attracts the attention of the young Imogene Grahame, Evalina's friend. Imogene develops a romantic attachment for Colville, after feeling sympathy for him when Evalina tells her that he has been disappointed in love. But she meets a young clergyman, Morton, and falls in love with him; she begins to understand the true nature of her feelings toward Colville. Imogene then breaks off her relationship with Colville, who marries Evalina at the end of the story.

**Ingelow, Jean** 1820–97. A native of Boston in Lincolnshire, Jean Ingelow became a professional writer after moving to London. She enjoyed considerable success with 25 books of verse, children's stories, and novels. Her *Mopsa the Fairy* (1869) was a children's favourite for a number of years and some of her poems were, until recently, popular anthology pieces. The most notable of these were 'The High Tide on the Coast of Lincolnshire, 1571' and 'Divided' from *Poems* (1863) and 'A Story of Doom' from the collection of that name (1867).

**Inge, William** 1913–73. Inge was born in Independence, Kansas, and educated at the University of Kansas. He taught in Missouri before becoming arts critic for the St Louis *Times* in 1943. His career as a playwright began with *Farther off from Heaven* (1947), first produced in Dallas, and was established with *Come Back, Little Sheba* (1950). *Picnic* (1953) won him the Pulitzer Prize and he continued to examine life in the Middle West with success in *Bus Stop* (1955) and *The Dark at the Top of the Stairs* (1958, a revised version of his first play). *A Loss of Roses* (1959), *Natural Affection* (1963), and *Where's*

*Daddy?* (1966) were less successful and Inge turned to writing novels. He died in 1973, apparently by suicide. His novels are *Good Luck, Miss Wyckoff* (1971) and *My Son is a Splendid Driver* (1972).

*Ingoldsby Legends, The* See **Barham, Richard Harris.**

*Inheritance, The* A novel by Susan Ferrier, first published in 1824.

The Earl of Rossville repudiates his son when he marries beneath him. When the son dies the earl admits his daughter-in-law and his granddaughter, Gertrude, to his presence; Gertrude is heiress presumptive to Rossville. Gertrude falls in love with Colonel Delmour, and when the earl dies she becomes engaged to him, against the advice of those who know him well and to the despair of her cousin, Edward Lyndsay, who loves her.

A coarse American stranger now appears on the scene and claims to be Gertrude's father. Against all protestations, his claim is eventually proved to be truthful: Gertrude's mother, despairing of children of her own, had adopted the child of a servant. Gertrude's 'inheritance' is therefore nullified. Colonel Delmour now displays his true character and abandons her but Edward Lyndsay stands by her and eventually wins her.

A less successful novel than *Marriage*, *The Inheritance* is nevertheless well characterized. Particularly successful is Miss Pratt, the jarring, nosey old gossip.

*In Memoriam A.H.H.* A poem by Alfred Tennyson, first published in 1850. (For the poet's friendship with Arthur Henry Hallam and the latter's death at the age of 22, see **Tennyson, Alfred, Lord**.) The first verses of the poem were written in the year of Hallam's death (1833) and Tennyson went on adding to them for years. In March 1850, pressed by his friends, he had the verses privately printed. The title was suggested by Tennyson's future wife, Emily Sellwood, and the poem known as *In Memoriam* was published anonymously in May. One alternative title was *Fragments of an Elegy*, which indicates the looseness of structure; Tennyson never claimed poetic unity for the verses. They were composed at different times in groups of differing extent, as the poet's feelings about the death of his friend ranged from his first violent grief to acceptance; resignation was followed by the return of resolution and will, the retrieval of purpose for his life, and a widening love and compassion for humanity. The last canto (CXXXI) is followed by an epilogue of 36 verses in the form of a prothalamion on the marriage of the poet's sister Cecilia to his friend Edward Lushington; the poem ends on a note of hope and happiness. The poem is written in octosyllabic four-line stanzas.

**Innocents Abroad, The:** *or The New Pilgrim's Progress.* An account by Mark Twain of his journey to Europe and the Levant on the steamship *Quaker City.* The book's origin was in the form of letters to the New York papers, *Tribune* and *Herald*, and the San Francisco *Alta California* and is in essence the narrative of a shrewd American in the Old World for the first time. In spite of Twain's obvious purpose to please his fellow Americans, there is a great deal of shrewd observation and humour to be found in the book.

**In Our Time** See **Hemingway, Ernest (Miller)**.

**International Episode, An** A story by Henry James, first published in the *Cornhill Magazine*, from December 1878 to January 1879, and in volume form in 1879.

Percy Beaumont goes to the USA on legal business; his cousin Lord Lambeth goes with him – he has nothing better to do. In Newport they meet Mrs Westgate and her sister, Bessie Alden. Lambeth is fascinated by Bessie, who is not only charming but frank and intelligent. But Beaumont takes it upon himself to keep Lambeth out of such an involvement and Lambeth is suddenly recalled to England. Later Bessie visits Europe with her sister and they are made aware of Lambeth's family's suspicion of Bessie as a title hunter. Lambeth, however, is charmed again by Bessie and really wants to marry her – but his world and his role in it provide the forthright American girl with increasing disillusion. This is traced with economy and wit and at the end of the tale, when both American and English characters are surprised by her rejection of a Duke's son, the reader understands Bessie perfectly.

This is one of Henry James's best stories. Bessie is a delightful heroine and there is a delicious interview with the Duchess, Lord Lambeth's mother.

**In the Midst of Life** A book of 19 stories by Ambrose Bierce, first published in 1891 under the title *Tales of Soldiers and Civilians.* More than half of the stories are concerned with soldiers in the Civil War; all of them could be called horror stories but, while they are reminiscent of Edgar Allen Poe, they pay more attention to the mental state the situations provoke. Bierce is also a master of the surprise ending. The author's reaction to the Civil War is reflected in many of them – he looked back to his life as a Union soldier with revulsion and those stories particularly carry remarkable force.

*Chickamauga* is the story of a deaf-mute child in the midst of the destruction and bloodshed attendant on the Union defeat at Chickamauga, when the child's home and family are wiped out. *A Horseman in the Sky* places a son on one side, as a Union soldier stationed near his own home in the South; on the other is his father, a Confederate cavalry officer. Their encounter leads to the son killing his father; his shot sends horse and rider to their deaths over a steep cliff. The most famous story in the book is *An Occurrence at Owl Creek Bridge*: a Southern planter, taken by the Union army, is summarily hanged at Owl Creek Bridge and the whole account of the victim's mind – the events that brought him to the rope and his desperate hope of escape – are confined to the interval between the tightening of the noose and the drop which kills him. The book also includes straightforward stories of terror and retribution – notably *The Middle Toe of the Right Foot*, which relates how a murderer, completely demoralized by the ghostly return of his victim, comes to his own death.

**In the Seven Woods** See **Yeats, William Butler**.

**In the Shadow of the Glen** See **Synge, J(ohn) M(illington)**.

**Intruder in the Dust** See **Faulkner William (Harrison)**.

**Iota** (*or* **Mrs Caffyn**) See **'New Women' novelists**.

**Ipomedon** A Middle English romance based on a 12th-century French original by the Anglo-Norman poet, Huon de Rotelande. (See **metrical romances**.) The romance exists in verse and prose versions, and tells of Ipomedon, Prince of Apulia, whose marriage with the Queen of Calabria has been arranged. Ipomedon goes incognito to the queen's court to woo her for himself. He wins her favour by his manly exploits and then for no explained reason departs. He returns to take part in a tournament when the queen is the prize, and wins the day only to depart again. The queen's domain is threatened by a neighbouring duke; Ipomedon, disguised as a fool, fights her battles and departs again. He claims her after further adventures when love is seen to be the proven reason for the match, rather than politic arrangement. The prose version of the romance is to be found in the Longleat Manuscript in the possession of the Marquis of Bath.

**Iras** One of the queen's attendants (the other is Charmian) in Shakespeare's *Antony and Cleopatra*. When there is no hope left, after Octavius' exit in Act V Scene 2, it is Iras who utters the unforgettable 'Finish good lady, the bright day is done, And we are for the dark.'

**Irena** The personification of Ireland in Book V of Spenser's *The Faerie Queene*, oppressed by Grantorto (unrest, rebellion) and succoured by Artegall (justice).

**Iron Heel, The** A novel of the future by Jack London, first published in 1907.

In a manuscript relating incidents which occurred seven hundred years before, the events leading to fascist totalitarianism in the USA are described. The Everhard Manuscript of 1932 relates how the industrial monopolies increase their power by cooperation and succeed in gaining control of the country. The all-powerful organization, the Iron Heel, establishes a caste system with an aristocracy of wealth, secret police, and subsidized 'unions', which exercise inflexible control over the workers. The opposition is driven underground; it is led by Everhard, a Californian who was brought to the cause by his wife, Avis, who tells the story in the manuscript.

The opposition, totally proscribed, often has recourse to terrorism. But it succeeds in preventing war with Germany by a general strike in both countries organized with the German trade unions. Eventually the conflict erupts in armed revolt – force can only be met by force. The manuscript ends with the execution of Everhard, but footnotes give the further information that the Iron Heel endured for three hundred years before being overthrown.

Jack London's novel – note the date of publication – has never enjoyed the fame of *Brave New World* or *1984* but, arguable literary qualities apart, it has greater claims than either as a forecast of things to come: the reader of the present knows that everything described actually came to pass. More disturbing is the point made in the book about the need for effective opposition to totalitarianism in any form.

**Irving, Washington** *c*.1783–1859. The son of a successful hardware dealer of New York city, Irving was the youngest of 11 children. His brothers, William and Peter, displayed literary interests but Irving was trained as a lawyer. Law held little interest for him and in 1803 he made a frontier journey through upper New York and into Canada that was much more to his taste. His brother Peter became editor of both the *Morning*

*Chronicle* and *The Corrector* and Irving's first writings were published in these. The pieces in the *Morning Chronicle* were satires on New York society in the form of letters written by 'Jonathan Oldbuck'. They were popular with readers and won Washington Irving his first recognition as a writer. Soon after, in 1804, to give his indifferent health a boost and to complete his education, he left for Europe, where he travelled until 1806.

Back in New York, Irving turned his attention exclusively to writing. With his brother, William, and his brother-in-law, J. K. Paulding, he produced a further series of satirical essays in 20 periodical pamphlets (1807–08), which were collected and published as a book in 1808. This was *Salmagundi*; and to reinforce his rising reputation as a wit and a man of society Irving created a comic Dutch-American, Diedrich Knickerbocker, under whose name he wrote *A History of New York* (1809). It enjoyed considerable success and Irving published three revised editions, the last one as late as 1848.

For some years following the publication of his burlesque *History* Irving was occupied in sundry literary activities and in the family business. In 1815 he went to England to take charge of the Liverpool branch, which was in difficulties; his efforts to restore it were not successful and it went into bankruptcy in 1818. Irving, who was impressed by the beauty of England, had made several journeys and some distinguished friends. One of these was Walter Scott, who encouraged him to start writing again, and the result, written under the pseudonym of Geoffrey Crayon, was *The Sketch Book* (1820), his most popular book and the one that made him a celebrity in Europe. He was soon able to number Byron and Thomas Moore among his friends. Another sketch book, *Bracebridge Hall* (1822), was equally popular.

After travelling in Germany and staying in Paris, Irving published *Tales of a Traveller* in London in 1824. This, his third sketch book, was rejected by public and critics alike; indeed the criticisms were so adverse that Irving wrote nothing for four years. Probably his public decided that he had lived on the reputation of his original *The Sketch Book* for long enough; certainly the three show a decline in quality and the last one could have been the work of an experienced hack. Irving accepted an appointment as a diplomatic attaché and spent the years from 1826 to 1829 in Spain. While he was there he researched the work of Spanish scholars and in 1828 published his *History of the Life and Voyages of Christopher Columbus*. He returned to London as secretary of the United States Legation in 1829 and, using his experience of Spain, published

Washington Irving's house at Sunnyside, his estate on the Hudson River near Tarrytown. Irving lived there from 1836 to 1842, and from 1846 until his death in 1859.

*A Chronicle of the Conquest of Granada* (1829) and a Spanish sketch book, *The Alhambra* (1832).

Irving returned to America in 1832 after an absence of 17 years. He received a considerable welcome since he was the first American writer to enjoy an international reputation. At home he made a journey to the Western frontiers and wrote *A Tour of the Prairies* (1835) and *The Adventures of Captain Bonneville, USA* (1837). Bonneville was an American soldier who obtained two years' leave to explore and trap in the Rocky Mountains. *Astoria* (1836) was written to a commission from the Astor family to record their fortune-making fur trade. Most of the remaining years of Irving's life were spent at Sunnyside, his estate on the Hudson River, and he went on writing until the year of his death. The most notable works of his last years were his massive five-volume *Life of Washington*, which had been in preparation since 1825, and his biography of *Oliver Goldsmith* (1840).

Though he spent more than a third of his life in Europe Washington Irving was the writer who put America firmly on the literary map. Opinions of his stature vary and no one would make extravagant claims for him now. But his services to American letters were immense and he was a writer of considerable grace and skill. He was also an excellent ambassador, in the cultural sense, from America to Europe.

*Isabella; or, The Pot of Basil*  A poem in *ottava rima* by John Keats, written in 1819 and first published in 1820. The poem is based on a story, the fifth one of the fourth day, in Boccaccio's

*Decameron*; like *The Eve of St Agnes* and *Lamia*, which were published in the same volume, it tells a story of love. The lady Isabella (Lisobeta in the original) of Florence falls in love with Lorenzo, a young man employed by her family. Her brothers, out of jealous pride and because they want to see Isabella married to some rich lord, persuade Lorenzo to go riding with them. They murder him in the forest outside the city and hastily bury his body; then they tell Isabella that they have sent him to another country on the family's business. But Lorenzo appears to her in a vision and tells her how he was murdered. Isabella, accompanied by her nurse, goes to the forest and finds the hastily dug grave; she cuts off

Isabella and the pot of basil. An illustration for Keats's poem by George Scharf, 1854.

the head and takes it home. She wraps it in a silken cloth and places it in a garden pot; she covers it with mould, which she plants with 'Sweet Basil, which her tears kept ever wet'. The basil flourishes, while Isabella wastes away, and her brothers wonder why. They steal the pot and are horrified at what they find in it; they flee from Florence now that their crime is known. Isabella, bereft of Lorenzo and the pot of basil, loses her reason and dies.

**Isabella** The chaste heroine of Shakespeare's *Measure for Measure*. She is about to take the veil when her brother Claudio is sentenced to death for his offence against the morality laws. She intercedes for him with Angelo and arouses his lust – she can exchange her virtue for her brother's life. Isabella refuses: she'd give her life 'As frankly as a pin' but her chastity? Never.

**Iseult** (*or* **Isoud, Ysoude, Ysolde**) See **Tristram**.

**Isherwood, Christopher (William Bradshaw)** 1904–  .   Christopher Isherwood was born at High Lane, Cheshire, and educated at Repton School and Corpus Christi College, Cambridge. He studied medicine briefly but gave it up to teach English in Germany. His first novel, *All the Conspirators* (1928), reflected the perennial conflict of the artist with the wishes of his family. The technique of the cinema influenced his second, *The Memorial* (1932), but he really began to attract attention with the striking series of episodes in *Mr Norris Changes Trains* (1935), telling of the rise of the Nazis in Germany, and his first collaboration with W. H. Auden, *The Dog Beneath the Skin* (also 1935), a metaphysical satire in verse and doggerel that was produced at the Westminster Theatre in 1936.

The collaboration with Auden continued with another play, *The Ascent of F6* (1936); F6 is a high mountain, the ascent of which will ensure the sovereignty of territory on either side. *Sally Bowles* (1937) was another Berlin story, and *Lions and Shadows* (1938) a memoir of his school days; *On the Frontier* (1938) was another play in collaboration with Auden. Isherwood and Auden visited China in that year and published a record of their journey in *Journey to a War* (1939). *Goodbye to Berlin* (also 1938) completed his fiction about Germany in the 1930s which is generally acknowledged as his best work.

Isherwood emigrated to the USA in 1939, where he wrote film scripts and became absorbed in Indian philosophy and religion. Among his later books are the novels *Prater Violet* (1945) and *The World in the Evening* (1954); a travel book on South America, *The Condor and the Cows* (1949); and *Ramakrishna and His Disciples* (1965). *Exhumations* (1966) is a miscellany of stories, essays, and verse.

**Ishmael** The part-narrator of Herman Melville's *Moby-Dick*. He is the only one to survive the final encounter with the great white whale.

*I Sing the Body Electric* A poem by Walt Whitman which first appeared, with no title, in the first edition of *Leaves of Grass* (1855). It was included as one of the *Children of Adam* sequences in the third edition of 1860 and titled in 1867. The poet celebrates the form of the body which, to him, is also a way of celebrating the soul.

*Islanders, The* A poem by Rudyard Kipling, included in the collection called *The Five Nations* (1903). It was first published in *The Times* not long before the end of the Boer War, which Kipling saw as having been almost lost through the smug confidence of the 'Islanders'. These were the English who went on blithely with their comfortable lives: 'Then ye returned to your trinkets; then ye contented your souls With the flannelled fools at the wicket or the muddied oafs at the goals'.

*Island in the Moon, An* See **Blake, William**.

*Israel Potter: His Fifty Years in Exile.* A novel by Herman Melville, first published in 1855. It is based on the anonymous *Life and Remarkable Adventures of Israel Potter* of 1824.

Israel Potter is a New England boy who, after a varied youth which includes a voyage on a whaler, joins the Revolutionary Army and is captured by the British at Bunker Hill. Taken as a prisoner to England, he escapes and finds work in England as a labourer. He is helped by American agents and becomes part of their secret service; he meets Franklin and John Paul Jones. The latter becomes his friend and Potter takes part in the battle in which Jones captures the British *Serapis*. Back in England, Potter becomes a labourer again to cover his tracks, marries, and settles down to family life.

In his old age he returns to America but he can find no trace of his family or his former home. He applies to Congress for a pension but is refused because there is almost no documentary evidence of his career. He dies in penury after dictating his memoirs.

The bleak account of his life by Israel Potter offered nothing to the reader beyond a record of facts. When Melville takes over, the hand of an artist transforms the story and students of the American Revolution will find the novel illuminating. The sea fight is a fine piece of extended narrative and there are memorable portraits of John Paul Jones and Benjamin Franklin. Notable too is the author's handling of a straightforward 'patriotic' novel; he is truthful, so neither Franklin nor Jones emerges as a gilt-edged hero – they are much more interesting than that. It has to be acknowledged that *Israel Potter* does not stand high among Melville's works. It lacks a true centre because the sheer size of John Paul Jones, for one, almost obliterates Israel Potter, to whose memory the author, mistakenly perhaps, tries to remain faithful.

**It is Never too Late to Mend**　A novel by Charles Reade, first published in 1856. The author had used some of the material in his play, *Gold!* (1853). To describe both the perils of a miner's life in Australia, and the dreadful fate of those sentenced to prison and transportation, the author tells two parallel stories. One concerns a young man who emigrates to Australia to earn £1,000 in the gold rush, necessary for his father's consent to his marriage; the other concerns the fate of a thief serving a vicious sentence, which Reade used as an attack on the prison system of his day.

**Ivanhoe**　A novel by Sir Walter Scott, his most popular work, published in 1819. For the first time Scott did not have the action taking place in Scotland – the setting is England, in the reign of Richard I.

Wilfred of Ivanhoe incurs the displeasure of his father, Cedric; he wants to marry Rowena, his father's ward, but Cedric wishes to marry her to Athelstane of the old Saxon blood royal. Rowena is descended from King Alfred and Cedric wants to see the Saxon line restored. Ivanhoe goes to the Holy Land with Richard I, whose brother, John, tries to oust him from the throne in his absence, depending on disloyal Norman barons for support. Richard is captured by Leopold of Austria on the way back from Palestine.

Richard reappears in England at the tournament at Ashby-de-la-Zouch where, as the Black Knight, he helps Ivanhoe defeat all comers, though he does sustain some wounds. His opponents are of John's party, among them Bois-Guilbert, the Templar. At the tournament Bois-Guilbert falls in love with the beautiful and courageous Rebecca, a Jewish girl enamoured of Ivanhoe. She nurses Ivanhoe when he is recovering from his wounds. Later in the story Rebecca and her father Isaac, Rowena and Cedric, and the wounded Ivanhoe are taken captive by Normans and held in Torquilstone Castle. The king and a Saxon force, with the help of Locksley (Robin Hood) and his band of outlaws, take the castle

Rebecca and Sir Brian de Bois-Guilbert. The frontispiece to *Ivanhoe* in the 1830 edition of The Waverley Novels.

and release the prisoners – with the exception of Rebecca, who has been carried off to Templestowe (the Templars' preceptory) by Bois-Guilbert.

Bois-Guilbert's design is halted by the arrival of the Grand Master of the Order but Rebecca is in danger of being charged with witchcraft. She demands trial by combat and Ivanhoe appears as her champion, opposing Bois-Guilbert, chosen as her accuser. In the encounter the latter falls dead, untouched by Ivanhoe's lance, a victim to his own passions. Rebecca perceives that Ivanhoe's real love is for Rowena, and at the end of the tale she departs from England with her father.

Scott was severely criticized for presenting Saxon–Norman enmity as persisting into the 12th century, when it was no longer an issue. But the medieval romance succeeds splendidly and the book's continued popularity is well deserved. An interesting feature is the introduction of Robin Hood as Locksley; one story of the outlaw does in fact give Locksley in Nottinghamshire as his birthplace.

**Ivory Tower, The**　An unfinished novel by Henry James. The setting is amongst people of great wealth in Newport, Rhode Island, where the wealthy Frank Betterman is dying. He proposes to make his great-nephew, Gray Fielder, his heir and Gray has returned after many years in Europe. Betterman would like his heir to make better use of the ill-gotten wealth. Other characters are Rosanna Gaw, daughter of a rich man once defrauded by Betterman and in love with Gray; Cissy Foy, who has her eye on the Betterman fortune and intends to marry Gray; and Howard Vint, who was rejected by Rosanna and is now in love with Cissy. He is, in fact, the man Cissy wants; she and Howard understand each other perfectly. Somehow, Gray's fortune is going to benefit both of them. But that is all of the novel that we have.

# J

*Jacke Uplande* An attack on the orders of friars by one of the supporters of John Wycliffe. John Bale, the 16th-century bibliographer, attributed it to Wycliffe himself but this has long been rejected. The attack was answered in *The Reply of Friar Daw Thopias*; the friar defends the religious orders and then attacks the Lollards in turn. This was answered in *The Rejoinder of Jacke Uplande*.

The three pieces have been dated by Thomas Wright (as 1401) and W. W. Skeat (as 1402). They are recognized as examples of the religious controversy of the time but are usually denied any merit as literature. Editions of all three were published by Thomas Wright in *Political Poems and Songs* (Vol 2, 1861) and by P. L. Heyworth (1968). W. W. Skeat's edition of *Jacke Uplande* appears in his *Complete Works of Chaucer* (Vol 7, 1897).

*Jacke Uplande, The Rejoinder of* See *Jacke Uplande*.

*Jack Juggler* (*A New Enterlued for Chyldren to Playe, Named Jacke Jugeler*). A comedy written in the late 1550s and first printed in 1562. It has been attributed to Nicholas Udall without much evidence and the true authorship is unknown. It is based on the *Amphitruo* of Plautus but considerably toned down since it was written to be acted by schoolboys at Christmas. Jupiter and Amphitryon are removed from the plot entirely and Mercury becomes the trickster Jack Juggler, who takes over the identity of Jenkin Careaway. The other characters are as English as the London street in which the action takes place: the maid is Alison Tripandgo, the mistress and master are Dame Coy and Master Bongrace. The play ends with a cautionary epilogue on the times.

*Jack Sheppard* See **Ainsworth, William Harrison** and **Sheppard, Jack.**

*Jacob Faithful* A novel by Frederick Marryat, first published in 1834.

Jacob Faithful's father is a Thames lighterman, and Jacob is born on board. His mother becomes gin-sodden and eventually, like Dickens's Mr Krook, dies of spontaneous combustion, an event which drives her husband, terrified, to leap overboard and get drowned. Kind friends do their best for the orphan boy and he is educated; Dominic Dobbs, his schoolmaster, recognizes that Jacob has the intelligence for better things but Jacob is withdrawn and proud, and suspicious of those who try to help him. His only real friend is young Tom Beazley, also of the river community. An old gentleman tries to befriend him and Jacob actually saves him from drowning.

Jacob stays on the river as a lighterman, and the book gives a lively picture of the life he leads and the adventures he meets. Then he falls victim to a press gang and is carried off to serve on a frigate. The turning point in his life and his attitudes comes when the old gentleman dies and makes Jacob his heir, providing him with security and the means of getting out of the navy.

Marryat was a strong opponent of impressment in the navy and wrote a powerful argument for its abolition which was published in 1822.

*Jacob's Room* See **Woolf, (Adeline) Virginia.**

**Jaggers, Mr** In Dickens's *Great Expectations*, the lawyer who acts for Miss Havisham and who brings to Pip the news of his 'expectations'.

**Jago, Richard** 1715–81. Jago was born at Beaudesert near Henley-in-Arden in Warwickshire and was a friend of William Somerville. He was admitted to Oxford as a servitor, and was ordained about 1739. He is remembered for his poem in four books called *Edge-hill, or The Rural Prospect Delineated and Moralised* (1767), which describes the prospect of Warwickshire observed at various times of day from the ridge where the battle took place during the Civil War.

**James I of Scotland, King** 1394–1437. James succeeded to the throne of Scotland as a boy of 11 – and was kidnapped in the same year on the way to France by one of Henry IV's sea captains. (This was a time of truce, strictly speaking – the war with England having proved inconclusive as far as the English were concerned, even after Bannockburn.) James remained a prisoner in

Henry V. He wrote *The Kingis Quair* while in England, the lady of the poem being Jane Beaufort, daughter of the Earl of Somerset, whom he married in 1424. He was assassinated at Perth in 1437 after a reign of 13 years.

Other poems have been attributed to King James but only *The Kingis Quair* can be called his with certainty. See also *Scottish anthologies and collections*.

**James, George Payne Rainsford** 1799–1860. A historical novelist who took Scott as his model but, having none of Scott's genius, was soon forgotten. He was an indefatigable worker – his novels and tales filled no less than 43 volumes, and he also poured out volumes of historical commentary and speculation. His style was parodied by Thackeray in *Punch* in 1850 in *Barbazure*, so he must have been popular enough to merit considerable attention in his own day. His first novel was *Richelieu: a Tale of France*, in 1829, and his last *The Man in Black: an Historical Novel of the Days of Queen Anne*, in 1860.

**James, Henry (Senior)** 1811–82. The son of a wealthy family in Albany, New York, Henry James suffered the loss of a leg following an accident when he was a schoolboy. His family were rigidly orthodox but the boy, much alone, was beginning to think for himself. He entered Princeton Theological Seminary in 1835 but withdrew after two years when he found he could not accept the Calvinism to which his family was bound. On a visit to Europe in 1837 he found a kindred spirit in the Scotsman Robert Sandeman, whose letters he edited for publication in the following years. In the 1840s James was drawn to the work of the Swedish mystic, Swedenborg; he also became the friend of Emerson and Thomas Carlyle. In 1864 he settled in Boston, after considerable travel between New York and Europe, and he lectured widely in the USA on his own particular philosophy for social reform. This philosophy was based on New England Transcendentalism with mystic overtones and a belief in the ideas put forward by the French social philosopher, Charles Fourier. James's ideas were, however, firmly rooted in the Christianity that he embraced after rejecting the Calvinistic form. His published works, among them *Christianity the Logic of Creation* (1857), *Substance and Shadow; or Morality and Religion in Their Relation to Life* (1863), and *Society the Redeemed Form of Man, and the Earnest of God's Omnipotence in Human Nature* (1879), were devoted to his religious beliefs but are not read now. He was the father of William and Henry James, both of whom owed much to their father's belief in a wide-ranging education.

**James, Henry** 1843–1916. The son of Henry James, the philosopher, and the younger brother of the more famous philosopher, William James. He was born in New York and, like his brother William, benefited greatly from his father's original ideas for his sons' education. Private tutors taught him until he was 12 and then the family went to Europe, staying there for three years. Henry's education continued in Boulogne, Paris, Geneva, and Bonn, and in Newport, Rhode Island, when the family returned to the United States. He entered Harvard Law School in 1862 but withdrew after a year; his interest in writing had, by now, taken precedence and he was receiving encouragement from Charles Eliot Norton, William Dean Howells, and others. His first essays into literature show an attempt at realism but soon, like his friend Howells, James began to regard fiction as an art – more than mere narrative and never to be debased by didacticism. His early reviews and critical essays were published in *The North American Review*, the *Nation*, and the *Atlantic Monthly*. James was, in the 1860s, becoming a spectator of life and an admirer of George Eliot and Nathaniel Hawthorne; psychological truth was the goal he was working towards. However, his first short novel – he had published some stories – was a product of his original interest in realism. This was *Watch and Ward*, published serially in the *Atlantic Monthly* in 1871 (and in volume form in 1878) and telling the story of a comfortable bachelor who falls in love with his ward as he watches her grow to womanhood. A farce, *Pyramus and Thisbe*, had appeared in 1869, when the author made his first considerable visit to Europe as an adult. He returned there in 1872 and stayed for two years; the most famous of the great American expatriates in literature was on the way to making up his mind about the intellectual climate that suited him best.

In 1875 Henry James published *A Passionate Pilgrim and Other Tales* and *Transatlantic Sketches*. He spent that year in Paris in the company of another expatriate, the great Russian writer Turgenev, and with the close acquaintance of Daudet, Flaubert, the Goncourts, and Zola. But James found Paris as wanting as the USA. His own country was essential to his art but he needed a point from which he could develop his detached observation of it and of Europe, so he settled in London in 1876.

*Roderick Hudson* (1876) was the first novel of this period; it concerns an American sculptor in

Rome and the failure of his artistic and personal life. **The American** (1877) was published in the following year and in it James makes a serious, though not wholly successful, attempt on the theme that was to prove so rewarding for him later – that of Americans in Europe and the gulf that seemed to divide the two cultures. **The Europeans** (1878) turns the situation round; two Europeans arrive in rural New England and the author studies the effect they have on their American cousins. *French Poets and Novelists* was also published in 1878. **Daisy Miller** (1878), the story of a charming and innocent American girl tripping lightly across convention in Europe, brought Henry James popular success and in the same year he published an excellent study of Nathaniel Hawthorne in the English Men of Letters series, a short novel called **An International Episode**, and *The Madonna of the Future and Other Tales*. Another short novel, *Confidence*, was published in 1880. For his next novel, **Washington Square** (1881), James returned to the American scene with a penetrating study of a plain girl's disillusion. The same year also saw the publication of the first of his novels to be acknowledged a masterpiece, **The Portrait of a Lady**. The Europe of the time and the characters, mostly Americans, who occupy its shifting scenes are drawn with the confidence of a master; he has explored the background thoroughly and he can make it serve the psychological study of Isabel Archer, the American girl in Europe who believes, in her youth and delight in life, that there is a marvellous fulfilment waiting for her. James's elegance and subtlety are a pleasure for readers and the high level of writing is sustained through Isabel's progress from her beginning as a girl who has the opportunity for everything – but chooses wrongly. Isabel emerges at the end of the novel with dignity, accepting her mistake, not just resigned to it – she is too intelligent and has too much character for that.

In 1883 James collected all his fiction together. There were 14 volumes of it; he was a short-story writer of considerable industry. He also dramatized *Daisy Miller*, published a book of short stories, *The Siege of London*, and a travel book, *Portraits of Places*. The following year, 1884, brought another trio of short stories, *Tales of Three Cities*, and 1885 another travel book, *A Little Tour in France*. A collection of early stories was also published as *Stories Revived* (1885).

Henry James returned to the novel in 1886 with first **The Bostonians** and then **The Princess Casamassima**. *The Bostonians* is a satirical study of reformers and philanthropists in New England, where women are self-consciously eman-cipated. *The Princess Casamassima* tells of social revolutionaries from both ends of the social scale and of the havoc wreaked on them by uncertainty of purpose. Neither novel was well received at the time. A short novel, *The Reverberator* (1888), pursues the theme of innocence abroad; **The Aspern Papers** (also published in 1888) is another short novel, relating how a critic tries to get his hands on the letters of a famous poet. A pre-occupation with the theatre at this time resulted in the four comedies published as *Theatricals* (1894–95) and in the novel **The Tragic Muse** (1890), a remarkable study of artistic life in London. The short stories continued: *A London Life* (1889), *The Lesson of the Master* (1892), *The Real Thing and Other Tales*, *The Private Life*, and *The Wheel of Time* (the last three all published in 1893). He failed in the theatre, his subtlety of motive and situation never overcoming his inability to write convincing dialogue or to encapsulate drama in a theatrical framework as opposed to the pages of a book.

The author was now a European by choice. He visited the USA of course, but less frequently, and the theme of the American in Europe was to continue to be a rewarding source of inspiration; three remarkable novels were to materialize from it in the near future. Meanwhile, there were more short stories – *Terminations* (1895) and *Embarrassments* (1896) – and essays. He also wrote *Partial Portraits*, containing 'The Art of Fiction' (1888), *Picture and Text* (1893), and *Essays in London and Elsewhere* (1893). *The Other House* (1896) is a novel that started life as a play; it was not a success in novel form. But in 1897 the master was back in form with the excellent short novel **The Spoils of Poynton** and the remarkable, if difficult (in many readers' opinion), **What Maisie Knew** – a world of adult dinginess seen through the eyes and mind of a little girl. *In the Cage* (1898) is another short novel, about a telegraph girl caught up (willingly) in the affairs of a rich couple. *The Two Magics* (1898) contains the fascinating **The Turn of the Screw**, one of the most famous stories of the uncanny in the English language, and in 1899 **The Awkward Age** was published in book form. **The Sacred Fount** (1901) is not regarded as a success even by Henry James's ad-mirers and he confessed to Howells that the novel had outgrown its original plan.

James had left London in 1896, the year after the failure of his play *Guy Domville*, and was now living in Rye, Sussex. It was to be his home for the rest of his life. He achieved, according to some critics, a masterpiece with **The Wings of the Dove** (1902) and another with **The Ambassadors** (1903). A volume of short stories, *The*

Henry James, 1913. Photograph by E. O. Hoppé.

*Better Sort* (1903), was followed by his last novel, which many critics regard as his finest work, **The Golden Bowl** (1904). Two were left uncompleted, **The Ivory Tower** and **The Sense of the Past**, and both were published posthumously (1917). Two further volumes of short stories were *The Altar of the Dead* (1909) and *The Finer Grain* (1910).

Henry James did not stop writing but his later years were saddened by the death of his brother, William, and by the coming of World War I. He became a British citizen in 1915, a gesture of allegiance to the country that had become his home. He published 11 more books and wrote three more plays. The books contained essays, lectures, and reviews; there was also a descriptive account of a journey in the USA, *The American Scene* (1907); and three autobiographical works, *A Small Boy and Others* (1913), *Notes of a Son and Brother* (1914), and *The Middle Years* (1917). Of his plays only *The High Bid* was produced and it was not a success (1908).

The author suffered a stroke in 1916 and died in the same year. James received the Order of Merit just before his death.

In his essay on Henry James in *Eight Modern Writers*, J. I. M. Stewart writes: 'Broadly speaking, James sees Americans as good and Europeans as beautiful; and his art in its ideal aspect is the Quest of a synthesis through an imagined order. Yet he never seems to be certain where to stop admiring a life lived in terms not of moral ideas but of style. Is not a high style, an aristocratic style, itself a sufficient morality? The answer, coming low but resonant from the farthest recesses of his creation, is an uncompromising No.' The qualification is important because, broadly speaking, Stewart is right and the realization of the theme, which occurs so often in Henry James's novels, was a rich resource that no other novelist exploited as well. With this must go the recognition that for many readers his work is not merely difficult, it is something rather worse; it was true in his own day and the present celebration of his writing is often a sore puzzle to those whose first encounter with him is in a novel such as *The Ambassadors* or *The Golden Bowl*. Special pleading should not be required for any novelist but it is true that an approach to Henry James has to be careful. *The Portrait of a Lady* and *The Spoils of Poynton* are easy to appreciate but his later work suffers too often from an arrangement of words that has to be studied to be understood. Equally daunting is the treatment of the theme – the ideas and perceptions that arise are taken so far into the upper air, in his perplexing style, that they almost vanish. The trouble was, as Marcus Cunliffe points out, that James had more to say as he grew older; he also lost touch with his audience, which had never been large. When his friend Edith Wharton, referring to the characters in *The Golden Bowl*, asked James 'Why have you stripped them of all the human fringes we necessarily trail after us through life?' he was surprised and perturbed: 'My dear – I didn't know I had!' he replied.

It is of course a tribute to Henry James that his work has generated mountains of comment and criticism. His best work is superb and the rest is worth the argument it has provoked; critics have not been, indeed they are not now, wanting who regard the last three novels as masterpieces of the novelist's art. But it is perhaps rather sad that the art that went into them pushed almost everything else out, including, in Edith Wharton's words, 'that thick nourishing human air in which we all live and move'. But they have considerable rewards – that must be understood, even if the way to the appreciation of their virtues has to be made through the works that led up to them.

A significant footnote to the career of Henry James is the great success enjoyed by adaptations of his novels and stories to the dramatic media. James, who never managed to write a successful play, provided the material for *Berkeley Square* in *The Sense of the Past*, for *The Heiress* in *Washington*

*Square*, and for *The Innocents* in *The Turn of the Screw. The Aspern Papers* was dramatized to excellent effect by Michael Redgrave; *The Portrait of a Lady*, *The Spoils of Poynton*, and, surprisingly, *The Golden Bowl* have made very good television serials. *The Wings of the Dove* and *The Ambassadors* were almost very good television plays, and *The Europeans* nearly a good film. There have been many others, the point being that Henry James, even at his most 'difficult', never lost sight of what the fiction writer must have first – a good story to tell.

**James, William** 1842–1910. The eldest son of the philosopher Henry James, William James was born in New York. His father had considerable means and very positive ideas about education; William and his brother Henry were taught in Europe and American by private tutors and encouraged to find their own way to a career. William studied painting first, then science, and then entered Harvard Medical School. He inter-

William James.

rupted his studies to accompany Louis Agassiz on an expedition to Brazil, finally taking his MD in 1869. A period of bad health followed and halted his as yet incomplete plans for practice or research; but a reading of Charles Renouvier, the French philosopher, helped order his thinking and he became an instructor in physiology at Harvard in 1872. He was to teach for 35 years, his interest shifting to psychology. In 1876 he opened a laboratory of psychology at Harvard – a pioneering venture. He married in 1878.

James spent the next 12 years of his spare time working on *The Principles of Psychology*, which was published in 1890. This is a classic in its field, even if later investigations – many of which it helped to inspire – have superseded it. The author continued to visit Europe regularly and was always in close touch with the leading minds of his time. A collection of essays was published as *The Will to Believe* (1897), in which he defined his position as that of a 'radical empiricist'. His international reputation increased when he was appointed Gifford Lecturer on Natural Religion at Edinburgh University from 1901 to 1902. His two sets of lectures there were published as *The Varieties of Religious Experience* (1902) and treat religion from the points of view of common sense and science, and as an area of psychological fact. He developed the concept of 'pragmatism' from the original idea of Charles Saunders Peirce and published his definition as *Pragmatism* (1907); the thesis that an idea only has meaning in relation to its consequences in feeling and action won him new followers everywhere but was also attacked. James published *The Meaning of Truth* (1909) in answer to his critics.

Though he retired from Harvard in 1907, where he had been Professor of Psychology (1889–97) and Professor of Philosophy (1897–1907), James continued to write and lecture; he was the most honoured philosopher in America. He published his metaphysical principles in *A Pluralistic Universe* (1909), the series of lectures he had delivered in Oxford in 1908. Posthumous publications were *Some Problems of Philosophy. A Beginning of an Introduction to Philosophy* (1911), edited by H. M. Kallen; *Memories and Studies* (1911), which was edited by his brother, Henry James; and *Essays in Radical Empiricism* (1912), edited by R. B. Perry. His son, Henry, edited his letters, *The Letters of William James* (1920), and R. B. Perry edited the *Collected Essays and Reviews* (1920).

William James was a remarkable man by any standards and his claim to the attention of posterity is threefold: as a pioneering psychologist, as a philosopher (whose influence on literature was considerable), and as an expositor of rare quality. The optimism and faith in human progress that inform his philosophy were reflected in his personal life; he had a distaste for pedantry, a hatred of war and injustice, and a healthy dislike of extremes. The thought of a fixed point of view from which to proceed was as abhorrent to him as the thought of philosophy as a purely intellectual pursuit.

**Jane Eyre** A novel by Charlotte Brontë, first published in 1847.

Jane Eyre is an orphan, and is in the care of her aunt, Mrs Reed. She is treated harshly and one day turns on her bullying cousin, John Reed. This leads to her being sent to Lowood Asylum, a charitable institution, where she spends a wretched girlhood in appalling conditions. (The school was modelled on Charlotte's memories of the dreadful school at Cowan Bridge which she attended, and where two of her sisters died.)

Jane escapes from Lowood when she gains the post of governess at Thornfield Hall. She has charge of Adèle, the illegitimate daughter of Edward Rochester, a man of scant courtesy and cynical humour. Jane is a plain girl with no pretensions to charm but she has wit and spirit and Rochester is drawn to her; he is moody and can be harsh – but Jane is attracted to him; they fall in love. Their marriage is prevented, at the last moment, by Richard Mason's disclosure that Rochester is already married – to Mason's sister, Bertha. The marriage took place in Jamaica; Bertha Mason's family had told Rochester nothing and he found himself tied to a madwoman. She is now kept in seclusion and under restraint at Thornfield Hall.

Jane, shattered by the truth, leaves the Hall. She wanders across the moors and collapses at the door of the Rev St John Rivers. She calls herself Jane Elliott. The Rivers sisters, Diana and Mary, are kind to her and St John gives her the post of mistress at the village school for girls. Later he discovers Jane's identity and she finds, to her delight, that she has a family – the Rivers are her cousins; when St John brings her news of a legacy, she insists on sharing it with them.

St John proposes to Jane. He is a strong character and a handsome man, and she is on the point of accepting him when she receives a powerful spiritual communication – Edward Rochester crying out for her. She hurries back to Thornfield Hall and finds it burned down – the poor mad wife had set fire to the house. Rochester, trying to save her, was badly burned; he is blind, among other things.

'Reader, I married him.' Thus the opening of the last chapter. Jane and Rochester settle down serenely and Jane undertakes the care and education of Adèle. Rochester's injuries are permanent, but he regains partial sight in one eye, enough to be able to look upon his first-born son.

*Jane Eyre* is a love story, told with unaffected skill, narrated by a woman with a directness that startled the Victorians. Jane was something new in fiction, a woman confronting men on equal terms; a woman, moreover, with no visual appeal but with something much stronger than that. Jane Eyre tells of her love with passion and frankness; Charlotte Brontë endows her with the capacity to speak as she feels. Her first published novel is the finest of Charlotte's works; she was never to reach this level of achievement again.

**Jane Shore, The Tragedy of** A tragedy by Nicholas Rowe, first produced in February 1714 and published in the same year. The play follows the fall from favour of Jane Shore, and her subsequent misfortunes. Edward IV fell in love with her; she was a goldsmith's wife and the daughter of a mercer of Cheapside. After the death of the king she became the mistress of Grey, 1st Marquess of Dorset, but fell victim to Gloucester when he became King Richard III. (She is 'that harlot strumpet Shore' in Shakespeare's *Richard II*, Act III Scene 4.) Richard had her charged with witchcraft and she was forced to endure public penance in 1483. She died in poverty about 1527. She is said to have saved Eton from destruction by Edward IV (it was founded by the Lancastrian Henry VI) and there are two portraits of her in the college.

**Janet's Repentance** See *Scenes of Clerical Life*.

**Japhet in Search of a Father** A novel by Frederick Marryat, first published in 1836. It was a departure for Marryat, his first novel without a maritime setting, and is in the form of an autobiography of a foundling, Japhet, and his struggles to achieve a place in the world.

**Jaques** The philosophical idler (as Hazlitt described him) of Shakespeare's *As You Like It*. He is a follower of the exiled duke. To him falls the celebrated 'seven ages of man' speech. His 'Why, 'tis good to be sad and say nothing' brings Rosalind's retort 'Why then 'tis good to be a post', in Act IV.

**Jason, The Life and Death of** A narrative poem in heroic couplets by William Morris, published in 1867. The story follows the classical myths and the *Argonautica* of Apollonius Rhodius. Morris's version gives the complete story, from the birth of Jason and his education by Chiron the centaur to the confrontation with the usurper Pelias and the embarkation for Colchis on the *Argo* (where Apollonius begins his version). The poet describes the voyage: the encounter with King Aeëtes and the meeting with Medea, the theft of the Golden Fleece and the flight of Jason and Medea, and the return voyage and its hazards (where Apollonius closes his version). The further adventures include the murder of Pelias by Medea and the flight to Corinth in the *Argo*, Jason's desertion of Medea for the daughter of the king of Corinth, and Medea's revenge and flight to the safety of Athens. Jason becomes an outcast wanderer and dies under the rotting timbers of the once proud *Argo*.

**Jeames de la Pluche, C.** The name assumed by James Plush, the aspiring footman of *Jeames's Diary*. See **Yellowplush Correspondence, The**.

**Jean-ah Poquelin** See **Old Creole Days**.

**Jebb, Richard Claverhouse** 1841–1905. Jebb was born in Dundee and educated at Charterhouse School and Trinity College, Cambridge. He became Professor of Greek at Glasgow University (1875) and at Cambridge; he was also the member for Cambridge University in Parliament during his later years. Jebb was a distinguished Greek scholar and published editions and translations of Theophrastus (1870), Sophocles (1883–96), and Bacchylides (1905); *The Attic Orators from Antiphon to Isaeus* (1876–80); and a biography of Richard Bentley for the English Men of Letters series (1882).

**Jefferies, (John) Richard** 1848–87. The son of a Wiltshire farmer, Jefferies was born at Coate. He became a journalist on the *North Wilts Herald* in 1866 and soon made a name for himself with the fine descriptive sketches of rural life for which he is best known. He had hopes of becoming a novelist and in fact published three novels between 1874 and 1877. But these were not successful and he went to London for a time, where he contributed a series of articles to the *Pall Mall Gazette*. These were collected as *The Gamekeeper at Home* (1878) and Jefferies enjoyed a popular success. The success continued with *Wild Life in a Southern County* and *The Amateur Poacher* (1879). His books on rural life were popular until he died and, his reputation secure, he returned to fiction with *Green Ferne Farm* (1880), which proved more successful than his earlier attempts. *The Dewy Morn* was published in 1884, *After London* in 1885 and his best, *Amaryllis at the Fair*, in 1887.

Jefferies' reputation, however, really rests on the three books which to some degree convey his own idiosyncratic philosophy; it happens that they also contain his best writing: *Wood Magic* (1881), **Bevis:** *The Story of a Boy* (1882), and *The Story of My Heart*, a quasi-autobiography (1883). He died at the early age of 39, at Goring-on-Sea.

**Jeffers, (John) Robinson** 1887–1962. Robinson Jeffers was born in Pittsburgh. His father was a theologian and classical scholar and spent much of his time in Europe. Jeffers's education was spread over Germany and Switzerland until the family settled in California when he was 16. He completed his education at Occidental College, California, studied medicine and forestry, and after marrying built a house at Carmel, in a setting which inspires most of his poetry. Jeffers's work is sombre, pessimistic, and misanthropic. The grandeur of the natural world, the recurring theme of his poetry and the one that invokes his strongest writing, is too good for the human race: the earth would be much improved without self-centred humanity spoiling it all the time. His first two collections, *Flagons and Apples* (1912) and *Californians* (1916), made little impression but he began to attract attention with *Tamar and Other Poems* (1924); thereafter he published regularly and his reputation grew. *Roan Stallion* (1925) was followed by *The Woman at Point Sur* (1927), *Cawdor* (1928), *Dear Judas* (1929), the volume of elegies *Descent to the Dead* (1931), *Thurso's Landing* (1932), *Give Your Heart to the Hawks* (1933), *Solstice* (1935), *Such Counsels You Gave to Me* (1937), *Be Angry at the Sun* (1941), *The Double Axe* (1941), and *Hungerfield* (1954). Many of Jeffers's title poems are verse narratives and his work includes English versions of Euripides' *Medea* and *Hippolytus*. 'The Eye', 'November Surf', and 'Hurt Hawks' are to be found in most anthologies of American verse.

**Jefferson, Thomas** *c.*1743–1826. The man who became the third president of the USA was born in Albemarle county, Virginia. His father was a civil engineer and a democrat who had married into the Randolph family. Jefferson was educated at the College of William and Mary at Williamsburg, where he excelled in classical languages and French and where he developed a lifelong interest in the natural sciences. After college he studied law and was called to the Bar in 1767. Two years later he entered the House of Burgesses, where he served until 1779, and for the rest of his life was actively involved in politics. He married Martha Skelton in 1772.

Jefferson was opposed from the beginning of his political life to the administration of the colonies by the British Parliament. In 1774 he published *A Summary View of the Rights of British America*, which was a brilliant exposition of his views, and gave him a leading place in the Revolutionary cause. He drafted the Declaration of Independence for the Continental Congress in 1775–76. In his own legislature of Virginia (he was governor from 1779 to 1781) he worked hard to make the ideals of the Declaration a reality. He was firmly opposed to the maintenance of a landed aristocracy and an established church and was an advocate of further education for all who desired it, with a free state library and state college. It was an uphill struggle since the legislators were chiefly representative of the land-owning class and opposed to reform. He foresaw the trouble that lay ahead if slavery continued (more than a hundred worked on his own land) but his plans for gradual abolition were implacably opposed.

During the War for Independence Jefferson suffered the loss of his wife and saw Virginia overrun by British troops. He declined a third nomination as governor and began work on *Notes on the State of Virginia*, which was completed in 1782 and published in 1784. He returned to public life in 1783 at the Continental Congress, where, among other things, he proposed the monetary system which the USA adopted and plans for the government of the Western territories. He was his country's ambassador to France (1784–89) and its first secretary of state. He became a staunch supporter of state rights in opposition to the federalist views of Alexander Hamilton, which he saw as too closely allied with moneyed interests.

Jefferson became Vice President in 1797, running second to John Adams, and President in 1801 in opposition to Aaron Burr – the decisive influence was Alexander Hamilton's, who, while a political opponent of Jefferson, held a low opinion of Burr. Jefferson served two terms as President and was responsible for the Louisiana Purchase (1803), which more than doubled the size of his country at a cost of four cents per acre, and for the historic expedition of Lewis and Clark, which explored the continent along the Missouri River and through the Rocky Mountains to the Pacific Ocean. He also used US naval power under the command of Stephen Decatur to put an end to the pirates of Tripoli as a menace to his country's shipping. He refused a third nomination in 1818 but his successors, James Madison and James Monroe, were both his friends and protégés and 'Jeffersonian' government continued in the USA for some time.

Jefferson founded the University of Virginia after his retirement from the Presidency. He is,

strictly speaking, a great figure in American history, like Benjamin Franklin, without enjoying Franklin's distinction of also being a great figure in literature. However, when he did write he wrote extremely well and his *Notes on the State of Virginia* is a fine statement of the reflections, hopes, and ideals of a great statesman. *The Papers of Thomas Jefferson* are being published by Princeton University Press under the editorship of Julian P. Boyd. The enterprise began in 1950 and has reached 20 volumes to date.

**Jeffrey, Francis** 1773–1850. Jeffrey, a lawyer's son, was born in Edinburgh. He attended Edinburgh High School, went on to Glasgow University and Oxford, and took a law degree at Edinburgh University. He was called to the Bar in 1794 and was one of a group of Edinburgh lawyers who strongly supported Whig ideas of reform. He was elected dean of the Faculty of Advocates in 1829 and Lord Advocate in the Reform ministry of 1830; he became MP for Edinburgh in 1832 and Lord of Session in 1834 as Lord Jeffrey. His contribution to literature was the founding, with Sydney Smith and Henry Brougham, of *The Edinburgh Review*.

**Jenkins, Winifred** Tabitha Bramble's maid in *Humphry Clinker* by Tobias Smollett. She falls in love with Humphry, who has become the party's postillion. When Humphry proves to be her employer's son, Winifred makes a sensible adjustment to her new status.

*Jennie Gerhardt* A novel by Theodore Dreiser, first published in 1911.

Jennie Gerhardt, a poor girl of Columbus, Ohio, is seduced by Senator Brander. He has promised marriage but his sudden death leaves her stranded; she has a daughter, Vesta, and eventually finds work in Cleveland as a lady's maid. In Cleveland she attracts Lester Kane, son of a wealthy manufacturer. He is forceful – and generous to her family, so Jennie's resistance to him gives way. She leaves Vesta in her mother's care and goes on a trip to New York with him; she does not tell him she has a baby daughter. After the New York trip Lester wants to marry Jennie – but his family opposes the match; he persuades Jennie to become his mistress and the liaison is successful, even when Lester is told of the existence of Vesta. The Kane family discovers the liaison but Lester refuses to give up Jennie. Then his father dies and his will reduces his son's inheritance drastically unless he renounces her.

Lester goes to Europe with Jennie and finds that she has limitations he was never aware of in the closed world of their relationship. He drifts away from her, becoming increasingly attracted to Letty Gerald, a woman of his own background. Then Jennie learns of the terms of the Kane will and insists that she and Lester must separate. Lester provides Jennie with a home but he marries Letty; he is soon back in the world of society and business. Jennie's daughter, Vesta, dies and Jennie adopts two orphan children to fill her life; but she still loves Lester Kane.

While his wife is absent Lester is taken ill. His condition becomes serious and he asks for Jennie, his only real love. She stays with him and nurses him until he dies – but she is never acknowledged by his family. She watches his funeral through the cemetery gates.

*Jenny* A ballad by Dante Gabriel Rossetti, begun in 1847 and eventually published in 1870 in *Poems by D. G. Rossetti*. Jenny is a prostitute and the poet regards her with great sympathy as a victim of her time and circumstances, scorned by her virtuous sisters and, more tellingly, by the men who use her. It is the only poem of Rossetti's that bears on the conditions of everyday life.

*Jerome, A Poor Man* A novel by Mary Wilkins Freeman, first published in 1897.

When Jerome Edwards' father disappears he is left, in his teens, as the only support of his mother and his sister, Elmira. His dogged integrity makes his path difficult but he earns the love of Lucina Merritt, a childhood friend. His sister Elmira falls in love with Lawrence Prescott, son of a wealthy doctor whose word is virtually law in the district. Jerome and Elmira are in the same dilemma – both their loves are members of wealthy families and there seems no hope for the future. During a flood Jerome suffers the loss of his mill, on which all his expectations were founded; then he loses an inheritance because of a promise he cannot bring himself not to honour.

All ends well for Jerome and Elmira, however, beginning with the relenting of Dr Prescott towards Lawrence's determination to marry Elmira.

Mrs Freeman never achieved the same level in her novels as she did in short stories. The best part of *Jerome, A Poor Man*, which is marred by its contrived plot, lies in the quality of the writing and the author's observation of New England life.

*Jerrold, Douglas William* 1803–57. Jerrold was born in London and spent part of his youth and early manhood as a sailor. One of his shipmates was Clarkson Stanfield (the scenic artist who was the son of an actor and an author); it was

as an author that Jerrold was to realize a very successful career. In 1827 his farce, *Paul Pry*, was staged at the Coburg and he became resident playwright there. A melodrama, *Fifteen Years of a Drunkard's Life* (1828), did equally well and he had a major success in *Black-eyed Susan* (Surrey Theatre, 1829). His next play was the melodrama *The Mutiny at the Nore* (Royal Pavilion, 1830), and *The Rent Day* (Drury Lane, 1832) was a drama, but he generally wrote comedy: *The Bride of Ludgate* (Drury Lane, 1831), *Beau Nash* (Haymarket, 1834), and *Time Works Wonders* (Haymarket, 1845).

In 1841 Jerrold became one of the original staff of a new weekly called *Punch* and from that date devoted most of his time to journalism. He was equally successful in his new role, signing his contributions 'Q'. His *Mrs Caudle's Curtain Lectures* (1845) helped to establish the paper's popularity and were published in book form (1846). Mrs Caudle is a nagging wife who always gets into her stride at bedtime, when her suffering husband is hoping to sleep. From 1852 until his death Jerrold edited *Lloyd's Weekly Newspaper*.

*Jerusalem* See **Blake, William**.

*Jesuits in North America in the Seventeenth Century, The* See **Parkman, Francis** and *France and England in North America*.

**Jewett, Sarah Orne** 1849–1909. The novelist and short-story writer of Maine was born and brought up in that state at South Berwick, near the border of New Hampshire and close to the harbour of York, which became the Deephaven of her early stories. A doctor's daughter, she often travelled with her father to farms and fishing towns and observed the decay that afflicted the once busy harbours when trade with the West Indies moved elsewhere. Farms were abandoned too; and one island was depopulated when its people joined the gold rush. Harriet Beecher Stowe's stories of New England life were the stimulus for Sarah Orne Jewett's first efforts; she decided to record the life of her own state and succeeded in having a story accepted by the *Atlantic Monthly* when she was 19. A collection of such pieces was published as *Deephaven* in 1877 and established her at once as a writer of considerable talent.

Annie Fields, the wife of the Boston publisher who had been editor of the *Atlantic Monthly*, became Sarah Orne Jewett's close friend and frequent visits to Boston were valuable to the writer; but she never lost her sense of perspective and always returned to South Berwick to write her books. She published two novels, *A Country*

Sarah Orne Jewett.

*Doctor* (1884) and *A Marsh Island* (1885), and further collections of stories: *A White Heron* (1886), *The King of Folly Island* (1888), *A Native of Winby* (1893), and *The Life of Nancy* (1895). In 1896 came the book that gave her a lasting place in American letters, **The Country of the Pointed Firs**. Her later work included two books for children, a historical romance, *The Tory Lover* (1901), and some poems that were posthumously published as *Verses* in 1916.

Sarah Orne Jewett's writing is crisp, assured, and memorable because her people and places are so skilfully observed. She was well read and her friendship with Annie Fields kept her in touch with the world of letters. She gave encouragement to the young Willa Cather, who was later to edit a collection of her stories and who placed her on a level with Hawthorne and Mark Twain. Annie Fields edited her friend's *Letters*, which were published in 1911.

**Jewkes, Mrs** Mr B.'s servant in *Pamela, or Virtue Rewarded* by Samuel Richardson. She abets her master's designs on Pamela's virginity and steals the latter's journal. Mrs Jewkes is 'a broad, squat, pursy, fat thing, quite ugly, if anything human can be so called: about forty years old'.

**Jew of Malta, The Famous Tragedy of the Rich** A tragedy in blank verse by Christopher Marlowe. It was first produced *c.*1590 and not published until 1633. The published text is believed to contain a number of alterations made during production and these are usually attributed to Thomas Heywood. The play was very popular and gave Edward Alleyn, the creator of Tamburlaine and Doctor Faustus, another great opportunity as an actor.

Barabas, a successful Jewish merchant of Malta, counts his riches and ponders on the prejudice of the Christians, their envy of his success, and their persecution of his people. He knows them for hypocrites – their religion is the excuse they use. Barabas longs for the power that would enable him to deal with his enemies.

The Turks demand tribute from Malta and the governor of the island decides to extract the money from the Jews. Barabas resists; his wealth is taken by force and his house confiscated – the governor turns it into a nunnery. He decides to revenge himself on those who have wronged him and embarks on a one-man campaign of destruction. Abigail, his daughter, has a Christian lover and he disposes of both of them. He poisons wells and destroys the entire nunnery, his former house, with poisoned porridge. But his plan to destroy the Turkish commander and his retinue at a banquet by means of a collapsible floor goes awry. He is betrayed and meets his death in a cauldron under the same floor.

The character of Barabas bears superficial resemblances to Shylock but in the course of the play he changes from a basically sympathetic character into a monster who is really incredible. Like Tamburlaine, Barabas is really the whole play, and Marlowe inevitably gives him marvellous things to say. The play is rarely revived.

**Jingle, Alfred** In Dickens's *The Pickwick Papers*, a strolling player who lives on his wits. He is first encountered at Rochester, where he nearly gets Mr Winkle involved in fighting a duel. He tries to elope with Rachael Wardle from Dingley Dell and crosses and recrosses the path of Mr Pickwick throughout the book. Their last encounter is in the Fleet Prison, where Jingle has finally come to grief as a debtor. Mr Pickwick's generous nature saves Jingle from total destitution.

**Jo** The crossing-sweeper of Dickens's *Bleak House* – an orphan child who has no memory of a home or parents. The only kindness he ever knows comes from poor little Guster, a slavey in the Snagsby household and an orphan like himself, and from the strange nameless scrivener who gives him food and money, when he has any. Jo's only way of thanking him is to sweep away the dust and leaves from the gate of the burial ground when his friend dies. Friendless and always half-starved, Jo is chivvied to his death by the lawyers and police in their enquiries.

***Joan of Arc, Personal Recollections of*** A historical novel by Mark Twain, first published in 1896 as the work of a supposed page and secretary to Joan, the Sieur Louis de Conte. The book follows the known facts of Joan of Arc's life and introduces a number of fictional characters to amplify the historical events.

**Jocelin de Brakelond** See **Brakelond, Jocelin de.**

**John, Don** The bastard brother of Don Pedro in Shakespeare's *Much Ado About Nothing*. Envious and spiteful, he engineers the plot to discredit Hero, so that Claudio jilts her on the wedding day.

***John Bull, The History of*** The collective title of a group of pamphlets by John Arbuthnot, published first in 1712 and rearranged for publication in Pope's and Swift's *Miscellanies* of 1727. John Bull, as an archetypal Englishman, makes his first appearance in literature in this work, an effective satire advocating the end of the war with France.

John Bull (England) and Nicholas Frog (Holland) are engaged in a lawsuit with Lewis Baboon (Louis XIV, Bourbon). Their case is fought and won by the attorney Humphrey Hocus (Marlborough). Then John Bull discovers an intrigue between Hocus and Mrs Bull (the Whig Parliament); Mrs Bull dies during the ensuing rumpus and John Bull marries again; the new Mrs Bull is the Tory Parliament and John Bull has spent a great deal in litigation, thereby losing the 'Plumbs' he had acquired by 'plain and fair dealing'. John Bull (naturally) is 'an honest plain-dealing Fellow' but is easily deceived by partners, apprentices, and servants. He honours his mother (the Church of England).

***John Buncle, Esquire, The Life and Opinions of*** See **Amory, Thomas.**

***John Gilpin, The Diverting History of*** A ballad by William Cowper, first published anonymously in *The Public Advertiser* in 1782. It was published in the same volume as *The Task* in 1785. Cowper heard the story of the linen draper John Gilpin from his friend Lady Austen and wrote his ballad on the subject the following day. The story, familiar to generations of schoolchildren, tells of John Gilpin of Cheapside and his wife, who decide to celebrate their wedding anniversary at The Bell, Edmonton. Mrs Gilpin and the children will travel by chaise and pair, while John Gilpin will proceed on horseback. But he loses control of his borrowed horse, which carries him ten miles farther, to Ware, and back again. The real John Gilpin was a citizen of London who owned land at Olney in Buckinghamshire, where Cowper lived for some years.

***John Halifax, Gentleman*** A novel by Dinah Mulock (Mrs Craik), first published in 1857. The hero is an orphan boy who, by his own industry and integrity, earns the friendship of one of his employer's sons, Phineas Fletcher. Phineas helps him to improve his education and John achieves a good position. He marries Ursula March, the heroine of the story. The point of the novel is that gentlemen are born, not made by claims of birth and wealth. It was the only work of the author to achieve a lasting success.

***John Inglesant*** A novel by Joseph Henry Shorthouse, privately printed in 1880 and published in 1881. The setting is the early 17th century.

John Inglesant, a young gentleman with a predisposition to mysticism, comes under the influence of a Jesuit emissary, who sees in the highly-wrought, sensuous young man excellent material for service in the religious intrigues of the later years of Charles I. Inglesant is strongly influenced by the community of Little Gidding, and the king's approval of it is a factor in his decision to undertake dangerous service in the Royalist cause. This involves delicate and secret negotiations to bring an Irish army into England: but when the plans come to light the king repudiates him. Inglesant's rectitude prevents him from exposing the king, even when he comes near to losing his head.

After the execution of the king, Inglesant makes his way to Italy, partly to be quit of England but also to find the Italian who murdered his brother. The author here moves the story of religious tension to Rome, where Inglesant witnesses the drawn-out intrigues that attend the election of a successor to Innocent X. He meets Molinos, the Spanish mystic who was ultimately condemned for the influence of his Quietism, and is drawn to the idea, temporarily, that human endeavour is futile except in devotion to God. The climax of the story comes with Inglesant's encounter with the murderer, now in his power. He renounces vengeance for himself and leaves him to God.

Shorthouse used passages from 17th-century books to reinforce his own imitation of contemporary style. This was not known when the book was published and Shorthouse's reputation suffered somewhat in consequence. But the novel remains a considerable achievement, a blend of political and religious history with a real understanding of the hero's mystical leanings.

***John Marr and Other Sailors,*** *with Some Sea-Pieces.* The sea poems of Herman Melville, first published in 1888. The poems are wide-ranging, nostalgic, and suggest a certain peace in the mind of the poet and novelist whose reputation had known extraordinary reverses. Among the best-known poems in the volume are 'John Marr' of the title, reflecting on a sailor, landbound now because of injury, and his memory of the life he once knew; 'The Berg', an apostrophe to a manifestation of natural forces; and 'To Ned', which recalls his friend Toby and their adventure in the Marquesas Islands.

**John of Salisbury**  See **Salisbury, John of.**

**Johnson, Edward** *c.*1598–1672. A chronicler of early Massachusetts, Edward Johnson was born in Canterbury and went to America with John Winthrop in 1630 to trade with the Indians for the Massachusetts Bay Company. He returned to England to fetch his family and settled, finally, in America in 1636. He was one of the founders of the town of Woburn in 1640, a captain of militia, and for the rest of his life an active figure in the affairs of the town.

Johnson's commitment to the life in a new world was absolute and, as a riposte to adverse comments from the old country on the way of life in Puritan New England, he began to write *A History of New England* in 1650. This was published anonymously in London in 1653 – actually dated 1654 – with the running title of *The Wonder-Working Providence of Sion's Saviour in New England.*

Johnson's work is a vigorous history of New England from 1628 to 1652, which presents the founding of the colony as a spiritual crusade: the settlers are crusaders who fight against both wilderness and unbelievers. It includes verse tributes, of no particular distinction, to people and events. The prose has an Elizabethan gusto that almost overcomes the wordiness and over-adornment. Its great value is as an expression of the feeling of the times; it is not regarded as an authoritative history.

**Johnson, Lionel Pigot** 1867–1902. Lionel Johnson was the son of an Irish army officer and was born at Broadstairs in Kent. He was educated at Winchester School and New College, Oxford, and became a literary journalist in London, writing for *The Athenaeum, The Spectator,* and other journals. Johnson made a name as a critic and became prominent in the Rhymers' Club; one of its members was W. B. Yeats and

Johnson was very interested in the Irish literary revival. He became a Catholic in 1891.

Johnson contributed to *The Books of the Rhymers' Club* and *The Yellow Book* and published his first collection, *Poems,* in 1895. *Ireland and Other Poems* (1897) was his only other collection published during his lifetime; like his contemporary, Ernest Dowson, he died of drink. His principal critical works were *The Art of Thomas Hardy* (1894) and the essays collected as *Post Linimium* (published posthumously, 1911) edited by T. Whittemore. *The Complete Poems* (1953), edited by I. Fletcher, contains more than 50 previously unpublished poems as well as the 12 which Johnson had contributed to *The Books of the Rhymers' Club* in 1892 and 1894. Johnson's best-known poem is 'The Dark Angel', a reflection of his struggles against the temptation that ruined him. 'By the Statue of King Charles at Charing Cross' is a familiar item in anthologies.

**Johnson, Samuel** 1709–84. Samuel Johnson was born in Lichfield in Staffordshire, where his father, a bookseller, was sheriff of the city. While a schoolboy he benefited greatly from being able to browse at will among his father's stock and he displayed an aptitude for Latin at an early age. He also knew his father's business reasonably well and never lost his ability to bind a book.

Johnson entered Pembroke College, Oxford, as a commoner in October 1728 and stayed until 1731. He left without taking a degree; but while at Oxford, for a Christmas exercise, he translated Alexander Pope's collection of hymns and prayers, *Messiah,* into Latin (published in J. Husbands' *A Miscellany of Poems by Several Hands,* 1731). After leaving Oxford Johnson returned to Staffordshire and taught for a time (1732) at the grammar school at Market Bosworth in Leicestershire. Later in the same year he went to live with his friend Edmund Hector in Birmingham, where he stayed for three years; it was in *The Birmingham Journal* that Johnson's first essays, now lost, were published. He also planned an edition of Politian (Angelo Poliziano), the 15th-century Italian humanist and classical poet, but his hopes came to nothing. However, it was in Birmingham that Samuel Johnson completed his first book, *A Voyage to Abissinia.* This was a translation from the French account of the travels of Father Jerome Lobo, the Portuguese missionary, and was published in 1735.

Johnson also married in that year. His wife was the widow of Harry Porter, a Birmingham friend. Elizabeth Porter was 46 – 20 years older than he. The newly married couple opened a school at Edial, near Lichfield, and one of Johnson's pupils was David Garrick. The enterprise did not succeed and the Johnsons decided to move to London in the summer of 1737 – Johnson hoping to earn a living with his pen. Garrick went to London with him, to work in the wine trade; he chose a different career for himself, as all the world knows. Samuel Johnson struggled to complete a tragedy, *Irene*, amid the upheaval of moving house, but it was not to be staged until 12 years later. An income for Johnson, who was living in Castle Street near Cavendish Square, came from Edward Cave who, under the pseudonym of Sylvanus Urban, had founded **The Gentleman's Magazine** in 1731. The monthly journal was wide-ranging and successful and Johnson was assured of a regular income and employment, contributing essays, poems, biographies, Latin verses, and comments on parliamentary reports. *London: A Poem in Imitation of the Third Satire of Juvenal* (1738) was published anonymously and received high praise from Alexander Pope.

In August 1743 the poet Richard Savage died in a Bristol prison. He had been Johnson's friend; he was apparently a man of considerable charm though his reputation was distinctly unsavoury. Savage's death was news and Edward Cave commissioned a biography from Johnson, who completed it by the end of the year. *An Account of the Life of Mr Richard Savage, Son of the Earl Rivers* (1744) was a great success and the difficulty of securing a career in letters seemed to be lessening. Johnson had meanwhile gained useful experience from the task of cataloguing the library of Edward Harley, Earl of Oxford, which had been purchased upon the earl's death by Thomas Osborne, a bookseller of Gray's Inn (1742); his already formidable knowledge of literature became immense. *An Essay on the Origin and Importance of Small Tracts and Fugitive Pieces* (1744) gives an outline of English pamphlets from the Reformation to the reign of Charles II. *Miscellaneous Observations on the Tragedy of Macbeth* (1745) indicated Johnson's intention of undertaking an edition of Shakespeare; but Warburton's 1747 edition obliged him to put it aside. He turned his concentrated attention to a subject which had been in his mind for years: a dictionary of the English language.

The publisher Robert Dodsley persuaded Johnson, who did not like the idea, to address his *Plan of a Dictionary of the English Language* (1747) to Lord Chesterfield, who acknowledged Johnson's great intentions and made him a small gift of money. Chesterfield, by his own admission, was usually indifferent to such compliments – his patronage was daily sought by numbers of people; but Johnson's great project interested

him very much. However, he was a busy man in the government and he had done what he could. Johnson embarked on the work which was to occupy him, on and off, for the next eight years.

*The Vanity of Human Wishes* (1749) is generally acknowledged as Johnson's most successful poem; the full title acknowledges his imitation of the tenth satire of Juvenal, and February of the same year saw the production of his tragedy, *Irene*, at Drury Lane. David Garrick had promised his friend and former teacher that he would produce the play as soon as he had power to. He played the part of Demetrius and persuaded the author to make some alterations. The play continued for nine performances – a respectable run in the 18th century – and Johnson earned a much-needed £200; Dodsley published the text and paid him another £100.

At work on his dictionary, Johnson took on another project for Edward Cave, a series of essays to be published twice weekly. This was to be **The Rambler**, which continued for 208 numbers, all but 5 written by Johnson himself. The range of the essays was wide and the quality remarkable; remarkable, too, was the fact that they were published anonymously. But Johnson was a man of little pretension; he knew that the authors of moral essays – there were a number of these – would be examined, and he also knew that 'a man writes much better than he lives'. But anonymity could not be sustained; Samuel Richardson, a great admirer, recognized the writer's identity and very soon it was known all over London. *The Rambler* continued from 1750 to 1752; Johnson's wife, Elizabeth (his Tetty, he called her), died on 17 March of that year. The apparently ill-starred marriage had been an important element in Johnson's life in spite of inevitable disharmonies. Tetty had been obliged to call a halt to their physical relationship – the demands of a husband 20 years her junior, whose 'amorous inclinations', according to Boswell, 'were uncommonly strong and impetuous', proved too much for her. Johnson was well aware of his own imperfections as a husband but his grateful affection never diminished; 26 years later, in his private diary, he wrote, 'Poor Tetty, whatever were our faults and failings, we loved each other . . .'

From March 1753, for the space of a year, Johnson contributed to John Hawkesworth's periodical *The Adventurer* and he wrote a life of Edward Cave for *The Gentleman's Magazine* when that publisher died in 1754. In 1755, after eight years' labour, was published – and its full title indicates its range – **A Dictionary of the English Language:** *In Which the Words are*

*Deduced from their Originals, and Illustrated in their Different Significations by Examples from the Best Writers. To Which are Prefixed A History of the Language, and an English Grammar*. Thomas Warton, Johnson's friend at Trinity College, Oxford, secured him an honorary degree of Master of Arts just before publication and this duly appeared on the title page. Lord Chesterfield, meanwhile, had retired; ill and growing deaf, he was using his enforced leisure to write his famous letters to his son. At some time during his work on the *Dictionary* Johnson had, apparently, waited on the patron he had not wanted – and been prevented from seeing him. There are no positive facts on record and the story remains a mystery; but one sure fact is that Johnson felt slighted and never forgave Chesterfield. When Chesterfield received news that Johnson's *Dictionary* was nearing completion he bestirred himself and wrote two essays recommending it, which were published anonymously in *The World*, Robert Dodsley's paper. Johnson was not pleased with the tone of the essays; he thought them unnecessarily waggish. He discovered that Chesterfield was the author – the letter that Johnson then addressed to Lord Chesterfield is one of the most famous in the language. What Johnson felt about patronage had, however, already been demonstrated in his *Dictionary*, where a patron is defined as 'Commonly a wretch who supports with insolence, and is paid with flattery'. The *Dictionary* was published again in 1756, in an abridged form, and in June of the same year Johnson issued *Proposals for an edition of Shakespeare*. But he was tired out, and whatever fame or distinction was his at this time he was earning a bare living from his work, no more. His earnings from the *Dictionary* were spent before the work was completed and he was sometimes near to serious debt, having to appeal to his friends for help. He had to work hard all the time – political articles, reviews, essays, lives of Sir Thomas Browne and Roger Ascham, and *The Idler* series of papers (1758–60) in *The Universal Chronicle*. His mother died while *The Idler* papers were in progress and Johnson published his novel *The Prince of Abissinia. A Tale* (1759), a didactic romance enquiring into the 'choice of life'. This became known as **Rasselas** after the posthumous edition of 1787.

Then George II, no patron of the arts, died, and George III ascended the throne. The new king, at the prompting of Lord Bute, awarded Johnson a pension of £300 a year. Free from the anxiety of supporting himself for the first time in his life, Johnson, now 53, went off to the west country for six weeks with his friend Joshua Reynolds (1762).

On 16 May 1763 Johnson visited Thomas Davies's bookshop in Great Russell Street about seven o'clock in the evening. In the tea parlour behind the shop he encountered a young Scot, to whom he was rather rude at first. However, the young Scot was not easily deterred and, after the conversation became more amiable, resolved to call on the great man, which he did, eight days later, at Johnson's chambers in the Inner Temple. He was cordially received and was asked to stay: posterity owes much to the persistence of James Boswell. Johnson and Reynolds founded The Club in 1764 (later called the Literary Club); Burke and Goldsmith were among the original members and Garrick, Boswell, and Charles James Fox came later. In January 1764 the Irish playwright, Arthur Murphy, a close friend of Johnson, persuaded his wealthy and cultured friends, the Thrales, to invite the great man to dinner – Murphy was trying to pull Johnson out of one of his frequent fits of depression. Henry Thrale and his wife, Hester, received Johnson in their town house at Southwark, where Thrale was a prosperous brewer. The friendship that resulted was to prove of enormous value. The generous and cultured husband and the tiny vivacious wife saved Johnson from a nervous breakdown at the beginning of their acquaintance, taking him off to their house at Streatham Park to recover his spirits. The Thrales' house, because of Johnson, became the meeting place of the London intelligentsia.

*The Plays of William Shakespeare* was published in eight volumes in 1765, with the *Preface* (*Mr Johnson's Preface to his Edition of Shakespeare's Plays*) appearing separately in the same year. *The Preface* is prized as a fine essay in criticism and has earned a permanent place in letters, while the edition of Shakespeare has long been superseded. It was, nevertheless, an advance in Shakespearean scholarship which owed much to what David Nicol Smith described as Johnson's 'imperturbable common sense' and 'robust honesty'. It was to be the last major enterprise of Samuel Johnson, who was now 56, but his influence was enormous; his every word was listened to and read with close attention. The political tracts, *The False Alarm* (1770), *Falkland's Islands* (1771), *The Patriot* (1774), and *Taxation no Tyranny* (1775), are remembered, as Nicol Smith observed, because Johnson wrote them; the same is true of the speech he wrote for his friend William Gerard Hamilton to deliver in parliament: *Considerations on the Corn Laws* (1766).

In August 1773 Johnson undertook the journey to Scotland with Boswell. Boswell had been pressing him to go for some time, eager to observe his friend in the country of his birth – and in its wilder reaches, too. The three months yielded two rewarding books. Johnson's *A Journey to the Western Islands of Scotland* (1775) is a series of absorbing reflections on a way of life completely strange to him. Then, at Easter 1777, a group of London booksellers waited on Johnson with a proposal that he write what he described to Boswell as 'little lives, and little prefaces, to a little edition of the English poets'. The 'little edition' was a venture to drive out rival editions of the poets being published in Edinburgh; it was to be elegantly presented and biographical prefaces by Samuel Johnson would give it superiority over others. Johnson accepted and enjoyed his work, which covered a period of four years at Streatham Park, with Hester Thrale helping him with copying and proof reading. *The Lives of the Poets* was published separately in 1781 and is considered by many scholars to be Johnson's masterpiece. Yet only 5 of the 52 lives the book contains were chosen by him, though no doubt he was listened to carefully by his sponsors. The decision to begin with Cowley is in itself enough to raise eyebrows; but the taste of the age is a factor which has to be considered and, within the limits imposed on him, Johnson achieved a miraculous balance of criticism and biography. He could not fail to be interesting as

Samuel Johnson. A detail from the unfinished portrait by J. Barry, c.1777. National Portrait Gallery, London.

a critic, and his intense curiosity about human behaviour made him an ideal biographer. He was by now the holder of two honorary doctorates, from Trinity College, Dublin (1765), and Oxford (1775), and these gave him his familiar title.

Henry Thrale died on the night of 3 April 1781, Johnson at his side. Thrale was 20 years younger than his friend, and his health had begun to break down with a stroke brought on by financial worry. His widow sold the brewery for a good sum – she had detested the business – and let the house at Streatham. She fell in love with Gabriele Piozzi, a singer and music teacher, and was in a torment of indecision about marrying him. Johnson became lonely and puzzled by the neglect of someone whose affection for him had always seemed so certain. In the middle of June 1783 Johnson received a letter from Hester Thrale announcing her impending marriage to Piozzi. He wrote her a furious and brutal letter, to which Mrs Thrale returned a dignified and cool reply, and all was over between them. Mrs Thrale was entitled to happiness; Johnson was old and lonely and suddenly put aside – his letter, unpardonable as it was, represented a howl of pain.

Johnson set off on a round of visits in July 1784. It was a farewell tour; he knew he had not long to live. He went to Lichfield, Ashbourne, Birmingham, and Oxford, returning to London in mid-November, dejected and suffering acutely from dropsy. In the last weeks of his life he destroyed his private papers; he died some time during the night of 13 December. On the 20th, he was buried in Westminster Abbey.

Samuel Johnson's career has almost been obscured by Boswell's fine biography – the artist is almost overpowered by the character. But Johnson was a literary artist of remarkable quality, the finest prose writer of the 18th century, unrivalled in the clarity of his expression. He was impatient with mere scholarship, recognizing how barren was the pursuit of learning for its own sake. His own erudition was prodigious (glance at any page of his *Dictionary*) but it was acquired while he was gaining his knowledge of life; he never made a separation between life and art. His direct and disciplined style is an object lesson to any aspiring writer.

Much of Samuel Johnson's work was published anonymously, as that of a man who was earning a living by his pen inevitably was in the 18th century. *A Bibliography of Samuel Johnson* was prepared by W. P. Courtney and David Nicol Smith and published in 1915 and 1925; this is being revised by J. D. Fleeman. A supplement, by R. W. Chapman and A. T. Hazen, was published in 1939.

'Vauxhall Gardens, 1784' by Thomas Rowlandson. Mrs Weichsel sings; in the ground-level box at the left are Johnson, Goldsmith, Boswell, and Mrs Thrale. Victoria & Albert Museum, London.

The first collected edition of Johnson's work (by Sir John Hawkins) appeared in 1787 and was added to regularly until 1792. Further material was added by Alexander Chalmers in 1806, 1816, and 1823. The edition in progress from Yale University Press, edited by A. T. Hazen and J. H. Middendorf, began in 1958 and supersedes all others; 10 volumes have appeared so far. Johnson's correspondence was edited by R. W. Chapman and published in 1952; Chapman also edited a useful selection, *Johnson. Prose and Poetry* in The World's Classics series (1962). Other recommended selections are *A Johnson Reader*, edited by E. L. McAdam and G. Milne (New York, 1964), and the Reynard Library, *A Selection*, edited by M. Wilson (1967).

**Johnstone, Charles** *c.*1719–*c.*1800.  Johnstone was born in Ireland and educated at Trinity College, Dublin. He practised as a lawyer in spite of his handicap of deafness. He went to Calcutta in 1782 and became a journalist; eventually he became a newspaper proprietor. Johnstone was the author of *Chrysal, or The Adventures of a Guinea* (1760–65), satirical episodes in the life of the times, related by a guinea passed from hand to hand. Within the framework of this clumsy device the author succeeds with several of the episodes, notably the scenes at the Hellfire Club and the successful manoeuvres of an ambitious wife on behalf of her clergyman husband.

Chrysal is the spirit of gold imprisoned in the guinea, who acts as narrator.

**John the Reeve**  A popular ballad of the 15th century, of unknown authorship. It tells of John, a sturdy villein who rides to court carrying a sword and a pitchfork. He succeeds there and is eventually knighted. The ballad was printed in David Laing's *Select Remains of the Ancient Popular Poetry of Scotland* (1822) but is identified as an English work by scholars of the period.

**John van Olden Barnavelt, The Tragedy of Sir**  A historical drama, concerned with contemporary events in the Netherlands, by John Fletcher and Philip Massinger. The play was first produced in 1619 but not published until 1883, when the manuscript was discovered in the British Museum by A. H. Bullen.

Barnavelt (Johan van Oldenbarneveldt), permanent Advocate of the United Provinces, is disturbed by the increasing power of the Prince of Orange and the army. He organizes opposition under the guise of a religious movement and conspires to raise companies of burghers to counter the strength of the army. The prince's agents discover the conspiracy, the companies are disbanded, and Barnavelt's principal associates captured; one of them, Leidenberch, confesses. The prince is in favour of moderation towards Leidenberch. Barnavelt, because of his eminence, remains free – but he visits Leidenberch and convinces him that his honourable course, now, is suicide. Leidenberch does kill himself. The prince is convinced that Barnavelt is dangerous and orders his arrest; Barnavelt is tried for treason and executed. The play is not faithful to history. Johan van Oldenbarneveldt was one of the architects of Dutch independence and prosperity; he was the loser in a struggle that involved both religious questions and the power of the princes. It culminated in the Synod of Dort and Oldenbarneveldt's principal antagonist was Prince Maurice of Nassau. The trial was highly irregular and the execution of the great advocate is regarded by most historians as judicial murder.

**Jolly Beggars, The** A verse cantata by Robert Burns. It was written before his first collection, called the Kilmarnock poems, was published in 1786, but was not included in that volume. It first appeared in a Glasgow chapbook of 1799. It is believed to have been inspired by a visit to Poosie Nansie's tavern in Mauchline, where Burns and two companions witnessed the uncaring gaiety of characters who, in the daily world, were wretched and beggarly. The songs pass from character to character, portraying them with great vividness; W. E. Henley described the effect as 'humanity caught in the act'.

**Jonathan Wild the Great, The Life of** A satirical novel by Henry Fielding, first published in his *Miscellanies* in 1743. Daniel Defoe had written two accounts of Wild's career in 1725, the year of his execution (*The Life of Jonathan Wild, from his Birth to his Death* and *The true and Genuine Account of the Life and Actions of the late Jonathan Wild . . . taken from his own mouth*), and Fielding's purpose was to question the values of his time by lauding the immense success of a notorious criminal. In a world where goodness counted for nothing, greatness had to be measured by success; Wild qualified for this no less than princes and politicians. Robert Walpole was the main target of the book.

Jonathan Wild is baptized by Titus Oates and while at school begins to display his disposition to wickedness. He then goes to work for Snap, warden of a sponging house (a bailiff's house, where arrested debtors were kept before going to prison), and soon learns the art of exploitation from his master. He also begins to show talent as a pickpocket. He becomes the head of a gang of thieves; he exploits them, too, securing discipline by denouncing to the law anyone who challenges him. The greater part of the proceeds always goes to Wild.

He marries Laetitia Snap, his former employer's daughter, and finds a ready-made victim in Heartfree, a jeweller, who attended the same school as himself. Heartfree is plundered and, unable to meet his obligations, is locked up as a bankrupt. Wild gets rid of Mrs Heartfree by a trick that sends her out of England and then accuses her husband of murdering her. Heartfree is almost on the scaffold before Wild is exposed and brought to justice. Wild goes to the scaffold himself with the demeanour of a great man. The black comedy is sustained throughout, and there is an excellent comic creation in Laetitia Wild, whose heart is as mean as her husband's but who pretends to virtue when it suits her.

*Jonathan Wild* is published in modern editions by The World's Classics and Everyman's Library. The latter volume, edited by George Saintsbury (1932), also contains *The Journal of a Voyage to Lisbon*.

**Jones, Henry Arthur** 1851–1929. Jones was born at Grandborough in Buckinghamshire and was the eldest son of a farmer. He began work at the age of 12 in drapers' shops; he then worked in a London warehouse and as a commercial traveller, using his leisure to extend his reading and further his education. He wrote a novel and some one-act plays, none of which were accepted; he eventually achieved a modest success with a domestic drama, *It's Only Round the Corner*, which was performed at the Theatre Royal, Exeter, in 1878, and later in London at the Strand Theatre, as *Harmony* (1884).

Jones made the drama his profession after 1878 and 45 full-length plays by him were staged in London and New York between 1878 and 1917. His *A Clerical Error* (Court Theatre, 1879) was produced by Wilson Barrett, for whom Jones and Henry Herman devised a spectacular melodrama called *The Silver King* (Princess, 1882). This was one of Barrett's most successful parts and the long run established Jones's reputation. He then turned to more serious theatre; he was interested in the drama of ideas and the drama as a vehicle for social criticism. With Herman he adapted Ibsen's *A Doll's House* as *Breaking a Butterfly* (Prince's, 1884) and in his own work displayed a talent for naturalistic dialogue and portrayal of character. However, it is now generally agreed that his drama lacked the firm philosophical basis that would have given his social and moral criticism a permanent place in the English theatre.

In his own day Jones was immensely successful and the leading players all appeared in his works. The most notable plays were *Saints and Sinners* (Vaudeville, 1884), *The Dancing Girl* (Haymarket, 1891), *The Case of Rebellious Susan* (Criterion, 1894), and *The Triumph of the Philistines* (St James's, 1895). *Michael and His Lost Angel* (Lyceum, 1896) was severely criticized because one of the central scenes contained the public confession of adultery by a priest. The star, Mrs Patrick Campbell, left the cast during rehearsals and the play was taken off after ten performances.

But Jones went on to further success with *The Liars* (Criterion, 1897) and *Mrs Dane's Defence* (Wyndham's, 1900). The last two plays are occasionally revived.

**Jones, James** 1921– . Jones was born in Robinson, Illinois, and served in the US Army in the Pacific from 1939 to 1944. In 1945 he submitted a novel to Maxwell Perkins, who returned it but encouraged Jones to persevere. His first novel is the one by which he is best known – *From Here to Eternity* (1951), a realistic story of army life in Hawaii on the eve of the attack on Pearl Harbor. Jones won the National Book Award and the novel became a best seller. His career continued with *Some Came Running* (1957), *The Pistol* (1962), *The Thin Red Line* (1962), *Go to the Widow-Maker* (1967), and *A Touch of Danger* (1973). *The Ice-Cream Headache* (1968) and *The Merry Month of May* (1971) are collections of short stories and *Viet Journal* (1974) is Jones's account of a visit to Vietnam. The author now lives in Paris.

**Jones, (Everett) LeRoi** 1934– . LeRoi Jones, who has adopted the name of Amiri Baraka, was born in Newark, New Jersey. Scholarships enabled him to study at Rutgers University, Newark; Howard University, Washington DC; and Columbia University. He served in the US Air Force from 1954 to 1956, and thereafter became actively involved in the Black rights movement. His first work was a play, *A Good Girl is Hard to Find* (produced 1958), and his first published poetry was *Preface to a Twenty-Volume Suicide Note* (1961). Since 1961 Jones has taught as well as being involved with the founding of a magazine, *Yugen*, and the Totem Press for the encouragement of young poets. He founded the Black Arts Repertory Theatre in Harlem in 1964. His career as a poet continued with *The Dead Lecturer* (1964), *Black Art* (1966), *A Poem for Black Hearts* (1967), *It's Nationtime* (1970), and *Spirit Reach* (1972). LeRoi Jones's commitment to the Black man's cause is total and his declared aim is socialist revolution. His criticism of modern America from a Black standpoint is powerfully expressed in his plays (the dates given are those of the first production): *Dante* (1961), *Dutchman, The Slave, The Baptism,* and *The Toilet* (1964), *Jello* and *Experimental Death Unit* (1965), *A Black Mass* (1966), *Arm Yrself and Harm Yrself, Slave Ship: A Historical Pageant,* and *Madheart* (1967), *Home on the Range* and *Police* (1968), *The Death of Malcolm X* and *Great Goodness of Life: A Coon show* (1969), *Bloodrites* (1970), *Junkies are Full of (Shhh)* and *BA-RA-KA* (1972), *The Creation of the New Ark* (1974), *Sidnee Poet Heroical* (1975), and *S-1* (1976).

**Jones, Sir William** 1746–94. Jones was born at Westminster; he was educated at Harrow School and University College, Oxford, and was judge of the High Court at Calcutta from 1783 until his death. A jurist and orientalist, Jones published several works on law and oriental languages but is best remembered for his mastery of Sanskrit and his insistence, in his essay in *Asiatic Researches* (1786), on its study as the common source of Greek and Latin. Jones's declaration, together with John Horne Tooke's advocacy of the study of Gothic and Anglo-Saxon (published in the same year), saw the birth of the science of comparative philology.

**Jonson** (*or* **Johnson**), **Ben** *c.*1572–1637. Benjamin Jonson was the posthumous son of a clergyman whose family came from the Scottish border. Jonson himself was probably born in Westminster. He was educated at Westminster School, where the headmaster was William Camden, who became his lifelong friend. Jonson had by this time acquired a stepfather, a master bricklayer for whom he worked from the time he left Westminster until 1591 or 1592. The years from then until 1597 are obscure but it is known that they included military service in Flanders as a volunteer and marriage in 1594. In 1597 he is

Ben Jonson. A detail from the portrait after A. Blyenberch. National Portrait Gallery, London.

identified as an actor and playwright in the service of Philip Henslowe; no work of Jonson's survives from this period, however.

Jonson fairly leaps into the records, both literary and criminal, in the following year. He had acted in Nashe's *The Isle of Dogs* (the play has not survived) in 1597 and, with the author and the rest of the company, had been summarily clapped into prison by the offended authorities. In 1598 Jonson and a fellow actor, Gabriel Spencer, quarrelled seriously enough for it to lead to a duel: Jonson killed Spencer on 22 September 1598 and only escaped the hangman because he had the wit to invoke an obsolete law by which he could claim benefit of clergy. While in prison he became a Roman Catholic but the conversion held no lasting conviction and he abjured it 12 years later.

The same year holds more importance for posterity in the literary records because it saw the production of Jonson's **Every Man in his Humour** by The Lord Chamberlain's Men at the Curtain Theatre in Shoreditch. (In the cast, playing the part of Knowell, was an actor named William Shakespeare, who became his friend, whom he criticized freely, and whom he loved and admired all his life.) Jonson was to make his dramatic purpose plain in the prologue to the revised edition of this play in 1616; it was the human comedy in the framework of his times: comedy 'would shew an Image of the times, And sport with humane follies, not with crimes'. The comedy was set in Italy originally but in the revision Jonson changed the setting to London – a change for the better, since he was a Londoner and knew his city very well. The play marked the beginning of Jonson's success; he had written *The Case is Alterd*, probably in 1597, but he was to leave it out of his published works, confirming the low estimate of its quality that is generally held.

The next two comedies, **Every Man out of his Humour** (1599) and **Cynthia's Revells,** *or The Fountaine of selfe-love* (1600), mark no advance. Nor does the third, **The Poetaster,** *or The Arraignment* (1601), in which Jonson's tedious assumption of superiority over his contemporaries, scarcely veiled in the first two, is given full exposure, with Marston and Dekker as the targets. This is all part of what is generally referred to as 'the war of the theatres', which is of minimal interest to the general reader; it did not produce good plays.

Jonson turned to tragedy in the classical manner in 1603 with **Sejanus, his Fall**, played at the Globe with Burbage and Shakespeare in the cast. He returned to comedy with *Eastward Hoe*

(written about 1604), collaborating with Marston and Chapman, in which all three authors offended the Scots. The Scots king, James I, gave them a short term of imprisonment but in spite of that he appreciated Ben Jonson. He was soon in favour at court and became its chief deviser of masques, beginning with *The Masque of Blacknesse*, which had Inigo Jones as designer.

The next period was Jonson's most successful as a playwright. **Volpone,** *or the Foxe* (1606), **Epicoene,** *or The Silent Woman* (1609), **The Alchemist** (1610), and **Bartholomew Fayre** (1614) are situation comedies – situation farces, perhaps, since his characters are firmly established types labelled by carefully chosen names. The comedies are constructed with great skill, building up to finely judged climaxes. *Volpone* and *The Alchemist* are still sometimes staged by England's national theatres. To this period a second classical tragedy, **Catiline his Conspiracy** (1611), also belongs.

The comic vein was not successfully maintained. **The Devil is an Ass** (*The Divell is an Asse*; 1616) presents the successful mixture of social satire and 'humours', but it lacked something and was not a success. Jonson, his livelihood secure in a pension from King James and acknowledged as

---

The frontispiece illustration for an 18th-century edition of Ben Jonson's *Bartholomew Fayre*.

poet laureate, turned his back on the theatre for the next nine years. The masques continued, however; he had begun using the form in 1603 with *The Satyr* and had written *The Coronation Entertainment* (1604) on King James's accession. *The Penates* was also written in 1604. His first court masque, *The Masque of Blacknesse* (1605), was followed by *Hymenaei* (1606) for the marriage of the Earl of Essex to Frances Howard. He wrote *The Masque of Beauty* and *The Hue and Cry after Cupid* in 1608 and *The Masque of Queens* in 1609. In the latter Jonson introduced the antimasque, adding ugliness to throw greater emphasis on beauty. He used an Arthurian setting for *Prince Henry's Barriers* (1610) and 'faeryland' for *Oberon, The Faery Prince* (1611). *Love Freed from Ignorance and Folly* (1611) and *Love Restored* (1612) both contain a new trend for masque, a note of humorous indecency. Jonson wrote 18 more masques but given the nature of this form – in which the text is hardly more than a libretto no matter what its quality – these are almost never revived. What survives are usually the songs and poems.

King James died in 1625 and Jonson was not so secure in the graces of King Charles. He quarrelled with Inigo Jones in 1631, after the production of the masque *Chloridia*, and fell out of favour at court. But the years since the relative failure of *The Devil is an Ass* had not been entirely occupied in the writing of masques. Jonson, a big robust man, seems to have had the energy of his size and somehow had managed to act as tutor to Sir Walter Ralegh's son while still a successful playwright; he spent a year in Europe with his young charge (1612–13). Later, Jonson travelled in Scotland (1618–19), where he visited William Drummond of Hawthornden, who kept careful notes of their conversation. He was honoured by Edinburgh, where he was made a burgess of the city, and by the universities of Oxford and Cambridge. He returned to the stage with *The Staple of Newes* (1625), which was well received, and became official Chronologer of London in 1628. Another comedy, *The Newe Inne* (1629), was a failure and though he wrote three more he did not enjoy another success on the stage. His health had begun to fail – he suffered a paralytic stroke in 1628 – and after his withdrawal from court he held a court of his own.

Ben Jonson's friends always outnumbered his enemies and they came from every level of society. He was always to be found at the Friday gatherings, begun by Ralegh at the Mermaid Tavern in Bread Street and later held at the Devil Tavern, where he exchanged views with Shakespeare, Donne, Chapman, Selden, Beaumont,

and Fletcher. The ageing Jonson was attended and listened to by Herrick, Carew, Sir John Suckling, and many others. Scholars and members of the cultured nobility were always among his friends. He died in 1637 and was buried in Westminster Abbey; a collection of elegies, *Jonsonus Virbius* (1638), contained tributes from 33 of his friends. His work had passed out of fashion but he was not forgotten; one of his admirers, whose name was Jack Young – all we know of him – inscribed the words 'O rare Ben Jonson' on his gravestone.

Although Jonson's principal fame lies in his contribution to English drama, during his life he was the acknowledged leader of a new generation of poets – 'of the tribe of Ben' as one of them put it. His poems were collected in **Epigrams** and **The Forrest** (both 1616) and **Underwoods** (1640), and he never regarded them, as later generations were to, as a minor part of a dramatist's work. Certainly his influence was great; he was the theorist and practitioner of classical forms and used them for direct poetic statement. He knew the work of the Latin prose writers as well as that of the poets – Martial, Catullus, Seneca, Quintilian, Horace, and Virgil; and to knowledge of their virtues and diversity he brought a genius for his own language. In the words of Douglas Bush, 'when he has learned the lessons of their wisdom and craftsmanship, he remains their peer and contemporary, not a tame "classicist" but his very own English self.'

The best-known of Jonson's prose works is **Timber;** *or Discoveries made upon Men and Matters*, a collection of notes and essays first published in 1640. He left an unfinished pastoral, *The Sad Shepherd*, from which comes the much-anthologized short poem 'Death and Love'.

While Jonson, in the opinion of his audience, rivalled and probably outshone his friend Shakespeare some of the time, it is beyond argument that his work has not a vast amount to offer modern audiences or modern readers. *The Alchemist* and *Volpone* are familiar – the latter chiefly owing to Sir Donald Wolfit's success in the title role – and there have been occasional productions of *Bartholomew Fayre* since World War II. A reading of *Epicoene, or The Silent Woman* may well leave one with a baffled feeling since it seems to be an anecdote about a man who hated noise, hammered out to last three hours. All these plays (the most highly praised of Ben Jonson's works) contain fine things but while they impress in various ways they also oppress in a strange way. The audience is almost instructed before the curtain rises about which actions and characters in the play are going to be funny: the *dramatis personae* bristle with names like Epicure Mammon, Dame Pliant, Morose, Waspe, Overdo, Politick Would–Be, Mosca, and Doll Common; then the characters and situations are examined at great length. It is not that the plays are very long; they are not, but the concentration and exploration of the 'humour' of each and every character is peculiarly tiring. It may be that we are, in the 20th century, too far removed from the life of Jacobean England and we find it difficult to appreciate Jonson's virtuosity in holding a mirror to his contemporaries. More important, perhaps, is Jonson's lack of kindness; there is not a single character in the whole of his work that we remember with affection. One only has to think of a minor character of Shakespeare's – the endearingly dotty Dogberry or the Old Shepherd in *The Winter's Tale* – to see why Shakespeare is so well known to us and why Jonson is not. Cleverness is not enough. The most famous of Jonson's plays is *Volpone* and that is the one that contains some memorable poetry.

The complete works of Ben Jonson were edited by C. H. Herford and P. and E. M. Simpson and published in 11 volumes (1925–52). The poems have been published in collections edited by B. H. Newdigate (1936), G. B. Johnston (1954), J. Hollander (1961), and W. B. Hunter (1963).

*Jorrocks' Jaunts and Jollities* See **Surtees, R(obert) S(mith)**.

*Joseph, The Selling of* See **Sewall, Samuel**.

*Joseph Andrews* A novel by Henry Fielding, first published in 1742. The full title is *The History of the Adventures of Joseph Andrews, and of his Friend Mr Abraham Adams. Written in Imitation of the Manner of Cervantes, Author of Don Quixote.* For the origin of the novel, see **Fielding, Henry**. The hero of Fielding's novel is the brother of Pamela Andrews, the heroine of Richardson's *Pamela*.

Joseph Andrews is a footman in Lady Booby's house in London. Both Lady Booby and her attendant, Mrs Slipslop, are anxious to seduce him; Joseph refuses the attentions of both and is dismissed. He decides to go back to his home and his sweetheart, Fanny. Also on the road is Parson Adams, the curate of the church near Sir Thomas Booby's country seat, hoping to get his sermons published in London. Joseph is knocked down, stripped by robbers, and carried to an inn, where he is found by Parson Adams. (The good parson has forgotten to bring his sermons, so he is making his way home, too.) Joseph and Parson Adams travel together and their way home is peopled by a rich assortment of characters: crooked innkeepers, privileged louts, brutish 'gentlemen', and clergymen who shame the cloth they wear.

The main characters, Joseph and Fanny, Parson Adams, Lady Booby, and Mrs Slipslop come together at the Boobys' country seat. Lady Booby is still pursuing Joseph with her spite but the arrival of Squire Booby, newly married to Joseph's sister, Pamela, saves him from further persecution. The story ends with the revelation that Joseph is not Pamela's brother, after all, but the son of people of consequence. He and Fanny are married at the end.

Fielding's bow to Cervantes in the title of this novel explains the form he chose but he hit on something else in its execution which proved to be of more importance. He put the life of ordinary people in England into the book and his range and observation helped him succeed as no one had before him. The argument between Parson Adams and Parson Barnabas in Chapter XVII (Book I) gives Parson Adams the line about a virtuous heathen being more acceptable to God than a vicious Christian and says as much about Fielding as it does about his character: he was much more interested in what people were than in the labels they wore and a broad cross-section of contemporary types is subjected to a searching examination. Parson Adams is the triumph of the novel, a remarkable creation of a good and guileless man who expects others to behave like the worthy, disinterested Christian he is himself. The result, inevitably, is that he is a victim of deceit every day of his life. But he is no fool; he is spirited and courageous and will have nothing to do with any doctrine that leads to rigidity or narrowness. In that he is, of course, the true follower of his God and emerges from every undignified and ridiculous adventure with his integrity intact.

*Joseph Andrews* has been published in numerous modern editions, including The World's Classics, Everyman's Library, the Modern Library, the Penguin English Library, the Oxford English Novels series, edited by Douglas Brooks (1970), which includes the text of *Shamela*, and the Wesleyan Edition of the *Works* of Henry Fielding, edited by Martin C. Battestin (1967).

*Joseph Vance* See **Morgan, William (Frend) de**.

*Journal of a Tour to the Hebrides with Samuel Johnson, The* This narrative, by James Boswell, of a journey undertaken by James Boswell and Samuel Johnson in 1773 was first published in 1785. The original manuscript, which was seen by Johnson and prepared for publication by Boswell with the help of Edmund Malone, was edited by Frederick A. Pottle and C. H. Bennett and published in 1961. This edition restored a previously unpublished third of Boswell's original. (For the progress of the tour, see *Journey to the Western Islands of Scotland, A*.) In contrast to Johnson's account, which reflects on life and manners with the insights to be expected from a man of such penetrating intelligence, Boswell's gives a fascinating description of the great man on a long and exhausting journey under adverse conditions. The book is a series of fascinating vignettes from which Johnson, who was 64 at the time, emerges with great credit.

Boswell's *Journal of a Tour* is published in a modern edition by R. W. Chapman in the Oxford Standard Authors series (1930), in a volume that also contains Johnson's *A Journey to the Western Islands*. The same edition is published in Oxford Paperbacks (1970). The Everyman's Library edition contains Boswell's *Journal*, edited by L. F. Powell (1955).

**Journal of a Voyage to Lisbon, The**  See **Fielding, Henry**.

**Journal of the Plague Year, A**  An account of the Great Plague of 1665 from an 'eyewitness' invented by Daniel Defoe, this historical reconstruction was first published in 1722. Defoe was born in 1660 and was a small child when the explosion of bubonic plague took place in London: he was also living outside London, in Stoke Newington – some four miles from Charing Cross – and could have no first-hand knowledge of the events so vividly described by 'H.F.', a saddler of Whitechapel, close to Aldgate. Defoe was a born journalist as well as a novelist of genius and both gifts are brought to serve his historical fiction. Scott, in 1834, wrote 'Had he not been the author of *Robinson Crusoe*, De Foe would have deserved immortality for the genius which he has displayed in this work.'

Defoe, using all the sources available to him from memoirs and official records (eyewitnesses are unlikely to have been available to him, over 60 years after the event), tells us, through the mouth of his narrator, of the spread of the plague from its beginnings in 1664 to the epidemic at its height in 1665; of the authorities' attempts to take effective measures against its spread; of the growing fear of the people and the flight of those who could get away; the symptoms of the dread disease, the death carts, the burials in large pits; the closing of plague-stricken houses and the banning of all assemblies; the effects of the plague with the paralysis of trade and crafts; and the stricken city with grass growing in the streets.

Defoe's account has been plundered by generations of novelists. Defoe himself, it seems clear, had read Thomas Dekker's *The Wonderful Yeare 1603*. *A Journal of the Plague Year* can be read in a paperback edition published in the Penguin English Library, with an introduction by Anthony Burgess.

**Journal to Stella**  'Stella' was Esther Johnson, the daughter of Lady Giffard's companion at Moor Park (see **Swift, Jonathan**). Swift, in his early twenties, became her tutor while she was still a child and the darling of Sir William Temple's household. The attachment that formed between Swift and Stella, as he called her, was the lasting one of his life. When Temple died he left Stella a little property in Ireland and she, with her companion, Rebecca Dingley, moved to Dublin where Swift had the living of Laracor. During his absences in England Swift kept the ladies informed of events, of his reflections on them, and his hopes for the future in a series of letters (1710–13) that have become known as his *Journal to Stella*. The *Journal*, often couched in – to the unwary reader – mystifying baby-talk because Stella lisped as a child, gives the clearest picture of Swift the man, relaxed and affectionate. There are no letters extant from Stella to Swift; he destroyed her letters after her death in 1728.

**Journey to the Western Islands of Scotland, A**  A narrative, by Samuel Johnson, of three months in 1773 spent travelling with James Boswell first published in 1775.

After welcoming him in Edinburgh, Boswell conducted his friend to St Andrews and Aberdeen, where Johnson was given the freedom of the city. Boswell took him to visit Lord Monboddo, the eccentric law lord, and then they travelled west by way of Banff to Inverness. From Inverness they proceeded on horseback to Glenelg and from there took a boat to Skye. After a lively time there, including a visit to Flora Macdonald, they set out for Mull; but a storm drove them to the island of Coll, where they were obliged to stay for two weeks. After Mull, their journey took them to Iona and thence to Oban. At Inverary they were guests of the Duke of Argyll, who generously provided them with good horses and made their journey much easier. At Glasgow University the faculty entertained Dr Johnson, and at the family seat Boswell's father, Lord Auchinleck, clashed with his famous guest. Boswell declined to record the details of the quarrel. Johnson departed for London from Edinburgh on 21 November. His account of the journey is, apart from the entertainment of reading his reflections on a (to him) completely alien society, a record of high value. It was a remarkable undertaking for a man of 64, in abominable weather and under exhausting conditions.

There is a modern edition of Johnson's *Journey* by R. W. Chapman, which also contains Boswell's *Journal of a Tour to the Hebrides*, in Oxford Standard Authors (1930) and Oxford Paperbacks (1970).

***Joviall Crew, A,*** *or The Merry Beggars.* A comedy by Richard Brome, first produced in 1641 and first published in 1652. The beggars of the title enjoy the kindness of Oldrents, a rich country squire. Oldrents suffers from melancholy, which depresses his two daughters; the most generous of men, he has been thrown into his gloomy frame of mind by a Gypsy's prediction that his daughters would one day become beggars. His steward, Springlove, was once a vagabond, and is seized with wanderlust every spring; he spends all his time with the beggars in Oldrents' barn. The two daughters find the beggars much better company than their melancholy father; with their lovers they join the beggars for a frolic. Two more who join the beggars are Justice Clack's niece and one of her uncle's clerks with whom she has run off. The rest of the play is a spirited and deftly handled comedy on the pursuit by Oldrents and Justice Clack and the eventual apprehension of the runaways and the beggars' band. The play, which is generally agreed to be Brome's best, is notable for its warmth and its pleasant view of human nature. It was the last play to be performed in London (at the Cockpit Theatre in Drury Lane) before the Puritans closed the theatres.

**Jowett, Benjamin** 1817–93. Jowett was born at Camberwell in London and educated at St Paul's School and Balliol College, Oxford. His brilliance as a scholar was acknowledged when he became a fellow of his college while still an undergraduate. He was ordained in 1845 and became Regius Professor of Greek in 1855. As a classical scholar he had few equals in his day.

The influence of Greek studies and his interest in German philosophy made Jowett a theological liberal and his *Epistles of Paul to Thessalonians, Galatians and Romans* (1835, revised 1855 and 1859) was notable for its fresh and original approach. His contribution to ***Essays and Reviews***, 'The Interpretation of Scripture' (1860), became the reason for angry debate and thenceforth his orthodoxy was under grave suspicion; he wrote no more on theological subjects. In the field of classical studies his translation of Plato (1871) became a classic; his Thucydides

followed in 1881 and the *Politics* of Aristotle in 1885. Jowett became Master of Balliol in 1870 and was active in the affairs of the college; he instituted many reforms in the interests of poorer students.

**Joyce, James (Augustine Aloysius)** 1882–1941. Joyce was born in Dublin. His father was a collector of rates, who moved his family to Bray when Joyce was five years old. In the following year (1886) Joyce was sent to Clongowes Wood College, a Jesuit school in Kildare. After his father's retirement in 1891 Joyce, a promising pupil, was admitted to the Jesuit Belvedere College in Dublin, and there he was bright enough to win several annual exhibitions. The money that went with the exhibitions was badly needed at home, where Joyce senior's pension did not go very far. While at Belvedere College Joyce began to write verse and prose and extended his reading considerably; he entered University College, Dublin, in 1898 and graduated in 1902.

While at University College Joyce wrote an essay, 'Ibsen's New Drama', which was published by *The Fortnightly Review* (April 1900). He visited London in the following month, hoping to find the offer of an appointment to a journal or review to follow university. He was studying modern languages while at University College but he found nothing promising in London beyond the interest shown by William Archer. In Ireland, after graduation, he cultivated the acquaintance of Yeats, Synge, Lady Gregory, George Russell, and others who were fostering the Irish cultural renaissance but, meanwhile, to study medicine, he went to live in Paris where he hoped to find work teaching English to support himself. He had quite a struggle; he could find no teaching in Dublin and it was not exactly plentiful in Paris. He was completely out of sympathy with the Irish cultural revival; but he and the moving spirits of that revival were out of sympathy with each other in any case. His precarious existence – he contributed some reviews to Dublin newspapers – embittered him; he had to borrow the fare back to Dublin in 1903 when he heard his mother was dying.

In Dublin in 1904 Joyce met a girl from Galway named Nora Barnacle. He began work on two books, one of short stories and one with an autobiographical background, and completed some poems. Some of the short stories were accepted by the periodical *Irish Homestead*, for a fee of £1 per story. He earned small sums for occasional book reviews and taught for a brief period. Then he borrowed what he could from

James Joyce, aged 22. Photographed by his friend, Constantine P. Curram, 1904.

his friends and left for the continent, hoping for an appointment as an English teacher in Zürich. He took Nora with him; their relationship endured even if Nora was never quite certain what Joyce's books were about. They eventually got around to marriage in 1931, to protect their children's rights. Joyce did not succeed in getting the post in Zürich, but he and Nora settled in Trieste, where he was employed by the Berlitz School of Languages in 1905.

*Chamber Music* (1907), a collection of short poems, was published in London and earned respectable reviews but it made no money for the author. Joyce, who was drinking heavily, suffered from a bad attack of rheumatic fever that was to provoke the eye trouble from which he suffered for the rest of his life. Nevertheless, he completed the book of short stories and added more chapters to the autobiographical novel. Two visits to Dublin, in 1909 and 1912, were the last that Joyce and Nora saw of Ireland.

After a dispute with the Irish publishers over some references to the British royal family, Joyce withdrew the book of short stories from them. Called *Dubliners*, it was published in London in 1914 and was well reviewed, but sales were few and it made no money. However it was read by Ezra Pound, who asked for some of the autobiographical novel that had been originally named *Stephen Hero*. Pound was so impressed that he arranged the publication of the novel in a magazine, *The Egoist*, edited by T. S. Eliot and Harriet Weaver, and *A Portrait of the Artist as a Young Man* appeared in 25 instalments (February 1914–September 1915). It was first published in volume form in 1916.

Joyce was obliged to leave Trieste during World War I and he moved to Zürich. He was fortunate in the active interest taken by friends in England, who secured him grants from the Royal Literary Fund and a Civil List grant in 1916 while he was working on his next book, *Ulysses*. The New York *The Little Review* accepted the new novel for serial publication, which began in April 1918 and continued until December 1920, when publication was stopped with the novel in the middle of the fourteenth episode: the editors of *The Little Review* were prosecuted for publishing obscene matter. American patrons gave donations to assist the author but he could not rely on them as an income and it was just as well, perhaps, that he was suddenly enjoying notoriety; his books began to sell. *Exiles* (1918), a play in three acts, was produced at the Münchener Theater, Munich, in 1919.

Joyce and Nora and their family moved to Paris in 1920 and it was their home between the two World Wars. Joyce was becoming famous: *The Egoist* had published some parts of *Ulysses* in 1919 before going out of circulation, and the complete novel was published in 1922. Harriet Weaver arranged for the book's importation and sale in England; the copies were seized by the Customs and those which reached New York were burned by the United States postal authorities. The book was banned in America until 1933, when a court ruling decided that although it was disgusting in many places it was not pornographic. But since 1918 it had been whispered that *Ulysses* was pornographic, and in England and the USA nothing sold a book faster, over or under the counter, than the hope on the part of the readers that it was indecent. By the time of the first complete and unexpurgated edition in England (1936) Joyce was a famous man indeed.

In 1923 Joyce began the composition of *Finnegans Wake*, which was published as *Work in Progress* in 12 instalments between 1928 and 1937. A new collection of poems was published as *Pomes Penyeach* in 1927. Joyce's eye condition worsened during these years and caused him great pain. Operations were essential and he emerged from them with seriously reduced vision. A domestic tragedy was the deteriorating mental state of his daughter, Lucia; it was diagnosed as schizophrenia in 1932. *Finnegans Wake* was published in 1939, and with the outbreak of World War II the Joyce family returned to Switzerland. James Joyce died on 13 January 1941 after an operation on a duodenal ulcer.

J. I. M. Stewart, referring to Joyce's extraordinary verbal virtuosity in *Eight Modern Writers* (The Oxford History of English Literature Vol XII, 1963) writes: 'Whether Joyce is in fact to be convicted of progressive artistic irresponsibility is a very hard question. But even if he is he remains, at least as a writer's writer, a very important figure indeed.' The question lies there: how important to literature is 'a writer's writer'? He is rarely one who rewards the reader. But Walter Allen, discussing *Ulysses* in *The English Novel* (1954) wrote: 'Joyce is a very great comic writer, a comic writer of the quality of Rabelais and Sterne. In my view this is the most useful point of departure from which to approach him.' Saving that nothing divides like a sense of humour, Allen's judgment is a fair one and the novel is full of rewards if the reader can stay the course from the first page to the last; it is an artistic whole and all of it must be read. The same critic deplores the fact that *Ulysses* and, to a greater extent, *Finnegans Wake*, has become an academic industry, and that references to 'the layman' seem necessary in a discussion of Joyce's work: Walter Allen proclaims himself a layman when he talks about *Ulysses*.

The layman is going to feel discouraged when he finds there is *A Skeleton Key to Finnegans Wake* (by J. Campbell and H. M. Robinson, 1944) available, which purports to help him read that very long and very difficult book. He is likely to leave it to J. I. M. Stewart's 'writers', and the thousands of English literature students who have found it a mine of thesis material. Laymen can avoid the millions of words written about Joyce to good purpose, and start at the beginning with *Dubliners*, a very rewarding book of short stories set in the Irish capital. *A Portrait of the Artist as a Young Man* is a striking novel about the progress of the artist, here called Stephen Dedalus, from childhood to university, to his eventual wrenching free from a stifling Catholic upbringing, to his hopes of an artistic career. Stephen Dedalus returns in *Ulysses* but the reader will find him in a totally different world. He and Leopold Bloom take the reader with them through this fascinating day in Dublin, described with enormous vitality, bawdy humour – and pathos. Dedalus and Bloom are essentially unhappy people. The difficulties of the novel soon become apparent and 'the layman' may well wonder why anyone should write like that. But by the end he will probably stop asking the question; there is no book like it in English nor one that has the same effect.

*Finnegans Wake* is Dublin night, after the Dublin day of *Ulysses*. The dreams and nightmares of H. C. Earwicker, the central character, present a shifting kaleidoscope of connections with his waking existence. There is a parade of vast erudition at the service of Joyce in his last experiment with language and an immense volume of allusions.

*Jude the Obscure* A novel by Thomas Hardy, first published in its complete form in November 1895. The first abridged form, called *Hearts Insurgent*, appeared in *Harper's New Monthly Magazine* (December 1894 to November 1895).

Jude Fawley is an orphan boy with a passion for learning. He even teaches himself some Latin and Greek, while earning his bread as a stonemason. His relations with Arabella Donn are a sensual pleasure, which he believes is how she regards them also – but she succeeds in trapping him into marriage. Jude is wretched in the marriage and drinks too much, and Arabella deserts him, leaving him with their son. Jude makes his way to Christminster (Oxford), returning to his love of learning. The atmosphere of Christminster, where he works as a stonemason, promises much but offers nothing in the end – the scholars have no interest in him whatever.

Jude meets his cousin Sue Bridehead, who works in a dreary religious shop and takes refuge from it in reading about Julian the Apostate in Gibbon's *Decline and Fall*. She is in fact well read and her intelligence attracts him. Jude falls in love with her, not understanding that she is neurotic. He keeps quiet when Sue marries Phillotson, an older schoolmaster. But Sue finds her husband physically repellent, eventually hiding in a cupboard from him. He is understandably puzzled when she quotes John Stuart Mill, and does not oppose her divorce when she leaves him for Jude. Jude himself – in spite of Arabella's return and her easy seduction of him on one occasion – manages to get a divorce also.

Jude and Sue (and Jude's unbalanced son) settle down together but Sue will not marry him, feeling an atavistic guilt. They have two children and Sue retreats into a morbid Christianity, while Jude moves in the opposite direction. Socially outcast, since they are unmarried, both go downhill: then Jude's son kills the two younger children and hangs himself, 'Done because we are too menny'. Sue returns to Phillotson and the embraces that revolt her. Jude dies of drink and debility.

*Jude the Obscure* seems to divide Hardy's readers; some regard it as a great tragic novel while others find it too contrived to be a success, with inconsistencies of character (e.g. Phillotson at the end, after his forbearance with Sue is emphasized in their early scenes) used to underline a point. But there can be no doubt that the essential Hardy was breaking through here – as the precursor of Lawrence – and one can only regret that his patience ran out. Jude and Sue Bridehead are victims of their times and circumstances just as much as they are of their birthright. Sue is baffled by her own sexuality, and her upbringing – in spite of her timid approaches to self-realization – sentences her, ultimately, to a wretched life. Jude is frustrated all his life, except in sensual terms: he wants more, much more, and everything in contemporary life conspires against him. Earnest and aspiring, his love for Sue suppressed when she marries Phillotson, Jude has no way of dealing with either her demands or her ambiguity when she descends on him again.

**Judith** An epic poem in Old English, written during the second decade of the 10th century. It is believed to have been a tribute to the valiant Lady Aethelflaed of Mercia, daughter of King Alfred, who took the field against the Danes with her brother Edward. A fragment of 350 lines – cantos 10, 11, and 12 – survives and is in the British Library. The fragment covers the murder of Holofernes, Judith's flight from the scene, the attack on the Assyrians, and their defeat. These surviving cantos are regarded as some of the finest poetry of the period.

A translation of the *Judith* fragment is included in G. Bone's *Anglo-Saxon Poetry* (1943).

**Julia** In Shakespeare's *The Two Gentlemen of Verona* she is Proteus's love. He forgets her when he meets Silvia but Julia disguises herself as a boy and follows him, becoming his page 'Sebastian', and an unhappy witness of his attempt on Silvia in Act V.

*Julia de Roubigné* See **Mackenzie, Henry.**

*Juliana* A short poem in Old English by Cynewulf, preserved in *The Exeter Book*. The subject is the martyrdom of Juliana, a Christian virgin, in the reign of Maximian (the persecution occurred in AD 303). The poem is based on a Latin original.

*Julian and Maddalo, A Conversation.* A poem by Percy Bysshe Shelley written during his visit to Venice in 1818 but not published until 1824, in *Posthumous Poems*. The 'conversation' is between Shelley (Julian) and Byron (Maddalo). Shelley had found Byron in a mood of bitter cynicism and the poem represents to some degree his reaction against this, though his own private life was then going through a difficult stage. *Julian and Maddalo* marked a distinct advance in Shelley's art; specialists in his work believe that this was because he was now dealing with real people and issues and not with distant ideals. The two poets discuss their views, and the poem contains the narrative of a mysterious Maniac whom they visit, whose mind has been unbalanced by a hysterically destructive woman. The Maniac, according to G. Wilson Knight's studies of the poet, represents the darker side of Byron's character, and the events which led to his self-imposed exile.

**Juliana (*or* Julian) of Norwich** *c.*1342–*c.*1413. Almost nothing is known of the life of this English mystic beyond the fact that she lived as an anchoress outside the walls of St Julian's Church in Norwich. According to her own account she received a series of visions, lasting five hours, on 8 May 1373. There were 15 revelations; another was received on the following day. Her meditations on these experiences were written 20 years later: *The Sixteen Revelations of Divine Love.* Juliana's reflections led her to the conclusion that Divine Love opens the way to solving all the problems of human existence. The *Revelations* can be read in several modern English versions.

*Julius Caesar, The Life and Death of* A tragedy by William Shakespeare. It was first produced *c.*1599 and published in the First Folio of 1623. The story comes from Sir Thomas North's English version (1579) of Plutarch's *Lives*, concentrating on the historical events of the year 44 BC.

Caesar is triumphant but distrust of his ambitions and jealousy of his achievements by those in high places runs against his popularity with the citizens. Both sentiments are voiced in the opening scene in which two tribunes, Flavius and Marullus, try to belittle Caesar's achievements to a crowd of citizens who are gathering to applaud the great man's appearance at the Lupercal festival. At the Lupercal the disaffection of Cassius and Brutus (both of whom were pardoned by Caesar after the defeat at Pharsalia) becomes clear. They learn from Casca that Caesar was offered a crown three times, and three times refused it.

The disaffection becomes a conspiracy and Brutus, uncertain of his motives and unhappily aware of Caesar's affection for him, joins it, persuaded that it is his duty to the republic. The conspirators murder Caesar – who has ignored all warnings – in the Capitol; Brutus strikes the final blow. Mark Antony comes late upon the scene and the conspirators immediately try to win him to their side. He lets them believe he is compliant but, left alone with the body of the murdered man, swears vengeance for his death.

Brutus addresses the citizens, attempting to justify the murder. Mark Antony brings Caesar's body to the Forum and follows Brutus in his address – which skilfully cuts the ground from under the conspirators' feet and turns the people against them. The lines are drawn: Brutus and Cassius flee the city and gather their forces, while Antony, Lepidus, and Julius Caesar's great-nephew, Octavius, form a triumvirate, organize a brutal proscription, and prepare for the war.

In the camp at Sardis the news of the triumvirate is brought and Brutus learns that his wife, Portia, is dead. But soon after he and Cassius have a violent quarrel over the latter's 'itching palm'. They are reconciled but the day of reckoning is near. Brutus plans to confront Antony's army at Philippi, against the advice of Cassius, a better soldier. The ghost of the murdered Caesar appears to Brutus and tells him 'thou shalt see me at Philippi'. Antony and Octavius win the battle and Brutus and Cassius kill themselves when defeat is certain.

*Julius Caesar* is devalued as a play for many people through having it thrust at them during their schooldays, which is a pity, because it is excellent theatre, compact and fast-moving. The parts that matter are all for men – Portia and Calpurnia are incidental – with the Roman mob, aroused by the brilliant oration Shakespeare wrote for Antony, playing a major part in Act 3, Scene 2. The three principals, Brutus, Cassius, and Antony, are subjected to searching examination; Shakespeare demonstrates vividly how much the course of history is determined by the character of those who take part in the events.

**Jungle Books, The**  See **Kipling, Rudyard.**

**Junius**  In *The Public Advertiser*, from 1769 to 1771, a series of letters appeared under the pseudonym 'Junius', which attacked public figures unsparingly. Scorn and personal invective

were directed at persons but the letters are shrewd and well judged when the author turns to political argument. The Duke of Grafton, Lord North, Lord Mansfield, and King George III were all targets of Junius; he entered the lists on behalf of John Wilkes and later attacked the Earl of Chatham and Barrington, the War Secretary. The identity of Junius has never been discovered, though Sir Philip Francis has for long been a favourite candidate. An edition of the *Letters* was published by Henry Sampson Woodfall, of *The Public Advertiser*, in 1772; the latest edition, by C. W. Everett, was published in 1927.

**Junius, Francis** (*or* **François Dujon**) 1589–1677.  Junius was born in Heidelberg and became librarian to Thomas Howard, 2nd Earl of Arundel. He was also tutor to Howard's son and became a friend of John Milton. A philologist and antiquary, he collected Anglo-Saxon manuscripts, which he later presented to the Bodleian Library in Oxford. He published *De Pictura Veterum* (1637) and an edition of Caedmon (1655) and wrote an *Etymologicum Anglicanum* (first printed in 1743), which was much used by Samuel Johnson while preparing his dictionary. Junius also gave his philological collections to the Bodleian and helped the Oxford University Press with the printing of Gothic, Anglo-Saxon, and Runic material.

The *Junius Manuscript XI* contains scriptural poems in Old English that Junius believed to be the work of Caedmon and published as such (Amsterdam, 1655). The manuscripts date from the 11th century but scholars reject the assumption that the poems are by Caedmon. See **Genesis**; **Exodus**; and **Daniel**.

**Junius Brutus**  In Shakespeare's *Coriolanus*, one of the tribunes opposed to the arrogant hero. With his fellow tribune, Sicinius Velutus, he rouses the plebeians against Coriolanus and secures his banishment, thus provoking the rage in him that makes him a traitor to Rome.

**Juno and the Paycock**  A tragedy in three acts by Sean O'Casey, first produced at the Abbey Theatre, Dublin, on 3 March 1924, and first published in 1925. The action of the play covers two months of 1922, and takes place in a Dublin tenement occupied by Jack Boyle and his wife, Juno, their daughter Mary, aged 22, and their son Johnny, two years younger. The civil war in Ireland followed the treaty which gave independence to Ireland – with the exception of the six Ulster counties which had succeeded in adhering to the UK. The diehard Republicans repudiated the treaty, maintaining that a united independent

Ireland had been the point of the rebellion. They were at war with the government of the Irish Free State which had accepted the treaty.

Mary Boyle, who reads Ibsen and belongs to a trade union, is reading a paper which reports the killing in an ambush of a neighbour's son, the Republican Robbie Tancred. Juno comes home and Mary reads some of the report aloud. Johnny, jumpy and neurotic, objects to the grim details and leaves the room. He is lame from a hip wound sustained during the Easter Rising when he was only 14; he has also lost an arm from a bomb explosion in the civil war. Jerry Devine, a Labour leader who has persuaded Mary to go on strike, enters with news of a job for Jack Boyle, Juno's useless husband who is nicknamed 'the Captain' because he once went to sea briefly. Jack Boyle spends all the time he can in pubs with his crony Joxer Daly, 'struttin' about like a pay-cock'. He is a man beyond redemption – work-shy, mendacious, cowardly, and vain. Juno is at her wit's end to know how to keep the house going but struggling is a part of her existence. Jack Boyle will dodge this offer of a job, that's for sure. Jerry, meanwhile, makes it plain that he wants Mary; it is also plain that Mary does not want him. She is more interested in Charles Bentham, a goodlooking teacher, who brings the great news that Jack Boyle has inherited a large sum of money from a relative. The will has been filed for probate, but on the strength of it Jack borrows from everyone, including their neigh-bour, Mrs Madigan.

---

O'Casey's *Juno and the Paycock* at the Royalty Theatre, London, in 1925 when the Abbey Theatre's production was first seen outside Ireland. Arthur Sinclair, seated, as Boyle; Sidney Morgan as Joxer.

At an evening during which Boyle's new pros-perity is vulgarly evident Charles Bentham, Joxer, and Mrs Madigan are guests. Mary echoes Charles's disapproval of the new gramophone, and it is plain that they have grown very close. Their conversation about ghosts relates to mur-der and Johnny reacts to it in nervous agitation and retires to his room, where he screams in terror at a vision of Robbie Tancred on his knees, bleed-ing from his wounds. He is consoled by his mother but the party is interrupted once more when Robbie Tancred's mother, who lives in the same tenement, passes on the stairs to go to receive her son's body. Juno, Mary, and Mrs Madigan offer what consolation they can; Mrs Tancred reflects sorrowfully on the like tragedy of her neighbour, Mrs Mannin – her son was a Free State soldier, killed in an ambush led by Robbie Tancred: 'An' now here's the two of us oul' women, standin' one on each side of the scales o' sorra, balanced by the bodies of our two dead sons.' And as the Boyles and a group of neighbours accompany Mrs Tancred to meet the cortège Johnny is left alone. A caller from the Republican Army startles him: he is to report to the Battalion Staff on the next evening, to answer questions about the ambush of Robbie Tancred.

Two months later Charles Bentham has left Mary, without a word, and gone to England. A tailor owed money by Jack Boyle has discovered that the will is wrongly drawn and Boyle has no expectations; the tailor comes to take away the clothes he made. Mrs Madigan seizes the gramophone, since Boyle cannot pay her what he owes. Mary is discovered to be pregnant; it is plain that Bentham knew about the will and deserted her. Johnny attacks his contemptible father, who hurries off to Joxer and the pub to escape him; then he attacks his mother for allow-ing Boyle to have his way since the day she married him. Jerry Devine, knowing that Bent-ham has gone, is hopeful that Mary will turn to him but turns away when he learns that she is pregnant. Johnny reproaches her; she could have deceived him and been safely married. Johnny is alone in the flat when two Republican Army men come for him; it was he who betrayed Robbie Tancred, and he is taken away, babbling his prayers.

Mrs Madigan brings the news to Juno, who turns her back on Boyle at last; she sends Mary to wait for her at her sister's, then they will look after each other and prepare for Mary's baby. She recalls Mrs Tancred; what does it matter whether Robbie and Johnny were diehards or Free Staters? In the end they are their mothers' poor sons, and gone for ever.

# K

**Katharina** The shrew of Shakespeare's *The Taming of the Shrew*. She is the elder of two sisters and her father would see her married first, before the younger and prettier Bianca (who is his favourite). Katharina's disagreeable character is explained by her feeling of neglect. ('They call me Katharine, that do talk of me'), and Petruchio's sycophantic flattery invokes a response, though her suspicions are hard to remove.

**Katharine** In Shakespeare's *Love's Labour's Lost*, one of the ladies in the Princess of France's suite. Dumain falls in love with her and when she leaves Navarre for a year of mourning for the death of the King of France, she tells him that she will return and 'Then, if I have much love I'll give you some.'

**Kavanagh, Patrick** 1905–67. Kavanagh, the son of a cobbler of Inniskeen in Monaghan, was self-educated. He worked at his father's trade and as a farm labourer until he was 34, when he went to Dublin to make a living as a freelance journalist. He was by that time a published poet, with his *Ploughman and Other Poems* (1936), and had also produced his autobiography, *The Green Fool* (1938). In Dublin Kavanagh supported himself by hack work and continued to publish his poetry: *The Great Hunger* (1942, revised 1966), *A Soul for Sale* (1947), and *Come Dance with Kitty Stobling and Other Poems* (1960); he also wrote an autobiographical novel, *Tarry Flynn* (1948). His circumstances changed for the better in 1955, when he was appointed to the staff of the board of Extra-Mural Studies at University College, Dublin. Further publications were *Collected Poems* (1964), *Collected Prose* (1967), and *Self Portrait*, a prose work (1964). With his brother, Peter Kavanagh, he founded *Kavanagh's Weekly*, a journal of literature and politics, in Dublin in 1952. It lasted for only 13 issues.

Kavanagh enjoyed a considerable reputation as an entertaining lyric poet with an excellent feeling for rhythm. He cultivated an image of himself as an eloquent and irascible character – a popular figure whom everyone wanted to meet.

**Keary, Annie** 1825–79. A writer of books for children, who is remembered for her retelling, with her sister Eliza, of Nordic myth, *The Heroes of Asgard* (1857). The stories emerge in a rather glamorous form, a long way from their cold and doomladen originals. But they did serve to introduce that rich source of story to English children. Annie Keary was also the author of adult novels, successful in their day, among them *Castle Daly* (1875) and *A Doubting Heart* (1879).

**Keats, John** 1795–1821. The son of a livery-stable keeper at Finsbury Pavement near the city of London, John Keats was born on 31 December 1795. His parents' means were not equal to their ambition to send him to Harrow and he was educated at Enfield Academy. While at school, where he learned some Latin, French, and history, the boy Keats suffered some emotional disturbance from the death of his father and his mother's second marriage, but he was fortunate in the kindness and friendship of the headmaster's son. Charles Cowden Clarke was eight years older than Keats, and he became a teacher himself; he introduced Keats to poetry and encouraged his interest.

Keats left school before he was 15. He was apprenticed to an apothecary in Edmonton in 1810, and served the five years necessary to qualify for the study of surgery at Guy's Hospital, where he went in 1815. Meanwhile he had begun to write poetry; 'Imitation of Spenser' belongs to 1813 and was probably his first completed work. He also continued his reading under the guidance of his friend Clarke. The Clarke family were admirers of Leigh Hunt's radical weekly, *The Examiner*, and when the Hunt brothers were imprisoned for libel Charles took the family's gifts of food and flowers to the jail. Keats, too, read *The Examiner* and continued to do so until his death. Clarke introduced Keats to Leigh Hunt.

By the time he was 21 Keats was determined to give up medicine but he was obliged to wait a little to ensure that his hopes of a small inheritance were not endangered. Hunt had published the sonnet 'O Solitude' in *The Examiner* on 5 May 1816, and was actively encouraging Keats in a career as a poet. At Hunt's house in Hampstead the young Keats met the painter, Benjamin Robert Haydon, William Hazlitt, and Shelley, who was three years his senior. Shelley admired Keats very much but his personality rather overpowered the younger man and they never became real friends. Leigh Hunt's influence was at once benign and dubious; he was helpful and believed in the young poet, but his standards were for Keats to aspire beyond rather than emulate.

Keats's first collection, *Poems* (1817), contained 17 sonnets, a form he used with great success; 'On First Looking into Chapman's Homer' was one of these. Another poem in this first collection was the remarkable 'Sleep and Poetry', which expresses his aspirations as a poet in search of the true image of beauty as the purpose of his art. The collection enjoyed no success in spite of excellences entirely due to Keats himself; the verse which shows the influence of Hunt was the lesser part.

The poet's search for beauty formed the subject of a work which occupied Keats for the best part of the next year. His friendship with John Hamilton Reynolds, an aspiring writer who admired him and helped counteract the influence of Hunt, was beneficial although the friendship did not last on account of Reynolds' jealousy. Reynolds had reviewed *Poems* (1817) in *The Champion*, and he hoped to interest Keats in an English version of Boccaccio, a project which was to have interesting consequences. **Endymion**, with its familiar opening lines, was published in 1818, after Reynolds had persuaded Keats to rewrite the preface. In this Keats asks pardon if he is seen to fail in his endeavour; what he felt when *Blackwood's Magazine* published a savage attack on him and his work can only be imagined. The author was John Gibson Lockhart, to whom it was not attributed at the time; the review was signed 'Z'. The magazine was anti-radical and Lockhart made the most of Keats's connection with Leigh Hunt; but his personal attack on Keats, repeated in subsequent issues, was unpardonable. John Croker Wilson, in *The Quarterly Review* (September 1818), also used the Hunt connection as an excuse to dismiss Keats as a 'copyist of Mr Hunt'. Keats was by then struggling against the consumption that cursed his family; his younger brother Tom was dying. (The brothers John, George, and Tom Keats were very close.) In November 1818 Keats met Fanny Brawne at the house of a friend; on December 1 Tom Keats died, just 19 years old.

John Keats could not marry Fanny Brawne. He had nothing to offer her apart from his love, and her family did not consider that enough. He made a resolution, in 1819, to come back to her when he had achieved some eminence as a poet. The project of an English version of Boccaccio provided him with a subject that suited his increasing power as a poet but the result, **Isabella; or, The Pot of Basil**, was one of his less admired poems. The poem was subtitled 'A Story from Boccaccio', and was completed in April 1818. By the end of that year his poetic genius was in full flow. He was at work on **Hyperion**; he commenced **The Eve of St Agnes** early in 1819. **La Belle Dame sans Merci**, 'The Eve of St Mark' (not completed), the great odes 'On a Grecian Urn', 'To a Nightingale', 'To Autumn', the dramatic poems *Otho the Great* and *King Stephen*, and **Lamia** all belong to 1819. By the end of the year he was dangerously ill.

A volume called *Lamia, Isabella, The Eve of St Agnes and Other Poems* was published in July 1820. Among the 'other poems' were the immortal odes and *Hyperion*. Keats's friend, Charles Armitage Brown, who looked after him when the poet was ill, did not realize the gravity of his condition and left for a holiday in Scotland in May. Although his condition was deteriorating, Keats went to stay with Leigh Hunt, and received a letter from Shelley inviting him to come and live in Italy. Keats's uncertainty about the other poet as a friend was reinforced by some criticism in the same letter of *Endymion* which, otherwise, Shelley praised. Then, after a letter from Fanny Brawne was mislaid in the perpetually disorganized Hunt household, Keats, in spite of Hunt's entreaties, walked to Hampstead to see her. He collapsed on the Brawne's doorstep on a July evening; Fanny and her mother took him in and nursed him for the month he remained in England. Keats knew he should go to a warmer climate and Italy – if not Shelley – was in his mind. The 1820 volume was receiving favourable attention and his publisher John Taylor (of Taylor & Hessey) speedily arranged for Keats to go to Rome for at least a year. Charles Armitage Brown was written to but returned from Scotland too late to accompany his friend. Fortunately there were always friends devoted to Keats's

John Keats. The charcoal drawing by the poet's friend Joseph Severn, who was with Keats during his last hours. Victoria & Albert Museum, London.

interests; William Haslam asked the painter Joseph Severn to go to Rome and Severn attended Keats with devotion to the harrowing end.

His death came in Rome on 23 February 1821. Keats knew the end was coming, and Severn held him in his arms as his life ebbed away; at least he died peacefully, having suffered appallingly since early December. He was buried in the Protestant cemetery in Rome, where Shelley's heart was also to be buried. Severn stayed on, trying to regain control of his shattered spirits by regular visits to Keats's grave whilst Taylor organized a subscription and paid off Keats's debts. Shelley wrote his famous elegy, *Adonais*, and implied that vicious reviews had helped to kill John Keats. Byron, on the contrary, believed that John Keats, the matchless poet, possessed too powerful a mind for that to be true. John Gibson Lockhart and John Wilson Croker had not made Keats's life any easier but a reading of the poetry written after their reviews shows that Byron was right. Fanny Brawne mourned him for several years. In a letter to Keats's sister Fanny in September 1820, she wrote: 'I am certain he has some spell that attaches them' (Keats's friends) 'to him, or else he has fortunately met with a set of friends that I did not believe could be found in the world.'

Keats's biographer Robert Gittings says of his poetry: 'What makes him different from any other poet is his extraordinary sensitivity to the impression of the moment, and his use of the day-to-day circumstances of life for poetry. He could and did transmute almost any experience into poetry, in an instantaneous and instinctive process.' He also comments on the poet's letters: 'His letters, undervalued or even regretted by the Victorians, now seem the counterpart of his poems. They are handbooks of poetical thought and practice; they show him as a man of ideas, a professional in technique, and a human creature whose tragic view of life was accompanied by stoutness of heart and a resilient sense of humour.'

The definitive edition of the poems is *The Poetical Works of John Keats*, edited by H. W. Garrod (Oxford English Texts, 1939, revised 1958). The same text is used in *The Poems of John Keats*, also edited by H. W. Garrod (Oxford Standard Authors, revised edition, 1956). *Complete Poetry and Selected Prose* is edited by H. E. Briggs (The Modern Library, New York, 1951). The Hampstead Edition of Keats, edited by H. B. and M. Buxton Forman, is the most complete (eight volumes, 1938). M. Buxton Forman's standard edition of Keats's letters has been superseded by *The Letters of John Keats 1814–1821*, edited by H. E. Rollins (1958). Among highly regarded biographers are W. J. Bate (1963), Aileen Ward (1963), and most recently, Robert Gittings (1968). *The Letters of Fanny Brawne to John Keats* (1937) was edited by F. Edgecumbe. Among numerous single-volume editions of the poems are those in Everyman's Library and Penguin English Poets.

**Keble, John** 1792–1866. Keble was born at Fairford in Gloucestershire, the son of a High Church minister, and was educated at Corpus Christi College, Oxford. A brilliant scholar, he became a fellow of Oriel College at the age of 19. While assisting his father at Fairford he published *The Christian Year* (1827) and became Professor of Poetry at Oxford in 1831. A leading figure in the **Oxford Movement**, he contributed nine of the *Tracts for the Times*, which affirmed the Movement's principles (hence Tractarianism, the Movement's early name). Keble published an edition of the *Works of Richard Hooker* (1836) and contributed a translation of St Irenaeus to the *Library of the Fathers* (posthumously published, 1872). His later sacred poetry included an English *Psalter* (1839) and *Lyra Innocentium* (1846). Keble became a parish priest at Hursley, near Winchester, in 1836 and never sought preferment. Keble College, Oxford, was founded in his memory in 1870. *The Christian Year*, which was immensely popular in the days when the English went to church, is a collection of poems for the Sundays and holy days of the year.

**Kelly, Hugh** 1739–77. Kelly was born in Killarney and his father kept a tavern in Dublin which became a favourite house for actors. Kelly was another one of the 18th-century playwrights who owed much to David Garrick. He came to London in 1760 and was for a time a dramatic critic; in this role he was cordially disliked by Bickerstaffe and Goldsmith. Kelly had extolled the great Garrick, and Garrick encouraged him to write plays; in fact he launched him on a successful career. George Colman was presenting Oliver Goldsmith's *The Good-Natur'd Man* at Covent Garden and Garrick, his rival and erstwhile friend, stole a march on him with a new play six days before, at Drury Lane on 23 January 1768. This was Kelly's *False Delicacy*, a sentimental comedy which enjoyed far more success than Goldsmith's play and was presented in translation in France and Germany; the published version sold 3000 copies in a single day. Of Kelly's five plays, only *The School for Wives* (Drury Lane, December 1773) is regarded as significant by students of the theatre, inasmuch as it showed a move away from sentimental comedy and an approach to the comedy of manners. Kelly's work is largely forgotten and has not been revived in the modern theatre.

**Kemble, John Mitchell** 1807–57. The son of Charles Kemble, the distinguished actor, John Mitchell Kemble was born in London and educated at Trinity College, Cambridge. His interest in philology was developed by further study at Göttingen with Jakob Grimm, who became his friend. He published *The Anglo-Saxon Poems of Beowulf* (1833–37) and a scholarly work on the early history of England, *Codex Diplomaticus Aevi Saxonici* (1839–48). His *The Saxons in England* (1849) advanced the theory that England's stability in a Europe racked by disturbance was due to the principles and institutions inherited from her Teutonic invaders. Kemble also published a collection of *State Papers, 1688–1714* (1857).

**Kemp, William** fl. 1600. Will Kemp was a member of the group of actors, the Lord Chamberlain's Men, which William Shakespeare and Richard Burbage joined in 1594. He was a short fat man with a considerable reputation as a clown and as a dancer of the jig with which some performances ended. He created the parts of Dogberry and Bottom but apparently fitted badly into the firm structure of Shakespeare's plays, being unwilling to discipline his comic gifts for ensemble playing. He also created the part of Falstaff in *Henry IV* and his departure from the company in 1600 may have been the reason why Falstaff did not appear in *Henry V*: it is believed that in an earlier draft of the play the fat knight went with the army to France. Kemp maintained his place as a public favourite by dancing from London to Norwich, a feat which proved a great success. He wrote his own account in *Kemps Nine Daies Wonder, Performed in a Daunce from London to Norwich* (1600).

**Kempe, Margery** c.1373–after 1433. Margery, daughter of John Brunham, mayor of King's Lynn in Norfolk, married John Kempe, a burgess of the same town, about 1393, and bore him 14 children. During her adult life she suffered a short period of insanity, after which she experienced several visions.

With her husband she went on a pilgrimage to Canterbury, and then the Kempes seem to have decided on a totally devout life, one that led Margery to exhibitions of tearful piety and a denunciation of all pleasure – which course she did not hesitate to recommend for everyone else. She was, naturally, heartily disliked. The Kempes took vows of chastity before the Bishop of Lincoln in 1413. In the same year Margery delivered a public rebuke to Arundel, Archbishop of Canterbury, who was an active persecutor of the Lollards, and then set off on a pilgrimage to the Holy Land. She visited the shrine at Compostela in 1417, and also made journeys to Norway and Danzig in 1433. Nothing is known of her life after that date.

Margery Kempe was illiterate and *The Book of Margery Kempe* was dictated. It describes her travels and mystical experiences; she enjoyed close communion with Christ and felt a growing compassion for the sins of the world. Her narrative is related in a homely direct style, giving a vivid impression of the speech of the time.

Selections from *The Book*, not very well chosen, were printed by Wynkyn de Worde (c. 1501), but the existence of a complete manuscript, in the possession of the Butler-Bowdon family, was not known until the 1930s. It was first published in a modernized version in 1936; the original text was published by the Early English Text Society (1940).

**Kendall, Henry C(larence)** 1839–82. Henry C. Kendall, of English and Irish descent, was born in Australia and worked as a clerk and general helpmeet to James Lionel Michael, a Sydney solicitor who had arrived in Australia to look for gold. Michael, a friend of John Everett Millais and a supporter of the Pre-Raphaelite movement, was the author of a long autobiographical poem, *John Cumberland* (1860), and he discovered his young clerk's poetical promise. Kendall's first poems were sent to Henry (later Sir Henry) Parkes, who published them in his paper, *The Empire*; Kendall's first collection, *Poems and Songs* (1862), was published when he was 21. Some new poems were published in London, in *The Athenaeum* on 27 September of the same year – the first recognition of an Australian poet by an English critical journal. Like other Australians of the period who found poetry their true medium, Kendall suffered from the lack of an Australian poetic tradition and echoes of English and American poets are clearly heard in his work. But at its best Kendall's work is a true realization of Australia and of the natural beauty which appealed to his lyric gifts. After 1862 his published volumes were *The Bronze Trumpet: A Satirical Poem* (1866), *Leaves from Australian Forests* (1869), *Songs from the Mountains* (1880), *Orara: A Tale* (1881), and *Poems* (1886).

***Kenelm Chillingly*** A novel by Bulwer-Lytton, first published in 1873. The eponymous hero is a young man of good family, bored and depressed by the falseness of the society he knows, who puts on humble dress and goes out into the world. He encounters the bullying farrier, Tom Bowles, who is pressing his unwelcome attentions on a village girl. Chillingly beats him in a fair fight and Bowles's character changes for the better. The beautiful Cecilia Travers wants to marry Chillingly but he falls in love with Lily, an uneducated girl, daughter of a felon. Lily, however, out of gratitude to him, promises herself to her guardian. She dies of heartbreak before her marriage and Chillingly's ideas, now that he has known happiness and grief in love, take on firm outlines. He will devote himself to the service of his fellow men in some honoured cause. The novel is an exposition of Bulwer-Lytton's criticism of the society of the time and in that respect is connected to his earlier book, *The Coming Race*.

**Kenilworth** A novel of Elizabethan England by Sir Walter Scott, first published in 1821.

Amy Robsart has been persuaded to marry the Earl of Leicester, who fears the queen's displeasure and keeps the marriage secret. Elizabeth's progress, which will bring her to Kenilworth, prompts Leicester to keep Amy at Cumnor Place, near Oxford, with Richard Varney (Leicester is his patron) as guardian. Amy's rejected suitor, Edmund Tressilian, believes that she is there as Varney's paramour and tries to persuade her to return to her father's house. Failing in this, he goes to the queen and charges Varney with seducing her: Varney, to protect Leicester, declares that Amy is his wife. Elizabeth orders Amy to appear before her at Kenilworth.

Varney has designs on Amy, and persuades Leicester that she should appear as Varney's wife. Amy, furious, goes to Kenilworth and confronts Leicester, who is now obliged to acknowledge her and earns the wrath of the queen. Varney then lies to Leicester about Amy and Tressilian, so the wretched earl orders Varney to take Amy back to Cumnor Place and kill her. Tressilian learns the true facts and races to Cumnor Place: but Varney has already contrived the accident that results in Amy's death.

Scott succeeds very well in presenting Elizabethan England and the novel is one of his major achievements. The queen's court, the young Walter Ralegh first coming to notice, Elizabethan revels – these are very well presented and the principal characters have enough credibility to keep the reader's interest.

**Kennedy, John Pendleton** *c.*1795–1870. Kennedy was born in Baltimore and educated at Baltimore College. He practised law for a time but gave it up fairly quickly for literature and, later, politics. *The Red Book* (1818) was a book of sketches, satirical essays, and poems, rather in the manner of Irving's *Salmagundi*. Under the pseudonym of Mark Littleton he published a Virginia sketch book, *Swallow Barn* (1832).

Kennedy's first novel, **Horse-Shoe Robinson**, was published in 1835 and another, *Rob of the Bowl*, in 1838. He knew Washington Irving and Oliver Wendell Holmes and sponsored Edgar Allan Poe. He received Thackeray during his visit to the USA and helped him with the background material for *The Virginians*.

Kennedy entered Congress in 1838 and became President Fillmore's secretary of the navy. He urged the expedition of Commodore Perry to Japan in 1853 and the second Arctic expedition of Elisha Kent Kane.

**Kennedy, Lady Laura** In Anthony Trollope's *Phineas Finn* she first appears as Lady Laura Standish, one of the ladies attracted to the charming Irish hero. She loves Phineas but marries Robert Kennedy. Phineas, strongly attracted, withdraws when she marries – but she has married Kennedy for his position and stays in love with Phineas. She pursues him further in *Phineas Redux*.

**Kennedy, Margaret** 1896–1967. The daughter of a barrister, Margaret Kennedy was born in London and educated at Cheltenham College and Somerville College, Oxford. Her first interest was history and her first book *A Century of Revolution* (1922). Her second was a novel, *The Ladies of Lyndon* (1923), which was well received; *The Constant Nymph* (1924) made her famous. The novel was dramatized by the author and Basil Dean (1926) and has been filmed three times. Margaret Kennedy's elegant style, cool wit, and skill at characterization made her novels welcome to discerning readers for three decades: *Red Sky at Morning* (1927), a sequel to *The Constant Nymph* called *The Fool of the Family* (1930), *Return I Dare Not* (1931), *A Long Time Ago* (1932), *Together and Apart* (1936), *The Midas Touch* (1938), *The Feast* (1950), *Lucy Carmichael* (1951), *Troy Chimneys* (1953, James Tait Black Memorial Prize), *The Oracle* (1955), *The Heroes of Clone* (1957), *A Night in Cold Harbour* (1960), *The Forgotten Smile* (1961), and *Not in the Calendar* (1964). For the theatre, Margaret Kennedy wrote *Come With Me* (1928, with Basil Dean), *Escape Me Never* (1933), *Autumn* (1937, with Gregory Ratoff), and *Happy with Either* (1948). *Jane Austen* (1950) is a critical biography and *The Outlaws on Parnassus* (1958) a study of the art of fiction.

**Kent, Earl of** In Shakespeare's *King Lear* he earns Lear's wrath by supporting Cordelia and is banished, but he remains loyal and enters Lear's service disguised as a commoner called Caius. At the end the old king does not recognize him.

***Kentucky Cardinal, A*** A short novel by James Lane Allen, first published in 1894. *Aftermath*, first published in 1896, is its sequel. The setting is the Blue Grass region of Kentucky.

The retiring, amiable Adam Moss is a nature lover and his garden is a refuge for migratory birds. The Cobb family move into the next house and disturb his seclusion; but he falls in love with the daughter, Georgiana. She is capricious and tantalizing – but she needs to feel sure of Adam, so asks him to capture and cage a Kentucky cardinal bird for her. Adam does so, in spite of himself, and the poor creature soon dies in captivity. A quarrel follows, but Georgiana has learned a lesson from the experience and both she and Adam understand each other now.

In *Aftermath*, Adam and Georgiana marry and enjoy an enviable happiness. Adam has learned to be less of a recluse and Georgiana has learned to appreciate his love for nature. Georgiana dies giving birth to their son but Adam finds that his devotion to the natural world helps him bear his loss.

**Ker, W(illiam) P(aton)** 1855–1923. Ker was born in Glasgow, where he attended the Academy before going on to Glasgow University. Later he went to Balliol College, Oxford, on an exhibition and became a fellow of All Souls College in 1879. His academic career was distinguished: Assistant in Humanity (Latin) at the University of Edinburgh, Professor of English Literature and History at University College, Cardiff, Professor of English Language and Literature at University College, London, and Director of Scandinavian Studies at London University. Ker's reputation as a teacher was of the highest; his special subject was medieval literature and his books on the subject, though few, were very influential: *Epic and Romance* (1897), *The Dark Ages* (1904), *Essays on Medieval Literature* (1905), and *English Literature: Medieval* (the Home University Library, 1912); *Collected Essays* (1925) was edited by C. Whibley. Ker also edited Berners' translation of Froissart's *Chronicle* (six volumes, 1901–03).

**Kerouac, Jack** 1922–69. John Kerouac was born in Lowell, Massachusetts, and attended local Catholic schools before going to Columbia University in 1941. He spent some time as a merchant seaman and in wandering round the USA before publishing the first of his semi-autobiographical novels, *The Town and the City* (1950), about a family in his home town, Lowell. *On the Road* (1957) is concerned with the Beat Generation (Kerouac was the first to use the term), its life style and its aimless search for

significant experience. The book identified Kerouac as the novelist of the Beats just as *Howl* had identified Allen Ginsberg as their poet. *The Subterraneans* (1958) and *The Dharma Bums* (same year), *Tristessa* (1960), *Big Sur* (1962), and *Desolation Angels* (1965) are all products of the Beat life style; *Doctor Sax* and *Maggie Cassidy* (both 1959) and *Visions of Gerard* (1963) are evocations of Kerouac's boyhood and *Satori in Paris* (1966) an account of the author's quest for his Breton ancestors. Among other books by Jack Kerouac are *Lonesome Traveller* (1960, travel sketches), *Mexico City Blues* (1959, verse), and *Book of Dreams* – the author's – (1961).

**Keyes, Sidney** See **poets of World War II**.

***Kidnapped*** and **Catriona** A novel and its sequel by Robert Louis Stevenson. *Kidnapped* was first published in 1886; *Catriona*, originally called *David Balfour*, appeared in *Atalanta* (December 1892 to September 1893).

An illustration from an edition of *Kidnapped*, published in 1887. Alan Breck survives the collision in the fog. Stevenson's novel was first published in 1886.

David Balfour, left in poverty on the death of his father, goes to his uncle, Ebenezer, for assistance. Ebenezer, an evil miser, has unlawfully seized the estate which belongs to David and tries to kill him. When the attempt fails he has David kidnapped, on a ship bound for the Carolinas.

On the voyage a man is picked up from a sinking boat: he is Alan Breck, a homesick Jacobite. When the ship is wrecked off the coast of Mull, David and Alan travel together – and witness the murder of Colin Campbell, the king's factor. Suspicion falls on them and they start a perilous flight across the Highlands. They make it to safety across the Forth, and the story ends with Ebenezer confronted and David restored to his rights.

In *Catriona* the young David is grown up and in love with Catriona, daughter of the renegade, James More. James Stewart of the Glens is accused – falsely, from political motives – of the murder of Colin Campbell. David, who with Alan Breck witnessed the murder, comes forward on his behalf and finds his own life and freedom threatened. The story is concerned with David's escape from the plot against him and with Alan Breck's (a wanted Jacobite) escape to safety in France.

Marginally less popular than *Treasure Island*, the two David Balfour novels reveal development in the author's art. To narrative skill is added truthful delineation of character and a convincing sense of Scottish history.

**Killigrew, Thomas** 1612–83. Born in London, Killigrew became page to King Charles I, and was in the suite of Prince Charles when he went into exile in 1647. At the Restoration the prince, now Charles II, made him groom of the bedchamber and Killigrew enjoyed the king's friendship all his life. Killigrew's career as a minor playwright was interrupted by the closing of the theatres in 1642, by which time he had written, among other pieces, the coarse and popular *The Parson's Wedding*. This was based on the Spanish of Pedro Calderón de la Barca and probably first produced in 1640. Revived after the Restoration, in 1664, it achieved mention in Samuel Pepys's diary as 'an obscene, loose play'. Restoration comedy took a new turn after the success of *The Parson's Wedding*.

However, like William D'Avenant, Killigrew holds a place in the history of English drama as one of those who did most to revive it after the Puritan interregnum. Charles II gave him a patent to open a playhouse, The King's House, in a disused tennis court in Vere Street. Meanwhile the new playhouse was being built in Drury Lane. D'Avenant's theatre, The Duke's House, was in Lincoln's Inn Fields. Killigrew's theatre burned down in 1672 but was rebuilt by Wren and reopened two years later. One of the first training-schools for actors was founded by Killigrew at the Barbican. He became Master of the Revels to Charles II in 1673. His brother, William, and his son, Thomas, both wrote plays whilst another son, Charles, took over the management of the Theatre Royal in 1671.

**Kilmeny, Bonny** See *Queen's Wake, The*.

**Kim** A novel by Rudyard Kipling, first published in 1901. The book was illustrated by Lockwood Kipling, the author's father, who is represented in the story as the curator of the museum at Lahore.

Kim (Kimball O'Hara) is the orphan son of a British soldier. Brought up by an Indian woman in Lahore, he lives the life of an Indian boy and is wise in the ways of the country. One day he encounters a Lama, come from Tibet to find the River of the Arrow, made holy by the Lord Buddha; the Lama will bathe in it and have his sins washed away, and he will be freed from the Wheel of Life. Kim learns all this after helping the Lama enter the Wonder House (the museum), and then listening to the Lama's conversation with the curator. He decides to wander wherever the Lama goes, a wonderful prospect; he will be the Lama's *chela* (disciple) and he will look after him. He takes the Lama to Mahbub Ali, horse-dealer and secret agent (the opposing power is Imperial Russia), who commissions Kim to deliver a message at Umballa on his way to Benares with the Lama.

At Umballa they are given hospitality by a planter. Kim delivers his message to Colonel Creighton at his bungalow, and overhears preparations for the movement of large numbers of troops. They continue their journey by way of the Grand Trunk Road (the fourth chapter is a fine set piece, giving a brilliant picture of the great highway and the diversity of people who travel on it), and at a halt the Lama and Kim see a troop of soldiers setting up camp. They are Kim's father's old regiment and the chaplain, Mr Bennett, recognizes Kim; before he can make himself scarce he is in the custody of Father Victor, the Roman Catholic chaplain, and his education is being planned. The Lama is sad at losing his *chela* but accepts it as a punishment; he will pay for Kim's education.

The regiment sets off for Umballa. Kim manages to send a message to Mahbub Ali, and he is not pleased at the thought of being sent to the best school in Lucknow. Mahbub Ali turns

An illustration by John Lockwood Kipling for his son Rudyard's novel, *Kim* (1901). 'On the Road.'

up and takes him to Colonel Creighton. Kim is aware of preparations for war and the colonel realizes that the boy could pass for an Indian. He will be useful as an agent; Kim goes to Lucknow with Colonel Creighton, and sends a letter to the Lama, telling him about the school.

During his holidays Kim insists on enjoying himself and, as an Indian boy, takes to the road again. He meets Mahbub Ali in Umballa and his part as an agent is more clearly outlined; the two go to Simla to see Lurgan, another agent. When he returns to school he travels with Hurree Chunder Mookerjee, going by way of the Grand Trunk Road. Kim is learning all the time, and three years pass; he spends his holidays on the road and with Mahbub Ali and Lurgan. Then he becomes an Indian boy for his journey to Benares to rejoin the Lama, and acquits himself well when his agent-identity is needed on the train. Next he and the Lama join Hurree Chunder Mookerjee on an expedition in the hill country of the north, where spies are active. The Lama is happy there – the high sharp air is his natural environment, and the hill people acknowledge him as a wise and holy man.

The Lama's status becomes very useful to Kim when the spies are identified and refuse to acknowledge the Lama. In the ensuing fight Kim gains the essential information and Hurree delivers the spies to Simla. The Lama's quest is successfully concluded when he finds what he believes to be his River of the Arrow. Kim's quest has yet to be defined, and his course to be run.

**King, Henry** 1592–1669. Henry King was the son of the Bishop of London, John King, who had ordained John Donne, and Henry himself became the older poet's devoted friend and admirer. He was educated at Westminster School and Christ Church, Oxford, and took his DD in 1625. He became Bishop of Chichester in 1642, only to be ejected from his see by the Parliamentary forces in the following year. He was obliged to live on the kindness of his friends until the Restoration, when Charles II gave him back his see. In his old age King was a lively preacher – often at court – and a steadfast opponent of Puritanism.

King is not regarded as one of the major poets of his day; he was in fact an 'occasional' one, often moved to write elegies on the passing of great men – Donne (he was Donne's executor), Ben Jonson, and Sir Walter Raleigh. He never published his work and it first appeared in book form anonymously, without his permission, in 1657. His output was not large but his best verse is often anthologized and does no dishonour to his masters, Donne and Jonson. His highest level is reached in his famous elegy on the death of

Anne Berkeley, his first wife, 'The Exequy: To his Matchlesse never to be forgotten Friend'.

**King, William** 1663–1712. A contemporary of Swift and John Arbuthnot, King was educated at Westminster School and Christ Church, Oxford; he became a lawyer. He held various minor posts in Ireland for six years (1702–08) and was appointed gazetteer (1711) after his return to England. Like Swift he was a High-Church Tory and contributed to the 'Battle of the Books' with *Dialogues of the Dead*, an attack on Richard Bentley written with Charles Boyle (1699). His first considerable piece was *Dialogue showing the way to Modern Preferment* (1690). King is a little-known writer of the late 17th and early 18th centuries, often praised by scholars of the period. Other works were *The Art of Cookery, in imitation of Horace's Art of Poetry* (1708) and burlesques and light verse collected in *Miscellanies in Prose and Verse* (1709) and *Useful Miscellanies* (1712).

**King and No King, A** A play by Francis Beaumont and John Fletcher, first produced in 1611 and first published in 1619.

After a long war between Iberia and Armenia victory goes to Arbaces, King of Iberia, in single combat against Tigranes of Armenia. Arbaces offers Tigranes his liberty and continued peace if he will marry Panthea, his sister. Tigranes declines, for he loves Spaconia. He sends her to Panthea; he hopes that Spaconia will enlighten Panthea and enlist her help in opposing the marriage. Panthea has grown up during Arbaces' absence at the war and when she appears her beauty disturbs not only Tigranes but her brother too. Arbaces tries to smother his incestuous passion; then he discovers that his feelings are reciprocated. The intervention of Gobrias, lord protector of the kingdom, reveals that the two are not related – he is Arbaces' father. The queen mother had despaired of bearing children and Gobrias had given her his infant son; Panthea was born to the late king and his queen six years later. There is no impediment to their union now; and Tigranes is also free to marry Spaconia.

**King Hart** (or **Heart**) A Scottish allegorical poem of uncertain date and authorship, for some time attributed to Gavin Douglas. It was probably written in the early decades of the 16th century, and is regarded as a finer work than the contemporary *The Palice of Honour* by Douglas. The allegory concerns the journey of a human soul – King Hart – to the point where he is at last free of the temptations of life and love and has mastered himself. But then, inevitably, his life is over and death is approaching. The poem was first printed in John Pinkerton's *Ancient Scotish Poems* (1786).

**King Horn** The earliest surviving Middle English verse romance, dating from the late 13th century and derived from an Old English source. (See **metrical romances**.) The son of King Murray and Queen Godhild of Suddene (the Isle of Man) is only spared during a Saracen raid because of his beauty. He is set adrift in a boat with his companions Athulf and Fikenhild, and they make landfall at Westernesse (probably the Wirral). Rymenhild, daughter of King Almair of Westernesse, falls in love with Horn, and the story follows the fortunes of the lovers. Fikenhild proves a false friend and betrays the lovers to King Almair; Horn is banished, but returns when Rymenhild is given in marriage to the treacherous Fikenhild. Disguised as a minstrel, he enters the castle and kills Fikenhild. He and Rymenhild live happily in the end, when he has turned the Saracens out of Suddene and recovered his kingdom. The story is clearly adapted from an older tale, with Saracens taking the place of Vikings as raiders. *King Horn* was edited by J. R. Lumby (1866) and revised by G. H. McKnight for the Early English Text Society (1901). A modern version by J. S. P. Tatlock was published in 1948.

**Kingis Quair, The** A poem by King James I of Scotland, written while he was the prisoner of Henry IV of England – probably 1423 or 1424, about the time of his marriage to Lady Jane Beaufort. The poem consists of 197 stanzas and shows the influence of Chaucer's *The Romaunt of the Rose*; it is also written in rhyme-royal, which Chaucer had first used. The poem was discovered and printed in 1783 by William Tytler.

The matter of the poem concerns the events that led to captivity, the royal prisoner's first sight of a beautiful lady walking in the castle garden and his falling in love with her; his dream-vision encounters with Minerva and Fortuna, and the promise given by Venus that his love will be realized. The title means The King's Quire or The King's Book.

**King John, The Life and Death of** A historical play by William Shakespeare. It was first produced c.1595 and the title role may have been played by Edward Alleyn. It was not published until the First Folio of 1623. The sources of the play were the chronicles of Raphael Holinshed and an anonymous chronicle play, *The Troublesome Raigne of King John*, which was once attributed to Shakespeare himself.

The matter of the play, which is regarded as an

early effort and a failure among Shakespeare's historical plays, is King John's determination to keep his throne in the face of his nephew's apparently stronger claim to it; Arthur of Brittany is the son of John's late older brother, Geoffrey, and has the support of the King of France. John's struggle with the pope is featured to a lesser degree; Magna Carta does not feature at all. John orders the blinding of Arthur and offers Hubert de Burgh a great bribe to carry it out; but in a memorable scene the boy's plea so moves him that Hubert spares his prisoner. But Arthur leaps to his death while attempting to escape his gaolers in a later scene, to the great grief of his mother, Constance.

The play ends with the death of King John at Swinstead Abbey. The best characterization in the play is generally agreed to be that of the bastard, Faulconbridge, who guards his country's integrity against everything, even a bad king.

**Kinglake, Alexander William** 1809–91. Kinglake was born at Taunton in Somerset and educated at Eton College and Trinity College, Cambridge. He went on to study law and became a successful barrister in 1837. He is best known as the author of *Eothen: or Traces of Travel brought Home from the East*, a narrative of his journeys in Egypt and the Near East. Kinglake, though very much the Englishman abroad, is a sympathetic observer and his book has considerable charm; the title is from the Greek and means 'towards the dawn'.

Kinglake contributed to *The Quarterly Review* and *Blackwood's Magazine* and visited the Crimea with the British Army. It was at the request of Lady Raglan, widow of the commander in chief, that he wrote *The Invasion of the Crimea* (1863–87), an exhaustive eight-volume history which is respected and referred to, but little read.

Editions of *Eothen* have been published in The World's Classics (1900) and in Everyman's Library (1908).

**King Lear** A tragedy by William Shakespeare, first produced *c*.1606, and printed in two slightly different versions in quartos of 1608. It was published in the First Folio of 1623. The source of the play is the chronicles of Raphael Holinshed, who probably drew it from Geoffrey of Monmouth's *Historia*, in which the story of Lear and his daughters was first written down. The story of Gloucester, so important to Shakespeare's plot, is based on a tale in Sidney's *Arcadia*.

The opening scene introduces the earls of Kent and Gloucester and Gloucester's bastard son, Edmund. Gloucester has more affection for Edmund than for his legitimate son Edgar. Edmund has a deep resentment of his half-brother, which he conceals, and is determined to dispossess him.

Lear is King of Britain and in his old age decides to divide his kingdom among his daughters Goneril, Regan, and Cordelia. Goneril's husband is Duke of Albany and Regan's is Duke of Cornwall; Cordelia's hand is sought by both the King of France and the Duke of Burgundy. Lear foolishly decides that the division shall be according to his daughters' affection for him and neither Goneril nor Regan are short of fulsome words. He awards each a third of his kingdom and then turns to Cordelia, who has been listening to her older sisters' glutinous declarations with growing revulsion. She replies, 'I cannot heave my heart into my mouth' and declares she loves her father as his daughter. The cantankerous old man does not succeed in bullying more out of her and divides the remaining third of the kingdom between Goneril and Regan. Kent upbraids the king for his stupidity; he sees the truth that lies with Cordelia. The enraged Lear turns him out of the kingdom – if he is discovered there after six days he will be put to death. Goneril and Regan are asked to maintain their father's state with a hundred knights a month, in turn. The Duke of Burgundy withdraws his suit, since Lear has withdrawn Cordelia's dowry, but the King of France loves her and accepts her for herself. Goneril and Regan, alone together, make it plain that their old and wilful father is not the sort of guest they would choose to maintain.

Edmund tricks his father (Gloucester) into believing that his lawful son, Edgar, is plotting his death. Edgar becomes a fugitive and adopts the mantle of an idiot, Poor Tom. Lear meanwhile, has become a tiresome nuisance at Goneril's and Albany's palace. Kent, in disguise, takes service with Lear and wins the old man's confidence at once in helping to deal with Goneril's insolent steward Oswald. Then Goneril makes it plain to her father that he and his knights and his fool are turning the palace into something 'more like a tavern or a brothel'. Lear calls his retinue and leaves in a rage; Goneril sends a letter to Regan to warn her. Regan will not have Lear; they meet at Gloucester's castle and Goneril arrives there too. Regan tells her father to dismiss half his train and finish his month with Goneril; but during the scene it becomes clear that neither sister will have him – unless he comes alone. Lear curses both of them and storms off into the night. Gloucester is uneasy about the treatment of the old man, who is now abroad in the stormy night without shelter. Edgar finds him in a hovel with Kent and the fool, his reason slipping. Gloucester confides his uneasiness to Edmund and hints at action to be taken; Edmund betrays his father's confidence to Cornwall.

Gloucester finds the king and guides him to shelter in the outhouse of his castle but later he has to bring warning that the old man's death is being plotted. Kent and the fool and some of Gloucester's knights hurry him away. Edgar ponders uneasily on the events that have brought a king so low.

A French army has landed in Britain and Albany and Goneril, Regan and Cornwall, their suspicions aroused by Edmund, are certain of Gloucester's complicity. When Oswald brings news that Lear, forewarned, has escaped to Dover and 'well-armed friends', Regan and Cornwall have Gloucester bound and they question him; then they blind him and mock him with the news that Edmund has betrayed him. An old tenant of Gloucester's leads him on the heath and gives him to the care of Poor Tom (Edgar). Gloucester entreats Poor Tom to take him to Dover; he does not know that the stranger is his son.

Cornwall dies of a wound inflicted by one of his servants who was appalled at the blinding of Gloucester. Albany is feeling increasingly cold towards the woman Goneril is proving to be. Edmund succeeds in attracting the favour of both Goneril and Regan. Lear meanwhile has reached Dover – thanks to Kent – and Cordelia is reunited with her father. Edgar brings his blinded father there safely and on the way encounters the evil Oswald and kills him in a fight. He finds that Oswald was carrying a letter to Edmund from Goneril, urging him to dispose of Albany. Lear meanwhile has lost control of his mind: but he is cared for by Cordelia and recovers.

Goneril with Albany and Regan with Edmund meet at the British camp near Dover; Goneril is jealous to see Edmund with her sister. Edgar, as Poor Tom, comes to the camp and gives Albany the letter Goneril sent to Edmund. Edmund himself, with the choice of one sister who is widowed and one who may well be widowed, decides to wait and see, and he objects to Albany's honourable approach to Lear and Cordelia, should they be defeated.

The British army is victorious and Lear and Cordelia are taken. Edmund gives the order for Cordelia to be murdered in her prison and is then confronted by Albany. Goneril and Regan are present and Regan is dying – Goneril has poisoned her. Albany challenges Edmund's honour in a public tournament and his champion is Edgar. Edmund is mortally wounded and Albany confronts Goneril with the proof of her treachery. Goneril kills herself and Edmund, dying, admits his guilt; he tells of the order to murder Cordelia but Albany is too late to countermand it.

Lear carries in the body of the dead Cordelia, watched by the others, who are shocked into silence ('Howl, howl, howl, howl! Oh, you are men of stones!'). He recognizes the faithful Kent and that is his only comfort – his enemies have even killed his poor fool, who kept to him in all his trials. He dies of grief. The kingdom, Albany decrees, shall fall to Edgar.

*King Lear* is most distinguished for its Olympian poetry, which is one reason why many lovers of Shakespeare find it more rewarding on the page than on the stage. The title role is stupendous and, while our most distinguished actors succeed in it in various ways, it is peculiarly elusive of sympathy in the theatre. The reason may be that Lear himself is a difficult man to sympathize with. The actor is given great opportunities to impress us; but very few to move us in the way that the fool does, or poor blinded Gloucester, who is another victim of himself. The subplot, in a curious way, is an essential buttress to the major theme, with the cold-blooded Edmund more in charge of events than anyone else.

The king, without the great poetry Shakespeare gives him, would be almost nothing, unless one is to see his tragedy in the fact that he is a remarkably stupid old man. He demands impossible statements from his daughters in the first scene and in reply is given words that only hypocrites could utter without blushing; the third daughter tells him the truth and he explodes in wrath. His behaviour is that of one who could never have *given* love in his life – he has always assumed it as his due and now he wants it weighed and measured. Goneril and Regan prove to be a nasty pair – but with such a father their dispositions are not hard to understand. After that, Lear does not so much fall as tumble in an untidy heap: he goes off with dire threats that are no more than bluster: 'I will have such revenges on you both that all the world shall – I will do such things – what they are yet I know not; but they shall be the terrors of the earth.' Then he goes out into the night and the storm – and into humility and a realization of human kindness, shown first to his unhappy, shivering fool. The sanity on to which he is holding so hard begins to slip. The poetry is what saves him from being merely pitiful; but the metamorphosis of Lear's character on the stage seems to defy convincing realization.

A remarkable creation is the fool, wry and truthful and as faithful as a dog. Shakespeare seems to forget him after the words 'And I'll go to bed at noon' in Act III Scene 6. The reference at the end, Lear's 'And my poor fool is hang'd!', seems to answer for his disappearance but he has been out of the play for more than two whole acts by then and the line could refer to Cordelia.

**Kingsley, Charles** 1819–75. The son of the vicar of Holne in Devonshire, Charles Kingsley was educated at King's College, London, and Magdalene College, Cambridge. His father's progress from one living to another made him familiar with various aspects of rural England and gave him a fondness for natural history. As a young man he was strongly influenced by the writings of Thomas Carlyle and by the friendship of Frederick Denison Maurice – who might be called the first Christian Socialist to formulate his ideas and to teach them. Kingsley's interest in reform was an extension of his thought at this stage in his life; his play-form expression of his religious ideas, *The Saint's Tragedy*, was published in 1848 and he published an essay on religion in *Fraser's Magazine* in the same year. Thereafter he was a regular contributor to *Politics for the People* and *The Christian Socialist*, for a time under the pseudonym of 'Parson Lot'.

His first published novel was **Alton Locke** (1850), though he had begun to work on another, **Yeast, a Problem**, before that. *Yeast* was serialized in *Fraser's Magazine* and then published in book form in 1851. *Alton Locke* was harshly received by both critics and politicians; Kingsley was, like Elizabeth Gaskell, unflinching in his criticism and like her he was a witness for his times. His own favourite among his books came next, **Hypatia** (1853), a historical novel of the conflicts in early Christianity and regarded by many as his finest work. By this time Kingsley was well established in his rectorship of Eversley in Hampshire, to which he had been appointed in 1844.

**Westward Ho!**, his most famous and successful – if not his best – historical novel, came in 1855, and a novel with a contemporary setting, *Two Years Ago*, in 1857. Between them came a re-telling of some Greek myths, **The Heroes** (1856), which has provided generations of school-children with their favourite versions of the adventures of Theseus, Perseus, and Jason. He also wrote a fair amount of verse, examples of which are to be found in every school anthology.

Kingsley was appointed Regius Professor of Modern History at Cambridge in 1860. He was pleased with the appointment and held it for nine years, though its responsibilities weighed on him increasingly. In 1864 he published, in *Macmillan's*

Charles Kingsley. A detail from the portrait by L. Dickinson, 1862. National Portrait Gallery, London.

*Magazine*, the review of Froude's *History of England, Vols 7 and 8*, which led him into conflict with John Henry Newman and was the impulse for the latter's *Apologia pro Vita sua*.

His last novel, **Hereward the Wake**, was published in 1865. **The Water Babies**, his 'Fairy Tale for a Land Baby' came out in 1863 and has been a favourite ever since. Other notable publications were *Glaucus: or the Wonders of the Shore* (1855), which developed from an article reflecting his interest in natural history, and a course of lectures, *The Roman and the Teuton* (1864). *Prose Idylls* (1873) is a felicitous and charming book of essays based on his observations at home and abroad; *At Last* (1871) is an account of a three-month visit to the West Indies – his mother's home – in 1869.

Charles Kingsley died in 1875, a Canon of Westminster and Chaplain to the Queen. All his life he was deeply concerned with social reform, but he was opposed, totally, to the idea of change brought about by force. Moral persuasion was the alternative he offered to Chartism and his first two novels reflect both this concern and the age of transition in which he lived. Less successful in these efforts than Elizabeth Gaskell, he found his real strength as a novelist in *Hypatia* and *Westward Ho!*, and in the little read *Hereward the Wake*.

**Kingsley, Henry** 1830–76. The younger brother of Charles Kingsley and the author of two novels set in Australia, **Geoffrey Hamlyn**

(1859) and *The Hillyars and the Burtons* (1865). Henry Kingsley was at Worcester College, Oxford, when some undisclosed trouble led to his departure without a degree. He went to Australia, where he spent five years, serving for some of the time in the Sydney mounted police. *Geoffrey Hamlyn* was published after his return to England. **Ravenshoe**, a romance, followed in 1862 and *Austin Elliott* in 1863. *Ravenshoe* was a popular success. Henry Kingsley became editor of the Edinburgh *Daily Review* in 1869 but left that position to report the Franco–Prussian War from the Prussian side. There were other novels, now forgotten; Henry Kingsley is not much read today. At his best he is a pleasing writer and he made very good use of the – at that time – exotic background of frontier Australia.

**Kingsley, Mary** 1862–1900. The daughter of a much-travelled as well as literary family, Mary Kingsley was niece to Charles and Henry Kingsley and was born in Islington, London. In 1893 she decided to explore. West Africa interested her most and her *Travels in West Africa* (1897) is the account of her journeys in the French and German colonies of Gabon and the Cameroons. Mary Kingsley died at Simonstown in 1900, of enteric fever, caught from the Boer prisoners she was nursing.

**King's Tragedy, The** A narrative poem by Dante Gabriel Rossetti, first published in 1881 in *Ballads and Sonnets*. The subject is the assassination of King James I of Scotland, related by Kate Barlass (Catherine Douglas). The king is warned by a spae-wife, who had a vision of him in a shroud. She warns him at the sea's edge and again at the Charterhouse in Perth, where the murderers eventually claim their victim. Kate Barlass makes a valiant but vain effort to hold the door against the killers; the bar has been removed and she thrusts her arm into its place.

**Kipling, Rudyard** 1865–1936. Rudyard Kipling was born in Bombay. His father, John Lockwood Kipling, came from a Methodist family and studied art and sculpture in London; he was recommended by Sir Philip Cunliffe-Owen for the post of Professor of Architectural Sculpture at the new Bombay School of Art. Kipling's mother (née Alice Macdonald) was also from a Methodist family and met her husband at a picnic at Lake Rudyard in Staffordshire. Their first child was a son and he was named Rudyard. Alice Macdonald's sister Agnes married Edward Poynter; her sister Louisa married Alfred Baldwin and became the mother of Stanley Baldwin, and her sister Georgiana married Burne-Jones.

In 1871 Kipling, aged six, and his three-year-old sister, Trix, were left in England at the end of their father's leave. Rudyard was to attend school and both children were put in the care of a Mrs Holloway in Southsea. The Kiplings seem to have done this without adequate preparation and the children found themselves apparently abandoned. The truth about this period in Kipling's life is obscure: the story 'Baa, Baa, Black Sheep' (1888) is ostensibly an account of cruelty and wretchedness suffered by the author but it is also highly sentimental about the parents, who would have been responsible. Trix was treated with indulgence and Rudyard with firmness, which must have seemed harsh to a boy who had enjoyed the pampered indulgence of English children in India. But Mrs Holloway succeeded in convincing the Macdonald aunts that she was a good housekeeper and a satisfactory foster-parent. Life at Southsea was relieved by visits to the Burne-Jones household at Fulham (where William Morris was a much-loved honorary uncle) and in Rudyard's case by voracious reading. This period resulted in permanent damage to Kipling's eyesight, noticed by Georgiana Burne-Jones, who sent for Alice Kipling. After a holiday, Trix returned to Mrs Holloway at Southsea and Rudyard went to the United Services College, a private school, at Westward Ho! in Devon.

At college Kipling emerged as a writer, contributing a large part of the contents of the school magazine. The headmaster, Cormell Price, was a friend of Morris and Burne-Jones and gave Kipling the run of the school library. Kipling read French without difficulty and developed a liking for American writers. He spent holidays with the Burne-Jones and Poynter aunts and cousins and would have liked to go to university. But it was beyond his father's means, and the United Services College was not equipped for the preparation of candidates for university scholarships. Kipling returned to India in 1882 and joined his parents at Lahore, where his father was now principal of the School of Art and Curator of the Lahore Museum. The United Services College and Kipling's schoolmates were later commemorated in *Stalky & Co.* (1899).

Kipling went to work as a journalist on *The Civil and Military Gazette*, which had the largest circulation in the Punjab. He learned to speak the vernacular with ease and could converse with the Indian people in every level of life: he listened to the conversations in the Punjab Club, where doctors, civil servants, army officers, traders, and engineers met every day. He also talked to the ordinary soldier, to the lasting benefit of his work. Summers were spent at Simla, and Kipling became a Freemason in 1885. In the following year the editor of the *Gazette*, Stephen Wheeler, was succeeded by Kay Robinson, who took Kipling off the conventional journalist's round and gave him the task of producing a weekly feature. This was to be a tale of local life in the Punjab and verse was used, Kipling declared, as something to fill up space. The 'fill-ups' launched his career; they were published by a Calcutta house. Kipling added more of these *Departmental Ditties* (1886) to succeeding editions, and no less than four were published and sold before he left India in 1889.

The stories, short and incisive, the result of a journalist's hard training combined with a genius for the form, were collected and published as **Plain Tales from the Hills** (1888). Kipling added eight stories to those from the *Gazette* and presented a round forty. Some are little more than anecdotes but many are memorable and demonstrate how clearly the author saw the remarkable world of Imperial India. 'Beyond the Pale', **Without Benefit of Clergy**, and 'The Story of Muhammad Din' are salutary tales in which Kipling is no apologist for his countrymen as overlords. *Plain Tales from the Hills* was a resounding success in India; so far his name was hardly known outside.

Meanwhile, Kipling was promoted to *The Pioneer*, a more important paper published in Allahabad, in 1887. He saw more of India, working in the heart of the country, and he travelled much more. He contributed further stories and travel articles from his journeys in what is now the United Provinces. The travel articles and additional similar material were eventually published as *From Sea to Sea* (1899). The tales were published in groups in the useful and popular Indian Railway Library, at a price of one rupee.

On *The Pioneer* Kipling was allowed greater space and his gifts developed rapidly. **Soldiers Three**, *The Story of the Gadsbys*, *In Black and White*, *Under the Deodars*, *The Phantom Rickshaw and Other Tales*, and *Wee Willie Winkie and Other Stories* were all published in 1888 and each averaged six or so stories. 'The Man Who Would be King' is one of the stories first published in *The Phantom Rickshaw*; 'Baa, Baa, Black Sheep' and 'The Drums of the Fore and Aft' first appeared in *Wee Willie Winkie*. *Soldiers Three* is the author's close look at the soldier – the private or ranker; no writer had done so before but sadly the stories are almost unreadable now. Kipling tried so hard to reproduce their speech in phonetic and syntactical exactitude that the effect is wearisome, leaving the storyteller's art too far behind. But his attempt impressed Lord Roberts, who asked Kipling to tell him more about the attitudes of the men in the barracks.

Kipling left India in the spring of 1889. He never lived there again but drew on the riches of the experience for many years. He travelled east from Calcutta and crossed the USA from San Francisco to New England, interviewing Mark Twain on the way. He landed at Liverpool in October and eventually found rooms in Villiers Street, off the Strand and near the Thames. He had a considerable income from his writing in India and was able to listen to Kay Robinson's suggestion that he flex his muscles in London. He had numerous family connections there, particularly on his mother's side, and a friend in his former boss in Lahore, Stephen Wheeler; Mowbray Morris, formerly of *The Pioneer*, edited *Macmillan's Magazine*. Kipling contributed poems to *Macmillan's* and commanded considerable attention with 'The Ballad of East and West'. His first story published in England was 'The Incarnation of Krishna Mulvaney' and soon he was being published regularly. Readers back from India remembered the Indian Railway Library collections and a London publisher realized that he had had *Plain Tales from the Hills* on his hands since 1888: a new star rose on the London literary scene.

The first collection Kipling published in London, **Life's Handicap** (1891), was a great success. The author was a member of the Savile Club and known to everybody in literary London. Among his friends were Andrew Lang, Henry James, Rider Haggard, and W. E. Henley; among his sponsors for membership to the Savile were Hardy, Edmund Gosse, George Saintsbury, Austin Dobson, and Sidney Colvin (whom Kipling disliked intensely but whose support, he knew, was valuable). The most important friendship of this period was that of Wolcott Balestier, a young American publisher who represented, in London, the house of J. W. Lovell & Co., Boston. Balestier was a hard-working publisher with drive and initiative, rather different from the slow-paced, privileged figures who dominated the London literary scene. Kipling, another hard worker and a creative artist who had succeeded entirely on his merits, took to Wolcott Balestier at once.

*The Light that Failed* (1891) was first published in *Lippincott's Magazine* and by J. W. Lovell & Co. to secure Kipling's copyright in the USA (he had been justly furious to discover that his stories were being pirated in the States). The novel is not a success and at the time was severely criticized by J. M. Barrie in *The Contemporary Review*. Barrie, a great admirer of Kipling's stories, perceived that Kipling had a genius for the particular; the world of his painter-hero, Dick Heldar, was imaginary, as were the people in it: 'His chief defect is ignorance of life. There is no sympathy with humanity, without which there never was and never will be a great novelist. With the mass of his fellow-creatures Mr Kipling is out of touch, and thus they are an unknown tongue to him.' But Kipling, meanwhile, was writing another novel in collaboration with Balestier. This was *The Naulahka, A Novel of East and West* (1892); the title should have been spelt 'naulakha', and it is not known why Kipling never corrected it. The novel told of an American engineer in India, searching for a fabulous jewel worth a fortune (*naulakha*). The novel was a commercial success but is not highly regarded now. At the end of 1890 Kipling's ill health, a legacy from his years in India, made a long sea voyage necessary. He left in 1891 and was in India when he learned of Balestier's death in Germany. Kipling returned to England and married Caroline Balestier (Carrie), his friend's sister, who was three years Kipling's senior. He commemorated Wolcott in a dedicatory poem in the collected volume of *Barrack-Room Ballads and Other Verses* (1892). ***Many Inventions*** (1893), which contains the striking ***Love-o'-Women***, was published while the Kiplings were living in the USA (in Vermont, where the Balestier family lived). The new collection was a triumph, his finest collection to date according to Saintsbury. *Barrack-Room Ballads* also earned a chorus of praise, though Lionel Johnson had a low opinion of the 'Other Verses' in the volume. Among the stories in *Many Inventions* were 'The Lost Legion', 'My Lord the Elephant', 'The Finest Story in the World' (a story of reincarnation, a subject that interested Kipling), 'His Private Honour', and 'In the Rukh', which first introduced Mowgli to readers, though in a different form from the figure that became so famous. 'One View of the Question' and 'Children of the Zodiac' demonstrated the art of a fine storyteller broadening his range.

Kipling built a house in Vermont – called Naulakha – and wrote *The Jungle Books* (1894 and 1895), which became classics. Mowgli, Toomai, Kaa, Bagheera, Rikki-tikki-tavi, and Akela are familiar names but the stories are perhaps better suited to adult readers, who tend, however, to regard them as tales for children.

The Kiplings returned to England in 1896 with their two daughters. Life in the USA suited them perfectly until relations with the Balestier family turned sour, as did, eventually, the American experience. But ***The Seven Seas*** (1896), a new collection of poems, raised his prestige higher than ever, both in England and the USA, where W. D. Howells and Charles Eliot Norton in particular gave Kipling the careful attention due to a major artist. *Captains Courageous* (1897), a moral tale of the Massachusetts fishermen and a spoiled rich man's son who falls among them, succeeded commercially since Kipling was the author but it is not highly regarded now. The spoiled boy, Harvey Cheyne, learns about life and acquires integrity just in time, before unearned riches ruin him completely. The fishing scenes are excellent but the didactic tone spoils it for modern readers.

Kipling became the youngest member of the Athenaeum at the age of 32, and was the friend of Milner, Rhodes, and Curzon; he dined at Balliol College and was given a rapturous reception by the undergraduates. He went to live in Rottingdean, where Burne-Jones and Kipling's aunt Georgiana lived, as well as the Stanley Baldwins. Kipling's only son, John, was born there in 1897. It was the high noon of the Empire, an excellent period for the young, brilliantly successful Kipling. But he was far too intelligent to believe that this apparently perfect world could endure; he had seen its citizens at their worst, as well as at their best, in India and he was a widely travelled man. Queen Victoria's Diamond Jubilee prompted his most famous poem, published in *The Times* as 'Recessional', which made him a respected national figure. It is doubtful if Kipling's contemporaries (Walter Besant and Edward Dowden are honourable exceptions) ever understood the poem. *Blackwood's Magazine* published a typically myopic review of Kipling's work in October 1898 in which J. H. Millar wrote that the poem 'took England by storm, and seemed to concentrate in itself the glowing patriotism of a Shakespeare, the solemn piety of a Milton, and the measured stateliness of a Dryden.' Millar ignored Kipling's warning that the responsibilities of Empire were overpowering and must never be forgotten, while subsequent history suggests that politicians did not hear the warning at all: 'If, drunk with sight of power, we loose Wild tongues that have not thee in awe, Such boastings as the Gentiles use, Or lesser breeds without the Law.' The 'lesser breeds', as George Orwell pointed out in 1942, referred not to those who did not know the Law but to those who did and refused to honour it.

Kipling and his family wintered in South Africa (1897–98) and were honoured by Rhodes and Milner. The next winter was spent in the USA, where Kipling's copyrights were being flouted and where his property in Vermont had to be sold since he had no intention of living there again. He fell ill in New York and the American press published progress reports that might have gratified him; but meanwhile his eldest daughter died of pneumonia and the family returned sadly to Rottingdean in 1899. *The Day's Work*, an undistinguished collection of stories, was published in 1898; *Stalky & Co.* and *From Sea to Sea* in 1899. The Boer War broke out in 1899 and the English suffered one humiliating defeat after another. Kipling wintered at the Cape in 1900; Lord Roberts took over the command and Kipling became a war correspondent: 'there happened to be a bit of a war on,' he wrote to an American friend, 'and I had the time of my life.' No one in the establishment, and certainly not Kipling, could have known that the high noon of Empire was passing. The 'bit of a war', of which Kipling the war correspondent saw virtually nothing at first hand, was not regarded as likely to tax the great Empire's competence and resources. But the war still went badly; Roberts was replaced by Kitchener; Baden-Powell had become a national hero through the siege of Mafeking, a town in no real danger and well stocked with food; the appalling concentration camps, at least, distressed Kipling because of the maladministration. Meanwhile he discussed the future of (British) South Africa with Rhodes, Jameson, and Milner. The Boers were to have no say in that future. Nevertheless, Kipling knew that incompetence and complacence had come close to losing the war. His poem **The Islanders** expressed his feelings clearly though it was the last of his works to criticize the establishment.

At the end of the century Kipling acquired a home of his own, Bateman's near Burwash in East Sussex, and here he settled down to write another novel, one that had been in his mind for years. **Kim** (1901) is acknowledged as Kipling's masterpiece in fiction, a fine panoramic novel with a problematic ending: the Lama's journey is completed; Kim's is not. But though Kipling failed to work out the two strands the novel is the finest written about the India of the British Empire. *Just So Stories* (1902) was begun in South Africa; it was a popular success and continued to be so for decades. *The Five Nations* (1903) was a collection of verse, in which 28 new poems appeared, many the result of his experiences in South Africa. Kipling was offered a knighthood, which he declined.

**Traffics and Discoveries** (1904) was a collection of 11 stories and 11 poems. The stories are a

An illustration by Rudyard Kipling for one of his *Just So Stories* (1902). 'How the Camel got his Hump.'

mixture of good and bad: when writing about the Boer War Kipling is neither clumsy nor without skill but his malicious, chauvinistic tone is unacceptable. The stories about Petty Officer Pyecroft do not quite succeed – Kipling seems not to have understood sailors – but 'Mrs Bathurst', 'They', and 'Below the Mill Dam' are Kipling at his best. **Puck of Pook's Hill** (1906) presents English history in stories beautifully contrived and told, and Kipling's historical sense is unerring. Pook's Hill is a real hill, visible from Bateman's, and the children to whom Puck appears, Dan and Una, were modelled on Kipling's children, John and Elsie.

In 1907 Kipling was offered the Nobel Prize for Literature. He was the first Englishman to be so honoured, and though he declined the numerous official laurels the English establishment wanted to bestow – even the Order of Merit – he was very pleased with this international recognition and accepted. *Actions and Reactions* (1909) contained eight stories and eight poems. Among the stories are the fine satire 'The Little Foxes', the ghostly-depression story 'The House Surgeon', and the repellent, condescending (in spirit if not in art) 'An Habitation Enforced'. *Rewards and Fairies* (1910) returns to Pook's Hill and the children are transported to other times by Puck. Kipling's fine poem 'The Way Through the Woods' appears in this book; so does 'If', which became so famous and over-quoted that the author grew heartily sick of it.

World War I was imminent and even at home, at the centre of the British Empire, things were not exactly calm. The Trade Unions, the determined Suffragettes, the Irish Home Rule movement – in fact anything that in any way threatened the Empire's smooth continuity deepened Kipling's conservatism. He was disappointed when his son John proved less than first-class officer material at Wellington School; the Royal Navy was closed to him because of weak eyesight. His father, like many men of his time, welcomed the outbreak of war – it was inevitable and justifiable. He persuaded his friend Lord Roberts to make John, not yet 17, a second lieutenant in the Irish Guards. Kipling went to France in 1915 and met the French war leaders; he also went to the front at Troyes, where little was happening. He never gained the least idea of what trench warfare was like. John Kipling, in October of the same year, was one of the 20,000 British soldiers who died at the Battle of Loos.

*A Diversity of Creatures* (1917) contained 14 stories and 14 poems. The famous **Mary Postgate** is in this volume, together with 'Swept and Garnished'. The latter, a fairly poisonous affair, is the sort of story that often appears during a war – especially when it is going badly. But 'Mary Postgate', superficially the same sort of story, is

Rudyard Kipling, 1923.

a fascinating work to have arisen from the current circumstances of Kipling's life and is one of his most memorable.

The uneasy peace after 1918 found Rudyard Kipling, the true-blue Tory, an unhappy reactionary. But life at Bateman's went on as before, apparently, with Rider Haggard and Stanley Baldwin as regular visitors. Kipling received honorary doctorates of literature from the universities of Edinburgh, Paris, and Alsace and was made Lord Rector of St Andrew's University in 1923. King George V became his friend. But Kipling was not happy in either the political or the literary climate (he detested Lytton Strachey's *Eminent Victorians*); he attended Hardy's funeral and thereafter saw Bloomsbury and the modern poets move into the ascendant.

Kipling's own work, meanwhile, continued with the collection of verses called *The Years Between* (1919), *Letters of Travel 1892–1913* (1920), *The Irish Guards in The Great War* (1923), and *Land and Sea Tales for Scouts and Guides* (1923). *Debits and Credits* (1926) contained 14 stories and 21 poems. 'Sea Constables' is a war story in which Englishmen behave with iron resolution, implacable justice, and of course good manners. **The Gardener** is also a war story, but moving and imaginative, one of his best, and 'The Eye of Allah' a well-told tale of a medieval artist, John of Burgos, and a primitive microscope. Best of all is **The Wish House**, about the compassionate gesture of a Mrs Ashcroft. *Thy Servant a Dog* (1930), a book of three stories concerning two Aberdeen terriers, Boots and Slippers, who relate the adventures, sold in great numbers but the cosy anthropomorphism did his reputation no good. *Limits and Renewals* (1932) contained 14 stories and 19 poems, among them the notable **Dayspring Mishandled**.

Kipling died on 18 January 1936, two days before his friend King George V. His ashes were interred in Poet's Corner in Westminster Abbey, at a ceremony packed with people, including the prime minister, his cousin Stanley Baldwin, generals, and admirals: there was no gathering of writers and intellectuals: it was as though a book was being closed after everyone had stopped reading. Fragments of autobiography were published posthumously as *Something of Myself* (1937).

Kipling's reputation went into eclipse after his death. His particular kind of patriotism had lost him the sympathy of the artistic and literary world some years before he died. Another war was imminent; Kipling's achievement as a writer was rejected along with his politics. In 1941 the

American critic Edmund Wilson reminded the literary world, at least, of Kipling's stature in an essay which later appeared in his *The Wound and the Bow*. The reading public had, as usual, made up its own mind and continued reading him anyway, and one distinguished critic, Bonamy Dobrée, had praised him consistently. Another American, T. S. Eliot, published *A Choice of Kipling's Verse* (1941), prefacing it with an oddly apologetic essay. Eliot, a major poet, was not to be ignored, and his *Choice* sent the reviewers scurrying around for something to say. The best essay came from George Orwell in 1942; he identified the reasons why Kipling irritated so often but pointed out that he had never courted favour. Orwell also drew attention to the remarkable fact that Kipling's verse, like it or not, never leaves the reader's mind completely – his score in a book of quotations is very high. Lionel Trilling's review of Eliot's *Choice*, however, in 1943, seems in retrospect the work of an uncertain critic. It was not until 1948 that C. S. Lewis, in *Kipling's World*, dealt with Kipling's work rather than his private life or his politics. Eliot, by 1957, was writing a new preface for his *Choice*, calling it 'In Praise of Kipling'.

Kipling's verse, in spite of Eliot's opinion, contains works that are difficult to read now. The utterances of the ranker, in barrack room or battle, do not gain from the carefully dropped aspirates and phonetic speech rendering, but must have been a revelation to the reading public of the *fin-de-siècle* period. Much of his verse is memorable and unique. His perceptive skill, in 'Chant-Pagan' for instance, is immediately plain; it speaks volumes about the mind of a soldier trying to settle down after a war. Kipling's stories speak for themselves, now that they are being judged as literature. They are among the best and it should be remembered that Kipling was a reporter; to attribute harshness and cruelty to the author is unjustifiable, for his account shows what the ranker's life was actually like. In *Kim*, his only successful novel, Kipling created an indisputable work of art from the episode of the British in India's history.

*Kipps* See **Wells, H(erbert) G(eorge)**.

**Kit-Cat Club** In the early 18th century a group of writers with Whig sympathies formed a club that met in the house of a pastry-cook, Christopher Katt, in Shire Lane, north of Temple Bar. The name was derived from Katt, whose mutton pies were called kit-cats. The secretary of the club for many years – and its solid centre – was the publisher Jacob Tonson, to whose house in Barn Elms the club eventually moved. Among its members were Sir Samuel Garth the physician, William Congreve, John Vanbrugh, Richard Steele, and Joseph Addison.

**Klein, A(braham) M(oses)** 1909– . A. M. Klein was born in Montreal, of an orthodox Jewish family, and was a barrister from 1933 to 1954. One of the 'Montreal Group', he is highly regarded as a poet in Canadian literary circles. Among his books of verse are *Hath not a Jew* (1940), *The Rocking Chair* (1948), and *The Second Scroll* (1951). Klein's poetry is not as yet well known outside Canada.

**Knickerbocker, Diedrich** See **History of New York, A** by Washington Irving.

**Knickerbocker Group** A group of writers in New York; the name was derived from *Knickerbocker's History of New York* by Washington Irving, who was one of their number. They were represented in **The Knickerbocker Magazine** and, apart from Irving, were most brightly adorned by the presence of William Cullen Bryant and James Kirke Paulding. Joseph Rodman Drake and Fitz-Greene Halleck were also in the group. Edgar Allan Poe criticized the group severely in his *The Literati of New York City*.

*Knickerbocker Magazine, The* A monthly literary magazine that was founded in New York in 1833 by Lewis and Willis Clark. The name was a bow in the direction of Washington Irving, and every American writer of any distinction, including Irving, contributed to it during its heyday: Longfellow, Hawthorne, Parkman, Hoffman, Whittier, Howells, Holmes, and Bryant were all

The cover design of *The Knickerbocker Magazine*, published from 1833 to 1865.

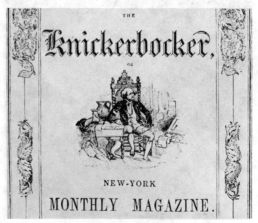

published in the *Knickerbocker*. The magazine continued until 1865.

**Knightley, George** The warm-hearted forthright bachelor of Jane Austen's *Emma*: one of Jane Austen's most attractive leading men. He is well aware of Emma's faults and helps her to an awareness of them. He marries her in the end.

***Knight of the Burning Pestle, The*** A comedy by Francis Beaumont, first produced in 1609 and first published in 1613. The play was once attributed to both Beaumont and Fletcher but has been named as Beaumont's work by E. K. Chambers.

At a performance of *The London Merchant* a grocer and his wife in the audience interrupt the play with a demand that their apprentice, Ralph, shall have a part in it. To fit Ralph's aspirations the play is interspersed with scenes written by the grocer himself and renamed *The Knight of the Burning Pestle*. Ralph becomes a 'grocer errant', with a burning pestle as his device, and has wild adventures that include the defeat of Barbaroso, a villainous barber. His scenes are a burlesque of romantic knight errantry. Interspersed with Ralph's histrionic pretensions is the main plot concerning another apprentice, Jasper, who is in love with Luce, daughter of the merchant who is his master. The merchant favours Humphrey, but Jasper carries off Luce when she is about to be married to his rival. Luce is brought back by her furious parents and locked up, so Jasper feigns death and gets himself taken to the house in a coffin. He appears to the merchant as a ghost and succeeds in gaining his consent for the marriage by frightening him.

Apart from the burlesque of chivalry, in which Ralph has lines of Shakespeare's to misquote, the contemporary theatre is satirized – particularly Heywood for his *The Four Prentises of London*. But the play's real strength is as a comedy of manners of the early 17th century.

***Knight's Tale, The*** See ***Canterbury Tales, The***.

***Knocking at the Gate in Macbeth, On the*** An essay by Thomas De Quincey, first published in *The London Magazine* in October 1823. The author, in the first paragraph, refers to the striking moment in the play (Act II, Scene 2), following the murder of Duncan and Lady Macbeth's 'If he do bleed, I'll gild the faces of the grooms withal, For it must seem their guilt', when the knocking at the south entry announces the arrival of Macduff and Lennox. He proceeds to analyse the effect and how Shakespeare's genius contrived it. De Quincey declared that he found

the answer while considering the deeds of the notorious murderer Williams, in Ratcliffe Highway in 1812. See also ***Murder Considered as One of the Fine Arts, On***.

**Knolles, Richard** *c*.1550–1610. An Elizabethan schoolmaster, Knolles was the author of *The Generall Historie of the Turkes, from the First Beginning of that Nation, Faithfully Collected out of the Best Histories*, first published in 1603. Knolles 'faithfully collected' to such good purpose that he earned the praise of Dr Johnson, Southey, and of Byron, who acknowledged the influence of Richard Knolles upon him.

**Knowles, James Sheridan** 1784–1862. Knowles was a relative of Richard Brinsley Sheridan; after trying various professions (teaching, the army, and medicine) he turned to the theatre and made his debut in his native Dublin at the Crow Street Theatre (1808). He wrote ballads and became a playwright, achieving prominence with *Virginius*, a tragedy written for Edmund Kean. Kean refused it so William Macready took it up and enjoyed a major success at Covent Garden (1820). Knowles' plays have not been revived: scholars regard them, in spite of their varied settings, as exercises in 19th-century domestic drama in black and white. Other successful plays by Knowles were *William Tell* (Drury Lane, 1825), the comedy *The Beggar's Daughter of Bethnal Green* (Drury Lane, 1828), *The Hunchback* (Covent Garden, 1832), *The Wife* (Covent Garden, 1833), and the comedy *The Love-Chase* (Haymarket, 1837).

**Knox, John** 1505–72. Knox was born at Haddington in East Lothian and educated at Glasgow and St Andrews. He took holy orders and practised as an ecclesiastical notary in his native town until about 1544, when he became a private tutor. About this time he came under the influence of George Wishart, the militant Lutheran, and took the Reformation as his cause. He was preacher at St Andrews in 1547, when the castle was captured by the French, and he spent two years in prison in France. He went to England upon his release and in 1551 became chaplain to Edward VI, assisting in the preparation of the Second Prayer Book. He fled from England upon the accession of Mary.

Knox met Calvin in Geneva and was for a short period (1554) pastor to the English congregation at Frankfurt. After his disputes with Richard Cox over matters of worship on Sundays he left Frankfurt and, after another visit to Geneva, was back in Scotland in 1555. He commanded considerable attention as a preacher but Protestants were not tolerated in Scotland during the regency of Mary of Guise and Knox returned to Geneva in 1556 to serve the English Church there. In Geneva he published several tracts, one of which was the deplorable *The First Blast of the Trumpet against the Monstrous Regiment* [rule] *of Women* (1558). He had been busy attacking the Catholics, Mary Tudor, and Mary of Guise; he now earned the detestation of the Protestant Elizabeth I, who had just succeeded to the throne of England. She refused him passage through her realm when he returned to Scotland in 1559.

Knox became the leader of the Reformation in Scotland and published the *Scottish Confession* in 1560 after the death of Mary of Guise. This was the confession of faith of the Reformed Church – and included the death penalty for attending mass. *The First Book of Discipline* was drawn up in the same year and contained a single proposal of lasting value – that for national education. But education required money and the Protestant lords drew their purse strings tight. Knox's *Treatise on Predestination* was published in Geneva in 1560; the idea that only the Elect had a hope of

salvation was the cornerstone of the beliefs of Calvin and Knox.

Mary Stuart ascended the throne of Scotland in 1561 and soon found herself in conflict with the author of the *Regiment of Women*. (It is, perhaps, worth noting that Knox, at 59, took a girl of 15 as his second wife; the 'regiment' of John Knox, husband, is interesting to contemplate.) However, Mary lost the throne in 1567 and the regent, Moray, supported Knox, who gave the sermon at the coronation of the infant James VI. Moray was assassinated in 1570. The last two years of Knox's life saw his political influence decline, but he left Scotland ready for the triumph of Presbyterianism.

Knox's contribution to literature is his *Historie of the Reformatioun of Religioun within the Realms of Scotland* in five books published in 1586. That he was a man of iron determination and a remarkable preacher scarcely needs saying and his *Historie* demonstrates his command of words. It also contains original documents and extracts from the works of others including Foxe. It is vivid history at its best; at its worst it is Knox presenting his own case and the reader may well find himself unable to take much at a time – the most exhausting of sermons does not run to five volumes.

The *Historie* was edited by W. C. Dickinson and published in two volumes in 1949.

John Knox. An engraving made in 1798 from a portrait painted during Knox's lifetime. National Gallery of Scotland, Edinburgh.

**Koestler, Arthur** 1905–83. Arthur Koestler, who was born in Budapest and educated in Vienna, wrote his first books in German. They were translated by various hands until Koestler achieved a grasp of English that enabled him to write the language himself, to the enrichment of the readers of his adopted country. The first step in his remarkable career was his decision to leave the University of Vienna for Palestine and a Zionist settlement. The experience was of brief duration and he returned to Europe to take up journalism; he became foreign editor of the Berlin *B. Z. am Mittag* in 1932. He had joined the Communist Party in 1931 and spent a year in the Soviet Union in 1933; he had to leave Germany when Hitler came to power and he went to Paris. This period of his life is vividly related in the autobiographical volumes *Arrow in the Blue* (1952) and *The Invisible Writing* (1954).

Koestler went to Spain to report the Civil War for French newspapers in 1936 and 1937. He was captured by the fascists and condemned to death; an exchange of prisoners by the International Red Cross saved his life and he wrote about his experiences in Spain in *Menschenopfer unerhört: Schwarzbuch über Spanien*, published in Paris in 1937 and translated in the same year as *Spanish*

*Testament.* In 1940 the German armies advanced on Paris. Koestler was interned as a suspect alien; his opposition to the Nazis was disregarded by those prepared to appease at all costs. He escaped and succeeded in leaving France at Marseilles, and reached England, where he was put into Pentonville Prison to be investigated. *The Scum of the Earth* (1941) is his account of those experiences and the first book he wrote in English.

After his experiences in Spain Koestler abandoned the Communist Party and he wrote a novel about a revolutionary of Roman times, *The Gladiators* (1939). The story of Spartacus was followed by *Darkness at Noon* (1940), one of the most famous books about Russian totalitarianism. Rubashov, one of the old guard of Bolsheviks in the creation of the revolution, is arrested during the purges of 1936. He is completely isolated and can only communicate with other prisoners by tapping out messages in morse code through the walls. In the intervals of various interrogations he reviews his career and his total allegiance to the Party, for which he sacrificed all humanity. Now he has been arrested through a confession extracted by torture from a younger colleague, but for what? Because the end justifies any means and the old guard can endanger the total autocracy of Stalin. So Stalin believes, and Rubashov's last interrogator, Gletkin, a tireless bureaucrat with no personal feelings, whose whole existence is governed by Party jargon, is the servant of the order now in the ascendancy. Rubashov's certainty that he is a victim grows and by degrees his mind moves away from political behaviour and revolutionary ideals. He is examining the dangers of what he has helped to create when he is taken out of his cell one morning and shot in the back of the head, while being marched along an underground corridor.

Koestler's third novel was written in English. *Arrival and Departure* (1943) examines the motives behind the actions of a Communist dealing with a wartime resistance group; a book of essays, *The Yogi and the Commissar* (1945), is a searching examination of the contemporary political scene, with particular attention to the ambitions of Russia and the nature of Communism. *Thieves in the Night* (1946), a novel about the hopes for a Jewish state, made excellent use of his experience of the Zionist experiment of his youth; *Promise and Fulfilment* (1949) is a historical account of the Jews in Palestine from 1917 to 1949. *The Age of Longing* (1951) is a novel set in the immediate future, in a society where the threat of nuclear extermination is ever present.

The work of Arthur Koestler is often mentioned in the same breath as that of George Orwell, who became his friend when he settled in England, and between them the two writers recorded much of the age of disillusion (1920–45). Koestler's immediate experience of events in Europe was of course greater than Orwell's but both men arrived at the same truth and would have none of the sentimental nonsense with which the Western Left surrounded its ideals. Koestler's autobiographical books and *Darkness at Noon* present a very clear picture of Europe in the 1930s and 1940s. Among other books by him are *The Sleepwalkers: A History of Man's Changing Vision of the Universe* (1959) and *The Act of Creation* (1964), in which he examines the parallels between artistic creation and advances in science.

***Kubla Khan:*** *or, A Vision in a Dream.* A poem by Samuel Taylor Coleridge, first published in 1816. In the preface Coleridge described how he came to write the poem and why it was never completed. 'In the summer of the year 1797, the author then in ill health, retired to a lonely farmhouse between Porlock and Lynton ... In consequence of a slight indisposition, an anodyne had been prescribed' (probably laudanum) 'from the effects of which he fell asleep in his chair at the moment he was reading the following sentence,

Arthur Koestler, 1959.

or words of the same substance, in Purchas's Pilgrimage: "Here the Khan Kubla commanded a palace to be built, and a stately garden thereunto. And thus ten miles of fertile ground were enclosed with a wall." The author continued for about three hours in a profound sleep ... ' Coleridge goes on to say that he composed two to three hundred lines in his sleep, and upon waking hastened to write them down. 'At this moment he was unfortunately called out by a person on business from Porlock, and detained by him above an hour.' Upon returning to his room Coleridge found that the remainder of the poem had passed from his memory, and the present 54 lines are all we have, but it is a remarkable fragment.

**Kulhwch and Olwen**   A Welsh prose romance found, in the earliest form, in *The White Book of Rhydderch*, a manuscript of the early 14th century. The story itself dates from about the 10th century; the material and the characters are even older. The story was included in her *The Mabinogion* (1838–49) by Lady Charlotte Guest, from the later manuscript known as *The Red Book of Hergest*.

Kulhwch (pronounced Keelhook) is Arthur's cousin and is doomed to remain unmarried unless he can secure the hand of Olwen, daughter of the giants' chieftain, Yspadadden. Kulhwch goes to Arthur for help and is given the assistance of Gwalchmei, Kai, and Bedwyr (Gawain, Kay, and Bedivere). The four attend on Yspadadden, who names 13 treasures as the price of Olwen's hand. Gaining the treasures involves the heroes in perilous quests which are successfully carried out. A feature of the romance is the appearance of Arthur and his court, the members of which are described with humorous comments on their characters. Some of them are also found in the dialogue between Arthur and Glewlwyd in *The Black Book of Carmarthen*, thus emphasizing the Welsh origin of the legends of Arthur.

The text of *Kulhwch and Olwen* is to be found in *The Mabinogion*, edited by Thomas and Gwyn Jones (Everyman's Library), and by Jeffrey Gantz (Penguin Classics, 1976).

**Kyd, Thomas** 1558–94.   The son of a scrivener, Kyd was born in London and educated at the Merchant Taylors' School at the same time as Edmund Spenser and under the same teacher, Richard Mulcaster. Later he practised as a scrivener before becoming a successful playwright. Not much is known about his life apart from his intimacy with Marlowe and his part – not altogether creditable – in the circumstances that led to his friend's murder. He seems to have been the target of Nashe in his preface to Greene's *Menaphon*; a sour reference from a 'university wit' to the other's lack of classical learning. Kyd had no need of Latin to score a major success with **The Spanish Tragedy**; Nashe was probably jealous.

A translation of Robert Garnier's *Cornélie* as *Pompey the Great, His Fair Corneliaes Tragedie* (1594) is the only other play that can definitely be accepted as Kyd's work, although it has been suggested that he was the author of a *Hamlet* and of an earlier version of *The Taming of the Shrew*. These suggestions arise from scholarly exercises and have no factual support; the *Hamlet* is offered as the basis for Shakespeare's revenge drama but Shakespeare need only to have looked at *The Spanish Tragedy*, which was the first play of that kind to achieve lasting success. The positive identification of Kyd as the author of *The Spanish Tragedy* rests entirely on a reference to him made by Thomas Heywood; none of the published versions carry his name. It was a favourite that lasted long enough with audiences to have been seen by Samuel Pepys in 1668.

**Kynaston, Sir Francis** 1587–1642.   Kynaston was the author of a romance in verse, *Leoline and Sydanis*, and the translator into Latin of Chaucer's *Troilus and Criseyde*. He opened an academy for young gentlemen and the sons of noblemen, the Museum Minervae, where they could learn the basics of science, languages, and courtly accomplishments.

**Kyng Alisaunder**   A Middle English verse romance of the 13th century. (See **metrical romances**.) The career of Alexander the Great is related in terms of a legendary hero of the Middle Ages: he is an invincible knight, in fact, and marvels and magic are encountered from the moment of his birth. *Kyng Alisaunder* was edited by G. V. Smithers for the Early English Text Society (1952–57).

# L

**Ladislaw, Will**   In George Eliot's *Middlemarch*, the young cousin of Edward Casaubon who has no patience with the latter's pretensions to scholarship. He also grows to love his cousin's wife, Dorothea – a development that brings out the worst in Casaubon.

**Lady Anna** A novel by Anthony Trollope, first published in the *Fortnightly Review* (April 1873 to April 1874). This is a short, straightforward, and altogether successful story, in which the spirited Lady Anna, daughter of an earl and an heiress, is successfully wooed and won by a hard-working tailor of Cumberland who earns 35 shillings (£1.75p) a week. Lady Anna resists her mother, the countess, and all her artistic and aristocratic friends, and marries her Daniel. Interestingly, Daniel Thwaite is a jobbing tailor, no more; there is no poet hidden beneath his working clothes. But he is dignified and honest and Anna responds to him. They marry in spite of everyone's opinions and depart for Australia.

**Lady Audley's Secret** A celebrated Victorian thriller, first published in serial form in *The Six-penny Magazine*, and in volume form in 1862. See **Braddon, Mary Elizabeth.**

**Lady Chatterley's Lover** A novel by D. H. Lawrence, first published in 1928. In this, his last novel, Lawrence returns to the English Midlands for a setting.

Connie Reid, an artist's daughter, has enjoyed a bohemian upbringing and healthy sex. She marries Sir Clifford Chatterley, a wealthy mine-owner, who returns from World War I severely wounded. He is paralysed from the waist down and sexually impotent. At the family seat, Sir Clifford lives an enclosed life and writes magazine stories; Connie helps him all she can though her father offers a low opinion of Sir Clifford's efforts. Observing his wife's restlesssness, Sir Clifford discusses with her the possibility of her bearing a child by another man to provide the estate with an heir and give her an outlet for her energies. When he gives up his writing and concentrates on managing his mines he becomes fascinated by business and technology and Connie feels completely stranded.

After a short and unsatisfactory affair with a young Irish playwright she becomes increasingly attracted to her husband's gamekeeper, Mellors, a man who had risen from the ranks to become an officer. He is separated from his wife: apparently the relationship failed in sexual matters. Sir Clifford objects to Mellors because of his lowly origins; the child he had suggested to Connie is now on the way but because of the father Sir Clifford refuses his wife a divorce. Connie and Mellors then go away together to make their own lives, while Sir Clifford becomes emotionally dependent on his nurse, a woman from the village.

Mellors says to Connie, at the end of the book: 'Sex is really only touch, the closest of all touch. And its touch we're afraid of. We're only half-conscious, and half-alive. We've got to come alive and aware. Especially the English have got to get into touch with one another, a bit delicate and a bit tender. It's our crying need.' How well the novel succeeds as an exposition of this tenet is arguable – and intensively argued over, and the notoriety of *Lady Chatterley's Lover* has almost blotted out recognition of its other qualities, which are undeniable. Industrial and social conditions in England after World War I, and the indefensible class structure, are examined with passionate concern, and it would be hard to find a more vivid picture of a mining town than Lawrence's description of Tevershall.

**Lady of Shalott, The** A poem by Alfred Tennyson, first published in 1832 and revised for the 1842 *Poems*. The theme was suggested by an Italian story, *Donna di Scalotta*, in *Cento Novelle Antiche* of the 14th century. Tennyson's ballad tells of a lady who lives in a castle on an island in the river which flows down to Camelot. The island is Shalott where, before a mirror which reflects the world, the lady weaves and sometimes sings. She is under a curse and never looks directly on the real world, which she weaves into her magic web. But she tires of this

Lancelot and the Lady of Shalott. An illustration by Dante Gabriel Rossetti for the Moxon *Tennyson*, published in 1857. Other illustrations were contributed by Millais and Holman Hunt.

– 'I am half sick of shadows' – and one day the sight of Sir Lancelot, proceeding to Camelot, provokes her to leave her loom and look down on Camelot. The mirror cracks and the curse takes effect. She knows she will die and writes her name on the prow of a boat which she finds by the island. She lies down in the boat and sings her death song as it carries her down to Camelot. The townspeople and the knights and ladies gather around her boat, wondering and fearful. Sir Lancelot muses on her beauty and commends her to God's grace.

The origin of the lady in the Italian story was in fact Elaine, the Maid of Astolat who loved Lancelot in vain in Malory's *Le Morte Darthur*, which Tennyson had not read when he composed his ballad. Elaine appears in *The Idylls of the King* in 'Lancelot and Elaine'.

***Lady of the Fountain, The***  A Welsh tale which appears in the manuscripts of *The White Book of Rhydderch* (early 14th century) and *The Red Book of Hergest* (late 14th century) and was translated by Lady Charlotte Guest in her *The Mabinogion*. The story of Owein (Uwaine) and the Lady of the Fountain arises from one told by Kynon at Arthur's court at Caer Llion (Caerleon). Kei (Kay), Gwalchmei (Gawain), and Gwenhwyvar (Guinevere) appear in the story and hear Kynon's tale of his adventure in a distant country at a mysterious fountain, and his encounter with a black rider. Owein sets out to find the fountain; he succeeds and defeats the black rider at the gate of a fortress. But the men of the fortress come to kill him: he is saved by a girl who gives him a ring to protect him with invisibility and takes him to a high chamber. On the next day he sees the funeral of the black rider and falls in love with his widow, who is called the Lady of the Fountain. The girl, Luned, agrees to help him woo her. The fountain is the key to the realm and the Lady will need a new champion to defend it. Luned then presents Owein, and the Lady knows that this is the knight who killed her husband. But she marries him as a brave champion and Owein becomes guardian of the fountain. Three years pass; Arthur and his knights come searching for Owein. At the fountain Kei challenges the black rider and is unhorsed; Gwalchmei tries next and is recognized by the black rider. Owein is his cousin and each would surrender to the other. But Arthur intervenes and accepts surrender for both, then persuades the Lady to allow Owein to return to Britain for three months. But he stays for three years, until a messenger arrives and tears the wedding ring from his finger, cursing him as faithless. Owein leaves Arthur's court and wanders through the world as an outcast, encountering many adventures (involving a lion, the girl Luned, and sundry villains) before returning to Arthur with the Lady of the Fountain. The adventures are confused and inconclusive, conveying a strong impression of imperfectly remembered stories from an ancient past.

***Lady of the Lake, The***  A romantic poem in the familiar six cantos that Scott had used for his first two poems, *The Lay of the Last Minstrel* and *Marmion*. It was first published in 1810. The lake is Loch Katrine and the lady is Ellen, daughter of the outlawed James of Douglas. The period is the early 16th century.

Roderick Dhu, the Highland chief, gives hospitality to James Fitz-James, a knight, in his home on Loch Katrine. Roderick and Malcolm are rivals for the hand of Ellen; she loves Malcolm. Threatened by the royal armies, Roderick summons his clans but Douglas, believing himself the cause for the royal army's approach, decides to go to Stirling where he will surrender himself to the king. Fitz-James returns and offers to give refuge to Ellen, and she declines – telling him she loves Malcolm. Fitz-James honours her, and before he withdraws gives her a ring which will secure the king's favour if she needs it. Fitz-James sets out for Stirling and meets Roderick on the road. They quarrel: Roderick is worsted in the ensuing fight and taken to Stirling as Fitz-James's prisoner. Ellen then arrives in Stirling to plead for her father, using the ring to gain audience. The king proves to be Fitz-James, the mysterious knight, and he pardons Douglas. Roderick dies of his wounds and Ellen marries her Malcolm.

This is the best of Scott's romantic poems. The story succeeds in keeping our interest, the characters are clearly delineated, and the poetic description of the Highlands is exquisite. Also memorable are Ellen's song, 'Rest, warrior, rest', and the beautiful funeral song, 'He is gone on the mountain'.

**Lady of the Lake, The**  Variously called Nimue, Nimiane, Vivien, and Vivienne, the Lady of the Lake is a strange, insubstantial figure, generally beneficent and a sort of guardian goddess who protects King Arthur in the stories surrounding him. In *Le Morte Darthur* the Lady of the Lake enters the story when she presents Arthur with his sword Excalibur, after Merlin takes him to the lakeside. Later she sends a damsel to Arthur's court; she is wearing a sword which is to go to the knight who draws it from the scabbard. This proves to be Balin. Then the Lady of the Lake comes to the court and demands payment from Arthur for his sword Excalibur: the price is Balin's head or the head of the damsel who brought Balin his sword. Balin kills her and then reveals that she is the sorceress who destroyed his family.

But Nimue, later in the story, is also called the Lady of the Lake. Merlin becomes besotted with her and to get rid of him she uses one of his own spells to imprison him under or inside a great stone.

In the French *Lancelot* it is the Lady of the Lake (Vivienne) who succours the infant Lancelot when his father is killed – hence his name, Launcelot of the Lake.

**Laertes** The son of Polonius in Shakespeare's *Hamlet*. He returns to Denmark when he hears of his father's murder and finds his sister, Ophelia, out of her mind. He plans revenge on Hamlet and Claudius is his willing prompter but he dies from the poisoned weapon intended for Hamlet.

**Lalla Rookh:** *an Oriental Romance.* Four narrative poems, with a connecting tale in prose, by Thomas Moore, first published in 1817. The romance enjoyed enormous popularity during the poet's lifetime and for most of the 19th century.

Lalla Rookh is the daughter of the Emperor Aurungzebe and is to be married to the King of Bucharia. Her journey to Cashmere from Delhi is enlivened by the stories told by Feramorz, a young poet from Cashmere, who joins her retinue. Also present is the self-important chamberlain Fadladeen, who vents his annoyance at mishaps on the journey by criticizing Feramorz's poetry. The four tales are as follows:

*The Veiled Prophet of Khorassan.* The beautiful Zelica mourns her lover Azim, believed to have died in battle. The impostor, Mokanna, poses as a prophet and, by promising Zelica admission to paradise, lures her into his house. Azim returns from the wars and finds Zelica married to Mokanna. The caliph raises a force to punish Mokanna as a blasphemer and Azim joins him. Mokanna is defeated, and kills himself, and Zelica looks for death also; she puts on the false prophet's veil. Azim, believing her to be Mokanna, kills her.

*Paradise and the Peri.* A peri was, according to Persian mythology, a beautiful but malevolent sprite. In later Islamic tradition peris are gentle spirits, the children of fallen angels who waft the pure in spirit to the gates of paradise. In Moore's poem the peri laments her exclusion from heaven, and is promised admission if she will bring the gift most dear to the Almighty to heaven's gates. She brings the blood of a young warrior who dies to free India from the tyranny

The Veiled Prophet of Khorassan. Engraving from a drawing by Richard Westall for Thomas Moore's *Lalla Rookh*, 1817.

of Mahmoud of Gazna: the gates remain closed. She brings the last sigh of an Egyptian girl who dies of grief when her lover succumbs to the plague: the gates remain closed. She brings the tear of a repentant criminal, wrung from him by the prayers of his child, and heaven's gates are opened to her.

*The Fire-Worshippers.* The Ghebers were the fire-worshippers of the ancient Persian religion, who resisted the advance of Islam. A young Gheber, Hafed, falls in love with Hinda, daughter of the emir Al Hassan of Arabia, who has come to crush the Ghebers. Hafed scales the eminence where Hinda has her bower and she falls in love with him, though she discovers his true identity when the Ghebers capture her. Al Hassan's army defeats the Ghebers and rescues his daughter from them, whereupon Hafed throws himself on a funeral pyre. Hinda drowns herself on the way back to her father's headquarters.

*The Light of the Haram.* Selim is the son of the emperor Akbar and his beloved wife is Nourmahal; they quarrel during the Feast of Roses in the Vale of Cashmere. Nourmahal is determined to win back her husband's love, and learns a magic song from the enchantress Namouna. At a banquet given by Selim she enters masked, and sings the magic song, thereby regaining her husband's love.

As Lalla Rookh's journey to Cashmere proceeds, she falls in love with the young poet. When she arrives at her destination she is delighted, and the chamberlain discomfited, to discover that the supposed poet is none other than her prospective husband, the King of Bucharia.

**Lamb, Charles** 1775–1834. Charles Lamb was the youngest surviving child of John and Elizabeth Lamb (four of their seven children died in infancy). John Lamb was a clerk to Samuel Salt, a lawyer, and general factotum in his house in the Inner Temple, where Charles Lamb was born and where he lived for 17 years. He went to school in Fetter Lane and later, through the influence of Samuel Salt, entered Christ's Hospital, where he became friends with another pupil – Coleridge. With his sister Mary (ten years his senior) he spent many holidays with his maternal grandmother, Mrs Field, who was housekeeper of Blakesware, a large country house at Widford in Hertfordshire. The owners were away when the children came to stay and the empty mansion with its extensive grounds was a paradise evoked to wonderful effect in his writings. Hertfordshire, the New River, and the River Lea had a permanent place in his affections.

Lamb left Christ's Hospital in 1789 and went to work for the East India Company three years later. He stayed in the same employment for 33 years; but the Lambs left the Inner Temple in 1792 and went to live in Holborn. Charles Lamb was encouraged to write by his friend Coleridge and Lamb's first sonnet was actually published in *The Morning Chronicle* over the initials S. T. C. on 29 December 1794. In the following year Lamb suffered a period of mental unbalance and was confined in the asylum at Hoxton for six

Christ's Hospital in 1784. Charles Lamb and Samuel Taylor Coleridge were schoolfellows there. Christ's Hospital, London.

weeks. He recovered and was never afflicted again, but there was mental instability in the family.

In 1796 Coleridge published *Poems on Various Subjects*, which included four sonnets by Lamb; in the same year tragedy struck. Mary Lamb, upon whom the care of the ill and helpless Mrs Lamb fell most heavily, killed her mother in a sudden fit of madness on 22 September. She was taken to a private asylum at Islington and Charles and his father moved to nearby Pentonville. Lamb found a safe lodging for his sister at Hackney when she was released from the asylum and spent all his weekends and holidays with her until 1799, when his father died. Charles became Mary's guardian, accepting total responsibility for her, and in 1800 was able to live in London again, in Chancery Lane. But he was never to stay in any place for very long; his sister's mental condition worsened without warning at intervals during the rest of his life. But apart from these intervals, Mary was mostly happy and active, shielded by her brother's selfless care. She survived him by 13 years; but without his presence her sanity, unhappily, did not.

Lamb's early published work consisted of *A Tale of Rosamund Gray and Old Blind Margaret* (1798) and occasional poems that appeared in books of verse by Charles Lloyd and Coleridge. One of Lamb's most famous poems, 'The old familiar faces', appeared in *Blank Verse* (1798) by Charles Lloyd and Charles Lamb. Lloyd, a friend and disciple of Coleridge, was a member of a Birmingham Quaker family. He and Lamb became friends but he was the wrong companion for a man whose mental resources were stretched to the limit. Lloyd was abnormally sensitive and jealous of the friendship between Lamb and Coleridge; he succeeded in causing a breach between them that was, fortunately, healed later but nevertheless harmed the friendship. In 1802 Lamb published his tragedy *John Woodvil*, of interest chiefly because it demonstrates the author's profound interest in Elizabethan and Jacobean playwrights. He had, meanwhile, made new friends; on a visit to Charles Lloyd at Cambridge he met Thomas Manning, a mathematician at Caius College, and George Dyer, an eccentric and delightfully simple man who was at Emmanuel College and later wrote some amiable verse. Manning was interested in everything and a man of inexhaustible good humour. These friends were only the first of a growing circle, for Lamb had a great capacity for friendship.

He was now contributing in a desultory way to newspapers: *The Albion*, *The Morning Chronicle*, and *The Morning Post* all published his work.

Charles Lamb. A detail from the portrait by William Hazlitt, 1804. National Portrait Gallery, London.

With these exercises and through a growing correspondence he practised the writer's craft, putting to use the love of literature that had begun in the chambers of Samuel Salt in the Inner Temple when he was a boy. In 1806, when Mary had recovered from a lapse, Lamb sent a farce called *Mr H.* for consideration by London theatre managers. It was produced at Drury Lane in 1807 but was not a success; even Lamb's admirers regard it as nonsensical. Manning left on a voyage for China but by now Lamb's circle included William and Dorothy Wordsworth, William Hazlitt, and William Godwin, who gave Lamb the idea for **Tales from Shakespeare**; this work gave Mary Lamb many happy hours of rewarding activity and proved for the first time that the master had a powerful appeal for the young. The book was published in January 1807 and has become a classic. Charles Lamb wrote *The Adventures of Ulysses* (1808) with a similar purpose, using Chapman's Homer for the story; though well done it never achieved the lasting success of *Tales from Shakespeare*. Charles and Mary published *Mrs Leicester's School* and *Poetry for Children* (1809) and Charles published *Prince Dorus* (1811), a fairytale in verse. After that he wrote no more for children and Mary's work,

too, came to an end. Charles had by then achieved something more ambitious.

*Specimens of English Dramatic Poets, who Lived About the Time of Shakespeare* (1808) ranges from Norton's and Sackville's *Gorboduc* to the plays of James Shirley, using Shakespeare as the implied standard of excellence by which they are judged. Lamb succeeded in restoring the work of a large group of forgotten playwrights, by careful selections from their plays and accompanying notes of remarkable quality. His life, meanwhile, suffered no little strain; his only regular income was the wages paid by the East India Company, where he laboured as a clerk day by day. Mary was his complete responsibility, which must have exhausted him. He began to write for journals in 1810: for Leigh Hunt's *The Reflector* and *The Examiner*, for *The Quarterly Review* (where the insufferable Gifford mangled his review of Wordsworth's *The Excursion*), and for *The Gentleman's Magazine. Confessions of a Drunkard* was published in *The Philanthropist* (1813) and reprinted in *The London Magazine* (1822). Lamb enjoyed his glass and his pipe and now turned his wit to give an account of this liking taken too far: he was justifiably annoyed when *The Quarterly Review* (Gifford again?) assumed the essay to be 'a genuine description of the state of the writer'. In 1817, when the Lambs were living in Russell Street, Covent Garden, Charles fell in love with the actress Fanny Kelly. He proposed to her in 1819; Miss Kelly refused him with graceful respect, and the possibility of marriage seems to have receded permanently.

*The Works of Charles Lamb* (1818), published by the Ollier brothers (Charles and James), included the two plays, *Rosamund Gray*, poems and sonnets, and essays carefully selected by the author. In 1820 Lamb contributed to *The London Magazine* an essay, *Recollections of the South-Sea House*. He had worked there briefly as his first job, before the lifetime's labour with the East India Company began. His brother John still worked for the South Sea Company and Charles, to spare him embarrassment, signed the essay 'Elia', the name of an Italian clerk who had also worked there. (John Lamb, however, died in October 1821.) Such essays were a popular feature of *The London Magazine* from August 1820 to December 1823 and in them Lamb, an experienced writer, found his true style. The first collection, *Elia: Essays which have appeared under that Signature in The London Magazine* (1823), contains the largest selection; the second, *The Last Essays of Elia* (1833), contains the remainder (see **Elia, The Essays of**).

By 1825 Lamb, now 50 years old, was very

tired: he secured his retirement from the East India Company with a decent pension that was arranged to provide for Mary in the event of his death. He had lost interest in his journalism, which now consisted chiefly of contributions to *The London Magazine* and *The New Monthly Magazine*. The Lambs adopted Emma, the orphan daughter of Charles Isola, a Cambridge friend, and spent summers in Enfield in Middlesex, not far from the River Lea and their much-loved Hertfordshire. Mary had a serious lapse in 1829 and Charles was obliged to surrender her to professional care for a while, something that always depressed him. The Lambs moved to Enfield in 1829 as soon as Mary recovered, and Emma married Gerald Moxon, the publisher, in 1830. In 1833 the Lambs moved, for the last time, to Edmonton. Moxon published *The Last Essays of Elia* in that year; it contained the remaining essays published in *The London Magazine* and a number that Lamb had written since then. In July 1834 Coleridge died and the loss was severe. In December Lamb sustained a fall while out walking and cut his face; he became infected with erysipelas and died on 27 July. Mary, who survived him by 13 years, lies buried in the same grave at Edmonton.

Lamb was a small man with a stammer; his gentle and engaging personality attracted Coleridge while they were still schoolmates. He was in fact a very much tougher spirit than Coleridge and shirked nothing in a life of gruelling responsibility. His essays, the best part of his work, reach a quality in prose writing remarkable even in an age that produced Hazlitt and Thomas De Quincey. Because of the subjects he chose, his writing now has less appeal; what appears charmingly whimsical in one age can seem merely cute in another, and Lamb's range is limited. With so much personal responsibility he could not muster much interest in the important questions of his time, and past pleasures and happiness form a large part of his matter. The lasting charm of his best essays lies in the style, the play of fancy, the gently ironic humour, and the warmth of his attitude towards his fellow men. His letters are almost as good and valuable for what they tell us of the lives of his friends.

The standard editions of Charles Lamb's works are those by E. V. Lucas but Lamb published so many pieces that work on a complete collection remains to be done. Lucas's six-volume edition of *Works* was published in a revised edition (1912). His edition of the *Letters* includes those of Mary Lamb (1935). A complete *Works* in two volumes was edited by T. Hutchinson (Oxford Standard Authors, 1908) and recommended selections are by A. C. Ward (1933), J. M. Brown (New York, 1949), J. E. Morpurgo (Pelican Books, 1949), and J. L. May (1953).

**Lament for the Makaris, The** A poem by William Dunbar, of uncertain date, written 'quhen he was seik' (when he was ill). 'Makaris' were 'makers' of poetry, and in this lament Dunbar pays tribute to his fellow poets, predecessors and contemporaries, and comments on the passing of man's endeavours. It is highly regarded by some critics for its discipline and restraint; but for others its principal value lies in the information it provides – sometimes the only information we possess – about Dunbar's contemporaries.

**Lamia** A poem by John Keats, written during 1819 and first published in 1820. The subject of the poem came from Burton's *The Anatomy of Melancholy*; Burton had found it in the *De Vita Apollonii* of Philostratus. It is written in rhyming couplets and, like *The Eve of St Agnes* and *Isabella* (which were published in the same volume), tells a story of love. In the Middle Ages *lamiae* were simply witches; in Greek mythology Lamia was the Libyan queen loved by Zeus. When her children are destroyed by the jealous Hera, Lamia, insane with grief, starts devouring the children of others. She joins the Empusae, children of Hecate, who in the guise of beautiful maidens lie with men and suck their blood while they sleep. In Keats's poem Lamia is transformed into a beautiful maiden by Hermes. She loves a young man of Corinth, Lycius, and he is captivated by her. He takes her to his house and summons his friends to a bridal feast. One of these is the old and wise Apollonius, who sees through Lamia's guise. She vanishes with a frightful scream; Lycius dies at the same moment.

**Lamming, George (Eric)** 1927– . Lamming was born and educated in a village in Barbados. He went to Trinidad when he was 19 and became a teacher, working there and in Venezuela. Lamming wrote in his spare time and some poems were published in magazines. In 1950 he went to England and earned his living as a factory labourer while working on his first book, *In the Castle of My Skin* (1953), which observes the end of colonialism and is based on his youth in Barbados. Through this and further semi-autobiographical novels the author examines the growing awareness of their identity by West Indian writers and intellectuals in the years following World War II, and the efforts to escape from an intellectually barren environment. His second novel was *The Emigrants* (1954), telling of the West Indies in England, their values displaced and their lives without focus in an alien climate; *Of Age and Innocence* (1958) and *Season of Adventure* (1960) followed. Lamming has published a volume of autobiography, *The Pleasures of Exile* (1960), and two further novels, *Water with Berries* (1971) and *Natives of My Person* (1972). *Water with Berries* uses motives from Shakespeare's *The Tempest*, but in Lamming's novel the power inherent in Caliban (Derek) is not successfully contained. George Lamming's short stories have not so far been published in a collected volume.

**Lamplighter, The**  A story by Charles Dickens about a crazy old astrologer searching for the Philosopher's Stone. It was first published in 1841.

**Lampman, Archibald** 1861–99. Lampman was the descendant of a Dutch family, who had left Pennsylvania during the American War of Independence and settled near Lake Rice in Ontario. His father was an Anglican clergyman and Lampman was born at Morpeth. He completed his education at Trinity College, Toronto, graduating in 1882. He taught for a time, unsuccessfully, and then went to work in the Post Office Department in Ottawa. He died of a heart condition at the age of 38. Though Lampman published only two small collections of verse during his lifetime, and his work is based on European models, he has a fair claim to be called the first Canadian poet of real stature. *Among the Millet* (1888) and *Lyrics of Earth* (1896) reflect his love of natural themes and the setting is Canadian. A broadening of interest is seen in *At the Long Sault*, the hitherto unpublished poems collected and edited by Lampman's friend, Duncan Campbell Scott (1943).

**Lancashire Witches, The**  See **Ainsworth, William Harrison**.

**Lancelot and Elaine**  See *Idylls of the King, The*.

**Land, The**  See **Sackville-West, V(ictoria Mary)**.

**Land of Heart's Desire, The**  See **Yeats, William Butler**.

**Landon, Letitia Elizabeth** 1802–38. Poet and novelist, who always wrote under her initials L.E.L. Her poems first appeared in 1821 and she continued to write verse until her early death at the age of 36. She was famous enough in her day to call for comment from Rossetti and Disraeli, and collected editions of her works were published in 1850 and 1873. She married George Maclean, governor of Cape Coast Castle in West Africa in 1838, and died there in the same year, from accidental poisoning. Her most successful novel was *Ethel Churchill* (1837).

**Landor, Walter Savage** 1775–1864. Landor came from a landed family of Warwickshire and was born at Ipsley Court; his father was a doctor. Landor was educated at Rugby School and Trinity College, Oxford, from where he was sent down in 1794 on account of his radicalism and his bad temper. He published his first book of *Poems* in the following year but suppressed the collection soon after. In the early 18th-century style, it was completely different from his next work, the exotic poem *Gebir*, in seven books on a half-Arabian, half-faery theme. Southey liked it but later Lamb called it gibberish, though he quoted from it in his own work. Landor published a Latin version, *Gebirus Poema*, in 1803.

Landor lived in the west of England and in Wales and served briefly as a volunteer in Spain. In 1808 he bought Llanthony Abbey in Monmouthshire; in 1811 he married Julia Thuillier. *Count Julian* (1812), a poetic tragedy with some fine passages of blank verse but little dramatic quality, was, Landor declared, never 'offered to the stage'. In 1814 his temper, eccentricity, and unacceptable behaviour led to a quarrel that forced him to leave Monmouthshire and he went to live abroad, chiefly in Florence, for the next 17 years. In 1824 he published the first series of ***Imaginary Conversations of Literary Men and Statesmen***, and four volumes were completed by 1829. It is the work by which he is best remembered. A trilogy of poetic tragedies began with *Andrea of Hungary* and *Giovanna of Naples* (1839) and was completed by *Fra Rupert* (1840). By this time Landor had quarrelled with his wife (1835) and left her in Italy. He lived in Bath until 1858, when he was obliged to leave England again after a libel action.

Landor's considerable output in verse is not well known beyond the handful of lyrics that appear in anthologies ('Lately our poets loiter'd in green lanes', 'Dying speech of an old Philosopher', 'Mother I cannot mind my wheel', 'Rose Aylmer', and 'To Ianthe') and he never found a satisfactory style. He was caught between two centuries and never quite succeeded in moving on as did his major contemporaries (*Gebir* was published in the same year as the *Lyrical Ballads* of Wordsworth and Coleridge). Other volumes of verse are *The Hellenics* (1847), the earlier *Poems from the Arabic and Persian*

(1800), and *Simonidea* (1806). *Idyllia Nova* (1815) and *Idyllia Heroica* (1820) are books of Latin verse.

Landor's output of prose is also considerable and valued more highly than his verse, though even the celebrated *Imaginary Conversations* is no longer a standard 'classic': there has been no new edition since that of R. H. Boothroyd (1936). Among his other prose works are *Imaginary Conversations of Greeks and Romans* (1853), *The Citation and Examination of William Shakespeare before The Worshipful Sir Thomas Lucy . . . touching deer stealing* (1834), *Pericles and Aspasia* (1836), and *Savonarola e il Priore di San Marco* (Italian, 1860). Landor wrote in Latin and Italian as easily as he wrote in English and a list of his complete works contains numerous titles in those languages. In Italy Landor became a close friend of Elizabeth Barrett (his poems to her were first printed in 1917) and of Robert Browning, who greatly admired him.

*The Complete Works: Prose* of Landor was edited by T. E. Welby (12 volumes, 1927–31). *The Complete Works: Poetry* was edited by S. Wheeler (four volumes, 1933–36).

**Lane, Edward William** 1801–76. Lane was born at Hereford and educated at Bath and at Hereford Grammar Schools. His great work was his *Arabic Lexicon*, which he compiled from original Arabic sources and published in five parts (1863–74). The work was continued after his death by S. Lane Poole. Lane also translated *The Arabian Nights* (1838–40) and *Selections from the Kur-ān* (1843).

**Lang, Andrew** 1844–1912. The son of the county sheriff-clerk of Selkirk, Lang attended the high school there and went on to Edinburgh Academy, the universities of St Andrews and Glasgow, and Balliol College, Oxford. He became a fellow of Merton College and settled in London in 1875. He earned his living as a journalist and a man of letters, and earned respect in various fields without achieving lasting distinction in any. He first appeared in print as a poet before leaving Oxford, with *Ballads and Lyrics of Old France* (1872). Further poetry appeared in *Ballades in Blue China* (1880 and 1881), *Helen of Troy*, a narrative poem in six books (1882), *Rhyme à la Mode* (1885), *Grass of Parnassus* (1888), *Ban and Arrière Ban* (1894), and *New Collected Rhymes* (1905). Lang liked using the old French forms, such as the rondeau, triolet, virelai, and ballade.

Lang's best work was done in the field of anthropology, which he approached through literature. As a Greek scholar he worked mostly on Homer, with a prose translation of Theocritus, Bion, and Moschus as an additional essay in 1880. As a historian he was chiefly concerned with events in Scotland but also produced a book on Joan of Arc, *The Maid of France* (1908). There was almost no literary form in which he did not engage: essays, reviews, literary controversy, plays, stories, bibliography, collections of fairy tales and fiction all form part of his collected works. Among his more notable publications in addition to those already mentioned were *The Odyssey of Homer done into English Prose* (with S. H. Butcher, 1879), *The Iliad of Homer done into English Prose* (with Walter Leaf and Ernest Myers, 1883), *Custom and Myth* (1884), *The Politics of Aristotle: Introductory Essays* (1886), *Books and Bookmen* (1886), *Myth, Ritual and Religion* (1887), *The World's Desire* (with H. Rider Haggard, 1890), *Homer and the Epic* (1893), *The Making of Religion* (1898), *The Homeric Hymns: A New Prose Translation* (1899), *A History of Scotland from the Roman Occupation* (1900), *The World of Homer* (1910), and *A History of English Literature from Beowulf to Swinburne* (1912).

Lang was the author of a number of notable and very readable historical monographs, among them *Prince Charles Edward* (1900), *The Mystery of Mary Stuart* (1901), *James VI and the Gowrie Conspiracy* (1902), and *John Knox and the Reformation* (1905). He published his first volume of retold fairy and folk tales in 1889 as *The Blue Fairy Book*. Eleven more volumes, known by the colours of the titles, followed and enjoyed great popularity. The last appeared in 1910 as *The Lilac Fairy Book*.

**Langland** (*or* **Langley**), **William** *c*.1331–*c*. 1399. Very little is known about the life of the man believed to be the author of **The Vision of William concerning Piers the Plowman**. Scraps of information elicited from the manuscripts of the poem have led to the assumption that he was born around 1331 at Cleobury Mortimer, about 30 miles from Shrewsbury. He was the son, possibly illegitimate, of Stacy de Rockayle (*or* Rokesle) of Shipton-under-Wychwood in Oxfordshire. His education was at the Benedictine school at Malvern, which prepared him for the church. He took minor orders but his marriage barred him from advancement. Some time before 1362 he went to London, where he earned a meagre living as a copyist and psalm singer. He began the composition of *Piers the Plowman* in 1362 and the expansion and revision of the poem occupied him until his death.

There was controversy in the early years of this century about the true authorship of *Piers the*

*Plowman*, as to whether it was the work of one author or, according to one theory, of five separate writers (see also **Piers the Plowman, The Vision of William concerning**).

The positive attribution of other work to Langland has not so far proved possible. Skeat, the distinguished editor of *Piers*, asserted that the fragment of another poem, *Richard the Redeless*, was to be found in the Cambridge manuscript of the B text. The title comes from the first line of the first *passus* (book) and the whole runs to 857 lines. However, a manuscript of 1750 lines, discovered in 1928, proved to contain the rest of the poem – one of Langland's time known as *Mum, Sothsegger*. See **Mum and the Sothsegger**.

**Lanier, Sidney** 1842–81. Lanier was born in Macon, Georgia, the son of an urban middle-class family. He was educated at Oglethorpe University and looked forward to a career as a musician. The Civil War blasted his hopes, however; he served in the Confederate army and was taken prisoner, spending four months in captivity at Point Lookout, Maryland. He returned home in 1865, his health wrecked. He had never been robust and one of the results of his privations was consumption.

In 1867 he published a novel, *Tiger-Lilies*, about his experiences and this decided him to use the rest of his life – he knew how uncertain that was – in writing and in music, his first love. He became a flautist with the Peabody Orchestra of Baltimore, lectured on English literature, and wrote poetry. His first book of *Poems* was published in 1877 and two years later the quality of his lectures secured him a position at Johns Hopkins University. *The Science of English Verse* (1880) presents his ideas on prosody, including his thesis that the laws governing verse and music are identical. His complete *Poems* was published in 1884 and the ballads and lyrics demonstrate his ideas in practice. The book was reissued with additions in 1891 and 1916.

Lanier's original lectures were collected and published in two volumes in 1902 as *Shakespeare and His Forerunners*; further lectures at Johns Hopkins were published as *The English Novel and the Principle of its Development* in 1883.

The importance of Sidney Lanier, who is not quite a major poet, lies in what he managed to achieve in his tragically short life and in his emergence as a poet of distinction from a background that hardly produced literature, much less poetry; the South was barren in that respect in Lanier's day. He might well have become a major poet, granted a longer life and the opportunity to mix with the poets who were beginning to be heard in the North. What he left us is original and full of beauty, if at times over-extravagant. He expresses an aching longing for a better future ('The Raven Days'); he knew that the passing of the old South was like an artificial light dying. In a short religious poem, 'A Ballad of Trees and the Master', he succeeds completely and in the long celebrated 'The Marshes of Glynn' he conveys the peace of wide skies and abundant nature – and the acceptance of the mystery contained therein.

**Lanthorne and Candle-Light:** *or The Bellmans Second Nights Walke, in which Hee Brings to Light a Broode of More Strange Villanies Than Ever Were Till This Yeare Discovered.* A pamphlet by Thomas Dekker, first published in 1608, the same year as its companion work, *The Belman of London*. See also **Belman of London, The**.

**Laodicean, A** A novel by Thomas Hardy, first published in *Harper's New Monthly Magazine* (December 1880 to December 1881).

The Laodicean (luke-warm person) is Paula Power, who vacillates about being baptized in the faith of her father, a Baptist. She also vacillates between a young architect, George Somerset, and Captain de Stancy, son of the family who once owned the castle in which Paula lives (her father is a successful railway contractor). She inclines to de Stancy, having a romantic disposition. Then Willy Dare, de Stancy's illegitimate son, attempts to discredit Somerset, and she decides on the architect. The castle, the restoration of which she has also been vacillating about, catches fire and burns down. There is a subplot involving Willy Dare and an ex-revolutionary, Abner Power.

Hardy was seriously ill while working on the later stages of his novel but, all allowances made, he has not succeeded in making his Laodicean interesting.

**Lardner, Ring(old Wilmer)** 1885–1933. Ring Lardner was born in Michigan and got his first job as a reporter in South Bend, Indiana. He worked in Chicago, and then in St Louis editing a baseball weekly. This led to his becoming a sports reporter for various newspapers and a syndicated columnist; he became famous through the imaginary letters of one Jack Keefe, a newcomer to a professional baseball team. These first appeared in *The Chicago Tribune* and were collected as *You Know Me, Al: A Busher's Letters* (1916). Lardner revealed a sharp-edged sense of humour and a remarkable ear for vernacular speech. Americans of every walk of life appeared in his stories, their utterances identifying their character accurately. Lardner's view of them is not sympathetic: he gives it without comment and none is needed after they have been presented and allowed to speak for themselves. In the *Bib Ballads* (1915) he demonstrated his talent for verse; *Gullible's Travels* (1917) is a collection of satirical stories; it was followed by more in *Treat 'em Rough* (1918). His only novel, *The Big Town*, was published in 1921.

Lardner had a large and enthusiastic following by the time he published the collection *How to Write Short Stories (with Samples)* (1924). Then the critics discovered him too: H. L. Mencken, Edmund Wilson, and Virginia Woolf wrote in praise of him. His friend F. Scott Fitzgerald wrote, 'Whatever [his] achievement was, it fell short of the achievement he was capable of, and this because of a cynical attitude towards his work.' Ring Lardner simply did not like the human race: Clifton Fadiman commented that if his characters are funny, then 'so is *Gulliver's Travels*'. Nevertheless, Lardner was master of his medium; nothing divides like a sense of humour and he made great numbers of readers laugh. His later works are the collections *What of It?* (1925), *The Love Nest* (1926), *Round Up* (1929), and *First and Last* (1934). *June Moon* (1929), written in collaboration with George S. Kaufman, was a successful comedy satirizing Tin Pan Alley. Robert Sherwood adapted the story *The Love Nest* for the stage in 1927. Lardner's *The Story of a Wonder Man* (1927) is a satirical autobiography.

**Larkin, Philip (Arthur)** 1922– . Larkin was born in Coventry, Warwickshire. He gained a scholarship to St John's College, Oxford, and published a volume of poems, *The North Ship* (1945), between his graduation (1943) and taking his Master's degree in 1947. The book had a small but appreciative readership and after Oxford Larkin became a university librarian. He has been in charge of the Brynmor Jones Library, University of Hull, since 1955. Two small collections were privately printed, *XX Poems* (1951) and *Poems* (1954), but ten years passed before his second volume was published, *The Less Deceived* (1955). Larkin's output has been modest but he is acknowledged as one of England's foremost poets. Other volumes are *The Whitsun Weddings* (1964, Queen's Gold Medal and the Arts Council Prize), *The Explosion* (1970), and *High Windows* (1974, Cholmondeley and Loines Awards). Larkin is the author of two novels, *Jill* (1946) and *A Girl in Winter* (1947). He is a feature writer on jazz and a collection of his articles are published as *All What Jazz?: a Record Diary 1961–1968* (1970). He

is the editor of *The Oxford Book of Twentieth-Century Verse* (1973).

**Larsen, Wolf** The ruthless but physically magnificent captain of the sealer, *Ghost*, in *The Sea-Wolf* by Jack London. He acknowledges no equal but is eventually defeated by a man who can survive only by learning how to challenge him.

***LaSalle and the Discovery of the Great West*** See **Parkman, Francis** and *France and England in North America*.

***Last Chronicle of Barset, The*** The last book in Anthony Trollope's Barsetshire series. The novel is mainly concerned with Josiah Crawley, the intractable, upright curate of Hogglestock.

Lord Lufton's agent, Mr Soames, loses a pocket-book containing a cheque for £20. Soames believes that he lost the pocket-book in Mr Crawley's house; later Mr Crawley cashes the cheque and uses the money to pay his bills. When he is called upon to explain, he first says that he received the money from Soames in payment of his stipend; then he says it was part of a gift from Francis (now Dean) Arabin, who is on his way to Jerusalem. But Arabin denies the statement and the distracted Crawley is committed for trial, unable to account for the money.

The bishop's wife, Mrs Proudie, is in the forefront of the persecution which now focuses on Crawley. Archdeacon Grantly's son, Major Henry Grantly, is in love with Crawley's daughter, Grace, and insists on becoming engaged to her in spite of his father's opposition; this leads to a serious breach between them. When the whole affair reaches a crisis it is resolved by Mrs Arabin (the former Eleanor Harding). She reveals that she was the unwitting cause of the trouble: she had slipped a cheque for £20 into the envelope containing Dean Arabin's gift – so the dean, when asked, could not account for the extra amount. The origin of the cheque itself went farther back: it had been stolen from Soames by a servant, and then paid to Mrs Arabin as money due to her. She in turn had used it to increase her husband's gift. Crawley's innocence established, he is appointed to the parish of the late Mr Harding. Archdeacon Grantly is completely won over when he meets Grace Crawley, and welcomes her as his daughter-in-law.

The story also contains the death of the dreadful Mrs Proudie and tells of Johnny Eames' ever-hopeful pursuit of Lily Dale.

Trollope, in his *Autobiography*, says that *The Last Chronicle of Barset* is his own favourite among the novels and many of his readers would agree with his choice. Josiah Crawley is a memorable character, whose very integrity daunts those who wish him well. There is a wonderful scene when, called before the bishop, he puts Mrs Proudie well and truly in her place, after she has obviously looked forward to bullying the hapless man. The archdeacon, with all his worldliness – and his wrong-headedness – is a very likable man and an affectionate father.

***Last Days of Pompeii, The*** A novel by Bulwer-Lytton, first published in 1834. The setting is Pompeii, just before the eruption of Vesuvius in AD 79, which obliterated that city and neighbouring Herculaneum. The chief characters are Ione and her lover Glaucus, two young Greeks, and the blind girl, Nydia, who cherishes a hopeless love for Glaucus. Ione is menaced by her guardian, Arbaces, whose regard for her is anything but paternal. The eruption is the great centrepiece; it is vividly done, but spoiled for modern readers by the implication that nasty pagans deserved no better. The blind Nydia saves the lovers by guiding them through the total darkness to the seashore.

***Last Man, The*** See **Shelley, Mary.**

***Last of the Barons, The*** A novel by Bulwer-Lytton, first published in 1843. The character described in the title is the Earl of Warwick, the 'Kingmaker', and the novel follows his career through the Wars of the Roses and ends with his death at the Battle of Barnet. Warwick's historical capricious desertion of the Yorkist cause is explained by an attempt on the honour of Anne, Warwick's sister, by the promiscuous Edward IV. Also portrayed is Lord Hastings, who deserts the beautiful (fictitious) Sibyll Warner.

***Last of the Mohicans, The*** A novel by James Fenimore Cooper, first published in 1826. It was the second of the *Leather-Stocking Tales* to be written and the second in order of events. The period is the mid-18th century; the French and their Indian allies are besieging the British in Fort William Henry on Lake George.

Cora and Alice Munro, with Major Duncan Heyward and the singing teacher, David Gamut, are on their way to Fort William Henry to join their father, the commander. Conducting them is the Indian, Magua, who in fact serves the French and plans to betray the group to the Iroquois. His plan is frustrated by Hawkeye and his Mohican friends, Chingachgook and his son Uncas – these are the only survivors of the Mohican chieftains.

Magua escapes from Hawkeye and the Mohicans and, with the help of an Iroquois band, captures the Munro girls. He wants Cora for himself but once more Hawkeye frustrates his plans; the girls are rescued and safely delivered to their father at the Fort. Eventually Munro is obliged to surrender the fort to Montcalm, who gives the English party a safe conduct; but this is no help when they are attacked by hostile Indians and the sisters are once again captured. This time they are separated; Cora is taken by the Delawares and Alice by the Hurons. Hawkeye discovers their whereabouts; Uncas is also a prisoner in the Huron camp and, with the help of Major Heyward, Alice and Uncas escape.

At the camp of the Delawares, where Cora is held, Uncas is welcomed by the old chief and made his successor; but Magua lays claim to Cora as his captive and this is acknowledged in tribal law – Uncas can do nothing. However, Magua is seen in his true colours when the tribe goes to war against the Hurons: he tries to desert, taking Cora with him. Uncas follows him but it is Magua who wins the ensuing fight and Cora is also killed. It is left to Hawkeye to avenge the death of his friend, the last of the Mohicans, and after he kills Magua the British party proceeds to the nearest settlement. But Hawkeye does not go with them: the frontier and the great unspoiled wilderness are his life.

***Last Puritan, The:*** *A Memoir in the Form of a Novel.* A novel by George Santayana, first published in 1935. The presenter of the story opens the 'memoir' in a prologue, where the chief character, Oliver Alden, is one of his students at Harvard who dies in World War I.

Peter Alden is rich and effete, a drug addict continually travelling in his yacht with a paid companion, Jim Darnley, and vaguely seeking some purpose in life. He has turned from the puritanical New England values held so rigidly by his brother, Nathaniel, and Nathaniel's narrow-minded wife, Harriet. Peter Alden's son, Oliver, is brought up by his mother, who is not interested in him, and by his governess, the sentimental Irma Schlote. Oliver grows up without love or friendship and in his own way tries to make the best of himself. He becomes interested in athletics and thus in achievement; soon he begins to question the values of his decadent family.

At the age of 17 Oliver accompanies his father on a cruise and finds a friend in Jim Darnley. Later, at Williams College, Oliver becomes a zealous student and sportsman; his puritan background is at work and he feels a commitment to give always of his best. Then Peter Alden commits suicide and Oliver finds Jim Darnley, who is sensual and self-seeking, a less rewarding friend than before. He finds a more sympathetic spirit in his cousin, Mario, whom his father has helped to support. Mario, educated in Europe, is an amiable hedonist; but he has a sincere liking for his cousin and respects his austere moral standards, though he deplores Oliver's cold courtship of their cousin Edith – a courtship Mario knows will come to nothing.

After graduating, Oliver goes on a world tour and in England is a guest of the Darnleys. He falls in love with Rose, Jim Darnley's sister – but Rose falls in love with Mario, who joined the army at the outbreak of war and who visits the Darnleys during his leave. Oliver's isolation – Rose's preference for Mario is plainly based on his vitality and lightheartedness – increases and his sense of inadequacy and tormented self-questionings begin to have a dangerous effect on him. Rose's love for Mario is one-sided; he does not realize the depth of her feelings and Rose is heartbroken. Oliver decides to enter the army and he asks Rose to marry him so that she will inherit his wealth – but she refuses him. Oliver goes to the war; he has no hope in anything and no faith in the future. He is killed in France and has left his money to the Darnleys.

Oliver Alden, reacting against the worthless existence of his own family, returns to the values of his puritan background and embraces them to such effect that devotion to purpose, gravity, singlemindedness, and moral austerity eventually destroy him. Even when he feels a desperate need to depart from those values and live a warmer life he cannot – his puritanism will not allow him to.

**Last Tournament, The**  See **Idylls of the King, The**.

**Latimer, Hugh** 1490–1555.  The son of a farmer of Thurcaston in Leicestershire, Latimer was educated at Cambridge. He became a fellow of Clare Hall in 1510 and a priest soon after. He was opposed to the idea of reform at first, but later became one of its most powerful advocates and in 1525 refused the request of Bishop West of Ely to preach a sermon against Luther. A Lenten sermon delivered before Henry VIII in 1530 won him the king's approval, and after the break with Rome he became one of Henry's advisers. He was appointed Bishop of Worcester in 1535.

Latimer, who was nothing if not steadfast, opposed the Act of the Six Articles of 1539 and was obliged to resign his see. He emerged from obscurity in 1548 when he preached the celebrated sermon 'Of the Plough' on New Year's Day. His preaching became famous; but Mary came to the throne in 1553 and Latimer was arrested. With Cranmer and Ridley, Bishop of London, he was taken to Oxford in 1554 to defend his heresy in a disputation with Catholic theologians and was excommunicated. He was examined again in the following year and refused to recant. He and Ridley were burned at the stake at Oxford on 16 October 1555.

A martyr for his beliefs, Latimer was not a gentle or saintly man in any way: he was pleased to preach at the burning of Katherine of Aragon's confessor, John Forrest (1538), and had complained to Cromwell that the poor man's confinement was not nearly harsh enough; he was wholeheartedly in favour of the slaughter of the family of Cardinal Pole. In literature he is remembered for his powerful sermons, written down by other hands. Latimer's style was direct and vivid, his speech a simple vernacular; theological subtlety is absent from his sermons. They were edited, with Latimer's miscellaneous writings, by G. E. Corrie and published by the Parker Society in 1845.

**latitudinarianism**  A term first applied in the 17th century to the outlook of those members of the Anglican clergy who, while conforming to the Church of England, held matters of ecclesiastical rules and organization and strict liturgical practice to be of little importance. This attitude also extended to their view of dogmatic 'truth'. In general, latitudinarian (it was a term of opprobrium) sympathies lay with Jacob Arminius and his rejection of strict Calvinist theology.

**Latter-Day Pamphlets**  See **Past and Present**.

**Laud, William** 1573–1645.  Laud is strictly speaking a figure of history rather than of literature. But his uncompromising Anglicanism, supported by his authority as Archbishop of Canterbury, led him to try and enforce his convictions by law, and this provoked much of the notable religious writing of the time. He overreached himself at the Convocation of 1640, when his proposals for permanent acceptance of the Anglican Church according to his own formula were treated with contempt by the growing party of dissent. The king ordered the suspension of the formula but Laud had already gone too far. In 1641 he was impeached by the Long Parliament for tyranny in matters of religion and sent to the Tower. His trial did not take place until 1644; it was a travesty, but by then there were few who would have defended him. The old man – he was 72 – was beheaded on Tower Hill on 10 January 1645 and died with unflinching courage.

A few of his sermons were published (1651) and a collection of his writings (1695–1700) but their literary value is slight. Of great interest to historians is *The History of the Troubles and Trial of William Laud*, written by himself in the Tower before his execution. It was edited by H. Wharton and published with Laud's diary (1695).

**Launce** The servant of Proteus in Shakespeare's *The Two Gentlemen of Verona*. His monologues to his dog Crab, who is never improved by his master's reproaches, are famous comic set pieces.

**Launcelot Greaves, The Life and Adventures of Sir** A novel by Tobias Smollett, first published serially in *The British Magazine*, from January 1760 to December 1761. It was first published in volume form in 1762. Smollett's fourth novel, it appeared eight years after the third, *Ferdinand Count Fathom* (1753). The author followed the model of *Don Quixote*, but the novel is mechanical and it is generally regarded as a poor example of Smollett's work. Sir Launcelot Greaves is an 18th-century Quixote, riding about England in armour with Timothy Crabshaw, his comic squire. The humour, in Smollett's case, is as harsh and violent as the rest of his work – far removed from Cervantes. The novel earns praise only for its picture of England before the Industrial Revolution and for its characters: Ferret, the rogue; Mrs Gobble, the justice's wife, and Captain Crowe, the naval knight-errant, who sounds like an early sketch for Jingle in Dickens's *Pickwick*. There is a modern edition of *Sir Launcelot Greaves* in the Oxford English Novels series, edited by David Evans (1973).

**Launcelot of the Lake** The most famous of all the knights of the Round Table was a comparative latecomer to the English Arthurian cycle. He was the subject of a 13th-century French prose romance, *Lancelot*, and does not reach major stature in English until the 14th-century English poem, *Le Morte Arthur*, which should not be confused with the book of Sir Thomas Malory. However, the story of Launcelot is substantially the same, if more detailed, in the later book.

He is Guenever's lover, and goes to the tournament at Winchester where Elaine of Astolat falls in love with him. Wounded, he is taken to Astolat and leaves his armour in the care of Elaine. When Gawain goes to Astolat, Elaine declares that she is Launcelot's love. But he does not return, and meanwhile Gawain has told the court what he learned at Astolat; Guenever is hurt and angry. Then Elaine's body is brought in a barge to Arthur's castle, with her letter saying that she

died of love. Launcelot and Guenever are reconciled but now Gawain's brother, Agravaine, betrays them to Arthur. They are surprised at night by 12 knights; Launcelot kills all of them except Mordred before escaping with Guenever.

Arthur and Gawain besiege Launcelot and Guenever in Launcelot's castle. There is a reconciliation between Arthur and Guenever, who is spared the sentence of death Arthur passed on her; but Gawain's bitterness against Launcelot, who has killed his brothers, prevents their reconciliation and he flees to Brittany, only returning after the fatal battle with Mordred that brings the end for Arthur.

Launcelot is the father of Galahad by another Elaine, daughter of King Pelles. His sins prevent him from ever seeing the Grail.

**Launfal, Sir** A Middle English verse romance of the 14th century based on the late 12th-century *Lanval* of Marie de France. (See **metrical romances**.) Launfal is also the subject of the 15th-century poem, *Launfal Miles*, by Thomas Chestre (fl. 1430). Launfal is a knight of the Round Table and, uneasy about the reputed misconduct of Guinevere, he retires from the court and lives in poverty in Caerleon. Tryamour, daughter of the faery King of Olyroun, falls in love with Launfal and enriches him; she will always come at his call, as long as he keeps their love secret. Launfal returns to Arthur's court and immediately Guinevere declares her love for him. He rejects her, telling her he already loves another lady, whose very maids are more beautiful than Guinevere. Having inadvertently betrayed his secret, Launfal is suddenly bereft of his wealth; then Guinevere charges him with trying to seduce her and he is brought to trial. He is charged to reveal, within a stated time, the name of his lady in order to disprove the charge against him. At the end of the time Tryamour appears and justifies her knight. She breathes into Guinevere's eyes and blinds her; then she and Launfal retire to the kingdom of Olyroun. The Middle English *Sir Launfal* was edited by W. C. Hazlitt (1875) and by A. J. Bliss (1960).

**Launfal Miles** See **Launfal, Sir.**

**Laurence, Friar** In Shakespeare's *Romeo and Juliet*, the Franciscan friar who agrees to perform the secret marriage of the young lovers and gives Romeo refuge in his cell after the deaths of Mercutio and Tybalt. He gives the potion to Juliet to prevent the marriage arranged by Capulet for his daughter to Paris and sends word to Romeo in Mantua. The message miscarries and Romeo believes Juliet dead. Friar Laurence is sympathetic to the young lovers and hopes their marriage may unite the warring families.

***Laus Veneris*** A poem by Algernon Charles Swinburne, first published in *Poems and Ballads* (first series, 1866). The poem is a celebration of the discovery of physical love. The speaker declares 'For I was of Christ's choosing, I God's knight' and feels the powerful force of his religion warring with his passion. His passion triumphs, even after his pilgrimage to Rome, and he surrenders to it, 'Until God loosen over sea and land The thunder of the trumpets of the night.'

***Lavengro,*** *The Scholar – the Gypsy – the Priest* and ***The Romany Rye*** A novel and its sequel by George Borrow, first published in 1851 and 1857, respectively. A Norfolk Gypsy, Ambrose Smith, called Borrow 'Lavengro', a Gypsy name for a philologist. Ambrose Smith was the original of the character in the novel called Jasper Petulengro. The 'Romany Rye' means the Gypsy gentleman.

The story is told in the first person by George, the son of an army officer, who travels from place to place with his father and is thus imbued with a wandering, restless spirit. During his wanderings he encounters a family of Gypsies, who become his friends, and a wandering girl, Belle (Isobel) Berners. What follows is a series of picaresque adventures which lead, ultimately, nowhere in particular, but the episodes strung together are related with remarkable verve, and Borrow had no rival in graphic power. These two qualities are the books' salvation, since the author cannot begin to establish a character – the narrator is not given one, and Belle Berners is ridiculous.

**Lavinia** The hapless daughter of Titus Andronicus in Shakespeare's play. She is raped by Tamora's sons, who cut out her tongue and chop off her hands so that she can't betray them. Her uncle Marcus shows her how to communicate and she is eventually avenged. But her father kills her thereafter to end the shame of her life.

**Law, William** 1686–1761. William Law was born at King's Cliffe, Northamptonshire, and educated at Emmanuel College, Cambridge. He became a fellow of Emmanuel in 1711, after being ordained. Law was a Nonjuror, refusing to take the Oath of Allegiance to George I, and as a result he was deprived of his fellowship and forbidden to take up any church appointment. His first published work, *A Sermon Preach'd at Harpingfield on Tuesday, July 7th, 1713*, had appeared the year before.

In 1717 Law published the first of *Three Letters to the Bishop of Bangor*, a reply to Bishop Hoadly's defence of the church's submission of loyalty to George I (*Preservative against the Principles and Practices of the Non-Jurors, 1716*). *Remarks on a Late Book entituled The Fable of the Bees* (1723) is a reply to the satire of Bernard de Mandeville; and in 1726 he wrote *The Absolute Unlawfulness of the Stage Entertainment*, which attacked the contemporary theatre.

In 1726 Law also published *A Practical Treatise on Christian Perfection* and in 1728 came *A Serious Call to a Devout and Holy Life*; these are the two books by which he is best known. They constitute a guide to the full practice of Christian ideals in everyday life, are written in clear vigorous prose, and carried a strong appeal in the simplicity of their teaching. *A Serious Call*, particularly, had great influence and Wesley declared that the beginnings of Methodism were to be found in it. Samuel Johnson also admired it very much. *The Case of Reason* (1731) was Law's answer to the deists; he saw total reliance on reason as a fundamental error, since both man and the universe are mysteries that admit of no explanation.

In middle life Law became intensely interested in the writings of the German Lutheran mystic Jakob Boehme, who was also to influence William Blake. However, William Law the mystic lost the loyalty of some of his former disciples and John Wesley became estranged from him. Among his mystical writings are *The Spirit of Prayer* (written in two parts, 1749 and 1750), *The Way to Divine Knowledge* (1752), and *The Spirit of Love* (again in two parts, 1752 and 1754).

From 1727 to 1737 Law was tutor to Edward Gibbon (the father of the historian) at Putney and remained the family's spiritual guide until 1740, when he returned to King's Cliffe with Hester Gibbon and a Mrs Hutcheson. There, with the help of the two ladies, he organized schools and almshouses and passed the rest of his life.

**Lawrence, D(avid) H(erbert)** 1885–1930. D. H. Lawrence was born at Eastwood, Nottinghamshire. He was a miner's son; his mother had been a schoolteacher and she aspired to refinement and a better future for her children. The conflict of interests in his home, between his uncultured father and his increasingly resentful mother coloured Lawrence's childhood. His mother succeeded in turning their five children away from their father and the unhappy man could hardly be blamed for the unpleasant scenes that sometimes occurred. When Lawrence was 12 he won a county scholarship which paid £12

Industrial Nottingham in 1901.

a year and gave him a place at Nottingham High School. The travelling – two hours from home and two hours back – was gruelling and the scholarship grant hardly covered the expenses. He did very well there but his constitution was sorely tried by the journey and his desire to shine, and he was ill during the last year.

Lawrence left school in 1901 and obtained a job as a junior clerk in Nottingham, working 12 hours a day for 6 days a week, and still making a long journey twice a day. After three months he was seriously ill, with pneumonia, and his mother asserted her possessiveness with double strength while nursing him through his long illness. He was 16 years old.

From 1902 to 1906 Lawrence worked as a pupil-teacher, first at Eastwood and then at Ilkeston. He had congenial company in the other apprentice teachers and his reading was extensive. His talent for drawing and painting developed and he was popular with the girls – they felt safe with him because he always behaved like a brother. Lawrence won a King's Scholarship at the end of 1904 and matriculated in 1905, qualifying for a period of study at Nottingham University College. He had to wait for a year, and save the £20 advance not covered by the scholarship, and did not enter the college until 1906. His first poems date from about this time, and he also began a novel. The college disappointed him badly, with its tired, conventional standards. He went along with them and in 1908 left it with several distinctions and a teacher's certificate. At the age of 22 he freed himself from his mother and from Nottingham and became a teacher at a boys' school at Croydon in Surrey. In 1909 he submitted some poems

to Ford Madox Hueffer of *The English Review* and these were published in the November issue. Hueffer was very impressed by Lawrence; he introduced him to literary London and Lawrence made the acquaintance of W. B. Yeats, Ernest Rhys, H. G. Wells, and Ezra Pound. Most important of all, Hueffer sent Lawrence's novel, now complete after concentrated labour, to William Heinemann who accepted it for publication. *The White Peacock* was published in 1911 and Lawrence, encouraged by the interest shown in his work before publication, gave up teaching

D. H. Lawrence in 1908, at Nottingham University College.

to make writing his career. Another attack of pneumonia brought a warning from a doctor that he was in danger of becoming consumptive.

Lawrence's second novel, *The Trespasser* (1912), was published in the same year as he completed the first draft of *Paul Morel*, and his poems were appearing in *The English Review*. He was asked for a collection of stories by another publisher, and a new mentor, Edward Garnett, was trying to arrange the publication of a volume of poems as well as the plays that Lawrence was also writing. But little money had come from all this and in March 1912 Lawrence consulted Ernest Weekley, his former teacher, about the hope of gaining a place in Germany as a teacher. Weekley was married to Frieda, daughter of Baron Friedrich von Richtofen, who had borne him three children, but was bored with her marriage to a dull, bookish husband. She had numerous affairs, and D. H. Lawrence was in a fair way to becoming one of these. He wanted more than that, and she fell in love with him. They eloped to Metz, then in German-occupied Lorraine, on 3 May 1912; they were married in 1914 after Frieda had been divorced.

*Sons and Lovers*, for many people the favourite of Lawrence's novels, was published in 1913. A new name had been found since Frieda had been rude about the original *Paul Morel* and had even written a skit on it. The rewritten novel demonstrated that Lawrence had now a better understanding of his father; he is consequently less 'His Mother's Darling', which was Frieda's description of Paul Morel. Lawrence's first published play was *The Widowing of Mrs Holroyd* (1914), which did not receive a professional production until 1926. *The Prussian Officer, and Other Stories* appeared in 1914; it contains the notable 'Daughters of the Vicar'.

A novel, *The Sisters*, which he began while in Europe with Frieda in 1913 eventually became two novels, and the first one was published in 1915 as *The Rainbow*.

Lawrence objected to World War I passionately, and saw the stated 'war aims' as humbug. He was right but no one in those days, with the exception of Shaw, agreed with him. Methuen, the publishers of *The Rainbow*, were prosecuted and the book was condemned; all copies were confiscated. Hardly anyone had a kind word to say for it; one review drew attention to the noble young men who were giving their lives for their country, in contrast to the dreadful creatures of Lawrence's novel. The tone of such reviews reflected the spirit of the times in England. The Lawrences were in need of money and were glad to be lent a house at Porthcothan in Cornwall by

J. D. Beresford. In 1916 Lawrence was exempted from military service as unfit. He was indeed very unwell but he completed *Women in Love*, the second novel of *The Sisters* material, *Twilight in Italy* (1916), *Amores: Poems* (1916), and the collection of poems called *Look! We have come through!* (1917). At the end of 1916 and all through 1917 the Lawrences were subjected to ridiculous and spiteful persecution: Frieda was the cousin of a German air ace; Lawrence was known as a subversive and antiwar writer. On 11 October 1917 the Lawrences were formally expelled from the county, and by December Lawrence was asking his friends to help him financially. Among those who did were Shaw and Arnold Bennett. His published work of this period – *New Poems* (1918), *Bay: A Book of Poems* (1919), and the play *Touch and Go* (1919) – brought him little. His frail constitution took another battering when he became one of the victims of the postwar influenza epidemic in February 1919. He left for Italy in November of that year; Frieda, after visiting her family in Germany, joined him in Florence a month later. He never lived in England again, and after Sardinia, Ceylon, Australia, Taos (New Mexico), and Mexico the consumption that had been threatening him for so long took hold after a serious illness at Taos. He returned to Europe in 1926, and moved from place to place in a hopeless endeavour to check his growing weakness. He died at a sanatorium at Vence, near Nice in the south of France, at the age of 44.

When he left England Lawrence's literary fortunes had taken an upward turn. Martin Secker became his publisher in England and there was competition for his work in America. *The Lost Girl* (1920) was awarded the James Tait Black Prize; *Women in Love*, finished during a period of wretchedness, was published in 1921, as was the fine travel book, *Sea and Sardinia*. *Aaron's Rod* followed in 1922, and at last Lawrence was earning a living from his work. A second volume of short stories (a form that suited Lawrence very well and drew from him some of his best work) was *England my England, and Other Stories* (1922); *The Captain's Doll: Three Novelettes* (1923) contains 'The Ladybird' and 'The Fox' with the title work. *Women in Love*, meanwhile, had provoked yelps of moral indignation from some reviewers but times had changed and no one thought of prosecution.

*Kangaroo* (1923) was written during a four-month stay in New South Wales, where Lawrence met Molly Skinner and with whom he collaborated on *The Boy in the Bush* (1924). *St Mawr* (1925, with 'The Princess') reflects the feeling, reinforced by a visit to England, that the country was heading for the end; *The Plumed Serpent* (1926) was inspired by his time in Mexico; *The Woman who Rode Away and Other Stories* (1928) expresses, in the title story, Lawrence's belief that regeneration was desperately needed by western civilization. *Lady Chatterley's Lover* was begun after Lawrence left England for Italy in 1926 and was first published in 1928, but not in England in its unexpurgated form until 1961, after a trial where the literary establishment closed ranks against the censor.

Among other works by Lawrence were *Movements in European History* (1921), a school textbook commissioned by the Oxford University Press and originally published under the pseudonym of Lawrence H. Davison: the 1971 edition contains a hitherto unpublished Epilogue; *Psychoanalysis and the Unconscious* (1921); *Studies in Classic American Literature* (1923); *David* (1926), a play which was produced at the Regent Theatre on 22 May 1927; the travel sketches, *Mornings in Mexico* (1927) and *Etruscan Places* (posth. 1932); *The Man Who Died* (posth. 1931), regarded by a few critics as his finest story and the collections of stories called *The Lovely Lady* (posth. 1932), and *The Tales of D. H. Lawrence* (posth. 1934). *The Complete Poems* of D. H. Lawrence were edited by V. de S. Pinto and W. Roberts (1964) and *The Complete Plays* appeared in 1965 (no editor credited). *The Letters of D. H. Lawrence* was edited by Aldous Huxley (1932) and *Mr Noon* (1984) appeared in *The Cambridge Edition of the Works of D. H. Lawrence*.

The disharmony of Lawrence's home, his parents' relationship, his mother's possessiveness and her contempt for the man she married influenced Lawrence profoundly. His mother's aspirations were his springboard but he came to see, belatedly, that his father's ill temper and drinking were the reactions of a hurt and rejected man. At the age of 22 Lawrence was without experience of physical love. He was class-conscious – rancorously so, and like many such men he found the middle classes the most worthy of his contempt. The more he saw of the world he lived in, the less he liked it. He suffered poverty and persecution; illness was to kill him in early middle age but Katherine Mansfield noted his passionate eagerness for life. These factors cannot be separated from Lawrence's novels: Ford Madox Hueffer told him that *The White Peacock* had every fault the English novel could have – but he added that Lawrence had genius. The same could be said of all of Lawrence's novels, with the exception of *Sons and Lovers*, and the rider is incontrovertible. He was always trying to say more than anyone else had said about

human relationships, and if he had been granted a longer life he might have discovered a consistent coherence and intelligibility of expression. He found it a lot of the time, and then achieved a level not found in any of his contemporaries.

**Lawrence, George Alfred** 1827–76. The author of *Guy Livingstone* (1857) was educated at Rugby and Balliol College, Oxford. His novels were in reaction to the virtuous, not to say pious, tone of some of the popular fiction of mid-Victorian times. It is interesting that he attended the same school as Thomas Hughes; he seems to have reacted with a rising gorge, and produced the muscular, immoral hero in opposition to Hughes and the muscular Christians currently in favour. *Guy Livingstone* was a great success, and Lawrence wrote in the same vein for another eight novels. He is almost unknown to modern readers.

**Lawrence, T(homas) E(dward)** 1888–1935. T. E. Lawrence was born at Tremadoc in Caernarvonshire, one of the illegitimate sons of Sir Robert Chapman and an engineer's daughter from Durham. He was educated at Oxford High School and Jesus College, Oxford, and went to the Middle East in 1911 as an archaeologist, working at Carchemish. In World War I he worked in the intelligence section of the Arab Bureau, and in 1916 went to the desert to organize the revolt of the Arab leaders against their Turkish overlords. After the war he attended the Versailles Conference (1919) with the Arab leaders, by which time he had become the almost legendary figure, Lawrence of Arabia. He retained the legend while renouncing a public and social life and began work on his account of the desert campaign. He was disillusioned with his country's policy in the Middle East and sought obscurity by enlisting in the Royal Air Force under the name of Ross; he was discovered and discharged, and rejoined under the name of Shaw. He was in the ranks until 1935, when he went to live in Dorset and died as a result of a crash at high speed riding a motor cycle. He had been awarded a fellowship of All Souls College, Oxford, in 1919.

*The Seven Pillars of Wisdom: A Triumph* was written three times (the first draft was lost on Reading station) and the published version came after George Bernard Shaw and his wife had carefully read and edited it. Charlotte Shaw had positive reservations about Lawrence's regard for truth but the book appeared in a very limited edition in 1926, with illustrations by Eric Kennington, at 30 guineas a copy. It focused a great deal of attention on a man who was seeking obscurity but Lawrence, as Philip Guedalla remarked, had a trick of 'backing into the limelight.' An abridgement, *Revolt in the Desert*, was published in the following year. A trade edition for general circulation, with five passages omitted, was published in 1935, after Lawrence's death.

*The Seven Pillars of Wisdom* was a great success because Lawrence of Arabia was a success, and because it presented a war in which a popular hero, with considerable modesty, explained his romantic and chivalrous contribution to it: it was a far cry from the squalid agony of the Western Front. But it was an acceptable volume of military history – subject, of course, to the criticism of other observers who gathered further facts about the desert campaign – despite the peculiar, old-fashioned prose. Time has rather damaged its popularity and it is not regarded so highly now.

Apart from contributions to early archaeological reports and occasional introductory essays Lawrence published a translation, *The Odyssey of Homer* (1932), and *The Mint* (1936). The first is a prose translation and was published in The World's Classics in 1955 with an introduction by C. M. Bowra. The second is a very peculiar book, first published in a limited edition subtitled 'Notes made in the RAF Depot between August and December 1922, and at Cadet College in 1925.' A trade edition was published in 1955 and the book, which was apparently meant to present Lawrence's experience of life in the ranks, makes an impression of ambiguity and – to put it mildly – of artistic uncertainty. It sank without trace in the climate of the 1950s. *The Letters of T. E. Lawrence* (1938) was edited by David Garnett.

**Lawson, Henry** 1867–1922. The son of a Norwegian sailor named Larsen who became a gold prospector, Lawson was born at Mudgee, New South Wales. He had an unhappy childhood (his parents eventually separated) which was exacerbated, at the age of nine, by deafness. He started to earn his living when he was 13. When his parents separated he went to Sydney with his mother, who launched a socialist periodical, *The Republican*, to which Lawson contributed his first writings. Like his contemporary, A. B. Paterson, he found his best form and outlet in *The Bulletin*. He went to live in the outback in the north of New South Wales in 1892 and the bush ballads and stories that resulted from his stay there became a popular feature of *The Bulletin* in the 1890s. Lawson was inclined to melancholy and this led to too much drinking. He married in 1896 and travelled to Europe and New Zealand. But

the best of Lawson's work was written by the turn of the century. After 1901 he seemed unable to recapture his laconic humour and fine balance and his later work is marred by sentimentality.

Lawson's first collection was *Stories in Verse and Prose* (1894) followed by *While the Billy Boils* (1896), *On the Track and Over the Sliprails* (1900), and *Joe Wilson and His Mates* (1901). A collection in three volumes, *The Stories of Henry Lawson*, was edited by Cecil Mann (1965).

**Layamon** (*or* **Lawemon** *or* **Laghamon**) fl. 1200. Layamon, whose name means 'Lawman', was, according to his statement in the preface to his verse chronicle *Brut*, a priest at Ernley (Areley Kings) on the River Severn in Worcestershire. His poem marks the movement away from the religious themes which had hitherto been the chief matter of English literature. His declared ambition was to tell the story of Britain from the time of the Flood, but he actually begins with the fall of Troy; he ends with the death of Cadwalader (689 AD). For material he travelled about England, and he gives as his sources Bede, the Latin books of St Albin and St Austin, and the *Roman de Brut* by the Norman writer Robert Wace of Jersey. The last named is the only really discernible influence in his work. Wace's *Brut* found its original in Geoffrey of Monmouth's *Historia Regum Britanniae*, and to this Layamon added numerous details which have been attributed to Breton, Norman, and Welsh sources. In

The building of Stonehenge, with Merlin's aid. An illustration from a 14th-century manuscript of a verse translation of Layamon's *Brut*. MS Egerton 3028, f.30. British Library.

addition, variant manuscripts of Wace existed and it seems likely that Layamon used whatever variants suited him. In spite of all this Layamon's *Brut* is highly prized as an early Middle English poem of considerable force and beauty, using the Old English alliterative line as well as the newly forged syllabic rhymed verse.

The content of Layamon's poem is of particular interest. For the first time in English Cymbeline, Lear, Arviragus, Cloten, and others make their appearance, together with Arthur, wearing the trappings of chivalry. The author could be said to have saved something priceless from the fast vanishing mythology of England and to have bequeathed to succeeding generations an imperishable hero.

Layamon's *Brut* was edited by F. Madden (1847) and by G. F. Brooke and R. F. Leslie for the Early English Text Society (Vol 1, 1963; Vol 2, 1978). Selections can be found in J. A. W. Bennett and G. V. Smithers, *Early Middle English Prose and Verse* (1968); K. and C. Sisam, *The Oxford Book of Medieval English Verse* (1970); and in G. L. Brook, *Selections from Layamon's Brut* (1963).

See also **Arthur, King**.

**Lay of the Last Minstrel, The** A romantic poem in six cantos by Sir Walter Scott, first published in 1805. It was the first of Scott's romances in this form. The story is told by an ancient minstrel, the 'last' of the title. The period is the middle of the 16th century.

The story tells of the lady of Branksome Hall, home of the Buccleuchs. She has lost her husband and blames his death on Lord Cranstoun, who is in love with her daughter Margaret. Margaret returns his love but the feud between the two families keeps them apart. Margaret's mother resorts to sorcery to revenge herself on Cranstoun, commissioning the dubious Sir William Deloraine to steal a magic book from the tomb of the alchemist Michael Scott in Melrose Abbey. Deloraine's encounter with Cranstoun after the theft serves to introduce the character of Gilpin Horner, Cranstoun's goblin page. This legendary Border character was the real inspiration of the poem (suggested to Scott by the Countess of Dalkeith); in spite of his wilful pranks, he is the agent for the reconciliation of the two families and the union of Margaret and Lord Cranstoun.

**Lays of Ancient Rome, The** Macaulay's poems about ancient Roman history were first published in 1842. The author had read *The History of Rome* by Barthold Niebuhr. The German historian suggested that Livy's history of early Rome, since it had no authentic historical sources, was based on traditional ballads. Macaulay's *Lays* are four ballads written with this idea in mind. 'Horatius' tells of the defence of the Sublician Bridge against the Etruscans by Horatius Cocles; 'The Battle of Lake Regillus' relates the Romans' defeat of the Latins (*c.*496 BC) with the divine aid of Castor and Pollux; 'Virginia' concerns the maiden slain by her father, Virginius, to save her from the lust of Appius Claudius; and 'The Prophecy of Capys' tells of the prophecy of the future greatness of Rome by the blind Capys to Romulus.

**Layton, Irving** 1912– . Layton was born in Romania but his family emigrated to Canada while he was still a baby. The family settled in Montreal and Layton studied agriculture before entering McGill University. He graduated in 1936 and served with the Royal Canadian Air Force during World War II. Layton was a teacher after the war and editor of *Preview*, an experimental literary magazine; he then became lecturer in modern poetry at Sir George William's College in Montreal. Layton's career as a poet began with *Here and Now* (1945). *In the Midst of My Fever* (1954), *The Bull Calf and Other Poems* (1956), *A Red Carpet for the Sun* (1959), *The Swinging Flesh* (1961), and *The Shattered Plinth* (1967) are among the 19 volumes of verse by him. Layton's early work was designed to oppose the austerity of the poetry being published in Canada at the time and was written to shock. His later work discloses his increasing resentment of social inequality and a deepening sensitivity.

**Leacock, Stephen Butler** 1869–1944. Stephen Leacock was born on the Isle of Wight and was seven years old when his family emigrated to Ontario, where they became farmers. Leacock was educated at Upper Canada College and the University of Toronto and he taught at his old school for eight years after graduating in 1891. After a period of study at the University of Chicago he became a lecturer at McGill University in 1901. Appointed head of the Department of Economics and Political Science in 1908, he remained in the post until he retired in 1936.

Leacock's first published work was *Elements of Political Science* (1906); he was known as a serious writer on economics and social science and as a biographer of Dickens and Mark Twain. But he is famous as a humorist, the author of *Literary Lapses* (1910), *Nonsense Novels* (1911), *Sunshine Sketches of a Little Town* (1912), *Arcadian Adventures with the Idle Rich* (1914), *Moonbeams from the Larger Lunacy* (1915), *Winnowed Wisdom* (1926), and *Laugh Parade* (1940). *How to Write* (1943) contains advice to young writers; *My Discovery of*

*England* (1922) was based on material gathered during his successful career as a lecturer. Leacock's stories and essays combine penetrating comment on society with a remarkable talent for the absurd. Leacock shared Mark Twain's gift for public speaking and his lectures at McGill were enormously popular with his students.

**Lear, Edward** 1812–88. Lear was the son of a stockbroker and was born in London. He was educated at home, chiefly by his sister Anne, but was obliged to start earning at the age of 15 when his father was imprisoned for debt. He had a natural talent for drawing and colouring and was engaged by the Earl of Derby, who kept a menagerie at Knowsley Hall; Lear produced the illustrations for a description of the contents. He became a successful artist and travelled as far as India and Ceylon. He spent his last years at San Remo in Italy.

While working at Knowsley Hall Lear wrote nonsense verses for the Earl of Derby's children; later he made nonsense drawings to accompany them. This singular talent, in a man who was generally unhappy and probably suffered from epilepsy, produced his most enduring work, though he is also recognized as an artist of considerable ability and as a rewarding travel writer.

Lear's verse was published as *A Book of Nonsense* (1846; enlarged 1861, 1863, 1870), *A Book of Nonsense and More Nonsense* (1862), *Nonsense Songs, Stories, Botany and Alphabets* (1871), *More Nonsense, Pictures, Rhymes, Botany, Etc.* (1872), and *Laughable Lyrics, a Fresh Book of Nonsense Poems* (1877). *Queery Leary Nonsense* (1911) contained new material and was compiled by Lady Strachey; *Teapots and Quails* (1953) contained

---

One of Edward Lear's illustrations for his *The Book of Nonsense*, 1846. 'There was an Old Man in a tree, who was horribly bored by a bee . . .'

unpublished fragments and was edited by P. Hofer and A. Davidson. *The Complete Nonsense of Edward Lear* (1947) was edited by Holbrook Jackson.

Lear's travel books include *Illustrated Excursions in Italy* (1846), *A Tour in Sicily* (1847), *Journal of a Landscape Painter in Albania, Illyria etc.* (1851), *Journal of a Landscape Painter in Southern Calabria* (1852), *Journal of a Landscape Painter in Corsica* (1870), and *Italian Journal* (1873–75). *The Letters of Edward Lear* (1907) and *Later Letters* (1911) were edited by Lady Strachey and are valued as a picture of his times. Lear's friend Tennyson wrote a poem in praise of him as artist and travel writer: 'To E. L. on His Travels in Greece' (1853).

***Leather-Stocking Tales***  The five novels by James Fenimore Cooper set in the early frontier period of American history. 'Leather-Stocking' is the nickname of the hero of the sequence, Natty Bumppo, who wears deerskin leggings. The plot sequence is different from the dates of composition and is as follows: **The Deerslayer**, **The Last of the Mohicans**, **The Pathfinder**, **The Pioneers**, and **The Prairie**. The hero is called by different names in the novels (Deerslayer or Bumppo in *The Deerslayer*, Hawkeye in *The Last of the Mohicans*, Pathfinder in *The Pathfinder*, Natty Bumppo or Leather-Stocking in *The Pioneers*, and simply 'the trapper' in *The Prairie*) but he is the same character and remarkably consistent all through.

***Leaves of Grass***  The first edition of *Leaves of Grass* was published by its author, Walt Whitman, in 1855. It contained 12 poems and a preface, which was omitted in later editions. The preface contained his ideas on poetry and among the poems were **Song of Myself** and **I Sing the Body Electric**.

The 1856 edition was increased by 21 poems, including **Crossing the Brooklyn Ferry** and **Song of the Broad-Axe**. The third edition, 1860, was a vastly increased one: 124 new poems, including the section of 45 called **Calamus**. Others first published in this edition were **Out of the Cradle Endlessly Rocking** and the **Children of Adam** group.

The fourth edition came out in 1867, after the Civil War. The poems already published as *Drum-Taps* (1865) and *Sequel to Drum Taps* (1865–66) were incorporated into this edition, so it contains the Civil War poems, the laments for Abraham Lincoln and 'Pioneers! O Pioneers!'.

The fifth edition of 1871 saw the addition of *Passage to India* and the sixth, of 1876, was in two volumes: the first was *Leaves of Grass* without the additions of 1871, which were transferred to the second volume, called *Two Rivulets*. The sixth edition was called the Author's or Centennial Edition and contained additional poems and Whitman's prose, including *Democratic Vistas*.

The seventh edition was published in Boston by James R. Osgood and Co and contained new poems – but the volume was considered indecent and official protests resulted in the book being withdrawn. That was in 1882, after Walt Whitman's work had been published in the USA for 27 years. A publisher in Philadelphia, Rees Welsh and Co, reissued the edition in the same year.

The eighth edition, of 1889, included the poems published as *November Boughs* (1888) and the poet's epilogue, *A Backward Glance O'er Travel'd Roads*. The ninth and final edition was prepared under Whitman's supervision; the poems of *Goodbye, My Fancy* (1891) and some new poems were added. The edition was completed in 1892.

The standard edition of *Leaves of Grass* is to be found in the *Complete Writings*, prepared by his executors and published in ten volumes in 1902.

**Lecky, William Edward Hartpole** 1838–1903. Lecky was the son of an Anglo-Irish landowner and was born near Dublin. He was educated at Cheltenham College and Trinity College, Dublin, and was intended for the Church. But writing interested him more and he was influenced by Henry Thomas Buckle's approach to history. *The Religious Tendencies of the Age* (1860) and *The Leaders of Public Opinion in Ireland* (1861) were published anonymously and attracted no attention. Lecky set out on travels in Europe in 1862.

*The Declining Sense of the Miraculous* (1863) became the first two chapters of *A History of the Rise and Influence of the Spirit of Rationalism in Europe* (1865), which argued with considerable force that progress is due to the spirit of rationalism and the tolerance demanded by reason and is always impeded by theological dogmatism and bigotry. The book made Lecky famous and he followed it with *The History of European Morals from Augustus to Charlemagne* (1869). *A History of England in the Eighteenth Century* (1878–90) was published in 8 volumes, which were extended to 12 (1892). The later volumes were devoted to Ireland, delivering a corrective to James Anthony Froude and his *The English in Ireland in the Eighteenth Century* (1872–74). Lecky also published some historical essays, *Democracy and Liberty* (1896) and *The Map of Life: Conduct and Character* (1899). From 1895 he sat in Parliament as MP for Trinity College: he opposed Home Rule for Ireland though his sympathies lay with the welfare and interests of that country.

*Lectures on the English Comic Writers*  See **Hazlitt, William.**

*Leda and the Swan*  See **Yeats, William Butler.**

**Lee, Alice**  The heroine of Scott's *Woodstock*. Loved by the hero, Everard, she is ardently pursued by the fugitive King Charles II, who has taken refuge at Woodstock after the Battle of Worcester.

**Lee, Nathaniel** *c*.1650–92.  The son of a clergyman and educated at Trinity College, Cambridge, Lee was a minor Restoration dramatist whose original ambition was to be an actor. Failing in this he turned to writing for the theatre, achieving enough distinction in his own day to enjoy the collaboration of John Dryden; indeed he was popular as well as successful and his work held the stage for over a century. He wrote in both rhymed and blank verse and among those who acted in his works were Thomas Betterton, John Philip Kemble, Sarah Siddons and Edmund Kean.

In spite of a real talent for poetic drama, Lee faded from the repertory because his tragedies began to seem overemphasized. He was a morbid writer and laced the action with mad avengers and bleeding corpses. Lee himself became insane, and, pathetically, died in Bedlam about the age of 40. He was the author of 13 plays and some occasional verse, written during a period of 15 years. Lee's plays are all concerned with an historical character or event: his first was *The Tragedy of Nero, Emperour of Rome* (1674), his last *The Massacre of Paris* (1689). The collaborations with Dryden were *Oedipus* (1678) and *The Duke of Guise* (1682).

The works of Nathaniel Lee were collected and edited by T. B. Stroup and A. L. Cooke (1954–55). The text of his *Sophonisba: or Hannibal's Overthrow* (1675) is included in Bonamy Dobrée's *Five Heroic Plays* (The World's Classics).

**Le Fanu, (Joseph) Sheridan** 1814–73. Sheridan Le Fanu was a descendant of Richard Brinsley Sheridan on his mother's side and was born in Dublin. He was educated at Trinity College and called to the Bar in 1839. But he had by then published his Irish ballads, 'Phaudrig Croohoore' and 'Shamus O'Brian', and eventually he turned to writing. He published more than 20 books – novels, short stories, and ballads, and the drama *Beatrice*. Much of his work was first published in the *Dublin University Magazine*, of which he became proprietor and editor in 1869.

He is best known for his novels and stories of mystery and terror, notably *The House by the*

*Churchyard* (1863), **Uncle Silas** (1863), and **In a Glass Darkly** (1872). The first is a ghost story, the second a crime story, and the third a celebrated collection of 'cases' on the unconscious workings of the mind which always succeeds in leaving the reader feeling uneasy. *The House by the Churchyard* probably offers the least to the modern reader; Le Fanu, either uncertain in his grasp or else following the conventions of contemporary fiction, crams his novel too full of 'characters' and incidents though the haunting, by a hand 'handsomely formed, and white and plump', is thoroughly nasty and almost makes the novel worth reading. The two later books, however, show a master craftsman at work.

**Legende of Good Women, The**  A poem in heroic couplets by Geoffrey Chaucer. The probable year of composition was 1387, after *Troilus and Criseyde* and before *The Canterbury Tales*. The form of the poem is Chaucer's familiar dream-vision.

In the Prologue the poet, after musing on the charm of 'daysyes', falls asleep in an arbour. In his dream he is visited by the God of Love and the Lady Alceste. The God of Love names him a heretic to love for writing about women as he has already done in *The Romaunt of the Rose* and *Troilus and Criseyde*. Alceste pleads for the poet, who is then permitted to sing in praise of women. He narrates the stories of nine heroines of antiquity, basing his tales on the *Heroides* of the Latin poet Ovid.

Chaucer appears to have put the poem down at a certain point and to have written no more. His disciple John Lydgate later implied that it bored the master to write so much of good women.

**Legend of Montrose, The**  A novel by Sir Walter Scott, in the third series of *Tales of My Landlord*, first published in 1819. The setting is the rising of the Highland clans, in favour of Charles I, against the Covenanters in 1644. Interwoven in the plot is the story of Allan M'Aulay, the nephew of a man murdered by Highland raiders calling themselves Children of the Mist, who seeks revenge on them. He rescues Annot Lyle from the raiders and falls in love with her. She loves the young Earl of Menteith, who responds but cannot marry her because of some unresolved mystery surrounding her birth. When this is cleared up, she is revealed to be the daughter of Sir Duncan Campbell, so her marriage to Menteith is possible. But Allan interrupts the wedding, stabs his rival, and then disappears.

The novel is more successful in its history than in its romance: the opposing characters of Montrose (for the king) and Argyle, and the events of the struggle, are far more interesting than the lovers' problems.

**Legend of the Holy Rood, The**  A version in Old English of the story of the Rood (the Cross) preserved in its oldest form in a manuscript in the Bodleian Library, Oxford. The manuscript dates from the 12th century but the legend is very much older. It is based on Jewish legends of the three seeds – cedar, cypress, and pine – which were given to Seth when Adam was on his deathbed. The seeds were buried with Adam, and the rods which grew from them were used by Moses to succour the Israelites during their wanderings. The Christian gloss offers the three rods to David as a vision of the Trinity: David plants the rods in a pool of bitter water and they grow into a mighty tree. The gloss goes on to make this the tree which provided the wood for the Cross. An edition of the Bodleian Manuscript was prepared by R. Morris and published by the Early English Text Society (1871).

**Legree, Simon**  The brutal and drunken planter who buys Uncle Tom in the auction in *Uncle Tom's Cabin*. He is a Northerner, from Vermont; the institution of slavery in the South provides him with not only a livelihood but with the opportunity to indulge all sides of his vicious nature.

**Lehmann, (Rudolph) John (Frederick)** 1907–  . John Lehmann was born at Bourne End in Buckinghamshire and educated at Eton College and Trinity College, Cambridge. His first published works were poetry, *A Garden Revisited and Other Poems* (1931) and *The Noise of History* (1934), and a travel book, *Prometheus and the Bolsheviks* (1937). He published a novel, *Evil was Abroad* (1938), and a further travel book, *Down River: A Danubian Study* (1939) before World War II. He had, meanwhile, started on his publishing career at the Hogarth Press with Leonard and Virginia Woolf (1938–46) and became the company's general manager. His periodical, *New Writing* (1936–41), did much to encourage promising young writers. In 1941 it amalgamated with *Daylight* and with Lehmann as editor continued the enlightened policy until 1946. *New Writing and Daylight* was associated with *Penguin New Writing*, with Lehmann as editor, throughout World War II and was of great importance to poets and writers in the armed services. He founded his own publishing house, John Lehmann Ltd, which he directed (1946–52), and the *London Magazine* in 1954.

Among other books by John Lehmann are his autobiographical volumes *The Whispering Gallery* (1955), *I am my Brother* (1960), and *The Ample*

*Proposition* (1966) and a readable and informative book on Virginia Woolf, *Virginia Woolf and her World* (1975). His *Collected Poems* was published in 1963.

**Lehmann, Rosamond (Nina)** 1903– . Rosamond Lehmann was born in London, the sister of John Lehmann and the actress, Beatrix Lehmann. She was taught at home before going to Girton College, Cambridge, the background of her first novel, *Dusty Answer* (1927). This was well received and the themes, developing womanhood and the subtle shades of emotional relationships, have served the author well in a successful career as a novelist. Her other books are *A Note in Music* (1930), *Invitation to the Waltz* (1932) and its sequel *The Weather in the Streets* (1936), *The Ballad and the Source* (1944), and *The Echoing Grove* (1953). Rosamund Lehmann is also the author of a play, *No More Music* (1939), *The Gipsy's Baby and Other Stories* (1946), and the autobiographical *The Swan in the Evening* (1967).

**Leland (*or* Leyland), John** *c.*1506–52. Leland was the first English antiquary. He was educated at St Paul's School and Christ's College, Cambridge. After further study in Paris he took holy orders and became librarian to Henry VIII some time before 1530. He was appointed King's Antiquary in 1533 and in the following year set out on six years of travelling, researching what he planned as 'The History of Antiquities of this Nation'. He described his intention to the king in a New Year's gift in 1545 (*The Laboryouse Journey and Serche of Johan Laylande, for Englandes Antiquitiees, Geven of Hym as a Newe Yeares Gyfte to Kynge Henry the VIII in the XXXVII Yeare of his Raigne*). But five years later, with none of his plan realized, Leland became insane. He left behind a mass of notes, which were to prove immensely useful to Holinshed, Stow, Bale, Harrison, and others, and were eventually published as *Itinerary* (nine volumes, 1710, edited by Thomas Hearne), and *Collectanea* (his notes in Latin, six volumes, 1715). Leland also wrote a Latin elegy on Sir Thomas Wyatt, *Naeniae in Mortem*, and *Assertio Inelytissimi Arturii Regis Britanniae* (1544), translated by R. Robinson in 1582 as *A Learned and True Assertion of the Life of Prince Arthure*. Leland claimed to have saved many valuable manuscripts during the dissolution of the monasteries. A recommended modern edition of his *Itinerary* is that by Lucy Toulmin Smith (1906–07).

**Lennox, Charlotte Ramsay** 1720–1804. Charlotte Lennox was born in New York, the daughter of the lieutenant governor, and went to England at the age of 15. She worked as an actress for a short time and then became a professional writer and novelist. *The Life of Harriot Stuart* (1750) was a sentimental novel of manners but she achieved success with her satire *The Female Quixote* (1752). She dramatized the novel as *Angelica: or Quixote in Petticoats* (1758). *The History of Henrietta* (1758) was dramatized as *The Sister* (1769). Other novels were *Sophia* (1762) and *Euphemia* (1790).

*The Female Quixote: or, The Adventures of Arabella* depicts a heroine whose world is conjured up from French romances of the previous century – a far more satisfying one for her than the real world. But reality keeps intruding and Mrs Lennox makes some successful comedy out of Arabella's conviction that all men are either suitors or ravishers.

**Leontes** The jealous King of Sicily in Shakespeare's *The Winter's Tale*. His jealousy is aroused when Hermione his wife successfully prevails on Leontes' friend, Polixenes, to prolong his stay with them. Polixenes' visit coincides with Hermione's expectation of a child and Leontes' sense of proportion deserts him. When Polixenes evades Leontes' plan to murder him and escapes, Leontes turns his rage on Hermione. The ill-used Hermione apparently dies in prison and Leontes orders Antigonus to abandon her baby daughter. The passage of 16 years occurs between the end of Act III and the beginning of Act IV in the play and Leontes is bowed down with grief and remorse when the second part, with its resolution, begins.

**Lepidus, Marcus Aemilius** The triumvir, with Mark Antony and Octavius Caesar, in Shakespeare's *Julius Caesar* and *Antony and Cleopatra*. He is called 'a slight unmeritable man, meet to be sent on errands' by Antony, but Octavius reminds him that Lepidus is 'a tried and valiant soldier' – which the historical Lepidus was and a loyal supporter of the fallen Caesar. He comes up against Octavius in the later play and is deprived of his triumvirate – an event referred to in Act III Scene 6.

**Lessing, Doris (May)** 1919– . Doris Lessing was born in Khermanshah in Persia, but grew up on a farm in what was then Southern Rhodesia. She had been twice married before she left Africa for England in 1949, taking with her the manuscript of a novel, *The Grass is Singing* (1950). This earned considerable praise, so did her next book, *This was the Old Chief's Country* (1951, short stories). Doris Lessing's second novel was *Martha Quest* (1952), the first part of a five-novel sequence, *The Children of Violence*, which reflects the author's experience of life in a constricting world where rigid convention and racial prejudice had to be resolutely withstood if individual integrity was to be preserved. The sequence follows Martha Quest through two unsuccessful marriages, her hopes of the Communist party, a dead-end life in Rhodesia, her departure for England, and a mental breakdown. The novels are *A Proper Marriage* (1954), *A Ripple from the Storm* (1958), *Landlocked* (1965), and *The Four-Gated City* (1969). While the sequence was in progress Doris Lessing also published *Five* (1953, short stories), *The Habit of Loving* (1957, short stories), *Going Home* (1957, a visit to Rhodesia), *Fourteen Poems* (1959), *In Pursuit of the English* (1960, the author's first year in London), the novel *The Golden Notebook* (1962), *A Man and Two Women* (1963, short stories), *African Stories* (1964), and the novels *Briefing for a Descent into Hell* (1971), *The Summer Before the Dark* (1973), and *The Memoirs of a Survivor* (1974).

**L'Estrange, Roger** 1616–1704. The son of Norfolk landowners, L'Estrange was an active Royalist and took part in the Civil War; he also spent some time in prison during the aftermath of the king's defeat at Naseby. After taking part in an abortive Royalist rising in Kent in 1648 he escaped to the Continent, where he first used his talents as a writer with political pamphlets against the army leaders and the Presbyterians. He contributed to the climate of opinion that led to the Restoration and in 1663 was appointed Surveyor of the Imprimery (of printing presses) and licenser of the press. L'Estrange published two newspapers, *The Intelligencer* and *The News*, from 1663 to 1666, but he had less success than Henry Muddiman, whose *London Gazette* ousted all rivals. Another paper published by L'Estrange was the *City Mercury*, which he founded in 1675. Soon after, however, he was obliged to leave England again; apparently his connection with the Popish Plot led to accusations against him. However, he was able to return in 1680 and published *The Observator* (1681–87), in which he attacked Titus Oates particularly and Dissenters and Whigs generally. He earned a knighthood in 1685.

The Revolution and the accession of William and Mary ended L'Estrange's career as a journalist; he was deprived of his office as Surveyor and imprisoned several times. In later life he supported himself by his translations, a field in which he had already enjoyed some success: among them were Erasmus' *Colloquies* (1680 and 1689), *The Fables of Aesop and other Eminent Mythologies* (1692), and the works of *Josephus* (1702).

*Letter Concerning the Sacramental Test, A* See *Argument against Abolishing Christianity, An.*

*Letters concerning Toleration* The first of John Locke's *Letters* was published in Latin (*Epistola de Tolerantia*) in Holland in 1689. *A Second Letter concerning Toleration* was published in 1690, as was the English version of the first; *A Third Letter for Toleration* followed in 1692. Locke, a convinced Christian and an empiricist, was the principal advocate for toleration and freedom of inquiry in the later 17th century. He wanted religious liberty for all except atheists and Catholics, and a national church that made possible the freedom of individual opinion which was every man's right; moreover, every man's knowledge was limited so he should not try to impose his opinion on his neighbour.

The exclusion of Catholics and atheists strikes a jarring note but Locke's proposed system must be regarded in its historical context. In Locke's time there were grounds for regarding Catholics as for the most part prepared to put their country second to their religion; they had for some time been known to conduct their operations from the sanctuary of a hostile country. Atheists were those who repudiated the accepted covenant with God: they could not, therefore, be trusted to honour the social contract.

*Letters from an American Farmer* The 'letters' by J. Hector St John de Crèvecoeur are in fact 12 essays depicting the conditions of rural life in America in the 18th century. The book was first published in London in 1782 and is recognized as a classic of its kind.

Crèvecoeur was a realistic farmer and a lover of nature at the same time. He could write vividly of the unpleasant realities of being a frontier farmer, and with considerable charm of the wild world around him. More than that, Crèvecoeur includes a thoughtful essay (the third) on the question 'What is an American?'. His reflections led him to the conclusion that an American is frequently the result of the quest for a new way of life, a completely different existence from the (often) oppressed one from which he has fled. In America a peasant could become a freeholder and new principles and aims were the business of men founding a new country.

The penultimate essay describes a visit to the botanist John Bartram in Philadelphia – Crèvecoeur was deeply interested in the cultivation of hitherto virgin land and introduced new crops, including alfalfa, to America. His last essay gives a memorable picture of the pioneer American farmer, menaced on the one hand by hostile Indians and on the other by the growing murmur of discontent that led, ultimately, to the Revolution.

**Letters on the Study and Use of History**  See **Bolingbroke, Henry St John, 1st Viscount**.

**Letter to Sir William Wyndham, A**  See **Bolingbroke, Henry St John, 1st Viscount**.

**Lever, Charles James** 1806–72. A once-popular novelist, Lever was the son of Anglo-Irish parents; he was born in Dublin and studied medicine at Trinity College. His first novel, *The Confessions of Harry Lorrequer* (1837), was enough of a success to persuade him to take up writing as a career. His novels were very popular in England, where readers were delighted to find, in Lever's pages, confirmation of their beliefs about Ireland and the Irish. Nevertheless, his light lively style seemed, at times, to be at the service of a considerable talent and a feeling for history, as in *Charles O'Malley* (1841). He lived in Italy from 1845 and became Consul at Trieste. Thackeray wrote a parody of his work in *Novels by Eminent Hands* (Mr Punch's Prize Novelists). Charles Lever wrote 37 novels and was a regular contributor to *Blackwood's Magazine*.

**Leviathan** *Or the Matter, Form, and Power of a Commonwealth Ecclesiastical and Civil*. Thomas Hobbes's great work of political philosophy was written while he was in exile in Paris and serving as tutor to the Prince of Wales, later Charles II. It was published in England in 1651.

According to Hobbes's theory of society the basis of government is consent. Eschewing all imagined – and therefore useless – ideals he argues from cause to effect and illuminates the realities of political power. Writing in a period when those who had won had as tender consciences as those who had lost, Hobbes was vilified by both sides, though he himself is completely innocent of moral criticism and proposes no perfect goal for attainment. He sees society as he sees man, from whom society stems, and he grants no man the right to assume for himself any quality other than that of mankind. Only man can govern man (the Church is granted no right to interfere); a sovereign or an assembly rules by consent and when the covenant breaks down the result is anarchy. The life of man, 'solitary, poor, nasty, brutish, and short', cannot be otherwise without this covenant, in which every man surrenders the right to please himself entirely in what he does.

Hobbes does not offer a new society for adoption by those hoping for a better world and his book is not a prescription for improvement. Nor does he propose a course of action for man should his sovereign or his assembly break the covenant, though he acknowledges that a broken covenant is cause for rebellion and disobedience to authority. But he was the first Englishman to subject political assumptions and traditions to a merciless examination. He wrote about political reality and he was vastly disliked for doing so by those in power or with aspirations to authority.

**Lewes, George Henry** 1817–78. Lewes was born in London and dabbled in various activities – business, the law, medicine, the theatre – before becoming a journalist, writing for *The Morning Chronicle* and *The Penny Encyclopedia*. In 1850 he became editor of *The Leader* with Leigh Hunt and later helped found the influential *The Fortnightly Review*, of which he was the first editor (1865). Lewes first met Mary Ann Evans (George Eliot) in 1851; he could not obtain a divorce but their liaison was established in 1854.

Lewes was the author of two novels and ten plays that are all forgotten, *The Life of Robespierre* (1849), a number of books on the contemporary theatre, and *The Life and Works of Goethe* (1855). He also wrote on philosophy: *A Biographical History of Philosophy* (1845) and *Problems of Life and Mind* (1873–79); he introduced the work of Auguste Comte to England in *Comte's Philosophy of the Sciences* (1853).

**Lewis, Alun**  See **poets of World War II**.

**Lewis, Meriwether** 1774–1809. The celebrated explorer was born in Albemarle, Virginia. As a soldier he served in frontier posts, where he learned the languages and customs of the Indian tribes he encountered. When his friend Thomas Jefferson became president Lewis was appointed his private secretary. It was Lewis's idea to search for a land route to the Pacific. The Louisiana Purchase was being negotiated at the time and Jefferson was in favour of Lewis's enterprise; he secured $2500 from Congress and Lewis was able to prepare his expedition. As co-commander Jefferson appointed William Clark, a soldier with experience of the Indians similar to Lewis's.

The expedition assembled in Illinois during the winter of 1803 and the following spring set off to travel up the Missouri River. After reaching its source the party crossed the Rocky Mountains in a long arduous portage to the west-flowing Columbia River, which took them to the Pacific just north of what is now the state of Oregon. Lewis and Clark were rendered invaluable service by the Shoshone Indian woman, Sacagawea. She was guide, interpreter, and liaison officer with the tribes encountered on their westward progress. The expedition returned overland and reached St Louis in September 1806.

Meriwether Lewis. Portrait by St Memin. Missouri Historical Society.

Lewis, though he was nominally co-commander with Clark, was the ultimate authority and his success was rewarded by his appointment as governor of the Louisiana Territory. He died in mysterious circumstances while on the way to Washington in 1809. Somewhere in Tennessee he was either murdered or committed suicide. Jefferson accepted that he had committed suicide.

Lewis and Clark both kept detailed journals of the expedition. These were edited by R. G. Thwaites in eight volumes, *The Original Journals of the Lewis and Clark Expedition* (1904–05).

See also **Clark, William.**

**Lewis, M(atthew) G(regory)** 1775–1818. M. G. Lewis, known as 'Monk' Lewis, was born in London, the son of a deputy secretary at the War Office. He was educated at Westminster School and Christ Church, Oxford, and went on to a diplomatic career. Whilst an attaché at the British Embassy at The Hague he wrote *The Monk* (1796), the only novel – or work of any kind – for which he is remembered, though his output in verse, drama, and fiction was considerable. He became a Member of Parliament in 1796, and inherited the family property in the West Indies,

which he visited twice and where he did his best to improve the conditions of the slaves. *The Journal of a West India Proprietor* (1834) is a highly regarded account and shows him to have been a sympathetic observer. Lewis numbered many of the foremost men of letters, including Scott, Byron, and Shelley, among his friends. He died of yellow fever on the voyage home from the West Indies.

**Lewis, (Harry) Sinclair** 1885–1951. Sinclair Lewis was born in Sauk Center, Minnesota, and completed his education at Yale from where he graduated in 1907. He worked as a journalist and copy editor and published his first novel, *Our Mr Wrenn*, in 1914. He wrote another four before gaining recognition with *Main Street* (1920). A satirical novel of the life of Gopher Prairie, Minnesota, 'its Main Street is the continuation of Main Streets everywhere'. The novel encapsulated life in a small town in the Middle West, which at the time of publication was arriving at a cultural coming-of-age. *Babbitt* (1922) satirizes the smug businessman of a small town; a Republican and Rotarian, he has achieved all he can in the town of Zenith. *Arrowsmith* (1925) is the story of an altruistic doctor and his struggles to stay free of money-grabbing fashionable medical practice and pursue his research; the novel was awarded the Pulitzer Prize. In *Elmer Gantry* (1927) Lewis satirized the religious shams of the USA. *Dodsworth* (1929), probably his best novel, is the story of a man who retires with a fortune while young enough to make a great deal of life. He goes to Europe with his pampered wife – and loses her. She is shallow and greedy for flattery and deceives herself into believing she is a woman of the world. She loses her long-suffering husband to another woman. The novel was adapted for the stage by the author and Sidney Howard and enjoyed a long run on Broadway. Lewis was awarded the Nobel Prize in 1930, the first American writer to receive the honour.

Sinclair Lewis wrote 12 more novels but he seemed to mark time in his work after *Dodsworth*, and time has not dealt kindly with the two novels which made his name. Their success was probably due to his skill as a narrator and certainly they offer a vivid picture of life in the Middle West; Lewis was the first postwar American novelist to bring it to the attention of an international audience. The 'satire' is anaemic because Lewis is not an analytic artist but rather an excellent reporter.

**Lewis, (Percy) Wyndham** 1884–1957. Wyndham Lewis was born on his father's yacht off the coast of Maine. His family was English and he was educated at Rugby School and the Slade School of Art, after which he spent some years in Paris. He earned a considerable reputation as a painter and he was very much of the avant-garde in London in the second decade of the 20th century (see **Pound, Ezra**).

Lewis's novels began with *Tarr* (1918), set in artistic circles in Paris before World War I; it is an intellectual comedy of art, life, and Teutonic romanticism embodied in Kreisler, a would-be artist with no talent. The first novel of a trilogy called *The Human Age*, *The Childermass* (1928), was not followed and completed until 1955, when *Monstre Gai* and *Malign Fiesta* appeared together. This remarkable fantasy takes place in a waste land outside heaven's gate where the remnant of mankind awaits its inquisition by the Bailiff. *The Apes of God* (1930) is a satire on art and literature in the London of the 1920s; the arts are a fashionable racket and Lewis is a formidable satirist. For many critics this is Lewis's best novel but his next, *The Revenge for Love* (1937), supersedes it in the opinion of others. It is political satire of the 1930s, when sentimental intellectuals rallied to causes they did not understand. Hardcaster, the Communist, does understand; Margot and her husband Victor come to do so: for these three who deal in realities the outcome is tragic. The background is the Spanish Civil War. *Self Condemned* (1954) was his last major novel and is semi-autobiographical. There is much of Wyndham Lewis in the character of Professor Harding who, unable to bear the insanity and cowardice engulfing Europe (the approach to World War II), resigns and retreats to Canada with his wife. The description of the hotel where they go to live is the world in microcosm. After a disastrous fire in the hotel and his wife's suicide Harding emerges and resumes life as a respected writer and teacher and the great universities of America welcome him. He accepts; he is still alive '. . . the Faculty had no idea that it was a glacial shell of a man who had come to live among them, mainly because they were themselves unfilled with anything more than a little academic stuffing.'

Lewis, a distinguished artist and art critic, brought a painter's technique to his novels and there is a remarkable precision about his word-pictures. He rejected the stream-of-consciousness technique, verbal antics transferred to paper, and the idea of sex as the prime mover of the universe; he had no patience with the contrived artlessness of some American writers, nor with what he saw as selective Christian piety. Virginia Woolf, James Joyce, D. H. Lawrence, Hemingway,

Wyndham Lewis, 1932. Self-portrait. National Portrait Gallery, London.

William Faulkner, and T. S. Eliot were all his targets at different times; but Eliot wrote a preface to the 1960 edition of Lewis's verse-satire, *One-Way Song* (1933). This celebration of individual will and consciousness opposed the surrender to inwardness and subjectivism which was so strong in the art of the 1920s and 1930s. Lewis saw it as flabbiness and smug exhibitionism and detested it, and in reaction was drawn briefly to fascism. But he recognized his error; the views expressed in *Hitler* (1931) were corrected when fascism came to power and he saw the theories translated into action (*The Hitler Cult, and How It Will End*, 1939).

Among Lewis's volumes of political and critical essays are *The Lion and The Fox* (1927), *Time and Western Man* (1927), *Men without Art* (1934), *The Mysterious Mr Bull* (1938), *America and Cosmic Man* (1948), and *The Writer and The Absolute* (1952). Short stories were collected in *The Wild Body* (1927) and *Rotting Hill* (1951); chapters of autobiography were published in *Blasting and Bombardiering* (1937) and *Rude Assignment* (1950).

***Lewis and Clark, The Journals of*** See **Lewis, Meriwether** and **Clark, William**.

**Leyden, John** 1775–1811. The son of a Border shepherd of Roxburghshire, Leyden was bright enough to complete his education at Edinburgh University and become a physician; later he became a specialist in Eastern languages. Like James Hogg, he was enlisted by Scott in the collection of *The Minstrelsy of the Scottish Border*, to which he contributed four versions of his own. He edited *The Scots Magazine* in 1802 and published a long reminiscent poem, *Scenes of Infancy*, in 1803, before going to India. He held the chair of Hindustani at the University of Bengal and published several translations of Indian and Malayan writings. He died of fever in Java at the age of 36, and earned a commemoration from Scott in Canto IV of *The Lord of the Isles*.

**Libel of English Policy, The** The 'libel' of the title does not in this case refer to a legal term but simply means 'little book'. *The Libel of English Policy* is a poem of unknown authorship, written in 1436 or 1437 and notable for its insight into the value of the command of the seas, whether for commerce or for defence. It cannot be doubted that the poem had considerable influence, in later decades if not at the time of its composition. Unremarkable as poetry, it is interesting not only for its main premise but for the author's knowledge of the trade of his time and for his exhortation to the English to remember that Ireland and Wales could be useful – as fortresses to protect England.

**Liberal, The** A periodical founded by Shelley and Byron in 1822 when they were both at Pisa. Leigh Hunt was brought from England as its editor. The first number appeared in September 1822; the fourth and last in July 1823. The death of Shelley in June 1822, before the first issue, did not help its prospects, since Byron and Hunt were incompatible.

**Liber Amoris:** *or The New Pygmalion.* See **Hazlitt, William.**

**Liberator, The** The weekly journal of the Abolitionists was founded by William Lloyd Garrison at Boston in 1831. He was its editor until 1865, when the Thirteenth Amendment abolished slavery throughout the USA.

Garrison's opposition to slavery was unequivocal. He was attacked and his press destroyed – vested interests in the North were as antagonistic to him as he was to slavery, which provided cheap materials for the North. The paper never had a circulation higher than three thousand (it was often less than half that) but passions were aroused by it to an extraordinary pitch in those who had something to lose: a law was passed forbidding its circulation among free Negroes; a reward was offered in South Carolina for information which led to the arrest of anyone guilty of circulating it; the Senate of Georgia passed a resolution offering another reward for the apprehension and arrest of Garrison himself. In 1835 a mob in South Carolina broke into the US Mail and seized copies of the weekly, which they burned along with effigies of its editor. The last issue was published on 18 December 1865 when the Thirteenth Amendment was ratified.

**Liberty, On** An essay by John Stuart Mill, first published in 1859. His most famous work, it has been translated into ten European languages and into Russian, Japanese, Chinese, Hebrew, and Persian. Mill examines the relationship of society to the individual: 'The subject of this Essay is . . . Civil, or Social Liberty: the nature and limits of the power which can be legitimately exercised by society over the individual. A question seldom stated, and hardly ever discussed, in general terms, but which profoundly influences the practical controversies of the age by its latent presence and is likely soon to make itself recognized as the vital question of the future.' In Mill's view 'the sole end for which mankind are warranted, individually or collectively, in interfering with the liberty of action of any of their number, is self-protection.' No man's own good, physical or moral, is sufficient warrant for the interference of society. Allowing for the state's essential regulation of trade and industry (in conformity with basic utilitarianism), 'Mankind are greater gainers by suffering each other to live as seems good to themselves, than by compelling each to live as seems good to the rest.'

**Life in London:** *or The Day and Night Scenes of Jerry Hawthorn and his Elegant Friend Corinthian Tom, Accompanied by Bob Logic, The Oxonian, in their Rambles and Sprees through the Metropolis.* A description of scenes of London life in the early 19th century, by Pierce Egan. It was illustrated by Robert and George Cruikshank and first published in 20 shilling parts (1820) and later in book form (1821).

Corinthian Tom is a Regency rake who shows his country cousin, Jerry Hawthorn, the life of London with his friend Bob Logic. The author presents Tom as an elegant and accomplished man-about-town, Jerry Hawthorn as an amiable rustic eager for adventure, and Bob as a man of wit and unfailing good humour. The book was enormously popular with young men who aspired to a dashing life and who probably indulged in a great deal of wishful thinking when they read it: it takes its three unpleasant characters

'Tom and Jerry in trouble after a spree.' An illustration by I. R. and G. Cruikshank for *Life in London* by Pierce Egan (1821).

through every variation of mindless and unprincipled debauchery. Thackeray confessed that when he read it as a young man he believed the three principals 'to be types of the most elegant, fashionable young fellows the town afforded' and their activities 'those of all high-bred English gentlemen'. Twenty years later he could find nothing to say in its favour, and George Cruikshank in later life admitted to leaving most of the work of illustrating Egan's dubious book to his brother Robert. The book is interesting for the picture it gives of the manners of the time and for its presentation of the slang affected by fashionable young men of the period. Egan seems to have had second thoughts about his characters as time passed: *The Finish to the Adventures of Tom, Jerry and Logic, in Their Pursuits through Life in and out of London* (1828) has Tom breaking his neck while hunting, his mistress Kate dying of drink, Logic dying from his excesses, and Jerry settling down in the country like a good boy. The illustrations are by Robert Cruikshank.

***Life of Samuel Johnson, LL D, The***   The rest of the title of James Boswell's biography, first published in 1791, is 'comprehending an account of his studies and numerous works, a series of his correspondence and conversations with many eminent persons, and various original pieces of his composition never before published, the whole exhibiting a view of literature and literary men in Great Britain for near half a century during which he flourished'. (For the author's friendship with his subject and the genesis of the biography, see **Boswell, James**.)

Boswell told Johnson of his intention to write the biography in 1773 but he had been carefully assembling material since his first meeting with Johnson ten years before. Boswell was a trained lawyer and John Butt points out that he used his legal skill to draw out Johnson and lead him to talk on a multitude of subjects. After Johnson died, Boswell had to tackle the task of making a book out of the enormous collection of records and papers at his disposal, and it is universally acknowledged that he produced a masterpiece. Lord Auchinleck, Boswell's father, once remarked in considerable irritation that his son was always pinning himself to the tail of somebody or other and any summary of Boswell's career bears this out. Johnson, fortunately, when Boswell grasped *his* tail, brought out the best in the restless and insecure young snob from Edinburgh and Boswell's *Life* is a recognition of that. It is infinitely more, of course; Boswell was a reporter of genius and his style is perfectly suited to his subject; Johnson is extraordinarily vivid in his pages – one would know him anywhere. No biographer writing in English ever served his subject better.

Modern editions of Boswell's *Life of Johnson* are numerous and include: G. B. Hill's edition (1887), with the *Journal of a Tour*, revised by

L. F. Powell (1939); the Everyman's Library edition by S. C. Roberts (1949); the Oxford Standard Authors edition by R. W. Chapman (1953), and The Penguin English Library edition (1969).

**Life on the Mississippi** Mark Twain's reminiscences were first published in 1883. The greater part of the first half (Chapters 4 to 22) was first published in *The Atlantic Monthly*. The three opening chapters constitute a history of the great river from its discovery by Hernando De Soto in 1541.

The first half covers the author's childhood, youth, and life as a river pilot, and gives a vivid picture of life on the Mississippi before the Civil War.

The second half was written seven years after the first and is an account of Mark Twain's return to the river 21 years later, and a trip to New Orleans from St Louis. The glamour of the great waterway has gone with the arrival of the railways and the author looks back, recalling George Washington Cable, Joel Chandler Harris, and Horace Bixby. He also dwells on the condition of the South, past and present, and attacks the influence of romanticism, particularly in the novels of Sir Walter Scott.

Chapter 3 contains a passage which was originally written for *Huckleberry Finn* but not used in the novel.

**Life's Handicap** A collection of 28 stories by Rudyard Kipling, first published in 1891. 'The Incarnation of Krishna Mulvaney', 'The Courting of Dinah Shadd', and 'On Greenhow Hill' tell more of the three privates, Mulvaney, Ortheris, and Learoyd. Among the others are the thrillers 'The Mark of the Beast', 'Bertran and Bimi', and 'The Return of Imray'. The volume is notable for the many stories dealing directly with Indian life. See also *Without Benefit of Clergy*.

**Life without Principle** An essay by Henry David Thoreau, posthumously published in *The Atlantic Monthly* in 1863. It is in essence a criticism of the way of life in the America of his day, where a man may be preoccupied to the point of obsession with the surface of existence and with acquisition in order to conform to the convention of society. There can be no true values in such a society; any thought, writing, or religion that emerges from it 'is not worth the dust of a puff-ball'.

**Light in August** A novel by William Faulkner, first published in 1932. It is concerned with Lena Grove and Joe Christmas, who are not directly concerned with one another. Lena is pregnant and making her way as best she can to Jefferson where she hopes to find Lucas Burch, her lover. But everyone she confides in knows that Lucas Burch has deserted her and will never marry her. She arrives in Jefferson just as a manhunt begins for a murderer, Joe Christmas. Joe is a supposed mulatto – but he might be White – turned over to an orphanage because his mother's father believes that her illegitimate child is part Negro. Grown up, he arrives in Jefferson where he is encouraged in a liaison with Joanna Burden, a White spinster. She, outwardly respectable, believes him a mulatto and conducts the affair in a furtive, hole-and-corner manner; he finds himself caught in a stew of lust and eventually kills her. Joe has nowhere to turn; he has no contact with humanity in either world, Black or White. He faces the mob which castrates and kills him because he is a Black man who, they want to believe, has raped and killed a virtuous White woman. In these circumstances Lena bears her baby, placidly and naturally, fulfilling her natural function as a woman.

**Light That Failed, The** See **Kipling, Rudyard**.

**Lilburne, John** 1615–57. The 'angry young man' of the early 17th century was the son of a Durham squire. A Leveller by conviction, he earned the wrath of the Royalist Anglican government for distributing unlicensed books, which were, inevitably, anti-episcopalian. The savage sentence that he earned from the Star Chamber in 1637 (he was flogged behind a cart from the Fleet to Westminster, pilloried, and then imprisoned at the age of 22) aroused enormous sympathy and helped the cause of king and bishops not at all.

Lilburne served in the Parliamentary army from 1642 but his refusal to subscribe to the covenant required by the New Model Army in 1645 earned him another term in prison where he wrote *England's Birthright Justified*. This and other tracts now earned him the wrath of the Parliamentarians; he was uncompromising in his criticism of all forms of repression and eventually he was charged with treason in 1649. He was acquitted, but later suffered banishment and ended his days as a Quaker.

Strictly speaking John Lilburne belongs more to history than to literature; but his life and career are a remarkable demonstration of the fear inspired by the written word in the minds of those in power, whether Royalists or Parliamentarians.

**Lilith** See **MacDonald, George**.

**Lilliburlero** The Earl of Tyrconnel went to Ireland in January 1686 as James II's Catholic lieutenant. Lord Thomas Wharton wrote a song to satirize the earl, using for its refrain a form of doggerel believed to have been used by the Irish when they rose against their Protestant overlords in 1641. 'Lero, lero, lilli-burlero; Lilli-burlero Bullen-a-la!'. The words were set to Wharton's catchy tune and became the kind of easily remembered nonsense that the army loved. An enormously popular song, it was of course anti-Catholic and was said to have sung James II out of his kingdom. The song is included in Percy's *Reliques of Ancient English Poetry* (1765), and the tune was once attributed to Purcell.

**Lillo, George** *c.*1693–1739.   George Lillo is believed to have been of Flemish and English parentage and was born in London. Not much is known of his life before he wrote for the theatre but his father was a jeweller and he may have followed that trade for a time. He wrote seven plays and an adaptation of the Elizabethan tragedy *Arden of Feversham* (Drury Lane, July 1759). Six of his plays were produced: *Sylvia: or The Country Burial*, a ballad opera (Lincoln's Inn Fields, November 1730), **The London Merchant: or The History of George Barnwell** (Drury Lane, June 1731), *The Christian Hero* (Drury Lane, January 1735), **The Fatal Curiosity** (Haymarket, May 1736), *Marina* (Covent Garden, August 1738), and *Elmerick: or Justice Triumphant* (Drury Lane, February 1740). *Britannia and Batavia*, a masque, was not performed. *Marina* was based on Shakespeare's *Pericles*.

The most successful of these works were *The London Merchant* and *The Fatal Curiosity*. *The London Merchant* is domestic prose tragedy and insists on the importance of high emotion in the life of ordinary people. It was based on an old ballad and, though it seems like barnstorming melodrama at this distance, it was to have considerable influence. The resemblance to Hogarth is not coincidental; the first important work of the master, *A Harlot's Progress*, appeared in the following year. *The Fatal Curiosity* was also a domestic tragedy, in more direct terms, based on an old Cornish story of murder. The same theme was used by Albert Camus in 1945; Lillo's influence in furthering domestic tragedy extended far beyond the bounds of England.

**Lilly, William** 1602–81.   A 17th-century astrologer, Lilly wrote a number of pamphlets containing 'Prophesies' and published an annual almanac from the year 1644. He is remembered as the author of *Monarchy, or no Monarchy, in England* (1651), the second part of which is called *Secret Observations on the Life and Death of Charles King of England*. He claims to have foretold the execution of the king but scholars generally agree that his biographical portrait is fair and accurate.

*Limits and Renewals*   See **Kipling, Rudyard.**

**Linacre, Thomas** *c.*1460–1524.   The Greek scholar and founder of the Royal College of Physicians was born at Canterbury and educated at Oxford; he became a Fellow of All Souls in 1484. Linacre learned Greek from Cornelio Vitelli (who was the first to teach it publicly in England) and later taught Greek to Thomas More. Linacre studied medicine in Italy under Angelo Poliziano and during the ten years he spent in that country extended his study of the classics. Upon his return to England he became a member of the group of friends and scholars that included Colet, More, and Erasmus; Henry VIII appointed him royal physician and both Wolsey and Archbishop Warham were among his patients.

In 1518 Linacre secured the royal charter for his college, which was designed to discourage quacks and regulate the practice of medicine. He founded chairs of medicine at Oxford and Cambridge. Linacre made no written contribution to English literature (his writing was chiefly concerned with translations from the Greek of Galen into Latin and the composition of a Latin grammar for Princess Mary) but as a representative of the Renaissance in England and of the forces of Christian humanism that led to the Reformation his influence on it was considerable.

*Linda Tressel*   A novel by Anthony Trollope, first published in *Blackwood's Magazine* (October 1867 to May 1868). It was published anonymously (see **Nina Balatka**).

The setting is Nuremberg and the story concerns Linda Tressel, a girl who loves her aunt, Madame Stanbach, who is also her guardian. The aunt is a good woman of strong Calvinistic principles and not a grain of charity. Aunt Stanbach decides that Linda, with not a grain of resolution to oppose her aunt's decisions, shall marry the vulgar and middle-aged Peter Steinmarc who, the aunt's character notwithstanding, has no time for religion. A contemporary critic called the novel 'so improbable and melancholy that it cannot be read with pleasure'. *The London Review* was convinced that the author of both this book and *Nina Balatka* was a woman.

*Lindisfarne Gospels*   A version of the Gospels in the Latin Vulgate text, written down by Eadfrith, Bishop of Lindisfarne, about 700. The bishop used the uncial script in an Irish style and tells us on the cover that his task was 'in honour of St Cuthbert'. The manuscript, on quarto vellum, contains an interlinear version in his own dialect by the Northumbrian priest Aldred, who

St Mark, as depicted in the 7th-century *Lindisfarne Gospels. Cotton MS Nero D. IV, f.93b.* British Library.

added his contribution about 950, long after the monks had been forced by Norse raiders to abandon Lindisfarne. The community was at this time in Chester-le-Street in County Durham. The beautifully illuminated openings to each gospel, and the beauty of the lettering, make the *Lindisfarne Gospels* one of the treasures of English art. The manuscript is in the British Museum.

**Lindsay, Lady Anne** 1750–1825. The daughter of the Earl of Balcarres, Anne Lindsay became Lady Anne Barnard by marriage and accompanied her husband to South Africa. Her journals were edited by D. Fairbridge in 1924 as *Lady Anne Barnard at the Cape, 1797–1802* and are a valuable source of information on the first English occupation of the Cape. Anne Lindsay is also known as the author of the ballad 'Auld Robin Gray' (1771) and the poem 'Why Tarries my Love' (1805).

**Lindsay, Sir David**  See **Lyndsay, Sir David.**

**Lindsay, (Nicholas) Vachel** 1879–1931. Vachel Lindsay was born in Springfield, Illinois. His parents wanted him to become a minister but he had different ideas, so did not complete his education at Hiram College. He left in 1900 to study art in Chicago and New York for several years, earning whenever he could, lecturing when the opportunity arose. He tramped across much of the United States and at this time began to write verse, which he would often barter for food and lodging. He found his inspiration in the broad range of American life.

Lindsay's first collection was *General William Booth Enters into Heaven and Other Poems,* published in 1913. The title poem had been published in Harriet Monroe's *Poetry* magazine and the Midwest movement was well under way. A new poet whose work was dramatic and displayed incisive rhythms, and whose vivid imagery arose from a broad American background, was welcomed. *The Congo and Other Poems* was published in the following year and *The Chinese Nightingale and Other Poems* in 1917. This collection is believed to represent his highest point of achievement in verse; he was prolific and published four more volumes but none of his later verse is held in the same esteem as the first three collections.

As a reader of his own poetry Lindsay became a popular figure and he tried to extend the popularity of poetry by presenting it in what he liked to call 'the higher vaudeville'. Inevitably, this method enjoyed only a limited success but Lindsay, in his younger days, had been preoccupied with the hope, which never quite left him, of becoming the great singer of everyman; he wanted to 'reconcile culture and manliness'. This sentimental idealism surfaced again in his *The Golden Book of Springfield* (1920); in it he offers a Utopia based on the 'Gospel of Beauty' on which he used to lecture before he gained recognition as a poet. As a poet Lindsay is at his best when he is giving expression to the America he has correctly perceived – authentic matter for endless poetry. His work deteriorated when the sharp focus failed and the best of his later work is contained in poems about childhood.

Lindsay had supported himself by his poetry readings – proof of his popularity in his best days. But his audiences dwindled as the years went by and inevitably his income was reduced. Emotional depression accompanied his receding popularity and he committed suicide in 1931. His last published work was a book of political essays, *The Litany of Washington Street* (1929). Lindsay's *Collected Poems* was published in 1923 and revised in 1925.

**Lindsay of Pitscottie, Robert** 1532–92. Robert Lindsay was a kinsman of Sir David Lyndsay and Pitscottie was near Sir David's estates in Fifeshire. Little else is known of him but he is remembered for his *The Historie and Chronicles* *of Scotland*, most of which was written some time before 1577. Robert Lindsay's *Historie* begins where the Latin *Historia Scotorum* of Hector Boece concludes, with the reign of James II, and ends with the accession of James VI to the throne of England (the history of the years 1565 to 1604 is by another hand).

Lindsay's *Historie* was loved by Sir Walter Scott and is generally admired by scholars as one of the few still readable books of that period in Scottish literature. Lindsay used as much direct information for his own period as he could find and gives the names of his informants. From Lindsay comes the famous account of James V on his deathbed, when he is brought the news that his heir, newly born, is a daughter: 'Adew, fareweill, it come with ane lass, it will pass witht ane lass.' His daughter was Mary, Queen of Scots.

*The Historie and Cronicles of Scotland* was edited by E. J. G. MacKay for the Scottish Texts Society and published in three volumes (1899–1911).

**Lingard, John** 1771–1851. Lingard was born in Winchester, the son of a Roman Catholic family, and was educated at the English College at Douai, which he entered in 1782. The revolutionary wars forced him to leave in 1793 and he completed his training for the priesthood at Crook Hall near Durham, taking holy orders in 1795. He taught natural and moral philosophy at Crook Hall and published *The Antiquities of the Anglo-Saxon Church* (1806, enlarged 1845). He spent most of his life after 1811 at Hornby, near Lancaster, making a successful journey to Rome in 1817 to negotiate the reopening of the English College. *The History of England from the First Invasion of the Romans to the Accession of William and Mary* (eight volumes, 1819–30) enjoyed considerable success; it was praised for its objectivity and careful use of original documents and for its balanced view of the Reformation. The history is not now read in its entirety but is continually mined by students: the scrupulousness which makes it dull reading makes it useful for study. Lingard was also the author of *A New Version of the Four Gospels* (1836).

**Lippard, George** 1822–54. A Philadelphia-born novelist who made a remarkable success writing novels about the iniquity and immorality of large cities by giving as many details of rape and seduction as the law permitted while deploring, of course, that such things could be. The most famous and successful was *The Quaker City* (1845), which told thousands of readers (thirty thousand a year for ten years) what dreadful things were happening to innocent girls in Philadelphia, especially those who fell among the rich and privileged. Lippard also wrote historical novels.

**Lismahago, Lieutenant Obadiah** The penniless and eccentric Scots soldier who joins Matthew Bramble's party in Durham in *Humphry Clinker* by Tobias Smollett. Tabitha Bramble marries him.

*Little Dorrit* A novel by Charles Dickens, first published in 20 monthly parts (December 1857 to June 1858).

Little Dorrit is Amy, the diminutive youngest child of William Dorrit. Dorrit lives in the Marshalsea prison for debtors – his children, perforce, live there too and Amy was actually born within its walls. The children go forth each morning to earn what they can and return to the Marshalsea at night. Little Dorrit and her father are befriended by Arthur Clennam, for whose mother Little Dorrit does sewing. Little Dorrit falls in love with him but keeps her feelings to herself because she gets no response from him, and he is middle-aged.

William Dorrit escapes the Marshalsea: he inherits a fortune and the family is suddenly rich. Little Dorrit's brother and sister show up badly in their new circumstances: they become arrogant and pretentious; and old Dorrit never really escapes the impression made on his character by 23 years in prison. Only Little Dorrit is unchanged.

Arthur Clennam, who had been generous to the Dorrits while fighting his own battles with bureaucracy, is in turn brought low and is sentenced to the Marshalsea, where he is found, sick and despairing, by Little Dorrit. She cares for him and Arthur in turn falls in love with her; but he is deterred from asking her to marry him by the reversal in their circumstances. His mother, the narrow-minded, humourless mistress of a gloomy house in which she lives in a single room as a paralytic (the paralysis is hysterical), shows no sympathy for her son in his troubles. The entry of Blandois, a villainous Frenchman, into the story helps to bring its various strands together and it transpires that the puritanical woman is not Arthur Clennam's true mother. Further, she had suppressed a codicil in a will, thereby contributing to the straits of the Dorrit family.

The main thread of the story, recounted in the foregoing lines, gives no hint of the complexity of Dickens's novel nor of the large cast of characters. The prison is the heart of the book and the author takes us outward from there to mount a sustained attack on the government departments of the day, staffed by obstructive officials who have no thought of serving people but use the departments to serve themselves, with no question in their minds that they could possibly be in error. Dickens calls his particular institution the Circumlocution Office but it could be any government department staffed with 'permanent' members comfortably settled there for life. It is a grim book; Dickens takes his reader through every level of society and spares no one, at any level. Dorrit, the debtor, the father of the Marshalsea because he has been there longest, is not a better man than Merdle, the immensely rich financier who proves a fraud and commits suicide. Dorrit is deplorable, never more so than in the horrible scene in the Marshalsea where he patronizes the honest old man Nandy, a pauper through no fault of his own, at a tea-party. The emphasis on personal responsibility throughout the long, dense novel is very strong.

A notable departure in *Little Dorrit* is the absence of the rich comic characters who have been, hitherto, a feature of Dickens. Flora Finching is a delight – but she is really the only one.

**Little Lord Fauntleroy**   A novel By Frances Hodgson Burnett, first published in 1886. It was adapted for the stage by the author in 1888.

The son of the Earl of Dorincourt alienates his father by marrying an American. The earl refuses to receive his daughter-in-law and after her husband's death she takes her son to New York, where she brings him up. He is called Cedric Errol, has long curls, is generous, affectionate, and loved by all in his modest neighbourhood, particularly by Mr Hobbs the grocer and Dick the bootblack. Then he becomes the heir of

Dorincourt and has to go to England with his mother, whom he always addresses as Dearest.

In England the old earl will not receive Dearest, who is obliged to live in a house near the Dorincourt seat. But Cedric wins the earl's love and soon influences him to behave benevolently to his tenants and other poor people. Then a strange American woman appears, claiming to be his real daughter-in-law, and she has a son for whom she claims the estate. She is eventually unmasked by Dick and Mr Hobbs, who journey all the way to England to discredit the impostor's claims.

The earl receives Dearest and the three generations settle down happily at Dorincourt, which Cedric, Little Lord Fauntleroy, will inherit.

**Little Gidding**   See **Ferrar, Nicholas**.

***Littlepage Manuscripts***   The trilogy of novels by James Fenimore Cooper about three generations of the Littlepage family in the state of New York. The sequence is **Satanstoe**, **The Chainbearer**, and **The Redskins**.

***Little Princess, The***   A novel by Frances Hodgson Burnett, first published in 1905. A shorter version, entitled *Sara Crewe*, had been published in 1887.

Sara is a rich girl and a favoured pupil in Miss Minchin's Seminary for Young Ladies. When her father is believed dead during the Boer War his fortune is lost too and Sara is reduced to the status of a slave in the garret, at the beck and call of her erstwhile school friends. But the story ends happily when her father returns; Sara, meanwhile, has proved she is a real little princess because she has risen above adversity.

***Little Women***   A novel by Louisa May Alcott, first published in two parts in 1868 and 1869.

Meg, Jo, Beth, and Amy are the daughters of March, an army chaplain in the Civil War. They live with their mother (Marmee) in a small New England community. Meg is pretty and would like to lead a gracious life; Jo is independent, unconventional, and wants to be a writer – she retires to the attic to practise her craft; Beth is a delicate girl with a fondness and some skill for music – she sometimes 'wept a little weep' over the keyboard of the battered old piano that is all she has to practise on; Amy is the youngest and a beautiful blonde child of 12. The story follows the girls' lives and their efforts to increase the family's small income. Jo emerges as the strongest character and is on the verge of success at the end of the first part. This part also establishes the girls' relationship with their neighbours, the Laurences, who are rather better off.

One of the illustrations by Birch for the 1889 edition of *Little Lord Fauntleroy*, by Frances Hodgson Burnett.

The second part (*Good Wives*) relates the girls' emergence into womanhood. Meg marries John Brooke, tutor of Mr Laurence's grandson, Laurie. Laurie himself falls in love with Jo; but she does not return his feelings and he goes to Europe, where he encounters Amy. Laurie and Amy fall in love and marry. The delicate Beth falls ill and dies. Jo becomes a successful novelist and later marries the professor, Dr Bhaer.

*Little Women* is a book of unaffected charm and gains much from the author's presentation of the background of the New England of the 1860s. The lives of the March girls and their children can be followed up in *Little Men* (1871) and *Jo's Boys* (1886).

**Lives of the Poets, The**  Samuel Johnson's biographical and critical study was first published as *Prefaces, Biographical and Critical, to the Works of the English Poets* (see **Johnson, Samuel**) in ten volumes (1779–81). The prefaces were published separately in four volumes in 1781. The intention had been to start with Chaucer but the ambitious scheme was reduced, in the event, and the starting point was Abraham Cowley. A total of 52 poets makes up the *Lives*, considered by many to be Johnson's most valuable work. His criticism is direct and vigorous and his approach is explained in his life of John Dryden: 'To judge rightly of an author we must transport ourselves to his time, and examine what were the wants of his contemporaries, and what were his means of supplying them.' The perspective of time, inevitably, makes some of Johnson's judgments seem rather strange, but they should be appreciated in the context of the author's times and the taste of the age.

A modern complete edition of Johnson's *Lives* is to be found in The World's Classics, in two volumes edited by Arthur Waugh (1906).

**Locke, David Ross**  See **Nasby, Petroleum V.**

**Locke, John**  1632–1704.  The son of a country lawyer, Locke was born at Wrington in Somerset, and educated at Westminster School and Christ Church, Oxford. He remained at Oxford to teach Greek and rhetoric and was influenced for the future by the work of René Descartes. He also studied medicine, though he did not take a degree until 1674, and was interested in the new experimental science being developed by Newton, Boyle, Harvey and others. In 1666 Locke became secretary to Lord Ashley (Anthony Ashley Cooper), later 1st Earl of Shaftesbury; he tutored the earl's son, and later his grandson. Shaftesbury was to earn the unenviable part of Achitophel in Dryden's celebrated satire, *Absalom and*

John Locke, 1685. Portrait by Sylvester Brownover. National Portrait Gallery, London.

*Achitophel*; Locke became a member of his household and shared his master's fortunes, acquiring a considerable knowledge of politics, trade, and the role of the monarchy. Meanwhile, he was given minor government appointments and maintained his connection with the University of Oxford. Locke spent the years between 1675 and 1679 in France, and was dismissed by the University when he was suspected of complicity in Shaftesbury's plots. Shaftesbury's fall came in 1682 and Locke fled to Holland in 1683, where he remained until 1689 and the accession of William and Mary. From 1691 until 1700 he was adviser on coinage to William III's government, and a member of the Council of Trade. He resigned when his health failed and died at his manor house of Otes in Kent.

Locke's earliest published work was the first of his **Letters concerning Toleration**, issued in Holland (1689) in Latin as *Epistola de Tolerantia*. The English version was published in 1690, as was *A Second Letter concerning Toleration*; *A Third Letter for Toleration* was published in 1692. **Two Treatises of Government** (1690) was followed a few weeks later by a book begun as a proposed reply, on a single sheet of paper, to the question 'what objects our understandings were, or were not, fitted to deal with'. This arose from Locke's discussion with some friends in 1671: nearly 20 years later the result of his brilliant examination of the question was published as an *Essay concerning Human Understanding*. It aroused enormous interest, not all favourable.

Locke's wide-ranging knowledge of economics was demonstrated in four essays on money (1692, 1695, and 1699); the future of learning was examined in *Some thoughts Concerning Education* (1693), and inevitably he gave interesting views in *The Reasonableness of Christianity as Delivered in the Scriptures* (1695). He published two replies to a host of attacks upon this work in his *Vindications* (1695 and 1697). His last years found him increasingly interested in religion and two posthumous publications were *A Paraphrase and Notes on the Epistle of St Paul to the Galatians* (1705) and *A Discourse on Miracles* (1716).

John Locke was a Fellow of the Royal Society from 1666, and in his investigation of the mind he followed the basic principles of the new experimental science, advancing his ideas upon a basis of ample evidence. His conclusions were influenced by his beliefs in religious toleration, in parliamentary democracy, and *laissez-faire* in commerce and trade. He detested the scholars' arrogance and their jargon which he called learned gibberish; the theological arguments of 15 centuries represented to Locke centuries of accumulated rubbish; men had minds of their own, and they should use them. Locke was a convinced Christian but his approach to his religion earned him a great deal of wrath from the Church. Remarkably, this philosopher who disregarded metaphysics stimulated to an extraordinary degree the minds of generations of later thinkers. Metaphysical speculation did not concern him: he appealed constantly to experience, from which reason and knowledge proceed. His *Essay concerning Human Understanding* is an essay by a great thinker on *how* to think.

**Locker, Frederick** 1821–95. Locker, who called himself Locker-Lampson on the occasion of his second marriage in 1885, was born in Greenwich and for a time served at Somerset House and at the Admiralty. He wrote verse after he left government service and published *London Lyrics* (1857), *Lyra Elegentiarium* (1867), a miscellany of verse and prose called *Patchwork* (1879), and the prose work *My Confidences* (published posthumously, 1896). Locker enjoyed comfortable means and his verse was a diversion; praised as elegant well-finished 'society verse', it is hardly known to the modern reader.

**Locker-Lampson, Frederick** See **Locker, Frederick**.

*Locksley Hall* A poem by Alfred Tennyson, written in 1837 and 1838 and first published in 1842. At the time of its composition the poet had emerged from acutely unhappy personal relationships within his own family and with the wealthy Rosa Baring, who entered into an arranged marriage with someone equally wealthy. The poem is in the form of a monologue: the speaker revisits Locksley Hall and recalls his love for his cousin, the shallow Amy who abandons him for a richer husband in accordance with her parents' wishes. The poet said '"Locksley Hall" represents young life, its good side, its deficiencies, and its yearnings.' It is a very romantic poem. 'Locksley Hall Sixty Years After' (1886) is also a dramatic monologue, in the same metre, and is addressed to 'my grandson' by the speaker of the earlier poem. After all his own struggles and disappointments he no longer envies the people of Locksley Hall and acknowledges that they have also served. The poet was 77 when he wrote the second poem, in which he dwells on the impermanence of human values and the question of what progress really is.

*Locksley Hall Sixty Years After* See *Locksley Hall*.

*Locrine, The Lamentable Tragedie of* A play first published in 1595 and once attributed to Shakespeare. Modern scholarship has named George Chapman as the more likely author but definite attribution is not possible.

The Locrine of the title is Logrin, King of Britain, mentioned by Geoffrey of Monmouth and Edmund Spenser (*The Faerie Queene*, Book I). Locrine's queen is Gwendolen, who watches with growing rage the king's infatuation with Estrildis, a German maiden. Estrildis had come to England with the invading Huns under King Humber, who had been defeated at the Battle of the River Abus – called the Humber thereafter. Estrildis bears Locrine a daughter and the tragedy's climax is reached when Gwendolen has mother and daughter drowned in the Severn.

**Lodge, Thomas** 1558–1625. Lodge was born in Lincolnshire. His father, Sir Thomas Lodge, became Lord Mayor of London and Lodge was sent to the Merchant Taylors' School, where one of his teachers was Richard Mulcaster. Later he attended Trinity College, Oxford, and studied law at Lincoln's Inn in 1578; but he abandoned law and embraced literature. In 1580 he published *Honest Excuses or A Defence of Poetry, Music and Stage Plays* in reply to Stephen Gosson's *The Schoole of Abuse* (see **Sidney, Sir Philip**). *An Alarum Against Usurers*, a warning to spendthrifts against moneylenders, followed in 1584 and was published with a romance, *The Delectable Historie of Forbonius and Prisceria*. Lodge's father, meanwhile, had gone bankrupt and Lodge, one of the University Wits, was obliged to fend for himself. He took part in freebooting expeditions to the Canary Islands (1588) and South America (1591) and went on writing to pass the time. *Scillaes Metamorphosis ... with Sundrie other Poems and Sonnets* came in 1589 and was reissued in 1610 as *A Most Pleasant Historie of Glaucus and Scilla*. This was a romance in verse treating a classical subject, anticipating Shakespeare's *Venus and Adonis*. **Rosalynde: Euphues Golden Legacie** (1590) was written during his first voyage and is Lodge's best-known romance – probably his finest work. It is based on the 14th-century *The Tale of Gamelyn* and was itself the basis for *As You Like It*; it was popular enough to be printed 12 times by 1642.

Lodge's next romance, *Euphues Shadow* (1592), was written during his voyage to South America; so was *A Margarite of America* (1596), an improbable tale of the love of a prince of Cuzco for the daughter of the King of Muscovy. Lodge's poetry, after *Scillaes Metamorphosis*, continued with *Phillis* (1593), a cycle of amorous sonnets from Italian and French originals, and *A Fig for Momus* (1595), satires and verse epistles on the Horatian model. His dramatic efforts contributed nothing to the development of the form. *The Wounds of Civill War* (1594) has a Roman republic setting; *A Looking Glasse for London and England* (1594) was written with Robert Greene.

In 1594 Lodge became a Catholic and his writing took a different turn. A devotional work, *Prosopopeia: Containing the Teares of the Mother of God*, and a treatise on the seven deadly sins, *Wits Miserie and the Worlds Madnesse*, were printed in 1596. He studied medicine at Avignon and obtained his MD in 1593. He obtained another at Oxford in 1603 and published *A Treatise of the Plague*. By this time he was active among the Catholics of London. He was obliged to retire to Europe in 1606 and lived in Brussels, where he was on good terms with the English ambassador. He was back in England in 1612, when he succeeded to his brother's estate and he became a member of the College of Physicians. Among his later works were translations of *Josephus* (1602) and *Seneca* (1614). *The Complete Works of Lodge* was edited by Edmund Gosse and published in four volumes in 1883.

**Logan, John** See **Bruce, Michael**.

*Logic, A System of, Ratiocinative and Inductive*. A treatise by John Stuart Mill, first published in 1843 (revised and enlarged editions were published in 1850 and 1872). In this book, which made the author's reputation as an original thinker, Mill formulated the inductive procedure of modern science while acknowledging the importance of deduction. He provides the procedure for the investigation of the causal relations of phenomena and assumes the causal principle: 'the belief we entertain in the universality, throughout nature, of the law of cause and effect, is in itself an instance of induction'. This is repeatedly verified by experience; if there were exceptions, we should probably have discovered them.

*Log of a Cowboy, The* The novel by Andy Adams, based on his own experience of a major cattle drive of the 1880s. It was first published in 1903. The drive is from the southern border of Texas over fifteen hundred miles northwest to the Blackfoot Agency of Montana. Under the veteran, Flood, a dozen cowboys move the Circle Dot herd across plains, along mountain trails, and over rivers. Every mile of the five months is vividly recalled from the author's own life as a cowboy and is unmatched as a record.

*London: A Poem in Imitation of the Third Satire of Juvenal*. By Samuel Johnson, first published in 1738. It is a powerful verse satire on the evils abroad in the capital, expressed in the reflections of a poet, Thales, who has turned his back on it for the sweeter air of the country. Johnson's satire is direct and deadly and every bit as disciplined as his prose.

**London, Jack** 1876–1916. Jack (really John Griffith) London was born in San Francisco and is believed to have been the illegitimate son of W. H. Chaney, an itinerant astrologer, and Flora Wellman, the daughter of an Ohio family. His mother married a John London soon after his birth. He grew up on the waterfront of Oakland; survival took most of his time and his schooling was, inevitably, intermittent. Much of his youth was spent on the wrong side of the law; he was, among other things, an oyster pirate and he spent a short time in prison as a vagrant. At the age of 17 he signed on a sealing ship which took him to the Arctic and Japan. He had, meanwhile, become a voracious reader and was familiar with most of the fiction to be found in the Oakland public library.

Depression had struck in the USA, however, and London was unable to find work of any kind when he returned. He joined the march on Washington, led by Jacob Sechler Coxey

(Coxey's Army) in 1894, to petition for relief. The petition yielded nothing for the deprived and London, who had just won first prize in a newspaper story competition, added the event to his rapidly expanding store of experience. The aspiring writer became, at the same time, an aspiring reformer. He discovered the Communist manifesto and from that time on (he was 20 years old) was an active socialist. London enrolled at the University of California in 1896 though, as it happened, he had really exhausted his potential for further education in preparing for it. He had read political sciences intensively, among other subjects. In 1897 he joined the Klondike gold rush carrying the works of Darwin and Milton in his pack.

London gained more experience of life in the raw in the Arctic. He gained little else, apart from time to read, and went down with scurvy, a frequent consequence of the miners' diet. He returned to Oakland in 1898 and began to write about his experiences. He was immediately successful; his work was accepted by the **Overland Monthly** in the West and *The Atlantic Monthly* in the East. His first collection, *The Son of the Wolf* (1900), made him famous: the reality of life in the North was something new and a steady output of work gave him distinguished visitor status when he visited England in 1902.

A successful and widely read author for the rest of his life, Jack London was in demand in the lecture circuit, reported the war between Russia and Japan for the Hearst papers, was a correspondent in Mexico, and voyaged in the South Seas and the Caribbean. He maintained a fine estate, Wolf House, in California. But for one so celebrated and rich (he earned more than a million dollars), he was an unhappy man who could not reconcile his own success with the things he had seen and endured. He spent lavishly, took drugs, and drank too much. His own survival suggested that Nietzsche was right; but his struggle and his own humanity drew him to Marx – yet he could write a novel that prophesied totalitarian despotism. Jack London died at the age of 40 and the evidence suggests that he took his own life.

The works of Jack London suffered what almost amounted to complete rejection by the critics for years, though he went on being read. Since World War II, however, he has been discovered by the scholars and his work is now being considered as literature. The crudeness of much of his writing is now acknowledged as being inseparable from the first-hand knowledge which London had of the life he describes.

London's first collection, *The Son of the Wolf,* was a book of stories which came from direct experience. This was also true of *The Cruise of the*

Jack London, 1905.

*Dazzler* (1902), for which he drew on his activities as an oyster pirate. **The Call of the Wild** (1903), a tremendous success, appeared in the same year as **The People of the Abyss**, which relied much on his observation of the slums of London. **The Sea-Wolf** (1904) is the story of a voyage on a sailing ship under a ruthless captain and *The Game* (1905) tells of a man fatally fascinated by the sport (boxing) in which he excels. In *Before Adam* (1906) London attempted to recreate a prehistoric community; the same year saw the appearance of **White Fang**, a sort of counter-novel to *The Call of the Wild* and equal to it in excellence. **Martin Eden** (1909) is more directly autobiographical than any of London's work but the accent is on his attempts to become a successful writer. *Burning Daylight* (1910) and *Smoke Bellew* (1912) see the author back in the Yukon, while his struggles with alcohol are reflected in *John Barleycorn* (1913).

The political questions which preoccupied Jack London were treated in his remarkable **The Iron Heel** (1907) and in *The Valley of the Moon* (1913). *The War of the Classes* (1905) was a treatise; another, *The Human Drift*, was published in 1917 after his death. *Jerry of the Islands*, another of London's stories about a dog, was also published after his death.

**London Lickpenny** An early 15th-century poem containing a vivid and satirical commentary on London life and London lawyers. It was attributed to John Lydgate until quite recently; the true author's identity is unknown.

**London Magazine, The** The earliest periodical to be called *The London Magazine* was published from 1732 to 1785 but the more famous monthly of the same name was published by Baldwin, Cradock, and Joy from January 1820 to June 1829. The first editor was John Scott: the magazine took advantage of the readership created by the success of *Blackwood's* and was to rival its circulation. The magazine's first great success was legitimate, rather than contrived like that of *Blackwood's*. The first instalment of Thomas De Quincey's *Confessions of an English Opium Eater* appeared in September 1821 and Charles Lamb's *Dissertation upon Roast Pig* was published exactly a year later. The staff of the magazine, apart from Scott, Lamb, and De Quincey, consisted of Hood, Hazlitt, and Miss Mitford. Poems by John Keats and John Clare were published by *The London Magazine*.

Rivalry between *The London Magazine* and *Blackwood's* led to abuse and Scott successfully exposed the careless libels of his rival. Eventually Lockhart and Scott agreed to seek satisfaction in a duel at Chalk Farm near Hampstead. The arrangements were badly handled and Lockhart returned to Edinburgh without having met Scott. But Lockhart's second, Jonathan Christie, insisted on deputizing for him, and Scott was mortally wounded in January 1821. He was succeeded by John Taylor, of the publishing house Taylor & Hessey.

**London Merchant, The: or The History of George Barnwell.** A tragedy by George Lillo, first produced at Drury Lane in June 1731 and published in the same year. The play is often called *George Barnwell* (the plot is based on an old ballad of that name). It is set in Elizabethan times and follows the downward path of an apprentice, seduced into evil ways by Millwood, a courtesan. Barnwell becomes her creature and even robs his employer, the honest merchant Thorowgood, whose moral probity is expressed in his observations to the upright apprentice Trueman. Eventually Millwood persuades Barnwell to murder and rob his uncle and for that crime the two of them are hanged.

Lillo's tragedy is written in prose and concerns the fortunes of ordinary people. The dialogue is often ridiculous but Lillo's attempt at least marked a beginning; drama had begun to move away from verse in the expression of tragic feeling. The

two factors make him an important figure in the development of English drama and he was to have considerable influence in France and Germany. He also succeeded in creating a real villainess in the depraved and passionate Millwood.

Modern editions of the play are published in The World's Classics (*Eighteenth-Century Tragedy*, edited by Michael R. Booth, 1965), and in W. H. McBurney's edition (Nebraska, 1965).

**London Prodigal, The** A play of unknown authorship, first published in 1605 and only of interest in that it was once attributed to Shakespeare. A comedy, it is concerned with the wayward young Flowerdale, the prodigal of the title, and how his constant and loving wife reclaims him.

**Longaville** In Shakespeare's *Love's Labour's Lost*, one of the lords attendant on the King of Navarre who accepts the withdrawal from the world. He falls in love with Maria, a lady attendant on the Princess of France. In the play he composes the sonnet in Act IV, which was also published in *The Passionate Pilgrime*.

**Long Day's Journey Into Night, A** See **O'Neill, Eugene (Gladstone).**

**Longest Journey, The** A novel by E. M. Forster, first published in 1907.

Frederick Elliot was orphaned at the age of 15. He hated his father and gave all his affection to his mother, though she was a reticent and distant sort of parent. He suffered from rickets as a child and is lame; his nickname is Rickie and when the novel opens he is an undergraduate at Cambridge. His friend Agnes Pembroke is engaged to marry Gerald Dawes, an 'athletic marvel' whom Rickie dislikes. He is, nonetheless, caught up in the romance of Agnes's engagement.

Rickie is ambitious to become a writer after graduating but publishers' comments have not been encouraging. Gerald Dawes is killed playing Rugby football and Rickie becomes engaged to Agnes, feeling that he cannot be a true substitute for Gerald in Agnes's life. After graduating he accepts a teaching post from Herbert, Agnes's brother, who is housemaster at Sawston, a minor public school. On a visit to his father's sister, Mrs Failing, Rickie discovers that her drunken amiable scapegrace of a nephew, Stephen Wonham, is in fact his half-brother, and he assumes that Stephen is his father's illegitimate son. He tells Agnes, and they agree to keep the matter secret even from Stephen himself.

Rickie and Agnes are married and Agnes is house matron at Sawston. She tries, without Rickie's knowledge, to persuade Mrs Failing to send Stephen away and keep him away, as a remittance man. Rickie finds himself disillusioned with Herbert as a teacher; he believes only in success and has no educational ideals. Stewart Ansell, Rickie's Cambridge friend, dislikes Herbert and Agnes and their attitudes and remonstrates with Rickie for giving way to them. Then Rickie discovers Agnes's attempt to persuade Mrs Failing and quarrels with her. Mrs Failing has in fact told Stephen the truth about his birth, and he goes to Sawston where he meets Ansell and reveals that he is Rickie's mother's illegitimate son. The Pembrokes assume that Stephen has come intending blackmail and try to buy him off. Ansell, outraged by the Pembrokes, reveals the secret and Rickie leaves his wife; he will devote himself to trying to make something of his half-brother. In the train on a visit to Mrs Failing, Stephen promises to reform, but he gets drunk again and falls across the lines at a level crossing. Rickie is fatally injured saving his life.

The title of the novel is from Shelley's *Epipsychidion*, the lines beginning 'Who travel to their home among the dead' and ending 'The dreariest and the longest journey go'.

**Longfellow, Henry Wadsworth** 1807–82. Longfellow was born in Portland, Maine. He was educated at private schools and at Bowdoin,

Henry Wadsworth Longfellow.

where one of his classmates was Nathaniel Hawthorne. After graduating in 1825 he was offered the chair in modern languages at Bowdoin, conditional upon a period of study in Europe. Accordingly, Longfellow spent the years from 1826 to 1829 in France, Germany, Italy, and Spain, where he was received by Washington Irving. He was at Bowdoin from 1829 to 1835, getting married in 1831. He contributed essays and sketches to many periodicals; he had published his first poem at the age of 13, in a Portland newspaper. Longfellow was highly regarded as a teacher and was offered the chair in French and Spanish at Harvard. In preparation for the new appointment and to refresh his knowledge Longfellow went to Europe again in 1835. His wife died in the same year.

Longfellow's exceptional linguistic abilities led him to the study of the Scandinavian languages and Icelandic; he was also interested in Finnish, which was then unknown outside northern Europe. It was during this second visit to Europe that he made the acquaintance of Thomas Carlyle. He settled in Harvard in 1836 at the beginning of a distinguished and influential career which lasted 18 years.

His writing career began with the publication of *Outre-Mer: A Pilgrimage Beyond the Sea* (1833–34), a sketch book rather in the manner of Washington Irving, whom he admired. In 1839 he published *Hyperion*, a romance interspersed with verse and prose from German sources which reflects his interest in German Romanticism but which has little to interest the modern reader. *Voices of the Night*, including 'A Psalm of Life', published in the same year, contains much that is representative of Longfellow at any stage of his career as a poet. *Ballads and Other Poems* was published in 1842 and contains many items which have remained fixed in the schoolroom curriculum though in their day they were immensely popular and helped to make their author famous. *Poems on Slavery*, also published in 1842, is an expression of the detestation of slavery which Longfellow shared with his distinguished New England contemporaries. With the exception of 'The Slave's Dream', however, the book does not offer anything to command a niche in the memory which distinguishes 'The Wreck of the Hesperus' and 'The Village Blacksmith'.

Longfellow married again in 1843. He had met Frances Appleton in Europe; her father was a wealthy mill owner and he presented the Longfellows with Craigie House. Frances and Longfellow had two sons and three daughters, and the family were contented and secure in the society of Cambridge. *The Spanish Student* (1843), a poetic drama, was warmly received and in 1847, with *Evangeline*, Longfellow turned to the early settlement of America for a subject – a scene which was to serve him well in the future. He was writing industriously now: *The Belfry of Bruges and Other Poems* (1845), a prose tale, *Kavanagh* (1849), more poems in *The Seaside and the Fireside* (1849) and *The Golden Legend* (1851), his version of a dramatic poem of medieval Germany by Hartmann von der Aue. He resigned from Harvard in 1854, admired and respected by pupils and colleagues and immensely popular with the public who read his poems.

In 1855 came the publication of *Hiawatha*, a long narrative poem about the North American Indian which, in spite of a metre borrowed from the epic of Finland, *The Kalevala*, is essentially romantic. The poem has been endlessly parodied – but it has not been forgotten and Longfellow's next work, *The Courtship of Miles Standish* (1858), was bought by 15,000 readers in the USA and Europe on the day of publication. His happy life was tragically disrupted when his wife died of burns after a fire in 1861. *Tales of a Wayside Inn*, published in book form in 1863, had been completed before the loss of his wife. He stopped writing for something like ten years, though he continued his association with James Russell Lowell and Charles Eliot Norton in the Dante Society, which was devoted to the translation of the Italian master.

In 1872 Longfellow published *Christus*, which included *The Golden Legend*, *The Divine Tragedy*, and *The New England Tragedies* as a religious dramatic cycle. He added to *Tales of a Wayside Inn* and wrote more poems, including the sequence of six sonnets, 'Divina Commedia', which is regarded by some as his best work. The last collections were *The Masque of Pandora* (1875), *Keramos* (1878), *Ultima Thule* (1880), and *In the Harbor* (1882). Longfellow visited Europe in 1868 and was honoured by the Universities of Oxford and Cambridge; Queen Victoria received him in private audience. A bust of him stands in the Poet's Corner of Westminster Abbey; he is the only American represented there.

During his lifetime Longfellow was almost unreservedly admired; his only detractor of any consequence was Edgar Allan Poe, who grumbled about his use of European sources. An amiable, hardworking, and for most of his life a happy man, Longfellow was rarely profound in his utterances. His translation of Dante is not respected; Longfellow simply could not reach the high imagination of the great Tuscan and the passionate expression was beyond him. He was a man of his time, with a tendency to moralize,

a New England scholar who did much to further interest in European culture. Posterity has judged his efforts in the other direction harshly but he did, nonetheless, succeed in interesting a great number of Europeans in America.

**Longman's Magazine**  See **Fraser's Magazine**.

**Longstreet, Augustus Baldwin**  1790–1870. Born in Georgia and educated at Yale, Longstreet was college president four times, newspaper editor, clergyman, and jurist. He is remembered for his *Georgia Scenes. Characters and Incidents etc. in the First Half Century of the Republic*, a collection of 18 humorous sketches first published in 1835. The most highly regarded of them display an acute eye for detail and a sharp ear for dialect, faithfully recording Georgian society at a particular time.

**Look Homeward, Angel**  See **Wolfe, Thomas (Clayton)**.

**Looking Backward: 2000–1887**  A novel by Edward Bellamy, first published in 1888.

Julian West, a Bostonian, falls into a hypnotic sleep in 1887 and wakes 112 years later. He finds himself in a new society in which the lot of man has been transformed by the reorganization of capital and the scrupulous provision of opportunity for the development of natural talent. Previously, uncontrolled private enterprise had encouraged waste, the squandering of resources, and extremes of wealth and poverty. This had given way to the better world in which Julian West awakens.

The basically utopian idea is managed with great skill: Bellamy not only considered his ideas with care but presented them with the ability of an experienced writer, demonstrating the vivid contrasts of the existing order (in which his hero falls asleep) with the world that could be brought about.

**Lord Jim**: *A Tale*.  A novel by Joseph Conrad, first published in *Blackwood's Magazine* (October 1899–November 1900) as *Lord Jim: A Sketch*, and in volume form in 1900.

Jim has no surname in the novel. The son of an English country parson, he trained as a merchant seaman and has become a mate on the *Patna*, a steamer. The *Patna* is carrying 800 pilgrims from an Asian port on their pilgrimage to Mecca when she strikes a submerged obstacle. The impact is hardly noticed but later Jim finds that the ship has been holed below the water line and the only bulwark, eaten away by rust, appears to be giving way to the pressure of the sea. When he reports this, the captain and the White officers shamelessly prepare to abandon ship and passengers and Jim yields to the temptation to go with them. When they are picked up by another ship the captain declares the *Patna* lost; Jim believes this because as the boat pulled away the *Patna*'s masthead was no longer visible. But when they land they discover that the *Patna* had been found, still afloat, by a French gunboat and safely towed into Aden harbour.

The officers are found guilty and their Master's certificates are cancelled. But only Jim had the courage to be present and face the Court of Inquiry, which is where the narrator, Captain Marlow, first encounters him. Marlow can see that there is more to Jim than the tragic lapse on the *Patna* implies, and he helps him get work ashore. But Jim's reputation dogs him and he goes from one job to another until Marlow, again, finds him a post as agent and manager of a remote trading-post, far up the river at Patusan.

Jim succeeds in gaining the trust and friendship of the chief, Doramin, and his son Dain Waris, who becomes his companion. The people call him Tuan (Lord) Jim. Cornelius, the worthless Malacca Portuguese whom Jim succeeds as head of the trading post, ill-uses his stepdaughter; Jim takes her under his protection as his nominal wife and her life is transformed, but she fears that one day he will go – all White men do. An evil ruffian, Gentleman Brown, arrives in Patusan in a stolen schooner, demanding provisions for his men. He plans to kill and loot but Jim frustrates his plan and shows him a clear way of retreat. Jim and the Patusans are betrayed by Cornelius, who reveals to Brown a channel by which he can attack. Brown returns by this and annihilates the Patusans guarding the river, among them Dain Waris. Doramin takes Jim's life in revenge for the White man's evil.

Jim is a representative figure; he has fallen into the abyss that yawns in front of most men in extreme situations and has been helped out of it, slowly and painfully, by the kindness of one who realizes that what happened to Jim could happen to any of us. But Brown undermines him by the association of guilt on Jim's part with his own wickedness. Jim allowed Brown a way of retreat when he should have destroyed him; but evil never really retreats and Jim is destroyed as a result.

**Lord Ormont and his Aminta**  A novel by George Meredith, first published in 1894.

Lord Ormont, elderly and disgruntled when he retires from the East India Company, meets Aminta Farrell in Madrid. He proposes to her and, in spite of the difference in their ages and her humble birth, is accepted. They marry at the embassy in Madrid and Ormont embarks with his young wife on a life of travel. Aminta, however, tires of this and he reluctantly agrees to return to London.

In London Aminta is put aside – Ormont will not present her to society. She becomes involved with a disreputable set, one of whom, the profligate Morsfield, is particularly spiteful and importunate. Meanwhile, Ormont acquires a secretary, Matie Weyburn, who proves to be a youthful admirer of Aminta's. Matie disposes of Morsfield and his obvious liking for Aminta persuades Ormont that Aminta should be given her proper position. But Aminta leaves him.

One day while bathing in the sea she meets Matie and the occasion decides their lives. Acknowledging their mutual attraction, they go to Switzerland in defiance of convention and open a school together. Ormont forgives them before he dies.

**Lorna Doone:** *A Romance of Exmoor.*  A novel by R. D. Blackmore, first published in 1869.

The time is the 17th century, in the reigns of Charles II and James II. The young John Ridd, an Exmoor yeoman, has lost his father – killed by the evil clan of Doone who inhabit a nearby valley and pursue a career of murder and theft. John, a man of great strength and stature, and his neighbours are determined to exact vengeance on the Doones, and the progress of the story has a further impulse in his love for Lorna, daughter of the head of the clan and the murderer of John's father.

John Ridd and his friends bring the Doones to account and he rescues the girl from them. It is then revealed that Lorna was stolen; she proves to be the daughter of a noble house. John is acutely aware of the difference in their positions but Lorna's love and faith in him do not waver. Later he is able to render valuable service both to the king and to a kinsman of Lorna's; his reluctance is overcome and the story ends happily for the young lovers. Monmouth's rebellion, the Battle of Sedgemoor, and Judge Jeffreys are part of the background of the story.

**Lorry, Jervis**  In Dickens's *A Tale of Two Cities*, the confidential clerk of Tellson's Bank and friend of the Manettes through all their trials.

**Lost Princess, The**  See **MacDonald, George.**

**Lothair**  A novel by Benjamin Disraeli, first published in 1870. It is regarded by some critics as his best, with a deftly-turned plot and brilliant dialogue.

Lothair is an orphaned nobleman of enormous

wealth. His guardians are Lord Culloden, and Grandison, a clergyman who embraces Roman Catholicism and rises so rapidly that he becomes a cardinal. Lothair reaches manhood after a Scots Protestant upbringing and joins Garibaldi's campaign in Italy. His wealth and influence make him a target for the Catholics; Cardinal Grandison, Clare Arundel and Monsignor Catesby combine to try and convert him. Lord Culloden, Lady Corisande and Theodora, the Italian girl who supports Garibaldi, resist their influence. In the campaign against the papal forces Theodora is killed: Lothair promises the dying girl that he will never enter the Roman Church. When Lothair himself is wounded at Mentana the cardinal renews his attempts at persuasion. Lothair, however, eventually returns to England, unconverted, and marries Lady Corisande.

The cardinal is probably Disraeli's best-realized character and the author's wit serves him well when he is demonstrating the cardinal's persuasive powers.

***Lotos-Eaters, The*** A poem by Alfred Tennyson, first published in 1832 and revised for the 1842 *Poems*. The theme of the poem is the episode in Book IX of *The Odyssey* when the sailors, returning home after the fall of Troy, make landfall after a strong wind carries them past the island of Cythera. In the strange land they are among people who eat only the fruit of the lotos plant. Some of the sailors eat it and are filled with a languorous content; they want to stay where they are: '. . .ah, why Should life all labour be? Let us alone. Time driveth onward fast, And in a little while our lips are dumb.' The poem, one of Tennyson's richest in verbal music, underlines the strong desire to withdraw from the ceaseless endeavour required of modern man and questions the values which enforce the struggle.

**Loveday, John** The eponymous hero of Thomas Hardy's *The Trumpet-Major*. Gentle and unselfish, he loses Anne Garland to his younger brother, Bob.

***Love for Love*** A comedy by William Congreve, first produced in April 1695, and published in the same year. Thomas Betterton and Anne Bracegirdle played the parts of Valentine and Angelica. In the modern theatre the comedy enjoyed a great success when John Gielgud revived it in 1942; it ran for well over a year.

Sir Sampson Legend has two sons, Valentine and Ben. Valentine, the elder, is a fashionable man–about–town whose extravagance has led him into serious debt. Ben is a sailor, and Sir

Valentine feigning madness, to the alarm of the lawyer, Buckram, in Act IV, scene 2 of Congreve's *Love for Love* (1695). An illustration for an edition published in 1791. Victoria & Albert Theatre Museum, London.

Sampson's wrath with Valentine's behaviour leads him to favour Ben. He will give Valentine enough money to pay his debts, no more, if he will sign a bond making Ben the heir. Valentine is in love with Angelica; she is wealthy but has not so far accepted him. Sir Sampson has arranged a marriage for Ben with Miss Prue, a foolish country girl. Valentine has no choice but to agree and the bond is prepared by Sir Sampson. But Valentine, realizing that he faces ruin, swallows his pride and pleads with his father, to no avail. When faced with signing the bond that will disinherit him he feigns madness to avoid doing so. Ben, meanwhile, has met Miss Prue; their dislike is mutual.

Angelica decides to intervene. She uses her charms to extract a proposal of marriage from Sir Sampson, and gets possession of the bond. Valentine, believing that she will marry his father, despairs and declares himself willing to sign the bond. Angelica then reveals her plot, declares her love for Valentine and tears up the bond.

The plot involves some diverting characters, one of the best being Jeremy, Valentine's resourceful servant. Ben, the younger brother, is his own man and will marry to please only himself, father and fortune notwithstanding. Mrs Frail, an amorous woman of the town, would be delighted to take Ben to bed; believing she has Valentine she finds herself married to Tattle, who has just disentangled himself from Miss Prue.

**Lovelace, Richard** 1618–58. More than any of his contemporaries, Lovelace best fits the popular image of a Cavalier poet. The son of a wealthy Kentish knight, he was handsome, graceful, and romantic. He was granted an honorary MA (Oxford) at the age of 18, and adorned the courtly and artistic life of London until, in 1639 and 1640, he took up arms for his king in the Bishops' Wars. The victory of the Covenanters made absolute Parliament's will in the matter, but Lovelace defiantly presented a petition for the retention of the bishops in 1642, earning himself seven weeks in the Gatehouse Prison in Westminster. He was released when he undertook to engage no more in Royalist activities.

Enforcedly idle, Lovelace spent his money on the king's behalf and his time, apparently, among the poets and wits of the day, but this period of his life is obscure and it is believed that some of it was spent abroad. He was certainly in England in 1648 when he was imprisoned again, for ten months, probably because of the activities of his family, whose efforts on the king's behalf he had so generously financed. He was freed after the execution of the king and spent the rest of his life in relative poverty. While in prison for the second time he prepared for publication the collection of verses called *Lucasta: Epodes, Odes, Sonnets, Songs, etc.* Another volume, *Lucasta: Posthume Poems by Richard Lovelace, Esq* was published by his brother a year after his death.

Lovelace is remembered for his poetry: his renown is well deserved even though his output was small, since a handful of perfect lyrics is a rare enough treasure. His work was almost forgotten until 1765, when Bishop Thomas Percy included the lovely 'To Althea from Prison' in his *Reliques of Ancient English Poetry*.

**Lovelace, Robert** The handsome and accomplished rake of *Clarissa* by Samuel Richardson. His plans for the seduction of Clarissa founder on the rock of her integrity and his desire for her becomes an obsession.

*Lovel the Widower* A story by W. M. Thackeray, first published in the *Cornhill* in 1860. Lovel has a nasty mother-in-law, Lady Baker, who lives with him, and a charming governess, Miss Prior, who was once a dancer. Lady Baker finds out about Miss Prior's past and high-handedly orders her out of the house. But Lovel rallies on Miss Prior's side and Lady Baker is completely routed when Lovel asks Miss Prior to marry him.

*Love-o'-Women* A story by Rudyard Kipling, included in the collection entitled *Many Inventions* (1893). It begins with the murder of a corporal by Sergeant Raines, a 'quiet and well-conducted sergeant': the corporal has seduced Raines' wife. Mulvaney, one of Kipling's 'soldiers three', recalls other such affairs; the principal one involves Larry Tighe, with whom Mulvaney served in the Black Tyrones. Tighe is called Love-o'-Women, a reference to his preoccupation with sex.

Mulvaney recalls Tighe at Silver's Theatre; in a satiated and regretful frame of mind, Tighe hopes to be killed in action. There was one woman in particular he remembers. Tighe survives some violent action but then becomes a victim of locomotor ataxia, a manifestation of the syphilis that kills him. His last meeting with 'the woman' discloses her in a brothel, where he dies in her arms. He calls her Aigypt (*Egypt* – Kipling's determination to reproduce the language of the ordinary soldier phonetically was consistent if not always convincing). She kills herself after his death and the two are buried in the same grave.

**Lover, Samuel** 1796–1868. A Protestant Irishman, Lover was born in Dublin. He made a success as a songwriter, best remembered for 'Rory O'More', and as a humorous novelist, who wrote in much the same vein as Charles Lever though his work is inferior. He was the author of several plays which were successful in their time, and of a number of stories of Irish life which, however, lack the truth and experience of those by William Carleton. Nevertheless, Lover enjoyed great success, and **Handy Andy** went on appearing in new editions for nearly 50 years after his death. *Rory O'More* (1836) was a novel developed from his ballad and was successfully dramatized in the following year. Lover's *Songs and Ballads* was published in 1839.

*Lover's Complaint, A* A poem in rhyme royal that was published with Shakespeare's *Sonnets* in 1609 and has been attributed to him. The date of composition is unknown. The 'complaint' comes from a girl who has been seduced and is unhappily aware that the young man, if he so wished, would have little trouble in seducing her again.

**Lover's Melancholy, The**   A romantic comedy by John Ford, first produced in 1628 and first published in 1629.

Eroclea, daughter of Meleander, is betrothed to Palador, a prince of Cyprus. Palador's father, however, has evil intentions with regard to Eroclea, so Meleander sends his daughter to Greece disguised as a boy to keep her out of harm's way. But, as a result, the old man brings disaster on his head; he is accused of treason, is cast into prison, and lapses into madness. Palador succeeds to the throne when his father dies and lives a sad life brooding over his lost love. Eroclea ventures back to Cyprus, taking the precaution of keeping her disguise; she is page to Menaphon, a courtier. Thamasta, Palador's cousin, falls in love with the page and Eroclea is forced to reveal her identity. She is restored to Palador, Meleander is freed and regains his sanity, and Thamasta settles for Menaphon.

**Love's Cruelty**   A tragedy by James Shirley, first produced in 1631 and first published in 1640. Hippolito has listened to his friend Bellamente praising the beauty and grace of his wife, Gloriana. He conceives a romantic passion for her and is determined it would be better for him if she remained unseen – he does not want to be tempted into betraying his friend. Gloriana is determined to meet him and her vanity leads her to visit Hippolito, without disclosing her identity. Disaster follows; the guilt of Hippolito when he learns who she is and Bellamente's grief at his wife's adultery lead to tragedy for all three.

**Love's Labour's Lost**   A comedy by William Shakespeare and generally agreed to be an early work. It was produced *c.*1595 and printed in a quarto in 1598. It was published in the First Folio of 1623. The story was invented by the playwright and owes nothing to any other positively identifiable source.

The framework of *Love's Labour's Lost* serves well enough for the beautifully executed comedy of love that the young Shakespeare devised. The situations are artificial, certainly, and the play divides the great man's admirers. Some find it tedious and contrived, others find it as rewarding as a Mozart symphony. It is, indisputably, one of the plays that must be seen in performance before any fair opinion can be offered.

Ferdinand, King of Navarre, and the three lords Berowne, Dumain, and Longaville have resolved to abstain from the company of women for three years; they will live in study and fasting. Then the Princess of France arrives in Navarre on an embassy, attended by her three ladies, Rosaline, Katherine, and Maria. The event obliges the four men to put aside their vows, which are soon abandoned altogether when they fall in love with the visiting ladies: Ferdinand with the princess, Dumain with Katherine, Longaville with Maria, and Berowne with Rosaline – the last-named pair being, perhaps, the most interesting. The ladies mock the men's conceits but the court proceeds to enjoy a high summer of dalliance, with other characters contributing the seasoning – Armado and his extravagant expression, Holofernes the pedantic teacher, Dull the constable, Nathaniel the curate, and Costard the clown. Then the King of France dies and the princess must leave. The ladies impose various penances on their lovers and promise to return to them in a year. The needs of the world will always intrude and time will show if love's labours have lost or won. The play ends with the owl and cuckoo song: the cuckoo's 'When daisies pied' and the owl's 'When icicles hang by the wall'.

**Loves of the Angels, The**   A poem by Thomas Moore, first published in 1823. The source of the poem was the *Koran*, and the tradition of the angels Harut and Marut, whose purpose is to tempt men and teach them sorcery. Moore elaborated this into the story of three fallen angels who loved mortal women. One of them loves Lea, but loses her when he reveals the word which will open the gates of heaven. Lea speaks the word and rises to the skies. Another loves Lilis; but when he comes to her in all the glory at his command she is consumed, like Semele by the glory of Zeus in the Greek myth. The third angel loves Nama, and for her sake lives among mortals. Their happiness on earth is imperfect but they look forward to immortality.

**Love's Sacrifice**   A tragedy by John Ford, first produced about 1627 and published in 1633.

The scene is Pavia, where the duke's favourite, Fernando, falls in love with the duchess, Bianca. She repulses him, but her feelings are awakened and she conceives a passion for him. She visits him in his chamber; she offers herself to him and declares that she will suffer overwhelming shame for her guilty passion – she will certainly kill herself before morning. This understandably persuades Fernando to master his passions and love her from a distance. He has other troubles, too; the duke's sister Fiormonda has been offering him her love, which he does not happen to want. She discovers his feelings for Bianca and, with the aid of D'Avolos, the duke's secretary, plants the seed of jealousy in her brother. A trap is laid for Fernando and Bianca and when they are found together the duke kills Bianca, though she was faithful to him. The duke is later convinced of her innocence by Fernando, who poisons himself at Bianca's tomb. The duke, overcome with remorse, gives orders that he shall be buried with his wife and his friend – and stabs himself.

*Loving*  See **Green, Henry.**

**Lowell, James Russell** *c.*1819–91. Lowell was born in Cambridge, Massachusetts, and graduated from Harvard in 1838. He studied law but found little fulfilment in it; he had written poetry of some distinction at Harvard but was uncertain about the possibility of pursuing it – or literature – as a career. His doubts were resolved by the influence of Maria White (herself a poet of some ability) whom he married in 1844. He published two volumes, *A Year's Life* (1841) and *Poems* (1844).

Lowell's wife also influenced his political beliefs and through her he became an active Abolitionist, publishing his views in the short-lived *Pioneer* (his own journal), the *National Anti-Slavery Standard*, and the *Pennsylvania Freeman*. His talents as a poet, critic, humorist, and political satirist all came to fruition, remarkably, in 1848. That year he published *Poems: Second Series*, **A Fable for Critics**, **The Vision of Sir Launfal**, and the first series of **The Biglow Papers**. He was 29 and his talents had reached their peak.

Maria Lowell died in 1853. In 1855 Lowell succeeded Longfellow as Professor of French and Spanish at Harvard and, like Longfellow, spent some time in Europe before taking up his appointment. He also followed the example of his predecessor in directing his students to a serious consideration of European literature. He remained professor until 1886 but in fact did little active teaching after 1876 and during that period published seven books of essays. Of more importance were his editorship of **The Atlantic Monthly** (1857–61) and, jointly with Charles Eliot Norton, of *The North American Review* (1864). Also important were the second series of *The Biglow Papers* (1867), which criticized England's part in the American Civil War, and his reflective poem **The Cathedral** (1869).

Lowell was the US minister in Spain (1877–80) and in England (1880–85). He was a popular American in England – a cultured and charming man who did much to interpret American aspirations and ideals for the Old World from which America sprang. He retired to Elmwood, his home in Cambridge, in 1885.

**Lowell, Robert** 1917–77. The great-grandson of James Russell Lowell, the poet was born in Boston and educated at Harvard University. After further study with John Crowe Ransom, Robert Penn Warren, and Cleanth Brooks, Lowell broke with the New England traditions of his distinguished family and became a Roman Catholic. He was a conscientious objector in World War II and served a prison term in 1943. He published his first collection of poems, *Land of Unlikeliness*, in the following year. His second, *Lord Weary's Castle* (1946), was awarded the Pulitzer Prize and spread his reputation to England. Since then Lowell had broadened his range considerably, with varying degrees of success, and had gradually moved from academic discipline to the free line that descends from Whitman. He had a fondness for dramatic monologue. His later volumes were *The Mills of the Kavanaughs* (1951), *Life Studies* (1959), *For the Union Dead* (1964), and *Now the Ocean* (1967). *Imitations* (1962) is versions from Baudelaire; *The Old Glory* (1965) is three verse plays based on stories by Hawthorne and Melville; *Prometheus Bound* (1967, with illustrations by Sidney Nolan) is a version from Aeschylus. His best-known poems, and those most frequently anthologized, are 'The Quaker Graveyard in Nantucket', 'As a Plane Tree by the Water', 'The Ghost', and 'The Drunken Fisherman'.

**Lowry, (Clarence) Malcolm** 1909–57. Malcolm Lowry was born in Wallasey in Cheshire. His father was a wealthy Liverpool stockbroker, whose life style Lowry rejected while at public school. He left school and sailed to China as a deck hand on a merchant ship, but was persuaded to complete his education at Cambridge University. His novel of seafaring, *Ultramarine*, was published in 1933. He married and became a wanderer and a drunk; he was in Mexico in 1939, when his wife divorced him. He acquired another wife and lived in a shack in Dollarton on the coast of British Columbia from 1940 to 1945. His second novel, *Under the Volcano*, appeared in 1947. He continued to write and drink and died at Lewes in Sussex in 1957. From a mass of work he left behind his volume of short stories *Hear Us, O Lord, from Heaven Thy Dwelling Place* (1961), *Selected Poems* (1962), a short novel, *Lunar Caustic* (1963), and *Dark as the Grave Wherein My Friend is Laid* (stories 1968) have so far been published. The autobiographical novel *Under the Volcano* has been highly praised. His *Selected Letters* were edited by Harvey Breit and Margerie Bonner Lowry (1966).

**Loyal Subject, The:** *or The Faithful General.* A play by John Fletcher, first produced about 1618 and published in 1706.

The loyal subject is the general, Archas. The new Duke of Muscovy dismisses him and gives command of the army to Boroskie, an incompetent soldier but a skilful flatterer. The general's son, young Archas, takes service with the duke's sister, Olympia, disguised as a girl and calling himself Alinda. Olympia warms to Alinda while the duke falls in love with 'her'. The duchy is attacked by the Tatars and Boroskie pretends he is ill to avoid fighting. The duke recalls Archas, who succeeds in defeating the Tatars – to the anger of Boroskie, who plants the seed of doubt in the duke's mind about Archas' loyalty. Evidence of disaffection in the army provokes the duke to having Archas arrested and tortured. The army mutinies on behalf of its commander and attacks the palace; but, prepared to desert to the Tatars, the soldiers respond to Archas, newly released from his sufferings by the repentant and disillusioned duke. Olympia, meanwhile, has dismissed Alinda, suspecting 'her' of responding to the duke's advances. Young Archas is now revealed and Olympia accepts him as her husband. His sister, Honora, becomes the duke's wife.

**Lucius** In Shakespeare's *Titus Andronicus* he is Titus' eldest son and asks for the sacrifice of the first-born son of the defeated queen, Tamora. This sets in motion the chain of murderous revenge with which the play is chiefly concerned. After the rape and murder of his sister, Lavinia, he flees from Rome and raises an army. He becomes emperor at the end of the play.

**Luck of Roaring Camp and Other Sketches, The** A collection of stories and sketches by Bret Harte, first published in 1870. They were originally published in *Overland Monthly* between 1868 and 1870. Among the most famous are the following.

*The Luck of Roaring Camp.* Cherokee Sal, a prostitute, is the only woman in the goldmining settlement of Roaring Camp. She gives birth to a son; the child is christened Thomas Luck (The Luck) but his mother dies. The tough hardened miners adopt the baby and he becomes a focus for their starved affections. Even Kentuck, the biggest and dirtiest of them, starts to wash and wear clean shirts so that he will not be denied the privilege of holding the baby boy. The camp prospers and the miners consider the possibility of attracting families to the town for the sake of The Luck and his future. But in the winter of 1851 floods engulf the camp. Kentuck makes a desperate effort to save the baby; they are both picked up by a rescue boat but The Luck, secure in Kentuck's arms, is already dead and Kentuck does not survive.

*The Outcasts of Poker Flat.* The outcasts, turned out of Poker Flat by its angry citizens, are the gambler John Oakhurst, the thief Uncle Billy, and the prostitutes Mother Shipton and The Duchess. Tom Simson and Piney, eloping, fall in with them; Tom Simson, the 'Innocent' of Sandy Bar, is delighted by the encounter because John Oakhurst had once shown him the generous side of his nature. But it is winter and the group are trapped by heavy snow in a loghouse while crossing the mountains. Uncle Billy steals the mules belonging to Tom and Piney, then deserts them. The rest, marooned with a few days' food, emerge in their true characters. All but one are doomed: but Mother Shipton starves to death so that Piney will have more food and Oakhurst takes his own life in the hope of giving Tom a chance of survival. Tom reaches Poker Flat to get help – but the rescue party arrives only to find the snow driven into the loghouse itself and The Duchess lying with her head on Piney's breast. Both of them are dead.

*Tennessee's Partner.* At Sandy Bar in 1854, Tennessee and his Partner work a mining claim. Tennessee is a dubious character; he is believed to be a thief although there is no proof. The Partner and Tennessee live in Poker Flat. The Partner had found a wife – but she had responded to Tennessee's advances and eloped with him. Then she had deserted Tennessee; he had gone back to his Partner and they returned, content, to living with each other. But Tennessee is apprehended as a thief and subjected to an impromptu trial. However, he refuses to testify on his own behalf and leaves all responsibility to his judges. The Partner offers his entire stake for Tennessee's life, innocently believing that if Tennessee is charged with stealing this will put things right. Tennessee is hanged on the following morning.

Tennessee's Partner waits patiently at the hanging tree with a donkey cart and a rough coffin. The body is handed over to him and he starts back to their claim, telling the curious and silent townspeople that any who 'care to jine in the fun'l, they can come'. Willy-nilly, most of them follow Tennessee's Partner and attend the simple burial – and hear an intensely moving farewell. Tennessee's Partner lives only until the next spring and dies in the happy conviction that Tennessee is waiting to welcome him.

*Miggles.* The story of an ex-saloon woman who, when one of her admirers, Jim, suffers a stroke, takes in the helpless man and becomes mother and nurse to him. She keeps a way station for stagecoaches and earns the admiration of all the men who meet her, if not the women. For company she has a pet bear, Joaquin, and a magpie, Polly.

**Ludlow, Edmund** 1617–92. MP for Wiltshire and an anti-Royalist, Ludlow was the son of a country gentleman, Sir Henry Ludlow. He joined the Parliamentary army at the outbreak of the Civil War and took part in the first battle, at Edgehill, in 1642. He became a lieutenant general in Cromwell's army and was a firm believer in the rightness of bringing Charles I to trial and to the scaffold.

A rigid Parliamentarian, Ludlow was later to be in bitter opposition to Cromwell – his participation in the rebellion had not been in order that one autocrat should replace another and he detested the idea of a Lord Protector in England. As a named regicide (he had signed the death warrant in 1649) his life was in mortal danger at the Restoration. He fled to Switzerland and settled at Vevey, where he wrote his *Memoirs*.

The value of Ludlow's memoirs, humourless and frankly anti-Royalist though they are, lies in their firsthand description of the great events and of his disillusion at what followed apparent success. On a personal level, his narrative of the days leading up to the Restoration, and the implications for himself, is extremely valuable. Ludlow, though lacking Clarendon's literary grace and historian's skill, should be read equally carefully by all students of the Civil War in England.

The *Memoirs* were first published in 1698–99; the standard edition is that of Sir Charles Firth (1894).

**Lufton, Lord Ludovic** The hero of Anthony Trollope's *Framley Parsonage*. Charming and generous, he falls in love with Lucy Robarts and resists his mother's opposition to the marriage. He also comes to the rescue when Mark, his friend and Lucy's brother, gets into trouble through his association with the profligate Mr Sowerby.

**Lumpkin, Tony** In Oliver Goldsmith's *She Stoops to Conquer*, the son of Mrs Hardcastle by a previous marriage. His mother dotes on him and he spends his time in idle pleasure, usually at the Three Jolly Pigeons. His mischievous misdirection of Marlow and Hastings sets the comedy of errors in motion.

**Lyall, Sir Alfred Comyn** 1835–1911. Lyall was born at Coulsdon in Surrey and entered the Indian Civil Service in 1856. He became Lieutenant Governor of the North-West Provinces and a member of the India Council, and founded the University of Allahabad in 1885. He was the author of *Asiatic Studies* (two series, 1882 and 1899, which dealt chiefly with Hinduism), *Warren Hastings: A Biography* (1889), *The Rise of the British Dominion in India* (1893), and *Tennyson* (for the English Men of Letters series, 1902). His *Verses Written in India* (1889) was revised, enlarged, and reprinted as *Poems* in 1907. Lyall enjoyed some reputation as a poet during his lifetime but his work is now largely unknown.

*Lycidas* John Milton's contribution to the memorial volume to Edward King, his friend and contemporary at Cambridge who was drowned in a shipwreck whilst returning to his home in Ireland in August 1637. Other contributors were John Cleveland and Henry More, and the volume was published in the following year.

Milton's nephew Edward Phillips tells us that his uncle was a close friend of King; but the poem itself conveys more about the author than about his subject. Milton was aware that the shipwreck was a sadly foolish affair – the sea was calm and the ship was only a few miles off Anglesey (the Mona of the poem) when it struck a submerged rock. The crew saved themselves but King, tragically, could not swim. He was apparently a young man of exceptional promise; Milton's elegy reflects on his untimely death and the poet, as a believer, ponders its meaning in Christian terms.

**Lydgate, John** c.1390–c.1450. Born in the village of Lydgate in Suffolk, John Lydgate was taken into the service of the Benedictine abbey at Bury St Edmunds, where he later became a monk. He was ordained a priest in 1397; how he spent the next 18 years of his life is unknown though there is reason to believe he spent part of that time in London. He returned to the abbey at Bury St Edmunds about 1415, remaining there until 1421, when he became Prior of Hatfield Broadoak in Essex. He received permission to return to Bury in 1432 and spent the rest of his life there. He was a friend of Chaucer's son Thomas, and an unabashed admirer of Chaucer himself.

Lydgate was typical of a certain product of monastic education and noble patronage (Humphrey, Duke of Gloucester, Henry V as Prince of Wales, and the Earl of Salisbury were among his patrons). He was erudite, able, and facile; the conditions of monastic life gave him security and access to libraries – a great boon in those days – and he could write about anything desired, rather in the manner of a master craftsman. Unfortunately he lacked the quality essential for a lasting place in the literature of

John Lydgate presenting his *Troy Book* to King Henry V. The book was written between 1412 and 1420. An illustration from *MS Cotton. Aug IV, f.1.* British Library.

England. However, it must be borne in mind that any large output of completed work was of some value before the days of printing, especially when much of the work was translation. The dissemination of knowledge in this way was of great importance.

His chief works are: the *Troy Book, or The History, Siege and Destruction of Troy* (1412–21), a poem of 30,000 lines which closely follows the Italian of Guido delle Colonne's *Historia, Destructionis Troiana*; *The Siege of Thebes* (1420), which is Greek tragedy filtered through French verse romance and elements from Boccaccio, and which has a Prologue in the manner of Chaucer; *The Pilgrimage of the Life of Man* (c.1428), a translation from the French of Guillaume de Deguileville described by C. S. Lewis as 'repellent and suffocating' for its great length and didactic tone; *The Fall of Princes* (1431–38), translated and enlarged from the French version of the Italian of Boccaccio's *De Casibus Virorum Illustrium*. There is a mass of shorter works including a version of *Aesop's Fables*, lives of saints, and verse tales.

Lydgate's output was something like 145,000 lines, and it was not without felicitous passages. But, as H. S. Bennett pointed out, he was a man of the cloister with no real experience of life: 'the limitations of his mind were coupled with an overwhelming facility of utterance and a very imperfect understanding of the problems of form and style.'

**Lydgate, Tertius** The ambitious young doctor of George Eliot's *Middlemarch*. His advanced ideas receive little sympathy in the provincial town and he makes a disastrous marriage with the beautiful Rosamond Vincy.

**Lyly, John** c.1554–1606. Lyly was probably born in Kent and is believed to have attended King's School, Canterbury. He completed his education at Magdalen College, Oxford, and went to London about 1576. Apart from his contribution to English letters he took part in public life, representing in succession Hindon, Aylesbury, and Appleby in Parliament (1589–1601). He entered the Marprelate controversy on the side of the bishops and contributed a pamphlet and some verses in 1589.

He published the first part of his **Euphues** in 1578: *Euphues: the Anatomy of Wit.* The second part, *Euphues and his England*, appeared in 1580, and the two were enormously popular – by 1630 25 editions had been printed. Lyly's first prose comedies were presented at court by his patron, the Earl of Oxford, in the years 1584 and 1585. These were *Alexander and Campaspe* and *Sapho and Phao*, acted by boys. They were followed by *Gallathea* (1588), *Endimion, the Man in the Moone* (1591), *Midas* (1592), *Mother Bombie* (1594), *The Woman in the Moone* (1597), and *Loves Metamorphosis* (1601). The players were always boys, usually from St Paul's School.

Lyly is forever associated with a style named after his book, which was the first prose novel in English. He was not the first to use this style but he was the first to use it with such a degree of art; 'euphuism' was the beginning of shape and balance in English prose and it had a host of imitators, the only one of any consequence being Thomas Lodge, who – with Peele and Lyly – formed the Oxford company of the 'University Wits'.

Lyly's comedies were soon forgotten. They were usually based on classical themes and he used lyrics freely – his own or others' is not certain – to give his boy players something to sing. But forgotten or not Lyly's comedies were historically important for his use of prose, establishing it as a medium for the play and giving comedy an immediacy and a range hitherto unknown. Lyly used prose with wit, subtlety, and grace, and out of his court entertainments there developed the great comedies of Shakespeare. Lyly departed from his usual light style in the last three plays: *Mother Bombie* was based on Terence and the pages, who would have been slaves in the original, control the outcome of the plot; *Loves Metamorphosis*, the shortest of his plays, contains no clowns and the comedy is given to the heroines; *The Woman in the Moone* is Lyly's only play in verse and was written for adult players. Lyly hoped to become Elizabeth I's Master of the Revels but he was disappointed in this, in spite of two petitions to the queen.

*The Complete Works of John Lyly* was edited by R. W. Bond and first published in 1902, reprinted in 1967.

**Lyndsay** (*or* **Lindsay**), **Sir David** *c.*1486–1555. Sir David Lyndsay was both the last of the Scots poets of the medieval tradition and the first modern poet of Scotland. His family was noble and David Lyndsay was at court in his youth. His birthplace has not so far been ascertained but it was at one or other of his father's estates, The Mount in Fifeshire or Garmyltont in East Lothian. At the court of James IV Lyndsay, as a young man, acted in a play performed for the king (1511), and in 1513 became usher to Prince James, then a baby. The prince became King James V at the age of one – after his father's death at Flodden – and he was to become a patron of his former usher, later his Lyon King of Arms (1542), on whose back he liked to ride when he was a boy.

Lyndsay married Janet Douglas in 1522 and inherited the estates (The Mount) in Fifeshire in 1524. He was unpopular with the greedy Angus family during their ascendancy during the king's minority, and from 1524 to 1528 was dismissed from the court. The Anguses lost the ascendancy to the equally greedy Douglases; but the king, still only 16, threw off their yoke and began to rule. Lyndsay was recalled (1528) and made a herald; the king sent him on embassies to the emperor and several times to France. Lyndsay composed a masque to welcome Mary of Guise to Scotland to become James's second wife in 1538 but no trace of this work survives.

Lyndsay had already written *The Dreme* before 1528, a *Complaynt to the King* about 1529, and *The Testament and Complaynt of our Soverane Lordis Papyngo* in 1530. *The Dreme* was not printed during the poet's lifetime; it is an allegorical lament on the condition of Scotland and is followed by an exhortation to the young king, at last his own master. Lyndsay employed the medieval dream-vision form and his Reformist sympathies are discernible in the lines describing purgatory. The *Complaynt to the King* is really an appeal to Lyndsay's lord to look to his servant's well-being; the lines recalling the king's childhood are notably warm and full of humour. Lyndsay, like Dunbar before him, made a point of attacking bad counsellors in his verse. His

Protestant sympathies were made plain in the *Testament* and *Complaynt*, which attacks the Church in Scotland for its worldliness and corruption. The poet is reduced – since polite terms had been exhausted – to putting his *Complaynt* into the mouth of a dying papyngo (parrot), who addresses it to his fellow courtiers. Birds of prey represent the monks and friars and the parrot rails at them for their avarice and hypocrisy. They in turn throw the blame onto the secular clergy and the Church, as a whole, is thoroughly damned by the time the poem is complete. It opens with a tribute by the poet to his predecessors and the list of names is of considerable historic interest.

The works between 1530 and 1542 include *Ane Publict Confession of the Kingis auld Hound callit Bagsche*, a dialogue between an old dog retiring from the king's service and a new pet just arrived, which satirizes the courtiers; *Deploratioun of the Deith of Quene Magdalene* (1537), which laments the death of Princess Madeleine of France, the king's first wife who was never crowned; and *Kitteis Confessioun* (1542), in which the Protestant poet attacks the Catholic confessional. Lyndsay's most celebrated work came after this period, the brilliant *Ane Pleasant Satyre of the Thre Estaitis in Commendation of Vertew and Vituperation of Vyce*, written between 1542 and 1546.

***Satire of the Three Estates*** is a morality play that, for its understanding of the stage as a medium, was a landmark in English literature. The work that followed, *The Tragedie of the Cardinall* (1546), is a dull poem on the murder of Cardinal Beaton but *The Historie of the Squyer Meldrum* is regarded as a successful tale in verse, in the manner of Chaucer, of the life of a likeable and bouncing laird who was a real person and the poet's friend. The *Dialog betuix Experience and ane*

Sir David Lyndsay reading the Prologue to his *A Dialog betuix Experience and ane Courteour* (c.1553). An illustration from an edition of 1566.

*Courteour* (*c*.1553), also called *Monarche*, is praised by C. S. Lewis but not highly regarded by other scholars.

To the end of his life Lyndsay was a fervent believer in the Reformation. His finest invective was directed against the Church but he never formally left it and may have hoped to see it transformed during his lifetime. He was one of those who encouraged John Knox to preach in public.

Various editions of Lyndsay were published by the Early English Text Society but that by Douglas Hamer, published in four volumes (1931–36), for the Scottish Texts Society, is regarded as the best. Hamer's *Bibliography of Sir David Lyndsay*, which is also highly praised, is included in his edition.

**Lyrical Ballads** A collection of poems by William Wordsworth and Samuel Taylor Coleridge, the first edition of which was published in 1798. The choice of poems each would contribute is described by Coleridge in Chapter 14 of his *Biographia Literaria*: 'During the first year that Mr Wordsworth and I were neighbours, our conversation turned frequently on the two cardinal points of poetry: the power of exciting the sympathy of the reader by a faithful adherence to the truth of nature, and the power of giving the interest of novelty by the modifying colours of imagination ... The thought suggested itself (to which of us I do not recollect) that a series of poems might be composed of two sorts ... In this originated the plan of the *Lyrical Ballads*; in which it was agreed that my endeavours should be directed to persons and characters supernatural, or at least romantic; yet so as to transfer from our inward nature a human interest and a semblance of truth sufficient to procure for these shadows of imagination that willing suspension of disbelief for the moment which constitutes poetic faith. Mr Wordsworth, on the other hand, was to propose to himself as his object to give the charm of novelty to things of every day, and to excite a feeling analogous to the supernatural by awakening the mind's attention from the lethargy of custom and directing it to the loveliness and the wonders of the world before us ... '

The first edition contained such poems as 'Lines written above Tintern Abbey', 'Simon Lee', 'The Rime of the Ancient Mariner', and 'The Nightingale': only four were by Coleridge, nineteen by Wordsworth. The *Lyrical Ballads* constituted a point of departure for English poetry, which had been stifled by the rigid conventions imposed upon it during the 18th century; the feelings of the heart were now escaping from the rule of the intellect. Cowper had looked in that direction but had no way, in his tragic life, of developing a method of expression, as Wordsworth and Coleridge did; the great Burns was a regional poet and used his own dialect. English literary circles however were not ready for the revolution; the Bristol bookseller Joseph Cottle, who published *Lyrical Ballads*, had to dispose of most of the 500 copies at a loss. But Wordsworth succeeded in retrieving the copyright and was approached by Longmans for a second edition in 1800. This includes additional poems by Wordsworth, among them 'Michael' and 'Ruth'; Coleridge added nothing. Wordsworth wrote a preface explaining his poetic principles, and extended this in 1802, in an appendix, *Poetic Diction*. This was ridiculed by the young Byron but Wordsworth's reputation increased rapidly from then on. W. J. B. Owen's edition of the 1798 edition of *Lyrical Ballads* was published in 1967.

**Lysander** Hermia's true love in Shakespeare's *A Midsummer Night's Dream*. She runs off with him rather than marry Demetrius at her father's insistence.

**Lyttelton, George, 1st Baron** 1709–73. Lyttelton was born at Hagley, Worcestershire, the country seat of his father, Sir Thomas Lyttelton. He was educated at Eton and Christ Church, Oxford, made the grand tour, and entered political life as Member of Parliament for Okehampton in 1735. In literature he is remembered as a minor poet and as a generous patron, the friend of Pope, Thomson, Henry Fielding, and William Shenstone. His poetry includes *Monody* (1747) to the memory of his wife, and *Dialogues of the Dead* (1760). He published *The History of the Life of Henry the Second* in four volumes between 1767 and 1771.

# M

**Mabbe, James** 1572–*c*.1642. Mabbe was educated at Magdalen College, Oxford. He became a fellow of his college and later a lay prebendary of Wells. His contribution to English literature consisted of his translations from the Spanish, which came after Thomas Shelton's fine *Don Quixote* in 1612. Mabbe's first translation was from Matheo Aleman, *The Rogue: or The Life of Guzman de Alfarache*, in 1622. This was followed by Fernando de Rojas' *Celestina* as *The Spanish Bawd* (1631) and Cervantes' *Novelas Ejemplares* as *Exemplarie Novells* (1640), the most famous of which is *The Spanish Ladye*.

**Mabinogion, The** Strictly speaking, a collection of *mabinogi*, or Welsh 'tales of youth'. The translation by Lady Charlotte Guest (1838–49) in her *Mabinogion* is of the four tales contained in the late 14th-century Welsh manuscript known as *The Red Book of Hergest*. The tales, known as the Four Branches of the Mabinogi, are different parts of the same myth retold by an 11th-century author-redactor. The principal hero is Pryderi, son of Pwyll, Prince of Dyfed; other figures are Rhiannon, the King of Annwyn (Hades), Gwawl (light – possibly a sun god), Matholwch, King of Ireland, and the Children of Llyr – the gigantic Bran, Branwen, and Manawyddan; and Math, Gilfaethwy, Goewin, Gwydion, Dylan, and Lleu Llaw Gyffes. The strands of ancient religious belief are clear.

Pwyll, Prince of Dyfed, exchanges his shape with Arawn, King of Annwyn, and kills Arawn's enemy; he becomes known as the Head of Annwyn. He returns to Dyfed and meets a woman on a white horse, Rhiannon, whom he wants to marry. But she is promised to Gwawl; Pwyll tricks Gwawl into a leather bag and only releases him after Gwawl gives up all claim to Rhiannon. A son, Pryderi, is born to Pwyll and Rhiannon; but on the night of his birth the baby is abducted and Rhiannon is suspected of having devoured him. However, after several years Pryderi is restored; the Lord of Gwent Is-coed, Teyrnon, had found the baby and cared for him. Pwyll dies and Pryderi succeeds him.

Bran, Branwen, and Manawyddan are the Children of Llyr. Branwen is given in marriage to Matholwch, King of Ireland. But during Matholwch's visit to Britain relations are soured by the malice of Evnisien, stepbrother of Bran and Branwen, and Branwen's life in Ireland is wretched. Bran invades Ireland on his sister's behalf and eventually defeats Matholwch. But it is a hollow victory and Bran, with his seven remaining men around him, dies of a wound from a poisoned spear. At his orders, his men cut off Bran's head and carry it to Britain; they bury it on the White Mount, the face towards France. (The White Mount is Tower Hill; the burial of Bran's head there would keep Britain free from invaders.) Branwen's son is murdered by Evnisien and Branwen dies of grief.

Manawyddan, the brother of Bran and one of the seven survivors, finds Bran's kingdom has been seized by Caswallawn. Pryderi was also one of the seven: he offers Manawyddan the freedom of his domain and his mother Rhiannon for a wife. Pryderi's wife is Kigva, and the four settle in Wales but seem to be dogged by misfortune. The people disappear from the land, and both Rhiannon and Pryderi fall victim to enchantment and vanish too. Manawyddan and Kigva live together but their crops are unaccountably ravaged just when they are ready for harvesting. Manawyddan watches all night at his last remaining croft, and sees hordes of mice carry off the ears of corn. One mouse is slow and clumsy and he catches it, intending to hang it over his land as a thief; but a wizard admits that he is responsible and pleads to save the mouse, who is his wife and pregnant, thus slow and easy to capture. He had worked the enchantments to revenge his friend Gwawl on Pwyll and his family. He has to remove the enchantments on the land and restore Rhiannon and Pryderi before Manawyddan will give him back his mouse-wife, who immediately becomes a woman.

Gwydion and Gilfaethwy, children of Don, are nephews of Math, Lord of Gwynedd and a wizard who rests with his feet in a virgin's lap. The girl is Goewin, and Gilfaethwy covets her. The brothers hear of the fine pigs which Arawn, King of Annwyn, has given to Pryderi. They offer him some apparently fine horses, greyhounds, and shields and Pryderi agrees to the exchange. But after the brothers leave the spell they used comes to an end and their barter proves to be no more than fungus. Pryderi declares war but is killed in single combat with Gwydion, who then contrives that his brother can take Goewin against her will. She pleads with Math, who turns the brothers into male and female animals. They couple and bear three young; Math takes the young and gives them human form and then decides that the two men have been punished enough and removes the spell. Gwydion recommends Arianrhod, daughter of Don, to Math. But when Math tests her virginity she drops a yellow-haired boy, and another whom Gwydion picks up and hides in a chest. The yellow-haired boy is Dylan, who becomes a child of the sea. Gwydion takes the other son and brings him up against Arianrhod's wishes; she will not give him a name and declares he will never have a human wife. On Math's advice Gwydion tricks her into naming the boy Lleu Llaw Gyffes – the Bright One of the Skilful Hand. Then Math and Gwydion conjure up a wife from flowers – Blodeuwedd. She is unfaithful to him with Goronwy, Lord of Peullyn, and plots his death. Lleu is wounded but escapes in the form of an eagle; Gwydion finds him and restores his human form. The faithless Blodeuwedd is turned into an owl. Goronwy sues for peace but Lleu kills him in single combat and thereafter reigns as Lord of Gwynedd.

In addition to the four *mabinogi*, *The Mabinogion* contains the texts of **Kulhwch and Olwen**, *The Dream of Maxen, Lludd and Llevelys*, **The Dream of Rhonabwy**, **The Lady of the Fountain**, **Peredur, Son of Evrawg**, and **Gereint and Enid**. In *Kulhwch and Olwen* and *The Dream of Rhonabwy* Arthur appears in a purely Welsh milieu. He also appears in *The Lady of the Fountain*, *Peredur, Son of Evrawg*, and *Gereint and Enid* but these are based on French originals and correspond to Chrétien de Troyes's *Le chevalier au lion*, *Perceval*, and *Erec* (late 12th century). The element of romance is present here with Arthur as the king of chivalric tradition rather than a king in an imperfectly remembered Celtic past.

**Macaulay, (Emilie) Rose** 1881–1958. Rose Macaulay was born in Cambridge. Her father, G. C. Macaulay, was a lecturer in classics at the university but his daughter completed her education at Oxford. She began her career as a writer with *Abbots Verney* (1906) but it was not until several novels and two books of verse later that she attracted both critical and popular interest with *Potterism* (1920). Her satirical view of vulgar journalism and commercialization was also her view of modern humanity in general and her tart intelligence combined with a Christian compassion to make her a very attractive writer. Between *Potterism* and World War II she completed 12 novels, of which the best known are *Told by an Idiot* (1923), *Orphan Island* (1924), *Crewe Train* (1926), *They Were Defeated* – a strikingly different period novel which many regard as her best (1932), *I Would be Private* (1937), and *And No Man's Wit* (1940).

*Told by an Idiot* is an excellent example of her work and tells of the Rev Aubrey Garden, who keeps losing his faith and finding another; he encounters Anglicanism and the Church of Rome before eventually finding his way to the Ethical Church, and on to another bout with Rome. His six children, who are named in accordance with his spiritual struggles, occupy the greater part of the book; the story follows them from 1879 to 1923 and records their views of their father's changes, which are not changes at all: there are no 'new' ideas in their lives or in his. The subject of *They Were Defeated* is the poet Robert Herrick, the vicar abhorred by the Puritans for his pleasure in the practice of his Anglican faith and his adherence to 'the cheerful middle English way'. Rose Macaulay's picture of the early 17th century is vivid and convincing and she introduces with effortless ease the characters of Sir John Suckling, John Cleveland, Abraham Cowley, and Henry More. *The World my Wilderness* (1950) and *The Towers of Trebizond* (1956), her two postwar novels, found her individual talent as bright as ever. She was made a DBE in 1958.

Rose Macaulay's nonfiction, apart from verse, included collections of essays: *A Casual Commentary* (1925), *Catchwords and Claptrap* (1926) and *The Writings of E. M. Forster* (1938), and the travel books *They Went to Portugal* (1946), *Fabled Shore: From the Pyrenees to Portugal* (1949), and *The Pleasure of Ruins* (1953). Her letters were edited by Constance Babington Smith as *Letters to A Friend 1950–1952* (1961), *Last Letters to A Friend 1952–1958* (1962), and *Letters to A Sister* (1964), which includes the fragment of a novel, *Venice Besieged*.

**Macaulay, Thomas Babington, 1st Baron** 1800–59. The son of Zachary Macaulay, a noted Scots Abolitionist and philanthropist, Macaulay was born at Rothley Temple in Leicestershire. Zachary Macaulay was a member of the Clapham Sect, whose members made much of his exceptionally bright and precocious son. Macaulay was educated at an evangelical school and entered Trinity College, Cambridge, in 1818, becoming a fellow in 1824. He became a barrister in 1826 but never practised. He had already begun a literary career with contributions to *Knight's Quarterly Review* (1823); this was followed in August 1825 by *Milton*, first of his series of brilliant essays for *The Edinburgh Review*. He was to become a familiar figure among the Whig set at Holland House, to the disappointment of his father who was well aware that Lady Holland's wealth came from West Indian plantations worked by slaves.

Macaulay's essays, which included political matters among their subjects, made him well known and brought him to the attention of political leaders. Lord Lansdowne offered him the pocket borough of Calne in Wiltshire and Macaulay entered Parliament in 1830. His speech in support of the Reform Bill in 1831 made him famous and he became Secretary of the Board of Control for India in the same year. In 1834 came the offer of a place on the East India Company's supreme council for India at the then enormous salary of £10,000 a year. Macaulay acquitted himself well in India, taking a leading part in the founding of an educational system and presiding over the committee which was formed to devise a workable criminal code. He continued to write for *The Edinburgh Review*: his famous essay *Francis Bacon*, published in July 1837 in the form of a review of Basil Montagu's edition of Bacon, demonstrates his brilliance as an essayist as well as his limitations as a critic. However, social and moral pronouncements on works of art were accepted in his day; Macaulay was listened to and his word could do considerable harm. His *Leigh Hunt* (January 1841) was a review of Hunt's *The Dramatic Works of Wycherley, Congreve, Vanbrugh and Farquhar* and resulted in the works of those playwrights being kept off the stage for decades.

Macaulay returned to England in 1838 with a plan for a history of England from the accession of William III (his Whig hero) to the French Revolution. Meanwhile he continued to write for *The Edinburgh Review* and he returned to Parliament as MP for Edinburgh, becoming Secretary of State for War (1839–41) and Paymaster of the Forces (1846–47). His experience of India was put to good use in *Lord Clive* (January 1840) and *Warren Hastings* (October 1841). A visit to Italy, combined with his admiration for Sir Walter Scott, resulted in Macaulay's first verse, *The Lays of Ancient Rome* (1842), which was an immediate success. In 1843 he agreed, because of the appearance of inaccurate pirated editions in the USA, to publish all the essays he wanted to preserve in a collected edition. *Critical and Historical Essays contributed to The Edinburgh Review* (1843) was widely bought and in the following year Macaulay devoted himself entirely to his history, except for the post of Paymaster-General – virtually a sinecure – which he accepted in 1846 and lost in 1847 with his seat in Parliament. He gained his peerage through the good offices of Palmerston in 1857 and died in 1859. He is buried in Westminster Abbey.

In the event Macaulay did not complete *The History of England from the Accession of James II*. The first two volumes appeared in 1849, two more in 1855; a fifth volume was prepared for the press by his sister Hannah, Lady Trevelyan (posthumously published, 1861). The history was immensely successful: Macaulay had said 'I shall not be satisfied unless I produce something which shall for a few days supersede the last fashionable novel on the tables of young ladies.' In fact, he wrote a best-seller and became world famous.

**Macbeth, Lady**  See *Macbeth, The Tragedy of.*

**Macbeth, The Tragedy of** A play by William Shakespeare, first produced *c.*1606 and published in the First Folio of 1623. The shortest of all Shakespeare's tragedies, it is known only in the Folio text (no quartos exist), which is believed to represent the acted version at the Globe. But the Folio text is acknowledged to be a faultily remembered copy by the scriveners and argument continues over the meaning of some passages. However, the heart of the play is intact and the short tragedy is a very rich one. Shakespeare would have been familiar with King James's preoccupation with witchcraft and could have read his *Daemonologie* (Edinburgh, 1597 and London, 1603). The historical Macbeth was documented by the Scottish chroniclers George Buchanan and John Leslie and by Raphael Holinshed. Banquo was a legendary ancestor of the Stuart kings.

A brief scene introduces the three witches, who announce their intention of meeting with Macbeth, King Duncan's general. Macbeth and Banquo have been conducting the war against the rebels and Macbeth, who is Thane of Glamis, has been victorious.

After leaving the field Macbeth and Banquo encounter the three witches on 'a blasted heath'. They know who Macbeth is, to his surprise; but they go on to address him as Thane of Cawdor, too. Then they tell him he will be king. To Banquo they offer less in immediate terms: 'Lesser than Macbeth, and greater' and 'Thou shalt get [beget] kings, though thou be none.' The witches vanish before they can be questioned further – and immediately after that the king's messengers meet Macbeth and Banquo. Macbeth is to receive the title and possessions of the Thane of Cawdor: Cawdor has proved a traitor in the rebellion and is under sentence of death. The first part of the witches' message is borne out, and Macbeth is pondering the rest. King? Duncan's throne is secure now and Malcolm, his heir, is alive and well. But Macbeth is already thinking of Malcolm as an obstacle to his eventual succession.

At Macbeth's castle in Inverness his lady awaits his return. Lady Macbeth reads his letter telling of the strange procession of events. Once the throne is apparently predestined she sets her sights on it at once, though she knows her husband is not the man 'To catch the nearest way'. When she learns that King Duncan will be a guest at the castle she makes up her mind and draws her husband with her. Macbeth murders Duncan; but the deed unnerves him – it is Lady Macbeth who finds resolution enough for both of them and attends to the details, which include throwing the blame on the king's grooms by smearing them with blood from the murder weapons. The murder is discovered by Macduff, and Malcolm and his younger brother Donalbain are uneasy when they learn that the only possible witnesses, the grooms, are dead. Macbeth has killed them – in fury at their crime, he says. The two princes escape from Scotland and Macbeth assumes the crown.

Macbeth's course is fixed now. He contrives the murder of Banquo, who would 'get kings', and his son, Fleance. But the son escapes and Macbeth is haunted by the ghost of Banquo. He seeks out the witches and learns that he must beware the Thane of Fife (Macduff) but he cannot be harmed by one 'of woman born' and that he will not be defeated until 'Birnam Wood . . . shall come against him'. Finally he is granted a vision of a line of kings and the last of them wears Banquo's face. Macbeth is baulked of a victim in Macduff – he has joined Malcolm in England, where the prince is raising an army to invade Scotland. Macbeth orders the slaughter of Lady Macduff and all her children.

Lady Macbeth's mind gives way. She sleepwalks and speaks of 'unnatural deeds'. Macbeth, with the invading army approaching, fortifies Dunsinane castle near Birnam Wood. It is there that Lady Macbeth dies, while the soldiers of Malcolm and Macduff use branches of the trees of Birnam Wood as camouflage for their assault on the castle. Macbeth's forces are defeated but he, remembering the witches' words, believes himself invulnerable. He is killed by Macduff, the opponent who was not 'of woman born' but 'was from his mother's womb untimely ripp'd'. Malcolm succeeds to the throne.

Macbeth and his lady used to be played by formidable middle-aged actors with booming voices but the parts are, more and more, entrusted to younger players and the tragedy in this grim and lowering play comes into clearer focus. Ambition for greatness tempts both of them into evil and with the murder of their guest they unloose the Furies. For Macbeth the consequences are devastating – he behaves with a savagery born of fear, desperately fending off retribution. Lady Macbeth is destroyed from within; her ambitions for her husband, quickened by his strange letter, prompt the murder and in the execution of it she does not betray weakness by a single tremor, knowing that if she does her husband will never carry out their plan. Nothing points the way to her mind's unbalancing but it is completely believable in the brief scene (her part is surprisingly short) that demonstrates it; she has lost her grip on the horrors she has tried to contain ('Yet who would have thought the old man to have had so much blood in him?'). Macbeth's instincts keep him struggling to the end ('Yet I will try the last'), even though he acknowledges that 'Life's but a walking shadow . . . a tale told by an idiot . . .'.

**MacDonagh, Donagh** See **MacDonagh, Thomas.**

**MacDonagh, Thomas** 1878–1916. MacDonagh was born in Tipperary and attended religious schools before going on to University College, Dublin. He taught for a time and was then appointed Professor of English Literature at Dublin. MacDonagh was a successful and, in his time, a well-regarded poet. He published *April and May, with Other Verse* and *Through the Ivory Gate* (1903), *The Golden Joy* (1906), *Songs of Myself* (1910), and *Lyrical Poems* (1913). Other works were a tragedy, *When the Dawn is Come* (1908), *Thomas Campion and The Art of English Poetry* (1913), and *Literature in Ireland* (1916). Another play, *Pagans*, was published posthumously (1920).

MacDonagh, as an Irish Volunteer, was a commander in the Easter Rising (1916) and was executed after it was suppressed. *Collected Poems* (1917) was published with an introduction by James Stephens.

His son Donagh MacDonagh (1912–68), born in Dublin, became a barrister and later a judge. He published *Twenty Poems* (1934), *Veterans and Other Poems* (1941), *The Hungry Grass* (1947), and *A Warning to Conquerors* (1968). In 1947 his play *Happy as Larry* was a considerable success in London and New York, and several others were performed on radio. Donagh MacDonagh edited *The Oxford Book of Irish Verse* (1958) with Lennox Robinson.

**MacDonald, George** 1824–1905. The Scottish novelist was born at Huntly in rural Aberdeenshire and educated at Aberdeen University. He was a tutor for a time and then, in 1850, became a Congregational minister at Arundel. After three years he was dismissed for 'heresy' – an offence which sounds incredible to modern ears. MacDonald was reacting to the Calvinism in which he was born, and had graduated to a less harsh religious belief; his reaction continued and he became more and more interested in a mystical interpretation of nature. He was to attack Calvinism vigorously in his novels.

After his dismissal from Arundel MacDonald earned his living by journalism and lecturing, until the influence of Byron's widow secured him academic respectability with a professorship of English literature at Bedford College in 1859. By this time he had published some verse and a narrative poem, *Within and Without* (1855), that earned some praise from Tennyson. The allegorical prose and verse *Phantastes: a Faerie Romance for Men and Women* was published in 1858. His first novel was *David Elginbrod* (1863), and he went on to write more than 20 more, most of them concerned with Scottish rural manners and Calvinistic restraints. They are no longer read and editions of them are hard to find.

MacDonald's enduring work is that which he wrote for children, notably *At the Back of the North Wind* (1871), *The Princess and the Goblin* (1872), *The Lost Princess* (1875), and *The Princess and Curdie* (1883). He was a friend of Lewis Carroll, and indeed *Alice in Wonderland* was read to him before publication, but his work for children was quite unlike his friend's – or indeed anyone else's until the time of Tolkien. The element that marks them is the fantasy of dream time and half-remembered things, which somehow stays close to truth. *Lilith: a Romance* (1895) was an allegorical fantasy in the vein of the earlier *Phantastes*.

**Macduff** Thane of Fife in Shakespeare's *Macbeth*. He finds the king dead in Macbeth's castle and, suspicious of the circumstances, does not attend Macbeth's coronation feast. The witches warn Macbeth to fear him but Macduff joins Malcolm in England before Macbeth can harm him. Macbeth slaughters Macduff's family but eventually falls to Macduff's sword. Macduff is the one 'not of woman born' whom Macbeth has to fear.

**Mac Flecknoe** A verse satire by John Dryden directed against Thomas Shadwell. The complete title is *Mac Flecknoe, or A Satyre upon the True-Blew-Protestant Poet, T.S.* Shadwell had written *The Medall of John Bayes* ('Bayes' refers to Dryden as the poet laureate) in answer to Dryden's *The Medall*. *A Satyre against Sedition* (see **Dryden, John**). Richard Flecknoe (*c.* 1600–78) was an Irish poet who had written a *Short Discourse on the English Stage* (1664), expressing disapproval. Dryden regarded him as 'the emperor of dullness' and Shadwell, as Mac Flecknoe, is his heir. He had already attacked Shadwell in the second part of *Absalom and Achitophel*.

Mac Flecknoe was first published in 1682 but is known to have been written some years earlier (probably 1678). Alexander Pope later acknowledged that he found the basic plan of *The Dunciad* in Dryden's satire.

**Mackenzie, Henry** 1745–1831. Mackenzie was a native of Edinburgh and was educated at Edinburgh High School and Edinburgh University. A lawyer by profession, he worked in London for a time and later became Comptroller of Taxes for Scotland. He published his first novel, *The Man of Feeling*, in 1771. *The Man of the World* followed in 1773, and *Julia de Roubigné* in 1777. Other activities of Mackenzie were a play, *The Prince of Tunis* (1773), and chairmanship of the committee which investigated James Macpherson's claims for the 'Ossian' poems. He also edited two periodicals, *The Mirror* (1779–80) and *The Lounger* (1785–86).

*The Man of Feeling* was popular in its day and gave Mackenzie a prominent place in Edinburgh literary life. Today it is regarded as a curiosity, representing a number of 18th-century elements in fiction but not displaying sufficient art to award it a lasting place. The life of the hero, Harley, is reconstructed from imaginary documents by an 'editor', the documents available dictating the events which shall be described. It resembles the de Coverley papers of Joseph Addiison but with a heavily sentimental tone. Harley gives vent to his feelings extravagantly – indeed he seems like a man out of control; but the times were extravagant and sensibility was the virtue most paraded. Mackenzie was a skilful and practised writer and the book was much admired by Robert Burns.

*The Man of the World* has a villain for its central character and possesses something like a plot; sensibility is demonstrated in the sufferings of the victims of Sir Thomas Sindall. Retribution overtakes Sir Thomas in the second half, when the heroine's brother, exiled by Sir Thomas's villainy, returns from life with the Cherokee Indians. A great deal of space is devoted to the picture of life among noble savages.

*Julia de Roubigné* is written in the epistolary form favoured by Samuel Richardson. Julia marries Montauban out of gratitude; a former lover, Savillon, returns to the scene. Julia and Savillon are perfectly innocent but Montauban believes the worst of their farewell to each other. He poisons Julia, then discovers that she was innocent, and poisons himself.

As a man of letters Mackenzie deserves praise for his recognition of the young Robert Burns and for his enthusiasm for Scott upon the publication of *Waverley*.

**Mackenzie, Mrs** The scheming widow of Thackeray's *The Newcomes*. She manoeuvres Clive Newcome into marriage with her daughter, Rosey, and makes life unendurable for Colonel Newcome when he loses his money.

**MacLeish, Archibald** 1892–1982. MacLeish was born in Glencoe, Illinois, and graduated from Yale before the USA entered World War I, in which he served. After the war he returned to university and took a further degree at Harvard. He published his first book of poems, *Tower of Ivory*, in 1917. After graduating from Harvard in 1919 he practised law for a few years but during the period 1923–28 he joined the group of Americans who had settled in Paris. His early poetry is subjective and recognizably in the same stream as that of T. S. Eliot and Ezra Pound: *The Happy Marriage* (1924), *The Pot of Earth* (1925), *Streets in the Moon* (1926), and *The Hamlet of A. Macleish* (1928). After his return to the USA a stronger consciousness of his own country and people is evident in *New Found Land* (1930), which contains his well known 'You, Andrew Marvell'; *Conquistador* (1932), an epic of the conquest of Mexico, which was awarded the Pulitzer Prize in 1933; and *Frescoes to Mr Rockefeller's City* (1933). MacLeish was also the author of some skilful and fluent verse plays: *Nobodaddy* (1925) was the first; the second, *Panic* (1935), dealt with the Wall Street crash and achieved production on the stage. *The Fall of the City* (1937) was written for radio and reached a wide audience in the USA and England; it is a denunciation of totalitarianism and MacLeish exploited the medium brilliantly. *Air Raid* (1938) was also written for radio.

Parallel with his career in letters was MacLeish's very active public life. After being editor of *Fortune* (1929–38), he became Librarian of Congress (1939–44), Assistant Secretary of State (1944–45), and Boylston Professor of Rhetoric and Oratory at Harvard (1949–62); he represented the USA in the organization of UNESCO. Among his later works are a verse play for radio, *The Trojan Horse* (1952), reflecting the contemporary fear of Red infiltration; *J.B.*, a verse play about a modern Job, which brought him his greatest success and a third Pulitzer Prize in 1958, his *Collected Poems* (1952) having won him his second; and *Herakles* (1967), a verse drama that explores the needs of human life in conflict with science and reason. *A Continuing Journey* (1968) is a collection of essays on the American scene since World War II.

**MacNeice, (Frederick) Louis** 1907–63. Louis MacNeice was the son of a Church of Ireland clergyman and was born in Belfast. He was educated at Marlborough School and Merton College, Oxford, and was a lecturer in classics at the University of Birmingham from 1930 to 1936. From 1936 to 1940 he was lecturer in Greek at Bedford College, London, and from then until his death at the age of 56 he was a feature-writer and producer at the BBC.

MacNeice's first collection of poems was *Blind Fireworks* (1929), published while he was still at Oxford, and he contributed four poems to *Oxford Poetry* in the same year. He contributed to *New Verse* in 1934 and published his second collection as *Poems* (1935). An Irishman and a scholar, MacNeice stood apart from his contemporaries and their proclaimed commitment to left-wing politics. He detested fascism but did

not believe that the answer to the extreme Right could be found in embracing the Left. His poetry is both personal and reticent; he eschewed symbolism and took his imagery from his surroundings – urban or rural, it provided him with continuing riches and he was publishing new poetry in the year of his death.

After his translation of *The Agamemnon of Aeschylus* (1936), his collaboration with W. H. Auden – *Letters from Iceland* (1937), and a play, *Out of the Picture* (1937), MacNeice resumed his poetry with *The Earth Compels* (1938), *Autumn Journal* (1939), *The Last Ditch* (1940), *Plant and Phantom* (1941), *Springboard* (1944), and *Holes in the Sky* (1948). *Goethe's Faust: Parts 1 and 2* (1951) is a translation by MacNeice of an abridged version; *Ten Burnt Offerings* (1952), *Autumn Sequel* (1954), *Visitations* (1957), *Solstices* (1961), and *The Burning Perch* (1963) were written during the course of a busy career that also produced several prose volumes and a number of works for radio during that medium's great days. *The Collected Poems of Louis MacNeice* (1966) was edited by E. R. Dodds. *One for the Grave: A Modern Morality Play* (1968) was produced at the Abbey Theatre, Dublin, in 1966.

Louis MacNeice's radio scripts were *Christopher Columbus: A Radio Play* (1944), *The Dark*

Louis MacNeice, 1946.

*Tower and Other Radio Scripts* (1947), *The Mad Islands and The Administrator* (1964), and *Persons from Porlock and Other Plays for Radio* (1969), which contains an introduction by W. H. Auden. MacNeice was the author of a single novel, published under the pseudonym of James Malone, *The Roundabout Way* (1932). Among his critical essays were *Modern Poetry: A Personal Essay* (1938), *The Poetry of W. B. Yeats* (1941), and *Varieties of Parable* (1965 – the Clark Lectures of 1963). *The Penny that Rolled Away* (1954) is a story for children; *The Strings are False* (1965) is the poet's unfinished autobiography.

**Macpherson, James** 1736–96. A farmer's son, Macpherson was born at Ruthven, in Inverness, and studied at Marischal College, Aberdeen, and at Edinburgh University. After that he became a teacher and in 1758 published a poem in heroic couplets called *The Highlander*. He had a knowledge of Gaelic poetry and knew the language, and when he met John Home while teaching at Moffat the playwright persuaded him to attempt some translations. *Fragments of Ancient Poetry Collected in the Highlands of Scotland and Translated from the Gaelic or Erse Language* was published in 1760 and was warmly received by Fergusson, Blair, Beattie, Robertson, and the rest of Edinburgh literary society. The preface told of the existence of a Gaelic epic, which Macpherson could recover for literature, given support and encouragement. The necessary money was found for him and he left for the Highlands, publishing the result of his labours as *Fingal, an Ancient Epic Poem* in six books in 1762 (with some shorter poems). *Temora, an Ancient Epic Poem* in ten books followed in 1763 (also with some shorter poems). The collection, the originals of which were attributed to a Gaelic poet named Ossian, was published in 1765. Its success was enormous and Macpherson's version was translated into every European language. Its greatest impact was in Germany, where Herder and Goethe admired it extravagantly.

However, some critics were dubious; Samuel Johnson and David Hume challenged the poems' authenticity and Macpherson was expected to produce the originals – which he failed to do; Irish scholars were equally sceptical. But the public were not interested in scholarly bickering: the poems of 'Ossian' gave them high romance from a misty Celtic past and they loved it; the *language* of a distant past was of little interest. The influence of 'Ossian' was immense; it helped turn attention to wild nature and man's place in it – a wondering curiosity about the (usually) doomed heroes and the epic battles laid the foundations of Romanticism. Scotland became a source of myth and romance and the way was prepared for Sir Walter Scott. Scott, incidentally, did not accept the claims made for the Ossian poems.

Macpherson became rich and thereafter wrote historical works: *An Introduction to the History of Great Britain and Ireland* (1771); *The History of Great Britain from the Restoration to the Accession of the House of Hanover* (1775) and *Original Papers: Containing the Secret History of Great Britain from the Restoration to the Accession of the House of Hanover* (also 1775), for which he was paid the, at that time, enormous sum of £3,000. A prose version of the *Iliad* appeared in 1773. He entered parliament in 1780, acquired the estate of Belville in Inverness, where he died, and was buried in Westminster Abbey.

Macpherson was wise to hold his peace and the success he enjoyed, both critical and popular, could be fairly said to justify his silence; he had written the version called *The Works of Ossian*, after all. Some 11 years after his death, in 1807, the Highland Society made the Gaelic originals available; but Macpherson's manuscripts had been destroyed. Subsequent investigations suggest that Macpherson certainly knew something about Gaelic poetry and there was, probably, a poet or bard named Ossian (Oisean). Out of what he found in Gaelic Macpherson fashioned his own poetry, in biblical language, using Celtic themes. He offended Irish scholars for ever, having no regard for Irish traditional poetry and even inventing the name Fingal, because he disdained the Irish Fionn. Nevertheless, the praise he earned was honestly won; he could have done nothing without possessing considerable poetic skill.

**Macro Plays, The**  See **morality plays**.

*Madame Delicieuse*  See *Old Creole Days*.

*Madame Delphine*  A short novel by George Washington Cable, first published in 1881.

Delphine Carraze is a quadroon who lives quietly in New Orleans with her daughter Olive, who is 17. Olive's father, who was White, left them his property when he died. Olive falls in love with the banker, Ursin Lemaitre, a White man who associates with the pirate Jean Lafitte. A marriage is arranged through Père Jerome; but Lemaitre's affairs come under investigation and he goes into hiding. His friends seize the opportunity to break off what they regard as his disastrous commitment to the daughter of a quadroon. Delphine then declares that Olive is not her daughter but the daughter of a White woman she was given to foster. Olive is heartbroken but her marriage is assured – she can look forward to happiness. Delphine later confesses to Père Jerome that she lied for her daughter's sake; she is granted absolution.

**Magee, William Kirkpatrick** 1868–1961. Magee wrote under the pseudonym of John Eglinton. He was born in Dublin and was a poet and essayist, coming to prominence in Ireland during the cultural revival. He became assistant librarian at the National Library in Dublin. Eglinton's prose is usually praised but neither his verse nor his essays are well known with the exception of *Irish Literary Portraits* (1935), which gives vivid sketches of his contemporaries, including W. B. Yeats, AE, and George Moore. His *A Memoir of AE* was published in 1937.

*Maggie: A Girl of the Streets* A novel by Stephen Crane. It was privately published in 1893 under the pseudonym of Johnston Smith. It was reissued after the success of *The Red Badge of Courage* and first published under the author's name in 1896.

In Rum Alley, a slum district on the east side of New York City, Maggie and Jimmie Johnson are the neglected and ill-treated children of a brutal father and a drunken mother. Jimmie finds work as a truck driver and is soon part of a tough crowd. The mother, now a widow, sinks into dipsomania and soon becomes well known to the police. Maggie labours in a sweat shop as a collar maker and falls in love with a friend of Jimmie's, the bartender Pete. He seduces her; in a display of drunken histrionics her mother disowns her.

Maggie has no one to go to except Pete and after a short time he abandons her. She tries to survive by becoming a prostitute but she has not the temperament for it nor the toughness; she drowns herself after a few months. This provides her dreadful mother with another opportunity for histrionics – grief-stricken now; but she allows her drinking cronies to persuade her to forgive her erring daughter.

*Maggie* is a bleak chronicle of the hopeless life of one girl in an environment from which she cannot escape. There is nothing for anyone's comfort in it; the environment makes the people and society made the environment of which she is a victim. The author knew well the background of his fine short novel.

**Maginn, William** 1793–1842. An Irishman from Marlboro's Fort, County Cork, Maginn was educated at Trinity College and was a schoolmaster in Cork before joining the staff of *Blackwood's Magazine* to form one of a gifted trio with Lockhart and Wilson. He is believed to have invented the *Noctes Ambrosianae* dialogues, which became such a popular feature of *Blackwood's*. His own contributions to the *Magazine* were under the pseudonym of Ensign O'Doherty. A brilliant journalist, Maginn went to London in 1823 and in 1830 helped Hugh Fraser to launch *Fraser's Magazine*, in which he published his *Homeric Ballads* and *Illustrious Literary Characters*. He was the model for Captain Shandon in Thackeray's *Pendennis*.

**Magwitch, Abel** The escaped convict of Dickens's *Great Expectations*, who is helped by the boy Pip, whose benefactor he later becomes.

*Maid Marian* A novel by Thomas Love Peacock, his fourth, first published in 1822. In contrast to his earlier novels, the author sets this one in a framework of historical romance, using the characters of Robin Hood, Richard I, and the rest for a satire on oppression and extreme doctrines of social order. It is perhaps most notable for the songs; the book itself is not one of Peacock's successes.

*Maid's Tragedy, The* The tragedy by Francis Beaumont and John Fletcher, first published in 1619.

Amintor of Rhodes is betrothed to Aspatia, daughter of the Lord Chamberlain, but the king orders him to marry Evadne, sister of his friend Melantius. On the wedding night Evadne refuses Amintor her bed – she is the king's mistress and intends to remain so. Melantius, puzzled by his friend's behaviour, learns the truth and he terrifies Evadne into repentance and to helping him against the king. Aspatia, after her rejection by Amintor, disguises herself as a boy, her brother, and provokes Amintor into fighting a duel with her; she is killed. Evadne kills the king on Melantius' orders and the Lord Chamberlain hands over the citadel to him. Evadne hopes to be accepted by Amintor now the king is dead and is so disappointed to find herself rejected that she kills herself. Amintor, discovering that he has killed Aspatia, kills himself. A new king makes honourable terms with Melantius, who – with all his friends killing themselves or each other – had been contemplating suicide.

Not surprisingly, the play is very rarely revived. There is no poetry in it strong enough to carry the plot or make the behaviour of Evadne and the king acceptable.

**Mailer, Norman** 1923–    . Mailer was born in Long Branch, New Jersey, grew up in Brooklyn, and graduated from Harvard in 1943. He served in the Pacific during World War II and used his experiences as the background for *The Naked and* *the Dead* (1948), an uncompromisingly harsh war novel which is also an abrasive comment on American society. The book made the author famous on both sides of the Atlantic. His view of society is again the theme of both *Barbary Shore* (1951) and *The Deer Park* (1955, dramatized in 1967). All of Mailer's subsequent work, whether fiction or documentary, is social criticism of some kind. *Advertisements for Myself* (1959) is a collection of stories, essays, and extracts from work formerly 'in progress', with linking autobiographical sketches. Among other books by Norman Mailer are the novels *An American Dream* (1965) and *Why are We in Vietnam?* (1967); *The Armies of the Night* (1968, National Book Award and Pulitzer Prize); *Miami and the Siege of Chicago* (1969); *The Prisoner of Sex* (1971); *Marilyn: A Biography* (with others, 1973); and *The Executioner's Song* (1979, Pulitzer Prize).

**Main-Travelled Roads**  A book of short stories about farm life in the Midwest by Hamlin Garland, first published in 1891. The title refers to the road of life, which in the author's view was monotonous and wearying in the rural USA which he knew. But the quality of the storytelling and the author's ability to convey the dignity of his farm people in their drab and straitened lives makes an impressive book.

**Maitland, Sir Richard** 1496–1586.  Sir Richard Maitland of Lethington became a judge in 1561 and about that time became blind. He served as judge and counsellor under James V, Mary of Scotland, and James VI. After he lost his sight he began to write satirical verse. He was deft and judicious and his 'Againis the Theivis of Liddisdail' is frequently found in anthologies of Scottish verse: it is a denunciation of Border raiders – one aspect of the troubled times that provided his material. Maitland is honoured as the foremost compiler, after George Bannatyne, of texts of Scots poetry. The Maitland manuscripts are now in the library of Magdalene College, Cambridge.

**Maitland Folio Manuscript, The**  See **Scottish anthologies and collections.**

**Maitland Quarto Manuscript, The**  See **Scottish anthologies and collections.**

**Makculloch Manuscript, The**  See **Scottish anthologies and collections.**

**Malaprop, Mrs**  In Sheridan's *The Rivals* she is the aunt of the heroine, Lydia Languish, and to some extent controls her niece's fortune. Mrs Malaprop has become famous for her misapplication of long words, since her understanding of their meaning is imperfect (for a character with a similar blind spot, see **Dogberry**), and 'malapropisms' take their name from her. The play abounds in examples; a famous one is 'No caparisons, miss, if you please. Caparisons don't become a young woman.'

**Malcolm**  In Shakespeare's *Macbeth*, Duncan's first-born and the heir to the throne of Scotland. Suspicious of the circumstances of his father's death while Macbeth's guest, he flees to England where Macduff joins him; they invade Scotland and defeat the usurper. It is Malcolm's strategy that takes Birnam Wood to Dunsinane.

**Malcontent, The**  A play by John Marston, with additions by Webster, first published in 1604. It may have been produced much earlier; some scholars give 1600 as the probable date.

Altofronto, the rightful Duke of Genoa, has lost his throne to the usurper, Pietro. He disguises himself and returns to the court as Malevole, a philosopher-buffoon who is accepted as one who will always speak his mind. At the court, meanwhile, his dubious ally, Mendoza, is Pietro's first minister; he has seduced Pietro's wife, Aurelia. He had little difficulty in doing so – Aurelia is promiscuous by nature. Malevole's assumed name and persona become more fitting to his observation of life: the former duke is now the malcontent.

Malevole confides to Pietro that his supposed friend, Mendoza, is conspiring against him and persuades him to go into hiding. Then he announces Pietro's death to the court. Mendoza seizes the opportunity to take the ducal throne for himself; he banishes Aurelia from the court. He also decides that Malevole must be removed; not only is he the rightful duke but as Malevole he is too ready to say what is better left unspoken.

Mendoza's plans include marriage with Maria, Altofronto's wife, and Altofronto goes to Pietro, as Malevole. He reveals his true identity and persuades the erstwhile usurper to help him remove the new one. The climax comes during a ball at the ducal palace, when Mendoza finds himself surrounded by his enemies.

*The Malcontent* is usually regarded as Marston's best play, a sardonic commentary on ambition, lust, and the reversal of fortune. The character of Altofronto–Malevole suffers from extravagant writing; when Marston lets him loose on his diatribes he seems to lose control of the character. The play is never revived now; with judicious cutting, however, it might prove a rewarding alternative to the Webster tragedies – almost the only Jacobean works that see the stage nowadays, though *The Changeling* and *The*

*Revenger's Tragedy* have made brief appearances and both have been well received.

**Malecasta** The lady of Castle Joyeous in Book III of Spenser's *The Faerie Queene*. Her name signifies that she is unchaste.

**Maleger** The phantom-like adversary of Prince Arthur in Book II of Spenser's *The Faerie Queene*. His strength comes from the Earth, his mother. Arthur has to lift him off the ground, like Heracles did Antaeus, to kill him.

**Malet, Lucas** 1852–1931. The pseudonym used by Charles Kingsley's daughter, Mary, for her published work, most of it fiction. Among her novels *The Wages of Sin* (1891) and *The History of Sir Richard Calmady* (1901) were very popular in their time.

**Mallet, David** *c*.1705–65. Originally called Malloch, the son of a Macgregor, Mallet was educated at Edinburgh University and went to London as a tutor in 1723. There he anglicized his name and succeeded in getting himself accepted in the circle of friends surrounding Alexander Pope, among whom was a fellow Scot, James Thomson. Mallet was a busy operator as well as a busy writer of tragedies and blank verse – now forgotten – and became Viscount Bolingbroke's literary executor. With Thomson he collaborated on a masque, *Alfred* (1740), which is now remembered only for 'Rule Britannia', contributed in fact by Thomson but claimed by Mallet as his. Mallet himself is remembered for *William and Margaret* (1723), which was the forerunner of Romantic verse and was developed from the fragment of an old ballad.

**Malmesbury, William of** *c*.1080–*c*.1143. William of Malmesbury was probably born near Malmesbury in the county of Wiltshire; he was educated at the abbey of Malmesbury and became its librarian. He probably spent some time at Glastonbury and travelled as much as the circumstances of his time permitted. He wanted to write and admired the work of Bede, whose successors had, he believed, fallen far short of the standards of the master. William himself is regarded as the best of the Anglo-Norman historians and was fortunate in having as patron Robert, Earl of Gloucester.

William of Malmesbury's chronicles give a history of England in two parts: *De Gestis Regum Anglorum* (449–1127) and *Historia Novella* (1125–42). The histories are highly valued and in addition give a remarkable impression of the mind of a learned and travelled man of the 12th century: for all his scholarship William was quite ready to believe reports of marvels and supernatural occurrences. However, his readiness to digress and reminisce adds much to the liveliness of his chronicles. In the *Gesta Regum* William gives two passages about Arthur, but unlike his near contemporary Geoffrey of Monmouth he is sceptical about the stories surrounding him.

Among William's religious writings are his *Gesta Pontificum Anglorum* and *De Antiquitate Glastoniensis Ecclesiae*. His *Historia Novella* was translated by J. Stevenson for *The Church Historians of England* (1853–56) and edited by William Stubbs (Rolls Series, 1888–89); K. R. Potter's edition and translation came in 1955. *De Gestis Regum Anglorum* was also translated for *The Church Historians of England* and edited by William Stubbs (Rolls Series, 1887).

**Malory, Sir Thomas** d. 1471. The author of *Le Morte Darthur* (Caxton's spelling) has been identified as Sir Thomas Malory, knight, of Newbold Revel in Warwickshire and Winwick in Northamptonshire. He seems to have been rather different from the 'gentle' knights of King Arthur's court: the evidence suggests a rip-roaring medieval rogue who was tried and imprisoned for a number of major crimes, including rape. (See E. K. Chambers, *English Literature at the Close of the Middle Ages*.) But the times in which Malory lived, the Wars of the Roses, were very disturbed and, as C. S. Lewis pointed out, the true character of a man is not easy to discern when the evidence exists in the records of his prosecutors. It is true that he was a prisoner during the compilation of his immortal work, and he appears to have been excluded from two general – probably political – pardons granted during the reign of Edward IV. He died on 14 March 1471 and was buried in the church of the Grey Friars in London.

**Malthus, Thomas Robert** 1766–1834. Malthus was born near Guildford in Surrey; his father was of independent means and had been a friend of Rousseau. Malthus completed his education at Jesus College, Cambridge, became a fellow of his college, was ordained, and became curate of Albury, Surrey, in 1798. In the same year he published his famous essay, *On the Principle of Population as it Affects the Future Improvement of Society*. Malthus had the benefit of a scientific education and he rejected the views of some of his philosophic contemporaries regarding human perfectibility. The more man prospered, he implied, the nearer he moved to further trouble; increasing population would outgrow the means of subsistence and some check was necessary.

Malthus published a second edition of his essay

in 1803: *The Principles of Population, A View of Its Past and Present Effects on Human Happiness*, in which his views seemed more optimistic; he had travelled extensively in Europe and thought that the advance of civilization and increasing 'morality' were modifying factors; morality in that context was a euphemism for voluntary birth control. But the harsh view of the first essay seems the one which posterity supports. Malthus's theory provoked a storm of controversy and was a powerful influence on 19th-century thought. His further writings are concerned with economics, notably *An Investigation of the Cause of the Present High Price of Provisions* (1800), *Observations on the effect of the Corn Laws* (1814), *The Principles of Political Economy* (1820), and *The Measure of Value Stated and Illustrated*.

**Malvolio** Olivia's steward in Shakespeare's *Twelfth Night*. He is 'of a rather overstretched morality' in Charles Lamb's words, and disapproves of the noisy Sir Toby and Sir Andrew, whom he regards, not without reason, as parasites. Withal he is stiff-necked and humourless, and his vanity makes it easy for his enemies to trick him into making a fool of himself. But Shakespeare contrives that the perpetrators will not be the better-liked for their treatment of this peculiarly defenceless and lonely man.

**Mammon, Cave of** The treasure house of the god of wealth in Book II of Spenser's *The Faerie Queene*.

**Man Against the Sky, The** A collection of poems by Edwin Arlington Robinson, first published in 1916. The title ode symbolizes mankind as a figure seen on a hilltop and the poet ponders on the endless and essential aspiration of man to more wisdom and awareness of the human condition. Also in this volume is 'Cassandra', an uneasy comment on the times.

**Man and Superman** Subtitled 'A Comedy and a Philosophy', a play in four acts by George Bernard Shaw. It was first produced in May 1905 at the Court Theatre, without the second scene of the third act. The first complete production using the whole text was in 1915, at Edinburgh. The play was published in 1903.

Ann Whitefield under her father's will has two guardians, the elderly and respectable Roebuck Ramsden and the reluctant John Tanner. Tanner is buzzing with forward-looking ideas, which Ramsden abhors: he refuses to act with Tanner, who in turn refuses to act for Ann, seeing her as an unscrupulous young woman with a genius for getting her own way. She does, in this case; she

*Man and Superman*. A scene from the first performance of Shaw's comedy in 1905 at the Court Theatre, London. Lillah McCarthy as Ann Whitefield, Granville Barker as John Tanner. Victoria & Albert Theatre Museum, London.

beguiles both men into accepting her as their ward. Ann's sister Violet is pregnant, and everyone reacts with various degrees of dismay, except Tanner. He proclaims that Violet is fulfilling a woman's true destiny: convention and respectability must be thrust aside in the light of that. Violet confounds him by indignantly proclaiming her respectability – she is married but was obliged to keep it a secret. Octavius, a sentimental poet, proposes to Ann, who blandly refers him to her guardian, Mr Tanner, who is to accompany the group, which includes Hector, Violet's husband, to Spain.

Tanner's chauffeur, 'Enry Straker, has spotted Ann's true intentions about Tanner. Ann has marked him for her own, and Tanner soon sees that 'Enry is right. He flees to Spain in his car with 'Enry; Ann sets off in pursuit, with the original party. Tanner, in the Sierra Nevada, falls asleep and dreams the scene that is sometimes not included and sometimes played separately as *Don Juan in Hell*. After the dream Tanner is joined by Ann Whitefield and the party from England. They all proceed to Granada, where Violet and Hector's marriage is eventually condoned by Hector's father. Octavius proposes to Ann again: she returns that her late father really wanted her to marry John Tanner – that must be the reason for the terms of the will – and her mother wants this, too. Her mother knows Ann very well; she understands that Ann will have Tanner and no power on earth will stop her. The final curtain comes down on his capitulation; he had no more chance of escaping from her than a mouse would from a python, only in this case the python is called the Life Force.

The play is a fine comedy, with excellent characterization and bubbling wit. Its implications are examined on another plane in the optional scene of Act III, called *Don Juan in Hell*. Tanner becomes Don Juan, Ann Whitefield is Dona Ana, Ramsden her father, and the brigand whose verses sent Tanner to sleep is the Devil. Ramsden comes from heaven to call on the Devil because heaven has proved to be so dull: 'Nobody could stand an eternity of heaven.' Ana, having declared that she will go to heaven to be happy, is warned by Juan that if she wants happiness she had better stay where she is. He intends to go there, though: Ana's father remarks that hell is 'a place where you have nothing to do but amuse yourself' and Juan wants something better than that. The Devil delivers a fine commentary on Man, who devotes his finest intelligence to finding new methods of destruction; but Juan returns that men, in spite of that, are amenable to ideas – that is how they will reach perfection and become supermen. Ana, who knows her true purpose as a woman, closes the scene with her declaration of belief in the future: 'I believe in the Life to come. A father – a father for the Superman!' Some of the scene is fine but some of it is numbing; the sheer weight of words in Juan's mouth seemed to worry the author, who has one character, Ana's father, remarking to him, 'I begin to doubt whether you will ever finish, my friend. You are extremely fond of hearing yourself talk.'

**Manciple's Tale, The** See **Canterbury Tales, The.**

**Mandeville, Bernard de** 1670–1733. Mandeville was a Dutchman, born at Dort and educated at the Erasmus School in Rotterdam. He took his medical degree at the University of Leyden and decided to practise in England after going there to learn the language. He was the author of some medical treatises in English and Latin but is remembered in English literature for his satirical writings, which display a remarkable command of colloquial English. These were written as a somewhat sour contradiction to the optimistic mood expressed by such philosophers as Berkeley and Shaftesbury. Such men were privileged and of comfortable means; optimism was infinitely more difficult for those who observed or experienced the harsher aspects of life. But Shaftesbury and Mandeville shared a detestation of Puritanism and Mandeville was a strong believer in the 'moral sense'; both men were empiricists, refusing to accept any 'system' of mental procedure, relying rather on common sense conclusions based on observation.

*The Grumbling Hive, or Knaves Turn'd Honest* (1705) was written in doggerel verse and reissued with prose commentaries as *The Fable of the Bees: or Private Vices, Public Benefits* (1714 and 1723); a second part was added in 1728. Both parts were published together in 1734. Other works by Mandeville are *A Modest Defence of Public Stews: or an Essay upon Whoring, as it is now Practis'd in these Kingdoms* (1724), *An Enquiry into the Causes of the Frequent Executions at Tyburn* (1725), and *An Enquiry into the Origin of Honour, and the Usefulness of Christianity in War* (1732). The definitive edition of *The Fable of the Bees* is by F. B. Kaye (1924).

Mandeville's mordant view of man aroused the wrath of the orthodox philosophers of his day. His idea of society as a hive wherein mankind thrives because of mutual greeds contained enough paradoxes to irritate them but they were never able to controvert them completely. Among those who tried were George Berkeley in *Alciphron* (1732) and William Law in *Remarks on a Late Book entituled The Fable of the Bees* (1723).

**Mandeville, The Travels of Sir John** A book purporting to be the account of his travels by a knight of St Albans, who left England in 1322 on a pilgrimage to Jerusalem and then travelled over much of the known world. In the framework of a guide for pilgrims to the Holy Land, the author relates tales and legends, romance and history, and geography and the world's marvels.

The earliest manuscript of the book that was to entertain generations of readers is in French and dated 1371. It originated in Liège, where John de Mandeville, knight of St Albans, was laid low by arthritic gout. At the suggestion of his physician,

Pilgrims arriving by ship (above); other pilgrims approaching a city gate. A 14th-century illustration for *The Travels of Sir John Mandeville. Add. MS 24189, f.8.* British Library.

John the Bearded, he wrote an account of his travels to enliven his enforced idleness. But scholarship has revealed that the book was compiled from the accounts of William of Boldensele, Friar Oderic of Pordenone, Vincent de Beauvais, and others. The identity of the author is not known for certain but he was probably Jean d'Outremeuse, who lived in Liège at the time of the book's appearance and was a writer of histories and fables in prose and verse. He must also have had access to an excellent library containing all the classics and books of travel and reference then known. Whoever the author, the book enjoyed a remarkable success and was translated into English, Latin, and German – and by 1500 into most European languages. The names of the translators into English are not known, but their praises are sung by scholars for their genuine contribution to English prose with a text that, in its handling of the language, marks an advance in smoothness and skill.

There was no Sir John de Mandeville but the account of his 'travels' was something new – it was entertaining. Its strong personal tone and interest in mankind, together with the projection of a vivid imagination prepared to utilize what the author found in the works of others (as far back as Pliny and Homer), are combined with the illusion of individual experience related in the first person.

Editions of *The Travels of Sir John Mandeville* have been edited by P. Hamelius for the Early English Text Society (1919–23) and by M. Letts for the Hakluyt Society (1953). The book can be read in modern English in an edition by M. C. Seymour (The World's Classics, 1967).

**Manette, Dr Alexander**   The prisoner of the Bastille, whose release marks the beginning of Dickens's *A Tale of Two Cities*. He nearly succeeds in saving his son-in-law, Charles Darnay, from the Revolutionary Tribunal.

***Manfred***   A dramatic poem by Lord Byron, first published in 1817. Byron told his publisher, John Murray, in a letter of 7 June 1820, that the awesome scenery of the Alps had inspired him to write *Manfred*; he stopped working on the third canto of *Childe Harold* in 1817 in order to write his dramatic poem. He was influenced by Goethe's *Faust*, the first part of which was published in 1808.

Manfred, guilty of some mysterious crime and an outcast from society, lives a solitary life in the Alps, tortured by remorse. He invokes the spirits of the universe but they do not offer him what he wants most – oblivion. He makes a vain attempt to kill himself and then calls up the Witch of the Alps, so that he can visit the realm of Arimanes and the spirits of Evil; but he refuses to submit to them. At his bidding they call up the dead and he encounters the shade of Astarte, the sister whom he loved and for whose death he is haunted by guilt. She tells him he will die on the next day; that is all. When the evil spirits come to claim him Manfred rejects his compact with them and they disappear. Though he dies at the time Astarte foretold, Manfred's resolution to remain master of his fate never falters.

**Mangan, James Clarence** 1803–49.   The son of a shopkeeper, Mangan was born in Dublin and was taught by a priest. He worked as a lawyer's clerk and later in the library of Trinity College and he contributed poems and translations to *The Dublin University Magazine*. Later he contributed verse to *The Nation*, the patriotic paper founded by Charles Gavan Duffy and Thomas Osborne Davis, and published *Anthologia Germanica*, translations from German poets (1845). *The Poets and Poetry of Munster* (1849) was called translations but is more correctly versions in English: Mangan knew no Irish and worked from prose translations. He contributed to *Romances and*

*Ballads of Ireland* (edited by E. Ellis, 1850) and left a version of the Irish satire *The Tribes of Ireland* by Aenghus O'Daly (published posthumously, 1852). Mangan was addicted to opium, drank too much, and died of cholera at the age of 46. His best-known poems, 'Dark Rosaleen' and 'The Nameless One', are usually found in collections of Irish verse.

A further volume of *The Poets and Poetry of Munster* was published by George Sigerson (1862). Unlike Mangan, Sigerson was a scholar and historian (he was also a doctor) and could draw directly from the original Irish, a language which was in grave danger of being lost forever. The work of dedicated enthusiasts eventually bore fruit and among those Sigerson holds an honoured place. His *Munster* volume contained careful metrical translations to accompany the original text, as did the more ambitious *Bards of the Gael and Gall* (1897). Among other works by George Sigerson were *Irish Literature* (with Charles Gavan Duffy and Douglas Hyde, 1894), *The Saga of King Lir* (1913), and *Sedulius: The Easter Song* (a translation, 1922).

**Man in Black, The** A character in Goldsmith's satirical *The Citizen of the World*. A humorous and kindly man, he becomes the mentor of the Chinese gentleman in London who is the citizen of the title. The Man in Black is regarded by scholars as a preliminary sketch for Dr Primrose in *The Vicar of Wakefield*.

**Mannyng of Brunne, Robert** fl. 1288–1338. Mannyng was a Gilbertine monk, born in Brunne (the present Bourne) in Kesteven, Lincolnshire. He spent some time at Cambridge and then probably the rest of his life in the priory of Sixille (the present Six Hills) near Market Rasen. He dedicated his **Handlynge Synne** to the Gilbertine fellowship of Sempringham, to which he had belonged for 15 years when he began work in 1303. Mannyng also translated the *Chronicle* of Peter Langtoft. Langtoft was canon of the Augustinian priory of Bridlington and, like William of Waddington (author of *Handlynge Synne*), wrote in French. His *Chronicle* covers the period from the arrival of the English to the reign of Edward I; Mannyng translated Wace of Jersey's version of Geoffrey of Monmouth for the earlier period and began his verse *Chronicle of England* with the arrival in Britain of the legendary Brutus. The text was edited by F. J. Furnivall as *The Story of England by Robert Mannyng* (Rolls Series, 1887).

**Man of Feeling, The** See **Mackenzie, Henry**.

**Man of Law's Tale, The** See **Canterbury Tales, The**.

**Man of Mode, The**, or *Sir Fopling Flutter*. A comedy by George Etherege, first produced in March 1676 and published in the same year. It was the author's third and last play and can be regarded as the first of the great Restoration comedies, in spite of having no real plot. It reflects society as seen through the brilliantly drawn personifications of its types, who come together and separate, forming new pictures and dissolving into further pictures. It is not concerned merely with the fashionable – even the shoemaker and the orange-woman are beautifully observed.

Among those present are the poet Young Bellair and his love Emilia; the old-fashioned Lady Woodvill and the fashionable and wise Lady Townley; Dorimant, the finest of fine gentlemen (the Earl of Rochester?) and his follower Medley; Harriet, beautiful and intelligent, who has the measure of Dorimant perfectly; Sir Fopling Flutter – a remarkable creation who, in Dryden's words, is a 'Fool so nicely writ, The Ladies wou'd mistake him for a Wit'. Dorimant's formidable wit makes him the major character in this passing parade; but he by no

Etherege's comedy, *The Man of Mode*, Act I, scene 1. Dorimant receiving Medley in his dressing room. Frontispiece to an edition of the play published in 1723. The play was first produced in 1676.

means has his own way entirely and the shoemaker makes short work of his attitudes in one scene. He has already discarded Loveit and Bellinda; Harriet is next on his list but this delightful heroine (if the play has a heroine at all) is more than a match for Dorimant, who falls in love with her.

**Man of the World, The** See **Mackenzie, Henry.**

**Mansfield, Katherine** 1888–1923. Kathleen Mansfield Beauchamp was the daughter of a successful businessman of Wellington, New Zealand, where she was born. She was sent to London in 1903 to complete her education at Queen's College, where she spent three years. At home in New Zealand she became a wide-ranging reader and began to write, trying verse and prose, and succeeded in having several *Vignettes* accepted for publication in the Australian monthly *Native Companion* (1907). In 1908 she left New Zealand for London, determined on a literary career. She had a small allowance from her father and supplemented this with the odd guineas earned by giving songs and recitations at parties; later she was helped financially by her friend Ida Baker. She seems to have led a rather bohemian life: she met, married, and left – on the day of her marriage – George C. Bowden in the space of three weeks. Then she found she was pregnant, though not by her husband of a few hours. Her mother travelled from New Zealand and installed her daughter in a hotel in Bavaria, then returned home. Kathleen suffered a miscarriage and returned to England in early 1910. Mr Bowden received her in his apartment in London and gave her lodging; to him Kathleen showed the Bavarian sketches she had written, and it was Bowden who suggested that she submit the stories to A. R. Orage, the editor of *New Age* (or 'No Wage' as the editor dubbed it). It made no money, paid its contributors a token fee if anything, and was nevertheless the liveliest weekly in London. Thus began her career as a short story writer of international repute, under the name of Katherine Mansfield.

Katherine Mansfield's relationship with *New Age* continued, and after meeting John Middleton Murry in 1911 her work began to appear in *Rhythm*, an *avant-garde* quarterly founded by Murry and Michael Sadleir in that year. Murry moved into Katherine Mansfield's flat near Gray's Inn in 1912, the same year Virginia Stephen married Leonard Woolf and Frieda Weekley (née von Richtofen) eloped with D. H. Lawrence. Mansfield and Murry did not bother to marry; they moved from place to place and, while Katherine Mansfield's reputation increased, her health deteriorated and the loss of her only brother in 1915 in World War I was a severe blow. She and Murry eventually married in 1918, but she was suffering from tuberculosis and died at Fontainebleau in 1922.

Katherine Mansfield is generally acknowledged as one of the finest short-story writers of the 20th century, and her work has been discussed by critics in the English-speaking world, France, and Germany ever since her death. The first collection was *In a German Pension* (1911), followed by *Prelude*, a story that was published singly in 1918 and marked her use of her own country and childhood as the source for some of her best work. 'Je ne parle pas français' (1919) and 'Prelude' were both included in *Bliss, and Other Stories* (1920); *The Garden-Party, and Other Stories* (1922) was the last collection published during her lifetime. Posthumous works were *Poems* edited by J. M. Murry (1923), *Something Childish, and Other Stories* (1924), and *A Fairy Story* (Stanford, 1932). Collections were published as *The Short Stories of Katherine Mansfield* edited by J. M. Murry (1937), and *The Collected Stories of Katherine Mansfield* (1945), which was an omnibus volume. A selection was edited by D. Davin, (The World's Classics, 1953). Murry edited *The Letters of Katherine Mansfield* (1928) and *Katherine Mansfield's Letters to John Middleton Murry 1913–1922* (1951).

**Mansfield Park** A novel by Jane Austen, begun in 1811 and first published in 1814.

Sir Thomas and Lady Bertram live at Mansfield Park. They have two daughters, Maria and Julia, and two sons, Tom and Edmund. Lady Bertram has two sisters, her neighbour Mrs Norris and Mrs Price – the wife of a marine officer with a family of young children. The Bertrams offer to take charge of one of these, and nine-year-old Fanny Price comes to Mansfield Park. Fanny is patronized by her cousins and bullied by the mean Mrs Norris but finds a friend in Edmund Bertram.

Later, Sir Thomas has to leave for the West Indies to look after his interests there. His children, on whom he has always impressed the need for manners and social (rather than moral) accomplishments, demonstrate the deficiencies in their upbringing as soon as their father has gone. Fanny, now in her teens, refuses to take part in the self-indulgent flirtations of her cousins.

Maria Bertram, engaged to Mr Rushworth, is attracted to Henry Crawford, whose sister Mary fascinates Edmund Bertram. But Maria decides after all to marry Rushworth, whereupon Henry turns his attentions to Fanny. He falls in love

**Map** 561

with her and proposes: Fanny turns him down and Sir Thomas, now back at Mansfield, is displeased at what seems foolishness – as a girl with nothing she was very fortunate to be chosen by Henry Crawford.

Fanny, depressed, goes to visit her own family in Portsmouth and finds the noise and disorder in her father's house depressing. In spite of herself, she longs to be back at Mansfield Park. Meanwhile Maria, now Mrs Rushworth, has run off with Henry Crawford. Julia has eloped with a Mr Yates. Edmund, who has taken orders, is still in subjection to Mary Crawford and still hopes to marry her. But she not only makes it plain that she is averse to marrying a clergyman, she lets Edmund know how tiresome she finds Henry's conduct – he could have arranged things better, so that exposure need not have followed.

Edmund and Fanny eventually find happiness together, and it is clear that the rest of the characters are unlikely ever to do so.

*Mansfield Park* is a novel apart in Jane Austen's work. There is a remarkable forthrightness that separates it from the exquisite comedy of *Pride and Prejudice* and *Emma* (her next novel) and suggests that the author, if she had lived to write beyond *Persuasion*, so to speak, might have produced a formidable work indeed. She presents us with a superficially attractive world and succeeds in making the Crawfords charming before we come to judge them: the Bertrams themselves have no magic but they have poise and elegance as well as individual weaknesses of character. Fanny, the girl from outside who remains detached, is homesick for Mansfield Park, nevertheless, when she leaves it to visit her family. The quiet and in some ways uninteresting Fanny is the author's means of exposing glamour's other side and making Edmund's and Fanny's retirement from the world seem preferable.

*Mansie Wauch, The Life of* See **Moir, David Macbeth.**

*Man that Corrupted Hadleyburg, The* The title story of a collection of essays and short stories by Mark Twain published in 1900. A stranger in Hadleyburg is offended by its citizens, who are fond of proclaiming how honest and upright their town is. By a device that arouses the greed of its most prominent men, who respond to the temptation, the stranger shows that this is not the case. The single one who becomes rich because of the device confesses it on his deathbed and the town's reputation is destroyed.

*Man Who Died, The* A story by D. H. Lawrence, first published as *The Escaped Cock* in Paris in 1929. Lawrence changed the title before he died and the present one was used in the 1931 edition. The man is Jesus, who emerges from his tomb and goes to live with some peasants outside Jerusalem. They keep a cock, which is confined. When he realises 'the necessity to live, and even to cry out the triumph of life' Jesus sets the cock free. He knows that his first mission to man was in error. He goes to the Lebanon with a priestess of Isis; in the temple she names him Osiris and heals the wounds of his terrible self-sacrifice. Her body becomes the symbol of regeneration and 'the great atonement' of his earlier life. The priestess conceives by him and wants him to abide with her in the temple but that is not his destiny; he goes forth into the world once more; he will return but for the present he knows, within himself, that he has sown the seed of his life and resurrection.

*Many Inventions* A collection of 14 stories and two poems by Rudyard Kipling, first published in 1893. Among the stories in the volume is 'The Disturber of Traffic', in which a lighthouse keeper, Fenwick, relates how another lighthouse keeper, Dowse, in the Flores Straits, went mad and played dangerous tricks on the ships seeking to pass; Dowse believes that the ships are harming the sea. He is taken off and eventually, back in Portsmouth, he recovers his reason. The story is an example of Kipling's scrupulous attention to the correct functioning of machinery. 'His Private Honour' is a strange tale of soldierly honour, the concern here of Private Ortheris, one of the 'soldiers three'; 'The Finest Story in the World' deals with reincarnation, and 'In the Rukh' presents Mowgli, of *The Jungle Books*, to readers for the first time. See also **Love-o'- Women**.

**Map (or Mapes), Walter** *c*.1140–1209. A Welshman from the border and a friend of Giraldus Cambrensis, Walter Map studied in Paris and afterwards became a clerk to Henry II. The king made him an itinerant judge and after Henry's death in 1189 he held various religious appointments, becoming Archdeacon of Oxford in 1197. He wrote his satirical miscellany *De Nugis Curialium* (*Of Courtiers' Trifles*) between 1181 and 1193. It is a commonplace book, containing reflections upon his life and times, the characters of those he knew, and a number of tales and anecdotes. From a historical point of view his book is most valuable for his reflections on the kings of the Norman dynasty, his description of Henry II, and his account of contemporary heresies. Included in *De Nugis Curialium* is the letter from Valerius to Rufinus on the folly of marrying (*Dissuasio Valerii ad Rufinum de non Ducenda Uxore*) once attributed to St Augustine and referred to by Chaucer's Wife of Bath in her Prologue. To Walter Map were attributed at one time some goliardic poems and a prose romance about Lancelot du Lac, but the *De Nugis Curialium* is the only work now attributed with certainty to him.

Editions of *De Nugis Curialium* are by T. Wright for the Camden Society (1850) and by M. R. James (1914). M. R. James's translation was published in 1923.

**Marble Faun, The**  A novel by Nathaniel Hawthorne, first published in 1860. In England it was published under the title of *Transformation*. The story is set in Rome.

Kenyon and Hilda are two Americans studying art in Rome. One of their friends is Miriam, a beautiful and rather mysterious girl, and through her they meet Donatello, Count of Monte Beni. He is a handsome, amoral, and warm-hearted man who resembles, facially, the Marble Faun sculpted by Praxiteles. Donatello falls passionately in love with Miriam; but he realises that Miriam has some undisclosed secret and that, after an encounter in the catacombs, she is being persecuted by some mysterious stranger who dogs her footsteps. On a moonlight walk above the Tiber with Miriam and her American friends Donatello is enraged to find the stranger following them; Miriam wordlessly encourages Donatello to kill the intruder. Hilda is a horrified witness.

Miriam and Donatello are now linked by their shared guilt but the weight of it proves too much for Donatello. Hilda, too, because she witnessed the crime but feels bound to silence for her friends' sake, is tormented by what has happened. Eventually Donatello, overcome by remorse, confesses his crime and Hilda, in contradiction to her Puritan training, finds relief in a Catholic confessional. Miriam disappears, still an enigma to those who knew her. At the end of the tale Hilda marries Kenyon.

**Marcus Andronicus**  Brother of Titus in Shakespeare's *Titus Andronicus*. Marcus discovers the mutilated Lavinia and teaches her how to communicate and it falls to him to proclaim Lucius, son of Titus, emperor at the end of the play.

**Mardi: and a Voyage Thither.**  An allegorical romance by Herman Melville, first published in 1849.

Taji, the narrator, deserts from a whaling ship with Jarl, an older seaman, in a whaleboat. They encounter the brigantine *Parki*, abandoned except for a Polynesian couple, Samoa and Annatoo, and the four live a contented life on board until the ship sinks during a storm and Annatoo is drowned. The three survivors take to the whaleboat and soon sight land on the horizon. An island boat comes into view; on board are a priest and a White maiden, Yillah, whom the priest intends to sacrifice. The boat is manned by the priest's sons. Taji is determined to rescue the girl and in doing so kills the priest. The three men and the girl reach the islands of Mardi, an earthly paradise; Taji is welcomed as a demigod and lives happily with Yillah. But three of the priest's sons are on their track and one day Yillah disappears. Mardi is no longer an earthly paradise to Taji and he sets out to find his lost love.

Accompanied by four Mardians, a king, a historian, a philosopher, and a poet, Taji embarks on his search, which takes them to many places that are observed and discussed. Dominora (Great Britain), Vivenza (the USA), and others are subjected to satirical examination in the manner of Swift. The travellers reach Serenia, ruled by Alma (Jesus), and the philosopher declares that his doctrine of love is the ultimate wisdom. But Taji observes that man ignores the doctrine and so they continue on their journey, though his companions call on him to give up his search. He discovers that Yillah was, after all, sacrificed in the whirlpool as the priest intended but he sails out into the ocean alone, still in search of what he has lost and followed by the priest's sons, who remain in pursuit.

**Maria** (i)  In Shakespeare's *Love's Labour's Lost*, one of the ladies of the Princess of France's suite. Longaville falls in love with her and she promises to return to Navarre after a year in France mourning the death of the king.

**Maria** (ii)  Olivia's maid in Shakespeare's *Twelfth Night*. She forges her mistress's hand in the letter to trick Malvolio into thinking Olivia favours him above his office. It is her suggestion that Malvolio is mad and results in his being confined in a dungeon. She marries Sir Toby Belch at the end of the play.

**Mariana**  Angelo's former betrothed in Shakespeare's *Measure for Measure*. Angelo had discarded her when her dowry was lost with her brother's shipwreck. Isabella and the duke arrange that she will be placed in Angelo's bed in place of Isabella and he is resigned to marrying her at the end.

**Marina**  The daughter of Pericles, Prince of Tyre, in Shakespeare's play of that name. Her virtue protects her when she is sold to a brothel keeper by pirates.

**Marino Faliero** A tragedy in verse by Algernon Charles Swinburne, first published in 1885. The subject is the same as that of Byron's tragedy of the same name (1821) but Swinburne uses the figure of the treasonous Doge of Venice, who rebels against the shackles of custom and tradition, as a symbol of liberty.

**Marino Faliero** A tragedy by Lord Byron, first published in 1821, when it was produced against his wishes at Drury Lane. It was one of two historical dramas set in Venice; the other, *The Two Foscari*, was published in the same year. Marino Faliero, Doge of Venice in the 14th century, is a haughty, over-proud old man, who has slighted Michele Steno, a gentleman of poor but distinguished family. Steno writes a gross lampoon on the Doge's chair of state; he is tried and punished by the Council of Forty but Faliero is furious at what he regards as a mild sentence. Faliero plots with some malcontents to overthrow the constitution of Venice and take his revenge on the council. But the plot is exposed and Marino Faliero is beheaded on the staircase of the Doge's Palace.

**Marius the Epicurean** A philosophical romance by Walter Pater, first published in 1885. The Greek philosopher Epicurus (341–270 bc) taught that the repose of the mind, which leads to the absence of pain, is the greatest good. Repose of the mind is achieved by virtue, which therefore must be pursued. The story is set in ancient Rome during the time of the Antonine emperors, the zenith of the empire's greatness. The life of Marius is followed from his childhood on his family's land to his education at Pisa and his adult life in Rome. The author examines Marius's response to the philosophical influences of his time, to the Roman religion, to the dreadful spectacles of the amphitheatre, and finally to the growing influence of Christianity. Marius does not become a Christian though he is strongly attracted by the high principles and commitment of his Christian friend Cornelius. Marius dies to save his friend's life and the Christian Church looks on him as a martyr.

**Marjorie Daw** The title story of a collection by Thomas Bailey Aldrich, first published in 1873.

John Flemming is the victim of a long illness and his friend Edward Delaney writes him letters to help pass the time. To make the letters interesting Delaney gives a glowing account of a neighbour, Marjorie Daw. Flemming, without having seen her, falls in love with the girl in his friend's letters; and Delaney insists that Marjorie Daw's feelings are the same. But when Flemming, partly recovered, insists on coming to meet the girl Delaney realizes he has succeeded too well in distracting his friend from his illness. He has to confess that Marjorie Daw does not exist.

**Markham, Gervase** *c.*1568–1637. Markham was a soldier and horseman who, after some years of fighting in the Netherlands, returned to England and became a writer on horsemanship, country pursuits, veterinary medicine, and the arts of war. He was an extremely busy writer and one critic, Douglas Bush, describes him as an industrious hack, while granting the long life which Markham's useful books enjoyed. *A Discource of Horsemanshippe* was published in 1593 and *Cavelarice: Or the English Horseman* in 1607. He supplemented it with a volume of veterinary information in 1610, *Markhams Maister-peece: Or What Doth a Horse-man Lacke*. Other books were *Cheape and Good Husbandry for the Well-ordering of all Beasts and Fowles* (1614), *Countrey Contentments* (1615), and *Markhams Faithfull Farrier* (1629). Markham also wrote a number of plays and published collections of poems. The performing horse mentioned by Markham in the title of *Cavelarice* was Marocco, famous throughout Europe. Shakespeare refers to him in the first act of *Love's Labour's Lost* as 'the dancing horse' of Armado's conversation with his page.

**Marlow, Young** Kate Hardcastle's suitor in *She Stoops to Conquer*. He mistakes her father's house for an inn and Kate for one of the servants. Reserved and tongue-tied in his own milieu, he is a different man when pursuing a servant girl.

**Marlowe, Christopher** 1564–93. Marlowe was the son of a shoemaker of Canterbury and was born in that city. He was educated at King's School, Canterbury, and at 17 (1580) went to Corpus Christi College, Cambridge; his entry to both institutions was by way of scholarships. Marlowe took his BA in 1584 and qualified for his MA in 1587. However the university withheld the degree because it was suspected that Marlowe wanted to become a Catholic and enrol in the English seminary at Rheims. But remarkably, the queen's privy council intervened and, rejecting the Catholic-convert story, declared that Marlowe had 'done her Majestie good service'. The good service was rendered in a secret mission abroad and Marlowe's MA was confirmed.

Marlowe lived as carelessly as his contemporaries Nashe and Greene. He was never their friend though he was, indisputably, a 'university wit' and was to prove the greatest by far. In London Marlowe lost no time in associating himself with the company of actors called The Admiral's Men; the admiral was the Earl of Nottingham, who had been Lord Howard of Effingham. At the same time he continued in the secret diplomatic service under Francis Walsingham, and it is possible that he needed whatever pay the service yielded in order to pursue a literary career. The Admiral's Men, with the great Edward Alleyn in the title role, presented his ***Tamburlaine the Great*** about 1587 and it was a resounding success. Marlowe was 23; he was dead before he reached his 30th birthday.

Marlowe's lifestyle was strangely at odds with his employment as an agent. He was free-thinking, atheistic, indiscreet, and in his love life frankly preferred his own sex: he was in many ways a typical Elizabethan and numbered among his friends Ralegh, Blount, Nashe, and Chapman. In 1592, when an outbreak of plague closed the London theatres, he went to stay with his patron Thomas Walsingham (brother of Francis) at Chislehurst. In the spring of 1593 Marlowe's friend and one-time room mate Thomas Kyd was investigated by the privy council; he was suspected of writing subversive pamphlets. The government men did discover some blasphemous and atheistical pamphlets and Kyd, confronted with them, declared that Marlowe was the

This portrait in Corpus Christi College, Cambridge, is believed to be a true likeness of Christopher Marlowe but proof has never been established.

author. The privy council ordered Marlowe to lodge in the environs of London – to be available should they want to examine him at any time.

Marlowe and three others arrived at a tavern in Deptford on the morning of 30 May 1593. That evening, in their room, they were gambling at backgammon and supper was served there. Soon after that there was an uproar in the room. One man, Ingram Frizer, was bleeding from head wounds; another was lying dead, fatally wounded by Frizer's knife. He was Christopher Marlowe. At the enquiry that followed Frizer declared that he had accidentally killed Marlowe in self-defence in a quarrel over the game. The other two, Robert Poley and Nicholas Skeres, supported everything Frizer said. All three men were dubious characters: Frizer was Thomas Walsingham's agent and a confidence trickster; Poley was a double agent who had rendered service to Francis Walsingham; Skeres had neither occupation nor abode. It seems certain that Marlowe's murder was coldly arranged. Indiscreet at the best of times, he could have been a dangerous liability to his masters if publicly arraigned.

The order of Marlowe's work can only be roughly decided. That it began while he was still at Cambridge is certain; his translation of Ovid's *Amores* is generally agreed to have been completed there and the first part of *Tamburlaine* also; the second part was written in the following year (1588). The first publication was in 1590 but Marlowe's name did not appear on the title page. ***Doctor Faustus*** was written and produced immediately after *Tamburlaine*, probably in 1589, but not published until 1604. ***The Jew of Malta*** was first produced about 1590 but not published until 1633 and then in a text that had been subjected to considerable alteration – probably by Thomas Heywood. ***Edward II*** was produced about 1592 and printed during the author's lifetime (published 1594, the year after the author's death), so we have a reliable text for Marlowe's best play.

*The Massacre at Paris*, a minor piece, was acted in 1593; the first printed text is undated but probably belongs to 1594. The subject was the massacre, on the eve of St Bartholomew in 1572, of the Protestants of Paris and the murder of the Duke of Guise. *The Tragedy of Dido* was the joint work of Marlowe and Thomas Nashe; published in 1594, it is the least regarded of Marlowe's works. The translation of the *Amores* of Ovid was first published in a book of *Epigrammes and Elegies* collected by Sir John Davies (1597); it is usually looked on as apprentice work and one to which Marlowe, with his imperfect Latin, was ill-suited. His translation of the first book of Lucan's *Pharsalia* (*Lucan's First Booke Translated*

*Line for Line*) was published in 1600 and C. S. Lewis believed it to be a late work and a new departure for Marlowe but one that promised great things. It was first entered at Stationers' Hall in 1593, the same year as the first two sestiads of the unfinished *Hero and Leander*, which was published in 1598. The famous 'The Passionate Shepherd to His Love' was first published in the anthology *The Passionate Pilgrim* (1599) but the text that appeared in *Englands Helicon* (1600) is the accepted one. The involvement or otherwise of Christopher Marlowe in the work of other Elizabethan playwrights and in the anonymous *Arden of Faversham* makes a pleasant exercise for scholars.

The grandeur and stupendous energy of Marlowe's verse gave English tragedy the instrument it needed. It did not make Christopher Marlowe a great playwright, though given the time he might well have subdued his extraordinary genius and made it serve the drama: as it was, within the tragically short span of his life, he was using the drama as a medium for his poetry. That he would certainly have discovered the method is demonstrated in *Edward II*, a fine historical tragedy but one in which what Ben Jonson called 'Marlowe's mighty line' is not much in evidence. What is in evidence are believable characters, an understanding of narrative, and a sense of history. *Tamburlaine* and the rest succeeded by the sheer force of the language (*Tamburlaine* also had the presence of the great Alleyn, who could handle the demands of it) but as plays they are all imperfect. Only a great poet could have given life to the great tragic fate-defying figures of Tamburlaine, Faustus, and Barabas; the developing dramatist had something more to learn. But genius could not be learned; Marlowe brought it to English drama and transformed it.

The two original poems of Christopher Marlowe are so beautifully finished that they only reinforce the regret one feels that he died so young. *The Passionate Shepherd* is too famous to need comment and the two parts of *Hero and Leander* – all we have – are a perfect expression of the pursuit of physical pleasure.

**Marmion, A Tale of Flodden Field**. Scott's second romantic poem, first published in 1808. It is in six cantos like his first, *The Lay of the Last Minstrel*. The Marmion of the title is a fictitious favourite of Henry VIII, who wants to marry the rich and beautiful Lady Clare. Clare, however, is betrothed to Sir Ralph de Wilton. There is another woman in Lord Marmion's life, Constance de Beverly, a renegade nun; but Marmion has tired of her. She follows him, disguised as a

page, and helps him forge a letter which will convict Ralph of treason: she hopes to recover Marmion but he betrays her and she is returned to her convent to be walled up alive. Ralph and Marmion then fight in the lists and Ralph is defeated and left for dead; but Clare flees to a convent to escape from Marmion. Ralph survives, goes to Scotland disguised as a palmer, and consults the Abbess of St Hilda, who is attended by Clare. The abbess has proof of Marmion's crime, which she received from the hapless Constance before she died. She entrusts the proof to the palmer, who can now reveal his true identity to Clare. The climax takes place at the Battle of Flodden, where Marmion is killed.

The poem has remarkable force and vividness, but it misses true greatness because the equivocal character which Scott sought to give Marmion is not successfully realized, and the scenes after Flodden are a lengthy anticlimax.

**Marmion, Shackerley** 1603–39. A friend of Sir John Suckling, Shackerley was, like him, a Royalist whose life was very short. He was the author of three plays, *Hollands Leaguer* (1632), *A Fine Companion* (1633), and *The Antiquary* (1634); the last-named is regarded as the best. His reputation, however, rests on his long poem, *Cupid and Psyche* (1637).

**'Marprelate, Martin'** During the years 1588 and 1589 there appeared in England a number of pamphlets from an 'underground' press that attacked the bishops and the Church as it was organized in England. The pamphlets appeared under the name of 'Martin Marprelate'. Two years before, in 1586, Archbishop Whitgift and the Star Chamber had decreed against Puritan pamphlets unless they had first been approved by the Church, and the Marprelate pamphlets were the most celebrated blasts against that establishment.

John Whitgift had been made archbishop in 1583 and he was as much against the Puritans as he was the Papists. There appeared in 1584, from the press of Robert Waldegrave, an anonymous tract called, from its running page title, *A Learned Discourse*; it was an effective attack on the established Church. The Dean of Salisbury, John Bridges, wrote *A Defence of the Government Established in the Church of Englande for Ecclesiasticall Matters* in reply; it was very long-winded and appeared in 1587. It was against this that the first Marprelate tracts were directed; after the decree of 1586 the tracts were signed with a pen name and clandestinely printed. John Penry, in 1587, had written *A Treatise Containing the Aequity of an Humble Supplication* and been promptly put into prison. A dialogue signed by John Udall, *The State of the Church of England* (1588), was published by Robert Waldegrave, who was silenced by the seizure of his press. But Waldegrave, by some means, contrived to go on printing in secret at East Molesey and the first of the famous tracts appeared in October 1588.

The title of the first tract begins 'Oh Read over D. John Bridges, for it is a Worthy Worke', and runs to 130 words. It is generally called *The Epistle* and was 'printed oversea, in Europe . . . at the cost and charges of M. Marprelate gentleman' (the christian name, Martin, appeared in the title). It promised an *Epitome*, which duly appeared in the same year. *The Epistle* was scandalous and lively in its attack on the bishops and was a huge success: the establishment set out to find the source and Waldegrave fled to Northampton, where he had friends in Sir Richard Knightley, Job Throckmorton, and John Penry's wife. Waldegrave managed to publish *The Epitome* in November 1588. Penry's house was raided in January 1589 and Waldegrave moved his press to the house of John Hales, a relation of Knightley's, in Coventry. The third Marprelate tract, on the ignorance of the bishops, is usually called *The Mineralls* and appeared in February. Meanwhile, in January 1589, an official reply to 'Martin Marprelate' had been written by Thomas Cooper, Bishop of Winchester, and called *An Admonition to the People of England*. The title was as lengthy as those on the tracts and referred to 'slaunderous untruethes ∴ by Martin the Libeller . . . to deface and descredite . . . the Church'. The fourth tract appeared in March, in reply: *Hay any Worke for Cooper*. The popularity of the tracts continued: theological argument against the condition of the reformed Church combined with spirited and often well-deserved abuse of its defenders made for lively reading.

But the sour side of Puritanism raised its head now, and frowned on its witty scurrilous champion. Robert Waldegrave took no further part in the controversy. A new printer had to be found and John Hodgkins printed the fifth tract, *Theses Martinianae* or *Martin Junior*, at Wigston House in Wolston, near Coventry, in July 1589. The sixth, *Martin Senior* or *The Just Censure and Reproofe of Martin Junior*, appeared in the same week and then Hodgkins decided to move his press to Manchester. The seventh and last tract appeared in September, hastily printed at Wolston before the move: *Protestatyon*, in which Martin Marprelate tells of the coming end of the bishops. But the end for the bishops was not yet: the Civil War and nearly 60 years were to pass before the Puritans became supreme. For the present it was

the end of 'Martin Marprelate'. Hodgkin and his assistants were caught and sent to London, where they were tortured to extract information from them.

Martin Marprelate *could* have been John Penry, or Job Throckmorton, or John Udall. But examples exist of writings by Penry and Udall and it seems impossible that either could have risen to the wit and ribaldry of the tracts. Throckmorton? He denied it absolutely – but then, his life was at stake. Was the writer, in fact, a Puritan? Not necessarily – adherents of the reformed Church in England could find plenty to criticize without wishing to go to Puritan extremes, and while Elizabeth herself supported Whitgift there were many – Burghley and Walsingham among them – who did not. John Penry was hanged in 1593, Udall ended his days in prison, and the question remains unanswered.

The man who destroyed the Martinists was Richard Bancroft (1544–1610), at that time Canon of Westminster. To him also fell the task of suppressing the flood of pro- and anti-Martinist tracts that the controversy unleashed. Among them were writings, under pseudonyms, by Richard Harvey, John Lyly, and Thomas Nashe but, remarkably, nothing by them reaches the level of the Martinist tracts. The tragedy, for English literature, was that the laughter went out of opposition to the established Church: the Puritans, frowning on their own champion, were stuck with a sour expression for ever. They did not appreciate the finest prose satires of the Elizabethan period any more than their opponents did. Richard Bancroft went on to become Bishop of London in 1597 and Archbishop of Canterbury in 1604.

**Marriage** A novel by Susan Ferrier, first published in 1818.

Lady Juliana, daughter of the Earl of Courtland, elopes with Henry Douglas, a penniless young officer. Her romantic illusions are stripped away quickly: Douglas's Highland home is a cheerless place, containing grim-faced aunts and five dull sisters. Then her expected child proves to be twin daughters. The couple move to London; there Henry gets into debt and is imprisoned. Upon his release he joins the army and goes to India, becoming separated from Lady Juliana permanently.

Lady Juliana's daughters, and their future, are now her main preoccupation: she is convinced that all her troubles are the result of an 'imprudent' marriage. One daughter, Mary, has been brought up in Scotland while the other, Adelaide, grows up in the Earl of Courtland's

London home. Mary rejects the ambitious marriage Lady Juliana wants her to make; Adelaide allows herself to be pushed into marriage with an elderly duke. Mary gives her heart to a man of her own choice and returns to Scotland with him to settle down contentedly. Adelaide, after less than a year of her prudent marriage, deserts the duke and runs off with a worthless man.

**Marriage à la Mode** A comedy by John Dryden, first produced in April 1672 and first published in 1673. There are two plots, and neither has any bearing on the other. One concerns Leonidas and Palmyra, daughter of the usurping King of Sicily; Leonidas is in fact the rightful heir and all ends satisfactorily for them. The other plot concerns Rhodophil and Doralice, married for two years and bored with each other. Rhodophil's friend Palamede has been ordered to marry Melantha but has meanwhile fallen in love with Doralice, not knowing that she is married to Rhodophil. Rhodophil pursues Melantha, not knowing that she is intended for Palamede; she is determined to be fashionable and her conversation is littered with French phrases, an affectation that has irritated Palamede beyond endurance. The quadrille is played out until each character discovers that he objects to the other's encroachments and that he wants his original partner after all.

**Marriage of Geraint, The** See **Idylls of the King, The**.

**Marriage of Heaven and Hell, The** A prose work by William Blake, usually dated 1790, which is a declaration of his revolt against the accepted values of his age. Swinburne, in *William Blake: A Critical Essay*, described it as the greatest of Blake's works. The six sections of satirical prose are prefaced by 'The Argument', a poem in which he declares that the paths of truth have been corrupted by false religion. Two of Blake's most quoted statements appear in this work: 'Jesus was all virtue, and acted from impulse, not from rules' and 'If the doors of perception were cleansed everything would appear to man as it is, infinite'.

**Marryat, Captain Frederick** 1792–1848. The son of a merchant in the West Indies trade, Marryat was born in London. He entered the navy in 1806 and served until 1830, reaching the rank of captain, and began to write just before his retirement. *The Naval Officer; or Scenes and Adventures in the Life of Frank Mildmay* was published in 1829. In an age when historical romances seemed to be the chosen field for novelists Marryat looks back to Smollett, and his

quality made a deep impression on the young Joseph Conrad.

Marryat's output was considerable and not much of it is read today. But he has narrative power and is good at character delineation; his knowledge of the sea and contemporary naval life is first-hand and – within the limitations imposed by the attitudes of the time – an authentic picture. He has become, strangely enough, a writer more associated with books for young people, and his gift for making the boyhood of his adult heroes so convincing has been partly responsible for this. He was an excellent writer for both age groups.

His best work is to be found in *Peter Simple* (1834), *Jacob Faithful* (1834), *Mr Midshipman Easy* (1836), and *Japhet in Search of a Father* (1836). His first book for young people, *Masterman Ready*, was published in 1841. Other notable titles for this readership are *The Settlers in Canada* (1844) and, most famous of all, *The Children of the New Forest* (1847).

**Marston** See **Croly, George**.

**Marston, John** *c.*1575–1634. Probably born in Coventry, Marston was the son of a Shropshire lawyer and an Italian mother. He studied at Brasenose College, Oxford, taking a degree in 1594, and then entered the Middle Temple to study law. However, when his father died he abandoned the law for literature and published two collections of verse satires in 1598: *The Metamorphosis of Pigmalion's Image* and *The Scourge of Villanie*. Some of the satires were directed against Joseph Hall, his literary rival.

Marston began to write for the theatre in 1599 – for the Children of (St) Paul's Company – and in 1601 revised a play of unknown authorship called *Histriomastix*, which touched on the 'war of the theatres' (see also **Jonson, Ben**). This was answered by Jonson in *The Poetaster*. *Satiromastix* (1601) was a retort from Marston and Dekker and *What You Will* (also written in 1601 but published 1607) is by Marston. The tedious (for modern readers) business was over by 1605 when Marston and Jonson, with Chapman, collaborated on *Eastward Hoe*.

Marston's first play was *Antonio and Mellida*; *Antonio's Revenge* was a sequel (both were published in 1602). *The Malcontent* (1604), which had additions by Webster, was a change of direction: the first plays had been revenge tragedies but this was a comedy. Believed to be his best play, it was dedicated to Ben Jonson. Another comedy, *The Dutch Courtesan* (1605), followed and in 1606 Marston published *The Parasitaster*, a comedy, and *Sophonisba*, a tragedy;

these last two are not highly regarded. The last play, *The Insatiate Countess* (1613), was a tragedy that was probably completed by William Barkstead.

In 1608 John Marston was imprisoned in Newgate. His offence remains unknown but by the end of that year he had turned his back on the theatre. In September of the next year he entered the church as a deacon and was ordained in December. He was given the living of Christchurch, Hampshire, in 1616 and in 1619 he married Mary Wilkes, daughter of one of King James's chaplains.

The plays of John Marston were collected and edited by H. H. Wood and published in three volumes (1934–39). His poems were edited by A. Davenport and published in 1961. Marston's work is uneven and it may have been his concern for the bald truth about human motives, the matter of his plays even in comedy, that drew him along a path of discovery leading eventually to his rejection of the theatre. He points the way to the murky horrors that were to become the preoccupation of the Jacobean theatre.

**Marston, John Westland** 1819–90. A native of Lincolnshire, Marston lived in London as a young man. He numbered Edmund Kean and William Macready among his friends and after publishing two critical essays on poetry became a playwright. *The Patrician's Daughter* may have been the first play in which poor people are shown as being good, at the mercy of wicked heartless aristocrats. It was a considerable success (Drury Lane, 1842) and Marston continued to write for the theatre until 1869. Among his successes were *Borough Politics* (Haymarket, 1846), *The Heart and The World* (Haymarket, 1847), a verse play, *Strathmore* (Haymarket, 1849), based on Scott's *Old Mortality*, and the comedy *The Favourite of Fortune* (Haymarket, 1866). Marston wrote dramatic criticism for *The Athenaeum* and a useful commentary, *Our Recent Actors* (1888). Marston's plays have not been revived.

**Marston, Philip Bourke** 1850–87. The son of the playwright John Westland Marston, Philip Bourke Marston was born in London and was blind from the age of three. He enjoyed a reputation as a poet but his work is little known to modern readers. He published *Song-tide and Other Poems* (1871), *All in All: Poems and Sonnets* (1875), and *Wind-Voices* (1883). *Garden Secrets* (1887), *For a Song's Sake and Other Stories* (1887), and *A Last Harvest* (1891) were published posthumously.

**Martin, Violet Florence** See **Somerville and Ross**.

*Martin Chuzzlewit* A novel by Charles Dickens, first published in 20 parts (January 1843 to July 1844).

Martin Chuzzlewit is a selfish young man – most of the Chuzzlewits are selfish – to the despair of old Martin Chuzzlewit, who is the head of the family. Old Martin has brought up an orphan girl, Mary Graham, and young Martin is in love with her. Young Martin is articled to Pecksniff, an architect, the archetypal Victorian hypocrite with a sharp eye for the main chance. Old Martin, in an excess of misanthropy, repudiates his grandson and gets Pecksniff to dismiss him.

Another Chuzzlewit, old Martin's nephew, Jonas, brings about his father's death out of greed and impatience and marries one of Pecksniff's daughters, Mercy (the other one is called Charity). He treats her brutally – partly in revenge because she looked down on him before he had his father's money, and partly because he is a natural bully and is soon bored with her. He becomes involved in the crooked schemes of Montague Tigg and succeeds in drawing the appalling Pecksniff into their dubious enterprises.

Young Martin, meanwhile, has sought his fortune in America with his servant, Mark Tapley. He is defrauded by the Eden Land Corporation of Cairo, Illinois, and nearly dies of fever in his penniless state. His saviour is the generous Mr Bevan, the Massachusetts physician, who sends him the money to pay for a passage home. Martin, a sadder and wiser young man, returns to England with Mark Tapley. He tries to make his peace with his grandfather. He finds him living in Pecksniff's house, apparently deferring to him on all matters. All young Martin can do is depart, apparently rejected, though the words of rejection come from Pecksniff.

The novel concludes with old Martin revealing his purpose in testing his grandson; Pecksniff is exposed for the self-seeking wretch that he is; Jonas murders Montague Tigg for fear of his secret being revealed and, when apprehended, poisons himself.

*Martin Chuzzlewit* at its best is Dickens at his greatest. Where it is not at its best (it can't be said to fail) it is hard to take, because of the author's persistence in telling us how good the good characters are; he should have just let them shine effortlessly, in contrast to the selfishness and mendacity of the principals – self-interest is the theme of the book, the impetus for old Martin's apparent cruelty. The chapters set in America are dull, too; they were probably devised to boost the feeble sales of the early numbers, and have proved such an irritant to some readers that they have been skipped, unread, in the reader's haste to get back to the fascinating events and characters in the main part of the book. Interestingly, those chapters offended the Americans even more than the author's *American Notes*.

It is impossible to add anything to the praise already earned by Dickens for his creation of Pecksniff and Sairey Gamp. Sairey is one of the great comic creations of English fiction and the impression she makes is heightened by the author's truthfulness. It was to women like these that nursing had to be entrusted in the days before Florence Nightingale. Pecksniff is a perfect example of Dickens's genius; he is placed in the author's time and speaks in Victorian tones but he is for all time – we are never without Pecksniffs.

**Martineau, Harriet** 1802–76. The daughter of a Norwich manufacturer and the sister of James Martineau, the philosopher. She began her writing career (she was a Unitarian) with religious subjects, *Devotional Exercises for the use of Young Persons* (1823) and *Addresses with Prayers and Additional Hymns for the use of Families* (1826). Later, she became interested in economics and earned a reputation as an original expositor – she used fiction to illustrate her theories and to advance her ideas for social reform: *Illustrations of Political Economy* (1832–34), *Poor Law and Paupers Illustrated* (1833), and *Illustrations of Taxation* (1834). A visit to the USA prompted the writing of *Society in America* (1837), which contains her comments on slavery, and *Retrospect of Western Travel* (1838). Later she wrote two novels, *Deerbrook* (1839) and *The Hour and the Man* (1841) – a historical novel with Toussaint L'Ouverture as its subject. An active journalist, she contributed regularly to *The Daily News* and the *Edinburgh Review*, and in 1841 published a book of stories for young people, *The Playfellow*. She was moving away steadily from her religious beliefs and in 1853 produced a condensed version of August Comte's *Cours de philosophie positive*. *A History of the Thirty Years Peace, 1815–45* appeared in 1849.

Harriet Martineau is always treated respectfully by historians of English literature for her contribution to various forms of writing, but she is almost unread today. Her *Autobiographical Memoir*, published posthumously (1877), is extremely valuable for its first-hand comments on her literary contemporaries.

**Martin Eden** A novel by Jack London, first published in 1909. There is a strong element of autobiography in the book.

Martin Eden is a labourer and a one-time sailor; his questing mind, however, has led him to educate himself and he aspires to a higher place in life. This is personified by Ruth Morse, college-trained and the daughter of a wealthy family. Martin works hard to succeed as a writer and his work reflects the influence of Herbert Spencer's ethical theories. His friend Russ Brissenden, a socialist poet, believes in his work but Martin has no success. When a newspaper calls him a socialist Ruth Morse deserts him.

Then one of Martin's books is a success; he acquires both fame and money and Ruth Morse seeks him out. But Martin realizes her true nature and turns away from her. His spirit is depressed and Russ's suicide lowers it even more. He finds himself an exile from his own class, having achieved distinction and a measure of wealth. The society he has reached despises him. He commits suicide on a sea voyage.

*Martin Eden* was not well received by the critics but it was a lasting success with readers. The critics declared that Martin's suicide was not believable; but Jack London invoked a remarkable response from great numbers of – particularly young – readers who aspired to a better condition of life and from many who recognized the dilemma that often accompanies a measure of success.

**Martin Faber** The first novel by William Gilmore Simms. It was first published in 1833 and published in revised form as *Martin Faber, the Story of a Criminal* in 1837.

Martin Faber marries Constance Claiborne in spite of the fact that he has seduced and deserted Emily, a village girl. Emily threatens to expose him; he strangles her and hides her body in the cleft of a rock outside the village. His raw nerves lead him to suspicions of Constance and their friend William Harding. Eventually he accuses Constance of having an affair with William.

William, his own suspicions aroused, reconstructs the murder of Emily and makes a painting of it which he hangs in the village gallery. Martin is obliged to accompany William and the villagers to the rocks, where blasting reveals Emily's body. Constance visits her husband, who has been sent to prison, and in a murderous rage he tries to kill her. But Constance is saved and Martin meets his end on the gallows.

**Martinus Scriblerus, Memoirs of** The intention of the members of the Scriblerus Club was to write a satirical work that would ridicule 'all the false tastes in learning, under the character of a man of capacity enough, that had dipped into every art and science, but injudiciously in each.' Only one volume, most of it by John Arbuthnot, was published, in the second volume of Pope's *Works* of 1741. The name Martinus Scriblerus was used as a pseudonym by Alexander Pope and, later, by George Crabbe. (See **Scriblerus Club**.)

Martinus, the son of Cornelius, an antiquary of Münster in Germany, is brought into the world, christened, and educated according to the teaching of the ancients. He grows up to become a physician, philosopher, and critic and sets out on his travels. An outline of his travels corresponds with those of Swift's Gulliver. The book closes at this point.

**Martyn, Edward** 1859–1924. Martyn was born in Galway and attended schools at Dublin and Windsor before going to Oxford. A prominent figure in the Irish cultural revival, he was one of the founders of the Irish Literary Theatre. The first works performed by the theatre were Yeats's *The Countess Kathleen* and Martyn's *The Heather Field* (1899), but Martyn's works have not held the stage. Among other plays by Martyn were *Maeve* (1899), *Grangecolman* (1912), and *The Dream Physician* (1914).

**Martyrs, The Book of** (*or Foxe's Book of Martyrs*)  See **Foxe, John**.

**Marvell, Andrew** 1621–78. The son of a clergyman, Marvell was born at Winestead, near Hull, and attended Hull Grammar School. Later he went on to Trinity College, Cambridge, where he spent eight years without making much impression as a scholar, coming down with a BA in 1641, the year of his father's death. Among his contemporaries at Cambridge were Crashaw and Cowley, and during those years Marvell considered becoming a Catholic but his father's counsel prevailed and he stayed in the Church of England.

After his father's death Marvell spent four years on the Continent. He was writing verse at this time: he contributed some commendatory verse to Lovelace's *Lucasta* and wrote an elegy on Lord Hastings, both published in 1649, the year of Charles I's execution. Marvell moved in Royalist circles and seems to have had Royalist sympathies at this time, but his politics probably suffered from the same lack of commitment as did his religious sympathies. 'An Horatian Ode upon Cromwell's Return from Ireland' was written in 1650 and has been highly praised. The poem contains, as well as fulsome praise of Cromwell, tender sympathy for Charles, warnings to the Scots, and contempt for the Irish whose country had provided a battlefield for the Royalists and Puritans of England. The ode has

Andrew Marvell. From a portrait by an unknown artist, c.1660. National Portrait Gallery, London.

been much analysed and the poet's view of Cromwell and the king has been widely discussed; debated also is the question whether or not the poem is as Horatian as Marvell's title claims. The general conclusion seems to be that it is.

In 1651 Marvell was appointed tutor to the daughter of Lord Fairfax, the Parliamentary general, who had retired to Nun Appleton in Yorkshire. In that pleasant setting (though a fine soldier, Fairfax had withdrawn from army and government and now liked growing roses) Marvell is believed to have written his best poetry. He stayed for two years and then became tutor to a ward of Cromwell's at Eton before taking up his post as Assistant Latin Secretary to the Commonwealth government in 1657, working with John Milton who became his friend. He became MP for Hull in 1659 and held the seat for the rest of his life. He never married.

Marvell had no difficulty in accepting the Restoration but to his credit he brought to bear all the influence he could on Milton's behalf when the blind, ageing poet was persecuted by the returning Royalists. Under the restored monarchy Marvell was secretary to an embassy to Scandinavia and Russia. He spoke often in the Commons in the cause of religious freedom and became a busy writer of satires and political tracts, in which he criticized the government of Charles II, railed at the continuing religious intolerance, and deplored the lamentable condition of England's forces in the war with the Dutch. Edmund Waller's *Instructions to a Painter* (a laudatory piece on the Navy, which was immediately trounced by the Dutch) provoked Marvell's wrath; his counterblast of the same name (1667) is a withering indictment of lazy and corrupt government. During the century after his death Marvell was known as a writer of sharp-edged satire and a defender of liberty: the ambiguity and uncertain loyalties of his younger years were gone.

His present stature owes much to the revival of interest in the early 17th-century poets, among whom he belongs in tone if not in time. Most of his verse was unpublished until 1681, when the *Miscellaneous Poems by Andrew Marvell, Esq* appeared, a collection of remarkable charm and wit and confident technique, most of it written while he was in Lord Fairfax's house at Nun Appleton. The 'Ode upon Cromwell's Return' was not included in the collection, published as it was in the Restoration climate. For the rest, in Marvell's comparatively small output there is not one poem that does not succeed. His pleasure in outdoor beauty is conveyed with a mixture of classical gravity and simple charm, supported by a flawless ear for word music – 'The Garden' is a classic example. 'To His Coy Mistress' is deservedly one of the most famous poems in the language, a lovely example of amorous persuasion that claims all things to be a setting for lovers – all things, that is, except time.

***Mary Barton,*** *a Tale of Manchester Life.* A novel by Elizabeth Gaskell, first published in 1848. The background of the story is the 'hungry forties' of the 19th century, when a series of bad harvests, beginning in 1837, coupled with taxation on imports of wheat, placed an impossible burden on the lower-paid workers. The Chartist movement and the Anti-Corn Law agitation arose out of these conditions and resulted in considerable strife.

One of the sufferers during the extreme conditions is John Barton, an upright man and a good worker. He has become an active trade unionist. His daughter, Mary, has attracted the attention of Henry Carson, her father's employer, and this flatters her. Hoping for a rich husband, she discourages the attentions of Jem Wilson, a young engineer. John Barton's fellow-workers, in despair at their condition, which the employers will do nothing to ease, decide to kill Henry Carson as a warning to his class. The lot falls to John Barton to commit the murder.

In the meantime Mary Barton has brought her emotions under control and, realizing that she loves Jem, sets out to break with Carson. At this point Carson is murdered – and suspicion falls on Jem, his rival for Mary. But Mary discovers that it was her father, John Barton, who shot Carson, and she is faced with a terrible choice.

Since she cannot betray her father's guilt Mary has to prove Jem's innocence: her father, meanwhile, is enduring acute mental anguish which Jem's acquittal does nothing to allay. At the end of the book John Barton, on the verge of death, confesses his crime to Henry Carson's vindictive old father, and succeeds in gaining his forgiveness.

The author painted a grim picture in *Mary Barton.* It was taken from life and, inevitably, it brought the Lancashire mill-owners to their feet to protest; they were supported by the press in London, which automatically took their side. But Elizabeth Gaskell had drawn attention to what was happening to men and women, and Thomas Carlyle was quick to make known his approval, both of the novelist and of the social commentator. As a novel *Mary Barton* was an unqualified success and the author found herself, almost at once, a literary celebrity of the first order.

***Mary Postgate*** A story by Rudyard Kipling, included in the volume entitled *A Diversity of Creatures* (1917). Mary Postgate is a middle-aged spinster, companion to Miss Fowler and devoted to Wyndham Fowler, her employer's orphan nephew, for whose upbringing she is largely responsible; he never displays any affection for her. During World War I the nephew is killed while training with the Royal Flying Corps, and Mary Postgate sees a child she knows die in a German bombing raid. She is carefully burning Wyndham's books and toys in the garden incinerator when she encounters a dying German airman from a crashed plane. She fetches a revolver, rather than help or a glass of water, and watches him die. Then she goes indoors and has a hot bath. She emerges, her employer remarks, looking 'quite handsome'.

**Masefield, John** 1878–1967. Masefield was born at Ledbury in Herefordshire. He was educated at King's School, Warwickshire, and then realized his ambition to go to sea. He was apprenticed on a sailing ship after his training on the *Conway*, and eventually became a junior officer on an Atlantic liner. An attack of ill health stranded him in New York and he took whatever work he could find; he was still only 19 when he returned to England in 1897. He was now determined to be a writer and had a number of pieces accepted by periodicals; he was engaged by the *Manchester Guardian* in 1898 and originated the 'Miscellany' column. Masefield's first collection of poems was *Salt-Water Ballads* (1902); he consolidated his position in contemporary literature with a notable volume of stories and sketches called *A Mainsail Haul* (1905).

Masefield's copious output included *Ballads* (1903), *The Tragedy of Nan and Other Plays* (1909), and *The Tragedy of Pompey the Great* (1910), and with the poems and plays came more short stories in *A Tarpaulin Master* (1907) and two novels, *Captain Margaret* (1908) and *Multitude and Solitude* (1909). He attracted wide attention with *The Everlasting Mercy*, a long narrative poem published in *The English Review* in 1911. Masefield's uninhibited colloquialism and near blasphemy made this work a literary sensation in those days. He told the story, in rhyming couplets in a first-person narrative, of the saving of the soul of Saul Kane, debauched and wicked, through the agency of Miss Bourne, a Quaker.

Masefield continued in this vein of narrative poetry with *The Widow in the Bye Street* (1912), *Dauber* and *The Daffodil Fields* (both 1913), and most notably in *Reynard the Fox* (1919). He published a great deal of verse during his long career and his vigorous and inventive quality, allied to a note of compassion, ensured his popularity. He became Poet Laureate in 1930 in succession to Robert Bridges and was awarded the Order of Merit in 1935; it is generally agreed that his best work was written before 1930.

Other plays by Masefield are *The Faithful* (1915), *The Trial of Jesus* (1925), *Tristan and Isolt* (1927), and *The Coming of Christ* (1928). He wrote several novels, among them *The Street of Today* (1911), *The Taking of Helen* (1923), *Sard Harker* (1924), *Oddtaa* (1926), and *The Bird of Dawning* (1933), and some very successful stories for young people including *Lost Endeavour* (1910), *Jim Davis* (1911), and *The Midnight Folk* (1927).

**Mason, Lady** In Anthony Trollope's *Orley Farm*, the lady whose inheritance of the farm is contested by her stepson, Joseph Mason. She enjoys the devotion of the elderly Sir Peregrine Orme.

**masque** The masque was a light form of dramatic entertainment, with music, dances, and lavish presentation, popular in the 17th century and usually played by amateurs. The extravagance entailed in such productions confined the masque to the court or the wealthy aristocracy and few exercises in the form proved to have lasting quality in spite of contributions by such poets and playwrights as Middleton, Jonson, Chapman, and Beaumont. The masque is believed to have come to England from the ducal courts of Italy.

**Massacre at Paris, The**, *With the Death of the Duke of Guise*. See **Marlowe, Christopher**.

**Massinger, Philip** 1583–1640. The son of an agent in the household of the earls of Pembroke, Massinger was born at Salisbury and studied at St Alban Hall, Oxford, though he did not go on to take a degree. He is identified as a playwright working for Philip Henslowe in 1613 and is believed to have been an actor before that. His name first appears on a published work in 1622 with **The Virgin-Martir**, which he wrote with Thomas Dekker (see **Dekker, Thomas**; **Fletcher, John**; **Middleton, Thomas**; and the following plays: *Sir John van Olden Barnavelt*; *Spanish Curate, The*; *Custome of the Countrey, The*; *Beggar's Bush, The*; and *Bloody Brother, The*).

Massinger wrote 16 plays that have survived as well as the number in which he collaborated with the writers already named, plus *The Fatall Dowry: A Tragedy* (1632) written with Nathan Field. The titles and publication dates of Massinger's plays are as follows: *The Duke of Millaine* (1623); *The Bond-Man* (1634); **The Roman Actor** (1629); *The Picture* and *The Renegado* (1630); *The Emperour of the East* and *The Maid of Honour* (1632); **A New Way to Pay Old Debts** (1633); *The Great Duke of Florence* (1636); *The Unnatural Combat* (1639); *Believe as you list* (1653); *The Bashful Lover*, *The Guardian*, and *A Very Woman* (1655); and **The City Madam** (1658). *The Parliament of Love* was not published until 1805.

Massinger was a skilful literary workman and like most of his contemporaries a very busy one. Only one of his plays, *A New Way to Pay Old Debts*, held the stage after the Jacobean period, though quality is not lacking in some of his other works. *The City Madam*, another comedy, is highly regarded but the bulk of his work is drama to order, in heavy historical settings. Massinger is notable among Jacobean playwrights in the expression of his own views in his works. He refused to join the chorus of vilification that was hurled at the Catholics (even by the otherwise generous and humane Dekker) and went so far as to draw a sympathetic Jesuit in *The Renegado*. He was courageous enough, too, to attack the all-powerful Duke of Buckingham in the character of Gisco in *The Bond-Man*. Massinger lies buried in the same tomb as John Fletcher in Southwark Cathedral.

Massinger's plays were collected and edited by W. Gifford and published in four volumes in 1805. A revised edition was published in 1840.

**Masson, David** 1822–1907. Masson, a stone-cutter's son, was born in Aberdeen. He was educated at the universities of Aberdeen and Edinburgh and became Professor of Rhetoric and English Literature at Edinburgh (1865–95). His literary career began unpromisingly, with some years of hack work for periodicals in Scotland. When he went to London his fellow Scot, Carlyle, introduced him to a higher level of journalism and Masson founded *Macmillan's Magazine* (1859); he was its editor until 1867. Masson's principal work is his exhaustive *The Life of John Milton, Narrated in Connexion with the Political, Ecclesiastical and Literary History of his Time* (seven volumes, 1859–94). Masson's *Life* takes into account everything Milton wrote and the seven volumes are indispensable for students.

Other works by David Masson include *Drummond of Hawthornden* (1873), *Chatterton* (1874), and *De Quincey* (1881, for the English Men of Letters series); *Essays Biographical and Critical, Chiefly on English Poets* was published in 1856. *Edinburgh Sketches and Memories* (1892), *Memories of London in the Forties* (published posthumously, 1908), and *Memories of Two Cities, Edinburgh and Aberdeen* (1911) give interesting pictures of Masson's career and the circles in which he moved. He was made Historiographer Royal for Scotland in 1893.

**Masterman Ready** A novel for young people by Frederick Marryat, his first written as such. It was published in 1841, and the writing was prompted by Marryat's children, who had read *Swiss Family Robinson* and knew that their father was a real expert in such matters. In Marryat's story the Seagrave family are wrecked on a desert island with their devoted Black nanny and the old sailor, Ready, the hero of the story.

**Master of Ballantrae, The:** *A Winter's Tale.* A novel by Robert Louis Stevenson, first published in *Scribner's Magazine* (November 1888 to October 1889).

Lord Durrisdeer has two sons. The older, the heir, calls himself the Master of Ballantrae; the younger is Henry Durie. In nature they are totally different: Henry is amiable and honest while Ballantrae, as the story unfolds, is revealed as completely evil.

Ballantrae joins Bonnie Prince Charlie; Henry is to stay at Durrisdeer as a supporter of King George. (The arrangement was not an uncommon one at the time: it ensured that, whichever side won, the estate would not be sequestrated.) Ballantrae disappears after the Battle of Culloden and is believed dead.

After many adventures, Ballantrae returns to Durrisdeer, a price on his head, and finds that Henry has succeeded to the estate; he has also married Alison Graeme, the heiress who was first wooed by Ballantrae. The rest of the story tells how the elder brother embarks on a prolonged and vicious persecution of the younger, whom he knows will never betray him. Henry loses his reason and both brothers come to an untimely death.

Stevenson, it is known, became bored with the progress of the novel. Unfortunately, it shows; it begins very well and promises much but the last quarter of the book unhappily suggests his eagerness to be finished with it.

**Master of Game, The** An elaborate treatise on hunting, translated from the French *Livre de la Chasse* of Gaston, Comte de Foix, by Edward, 2nd Duke of York, about 1406. It was a popular hunting manual with those who could hunt on the same scale as the duke, who added some chapters to the original. Its value in the development of English prose is small, since it is chiefly concerned with technicalities.

**Masters, Edgar Lee** 1868–1950. Though he was brought up in Illinois and his name became identified with the state, Masters was born in Kansas. He was a lawyer by profession, in Chicago, where he practised from 1891 to 1920, and he wrote poetry with no particular success though he published *A Book of Verses* (1898) and a blank verse drama, *Maximilian* (1902). He became famous in 1915 with *Spoon River Anthology*, a book of epitaphs in free verse about the lives of those buried in a cemetery in rural Illinois. The expression is direct and simple; but there is much wry unromantic observation of life in Spoon River, the representative community whose two hundred members speak in the book. It seems to have been a place of mostly unhappy people but Masters' success implied immediate recognition from his readers.

Masters was never to repeat the success of *Spoon River Anthology* because he never found a subject so perfectly suited to his free verse style and his vein of irony. However, he commanded attention and published, among a number of books, several more collections, three dramatic poems (*Lee*, 1926; *Jack Kelso*, 1928; *Godbey*, 1931), three novels based on his own youth (*Mitch Miller*, 1920; *Skeeters Kirby*, 1923; *Mirage*, 1924), and a biographical study of Abraham Lincoln, *Lincoln the Man* (1931), which was hostile and belittling.

In 1924 Masters returned to the scene of his initial success in *The New Spoon River*. This was an uncompromising attack, using the same method, on the urban life that now prevailed in an America changed out of all recognition. Sentimental regionalism was hurried out of American literature by writers like Edgar Lee Masters and Hamlin Garland and the way opened for a different, harsher look at life in the Midwest.

**Mather, Cotton** *c*.1663–1728.   The son of Increase Mather, he entered Harvard at the age of 12 and seems to have been regarded by his fellows as a prig. He gained his MA at the age of 18 and then became his father's assistant at the Second Church of Boston. He was in complete charge during his father's mission to England in 1692 and looked like becoming a preacher of remarkable force. At the same time he was quite capable of supporting his father's political interests in Massachusetts and was a staunch supporter of Sir William Phips, the governor who took office when Increase Mather succeeded in obtaining a new charter for the colony.

It was Phips who instituted the Salem witchcraft trials, in which Cotton Mather was intensely interested and about which he wrote two appalling books: in 1689 after a minor 'outbreak' (*Memorable Providences, Relating to Witchcrafts and Possessions*), and in 1693 (*The Wonders of the Invisible World*), following what was virtually a reign of terror.

Paradoxically Cotton Mather was as interested in scientific enquiry as his father, Increase Mather, and was elected to the Royal Society in 1714. His library numbered 2000 volumes, he was very widely read, and in his last years he urged tolerance in the ministry in his *Manductio ad Ministerium* (1726). He was an indefatigable writer (more than 450 works) and believed himself to be the political and religious leader of Massachusetts. His arrogance did not make him popular: Robert Calef published a powerful and carefully reasoned attack on his *The Wonders of the Invisible World* and people did not forget that the witchcraft hysteria began to subside when it threatened to involve the Mather and Phips families.

Nevertheless there is quality in Mather's writing, which included a translation of the Psalms and a biography of his father. His massive diary was published in seven volumes by the Massachusetts Historical Society.

**Mather, Increase** *c*.1639–1723.   The son of Richard Mather, an English minister who was suspended because of his Puritanism and who emigrated to Massachusetts in 1635. Increase Mather was a first-generation New Englander, educated at Harvard and later at Trinity College, Dublin, where he gained his MA. He spent some years in England, where he preached in Congre-

Increase Mather. The frontispiece to his *Cases of Conscience Concerning Evil Spirits*, 1693.

gational churches, but the Restoration brought the return of Anglicanism and he was obliged to return to Massachusetts. He became the teacher of the Second Church in Boston and a Fellow of Harvard and married the daughter of John Cotton, the Puritan leader.

A leading spirit in the affairs of early Massachusetts, Increase Mather headed a mission to England that gained a new charter for the colony – and a new governor in the person of Sir William Phips. Mather was an advocate of scientific enquiry and an early champion of inoculation to fight smallpox. In 1693 he published his *Discourse Concerning Comets*, which gave him a place in the forefront of astronomical investigation in his day. But as a dedicated Puritan he was committed to the support of Phips, who instituted the infamous witchcraft trials at Salem in 1692. Mather did make it clear (a year later, when many other voices had already been raised against the persecutions) that he disapproved of the emphasis of the prosecution on 'spectral evidence' in his *Cases of Conscience Concerning Evil Spirits*. But his influence might have helped save the lives of 20 people if he had spoken when it really mattered.

He wrote over a hundred books, in a strong direct style, on secular and sacred themes. Some of them have authentic value for students of early American history, notably *A Brief History of the Warr with the Indians* (1676) and *A Relation of the Troubles which have happened in New-England by reason of the Indians there* (1677). The rest are of interest to students of the Puritan mentality.

**Matthew's Bible**  See **Coverdale, Miles.**

**Matty, Miss (*or* Mathilda Jenkyns)**  In Elizabeth Gaskell's *Cranford*, the daughter of the former rector and sister of Miss Jenkyns (Debōrah), who disputes with Captain Brown the quality of the newly famous writer, Boz. Miss Matty is a sweet little woman, who once loved Mr Thomas Holbrook but was prevented from marrying him by her family's hidebound notions, Holbrook's station being lower than theirs. Miss Matty's reunion with her brother, Peter, and her restored security, bring *Cranford* to a happy end.

**Maturin, Charles Robert**  1782–1824.  Of Huguenot descent, Maturin was born in Dublin and, after his education at Trinity College, took holy orders. His first book was *The Fatal Vengeance* (1807) and he also wrote a number of tragedies, one of which was produced with great success at Drury Lane by Edmund Kean (*Bertram*, 1816). The other tragedies, *Manuel* (1817) and *Fredolfo* (1819), were not successful. He did better with his novels: *The Wild Irish Boy* (1808), *The Milesian Chief* (1811), *Women, or Pour et Contre* (1818), and *The Albigenses* (1824). Most successful of all, and still read, was **Melmoth the Wanderer** (1820), one of the better examples of the current literary vogue for tales of terror.

**Maud**  A poem by Alfred Tennyson, first published in 1855. The nucleus of the poem was 'Oh! that 'twere possible', which was first called simply 'Stanzas' and was published in *The Tribute* in 1837. Years later, it has been suggested, the poet's friend Sir John Simeon asked him to weave a story around the poem; but the poet had been thinking of that for some time, according to his son, Hallam Tennyson, and the result is based to a considerable extent upon events and characters in the poet's life. The poem 'Oh! that 'twere possible' is in Part II (IV) of *Maud*, which is written in a variety of metres and was called *Maud: A Monodrama* by Tennyson in 1875. The narrator's precarious mental balance was something which the poet had observed at first hand in his brothers Edward and Septimus who later became insane.

The narrator has been left an orphan; his father committed suicide after ruin in an unstable speculation encouraged by a wealthy neighbour and his mother had died in poverty. The young man broods in the lonely old house over his parents' fate and the wretchedness of contemporary life; he is a prisoner of his own misery and hatred. The wealthy neighbour returns and with him is his beautiful daughter, Maud. The narrator and she had been playmates; now he falls in love with her. But her brother despises him: 'And curving a contumelious lip, Gorgonised me from head to foot With a stony British stare.' And there is a 'new-made lord' seeking her hand. The narrator wins her love but the brother's hostility leads to a fatal duel in which the brother is killed. The young man flees the country, and he descends into madness when he hears that Maud has died. His recovery and adjustment to life are brought about by service to his country in war. The narrator's closing verses (Part III) suggest that war, for some men in some circumstances, provides a better opportunity for salvation than a peace in which many knew little more than poverty and injustice; in the narrator's case it is salvation from madness and despair.

Dante Gabriel Rossetti's sketch of Tennyson reading his poem, *Maud*, in 1855. City of Birmingham Museum and Art Gallery.

The conclusion brought down wrath on Tennyson's head but conversations with men who enlisted for the Crimea might have enabled the critics to understand. The conclusion of Maud fails because the narrator's recovery is shirked: he moves from madness to sanity with nothing in between. But among the great passages of the poem are the brooding obsession conveyed in the opening, the fine and justly famous lyrics, and the whole of Part II with its powerful images straight from a deranged mind.

**Maugham, W(illiam) Somerset** 1874–1965. The youngest of six brothers, Somerset Maugham was the son of a solicitor to the British embassy in Paris. His mother died when he was eight and his father when he was ten, and Maugham was sent to England in 1884, to the care of his uncle, the Rev. H. M. Maugham, Vicar of All Saints', Whitstable, in Kent. He was educated at King's School, Canterbury, where his stammer made his life wretched among teachers and pupils alike. Two breaks from this background had an important influence on his later career: one in the south of France, for his health, gave him a liking for French literature, particularly the short stories of Guy de Maupassant; the other was a year spent at Heidelberg in the early 1890s, where he read philosophy at the university and acquired an interest in art and the theatre. Upon returning to England he rejected his uncle's wish that he enter the church and chose medicine instead. He studied at St Thomas's Hospital in Lambeth, where he saw the harsh side of life at close quarters, and became a doctor in 1897. However, he made no immediate practical use of his qualifications; a small private income allowed him to travel in Europe and he settled in Paris in 1898.

His experience of life in London had given him the material for his novel *Liza of Lambeth*, published in 1897. He now lived in Montparnasse among writers and painters, and pursued a literary career. He wrote seven novels, a volume of short stories, and a travel book about Andalusia. He had two plays tried out in London in 1903 and 1904 and then achieved success as a playwright with *Lady Frederick* at the Court Theatre in October 1907. *Jack Straw*, a farce, followed at the Vaudeville Theatre, March 1908; another farce, *Mrs Dot*, opened at the Comedy Theatre in April of the same year and a melodrama, *The Explorer*, at the Lyric Theatre in June. With four plays running simultaneously in London the playwright W. Somerset Maugham was a resounding success.

The novelist achieved distinction with an

Somerset Maugham, 1911. Photograph by E. O. Hoppé.

autobiographical novel, *Of Human Bondage* (1915). This is the story of Philip Carey, who has a club foot and who attends King's School, Tercanbury; who rejects the idea of the ministry and who studies in Heidelberg and later becomes a doctor; who becomes obsessed with a vulgar waitress, Mildred Rogers, who goes to a bad end, etc. But the novel succeeds because of its unflinching honesty and its devastating account of loneliness, the most tragic of all human conditions. During World War I Maugham was an agent for the intelligence service, and subsequently he travelled extensively. His brilliantly successful career in fiction and drama continued and his 11 subsequent novels included *The Moon and Sixpence* (1919), an excellent presentation of the Gauguin case in the person of Strickland (not meant to be the French painter himself), a stockbroker who deserts wife, work, and family after 17 years to become a painter. Everything is subordinated to his passion for his art and he regards love as a tiresome intrusion upon it. He dies of leprosy in the South Seas, leaving behind the pictures that make his name famous. *Cakes and Ale* (1930), perhaps his best novel, is a witty and malicious comedy of literary England in the early decades of the 20th century, told in the first person by a novelist, Ashenden. The pushing and self-advertising novelist Alroy Kear wants to get at the details of the early life of Edward Driffield, an eminent novelist whose biography Kear has been commissioned to write. Ashenden had known Driffield and his first wife Rosie, a barmaid; Rosie, the skeleton in the cupboard of Driffield's life, is Kear's stumbling block – he is not honest enough to be given the facts that Ashenden gives the reader. Rosie is a wonderful character – affectionate, amoral, and generous. The narrator is obviously Maugham but he denied what so many readers were quick to conclude: that Alroy Kear was founded on Hugh Walpole and Edward Driffield on Thomas Hardy.

As a playwright Maugham enjoyed a remarkable run of success until 1933, after which, with the production of *Sheppey*, he gave up writing for the theatre. Among his plays, between 1908 and 1933, were (the dates given are those of the first production) *The Tenth Man* (Globe Theatre, February 1910), *Our Betters* (Hudson Theatre, New York, March 1917), *The Circle* (Haymarket Theatre, March 1921), *The Letter* (from his short story: Playhouse Theatre, February 1927), and *For Services Rendered* (Globe Theatre, November 1932).

Maugham's fine short stories were published in various collections, starting with *Orientations* (1899) and ending with *Creatures of Circumstance* (1947). Some of them – 'Rain', 'The Letter', 'Red', 'Episode' – are among the best in the language though the critics, as is often the case, limped behind the reading public in their acknowledgement of them. All the stories have been collected in three volumes, *The Complete Short Stories* (1951); all the plays the author wished to preserve can be read in *Collected Plays* (1931). Maugham's extensive travels are the subject of *The Land of the Blessed Virgin* (1905), *On a Chinese Screen* (1922), *The Gentleman in the Parlour* (1930), and *Don Fernando* (1935). His personal views on life and art can be found in *The Summing Up* (1938), *Strictly Personal* (1942), *Ten Novels and Their Authors* (1948), *A Writer's Notebook* (1949), *The Vagrant Mood* (1952), and *Points of View* (1958). Maugham was a storyteller of genius with a sardonic view of human behaviour, anti-romantic and mercilessly observant, with unrivalled skill in realizing the climax of a story.

**Maurice, (John) Frederick Denison** 1805–72. Frederick Denison Maurice was born at Normanstone, near Lowestoft in Suffolk. His father was a Unitarian minister and his family were disputatious; his boyhood was spent with religious wrangling continually within hearing.

He entered Trinity College, Cambridge, in 1823. In 1825 he moved to Trinity Hall with his friend John Sterling but there he was excluded from both degree and fellowship because he refused to subscribe to the Thirty-Nine Articles. Maurice went to London; he was an advocate of social reform and wrote against the materialism of Bentham and James Mill. He was also ready to accept the Anglican faith and went to Exeter College, Oxford, in 1830. He was ordained in 1834 and appointed to the curacy of Bubbenhall in Warwickshire. Maurice, whose original intention had been to study law, did not forego his belief in social reform and successfully combined it with his adherence to the Church. He declared that true socialism was the necessary result of sound Christianity.

Maurice was appointed chaplain to Guy's Hospital in 1836, and while there he wrote *The Kingdom of Christ* (1838), a plea for religious unity that was generally misunderstood. He became Professor of English Literature and History at King's College, London, in 1840 and six years later Professor of Theology in the college's new Theological School. He worked for the application of Christian principles to social reform and this led to the formation of the Christian Socialist group and his association with J. M. F. Ludlow, Thomas Hughes, and Charles Kingsley. *Theological Essays* (1853) brought him into conflict with the establishment once more by questioning accepted doctrine, and he was dismissed from King's College. Two years before he died Maurice was appointed Knightsbridge Professor of Moral Philosophy at the University of Cambridge.

Maurice's lasting memorial is The Working Men's College, London, which arose from the organization of evening classes and was firmly established in 1854. He was a dedicated man who practised what he preached and had little time for biblical criticism or theological theorizing; the mainspring of all his Christian belief and teaching was a God of Love. His friend Tennyson asked him to be godfather to his son Hallam in 1852. The poet's well-known lyric to Denison after his dismissal from King's College was published in January 1854 ('To the Rev F. D. Maurice'). Among other works are *The Religions of the World* (1847), an early essay in the study of comparative religion, and *What is Revelation?* (1859), an attack on H. L. Mansel and his idea that the human intellect depended upon supernatural revelation alone for the knowledge of the nature of God.

**May, Thomas** 1595–1650. May was born in Sussex and educated at Sidney Sussex College,

Cambridge. He was one of the many admirers of Ben Jonson and Jonson himself praised May's translations of Lucan's *Pharsalia* (1627) and Virgil's *Georgics* (1628). Two earlier efforts by May, *The Heir* and *The Old Couple* (both *c*.1621), were undistinguished comedies; he also wrote three undistinguished tragedies, *Antigone, the Theban Princess* (*c*.1626), *Cleopatra* (1626), and *Julia Agrippina* (1628). His translations from the Latin, which are regarded as his best work, continued with *Selected Epigrams of Martial* (1629) and a further instalment of Lucan, *Continuation* (1630). But his next works were very long and practically unread historical narrative poems, *The Reigne of King Henry the Second* (1633) and *The Victorious Reigne of King Edward the Third* (1635).

May was a Puritan and embraced the parliamentary cause during the Civil War. He became secretary to the Long Parliament and his *History of the Parliament in England: which began November the Third, 1640, with a short and necessary view of some precedent yeares* (1647) is a valuable historical document.

**Mayhew, Henry** 1812–87. Mayhew, the son of a solicitor, was born in London. He was sent to Westminster School but ran away to sea and travelled to India and back before entering his father's office. But the law had no appeal for him and he turned to journalism. A friend from his schooldays, Gilbert Abbott à Beckett, launched *Figaro in London* in 1831, and Mayhew worked on the illustrated comic weekly as joint editor. He became editor three years later.

Mayhew enjoyed success with a farce called *The Wandering Minstrel* (1834), which was produced at the Fitzroy Theatre. In 1841 he was one of the original founders of *Punch* but a change in the financial control of this periodical led to Mayhew's departure in 1846. He was by then well established as a journalist and in 1849 published the first instalments of *London Labour and the London Poor* in *The Morning Chronicle* as 'Labour and the Poor'. The great survey appeared for a year in the paper and then independently in weekly parts. This first collection appeared in volume form in 1851; a further four volumes followed (1861–62). The fourth volume dealt entirely with those who lived outside the law – the large class of professional defaulters and offenders in London – and this was published in a separate enlarged volume (1864).

In 1856 Mayhew began to issue a concurrent series called *The Great World of London* in monthly instalments, nine of which were published as a volume at the end of that year. *The Criminal Prisons of London*, which Mayhew as social critic

Women and children at work salvaging material in a London dust yard. From a sketch made on the spot for *London Labour and The London Poor* by Henry Mayhew, published in 1851.

considered his most important work, was incorporated with *The Great World of London* and the volume published as *The Criminal Prisons of London and Scenes of Prison Life* (1862).

Mayhew was a busy journalist and editor but managed to travel as well. His *The Rhine and its Picturesque Scenery* (1856) and *German Life and Manners as seen in Saxony* (1864) are valuable as contemporary accounts. He was the author of a score of other books but is best remembered for his work on London. He went almost unnoticed by the literary establishment: his name is just mentioned in *The Cambridge History of English Literature* (Vol. 14, 1916) in connection with *Punch*. Mayhew deplored the condition of the great mass of Londoners and was a fierce critic of the Victorian morality that had led to it. The reporting is not entirely by him and careless passages can be found; but when it is good, as most of it is, it is vigorous and immediate and lingers in the mind. It was not until the 1940s, when interest in social studies was stimulated by World War II, that Mayhew was rediscovered. No complete edition has been undertaken but valuable sections have been published as *The Street Trader's Lot* edited by S. Rubinstein (1947); *Mayhew's London* (1949), *London's Underworld* (1950), and *Mayhew's Characters* (1951) were edited by Peter Quennell.

**Mayne, Rutherford** 1879–1967. Rutherford Mayne was the pseudonym used by Samuel J. Waddell when he acted and wrote for the Ulster Literary Theatre and the Abbey Theatre, Dublin. Born in Japan and educated in Belfast, he made a fair contribution to the Irish theatre with *The Turn of the Road* (published 1907), *The Drone*

(1909), *The Troth* (1909), *Red Turf* (1912), *Phantoms* (1923), *Bridgehead* (1939), and *Peter* (1944). Mayne examined a particular Ulster situation in *The Turn of the Road*, in which a genuine artistic temperament is stifled by the Protestant prejudices of the province. *The Drone* presents a familiar Irish figure, the man with the gift of the gab who never faces reality but manages to survive nevertheless.

**Mayor of Casterbridge, The** A novel by Thomas Hardy, first published in weekly instalments in the *Graphic* and *Harper's Weekly* (USA) from 2 January to 15 May 1886.

A hay trusser, Michael Henchard, gets drunk at a fair and auctions his wife and child. A sailor, Newson, buys them for five guineas.

When he comes to his senses Henchard forswears drink for 20 years and his energetic application to work brings its reward. He becomes rich and respected enough to become Mayor of Casterbridge. After 18 years his wife comes to Casterbridge with her daughter, Elizabeth-Jane; Newson is presumed lost and she is reunited to Henchard. The echo from the past is like Nemesis: Henchard is soon in a web of troubles provoked by wrong-headed actions. He quarrels with his assistant, Donald Farfrae, for whom he had a high regard. Then Mrs Henchard dies and he learns that Elizabeth-Jane, whom he had assumed was his child, is in fact Newson's daughter. Farfrae sets up in business on his own and soon rivals Henchard – he also wins the hand of the woman Henchard had hoped to marry.

His business goes to ruin, and the story of what happened at the fair, nearly 20 years before, becomes known in Casterbridge. Henchard takes to drink, and his only comfort is Elizabeth-Jane. But Newson comes back from the sea and claims his daughter, and Henchard is alone. He dies wretchedly in a hut on Egdon Heath.

Casterbridge is Dorchester, and Hardy presents a vivid picture of it in the 19th century. His novel is one of his best, astonishingly, since it was written to order, week by week. But it survives some bad patches because of the portrayal of the doomed Henchard: he is like Saul in the Old Testament, granted a short period in the light, until the grace of the Lord departs from him.

**Mazeppa** A poem by Lord Byron, first published in 1819. It is based on a story related by Voltaire in his *Histoire de Charles XII* (1731). In the poem the Swedish king, Charles XII, and his officers are resting after their defeat at Pultowa (1709). They listen to the story related by Mazeppa, a former commander (*hetman*) of the eastern

Ukraine who has abandoned Peter the Great to fight with the Swedes. Mazeppa, born c.1645 of a noble Polish family, was page to the king of Poland, Casimir V. He had a love affair with the wife of a wealthy merchant and this was discovered. As punishment he is bound naked across the back of a horse, which is whipped into madness and gallops away with him. The poor animal races across rivers and through forests with its semiconscious burden and eventually falls dead on the plains of the Ukraine. Mazeppa is rescued and restored by the local people, and becomes their leader. He seizes the opportunity presented by the Swedish invasion to desert and make his way west. Ivan Stepanovitch Mazeppa is also the subject of Pushkin's *Pultowa*.

**McCarthy, Mary (Therese)** 1912– . Mary McCarthy was born in Seattle, and after being orphaned at the age of six was brought up by relatives and sent to Catholic schools. She completed her education at Vassar in 1933 and became a critic and reviewer. Her work appeared in *The New Republic*, *The Partisan Review*, and *The Nation* and she published a collection of short stories in 1942, *The Company She Keeps*. Another collection, *Cast a Cold Eye* (1950), included *The Oasis* (called *A Source of Embarrassment* in England), which had appeared separately in 1949. Mary McCarthy's other novels are *The Groves of Academe* (1952), *A Charmed Life* (1955), *The Group* (1963, a best seller), and *Birds of America* (1971). She is also the author of *Sights and Spectacles* (1956, theatre reviews), *Venice Observed* (1956), *Memories of a Catholic Girlhood* (1957), *The Stones of Florence* (1959), *On the Contrary* (1961, essays), *Vietnam* (1967), *Hanoi* (1968), *The Writing on the Wall* (1970, essays), *Medina* (1972), *The Mask of State: Watergate Portraits* (1974), and *The Seventeenth Degree* (1974).

**McCullers, Carson** 1917–67. Carson McCullers, née Smith, was born in Columbus, Georgia, and completed her education at Columbia University, New York. She published her first novel, *The Heart is a Lonely Hunter* (1940), when she was 23. Set in a small Southern town, it is the story of a deaf-mute, John Singer; he becomes the focus of four lonely people who create in him the image of their own desires. Singer himself is reduced to an agony of isolation when the one person he cares for is taken away from him and confined in a mental hospital; but he is a person of infinite gentleness and even in his loneliness he contributes to the happiness of others. When his friend dies in the mental hospital his own reason for living dies too, and he kills himself. Carson McCullers's prose is deceptively simple; but the effect it makes could not be achieved without infinite pains. Nor do her principals move in isolation; they are part of the life of a small town which is rendered in concrete detail. The novel diffuses an aching poetic pity for the spiritual isolation that underlies the human condition. *Reflections in a Golden Eye* (1941), by contrast, is a novel of violence set in a Southern army camp. The characters are indeed no more than reflections whose behaviour should explain them; but between them they exhibit enough hang-ups to fill a textbook.

Five years passed before Carson McCullers's next novel, *The Member of the Wedding* (1946). The girl Frankie is 12 years old and undergoing one of those heartbreaking periods of loneliness known to every child, when she seems to belong nowhere and to no one. When her soldier brother announces his forthcoming marriage she is alive with excitement – she will become a member of the wedding. She has no idea of what being married consists and of course she cannot be part of it. But for Frankie the bad time passes; she makes a bosom friend and becomes Frances instead of Frankie. For the others, John Henry, the boy next door, and Berenice, the Black cook, who provide the sounding-panels of the girl's story, the bad time does not pass. Berenice is a wonderful

Carson McCullers, 1944. Detail from the portrait by H. V. Poor.

character; the whole range of human experience seems represented in her. *Clock Without Hands* (1961) deals with desegregation in the South, centred on a small town in Georgia. The title refers to the term of life left to the druggist, Malone. He is dying of leukaemia and the action occurs during that term; it encompasses the reactions of the townspeople and the violent death of the blue-eyed Black man, Sherman, at the hands of a mob of poor Whites. Mrs McCullers gave the novel, which benefits enormously from her unambiguous narrative style, an extra quality by setting it in the vision of a man isolated from events by his awareness of his coming death. *The Ballad of the Sad Café* (1951) is a collection of short stories and each one shows the author as mistress of her craft. The title story is, for many critics, Carson McCullers's masterpiece. It relates how Miss Amelia and her Cousin Lymon turn her house into a café, which makes a centre of warmth in a small Georgia mill town where 'If you walk along the main street on an August afternoon there is nothing whatsoever to do.' Miss Amelia had turned out her handsome sadistic husband Marvin after ten days of marriage; he wound up in prison. The arrival of Cousin Lymon gives her a focus of affection and the café comes into being. Marvin leaves prison and comes back to the town, and Miss Amelia loses Cousin Lymon to him. She hopes he will come back, but after four years she has the café boarded up and retires indoors. Now there is absolutely nothing to do in the town, apart from listening to the singing of the 12 men in the chain gang. The story is indeed as timeless as a ballad.

Carson McCullers suffered a series of strokes while still in her twenties and the rest of her life was a struggle with physical affliction. A collection of unpublished stories was published posthumously as *The Mortgaged Heart* (1971). *The Member of the Wedding* was dramatized in 1950; *The Ballad of the Sad Café* in 1963.

**McDiarmid, Hugh** 1892–1978. The pseudonym of Christopher Murray Grieve, who was born in Langholm, Dumfriesshire. While taking a teacher-training course in Edinburgh he decided to become a journalist; he also joined the ILP, worked for the Fabian Society, and contributed his first pieces to *New Age*. He served in World War I in the RAMC, and afterwards earned a meagre living as a journalist in Montrose, Liverpool, and London until his health broke down in 1933. He worked on the Clyde during World War II, and was awarded a Civil List pension in 1950.

McDiarmid was one of the founders of the

Scottish Nationalist Party in 1928 and he is best known as a Scottish nationalist poet. He joined the Communist Party in 1934 but was expelled from it in 1938 because he continued to be a Scottish Nationalist. His first poem to be published was *Sangschaw* (1925) and his first collection was *First Hymn to Lenin and Other Poems* (1931). *Collected Poems* was published in 1962 and meanwhile McDiarmid, a prolific poet and journalist, had worked for a renascence in Scottish letters by trying to establish a distinctly contemporary Scots poetry. McDiarmid's poems are beginning to find their way into anthologies, notably 'O Wha's the Bride?' and 'At My Father's Grave'.

**McKay, Claude** 1890–1948. McKay was born in Jamaica and emigrated to the USA in 1912. Through a meeting with Max Eastman, the Marxist critic and magazine proprietor, McKay became editor of Eastman's *The Liberator*, and for literary New York in the prewar years he became the connection between Harlem and the Greenwich Village intellectuals. He was the precursor of the growth of West Indian letters in the decades following World War II. His first published book was a collection of poems, *Songs of Jamaica* (1912), which attracted favourable attention. Ten years passed before his second, *Harlem Shadows* (1922), and another six before his next book, a novel. *Home to Harlem* (1928) tells of a Black soldier's return to America after serving in France. The next year brought *Banjo* (1929), a novel of the Marseilles waterfront where McKay worked for a time. *Banana Bottom* (1933) examines the dilemma of a Black girl who has been educated in England and has then gone back to Jamaica: racial traditions and attitudes, half-forgotten, make her readjustment a painful process and the author writes from first-hand experience. McKay published his autobiography, *A Long Way From Home*, in 1937 and a study of the community, *Harlem*, in 1940.

**Meaning of Truth, The** See *Pragmatism* and **James, William.**

**Measure for Measure** A play by William Shakespeare that is listed with the comedies in the First Folio. It was first produced *c.*1604 and published in the First Folio of 1623. The immediate source of the play was *Promos and Cassandra* (1578), a translation by George Whetstone of *Epitia*, a play by Giraldo Cinthio based on one of the stories in his *Hecatommithi* (1565).

The scene is Vienna, and the duke, Vincentio, is about to depart for Poland. He gives charge of the state to Angelo and impresses on him that he has complete authority. The duke then goes to

Friar Thomas to whom he explains that certain laws concerning morals have been allowed to slip; he believes them harsh but he knows that Angelo will enforce them. He disguises himself as a friar to observe the effect of the laws' enforcement. Angelo meanwhile, has been enforcing them fervently – Claudio has been waiting for the dowry to make possible his marriage to Juliet; they have been impatient and now Juliet is pregnant; Claudio is arrested and will lose his head for seduction. Claudio sends word to his sister Isabella, a novice, asking her to help him. Isabella hurries from the convent but she finds Angelo immovable; but she makes another attempt and discovers that her beauty has aroused Angelo. She is shocked to hear him propose a price – she must yield to Angelo in exchange for her brother's life. She refuses.

Isabella goes to the prison; the duke is there in his disguise and overhears Isabella and Claudio. Isabella relates what happened with Angelo; for her brother she would give her life – but never her chastity. Claudio pleads with her to yield to Angelo; Isabella is outraged and storms out of the cell.

The duke now takes an active part in the affair. He tells Isabella of Mariana, whom Angelo should have married. He left her when her dowry was lost but she still loves him. So Mariana will be taken to the bed of Angelo, who will believe he has Isabella. Angelo nevertheless orders the execution of Claudio to proceed but this is prevented by the duke. Angelo is confronted on the following day when the duke returns to Vienna; his villainies are unmasked but everything is arranged neatly. Claudio gets his life and Juliet, Angelo gets forgiveness and Mariana. Isabella keeps her chastity and gains the love of the duke.

One could speculate endlessly about Shakespeare's intentions. A great issue is raised in this sombre play: the issue of a moral law that, however much at variance it may be with basic human impulses, is nonetheless essential to society – the alternative is moral anarchy. The creation of the two protagonists to highlight the dilemma is brilliant; they both lack experience and charity and so both of them are deadly. Isabella's moral superiority could blast the leaves off a tree but she has not one grain of feeling for others beyond her duty to her brother – and that is measured to the inch. It does not occur to her to keep Angelo's proposal from her brother; the wretched Claudio is suddenly made aware of a faint hope of life after he has nerved himself to accept death and the hope unmans him. Angelo is a very mean creature indeed; he has discarded Mariana because he can't have her dowry – though he insists, in Act V, that 'her reputation was disvalued in levity', as if that were a good reason. He will take Isabella if he can and then kill her brother anyway. The duke is a device, a necessary symbol of authority who can set the events in motion; but he is not credible either in his guises or his motives. Mariana is a poor thing; if she would take Angelo after all that has transpired she would take him if he had horns and a tail. The mind boggles at the thought of their married life.

The play holds the stage and a first viewing is an arresting experience – for two-thirds of its length. The scenes between Isabella and Angelo and Isabella and Claudio are memorable, and the spectator will be expecting a memorable resolution to the issue raised. But there isn't one; Shakespeare seems to have begun to exercise his brilliant mind on enduring questions and then been defeated by the need to bring the curtain down. He was a working dramatist, it should be remembered, writing at high speed and with no opportunity to revise.

**medieval drama** See **miracle plays**.

**Medwall, Henry** c.1462–1502. Almost nothing is known of the life of Henry Medwall beyond his work – much of which is lost – and his post as chaplain to Cardinal Morton. He was ordained an acolyte in 1490 and is believed to have been a member of, or connected with, a noble family since various livings were granted to him by the Crown. His last living was at Calais after Cardinal Morton's death in 1500. His surviving works are a morality, *Nature* (printed in 1530), and *Fulgens and Lucrece*, the first completely secular play in English. It was first performed about 1497 and first printed between 1512 and 1516.

*Melibeus, The Tale of* See *Canterbury Tales, The*.

*Melincourt, or Sir Oran Haut-ton*. Thomas Love Peacock's second novel, first published in 1817. Generally regarded as both more ambitious and less successful than his first, *Headlong Hall*, it attacks both the enthusiasms and reactions of the period after Waterloo, including the current glib enthusiasm for 'progress'. Rich Mr Sylvan Forester has educated the orang-outang of the title – so that he appears to be a charming gentleman who plays the flute – and has bought a baronetcy and a seat in Parliament for him. Among Peacock's targets in this book are Southey (Mr Feathernest), William Gifford (Mr Vamp), Coleridge (Mr Mystic), and Wordsworth (Mr Paperstamp).

*Melmoth the Wanderer* A novel of mystery and terror by Charles Robert Maturin, first published in 1820. The theme is the bargain with Satan, with the variation that the debt can be transferred if another can be persuaded to take it on. In the novel the bargain takes place in the 17th century.

The story opens with Melmoth still alive: he recounts in six different episodes his attempts to persuade someone else – someone in terrible straits – to take over his dreadful debt so that he can find relief. One possibility is a man in a lunatic's cell, another is a victim of the Inquisition, a third sees his children dying of hunger; then there is Melmoth's wife Isadora . . . but no one will change places with him. Melmoth is doomed by the bargain he has made.

Melmoth was the name taken by Oscar Wilde when he went into exile after his release from prison; for a Christian name he adopted Sebastian, suggested by the arrows of his convict garb.

**Melmotte, Augustus** The central character of Anthony Trollope's *The Way We Live Now*. He is an unscrupulous financier who is determined to keep his hard-won place at the fringe of society at any cost. His daughter, Marie, is to a considerable extent the reason for his downfall, since she has enough of his ruthless character to resist him.

**Melville, Herman** 1819–91. Herman Melville was born in the same year as Walt Whitman and died the year before Whitman died. But the two greatest figures of 19th-century American literature never met, though New York was, at times, common ground for both men.

Melville (originally Melvill) was descended, on his father's side, from a Scots gentleman who had been knighted by James VI. His father was the second son of Thomas Melvill, one of the 'Mohawks' of the Boston Tea Party. Melville's mother was the daughter of the Revolutionary hero General Peter Gansevoort, so the author was, like Whitman, a mixture of Dutch and British stock. He was the third of eight children and born in New York City.

Melville's father was a successful importer for a time, but his business failed in 1830 and the family moved up river to Albany, where his father found work. He died two years later and his two eldest sons, Gansevoort and the 11-year-old Herman, had to leave school.

An uncle found Herman a job as a clerk in the New York State Bank, where he remained for two years. Later he worked for his brother Gansevoort in the store, which was all his father had left the family and which now had to support them, and sought to complete his education by supplementary classes. He succeeded in gaining

Herman Melville.

a teaching post in a rural district but was only able to hold it for three months. He was already, in such leisure time as he had, trying his hand at writing.

The store failed in the economic depression of 1837. The family moved to Lansingburgh, where Gansevoort found work and Herman took an engineering course with hopes of employment on the Erie Canal. When no job materialized he signed on the *St Lawrence*, a trading ship, for the round trip to Liverpool; he was 19 and the year was 1839. At this time Melville had no thoughts of the sea as a career; he weathered the experience of life in the forecastle as a youthful apprentice and left the ship when she returned to the USA. He was obliged to become a sailor again, however, having failed to find a position for himself ashore where his brother's efforts were all that served to keep his family housed and fed. He joined the *Acushnet* at New Bedford, Massachusetts. It was a whaling ship with a callous commander, Pease – and the sort of crew such a man deserved. Melville, with his friend Richard Tobias (Toby) Greene, deserted the ship in the Marquesas Islands and Melville lived among the islanders for a month. He secured a berth on the Australian whaler the *Lucy Ann*, but conditions on board were so bad that the crew mutinied, joined belatedly by Melville, and they all ended up in prison in Tahiti. The

author was quickly set free, however, and obtained employment working in the fields. This experience of Pacific island life lasted another month: Melville cast a sharp eye on the contrast between the islanders and the men from the civilized world; his conclusions were not in favour of the 'civilized'.

Perhaps it was inevitable that a whaler, again, should facilitate Melville's departure. He now had some experience and was given a berth on the *Charles & Henry*, out of Nantucket, but was discharged at Lahaina in Hawaii in May 1843. The ship proceeded to Japan but Melville, for nearly four months, lived on his wits in Honolulu. The US consul could have found him a berth on any number of whaling ships but he would have no more of them. There is reason to believe that he considered staying in Hawaii, but some further reason or reasons unknown to us persuaded him to enlist as an ordinary seaman in the US Navy. He served on the *United States* and a long voyage home brought him to Boston in October 1844. He was paid off there and returned to his family, aged 25 – but with enough experience for two lifetimes.

Melville found his brother Gansevoort prosperous and his home comfortable; the wandering brother was home and the family would listen enthralled to his stories. He would have to write them down, obviously, and the first story he completed was about the time spent among the Marquesas Islanders. The novel which emerged was *Typee* but one publisher – Harpers – rejected it on the grounds that the adventure it related could not possibly be true. In the same year Gansevoort was appointed Secretary to the US Legation in London and he took his brother's book with him to England. John Murray bought it for publication in Britain and that encouraged G. P. Putnam to take it for the USA. It appeared in 1846 and was highly commended for its narrative power and pictures of pagan life. Nathaniel Hawthorne's praise, particularly, meant much to the new writer. Tragically, the same year saw the death of the steadfast and hard-working Gansevoort, leaving Herman as the head of the family.

*Omoo* (1847), Melville's next book, was accepted by his publishers with a degree of uneasiness. *Typee* had been attacked by missionary societies and those who could not see how the arrival of the White man and his gods – as well as his God – could be anything but a blessing for pagan 'natives'. Worse, some people declared the whole account a fiction even though Toby himself, Richard Tobias Greene, wrote to a newspaper in Buffalo to deny he was merely a figment of Herman's imagination. *Omoo*, which pointed to the failure of missionary work in Tahiti, brought renewed attacks. Melville's editor, Evert Duycinck, persuaded him to allow a revised (emasculated) edition of *Typee* to be published in 1849; the author's original text was not to be seen again until 1922. In August 1847 Melville married Elizabeth Shaw, daughter of the Chief Justice of Massachusetts, and in the same year he accepted Duycinck's offer of regular reviewing for *The Literary World*. He began work on a new book, **Mardi**, and meanwhile (25 March 1848) wrote an acid letter to John Murray. The English publisher had asked for 'documentary evidence' of Melville's sojourn in the South Seas: the author, understandably, was both angry and offended. *Mardi* was published by Richard Bentley in Britain in 1849. The book was not well received; it reinforced the theme of his earlier two by making the narrator a Polynesian, the White man's conscience was wounded once more, and Melville's forecast that the lifestyle of the Southern states could produce a battlefield provoked positive scorn.

*Mardi* had taken a long time to write; now, with remarkable speed, Melville wrote two sea stories, **Redburn** (1849) and **White-Jacket** (1850). *Redburn* was based on his first voyage as an apprentice seaman, *White-Jacket* on his term on a man-of-war. He was now living in Massachusetts, where he had bought a farm and where he became friends with Hawthorne, whom he admired. He visited England in 1849. *Redburn* and *White-Jacket* were well received, and a letter thanking Richard Henry Dana for his praise (Dana was one of those campaigning against the practice of flogging in the US Navy) mentions 'the whaling voyage' – 'I am half way in the work ... It will be a strange sort of a book ...'. Another book already begun (**Pierre**) was laid aside. Melville's essay, *Hawthorne and His Mosses*, was prompted by Evert Duycinck and appeared in *The Literary World* about this time.

Melville's friendship with Hawthorne and the intensive reading he had been able to enjoy since returning from the sea were strong influences in the shaping of the book about 'the whaling voyage'. Hawthorne's work, which acknowledged how many Calvinistic shadows overlay the mind of Americans, encouraged him to look farther into the motives of his fellow men; the whaling voyage became a peg on which to hang his most ambitious book, one of the great novels of the 19th century. **Moby-Dick** was published in 1851 and was dedicated to Hawthorne. The American publisher was Harpers, who had turned down Melville's first book; the British publisher was Bentley. But the book was not well received. The next, *Pierre* (1852), was simply disliked, and any hope of revaluation of its metaphysical approach was lost when a fire at the publishers in 1853 destroyed the plates of Melville's books as well as the greater part of the bound stock. Nathaniel Hawthorne moved away, to Concord, and the discouraged and lonely Melville now found himself without the active support of his family and friends. The critics dismissed *Moby-Dick* as the work of an unbalanced mind; *Pierre* encouraged them in their opinion. Melville was 33 and exhausted; his wife Elizabeth sought some way of relieving the pressure which writing imposed on him, for it was his writing that supported his family. Her appeals were heard by his friends; both Richard Henry Dana and Nathaniel Hawthorne tried to secure him a consulship from President Pierce. But Melville had never sought political favour and Pierce did not respond.

Apart from stories for magazines Melville published nothing more until 1855, when **Israel Potter** appeared. It was a novel set during the American Revolution and based on an existing 'life' by an unnamed author. It is an odd book; when it is Melville it is good, when it is Potter it is unremarkable. The following year saw the publication of his striking short stories in **The Piazza Tales**, and his novel **The Confidence-Man** (1856) adds a sharp edge of satire to the disillusion that his work expressed at this time. His health was none too good and in 1856 his father-in-law sponsored a tour of Europe and the Near East. Melville hoped for a consulship from Lincoln but that did not materialize and he devoted the next phase of his life – the Civil War – to writing poetry. He was given the post of Inspector of Customs in 1866 and worked there until he retired in 1885. **Clarel** (1876), a long poem on the search for faith, occupied his spare time in the 1870s. He wrote no more prose apart from **Billy Budd**, which was completed just before his death but not published until 1924. Melville's last years were spent in complete obscurity and his death in 1891 was hardly noticed.

The rediscovery of Herman Melville began in the 1920s and, once begun, seemed to become almost an industry for scholars and students. The reader of today can feel grateful for his restoration and the reintroduction of so much of his work.

Melville did not achieve consistent greatness as a poet but he wrote memorable pieces such as 'Misgivings' in **Battle-Pieces and Aspects of the War** (1866), **John Marr and Other Sailors** (1888), and **Timoleon** (1891). A further 80 short poems first appeared in the collected edition of his works in 1924.

His magazine pieces were published as *The Apple-Tree Table* (1922) and *Journal of a Visit to Europe and the Levant, October 11, 1856–May 6, 1857* (1935).

**Melville, Rev. James** 1556–1614. An active supporter of the Reformation, Melville became Professor of Oriental Languages at New College, St Andrews, but was obliged because of his cantankerous nature to flee to England. He returned to St Andrews in 1585 but was soon in trouble again, quarrelling with Bishop Adamson. Eventually he incurred the wrath of the king. His *Diary of Mr James Melville, Minister of Kilrenny in Fife* is valued by scholars of the religious troubles of the period.

**Melville, Sir James** 1535–1617. Sir James Melville of Halhill became page to Mary of Scotland while she was Queen of France and still only 14 years old. He continued in her service when she returned to Scotland, as privy-councillor and as a diplomat. His *Memorials* disclose a writer of considerable grace and they are a valuable record of Mary's reign and of Melville's encounters as her ambassador, particularly with Elizabeth I.

**Member of the Wedding, The** See **McCullers, Carson**.

**Memoirs of a Cavalier: or A Military Journal of the Wars in Germany, and the Wars in England, from the year 1632 to the year 1648.** A novel by Daniel Defoe written in the first person and first published in 1720.

The cavalier is Andrew Newport, an English gentleman (born in 1608), who travels in Europe as a young man in 1630. His travels take him to Vienna and he accompanies the imperial army during the Thirty Years War. He is present at the sack of Magdeburg (a remarkable piece of 'reporting' by Defoe) and after it joins the army of the opposing forces led by Gustavus Adolphus, the King of Sweden. After the king's death at the Battle of Lützen in 1632 he returns to England and as a Royalist colonel serves King Charles I, taking the narrative to the Battle of Naseby and the end of the Civil War.

Sir Walter Scott, in 1834, observed that 'the high-born Cavalier' speaks the same language as Robinson Crusoe and shows no more knowledge of society than the famous castaway; 'only he has a cast of the grenadier about him, as the other has the trim of a seaman.' In the same essay; 'De Foe's genius has shown, in this and other instances, how completely he could assume the character he describes.' The Earl of Chatham, reading *Memoirs of a Cavalier*, was convinced that a Colonel Andrew Newport's memoirs were what the book contained and took some persuading that he was in fact reading a historical fiction by Daniel Defoe.

**Memoirs of a Woman of Pleasure** (*Fanny Hill*). See **Cleland, John**.

**Memoirs of Miss Sidney Bidulph** See **Sheridan, Frances**.

**Memoirs of My Life and Writings** Edward Gibbon's memoirs, first published in 1796 two years after his death, existed in a group of seven rough drafts, written at various dates between 1788 and 1793. From these, which were not strictly chronological and went as far as Gibbon's departure from Lausanne after the death of his friend Georges Deyverdun in 1789, Lord Sheffield devised the familiar volume of memoirs. The complete text of Gibbon's original manuscript was not published until a century later, when John Murray's *The Autobiographies of Edward Gibbon* revealed how rewarding they are.

One of the best of 18th-century autobiographies, it can be read in entirety in The World's Classics, edited by J. B. Bury (1907), and Everyman's Library, edited by Oliphant Smeaton (1911).

**Men at Arms** The first volume of the trilogy *Sword of Honour*. See **Waugh, Evelyn (Arthur St John)**.

**Mencken, H(enry) L(ouis)** 1880–1956. H. L. Mencken was born in Baltimore and lived there for most of his life. His career as journalist, critic, and essayist began on a local newspaper in 1899; his formal education went only as far as high school. He became editor of the *Evening Herald* in 1905 and served on the staff of the *Evening Sun* for the rest of his life, including a period as war correspondent in Germany in 1916–17.

His career as a literary critic began in 1908 on *The Smart Set*, a lively New York periodical of which he later became coeditor with George Jean Nathan from 1914 to 1923. He and Nathan founded *The American Mercury* in 1924, which Mencken edited until 1933. He published critical works, including books on Shaw and Nietzsche, several books and essays, and became famous with the first edition of his *The American Language* in 1919. This study of the English language as used and developed in the United States was issued in revised volumes three times and supplementary volumes were added, the last in 1948. His essays were collected into six volumes called *Prejudices*, the first published in 1919 and the last in 1927.

Mencken's great contribution to the American literary scene lay principally in his qualities as a reporter, journalist, and editor. He was perhaps the best all-round newspaperman the United States produced in the early 20th century, though his political blind spots are now notorious and his criticism of poetry of little value. But he was a passionate man of the New World and had no patience with the pretensions of the old one. World War I had drawn attention to the failure of supposedly democratic institutions and Mencken, in the decade which followed, was a merciless critic though, finally, his comments ceased to have real value. This was proved when he failed to see that the Depression existed until his country was prostrated by it. His advocacy of indigenous American culture and civilization was another matter and writers such as Theodore Dreiser, James Branch Cabell, Sherwood Anderson, and Sinclair Lewis owed much to his praise.

Mencken was, perhaps, as a critic of everything in America, too ready to cause controversy. But he did demonstrate to his countrymen that nothing should ever be regarded as above criticism – he had as little patience with American gaucheries as he had with European patronage. His famous *The American Language* is brisk and lively, a fine journalist's presentation of the conclusions of the professional students of language – and it has been criticized on that account. The conclusion is inescapable, nevertheless, that its legions of readers would never have responded to a book by a scholar and written in scholarly terms. He published three volumes of autobiography: *Happy Days* (1940), *Newspaper Days* (1941), and *Heathen Days* (1943).

**Menenius Agrippa**  The patrician friend of the hero in Shakespeare's *Coriolanus*. He feels the same contempt for the plebeians as Coriolanus but he warns his friend that his openly proclaimed superiority is making enemies for him. His appeal (Act V Scene 2) to the traitorous Coriolanus is rejected.

**Menologium**  A poetic calendar prefixed to Version C of the *Anglo-Saxon Chronicle*. Valued as one of the few examples of nature poetry in Old English, it follows the progression of the seasons. *Menologium* was edited with a translation by S. Fox (1830).

**Men Without Women**  See **Hemingway, Ernest (Miller)**.

**Merchant of Venice, The**  A comedy by William Shakespeare. It was first produced *c.*1596, very likely in the same season as *A Midsummer Night's Dream* and printed in a quarto in 1600. It was published in the First Folio of 1623. The source of the play was the story in *Il Pecorone* by Giovanni Fiorentino, of which there was more than one English version available in Shakespeare's day. The casket story came from the *Gesta Romanorum*, which was known in the English translation printed by Wynkyn de Worde.

Antonio, a merchant of Venice, is worrying about the return of his ships, in which his fortune is invested, when his friend Bassanio asks him for the loan of a sum of money. Bassanio hopes to marry Portia, the heiress of Belmont, and he requires the sum for his journey and for the means to make a suitable impression on the lady. Antonio has no money to hand until his ships return; but he can give his bond for Bassanio to borrow it. Bassanio asks the wealthy Shylock, a Jew of Venice, for 3000 ducats. Shylock detests Christians and particularly Antonio, because his open-handedness keeps down the rate of usury. Antonio dislikes him as much – but is prepared to do business with him. When Shylock asks for a pound of flesh if the debt is not met in three months, Antonio agrees – he is certain that his ships will have returned in two months and he overbears Bassanio's protests.

Bassanio goes to Belmont and successfully chooses the right casket in the test set in Portia's father's will for his daughter's suitors. They are married and his friend Gratiano marries Portia's maid, Nerissa. Another friend, Lorenzo, is enamoured of Jessica, who is Shylock's daughter. Upon their marriages, Portia and Nerissa each give their husbands a ring that they swear they will never part with.

Antonio's ships do not return in time and Shylock demands his bond. The case is heard before the Duke of Venice and an advocate and his clerk come to defend Antonio: they are Portia and Nerissa in disguise and unknown to their husbands. Portia makes her celebrated plea for mercy and Bassanio offers to pay a huge sum if Shylock will withdraw. Shylock is implacable: he made a bond with Antonio and he must have his pound of flesh. But Portia warns him that flesh is all – he must not shed one drop of blood in the taking. Shylock is defeated and, already crushed by his daughter's elopement with the Christian Lorenzo, accepts Antonio's settlement and conditions. The advocate and clerk, in response to their gratitude, extract from Bassanio and Gratiano the rings they forever swore to keep and Portia and Nerissa have a lively time taking them to task at the close of the play.

*The Merchant of Venice* will never cease to be played while there is an actor who can tackle the great part of Shylock. That does not mean it is always played convincingly but Macklin, Kean, Macready, Irving, Gielgud, and Olivier have offered celebrated – and different – interpretations of it. Shylock is a villain, unmistakably, but Shakespeare makes him human and puts his audience on the knife edge between sympathy and rejection. Of the other characters only Portia stays in the mind; a charming creation and one can wonder what she – or the melancholy Antonio who loves him so unreservedly – can find in the character of Bassanio. Gratiano, on the stage so much of the time, 'speaks an infinite deal of nothing' in the words of his friend.

**Merchant's Tale, The** See **Canterbury Tales, The.**

**Merchant's Tale, The Second** See **Beryn, The Tale of.**

**Mercilla** In Book V of Spenser's *The Faerie Queene*, a maiden queen who represents Elizabeth I. Her adversaries are the Soudan (Philip II of Spain) and Duessa (Mary of Scotland).

**Mercutio** Romeo's friend in Shakespeare's *Romeo and Juliet*. A kinsman of the Prince of Verona, he becomes a victim of the strife between the houses of Montague and Capulet when Romeo, in love with Juliet, refuses Tybalt's challenge. Mercutio takes the challenge and is killed by Tybalt when Romeo tries to intervene. Mercutio's view of love (the Queen Mab speech, Act I Scene 4) is in direct contrast to the trancelike ecstasy of Romeo; he is the realist of the play.

**Meredith, George** 1828–1909. The son of a naval outfitter of Portsmouth, George Meredith received part of his education in Germany at the Moravian School at Neuwied. His father's extravagance deprived him of such expectations as he might have looked forward to, and he was articled to a London solicitor at the age of 17. However, he was soon more interested in writing than in the law and was publishing poems and articles with some success by the time he married, in 1849. His wife was the widowed daughter of Thomas Love Peacock, Mary Ellen Nicolls.

Widely read in the classics and in German and French literature, Meredith enjoyed the friendship of Peacock, Swinburne, and Rossetti and was well aware that literature would only provide a precarious living. His wife deserted him in 1858, taking their son, and went abroad with the painter, Henry Wallis. In 1860 Meredith settled down to weekly journalism for the *Ipswich Journal* and to reading for Chapman & Hall; in the latter capacity he gave encouragement to the young Thomas Hardy and to George Gissing. His wife died in 1861, leaving him free to marry Marie Vulliamy. The Merediths moved to Flint Cottage at Box Hill in Surrey in 1864; it was to be his home for the rest of his life.

His first published book was *Poems* (1851), which contained the first version of 'Love in the Valley'. Next came two fantasies, *The Shaving of Shagpat* (1856) and *Farina* (1857), and in 1859 his first novel, **The Ordeal of Richard Feverel.** **Evan Harrington**, an autobiographical novel, appeared in 1861, and this was followed by his second volume of poetry, the one that gave him a permanent place as a poet, **Modern Love** (1862).

Beginning in 1864, Meredith published a steady flow of novels over the next 20 years. **Sandra Belloni** – first called *Emilia in England* – (1864), **Rhoda Fleming** (1865), **Vittoria** (1867), **The Adventures of Harry Richmond** (1871), Beauchamp's Career (1876), **The Egoist** (1879), and **The Tragic Comedians** (1880). Another volume of poetry, *Poems and Lyrics of the Joy of Earth*, appeared in 1883, and the novel **Diana of the Crossways** two years later.

*The Egoist* was a critical success and *Diana of the Crossways* was also a popular success; by now Meredith was an honoured figure. He had written in his own way always but now he seemed to write only for himself – **One of our Conquerors** (1891), **The Amazing Marriage** (1895), and **Lord Ormont and his Aminta** (1894), see his epigrammatic style, his endless elliptical sentences, and his overplotted narratives taken to the point of obscurity. His critical *Essay on Comedy and the Uses of the Comic Spirit* (1897) is, in contrast, a highly regarded study of the role of comedy in literature.

Further volumes of poetry were published: *Poems and Ballads of Tragic Life* (1887), *A Reading of Life* (1909), and *Last Poems* (1909). There were also a number of short stories. Meredith has never been a popular novelist (apart from the transitory success of *Diana of the Crossways*) and is unlikely to become one. At his worst he is a bore, parading his linguistic accomplishments with a pompous conceit that is simply fatiguing. At his best he is dazzling and subtle and his verbal precision makes his prose sing – he was, it must be remembered, an accomplished poet. All his qualities and his faults are tethered to his times (*The Ordeal of Richard Feverel* was published in the same year as *Adam Bede*) and his exhausting cleverness would have to yield far more than it does to keep the modern reader interested in novels that are essentially Victorian in their view of life.

**Meres, Francis** 1565–1647. A Cambridge antiquarian, clergyman, and teacher, Francis Meres published a commonplace book in 1598 called *Palladis Tamia; Wits Treasury*. In the book he collected a great number of anecdotes and quotations. In one section he lists the great writers of antiquity; this is followed by *A Comparative Discourse of our English Poets with the Greeke, Latine and Italian Poets*, which is notable because it names and praises, beyond the work of 80 other English poets, William Shakespeare's works and gives us priceless evidence of how well his plays were known to a contemporary in 1598. Meres names 11 plays by Shakespeare that are known to us. These are *The Two Gentlemen of Verona, The Comedy of Errors, Love's Labour's Lost, A Midsummer Night's Dream, The Merchant of Venice, Richard II, Richard III, Henry IV* (Part I and Part II), *King John, Titus Andronicus*, and *Romeo and Juliet*. He also names one, *Love's Labours Wonne*, which has puzzled scholars ever since (see **Shakespeare, William**). Meres prefaces his references with the words 'witnes his', which indicates that he was selecting plays for mention – he probably knew many more than the ones he names.

**Merle, Madame** In *The Portrait of a Lady*, by Henry James, Madame Merle is the agent behind Isabel Archer's marriage to Gilbert Osmond. Her poise and sophistication make it easy for her to influence Isabel, who has no idea that she is being manipulated.

**Merlin** The magician of the Arthurian legends makes his first appearance in Nennius' *Historia Britonum*, in which he is Ambrosius, a boy without a mortal father. He explains to King Vortigern that his attempts to build a citadel will fail because two dragons live under the site and swallow the stones. The dragons, one white and one red, are discovered, and they fight. The red dragon wins and this means, says the boy, that the Britons will prevail over the Saxons. Geoffrey of Monmouth identified Ambrosius with Merlin, who arranges the union of Igraine and Uther Pendragon of which Arthur is the fruit; it is he who brings the great stones from Naas in Ireland for the building of Stonehenge. The element of ancient myth and magic became an inseparable part of the Arthurian cycle, which was later transformed into a paradigm of knightly chivalry. Merlin was developed in the French or Breton romances, *Merlin* and *Suite de Merlin*, and in an English version of yet another, *Arthour and Merlin*, translated at the beginning of the 14th century. This gives Merlin the devil as a father, and makes a reference to his entrapment by the wiles of Nimue, a story also told in Malory's *Le Morte Darthur*.

In Welsh literature there is a bard Myrrdhin (Merlin), to whom is attributed a group of patriotic poems.

**Merlin and Vivien** See *Idylls of the King, The*.

**Merrilies, Meg** The Gypsy woman of Scott's *Guy Mannering*. She recognizes Harry Bertram as the lost heir of Ellangowan and helps him to regain his inheritance, defeating the designs of the evil lawyer, Glossin. Keats's poem, 'Old Meg', is about Meg Merrilies.

**Merry Devil of Edmonton, The** A romantic comedy first published in 1608. It was found in a volume of Shakespeare in the library of Charles II and for a time was assumed to be one of Shakespeare's plays. Charles Lamb attributed it to Michael Drayton but it is now acknowledged to be of unknown authorship. The play has a rural setting (Edmonton in those days lay some 13 kilometres (8 miles) from London) and is chiefly concerned with Sir Arthur Clare's objections to the marriage of his daughter Millicent to Raymond Mounchensey. The young couple are helped in their elopement by the kind magician of Edmonton, Peter Fabel. The only part magic has in the play actually takes place in the prologue. Peter Fabel has made a compact with the Devil and his time is up; the Devil comes to collect, but Fabel tricks him into a magic chair, which holds him fast until he agrees to a new deal.

**Merry Wives of Windsor, The** A comedy by William Shakespeare. It was first performed in 1597, before Elizabeth I, and written as an entertainment for the installation of the Knights of the Garter, though it was played not at Windsor but at Westminster on St George's Day. The plot is original as far as can be ascertained, though the situations are time-honoured in comedy. A story persists (first told by John Dennis, the 18th-century critic) that the queen commanded the play because she wanted to see the fat knight in love. But she would not see Falstaff in love, least of all in this play, where his interest in the ladies is prompted by the hope of sponging on them. The play has a particular interest, especially as an early work, in that the characters are, with the exceptions of Fenton and Falstaff, ordinary people: successful and prosperous, certainly, but plain folk who attend to their business and manage their households. In contrast, Fenton and Falstaff are a dubious pair of 'gentlemen'. The play was first printed in a quarto in 1602 and published in the First Folio of 1623.

Falstaff, now on his uppers, is lodging at the Garter Inn at Windsor. He knows that Mistress Ford and Mistress Page control their husbands' purses and decides to woo them. His followers, Nym and Pistol, object to carrying letters for him and he throws them out, but the letters are delivered, one to each lady. The disgruntled Nym and Bardolph tell Ford and Page what Falstaff is up to. As it is, the ladies are friends and compare letters. They decide to have the laugh on Falstaff.

Anne Page is wooed by the dashing young gentleman, Fenton; he too is impoverished and Anne would be a good match for him; but he has fallen in love with her and confessed all. Anne loves him but her parents have other suitors in view. Mistress Quickly, servant to Dr Caius (who is one of Anne's suitors), plays go-between in the various adventures that befall. Falstaff has to hide in a laundry basket in Ford's house; he is covered with foul linen and thrown into a muddy ditch. He is soundly thrashed by Ford while disguised as a woman. Eventually Ford is let into the secret and a final assignation is made for Falstaff at Herne's Oak in Windsor Forest. Page hopes to take advantage of the occasion to pair his daughter off with Slender, nephew of Justice Shallow. Falstaff is thoroughly cowed at the end of the adventure, having been punched and pinched by 'fairies' organized by the two families. Anne slips away during the proceedings to Fenton and persuades her parents to accept him in the end. Falstaff is forgiven and taken home to a fireside and a hot posset.

Shakespeare in *The Merry Wives* is master of his craft. The play has a confident pace and a perfect structure: the details – Ford's masquerade as Master Brooke, the love affair of Anne and Fenton, the unwanted suitors – fit perfectly into the larger design. The play can be confusing for Shakespeare's admirers who try to relate Falstaff and his cronies, and Mistress Quickly, to the characters in the history plays. He was simply using a ready-made set of characters in a play written to order for a particular occasion.

**metaphysical poets** The general reader with a liking for poetry who feels puzzled by this description and consults a dictionary hoping to find clarification, is likely to feel even more puzzled after doing so. And he could be pardoned for wondering why such a label could be used for John Donne and George Herbert, for instance, but not for John Milton.

The term 'metaphysical' was first used in an undated letter by William Drummond of Hawthornden, complaining about poets who used what he described as new metaphysical ideas and scholastical quiddities. In 1693 Dryden wrote of Donne: 'He affects the Metaphysics ... in his amorous verses, where nature only should reign; and perplexes the minds of the fair sex with nice speculations of philosophy, when he should engage their hearts, and entertain them with the softnesses of love.' Some 90 years later Samuel Johnson, in his essay on Abraham Cowley, wrote 'about the beginning of the seventeenth century appeared a race of writers that may be termed the metaphysical poets.'

The label was, therefore, applied to poets who were not consciously writing 'metaphysical' poetry but who were using, as do the poets of every age, the presuppositions and philosophical beliefs of their time. In the early 17th century philosophic and religious ideas were inseparable. In thought, Samuel Johnson's age was far removed from that of Donne, while Dryden used the word 'metaphysics' to make an unfavourable comment. Unfortunately the use of this term continues to confuse the reader who may expect to find it applied to a school or a specialized group of poets when it more properly refers to a period in literature where values were changing. The poetry of the time reflected those changes, and a more sensible, if more cumbrous label would be 'early seventeenth-century poets'. Metaphysical poetry can be found in Shakespeare and Ben Jonson and in the work of many poets never called 'metaphysical'. Helen Gardener, in the introduction to her fine *The Metaphysical Poets* says: 'I am aware that I have included in this collection some poems whose presence under its title may be challenged. If I had the space I could defend them all on one ground or another, though my defence would of course have to take the form of "All these poems are metaphysical, but some are more metaphysical than others".'

**metrical romances** After the Norman Conquest the heroic literature of Anglo-Saxon England simply faded away; the conditions which produced it no longer existed and for some time the written language of England was Latin. In the wider world the bards and gleemen who entertained in warriors' halls and in market places were giving way to the minstrels, whose appeal was much wider. In the south the troubadours were bringing to oral literature a refinement it had not known before: a new form of story-poem, a romance in metre, began to emerge. It made its way to England from France, which by the 12th century was the home of lyric and romance; there the heroic *chansons de geste* which the knights had listened to had been supplanted by something which both knights and ladies could read. The impact of the East was profound: new subjects as well as new rhyming forms were serving Romance. French literature dominated western Europe; the stories of Charlemagne, Roland, and the rest ('the matter of France') had become known abroad; whilst from Wales and Brittany the Arthurian legends ('the matter of Britain') had been seized upon and used with consummate artistry. Alexander, the heroes of Troy, and the characters of Ovid ('the matter of Rome', i.e. of the classical world) became subjects for medieval romance as did traditional tales of ancient origin.

The beginnings of the English novel are to be found in the English metrical romances, which themselves arose from the French form and were industriously produced by anonymous authors for about three hundred years (1200–1500). The English romance is more concerned with incident and less with courtly love than is its French counterpart: but it is truly Romantic in its remoteness from reality. Time and place have no importance since its sole concern is with the ethos of medieval chivalry: thus knights are always valiant, ladies are virtuous and always beautiful; enchantresses and evil Saracens abound; descriptions of stupefying exactitude, alongside exhaustive catalogues, are a common feature. The appearance of an alewife or plowman would contribute a breath of fresh air – but workers have no place in Romance. The English metrical romances are of enormous interest to scholars but unrewarding, on the whole, for the general reader. A number survive; for details of the more notable romances see: *Otuel, Sir*; *Roland and Vernagu*; *Ferumbras, Sir*; *Havelok the Dane, The Lay of*; *King Horn*; *Guy of Warwick*; *Bevis of Hampton*; *Gest Hystoriale of the Destruction of Troy*; *Kyng Alisaunder*; *Richard Coeur de Lion*; *Flores and Blancheflour*; *Barlaam and Josaphat*; *Athelston*; *Seven Sages of Rome, The*; *Launfal, Sir*; *Orfeo, Sir*; *Golagros and Gawain*; *Ywain and Gawain*; *Awntyrs of Arthure at the Terne Wathelyne, The*; *Morte Arthur, Le*; *Morte Arthure*; *Ipomedon*; *Amis and Amiloun*; *Cleges, Sir*; *Squire of Low Degree, The*; and *William of Palerne*.

**Mew, Charlotte** 1869–1928. Charlotte Mew, the daughter of an architect, was born in Bloomsbury, London. Her father died young and his four children had to fend for themselves; two of them were unbalanced and spent the greater part of their lives in institutions. Charlotte and her sister struggled on and Charlotte's first poems were published in *The Yellow Book*.

Her first collection was *The Farmer's Bride* (1916). Another edition was published, with 11 new poems, in 1921 and appeared in the USA in the same year as *Saturday Market*. She was admired by Thomas Hardy, who helped secure her a small Civil List pension in 1923. But the loss of her sister was the last blow in a life of grief and poverty and she committed suicide in 1928. *The Rambling Sailor* was published posthumously (1929).

**Mexico, A History of the Conquest of** See **Prescott, William Hickling.**

**Meynell, Alice** 1847–1922. Alice Thompson was born at Barnes, then in the county of Surrey, and spent much of her childhood in Italy. She was educated by her father, who numbered many writers among his friends, and she began to write poetry while still a girl. Friends such as Tennyson, the Brownings, Ruskin, Dickens, and George Eliot encouraged her and her published work is generally acknowledged as of high quality though the quantity is not large. She became a Catholic in 1872 and as Alice C. Thompson published her first collection, *Preludes* (1875), before her marriage to Wilfred Meynell in 1877.

Alice Meynell assisted her husband in the publication of his Catholic periodical, *Merry England*, to which she contributed a number of critical essays, and helped in the rescue of Francis Thompson from destitution. *Poems* (1893), *Other Poems* (1896), *Later Poems* (1901), *A Father of Women and Other Poems* (1917), and *Last Poems* (published posthumously, 1923), together with the *Collected Poems* of 1912, completed her poetic output. The poems written in the last decade of the 19th century are unattractive to the modern reader in their refined sadness and vein of piety; in the 20th century her work became stronger in tone while maintaining the fastidious style but she is not read much today. The sonnet 'Renouncement', one of her early poems, is probably her best known.

Alice Meynell also published *The Life and Work of Holman Hunt* (1893, with W. Farrar), *John Ruskin: A Biography* (1900), and several volumes of critical essays. Collections of her work have been edited by Frederick Page, *The Poems: Complete Edition* (Oxford Standard Authors, 1940), and by her son Francis Meynell, *The Poems* and *Essays* (The Centenary Edition, 1947).

**Micawber, Wilkins** David Copperfield's landlord when he first arrives in London to work for Murdstone & Grinby. A jaunty improvident good-natured man, he is always optimistic about something turning up to extricate him from his difficulties. He helps Traddles to expose the villainy of Uriah Heep.

***Michael*** A pastoral poem by William Wordsworth, written in 1800. Michael is a shepherd whose only child is Luke, a son born to him late in life. When Luke is 18 Michael sends him to his kinsman, a merchant, to learn a trade and prosper. Michael has been obliged to forfeit half his land, which was surety for a brother who fell on hard times. It breaks Michael's heart to be separated from his son; but he hopes Luke will prosper and, returning, retrieve the land which is his birthright. Before he leaves Luke is taken by his father to lay the first stone of a sheepfold, as a token of faith in his return in better times. But Luke falls into evil ways in the city and eventually flees abroad. Michael ends his days without his son, the sheepfold unfinished. He goes there from time to time, but can never find the heart to lift another stone.

**Michael, James Lionel** See **Kendall, Henry C(larence)**.

***Michaelmas Terme*** A comedy by Thomas Middleton, first published in 1607, about a Jacobean 'loan shark' who unwittingly brings about his own downfall.

Easy, an amiable gentleman of Essex, falls into the hands of Ephestian Quomodo and his attendants and confederates, Falselight and Shortyard. Quomodo succeeds in tricking Easy out of his estates in Essex and gloats over his new prospects as a gentleman landowner. He feigns death because he wants to know if his wife and son will prove equal to their new status.

But meanwhile Quomodo's wife has fallen in love with the pleasant gentleman from the country and as soon as she becomes a 'widow' accepts Easy as her husband. Quomodo's son, far from being grieved at the death of his father, proves to be unmoved; the furious Quomodo discovers that he has earned little filial respect. He is brought down completely by being tricked into signing a document that frees Easy from obligation to him and gets him back his land.

***Michael Robartes and the Dancer*** See **Yeats, William Butler**.

***Microcosmographie*** See **Earle, John**.

***Middlemarch, a Study of Provincial Life***. A novel by George Eliot, first published in four volumes (1871–72).

Middlemarch is a provincial town, and the scene is laid in the first half of the 19th century.

One part of the novel is concerned with Dorothea Brooke, idealistic and ardent, who seeks dedication to some worthy cause. She believes she has found it in her marriage to Edward Casaubon, an elderly pedant who is devoted to the immense task of writing a 'Key to all the Mythologies'. She is rapidly disillusioned; he spends their honeymoon on tireless research and reveals a temperament of extraordinary selfishness.

The other part of the novel is the story of Tertius Lydgate, the ambitious doctor who yearns for scientific discovery and who strives, against the uneasy reactions of his patients, for reforms in medical practice. He falls in love with Rosamund Vincy, and discovers too late that his wife is interested in nothing but the effect her person makes. To this preoccupation she makes everything else secondary – her husband's career, even his solvency.

The two parts are blended in the setting of Middlemarch and the characters come and go in each other's lives. Rosamond's brother, Fred, is loved by Mary, the daughter of Caleb Garth the builder. He has expectations, and is conscious that in Middlemarch his neighbours regard him in that light. The Garth family, on the other hand, are of rare integrity and prove to be the saving of the young man, whose expectations come to nothing. Rosamond flirts with Will Ladislaw, a young cousin of Casaubon, whose regard for Dorothea grows steadily from their first meeting in Rome. Will is regarded with increasing suspicion by Casaubon, who goes to spiteful lengths, in his will, to try and stop his cousin and Dorothea from ever marrying. It is Will who disillusions Dorothea about the worth of Casaubon's work; he is also the single character who knows that the world outside Middlemarch has very different standards and will have little patience with the pretensions of the Casaubons and Rosamond Vincys. At the end of the story Dorothea and Will do marry, in spite of the fact that Casaubon's will deprives Dorothea of her fortune if they do.

The canvas is broad, and the characters numerous; the novel is one of the finest in the language and George Eliot's greatest work. Her control of the manifold strands of her story never weakens and neither does her observation of a provincial town. She knew that sort of world intimately, and had the experience of the greater one to provide the detachment essential to her design.

***Middle Toe of the Right Foot, The*** See ***In the Midst of Life***.

**Middleton, Conyers** 1683–1750. The son of the rector of Hinderwell, near Whitby in Yorkshire, Middleton became a fellow of Trinity College, Cambridge, where he had been educated, and head of the University Library in 1721. Middleton published a *Life of Cicero* (1741) but is best remembered for his *A Free Inquiry into the Miraculous Powers which are supposed to have existed in the Christian Church through several successive Ages* (1748). Middleton examined – and rejected – the evidence for post-apostolic miracles in the lives of the saints and during Church history. Coming from a clergyman, his book caused considerable disturbance and demonstrated that some of the principles of the deists could find sympathetic response in the ranks of the established Church.

**Middleton, Thomas** *c.*1580–1627. The son of a master bricklayer, Middleton was probably born in London after his family settled there. He entered Queen's College, Oxford, in 1598 having already published *The Wisdom of Solomon Paraphrased* (1597), a poetic expansion of material from the Apocrypha. Other early works are *Micro-Cynicon* (1599), an attempt at formal satire in the manner of Persius and Juvenal, and a tragic complaint, *The Ghost of Lucrece* (1600). The poems are generally dismissed by scholars as apprentice works; but two pamphlets published in 1604, *The Ant and the Nightingale* and *The Black Book*, which are satirical comments on social evils, are more successful.

Details of Middleton's life are scarce but he is known to have been in London by 1602, working for Philip Henslowe. He also married about that time; his wife, Maria Marbeck, was the sister of one of The Admiral's Men company of actors. Middleton, while writing busily for Henslowe, was also turning out plays for the children's companies and his manifold activities have made correct documentation impossible. It is known that one of his tasks for Henslowe was to write a prologue and epilogue for Greene's *Friar Bacon and Friar Bungay*. For the children's companies (1602–08) he wrote the sharp-edged comedies of London life that are among his best work. When those companies began to decline he wrote for the professional adult companies and from about 1613 pageants for the City of London. In 1620 he became Chronologer of the City of London and was thus assured of a livelihood.

Like many of the working playwrights of the time Middleton wrote much that has not survived; some work that would probably be accounted mere hack writing, and much – probably more than we know – in collaboration with other playwrights. Some of the work known to be Middleton's is of remarkable quality, among the finest plays of the Jacobean stage. The closest we can approach to documentation is to follow the dates of the published plays and collaborations. The most notable are *Michaelmas Terme* (1607), *A Tricke to Catch the Old-One* (1608), *A Faire Quarrell* (1617), *A Game at Chess* (1625), *A Chast Mayd in Cheape-side* (1630), *The Changeling* (with William Rowley, 1653), and *Women Beware Women* (1657).

Other plays by Middleton are *Blurt master-constable* (doubtful – some scholars attribute it to Dekker – 1602), *The Honest Whore*, Part 1 (mostly Dekker, 1604), *The Phoenix* (1607), *The Familie of Love* (1608), *A Mad World, My Masters* (1608), *Your Five Gallants* (*c.*1608), *The Roaring Girle* (with Thomas Dekker, 1611), *The Widdow* (with Ben Jonson and John Fletcher, 1652), *The Spanish Gipsie* (with William Rowley and John Ford, 1653), *The Old Law* (with Philip Massinger and William Rowley, 1656), *No Wit like a Woman's* (with James Shirley, 1657), *More Dissemblers Beside Women* (1657), *The Mayor of Quinborough* (1661), *Anything for a quiet life* (1662), and *The Witch* (not published until 1778).

Middleton, whose character is unknown, displays no hint of his personality in his dramas or comedies: 'He has no point of view', T. S. Eliot wrote in his *Elizabethan Essays* (1934), 'He is merely the name which associates six or seven great plays.' His dialogue is sharp; his character drawing excellent; his stagecraft, in the best plays, unerring. Of particular interest are the colours of Middleton's work; they are sombre, even in his comedies, and suggest that he was acutely aware of the sinister undercurrent in Jacobean life.

The standard edition of Middleton is the eight-volume *The Works of Thomas Middleton* (1885–86) edited by A. H. Bullen. The two-volume selection in the Mermaid series contains ten plays: the first volume was edited by Swinburne (1887) and the second by Havelock Ellis (1890).

***Midshipman Easy, Mr*** A novel by Frederick Marryat, first published in 1836.

Nicodemus Easy is a rich man with egalitarian ideas and these he instils into the mind of his son, Jack. Jack Easy goes to sea as a midshipman and is soon in trouble; naval discipline and egalitarianism do not mix. But his commander is a humane and sensible man and Jack finds good friends in Edward Gascoigne, a fellow midshipman, and the Ashanti sailor Mesty, and he begins to realize that being heir to a fortune bestows privileges of its own which have nothing to do with egalitarianism.

Midshipman Easy's story, and his growth to intelligent and resourceful manhood, is a variation of the theme of *Peter Simple* but the variation is good enough to stand beside it. Notable characters are the lieutenant, Pottyfar, who dies of his own medicine which is meant to cure everything, and the bosun, Biggs, who puts duty before everything.

### Midsummer Night's Dream, A

A comedy by William Shakespeare. It was first produced *c.*1596 and printed in a quarto in 1600. It was published in the First Folio of 1623. The sources include Plutarch and Chaucer (Theseus and Hippolyta) and Ovid (Titania, Pyramus, and Thisbe); Oberon comes from a 13th-century *chanson de geste* that Berners had translated in 1534. The rest is Shakespeare's invention.

Theseus, Duke of Athens, is planning his wedding to Hippolyta, the Amazon queen, when into his presence comes Egeus with his daughter Hermia and two young men, Lysander and Demetrius. Egeus has ordered Hermia to marry Demetrius; she refuses because she loves Lysander. Theseus orders her to obey her father – and the law, which supports him. She is given four days to obey; the penalty is either death or for ever to remain unwed.

Hermia's friend Helena loves Demetrius and Hermia confides in her: she and Lysander are going to flee from Athens so that they can marry and they will meet in a wood near the city. But Helena tells Demetrius and he sets off after them, with Helena following. All four come to the wood at night; the wood is inhabited by fairies.

Oberon, king of the fairies, quarrels with his queen, Titania, over a changeling boy and Oberon tells the sprite Puck to bring him a magic flower. He drops the juice on Titania's eyes and she will love the first creature she sees upon waking. Then Oberon hears Demetrius scolding Helena for having followed him and, to reconcile them, tells Puck to use the flower on Demetrius' eyes. But Puck mistakes his man and uses it on Lysander – who promptly falls in love with Helena. Oberon tries to correct the error and uses it on Demetrius; so both men are in love with her and prepared to fight over her.

Bottom the weaver and his friends Quince, Snug, Flute, Snout, and Starveling have come to the wood to rehearse a play for the duke's wedding. While Bottom sleeps, Puck mischievously gives him a donkey's head: Titania wakes and falls in love with him. Oberon is confounded to discover his wife in love with such a creature and

Pyramus and Thisbe, from a woodcut in an edition of Ovid's *Metamorphoses* published in 1538. Bottom and his companions act the story of the lovers to celebrate the marriage of Theseus and Hippolyta at the end of Shakespeare's *A Midsummer Night's Dream*.

demands the changeling boy from her again; this time she yields and he releases her from the charm. It is Oberon who orders Puck to shroud the sleeping mortals in a mist and, having brought them unknowing to the same spot, makes sure that they will find their true loves when they wake.

In the morning the four young people are found by Egeus and the duke and are rightly paired: Demetrius wants Helena and Hermia and Lysander can marry each other. Bottom wakes up with his own head and hurries off to gather his friends for the play 'Pyramus and Thisby', which is duly given at the wedding of Theseus and Hippolyta.

*A Midsummer Night's Dream* is an exquisite play. The charm of each of the three strands is sufficient to make three plays and here they are blended with effortless skill. Yet there is no cloying sweetness; the observation is wry but there is warmth and humour and humanity, and Bottom is a great creation, the unpretentious and contented man who is never out of countenance in any world. The character is sometimes played as a buffoon, which is quite wrong.

### Miggles

See *Luck of Roaring Camp and Other Sketches, The*.

### Mill, James

1773–1836. A shoemaker's son, Mill was born at Northwater Bridge near Montrose in Angusshire. Through the patronage of Sir John Stuart, Mill was educated for the church at Edinburgh University and received a licence to preach in 1798. Mill went to London in 1802 and soon lost interest in theology; he turned to journalism and became editor of *The London Journal* in 1803. He published some pamphlets on commerce and education, contributed to *The Edinburgh Review*, and also edited *The St James's Chronicle*. He developed an interest in the administration of India, a country he had never seen, and began to work on a study of it in 1806. He became a friend and disciple of Jeremy Bentham about this time; it proved to be the decisive influence of his life.

*The History of British India* (three volumes) was published in 1817 and made a considerable impression. He was offered, and accepted, the post of Assistant to the Examiner of Correspondence in the India Office in 1819, and became head of the department in 1830. His interests at home were in the field of radical politics and besides Bentham his friends and associates were Henry Brougham and David Ricardo. He published *The Elements of Political Economy* (1821), *An Analysis of the Phenomena of the Human Mind* (1829), and *A Fragment on Mackintosh* (1835), as well as a number of essays and articles on similar subjects.

*The History of British India* was called the greatest historical work since Gibbon by no less a critic than Macaulay. Mill's aim, where India was concerned, was to ensure the country a good system of judicial procedure. Posterity does not agree with Macaulay and the book is not read any more. Ian Jack's comment puts the case perfectly: 'Mill seems to set himself deliberately to damp . . . interest in Hindu civilisation . . . and the result is a sort of intellectual steam-roller which crushes flat the whole complex structure of traditional Indian society as well as the flagrant abuses of the [East-India] Company and its agents . . . human nature and human history are too subtle and complex to be treated in this manner.' Mill's *Analysis*, with his theory of association, gave Bentham a psychological basis for his Utilitarianism. The *Fragment* was Mill's reply to Sir James Mackintosh's *Dissertations on the Progress of Ethical Philosophy*.

Mill seems to have been a stern and practical man, lacking warmth and charity in the small change of life, no matter how far-seeing he was. His brilliant son, John Stuart Mill, has given us a grim picture of him and Jeremy Bentham said that he was motivated 'less from love to the many than from hatred of the few.'

**Mill, John Stuart** 1806–73. The son of James Mill, John Stuart Mill was born in Pentonville, London, and was extensively and rigorously educated by his father. By the time he was 14 he had reached an advanced level in Latin, Greek,

logic, history, and economics. At 17 he was appointed to a clerkship at India House and formed the Utilitarian Society for the discussion of Benthamite philosophy. In 1824 Mill began his career in literature and philosophy with contributions to the utilitarian journal *The Westminster Review*; his father, at the same time, demanded his services in editing the works of Jeremy Bentham for publication: his edition of Bentham's *Treatise upon Evidence* was published in 1825 when he was 19. It is perhaps not surprising that Mill was to experience a lessening of enthusiasm for Bentham's philosophy as the years passed; he suffered a nervous breakdown in 1826 and another in 1836. His grim parent died in that year and he was finally free to broaden his intellectual experience.

Mill published an essay, *Bentham*, in *The London and Westminster Review* (1838) which marks his departure from strictly utilitarian philosophy. His *Coleridge* (1840) in the same journal signified his growing interest in the Romantics and the importance of the emotions and his further distance from the Enlightenment philosophy personified by Bentham. Mill continued his journalism and his contributions to periodicals and newspapers attracted the attention of Thomas Carlyle but their characters were not compatible and the friendship did not flourish. (See also **Carlyle, Thomas**.)

In 1843 Mill published his *A System of Logic, Ratiocinative and Inductive*. The next year saw the publication of *Essays on Some Unsettled Questions of Political Economy*, the product of discussions with his father and first written about 1830. More important was *Principles of Political Economy* (1848), which takes the views of both Adam Smith and David Ricardo some stages further. Mill had carefully studied their works and he expanded their theories to fit a more rapidly changing society, where the existing system of distribution was proving inadequate and where the industrial proletariat was increasing year by year.

Mill married Harriet Taylor in 1851. Their liaison had been in progress for 20 years and Harriet was an important influence on his intellectual development. Her husband had fully acknowledged the attachment even when society had disapproved, and his death left Harriet free to marry. The two enjoyed a brief six ' years together; Mill's love and esteem were made plain in his dedication to her memory of the famous *On Liberty* (1859). In the previous year the East India Company was dissolved and Mill, who had become head of the Examiner's Office, received a pension more than equal to his needs. The first

John Stuart Mill. A detail from the portrait by G. F. Watts, 1873. National Portrait Gallery, London.

two volumes of collected essays, *Dissertations and Discussions* (1859), was followed by *Considerations on Representative Government* (1860), in which Mill examined the political creeds of his time. *Utilitarianism* (1863) is his examination of, and commentary on, the principles of Jeremy Bentham's philosophy. He entered Parliament in 1865 as MP for Westminster and served until 1868. *The Subjection of Women*, which obviously owed something to Harriet, was published in 1869 and Mill retired from public life. He spent many of his remaining years at Avignon in Provence, where Harriet was buried and where he died. His *Autobiography* was published in 1873, the year of his death.

The philosophy of John Stuart Mill stems from Jeremy Bentham and James Mill but he tempered their ideas with humanitarianism. He understood, as his predecessors of the Age of Reason had not, the vital factors of individual thought and action and he emphasized their importance. Social and political thought could not be separated, in Mill's view, and he presented his conclusions with eloquence and power, moving towards socialism and foreseeing the issues that were to emerge in the modern industrialized world. Among the reforms he advocated were the emancipation of women, proportional representation, the development of farm cooperatives, and the organization of labour.

Other works by John Stuart Mill were *Considerations on Representative Government* (1861), *Auguste Comte and Positivism* (1865), *An Examination of [Sir William] Hamilton's Philosophy* (1865), *Inaugural Address* (1867), upon his installation as Lord Rector of the University of St Andrews and notable for Mill's views on university education, *England and Ireland* (1868), and *Chapters and Speeches on the Irish Land Question* (1870). Further collections of essays as *Dissertations and Discussions* were published in 1867 and 1875. *The Collected Works* was edited by F. E. L. Priestley, F. E. Mineka, and J. M. Robson (Toronto, 1963, still in progress). *On Liberty, Representational Government,* and *The Subjection of Women* are published together (Oxford Paperbacks, 1975); in the same series is Mill's *Autobiography* edited by Jack Stillinger (1971). *Utilitarianism* is published in Everyman's Library (1950), and *On Liberty* in Penguin Books (1966).

**Miller, Arthur** 1915– . The son of a Jewish manufacturer whose business failed in the Depression, Miller was born in New York City. He worked at a number of odd jobs after leaving school, and attended a course in journalism at Michigan University when he was 19. He succeeded in making a living writing radio scripts and worked briefly for the Federal Theatre project. During World War II he worked as a fitter in the Brooklyn Navy Yards and had his first play, *The Man Who Had All the Luck*, produced in 1944. It was not a success but his second, *All My Sons* (1947), dealing with the emotional aftermath of the war, was favourably received. Miller established himself with *Death of a Salesman* (1947), a modern tragedy about an ordinary man betrayed by the hollow values which are all he knows. In his next play, a powerful drama of the hysterical witch trials in Salem in 1692 entitled *The Crucible* (1953), Miller drew an unmistakable parallel with MacCarthy and his contemporary witch hunt, the product of modern hysteria. The author was himself ordered to appear before that infamous tribunal but he refused to comply with the demand that he incriminate others.

Miller's subsequent plays have been less successful. They include *A View From the Bridge* and *A Memory of Two Mondays* (both 1955), *After the Fall* (1964), *Incident at Vichy* (1965), and *The Creation of the World and Other Business* (1972). He is the author of one novel, *Focus* (1945), about American urban antisemitism. Miller was awarded the Pulitzer Prize for *Death of a Salesman*.

**Miller, Henry** 1891–1980. Miller was born in New York City, brought up in Brooklyn, and worked for Western Union until 1924, when he decided to make writing his career. He went to live in Paris in 1930, and published *Tropic of Cancer* in 1934. This is a book of episodes related in the first person, based on the author's experience of life in Paris as a poor aspiring writer. Mordantly funny and uncompromisingly bawdy, its sexual frankness prevented its publication in the USA and England until long after World War II; nevertheless it was widely read and gave encouragement to many younger writers chafing under conventional restraints. In the same vein are *Black Spring* (1936) and *Tropic of Capricorn* (1939). Miller went to Greece in 1939 and published his impressions in *The Colossus of Maroussi* (1941), an unconventional travel book in which people are of more importance than places. Many critics regard it as his best work. Miller returned to the USA in 1940 and travelled extensively during the next few years. *The Air-Conditioned Nightmare* (1945) and *Remember to Remember* (1947) record his unease about the condition of life in his own country, and his belief that the artist and the individual may prove its salvation. He spent the rest of his life at Big Sur on the coast of California. Among Henry Miller's other works are *The Books of my Life* (1952), *The Time of the Assassins: A Study of Rimbaud* (1956), and the novel sequence called *The Rosy Crucifixion*: *Sexus* (1945), *Plexus* (1949), and *Nexus* (1960).

**Miller, Joaquin** 1841–1913.  Cincinnatus Hiner (Heine?) Miller was born in Liberty, Indiana, and was given the nickname 'Joaquin' after his first literary effort, which was a defence of the Mexican bandit, Joaquin Murietta.

Miller's early life reads like the script of a television series and it is likely that accounts of a hectic past suited him very well, true or not. However, it is quite believable that he travelled West in a covered wagon, lived in frontier Oregon – just like a number of other people – and lived with Digger Indians in northern California. He acquired sufficient education in Portland to become a lawyer in 1860 and eventually went to San Francisco with literary ambitions. He had published poems in 1868 (*Specimens*) and in 1869 (*Joaquin et al*).

Miller went to London in 1870 and published *Pacific Poems* at his own expense. The book made a great impression and Rossetti took an active interest in this 'Byron of Oregon'. A frontier poet was a fascinating novelty in England and *Songs of the Sierras* (1871), which Rossetti helped him prepare for publication, made him famous. He returned to America soon after and, though he continued to write and publish poetry, gradually lost his reputation as it became clear that his talent was not rich and varied enough to maintain his original success. He also wrote plays, of which the most successful was *The Danites of the Sierras*, on a Mormon theme (1877); several novels; and an autobiography, *Life Among the Modocs* (1873). Miller's poems 'Kit Carson's Ride' and 'Columbus' were learned by thousands of schoolchildren in the USA.

*Miller's Tale, The*  See *Canterbury Tales, The.*

**Millin, Sarah Gertrude** 1889–1968.  Sarah Gertrude Millin, née Liebson, was born and educated in Kimberley, South Africa. Her husband became a judge of the Supreme Court of South Africa, and she published her first novel, *The Dark River*, in 1920. She was the author of several novels which are generally regarded as a major contribution to fiction by a South African during the inter-war period, among them *Adam's Rest* (1922), *God's Stepchildren* (1924), *Mary Glenn* (1925), and *The Sons of Mrs Aab* (1931). Her novels have been praised for the awareness they display of the realities and complexities of the racial conflict, a subject she explored further in *The South Africans* (1926, revised 1934). Mrs Millin was honoured by Witwatersrand University for her historical books, among them biographies of *Rhodes* (1933) and *Smuts* (1936).

*Mill on the Floss, The*  A novel by George Eliot, first published in 1860.

The mill of the title – Dorlcote Mill – lies on the river Floss. Tom and Maggie Tulliver are the miller's son and daughter and as children are very close. But Tom develops into a prig and a moral bully; Maggie is intelligent and perceptive, a girl of great sensibility, responsive to beauty. Unfortunately, she worships her brother, who is too self-centred to try and understand her.

Philip Wakem, the son of a neighbouring lawyer, suffers from a malformed back, but his appreciation of the same things gives him a bond with Maggie, though her father has a strong dislike of Philip's father, the clever lawyer. When Tulliver is involved in litigation, Wakem acts for the other side, and the case goes against Maggie's father. Bankrupt as a result, Tulliver's dislike of Wakem turns to bitter hatred: Tom turns on Maggie for her friendship with Philip and, with his obvious rectitude and demonstrable loyalty to his father, persuades her to stop seeing Philip.

Tulliver knocks Wakem off his horse outside Dorlcote Mill and thrashes him. This aggravates the strain under which the miller has been living, and soon after the incident he dies, Tom becoming head of the family. Maggie goes to St Ogg's, the nearby town, to stay with her cousin Lucy, who is to marry Stephen Guest. Stephen and Maggie are drawn to each other but Maggie is acutely conscious of the loyalty she owes to Lucy. However, Stephen falls in love with Maggie and his irresponsible behaviour during a boating party on the Floss leads to her being compromised.

Tom Tulliver turns his sister out of the house, and the townspeople of St Ogg's, especially the women, pounce on the scandal and ostracize her. Lucy and Philip, by contrast, are generous and understanding but they are only two in a close community. Then her aunt, Mrs Glegg, remonstrates firmly with Tom and the warm-hearted rector, Dr Kenn, gives her the post of governess to his children.

During the autumn of that year, the heavy rains threaten floods. Dr Kenn is pressed by his parishioners to consider the wisdom of having Maggie to teach his children, and in despair suggests that Maggie leave St Ogg's for a time, and become governess to one of his colleagues. Then the flood rises, and Maggie knows that the mill will be submerged. She takes a boat and finds her brother there (her mother is safely out of the way). They take to the water, with the intention of helping others if they can; and in a brief flash of happiness are restored to their childhood affection. But they drown in the flood, hurled by the current into a great mass of floating debris.

*The Mill on the Floss* displays both an intensification of the author's gifts – and a flawed construction that spoils it for many readers. Its saving grace – and it deserves judgment on the highest level – is the way it catches a time and place forever. George Eliot's book is as fine an evocation of rural England in the mid-19th century as *Adam Bede*, and like that book has many outstanding portraits of country people: the Dodsons, Tulliver and the packman, good kind Bob Jakin; Aunt Glegg and Aunt Pullet, sisters but poles apart. The two principals, Tom and Maggie, strain credibility, the one so detestable, the other so idealized. But their childhood is beautifully done, a triumph for the author. The story ends in a rush that suggests too drastic a solution to the impasse in which the principals are caught. But the quality of the whole outweighs the faults of its parts.

An illustration by W. J. Allen for George Eliot's *The Mill on the Floss* (1860). Maggie and Tom meet their deaths in the flood.

**Milman, Henry Hart** 1791–1868. The son of a fashionable physician, Milman was born in London and educated at Eton College and Brasenose College, Oxford. He won the Newdigate Prize for poetry and the Chancellor's Essay Prize and was made a fellow of his college in 1814. His career as a poet began with *Fazio: a Tragedy* (1815) and *Samor: Lord of the Bright City* (1818). Milman was ordained in 1816 and appointed rector of St Mary's, Reading, in 1818. He continued to write dramatic poetry: *The Fall of Jerusalem* (1820), *The Martyr of Antioch* and *Belshazzar* (1822), *Anne Boleyn* (1826), and *Nala and Damayanti and Other Poems* (translations from Sanskrit, 1835). His considerable learning was employed in translations from classical Greek with his versions of *The Agamemnon* of Aeschylus and *The Bacchae* of Euripides (1865).

As a poet Milman is practically forgotten now, though he was Professor of Poetry at Oxford (1821–31) and honoured in his day. As a church historian his reputation stands high, however. *The History of the Jews* (1838–42), *The History of Christianity from the Birth of Christ to the Abolition of Paganism in the Roman Empire* (1840), *A History of Latin Christianity, including that of the Popes to Nicolas V* (1854–55), *The Life of Thomas à Becket* (1860), and *The Annals of St Paul's Cathedral* (posthumously published, 1868) form an impressive body of work, presenting their subjects with a freshness that probably owed something to Gibbon, whom Milman much admired. Sir Robert Peel made him rector of St Margaret's, Westminster, in 1835 and he became dean of St Paul's in 1849. Milman produced an edition of Gibbon's *Decline and Fall* (1838–39) and wrote *The Life of Edward Gibbon, with Selections from his Correspondence* (1839).

**Milnes, Richard Monckton, 1st Baron Houghton** 1809–85. Milnes was the son of a wealthy Yorkshire family. While at Trinity College, Cambridge, he was a member of the group called the Apostles, which also included Tennyson and Arthur Hallam. He published collections of verse in *Memorials of a Tour in some parts of Greece* (1834) and became MP for Pontefract in 1837. During an active life he published five collections of verse but remains unknown as a poet. He was a patron of letters and a generous host; most men of letters in Europe and the USA were guests at his home, Fryston Hall in Yorkshire, during his lifetime. He is best remembered for his championship of John Keats and his publication of *Life, Letters and Literary Remains of John Keats* (1848). Milnes became a peer in 1863.

***Milton, A Poem in Two Books*** See **Blake, William**.

**Milton, John** 1608–74. Milton was the son of a scrivener, also named John, who had been disinherited by a wrathful father for abandoning his Catholic faith and turning to the Church of England, but who managed nevertheless to earn a comfortable living. He was also an accomplished musician. The poet was born in London, in Bread Street off Cheapside, and went to St Paul's School. Later he went to Christ's College, Cambridge, where his remarkable looks and steadfast refusal to be as gay a young dog as his fellows led to his being dubbed 'the lady of Christ's'.

An exceptional scholar, the young Milton was in trouble soon after arriving because he demanded a broader curriculum than was available; but he settled down and developed further the Greek and Latin at which he was already adept. He also took private tuition in Hebrew and at the age of 20 produced a group of sonnets in Italian. He had been writing poetry in English and Latin since he was 17, but the first true indication of his

exceptional gifts came at Christmas in 1629, when he wrote his ode 'On the Morning of Christ's Nativity'. An indication of his character comes with the contemporary piece 'The Passion', which was begun but 'This Subject the Author finding to be above the years he had, when he wrote it, and nothing satisf'd with what was begun, left it unfinisht.' By the age of 21 Milton, having refused a career in the Church – he was highly critical of the Anglican clergy – was dedicated to poetry.

The elder Milton had meanwhile retired to Horton in Buckinghamshire and his son joined him there, having left Cambridge in 1632 after taking his MA. He had spent his vacations there (*L'Allegro* and *Il Penseroso* were written during these vacations) and now he settled down contentedly to a long period of absorption in the classics, broken here and there by appearances in the artistic England of the 1630s. His short poems show his love of music and his interest in Italian poetry; more important were the invitations from his friend Henry Lawes to write the texts for *Arcades* (1633) and for *A Maske presented at Ludlow Castle 1634: on Michaelmasse night*. The former was a pretty entertainment presented to the Countess Dowager of Derby; the latter a full-scale pastoral better known as **Comus**. **Lycidas**, the immortal elegy that was Milton's contribution to the volume on Edward King, was written in 1637.

In the spring of 1638 he set off on a journey to Europe, intending to visit Italy, Sicily, and Greece. Italy and its associations with the past made a deep impression on Milton and he in turn seems to have impressed the Italians. He made friends easily, his path no doubt made smoother by his friendship, in England, with Charles Diodati, a school friend whose father was an Italian settled in London. In Naples his host was Giovanni Batista Manso, who had been Tasso's patron; in Florence he visited the aged and blind Galileo in prison. Another meeting was with Hugo Grotius, the great jurist. But his Italian sojourn was to be the extent of the poet's European experience: events were stirring in England and he started home in 1639, arriving back in August.

Milton had looked forward to seeing Diodati and sharing with him his experience of Italy and his plans for the future (a letter mentions his hopes of undertaking an epic work) but his friend had died during his absence and Milton mourned him in the Latin elegy *Epitaphium Damonis*. It was to be his last ambitious poem for some time.

He settled down in London in Aldersgate Street and undertook the teaching of his nephews, John and Edward Phillips, sons of his sister Anne and the source of a great deal of information on the poet's life. Other pupils joined them but the events that had persuaded Milton to return from Italy began to occupy him more and more. That he was a man of strong will he had already shown as a student; that he was also one of strong principles with a genius for expression he was about to demonstrate. During the events of the next 20 years John Milton was bound to be heard but, incredibly, he was lost to poetry almost all that time. His convictions were clear and, as a Protestant, he saw the Reformation as having freed the minds of Englishmen from the tyranny of Rome; the Anglican Church seemed to be a new tyranny, imposing new restrictions on their freedom to worship. Having defied the pope, were Englishmen to submit to bishops? Consequently Milton was anti-episcopalian and also anti-Royalist, for the imposition of a church that denied freedom of religion was the king's doing. Charles I himself had already shown that he was prepared to deny his subjects other freedoms too, and the opposition to king and bishops was led by the Parliamentary party. Milton's first contribution to the conflict was in defence of Thomas Young, his old tutor, a busy pamphleteer against episcopacy: *Of Reformation touching Church Discipline in England* (1641). This was quickly followed by *Of Prelatical Episcopacy*, and the *Animadversions upon the Remonstrant's defence against Smectymnuus* (1642).

Milton married Mary Powell, the daughter of Oxford Royalists, in, probably, May 1642. Within a year Mary had left him and returned to her parents' house. The reason for this separation is not known and much speculation has taken over – novels have even been written laying the blame either on Mary or on Milton. Certainly their backgrounds were different; moreover Mary was half Milton's age and possibly a light-hearted girl who proved to be the wrong choice for the cultured, intense man so committed to the Parliamentary cause. That Milton was shocked by her desertion seems certain and he received her back in 1645. He also received her family following the fall of Oxford, a Royalist stronghold, to the Parliamentary forces. The marriage resumed and Mary bore him four children before she died in 1652.

The crisis of his marriage resulted in four carefully considered pamphlets on divorce (1643–45). Milton argued that since marriages do break down, some irretrievably, divorce should be allowed. But now the party he had espoused turned its wrath on Milton. Parliament had succeeded in abolishing the Star Chamber in 1641 and the press was free. The result was an avalanche of controversial literature and the Parliamentary party, no less than king or church, soon displayed its own aversion to liberty of opinion by reimposing restraints on printing in 1643. Milton had published without a licence and divorce was not popular with the Puritans. All this moved the poet to his most celebrated prose work, the *Areopagitica* (1644). But his eloquence was wasted; another 50 years passed before the press was free in England.

The first published poetry came in 1645 as *Poems of Mr John Milton, both English and Latin, Compos'd at several times.* The elder Milton died in 1646 and the poet's circumstances became more comfortable; he gave up teaching entirely. A little poetry was written about this time, notably his 'On the new forcers of Conscience under the Long Parliament', which shows that Milton's loathing of religious intolerance, whether practised by Anglican or Puritan, remained unshakable: '*New Presbyter* is but *Old Priest* writ Large.' But the comparative peace of these years came to an end with the execution of Charles I in 1649. While his trial was being arranged Milton had prepared *The Tenure of Kings and Magistrates*, and it was published immediately after the king's death. His view was that the first duty of kings and magistrates was the good of the people; in this lay their authority, and the covenant must be kept. If the covenant had been broken it was right that they be called to account and deprived of their office if found at fault; they should not escape death if their offences deserved it. But the manner of the king's trial, the purging of the Commons, and the court's refusal to allow the king to speak after sentence alienated many of Parliament's own supporters. The execution itself provoked a reaction that swept through England and Europe: Charles I came to be regarded as a saintly martyr.

The publication of *Eikon Basilike* (Royal Image), purporting to be a set of meditations by the king, followed immediately after the execution; the book was at once widely bought and read. Milton, as writer of *The Tenure of Kings*, was chosen to write a reply and *Eikonoklastes* (Image Breaker) was the result. Whatever its virtues or the strength of its case it had little effect: two editions were published in England and one in France whilst no fewer than 50 editions of *Eikon Basilike* were published in a single year. More serious for Milton for the future was the war of words that followed. Whilst the poet's vindication of the English people's defence of their freedom was well-argued and forceful, blast and counterblast grew more abusive and bitter.

The same eventful year, 1649, saw the appointment of Milton as Latin secretary to the Council of State. In 1652 his wife Mary died, and a further blow followed when his already strained eyesight gave out and total blindness descended. He kept his post, continuing his work with assistants, and took a new wife in 1656. This second marriage, to Catherine Woodcock, was apparently happy but Catherine died in childbirth in 1658. She is the subject of the sonnet beginning 'Methought I saw my late espoused Saint'.

The life of this remarkable man now took on a quieter tone but his intellect and vigour were unimpaired. Still hopeful, in spite of his own and his fellow countrymen's disillusion with the Commonwealth, that a free commonwealth could be achieved, he wrote on in support of his hopes to the very eve of the Restoration. Charles II and the Royalists lost no time in taking revenge on the surviving regicides and in punishing their associates but Milton was spared because he was of little importance: the English wanted a king and the poet could not influence them. He lost a large portion of his property and his living was now more modest. But he was not in any difficulty and was able to return to the privacy he had lost 20 years earlier. His third marriage, in 1662, was to Elizabeth Minshull and they moved to a house in Cripplegate.

John Milton. A detail from the frontispiece to the 1668 edition of *Paradise Lost*. The poem was first published in 1667.

At the age of 59 Milton published *Paradise Lost*, the epic poem that he had wanted to write since he was a young man. He had then considered King Arthur as a possible subject but the one he eventually chose – the Fall of Man – was infinitely more challenging. He wrote in blank verse and succeeded in carrying out his great design. *Paradise Regained*, apparently suggested to him by a chance remark of his Quaker friend Thomas Ellwood, was published in 1671; the superb *Samson Agonistes* in the same year. His prose works also included a *History of Britain* (1670) and a *History of Moscovia* (1682). A lost *De Doctrina Christiana* came to light in the 19th century; this contains some intensely interesting matter, showing that the author of the only great biblical epic in the English language never ceased his search for a completely satisfying Christian creed.

Milton spent the rest of his life at Cripplegate, apparently content. He was a sociable man and no abstainer from the small pleasures of life. His visitors – and there were many, both from home and abroad – could enjoy tobacco, wine, and stimulating conversation. Marvell and Dryden were frequent callers. He was on the best of terms with his numerous relatives, many of whom were Catholic and Royalist. His last years were troubled by gout, which brought about his death. He was buried next to his father at St Giles' Church, Cripplegate.

The reputation of Milton has suffered from more critical vagaries than that of any poet of similar stature: but it is upon his stature as a poet that criticism eventually founders. His personal life, his public declarations, his involvement in the stormy history of his times – all have been searched for faults of character, inconsistency, and hypocrisy, as if his shortcomings as a man could reduce the quality of his work. But a great deal is known about the man: he was neither intolerant nor uncompromising except in his belief that all men should have freedom to think, speak, and worship. In this he was very much a son of the Reformation; but he was far removed from the sour-faced Puritan pictured by his detractors, who overlook the evidence of the poetry produced by this true descendant of the Renaissance.

The first major critic of Milton as a poet was Samuel Johnson in *The Lives of the Poets*. Johnson's interest in the personality as well as the poetry is one of the virtues of his book, and being a High-Church Royalist, he could not be expected to be sympathetic to the man. He was moreover writing in an age separated from Milton's not only by years – they were not so very many

– but by great changes in the life and literature of England; the omission from his book of Andrew Marvell and Robert Herrick is an indication of his views. But the poets who came after Milton, from Dryden to Robert Bridges, extolled his genius. In our time T. S. Eliot attacked him (1932 and 1936), as did F. R. Leavis (1933), John Middleton Murry (1938), and Robert Graves (1943, 1949, and 1957). Leavis did not, however, like the others, decry Milton as a man. The shade of the great poet must have been amused when in a later essay (1952) Leavis described Milton as a great genius, then criticized Eliot who in his British Academy lecture (*Milton*, 1947) spoke of his subject favourably, in contrast to his earlier views. Milton himself survives all critical attacks: as a poet he is among the greatest in the English language.

*Mingo, and Other Sketches in Black and White*. A collection of stories by Joel Chandler Harris, first published in 1884.

The title story, *Mingo: A Sketch of Life in Middle Georgia*, tells of the Negro servant, Mingo, who remains with his mistress when she marries beneath her into a poor White family. She loses her husband in the Civil War and then dies herself, leaving a child. Mingo remains to care for the child at the farm, which belongs to his mistress's good-natured but coarse mother-in-law.

A notable contrast is *At Teague Poteet's*. Teague Poteet is a Georgia backwoodsman and moonshiner who has successfully evaded the Civil War conscription. He marries Puss Pringle and they have a daughter, Sis. Philip Woodward, the excise agent, comes to investigate the moonshiners, falls in love with Sis Pringle, and resigns his commission; he also helps the backwoods people outwit the federal officers. Teague and Puss grieve the loss of their daughter when Philip takes Sis to the city to marry her; but are consoled by the thought that their daughter's husband-to-be is 'somebody'.

**Minot, Laurence** d. *c*.1352. Almost nothing is known of Laurence Minot apart from his name, though his work suggests that he was a Yorkshireman. He is best described as a war poet of the Middle English period, of the years 1333–52, from the Battle of Halidon Hill to the taking of Guisnes in the Hundred Years' War. The 11 poems include celebrations of the battles of Sluys and Crécy and the siege of Calais, and Laurence Minot is adept in the use of both rhyming and alliterative verse. He is unblushingly chauvinistic: an English king, here Edward III, is the best of all possible monarchs and English soldiers are all in-vincible fighting men. Minot evinces no gallantry and little compassion (the burgesses of Calais arouse a fleeting pity); the enemy is in all respects contemptible and there to be slaughtered. The poems have considerable energy and vigour; they are the war songs of a winning side. Laurence Minot's poems were edited by T. Wright for the Percy Society (1849) and by M. Konrath for the Early English Text Society (1902).

**miracle plays** When the classical world perished the theatre perished with it. The early Christian fathers could not be expected to approve of the degenerate Roman theatre, which was quick to lampoon the new religion in the coarsest terms: whether they would have approved of even the loftiest form of Greek tragedy is equally unlikely – as unlikely as the possibility of a new theatre ever coming into being.

Paradoxically, the new theatre began in the same way as the ancient theatre had: it grew out of religious ritual. And it was indeed a new theatre – not a trace of the classical theatre survived in the medieval world, though incidental resemblances were bound to occur. Exactly how the mystery play arose – from chanted responses, from simple religious pageantry of the kind seen in any Catholic country at Christmas, or as a spontaneous elaboration of the drama inherent in the Christian story – is a subject about which argument continues. But the nature of medieval drama indicates its origins.

Miracle plays were common in France long before they became familiar in England; the earliest surviving English miracle play is *The Harrowing of Hell*, which dates from about the end of the 13th century. It is not a play in the familiar sense, merely a recitation piece for more than one voice. The text is in Anglo-Norman French. English-language mystery plays were certainly being performed in most parts of England by the middle of the 14th century, usually on the occasion of the great church festivals – Easter, Pentecost, Christmas – but chiefly at Corpus Christi. The performances were the charge of the town corporations; as the form developed and the plays became progressively more elaborate, the various guilds of craftsmen were given charge of individual scenes, often on movable stages.

The growth of these plays continued into the 16th century, by then acquiring the elements that were later transferred into the drama proper: the words of the observer, the comic byplay, the recognition that life, even in matters of worship, can sometimes be light-hearted. The authorship of the principal mystery plays is as much a matter for argument as is the true origin of the form. Those texts that survived and have been collected are grouped under the names of the towns in which they are believed to have been performed – York, Chester, Coventry, and Wakefield. One play has survived from Newcastle and one from Norwich.

The earliest group, or cycle, is believed to be that from Chester and was performed at Pentecost (Whitsuntide). The plays are believed to have been the work of a single author (who may have been Ranulf Higden) and number 25 in all, covering the principal events from the Fall to the Nativity and moving on to the Resurrection.

The York cycle, no less than 48 plays, began at 4.30 on the morning of Corpus Christi and lasted throughout a single crowded day. Also performed at York, every tenth year, was the 'Creed' play, given at Lammastide instead of Corpus Christi. This gave a dramatic representation of the Apostles' Creed, the articles of the Faith.

The Wakefield cycle (also called The Towneley Plays because the manuscript belonged to the Towneley family of Towneley Hall near Burnley in Lancashire) was given at Corpus Christi (it was given at Whitsuntide in one year). There are 32 plays in the Wakefield cycle, and 5 plays have been identified as directly borrowed from the York cycle.

The Coventry cycle is represented by only 2 surviving plays out of a possible 10, each of which was performed in a different place, in sequence, in the city. The occasion was Corpus Christi.

The single play we have from Newcastle was also played at Corpus Christi, after the religious services and processions, and tells the story of Noah and the making of the ark. The Norwich play concerned the creation of Eve and the Fall.

Another cycle of mystery plays that has survived is the *Ludus Coventriae sive Ludus Corpus Christi* – the name mistakenly given to a manuscript of 1468 by Sir Robert Cotton when his librarian Richard James brought him the manuscript. But research has shown that while Sir Robert had reasons for believing it to be a cycle of plays given in Coventry at Corpus Christi, it was in fact a cycle from another city and not played on that festival day. The language is closer to the East Anglian than the Midland speech of the time, and the cycle seems to be of a later date than the others.

There were single plays which dealt with the lives of the saints and events of the New Testament narrative; the most complete survival of these is *The Play of Mary Magdalene*, which purports to give an account of her life after the Resurrection.

**Miracles, On** An essay by David Hume, which was first published in *An Enquiry Concerning Human Understanding* in 1748.

Hume's famous sceptical essay proceeded from the assumption that no dead man, in any age or in any place, had ever been observed coming to life again. The scriptures, obviously, could have no place in his argument, since belief in miracles was an article of faith in the truth of the scriptures themselves. The 'historical evidence' for miracles could be brushed aside, since the possibility of a miraculous event was no stronger than the possibility of its being an event falsely reported. 'It is contrary to experience that a miracle should be true, but not contrary to experience that testimony should be false.'

The essay contains Hume's memorable comment on religious faith as a factor in the acceptance of the miraculous. 'The Christian religion not only was at first attended with miracles, but even at this day cannot be believed by any reasonable person without one. Mere reason is insufficient to convince us of its veracity; and whoever is moved by faith to assent to it, is conscious of a continued miracle in his own person, which subverts all the principles of his understanding, and gives him a determination to believe what is most contrary to custom and experience.'

**Miranda** Daughter of Prospero, the exiled Duke of Milan in Shakespeare's *The Tempest*. She falls in love with the shipwrecked Ferdinand, son of the King of Naples; he is the first man, apart from her father and the repulsive Caliban, whom she has ever seen. But her love is part of Prospero's design.

**Mirror (Myrroure) for Magistrates, A** In 1555 the printer John Wayland published an edition of Lydgate's translation of Boccaccio, which is commonly known as *The Falls of Princes*. Wayland intended to add further 'falls' to include English princes and an announcement of this closes the book. The additional texts did not appear and it is assumed that those in power disliked the idea and forbade the publication. However, in 1559, 19 such moral tales did appear as *A Myrroure for Magistrates*, edited by William Baldwin and presented as examples of the fatal mistakes of those who had known greatness, ending with the death of Edward IV. The second edition (1563) was enlarged to 25 but the third (1574), edited by John Higgins, went back to earlier times and added a number of obscure Roman-British figures. The next edition (1578) included more

English characters and the book continued with great success for 50 years; total characters examined numbered 98. Among those whose careers were described, usually in very bad verse, were Jane Shore, Buckingham, Eleanor Cobham, and the Duke of Gloucester. Exceptions to the low level of verse are Thomas Churchyard's *The Complaint of Shore's Wife*; *A Lamentacion Upon the Death of Kinge Edwarde the 4*, which some scholars believe to have been written at some time by John Skelton; *Hastings* by John Dolman; and the *Induction* and *The Complaint of Henry Duke of Buckingham* by Thomas Sackville.

*A Mirror for Magistrates* has little to recommend it as literature, except for the contributions named above. But it was very popular and the chronicle poem found true success in the hands of Sackville, as we have seen, and in those of Michael Drayton, Samuel Daniel, and others. The chronicle play is perhaps even more important, and over 30 of the subjects in the *Myrroure* were used by dramatic poets.

**Misfortunes of Arthur, The** A tragedy by Thomas Hughes, first performed by the Gentlemen of Gray's Inn for Elizabeth I at Greenwich in 1588. It was published in the previous year. Thomas Hughes of Gray's Inn had been a fellow of Queen's College, Cambridge, and the full title of the play, *The Misfortunes of Arthur (Uther Pendragons Sonne) Reduced into Tragicall Notes* gives a hint of the form. It begins with the begetting of Arthur on Igerna by Uther and in five acts and an epilogue traces the story of King Arthur's reign and death. The play is not a notable example of early 16th-century tragedy; the blank verse is respectable and shows that it was continually improving in its use for drama, but Marlowe's *Tamburlaine* had been produced a year before and completely new standards had been set.

**Misfortunes of Elphin, The** A novel by Thomas Love Peacock, first published in 1829. Like his earlier *Maid Marian* this book is set in the past, prompted in this case by Peacock's fondness for Wales. The background is Arthurian legend, and the story deals with Elphin's loss of much of his kingdom to the encroaching sea and his imprisonment by a powerful neighbour because he will not acknowledge that his neighbour's wife is more virtuous and lovely than his own. Taliesin, Arthur, and Guinevere are all characters in this light-hearted romance; a notable invention is Prince Seithenyn, charged with maintaining the sea walls but usually too drunk to prevent the loss of much of Elphin's land. The book contains 14 songs, many of them fine translations or adaptations of traditional poetry, but the total effect is spoilt by Peacock's failure to stay within his frame of reference: his comparisons of life in the past with that of his own time are intrusive.

**Misogonus** A comedy that was acted at Trinity College, Cambridge, between 1568 and 1574 and first printed in 1577. It was a variation on the prodigal son theme, popular with playwrights of the time. The author's identity is not known with certainty but evidence points to Anthony Rudd (c.1549–1615), who became Bishop of St David's in 1594. His career didn't advance further – in a sermon in 1596 he riled the queen by referring to her wrinkled age.

In this version of the theme the prodigal son is the one who stays at home. Misogonus is vicious and debauched and wastes the substance of his father Philogonus. The virtuous son, Eugonus, is long-lost and the elder; his return home brings about the repentance of the wicked Misogonus. The play is notorious for its coarseness and the elaborate scenes of Misogonus's dissipation.

**Mister Johnson** See **Cary, (Arthur) Joyce (Lunel)**.

**Mitchell, Margaret** See *Gone with the Wind*.

**Mitchison, Naomi (Margaret)** 1897– . The daughter of the physiologist J. S. Haldane, Naomi Haldane married G. Richard Mitchison, a barrister, in 1916. She studied science but turned to writing, and chose the world of Greece and Rome as the setting for her most successful fiction. During a long career she has published some seventy books but the novels and stories of the decade 1923–33, evoking classical times, are acknowledged to be her best work. Though she admitted to having little Latin and no Greek beyond the alphabet, Naomi Mitchison made excellent use of histories and scholarly translations in English, French, and German. Her direct narrative style, avoidance of sentimentality, and dialogue free of archaisms confer a rare quality on *The Conquered* (1923), *When the Bough Breaks* (1924, short stories), *Cloud Cuckoo Land* (1925), *Black Sparta* (1928, short stories), *Barbarian Stories* (1929), *The Corn King and The Spring Queen* (1931), and *The Delicate Fire* (1933, short stories). *The Blood of the Martyrs* (1939) is an original and moving novel of the early Christians in Rome. *Anna Comnena* (1928) is a biography of the Byzantine princess and historian of the 12th century AD.

**Mitford, Mary Russell** 1787–1855. Mary Russell Mitford was the daughter of a country doctor of Alresford, Hampshire, who ruined his family by his extravagance. Mary supported her family with the money she earned as a writer. She had ambitions to be a dramatist and a poet, and indeed published both plays and poems, but she is best known as a miniaturist and most successful in that form. *Our Village: Sketches of Rural Life, Character and Scenery* began as a series of contributions to *The Lady's Magazine* in 1819 and appeared in five volumes between 1824 and 1832. The village she wrote of was Three Mile Cross, near Reading, and Miss Mitford makes it a wholly charming place. In this she is slightly suspect but she is after all selecting what aspects will interest her readers. Reading itself is the town in her *Belford Regis, Sketches of a Country Town* (1835).

Miss Mitford's fiction (*Atherton, and Other Tales*, 1854) has no distinction and her plays, with the exception of *Rienzi* (1828), did not enjoy much success. However, her *Recollections of a Literary Life* (1852) is bright and gossipy and contains interesting chapters on her contemporaries.

**Mitford, Nancy (Freeman)** 1904–73. Daughter of the 2nd Baron Redesdale, Nancy Mitford was born in London and educated privately. Her early novels – *Highland Fling* (1931), *Christmas Pudding* (1932), *Wigs on the Green* (1935), *Pigeon Pie* (1940) – were amusing and slight. With *The Pursuit of Love* (1945) she enjoyed a great success with an elegant and witty satire on her own class. *Love in a Cold Climate* (1949) and *The Blessing* (1951) were equally successful but she seemed to lose her touch with *Don't Tell Alfred* (1961). However her gifts as a writer were very much in evidence in her biography *Madame de Pompadour* (1954). Voltaire's liaison with the Marquise du Châtelet was a less happy choice of subject (*Voltaire in Love*, 1957) but Louis XIV, in *The Sun King* (1966), suited her perfectly and the book was a best seller. Nancy Mitford lived in Paris from 1945 and her translation of André Roussin's comedy *The Little Hut* (1953) ran for months in London. Her last biography was *Frederick the Great* (1970). With A. S. C. Ross she edited and contributed to a delightful trifle called *Noblesse Oblige* (1956), a book of satirical essays by various writers on English snobbery.

**Mitford, William** 1744–1827. Mitford was born in London and completed his education at Queen's College, Oxford. He served in the Hampshire militia at the same time as Edward Gibbon and published a treatise on England's military strength. Gibbon suggested to Mitford a subject for a history, one which had not so far engaged the attention of English historians – Greece. Mitford published *The History of Greece* in five volumes (1784–1818). It was a pioneer work and has long been superseded, but it demonstrated that Mitford understood his theme and the *History* was praised by Macaulay, who, at the same time, grumbled about his style. Mitford was a member of the family whose name was to become well known to 20th-century readers; his brother Lord Redesdale added a life of William Mitford to the 1822 edition.

**Mittelholzer, Edgar (Austin)** 1909–65. Mittelholzer was born in New Amsterdam, Berbice County, in what was then British Guiana. He joined the Royal Navy in Trinidad in 1941, the same year his first novel was accepted for publication – he had been writing unsuccessfully for 12 years. *Corentyne Thunder* went almost unnoticed and the stock was destroyed during the air raids on London; but it was the first sign of the remarkable flowering of talent in the West Indies and Guyana after World War II. The author went to London in 1948 to work for the British Council and took with him the manuscript of *A Morning at the Office* (1950), an unsparing appraisal, in microcosm, of the colour-based society from which he had *escaped* (the word was also used by George Lamming). The novel was a considerable success with the critics and helped focus attention on the West Indian writers who followed. In a short career Mittelholzer's output was considerable: *Shadows Move Among Them* (1951), *Children of Kaywana* (1952), *The Weather in Middenshot* (1952), *The Life and Death of Sylvia* (1953), *The Harrowing of Hubertus* (1954), *My Bones and My Flute* (1955), *Of Trees and the Sea* (1956), *A Tale of Three Places* (1957), *Kaywana Blood* (1958), *The Weather Family* (1958), *A Tinkling in the Twilight* (1959), *Latticed Echoes* (1960), *Eltonsbrody* (1960), *Thunder Returning* (1961), and *The Mad Macmullochs* (1961) are the titles of his West Indian novels. His later ones have a European setting and are of less interest. Mittelholzer wrote two nonfiction books, *With a Carib Eye* (1958) and his autobiography, *A Swarthy Boy* (1963).

***Moby-Dick:** or The Whale.* Herman Melville's novel was first published in 1851. The hyphenated form was given on the title page, but throughout the book the whale is called Moby Dick. The original title was *The Whale*: Melville notified Richard Bentley, his British publisher, of the change when he sent him the proofs, but it appeared in London in 1851 with the original title. Harper and Brothers published it as *Moby-Dick*. The destruction of a ship by a sperm whale had been documented already by J. N. Reynolds in *The Knickerbocker Magazine* in 1839, when the whale had been called Mocha Dick – an albino giant carrying a scar on his great head from a previous attempt to kill him. Melville, while

A detail from 'Pêche du Cachalot', an aquatint after Garneray, 1850. Melville describes the incident in Chapter 56 of *Moby Dick*. National Maritime Museum.

serving on the whaler *Acushnet*, met a seaman whose father, Owen Chase, had been first mate on the *Essex*, which had been sunk by a whale in 1820.

'Call me Ishmael', one of the most famous openings in the history of the English novel, introduces the narrator, a sea-going boy who is alone in the world. He goes to New Bedford and signs on for a voyage on the whaler *Pequod*. He has to share a bed at the Spouter-Inn with the harpooner, whom he has not yet seen. When he does see him he is terrified by the knowledge that the harpooner has eaten human flesh: he is also hideously tattooed. But he finds that the harpooner, Queequeg, is much more than his exterior suggests and soon they become devoted comrades. He also discovers that Queequeg, a Polynesian, is a king's son. Before sailing, the two friends attend the seamen's chapel to get out of the rain and hear Father Mapple's sermon – a remarkable set piece by Melville.

The *Pequod*, commanded by Captain Ahab, sails on Christmas Day. Ahab is minus a leg – lost to the great white whale, Moby Dick. He pledges the crew to his own paranoia and the whaling voyage becomes transformed into Ahab's determination to conquer the whale. The principal characters are revealed in their reactions: the chief mate, Starbuck, a humane and experienced seaman, is repelled; the second mate, Stubb, takes life as it comes, even a captain with a fixation; Flask, the third mate, sees whales as creatures to be killed for a living, no more. The harpooners are Queequeg, the Indian Tashtego, and the magnificent Black man Daggoo, before whom a White man 'seemed a white flag come to

beg truce of a fortress'. The cabin boy, Pip, is also Black; he is the only one for whom Ahab seems to have any human feeling.

The voyage proceeds and the business of whaling is pursued. Pip is unbalanced by terror during a hunt, when the *Pequod* rams one of its own whaleboats. (The author, meanwhile, gives the reader a striking account of the creature it is the crew's business to kill.) Ahab pores over charts trying to guess the whereabouts of Moby Dick from the season's feeding grounds. Queequeg has a coffin made for himself; his people are buried in canoes and a coffin is a White man's 'canoe'. In the South Pacific Ahab learns from another whaler, the *Samuel Enderby*, that Moby Dick has been sighted; he sets off in a frenzied pursuit to which everything is sacrificed and which misfortune accompanies. The compass needle goes out of true; a man is lost overboard; another ship, the *Rachel*, has lost a boat and the captain's son is one of its crew – Ahab refuses to help in the search. Starbuck is tempted to kill Ahab for that. Pip, the half-mad cabin boy, begins to show the love he has always felt for the captain and almost elicits a response. But it is too late for Ahab; he pauses to reflect on his own actions and cannot understand them. Then he sights the great white whale.

Ahab is in the whaleboat on the first day of the chase. Moby Dick breaks it in two. On the second day the whale attacks the boats as soon as they move off from the ship. Ahab's boat is flung into the air by Moby Dick, who, in spite of harpoons in his flesh, simply surfaces below it; the captain's whalebone leg is snapped off. Ahab resumes the chase on the third day, in spite of Starbuck and the presence of sharks. Moby Dick surfaces, harpoon lines dangling from his great body and smashes the bows of the mate's boat. Ahab keeps to the hunt and the whale seems to wait for him. Ahab makes a strike – then Moby

Dick charges the *Pequod*, where the other boats are waiting, and smashes her sides. The ship begins to sink; Ahab's last cast is with a fouled line and the harpoon takes him with it. The *Pequod* goes to the bottom, taking the boats with her in the enormous suction. The only survivor is Ishmael, drifting in the sea after his whaleboat is smashed. He is drawn inexorably to the vortex but Queequeg's coffin shoots to the surface and he clings to that. He is rescued by the *Rachel*, which is still searching the ocean for the lost boat.

An outline of the narrative gives no hint of the riches to be found in Melville's great novel. Melville has hardly a rival (Conrad, perhaps) as a writer of the sea and on that level alone the book is magnificent. The ship and the seamen; the living and eternally moving oceans; the tiny creatures in small vessels who brave the element's surface to hunt one of its noblest creatures – all this is brought as close as a breath on the reader's face. The whales themselves are realized superbly; the great creatures have never been depicted with such care or the economics of the hunt in the 19th century examined so coolly. It has been stated that the narrative is halted arbitrarily so that Melville's exposition can be given room: but some of the power of the novel lies in the exposition, which contributes so much to the reader's understanding.

But *Moby-Dick* is more than a fine maritime adventure story, just as Ahab is far more than a glowering monomaniac. The book's action and setting provide a picture, in rich detail, of a world that, even as Melville wrote, was coming to an end. Ahab is a sea captain, wise in the ways of his craft and the element in which he moves, and the reader is kept aware of this. Ahab is a surprisingly humorous character, many-sided, like the book. He is aware of his obsession yet cannot defeat it; he is fond of Pip but refuses to accept the idea that the boy is fond of him because he cannot allow affection to interfere. Queequeg has been dismissed as another of the 'noble savages' of Melville's imagination but the criticism is shallow; Queequeg is different from the people Ishmael (Melville?) has known before and he *is* noble, and fearless – and original.

**Modern Chivalry,** *or the Adventures of Captain John Farrago and Teague O'Regan his Servant*. A novel by Hugh Henry Brackenridge, first published in instalments (1792–1815). A one-volume edition, edited by C. M. Newlin, was published in 1937. The novel has no real plot; it is a satirical account of episodes in the lives of two characters in the America which came into being when the War of Independence was won. Brackenridge's literary ancestors were Cervantes and Swift.

Captain John Farrago sets out with his servant, Teague O'Regan, from his farm in western Pennsylvania. The object of his journey is to observe his country and the life and manners of the time. Farrago is a democrat, part Jeffersonian but inclining to the ideas of Thomas Paine. O'Regan is a red-headed long-legged Irishman of no accomplishment whatever – but with a stupendous self-assurance that acts as a magnet to silly people. The character of O'Regan gives the author a fine mirror for his comments on the self-seeking opportunism and ham-fisted administration that he experienced during his legal career.

O'Regan moves higher and higher in society and is appointed collector of the excise tax on whisky (see also **Brackenridge, Hugh Henry**), which leads to his being tarred and feathered. In this condition he is captured as an exotic animal and examined by a Philosophical Society, which sends him to France. When he gets there O'Regan has lost most of his tar and feathers; he has also lost most of his breeches and the French welcome him as a 'sans-culotte'. When he returns to America Farrago has completed his journey and O'Regan joins him in the formation of a new frontier state. In this last section Brackenridge puts his ideas for the development of democracy into the mouth of Farrago, who has been considerably enlightened by what he has observed. The principal evil of society, he believes, is the aspiration to office for its own sake by men without the essential qualifications.

*Modern Chivalry* is hardly known nowadays but it was the first work of fiction which was essentially American, in spite of the influences which can be found in its construction. Backwoods life and the *tone* of life in what was largely a frontier state were presented for the first time in American fiction.

**Modern Love**   A sequence of 50 poems, each of 16 lines, by George Meredith, first published in 1862. It traces the decline of passion and the disintegration of a marriage as the result. Jealousy and discord fill the space left in two ill-suited lives, leading to tragedy after separation.

**Modern Painters**   John Ruskin wrote the first part of his treatise as an essay, *A Reply to Black-wood's Criticism of Turner*, in 1836. He extended his defence of Turner, wrote a counter-criticism of the aesthetic ignorance prevailing in England, and expounded his views of the principles of art. The first volume (1843) was published when Ruskin was 24. The second volume (1846) continues on the subject of the function of the imagination in art. The third volume (1856) begins with an essay on 'the Grand Style' and idealism and continues with the development of the appreciation of landscape painting in the history of the civilized world, beginning with the art of classical Greece. The volume concludes with an essay on the Crimean War. The fourth volume (also 1856) deals with colour, illumination, and natural forms (clouds, the movement of water, plant life) and contains the well-known passage on the church tower at Calais. The fifth and final volume (1860) continues the discussion of landscape and the four orders of landscape painting: Heroic, Classical, Pastoral, and Contemplative. Ruskin describes the Venice of Giorgione and the London of Turner, closing with a lament for Turner (who died in 1851).

*Modern Painters* was edited by L. Cust (Everyman's Library, 1907).

*Modest Proposal, A, for preventing the Children of Poor People from being a Burthen to their Parents, or the Country, and for making them Beneficial to the Publick.* A pamphlet by Jonathan Swift. First published in 1729, it is the most celebrated of Swift's protests against the treatment of Ireland by the English.

Swift knew better than anyone in England how appalling the condition of the Irish peasantry was; he knew also that during the suppression of Tyrone's rebellion and, indeed, more than once during the century past, the starving Irish had been reduced to cannibalism. His 'modest proposal', presented with chilling force in the blandest of reasonable voices, was quite simple: there were too many children, they had no future, so why not use them as food? 'Infants' Flesh will be in Season throughout the Year.' And if his proposal was adopted there would be no need to worry about the old or ill: '. . . they are every Day dying, and rotting, by Cold, and Famine, and Filth, and Vermin' in any case. His modest proposal would ensure that there would be no more of them. The targets are unmistakable: '. . . this food will be somewhat dear, and therefore very proper for landlords, who, as they have already devoured most of the Parents, seem to have the best Title to the Children.' 'Men would become as fond of their wives during the time of their pregnancy, as they are now of their mares in foal, their cows in calf, or sows when they are ready to farrow . . .'

The pamphlet is a masterpiece of controlled rage and in the modern world – exploding with people – it carries uncomfortable echoes.

**Moir, David Macbeth** 1798–1851. A Scots novelist who wrote much in the manner of his friend, John Galt. Moir was a doctor in Musselburgh and contributed regularly to *Blackwood's Magazine* and other periodicals, signing his work with the Greek capital, delta.

Moir's best-remembered book first appeared in parts in *Blackwood's* and was published in volume form in 1828. This was *The Life of Mansie Wauch, Tailor in Dalkieth*, an imaginary autobiography by a small-town tailor, which contains much wryly humorous observation. The book is dedicated to John Galt. A later edition, in 1839, was illustrated by Cruikshank.

Moir was a friend of Thomas De Quincey and probably discussed the effects of opium with him. He also published a history of medicine.

**Molesworth, Mary Louisa** 1839–1921. Mary Louisa Stewart married Major Richard Molesworth in 1861. She began to write after the loss of two of her children and published four novels for adults, now forgotten. She began to write for children at the suggestion of an artist friend, Sir Noel Paton, and found the level which suited her best. Later her talents were to be her family's support, since her husband had suffered a head wound in the Crimean War and his condition deteriorated as the years went by. She became so popular that Macmillan made a practice of publishing a book by Mrs Molesworth every Christmas, with illustrations by the best artists of the day. Swinburne accorded her the highest praise.

Mrs Molesworth wrote for young children; her work has, unlike that of many of her contemporaries, a lasting quality and can be read with pleasure by children today. She wrote no less than 101 books before she put down her pen in 1911. Among the best are *The Cuckoo Clock* (1877), *The Tapestry Room* (1879), *The Adventures of Herr Baby* (1881), *The Children of the Castle* (1890), *The Carved Lions* (1895), *Peterkin* (1902), *The Little Guest* (1907), and *The Story of a Year* (1910).

*Moll Flanders, The Fortunes and Misfortunes of the Famous* A novel by Daniel Defoe, first published in 1721. The title page of the first edition continues '&c. Who was born in Newgate, and during a life of continu'd Variety for Threescore Years, besides her Childhood, was Twelve Year a Whore, five times a Wife (whereof once to her own Brother), Twelve Year a Thief, Eight Year a Transported Felon in Virginia, at last grew Rich, liv'd Honest, and died a Penitent. Written from her own Memorandums.' For many scholars and readers *Moll Flanders* is Defoe's greatest novel. The text of the first edition is available in the excellent The World's Classics edition, which contains an introduction by Bonamy Dobrée.

Moll Flanders is born in Newgate prison, where her mother is under sentence of death on the gallows for 'having an opportunity of borrowing three pieces of fine holland of a certain draper in Cheapside.' The hanging is delayed because 'being found quick with child, she was respited for about seven months' and then her sentence is commuted to transportation to the Virginia plantations. The abandoned child is fortunate to be taken in by the mayoress of Colchester, from whom she passes to another gentlewoman who gives her an education; but the son of the house seduces her. She leads an adventurous love life and eventually marries. She visits Virginia with her husband and finds her mother – and discovers that her husband is in fact her brother. She leaves him and her children and goes back to England, where she falls among bad companions and eventually finds herself destitute.

Moll descends into the underworld. She becomes an expert and successful thief and for a while enjoys life; but inevitably she is caught and, like her mother, transported to Virginia. On the ship is one of her former husbands, who had been a highwayman, and they renew their liaison. Moll and her lover prosper in Virginia; she also inherits a plantation from her mother. When their sentence runs out, Moll and her husband return to England, where in comfort and serenity Moll looks back from the age of 70 over 'the wicked lives we have lived'.

It is not enough to say that *Moll Flanders* is a remarkable creation; she is that rare character, a completely realized one, and she exists in a setting that Defoe evoked better than anyone else. One of the most interesting things about her is the way she lives completely in the moment (that is one of the reasons for her survival) and keeps the reader's understanding – he may not approve but that is a different matter. And Moll does not tell us everything, as might be imagined from an outline of the narrative: she is all woman and tells us only what she wants us to know.

**Monastery, The**  A novel by Sir Walter Scott, first published in 1820. The setting is the monastery of Kennaquhair (based on Melrose Abbey) in the time of Elizabeth I.

An English knight, Sir Piercie Shafton, takes refuge in Scotland – he has been intriguing for the Catholic cause in England. The Abbot of Kennaquhair lodges him with his tenant, Simon Glendinning. The Glendinning sons are both in love with Mary Avenel, an orphan girl who is given a home by the kind and hospitable Simon. Edward is quiet and studious, Halbert is spirited and gallant; Mary prefers the latter.

Shafton, arrogant and vain, provokes Halbert who leaves him for dead after a duel. The White Lady of Avenel, a beneficent ghost, restores Shafton to life, and Halbert enters the service of the Earl of Murray, where he prospers. Mary marries Halbert and Edward becomes a monk.

The novel is one of Scott's least successful. The supernatural is a clumsy innovation, and the slight plot cannot carry the weight of the book. Scott's background characters – Abbot Boniface, and the reformer, Henry Warden – are more interesting than his lovers and their troubles.

**Monk, The**  A novel by M. G. ('Monk') Lewis, first published in 1796. The monk of the title is Ambrosio, superior of the Capuchins in Madrid and respected for his saintly life. A young and wanton noblewoman, Matilda de Villanegas, falls in love with him and, disguised as a boy, enters the abbey as a novice. She succeeds in corrupting him and after that his fall from grace is irreversible. He falls in love with one of his penitents and invokes evil forces to help gain his way with her. After rape he goes on to murder and is eventually discovered and handed over to

'Almighty God! – My mother!' Frontispiece engraving to Vol. III of the 1807 edition of *The Monk* by M. G. Lewis. The novel was first published in 1796.

the Inquisition. Following Matilda's example he bargains with Lucifer for his freedom; the Devil gets the best of it as usual, by transporting him to a desolate waste where freedom is all he will have. Ambrosio, too late, repents his wicked folly; Lucifer, enraged, hurls him against the rocks and leaves him to die. *The Monk*, one of the most famous gothic novels of the late 18th century, was notorious in its day for its strong sexual element, and an expurgated edition was issued in 1798 as *Ambrosio: or The Monk*. There is a modern edition by Howard Anderson (The World's Classics, 1981).

**Monk's Tale, The** See *Canterbury Tales, The.*

**Monmouth, Geoffrey of** *c.*1100–54. The son, it is believed, of Breton parents, Geoffrey was born at Monmouth and studied at Oxford. He probably became a Benedictine monk. His patron, Robert, Earl of Gloucester, may also have been his employer and Geoffrey became Archdeacon of either Monmouth or Llandaff by 1140. He was promoted to the see of St Asaph in 1152.

Geoffrey's *Historia Regum Britanniae*, probably completed by 1148, was in preparation as early as 1139. The *Prophetia Merlini* (*Merlin's Prophecies*) is the last of the seven books; the *Vita Merlini*, written in Latin hexameters, is attributed by some scholars to Geoffrey but his authorship is denied by others. The first six books were dedicated to Robert, Earl of Gloucester; the seventh to Alexander, Bishop of Lincoln.

The *Historia Regum Britanniae*, the most significant book of the 12th century, was being rejected as historical nonsense before the century ended; William of Newburgh, in the preface to his *Historia Rerum Anglicarum*, denounces Geoffrey in positive terms. But if Geoffrey did nothing for history he did a great deal for romance. He wanted to give life to the period before the Christian era, as well as to the dark periods after Christ, and was enabled to do so by means of an ancient book 'in the British tongue' which was given to him by Walter, Archdeacon of Oxford, who had brought it from Brittany. The epilogue to the *Historia* contains an impudent warning to other historians – he names William of Malmesbury and Henry of Huntingdon – not to try and write about the kings of ancient Britain: only he, who possessed the book from Brittany, possessed the knowledge. No amount of research has discovered the identity of the mysterious book, access to which seems to have been granted only to Geoffrey. He could have possessed Welsh documents which have not survived; British traditions were there for all, and

An illustration from Geoffrey of Monmouth's *Prophetia Merlini* in a 13th-century manuscript. Merlin, standing on a cloud, shows his prophecy to Vortigern. *MS Cotton Claudius B. VII, f.224.* British Library.

he certainly drew on Bede and Nennius. The result is prose romance rather than history: but it gives us Brutus (Brute) as the founder of the British race at Troynovant (London) and his successors, including Bladud, Lear, Gorboduc, Old King Cole (Coel), Cymbeline, Lud, and Vortigern. Most important of all he took the outlines of the story of Arthur and fashioned England's great romantic hero.

Geoffrey's *Historia* was translated into Anglo-Norman verse by Robert Wace of Jersey and Geoffrey Gaimar within a year of the author's death; Layamon, about fifty years later, gave us the stories in Middle English, having used Wace's French version. High romance is welcome in any age, and the tale of Arthur has continued to haunt the English imagination.

*Historia Regum Britanniae* was edited by J. A. Giles (1844). Modern translations are by C. W. Dunn (1958) and Lewis Thorpe (Penguin Classics, 1966): both are entitled *Geoffrey of Monmouth's History of the Kings of Britain.*

**Monro, Harold (Edward)** 1879–1932. Harold Monro was born in Brussels and educated in England at Radley School and at Cambridge. A poet himself, Monro launched *The Poetry Review* and opened his Poetry Bookshop in Bloomsbury in 1912. The Poetry Bookshop published the anthologies of contemporary verse edited by Edward Marsh and entitled *Georgian Poetry*. The bookshop became a meeting place and in some cases a haven for poets in all stages of their careers; Rupert Brooke, Robert Frost, and others gave readings and Charlotte Mew's poems were published there. Monro's generosity and catholic taste cost him a great deal of money and many aspirants had reason to be grateful to him. He also founded and edited *The Monthly Chapbook* (1919–25). Monro's *Collected Poems* (1933) was given a critical note by T. S. Eliot.

**Monroe, Harriet** 1860–1936. Born in Chicago, Harriet Monroe first attracted attention as a poet with her *Columbian Ode*, written for the World's Columbian Exposition in Chicago in 1892. She also published *Valeria and Other Poems* (1892), *You and I* (1914), and *Chosen Poems* (1935). Respected as a poet, her lasting contribution to English literature was her founding (1912) and editorship of *Poetry: A Magazine of Verse*, which gave positive encouragement to the new poetry that, in England, was to have a more difficult time getting off the ground. Her London editor was Ezra Pound, who directed T. S. Eliot to Harriet Monroe when her English near-namesake, Harold Monro, rejected Eliot's early work. Ezra Pound, T. S. Eliot, Carl Sandburg, H. D. (Hilda Doolittle), Edgar Lee Masters, Hart Crane, Robert Frost, and Edwin Arlington Robinson are some of the poets who owed much to Harriet Monroe. She wrote *A Poet's Life: Seventy Years in a Changing World* (1937), one of the best books on the Chicago school and the 20th-century revolution in literature.

*Monster, The: and Other Stories*. Short stories by Stephen Crane, first published in 1899.

The title story is set in Whilomville, a fictional small town in New York State, and concerns the characters which Stephen Crane also used in his *Whilomville Stories*. Dr Trescott's Black servant, Henry Johnson, rescues the doctor's son from death in a fire but Henry himself suffers terribly; he is badly disfigured and the balance of his mind is wrecked. The doctor and his family are the only refuge he has. The people of Whilomville display a collective lack of human sympathy; the 'monster' Henry Johnson has become fills them with revulsion and they slowly ostracize the doctor, his family, and his practice. Dr Trescott is ruined because he adheres to an ethical principle.

*The Blue Hotel* is a classic murder story which has been imitated scores of times. There is a quarrel at a bar in a small town in Nebraska and it leads directly to murder. The victim is both stupid and suspicious, while the perpetrator is morally innocent but goes to a penitentiary nevertheless. But why the murder should ever have happened is the point of the story; the author's analysis of the chain of events which lead to the quarrel in the bar show that the real cause is circumstance, which neither victim nor murderer could have escaped.

**Montagu, Elizabeth** 1720–1800. Elizabeth Robinson was the daughter of a Yorkshire family and married the grandson of the first Earl of Sandwich, Edward Montagu. In her houses in London, at Hill Street and Portman Square, she introduced the fashion for intellectual discussion as an alternative to the accepted diversion of card playing. She was immensely rich and her salon, a personal indulgence, was in rivalry with those of Mrs Vesey, Mrs Chapone, and other society ladies. Elizabeth Montagu was the original bluestocking and a gathering at her house is described in Boswell's *Life of Johnson*; Johnson admired her conversation. She published her *Essay on the Writings and Genius of Shakespeare* in 1769, in reply to Voltaire's strictures on the dramatist's work, and contributed the last three pieces in Lyttelton's *Dialogues of the Dead* (1760). Other frequenters of Elizabeth Montagu's salon were Edmund Burke, Joshua Reynolds, and William Wilberforce, and her correspondence is of considerable interest. It was published in two parts: E. J. Climenson's collection (1906) goes up to 1761; R. Blunt's (1923) from 1762 to 1800.

**Montagu, Lady Mary Wortley** 1689–1762. Lady Mary Pierrepoint, the eldest daughter of the 1st Duke of Kingston, was born in London. She received her education at home and was better taught than most of her contemporaries. In 1712, in the face of her father's opposition, she married Edward Wortley Montagu, who became English ambassador to Constantinople in 1716. At the time of their marriage Montagu was a Member of Parliament and after the accession of George I held various offices. He was a friend of Joseph Addison and the Montagus became well known in court and literary circles. Lady Mary's friendship with Alexander Pope probably began about this time.

The Montagus travelled to Constantinople by way of Vienna and Lady Mary stayed in Turkey until 1718. A keen observer and a lively correspondent, she took the trouble to learn Turkish and wrote letters home that gave a fascinating account of life in the Ottoman court. She also encountered the practice of inoculation against smallpox and introduced it, despite considerable opposition from the medical profession, to England, where she became a prominent figure in literary and intellectual circles. The quarrel with Pope, the reasons for which are not known, occurred about 1723; he was very spiteful about her in his verse more than once after that. Lady Mary, meanwhile, continued to be a lively correspondent, writing chiefly to her sister, Lady Mar, in Paris. In 1738, though still married to and on good terms with Montagu, she left England and went to live abroad. Her daughter had married Lord Bute and Lady Mary's letters from abroad are mostly addressed to Lady Bute; Lady Mar, her sister, was by this time tragically afflicted with melancholia.

Lady Mary lived in various places in France and Italy, including Avignon and Lago d'Iseo, until her return to England in 1762 at the persuasion of her daughter. She died at her daughter's house in the same year.

The author of some spirited verse pictures of contemporary society called *Town Eclogues* (1716) and *Court Poems by a Lady of Quality* (also 1716), as well as occasional verses and a handful of essays, Lady Mary Wortley Montagu earned a place in English literature with her letters, the first collection of which was published in 1763, the year after her death. *Letters during Mr Wortley's Embassy to Constantinople* was followed by another volume in 1767. The definitive collection is by Robert Halsband, *The Complete Letters of Lady Mary Wortley Montagu* (three volumes, 1965–67). Halsband's biography, *The Life of Lady Mary Wortley Montagu*, was published in 1956.

**Montague**  The Veronese family of Shakespeare's *Romeo and Juliet*, enemies of the Capulets. Romeo is a Montague.

*Montcalm and Wolfe*  See **Parkman, Francis** and *France and England in North America*.

**Montgomerie, Alexander**  *c*.1545–*c*.1611. Montgomerie was related to the Earls of Eglintoun on his father's side; through his mother, who was Lady Margaret Fraser, he was related to James VI, who became his patron in 1577. Montgomerie was brought up in Calvinist beliefs but became a Catholic, probably after a visit to Spain. This did him no harm at the court of James, especially after the king, smarting at the humiliation of being kidnapped by Protestant lords in 1582, reassembled his court with a careful counterbalance to the Protestant faction. Montgomerie seems to have stayed in favour with the king until about 1584, turning out sonnets that pleased and receiving money from the see of Glasgow which, for the time being, was in the possession of the Duke of Lennox, the king's

cousin. In 1586 he went abroad and became involved in unsuccessful Catholic plots, one of which involved the capture of Ailsa Craig as a base for a Spanish invasion. He is believed to have died, or been killed, about 1611 but the possibility exists that he found sanctuary with the Scottish Benedictines.

Montgomerie wrote 70 sonnets, translated 'certayne Psalmes of the kinglie próphete David', and amused King James with *The Flytting betwixt Montgomerie and Polwart*. (Flytting or flyting was a sort of poetic contest, as old as the Celtic bards. Polwart was Sir Patrick Hume of Polwart, Montgomerie's rival.) He is best remembered for *The Cherrie and the Slaye* (sloe), a poem of 114 quatorzains (14-line verses), which once enjoyed great popularity in Scotland and was translated into Latin. The earliest text is dated 1597. The cherry represents the fruits of heaven, the sloe the tart but easily accessible Reformed religion – Montgomerie's heaven was a Catholic one and much harder to attain. The poet uses allegory but not the dream-allegory so familiar in the work of his predecessors; the debate is an internal one and the voices of Courage, Hope, Dread, Despair, Reason, Wisdom, and the rest all have their say. The poet attains his heaven and voices some sharp criticism of his former royal patron by the way.

Montgomerie's poems were edited by J. Cranstoun in 1887 and a supplementary volume edited by G. Stevenson followed in 1910. Both were published by the Scottish Texts Society.

**Montgomery, L(ucy) M(aud)**  1874–1942. L. M. Montgomery was born and educated on Prince Edward Island in eastern Canada. She became a teacher and enjoyed a modest success with contributions to periodicals; later she married Ewen Macdonald, a Presbyterian minister, and settled in Toronto. *Anne of Green Gables* (1908), her first book for girls, was an immediate success. It began as a serial for a Sunday school paper; Mrs Macdonald, the minister's wife, was asked to write something for it and she drew on memories of her girlhood and schooldays on Prince Edward Island. She repeated her success with *Anne of Avonlea* (1909) and became a worldwide favourite with girls with a series of books in the same vein.

*Mont Saint-Michel and Chartres*  A study by Henry Brooks Adams, first printed privately in 1904 and published in 1913. The book is subtitled *A Study in 13th Century Unity* and is one of the aspects of civilization that the author uses to illustrate his philosophy of history. (The other is found in *The Education of Henry Adams*.) The exact period of this study is 1150–1250, when Adams believed that western man 'held the highest idea of himself as a unit in a unified universe'. Faith informed everything, not only religion but also the arts and philosophy, and the author takes as his starting point the 12th-century Norman architecture of Mont St Michel. The period closes with the completion of the great gothic cathedral of Chartres in sight; the Virgin of Chartres is the symbol of unity of religion and intuition with reason and science. The unity begins to disintegrate with the coming of St Thomas Aquinas and his system of metaphysics, which insisted that reason must be applied to religion.

**Moody, William Vaughn** 1869–1910. The playwright and poet was born in Indiana and educated at Harvard, from where he graduated in 1893. He taught English at Harvard and at the University of Chicago. Moody's first published work was a poetic drama, *The Masque of Judgment* (1900); its theme was the conflict that must arise between the rightful exercise of man's free will and the obedience that he owes to an acknowledged God. His next work was a volume of lyrics, *Poems* (1901), which contains some powerful comments on the exercise of power; two of the poems are often to be found in anthologies, 'Gloucester Moors' and 'An Ode in Time of Hesitation'. A second poetic drama, *The Fire Bringer* (1904), has the story of Prometheus as its theme and a third, which would have made a trilogy on the aspirations and destiny of man, was left unfinished when Moody died at the age of 41. The third play was *The Death of Eve*; here the theme was the reconciliation of God and man through the creation of woman. No part of the trilogy has ever been produced. However, Moody's play *A Sabine Woman* (1906) was produced as *The Great Divide*, achieving enormous success in New York. It was staged in London in 1909, the year when Moody's *The Faith Healer* was first produced.

Moody's short career was of considerable importance to the American theatre. For some time it had existed on adaptations from fiction and imported works and was in need of more serious work from native writers. *The Great Divide* contrasts the attitude of a woman brought up with the inhibitions of a puritan background with the freethinking pragmatism of a frontier man. *The Faith Healer* was less successful. The play deals with a more exalted subject: the effect of earthly love on a faith healer. Love deprives the faith healer of his powers; he only recovers them when he sublimates his personal love for

the broader mission as a healer in a world that needs him.

**Moon and Sixpence, The** See **Maugham, W(illiam) Somerset**.

**Moonstone, The** A novel by Wilkie Collins, first published in *All the Year Round* (January to November 1868).

At the siege of Seringapatam an English officer, John Herncastle, steals a great diamond from the forehead of an image of the moon god, killing the three Brahmins who guard it.

On her 18th birthday, according to the dispositions of a will, the moonstone is given to Rachel Verinder. It is stolen that same night. Rachel's lover, Franklin Blake, takes it from her cabinet while under the influence of opium. She sees him take it, but while she doesn't want him charged neither does she want any more to do with him. The moonstone has disappeared – but Blake has no knowledge of his theft, and he hasn't got it. Three Indians, purporting to be jugglers, have been seen near the house. Sergeant Cuff (one of the first detectives in English fiction) takes part in solving the mystery.

Blake's rival for the affections of Rachel Verinder, Godfrey Ablewhite, had taken the moonstone from the unconscious Blake, then he found the three Indian 'jugglers' on his track. At the resolution of the mystery, Ablewhite is murdered, the moonstone is recovered by its rightful owners, and all's well between Miss Verinder and Blake.

**Moore, Edward** 1712–57. The third son of a dissenting minister, Moore was born at Abingdon in Berkshire. Fatherless at the age of ten, he became the ward of an uncle, John Moore, a schoolmaster of Bridgwater in Somerset, and was apprenticed to a London linen draper. He followed the same trade when he came of age, without much success, and turned to writing. *Fables for the Female Sex* (1744) contained contributions by Henry Brooke and enjoyed a modest success; Brooke also contributed the prologue to Moore's first essay in drama, *The Foundling* (Drury Lane, February 1747). *The Foundling* was a comedy and it was not well received; *Gil Blas* (Drury Lane, February 1751) was based on episodes from Le Sage and did better, and Moore enjoyed a real success with *The Gamester* (Drury Lane, February 1753), though David Garrick brought his considerable experience to help make it stageworthy.

Through the influence of Lord Lyttelton, Moore became editor of *The World* in 1753; this was a weekly journal which satirized current society and boasted contributions from Lord Chesterfield and Horace Walpole. The journal thrived until Moore was forced, through ill health, to relinquish the editorship. He died in London at the age of 45, and his son, Edward, became the ward of Lord Chesterfield.

*The Gamester* followed the trend set by George Lillo in offering domestic tragedy in prose. However, no playwright had yet discovered how to convey feeling and emotion without using inflated language and no one should look for the natural language of the time in plays like this. Nevertheless, the trend was there and the play was to influence the development of drama. *The Gamester* is a tragedy with the consequences of Beverley's hopeless addiction to the gaming table as its theme. Henry Fielding's *Amelia*, published two years before, had explored the same subject.

**Moore, George Augustus** 1852–1933. George Moore was born at Ballyglass in Mayo, the son of an Irish MP who was also the proprietor of a racing stable. He was educated at Oscott College in Birmingham and intended for a career in the army; but his father died when he was 18 and that enabled him to follow his inclinations towards a career in the arts. He spent ten years in Paris, studying painting but being drawn more and more towards literature. He went to live in London in 1880, where he published poems, plays, essays, his autobiography *Confessions of a Young Man* (1888), and seven realistic novels which clearly displayed the influence of Zola: *A Modern Lover* (1883), *A Mummer's Wife* (1885), *A Drama in Muslin* (1886), *A Mere Accident* (1887), *Spring Days* (1888), *Mike Fletcher* (1889), and *Vain Fortune* (1891). He achieved a major success with *Esther Waters* (1894), generally acknowledged as his finest work.

Moore's knowledge of painting led him to become art critic of *The Speaker* and he published *Modern Painting* in 1893. He opposed the Boer War and returned to Ireland in 1899. He had been brought up as a Catholic and educated as one; he now became a Protestant and was caught up in the Irish cultural revival, particularly in the growing pains of the Irish National Theatre. The years in Ireland are the subject of the trilogy of reminiscence called *Hail and Farewell* (1911–14): it first appeared as *Ave* (1911), *Salve* (1912), and *Vale* (1914). Some of the people recalled in Moore's pages were annoyed by the book but it stands high among 20th-century autobiographies and is a delight to read. Among other works published in the years between publication of *Esther Waters* and 1911, when Moore returned to

'George Moore au Café' by Edouard Manet, 1879.

London, were two collections of stories, *Celibates* (1895) and *The Untilled Field* (1903); the novels *Evelyn Innes* (1898) and *Sister Theresa* (1901); and *Reminiscences of the Impressionist Painters* (1906).

In London Moore went to live in Ebury Street, near Victoria Station, and made it his home for the rest of his life, acquiring a reputation as a literary sage. His later stage as a writer began with the elaborate and painstaking **The Brook Kerith** (1916), a novel about Jesus. Among other works of this period were the short stories *A Story-teller's Holiday* (1918); the essays *Conversations in Ebury Street* (1924); a translation from the Greek, *Daphnis and Chloe* (1924); the novels *Héloïse and Abélard* (1921) and *Aphrodite in Aulis* (1930); and the plays *The Making of an Immortal* (1927) and *The Passing of the Essenes* (1930), which was a revised version of the earlier *The Apostle* (1911).

**Moore, Julia A.** 1847–1920. 'The Sweet Singer of Michigan' was a lady who published a book of bad verse called *The Sweet Singer of Michigan Salutes the Public* in 1876 and another, *A Few Words to the Public with New and Original Poems*, in 1878. People read the verse because it was famously bad – rather like the trendy popularity that was earned, posthumously, by the work of William McGonagall in England during the 1960s.

**Moore, Marianne (Craig)** 1887–1972. Marianne Moore was born in St Louis, Missouri, and educated at Bryn Mawr. She became a shorthand teacher and then worked in the New York Public

Library (1921–25). During this period her poems were published in the English magazine *Egoist*, and her first collection, *Poems* (1921), was selected from the magazine without her knowledge. She prepared the second, *Observations* (1924), herself. T. S. Eliot introduced her *Selected Poems* (1935), which was followed by *The Pangolin and Other Verse* (1936), *What Are Years?* (1941), and *Nevertheless* (1944). Her *Collected Poems* (1951) won her a Pulitzer Prize. Her poetry is marked by an unconventional but disciplined use of metrics and a cerebral ironic attitude. 'Melancthon' is a characteristic example of her work. Later books by Marianne Moore are her verse translation, *The Fables of La Fontaine* (1954), and the collections of verse, *Like a Bulwark* (1956), *O To Be a Dragon* (1959), *The Arctic Fox* (1964), and *Tell Me, Tell Me* (1966). She was editor of *The Dial* from 1925 to 1928.

**Moore, Thomas** 1779–1852. Thomas Moore, a grocer's son, was born in Dublin. He was educated at Whyte's School, and took advantage of a slight relaxation of the laws against Catholics to enter Trinity College, Cambridge, where he first began to write verse. In 1799 Moore went to London to study law at the Middle Temple, and published his first work in the following year: *Odes of Anacreon Translated into English verse, with Notes* (1800). A volume of amorous verses, *The Poetical Works of the Late Thomas Little, Esq* (1801), were full of a young man's improprieties and he revised them later; the title refers to Moore himself, a small man.

He was, meanwhile, a remarkable success in London. He possessed a sweet singing voice and considerable charm and was welcome everywhere; his poetry was popular and widely read. In 1803 he was appointed Admiralty Registrar in Bermuda; but he lightheartedly left his deputy in charge and took the opportunity to travel in Canada and the United States, returning to England during 1804. He was later to regret his negligence. *Epistles, Odes and Other Poems* (1806) was severely criticized by Francis Jeffrey in *The Edinburgh Review*; rather more for its moral tone than for its literary quality. Moore was furious but the review did no harm to his sales and he not only became a contributor to the review but was later offered the editorship.

Moore published *Corruption and Intolerance: Two Poems with Notes, addressed to an Englishman by an Irishman* in 1808; but serious satire was not within his range. He was later to do quite well with light satire in *Intercepted Letters; or The Twopenny Post Bag, by Thomas Brown the Younger* (1813); meanwhile he was preparing the work which proved his most enduring and secured his reputation during his lifetime. The ten parts of *A Selection of Irish Melodies* were published from 1808 to 1834. Moore had a keen instinct for the taste of a public wealthy enough to afford a piano and scores, and likely to enjoy a comfortable sentimental view of Ireland. An example of his judgment is 'The Last Rose of Summer'. The original air was used by R. A. Millikin in the late 18th century for his song 'The Groves of Blarney'; but it was old even then and had originally belonged to a song called 'Castle Hyde'. Thomas Moore's version was purloined by the German composer Flotow for his opera, *Martha* (1847) and it became famous the world over. (Flotow, incidentally, never acknowledged the origin of his celebrated aria.) The accompaniments of Moore's songs were arranged chiefly by Sir John Stevenson, and the lyrics were published separately in 1821.

Moore became Byron's friend after the latter returned to England from the eastern Mediterranean in 1811 and the friendship endured. In December 1814 the publisher Longman commissioned Moore to write a romantic poem. Scott's *Rokeby* had been published the year before and Longman wanted something of the same length and hoped for a similar success. *Lalla Rookh; an Oriental Romance* was not only romantic but exotic, and Byron had already created a large public for such a combination. Moore certainly earned the enormous sum of £3000 which Longman paid him. *The Fudge Family in Paris, edited by Thomas Brown the Younger* (1818) continued the vein of light satire which Moore had successfully exploited in 1813.

In 1819 Moore's deputy in Bermuda misappropriated £6000, and the responsibility fell on Moore himself. He left England with Lord John Russell for a visit to Italy and stayed away until the debt to the Admiralty was paid, returning in 1822. *The Loves of the Angels* was published in 1823 and was financially as successful as *Lalla Rookh*, though an inferior work. Like the earlier poem it used an exotic eastern original as its basis.

While in Italy Moore spent some time with Byron in Venice. Byron had written his memoirs and he entrusted the manuscript to Thomas Moore. After Byron's death in 1824 his publisher, John Murray, and Byron's conventional and possessive friend John Cam Hobhouse persuaded Moore to agree to the destruction of the memoirs which were burned in the fireplace of Murray's drawing-room at Albemarle Street. Moore has been severely criticized by posterity and certainly many vexing questions about Byron's personal life will never be answered. But it should be remembered that Moore could have made a great deal of money from the publication of the memoirs; that he probably understood Byron far better than did the circumspect Hobhouse or Murray – a hardheaded businessman who was doing very well out of Byron's works; and that the English public, who would have devoured 'scandalous' disclosures about Lord Byron, might have suffered a severe fit of morality as a result. As it was, Moore served his friend's memory very well in *Letters and Journals of Lord Byron, with Notices of his Life* (1830). Macaulay declared that 'it deserves to be classed among the best specimens of English prose which our age has produced.'

Other works by Moore include his lives of Sheridan (1825) and Lord Edward Fitzgerald (1831); a novel, **The Epicurean** (1827); *The Fudges in England* (1835), and *The History of Ireland* (1835–46). He remained a celebrated and popular figure for the rest of his life, and he was awarded a Civil List pension in 1850, when his mental powers began to fade. His married life was happy (Bessie Dyke was a pretty actress he met in 1811) and he seems to have been liked by everyone. Though not a great poet he was a fine songster, and is worth cherishing for that.

*The Memorials, Journal and Correspondence of Thomas Moore* was edited by Lord John Russell (eight volumes, 1853–56).

**Moore, Thomas Sturge** 1870–1944. Moore, the brother of the Cambridge philosopher G. E. Moore, was born at Hastings in Sussex. Indifferent health brought his schooling to an early end but he succeeded as a wood engraver and later became an art historian, publishing studies of painters: *Albrecht Altdorfer* (1900), *Albrecht Dürer* (1905), *Correggio* (1906), and *Charles Ricketts* (1933). He became a close friend of W. B. Yeats and designed the covers of some of Yeats's volumes of poetry. Moore also wrote poetry, much of it on classical themes, that was cordially received by the critics but generally ignored by the public. *The Poems of T. Sturge Moore* contained most of his work (four volumes, 1931–33).

**Moral and Political Philosophy, The Principles of** William Paley's exposition, which was published in 1785, is indebted to Abraham Tucker's *The Light of Nature Pursued*. Paley systematized the principles of Tucker's immense and diffuse book and presented them with order and clarity. Paley's presentation of theological utilitarianism is firmly grounded in the Christian religion and his ethical system requires the ac-

knowledgment of rewards and penalties after life. His skill as an expositor made his book very widely read in academic circles for a number of years.

*Moral Essays* Four poems by Alexander Pope, written in the form of epistles. The use of ethical questions as material for verse was inspired by the poet's friend, Lord Bolingbroke. The first epistle was addressed to Lord Burlington, *Of the Use of Riches* (1731); the second, addressed to Lord Bathurst, was also called *Of the Use of Riches* and extended the theme (1732); the third, addressed to Lord Cobham, was called *Of the Knowledge and Characters of Men* (1733). The fourth epistle, *Of the Characters of Women*, was published in 1735 and was very rude about Lady Mary Wortley Montagu, who appears as 'Sappho'; it was addressed to Pope's friend Martha Blount.

**morality plays** The morality plays of the late Middle Ages were to some degree plays about Man, while the mystery plays were celebrations of God in the life and death of Jesus; the tone of the pulpit informed the morality play while the mystery play drew its inspiration from the liturgy. The form of the morality play was usually allegorical, with abstractions such as Mercy and Justice representing the forces which opposed others such as Envy and Lust in the progress of Man through life. The earliest morality play of which we have any knowledge from records is the *Pater Noster* play, which may have been the work of John Wycliffe and was performed at York. The earliest manuscript we possess, of a morality called *The Pride of Life*, is imperfect and may date back as far as the end of the 14th century. The most remarkable collection is *The Macro Plays* (so called after the former owner of the manuscripts) and may have come from the Abbey of Bury St Edmunds. The three plays in the collection are *Mankynde* (*c*.1473), *Wisdom, who is Christ* (*c*.1460), and the earliest and most elaborate, *The Castell of Perseverance* (*c*.1425). The most famous morality belongs to the whole of western Europe: **Everyman** (1495) was an English version of the Dutch *Elckerlijk*. It enjoyed a new fame in the German verse translation, *Jedermann* by Hugo von Hofmannsthal (1911), and this became the opening item of the Salzburg Festival each year in Max Reinhardt's celebrated production.

The morality play did not die with the Middle Ages – indeed examples abound right up to 1550; but by then the form had become flexible enough to be used for satire and comedy and for abstraction to give way to character.

***Morall Fabillis of Esope the Phrygian, The*** A version of the fables which, during the Middle Ages, were attributed to Aesop, written in rhyme-royal by Robert Henryson. The first printed edition is dated 1570. The classical basis of the work was much used and familiar but Henryson's version keeps story and moral separate, and the didactic element, obtrusively strong in other versions, does not spoil the tale. Another notable factor in Henryson's version is his familiarity with nature and his sharp observation of country life.

***Morals and Legislation, Introduction to the Principles of*** Jeremy Bentham's exposition of his theory of Utility applied to ethics and politics was written and printed for private circulation in 1780. It was first published in 1789.

Bentham goes directly to the matter for discussion: that the interests of the individual and the interests of the community are sometimes at variance and the problems for the application of the law lie in this divergence. 'Nature has placed mankind under the governance of two sovereign masters, pain and pleasure.' They 'point out what we ought to do, as well as determine what we shall do. On the one hand the standard of right and wrong, on the other the chain of causes and effects' are immutable; 'They govern us in all we do, in all we say, in all we think . . .' The standard by which the worth of a law is measured is 'The principle of Utility', which also recognizes the subjection of man to the immutable standards, 'and assumes it for the foundation of that system the object of which is to rear the fabric of felicity by the hands of reason and of law'. The true purpose of law and education should be to make sufficiently strong inducements for the individual to subordinate his own happiness to that of the community.

**Mordred** The name is given thus in Malory's *Le Morte Darthur* but is encountered as Modred in some versions of the stories. He is Arthur's son by his incestuous union with his half-sister Morgause, Queen of Orkney, and one of the knights who surprises Launcelot and Guenever in their guilty love. He attempts to usurp the kingdom in Arthur's absence and tries to force Guenever to be his wife. He falls in the final battle when Arthur is also mortally wounded.

Mordred, like Gawain, can be identified in Welsh mythology in which he is Medrawt, a god of darkness.

**More, Hannah** 1745–1833. The youngest of five sisters, Hannah More was born at Stapleton in Gloucestershire; her father was a schoolmaster and her sisters kept a boarding school in Bristol. At her sisters' school Hannah received an excellent education, learning Spanish and Italian as well as French and Latin. She acquired material independence through the prevarication of a Mr Turner, to whom she was engaged at the age of 22. Turner never got as far as marrying her; eventually he settled £200 a year on her and went his way. Her first publication was a pastoral play for schools, *The Search after Happiness* (1773), and she went to London in the following year. Hannah More was fortunate in making an impression on Joshua Reynolds and his sister, and through them in finding an entrée into London literary society – Johnson, Garrick, Walpole – and the bluestocking salons of ladies like Elizabeth Montagu. Her particular friends in London were the Garricks; Miss More's comments on the great man's acting were obviously the right ones, and her tragedy, *Percy*, was produced by Garrick in 1777. She was the author of poems, religious tracts, and a didactic novel, *Coelebs in Search of a Wife* (1808). The movement from drama and poetry into works concerned with ethical principles came after the death of Garrick, which affected her deeply, and she was remarkably successful. The Religious Tract Society was formed to continue her work and she was a tireless helper in Wilberforce's anti-slavery campaign. She continued her philanthropic work, aided by her sisters and her income from her writings, after she retired to Bristol. Her correspondence with her distinguished friends continued and is the principal reason that she is remembered; her other work has not stood the test of time. Hannah More's selected *Letters* were edited by R. B. Johnson and published in 1925.

**More, Henry** 1614–87. A prominent Cambridge Platonist, Henry More was born at Grantham, Lincolnshire, and was educated at Eton College and Christ's College, Cambridge. He became a fellow of his college in 1639, and stayed there for the rest of his life, refusing the offers of rich preferments made after he received holy orders. More's family tended to Calvinism; More himself remained a steadfast supporter of the Church of England and was Royalist in sympathy during the Civil War. Like his fellow Platonist Cudworth he opposed the materialism of Thomas Hobbes, and eventually rejected the philosophy of René Descartes for the same reason. More was an industrious writer, expounding his ideas in both verse and prose. *Psychozoia Platonica* (1642) was enlarged and included in *Philosophical Poems* (1647) as *A Platonick Song of the Soul. An Antidote against Atheism*

(1652); *Enthusiasmus Triumphatus* (1656), an effective denunciation of Puritan 'enthusiasms' (extravagant claims for their faith and religious practices) and *The Immortality of the Soul* (1659) are amongst his works. More was a writer of considerable quality but his work does not have wide appeal. The Cambridge Platonists are, inevitably, of more interest to students of 17th-century philosophy and religious controversy than to lovers of English literature.

**More, Thomas** 1478–1535. The son of a London lawyer, Sir John More, who later became a judge, Thomas More was brought up in the household of Cardinal Morton, where he served as a page, and educated at St Anthony's School. At the age of 14 he entered Canterbury Hall, Oxford (later incorporated into Christ Church) and there began the study of the classics to which he was devoted all his life. He began to study law in 1494 and was called to the bar in 1501, living meanwhile among the austere Carthusians of London, testing his religious vocation. He apparently found himself wanting; the law was to be his career.

More entered Parliament in 1504 and married in 1505. His home in Chelsea became a centre of intellectual life; he had been a friend of Erasmus since 1499 and had learned Greek from William Grocyn; Holbein was his guest, John Colet was another friend. In Parliament he successfully opposed the financial demands of Henry VII in 1504, and with the accession of Henry VIII in 1509 began his brilliant public career. He became Under-Sheriff of London in 1510 and soon attracted the king's attention; he was sent on a diplomatic mission to Flanders in 1515 (he completed Book II of *Utopia* there), and became Privy Councillor and Master of Requests in 1518. He accompanied Henry to the Field of the Cloth of Gold and was knighted in the following year (1521). The king's favour seemed to be limitless: his friend and counsellor became Speaker of the House of Commons (1523), Chancellor of the Duchy of Lancaster (1525), and finally Lord Chancellor to succeed Wolsey in 1529. Thomas More was now 51; his first wife, Margaret Colt, had died in 1511 and he had married Alice Middleton in the same year.

In spite of the intellectual climate of his Chelsea home, and his brilliant career, More's life was disciplined and his religious convictions remained unshakable. The company of distinguished friends all shared the conviction that reforms were sorely needed in the church; it fell to More and the old and frail John Fisher to be witnesses on behalf of that church. Henry VIII, anxious

about the future of the dynasty, found his wife of 20 years, Katherine of Aragon, an encumbrance; there was no male heir and Katherine was now 44. Henry, who was opposed to Luther's Reformation, found his wishes for a 'legitimate' divorce thwarted at every turn. Katherine herself was immovable; her nephew was the Emperor Charles V and the pope, Clement VII, preferred to stay on the strongest side – the emperor's. Henry, after years of fruitless negotiations that brought about Wolsey's downfall, eventually repudiated papal authority. The king became head of the Church in England in 1531. Cranmer became Archbishop of Canterbury and proceeded in accordance with the king's wishes. Henry's marriage was declared invalid in 1533 and he married Anne Boleyn five days later.

More resigned his chancellorship in 1532 and lost nearly the whole of his income in doing so. He had opposed Martin Luther, but he also opposed Henry in the matter of his divorce. In 1534 he refused to take the oath on the Act of Succession, which made Henry's and Anne's children the legitimate heirs to the crown, and was imprisoned in the Tower. He remained there for 15 months, until a charge of treason was brought against him on 1 July 1535 for having opposed the Act of Supremacy (1534), which made the

Thomas More. The portrait by Holbein. Royal Library, Windsor Castle.

king head of the Church. More was beheaded on Tower Hill on 6 July, 14 days after John Fisher's death and on the same spot. He was canonized by the Catholic Church in 1936.

The young Thomas More wrote some English verse, including a Lamentation on the death of Elizabeth, Henry VII's queen, the humorous poem 'How a Sergeaunt wolde lerne to be a frere', and the verses for the *Book of Fortune*. The famous **Utopia** (1516) was written in Latin but has found a place as a classic book in English literature, unlike the controversial writings in the same language that were directed against Luther and William Tyndale. On the same theme was his *Dialogue* (1528), written in English and dealing with the author's handling of an imagined Messenger who presents the case for Luther. The *Historia Ricardi Tertii* (1514) is a history of the reign of Richard III, which no doubt pleased his Tudor king and may owe something to More's early association with Cardinal Morton. More began an English version, which remained unfinished by him, but the complete **History of King Richard III** can now be read in English and its influence on Shakespeare's play is obvious. Less well known are his *Lyfe of Johan Picus, Erle of Myrandula* (1510) – a biography of Pico della Mirandola, the Italian humanist and philosopher, which is rather more concerned with the man's ideals than with his life – and a series of books providing further opposition to Tyndale, at the request of the Bishop of London, including *The Supplycacyon of Soulys* (1529), *A Confutacyon of Tyndale's Answere* (1532), *The Debellacyon of Salem and Byzance* (1533), and *The Answere of the Poysoned Book*.

In the shadow of the scaffold More wrote **A Dialoge of Comfort against Tribulacion** (published posthumously in 1553) in the form of a conversation between two Hungarians who see the possibility of death at the hands of the advancing Turks. This is regarded as his noblest work, the mind of a warm and generous man expressing, in the finest prose of his time, the expectation of dreadful pain and his thoughts on how he could prepare to face it. (The punishment for the charge on which More was condemned was barbarous. He would have been hanged and quartered after being dragged to the scaffold. But the king allowed him, in the end, to die by the axe.) The subject is grim, and the reader is never unaware of the ordeal in the writer's mind; but More did not earn generous tributes from Erasmus for nothing. The *Dialoge* also discloses a man of humour and kindness. Of less value is the *Treatise on the Passion*, which was completed from More's Latin text by his daughter, Margaret Roper.

Memoirs of Thomas More were written by his son-in-law, William Roper, and by Nicholas Harpsfield. These were published by the Early English Text Society in 1932 (Harpsfield) and 1935 (Roper) in editions prepared by E. V. Hitchcock. A highly regarded modern biography is *Thomas More* by R. W. Chambers (1935). More's *Complete Works*, in 14 volumes, are being published by Yale University Press (begun in 1965).

**More, Sir Thomas** A play that has been dated *c.* 1595 but for which there is no evidence of production. A manuscript exists and is preserved in the British Museum and the play's great interest lies in the identification of Shakespeare's handwriting and the proof of his contribution to a play by many hands – the others are Anthony Munday, Henry Chettle, Thomas Heywood, and Thomas Dekker.

The play is based on the main events of More's life, well chronicled by this date, from his rise to favour, through his friendship with Erasmus and the opposition to the king, to his fall and death on the scaffold. Henry VIII does not appear in the play. There has been no professional production of *Sir Thomas More*, which is regarded as the best of the Shakespeare apocrypha. It was first published in 1844.

**Morgan, William (Frend) de** 1839–1917. William de Morgan was an artist in ceramics and stained glass whose work is highly regarded nowadays, particularly by those with a special interest in art nouveau. He did not, as an artist, prosper greatly during his lifetime but made a new career, at the age of 67, as a novelist with the publication of *Joseph Vance* (1906). He went on to write seven more books and many readers found them rewarding, with their echoes of the style of Trollope and Dickens. He is often dismissed as no more than a name for the records but *Joseph Vance* was issued in The World's Classics in 1954, with an excellent introduction by A. C. Ward. Other novels were *Alice-for-Short* (1907), *It Can Never Happen Again* (1909), and *A Likely Story* (1911).

**Morgan le Fay** In the Arthurian cycle a strange equivocal figure regarded by some mythographers as an aspect of Nimue and the Lady of the Lake. In one version of the story of Arthur it is she who tells him of Guenever's love for Launcelot. Generally she is an enchantress possessing dark powers – Morgan le Fée – and is Arthur's enemy. Yet in some versions it is Morgan who takes Arthur to Avalon to be healed of his wounds after the last battle. To the 12th-century chronicler Giraldus Cambrensis, writing of Arthur, Morgan was a noble woman of the region (of Glastonbury) who arranged for her kinsman Arthur to be taken to Avalon (Glastonbury) to be tended after the final battle at Camlan. She is Arthur's sister in *Le Morte Darthur*, and still possesses the magical powers with which she must originally have been endowed in early romance and mythology. Her strange presence as one of the three ladies who comes to take the dying Arthur away in a ship, identifies her firmly as a figure from the pre-Christian tradition.

Malory's Morgan le Fay, Arthur's sister, is married to King Uriens. She tries to kill Arthur with the help of Sir Accolon, her lover, stealing Arthur's sword Excalibur to help him. Then she can kill Uriens without opposition and take Accolon as her consort. Her designs are frustrated by the Lady of the Lake and Uriens' son Uwaine. Accolon is killed and Morgan flees to her own country, and in one last attempt on Arthur's life sends him a magnificent cloak; but the Lady of the Lake, once more, warns him that it will kill him if he wears it – it is poisoned, like the one devised by Medea in Greek mythology.

Morgan le Fay appears as Morgana in Ariosto's *Orlando Furioso* and in Boiardo's *Orlando Innamorato* as well as in *Ogier the Dane*, one of the stories of the Charlemagne cycle. In Irish myth she is the Morrigan, the goddess of death.

**Moriarty, Professor** In Sir Arthur Conan Doyle's Sherlock Holmes stories (up to 1893), the great detective's principal adversary. He perishes in the Reichenbach Falls in Switzerland in *The Final Problem* and takes Holmes with him on his fall to death.

**Morier, James** *c.*1780–1849. The son of the Consul General of the Levant Company, James Morier was born at Smyrna. He was educated at Harrow and returned to Turkey afterwards. He entered the diplomatic service in 1807 and went with Sir Harford Jones's mission to Persia. In 1812 he published his *Journey through Persia, Armenia and Asia Minor*, and in 1818 the more notable *Second Journey through Persia*; Morier knew the language and was really at home with the people of Persia. His book was published about the time he retired and he made use of his unique experience to write **The Adventures of Hajji Baba of Ispahan** (1824), a picaresque romance which presented real people in a setting both exotic and authentic. Morier wrote other novels and they are all forgotten – but *Hajji Baba* is a real success and deserves to be better known.

**Morland, Catherine** The heroine of Jane Austen's *Northanger Abbey*. Catherine discovers that her preoccupation with the imaginary world of the gothic romance can lead her into acute embarrassment.

**Morley, Henry** 1822–94. Morley was born in London, studied medicine at King's College, London, and practised for a time before turning to journalism. He contributed to Dickens's *Household Words* and *All the Year Round*, edited *The Examiner*, and published a number of now forgotten translations, biographies, and miscellanies. Morley, who became Professor of English at University College, London, was active in the field of adult education and produced valuable editions of English classics in cheap formats: *Cassell's Library of English Literature* (1875–81) and *Cassell's National Library* (begun 1886). His ambitious history of English literature was begun in 1887 and called *English Writers*: 20 volumes were projected, of which Morley completed 11, taking his subject as far as Shakespeare before he died.

**Morley, John, 1st Viscount** 1838–1923. Morley, a doctor's son, was born at Blackburn in Lancashire. He was educated at Cheltenham College and Lincoln College, Oxford; he studied law and was called to the Bar but decided to practise journalism instead. He knew John Stuart Mill and George Meredith and contributed to *The Saturday Review*; later he became editor of *The Fortnightly Review* (1867) and *The Pall Mall Gazette* (1881).

Morley entered politics in 1883, when he became MP for Newcastle. He was a staunch supporter of Gladstone and held office as Chief Secretary for Ireland (1886 and 1892), Secretary of State for India (1905), and Lord President of the Council (1910). His principal contribution to literature was as a biographer: *The Life of William Ewart Gladstone* (1903) is his best-known work. Others were *Voltaire* (1872), *Rousseau* (1873), *The Life of Richard Cobden* (1881), and *Oliver Cromwell* (1900). Collections of essays contributed to *The Fortnightly Review* were published as *Critical Miscellanies* (four series, 1871–1908). Morley was editor of the English Men of Letters series, to which he contributed *Edmund Burke* (1879); among his other publications were *Diderot and the Encyclopaedists* (1878), his Romanes Lectures, *Machiavelli* (1897), and two collections of speeches on Indian affairs (1908 and 1909).

**Morris, Dinah** In George Eliot's *Adam Bede*, the young Methodist preacher loved by Seth,

Adam Bede's brother, to whom Adam is increasingly drawn after Hetty's flight. The character for Dinah was suggested by the experiences of Elizabeth Evans, the author's aunt who was also a Methodist preacher.

**Morris, William** 1834–96. Morris was born at Walthamstow near London, the son of middle-class parents of comfortable means. He was educated at Marlborough School and at Exeter College, Oxford. Interested in medieval antiquity and stirred by the teachings of the Oxford Movement, he intended to study for the Church. At Oxford he met Edward Burne-Jones, who became his lifelong friend and helped to extend his appreciation of the medieval world to its literature. Burne-Jones had also intended to enter the Church and he in turn was influenced by Morris's enthusiasms. Both men were strongly influenced by the work of Carlyle and Ruskin and they renounced the Church in 1855.

Morris studied architecture under George Edmund Street and married Jane Burden in 1859. The Red House at Bexley Heath was designed for the newly married couple by Philip Webb. The furniture and appliances were specially designed in reaction to the prevailing ugliness of the age. In 1861 Morris launched the company of decorative artists (Morris, Marshall, Faulkner & Co) which over a period of 30 years helped effect a complete revolution in public taste. Morris reacted against both external ugliness and the ugliness of mid-century commercialism and labour relations. He became a socialist, and though the roots of his socialism lay in his love of beauty, he was tireless in pursuit of his ideals.

William Morris's literary career began with the publication of *The Defence of Guenevere and Other Poems* (1858). The work of Morris and his friends had been given an outlet in *The Oxford and Cambridge Magazine*, which ran for one year (1856). The journal had achieved nothing notable apart from publishing three contributions by Dante Gabriel Rossetti. Morris included some poems from this period in his first collection but *The Defence of Guenevere and Other Poems* was not well received. It is now regarded as the work of a poet in search of a means of expression, using various metres and rhythms with incomplete success but achieving definite beauty and force. *The Life and Death of Jason* (1867) was, by contrast, a narrative poem in couplets, carefully controlled from first line to last. Morris's master in the form was Chaucer but there is little of romance, in the medieval sense, in the love of Jason and Medea. Morris is more truthful, and their relationship moves nearer to that of the Greek myth. This book received more favourable notices than his first.

*The Earthly Paradise* (1868–70) was published in three volumes and contains 24 tales in verse. The model again is Chaucerian, with a prologue to set the scene and provide the subject for the linking narratives; 12 tales are told by the travellers and 12 by the hosts. The stories come from a wide range of sources, chiefly, and most strikingly, classical and Norse. *The Earthly Paradise* enjoyed great success with the public, who made the acquaintance of unfamiliar timeless stories in an enjoyable form. The retelling of the Icelandic *Laxdaela Saga* (The Lovers of Gudrun) is regarded as one of the most effective parts of *The Earthly Paradise*. Morris had worked with Eirík Magnússon on translations of Icelandic sagas in 1869 and 1870 and he paid his first visit to Iceland in 1871. He saw at first hand the scenes of those great sagas that interested him so profoundly, and this led to his most ambitious work.

Meanwhile he completed and published the verse morality *Love is Enough or The Freeing of Pharamond* (1873) and his translation of Virgil's *Aeneid* (1875). **The Story of Sigurd the Volsung and The Fall of the Niblungs** was published in 1876. An epic in four books, opening with the story of Sigmund, it proceeds to the tale of Sigurd and the final conflict in the hall of Atli. (This is the story of the *Volsunga Saga*, famous in another version as the German *Nibelungenlied*, in which Sigurd is called Siegfried and Atli–Attila the Hun–is called Etzel.) To relate his version Morris employed an anapaestic couplet of his own devising with six beats to the line. He used this again in his translation of Homer's *Odyssey* (1887).

Morris's last book of original verse was *Poems by the Way* (1891); but he found time in his busy life as an active and successful designer to write prose, to promote his ideas on social reform, to found the Kelmscott Press, which gave printing and book design a new direction, and to work on translations of medieval and Old English poems and further Icelandic sagas. He also founded the Society for the Protection of Ancient Buildings. His socialism led to two prose romances, *The Dream of John Ball* (1888) and the Utopian *News from Nowhere* (1891), and to a number of essays, pamphlets, and printed lectures. Stories in prose continued with *The House of the Wolfings* (1889), *The Roots of the Mountains* (1890), *The Story of the Glittering Plain* (1891), *The Wood beyond the World* (1895), and *The Well at the World's End* (1896). *The Water of the Wondrous Isles* and *The Sundering Flood* were published posthumously (1897).

Morris's translations, in addition to his *Aeneid* and *Odyssey*, were *Grettis Saga: The Story of Grettis the Strong* (1869), *Volsunga Saga: The Story of Volsungs and Niblungs* (1870), *The Northern Love Stories and Other Tales* (1875), and *The Saga Library* in five volumes (1891–95), all in collaboration with Eirík Magnússon; *The Order of Knighthood* and *The Tale of King Florus and the Fair Jehane* (1893); *Of The Friendship of Amis and Amile* and *The Tale of the Emperor Coustans and of Over Sea* (1894); and *The Tale of Beowulf* with A. J. Wyatt (1895).

William Morris died at Kelmscott House, on the Thames at Hammersmith, at the age of 62. One of his doctors said that he had died of 'simply being William Morris and having done more work than most ten men'. He was buried at Kelmscott in Oxfordshire, where he lived in the manor which he rented for a number of years. (Jane Morris bought the property after his death and it now belongs to the Society of Antiquaries.) Morris's influence in design was enormous and spread across Europe. His dislike of Victorian printing revolutionized book design and led to clear typefaces and wider margins. As a social critic he advocated restrictions on mendacious advertising and legislation for clean air. In his lifetime, however, he was best known as a poet: he was asked to succeed Matthew Arnold as Professor of Poetry at Oxford and to succeed Tennyson as poet laureate. He declined both

'A view of the Manor House at Kelmscott, in Oxfordshire, from the garden gate.' From *Gossip about an Old House on the Upper Thames* by William Morris (1895).

honours. Today he is better known as a designer and socialist, while his poetry is hardly known. Swinburne described his style in *The Earthly Paradise* as 'spontaneous and slow' and it is also true that Morris's social conscience finds no echo in his poems or his prose romances. But these were not just a refuge from the harsh and ugly world that he wanted to change: his inspiration lay in his preoccupation with beauty, which led to his desire to effect social change.

*The Collected Works of William Morris* was edited by May Morris, the poet's daughter (24 volumes, 1910–15). A new edition of this, the most comprehensive source of the poetry, prose, and other writings, was published in New York (1966). The single-volume *Prose and Poetry 1856–1870* (Oxford Standard Authors, 1920) was based on May Morris's edition. A modern selection was made by Asa Briggs: *William Morris: Writings and Designs* (1962). The standard biography is J. W. Mackail's *The Life of William Morris* (1899). A modern one, using unpublished letters, is by Philip Henderson: *William Morris: His Life, Work and Friends* (1967).

**Morrison, Arthur** 1863–1945. The son of an engine fitter, Arthur Morrison was born in Poplar, and spent most of his life in the east London in which his stories are set. He became clerk to trustees administering the People's Palace in Mile End Road, where he met Walter Besant, who was probably the man who appointed him sub-editor of the (People's) *Palace Journal*. Afterwards he became a freelance journalist, and in 1891 an article in *Macmillan's Magazine* called 'A street' brought him to the notice of W. E. Henley, who invited Morrison to write a series for *The National Observer*. These were the stories published as *Tales of Mean Streets* (1894), with 'A street', in a revised form, as the introduction. *A Child of the Jago* (1894) and *The Hole in the Wall* (1902) complete the trio of books which are his finest work.

Morrison's importance lies, first, in his qualifications. Unlike Dickens, Gissing, or Kipling he was writing from the inside; he knew at first hand the world he described. Secondly, he presents the working people and criminals of the slums in terms of their own values and attitudes to life, and refuses absolutely to declare a moral position of his own. He delivered a forceful answer to those critics who thought he should: '. . . for how do they know whether I weep or not? No: their wish is not that I shall weep, but that I shall weep obscenely in the public gaze. In other words that I shall do their weeping for them, as a sort of emotional bedesman.' The world which Morrison described – much of it survived until World War II – resembled an enclosed jungle, and Morrison makes the point again and again that the monotony and the precarious respectability of working-class life in the East End was always at risk, and that a step downward was straight into the abyss.

The abyss was vividly described in *A Child of the Jago*, which earned high praise from H. G. Wells and, later, V. S. Pritchett. The Jago (Morrison's name for the Old Nichol) was an area in Bethnal Green, close to Shoreditch, which Morrison knew well. It was duplicated in other parts of London, such as Hackney, Stepney, and Bermondsey – the old Gorbals in Glasgow was much the same – and represented a sort of last ditch retreat, an area which was so far down that it contained only dregs and which had firmly defined boundaries. Dicky Perrot lives and dies in this jungle, where his father had come when he lost his job as a plasterer – and found that he preferred to live as a big man there (by defeating his challengers) rather than have the monotonous respectability of his former life. *The Hole in the Wall* is the name of a pub in Wapping where the young hero is taken by his grandfather to live when his mother dies. While he waits for news of his father who is at sea, he becomes aware of the tightrope his grandfather, Captain Kemp, walks between two worlds – a pub owner in Wapping could not remain untouched by the worst, no matter how much of the better he wanted for his grandson. The violence which is part of the fabric of life in the Jago, and therefore accepted as normal soon after the book is opened, is, in *The Hole in the Wall*, part of the world outside, and consequently more shocking when it occurs. The blind man's revenge, with a bucket of quicklime on the desolate marshes near the River Lea, is unforgettable. The stories in *Tales of Mean Streets* extend the view of life east of Aldgate: we read of the woman who, given money by a sympathetic doctor, does not spend it on medicine – she keeps it so that she can face the neighbours with a decent funeral; the factory girl who in three short years becomes bride, ill-used wife, and prostitute, at her husband's orders, and accepts what is inevitable in her world; and the respectable women, mother and daughter, who die of starvation keeping up a front of respectability. There are no miracles and no transformations – social ambitions of any kind are beyond their range of thought. Morrison relays all this in a terse straightforward style that looks ahead several decades.

Morrison also wrote the detective stories *Martin Hewett, Investigator* (1894), *Chronicles of Martin Hewett* (1895), and *Hewett: Third Series* (1896). More interesting than these, and equally little known, is a novel of witchcraft and smuggling in the time of the Napoleonic Wars, *Cunning Murrell*, set on the Essex shore of the Thames estuary and published in 1900. It was reissued in 1977 by the enterprising Boydell Press of Ipswich.

Morrison collected Japanese prints and paintings and published *The Painters of Japan* in two volumes (1911). His collection was left to the British Museum when he died.

**Morte Arthur, Le**  A Middle English romance of the late 14th century, in rhyming stanzas. (See **metrical romances**.) The source of the poem is the French *La Mort le Roi Artu*, the last part of the 13th-century prose *Lancelot*. It is the first appearance, in English romance, of Launcelot rather than Gawain as the principal figure of the Arthurian stories. Malory is also much closer to French sources than to English in his elevation of Launcelot's part in his *Le Morte Darthur*. In the Middle English poem he is the lover of Guinevere and is loved by Elaine of Ascolot (Astolot – Guildford in Surrey). But Launcelot remains true to his love for Guinevere (see **Launcelot of the Lake**) and he and the queen are reconciled. But they are betrayed by Agravain, Gawain's brother, and surprised by a party of knights. Launcelot fights his way out and kills Agravain and most of the others; only Modred escapes. Guinevere is sentenced to the stake but meanwhile she and Launcelot have escaped to his castle, Joyous Gard, where they are besieged by Arthur and Gawain. Launcelot restores Guinevere to Arthur when he revokes the sentence and retreats to Brittany; Arthur and Gawain pursue him. Launcelot wounds Gawain in combat, but Arthur and Gawain are forced to return to Britain when news comes that Modred has seized the kingdom and is trying to gain possession of the queen. During the first battle at Dover Gawain is killed, but Modred is forced to retreat to Cornwall as the fighting goes against him. In the final confrontation Arthur and Modred mortally wound each other and Arthur, after returning Excalibur to the lake, is borne away to Avalon. Launcelot, belatedly coming to help Arthur and hearing of his death, goes to Guinevere. But she has taken the veil, and Launcelot becomes a priest. He guards Arthur's grave, and upon dying is carried to Joyous Gard. Guinevere is buried with Arthur at Glastonbury.

Malory's treatment of this story in *Le Morte Darthur* is substantially the same but it is only one part of his great work. See **Morte Darthur, Le**; **Arthur, King**; **Gawain**; **Guenever**; **Mordred**; and

**Lady of the Lake, The**. The text of *Le Morte Arthur* was edited by G. A. Panton for the Roxburghe Club (1819), by F. J. Furnivall (1864), by J. D. Bruce for the Early English Text Society (1903), and by S. B. Hemingway (New York, 1912). L. A. Paton's modern version in *Arthurian Chronicles* was published in Everyman's Library (1912).

***Morte Arthure*** A Middle English romance in alliterative verse of the 14th century. (See **metrical romances**.) The unknown author (some have attributed the work to the Scottish poet Huchoun of the Awle Ryale) follows the later history of Arthur as told by Geoffrey of Monmouth, with additions from other sources and from his own imagination. The poem begins with Arthur turning back from Rome, proceeds to the struggle with Modred, and ends with Arthur's death and his burial at Glastonbury. (See **Arthur, King**.) The text of *Morte Arthure* was edited for the Early English Text Society by G. G. Perry (1865), revised by E. Brock (1871), and by M. M. Banks (1900). A. Boyle's modern version in *Arthurian Chronicles* was published in Everyman's Library (1912).

***Morte Darthur, Le*** The printing of *Le Morte Darthur* was completed by William Caxton in 1485. It carries no title but the name by which it is known comes from the printer's note at the end: 'Thus endeth this noble and joyous book entitled Le Morte Darthur . . . . Which book was reduced into English by Sir Thomas Malory, knight . . . . and by me divided into twenty-one books.' Caxton's printed edition was for over 400 years the only text to which scholars could refer; it was the original, printed, as Caxton says in his Preface, '. . . after a copy unto me delivered.' No manuscript was known, and the only perfect surviving copy of Caxton's edition is in the Pierpont Morgan Library in New York. It was not known whether the text Caxton used was in the hand of Malory or the work of a copyist, but it raised a number of questions – the spelling of the title and the division into books that had little respect for narrative and continuity, to name only two – which occupied scholars for a great many years. Then in 1934 W. F. Oakeshott discovered a manuscript that could be dated 1475, in Winchester College, in a safe in the Warden's bedroom. Examination showed that while it was not Malory's own manuscript it was older than Caxton's printed edition and different enough to make a new edition essential. There are 8 books in the Winchester Manuscript; Caxton's has 21. The fifth book was seen to have been arbitrarily altered, while Malory's colophons, or

comments, at the end of each book had been left out except for the one at the very end. W. F. Oakeshott modestly declined, despite the urging of Sir Frederic Kenyon, to undertake a new edition of the text, yielding the task to Eugène Vinaver whose 'unrivalled knowledge of Malory's French sources' gave him 'unrivalled equipment as Malory's editor.'

Eugène Vinaver's first edition of Malory was published in 1947 and a revised – now regarded as definitive – edition in 1967. He has established that Malory, while certainly working from French texts in the main, was obviously acquainted with English sources and traditions. The condition of England in Malory's day, already referred to, may have been a strong influence on his work. The world of *Le Morte Darthur* is a world which, in humanitarian terms, one hopes did not exist. Possibly it did: an aristocratic ideal in which an ideal king headed a court of chivalrous knights may well have been a dream in the medieval mind, but it could only have been a dream for the privileged. But Malory was a great storyteller; he left a superb book that encompasses and unifies the great tales surrounding the figure of Arthur, the king who may have been a champion of the British people when these islands were abandoned by their Roman overlords and when the mounted soldier – the knight – was the most highly prized fighter. The period of the historical Arthur gave rise to the marvellous and mysterious elements that form part of the book's undying magic. Pre-Christian beliefs and traditions abound, from the ancient theme of the sword that only the true man can

---

An illustration from Wynkyn de Worde's 1529 edition of Malory's *Le Morte Darthur*. Frontispiece to the 21st Book: 'How Sir Mordred presumed and took on him to be King of England, and would have married the Queen.'

recover, to the wound that will not heal, the poisoned garment, and the Grail theme itself – the origin of which is, according to one scholar, old enough to be traced back to the Vedas. Interestingly, the historical Arthur existed between two worlds – the ordered world of Rome, of which he was the last echo, and the chaos that was about to descend. Malory, too, comes at the end of a world – the medieval one; *Le Morte Darthur* was printed in the year the first Tudor king ascended the throne of England.

The eight books of the Winchester Manuscript are, in brief: *The Coming of Arthur, The War with Rome, Launcelot, Gareth, Tristram, The Sangreal* (the Holy Grail), *The Knight of the Cart* (concerning Launcelot – the real hero in Malory's version), and *The Death of Arthur*.

For the principal elements of the story see also **Arthur, King**; **Bors de Ganis**; **Galahad**; **Gawain**; **Grail, the**; **Guenever**; **Igraine**; **Launcelot**; **Merlin**; **Mordred**; **Morgan le Fay**; **Nimue**; **Percival**; **Tristram**; and **Uther Pendragon, King**.

**Morton, Thomas** *c.*1764–1838. A minor Georgian playwright, Morton was born at Durham. He studied law at Lincoln's Inn, and had his first production with an adaptation of Jean-François Marmontel's *Les Incas* (1777) as *Columbus* at Covent Garden (1792). He was the author of 18 plays, including *Speed the Plough* (1800), which introduced the character of Mrs Grundy (referred to, not seen) as the self-conscious embodiment of English respectability. Morton's work lay in the field of sentimental comedy, popular at the time and now mostly forgotten.

**Moth** Don Armado's page in Shakespeare's *Love's Labour's Lost*, and the name of one of the fairies in *A Midsummer Night's Dream*.

**Motherwell, William** 1797–1835. Born in Glasgow and educated at Glasgow University, Motherwell published a collection of *Minstrelsy Ancient and Modern* (1827), and a collection of his work, *Poems Narrative and Lyrical* (1832). His ballad 'Jeanie Morrison' was popular but Motherwell is not highly regarded among Scots poets. He and James Hogg collaborated in an edition of the works of Robert Burns, published in five volumes, between 1834 and 1836.

**Motley, John Lothrop** *c.*1814–77. The son of a prosperous New England family, Motley was born in Dorchester, Massachusetts. He graduated from Harvard in 1831 and then studied for two years in Germany. After touring on the continent he returned to America to marry and to study law at Boston. He published two novels, of no particular merit, in 1839 and 1849 but the important part of his life was his diplomatic service in Russia, his increasing interest in historical studies and his preparation for writing one of his own.

This study was his celebrated *The Rise of the Dutch Republic*, which was published in 1856 after nine years' work in the USA, Holland, and Germany. The history was warmly received and was soon being translated into the principal European languages. Motley followed this work, which ended with the death of William of Orange, with the years up to the truce of 1609 (*The History of the United Netherlands*, two volumes in 1860 and two in 1867 – he was his country's minister to Austria during the years between). A further history from 1609 to the Thirty Years' War, *The Life and Death of John of Barneveld*, was published in 1874. Another instalment, to complete the history to the year 1648, was planned but Motley died before the work had proceeded very far.

Motley's histories are detailed and conscientious but, at the same time, they are didactic and at times he overdramatizes. He presents the triumph of the Reformation–inspired Protestantism represented by a small heroic country in conflict with the powerful and evil Catholics: William of Orange and Philip of Spain are hero and villain, respectively, in *The Rise of the Dutch Republic*. But Motley's work is honoured, if with certain reservations, and, like that of Prescott a few years before, was a definite contribution to the development of American literature.

**Motteux, Peter Anthony** 1660–1718. Motteux was a busy writer and journalist who made his home and career in England in 1685. He was from Rouen, in Normandy, and is known, appropriately, as the translator of the portion of Rabelais that Sir Thomas Urquhart left unfinished in his translation of the same year (1693). He edited *The Gentleman's Journal*, a periodical modelled on *Le Mercure Galant*, from 1691 to 1694. This was a news magazine that also published miscellaneous prose on a number of subjects and occasional verse; it was in many ways the precursor of the modern magazine. Motteux published his version of Cervantes' *Don Quixote* in 1703.

***Mourning Becomes Electra*** See **O'Neill, Eugene (Gladstone)**.

***Mourning Bride, The*** A tragedy by William Congreve, his only essay in the form, first produced in February 1697 and published in the same year. The play was a considerable success and provided a fine part for a tragic actress; the part of Zara was created by Elizabeth Barry.

Alphonso, Prince of Valencia, is captive to his

enemy, Manuel, King of Granada. Manuel's daughter Almeria is secretly married to Alphonso. Manuel discovers their secret and orders the murder of Alphonso; he also plans to impersonate his prisoner in his cell, so that he will have an opportunity of mocking his daughter, who believes she can save Alphonso. His plan misfires and Manuel is killed in place of his victim. The body is decapitated and Zara, a Moorish queen who is also a captive in Granada, believes that the victim is Alphonso, whom she loved, and kills herself in grief. A revolt in Granada releases the true Alphonso who is reunited with Almeria.

The play has not been revived but contains two famous quotations: 'Music has charms to sooth a savage breast' and 'Heav'n has no rage, like love to hatred turn'd, Nor Hell a fury, like a woman scorn'd'.

***Moveable Feast, A*** See **Hemingway, Ernest (Miller)**.

***Mr Scarborough's Family*** A novel by Anthony Trollope, first published in *All the Year Round* (May 1882 to June 1883). In volume form it appeared in 1883, the year after the author's death.

Mr Scarborough has two sons, and uncertain of their development as responsible characters, marries the same woman twice – the second time after the birth of Mountjoy, his eldest son. He can, if necessary, proclaim his second son Augustus his heir if he finds him more promising. All this gives his attorney, Mr Grey, a dreadful time. Mountjoy disappoints his father by becoming involved with moneylenders but then Augustus does it too – only he is too wily to be caught by them. Much of Mr Scarborough's last weeks alive are spent trying to frustrate the rapacity of Augustus, who is now his heir.

The novel is rather long for the story it tells, but the characterization is excellent. Particularly good are the honest sweet-natured Mr Grey; his daughter Dolly, who declines to marry because all the men she meets compare unfavourably with her father; and Dolly's vulgar cousin Amelia, who is so silly that she feels honoured by the insolent familiarity of a Russian prince.

***Mrs Caudle's Curtain Lectures*** See **Jerrold, Douglas William**.

***Mrs Dalloway*** See **Woolf, (Adeline) Virginia**.

***Mrs Warren's Profession*** A play in four acts by George Bernard Shaw. It was refused a licence by the Lord Chamberlain but was produced for private performance by the Stage Society in January 1902; it was published in 1898. The first public performances did not take place until 1925.

Vivie Warren, after a fine scholastic record at Cambridge, is working with her friend Honoria Fraser, an actuary in Chancery Lane. Vivie lives in Surrey, where her mother visits her. Mrs Warren, who spends most of her time in Europe, is accompanied by Sir George Crofts and Mr Praed. Later callers are the Rev Samuel Gardner and his son Frank, with whom Vivie is on friendly terms, no more. He would like to marry her, but so would Crofts.

That night Mrs Warren, prompted by Crofts, makes it clear that Vivie must be prepared to see more of him. Vivie refuses to acknowledge her mother's moral authority and in the clash that follows she discovers what Mrs Warren's profession is: to escape from poverty and exploitation she and her sister Liz (now living in gentlewomanly retirement in Winchester – near the cathedral) took up prostitution and now Mrs Warren runs a chain of brothels in the capitals of Europe. The stunned Vivie wants to know who her father was: Mrs Warren is unable to tell her – it could be the Rev Samuel Gardner.

Vivie rejects Crofts when he proposes; he is spiteful at being refused, pointing out that her education was made possible by his generous investment in Mrs Warren's business. She refuses Frank too, and the money her mother can provide in generous measure. She will work with her friend Honoria, and the final curtain leaves her happily immersed in actuarial calculations.

Shaw's play is a fine piece of theatre and the characters of the two women are vividly contrasted. Mrs Warren is uncompromisingly drawn; she is a successful 'madame' and her vulgarity and toughness are plain. Vivie is tough but limited in her response to what she has discovered; she is shocked – but there is no compassion in her reaction. Shaw, the social critic writing at the end of the 19th century, 'is concerned to show prostitution, as he was concerned to show the slums [in *Widowers' Houses*], in its aspect as an economically determined disorder' (J. I. M. Stewart: *Oxford History of English Literature*, Vol XII).

***Mr Weston's Good Wine*** See **Powys, T(heodore) F(rancis)**.

***Mucedorus, The Comedie of*** A play of unknown authorship first published in 1598. It was discovered in a volume of Shakespeare in the library of Charles II and the possibility was once considered (and is now totally rejected) of it being an early work of Shakespeare's. The story concerns the efforts of Mucedorus, Prince of Valencia, to discover the virtues of Amadine, daughter of the King of Aragon. In the process he falls in love with her, saves her life on two occasions, and successfully overcomes the king's objections to him as a husband for his daughter.

***Much Ado About Nothing*** A comedy by William Shakespeare first produced *c.*1598–99 and printed in a quarto in 1600. It was published in the First Folio of 1623. The part of Dogberry was created by Will Kemp. The source of the plot was a story that was already familiar and had appeared in the works of Ludovico Ariosto and Matteo Bandello.

Leonato, Governor of Messina, is host to Don Pedro, Prince of Arragon. In Don Pedro's suite are Claudio and Benedick, and Claudio falls in love with Leonato's daughter, Hero. Benedick and Leonato's niece Beatrice, are hard put to stay out of each other's way but their contacts seem to be for the pleasure of engaging in witty repartee at each other's expense. Don John, bastard brother of Don Pedro, hates Claudio and plans to wreck his forthcoming marriage to Hero. Beatrice and Benedick meanwhile, are manoeuvred into love by their friends; Don Pedro and Claudio, in Benedick's hearing, discuss the love that Beatrice secretly feels for him and the same sort of conversation is held for Beatrice's benefit. Happily, the plan works.

Don John proceeds with his design. At midnight, before the wedding day, his servant Borachio is shown to Don Pedro and Claudio apparently conversing with Hero; but the 'Hero' is the maid, Margaret, dressed in Hero's clothes. Borachio testifies that these encounters are frequent. At the church Claudio rejects his intended bride and the baffled, unhappy girl falls in a swoon. Friar Francis, sure of Hero's innocence, persuades Leonato to give out news that she is dead; this will at once raise doubts about her guilt. Beatrice, outraged at the dishonour to her cousin, demands that Benedick kill Claudio.

Benedick, on Beatrice's behalf, challenges Claudio and leaves Don Pedro's suite. Don Pedro and Claudio are pondering this when Dogberry, the constable, hauls in Borachio. The villain has been boasting of Don John's evil trick – and been overheard. The plot is revealed, to the dismay of Don Pedro and Claudio, who seek some way of making amends. Leonato forgives, Hero and Claudio are brought together again, and Beatrice and Benedick marry. Don John has been apprehended and is being brought back under armed guard – but that will do for another day.

Beatrice and Benedick are originals; they do not appear in the sources, which are concerned with the Hero–Claudio theme. They are wonderful creations and their crisp and witty exchanges a delight to listen to. They might be exhausting to live with, so it is right they should marry each other. Dogberry is an unfailing delight, a gift for a skilful comedian. Don Pedro is a strange figure, one who has the respect and liking of all but who betrays his princely loneliness in his sudden proposal to Beatrice. Hero and Claudio will do nicely to hang the story on and, for the rest? A play that has wit, warmth, and elegance and moves at a lively canter from the first curtain.

**Muddiman, Henry** b. 1629. Almost nothing is known of Henry Muddiman's personal life. However, he had been a pensioner at St John's College, Cambridge, and was a schoolteacher when, through the influence of General Monck and the patronage of Sir John Williamson, he was chosen to write a third news sheet under the Rump Parliament in 1659. The two already in existence were in the hands of two journalists, Marchamont Nedham and Oliver Williams, while Muddiman had no experience whatever. But he was remarkably successful and his *Oxford Gazette*, which began publication in 1665, was the ancestor of the *London Gazette*. See also **seventeenth-century journalism**.

**Muir, Edwin** 1887–1959. A native of Orkney, Muir left the island at the age of 14 when his father was evicted from his farm. The family managed as best they could in the Glasgow slums. Edwin Muir worked at a variety of clerical jobs and meanwhile educated himself thoroughly; he taught himself German and the poetry of Heine was to have a distinct influence on his early poetry. In 1919 Muir, who had been contributing to *New Age*, married and went to London; he became assistant to the editor A. R. Orage, and began to write for *The Athenaeum*, *The New Statesman*, and *Freeman*. His first books were collections of essays: *We Moderns: Enigmas and Guesses* (1918) reprinted from *New Age*, and *Latitudes* (1924) reprinted from the others. The Muirs – his wife Willa was a Shetland girl and a scholar of German – lived in Europe from 1921 to 1927, first in Prague and then in France; they returned to Scotland in 1927.

Edwin Muir's *First Poems* (1925) was followed by *Chorus of the Newly Dead* (1926) and his poetry appeared at intervals until 1956. *The Labyrinth* (1949), one of his most admired poems, reflects the poet's divided spirit, haunted by the pastoral northern setting of his childhood and doing his best to come to terms with the modern soulless world in which he must live so that he can work. As a poet he ignored the directions of modern poetry; his work is that of a sinewy romantic and earned the praise of the great modern, T. S. Eliot. Eliot wrote the preface to Muir's *Collected Poems 1921–1958* (1960), and edited a selection in 1965.

Muir's critical essays earned him a high place in modern English letters: *Transition: Essays on Contemporary Literature* (1926), *The Structure of the Novel* (1928), *Scott and Scotland* (1936), *Essays on Literature and Society* (1949), and *The Estate of Poetry* (published posthumously, 1962 – the Charles Eliot Norton lectures, 1955–56). Willa and Edwin Muir were responsible for some fine translations from the German: Hermann Broch, Lion Feuchtwanger, Gerhart Hauptmann, and, most notably, Franz Kafka. Edwin Muir's autobiography was first published as *The Story and the Fable* (1940), and in the revised version as *An Autobiography* (1954). He was the author of three novels: *The Marionette* (1927), *The Three Brothers* (1931), and *Poor Tom* (1932).

**Mulcaster, Richard** *c.*1530–1611. The first headmaster of the Merchant Taylors' School, Mulcaster was educated at Eton during Nicholas Udall's headship and at Oxford and Cambridge. He was in charge of the Merchant Taylors' for 25 years (1561–86) and became high-master of St Paul's School in 1596. Mulcaster published his theory of education in two short books, *Positions Wherein those Circumstances be Examined Necessarie for the Training up of Children* (1581) and *The First Part of the Elementarie, which Intreateth of Right Writing of our English Tung* (tongue) in 1582, which contain volumes of good sense. Mulcaster was well ahead of his time and a strong advocate of education for girls. His contribution to English literature lies in his insistence on the use of his native language: he gave due honour to the classics and Renaissance Italian but declared that English had no superior as a medium for expression. His influence was profound and among his pupils were Lancelot Andrewes, Thomas Kyd, Edmund Spenser, and Thomas Lodge. Mulcaster published Latin verse, *Cato Christianus* (1600); Latin and English verse in the year of Queen Elizabeth's death, *In Mortem Serenissinae Reginae Elizabethae* (1603); and English versions from the Latin of the same book.

**Müller, (Friedrich) Max** 1823–1900. The son of the German poet Wilhelm Müller, Max Müller was born in Dessau and educated at Leipzig. He went to England in 1846 and settled at Oxford and was commissioned by the East India Company to publish an edition of the Sanskrit *Rig Veda*, the principal of the four Vedas (the ancient sacred books of the Hindus). The first part appeared in 1849 and the work was complete

in 1873. Meanwhile he became a naturalized British subject as Frederick Max Müller and was appointed Taylorean Professor of Modern Languages at the University of Oxford; he became a curator of the Bodleian Library (1856) and Professor of Comparative Philology (1868). In addition to his great distinction as a philologist Max Müller was a scholar of comparative religion and mythology; from 1875 he was editor of *The Sacred Books of the East*, the highly valued series of translations of the scriptures of Eastern religions. Other books by Max Müller are *A History of Ancient Sanskrit Literature* (1859), *Lectures on the Science of Language* (1861–64), *Rig-Veda-Sanhita: the Sacred Hymns of the Brahmins Translated and Explained* (1869), and *The Origin and Growth of Religion, as Illustrated by the Religions of India* (1878). His *A Sanskrit Grammar for Beginners*, a standard work, was first published in 1866.

**Mulock, Dinah Maria** (*or* **Mrs Craik**) 1826–87. A Victorian writer of novels and of stories and verse for children. She was also one of the numerous ladies of Victorian times who could be classed as a 'lesser poet'. She is remembered as the author of ***John Halifax, Gentleman***.

***Mum and the Sothsegger*** An alliterative poem dealing with the misrule of Richard II, written at about the same time as *Piers the Plowman* (1360–1400). It was known for some time as a fragment that occurred in the B text of *Piers the Plowman* in the Cambridge Manuscript. Its first editor was Thomas Wright (1838), who called it *A Poem on the Deposition of Richard II*. W. W. Skeat, in his editions of 1873 and 1886, called it *Richard the Redeless* from the opening words of the first *passus* (book).

The Cambridge fragment contained 857 lines and Skeat believed it to be the work of William Langland. However in the early years of the 20th century the scholar Henry Bradley identified its correct name from a 16th-century note, and *Mum, Sothsegger* (Hush, Truthteller) is the name recorded in the bibliography of John Bale (1548). Another manuscript of 1750 lines, apparently part of the same poem, was discovered in 1928, and the whole published in 1936 as *Mum and the Sothsegger*. It is not now believed to be the work of Langland.

**Munday** (*or* **Mundy**), **Anthony** 1553–1633. Munday was born in London, the son of a freeman of the Merchants' and Drapers' Companies. He was a boy actor for a time and was later apprenticed to a printer. In 1578 he became a government agent in Europe, spying on the activities of exiled English Catholics, and succeeded in entering the English College in Rome under an assumed name. Munday's first literary activity was as an anti-Catholic pamphleteer, basing his writings on his own knowledge and experiences. He was rewarded with a court appointment and later became Messenger of the Chamber.

Munday was a prolific writer of pamphlets, lyrics, and ballads and translated *Amadis de Gaule* into English (1590). He became official poet and pageant writer for the City of London during the reign of James I – to the annoyance of Ben Jonson, who wanted the appointment for himself and who had satirized Munday in *The Case is Altered* (*c.*1598). Munday was also satirized in the anonymous *Histriomastix* (1589), where he is called Posthaste – the explanation lies in Munday's busy activities as a playmaker for Philip Henslowe from 1594 to 1602 and as a theatrical hack who seems to have had a hand in a number of plays. Most of these are lost but it is known that he was part author of *Sir Thomas More* and *Sir John Oldcastle*. Munday's identifiable surviving works are *John a Kent and John a Cumber* (*c.*1594); *The Downfall of Robert, Earle of Huntington, Afterward called Robin Hood of Merrie Sherwodde*; and *The Death of Robert, Earle of Huntington* (1601). The last two were both written in collaboration with Henry Chettle. *Fedele and Fortunio* (1585) is believed to be Anthony Munday's.

Munday was a minor Elizabethan whose chief interest lies in his long and busy life and in his connection with the theatre of his time. Scholars have found incidental felicities in his works but none of them hold the stage.

**Munera Pulveris** The title of an unfinished treatise by John Ruskin. He was invited to contribute to *Fraser's Magazine* by James Anthony Froude, the editor, and six essays on the elements of political economy were published (June 1862–April 1863). However, the same fate attended the series as had *Unto this Last* (See also **Unto this Last**): bourgeois readers became angry and the proprietors (Longmans) became worried; Froude was told not to publish any more. The six essays were published in book form in 1872. Ruskin's title means 'gifts of dust' and he offers 'an accurate analysis of the laws of Political Economy'. He opens by giving definitions of terms connected with his subject, the most important being Wealth. He seeks to define its true nature as the life-giving power of things, not merely something which governs exchange and market rates. *Munera Pulveris* was edited by Oliver Lodge with *Unto this Last* and *The Political Economy of Art* (Everyman's Library, 1907).

**Munro, Hector Hugh** See **Saki**.

**Munro, Hugh Andrew Johnstone** 1819–85. Munro was born at Elgin, Morayshire, and educated at Shrewsbury School and Trinity College, Cambridge. He was a distinguished Latin scholar and his edition of Lucretius with his translation (1860–64) remains standard. His *Criticisms and Elucidations of Catullus* was published in 1878.

**Murder Considered as One of the Fine Arts, On** An essay by Thomas De Quincey, first published in *Blackwood's Magazine* (February 1827). A second part was published in the same magazine in 1839 and the whole essay appeared in Volume IV of *Selections Grave and Gay* (1854). The essay is sardonic in tone and was prompted by the Williams murders in Ratcliffe Highway, a street notorious for its vicious crimes, which ran through Wapping parallel with the River Thames. (The street is now called The Highway, and runs from just below Tower Bridge to Shadwell Park.)

**Murder in the Cathedral** A religious verse drama by T. S. Eliot, first produced at the Chapter House of Canterbury Cathedral during the Canterbury Festival of 1935, and first published in the same year. The play follows the events in Canterbury after Becket's return in AD 1170.

A Chorus of Women lament the absence of their archbishop and the people's helplessness in the schism between church and state. A herald announces to them, and to the priests, that Becket is returning; the news is welcome but all, save the second priest, are fearful of King Henry II's reconciliation with Becket and wonder if it is to be trusted. Becket enters; he is not hopeful of peace but he is determined to resolve the crisis, though he knows it may cost him his life. The Four Tempters, in a long scene, illustrate the conflict his decision provokes within himself – the temptation to seek martyrdom is powerful. Becket realizes that the only course he can follow is to offer his life to 'the Law of God above the Law of Man.' The Christmas morning sermon of 1170 makes his position clear. Four days later the King's Four Knights arrive and charge Becket with rebellion; he is ordered to depart from England. He refuses, and the abusive knights warn him they will come again. The priests try to persuade Becket to barricade himself in the cathedral. He refuses, and orders them to unbar the door and open it. The knights return, half drunk, and murder him; then they address the audience in turn with a justification of their deed. After they withdraw the stage is left to the priests, who offer thanks to God for having given another saint to Canterbury.

***Murders in the Rue Morgue, The*** A story by Edgar Allan Poe, first published in 1841 by *Graham's Magazine* in Philadelphia. It was his first story of ratiocination and is generally regarded as the first detective story – presenting the first detective in the character of C. Auguste Dupin. Dupin is possessed of extraordinary analytical powers and undertakes to solve the mystery of the murders of Mme L'Espanaye and her daughter – a crime of remarkable brutality but with no apparent motive. Dupin examines, questions, and analyses; then he concludes that the killer must have been an ape. An advertisement produces a seaman, who tells the detective that he brought an orang-outang to Paris to sell but the creature escaped. The ape is recaptured and sent to the menagerie at the Jardin des Plantes. Dupin is proved right and a wrongfully suspected man is released.

**Murdoch, (Jean) Iris** 1919– . The daughter of an Anglo-Irish family, Iris Murdoch was born in Dublin. She was educated at Badminton School, Bristol, and Somerville College, Oxford, and taught philosophy for some years. Her first book, a critical study called *Sartre: Romantic Rationalist* (1953), was well received but with her second, *Under the Net* (1954), she embarked on a career as a novelist. Her fourth novel, *The Bell* (1958), made her famous and established the method, for which she is celebrated, of juxtaposing the ordinary with the extraordinary and leaving the reader to decide which level of reality he is being offered. Narrative skill and a talent for irony ensure Iris Murdoch a large readership. In addition to those novels mentioned she is the author of *The Flight from the Enchanter* (1956), *The Sandcastle* (1957), *A Severed Head* (1961), *An Unofficial Rose* (1962), *The Unicorn* (1963), *The Italian Girl* (1964), *The Red and the Green* (1965), *The Time of the Angels* (1966), *The Nice and the Good* (1968), *Bruno's Dream* (1969), *A Fairly Honourable Defeat* (1970), *An Accidental Man* (1971), *The Black Prince* (1972), *The Sacred and Profane Love Machine* (1974), *A Word Child* (1975), *Henry and Cato* (1977), *The Sea, The Sea* (1978, Booker Prize), and *Nuns and Soldiers* (1980). Iris Murdoch is the author of three plays, *The Servants and the Snow* (1970), *The Three Arrows* (1972), and *Art and Eros* (1980). Other books are *The Sovereignty of the Good* (1971) and *The Fire and The Sun: Why Plato Banned the Artists* (1977).

**Murphy, Arthur** 1727–1805. Born in Clomquin, Roscommon, Murphy was an Irish lawyer who came to London to follow an actor's career and received encouragement from Samuel Foote.

He persevered and actually played Othello at Covent Garden in 1754 but never became a favourite with audiences. In 1756 he became a playwright and displayed remarkable ease in turning out farces. He adapted Voltaire's tragedy *L'Orphelin de la Chine* for the English stage in 1759 and went on to write successful comedies in the manner of Molière: *The Way to Keep Him* (1760), *All in the Wrong* (1761), *The School for Guardians* (1767), and *Know Your Own Mind* (1777). Among his tragedies were *The Grecian Daughter* (1772) and *Alzuma* (1773).

Murphy was a good craftsman and his work found a ready public. He was not original and his plays are not revived but his treatment of stage comedy was a phase in its development which found its finest expression in Sheridan and the 18th-century comedy of manners. Murphy was a friend of Samuel Johnson and Samuel Rogers and the first editor of Henry Fielding.

***Muses' Looking-Glass, The*** A play by Thomas Randolph, first performed in 1632 and first published in 1638. It is a defence of the dramatist's art in play form and is considered Randolph's best work by scholars of the period. Two Puritans, Bird and Flowerdew, sell posies and feathers in the Blackfriars playhouse; but at the same time they proclaim their abhorrence of theatres and all their works. Roscius joins them, persuades them to attend the play with him, explains the action of the piece as it proceeds, and eventually converts them to a more intelligent view. Roscius was a celebrated comic actor of republican Rome; his full name was Quintus Roscius Gallus.

**Musidorus** In Sir Philip Sidney's *Arcadia*, one of the two royal cousins who finds his way to the forest of Arcadia after being shipwrecked. The other cousin is Pyrocles.

**Myers, L(eopold) H(amilton)** 1881–1944. L. H. Myers was born in Cambridge and educated at Eton and Cambridge University, which he left upon the death of his father in 1901. A legacy in 1906 gave him independence and, except for service at the Board of Trade in World War I, he devoted all his time to becoming a writer. His first published work was a verse play, *Arvat* (1908), and his first novel was *The Orissers* (1922), which took him 13 years to write. The novel is basically the story of the struggle for possession of the family seat, Eamor, between the Maynes and the Orissers. The Orissers are in possession at the end of the book but the struggle has really been between the worlds of the Maynes and the Orissers, whose moral superiority John

Mayne cannot undermine. But the Orissers, by their very nature, are isolated from the world and Myers has stated a dilemma which he does not offer to resolve. After *The 'Clio'* (1925), in which a group of socialites are found on a yacht bound for a testing time in the jungle, Myers published *The Near and the Far* (1929), the first of a sequence of novels set in the court of the Moguls in India. Myers was not writing a historical sequence but using the setting of a past society for his exploration of the problems of the present. The young prince, Jali, is subjected to the influence of all the illusions which can 'intercept and corrupt the light of nature'. The illusions are embodied in both individual characters and in the structure of society: the novels follow the prince's progress and describe the guidance shown him by the guru. Myers was casting a jaundiced eye on Bloomsbury in his comments on Prince Daniyal, heir to Akbar, and his Pleasaunce of the Arts, a cultural elite the members of which nourish themselves with the belief that they are of breathless interest to a 'solid, shockable world of decorum and common sense. They had to believe that a great ox-like eye was fixed upon them in horror. Without this their lives lost their point.' The other books of the sequence are *Prince Jali* (1931), *The Root and the Flower* (1935), and *The Pool of Vishnu* (1940). The sequence was published as a single volume in 1940 as *The Near and the Far*.

**My Favorite Murder** See *Can Such Things Be?*

**My Last Duchess** A poem by Robert Browning, first published in *Dramatic Lyrics*, one of the *Bells and Pomegranates* series, in 1842. The poem is in the form of a monologue delivered by Alfonso II, Duke of Ferrara, to the envoy of the Count of Tyrol, whose daughter the duke seeks as his second wife. The duke's arrogant and cruel nature is revealed by his comments on his first wife, whose innocent character also emerges from them. The envoy's growing distaste and restlessness is subtly conveyed, although the poem is quite short, no more than 56 lines.

**mysteries, medieval** See **miracle plays.**

**Mysteries of Udolpho, The** A novel by Ann Radcliffe, first published in 1794. The setting is Gascony and the Italian Apennines at the end of the 16th century. Emily de St Aubert is a beautiful girl of Gascon family; after losing her parents, she becomes the ward of her tyrannical aunt, Madame Cheron. Madame Cheron marries Montoni, a sinister character, and disapproves of Emily's attachment to the Chevalier de Valen-

court, whose means are too moderate for the aunt's ambitions. Emily is carried off to the Montoni castle, Udolpho, in the Apennines, where frightening and apparently supernatural occurrences are frequent. Montoni's cruelty brings about the aunt's death and he then turns his attentions to Emily. The heroine succeeds in escaping, however, and returns to Gascony, where she eventually wins her chevalier. The evil Montoni, who has been pillaging the countryside from his sinister castle, is captured and brought to justice.

*The Mysteries of Udolpho* is edited by R. A. Freeman (Everyman's Library, 1931) and Bonamy Dobrée (Oxford English Novels, 1966).

# N

**Nabokov, Vladimir** 1899–1977. Nabokov was born in St Petersburg and left Russia with his family after the Revolution. He completed his education at Trinity College, Cambridge, in 1922 and published some poems in Russian in 1923. For some 15 years Nabokov published fiction in Russian as V. Sirin and some of these novels were translated after his first successful novel in English, *The Real Life of Sebastian Knight*, appeared in 1941. Among them were *King, Queen, Knave* (1928, English 1968), *The Luzhin Defence* (1929, in English *The Defence*, 1964), *The Eye* (1930, English 1965), and *Camera Obscura* (1932, English 1938, called *Laughter in the Dark* in the USA). Nabokov went to the USA in 1940, taught at various colleges, and became a citizen in 1945. He was Professor of Russian Literature at Cornell (1948–59). *Bend Sinister* (1948) and *Pnin* (1957) made him better known and were followed by *Lolita* (1958), which made him famous. The novel had been published in Paris in 1955 and was already celebrated when the first American edition appeared. A farcical novel about a middle-aged man's infatuation for a 12-year-old American girl, it is also a sharp-edged satire on American life, experienced through a lunatic pilgrimage across the States. Nabokov moved to Switzerland in 1959 and spent the rest of his life there. He was an authority on lepidoptera and was granted a Harvard Fellowship for further study in the subject. Among his other books were *Pale Fire* (1962), *Ada or Ardor: A Family Chronicle* (1969), *Speak Memory: An Autobiography* (1967), *Poems and Problems* (1971), and a translation of Pushkin's *Eugene Onegin*, with commentary (four vols, 1964–76).

**Naipaul, V(idiadhar) S(urajprasad)** 1932– .
V. S. Naipaul is the eldest son of Seepersad
Naipaul, an emigrant from India to Trinidad
who became a successful journalist and wrote a
book of short stories with the decline of cultural
identity as a result of exile as its theme (*Gurudeva
and Other Indian Tales*, 1943). The same theme
provides one aspect of the work of his son, who
examines the implications in greater detail and in
a wider perspective. V. S. Naipaul attended
Queen's Royal College and won a scholarship to
University College, Oxford, where he took a
degree in English. He worked for the BBC as an
editor for *Caribbean Voices* and for *The New
Statesman* as a reviewer, and published a satirical
novel, *The Mystic Masseur* (1957, John Llewellyn
Rhys Prize). *The Suffrage of Elvira* (1958, Somerset Maugham Award – Elvira is a place) and
*Miguel Street* (1959) followed and Naipaul's
growing reputation was sealed with *A House for
Mr Biswas* (1961). *The Middle Passage* (1962) was
the result of a journey through the Caribbean; it
confirmed the author's view of the West Indies as
a region of the displaced, with no alternative culture to aspire to. Another novel, *Mr Stone and the
Knights Companion* (1963, Hawthornden Prize),
was followed by *An Area of Darkness* (1964):
Naipaul had gone to India but found the mother-
land was no place for him – a country stranded
between the past to which it could not return and
the present for which it was unprepared. The
subject is examined further in *India: A Wounded
Civilization* (1977). Other books by V. S.
Naipaul are the novels *The Mimic Men* (1967, W.
H. Smith Award), *Guerrillas* (1975), and *A Bend
in The River* (1979), *A Flag on the Island* (1967,
stories), *The Loss of El Dorado: A History* (1965),
*In a Free State* (1971, three stories with a prologue
and an epilogue, Booker Prize), *The Overcrowded
Barracoon* (1972, essays and journalism), *The
Return of Eva Perón* (1980), and *Among the
Believers: An Islamic Journey* (1981).

**Nairne, Carolina, Baroness** 1766–1845. Carolina Oliphant was the daughter of a Jacobite
family of Perthshire. She married Major William
Nairne, who became 5th Baron Nairne in 1824.
She is remembered as a songwriter and song
collector: in the former activity her Jacobite sympathies are plain, in the latter her tendency was to
refine the robust lyrical strength of Scotland
which remained intact in the hands of Robert
Burns. Most of her work was contributed to *The
Scottish Minstrel* (1821–24), anonymously; it was
collected after her death and published as *Lays from
Strathearn* (1846). Among her songs were 'Will ye
no Come Back Again?', 'The Auld Hoose', 'The

Rowan Tree', 'The Land o' the Leal', 'The Laird of
Cockpen', and 'Caller Herrin'.

**Nancy** In Dickens's *Oliver Twist*, the hapless
victim of Bill Sikes when she tries to help Oliver.
She is a thief in Fagin's service, corrupted by him
while a child, and fears and detests him. She
knows she is doomed and says as much to Rose
Maylie.

**Nasby, Petroleum V.** 1833–88. The pseudonym of David Ross Locke, who was born in
New York and became a successful journalist in
Ohio. The first letter from 'Petroleum Vesuvius
Nasby' appeared in the *Jeffersonian* in the town of
Findlay in March 1861 and the letters' success
continued until the end of the Civil War. The
purpose was to ridicule the South and the Confederate cause by loudly proclaiming their rightness in the silliest possible way. (There were a
number of sympathizers in the North, or opponents of the war in any case, who were called
Copperheads.)

A humorist in the style of Artemus Ward and
Josh Billings, Nasby successfully exploited the
vein until his death. He became editor, and later
owner, of the Toledo *Blade* in 1865. The Nasby
letters were popular with Abraham Lincoln and
were issued in several collections. The author
also wrote a political novel, *The Demagogue*
(1881).

**Nashe, Thomas** 1567–*c*.1601. Nashe was one
of the University Wits and, with the exception of
Marlowe, whom he admired extravagantly, the
brightest of them. He was the son of a Lowestoft
preacher and was educated at St John's College,
Cambridge. His first published work was a
preface to the *Menaphon* (1589) of his friend,
Robert Greene, which replied to an attack on
Greene by Gabriel Harvey and provides an
interesting review of the literature of the day.
Nashe had travelled briefly in Italy and France
with Greene and Peele after leaving Cambridge
and settled in London in 1588.

In 1589 Nashe also published *The Anatomie of
Absurditie*, taking his review further and attacking the Puritanism of Philip Stubbes' *The
Anatomie of Abuses*. Nashe's detestation of
Puritanism and his high-spirited combativeness
drew him into the Martin Marprelate
controversy. Using the pseudonym Pasquil he
wrote three pamphlets and under his own name
a counterattack on Richard Harvey, the
astrologer brother of Gabriel Harvey. He continued the attack in **Pierce Penilesse, his
Supplication to the Divell** (1592), a prose satire
that was printed three times in that year and was

also translated into French. It is the most vivid of Elizabethan pamphlets and a fine piece of report-ing. In *Strange Newes, of the Intercepting Certaine Letters* (1593) Nashe returned to the defence of Robert Greene, who had been attacked again by Gabriel Harvey; he counterattacked three years later with a pseudobiography of Harvey in *Have with You to Saffron-Walden* (1596), but mean-while, in 1593, he also published *Christs Teares over Jerusalem*, which gave expression to his religious doubts and repentance. *The Terrors of the Night* (1594) is an oddly ambiguous denuncia-tion of demonology and the interpretation of dreams and the same year saw the publication of **The Unfortunate Traveller;** *or the Life of Jacke Wilton*, a spirited piece of fiction set in the reign of Henry VIII.

In 1597 Nashe, Ben Jonson, and others collaborated in a comedy, *The Isle of Dogs*, which was staged by the Earl of Pembroke's company at the Swan Theatre in Bankside. The satire of existing institutions was so savage that it caused all theatres in London to be closed, while authors and players were imprisoned in the Fleet. *Nashes Lenten Stuffe: The Praise of Red Herring* (1599) was written to repay the hospitality shown the author by the people of Yarmouth and is in a burlesque vein, with vivid pictures of a fishing town.

*A Pleasant Comedie Called Summers Last Will and Testament* was published in 1600 and is the surviving dramatic work by Thomas Nashe. It was acted in 1592, probably for Archbishop Whitgift by members of his household. The 'Summers' of the title is not the season but Will Summers, Henry VIII's celebrated jester. The entertainment's theme is the yielding of summer to autumn in the cycle of the seasons and contains the celebrated lyric 'Adieu, farewell, earth's bliss'.

Little is known of the life of this exuberantly gifted writer. He enjoyed the patronage of Sir George Carey for a short time in his 20s, and was his guest at Carisbrooke Castle for a year (1592–93). He lodged at the Dolphin, Cam-bridge, in 1595, and after that lived with the prin-ter John Danter for a period, the extent of which is not known. The authorities frowned on him for *Christs Teares over Jerusalem* in 1594 and, as we have seen, put him in prison for some months for his contribution to *The Isle of Dogs*. In 1601 he was known to be dead, but it is not known how he died or where. He would have been 34 years old in that year.

R. B. McKerrow's edition of the works of Thomas Nashe was published in five volumes (1904–10). It includes a commentary and is regarded as the best edition. It was reprinted in 1958 with corrections and supplementary notes by F. P. Wilson.

**Nathaniel, Sir**   The curate of Shakespeare's *Love's Labour's Lost* who hangs on every word uttered by Holofernes, whose erudition he ad-mires. Costard the clown defends his gentle character when the court laughs at him.

*Native Son*   See **Wright, Richard**.

*Natural History of Religion, The*   One of the *Four Dissertations* by David Hume, published in 1757.

Hume had attracted wide attention with his essay *On Miracles*, which had appeared in his *An Enquiry Concerning Human Understanding* nine years before. In the present essay he examines the theoretical argument that leads to theism (the acceptance of a transcendent and personal God, a creator and preserver), and the mental processes from which religion has arisen. Hume main-tained that religion came into being from a con-cern with the events of life, 'from the incessant hopes and fears which actuate the human mind', and insisted that polytheism preceded theism in the development of religious belief – the latter was not necessarily the highest form of religion. The existence of God cannot be proved by reason.

A modern edition of the dissertation by H. E. Root was published in 1956, and it is contained in *The Natural History of Religion and Dialogues concerning Natural Religion*, edited by A. Wayne Calver and John Valdimir Price (1976).

*Nature*   Emerson's first published book, a development of his early lectures, was published in 1836. The main principles of Transcendental-ism are expressed in the book, which postulates (in the Introduction) the need for 'an original relation to the universe' and rejects timeworn attitudes to God and nature. He gives the uses of nature as commodity, beauty, language, and discipline, and sees nature as the expression of the divine will.

*Naulahka, The*   See **Kipling, Rudyard**.

*Naval Officer, The*   See **Marryat, Captain Frederick**.

**Neal, John** *c.*1793–1876. The son of a Quaker family, Neal was born in Portland, Maine. He began to write when he was studying law in Baltimore and from then on his output was con-siderable. He had published a number of novels and poems by 1823, when he published an epis-tolary novel called *Randolph*. The novel con-tained some lively criticism of contemporary

English and American writers and an attack on William Pinckney, the Baltimore politician. Pinckney's son challenged Neal to a duel but he refused the challenge and sailed for England. He lived in London from 1824 to 1827 and in a series of contributions to *Blackwood's Magazine* did much to arouse interest in American literature. The essays were reprinted as *American Writers* (1937).

Neal advocated the use of American themes and speech rhythms in fiction and a vernacular literature which would be judged on its own terms. Of his voluminous writings perhaps the most notable are the novels *Rachel Dyer* (1828), about the Salem witch trials, and *The Down-Easters* (1833), a rather overblown romance but with the virtue of a carefully depicted background of New England life.

**Neale, John Mason** 1818–66. Neale was born in London and educated at Sherborne School and Trinity College, Cambridge. A convinced High Church man, Neale was in sympathy with the Oxford Movement and opposed to liberal tendencies in the Church of England. With his friend Benjamin Webb he founded the Cambridge Camden Society in 1839 for the study of ecclesiastical art. He was the author of *A History of the Holy Eastern Church* (1847–50) and a number of hymns that were eventually collected and published as *Collected Hymns, Sequences and Carols* (1914), edited by M. S. Lawson. Among them are 'O happy band of pilgrims', 'Art thou weary', 'Good Christian men, rejoice', 'Good King Wenceslas', and 'Jerusalem the golden'. Many of Neale's hymns were translated from Greek and Latin originals.

***Near and the Far, The*** See **Myers, L(eopold) H(amilton)**.

**Nell (Trent), Little** The heroine of Dickens's *The Old Curiosity Shop*. She looks after her grandfather, who runs the shop and loses it to Daniel Quilp. She flees with her grandfather to escape Quilp and dies of exhaustion despite the good will of many people on the road and the efforts of Kit Nubbles to find and help her.

**Nennius** (*or* **Nynnian**) fl. 796. A Welshman, Nennius lived on the border of Mercia and was probably taught by Elbod, Bishop of Bangor. He was the compiler of the collection of historical notes known as ***Historia Britonum***, of which he was at one time believed to have been the author.

**Nesbit, E(dith)** 1858–1924. E. Nesbit was born in London, the youngest of six children in a comfortably-off family. She spent some of her schooldays on the Continent and some in Kent; the latter provided her with the happy memories of holidays and adventures that she evoked with such success in her books. The holidays probably seemed doubly golden in retrospect: her widowed mother's income was severely reduced and the family moved to a small house in London. She married Hubert Bland, a Fabian journalist, in 1880 and he lost all his capital in an unlucky investment. E. Nesbit, like so many before her and so many since, first wrote from necessity – anything that would pay.

Her first real success came with *The Treasure Seekers*, which had begun as a single contribution to the *Illustrated London News* for Christmas 1897, another to *The Pall Mall Magazine* for April 1898, and finally as a serial in *The Windsor Magazine*. It was published as a book for Christmas in 1899 and earned high praise from Andrew Lang.

E. Nesbit's best work – only a small part of her total output (something like a hundred books) – is for children: it retains its public and continues to be read. Notable titles apart from *The Treasure Seekers* are *The Would-be-Goods* (1901), *The Phoenix and the Carpet* (1904), *The New Treasure Seekers* (1904), *The Railway Children* (1906), *The Wonderful Garden* (1911), *The Magic World* (1912), and *Five of Us – and Madeline* (1925).

***New Atlantis, The*** A philosophical treatise in the form of a visit to an imaginary island by Francis Bacon. It was left unfinished and was published in 1626, the year of the author's death. The imaginary island is called Bensalem and is somewhere in the Pacific. The social conditions are described and there is an account of an ideal college called Solomon's House, dedicated to natural philosophy.

***New Bath Guide, The*** See **Anstey, Christopher**.

**Newbolt, Sir Henry** 1862–1938. Newbolt was born at Bilston in Staffordshire and was educated at Clifton School, for which he seems to have had an extravagant regard, before proceeding to Oxford. After university he became a barrister. He published his first work, *A Fair Death* (1882), anonymously. A novel, *Taken from the Enemy* (1892), was followed by *Mordred: A Tragedy* (1895); success came with *Admirals All and Other Verses* (1897), which ran through 21 editions in two years. Newbolt was editor of *The Monthly Review* (1900–04) and enjoys the credit for first publishing the work of Walter de la Mare. *Songs of the Sea* (1904) consolidated his success, which continued with *Clifton Chapel and Other Poems* (1908) and *Songs of the Fleet* (1910).

During World War I Newbolt was Comptroller of Telecommunications and he was also an official war historian. He was awarded a knighthood in 1915 and became a Companion of Honour in 1922.

Newbolt was extravagantly praised during his lifetime and went on publishing poetry until 1931. Praise ceased after World War II, perhaps because it became difficult for readers to appreciate aspects of a bygone world that Newbolt habitually depicted in unreal terms. That he was an excellent craftsman cannot be denied: 'Drake's Drum', first published in *The St James Gazette* (1896), remains a favourite ballad. His 'Vitae Lampada', however, now seems repellent: in this and other verses in *Clifton Chapel*, Newbolt blandly presented his readers with the popular image of the public schools. He was at his most successful in the short ballad form, as in 'The Fighting Temeraire' and 'He fell among thieves'.

**Newburgh, William of** 1136–1208. A Northumbrian chronicler of the Anglo-Norman period, William, Canon of Newburgh, wrote a valuable contemporary history (1066–1198) entitled *Historia Rerum Anglicarum*.

William of Newburgh's *Historia* was edited by R. Howlett and published in *Chronicles of the Reigns of Stephen, Henry II and Richard I* (Rolls Series, 1886). It was translated by J. Stevenson for *The Church Historians of England* (1853–56).

**Newcastle, Margaret, Duchess of** 1623–74. Margaret Lucas married, in 1645, the Marquis of Newcastle, William Cavendish, who was one of the wealthiest peers of England (his losses in the Civil War are said to have amounted to over £900,000). She had been a maid of honour to Queen Henrietta Maria.

Newcastle served the king faithfully as governor of the Prince of Wales but was dismissed by him when Charles I wanted to show clean hands to Parliament at the time of the alleged Army Plot to rescue Strafford. Newcastle's name had been mentioned in connection with the plot. Eventually he went to Paris in the queen's suite when she left England at the king's insistence. He was made Duke of Newcastle at the Restoration.

The Duchess of Newcastle was an indefatigable writer but only her biography of her husband, *The Life of William Cavendish, Duke of Newcastle* (1667), has any value. Pepys thought the book ridiculous but it remains a notable document of the time, reflecting the other side of the conflict described by Lucy Hutchinson. Margaret's tendency to gossip is one of the book's distinguishing qualities – at a time when the most personal matters were rarely written about she gives us, inadvertently, some illuminating glimpses of their private lives. Charles Lamb, writing over a century after Pepys, praised the book extravagantly.

**Newcome, Ethel** The hero's cousin in Thackeray's *The Newcomes*. Clive Newcome falls in love with her but her wealthy, arrogant family are determined that she shall marry someone of exalted rank. She loves Clive, however, and finds the resolution to resist their bullying.

**Newcome, Colonel Thomas** The hero's father in Thackeray's *The Newcomes*. Not overburdened with brains, Colonel Newcome is the soul of honour and a gentleman through and through. His death scene is a famous set piece in Thackeray.

**Newcomes, The** A novel by W. M. Thackeray, first published in 24 parts (October 1853 to August 1855), 'edited by Arthur Pendennis, Esq.' and called 'Memoirs of a most respectable Family'.

Clive is the son of Colonel Thomas Newcome, a simple gentleman of the highest honour. Clive loves his cousin Ethel, whose father, Sir Brian Newcome, is a wealthy banker. The union of Clive and Ethel is opposed by most of her relatives – chiefly her mean, snobbish brother Barnes and her grandmother, the Countess of Kew. Yielding to the pressure of her family, Ethel becomes engaged to her cousin, Lord Kew, and then to the spineless and callow Lord Farintosh: but her own character asserts itself and she refuses both of them finally.

Clive, despairing of Ethel, is manoeuvred into marriage to her daughter by Mrs Mackenzie, a scheming widow. Rosey Mackenzie proves to be a brainless girl and no fit wife – the house is dominated by Mrs Mackenzie. Then Colonel Newcome loses his fortune and in the poverty-stricken circumstances that follow is bullied and reproached by the vindictive Mrs Mackenzie to such a degree that the poor bewildered old soldier takes refuge in the Greyfriars almshouse.

Rosey Newcome dies, leaving Clive free, but Colonel Newcome dies, too, in a protracted deathbed scene that reads more like Dickens than Thackeray. Clive's fortunes are restored by the discovery of a will, and he is presumably free to marry Ethel.

*The Newcomes* was once a very popular novel but it is hardly read nowadays. In spite of Thackeray's success with the characters of the colonel and Ethel Newcome he overdraws both Barnes Newcome and Mrs Mackenzie, making them so awful as to be unbelievable. The Countess of Kew, however, is an excellent example of the arrogant and unscrupulous woman of position Thackeray drew so well.

**New Criticism, The**  See **Ransom, John Crowe**.

*New England Nun and Other Stories, A*  The second collection of New England short stories by Mary Wilkins Freeman, first published in 1891. The following are the most memorable.

*A New England Nun.* The central character is Louisa Ellis, who is left for 14 years by her fiancé when he goes to Australia to seek his fortune. When he returns, having made his fortune, he finds he has lost Louisa. She is so content with her present life and its subtle domestic order that she has no wish to disturb it.

*A Gala Dress* is an anecdote, skilfully kept within the bounds of humour, about two maiden ladies who never appear at village functions together. A nosy gossip discovers that they can only afford one fine dress, which they take turns to wear.

*Sister Liddy* takes place in an almshouse, where poor crippled old Polly Moss, who has absolutely nothing, derives a certain contentment from describing her sister Liddy, whose exceptional beauty and accomplishment has opened the world to her. But Liddy only exists in Polly's mind.

*Life Everlastin'* is the story of Luella Norcross, a strong-minded humanitarian, who has been a proclaimed agnostic all her adult life. She befriends a wanted murderer and the experience brings her back to an acknowledgment of God.

*Newgate Calendar, The, or Malefactors' Bloody Register.* A biographical record of notorious criminals first published in 1774; it dealt with celebrated crimes from 1700 and ran to five volumes. In 1824 the lawyers, Andrew Knapp and William Baldwin, published *The Newgate Calendar, comprising interesting memoirs of the most notorious characters* in four volumes. They followed this, in 1826, with six volumes of *The New Newgate Calendar.* Knapp and Baldwin, in their preface to the earlier series, suggest that their labours were connected with the current protests about the severity of the law, but it is generally agreed that they knew they had a ready-made public who, in large numbers, bought and read their volumes in horrified fascination. George Borrow was one of Knapp's and Baldwin's staff of compilers. The last of the series was C. Pelham's *Chronicles of Crime, or the New Newgate Calendar* (1886).

*New Grub Street*  A novel by George Gissing, first published in 1891. It depicts the literary world of Gissing's day and the author stresses that self-advertisement has a far better chance of bringing success than any amount of artistic endeavour.

Edwin Reardon is the author of two fine books; he is hampered by poverty and an unsympathetic wife. Jasper Milvain is a reviewer, facile and selfish. Alfred Yule is a rancorous and sarcastic scholar, whose learning goes unappreciated, and whose daughter, Marian, falls in love with Jasper Milvain. Jasper decides to marry Marian when he learns that she has expectations of a legacy. When the legacy does not materialize, he withdraws from the engagement. Reardon's wife, Amy, deserts him; this and his failure as a writer send him to his grave. Jasper marries the widowed Amy and becomes a success.

A multitude of other characters also help to represent the literary world. Two of the best are Biffen, who is earnestly polishing a novel of absolute realism, called 'Mr Bailey, Grocer', and Whelpdale, a literary failure who becomes an Adviser to Literary Aspirants and achieves success in thinking of the best name for a magazine full of scraps – a reference to *Tit-Bits*, which had first appeared in 1881.

**Newman, John Henry** 1801–90.  The son of a banker, Newman was born in London and was educated privately before going to Trinity College, Oxford, in 1817. He became a fellow of Oriel College in 1822 and was ordained in 1824; he was appointed vice-principal of Alban Hall in 1825 and vicar of St Mary's, Oxford, in 1828. Newman became closely involved with the **Oxford Movement** at the beginning (1833) and was soon its leader. But from 1839 he began to have doubts about the claims of the Anglican Church. In his tract number 90, the last of the Movement's *Tracts for the Times* (1841), he advocated the interpretation of the Thirty-Nine Articles in accordance with the Council of Trent (1545). Uproar followed and Richard Bagot, Bishop of Oxford, imposed silence on the author. Newman gave up his position in Oxford and by 1842 had retired to nearby Littlemore. In October 1845 he was received into the Roman Catholic Church. Newman was made a cardinal by Pope Leo XIII in 1877.

Newman's career really belongs to religious history and most of his writing is concerned with Christian controversy. Though the occasion of the controversy is past some of his work has lasting value. *The Idea of a University* (1852) contains ideas that transcend religion, notably that universities should exist to train the mind rather than to diffuse existing knowledge. The famous

*Apologia pro Vita Sua* (1864) was written in answer to Charles Kingsley (see **Kingsley, Charles**). With its combination of frankness and delicacy it had a wide appeal and has become a classic of spiritual autobiography. His poem *The Dream of Gerontius* (1866) has earned extra celebrity as the text of Elgar's oratorio. Two novels, now forgotten, are *Loss and Gain* (1848) and *Callista* (1856). In 1854 Newman was appointed the first rector of the Catholic University in Dublin, which he helped to found.

**Newsome, Chad**   The object of Lambert Strether's visit to Paris in *The Ambassadors*, by Henry James. Chad displays no eagerness to return to Massachusetts and the family business, and soon he has Strether sharing his point of view.

**Newton, Isaac** 1642–1727.   Newton was born at Woolsthorpe near Grantham in Lincolnshire, and educated at Grantham Grammar School and Trinity College, Cambridge. He succeeded his teacher, Isaac Barrow, as Lucasian Professor of Mathematics in 1669. The years before that (1664–66), during a university interregnum, were spent in his home at Woolsthorpe and saw the beginning of his scientific enquiries, leading to his theories of gravitation and the spectrum and the development of the calculus – the instrument he used to discover the results he published in *Philosophiae naturalis principia mathematica* (The Mathematical Principles of Natural Philosophy) in 1687. A milestone in the history of science, Newton's *Principia* demonstrated the principle of universal gravitation. His first communications to the Royal Society on light and colour were made in 1672; his *Opticks* (1704) makes him the founder of the modern science of optics. To this book was attached *Method of Fluxions* – the Newtonian calculus, which anticipated Gottfried Leibniz in the same field and was the source of a bitter dispute between them over priority of invention.

Newton has been called the greatest of all scientists. He was honoured generously during his lifetime: he was the university's representative in parliament twice (1689 and 1701); President of the Royal Society (1703 until his death); Warden of the Mint (1696) and Master in 1699; he received a knighthood from Queen Anne in 1705.

***New Way to Pay Old Debts, A***   A comedy by Philip Massinger, first produced before 1626 and first published in 1633.

Sir Giles Overreach, a monster of greed, has succeeded in gaining possession of the property of Frank Wellborn, his prodigal nephew. Reduced to poverty and treated with contempt, Wellborn finds a friend in Lady Allworth, a rich widow; Wellborn had given useful service to her late husband. Lady Allworth lets it be known that she intends to marry Wellborn. Overreach is delighted at the prospect and is prepared to advance him money. Lady Allworth's stepson, Tom, is in love with Sir Giles' daughter, Margaret; but she is intended for Lord Lovell. Tom Allworth is Lord Lovell's page, so not considered a good enough prospect for Sir Giles; but his employer is sympathetic and enters the plot on the young people's behalf. Sir Giles is tricked at the wedding ceremony – the bridegroom proves to be the page, not the Lord, and Sir Giles' rage unbalances him. The news that his claim to his nephew's property cannot be upheld drives him right over the edge and he is carried off to Newgate. A happy match is made between Lady Allworth and Lord Lovell; and Wellborn takes a commission in Lord Lovell's regiment.

The character of Overreach was based on that of a contemporary villain, the extortioner Sir Giles Mompesson. It was a favourite part with powerful actors such as Garrick, Kemble, Kean, Phelps, and Booth. In the modern theatre the part is associated with Sir Donald Wolfit. Unfortunately, the play, which owes its continued life to the character of Overreach, is rather unbalanced by it – becoming almost a one-man show for an actor who must be capable, if he is to attempt the part, of overpowering the rest of the company.

**'New Women' novelists**   Towards the end of the 19th century, through the influence of higher education and with their insistence on being included in the professions, English women were strongly influenced by Henrik Ibsen and John Stuart Mill. The movement for the enfranchisement of women had begun and the novel was a useful medium for the expression of these ideas.

Among those works that made their mark were Sarah Grand's (Mrs David C. M'Fall) *The Heavenly Twins* (1893), 'George' Egerton's *Discords* (1895), Iota's (Mrs Caffyn) *A Yellow Aster* (1894), and Elizabeth Robins's *The Convert* (1907).

A curiosity of the genre was *The Woman who Did* (1895), about a woman who rejected the belief that formal wedlock was essential for rewarding relationships between men and women. The author was a man, a Canadian novelist named Grant Allen.

Unfortunately, the writers who made their contribution to this movement in fiction were not outstandingly gifted and their work is forgotten. Mrs Humphry Ward, who firmly opposed their ideas, was a better writer.

***Nicholas Nickleby*** A novel by Charles Dickens. It was first published in 20 monthly parts (April 1838 to October 1839) under the pseudonym of Boz and in volume form in 1839.

Nicholas Nickleby, his sister Kate, and his mother are left penniless when Mr Nickleby dies. They appeal to Ralph Nickleby, the dead man's brother, who is both greedy and unscrupulous and who is not pleased at his nephew's lack of subservience. Kate is apprenticed to a dressmaker, Madame Mantalini. Nicholas is sent to teach at Dotheboys Hall, where 40 boys are supposedly given full board and taught by Wackford Squeers. In reality, Squeers starves and ill-treats them, knowing them to be the children of uncaring parents.

Nicholas is horrified at what he discovers, particularly at Squeers' vicious treatment of Smike, a half-witted orphan left on his hands, who is made to work night and day. Smike tries to run away; when he is brought back, Squeers sets out to flog him in the presence of the whole school. Nicholas finds this more than he can bear and thrashes Squeers into insensibility; then he and Smike leave Dotheboys Hall and work where they can – for a while with Vincent Crummles and his band of actors.

Kate Nickleby, meanwhile, is exposed to the advances of Ralph Nickleby's friends and business associates, among them the vicious Sir Mulberry Hawk. But they are no match for the resolute Kate, who treats Hawk with contempt. Ralph Nickleby, receiving news from Squeers, tries to intimidate Kate and her mother by his representation of Nicholas's character – but Nicholas arrives back in London with Smike and confronts his uncle.

The return of Nicholas precipitates a number of events. He breaks Sir Mulberry's head for him; he encounters the Cheeryble brothers, who take him into their business and their hearts; he meets Madeline Bray, another of Ralph Nickleby's intended victims – he wants to marry her to the revolting old usurer, Gride – and falls in love with her; and finds an ally in Newman Noggs, Ralph Nickleby's eccentric clerk.

Squeers and Nickleby try to injure Nicholas through Smike; their plans come to nothing but Smike, ill-used and frail, dies with Nicholas at his side. Newman Noggs and the Cheeryble brothers frustrate the villains' designs completely, and when they disclose that Smike is his own son Ralph Nickleby hangs himself.

*Nicholas Nickleby* is usually accorded a higher place in Dickens's work than *Oliver Twist* but the assessment is debatable. Some of the characterizations are excellent – Mrs Nickleby, Vincent Crummles, Newman Noggs, Wackford Squeers – and the scenes at Dotheboys Hall are chillingly vivid. The world of the strolling players is Dickens the comic writer at his best – but the rest of the characters, on whom the weight of the story rests, are pasteboard and often speak in melodramatic tones. Once begun, however, it is, like all of Dickens's novels, hard to put down.

'The internal economy of Dotheboys Hall.' Mrs Squeers dosing the boys with brimstone and treacle. An illustration by Phiz for *Nicholas Nickleby*.

**Nicholson, Norman (Cornthwaite)** 1914– . Norman Nicholson was born in Millom in Cumberland and has lived there all his life. He was educated locally, and published his first poems in 1943 in a volume shared by Keith Douglas and J. Hall (*Selected Poems*). *Five Rivers* (1944) was awarded the Heinemann Prize and in the following year Nicholson became a fellow of the Royal Literary Society. *Rock Face* (1948) and *The Pot Geranium* (1954) are further collections of poems, and confirm his identity as a modern Christian Lakeland poet. *The Old Man of the Mountains* (1946), *Prophesy to the Wind* (1950), *A Match for the Devil* (1955), and *Birth by Drowning* (1960) are verse plays; *The Fire of the Lord* (1944) and *The Green Shore* (1947) are novels.

Nicholson edited *An Anthology of Religious Verse, Designed for the Times* (1942), and selections of Wordsworth (1949) and Cowper (1951). His volume of critical essays, *Man and Literature*

(1943), is an excellent guide to 20th-century writers and contains illuminating essays on Eliot's *The Waste Land* and the novels of Franz Kafka.

**Nickleby, Mrs**  The hero's mother in *Nicholas Nickleby*. A featherbrained woman who continually recalls her better days, she was a caricature of Dickens's own mother – an unjust one, according to some of his contemporaries. But she is a remarkable comic creation.

**Nicolay, John George**  1832–1901.  See **Hay, John Milton.**

**Nicolson, Sir Harold (George)**  1886–1968. The son of Sir Arthur Nicolson, the English chargé d'affaires in Teheran, Harold Nicolson was born in that city. He was educated at Wellington School, and went on to Oxford before joining the diplomatic service, in which he served in Madrid, Constantinople, Teheran, and Berlin. He married V. Sackville-West in 1913, and eventually resigned from the service when he was 43. He had, meanwhile, begun his literary career with a study, *Paul Verlaine*, and a novel, *Sweet Waters*, both published in 1921. There followed *Tennyson: Aspects of his Life, Character and Poetry* (1923), *Byron; The Last Journey* (1924), *Swinburne* (1926, for the English Men of Letters series), *The Development of English Biography* (1927), and *Some People* (1927). His book on Tennyson was an important contribution to the revaluation of the great Victorian poet.

Nicolson's lucid, elegant style makes his prose a pleasure to read. Among his later books were a novel, *Public Faces* (1932); a study of Curzon, the statesman, *Curzon: The Last Phase 1919–1925* (1934); *The Congress of Vienna: A Study in Allied Unity 1812–1822* (1946); the highly praised official biography *King George the Fifth: His Life and Reign* (1952); and a biography of the French critic *Sainte-Beuve* (1957). He was MP for West Leicester (1935–45) and was knighted in 1953. His diaries, which give an interesting picture of political life between the two World Wars, have been edited by his son Nigel Nicolson: *Diaries and Letters* (3 vols, 1966–68).

**Nigger of the Narcissus, The:** *A Tale of the Sea*. A novel by Joseph Conrad, first published in 1897.

The sailing ship *Narcissus* is being prepared for the voyage home to London from Bombay and the First Mate, Baker, is mustering the crew. Among them are Singleton, a veteran seaman, Craik, a religious fanatic from Belfast, and Donkin, a work-shy Cockney scrounger. The last arrival is Wait, a gigantic Black from St Kitts.

The *Narcissus* has only begun the voyage home when Wait goes sick with a racking cough and takes to his bunk. He is believed by the crew to be a dying man and his presence dominates the ship: the veteran Singleton prophecies that Wait will die when they sight land. The ship runs into a gale and nearly capsizes. Wait, now in the sick bay, has to be literally hacked out of it when the vessel heels over; he simply abuses his rescuers. After the gale the *Narcissus* is becalmed and the crew blame all the misfortunes of the voyage on Wait. Craik terrifies him by preaching hell-fire at him and Wait declares that he is well and ready to resume his duties. Captain Allistoun is convinced that Wait was shamming all along and orders him to remain off deck. The crew, incited by of all people the work-shy Donkin, become mutinous over the captain's decision but Allistoun is a strong man and calms them; he also deals with Donkin, who wielded a belaying-pin. Wait dies, as Singleton predicted, when they sight land, and he is buried at sea. *The Nigger of the Narcissus* is a magnificent story of life at sea, one of the finest of its kind, centred on the presence of a disruptive character on board during the voyage home.

**Night in Acadie, A**  The second collection of short stories by Kate Chopin, first published in 1897. 'Acadie' refers to the former French colony of Acadia, which now corresponds roughly to the Canadian province of Nova Scotia. The French settlers dispersed rather than take the oath of allegiance to the British and many of them resettled among the French Creoles of Louisiana. They were called 'Cajuns' in Louisiana and were easily distinguished from the Creoles.

Among the stories in this volume is *Nég Créol*, a cold and searching rebuttal of the sentimental view of their former slaves held by many southern families. *Athenaise* is about a young wife who twice runs away from her husband. After the first flight she is brought back by her husband. On the journey home they pass an oak tree where her father-in-law had recaptured a fleeing slave. She cuts the second flight short herself, realizing that she is pregnant. She is as much a slave, as a wife and mother-to-be, as the runaway captured by the oak tree. However, she surrenders to her condition and thus achieves a certain peace. *Regret* tells of Mamzelle Aurelie's realization, through the accident of having to look after a neighbour's children, that her sturdy independent farmer's life suffers badly from the lack of something she never believed she wanted.

**Nightmare Abbey**  A satirical tale by Thomas Love Peacock, first published in 1818, the target in this case being Romanticism. There is more plot than in Peacock's first novel, *Headlong Hall*, but it is little more than a framework, though description and narrative are better served. The most important characters are Mr Cypress (Byron), Mr Scythrop (Shelley), and Mr Flosky (Coleridge). Shelley bore his friend no malice for the caricature of him in the book.

*Night Rider* See **Warren, Robert Penn**.

*Night Thoughts* (*The Complaint, or Night Thoughts on Life, Death and Immortality*). A didactic poem in nine books and some 10,000 lines, in blank verse, by Edward Young, first published between 1742 and 1748. The first book is concerned with reflections by the poet on life, death, and immortality; the following seven form a soliloquy, addressed to the worldly Lorenzo, who is exhorted to turn to Faith and the good life; the final book is entitled 'The Consolation' and includes a vision of the Day of Judgment, a contemplation of eternity, a survey of the firmament, a last exhortation to Lorenzo, and an invocation to the Deity.

**Nimrod** See **Apperley, Charles James**.

**Nimue** See **Lady of the Lake, The**.

*Nina Balatka* A novel by Anthony Trollope, first published in *Blackwood's Magazine* (July 1866 to January 1867). This book and *Linda Tressel* were published without Trollope's already famous name appearing on the title page. The author wanted to see if he 'could obtain a second identity', having made one mark by ability, to make another. 'It seemed to me that a name once earned carried with it too much favour.' His belief was borne out: discerning critics praised the book but few readers paid attention to the 'anonymous' author's work.

The setting of the novel is Prague and its subject is the love of Nina Balatka for Anton Trendellsohn. Anton is a Jew and Nina's family set their faces against her marrying him: Anton's family are just as strongly opposed to his marrying a Christian. A striking character is the beautiful Rebecca Loth, the Jewish girl who had been intended as a wife for Anton. Her scene with Nina, when she confronts the Christian girl, with unsentimental truthfulness, about the consequences for her and Anton if they marry, and alienate both their communities, is the best part of the book.

**Nin, Anaïs** 1903– . The daughter of the composer Joaquin Nin, Anaïs Nin was born in Paris and taken to live in the USA at the age of nine. From her eleventh year, when her father deserted his family, she kept a journal, and she spent some time in Europe before World War II. Her first book was *D.H. Lawrence, An Unprofessional Study* (1930). Her interest in psychology – she was a patient and associate of Otto Rank's – underlies her fiction, which began with *The House of Incest* (1936) and *Winter of Artifice* (1939). In 1940 she returned to America where, not being able to find a publisher, she became her own for *Under a Glass Bell* (1944, short stories) and *This Hunger* (1945, short stories). A novel, *Ladders of Fire* (1946), was her first book to be accepted by an American publisher. Among other books by Anaïs Nin are *Children of the Albatross* (1947), *The Four-Chambered Heart* (1950), *A Spy in the House of Love* (1954), and *Cities of the Interior* (1959). *Realism and Reality* (1946), *On Writing* (1947), and *The Novel of the Future* (1965) are critical studies. *The Diary of Anaïs Nin* was edited by Gunther Stuhlmann and published in five volumes (1966–74, called *The Journals of Anaïs Nin* in England).

*Nineteen Eighty-Four* See **Orwell, George**.

**Nipper, Susan** Florence Dombey's maid in Dickens's *Dombey and Son*. She is dismissed by Mrs Pipchin when that sour old woman takes over the running of Dombey's household. She is married to Toots at the end of the story.

*Noctes Ambrosianae* A series of imaginary conversations at Ambrose's Tavern in Gabriel Road, Edinburgh. The 'Ambrosian Nights' conversations appeared in *Blackwood's Magazine* from 1822 to 1835 and the idea for them is believed to have been William Maginn's. Those supposedly taking part were the Ettrick Shepherd (James Hogg) and 'Christopher North' (John Wilson). Wilson was the author of the greatest number (41 of the 71 published); the others were by Lockhart, Hogg, and Maginn. The *Noctes Ambrosianae* were a favourite feature of *Blackwood's* and contributed to its success.

**Noggs, Newman** The eccentric clerk of Ralph Nickleby in Dickens's *Nicholas Nickleby*. He befriends the family to the extent of his limited powers because Nicholas's father had been kind to him. He has the measure of his villainous employer and helps to bring him down.

**Nonjurors** This was the name given to those ministers of the Church of England who refused to take the Oath of Allegiance to William and Mary in 1689 – they had given their oath to the deposed King James II and his successors and could not lawfully break it. Among them were the Archbishop of Canterbury, William Sancroft, and seven other bishops.

**Norman Conquest**   The Normans under Duke William became masters of England on 14 October 1066. The historical fact is precisely dated but the temporary eclipse of the English language was a continuous process, and when English re-emerged it was transformed and strengthened. The principal reason for its eclipse was the simple one that the rulers' language was French and their documents were written in Latin, the scholar's language of western Europe. English did not by any means disappear: it remained the language of the people and the **Anglo-Saxon Chronicle** was continued in the vernacular until the end of the Norman dynasty, but English did not reappear as a literary language until the beginning of the 13th century.

In England, meanwhile, powerful influences came to bear on life and thought; the Conquest brought to England something more than alien rule. In George Sampson's words, 'It was the coming not, indeed, of romance, for we had that before; but it was the coming of Romance.' A highway was opened from the south and European scholars brought with them a new richness of culture and learning; the English were obliged to learn the language of their new masters, and in doing so refreshed their own. It became more flexible and expressive, and from tentative beginnings in the 13th century was ready, in the 14th, for the genius of Chaucer.

**Norris, Frank**   1870–1902.   Benjamin Franklin Norris was born in Chicago but his family moved to San Francisco when he was 14. He studied in Paris, where he wrote medieval romances in his spare time. He was at the University of California from 1890 to 1894 and, under the influence of Zola's novels, began to move towards realism in his writing. He had been mildly successful with occasional pieces and his first novel, *McTeague*, was eventually published in 1899. It tells of the descent of a man of limited intelligence into primitivism when his precariously assembled world is brought down through the greed and spite of others. Meanwhile Norris moved from California to Harvard, where he continued work on his novel and began work on another. He visited South Africa in 1895, hoping to find material for travel sketches. But there was fighting between the English and the Boers so instead he reported the conflict for *Collier's* magazine and the San Francisco *Chronicle*. After being captured by the Boer forces he was deported from the country. He returned to San Francisco and joined the staff of a magazine called *The Wave*.

*Moran of the Lady Letty*, a sea story, was

Frank Norris.

serialized in the magazine and published in 1898. *A Man's Woman*, a romantic adventure story, was published in 1900. Other contributions to *The Wave* were published in later years as *The Joyous Miracle* (1906), a novelette, and the short story collections, *A Deal in Wheat* (1903) and *The Third Circle* (1909). Norris went to Cuba in 1898 to report the Spanish–American War for *McClure's Magazine* and on his return went to work for the publishers, Doubleday, who published *McTeague* in that year along with Norris's love story, *Blix*.

Norris had been observing events in the USA with close attention and he now concentrated his energies on a trilogy, *The Epic of the Wheat*, in which he would comment on those events. The first book, **The Octopus** (1901), describes the struggle between farming and railroad interests in California. The author died tragically in the following year after an appendix operation and the second novel, **The Pit**, was published posthumously in 1903; the third part, **The Wolf**, was never written. This was a real loss: *The Pit*, which concerns the manipulation of the wheat market in Chicago, had maintained the high standard of *The Octopus* and the third volume was to tell of a wheat famine in Europe. *The Octopus* and *The Pit* are acknowledged as Frank Norris's best work. Further posthumous publications were *The Responsibilities of the Novelist* (1903), a book of essays that is not highly regarded now, and the novel which he had begun at Harvard in 1895, *Vandover and the Brute* (1914).

Frank Norris was only 32 when he died and a

positive attitude does not emerge from his writing. In spite of his realism and the radicalism which is plain in parts of his proposed trilogy, his work has an intrusive romantic quality. There is a tendency toward a determinism that cancels out some of Norris's most arresting sequences – the reader is first made to feel but then given to understand that there is really no point at all in feeling. But the confusion was probably due to his age; his narrative power is remarkable and, given the time, he might well have become a major American novelist.

**Norris, John** 1657–1711. The last of the Cambridge Platonists, Norris was educated at Winchester and Exeter College, Oxford. He became a fellow of All Souls' College. He was a supporter of Nicholas Malebranche, the French philosopher who combined the ideas of René Descartes with a Platonic mysticism. His chief work was the elaborate *Essay towards the Theory of the Ideal or Intelligible World* (two parts, 1701 and 1704), which contains his criticism of the empiricist John Locke's *Essay concerning Human Understanding*.

**Norris, Mrs** The malicious bullying aunt of Jane Austen's *Mansfield Park*, who extols charity and helpfulness but is far too selfish and corrupt to act according to those precepts herself.

**North, Christopher** See **Wilson, John**.

**North, Sir Thomas** *c*.1535–*c*.1601. The younger son of Edward, first Baron North, is believed to have been educated at Peterhouse College, Cambridge, before entering Lincoln's Inn in 1557. He became a freeman of Cambridge in 1568 and was knighted by Queen Elizabeth in 1591. He became JP for Cambridgeshire in 1592 and was awarded a royal pension in 1601. North travelled in France and it was by working from a French version of a Spanish book that he made his mark as a translator into English. The book was Antonio de Guevara's *El Relox de Principes*, which North published as *Diall of Princes* in 1557. He added Guevara's *Aviso de Privados* as an additional book in 1563. The famous 'Englishing' of Plutarch's lives was also from French – Jacques Amyot's 1559 translation from the Greek. *The Lives of the Noble Grecians and Romanes* (1579), for all its many faults, including North's compounding of Amyot's errors with more of his own and his lack of historical sense, was a priceless book for the Elizabethans to have. North gave them a rich storehouse from antiquity in lively, readable English prose and provided Shakespeare with the stories for a number of his plays.

*North American Review, The* A New England quarterly first published in 1815 in Boston and edited by William Tudor. Later it became a monthly and continued until 1939. As a monthly its editors included Charles Eliot Norton, James Russell Lowell, Henry Adams, and Henry Cabot Lodge. In 1878 publication was moved to New York, where, away from the New England atmosphere, it extended its range to include writing on social and political matters. The authors whose works were printed in *The North American Review* make an impressive list and include Emerson, Washington Irving, Longfellow, Francis Parkman, Whitman, Mark Twain, Henry James, Tolstoy, D'Annunzio, H. G. Wells, Maurice Maeterlinck, and Alan Seeger. After World War I the magazine's readership diminished considerably and it became a quarterly again.

*North and South* A novel by Elizabeth Gaskell, first published in serial form in *Household Words*, from September 1854 to January 1855, and in volume form in 1855. The north and south of the title are the 'satanic mills' of the north and the leisured life of London society and rural Hampshire. Mrs Gaskell began writing it early in 1854, while *Hard Times* was being serialized, also in *Household Words*.

The Rev Hale, feeling that his life as a minister in comfortable – affluent, even – circumstances calls for too little from him, goes to the grim industrial city of Milton where, in modest circumstances, he will live by teaching mill owners with aspirations. His wife and his daughter, Margaret, go with him. Margaret Hale detests trade of any kind but she soon discovers that the reality behind it all arrests and challenges her: her true character begins to emerge. Her mother never changes but Margaret's lively mind inevitably leads her to examine the industrial way of life. She moves to the side of the workers and soon confronts John Thornton, the mill owner who is the employers' leader, and his tough, practical mother.

John Thornton, not in sympathy with Margaret's argument for a humane approach to his workers' problems, is nevertheless strongly drawn to her. She is beautiful and has a dignified certainty that irritates his confidence. When he is attacked by a mob of strikers, Margaret's courage in protecting him convinces him that his feelings are reciprocated, and he proposes to her. Margaret rejects him so coldly and firmly that he is deeply hurt. Later he sees her with another man and is shocked by her denial that this could be true. The knowledge that she has lied to him turns him away from her. The man was Margaret's brother Frederick who, in danger of arrest, had sought her out; she was protecting him.

Thornton's attitudes to the workers do not bring him further prosperity and he is made to realize the need for the warmer approach that Margaret advocated. For her part, Margaret has been deeply affected by her fall in Thornton's estimation and begins to appreciate how much his regard matters to her. The two come together at the end of the novel.

*North and South* uses the background of industrial relations, some years on, that served Elizabeth Gaskell so well in *Mary Barton*. This time the approach is strikingly different: the two sides are really both middle class; one from a background of middle-class values and upbringing and the other from arrival there through success in 'trade'. The contrasts – John Thornton and Margaret Hale, Mrs Thornton and Mrs Hale – are finely done and the best of *North and South* demonstrates the author's advance as a novelist. It was Mrs Gaskell's first attempt at writing a novel to order. Unfortunately, the need for regular instalments harassed her dreadfully and the results discouraged Dickens, who had asked her for the book. In spite of that, it is a remarkable novel. The slow beginning and Elizabeth Gaskell's inability to create a 'crisis' each week give way to her narrative gifts, her unerring evocation of the industrial background, and her use of it to deepen the reader's interest in the love of John Thornton for Margaret Hale.

**Northanger Abbey** A novel by Jane Austen which was begun in 1798 and accepted by a publisher in 1803 under the original title, 'Susan'. He did not issue it, however, and Jane Austen retrieved the manuscript in 1816. It was published posthumously in 1818.

Catherine Morland goes to Bath for the season as the guest of Mr and Mrs Allen, and there she meets the eccentric General Tilney, his son Henry, and his daughter Eleanor: Henry and Catherine fall in love. Catherine's friend Isabella Thorpe has a silly brother who gives General Tilney an exaggerated account of Catherine's wealth; the general approves of her and invites her to Northanger Abbey, the Tilney's medieval home.

Catherine, who has read too many of Mrs Radcliffe's gothic novels, imagines a gruesome secret at Northanger Abbey, one which involves the general. When her suspicions are revealed, by Henry, to have no more substance than that which her imagination provides, Catherine is deeply humiliated. But when she recovers her

'Tales of Wonder!' by James Gillray, 1802. Catherine Morland, the heroine of *Northanger Abbey*, was an assiduous reader of gothic novels. British Museum Print Room.

balance – Henry loves her, and the elegant and pretty Eleanor has become her friend – it is soon upset again by her almost being ordered out of the house by the general. Meanwhile, Henry's brother, Captain Tilney, has been flirting with Isabella Thorpe, who is engaged to Catherine's brother. Catherine's friendship with Isabella ceases abruptly; the engagement ceases also and Captain Tilney drops Isabella.

Catherine returns home, and is soon followed there by Henry. The general has ordered him to have no more to do with Catherine but Henry refuses, demanding an explanation – which is that Isabella's brother has met the general in London, and in a spiteful mood represents Catherine as a penniless girl, implying that they were all deceived. The general, believing the worst of Catherine, got rid of her as soon as he could. Now, however, restored to a sensible humour by the truth, and by Eleanor's marriage to a viscount, he gives Henry his blessing.

*Northanger Abbey* is Jane Austen's shortest novel and it proceeds at a lively pace. With the skill and grace that characterizes her major novels (she referred to it as 'this little work') she presents a normal, '*almost* pretty' girl, with a lively imagination and a fondness for gothic romances, who discovers that the real world can deliver more than enough shocks of its own.

**North Briton, The** A political weekly founded by John Wilkes in 1762 and run with the help of Charles Churchill. Lord Bute's paper, edited by Tobias Smollett, was called *The Briton*, though proprietor and editor were Scots. Wilkes's name for his weekly was carefully chosen: *The North Briton* was supposed to be edited by a Scot, one who saw reason for rejoicing in the ascendancy of the 'North Britons' in powerful positions. The paper was suppressed after Wilkes, in no. 45, exposed himself to prosecution for libel. See **Wilkes, John**.

***Northern Lasse, The***   A comedy by Richard Brome, first produced about 1629 and first published in 1632. The northern lass of the title is Constance, who sends a letter to her love, Sir Philip Luckless, in London. The letter arrives as Luckless is about to marry the wealthy widow Fitchow; but he mistakes the sender, believing the letter is from a lady of dubious morals, also named Constance. He ignores the letter and marries the widow – and then discovers his mistake. The comedy concerns the efforts of Luckless to extricate himself from his marriage; and the widow's counterintrigues to prevent him. All ends well for Luckless and his Constance.

***Northward Hoe***   A comedy by Thomas Dekker and John Webster, produced about 1605 and first published in 1607. The plot concerns the efforts of Greenshield to seduce Mistress Maybury, who rejects him. He tries to convince her husband that she is unfaithful by producing a ring he has stolen from her. Maybury, convinced of her innocence, takes his revenge upon Greenshield with the help of the old poet, Bellamont. The character of Bellamont is an amiable caricature of the authors' fellow playwright, George Chapman.

**Norton, Caroline Elizabeth Sarah** 1808–77. Caroline Sheridan was a granddaughter of the playwright Sheridan; she married the Hon C. G. Norton in 1827. She published *The Sorrows of Rosalie: A Tale with Other Poems* (1829) and enjoyed a considerable success. She divorced Norton when he sued her for her earnings as a writer and subsequently gave much of her time in active support of the Married Women's Property Act. The success in carrying this badly needed measure into law was largely due to her. Caroline Norton's career was the model for George Meredith's novel *Diana of the Crossways* (1885). She married Sir William Stirling-Maxwell in 1871. As a poet Caroline Norton is forgotten, though 'The Arab's Farewell to His Steed' and 'I do not love thee' were until recently popular anthology pieces.

**Norton, Charles Eliot** 1827–1908.   The son of the Biblical scholar Andrews Norton, Charles Eliot Norton was Professor of History of Fine Art at Harvard from 1873 to 1898. A regular contributor to the *Atlantic Monthly* and coeditor of *The North American Review*, he also helped to found *The Nation* in 1865. Norton was a frequent visitor to Europe and had a wide range of friends among writers and artists on both sides of the Atlantic. His *Letters*, published in 1913, are a valuable document of intellectual life in Massachusetts in the latter half of the 19th century and of his own critical attitude: they are also entertaining and informative. Other books by Charles Eliot Norton are a prose translation of Dante's *The Divine Comedy* (1891–92), editions of Donne's poetry (1895), the early letters of Thomas Carlyle (1886), and *Notes of Travel and Study in Italy* (1860).

**Norton, Thomas** 1532–84. The son of a wealthy London citizen Norton entered the Inner Temple in 1555. He was a zealous Protestant and translated Calvin's *Christianae Religionis Institutio* into English (1561), and his wife was one of the daughters of Thomas Cranmer. A successful lawyer, he became counsel to the Stationers' Company in 1562 and Remembrancer to the City of London in 1570.

During his years at the Middle Temple he became friends with Thomas Sackville (later Earl of Dorset) and this led to their collaboration on the tragedy **Gorboduc**, which was acted before Elizabeth I at the Inner Temple Hall in 1562.

***Nostromo: A Tale of the Seaboard***.   A novel by Joseph Conrad, first published in *T. P.'s Weekly* (January–October 1904) and in volume form in the same year.

In the South American republic of Costaguana the most important resource is the silver mine of San Tome. This is inherited by Charles Gould; the Goulds have been settled in Costaguana for generations and Charles returns from England, after completing his education, with an English wife. They move into the Gould mansion in the port and capital, Sulaco. Gould's father had died of the strain imposed by trying to deal with successive revolutionary governments, who regard the mine as something to plunder. Charles Gould obtains backing from North America and re-opens the mine, making it pay by going along with the expected corruption in the country's official circles. He also backs Ribiera, a president who seems to promise better and more humane rule for Costaguana. In Sulaco the foreman of lightermen is the much-respected Nostromo, a Genoese, who is trusted by both the wealthy and the workers: both sides know he is incorruptible. He lives in the house of his fellow Genoese, Giorgio Viola. The town's newspaper, which supports Ribiera, has been founded and is edited by Martin Decoud. Returned from Europe, the dilettante Decoud was persuaded to his course by Avellanos, one of Ribiera's supporters.

Avellanos' daughter, Antonia, and Decoud are in love.

Ribiera's regime is overturned in a military coup and the president manages to escape on board a steamer. There is a large consignment of silver in the port and the rabble is out of hand; it must be loaded on to a lighter and transferred to a European ship. The task is entrusted to Nostromo, who is given Decoud as his helper. The two men move out at night and head for the Isabel Islands, where Nostromo intends to wait until the steamer is sighted. An encounter with a rebel ship damages the lighter; Nostromo is forced to run it aground on Great Isabel and bury the silver. Decoud remains on the island with the silver while Nostromo, shaken by the near disaster of the mission, succeeds in getting back to Sulaco, where his courage and intelligence are hastily made use of and the political situation is reversed. Gould can see prosperity returning with a stable government under Ribiera, but when the silver is remembered it is discovered that the hapless Decoud, isolated in Great Isabel, has given up hope and drowned himself in circumstances which make it appear that the silver was lost at sea.

Nostromo, a man whose integrity was founded on his pride in his capabilities, realizes that to his employer, Captain Mitchell of the steamship company, and to Gould, the owner of the silver, he is no more than a useful tool; he lets them believe that the silver is lost. With the coming of stability the mine prospers and Gould's wife sees it become an obsession with her husband and spoil their relationship. A lighthouse is built on Great Isabel and Georgio Viola becomes keeper; he moves to the island with his wife and two daughters. Nostromo, affianced to Linda Viola, has been enriching himself; he has bought a trading schooner and he visits the island secretly to take away a few ingots at a time. He falls in love with Linda's sister, Estelle, and one night he is shot by his old friend Giorgio, who is on the lookout for an intruder. While he lies dying in the hospital of Sulaco he sends for Mrs Gould and offers to tell her where the supposedly lost silver lies hidden. She does not wish to hear – the hateful silver is not missed by anyone now. The novel closes with the unhappy certainty that the peace of a state in which the hopes of continued stability depend on circumstances which favour private gain is not likely to continue for long.

**Novum Organum:** *Summi Angliae Cancellarii Instauratio Magna.* A philosophical treatise in Latin by Francis Bacon, first published in 1620. It forms the second part of *Instauratio magna.* See also **Bacon, Francis.**

Bacon in this book takes the ideas of *The Advancement of Learning*, gives them a systematic exposition, and offers a method of extension of knowledge. He rejects the deductive method, the syllogism, which was based on abstraction, in favour of observation and experiment – an inductive method. He describes the defects to which the human mind is subject and which must be acknowledged and overcome, the 'idols' which prevent man from attaining essential knowledge. He lists them as *Idola tribus* (the idols of the tribe), *Idola specus* (the idols of the cave), *Idola fori* (the idols of the market-place), and *Idola theatri* (the idols of the theatre). From each of these comes an inherited preconception and the first stage to learning must be the rejection of it. This done, he offers a method of interpreting nature by three inductive methods.

Bacon's 'New Instrument' was imperfect in many respects but it was a milestone in natural philosophy and his principles of investigation were correct.

**Nubbles, Kit** The awkward, honest lad employed as the errand-boy in *The Old Curiosity Shop* by Charles Dickens. He is devoted to Nell and does his best to help her and her grandfather, thereby earning the hatred of Quilp, who nearly succeeds in framing him. At the end of the story he marries Barbara, the Garlands' pretty housemaid.

**Nun's Priest's Tale, The** See **Canterbury Tales, The.**

**Nurse** In Shakespeare's *Romeo and Juliet* she has no name but is a major character. She has looked after Juliet since she was a baby and she acts as go-between for her and Romeo. She finds Juliet apparently dead in Act IV Scene 5.

# O

**Oak, Gabriel** In Thomas Hardy's *Far from the Madding Crowd*, the shepherd who loses his flock and goes to work for Bathsheba Everdene, the heroine of the story.

**Oberon** The king of the fairies in Shakespeare's *A Midsummer Night's Dream*. He quarrels with Titania over a changeling boy and puts a charm on her. The result is that she falls in love with Bottom, given an ass's head by Puck.

**O'Brien, Edna** 1932–  . Edna O'Brien was born in Tuamgraney in Clare, Ireland. She was educated at Scarriff, nearby, and at Loughrea in

Galway. Later she studied pharmacy in Dublin and she is a Licentiate of the Pharmaceutical College of Ireland. Her first novel was *The Country Girls* (1960), followed by *The Lonely Girl* (1962) and *Girls in Their Married Bliss* (1964). Her later work is darker in tone and reflects both her experience of a harsh and rigidly conventional background and her objection to the position of women not only there but in the apparently more liberated society of England. But while her attitudes have been criticized the quality of her writing has always been praised. Her later books are *August is a Wicked Month* (1965), *Casualties of Peace* (1966), *The Love Object* (1968, short stories), *A Pagan Place* (1970), *Night* (1972), *A Scandalous Woman and Other Stories* (1974), *Mother Ireland* (1976, travel report), *Johnny I Hardly Knew You* (1977), and *Mrs Reinhardt and Other Stories* (1978, called *A Rose in the Heart* in the USA).

**O'Brien, Fitz-James** *c.*1828–62. Irish born, Fitz-James O'Brien went to the USA in his 20s. He was already an experienced journalist but his reputation as a writer was made in the USA, where his short stories were highly regarded. He fought in the Civil War and died of wounds sustained at the Battle of Bloomery Gap. O'Brien's most famous short story is *The Diamond Lens* (1858), which tells of an inventor who produces a powerful microscope. By means of this he is able to see a sylphlike creature in a drop of moisture and becomes obsessed with it. His other stories were also written in this fantastic vein. He was a successful playwright (*The Gentleman from Ireland*, 1854) and wrote verse. O'Brien's *Poems and Stories* were collected by his friend William Winter and published in 1881.

**O Captain! My Captain!** Walt Whitman's most famous poem was first published in *Sequel to Drum Taps*, which became part of the fourth edition of *Leaves of Grass* (1867). It was one of two laments for Abraham Lincoln and in fact the poet himself thought far more of the other – 'When Lilacs Last in the Dooryard Bloom'd'. But the shorter poem attained more popularity because of its conventional form, which demanded less of the reader. In it the poet tells of the ship coming home safely, though the captain who brought it home (Lincoln) lies 'Fallen cold and dead'.

**O'Casey, Sean** 1880–1964. Sean O'Casey (Shaun O'Cathasaigh) was born in Dublin, the youngest in a large Protestant family struggling to exist in the slums. He suffered from bad eyesight and this blighted even the elementary education which was all he ever knew. He did not read properly until he was 13 and after that he read everything he could lay hands on. For most of his early working life he laboured on the roads. Meanwhile he learned Gaelic, became an active trade unionist, helped to organize the Irish Citizen Army (1914), took part in the Easter Rising (1916), and wrote three plays which were rejected by the Abbey Theatre. Then **The Shadow of a Gunman** was produced there in April 1923, and O'Casey's skill in the dramatic treatment of the lives of the urban poor, involved in momentous events, made his reputation. *Kathleen Listens In: A Phantasy in One Act* was produced at the Abbey in October 1923, and **Juno and The Paycock** in the following March. The play's success was repeated in London in 1925 and it is now acknowledged as one of the major works of 20th-century English drama.

**The Plough and the Stars** was produced at the Abbey in February 1926 and caused a riot in the house. The Irish proved remarkably sensitive about themselves in the face of O'Casey's tragic irony, just as, not 20 years before, they had in the face of Synge's comic irony. The truth of both Synge's and O'Casey's work was plain to W. B. Yeats, who rose in wrath to confront the audience; but relations between O'Casey and Yeats were to founder on another play of O'Casey's. The reception of the moving and memorable *The Plough and the Stars* embittered the author, who went to live in England; he stayed there for the rest of his life.

O'Casey's plays of life in the Dublin slums during the Easter Rising and the civil war were a new departure in the theatre: the violence

Sean O'Casey at a rehearsal of *The Plough and the Stars* in 1926. The playwright in conversation with actress Ria Mooney, who played the prostitute Rosie Redmond.

which erupts into the poorest homes; the comedy of everyday life observed with a merciless eye, in juxtaposition to the tragedies arising from the identification of humble men with a cause which puts their lives in pawn, and the women who wait and pray and support them. O'Casey's characters have no lilting poetic language for their utterance but they have the poetry of truth, and O'Casey's characterization is faultless. The three plays deal with the chief phases of the Irish 'troubles'. The Easter Rising is the subject of *The Plough and the Stars*, the suppression of the Irish guerrillas by the British forces of *The Shadow of a Gunman*, and the Civil War of *Juno and the Paycock*. The last-named is perhaps the most famous but it is also the one which defies successful revival because the part of Jack Boyle, the paycock, is so difficult to play. It seems tailored to fit the talents of a particular sort of Irish actor and no other kind can make it convincing. The finest play of the three is *The Plough and the Stars*.

In 1928 Yeats rejected O'Casey's new play, *The Silver Tassie*, for production at the Abbey Theatre and set off a literary feud which continued for decades. The play, an expressionist anti-war tragi-comedy, was staged in London in 1929 and was received with respect. *Within the Gates* (London, 1934) and *The Star Turns Red* (London, 1940) were also received with respect. It was not until 1943 that another play by Sean O'Casey, *Red Roses for Me*, was given its first performance in Dublin, at the Olympia Theatre on 14 March. By then O'Casey's particular genius, which had responded to a particular Irish urban way of life, had dried up. He was now writing in standard English about issues in standard socialist abstractions. *Red Roses for Me* is set in Dublin; but the Dublin he knew was not present in the audience, which came from a Dublin changed out of recognition. *Purple Dust* (Newcastle-on-Tyne, 1943), *Oak Leaves and Lavender* (London, 1947), and *Cock-a-Doodle Dandy* (Newcastle-on-Tyne, 1949) were followed by the anti-clerical *The Bishop's Bonfire* (Gaiety Theatre, Dublin, 1955). At the Dublin Festival of 1958 O'Casey's *The Drums of Father Ned*, another play to displease the church, led to the Archbishop of Dublin's refusal to inaugurate the festival. O'Casey withdrew the play (Samuel Beckett also withdrew his work, in sympathy) and thereafter discouraged professional productions of his work in Ireland.

O'Casey's later plays were not successful in the theatre but attention was paid by the critics, a minority of whom praised them. But the truth seems to have been that O'Casey needed his own ground to work upon, and some of that, fortunately, comes through with arresting clarity in his volumes of autobiography: *I Knock on the Door* (1939), *Pictures in the Hallway* (1942), *Drums Under the Windows* (1945), *Innishfallen, Fare Thee Well* (1949), *Rose and Crown* (1952), and *Sunset and Evening Star* (1954).

**Occam (*or* Ockham), William of**  See **William of Occam**.

**Occleve, Thomas** *c*.1368–*c*.1426. The name is sometimes spelled Hoccleve and may be a placename in origin, possibly Hockliffe in Bedfordshire, but very little is known about Occleve's early life. His working life as a clerk in the Privy Seal office was spent in London. His employment is recorded as having begun in 1378 and ended in 1425. He had a very small income of £4 (whatever that was worth in medieval England) and had aspired to a benefice. He was always short of funds, since he spent most of his nights in dissipation. This much is known of his life from his own words, contained in verses to Sir Henry Somer, pleading that the payment of his yearly pension be expedited. Generally Occleve seems to have lived for the day, even though he married; he enjoyed no security of the kind known to Chaucer or to his contemporary Lydgate. He was at last granted a small benefice from a Hampshire priory in 1424 but it is not known how long he lived to enjoy it.

He hoped to augment his income with his verse: those writings that can be attributed to him with certainty (the canon is not established) are hopefully addressed to Henry, Prince of Wales (later Henry V), the Duke of Gloucester, the Duke of Bedford, the Duke and Duchess of York, and John of Gaunt among others.

Unlike his contemporary Lydgate – a man cut off from society – Occleve was very much in the world; but, no more than Lydgate did he leave any lasting impression on the literature of England. His was one of the voices of the time, immediate – and limited. There is nothing profound in the work of Thomas Occleve: he is the 'average poet' of medieval London and a fair representation of his life and times emerges from his work, the best of which is considered to be his *Ars Secondi Mori*.

Occleve's other chief works are the autobiographical poem *La Male Regle* (1406), *Regiment of Princes* (1412), a translation of the *De Regimine Principum* of Aegidius Romanus, and two verse tales from the *Gesta Romanorum* (1421). His *Regiment of Princes* contains Occleve's tribute to Chaucer, whom he admired without reservation. Those works attributed with certainty to Occleve were collected and edited by F. J. Furnivall for the Early English Text Society (1892–97).

**Occurrence at Owl Creek Bridge, An** See *In the Midst of Life*.

**Ochiltree, Edie** The old bedesman of Scott's *The Antiquary*. One of Scott's most successful characters, he is as tough as an oak tree in spite of his age, a storehouse of local information, and a man of great common sense. Both shrewd and kind, he helps Lovel expose the scoundrel Dousterswivel and also helps him to discover the truth of his own origins.

**O'Connor, Flannery** 1925–64. Flannery O'Connor was born in Savannah, Georgia. She was educated at the Women's College of Georgia and also studied at the Writer's Workshop in the University of Iowa. During a short career she made a strong impression with her strange God-obsessed novels and stories. How she might have developed cannot be conjectured but the small body of work she has left makes her early death a matter for regret. She wrote two novels, *Wise Blood* (1952) and *The Violent Bear it Away* (1960), and two books of short stories, *A Good Man is Hard to Find* (1955, called *The Artificial Nigger and Other Stories* in England) and *Everything that Rises Must Converge* (1965). Flannery O'Connor's *Complete Stories* was published in 1971.

**O'Connor, Frank** 1903–66. The pseudonym of Michael Francis O'Donovan, who was born in Cork and educated there at the Christian Brothers School. In the Civil War he fought on the Republican side and served a prison sentence in 1923; he used the time for extensive reading. Later he worked as a librarian in Cork and began to write, first in Gaelic. His stories in English were first published by AE in *The Irish Statesman* and the first collection was *Guests of the Nation* (1931). Collections appeared at regular intervals and his reputation increased with each one: *The Saint and Mary Kate* (1932), *Bones of Contention* (1936), *Three Old Brothers* (1937), *The Big Fellow* (1937), *Crab Apple Jelly* (1944), *The Common Chord* (1947), *Traveller's Samples* (1950), *Domestic Relations* (1957), and *My Oedipus Complex* (1963). *The Wild Bird's Nest* (1932), *Lords and Commons* (1938), and *The Little Monasteries* (1963) are translations of Irish verse. During the 1930s O'Connor went to work in Dublin, where W. B. Yeats, who admired his work enough to compare him to Chekov, persuaded him to become a director of the Abbey Theatre and encouraged him to write plays. O'Connor resigned from the Abbey during the censorship quarrels of 1958 and spent the rest of his life in the USA. Among his other works are the plays *In the Train* and *The Invincibles* (1937), *Moses' Rock* (1938), *Time's Rocket* (1939), and *The Statue's Daughter* (1940); a novel, *Dutch Interior* (1940); and two volumes of autobiography, *An Only Child* (1961) and *My Father's Son* (1968, posthumous). O'Connor's critical essays are published in *Towards an Appreciation of Literature* (1945), *The Art of the Theatre* (1947), *The Mirror in the Roadway: The Modern Novel* (1957), *Shakespeare's Progress* (1960), and *The Lonely Voice: The Short Story* (1963).

**Octavia** The sister of Octavius Caesar in Shakespeare's *Antony and Cleopatra*. She is married to Antony as part of the peacemaking process between her brother and Antony and she is devoted to her husband. But Antony goes back to Cleopatra and the breach between the two men becomes irreparable.

**Octavius Caesar** In Shakespeare's *Julius Caesar* and *Antony and Cleopatra*, the great-nephew of Caesar who becomes, after Caesar's murder, a triumvir with Mark Antony and Lepidus and takes part in the defeat of Brutus and Cassius at Philippi. In the later play he views Antony's relations with Cleopatra with uneasiness and, to keep the ruling triumvirate strong, gives his sister Octavia in marriage to Antony. He deprives Lepidus of his triumvirate and is then obliged to make war on Antony and Cleopatra. Octavius wins in the end and becomes sole master of the Roman world. He is the cool, far-seeing politician – not likable, but better fitted than Antony for the great undertakings their positions imply.

**Octopus, The:** *A Story of California*. A novel by Frank Norris, first published in 1901. It is the first part of his uncompleted trilogy, *The Epic of the Wheat*.

The octopus of the title is the powerful Pacific and Southwestern Railroad that in the course of the story strangles the wheat farmers of California. Opposition by the farmers is led by Magnus Derrick, who owns a large ranch near Bonneville. The railroad is the most powerful vested interest and dominates the state government, gains total control of the town of Bonneville, and is behind the movement of all prices and interest rates. Many of the wheat farmers hold their land on option from the railroad, which can dispossess them at will. Freight rates can be manipulated to ruin farmers if the railway interests want their land and the wheat may be purchased at rock bottom prices. Magnus Derrick's direct opponent is the railroad agent Behrman, who eventually dies in the wheat he has plundered from the ruined and dispossessed farmers, wheat that he was intending to sell at a huge profit. Derrick himself is ruined when the railroad succeeds in bribing his son Lyman, a lawyer on the state commission, to act against the farmers' interests.

Other characters are Dyke, the railroad engineer who wants to be a farmer, and Shelgrim the railroad president, who blandly tells the protesting poet, Presley, that what has happened is really nothing to do with people – it is all a matter of economic forces and the law of supply and demand.

**Odd Women, The** A novel by George Gissing, first published in 1893. The 'odd women' of the title are those women of Victorian society who are helpless in the face of change. The Madden sisters are a respectable doctor's three daughters. He is, however, improvident, and his death leaves them stranded with very little money and no training of any kind. The loneliness and poverty of the sisters in London lodgings and their desperate maintenance of middle-class respectability – Virginia has found a secret consolation in gin – is conveyed with considerable pathos. In contrast to the Madden sisters is Rhoda Nunn, an active feminist who finds a role in life in preparing women for some fate other than marriage.

**Odets, Clifford** 1906–63. Clifford Odets was born in Philadelphia and brought up in New York. After leaving high school he found work as an actor in radio, and later with the Theatre Guild. He joined the Group Theatre in 1930 and used his spare time as an actor to write. He achieved a striking success in 1935 with *Waiting for Lefty*, a short play about the New York taxi-drivers' strike, in which he made full use of European expressionistic technique. In the same year three more of his plays were produced on Broadway: *Till the Day I Die*, about the Communist opposition to the Nazis in Germany; *Paradise Lost*, depicting a middle-class family's reaction to the Depression; and, most memorably, *Awake and Sing!* This is a picture of a poor Jewish family, the Bergers, living in the Bronx. The father is a failure and the household is dominated by Bessie, the mother. Her father, Jacob, encourages his grandson, Ralph, to find a life that is really his. Hennie, Ralph's sister, after an agony of guilt and floundering and a hasty marriage to conceal her pregnancy, eventually yields to the man who has always loved her, the passionate, disabled war veteran Moe. Bessie's eternal preoccupation is with the present; Jacob, a figure of the past, looks to the future in the person of Ralph and commits suicide so that Ralph may collect the insurance and look for his

own identity. But tomorrow already belongs to Ralph; by the end of the play he is strong enough to see it and he leaves the money with his family. Odets's next play, *I Can't Sleep* (1936), was less impressive, but he enjoyed another success with *Golden Boy* (1937), the tragedy of a promising musician who finds a rapid way to success and wealth as a boxer.

Odets's later plays, *Rocket to the Moon* (1938), *Night Music* (1940), and *Clash by Night* (1941), were surpassed by *The Big Knife* (1948), which made excellent use of his experience of Hollywood. *The Country Girl* (1950), probably the biggest commercial success of his career, is a domestic drama. *The Flowering Peach* (1954) is based on the biblical story of Noah.

**Officers and Gentlemen** The second volume of the trilogy *Sword of Honour*. See **Waugh, Evelyn (Arthur St John)**.

**Of Human Bondage** See **Maugham, W(illiam) Somerset**.

**Of Time and the River** See **Wolfe, Thomas (Clayton)**.

**O'Grady, Standish James** 1846–1928. Standish O'Grady was born at Castletown Berehaven in Cork, Ireland. He was educated at Tipperary Grammar School and Trinity College, Dublin. Later he studied law and was called to the Bar but never practised, preferring the world of letters. His chosen field was the epic past of Ireland. His scholarly research and his clear, lucid prose give him an honoured place in the rediscovery of Ireland's historical and poetic heritage, almost obliterated by centuries of occupation. His two-volume *History of Ireland* (1878 and 1880) aroused considerable interest and had great influence on the poets. *The Early Bardic Literature of Ireland* (1879) also helped inspire the Irish revival.

O'Grady was criticized for the romantic ardour of his history and his next work, *A History of Ireland: Critical and Philosophical* (1881) was an attempt to correct this tendency; but it was the romance of the past, not the plain facts, which inspired O'Grady and after one volume he abandoned it. He wrote some political essays also, but of more lasting interest were his novels and the retelling of epic stories from his history. *Red Hugh's Captivity* (1889) and *The Flight of the Eagle* (1897) are a novel and sequel about Ireland in the days of Elizabeth I; Irish myth is the matter of *Cuculain: An Epic* (1882), *Finn and his Companions* (1892), *The Coming of Cuculain* (1894), and *The Departure of Dermot*, *The Triumph of Cuculain*, and *The Passing of Cuculain* (all 1917). *The Bog of Stars* (1893) is a collection of stories about Ireland in the 16th century; *Hugh Roe O'Donnell* (1902) is a play set in the same period.

**Old Bachelor, The** William Congreve's first play, a comedy, was produced in March 1693 and published in the same year. Its success on the stage was aided considerably by the presence of Anne Bracegirdle and Thomas Betterton.

The old bachelor of the title is Heartwell, who maintains a pose of despising women. But he falls in love with Silvia and is persuaded to marry her, only to discover that she is Vainlove's discarded mistress. He is later intensely relieved to discover that the parson who married them is Vainlove's friend Belmour, in disguise to pursue an intrigue with Laetitia Fondlewife, already married to an uxorious old banker. Heartwell is still a bachelor, and a husband is found for Silvia in the person of Sir Joseph Wittol, a foolish old man deceived into believing he is marrying the wealthy Araminta. His companion, the bully, Captain Bluffe, is similarly deceived into marrying Silvia's maid.

**Oldbuck, Jonathan** The antiquary of Sir Walter Scott's novel *The Antiquary*, who is devoted to the study of coins and medals. Beneath his façade of irritability and misogyny he is a generous and kindly man of great learning. Scott drew much of his character from a boyhood friend, George Constable, and there is much of Scott himself, also, in Jonathan Oldbuck.

**Old Creole Days** A book of stories of life in 19th-century New Orleans by George Washington Cable, first published in 1879. The following four stories are particularly notable.

The *Café des Exiles* belongs to the amiable, elderly M. D'Hemecourt and is the centre of a smuggling plot. The leader is Major Galahad Shaughnessy, who is so determined to be clever that his plans come to nothing. However, he does win Pauline D'Hemecourt.

In *Jean-ah Poquelin* the character in the title, a slave trader, retires suddenly to his house in the suburbs. His acquaintances are puzzled – and also wonder about the disappearance of Jacques Poquelin, his brother. The house declines, the grounds become a wilderness, trespassers are fiercely discouraged, and everyone believes the worst of Poquelin. Then he dies – and Jacques is discovered in the house, an aged and helpless leper whom his brother had concealed and cared for all those years.

'*Tite Poulette* is Madame John's daughter and their neighbour, Kristian, a young Dutchman, falls in love with her. He champions Poulette in a quarrel and suffers injury on her behalf; she nurses him back to health. When Kristian proposes Poulette tearfully refuses him, explaining that her mother is part Negro. But the story ends happily when Madame John reveals that Poulette is her foster child – she took care of the child when her White parents died during her infancy.

*Madame Delicieuse* is engaged to Dr Mossy, a forward-looking young man who champions scientific advance. But Dr Mossy will not marry her because of the long-standing quarrel with his father, General de Villivicencio. The General is a hidebound old soldier with his head stuffed full of old Creole notions of honour; he has disinherited his son. The story relates how Madame Delicieuse uses her wits to bring about a reconciliation between father and son, making her marriage possible.

**Old Curiosity Shop, The** A novel by Charles Dickens, first published as a weekly serial in *Master Humphrey's Clock* (April 1840 to February 1841): the original narrator was Master Humphrey. It was first published in volume form in 1841.

Little Nell (Nell Trent) lives in the shop of the title with her grandfather, the proprietor. A prey to grasping relatives, the grandfather is also a gambler. In the hope of repairing his ruined finances and providing for Nell, he borrows money from Daniel Quilp, the evil dwarf, moneylender and smuggler, who has designs on Nell and has convinced himself that her grandfather is a rich miser. The grandfather loses the borrowed money also, and he and Nell flee to the country – he cannot possibly repay his debts. Quilp seizes the shop and sets out in pursuit of them, determined on revenge.

Nell and her grandfather roam the countryside, reduced to beggary, and in the course of their wanderings meet a number of arresting characters. Kit Nubbles, errand-boy of the curiosity shop and devoted to Nell, does his best to find and help them. He becomes a victim of Quilp's hatred, which nearly succeeds in getting him framed and transported. Nell's great-uncle, returned from abroad, is anxious to help them, too, but he only traces their whereabouts when it is too late. Nell dies, exhausted by their troubles, and her grandfather dies too, soon after. Quilp, trying to evade arrest, falls into the Thames near his wharf on the south bank and drowns. Kit is set free when Quilp's infamy is exposed and marries a pretty housemaid.

*The Old Curiosity Shop* is often dismissed as a particularly glutinous example of Dickens at his sentimental worst, and it is true that Nell and her grandfather are hard to swallow. But it is no worse – or better – in that respect than *Nicholas Nickleby*. Indeed, the book is better than its reputation, as will be discovered by those who take the trouble to read it. The wanderings of Nell and her grandfather are a framework for the presentation of some fascinating characters – creations which show Dickens at his imaginative best. Quilp is a marvel of nastiness – he is evil with such gusto, as evidenced in the scenes at his home, with his unfortunate spouse a permanent victim of his sadism.

**Old Fortunatus, The Pleasant Comedie of** An allegorical play by Thomas Dekker, first produced before Elizabeth I on Christmas night, probably in 1598. It was first published in 1600. The source of the play was the story in the German *Volksbuch* (1509), which was dramatized by Hans Sachs in 1553.

An old beggar, Fortunatus, encounters the goddess Fortune. She offers him long life, wisdom, strength, health, beauty, or riches. He decides to take the last and is endowed with a purse that will yield ten pieces of gold at any time. He goes on his travels with his sons and frequently encounters both Vice and Virtue. During his travels he gains possession of the miraculous hat of the Soldan of Turkey, which takes the wearer wherever he wants to go. But Death takes Fortunatus; the purse and hat go to his son, Andelocia, who eagerly follows the same way of life as his father – and comes to grief when Fortune withdraws the purse and the hat. He has learned nothing and without Fortune's favour can make nothing of his life.

**Oldham, John** 1653–83. The son of a Nonconformist minister, Oldham was born in Shipton-Moyne in Gloucestershire. A minor Restoration poet and translator, Oldham impressed his contemporaries, Dryden among them. They regarded him as a poet of great promise whose untimely death from smallpox was a great loss to literature. Oldham was educated at Tetbury Grammar School and St Edmund Hall, Oxford, and after taking his degree in 1674 earned his living as a teacher.

Oldham's chief works were satires: *A Satyr upon a Woman, who by her Falsehood and Scorn was the Death of my Friend* (1678), *A Satyr against Vertue* (1679) and four *Satyrs upon the Jesuits* (1681). The manner is confident, the matter – particularly in the last-named – deplorable. Oldham began his satires the year after the 'Popish Plot' of Titus Oates, and they demonstrate, in rhymed couplets, how far mindless vituperation can go. Perhaps Dryden's tribute was earned by

Oldham's other works: the ode *Upon the Works of Ben Jonson*, the satires in the manner of Horace, and the two translations from Juvenal. His *Poems and Translations* appeared in 1683, the year of his death, and he was widely read until the early 18th century.

**Old Maid, The** A short novel by Edith Wharton, one of the *Old New York* series, first published in 1924. (The others in the volume were *False Dawn*, *The Spark*, and *New Year's Day*.) *The Old Maid* was dramatized by Zoe Akins in 1935 and also became a celebrated film (1939).

The cousins, Charlotte and Delia Lovell, are both in love with Clem Spender but it is Charlotte he really cares for. Delia marries the wealthy Jim Ralston and after Clem's death Charlotte bears his daughter. The illegitimate child is taken by Delia and brought up as her own; Delia is bound by convention and in the circumstances has no trouble in overbearing Charlotte's wishes. But later she also bullies Charlotte into breaking her engagement with Joseph Ralston. Charlotte takes her place in Delia's household as a maiden aunt whom her daughter, Tina, not knowing the truth, finds rather tiresome and humourless. When Tina's marriage is about to take place Charlotte's feelings nearly get the better of her and there is a bitter scene with Delia on the night before the wedding. After the ceremony the cousins are alone and Delia acknowledges that she had been wrong to interfere in Charlotte's life; everyone has the right to love and suffer in their own fashion. The two women, reconciled, settle down to a peaceful old age.

**Oldmixon, John** 1673–1742. The son of a long-established Somerset family, John Oldmixon was born at Axbridge and later succeeded to the manor of Oldmixon near Bridgwater. He was educated privately with Humphrey, the young brother of Admiral Blake, in the admiral's household. His first works were poems, which are now forgotten. But his career as a historian began with *A Complete History of England, with the Lives of all the Kings and Queens thereof to the Death of William III*, which he edited. It was published in 1706 (with additions in 1716).

Oldmixon's first real contribution was *The British Empire in America* (1708), the first history of that kind. It is not highly regarded now, relying overmuch on the accounts of others, but it filled a need at the time. *The Secret History of Europe* (written in four volumes, 1712–15) was unsparing in its criticism of the Tory party and its willingness to reach agreement with the French – Oldmixon was a dedicated Whig. *The Critical History of England* (two volumes, 1724–26) has a title the length of a paragraph explaining that his intention is to correct the work of historians whom he regarded as guilty of bias; Clarendon, Gilbert Burnet, and Laurence Echard are named. To the third edition of the *Critical History* (1727) Oldmixon added an *Essay on Criticism* that revealed his own bias, a fierce anti-Tory one, and he became the target for Pope and the other Tory wits. *The History of England during the Reigns of the Royal House of Stuart* (1730) is regarded by some scholars as his best work; it states at length the reason for believing that the Oxford editors of Clarendon's *History* meddled with the text for political reasons.

**Old Mortality** The second of Sir Walter Scott's *Tales of My Landlord*, published in 1816.

The title is the nickname of Robert Paterson who, at the end of the 18th century, wandered round Scotland caring for the graves of the Cameronians, strict Covenanters. His stories of the Covenanters form the basis of the novel, one of the principal characters being Graham of Claverhouse, who led the king's forces against them.

The hero of the story is Henry Morton, who shelters Burley, an old friend of his father, not knowing him to be guilty of having taken part in the murder of the Archbishop of St Andrews. Morton's narrow escape from execution, and his anger at the suppression of his countrymen, lead him to join the Covenanters, though he does not share their religious extremism.

Against this background are set the vicissitudes of Morton's love for Edith Bellenden of a royalist family. His rival is the honourable Lord Evandale, who helps save Morton's life, at Edith's plea, when Morton is arrested after the murder of the archbishop. Later, when William III comes to the throne and Morton, banished after the defeat of the Covenanters at Bothwell Bridge, returns to England, Edith has given him up for dead and is about to marry Evandale. But Evandale is attacked by a band of religious fanatics and, in spite of Morton's desperate intervention, is killed.

**Old Regime in Canada, The** See **Parkman, Francis** and *France and England in North America*.

**Old St Paul's** See **Ainsworth, William Harrison**.

**Old Wife's Tale, The** A play in prose by George Peele, first published in 1595. It is usually regarded as Peele's best dramatic work. The old wife of the title is the narrator, encountered by three strollers in a forest.

Delia has been stolen by the wicked magician Sacrapant and her two brothers are searching for her. But the brothers also fall victim and a gallant knight, Sir Eumenides, sets out to rescue them. Sir Eumenides is aided in his quest by Jack's ghost – Jack was a poor man and when he died Sir Eumenides had borne the cost of a dignified funeral for him. The quest is successful, the magician defeated, and Delia and her brothers rescued. Milton used the basis of the plot for his masque *Comus*.

The whole play is a satire on the romantic drama of the time, parodying all its absurdities and unreal characters. See also **Knight of the Burning Pestle, The**.

**Old Wives' Tale, The** See **Bennett, (Enoch) Arnold**.

**Oliphant, Laurence** 1829–88. The son of the chief justice of Ceylon, Sir William Oliphant, Laurence Oliphant became a barrister but was chiefly interested in travel and adventure. He earned a considerable reputation with his accounts of his journeys, beginning with *Journey to Khatmandu* (1852). *The Russian Shores of the Black Sea* followed in 1853 (later he was consulted as an authority upon the outbreak of the Crimean War). He was Lord Elgin's secretary in the USA and Canada (1853–54) and published *Minnesota and the Far West* in 1855. As a correspondent for *The Times* he covered certain aspects of the Crimean War, the Indian Mutiny, and the Risorgimento.

Oliphant accompanied Lord Elgin to the Far East, published a *Narrative of the Earl of Elgin's Mission to China and Japan in the Years 1857, 58, 59* (1859), and sent dispatches to *The Times* from the Franco-Prussian War. To all this can be added a satirical novel about London life, *Piccadilly*, which was published in *Blackwood's Magazine* in 1865.

In 1867 Oliphant became so besotted with an American 'prophet', Thomas Lake Harris, that he surrendered all his property to him. He went to America with Harris, and with his first wife produced a weird book called *Sympneumata*, which they both believed to have been dictated by a spirit. With his second wife he founded a community of Jewish immigrants at Haifa, where he wrote several mystical works. But for all his later eccentricities, Oliphant deserves to be remembered as one of the most remarkable travel writers his age produced. *Episodes of a Life of Adventure* was published in 1887, after appearing in *Blackwood's Magazine*.

**Oliphant, Margaret** 1828–97. A Scotswoman of Edinburgh, Margaret Wilson married her cousin, the artist William Oliphant. She published her first novel in 1849, and after her death two volumes of short stories were published. Over 100 books, not all of them novels, were published during her lifetime, not to mention over 200 contributions to *Blackwood's Magazine*. From a series of novels she called *Chronicles of Carlingford*, which deal with Scottish life, she has been praised for *Miss Marjoribanks* (1866) and *Salem Chapel* (1863). Her *Annals of a Publishing House: William Blackwood and his Sons* (1897) is a useful book for students of English literature, and *A Beleaguered City* (1880) is a well-fashioned occult novel.

Margaret Oliphant was more than a remarkably prolific writer: she wrote to some purpose about life in her day and often with considerable skill. However, she had talent rather than genius and her books were forgotten after she died.

**Oliver**  In Shakespeare's *As You Like It*, the elder brother of Orlando and Jaques de Boys. He maltreats Orlando, his youngest brother, and tries to have him killed. Orlando saves his life in the Forest of Arden and the brothers are reconciled. Oliver falls in love with Celia and marries her at the end of the play.

***Oliver Twist:** or, the Parish Boy's Progress.* A novel by Charles Dickens. It was first published in *Bentley's Miscellany* (January 1837 to January 1838) in monthly parts. The first book form appeared in 1838 in three volumes: in both cases it was published under the pseudonym of Boz. Unlike its predecessor, *Pickwick*, it is a true novel and not a series of loosely connected episodes.

A pauper's child, Oliver Twist is actually born in the workhouse, his mother having been picked up half-dead in the street and carried there, where she dies giving birth to him. Until he is nine Oliver is placed in the care of Mrs Mann in a 'branch workhouse', then he is taken by Bumble, the parish beadle, to the workhouse proper. After daring to 'ask for more', Oliver is apprenticed to an undertaker where he is no better used than in the workhouse. He runs away and eventually gets to Barnet, where he is picked up by the Artful Dodger (Jack Dawkins) and taken to Fagin's den in Saffron Hill. Fagin has a stable of boys being taught to steal: his associates are Bill Sikes, a coarse and brutal burglar, and Sikes's companion Nancy. Fagin is also a receiver.

Oliver is rescued by the benevolent Mr Brownlow, but the gang kidnap him; they have a special interest, prompted by the villain Monks, in keeping him. They send him on a burgling enterprise of Bill Sikes's but the thieves are surprised and the hapless Oliver suffers a

'Oliver introduced to the respectable Old Gentleman.' George Cruikshank's illustration for *Oliver Twist* depicts Fagin, the Artful Dodger and, right, Oliver.

gunshot wound. The lady of the house, Mrs Maylie, is horrified to find that the wounded 'thief' is only a child; she and Rose, her adopted daughter, take care of Oliver.

Nancy, meanwhile, has learned that there is something about Oliver's origins that Monks wants to suppress. Trying to help the boy, she visits Rose Maylie and warns her that Fagin is being bribed by Monks to persist in Oliver's degradation and that there is some relationship between Rose herself and Oliver. With the help of Mr Brownlow enquiries are begun. Nancy's actions are discovered by the gang and Bill Sikes murders her in his rage at her apparent betrayal. In the hue and cry that follows, Sikes hangs himself accidentally and Fagin and the rest are taken. Monks is investigated by Mr Brownlow and his motives are at last revealed. He is Oliver's half-brother and greedily seeks their whole inheritance for himself. Rose Maylie is Oliver's aunt – her sister was Oliver's mother. Fagin is hanged at the end of the story and Oliver is adopted by Mr Brownlow.

Dickens was writing *Oliver Twist* while he was still working on *Pickwick* and also occupied with his manifold duties as editor of *Bentley's Miscellany*. It is, inevitably, an imperfect book – the arm of coincidence is nearly torn from its socket – but it is a marvellous book. There is scarcely a character that doesn't stay in the mind and the great set pieces – the introduction of Oliver to Fagin's den, the murder of Nancy, the hue and cry for Bill Sikes, and Fagin's last hours in the condemned cell – have hardly been equalled in his other works; his picture of life in the workhouse is unforgettable, too. Dickens's exposure of the reality behind the infamous Poor Law of 1834 and the London that lay outside the knowledge of society was something new, and new also was the total absence of any redeeming glamour in the lives of the criminals.

**Olivia** In Shakespeare's *Twelfth Night*, the countess wooed by Orsino to no avail. She falls in love with 'Cesario', who is Viola in disguise, but later settles for Viola's twin brother, Sebastian. Her steward, Malvolio, is deceived into thinking that Olivia regards him with favour and to her amazement comes to woo her.

**Omoo**, *a Narrative of Adventures in the South Seas*. Like its predecessor, *Typee*, this is a fictional narrative by Herman Melville with the same proportion of fact to imagination. It is a sequel to *Typee* and was first published in 1847.

The narrator, Tom, picked up from the sea after his flight from the Marquesas, is signed on to the *Julia*, the ship whose boat rescued him. The ship is short-handed and he is told he can sign off at the next port. The *Julia* proves to be hardly seaworthy, however, and the captain is ill and unstable. Tom makes friends with the mate, Jermin, and with the erudite experienced Dr Long Ghost. In Tahiti the crew refuse to take the ship to sea again; they are imprisoned in Papeete and a new crew is found, but the former crew believe she is doomed. Tom and the doctor find the Tahitians resentful and unfriendly but they manage to find work on a plantation in Imeco. Field work, however, is not to their liking and they resort to beachcombing, at the same time exploring and observing the people. In the end the doctor stays in Tahiti while Tom ships out on the whaler *Leviathan*.

With this book Melville brought down in full measure the wrath which had been hovering over his head since *Typee* was published. That he was a gifted storyteller was acknowledged but, perhaps even more than in his first book, it was obvious in *Omoo* that the degraded condition of the islanders was the consequence of the White man's intrusion.

**Once I Pass'd Through a Populous City** A short poem by Walt Whitman, in the *Children of Adam* group, first published in the third edition of *Leaves of Grass* (1860). The city concerned is New Orleans, where the poet worked for a time on the newspaper the *Crescent*, and the poem speaks of a brief passionate encounter. The manuscript refers to a man but the published version to a woman ('of all that city I remember only a woman'). The lines are memorable so the point is hardly relevant except to those determined to know about Walt Whitman's sexual preferences.

See **Children of Adam**.

**O'Neill, Eugene (Gladstone)** 1888–1953. Eugene O'Neill, the son of James O'Neill, a popular romantic actor, and the actress, Ellen Quinlan, was born in New York City. He attended Catholic schools and with his brother was often exposed to an unsettled life when his parents went on tour and took their children with them. O'Neill went to Princeton in 1906 but only stayed for a year; he drifted from one job to another, gaining a brief experience of newspaper work and, of great importance, the life of a seaman. His voyages to South America and South Africa brought him into contact with stevedores, derelicts, and outcasts from all walks of life, and later furnished him with characters for his work. He was married in 1909 and divorced in 1912; in the same year he was discovered to have tuberculosis and spent six months in bed. During this period he discovered what he really wanted to do; he completed two full-length plays and eleven one-act plays during the next two years. In 1914, at the age of 26, he joined George Pierce Baker's drama workshop at Harvard, and in the following year worked at the Wharf Theatre in Provincetown, Cape Cod. The Provincetown Players gave the first performances of O'Neill's work, the one-act plays of a sailor's life called *Bound East for Cardiff* (1916), *The Long Voyage Home* (1917), and *The Moon of the Caribbees* (1918). By then the Players were performing in New York and in 1920 mounted the first production of O'Neill's full-length play *Beyond the Horizon*, a domestic drama set on a New England farm, with the sea as an ever-present influence on the lives of the two brothers, Robert and Andrew Mayo, who love the same woman.

*Beyond the Horizon* won the Pulitzer Prize and confirmed that an essentially American theatre had come into being. O'Neill became a director of the Provincetown Players, and with Robert Edmond Jones managed the Greenwich Village Theatre (1923–27). He was also one of the founders of the Theatre Guild; but by degrees he withdrew from these activities and devoted all his time to the playwright's craft. Meanwhile, three more of his plays had been produced in 1920: *Diff'rent*, *Chris Christopherson*, and *The Emperor Jones*. The last named, an expressionistic drama about the disintegration of the personality of a Black dictator in flight, proved a lasting success. *Chris Christopherson* was rewritten and, as *Anna Christie* (1921), won another Pulitzer Prize; it is the story of a waterfront prostitute's attempt to escape from her degrading life. *Gold* (1921), *The Straw* (1921), and *The First Man* (1922) were followed by another successful expressionistic drama, *The Hairy Ape* (1922), the story of Yank, a stoker brutalized by his work, who comes to realize that another world exists. His attempts to communicate with it fail; the only creature he feels kinship for is the imprisoned ape in the zoo. He frees it from its cage and he is killed by it.

O'Neill returned to naturalism in *All God's Chillun Got Wings* (1924), the tragedy of a thoughtless White woman who marries an ambitious and intelligent Black man as an escape from her own problems. He enjoyed a major success with *Desire Under the Elms* (also 1924), a Zola-esque drama set in a New England farmhouse in 1850. He followed this with a romantic play, *The Fountain* (1925), about the explorer Ponce de Leon and the legend of a fountain of youth. *The Great God Brown* (1926) examines the concept of multiple personality. The actors wore masks for the faces they presented to the world, and only removed them when the character was alone or in the presence of sympathetic companions. Brown, the materialist, loves Margaret, who marries Brown's friend Dion, who seeks consolation from Cybel, a prostitute, when he fails as a painter. The only one without a mask is Cybel; when Dion dies in Brown's presence Brown takes his mask and wears it and Margaret marries him. After Brown's death Margaret devotes her life to her children and her memory of Dion, a man she only knew by the mask he wore. *Lazarus Laughed* (1927) and *Marco Millions* (1928) were followed by *Strange Interlude* (also 1928). This two-part, nine-act drama won another Pulitzer Prize for O'Neill and proved his readiness to experiment. He gives his characters elaborate asides to reveal what they are thinking, as opposed to what they say in their dialogue with each other. The plot is a narrative of some length, realized in dialogue, of the love life of Nina Leeds. It is nevertheless a powerful piece of theatre and was successfully revived by the Theatre Guild during the 1960s. *Dynamo* (1929) marked O'Neill's brief return to expressionistic theatre.

In 1931 came *Mourning Becomes Electra*, O'Neill's modern version of Aeschylus' *Oresteia*, set in New England in the aftermath of the Civil War. It has been much admired and O'Neill made a courageous essay into a difficult field. The 19th-century setting posed difficulties of its own: the atavistic terror of nemesis which torments Orestes is expressed in Aeschylus by the invocation of the Furies. There is no modern equivalent and Orin, in the third part of O'Neill's play, comes dangerously near to becoming a self-pitying bore. The incestuous proposal made by Orin to Lavinia (Electra) is completely alien to Aeschylus. But the play really fails, in its own terms, because the author could not rise to the stupendous theme; he had not the language for its expression. His next play was a complete departure, a successful comedy about youth and the awakening to adulthood called *Ah, Wilderness!* (1933). An unsuccessful play about faith, *Days Without End* (1934), was the last work of O'Neill's to be staged for some years; the playwright withdrew to concentrate on further work and refused to let any of it be staged until 1946. *The Iceman Cometh*, his first play to be seen for 12 years, reaffirmed his position as America's leading playwright. It is a tragedy of disillusion and the coming of death, set in a bar in the Bowery. O'Neill was awarded the Nobel Prize in 1936.

*A Moon for the Misbegotten* (1947) was the last of his plays to be staged during the author's lifetime. It is a long play about the tragic, frustrated love of an alcoholic and a farm woman, with a built-in philosophical discussion of faith. It was not well received, and O'Neill's last years were unhappy. His son committed suicide and he was estranged from his daughter Oona when she married Charlie Chaplin, a man her father's age, when she was 18. A progressively crippling disease made it impossible for him to go on writing. The first of his plays to be produced posthumously was *A Long Day's Journey*

Eugene O'Neill.

A scene from *A Long Day's Journey into Night* at the Helen Hayes Theatre, New York, in 1956. Jason Robards Jun. and Bradford Dillman as the Tyrone sons.

*into Night* (1956), a superb autobiographical play about his own family, here called Tyrone. The story of his mother, who became addicted to morphia through the careless attendance of a slovenly doctor, is intensely moving; this and the part of the elder Tyrone present a marvellous challenge to gifted actors. Two parts of an unfinished cycle have also been produced: *A Touch of the Poet* (1958) and *More Stately Mansions* (1967). *A Moon for the Misbegotten* was revived in 1973 and was a remarkable success. Eugene O'Neill's work is uneven. He was not afraid to experiment and sometimes he did not succeed in his intentions; sometimes he overreached himself, but even his failures are worth attention – nothing he wrote was ever dull. His position as America's greatest playwright is unchallenged.

**One Kind of Officer** See *Can Such Things Be?*

**One of our Conquerors** A novel by George Meredith, first published in 1891.

Nesta Victoria is the daughter of Victor Radmor and Natalia Dreighton. Her father is prosperous and lively; her mother timid and anxious. Nesta has many suitors, the most eligible of whom is the Hon Dudley Sowerby, heir to an earldom. Then Nesta learns that she is illegitimate: her father's lawful wife is a rich elderly woman and Natalia was her young companion. Nesta's parents took the only course open to them, which was to live out of wedlock.

Sowerby, his ardour dampened, is also critical of Nesta's befriending of the hapless Mrs Marsett, the mistress of an army officer. Nesta persists and it causes the final breach between them.

Natalia is also unhappy about her daughter's friendship and – her own background in mind – falls ill during this crisis and dies. Victor receives news that his wife is dead also, within a few hours of Natalia's passing. The cruel irony of this, and the loss of Natalia, unhinge his mind.

Victor lives for a few years. Nesta eventually marries a more worthy suitor, Dartrey Fenellan.

**Open Boat, The:** *and Other Tales of Adventure.* Short stories by Stephen Crane, first published in 1898.

*The Open Boat* is based on the author's experience after being shipwrecked off the coast of Florida at the end of 1896. Four men escape the shipwreck in a dinghy: captain, ship's cook, oiler, and a journalist. When they come within reach of a shore the dangerous surf prevents them from landing – they have to drift at sea for the rest of the day and through the night, hoping that help will reach them. The following day they make a determined effort to land and three of them make it ashore. The fourth, the oiler, is drowned in the attempt. Within this outline the author presents a moving picture of the closeness the four experience in their situation and a powerful feeling of the inexorable sea from which they must escape, or die.

Also to be found in this volume is *The Bride Comes to Yellow Sky.* Scratchy Wilson is a gunfighter from the old frontier days and he has an unresolved quarrel with the sheriff of Yellow Sky, Jack Potter. The sheriff brings his wife to Yellow Sky and Wilson is waiting for him, guns ready, to resolve the quarrel. But Potter is not carrying a gun. There can be no fight and Wilson begins to realize that the 'old West' is no more.

**Ophelia** The pathetic daughter of Polonius in Shakespeare's *Hamlet.* She loves Hamlet but she is helpless when he starts behaving strangely and shattered when he abuses her (Act III Scene 1). The murder of her father leaves her abandoned; her brother Laertes is in France and Hamlet does not spare a thought for her. She goes mad and drowns accidentally.

**Ordeal of Richard Feverel, The** A novel by George Meredith, first published in 1859.

Sir Austin Feverel, deserted by his wife, brings up his son Richard in his own way. He educates the boy at home, believing all schools to be corrupt, and thinks that he can make his son a man of exceptional quality. But when Richard reaches adolescence he confounds his father by falling in love with Lucy Desborough, niece of a local farmer. Sir Austin acknowledges her quality but opposes the match because of Lucy's humble birth, and the two young people have to marry in secret.

Richard is devoted to his father, who now ruthlessly manipulates the boy's feelings to separate him from Lucy. Sir Austin sends Richard to London, where his friend Lord Mountfalcon, who has designs on Lucy, puts Richard in the path of a 'fallen' woman of considerable allure. Thinking to redeem her, the innocent Richard is seduced with ease. He prolongs his absence and goes abroad, ashamed of his infidelity. He then learns that he is a father; moreover, Sir Austin is reconciled to Lucy as his daughter-in-law through the good offices of Richard's uncle, Wentworth. Richard hurries home and now he discovers Lord Mountfalcon's villainy. Just when happiness seems to be within his grasp, Richard challenges Mountfalcon to a duel and is seriously wounded. The events prove too much for Lucy, who dies after a period of madness.

**Ordericus Vitalis** *c.*1075–1143. The son of Norman parents, Ordericus was born in Shropshire but spent most of his life in the monastery of St Evroul in Normandy. He spent 20 years working on his *Historia Ecclesiastica* in 13 books, the history of the church down to 1141. Fortunately Ordericus was, for his time, a travelled man of wide interests. That he views events from the seclusion of the cloister does not reduce the value of his *Historia* or of the information it provides: in spite of inaccurate chronology and confused arrangement it is regarded as the fullest account of Norman history in both England and France up to the sixth year of Stephen's reign.

The standard modern edition of the *Historia* of Ordericus is by A. le Prévost (Paris, 1838–55). There is also T. Forester's translation (1853–56) and a modern edition and translation by Marjorie Chibnall (1969–78).

**Oregon Trail, The** The narrative of Francis Parkman's journey in 1846, first published in serial form in *The Knickerbocker Magazine* in 1847. In volume form it first appeared as *The California and Oregon Trail* in 1849 but in later editions the original title was retained.

Parkman and his companion, his cousin Quincy Adams Shaw, set out from St Louis by steamboat in April 1846. They continued their journey on horseback, sometimes in the company of other travellers and with occasional help from guides, along the route to the Pacific as far as Fort Laramie in Wyoming. They encountered emigrants, Indians, hunters, and trappers, experienced storms, took part in buffalo hunts, and talked with seasoned frontiersmen. Parkman

An illustration by Frederic Remington for Parkman's *The Oregon Trail*. 'The Hunting Camp'.

became separated from Shaw when, in a Sioux encampment, he heard that a war party was preparing to attack the Snake tribe. He was eager to join the war party and somehow Shaw was left behind. Parkman did not see a battle but lived with the Sioux for several weeks. His account of them is one of the best things in a fine book and a tribute to the remarkable courage of a man who never enjoyed physical well-being. The Sioux, as tough as any men on earth could be, came to respect the paleface in their midst and told him much about their way of life.

After returning to Fort Laramie, Parkman set out on the return journey with Shaw, which they completed in August. Parkman's frail health broke down completely after their return and his classic narrative was written down by his cousin from his dictation.

**Orfeo, Sir** A verse romance in Middle English of the 14th century. (See **metrical romances**.) The classical myth of Orpheus and Eurydice is placed in a Celtic setting, where Queen Heurodys is carried off to the world of faery. King Orfeo, disguised as a minstrel, searches for her and brings her back to the ordinary world with the beauty of his wonderful melodies. *Sir Orfeo* was edited by D. Laing (1822), W. C. Hazlitt (1875), and A. J. Bliss (1966). Modern versions are by E. E. Hunt (1910) and F. Montagu (1954).

**Orinda** See **Fowler, Katherine**.

**Orlando** The hero of Shakespeare's *As You Like It*. He is the youngest brother of Oliver, who maltreats him and tries to have him killed. He loves Rosalind and does not know her when he meets her disguised as Ganymede in the Forest of Arden.

**Orlando** See **Woolf, (Adeline) Virginia**.

**Orley Farm** A novel by Anthony Trollope, first published in 20 monthly parts, from March 1861 to October 1862.

Orley Farm is part of the estate of Sir Joseph Mason. Late in life Sir Joseph remarries and a son, Lucius, is born. When he dies Sir Joseph's will leaves the bulk of his estate to his son Joseph (by his first wife) and, in a codicil, Orley Farm to Lucius. Joseph contests the validity of the codicil but the law upholds it, and the widowed Lady Mason and her son Lucius live there in comfortable circumstances for 20 years. Then one of Lady Mason's tenants, an attorney of dubious character, is given notice to quit. The attorney, Dockwrath, feels unjustly used and determines to get his own back on Lady Mason.

Dockwrath proceeds to reopen the matter of the codicil, and Joseph Mason is arrested by the attorney's discovery that there was another document, signed on the same day as the codicil. The witnesses declare that they signed only one document – though the signatures on both that and the codicil are the same. Lady Mason's friends rally round to support her, and her elderly

'Guilty.' Lady Mason confesses her forgery to Sir Peregrine Orme in *Orley Farm*. An illustration by John Everett Millais in Vol. II of Trollope's novel, 1862.

lover, Sir Peregrine Orme, will not swerve from his belief in her probity. Everything points to forgery, however, and Lady Mason is plainly under severe strain.

The case is brought: Mr Chaffanbrass appears for Lady Mason and all goes in her favour. But her apparently unshakable resolution breaks down after the trial, and she confesses everything to Sir Peregrine Orme. Orley Farm reverts to Joseph Mason.

The characters of Joseph Mason and his stepmother, Lady Mason, so sharply contrasted, are consistent and totally believable; so are the former's resentment, smouldering for 20 years, and the strain on the latter, held at bay for the same period until her resolution is exhausted. The commercial travellers (bagmen), Kantwise and Moulder, are fascinating representations of one level of the commercial life of the period.

**Ormulum** A poem of 10,000 lines in Middle English by an Augustinian monk named Orm (*or* Ormin) who was thought to have lived in the east Midlands in the first half of the 13th century. In response to the wishes of 'brother Wallterr' the author turns into English paraphrases all the gospels for the ecclesiastical year, adding to each an exposition in English. The author completed 30 paraphrases. The *Ormulum* is not highly regarded as poetry and is of interest chiefly to scholars for the light it sheds on the evolution of the English language and literary form. The line is of 15 syllables without rhyme or alliterative ornament. Editions of the *Ormulum* are by R. M. White (1852) and R. Holt (1878).

**Oroonoko,** *or The Royal Slave.* A novel by Aphra Behn, first published *c*.1678 and included in *Three Histories* (1688). It was adapted for the stage by Thomas Southerne in 1695 and enjoyed considerable further success.

Oroonoko, the grandson and heir of an African king, loves the beautiful Imoinda, daughter of the king's general. But the old king himself falls in love with Imoinda and commands that she be taken to his harem. When he discovers that she loves his grandson the infuriated old man has her sold as a slave. Later the grieving Oroonoko is captured by an English slaver and sold in Surinam. There he finds his Imoinda, also a slave.

Oroonoko rouses the other slaves and inspires them to make an escape from their dreadful existence. They are hunted, and eventually induced to surrender to Byam, the deputy governor, on promise of a pardon. But Byam, once he has Oroonoko in his hands, has him flogged. Determined to exact payment from Byam, Oroonoko realizes that he will not escape the consequences of killing him. At the same time he knows what will happen to Imoinda when he is no longer there to protect her. Imoinda understands and serenely surrenders her life to Oroonoko. Oroonoko is discovered by her body; he is prevented from taking his own life and executed with savage cruelty.

In Southerne's dramatized version Byam is motivated by his passion for Imoinda, and there is a comic subplot.

Mrs Behn's novel was the first expression in English literature of sympathy for the plight of slaves. The influence of the theatre is shown in the hero's passionate speeches, which read like declamations for a heroic actor, and in the inviolable nobility of Oroonoko and Imoinda. Oroonoko himself is not only noble but cultured, in a European and therefore implausible way. Yet, accepting the literary conventions of Aphra Behn's time, the novel succeeds as a romance against a background of oppression wielded by her fellow Christians. The author claimed first-hand knowledge of her setting and there is no way of actually disproving this claim though some scholars have found 'her' Surinam in George Warren's *Impartial Description of Surinam* (1667).

**Orphan, The,** or *The Unhappy Marriage*. A tragedy by Thomas Otway, first produced in February or March 1680 and published in the same year. The principal parts were played by Thomas Betterton and Elizabeth Barry.

Acasto has brought up Monimia, the orphan daughter of a friend, with his own twin sons, Castalio and Polydore. Monimia's brother Chamont is a soldier. The twin brothers have both fallen in love with Monimia; she loves Castalio, but from consideration of Polydore's feelings Castalio pretends indifference. Chamont, visiting his sister, believes that Monimia's disturbed emotions can be blamed on one of the brothers but his questions annoy her. Castalio declares his love, and he and Monimia are secretly married.

Polydore does not know of the secret marriage; he overhears his brother arranging to meet Monimia during the night and contrives to take his brother's place. Monimia accepts him, and Castalio, arriving later, finds himself barred from his wife's room. The deception is eventually revealed by Charmont, and the three unhappy lovers kill themselves.

**Orpheus and Eurydice**  A version of the Greek myth by Robert Henryson the 15th-century Scottish poet. The story is based on Ovid but Henryson's distinctive Scottish flavour informs the work, which is vividly related and includes a memorable picture of a medieval Hell. The poem was first printed in 1508.

**Orsino**  The lovelorn Duke of Illyria in Shakespeare's *Twelfth Night*. The object of his love is Olivia, who doesn't want him. Viola, disguised as Cesario, becomes the duke's page.

**Orwell, George** 1903–50.  The pseudonym of Eric Arthur Blair, the son of a civil servant in India. He was born in Bengal, and at school in England won a scholarship to Eton College, about which he wrote in one of his essays. He was acutely conscious of the air of wealth and privilege that surrounded most of his schoolfellows. However, he did well there, and then joined the Indian Civil Police in Burma in 1922. He returned to Europe in 1927; he had acquired a loathing of colonialism and he turned to writing as a career. He went to Paris, hoping to be able to live by teaching while practising his craft. As it was he nearly starved and after 18 months made his way back to England as best he could. A further period of destitution followed until his work was accepted by *The Adelphi* in 1930, and he became a regular contributor until 1935. His first book was the autobiographical *Down and Out in London and Paris* (1933), a vivid comment on the reality of deprivation. A horrifying footnote appeared in the essay 'How the Poor Die', which described his experience of a charity hospital in Paris. His experience of social injustice inevitably led to social criticism; but in Orwell's case it was a matter of personal conviction – he never gave his allegiance to a political party.

*Burmese Days* (1934), his first novel, enabled him to leave London and become a modest shopkeeper in the country. *A Clergyman's Daughter* (1935) and *Keep the Aspidistra Flying* (1936) followed. Then the Left Book Club commissioned a book on unemployment in Lancashire and Orwell produced *The Road to Wigan Pier* (1937). It did not please its sponsors, who got a book that bowed in no one's direction, not even that of the Left. In 1936 Orwell went to the Spanish Civil War. He fought with the *Partido Obrero de Unificación Marxista* (POUM), a group of Communist worker-democrats. In *Homage to Catalonia* (1937) Orwell told of the destruction of the POUM and its leaders by the Comintern. Stalin's sort of 'Communism' brooked no rivals, as Victor Serge, Trotsky, Arthur Koestler, and many others testified. Orwell was vilified by the fashionable and sentimental Left in England, who knew nothing of the truth and had no desire to be told it. His next book was a novel, *Coming*

*Up for Air* (1939), a sardonic picture of England on the eve of another war.

Orwell had been wounded in Spain. Back in England he became a regular contributor to *Time and Tide* (1936–43) and published his first collection of essays, *Inside the Whale*, in 1940. From 1943 to 1946 he contributed regularly to *The Observer* and *The Manchester Evening News*; he was literary editor of *Tribune* (1943–45) for which he wrote a weekly column until 1947. He speculated on a coming social revolution in England in *The Lion and the Unicorn* (1941) and in the same year wrote the foreword to Joyce Cary's *The Case for African Freedom*. Then in 1945 he published *Animal Farm* which, after rejection by T. S. Eliot, and much hesitation on the part of the eventual publishers, made Orwell world famous.

Orwell had become increasingly pessimistic about affairs at home and abroad, and his constitution had been seriously weakened by the years of deprivation and his experiences in Spain. He saw Stalin and his ambitions clearly and in his short, simple, and frightening book he described the defeat of a revolution and the crushing of hope. There is almost unbearable pathos in the final sacrifice of Boxer, the gallant unquestioning shire horse who believes that if he works a little harder for the revolution all will be well. When his body is at last broken he is sent to the knacker's yard, and the other animals by then are too discouraged and exhausted to understand the iniquity of his fate. The last horror is when the pigs, triumphant, start practising how to walk upright in imitation of the masters they have overthrown. 'All animals are equal, but some are more equal than others' has passed into every modern book of quotations and is a devastating comment on left-wing totalitarianism.

*Critical Essays* (1946) contains the fine essays on Rudyard Kipling and James Burnham and the Managerial Revolution; this was followed by *The English People, Politics and The English Language* (both 1947), and *Nineteen Eighty-Four* (1949). In this, his last novel, Orwell once more caught the world by the ear with his picture of a totalitarian future. The Right gave it a bland welcome as a criticism of the Left but the Right was throwing stones from inside its own glass house: Orwell was condemning totalitarianism of every kind. The apparently indestructible bourgeois English character which he had identified in his prewar studies, the lack of a proletariat eager to follow a red banner, were already familiar themes. But an English public at the mercy of a computerized bureaucracy which hoarded secret information about every man, woman, and child, was a new threat. Where people were not willing to go they could be sent without knowing what was happening to them: Orwell described their destination. He died in the following year. A book of essays, *Shooting an Elephant*, was published in 1950 and another, *England, Your England*, posthumously (1953). *The Collected Essays, Journalism and Letters of George Orwell*, edited by Sonia Orwell and I. Angus (four vols, 1968), contains over 200 pieces of uncollected journalism, four poems, and diaries and notebooks.

**Orygynale Cronykil, The** See **Wyntoun, Andrew of.**

**Osbaldistone, Rashleigh** The malevolent schemer of Scott's *Rob Roy*. He plots the death of Francis Osbaldistone when Diana Vernon plainly prefers the hero's attentions to his own. His treachery to the Jacobite cause leads to his death at the hands of Rob Roy.

**Osborne, Dorothy** 1627–95. The wife of Sir William Temple, whose letters to him before their marriage were first published in 1888; a new edition by G. C. Moore Smith appeared in 1928. See **Temple, Sir William.**

**Osborne, John (James)** 1929– . Osborne was born in London and educated at Belmont College in Devon. He became an actor in 1948, and while appearing in the provinces wrote plays in his spare time. Two of these were written in collaboration and later published, *The Devil Inside Him* (1950, with S. Linden) and *Personal Enemy* (1955, with Anthony Creighton). *Look Back in Anger* (1956) was produced by the English Stage Company at the Royal Court Theatre in Chelsea and playwright and company made each other famous. Osborne's career continued with (the dates given are of publication) *The Entertainer* (1957), *Epitaph for George Dillon* (1957, with Anthony Creighton), *The World of Paul Slickey* (1959, musical comedy), *Luther* (1961), *A Subject for Scandal and Concern* (1962), *Plays for England – The Blood of the Bambers and Under Plain Cover* (1963), *Inadmissible Evidence* (1964), *A Patriot for Me* (1966), *The Hotel in Amsterdam* and *Time Present* (1968), *Very Like a Whale* (1970), *West of Suez* (1971), *The Gifts of Friendship* and *A Sense of Detachment* (1972), *A Place Calling Itself Rome* (1973), *The End of my Old Cigar* and *Watch it Come Down* (1975), and *You're not Watching me, Mummy* and *Try a Little Tenderness* (1978). John Osborne has also made adaptations of plays by Ibsen and Lope de Vega. He published the first volume of his autobiography, *A Better Class of Person*, in 1981.

**O'Shaughnessy, Arthur William Edgar**
1844–81. A minor poet of the 1870s, O'Shaughnessy was born in London and educated privately. His working life was spent in the British Museum Library and the Natural History Museum, where his subjects were fish and reptiles. He knew Rossetti and some of the Pre-Raphaelites, who were the chief influences in his poetry. He published *An Epic of Women and Other Poems* (1870), *Lays of France* (1872), *Music and Moonlight* (1874), and with his wife E. O'Shaughnessy, a volume of verse for children, *Toyland* (1875).

**Osmond, Gilbert** The man whom Isabel Archer marries in *The Portrait of a Lady*, by Henry James, against the advice of all her friends, who perceive that he is a conceited and selfish snob. Isabel has to discover for herself that, as a husband, he is even worse.

**Ossian** See **Macpherson, James**.

**Oswald** Goneril's steward in Shakespeare's *King Lear* and the would-be murderer of the blind Gloucester. Edgar kills him and finds Goneril's letter to Edmund in his purse. Oswald is a remarkably well-drawn portrait of an insolent servant: his interests dictate his behaviour to the last degree.

**Oswald, St** d. 992. Oswald was a nephew of Odo, Archbishop of Canterbury, and a Benedictine monk. He was appointed Bishop of Worcester by King Edgar on the recommendation of Dunstan, and with Dunstan and Aethelwold did much to help bring about the revival of learning during the reign of the enlightened King Edgar. He had been ordained at Fleury on the Loire and had visited Rome: he was able to persuade many scholars to come to England from the continent.

***Othello, the Moor of Venice*** A tragedy by William Shakespeare, first produced *c.*1604 and printed in a quarto of 1622. It was published in the First Folio of 1623. The source of the play is a story in the *Hecatommithi* of Giraldo Cinthio (1565).

The Venetian, Roderigo, and Iago, a tried and trusted soldier in the service of Othello, a general in the service of Venice, both harbour grudges against the Moor. Roderigo wanted Desdemona, who has secretly married Othello, and Iago's claim to preferment has been set aside in favour of the younger Michael Cassio, a Florentine whom Othello has made his lieutenant. Iago is bitterly resentful: he has no more than the rank of ancient (ensign, standard-bearer) as a reward for his years of service. Roderigo is a silly man, easily

influenced; Iago is cunning and dangerous. They go, at Iago's suggestion, to rouse Brabantio, the Venetian senator, and tell him that his daughter Desdemona has run off and even now 'an old black ram is tupping (his) white ewe.' Iago then leaves the scene to Roderigo.

Brabantio orders the arrest of Othello for abducting his daughter. Othello denies the charge: he loves Desdemona and she returns his love and Desdemona's words bear out all he says. Brabantio, with some reluctance, acknowledges the match, while news is brought that the Turks are planning to attack Cyprus. Othello sets off to command the Venetian forces and his wife goes with him. Iago meanwhile has encouraged Roderigo to believe he has a chance of gaining Desdemona – and of cuckolding Othello.

In Cyprus the chief characters are assembled: Othello and Desdemona, Cassio, Roderigo, and Iago and his wife Emilia. The Turkish attack is defeated and Othello's honour stands high. Iago tells Roderigo that Desdemona is lusting after the handsome and youthful Cassio. Roderigo is easily persuaded to fall in with Iago's plan to discredit the man. Cassio, who has no reason to distrust Iago, is readily deceived and provoked into apparently mutinous behaviour and Othello deprives him of his lieutenancy. Iago advises Cassio to plead with Desdemona to intercede on his behalf and at the same time convinces Emilia that Cassio's pleading should be heard. Emilia helps to persuade Desdemona to act on Cassio's behalf; the well-meaning and innocent lady promises to help.

Iago, with Othello, wonders aloud why Cassio should be with Desdemona. Othello pays no attention and listens with indulgence to her plea for the lieutenant's reinstatement. He can refuse her nothing and promises to attend to the case. Iago refers again to Desdemona and Cassio: his innuendo is skilful enough to set Othello wondering and he seizes his opportunity to drive the seed of jealousy deep – contriving at the same time to convince Othello of his honest motives. When Iago is gone and Desdemona comes upon the scene he explains his distracted manner by saying his head aches. Desdemona offers her handkerchief but Othello declines: 'Your napkin is too little.' Desdemona loses the handkerchief, which is found by Emilia. Emilia remembers that it was Desdemona's first remembrance from Othello; but Iago takes it from her before she can give it back to its owner. Then he puts the handkerchief with Cassio's possessions.

Iago increases the pressure on Othello and provokes him to the limit – 'Villain, be sure thou prove my love a whore' – but Iago tells of

Cassio's troubled sleep and the name of Desdemona on his lips – and what is he doing with a handkerchief that was certainly Desdemona's? And the next time Othello speaks to his wife she insists on pleading Cassio's cause. Where is the handkerchief he gave her? She does not have it with her. Othello orders her to find it and bring it to him. Emilia is an uneasy witness to this scene.

Cassio has given his mistress, Bianca, a handkerchief he has found among his clothes, asking her to take out the embroidery. Bianca, Iago insists, loves Cassio and wants to marry him. He encourages Cassio, in Othello's hearing, to speak slightingly of her regard, having led Othello to believe it is Desdemona they are talking about. Then Bianca arrives on the scene and demands to know where Cassio got this handkerchief. It is plainly another woman's. Othello humiliates Desdemona in the presence of the Venetian emissaries and then cross-examines Emilia about his wife's conduct; but that yields nothing for his suspicions and he turns his wrath directly on the bewildered and terrified Desdemona. Iago sets Roderigo to kill Cassio but the plan goes awry and Iago kills Roderigo in order to stop him from speaking.

Emilia, despatched to Othello to tell him of the affray, arrives to discover that he has killed Desdemona. She was, he says, betraying him with Cassio: Iago told him so. The horrified Emilia calls the Venetian emissaries, who arrive with Iago, and Emilia tells the truth about the handkerchief and what she now perceives is her husband's treachery. Iago kills her and succeeds in escaping from the chamber, but he is brought back a prisoner, and the wounded Cassio also. Letters have been found on Roderigo's body that convict Iago beyond a shadow of a doubt. Othello, his spirit broken beyond recovery, kills himself.

Of all Shakespeare's great tragedies, Othello is the most notable for its pathos. Othello himself is a great creation, an honest man willing to believe in honesty. His love is absolute and it is agonizing to see it breaking down. He believes Iago honest and Desdemona true; there is nothing to show him that Iago is false but he is shown many reasons for believing Desdemona is faithless. His anguish, as Coleridge observed, lies in 'the struggle *not* to love her'. If he loved her less he could reject her, though not without pain; it is the fall from grace that tears him to pieces. And just as Othello is an honest man Iago is a mean one to the depths of his soul; he knows very well how jealousy and doubt can be made to work.

Shakespeare has portrayed brilliantly a man who has felt the bitterness of envy every day of his life. The characters of Desdemona and Emilia are overshadowed by Othello and Iago but they are excellently portrayed. Desdemona is just the kind of warm and uncomplicated girl who would love the honest and great-hearted Moor and spirited enough to marry him in the face of parental disapproval. Emilia is a passive character for the first half of the play, but see how she springs, a completely rounded woman, into the action at Othello's reference to her husband: 'Ay, 'twas he that told me on her first. An honest man he is, and hates the slime that sticks on filthy deeds.' Emilia had doubts enough about the man she married; she has no doubts now and nothing will stop her from revealing the truth.

*ottava rima* A verse of 8 lines, each with 11 syllables, Italian in origin and much used by Torquato Tasso, Ludovico Ariosto, Luigi Pulci, and other Italian masters. The rhyme scheme is abab, abcc. Byron adapted the *ottava rima* to English usage but used a 10-syllable line instead of the original 11.

*Otuel, Sir* A Middle English verse romance, based on an Old French source. (See **metrical romances**.) During a Saracen attack on France the Saracen emissary Otuel insults Charlemagne and is immediately challenged by Roland. A combat ensues, during which Charlemagne offers up prayers. In answer a white dove alights on Otuel's shoulder. He capitulates and becomes a Christian knight and one of Charlemagne's paladins. *Sir Otuel* was edited by J. Maidment for the Abbotsford Club (1836) and by S. J. H. Herrtage for the Early English Text Society (1880 and 1973).

**Otway, Thomas** 1652–85. The first considerable tragic poet of the Restoration after Dryden, Thomas Otway was born at Trotton in Sussex. He was educated at Winchester School and Christ Church, Oxford, and at first hoped to be an actor. But an unsuccessful appearance in 1670 in a play by Aphra Behn was the beginning and end of his acting career. He became a playwright and his first work, *Alcibiades*, was produced in 1675. Otway was in love with the actress Elizabeth Barry and the part she played helped establish her. The play itself, a tragedy in rhymed verse, has not held the stage and has no reputation among scholars.

Otway was more successful with his next work, *Don Carlos, Prince of Spain* (1676), based on a romantic fiction about the mad son of Philip II by the French writer Saint-Réal. (Saint-Réal's romanticization was also the source of Schiller's

Thomas Otway. A detail from the portrait attributed to Soest (undated) in the Poet's Parlour at Knole, where hang several paintings of Restoration poets.

tragedy and therefore of Verdi's opera.) This was followed (1677) by two versions from the French, Racine's *Bérénice* as *Titus and Berenice* and Molière's *Les Fourberies de Scapin* as *The Cheats of Scapin*, and by a comedy, *Friendship in Fashion* (1678). Comedy was not Otway's forte and the author's prospects seemed poor. He had sought patronage, in the manner of his time, with indifferent success. Lord Buckhurst and the Earl of Rochester extended some short-lived favour. Elizabeth Barry did not return his love and became Rochester's mistress, though she was to enjoy great success in Otway's plays. Otway went to Flanders for a year with the army in 1678.

Upon his return to England Otway looked like achieving real eminence. After an unwise attempt to adapt Shakespeare's *Romeo and Juliet* (1679) he wrote **The Orphan,** *or The Unhappy Marriage* (1680), a tragedy in blank verse, which gave Elizabeth Barry a splendid opportunity and proved to be Otway's greatest success. He surpassed it two years later with **Venice Preserv'd,** *or A Plot Discover'd* (1682), his masterpiece and the outstanding tragedy of the Restoration theatre. Mrs Barry played Belvidera and enjoyed another success, predictably, since Otway's heroines were written for her. But in spite of his newly found esteem Otway did not prosper and

was leading a dissipated life; he was destitute when he died at the age of 33.

*Venice Preserv'd* was revived in 1953 with notable success. The play endures because Otway eschewed the Restoration 'heroick' tone and reached backward to Elizabethan and Jacobean traditions. The psychological credibility of his characters and his ability to appeal directly to the emotions of the audience are unique in this period and indeed in Otway's own work, with the possible exception of *Don Carlos*. *The Orphan* has not been revived but the force of *Venice Preserv'd* on the stage arouses considerable interest in the earlier play's potential. Otway wrote another comedy, *The Soldier's Fortune* (1680), produced in the same year as *The Orphan*; he also contributed to a translation of Ovid's *Epistulae* (1680), and wrote some occasional verse.

The complete works of Thomas Otway were collected and edited by J. C. Ghosh (1932).

**Ouida** 1839–1908. The pen name of Marie Louise de la Ramée, daughter of a French father and an English mother. She was born at Bury St Edmunds. 'Ouida' was a childish corruption of her name, Louisa, and her first published works were short stories contributed to *Bentley's Miscellany*. Like George Alfred Lawrence she reacted against the moral tone of the times. Unfortunately, she was no better a novelist than Lawrence and though she had a strong narrative gift she knew little of the worlds she often chose to write about. The most famous example is *Under Two Flags* (1867), about the well-born young Englishman in the Foreign Legion. However, she was very popular, and her hot-house romanticism was imitated for years – and still is – by ladies of inexhaustible industry who know little more than Ouida of the passion or heroism they write about so glibly. Ouida's narrative gift brought good moments to *Under Two Flags*, and to *Held in Bondage* (1863), *Strathmore* (1865), *A Dog of Flanders* (1872), *In Maremma* (1882), and *Two Little Wooden Shoes* (1874).

**Our Mutual Friend** A novel by Charles Dickens, first published in 20 monthly parts (May 1864 to November 1865). It was his last completed work.

Gaffer (Jesse) Hexam, a river scavenger, hauls a body out of the Thames and to the revulsion of his daughter, Lizzie, robs the corpse while towing it in. The papers found on the body identify him as John Harmon, the returning son of a harsh old dust contractor. Conditional to inheriting his father's estate, John Harmon was to have married Bella Wilfer, whom he had never seen.

The inheritance goes by default to Mr Boffin,

former foreman to old Harmon, and Bella Wilfer's adoptive father. Boffin hires a secretary, Rokesmith, who is obviously interested in Bella, but she is spoiled by her taste of affluence and rejects him with contempt.

Gaffer Hexam, meanwhile, is drowned in the Thames. Lizzie has attracted the attention of Eugene Wrayburn, the barrister in the Harmon case. Now she comes to London to work to support herself and her brother Charley. Charley is at school being taught by Bradley Headstone – indeed, he is bright and ambitious enough to be Headstone's protégé; greedy for himself, he is half-ashamed of his sister. Her loveliness attracts the attention of the schoolmaster, however.

Boffin's wife discovers the true identity of Rokesmith. He is John Harmon who, returning from abroad, confided to the mate of the ship that he was going to conceal his identity until he had made up his own mind about the wife chosen for him. The mate attempted to murder Harmon after stealing his money and papers but was in turn waylaid. Harmon survived the attempt and changed his name. The mate's body was recovered from the river and the papers suggested it was John Harmon. The Boffins decide that, for the son of their old master, Bella will have to be tested – and Boffin presents himself henceforth as someone to whom only the possession of money has meaning. He becomes rapacious and miserly.

Lizzie Hexam is rejected by her loathsome brother, courted by Wrayburn, and longed for by Headstone. She finds a friend in Riah, a gentle old Jew. Headstone, in a jealous rage, sets out to murder Wrayburn, but he is suspected by Charley Hexam, who immediately forsakes him. Worse, he is blackmailed by Riderhood, a waterside villain. Driven to the verge of madness, Headstone kills Riderhood and himself in the river while Wrayburn, tended by Lizzie, recovers from the attempt on his life.

Bella Wilfer, to the Boffin's delight, recovers her true nature and revolts against the greed and mendacity she seems to see all round her, and John Harmon discloses his identity. The two stories are loosely connected throughout the novel, and brought together at the end, with the introduction of a rich gallery of characters such as the parvenu Veneerings, Jenny Wren, the dolls' dressmaker, and Betty Higden, the spirited old woman haunted by the fear of being taken to the workhouse.

Dickens's last completed novel was worthy of the master: it is one of his best. The atmosphere of the river is pervasive and powerful as is the pursuit of money and advancement seen at every level of the social scale. More important, there is an exploration of the characters' psychology in the Hexam–Wrayburn–Headstone part of the book that makes one regret all the more that *Edwin Drood* was not completed. The Harmon–Boffin–Wilfer part looks forward to the possibility of a change of direction for the great novelist which, tragically, he did not survive to pursue. Headstone, the jealous tragic schoolmaster, is a particularly striking character, a man who is indeed his own executioner.

***Our Village*** See **Mitford, Mary Russell.**

***Outcasts of Poker Flat, The*** See ***Luck of Roaring Camp and Other Sketches, The.***

***Out of the Cradle Endlessly Rocking*** Walt Whitman's poem received its present title in 1871. He first called it 'A Word Out of the Sea', in the third edition of *Leaves of Grass* (1860). One of Whitman's finest poems, it tells of a boy's experience on the shore of Long Island, where he listens to a bird calling to its mate and hears the answering cry. Then one night there is no answer and the bird's call becomes one of sorrow. The boy awakens to a knowledge of love and death – and an awareness of what will be the subject of his songs.

***Overland Monthly*** Founded in 1868 and published in San Francisco, *Overland Monthly* was intended to give California and the West a serious magazine and review of the same level of quality as those of New England and the Atlantic states. For the first two-and-a-half years it was edited by Bret Harte, to whom its notable early success can be credited. The magazine in its original form continued until 1875. It was revived in 1883, but the second *Overland Monthly* was simply an imitation of the original although it lasted until 1933 and was the first publisher of Jack London.

**Owen, John** 1564–1622. John Owen was a Welshman educated at Winchester School and New College, Oxford. He was a fellow of New College for some years and then became a teacher. Owen wrote in Latin and achieved fame with his four books of epigrams, mostly in couplets, on characters, institutions, imaginary personages, and works of literature. The volumes of *Epigrammatum Joannis Owen cambrobritanni* of 1607 and 1612 were compared to those of the Latin master, Martial. The first translation into English was by John Vicars in 1619, and the epigrams achieved considerable fame in Germany and France.

**Owen, Wilfred (Edward Salter)** 1893–1918. Wilfred Owen was born at Oswestry in Shropshire. He was educated at Birkenhead Institute and London University, and at the age of 20 became tutor to a French family living near Bordeaux. Two years later, in 1915, he volunteered for the army and served on the western front when trench warfare and soldiers' conditions were at their worst. He was invalided out in 1917, a nervous and battle-shocked wreck, but he recovered and returned to France with a commission. He won a Military Cross, and was killed on 4 November 1918, a week before the armistice.

Wilfred Owen was drawn to poetry in his childhood and his early work shows the influence of Keats, to whose art he was devoted. He was a romantic at the time he became a soldier. In 1915 he wrote, 'There is a fine heroic feeling about being in France.' But the shocking reality changed his attitudes and stifled his poetry. While convalescing in 1917 he met Siegfried Sassoon and the two poets became friends: Owen followed Sassoon's example in telling the truth about war.

Among his papers was found a draft preface to a future volume of poems: 'This book is not about heroes. English poetry is not yet fit to speak of them. Nor is it about deeds, or lands, nor anything about glory, honour, might, majesty, dominion, or power, except War. Above all I am not concerned with Poetry. My subject is War, and the pity of War. The Poetry is in the pity.' The need to be truthful about the terrible experience called upon a poetic gift that marks Wilfred Owen as the greatest of the English war poets: see 'The Chances', 'Anthem for Doomed Youth', 'Exposure', 'Strange Meeting', 'Futility', 'Disabled', and the rest. His close-up, concentrated view makes some of his poems almost unbearable but his compassion for his fellow men informs every one of them. No one could ever write war poetry like that of Brooke or Grenfell again.

Edith Sitwell published seven of Wilfred Owen's poems in her anthology of contemporary verse, *Wheels*, in 1919. *Poems* (1920) was introduced by Siegfried Sassoon; a second edition, with additional poems and a memoir by Edmund Blunden, was published in 1931. Blunden's memoir was included in *The Collected Poems of Wilfred Owen* (1963), edited by C. Day Lewis. Harold Owen's memoir of his brother, *Journey from Obscurity*, was published in three volumes, 1963–65. Jon Stallworthy's biography, *Wilfred Owen*, was published in 1974; *The Collected Letters* (1967) was edited by Harold Owen and John Bell.

**Owenson, Sydney** 1783–1859. Afterwards Lady Morgan, Sydney Owenson was a lively Irish writer of poetry, fiction, and commentaries on France and Italy. Byron praised her *Italy*, but both her books of continental experience aroused the wrath of the critic and arch-Tory, John Wilson Croker. Her *The Wild Irish Girl* (1806) was a very popular novel in its time.

**Owl and the Nightingale, The** A poem in Middle English, in octosyllabic couplets, of some 2000 lines, composed about 1250. The authorship has been attributed to Nicholas de Guildford, of Portisham in Dorset, or to his fellow cleric, John de Guildford. The former is named in the poem and referred to in the third person, while the latter is known to have been a poet of the period. The poem is a debate between the wise owl and the gay nightingale on the benefits they confer on man: the owl is the religious poet and the nightingale the poet of love. The poem is notable for the characterization of the two principals, for its appreciation of the beauties of nature, and for the glimpses of contemporary life.

There are numerous editions of *The Owl and the Nightingale*, beginning with J. Stevenson's for the Roxburghe Club (1838); J. W. H. Atkins also gives a translation in modern English (1922). G. Eggers' translation was published in 1955. The edition by N. R. Ker (Early English Text Society, 1963) gives facsimiles of the manuscripts in Jesus College, Oxford, and the British Library. The poem is also edited by Brian Stone (Penguin Classics, 1970).

**Oxford Movement** A movement within the Church of England that sought to restore to it the High Church ideals of the 17th century. One of the immediate causes was the Catholic Emancipation Act of 1829; another was the Reform Bill (1832) and the plan to suppress ten Protestant bishoprics in Ireland. But the decline of church life and the spread of liberalism in theology was causing concern to many churchmen. The first declaration was John Keble's sermon at Oxford in 1833 'On National Apostasy', and the formative years were from then until 1845, when John Henry Newman, William George Ward, and Frederick William Faber entered the Roman Catholic Church. But the momentum continued and the Movement exerted considerable influence on the standard of worship in the Church of England and on the range of its social activities. Among the leaders were Edward Bouverie Pusey, R. W. Church, R. H. Froude, and R. I. Wilberforce. The aims of the Movement were published in *Tracts for the Times*, the first of which was by Newman in 1833. The last was by Newman also (number 90 in 1841), and caused a storm because it demonstrated that the author was moving closer to Rome.

# P

**Pacing Mustang, The** A legendary wild horse of the American frontier, a superb stallion of great strength and beauty, and untamable. In Melville (*Moby Dick*) he is white; in Seton (*The Pacing Mustang*) he is black. He occurs in Emerson Hough's novel *North of 36* and as far back as 1832 Irving refers to him in his *A Tour of the Prairies*.

**Page** The husband of Meg Page and friend of Ford in Shakespeare's *The Merry Wives of Windsor*. He laughs at Falstaff's impudence but cannot persuade Ford to do the same. He takes part in the final discomfiture of the fat knight in Windsor Forest but afterwards, being a good-natured man, he invites him to his fireside for a hot posset. His wife calls him George.

**Page, Anne** The daughter of Meg and George Page in Shakespeare's *The Merry Wives of Windsor*. Her father wants her to marry Slender, Justice Shallow's cousin, while her mother would prefer the Frenchman, Dr Caius. Anne prefers Fenton, and gets him with her father's blessing in the end.

**Page, Mistress** One of the merry wives of Windsor in Shakespeare's play of that name. Meg Page is Alice Ford's friend and ally in the discomfiture of Falstaff and the originator of the final baiting of him in the forest at Windsor.

**Page, Thomas Nelson** *c*.1853–1922. Page was a Virginian lawyer, born in Hanover, who gave up the law after nine years of successful short-story writing. The first of many collections of stories was *In Ole Virginia* (1887). A prolific writer, Page was preoccupied with the Old South and its way of life – to which he ascribed all grace and virtue. He wrote a number of novels in the same vein, of which the first was *On New-found River* (1891). *Red Rock* (1898) was a story about the reconstruction of the South and very popular with his readers – it tells of the oppressive military rule endured by the Southern people. Page could render the Negro speech of Virginia with accuracy and he used it, inevitably, as a further illustration of his favourite theme. *Befo' de War* (1888) is a book of verse in dialect and Page also wrote an admiring biography, *Robert E. Lee, Man and Soldier* (1911). He gave up his literary career when he became the US ambassador to Italy in 1913.

**Paine, Thomas** 1737–1809. Paine was the son of a Quaker small farmer and corset-maker of Thetford in Norfolk. His father provided him with some schooling but he was obliged to work at his father's trade from the age of 13. He became an excise officer at the age of 24 but was dismissed eventually as an agitator; he had fought for an increase in excisemen's pay in his *The Case of the Officers of Excise* (1772). He went to London to plead the excisemen's case and there met Benjamin Franklin, with whose advice and help Paine was able to start again in America. He arrived in Philadelphia in 1774. Behind him were two failed marriages and a variety of occupations held before he became an excise officer.

In America Thomas Paine the writer and radical emerged; the climate of the energetic, aspiring society was the right one for his talents. He contributed to, and became editor of, *The Pennsylvania Magazine*, attacking the institution of slavery and advocating independence. His pamphlet, *Common Sense* (1776), demanded an immediate declaration of independence (it came six months later); it appeared in January and had sold over 100,000 copies by March. Paine was opposed by William Smith, writing as 'Cato' in *The Pennsylvania Gazette*. He replied to Smith in *The Pennsylvania Packet* as 'Forester'.

During the War of Independence Paine served in Washington's army and continued his political journalism: *The American Crisis* was a series of pamphlets, published between December 1776 and April 1783. He became secretary to the Congressional Committee on Foreign Affairs in 1777, but was forced to resign in 1779 after bringing an ill-founded charge of corruption against Silas Deane. He wrote *Public Good* in 1780, reiterating the case for federal union made in *Common Sense* and objecting to the Virginia Plan, and in 1781 executed a successful mission to France. After that Paine withdrew to the farm in New Rochelle which the state of New York had given him and worked on his plans for an iron bridge. *Dissertations on Government* (1786) was his single political work during this period; it was an attack on paper money and the danger of inflation.

Paine went to Europe in 1787 to promote his iron bridge. It aroused interest in England, where new technology was taking giant strides, and a model was exhibited in 1791. The bridge was never built but events in France provided a new channel for Paine's energies. He replied to Edmund Burke's *Reflections on the Revolution in France* with **The Rights of Man**, published in two parts in 1791 and 1792. The two tracts, powerfully argued and widely circulated, were called seditious and he fled to France. In his absence he was tried for treason and sentenced to banishment. In Paris the revolutionary Assembly made him a citizen of France (1792) and a member of the Convention; but he was a moderate republican, a Girondist, not a Jacobin, and he opposed the execution of the king. He nearly went to the guillotine when the Jacobins began to slaughter their opponents. His French citizenship was taken from him and he was then arrested as an enemy Englishman. He believed himself the victim of a plot and saw the conservative American minister as his chief enemy. The verdict of history is rather in Gouverneur Morris's favour. He knew that Paine in prison was comparatively safe because he was forgotten. Once at large, Paine's case might be re-examined and he might well find himself on the way to death in a tumbril. He remained in prison until the Terror was past and Morris's successor, Monroe, could secure his release (1795); then he returned to the Convention. His *A Letter to George Washington* (1796) accused the president and Morris of plotting against him. The years which Paine had spent in prison (1793–95) saw the completion of his most famous work, the great attack on accepted religious beliefs called **The Age of Reason**.

Thomas Paine returned to the United States in 1802 and found that *The Age of Reason* had made

Thomas Paine. A detail from the portrait by August Millière after an engraving of 1793. National Portrait Gallery, London.

him unwelcome to many he had believed his friends. How seriously he was regarded is shown by the quarrel which ensued between John Quincy Adams and Thomas Jefferson when the latter championed *The Rights of Man*. Paine suffered ostracism – the man who led the way to independence was now shunned as a radical free-thinker and an atheist. He was accused of every antisocial crime and when he died on his farm at New Rochelle the worthies refused him burial in consecrated ground.

Ten years later William Cobbett, in America to escape his creditors, went to New Rochelle. When he returned to England he took the remains of Thomas Paine with him, hoping to erect a monument at the grave he planned, though Paine had wanted to be buried on his farm. Cobbett was not allowed to reinter the coffin, however, and after his death the remains of Thomas Paine disappeared.

Paine is not remembered as a stylist; his ability with words suited his purpose and what he had to say was infinitely more important than how he said it. Despite our reservations about vulgarity or the rare occasions when he becomes a little too rhetorical, Paine can be seen to have possessed the gifts required to express the new ideas; he is clear, unaffected, warm, and forceful. He did not merely oppose, he offered an alternative and saw the changes he advocated in terms of humanity, not just society or country. 'My country is the world, and my religion is to do good.'

A modern edition of Paine's *Complete Writings* was edited by P. S. Foner and published in two volumes in 1945. *Common Sense* was published in Penguin Books (1976).

**Painter, William** *c.*1540–94. Painter, a school-master at Sevenoaks, Kent, found a patron in the Earl of Warwick and through his influence became Clerk of Ordnance in the Tower of London. He had been educated at St John's College, Cambridge, but had not taken a degree. In English literature he is known as a translator. He published two volumes of tales in 1566 and 1567 translated, and sometimes retold, from Greek, Latin, and contemporary Italian and French. The two collections were dedicated to his patron and are usually called *The Palace of Pleasure (The Palace of Pleasure: Pleasaunt Histories and Excellent Novelles)*. Over a hundred tales are contained, including works by Herodotus, Plutarch, Livy, Boccaccio, Bandello, and Marguerite of Navarre, and range from anecdotes to short novels. The volumes provided a rich source for the Elizabethan dramatists and a modern edition was published in four volumes in 1930, edited by H. Miles.

*Pair of Blue Eyes, A*  A novel by Thomas Hardy, first published in *Tinsley's Magazine* (September 1872 to July 1873).

The blue eyes belong to Elfride Swancourt, daughter of the vicar of Endelstow. To restore the church tower comes Stephen Smith, a young architect. Elfride falls in love with him but the vicar, discovering that Stephen's parents were humble folk, opposes the marriage. Elfride, at first agreeable to the idea that they run away to marry, later vacillates and their plans come to nothing.

Stephen goes to India, hoping to make money; then he will try again. In his absence Elfride saves the life of Henry Knight on a cliff. Knight was formerly Stephen's friend and patron. Henry and Elfride become engaged; but he proves to be a man of impossible rectitude – and stupendous conceit, the modern reader might conclude – and he approaches Elfride unblemished. He insists that his chosen be unblemished, also. Mrs Jethway tells Knight of Elfride's earlier involvement with Stephen and Knight abandons Elfride with harsh words, leaving her heartbroken.

Later Stephen and Knight meet again. Their conversation reveals to Stephen that Elfride could still be free, to Knight that he has been something less than kind. The two hurry down to Cornwall by train. But the same train carries the corpse of Elfride, being taken home for burial. She had married a widowed nobleman but neither his devotion nor his children's affection could save her decline.

**Paley, William** 1743–1805.  Paley was born at Peterborough and completed his education at Christ's College, Cambridge. His abilities were soon recognized and led to him becoming a lecturer, a senior wrangler at the age of 20, and a fellow of Christ's College in 1766. His lectures on ethics were expanded and published as *The Principles of Moral and Political Philosophy* (1785). *Horae Paulinae* (1790) sought to demonstrate the historical truth of the New Testament by a close examination of the life and epistles of St Paul. *A View of the Evidences of Christianity* (1794) was widely read. It offered little that was not already known to scholars but Paley's lucid prose and excellent presentation made its contemporary popularity well deserved. *Natural Theology* (1802) offered a more intensive examination of certain features of the *Evidences*.

Paley's advance as an 18th-century churchman was hindered by the latitudinarianism of his younger days, in spite of his ability. He became Rector of Musgrave in Westmorland in 1776 and Archdeacon of Carlisle in 1782.

**Palgrave, Sir Francis** 1788–1861.  Palgrave was a Jewish solicitor whose original name was Cohen. He was born in London and upon his marriage in 1823 became a Christian and adopted the name of Palgrave. He became a historian through his interest in national records and published *A History of the Anglo-Saxons* in 1831. This was followed by *The Rise and Progress of the English Commonwealth* (1832), *An Essay on the Authority of the King's Council* (1834), *Truths and Fictions of the Middle Ages: the Merchant and the Friar* (1837), and *The History of Normandy and of England* (1851–64). Palgrave became Deputy Keeper of the Records (1838–61). His work is difficult to read and consequently rather neglected but he helped promote the closer study of English medieval history.

**Palgrave, Francis Turner** 1824–97.  Son of the historian Sir Francis Palgrave, the poet and anthologist was born at Great Yarmouth and educated at Charterhouse School and Balliol College, Oxford. Palgrave was made a fellow of Exeter College and became a civil servant after leaving Oxford. He was vice-principal of Kneller Hall Training College (1850–55) and assistant secretary of the Education Department when he retired. A minor poet, Palgrave published a dozen books of verse which are now forgotten but he is remembered chiefly as an anthologist. *The Golden Treasury* (1861), compiled with the help and advice of his friend Tennyson, is probably the most famous anthology of poems and lyrics in the English language. It is, however, a typically 'Victorian' production and its pride of place as a school poetry book was a mixed blessing. The book changed with The World's Classics edition of 1907, which carried additional poems, and the 1928 edition included more work by contemporary poets. Further contemporary poems were included in The World's Classics edition of 1941. Finally, a complete Fifth Book was added to the existing four by John Press (Oxford Standard Authors, 1964), bringing the famous anthology up to date. The same text is used in The World's Classics edition (1964).

*Palice of Honour, The*  An allegorical poem by Gavin Douglas, of 2166 lines, dedicated to King James IV of Scotland. Using the familiar dream-vision form of the medieval courtly poem, the poet describes his allegorical journey on the path to honour. In his encounter with Venus he receives from the goddess a book to translate; this suggests that Douglas's version of the *Aeneid* (1513) was in his mind for some time. *The Palice of Honour* was completed about 1501. See **Douglas, Gavin**.

*Palladis Tamia*  See **Meres, Francis.**

**Palliser, Lady Glencora**  In Anthony Trollope's *Can you Forgive Her?* she first appears as Lady Glencora McCluskie, in love with Burgo Fitzgerald. But she is an heiress and her family bully her into marrying the upright but insipid Plantagenet Palliser. Lady Glencora is one of the author's most attractive characters; she is never completely reconciled to the marriage, which was not of her choosing, but achieves a measure of content with Palliser, who earns her respect and liking, if little more. Her last appearance in the Palliser novels is in *The Prime Minister.*

**Palliser, Plantagenet**  One of Anthony Trollope's characters who, after making a brief appearance in *The Small House at Allington*, becomes a principal in *Can you Forgive Her?* where he is chosen for Glencora McCluskie by her family. He succeeds to the title when his uncle (the Duke of Omnium) dies, and becomes prime minister for a short period. The political novels by Trollope are often called the 'Palliser' novels and the sequence runs, *Can you Forgive Her?*, *Phineas Finn*, *The Eustace Diamonds*, *Phineas Redux*, *The Prime Minister*, and *The Duke's Children.*

**Paltock, Robert** 1697–1767. Paltock was born in the parish of St James, Westminster, and became a lawyer, practising at Clements Inn. He is remembered for a novel of fantasy, *The Life and Adventures of Peter Wilkins* (1751). The hero is shipwrecked in the far south and reaches a country inhabited by people who can fly by means of an outer silk-like skin which spreads out to enable them to become airborne. One of these, the beautiful Youwarkee, drops out of the sky by Wilkins's hut and he falls in love with her. He marries her and rises to importance in the kingdom. The descriptions of flight are very well done but the novel, on the whole, has not sufficient art in its presentation and is no longer read. It was admired by Robert Southey and Leigh Hunt.

*Peter Wilkins* is published in modern editions in the Oxford English Novels series, edited by C. F. Bentley (1973), and in Everyman's Library.

**Pamela**  In Sir Philip Sidney's *Arcadia*, the king's daughter loved by Musidorus.

*Pamela, or Virtue Rewarded.*  A novel by Samuel Richardson, first published in 1740–41. It was his first novel and, like the two which followed, used the epistolary form and parts of a journal. (See **Richardson, Samuel**, for the origin of his method.)

'Pamela asks Sir Jacob Swinford's blessing.' Richardson's *Pamela* was published in 1740; Joseph Highmore's series of twelve illustrations from the novel was completed in 1745. Tate Gallery, London.

Pamela Andrews is a maidservant aged 15 and at the beginning of the story her mistress has just died. The lady's son, Mr B., lusts after her and takes advantage of her isolation to press his attentions; his servants, Mrs Jewkes and Monsieur Calbrand, abet him. Pamela repels his advances but the fact that she has been falling in love with him makes his behaviour even harder to bear. There is no sympathy for her plight; her case is described by one parson to another as both 'common and fashionable'. In the end Mr B.'s persistence drives Pamela from the house, back to her parents. Before she reaches home a letter arrives from Mr B., asking her to return. His pursuit continues although his determination is wearing thin. Pamela's resolution remains unshaken, however, and at last, to her joy, Mr B. asks her to marry him. He has, in fact, read parts of Pamela's diary (stolen by Mrs Jewkes) and this has influenced his behaviour.

The second part of the novel relates how Pamela persuades Mr B.'s family to accept her in spite of her humble origins; how she retains the respect of the class to which she formerly belonged; how she comports herself when she has to meet one of Mr B.'s bastards by a former mistress; and how she saves Mr B. from sinning with an amorous dowager countess.

*Pamela*, to take the unkindest view, could be called the 18th-century equivalent of those modern novels that stay on the bestseller lists for months and then go into paperback in a deal that sets an annual record price. The author might be surprised at how his heroine looks in the 20th century. But he has to be judged in the moral context of his own time and then Pamela's resolution could only have been applauded: she is, after all, in love with her would-be seducer. What is more significant is that she holds her ground despite the accepted standards of her social background – and wins. She was celebrated by readers in nine languages.

That *Pamela* did not convince all readers is shown by the skits which soon appeared. The most famous was published in the following year: *An Apology for the Life of Mrs Shamela Andrews* (1741), the first venture into fiction by none other than Henry Fielding. Fielding's *Joseph Andrews* (1742) is also partly a skit on *Pamela*, with the sexes transposed.

**Pandarus** Cressida's uncle in Shakespeare's *Troilus and Cressida* and the go-between for Troilus in his wooing of Cressida. Pandarus in Shakespeare is different from his previous appearances in literature, beginning with Homer: here there is a distinctly lewd tinge to his character. He is a sort of unpaid pimp, but harmless enough, and reflects the moral atmosphere of the play.

**Paracelsus** A dramatic poem by Robert Browning, first published in 1835. It is based on the life of the Swiss doctor, alchemist, and philosopher (1493–1541) whose real name was Aureolus Philippus Theophrastus Bombastus von Hohenheim. He was the declared enemy of everything in the contemporary accepted practice of medicine, which was mostly based on the knowledge of the ancients. In Browning's poem Paracelsus is a man determined from his earliest years to search out true knowledge. Festus and his wife Michal, his friends, are worried by his arrogance and try to dissuade him, but he goes forth into the world. In Constantinople he meets the poet Aprile. Paracelsus is despondent because the final truth eludes him; through Aprile he learns that man must love as well as know. Aprile is dying, but Paracelsus continues his quest. Five years later Festus goes to Wittenberg to meet Luther. At Basle he finds Paracelsus, now a professor and successful physician. But he is disillusioned; he has tried to follow the example of Aprile but has found the desire for knowledge a continuing torment. He becomes discredited at Basle and is dismissed as a charlatan. Festus finds him half-crazed but determined to retrieve his reputation. But he dies at Salzburg in the hospital of St Sebastian, delirious but aware of why ultimately he failed. His great learning did not suffice for he had not discovered the secret now known to him: love becomes the means of knowledge and intelligence the instrument of love. He

dies with this new awareness, believing that 'It is but for a time: I press God's lamp Close to my breast; its splendour, soon or late, Will pierce the gloom: I shall emerge one day.'

**Paradise Lost** John Milton's epic poem was first published in August 1667. The first edition was in 10 books. A revised edition was published in 1674 with the 10 books rearranged as 12. The poet had expressed his ambition to write an epic nearly 30 years before, and lists exist that name some possible subjects, including Samson, King Arthur, and Macbeth. *Paradise Lost* was begun in 1658 and completed in 1663. Publication was delayed by both the Great Plague and the Great Fire.

*Book I.* Satan and the rebel angels have been driven out of Heaven and are disclosed lying in the burning lake. Satan rouses his followers and tells them there is hope of regaining Heaven. He orders them into legions, naming the leaders and telling them of a new world being created

Frontispiece illustration by Sir John Baptist Medina for Book I of the fourth edition of Milton's *Paradise Lost*, 1688.

somewhere in the utter darkness of Chaos. Then he summons a council and the palace of Satan, Pandemonium, is built.

*Book II.* Satan and his followers debate whether or not to wage another war at once to regain Heaven. They finally decide to investigate the new world: Satan himself will go. He passes through Hell Gates and journeys into the realm of Chaos.

*Book III.* God observes Satan's journey to the newly created world and tells of the future: how Satan will succeed in bringing about the Fall of Man and how God will punish Man for yielding to temptation. The Son of God offers himself as a ransom for Man, to answer for his offence and undergo his punishment. To rejoicing in Heaven, God accepts him, and ordains his incarnation on a future day. Satan meanwhile has reached the outer rim of the universe; he passes the Limbo of Vanity and arrives at the Gate of Heaven, where he changes his form to deceive Uriel, Guardian of the Sun. From him he learns the whereabouts of the new world, and about Man, the creature God has placed there.

*Book IV.* Satan arrives on earth and finds the Garden of Eden, where he observes Adam and Eve. They speak of the Tree of Knowledge and Satan decides to base his temptation on this. But meanwhile Uriel has heard that one of the fallen has escaped from Hell, and of the shape which sought knowledge of the world from him. He warns Gabriel, who in Eden finds Satan at Eve's bower, trying to tempt her in a dream. The tempter is ejected.

*Book V.* Eve awakens, troubled by her dream of temptation, and is comforted by Adam. God sends Raphael to Adam: so that Man may know the nature of his enemy and the need for obedience to God, Raphael tells him of Satan's revolt in Heaven. Satan had gathered many to hear him and had proclaimed his resistance to the supreme authority of God. Only one of those who heard, Abdiel, opposed Satan and refused to embrace his cause.

*Book VI.* Raphael continues his narrative. Michael and Gabriel command the hosts of Heaven but it is the Son of God who decides the outcome. He orders his angels to hold, then from the centre he charges straight into Satan and his legions, driving them to the wall of Heaven, and down from there into the Deep of Hell.

*Book VII.* Adam asks Raphael about the making of the world. The archangel tells him that God, after the defeat of Satan, decided upon another world, from where Man may aspire to Heaven. He sends His Son to perform the Creation in six days.

*Book VIII.* Adam asks for knowledge of the celestial bodies and Raphael tells him that his first need is for knowledge of his own world. Adam then talks to him of Eve and of the passion she arouses in him. The archangel warns him to attend also to his higher instincts, lest he subordinate these to his love for Eve. Then Raphael departs from Eden.

*Book IX.* Eve suggests to Adam that they labour separately in the Garden. Adam is uneasy as, if separated, they could be tempted more easily. Eve says they can do more work on their own; she is hurt that he doubts her strength to resist temptation. Adam weakens and, reassuring himself that awareness adds strength, allows her to persuade him. Satan meanwhile has returned to Eden as a mist by night, and has entered into a sleeping serpent. He finds Eve alone and speaks flatteringly to her, extolling her beauty. Eve is curious that the creature has the gift of speech. He tells her he gained it by eating of a certain fruit from a tree in the Garden. She asks to be shown the tree; at once she recognizes the Tree of Knowledge and turns away but the serpent says she will not die from the fruit – if it did not kill a serpent, what has she to fear? The fruit gives Life to Knowledge. At length he weakens her resolve and she eats of the fruit. Then Satan, his design accomplished, slips out of the Garden. Eve, feeling transformed in awareness, takes more of the fruit and goes with it to Adam who sees at once that she is lost; he eats of the fruit also in order to share her transgression – they will fall together. Their innocence departs: they look for cover from their nakedness and soon are quarrelling bitterly.

*Book X.* After the transgression, the guardian angels return to Heaven. The Son of God goes to Eden to deliver the judgment on Adam and Eve (as known from the Book of Genesis). Before he leaves the Garden he clothes them, out of pity for their shame in their nakedness. Satan has returned triumphant to Hell; henceforth a path is open for Sin and Death to enter the world of Man. Adam and Eve approach the Son of God in repentance and supplication, begging for mitigation of the doom pronounced upon their children.

*Book XI.* The Son of God intercedes with the Father. God hears His Son but declares that Adam and Eve must go from Eden. Michael and a Band of Cherubim come to the Garden; Michael tells them they must now go into the world, which he shows Adam from the crest of a hill. Adam is also shown what will happen in the world until the time of the Flood.

*Book XII.* Michael continues his account of the world, telling of Abraham and of the Messiah promised in the Son's intercession. Adam is comforted by these revelations; he wakes the sleeping Eve and Michael leads them from the Garden.

*Paradise Lost* shows us how familiar Milton was with classical literature, but he succeeds in keeping his chosen subject within its biblical and Christian frame of reference. He has been criticized for glossing over the new ideas of the times (e.g. in the ambiguous exchange between Adam and the archangel in Book VIII), particularly since he knew perfectly well of Galileo's support of Copernican theory, and had himself visited Galileo in his lifetime. But within his framework this has no relevance, and the archangel's words indicate that astronomical controversy has no bearing on Man's salvation. Adam and Eve are very human and credible in Milton's epic, whilst in Satan, who requires the stature to be no less than the opponent of God himself, the poet has created one of the great figures of world literature.

**Paradise Regained** John Milton's second long poem was published in 1671. It is not the same length as *Paradise Lost* and is often thought of as a sequel to it. This is a mistake: the content is completely different and does not call on Milton's gift for epic grandeur. The principal is the Son of Man – the second Adam – and while his adversary is again the tempter the weapons used are subtle and cunning arguments supported by the vision of this world's power and riches.

*Book I.* Jesus, with many others, hears the call of John, and goes to Bethabara on the Jordan. He is baptized, and the Father's voice from Heaven proclaims his beloved Son. Satan is alarmed, seeing his dominion over Man threatened, and he calls his fallen brethren and tells them he will outwit the Son of God. In the guise of an aged countryman he approaches Jesus, fasting in the desert. He tells Jesus that he recognizes the man who was baptized at the Jordan ford: if he is the Son of God, why does he not make bread of the stones in that desert place? But Jesus recognizes the tempter and resists him; Satan disappears as night falls.

*Book II.* Mary awaits her son's return from the Jordan, unaware that he is in the desert. Satan returns to his fallen brethren to confer with them. Jesus wakes, his hunger heavy upon him, and is confronted by the tempter, now in the guise of a man of wealth. Again he tries his temptations, this time with a richly laden table and the finest wine. Waiting to serve are comely youths and maidens and 'all the while Harmonious Airs were heard.' All this is rejected, and disappears. Satan

then tells him that all the riches of the world will be at his disposal if Jesus will listen to him – riches aid the most ambitious designs. Jesus refutes him: the empires of the earth have come and gone 'In height of all their flowing wealth dissolved.'

*Book III.* Satan persists: he tells Jesus he is born to the kingdom of David – yet Judea is under the Roman yoke. Will he not perform his duty and free his country? Jesus answers that he is under his Father's rule and knows the tempter seeks his destruction. Satan retorts that Jesus knows nothing but the meanest aspects of life; he takes him to a high mountain to show him the eastern kingdoms of the earth. He will ally any of these, he says, to Jesus and will restore to him the kingdom of David.

*Book IV.* Satan takes Jesus to the other side of the mountain, and looks west to where the Roman oppressor rules supreme, with the evil Tiberius in power. Satan will help Jesus overthrow him. But who, asks Jesus, made him evil? He rejects the argument of Satan, and also turns his back on the brilliant society of Athens. Satan, having failed, returns Jesus to the desert as the second night falls. On the third day Satan makes his last try, tempting Jesus (as in the Gospel narrative) to prove his godhead. He takes him to the Temple, and sets him on the pinnacle, exhorting him 'Cast thyself down. . .' Jesus tells him he shall not tempt 'the Lord thy God'. Satan, defeated, falls back into the pit and angels come to bear Jesus away.

**Paradyse of Daynty Devises, The** An anthology of works by poets of the early part of the 16th century. It was collected by Richard Edwards (1523–66), a playwright of the time, and published in 1576 after Edwards' death. The poets in the volume are not major figures, the most considerable one being Thomas Vaux.

**Pardoner's Tale, The** See **Canterbury Tales, The.**

**Paris** Juliet's betrothed in Shakespeare's *Romeo and Juliet*, a kinsman of the Prince of Verona. Romeo kills him when he comes upon him taking flowers to Juliet's tomb.

**Paris, Matthew** *c.*1200–59. Matthew Paris was a Benedictine monk of St Alban's Abbey in Hertfordshire, which he entered in 1217. He is believed to have been of English birth and was educated in Paris. He referred to himself as Matheus Parisiensis, but his true surname is not known. During his adult life he made two journeys to France and visited Norway; otherwise he spent his days at St Albans, where in 1236 he succeeded Roger of Wendover as chronicler to

An illustration from a manuscript of Matthew Paris's *Chronica Majora*, c.1250. At the battle of the Horns of Hattin Saladin seizes the True Cross from Guy of Lusignan. *MS 26. f279,* Corpus Christi College, Cambridge.

the abbey. He was skilled in the arts of drawing and painting and was also a goldsmith and silversmith. His work as a chronicler was helped immeasurably by the high esteem in which the abbey of St Albans was held. Persons in high places were frequent visitors, including King Henry III and his brother, the Earl of Cornwall. His visit to Norway was on a mission of reform to the Benedictines of Holm on behalf of Pope Innocent IV.

Matthew's *Chronica Majora* is an edition of Roger of Wendover's work up to the year in which Matthew succeeded him. From 1236 the work becomes his own, and these 23 years of contemporary history place Matthew Paris as the finest of 13th-century chroniclers. He is the most vivid and comprehensive, being interested in everything that happened in the great world outside England. He is also unhesitatingly critical of those in high office – nobles, kings, and pope. Nevertheless, he retained the favour of Henry III throughout his life. Matthew's *Historia Anglorum sive Historia Minor* is an abridgment of the *Chronica Majora,* summarizing the events of the years 1200–50.

The *Chronica Majora* was edited by H. R. Luard (Rolls Series, 1872–83). The *Historia Minor* was edited by F. H. Madden (Rolls Series, 1866–69) and contains a biographical preface in volume 3; there is a translation by J. A. Giles (1852–54).

**Parker, Dorothy** 1893–1967. Dorothy Parker, née Rothschild, was born in West End, New Jersey, and grew up in New York. Educated at a girl's school in Morristown, New Jersey, and a Catholic convent school in New York, she began her career when some poems were accepted by the magazine *Vogue,* in 1916. She later worked as an editor on *Vogue,* and then became dramatic critic of *Vanity Fair.* She wrote book reviews for *Esquire* and *The New Yorker* and acquired a

reputation for sardonic wit. Her first collection of verse, *Enough Rope* (1926), made her famous. *Sunset Guns* (1928) and *Death and Taxes* (1931) maintained the same level of quality, and her poems were collected in the volume *Not so Deep as a Well* (1936). She was equally successful in her short stories and sketches, *Laments for the Living* (1930) and *After Such Pleasures* (1933), which were collected in *Here Lies* (1939).

Dorothy Parker collaborated with Elmer Rice on the play *Close Harmony* (1929) and with Arnaud d'Usseau on *Ladies of the Corridor* (1953). Her verses and stories are models of economy and craft. With the caustic wit and wry observation go a human sympathy which can, in stories like 'Big Blonde' and 'Clothe the Naked' achieve an unexpected poignancy. *The Portable Dorothy Parker* (USA, 1973) contains a generous supplement of previously unpublished reviews, stories, and articles selected by the author's friend and executrix, Lillian Hellman. It was published in England in the same year as *The Collected Dorothy Parker.*

**Parker, Matthew** 1504–75. Queen Elizabeth's Archbishop of Canterbury was a product of Corpus Christi, Cambridge, where he became a fellow in 1527. He was an early supporter of the Reformation in England, though he favoured moderation; he enjoyed ecclesiastical advancement in the reigns of Henry VIII and Edward VI (he married during this reign) but was deprived of all when Mary became queen. He lived in obscurity until 1559, when Elizabeth chose him for the see of Canterbury, though he was reluctant to undertake this highest office of the Reformed Church.

Parker's was an important voice in the formulation of the Thirty-Nine Articles, which fixed the form of the Church of England; he was an active member of the group of scholars who produced **The Bishop's Bible** and he published his *Advertisements,* or Church procedure, in 1566. These brought him into conflict with the Puritans, because the wise and moderate archbishop refused to sweep away every vestige of the old Church practices.

In English literature we are indebted to Parker for his scholarship. He published valuable editions of Aelfric and of the Anglo-Saxon and medieval chroniclers, such as Matthew Paris, Thomas of Walsingham, Gildas, and Asser. His collection of manuscripts, which is of enormous value, is now in the library of his college, Corpus Christi, and he was a generous benefactor of the college and of the university generally. He published a considerable Latin work, *De Antiquitate*

*Ecclesiae et Privilegiis Ecclesiae Cantuarensis cum Archiepiscopis eius lxx* (1572), and founded the First English Society of Antiquaries in the same year.

**Parkes, Sir Henry** 1815–96. Parkes was born in Birmingham and emigrated to Australia at the age of 24. He worked as a farm labourer near Sydney for a time and then returned to his original craft, which was that of an ivory turner. Success enabled him to found a liberal newspaper, *The Empire*, and he made a successful career in politics also, becoming Prime Minister of New South Wales. He was one of the moving spirits behind the forming of the Australian Federal Commonwealth, which came into being in 1901, five years after his death. Parkes wrote poetry as a recreation and encouraged the art of poetry in Australia. Of his five volumes of verse the most highly regarded is *Murmurs of the Stream* (1857). Other books by him were *Australian Views of England: Eleven Letters, 1861 and 1862* (1869) and *Fifty Years in the Making of Australian History* (1892).

**Parkinson, John** 1567–1650. A botanist and herbalist of the royal gardens, Parkinson published *Paradisi in Sole Paradisus Terrestris, or a Garden of all Sorts of Pleasant Flowers which our English Ayre will Permitt to be Noursed up* (1629) and a massive herbal, *Theatrum Botanicum* (1640), which dealt with nearly 4000 plants. The book contains 2600 illustrations.

**Parkman, Francis** *c.*1823–93. Regarded by many scholars as America's foremost historian, Parkman was the son of an old-established New England family and born in Boston. He graduated from Harvard University in 1844 and completed his law studies in 1846 but never applied for admission to the bar.

Parkman found that the neighbouring wilderness (as it was in those days) held a fascination for him that increased with every excursion he was able to make into it during his vacations from college. He suffered from poor health: a chronic nervous disorder led to periods of complete debilitation and psychosomatic blindness. He always felt at his best in his beloved wilderness and while delving into the origins of America. So, in 1846, he set out from St Louis on the 1700-mile journey, much of it on horseback, along the Oregon trail of the pioneers. He mingled with frontiersmen and trappers, lived with the Indian tribes he encountered, and made notes of all his experiences. He journeyed as far as Wyoming.

Unhappily, his constitution proved unequal to his exertions and his health broke down on his return. He dictated his account of the journey to his companion, his cousin Quincy Adams Shaw, and produced a classic – **The Oregon Trail** (1849). Against almost impossible odds – he was at times incapable of composing more than a few lines at a time, depending very much on being read to and dictating his words – he wrote his *History of the Conspiracy of Pontiac* (1851). This was a history of the French war in Canada and highly praised; a novel called *Vassal Morton* followed in 1856. But his health was not improving and Parkman went to Europe in search of treatment in 1858. He stayed for a year and became interested in horticulture. In spite of his afflictions he became an authority in the subject, publishing *The Book of Roses* (1866) and being appointed Professor of Horticulture at Harvard in 1871.

But his real interest lay in the history of America. By a great effort of will he had forced his flagging constitution to grapple with the problem and he had returned to the subject: he published *Pioneers of France in the New World* in 1865. His great **France and England in North America** was on the way. Parkman wrote nine volumes to cover the whole conflict between France and England, going back to the events before the period of his *Conspiracy of Pontiac* for additional material to make his history complete.

In spite of the tendency, common to American historians of the time, to see the emergence of liberty as the result of right (Protestant democracy) succeeding over wrong (Catholic despotism) Parkman was a scrupulous researcher in the tradition of German historical method. He also took endless trouble to visit the scenes where events took place whenever possible and whenever his health permitted it, and the result is a faultless representation of the facts. His literary craftsmanship, as demonstrated in *The Oregon Trail*, makes his history vivid – he was a genuine resurrector of the past.

Parkman's *Journals* were published in 1948, edited by Mason Wade, and threw new light on the life of a remarkable man.

**Parlement of Foules, The,** *or The Parlement of Briddes* (The Parliament of Fowls). *The Parlement of Foules* is an allegorical fantasy of 700 lines in rhyme royal by Geoffrey Chaucer, composed during the later part of the 'second period' of the poet's work. The dream-vision method employed by Chaucer as a device for storytelling is used here.

The poet is taken to a beautiful park where he sees 'Nature, the vicaire of the almyghty Lord'. It is St Valentine's Day and the birds are gathering to

'The Assemble of Foules.' An illustration for *The Parlement of Foules* in R. Pynson's edition of Chaucer's *Works*, 1526.

choose their mates. The poet relates how three royal eagles court a beautiful 'formel' (female), and all the other birds – geese, sparrows, doves – declare their needs and preferences so insistently that it exercises all of Nature's authority to keep order. The royal eagles have to abide by Nature's decision to leave the choice to the formel, who will have a year in which to make up her mind. The noise made by the birds' departure wakes the poet from his dream.

**Parlement of the Three Ages, The**   An alliterative poem of the time of Edward III (see **Wynnere and Wastoure**). The speaker of the poem, after hunting in a wood, falls asleep and dreams of three men: Youth clad in green, Middle-Age in grey, and Age in black. The matter of the poem is the argument of the three concerning the advantages and disadvantages of the age each represents. The speaker of the poem awakes after Age has declared that all is vanity and hears the bugle of Death summon him.

**Parnassus Plays, The**   In about 1600 two plays were produced at St John's College, Cambridge: *The Pilgrimage to Pernassus* and *The Returne from Pernassus*; the second play was in two parts and its second part is called *The Scourge for Simony*. The three have become known as *The Parnassus Plays*

and the authorship remains unknown though they have been attributed to John Day. *The Pilgrimage* is allegorical and traces the journey of Philomusus and his cousin Studioso to Parnassus by way of the Trivium (logic, grammar, and rhetoric) and Philosophy. They encounter Madido, the votary of wine, Amoretto, the voluptuary, and Ingenioso, who has forsaken the struggle and burned his books. The cousins resist temptation and diversion – and reach their goal. *The Return* is satirical and shows the characters on their way back to London, learning how difficult it is to survive. They are obliged to take humble jobs, though they try the accepted forms of attempting to secure a patron or gull the tradesmen. Eventually they are reduced to being shepherds. The satire continues in *The Scourge for Simony* and surveys the literary and academic scenes. The separation of town and gown is considered and Brackyn, the Recorder of Cambridge, is subjected to a fair amount of abuse (he also suffers in **Ignoramus**). The merits of contemporary poets are satirically examined, Shakespeare and Ben Jonson among them; Will Kemp and Richard Burbage appear as characters.

A modern edition of *The Parnassus Plays* is that by J. B. Leishman, prepared from the manuscript and published in 1949.

**Parnell, Thomas** 1679–1718.  A minor though mildly influential poet of the early 18th century, Parnell was born in Dublin, the son of an Anglo–Irish family. He was educated at Trinity College and became a canon of St Patrick's Cathedral in 1702 and Archdeacon of Clogher in 1706. He went to London in 1712. Two allegorical essays that Parnell contributed to *The Spectator* attracted the attention of Swift, who became his friend and introduced Parnell to his circle of acquaintances.

Parnell attempted several forms and succeeded best writing reflective poems in a religious tone. During his lifetime he published almost nothing apart from *An Essay on the Different Styles of Poetry* (1713) and his contribution to Pope's *Iliad*, *An Essay on the Life of Homer*. Parnell accepted the living of Finglass in 1716, which obliged him to return to Ireland. But the decision seems to have been unwise and two years later he was dead, apparently of melancholy. His friend Pope prepared a selection of Parnell's work for publication and it appears as *Poems on Several Occasions* (1722).

Among the poems by Parnell to which respect is accorded are 'A Nightpiece on Death', an early example of the 'graveyard' poem that was taken to its highest point by Thomas Gray; 'A Hymn to Contentment'; and 'The Hermit', based on a story in the *Gesta Romanorum*. He also translated the Latin *Pervigilium Veneris* into English verse.

**Parolles** Bertram's unprincipled and cowardly friend in Shakespeare's *All's Well that Ends Well*. He represents a moral irresponsibility which is all too attractive to the weak Bertram.

**Parr, Samuel** 1747–1825. Parr was born at Harrow-on-the-Hill, Middlesex, and educated at Harrow School and Emmanuel College, Cambridge. He became perpetual curate of Hatton in Warwickshire and assembled a considerable library of 10,000 volumes. Parr was a Latin scholar of distinction and wrote the epitaph on Samuel Johnson in St Paul's Cathedral. An argumentative Whig and literary man, he is now regarded as a pale imitation of Johnson. His writings were collected and published (eight volumes, 1828) and he is the subject of Thomas De Quincey's essay 'Dr Samuel Parr, or Whiggism in relation to Literature'.

**Parson's Tale, The**  See **Canterbury Tales, The**.

**Parson's Wedding, The**  A comedy by Thomas Killigrew, written before the closing of the playhouses in 1642 and first produced about 1640. It was first published in 1664, the year in which it was revived. Based on an original (and presumably quite different) work by the Spanish playwright Calderón, Killigrew's play is a coarse and uninhibited comedy of sex with its extremes of behaviour personified by the parson and Lady Love-all, an old 'stallion-hunting widow'. Mistress Pleasant, her rich young aunt, and their two suitors occupy the rest of the play. Killigrew enjoyed a considerable success and Restoration playwrights were quick to follow with the same sort of subject and treatment. The play is included in *Six Caroline Plays* edited by A. S. Knowland in The World's Classics.

**Partisan, The**  A novel by William Gilmore Simms, first published in 1835. The story is set in South Carolina during the War for Independence.

Davis, a settler in Dorchester, and Hastings, a British officer, are both in love with Bella Humphries and quarrel over her. Davis and Dick Humphries, Bella's brother, join the forces of Robert Singleton, the patriot leader, who is a friend of Davis and who takes his side against Hastings.

Singleton is in love with Katherine Walton, whose father is a British colonel but who also joins Singleton. The story follows the events leading to the Battle of Camden, which results in a disastrous setback for the Americans. Historical figures mentioned include Horatio Gates, Francis Marion, and Baron Johann De Kalb. The tale ends happily for Davis and Bella, and Singleton and Katherine.

**Passage to India, A**  A novel by E. M. Forster, first published in 1924.

Adela Quested visits India with Mrs Moore. She wants to see the latter's son Ronny in his working environment before making up her mind about marrying him. He is a city magistrate at Chandrapore, and he is not too happy with his mother's and Adela's lively interest in the Indians; nor are the established officials and their wives. One night when she visits a mosque Mrs Moore encounters Dr Aziz, assistant to the British Civil Surgeon at the Chandrapore hospital. Mrs Moore gains an agreeable impression of the young doctor, and Adela likes him too when she meets him. They accept his invitation to join a party to visit the caves in the Marabar Hills; also in the party will be Cyril Fielding, principal of the government college and a close friend of the doctor's.

At the Marabar Caves the ladies are escorted by Aziz, Fielding having missed the party's train and following on the next. Mrs Moore finds the caves overpowering with their oppressive, booming echoes and steps outside. Adela and Aziz continue. When Aziz pauses to light a cigarette he loses Adela. He learns, after some anxious moments, that Miss Quested has left with Miss Derek, a nurse, having rushed out of the caves in a distraught condition. Aziz finds Fielding with Mrs Moore, and the three return to Chandrapore. Aziz is arrested at the station and charged with trying to assault Adela Quested.

The English close ranks, ready and willing to believe Aziz guilty of assaulting an English-woman; only Fielding and Mrs Moore believe him innocent. Fielding is turned out of the Club for championing Aziz. Mrs Moore's health deteriorates rapidly and she has to leave for England before the trial. Feelings run high in Chandrapore and the trial is a stormy affair; but by then Adela has summoned her wits, and after tracing the events of the day the clouds in her mind disperse and she admits frankly that she was mistaken. The English ostracize her at once. Ronny, having succeeded in gaining her hand, now breaks off the engagement. Mrs Moore dies on the voyage home, and the friendship of Aziz and Fielding is seriously damaged. Adela returns to England. Like Mrs Moore, she had been too curious about India too soon, and been overpowered at the Marabar caves.

**Passing of Arthur, The**  See **Idylls of the King, The**.

**Passionate Pilgrime, The**  See **Shakespeare, William**.

**Passionate Shepherd to His Love, The**  The famous poem by Christopher Marlowe beginning 'Come live with me and be my love', which sings of love in an idyllic strain in a world of perpetual summer. Sir Walter Ralegh wrote a witty reply in *The Nymph's Reply to the Shepherd*, in which the nymph seeks assurance that the shepherd's love is more than a summer's dalliance: 'But could youth last and love still breed, Had joys no date nor age no need. . .'.

**Passtyme of Pleasure, The**  See **Hawes, Stephen**.

**Past and Present**  An essay by Thomas Carlyle, first published in 1843. Written in under seven weeks, it was a powerful statement in criticism of conditions in England. The lot of workers was at its worst and Carlyle, who had published *The French Revolution* in 1837, pointed to the abyss into which England, too, could stumble. He questioned the idea of 'progress' as it was conceived in his time, contrasting it with the condition of life in 12th-century England. His source for the latter was the chronicle of Jocelin de Brakelond, discovered by the Camden Society a few years before, which described the social life and a monastic community at the turn of the 13th century. Carlyle posed the question of whether the serf of those days was really worse off than the 'free man' of the 1840s, who worked cruelly long hours and was more expendable than the meanest farm animal.

Carlyle saw as the real answer the 'strong man', to rule and put an end to the rottenness of the state, instead of the democratic process. In *Latter-Day Pamphlets* (1850) he expressed his criticisms of particular institutions in a fiercer attack that also denounced philanthropy and the measures which well-intentioned people were taking to alleviate the harshness of most people's lives. His strident insistence on the 'strong man' was, at the same time, so badly expressed that he seemed to be advocating a doctrine of Might being Right, and the book, consisting of eight pamphlets, alienated many of Carlyle's friends.

See also **Brakelond, Jocelin de**.

**Paston Letters**  The letters of the wealthy Paston family of Norfolk for the years 1422–1509 are of enormous value as a straightforward personal account of three generations of their life and times, spanning the reigns of Henry VI, Edward IV, Richard III and Henry VII. Domestic life, leisure habits, social occasions, and what educated people read; business matters and the process of law; and the violence which prevailed in England in those troubled times – all can be found in the letters of the Paston family.

The letters were first published in a two-volume selection made by John Fenn in 1787. They had arrived in Fenn's possession after passing through various hands, beginning with Peter Le Neve, an antiquary, to whom they were sold by the 2nd Earl of Yarmouth (1652–1732), the head of the Paston family. Fenn presented the manuscript of the letters of the two volumes to the Royal Library when George III displayed interest in his publication and awarded him a knighthood. Another two volumes of Paston letters were published in 1789; a fifth followed in 1825.

The originals were lost for a number of years and not completely reassembled until 1889. The edition prepared by James Gairdner (6 volumes 1904, republished 1965) is valued for its thoroughness and for Gairdner's introduction. Virginia Woolf devoted an essay to the subject in *The Common Reader*. A new edition of all the correspondence has been prepared by Norman Davis (Part I 1971, Part II 1976).

**pastoral**  A term usually used to describe a romance or play of straightforward thought and action in a country setting. Examples are Sidney's *Arcadia*, Fletcher's *The Faithful Shepherdess*, Shakespeare's *As You Like It*, and Milton's *Comus*. The form came to England through Italian and Spanish examples, which themselves looked back to the Greek writers of Sicily, particularly Theocritus.

**Pastorella**  In Book IV of Spenser's *The Faerie Queene*, the shepherdess who is loved by Coridon and who falls in love with Sir Calidore. She proves to be of 'gentle' birth.

**Patchen, Kenneth**  1911–72. Patchen was born in Niles, Ohio. He spent one year at the University of Wisconsin and then, at the age of 17, went to work in a steel mill. He published his first volume of poetry in 1936, *Before the Brave*. Patchen's work is not confined to any one form and embraces love poetry, satire, fantasy, and social criticism; many of his works have been illustrated by the poet himself. Among his other volumes are *First Will and Testament* (1939), *The Teeth of the Lion* (1942), *Cloth of the Tempest* (1943), *An Astonished Eye Looks Out of the Air* (1945), *Pictures of Life and of Death* (1946), *Red Wine and Yellow Hair* (1949), *To Say if You Love Someone* (1949), *Hurrah for Anything* (1957), and *Because It Is* (1959). Patchen's prose works include the surrealist allegory *The Journal of Albion Moonlight* (1941), the satirical novel *Memoirs of a Shy Pornographer* (1945), and the novels *Sleepers Awake* (1946) and *See You in the Morning* (1948). His prose poems are collected as *Panels for the Walls of Heaven* (1947) and *The Famous Boating Party* (1953). In 1951 Kenneth Patchen had to undergo major spinal surgery and was incapacitated for the last two decades of his life. But he continued to write poetry until his death in January 1972. *Collected Poems* (1968), *Aflame and Afun of Walking Faces: Fables and Drawings* (1970), *There's Love All Day: Poems* (1971), *Wonderings* (1971), and *In Quest of Candlelighters* were his later works.

**Pater, Walter Horatio** 1839–94. Pater, the son of a doctor who was formerly a Roman Catholic, was born in London. He was educated at King's School, Canterbury, and entered Queen's College, Oxford (1858), where he studied Greek philosophy under Benjamin Jowett. Pater had met John Keble in 1855 and had become interested in the Oxford Movement. At Oxford and during visits to Germany he grew sceptical and lost interest in the Church. Pater became a fellow of Brasenose College in 1865, and a visit to Italy in the same year stimulated his interest in the Renaissance. In England he acquired an interest in the Pre-Raphaelites and the works of Swinburne and in the 'art for art's sake' principle, which was to inform so much of his work.

Pater's literary career began with a notable essay on Johann Joachim Winckelmann contributed to *The Westminster Review* (1867). A regular contributor to periodicals, he published a collection of essays, *Studies in the History of the Renaissance* (1873). This gave him a firm reputation as an aesthete and scholar though the concluding essay, which declared that the love of art for art's sake was the highest form of wisdom, was attacked by several critics and dropped from the next edition (1877). Pater lived in Oxford when he was not travelling and he was at the centre of an earnest aesthetic group. His views on Renaissance and classical art were published in *The Academy*, *The Athenaeum*, *The Pall Mall Gazette*, *The Contemporary Review*, and other journals, and commanded attention.

*Marius the Epicurean* (1885) is a philosophical romance; *Imaginary Portraits* (1887) is a collection of published essays; *Appreciations* (1889) contains his judgments of some English writers, including Shakespeare. *Plato and Platonism* (1893), a series of lectures that continues in the manner of his first published collection, represents the aesthetic of a remarkable prose stylist who had withdrawn from the ordinary world and looked forward to nothing. 'Aestheticism' – the doctrine that fine art acknowledges no moral standards and has no regard for the progress of everyday life – was challenged by Sainte-Beuve, Ruskin, William Morris, and Tolstoy.

*Paternoster* A poem in Middle English dated about 1170, of some 300 lines in rhyming couplets. It is a lengthy paraphrase of the Lord's Prayer, written for homilectic purposes and, though influenced by Latin models, notable as an early example of vernacular poetry. The poem was edited by R. Morris (Early English Text Society, 1867).

**Paterson, A(ndrew) B(arton)** 1864–1941. A. B. Paterson was the son of a landowning family of New South Wales. He was educated in Sydney and later trained for the law. He practised as a solicitor in Sydney until the Boer War, when he became a war correspondent. In 1904 he edited a Sydney newspaper but from 1908 until World War I he spent his time on the land. He served with distinction in the war and settled down afterwards in Sydney.

Apart from his activities as a journalist Paterson was the author of some novels; but he is famous for the ballads he contributed to *The Bulletin*, the widely read Sydney paper founded in 1880 by J. F. Archibald and John Haynes, while still practising as a solicitor. He published a collection of ballads and longer narrative poems as *The Man from Snowy River* (1895) and became a best seller. He also collected authentic bush ballads and published an anthology, *Old Bush Songs*, in 1905. The slangy language and infectious rhythms make Paterson's own poems, and the ones he collected, immediately memorable. Everyone in the English-speaking world knows 'Waltzing Matilda', which he adapted from a traditional source. His nickname, Banjo Paterson, comes from his pseudonym in *The Bulletin* – his ballads were by 'The Banjo'. Paterson's *Collected Verse* was published in 1921.

*Pathfinder, The; or, The Inland Sea.* A novel by James Fenimore Cooper, first published in 1840, it was the fourth of the *Leather-Stocking Tales* to be written and the third in order of events. The period is the mid-18th century and the centre of the action is Oswego, the British fort on Lake Ontario.

Mabel Dunham is making her way to Oswego to join her father, with a group consisting of her uncle, Charles Cap, a Tuscarora Indian named Arrowhead and his wife Dew-in-June, the scout Pathfinder, Chingachgook the Mohican chief, and Jasper Western the sailor, whom the French called Eau-douce. The party is harassed by Iroquois and in one skirmish Arrowhead and his wife disappear; the rest of the party arrive safely at the fort. Mabel, with her father, her uncle, Pathfinder, and Lt Muir (who wants to marry Mabel), proceeds on Jasper Western's boat, *Scud*, to relieve a post in the Thousand Islands. But Jasper is under suspicion of disloyalty to the English and is sent back to Oswego, while Dunham and his force set out to attack French supply boats.

Then Dew-in-June arrives, with the warning that Arrowhead, at the head of an Iroquois force, is leading an attack on the post. Cap and Lt Muir are taken prisoner and Dunham is wounded. Mabel defends the blockhouse and implores Pathfinder to protect her father, offering him her hand. Dunham approves of the scout's obvious attraction to his daughter.

The Iroquois are eventually routed by Pathfinder and Chingachgook, and Lt Muir arrests Jasper Western as a traitor – to the despair of Mabel who, in spite of her desperate promise to Pathfinder, has been in love with Jasper for some time. But the story is resolved by the unmasking of Muir as the real traitor; it is Arrowhead who kills him. Dunham dies and Pathfinder, realizing the truth, relinquishes Mabel to Jasper.

**Patience** An alliterative poem of the late 14th century, *Patience* is the third and shortest poem in the Cotton Nero A.X manuscript. (See *Pearl*.) The poem is a paraphrase of scripture, told in terse and vivid style and using the story of Jonah to make the point of the title. *Patience* was edited by R. Morris for the Early English Text Society (1864), by H. Bateson (1912 and 1918), and by I. Gollancz (see *Pearl*). A. C. Cawley and J. J. Anderson's edition contains the four poems of the Cotton manuscript (Everyman's Library). Brian Stone's translation appears in *Medieval English Verse* (Penguin Classics, 1964).

**Patient Grissil, The Pleasant Comedie of** A play by Thomas Dekker, written in collaboration with Henry Chettle and William Haughton and first published in 1603. The story is based on Chaucer, who in turn based it on Boccaccio (see *The Clerk's Tale* in the entry for **Canterbury Tales, The**). The play is remembered for Dekker's beautiful songs 'Art thou poore yet hast thou golden Slumbers? O sweet content!' and 'Golden slumbers kiss your eyes'.

**Patmore, Coventry Kersey Dighton** 1823–96. Coventry Patmore was born in Woodford, Essex, and educated privately. He became an assistant in the Department of Printed Books at the British Museum and published his first *Poems* (1844) at the age of 21. Patmore, who numbered Ruskin and Tennyson among his friends, now attracted the attention of Rossetti and Holman Hunt though his work had not pleased the critics. He was one of the original contributors to *The Germ* and published *Tamerton Church Tower and Other Poems* (1853) before becoming well known with *The Betrothal* (1854), the first book of **The Angel in the House**. *The Espousals* (1856), *Faithful for Ever* (1860), and *The Victories of Love* (1862) completed the work by which he is best known. The critics were again displeased but the domestic epic enjoyed considerable popularity.

Patmore became a Catholic in 1862 and *The Unknown Eros and Other Odes* (1877) displayed elevated intentions (Patmore had moved from domestic love to its metaphysics), which were not expressed with complete success. However, 'Magna est Veritas' and 'A Farewell' are to be found in good anthologies of English verse, as are some of the lyrics from *The Angel in the House*. Among other works by Coventry Patmore were *Amelia* (1878) and *The Rod, The Root and The Flower* (1895), meditations on religious subjects. *Works: A New Uniform Edition* was published in five volumes (1897). Patmore was a regular contributor to *The Fortnightly Review*, *The St James Gazette*, and *The Edinburgh Review*.

**Paton, Alan Stewart** 1903– . Alan Paton was born in Pietermaritzburg and educated at the University of Natal. He was a teacher from 1924 to 1935 and was then appointed principal of the reformatory for African boys. After 13 years, during which he visited Europe and the USA to examine the problems of young offenders in other countries, Paton resigned and devoted himself to writing.

*Cry the Beloved Country* (1948) made him famous in the English-speaking world and very unpopular with the supporters of apartheid. A passionate and moving story, it relates how a Zulu country parson goes to Johannesburg to see his son and his sister and how he discovers what the environment has done to them. Paton allows the strange lyricism of Zulu speech to make its effect and the language of the novel is poetic. The novel itself is an angry protest against the condition of the Africans and the White man's laws that brought it about.

*Too Late the Phalarope* (1953) was in the same vein but more controlled and *Debbie Go Home* (short stories, 1961) drew on his experiences as principal of the reformatory. Among his nonfiction books are *The Land and People of South Africa* (1955), *South Africa in Transition* (1956), and *Hope for South Africa* (1958). *Ah, But Your Land is Beautiful* (1981) is Alan Paton's third novel and tells of the 1950s in South Africa, when passive resistance began and active protest was first heard.

**Paulding, J(ames) K(irke)** 1778–1860. J. K. Paulding was born in the state of New York and grew up in Tarrytown, close to Washington Irving and his family. His sister married William Irving and Paulding became involved in the literary activities of the Irving family. The success of *Salmagundi* inspired Paulding to pursue an active writing career of his own and in 1812 he published *The Diverting History of John Bull and Brother Jonathan*, written in the comic vein used by Irving for his *History of New York*. He satirized English romanticism in *The Lay of the Scottish Fiddle* (1813) and extolled the American spirit in a long poem called *The Backwoodsman* (1818). He became famous with little effort in America by continuing to write in that style.

Paulding served on the Board of Navy Commissioners (1815–23) and later became Secretary of the Navy (1838–41). His output was considerable and included realistic tales (*The Tales of the Good Woman*, 1829, and *The Book of St Nicholas*, 1836) and novels (*Konigsmarke*, 1823, *The Dutchman's Fireside*, 1831, *Westward Ho!*, 1832, and *The Puritan and His Daughter*, 1849).

**Paul Ferroll** A novel by Mrs Archer Clive (1801–73), first published in 1855. Mrs Clive was a minor poet and novelist who is remembered for this one book, which anticipates the crime stories of Wilkie Collins – the first true practitioner in the form in England. *Paul Ferroll* is not a detective story, since the crime and the perpetrator are known to the reader from the beginning.

Paul Ferroll murders his malignant and domineering wife who had, by a clever trick, prevented his marriage to the woman he really loved. He manages to get away with the murder and marries the woman he always wanted. They enjoy 18 years of happiness before Paul, to save innocent suspects, confesses to the crime.

The book was followed by a less effective sequel, entitled *Why Paul Ferroll Killed his Wife* (1860).

**Paulina** In Shakespeare's *The Winter's Tale* Hermione's loyal and devoted friend. She refuses absolutely to withdraw in her defence of Hermione and allows Leontes to believe his wife has died in prison. Paulina's husband is Antigonus,

whom she loses through Leontes' deeds during his jealous rage.

**Paul's Walk** By the early 17th century St Paul's Cathedral had largely ceased to be a sacred building – it was even used as a market at one time. The central aisle, known as Paul's Walk, was a promenade, a place of business and assignation and a gossip exchange. Frequenters were described as 'Paul's men', a reference encountered in Elizabethan and Jacobean drama.

**Payne, John Howard** 1791–1852. The American playwright was born in New York City and showed an interest in drama while still a child. He was publishing his own theatrical reviews, *Thespian Mirror* and *The Pastime*, before he was 20. He wrote *Julia, or the Wanderer* (1806) and adapted *Lovers' Vows* (*Das Kind der Liebe*) from Kotzebue (1809). Both were produced and Payne had meanwhile made his debut as an actor. However, the public reacted against their prodigy and the erstwhile boy wonder found himself out in the cold. His friends collected a fund to send him to Europe to seek a new career in 1813.

In England Payne was reduced to theatrical hackwork until Edmund Kean decided to produce his *Brutus: or The Fall of Tarquin* in 1818. The production was a success and on the strength of it Payne leased Sadler's Wells Theatre. He had, during his lean years, become friends with François-Joseph Talma, the great French actor, and on a visit to Paris he had been given the freedom of the Comédie-Française; he had reason to feel confident about the future. But he was no manager and his tenure of the Wells led him to prison for enormous debts. The successful production of *Thérèse, the Orphan of Geneva* (1821), which he had adapted from a French original, rescued him from perdition and he fled to Paris as soon as he was released – there were still outstanding debts.

Payne returned to London in 1823 and was fortunate in his friendship with Henry Irving, with whom he collaborated in several successful plays, notably *Charles the Second* (1824) and *Richelieu* (1826). He also edited a weekly, *Opera Glass*, but fortune eluded him and he returned to New York in 1832 with an increased reputation but little more. Payne's uncertain career took another strange turn when he decided to write about the Cherokee Indians and collected 14 volumes of notes. Little of this work was ever used and it was not until his appointment as US consul at Tunis (1842) that he attained any kind of security, though he never succeeded in paying his debts. To the end of his life he was planning great literary and dramatic ventures.

John Howard Payne was a curious figure; he is credited with 50 or 60 plays but it is difficult to find something original in them or to find, for that matter, much that had any life off the boards. But he had some influence in the development of the American theatre and that should be remembered. His only claim to present fame is that he wrote the lyrics for Henry Bishop's song 'Home Sweet Home', the result of Bishop's use of *Clari: or The Maid of Milan* (1823) for the opera stage.

**Peacham, Henry** *c*.1576–*c*.1643. A writer of essays and 'characters', Peacham is best remembered for *The Compleat Gentleman* (1622), a volume of advice to young men about to enter the world. It is often regarded as presenting the ideal picture of a young cavalier and it covers a remarkable number of subjects from manners to art, poetry, and heraldry. The heraldic definitions in the 1661 edition were to prove enormously valuable to Samuel Johnson when he came to compile his dictionary. Other books by Peacham were *Coach and Sedan* (1636), *The Truth of Our Times* (1638), and *The Art of Living in London* (1642). His treatise on art, *Graphice*, was first published in 1606 and appeared in many subsequent editions as *The Gentleman's Exercise*.

**Peacock, Thomas Love** 1785–1866. The son of a London merchant, Peacock was born in Weymouth and received no schooling beyond the age of 16, when he came to London. He taught himself Greek, Latin, French, and Italian so well that he enjoyed reading those languages and despised all his life the scholastic method that seemed to remove all the pleasure from such studies. For many years he lived on his allowance, having no desire to join his father's business.

He began to write poetry when he was 16 and was making his name by the time he met Shelley in 1812, having published two volumes of verse, in 1806 and 1810. His friendship with Shelley grew closer and he accompanied him and his first wife, Harriet Westbrook, to Edinburgh. He was Shelley's confidant during the break with Harriet and later during the elopement with Mary Godwin. He remained his intimate friend for the rest of Shelley's short life, and the friendship no doubt stimulated the writing of his *The Four Ages of Poetry* in 1820, an essay important enough to provoke Shelley into a reply.

The sequence of novels by which Peacock is best remembered began in 1816, with the publication of **Headlong Hall**. Then came **Melincourt** (1817) and **Nightmare Abbey** (1818). In 1819 he entered the service of the East India Company and remained there until 1856; he was their chief examiner of correspondence. He married in 1820 and returned to his novels in 1822 with **Maid Marian**. **The Misfortunes of Elphin** (1829) is set in Wales: his wife, Jane Gryffydh, was a Welsh girl and he developed a great liking for the country. **Crotchet Castle** was published in 1831 and **Gryll Grange**, the last and the most accomplished, in two parts in 1860 and 1861. The fact that he never wrote a life of his friend Shelley is to be regretted but he did contribute a memoir to *Fraser's Magazine*, which corrected the misrepresentations of such men as Trelawny, Middleton, and Hogg and defended the memory of Harriet Shelley.

Peacock's novels have never achieved real popularity. They are satirical tales with almost no plot, remarkable for their witty conversations, which reflect the author's view of the intellectual and social cross currents of his time. Their quality is undeniable; Peacock's prose style is impeccable and his satire is lethally accurate. Shelley praised his friend's opposition to every kind of tyranny – and was himself a target in *Nightmare Abbey* when the author satirized the Romantics. Peacock's spokesman, Mr Hilary, says: 'To represent vice and misery as the necessary accompaniments of genius is as mischievous

Thomas Love Peacock. From the portrait by H. Wallis, 1858. National Portrait Gallery, London.

as it is false.' It needed saying then; the need is still with us. A notable feature of the novels is the number of songs that Peacock scattered throughout them. An accomplished versifier, he achieves real beauty in short pieces.

***Pearl*** An alliterative poem of the later half of the 14th century. Composed in octosyllabic 12-line stanzas, it is one of four works contained in a single manuscript in the British Library (Manuscript Cotton Nero A.x). The other works are *Cleanness*, *Patience*, and *Sir Gawain and the Green Knight*; all four poems are illustrated by drawings. The dialect of the poems, which are probably by the same hand, has been identified as northwest Midland; the authorship remains unknown. The poem, which is in 20 sections, is essentially a lament: the Pearl lost by the poet is a baby daughter of less than two years old. He wanders in the garden where she lies buried, and falls asleep. In his dream he finds himself by a stream in a strange land. On the far side of the stream is a beautiful maiden in white, her gown decorated with pearls. He recognizes his lost child, grown to maturity. She reproaches him for grieving too much: her state is blessed. From this point (Section X) the poem takes the form of a

An illustration from the late 14th- or early 15th-century manuscript of *Pearl*. The poet sleeps by the river. *MS Cotton Nero A. x, f.41*. British Library.

religious allegory. At the end (Section XX) the poet tries to cross the stream to join his Pearl but wakes in the garden. The theme of spiritual crisis and reconciliation to loss is raised to the highest level of expression in one of the acknowledged masterpieces of English medieval poetry.

A facsimile of the manuscript Cotton Nero A.x containing *Pearl* and the other three poems was edited by I. Gollancz and published, with his translation, by the Early English Text Society (1921). Other editions of *Pearl* are by S. P. Chase (Boston, 1932), E. V. Gordon (1953), M. V. Hillman (New York, 1961), and by A. C. Cawley and J. J. Anderson in the Everyman's Library edition, which contains the four poems of the Cotton manuscript. There are numerous translations, including those by R. S. Loomis in *Medieval English Verse and Prose* (New York, 1948) and Brian Stone in *Medieval English Verse* (Penguin Classics, 1964).

**Pearson, John** 1613–86. Pearson, who became Bishop of Chester in 1673, was born at Great Snoring, Norfolk, educated at Eton and Queen's College, Cambridge, and ordained in 1639. A Royalist, he lived quietly in London during the Commonwealth, and became Master of Jesus College at the Restoration (1660), Lady Margaret Professor of Divinity (1661) and Master of Trinity College, Cambridge (1662). Pearson is acknowledged as the most learned and profound divine of an age when erudite divines were fairly thick on the ground. His *Exposition of the Creed* (1659), developed from a series of sermons delivered at St Clement's, Eastcheap, was for long a standard work in English divinity studies.

**Pecksniff, Mr (Seth)** The self-seeking hypocrite of Dickens's *Martin Chuzzlewit*. According to Forster, the author's friend and biographer, the conception of Pecksniff was the origin of the book. He hopes to marry Mary Graham, old Martin's adopted daughter, and brings about his own downfall by trying to separate the old man from his reformed grandson, young Martin.

**Pecock, Reginald** *c.*1395–1461. Pecock was born in Wales and educated at Oxford, from where he graduated as a Doctor of Divinity. He was elected a fellow of Oriel College about 1417 and became a priest in 1421. After a period as Rector of St Michael Royal, London, and as Master of Whittington College, he became Bishop of St Asaph (1444) and later of Chichester (1450). He enjoyed the patronage of Humphrey, Duke of Gloucester.

Pecock's importance in the history of English religion is possibly as great as his contribution to English literature, though his importance in both fields was eclipsed by that of his successors, as the work of innovators so often is. Pecock's significance as a writer of English prose dates from before his appointment to a bishopric. He was violently opposed to the Lollards and determined that argument in such matters should be available for examination to all – not just to those who read and argued in Latin. He forced his polemics into English, at that time a prose language ill-suited to the expression of his views. The result, with its pleonasm, its invented words, and anglicized foreign words, makes him unreadable now, but he did give English prose a sharp push forward as a medium of expression.

Bishop Pecock sought to bring the Lollards back to the fold with reason. But his opposition to them rested heavily on his convictions regarding episcopal privilege and papal authority, and he was thoroughly disliked by the people of London where Lollard sympathies were strong. In 1457 he wrote *The Repressor of Overmuch Wijting* (blaming) *of the Clergy*, embodying his opposition in a book of disciplined prose and carefully reasoned argument: but reasoned argument was the last thing that bishops, jealous of their privileges, would welcome. Papal authority was already quite strong enough for them. Pecock was, moreover, attached to the Lancastrian side, and one of his pamphlets, addressed to the Mayor of London, gave the mayor (a Yorkist) fuel for attack should he choose to regard the pamphlet as seditious. Archbishop Bourchier was also a Yorkist, and soon Bishop Pecock was charged with, and found guilty of, heresy. He had the choice of recanting or being burned alive. In public at Paul's Cross, in front of a huge crowd, Pecock gave his works to the public executioner to be burned. Then he was taken to confinement in Thorney Abbey, where he died a year or two later. He had no friends; he was intolerably proud of his erudition, and both sides of the religious controversy of his time found – indeed searched for – something to beat him with.

No exact dates can be given for the composition of Pecock's other works. *The Repressor*, with an introduction and bibliography by its editor, C. Babington, was published in 1860 and is regarded as the standard work on Pecock and his writings. His other surviving works are: *The Donet* (his attempt to frame a creed for believers), *The Follower to the Donet*, a reduction of those two books in *The Poor Men's Mirror* (in the hope of reaching a wider audience), *The Book of Feith*, and *The Reule of Cristen Religioun*.

**Pedro, Don**  The Prince of Arragon on a visit to Messina in Shakespeare's *Much Ado About Nothing*. Benedick and Claudio are members of his suite. He takes an active part in the plans for Claudio and Hero and Beatrice and Benedick, but he is convinced that Hero is playing Claudio false in Act III.

**Peebles, Peter**  In Scott's *Redgauntlet*, the pathetic, half-crazy litigant who haunts the Edinburgh courts.

**Peele, George**  1558–97.  The son of a London salter, Peele was educated at Christ's Hospital and Christ Church, Oxford. He also spent some time at Broadgates Hall (now Pembroke College). He paid two visits to London and lived in his aged father's retreat in the precincts of Christ's Hospital. On the second visit (1579) he was ejected by the school governors because they believed an able-bodied student should look after himself. A 'university wit' from Oxford, he lived in London from 1581 – on whatever he could earn at playwriting and acting, which in his case may have provided a steady income. He was certainly industrious and apart from his plays wrote a number of lyrics and poems for occasions.

The plays that survive are **The Araygnement of Paris:** *A Pastorall* (1584), **The Famous Chronicle of King Edward the First** (1593), **The Battel of Alcazar** (1594), **The Old Wife's Tale** (1595), and **The Love of King David and Faire Bethsabe** (1599). The dates given are those of the first printings.

Among Peele's poems are *Polyhymnia* (1590), upon the retirement of Sir Henry Lee, which contains the celebrated lyric 'Farewell to Arms'; *The Honour of the Garter* (1593), addressed to the Earl of Northumberland upon his admission to the order; and *Anglorum Feriae* (1595), to Queen Elizabeth on the 37th anniversary of her accession. The lyrics in Peele's plays are very attractive and are often found in anthologies.

**Peggoty, Clara**  David's nurse in Dickens's *David Copperfield*. She and her family play a large part in the story: her brother, Daniel, is a Yarmouth fisherman who lives in a wonderful upside-down ship of a house; Emily is his niece by marriage, and is seduced by the unprincipled Steerforth; Ham is Daniel's nephew, and loves Emily. Ham is tragically drowned when trying to rescue Steerforth from the sea.

**Peg Woffington**  A novel by Charles Reade, first published in 1853. It was based on the play, *Masks and Faces*, by Charles Reade and Tom Taylor. The story concerns one of the conquests of the famous Irish actress Margaret Woffington, who lived for a time with David Garrick. The conquest in this novel is Ernest Vane, a wealthy man who has, unknown to her, recently married. Vane's wife, Mabel, fearful of losing him to her rival, prays to a portrait of Peg Woffington. The portrait, however, is not what it seems: Peg has cut out the face and placed herself there to fool a party of critics come to scoff, since the portrait is by a poor scene painter. She hears the plea, and forswears her conquest – betrayed by a tear she cannot hold back.

***Pelleas and Ettarre*** See ***Idylls of the King, The***.

***Pendennis, The History of*** A novel by W. M. Thackeray, first published in 24 parts (November 1848 to December 1850).

Arthur Pendennis is apparently a frank and engaging character but is really a selfish and conceited young man. At university his extravagance gets himself and his mother into financial difficulties, from which they are rescued by Laura Bell. Laura is the daughter of a former admirer of Mrs Pendennis and has been adopted by that lady. Laura also helps Arthur to embark on a literary career in London: Mrs Pendennis has hopes of Arthur marrying Laura but they are more like brother and sister in their relationship.

Major Pendennis, who has already extricated Arthur (his nephew) from a silly entanglement with an Irish actress, is encouraged by Arthur's interest in Blanche Amory, daughter of Lady Clavering by her first husband. He discovers that Amory is a former convict, now masquerading as Colonel Altamont; but the major favours the match nonetheless, ambitious for his nephew. Arthur has in fact proposed to Laura at his mother's prompting. Laura is too intelligent not to perceive the reason and firmly rejects him. She is, in any case, increasingly drawn to George Warrington, who shares chambers with Arthur.

After all sorts of disclosures concerning George Warrington, Blanche Amory, and her father, Arthur and Laura do marry, thanks to the realization by Major Pendennis of exactly the kind of world his ambitions for his nephew would place him in. Arthur succeeds as a writer.

An outline of the plot of *Pendennis* exposes the book's weakest quality. Arthur Pendennis and his mother are the sort of characters the reader feels an urge to slap: Arthur for his selfishness; his mother for her saintly indulgence of him. But Thackeray succeeds in making a whole which is greater than its parts: he knew from his own experience the temptations which beset an indulged young man at university and he knew the world of London journalism in which Pendennis em-

barks on a career. Arthur Pendennis is in many ways the least of *Pendennis*; while the story is his own biography, written in the third person, it is Thackeray the storyteller who keeps the reader interested, from situation to situation and from one character to another. Among the more notable ones are the Irish Captain Costigan, George Warrington (whose ancestors appear in *The Virginians*), Blanche Amory and her mother, Lady Clavering, and Captain Shandon of the *Pall Mall Gazette*.

***Peninsular War, The History of the*** The title commonly given to *The History of the War in the Peninsula and the South of France from the year 1807 to the year 1814*, by Sir William Francis Patrick Napier (1785–1860), published in six volumes (1828–40). An abridgment, *English Battles and Sieges in the Peninsula*, was published in 1852. Napier served with Sir John Moore in Spain in 1808 and subsequently during the rest of the war, and much of his book is eye-witness reporting. It is highly regarded as military history and was warmly praised by the Duke of Wellington.

**Penn, William** 1644–1718. The son of Admiral William Penn, who captured Jamaica from the Dutch, Penn was born in London. He was sent down from Christ Church, Oxford, in 1661 because he refused to conform to the rules of the restored Anglican Church. After travelling for some years he entered Lincoln's Inn (1665); but he was soon a convinced Quaker and published a defence of his new faith in *The Sandy Foundation Shaken* (1668). This attacked both orthodox and Calvinistic doctrines and resulted in his imprisonment in the Tower.

During his imprisonment Penn wrote *No Cross, No Crown* (1669), now a recognized classic of Quaker literature. He had meanwhile become interested in the foundation of a colony in America. The death of his father left him financially secure, and a debt to his father by the crown was settled by a grant of land in the New World. Penn named it Pennsylvania and hoped to establish liberty of conscience for all settlers, whether Quakers or not. After establishing the colony, Penn returned to England in 1684, and wrote a loyal address to James II and a pamphlet (1687) expressing gratitude for the Declaration of Indulgence.

When James II lost his throne Penn continued their lifelong friendship and, inevitably, fell foul of the new regime under William and Mary. He was accused of treason and deprived of the governorship of Pennsylvania. In his enforced leisure (he was not imprisoned) he wrote *Some Fruits of Solitude* (1692): as literature, this is the best of his writings. Pennsylvania was annexed to New York until 1694, and Penn spent his time in England preaching and writing.

Difficulties in Pennsylvania brought about his return and, after restoring order, he wanted to retire there (1699–1701). But legislation to make it a Crown Colony was proposed in 1701 and he returned to England to oppose the plan. His last years were troubled: his steward had successfully swindled him, Penn was imprisoned for debt (1707–08) and became alienated from his eldest son. He suffered a stroke in 1712 and took no further part in public life.

Penn wrote a great deal, being a man of tireless energy, but only the above works are of interest to scholars. An advocate of tolerance, a courageous and stubborn upholder of human rights, he was noted for his gentleness and sweet temper and was a worthy representative of the distinguished movement he espoused. His contribution to literature, though small, is worthwhile.

**Penseroso, Il** The companion poem to *L'Allegro*, this was also composed by John Milton in 1632 during the vacations from Cambridge spent at his father's house at Horton. The title is a misspelling – Milton's Italian slipped up here and he never seems to have made the correction to *Il Pensieroso*, which means 'the contemplative'. In this invocation Milton celebrates the pleasures of solitude and quietness, and the opportunity to dwell on the quality of music, drama, and poetry.

**People, Yes, The** A poem by Carl Sandburg, first published in 1936. It is, as the title implies, a celebration of Americans and the poet had a wide range of experience to draw upon. His emphasis lies on the indestructible quality of the ordinary man and woman on whom the nation ultimately depends and who go on – even if at times they falter – stumbling towards a world where some social justice may in the end prevail. Carl Sandburg uses every level of language and his images are striking. There are caustic references to big business, which seemed to have learned nothing from the Depression, as well as moving, apparently simple, lines which underline the intense bitterness of the experience for its victims:

'He walks and walks and walks
and wonders why the hell he built the road.'

**People of the Abyss, The** Jack London's account of the London slums which he investigated in 1902. The abyss of the title was the degraded level of urban life in which great numbers of the proletariat existed. The conditions stifled any hope of betterment but the abyss was the consequence of capitalism – and essential to its continuance. The book was written in seven weeks and published in 1903. While the reporting of the shocking conditions is accurate and truthful London has been criticized for showing only one side of slum life, implying the complete absence of aspiration. It is, nevertheless, a valuable social record.

**Pepys, Samuel** 1633–1703. Samuel Pepys was the son of a London tailor, John Pepys. He was educated at St Paul's School and Magdalene College, Cambridge, graduating in 1654. In the same year a kinsman of his father, Sir Edward Montagu (later 1st Earl of Sandwich), employed him as a secretary, and in 1655 Pepys married Elizabeth le Marchant de St Michel, daughter of a Huguenot family. Montagu commanded the fleet which brought Charles II back to England at the Restoration, and he proved a good master to Pepys, helping his advancement in the Navy Office. Pepys, a hardworking and perceptive man, rose steadily, his own efforts justifying Montagu's confidence. He also impressed the Duke of York, through whose favour he became Secretary to the Commissioners of the Admiralty in 1673. He had meanwhile given sterling service as Clerk of the Acts, Surveyor-General of the Victualling Service (for which the navy had cause to be very grateful), MP, Justice of the Peace, and Fellow, later President, of the Royal Society. His years as Secretary of the Navy were of inestimable value; he was, as Arthur Bryant rightly described him, the 'Saviour of the Navy'.

In 1678 Pepys became one of the victims of the hysteria attendant upon the discovery of the supposed 'Popish Plot'. He was accused of complicity and sent to the Tower in 1679 but not even manufactured evidence could produce a convincing case against him and he was released in 1680. He had been deprived of his office, but in 1683 he accompanied Lord Dartmouth to Tangier and kept an interesting journal of the experience. He regained his secretaryship in 1684. He was a passionate believer in the value of the navy to England and he set to work anew with a campaign for naval reform. But James II abdicated in 1688 and Pepys was obliged to resign. The government of the new king decided he must be an enemy of the state, since he had been loyal to James, and imprisoned him in the Gatehouse in Westminster. He was 56 and held no further office during his remaining years. After his release from the Gatehouse he wrote his *Memoires of the Navy* (1690) and in 1700 retired to Clapham

Samuel Pepys. Portrait by John Hayls, 1666. National Portrait Gallery, London.

Common, to the comfortable house of his old friend and clerk, William Hewer. He remained actively interested in experimental science and maintained a lively correspondence with his friends in the Royal Society. George Hickes, the nonjuring Dean of Worcester, was another friend, and he was present when Pepys died in 1703. The abdication and flight of King James had left Pepys with outstanding unpaid earnings of over £28,000; William and Mary did not honour the debt.

Pepys was an enthusiastic collector of broadside ballads, and after his death his collection, with his personal papers, went to his old college, Magdalene, at Cambridge. The publication of the diary of his friend, John Evelyn, disclosed a number of references to Samuel Pepys who 'was universaly beloved, Hospitable, Generous, Learned in many things . . . . Mr Pepys had ben for neere 40 years, so my particular Friend.' Evelyn was ill when Pepys died and regretted not being able to be his pallbearer. The Pepysian Library at Magdalene College contained six mysterious volumes written in shorthand. W. R. Gurney, stenographer to Parliament, declared the volumes indecipherable, but an undergraduate, John Smith, undertook the work and succeeded in deciphering them. The debt owed to Smith by literary scholars and historians is

incalculable, though the name of Lord Braybrooke, the editor, appears in the first edition (1815).

The diary of Samuel Pepys is unique. Pepys was writing for and about himself, in shorthand, and there he is, the complete man, having lain quietly at rest for nearly 150 years. His diary is quite different from that of Evelyn, a gentleman who never committed his own private self to paper. Pepys was a commoner making his way in the world and he was certainly not hiding himself from himself. Astonishingly, the most famous diary in the English language covers only nine years. Pepys began it on 1 January 1660 confiding to its pages the excitement and intellectual curiosity of the Restoration world and his reactions to it. His diary is also an unabashed record of his own progress, and a fascinating testimony of his wonder at the lives lived by his betters. He was obliged to abandon his diary in May 1669 because of failing eyesight. Posterity is the richer for the comparatively brief period during which this remarkably endearing man and devoted public servant wrote so candidly about himself and his world.

A new edition of the whole diary is in progress, freshly deciphered by W. Matthews, edited by R. Latham and W. Matthews. The first three volumes were published in 1970. Shortened versions have been edited by O. F. Morshead (1926) and J. P. Kenyon (1963). *The Account of the Preservation of King Charles II after the Battle of Worcester*, dictated to Pepys by the king in 1680, is available in a modern edition by W. Rees-Mogg (1954). *The Tangier Papers* was published by the Navy Records Society (1935). The letters of Samuel Pepys are collected in editions by J. Smith (1841), J. R. Tanner (1926 and 1929), R. G. Howarth (1932), E. Chappell (1933) and Helen T. Heath (1955). The standard biography is by Arthur Bryant: *Samuel Pepys, the Man in the Making* (1933), *The Years of Peril* (1935), and *The Saviour of the Navy* (1938).

**Perceval** Variously spelled, as are the names of all the Arthurian heroes, Perceval appears as Percival, Percivale, Peredur, and Percyvelle. As a knight concerned with the Grail he first appears in the 12th-century French *Perceval* or *Le Conte del Graal*. In the 14th-century Welsh *Mabinogion* he is Peredur, son of Efrawg, a doughty youth who achieves knighthood by valour. Malory in *Le Morte Darthur* combines the two elements and Perceval, one of his noblest knights, is one of the three who alone are able to achieve the quest for the Grail. (Bors and Galahad are the others.) He dies content after seeing it.

Perceval is also found in German romance in the 13th-century *Parzival* of Wolfram von Eschenbach.

**Percy, Thomas** 1729–1811. Percy, whose name was originally Piercy, was the son of a grocer of Shropshire and was educated at Bridgnorth Grammar School and Christ Church, Oxford. After being ordained he became vicar of Easton Mandit in Northamptonshire, then chaplain to the king and the Duke of Northumberland; later he was made Dean of Carlisle (1778) and Bishop of Dromore in Ireland (1782). None of his duties could have been very onerous; certainly the king allowed him the leisure to pursue his antiquarian and literary interests. His enquiring mind pleased Samuel Johnson, who declared that Percy was a man 'out of whose company I never go without having learnt something.'

Percy's interest in ancient and foreign poetry was first expressed in works from the Chinese, which he found in European translations: *Hau Kiou Choaan, or The Pleasing History* (1761) was the first English version of a Chinese novel. The great success of Macpherson's Ossianic poetry stimulated him to publish *Five Pieces of Runic Poetry Translated from the Islandic Language* in 1763 (taken, in fact, from an existing Latin version) and to begin the collection that became famous as **Reliques of Ancient English Poetry** (1765). Percy's transference of interest to his own country's literary antiquity was to prove of great influence and value, while his own poetry is of little interest.

**Percy Folio, The** A 17th-century manuscript that Thomas Percy acquired from Humphrey Pitt of Shifnal in Shropshire. Percy drew most of the ballads for his *Reliques of Ancient English Poetry* from it. It contained material of every kind, including an allegorical alliterative poem, 'Death and Liffe', of the 14th century, but its importance lies in its preservation of ballad poetry. *The Percy Folio* is now in the British Museum and was edited for publication by F. J. Furnivall and J. W. Hales (1867–68).

**Perdita** The child of Leontes and Hermione in Shakespeare's *The Winter's Tale*. She is born in prison, during her mother's humiliation at the hands of the jealous Leontes, and Paulina takes the baby girl to Leontes, hoping to soften his heart. But Leontes has the child left to die on the seacoast of Bohemia, where she is found and cherished by a kindly shepherd. The king's son, Florizel, falls in love with her.

**Peredur, Son of Evrawg** A Welsh tale which appears in the manuscripts of *The White Book of Rhydderch* (early 14th century) and *The Red Book of Hergest* (late 14th century) and was translated by Lady Charlotte Guest in her *The Mabinogion*. It tells part of the same story as the *Perceval* or *Conte del Graal* of Chrétien de Troyes (late 12th century) but it contains few of the elements which Chrétien introduced and made into one of the most haunting stories in western literature. *Peredur*, the story of a doughty champion, is an ancient folk tale set in the Britain of Arthur and his court.

Peredur is the only surviving son of Earl Evrawg, who squandered the lives of himself and his other sons in war. His widow takes Peredur and some of her women with their children to live in the wilderness. But one day some knights, including Gwalchmei and Owein (Gawain and Uwaine), ride by and Peredur is determined to join them. His mother is deeply grieved but she makes him promise to go to Arthur, the best of men, and serve him. He listens to her advice then mounts his horse and departs; he wears rustic clothes and carries a handful of darts. After two days of wandering he comes to a chapel-like pavilion where a beautiful girl sits. There he eats from the table and the girl gives him a gold ring from her finger. The knight of the pavilion returns and sees the strange hoofprints. He charges the girl with being faithless and sets off after Peredur.

At Arthur's court a strange knight has appeared and insulted Gwenhwyvar (Guinevere). The knights have not taken up the strange knight's challenge, believing that only one possessing magic powers would have dared insult the queen. Peredur arrives to become a knight, and the court is glad to have someone to mock to relieve their feelings; Kei (Kay) bullies him into challenging the strange knight. Owein upbraids Kei for his behaviour and goes out after Peredur, only to find the latter dragging in the body of the strange knight, whom he has killed with a dart. Owein tells Peredur to take the strange knight's armour and present himself to Arthur. Peredur vows service to Arthur but refuses to return to the court until he has settled accounts with Kei. After his departure he meets and vanquishes many challengers, sending his adversaries to the court to tell Kei what befell them. He comes to a castle and there meets a grey-haired lord who reveals himself as Peredur's uncle, his mother's brother. He advises Peredur not to question if he sees something strange: he must wait to be told what it means. He meets another uncle at a fortress and sees a spear carried into the hall, while from the blade of the spear blood flows continually. Peredur also sees a bleeding head carried on a platter, but does not ask the meaning of these strange sights; his uncle does not tell him.

After many adventures, settling accounts with Kei, and winning the friendship of Gwalchmei, Peredur is accepted and honoured at Arthur's court. One day a hag riding a mule comes to Caer Llion (Caerleon) and upbraids Peredur: had he asked what the bleeding spear and head signified the kingdom would be at peace. After she leaves Peredur sets out to find her. He travels for a year and then meets a priest who upbraids him for being armed – it is Good Friday. Eventually Peredur finds the Fortress of Marvels and the messenger who had appeared as a hag. The bleeding head was that of Peredur's first cousin, murdered by the evil Hags of Gloucester. Peredur kills the Hags and peace and order are restored.

The spear, which became so important in the legend of the Grail, is not explained in the rather hasty summing-up at the end of Peredur's adventures and has no mystical significance here.

***Peregrine Pickle, The Adventures of*** A novel by Tobias Smollett, first published in 1751. Smollett's second novel, it follows the picaresque form of *Roderick Random*, his first. The full title is *The Adventures of Peregrine Pickle, in which are included Memoirs of a Lady of Quality*. The *Memoirs* were an interpolation, as Chapter LXXXI, by the notorious Viscountess Vane (1713–88): they occupy some 150 pages of the first edition and contribute nothing to the novel. It is generally assumed that Smollett, who has never earned praise as a literary craftsman, received a considerable fee for consenting to the inclusion. Peregrine Pickle, as a character, differs from his predecessor, Roderick Random, in being privileged and of considerable means. He is also the abettor of incidents of varying degrees of nastiness, whereas Roderick was usually the victim.

Peregrine Pickle is brought up by his aunt, Grizzle Pickle, and has been educated by private tutors, at Winchester, and at Oxford. Aunt Grizzle marries Commodore Hawser Trunnion, a one-eyed naval veteran whose country house is ordered like a man o'war and defended like a garrison with a drawbridge and moat. His companion is one-legged Lieutenant Jack Hatchway. Going to be married, Trunnion travels on horseback, finding his way by compass. Peregrine's adventures are mostly prompted by lust; he is apparently in love with Emilia Gauntlet, sister of a friend, but he stoops to trying to get

Frontispiece illustration to Vol. 1 of an edition of *Peregrine Pickle* published in 1769. Commodore Trunnion aims a blow at Jack Hatchway with his stick; Hatchway deflects it with his wooden leg. Smollett's novel was first published in 1751.

his way with her by drugging her. In Paris he fights a duel, is imprisoned in the Bastille, and rescued by the English ambassador. In England he plays tricks on the physicians of Bath, dissipates his fortune in politics, and is clapped into the Fleet Prison for his political journalism. Then his father, Gamaliel Pickle, dies and Peregrine inherits his fortune. His release from the Fleet is obtained and Emilia forgives him. He is, the author maintains, a sadder and wiser man. It is impossible to care, one way or the other.

*Peregrine Pickle* displays even more vitality and inventiveness than *Roderick Random*. It is also more unpleasant, both in the episodes which make up the narrative and in the preoccupation with scatological details. The book is much longer than its predecessor but it shows an advance in the presentation of character. Hawser Trunnion, if the modern reader can endure his excessive use of maritime metaphor (this was a novelty in Smollett's time), is an original creation and he grows in stature as the story progresses. His death scene is affectingly handled.

Modern editions of *Peregrine Pickle* are published in Everyman's Library and in the Oxford English Novels series, edited by James L. Clifford (1964).

**Peres the Ploughman's Crede** A poem that came after and was clearly influenced by *Piers the Plowman*. W. W. Skeat assigned the date of its composition to the last decade of the 14th century. It is distinguished for its forthright satire and descriptive power. The speaker is in quest of someone to teach him what to believe. He visits each order of friars; but each one abuses the others and each tries to persuade him to contribute to their order and stop troubling about his creed. But he sees their worldliness and self-seeking and continues his search. At last he meets an honest ploughman, who delivers a bitter attack on all the orders of friars and teaches the searcher his sought-for creed.

W. W. Skeat's edition was published by the Early English Text Society (1867).

**Pericles, Prince of Tyre** A romantic play by William Shakespeare, first produced *c*.1608, and included in the Third Folio of 1664. It is agreed by scholars that the play is not entirely Shakespeare's work. The plot is based on the 'Apollonius of Tyre' story in John Gower's *Confessio Amantis* and Gower himself appears as Chorus. The author of the first two inferior acts is believed to have been George Wilkins, who worked for the company at the Globe.

While in Antioch Pericles, Prince of Tyre, guesses that King Antiochus has an incestuous love for his daughter. The wrath of Antiochus pursues Pericles and he leaves Tyre to escape it. He is shipwrecked on the shore of Pentapolis and is the only survivor from the ship. But in Pentapolis fortune favours him. In a tournament he wins the hand of Thaisa, daughter of King Simonides. Meanwhile, Antiochus dies and Pericles' faithful minister, Helicanus, urges him to return – otherwise the people will force the throne on Helicanus. Pericles and Thaisa set sail for Tyre. Thaisa is with child and gives birth to a daughter during a storm. Thaisa's condition afterwards leads everyone to believe her dead, so they place her body in a chest and confide it to the sea. It is washed ashore at Ephesus, where a physician, Cerimon, opens it and revives Thaisa. She, believing her husband dead, becomes a priestess of Diana. Pericles leaves his infant daughter Marina in the care of the governor of Tarsus, Cleon.

Sixteen years pass and Dionyza, wife of Cleon, becomes jealous of Marina's beauty and tries to kill her. But Marina is carried off by pirates and sold to a brothel in Mytilene; Pericles is told that his daughter has died. On Mytilene, Marina confounds the brothel keepers because her innocence and purity save her from indignity. The governor, Lysimachus, falls in love with her and then Pericles arrives in Mytilene. The ecstatic father and daughter are reunited and Pericles is granted a dream that guides him to Ephesus and his long-lost wife. Marina marries Lysimachus and the guilty pair, Cleon and Dionyzia, are burned in their palace for their intended crime.

**Pericles and Aspasia** See *Imaginary Conversations of Literary Men and Statesmen*.

**Perkin Warbeck** A tragedy by John Ford. The play was first published in 1634 but there is no record of its first production.

The historical facts of Warbeck's imposture as Richard, Duke of York (the younger son of King Edward IV), are closely followed. Warbeck (de Werbecque) was the son of a burgess of Tournai. He came to notice during the reign of Henry VII and succeeded in gaining support for a time. The play deals with his arrival at the court of James IV of Scotland, his marriage to Lady Katherine Gordon, and the events surrounding the treason and execution of the disaffected Sir William Stanley in London. James IV leads an expedition to England in support of Warbeck, but deserts him when the Tudor king offers forceful resistance. Warbeck's last attempt sees him landing in Cornwall; but the support he had hoped for is not forthcoming and the play follows his capture and eventual execution. In Ford's play he maintains his royal origins to the end. The love and loyalty of Lady Katherine are movingly portrayed.

**Perlis to the Play** A popular Scottish poem once attributed to King James I of Scotland. See **Scottish anthologies and collections**.

**Persuasion** Jane Austen's last novel. It was published posthumously in 1818. It was written in 1815–16, when her health was failing, and it is possible that revision would have improved certain incidents, or even deleted them. But as it stands it makes strong claims of its own: it is notable for the beautifully drawn character of Anne Elliot and for the tenderness of her love for Wentworth. Jane Austen conveys very well the demands that have been made on Anne and makes us understand why she acknowledged their validity. This novel gives us a further glimpse of the author of *Mansfield Park*, in contrast to the high comedy of *Pride and Prejudice* and *Emma*.

Anne Elliot, engaged to Frederick Wentworth, a young naval officer, was persuaded by her godmother, Lady Russell, to break the engagement because of his lack of fortune, which made him unacceptable to her father, Sir Walter Elliot, and because he was brilliant and headstrong – too forceful a character for Lady Russell. Now Anne is 27 and her looks are faded.

Sir Walter's extravagant way of life forces economies on him and he lets his house to Admiral and Mrs Croft. This brings Anne and Wentworth into contact again: Mrs Croft is Wentworth's sister. Wentworth has had a successful career and is now a rich man. Anne's younger sister Mary is married to Charles Musgrove, who has two sisters, and Wentworth becomes involved with Louisa Musgrove. Anne's presence disturbs him, however, and they are both aware that their former love for each other is reviving. But an accident to Louisa at Lyme Regis, for which Wentworth feels himself responsible, draws him further away from Anne, who has gone to Bath with her family.

Louisa, however, becomes engaged to Wentworth's friend, Captain Benwick, and Wentworth follows Anne to Bath. There he finds that Anne is being wooed by William Elliot, her cousin, and that Mrs Clay, companion to Anne's elder sister, has designs on Sir Walter. But William Elliot is, at the same time, carrying on an intrigue with Mrs Clay.

The novel ends with the exposure of William Elliot's character and Wentworth's becoming aware that Anne's love has remained constant. He asks for her hand again and this time she accepts him gladly.

**Peru, A History of the Conquest of** See **Prescott, William Hickling.**

**Peter Simple** A novel by Frederick Marryat, first published in 1834, and generally regarded as his best.

Peter, the simple of the title, is sent off to sea because his family are not sure what else to do with him. At first he lives up to his reputation and seems prone to ludicrous misadventures. But the sea proves to be the right place for him and his encounters with Captain Savage, a fine seaman and commander, Chucks the bosun, who aspires to higher things and ends up as a Danish count, and the warm-hearted and brave Irishman, Terence O'Brien, help Peter to realize himself. He proves to be an able and courageous officer and wins the hand of a charming girl.

**Peter Wilkins, The Life and Adventures of** See **Paltock, Robert.**

**Petruchio** In Shakespeare's *The Taming of the Shrew*, a Veronese gentleman who comes to Padua looking for a rich wife. Having ascertained how much the disagreeable Katharina is worth, he decides she is worth the effort of taming and marries her.

**Pettie, George** 1548–89. Pettie was an Elizabethan translator and is remembered for his 12 tales, which were published without his permission in 1576 and entitled – also without his permission – *The Petite Pallace of Pettie his Pleasure*. The book proved very popular and went on being printed. Its originals, with one exception, are from Ovid and Livy. His style is rhetorical and adorned, looking forward to John Lyly, and is called 'euphuism'.

**Peveril of the Peak** A novel by Sir Walter Scott, first published in 1822. The period is the reign of Charles II.

Julian Peveril and Alice Bridgenorth are in love. Their fathers are old friends, despite their differences in outlook: Sir Geoffrey Peveril is a Royalist while Major Bridgenorth is a Puritan. Julian Peveril, in the employ of the Countess of Derby, who rules the Isle of Man, arrives back in England on her service. The supposed 'Popish Plot', the invention of the evil Titus Oates, has reawakened bitter religious strife and Julian finds his father placed under arrest, by his erstwhile friend Bridgenorth, as a suspected Papist. Julian is arrested, too. Alice has been sent for safety to Bridgenorth's brother-in-law, Edward Christian. Christian is contriving with Chiffinch, Charles II's pander, to bring Alice to the king's notice but she falls into the hands of the Duke of Buckingham. Julian and his father have meanwhile escaped – with the help of Derbyshire miners – and Fenella, who is Christian's daughter by a Moorish woman, helps Alice escape. Fenella herself is in the household of the Countess of Derby, as a deaf-mute, to help her father discover the countess's part in the murder of Christian's brother.

It will be plain that the story is overcomplicated, and part of its excessive length is due to Scott's self-confessed preoccupation with the scenes at court, which he wrote with pleasant ease. He was in bad health while the work was in progress and in spite of the excellent characterizations of Charles II, the Duke of Buckingham, Titus Oates, Colonel Blood, and the rest the book cannot be regarded as a success.

**Phantastes** See **MacDonald, George.**

The title page illustration for Beaumont and Fletcher's *Philaster*, 1620. The original spelling is no longer used.

***Philaster,** or Love Lies A-Bleeding*. A play by Francis Beaumont and John Fletcher, first produced in 1611 and first published in 1620.

Philaster is the rightful heir to the throne of Sicily but the kingdom has been taken by the King of Calabria. He is obliged to live in the usurper's court. He and Arethusa, the usurper's daughter, are in love and Philaster places his page, Bellario, in Arethusa's service as his go-between. A marriage is arranged between Arethusa and the Spanish prince, Pharamond; but Arethusa is able to reveal that Pharamond has been amusing himself with Megra, a lady of the court, and the marriage is called off. Pharamond gets his revenge with the accusation that Arethusa has been conducting an affair with Bellario. Philaster believes the story and, distracted, alters his intention to kill himself to an intention to kill the 'guilty' pair. He is arrested and entrusted to the custody of Arethusa, who promptly marries him, thereby saving his life. Her honour is shown to be intact when it is revealed that Bellario is a girl, daughter of a Sicilian nobleman who, infatuated with Philaster, had disguised herself as a boy to be his page. The usurper is overthrown and Philaster is restored to his inheritance.

***Philip, The Adventures of*** The last complete novel of W. M. Thackeray. It was first published in 20 serial parts in the *Cornhill* (January 1861 to August 1862). It was developed from an earlier tale, *A Shabby Genteel Story*, first published in four parts in *Fraser's Magazine* in 1840.

Dr George Firmin, a fashionable London physician, has gone through a form of marriage as a young man, with Caroline, the daughter of a lodging-house keeper. He has deserted her and then married again: his son is the Philip of the title and the novel concerns his fortunes and misfortunes. It is generally regarded as a failure, with a contrived ending (the discovery of a will which provides the hero with a legacy). The characters, too, are poor shadows of earlier creations.

**Philips, Ambrose** *c.*1675–1749. A fellow of St John's College, Cambridge, and a friend of Addison, Philips is remembered chiefly because so many other writers of the time were rude about him. He was the author of a version of Racine's *Andromaque* called *The Distrest Mother* (1712) and in 1723 published *A Collection of Old Ballads*, one of the first of its kind. Philips' *Pastorals* were published in Tonson's *Miscellany* in 1709; Pope's were also published in the same issue. Pope believed that Philips had been malicious about him in the coffee houses and attacked the latter's *Pastorals* in *The Guardian*. Infinitely more gifted, he successfully demolished Philips' reputation as a poet. Henry Carey referred to Philips as 'Namby-Pamby' for the quality of his poems written for the children of the nobility; this sobriquet introduced a new term to the language, though Samuel Johnson found Philips' verses for children his most pleasing work. John Gay parodied Philips' *Pastorals* in *The Shepherd's Week*.

**Philips, John** 1676–1709. Philips was educated at Winchester and Christ Church, Oxford, and was intended for a medical career. However, he turned to literature and is remembered as a poet who wrote blank verse during a period when the couplet was the fashionable form. *The Splendid Shilling* (1701) is in burlesque Miltonic verse and contrasts the wellbeing of the man who possesses a shilling with the privation of being a poet. A Tory, Philips was persuaded by Harley and St John (later, Lord Bolingbroke) to write a blank-verse poem, *Blenheim* (1705), as a counter to Addison's *The Campaign* (1704) on the same subject. The piece is a failure but *Cyder, a Poem in Two Books* (1708) is a successful essay in blank verse in the manner of the *Georgics* of Virgil. Concerned with apples and cider, the poem contains some felicitous passages on country life.

**Philips, Katherine** See **Fowler, Katherine**.

**Phillips, Stephen** 1868–1915. Phillips was born near Oxford and became an actor at the age of 17, working with Benson's company until 1892. Next he became a teacher and published several books of verse. Though not now regarded as a poet of particular quality, he was very successful in his day. *Poems* (1898) won the 1000-guinea prize offered by *The Academy*, and George Alexander asked him for a verse play for the

St James's Theatre. Phillips published *Paolo and Francesca* (1899), which Alexander produced in 1902 with considerable success. Tree produced his next play, *Herod*, at Her Majesty's (1900) and Phillips was for a time the most successful English dramatist with public and critics alike. *Ulysses* (1902), *Nero* (1906), and *Faust*, with J. Comyns Carr (1908), were all produced at His Majesty's but after that his work, which had been taking on grand-opera dimensions, ceased to appeal. *Iole* (Cosmopolis, 1913) and *The Sin of David* (Savoy, 1914) were failures. Phillips had been extravagantly overpraised and his work could not live up to the level on which the critics had placed it. *Paolo and Francesca* is occasionally revived.

**Philoclea** In Sir Philip Sidney's *Arcadia*, the king's daughter who falls in love with Pyrocles, having seen through his woman's disguise.

**Philotas, The Tragedy of** A tragedy in blank verse by Samuel Daniel, first published in 1605. The subject is the execution of Philotas, the son of Alexander's great general, Parmenion. Philotas is a favourite with the Macedonians but at the same time is boastful and presumptuous. Alexander is suspicious of him and, when it is proved that Philotas has concealed knowledge of a conspiracy against him, has him put to death.

Daniel was obliged to defend himself against the charge of sympathy with Essex, who had been executed for treason in 1601.

**Philotus** A play of unknown authorship that was probably written about 1600. The earliest known text is the one printed by Robert Charteris (Edinburgh, 1603), and it represents the only complete survival of Scottish drama apart from the *Thre Estaitis* of Sir David Lyndsay. The theme is the attempt of two old men, Philotus and Alberto, to marry young and pretty girls, and how their plans are frustrated by the girls, Emilie and Brisilla, with the aid of their lovers.

**Phineas Finn** A novel by Anthony Trollope, first published in *St Paul's Magazine* (October 1867 to May 1869). This is the second of the 'Palliser' novels, though the third in which the Pallisers make an appearance (*The Small House at Allington* is the first).

Phineas Finn is a penniless young Irishman who secures a seat in Parliament and goes to London; his sweetheart, Mary Flood-Jones, waits for him in Ireland. Phineas, in London, proves irresistibly charming and soon he is amorously entangled with Violet Effingham, Lady Laura Standish, and Madame Max Goesler, a beautiful and wealthy widow. Phineas is hardly a philan-

'You don't quite know Mr Kennedy yet.' Phineas Finn and Lady Laura Standish at Lord Brentford's. An illustration by John Everett Millais for Trollope's *Phineas Finn*, 1869.

derer; he is warm as well as light-hearted, and responsive to beauty. He is also fundamentally honest and does not make capital of his considerable attraction for women.

The women with whom Phineas becomes closely associated are an equal part of the novel and their fortunes are recounted along with his. Lady Laura is generous in her patronage of Phineas – but marries Robert Kennedy, so Phineas muffles his feelings. Kennedy's position and influence, and his attraction to Laura, persuaded her to marry him; he proves to be a cold and fussy prig and she soon grows to loathe him. She leaves him and is then peevish because Phineas, having withdrawn, keeps his honourable distance. Violet marries Lord Chiltern, a wilful and stormy man who is as likely to exchange hard words with those closest to him as he is to embrace them a moment later. He is frank and generous, without malice or pretence of any kind. Madame Max Goesler (Marie) is the only one with enough sophistication to be mistress of her feelings and she is the best of the ladies.

Phineas's story takes him through a rapid rise

in Parliament as well as through his entanglements. He becomes Under-Secretary for the Colonies but quarrels with the government and resigns. He returns to Ireland, marries his Mary – and waits there quietly until Trollope brings him back on stage, where meanwhile Plantagenet Palliser and Lady Glencora have also been active. The characters in Parliament are believed to have been largely modelled on real people. Trollope himself stated that three of the principals, Daubeny, Gresham, and Turnbull, were based on Disraeli, Gladstone, and John Bright respectively.

**Phineas Redux**  A novel by Anthony Trollope, first published in the *Graphic* (July 1873 to January 1874). This is the fourth of the 'Palliser' novels though, once again, the central character is neither Lady Glencora nor Plantagenet Palliser.

Phineas Finn is now a widower, his pretty Mary having died in childbirth. He has also lost his father and, in the middle of his depressed state, finds the promptings of friends and former parliamentary colleagues irresistible. He has a small legacy from an aunt, so he returns to Westminster. The ladies with whom he had been entangled are soon back on the scene – with the exception of Violet, Lady Chiltern, though her liking for him is strong and, like Lady Glencora, she is more than willing to further his career. Marie Goesler's serene self-control is in evidence; but Lady Laura Kennedy is hysterical and importunate.

Phineas has an enemy in Mr Bonteen, a rival politician. Mrs Bonteen's house guest is Lady Eustace – now separated from her dubious husband and longing to be free of him. Phineas almost secures a seat in the Cabinet; but Bonteen is murdered in the street after an exchange with Phineas at his club: Phineas is charged with his murder and brought to trial.

Mr Chaffanbrass defends Phineas. Marie Goesler uses her wits and her wealth to gather essential evidence. Lady Laura Kennedy proclaims her belief in the innocence of Phineas Finn.

The trial is a fine set piece, and Trollope traces the effect of the prolonged strain on Phineas, an honest and gentle man who would never willingly harm a soul. He is acquitted and breaks down completely after the trial. The story ends with Marie Goesler winning the hand of Phineas and Lady Eustace being asked to leave Mrs Bonteen's house. Phineas refuses office in the new Cabinet, thoroughly disillusioned by what he has seen of political life. Palliser is Chancellor of the Exchequer in this book and in *Phineas Finn*.

**Phoenix, The**  A poem of 677 lines in Old English, preserved in *The Exeter Book*. Probably based on the *De Ave Phoenice* of Lactantius, it is notable as an essay by an early English poet in the creation of an imaginary world.

**Phoenix and the Turtle, The**  A poem by William Shakespeare, contributed to the appendix of *Loves Martyr: or, Rosalins Complaint. Allegorically shadowing the truth of Love, in the constant Fate of the Phoenix and Turtle* by Robert Chester (1601). Chester's work is regarded as valueless now but interest in it continues because such poets as Jonson, Chapman, Marston – and Shakespeare – were persuaded to contribute to it. The turtle is of course a turtle dove, which is consumed in the fire with its love, the phoenix. Thus love is reason enough for complete surrender to the destiny of another.

**Phoenix Nest, The**  A miscellany of poems first published in 1593. It contains work by Nicholas Breton (N. B. Gent) and Thomas Lodge (T. L. Gent). The title page proclaims the work of 'rare and refined Noble men, worthy Knights, gallant gentlemen' but apart from the two poets who can be identified only two or three anonymous lyrics are considered to be of rare quality. A modern edition was edited by H. E. Rollins (1931).

**Physician's Tale, The**  See **Canterbury Tales, The**.

**Piazza Tales, The**  A volume of short stories and sketches by Herman Melville, collected and first published in 1856. The 'piazza' was the green open space in front of Melville's farmhouse at Pittsfield, Massachusetts. The stories and sketches originally appeared in *Putnam's Monthly Magazine* and *Harper's New Monthly Magazine*. The most famous of them are the following.

In *Bartleby, the Scrivener*, a Wall Street lawyer hires a copyist, Bartleby, a pale and withdrawn character who keeps to himself, declining to accept any work but the copying he was engaged for – 'I would prefer not to'. His employer finds him strangely touching and does his best to be kind but, with the awful obstinacy of the weak, Bartleby resists kindness as much as any other interference. Soon he is living in the office where he should work. Then his employer moves to another building and the new tenant has Bartleby arrested as a vagrant. Bartleby dies in prison within days, resisting to the end the attempts of his erstwhile employer to help him. The lawyer later hears a report that Bartleby had spent all his previous working life in the Dead Letter Office in Washington; a change of administration had deprived him of his post. The lawyer ponders on the relevance of this to the character of his strange copyist, who would 'prefer not to'.

The story of *Benito Cereno* takes place in 1799. Captain Delano puts in to an uninhabited island off the coast of Chile for water. Another ship is there already, in distress, and Delano goes aboard, taking water and supplies. He finds the commander, Don Benito Cereno, down with fever. In attendance is his Black slave, Babo, whose care and watchfulness can only be called extravagant. Delano finds Cereno's behaviour strangely equivocal. He also finds the crew, all of whom are Black, disorderly. In spite of Babo's solicitude Cereno seems incapable of meeting a commander's duty. He tells Delano that he is bound for Lima, out of Buenos Aires, with a crew of 50 and a cargo of 300 Black slaves owned by one Aranda. They encountered a violent storm round the Horn and many of the crew were lost; disease killed the rest. Delano, puzzled by his encounter, and wondering if some treachery is at work, promises further aid and boards his boat to return to his own ship. Then there is a disturbance and Cereno leaps into the boat, followed by Babo. To Delano's astonishment Babo goes for Cereno with a dagger. Delano and his men save Cereno and the boat pulls away, just as a mass attack from the Black crew seems imminent.

Cereno tells Delano the truth now. Babo had led a slave mutiny and Cereno was their prisoner. He was to take the ship to Africa but had succumbed to fever. The arrival of the US ship had brought the possibility of another seaman to take the ship to Africa. The slaves had planned to seize Delano's ship and Cereno's desperate flight had been the only way to warn him. Delano succeeds in capturing the slave ship and then proceeds to Lima, where Babo is executed. Cereno spends his remaining few years in a monastery.

Melville found the original events in the *Narratives of Voyages and Travels of Amasa Delano* (1817). His story is a fine essay in mystery, with the figure of Cereno transformed from the original to portray a good man's dilemma when he feels inextricably bound in a web of evil.

Ten sketches under the title *The Encantadas, or Enchanted Isles* were first published as a magazine contribution under the pseudonym, Salvator R. Tarnmoor. Seven sketches concern the Galapagos Islands – the Encantadas of the title – and the rest are accounts of people who lived there: a Creole from Cuba who acquires title to Charles's Isle and rules it like a tyrant until the other people throw him out; a hermit, on Hood's Isle, who enslaves deserting sailors until he is overcome by their captains; and the most con-

siderable – the account of Hunilla, a Chola Indian woman marooned on Norfolk Island, who is eventually rescued by an American ship. It is a fine short story, with implications that go far beyond the narrative.

**picaresque** The Spanish word *picaro* or *picarón* became picaroon in English. Originally a *picaro* was a character from low life, living on his wits and often a scoundrel, but the term came to be applied to anyone at odds with society. The *picaro* first appeared in fiction in *Lazarillo de Tormes* (1554), an anonymous novel. *Guzman de Alfarache* (1559) by Mateo Alemán was widely read and translated and the *picaro*, common to all countries, was to appear in the literature of all western Europe eventually. The picaresque novel is the episodic narrative of the progress of the *picaro* but the term is rather loosely applied: *Don Quixote* is told in the picaresque *form* but is a satirical romance; Le Sage's *Gil Blas* (1715–35) and Hans Jacob Christoph von Grimmelshausen's *Der Abentheurliche Simplicissimus Teutsch* (1669) are more correctly picaresque novels. The tradition in English literature begins with Nashe's *The Unfortunate Traveller* (1594) and can be found in Defoe (*Moll Flanders*), Smollett, Fielding, and Dickens.

**Pickering, John**  See **Puckering, Sir John.**

**Pickwick, Samuel**  The hero of Dickens's *The Pickwick Papers*. He is Chairman of the Pickwick Club and Proposer of the Corresponding Society as well as one of its four members. An indication of the impact Dickens made with the creation of this immortal character can be found in the author's obituary in the *Illustrated London News*. It refers to the 'high-flown affectation of classic and aristocratic elegance' current at the time of Pickwick's creation and goes on to describe how 'Mr Pickwick, of Goswell Street, in his gaiters and spectacles, with Sam Weller at his heels toddled forward and took possession of the stage'.

***Pickwick Papers, The*** (*The Posthumous Papers of the Pickwick Club*, Edited by Boz).  The original proposal to Dickens from Chapman & Hall was for a serial relating the adventures of the Nimrod Club, accompanied by sporting prints, in the manner of Surtees. Dickens pointed out that he was no great sportsman, and persuaded the publishers to let him choose his own subject. The project nearly foundered when the illustrator, Robert Seymour, committed suicide, but Dickens pressed the publishers to find another artist – the contract was of great importance to him as a newly married man. Cruikshank, the illustrator of *Sketches by Boz*, was too busy and Thackeray was found wanting. The commission went to a friend of Thackeray, the 20-year-old Hablot Knight Browne, who adopted the pseudonym of Phiz.

The first numbers of *Pickwick* were not a success. In the fourth, however, Sam Weller made his entrance and there was an upsurge in sales thereafter: favourable notices were written and readers began to send in orders for back numbers. Dickens asked for an increase in his payment, which to their credit Chapman & Hall gave him at once. *Pickwick* became such a success that 40,000 copies were sold each month. Publication was from April 1836 to November 1837. The first volume form was published in 1837.

*Pickwick* is a novel in the loosest sense, relating the adventures of the four members of the Corresponding Society of the Pickwick Club – Pickwick, Tupman, Winkle, and Snodgrass. These adventures are interspersed with other tales related by various characters they encounter. It is the favourite of many Dickens lovers, and it is a comic book of the highest order; but it is not a comedy – there is almost no examination of the deeper springs of laughter and, perhaps in compensation, there is almost none of the sentimentality we encounter in his later work.

See **Bardell, Mrs**; **Buzfuz, Serjeant**; **Hunter, Mrs Leo**; **Jingle, Alfred**; **Pickwick, Samuel**; **Snodgrass, Augustus**; **Trotter, Job**; **Tupman, Tracy**; **Wardle, Mr**; **Wardle, Rachael**; **Weller, Sam**; **Weller, Tony**; and **Winkle, Nathaniel**.

*Picture of Dorian Gray, The*  A novel by Oscar Wilde, which began as a serial in *Lippincott's Magazine* in 1890 but was not completed. The complete novel was first published in 1891 and was Wilde's first real success.

Dorian Gray is a beautiful young man; that he is much sought after he accepts without question. He sits for his portrait by Basil Hallward and comes under the influence of the witty, heartless aesthete, Lord Henry Wooton. The finished portrait makes Dorian conscious of the transitory quality of his own youth and good looks whereas the portrait will always be beautiful. He wishes his soul away, praying that the picture will age – and he remain as he is now.

Tutored in the satisfaction of the senses through Lord Henry's influence, Dorian is soon guilty of heartless cruelty to Sybil Vane, a young actress he has fallen in love with. Sybil kills herself and Dorian's reaction is one of disdainful impatience. Then Lord Henry sends him a novel which fascinates him: 'It seemed to him that in exquisite raiment, and to the delicate sound of flutes, the sins of the world were passing in dumb show before him.' Dorian's corruption is complete – and he remains beautiful and untouched by age. The years pass, and one evening Basil Hallward calls on him, asking him to refute the evil things which are being said about him. Dorian takes him to an upper room, and shows him the portrait: it has turned into a portrait of the real Dorian – ageing, gross, and corrupt. In a frenzy of rage he murders Hallward, the originator of the portrait.

Ultimately, after a short life of total selfishness, corruption of others, and an indulgence in esoteric and erotic pleasures, Dorian longs for the person he used to be. He attacks the portrait, thinking to destroy it. But the portrait reverts to one of a young man of remarkable beauty, while the man found dead on the floor with a knife in his body is old and evil-looking.

The novel is prefaced by 22 aphorisms on art and the artist. Some are interesting, some are not, but two comments on Wilde's own times are memorable: 'The nineteenth-century dislike of Realism is the rage of Caliban seeing his own face in a glass' and 'The nineteenth-century dislike of Romanticism is the rage of Caliban not seeing his own face in a glass.'

*Pictures from Italy*  The account by Charles Dickens of his tour of Italy in 1844. He travelled through France to Genoa, and his description of

'The Break-Down.' Pickwick and Mr Wardle, in pursuit of Jingle and Rachael Wardle, are wrecked when the chaise loses a wheel. An illustration by Phiz for *The Pickwick Papers*.

the coaching trips which took him from place to place for five months is full of wonderful observations of his fellow-men. A born reporter, he has left a vivid picture of Italy in the 1840s: carnival in Rome, Venice a dead city that holds little for him, Pompeii, Naples, and Vesuvius. His account of a public execution in Rome is remarkable – his emotional reaction is held firmly in control but revulsion at the whole proceeding is implicit in every line. The sketches first appeared in *The Daily News* as traveller's reports and were published in volume form in 1846.

**Pied Piper of Hamelin, The**  A poem by Robert Browning, first published in *Dramatic Lyrics*, one of the *Bells and Pomegranates* series, in 1842. The event described in the poem was believed for a long time to have actually taken place. But Sabine Baring-Gould, in *Curious Myths of the Middle Ages* (1866–68), reported that similar legends are told of other places. It is generally believed now that the story is connected with the Children's Crusade, when 20,000 children left their homes to follow Nicholas of Cologne and, for the most part, perished without ever reaching the Holy Land. *The Pied Piper of Hamelin* is probably Browning's most famous poem. The town is infested with rats and the people threaten to unseat the mayor and corporation, who have no idea what to do. A stranger seeks entrance to the town hall: '. . .the strangest figure! His queer long coat from heel to head Was half of yellow and half of red'. The Pied Piper offers to get rid of the rats for a thousand guilders. He succeeds; all the rats follow his piping and he leads them to the River Weser, where the hordes plunge into the water and drown. The people rejoice and the mayor and corporation prepare to remove every trace of the rats which have plagued them for years. The Pied Piper comes to claim his agreed reward; but the mayor and corporation, now rid of the rats, rudely refuse to pay. The Piper's revenge is to play another tune, '. . .such sweet Soft notes as yet musician's cunning Never gave the enraptured air', which now bewitches the children of Hamelin. They dance along behind the Pied Piper, who leads them to Koppelberg Hill where 'A wondrous portal opened wide'. The children follow the Piper into the hillside, the portal closes behind them, and they are never seen again. In the closing lines of the poem it is related that the children emerged in Transylvania, where their descendants can still be found. Browning gives a precise date for the disappearance of Hamelin's children: 22 July 1376.

**Pierce Pennilesse, his Supplication to the Divell**  A prose satire by Thomas Nashe, published in

1592. It takes the form of a complaint to the Devil about the vices of the time, including drunkenness – which in Nashe's view had become fashionable through England's association with the Netherlands – and is directed mainly against Nashe's enemies in the Marprelate controversy. In general terms it throws interesting light on the life and customs of Nashe's time; the vigour, coarseness, and cruelty are vividly described.

**Pierre:** *or The Ambiguities.*  A novel by Herman Melville, first published in 1852.

Mrs Glendinning, a wealthy widow, lives in upstate New York with her 19-year-old son Pierre. Pierre is engaged to the blonde beauty Lucy Tartan. She is from a prominent family and has Mrs Glendinning's approval. Into Pierre's life, however, comes Isabel, who was born abroad and whom Pierre is persuaded is his half-sister, sired by his father during a journey to Europe. Pierre knows that his mother will never accept a girl whose existence exposes her husband's behaviour. Indeed Pierre has already seen her join her neighbours when they close ranks against Delly Ulver, a 'fallen' girl. To give Isabel some measure of protection he takes her to New York, allowing everyone to believe that he and the girl have eloped. He also takes Delly and asks his cousin, Glen, with whom he had shared a boyish David and Jonathan devotion, to lend him his house. But on learning the truth, Glen cuts him dead. With almost no money, Pierre writes to earn a living. But the novel which results from his exhaustive efforts is refused by all the publishers who read it.

Lucy Tartan, meanwhile, has come to New York looking for Pierre. Isabel shows jealousy at Lucy's appearance and Pierre's true feelings about his half-sister become clear to him. Lucy's brother and his cousin Glen confront Pierre; Glen attacks him with a whip and Pierre shoots him dead. He is marched off to prison and Lucy discovers from Isabel her true relationship to Pierre. She falls in a heap, dead. Pierre's mother dies of grief. Pierre and Isabel take poison in Pierre's prison cell.

It is easy to see why this improbable sequence of events was so disliked, and whatever Melville's intentions the result of his labours is a mess. He seems to have set out to explore, from a certain standpoint, the ambiguities which exist in all close relationships and to have dredged his unconscious for the real psychological truth. Essays have been written about the book and its meanings vis-à-vis Melville himself: it would be simpler to note that a reading is not a waste of time, given the mind and art of Herman Melville, but that as a whole the book must be considered a failure.

### Piers the Plowman, The Vision of William concerning

An allegorical alliterative poem written in Middle English, probably between 1360 and 1400, by William Langland. Three manuscripts exist: the first, A (1362), is the shortest with 2567 lines; B (1377) expands the first version to 7242 lines; C (*c*.1393) contains 7357 lines in 23 *passus* (books).

The several visions of William the storyteller are seen in a dream. He falls asleep 'Ac on a may morwening on Malverne hulles' and meets 'Al the welthe of this worlde and the woo (woe) bothe' in the guise of a crowd of people in a field in a valley. To the east is a high cliff on which stands a tower; to the west the Dale of Death and a deep dungeon. Every kind of person is to be met in the field – the mendacious and greedy, the false-hearted and mean-spirited and hypocritical, as well as the honest, the hardworking, and the truly charitable.

From the high cliff comes a beautiful woman who explains to the storyteller that the tower is the dwelling of Truth while the dungeon is the house of Wrong. But who is she? She replies that he should know her – she is Holy Church. He beseeches her to tell him how to believe so on Christ as to do His will. She tells him to love his lord and to follow him in loving-kindness, else there is no merit in piety, chastity, or faith. Without works these are meaningless: that is truth, the most precious thing asked by Our Lord. She shows him where stands Lady Meed (who seeks reward) richly arrayed, preparing to marry False. The two were brought together by Favel (duplicity) and Guile prepared her; Liar oversaw it all. Holy Church warns the storyteller to keep himself from them if he would know his Lord, and then she leaves.

The marriage of Meed and False takes place in gorgeous settings. There follows a sharp and bitter satire on the vices and their opposing virtues. Theology objects to the wedding and the whole company goes to London to appeal to the King, while Civil Law and Simony distribute bribes to officers and witnesses. Wit and Wisdom follow on the heels of Reason; Peace is advised to seek the help of Meed. Finally the King listens to Reason, and Love laughs Meed to scorn. The King takes Reason and Conscience as his advisers. Meed is clearly shown as an influence whose corruption pervades everything, even those who profess to serve Holy Church. The lawyers emerge as those most influenced by her. The first vision ends there.

In the second vision the field is back in the dreamer's sight. Conscience urges the people to look into their hearts and perceive their own faults. The people yield to his pleading and there is a remarkable parade of the Seven Deadly Sins. The people acknowledge that the only goal for good men is St Truth – but how can they find their way to him? They try to attain the tower on the high cliff, crossing valleys and hills until, exhausted, they meet a man in the clothes of a pilgrim. He has been to many Holy Places and carries many relics. But he does not know St Truth. It is at this point in the poem that the ploughman Piers makes his appearance. 'Ich knowe hym...' he says, 'Ich have yben his folwer al this fourty wynter.' He has been directed to him by Conscience and Kind-Wit.

The people offer him money to show them the way: he refuses – Truth would love him the less if he sought reward – but tells them how to get there. The way is marked by symbols of Christ's counsel, and at the Tower they will meet Grace, who keeps the gate, and the sisters Abstinence, Humility, Charity, Generosity, Chastity, Patience, and Peace. Unless the people are kin to one of these they can gain no entrance. Many people despair, knowing they are kin to none of them, but Piers reassures them: there is a maiden who has power over them all. She is Mercy and kin to them all – the sinful included – and with the help of her Son they may all gain the grace that will assure them entry.

The people implore Piers to guide them there, but he tells them that his little piece of land is unploughed and he must first see to his labours. Help to get the work done is offered at once but there are few honest men among those who come forward. Idlers and wasters are among them, and greedy men who grab too much of the food. Many sit around pleading that they are lame and blind and ill. Piers turns for advice to Hunger, who seizes Waster by the maw and nearly throttles him. Then he thrashes the other villains and tells Piers that those who shirk from honest work should get nothing, but the needy and unfortunate should be helped. Truth hears of these events and sends to Piers the assurance that he and all honest men – even kings who rule well – shall have Pardon. Men of law have the least chance of it since few of them will plead any man's cause, however just, without the promise of money. A priest then questions the value of the Pardon. While he and Piers are disputing the sleeper wakes and finds it is noon on the Malvern hills. The second vision is finished (*passus* 8).

It will be clear from this account of roughly the first third of the poem that the honest ploughman is Everyman seeking the way to salvation. The poem continues with the pilgrimage to Truth. The dreamer, William, sees the Crucifixion, Christ's triumph over death, and the establishment of Holy Church. Christ's challenge to human evil is made in human form and he takes on the humanity of Piers, who has in his pilgrimage borne witness to the Christian virtues and is prepared for the supreme encounter. He participates in the victory – and the sleeper wakes. He finds to his grief that his world is unchanged. The struggle never ceases.

That the author was a man of remarkable wit and humanity as well as a fine poet is plain in every line of this remarkable work. The 14th century in England produced Langland, Chaucer, and John Wycliffe but for the plain man the times were harsh. The revolt of the peasants against the oppression, injustice, and ecclesiastical corruption of the Middle Ages took place before Langland's third manuscript (C) was begun: it would be fair to assume that he had

---

'And as I lay and lened and loked in the wateres, I slombred in a slepying.' An illustration from a manuscript of the second version (B) of *Piers Plowman. MS 201 f.1*. Corpus Christi College, Oxford.

observed its beginnings when he began to write the first, around 1360. His astute observation of these times and of his fellow men is expressed in allegory and written in alliterative verse but his range of effects is remarkable, fully equal to his attempt to show that the search for truth is the way to salvation. Langland's frame of reference is Christianity and his poem was widely read. Piers became a symbol of protest in his own age and he is not without relevance in ours. But more important, perhaps, is the poem itself: despite untidiness and the evidence of too much editing it is a great one, vivid and moving. Only Chaucer wrote greater work in the language of Middle English.

The most famous edition of *Piers Plowman* is that of Walter William Skeat (1866), to whom must also be ascribed the assumptions concerning the author's life. These were challenged by the American scholar, J. M. Manly, in the *Cambridge History of English Literature* (Vol 2, 1908). Manly decided that five different authors were involved in the poem's composition, pointing out differences in diction and method, as well as matter, to support his theory. His statement led to considerable argument and the Early English Text Society published *The Piers Plowman Controversy* (1910). Manly's theory found little favour, however, and the case for the single authorship of William Langland (*or* Langley) is generally accepted now. For readers who feel unequal to the Middle English of the original there are versions in modern English, notably by D. and R. Attwater (Everyman's Library) and by J. F. Goodridge (Penguin Classics). The best selection in modern verse is that by Nevill Coghill (1949).

*Pike County Ballads and Other Pieces.* A book of poems by John Hay, written in the dialect of frontier Illinois, the Pike County of the 1850s where Hay spent his childhood and youth.

*Pilgrim's Progress, The, from this World to that which is to come.* John Bunyan's Christian allegory was begun while he was a prisoner in Bedford Gaol in 1675, and Part I was published in 1678. This was subsequently revised and the complete text appeared in the third edition (1679). Part II was published in 1684.

In Part I the story opens with the author's dream, in which he sees Christian with his burden reading a book, which relates a prophecy that his city will be destroyed. Evangelist tells him to leave the City of Destruction and journey to the Wicket-gate; beyond the gate is the way to the Celestial City. Christian cannot persuade his family to accompany him and he sets off alone, his burden of sin heavy on his back. He wanders into the Slough of Despond, where he nearly succumbs because of the weight of his burden. He is rescued by Help and meets Mr Worldly Wiseman, who urges him to give up his perilous quest: Legality can remove his burden from him and he can settle down in Morality, a comfortable village nearby. Christian is tempted but Evangelist reappears and rescues him. He proceeds to the Wicket-gate, which is opened for him by Mr Good-will. The straight and narrow path to the Celestial City is revealed and Christian's pilgrimage continues. He comes to the Cross where his burden of sin falls from his back and he meets the personifications of various faults, who either have no desire to go to the city or else try to find an easy way to it instead of passing through the Wicket-gate. The way is going to be hard and Christian knows that he has many trials to face before he crosses the River of Death and reaches salvation on the other side, but he has at different times the help and encouragement of various characters who personify the virtues. Prudence, Piety, and Charity guide him from the House Beautiful to the Delectable Mountains – but to reach them he must pass through the Valley of Humiliation where he fights with Apollyon, one of Satan's fallen companions. He makes his way successfully through the Valley of the Shadow of Death, which swarms with creatures of the Pit, and meets another pilgrim, Faithful. They go on to Vanity Fair, which Evangelist has warned them about, and here Faithful is put to death. Christian escapes and is joined by a new companion, Hopeful, who witnessed the fate of Faithful and is inspired to seek the Celestial City also. They fall into the hands of Giant Despair but Christian uses the key called Promise to release them from Doubting Castle, and so on.

Bunyan's characters and places have passed into the possession of many more than his English readers – his book has been translated into over a hundred languages. Many who have not read *The Pilgrim's Progress* are familiar with the 'Slough of Despond' and 'Vanity Fair'. Bunyan was writing at a time when the rich, with elegance and wit, enjoyed much that was trifling. The masses had only the Bible and a number of improving books – it was an age when people were perhaps too concerned with the good of their souls – but little to enjoy. Bunyan's down-to-earth, direct style combined with his extensive reading of the Bible to create an allegory of man's search for salvation, and he produced a masterpiece, which gave both pleasure and reward.

Part II of *The Pilgrim's Progress* tells how Chris-

Christian climbing the Hill Difficulty. An illustration from the 1695 edition of *The Pilgrim's Progress*.

tian's wife, Christiana, follows her husband to the city after being inspired by a vision. She is accompanied by her children and a neighbour, Mercy, and escorted by Great-heart who is their protector on their perilous journey. Their pilgrimage is far less interesting since the reader knows what they will encounter, and they have Great-heart to help them through their trials. However the author's strength as a writer makes many passages in this gentler chronicle memorable and the small change of the domestic scene is presented with humour and warmth.

**Pinero, Sir Arthur Wing** 1855–1934. Pinero was born in Islington, London, and was intended for the law. He enjoyed amateur acting and eventually abandoned the law, becoming a professional in 1874 at the Theatre Royal, Edinburgh. He was an actor for ten years and began to write for the stage during that period, making his mark as a playwright with a comedy, *Two*

*Hundred a Year* (Globe Theatre, 1877). His work became fashionable with *The Money Spinner* (St James's, 1881). Popular success began with his farce *The Magistrate* (Court, 1885) and continued at the same theatre with *The Schoolmistress* (1886), *Dandy Dick* (1887), and *The Cabinet Minister* (1890). Pinero's farces are brilliantly contrived and have held the stage. *Sweet Lavender* (Terry's, 1888) demonstrated that his gifts extended to true comedy and he next entered the field of serious drama with *The Profligate* (Garrick, 1889).

It was as a serious playwright that Pinero scored his greatest success: *The Second Mrs Tanqueray* (St James's, 1893) made a star of Mrs Patrick Campbell and gave fashionable London a play to talk about. The elegant settings, recognizable milieu, and well-constructed plot – the heroine's dubious past, the inevitable tragedy, and the reconsideration of her true nature – all of this was finely done and Pinero's success helped to broaden the scope of the drama in England in the later decades of the 19th century. His stagecraft ensures that his work is often revived.

Pinero wrote more than 40 plays and was knighted in 1909. Apart from his farces and the plays already mentioned his greatest successes were *The Notorious Mrs Ebbsmith* (Garrick, 1895); *Trelawney of the Wells* (Court, 1898), a comedy about the stock theatre where Pinero learned his trade; *The Gay Lord Quex* (Globe, 1899), considered by many to be his best comedy; *Iris* (Garrick, 1901); *His House in Order* (St James's, 1906); and *The Thunderbolt* (St James's, 1908).

**Pinter, Harold** 1930– . Pinter was born in London and educated at Hackney Downs Grammar School. Like his contemporary, John Osborne, he was an actor (as David Baron) before becoming a playwright. His first play to be performed was the one-act *The Room*, at Bristol University Drama Department in 1957. His first major success was the full-length *The Caretaker*, in 1959. Other plays by Harold Pinter (the dates given are of publication) are *The Birthday Party* (1958), *A Slight Ache* (1959), *The Dwarfs*, *The Dumb Waiter*, *The Night Out*, and *Night School* (1960), *The Collection* (1961), *The Lover* (1963), *Tea Party*, *The Homecoming*, and *Eight Revue Sketches* (1965), *The Basement* (1967), *Mac – A Memoir* and *Landscape* (1968), *Sketches by Pinter* and *Night* (1969), *Old Times* (1971), *Monologue* (1973), *No Man's Land* (1975), *Betrayal* (1978), and *The Hothouse* (1980). Pinter published *Poems and Prose 1949–1977* in 1978 and his adaptation for film of Proust's *A La Recherche du Temps Perdu* as *The Proust Screenplay* in 1977.

*Pioneers, The; or, The Sources of the Susquehanna.* A novel by James Fenimore Cooper, first published in 1823. It was the first of the *Leather-Stocking Tales* to be written but it is the fourth in order of events. The period is the decade which followed the War for Independence.

Judge Temple is a Quaker, a retired merchant, and one of the principal landowners in Otsego County in the frontier region of New York state. The land he owns was once the estate of Major Effingham, a loyalist who was lost in the recent war. The major's son Edward was Temple's friend, and before leaving to fight in the War of Independence he confided the care of his money and possessions to Temple. Temple went to fight also – but on the opposite side. Edward Effingham did not return to his father's land after the war, and when loyalist estates were confiscated and put up for sale Temple bought the former Effingham lands.

While hunting deer, Temple accidentally wounds Oliver Edwards, the companion of the frontiersman Natty Bumppo, who is called Leather-Stocking because he wears deerskin leggings. The judge and his daughter, Elizabeth, befriend Edwards and he becomes their overseer; but he maintains his friendship with Bumppo and with old John Mohegan, whom everyone knows is the Mohican chief, Chingachgook. It is suspected that Edwards is the chief's son and soon Elizabeth and her friends are disdaining his company.

Bumppo is arrested for shooting deer out of season and spends a short term in prison. Elizabeth goes to visit him in his cabin upon his release but is caught in a forest fire on her return. Edwards saves her; Bumppo saves his friend Chingachgook but the old chieftain dies. Elizabeth realizes that she loves Edwards.

A party searching for Elizabeth comes upon a demented old man and it transpires that he is Major Effingham, still alive. Natty Bumppo had worked for the major and taken care of him when he was dispossessed. Edward Effingham had returned to England after the defeat, and when he died his son, Oliver, had gone to Otsego to find his grandfather, who would be destitute without Edward's support. As Oliver Edwards he had found his grandfather, and like him was given protection by Chingachgook by adoption into the tribe. Temple is able to prove to Oliver that he had always kept faith with Edward Effingham and he settles half his estate on Oliver. Elizabeth and Oliver are betrothed at the end.

*Pioneers of France in the New World*  See **Parkman, Francis** and *France and England in North America*.

**Pip** (*or* **Philip Pirrip**) The narrator of Dickens's *Great Expectations* and the central character. As a small child he cannot pronounce his surname and becomes, simply, Pip.

**Pippa Passes** A dramatic poem by Robert Browning, the first of the series called *Bells and Pomegranates*. It was first published in 1841. Pippa, a girl of Asolo, a small town in Italy, is a silk winder enjoying her yearly holiday. She wanders through the town, singing her songs and thinking about the four people she innocently believes to be the most blessed – Ottima, Phene, Luigi, and the Bishop. But Ottima and her lover, Sebald have murdered Ottima's husband. Phene's husband, Jules, a sculptor, is disillusioned with his bride; she is an ignorant girl, no fit wife for an artist, and he is going to put her aside. Luigi is a patriot and plans to kill the Austrian emperor, not knowing that the police are already planning to arrest him. The Bishop is actually intending Pippa's death; she is the child of his murdered brother, whose wealth the Bishop has taken for himself. Pippa passes, singing her songs, and the four characters are affected in different ways by what they hear. She makes her way home at sunset, unaware that her last song has awakened the Bishop's conscience and changed her life. The most famous of Pippa's songs are 'The year's at the spring', overheard by the guilty lovers, and 'A King lived long ago', which spurs Luigi to action and saves him from arrest.

**Pirate, The** In this novel Sir Walter Scott returns to Scotland for the setting of his story. It was first published in 1822.

In a remote part of Zetland (the Shetlands) lives the misanthropic Basil Mertoun, and his amiable and attractive son Mordaunt. Their landlord is the wealthy Magnus Troil: he has two daughters, Minna and Brenda, who are on happy terms with Mordaunt, who spends much time with them and is their father's frequent guest. But when a buccaneer, Cleveland, is wrecked on the coast and Mordaunt rescues him, Minna falls in love with him. Mordaunt and Cleveland develop a hatred for each other and Mordaunt finds himself less than welcome at his landlord's house. Brenda, however, remains true to their friendship and he grows to love her. Eventually the pirates and Cleveland attempt to capture Magnus and his daughters but Mordaunt raises the alarm and they are rescued by a frigate. Minna and Cleveland (who proves to be half-brother to Mordaunt) are thus parted for ever. Mordaunt and Brenda find a happy ending.

**Pisanio** Posthumus' servant in Shakespeare's *Cymbeline*, left behind when his master is banished. Posthumus tells him to kill Imogen, believing her faithless, but he will not do it and persuades her to adopt a boy's disguise, and it is as 'Fidele' that she encounters her brothers in the forest.

**Pistol** Falstaff's ancient (ensign) in Shakespeare's *Henry IV* Part 2. He marries Mistress Quickly in that play and appears to have the same intention in *The Merry Wives of Windsor*. In *Henry V* he tries conclusions with Fluellen, the doughty Welsh captain, who thrashes him and forces him to eat a raw leek. Pistol, apart from being a coward, is a despicable character, as his last speech reveals ('Doth Fortune play the huswife with me now?').

**Pit, The:** *A Story of Chicago.* A novel by Frank Norris, first published in 1903, the year after the author died. It is the second part of his uncompleted trilogy, *The Epic of the Wheat*. The pit of the title is the Chicago stock exchange, where Curtis Jadwin has become a leading speculator and hopes to gain a corner in the wheat market. Jadwin has won the hand of Laura Dearborn despite strong competition from rival suitors, among them the artist dilettante Sheldon Corthell; but his obsession with money and the operations of the pit leads him to neglect her, so she drifts into an affair with Corthell. Jadwin gains a monopoly of wheat stocks but his coup goes for nothing when growth and harvest in the West greatly increase the supply: he has been brought down by natural forces. In the end Laura returns to him; his health has broken down and his wealth is gone but they are hopeful of the future.

**Plain Dealer, The** A comedy by William Wycherley, first produced in December 1676, and published in 1677. The source of the play is Molière's *Le Misanthrope*. The most mordant of Wycherley's four plays, it is regarded by many as his finest. His friend John Dryden described it as 'one of the most bold, most general, and most useful satires which has ever been presented on the English theatre'.

The plain dealer of the title is the misanthropic Manly, a sea-captain who believes that only his friend Vernish and his betrothed Olivia are sincere. He returns from the Dutch wars to find that Olivia has married another and has no intention of returning the money he left in her care. Manly uses his page as a go-between in his vengeance on Olivia. Part of his plan is to dishonour her, but he does not know that his page is a girl, Fidelia, who has always loved him and has followed him to the war in disguise. Olivia is charmed by the page and makes an assignation with him. Manly accompanies Fidelia thinking his plan successful and intending to expose Olivia. But Olivia's husband, none other than the supposed friend Vernish, arrives on the scene. In the scuffle that follows Fidelia is wounded and her disguise discovered. Manly is touched by her devotion and sees the worthlessness of his obsession with Olivia. Fidelia wins her man.

The play held the stage until the end of the 19th century, and was revived by the Renaissance Society of London in 1925, but it is rarely seen in the modern theatre. It has a cast of excellently drawn characters and many fine scenes but Manly is a difficult central character: in spite of all his 'plain dealing' he seems rather foolish and is won in the end by the romantic revelation of Fidelia's devotion. One of the characters observes 'we fail not to quarrel with (the world) when anything crosses us, yet cannot part with't for our hearts', a truth the rigid plain dealer could never understand. The widow Blackacre, tirelessly litigious, and her Lumpkin-like son, Jerry, provide a great deal of fun.

*Plain Tales from the Hills* A collection of stories by Rudyard Kipling, first published in 1888. The book contains 40 stories, 32 of which had first appeared in *The Civil and Military Gazette*, the paper that the author worked upon in Lahore. They are sketches of life in the Punjab in that period and deal with the English civilians and soldiers and their womenfolk, and the Indian people with whom they come in contact. Among them are 'Thrown Away', which tells of a young man who comes to India from Sandhurst and is defeated by both India and active service life: he commits suicide after being rebuked by his colonel. 'The Bronckhorst Divorce-Case' tells of an attempt by a despicable man to divorce his wife; the attempt fails and the wretched marriage resumes. 'By Word of Mouth' is the story of an appointment with nemesis, brought to a bereaved doctor by his servant, Ram Dass. 'The Gate of a Hundred Sorrows' describes an opium den and its pathetic patrons. 'A Bank Fraud' tells of a good man's unfailing kindness to a subordinate when the other is mortally ill: the subordinate is disagreeable and inefficient but his superior's goodness never weakens. 'The Bisara of Poree' tells of a sinister talisman, only beneficial if the possessor has acquired it by theft, and 'Beyond the Pale' of the fate of the young Indian widow, Bisesa, who becomes involved in an affair with an Englishman. Kipling's 'soldiers

three' make their appearance in some of the stories in this collection.

**Plath, Sylvia** 1932–63. Sylvia Plath was born in Boston, Massachusetts. She was educated at Smith College and in 1956 went to Newnham College, Cambridge, on a Fulbright Fellowship. In the same year she met and married the English poet Ted Hughes. After taking her MA at Cambridge in 1957 Sylvia Plath and her husband went to the USA. She taught at Smith College and her husband at the University of Massachusetts. They gave up teaching in 1959 and, after a tour of the USA and Canada, returned to England where their children (a son and a daughter) were born. They separated in 1962 and Sylvia Plath lived with her children near Chalk Farm in northwest London until February 1963, when she committed suicide. Her single novel, *The Bell Jar* (1963), was published under the pseudonym of Victoria Lucas barely three weeks before her death; it is a fictionalized account of a nervous breakdown she suffered in college. Sylvia Plath wrote poetry from the time she was a child – over 200 juvenile poems are listed and 50 are published in *Collected Poems* – and her first volume, *A Winter Ship* (1960), was published anonymously. *The Colossus* (1960) was the first to bear her name. The posthumous volumes are *Ariel* (1965), *Crossing the Water* (1971), and *Winter Trees* (1972). *The Bell Jar* was republished under her own name in 1966. *Collected Poems* (1981) was edited by Ted Hughes. A play for radio, *Three Women* (1968), was first broadcast in 1962. *The Art of Sylvia Plath: A Symposium* (1970) was edited by Charles Newman and contains a bibliography.

*Playboy of the Western World, The* A comedy by J. M. Synge, first produced at the Abbey Theatre, Dublin, in 1907, and first published in the same year.

The story takes place in a country tavern – a shebeen – on the coast of Mayo, owned by Michael James Flaherty. His daughter Margaret, called Pegeen Mike (Flaherty is always called Michael James) will be alone while her father attends Kate Cassidy's wake. She and Shawn Keogh will marry if they can obtain the necessary dispensation required because they are cousins. Meanwhile Shawn is very circumspect and afraid of the priest's disapproval, which, to Pegeen's intense irritation, makes him nervous about staying alone with her that night while her father is away. Michael James and his friends join them in the bar and tell of a stranger who has been heard moaning in the dark. Shawn earns the contempt of all for his reluctance to stay with Pegeen. After he leaves a stranger, pale and weak and dirty, arrives.

He is Christy Mahon. He seems wrapped up in his misery and afraid of the police, and they are astonished when he confesses to having killed his father and to have been running for 11 days. Even Pegeen is convinced, and everyone is fascinated by the presence of a murderer: how did he commit his terrible crime and how was he provoked to it? His father ordered him to marry the Widow Casey, more than twice his age. Her circumstances were comfortable compared to Mahon's, who would gain by the marriage. Christy had brained his father in the potato field and buried him there. To the men Christy becomes a romantic refugee; to the girls and Pegeen and the Widow Quin he is rather more. Michael James gives Christy a job in the shebeen and everyone assures him he is safe. Shawn is obliged to take a back seat, while Christy proves adept at the village games, and the Widow Quin – handsome, self-sufficient, and still young – enters the lists for his hand; but Christy has been marked down by Pegeen. He is riding high when his father turns up, with a bandaged head. Christy hides behind the door while Mahon tells his tale to the Widow Quin. Christy, his son, is idle, useless, and even afraid of girls.

Mahon returns to the shebeen as the neighbours return from the wake. The Widow Quin persuades him to go again and not to believe that the young man he saw win the mile race is his son. Michael James is persuaded that Christy would be a more worthy son-in-law than

Sara Allgood as Pegeen Mike and Arthur Shields as Christy Mahon in J. M. Synge's *The Playboy of the Western World* at the Abbey Theatre, 1907.

Shawn, and gives his blessing to Pegeen and Christy when Mahon rushes in, not to be fooled this time. He knocks Christy down and starts to beat him with a stick. The worm turns – Christy, emboldened by the status he briefly enjoyed, turns on his father and chases him out of the door, and to everyone's horror strikes him down again. The resolution of the comedy turns on the transformation of Christy, and the apparent indestructibility of Mahon, who returns yet again. Christy goes home with his father, having at last earned his respect. Shawn turns to Pegeen; he has received the dispensation and the storm is over. But Pegeen rejects him with a box on the ear: he is a poor substitute for the playboy of the western world.

***Plimmoth* (or *Plymouth*) *Plantation, History of***
William Bradford began his history about ten years after the landing of the Pilgrim Fathers from the *Mayflower* in 1620. It occupied him for 20 years, most of that period being spent in the position of governor of the Plymouth colony. When Bradford died, the manuscript – possibly not intended for publication – went to his nephew, Nathaniel Morton. It provided him (and Thomas Prince and Thomas Hutchinson) with material for historical works, and then disappeared during the War for Independence. It was discovered in the Bishop of London's library in 1855. The bishop returned it to the Commonwealth of Massachusetts and the entire work was published in 1856.

In spite of its tone – the Leyden community has, in Bradford's retrospective account, a disturbing air of having been God's own – the *History* is an invaluable source of information. The first part begins with the separatist movement in England, the flight to the Netherlands, and describes the momentous voyage. The second part is, in effect, the annals of the Plymouth colony from 1620 to 1646 and describes every aspect of pioneer life – the hardships, relations with the Indians, and the social and religious problems that arose year by year as the colony strove for permanence. The prose is vigorous and grave, and Bradford's wry observations of his fellow men provide a welcome touch.

**Plomer, William Charles Franklyn** 1903–73. Born in the northern Transvaal, William Plomer was sent to England to be educated at Rugby School. He returned to South Africa, where he became first a farmer and then a trader and wrote a novel, *Turbott Wolfe* (1925). A book written out of anger and contempt for racial discrimination, *Turbott Wolfe* gave a sharp corrective to most people's view of the British dominion in South

Africa, where inevitably neither book nor author was very popular. In the following year Plomer and Roy Campbell founded the literary journal *Voorslag* (Whiplash), which lasted for a single year but gave both writers a further platform from which to proclaim their criticisms of the administration. Plomer left South Africa. After two years in Japan he settled in England in 1929. Other works by William Plomer concerning South Africa are the collection of three short novels and seven stories called *I Speak of Africa* (1927) and a discerning biography, *Cecil Rhodes* (1933).

William Plomer's work, outside the context of South African experience, consists of poems, novels, and short stories of high quality and deserves to be better known. He is unsentimental, witty, wryly observant, and elegant in expression; but there is always warmth and tolerance present. The voice is that of a man who has seen much but is not didactic: the statement, made with humour and intelligence, is enough. He respects his readers.

*Paper Houses* (1929), *The Child of Queen Victoria* (1933), *Curious Relations* (1945), and *Four Countries* (1949) are collections of short stories. *Sado* (1931), *The Case is Altered* (1932), *The Invaders* (1934), and *Museum Pieces* (1952) are novels. He has also published *Collected Poems* (1960), *Double Lives* (1943) – an autobiography, and *At Home: Memoirs* (1958). Plomer wrote the libretti of four of Benjamin Britten's operas: *Gloriana* (1953), *Curfew River* (1964), *The Burning Fiery Furnace* (1966), and *The Prodigal Son* (1968).

**Plough and the Stars, The** A tragedy in four acts by Sean O'Casey, first produced at the Abbey Theatre, Dublin, on 8 February 1926, and first published in the same year. The action of the play covers one day in November 1915 and Easter Week 1916. The setting is the Dublin slums and the title refers to the banner of the Irish Citizen Army.

In a tenement in Dublin Jack and Nora Clitheroe occupy two rooms. Nora is possessively in love with her husband, a bricklayer with ambitions to be an officer in the Citizen Army. In the same tenement are Peter Flynn, Nora's uncle and a supporter of the independence movement; Covey, Jack's cousin, who is much more interested in a social revolution than any other kind; Fluther Good, a carpenter; Mrs Gogan, a charwoman with a daughter, Mollser, dying of consumption; and Bessie Burgess, a street fruit-vendor who lives on the attic floor. Bessie has a son in the British army. She has little time for Nora Clitheroe and her airs; she has known poverty all her life and she drinks when she can. She is the strongest character in the play. The first act tells how Jack is estranged from Nora when he discovers that she burned a letter bearing his appointment as Commandant in the Citizen Army. He leaves with Captain Brennan and Nora is left with Mollser, who is frightened of being alone, certain that when she is she will die.

The second act takes place in a pub an hour later. Peter, Fluther, Covey, Mrs Gogan, and Bessie Burgess react in their different ways to the inflammatory speeches of Irish patriots addressing a crowd outside. Bessie and Mrs Gogan quarrel and the barman ejects them before they start to have a real fight. Clitheroe, Brennan, and Lieutenant Langon are blazing with enthusiasm and in a fever for action.

In the third act the time is Easter Week 1916 and the scene is the street outside the tenement. Mollser sits in a chair in the spring sun, listless under her mother's fussing. Gunfire has been heard through the night; Nora, who is pregnant, is frantically searching the barricades for Jack; Peter, Covey, and Fluther have been looking for her. Peter and Covey return and report on the fighting in the centre of the city. Bessie leans out of her attic window to comment scathingly on their reaction to events, and then Fluther is seen helping Nora along the street. Nora is completely single-minded in her purpose: she wants her husband, and has endured scorn and contempt from others in her night-long search. Mrs Gogan helps her inside. Bessie, on the way out, stops to give Mollser a mug of milk to drink. The booming of artillery adds a note of doom; Peter and Covey nervously play pitch-and-toss. Bessie rushes back, her arms full of goods – the shops are being looted. She stops long enough to help the sinking Mollser into the house and then everyone, except the timorous Peter, rushes off to loot whatever they can. When they return, laden with goods, rifle fire provokes a hasty retreat into the house. Brennan arrives, supporting Langon, who is mortally wounded. Jack, who has been covering their retreat, hurries after them, but Nora sees him and rushes to him. She clings to him hysterically, determined to keep him with her. From the attic floor window Bessie resumes her comments on the retreating 'heroes'. Jack is forced to throw Nora from him to help Brennan with the dying Langon and they leave. Bessie observes the scene in the street, and after a moment she comes down and carries the prostrate Nora into the house.

The last act takes place in Bessie's attic rooms. Nora has been delivered of a stillborn child, which lies in the same coffin as the body of poor Mollser. Bessie is looking after her while Fluther, Covey, and Peter play cards by candlelight. There is sniping going on and the British Army has warned everyone to stay away from the windows. Brennan arrives with the news that Jack is dead. Nora emerges from the bedroom in a demented condition, not knowing where she is. An English corporal arrives with Mrs Gogan to oversee the taking away of the coffin, and Brennan hastily becomes one of the card players. Later the men are rounded up for summary confinement while the snipers are located. The last part of the tragedy is played when Nora starts to lay the table for tea, imagining Jack will be coming home from work, while Bessie falls into an exhausted sleep in a chair. Firing from the street sends Nora to the window; she flings it open and screams for Jack. Bessie struggles to get her away from the window and it is Bessie who is killed, by two rifle shots.

The events of Easter 1916 were not popular with the greater part of the people of Dublin. Indeed most people were frankly scornful and angry at the havoc caused by a few extremists. The poor of Dublin, many of whom had menfolk in the British army, saw no relief from their own condition in those events, and the looting is part of recorded history. However, the executions which followed the rising and the brutal suppression by the Black and Tans alienated the Irish completely and the Irish Free State came into being in December 1921. By 1926, when the play was produced, the Irish were exceedingly angry with O'Casey's truthful account of ordinary people at the centre of great events.

**Ploughman's Tale, The** This poem was first published as the work of Chaucer in the 16th-century *Workes of Chaucer*, edited by W. Thynne. This attribution was later rejected and for a time the poem was believed to be the work of the poet of *Peres the Ploughman's Crede*, but examination indicated that it was written by a different hand. Moreover the parts that resembled the other poem were proved by Henry Bradley to have been added during the 16th century. But it has been acknowledged by both Bradley and W. W. Skeat that the poem does contain authentic 14th-century lines. The poem is in rhymed stanzas; the originals are the work of a Lollard poet while the additions adapt the matter of the poem to the religious controversy of the later age. The poem was edited and published by Thomas Wright in *Political Poems and Songs* (Vol 1, 1859). W. W. Skeat's edition appears in his *Complete Works of Chaucer* (Vol 7, 1897).

**Plumed Serpent, The** A novel by D. H. Lawrence, first published in 1926.

Kate Leslie is a disillusioned woman and a compulsive traveller since the death of her second husband, who had played a part in the Irish rebellion. She feels the need for a new spirit in the world; gods unknown are needed to put the magic back into life. The story opens at a bull-fight in Mexico. She finds it disgusting, representative of the degeneration and near chaos of modern Mexico. Then she meets Don Ramon Carrasco, who is a scholar as well as a political leader and who is determined to change things in his country. He intends to dispose of Christianity and revive the gods of Mexico. Quetzalcoatl, the plumed serpent, will preside and Don Ramon will represent him.

Closest to Don Ramon is his general, Cipriano, who is bound by unswerving devotion. Pure Indian, he makes a powerful impression on Kate Leslie, who sees in him the manifestation of primeval sex. He is also completely strange in her experience and this reinforces the attraction she feels. Cipriano responds to Kate, and it is because of him that she embraces Don Ramon's cause, though she soon becomes aware that the relationship of the two men to each other is more important than Cipriano's response to her. However, she becomes the 'woman of the man', Cipriano, who is elevated to godlike status by Don Ramon – Quetzalcoatl choosing his war god, Huitzilopochtli. Don Ramon rises to lead the people and the cult spreads over Mexico. Kate witnesses blood sacrifices performed by Cipriano and is taken to a disused Christian church, now a temple. He names her Malintzi, bride of Huitzilopochtli, and possesses her among the idols. She accepts both blood sacrifices and pagan nuptials, and eventually submits to everything ordered by Cipriano, including absolute passivity in their physical relationship.

Lawrence seems to be trying to assert that long-buried wisdom exists, and that its recovery will put the world to rights. This was his penultimate novel and his letters suggest that after the book was published he repudiated the ideas he expressed in it.

**Pocahontas** The daughter of the Powhatan chief, Wahunsonacock, who saved the life of Captain John Smith in 1607. See **Smith, Captain John** and *My Lady Pokahontas*, the novel by J. E. Cooke.

**Podsnap, John** In Dickens's *Our Mutual Friend*, the smug and self-important representative of 'society'.

**Poe, Edgar Allan** *c.*1809–49. The son of a family of actors, Poe was born in Boston. His father died in the year following Poe's birth and his mother cared for her three children (there was another son and a daughter) on her own, taking them from town to town until she died in 1811 at Richmond, Virginia.

Edgar was taken into the home of a childless Richmond merchant, a Scotsman named John Allan. Though he was never formally adopted, Edgar Poe inserted his guardian's name into his own in 1824 and used it for the rest of his life. He was educated at a private school in England (the Allans were there from 1815 to 1820) and went on to the University of Virginia. By this time Allan had become rich (through an inheritance) and was unfaithful to his wife. He was out of sympathy with his foster-son and refused to give him an allowance while at college. He also insisted that Edgar study law and quarrelled with him when he incurred gambling debts. After one of these quarrels Poe absconded. He went to Boston, where he paid for the publication of *Tamerlane and other Poems*. His work found no public, however, so he enlisted in the US Army in 1827. Meanwhile, Mrs Allan was dying in Richmond and she pleaded with her husband on Poe's behalf. John Allan went so far as to secure a place at West Point for Poe and gave him a small allowance to live on while waiting. He stayed with his father's sister, Mrs Maria Clemm, in Baltimore and published *Al Aaraaf* in 1829. Poe went to West Point in 1830 but was thrown out in the following year for gross neglect of duty. John Allan remarried and there was no hope of a permanent reconciliation with his foster-son; Allan's will, when he died, had nothing in it for Poe.

Poe went to New York and published *Poems by Edgar A. Poe* in 1831. He then went back to Baltimore and Mrs Clemm, living there until 1835. His third book of poems showed an advance in confidence. The first two were fashionably romantic while the third contained an introduction to verse which was romantic in Poe's own way. In Baltimore he began to sell his short stories and one of these, *MS Found in a Bottle*, was noticed by J. P. Kennedy, who found Poe an editorial job on the *Southern Literary Messenger*. But the proprietors were obliged to sack him because he drank too much. In 1835 he married his cousin Virginia, who was 13 years old.

Poe was taken back on to the staff of the *Messenger*. Whatever his faults his stories and poems were arresting and original; he was also an excellent, if abrasive, literary critic. He moved to Richmond with his child-wife and his aunt, remaining on the *Messenger* until 1837, when the proprietors' patience ran out again. But Poe had certainly increased the magazine's circulation; he had also published six more poems, three more short stories, and an unfinished tragedy, *Politian*. He moved his family to New York (1837–38), where he survived on hack work but managed to publish *The Narrative of Arthur Gordon Pym*, and then moved again, to Philadelphia, where he became coeditor of *Burton's Gentleman's Magazine* (1839–40), which published a number of his stories including *The Fall of the House of Usher*. In 1840 he published *Tales of the Grotesque and Arabesque*, his first collection, including *Berenice* and *Ligeia*. He planned to publish his own magazine. Meanwhile he moved from *Burton's* to become literary editor of *Graham's Magazine* (1841–42). He became acquainted with the poet T. H. Chivers, whose work resembled Poe's enough to lead to him being accused of plagiarism after Poe's death. Among Poe's contributions to *Graham's Magazine* were **The Murders in the Rue Morgue**, *A Descent into the Maelstrom*, *The Masque of the Red Death*, *The Imp of the Perverse*, and a critical essay, *The Philosophy of Composition*. A New York magazine published *The Mystery of Marie Roget* in 1843 and he won a hundred-dollar prize for **The Gold Bug**, published in a Philadelphia magazine.

Poe was in New York again in 1844. He wrote 'The Raven' in that year and worked on the *New York Mirror* as literary critic – a job that lasted for one year and saw the beginning of his attacks on Longfellow. These critical attacks continued in 1845 when Poe became proprietor of the *Broadway Journal* for a year. This short period was notable for the appearance of several stories, including *The Pit and the Pendulum*, **The Tell-Tale Heart**, *Eleanora*, and **The Premature Burial**. The collection *Tales* (1845) included *The Black Cat* and *The Purloined Letter*; 1845 also saw the publication of *The Raven and Other Poems*.

Poe's income was, inevitably, erratic – like his ability to keep a job. He worked on *Godey's Lady's Book*, where his critical essays on *The Literati of New York City* provoked one of his targets, T. D. English, to attack him in print. Poe won a libel action but, in spite of this, he found it difficult to maintain his home and the family nearly starved in the house at Fordham where they lived. Virginia died of tuberculosis in the winter of 1846 and Poe, his condition of mind and body swinging between extremes of euphoric drunkenness and neurotic depression, sought consolation with different women. He became involved with the poet Sarah Whitman and the

Mrs Richmond of his poem 'For Annie' – but his disordered mind could not deal with his problems: he attempted suicide. Yet during the years between Virginia's death and his return to Richmond in 1849 he completed 'Ulalume', a ballad expressing his grief for Virginia, *The Domain of Arnheim*, and 'The Bells'; he was also working on his metaphysical prose poem, *Eureka*.

On his return to Richmond Poe made a serious effort to control his drinking and completed the celebrated **Annabel Lee**. He re-encountered an early love, now a widow, a Mrs Shelton who had been a neighbour of the Allans. They planned their marriage and Poe went north to fetch Mrs Clemm. On the way he stopped in Baltimore, where he fell among doubtful company and was discovered, after five days, in an alcoholic stupor. He died four days later and was buried beside Virginia in Baltimore.

Edgar Allan Poe's influence on the literature of the 19th century and after is astonishing. This most romantic of writers – as he seems to us now – was Baudelaire's idol. At the same time his work was translated into Russian and praised by Dostoevsky years later for its realism. His stories, usually published now as *Tales of Mystery and Imagination*, vary in quality to a remarkable degree and it is difficult in the 20th century not to smile at *The Black Cat* or *The Fall of the House of Usher* (though it is quite easy to feel revolted by *The Facts in the Case of M Valdemar*). At the same time there are few stories to rival *The Tell-Tale Heart* and *The Premature Burial*. Poe's stories of ratiocination also brought a new literary form into being – the detective story. Dupin was the first in a long line of languorous, aristocratic amateurs who always outpolice the police.

Poe is regarded by many as the first American poet, an original singer whose voice is his own, even if his impulse came from the great romantics of Europe. Baudelaire's description of him as an 'étoile de la première grandeur' in the melancholy sky of modern poetry was the tribute of a French master and one not accorded him by English and American contemporaries. Emerson dismissed him as 'the jingle man' and certainly there is a weary, singsong repetition in his lyrics that can be very tedious. But Lowell's comment that he was 'three-fifths genius and two-fifths sheer fudge' is a more telling and possibly truthful tribute than a first glance may suggest. The French had no doubts about him as a poet or a prose writer and his influence helped to set in motion the poetry of the Symbolistes. Baudelaire was the translator of Poe's critical essays, and Poe's theory of poetic unity being one of mood or emotion (his critics complained that his poetry is a sustained tone, dominated by an atmosphere) was studied and accepted. The French poet's translation of the Tales (*Histoires Extraordinaires*) also started something, as a look at the morbid romanticism of the stories of Barbey d'Aurevilly, Villiers de l'Isle Adam, and others will show. At a further remove, Poe's influence can be also found in the sentimental aestheticism of Huysmans's *A rebours*.

Edgar Allan Poe himself was paid his finest tribute by a great writer in his own language whose symbolism was a natural part of his poetic self – W. B. Yeats. He considered Poe to be 'always and for all lands a great lyric poet'.

**Poema Morale (or Moral Ode)**   A sermon-poem of the first half of the 13th century, evidently popular since a number of manuscripts have survived. It is the first known example in the English language of the use of the Latin catalectic tetrameter form – 14-syllable rhymed couplets. Editions of *Poema Morale* are by F. J. Furnivall in *Early English Poems* (1862) and R. Morris for the Early English Text Society (1869).

**Poetaster, The,** or *The Arraignment.*   A satire by Ben Jonson, first produced in 1601 and published in 1602. The point of the satire is Jonson's view of his contemporaries and it is played out at the court of the Emperor Augustus. A thin storyline concerns the efforts of Crispinus (Marston) and Demetrius (Dekker) to defame Horace (Jonson). See also **Jonson, Ben.**

**Poetical Rapsody, A**   The full title of this, the last of the Elizabethan anthologies, was *A Poetical Rapsody Containing diverse Sonnets, Odes, Elegies, Madrigalls and other Poesies, both in Rime and Measured Verse.* It was collected by Francis and Walter Davison, both of whom contributed to it, and first published in 1602. It contains pieces by Ralegh, Greene, Wotton, Sidney, Spenser, Donne, and Campion. There are modern editions by A. H. Bullen (1891) and H. E. Rollins (1932).

**Poetical Sketches**   This was the first collection of William Blake's lyrics and was published in 1783. The expense was borne by the artist John Flaxman and the Rev Anthony Mathew and his wife: Mrs Mathew's drawing-room was a centre where artists and writers gathered. The poems were composed between Blake's 12th and 20th years and include 'To the Muses', 'The Passions', 'Fair Elenor', and 'My silks and fine array'.

**Poetry: A Magazine of Verse**   See **Monroe, Harriet.**

**Poetry Bookshop** See **Monro, Harold (Edward)**.

**poets of World War II** It is generally agreed that World War II, unlike World War I, did not produce poets of the level of accomplishment of Wilfred Owen, Isaac Rosenberg, or Edward Thomas. But three of notable promise who died in the conflict were Alun Lewis, Keith Douglas, and Sidney Keyes.

Alun Lewis (1915–44) was born in Aberdare, Glamorganshire, the son of a schoolmaster, and was educated at the University of Aberystwyth. A lieutenant in the army from 1942, he was killed in Burma. His first work was published in that year: the volume of short stories about army life called *The Last Inspection* and *Raider's Dawn and Other Poems*. Posthumous work was published as *Ha! Ha! Among the Trumpets: Poems in Transit* (1945), to which Robert Graves contributed a foreword, and *In the Green Tree* (1948), which contained his letters from India and six short stories. For the latter A. L. Rowse wrote a preface and Gwyn Jones a postscript. The beautiful 'All Day it has Rained ...' can be found in most anthologies of modern verse.

Keith Douglas (1920–44) was born in Tunbridge Wells, Kent, and educated at Christ's Hospital and Oxford, but his student days were cut short by the outbreak of war. By 1941 he was a tank commander, serving in North Africa. He survived that but was killed in Normandy three days after the Allied invasion of Europe. Douglas had written poetry since he was 16 and his early work was published in *Augury: An Oxford Miscellany of Verse and Prose* (1940). More mature and coldly angry poems were published in *Alamein to Zem Zem* (1946), and *Collected Poems* appeared in two editions, edited by J. Waller and G. S. Fraser (1951) and with an introduction by Edmund Blunden (1966). A notable *Selected Poems* was edited and introduced by Ted Hughes (1964). 'How to Kill' and 'Vergissmeinnicht' are familiar anthology pieces.

Sidney Keyes (1922–43) was born in Dartford, Kent, and his days as a student were cut short, like those of Keith Douglas, by the outbreak of war. He was killed in Tunis, the youngest of the three poets at the time of his death. Six of his poems were published in *Eight Oxford Poets* (1941). *The Iron Laurel* (1942), *The Cruel Solstice* (1943), and *Minos of Crete: Plays and Stories* (1948) complete the list of his work. *Collected Poems* (1945) was edited and contains a memoir and notes by the poet's Oxford friend, Michael Meyer. Keyes's poems are not anthologized as frequently as those of Lewis or Douglas but such poems as 'The Wilderness', 'The Foreign Gate', and 'Against a Second Coming' demonstrate how rich his promise was.

*Pokahontas, My Lady: A True Relation of Virginia*. A novel by John Esten Cooke, first published in 1885.

The story of John Smith and Pokahontas is told in this romance by Amos Todkill, a member of Smith's company. He relates how Smith was captured by the Indians, the events of his captivity, and his rescue by Pokahontas. Amos continues the story with Pokahontas being given in marriage to John Rolfe after Smith's death has been reported. Rolfe and his Indian princess leave for England, where Smith reappears and finds Pokahontas again; but she is now another man's wife. Smith meets William Shakespeare, who tells him that Virginia provided the sources for *The Tempest*. The novel ends with the death of Pokahontas, just as she and Rolfe are preparing to return to America.

*Political Economy, Principles of* See **Mill, John Stuart**.

**Polixenes** The King of Bohemia and Leontes' lifelong friend in Shakespeare's *The Winter's Tale*. Leontes convinces himself that Polixenes has betrayed him with his wife, Hermione, and tries to have him murdered. Polixenes escapes, warned by Camillo. Polixenes opposes his son's marriage to Perdita, believing her to be of low birth.

**Pollexfen, Sir Hargrave** The arrogant and wealthy baronet of *Sir Charles Grandison* by Samuel Richardson who makes an attempt on the virtue of Harriet Byron. His intended victim is rescued by Grandison.

*Polly* This musical play, or ballad opera, by John Gay is a sequel to *The Beggar's Opera*. Performance was banned by the government – by Robert Walpole, that is – so the published version (1729) attracted great interest and probably made far more money for the author than the successfully produced and popular *The Beggar's Opera*. The play was eventually staged in 1777 by George Colman at the Haymarket in an adapted version that was not a success. It is generally regarded as inferior to *The Beggar's Opera*. The mixture was thicker and heavier. *Polly* is almost never revived.

Polly and Macheath have been separated by the sentence of transportation on Macheath to the West Indies. She goes there to find him but he has escaped from the plantation where he was a bondman and is believed to be dead. Polly, upon arrival in the Indies, stays in the house of a planter,

Ducat, who soon makes her a prisoner in the hope of realizing his lustful ambitions. An attack by pirates gives Polly a chance to escape; she puts on men's clothes, joins the loyal Indians, and takes part in the defeat of the pirates. She takes their leader, Morano, prisoner and hands him over to justice – but then discovers that he is none other than Macheath. But Polly cannot save him from the scaffold and at the end of the play she marries an Indian prince.

**Polonius**  The sly and busy but not very intelligent old councillor in Shakespeare's *Hamlet*. Father of Ophelia, he believes that Hamlet's erratic behaviour is due to his love for her and reports the prince's actions to Claudius and Gertrude. Trying to overhear the argument between Gertrude and Hamlet, he hides behind the arras in the queen's chamber. He betrays his presence and Hamlet kills him, believing him to be Claudius. Laertes is Polonius' son.

**Polychronicon**  See **Higden, Ranulf** and **Trevisa, John.**

**Poly-Olbion**  Michael Drayton's enormous poem was published in two parts, in 1613 and 1622. The first part consisted of 18 songs, the second of 12. None of the 30 songs is less than 300 lines and the longest are of 500. The whole poem is a celebration of England. The reader is taken on a tour of the country and its physical beauties, reminded of its glorious history, and told of the richness of its the natural life. Drayton was a countryman, of yeoman stock from the same county as William Shakespeare, and deeply patriotic; and while the level of *Poly-Olbion* is necessarily uneven its finer songs are part of the great Elizabethan tradition.

The first 18 songs were 'illustrated' (annotated) in prose by John Selden, the jurist and antiquarian.

**Pomfret, John**  1667–1702.  Pomfret was educated at Queen's College, Cambridge, and became rector of Maulden in Bedfordshire. He wrote a number of poems, one of which enjoyed great popularity and ensured Pomfret's inclusion in Johnson's *Lives of the Poets*. This was *The Choice or Wish* (1700), in which the poet describes the kind of life and modest income that he would choose for a contented life: 'Near some fair Town, I'd have a private Seat . . .'.

**Pontifex, Ernest**  The central character of Samuel Butler's *The Way of all Flesh*, the archetypal victim of a repressive Victorian Low-Church upbringing.

*Poor Richard's Almanack*  Benjamin Franklin launched his almanac in Philadelphia in 1733 and it continued until 1758. It was fundamentally a calendar and basic astronomic data book similar to all almanacs. However, the general form had broadened considerably in America and by Franklin's time almanacs were much more like popular magazines, carrying information on all sorts of subjects as well as humorous articles. Franklin wrote his almanac under the pseudonym of Richard Saunders, a figure which, with his wife Bridget, became very popular in the America of the time. The couple imparted Franklin's brand of wisdom and humour and the almanac continued in this style until 1748, when Franklin ceased to write it himself. Thereafter it was called *Poor Richard Improved*. Franklin sold the almanac in 1758 but it remained popular and continued to be published until 1796.

**Pope, Alexander**  1688–1744.  Alexander Pope was the son of a London linen merchant who was old enough to be contemplating his retirement from the city and his Lombard Street house when his son was born. The family, which was Roman Catholic, spent a little time in Hammersmith, where an aunt taught the infant Alexander to read. Pope spent brief periods at Catholic schools but his education was erratic. He was taught the rudiments of Greek and Latin by a priest and, from the year 1700, when the family moved to Binfield in Windsor Forest, he could be said to have been self-educated. The process was to leave some gaps in his knowledge of English literature, as Bonamy Dobrée has pointed out. His learning was of his own choice and, inevitably, the precocious and often ailing boy could not have been expected to choose judiciously all the time. The year 1700 was also the year of his first serious illness; he was to suffer from ill health for the rest of his life and eventually he was crippled by a tubercular spine.

Pope began to write poetry during his boyhood; his 'Ode on Solitude' was a product of his twelfth year. He read and wrote constantly and cultivated the friendship of older men, among them William Walsh, Henry Cromwell, and Sir William Trumbull, who encouraged him and were willing to read and criticize his work. *The Pastorals* were written during his teens and were no doubt well read in manuscript before the publisher, Jacob Tonson, invited Pope to publish them in his *Miscellany* (volume VI) in 1709. The poems demonstrate Pope's mastery of metre though they are, inevitably, rather more to be admired as successful exercises in an accepted form than as memorable poems. But at the time of their publication Pope was working on *An Essay on Criticism*, the remarkable essay in couplets that made him famous when it was published in 1711. *Messiah* and *The Rape of the Lock* were published in 1712. The first of these was completely eclipsed by the second, which confirmed his promise and established him as a poet of the first rank. *Windsor Forest*, published in 1713, extended the range of his friendships in London, where he was now living. He had been a young admirer of William Wycherley and had rendered the crotchety old playwright very useful service. His reward was an introduction to literary London; his gifts ensured the attention of Addison and, later, Swift. He became a member of the Scriblerus Club and contributed to Gay's and Arbuthnot's play *Three Hours after Marriage* (1717), though he did not otherwise venture into the dramatic form.

Meanwhile, the ambitious project of a translation of Homer had been in Pope's mind. He published his ideas for it as early as 1713 and the first instalment of the *Iliad* appeared in 1715. Written in heroic couplets, the work (finished by 1720) is acknowledged as a great poem, one of the masterpieces of the period. It is not Homer but, as Richard Bentley pointed out, it is a fine poem; and that can be said of few translations. While engaged on this exacting task Pope issued, in 1717, a volume of *Works* that included a translation of Chaucer, a reworking of that poet's *The House of Fame*, the 'Ode for Music on St Cecilia's Day', and two love poems, 'Eloisa to Abelard' and 'Elegy to the Memory of an Unfortunate Lady'. The three *Epistles* in the volume include two addressed to Teresa Blount. They were later transferred to her younger sister, Martha, who was to remain the poet's affectionate friend for the rest of his life. To this period also belongs the beginning of his friendship with Lady Mary Wortley Montagu – a friendship that did not survive a quarrel (the cause for it is obscure) in 1723, which led to Pope's contemptuous lines about her in the first satire of his *Imitations of Horace*.

The translation of the *Iliad* was sold on subscription and was so successful that the poet became financially independent. He also became the acknowledged head of English letters and brought Homer within reach of many to whom Greek epic poetry had been, hitherto, a scholastic labour and little more. Pope was now a sought-after figure and the guest of noblemen. He bought the villa in Twickenham that was to be his home for the rest of his life. The *Odyssey* followed the *Iliad* and was completed in 1726 with the assistance of Elijah Fenton and William

Alexander Pope. A detail from the portrait, c.1727, from the studio of M. Dahl. National Portrait Gallery, London.

Broome. Pope enjoyed another success, which might have consoled him for the comparative failure of his edition of *Shakespeare's Works* (1725). Unfortunately the enterprise, undertaken to a commission from Jacob Tonson, provoked a pamphlet from Lewis Theobald, *Shakespeare Restored* (1726), which pointed out Pope's errors and his failings as a Shakespearean scholar. Pope nursed a bitter grudge against Theobald that was to find expression, with a number of other grudges, in *The Dunciad*. The poet's poor health and permanent disability could not have made for a sweet temper but his disposition does seem to have been notoriously prickly. He also quarrelled with William Broome and wrote insulting lines about him in the *Miscellany* of 1727. On the other hand Pope was a good friend to Swift, inviting him to England in 1725 and making sure that he was properly welcomed, as well as arranging for the publication of *Gulliver's Travels*.

The circle of Pope, Swift, Gay, Lord Oxford, Arbuthnot, and Bolingbroke agreed to publish a *Miscellany*, of which two volumes appeared in 1727 and a third in 1728. The first version of the satire *An Epistle to Dr Arbuthnot* (1735) appeared in 1727 in the *Miscellany*. More important was *Martinus Scriblerus peri Bathous: or The Art of Sinking in Poetry*, which insulted not only Broome but

'An exact Draught and View of Mr Pope's House at Twickenham.' Detail from an 18th-century engraving. Society of Antiquaries, London.

Ambrose Philips, Lewis Theobald, and John Dennis. The prose essay examines bathos and Pope uses the work of his literary enemies to illustrate his theme. The piece was brilliantly carried through and the victims' angry retorts soon appeared. Pope was in fact sharpening his teeth. Theobald's successful criticism of 1726 rankled so much that it inspired *The Dunciad*, consisting of three books that were published in 1728. A satire on dullness, it presents Theobald as its hero. An enlarged edition came in 1729 and an additional book, *The New Dunciad*, in 1742. The complete *Dunciad* was published in 1743 and by that time Pope's spite was aimed at Colley Cibber, the poet laureate, who was made hero in place of Theobald. A tiresome literary war ensued, of interest to students of Alexander Pope's life and times but not to many others. Pope began the *Grub Street Journal* to give himself an outlet for his attacks and replies, wasting his energies thus until the influence of his friend Lord Bolingbroke drew him back to better things.

**Essay on Man** (1733–34) consists of four epistles; he also wrote four **Moral Essays** (1731–35). Neither effort is wholly successful as sustained philosophical poetry but both have their rewards. Pope was a poet of genius and his remarkable gifts are always present. The miscellaneous satires, *Imitations of Horace*, began to appear in 1733. The idea came from Bolingbroke and proved a felicitous one. Pope's 11 translations and adaptations to the 18th-century scene of Horace's *Odes*, *Epistles*, and *Satires* contain some of his finest poetry. *An Epistle from*

*Mr Pope to Dr Arbuthnot* (1735), dedicated to the poet's dying friend, the physician John Arbuthnot, was placed by Bishop Warburton, Pope's friend and editor, at the beginning of the satires and called *The Prologue*. An *Epilogue* was made from *One Thousand Seven Hundred and Thirty Eight: a Dialogue something like Horace* (1738).

Pope's later years were partly occupied with the preparation for publication of his earlier correspondence – something new in English letters. Unfortunately, however, he edited and altered his letters to such a degree that the contemporary literary scene was misrepresented. The chief value of them is to throw light on Pope's character and thoughts, but the whole proceeding was dishonest and Pope compounded it by trying to make it appear that the correspondence was published without his permission.

After his death Pope's work was devalued, dismissed as technically brilliant but without warmth or feeling. The poet himself was regarded as a spiteful and malicious character who, for the most part, employed his skill to injure. A real examination yielded something different, as Byron, a great Romantic poet, was quick to proclaim. Nevertheless, the Romantic era would have none of Pope's relatively parochial world. His poetry was different, certainly, and nearly two centuries were to pass before its rehabilitation began. A distinguished name in the process is that of Edith Sitwell. Her *Alexander Pope* (1930) honoured both subject and advocate and drew attention to the remarkable skill with which he used apparently rigid forms and yet achieved, within them, an extraordinary range of expression. Pope is not a popular or well-loved poet by any means, but he is a highly honoured one, the true poetic voice of his time. *The Twickenham Edition* of his works, edited by John

Butt, is the accepted modern one (11 volumes, 1961–70), and an excellent single volume is Herbert Davis's in the Oxford Standard Authors edition. *The Correspondence*, edited by G. Sherburn, was published in five volumes in 1956 and some of the prose works, edited by Norman Ault, in 1936.

Alexander Pope seems to have been a complicated, quarrelsome, jealous, and frankly spiteful man. He seems also to have been, according to his friends, a generous man, spontaneously kind, and notably liberal to those servants of whose attention he was constantly in need. His illnesses in youth stunted his growth – he was no more than 1.4m (4ft 6in) tall – and he was plagued by headaches. So much of the bad side of his character can be understood, if not easily forgiven. His character does not detract from his achievement and if, at times, his ill health and frustrations provided the impulse for his work, posterity should be grateful for all the facets of the character of a sorely tried man who was also a great poet.

**Poretta, Clementina della** The noble Italian lady to whom the hero is promised in *Sir Charles Grandison* by Samuel Richardson. Clementina, because of her faith, surrenders him to her rival, Harriet Byron.

**Porson, Richard** 1759–1808. Porson was born at East Ruston near the coast in Norfolk, the son of the parish clerk. His bent for scholarship was recognized and through the help of patrons Porson was educated at Eton College and Trinity College, Cambridge, and was appointed Regius Professor of Greek at Cambridge in 1792.

Porson's quality as a writer of English was first displayed in *Letters to Archdeacon Travis* (1788–89). Travis was one of the critics of Gibbon. Porson dealt with his strictures, which were based upon the acceptance as historical truth of a passage in the First Epistle of St John (V.7.). Porson's sense of humour is evident in the *Letters*, in which he also offers some criticism, better founded than Travis's, of Gibbon's great work. His reputation as a classical scholar stands very high: he advanced the study of Greek by his elucidation of idiom and usage and by his knowledge of Greek prosody. Porson edited four plays of Euripides: *Hecuba* (1797), *Orestes* (1798), *The Phoenician Women* (1799), and *Medea* (1801).

**Porter, Anne Maria** 1780–1832. The younger sister of the more successful Jane Porter and, like her, a writer of romances. Her output was large but her works are now forgotten, and she is perhaps most interesting in that she began to write at the age of 12 and probably gave her sister the impulse to emulate her. Her novel of the French Revolutionary war, *The Hungarian Brothers* (1807), was a popular success.

**Porter, Jane** 1776–1850. One of two sisters (see **Porter, Anne Maria**) who wrote historical romances and enjoyed considerable success in their day. Jane was the elder and the more successful of the two. Her *Thaddeus of Warsaw* (1803) was enormously popular and *The Scottish Chiefs* (1810) was translated into Russian and German. She also wrote plays, but these met with no success.

*Thaddeus of Warsaw* is one of the earliest examples of the historical novel, though the setting itself was more romantic than the date, which was not so far removed from the author's time. The hero, Thaddeus, apparently a member of the Sobieski family, accompanies the Polish patriot army against the occupying Russians. The Poles are defeated, the Sobieski castle is destroyed, and Thaddeus, an exile, arrives in England. There he suffers hardship and deprivation, until he proves to be none less than the long lost son of an English gentleman.

*The Scottish Chiefs* is more ambitious and more successful. Jane Porter knew her Scotland far better than she did her Poland. The story opens with the murder of Wallace's wife by Heselrigge, the English governor, when he tries to make her divulge her husband's whereabouts. It continues with the career of the ill-fated Wallace and his barbarous execution by the English, and closes with the triumph of Bruce at Bannockburn.

**Porter, Katherine Anne** 1890–1980. Katherine Anne Porter was born in Indian Creek, Texas, into a family which claimed Daniel Boone as one of its ancestors. She attended convent schools and grew up chafing under the traditions and values of her Southern family. These provided the background for much of her fiction but she rejected them for herself and went to work for a newspaper in Denver, Colorado. Later she began to travel and lived in Mexico and Europe for a number of years. Her first book was a collection of short stories, *Flowering Judas* (1930, enlarged edition 1935), and her keen observation, spare economic style, and unsentimental view of humanity commended her to the critics. During a long career her output was not large but she was honoured to a remarkable degree by academic America. She was also the recipient of the O. Henry Award, the Pulitzer Prize, and the National Book Award. *Hacienda* (1934) and *Noon Wine* (1937) are short novels; *Pale Horse, Pale Rider* (1938) contains *Noon Wine* and two other stories; *The Leaning Tower* (1944) contains nine stories. *Ship of Fools* (1962), 20 years in the writing, is an allegorical novel. Among other works by Katherine Anne Porter are the essays *What Price Marriage* (1927) and *A Defence of Circe* (1955), *The Days Before* (1952 and 1970, essays and occasional writings), and *The Never-Ending Wrong* (1977), a memoir of the infamous Sacco and Vanzetti trial and execution (1920–27). *The Collected Stories* was published in 1967.

**Portia** (i) The heroine of Shakespeare's *The Merchant of Venice*. She marries Bassanio when he passes the suitors' test laid down in her father's will. She brings her wits to bear on Shylock's bond when Bassanio's friend Antonio looks like becoming its victim, appearing in the court disguised as a lawyer.

**Portia** (ii) The wife of Brutus in Shakespeare's *Julius Caesar*. She kills herself before the Battle of Philippi in the play. The historical Portia (Porcia, daughter of Cato of Utica) killed herself after Brutus' death.

***Portrait of a Lady, The*** A novel by Henry James, first published in serial form in the *Atlantic Monthly* and *Macmillan's Magazine*, from October 1880 to November 1881, and in volume form in 1881.

Isabel Archer, of Albany, becomes the protégée of her wealthy aunt, Lydia Touchett. Mrs Touchett is the wife of an American banker in England. She has a son, Ralph, who is an invalid and, being a mildly eccentric woman, comes and goes as she pleases. She leaves Isabel on their arrival at the Touchett home, Gardencourt, and Isabel is received by benign old Mr Touchett and Ralph. A guest on that occasion is their neighbour, Lord Warburton. Isabel is penniless and an orphan; but she is intelligent, charming, and independent – she has turned down a rich young American, Caspar Goodwood, who wanted to marry her.

Ralph and Isabel become friends; Lord Warburton becomes enamoured. Ralph knows he can offer Isabel nothing but he persuades his father to provide for Isabel in his will. Meanwhile he becomes Isabel's confidant. She declines a proposal from Lord Warburton and a second one from Caspar, who has followed her to England. When Mr Touchett dies Isabel finds herself rich and goes to the continent with Mrs Touchett and her friend, Madame Merle.

Madame Merle has made a strong impression on Isabel. Sophisticated and accomplished, she is obviously in complete charge of her life; but along with all her gifts she is also a manipulator of remarkable skill and Isabel does not realize that. In Florence she introduces Isabel to Gilbert Osmond, a widower of middle age with a daughter of 15, Pansy, who has been educated by nuns and is incredibly docile and dutiful. Isabel is very impressed with Osmond's taste and intellectual detachment and, in spite of the advice of Caspar, Ralph, Mrs Touchett, and other friends, accepts his proposal and marries him. She discovers him to be a selfish and sterile dilettante who married her for her money. He becomes aware that Isabel, after a few years of marriage, understands him perfectly and he hates her for that. Isabel is also certain that Madame Merle was part of the manoeuvring that resulted in the match but she cannot understand what her motive could have been. She makes the best of her life and is at least able to bring warmth and friendship to Pansy.

Lord Warburton comes to Italy and is a frequent visitor to the Osmond home. He takes an interest in Pansy and persuades himself that he wants to marry her. The thought pleases Madame Merle and Osmond very much – Warburton is very wealthy – and they urge Isabel to use her influence on Warburton's behalf. But Isabel discovers that Pansy does not want him. She also realizes that the attraction for Warburton is really herself, so she sends him away. Osmond is furious and his hatred of his wife reaches new depths; he stupidly accuses her of having an affair with Warburton. When Isabel hears that Ralph is dying she prepares to depart for England to be with him: Osmond forbids her to go. It is at this point that Isabel discovers that Madame Merle is Pansy's mother and she at last understands the woman's part in her marriage to Osmond. (Osmond would never have married Madame Merle – she was penniless.)

Isabel goes to England after a final confrontation with Madame Merle and is by Ralph's side when he dies. Caspar makes a last attempt to gain Isabel but, while she admits his attraction for her, she denies him – and returns to Italy. She has made a mistake and it seems to her that she must live with it – she can use her energies on Pansy's behalf.

For many readers and critics this is Henry James's masterpiece, a novel that has a rightful place in any gallery of great fiction. The story itself is fascinating and the ending, with Isabel's return to the Osmond palazzo and the life that will be a continued struggle with a mean and ridiculous husband, is consistent with the conduct of the lady whose portrait this is. Isabel is offered everything and given much, except a call on her resources – mental, emotional, and material – that will enable her to realize herself fully. She believes that she has received such a call when she is cultivated by Gilbert Osmond. So convinced is she that the counsel of her friends, much more experienced than she, is disregarded – and she learns too late how dreadful a mistake she has made. The book is also distinguished for its character drawing. Beside Isabel are the wilful and generous Lydia Touchett; the vital – too vital and demanding for Isabel – young American Caspar Goodwood; the handsome Lord Warburton – the 'radical peer' whose demands are of a different kind but are as discouraging to Isabel as those of Caspar; and the affecting, sweet-tempered Ralph, through whose eyes the character of Gilbert Osmond is remorselessly examined. Osmond himself is a masterpiece, a loathsome man whose full moral squalor is conveyed with effortless skill. Serena Merle, his victim and his creature, is equally well drawn and suddenly revealed, in the chattering malice of Osmond's sister, to be a wretched woman behind her accomplished and confident façade.

*Portrait of the Artist as a Young Man, A* An autobiographical novel by James Joyce, first published in serial form in *The Egoist* (February 1914–September 1915) and in volume form in 1916. The earlier work from which *A Portrait* was developed, *Stephen Hero*, survived in part and was published in 1944, edited by T. Spencer. The style of the novel predates the author's experiments in prose but the presentation of a Catholic upbringing, and the author's reaction to it, is original and arresting. His alter ego is Stephen Dedalus, whose intellectual, moral, and religious development is followed from babyhood to the completion of his education at Trinity College. He is unathletic and has defective vision and at times he seems to be earning punishment just for those reasons; but he stubbornly holds on to the core of his identity, which is often in danger of being submerged. The many levels of convention in Stephen's world are dictated by the family, the Catholic religion, and Irish nationalism. The book moves from experience to experience: there is a brilliantly written scene describing a quarrel between the supporters of Parnell, the Irish leader (recently dead – Joyce would have been nine years old), who abuse the priests as his destroyers, and the anti-Parnellites who see his fall as God's just punishment for adultery. Stephen, at the Jesuit school, suffers at the hands of the stupid and brutal Father Dolan. Moving into adolescence, his sense of sin and the fear of eternal punishment is exacerbated by his teachers. His identity asserts itself and he

rejects the suggestion that he should train for the priesthood. At Trinity College he moves towards the wider and more rewarding world of literature, philosophy, and aesthetics. At the close Stephen has rejected the claims of family, church, and society and is about to leave Dublin for Paris to embrace the world of art.

**Posthumus Leonatus** A poor but worthy man brought up at the court in Shakespeare's *Cymbeline*. He falls in love with the king's daughter, Imogen, and they marry secretly. The angry Cymbeline banishes him and he goes to Rome, where Iachimo convinces him that Imogen is faithless. He is reunited with her at the end of the play.

**Pound, Ezra (Weston Loomis)** 1885–1972. Ezra Pound was an only child and was born in Hailey, Idaho. His family moved to Pennsylvania when he was four years old and settled in Wyncote near Philadelphia. Pound enrolled at the University of Pennsylvania at the age of 16. He studied poetry and also wrote it. A friend he made there, the poet William Carlos Williams, recalled him writing a sonnet each day though he never preserved the poems of those years. In 1903 Pound went to Hamilton College in New York State, where he studied Anglo-Saxon, the Romance languages, and medieval history. About 1904 he began to consider the writing of a long epic poem, and in 1906 became a Harrison Fellow in Romanics at the University of Pennsylvania. He taught briefly at Wabash College in Crawfordsville, Indiana, and was asked to leave there after an incident concerning his hospitality to a young actress. Pound was dissatisfied with academic life anyway and the episode seems to have made up his mind. He sailed for Europe in February 1908 and went to live in Venice. He did not return to America for 40 years, and when he did the circumstances were tragic.

In June 1908 Pound published his first collection of poems, *A Lume Spento* (With Tapers Quenched), in Venice. He paid the costs himself and was determined, he wrote to his parents, to get it published in the USA – even if he had to write fake reviews of it. In September of that year he went to London; he wanted to renew his acquaintance with W. B. Yeats, whom he first met in 1903 during Yeats's lecture tour of the USA. He did; he had a talent for promoting himself and in a short time was mixing with T. E. Hulme, Ford Madox Hueffer, James Joyce, and Wyndham Lewis. Hueffer published his 'Sestina: Altaforte' in *The English Review* in 1909. Two collections of Ezra Pound's poems, *Personae* and

*Exultations*, were also published in 1909 and he enjoyed a distinct success with the critics. *The Spirit of Romance* (1910), a book of critical essays adapted from lectures, demonstrated further the broad erudition suggested by his poems. His knowledge of medieval literature, Provençal singers and troubadour ballads provided the basis of his poetic forms. *Provença* (1910) and *Canzoni* (1911) were collections in the same vein, with a tendency to esoteric lore being used for its own sake.

The Imagist movement in poetry, dedicated to the use of the language of common speech, the creation of new forms of rhythm, absolute freedom in the choice of subjects, and the evocation of sharp and clear poetic images, attracted Pound to its ranks in 1912. The movement arose from the aesthetic philosophy of T. E. Hulme and one of its American enthusiasts was Pound's friend and fellow poet, H. D. (Hilda Doolittle). Pound prepared an anthology of his own work and that of Richard Aldington, H. D., and F. S. Flint, with contributions by Amy Lowell, William Carlos Williams, James Joyce, and others, and published it as *Des Imagistes* (1914). His own work had been moving in that direction, with *Ripostes* (1912). He published a translation of *The Sonnets and Ballate of Guido Cavalcanti* in the same year, and also established a positive connection with Harriet Monroe and her Chicago magazine, *Poetry*. It was through this that Pound was able to promote the talents of his contemporary, T. S. Eliot, and he also championed Joyce, Robert Frost, Rabindranath Tagore, and his friend William Carlos Williams. A direct influence on Pound himself was the sculptor Henri Gaudier-Brzeska, through whom he became active in trying to bring the arts together. From their association came the short-lived movement called Vorticism, in which painting was represented by Wyndham Lewis. The movement's journal, *Blast*, survived for two issues, in 1915.

Pound published *Cathay* (1915), versions from the Chinese based on notes by the American scholar Ernest Fenollosa, *Lustra* (1916), *Homage to Sextus Propertius* (1917), and *Quia Pauper Amavi* (1919), which contained the first three cantos of a poetic human comedy. An epic poem had been in his mind since his student days but the form had taken ten years to evolve. He had begun the cantos before the Vorticist period, probably in 1914. By 1919, however, he had lost favour with the critics, and the conduct of the war had disillusioned him about England. These feelings, and the poet's recurring dilemma in a world of false values, are the matter of *Hugh Selwyn Mauberly* (1920). He and his wife Dorothy (née Shakespear – they were married in 1914) went to live in Paris in 1921, where he made friends with Ernest Hemingway, Cocteau, e. e. cummings, Ravel, Gertrude Stein, and most of the intellectuals of that period. He worked through the first draft of *The Waste Land* with T. S. Eliot and the result became a 20th-century classic. He moved on from Paris to Italy in 1924, and made a home in Rapallo. *A Draft of XVI Cantos* (1926) represented his resumption of work on the continuous poem begun in 1914.

*Personae: The Collected Poems of Ezra Pound* was published in 1926; T. S. Eliot edited a *Selected Poems* in 1928. *A Draft of XXX Cantos* (1930) continued Pound's sequence, which was extended with *Eleven New Cantos* (1934), *Cantos LII–LXXI* (1934), and *The Fifth Decad of Cantos* (1937). He had, meanwhile, met Mussolini in 1933 and the Italian dictator's imposition of order on Italy had impressed him favourably. His involvement with fascism is a subject for biography and cannot be dealt with in a brief entry. He alienated many friends during his visit to the USA in 1939 and when he wanted to return in 1941 he

Ezra Pound, 1918. Photograph by E. O. Hoppé.

was denied permission. He began to broadcast for the Axis from Rome in the same year. He was arrested by partisans in April 1945 and delivered to the American authorities. In November, in Washington, he was declared unfit to stand trial for treason and confined to St Elizabeth's Hospital.

In spite of the harsh conditions of his confinement in the American forces disciplinary centre at Pisa, Pound returned to poetry and wrote a set of cantos there. He went on working at the hospital in Washington, and was visited by T. S. Eliot, Conrad Aiken, Robert Lowell, William Carlos Williams, e. e. cummings, and others. Oddly enough, his poetry was being appreciated as never before and *The Pisan Cantos* (1948) was awarded the Bollingen Prize in Poetry, a decision which caused an uproar and led to the Library of Congress relinquishing the administration of the prize, which thereafter passed to Yale University. The sequence of cantos was completed with the publication of *Section: Rock Drill: 85–95 de los Cantares* in 1955 and *Thrones: 96–109 de los Cantares* in 1959. *The Cantos of Ezra Pound* was published in 1964.

Pound's confinement in a hospital for the insane came to an end in 1958. Among those actively engaged on his behalf were T. S. Eliot, Robert Frost, Archibald MacLeish, Dag Hammarskjöld, and Congressman Usher Burdick. He returned to Italy in June 1958; he was old and ill but he outlived his contemporaries. He died in Venice at the age of 87, uncertain of his achievements. He is honoured by scholars as one of the makers of modern poetry, one of those who insisted on the retention of discipline in the composition of free verse, and one who could use archaic and modern forms to excellent purpose. His extraordinary erudition, which embraced Chinese poetic tradition in addition to European, frequently makes a pedagogue of the poet and prevents the celebrated *Cantos* from being a complete success. But the finest sequences, found in every anthology of modern verse, are testimony to Pound's poetic genius.

The most influential man of letters of his generation, Pound left some important works of criticism, among them *Pavannes and Divisions* (1918), *Instigations* (1920), *Indiscretions* (1923), *How to Read* (1931), *Polite Essays* (1937), and *A Guide to Kulchur* (1938). *Gaudier-Brzeska: A Memoir* was published in 1916, his versions from the Chinese, *The Classic Anthology Defined by Confucius*, in 1954, and his translation of Sophocles' *The Women of Trachis* in 1956.

**Powell, Anthony (Dymoke)** 1905– . Anthony Powell, the son of a serving army officer, was born in London but spent much of his childhood at army bases. He was educated at Eton College and Balliol College, Oxford, and then went to work for a London publisher. His first novel was *Afternoon Men* (1931), a precisely judged satire of the bohemian world and the futile foolishness of those inhabitants of Chelsea and Bloomsbury who feel their existence justified by mere aspiration. Meanwhile their slovenly existence continues, without purpose, with aimless promiscuity and dependence on drink. Powell's description is done with remarkable economy and a fine ear for speech. *Venusberg* (1932), *From a View to a Death* (1933), the privately printed verse satire *Caledonia: A Fragment* (1934), *Agents and Patients* (1936), and *What's Become of Waring?* (1939) complete his first group of works. In *What's Become of Waring?* Powell makes excellent use of his publishing background and tells of a travel writer, Waring, upon whose works the publishers, Judkins & Judkins, depend for prosperity. The death of Waring and the search for a suitable biographer provide the basis of the story. The investigations into Waring's life reveal facts that threaten to undermine Judkins & Judkins, and Powell's polished economy of style makes for incisive social comedy.

After serving in World War II in the Welch Regiment and the Intelligence Corps Powell published a biographical study, *John Aubrey and His Friends* (1948), and edited a selection of Aubrey's *Brief Lives* (1949). His first fiction after the war was the beginning of a novel sequence, *A Dance to the Music of Time. A Question of Upbringing* (1951) introduces the narrator, Nicholas Jenkins, and his life at Eton and Oxford. The world of Jenkins expands in the novels that follow and is seen through his eyes. His own life takes place off-stage, as it were, but as a selective recorder with a subtle style and an unerring nose for crucial facts about people he is the perfect medium for Powell's recall of a now mature generation of writers, businessmen, scientists, and respectable hustlers. The sequence continued with *A Buyer's Market* (1952), *The Acceptance World* (1955), *At Lady Molly's* (1957), *Casanova's Chinese Restaurant* (1960), *The Kindly Ones* (1962), *The Valley of Bones* (1964), *The Soldier's Art* (1966), *The Military Philosophers* (1968), *Books do Furnish a Room* (1971), *Temporary Kings* (1973), and *Hearing Secret Harmonies* (1975).

***Power and the Glory, The*** See **Greene, (Henry) Graham**.

**Powys, John Cowper** 1872–1963. The son of a clergyman, John Cowper Powys was born in Derbyshire and educated at Sherborne School and Corpus Christi, Cambridge. His early reputation was that of a poet and essayist, with *Odes and Other Poems* (1896), *Poems* (1899), *Visions and Revisions: A Book of Literary Devotions* (1915), and *Suspended Judgements* (essays 1916) and other books. He lectured in the USA from 1904 to 1934, and approached his later career in fiction through a group of romances: *Wood and Stone* (1915), *Rodmoor* (1916), and *Ducdame* (1925). His career as a novelist really began with *Wolf Solent* (1929) and was consolidated with *A Glastonbury Romance* (1932) when he was 60 years old. *Weymouth Sands* (1934), *Maiden Castle* (1936), and *Morwyn: or The Vengeance of God* (1937), were followed by the historical novels *Owen Glendower* (1940) and *Porius: A Romance of the Dark Ages* (1951). *The Inmates* (1952), *Atlantis* (1954), *The Brazen Head* (1956), and *All or Nothing* (1960) complete the list of his novels. *Homer and the Aether* (1959) is an adaption of the *Iliad*.

**Powys, Llewellyn** 1884–1939. The youngest of the three Powys brothers to become writers, Llewellyn was born in Dorchester and educated at Sherborne School and at Corpus Christi, Cambridge. He lectured in the USA but was discovered to have tuberculosis when he returned in 1909. He lived in Switzerland and in East Africa with his brother William, not returning to England until 1920. He spent another five years in the USA, and the remainder of his life in Switzerland. Among his books were *Ebony and Ivory* (1923) and *Black Laughter* (1924), sketches and stories of life in East Africa, a biography, *Henry Hudson* (1927), the novels *Apples Be Ripe* (1930) and *Love and Death: An Imaginary Autobiography* (1939), and several collections of philosophical essays.

**Powys, T(heodore) F(rancis)** 1875–1953. T. F. Powys was the younger brother of John Cowper Powys and was born in Dorset. He was educated in Dorchester and spent his whole life in the Dorset countryside, the setting for his novels, which have a dark strain conflicting with the deeply religious character of the author. His first published work was *An Interpretation of Genesis* (1907), and his first fiction appeared in a collection of stories called *The Left Leg* (1923). His first novel, *Black Bryony*, was published in the same year. Of the seven novels which followed the best known is *Mr Weston's Good Wine* (1927), and he published several more collections of short stories, including *Feed my Swine* (1926), *The House with the Echo* (1928), *Fables* (1929), *The White Paternoster and Other Stories* (1930), *Captain's Patch* (1935), and *Bottle's Path* (1946). *Mr Weston's Good Wine* is an allegory

of love and death in a realistic and sensual framework, starting with the arrival of the purveyor of good wine, Mr Weston, at the village of Folly Down. With him is his assistant, Michael. The visitor and his archangel know all about the village people who form the list of their potential customers.

**Poyser, Mrs** In George Eliot's *Adam Bede*, the wife of farmer Martin Poyser and aunt to Hetty Sorrel. She is one of George Eliot's most successful characters, a countrywoman of the Midlands in the 19th century seen in the round.

**Praed, Winthrop Mackworth** 1802–39. The son of a lawyer, Praed was born in London and educated at Eton and Trinity College, Cambridge, where he became a fellow and was twice winner of the Chancellor's Prize for English verse. He entered Parliament after becoming a lawyer, and was made Secretary of the Board of Control in Sir Robert Peel's government. His promising career was cut short by his early death. Praed's literary talents were manifest while he was still at Eton, where he founded *The Etonian*. He is remembered as a humorous poet but his range was confined to that and his work is hardly known now. *The Poetical Works* of Winthrop Mackworth Praed were first collected by R. W. Griswold (1844). Probably his best-known poems are 'Goodnight to the Season' and the comic-macabre 'The Red Fisherman'.

***Pragmatism:*** *A New Name for Some Old Ways of Thinking*. A volume containing the lectures by William James delivered at the Lowell Institute of Boston and at Columbia University. It was first published in 1907. The theme of the lectures is James's exposition of pragmatism, to which he had been turning throughout his career as a philosopher. He proposed it as a mediating system; rationalism and empiricism were proving inadequate in 'the present dilemma in philosophy'. 'A pragmatist', William James stated, 'turns away from abstraction and insufficiency, from verbal solutions, from bad *a priori* reasons, from fixed principles, closed systems, and pretended absolutes and origins.' The principle as expounded by James was the form to which the ideas of Peirce, Bergson, and F. C. S. Schiller had been moving. After James it was taken farther by John Dewey. Basically the principle is that every truth has practical consequences; these are a test of its truthfulness. Truth is, therefore, relative and the proof of a fact is an account of how that fact has come to be accepted by justifying itself in practical results – it is not an act of pure reason. The real should be investigated according to the values developed as a result of its being known.

James amplified and reasserted these basic principles two years later in *The Meaning of Truth* (1909), which was a reply to the critics of *Pragmatism*.

**Prairie, The** A novel by James Fenimore Cooper, first published in 1827. It was the third of the *Leather-Stocking Tales* to be written but it is the last in the order of events. The time is the opening of the 19th century and the setting is the great plains of America where the frontier is moving farther and farther to the west.

The trapper (Natty Bumppo) has moved with the frontier and is now in his eighties but is still an outstanding frontiersman. He has his rifle, Killdeer, and his hound, Hector. He meets an emigrant wagon train and gains an unpleasant impression of its leaders, Ishmael Bush and his brother-in-law, Abiram White, and is puzzled by the confinement of a woman in a covered wagon, who nonetheless has an attendant, Ellen Wade. One of the emigrant party is the bee-hunter Paul Hover, who is in love with Ellen. The trapper's wisdom enables the train to evade an Indian raiding party; then he guides it to a safe camp.

At this point a young soldier joins the camp and the trapper is overjoyed to recognize Duncan Uncas Middleton, a descendant of his friend Duncan Heyward (in *The Last of the Mohicans*). Duncan is on a mission for the army but he is also seeking his betrothed, Inez de Certavallos, who has been kidnapped and is being held for ransom. The trapper remembers the confined woman, who proves to be Inez. They rescue her and then the trapper, Duncan, and Inez, and Ellen and Paul, leave the wagon train to put as much distance as possible between themselves and the evil leaders.

The five endure a prairie fire, a buffalo stampede, and capture by the Sioux. A Pawnee raid on the Sioux frees them but Ishmael Bush catches up with them and accuses the trapper of the murder of one of his men. There has indeed been a murder but the guilty man proves to be Abiram White. The arrival of Duncan's soldiers finally provides the party with safety, with the trapper's Pawnee friends watching quietly.

The end of the tale brings the frontiersman's life to a close. He yields peacefully to his years and dies on the prairie, surrounded by his friends of both races.

**Pratt, E(dwin) J(ohn)** 1883–1964. E. J. Pratt was born in Newfoundland and educated in St John's and at Victoria College, University of Toronto. He was Associate Professor of English

at the University of Toronto in 1920. Pratt was the son of a Methodist minister and was himself ordained before setting his career in another direction. His early years in Newfoundland put him into close proximity with the hazardous lives of the fishermen, and both elements are present in his work. Among his books of poems are *Newfoundland Verse* (1923), *The Witches' Brew* (1925), *Brebeuf and his Brethren* (1939), and *Towards the Last Spike* (1952). Pratt's *Collected Poems* was published in 1944.

**Prelude, The** An autobiographical poem by William Wordsworth. The poet began to write it in 1799 and it was completed in 1805. Wordsworth revised the 14 books continually and the poem was not published until 1850, just three months after he died. Ernest de Selincourt's edition of 1926 contained the original versions, from the manuscripts, as well as the 1850 edition. *The Prelude* was intended as a preparation for an even more ambitious work. In the poet's own words he set out 'to record, in verse, the origin and progress of his own powers, as far as he was acquainted with them'. The more ambitious work was *The Recluse*, a philosophical poem addressed to his friend Coleridge. *The Prelude* 'conducts the history of the author's mind to the point when he is emboldened to hope that his faculties were sufficiently matured for entering upon the arduous labour which he had proposed to himself'. This 'arduous labour', *The Recluse*, was only completed as far as its first part, called *The Excursion*. *The Prelude* is a portrait of the artist and a unique study of the influences that contributed to his development as a poet. The poem, generally regarded as Wordsworth's masterpiece, was given its title by his widow, Mary.

**Premature Burial, The** A story by Edgar Allan Poe, first published in the *Broadway Journal* in 1845. It is a sustained essay in terror, related by a man subject to catalepsy who has a fear of being buried as a dead man while in the grip of the condition. After experiencing, accidentally, something very like a premature burial he manages to shake off his morbid preoccupations and his health recovers.

**Pre-Raphaelite brotherhood** A group of artists and writers formed in 1848 in reaction to the existing conventions in art and literature. They wanted a return to simple sincerity and believed that this was to be found in the art of the early Italian artists before Raphael, whose technique was the model of the academicians. Most of the brotherhood were concerned with painting. The founders were D. G. Rossetti, William Holman

'Cordelia' by Ford Madox Brown. One of the illustrations published in *The Germ*, the short-lived periodical published by the Pre-Raphaelite Brotherhood in 1850 to propagate its views.

Hunt, and John Everett Millais but literature was represented in the poetry of Rossetti and, to a lesser degree, of the sculptor, Thomas Woolner. F. G. Stephens and William Michael Rossetti were art critics; the seventh member was the painter James Collinson. The brotherhood launched a periodical to propagate its views: *The Germ, Thoughts towards Nature in Poetry, Literature and Art*. The first number appeared in January 1850 but only four were published, most of the work devolving on D. G. Rossetti, some of whose poems first appeared in it. A notable champion of the movement was John Ruskin.

**Prescott, William Hickling** *c*.1796–1859. Prescott was born at Salem, Massachusetts, of rich parents, and educated at Harvard. While at Harvard he suffered severe damage to his sight during a students' game – he was struck in the eyes by a hard crust of bread. He lost the sight of one eye completely and sustained serious damage to the other but he went on to take his MA and was determined to follow a literary career. His parents sent him to Europe for two years, from 1815 to 1817, and while there his interests became focused on historical studies – particularly on the initiative of the Spaniards in America. He published some essays and in 1829 began the preparation of his first history.

*A History of Ferdinand and Isabella* was published in three volumes in 1838 and Prescott was encouraged by the reception it received. The following year he began to prepare **A History of the Conquest of Mexico**, which was published in 1843 and made him famous. *A History of the Conquest of Peru* followed in 1847 and the cycle was

nearing completion with *A History of the Reign of Philip the Second* when the author died. Three volumes were published of this last work (1855–58); Prescott had intended to write four.

Prescott's *Conquest of Mexico* is an epic historical adventure, but carefully researched through the material available to him at the time. Prescott was also careful to present the tragedy inherent in the advance of the conquistadors and he possessed considerable narrative power and a gift for portraying character. His careful examination of sources and his ability to organize the results provided a model for aspiring historians in America.

During a visit to Europe in 1850 Prescott was honoured by the University of Oxford and received by Queen Victoria. An abridgment of his great three-volume *Conquest of Mexico*, edited by C. H. Gardiner, was published in 1867.

**Preston, Thomas** fl. 1570. Nothing is known of the life of the author of *Cambises* though he has often been confused with his namesake who was vice-chancellor of Cambridge University and actively opposed to the presentation of plays there.

*A Lamentable Tragedy mixed full of Mirth conteyning the Life of Cambises, King of Percia* (1569) is notable as a fully fledged historical drama that owes nothing to the morality plays. It is full of verbal bombast and Shakespeare gives Falstaff a reference to it: 'for I must speak in passion, and I will do it in King Cambyses' vein' (*Henry IV*, Part 1 Act 2). Preston may have been the author of the heroical romance *Sir Clyomon and Sir Clamydes*.

**Price, Fanny** The heroine of Jane Austen's *Mansfield Park*, the modest little cousin taken into the wealthy household of the Bertrams.

**Price, Richard** 1723–91. Price was born at Tynton in the parish of Llangeionor in Glamorgan and became a Unitarian minister in London. In 1758 he published *A Review of the Principal Questions in Morals*, which postulated that the rightness and wrongness of any action belonged to that action intrinsically. He was in opposition to the 'moral sense' view of ethics and the writings of Shaftesbury and Francis Hutcheson.

Price also became a distinguished writer on politics and economics. He advocated the reduction of the national debt in *An Appeal to the Public on the Subject of the National Debt* (1772) and strongly supported the American movement to independence in *Observations on the Nature of Civil Liberty, the Principles of Government and the Justice and Policy of the War with America* (1776).

He supplemented the *Observations* with further material in 1777 and 1778 and became the close friend of Benjamin Franklin. In 1783 he was awarded an honorary D.Litt. by Yale University. In 1778 he was invited by Congress to live in America.

The next revolution, in France, was the occasion for *A Discourse on the Love of our Country* (1789): 'After sharing in the benefits of one Revolution, I have been spared to be a witness to two other Revolutions, both glorious.' Price's *Discourse* provoked Edmund Burke to write his *Reflections on the Revolution in France*, which was published in the following year.

**Pride and Prejudice** A novel by Jane Austen, first published in 1813. It was begun in 1796 and completed the following year under the title 'First Impressions'. Jane's father offered it to a publisher in this form but it was refused. Sixteen years later, after careful revision and with a new title, it was an immediate success.

Mr and Mrs Bennet of Longbourn have five daughters but no son, and in the absence of an heir the property, entailed, will pass to William Collins, a rector under the patronage of Lady Catherine de Bourgh of Rosings in Kent. Near Longbourn is Netherfield, and the house is taken by Charles Bingley who comes to live with his sisters and his friend, FitzWilliam Darcy. Bingley falls in love with Jane Bennet but Elizabeth Bennet frankly dislikes Darcy and his superior airs. Her dislike is increased when George Wickham, a handsome young militia officer, tells of his unjust treatment by Darcy: he is the son of the late steward of Darcy's estate. For their part, the Bingley sisters and Darcy find Mrs Bennet and the younger sisters coarse and unacceptable and prevail upon Bingley to detach himself from Jane Bennet.

Mr Collins, meanwhile, has proposed to Elizabeth – a match which would mitigate the hardship caused by the entail. When Elizabeth refuses him Mr Collins proposes to her friend, Charlotte Lucas, who accepts him. Elizabeth goes to stay with the newly married couple and finds that Darcy is in the neighbourhood, visiting his aunt, Lady Catherine. Darcy falls in love with Elizabeth and proposes to her, but his manner betrays that he is doing so in spite of himself. Elizabeth rejects him and takes the opportunity to reproach him for his treatment of Wickham and for separating Jane and Bingley. Darcy withdraws, and in a letter protests that he was never convinced that Jane loved Bingley, who would in that case have been unwise to ally himself to a family like the Bennets. As for Wickham, he exposes him as an adventurer – one of his victims might have been Darcy's sister, 15-year-old Georgiana, if Darcy had not discovered his designs.

Elizabeth leaves for a journey with her aunt and uncle, the Gardiners, and while in Derbyshire they visit Pemberley, Darcy's estate, believing him to be absent. But he is there with Georgiana and welcomes them, and his charm and grace impress Elizabeth. Then comes the news that her sister Lydia has eloped with George Wickham.

It is Darcy who traces the runaways and makes it possible for them to marry (they have no means of their own). Bingley renews his courtship of Jane, and Darcy, in spite of the insolent interference of Lady Catherine, persists in his wooing of Elizabeth. The story ends with Jane happily married to Bingley and Elizabeth to Darcy.

**Priestley, J(ohn) B(oynton)** 1894–1984. J. B. Priestley was a schoolmaster's son born in Bradford, where he was educated. He served in the army during World War I, and was wounded three times. After the war he went on to further study at Trinity Hall, Cambridge, and became a journalist in London in 1922. He had already published a book of verse, *The Chapman of Rhymes* (1918), a collection of occasional pieces mostly written for *The Cambridge Review* as *Brief*

A scene from *The Good Companions* at His Majesty's Theatre, 1931. J. B. Priestley's novel was dramatized by the author and Edward Knoblock and enjoyed further success. The players were, left to right, Adèle Dixon, John Gielgud, Deering Wells, and Lawrence Baskcomb. Victoria & Albert Theatre Museum, London.

*Diversions* (1922), and a collection of contributions to various papers as *Papers from Lilliput* (also 1922). Priestley enjoyed remarkable success as a contributor to *Challenge*, *The London Mercury*, *The Saturday Review*, and other journals and his early books were collections of these pieces. *George Meredith* (1926) and *Thomas Love Peacock* (1927) for the English Men of Letters series and *The English Novel* (1927) furthered his reputation and his first novel, *Benighted* (1927, *The Old Dark House* in the USA) was a success. The second, *Farthing Hall* (1929), was written in collaboration with Hugh Walpole.

Priestley's third novel, *The Good Companions* (1929), was a popular success and won him the James Tait Black Prize. This story of three people who, at crises in their lives, are involved with a concert party which becomes 'The Good Companions' troupe is immensely readable, full of warmth, and a rewarding picture of life in England at the time. It was dramatized by the author in collaboration with Edward Knoblock, and opened at His Majesty's Theatre in May 1931. Its success in the theatre was to have consequences for Priestley's further career. *Angel Pavement* (1930), his next novel, is regarded by many critics as his best but its depressing theme, the spoiling of a group of lives briefly lifted out of hopelessness by the arrival of a confidence man, prevented it from being popular. It is a well-fashioned variation of the pessimism which informed so much of the fiction of the 1930s. Priestley's next popular success came with a play, *Dangerous Corner* (Lyric Theatre, 1932), about a group of people who fail to negotiate a dangerous corner in their lives. A chance remark about a cigarette box opens up a disturbing chapter of personal history and Robert Caplan's insistence that the truth should always be told destroys him in the end. The action of the play is continuous and confined to a single drawing-room set; the mounting tension is finely managed.

Priestley wrote some 60 further books of essays, literary criticism, travel, fiction, and autobiography, and over 40 plays. Among his more successful works were the plays *Laburnum Grove* (Duchess Theatre, 1933), *When We are Married* (St Martin's Theatre, 1938), and *The Linden Tree* (Duchess Theatre, 1947), *English Journey* (1934), subtitled 'being a rambling but truthful account of what one man saw and heard and felt and thought during a journey through England during the autumn of the year 1933', and *Britain Speaks* and *Postscripts* (1940), the published texts of his wartime broadcasts.

**Priestley, Joseph** 1733–1804. A native of Fieldhead in Yorkshire, Priestley was educated at Batley Grammar School and at Heckmondwike. He was interested in chemistry as a schoolboy and was to earn a considerable reputation as a scientist; but meanwhile he was trained for the Presbyterian ministry at Daventry Academy. He became minister at Needham Market, Suffolk, in 1755, and at Nantwich in Cheshire in 1758, where he opened a school. Priestley's views became increasingly unorthodox and after a period as tutor of languages at Warrington Academy he accepted the appointment of minister of Mill Hill Chapel, an unorthodox church in Leeds (1767). At this time he founded an irregular periodical, *Theological Repository*, which expressed his own views and aroused considerable hostility. Priestley favoured the autonomy of the individual congregation and saw no objection to the proliferation of sects. He attacked the principle of an Established Church and demanded complete toleration for Roman Catholics.

In 1772 Priestley became librarian to Lord Shelburne, an appointment that gave him leisure to pursue his talents as a scientist. His first published work was *The History and Present State of Electricity* (1767); the next was to reach a wider audience. *An Essay of the First Principles of Government* (1768) presented the first statement of the idea, developed later by Jeremy Bentham, 'that all people live in society for their mutual advantage' and the happiness of the majority is 'the great standard by which everything relating to that state must finally be determined.' During his period with Lord Shelburne, Priestley published *Institutes of Natural and Revealed Religion* (1772–74), *Disquisitions relating to Matter and Spirit* and *A Harmony of the Evangelists* (both 1777). In 1780 he moved to Birmingham and became a minister of the New Meeting Society.

*A History of the Corruptions of Christianity* (1782) was widely read and widely resented, and *A History of Early Opinions concerning Jesus Christ* (1786) provoked an attack from Samuel Horsley, Bishop of St Asaph. Priestley denied the infallibility and the accepted impeccability of Jesus, though he held throughout his life to a belief that Jesus was the Messiah. He also believed in the mission of Moses.

In 1791 Priestley became one of the founders of the Unitarian Society, and in his *Letters to Edmund Burke* defended the French Revolution. His celebration of the fall of the Bastille provoked an attack from a mob which wrecked his house. He went to London and for three years was morning preacher at Gravel Pit Chapel near the River Lea in Hackney. He went to America in 1794 and spent his remaining years at Northumberland, Pennsylvania.

Among Priestley's scientific works were *The History and Present State of Discoveries relating to Vision, Light and Colours* (1772) and *Experiments and Observations on Different Kinds of Air* (1774–77).

***Prime Minister, The***   A novel by Anthony Trollope, the penultimate volume of the 'Palliser' series. It was first published in eight monthly parts (November 1875 to June 1876). Plantagenet Palliser and Lady Glencora now move to the centre of the stage and Palliser, nephew and heir to the Duke of Omnium, reaches the summit of his career. Trollope was very pleased with his portraits of Lady Glencora and Palliser – indeed he regarded them as his finest work; but he acknowledged that his book was not loved by the reading public.

Time passes. Plantagenet Palliser, now Duke of Omnium, has a son and heir: his loveless marriage (Glencora would never have married him without her family's bullying, while Palliser – as we are shown him – is unlikely to know what love means at any time of his life) has settled into a sort of comfortable friendship. His career, however, founders: he cannot perceive that the country has to be helped to improve. He can just hold his own in the face of his political opponents. Change, therefore, will have to come gradually, and be gently directed. Inequalities in society will, inevitably, be ironed out since that must be the goal of men of good will in high office. This amelioration will not, however, affect the wealth or status of people like Plantagenet Palliser, Duke of Omnium, who, in the words of one character, 'loved his country dearly, and wished her to be. . .first among nations'.

The modern reader may well boggle at all this, and wonder how the author thought such a man as Palliser, even in the 1870s, could hold the sympathy of his readers. In his introduction to The World's Classics edition, L. S. Amery points out that Trollope's views were projected on to Palliser. Trollope had once tried to stand for Parliament, and had hated the experience – he was left with a strong dislike of politics and politicians: politicians should be more honourable and disinterested. But they are not and this prime minister has but a short term in office.

Lady Glencora, Duchess of Omnium, also sets herself to play the political game – in her own way, which is unlike her husband's. She does it in his interests. However, the difference in their temperaments is not merely a stumbling block but an obstacle that no amount of good intentions can overcome. Interwoven with the lives of the Pallisers is the story of the pretty Emily Wharton and Ferdinand Lopez, an upstart politician, and their joyless marriage. Phineas Finn and his wife, Marie, move in and out of the story, and Glencora makes her last appearance in Trollope's pages.

***Primrose, Dr***   The narrator and eponymous hero of *The Vicar of Wakefield*, by Oliver Goldsmith. Amiable and kind, he is without wisdom; but his simple goodness enables him to bear considerable reverses with fortitude and resignation.

***Prince and the Pauper, The***   A historical novel for the young by Mark Twain, first published in 1882.

During the last years of Henry VIII's reign, Prince Edward encounters a pauper boy, Tom Canty, and is fascinated to see that he possesses, in appearance at any rate, an exact twin. He persuades Tom to change clothes with him – and is then chased from the palace by mistake. The pauper boy is treated as a prince. Prince Edward wanders through London in rags. He finds Tom's family, but he is ill-treated and runs away. A disinherited knight, Miles Hendon, takes pity on the boy, whom he believes – from his repeated claim to royal birth – to be unbalanced. In Miles's company Edward sees at first hand the wretchedness of the poor and the cruelty of the law. Tom, meanwhile, has made the best of his situation and is trying to be a prince. The king dies and Tom is being prepared for his coronation. Edward makes his way to Westminster Abbey to Tom's relief. The prince's identity is finally established when he alone can reveal the whereabouts of the Great Seal, which is missing – Tom had been using it, not knowing what it was, to crack nuts. The prince becomes King Edward VI, and during his brief reign does his best to keep in mind the lessons of his own days as a pauper.

***Prince's Progress, The***   An allegorical poem by Christina Rossetti, first published in 1866. A princess awaits her bridegroom. The prince sets out, confident and happy, to claim his bride, travelling a long and arduous road. He yields to temptation on the way, seeking mere comfort at first and then turning to one pleasing distraction after another. When he arrives he finds that the princess has died of despair while awaiting him.

***Princess, The***   The full title of Tennyson's poem is *The Princess, A Medley*. It was first published in 1847 and enlarged for the third edition (1850) by the addition of six more of the celebrated lyrics acknowledged as some of Tennyson's most beautiful verse. The poem tells how a group of friends at a picnic in the ruins of a medieval abbey exchange banter about women's rights. They then agree to tell a story, each one picking up the narrative where the last speaker stops. The story which emerges is set in no particular time or place and concerns Princess Ida, daughter of King Gama, who supports the rights of women. She rejects marriage and opens a university for women. Her erstwhile betrothed, a neighbouring prince, gains admission with his friends Florian and Cyril, disguised as girls. They are detected by Lady Psyche and Lady Blanche, two of the tutors, who conceal their knowledge; but they are recognized by Princess Ida when the prince saves her from drowning. After a battle between the army of the prince's father and that of King Gama, when the three young men are left lying on the field, womanly pity prompts the care of the wounded. The university becomes a hospital and the prince wins his princess.

Tennyson was interested in the subject of women's rights and how rich a field lay open to women if their capacities could be fully developed and restrictions removed. At the same time, he maintained, any movement towards that realization must acknowledge woman's true nature. The poem was not a critical success but the public liked it very much and it sold extremely well. The lyrics which Tennyson added to the 1850 edition were: 'As through the land at eve we went', 'Sweet and low', 'The splendour falls on castle walls', 'Thy voice is heard through rolling drums', 'Home they brought her warrior dead', and 'Ask me no more'. The five which had already appeared in the original version are the exquisite blank-verse 'Tears, idle tears', with 'O Swallow, Swallow', 'Our enemies have fallen', 'Now sleeps the crimson petal', and 'Come down, O maid, from yonder mountain height'.

**Princess and Curdie, The**  See **MacDonald, George.**

**Princess and the Goblin, The**  See **MacDonald, George.**

**Princess Casamassima, The**  A novel by Henry James, first published in serial form in the *Atlantic Monthly*, from September 1885 to October 1886, and in volume form in 1886.

An orphan boy, Hyacinth Robinson, is taken in and brought up by Miss Pynsent, a quiet little spinster in the Pentonville district of London, who makes a living as a dressmaker. He only saw his own mother once, when she was dying in the prison to which she was condemned for the rest of her natural life for the murder of his father, 'Lord Frederick'. Miss Pynsent (Pinnie) numbers among her friends Anastasius Vetch, a musician who hopes that things will improve for the

working man, and Eustache Poupin, a French communist in exile and a bookbinder by trade. Hyacinth is apprenticed to Poupin and while he is learning his trade is caught up in the movement toward revolution. The boy's contemporary, Paul Muniment, is a full-scale revolutionary by the time he grows up and Hyacinth is carried with him, pledging his life for the cause.

Christina, the Princess Casamassima, is separated from her husband (see **Roderick Hudson**) and in London finds the revolutionary movement an outlet for her energies. She sees in Hyacinth a responsive spirit. He is artistic, and fastidious, and his sympathy for the poor is profound – but his dilemma is real while hers is questionable. Hyacinth longs for the fine things to be brought within the reach of everyone who aspires to them. He does not want everything to be reduced to pieces willy-nilly so that everyone will have: merely having, he feels, is not enough.

When his beloved Pinnie dies, Hyacinth uses his small legacy to travel. He returns with his horizons enlarged and a conviction that revolution, whatever it may accomplish, will not change him. But meanwhile he is committed to the movement. Paul Muniment calls upon him to carry out the assassination of a duke and Christina decides to intervene, knowing what a shocking demand the proposed murder is on Hyacinth. But her intervention is mixed with a desire to be more clearly accepted by the revolutionaries and her way is to try and beguile Paul. Paul refuses to intervene and the call stands. Meanwhile Hyacinth feels that both of them have betrayed him. Christina then offers to substitute herself for Hyacinth; but when she goes to him to tell him the news it is too late. He has given up in despair and killed himself.

So many things are good about *The Princess Casamassima* that it seems unfair to light upon its principal fault as a first comment. But the book is, simply, too long and the tragic dilemma of Hyacinth Robinson is dwelt on so much that the reader is in danger of being exhausted by it. The reader who is not is fortunate, because he will have a masterpiece to treasure – the novel at its best is of a quality rarely found. Henry James's London is vividly drawn and populated by real people: Millicent Henning, the warm-hearted Cockney girl; Captain Sholto, the hanger-on of the bountiful Lady Aurora who finds Millicent a very rewarding contact with the proletariat; Anastasius Vetch, who would like to enjoy life in a gentle way and hopes it may one day be possible; Paul Muniment, the single-minded revolutionary whose esteem for the poor is meagre; the unpleasant invalid, his sister Rose, who esteems herself; and the endearing little Pinnie, who cares for the orphan boy. Christina, who became a princess in an earlier novel, is present among the revolutionaries because of her personal discontent. It is her presence that helps drive Hyacinth Robinson into a crisis that he cannot resolve. Hyacinth himself is a memorable character, one of real tragic stature. Henry James, the novelist of high life in two continents, demonstrates his range in this book. The London of the 1880s is vividly presented and the range of characters is a triumph.

**Princess of France** In Shakespeare's *Love's Labour's Lost*, she visits Navarre, where King Ferdinand falls in love with her in spite of his vow of withdrawal from the pleasures of the world. When her father dies she exacts a promise of true withdrawal 'To some forlorn and naked hermitage' while she spends a year in mourning.

*Principles of Psychology, The* William James's great work was published in two volumes in 1890. The author had established the first psychological laboratory in the USA in 1876 and made a science of what had been hitherto termed 'mental philosophy'. The publication of *The Principles of Psychology*, a work that had occupied James for 12 years, was of enormous importance because it established the functional approach. James maintained that mind is a function of the body, the physical organism, so the individual adjusts to environment. The mind is the instrument that controls choice, effort, and free will to make an adjustment modified by deterministic factors such as heredity and biology.

**Pringle, Thomas** 1789–1834. Pringle was born at Kelso in Roxburghshire and completed his education at the University of Edinburgh. He published *The Institute: A Heroic Poem* (1811) and founded *The Edinburgh Monthly Magazine* (1817). *The Autumnal Excursion* (1819) was published in the same year that he accepted, because of financial difficulties, the post of government librarian at Cape Town. He spent six years in South Africa, where he opened a school and founded a periodical, *The South African Journal*. This led to his dismissal by the governor, who objected to Pringle's politics and rejected his hopes of bringing the country's various cultural groups together. Pringle left South Africa in 1826 and settled in London with his family. He devoted his energies to the Anti-Slavery Society, working closely with Wilberforce and Clarkson, and to giving the first authentic breath of South Africa to English literature. His poems were published in *Ephemerides* (1828) and *African Sketches* (1834).

*The History of Mary Prince, a West Indian Slave* (1831) and *Narrative of a Residence in South Africa* (1835) reinforce the humanitarian tone of his poems, which were admired by Coleridge and Tennyson.

**printing in England** See **Gutenberg, Johann** and **Caxton, William.**

**Prior, Matthew** 1664–1721. The son of a joiner, Matthew Prior was born near Wimborne Minster, in Dorset. His education was sponsored by the Earl of Dorset, who found the young Prior working in his uncle's tavern near Charing Cross. Lord Dorset, impressed by the boy, sent him first to Westminster School and then to St John's College, Cambridge. While an undergraduate Prior collaborated with Charles Montagu (the Earl of Halifax) on a satire on Dryden's *The Hind and the Panther* called *The Hind and the Panther Transversed to the Story of the Country and the City Mouse* (1687).

Prior was a man who wrote verse with remarkable ease and he seems to have had a similar ability in making friends. He became a successful diplomat after a useful parliamentary career; he became Under-Secretary of State and Commissioner for Trade and Plantations while continuing to write verse. Originally a Whig in politics, Prior, like Swift, gradually identified himself more with the Tories, acting with Lord Harley and Henry St John, Viscount Bolingbroke. In 1711 he went to Paris as plenipotentiary to initiate the peace talks that led to the Treaty of Utrecht, which became known in English political circles as 'Matt's Peace'. The accession of George I brought the Whigs back to power and the high feelings provoked by the war during the last part of Queen Anne's reign had left a legacy of bitterness. Prior was arrested and spent two years in prison with the threat of impeachment hanging over him. But he was released with his personal and political honour intact. Harley's son gave Prior £4000 to enable him to buy Down Hall in Essex. When he died Prior was honoured with a grave in Poet's Corner in Westminster Abbey.

Matthew Prior's work appears in anthologies but is not really well known. He excites the admiration of literary scholars for his range and grace in epigram, light satirical narrative, and humorous ballad. He was also a master of familiar verse and the author of pretty poems addressed to children. Among his more ambitious efforts are *Henry and Emma, a Poem, Upon the Model of the Nut-Brown Maid. Alma, or The Progress of the Mind* and *Solomon on the Vanity of the World* both examine the vanity of worldly concerns. Matthew

Prior's verses were first published in *Poems on Several Occasions* (1709). A subscription folio edition of his *Poems* was organized by his friends and published in 1718. A modern edition of Prior's works is *The Literary Works* edited by H. Bunker Wright and M. K. Spears (1959).

**Prioress's Tale, The**  See **Canterbury Tales, The.**

**Prisoner of Zenda, The**  A novel by Anthony Hope, first published in 1894.

Rudolf Rassendyl, an Englishman, is travelling in Ruritania. Two of the king's aides, Colonel Sapt and Fritz von Tarlenheim, come upon him and are arrested by his extraordinary likeness to the king, soon to be crowned. The story tells how they prevail on him to impersonate the king when the monarch is kidnapped by Black Michael and Rupert of Hentzau, who intend to usurp the throne. Rassendyl agrees, is successfully crowned with the Princess Flavia, and helps to rescue the king. Rassendyl has fallen in love with Flavia but at the end of the story he surrenders her and departs.

*Rupert of Hentzau* (1898) takes the hero back to Ruritania. The queen is leading an unhappy life with the dissolute king and Rupert of Hentzau, who had survived the former plot, now reappears, determined to undermine the throne by attacking the queen. His new plot is defeated, he is killed, and Rassendyl has an opportunity of ousting the king and marrying Flavia. Before he can come to a decision, he is assassinated by Rupert's younger brother.

**Pritchard, Katherine Susannah** 1884–1969. The daughter of a journalist, Katherine Pritchard was born in Fiji, spent her childhood in Tasmania, and was educated in Melbourne. She worked as a journalist in Melbourne and then went to London, where she spent six years as a freelance journalist and published her first novel, *The Pioneers* (1915). In Australia she took pains to familiarize herself with the background of her novels, travelling the continent and observing the life she depicts with such care. The life of teamsters is featured in *Working Bullocks* (1926); the life of a cattle station and a relationship with an Aboriginal girl in *Coonardoo* (1929), her best novel; and circus life in *Haxby's Circus* (1930). Her trilogy of novels about the goldfields, *The Roaring Nineties* (1946), *Golden Miles* (1948), and *Winged Seeds* (1950), are set in Western Australia, where she eventually made her home.

**Pritchett, V(ictor) S(awdon)** 1900–  . V. S. Pritchett was born in Ipswich and educated in London at Dulwich College. He worked at various things from 1916 until 1923, when he became a journalist. He was literary critic of *The New Statesman* for 20 years and a director from 1946 to 1978. His first book was a travel report, *Marching Spain* (1928); his first novel, *Clare Drummer*, followed in 1929 and his first volume of short stories, *The Spanish Virgin and Other Stories*, in 1932. While he is most successful as a critic and short-story writer, Pritchett's range is wide and he has also published travel books and biographies. Among his best known works are *Dead Man Leading* (1937, novel), *You Make Your Own Life* (1938, short stories), *In My Good Books* (1942, reviews), *It May Never Happen* (1945, short stories), *The Living Novel* (1946 and 1964, essays), *Mr Beluncle* (1951, novel), *The Spanish Temper* (1955, travel), *When My Girl Comes Home* (1961, short stories), *The Working Novelist* (1965, reviews), *A Cab at the Door* (1968, memoir), *George Meredith and English Comedy* (1970), *Balzac* (1973), *The Camberwell Beauty* (1974, short stories), and *Turgenev: The Gentle Barbarian* (1977). V. S. Pritchett was knighted in 1975.

**Private Lives**  See **Coward, Noël (Pierce)**.

**Private Papers of Henry Ryecroft, The**  A novel by George Gissing, first published in 1903. It takes the form of a journal kept by a recluse, a writer who strove for success to no avail and was enabled, by means of a legacy from a friend, to withdraw from his literary labours in London.

The private papers are the personal essays in his journal, reflecting on his present content and his good fortune in escaping from a literary drudgery that brought him almost no reward. The form enables Gissing to indulge in psychological exploration and that aspect of the book is what has pleased Gissing's admirers. In other respects it is a literary oddity, a beautifully written statement of what form his withdrawal should take – if Gissing could have afforded a withdrawal.

**Procter, Bryan Waller** 1787–1874.  Procter was born in Leeds, Yorkshire, and educated at Harrow, where Byron was one of his schoolfellows. He became a successful lawyer in London and eventually a Commissioner in Lunacy. Procter began to write in 1815 as a contributor to the *Literary Gazette* and thereafter wrote industriously throughout a long life as 'Barry Cornwall'. His work had no lasting value, though it was popular during his lifetime, and he numbered Lamb, Hunt, Hazlitt, and Dickens among his friends.

**Professor, The**  This was Charlotte Brontë's first completed novel but it was rejected, while her sisters' *Agnes Grey* and *Wuthering Heights* found acceptance. It was published after her death, in 1857, with a preface by her husband, Arthur Bell Nicholls. The subject is the experience which Charlotte was later to use with such success in *Villette*: in this first attempt she transposed the sexes. William Crimsworth goes to Brussels as a scholmaster and falls in love with a fellow-teacher, an Anglo-Swiss girl. But Crimsworth is modelled on Heger, who became the model for Paul Emanuel, and the influence which makes the story work in the later novel is, in this first attempt, exercised by the emigrant teacher.

*Progress and Poverty* See **George, Henry**.

*Project for the Advancement of Religion* See *Argument against Abolishing Christianity, An*.

*Prometheus Unbound* A drama in four acts by Percy Bysshe Shelley, first published in 1820. It was written in Rome and inspired by the Greek tragedy of Aeschylus but Shelley substitutes the Latin Jupiter for the Greek Zeus, and rejects the reconciliation of Prometheus and Zeus as told in the Greek myth. (This is not in Aeschylus; only the first part of his tragedy survives.) In Shelley's drama Prometheus has been chained to the rock for his defiance of Jupiter, symbol of evil and intolerance. Prometheus is supported by his mother, Earth, and by the thought of his bride Asia, the spirit of nature. Jupiter is overthrown by the Primal Power, Demigorgon; Prometheus is unchained by Hercules, symbol of strength. The supremacy of love follows: thrones and altars, prisons and judgment-seats become things of the past, and all men are equal and free.

*Proposal for the Universal Use of Irish Manufactures* The first of Jonathan Swift's pamphlets relating to Ireland was published in 1720 when Swift, who never regarded himself as an Irishman, was moved to indignation at the treatment of Ireland by England. His indignation grew into a finely controlled rage but in this first pamphlet he proposes that the home-produced cloth of Ireland – devalued because the English in Ireland regarded it without justification as inferior – should be promoted as an industry and that imported fabrics from England should be boycotted. Swift's efforts in this matter were not helped by the well-to-do Irish, who frequently followed the English line for snobbish reasons.

*Proprietatibus Rerum, De* See **Bartholomaeus Anglicus** and **Trevisa, John**.

**Prospero** The rightful Duke of Milan in Shakespeare's *The Tempest*. From his mysterious island he exercises his magic arts to confound his enemies and regain his dukedom.

**Pross, Miss** Lucie Manette's maid and nurse in Dickens's *A Tale of Two Cities*. She kills Thérèse Defarge when the latter tries to stop Lucie and her family from leaving Paris during the Terror.

**Proteus** One of the two gentlemen of Verona in Shakespeare's play of the same name. He lusts after Silvia, the chosen of his friend, Valentine, and forgets his own love, Julia. His attempt on Silvia is frustrated by Valentine's arrival on the scene.

*Prothalamion* The title of Spenser's poem of 1596 was one that he contrived for an espousal song (see *Epithalamion*) and was composed for the daughters of the Earl of Worcester, Elizabeth and Katherine, who celebrated a double wedding. It is not as fine a poem as *Epithalamion*, perhaps because it lacked the joy of a personal celebration but it contains beautiful music. The verse that begins with the line 'With that, I saw two Swannes of goodly hewe' is an example.

**Proudie, Mrs** In Anthony Trollope's Barsetshire novels, the new bishop's wife. She has her husband under her thumb and uses her position to bully anyone who will submit to it. A leading lady on a provincial stage, she is a vulgar woman who, at the last, becomes aware how mean her tyranny over others has been.

*Provok'd Wife, The* A comedy by John Vanbrugh, first produced in May 1697 and published in the same year.

Sir John Brute is a coward and a bully whose wife suffers greatly. Lady Brute has a devoted admirer, Constant, but she has remained true to her marriage vows. Constant's friend Heartfree has always declared his indifference to women, but falls in love with Bellinda, Lady Brute's niece. Bellinda persuades her aunt to join her in a lighthearted frolic, a meeting with Heartfree and Constant in Spring Garden whilst Sir John is out drinking. Lady Brute finds Constant's attentions persuasive and is about to yield when the jealous and spiteful Lady Fancyfull intrudes upon them. The two couples hurry away from the Garden and repair to Lady Brute's house, where they sit down to cards. Sir John Brute, meanwhile, has been indulging in drunken and vulgar behaviour with Lord Rake and Colonel Bully, and has taken a parson's gown from a poor tailor. He is wearing it when he is arrested for brawling. The magistrate dismisses him and he lurches off home unexpectedly early. Constant and Heartfree hide in a closet, where he discovers them. But he is outfaced by Constant and accepts that the two men are present because of Heartfree's forthcoming marriage to Bellinda, though he is

Sir John Brute brawling with the watchman in Act IV, scene 1 of Vanbrugh's *The Provok'd Wife*. An 18th-century illustration. Victoria & Albert Theatre Museum, London.

sure in his own coward's mind that he has been cuckolded. Lady Fancyfull does her best to make mischief but fails because her fellow conspirator Rasor, Sir John Brute's valet, baulks at the extent of her spite. The play ends with Bellinda's marriage to Heartfree.

**Provost, The** A novel by John Galt, first published in 1822.

The book is told in the first person by the provost (mayor), Mr Pawkie, who has three times reached the office and smugly relates his progress through public life. He has a sharp ear for the public voice and takes care to follow it. He carefully serves his own interests – why not? – when serving the community; he resents the free expression of opinion by the press and is careful to see that his retirement is marked by a presentation. The speech in his honour is written by himself.

Mr Pawkie is the representative politician, the kind that modern readers are unhappily familiar with. He could as easily be a cabinet minister as a provost. This is Galt's best book, a successful essay is sustained irony, and it could be read with profit by every retiring politician who contemplates writing his memoirs.

**Prynne, William** 1600–69. The Puritan pamphleteer was born in Somerset and attended Bath Grammar School. Later he went to Oriel College, Oxford, and then studied law at Lincoln's Inn; he was called to the bar in 1628. A fanatical Puritan, Prynne published a 'pamphlet' of over a thousand pages, *Histrio-Mastix* (1632), attacking the playhouses. Archbishop Laud decided that the work contained veiled attacks on Henrietta Maria and King Charles (the queen had

taken part in a masque) and Prynne was sentenced by the Star Chamber in 1634 to life imprisonment, a huge fine, loss of his law and university degrees, and the pillory, where his ears were cut off.

Prynne was freed by the Long Parliament in 1640 and emerged as a hero. He was to see his prosecutor, Laud, impeached, sent to the Tower, and beheaded after a grossly unfair trial in which Prynne took an active part. He was also to have the satisfaction of seeing the theatres closed in 1642. In 1648 he became MP for Newport and, surprisingly, opposed the trial and execution of Charles I. He became therefore a victim of Pride's Purge and suffered more imprisonment, but he continued as an MP and was usually involved in opposition to something – the Commonwealth Army, the Rump Parliament, Milton's views on divorce – until in 1660 he brought in the bill dissolving parliament for the restoration of the monarchy. Prynne was an active supporter of monarchy as well as being a convinced Puritan. Charles II made him Keeper of the Tower Records and Prynne wrote on busily until the end of his days. He was the author of no less than 200 pamphlets.

**Psalms** (in English). See **Psalters** and *Gude and Godlie Ballatis, The*.

**Psalters** The Book of the Psalms in the Old Testament became as rich and beautiful a source of public and private prayer for the Christians as for the Jews. The Reformed Church in England, seeking a substitute for the popular hymns of the Catholic services, turned to the Psalms and some of these were translated into English verse by Thomas Sternhold, a member of Henry VIII's household, in 1548. Sternhold died in the same year and John Hopkins, a Suffolk clergyman, republished Sternhold's, with the addition of some of his own, in 1549.

Hopkins continued his work, and others helped; *The Whole Booke of Psalmes* was published in 1562. It was in verse and it was added to the Prayer Book. Melodies to which the Psalms could be sung were also published. Whittingham's Geneva translation (1559) was an alternative Calvinistic version. This was the ancestor of the Scots Psalter of 1564.

*Pseudodoxia Epidemica, or Enquiries into very many received Tenents and commonly presumed Truths*. Commonly known as *Vulgar Errors*, Sir Thomas Browne's second book, published in 1646, is his most considerable. In an age of scientific enquiry (this was the time of Francis Bacon) and of little productive experiment, many people tried to find a new approach to knowledge. Much speculation found its way into print and, inevitably, much was merely fanciful. Browne's ceaseless curiosity about the world combined with his keen observation to produce a more notable exercise, which of course had also the inestimable benefit of his remarkable prose style.

The book is an enquiry, as the title states, and in some respects is scientifically more sound than the work of Bacon. According to Browne much 'error' was due to the credulous acceptance by many of the false deductions of others, i.e. man is by nature easily imposed upon by the authoritarian tone and ultimately (Browne was a Christian believer) he yields to the endeavours of Satan. This conclusion does not, however, invalidate the value and charm of Browne's book. He genuinely believed that the world was the creation of a loving God and that man should know the truth about it. He covers a wide range of subjects, and while many of his examples may seem laughable to the 20th-century reader they should be considered in their historical context. Many more examples compel respect and the whole book is informed with Browne's wit and gentle irony.

**Public Advertiser, The**  *The London Daily Post and General Advertiser*, which began in 1752, ceased publication in 1798 and was amalgamated with John Newbery's *The Public Ledger*. The new paper was *The Public Advertiser*, which published home and foreign news and a great deal of political correspondence. John Wilkes and John Horne Tooke, formerly friends, carried on a dispute in its pages. Junius's famous letters were also published in the paper, whose most illustrious editor was Henry Sampson Woodfall, from 1758 to 1793.

**Puck (*or* Robin Goodfellow)**  In the service of Oberon in Shakespeare's *A Midsummer Night's Dream*, Puck is a mischievous sprite out of English folklore. He works a charm on Lysander in mistake for Demetrius, and mischievously gives Bottom an ass's head. He frightens Bottom's friends out of the enchanted wood.

**Puckering, Sir John**  1544–96.  Sir John Puckering is identified as the 'John Pickering' who wrote *Horestes*, a play which is itself identified as the *Orestes* acted at court in 1567 or 1568. Puckering was a lawyer of Lincoln's Inn who later became Lord Keeper of the Seal and who was an implacable enemy of Mary of Scotland.

The young Puckering's *Horestes* was published just before it was produced and was a distinct advance on the bombastic ineptitudes of contemporary works of the same period such as *Cambises*

and *Appius and Virginia*. There are still hangovers from the morality plays in the characters who personify Vice, Revenge, and Nature; but the action develops steadily and the utterances of the principals approach the correct mixture of poetry and credibility.

**Puck of Pook's Hill**  A collection of stories for children by Rudyard Kipling, first published in 1906. To the children Dan and Una, who are acting a version of *A Midsummer Night's Dream*, Puck appears in person from Pook's Hill (near Bateman's, Kipling's home in Sussex). Puck shows them the past of England, including episodes from Saxon times, the Battle of Hastings, sea voyages in the 11th century, the wardenship of Pevensey Castle in Henry I's reign, the days of the Romans' rule, and the importance of Hadrian's Wall.

*Rewards and Fairies* (1910) is in the same vein. Both volumes contain verse and the second book contains both the charming short poem 'The Way Through the Woods' and the famous 'If'. The stories range over Norman romance, shipbuilding, Queen Elizabeth I, the era of the Napoleonic Wars, the American War of Independence, the early missionaries in England, the Plague, and the Armada.

**Pudd'nhead Wilson**  The full title of Mark Twain's novel is *The Tragedy of Pudd'nhead Wilson, and the Comedy, Those Extraordinary Twins*. It was first published in 1894 and dramatized in the following year by Frank Mayo. The 'tragedy' of Wilson is that he is both wise and eccentric – and regarded as a fool by his fellow townsmen, who have dubbed him 'Pudd'nhead'.

The setting is Dawson's Landing, Missouri – the same place on the Mississippi as the St Petersburg of Tom Sawyer and Huckleberry Finn; that is, the Hannibal of the author's early years but this time subjected to a colder scrutiny. The period is the 1830s, long before the Civil War and Abolition.

Percy Driscoll is a prosperous slave owner in Dawson's Landing, whose wife dies a week after giving birth to his son, Tom. One of Driscoll's slaves is the beautiful Roxana (Roxy), one sixteenth Black 'and that sixteenth didn't show'. On the day Tom is born Roxy also bears a child, the son of a Virginian. The infant Tom is given to Roxy to nurse with her own baby and there is no difference in the babies' colour. For that matter there is no discernible difference in their appearance either. Roxy's baby is called Chambers.

Roxy knows that her baby will never be hers. As a slave child he can be taken and sold at her owner's pleasure. She switches the babies' identities: her own son becomes Tom Driscoll and Driscoll's son becomes Chambers, a slave.

Percy Driscoll's brother, Judge Driscoll, adopts the false Tom. His 'nephew' grows up to be a spoiled waster and a coward. To pay his gambling debts he decides to sell Roxy: she reveals the truth of his birth but it means nothing to him that she is his mother and he sells her anyway. But Roxy escapes from her new owners and starts to blackmail him.

The false Tom robs the judge, his guardian. Then he steals a knife from Luigi, one of Italian twins with whom the judge had once fought a duel, and murders the old man. Both Italians are charged with the crime and their advocate is David (Pudd'nhead) Wilson who, apart from being a lawyer, is interested in the use of finger-prints in evidence. He successfully establishes Luigi's innocence. More, he establishes the true identity of the supposed Tom Driscoll. The true Tom, who has been brought up as Chambers, as a slave, is appointed to his rightful place, while the true Chambers is returned to his owner, who immediately sells him. Roxy is left prostrated with sorrow while Tom enters a society of which he knows nothing and into which he will take a lifetime's conditioning as a slave. Wilson is accepted as a wise man and a valued citizen in a community where life is conditioned by the institution of slavery and with whose values, the reader can only presume, he is now going to live quite comfortably.

*Pudd'nhead Wilson* has been called 'Twain's second masterpiece' by R. C. Churchill and 'the masterly work of a great writer' by F. R. Leavis. While that estimate of Twain is acceptable the estimate of the novel is more problematical. An outline of the plot conveys the tragic irony but has to leave out the small change, so to speak. This led Van Wyck Brooks to call it 'an absurd and unholy mixture of tragedy and farce'. It is not a masterpiece but, like *Huckleberry Finn*, rises to that level at its best, when it is a powerful commentary on the institution of slavery and the mentality of the South. Wilson is, as Leslie Fiedler wrote, no more than an adult Tom Sawyer in his big moments – but Roxy is a memorable creation, beautiful and proud, imprisoned in a world where she has no more status than a farm animal.

**Punch's Prize Novelists, Mr**  A series of parodies by Thackeray of the popular novelists of his day, published in *Punch* in 1847. His subjects were Disraeli, Bulwer-Lytton, G. P. R. James, Charles Leger, J. Fenimore Cooper, and Catherine Grace Gore.

**Purchas, Samuel** *c*.1575–1626.  The acknowledged successor of Richard Hakluyt was born at Thaxted in Essex and educated at St John's College, Cambridge. He was vicar of a parish on the Thames estuary for ten years and then became rector of St Martin's, Ludgate, for the remaining 12 years of his life. He assisted Hakluyt in his later years and some of the collected material was left with him. He had published work of his own before moving to a London living: *Purchas his Pilgrimage, or Relations of the World and the Religions Observed in all Ages* (1613). *Purchas his Pilgrim: Microcosmus, or the Histories of Man* (1619) was a similar work. His contribution to the literature of travel is contained in the extensive *Hakluytus Posthumous, or Purchas his Pilgrimes: Contayning a History of the World, in Sea Voyages and Lande Travells by Englishmen and Others* (1625).

While it is generally regarded as inferior to the work of the great Hakluyt, Purchas's work is very valuable and contains some fine things, notably the account by William Adams of his journey to Japan and his residence there. Purchas's book is in two parts: the first deals with the Mediterranean and the East; the second with the Northwest Passage, Russia (Muscovy), the West Indies, and Florida.

*Hakluytus posthumous* was reprinted by the Hakluyt Society in 20 volumes (1905–07).

**Puritan, The,** *or The Widow of Watling Street.*  A comedy of unknown authorship, first published in 1607 with the author given as 'W.S.' on the title page. The attribution to Shakespeare is rejected now though some detected the hand of his contemporary, John Marston. The story concerns the efforts of Captain Idle and George Pye-board to win the hands of a Puritan widow and her daughter, and ridicules the Puritans' attitude to life.

**Pusey, Edward Bouverie** 1800–82.  Pusey, one of the leaders of the **Oxford Movement**, was born at Pusey in Berkshire. He was educated at Eton College and Christ Church, Oxford; he became a fellow of Oriel College in 1823. Further studies took him to Göttingen and Berlin and he studied Hebrew and Arabic. He was ordained in 1828 and became Regius Professor of Hebrew and Canon of Christ Church. His attachment to the Movement was confirmed by his contribution of number 18 of *Tracts for the Times* in 1834; he contributed three more numbers in 1836. He became the leader of the Movement when John Henry Newman withdrew.

**Puttenham, Richard** *c*.1529–*c*.1590.  *The Arte of English Poesie* was published anonymously in

1589 and has been attributed to Richard or George Puttenham. Both were nephews of Sir Thomas Elyot. George was educated at Christ's College, Cambridge, and the Middle Temple. The editors of the edition of 1936, G. D. Willcock and A. Walker, name him as the author in the light of the available evidence. The book probably dates from the 1570s.

*The Arte of English Poesie* is interesting as a discussion and description of English poetry at a time when work of true stature still lay in the future.

**Pye, Henry James** 1745–1813. Pye was poet laureate from 1790 and his successor was Robert Southey. He published a number of poems, plays, translations from the classics, and critical essays. None of his works has been reprinted since 1822.

**Pygmalion** A romance in five acts by George Bernard Shaw, first produced in German in

Mrs Patrick Campbell as Eliza Doolittle in the first London production of *Pygmalion* at His Majesty's Theatre, 1914.

Vienna in 1913. The first English production was by Tree at His Majesty's Theatre in 1914 with Mrs Patrick Campbell, for whom the part was written, as Eliza Doolittle. The film version of 1938, which Shaw approved, had a different ending with Eliza and Higgins finally coming together. This version was made into *My Fair Lady* (1956), probably the most successful musical comedy since World War II. The comedy turns on a professor of phonetics, Henry Higgins, and his remark to Colonel Pickering that he could pass off a Cockney flower girl, Eliza Doolittle, as a duchess in a few months, by teaching her how to speak properly. Her present English, he had told her rudely, would keep her in the gutter all her life. Eliza calls on Higgins and offers him a shilling a lesson to be taught how to speak like a lady in a flower shop. She is taken by Higgins into his house for six months to be transformed. Eventually he is able to present her as a great lady, with some very funny scenes on the way. Eliza develops as her presentation does and emerges as a beautiful woman of increasing sensitivity. But to Higgins she is a successful experiment, no more. The play, as originally written, ends with Eliza asserting her identity as a human being and rejecting Higgins on every level. Other notable figures in the comedy are Mrs Higgins (the professor's mother) and Eliza's dustman father, who gets £5 from Higgins to go away and forget his scruples about his daughter living in a strange man's house.

**Pynchon, Thomas** 1937– . Pynchon was born in Glen Cove, Long Island, New York and graduated from Cornell University in 1958. He worked for a time at the Boeing Aircraft Corporation in Seattle but little else is known about his life – he avoids interviews – beyond his liking for Mexico. His first novel, *V.* (1963, Faulkner Award), is a long dark-toned fantasy – Pynchon's preferred medium for depicting American life in the latter half of the 20th century. Other novels are *The Crying of Lot 49* (1966, Rosenthal Memorial Award), *Gravity's Rainbow* (1973, National Book Award), and *Mortality and Mercy in Vienna* (1976). *Low-Lands* (1978) is a book of short stories.

**Pyrochles** In Book II of Spenser's *The Faerie Queene*, the adversary of Sir Guyon and brother of Cymochles. He is aided by Archimago and eventually killed by Prince Arthur.

**Pyrocles** In Sir Philip Sidney's *Arcadia*, one of the two royal cousins (the other is Musidorus) who finds his way to the forest of Arcadia after being shipwrecked.

# Q

**Quadroon, The** A novel by Mayne Reid, first published in 1856. It was successfully dramatized by the author.

An Englishman, Edward Rutherford, is travelling in Louisiana. On a steamboat trip the boiler explodes; Rutherford saves the beautiful Creole girl Eugenie Besançon and her quadroon slave, Aurore, from drowning. Eugenie falls in love with him but he has fallen in love with Aurore; however, Eugenie selflessly does her best to help Edward secure Aurore's freedom.

Eugenie is cheated out of her estate by Gayarre, the trustee, and the slaves are to be sold at auction. She helps Edward obtain the money to buy Aurore; but he is outbid at the auction and in desperation he kidnaps her. Edward is arrested and charged but at his trial Gayarre's embezzlement is discovered and the story ends happily for Edward and his Aurore.

**Quarles, Francis** 1592–1644. A prolific poet and prose writer of the early 17th century, Quarles was born in Essex, the son of a surveyor-general of victualling for the navy. He was educated at Christ's College, Cambridge, and Lincoln's Inn, and found favour at court; he was part of the Princess Elizabeth's suite when she travelled to Germany to marry the Elector Palatine. A staunch Royalist, he wrote pamphlets in defence of King Charles I, and like many of his kind suffered for his convictions when the Parliamentary party came to power; his property was sequestered and his manuscripts destroyed. He married in 1618 and was the father of 18 children, 9 of whom survived. At his death in 1644 his wife and children were left in poverty.

From the mass of work he left (three volumes in Grosart's edition of 1880) the most highly regarded is his *Emblems* (1635), which became the most popular book of verse of the century. His *Enchiridion* (1640–41), a book of aphorisms, was almost as popular. Quarles's verse is direct and appealing but he never achieves true greatness: his popularity in his own times is easy to understand but posterity is a sterner judge and he is little read today.

**Quarterly Review, The** A right-wing rival of *The Edinburgh Review*, *The Quarterly Review* was founded by John Murray, the second John Murray of the distinguished publishing house, in 1809. The first editor was William Gifford and its guiding principles were suggested by Sir Walter Scott, a keen supporter of the venture. The first number appeared in February 1809, and the editors who succeeded Gifford were Sir J. T. Coleridge, the poet's nephew, and J. G. Lockhart. Sir Walter Scott, George Canning, Robert Southey, Samuel Rogers, Gladstone, Lord Salisbury, and Sir John Barrow were among the more distinguished contributors. The first praise of Jane Austen (from Scott, reviewing *Emma*) appeared in *The Quarterly Review*; so did Scott's review of his own *Tales of My Landlord*, a notable piece of lighthearted writing from the great man. A reviewer whose name dimmed the lustre of a notable journal was John Wilson Croker, for his savage review of John Keats's *Endymion* in 1818.

**Queen Mab;** *A Philosophical Poem*. A poem with prose notes by Percy Bysshe Shelley, first printed and circulated (but not published) in 1813. Written when Shelley was 18, it is more notable as an expression of his beliefs than as a finished poem, though it shows more than a hint of the poet he was to become. He prefaced it with quotations from Voltaire, Lucretius, and Archimedes. The fairy queen, Mab, carries off the spirit of a maiden, Ianthe, in her celestial chariot. Ianthe is shown a vision of the world's past history and Mab tells her why the people live in such a wretched condition. Shelley's thoughts on human institutions are spoken by Queen Mab: marriage, trade, Christianity, kings, priests, and statesmen are exposed to the poet's censure. The poem carries a message of hope for a better world in the future. It was not published because Thomas Hookham, who arranged the printing at Shelley's expense, was justifiably afraid of prosecution. The poet said plainly that the Christian religion contributed much to the total of human suffering, that marriage and contemporary morals encouraged the worst sort of hypocrisy, and that 'God' was a projection of the cruelty and arrogance of man himself. The poem became a favourite with 19th-century radicals.

**Queen of Britain** In Shakespeare's *Cymbeline* she has no given name. Cymbeline's second wife, she has ambitions for her unattractive son, Cloten, to become king with Imogen as his wife. When her plans come to nothing she dies insane; her deathbed ravings reveal that she only married the king from ambition and 'abhorred' his person.

**Queen's Wake, The** A 'legendary poem' by James Hogg, first published in 1813. The term 'wake' is used, in this case, in the sense of a feast on the occasion of a church dedication, not as a vigil before burial. The queen is Mary of Scotland and the scene is Holyrood, August 1561.

Assembled are 17 bards, including David Rizzio, summoned by the Earl of Argyle to compete in song; 13 of them relate verse tales, comic, mystical, martial, and eerie. Of these two are regarded as Hogg's finest poems, 'Bonny Kilmeny' and 'The Witch of Fife'.

'The Witch of Fife' is the 8th bard's tale. A suspicious husband questions his wife about her nocturnal activities and learns that she is a witch. His censure is tempered by the realization that she and her friends can gain access to the Bishop of Carlisle's cellars, and he asks her to initiate him. She refuses but her husband spies on her and learns the essential 'word'. Using it, he sails up the chimney and finds himself transported to the bishop's cellars. Unfortunately he drinks himself insensible, is apprehended, and sentenced to be burned. He is saved when his wife flies in from Fife, puts a red cap on his head, and reminds him of the word. He flies away to freedom. The ending was suggested to Hogg by Sir Walter Scott.

'Bonny Kilmeny' is the 13th bard's tale. Kilmeny wanders in the glen, listening to the birds and picking berries. She disappears and is believed to be dead; but she returns after seven years. In her long trance she had been transported to 'a land of light' from where she could see the world, and all that happens there. She has asked to return so that she can tell of what she has seen; she is transformed and has a mysterious influence on all around her. She stays for a month and a day, and then returns once more to the glen and vanishes for ever.

**Queequeg** The Polynesian harpooner of Herman Melville's *Moby-Dick*. He terrifies Ishmael when they share a bed at the Spouter-Inn, with his idol, his tattooed face, and the shrunken human head he carries in a bag. But he is a king's son and in spite of his strangeness Ishmael and he become very close: '. . . how elastic our stiff prejudices grow when once love comes to bend them.'

**Quentin Durward** A novel of 15th-century France by Sir Walter Scott, first published in 1823.

King Louis XI of France matches his considerable wits against Charles the Bold, Duke of Burgundy, whose devouring ambitions are a continual threat to crown and country. Louis enlists the aid of William de la Marck, the Wild Boar of the Ardennes, to incite a revolt against the duke in Liège. Quentin Durward, a young Scot in the king's guard, is sent to conduct the Burgundian heiress, Isabelle de Croye, to the protection of the Bishop of Liège to save her from marriage to Count Campo-Basso, an Italian in the service of

the duke who wants to be sure that Isabelle's wealth stays within his dukedom. The two stories blend well: de la Marck proves an unwise choice as an ally and he is eventually killed by Quentin. Isabelle's and Quentin's journey is beset by dangers – many of them provoked by the duke but complicated by de la Marck's villainous nature; the murder of the Bishop of Liège threatens not only Isabelle's safety but also the king's careful plans for controlling the duke's ambitions. The story ends happily: King Louis outwits the duke and Quentin Durward wins the hand of Isabelle.

**Quickly, Mistress** The hostess of the Boar's Head tavern in Eastcheap in Shakespeare's *Henry IV* and *Henry V*. She is a frequent victim of Falstaff's dishonesty in *Henry IV* but plainly nurses a soft spot for him. In *Henry V* she has married Pistol and it falls to her to describe so movingly how Falstaff dies.

In *The Merry Wives of Windsor* Shakespeare introduces her as Dr Caius' housekeeper, who plays go-between for Mistress Ford and Mistress Page in their tricks on Falstaff. She is the same sort of character as she is in the histories but obviously, in their first scene, she and Falstaff are strangers to each other. Her death 'i' the 'spital of a malady of France' is mentioned by Pistol in Act V of *Henry V*.

**Quiet American, The** See **Greene, (Henry) Graham**.

**Quiller-Couch, Sir Arthur** 1863–1944. Sometimes known by his pen-name, 'Q', Quiller-Couch was born in Bodmin and completed his education at Trinity College, Oxford. He became the first King Edward VII Professor of English Literature at Cambridge in 1912.

His first published work, as Q, was for the *Oxford Magazine*. Later he became a journalist, wrote novels and short stories, and in 1892 went to live in Fowey where he stayed for 20 years, living as a freelance writer and undertaking the celebrated anthologies for the Oxford University Press: *English Verse* (1900), *Ballads* (1910), and *Victorian Verse* (1912); *English Prose* came in 1925. *On the Art of Writing* (1916) and *On the Art of Reading* (1920) contained his lectures and enjoyed great popularity for a number of years.

Quiller-Couch used his Cornish background for his fiction: *Dead Man's Rock* (1887), *Troy Town* – the town is Fowey – (1888), *The Splendid Spur* (1889), and *The Ship of Stars* (1899), among others. He was knighted for political services (he had been much involved with the Liberal *Leader*) in 1910.

**Quilp, Daniel** The evil dwarf of Dickens's *The Old Curiosity Shop*. He is a moneylender and a smuggler and is determined on revenge when Nell's grandfather cannot repay the money he has borrowed from him. He bullies his wife and has designs on Nell. At the end of the story, he drowns in the Thames while trying to evade arrest.

# R

**Radcliffe, Ann** 1764–1823. Born in London, Ann Ward married William Radcliffe, proprietor and editor of *The English Chronicle*, in 1787. Her uncle, Thomas Bentley, was partner to Josiah Wedgwood, and Mrs Radcliffe grew up in an artistic and cultured society. Her response to dramatic landscape in fashionable painting is reflected in her novels and became more romantic as her career progressed. Her first novel, *The Castles of Athlin and Dunbayne: a Highland story* (1789), was followed by *A Sicilian Romance* (1790), *The Romance of the Forest* (1791), **The Mysteries of Udolpho** (1794), *The Italian* (1797), and *Gaston de Blondeville* (published posthumously, 1826). She wrote some poetry that appeared in her novels and was later collected and published (1834); *A Journey through Holland and the Western Frontier of Germany* (1795) is made notable by her talent for visual description.

Ann Radcliffe's novels were fashionable gothic mysteries of the kind Jane Austen satirized so effectively in *Northanger Abbey*. But she was a better writer than her contemporaries: both Scott and Byron learned something from her skilful evocation of atmosphere. Her novels are little read now and her endings are disappointing; in essentials, Ann Radcliffe was a late-18th-century writer of romantic thrillers and such works are rarely readable out of their time. *The Mysteries of Udolpho* has, however, outlived her other novels, and is usually found in popular editions of English classics.

**Radigund** The queen of the Amazons in Book V of Spenser's *The Faerie Queene*. She captures and unmans Artegall until he is rescued by Britomart.

**Rainbow, The** A novel by D. H. Lawrence, first published in 1915.

The novel begins in 1840, introducing the Brangwen family of Marsh Farm on the Nottinghamshire–Derbyshire border. Tom Brangwen takes over the farm when his father dies; he is the younger son but his brother Alfred has become a lace designer in Nottingham. Tom marries Lydia, a widowed Polish exile with a daughter named Anna. He has two sons by Lydia, Tom and Fred, and after that his life with Lydia turns sour; he becomes fonder of Anna. Anna falls in love with Alfred Brangwen's son, Will. Tom is distressed but he reconciles himself to the marriage and leases a cottage for the young couple.

The honeymoon is an extravagant success but the powerful physical attraction Anna and Will hold for each other is destructive, particularly for a character like Will, who feels his identity threatened by his surrender to it. He tries to assert himself as a husband and head of his house; he is a church-goer and choirmaster; he bores Anna and then alienates her. She retaliates as best she can within the framework of their marriage but the powerful sexual attraction persists, and Anna bears five daughters and a son. The firstborn, Ursula, becomes attached to her father; her sister Gudrun, who goes to the same grammar school, lives in the shadow of her strong and free-willed sister.

Ursula falls in love with Anton Skrebensky, a Polish exile whose family are related to Lydia Brangwen's. Anton is a glamorous figure to Ursula and seems to represent a wider and more interesting world; but he answers to many conventional notions nonetheless. While he is serving in the Boer War Ursula is tormented by awakened sexuality and enters a lesbian relationship with her class mistress. After matriculating Ursula spends two wretched years as a teacher, then she goes to college to study for a degree. Anton returns; Ursula abandons herself to him; her studies go by the board and she fails to get her degree. Anton asks her to marry him but Ursula has learned that a relationship cannot exist only on sexual attraction and she has exhausted that. She rejects Anton, who has to leave for service in India. Then she believes that she is pregnant and she writes to him, changing her decision. He replies, telling her that he has married someone else, and she discovers her pregnancy to be a false alarm. The novel's title refers to the rainbow seen by Ursula at the end of the book, arching over the ugly collieries and giving hope of better things.

See also **Women in Love**.

**Ralegh** (*or* **Raleigh**), **Sir Walter** *c.*1552–1618. The first spelling given is that used by the subject after 1584. He had used various spellings before that, and the correct pronunciation is indicated in the 'Rauley' he used in his youth.

Ralegh was born at Hayes Barton in Devonshire and educated at Oriel College, Oxford, after a brief period as a soldier with the

Huguenots in France. His name appears in the register of the Middle Temple in 1575 but he is not known to have practised law. Some verses of his preface Gascoigne's *The Steel Glas* (1576) and it is assumed that he moved in literary circles. Ralegh and his brother Carey planned to outfit a fleet of ships with their cousin, Sir Humphrey Gilbert, for a voyage of discovery, but their plans came to nothing and in 1580 Ralegh was busy in Ireland, taking part in what he and other Elizabethans believed to be the settlement of a colony.

When he returned to England in 1581 Ralegh attended court and immediately came to the attention of the queen. His obvious ability and personal charm made him a favourite of Elizabeth's; he was given the wine trade monopoly in 1583 and knighted in 1584; he was made warden of the West Country tin mines in 1585 and awarded extensive estates in Ireland; in 1587 he became Captain of the Guard, an office that involved constant attendance on the queen.

Ralegh's proud bearing, his learning, and his handsome presence made him as many enemies at court as it made him friends in other walks of life and he never held a position of power. The two expeditions that he organized for the settlement of Virginia, in 1584 and 1587, both ended in disaster. By 1589 there was a new favourite at court, the Earl of Essex, and Ralegh retired to his estates in Ireland, where he was the neighbour, and soon the close friend of Edmund Spenser, whose work on *The Faerie Queene* he did much to encourage.

In 1590 Essex incurred the queen's displeasure by his marriage to Frances Sidney and Ralegh returned to court. He was given an estate at Sherborne in 1592 and in the same year set out on a privateering expedition. But Elizabeth, meanwhile, learned that he had married Bess Throckmorton, one of her maids of honour, without her permission. Ralegh was recalled and shut up in the Tower (together with his wife) by the queen, but at the end of the year his expedition returned with rich booty and he was released to supervise the division of the spoils. However, he was not re-admitted to court.

Ralegh sat in parliament and mingled with the writers and scholars of a group dubbed the 'school of night' because their advanced opinions were looked on with suspicion. Among them were Thomas Harriot, Christopher Marlowe, and George Chapman. He is believed to have suggested the gatherings at the Mermaid Tavern in Bread Street, where Ben Jonson, Shakespeare, Beaumont and Fletcher, and John Donne met and talked on Fridays. Ben Jonson became tutor to Ralegh's son.

Sir Walter Ralegh and Arrowmaia, King of Guyana, during Ralegh's second expedition to the Orinoco, 1616. From Theodor de Bry's *Americas*, 1590–1623.

In 1595 Ralegh and Laurence Keymis embarked on an expedition to find El Dorado. They never found it, of course, but they sailed 480 kilometres (300 miles) up the Orinoco River into the interior of Guyana and they did bring home some gold. The following year Ralegh commanded a squadron in the raid on Cadiz and in 1597, during the expedition against the Azores, captured Fayal without waiting for Essex to join him. That a violent quarrel ensued was well known and Ralegh's enemies made the most of it, especially when, as Captain of the Guard, he was obliged to oversee the execution of Essex in the Tower in 1601.

Two years later, with the accession of James I, Ralegh's fortunes took a downward turn from which they never recovered. James's correspondent at the Tudor court had been Lord Henry Howard, who hated Ralegh and attributed every villainy to him. The new monarch kept Robert Cecil, described by Godfrey Davies as a supreme mediocrity, as his chief minister and dismissed Ralegh from his post as Captain of the Guard, at the same time depriving him of his trade monopoly. Later Ralegh was wrongfully accused of complicity in Cobham's plot to dethrone James in favour of Arabella Stuart. This was a charge of treason; Ralegh was convicted and condemned to death but he was reprieved and confined to the Tower – an imprisonment lasting 13 years.

In 1611 Sir Thomas Roe's expedition to South America returned with the intelligence that the Spaniards were maintaining a base in the area from where Ralegh had brought gold-bearing ore in 1595. Ralegh, from the Tower, had petitioned for his release with the claim – based chiefly on hope – that he and Laurence Keymis could bring gold to England. King James was fearful of war with Spain but he was very greedy for gold. Ralegh was released from the Tower in 1616; in the following year, with the warning that in no circumstances must he infringe Spanish sovereignty, he returned to Guyana with Keymis. But there was no gold and Keymis, after wandering around in the jungles of the Orinoco (Ralegh was at the coast, laid low with fever) made camp a few miles from the Spanish base at San Thomé – convinced that where the Spaniards were there must be gold. Hostilities broke out; the English, led by Ralegh's son, took the base from the Spaniards. Young Ralegh was killed in the action. Keymis committed suicide after bringing the news of the engagement to Ralegh, who returned to England with the certainty of death hanging over him. King James, at the prompting of the Spanish ambassador, set the process in motion and on 28 October 1618 the original sentence of 1603 was invoked. The last of the great Elizabethans was beheaded on the following morning outside Westminster Hall.

It is as a great Elizabethan, a representative of a remarkable period in English history and English literature, that Ralegh merits so much attention. He was an arrogant, rash, overproud adventurer in a world in which such men could prosper. But they required much more than personality and good looks – Elizabeth's powerful intelligence would demand much more. And while Ralegh's pride made him foolish he was also enterprising, courageous, and immensely cultured; his friendship for and patronage of the poets and intellectuals of his time is famous. He was, in fact, very much one of them, with an enquiring mind and uncommon literary ability.

Few of Ralegh's poems were published during his lifetime and certain identification is difficult. Less than 50 are acknowledged as being his, and these include the verses that prefaced Gascoigne's *The Steele Glas*, the fragment of a poem, *Cynthia*, addressed to Elizabeth, and the introductory sonnet he wrote for Spenser's *The Faerie Queene*. Their quality ensures their survival; 'The Nymph's Reply to the Shepherd' (his answer to Marlowe's 'The Passionate Shepherd'), 'The Passionate Man's Pilgrimage', 'The Lie', and the famous epitaph beginning 'Even such is Time, which takes in trust' are essential inclusions in any anthology.

Ralegh's first published prose did not bear his name; it was a tract entitled *A Report of the Fight about the Iles of the Acores* in 1591, which told of his kinsman, Grenville, and the *Revenge*. Richard Hakluyt reprinted the piece in his *Voyages, Vol II* and named the author. After his first voyage to Guyana Ralegh's enemies hoped to discredit him by loudly expressing doubt that he had been to Guyana at all. Ralegh wrote his account of the expedition, *The Discoverie of the Large, Rich and Beautiful Empyre of Guiana*, and published it in 1596. It proved very popular, an adventure story excellently told; three editions were printed in that year and it was translated into German, Dutch, and Latin.

At the age of 50 or thereabouts, a prisoner in the Tower, Ralegh began to write *A History of the World*, which was intended to be a book for everyone, not merely scholars. In 1614 he published the first part, a large folio volume that began with the creation and reached the fall of Macedon and the growing power of Rome. It is famous for its clear strong English prose and the scrupulous acknowledgment of the authors he studied. No less than 13 editions appeared in the 17th century.

There are other pieces; ten have been attributed to Ralegh with certainty, another ten are believed to be his, and five are known of but are not extant. Ralegh's poems were collected by A. M. C. Latham in 1951, but the last complete edition of his *Works* is the one of 1829, reprinted in New York in 1965, by W. Oldys and T. Birch.

**Raleigh, Walter Alexander** 1861–1922. Walter Raleigh was born in London and enjoyed a varied academic career after completing his education at the universities of Edinburgh and Cambridge. He was Professor of English at Aligarh in India (1885), at the University of Liverpool (1890), and at the University of Glasgow; he became Professor of English Literature at Oxford University in 1904. After World War I Raleigh was chosen to write the official history of the RAF, but he died after completing the first volume (1922). A respected critic in his day, he was the author of, among other books, *The English Novel: From the Earliest Times to the Appearance of Waverley* (1891), *Robert Louis Stevenson* (1895), *Milton* (1900), *Wordsworth* (1903), *Shakespeare* (for the English Men of Letters series, 1907), and *Six Essays on Johnson* (1910). Raleigh was knighted in 1911.

**Ralph of Diceto** See **Diceto, Ralph de.**

*Ralph Roister Doister* A comedy by Nicholas Udall. There are conflicting views about the date of its composition. One theory is that it belongs to Udall's tenure as headmaster of Eton, as a variation on the Latin play that was traditionally performed at Eton every year. Udall's knowledge of Plautus and Terence was comprehensive and their influence on this play is marked. That would place it before 1541, when Udall was dismissed from Eton. Another theory, supported by a reference from another writer, Thomas Wilson, in 1554, suggests a date that fits better with the time when Udall was tutor in the Bishop of Winchester's household. A third theory suggests that it was written while Udall was headmaster of Westminster School but there is really no support for it. The only known printed copy of the play (*c*.1566) contains no title page and thus no information or dates.

The comedy is written in rhyming doggerel and the plot is of the simplest. The action takes place in a street, before the house of Christian Custance, a widow betrothed to the absent merchant Gawyn Goodluck. Matthew Merrygreek, a hanger-on of Ralph Roister Doister's, encourages Ralph to woo Custance, who is a woman of means. Ralph is a vain and stupid braggart and ready to believe that she will yield to him. His suit meets with no success whatever and he stupidly tries to take her by storm. But the spirited Custance and her loyal household put Ralph and his men to rout. Gawyn returns to his Custance soon after and the play ends happily. A notable feature of the play is the presence of homely English maidservants with names like Meg Mumblecrust and Tib Talkapace, who deliver pithy comments on the behaviour of the principals.

***Ram-Alley*** or *Merrie Trickes*. A comedy first produced about 1609 and set in a disreputable area of the City of London. Ram Alley was where Mitre Court now stands in Fleet Street. The author was Lording Barry, of whom nothing is known beyond the fact of his authorship of this single play. Its coarseness had a strong popular appeal and it was published in 1611.

***Rambler, The*** A periodical published twice weekly by Edward Cave and written by Samuel Johnson. The total of 208 numbers ran from 20 March 1750 to 14 March 1752 and contained essays on all subjects with the object of instructing readers; Johnson also worked toward the refinement of the English language. He wrote all but five numbers: the others were contributed by Samuel Richardson, Elizabeth Carter (two numbers), Hester Chapone, and Catherine Talbot. After a modest beginning *The Rambler* became a great success. It was published anonymously but Samuel Richardson recognized the style (he was a great admirer of Johnson) and the author's identity was soon known all over London. In its collected form it reached ten editions during Johnson's lifetime. A 19th-century periodical directed by Lord Acton and J. H. Newman was also called *The Rambler*, before the name was changed to *The Home and Foreign Review*.

**Ramsay, Allan** 1686–1758. Ramsay was born at Leadhills, Dumfriesshire. He went to Edinburgh as a wigmaker's apprentice and became a journeyman wigmaker. His interest lay in literature, however, and he was to do more than anyone to cure Scottish poetry of the depression into which it had been cast by the ascendancy of the Kirk.

Ramsay founded the Easy Club in 1712, for the exchange of ideas and the promotion of conversation, and published occasional poems in periodicals and broadsheets from 1713. He became a bookseller in 1718, began to publish collections of his poems from 1721, and in 1724 began the publication of *The Tea Table Miscellany*, which continued until 1737. The *Miscellany* collected the texts of Scots songs and ballads that had survived the depression and the collection was to provide Burns and other later Scottish writers with the impetus for their work.

Allan Ramsay, c.1739. Self-portrait. National Portrait Gallery, London.

It has been said, however, that Ramsay indulged in 'improvements' that deprived succeeding collectors of the original texts.

In 1724 Ramsay published *The Ever Green, being a Collection of Scots Poems, wrote by the Ingenious before 1600*. The volume presented the work of such poets as Robert Henryson and William Dunbar from the Bannatyne Manuscript and provided further stimulus to the revival of Scots secular poetry. Ramsay also published a broadside edition of *Christis Kirk on the Grene* (attributed to James I of Scotland) in 1718 but ill-advisedly added two cantos of his own. His *Collection of Scots Proverbs* (1736) has also been adversely criticized for his readiness to change the originally coarse and vital expressions to something more 'acceptable'. Nevertheless, Ramsay's services to the intellectual revival of Scotland, centred in Edinburgh, were considerable. His own best work is to be found in his *Poems* (1728). *The Gentle Shepherd* (1725), a pastoral drama, was also staged as a ballad opera with Scots airs.

Ramsay founded the first circulating library in Great Britain in 1728 and succeeded in opening a playhouse in Carruber's Close in Edinburgh in 1736 – though this was closed by Walpole's Licensing Act of the following year.

The complete *Works* of Allan Ramsay were published by The Scottish Text Society in four volumes (1951–61) and edited by B. Martin, J. W. Oliver, A. M. Kinghorn, and A. Law.

**Randolph, Thomas** 1605–35. A minor Caroline playwright and poet, Randolph was born at Daventry in Northamptonshire. He was educated at Westminster School and at Trinity College, Cambridge, where he became known as an accomplished versifier in English and Latin. Randolph became a fellow of Trinity College in 1629 and wrote two plays that were performed at Cambridge: *The Conceited Pedlar* and *Aristippus, or the Joviall Philosopher* (both 1631). In March of 1632 King Charles I visited Cambridge and attended a performance of Randolph's *The Jealous Lovers* by the men of Trinity. He went to London in the same year and became a disciple of Ben Jonson; he wrote **The Muses' Looking-Glass**, his best work, in that year also. Other works include a pastoral, *Amyntas* (published 1638), and an adaptation from Aristophanes called *Hey for Honesty* (published 1651). Randolph died of smallpox at the age of 29. His works were collected by William Hazlitt and published in 1875.

**Ransom, John Crowe** 1888–1974. A native of Tennessee, Ransom was born in Pulaski and educated at Vanderbilt University in Nashville, Tennessee, and, as a Rhodes Scholar, at Oxford. In 1914 he became Professor of English at Vanderbilt where he taught until 1937; his first poems were published during this period. After Vanderbilt Ransom taught at Kenyon College, Ohio, where he founded the *Kenyon Review*, which became one of the most influential academic reviews in America. Ransom was one of the group of Southern conservative writers who stood for the traditional agrarian values when industrialism was widely believed to be the answer to the South's problems (among others were Allen Tate, Donald Davidson, Laura Riding, and Robert Penn Warren). They became known as the 'Fugitives' from their contributions to the poetry magazine *Fugitive*, published in Nashville from April 1922 to December 1925. Ransom was later associated with the 'New Criticism', which insisted on a literary work being judged as a complete experience in itself; no consideration of circumstance on the part of the creator was admissible in a review of it.

Ransom's first book of verse was *Poems about God* (1919). *Chills and Fever* (1924) and *Two Gentlemen in Bonds* (1927) followed and most of his poetry was written by then. *Selected Poems* (1945) is Ransom's own selection of his work. His critical writings are contained in *God Without Thunder* (1930), *The World's Body* (1938), and *The New Criticism* (1941). Ransom edited *I'll Take my Stand: The South and the Agrarian Tradition* (1930), a statement by 12 of the Southern writers of the Fugitive Movement.

**Rape of Lucrece, The** A poem by William Shakespeare, his second published work and like *Venus and Adonis* dedicated to Henry Wriothesley, Earl of Southampton. The matter of the poem is the passion of Sextus Tarquinius, son of the King of Rome, for Lucrece, the virtuous wife of Collatinus, and how he satisfies that passion by violence. Lucrece tells her father Lucretius and her husband of the outrage and then kills herself. The rape of Lucrece leads to the expulsion of the Tarquin kings from Rome. The poem is written in seven-line stanzas and is introduced by an 'Argument'. In spite of over-amplification of states of mind the poem has considerable tragic force.

**Rape of the Lock, The** A poem by Alexander Pope, first published in two cantos in Barnaby Lintot's *Miscellany* in 1712. The poet enlarged it to five cantos and published the new version in 1714. The subject was suggested to Pope by John Caryll; Lord Petre, a 20-year-old Catholic peer, admired Arabella Fermor and one day snipped off a lock of her hair. The families were estranged

An engraving by M. van der Gucht for the second edition of *The Rape of the Lock*, 1714. Belinda, shorn of a lock of hair by her admirer, is comforted by her friends.

and Caryll suggested that a poetic pleasantry from Pope, who knew them, would effect a reconciliation. In the event neither Miss Fermor nor Lord Petre seems to have been particularly pleased by the expanded form of the poem; but the public was and Pope's reputation was established. He found the idea of a mock-heroic poem in the French *Le Lutrin* (1674–83) by Nicholas Boileau-Despreaux. Arabella Fermor is represented by the character of Belinda, who is depicted at her toilet, at cards, and sipping coffee when her admirer cuts off a lock of hair. Belinda's wrath is described along with her demands that the lock be restored. Eventually it is wafted into the heavens to become a new star.

Miss Fermor agreed to the publication of the poem in its original form. Pope expanded it against the advice of Joseph Addison, who admired the original very much, and thereby offended Miss Fermor, who had had quite enough exposure of her affairs for the amusement of the public.

***Rasselas*** A philosophical romance by Samuel Johnson, first published under the title *The Prince of Abissinia. A Tale* in 1759. The 1787 edition carried the title *The History of Rasselas, Prince of Abissinia. A Tale*. Johnson had translated Father Jerome Lobo's *A Voyage to Abissinia* in 1735 and thus had a ready-made exotic background (the fashion in the 18th century – Voltaire's *Zadig* is another example) for a moral tale. He had been considering such a work during his mother's last illness; when she died he had to find some means of settling her debts and providing for a decent funeral. He concluded an agreement with the printer William Strahan and wrote *Rasselas*, he told Joshua Reynolds, in the evenings of *one week*. It was an immediate success. An odd coincidence was the almost simultaneous publication of Voltaire's similar, but ultimately more celebrated, *Candide*; but the difference in tone between the two books is striking.

Rasselas, son of the Emperor of Abissinia, is weary of the comforts and pleasures of existence in his 'happy valley'. With his sister Nekayah and the aged philosopher Imlac, he escapes from it and goes to Egypt, where they study other men in various conditions of life. There is hardly any incident to support the observations, which are made with Johnson's usual wisdom, humour, and humanity. Rasselas is convinced that earthly happiness can be found, somewhere; but he does not find it. The monks who follow St Antony have one certainty – hardship, which they endure without complaint; the hermit has another – solitary life is miserable and there is no certainty that it will be devout. The prosperous man lives in fear of the Bashaw, the Sultan's minister; the Bashaw lives in fear of the Sultan; the Sultan is tortured by suspicion of everyone.

Every example shows the three that they must guard against a romantic outlook, too much reverie, and too much imagination; not to trust too much in philosophical speculation and scientific discovery – there is no easy way to contentment. They return, sadder but certainly wiser, to their valley in Abissinia.

***Rattlin the Reefer*** A novel by Edward Howard, first published in 1836. Howard was a shipmate of Captain Marryat and the story is in the same vein as Marryat's celebrated novels of the sea but without the same warmth and humour. However, Marryat thought enough of his friend's work to prepare it for publication and the titlepage carried the statement 'Edited by the author of *Peter Simple*.' This led many people to believe that the author was Marryat himself.

**Rauf Coilyear, The Taill of** A 15th-century Scottish poem of unknown authorship. No manuscript exists but the poem is known from a copy printed at St Andrews in 1572, and the probable date is deduced from mentions by Gavin Douglas and William Dunbar. It is a contribution to the cycle of poems derived from the legends of Charlemagne, and while the setting is France, the flavour is Scottish.

Charlemagne is separated from his suite during a storm. Rauf (Ralph), a charcoal-burner, finds him in the storm and offers him a night's lodging. Rauf is an independent and plainspoken man who has no idea of the identity of his guest. Charlemagne is treated hospitably but with a freedom and equality characteristic of his host. At one point Rauf knocks him flat with a clout under the ear when Charlemagne argues with him over precedence. Rauf, disconcerted when he later discovers who it is that spent the night in his house, is knighted by his king and appointed a marshal of France. Other characters are Roland and Rauf's wife Gyliane.

A modern version of the poem, *Ralph the Collier*, was made by B. J. Whiting (New York, 1942).

**Ravenshoe** A novel by Henry Kingsley, first published in 1861. Part of the book is set in the Crimean War, in which Charles Ravenshoe, the son of a wealthy Catholic family, is seeking obscurity after a series of blows connected with the mystery of his birth. The mysteries are complicated by the inexplicable neglect of a Jesuit confessor to tell the whole truth, and by the remarkable villainy of Charles's supposed friend Lord Welter – a sort of quadruple-dyed Steerforth. Charles Ravenshoe survives Balaclava and returns to England a broken man. However, he is succoured by friends, the mystery of his birth is cleared up, and all ends well for him.

**Reade, Charles** 1814–84. The son of a well-to-do Oxfordshire family, Charles Reade was educated at Magdalen College, Oxford, and at Lincoln's Inn. He was called to the Bar but never practised, spending much of his time trying to write for the stage. His first attempts at comedy met with little success – indeed, he was 38 before he achieved real celebrity with *Masks and Faces* (1852), on which he collaborated with Tom Taylor. On the advice of his friend, Laura Seymour, he turned this story of David Garrick and Peg Woffington into a novel, (**Peg Woffington**, 1853), and he was to succeed much better with his fiction, as it turned out, than with his plays. However, it should not be forgotten that, in contemporary terms, he achieved considerable fame

with *The Courier of Lyons* (1854), which was a favourite vehicle for Henry Irving and Sir John Martin-Harvey as *The Lyons Mail*. Less successful was his dramatization of Tennyson's *Dora*, but *Drink*, his adaptation of Zola's *L'Assommoir*, with Charles Warner, was a great success in 1867.

Reade is best known as a novelist. He was an excellent storyteller and used the novel to attack many of the abuses of his day, compiling documentary evidence in large ledgers which he indexed with painstaking care. Thus he could quote precedents for all the horrors that appear in his books, when he describes prison life, lunatic asylums, marine insurance malpractice, or trade-union victimization. Inevitably, his crusading novels are little read nowadays, nor for that matter is the bulk of his work well known. But he made a definite place for himself with, surprisingly, a historical novel of the time just before the Reformation: **The Cloister and the Hearth** (1861) stands high among English fiction classics. His most notable novels in his more familiar vein are **It is Never too Late to Mend** (1856), **Hard Cash** (1863), **Griffith Gaunt** (1866), and **A Terrible Temptation** (1871).

Other novels by Charles Reade are *Christie Johnstone* (1853), *The Course of True Love* (1857), *The Autobiography of a Thief* (1858), *Jack of all Trades* (1858), *Love me Little, Love me Long* (1859), *Foul Play* (with Dion Boucicault, 1869), *Put Yourself in his Place* (1870), *A Hero and a Martyr* (1874), and *The Wandering Heir* (1872).

**Reade, William Winwood** 1838–75. The explorer William Winwood Reade was a nephew of Charles Reade, the novelist and playwright. He published accounts of his expeditions in West and South-West Africa in *Savage Africa* (1863) and *The African Sketch-Book* (1873). *The Story of the Ashantee Campaign* (1874) derives from his experiences during the Ashanti War as correspondent for *The Times*. Reade also wrote the once-popular *The Martyrdom of Man* (1872), a sketch of history which expressed his criticism of accepted religious beliefs.

**Rebecca** The daughter of Isaac of York in Scott's *Ivanhoe*. One of the author's most successful heroines, beautiful and resolute, she completely overshadows the gentle Rowena, whom Ivanhoe eventually marries.

**Recessional** See **Kipling, Rudyard**.

**Recollections of the Lake Poets** Thomas De Quincey's 'Lake Reminiscences', as they were first called, were written for *Tait's Magazine*, in five separate articles (1839–40). De Quincey recalls, from the years he spent at Grasmere

(1809–19), the characters and work of Coleridge, Wordsworth, and Southey. In spite of many inaccuracies the book is valued for its criticism and as a contemporary account. The reminiscences, in collected form, were edited by Edward Sackville-West as *Recollections of the Lake Poets* (1948), by J. E. Jordan as *Reminiscences of the Lake Poets* (Everyman's Library, 1961), and by David Wright (Penguin English Library, 1970).

**Recruiting Officer, The**  A comedy by George Farquhar, first produced in April 1706, and published in the same year. Farquhar had been commissioned as a recruiting officer himself, to raise a company for the War of the Spanish Succession. He was active in Lichfield and Shrewsbury, and sets his comedy in a country town instead of in the then almost compulsory atmosphere of fashionable London. The play was a great success when revived by the National Theatre of London in 1964.

The story is very slight; it is Farquhar's genius for invoking laughter that makes the play so successful. In a country town the recruiting officer, Captain Plume, secures recruits by making love to the women: their swains give up and, disillusioned, join the army. Plume's sergeant, Kite, is equally successful in his pose as an astrologer. Justice Ballance's daughter Sylvia is in love with Plume but has promised her father not to marry without his consent. She disguises herself as a man and is arrested for misbehaviour. Justice Ballance hands the 'young man' over to Plume for the army.

Another character is a rival recruiting officer, Captain Brazen, who has an eye for the rich Melinda. He boasts of valorous deeds in battles the world over – but instead of a rich wife he gets her maid. Sylvia's identity is revealed to Plume at the appropriate moment.

**Red Badge of Courage, The:** *An Episode of the American Civil War*.  A novel by Stephen Crane, first published in 1895.

The 'red badge' of the title is a wound – the mark of the soldier who has fought. In the novel an uneducated farm boy (Henry Fleming, though his name is not given to the reader until the story is half-told) is a soldier in the Union (northern) army. He is anxious to show himself as a patriot and a fine soldier and, with his comrades, tends to bluster, something that comes easily to untried soldiers. Comes the day of battle and he is thrust into a reality he could never have imagined. A fellow soldier strikes him accidentally with the butt of his gun: he sees his friend Jim die. Overcome by fear he runs from the field and hides in the forest. He returns to the lines with the wounded, wearing his red badge – ironically the blow from the gun butt has drawn blood. In the following day's battle he is simply part of the machine that fights and, in a charge, automatically picks up the regiment's colours when they fall from another's hands. He is, for the moment, a hero. He is also without illusions about war and heroism.

The setting of the novel is the Battle of Chancellorsville in May 1863, in Virginia, where Stonewall Jackson was killed – accidentally, by a shot from one of his own men. Stephen Crane had no experience of war when he wrote the book and he drew its background from his own reading. Ambrose Bierce had written some fine short stories from direct experience but Stephen Crane was the first American novelist to use the Civil War to examine the mind of a man in the experience of battle. (The Civil War was also the first war in history reported directly by the use of photographs as well as words.) The mind of Henry Fleming is vividly conveyed, the scenes of battle totally convincing; both achievements were essential to the success of this fine short novel and the author's artistry proved equal to them.

**Red Book of Hergest, The**  See **Mabinogion, The**.

**Redburn:** *His First Voyage*.  A novel by Herman Melville, first published in 1849. In this novel Melville drew upon his experiences during his first trip as an apprentice seaman in 1837.

The son of an impoverished New York family, Wellingborough Redburn goes to sea. As a ship's boy on the *Highlander* he encounters a sort of equivocal kindness from Captain Riga; but when the ship sails the captain withdraws to his cabin, leaving the command to his mate. The crew treat Redburn with contempt and he endures a gruelling six-week voyage to Liverpool, isolated and experiencing little kindness from anyone. When the ship reaches Liverpool he explores the city and sees the appalling conditions of the poor (beggars, unknown in New York, abounded in Liverpool), and the iron barriers of class. However, he encounters a spendthrift young aristocrat, Harry Bolton, who takes a liking to him and takes him to London. Harry's riotous behaviour and excesses shock Redburn – and lead to Harry being obliged to take a berth on the *Highlander* too. The return voyage, with cholera on board, a shortage of food, and the inescapable presence of the evil Jackson, a degenerate veteran seaman, is even worse than the eastward crossing and both Redburn and Harry are cheated by Captain Riga at the end of the voyage.

Melville did not regard Redburn as one of his better books but as a sea story it stands very high. John Masefield, Robert Frost, and Van Wyck Brooks held it in high esteem and it is notable how effortlessly the ship becomes, on Redburn's first sight of her, as vivid as a principal character.

**Red Cross Knight** In Spenser's *The Faerie Queene*, Book I, the knight of holiness and St George of England. He represents the Anglican Church and is parted from Una (true belief) by the villainy of Archimago (hypocrisy). Duessa (the Roman Church) leads him to the House of Pride, where he drinks from enchanted waters, loses his strength, and becomes the prisoner of Orgoglio (pride). Prince Arthur rescues him and kills Orgoglio, and Una takes her knight to be healed in the House of Holiness.

*Redgauntlet* With this novel, published in the same year as the disastrous *St Ronan's Well* (1824), Sir Walter Scott returned to a historical setting – and to his best form. The background of the story is the supposed return of the Young Pretender, after the defeat of '45, to make one more attempt on the throne.

Herries of Birrenswork (Sir Edward Redgauntlet) is a fanatical Jacobite and in the plans for his cause he kidnaps his nephew Darsie Latimer. Darsie is Sir Arthur Darsie Redgauntlet, the head of the house, and Sir Edward hopes to force the family to support his design. Darsie's friend, Alan Fairford, sets out to rescue him, and the adventures of the two, against the ignominious failure of Sir Edward's hopes, form the substance of the novel. In the end Sir Edward is forced to flee abroad (where he becomes a prior) and Prince Charles Edward's hopes are at an end.

Scott tells his story in the form of letters and the novel succeeds on every level. A famous feature of the book is 'Wandering Willie's tale', a classic ghost story, and the characters – Nanty Ewart, Wandering Willie, Peter Peebles, and the rest – are beautifully drawn.

*Redskins, The; or, Indian and Injin.* A novel by James Fenimore Cooper, first published in 1846. It was the third novel in the trilogy called the *Littlepage Manuscripts*.

The period is the 1840s and much of the land in New York State is owned by absentee landlords who simply draw unceasing revenue from the rents and produce in the manner of European aristocrats. This provokes a popular rising (the Anti-Rent War) and bands of angry farmers, disguised as 'Injins', raid the homes of wealthy families. Hugh Littlepage and his uncle Roger, disguised as German pedlars, visit their estate at Ravensnest to investigate the activities of the Injins. They are recognized by Susquesus, the old Onondaga scout, and the Black servant, Jaap, and take the two men into their confidence.

Susquesus is awaiting the arrival of a group of western Indians who are coming for a tribal conference. They arrive and then a band of anti-renters dressed up as Injins arrives at Ravensnest. The real leader is Seneca Newcome, a lawyer, who had hoped to fix a marriage for his daughter with Hugh Littlepage. But Hugh is in love with Mary Warren, the rector's daughter, and has rejected Newcome's proposal. Hugh and Mary, with Susquesus and his Indians, frustrate Newcome's design, which is to encourage the anti-renters to set fire to the estate. The forces of law arrive in time, and when order is restored Hugh marries Mary Warren.

Cooper's narrative contrasts the natural dignity of Susquesus and the Indians with the rabble of 'Injins'. The agrarian unrest called the Anti-Rent War lasted from 1839 to 1846. Eventually the old laws of land tenure, which the Dutch and the English had brought with them from Europe, were completely revised.

**Reed, Talbot Baines** 1852–93. The author of a number of school stories for boys, which emphasized the bright side of public-school life and lent a spurious glamour to the idiotic shibboleths and traditions of some public schools. They were immensely popular with boys in the same way as the magazines *The Gem* and *The Magnet* of much later days and, like them, read mostly by boys who did not attend public schools. Reed's most popular titles were *The Fifth Form at St Dominic's* (1887), *Cock House at Fellsgarth* (1891), and *The Master of the Shell* (1894).

**Reeve, Clara** 1729–1807. Clara Reeve was born in Ipswich, Suffolk. She wrote the second English novel of terror to follow Walpole's *The Castle of Otranto*, which had appeared 12 years before: *The Champion of Virtue* (1777). She acknowledged her debt to Walpole but criticized his performance; her own ambitions were more modest but her achievement greater. *The Champion of Virtue: A Gothic Story* was revised and republished as *The Old English Baron* and went through 10 editions by 1800. Her other novels were *The Two Mentors* (1783), *The Exiles* (1788), *The School for Widows* (1791), *Memoirs of Sir Roger de Clarendon* (1793), and *Destination* (1799). Clara Reeve also published a critical dialogue, *The Progress of Romance* (1785). A modern edition of *The Old English Baron* was published in Oxford Paperbacks, edited by James Trainer (1967).

*Reeve's Tale, The* See *Canterbury Tales, The.*

*Reflections on the Revolution in France* See **Burke, Edmund.**

*Reformation in England, Annals of the* See **Strype, John.**

**Regan** The second daughter of Lear in Shakespeare's *King Lear*, married to the Duke of Cornwall. She rejects the old king as completely as her sister Goneril and is an eager witness of the blinding of Gloucester by her husband. Regan is attracted to Edmund and becomes her sister's rival; when her husband dies of his wounds she seems to have the better chance and is prepared to have Goneril murdered. However, Goneril murders her first.

*Rehearsal, The* A burlesque by George Villiers, 2nd Duke of Buckingham, assisted by Thomas Sprat, Martin Clifford and Samuel Butler, it was first produced at Drury Lane in December 1671 and first published in 1672.

Bayes takes his friends, Smith and Johnson, to watch rehearsals of his new heroic tragedy. Passages from this, with comments from Bayes and his friends, make up a satire on D'Avenant and Dryden: their laureateships are represented by Bayes (hence the name) and their heroic tragedies are skilfully ridiculed.

See also **Dryden, John** and *Critic, The.*

**Reid, (Thomas) Mayne** 1818–83. Mayne Reid was born in Ireland and went to the USA in 1840. After a varied and adventurous career, which included service with the US Army in the Mexican War and extensive travel across the length and breadth of America, he returned to Europe and lived in England. In 1850 he published *The Rifle Rangers*, a romantic adventure that was immensely popular. It was just one of something like 90 books, most of which were concerned with American frontier life. He knew the background at first hand and his work was immensely popular with young readers. Other titles are *The Scalp Hunters* (1851) and *The Boy Hunters* (1852). Reid spent a further three years in the USA from 1867 to 1870.

*The Quadroon* (1856) was successfully dramatized by the author and was the basis of Dion Boucicault's *The Octoroon* (1859).

**Reid, Thomas** 1710–96. The Scottish philosopher was born at Strachan, Kincardineshire. He was the parish minister's son and completed his education at Marischal College, Aberdeen. He was Professor of Moral Philosophy at King's College, Aberdeen, from 1752 to 1764, when he succeeded Adam Smith in the same chair at Glasgow University, where he stayed until 1781. Reid's first publication was *An Essay on Quantity* (1748) but he made his mark with *An Inquiry into the Human Mind on the Principles of Common Sense* (1764). *Essays on the Intellectual Powers of Man* (1785) and *Essays on the Active Powers of Man* (1788), his later works, confirmed him as the founder of the 'common sense' school of philosophy, in ranging the principles common to the understanding of all rational men against the scepticism generated by philosophers like Locke, Berkeley, and Hume who could not, he insisted, produce any evidence for their assumptions. Reid's rhetorical prose style has confined his readership to students of philosophy and no modern edition of his work exists.

*Relapse, The, or Virtue in Danger.* A comedy by John Vanbrugh, first produced in November 1696 and first published in the following year. The plot is derived from the situation in the last act of Colley Cibber's play, *Love's Last Shift*, using the same characters, Loveless and Amanda.

Loveless, a reformed libertine, lives in the country with his wife Amanda. When they have to visit London Loveless falls from grace again with the beautiful Berinthia, a widow who usually gets what she wants. One of Berinthia's former lovers, Worthy, encourages her seduction of Loveless. He is attracted to Amanda and hopes she will yield to him when her husband proves unfaithful. He is disappointed: Amanda is a better woman than that. This is the main plot; the subplot is the more substantial part of the play.

Sir Novelty Fashion, the epitome of the fashionable gentleman, has bought himself the title of Lord Foppington. He is about to enter an arranged marriage with Miss Hoyden, daughter of a country squire, Sir Tunbelly Clumsey; neither father nor daughter have set eyes on him. Young Fashion, Foppington's young brother, has gone through his money and asks his brother for help. Foppington rudely rejects his brother's appeal and Fashion is determined on revenge. He goes to Sir Tunbelly's house and presents himself as Foppington. Miss Hoyden, an heiress, would marry the young man the following morning but Sir Tunbelly insists that she wait at least for a week. Seeing the dangers in delay, Fashion bribes Nurse and Parson and a secret marriage takes place at once. When Foppington arrives he is treated as an imposter, and his dignity suffers some rude shocks until an acquaintance vouches for him. Fashion slips away undetected and Nurse, Parson and Miss Hoyden decide to hold their peace. Miss Hoyden is married to Foppington and goes to London with him. Young Fashion now comes forward to claim his bride, and makes Nurse and Parson admit the earlier true marriage. Foppington loses a wealthy wife and Miss Hoyden loses a title; but she settles for Fashion in the end, for he is a lord's brother, after all.

*Religio Laici, or A Layman's Faith.* A poem by John Dryden, first published in 1682, and printed three times in that year. There is a prose preface which serves as a gloss on the expression of faith which is the poem's purpose. He supports the Christian religion and enquires what a Christian should believe to be sure of being saved. He argues against deism (the belief that man could, by the use of reason, infer the existence of a Creator from the design of the universe), and in favour of the study of the Bible as the true means of knowing God. The second part of the poem is regarded as less successful; here Dryden argues for the Anglican Church against the Catholic Church. The impulse for the poem is believed to have been the translation into English, by Henry Dickinson, of Richard Simon's *Histoire critique du Vieux Testament* (1679). Dryden agreed with Simon's insistence that the word of God must be retrieved from the centuries of commentary which overlaid it; but he could not agree with the claims of Simon, a Roman Catholic, for the Catholic tradition. The work is highly regarded as an example of Dryden's poetic art, and as a statement of the moderate Anglican's position during the Restoration period.

*Religio Medici* Sir Thomas Browne's first book, written for his 'private exercise and satisfaction'. It is basically an affirmation of his faith but Browne's enquiring mind roams over a number of subjects connected with religion, linking these to his personal faith. His remarkable learning is evident throughout and the whole work is realized in the finest prose, with the additional gift of two beautiful prayers written in verse.

Browne's world was a continuing source of interest, of inexhaustible treasures for the searching mind. It was God's creation, he firmly believed, but on that account no less rich and rewarding even to a man of his sceptical enquiring nature. His own reflections – conclusions he would never have claimed – are a statement of the mysteries of the universe, while his wit and common sense prevented him from indulging in mystical vapours.

The manuscript of the book was widely circulated, falling into the hands of a printer who published it without the author's permission (1642). Sir Kenelm Digby, a scientific amateur who became a member of the Royal Society, read a copy of this imperfect edition and rapidly made *Observations* on it, publishing them in 1643. Browne at once, in the same year, published his own edition, improving considerably on the earlier private edition.

*Reliques of Ancient English Poetry* A collection of songs, ballads, metrical romances, and sonnets, published by Thomas Percy in 1765. The ballads were drawn from the manuscript now known as *The Percy Folio* and edited for the *Reliques*. Some of the pieces in the collection are very old while others are as late as the early 17th century; the subsequent editions of 1767, 1775, and 1794 contained additional matter. Percy's editing of the material would not be acceptable now but the collection was an important step towards the revival of ballad poetry and restored interest in the older English forms. The English romantic poets acknowledged their debt to Thomas Percy.

**Renault, Mary** 1905– . The pseudonym of Mary Challans, a doctor's daughter who was born in London and educated at St Hugh's College, Oxford. She became a nurse in 1936 and published her first novel, *Purposes of Love* (called *Promise of Love* in the USA), in 1939. Her life as a nurse provided the background of her early novels: *Kind Are Her Answers* (1940), *The Friendly Young Ladies* (1944, called *The Middle Mist* in the USA), *Return to Night* (1947), and *North Face* (1948). The sale of *Return to Night* to a major film studio (the film was never made) enabled her to live in South Africa and devote all her time to writing. *The Charioteer* (1953), her story of servicemen and homosexuality during the war, made use of her medical experience and for many critics remains her best novel. Her first novel of life in ancient Greece was *The Last of the Wine* (1956); for her next she turned to the myth of Theseus and with *The King Must Die* (1958) enjoyed a major success with critics and public alike. *The Bull from the Sea* (1962) concluded the Theseus story. Other novels by Mary Renault are *The Lion in the Gateway* (1964, for young people); *The Mask of Apollo* (1966); three novels about the life and death of Alexander, *Fire from Heaven* (1970), *The Persian Boy* (1972), and *Funeral Games* (1981); and *The Praise Singer* (1978). *The Nature of Alexander* (1975) is a historical study.

*Representative Men* A book of essays by Ralph Waldo Emerson based on his lectures and first published in 1850. The first essay presents the idea that humanity, from time to time, is presented by exceptional men who express to a greater degree than their fellows the spirit of God: but the possibility is inherent in all and the exceptional man is an example to all men. Emerson's six representative men are Plato, Swedenborg, Montaigne, Shakespeare, Bonaparte, and Goethe.

***Reprinted Pieces*** A collection of occasional pieces by Charles Dickens which first appeared in *Household Words* (1850–1856). It was first published in volume form in 1868.

***Responsibilities*** See **Yeats, William Butler**.

***Return of the Native, The*** A novel by Thomas Hardy, first published in *Belgravia* (January to December 1878).

The scene is Egdon Heath, where Damon Wildeve, a publican who used to be an engineer, keeps two women in love with him while making up his mind. They are Thomasin Yeobright and, a contrasting character, the sharp and restless Eustacia Vye, a born romantic who, like Emma Bovary, longs to know a great passion. Damon marries Thomasin, who rejects the adoring Diggory Venn. Thomasin's cousin, Clym Yeobright, returns to Egdon Heath; he has been working as a diamond merchant in Paris but his occupation seemed useless and now he is going to teach and serve his fellow men. He falls in love with Eustacia.

Eustacia marries Clym – she hopes she can persuade him to go back to Paris and take her away from Egdon Heath. But Clym's eyesight fails, tried too much by his previous occupation and his intensive studying. He works as a furze cutter rather than be idle. Eustacia becomes Damon's mistress and she is also the unintentional cause of the death of Clym's mother. Clym discovers that Eustacia and Damon are lovers and after a violent scene she leaves him to run off with Damon. But during their flight the two lovers are drowned. Thomasin marries Diggory Venn, and Clym becomes an itinerant preacher, feeling an obscure guilt for the death of Eustacia and his mother.

Hardy nearly spoils an otherwise remarkable novel by insisting on helping the fates, who have us all at their mercy, play nasty tricks on his characters; while Clym is enough of a prig, and Diggory enough of a saint, to forgo much of our sympathy. The twin triumphs of the book are Eustacia – rebellious, passionate, longing for another sky and different air – and Egdon Heath itself.

***Revenge for Love, The*** See **Lewis, (Percy) Wyndham**.

***Revenger's Tragedy, The*** A tragedy by Cyril Tourneur. There is no record of the first performance and it was first published in 1607 without an author's name on the title page. However, scholars of English drama attribute the play to Tourneur on the evidence of his style and on the positive identification of a later and much inferior work called *The Atheist's Tragedy*, published in 1611.

Vindice is determined on the destruction of the duke and his evil court. He watches them pass by, holding in his hand the skull of his dead betrothed, Gloriana, whom the duke had poisoned when she refused his advances. His father, also, had died after the duke's rejection of him. His brother Hippolito is at court in the service of the duke's son Lussurioso (the play is littered with allegorical names) and introduces Vindice to him as an experienced pander. The brothers have assumed disguises.

Lussurioso commissions Vindice to procure a pretty virgin for him: the girl proves to be Vindice's own sister, Castiza. At court, meanwhile, the duke's bastard son, Spurio, has aroused the lust of the duchess. She is the duke's second wife and has three sons of her own: the dukedom is very much part of their ambitions and two of them plot feverishly against Lussurioso, the heir. An ill-judged attack on the duke and duchess by Lussurioso (prompted by Vindice, who knows of the duchess's passion for Spurio) nearly costs the heir his head. The duchess's sons plot to hasten the execution but only succeed in getting their younger brother, in prison for rape, beheaded instead.

In the meantime Vindice and Hippolito, in disguise, visit their mother Gratiana and offer her gold for her daughter on behalf of the duke's son. The gold corrupts her and the horrified Castiza finds herself sold; her mother tells the brothers the duke's son 'shall be most welcome when his pleasure conducts him this way'.

Vindice, at court, succeeds in killing the duke with Hippolito's help; they keep him alive long enough for him to discover that his wife and his bastard son have cuckolded him. Lussurioso, furious with the disguised Vindice over the embarrassing attack on the duke and duchess, dismisses him. But Hippolito has a brother, has he not? So Vindice returns to his service, out of disguise. His first order from Lussurioso is to kill the pander (himself); so he and Hippolito dress the duke's body in Vindice's former disguise to make it seem that the murderer was the pander who has now indeed been killed. The duchess's two sons learn of her liaison with Spurio and are determined to kill him.

The brothers' plan succeeds and Lussurioso, in their presence, proclaims the murderer's 'identity'. The court hurries on to the scene: the new duke determines to banish the duchess; Spurio determines to keep an eye on the main chance; the duchess's sons resolve to kill Spurio without delay; and each son becomes jealous of the other's aspirations to the dukedom. Vindice and Hippolito recruit the discontented courtiers in a conspiracy.

Lussurioso announces at a banquet with three of his favourites that the duchess is banished, that Spurio is doomed – and the duchess's sons also. Vindice, Hippolito, and two conspirators enter, masked as if for revels; they kill the four at table and depart. The rest of the court arrive on the scene and find the new duke murdered. One of the duchess's sons proclaims himself duke, whereupon the other kills him. He in turn is killed by Spurio, who is killed by a furious courtier.

Vindice and Hippolito, with their associates, Piero and Antonio, return to the scene and Antonio is proclaimed duke. The brothers confess that it was they who killed the old duke – and at once their lives are forfeit; Antonio cannot risk their dangerous presence in his duchy.

An outline of the plot makes *The Revenger's Tragedy* sound like an extravaganza of villainy – everyone who is not vengeful is evil; most characters are both. Nevertheless the play succeeds, as was demonstrated in a fine revival by the Royal Shakespeare Company in 1966 and 1969, when Ian Richardson gave a superb account of Vindice. To gain his revenge on a festering society Vindice has to enter it and act according to its values; but the truth of Tourneur's masterpiece shows that, after revenge, there is no world left for Vindice and Hippolito to inhabit. The play moves at great speed, one vivid scene following another until the bloody climax; it is delivered in sharp-edged dialogue with passages of poetry.

**Review, The** A periodical founded by Daniel Defoe with the help of Robert Harley, Earl of Oxford, on 19 February 1704, upon Defoe's release from prison. It was first called *A Weekly Review of the Affairs of France, Purged from the Errors and Partiality of News-Writers and Petty-Statesmen, of all Sides*. It had become *The Review* by 11 June 1713, the year it closed, when Defoe went to prison for the second time. After the first six weekly issues it came out twice weekly and from 22 March 1705 was appearing thrice weekly. It was written entirely by Defoe himself, an incredible feat since he was often in Scotland as Harley's agent during the paper's existence. *The Review* offered well-informed comment on the affairs of Europe (England was at war with France), dealt with aspects of the social life of the day, and kept its readers informed on commerce and trade. Nonpartisan, Defoe gave his opinion on political topics and thus became the first leader writer of the English press.

**Revolt of Islam, The** A poem by Percy Bysshe Shelley, in Spenserian stanzas, first published in 1818. Written in 1817, it was originally called *Laon and Cythna*; the principal characters, who become lovers, are brother and sister. Charles Ollier, who published the revised poem, persuaded Shelley to change the relationship. The condition of England, two years after Waterloo, was harsh for working men and their families; many industries had ceased and large numbers of returned soldiers were treated as vagabonds by the authorities. The Shelleys, living at Marlow, tried to help local people in need and were disapproved of by the middle-class and comfortable. *The Revolt of Islam* was provoked by contemporary circumstances but the poem was too obscure and difficult, and its principals too far from being recognizable human beings to reach a large number of readers. Ian Jack comments, in *English Literature 1815–32*, 'One sometimes wonders whether Shelley ever met any ordinary men and women.'

The poem is set in Islam where Cythna, a maiden dedicated to the freedom of her sex from harsh laws, joins forces with Laon, another revolutionary. They unite the people in revolt and for a time succeed; but the ruling tyrants, with reinforced armies, crush the revolt and lay waste the land. Famine and pestilence follow, and at the instigation of a priest Laon and Cythna are burned alive as a sacrifice.

**Rewards and Fairies** See *Puck of Pook's Hill*.

**Reynolds, John Hamilton** 1794–1852. Reynolds, a schoolmaster's son, was born at Shrewsbury in Shropshire and educated at Shrewsbury and St Paul's schools. He worked for an insurance company and published his first poems, *Safie* and *The Eden of Imagination*, at the age of 19. He moved from insurance to law but in 1815 became a contributor to the periodical *The Champion*. He met John Keats in 1816 and the two became friends; in the same year Reynolds published *The Naiad: A Tale, with Other Poems*. At the end of 1816 an article in *The Examiner* hailed Shelley, Reynolds, and Keats as the most promising poets of the day. Reynolds published further poems, of which *The Garden of Florence* (1821) is the most highly regarded, and collaborated with Thomas Hood in *Odes and*

*Addresses to Great People* (1825). But his promise was never realized and his poetry is forgotten now.

**Reynolds, Joshua** 1723–92. The great English portrait painter was born at Plympton, Devonshire, where his father, a former fellow of Balliol College, Oxford, was headmaster of the grammar school. The friend of Burke, Johnson, Goldsmith, and David Garrick, he has earned a place in English letters with his *Discourses* on the principles of art, which he delivered to the students of the Royal Academy of Arts between 1759 and 1790. Reynolds was the first president of the Royal Academy (1768) and was knighted in 1769.

A notable edition of the *Discourses* is Roger Fry's (1905). Reynolds's *Letters* were edited by F. W. Hilles and published in 1929.

*Rhoda Fleming* A novel by George Meredith, first published in 1865.

Fleming, a Kentish yeoman, has two daughters: proud and wilful Rhoda and gentle soft Dahlia. He has an assistant, Robert Eccles, strong and upright, who loves Rhoda. Edward Blancove, son of a rich banker, seduces Dahlia and then deserts her; Robert sets out to see that Blancove does right by Dahlia. Blancove hires a ruffian, Sedgett, who waylays Robert and knocks him unconscious. But Robert finds Dahlia, who has hidden herself. Blancove will not marry her but he offers Sedgett a bribe to do so. The Flemings will then see Dahlia in wedlock. Rhoda, who has refused to believe in Dahlia's 'sins' until obliged to, now forces the helpless Dahlia to accept this squalid and humiliating way out.

Robert, appalled, tries to prevent the marriage but the best he can do is to kidnap Dahlia as the bridal group are leaving the church. He then keeps Sedgett away by force and the hiatus gives him enough time to discover that Dahlia's 'husband' already has a wife. The wretched girl, terrified of Sedgett, tries to poison herself. Blancove is now willing to marry her but her recovery has changed Dahlia and she rejects him. Rhoda, her wilfulness diminished by the tragic events, marries Robert at the end of the story.

**rhyme-royal** A seven-line stanza form that first appeared in English poetry when used by Chaucer in his *Complaint unto Pity*. It was used by King James I of Scotland (1394–1437) for *The Kingis Quair* and thus became known as rhyme-royal: but there is little doubt that the king found his example in the great English poet. The rhyme sequence is *ababbcc* and the line is decasyllabic. The form remained unchallenged until the time of England's next major poet, Edmund Spenser.

**Rhymers' Club** The name adopted by a group of young writers of the late 19th century who met at Ye Olde Cheshire Cheese in Wine Office Court off Fleet Street, in the City of London. They published two volumes of their poetry, *The Books of the Rhymers' Club* (1892 and 1894), and regarded Oscar Wilde as their mentor. Among them were Ernest Dowson, Lionel Johnson, John Gray, W. B. Yeats, Richard le Gallienne, and John Davidson.

**Rhys, Jean** 1894–1979. Jean Rhys was born and brought up on the island of Dominica in the West Indies. Her father was Welsh, her mother Creole, and she went to live in Europe when she was 16. She studied for the stage and was an actress, briefly; she divided her time between London and Paris and observed the bohemian life of Anglo-Saxons in Montparnasse. She met Ford Madox Ford in Paris; he encouraged her to write and wrote a preface to her first book of short stories, *The Left Bank* (1927).

Before World War II Jean Rhys published *Postures* (1928; *Quartet* in the USA), *After Leaving Mr Mackenzie* (1931), *Voyage in the Dark* (1934), and *Good Morning, Midnight* (1939). Her novels enjoyed critical praise but no popular success, and her work disappeared from view for over 20 years, until she published a new novel, *The Wide Sargasso Sea* (1966), a sombre and unsentimental life of the first wife of Mr Rochester before he meets Jane Eyre. Renewed attention brought the republication of her prewar fiction, and new short stories appeared in the collection *Tigers are Better-Looking* (1968). Jean Rhys is the novelist of women's mistrust of men, born of the incomprehension of the nature of women by men. She is objective and compassionate at the same time; the chief characters of her novels and stories are victims, and her unique talent retains the reader's interest in them.

**Ricardo, David** 1772–1823. A successful businessman, Ricardo was the son of a Dutch Jewish family and was born in London. After making a fortune on the Stock Exchange Ricardo devoted himself to the study of economics, to which he had been drawn through reading Adam Smith. He began to write with the encouragement of James Mill and his best-known work is *On the Principles of Political Economy and Taxation* (1817). This is concerned with the forces controlling the distribution of wealth and contains his theory of rent, which maintains that the better and more productive the land the higher the rent charges will be. Rent will become artificially high, providing a powerful argument in favour of free and unrestricted imports.

**Rich, Barnabe** *c*.1540–1617. Rich was a professional soldier who served with distinction in the last struggle for Calais during the reign of Mary and in the Netherlands, rising to the rank of captain. His literary career began in 1574 with a story, *A Right Exelent and Pleasaunt Dialogue, Betweene Mercury and an English Souldier*, one of many pieces intended to make the people aware of the soldier's condition and the country's ultimate dependence on an adequate army. Among others were the pamphlets *Allarme to England* (1578), *A Path-way to Military Practise* (1587), and *A Souldiers Wishe to Britons Welfare* (1604). *Riche his Farewell to Militarie Profession* (1581) contains eight inset stories, among them *Apolonius and Silla*. This was from the French of François de Belleforest, who translated it from the Italian of Matteo Bandello: it became *Twelfth Night* when Shakespeare used the story. Other fictions by Rich are *The Straunge and Wonderfull Adventures of Don Simonides* (1581), *The Second Tome of the Travailes and Adventures of Don Simonides* (1584), and *The Adventures of Brusanus, Prince of Hungaria* (1592). He wrote a number of other pamphlets, continuing to within two years of his death, many of them on the condition of Ireland.

**Richard II, The Life and Death of** A historical play by William Shakespeare. The events directly precede those of the two parts of *Henry IV* and the source is acknowledged to be the chronicles of Raphael Holinshed. Also acknowledged is the influence of Marlowe's *Edward II*, which had been produced about two years before. *Richard II* was first produced *c*.1595 and printed in a quarto in 1597. It was published in the First Folio of 1623.

The play opens with the conflict between Mowbray and Bolingbroke. (Mowbray was Duke of Norfolk: Bolingbroke was Earl of Hereford and John of Gaunt's son. The play can sometimes be confusing to audiences when both men are referred to by either name – the king refers to Bolingbroke as 'Henry Hereford' in his first speech.) The king orders them to settle their differences in a duel at Coventry, then he arbitrarily stops the duel and banishes both of them. Upon the death of John of Gaunt, Richard confiscates Bolingbroke's inheritance to finance his war in Ireland; but during his absence Boling- broke invades England. The king, upon his return, finds himself opposed and withdraws to Flint Castle but eventually surrenders to Boling- broke, who proceeds to London with Richard in his train. The deposition of King Richard, one of the most famous scenes in Shakespeare, follows and then Richard is confined in Pomfret Castle. Bolingbroke then ascends the throne as Henry IV (the first Lancastrian king); but he is scarcely crowned before the news of the murder of Richard by Sir Pierce of Exton is brought to him at Windsor. The play closes with Bolingbroke secure in the crown but afraid in his conscience, knowing that his own security demanded Richard's life. The play is rich in poetry and the characters of Richard and Bolingbroke skilfully contrasted. A notable character is the ageing and honorable John of Gaunt, Duke of Lancaster.

**Richard III, The History of King** See **More, Thomas**. Modern editions of the English version are by R. S. Sylvester (1964) and Paul Murray Kendall (1965).

**Richard III, The Life and Death of** A historical play by William Shakespeare, following directly on the events of the trilogy *Henry VI*. It was first produced *c*.1594 and printed in a quarto in 1597. It was published in the First Folio of 1623. The source was probably the same as that of the tri- logy, the chronicles of Raphael Holinshed, which included More's life of Richard III by this date. The title role is a fine vehicle for a great actor and Burbage was the first of these: his suc- cessors include Garrick, Kean, Irving, and Olivier.

Richard, Duke of Gloucester, celebrates the triumph of the house of York. His brother is king (Edward IV) and Richard intends to have the crown – but he must first clear the way to the succession. He woos Anne, widow of the Lancastrian Prince of Wales (whom he killed at Tewkesbury) and contrives the imprisonment in the Tower of his brother Clarence, whom he then has murdered. When Edward IV dies he conspires with Buckingham to seize the boy king Edward V and his brother and then keeps them confined in the Tower. Hastings is accused of treason and witchcraft and summarily executed when Richard suspects his opposition. He becomes king with the help of Buckingham and orders the murder of the boy king and his brother, 'those bastards in the Tower'. Believing himself secure, and with Anne, his neglected wife, now dead, he proposes to marry his niece Elizabeth, the daughter of Edward IV. But he alienates Buckingham by his ingratitude ('I am not in the giving vein today') and when the Earl of Richmond, the Lancastrian claimant to the throne, lands in England, Buckingham raises a force in support. Buckingham is taken and executed but Richard is defeated and killed at Bosworth Field (1485) by Richmond, who becomes king as Henry VII.

**Richard and John of Hexham**  See **Hexham, Richard and John of.**

*Richard Coeur de Lion*  A Middle English verse romance of the 14th century. (See **metrical romances**.) The unknown author makes an English king the subject of marvellous knightly adventures; he is, inevitably, of strange birth – his mother is the enchantress Cassodorien, not Eleanor of Aquitaine. Philip Augustus and the French are treated with scorn; Richard kills a lion in his German prison; he feeds on Saracens and offers the same dish to Saladin's emissaries. However, St George is on his side, and the glory of the fighting hero at the Crusades is the theme of the romance. The text was edited by D. Laing, W. B. Turnbull, Owen Miles, and others (1837). A modern version by B. B. Broughton appeared in *Richard the Lion-hearted and other Medieval Romances* (New York, 1966).

**Richard de Bury**  See **Bury, Richard de.**

**Richard of Devizes**  See **Devizes, Richard of.**

**Richardson, Dorothy M(iller)** 1873–1957. Dorothy M. Richardson was born in Abingdon, Berkshire, and after attending local schools worked as a teacher and as a clerk. She married a painter, Alan Odle. She was the author of *The Quakers Past and Present* (1914) and *Gleanings from the Works of George Fox* (1914) before publishing the first volume, *Pointed Roofs* (1915), of her 12-novel sequence entitled *Pilgrimage*. This is known to students of the English novel because the author was the first novelist, antedating Joyce and Virginia Woolf, to use the interior monologue or stream-of-consciousness. But the attention gained by Dorothy M. Richardson has been confined to specialists and her work is largely unknown to the general reader. The sequence deals with the life (in the mind) of Miriam Henderson, and is followed through *Backwater* (1916), *Honeycomb* (1917), *Interim* (1919), *The Tunnel* (1919), *Deadlock* (1921), *Revolving Lights* (1923), *The Trap* (1925), *Oberland* (1927), *Dawn's Left Hand* (1931), *Clear Horizon* (1935), and *Dimple Hill* (1938).

**Richardson, Henry Handel** 1870–1946. The pseudonym of Ethel Florence Richardson, who was born in Melbourne in Australia. She was educated at the Melbourne Presbyterian Ladies College, where she displayed a talent for music that led to further study at the Leipzig Conservatorium. At Leipzig she met John George Robertson, whom she married, and who became Lecturer in English at Strasbourg (1896–1903). Ethel Florence Richardson gave up the study of music when she realized that she did not have the temperament to be a performer and turned to literature. She was widely read and a great admirer of Flaubert, whose influence she acknowledged as the strongest in her own work.

Adopting the pseudonym of Henry Handel Richardson, she successfully used music as the theme for her novel *Maurice Guest* (1908). Her own adolescence provided the background for *The Getting of Wisdom* (1910) and music, again, for *The Young Cosima* (1939). She lived in Strasbourg until 1904, when her husband became Professor of German Language and Literature at the University of London. They made their home in London, and she moved to Sussex after his death. Henry Handel Richardson only revisited Australia once – to ensure the authenticity of the background of *Australia Felix* (1917). This was the first part of a trilogy which was completed in *The Way Home* (1925) and *Ultima Thule* (1929). The trilogy was published as ***The Fortunes of Richard Mahony*** (1930) and earned her top rank among Australian novelists. She left an autobiography, *Myself when Young* (1948), which was published after her death.

**Richardson, Samuel** 1689–1761.  A native of Derbyshire, Richardson was the son of a joiner who hoped that Samuel would be able to enter the Church. His hopes were frustrated by poverty and Richardson's education was only sketchy; at the age of 17 he was sent to London to become a stationer's apprentice. He learned the printing business and by the time he was 30 he owned his own printing and stationery company. He had, meanwhile, married his employer's daughter.

Richardson prospered. His premises in Fleet Street contained the house where he lived, his printing room, and his stationer's shop. He became the father of six children by his first wife, Martha Wilde; he took a second wife, Elizabeth Leake, after her death and sired six more. Only four survived. His business required larger premises and he moved to Salisbury Court, where he spent the rest of his life. He was the printer of the Tory periodical *The True Briton*, the *Journals* of the House of Commons, volumes of law reports, and the newspapers *Daily Journal* and *Daily Gazeteer*. He became Master of the Stationers' Company in 1754.

When Richardson was 50, in 1739, he was approached by two friends, the booksellers Rivington and Osborne, to prepare a manual of letter writing, providing models for people little used to epistolary communication. The manual was published eventually, in 1741, as *Letters written to and for Particular Friends, on the most important Occasions, Directing not only the requisite Style and Forms to be observed in writing Familiar Letters; but how to think and act justly and prudently, in the common Concerns of Human Life*, and it was while Richardson was considering the problems which could face a pretty girl working as a servant that he conceived the idea of a novel told in the form of letters. The novel took shape faster than the manual; **Pamela**, *or Virtue Rewarded* was published in two volumes in 1740 and completed with two more in the following years. The book was a remarkable success; at the age of 51 Samuel Richardson had found a means of expression which suited him perfectly. It also suited his readers; the epistolary form may seem impossibly contrived, especially if it purports to be a servant girl telling her story; but it was a new approach and 18th-century readers were not irritated by the contrivance.

**Clarissa**, *or, The History of a Young Lady* was Richardson's next novel and it is notoriously long. The first two volumes appeared in 1747 – five more completed the work in 1748. But the novel was a greater success than *Pamela*; it was also more truthful and uncompromising and the fortunes and misfortunes of Clarissa Harlowe were followed with breathless interest on the

Samuel Richardson, c.1747. A detail from the portrait by Joseph Highmore. National Portrait Gallery, London.

continent as well as in England. (Richardson had gained a European reputation with *Pamela*, which was translated into French, Dutch, German, Danish, Italian, Russian, and Spanish. It was translated into Welsh in 1818.)

**The History of Sir Charles Grandison** was Richardson's third novel and as lengthy as *Clarissa*. In spite of considerable virtues, the book has not the overall quality of the first two. Richardson, after concentrating on two good women, attempted to portray a good man, and failed to bring him to life. But that is the verdict of posterity; it enjoyed a great success in Richardson's day and Jane Austen loved it.

The three novels – *Clarissa*, particularly – give Richardson an honoured place in the history of the English novel but he is hardly known to modern readers. His obsession with sexual 'respectability' is unacceptable, for one thing; virtue's reward, in Pamela's case, is a wedding ring – a cynical view might be that she got her asking price. The enormous length of the novels, too, so welcome in that age, now seems unendurable. There are rich rewards, however, for those who can stay the course: Richardson's writing is straightforward and idiomatic and he is remarkably subtle in conveying the lubricious characters of Mr B., whom Pamela brings to the altar, and Lovelace, whose pursuit of Clarissa ends in tragedy. More important, perhaps, Richardson was the chronicler of his age – as much as was Fielding (whom he resented bitterly for *Joseph Andrews*). Girls like Pamela were virtually helpless and Richardson's early years had acquainted him with privation. The class structure was rigid; while he was no radical critic of the social order, Richardson's view of morality was that it allowed of no privilege and he shows the triumph of virtue against authority. His great popularity in his time is partly explained by this attitude and partly by his painstaking description of ordinary life. His novels are sentimental but not romantic; his audience could recognize their own world in every chapter. How much of his success was due to another aspect of his work, his obsession with sex, is hard to say. Whatever the reasons, he did succeed. The epistolary form, which a later age is bound to find ludicrous at times (when did Pamela, a servant, find the time to write such immensely long letters?); the inordinate length (to cover the action of *Clarissa*, which takes place within a year, Richardson wrote the longest novel in the language); the author's uncertainty in handling scenes in high society (Richardson had no acquaintance with it) – certainly he can be criticized on these grounds. But the form he chose gave his novels immediacy, a feeling of the present; and their great length gave him time to create characters at a high level of credibility and to demonstrate in detail the course his characters would follow: the reader is convinced that Lovelace could behave in no other way and that Clarissa's fate was inevitable. Richardson brought to English fiction a consideration of motive, an examination of emotion, and complete consistency in allowing his characters to be themselves: the author offers no comment whatever. His influence as a novelist was enormous; natural feelings and emotions had become the matter of imaginative fiction.

Richardson's other works are forgotten. He would not, one imagines, have had much time for other works; he was a busy and successful printer as well as a novelist. Yet the three novels were completed between 1740 and 1754 and Richardson lived on to a comfortable 72. He had legions of female admirers, at whose behest he wrote about a good man, for a change, in his third novel, and he was the friend of many contemporary men of letters, including Edward Young and Samuel Johnson. He was generous to Johnson in his troubles and assisted him financially. It was Johnson who said of his work (to Boswell) '. . .if you were to read Richardson for the story, your impatience would be so much fretted that you would hang yourself. But you must read him for the sentiment'.

Richardson's novels can be read in a modern edition published by the Shakespeare Head Press in 18 volumes, between 1929 and 1931. *Pamela* and *Clarissa* are both in Everyman's library, and *Sir Charles Grandison* in the Oxford English Novels series, edited by Jocelyn Harris (1972).

**Richard the Redeless**  See **Mum and the Sothsegger**.

**Richardus Tertius**  A play in Latin after the manner of Seneca by Thomas Legge (1535–1607), Master of Caius College, Cambridge, produced at St John's College in 1580. It is believed to have had considerable influence on Robert Greene and Christopher Marlowe. The wooing scenes in Shakespeare's *Richard III* (Acts I and IV) have no basis in Holinshed, the acknowledged source of the play, but are anticipated by Thomas Legge in his Latin tragedy.

**Riderhood, Rogue**  The evil, blackmailing waterman of Dickens's *Our Mutual Friend*.

**Riders to the Sea**  See **Synge, J(ohn) M(illington)**.

**Riding, Laura**  1901–  .  Laura Riding (née Reichenthal) was born in New York City and completed her education at Cornell University. She was associated with the 'Fugitive' group of Southern writers, but she left the USA in 1925 and lived and worked in Europe until 1939. In England she worked closely with Robert Graves and published her first poems, *The Close Chaplet*, in 1926. She established the Seizin Press in Majorca in 1927 and edited the literary magazine *Epilogue* from 1935 to 1938 with Robert Graves, with whom she also collaborated on *A Survey of Modernist Poetry* (1927). She is the author of two historical novels, *A Trojan Ending* (1937) and *Lives of Wives* (1939), and a book of essays, *Contemporaries and Snobs* (1928). Her *Collected Poems* was published in 1938.

**Rienzi,** or *The Last of the Tribunes*.  A novel by Bulwer-Lytton, first published in 1835. It is based on the career of Cola di Rienzi, who is represented by one modern writer (Maurice Druon) as a blood relative of the Valois kings. He appeared in Roman politics in the 14th century and succeeded, for a brief period, in breaking the power of the nobility and establishing a republic on ancient lines. He was overthrown and after seven years' exile regained power as a senator before being assassinated. Bulwer-Lytton's characters include Irene, Rienzi's sister, who is loved by Adrian Colonna, whose patrician father meets his death at the hands of Rienzi.

**Rievaulx, Aelred (**or **Ethelred) of**  d. 1167. Aelred of Rievaulx was a Cistercian monk and writer in Latin. He has a place among chroniclers of the Anglo-Norman period for his account of the Battle of the Standard at Northallerton in Yorkshire in 1138, during the reign of King Stephen, when David, King of Scotland, who supported the Empress Matilda, invaded England. Aelred was a friend of King David and his account purports to give the words spoken by the rival leaders before the battle commenced. Richard of Hexham, whose monastery in Northumberland lay close to the action, gives a fuller and less biased account. (See also **Hexham, Richard and John of**.)

Aelred of Rievaulx's *Relatio de Standardo* was edited by R. Howlett and published in *Chronicles of the Reigns of Stephen, Henry II and Richard I* (Rolls Series, 1886).

**Rights of Man, The**  A political tract by Thomas Paine, published in two parts, in 1791 and 1792. It was written in reply to Edmund Burke's *Reflections on the Revolution in France*, published in 1790. Paine defended the Revolution and provoked the English establishment to such a degree that it passed a law against seditious publications. He fled to France to escape prosecution.

Paine's springboard is the theory of the social contract. Sovereignty is inherent in the will of the majority and should be reaffirmed by each generation; no generation has any right to bind its successors to its own order. The social contract should be embodied in a formal constitution; where that did not exist authority – and therefore tyranny – prevailed, without fear of contradiction. The purpose of government should be the freedom and security of the individual; the rights of man include the maximum freedom of thought and action compatible with the rights of others.

In the second part Paine compares the constitutions of the United States and the new France with English institutions, to the latter's disadvantage. But the work is most interesting in the radical constructive policy which it outlines. Paine advocated, among other things, a tax on income above a certain level, pensions for the aged, the promotion of free education for the poor, family allowances, and the limitation of armaments by treaty.

Modern editions of *The Rights of Man* are published in Everyman's Library (1915) and the Penguin English Library (1969).

**Riley, James Whitcomb** 1849–1916. The poet of Indiana did not make a real connection with letters until, after working at various jobs, he began to contribute pieces to the Indianapolis *Journal* in 1877. His connection with the paper lasted for eight years and secured his reputation as a regional poet in a sentimental, whimsical, and kindly vein. The most successful published collection was *The Old Swimmin'-Hole and 'Leven More Poems* (1883). Riley also wrote *Afterwhiles* (1887), *Pipes o' Pan at Zekesbury* (1888), and *Poems Here at Home* (1893). His most famous poem was 'Little Orphant Annie'.

**Ring and the Book, The** A poem by Robert Browning, first published in four volumes (1868–69). The poem is in 12 books and runs to 21,000 lines of blank verse. It was begun in Florence about 1864, after Browning discovered the facts of the story in an old book he bought in the market place in 1860. He made further investigations into the story and worked on the poem intermittently for a number of years, completing other poems meanwhile.

The events took place in Rome towards the end of the 17th century. Count Guido Franceschini, an impoverished nobleman of Arezzo, sought an advantageous marriage, having tried unsuccessfully to find some lucrative office in Rome. He discovered the Comparini family, property owners advanced in years and with only a daughter, Pompilia, to inherit. The girl was only 13, but Franceschini's rank was much higher and Violante Comparini arranged a marriage for her daughter with the nobleman, who was not exactly truthful about his estates in Arezzo. The Comparini's delivered their daughter to Arezzo but soon hastened away from the poverty-stricken Franceschini home. Pompilia led a wretched life; her husband was cruel and his younger brother frankly lustful. She appealed to the archbishop and the governor of the province but they did nothing for her. Her only help came from a young canon, Giuseppe Caponsacchi, whom she persuaded to take her back to her parents in Rome. Franceschini pursued and caught them and had Pompilia confined to a convent. She was pregnant, and when she was taken to her parents' house to await the birth of her child Violante Comparini confessed the truth of her daughter's origins: Pompilia was not Violante's child, for unknown to her husband the childless woman had bought a baby in the slums of Rome. The enraged Franceschini hired four accomplices and, using Caponsacchi's name to gain admittance to their house, murdered the Comparinis. Pompilia died later of her wounds. Franceschini was arrested and tried with his four accomplices. He had received minor orders earlier in life and appealed to the pope, Innocent XII, for special privilege as a cleric. His plea was rejected; he was beheaded and his accomplices hanged on 22 February 1698.

The 'Book' of the title was the volume Browning discovered in the market place in Florence. The 'Ring' is the 'gold' the poet sought – the real truth behind the facts of the case and the testimony given at the trial. The 12 books of the poem begin with Browning's account of his sources, opening with a fine 'Invocation' to his late wife. This is followed by the gossip of those in Rome favourable to Count Guido; of those favourable to the hapless Pompilia; the comments of an impartial observer (Tertium Quid); Guido's defence; the evidence of Giuseppe Caponsacchi; Pompilia's deathbed account of her own life; the statement for the defence; the statement for the prosecution; Pope Innocent's soliloquy on the nature of evil and the fallibility of human judgment and his decision to let the sentence stand; Guido's abject cowardice when he realizes he is doomed; and the pope's intervention to prevent the convent from claiming Pompilia's property.

The finest parts of the poem are generally agreed to be the dramatic monologues delivered by the characters; less successful are the detailed legal arguments scrupulously rendered by Browning.

**Ripley, George** 1802–80. The New England religious thinker and writer was born in Massachusetts and educated at Harvard. He went on to the Harvard Divinity School and in 1826 began a 15-year ministry at Boston Unitarian Church. He became editor of the Unitarian *Christian Register*, in which he displayed his preoccupation with contemporary German transcendental thinking. He was criticized by the biblical scholar Andrews Norton, who saw Ripley's expressed views as dangerously loose. His *Discourses on the Philosophy of Religion* (1836) drew further fire from Norton; Ripley replied in *Letters on the Latest Form of Infidelity* (1840): 'infidelity' was the term used by Norton to describe Ripley's religious liberalism.

In 1838 Ripley, with F. H. Hedge, began to edit *Specimens of Foreign Standard Literature* (14 volumes, 1838–42), which stimulated American interest in idealistic philosophy; it also published contributions from the New England Transcendentalists, who found the origins of their own ideas in the journal. Ripley resigned from the ministry in 1841 and helped to launch *The Dial* as well as organize the Brook Farm community. He edited the community's weekly, *The Harbinger*, and continued to publish it after the community failed (1845–49).

Ripley became the New York *Tribune's* book reviewer in 1849 and continued in that position until 1890, contributing work of distinction. He was a frequent visitor to Europe and made the acquaintance of many thinkers and writers. With Bayard Taylor he edited *A Handbook of Literature on the Fine Arts* (1852) and with C. A. Dana, the *New American Cyclopedia* (16 volumes, 1858–63).

**Rip van Winkle** See **Sketch Book, The** by Washington Irving.

*Rise of Silas Lapham, The* A novel by William Dean Howells, first published in 1885.

A self-reliant businessman, Colonel Silas Lapham has risen from his farm in Vermont to wealth and success as a paint manufacturer, though his methods of achieving success might not always bear close examination. He moves to Boston, builds a mansion on Beacon Hill, and urges Persis, his wife, and their daughters, Irene and Penelope, to take the place in society to which his wealth, he believes, entitles them. He looks forward to a new life, and thinks back on his old one with increasing moral discomfort. Persis, however, is hopelessly at sea with Boston

society, though it happens that a representative of it, Tom Corey, takes a position in the Lapham company and falls in love with Penelope. Penelope is unhappy, though she loves Tom, because of the differences in their social standing; complications arise when her younger sister Irene convinces herself that Tom is in love with *her*. Penelope refuses Tom's proposal of marriage and does not attend the Coreys' dinner party, to which her family is invited and at which her father gets drunk, revealing himself as a social barbarian.

Silas has, meanwhile, been speculating and this has turned out badly. Facing bankruptcy, he is urged by his former partner, Rogers, to sell a milling property to an interested English syndicate. The sale would save Silas from ruin – but he knows the property will soon become worthless; its purchase would mean disaster to the syndicate. After a struggle with himself, Silas resists the temptation. Bankrupt, but morally restored, he returns to Vermont with his wife and Irene. Penelope and Tom are married and run off to Mexico, where they will be spared the tiresome social distinctions that nearly separated them in Boston.

Howells' best novel, *The Rise of Silas Lapham* is a beautifully observed comedy of Boston life. Warmth and wit are allied in his presentation of the *nouveau riche* Silas and his aspirations and in the monumental self-assurance of the Coreys, an old Boston family from whom, aspiration no longer being necessary, inspiration has largely departed.

*Rivals, The* A comedy by Richard Brinsley Sheridan, first produced at Covent Garden in January 1775, and published in the same year. It was Sheridan's first play and he was not by any means convinced of its success the night it opened. However, after he had tightened up the text and Lee, who according to one critic gave a bad performance as Sir Lucius O'Trigger, had been replaced by Clinch, the play settled down to a prosperous run. The action takes place at Bath.

Captain Absolute has assumed the character of Ensign Beverley. The heir to a baronetcy, Absolute has fallen in love with Lydia Languish, who is romantic enough to imagine a man of modest means, for example, an ensign on half-pay, more worthy of her love than a rich man. Unfortunately, Lydia's aunt, Mrs Malaprop, has no time for the beggarly 'Ensign Beverley', and Lydia will lose half her fortune if she marries without her aunt's consent. Then Sir Anthony Absolute, the baronet, arrives in Bath with proposals for his son's marriage: he thinks Lydia

Act IV.—Scene 2

An 18th-century illustration for *The Rivals*. Sir Anthony Absolute and his son, Captain Absolute; Lydia Languish and her aunt, Mrs Malaprop, in Act IV, scene 2. Victoria & Albert Theatre Museum, London.

Languish would be a good wife for Captain Absolute and Mrs Malaprop is delighted.

The captain is not sure what to do and his indecision is further compounded by his having a rival, Bob Acres (more exactly, Ensign Beverley's rival). The bellicose Sir Lucius O'Trigger incites Bob Acres to challenge Beverley, and Acres asks Captain Absolute to deliver the challenge. Meanwhile, Mrs Malaprop looks fondly on Sir Lucius; he imagines, however, that her letters are from Lydia and decides to enter the field himself. Finding the captain in his way, he challenges him.

Bob Acres, who has no real desire to fight with anyone, discovers the identity of 'Ensign Beverley' and resigns his hopes of Lydia; Sir Lucius discovers who is the true writer of the letters when Mrs Malaprop arrives on the scene; Lydia, annoyed at the loss of her romantic illusions, quarrels with Captain Absolute. However, she forgives him, and the play ends happily. A subsidiary plot tells the story of Lydia's friend, Julia Melville, and her love affair with the jealous Faulkland.

**Rivers, Rev St John**  In Charlotte Brontë's *Jane Eyre*, the handsome and strong-minded cousin who almost wins Jane's hand. When she chooses Rochester, he devotes himself to missionary work in India.

**Road to Ruin, The**  A comedy by Thomas Holcroft, first produced at Covent Garden in February 1792, and published in the same year. It was translated and played in Holland, Denmark, and Germany. Harry Dornton's extravagance causes a run on his father's bank and brings it close to ruin. In love with Miss Warren, he resolves to save the house by marrying the girl's wealthy mother, an unpleasant woman who surrounds herself with sycophantic admirers. Among these is Goldfinch, heavily in debt from his idle fashionable way of life, who is determined to marry Mrs Warren himself. In the end the bank is saved by the genius of Old Dornton's chief clerk, the grim old Mr Sulky. Harry, a reformed character, is able to marry Miss Warren, while her odious mother is disinherited by the discovery of a new will.

**Roaring Girle, The,** *or Moll Cutpurse*.  A comedy by Thomas Middleton and Thomas Dekker, first produced in 1610 and first published in 1611. Moll Cutpurse was a thief and forger whose real name was Mary Frith. The play is a comment on her notoriety – she was not apprehended until 1612, when she was sentenced to perform public penance at St Paul's Cross as part of her punishment.

Sebastian Wentgrave and Mary Fitzallard are betrothed but Sebastian's father, Sir Alexander, is both mean and mean-spirited; he forbids the match. To force his hand Sebastian pays court to the notorious Moll Cutpurse. Moll herself is touched by the young lovers' plight; she agrees to follow Sebastian's scheme and also to be his means of contact with Mary. Sebastian announces that he has fallen in love with Moll Cutpurse and must marry her. The distracted old villain, Sir Alexander, sends his unpleasant servant Trapdoor to worm his way into Moll's confidence and then betray her. But Trapdoor is unequal to the task and Moll and Sebastian extract Sir Alexander's consent by a carefully staged wedding; the alternative – Sebastian's marriage to Mary – is infinitely preferable.

The play, which was revived in the modern theatre in 1983, is an interesting example of the way a character outside the law can invoke a sympathetic response from both playwright and public. There is no attempt to make the underworld attractive or romantic but, for that matter, no attempt either to tell the truth about it. The most vivid scenes, as might be expected since Dekker is involved, are the ones that depict the life of the London streets.

**Robarts, Mark**  In Anthony Trollope's *Framley Parsonage*, the young clergyman who disappoints his patroness, Lady Lufton, when he is led into an extravagant way of life through his association with Mr Sowerby and the Duke of Omnium.

**Robbery Under Arms**  See **Boldrewood, Rolf.**

**Robene and Makyne**  A poem by Robert Henryson telling of a rustic wooing amid the flocks on a green hill. It was written in the late 15th century but not printed until 1765. The moral of the poem is: 'The man that wilt nocht when he may/ Sall have nocht when he wald.'

**Robert Elsmere** A novel by Mrs Humphry Ward, first published in 1888. The story concerns a young clergyman, Robert Elsmere, whose convictions force him to leave the Church – he can no longer accept the insistence on miraculous and divine elements and believes that Christianity should be more concerned with man on earth. His changing faith alienates his wife, Catherine, who cannot forsake her established beliefs. Elsmere, at the end of the story, has come to terms with himself, and is practising his Christianity in active benevolence in a foundation he has established in the East End of London.

The novel is dedicated to Thomas Hill Green, the Oxford social philosopher whose work the author admired.

**Robert of Gloucester** See **Gloucester, Robert of.**

**Robert of Torigni** See **Diceto, Ralph de.**

**Robertson, Thomas William** 1829–71. Robertson, one of 22 children, was the son of an actor and born at Newark-on-Trent. His sister Madge became the great actress Madge Kendal. Tom Robertson acted as soon as he was old enough to learn dialogue and grew up as actor, stage manager, songwriter, and journeyman playwright; he was the model for Tom Wrench in Pinero's *Trelawny of the Wells.* His first real success was *David Garrick* (Haymarket, 1864), an adaptation from the French that provided an excellent vehicle for Edward Sothern. Robertson's next play, *Society,* presented by the Bancrofts at The Prince of Wales (later called The Scala) in 1865, opened a new direction in English drama, that of the realistic domestic interior where everything was immediately recognizable to the audience. *Society* was a success and established both Robertson as a playwright and the Bancrofts as managers.

*Ours* (1866), *Caste,* his most famous play (1867), and *Play* (1868) were all presented by the Bancrofts at The Prince of Wales and represent his best work. He wrote 22 plays in all but enjoyed his success for only seven short years, dying at the age of 42. He made a definite mark on English drama, his naturalism being a great advance. *Caste* does not offer a solution to the human problem it presents but is an excellent play that is frequently revived.

**Robertson, William** 1721–93. Robertson was the son of a minister and became a minister. He was born at Borthwick in Midlothian and educated at Edinburgh University. He ministered at Gladsmuir and Edinburgh and became Principal of Edinburgh University in 1762. The following year Robertson became Moderator of the General Assembly of the Church of Scotland, and was appointed Historiographer for Scotland.

Robertson's place in English letters is assured; he was a historian who wrote in a pleasant easy style which makes history a pleasure to read, and whose narrative power is equal to the recounting of great events. His first publication was in fact a sermon, *The Situation of the World at the Time of Christ's Appearance* (1755); his first history came four years later: *The History of Scotland during the Reigns of Queen Mary and of King James VI . . . with a Review of the Scotch History previous to that period* (1759). The book was well received and widely read, and led to Robertson's appointments as Principal and Historiographer. His next history came after a decade; *The History of the Reign of the Emperor Charles V* (1769) earned Robertson the largest sum so far paid for a historical work, £4,500 – an incredible figure for that time. The book also earned Robertson great fame in Europe; it was translated into French in 1771 and brought high praise from Voltaire; the Empress Catherine II of Russia sent Robertson a gold snuff-box and assured him that she never travelled without his book. *The History of America* (1777) is actually the history of the discovery and settlement of America; his last work was *An Historical Disquisition concerning The Knowledge which The Ancients had of India* (1791).

As a historian Robertson, like his friend and contemporary David Hume, has been superseded. Also, like Hume, he is careless about sources at times; but it has to be borne in mind that many sources were simply not available to them. Robertson's style improved as his histories continued and his description of Columbus's voyage and landfall is magnificently done. His work was admired by Edward Gibbon.

**Robins, Elizabeth** See **'New Women' novelists.**

**Robinson, Edwin Arlington** 1869–1935. The New England poet was born at Head Tide, Maine, in the same year as the Midwest poet Edgar Lee Masters. He was brought up in the town of Gardiner, Maine, which provided the background (Tilbury Town) for his most enduring work. Robinson's family life was marred by the death of his mother and the failure of the family's fortunes; in addition, his father's cranky interest in spiritualism was not much help to a son to whom life seemed to be a succession of misfortunes. Robinson had to leave Harvard in 1893 and he found work in New York City. He published his first collection of poems, *The Torrent and the Night Before* (1896), at his own expense, even though his work was actually ill paid and he could not really afford such a step. He was shy, withdrawn, and drank too much for one in his straitened circumstances. But his fortunes began to change in the following year when *The Children of the Night* (1897), a revision of his first collection with some additional poems, gained some acknowledgment from the critics. Robinson's third book was *Captain Craig* (1902) and with that he found a public – and a helper in Theodore Roosevelt, who had been impressed by *The Children of the Night*. The president helped Robinson secure a post in the New York Custom House, which improved his circumstances considerably.

Robinson worked at the Custom House until 1910, when he published *The Town Down the River*, which was successful enough to allow him to become a full-time poet. He spent his summers at the artistic colony established by Mrs Edward MacDowell at Peterboro, New Hampshire, and wrote most of his poetry there. His next collection was *The Man Against the Sky* (1916) and the following year he published the first part of his Arthurian trilogy, *Merlin*. *Lancelot* followed in 1920 but the third part, *Tristram*, did not appear until 1927. Meanwhile he published *The Three Taverns* (1920) and *Avon's Harvest* (1921). Robinson also published a volume of *Collected Poems* in 1921 and it was awarded the Pulitzer Prize the following year.

The verse flowed steadily from his pen until the year he died: *Roman Bartholow* (1923), *The Man Who Died Twice* (1924, also winner of the Pulitzer Prize), *Dionysus in Doubt* (1925), *Cavender's House* (1929), *The Glory of the Nightingales* (1930), *Matthias at the Door* (1931), *Nicodemus* (1932), *Talifer* (1933), *Amaranth* (1934), and *King Jasper* (1935). Robinson published his sonnets in a volume *Sonnets 1889–1927* in 1928.

Robinson enjoyed real success by the 1920s though his style was substantially the same as when he first began to write; the public moves more slowly than the literary world and he was not too 'modern' to earn immediate and grateful appreciation from a large number of readers. But his work did not develop sufficiently for interest in him to remain at the same level and his reputation is rather less, now, nearly 50 years after his death. But very good things can be found in his work; he used existing forms and his intelligence and craftsmanship are evident; his observation is keen, and often ironic, and he is never romantic or sentimental. He is chiefly concerned with human relationships and the human condition, with the emphasis on the individual – in this he is the true heir of the New England tradition.

**Robinson, (Esme Stuart) Lennox** 1886–1958. Lennox Robinson was born in the county of Cork and became associated with the Irish theatre in his early twenties. *The Clancy Name*, a one-act play, was produced at the Abbey Theatre in 1908 and he was manager of the company from 1910 to 1914 and from 1919 to 1923. Robinson was manager of the Abbey Theatre during the tour of the USA (1911), which made it famous outside Ireland. He was also a successful playwright, the author of over 20 plays that mirrored the changes in Irish life both before and after the Easter Rising of 1916. The best known of these are *The Whiteheaded Boy* (1916), a comedy that was a success in both London and New York, *The Lost Leader* (1918), *Crabbed Youth and Age* (1922), *The Big House* (1926), *The Far-Off Hills* (1928), and *Church Street* (1934). Robinson's contributions to dramatic history and criticism include *The Irish Theatre*, a collection of lectures (1939) and his autobiography *Curtain Up* (1942). With Donagh MacDonagh he edited *The Oxford Book of Irish Verse* (1958).

*Robinson Crusoe* (*The Life and Strange Surprising Adventures of Robinson Crusoe, of York, Mariner. Written by Himself*). Defoe's immortal romance, first published in 1719, was based on the story of Alexander Selkirk, the sailing master of the privateer *Cinque Ports Galley* in Dampier's expedition of 1703, who decided to stay on the remote island of Juan Fernandez in the Pacific, off the coast of Chile, after quarrelling with his captain, Thomas Stradling. Selkirk was alone on the island from 1704 until 1709, when Woodes Rogers commanded another privateering expedition in which Dampier served as pilot. Selkirk was rescued from his island solitude; and both Rogers and Dampier published journals of their travels. Selkirk had run away to sea and Defoe's hero begins his adventures in the same way, leaving his family and forgetting the precepts taught him with such care in order to answer a 'burning lust of ambition for great things'.

As a mariner Crusoe has a number of adventures, including capture by Barbary pirates and a period as their slave, and the saving of his life by the Moorish boy, Xury, whom he sells for a good price to a Portuguese trader. The shipwreck off South America leaves him entirely alone, to survive as best he can. He salvages everything from the wreck that may prove useful; he builds a house of sorts, and a boat, and domesticates the island goats. He keeps a scrupulous record of what happens – the passing of days and the sudden shocked discovery that he may not be alone on the island after all. Cannibal natives come to his island and he saves the life of one of them, whom the others were going to kill; he calls him Friday from the day on which the event occurred and makes him his servant. When a ship at last approaches the island it proves to be an English one, with a mutinous crew. Crusoe subdues the mutineers and escapes from the island. According to his reckoning, he has been on the island for 28 years, 2 months, and 19 days.

An outline of the great adventure gives no idea of the flavour of the book or the character of Crusoe. *Robinson Crusoe* was not the first novel in the English language but it would not be too much to say that it was the first great one. Just as

---

'Robinson Crusoe saving his goods out of the wreck of the ship.' An illustration from an edition of Defoe's novel published in 1726. *Robinson Crusoe* was first published in 1719.

Defoe was a great original so is his character. What is remarkable about Crusoe is his matter-of-factness; in his extraordinary situation how would a sturdy self-reliant man of the early 18th century behave? As Robinson Crusoe does, we are convinced. He is resourceful, observant, frightened, and horribly alone; he is not romantic, he does not indulge in metaphysical speculation – in fact he is well aware that God's matters are perfectly straightforward (Defoe was a Dissenter, after all). Defoe makes his reader vividly aware of Crusoe's responses to everything, of the day-by-day progress of his life, such as it is, and his passionate prayers when the shadow of despair comes near. But Crusoe has little time for bouts of despair; he has to make pots out of clay, discover that turtles provide delicious food, and learn how to protect his skin from the sun until he becomes accustomed to it – he has to survive in terms that strike a chord in every reader. Coleridge was right when he said that Crusoe was 'the universal representative, the person for whom every reader could substitute himself'.

Defoe continued the story in *The Farther Adventures of Robinson Crusoe: being the Second and Last Part of his Life*, which was also published in 1719. One of the 'farther' adventures is his return to the island with Friday, the attack by savages in a fleet of canoes as he leaves the island, and the death of Friday in the encounter. *The Serious Reflections during the Life and Surprising Adventures of Robinson Crusoe, with his Vision of the Angelick World* was published in 1720. It is a moralistic work by a man of considerable personal experience who was also a well-educated and thoughtful Dissenter. There is much of interest in it but only committed students of Defoe ever get around to reading it. Particularly rewarding, in the light of *Robinson Crusoe*, is the first chapter, 'Of Solitude'.

**Rob Roy** A novel by Sir Walter Scott, set in the north of England in the early 18th century, first published in 1817.

It concerns the adventures of Francis Osbaldistone, banished from London by his father, a successful merchant, because Francis will not work in his father's business. At the house of his uncle, Sir Hildebrand, he meets Rashleigh his youngest son, both greedy and malicious, and Diana Vernon, Rashleigh's cousin on whom he has designs. When Francis is favourably received by Diana, Rashleigh determines to destroy him. He is already plotting to ruin Francis's father. At the prompting of Diana, Francis goes to the Highlands, accompanied by Bailie Nicol Jarvie, to seek the help of Rob Roy MacGregor, the out-law. In the Highlands Francis witnesses a clash between clansmen and the king's troops and Rob Roy's escape. With the help of the spirited Diana and Rob Roy, Francis is able to unmask Rash-leigh's villainy and regain the money which the latter has embezzled from Francis's father. Rash-leigh, who dabbles in everything, knows some-thing about the Jacobites and betrays them to the government. For this final wickedness Rob Roy kills him.

Rob Roy was a historical character. A drover, he became a powerful and dangerous outlaw when he and his clan were proscribed as Jacobite sympathizers. He was a ruthless opponent of the government but he was famous for disinterested kindness and his partisanship on behalf of the oppressed. In 1716 he came under the protection of the Duke of Argyle and assumed the name of Campbell.

**Robson, Sylvia**   The heroine of Elizabeth Gas-kell's *Sylvia's Lovers*. Her bitter experience of a loveless marriage is followed by total disillusion in the man she really loves. Pity for the husband she despises eventually brings her some degree of resignation.

**Rochester, Edward**   The hero of Charlotte Brontë's *Jane Eyre*. The master of Thornfield Hall, he engages Jane Eyre as governess for his illegitimate daughter, Adèle. He falls in love with her, and keeps from her the secret of his first marriage – from which there is no release. A catastrophic fire at the Hall resolves the impasse, though it leaves him blind and maimed.

**Rochester, John Wilmot, 2nd Earl of** 1648–80. Rochester was born at Ditchley near Woodstock, and spent a year (1660–61) at Wad-ham College, Oxford. He continued his educa-tion with a tour of Europe, and returned to fight, with notable courage, with the navy during the second Dutch War. His wit made him a favourite with Charles II but his dissolute behaviour and unbridled tongue forced the king to banish him from court on several occasions. Nonetheless he retained the favour of Charles, who liked having witty and attractive people around him. Roches-ter married Elizabeth Malet, a wealthy heiress, in 1667 but did not change his way of life. He was an erratic and unpredictable patron of poets and dramatists. Dryden's comfortable acceptance of success irritated Rochester so much that he set up John Crowne as a rival, and for some time Rochester was believed to have hired three men to waylay and thrash the elderly poet in Covent Garden in 1679. He quarrelled with the Earl of

Mulgrave, who challenged him to a duel; Rochester succeeded in wriggling out of the engagement. His health broke down in 1679 and by the age of 32 his way of life looked like being his downfall. He asked Gilbert Burnet, formerly the king's chaplain, for advice and instruction, and died a penitent in the following year.

Rochester was a minor poet of attractive qual-ity. His satirical work is his most accomplished, notably *A Satyr against Mankind* (1675). But little of his work was published during his lifetime though some poems circulated in manuscript. Burnet's account of his conversations with Rochester during the last months of the latter's life were published soon after Rochester's death, and two editions of his collected *Poems on Several Occasions* appeared (1680 and 1691). *Collected Works* was edited by John Hayward (1926), *Poems by John Wilmot, Earl of Rochester* by Vivian de Sola Pinto (1953) and *Complete Poems* by D. M. Vieth (1968).

***Roderick Hudson***   A novel by Henry James, first published as a serial in the *Atlantic Monthly*, from January to December 1875, and in volume form in 1876. The author revised it for its publication in England in 1879.

Roderick Hudson, an amateur sculptor, is taken to Europe by Rowland Mallet, a wealthy connoisseur who is deeply impressed by Roderick's talent. In Rome he introduces Roderick to his circle, which includes the French sculptor Gloriani. Rowland, an appreciator, sees Roderick as a creator; Gloriani is certain that the young American's talent exists only in the present and will never develop. But his opinion does not disturb Roderick, who seems to bear out Rowland's hopes by producing fine work in spite of sterile intervals and his dependence on others for stimulus.

Then Roderick meets Christina Light, daugh-ter of an American widow living in Europe; he is fascinated by her and deserts his work com-pletely, to the despair of Rowland. To try and force Roderick back to reality, Rowland brings Roderick's mother and fiancée from New Eng-land. Roderick's fiancée is Mary Garland, to whom Rowland is also attracted. The arrival of Mrs Hudson and Mary seems to work for a while; Roderick executes a fine bust of his mother but then Christina, urged by her am-bitious mother, marries Prince Casamassima – and Roderick comes to a complete stop.

Rowland is helpless in the face of Roderick's infatuation but he does arrange a visit to Switzer-land for Mary, Mrs Hudson, Roderick, and him-self. Unfortunately Christina is there too and

Roderick borrows money from Mary so that he can follow her. This provokes Rowland to a furious outburst that, while it reveals Rowland's dependence on him, takes Roderick by surprise. He is a natural egoist and cannot see that something may be given to him other than to please the giver, who thereby (in his eyes) also receives. His nature cannot, for that matter, accept that Christina has completely rejected him and she is obliged to do so again, in Switzerland. Roderick dies in a thunderstorm in the mountains and there is no way of knowing whether he fell to his death or if he jumped. Rowland and Mary now have nothing for each other; the real link was Roderick, whom they both loved.

**Roderick Random, The Adventures of**  A picaresque novel by Tobias Smollett, who modelled it on Le Sage's *Gil Blas*. It was Smollett's first novel, first published in 1748. The story opens in Scotland.

Roderick Random's father disappears and the boy is left in the care of his grandfather, who ill-treats him and leaves him penniless when he dies. Roderick is befriended by his uncle, Tom Bowling, a lieutenant in the navy, and decides to go to London to make his fortune; an old school friend, Hugh Strap, accompanies him as valet. The journey bristles with crude adventures and most of the characters they encounter seem to be rogues of one kind or another. In London, Roderick qualifies as a surgeon's mate but discovers that a bribe is what he needs to secure a commission, not qualifications. He becomes assistant to a French apothecary – and is seized by the press gang.

Forced into service as a common sailor on the man o'war *Thunder*, Roderick proves his qualifications and becomes a surgeon's mate, after all. The *Thunder* takes part in the siege of Cartagena (1741) and Roderick suffers all manner of humiliations and misadventures. On return to England he is shipwrecked and robbed and, lying naked on the shore, is found and succoured by a middle-aged woman poet, whose footman he becomes. He falls in love with the poet's niece, Narcissa, but the presence of suitors of considerable means obliges him to leave. He is kidnapped by smugglers and taken to France, where he finds his uncle Tom Bowling and a Monseiur d'Estrapes, who is his old friend Hugh Strap. The two return to London in their original partnership: Strap sets up Roderick, acts as his valet, and is going to aid and abet Roderick's design to marry an heiress.

Melinda Goosetrap is a likely quarry, but her mother is not impressed. At Bath, Roderick

The frontispiece to Vol. II of *Roderick Random*, 1748. Roderick discovers his long-lost uncle, Tom Bowling, in a tavern.

meets Narcissa again. He loses all he has at the gaming tables and, returning to London penniless, is thrown into a debtors' prison. Tom Bowling finds him there, obtains his release, and takes him aboard his own ship as a surgeon for a trading trip. During the voyage they encounter a wealthy trader, Don Roderigo; he proves to be Roderick's father, who had been disinherited by the evil grandfather and had left the country to make his fortune. They return to England and Roderick marries Narcissa. Strap marries her maid, Miss Williams. Roderick repurchases the family estate and has a rewarding time snubbing those relatives who, formerly, had put him down as an impecunious dependant.

There is hardly a pleasant episode in the whole narrative and the author displays an obsession with filth and violence. But the sheer vitality of the writing and the vivid, albeit grotesque, portrayal of life in London, in the navy, and, in the later chapters, in fashionable England, hold the attention even while the reader's sympathy is never wholly engaged.

*Roderick Random* is published in modern editions in The World's Classics, Everyman's Library, and in the Oxford English Novels series, edited by Paul-Gabriel Boucé (1968).

**Roderigo** The silly Venetian rejected by Desdemona in Shakespeare's *Othello*. He becomes the easy tool of Iago, who persuades him to continue his pursuit of Desdemona and to regard Cassio as his chief rival. He tries to kill Cassio but is himself killed; letters containing proof of Iago's guilt are found on his body.

**Roderigo, Don** The wealthy, apparently Spanish trader encountered by the hero and Tom Bowling in *Roderick Random* by Tobias Smollett. He turns out to be Roderick's long-vanished father.

**Roethke, Theodore** 1908–63. Roethke was born in Saginaw, Michigan, and educated at Michigan University. After further study at Harvard he taught English at various universities and published his first book of poems, *Open House*, in 1941. The volume of his work was small but Roethke maintained a consistently high level from the lyrics of his first verse to the mystical strain of his later work. His second collection was *The Lost Son* (1948), followed by *Praise to the End* (1951) and *The Waking* (1953, Pulitzer Prize). The range of his work was demonstrated in a selection called *Words for the Wind* (1958), for which he was awarded the Bollingen Prize in Poetry. *I am! Says the Lamb* (1961) was the last collection published during his lifetime; a posthumous volume, *The Far Field*, was published in 1964. Theodore Roethke's essays and lectures were edited by R. J. Mills and published as *On the Poet and His Craft* (1965).

**Roger of Hoveden** See **Hoveden, Roger of.**

**Roger of Wendover** See **Wendover, Roger of.**

**Rogers, Samuel** 1763–1855. The son of a banker, Rogers was born at Stoke Newington, then just north of London. His affluence (he succeeded to his father's fortune) gave him the opportunity to indulge his fancy for writing poetry. His work has not lasted and he is remembered chiefly as a generous patron at whose table the cultured elite of London was always welcome. He commissioned Turner as illustrator for an edition of his *Italy* (1822–28), for which he had followed Childe Harold's footsteps as a tribute to Byron. He was offered the laureateship on the death of Wordsworth but declined. Among his poetical works are *Ode to Superstition* (1786) and *The Pleasures of Memory* (1792); both are distinctly 18th-century in feeling while *Columbus* (1810)

and *Jacqueline* (1814) show him adjusting comfortably to the Romantic movement. *Recollections of the Table-Talk of Samuel Rogers* (1856; edited by Alexander Dyce) and *Recollections* (1859; edited by William Sharpe) are useful for information on the artistic life of the period.

**Rogers, Woodes** d. 1732. A captain in command of two privateering ships, the *Duke* and *Duchess*, during an expedition to the Pacific (1708–11), Rogers wrote a vivid account in his journal, published as *A Cruizing Voyage Round the World* (1712). His pilot was William Dampier, and Rogers tells of the seizure of Guayaquil in Ecuador from the Spaniards, who were forced to ransom the city, and the capture of a galleon from Manila. Also related is Rogers' visit to the island of Juan Fernández, where they found 'a man clothed in goat-skins, who seemed wilder than the original owners of his apparel. His name was Alexander Selkirk'. Nothing is recorded of Rogers' early life. He was Governor of the Bahamas (1718–21 and 1729–32) and was chiefly responsible for the suppression of piracy. See also **Dampier, William** and *Robinson Crusoe*.

*Roland and Vernagu* A Middle English verse romance, based on an Old French source. (See **metrical romances**.) While Charlemagne's army is fighting in Spain, Roland meets Vernagu in combat. Vernagu is the giant black champion of the Sultan of Babylon; the story tells of the prolonged combat and of Roland's chivalrous behaviour when his opponent is overcome with fatigue. *Roland and Vernagu* was edited by J. Maidment for the Abbotsford Club (1836) and by S. J. H. Herrtage for the Early English Text Society (1880 and 1973).

**Rolle of Hampole, Richard** *c.*1295–1349. The English mystic Richard Rolle was born at Thornton-le-Dale, near Pickering in Yorkshire, and studied at Oxford. He left at the age of 19 with a knowledge of Latin, and records at the Sorbonne suggest that he completed his studies as a master and a priest in Paris. From about 1326 he occupied a hermit's cell on the estate of John Dalton, whom he had known at Oxford. After about four years there he moved to another cell at Ainderby near Northallerton, where his friend Margaret Kirkby lived a similar life. His last years were spent at Hampole near Doncaster, near a convent of Cistercian nuns whose spiritual guide he became. The nuns sought his canonization after his death but they were unsuccessful, though an office for his festival was composed and a record made of miracles ascribed to his saintly influence.

Rolle was one of the first religious writers to use his own language as well as Latin. Remaining aloof from the world around him, he spread his teaching through the written word: his message was basically that all men can realize the personal bond with God, as he had, by contemplation of God through love. But he did acknowledge that for most men life was an active business; he sought in his writing to teach them the spirit in which to live.

Among his English works are *The Psalter, or Psalms of David and certain Canticles, with a Translation and Exposition in English*, edited by H. R. Bramley (1884); *Ego dormio et cor meum vigilat, the Form of Living, Meditations on the Passion*; and, sometimes attributed to him, *The Pricke of Conscience*, a summary of medieval theology.

*The English Writings of Richard Rolle* was edited by H. E. Allen (1931, revised 1963). In this the *Psalter* is represented by excerpts.

**Rolliad, Criticisms on The** After the success of William Pitt and his followers in the election of 1784, a series of political satires appeared in *The Morning Herald* and *The Daily Advertiser* in that year. The satires took the form of reviews of an imaginary epic called *The Rolliad*. John Rolle was a Tory MP and one of Pitt's supporters; the epic narrated the adventures of his heroic ancestor, the Norman Duke Rollo. The authors, members of the Whig club the Esto Perpetua, included General Richard Fitzpatrick, Lord John Townshend, the antiquary George Ellis, and French Laurence, Regius Professor of Civil Law at Oxford. The *Rolliad* satires were followed by *Political Eclogues*, in which Pitt and his followers appeared as Virgilian shepherds. The death of the poet laureate, William Whitehead, in 1785 prompted further satire against the Tories from the same group in the form of *Probationary Odes* for the vacant laureateship.

**Rolls Series** The publication of 'The Chronicles and Memorials of Great Britain and Ireland from the Invasion of the Romans to the Reign of Henry VIII' was authorized by the government in 1857. The suggestion was made by archivist Joseph Stevenson and recommended by the Master of the Rolls, Sir John Romilly. Some hundred chronicles and histories were published in the Rolls Series by 1914, edited by the most eminent historians of the time.

**Roman Actor, The** A tragedy by Philip Massinger, first produced in 1626 and first published in 1629. Highly regarded in its time and praised by Massinger's contemporaries, the author considered the play to be his best work. It has not been revived in the modern theatre. The plot is based on Suetonius, which Massinger could have read in Philemon Holland's translation.

The emperor Domitian conceives a passion for Domitia Longina, wife of the senator Aelius Lamia; Domitia is taken from her husband and is made empress. Domitian is intensely jealous; but Domitia does not care for the emperor and falls in love with an actor, Paris. Unfortunately she betrays herself at a performance in which Paris plays a character who threatens suicide when his love rejects him. Domitian is brought information by his wife's enemies; he surprises her with Paris and kills the actor with his own hands. Domitia, in a following scene, heaps contempt on the emperor and abuses him for his subservience to his passions; but he cannot bring himself to harm her. However, he adds her name to a list of the proscribed – someone else will kill her. Domitia discovers the proscription while he sleeps and she hastily summons those named along with her. Domitian is tricked into leaving the protection of his tribunes by one of the conspirators, Parthenius, with the promise of news of a victory in the east. Among the six who strike him down are Domitia, his niece Julia, and his cousin Domitilla.

**Roman Republic, The History of the Progress and Termination of the** A survey of Roman history from its origins to the end of the Republic by Adam Ferguson, first published in 1783. In an age of great historians Ferguson's contribution provided an account of the events that led to the subversion of the Republic and the establishment of the Empire, an institution that bore the seeds of its own destruction – and gave Edward Gibbon the theme for his great work. Ferguson writes well and at times his narrative of events is powerful; however, research has increased the knowledge available to historians and his book has been superseded.

**Romany Rye, The** See *Lavengro*.

**Romaunt of the Rose, The** A translation of *Le Roman de La Rose*, a French verse romance of the 13th century by Guillaume de Lorris (the first 4067 lines) and Jean de Meung (the greater part, 22,047 lines), who wrote his extension about 40 years after de Lorris's work. The English version (7700 lines) is of the first part and of some of the extension. Much of this has been attributed to Geoffrey Chaucer.

The first part is a tale of courtly love in which the rose symbolizes the lady. The poet would pluck a rose but, though invited into the garden by Idleness, finds that the rose is closely guarded.

He surrenders himself to the God of Love, who instructs him, but Jealousy builds a castle that surrounds the rose. The second part continues within the allegorical framework but the second poet substitutes satire for reverence: his tone is harsh and cynical and his targets are women, religion, and the social order.

**Romeo and Juliet**   A tragedy by William Shakespeare. This was his first romantic tragedy, vastly different from the gory horrors of *Titus Andronicus*, and was first produced *c*.1595. It was printed in a quarto of 1597 and again in 1599 with the authentic text; it was published in the First Folio of 1623. The source of the play was *The Tragicall Historye of Romeus and Juliet* by Arthur Brooke (1562), which in turn was based on a story by the Italian, Matteo Bandello. Variations of the tale were found in the work of a number of Bandello's contemporaries.

The scene is Verona, where the two principal families, Capulet and Montague, are sworn enemies. After a bloody brawl in the streets the Prince of Verona tells the heads of the two houses to keep the peace in future – or pay with their lives. Capulet, after further strictures laid down by the prince for him and Montague, decides that it should not be hard for two old men to keep the peace. He announces a ball; Count Paris seeks the hand of his daughter Juliet and Capulet encourages the match – if two more years may pass. His daughter is not yet 14.

Romeo, Montague's son, hears of the feast at the Capulet house and knows that Rosaline will be there. He goes to the feast in disguise; but the sight of Juliet drives all thought of Rosaline from his mind. Romeo and Juliet are in love from the moment they see each other. He waits under her window after the feast and they arrange a secret marriage. Juliet confides in her nurse and Romeo persuades Friar Lawrence to perform the ceremony. That night is theirs but the day has been disastrous: Romeo's friend, Mercutio, a kinsman of the Prince of Verona, meets Tybalt (related to Juliet on her mother's side), who is looking for a quarrel – he had been infuriated at the Capulets' feast at seeing Romeo present. His quarrel with Mercutio leads to a fight. Romeo comes upon the scene but cannot prevent it. Tybalt kills Mercutio and Romeo kills Tybalt. Romeo is banished from Verona and leaves for Mantua after consummating his marriage; he and Juliet depend completely on the counsel of Friar Lawrence, who intends to make the marriage public at the first opportune moment.

Capulet insists on Juliet's marriage to Count Paris and the desperate Juliet consults the friar.

He gives her a potion to drink on the eve of her wedding; it will render her apparently dead 'for two and forty hours'. He will warn Romeo, who will await her recovery in the vault and then take her to Mantua. But Friar Lawrence's message does not reach Romeo before news of Juliet's 'death' and in despair he buys poison. But he goes to the Capulets' vault for a last sight of Juliet. He encounters Count Paris there and kills him; then he kisses Juliet for the last time and drinks the poison. Juliet awakes and finds him dead, the poison vial still in his hand. She kills herself with his dagger. The sequence of events is related to the prince, Capulet, and Montague by Friar Lawrence and Balthasar, Romeo's servant. The tragedy reconciles the two families.

This is the most famous of all Shakespeare's plays and the tragic children (that, after all, is what they are) have become the world's most famous lovers. The play itself almost defies criticism; the work of a young man who conveyed to perfection the soaring ecstasy of a first passionate love. The story works, the characters are all believable, and the poetry is lovely – it is quoted endlessly, and it never loses its charm.

**Romola**   A novel by George Eliot, first published in the *Cornhill Magazine* (July 1862 to August 1863). The setting is Florence at the end of the 15th century, and the story is woven into the historical events surrounding the downfall of the Medici and the rise and fall of Savonarola.

Into the lives of the blind scholar, Bardo, and his daughter, Romola, comes the clever and charming young Greek, Tito Melema. Tito is completely ruthless and self-seeking but his charm wins him the friendship of Bardo and Romola becomes his wife. When, a short while after their marriage, Tito is revealed as having betrayed Bardo's trust in him, the full depth of his villainy comes to the surface. He has tricked a peasant girl, Tessa, into a mock marriage; he has robbed Baldassare, who was the benefactor of his childhood, and abandoned him in prison. Now he is capitalizing on the political strife in the city by playing a double game, trying to keep the confidence of both sides. Romola, who looks to the austere Savonarola for guidance, believes in his counsel even in the face of papal wrath: her disillusion in her marriage is paralleled by her disillusion in Savonarola when his high prophetic mission becomes a religious tyranny. Tito is eventually killed by Baldassare when the old man escapes from prison. Romola finds some consolation and peace in serving others and caring for Tessa and her children by Tito.

*Romola* was written after some very hard work

'The Painted Record.' One of Sir Frederick Leighton's illustrations for *Romola*, first published in the *Cornhill Magazine*, July 1862–August 1863. Romola visits the painter Piero de Cosimo to look at the unfinished portrait of her father, and is surprised to see also a sketch of her husband, Tito.

by George Eliot on the Florence of the Renaissance. The city of Machiavelli, Savonarola and the Medici was researched with scrupulous accuracy and the historical events were exhaustively studied before she wove the tale of Romola and the appalling Tito around them. The novel is impressive – and oddly unsatisfactory. Romola is an interesting heroine because she is a George Eliot heroine, not because she is a girl of 15th-century Florence. The city is superbly presented, but the invented characters do not seem to quite belong there.

**Rookwood**   See **Ainsworth, William Harrison** and **Turpin, Dick.**

**Rosalind**   The heroine of Shakespeare's *As You Like It*. The daughter of the exiled duke, she falls in love with Orlando, the son of a supporter of her father's. The usurping duke banishes her from court and she goes to the Forest of Arden, disguised as a man, to look for her father. She takes the name of Ganymede and remains unrecognized by Orlando, who confides to the 'young man' how much he loves Rosalind.

**Rosaline**   In Shakespeare's *Love's Labour's Lost*, one of the ladies in the Princess of France's suite. Berowne falls in love with her and when she has to leave Navarre she charges him to be witty for the sake of others, rather than to satisfy his own conceits.

**Rosalynde: Euphues Golden Legacie**   A pastoral romance by Thomas Lodge, first published in 1590 and written during the author's voyage to the Canary Islands in 1588. The basis of the story is to be found in the 14th-century *The Tale of Gamelyn* and Lodge's version was used by Shakespeare in *As You Like It*. The differences are the emphasis, by Lodge, on the ill-treatment of the younger brother by the elder and on the restoration of the rightful duke by force of arms. The names are sometimes different: the younger brother is Rosader, the elder is Saladyne, Celia is Alinda. The characters of Jacques and Touchstone are originals in *As You Like It*.

**Rosciad, The**   See **Churchill, Charles.**

**Rose and the Ring, The**   A comic fairy tale written and illustrated by W. M. Thackeray, first published in 1855 under the pseudonym of Michael Angelo Titmarsh. Fairy Blackstick gives each of her goddaughters, King Savio's wife and King Pedella's wife, a present – a magic rose and ring that render their wearers irresistible. Savio's wife gives birth to Prince Giglio, whose throne is later usurped by his uncle, Valoroso. Giglio doesn't mind too much, as long as he has enough clothes, horses, and money – and can pay court to his cousin, Angelica. She, however, favours Prince Bulbo, son of King Padella, who has usurped the throne of King Cavolfiore, causing the rightful princess, Rosalba, to wander from the palace, get lost in the forest, and re-emerge in the plot as Betsinda, lady's maid to Angelica. After many changes in the ownership of the magic gifts and some interventions from Blackstick, all ends well, with Giglio marrying Betsinda-Rosalba and Bulbo his Angelica.

**Rose Mary**   A narrative poem by Dante Gabriel Rossetti, first published in *Ballads and Sonnets* (1881). Rose Mary seeks the truth in a magic stone, a beryl which vouchsafes it to the pure. She sees that her lover is in danger and he is warned; but her lover is faithless and this leads to his death. Rose Mary is not without sin and her fault has allowed the spirits of evil to enter the stone: they have concealed the truth about her lover. Rose Mary breaks the stone with her father's sword, the spirits are cast out, and her soul is saved; but she dies with the breaking of the stone.

**Rosenberg, Isaac** 1890–1918. Isaac Rosenberg was born in Bristol of Russian–Jewish parents, but grew up in Whitechapel in East London where he attended council schools. He was apprenticed as an engraver and studied art at the Slade School, and his friends included Mark Gertler, John Rodker, and other Jewish artists and writers. His paintings have an affinity with the French post-impressionists; his poetry looks beyond the Georgians though that is the period to which he belongs.

Rosenberg's first poetry appeared in magazines and privately printed leaflets. His first volume was *Night and Day* (1912); *Youth* (1915) and *Moses: A Play* (1916, some poems appearing in the volume) completed his published work; he was killed in action in 1918. His *Collected Works: Poetry, Prose, Letters and Some Drawings* (1937) was edited by Gordon Bottomley and D. W. Harding and had a foreword by a war poet who survived the conflict, Siegfried Sassoon. *The Collected Poems* were issued separately in 1949. Isaac Rosenberg is one of the World War I poets whose early death is most deeply regretted. 'Dead Man's Dump', 'Break of Day in the Trenches', and 'Midsummer Frost' are much anthologized poems that give a fair idea of his quality.

**Rose of Dutcher's Coolly** A novel by Hamlin Garland, first published in 1895.

Rose Dutcher is a motherless girl who is brought up by her father on his farm in Dutcher's Coolly in Wisconsin. Her father is a simple and affectionate man but Rose is restless in the confined life of the farm. She dreams of becoming a writer and confides in Dr Thatcher, a physician from Madison, who lives at the farm while Rose attends the state university. Rose is a distinguished student and after graduation she leaves the farm, in spite of her father's grief at losing her. She goes to Chicago and the novel traces her development as a woman and a writer – and the impact on her of cultured and sophisticated minds.

Rose Dutcher is a representative heroine for Hamlin Garland, one who rebels against the monotony and depression of spirit that he saw was often the lot of girls on lonely Midwest farms.

**Ross, Alexander** 1591–1654. One of the circle of writers who enjoyed the patronage of Edward Benlowes, Ross is remembered as a remarkably disputatious scholar. He also wrote – perhaps incidentally – some charming verse in his presentations of mythology in the form of allegory in *Mel Heliconium* (1642) and *Mystagogus Poeticus* (1647). Posterity has disposed of Ross but in his day he felt able to oppose the teachings of Sir Kenelm Digby, Hobbes, and Galileo, and the speculations of Sir Thomas Browne.

**Ross, Alexander** 1699–1784. Ross was born at Kincardine O'Neil in Kincardineshire and was educated at Aberdeen University. He became a teacher at Lochlea in Angus and is remembered for a single work, the pastoral *Helenore, or the Fortunate Shepherdess* (1768), published when the author was in his seventies. The poem is written in the dialect of north-east Scotland and contains some fine scene painting and effective lyrics.

**Rossetti, Christina Georgina** 1830–94. The sister of Dante Gabriel and William Michael Rossetti and the youngest of the three, Christina was born in London and educated at home by her mother. She showed promise as a poet before her brother, and her grandfather had small collections printed when Christina was 12 and 15. She was a delicate and devout girl – the latter quality is clear in her poetry – and spent much of her life inside the family circle. She might have married the painter James Collinson but he became a Catholic and Christina was too staunch a Protestant to continue with their engagement.

Christina Rossetti's lyrics 'An End' and 'Dream Lane' were published in the first number of *The Germ* (1850) under the pseudonym 'Ellen Alleyne'. She contributed further poems both to *The Germ* and to other periodicals. Her first collection was **Goblin Market** *and Other Poems* (1862), which gave her the first literary success of the Pre-Raphaelites. ***The Prince's Progress** and Other Poems* (1866) was published in the same year that she rejected another proposal of marriage and her poems thereafter convey her increasing preoccupation with the rejection of earthly allurements. *Sing Song: A Nursery Rhyme Book* (1872) was illustrated by Arthur Hughes. *A Pageant and Other Poems* (1881) contains the sonnet sequence 'Monna Innominata', which is filled with a sense of the claims of divine love over human passion. By this time her health was bad enough to make her a complete invalid. *Time Flies: A Reading Diary* (1885) contained 130 poems and thoughts for each day. *The Face of the Deep: A Devotional Commentary on the Apocalypse* (1892) also contained poems and verse fragments and was the last original work published during her lifetime. The posthumous *New Poems, hitherto*

The Rossetti family, 7 October 1863, photographed by Lewis Carroll. Left to right; Dante Gabriel Rossetti, Christina Rossetti, Frances Rossetti (mother), and William Michael Rossetti.

*Unpublished and Uncollected* (1896) was edited by her brother W. M. Rossetti.

The range of Christina Rossetti's verse was limited by her preoccupations but within her limits she achieved more than had any English poet of her sex. Elizabeth Barrett Browning, her near contemporary, had more intellectual force and a wider range but Christina Rossetti had a far better instinct for verbal music and it informs everything she wrote. The standard edition of her work is *Collected Poems* (1904, reprinted 1968) edited by W. M. Rossetti, who contributed a memoir. Her poems are to be found in most anthologies of English verse. The best known are probably 'Goblin Market', 'Spring Quiet', 'Eve', 'A Birthday', 'When I am dead, my dearest', 'Uphill', the carol 'In the bleak mid-winter', and the sonnet 'Remember'.

**Rossetti, Dante Gabriel** 1828–82. The son of Gabriele Rossetti, a royalist exile from Naples, Dante Gabriel Rossetti was born in London. Gabriele Rossetti became Professor of Italian at King's College, London, and his children were bilingual in English and Italian. Dante Gabriel received his education at home and at King's College School. He later studied art and was at the Antique School of the Royal Academy for a time. There he was restless and dissatisfied with the conventional academic approach, a feeling he shared with two fellow students, John Everett Millais and William Holman Hunt. From their discontent the Pre-Raphaelite Brotherhood was born, and Rossetti founded the short-lived journal, *The Germ*.

Rossetti's poems were first published in *The*

*Germ*, notably the first versions of **The Blessed Damozel**, 'My Sister's Sleep', and the sonnets on paintings by Memling, Mantegna, Giorgione, and Ingres. He did not publish a volume until 1861; this was *The Early Italian Poets*, a group of translations from the Italian, including a prose version of Dante's *La Vita Nuova*. The book was later revised and republished in a new arrangement as *Dante and his Circle* (1874). Rossetti had not ceased to write original poetry, however, though most of this remained unseen for a number of years. In 1850 he fell in love with Elizabeth Siddal, the milliner's assistant who became the most famous model of the Pre-Raphaelite painters. They could not afford to marry until 1860 and meanwhile Rossetti published 'The Burden of Nineveh', 'The Staff and Scrip', and a revised version of 'The Blessed Damozel' in *The Oxford and Cambridge Magazine* (1856). Elizabeth took laudanum regularly because she was tubercular and used it against the symptoms of her illness; she died of an overdose in 1861. Rossetti copied all his unpublished poems into a manuscript book and it was buried with her; he destroyed the other copies.

Rossetti settled in Chelsea and for the next few years was chiefly occupied with his painting. He was troubled by Elizabeth's death, fearing it might have been suicide. In 1869 he yielded to his friends' persuasion and gave consent for the exhumation of the poems which had lain in Elizabeth's grave for the past seven years. *Poems by D. G. Rossetti* (1870) established him as a poet in England. The volume included **Sister Helen**, **Eden Bower**, 'The Stream's Secret', **Jenny**, 'Love's Nocturne', and part of the sonnet sequence called **The House of Life**. Rossetti was not immune from adverse criticism and this is believed to have affected his already precarious nervous stability. He lived with William Morris at Kelmscott Manor from 1871 to 1874, trying to impose some order on his life for his health's sake, but during that period he began to take chloral to combat insomnia. In spite of the further damage this inflicted on him – he began to suffer from delusions of persecution – he wrote enough poetry to publish a second collection, *Ballads and Sonnets* (1881), which contained the rest of *The House of Life* sonnets, **Rose Mary**, **The White Ship**, and **The King's Tragedy**.

Rossetti translated Gottfried Burger's *Lenore* and Hartmann von Aue's *Henry the Leper* from the German and Villon's *Ballade des dames du temps jadis* from the French. The prose tale *Hand and Soul*, purporting to be the biography of an Italian painter of the 13th century, appears in the first issue of *The Germ*; another, *St Agnes of the*

*Intercession*, was never completed. *The Collected Works* (1886) of D. G. Rossetti and *Poems of Rossetti* (1904), with illustrations from his own pictures and designs, were edited by his brother W. M. Rossetti. The standard edition, *Works* (1911), was also edited by W. M. Rossetti and this provided the text used in *Poems and Translations 1850–1870* (Oxford Standard Authors, 1913). *The Letters of Dante Gabriel Rossetti* was edited by Oswald Doughty and John Robert Wahl (four volumes, 1965–67).

**Rossetti, William Michael** 1829–1919. The younger brother of Dante Gabriel Rossetti. Born in London, he was closely associated with his brother in the movement called the Pre-Raphaelite Brotherhood and edited its short-lived journal, *The Germ*. An art critic for *The Spectator*, his reviews were collected and published as *Fine Art, chiefly Contemporary* (1867). W. M. Rossetti published a blank verse translation of Dante's *Inferno* (1865), *Lives of Some Famous Poets* (1878), *A Life of John Keats* (1887), *D. G. Rossetti: his Family Letters, with a Memoir* (1895), and *Pre-Raphaelite Diaries and Letters* (1900).

**Roth, Philip** 1933– . Roth was born in Newark, New Jersey, and educated at Bucknell University, Pennsylvania, and at the University of Chicago. His first book, *Goodbye, Columbus* (1959), contained a novella and five short stories and won him the National Book Award. Jewish-American life and modern American life generally are the subjects of his comedies of manners, which continued with *Letting Go* (1962), *When She was Good* (1967), *Portnoy's Complaint* (1969), *The Breast* (1972), *The Great American Novel* (1973), *My Life as a Man* (1974), and *The Professor of Desire* (1977). *Our Gang* (1971) is a satire on the Nixon administration, and *Reading Myself and Others* (1975) a collection of essays.

**Roughing It** A book of autobiographical episodes by Mark Twain, covering his days in the West. It was first published in 1872 and includes descriptions of a journey from St Louis to Nevada, a visit to the Mormon community in Utah, and life and adventures in Virginia City and San Francisco. The personality of the author pervades every episode and a vivid many-sided picture emerges of the West in the 1860s.

**Round Table, The** See **Hazlitt, William.**

**Rousillon, Countess of** In Shakespeare's *All's Well that Ends Well*, the mother of Bertram. Helena is her ward and the countess regards her as a suitable match for her son.

**Rowe, Nicholas** 1674–1718. Rowe was born in London and educated at Westminster School. Later he entered the Middle Temple and qualified as a barrister, but he became a man of means when his father died (1692) and decided on a literary career; his friendship with Joseph Addison and Alexander Pope would certainly have influenced him. His first play was *The Ambitious Stepmother* (1700); *Tamerlane* (1701) was more successful, and *The Fair Penitent* (1703; see **Fatal Dowry, The**) brought him celebrity. However, his next effort – a comedy, *The Biter* (1704) – proved that Rowe had no talent for the form. He returned to tragedy with *Ulysses* (1705), *The Royal Convert* (1707), and had a major success with **The Tragedy of Jane Shore** (1714). His last play was *The Tragedy of Lady Jane Grey* (1715).

Rowe, the last Restoration and the first 18th-century playwright was simply a skilful professional working within contemporary dramatic conventions. The impulse that flared into life with Otway's *Venice Preserv'd* was an isolated one and while Rowe was a better dramatist than his contemporaries he proved not quite good enough for posterity. His tragedies had a moral tone lacking in the drama of the previous fifty years, but they are none the better for the inclusion.

Rowe performed useful service with his painstaking edition of Shakespeare's plays. He divided them into acts and scenes and provided stage directions; he worked on the text to remove corruptions and make it more intelligible. His edition (1709) was the first since the First Folio and Rowe deserves our gratitude. Rowe was also distinguished by his fine translation of Lucan's *Pharsalia* (1718), highly praised by Samuel Johnson. He was poet laureate from 1715.

**Rowlands, Samuel** *c.*1570–*c.*1630. Nothing is known for certain of the life of Samuel Rowlands, not even the exact dates of his birth and death. It is possible that he was a cooper of East Smithfield who was also a churchwarden and wrote in his spare time. He is remembered (chiefly by scholars) as a writer of verse and prose satires, though he also wrote religious poems, notably *The Betraying of Christ: Judas in Despaire* (1598), *A Sacred Memorie of the Miracles Wrought by Jesus Christ* (1618), and *Heavens Glory, Seeke it; Hearts Vanitie, Flye it; Hells Horror, Fere it* (1628). Among his satires, comments on the manners of his time, are *The Letting of Humors Blood in the Headvaine* (1600), *Tis Merrie when Gossips Meete* (1602), *Looke to it, for Ile Stabbe ye* (1604), *Hell's Broke Loose* (1605), and *Democritus: Or Doctor Merry-Man his Medicines against Melancholy Humors* (1607). *A Terrible Battell betweene the Two*

*Consumers of the Whole World; Time and Death* (1606) is a dialogue in verse, and *The Famous Historie of Guy Earle of Warwick* (1608) a comic ballad. *The Melancholie Knight* (1615) is a verse monologue which ridicules nostalgia for a romantic past.

**Rowlandson, Mary** *c.*1635–78. Mary White was the daughter of an early settler in Massachusetts, John White, who prospered and became a leading citizen of the town of Lancaster. She married Joseph Rowlandson, a Congregational minister, in 1656. During the war with the Indians called King Philip's War the Narraganset tribe attacked Lancaster, and on 10 February 1676 Mary and her three children were abducted. The youngest child died, but Rowlandson succeeded in ransoming his wife and two surviving children after nearly 12 weeks.

Mary Rowlandson wrote an account of her experiences and this was published in Cambridge, Massachusetts, in 1682: *The Soveraignty and Goodness of God, Together with the Faithfulness of His Promises Displayed; Being a Narrative of the Captivity and Restauration of Mrs Mary Rowlandson.* In spite of its discouraging title the *Narrative,* written in clear unadorned prose, became a classic of early American literature and has so far appeared in no less than 30 editions. It has been plundered by novelists in search of the true background of the lives of the early settlers.

**Rowley, William** *c.*1585–*c.*1642. Rowley is best known for his collaboration with other playwrights (see **Middleton, Thomas; Heywood, Thomas; Ford, John; Dekker, Thomas;** and **Webster, John**) since the plays known to be his own works are undistinguished. Nothing is known of Rowley's birth or his life beyond his identification as an actor with The Queen's Men before 1610 and with The King's Men at the Globe in the 1620s. Rowley's known plays are *A New Wonder* (1632), *All's Lost by Lust* (1633), *A Match at Midnight* (1633), and *A Shoomaker a Gentleman* (1638).

**Roxana** A novel by Daniel Defoe, first published in 1724. The full title of the original edition is *The Fortunate Mistress: or A History of the Life and Vast Variety of Fortunes of Mademoiselle de Beleau, afterwards call'd the Countess de Wintselsheim, in Germany, being the person known by the name of the Lady Roxana, in the time of King Charles II.* The story is told in the first person, the narrator being Mlle Beleau herself.

The daughter of Huguenot refugees in England, the heroine is beautiful and ambitious for a more glamorous life. She deserts her husband, a London brewer, and their five children after her profligacy has ruined him. Her life from that point becomes the progess of an expensive courtesan – in plain language, a highly paid whore – and she moves from 'protector' to 'protector' in England, Holland, and France. She becomes very rich and, after performing a Turkish dance before the king, is called Roxana, a vague reference to the widow of Alexander the Great. Throughout her progress to wealth Roxana is accompanied by her loyal maid Amy. Eventually she marries a Dutch merchant of considerable means.

Roxana is apparently secure; but a girl appears who displays an unwonted curiosity about this rich wife of a rich merchant. Roxana discovers that the girl is her daughter by the man she callously deserted. Maternal feelings are belatedly aroused in Roxana but she dares not acknowledge her daughter. Amy promises to get rid of the girl and fails; she tells her mistress, to the latter's apparent horror, that she will kill her if that is the only way to silence her enquiries. But Roxana, in spite of her protestations, would be intensely relieved to be rid of the girl. Amy disappears and then the girl disappears. Roxana has to accompany her husband to Holland without knowing whether Amy has murdered her daughter or not. If the girl has escaped murder she may well be spreading the truth about her mother's past. Then Amy joins Roxana in Holland but says nothing about the outcome of her intentions. Roxana is left in a mire of misery and apprehension, until it becomes clear that her husband knows the truth. He dies soon after and from their joint wealth Roxana is bequeathed a mere pittance. Her path then is a descent into poverty, debt, and remorseful penitence.

Leslie Stephen, writing in 1868, considered the ending too simple a solution of the situation in which Roxana, as a result of her life's conduct, finds herself when her daughter appears, threatening both her security and, if Amy's threatened action was carried out, her own life. Certainly a fascinating dilemma is posed, and then apparently shirked, by the pat solution of her husband's knowledge of her iniquity. Defoe's strength lay in his narrative power; psychological examination of character in the novel had not yet come to English literature.

**Roxy** A novel by Edward Eggleston, first published in 1878. The story is set in the early 19th century in Indiana at the time of the campaign against the Indian forces of Tecumseh in 1811. The campaign, however, is not part of the main story.

Roxy Adams is ambitious to travel in Texas and carry Methodism to the settlers. Then she discovers that her husband, Mark, has become involved in an affair with Nancy Kirtley; Nancy is a poor White, a member of the shiftless fringe at the edge of the pioneer community. Mark is easily distracted and Roxy's aspirations have left him plenty of opportunities. Roxy realizes where her responsibilities lie. She visits Nancy and undertakes to adopt her unborn baby, which is Mark's. Then she settles down to her life in Indiana as Mark's wife.

**Rubáiyát of 'Omar Khayyám, The**   Omar Khayyám (Omar the tent-maker) was a Persian poet and astronomer who was born *c.*1050 in Naishapur and died in 1123. Omar's original quatrains (*rubáiyát*) were independent verses. In his famous version (first edition, 1859) Edward Fitzgerald found a continuing theme and his quatrains were assembled with it in mind. His verses contain the poet's reflections on the mysteries of existence and the wisdom of enjoying this life to the utmost. Fitzgerald's Rubáiyát has been translated into most European languages and into Latin, Hebrew, Irish, Afrikaans, Sanskrit, Swahili, Welsh, Romany, and Yiddish. See also **Fitzgerald, Edward**.

**Ruggle, George**   See *Ignoramus.*

**Ruin, The**   A poem of 35 lines in Old English, known only from a torn fragment preserved in *The Exeter Book.* The poem describes the ruin which is all that remains of a once proud castle or city, and scholars believe that it must refer to something Roman – possibly the city of Bath since the bathing halls of the place are mentioned. But no true identification is possible. The fragment was last translated by H. Massingham and published in the *Times Literary Supplement* (1966) and a translation is included in C. W. Kennedy's *An Anthology of Old English Poetry* (1960).

**Rules by which a Great Empire may be reduced to a Small One**   A satirical essay by Benjamin Franklin published in the London *Public Advertizer* in 1773 and criticizing Britain's dealings with her colonies in America. The 'rules' are addressed to a minister who wants to reduce the extensive dominions he has to govern. In essence the advice Franklin gives is for him to govern in the way that Britain governs in America: adherence to such rules will ensure the loss of a great part of the minister's responsibilities.

**Runyon, (Alfred) Damon** 1884–1946. Damon Runyon was born in Manhattan, Kansas, grew up in Pueblo, Colorado, and was contributing pieces to local newspapers while still at school. He enlisted for the Spanish-American War at the age of 14 and returned to journalism when it was over. His first New York job was as a sports writer on *The American* in 1911. During World War I Runyon became a war correspondent for the Hearst papers, and stayed on them as a columnist after the war. The New York scene provided the material for his unique vernacular humour: athletes, show people, gamblers, hustlers, crooks, and their women were transformed into types inseparable from Runyon's name and inimitable style, which uses the present tense throughout and eschews contractions: 'It is well known to one and all that I am one of the greatest horse players in New York, and will be a very rich guy if it is not for crooked jockeys riding the horses different from the way I dope them.' Collections of Runyon's stories are *Guys and Dolls* (1932), *Blue Plate Special* (1934), *Take it Easy* (1938), *Runyon à la Carte* (1944), and *Runyon on Broadway* (1950). Runyon, in collaboration with Howard Lindsay, wrote a farce, *A Slight Case of Murder* (1935), which had a successful run on Broadway.

**Rupert of Hentzau**   See *Prisoner of Zenda, The.*

**Rural Rides**   Descriptions of some parts of rural England, collected by William Cobbett. The Napoleonic Wars had left agricultural England in acute distress and this was aggravated by the effects of the Industrial Revolution. The government's Agricultural Committee, in 1821, proposed remedial measures but Cobbett disagreed with those. The committee was – inevitably, in those days – composed largely of landlords, and Cobbett decided to gather firsthand information to support his disagreement with the committee's proposals. The first volume collected the *Rides* published in *Cobbett's Political Register* between 1821 and 1826 and appeared in 1830. Later editions included material from the *Register* up to 1834.

*Rural Rides* are exactly what the title says. Cobbett travelled on horseback to be sure of access: 'My object was . . . to see the *country*; to see the farmers at home, and to see the labourers in the fields; and to do this you must go either on foot or on horseback [to] get about amongst byelanes and across fields, through bridle-ways and hunting-gates.' Cobbett could be described as vain, prejudiced, and opinionated and there is evidence of all three in *Rural Rides*. But the book deserves its status as a classic; the picture it presents of rural England at the beginning of the 19th century brings a vanishing world to the mind's eye with great clarity.

A modern edition of *Rural Rides* edited by G. D. H. and Margaret Cole contains material from the *Register* not included before (1930 and 1958). The Everyman's Library edition of 1957 has a preface by Asa Briggs and the Penguin English Library volume is edited by George Woodcock (1974).

**Rushworth, John** See **seventeenth-century historical collections**.

**Ruskin, John** 1819–1900. Ruskin, the son of a wealthy wine merchant, was born in London. His early education was received from his parents and tutors and he travelled with his parents in France, Switzerland, and Italy during his youth. He entered Christ Church, Oxford, in 1836 and won the Newdigate Poetry Prize in 1839 with 'Salsette and Elephanta'.

Ruskin's parents intended a church career for their son and hoped to see him become a bishop. His upbringing was sheltered and his education of the finest – humane, literary, and artistic; it was of course deeply religious also and this was an influence he later rejected. The Authorized Version of the Bible was read constantly in his mother's company and Ruskin knew exactly what he was rejecting; but he loved the language of the Bible and this influenced his prose style. His mother, who also taught him to draw, was overprotective right into his manhood, and his marriage to Euphemia (Effie) Chalmers Gray was a failure. But his upbringing and the opportunity to travel fitted him very well for his calling as critic, for whom artistic, ethical, and social concerns were equal.

The first published writings of John Ruskin were contributions to London's *Magazine of Natural History* and poems published in *Friendship's Offering* (1834). In 1835, incensed by an attack on the painter Turner in *Blackwood's Magazine* (whose critics seem to have had a genius for being wrong), Ruskin wrote an essay in Turner's defence. This was the germ of his first volume (it became many volumes) of art criticism, **Modern Painters:** *Their Superiority in the Art of Landscape Painting to all the Ancient Masters proved by Modern Artists, especially those of J. M. W. Turner.* The first volume (1843) was 'by a graduate of Oxford'; Ruskin did not put his name to the work until 1851. After 17 years of constant travel in the study of art in Europe his *Modern Painters* was completed in five volumes (1860). *The Seven Lamps of Architecture* (1849) and the three volumes of **The Stones of Venice** (1851–53) were illustrated by Ruskin; these were by-products of this period, as was that oddity in Ruskin's published work, the children's story

*The King of the Golden River* (1851). Ruskin began his *Modern Painters* by defending the work of a great artist; he felt a strong need to dispel the clouds of ignorance and insensitiveness overhanging England. He rejected the Christian ministry but became a remarkable preacher and teacher. His letters to *The Times* defending the Pre-Raphaelites (1850) were collected and published as *Pre-Raphaelitism* (1851). He lectured tirelessly in addition to writing and travelling.

As a lecturer Ruskin saw a great deal of England and was appalled by it. Commercial prosperity was evident but so too were poverty and wretchedness; even where the swarming workers were not in want they lived in ugliness and survived through exacting labour. The economic doctrines of Ricardo and the utilitarians appalled him too with their lack of humanity. John Stuart Mill rejected them for the same reason. In 1860 Ruskin began to write a series of essays 'on the first principles of political economy' for *The Cornhill Magazine*, of which Thackeray was editor. His eloquent demonstration of the moral and aesthetic objections to uncontrolled industrial development roused such a storm of indignation that after four essays had been published (August–November) Thackeray was ordered by the proprietors to stop publication: triumphant moneymakers in Victorian England refused to let themselves be criticized. Ruskin published similar essays in *Fraser's Magazine* and the same thing happened; after six had appeared (June 1862–April 1863) James Anthony Froude called a halt. The essays from *The Cornhill* were published as **Unto this Last** (1862) and those from *Fraser's* as **Munera Pulveris** (1872). Ruskin's range was remarkable: *Sesame and Lilies* (1865) is concerned with literature and the place of women in society; *The Crown of Wild Olive* (1866) with war, work, and false ideals of wealth; *The Ethics of the Dust* (1866) with crystallography; and *The Queen of the Air* (1869) with, among other things, the myths of the Greek sky gods.

In 1869 Ruskin was appointed the first Slade Professor of the Fine Arts at Oxford and stayed until 1879 (he returned in 1883 for another year). He passed on his ideals to his students; his success in doing so is suggested by his ability to persuade them to undertake hard practical work like road-making. He founded the Guild of St George in 1871, the members being pledged to give a tithe (a tenth) of their fortunes to philanthropic purposes. Ruskin practised what he preached: he inherited a large fortune from his father and spent it all on good works before he died. In 1871 also he settled at Coniston, in the Lake District, and began a series of 96 letters, issued monthly, addressed to the workers and labourers of Great Britain and known as **Fors Clavigera**. His industry was prodigious; the titles so far mentioned are his most important works but represent only a quarter of his published output. *Notes on the Construction of Sheepfolds* (1851), *The Elements of Perspective* (1859), *Notes on the General Principles of Employment for the Destitute and Criminal Classes* (1868), and *Proserpina: Studies of Wayside Flowers* (1879) indicate how much lay within his grasp.

His health began to give way in 1878 and he resigned his professorship in the following year. He returned briefly (1883–84) but it was too much for him and he retired to Coniston. During his last years he embarked on his autobiography, *Praeterita*: three volumes appeared (1885–89) but he never completed it. He lies buried at Coniston, where he died.

As art critic, economist, and social reformer Ruskin taught his countrymen a great deal, using splendid prose that moved toward simplicity during his career. The general appreciation of fine art in England began with him, and he made it clear that art is the possession and expression of a whole people, not the privilege of the wealthy few. Art is an expression of the spirit, of man's pleasure in the forms and laws of nature; the more he explored that spirit the more Ruskin was

John Ruskin, c.1875. A detail from a photograph by Lewis Carroll.

shocked by the mid-Victorian world and its pursuit of worldly goods. The step from *Modern Painters* to *Unto this Last* was not really a large one; the economist and social reformer can be discerned in the writings of the art critic. Like John Stuart Mill he brought humanity into economics, and indeed humanity inspires all of Ruskin's work. The volume of his work is intimidating; the publication of *The Works of Ruskin: Library Edition* (1902–12), edited by E. T. Cook and A. D. O. Wedderburn in 39 volumes, probably discouraged many readers. Much that he wrote is now unacceptable but much more is interesting, rewarding, and provocative. It is fascinating to read 'I hold it indisputable, that the first duty of a State is to see that every child born therein shall be well housed, clothed, fed and educated, till it attain years of discretion. But in order to the effecting this the Government must have an authority over the people of which we now do not so much as dream' and to remember that Ruskin wrote it in 1867 in *Time and Tide by Weare and Tyne*.

**Russe Common Wealth, Of the**  An account by Giles Fletcher, Senior, of Russia and its people. Fletcher was Elizabeth I's ambassador to Russia and secured a favourable trade agreement. He presented the manuscript of his account to the queen in 1589 and it was published by Hakluyt in 1598. It is short on geography but rich in information and was widely read. The full title is *Of the Russe Common Wealth: Or Maner of Government by the Russe Emperour, with the Manners and Fashions of the People of that Countrey*. The first complete version of the text was E. A. Bond's edition for the Hakluyt Society in 1856. The 'Emperour' of the title was Feodor, son of Ivan the Terrible, but the real ruler of Russia at the time was Boris Godunov. A number of modern editions of Fletcher's account have been published, the latest by L. E. Berry and R. O. Crummey in 1969.

**Russell, Bertrand Arthur William, 3rd Earl** 1872–1970.  Bertrand Russell was born at Trelleck in Wales, and after private education went on to study mathematics and moral sciences at Trinity College, Cambridge. He was a distinguished scholar and became a fellow of Trinity in 1895. He published his first book a year later, *German Social Democracy* (1896), folowed by *An Essay on the Foundations of Geometry* (1897), demonstrating his skill as an expositor in his two chosen fields. He was to become world-famous for his application of mathematical reasoning to the solution of ethical and political problems.

Russell was also a humanist reformer and

opposed to dogmatism of any kind. For the fullest development of creative faculties, essential to human progress, he insisted on freedom of thought and utterance. His pacifism, the logical outcome of his views, led to imprisonment during World War I and the temporary deprivation of his fellowship. After World War II he became one of the leaders of the anti-nuclear movement. During his long career he published a great deal, much of it in the form of pamphlets and printed speeches that questioned policies or protested about them. But his principal works on mathematics and philosophy gave him a high place in both fields: he was awarded the Order of Merit (1949) and the Nobel Prize for Literature (1950). Among his works were *A Critical Exposition in the Philosophy of Leibnitz* (1900), *Principia Mathematica* (three vols, 1910–13), *Our Knowledge of the External World as a field for Scientific Method in Philosophy* (1914), *The Practice and Theory of Bolshevism* (1920), *The ABC of Atoms* (1923), *The ABC of Relativity* (1925), *Why I am not a Christian* (1927), *Power: A New Social Analysis* (1938), *A History of Western Philosophy* (1945), *Unpopular Essays* (1950), *Human Society in Ethics and Politics* (1954), and *The Wisdom of the West* (1959). Russell was the author of two collections of short stories, *Satan in the Suburbs* (1953) and *Nightmares of Eminent Persons* (1954). *The Autobiography of Russell* was published in three volumes (1967–69).

**Russell, George William** 1867–1935. Russell, best known under the pseudonym 'AE' (or 'A.E.'), was the son of a Protestant Irish family and was born at Lurgan in Armagh. He had ambitions to be a painter, and while working in Dublin attended evening classes at the Metropolitan School of Art. One of his teachers was John Butler Yeats; W. B. Yeats was a pupil and he became a friend of Russell's, sharing an interest in theosophy and mysticism. The influence of Yeats turned Russell from art as a career to literature, and he published a volume of poems, *Homeward: Songs by the Way* (1894). Several small books of poetry and a play, *Deirdre* (1903), gave him a place in the Irish cultural revival and he also became interested in public affairs.

Russell became associated with the Irish Agricultural Organization Society and edited its journal, *The Homestead*, from 1906 to 1923. The journal merged with the *Irish Statesman* in 1923 and Russell continued as editor until 1930. He continued to write verse, and as poet and journalist became a prominent figure, actively involved in agrarian and political matters. Russell left Ireland after 1930; he was not convinced, in spite of his work for and position in Ireland, that the separatist policy was the best one and he was saddened by the outcome of events. He published a great deal of poetry and thoughtful essays on current affairs. He was a respected figure but his reputation has not stood the test of time, his poetry now being hardly known. The pseudonym AE was intended to be Aeon; a printer's error resulted in AE, which he settled for. An edition of Russell's *Collected Poems* was published in 1935.

***Ruth*** A novel by Elizabeth Gaskell, first published in 1853.

Ruth Hilton, a seamstress, attracts the attention of Henry Bellingham, a country gentleman, while she is in attendance on the ladies at a county ball. She falls in love with him and he has no trouble persuading her to go away with him. In Wales he falls ill and his mother is sent for; Ruth, an encumbrance to him now, and pregnant, is dismissed with £50. She decides to commit suicide but is saved by Thurston Benson, a dissenting minister who is on holiday in Wales with his sister Faith.

Ruth responds to the generous-hearted Bensons and goes with them to Thurston's northern parish, Eccleston. There she is to be known (the idea is Faith Benson's) as a widowed relative, Mrs Denbigh, and there her son is born. She studies with Thurston, is absorbed in her son's upbringing, and finds herself a place in the community. When her son is old enough, she takes a post as daily governess with the Bradshaws, Thurston's most prominent parishioners.

Then Bellingham reappears in Ruth's life, as a parliamentary candidate for Eccleston. He finds her a woman of mature warmth and grace and wants her again. He discovers the existence of their son, Leonard, and proposes marriage. She refuses him: she loved him once; ten years later she can only wonder that she ever did. Soon after this the Bradshaw family learn the truth about Ruth's past, and both Ruth and the Bensons find they are among the Pharisees.

Leonard takes the news of his parentage badly, but the family doctor has taken a liking to the boy and offers to take him as a ward and a pupil. Meanwhile the Bradshaws' spite has deprived Ruth of her good name and impoverished the Bensons. Ruth comforts herself with the certainty that her son's future is assured and volunteers as a nurse when cholera breaks out in Eccleston. The sufferers come to regard her as an angel of mercy and kindness, and one of them is Henry Bellingham. She dies of the disease herself, deeply mourned by those who really knew her.

The effect of *Ruth*, at the time of its publication, cannot easily be imagined now. Elizabeth Gaskell wanted to write the story of one good woman in an era when the gross hypocrisy of Victorian conventions left those outside the educated class with no recourse to moral or social justice of any kind. The author knew many girls like Ruth Hilton and in her own way she drew the attention of that class to its own appalling lack of Christian humanity. The storm broke over the author's head within days of publication. The book was burned and withdrawn from circulating libraries: one periodical deplored what it called her 'loss of reputation', and she was looked at askance by her conventional acquaintances. The opinions that mattered to her were soon heard, however: they came from Charles Kingsley, Frederick Maurice, Charlotte Brontë, Dickens, Lord Houghton, Florence Nightingale and Elizabeth Barrett Browning amongst others. *Ruth* is very much a book of its time and is hard to read now, but Elizabeth Gaskell exposed a social evil by writing about one individual with compassion.

**Rutherford, Mark**  See **White, William Hale.**

**Rymer, Thomas** 1641–1713.  The son of a Puritan country gentleman executed for treason in 1664, Rymer was born in Yafforth in Yorkshire. He was educated at the Free School in Northallerton and Sidney Sussex College, Cambridge. Later he took law and was called to the Bar at Gray's Inn.

Rymer's first critical essay was his preface to a translation of René Rapin's *Réflexions sur la Poétique d'Aristote* (1674). *The Tragedies of the Last Age Consider'd* (1678) was praised by Dryden but *A Short View of Tragedy* (1693) found him attacking Shakespeare. He was entitled as a critic to attack anyone's work if he could support his case; but his *Short View* earned him ridicule and he brought down even more scorn with his own unsuccessful tragedy, *Edgar, or The English Monarch* (1678).

Rymer was appointed historiographer royal in 1692, and undertook the task of collecting English treaties, covenants, and similar documents. His *Foedera* (20 volumes, 1704–35) earned him the thanks of generations of scholars.

# S

**Sacheverell, Henry** 1674–1724.  Sacheverell was born at Marlborough in Wiltshire and attended Marlborough Grammar School. Later he went to Magdalen College, Oxford, and became a fellow in 1701. In 1705 he became a chaplain of St Saviour's in Southwark (now Southwark Cathedral) and established a reputation as a preacher against toleration. On 5 November 1709, at St Paul's, he launched an attack on Bishop Burnet in a sermon before the Lord Mayor; Burnet was a latitudinarian and represented the opposite side. In December 1709 Sacheverell's sermons were condemned as seditious by the Commons, and he was banned from preaching for three years. But religious feeling in England at that time was feverish and Sacheverell became, for many, a popular hero. When he returned to the pulpit he addressed a packed church at St Saviour's, and the Tory party, which had been in opposition, was now in power. Queen Anne presented Sacheverell with the living of St Andrew's, Holborn. Sacheverell was the champion of the High Church and the Tory party and wrote pamphlets in their support.

**Sackville, Thomas, Earl of Dorset** 1536–1608. Sackville followed his father, Sir Richard Sackville, in the study of law. After Oxford (Hart Hall) and Cambridge (St John's College) he entered the Inner Temple and became a barrister. While at the Inner Temple Sackville collaborated with Thomas Norton in the composition of *Gorboduc*, a blank verse tragedy (the first in English) in the style of Seneca, which was first performed in 1561, and composed the *Induction* and *The Complaint of Henry Duke of Buckingham*, his contributions to the 1563 edition of *A Mirror for Magistrates* and now acknowledged to be the best part of that book. Verses from the *Induction* often appear in anthologies.

Sackville had entered Parliament in 1558 and was awarded his peerage by Elizabeth I in 1567, becoming Lord Buckhurst. Later he became Earl of Dorset in recognition of his many services to the state: he served as ambassador to the Netherlands, as commissioner at state trials (he announced the death sentence to Mary of Scotland), as Lord Treasurer, and as Chancellor of the University of Oxford.

**Sackville, Charles, 6th Earl of Dorset** 1638–1706.  Like his contemporary Rochester, Sackville was a court poet of the Restoration and fashionably dissolute. However, he lived to become a sober man of public affairs. He was praised by Dryden, among others, for his wit but his reputation now is very flimsy. His poems were published in 1701 and include some personal satires and some pleasant songs. His 'Song. Written at Sea in the First Dutch War (1665) the night before an Engagement' is a much-anthologized ballad perhaps better known by its first line 'To all you ladies now at land'.

**Sackville-West, V(ictoria Mary)** 1892–1962. V., or Vita, Sackville-West was born at Knole, the great house in Kent which had been the seat of the Sackvilles since the 16th century, and she was educated there. She married a diplomat, Harold Nicolson, in 1913 and travelled with him to Persia and other countries. Her first published work was a collection of verses, *Poems of West and East* (1917), followed by a novel, *Heritage* (1919). Then came another volume of poetry, *Orchard and Vineyard* (1921), as well as novels, short stories, and various prose works, but her work was not well known until publication of her long poem *The Land* (1926), which was awarded the Hawthornden Prize. Her finest poetic achievement, *The Land* is a realistic pastoral set in the Weald of Kent; in varied metres it details the progress of the seasons and, while celebrating the beauty of the natural world, acknowledges the continuing struggle of man with nature to wrest a living from the soil.

V. Sackville-West was the author of some 50

Vita Sackville-West, 1916. A detail from a photograph by E. O. Hoppé.

books altogether and a small group of these has given her a high place among the English writers of the first half of the 20th century. *Knole and the Sackvilles* (1922, revised 1958) is an account of her family and the family home; *The Eagle and The Dove, A Study in Contrasts* (1943) examines the two saints Teresa of Avila, the Spanish mystic, and the French Thérèse of Lisieux, 'The Little Flower'; *Daughter of France* (1959) is a biography of La Grande Mademoiselle. She was the author of several novels, of which *All Passion Spent* (1931) has been accorded the most praise. It is an elegant study of the 88-year-old Lady Slane, who upon her husband's death fends off the attentions of her children in order to live her own life in twilit calm in a small house in Hampstead. There she is sought out by the wealthy Fitzgeorge, who has loved her all his life and remained a bachelor because of her. Lady Slane has trouble remembering when they met, but Fitzgeorge becomes a regular and welcome visitor until his sudden death. He leaves her a large annual income and a collection worth millions; immediately, to the annoyance of her family, she passes on the income to hospitals and the collection to the nation. Her action brings her the gratitude of her great-granddaughter, Deborah; released from wealth, she can follow her career in music (Lady Slane had wanted to be an artist before she married) and marry whom she likes.

V. Sackville-West was an expert and passionate gardener, an art she practised at Sissinghurst, her married home, and about which she wrote with great success in a weekly column in *The Observer*. The contributions were published in several collections (1951, 1953, 1955, and 1958). V. Sackville-West was the model for *Orlando* (see **Woolf, Virginia**).

***Sacred Fount, The*** A short novel by Henry James, first published in 1901. The theory of the 'sacred fount' comes to the mind of the narrator while he is a guest at a weekend party at Newmarch, an English country house. He observes that Grace Brissenden is much older than her husband, Guy, and that after a few years of marriage she seems to be the more youthful and energetic – Guy is the fount from which she draws her new vitality and he seems correspondingly devitalized. The narrator seeks to apply this theory to another guest, Gilbert Long, who once seemed dull-witted but now seems witty and a man of the world. The question the narrator wants answered is who is the fount from whom Gilbert has benefited? He decides that it must be May Server, an attractive woman who seems to be concealing some emotional disturbance. The narrator further decides that Gilbert and Grace, the strong ones, are drawing closer and so are May and Guy, the weak ones. But Grace, whom he has taken into his confidence in the matter of Gilbert and May, eventually tells him he is crazy and has imagined the whole thing. The reader is left uncertain as to whether Grace is lying or whether the narrator's theory is being exposed as absolute nonsense.

Henry James told William Dean Howells that *The Sacred Fount* had originally been conceived as a short story and admitted that it had occurred to him to leave it unfinished. Many of James's admirers wish that he had left it – or else adhered to his intention of writing a short story. Sexual musical chairs is an ideal subject for comedy but this is not comedy; nor is it social commentary or drama. The theory itself is obviously dotty in the terms presented here and the narrator (peeping Tom would be a better description) is thoroughly disagreeable. Grace Brissenden might have been lying to the narrator; but if she is not, the society presented here is carrying emotional cannibalism too far for it ever to be made believable.

**Sailing to Byzantium**   See **Yeats, William Butler.**

**Saint Joan**   A Chronicle Play in Six Scenes and an Epilogue, by George Bernard Shaw, first produced at the Garrick Theatre, New York, in December 1923. The first production in England was at the New Theatre, London, in March 1924. It was first published in 1924. The part of Joan was created by Sybil Thorndike.

The play follows the fortunes of the girl from Lorraine, from her first encounter with Robert de Baudricourt, to her first encounter with the Dauphin at Chinon, and her subsequent fortunes after she leads the assault on the English and raises the siege of Orleans. After her victory her faith in her inspiration raises the suspicion of heresy: the Earl of Warwick seizes on this. The Bishop of Beauvais and John de Stogumber see her as a girl who may be in error but whose soul can be saved; Warwick sees her as a dangerous enemy to be extinguished. When Joan is taken by the Burgundians she is sold to Warwick, who hands her over to the Church. She is tried for heresy and, terrified by the threat of burning, signs a recantation of her belief in the voices that inspired her. But the alternative sentence is worse – perpetual imprisonment. Joan destroys her recantation and they hurry her out to the stake.

The Epilogue deals with the nullifying of the Church's verdict of 1431, and the canonization of Joan of Arc. This play is Shaw's most generally praised dramatic work, with a fine part which has been essayed by every distinguished actress since Sybil Thorndike's great performance in the first production.

**Saintsbury, George** 1845–1933.   Saintsbury was the son of a dock superintendent in Southampton, where he was born. He was educated at King's College School, London, and Merton College, Oxford. He taught for a number of years and wrote reviews for *The Academy*, gaining attention with his notices of the work of French writers, especially Baudelaire, in 1875.

Saintsbury's first book was *A Primer of French Literature* (1880); *A Short History of French Literature* (1882) was a standard book for students for decades, and *Specimens of French Literature from Villon to Hugo* (1883), *Essays on French Novelists* (1891), and *A History of the French Novel to the Close of the Nineteenth Century* (1917–19) were others on the subject. But Saintsbury's range of reading was enormous; his books on English literature and on the history of criticism extend from 1881 to the year of his death. Among them were *Dryden* in the English Men of Letters series (1881), *Essays in English Literature 1780–1860* (two series, 1890 and 1895), *A Short History of English Literature* (1898, last reprinted in 1960), *A History of Criticism* (1900–04), *Minor Poets of the Caroline Period* (1905–21), *A History of English Prosody* (1906–10), *The English Novel* (1913), and *The Peace of the Augustans* (1915).

Saintsbury contributed 21 chapters to *The Cambridge History of English Literature* and was Professor of Rhetoric and English Literature at the University of Edinburgh (1895–1905). Saintsbury was also a wine fancier and his *Notes on a Cellar Book* (1920) is acknowledged as a classic of its kind.

**Saki** 1870–1916.   The pseudonym of Hector Hugh Munro, the son of an inspector general in the Burma police. He was born in Akyab on the Bay of Bengal and from the age of two was brought up by two maiden aunts in Devonshire. He was educated at a school in Exmouth and at Bedford Grammar School, and travelled in Europe with his father after the latter's retirement. He followed his father in the Burma police in 1893 but his health was not equal to it; he settled in London in 1896 and took up writing, contributing political satires to *The Westminster Gazette* (collected in *The Westminster Alice*, 1902). His first published book was his only one in a serious vein, *The Rise of the Russian Empire* (1900).

In 1902 Munro became correspondent for *The Morning Post* in the Balkans and eastern Europe, and was in St Petersburg at the time of the 1905 revolution. He returned to England in 1908, by then a successful journalist and short-story writer whose work first appeared in *The Westminster Gazette*. The first collection, *Reginald*, had been published in 1904. Two more collections, *Reginald in Russia and Other Sketches* (1910) and *The Chronicles of Clovis* (1912) followed, and then two novels, *The Unbearable Bassington* (1912) and *When William Came* (1914), the latter an acid fantasy with the subtitle *A Story of London under the Hohenzollerns*. Another collection of stories, *Beasts and Superbeasts*, was published in the same year. At the age of 44 Munro enlisted in the Royal Fusiliers and was killed on the Western Front in November 1916. He had refused a commission.

Munro's background was rather like Kipling's, as was his reaction to Edwardian society, which he saw as a coarse-grained world full of selfish and useless people. But Munro's talent and that of Kipling could not be farther apart; his deft and economical stories, with their sharp-edged wit and elegant malice, are unique. Two collections of stories and sketches were published posthumously, *The Toys of Peace and Other Papers* (1919) and *The Square Egg and Other Sketches* (1924). The last-named contains a biography of Ethel Munro, the author's sister. Munro's pseudonym comes from the last stanza of the *Rubáiyát of 'Omar Khayyám*: Saki is the name of the cup-bearer.

**Saladin** Sala-ed-Din Yusuf ibn Ayub (1137–93) plays an important part in Scott's *The Talisman*. He became Sultan of Egypt about 1174 and earned a reputation as a courageous and chivalrous adversary. He was a Kurd by birth, and apparently displayed no fanaticism or any particular piety, in spite of the nature of the Crusades.

*Salathiel* See **Croly, George.**

**Salinger, J(erome) D(avid)** 1919– . J. D. Salinger was born in New York City and educated at Valley Forge Military Academy, New York University, and Columbia University. He published short stories in *The Saturday Evening Post* and other magazines (not collected) during the early 1940s and served in the US infantry during World War II. His first novel was *The Catcher in the Rye* (1951), narrated by a teenage schoolboy in rebellion against the dubious values of the adult world; the book conveys a strong vein of compassion for the untainted innocence of children. The novel made Salinger world-famous but his admirers have had little from him since then. He published a volume of stories written since 1948, *Nine Stories* (1953, called *For Esmé – with Love and Squalor* in England), in which members of the Glass family appear as characters. *Franny and Zooey* (1961) contains two stories about a brother and sister of that family; Buddy Glass is the narrator of *Raise High the Roof Beam, Carpenters* and *Seymour: An Introduction* (both 1963).

**Salisbury, John of** *c.*1115–80. Born at Salisbury in Wiltshire, John studied in Paris, learning logic from Peter Abelard for two years. He spent the next three studying Latin literature and grammar, probably at Chartres, and returned to Paris about 1141. At the Council of Rheims (1148) his acquaintance with Bernard of Clairvaux led to his appointment at Canterbury, where he served the archbishops Theobald and Thomas Becket, and went on missions to Rome. John supported Becket in his quarrel with Henry II, and was at Canterbury on the night of 29 December 1170 when Becket was murdered. He spent his last years as Bishop of Chartres (from 1176).

John of Salisbury's principal works are *Policraticus* or *De Nugis Curialium, et Vestigiis Philosophorum*, a collection of miscellanies which throws valuable light on the cultivated thought of western Europe in the 12th century; *Metalogicus*, in praise of logic and containing the first medieval examination of Aristotle's *Organon*; *Historia Pontificalis*, an ecclesiastical history (1148–52); and lives of Anselm and Becket, his mentor. His *Letters* were collected and edited by John himself soon after 1170.

John of Salisbury's complete works (*Opera Omnia*) were collected and edited by J. A. Giles (1848). *Historia Pontificalis* was edited and translated by Marjorie Chibnall (1956); R. L. Poole's edition was published in 1927. *Policraticus* was edited by C. C. J. Webb (1929); Webb also wrote a biography, *John of Salisbury* (1932); J. P. Pike's translation of *Policraticus* was published as *Frivolities of Courtiers and Footprints of Philosophers* (1938). *The Letters of John of Salisbury* were edited and translated by W. J. Millor and C. N. L. Brooke (1979).

*Salmagundi; or, The Whim-Whams and Opinions of Launcelot Langstaff, Esq and others.* A series of satirical essays and poems by Washington and William Irving and J. K. Paulding that were first published in 20 periodical pamphlets from 24 January 1807 to 25 January 1808. They were issued in book form in 1808. The three authors used a variety of pseudonyms in the same manner as *The Spectator* of 18th-century London, representing members of an imaginary club.

The essays covered aspects of life in contemporary New York and the political tone favoured aristocratic federalism in opposition to Jeffersonian democracy. A further series of *Salmagundi* papers, of which J. K. Paulding was the sole author, was published from May 1819 to September 1820.

**Sampson, Dominic** Harry Bertram's simple-minded and graceless tutor in *Guy Mannering*, before little Harry is kidnapped.

*Samson Agonistes, A Dramatic Poem.* The Agonistes of the title of John Milton's poem, published in 1671, is a reference to Samson as an athlete or a wrestler. The subject is Samson's last days of life as the Philistines' prisoner 'Eyeless in Gaza at the Mill with slaves'.

On a festival day when work ceases Samson is brought into the open air, where he reflects on his fate: 'O dark, dark, dark, amid the blaze of noon'. The men of Dan, his tribe, find him there and try to comfort him and his aged father Manoa also comes to him and tells him he will attempt to ransom him from the Philistines, who have made this day a festival to celebrate their deliverance from Samson. The news torments Samson: he feels his fate is deserved and he cannot look forward to freedom as he is, blinded and brought low. Manoa, nevertheless, goes ahead to treat with the Philistines for his son's freedom.

The next one to come is none other than Dalila. She pleads for forgiveness for her part in his downfall, saying she will do all in her power to lighten his sufferings. He treats her with scorn: she knows she is guilty – does she now seek exoneration? She replies that she is like all women: she feared he would not keep her – had he not abandoned another for her? She had found his weakness: *her* weakness used it. She wants him to return to her but he rejects her with contempt and will not let her so much as touch him. She departs, declaring that she is now honoured above all women for her part in his defeat and she will leave him to his lot. The Chorus watch her go and observe that her new pride is assumed. She lost her true pride with her falseness to Samson.

But now there comes a violent giant of a man, Harapha the Philistine, a bully who taunts the fallen Samson. He is disposed of by Samson's furious defiance: blind, and in chains, he will prove Harapha a coward. Harapha is forced to retire, declaring he will not stoop to combat with a blind man, but also muttering that Samson will rue his boldness. The Chorus praise the hero's unquenchable spirit, but are disturbed to see a Philistine officer approaching. The officer's news is that the Philistines want a demonstration of Samson's superhuman strength at the festival of their god Dagon.

Samson refuses; the officer warns him not to rouse the wrath of his captors. Samson dismisses him, and the Chorus voice their unease at what may happen to him now. But Samson, his strength renewed with his hair regrown, has come to a decision. When the Philistine officer returns with orders to have him dragged through the streets to the temple he says there is no need for force, he will come. The Chorus watch him go and at once Manoa hurries in to seek his son. The Philistines have relented, he says, and will accept a ransom but his words are interrupted by the great shouting in the streets, as the Philistines behold their enemy in chains. Manoa will reduce himself to absolute poverty, if necessary, to find the ransom. His exchanges with the men of Dan are halted again by a louder uproar, and they wonder what this can mean. The poem ends with the Messenger's arrival and his narrative of the destruction of the temple and Samson's death.

*Samson Agonistes* is cast in the form of a Greek tragedy, with the action encompassed in the exact time of the words. The poetry is magnificent, Samson's humanity movingly defined, and while Milton never intended it for the stage it has been performed with success. Handel composed an oratorio using Milton's poem as the basis of the libretto; this too was staged with considerable success by the Royal Opera in 1958.

**Sandburg, Carl** 1878–1967. Carl Sandburg was the son of Swedish immigrants and was born in Galesburg, Illinois. He had little formal education and earned his living as an itinerant labourer wherever work could be found. He served in the Spanish-American War and afterwards worked his way through Lombard College in his native town, graduating in 1902. He found work as a journalist and as a copywriter in advertising; he also became involved in the Social-Democratic Party as an organizer and was secretary to the socialist mayor of Milwaukee from 1910 to 1912. He married in 1905.

Sandburg's career as a poet began with a privately printed pamphlet in 1904. But it came to no one's notice and he remained unrecognized until 1914, when some of his work was published by Harriet Monroe in her *Poetry: A Magazine of Verse*. One of the poems was his famous 'Chicago' and Sandburg found himself in the forefront of the flourishing school of literature of the Midwest that was centred in the USA's second city. *Chicago Poems* was published in 1916 and Sandburg's celebration of the life of the Midwest and the people of the great sprawling, vital – and brutal – city had begun. His work owed much to Whitman and the poetic form that he had introduced and Sandburg shared Whitman's wonder at the range of sensation that life

Carl Sandburg, 1956.

offered. Sandburg saw everything as a subject for poetry. His reputation was made with that first volume and strengthened by **Cornhuskers** (1918), **Smoke and Steel** (1920), which contains his poem on John Brown, 'Ossawatomie', *Slabs of the Sunburnt West* (1922), and *Good Morning, America* (1928). The last-named volume's title poem was delivered at Harvard University.

**The People, Yes** (1936), in spite of its optimism and faith in the enduring qualities of ordinary working people, is darker in tone; the Depression had coloured the utterances of poets. Sandburg's *Complete Poems* (1950) was awarded the Pulitzer Prize.

Apart from his poetry Carl Sandburg was responsible for a compilation of folk songs and ballads, *The American Songbag* (1927), and three books for children, *Rootabaga Stories* (1922), *Rootabaga Pigeons* (1923), and *Potato Face* (1930). But his most famous prose work is his biography of Abraham Lincoln: *Abraham Lincoln: The Prairie Years* (1926) and *Abraham Lincoln: The War Years* (1939). This brought him another Pulitzer Prize and was abridged in one volume by the author in 1954. He also used selections from it for his picture of the Civil War, *Storm Over the Land* (1942). Sandburg recalled his own youth in *Always the Young Strangers* (1952).

**Sanderson, Robert** 1587–1663. One of the subjects of Izaak Walton's *Lives*, Sanderson (an Anglican) was among the many Caroline divines who published books of religious casuistry. He was a popular preacher and became a bishop at the Restoration. He was also the author of the Preface to the revised *Book of Common Prayer*.

**Sanditon** A novel which Jane Austen worked on during the early months of 1817. She died in July of that year and what we have seems to be part of a first draft. The scene is set – Sanditon is an attractive seaside village rapidly developing into a resort. A number of characters are introduced: Mr Parke, the speculator; his busybody hypochondriacal sister, Diana; Charlotte Heywood, the Parkers' pretty guest at Sanditon; Sidney Parker; and the Denhams. Charlotte is possibly the intended heroine but one can only speculate about the form the novel would have taken.

**Sandra Belloni** A novel by George Meredith, first published in 1864 as *Emilia in England*.

Emilia Sandra Belloni, a simple Italian girl with a fine voice, leaves her wretched home and disreputable father and is taken up by the Pole family. Pole is a city merchant with three aspiring daughters and a spineless son, Wilfred. A business ally of Pole, a wealthy Greek named Pericles who has a passion for fine voices, tries to persuade Emilia into taking musical training in Italy under his direction. But Emilia and Wilfred have fallen in love and she resists Pericles's persuasions even when he tries to bully her.

Pole is involved in speculation by Pericles and brought to the verge of ruin. He casts about feverishly for a solution to his troubles; one way would be to win Lady Charlotte Chillingworth, a rich woman, for Wilfred. The wretched young man is more than willing but Lady Charlotte sees him for what he is, as do Merthyr Powys and his sister, who have taken a liking to Emilia. Charlotte exposes Wilfred to the girl – and nearly breaks her heart. The Powyses take Emilia under their wing.

To save the Poles – to whom, in spite of everything, she owes much – Emilia persuades Pericles to part with a large sum of money by agreeing to go to the conservatory at Milan. She departs, and both she and Merthyr look forward to her return and their probable marriage.

The story continues in Meredith's later novel, **Vittoria**.

**Sandys, George** 1578–1644. Best known for his translations from the Latin, Sandys was educated at St Mary Hall, Oxford, and travelled widely in Italy and the Levant. He published a widely read account in *A Relation of a Journey Begun an. dom. 1610: Foure Bookes Containing a Description of the Turkish Empire, of Aegypt, of the Holy Land, of the Remote Parts of Italy, and Ilands Adjoyning* (1615).

In 1621 Sandys went to America as treasurer of the Virginia Company for five years and used his leisure to translate the *Metamorphoses* of Ovid, in couplets. It was published in 1626, and his trim regular verse form was much admired by younger poets. In 1632, in a later edition, he added *The Aeneid, Book I,* translated in the same style. A verse exercise of another kind was *A Paraphrase upon the Psalmes of David, and upon the Hymnes Dispersed Throughout the Old and New Testaments* (1636). Another verse translation was from the Latin of Hugo Grotius, *Christ's Passion: A Tragedie* (1640); his last work was the verse *A Paraphrase upon the Song of Solomon* (1641). Sandys is admired not for his poetry but for his technique; his verse is regular and neat and the compact forms had considerable influence on English verse in his time.

**Santayana, George** 1863–1952. The long-lived American philosopher was born in Madrid. He was taken to the USA at the age of eight when his family moved there. (The original form of his name was Jorge Ruiz de Santayana y Borrais.) He was brought up in Boston and educated at Harvard, graduating from there in 1886. After further study in Germany and England he was awarded his PhD from Harvard in 1889 and became Professor of Philosophy there in the same year. He stayed until 1912, when he returned to Europe to live.

Santayana published poetry and a highly regarded novel, **The Last Puritan** (1935), but the main body of his work contains his philosophy, written in lucid and attractive English prose – his style extended his readership well beyond those chiefly interested in philosophy. The absence of pedantry and jargon is deliberate and, while the result is sometimes a lack of precision, the writing is rich and persuasive. *The Life of Reason* was a five-volume study (1905–06) of reason in everyday life, science, art, and literature; Santayana offers the conclusion that the only reality is matter itself and that all else arises from man's experience of, and response to, matter. He took this idea further with *The Realms of Being,* which began with an introductory volume, *Scepticism and Animal Faith* (1923), and eventually covered four volumes (1927–40). The objects of our thoughts are called essences and these are responses to material events in our (animal) world; logical analysis may lead to complete scepticism

but animal faith persists. True perception of the objects of our thoughts results in knowledge.

Santayana's work includes three studies dealing with American life: *Philosophical Opinion in America* (1918); *Character and Opinion in the United States* (1920), on the conflict of idealism and materialism; and *The Genteel Tradition at Bay* (1931), a criticism of the 'new humanism', which he saw as rejecting too much of value from the past while attempting a movement toward what he saw as a universal scale of values. Santayana was, he insisted, a materialist; he had put forward his theory in *The Life of Reason* and furthered it in *The Realms of Being,* that it is from man's response to matter that his aspirations and achievements arise.

Among Santayana's other works were *Three Philosophical Poets* (1910), which studies the work of Lucretius, Dante, and Goethe; *Egotism in German Philosophy* (1916), a criticism of German idealism and romantic wilfulness (Santayana published a revised edition of this book during World War II, in 1940); *Soliloquies in England* (1922), an examination of the Anglo-Saxon character; and *The Last Puritan* (1935), the only novel by Santayana, in which his philosophy is applied to fictional characters in New England. *The Idea of Christ in the Gospels* (1946) is both an interpretation of the Gospels and an examination of the idea of God in man.

From 1920 Santayana lived chiefly in Rome and he died there at the age of 89, cared for by the sisters of a convent nursing home. His memoirs, *Persons and Places,* were published in three books: *The Backgrounds of My Life* (1944), *The Middle Span* (1945), and *My Host the World* (1953).

**Sapienta Veterum, De** A group of short discourses by Francis Bacon on 30 characters of classical mythology. It was first published in 1609 and translated as *The Wisdom of the Ancients* by Sir Arthur Gorges in 1619. In many respects it is a companion book to Bacon's celebrated *Essays* and an illustration to the progress of his thinking between *The Advancement of Learning* and *Novum Organum.* His interpretations of classic myth are very much the product of his particular views on science, morals, and politics and provides fascinating thoughts on Pan, Prometheus, Cassandra, Oedipus, and many others.

**Sapphira and the Slave Girl** A novel by Willa Cather, first published in 1940. In this novel Willa Cather makes use of her family's Virginia background and tells of events in the old South.

Henry Colbert is a prosperous miller, his wife Sapphira is a jealous invalid. Their mulatto slave,

Nancy, is the daughter of a White artist and a Black servant. Henry is unfailingly kind to Nancy – Sapphira resents this and begins to persecute the girl. In an effort to discredit Nancy completely Sapphira invites her nephew for a visit, knowing he is the kind of man who will regard Nancy as fair game.

But Nancy resists and places herself under the protection of the Colberts' daughter, the widowed Rachel Blake. Rachel is cool to her arrogant and proud mother; she is a humane and generous woman and helps Nancy to escape from the South to Canada by way of the underground railroad. Sapphira suspects Rachel and they are estranged, only coming together, formally, over the death of a favourite grandchild.

Nancy returns to visit her mother and Rachel 25 years later. The Civil War has been fought and she is a free woman, even in Virginia. Rachel finds her poised and at peace, happy in her life as housekeeper to a wealthy Canadian family.

**Sardanapalus** A tragedy by Lord Byron, first published in 1821. It was written in 1820 while Byron was at Ravenna and produced by Charles Kean at Drury Lane in 1834. The tragedy was based on the history of Diodorus Siculus and the events took place about 640 BC. Belesus, a Chaldean soothsayer, and Arbaces, a governor of Media, organize a revolt against the king of Assyria, Sardanapalus. The king is luxury-loving, cynical, and good-natured; he is also courageous. The revolt rouses him to action, and with the encouragement of the beautiful Myrrha, his Greek slave whom he loves, he leads his army into battle. But in spite of his valour the fighting goes against him and he has to retreat to his palace. He makes provision for the safe withdrawal of Zarina, his queen; then he prepares a funeral pyre around his throne, and perishes upon it with Myrrha and his supporters.

**Sargeson, Frank** 1903– . A New Zealand writer whose avowed aim was to reveal his country not only to the rest of the English-speaking world but also to his own countrymen also, Sargeson was born at Hamilton in North Island. He qualified as a solicitor but worked at a number of jobs, becoming acquainted with all levels of society and reacting sharply against bourgeois values. The depression sharpened his sympathies with those who suffered most from it and his first stories were published in the 1930s, in the Auckland periodical *Tomorrow*. His first collection of stories, *Conversations with My Uncle* (1936), demonstrated his skill at using the verbal style of the ill-educated and semi-literate without the loss of truth and pathos. Sargeson's *Collected Stories*

was published in 1965; he is also the author of *I Saw in My Dream* (1949), *I For One* (1956), and *Joy of the Worm* (1969).

**Sartor Resartus** A philosophical and autobiographical essay by Thomas Carlyle. It was first published in *Fraser's Magazine* (November 1833–August 1834). In book form it was first published in the USA with a preface by Emerson and the subtitle 'The Life and Opinions of Herr Teufelsdrockh' (1836). (*Teufelsdrockh* means Devil's Dung.) The first publication in book form in England was in 1838. The original title means 'the tailor re-tailored'.

In the first part the author considers the universe: all symbols, forms, and institutions are 'a large suit of clothes which invests everything' and which are, therefore, impermanent. The second part is the biography of Diogenes Teufelsdrockh, Professor of Things in General at the University of *Weissnichtwo* (I know not where). The professor (Carlyle) describes his own spiritual trials; his denial of kinship with The Everlasting No (the Devil, the spirit that denies), The Centre of Indifference, and The Everlasting Yea. The third part of the book is a criticism of various aspects of life in England. Carlyle's birthplace, Ecclefechan, is represented by the village of Entepfuhl, and the university described represents Edinburgh.

**Sassoon, Siegfried (Lorraine)** 1886–1967. Siegfried Sassoon was born in London and educated at Marlborough Grammar School and Clare College, Cambridge. He was sent down from Cambridge without a degree, being more interested in sport and poetry than in his studies, and divided his time between the country, where he hunted, and London, where he published 11 small collections of poems, including a parody of Masefield's *The Everlasting Mercy* called *The Daffodil Murder* (1913). Sassoon enlisted at the outbreak of World War I and went to France as a second lieutenant.

Sassoon acquitted himself with honour; he was wounded twice and awarded the Military Cross but acquired a sharp loathing for those responsible for the dreadful and stupid waste of young lives in indescribable conditions. He was invalided home in 1917 when he met Robert Graves and Wilfred Owen and, as a protest, announced publicly his refusal to serve again. Instead of being court-martialled, as he expected, he was sent to a sanatorium. His views changed when he came to believe that he was betraying his fellow soldiers in France. He was posted to Palestine, and then sent back to France; he was wounded a third time and finished the war as a captain.

*Counter-attack* (1918, before the armistice) was the first volume of antiwar poems and it is Sassoon's most memorable volume. 'The General', 'The Dug-Out', 'Base Details', 'Attack', and the other poems in the book are the product of an outraged moral sensibility and the effect is often shattering. His later poems, in spite of their quality, do not have and probably could not have the same force. Sassoon's prose works are nostalgic in tone and elegantly written: *The Memoirs of a Fox-Hunting Man* (1928), *The Memoirs of an Infantry Officer* (1930), *Sherston's Progress* (1936), *The Old Century* (1938), *The Weald of Youth* (1942), and *Siegfried's Journey* (1945). *The Collected Poems 1908–1956* was published in 1961.

**Satanstoe** A novel by James Fenimore Cooper, first published in 1845. It was the first novel of the trilogy called the *Littlepage Manuscripts*.

Satanstoe is the Littlepage estate in Westchester county, New York. Captain Hugh Littlepage runs the estate that his grandson Corny (Cornelius) will inherit. The time is the 18th century and Cooper uses Corny's visit to New York city to give a vivid description of it at that time. Corny makes friends with Jason Newcome, the Yankee schoolmaster, and the Dutch–American Dirck Follock. He falls in love with Dirck's cousin, Anneke Mordaunt.

Corny and Dirck are sent by their families to Albany to survey large land grants where they hope to settle tenant farmers; Mr Worden, Corny's tutor, and Jason Newcome accompany them. Anneke's family, the Mordaunts, are in Albany too – with the same ambitions – and Major Bulstrode, another admirer of Anneke's. Anneke's companion, Mary Wallace, is loved by Guert Ten Eyck of Albany, who befriends the newcomers. Dirck and Corny go to work at Mooseridge, the Littlepage frontier estate.

The French and Indian wars break out and affect the destinies of each of the characters and the author describes the defeat at Ticonderoga and the Indian attack on the Mordaunt estate, Ravensnest, during which Guert is killed. Anneke marries Corny at the close of the story, which is continued in **The Chainbearer**.

**Satchell, William** 1860–1942. Satchell was born in London and completed his education at Heidelberg. He emigrated to New Zealand in the 1880s and settled near Auckland; he published his first novel of New Zealand life, *The Land of the Lost*, in 1902. Others were *The Toll of the Bush* (1905), *The Elixir of Life* (1907), and the highly praised *The Greenstone Door* (1914), a novel about Anglo-Maori relations.

**Satiromastix** A comedy by Thomas Dekker, possibly with contributions by John Marston. First published in 1602, it was a reply to Ben Jonson's *The Poetaster* in the 'war of the theatres' in which Jonson modestly assigned himself the role of Horace. In *Satiromastix* Horace's vanities are satirized and ridiculed by Crispinus (Marston) and Demetrius (Dekker).

**Saturninus** The Emperor of Rome in Shakespeare's *Titus Andronicus*. He wants Titus' daughter Lavinia but she is claimed by his brother, Bassianus, and he marries Tamora, recently defeated queen of the Goths.

**Satyrane, Sir** In Book I of Spenser's *The Faerie Queene* he fights with Sansloy (lawless) and enables Una to escape. He is the son of the nymph Thyamis and a satyr.

**Savage, Marmion** 1803–72. An Anglo-Irish novelist, popular in his day. He was the author of six novels, among them a satire on the Young Ireland party, *Falcon Family* (1845), which is usually regarded as his best. Most of his work was written in London, where he was editor of *The Examiner*.

**Savage, Richard** *c.*1696–1743. Richard Savage claimed to be the illegitimate son of the 4th Earl Rivers and the Countess of Macclesfield. He convinced his friend Samuel Johnson, at any rate, and Dr Johnson wrote a sympathetic biography of Savage in his *Lives of the Poets*. Savage himself wrote a poem called *The Bastard* (1728), which was a censure on his supposed mother; but the general conclusion of modern scholars is that Savage was a man of humble birth. His life would make an interesting thesis for students who subscribe to Freudian psychology, since he seems to have made a career out of being rejected.

Savage's first work was a poem, *The Convocation* (1717), and it was followed by the comedy *Love in a Veil*, produced in 1718, and *The Tragedy of Sir Thomas Overbury*, produced in 1723. His poetry is forgotten except for *The Wanderer* (1729), though Queen Caroline paid him a pension for celebrating her birthday with an annual ode. Savage was involved in a tavern brawl in 1727 and found guilty of killing a man in the course of it. He was pardoned, however, and died in a debtors' prison in Bristol.

*The Wanderer*, a poem in five cantos, is a long, rambling, derivative, and contemplative work on the nature of Man, God, and Nature. Johnson called it 'a heap of shining materials thrown together by accident.' Saintsbury called it tinsel.

**Savile, George, Marquess of Halifax** 1633–95. George Savile was the son of a Yorkshire baronet and entered parliament in 1660. A man of independent politics, he became Viscount Halifax in 1668, Earl in 1679 and Marquess in 1682. He led the opposition to Shaftesbury in the House of Lords and carried the house with him (see **Dryden, John**). His influence at court waned with the accession of James II, whom he had criticized freely. As chairman of the committee of peers it fell to Halifax to ask William and Mary to accept the throne of England in 1689. The last office he held before retirement was Lord Privy Seal.

In literature Halifax is remembered for his political tracts and essays, most notably *The Character of a Trimmer* (1688), a highly praised and bold pamphlet which contains a famous passage in praise of truth. The main body of his work is to be found in *Miscellanies* (1700), and *A Character of King Charles the Second: And Political, Moral and Miscellaneous Thoughts and Reflections* (1750) both published after his death.

**Savile, Sir Henry** 1549–1622. Savile was secretary in the Latin language to Elizabeth I and was one of the scholars commissioned to prepare the Authorized Version of the Bible. Educated at Brasenose College, Oxford, he became a fellow, and subsequently Warden of Merton College; he also became Provost of Eton. Savile is remembered as a translator of part of the histories of *Tacitus* (1591) and the *Cyropaedia* of Xenophon (1613). He was also responsible for a notable edition of St John Chrysostom (1610–13). Savile left a collection of manuscripts to the Bodleian Library, which he helped to found, and established the Savilian professorships of geometry and astronomy at Oxford.

**Scarlet Letter, The** A novel by Nathaniel Hawthorne first published in 1850 and developed from an incident which the author described in his short story *Endicott and the Red Cross* (1837). The book contains an introductory essay describing the author's work at the Custom House in Salem and how he supposedly discovered the letter cut from red cloth and the documents relating to the heroine. The time is the 17th century and the scene is Puritan New England.

The story opens with Hester Prynne, a young married woman, being brought forth from prison to stand exposed as an adulteress on the public pillory for three hours. She carries a baby in her arms and, refusing to name her lover, is condemned to wear a scarlet letter 'A', signifying adulteress, for life. Among the crowd gathered around the pillory is her elderly husband, an English scholar, who had sent Hester to Boston to prepare a home for them. He had been captured by Indians and now, two years later, he sees her for the first time since leaving England. After her sentence Hester retires to the outskirts of the town with her baby. Her independent spirit enables her to bear the 'good' people's ostracism and by degrees she becomes known to the unfortunate as a generous and helpful woman to whom they can turn when in need.

Prynne assumes the name of Roger Chillingworth and extracts a promise from Hester to conceal his identity. He presents himself in Boston as a doctor and sets out to find Hester's lover. His dogged persistence eventually rewards him with the knowledge that Arthur Dimmersdale, a revered and apparently saintly young minister, is the father of Hester's child. Dimmersdale's courage had failed him and when Hester had refused to name him he had allowed the wrath of the Puritan community to fall on her alone. He has tortured himself with guilt for years and done private penance but cannot face a public confession. Now Chillingworth (Prynne) adds to his torment: he has Dimmersdale at his mercy and gloats over his victim. The power Chillingworth feels corrupts him completely and he puts aside everything but his continuing revenge.

Hester tries to persuade Dimmersdale to flee from Boston and go with her to Europe but seven years of inward agony have broken him. He sees flight as yielding further to temptation. Finally, he summons the people to the same pillory. His last act is to confess publicly and he dies on the pillory in the presence of Hester and their child, Pearl, and Hester's husband. Chillingworth dies within a year, deprived of the driving force of his degraded existence and leaving considerable wealth to Pearl. Hester takes her daughter and they leave for Europe, where Hester achieves contentment in continuing to work for the good of others.

**Scenes of Clerical Life** A volume, published in 1858, containing George Eliot's first fiction – three tales originally published in *Blackwood's Magazine*.

*The Sad Fortunes of the Revd Amos Barton.* Amos Barton is the curate of Shepperton, a hardworking, conscientious man but one with little learning or charm. His parishioners have no particular liking for him and the living offers him and Milly, his wife, little in the way of physical ease. Milly, a gentle and beautiful woman who works all hours to help her husband, also has children to care for and a house to run. Eventually she succumbs to the unending labour and dies – and at last the parishioners begin to feel some concern for Amos Barton and his children. He gains their liking but he is haunted by the thought that he had not cherished his wife enough.

*Mr Gilfil's Love-Story*. The setting of the second tale is also Shepperton, in the years before Amos Barton became curate. The incumbent is Maynard Gilfil, who loves Tina (Caterina), the adopted child of Sir Christopher Cheverel. Cheverel's heir is his nephew, Anthony Wybrow, who has captured Tina's affections; but for him it was no more than dalliance, and he obeys his uncle's instructions to marry wealthy Beatrice Assher. Tina's health breaks down but she seems to recover through the loving kindness shown by Maynard Gilfil. She marries him – but it is no solution for her, and she dies within a few months of the ceremony.

*Janet's Repentance*. The Rev Edgar Tryan arrives in the manufacturing town of Milby and finds it sunk in religious apathy, dominated by the bullying, drunken lawyer, Dempster. Dempster's wife, Janet, has also taken to drink – her only escape from her husband's brutality. Neither of the Dempsters has any sympathy with Tryan's attempts to reawaken the community but Janet discovers that Tryan is someone who also carries a burden of pain. When she suffers a final outrage at the hands of Dempster she turns to Tryan, and under his influence begins her struggle to defeat her craving for alcohol. Dempster, meanwhile, succumbs to drink and Janet's self-conquest parallels Tryan's growing physical weakness. His death from consumption leaves Janet grieving, but resolute and strengthened, determined to be of use to the world.

The tone of George Eliot's first book can be taken from the title and, inevitably, it is religious. But the author's gifts found their first expression in these stories and it should be remembered that clerical life in a provincial setting was familiar to her, providing the materials to which she added a remarkable ear for dialogue and a natural talent for characterization.

**Scholar-Gipsy, The**  A poem by Matthew Arnold, first published in 1853 in *Poems: A New Edition*. The origin of the poem is in *The Vanity of Dogmatizing* (1661) by Joseph Glanvill, who retold an old legend. In Arnold's poem the speaker has Glanvill's book beside him and is inspired to follow the example of the scholar-gipsy. The poet weaves a song in praise of country life into the fabric of his poem and expresses envy of one born 'Before this strange disease of modern life, With its sick hurry, its divided aims, Its heads o'ertaxed, its palsied hearts, was rife'.

**School for Scandal, The**  A comedy by Richard Brinsley Sheridan. It was first produced at Drury Lane in May 1777, and published in 1780. The play was not complete even after the first night had been announced and the author was altering and polishing it almost until the curtain rose. Sir Peter Teazle was played by Thomas King and Lady Teazle by the brilliant and beautiful Frances Abington.

Sir Peter Teazle, past his prime, has married a young wife. Lady Teazle is fresh from the country and, dazzled by London society, is extravagant and immensely flattered by the attention she receives. A great deal of this comes from Joseph Surface, but he is simultaneously courting Maria, Sir Peter's ward, for her fortune. His brother, Charles Surface, is in love with Maria and she with him, but the corrupt and hypocritical Joseph has managed to convey to Sir Peter that Charles is paying attention to Lady Teazle. The direction of the innuendo and scandal is chiefly in the hands of Lady Sneerwell and her deplorable friends: Sir Benjamin Backbite, his uncle Crabtree, and Mrs Candour. Lady Sneerwell wants Charles Surface and this gives added impulse to her spite; she puts about stories discrediting his character to Maria and encourages Joseph Surface in his pursuit of her. Poor Maria is also being pursued by Sir Benjamin Backbite.

Sir Oliver Surface, a friend of Sir Peter Teazle and a man of great wealth, arrives home from Bengal and decides to find out for himself what sort of characters his nephews Charles and Joseph are. He visits Charles as a moneylender; Charles promptly sells him the family portraits – all but one: the portrait of his uncle. 'No, hang it! I'll not part with poor Noll. The old fellow has been very good to me ... I'll keep his picture while I've a room to put it in.' So Sir Oliver is sure of Charles's good heart.

Joseph Surface persuades Lady Teazle to visit him and does his best to seduce her. Sir Peter arrives unexpectedly; he believes Joseph to be his friend and confides his uneasiness about Lady Teazle and the scandal linking her name with Charles. Then Charles himself turns up. Lady Teazle has taken refuge behind a screen which Charles inadvertently knocks over; Sir Peter finds his wife concealed in Joseph's house. Charles is exonerated and Joseph's hypocrisy exposed.

Sir Oliver Surface, in the guise of a poor relation, calls on his nephew Joseph. Joseph Surface not only pleads poverty but blackens the character of both his 'absent' uncle and his brother Charles. The comedy ends with Charles and Maria united and the Teazles reconciled.

A mezzotint of 1783 of the famous screen episode in Act IV, scene 3 of *The School for Scandal*. Sheridan's comedy was first produced in 1777. Victoria & Albert Theatre Museum, London.

The skill with which the plot is handled and the sparkling dialogue make this one of the great English comedies. The screen scene was greeted with thunderous applause at its first performance and it remains one of the liveliest in theatre history, a brilliantly contrived climax.

**Schoolmistress, The** A poem by William Shenstone, first published in 1737 and revised twice, in 1742 and 1748. Shenstone's first lessons were received in a local dame school, and the teacher, Miss Sarah Lloyd, became the subject of his most successful poem. The tone is affectionate, though it does not escape a note of condescension. The virtue of the poem lies in its successful balance of observation and sentiment. Shenstone's poem anticipated Goldsmith's *The Deserted Village*, which was published in 1770.

**Schreiner, Olive Emily Albertina** 1855–1920. Schreiner was born in Basutoland of German-English parentage and was largely self-educated. She worked for some years as a nursery governess with a Boer family and during that time wrote a novel. She went to England in 1881 and took the manuscript with her; it was published in 1883 as *The Story of an African Farm* and the name of the author was given as Ralph

Iron. The novel deals with the struggles of a girl, Lyndall, imprisoned in the ironbound conventions of Boer life, to attain independence of action and belief. The farm is an ostrich farm in the veld and the picture of life there is vivid and unsparing in its details, in spite of the deceptively quiet tone. The book became famous throughout the English-speaking world and was severely criticized for its feminist and anti-Christian outlook – factors that made it notorious when the author's identity became known.

The emancipation of women was of immense importance to Olive Schreiner and she was a lifelong friend of Havelock Ellis. She returned to South Africa in 1889 and married Samuel Cronwright, a politician, in 1894. Her own interest in politics was on behalf of women's rights and she was the author of a number of pamphlets. A second novel, *Trooper Peter Halkett of Mashonaland* (1897), was concerned with Rhodes and the early White settlers in Rhodesia and was decidedly critical of them. A third, *From Man to Man* (published posthumously, 1926) was left unfinished when she died.

**Scoggin, his Jestes** An example of the collections of jests or jokes that were popular in 16th-century England. It dates from about 1565 and was printed in 1613. John Scoggin (*or* Scogan *or* Skoggan), to whom the jests are attributed, was the court jester of Edward IV.

**Scot, Michael** *c*.1175–*c*.1234. A medieval scholar of Scottish birth, Scot studied at Oxford and in Paris; he was appointed to the brilliant court of Frederick II of Hohenstaufen at Palermo some time before 1209. At Palermo he learned Arabic and so impressed Frederick that the emperor sent him to the universities of Europe to make better known Aristotle's works on animal life, which he translated into Latin from Arabic abstracts at Toledo. His great learning – he was a physician and an astrologer – led to his being credited with skill as a magician and he appears as such in Dante's *Inferno* and Sir Walter Scott's *The Lay of the Last Minstrel*. Scot's works include *Liber Physiognomiae* and *Quaestio Curiosa de Natura Solis et Lunae*, but much remains in manuscript and awaits publication. He is believed to have returned to Lowland Scotland and to have died there.

**Scot (*or* Scott), Reginald** *c*.1538–99. Reginald Scot was a Kentish man who became MP for New Romney in 1588. He was educated at Hart Hall, Oxford. He was the author of *A Perfite Platforme of a Hoppe Garden* (1547) and of the celebrated *The Discouerie* [Discovery] *of Witchcraft*

(1584). Scot was making an enlightened humanitarian protest in an age full of ignorance and superstition. He attacked the judicial processes as well as all forms of credulity and used scripture to support his case against those who delighted 'to pursue the poore, to accuse the simple, and to kill the innocent'.

Unfortunately, Scot was a product of his age and acknowledged 'naturall magicke' – the resources of scientific enquiry were not available to him. Worse, he got carried away and his description of the things he rejected became so detailed that he unknowingly produced a magician's manual in a book of enormous size. It was added to in 1665 by an anonymous writer who was obviously an industrious warlock himself and who simply extended the range of the magician's 'craft'. Many years were to pass before Reginald Scot's protest was reinforced.

Editions of *The Discouerie of Witchcraft* were published by B. Nicholson in 1886 and by Montague Summers in 1930.

**Scott, Alexander** *c*.1525–*c*.1584. Scott was probably the younger son of Alexander Scott, prebendary of the Chapel Royal at Sterling, according to the antiquary and bibliographer David Laing. He wrote lyrics (36 are preserved in the Bannatyne manuscript), mostly about love. Some of these are notable for their successful expression of deep feelings; others are cynical and astringent. Scott also translated two of the Psalms. A selection of Scott's work was published by W. MacKean in 1887.

**Scott, Duncan Campbell** 1862–1947. Scott was born in Ottawa. His father was a Methodist minister and the family lived in various places in Ontario and Quebec. Scott completed his education in the city of Quebec and entered the Department of Indian Affairs in Ottawa in 1879; he was head of the department from 1917 until he retired in 1935.

In Ottawa Scott became friends with Archibald Lampman, who encouraged him to write, and his first book of verse, *The Magic House*, appeared in 1893. A volume of short stories, *In the Village of the Viger* (1896), followed and he published seven more volumes of verse during his lifetime, including *New World Lyrics and Ballads* (1905), *Beauty and Life* (1921), *The Green Cloister* (1935), and *The Circle of Affection* (1947). A second volume of short stories, *The Witching of Elspie*, was published in 1923.

**Scott, Sir Walter** 1771–1832. Walter Scott was born in Edinburgh, the son of a Calvinist lawyer. As a boy he suffered from infantile paralysis and he limped for the rest of his life. His illness necessitated a long period of convalescence at Kelso in Roxburgh; his family's roots were in the Border country and much of his time there was spent in the company of his uncle, Thomas Scott. The young Scott would listen with enthralled interest to his uncle's stories of the past and to the stories of elderly people who had time – and memories – at the disposal of their eager listener. Scott was educated at the Royal High School in Edinburgh and at the university; he was called to the Bar in 1792. He spent much of his leisure exploring the Highlands and the Border country; in spite of his early frailty he became an enthusiastic rider and his limp never deterred him from extended walks. His interest in Border tales and ballads deepened and he became interested in the romantic poetry of Italy and France. Another enthusiasm was for the German poets of his time: he published (anonymously) translations of Burger in 1796 and of Goethe in 1799.

In the same year Scott was appointed Sheriff Deputy for Selkirkshire. He had married in 1797 and he settled in the Border country for the rest of his life. He lived at Ashestiel, on the Tweed, and became clerk to the Court of Session in 1806. He bought Abbotsford in 1811 and was created a baronet in 1820. In 1826 came the collapse of the Ballantyne printing house (he had been a friend of James Ballantyne since they were schoolboys together) in which he was concerned, and Scott, who lived to the limit of what had seemed an immense income, was suddenly faced with tremendous debts. He spent the rest of his life working to acquit the crushing obligation and to his eternal honour it was eventually discharged –

Abbotsford, the house near Melrose in Roxburghshire which Scott built for himself between 1817 and 1824. He purchased the estate in 1811. From an engraving dated 1833.

most of it during his lifetime, the remainder by the sale of his copyrights after his death.

Scott's career as a writer could be said to have passed its first stage with his translations from the German. His intense interest in the oral literature of the Border prompted the next stage, assisted by his friendship with James Hogg, John Leyden, and William Laidlaw (who became his steward). The collection of Border songs, with ballad imitations by Scott and others, was published in 1802 as *Minstrelsy of the Scottish Border*. The book was a revelation of poetic content which was in serious danger of being lost. The ascendancy of the Kirk, the Jacobite cause, and the repression which followed – these and other factors in Scottish history had almost obliterated the romance of Scotland's past. The book also led to the study of other disappearing traditions in literature, which paved the way for the great ballad collections that followed.

Scott's original work marks the third stage of his career. **The Lay of the Last Minstrel**, published in 1805, is a romance in verse set in the Border and told by an old minstrel, the last of his race. **Marmion**, published in 1808, is a historical romance that culminates in the defeat at Flodden in 1513; in **The Lady of the Lake** (1810), the subject is not the Arthurian lady but Ellen, of Loch Katrine. These were successful commercially as well as artistically but *Rokeby* (1813) was a commercial failure. It contains two immortal songs, 'Brignall Banks' and 'A weary lot is thine, fair maid', but the setting, in England during the Civil War, was not the happiest choice for Scott. There were other poetic romances but it seems that Scott recognized the form was no longer for him. Byron, no less, was using it and more successfully, giving his material a passionate intensity of tone that Scott, who made no attempt to reach emotional depth, could not emulate.

Scott had already begun, as long ago as 1805, to write fiction. Now he completed and published **Waverley** (1814). He was over 43, with a great reputation as a poet, and fiction was not, in 1814, highly regarded. So he published it anonymously, achieved a major success, and published novel after novel with the inscription 'By the author of *Waverley*'. He wrote novels for only 18 years, reaching an astonishing output which achieved on the whole an astonishing success. Artistically, the level is remarkable: he was the first novelist to really succeed in historical romance and his gallery of vivid characters is rivalled only by Dickens; indeed, Dickens might have benefited from his example – Scott never overdraws a character. He had a poet's eye for a scene, too, and presented the 'look of things' as

Sir Walter Scott, 1820. A detail from the portrait by Sir Thomas Lawrence, which was not completed until 1826. The Royal Collection.

it had never been done by any novelist before him, and the people of the past, in Scott, are recognizable human beings.

In sequence of publication his novels were: *Waverley* (1814), **Guy Mannering** (1815), **The Antiquary** (1812), **The Black Dwarf** and **Old Mortality** (*Tales of My Landlord*, 1816), **The Heart of Midlothian** (*Tales of My Landlord*; second series, 1818), **Rob Roy** (1818), **The Bride of Lammermoor** and **The Legend of Montrose** (*Tales of My Landlord*; third series, 1819), **Ivanhoe** (1820), **The Monastery** (1820), **The Abbot** (1820), **Kenilworth** (1821), **The Pirate** (1822), **The Fortunes of Nigel** (1822), **Peveril of the Peak** (1822), **Quentin Durward** (1823), **St Ronan's Well** (1824), **Redgauntlet** (1824), **The Betrothed** and **The Talisman** (*Tales of the Crusades*, 1825), **Woodstock** (1826), *The Highland Widow, The Two Drovers, The Surgeon's Daughter* (**Chronicles of the Canongate**, 1827), *The Fair Maid of Perth* (*Chronicles of the Canongate*, second series, 1828), **Anne of Geierstein** (1829), **Count Robert of Paris** and **Castle Dangerous** (*Tales of My Landlord*; fourth series, 1832).

Such an output would be creditable in any writer of Scott's quality, and this is without mention of several other verse romances which were not successful. But there was much more: at least four dramas, editions of Dryden (1808) and Swift (1814) with biographies, *Border Antiquities of England and Scotland* (1814–17), *Provincial Antiquities of Scotland* (1819–26), *The Life of Napoleon Buonaparte* (1827), *Tales of a Grandfather* (1828–30), *A History of Scotland* (1829–30), and essays on chivalry, romance, and the drama for the *Encyclopaedia Britannica* – and even these are only part of his complete works.

In the opinion of those who knew him, Scott was a charming and generous man. He may have been too generous; certainly he was a great spender. His ambitions ran to a great house and a great estate as well as a great name, and he was no doubt less than wise in his investments. But it took a man of enormous courage to meet the challenge he faced after the crash of 1826. The urgent compulsive writing, however, prevented Scott from revising his work and it would probably have benefited enormously if he had had more time. At his best he is superb and he was enormously popular in Europe. Less read now than at any time since the end of the 19th century, Scott nevertheless has always received serious critical attention and it is by no means unlikely that he will be widely read again.

**Scottish anthologies and collections** While much of Scottish poetry followed the example of *The Kingis Qùair*, which itself followed the example of Chaucer, the poetry so well known in this tradition represents an 'imported' form. The native poetry of Scotland flourished alongside it and is usually called Middle Scots, and in its finest and final phase is found in the work of William Dunbar. Most of the poetry called Middle Scots is anonymous and its preservation is due to the work of antiquaries who collected much of it. These collections comprise the following.

*The Makculloch Manuscript* (1477). A collection of Scots pieces written in the flyleaves and blank pages of a collection of lecture notes in Latin at Louvain, the manuscript is now in the library of the University of Edinburgh.

*The Gray Manuscript* (c.1500). James Gray was notary public and priest of Dunblane, and the Scots pieces are interpolated in the manuscript, which is in the National Library of Scotland.

*The Asloan Manuscript* (c.1515). This was collected by John Asloan and is now in the possession of Lord Talbot. It formerly belonged to the Boswell family.

*The Bannatyne Manuscript* (1568). Now in the National Library of Scotland, this is the work of George Bannatyne.

*The Maitland Folio Manuscript* (c.1580). This was compiled by Sir Richard Maitland of Lethington and is now in the library of Magdalen College, Cambridge.

*The Maitland Quarto Manuscript* (1586). The work of Marie Maitland, Sir Richard's daughter, this manuscript is in the library of Magdalen College, Cambridge.

The earliest known specimens of Scots printing, *Chepman and Myllar's Prints*, also contributed to the survival of the native poetry. Walter Chepman and Andrew Myllar produced printed sheets independently in 1508; the sheets have been bound together and are in the National Library of Scotland.

**Scottish Chiefs, The**  See **Porter, Jane**.

**Scottish literature, early**  The earliest identifiable Scottish literature is in the form of some unremarkable verses on the death of King Alexander III (1286). After the struggle with the English and the victory at Bannockburn (1314), Scotland was a country that needed to be remade; soon after this (c.1320) John Barbour was born. He wrote his *The Bruce, or The Metrical History of Robert I King of Scots* about 1375, and Scottish literature could be said to have begun. The language was English (Inglis), the 'Scots' language being that now known as Gaelic. 'Scots' was spoken in the north and west but the language of the court and the scholars was English.

**Scotus, John Duns**  See **Duns Scotus, John**.

**Scriblerus Club**  Formed about 1713, the members of this association were Alexander Pope, Jonathan Swift, Lord Oxford, John Arbuthnot, William Congreve, John Gay, Thomas Parnell, and Francis Atterbury. They undertook the compilation of the *Memoirs of Martinus Scriblerus*. See also **Martinus Scriblerus, Memoirs of**.

**Scrooge, Ebenezer**  The sour, stingy old employer in Dickens's *A Christmas Carol*. He becomes a reformed character when the ghost of his late partner, Marley, shows him the consequences of his actions.

**Scudamour, Sir**  In Book IV of Spenser's *The Faerie Queene*, he is married to Amoret, who is abducted by Busirane on the wedding day.

**Seafarer, The**  A poem of just over 100 lines in Old English, preserved in *The Exeter Book*. The speaker reflects on the hardship of his seaman's life, especially during winter voyages. But after a third of the poem the complaint changes to praise of the attractions of a life at sea. Scholars have suggested that the original poem, or minstrel's tale, may have been a dialogue between an old seaman offering a warning and a young man who feels the lure of a seagoing life. The final third of the poem takes on a pious tone, comparing heaven's rewards with transitory earthly pleasures.

The contradictions of the first two-thirds of the poem could, as George Sampson noted, be resolved by accepting the early complaints as the words of a seafarer who knows perfectly well how harsh his life can be, but would live no other. There is a fine modern version of the poem by Ezra Pound, first published in his *Ripostes* (1912), and a translation by C. W. Kennedy in *An Anthology of Old English Poetry* (1960).

**Seagrim, Molly** The gamekeeper's daughter in *Tom Jones* by Henry Fielding. She enjoys sexual romps with Tom and others, and nearly succeeds in getting Tom to the altar when she finds herself pregnant.

**Seasons, The** A poem in blank verse by James Thomson, consisting of four books (one for each season) and a final Hymn. The first book was *Winter*, published in 1726; *Summer* followed in 1727, *Spring* in 1728, and *Autumn* and the closing *Hymn* in 1730. The whole was carefully revised, possibly with the help of the poet's friend Alexander Pope, and the new version published in 1744. Thomson acknowledged his debt to the *Georgics* of Virgil in the forming of his poem. The title of each book indicates the content, and each one contains some story or anecdote which relates the season to humanity. *Winter*, for instance, tells of a wayfarer dying in a snowdrift, and life in town and village; *Spring* contains praise of nuptial love and an idyllic picture of an angler; *Summer* tells the stories of Celadon and Amelia and Damon and Musidora; *Autumn* relates a story based on the Book of Ruth and condemns the barbarity of hunting. The overall picture is of the world progressing through the seasons, rounded off by a hymn to Nature.

**Sea-Wolf, The** A novel by Jack London, first published in 1904. In this novel the author turned from the subject of the North and the gold rush towards his experience as a seaman on board a sealer.

During a fog there is a collision in San Francisco Bay; the sealing ship, *Ghost*, runs down a ferry boat and one of the passengers, Humphrey van Weyden, is flung overboard. He is picked up by the *Ghost* and pressed into service by the captain, Wolf Larsen. Van Weyden is a literary critic and a stranger to hardship; Larsen is magnificent and powerful – van Weyden is fascinated by him while at the same time repelled by his ruthlessness.

The *Ghost* reaches the sealing grounds off Japan. A woman castaway from a sea disaster is rescued by the ship; she is a poet, Maude Brewster, and almost at once she becomes the object of Larsen's attentions. She finds a sympathetic response in van Weyden, Larsen's opposite. The struggle between these two is hopelessly unequal and van Weyden and Miss Brewster flee from the ship. They reach a deserted island – but ironically the *Ghost*, with Larsen on board, is driven ashore there. Larsen has been deserted by his crew. The ship has been dismasted and Larsen is blind; he is suffering from cerebral cancer. Van Weyden and Miss Brewster manage to make the *Ghost* seaworthy again and set out for civilization: van Weyden has realized himself through adversity and wins through, while Larsen, unchanged and defiant to the end, dies on the island.

*The Sea-Wolf* was enormously successful and had an advance sale, before publication, of forty thousand copies. It was severely criticized by Ambrose Bierce for the introduction of the love interest, which London had to try (and failed) to make believable within the proprieties of the time and was in conflict with his own experience. But the book is remarkable in its evocation of a voyage on a sealer and Wolf Larsen is a memorable character.

**Sebastian** Viola's twin brother in Shakespeare's *Twelfth Night*. He is believed lost at sea and when he arrives in Illyria is mistaken for Viola, who has been masquerading as a man (Cesario). Olivia falls in love with him, believing him to be Cesario.

**Second Coming, The** See **Yeats, William Butler**.

**Second Nun's Tale, The** See *Canterbury Tales, The*.

**Secret Agent, The:** *A Simple Tale*. A novel by Joseph Conrad, first published in the New York weekly *Ridgeway's* (October 1906–January 1907) and in volume form in 1907.

Adolf Verloc runs a dubious paper and stationery shop in Soho, and lives comfortably with his wife Winnie and her weak-minded brother Stevie. Verloc is in fact a double agent, working for an international anarchist group as well as for a foreign power. The group uses his shop as a rendezvous, and Verloc does profitable business selling their secrets to the foreign power, which eventually disturbs Verloc's quiet life by insisting that he contrive a bomb outrage at Greenwich Observatory, which will certainly be blamed on the anarchists.

Verloc decides to use Stevie, who is devoted to him, to plant the bomb; but the boy stumbles in

Greenwich Park on his way to deliver the bomb and it explodes prematurely. In the fragments, which are all that is left of Stevie, the police find the address in Soho: Winnie's protectiveness had led her to sew an address tag on his clothes, and she recognizes it. She had married Verloc to secure protection for Stevie, and she is stunned. She has always made a point of being incurious about her husband's activities, and Verloc has always believed that she married him for himself. He misguidedly suggests that it would have been far worse for Winnie if she had lost her husband. She kills him with a carving knife and tries to flee to the Continent with Ossipon, one of her husband's associates. Ossipon had been attracted to Mrs Verloc and had believed that the bomb victim was Verloc himself. When he learns the truth he coldly abandons her on the journey after robbing her. Mrs Verloc drowns herself in the Channel.

*Secret Garden, The*  A novel by Frances Hodgson Burnett, first published in 1910.

Mary Lennox is a spoiled child who returns to England from India and goes to live in her uncle's house on the Yorkshire moors. She is used to having her own way but here she is faced with the disagreeable fact that she is going to have to amuse herself and, after some bumpy patches, becomes friends with a local boy named Dickon. Mary finds a small garden through a locked door in the main wall. The garden has been neglected for years and she plans its restoration with Dickon's help. She also discovers that she has a young cousin living in the house, an invalid boy named Colin. Mary and Dickon's efforts to restore the secret garden stir Colin into life; he recovers as well as the garden. At the end of the story Mary has come a long way from the spoiled and petulant girl who arrived from India.

*Secret Love, or The Maiden Queen.*  A comedy by John Dryden, first produced in February 1667 and first published in 1668. The play was a favourite of Charles II and enjoyed considerable success. The king's fondness for the piece may have lain in its theme, that of a monarch in love with a subject, in this case however, the monarch is a queen. She is in love with Philocles, who is in love with Candiope but whose feelings for his sovereign lady might also be love. Another couple, Celadon and Florimel, have the better part of the comedy with their witty raillery, being modelled on the principals of *Much Ado About Nothing*. Nell Gwynne played Florimel and enchanted Samuel Pepys with her performance.

**Sedley, Amelia**  The 'good' girl in Thackeray's *Vanity Fair*, her only real virtue is that she shows

kindness to Becky Sharp at Miss Pinkerton's academy and after. Otherwise she is silly, clinging, and in times of crisis apt to rely on spurious feminine helplessness.

**Sedley, Sir Charles** *c*.1639–1701.  Sedley, the younger son of a baronet, inherited the title when his elder brother died. He spent some time at Wadham College, Oxford, but left without taking a degree. He settled down to life in London and for something like ten years was a notorious debauchee. He began to lead a more adult life when he became MP for Romney (*c*.1668); he was later an active parliamentary speaker, and became something of a patron of men of letters. Sedley was the author of some lyrics, two forgotten tragedies, and three comedies, two of which were adapted from French originals. *Bellamira, or The Mistress* (1687) based on a comedy by Terence, is regarded as his best work.

**Sedley, Jos** (*or* **Joseph**)  The fat and stupid nabob of Thackeray's *Vanity Fair*. He would have been happy to have married Becky Sharp – but he is diverted from this by George Osborne. He is Amelia Sedley's brother.

**Seeger, Alan** 1888–1916.  The son of an old New England family, Alan Seeger was born in New York and graduated from Harvard in 1910. He wrote poetry while at college and some of his verse appeared in the *Harvard Monthly*. He apparently found life in America unsatisfying after completing his education and two years later departed for Paris. France was his home from 1912, and upon the outbreak of World War I he enlisted in her defence, joining the Foreign Legion. Seeger was a soldier of some distinction and was killed in 1916 at Belloy-en-Santerre during the Battle of the Somme. He was awarded the Croix de Guerre and the Médaille posthumously.

Alan Seeger's *Collected Poems* was published in the year of his death, with an introduction by William Archer; his *Letters and Diary* was published in 1917. His famous 'I Have a Rendezvous with Death' was first published in the *North American Review* in October 1916. His other poems, such as 'Ode to Antares', Sonnet VIII ('Oh, love of woman, you are known to be') and 'Ode to Natural Beauty' are strongly romantic in tone.

**Seeley, John Robert** 1834–95.  The son of the publisher R. B. Seeley, John Robert Seeley was born in London and educated at the City of London School and Christ's College, Cambridge. He became Professor of Latin at University

College, London (1863–69), and Professor of Modern History at Cambridge in 1869. Seeley's inaugural lecture at London was *Classical Studies as an Introduction to the Moral Sciences* (1864); his interest in Christian ethics found further expression in *Ecce Homo* (published anonymously, 1865), which quickly became famous. Seeley's historical works, *The Expression of England* (1883) and *The Growth of British Policy* (1895), expressed the view that England's assumption of empire was Christian and ethical, therefore inevitable. *The Life and Times of Stein: or Germany and Prussia in the Napoleonic Age* (1878) was a study of the German statesman and made Seeley popular in Germany.

*Sejanus, his Fall* A tragedy by Ben Jonson, first produced in 1603 and first published in 1605. The first performance was given by The King's Men at the Globe Theatre and the cast included Richard Burbage and William Shakespeare. The play, which is rarely revived, follows the events of Roman history through the career of Lucius Aelius Sejanus, favourite of Tiberius, who leaves him in charge of Rome while he spends more and more time on his island, Capri. Sejanus aspires to the purple and poisons the emperor's son, Drusus; he has seduced – and hopes to marry – Drusus' widow, Livia (historically, Livilla). He also succeeds in discrediting Agrippina, the widow of the great soldier Germanicus (he was Tiberius's nephew and adopted son), but the old man grows suspicious; and Naevius Sertorius Macro, the ambitious commander of the Praetorian Guard, is more than willing to supplant Sejanus. Eventually Tiberius denounces Sejanus to the Senate; he is arrested and put to death.

*Selborne, The Natural History of* See **White, Gilbert**.

**Selden, John** 1584–1654. The son of a Sussex yeoman, Selden became a lawyer and was keeper of the records at the Inner Temple. He entered Parliament in 1623, having acquired meanwhile a certain fame as the author of a *History of Tythes* (1618), which angered the church authorities. No lover of the episcopacy, Selden was no lover of Puritanism either, though he was, like many of the better minds of his time, a sharp opponent of the crown's prerogative. His clear detached criticism often earned him the ill will of both sides and he had no patience with Parliamentarians who fought to displace princes, only to assume princely powers. He withdrew from public affairs before the trial of Charles I.

His most notable work is the posthumous *Table Talk: being the Discourses of John Selden Esq*

*. . . relating especially to Religion and State*, which was collected by his amanuensis Richard Milward and published in 1689. A jurist and scholar of considerable distinction, Selden pronounces upon matters of law, personal freedom, and the motives of authority in crisp direct English, leaving a book that transcends his times.

Selden was a friend of Ben Jonson and was admired by Milton; he contributed notes ('illustrations') to the first 18 cantos of Drayton's *Poly-Olbion* and was also the author of books on antiquities and on law. In 1635, in *Mare Clausum*, he disputed the principle of sovereignty on the high seas with Hugo Grotius.

*Self Condemned* See **Lewis, (Percy) Wyndham**.

*Self-Help* See **Smiles, Samuel**.

**Sempill, Robert** *c*.1595–*c*.1665. A gentleman of Renfrewshire, Sempill was educated at Glasgow University. He fought for the king during the Civil War and was an active figure in the move toward a Restoration. In literature Sempill was one of the links between the old school of Scots secular verse and its recovery from the blight of the Kirk with the work of Allan Ramsay. Sempill's output was small and he is best known for *The Life and Death of Habbie Simson, Piper of Kilbarchan*, a mock elegy in a familiar Scots tradition.

*Sense and Sensibility* Jane Austen's first published novel (1811). It began as a story, 'Elinor and Marianne', which Jane read to her family in 1795. She began to rewrite the story in 1797, but at the same time was also drafting the first sketches for *Pride and Prejudice* and *Northanger Abbey* and working on a story, 'The Watsons', which was never completed.

The Dashwoods of Norland Park, in Sussex, have a life interest in the estate while Henry Dashwood lives: when he dies it passes to John Dashwood, his son by his first marriage. Henry Dashwood recommends his second wife and his daughters to John when he dies. But John and his wife are selfish and, encouraged by Mrs Ferrars, John's mother-in-law, defeat his father's wish. Mrs Henry Dashwood and her daughters retire to a cottage in Devonshire. Elinor Dashwood and Mrs John Dashwood's brother, Edward Ferrars, feel a mutual attraction but Elinor feels an odd constraint in Edward's relations with her.

In Devonshire, Marianne Dashwood falls passionately in love with John Willoughby, charming and penniless, and is deeply distressed when he suddenly leaves for London. Elinor and Marianne go to London, too, at the invitation of their friend Mrs Jennings, and Marianne now finds Willoughby indifferent to her. Her importunities finally provoke an insolent letter from him, announcing his forthcoming marriage to an heiress. Elinor, meanwhile, has learned that Edward Ferrars has been secretly engaged to Lucy Steele for four years. Elinor's self-control enables her to conceal her distress.

It is Edward's dependence on his mother that made him conceal his engagement and now Mrs Ferrars, learning of it, dismisses him and settles her property on his silly young brother Robert. Edward, who intends taking orders, now has a small living offered him by Colonel Brandon, a quiet worthy man who has long been an admirer of Marianne. But now Lucy transfers her attention to Robert and marries him instead. Edward, at last free of a commitment he deeply regretted, proposes to Elinor and she accepts him. The staunch and generous Colonel Brandon wins Marianne, who is brought to see that her passionate sensibility would hardly make for happiness.

*Sense and Sensibility* is not Jane Austen's most popular book nor, her admirers acknowledge, is it her best. Lord David Cecil's comment, in his introduction to The World's Classics edition, could not be improved upon: 'Now any art so disciplined and vigilant [as Jane Austen's] cannot be perfected in a day. And for this reason *Sense and Sensibility* is not likely to be her best book. For it was her first.'

**Sense of the Past, The**  An unfinished novel by Henry James. It is a fantasy in which a young American, Ralph Pendrel, inherits a house in London and steps into the past by changing places with the portrait of an ancestor. The theme was developed and made into a play called *Berkeley Square*, by J. L. Balderston and J. C. Squire, which enjoyed considerable success.

**Sentimental Journey Through France and Italy, by Mr Yorick, A**  A novel by Laurence Sterne, his second and last, first published in 1768. Sterne travelled in France and Italy for his health's sake – he was consumptive – and based the novel on his experiences. He only completed the first part, concerning France, and died in the year of its publication. His pseudonym, Mr Yorick, was familiar to his readers as a character in *Tristram Shandy*, and Sterne refers to the characters in that book. The story of Maria, the 'disordered maid' of Moulines from Volume IX of *Tristram Shandy*, is recalled when Yorick passes that way in the later book. He travels from Calais to Rouen, on to Paris, through the Bourbonnais, and on to the road for Lyons, where the narrative suddenly stops. A striking feature of the book – and the times – is that France and England are at war. The book ambles from incident to incident and the author observes life from a privileged position, as his effortless entrée to smart circles indicates. Sterne's ability to convey shades of feeling make the short book intensely alive, despite the triviality of most of what occurs. 'The book relies for its effect entirely on Sterne's ability to buttonhole his readers', as A. Alvarez observes in his introduction to the Penguin English Library edition. Another modern edition of *A Sentimental Journey* is published in The World's Classics, with an introduction by Virginia Woolf.

**Sentiments of a Church of England Man, The**  See *Argument against Abolishing Christianity, An*.

**Serious Call to a Devout and Holy Life, A**  See **Law, William**.

**Service, Robert William** 1876–1958.  Robert William Service was born in Preston in Lancashire and emigrated to Canada in 1897. He had worked in a bank but in the New World he lived rough on the Pacific coast and Vancouver Island for eight years. In 1905 he went to work for a Canadian bank, which sent him to the far north to a branch in Yukon Territory. The Klondike gold rush was in progress and Service's experience of the wilderness, and the influence of Kipling, gave him the impulse for *Songs of a Sourdough* (1907). A 'sourdough' is a veteran of the northwest wilderness; survival of a winter or two in Alaska and the Yukon entitled any man to call himself one. The critics sniffed at Service's lack of literary sophistication but an eager public gave him a great success: 2,000,000 copies had been sold by 1940.

*Rhymes of a Rolling Stone* (1912) was published after Service had become the European correspondent of a Toronto newspaper; *Rhymes of a Red Cross Man* (1916) when he was an ambulance driver with the Canadian army in France during World War I. He continued to exploit his talent for 'pop' lyrics and ballads successfully in *Ballads of a Bohemian* (1920), *Bar-Room Ballads* (1940), *Rhymes of a Roughneck* (1950), *Lyrics of a Lowbrow* (1951), and *Rhymes of a Rebel* (1952). 'The Shooting of Dan McGrew' is a famous example. Service also published novels – *The Trail of '98* (1910), *The Pretender* (1915), *The Roughneck* (1923), and *The House of Fear* (1927) – and two volumes of autobiography, *Ploughman of the Moon* (1945) and *The Harper of Heaven* (1948).

**Seton, Ernest Thompson** 1860–1946.  Seton was born in South Shields, Durham, and his name was originally Ernest Seton Thompson.

He went to Canada with his emigrant family when he was still a child and was educated in Toronto. Seton studied art in London at the Royal Academy and later became a government naturalist in Manitoba. He founded the Boy Scouts of America and the Woodcraft League and wrote a great number of books on wildlife, which enjoyed a great success. Among his books, which he illustrated himself, were *Wild Animals I Have Known* (1898), *Biography of a Grizzly* (1900), *Lives of the Hunted* (1901), *Wild Animals at Home* (1913), and *The Arctic Prairies* (1911).

**Settle, Elkanah** 1648–1724. The target of Dryden's satire in the second part of *Absalom and Achitophel* (Settle is Doeg and Shadwell is Og), Settle wrote *Cambyses, King of Persia* while at Oxford. His chief claim to remembrance, unfortunately, lies in the scorn of Dryden and later, of Alexander Pope. Settle's career in the theatre began in the London city fairs, where he staged drolls (short comic scenes usually based on scenes from well-known plays) in booths as sideshow entertainment; drolls were a popular feature of the fairs. *Cambyses* was produced at the Lincoln's Inn theatre in 1666 and published in 1671, and Settle was helped by the Earl of Rochester, Dryden's enemy, in the production of *The Empress of Morocco* (1673). The play, as elaborate and heroic as Dryden's work in the same vein, enjoyed a healthy success with Thomas Betterton in the cast and was published in the same year.

Encouraged by his reception Settle became a writer of tragedies but none had lasting value; 15 were produced, the last in 1718. But true success was never again his and in the last years of his life he returned to staging drolls at the London fairs, being designated City Poet, and staging pageants on Lord Mayor's Day. He died in poverty in the Charterhouse.

Settle devised the libretto, based on *A Midsummer Night's Dream*, for Purcell's opera *The Fairy Queen*. *Settle: His Life and Works* by F. C. Brown, was published in 1910, (revised 1933). The text of *The Empress of Morocco* is included in *Five Heroic Plays*, edited by Bonamy Dobrée (The World's Classics).

**Settlers in Canada, The** A novel for young people by Frederick Marryat, telling of the adventures of the Campbell family when they settle on the shores of Lake Ontario. It was first published in 1844.

***Seven Deadly Sinnes of London, The,*** *Drawne in Seven Severall Coaches Through the Seven Severall Gates of the Citie, Bringing the Plague with them.* A

pamphlet by Thomas Dekker, first published in 1606. It is a remarkable account of Dekker's own city; written in the form of an address like a medieval sermon, it evokes the London of the early 17th century with a vividness that looks forward to Defoe. Dekker is not sentimental about his London: 'the wealthiest, but the most wanton ... attir'de like a Bride ... but there is much harlot in thine eyes. Thou sitst in thy Gates heated with Wines, and in thy Chambers with lust.'

***Seven Lamps of Architecture, The*** John Ruskin's essay on architecture was written while the author was still working on *Modern Painters* and first published in 1849. The seven lamps of the title refer to the lamps of Sacrifice, Truth, Power, Beauty, Life, Memory, and Obedience, the leading principles of architecture, of which the noblest style, in Ruskin's findings, is Gothic. The work was edited by S. Image for Everyman's Library in 1907.

***Seven Pillars of Wisdom, The*** See **Lawrence, T(homas) E(dward)**.

***Seven Sages of Rome, The*** A Middle English verse romance of the early 14th century. (See **metrical romances**.) The story is of eastern, probably Arabic, origin and found its way to England through Latin and French versions. The form of connected verse stories was later used by Chaucer to fine effect in *The Canterbury Tales*. Diocletian, Emperor of Rome, has entrusted the education of his son Florentine to seven sages. Diocletian's wife is the son's stepmother and she lusts after him. He spurns her, so she tells the emperor that his son has tried to seduce her. She then casts a spell on Florentine so that for seven days he remains silent. He is sentenced to death, and she proceeds to malign his character to show what an unsuitable heir he would be, countering the evidence of his worth offered by Florentine's tutors, the seven sages. The sages each relate a story of the perfidy of ambitious women; she retaliates with seven tales of the wickedness of counsellors. But at the end of seven days Florentine is once more able to speak and his stepmother is exposed. She is sent to the stake. *The Seven Sages* was edited by D. Laing for the Bannatyne Club (1837), by T. Wright for the Percy Society (1845), by K. Campbell (Boston, 1907), by W. Craigie for the Scottish Text Society (1924), and by K. Brunner for the Early English Text Society (1933).

***Seven Seas, The*** A book of verse by Rudyard Kipling, first published in 1896. The collection contains 60 poems, among them 'McAndrew's

Hymn', 'The "Mary Gloster"', 'The Native-Born', and 'A Song of the English'.

## seventeenth–century historical collections
The collections of state papers are among the principal sources of published information for students of the period. John Rushworth's *Historical Collections* (eight volumes, 1659–80) deals with events from 1618 to 1641. Rushworth was clerk-assistant to the Commons and made his own notes during such events as the trial of Strafford and the execution of Archbishop Laud. *The Collection of the State Papers of John Thurloe* (seven volumes, 1742) covers the last years of the reign of Charles I and continues to the Restoration. Thurloe was Cromwell's friend and secretary to the council of state and the collection is the chief source of information on the Protectorate. *The Calendar of the Clarendon State Papers* (four volumes, 1872–1932) was preserved in the Bodleian Library and the first part published in the 19th century. Clarendon was Charles II's chief minister and Lord Chancellor. *The Letters and Speeches of Oliver Cromwell* were collected by Thomas Carlyle (1845). *The Court and Times of James I* is the subject of Thomas Birch's letters and reports (1848). *Memorials of the Civil War* is a personal account by Lord Fairfax, the most sympathetic figure on the Parliamentary side (1849), and *The Fairfax Correspondence* was published in four volumes (1848–49).

## seventeenth–century journalism
Printed journalism in England might be said to have sneaked into existence. The dissemination of news was chiefly through letters and men in high places often retained 'intelligencers' to keep them informed of events. This was particularly true of ambassadors and commanders who needed to know how events were progressing at home. Printing, hardly more than a century old, was not an advantage that the mighty intended the masses to possess – those in power were well aware of its value and held to it as a privilege that they might withhold or bestow at will. The first evidence of journalism is the broadside ballad, a crude statement, often in verse and printed on one side of a single sheet, relating some startling event.

The broadside ballad slowly expanded to become a pamphlet but these too were 'occasional' and the first periodical pamphlet was printed in Amsterdam. The first Englishman to publish them, Thomas Archer, was imprisoned in 1621. His pamphlets gave news of foreign wars and in spite of Archer's imprisonment others soon followed his example, until the crown, which controlled printing through the Star Chamber, forbade the printing of news from foreign countries. However, a monopoly for the printing of foreign news was granted to Messrs Butter and Bourne in 1638 and the first issue of the news was dated 20 December of that year.

The Long Parliament abolished the Star Chamber in 1641 but the Parliamentarians had no intention of letting the masses read and write what they liked. A certain Henry Walley, clerk to the Stationers' Company, was made licenser and the Parliamentary party lost no time in pouring out dozens of propaganda sheets.

After Cromwell's death the Council of State gave Oliver Williams and Marchamont Nedham official sanction for a twice-weekly newsletter. Another journalist of far greater importance to England, Henry Muddiman, was also given permission to publish news at the request of General Monck, under the patronage of Sir John Williamson. In 1659 Muddiman started the twice-weekly *The Parliamentary Intelligencer*, and next he published the weekly *Mercurius Publicus*: these became an important political feature of the time. The Restoration followed in 1660, and when the court fled from London during the plague of 1665 it resided at Oxford, where Muddiman (again under the patronage of Sir John Williamson) published the *Oxford Gazette*. This became the *London Gazette* when the court moved back to London and it was still in circulation three centuries later.

An invaluable advantage secured by Muddiman was the grant of free postage to his contributors. Anyone, anywhere in England, could send information to the *London Gazette* free of charge. The public's need for news was at last acknowledged and journalism was born in England.

## seventeenth–century verse romances
Mainly the work of minor poets, the romances of this period were an attempt at storytelling in the form available to those writers: there was as yet no suitable prose style available, while the drama had requirements that none of them could meet. Such writers could be said to have been trying to feel their way to romantic fiction; but the demands of poetry required greatness of the level of Chaucer, Spenser, and Shakespeare, and except for an occasional felicitous lyric most of these 17th-century attempts have been forgotten.

See also **Chamberlayne, William**; *Thelma and Clearchus*; **Kynaston, Sir Francis**; **Hannay, Patrick**; **Marmion, Shackerley**; *Chaste and Lost Lovers, The*; *Pleasant Historie of Albino and Bellama, The*; and *Arnalte and Lucinda*.

**Sewall, Samuel** c.1652–1730. The son of New England settlers, Sewall was born in England when his family returned there. He went back to Boston when he was nine years old and received his education at Harvard, graduating in 1671 and soon after becoming a fellow. In 1676 he married the daughter of John Hull, a man of considerable wealth, and this enabled him to enter public life. He gave valuable help to Increase Mather's mission to William III to recover the Massachusetts charter and was a councillor from 1691 to 1725. In 1692 he became a special commissioner at the Salem witchcraft trials.

Sewall was one of those who lived to regret his participation in those infamous proceedings and was in fact the only one of the nine judges to make a public confession of error (1697). Thereafter, he went on to become a humane and liberal jurist; he was chief justice of the Superior Court of Judicature from 1718 to 1728. His first notable published work was *The Selling of Joseph* (1700), his third publication and the first antislavery tract to appear in America. It is in the form of a lawyer's brief, with the authority of Scripture to lend strength to its case. *A Memorial Relating to the Kennebeck Indians* (1721) argues the case for more humane treatment of Indians. But his greatest contribution to New England literature is his invaluable *Diary*, which was published by the Massachusetts Historical Society and which deals with the years 1674–77 and 1685–1729. This is intimate and detailed, giving a vivid picture of day-to-day life and revealing Sewall's own character with remarkable honesty.

**Seward, Anna** 1747–1809. Born at Eyam in Derbyshire, Anna Seward became a lady of Lichfield in Staffordshire when she inherited her father's money. She was the centre of a literary circle of no great distinction and a busy writer of poems and letters. She met Samuel Johnson frequently and, though not an admirer, gave Boswell very useful information. She bequeathed her poems to Sir Walter Scott, who published them with a memoir: *Poetical Works* (1810). Her letters, which were carefully written for publication, appeared in six volumes: *The Letters of Anna Seward, 1784–1807* (1811). Anna Seward was called the Swan of Lichfield by her admirers but her poetry is no longer read.

**Sewell, Anna** 1820–78. The daughter of a family of Norfolk Quakers. Her mother wrote verse and stories for children, sometimes assisted by Anna Sewell, a semi-invalid incapacitated as a result of a childhood accident who nevertheless managed to get about through her skill at managing a pony and trap. But her health continued to fail and she was a complete invalid at the age of 50. She spent the next six years writing *Black Beauty*, which was published at Christmas in 1877. Anna Sewell lived just long enough – she died in the following April – to know of its great success.

*Black Beauty* is the classic horse story, following the animal's life from its days as an exquisite foal, through all sorts of vicissitudes. It is a perennial favourite, an animal story that has seldom been bettered.

**Shadow of a Gunman, The** A tragedy in two acts by Sean O'Casey, first produced at the Abbey Theatre, Dublin, on 12 April 1923, and first published in 1925. The action of the play occurs during a few hours in a tenement room in Dublin in 1920.

Donal Davoren is sharing the room with Seamas Shields, a pedlar. He is the focus of considerable interest because nothing is known about him – many believe him to be on the run from the British. Minnie Powell, a girl in the tenement who earns her own living (her parents are dead), is enchanted with him because he works at a typewriter and knows a great deal of poetry; but she too is convinced that he is a gunman on the run. Donal finds her charming and lets her keep her illusions about him. Other people in the tenement call with protestations of undying loyalty (Tommy Owens) and appeals to the authority which will, one day, rule in Ireland and which is personified by Donal (Mrs Henderson and Mr Gallogher). At the end of the first act they hear news of an ambush at Knocksedan. Donal is disturbed; Seamas's friend Maguire, who went to Knocksedan that day, has been named as a casualty. He had dumped his bag in Seamus's room before leaving.

In the second act Donal is trying to write; Seamus deplores Maguire's death – if he had gone with Seamus he'd still be alive. But Seamus is very jumpy on his own behalf and admits to knowing that the carpenter's shop in the mews behind the house is used by the IRA. A burst of gunfire startles both men and Mrs Grigson, another tenant, comes to air her fears about her drunkard husband, always in danger of being shot through being caught out after curfew. Grigson arrives home safely, very drunk and, inevitably, very boring, determined to assure Donal that he has nothing to fear from Grigson. A British army vehicle draws up outside the house and Donal realizes that a great many people believe he is a gunman on the run. Firing is heard from the street; Donal searches frantically for the letter pressed on him, addressed to the Irish Republican Army, by Mrs Henderson and

Mr Gallogher. The Grigsons depart and Donal and Seamus discover to their horror that Maguire's bag is loaded with Mills bombs. Minnie rushes in to say the house is surrounded; if it's the British Army it will be bad enough, if it's the Black and Tans, God help them. Minnie takes the bag and hurries away with it to hide it in her room as the thunder of rifle butts sounds on doors and windows are smashed.

It is the Black and Tans. Minnie's room is searched, the bag is found, and Minnie is dragged out, loyally defending the republic and Donal. It is Minnie who dies; farther down the street the truck is ambushed and she is shot while trying to escape. Donal, the gunman who never was, is left with his shame as the curtain descends.

**Shadowy Waters, The** See **Yeats, William Butler.**

**Shadwell, Thomas** *c.*1642–92. Shadwell was born in Norfolk and was a lawyer's son. After Cambridge, where he attended Caius College, he entered the Middle Temple to study law but abandoned it for a literary career. Shadwell proclaimed Ben Jonson as his master and in his time he was a successful dramatist. Many modern critics believe his work underrated, and certainly his reputation was not helped by his former friend Dryden's peculiarly spiteful attack on him (see **Dryden, John** and *Mac Flecknoe*). However, while Shadwell's work is certainly better than Dryden claims, he did nothing that was not better done by his contemporaries. When Dryden was deprived of his positions as poet laureate and historiographer royal these were conferred on Shadwell.

Shadwell was the author of 14 plays, two operas (he was also a musician), one adaptation from Shakespeare, various replies to John Dryden, and some poems in his duty as poet laureate. His dramatic works are *The Sullen Lovers* (based on Molière, 1668), *The Royal Shepherdess*, an opera (1669), *The Humorists* (1670), *The Miser* and *Epsom Wells* (1672), *The Tempest*, an opera based on Shakespeare's play (1674), *Psyche* and *The Libertine* (1675), *The Virtuoso* (1676), *Timon of Athens*, an adaptation (1678), *The Woman-Captain* (1679), *The Lancashire Witches* (1681), *The Squire of Alsatia*, which was highly praised by Macaulay and Scott (1688), *Bury Fair* and *The Amorous Bigotte* (1689), *The Scowrers* (1690) and *The Volunteers* (1692).

Shadwell's complete works were edited by Montague Summers (five volumes, 1927).

**Shaftesbury, Anthony Ashley Cooper, 3rd Earl of** 1671–1713. Grandson of the 1st Earl of Shaftesbury, who became the 'Achitophel' of Dryden's *Absalom and Achitophel* (1681), Shaftesbury was born in London and educated at Winchester College under the supervision of John Locke, who had been physician and secretary to his grandfather. After travelling in Europe Shaftesbury entered Parliament, inheriting the title in 1700; he retired from public life through ill health and in 1711 went to live in Naples, where he died. After withdrawing into private life Shaftesbury devoted himself to moral philosophy. He rejected the bleakness of Hobbes and Locke but at the same time questioned the dogma of religion; the Cambridge Platonists were his philosophical and literary ancestors.

Between 1698 and his death Shaftesbury wrote a series of philosophical essays including *An Inquiry Concerning Virtue* (1699), *A Letter Concerning Enthusiasm* (1708), *The Moralist* (1709), and *Soliloquy, or Advice to an Author* (1710). He collected his writings in *Characteristics of Men, Manners, Opinions, Times* (1711), which contained further reflections and essays on new subjects. A carefully revised text was published in 1714; his unfinished *Second Characters, or the Language of Forms* was edited by B. Rand and published in 1914.

Shaftesbury's prose presents no difficulties to the reader and his moral philosophy has no need of technicalities. He disliked religious controversy and regarded it as valueless; he used ridicule against superstition, but thought the use of ridicule as the sole weapon for argument detestable. At a time when many people were dismayed by the rival – and sometimes stridently argued – claims of philosophers, deists, and religious dogmatists, Shaftesbury's 'moral sense' had a very strong appeal and his work was widely read.

**Shakespeare, William** 1564–1616. The son of John Shakespeare, a glove maker and leather craftsman, William Shakespeare was born, as all the world knows, at Stratford-upon-Avon in Warwickshire. His birth date was probably 23 April, a surmise following his baptism on 26 April at Holy Trinity Church in Stratford. His education was almost certainly received at Stratford Grammar School, which he could have attended without fees as the son of an alderman of the town, which his father was by this time. John Shakespeare's fortunes took a downward turn while Shakespeare was in his teens, and William's obligatory marriage at the age of 18 (1582) to Anne Hathaway (she was pregnant), who was eight years his senior, make the 'lost' years of Shakespeare's life a matter for endless speculation. His first child, a daughter, was born within six months of his marriage, and twins, a son and daughter, two years later (1584). But

Shakespeare, by an unknown artist. Known as the Chandos portrait, the painting is undated and hangs in the National Portrait Gallery, London.

while Anne stayed all her life in Stratford her husband is not accounted for until eight years later, when he appears in London as an actor and playwright with a growing reputation. The explanation is probably that he was doing whatever work he could to maintain the home in Stratford to which he always returned.

The date 1592 was marked by Robert Greene's posthumous *Groatsworth of Wit*, which refers to a scene from *Henry VI Part 3*, and to 'Shakescene', and rudely calls the author an 'upstart Crow'; a mere actor who had the impudence to write a successful play when university-trained writers like himself and his friends were better qualified by far. Shakespeare was plainly then the author of the second and third parts of *Henry VI* by 1591; the first part followed in 1592, and *Richard III* completed the tetralogy in 1593 – and Richard Burbage became famous in the great part. *Titus Andronicus*, in spite of attempts to deny it to Shakespeare, is firmly named as his by Francis Meres and was probably played in 1593 by Edward Alleyn, no less. At this period, in the wake of the plague of 1592 and the closing of the theatres, comes Shakespeare's two poems, *Venus and Adonis* (1593) and *The Rape of Lucrece* (1594), both dedicated to the Earl of Southampton, a patron of literature in whom Shakespeare probably had hopes for the future.

Exactitude in the dating of Shakespeare's plays is virtually impossible and approximation has to serve in a brief survey. Among his early works (*c*.1590–*c*.1595) were the comedies *The Comedy of Errors*, *Love's Labour's Lost*, *All's Well that Ends Well*, and *The Taming of the Shrew* (concerning *Love's Labour's Wonne*, mentioned by Francis Meres, see *Love's Labour's Lost*). *The Two Gentlemen of Verona* and *King John* are usually assigned to this period also. Shakespeare was by this time a member with Richard Burbage of the company called The Lord Chamberlain's Men (Edward Alleyn was with The Admiral's Men) and he was to spend the rest of his working life with them. It is difficult to imagine how he combined the work of actor, playwright, and businessman (to some extent the company shared the receipts); but by 1599 he had written *Romeo and Juliet*, *Richard II* (the beginning of another historical tetralogy), the two parts of *Henry IV*, *Henry V*, *Much Ado About Nothing*, *A Midsummer Night's Dream*, *The Merchant of Venice*, and *The Merry Wives of Windsor*. During this period Shakespeare's fortunes seem to have set fair and he lived in Bishopsgate. He was confident enough in 1596 to pursue the grant of a coat-of-arms to his father. He succeeded, but tragically his own son died in the same year and what was to become the greatest name in English literature was never passed on. In 1597 Shakespeare was able to buy a fine house in Stratford, New Place.

During the 1590s Shakespeare, as a working playwright, probably did his share of the 'play-doctoring' of those days. Dekker and Heywood have left evidence of how commonplace the practice was and it has always been an obstacle in establishing satisfactory texts for the works of Marlowe. One instance of Shakespeare's help in mending a play has been verified to the satisfaction of most scholars in the manuscript of Anthony Munday's *Sir Thomas More*; but it is likely that many more instances have simply not come to light.

Usually dated towards the end of the 16th century – or the close of it – are *As You Like It* and *Twelfth Night*, often cited with *Much Ado About Nothing* as the summit of Shakespeare's comedy, and certainly it would be hard to find anything in English drama that approaches their exquisite quality. The company was now playing in its new theatre on Bankside, the Globe. *Julius Caesar* belongs to this period, *Troilus and Cressida* probably to the first year of the new century. In 1601 the company earned the wrath of Elizabeth I: the supporters of the Earl of Essex commissioned a performance at the Globe and to

D. Loggan's 'A Prospect of London as before the Fire.' The South Bank is in the foreground and the theatres are clearly seen.

the company's surprise asked for a revival of *Richard II*. It was played on Saturday 8 February, and The Lord Chamberlain's Men were paid 40 shillings. On the next day Essex, supported by a few friends, of whom the Earl of Southampton was one, rebelled against the queen – who understood only too well why the play chosen was *Richard II*. The deposition of a sovereign, ostensibly for the country's good – to be offered as a public spectacle at a time of disaffection, was not to be borne. Fortunately for them, the company were able to convince the commissioners that they had been no more than a band of players hired by a company of noblemen.

Shakespeare's next play may have been – but again, approximation is the best we can do – the most discussed work ever written for the theatre, **Hamlet**. **Measure for Measure**, that peculiar 'comedy', belongs to the same period, the closing years of Elizabeth's reign. King James released Southampton from the Tower (Essex had been beheaded) and granted a royal patent to The Lord Chamberlain's Men; they were now The King's Men and their prospects were bright. For one thing, they were completely freed from the threat of local harassment from authorities who might disapprove of their work. The second name on the list of members was William Shakespeare. An outbreak of plague in the same year closed the theatres but The King's Men played at Wilton House, Somerset House, and Whitehall.

The next few years, from 1604 to about 1608, found Shakespeare's extraordinary genius at its height: it is staggering to think that **Othello**, **King Lear**, **Macbeth**, **Antony and Cleopatra**, and **Coriolanus** belong to this brief period, as do the inferior **Timon of Athens** and **Pericles**.

In 1608 The King's Men acquired another theatre, an indoor one for their winter seasons, at Blackfriars. Beaumont and Fletcher began to write plays for the company and Fletcher was later to collaborate with Shakespeare himself. The great man was entering his last phase: **Cymbeline**, **Henry VIII** (with help from John Fletcher), **The Winter's Tale**, and the lovely swan song, **The Tempest**. On 29 June 1613 there was a spectacular performance of *Henry VIII* at the Globe, and during the king's entrance to Wolsey's entertainment (Act 1, Scene 4) the theatre thatch caught fire. The house was destroyed within an hour but no lives were lost and the actors rescued everything they could: they saved the manuscripts of Shakespeare's plays.

Work began at once on a new playhouse but Shakespeare took no part in it or in the company. He retired to Stratford, where he was now a landowner, and three years later, in March of 1616, became seriously ill. There is a story that he drank too much with his friends Ben Jonson and Michael Drayton and contracted a fever following a party. He made his will on 25 March and died a month later, at the age of 52. He was buried in Holy Trinity Church, Stratford, where the monument to him can be seen in the chancel.

Two of Shakespeare's poems have already been mentioned. The matchless **Sonnets** were published in 1609, with **A Lover's Complaint** added to the volume. *The Passionate Pilgrime*, a small group of poems, was published by William Jaggard in 1599 as 'By W. Shakespeare', and two of them reappear in the collected *Sonnets* (138 and 144) so there is little doubt that some of the poems are from the master's hand – three of them are from *Love's Labour's Lost*. **The Phoenix and the Turtle** (1601) was Shakespeare's contribution to the theme of *Love's Martyr* by Robert Chester (1601). Other contributors were Marston, Jonson, and Chapman.

When Shakespeare died some of his plays had been printed in unauthorized quartos – Shakespeare himself had made no effort to have his plays published. They belonged in fact to the company, The King's Men, but the pirated editions in faulty texts may have provoked Shakespeare's friend and rival Ben Jonson to include his own plays among his published works in 1616. William Jaggard, who had published the poems in *The Passionate Pilgrime* without Shakespeare's consent, rightly believed that there was a market for the plays and he published six of them (and three not by Shakespeare) in quartos in 1619. Shakespeare's friends in the company took action and two of them, John Hemmings and Henry Condell, began the work of preparing an edition of the plays from the scripts and prompt books. The fair copy was made by the company's scrivener Ralph Crane, and seven years after his death the plays of William Shakespeare were published in the great First Folio of 1623. The gratitude owed by lovers of literature to Hemmings and Condell is incalculable; without their efforts 20 of the plays could have been irretrievably lost.

Four editions of the First Folio were published (1623, 1632, 1664, and 1685) and the first scholarly edition came in 1709. This was by Nicholas Rowe, who worked from the Fourth Folio. Rowe made the first attempt to divide and locate the scenes correctly, as well as the entrances and exits; he also gave each play its *dramatis personae*. He was the first; his successors are legion. Of the modern editions notable for various excellences may be mentioned *The Arden Shakespeare* (edited by W. J. Craig and R. H. Case and revised by Una Ellis-Fermor and H. F. Brooks); the *New Variorum Shakespeare* from Philadelphia, prepared by Howard Furness and Howard Furness Jr in facsimile reprints of the quartos and folios; *The New Cambridge Shakespeare* edited by R. B. McKerrow; and the single-volume editions by Peter Alexander and Charles Jasper Sisson.

Comment on the work of William Shakespeare cannot amount to much more than a small addition to the hymns of praise sung by generations. Ben Jonson criticized his friend freely and jibed at his lack of classical learning; but he declared 'I loved the man, and do honour his memory, on this side idolatry' and 'There was ever more in him to be praised than pardoned'. He spoke for more of us than he could ever have guessed when he said of Shakespeare that 'He was not of an age, but for all time'. There is nothing one can add: every admirer has some treasured memory of magnificence, of pathos, of warmth and humour, of needle-sharp wit, of aching resignation. And performances go on yielding marvels undiscerned in the glorious symphony of words the great plays offer at first attendance. Only Shakespeare has riches enough to bestow them on the smaller parts; thus, the lesser of Cleopatra's maids can utter the shattering 'Finish, good lady; the bright day is done, And we are for the dark'. But that is just one line in one play – the Shakespeare canon teems with unforgettable music.

Withal he seems to have been a quiet man in an age when spectacular characters thrived. One can only marvel at his range of expression and wonder what experiences could have lain at the heart of the greatest poetry in the English language.

**Shakespeare apocrypha** The reputation of William Shakespeare was such that during his lifetime works were being offered as his in which he had no part whatever. It is acknowledged that he contributed, as a working playwright, to the works of others and occasional contributions by other hands have been noted in his own. C. F. Tucker Brooke's study *The Shakespeare Apocrypha* (1908) named no less than 42 plays attributed to the great man but there are only two – *Sir Thomas More* and *The Two Noble Kinsmen* – that contain positive evidence or historical proof of Shakespeare's involvement.

See ***More, Sir Thomas***; ***Two Noble Kinsmen, The***; ***Arden of Feversham, The Tragedy of Mr***; ***Thomas, Lord Cromwell***; ***London Prodigal, The***; ***Puritan, The***; ***Yorkshire Tragedy, A***; ***Merry Devil of Edmonton, The***; ***Mucedorus, The Comedie of***; ***Edward III, The Raigne of***, and ***Locrine, The Lamentable Tragedy of***.

***Shamela Andrews, An Apology for the Life of Mrs*** See ***Pamela*** and **Fielding, Henry**.

**Shandon, Captain** The founder of the *Pall Mall Gazette* in Thackeray's *Pendennis*. The author based his character on William Maginn, who founded *Fraser's Magazine*.

**Shandy, Walter** The hero's father in *Tristram Shandy* by Laurence Sterne. He is very familiar with current scientific theories and is always looking for ways to apply them. He is exasperated by his wife's complete lack of interest in his ideas: 'That she is not a woman of science . . . is her misfortune; but she might ask a question.'

**Sharp, Becky (*or* Rebecca)** The central character of Thackeray's *Vanity Fair*. The daughter of a penniless artist and a French dancer, she is an articled pupil who teaches French at Miss Pinkerton's academy for young ladies. Her contempt for the school and for Miss Pinkerton's pretensions are depicted vividly in the opening chapters; so is her determination to make a place for herself in an unsympathetic world.

**Shaw, George Bernard** 1856–1950. Shaw was born in Dublin, the only son and youngest child of parents who had, by the time he was able to comprehend such things, no affection left for each other. His mother, who sang, took lessons from George Vandaleur Lee, and the Shaws and Lees became a joint household when Shaw was ten years old. He began to acquire the knowledge and appreciation of music and the singer's art that proved so valuable in his career as a journalist; his formal education was completed at a day school, which he left at the age of 15. Shaw worked for an estate agent in Dublin and did well, but when George Vandaleur Lee went to London Mrs Shaw went also; Shaw was ambitious to write and he went there when he was 20. Mrs Shaw became a singing teacher and her son had an allowance of £1 a week from his father. Mother, son, and two sisters settled down in London.

Shaw spent a great deal of time in the British Museum Reading Room and became actively interested in socialism. His studies in the library were so diverse – from Karl Marx to operatic scores – that they attracted the interest of another reader, William Archer, and a lifelong friendship began. Archer was both encouraging and generous; he introduced Shaw to profitable journalism by giving him some of his own work, as book reviewer for the *Pall Mall Gazette* (1885–88). As a journalist Shaw was a distinct success; he became art critic for *The World*, music critic for *The Star* as 'Corno di Bassetto', and theatre critic for *The Saturday Review* in 1895 under Frank Harris. His name was now well known and his income was steady. His interest in socialism found a constructive outlet in the Fabian Society, which he joined in 1884; he became a notable speaker and pamphleteer. He had, meanwhile, written four novels but had found a publisher for only one, *Cashel Byron's Profession* (1886). In 1885 William Archer had suggested that they collaborate on a play but nothing came of it. Shaw shared Archer's interest in Henrik Ibsen, however, and in 1891 published a critical study entitled *The Quintessence of Ibsenism*.

Ibsen's plays, in English, were being performed by the Independent Theatre Society, directed by J. T. Grein. Shaw suggested to Grein that he complete one of the projects which had foundered in the abortive collaboration with Archer; Grein agreed, and produced the result, **Widowers' Houses**, in 1892 (1893 was the date of publication). It was a far cry from Ibsen, whom he so much admired; Shaw admitted frankly that he had laid 'violent hands' on a conventional well-made play to turn it into a 'realistic exposure of slum landlordism, municipal jobbery, and the pecuniary and matrimonial ties between them' and the result, he declared, was 'revoltingly incongruous'. It was his privilege to describe his work thus but it was the first expression of his dramatic genius. It was published with a preface, the first of a series of provocative essays which are almost as famous as the plays themselves.

Shaw's plays cover a period of nearly sixty years: *Arms and the Man, Candida, The Man of Destiny, You Never Can Tell* (1898, in *Plays Pleasant*); *Widowers' Houses*, **Mrs Warren's Profession**, *The Philanderer* (1898, in *Plays Unpleasant*); *The Devil's Disciple, Caesar and Cleopatra, Captain Brassbound's Conversion* (1901, in *Three Plays for Puritans*); **Man and Superman** (1903); *How He Lied to Her Husband, John Bull's Other Island, Major Barbara* (1907); *The Doctor's Dilemma, Getting Married, The Shewing-up of Blanco Posnet* (1909); *Misalliance, The Dark Lady of the Sonnets, Fanny's First Play* (1914); *Overruled, Androcles and the Lion,* **Pygmalion** (1916); **Heartbreak House**, *Great Catherine, Playlets of the War* (1919); **Back to Methuselah** (1921); **Saint Joan** (1924); *The Apple Cart* (1930); *Too True to be Good, On the Rocks, Village Wooing* (1934); *The Six of Calais* (1936); *The Simpleton of the Unexpected Isles* (1935); *The Millionairess* (1936); *Cymbeline Refinished, Geneva, In Good King Charles's Golden Days* (1939); *Bouyant Billions, Shake v. Shaw,* and *Farfetched Fables* (1950).

The greatest playwright in the English language of the 20th century, Shaw brought his brilliant mind to bear on social, political, and

George Bernard Shaw, 1945.

Shaw (right) rehearsing *Androcles and the Lion* with Lillah McCarthy and Granville Barker. St James's Theatre, London, 1913. Victoria & Albert Theatre Museum, London.

---

metaphysical questions; he often aroused hostile comment but his genius for paradox and argument ensure that his best plays, which may be said to have ended with *The Apple Cart* (produced in 1929), are constantly revived. They set the mind ticking furiously; after a performance there is a compulsion to read the preface just for the pleasure of listening to the argument continued.

Shaw married Charlotte Payne-Townshend in 1898. She was a wealthy woman of 34 whom Beatrice Webb induced to part with £1000 for the library of the London School of Economics, where she met Shaw in 1896. The marriage was a success, though childless and apparently lacking in passion, a quality notably absent from Shaw's work. He continued to write and speak about socialism throughout most of his career: *An Unsocial Socialist* (1887), *Socialism and Superior Brains* (1909), *The Intelligent Woman's Guide to Socialism and Capitalism* (1928), and *Everybody's Political What's What* (1944). *The Adventures of the Black Girl in Search of God* (1932) he describes as a parable; *The Perfect Wagnerite* (1898) is a fascinating commentary on Wagner's *Ring* (the reader must be prepared, however, for some idiosyncratic spelling of some characters' names). Shaw's other novels were eventually published but they are not highly regarded: *Love Among the Artists* (1900), *The Irrational Knot* (1905), and *Immaturity* (1930).

Of lasting interest are Shaw's letters. *The Collected Letters*, edited by Dan H. Laurence, is in progress but only one volume has been published so far (1965). Notable collections, meanwhile, are *Ellen Terry and Bernard Shaw: A Correspondence*, edited by C. St John (1931), *The Correspondence Between Shaw and Mrs Patrick Campbell*, edited by Alan Dent (1952), and *Bernard Shaw's Letters to Granville-Barker*, edited by C. B. Purdom (1956).

**Shaw, Henry Wheeler**   See **Billings, Josh**.

**Sheffield, John, 1st Duke of Buckingham and Normanby** 1648–1721. A court poet of the Restoration, Sheffield left no work of any quality. He wrote two satires and some occasional poems; he was an admirer and friend of Dryden, and an enemy of Rochester. Rochester blamed Dryden for the couplets ridiculing him in Sheffield's *An Essay on Satire* (1679). Sheffield erected the monument to Dryden in Westminster Abbey.

**Shelley, Mary** 1797–1851. The daughter of William Godwin and Mary Wollstonecraft, Mary Godwin was brought up with the Clairmonts, the children of her stepmother. She met Shelley in May 1814 and in July of that year she went to Europe with him. Shelley married her in 1816 when his first wife committed suicide. In that same year, in Switzerland, Byron made the suggestion that all three should write a ghost story – a suggestion that produced a classic novel, *Frankenstein*, the work by which Mary Shelley will always be remembered.

She wrote other novels after Shelley's death in Italy in 1822: *Valperga* (1823), *Perkin Warbeck* (1830), and two which are really in defence of her husband (*Lodore* in 1835 and *Falkner* in 1837). Her most notable, after *Frankenstein*, was in a similar vein but using the destruction of mankind by a plague as the theme – *The Last Man* (1826). Apart from her fiction she wrote a large number of occasional pieces for periodicals and published an edition of Shelley's poems.

**Shelley, Percy Bysshe** 1792–1822. Shelley was the grandson of a baronet and his family were squires in Sussex. He was born in that county, at Field Place near Horsham, in the year which saw the deposition of Louis XVI and the imprisonment of the French royal family: he could be called a child of revolution. Near Shelley's home there was a small lake, and the poet's love of boats and water was acquired when he was a boy. He was educated at Syon House Academy and Eton, and went up to Oxford in 1810, to University College. At Eton Shelley was deeply influenced, not by his teachers, but by his friendship with Dr James Lind. Physician to George III, an enthusiast for the radical scientific thought of the close of the 18th century, and widely travelled, Lind lived nearby at Windsor and took a liking to the boy Shelley, who had mastered Latin and Greek and was now rather bored with them. Science, on the other hand, fascinated him. Dr Lind encouraged Shelley to study modern languages and directed his reading into more rewarding channels; Lucretius, Condorcet, Thomas Paine, and William Godwin were the most important of the philosophers whose writings he absorbed.

While still at Eton Shelley wrote two wild youthful romances: *Zastrozzi* (1808) and *St Irvyne, or the Rosicrucian* (1810). These were very gothic and of no particular worth but in 1810, just before he went to Oxford, Shelley published his first poetry in collaboration with his sister Elizabeth. *Original Poetry by Victor and Cazire*, though of little worth, marks the beginning of Shelley's career as a poet.

His first friendship at Oxford proved to be a lasting one; Thomas Jefferson Hogg has given posterity a vivid picture of the youthful Shelley in his *The Life of P.B.S.* (1858), and he was steadfastly loyal to him in 1811 when Shelley got into trouble. *The Necessity of Atheism* was a pamphlet in which Shelley declared that the existence of God was not proven and that there was no evidence in support of such a belief; free enquiry into the matter was necessary. Shelley, and then Hogg, refused to answer questions put by the Master and Fellows of University College and both were expelled. Shelley's father tried to separate him from Hogg, whom he felt was much to blame, and refused to support his son unless he returned home and took religious instruction. Shelley, the heir to a large fortune, rejected it in favour of his freedom and a small annuity. His friend Hogg was reconciled with his own family and returned to them, at York, to study law. Shelley, alone in London and 19 years old, was attracted to Harriet Westbrook, a pretty girl of 16 who was at school with his sisters. He ran off to Edinburgh with her and they were married in August 1811. Shelley's father, who was perfectly willing to support bastards, would not support a misalliance, and stopped his son's annuity. He restored it in December; but money was a problem which dogged Shelley for the rest of his short life since he refused to make the compromises that would have gained him material security and, later, affluence. This was not a mature decision: in the ordering of his life Shelley never reached maturity but left disorder wherever he trod.

At the close of 1811 Shelley met Southey, by then aged 38. Shelley had always admired Southey's poetry but he took him to task about his politics. Like Wordsworth and Coleridge, Southey had welcomed the idea of revolution in thought, politics, and poetry. But the reality was another matter and all three became reactionaries; Byron and Shelley were counter-reacting against such attitudes as theirs. Shelley and Southey liked each other, and Southey believed that Shelley would eventually settle down; more important, Shelley heard from Southey that William Godwin was now living in London. Shelley wrote to him at once, and meanwhile went on with a marriage that he should never have undertaken; the excitement had cooled, and Shelley could no more develop an adult approach to marriage than he could to money.

In 1812 Shelley went to Ireland. He spent seven weeks there and saw the appalling condition of the poor; he addressed a public meeting and with Harriet's help distributed pamphlets. The fervent young radical achieved nothing and returned to England in April to live at Lynmouth on the north coast of Devon. Chaos, however, seemed always to follow Shelley. Elizabeth Hichener, a Sussex schoolmistress ten years older than he, was invited to join the household: she had hopes of which Shelley was ignorant and he was eventually obliged to pay her to go away. The pamphlet, *A Declaration of Rights*, which he had written and had printed in Dublin, was distributed from balloons and put into large numbers of bottles to be picked up from the sea. Shelley's servant Dan Healey was arrested in Barnstaple for posting an advertisement for it; he was imprisoned for six months. Another pamphlet, *A Letter to Lord Ellenborough* (June 1812), defended Daniel Eaton, who had published the third part of Thomas Paine's *The Age of Reason* and been sentenced by Ellenborough, in a travesty of a trial, to 18 months in prison and the pillory once a month. Shelley was right: Eaton had been unjustly imprisoned, and the pamphlet's declaration that the word of God did not need protection by the law is incontestable. But this was 1812 and authority was terrified of radical opinions. Dan had to stay in prison, as did Daniel Eaton; Shelley did his best for his servant, contributing a weekly sum to make his imprisonment easier (Shelley, who never had enough money, was, like Byron, unstintingly generous). He had, meanwhile, begun work on a poem to be called **Queen Mab**.

Shelley's friendship with William Godwin developed and the Shelleys were frequent visitors to the Godwin house at Holborn; Harriet probably did her best to stay in the conversations that must sometimes have been difficult for her to comprehend. Thomas Love Peacock met the Shelleys in that year and was drawn to Harriet, now pregnant with her first child. Another acquaintance was the health fanatic, John Newton, and in 1813 Shelley published an essay, *A Vindication of Natural Diet*. The same year saw the completion and printing of *Queen Mab*. Thomas Hookham printed 250 copies at the poet's expense but refused to publish it for fear of prosecution. A mixture of allegory and polemic, it was to become famous for its attack on the established order, but meanwhile fewer than a hundred copies were privately distributed. In 1813 also Harriet bore a daughter, Ianthe. But all was not well, though another child was soon on the way. Shelley discovered that the Scottish marriage was not legal and he and Harriet were married again in England, probably at her family's insistence. But Shelley was out of love with Harriet, and attracted by Cornelia Boinville. Cornelia was promptly removed by an alarmed fiancé, and Shelley then met Mary Godwin, daughter of Mary Wollstonecraft and as romantic as Shelley. They fell in love at once and Shelley, who regarded sexual liberty as part of his revolutionary creed, wrote to Harriet and told her. The distraught and pregnant Harriet retreated to her father's house. Mary, accompanied by Jane Clairmont (for an explanation of their relationship see **Godwin, William**), met Shelley in order to elope with him. In the excitement of the moment Shelley suggested that Jane accompany them and she was delighted to agree.

Jane Clairmont decided to call herself Claire some time in 1815, and under that name she was to prove a dubious factor in the lives of Shelley and Mary. Mary was to regret the inclusion of Claire in the elopement party: Shelley was to find her attractive enough and willing to endorse his belief in sexual freedom. (She had no trouble later in seducing the confused and unhappy Byron at a low point in his life.) Shelley's son Charles was born to Harriet in November 1814; a daughter by Mary was born prematurely in February 1815 and died, unnamed, in March. One touch of order had been imposed by Shelley's father in 1814; to put a stop to Shelley's reckless borrowing on the expectations of the family estate he paid off his son's debts and granted him £2000 a year, of which £200 was paid directly to Harriet.

But Shelley's private life continued as a confusion of commitments; he was fortunate in Mary and in the friendship of Thomas Love Peacock, but personal grief seems to have been the lot of women connected with him. It is difficult to blame Shelley; he was attractive to women and they were apparently willing to accept him and his attitudes; however, the unfortunate Harriet drowned herself in the Serpentine in 1816. Shelley and Mary were married soon after and Mary, a much tougher woman, weathered the strain of his attraction to Jane Williams and Emilia Viviani, and the presence of Claire. Harriet's suicide led to Chancery proceedings initiated by Eliza Westbrook, her sister, which took up much of 1817. Shelley was deprived of the custody of his two children and in March 1818 left England for the last time.

In Italy Shelley visited Venice, Rome, Naples, and Leghorn and settled for a while at Pisa. (See **Byron, George Gordon, Lord** for the friendship between them, renewed at this time.) New friends were made: Edward Williams and Trelawny; old friends like his cousin Tom Medwin and Hogg turned up. Leigh Hunt and his family came out from England and Shelley, now at Spezia, sailed up to Leghorn with Edward Williams, a young English sailor named Charles Vivian, and Captain Daniel Roberts who had built the boat (called *Don Juan* by Byron) to welcome them. Five days later Shelley, Williams, and Vivian left to sail back to Spezia on a sultry afternoon. A storm arose during the evening and the boat sank about ten miles out from Viareggio, some distance south.

The bodies were washed ashore ten days later, on 17 July 1822. Shelley's was identified by his

Shelley. A detail from the portrait by Amelia Curran, 1819. National Portrait Gallery, London.

clothes and the copy of Keats's poems which he had borrowed from Leigh Hunt. In accordance with quarantine laws against the plague the bodies had to be burned. Trelawny took charge; Hunt and Byron had hurried down upon hearing the news. Shelley's heart and ashes were collected by Trelawny; the ashes to be buried in the Protestant cemetery in Rome where Keats had been buried the year before and the heart to be returned to England.

Had Shelley lived longer than thirty years his poetry might have reached an extraordinary level of quality. But not necessarily, and while a brief outline gives a hint of the chaos of his life a full biography should be studied for a complete picture; the outline has to serve to explain how he was regarded by contemporary society. His revolutionary fire might have found a positive direction if he had lived; his anger about injustice and inequality was genuine but his idealism was vague – he could not move from London to Lynmouth without a servant and was a total stranger to physical labour. The appalling mess which was his private life left casualties enough, too; sexual liberty was a fine ideal but Shelley was the male partner and the biological consequences had to be reckoned with in those days, when contraception was unknown. The most one can do in his favour is to believe that he was sincere, in his own ineffectual way. The poet Shelley is another matter; his finest work is that of a great lyric poet and it is better to judge him by that than to bewail the fact that a lot of his work is unsatisfactory, flawed by his inability to look closely at human feelings. He seemed unable to move his sights away from a glamorous horizon where a more suitable world existed if only mankind could reach it. Thomas Love Peacock sincerely believed that Shelley's poetry would have developed for the better; however, he regretted 'the want of reality in the characters with which he peopled his splendid scenes, and to which he addressed or imparted the utterance of his impassioned feelings. He was advancing, I think, to the attainment of this reality.' Peacock was Shelley's friend as well as his critic: 'It would have given to his poetry the only element of truth which it wanted; though at the same time, the more clear development of what men were would have lowered his estimate of what they might be, and dimmed his enthusiastic prospect of the future destiny of the world.'

After *Queen Mab* (1813) Shelley published no poetry for two years. **Alastor,** *or The Spirit of Solitude* was published in 1816. The same year, in Switzerland, saw the beginning of his friendship with Byron and the completion of 'Mont Blanc' and 'A Hymn to Intellectual Beauty'. *Laon and Cythna* was written at Marlow in 1817 after he returned to England; he revised the poem and published it as **The Revolt of Islam** (1818). Shelley was back in Italy in 1818 and there he translated the *Symposium* of Plato and worked on further poems published as *Rosalind and Helen: a Modern Eclogue with Other poems* (1819). At Este, at Byron's villa, he wrote 'Lines Written in the Euganean Hills' and at Venice, where he visited Byron, **Julian and Maddalo.** Also in 1818 he started work on **Prometheus Unbound**, which was finished in Rome during 1819 and published in 1820 as *Prometheus Unbound: a Lyrical Drama in Four Acts, with Other Poems.* At Naples, before he went on to Rome at the end of 1818, Shelley composed 'Stanzas Written in Dejection, near Naples'.

While in Rome Shelley heard the news of the Peterloo affair and wrote his indictment of Castlereagh's administration, *The Masque of Anarchy*, not published until 1832. **The Cenci** (1819) was also written at this time. The Shelleys were living in Pisa in 1820 and there Shelley wrote some of his most famous lyrics, including the odes 'To the West Wind' and 'To a Skylark'. *Oedipus Tyrannus, or Swellfoot the Tyrant* (1820) satirized in dramatic form George IV's marital squabble with Queen Caroline; other poems of this productive period were 'The Sensitive Plant' and 'A Letter to Maria Gisborne'. **Adonais** (1821) is *An Elegy on the Death of John Keats*; *Epipsychidion* (1821) was addressed to Emilia Viviani. Unfinished at the time of Shelley's death were a drama, *Charles I*, the poem **The Triumph of Life**, and some philosophical essays begun in 1815: *On Love, On Life, On Metaphysics, On Morals, On a Future State,* and *On Christianity.* Other prose works by Shelley were *A Refutation of Deism* (1814) and **A Defence of Poetry** (1821). Two collections of poems appeared after Shelley's death: *Poetical Pieces* (1823) and *Posthumous Poems* (1824). The first authoritative edition of Shelley, *The Poetical Works*, with a preface and valuable notes, was that of Mary Shelley (four volumes, 1839).

*The Complete Poetical Works* of Shelley, edited by Neville Rogers, is in progress; the two volumes published so far cover the years up to 1817 (Oxford English Texts). Neville Rogers also produced a valuable study, *Shelley at Work* (1956), and a volume of Shelley's early minor poems, *The Esdaile Poems* (1966). The complete poems are edited in a single volume by Thomas Hutchinson, revised by G. M. Matthews (Oxford Standard Authors, 1970). Shelley's *Letters* are collected and edited by F. L. Jones (1964). *Shelley's Prose* is edited by D. L. Clark (Albuquerque, 1954).

**Shenstone, William** 1714–63. Shenstone was born near Halesowen in Worcestershire. He received his first lessons at a dame school and then attended Solihull Grammar School. He was at Pembroke College, Oxford, with Samuel Johnson, though he did not take a degree. At the age of 21 Shenstone inherited a small estate, The Leasowes, with a small income, and he proceeded to turn the grounds of The Leasowes into a show garden; he became the leading exponent of the artificial style of landscape gardening. 'Nothing aroused Shenstone's indignation more,' said Samuel Johnson, 'than to ask if there were any fishes in his water.' The tendency to contrivance is evident in Shenstone's poetry, even in *The Schoolmistress* (1737), usually acknowledged as his most successful piece. 'I meant to skreen the ridicule which might fall on so *low* a subject . . . by *pretending* to *simper* all the time I was writing,' he wrote to Lady Luxborough. His correspondence was plainly intended as a literary production but is rather less interesting than he probably thought it was.

*Poems upon Various Occasions* (1737) was published anonymously. *The Judgement of Hercules, A Poem* (1741) was followed by a recast version of *The Schoolmistress*, which had appeared in the 1737 collection; a third and final version was published in Robert Dodsley's *A Collection of Poems by Several Hands* (1748). Shenstone also wrote miscellaneous poems – elegies, ballads, and songs. *Jemmy Dawson*, a ballad about a supporter of the Young Pretender who was executed for treason, is the best known of these. The shorter poems are frequently found in anthologies.

Shenstone was a minor poet but he could as easily be under- as over-rated. *The Schoolmistress*, in spite of the uncertainty of approach, is a minor classic, and *Jemmy Dawson* enjoyed great popularity. There is no modern collected edition of Shenstone but his *Letters* have been edited by M. Williams (1939) and D. Mallam (also 1939).

**Shepheardes Calender, The**  The first important work of Edmund Spenser (1579). It is a set of 12 eclogues, one for each month of the year, and follows the tradition of allegory in the pastoral form. The models were, variously, the works of Theocritus, Virgil, the French poet Clement Marot, and the Italian Mantuan (Johannes Baptista Spagnola) but Spenser used a variety of metres and freely included archaic words from the poetry of earlier centuries (his friend Sidney complained about the 'rusticke' language as, later, did Ben Jonson). The poem carries a commentary written by E. K. (Edward Kirke), a

'Januarye.' A woodcut from the first edition of Spenser's *The Shepheardes Calender*, 1579. Colin Cloute, the shepherd boy, compares the bleak season with the bleak progress of his love for Rosalinde. Each month of the poem is illustrated by a woodcut.

friend of Spenser's from his Cambridge days, and opens and closes with 'complaints' by Colin Cloute (the poet himself). The others are dialogues between shepherds and range over the subjects of love, Elizabeth I (Elysa), religion, behaviour, and the low regard in which poetry is held; there is a lament for a high-born lady and a singing contest.

**Shepherd, Old**  In Shakespeare's *The Winter's Tale*, he finds the abandoned baby, Perdita, on the seacoast of Bohemia. He cherishes her and brings her up as his own, but brings down the wrath of King Polixenes on his head upon daring to see his foster-daughter a fit wife for the king's son. He flees to Sicily with the young lovers and Camillo, where he is well rewarded by Perdita's true father, Leontes.

**Shepherd's Calendar, The**  John Clare's best-known poem was first published in 1827. The idea came from his publisher, John Taylor, in 1823 and the work was completed in 1824. But Taylor, having labelled Clare a 'peasant poet', wanted him to write like every other versifier and the poem he published was a mutilated version of the original. (See **Clare, John**.) The original text of the poem, from the poet's manuscripts, was published by Eric Robinson and Geoffrey Summerfield (1964) and its remarkable quality was revealed for the first time. The poem follows the procession of the months in rural England, from January (in two parts, 'A Winter's Day' and 'Cottage Evening') to December ('Christmas'). The pictures are vivid, the verse felicitous and simple. It is one of the most accessible of all great English poems.

**Shepherd's Life, A:** *Impressions of the South Wiltshire Downs.*  W. H. Hudson's account of life around Salisbury Plain before the automobile age was first published in 1910.

Hudson's observations of the wildlife of the county, both flora and fauna, together with his arresting stories about dogs, in themselves make the book worth reading; but the recollections of a shepherd in addition make it a classic of country life from about 1840 to the first years of the 20th century. The shepherd, Caleb Bawcombe, is in his eighties and from early boyhood has tended his master's flocks on the downs; he would not wish for a different life if one was offered him. He trained his sheepdogs, his only company, to the level of almost human response. It is chiefly from Caleb's memories that the vivid parade of human characters is drawn – the villagers and Gypsies, employers of every quality from good to tyrannical and greedy, and deer stealers, poachers, and machine wreckers. The author's wrath is aroused most by gamekeepers, to whom everything is subordinate to the care of pheasants and game birds, which are reared with extravagant care so that they may be destroyed.

**Shepherd's Week, The** A series of six eclogues by John Gay, first published in 1714 and written in mock-classical style. Designed as a parody of the *Pastorals* of Ambrose Philips, they present shepherds and milkmaids in a realistic way, leading hard and graceless lives instead of enjoying the totally imaginary golden age of Philips, where all was dainty and spring was eternal. Gay's skillful and humorous parodies survive on their own merits.

**Sheppard, Jack** A thief and highwayman, Sheppard was the son of a London carpenter. He was born in 1702, orphaned in childhood, and brought up in Bishopsgate workhouse. He was hanged at Tyburn in 1724. He is the subject of a novel by Ainsworth and of tracts by Daniel Defoe. See also **Ainsworth, William Harrison.**

**Sheridan, Frances** 1724–66. The mother of Richard Brinsley Sheridan, Frances Chamberlaine was born in Dublin and married actor-manager Thomas Sheridan in 1747. The couple lived in Dublin and Frances worked on a novel called *Eugenia and Adelaide*. They were obliged to return to London in 1754 when Thomas Sheridan's enterprises failed and there Frances met Samuel Richardson. Richardson, at the height of his success, read the unpublished novel and advised Frances to go on writing.

*Memoirs of Miss Sidney Bidulph* (1761) launched her successfully as a novelist and it was followed by three plays, *The Discovery* (1763), *The Dupe* (1764), and *A Trip to Bath* (1765). *The History of*

*Nourjahad* (1767) was another novel. Frances Sheridan's plays were produced at Drury Lane – *The Discovery* by David Garrick – but were not published until 1902. *Eugenia and Adelaide* was published posthumously, in 1791.

*Memoirs of Miss Sidney Bidulph. Extracted from her own Journal* was heavily influenced by Richardson's *Pamela*. Poor Miss Bidulph endures such agonies of love and jealousy and reaches such a pit of misery at the end that Samuel Johnson questioned Frances Sheridan's moral right to make her readers suffer so much. However, the novel was popular and was translated into French and German. A sequel, *Continuation of the Memoirs* (1767), recounts Miss Bidulph's further tribulations and staggers on inexorably to her death.

**Sheridan, Richard Brinsley** 1751–1816. The son of Thomas and Frances Sheridan, the playwright was born in Dublin and educated at Harrow. He was intended for the law, but while at his father's house in Bath became involved with Elizabeth Linley, a beautiful singer who was trying to escape the attentions of a Major Mathews. He helped Miss Linley escape her persecutor by escorting her to the continent and fought two duels on her behalf with the unpleasant

Sheridan. From the portrait by J. Russell, 1788. National Portrait Gallery, London.

Mathews. He fell in love with her in the process and they were married in 1773.

The Sheridans went to London in the same year. Sheridan's father was an actor–manager and his mother was a writer of some note (see **Sheridan, Frances**) so it was perhaps inevitable that he should seek a living in the theatre. He was 24 when his first play, *The Rivals*, was produced at Covent Garden (1775). It had an uncertain start but with improvements to the text soon became a success, and he scored again, twice, in the same year with a farce, *St Patrick's Day; or, The Scheming Lieutenant*, and a comic opera, *The Duenna*, which had music by his father-in-law, Thomas Linley.

In 1776 Sheridan was able to buy David Garrick's share in Drury Lane and went into management. His revision of Vanbrugh's *The Relapse*, *A Trip to Scarborough*, gave him another success in 1777 but, even more notable, it was the year of the first production of *The School for Scandal*, one of the great comedies of the English language. *The Critic* (1779), his satire on the theatre, exploited the idea used with some success by George Villiers, 2nd Duke of Buckingham, in *The Rehearsal* in 1671. Sheridan wrote other minor pieces as contributions to theatre entertainments but the only full-length play he was concerned with after 1779 was an adaptation of August von Kotzebue's tragedy *Pizarro* (1799), which was a great success with the public as a patriotic spectacle.

Unfortunately for English comedy Sheridan became interested in politics and entered parliament in 1780 with the help of the Duchess of Devonshire and the expenditure of £1,000. He was a politician for more than 30 years, until 1812, when he was defeated in an election. He became close friends with the Prince of Wales, and was a notable orator – Edmund Burke's only real rival. He supported the impeachment of Warren Hastings. His theatre holding taxed his resources severely when Drury Lane had to be rebuilt – the house was 120 years old. The new theatre opened on 12 March 1794 and a safety curtain was installed as a precaution against fire. Sheridan left much of the management to others and he was often dangerously near bankruptcy. The theatre caught fire on 24 February 1809 and was completely destroyed. Sheridan's last years, deprived of both parliament and the theatre, were sad and comparatively comfortless, though good friends did their best to keep him from actual want. He lies buried in Westminster Abbey.

Sheridan wrote nothing that was new in the theatre, though like Goldsmith he avoided the

The interior of Drury Lane Theatre in 1813, rebuilt after the fire of 1809. Engraving by W. Hopwood. Victoria & Albert Theatre Museum, London.

sentimentality which keeps most plays of the 18th century from being revived. Sheridan knew the play-going public very well – and knew that nothing pleased them better than seeing themselves on the stage. In his plays a leisured and privileged elite is portrayed in all its artificiality, in a world where the social intercourse of the intellectually idle becomes a pointless and sterile competition, creating layers of jealousy and malice which surface when a crisis occurs. There are hints of this in *The Rivals*, which is otherwise a 'laughing comedy' like Oliver Goldsmith's *She Stoops to Conquer*. In *The School for Scandal* Sheridan has the last word on the psychology of the contemporary world of fashion.

The standard modern edition of Sheridan is *The Dramatic Works of Richard Brinsley Sheridan*, edited by Cecil Price (1973) in the Oxford English Texts series. The same editor was responsible for *The Letters of Richard Brinsley Sheridan*, published in 1966.

**Sherlock, Thomas** 1678–1761. Sherlock was born in London and became Bishop of London in 1748 after having held the same office in Bangor (1728) and Salisbury before that. He established a reputation as a preacher and while Master of the Temple opposed Benjamin Hoadly in the 'Bangorian controversy' (both men were Bishop of Bangor at different dates). His exercise in Christian apologetics, *The Trial of the Witnesses of the Resurrection of Jesus* (1729), is his most notable published work. Sherlock earned a reputation for being athletic as well as studious. A fine swimmer, he became the 'Plunging Prelate' of Pope's *The Dunciad*.

**Sherlock, William** 1641–1707. Sherlock was born in Southwark, and educated at Eton and Peterhouse College, Cambridge. He became Master of the Temple and Dean of St Paul's, and belongs more to ecclesiastical than literary history though his published sermons were much admired by Macaulay. During the Revolution which saw the abdication of James II, Sherlock was a nonjuror, and published his *Practical Discourse concerning Death* in 1689. In the following year he decided to take the oath to William and Mary and also published a *Vindication of the Doctrines of the Trinity and of the Incarnation*. Both his action and his book made him the target of a chorus of attacks and his appointment as Dean of St Paul's in 1691 exposed him further. Macaulay gave Sherlock the credit for having made a carefully reasoned decision influenced by thoughts of the ultimate peace of the kingdom; but Sherlock's contemporaries, who knew him better, thought otherwise. He suffered most from the skilful and witty attacks of Robert South, rector of Islip in Oxfordshire. Sherlock's sermons were published in 1719.

**She Stoops to Conquer,** *or The Mistakes of a Night*. A comedy by Oliver Goldsmith, first produced at Covent Garden in March 1773, and published in the same year. The episode of the travellers mistaking a private house for an inn was based on a similar incident in the author's youth.

Mr and Mrs Hardcastle have a daughter, Kate; Mrs Hardcastle also has a son, Tony Lumpkin,

*She Stoops to Conquer* at Covent Garden, 1773. From a mezzotint after Thomas Parkinson who depicted the incident from the last act in 1779. The characters, left to right, are Mr Hardcastle, Mrs Hardcastle, and Tony Lumpkin. Victoria & Albert Theatre Museum, London.

by a former marriage. Sir Charles Marlow has proposed a match between his bashful and reserved son and Kate Hardcastle; young Marlow and his friend Hastings accordingly make the journey to visit the Hardcastle home. They lose their way and arrive at a tavern, the Three Jolly Pigeons, a favourite haunt of the mischievous and dissolute Tony Lumpkin. Lumpkin directs them to an inn which is in fact Mr Hardcastle's house. The scene is expertly laid for the superb comedy that follows – young Marlow thinks Kate is one of the servants, and Kate's friend Constance Neville falls in love with Hastings. Mrs Hardcastle, who dotes on her oafish Tony, intends a match for him with Constance, and is thoroughly displeased. Marlow, so 'bashful and reserved' with the ladies, proves a rather different man when he falls in love with the servant (Kate). Sir Charles Marlow's arrival puts everything to rights.

*She Stoops to Conquer* is one of the great English comedies and succeeds on every level. The characterization is faultless and Kate Hardcastle is a charming and spirited heroine, who knows exactly what she is doing. The play bears out the promise of Goldsmith's first play, *The Good-Natur'd Man*, and moves away completely from the sentimental comedy that was in vogue in the contemporary theatre and much favoured by David Garrick.

**She Wou'd if She Cou'd** A comedy by George Etherege, first produced in February 1668 and published in the same year.

Sir Oliver Cockwood and his lady, with Sir Joslin Jolley and his pretty nieces Ariana and Gatty, come to London. Lady Cockwood speaks much of virtue but intends to indulge in amorous adventures; Ariana and Gatty intend to flirt with London gallants; Sir Oliver and Sir Joslin are bent on dissipation. The two families lodge in St James Street. Courtall and Freeman, two young men of the town, are charmed by Ariana and Gatty; Lady Cockwood is charmed by every good-looking man within range (Courtall describes her as 'a ravening kite') whilst the senior knights are happy to roister while they can. Courtall and Freeman escort the girls to The Bear in Drury Lane to enjoy some dancing; Lady Cockwood goes too. To The Bear also come Sir Oliver and Sir Joslin; Sir Oliver gets drunk and dances with his wife – not knowing, in his condition, who she is, nor quite sure how things are going: the resulting uproar is resolved when the ladies leave.

Freeman goes to St James Street; he has decided to 'console' Lady Cockwood. Courtall arrives and Freeman hides in a cupboard; Sir Oliver comes home and Courtall hides under the table, only to be discovered when Sir Oliver drops a china orange, which rolls underneath it. Both young men are eventually discovered and all ends peaceably. The girls accept the young men, Sir Oliver and Sir Joslin decide they have had enough of a holiday, and Lady Cockwood that she has had enough of the great adventure.

This, Etherege's second play, has no more plot than a 20-minute script could support; its achievement lies in the quality and wit of the dialogue, and in the creation of Ariana and Gatty, two deliciously high-spirited and intelligent heroines.

**Shipman's Tale, The** See *Canterbury Tales, The.*

**Ship of Fools, The** See **Barclay, Alexander.**

**Shirley** Charlotte Brontë's second published novel; it appeared first in 1849. The setting is Yorkshire at the time of the Luddite riots, in the later phases of the war against Bonaparte. The wool industry of England was paralysed when exports came to a halt and at that time the introduction of machinery was seen as its death knell by many workers in the industry. Charlotte Brontë's father, Patrick Brontë, had once been appointed to the parish of Hartshead-cum-Clifton, near Dewsbury, when a riot resulted in 14 men being hanged.

Robert Gerard Moore, mill-owner, is determined to instal labour-saving machinery. He is undeterred by the opposition of the workers, who first attempt to destroy the mill in protest, and later attempt to kill him. Robert's brother, Louis, is tutor to the wealthy Keeldar family and Robert sees that marriage to Shirley Keeldar would enable him to weather the financial embarrassment of the troubled times, even though he loves Caroline Helstone, the rector's niece.

Shirley rejects him with contempt; she knows he doesn't love her. Then the wars at last come to an end and Robert is freed of his difficulties. The devoted Caroline accepts him, and Shirley, meanwhile, is drawn to Louis more and more.

The best parts of *Shirley* are the opening chapters and the characterization of the eponymous heroine, who was modelled on the author's sister Emily. The last third of the book (Charlotte Brontë, like many writers of her time, was a victim of the three-volume convention), moves the story to Shirley and Louis and, though the growing love between them is well done, one feels the material is being padded out. Robert Moore was based on William Cartwright, who

was decorated for his part in the historical defence of Rawfold's Mill.

**Shirley, James** 1596–1666. Shirley was the last in the line of dramatists who graced the Elizabethan, Jacobean, and Caroline stages; he also survived the closing of the theatres – and the Commonwealth itself – though he ceased to write for the theatre when the Puritans decided that people were deriving too much pleasure from it for the good of their souls. (See **closure of the playhouses.**)

Shirley was born in London and attended the Merchant Taylors' School; later he went to St John's College, Oxford and St Catherine's Hall, Cambridge. He took holy orders and after leaving Cambridge became headmaster of St Alban's Grammar School. In 1625 he became a Roman Catholic – and was obliged to relinquish his position. He had married in the meantime and, obliged to earn a living, turned to the theatre. Shirley enjoyed a steady success for ten years and in 1636, during an outbreak of the plague, went to Dublin. He continued to write for the stage; the first theatre in the Irish capital, in St Werburgh Street, had opened in 1635. He returned to London in 1640 and was the principal dramatist for The King's Men at the Globe until the Puritans closed the theatres in 1642.

A Royalist, Shirley followed the Earl of Newcastle during the Civil War and returned to teaching after the defeat. He published his verse in 1646 and was the author of some masques. Shirley was in London when the Great Fire broke out and both he and his wife died as a result of their privations following the ordeal.

Shirley was the author of 31 plays that have survived. The quality is inevitably variable and among the playwrights of the period he cannot be considered in the first rank. Nevertheless his place is a distinguished one; he maintained a high level in his work, particularly in his comedy, even if he lacked the spark of genius that would make his work live on the stage today. His plays have not been revived.

Shirley's first work for the stage was a comedy, *Love Tricks: or the Schoole of Complement* (1625). From the considerable output that ensued the following may be mentioned: *The Traitor* and *Love's Cruelty* (both 1631), *Hyde Park* (1632), *The Gamester* (1633), *The Imposture* (1640), *The Cardinall* (1641), and *The Sisters* (1642). Shirley's verse is undistinguished except for the funeral chant delivered over the body of Ajax in *The Contention of Ajax and Ulisses for the Armor of Achilles* (1659), a dramatic entertainment written for private performance. The much-anthologized piece opens with the lines 'The glories of our blood and state Are shadows, not substantial things'.

*The Dramatic Works and Poems of James Shirley*, edited by W. Gifford and A. Dyce, was published in six volumes in 1833.

**Shoemaker's Holiday, The,** *or The Gentle Craft*. A comedy by Thomas Dekker, first produced at the Rose Theatre on Bankside at the end of 1599 and acted before Elizabeth I on the evening of New Year's Day, 1600. It was first published in 1600. For the source of the plot, see **Deloney, Thomas.**

Rowland Lacy, a kinsman of the Earl of Lincoln, loves Rose, daughter of the Lord Mayor of London; the earl disapproves and sends Lacy off to France to command a company of soldiers in the war. Lacy lets the company go without him and, presenting himself as a Dutch shoemaker, goes to work for Simon Eyre, who makes the shoes for the Lord Mayor's family. From this base he pursues his longed-for marriage to his Rose and succeeds in the face of the earl's objections, the Lord Mayor's objections, and the fact that he is a deserter from the colours.

The little love story of Lacy and Rose is the reason for the audience's introduction to Simon Eyre and his wife, Margery, and the bustling rowdy household of journeymen and apprentices. Simon and Margery complement each other perfectly: he is a larky high-spirited man and she is a comfortable loving woman who appreciates her husband's hard commonsense; when he becomes Lord Mayor she is quite prepared to be glamorous as his Lady. Margery also takes the household in her stride: she is never really in control of it but it is none the worse for that. Another love in the play portrayed with considerable warmth is that of Simon's journeyman, Ralph, and his wife, Jane. Ralph is called to the colours in spite of Simon's attempts to keep him out of the army; and a wealthy suitor, Hamond, has great hopes of Jane in her husband's absence. Jane will have none of him: but then news is brought of Ralph's death and Hamond wants to marry her. She consents – but Ralph, lame and in rags, returns and she throws herself into his arms. Lacy is forgiven by the king at the end of the play.

A memorable character is the journeyman Firk, as good a man as any and well-versed in how to deal with his supposed 'betters'. The scene and the sense of Dekker's play is Cockney London and Firk is one of its unchanging features. The playwright drew his pictures from life.

**Shoreham, William of** fl. 1325. William of Shoreham, in Kent, was vicar of Chart near Leeds (in Kent) and the author of seven poems in Middle English preserved in a single manuscript in the British Library. The poems are homilectic and deal with the Sacraments, the Psalms, the Ten Commandments, the Seven Deadly Sins, two poems to the Virgin Mary (one a translation from Robert Grosseteste), and the evidences of Christianity. William of Shoreham's poems are highly regarded by scholars of Middle English verse; they were edited by T. Wright for the Percy Society (1849) and by M. Konrath for the Early English Text Society (1902).

**Shorthouse, Joseph Henry** 1834–1903. The son of a Quaker family of Birmingham, Shorthouse was a chemist in his father's business. He became an Anglican following his interest in mysticism and was preoccupied with the contemporary tensions between Anglicans and Roman Catholics and the results of the Oxford Movement. This preoccupation is the matter of the one novel by which his name is remembered, *John Inglesant* (1881, but privately printed the year before). His other works, novels, and *The Platonism of Wordsworth* (1882), are now no more than entries in bibliographies but *John Inglesant* deserves attention. Shorthouse edited, and contributed an essay to, an edition of George Herbert's *The Temple* in 1882.

**Shylock** The wealthy Jew of Shakespeare's *The Merchant of Venice*. Antonio, who despises him, wants to borrow a large sum from him and Shylock seizes the opportunity to bind Antonio to yielding a pound of flesh if he cannot pay the debt on time. Shylock invokes the bond, only to be confounded by Portia's wit in the courtroom. Shylock loses half his wealth and his daughter Jessica elopes with Lorenzo, a Christian, plundering her father's coffers to do so.

The character of Shylock, in the hands of Shakespeare, towers above the lamentable prejudice of late Elizabethan England. He also towers above the other characters in the play, whose behaviour prompts Shylock's memorable speech in Act III, ending with 'The villainy you teach me I will execute; and it shall go hard but I will better the instruction.'

**Sicinius Velutus** One of the tribunes opposed to Coriolanus in Shakespeare's play of that name. With his fellow tribune Junius Brutus he secures the banishment of Coriolanus, which leads to the latter becoming a traitor to Rome.

**Sidgwick, Henry** 1838–1900. The son of a schoolmaster, Sidgwick was born at Skipton in

Yorkshire. He was educated at Rugby School and Trinity College, Cambridge, where he became a fellow. He was appointed Professor of Moral Philosophy at Cambridge in 1883. Sidgwick was a follower of John Stuart Mill and also leaned towards the Common-Sense School of Thomas Reid in his enquiries into the question of man's knowledge of the external world. His reputation as a philosopher is in the field of ethics but more as an analyst and critic than as an original thinker. His chief publications are *The Ethics of Conformity and Subscription* (1870), *The Methods of Ethics* (1874), *An Outline of the History of Ethics* (1886), *The Scope and Limits of the Work of an Ethical Society* (1900), *The Principles of Political Economy* (1883), and *The Elements of Politics* (1891).

**Sidney, Sir Philip** 1554–86. Philip Sidney was not knighted until four years before his death but he was from a family whose connections were among the most exalted in the reign of Elizabeth I. He was born at Penshurst Castle, the family home in Kent. His father was Sir Henry Sidney, his mother the sister of the Earl of Leicester. Sidney's sister Mary became the Countess of Pembroke when her husband, William Herbert, succeeded to the title. Another uncle, Ambrose Dudley, was Earl of Warwick.

Sidney was taught at home by his mother until he was old enough to attend Shrewsbury School, which he entered with his friend Fulke Greville. From there he went to Christ Church, Oxford, but left in 1571 without taking a degree and in the following year left for Europe in the party of his uncle, Leicester. He visited France – where he became Gentleman of the Bedchamber to King Charles IV – Austria, Venice – where he met Veronese and Tintoretto – Padua, and Genoa; he met the scholars Petrus Ramus and Hubert Languet. On his return he served in Ireland with his father, who was three times Lord Deputy. In England again (1576) he met the first Earl of Essex and his daughter, Penelope, who was to inspire the sonnet-sequence *Astrophel and Stella*. Penelope's brother Robert was to become the Earl of Essex who was beheaded but who should also be remembered as the friend of Edmund Spenser, who became Sidney's friend when working in Leicester's household. However, Penelope Devereux married Lord Rich, and Sidney married Frances Walsingham in 1582, the year he was knighted.

He had, meanwhile, become one of the brighter adornments of Elizabeth's court and was entrusted with diplomatic missions. In 1578 he wrote a masque, *The Lady of May*, for the queen's

Sir Philip Sidney. Portrait by an unknown artist. National Portrait Gallery, London.

visit to Leicester House, and in the same year, after a quarrel with the Earl of Oxford, left the court in temporary disfavour and went to stay with his sister Mary, for whose entertainment he composed his *Arcadia*, a prose romance of which, in spite of its subsequent fame, he had no great opinion. At this time too (1580) he probably wrote *The Apologie for Poetrie*.

In 1584 Sidney became Joint Master of Ordinance with the Earl of Warwick. He contemplated joining Drake's expedition to the West Indies but was sent to the Netherlands as Governor of Flushing in 1585. A year later in September, during an attack on a Spanish force for the relief of Zutphen, his thigh was smashed by musket shot and he died of his wounds. He was 32 years old, and a year later the queen spoke of him as 'Sir Philip Sidney whose life I should be glad to purchase with many millions'. Elegies on the death of Sidney were written by Spenser and Michael Drayton.

Sir Philip Sidney was a cultured, courteous, and courageous man – everything a man should be when the term 'aristocrat' is applied to him. His work was not published in his lifetime though the manuscripts were circulated, in the fashion of the day, and widely read. Sidney's appearance in English poetry is sudden, brilliant, and brief. He is often bracketed with his friend Spenser – but only because they were contemporaries; if Spenser had died at 32 we would only have *The Shepheardes Calender* and a few short poems. But though Sidney's poetic legacy is small enough his work, in C. S. Lewis's words, 'rises out of the contemporary Drab almost as a rocket rises: Spenser climbed slowly and painfully', and Lewis points out that Sidney's work was done before Spenser had published anything of comparable value. His *Astrophel and Stella* is the acknowledged first among Elizabethan sonnet sequences and its influence was profound. The *Arcadia* and *The Apologie for Poetrie* are little read now except by scholars; the former because, like Spenser's *The Faerie Queene*, it is bewilderingly intricate though it contains fine things, and the latter because the time for that Apologie (defence) is long past.

The standard modern edition of Sidney's collected works was published at Cambridge (1912–26) by A. Feuillerat. Sidney's letters were added to the edition in 1923–26.

**Sigerson, George** 1839–1925. See **Mangan, James Clarence**.

*Sigurd the Volsung and the Fall of the Niblungs, The Story of* An epic in four books by William Morris, first published in 1876. The story is told in anapaestic couplets and is based upon the Icelandic *Volsunga Saga*. The first book tells the story of Sigmund; the other three of Sigmund's son Sigurd.

King Volsung's daughter Signy is married to Siggeir, the cruel and treacherous king of the Goths. Signy's brother Sigmund and Siggeir hate each other. Siggeir brings about the death of Volsung and his family and seizes his kingdom, but Sigmund's great strength enables him to escape. Signy, to preserve the line of the Volsungs, changes shape with a witch maiden and visits Sigmund in the forest. He begets a son with her, not knowing she is his sister, and she returns to the Goths' hall where her son Sinfiotli is born. When Sigmund and his son attack the Goths and burn the hall of King Siggeir, Signy perishes with her husband, knowing her design is fulfilled. Sigmund regains his kingdom and marries Borgild. Sinfiotli dies of poison administered by Borgild: Sinfiotli had killed her brother Gudrod in a quarrel over battle spoils. Borgild is turned out and Sigmund marries Hiordis, daughter of an island king. Sigmund dies in battle and Hiordis, expecting a child, finds refuge with King Elf.

A son is born to Hiordis and he is named Sigurd; Hiordis then marries King Elf. Sigurd is tutored by Regin, the old and wise dwarf smith, and given a fine horse, Greyfell. Regin tells him of the gold treasure guarded by his brother Fafnir, who has assumed the shape of a great serpent. The gold was a ransom paid by the gods for the killing of their third brother, Otter; it includes the magic ring of Andvari that Regin covets, though he does not tell Sigurd that – he is simply proposing a great adventure. Regin reforges the fragments of Sigmund's sword, which had been a gift from Odin. Sigurd kills the serpent. A drop of blood from its heart enables him to understand the birds. He learns that Regin wants total mastery of the world; he has secured the treasure and Sigurd has seen him drink the serpent's blood: henceforth all gods and men will be enslaved by him. Sigurd cuts off Regin's head and rides forth on Greyfell with the treasure, which includes Andvari's ring and the magic Helm of Aweing. He comes upon the sleeping Brynhild surrounded by a wall of fire. She is an earth woman who became a Valkyrie and was cherished by Odin; but she disobeyed him and her punishment was to sleep. She would love the man who wakened her. She loves Sigurd and they plight their troth; he gives her the ring of Andvari. Brynhild will wait for him in her homeland, Lymdale, while he goes in quest of glory.

Gudrun, princess of the Niblung house, dreams of a golden falcon from the north. She visits Brynhild, wisest of women, to ask her what it means. Brynhild tells her of Sigurd the Volsung, the glorious warrior of the north, and explains Gudrun's dream as that of a royal maiden who will love and lose, as is often the fate of the daughters of kings. Sigurd falls in with the Niblungs and is welcomed to their hall. Gudrun falls in love with him and Queen Grimhild gives Sigurd a potion in a cup of wine. He forgets Brynhild and marries Gudrun; the king of the Niblungs dies and is succeeded by Gunnar, Gudrun's brother. Gunnar must have a wife, and Queen Grimhild tells him of Brynhild. She lives in a gold hall on the Hindfell close by Lymdale but she is surrounded by fire. Sigurd, by means of the Helm of Aweing, takes Gunnar's shape and enters the flames to secure her. Brynhild gives the ring to 'Gunnar' and accepts a ring from him, and the next day he conducts her to the Niblung princes. She is married to Gunnar; when she sees Sigurd's ring being worn by Gudrun she asks why she has the ring Brynhild gave her brother. Gudrun replies that Sigurd gave it to her. Brynhild realizes that she has been tricked as well as forsaken and she intimates to Gunnar that she knows the story of her wooing. Soon she provokes him enough, as a warrior without glory of his own, to arrange the killing of Sigurd the Volsung. The deed is carried out by his brother Guttorm; Brynhild kills herself to join Sigurd in death.

Gudrun has withdrawn to the forest. Atli, king of the Eastlands (Attila the Hun), seeks her hand. Grieving for Sigurd, Gudrun sees a way of avenging his murder. She marries the ruthless Atli and tells him how she was betrayed and about the treasure that Sigurd brought to the Niblungs. Atli is tempted and invites Gunnar and the Niblungs to his domain; he traps them in his castle and Gudrun tells them they will die that day. Atli demands Sigurd's treasure; they refuse, and in the battle which follows the Niblung house is extinguished. Gudrun, her purpose achieved, kills Atli and herself.

The figure of a different Gudrun provided the centre of another of Morris's poems, 'The Lovers of Gudrun' in *The Earthly Paradise*. She is the central figure of the *Laxdaela Saga* and should not be confused with the Niblung princess. The German *Nibelungenlied* uses part of the same story as the *Volsunga Saga* but tells it in a historical setting of the Dark Ages without the old pagan associations. The libretto of Wagner's *Der Ring des Nibelungen* adapts the *Volsunga Saga* but stops at the death of Siegfried and Brünnhilde (Sigurd and Brynhild). The characters have German names in Wagner, and Hogni, a minor character in the original, is elevated to the major villain, Hagen, in the opera.

**Sikes, Bill** The coarse and brutal burglar of Dickens's *Oliver Twist*. He murders Nancy and tries to kill his wretched devoted dog, believing correctly that the dog will be identified and followed by his pursuers. He accidentally hangs himself trying to escape.

**Silas Marner,** *the Weaver of Raveloe*. A novel by George Eliot, first published in 1861.

Silas Marner is a weaver in the village of Raveloe. Some 15 years before he had been a trusted member of a religious community, and had been turned away in disgrace, believed guilty of theft. He knows who is guilty; it is his closest friend, and the shock drives him away to seek obscurity. He can no longer believe in anything; at Raveloe he simply works and hoards the money he earns. One winter night the money is stolen from him.

The squire's son, Godfrey Cass, is in love with Nancy Lammeter, but is secretly married to Molly Farren, a sluttish girl from the neighbouring town. His young brother, Dunstan Cass, knows his secret and, being without principles of any kind, is calmly blackmailing his brother. Then he hears that the weaver, Silas Marner, has a small hoard of money. He robs the weaver and disappears. Molly Farren, in a haze of opium, takes her infant daughter and walks through the snow to the squire's house, determined to confront the Cass family with her status. The opium overcomes her and she dies in the snow. The child crawls into the nearest refuge: it is the weaver's cottage, where Marner is still trying to come to grips with the theft of his money. The child awakens his stifled humanity and in his care for her he finds his place among his fellow-men once more. He calls the child Eppie, and is helped in her upbringing by kind Dolly Winthrop, the wife of the village wheelwright.

Eppie grows up; she and the only father she knows – Silas Marner – are familiar, well-liked people in the village. Near their cottage a pond is drained, and in it is found the skeleton of a man who is identified as Dunstan Cass. With the skeleton is the money stolen from Silas Marner 16 years before. The shock provokes Godfrey Cass to tell Nancy, now his wife, the truth about his former marriage and the identity of Eppie. He acknowledges her as his daughter and tries to claim her, but she refuses him and will not leave Silas, who she loves as her true father. The story ends with Eppie's marriage to Aaron, Dolly Winthrop's son.

*Silas Marner* is a novel of remarkable quality. Idyllic, certainly, but nowhere does it strain belief or offer coincidence as a resolution. Nor does it attempt to give final balm to Silas's bitter grievance – he is a man deeply wronged and he learns to bear it, strengthened in the new purpose his life is given when the infant girl crawls into his cottage. There is not a superfluous line in the narrative and the book has *charm*, a quality rarely found in the work of the great Victorian novelists.

**Silver, Long John** In Robert Louis Stevenson's *Treasure Island*, the pirate who, in the guise of a sea cook, joins the *Hispaniola*, which sets sail in quest of the treasure. Jim Hawkins finds him a congenial shipmate.

**Silvia** Valentine's love in Shakespeare's *The Two Gentlemen of Verona*. She is the Duke of Milan's daughter and her father intends her for Thurio. Her plan to elope with Valentine is betrayed to the duke by Proteus, who also wants her.

**Simeon of Durham** See **Durham, Simeon of.**

**Simms, William Gilmore** 1806–70. The son of a storekeeper, Simms was born in Charleston, South Carolina. His parents separated and he spent his childhood and youth in straitened circumstances. He became a lawyer after intensive private study and believed that he had a future as a poet. He wrote five books of Byronic verse, practised law, and was editor of the Charleston *City Gazette*. He moved to New York in 1832 and his first novel, **Martin Faber**, was published in the following year. This was a crime story influenced by the work of William Godwin, but he struck the vein which really suited him with his next book, **Guy Rivers** (1834), a Southern romance. In 1835 he published **The Yemassee**, about the confrontation of White man and Red man, and **The Partisan**, a romance of the American Revolution. These three themes were to form the matter of some eight novels; he enjoyed considerable success and, with the publication of the first three, returned to the South.

Simms, who had played no social role, seemed to regard South Carolina's institutions and society as worthy of his tireless support. Not content with being the only Southern novelist who was widely read, he edited the *Southern and Western Magazine and Review*, *The Southern Quarterly Review*, and *Russell's Magazine*, and wrote a *History* of his state (1840) and a *Geography* (1843). He made himself a promoter of Southern literature, became a planter, and wrote essays and delivered speeches in defence of slavery. He was ruined by the Civil War.

A successful novelist in his lifetime, Simms' is most notable, perhaps, for his successful exploitation of purely American themes and for his ability to portray the humble life of the South as well as the romantic 'aristocracy'. He did much to encourage the writers of the South, including Edgar Allan Poe, and while his own work was praised by a writer as distinguished as George Washington Cable it was also to provoke sour comments from Mark Twain, who considered much of it as inferior work in the style of Walter Scott. Simms did not maintain a high standard through all his large output – it simply did not grow in stature from its promising beginnings. But he has to be considered in the context of time and place: Mark Twain's criticism may be just but it remains unarguable that a tradition of fiction in any country has to grow – and Simms made a definite contribution. He also deserves considerable credit for helping to establish a climate for writers in which their work would be published and read – and ultimately achieve distinction.

**Simple Story, A** A novel by Elizabeth Inchbald, first published in 1791. The story concerns Dorriforth, a priest, and his ward, the worldly and flirtatious Miss Milner, who falls in love with him. He loves her, but because of his calling they both conceal their feelings. Dorriforth inherits a peerage and is released from his vows; he becomes Lord Elmwood, and marries his erstwhile ward. Lady Elmwood's basic weakness of character leads to an affair with a former suitor, Sir Frederick Lawnley, and Elmwood banishes her from his house with their daughter, Matilda. Lady Elmwood dies of remorse and Matilda is left unprotected. Elmwood's feelings are brought back to life when Matilda is abducted by a shallow libertine and he restores her to her home and position. Another priest, Father Sandford, who succeeds Dorriforth as a spiritual guide, plays an important part in the course of the novel, which is frankly didactic, but notable for the author's attempt to portray emotions honestly.

A modern edition of *A Simple Story* was edited by J. M. S. Tompkins (1967) and published in the Oxford English Novels series.

**Simpson, Louis (Aston Marantz)** 1923– . Born in Jamaica, Simpson studied at Murro College in Jamaica before service with a US airborne division in World War II. He completed his education at Columbia University and worked in publishing until 1955, when he returned to Columbia as an instructor. He was Professor of English at the University of California from 1959 to 1967 and now teaches at New York University. Simpson's first volume of poetry was *The Arrivistes: Poems 1940–1949* (Paris, 1949). His next work was *The Father Out of the Machine: A Masque* (1951) and more poetry followed with *Good News of Death and Other Poems* (1955). A play, *Andromeda* (1956), was followed by *A Dream of Governors* (1959), the novel *Riverside Drive* (1962), and *James Hogg: A Critical Study* (1962). Simpson was awarded the Pulitzer Prize for *At the End of the Open Road: Poems* (1963). He is also the author of *An Introduction to Poetry* (1967), *Three on the Tower* (1975 essays on Pound, Eliot, and Williams), *A Revolution in Taste: Studies of Dylan Thomas, Allen Ginsberg, Sylvia Plath and Robert Lowell* (1978), and the volumes of poetry *Adventures of the Letter I* (1971) and *Searching for the Ox* (1977).

**Sister Carrie** A novel by Theodore Dreiser. It was accepted for publication by the novelist Frank Norris for the New York publishing house, Doubleday – but the publisher's wife read it before publication and complained that it was immoral, with the result that only a token edition was printed (1900). It was never advertised and the author's career seemed blighted almost before it began. The novel was reissued in 1912, after the publication of Dreiser's second novel, *Jennie Gerhardt*.

Carrie Meeber is a country girl, who has come to Chicago to find work, and is living with her sister and brother-in-law. She can only find irregular ill-paid work, and in a period of unemployment and low spirits becomes the mistress of Charles Drouet, a salesman. But while her material condition improves, her esteem for Drouet declines. Drouet's friend, George Hurstwood, a restaurant manager, is successful, middle-aged, and married; compared to Drouet he is intelligent and cultured – he and Carrie fall in love. Hurstwood embezzles a sum of money and then persuades Carrie to elope with him. In New York he opens a saloon and their liaison continues for about three years. Carrie, meanwhile, has acquired a degree of poise and her natural intelligence leads her to steady improvement; Hurstwood, his life somewhat crippled now, begins to decline and proves unable to deal with financial reverses. Reduced to poverty, their relationship suffers and Carrie becomes a chorus girl to support them. She makes an impression in a small part and begins what is to become a successful career; Hurstwood loses his grip completely and does not even try to find work. Eventually Carrie deserts him, unable to carry the burden which he has now become. Hurstwood ends up on Skid Row, a drunken beggar who eventually kills himself. Carrie knows nothing of this; she rises in her profession and becomes a sought-after leading lady in musical comedy. She is successful and enjoys a material well-being beyond her dreams. At the same time, however, she is aware of a hollowness in her success, because she is alone.

**Sister Helen** A poem by Dante Gabriel Rossetti, first published in 1870 in *Poems by D. G. Rossetti*. In semi-dramatic form the poem tells the story of a woman betrayed by her lover. She makes a waxen image of him and melts it, thereby destroying him. Her young brother questions 'Sister Helen' about her actions and the appearance of those who plead for the lover's life. An unearthly chorus laments her course – 'O Mother, Mary Mother' – but cannot halt it, and Helen loses her own soul by it.

**Sisters, The** A comedy by James Shirley, first produced in 1642 and first published in 1652. The sisters are the presumptuous and haughty Paulina and the unassuming and modest Angellina. A bandit chief, Frapolo, comes to the house, masquerading as a fortune teller; he tells Paulina that she is destined to marry a prince. He next appears as the Prince of Parma – and Paulina marries him without hesitation. Then the real prince appears on the scene and falls in love with Angellina.

Frapolo is exposed and Paulina is discovered to be a changeling, the daughter of a peasant.

**Sitwell, Edith (Louisa)** 1887–1965. Edith Sitwell was the eldest child of Sir George and Lady Ida Sitwell and was born at Scarborough in Yorkshire. She was educated at home, in an environment where warmth and sympathy were scarce – her father was a self-centred eccentric and she did not conform to her mother's idea of a fashionable woman's daughter. Her father decreed that her curving spine and the slightly crooked bridge of her nose should be corrected by iron frames and she was imprisoned in these every night. The richness of the great house in Derbyshire, Renishaw Hall, and the beautiful gardens were not sufficient compensation for a childhood blighted by loneliness and parental disapproval. She was grateful for the kindness of servants and the companionship of her brothers Osbert and Sacheverell – when she was permitted it. *The Sleeping Beauty* (1924) and *Colonel Fantock* (1926), two of her most beautiful early poems, evoke this period of her life.

A natural liking for music and poetry were conventionally approved – and firmly guided into 'acceptable' channels; Edith Sitwell discovered Shakespeare, Pope, Yeats, and Swinburne for herself and responded to music and the beauty of design in nature. The engagement of Helen Rootham as her governess during her adolescence changed her life. Miss Rootham was an accomplished young woman who appreciated the quality of her pupil and introduced her to French Symbolist poetry and, particularly, the work of Rimbaud. The new governess accompanied Edith Sitwell to concerts and on visits to European capitals and encouraged her aspirations. She went with her to London when she was at last allowed to leave Renishaw Hall (1915).

For a brief period, Edith Sitwell worked as a clerk in a government office. Then she decided to make literature her career, and printed a slim booklet of ten pages at her own expense. This was *The Mother and Other Poems* (1915), her first published work. In 1916 she contributed seven poems to a joint effort with her brother Osbert, who was invalided home from the front in that year, called *Twentieth Century Harlequinade and Other Poems*, and founded and edited *Wheels*, an annual which ran until 1921 and published contemporary verse. The contributors were usually young and innovative, forward looking, and reacting against Georgian poetry. The first poems of Wilfred Owen to be published appeared in *Wheels* in 1919. Her own career as a poet continued meanwhile with *Clown's Houses* (1918) and *The Wooden Pegasus* (1920), and she made friends with Aldous Huxley, T. S. Eliot, Harold Acton, Roger Fry, Virginia Woolf, and Cecil Beaton, who found in her striking elegance of feature the perfect subject for photography.

*Façade* (1922) made Edith Sitwell, already famous, almost notorious when her verses, written in collaboration with the composer, William Walton, for an entertainment for voice and orchestra, were heard at the Aeolian Hall in London in June 1923. At the centre of hostile and reactionary criticism, Edith Sitwell and her two brothers gave battle and more than held their own. But one result was the sort of observation made by F. R. Leavis and often quoted, that the Sitwells belonged to the history of publicity rather than to that of literature. However, Edith Sitwell's work continued to be published and discussed and *Bucolic Comedies* (1923), *The Sleeping Beauty* (1924), *Troy Park* (1925), *Elegy on Dead Fashion* (1926), *Poem for a Christmas Card* (1926), and *Rustic Elegies* (1927) confirmed her position in English poetry. *Gold Coast Customs* (1929) was something new, a denunciation of fashionable extravagance set in juxtaposition with the savage rites of Gold Coast tribes. A powerful poem, it was the first expression in her work of a religious and social sense which was to deepen with the years.

In 1930, badly in need of money to care for a very ill Helen Rootham, Edith Sitwell turned to prose and journalism to earn it. Apart from her contributions to several newspapers she published a study, *Alexander Pope* (1930), which contributed much to the rehabilitation of that poet; *Bath* (1932), *English Eccentrics* (1933), *Aspects of Modern Poetry* (1934); a biography, *Victoria of England* (1936), and her single novel, *I Live Under a Black Sun* (1937), which drew extravagant praise from, among others, Evelyn Waugh, L. P. Hartley, and Wilfred Gibson. The novel is founded on the affairs of Jonathan Swift, Stella, and Vanessa. Her poetry, with the exception of occasional pieces, was not resumed until after Helen Rootham died in 1938.

*Street Songs* (1942), *Green Song and Other Poems* (1944), and *The Song of the Cold* (1945) demonstrated that the poet of *Gold Coast Customs* had responded to the challenge of expressing her grief at the horrors of war and the unforgivable – because it could be remedied – misery of poverty. *The Shadow of Cain* (1947), provoked by an eyewitness account of the first nuclear bomb on Hiroshima, was two years in the writing. *The Canticle of the Rose* (1949), *Poor Men's Music* (1950), *Gardeners and Astronomers* (1953), and

*Music and Ceremonies* (1963) completed her published poetry. *Collected Poems* was published in 1954. Among her prose works were two notable books on the life and reign of Elizabeth Tudor, *Fanfare for Elizabeth* (1946) and *The Queens and the Hive* (1962); an appreciation of the poetry of the USA, *The American Genius* (1951); an anthology, *The Atlantic Book of British and American Poetry* (1958), and a volume of autobiography, *Taken Care Of* (published posthumously, 1965).

When she died at the age of 77 Edith Sitwell was one of the most celebrated of Englishwomen. She had earned the praise of W. B. Yeats as a young poet; as a mature one she had been awarded honorary doctorates by no less than four universities; she became a Dame of the British Empire in 1954; a television interview, *Face to Face*, had made millions of people aware of a major poet with an arresting personality; her 75th birthday concert at the Royal Festival Hall had brought a packed house and the cultural elite of England out in attendance. An unfailingly courteous woman, she reserved her considerable and waspish wit for her critics, and was generous to younger poets – the most notable of whom was Dylan Thomas – in whose gifts she believed.

Edith Sitwell, 1950.

**Sitwell, Osbert** 1892–1969. The elder son of Sir George and Lady Ida Sitwell and the brother of the poet Edith Sitwell, Osbert Sitwell was born in London and spent much of his childhood and youth at the family home, Renishaw Hall in Derbyshire. He was educated at Eton College, which he detested, and held a commission in the Grenadier Guards from 1912 to 1919. He served in World War I until he was invalided home in 1916; in that year his first poems appeared with some of his sister's in *Twentieth-Century Harlequinade and Other Poems*. Another joint publication was *Poor Young People* (1925), which also included poems by his younger brother Sacheverell, and by then he was committed, with his sister and his brother, to fighting philistinism and the national indifference to the arts. He published verse at regular intervals and it was collected in *Collected Satires and Poems* (1931), *Wrack at Tidesend* (1952), and *On the Continent* (1958). His fiction began with the volume of short stories, *Triple Fugue* (1924), and continued with a notable novel, *Before the Bombardment* (1926), *The Man Who Lost Himself* (1929), *Miracle on Sinai* (1933), *Those Were the Days* (1938), *Open the Door* (1941, short stories), and *A Place of One's Own* (1941). He was a prolific essayist and published a number of collections, and in 1944 the first volume of his highly-praised autobiography, *Left Hand, Right Hand!* (1944). The succeeding volumes were *The Scarlet Tree* (1946), *Great Morning* (1947), *Laughter in the Next Room* (1948), and *Noble Essences* (1950). Osbert Sitwell's *Collected Short Stories* was published in 1953. He became the fifth baronet when his father died in 1943.

**Sitwell, Sacheverell** 1897– . The youngest child of Sir George and Lady Ida Sitwell and the brother of Edith and Osbert Sitwell. Like his brother Osbert he was educated at Eton College and served with the Grenadier Guards in World War I. Though a little less in the front lines of literary controversy than his sister and brother, he made his own claim to distinction as, first, an accomplished poet. His first published poetry was *The People's Palace* (1918) and he contributed to *Poor Young People* (1925) with his brother and sister. *Collected Poems* (1936) has an introductory essay by Edith Sitwell; *Selected Poems* (1948) contains some unpublished poems and a preface by Osbert Sitwell.

Sacheverell Sitwell made a notable debut as a critic of art and architecture with *Southern Baroque Art* (1924). Several such volumes followed, among them *German Baroque Art* (1927), *The Gothick North* (1929–30, three

volumes), *Conversation Pieces* (1936), *Narrative Pictures* (1937), and *British Architects and Craftsmen* (1945). A widely travelled man, he wrote about his experiences in *Roumanian Journey* (1938), *Mauretania* (1940), *The Netherlands* (1948), *Spain* (1950), and many other books, and published an excellent romantic biography, *Liszt*, in 1934. His lively wide-ranging essays on art, music, travel, and other subjects form the contents of several other prose volumes, notably *The Dance of the Quick and the Dead* (1936), *Sacred and Profane Love* (1940), *Primitive Scenes and Festivals* (1942), *Splendours and Miseries* (1943), and *Cupid and the Jacaranda* (1952). Sacheverell Sitwell became the sixth baronet upon the death of his brother in 1969.

**Skeat, Walter William** 1835–1912. An architect's son, Skeat was born in London. He was educated at King's College School, Highgate School, and Christ's College, Cambridge, where he became a fellow in 1860. He entered the ministry and practised as a curate for a time, but ill-health obliged him to give up and he returned to Christ's College as a lecturer in mathematics. His other interest, early English texts, was pursued privately but led eventually to his great reputation. He edited texts for The Early English Text Society, The Chaucer Society, The Scottish Text Society, and The English Dialect Society (which he founded). His edition of *The Vision of William concerning Piers the Plowman* (1867–85) was authoritative for a number of years, and *The Complete Works of Geoffrey Chaucer* (1894–97) remains standard, other editions being invariably measured by it. He was appointed Elrington and Bosworth Professor of Anglo-Saxon at Cambridge in 1878.

Skeat's study of the English language was scientific with a historical basis; his published works as a philologist and etymologist are classics, including *An Etymological Dictionary of the English Language* (1882), *A Concise Dictionary of Middle English* (1888), *A Primer of Classical and English Philology* (1905), and *The Science of Etymology* (1912). Skeat was the author of numerous essays and reviews and was interested in the etymology of English place names. Among other early works edited by Skeat were John Barbour's *The Bruce* (1870–89), *The Holy Gospels in Anglo-Saxon, Northumbrian and Old Mercian versions* (1871–87), *Aelfric's The Lives of the Saints* (1881–1900), and *The Kingis Quair* (1884). His edition of *The Poetical Works of Thomas Chatterton* was published in 1871.

**Skelton, John** *c*.1460–1529. Details of Skelton's life are scarce, and although it is known that he was born in Norfolk the date of his birth is as likely to have been *c*.1464 as *c*.1460. He was educated at both Oxford and Cambridge and he is mentioned by William Caxton as a translator from the Latin. He also wrote Latin verse that displays an easy facility in that language. He was honoured as *poeta laureatus* by both universities – some time before 1490 by Oxford and in 1493 by Cambridge; he took holy orders in 1498. Skelton was at court by this time and was made tutor to Prince Henry. He met Erasmus in 1499. He had become rector of Diss in Norfolk by 1502 and probably held the living until about 1511; his best work belongs to this period. His former pupil became King Henry VIII in 1509 and Skelton was apparently secure at court in spite of his outspoken criticism of courtiers and court life in his early work *The Bowge of Courte* (1498–99).

He described himself as *orator regius* from 1512 and he was to a certain extent a court – that is the king's – poet, as can be seen in the ballads written against the Scots. Not all of Skelton's work survives; indeed we possess only a little of it if his own account (in the *Garlande of Laurell*, 1523) is to be believed. The first considerable work is *The Bowge of Courte* already mentioned. (The word bowge meant the provisions or allowances made to minor officials at court.) It is a work that looks back to the Middle Ages and is in the dream allegory form, introducing a character into the peculiar world that is the court; in this case the court of Henry VIII. The dangers to be encountered there are personifications whose names, such as Disdain, Suspect, and Danger describe them. *Phylyp Sparowe* (before 1509) is a lament by a girl, Jane Scroupe, for her pet sparrow killed by a cat. *Ware the Hawk*, *Epitaphe*, and *The Tunnyng of Elynour Rummyng* are all from Skelton's period at Diss and the last-named is the best known. Elynour Rummyng is an alewife of Leatherhead and the poem is a remarkable description of her ale house and her customers, coarse, lively, and humorous (there was a real Alianora Romyng who was charged with giving short measures in 1525). *A Ballade of the Scottysshe King* belongs to 1513 – the year of the Battle of Flodden, which it celebrates.

*Collyn Clout* and *Why Come Ye Nat to Court?* are both dated 1522. The first details the grievances of a vagabond against churchmen, the second is a direct attack on Wolsey himself and the all-powerful position he held. *Speke, Parot* had appeared in the previous year and one version (two divergent texts are known) is also an attack on the cardinal. Skelton had gone too far and to escape Wolsey's wrath he was obliged to go into sanctuary in Westminster. But he found a new patron in the Countess of Surrey. *A Goodly Garlande or Chapelet of Laurell* (1523) is addressed to her. It is an allegory full of praise of the poet himself and describes his crowning among the great poets of history. Skelton was also the author of a vast morality play called *Magnyfycence* (1515), which is full of tedious moralizing and is not admired, and his Latin translations include Diodorus Siculus.

Skelton is described by most scholars as the only real poet of his time – the long period between the poets of the Middle Ages and the times of Wyatt, Surrey, Sidney, and Spenser. He was a priest and a staunch adherent of the old faith, as his comments on the reformers in *Collyn Clout* demonstrate. But he was anything but dainty and his short and bouncy metre (chiefly three beats in a line, sometimes five), his inexhaustible capacity for rhyme, and his talent for invective have kept his work alive. He was not capable of a broad view and no one with a real sense of humour or humanity could have written the *Garlande of Laurell* or *A Ballade of the Scottysshe King*. Nevertheless, his is an original and refreshing voice after the dullness of the late Middle Ages, even if he cannot be regarded as a major English poet. *The Complete Poems of John Skelton* was edited by P. Henderson (modernized spelling) in 1931. The latest revised edition appeared in 1964.

**Sketch Book, The** Washington Irving's book of tales and essays was written while he was in England, after the failure of his family's business in Liverpool. Walter Scott encouraged him to start writing again – and this first sketch book has proved to be the most enduring of all his works. It was written under the pseudonym of Geoffrey Crayon, Gent. and issued serially in the USA in 1819–20. It was first published in book form in England in 1820.

Much of the book is taken up with an American visitor's impression of English places and occasions; but the six chapters of American matter, which include *Rip van Winkle* and *The Legend of Sleepy Hollow*, may be said to have given the book its lasting fame and ensured its status as a classic. There was enough in the volume to interest and stimulate readers on both sides of the Atlantic and to make Irving famous in both worlds.

*Rip van Winkle* tells the story of an amiable rather lazy Dutch-American who lives in a village on the Hudson River in the years before the American Revolution. One day he goes hunting in the Catskill Mountains with his dog – and meets a strange dwarflike person dressed in the Dutch fashion of a bygone age. He helps the stranger, who is struggling with a keg, and joins him at a silent party of similar dwarfs playing ninepins. He is given drink from the keg and falls asleep. When he wakes up he finds himself an old man; 20 years have passed, the Revolution has succeeded, and his nagging wife is dead. He finds a home with his daughter, who is now married and has children of her own, and his amiable disposition finds him new friends. The author makes much of the contrast that the new world presents to Rip, after the one that vanished while he slept. The story was adapted for the stage by Joseph Jefferson and Dion Boucicault in 1865 and played with enormous success by Jefferson for nearly 40 years.

*The Legend of Sleepy Hollow* was based on a German original and in Irving's version takes place on the Hudson River among the Dutch-American folk of Sleepy Hollow in the years after the Revolution. It is a simple story about an assertive Yankee schoolmaster, the lanky Ichabod Crane, who pursues Katrina Van Tassell, the daughter of a rich farmer. His rival is Brom Van Brunt, a local hero and a fine horseman. At an autumn quilting party at the Van Tassell farm Brom and his friends tell the story of a headless horseman who haunts the neighbourhood. Katrina has to discourage Ichabod Crane's attentions at the party. On the way home on a borrowed carthorse Crane is pursued through the woods by a headless horseman carrying a round object, which he hurls at Crane's head.

Crane disappears from Sleepy Hollow and a pumpkin is found lying on the way taken home by him. Katrina marries Brom and the tale of Ichabod Crane and the headless horseman becomes a legend in Sleepy Hollow.

**Skimpole, Harold** In Dickens's *Bleak House*, an acquaintance of John Jarndyce. 'He was a bright little creature . . . and there was a perfect charm in him.' His charm is his way of being apparently helpless and baffled by life; in fact he is totally selfish and will betray any of his friends for his own advantage.

**Slick, Sam** See **Haliburton, Thomas Chandler**.

**Slipslop, Mrs** Lady Booby's attendant in *Joseph Andrews* by Henry Fielding. Like her mistress, she is keen to seduce Joseph, the footman, and, also like her mistress, becomes very spiteful when Joseph turns her down.

**Slop, Dr** The irascible Catholic doctor of *Tristram Shandy* by Laurence Sterne. In his eagerness to demonstrate a new kind of obstetrical forceps he spoils Tristram's nose – to the despair of Mr Shandy, who believes that big noses are a characteristic of great men.

**Slope, Obadiah** The ambitious and intriguing chaplain of Anthony Trollope's *Barchester Towers*. He is bested by Mrs Proudie, the bishop's wife, and brought down by his infatuation with Madeline Vesey-Neroni.

**Sloper, Catherine** The central character of *Washington Square*, by Henry James. A plain and subdued girl, Catherine is patronized by her rich and successful father, who effortlessly disposes of her suitor, the penniless Morris Townsend.

**Slough of Despond** In John Bunyan's *The Pilgrim's Progress*, the place where Christian wanders after deciding to set out on his pilgrimage. It is a mire where doubts and apprehensions settle and Christian, with the weight of his sins to carry, nearly succumbs but is rescued by Help.

**Sly, Christopher** The drunken tinker of the Induction to Shakespeare's *The Taming of the Shrew*, who witnesses the play that follows. The playwright seems to have forgotten him after the first two scenes – he does not even appear in an epilogue.

***Small House at Allington, The*** A novel by Anthony Trollope – the penultimate Barsetshire story – first published in 1864.

The Small House is the house of Bell and Lily Dale and their mother, adjacent to the Great House, the home of Squire Dale, their uncle and an embittered old bachelor. To Allington comes Adolphus Crosbie, a good-looking man who is a rising government official. He courts Lily Dale and she falls in love with him; they become engaged, to the grief of Johnny Eames, a government clerk who worships Lily. But Crosbie is disturbed to find out that Lily has no fortune to look forward to, in spite of her uncle's wealth. When he is a guest at Courcy Castle he is seduced by the aristocratic world and proposes to Lady Alexandrine de Courcy. She accepts him and he jilts Lily.

Johnny Eames, beside himself, goes to Crosbie and thrashes him. But the marriage goes forward and proves to be disastrous; Crosbie is well served for his mean and selfish actions. Johnny, meanwhile, has made a favourable impression on Lord de Guest, who helps him in his career. He feels secure enough to propose to Lily; but, sadly, she is still obsessed with Crosbie and refuses him. Her sister, Bell, also refuses a suitor, her cousin Bernard who is her uncle's choice. Bell wants to make her own choice – Dr Crofts. Relations between Great House and Small House are completely estranged: the squire's heir is Bernard – and Bell was to have been appropriated as a suitable wife. The story closes, however, with a reconciliation; Mrs Dale goes on living at the Small House, Bell marries Dr Crofts, but Lily remains unmarried. Lady Dumbello (Griselda Grantly) makes an appearance in this novel, as does Plantagenet Palliser.

**Smart, Christopher** 1722–71. The son of a steward on Lord Vane's estate, Smart was born at Shipborne in Kent. At the age of 11, when his father died, he went to live in Durham, and became a protégé of Lord Barnard of Raby, who was related to Lord Vane. He sponsored Smart's entry into Pembroke College, Cambridge, of which he became a fellow in 1745. Smart had made a reputation at Cambridge with his Latin verse and in 1747 he took his MA and published his first English verse. About this time his erratic behaviour gave cause for concern; he was arrested for debt but his friends came to the rescue and 1748 found him back, apparently secure once more, at Pembroke College. In 1749, however, Smart left Cambridge for London, where he worked as a journalist for John Newbery, the publisher of *The Mid-Wife, or The Old Woman's Magazine* and *The Student, or Oxford and Cambridge Monthly Miscellany*.

Smart won the Seatonian Prize for sacred poetry no less than five times, with *On the Eternity of the Supreme Being* (1750), *On the Immensity of the Supreme Being* (1751), *On the Omniscience of the Supreme Being* (1752), *On the Power of the Supreme Being* (1753), and *On the Goodness of the Supreme Being* (1755). His first collection was *Poems on Several Occasions* (1752), which included the didactic nature poem *The Hop Garden*, notable for its fresh and touching recollection of childhood. *The Hilliad* (1753) was a satire on the quack doctor John Hill. In 1756 Smart published his *Hymn to the Supreme Being on Recovery from a Dangerous Fit of Illness*, which marked the onset of the tragic insanity which was to darken his later years. In 1756, also, he published his prose translation *The Works of Horace*.

During the next seven years the hapless poet was forcibly confined at intervals in St Luke's Hospital. He wrote poetry in his madness, which was not published for nearly 200 years, but 1763 saw the publication of his most celebrated work, *A Song to David*, which made no particular impact at the time. *A Translation of the Psalms of David*, *Hymns and Spiritual Songs for the Fasts and Festivals of the Church of England* (both 1765), and *The Parables of Our Lord and Saviour Jesus Christ, done into familiar verse, For the Use of Younger Minds* (1768) were probably his last published works. The sorely tried man was imprisoned for debt in 1770; he wrote *Hymns for the Amusement of Children* in prison, and died in the following year. His preoccupation with religious subjects was reflected in Smart's mental condition – his insanity took the form of religious mania. The most notable work of his confinement was *Jubilate Agno*, which was edited by W. T. Stead in 1939 and published as *Rejoice in the Lamb*. *A Song to David* is an expression of religious ecstasy and generally acknowledged by scholars as unique among the lyrical poems of the 18th century. Christopher Smart remains, on the whole, a scholar's poet; in spite of his obvious gifts, his chosen subject keeps him at a distance from most general readers.

The recommended modern editions of Smart's work are *Collected Poems* edited by N. Callan (1949) and R. E. Brittain's selected *Poems by Christopher Smart* (1950).

**Smectymnuus** A portmanteau name of five Puritan writers against episcopacy: S. Marshall, E. Calamy, T. Young, M. Newcomen, and W. Spurstow. See also **Milton, John**.

**Smedley, Francis Edward** 1818–64. Smedley was an afflicted man, a cripple from childhood with a love of sport. He succeeded as a writer of pleasant novels which blended romance with sport and adventure. They were regarded highly enough to be illustrated by Phiz and Cruikshank, though they are forgotten now. The most popular was *Frank Farleigh: or scenes from the life of a private pupil* (1850). Others were *Lewis Arundel* (1852) and *Harry Coverdale* (1855).

**Smike** The pathetic waif of Dotheboys Hall in *Nicholas Nickleby*. Apparently an orphan left on the hands of the Squeers family, he is subjected to continual cruelty until Nicholas intervenes. Smike's origins are revealed in the closing chapters of Dickens's novel.

**Smiles, Samuel** 1812–1904. Smiles was born in East Lothian, near Edinburgh, and attended Haddington High School before going to Edinburgh University to study medicine. He became a doctor and later a journalist and company secretary in the expanding railway business. He had definite ideas on social and political reform combined with a strong belief in the doctrine of self-interest. His ideas emerge clearly in his biographies of successful men of the industrial age: *George Stephenson* (1857), *The Lives of the Engineers* (1867, extended 1874), and *Josiah Wedgwood* (1894). He is best known for *Self-Help: With Illustrations of Character and Conduct*

(1859), which sold in enormous numbers and was translated into several languages. Smiles continued his effective role as a popular moralist with *Character* (1871), *Thrift* (1875), and *Duty* (1880). A centenary edition of *Self-Help* was published with an introduction by Asa Briggs (1958).

**Smith, Adam** 1723–90. Adam Smith, the son of a customs controller, was born at Kirkcaldy in Fifeshire. He was educated at Glasgow University, where one of his teachers was Francis Hutcheson, and at Balliol College, Oxford, gaining his place by winning a Snell Exhibition. He spent six years at Oxford though he was hard put, later, to find any praise for an institution that confiscated his copy of David Hume's *A Treatise of Human Nature*. However, he did appreciate the college's fine library. After Oxford he spent two years at home and then gave a course of lectures on literature and rhetoric in Edinburgh under the patronage of Lord Kames. He was appointed Professor of Logic at Glasgow in 1751 and of Moral Philosophy in 1752; he published **The Theory of Moral Sentiments** in 1759. This work, based on a group of lectures, brought him considerable notice, and he was made a Doctor of Law by Glasgow University.

Smith left the university in 1763, and early in the following year accompanied the young Duke of Buccleuch to Europe as his tutor. They were away for two years and Smith made the acquaintance of Jean d'Alembert, Voltaire, La Rochefoucauld, Claude-Adrien Helvétius, and François Quesnay, whose system of political economy impressed him very much. In Toulouse, to pass the time, Smith began to write his own book of political economy.

After returning from Europe Smith settled down at Kirkcaldy and continued work on the book he had begun to write in Toulouse. He intended to dedicate it to François Quesnay; the French economist and his associates, the physiocrats, were held in high esteem by Smith. **An Enquiry into the Nature and Causes of the Wealth of Nations** was published in 1776 and was immediately greeted by a letter of praise from Smith's friend David Hume. It proved to be one of the most important works of economic theory ever written.

In the following year Smith was editing David Hume's autobiography for posthumous publication and he was appointed Commissioner of Customs in Edinburgh in 1778. He was elected Rector of Glasgow University in 1787 and died in Edinburgh in 1790. His name is forever associated with a single book – one of the most famous in history – though a volume of essays was collected by Dugald Steward and published with the memoir *Essays on Philosophical Subjects* (1795), and two collections of lectures dating from 1762 and 1763 were edited by E. Cannan (1896) and J. M. Lothian (1963).

Smith did not, apparently, possess the amiable charm of his friend Hume and he was notoriously absent-minded. His later style is blunt and direct, probably because of his habit of dictating, when he would walk around the room. If he lacks literary elegance, he lacks nothing in clarity; he was an expositor of genius.

**Smith, Alexander** 1830–67. Smith was born in Kilmarnock, Ayrshire, and earned his living as a lace-pattern designer in Glasgow. He published *Poems* (1853), which contained 'A Life Drama'; this was highly praised but he was satirized by William Aytoun in *Firmilian* (1854). *Sonnets on the War* (1855) was written with Sydney Dobell (the war was the Crimean); *City Poems* (1857) followed and contains what is usually regarded as his best poem, 'Glasgow'. *Edwin of Deira* (1861) was his last volume of verse. Smith was falsely accused by some reviewers of plagiarizing the work of other poets, including Tennyson, and thereafter only published prose. *Alfred Hagart's Household* (1866) is a novel, *Dreamthorp* (1863) and *Last Leaves* (published posthumously, 1868) are collections of essays, and *A Summer in Skye* (1865) is a highly regarded description of the island and its people.

**Smith, Charlotte** 1749–1806. Born Charlotte Turner in London, in 1765 she married a merchant in the West Indian trade. Smith, however, was improvident and after the ruin of his business in 1782 was imprisoned for debt. Charlotte Smith became a writer and her first published work was an English version of Prévost's *Manon Lescaut* (1785). She went on to make a living as an industrious writer and translator and is remembered chiefly as a novelist; her ten romances were well-told stories and most were translated into French. Two of them, *Emmeline, the Orphan of the Castle* (1788) and *The Old Manor House* (1793), were edited with an introduction by Anne Henry Ehrenpreis (Oxford English Novels, 1971 and 1969 respectively). In her day Charlotte Smith also received respectful praise as a poet.

**Smith, Goldwin** 1823–1910. Smith was born in Oxfordshire and educated at Eton College and Christ Church, Oxford. He was appointed to the Commission on National Education (1858) and became Regius Professor of Modern History (1859). He acquired a considerable reputation as an educational reformer and a political journalist when he published *The Empire* (1863), in which he advocated the separation of the colonies and their establishment as states independent of England. Smith resigned from Oxford in 1866 and went to the USA to become Professor of History at Cornell University. He eventually settled in Toronto in 1871. Smith distrusted imperialism when it seemed to have become a permanent force in the affairs of nations; he was perhaps more interesting as a political controversialist than as a historian though he earned respect in both fields during his lifetime. Other books by Goldwin Smith were *Irish History and Irish Character* (1861), *Three English Statesmen* (1867), on Pym, Cromwell, and Pitt, and *The United Kingdom; A Political History* (1899). He wrote *Cowper* for the English Men of Letters series (1880).

**Smith, Harriet**   The pretty, rather silly, girl who becomes the protégée of Emma Woodhouse in Jane Austen's *Emma*.

**Smith, Captain John** *c.*1580–1631.   The most romantic figure in the history of Englishmen in the New World was born in Willoughby, Lincolnshire. He was apprenticed to a merchant but when his father died in 1596 he left home to seek his fortune as a soldier. He served in the Netherlands and on the borders of Hungary with the Austrian army fighting the Turks. He was captured and taken to Constantinople, to serve as a slave to a Turkish pasha: the pasha's wife, fortunately, fell in love with him and selflessly helped him reach the court of her brother, which lay somewhere farther to the east. From there he was able to escape back to England; he returned about 1604, bringing with him a coat of arms that had been awarded him for valour as a soldier. The remarkable thing about this account, written by Smith himself (*The True Travels, Adventures and Observations of Captain John Smith in Europe, Asia, Africa and America*, published in 1630), is that however far-fetched and romantic it sounds – it was rejected as pure romance by many – it has proved to be true in every detail that can be checked.

Smith was involved in the foundation of the Virginia Company and went with them to Jamestown, arriving in 1607. He was active in exploration and in the essential trade with the Indians for food and on one expedition was captured by the Powhatan chief, Wahunsonacock. This was the celebrated adventure that involved Pocahontas, the chief's daughter who successfully pleaded for his life. When he returned to the colony in January 1608, the loss of two men gave his rivals on the council an opportunity to charge him with responsibility for their deaths. He was sentenced to death – but the arrival of a ship from England, commanded by his friend Christopher Newport, saved him from the gallows. Newport restored order in the colony (it was suffering badly from dissension in a badly ordered council) and Smith resumed his rightful place. He also continued his explorations, along the rivers Rappahannock and Potomac and in the region of Chesapeake Bay.

Smith became president of the colony but his administration did not escape criticism. He left for England in October 1609, suffering from severe injuries sustained in a gunpowder explosion. He was denied further employment by the Virginia Company but a group of London merchants sent him to explore to the north of Virginia, in the region that he named New England in his map of 1616 – the name it has borne ever since. Smith disappointed his backers because he didn't bring them gold; he was interested chiefly in exploration and colonization – what profit a new colony yielded would depend entirely on what it would produce. He found a new supporter in Sir Arthur Gorges, Ralegh's friend and co-commander, but his hopes for New England came to nothing. The Puritans, who eventually made New England their own, decided that Smith fell short of their character requirements and declined to listen when he tried to interest them in the project. Smith was obliged to give up; he settled down in London and began to write more about the colony that was his principal interest. His pamphlet of 1608 had given the first authentic account: *A True Relation of such Occurrences and Accidents of Noate as hath hapned in Virginia since the First Planting of that Colony*; he had published *A Map of Virginia, with a Description of the Countrey, the Commodities, People, Government and Religion* in 1612.

Smith published his account of his voyages to New England under Gorges' patronage in *A Description of New England: Or the Observations and Discoveries of Captain John Smith in the North of America 1614; with the Successe of Six Ships that went* (1615). This was followed by what was virtually a statement of his own achievements and a plea for further support: *New Englands Trials: Declaring the Successe of 26 Ships Employed thether within these Six Yeares: With the Benefit of that Countrey by Sea and Land* (1620). *The Generall Historie of Virginia, New England and the Summer Isles* (1624) is his most famous book, an extensive reworking of his earlier writings together with the story of Pocahontas. Other works were a manual for seamen, *The Seaman's Grammar*

(1626), and a manual for colonists, *Advertisements for the Unexperienced Planters of New England, or any where; with the Yearely Proceedings of this Country in Fishing and Planting, since the Yeare 1614* (1631).

**Smith, John Thomas** 1766–1833. Smith, who became Keeper of Drawings and Prints in the British Museum, was born in London in a hackney carriage, on a journey from Seven Dials to Great Portland Street. His father worked in the studio of the sculptor Joseph Nollekens, who was notoriously stingy and left a huge fortune when he died. Smith's biography, *Nollekens and his Times* (1828), is remarkable for its vivid detail and malicious candour. He was also the author of *A Book for a Rainy Day, or Recollections of the Events of the years 1766–1833*, which is a mine of information on the artistic and literary life of the period. It was published posthumously (1845).

**Smith, Logan Pearsall** 1865–1946. A member of a Philadelphia Quaker family, Smith was born in Millville, New Jersey, and educated at Harvard and Oxford. He had independent means and decided to settle in England, where he earned a reputation as an essayist with an elegant and witty style, a lexicographer, and a bibliographer. He prepared editions of various authors, including John Donne, and published a biography of Sir Henry Wotton in 1907. Smith's most notable work of criticism is *Milton and His Modern Critics* (1941), in which he attacks T. S. Eliot and Ezra Pound for their attacks on Milton's reputation. *Unforgotten Years* (1938) is his autobiography and describes his Quaker boyhood, his experiences as an expatriate American with some interesting observations on American letters, and his acquaintance with Walt Whitman. His aphorisms and essays were collected in *All Trivia* (published in 1933, with a revised edition in 1945) and *Reperusals and Re-collections* (1936). Smith also published some poems and short stories.

**Smith, Sydney** 1771–1845. Smith was born at Woodford in Essex, and was educated at Winchester and at New College, Oxford. He was ordained and became a fellow of his college and, while waiting for a living, went to Edinburgh as a tutor. While in Edinburgh Smith became friendly with a group which included Francis Jeffrey and Henry Brougham, and with them founded **The Edinburgh Review** in 1802. He was a wit as well as a humanitarian, and his contributions greatly helped to ensure the success of *The Edinburgh*. Smith went to London in 1803 and became a popular lecturer on moral philosophy at the Royal Institution; he was also a member of the Whig circles at Holland House, where his conversation was eagerly sought. In 1807 Smith published *The Letters of Peter Plymley on The Subject of the Catholics to My Brother Abraham who Lives in the Country*, a remarkable attack on traditional religious prejudice. Smith brought his generous humanity and wit to bear against the exploitation of children as chimney sweeps, the transportation of convicts, the Corn Laws and Game Laws, the prison system, and the condition of Ireland.

Smith was awarded the living of Foston near York in 1808 and of Combe-Florey in Somerset in 1828; he was made Canon-Residentiary of St Paul's in 1831. *Selected Writings of Sydney Smith* was edited by W. H. Auden (1956); *Selected Letters of Sydney Smith* was edited by N. C. Smith (The World's Classics, 1956).

**Smith, William Robertson** 1846–94. Smith was born at Keig in Aberdeenshire and studied at the universities of Edinburgh, Bonn, and Göttingen. He became Professor of Oriental Languages and Old Testament Exegesis at Free Church College, Aberdeen, in 1870. In 1875 Smith's contributions on biblical subjects to the ninth edition of the *Encyclopaedia Britannica* aroused the anger of the establishment. Smith's scholarship was advanced and so was the nature of his essays; the General Assembly of the Free Church declared that Smith was undermining belief in the 'inspiration of the Bible'. He was removed in 1881; in the same year he published *The OT in the Jewish Church*. *The Prophets of Israel* appeared in the following year and *The Religion of the Semites* in 1889. After 1881 Smith lived at Cambridge; he became a fellow of Christ's College in 1885.

***Smoke and Steel*** A collection of poems by Carl Sandburg, first published in 1920. The title poem describes the great steel plants of the United States, the awe-inspiring spectacle they present, and the human lives they devour. 'Broken-Face Gargoyles' acknowledges Sandburg's artistic imperfection in a touching and memorable poem and 'Ossawatomie' evokes the memory of John Brown.

**Smollett, Tobias George** 1721–71. The son of Sir James Smollett, judge and member of both English and Scottish parliaments, Tobias Smollett was born at Dalquhurn in Dunbartonshire. He was educated at Dumbarton School and Glasgow University, where he studied medicine, and became a surgeon and apothecary's apprentice. At the age of 18 he went to London, taking with him a tragedy, *The Regicide*, which he hoped to have accepted for production. However, no one would accept his play and the refusal seems to have soured his attitude towards the theatre managers of the time. He obtained a commission as surgeon in the navy and sailed with Admiral Vernon's fleet to the attack on Cartagena which failed. Smollett left the West India Fleet, and the navy, in Jamaica, where he stayed for four years. He married Anne Lascelles, a lady from Jamaica of considerable means, in London in 1747.

Smollett had established himself as a surgeon in Downing Street, meanwhile, and wrote nothing until 1745, when he wrote a poem after Culloden called 'The Tears of Scotland' and some forgotten verse and verse satires. *The Adventures of Roderick Random*, a picaresque novel based, to some extent, on his own experiences, and using for a model Alain-René Le Sage's *Gil Blas*, was published in 1748 and made Smollett famous. His view of the world was that it was both cruel and coarse, and he said so without mincing words. Smollett's novel is cruel and coarse but it jumps with vitality and displays the author's skill at sketching his characters in a few sharp words.

His eminence enabled Smollett to publish *The Regicide* (1749), with a bilious preface about those who had not discerned its virtues. No one could discern its virtues at this date, either; it was never staged. In the same year he published an English version of *Gil Blas*, and in 1750 took his degree as MD at Marischal College in Aberdeen. A journey to Paris with his friend Dr John Moore gave him the material for a second novel, which was published as *The Adventures of Peregrine Pickle* (1751). This is Smollett's longest book and considered his best by many scholars. The mixture is the same as for *Roderick Random* but Smollett's talents are sharper and he created a major character in Commodore Trunnion. The first edition of *Peregrine Pickle* contained attacks on some of the people who had not the wit to appreciate his brilliance as a budding playwright: David Garrick, Colley Cibber, Lord Lyttelton, and John Rich. More puzzling was his attack on Henry Fielding; it was probably plain jealousy. Or Smollett's rancorous disposition may have convinced him that his character Strap was plagiarized by Fielding from *Roderick Random* for use as Partridge in *Tom Jones*. Fielding retorted in two numbers of *The Covent Garden Journal*; Smollett probably returned as an answer (there is some doubt about the attribution) *A Faithful Narrative of the Base and Inhuman Acts that were lately practiced upon the Brain of Habbakuk Hilding* (1752), a vicious and lewd performance that, if he

was the author, he learned to be ashamed of; at any rate, he praised Fielding in his *History* of 1765.

Smollett moved to Bath and continued to practise as a doctor. But he did not attract patients, so he wrote a pamphlet declaring that the waters had no particular virtue and returned to London. He lived in Chelsea and settled for literature. *The Adventures of Ferdinand Count Fathom* (1753) was his next novel, and it is generally regarded as one of his lesser works; he could not maintain the consistent irony required for the portrayal of villainy, in which, oddly enough, he seems to be apeing Henry Fielding, of all writers. It was his last novel for some years; he spent far beyond his income and his wife's fortune was not at his disposal. He organized a group of hacks and directed them in the rapid production of ready-made books; he was successful and his book factory was profitable. About this time he seems to have forgiven David Garrick for not appreciating his dramatic genius; certainly Garrick was among those who visited his Chelsea house. Others were Laurence Sterne, Samuel Johnson, and Oliver Goldsmith. He published a version of *Don Quixote* (1755), which was a reworking of an early translation of 1742, and in 1756 became editor of *The Critical Review*. Garrick staged his comedy *The Reprisal, or the Tars of Old England* with considerable success at Drury Lane (1757).

*A Complete History of England* occupied Smollett from 1757 to 1765, though not exclusively. In 1759 he spent three months in prison for libelling Admiral Sir Charles Knowles in *The Critical Review*, and in 1760 his fourth novel, *The Life and Adventures of Sir Launcelot Greaves*, began to appear in instalments in *The British Magazine*. It was published in book form in 1762. In the same year Smollett became editor of *The Briton*, a newspaper which was founded to support the policies of Lord Bute. But he was not a success as a polemical journalist, and Bute was not a man to reward those who worked on his behalf, even when their health gave way, as Smollett's did, in 1763. A harsher blow was the loss of his daughter Elizabeth, whom he adored. In the autumn of 1764 he went to Europe with his wife and travelled in France and Italy, returning to England in the middle of 1765. *Travels through France and Italy* (1766) finds Smollett back in his best form, as cantankerous and splenetic as ever but with an authentic traveller's eye for the places, people, and customs he encountered. He met Laurence Sterne in Italy and turned up later as a character in *A Sentimental Journey*.

In 1766 Smollet visited his homeland and was made much of in Edinburgh. Later he visited Bath as a patient, notwithstanding his spiteful denigration of the spa in 1751. He probably gathered material for *Humphry Clinker* during this time, but meanwhile he published *The History and Adventures of an Atom* (1769), a satire on English public affairs from 1754 to the time of publication. The tone can be imagined, Smollett being Smollett. 'The *Travels* of Lemuel Gulliver', wrote Harold Child in 1913, 'are fragrant beside it.' His health obliged him to leave England again at the end of 1769; he settled in a villa at Monte Nero near Leghorn, and there he wrote his last novel.

***The Expedition of Humphry Clinker*** (1771) found Smollett in a different mood. He was not mellow, exactly, but he seemed to be learning that he was, like the rest of his fellow men, an object of humour. This epistolary novel is usually acknowledged as his best work and Lismahago, the Scottish soldier, as one of his best characters. Smollett died in September 1771 and lies buried in the English cemetery in Leghorn. His 'Ode to Independence' was published after

Smollett. A detail from a portrait by an unknown artist, c.1770. National Portrait Gallery, London.

his death. Smollett was not a poet of any distinction but he *may* have been a political thinker. In 1795 there appeared a curious pamphlet bearing his name, called *Wonderful Prophecies, particularly those worthy of notice, by Richard Brothers, and a memorable prophecy of Dr Smollett, just before his death*. The pamphlet foretold the American War of Independence and the French Revolution. But its attribution remains uncertain.

Smollett, removed from the English scene while writing his last novel, may have been influenced in his affection by a backward glance; he was probably not softening in his attitudes through age (a softening is discernible) because, like Fielding, he was relatively short-lived and, as in the case of Fielding, the reader must regret that. The sheer nastiness of his first three novels, with their cruelty and totally unlikeable characters, will prevent modern readers from going to Smollett for a view of 18th-century life because, for all their gusto, their abundant vitality, they lack a sympathetic emotional connection of any kind and the reader is simply never involved. That Smollett knew his public seems plain and his success is a chilling indication of the tone of 18th-century England. Like it or not, the force of his writing conveys an uncomfortable feeling of truth: not the whole truth, of course. In comparison with Richardson and Fielding, his contemporaries, Smollett's representation of life is narrow, and although his novels were written in the picaresque form which produced masterpieces in *Don Quixote* and *Gil Blas*, Smollett did not have the humane and generous temperament of Cervantes and Le Sage, so there is nothing warm or consolatory about his fiction until the time of *Humphry Clinker*. Even in that novel his insistence on what is unattractive about a character can be both boring and depressing. It has to be admitted, however, that Smollett was a fine writer. It was as well that the theatre had no place for his aspirations as a tragic dramatist; he turned to fiction eventually, and enriched it considerably. His invention is tireless and his narrative power remarkable; his prose is lean, tough, and direct, and his influence on later writers is clear. He is also the first English novelist to portray the life of a seaman. *Pickwick* is not far from *Roderick Random*, though of course the Victorian tone is completely different; Dickens had a great fondness for Smollett's work and also his talent for caricature.

Collected editions of Smollett's works were published in 1895, edited by George Saintsbury, by the Shakespeare Head Press, from 1925 to 1926, and by G. H. Maynadier (New York, 1902–11). Numerous modern editions of the separate novels are available (see individual entries).

**Sneerwell, Lady** In Sheridan's *The School for Scandal*, the centre of an idle and leisured group whose principal activity is spiteful gossip and sometimes active malice. Lady Sneerwell wants Charles Surface but he is in love with Maria; Lady Sneerwell does her best to discredit Charles to Maria, while encouraging his brother Joseph to pursue the girl.

**Snobs of England, The,** by *One of Themselves*. A series of papers by W. M. Thackeray, describing the range of English snobs. It appeared in *Punch* in 1846–47, and was republished as *The Book of Snobs* in 1848.

**Snodgrass, Augustus** One of the four members of the Corresponding Society of the Pickwick Club, who undertakes to send in occasional papers for the pleasure of the club members. Hence *The Pickwick Papers*, of Dickens's novel.

**Snow-Bound** John Greenleaf Whittier's poem of winter life in Massachusetts was first published in 1866. It contains vivid word pictures of his memories of life on his Quaker father's farm, when snowstorms would blanket the world and the isolated farming community would proceed with its own busy life. The long evenings by the fireside would bring accounts of adventures the elders knew as settlers.

Whittier wrote the poem after the death of his much-loved sister Elizabeth, to recall his childhood and probably to reconcile himself to his loss. It is considered by many to be his best work.

**Snow, C(harles) P(ercy)** 1905–80. C. P. Snow was born in Leicester and attended Alderman Newton's School before going on to Leicester University College to study science. At Christ's College, Cambridge, he took a PhD for research in physics, was made a fellow of his college in 1930, and tutored in science from 1935 to 1945. During World War II he served as a scientific adviser and was a Civil Service Commissioner from 1945 to 1960. He was knighted in 1957 and became Parliamentary Secretary to the Ministry of Science and Technology in 1964 with a seat in the House of Lords as Baron Snow of Leicester. Snow's first novel was *Death Under Sail* (1932), a detective story; the second, *The Search* (1934), looks forward to his later work with its concern with power and the ethics of science. The sequence called *Strangers and Brothers*, for which he is best known, began in 1940 with a novel of that name and continued, after a wartime interval, with *The Light and the Dark* (1947), *A Time of Hope* (1949), *The Masters* (1951, James Tait Black Memorial Prize), *The New Men* (1954), *Homecomings* (1956), *The Conscience of the Rich* (1958), *The Affair* (1960), *The Corridors of Power* (1964), *The Sleep of Reason* (1968), and *Last Things* (1970). Snow's Rede Lecture, *The Two Cultures and the Scientific Revolution* (1959), examined the growing separation between the humanities and science, and pointed out the dangers of this as well as the benefits which could result if the two cultures acknowledged that each had something to teach the other. *Science and Government* (1961, Godkin Lectures at Harvard) examines the scientist's vocation and the factor of power involved in government-sponsored research. *Public Affairs* (1971) examines the dangers and benefits of advanced technology, and *A Variety of Men* (1967) is a group of biographical studies. Other novels by C. P. Snow are *New Lives for Old* (1933), *The Malcontents* (1972), and *In Their Wisdom* (1974). He was married to the novelist Pamela Hansford Johnson.

**Social Contract, The** See *Two Treatises of Government*.

**Sohrab and Rustum** A poem by Matthew Arnold, first published in 1853 in *Poems: A New Edition*. The subject of the poem is an episode in the Persian epic, the *Shah Nameh* of Abul Kasim Mansur Firdausi (*c*.950–1020). Sohrab was the son of the hero Rustum, born while his father was away at war. His mother feared that he would grow up to spend his life fighting and sent a message that she had borne a girl. Then she returned to her own country with her son, who nevertheless grew up to be a warrior in the Tatar armies. When the Tatars attack Persia Sohrab challenges the bravest of the Persians to meet him in single combat. This proves to be an old warror who is still the Persian champion, and the fight begins. During the struggle the old warrior calls his own name, 'Rustum!', and Sohrab realizes he is fighting his father. He recoils and his opponent strikes him down. Sohrab reveals his identity through the seal pricked on his arm but he dies at his father's feet.

**Soldiers Three** A collection of 13 stories by Rudyard Kipling, first published in 1888. The soldiers are Mulvaney, an Irishman, Ortheris, a Cockney, and Learoyd, a Yorkshireman; the three had appeared in stories already published in *Plain Tales from the Hills*. Among the stories in this volume, which presents the long-service private in India as the central character, are 'The God from the Machine', in which a colonel's daughter is saved from dishonour; 'The Big Drunk Draft' in which Mulvaney, retired and working in India, gives excellent advice to the young officer in charge of a new draft; and 'Black Jack', in which Learoyd and Ortheris hear how Mulvaney foiled a plot to murder Sergeant O'Hara. The soldiers appear again in other collections of stories by Kipling.

**Soliloquy of the Spanish Cloister**   A poem by Robert Browning first published in *Dramatic Lyrics*, one of the *Bells and Pomegranates* series, in 1842. The poem is in the form of a soliloquy by a spiteful monk who envies the innocent happiness of his fellow monk, Brother Lawrence, and tries to lead him into sin. He seems unaware that every one of his own thoughts is also a sin.

**Somervile (*or* Somerville), William**   1675–1742. Somervile was a country gentleman of Edstone near Henley-in-Arden, Warwickshire. He was educated at Winchester School and New College, Oxford, where he became a fellow, and the hobby of his leisured life was the study and composition of poetry. *The Chace* (Chase), published in 1735, a poem in blank verse in four books, is mainly about hunting in its different forms; *Field Sports* (1742) is about hawking and *Hobbinol* (1740) is a mock-heroic account of rustic May games in the Vale of Evesham. *The Chace* was to become the favourite of Mr Jorrocks in Surtees's novel *Handley Cross*.

**Somerville, Edith Anna Oenone**   See **Somerville and Ross.**

**Somerville and Ross**   The joint pseudonym of Edith Anna Oenone Somerville (1858–1949) and Violet Florence Martin (1862–1915), cousins. Edith Somerville was born in County Cork and studied art in London and Paris; Violet Martin was born in County Galway and was educated in Dublin. Edith Somerville enjoyed some success as an artist, exhibiting from 1920 to 1938 but her literary career in collaboration with her cousin began as early as 1889, when the first book by Somerville and Ross, *An Irish Cousin*, was published. The two ladies are successful representatives – and at one time exceedingly popular ones – of the Anglo-Irish tradition of exploiting the humours of the true Irish in relation to the owners of the big houses and estates.

Other novels were *Naboth's Vineyard* (1891) and *The Real Charlotte* (1894); *In the Vine Country* (1893) related travels in France, and *Through Connemara in a Governess Cart* (1893) travels in the west of Ireland. *The Silver Fox* (1898) is a novel, and the enormously popular *Some Experiences of an Irish RM* (1899) contains stories about a resident magistrate in Ireland. *Beggars on Horseback* (1895) told of a riding tour of North Wales. *A Patrick's Day Hunt* (1902), *All on the Irish Shore* (1903), and *Further Experiences of an Irish RM* (1908) continued the short stories of Irish life; *Dan Russell the Fox* (1911) is a novel, the last collaboration before Violet Martin died.

Edith Somerville's later works were published under the familiar pseudonym and included *In Mr Knox's Country* (1915), *Mount Music* (1919), *The Big House of Inver* (1925), *The Sweet Cry of Hounds* (1936), and *Sarah's Youth* (1938).

**Song of Los, The**   See **Blake, William.**

**Song of Myself**   Whitman's celebrated poem was at first untitled and introduced the first edition of *Leaves of Grass* (1855). It was given its present title in 1881 and was a happy choice because it is Whitman's declaration of himself. He embraces the idea of universality and proclaims that all things are equal in value. He accepts evolution but clings also to a pantheistic belief; he applauds scientific progress but new facts are, for him, a way to further knowledge of 'Myself' (that is, knowledge of all the mysteries of existence) – 'Do I contradict myself? Very well then I contradict myself, (I am large, I contain multitudes)'.

**Song of the Broad-Axe**   Whitman originally called his poem 'Broad-Axe Song' and published it in the second edition of *Leaves of Grass* (1856). In it the poet celebrates the axe as a tool for the pioneers, in contrast to its former use as a weapon by men against men.

**Songs of Innocence and of Experience**   *Songs of Innocence* by William Blake was first published in 1789; the poems are a remarkable expression of spontaneous sympathy with all living things and a belief in the presence of universal love. The 'Introduction' is the famous song beginning 'Piping down the valleys wild', which announces the theme; among the 'happy songs' that follow are 'The Lamb', 'The Little Black Boy', 'Holy Thursday', 'A Cradle Song', 'The Divine Image', and 'A Dream'. During the years up to 1794, when Blake published another edition with additional poems 'Shewing the Contrary States of the Human Soul', the other aspects of life had produced a feeling of disenchantment, plainly discerned in the lines of the motto: 'The Good are attracted by Men's perceptions And think not for themselves; Till Experience teaches them to catch And to cage the Fairies and Elves.' The poems demonstrate the change of mood, most strikingly in 'The Tiger'; this looks at the same world of creation that produced 'The Lamb' of *Songs of Innocence*, and 'Holy Thursday'. Other

Blake's illustration for his *Songs of Innocence*, 1789. British Museum Print Room.

poems in *Songs of Experience* are 'The Clod and the Pebble', 'A Poison Tree', 'A Little Boy Lost', and 'The Chimney-Sweeper'. *Songs of Experience* was never published as a separate book; the full title of the 1794 edition is *Songs of Innocence and of Experience shewing the Two Contrary States of the Human Soul*.

**sonnet** An Italian verse form that first appeared in the 13th century, and was first imitated in English by Wyatt and Surrey. The sonnet sequence was first attempted by George Gascoigne in *A Hundredth Sundrie Flowers* (1573), and soon became a fashionable literary habit, brought to greatness in the work of Sidney, Spenser, and Shakespeare. The English sonnet owed less to the original Italian form than to the contemporary French development of it introduced by Clement Marot and used with skill and refinement by Ronsard, Joachim du Bellay, and Philippe Desportes.

A sonnet consists of 14 lines, sometimes with a pause after the octave or first 8 lines. The Elizabethan sonnets follow the rhyme scheme abab, cdcd, efef, gg.

**Sonnets, Shakespeare's** The 154 sonnets were first published in 1609. The title page read *Shakespeares Sonnets. Never before Imprinted. At London by G. Eld for T. T.* The initials belonged to the publisher Thomas Thorpe, who printed a dedication that opened 'To the onlie begetter of these insuing sonnets Mr W. H. all happinesse', which provided a happy hunting ground for hundreds of scholars in their quest for the identity of Mr W. H. The young man, 'the onlie begetter' who inspired the sonnets, is the principal subject of the sequence from the beginning to sonnet 126; a break occurs in that sonnet, which is incomplete. The page in the 1609 edition also shows definite signs of resumption in the printing with sonnet 127, which begins the group concerning the Dark Lady. She occupies the sequence 127–152 and the cycle closes with two sonnets on conventional themes. The *Sonnets* seem to tell us that Shakespeare experienced an emotional attachment to another man, that he was deeply hurt by the other's response to a third man, a rival poet (sonnets 80–86), and was in the grip of bitter jealousy by sonnet 126, which he never completed. The identities of Mr W. H., the rival poet, and the Dark Lady remain unknown, despite some weird theories and volumes of speculation.

The *Sonnets* remain, and everyone who appreciates poetry should be grateful to the inspirers, whoever they were. It is not known when they were written, only that two (138 and 144) had already been published in the unauthorized *The Passionate Pilgrime* in 1599. But their placing in the later part of the sequence is not sufficient evidence that they were lately composed. Nor can simple psychological assumptions be made; the belief that emotional immaturity suggests a date for the sonnets' composition is contradicted by the warning to the young man (126) that he too will age.

All that can be reasonably assumed from the sonnets themselves is that they were composed over a period of some years, and some of the fascination of these matchless poems lies in this. It accounts for the remarkable range of feelings expressed in them – they are first and foremost love poems, arguably the greatest ever written. They do not have to be read as a sequence: the *Sonnets* can be opened anywhere and riches will be found: they would have made Shakespeare immortal if he had not written a single play.

**Sonnets from the Portuguese** Elizabeth Barrett Browning's group of sonnets was first published in *Poems* (1850). The models used by Mrs

Browning are believed to be the sonnets of Luis de Camoens (1524–80) addressed by the Portuguese poet to a lady named Catarina; one of the poems in the same volume is 'Catarina to Camoens'. The sequence of 44 sonnets was begun in the spring of 1846, the year of the poet's marriage to Robert Browning, and was inspired by her love for him. The most famous is sonnet 43: 'How do I love thee? Let me count the ways'.

**Son of the Middle Border, A** The first part of an autobiography by Hamlin Garland. It was first published in serial form in 1914 and issued as a book in 1917.

This book tells of the emigration to the West, after the Civil War, of the author's forebears, his family background, and his childhood and young life among the frontier farmers of South Dakota. The narrative continues to the author's 33rd year. It includes his decision to go to Boston and his struggles to establish himself as an author.

The book is the first of the four which are usually regarded as Hamlin Garland's best work. The next volume, *A Daughter of the Middle Border* (1921), deals with the author's marriage and was awarded the Pulitzer Prize. *Trail-Makers of the Middle Border* (1926) tells of the author's father and his migration from Maine to Wisconsin. *Back-Trailers of the Middle Border* (1928) relates the author's career as a writer.

**Sons and Lovers** A novel by D. H. Lawrence, first published in 1913, and based on his own life up to the time of his mother's death.

The mother in the novel is Gertrude Coppard, who becomes a schoolteacher to escape her harsh and overbearing father. She is fascinated by the miner, Walter Morel, whose earthy liveliness is in complete contrast to the Puritan atmosphere of her own home. She marries him and for a time is completely happy with him; but Morel is a heavy drinker and a liar, sometimes brutal, and he resists her efforts to change him. Mrs Morel concentrates all her energies on her children, three sons and a daughter, and seeks some stimulus for her mind at the Co-operative Women's Guild. Her eldest son, William, goes to work and brings a little more money into the home; later he goes to London where he becomes interested in a shallow girl and wastes his money on her. William dies in London, of pneumonia, and Mrs Morel is stunned for a time. Then her second son, Paul, falls ill and she nurses him through it. Her ambitions for William are now concentrated on Paul, and the whole household is imbued with her aspirations; Walter Morel is scorned by his wife and children and simply excluded.

Paul Morel goes to work as a junior clerk in Nottingham. In his leisure he paints, and enjoys some success; he also falls in love with Miriam Leivers, a farmer's daughter, and Mrs Morel is not pleased about that. She asserts her claim on Paul – and he is helpless: 'I never shall meet the right woman while you live.' However, his relationship with Miriam persists to physical intimacy, which is predictably disastrous, and eventually Paul enters into a liaison with Clara Dawes, a married woman. With Clara he discovers authentic physical passion; but that becomes the whole point of their relationship, which in any case has no real future. And Paul is powerfully drawn to Clara's husband – an attraction which the author leaves in the air, though Paul goes so far as to almost invite violence from Baxter Dawes.

Paul's mother dies after a long and painful illness; he gives her an excessive dose of morphia to relieve her suffering towards the end. After her death Paul sets out to make his own life; he suggests marriage to Miriam but both of them realize that the shadow of his mother is too strong and Paul goes off alone.

**Sordello** A poem by Robert Browning, first published in 1840. The action takes place during the early 13th century against the background of the struggles for supremacy between Guelphs (adherents of the pope) and Ghibellines (supporters of the emperor). The lord of Vicenza, Eccelino, has been driven from his city. His wife Adelaide owes her life and that of their baby son to the brave Elcorte, an archer. Sordello is the son of Retrude, wife of one of Eccelino's allies, Salinguerra; she also escaped from the city but died in giving birth to him. Adelaide, who does not want a rival to her own son, passes off Sordello as the son of Elcorte and makes him her page. He becomes a poet and enjoys a triumph over the troubadour Eglamor. During a political crisis Sordello's true identity comes to light; his father Salinguerra and his love Palma (daughter of Eccelino) urge him to take the high place which is rightfully his. But Sordello is torn between his vocation as a poet and the duties of his birthright and he dies in the struggle to decide. This poem has always been one of the most difficult of Browning's to interpret. See **Browning, Robert**.

**Sorrel, Hetty** In George Eliot's *Adam Bede*, the pretty, thoughtless niece of Martin and Mrs Poyser who is loved by Adam Bede – but who spurns him because she hopes to marry Arthur Donnithorne. Seduced by the latter, she bears his child, and is condemned to death for its murder.

**Sound and the Fury, The**  A novel by William Faulkner, first published in 1929. The story is told in four parts, three through the minds of the Compson brothers; the fourth part is an objective narrative. Each part narrates the happenings of a single day, with an excursion into the past for Quentin Compson. The first part is told by Benjy Compson, an imbecile of 33. His narrative is illumined by what follows and, while Benjy's account is a writer's tour-de-force it is also questionable, since he is deaf and dumb. How would he know any of the words attributed to him? The second part is Quentin's, his last day at Harvard, and tells us of the decay of the Compson family: the posturing useless father, who has caused the mother to retreat into illness; Quentin's sister Caddy (Candace), a nymphomaniac who has been married off because she is pregnant and whom Quentin loves hopelessly; the sale of Compson land to pay for Quentin's education, and his brother Jason, who is hard-headed and dishonest. Quentin kills himself at the end of the day. The third part is Jason's. He has seen his family for what it is and it is only through him that they have a hope of survival. He is coarse, greedy, and determined. He will put Benjy into a home. The fourth part brings the Compsons into the open and the Black people of the household occupy the centre. Dilsey, the old cook, and her children are where the human values of the novel reside and the last part sets the degeneration of the White family in perspective.

**Soutar, William** 1898–1943. William Soutar was the son of a joiner and was born in Perth. During World War I he served in the navy and contracted a spinal infection, which turned him into an invalid soon after graduating from Edinburgh University in 1923. Soutar wrote most of his poetry between 1929 and his death, working on the same lines as Hugh McDiarmid – to establish a distinctly contemporary Scots poetry. His work, not well known outside Scotland, began with the publication of *Gleanings by an Undergraduate* (1923) and closed with the posthumous *The Expectant Silence* (1944). Most of his poetry is collected in the 1948 *Collected Poems*, edited and with an introductory essay by Hugh McDiarmid, and *Poems in Scots and English*, edited by W. R. Aitken (1961). An autobiographical volume, *Diaries of a Dying Man* (1954), was edited by A. Scott.

**South, Robert** 1634–1716. South was born in London, the son of a merchant, and attended Westminster School at the same time as John Dryden. He went on to Christ Church, Oxford, and was ordained in 1658. In 1660 South became chaplain to the Earl of Clarendon, who procured for him the degrees of BD and DD in 1663. South became famous for his sermons; he was Public Orator to the University of Oxford from 1660 to 1667 and used his considerable wit to excellent effect. 'Piety', he declared, 'engages no Man to be dull.' He had no patience with dissenters and was listened to with considerable pleasure by Charles II. In 1676 South went to Poland as chaplain to the English ambassador, and sent back vivid impressions of the country in a letter to his friend Edward Pococke. He became rector of Islip in Oxfordshire in 1678, and opposed the Toleration Act of William and Mary (1689), which gave freedom of worship to dissenters in an attempt to unite all Protestants against the deposed Catholic king, James II. South delivered a brilliant attack on William Sherlock in *Animadversion on Mr Sherlock's Book* (1693) and *Tritheism Charged* (1695). South's sermons were collected and published in seven volumes in 1823.

**South English Legendary, The**  A collection of the lives of the saints made at Gloucester and also called *The Southern Legend Collection*. It was written about the end of the 13th century but the character of the collection suggests that it had been in preparation for some time. Some of the contributions may have been written by Robert of Gloucester; they vary considerably in style and quality and include saints of most countries, including St Francis of Assisi and St Dominic. Particular interest, however, attaches to the native saints, such as Kenelm, Brendan, Patrick, and Thomas of Canterbury. There is a vivid account of Thomas's career and murder. The text was edited by F. J. Furnivall (1862), by C. Horstmann (1887), and by C. d'Evelyn and A. J. Mill for the Early English Text Society (1956–59).

**Southerne, Thomas** 1659–1746.  Southerne was born near Dublin, and educated at Trinity College, Cambridge. He came to London to study law at the Middle Temple in 1678; he became the friend of John Dryden and it seems, inevitably, (the inns of court being the springboard for a number of aspiring dramatists) a playwright. Southerne wrote prologues and epilogues for some of Dryden's plays and his own first work was *The Loyal Brother: or The Persian Prince* (1682) a tragedy. His next was a domestic drama, *The Disappointment: or The Mother in Fashion* (1684) and much more successful. Southerne accepted a commission in the army in the following year, but with the abdication of James II his military career came to an end (1688), and he returned to the theatre with *Sir Anthony Love: or The Rambling Lady* (1690).

Southerne wrote seven more plays, the last as late as 1726, but undistinguished except for two dramatizations of novels by Aphra Behn, *The Fatal Marriage: or The Innocent Adultery* (1694) and *Oroonoko* (1695). His plays have not been revived.

**Southern Legend Collection, The** See *South English Legendary, The*.

**Southey, Robert** 1774–1843. Southey was a linen draper's son and was born in Bristol. His father, who was not successful in business, died while Southey was a child; his mother's family took an interest in the precocious boy and an uncle, Thomas Hill, sent him to Westminster School. Southey made useful friends there and, like most of his intelligent contemporaries, was caught up in the exciting climate of ideas sparked off by the Revolution in France. He was expelled from Westminster in 1792, when he wrote a denunciation of whipping in the school magazine, and went on to Balliol College, Oxford, in the same year. He did nothing at university except become involved with Coleridge in sentimental idealism, proposing a miniature republic called a Pantisocracy. He left Oxford in 1794 without a degree and married Edith Fricker in 1795. His behaviour at Oxford had strained relations with another benefactor, his aunt Miss Tyler, in whose house he lived; his marriage provoked an irreparable breach and Miss Tyler closed her house to him. Leaving his wife in England, Southey joined his uncle, who was English chaplain in Lisbon, and during the two years he spent there became interested in the literature of Spain and Portugal.

Southey's published work by this time included part of an historic drama, *The Fall of Robespierre* (1794), of which Coleridge wrote Act 1, Southey Acts 2 and 3; an early volume of *Poems* (with Robert Lovell, 1795); and a blank-verse epic poem, *Joan of Arc* (1795). Upon his return to England he published further *Poems* (1797) and *Letters Written During a Short Residence in Spain and Portugal*. Living partly in Bristol and partly in London, he tried to settle to a career in law. He suffered total disenchantment with the ideals of the Revolution and was to admit later that he had no head for politics. He paid a second visit to Lisbon, this time with his wife, in 1800, and led an unsatisfactory literary life writing verse and reviews for papers and periodicals; he spent a year in Dublin as secretary to the Chancellor of the Irish Exchequer. Eventually, through the generosity of his friend Charles Wynn, who gave him an annuity of £160, he was able to settle in Keswick in Cumberland. Coleridge was also at Keswick (his wife, Sara, was Edith Fricker's sister) and Wordsworth at Grasmere; Southey became known as one of the 'Lake School', which in fact never actually existed. He stayed in Keswick for the rest of his life, an affectionate father with a growing family and a remarkably extensive library. He worked hard and contributed to the support of the widow and family of his friend Robert Lovell; without Southey, Coleridge and his family would often have been in severe straits. In 1807 he received a government pension of £200 a year and immediately relinquished the annuity from Charles Wynn. He became poet laureate in 1813, and Peel secured him a further pension, in 1835, of £300 a year, making his last years materially comfortable. He was an honourable man with the best intentions and high ambitions. His talents were considerable; much of his poetry and prose testifies to that and he was praised by men like Scott and Macaulay – and even by Byron and Hazlitt, who detested him. Posterity does not acknowledge the honour in which he was held in his own day but he deserves better than the dismissal so often accorded him.

Southey's output was enormous and his more popular short poems are known in every school ('After Blenheim', 'The Scholar', 'The Inchcape Rock', and 'God's judgement on a wicked Bishop', the cautionary tale of the nasty cleric who was devoured by rats) and mention must be made of some of the more ambitious poems, which are no longer read. *Thalaba* (1801), *Madoc* (1805), *The Curse of Kehama* (1810), *Roderick, the Last of the Goths* (1814), and *All for Love* (1829) are verse romances set in, respectively, the land of the Arabian Nights, Aztec Mexico, India (presumably), Visigothic Spain, and the 4th-century Christian East. In 1808 Southey became a regular contributor to *The Quarterly Review* and from an article in that journal developed his *The Life of Nelson* (1813). Another notable biography was *The Life of Wesley* (1820), and he published an edition of Cowper with a biography (1833–37). His principal historical works are *The Lives of the British Admirals* (1833–40), *The History of Brazil* (1810–19), and *The History of the Peninsular War* (1823–32). He translated *The Chronicle of the Cid* from the Spanish (1808). Of his miscellanies the best known is *The Doctor* (1834–37), which gave children 'The Story of the Three Bears'. *Wat Tyler*, a short drama in verse, was written in three days during his idealistic youth in 1794. A stolen copy was published without his permission in 1817 and its crude and ill-considered politics, expressed in bad blank verse, led to an attack on him in the House of Commons. His poem as poet laureate (he found the office onerous) on the passing of King George III (1821) provoked Byron's masterpiece of parody with the same title, *The Vision of Judgement*. Southey's letters are highly valued for his excellent prose style, which Coleridge admired without reserve, and as a mine of information concerning an important period in English literature and history. A complete definitive edition is still lacking but meanwhile there is *The Life and Correspondence of the late Robert Southey* (1850) by C. C. Southey, the poet's son, *Selections from the Letters of Southey* (1856) by J. W. Warter (the poet's son-in-law), and *The Correspondence of Southey with Caroline Bowles: to which are added Correspondence with Shelley* (1881) by E. Dowden. Caroline Bowles was the poet's second wife.

**Southwell, Robert** *c.*1561–95. The Catholic poet and martyr was a native of Norfolk. His family were staunch adherents to the old faith and Southwell was educated at Douai and Paris. His teachers were Jesuits and he entered the order himself in 1580, becoming a priest in 1584. After two years as prefect of studies at the English College in Rome he was sent on the mission to England. For six years he moved about, usually concealed by Catholic families and under a variety of names. Southwell was a successful missionary until Anne Bellamy, a Catholic who was enamoured of the infamous Richard Topcliffe (Burleigh's agent), betrayed him and her family. Southwell was held and tortured at the Gate House, Westminster; later he was imprisoned in the Tower. After three years of atrocious treatment – Topcliffe had authority to extract information from his prisoners by any means he cared to use – Southwell was hanged and quartered at Tyburn as a traitor. He was canonized in 1970.

Southwell's prose was written in the year before his betrayal and was intended for the comfort and support of the persecuted Catholics in England. His poetry, which was probably written during his years in prison, was published immediately after his death in 1595. *Saint Peters Complaint: Other Poemes* was widely read; three printings appeared in 1595 and the same was true of *Moeniae*, published in the same year. Southwell's poetry, inevitably, is small in volume and always religious in content. It is not well known, with the exception of *The Burning Babe*, which is often anthologized, but the level is high and his tone anticipates the religious poetry of the early 17th century.

**Soyinka, Wole** 1934–　. Akinwande Oluwole Soyinka is the son of a schools inspector and was born at Abeokuta in western Nigeria. He studied at the Unversity of Ibadan and completed his education in England at Leeds University. He also studied the theatre in England, a prelude to his active interest in Nigerian theatre. He returned to Nigeria in 1960 and lectured at the University of Ife until he was imprisoned during the Nigerian Civil War. He returned to the university as Research Professor of Drama and is now Professor of Comparative Literature. Soyinka founded the Orisun Theatre and has also managed a company of touring players. His published plays are *The Swamp Dwellers* (1958), *The Lion and the Jewel* and *The Invention* (1959), *A Dance of the Forests*, *The Trials of Brother Jero*, and *Camwood on the Leaves* (1960), *The Strong Breed*, *Kongi's Harvest*, and *Before the Blackout* (1964), *The Road* (1965), *Madmen and Specialists* (1970), *Death and the King's Horsemen* (1976), and a version of *The Bacchae* of Euripides (1973), which was produced at the National Theatre, London. Wole Soyinka is the author of two novels, the satirical *The Interpreters* (1965) and *Season of Anomy* (1973), a grim allegory of the outlook for Nigeria after the Civil War. His own experiences are related in *The Man Died: Prison Memoirs* (1972) and his poems are published in *Idanre* (1967), *A Shuttle in the Crypt* (1972), and *Ogun Abibiman* (1977). Other books are a translation into English of D. A. Fagunwa's *Forest of a Thousand Daemons* (1968), *Poems of Black Africa* (1973, called *An Anthology of Black Verse* in the USA), and *Myth, Literature and the African World* (1976).

**Spanish Curate, The** A comedy of intrigue by John Fletcher and, probably, Philip Massinger, first produced in 1622 and first published in 1718. The play's title comes from the subplot in which a rich young man, Leandro, seeks an intrigue with Amaranta, the beautiful wife of the jealous lawyer Bartolus. To further his designs he plays on the cupidity of the priest and his sexton and, with their help, on the cupidity of Bartolus. The main plot follows the machinations of Violante, mistress of Don Henrique, and how her schemes lead to her own downfall – Don Henrique is reconciled to his wife Jacinta; and Violante ends up in a nunnery.

**Spanish Gypsy, The** See **Eliot, George.**

**Spanish Tragedy, The: or Hieronimo is Mad Againe.** A tragedy in blank verse by Thomas Kyd, produced *c.*1589 and first published in 1592. It was the first play to use revenge as the

The title page illustration of an edition of Kyd's *The Spanish Tragedy* published in 1633. The play was first acted *c.* 1589 and first published in 1592.

motive for the plot and was to have a number of successors; the most celebrated is Shakespeare's *Hamlet*.

Hieronimo is a marshal of Spain at the time of his country's victory over Portugal in 1580. His son Horatio and his nephew Lorenzo captured Balthazar, son of the Viceroy of Portugal, during the war and now Balthazar is courting Bel-imperia, Lorenzo's sister. Lorenzo favours the match and so does the King of Spain for political reasons but Bel-imperia loves Horatio. Lorenzo and Balthazar surprise the two lovers in Hieronimo's arbour at night: they murder Horatio and hang his body to a tree. Bel-imperia escapes but Hieronimo, hearing the disturbance, finds his son's body and is beside himself with grief. He ascertains the murderers' identities and plots their destruction with Bel-imperia. To accomplish this he engages them to take part in a play, with himself and Bel-imperia, to be acted before the court. In the play within a play revenge on Lorenzo and Balthazar is carried out successfully; Hieronimo and Bel-imperia take their own lives when their purpose is fulfilled.

The resemblance of *Hamlet*, in more than one respect, to Kyd's tragedy is obvious. The play was revised in different productions, probably by Ben Jonson, though Charles Lamb detected the hand of John Webster. The play, thought to be unacceptable to modern audiences in its horrors and excesses, was immensely important in the development of English drama and was successfully revived in 1982. The extravagant style did not prevent audiences of a later day enjoying it but its success lay much more in the author's grasp of what was dramatic; he drove the plot forward relentlessly and in Hieronimo created a new kind of hero, one who lacks certainty in his motives and communes with himself when examining his doubts.

**Spark, Muriel (Sarah)** 1918– . Muriel Sarah Camberg was born in Edinburgh, where she was educated at Gillespie's School for Girls. She married S. O. Spark in 1938 and during World War II worked in political intelligence at the Foreign Office. Muriel Spark became editor of *Poetry Review* in 1947 and published a volume of poems, *The Fanfarlo*, in 1952. After several books of literary criticism, some of them in collaboration with Derek Stanford, she published her first novel, *The Comforters* (1957). With *Memento Mori* (1959) and *The Ballad of Peckham Rye* (1960) she made a name as a satirical novelist: her books adapted neatly for radio and this helped to make her well known. Other novels by Muriel Spark are *The Bachelors* (1960), *The Prime of Miss Jean Brodie* (1962), *The Girls of Slender Means* (1963), *The Mandelbaum Gate* (1965), *The Public Image* (1968), *The Driver's Seat* (1970), *Not to Disturb* (1971), *The Hothouse by the East River* (1972), *The Abbess of Crewe* (1974), *The Takeover* (1976), *Territorial Rights* (1979), and *Loitering with Intent* (1981). Her short stories and poems are collected in *Collected Stories I* and *Collected Poems I* (both 1967).

**Spasmodic School** The description given by William Aytoun to the work of Philip James Bailey, Sydney Dobell, and Alexander Smith: poets whose work seemed to him to be executed in verbal spasms over which they had no control. The resulting poems were in fact concerned with challenging themes to which their talents were unequal. Aytoun parodied their 'spasms' in his mock tragedy *Firmilian* (1854).

*Specimens of English Dramatic Poets* See **Lamb, Charles**.

*Spectator, The* The periodical founded by Richard Steele and Joseph Addison which they conducted jointly from 1 March 1711 to 6 December 1712, a total of 555 issues. Addison revived *The Spectator* in 1714 for a further 80 issues. Unlike *The Tatler* it appeared daily; it was chiefly the work of Addison and Steele but among other contributors were Alexander Pope, Thomas Tickell, Ambrose Philips, Laurence Eusden, and Eustace Budgell.

The periodical was presented as the work of a small club of representative gentlemen from different walks of life: Sir Andrew Freeport, commerce; Captain Sentry, the army; Will Honeycombe, the townsman; and a lawyer and a clergyman, both anonymous. Sir Roger de Coverley was the country gentleman.

Addison said '. . . I shall be ambitious to have it said of me, that I have brought Philosophy out of Closets and Libraries, Schools and Colleges, to dwell in Clubs and Assemblies, at Tea-Tables, and in Coffee-Houses.' It is acknowledged that he raised the intellectual level of the rising middle class in the early 18th century. He never exercised the minds of his readers to any great degree but he had a remarkable talent for putting the best ideas of his time within their reach. 'Mr Spectator' was the detached observer, as Addison stated, and did not meddle 'with any practical part in life'. In Bonamy Dobrée's words: 'He is, therefore, always a little aloof; his universal benevolence may seem to us priggish, but for his time this was a merit. He is the perfect representative of what the age was trying to be, the man who more than anybody else helped society to go the way it wanted to go . . . ' (*Oxford History of English Literature*, Vol. VII). See also **Addison, Joseph** and **Steele, Richard**.

**Speculum Meditantis**  See **Gower, John**.

**Speed, John** *c*.1552–1629. Like his near contemporary and fellow-historian John Stow, Speed was a tailor by trade but he found a post in the custom house in 1598. In 1607 he began to work on the maps of England for which he is famous. These were of English counties and, with the encouragement of William Camden, Sir Robert Bruce Cotton, and others, he wrote a history to supplement his atlas. The antiquarian and topographical atlas was called *The Theatre of the Empire of Great Britaine* and was published in 1611; the history, *The History of Great Britaine*, was published in the same year. The history is recognized as being conscientious and painstakingly researched but Speed's maps have more lasting value as contemporary documents.

A modern edition, *John Speed's England. A Coloured Facsimile of the Maps and Text*, was prepared by J. Arlott and published in four parts (1953–54). A selection by E. G. B. Taylor of 40 plates was published by Penguin Books in 1951.

**Speke, John Hanning** 1827–64. Speke was Richard Burton's companion on two expeditions to explore East Africa. They went to Somaliland (1854) and to the interior (1857–59); they discovered Lake Tanganyika in 1858. Speke continued after Burton's physical condition obliged him to withdraw to Tabora, and discovered Lake Victoria. His intuitive assumption that this was the source of the Nile had no supporting evidence but he was proved right. Speke's *Journal of the Discovery of the Source of the Nile* was published in 1863.

**Spencer, Herbert** 1820–1903. Spencer was born in Derby, the son of Methodist parents. He received his early education from an uncle who was a clergyman and he was later trained as a railway engineer. He became more interested in writing and philosophy and gave up engineering completely to become a journalist. Spencer became a subeditor on *The Economist* in 1848 and made the acquaintance of Thomas Huxley and George Eliot. He published *Social Statics: or The Conditions Essential to Human Happiness Specified*, the first statement of his evolutionary philosophy, in 1851. This was earlier than Darwin, and Spencer was to apply the same evolutionary principle to all areas of human development. Later he was closely associated with Huxley in the controversy that led to the acceptance of Darwin's conclusions.

*A New Theory of Population* (1852), *Over-legislation* (1854), *Railway Morals and Railway Policy* and *The Principles of Psychology* (1855), *Essays Political, Scientific, and Speculative* (first series, 1858), and *Education: Intellectual, Moral and Physical* (1861) led the way to his great ten-volume *A System of Synthetic Philosophy*, in which all phenomena are interpreted according to the principle of evolutionary progress. The work occupied Spencer from 1860 to 1896 and consists of *First Principles of a New System of Philosophy* (Vol. 1, 1862), *The Principles of Biology* (Vols. 2 and 3, 1864–67), *The Principles of Psychology* (Vols. 4 and 5, a revision of the 1855 book, 1870–72), *The Principles of Sociology* (Vols. 6, 7, and 8, 1876–96), and *The Principles of Ethics* (Vols. 9 and 10, 1879–93). Separate parts were frequently reprinted and translated into many European languages, *The Data of Ethics*, from the first volumes of *Sociology*, most frequently of all. Other works are *The Classification of the Sciences* (1864), *The Man versus The State* (1884), and *The Factors of Organic Evolution* (1887). *Essays Scientific, Political and Speculative, Second Series* was published in 1863, and Spencer's *Autobiography* in 1904, the year after his death.

As an educational theorist Spencer was particularly influential with his *Education: Intellectual, Moral and Physical*. He argued that the most useful education would have science as its principal instrument, thereby preparing children best for the world. He rejected the widely held assumption that the teaching of the classics provided an intellectual discipline and that art and the humanities were the proper basis for education.

**Spender, Stephen (Harold)** 1909– . Stephen Spender was born in London and was the son of the political journalist and biographer Harold Spender. He was educated at University College School, London, and University College, Oxford. Between the two World Wars he travelled much on the Continent and lived at intervals in Germany, his mother's country. In the 1930s he was one of a group of left-wing poets and wrote *Forwards from Liberalism* (1937) for the Left Book Club. However, like many writers of the time, he might be said to have been turned back by the unacceptable manifestation of the left-wing power in its ascendancy.

Spender's first published poetry was written when he was 18: *Nine Experiments* (1928). He made his reputation with *Poems* (1933); *Collected Poems 1928–1953* was published in 1955, since when he has published no new poetry. A poetic tragedy, *Trial of a Judge*, was produced and published in 1938. Spender took part in presenting translations of the following: Federico Garcia Lorca, with J. L. Gili (*Poems*, 1939); Rainer Maria Rilke (*Duino Elegies*, with J. B. Leishman, 1939, and *The Life of the Virgin Mary*, 1951); Paul Eluard, with Frances Cornford (*Le dur desir de durer*, 1950); Friedrich von Schiller (*Mary Stuart*, 1959); Georg Buchner (*Danton's Death*, with G. Rees, 1939); Ernst Toller (*Pastor Hall*, with H. Hunt, 1939); and Frank Wedekind (*Five Tragedies of Sex*, with F. Fawcett, 1952). Spender is the author of short stories – *The Burning Cactus* (1936), a novel – *The Backward Son* (1940), and two short novels – *Engaged in Writing* and *The Fool and the Princess* (1958). His autobiography *World within World* (1951) is a rewarding book for those who wish to know more about the literary and intellectual world of the 1930s.

Stephen Spender was coeditor with Cyril Connolly of *Horizon* from 1940 to 1941 and coeditor with Irving Kristol of *Encounter* from 1953 to 1965. He withdrew from the editorial board of the latter with Frank Kermode in 1967 upon the discovery that part of the original funds to launch the magazine had come from the CIA, behind the cover of 'The Congress of Cultural Freedom'.

**Spenser, Edmund** 1552–99. Edmund Spenser's father was John Spenser, a journeyman in the art of clothmaking, who was (his son maintained) connected with the noble family of Spencer in Northampton. Edmund attended the Merchant Taylors' School from 1561 to 1569. The headmaster was Richard Mulcaster, a teacher of formidable quality and a man with a passionate devotion to the possibilities of English as a literary language; the schoolboy Spenser was already practising the poet's craft as Mulcaster's

Spenser. Engraving by J. Thomson from an original painting.

pupil. In 1569 Spenser went to Pembroke Hall, Cambridge, as a sizar, and during his second year became friends with Gabriel Harvey, newly elected a fellow. The friendship endured though Harvey had no real sympathy with Spenser's work and sometimes ridiculed it.

Spenser, in his first year at Cambridge, contributed epigrams and sonnets, translated from French and Italian, to S. John van-der Noodt's anthology *A Theatre Wherein be Represented as wel the Miseries and Calamities that Follow the Voluptuous Worldlings*. He took his BA in 1573 and his MA in 1576, and two years later became secretary to the Bishop of Rochester, John Young. A year after that (1579) he found through Harvey's influence a place in the Earl of Leicester's household and became friends with Philip Sydney, who was Leicester's nephew. In the same year he married Machabyas Child and completed **The Shepheardes Calender**, which he dedicated to his new friend.

Sidney was full of praise, though he had reservations about his friend's 'rusticke' language, which was a criticism made by many scholars. But Spenser's gifts were plain; a poet of remarkable quality, a man who could make music with words. In 1579 Spenser, Sidney, Edward Dyer, Gabriel Harvey, Fulke Greville, and other friends formed a literary club called the Areopagus. Spenser completed some of his shorter poems in 1579–80; these were not published until some years later. He began work on *The Faerie Queene* and became secretary to Lord Grey de Wilton, who became Lord Deputy of Ireland. Spenser arrived in Dublin in August 1580 and lived in Ireland for 18 years, successively at Enniscorthy, Dublin, Kildare, and at Kilcolman Castle in the county of Cork, which he leased in 1586.

The first three books of *The Faerie Queene* were completed at Kilcolman and published in 1590 during a visit to England. Spenser had meanwhile become friends with Ralegh, his neighbour in Ireland, to whom he addressed a prefatory letter declaring his intention of singing the praises of England and Elizabeth. The work was designed to be in 12 books. In the meantime his friend Sidney had died of wounds sustained at the Battle of Zutphen in 1586. Spenser's *Astrophel* is a pastoral elegy in Sidney's memory.

Spenser had gone to England under Ralegh's wing and had hoped that *The Faerie Queene*, if favourably received, might help him gain a higher post. The poem did succeed and Elizabeth I expressed her pleasure (she awarded him a pension), but the poet did not realize his hopes and returned to Ireland and Kilcolman Castle. While in England his shorter works were collected into a volume by the printer of the first three books of *The Faerie Queene*, W. Ponsonbie, and called *Complaints, Containing Sundrie small Poemes of the World's Vanitie* (1591). This includes 'The Ruines of Time', 'The Teares of the Muses', and 'Mother Hubberd's Tale'. In the same year Spenser published *Daphnaida: an Elegie upon the Death of the Noble and Vertuous* [Lady] *Douglas Howard*, a poem in Chaucerian style that is not regarded as a success. Back in Ireland, he dedicated to Ralegh in 1591 the poem that recounts his visit to London, his hopes, and his reflections upon returning, **Colin Clouts Come Home Againe** (1595). Spenser returned to pastoral in this autobiographical poem; meanwhile his work in romance (*The Faerie Queene*) continued and in 1592 came a work that is often attributed to him, a pseudo–Platonist dialogue called *Axiochus*. The author is given as 'Edw. Spenser' but the attribution is denied by many scholars on stylistic grounds.

In 1594 Spenser married for the second time. Elizabeth Boyle was an Irish lady and is regarded as the inspiration of the sonnet sequence **Amoretti** (1595), and the famous marriage ode, **Epithalamion** (1595) – Spenser's finest lyrical achievement. Three more books of *The Faerie Queene* appeared in the edition of 1596, giving us books I–VI; no more appeared during Spenser's lifetime. **Prothalamion** (1596) was a betrothal ode, written for the double plighting of Elizabeth and Katherine Somerset, the daughters of the Earl of Worcester, and *Fowre Hymnes* (Four Hymns, 1596), are meditations on love. Spenser had visited London again in 1595 and this time he stayed for two years – but to no better purpose than before. He was back at Kilcolman in 1597 and became Sherriff of Cork in 1598. In October of the same year Ireland rebelled, under the leadership of Tyrone, and Kilcolman Castle was attacked and burned. Spenser and his family succeeded in reaching safety in the city of Cork and were in London at the end of the year. Spenser died a year later, he and his family in reduced circumstances.

Spenser was buried in Westminster Abbey, the expenses borne by the Earl of Essex. Elizabeth I ordered a monument to him, but one was not executed in her lifetime. The Countess of Dorset provided one in 1620 that bore incorrect dates and the inscription 'The Prince of Poets in His Tyme'. The monument was restored in 1778 and the dates corrected and it can be seen in the Abbey. It is likely that part of the later books of *The Faerie Queene* were lost in the burning of Kilcolman. All that survives are the 'Two Cantos of Mutabilitie', which are part of the 'Legend of Constancie', and these were printed in the posthumous edition of *The Faerie Queene* of 1609. Also published after his death was the prose dialogue *A Veue of the Present State of Ireland*. This was written in 1596 and entered at Stationers Hall in 1598, but it was not published until 1633, by Sir James Ware in Dublin.

Spenser's character is hard to discern but the occasional reflections of his life that occur in his poetry, in *Colin Clouts Come Home Againe*, and in the confusions of purpose in the design of *The Faerie Queene*, suggest that he might have left us richer if he had been less concerned with preferment at court. C. S. Lewis saw a distinct falling-off in his poetry during his first visit to London and it is hardly possible to disagree with him that in *Colin Clouts Come Home Again* 'we find Spenser restored to poetical health'. The poet was indeed a disappointed man at the end of his life, though one could reasonably assume that he loved his Elizabeth and was pleased with the favour shown by 'that sacred Saint my soveraigne Queene'. But he aspired to more; since he was a young man he had moved near the world of the illustrious and Ralegh and Essex had become his friends. The court of his sovereign queen, no matter what reservations are expressed in *Colin Clouts* and 'Mother Hubberd's Tale', was a longed-for goal that Spenser never attained.

Spenser is commonly acknowledged the first major poet in English since the death of Chaucer. The teaching of Richard Mulcaster and his advocacy of his own language was thoroughly learned by his pupil, Spenser, who proceeded to 'garnish it with eloquence and . . . enrich it with learning'. He used classical shapes but the music in which he clothed them was English, used as it had not been used for 200 years. The richness of Elizabethan poetry began with Spenser. It is in this that his greatness lies.

The prose dialogue, *A Veue of the Present State of Ireland* is a curiosity, expressing a 'veue' that was unhappily shared by many Englishmen and resisted by the Irish without cease. The estate of Kilcolman, 3000 acres, provided Spenser with a comfortable living, after it was taken from its rightful owner, and the poet's view is that of the conqueror's and therefore, in that stage of history, fair enough. Spenser was one of many Englishmen getting all they could out of what they regarded as a colony, which resulted in centuries of tragic strife.

A recommended edition of Spenser's complete poetical works is the one-volume edition in the Oxford Standard Authors, edited by J. C. Smith and E. de Selincourt.

**Spenserian stanza** Spenser invented his own stanza for *The Faerie Queene*. It consists of eight lines of five feet, followed by a ninth of six. The rhyme scheme runs abab, bcbc, c.

*Spirit of the Age, The:* or *Contemporary Portraits.* See **Hazlitt, William.**

*Spiritual Quixote, The,* or the Summer's Ramble of Mr Geoffry Wildgoose: a Comic Romance. A novel by Richard Graves, first published in 1772.

Geoffry Wildgoose, a young man of property in the Cotswolds, is enthusiastic about Methodism. He sets forth with the village cobbler, Jerry Tugwell, on a summer tour to preach the gospel and meet his hero, George Whitefield. On this Quixotic base, with Jerry Tugwell as his Sancho Panza, Geoffry Wildgoose encounters life on the road in 18th-century England. The Methodists generally and Whitefield in particular are satirized (Graves was at Pembroke College with Whitefield): Graves was perpetually irritated by the conviction that the Methodists were showing the parish clergy a better way of doing their job. He also makes a great deal of the collision of Whitefield and John Wesley. The picture of English life is valuable: inns, roads, the interest in open-air preachers, are carefully described. Graves writes extremely well and rarely raises his voice.

A modern edition of *The Spiritual Quixote* is published in the Oxford English Novels series, edited by Clarence Tracy (1967).

*Spoils of Poynton, The* A short novel by Henry James, first published in the *Atlantic Monthly*, from April to June 1896, under the title of *The Old Things*. As *The Spoils of Poynton* it was first published in 1897.

Poynton Park is the home of Owen Gereth; his mother, an antiques connoisseur, has arranged it with faultless taste and filled it with fine furniture and *objets d'art*. Mrs Gereth visits the home of the Brigstock family, Waterbath, because Owen is interested in Mona Brigstock, the eldest daughter. She is appalled by the tastelessness of Waterbath and the Brigstock family: even the wallpaper in her bedroom keeps her awake at night. She finds a kindred spirit in Fleda Vetch, a girl also visiting the Brigstocks; she takes her to Poynton Park and is gratified when Fleda is moved by its beauty. Mrs Gereth is hopeful that Owen will respond to the girl; he does not – but she falls in love with him.

Owen decides to marry Mona Brigstock and it is soon clear what Mrs Gereth thinks of his choice. Owen enlists Fleda's aid in persading his mother to leave the house and Mrs Gereth moves to the dower house; but she takes the most prized pieces with her. Owen, who has grown closer to Fleda, is threatened with rejection by Mona if the 'spoils' are not returned by Mrs Gereth. Mrs Gereth, in spite of Fleda's urging, will not budge. Fleda is becoming aware that Owen is more and more attracted to her; she is also aware that she could encourage Mrs Gereth to keep the spoils and thereby see Mona carry out her threat to break off the engagement. But she will not manoeuvre Owen and waits for him to declare himself. He does, eventually, but she will not marry him until he frees himself from Mona.

At the dower house, Fleda learns that Mrs Gereth is certain now that Owen will not marry Mona; she has gone so far as to return the spoils to Poynton, happy that one day Fleda will have them to care for. But Owen is no match for Mona; she has learned that the spoils have been returned to Poynton and when Owen arrives at Waterbath to break the engagement she has him tied, thrown, trussed, and married to her in no time. Mrs Gereth and Fleda Vetch have lost everything. From Owen Gereth, travelling abroad with Mona, there comes a letter to Fleda one day asking her to choose from Poynton for herself whatever object she would most like to possess. Fleda is a long time making up her mind to go to Poynton Park but when she does go she arrives just as the house and its contents go up in flames.

There is no explanation offered to the reader about the fire at Poynton; it simply happens, as such things do. The stationmaster offers Fleda more than one possible explanation for the accident, if accident it is. Its cause does not matter, anyway, but there is a pleasant satisfaction at the close of this delightful book, in the thought that the coarse and greedy Mona will be deprived of the great house and the contents that, to her, are objects of value; they mean nothing else. Mrs Gereth's possessiveness is almost as bad; saving her the grace that the beautiful things exist at Poynton only because of her faultless taste she is not a very nice woman and her regard for Fleda (where, one may pause to wonder, did James ever find such a name?) arises directly from the fact that they have similar taste. Fleda is certainly a nicer girl than Mona but that would be plain to anyone. The author, with his unrivalled subtlety, suggests that what happens to the Gereths, mother and son, does rather serve them right. Owen is both spineless and foolish; a woman like Mona would be able to bring him down with little trouble while a woman like Fleda, unfortunately, would be quite likely to fall in love with such a man. Fleda, in fact, proves to be a bad choice of ally for Mrs Gereth; her personal standards are too high for her ever to engage in such an affair as the spoils of Poynton with any hope of success.

*Sponge's Sporting Tour, Mr*   See **Surtees, R(obert) S(mith).**

*Spoon River Anthology*   See **Masters, Edgar Lee**.

**Spottiswoode, John** 1565–1639.   At the beginning of his career Archbishop Spottiswoode was a firm Presbyterian but the growing contention between king and kirk changed his attitude and his sympathies. He came to England with King James I, who made him Archbishop of Edinburgh (1603) and Archbishop of St Andrews (1615). He became a firm opponent of the Presbyterians though he was not always in agreement with the policies of Charles I. In literature he is remembered for his *The History of the Church of Scotland* taken to the year 1625 and giving an account which is fair to both sides. It was posthumously published (1665).

*Spy, The, A Tale of the Neutral Ground*.   A novel by James Fenimore Cooper, first published in 1821. It was dramatized by C. P. Clinch in 1822 and concerns the adventures of Harvey Birch, a spy who works for George Washington during the years of the Revolution and the War for In-

dependence. The 'neutral ground' is Westchester county in New York state and the story is full of incident, complicated by the fact that Birch poses as a spy on the loyalist side and by Washington's appearances in disguise as 'Mr Harper'. *The Spy* was Cooper's first successful novel.

**Squeers, Wackford**   The vicious headmaster of Dotheboys Hall in Dickens's *Nicholas Nickleby*. His family are as evil as he is and treat the boys as badly. Squeers is thrashed by Nicholas for his treatment of Smike.

*Squire of Low Degree, The*   A Middle English verse romance of the early 14th century. (See **metrical romances**.) A squire of modest birth falls in love with the King of Hungary's daughter. He tells the princess of his love and she promises to marry him when he becomes a knight of renown. Their meeting is witnessed by a villainous steward, and the squire kills him. He is thrown into prison and the princess is inconsolable. The king relents and releases the squire, who sets forth on knightly adventures. He achieves renown and at the end of the tale returns to claim his princess. *The Squire of Low Degree* (*The Squyr of Lowe Degre*) was edited by W. C. Hazlitt (1866), W. E. Mead (Boston, 1904), and J. D. McCallum in *English Literature: the Beginnings to 1500* (New York, 1929).

*Squire's Tale, The*   See **Canterbury Tales, The**.

**Stanley, Sir Henry Morton** 1841–1904.   Stanley's real name was John Rowlands. He was born in Denbigh in Wales and was put into a workhouse at the age of six when his father, a farmer's son, died of drink. He stayed there until he was 15, when he signed on as a cabin boy in Liverpool and sailed to New Orleans, where he jumped ship. He was fortunate in encountering an English cotton merchant named Henry Stanley, who adopted the tough, enterprising boy. Rowlands took the name Henry Stanley but quarrelled with his benefactor within a year. (The 'Morton' was his own invention, conforming to the American fad for three names.) After numerous adventures, and fortunate in the forbearance and generosity of Stanley, he eventually found his true metier as a journalist.

Stanley's assignment by James Gordon Bennett Jnr, the proprietor of the *New York Herald*, to find the Scottish missionary and explorer David Livingstone, was successfully accomplished and made Stanley world-famous. His own remarkable career as an explorer included the tracing of the great Congo (Zaïre) River from its source to its mouth, thereby throwing light on huge areas of the Dark Continent. Some of his experiences can be read in *How I found Livingstone* (1872), *Through the Dark Continent* (1878), and *In Darkest Africa* (1890). Stanley eventually resumed English citizenship and was knighted in 1899.

**Stanley, Thomas** 1625–78. A descendant of the Stanley family who rose to prominence with the accession of Henry VII, Thomas Stanley wrote a *History of Philosophy* (1655–62), which was an early and commendable effort at popularization. He prepared an edition of Aeschylus (1663) and translated the work of Anacreon, Moschus, Bion, and other classical poets. Stanley was also the author of some little-known original poems, which were collected in 1650.

**Stant, Charlotte** The beautiful and penniless woman who becomes the wife of the rich Adam Verver in *The Golden Bowl*, by Henry James. She was, years before, in love with the impoverished Italian prince, Amerigo, who is now the husband of Maggie, Adam Verver's daughter. She and Amerigo embark on an affair during the course of the story.

**Starbuck** The first mate on board the *Pequod* in Herman Melville's *Moby-Dick*. His level-headed humanity proves powerless against Captain Ahab's mania for revenge.

**Steele, Richard** 1672–1729. The founder of *The Tatler* was born in Dublin and went to Charterhouse School before going to Merton College, Oxford. His schoolfellow at Charterhouse was Joseph Addison, his exact contemporary, who was later to be his collaborator. After Oxford, Steele became a cadet in the Life Guards; he wrote a poem on the funeral of Queen Mary in 1694, which he dedicated to Lord Cutts, colonel of the Coldstream Guards. The colonel made Steele his secretary and obtained the rank of captain for him.

Steele, who was something of a rake, seems to have had a strong sense of guilt about his dissipations and was bent on turning others from the downward path. His *The Christian Hero: an Argument proving that no Principles but those of Religion are sufficient to make a great man* (1701) needs no explanation beyond its title; Steele's admirers insist that the author knew very well where the right path lay, despite his failure to stay on it himself. Certainly he is one of the representative voices of the more restrained post-Restoration mood. His next work was for the theatre: *The Funeral, or Grief à-la-Mode*, a comedy, was produced at Drury Lane in 1701 and demonstrated the triumph of virtue and the downfall of a greedy widow. Two more comedies followed, *The Lying Lover* (1703) and *The Tender Husband* (1705), but in spite of being a successful playwright Steele had not found his true metier. In 1706 he accepted the appointment of gentleman waiter to Prince George, Queen Anne's consort, and became gazetteer, an official government writer, in 1707. Finding his inspiration in the lively conversations of the coffee-house gatherings that had become fashionable in London by then, Steele founded *The Tatler* in 1709 with help from Swift and with a pseudonym, 'Isaac Bickerstaff', borrowed from him to use as editor. One of his contributors was Joseph Addison and the thrice-weekly periodical was a considerable success until 1712, when Steele probably ran out of stamina. He had, nevertheless, founded another periodical with Addison in 1711, called *The Spectator*, which enjoyed 22 months of lively success – but it was more Addison's paper than Steele's.

Steele, a Whig in politics, lost his post as gazetteer when the Tories attained power in 1710 and held no government appointment again until the accession of George I in 1714. Meanwhile, he continued his career as a journalist: *The Spectator* was followed by *The Guardian*, to which Pope, Berkeley, and Addison contributed, and *The Englishman* (1713–14). He also became MP for Stockbridge in 1713 but his pamphlet *The Crisis*, in favour of the Hanoverian succession, brought a counterblast from Swift and led to Steele's expulsion from the Commons on 18 March 1714.

The Hanoverian succession in the same year, of course, restored his fortunes. He became supervisor of the Theatre Royal, Drury Lane, a Justice of the Peace, Governor of the Royal Stables, and Deputy Lieutenant of Middlesex; he was knighted in 1715. He was the editor of *Theatre* and *The Plebeian*, provoking in the latter a controversy over Sunderland's Peerage Bill that led to a break with Addison, who opposed him in his own paper, the *Old Whig*. Steele was one of those who warned against the investment mania that led to the South Sea Bubble. His last work is often called his best; this was a comedy, *The Conscious Lovers* (1722), based on the *Andria* of Terence, and held the stage for a number of years. Financial difficulties forced Steele to leave London in 1724 and he died at Carmarthen, in Wales, soon after a stroke.

Steele, like his precursor Defoe, wrote most of his most famous periodical himself. The period was a very disturbed one, with political excitement running at a very high pitch between Whig and Tory, the enormously expensive cost of the wars in Europe lying heavily on the nation in the aftermath of Marlborough's victories, and the question of the succession making everyone nervous at the possibility of another Catholic Stuart laying claim to the throne. At such a time good journals reached an eager public and Steele and Addison were the right men for their times. Steele's journalism was a commentary on civilized life and he touched on most aspects of it; he also introduced something no one had considered hitherto – a consideration of women's life. He invented a woman editor called Jenny Distaff and through 'her' he brought a connection with family life into his periodical. In his 'Isaac Bickerstaff' character as editor Steele revealed a genius for journalism, appealing to a very wide readership and covering every subject (including the news of the day) that aroused his apparently inexhaustible curiosity. *The Tatler* of Richard Steele is almost impossible to read now but in his day it was exactly what was required. It was for the literate enquiring public, not for any literary or political clique. With Defoe, Steele, and Addison journalism in England was off to a flying start.

**Steerforth, James** In Dickens's *David Copperfield*, the handsome and charming seducer whom David idolizes after being his friend at Creakle's school. Shallow and selfish, he leads Emily astray, and when he tires of her, brutally suggests that she marry his servant. He dies in a shipwreck off Yarmouth.

**Stein, Gertrude** 1874–1946. Gertrude Stein was born in Allegheny (now part of Pittsburgh), Pennsylvania. She was educated at Radcliffe College, where she was a student of William James, and began premedical studies at Johns Hopkins University, Baltimore. She relinquished these in 1902 and moved to Europe; from 1903 until she died she made her home in Paris, from 1907 with her friend and companion Alice B. Toklas. In Paris Gertrude Stein became interested in modern art movements, and championed the then unknown Picasso, Braque, Matisse, and Juan Gris. Her salon became famous and by the 1920s it was a meeting place of European culture and numbers of expatriate Americans – the 'lost generation' as she called them: Sherwood Anderson brought Ernest Hemingway who brought Scott Fitzgerald and so on.

In literature Gertrude Stein is important as an innovator. Her work is little read now but her early *Three Lives*, stories which presented the characters of three women through their thoughts, demonstrates the effort towards fundamental clarity which marks her work at that stage. It was written in 1909. The fiction writers

of the 1920s were strongly influenced by Gertrude Stein, but the extension of her ideas led eventually to a blind alley of verbal eccentricity which she painstakingly reproduced on paper. Among her difficult works are the enormous fictional history *The Making of Americans* (1925) and the Cubist verse portraits, *Tender Buttons* (1914). More approachable are the chapter of autobiography, *The Autobiography of Alice B. Toklas* (1933), a rewarding glimpse of her Paris life; *Everybody's Autobiography* (1938), further reminiscences of Paris and of her lecture tour in America, and *Paris France* (1940).

During World War II Gertrude and Alice remained in France, and she published *Wars I Have Seen* in 1945, a book of droll personal observations which did not suit the climate of the time but which should be reissued. The arrival of American soldiers in Paris resulted in the flat in the Rue Christine becoming a place of pilgrimage. *Brewsie and Willie* (1946), her last book, tells of the lives of American soldiers in France during and immediately following World War II.

Alice B. Toklas, who was born in San Francisco and who first met Gertrude Stein in Paris in 1907, published her autobiography, *What is Remembered*, in 1963.

**Steinbeck, John** 1902–68. John Steinbeck was born in Salinas, California, and attended Stanford University to study marine biology. He did not take a degree, and worked at various jobs before deciding to become a writer. His career began with a romantic novel about the buccaneer Sir Henry Morgan called *Cup of Gold* (1929). His next book was a collection of stories portraying the people in a farm community, *The Pastures of Heaven* (1932), and his second novel was *To a God Unknown* (1933), about a California farmer whose religion is a pagan belief in fertility and who sacrifices himself on a primitive altar to bring an end to drought. *Tortilla Flat* (1935) brought Steinbeck to prominence, with its well-realized picture of life among the *paisanos* in the 'uphill district above the town of Monterey'. The tone of his work changed with *In Dubious Battle* (1936), a powerful novel about a strike among migratory workers in the California fruit orchards, and *Of Mice and Men* (1937), the story of two itinerant farm workers who yearn for some sort of home. Steinbeck became the novelist of the rural proletariat, which in the grim years of the 1930s often existed just on the edge of survival.

*The Long Valley* (1938), 13 stories set in Salinas Valley, was followed by **The Grapes of Wrath**

(1939), his finest work and the high point of his career. This novel of a family fleeing from the dust bowl of Oklahoma to what they hope will be a better life in California was awarded the Pulitzer Prize in 1940 and became one of the classic American films. Steinbeck's career continued with *The Moon is Down* (1942), a short novel about Norwegian resistance to the Nazi occupation; *Cannery Row* (1944), in which he returned to the *paisanos* of Monterey; and *The Wayward Bus* (1947), in which the passengers on a stranded bus in California become a microcosm of contemporary American frustrations.

Steinbeck's nonfiction includes *Bombs Away: The Story of a Bomber Team* (1942); *The Log of the Sea of Cortez* (1951); the selection of his despatches as a war correspondent, *Once There Was a War* (1958); and his book about rediscovering his own country, *Travels with Charley* (1962). Among other novels were *The Pearl* (1947), *East of Eden* (1952), *Sweet Thursday* (1954), and *The Winter of Our Discontent* (1961). John Steinbeck was awarded the Nobel Prize in 1962.

**Stephen, Sir Leslie** 1832–1904. The son of Sir James Stephen, Under-Secretary of State for the Colonies, Leslie Stephen was born in London. His older brother was Sir James Fitzjames Stephen, a distinguished jurist. Stephen's family were members of the group of practical and benevolent Christians known as the Clapham Sect, one of whom was William Wilberforce; Sir James Stephen was himself actively involved in the abolition of slavery. Leslie Stephen was educated at Eton College, King's College, London, and Trinity College, Cambridge. He was ordained and became a hearty Christian tutor. Also an enthusiastic mountaineer, he edited *The Alpine Journal* (1868–71) and published *The Playground of Europe* (1871), a collection of essays on mountaineering. His reading meanwhile had embraced Kant, John Stuart Mill, and Herbert Spencer; he left the chuch in 1870, becoming an agnostic.

Stephen's literary career began in 1864 when he went to London and contributed to periodicals including *The Saturday Review* and *Fraser's Magazine*. These contributions were published in collections, *Hours in a Library* (1874, 1876, and 1879). He wrote a statement of his agnostic position, *Essays on Free Thinking and Plain Speaking* (1873); his *Agnostic's Apology* was published in *The Fortnightly Review* for June 1876. *A History of English Thought in the Eighteenth Century* (1876), generally regarded as his most important work, is a study of the principal writers of the deist controversy and the utilitarian and intuitional schools of philosophy. He returned to the subject

in *The English Utilitarians* (1900) and published *The Science of Ethics* in 1882.

*Samuel Johnson* (1878), *Alexander Pope* (1880), *Swift* (1882), *George Eliot* (1902), and *Thomas Hobbes* (1904) were contributions to the English Men of Letters series. Stephen was editor of *The Cornhill Magazine* (1871–82); in 1882 he accepted the editorship, offered by George Smith of Smith, Elder of the *Dictionary of National Biography*. He oversaw the first 26 volumes and contributed many entries himself, particularly for the 18th and 19th centuries. He continued to contribute to the dictionary after giving up the editorship. Stephen's wife was Thackeray's youngest daughter, Harriet Marian, and he was the model for Vernon Whitford in Meredith's *The Egoist*. Virginia Stephen, his youngest daughter, became famous as Virginia Woolf.

**Stephen Hero**  See **Joyce, James (Augustine Aloysius)** and *Portrait of the Artist as a Young Man, A.*

**Stephens, James** 1882–1950.  Stephens was born in the Dublin slums and such education as he had he found for himself. He was employed in an office and wrote in his spare time, working at stories and poems with no success until a meeting with George Russell (AE). Russell encouraged him and helped arrange the publication of his first collection of poems, *Insurrections* (1909). *The Lonely God and Other Poems* (1909) followed, and in 1911 his novel *The Charwoman's Daughter* was published in *The Irish Review*. In 1912 **The Crock of Gold**, a prose fantasy, made him famous and thereafter he was able to make a living as a writer. *The Charwoman's Daughter* was published in book form in the same year; a humourous idyll of the Dublin slums, it differed very much from *The Crock of Gold* and *The Demi-Gods* (1914), another fantasy, typical of the work with which his name is generally connected.

Stephens studied Irish literature and mythology and contributed to the revival of interest in the Gaelic language; he was also a busy journalist and an active Sinn Feiner, and edited the poems of his friend and colleague Thomas MacDonagh when the latter was executed after the Easter Rising. However, he opposed Irish neutrality in World War II. Two editions of *Collected Poems* by James Stephens were published in 1926 (enlarged 1954). Volumes of short stories were *Here are Ladies* (with poems, 1913), *In the Land of Youth* (1924), *Etched in Moonlight* (1928); *Deirdre* (1823) was a novel based on a famous Celtic subject. Among other works by James Stephens were *The Insurrection in Dublin* (1916), *Irish Fairy Tales* (1920), and several essays on poetry.

**Sterne, Laurence** 1713–68. The son of a junior army officer, Sterne was born at Clonmel in Tipperary, and spent his early years in various garrison towns. He went to school in Halifax for eight years and was left penniless when his father died in Jamaica in 1731. Fortunately, Sterne's parents were well connected and he was able, through the good offices of a cousin, to enter Jesus College, Cambridge, as a sizar or poor scholar. One of his friends at Cambridge was a young landowner, John Hall-Stevenson, a wit with a liking for pornography who turns up as a character in *Tristram Shandy*. Sterne took his degree in 1737 and was ordained soon after; the Church was a well-used refuge, then, for young men with no income or prospects. Family connections secured him the living of Sutton-in-the-Forest, in Yorkshire, and later he was made a prebendary of York Minster.

Sterne married Elizabeth (Eliza) Lumley in 1741; her family connections secured him the benefice of Stillington, and that was where he lived. The marriage was an unhappy one for Elizabeth Sterne; her husband was soon embarking on a series of sentimental love affairs and she became unbalanced in 1758. However, Sterne seems to have had a great affection for his only child, his daughter Lydia.

In his spare time (he seems to have had a considerable amount of it) Sterne read a great deal and contributed occasional pieces to Yorkshire journals. His first book was published when he was 46, a short allegorical tale called *A Political Romance* (1759). In the same year he started work on **Tristram Shandy**, and read portions of it to his friends at Skelton Hall, the home of John Hall-Stevenson. The first two volumes were published in London in 1760 and made Sterne famous. Further volumes came out in 1761, 1762, 1765, and 1767.

His newly found fame brought Sterne to the attention of influential people; and the perpetual curacy of Coxwold was given to him in 1760. He was now in a position to travel and he needed to do so – Sterne was consumptive and, with the exception of two years in Toulouse with his daughter and his melancholy wife (1762–64), he spent the rest of his life either travelling in warmer countries or living the life of a London celebrity. He began to publish his sermons as *The Sermons of Mr Yorick* in 1760 (Parson Yorick was a character in *Tristram Shandy*) and further volumes followed in 1766 and 1769. His name was sufficient to make them a success. **A Sentimental Journey** (1768) was the result of a seven-month tour of France and Italy in 1765; the book tells of the French part of his travels.

Laurence Sterne. A detail from the portrait by Joshua Reynolds, 1760. National Portrait Gallery, London.

Sterne died in 1768. The year before he had become involved with Mrs Eliza Draper, the wife of an East India Company officer. His letters to her were published after his death, with Mrs Draper's permission, as *Letters from Yorick to Eliza* (1773). Mrs Draper proved a good friend to Elizabeth and Lydia Sterne: the author, when he succumbed to pleurisy in his lodgings in Old Bond Street, was insolvent; his family was relieved through subscriptions collected by Mrs Draper and John Hall-Stevenson.

On the strength of two books – and one of those is little more than a fragment – Laurence Sterne became one of the key figures of English fiction. His contemporaries Richardson, Smollett, and Fielding in their different ways attempted a likeness of reality and the form they chose for their narratives was the relation of past events arranged in careful progression. The novel was comfortable in that form and but for Sterne might have remained in it indefinitely; he demonstrated its Protean possibilities. He wrote: 'Writing, when properly managed, is but a different name for conversation.' He might have said also that authentic conversation is not like the ordered progression presented in drama and in most fiction; it is full of bumps and stops, digressions and apparent irrelevancies. His famous novel was a point of departure in fiction because it was the result of remarkable skill and painstaking care in ordering an apparently disordered narrative, demonstrating the truth of Locke's theory that the association of ideas is an irrational process. Sterne's revolutionary approach to the novel would not, in itself, have made him memorable or had such an enormous influence; but he used it to convey his own humorous view of life and to express shades of feeling with great subtlety. He was a humorist and sentimentalist both and his heirs are legion. He betrays a peculiar dinginess of mind; but it is part, for better or for worse, of a novelist of genius. Sterne is prurient, certainly, but if he can be criticized it is not on those grounds. Attitudes change from period to period and grounds for censure of Sterne's handling of sex and sentimentality are dictated by the moral atmosphere of the times in which his critics are writing. His characters are instantly and delightfully recognizable; My Uncle Toby, My Father, Corporal Trim, Widow Wadman, Yorick, Dr Slop, and the rest belong in the gallery of great fictional characters.

**Steuart (or Steuart-Denham), Sir James** 1712–80. Born in Edinburgh, Steuart was a Jacobite who returned from a long exile in 1763. He had travelled extensively in Europe and had paid close attention to the different ways of ordering society which he encountered in the countries he visited. His reflections, after returning home, were published in *An Inquiry into the Principles of Political Economy* (1767). His book has no claim to literary merit but in some respects it looks forward to the great work of Adam Smith, who knew Steuart and his book, which opens with 'Man we find acting uniformly in all ages, in all countries, and in all climates, from the principles of self-interest, expediency, duty and passion.' (See *Wealth of Nations, An Enquiry into the Nature and Causes of, The*.)

**Stevenson, Robert Louis (Balfour)** 1850–94. The son of a prosperous Presbyterian engineer, Robert Louis (originally Lewis) Stevenson was born in Edinburgh. He was educated at Edinburgh University and was expected to become an engineer like his father. But the young Stevenson wanted something else and his father agreed to his becoming a lawyer. He began to write in his teens, and several occasional pieces were published by the time he was admitted advocate in 1875.

Stevenson was a delicate child; at the same time he was a spirited one, and by the time he reached manhood he was in reaction against his father's Calvinism. His declaration of his agnosticism, when he was 23, led to a breach with his parents which, in spite of strenuous surface amiability, took a long time to heal. That same year, 1873, his respiratory weakness became serious and while in London, where he met

Sidney Colvin, he was advised to go to the Mediterranean. At Menton, Colvin introduced him to Andrew Lang, and the writer in Stevenson found a climate, in more than one sense, that really suited him. His father gave him a small allowance, and soon his pieces were being published in the *Cornhill Magazine* and the *Portfolio*; readers began to look for contributions by 'R.L.S.'. His circle of friends grew; Stevenson had great charm and both W. E. Henley and Edmund Gosse were anxious to help.

His first books were the result of his travels, first by canoe on the canals of France and Belgium (*An Inland Voyage*, 1878), and later after rambling in Languedoc (*Travels with a Donkey in the Cevennes*, 1879). In 1876 at Brez-sur-Loing, near Fontainebleau, Stevenson met and fell in love with Fanny Osbourne, an American woman with three children. When she left for California to institute divorce proceedings (her husband had deserted her), Stevenson followed, travelling steerage; he was determined to marry her. Against all the odds – she was 10 years his senior – Stevenson's marriage was ideally happy, and Fanny won the blessing of Stevenson's parents. His father settled an income on him and he was relieved of anxiety on that score; but for the next few years his health kept him moving from one resort to another to stay in the sun. From this period date the collections *Virginibus Puerisque* ('for girls and boys'; 1881), *Familiar Studies of Men and Books*, and *The New Arabian Nights* (1882). Then his 12-year-old stepson, Lloyd Osbourne, began to draw a map of a desert island while the family were staying at Braemar. Stevenson helped him, giving names to the physical features, and that day started to write the book which made him famous – *Treasure Island* (1883); it was originally called *The Sea Cook or Treasure Island*. Another novel which appeared simultaneously, in serial form, was *The Black Arrow*, enormously popular with young readers of the time but not appearing in book form until 1888. In France once more, at Hyères, because of his health, he wrote among other things *A Child's Garden of Verses* (1885). At Bournemouth he became friends with Henry James, and in 1886 published *Kidnapped* and *The Strange Case of Dr Jekyll and Mr Hyde*.

Stevenson's father died in 1887, and in August his son, now financially secure, left England with his family. They settled in Samoa, where his interest in the South Seas was reflected in *The Beach at Falesa* (1892), *A Footnote to History* (1892), and *In the South Seas* (1896). The author died suddenly at the age of 44, but the years between 1887 and 1894 had been productive, seeing the publication of **The Master of Ballantrae** (1889), *Catriona* (1893; the sequel to *Kidnapped*), and, in collaboration with Lloyd Osbourne, *The Wrong Box* (1889), *The Wrecker* (1892), and *The Ebb-Tide* (1894). Left unfinished were *St Ives* (completed by Quiller-Couch) and **Weir of Hermiston**, a fragment which suggested that a fine writer was within reach of becoming a great one, when death intervened.

In addition to the titles already listed, Stevenson wrote a mass of short pieces and some fine short stories, notably 'Thrawn Janet' and 'Markheim'. Collections include *The Silverado Squatters* (1883), *Prince Otto* (1885), *The Merry Men* (1887), *Memories and Portraits* (1887), *Across the Plains* (1892), and *Island Night's Entertainment* (1893) and a further collection of poems, *Underwoods* (1887).

Robert Louis Stevenson is usually – with the exception of *The Strange Case of Dr Jekyll and Mr Hyde* – fixed in readers' minds as the author of great adventure stories for younger readers. He is that, certainly, and with few rivals, but he has much to offer adult readers, who would be well rewarded for getting to know him better.

**Stewart, Dugald** 1753–1828. Stewart was born in Edinburgh and attended Edinburgh High School. He completed his education at Edinburgh and Glasgow Universities and became Professor of Moral Philosophy at Edinburgh in 1785. He remained there until 1810 and during those years his lectures did much to encourage a distinguished generation of Scottish writers and philosophers. A philosopher himself, he was a disciple of Thomas Reid; however, the 'popularizing' element of his teaching reveals a lack of depth. Among his pupils were James Mill, Sir Walter Scott, Henry Brougham, and Sydney Smith. His philosophical works include *The Elements of the Philosophy of the Human Mind* (1792–1827), *Outlines of Moral Philosophy* (1794), and *The Philosophy of the Active and Moral Powers* (1828).

**Stickney, (Joseph) Trumbull** 1874–1904. Trumbull Stickney was born in Switzerland. He graduated from Harvard in 1895 and returned to Europe and was one of the first Americans to receive a doctorate in literature from the Sorbonne. He taught at Harvard, like his friend William Vaughn Moody, and died at the age of 30 from a brain tumour.

Stickney shared Moody's interest in Greek literature; his *Prometheus Pyrphoros* was published in 1900, four years before his friend's exploration of the same theme in *The Fire Bringer*. Stickney's *Dramatic Verses* was published in 1902 and a collection of his verses was published by his friends in 1905.

**Stillwater Tragedy, The** A novel by Thomas Bailey Aldrich, first published in 1880.

In the New England village of Stillwater a wealthy miser, Lemuel Shackford, is brutally murdered. His nephew Richard, his ward, inherits the Shackford wealth and becomes engaged to Margaret Slocum. Margaret's family own the Marble Yard and Richard becomes an executive there; he suppresses a strike fomented by the labour leader Torrini and Richard's former friend, Durgin. Richard then has to visit New York on business and before leaving he advertises a reward for the apprehension of Shackford's murderer. The case is being investigated by the detective Edward Taggett.

Taggett's diligence uncovers evidence that unfortunately points to the absent Richard; but Margaret steadfastly believes him innocent. Richard returns to Stillwater, where Torrini is dying, and does his best for his former adversary. Torrini, out of gratitude, reveals his part in the events that led to Shackford's murder and Taggett's evidence has to be reinterpreted. The guilty man proves to be Durgin and Richard gives the reward money to Torrini's family. Margaret's faith is justified – and she and Richard marry.

**Stoddard, R(ichard) H(enry)** 1825–1903. R. H. Stoddard was born in Massachusetts, the son of poor parents. He educated himself while working as an iron moulder and published a collection of romantic verses, *Poems*, in 1852. Nathaniel Hawthorne gave him help and encouragement; it was through Hawthorne that Stoddard found more congenial work as inspector of customs in New York. He wrote reviews for the *New York World* for 20 years and eventually became editor of the *Mail and Express*, a post he kept until he died.

Stoddard enjoyed a reputation as a poet during his lifetime but it has not endured. He and his wife Elizabeth maintained a literary salon in New York from about 1870 and Stoddard befriended Herman Melville, who was at that time almost forgotten. He also published an edition of Edgar Allan Poe, whom he had known in former days – but he added a memoir that was critical of the poet's character. Stoddard published his autobiography, *Recollections Personal and Literary*, in 1903.

**Stones of Venice, The** A treatise by John Ruskin published in three volumes, *The Foundations* (1851) and *The Sea Stories* and *The Fall* (both 1853), and illustrated with drawings by the author. According to Ruskin, '*The Stones of Venice* had, from beginning to end, no other aim than to show that the Gothic architecture of Venice had risen out of, and indicated in all its features, a state of pure national faith, and of domestic virtue; and that its Renaissance architecture had arisen out of, and in all its features indicated, a state of concealed national infidelity, and of domestic corruption.' The sixth chapter of the second volume contains the famous *On the Nature of Gothic: and herein the True Function of the Workman in Art*, in which Ruskin the art critic becomes a critic of society also. It was published separately in 1854.

*The Stones of Venice* was edited by L. M. Phillips (Everyman's Library, 1907).

**Stonor Letters**  Though less famous than the *Paston Letters*, the correspondence of the Stonor family from 1290 to 1483 is equally rewarding for students of the period, not only for the immediate information conveyed about their life and times but also for their *tone*: neither the Pastons nor the Stonors were writing for anyone but each other.

*The Stonor Letters and Papers 1290–1483* were edited by C. L. Kingsford for the Camden Society (1919), followed by a supplementary collection for the years 1313–1482 (1924).

**Stoppard, Tom**  1937–   . Stoppard was born in Zlin in Czechoslovakia, taken to Singapore as an infant, and then to England in 1946, where he completed his education. He worked as a journalist in Bristol from 1954 to 1963, latterly as a freelance while he wrote plays. *A Walk on the Water* was televised in 1963 and revised twice as *The Preservation of George Riley* (1964) and *Enter a Free Man* (produced 1968). *The Gamblers* was produced in Bristol in 1965 and *Tango*, an adaptation from the Polish of Slavomir Mrozek, in London in 1966. *A Separate Peace* (TV, 1966) was followed by *Rosencrantz and Guildenstern are Dead* (Edinburgh, 1966, revised for the National Theatre, 1967), which made Stoppard famous and won awards in England and America. His career continued with (the dates given are of the first production) *Albert's Bridge* (radio, 1967), *Teeth* (TV, 1967), *Another Moon Called Earth* (TV, 1967), *The Real Inspector Hound* (1968), *Neutral Ground* (TV, 1968), *After Magritte* (1970), *Where Are They Now?* (radio, 1970), *Doggs Our Pet* (1971), *Jumpers* (1972), *Artists Descending a Staircase* (radio, 1972), *Travesties* (1974), *Dirty Linen* and *New-Found-Land* (1976), *Every Good Boy Deserves Favour* (1978), *Professional Foul* (radio, 1978), *Night and Day* (1978), and *Undiscovered Country* (1980). Tom Stoppard is the

author of a single novel, *Lord Malquist and Mr Moon* (1966); his adaptation of Lorca's *The House of Bernarda Alba* was produced in London in 1973.

**Storm, The**  A short story by Kate Chopin, written in 1898 but never published. It remained among her papers until Per Seyersted's edition of her complete works was published in 1969.

Calixta sits at home sewing. Her husband Bobinôt has taken their son for a walk and when a storm breaks they take shelter in a store. Bobinôt buys a can of shrimps for Calixta, who is very fond of them. The storm sends Calixta hurrying into the garden to bring in some washing; Alcée, a former beau, is riding by and he takes shelter in her house when the storm breaks. He had wanted her passionately in their younger days five years before; but she had been inviolable and he had conquered his desire, though not with any help from her. The storm rages outside while they fall on one another.

After the storm Alcée rides away, bidding her a warm and affectionate adieu. She waves to him, blooming and contented. Alcée writes to his wife, offering her a further month's vacation with the children. Bobinôt returns home, bringing Calixta a can of shrimps. She is preparing supper and is delighted to have her husband and son home after the storm.

Alcée's wife receives her husband's letter and is delighted to think that she can stay away from him for another month. The storm is over and everyone is happy.

**Story of a Bad Boy, The**  A novel by Thomas Bailey Aldrich, first published in 1870 (dated 1869). The book is based on the author's boyhood in Portsmouth, New Hampshire, the Rivermouth of the novel, and begins in New Orleans where the central character is staying with relatives. On the way home by sea to Rivermouth, New Hampshire, young Tom Bailey becomes friends with an old seaman, Sailor Ben. Tom's maternal grandfather and his maiden great-aunt, Miss Abigail, live with the family and contribute to the interest of life in Tom's home in Rivermouth. The house and family are looked after by Kitty Collins, the Irish maid to whom all are devoted. The novel describes Tom's parents and recounts his childhood, his schooldays, his friendships (the 'Rivermouth Centipedes'), and his delight at meeting Sailor Ben again. When Ben pays a visit to Tom's home he proves to be Kitty's long-lost husband.

The book closes when Tom's father dies, and the boy has to think of work and how to earn his living. It is a charming evocation of boyhood in a country which might have been expressly created for the delight of a high-spirited boy.

### Story of a Country Town, The  A novel by E. W. Howe, first published in 1883.

The story is told by Ned Westlock, the son of a secretive stern Bible-quoting minister-farmer. John Westlock's religious gatherings each Sunday are the only focus for the neighbours in the Midwestern farming community and their harshness is accepted. The important people in young Ned's life are Jo Erving, his mother's young brother, who works on the Westlock farm, the young schoolteacher Agnes Deming, and the miller Damon Barker, to whom Jo is later apprenticed. It is Damon who makes Ned aware that there is a rich and varied world outside.

Jo falls in love with Mateel Shepherd and feels an increasing dislike for Clinton Bragg, a friend of the Shepherd family. Then, to everyone's surprise, John Westlock leaves the land and moves his family to the country town Twin Mounds. Westlock trades in land and buys the local newspaper and Ned helps him to edit it. Jo builds a mill and a home of his own; he is also accepted by Mateel Shepherd.

Then John Westlock elopes with Damon's sister; Ned's mother becomes ill with worry and Ned keeps the paper going on his own. Damon himself turns out to be the father whom Agnes Deming never knew and she goes to her new home at Damon's mill. Ned's mother dies just before his father comes back, alone. The return is brief; John Westlock is a man without resolution or purpose now and soon disappears again.

Jo has been prospering but now he discovers that Mateel and the hated Clinton Bragg were once lovers. His insane jealousy leads to the death of Mateel and he murders Bragg. He surrenders to the police but commits suicide. Ned and Agnes marry and settle down happily. Thus the life of the country town continues.

E. W. Howe's novel captures perfectly the tone of a tired old man looking back on life – the author had not reached 30 when he wrote it. The note of bitterness is strong and the disillusion with what life's reward has been is almost palpable – under endless skies and surrounded by immense distances the life in his country town is close, stifling, and arid. Ned Westlock knows there is more to life but he has never achieved more; and he notes wryly how many of the people who come to the West are those without hopes in the places they have left.

### Story of an African Farm, The  See **Schreiner, Olive Emily Albertina.**

### Story of My Heart, The  See **Jefferies, (John) Richard.**

### Stow, John 1525–1605.  John Stow was a London tailor and a freeman of the Merchant Taylor's Company from 1547 but from 1560 he indulged his passion for historical manuscripts and records and spent the rest of his life and all his money in collecting, transcribing, and chronicling. He never learned to ride and travelled about England on foot, looking for antiquities. Stow was suspected of being a Catholic and being in possession of dangerous – Catholic, that is – writings and on three occasions was summoned to appear before ecclesiastical courts. He spent so freely in his quest for additions to his library that he was sometimes obliged to live on charity.

Stow published editions of Chaucer (1561), Matthew of Westminster (1567), Matthew Paris (1571), Thomas Walsingham (1574), and the second edition of Holinshed (1585). His further notes on Chaucer were printed by Thomas Speght in 1598. His fame rests on his own writing, nonetheless: *A Summarie of Englysh Chronicles* (1565), *The Chronicles of England from Brute unto this Present Yeare of Christ 1580* (1580), and *A Survay of London* (1598). Stow took the trouble to research his facts and wrote in plain straightforward prose. His *Summarie* is in the form of annals, with the results of his diligent examination of records adding useful information. The *Chronicles* is his own history (the 'Brute' of the title is the legendary Trojan Brutus, who founded a new kingdom – Britain). It was dedicated to the Earl of Leicester and was widely read; six editions were printed by 1631 and it became known as *The Annales of England* after the second edition of 1592.

*A Survay of London* is his most famous book and the most highly regarded. It is an invaluable source of information on the history and customs of the city and provides details found nowhere else. John Strype, another antiquary, brought it up to his own times in 1720 and corrected the original text. A modernized and annotated edition was published by C. L. Kingsford (1908), and the Everyman's Library edition of H. B. Wheatley (1912) was revised in 1960.

### Stowe, Harriet (Elizabeth) Beecher 1811–96.
Harriet Beecher was the daughter of a Presbyterian anti-Catholic anti-liquor fire-eating minister of Litchfield and Boston, Lyman Beecher. Her childhood was lightened by the friendship of her warmly liberal uncle, Samuel Foote, and by her wide-ranging interest in books. Beecher took his family to Cincinnati in

1832, where Harriet did some teaching and tried her hand at writing sketches of New England life. It was there, on the Midwestern frontier, that she first learned about the 'Underground Railway' through which slaves reached freedom. She married a teacher at her father's seminary, C. E. Stowe, in 1836, and on a visit to Kentucky saw slavery at first hand. The Stowes returned to the East in 1850 when Stowe joined the faculty of Bowdoin College. Harriet was the mother of seven children by this time and she had, meanwhile, continued writing didactic and religious trifles. Her increasing interest in slavery led to the writing of a novel.

**Uncle Tom's Cabin** was published in 1852 and was a tremendous success, not only in America: Palmerston read it three times and Gladstone was moved to tears by it. It would be doing Harriet less than justice to call her book a tract that appeared at exactly the right time. Her experience of the South was second-hand and there is a tendency in the 20th century to impute the book's success to the fashionable protests of the 1850s. There was indeed plenty of protest, as library records show. The indefensible Fugitive Slave Law of 1850 was provocative enough, in any case, to have unleashed a storm of books but Harriet's was read by an enormous public, which the others were not, because it has narrative power, some excellent characterization, and the degree of passion necessary to involve the reader. The quality of her writing is indisputable, while it also remains true that nowhere does Mrs Stowe, a respectable New England lady, depart from her own standards of propriety and behaviour.

As the issue was so topical Harriet was, inevitably, attacked by those who thought that slavery was a right and proper thing. Both the slave owners of the South and the manufacturers of the North, who enjoyed great profits as a result of cheap materials, impugned the accuracy of the book, and in 1853 the harassed author published *A Key to Uncle Tom's Cabin*, which documented her sources. **Dred:** *a Tale of the Great Dismal Swamp* (1856) was a further essay in antislavery fiction but it is hardly known nowadays. It is an interesting work, emphasizing the demoralizing influence to which those who kept slaves subjected themselves.

Harriet Beecher Stowe paid a second visit to England – where she was an honoured guest – in the 1850s and was received by Queen Victoria. On a third visit in 1869, Harriet, proper woman that she was, met and defended Lady Byron. The poet's widow gave Harriet the information that she published in *Lady Byron Vindicated* (1870),

charging the late poet with incestuous relations with his half-sister, Augusta Leigh. Whereupon the English, whose fit of morality in 1816 had driven one of Britain's great poets into permanent exile, decided that Mrs Harriet Beecher Stowe was scandalmongering; she lost a great many readers in England.

Her career had, meanwhile, proceeded. She wrote fiction with a New England setting: *The Minister's Wooing* (1859), *The Pearl of Orr's Island* (1862), *Oldtown Folks* (1869), and the stories in *Sam Lawson's Oldtown Fireside Stories* (1872) and *Poganuc People* (1878). In addition there was miscellaneous fiction and *Religious Poems* (1867).

Harriet's success brought financial security to the Stowes. Her husband left Bowdoin College and the family moved to Hartford, Connecticut (where a neighbour was Mark Twain), and after the Civil War to Florida. She grew more and more disenchanted with the Calvinism of her father and eventually deserted it. She was disappointed in what became of her children: she lost a son in a drowning accident in 1857 and another became a drunkard; two of her daughters (twins) remained unmarried but another became a morphine addict. Harriet's life in Florida is described in *Palmetto Leaves* (1873).

**Strachey, (Giles) Lytton** 1880–1932. Lytton Strachey, the son of Sir Richard Strachey, a general and civil engineer who served in India, was born in London. He was educated at Leamington College and Liverpool University, where he read history, and at Trinity College, Cambridge. The friendships of his Cambridge days – with John Maynard Keynes, E. M. Forster, Leonard Woolf, Clive Bell, and the rest – continued in his professional life and into the Bloomsbury Group of which he was a notable figure. After Cambridge, from 1904 to 1914, Strachey reviewed books in *The Spectator*: he had published two collections of verse, *Prolusiones Academicae* (1902) and *Euphrosyne* (1905) and won the Chancellor's Medal for 'Ely: An Ode' but he then abandoned poetry. His first book, *Landmarks in French Literature* (1912, for the Home University Library series), revealed an excellent critic and a prose stylist of uncommon quality.

Strachey was a conscientious objector during World War I, and six years passed before he published another book. *Eminent Victorians* (1918) looked at the careers of Florence Nightingale, Cardinal Manning, Dr Thomas Arnold, and General Gordon; the book consisted of four essays in iconoclasm and was a popular sensation in a period which was busy shrugging off a heritage only a few years old. Strachey made his purpose plain in his introduction: biography is an art, and the biographer as an artist must select and arrange, not merely accumulate and reproduce a great mass of material. It would be difficult to argue against that but Strachey's irony and his talent for casting light into obscure places resulted in caricature. It is wonderfully readable and illuminating as well as provocative of further study. Unfortunately the book let loose a host of less gifted imitators, who thought that the whole art of biography was to be found in Strachey's book.

*Queen Victoria* (1921) at times reads like a novel; in the writing the author seems to have been seduced by his subject and a reluctant admiration replaces the mordant irony. A book of critical essays came next, *Books and Characters, French and English* (1922), and a play about the end of the Manchu dynasty, *The Son of Heaven*, which was played for two nights at the Scala Theatre, London (July 1925). *Elizabeth and Essex: A Tragic History* (1928) is a readable and interesting account but the character of the great Tudor monarch is not well realized. The remainder of Strachey's works are collections of critical essays, in which some of his best work is to be found: *Portraits and Miniatures* (1931); *Characters and Commentaries* (1933) which contains his notable essay on Alexander Pope, first published in 1925; and *Spectatorial Essays* (published posthumously, 1964), a collection of his reviews published in *The Spectator* (1904–14).

**Strap, Hugh**  The hero's school-friend who agrees to act as his valet in *Roderick Random* by Tobias Smollett. When he prospers, in Paris, he calls himself Monsieur d'Estrapes.

*Streetcar Named Desire, A*  See **Williams, Tennessee**.

**Strether, Lambert**  The first and principal emissary in *The Ambassadors*, by Henry James. He is sent to Paris by the rich Mrs Newsome to persuade her son to return to America and the family business. Strether finds his mission infinitely more complex than he had thought; he also finds that the environment Mrs Newsome's son has chosen is dangerously seductive.

**Strickland, Agnes**  1796–1874. Agnes Strickland, born in London, was the daughter of a landed family and began her literary career as a poet. Later she turned to fiction with a historical basis for children and eventually to the short biographies for which she is remembered: *The Lives of the Queens of England from the Norman Conquest* (1840–48) and *The Lives of the Queens of Scotland, and English Princesses* (1850–59). Agnes Strickland was a popularizer; though her books

were popular and very useful to teachers for many years she is hardly read now.

*St Ronan's Well*  A novel by Sir Walter Scott, first published in 1824. The setting is his own time – a departure for Scott – at the fashionable spa of St Ronan's Well, and Scott makes excellent use of the opportunity to describe the idle and self-centred society which frequents it. The story itself concerns two half-brothers, the sons of the late Earl of Etherington: the younger bears the title and is called Etherington, the elder is called Francis. The girl is Clara Mowbray, daughter of the laird of St Ronan's who is addicted to gambling. The brothers hate each other and the narrative proper begins with one improbability (Clara and Francis are going to be married secretly, at midnight; Etherington gets there first and impersonates his brother, so poor Clara is married to a man she loathes) and continues with many more, with poor Clara going off her head in the end.

Not even Scott's skill at characterization can save the book. Meg Dods, the down-to-earth landlady, and Mr Touchstone, the nabob with a nose for intrigue, are up to the author's best level but the novel is a failure.

**Strype, John**  1643–1737. The historian of the English Church was born in London and attended St Paul's School. He went on to Jesus College, Cambridge, but disliked the way religion was practised there and transferred to St Catherine's Hall. After Cambridge he became curate and lecturer at Leyton in Essex (1669) and from 1689 to 1724 added a lectureship at Hackney to his activities. He was given the sinecure of West Tarring in Sussex in 1711.

Strype made a remarkable collection of Tudor documents that are now in the British Museum. It is the documentary evidence in Strype's work that makes it important – as a writer he was without grace and the arrangement of his material is clumsy; he also made mistakes in his reading of documents. But Strype's works remain authoritative. The first of them was *Memorials of Thomas Cranmer* (1694). Works on the lives of Sir Thomas Smith (1698), John Aylmer (1701), and Sir John Cheke (1705) were followed by his magnum opus, *Annals of the Reformation and Establishment of Religion, and other Occurrences in the Church of England, during the first twelve years of Queen Elizabeth's Reign* (four volumes, 1709–31). Lives of Edmund Grindal (1710) and John Whitgift (1718) were also written while work proceeded on the *Annals*. Strype's *Ecclesiastical Memorials Relating chiefly to Religion and the Reformation of it under Henry VIII, Edward VI and Mary* was published in 1721.

Strype also edited and extended Stow's *Survay* as *A Survey of the Cities of London and Westminster*, adding a life of John Stow (1720, with a much enlarged edition in 1754).

**Stubbes, Philip** *c*.1555–91. The early years of Philip Stubbes are closed to us; his birthplace is unknown and the date of his birth is conjecture. It is known, however, that he studied at both Cambridge and Oxford and became a printer; he wrote verse of no merit. In 1583 Stubbes published *The Anatomie of Abuses*, a dialogue in which Philoporius, a traveller returned from seven years in Ailgna (England), discusses the people of that country with Spudeus. He tells him that the English people have fallen into wickedness – they profane the Sabbath in 22 different ways; they neglect the poor; usury is practised; a poor man cannot have his children properly educated; they attend playhouses; and generally they behave in wicked and irresponsible ways.

By some strange chance Stubbes has been regarded as an attacker of the playhouses and a contributor to their eventual closure; a detestable sort of Puritan, in fact. The reason probably lies in the fact that Nashe delivered a reply some years later in *The Anatomie of Absurditie* (1589); this stressed the attack on the theatre, which was a small part of Stubbes' work. But Stubbes attacks bear baiting, hunting for sport, and the unspeakable prisons every bit as strongly, emerging as an oddly likable, if rather stiff-necked, man. He adored his wife, whom he lost in childbirth and eulogized in the widely read *A Christall Glass for Christian Women* (1590). The wide-ranging criticism of society contained in *The Anatomie* has left us a valuable account of popular amusements in Elizabethan London.

**Stubbs, William** 1825–1901. Stubbs was born at Knaresborough in Yorkshire and attended Ripon Grammar School. Through the influence of Bishop Longley he was nominated as a servitor and enabled to enter Christ Church, Oxford. He became a fellow of Trinity College in 1848. Stubbs became rector of Navestock in Essex in 1850 and during his 16 years there he increased his remarkable historical knowledge and became interested in the publication of the Rolls Series, to which he made his first contribution with *Registrum Sacrum Anglicanum* (1858), which tabled the course of ecclesiastical succession in England. In 1866 he was made Regius Professor of Modern History at Oxford.

Stubbs contributed no less than 19 volumes to the Rolls Series, including the *Chronicles and Memorials of Richard I* (1864), the *Gesta Regum*

(1867) and *Historia Novella* (1885) of William of Malmesbury, *The Memorials of St Dunstan* (1874), and *Historical Works of Gervase of Canterbury* (1879). His most celebrated works are *Select Charters and Other Illustrations of English Constitutional History* (1870) and *The Constitutional History of England* (1873–78), which take the subject to the accession of the Tudors and have become historical classics. Stubbs became a canon of St Paul's in 1879, Bishop of Chester in 1884, and Bishop of Oxford in 1889. He was also the joint author, with A. W. Haddan, of *Councils and Documents Relating to Great Britain and Ireland* (1869–73). Stubbs was a devoted follower of the Oxford Movement.

**Studs Lonigan** See **Farrell, James T(homas).**

**Sturt, George** See **Bourne, George.**

**Subjection of Women, The** An essay by John Stuart Mill, first published in 1869. 'The object of this Essay is to explain, as clearly as I am able, the grounds of an opinion which I have held from the very earliest period when I had formed any opinions at all on social or political matters, and which, instead of being weakened or modified, has been constantly growing stronger by the progress of reflection and the experience of life: That the principle which regulates the existing social relations between the two sexes – the legal subordination of one sex to the other – is wrong in itself, and now one of the chief hindrances to human improvement; and that it ought to be replaced by a principle of perfect equality, admitting no power or privilege on the one side, nor disability on the other.'

**Such Is Life** See **Furphy, Joseph.**

**Suckling, Sir John** 1609–42. A Cavalier poet, Suckling's short life was so crowded with activity that the amount of his literary output is remarkable. The son of an old Norfolk family, he seems to have taken his education none too seriously: he left Cambridge without graduating and spent a year at Gray's Inn. His father died when Suckling was 18, and this gave him freedom to seek what adventures he pleased. He was a member of the expedition to the Île de Ré (1627), was in the Netherlands (1629–30), and served under Gustavus Adolphus of Sweden (1631–32). He was knighted in 1630.

A staunch Royalist, Suckling took up arms on the king's behalf in 1639 and 1640 and is believed to have been active in a plot to free the Earl of Strafford from the Tower. It was to the Parliamentary party's advantage to make a 'plot' of the affair and Suckling fled to Paris, where he died in the following year – by his own hand according to John Aubrey.

Suckling was the author of three plays – *Aglaura*, *The Goblins*, and *Brennoralt* – which have never been revived but which contain some good lyrics, notably 'Why so pale and wan, fond lover?' His best work, indeed, is in the form of short pieces, occasional verses and songs, and in the delightful 'A Ballad upon a Wedding'. His expression is direct and robust, reflecting to some degree his lively, pleasure-loving, and tragically short life. His first published collection was *A Session of the Poets* (1637). *Fragmenta Aurea. A Collection of all the Incomparable Pieces, written by Sir John Suckling. And published by a Friend to perpetuate his memory* appeared posthumously (1646).

**Sumer is i-cumen in** (*Summer is a-coming in*). The opening line of a Middle English poem believed to be the earliest surviving lyric in English, from the first half of the 13th century; the music to which it was sung still exists. It is in the form of a round for six voices, a rare and valuable survival of a form probably common during the period. The song is preserved in the Harleian manuscript 978 in the British Library. The author is unknown. The poem is usually called *The Cuckoo Song* in anthologies.

**Summer is a-coming in**  See **Sumer is i-cumen in**.

**Summerson, Esther**  The heroine of Dickens's *Bleak House* and part-narrator of the story. Apparently an orphan, the mystery of her birth is revealed during the narrative. She marries the young doctor, Allan Woodcourt.

**Summoner's Tale, The**  See **Canterbury Tales, The**.

**Sun Also Rises, The**  See **Hemingway, Ernest (Miller)**.

**Sunday Under Three Heads**  A 'little pamphlet' by 'Timothy Sparks' addressed to the Bishop of London on the right of ordinary people to spend their day of rest in whatever way pleased them best. It was written by Charles Dickens and first published in 1836.

**Surface, Charles**  The amiable rake, good at heart, in Sheridan's *The School for Scandal*. He is in love with Maria, Sir Peter Teazle's ward.

**Surface, Joseph**  In Sheridan's *The School for Scandal* the brother of Charles Surface. He is quite ready to blacken anyone's character for his own purposes, and intends to marry Maria, who loves Charles, for her money.

**Surgeon's Daughter, The**  See **Chronicles of the Canongate**.

**Surrey, Henry Howard, Earl of** 1517–47. Surrey was the son of Thomas Howard, who became 3rd Duke of Norfolk in the reign of Henry VIII. He was educated in England and France and was the chosen friend and companion of Henry's bastard son, the Duke of Richmond. He married Frances Vere, daughter of the Earl of Oxford, in 1532. During the Pilgrimage of Grace in 1536 he served in the king's army under his father's command and for brawling with an officer was imprisoned at Windsor in 1537; Surrey heard the man repeat a rumour that he sympathized with the rebels. However, he was not really out of favour at court and was put in charge of the realm's defences in Norfolk in 1539, won honour at a tournament in 1540, and was made Knight of the Garter in 1541. But he earned more time in prison for his riotous behaviour and brawling in 1542 and 1543.

Surrey's pride and his quarrelsome disposition helped to put his family's future in pawn. The Howards, representing the Catholic nobility, helped to bring about the disgrace and death of Thomas Cromwell. The Seymours, also enemies of the Howards, were growing in influence towards the end of Henry's reign and Surrey was superseded as commander of Henry's forces in

Henry Howard, Earl of Surrey. The portrait drawing by Holbein. The Royal Library, Windsor.

Earl of Surry

France by Edward Seymour. Surrey resented this bitterly; he had once assaulted Seymour at Hampton Court and had been in danger of losing his right hand – the punishment for striking another in the king's presence. He was saved by the intercession of none other than Thomas Cromwell, the man whom the Howards – and particularly Surrey's father, the Duke of Norfolk – pursued so implacably. The Seymours and their friend Sir Richard Southwell, who had once been Cromwell's friend, had little difficulty, given Surrey's pride and indiscretion, in bringing the Howards down. They were helped immeasurably by Surrey's insistence on coupling the royal arms with his own, claiming his right through his descent from Edward I. The Duke of Norfolk and the Earl of Surrey, father and son, were arrested in December 1546 and indicted for high treason the following January. Surrey was beheaded on Tower Hill on 19 January; his father's execution was fixed for the 28th. Norfolk kept his head because the king died during the previous night.

Surrey was 14 years younger than Wyatt, whom he admired unreservedly and who showed him the way to poetry of precision and elegance in the English language. His models were the same as Wyatt's – the Italian school and Petrarch and his poetry displays a finish and smoothness that made him more popular than Wyatt with the Elizabethans. His sonnets were in the form that Shakespeare used to perfection. What Surrey does not achieve in the same measure as Wyatt is strength – his love poems are cool statements rather than declarations; but his grace and his skilful use of classical models show him to be the poetic ancestor of Sir Philip Sidney. English poetry is indebted to Surrey also for his introduction of blank verse, a form that he probably found in Italy. His use of it can be seen in his translations of Books II and IV of Virgil's *Aeneid*, which – despite any imperfections or unevenness – remain a landmark and led on to Marlowe, Shakespeare, and Milton.

*Tottel's Miscellany* of 1557 (see **Tottel's Miscellany** and **Wyatt, Thomas**) contained 40 poems by Surrey, and the earliest known edition of his Virgil survives in a single copy, undated, from about the year 1554. It is called *The Fourth Boke of Virgill, Intreating of the Love between Aeneas and Dido Translated into English and Drawne with a Strange Meter by Henrye Howard Earl of Surrey Worthy to be Embrased*. The two books are found in *Certain Bokes of Virgiles Aeneis Turned into English Metre, by Henry Earle of Surrey* (1557).

The most recent edition of Surrey's *Works* is that by Emrys Jones (1964).

**Surtees, R(obert) S(mith)** 1805–64. R. S. Surtees was born in the county of Durham and was for a time an unsuccessful lawyer. The second son of a landowner, he was personally secure and was able to launch *The New Sporting Magazine* with Rudolf Ackermann in 1831. He remained editor until 1856, meanwhile contributing the comic papers which appeared, in 1838, as a book entitled *Jorrocks' Jaunts and Jollities*, with coloured plates by Henry Alken, and later revised and enlarged with illustrations by H. Allen (1864).

Jorrocks, the sporting grocer, was a success and Surtees gave his public more in *Handley Cross, or the Spa Hunt* (1843, as *Handley Cross: Mr Jorrocks' Hunt* with pictures by John Leech, 1854). There followed *Hillingdon Hall, or the Cockney Squire* (1845), *The Analysis of the Hunting Field* (1845), *Hawbuck Grange: or the Sporting Adventures of Thomas Scott, Esq.* (1847, with illustrations by Phiz), *Mr Sponge's Sporting Tour* (1853, with illustrations by John Leech), *Ask Mamma: or The Richest Commoner in England* (1858, with illustrations by John Leech), *Plain or Ringlets?* (1860, with illustrations by John Leech), and *Mr Facey Romford's Hounds* (1865, with illustrations by Phiz and John Leech).

Surtees' reputation as a comic writer has remained highest, inevitably, with those readers who 'ken John Peel'. His canvas is small compared to that of Dickens, his contemporary, but as a creator of humorous characters and comic speech he runs him close and deserves to be better known. That is not to suggest that he was a novelist of anything like the same quality: Surtees was careless about the ingredients of a story that did not interest him and his books are loose and rambling. But the fun in them arises directly from human nature and the stories are told with irresistible bounce and energy.

'Hercules "takes" a Draper's Shop.' An illustration by John Leech for Surtees' *Mr Sponge's Sporting Tour*, 1853.

**Swift, Jonathan** 1667–1754. Swift was the grandson of a Royalist vicar of Yorkshire, whose three sons sought their fortune in Ireland after the Restoration settlement. One of the sons, Jonathan, married Abigail Erick (or Herrick), daughter of a Leicestershire family, and obtained a legal post in Dublin. He died before his expected child was born; this was Jonathan Swift who, though born in Dublin, educated at Kilkenny School, and a graduate of Trinity College, could declare at one stage of his life: 'I am not of this vile country, I am an Englishman.' But the 'vile country' was to become his passionate concern.

From his birth, on 30 November 1667, Swift's nurse doted on the baby boy and, being obliged to return to her home in Whitehaven, in Cumberland, on family matters, took her charge with her rather than have him out of her sight. She proved the best of foster mothers and when young Jonathan returned to Dublin at the age of three he was able to read. But soon after that his mother returned to her family in Leicestershire, leaving him in the care of his uncle Godwin. So his start in life was not exactly auspicious; he was a virtual orphan from his fourth year. His uncle sent him to Kilkenny, the best school in Ireland (Congreve was a fellow pupil), and at 14 Swift entered Trinity College as a pensioner. He was guilty of bad behaviour there and was only awarded his degree *speciale gratia*; he felt as complete a contempt for the teaching at Trinity as Milton had felt for that at Cambridge 50 years before.

Swift said later that his uncle 'gave him the education of a dog' but Godwin himself was in straitened circumstances and probably did his best. But Swift wanted Oxford, not Dublin, and complained of 'the ill-treatment of his nearest relations'. In 1689, when James II landed in Ireland and the country was plunged into turmoil, Swift left for England to stay with his mother's family in Leicestershire. He had been preparing for his MA at Dublin but had only his bachelor's degree when he arrived in England. He obtained employment in the house of Sir William Temple at Moor Park, near Farnham, Surrey. Temple's father had been head of the Irish Bar and had been kind and helpful to the Swifts.

Swift became secretary to Sir William Temple and probably hoped that the connection would help him along in the world. Temple did send Swift to William III on one occasion but nothing came of it; he also sent him to Ireland with a letter of recommendation to the Secretary of State. Nothing came of that either, and Temple invited Swift back to Moor Park. He returned there in 1691, visiting his mother on the way and stopping at Oxford to visit friends. He took his MA from Hart Hall, to give himself the qualification to enter the Church – it was not what he really wanted but he knew it was a way to independence if he could find no other.

The peace and order of Moor Park, as well as Temple's wide connections, proved beneficial to Swift, who practised the art of poetry during his leisure. He began to write Pindaric odes in the manner of Abraham Cowley; one of them was published in the *Athenian Mercury* and, according to Samuel Johnson, provoked John Dryden's remark: 'Cousin Swift, you will never be a poet.' (Dryden and Swift were related.) Swift, meanwhile, had been given the tutoring of a fellow dependant at Moor Park. This was the eight-year-old daughter of Lady Giffard's companion; Lady Giffard was Temple's sister. Esther Johnson, 'Stella', was to prove one of the lasting attachments of Jonathan Swift's life. But meanwhile he took the step that promised some kind of advancement – something which did not seem to be forthcoming through his association with Temple. Swift was ordained in 1694 and Temple helped him obtain the prebend of Kilroot, near Belfast. Swift was back in Ireland again; he was 27 years old and he had had to appeal to Temple for a testimonial, since so much time had elapsed since he took his degree. However, he obtained a licence for nonresidence at Kilroot and was back at Moor Park two years later, after an abortive attempt to arrange a marriage with a lady named Jane Waring.

Swift was on a happier footing at Moor Park now, since he had independent, if rather slender, means. He put Temple's papers in order and wrote *The Battle of the Books* in 1697, when Temple became involved in the 'Phalaris' controversy (see **Temple, Sir William**).

Sir William died in 1699 and Swift was without a patron. He returned to Ireland, to Dublin this time (he had resigned the living of Kilroot) as chaplain to Lord Berkeley, the new Lord Justice of Ireland. He had failed utterly to obtain a living in England and Temple's influence died so completely with his death that there has been speculation as to just how much effort he had put into helping Swift. Whatever the truth, Swift honoured Temple's memory without reserve for the rest of his life. He obtained the living of Laracor and Stella joined him in Dublin with her chaperone, Miss Rebecca Dingley. Stella had been left a little property in Ireland in Temple's will.

In 1704 Swift published *The Battle of the Books*

in the same volume as *A Tale of a Tub*. The former gave him an excellent opportunity to attack pedantry and the latter was a satire on the religious contentions of the time, with some digressions into other matters but with particular force in its attacks on fanaticism. Swift spared no one and the book was to be held against him later, when he hoped desperately for a preferment that would enable him to escape from Ireland. Other works, a few years later, were pamphlets on religious questions, including the *An Argument against abolishing Christianity* and *Letter concerning the Sacramental Test*. Swift's brilliant irony was simply too much for the establishment – the author was not the man to lean down from his intellectual heights and the establishment, unfortable, would not admit him. Meanwhile he was a regular visitor to England and his publication of the memoirs of Sir William Temple gave him a place in the literary scene. He became friends with Addison, Steele, Pope, and Congreve; Addison and Steele, particularly, admired and liked him. He was disillusioned with Whig policies and his pamphlets demonstrate his conviction that the party was ill-disposed toward the Church; he could not tolerate its association with Dissenters who, to him, were of the stamp of the fanatics who had brought England into a Civil War. The Tories, now bending their energies in an effort to conclude the war with France, were to benefit from two fine peace pamphlets from Swift (1711); but his preferment did not come about. His orthodoxy was doubtful and Queen Anne was hostile to him; many highly placed and influential friends, who welcomed the brilliant man as their guest, somehow failed – or simply did not try hard enough – to secure him advancement. And that was what Swift wanted above all; it must have tormented him to see the steady rise of dull, if perhaps acceptable, men. A diversion occurred during this period when he successfully confounded the pretensions of John Partridge, a cobbler who claimed to be an astrologer. Under the pseudonym 'Isaac Bickerstaff', Swift published a parody of Partridge's almanac in which he predicted the astrologer's death. Steele adopted the name of Bickerstaff when he founded *The Tatler* in 1709.

In 1713 Swift, who had taken his DD in 1701, became Dean of St Patrick's Cathedral in Dublin. It was the highest position to which he was ever to rise and it established him in Ireland for the rest of his life. Within the confining circumstances of a minority church – the Protestants in Ireland were between the Catholic majority in the country as a whole and the Presbyterian leanings strong in the north – Swift rendered excellent

Jonathan Swift. A detail from the portrait by Charles Jervas, c.1718. National Portrait Gallery, London.

service. He was mourned at his passing by Protestants and Catholics alike; his powerful pen had proved to be a great force working on their behalf.

About 1710 Swift began his *Journal to Stella*, the series of letters to Esther Johnson and Rebecca Dingley that tells us so much about his life and his feelings. There was another woman in his life by now, another Esther, oddly enough. This was Esther Vanhomrigh ('Vanessa'), who fell in love with him; he did not return such feelings but Vanessa, only 20 years old to Swift's 43, followed him to Ireland when her parents died. Swift's feelings towards her are depicted in his poem, *Cadenus and Vanessa*, written about 1713. He also published various political pamphlets during the years 1713 and 1714 in support of the Tory ministry but the death of Queen Anne and the ascendancy of the Whigs came in 1714; he retired to Dublin, briefly returning at the invitation of Pope and becoming involved in the activities of the Scriblerus Club with Pope, Gay, Arbuthnot, and the others. But he was soon back in Dublin; the Whig policies were unfair to Ireland – and Swift was opposed to injustice and unfair dealing of any kind.

His most notable efforts on behalf of Ireland were *Proposal for the Universal Use of Irish Manufactures* (1720) and the famous *Drapier's Letters* (1724), which frustrated the hopes of making an easy fortune through debased 'small money' for Ireland called 'Wood's ha'pence'. About 1720 Swift began work on another book, which was to become one of the most famous in English literature.

In 1723 Esther Vanhomrigh seems to have provoked a crisis in her relations with Swift. His honourable behaviour and continued solicitude for her well-being, and his genuine esteem of her, were simply not enough for the woman who was in love with him. One theory advanced by Swift's biographers is that he and Stella had contracted a secret marriage, a matter of securing their independence from other encroachments, though they were never 'married' in the physical sense. Vanessa learned of this and wrote to Stella, who sent the letter to Swift. The breach caused by Vanessa's behaviour was final for Swift – and possibly fatal for Vanessa. She died in June 1723 and never mentioned Swift in her will, which she made the month before her death.

Swift went to London in 1726. He visited his friends Pope and John Gay but his chief purpose was to deliver a letter of remonstrance on Irish affairs to Walpole, the Prime Minister. Swift and Walpole disliked each other at once and Swift's efforts achieved nothing. Stella died in January 1728 and Swift, while still continuing to work, was beginning to succumb to the condition that had plagued him from his 23rd year. This has now been diagnosed by modern medicine and is called Ménière's disease, a disturbance of the inner ear that causes vertigo and nausea. There was no treatment for it in Swift's lifetime and his fortitude must have been extraordinary. *Gulliver's Travels*, probably the most misread classic of English literature, was published in 1726, *The Grand Question Debated* in 1729, and *Verses on his own Death* in 1739. He continued to correspond with his friends in London and was venerated by the people of Dublin. He spent a third of his income on charities and saved what he could to found St Patrick's Hospital, a charitable institution that was opened in 1757.

Swift was to depart from the world, in a sense, before he died. He suffered from a brain tumour and no mental constitution, however strong, could go on fighting his combined disabilities. He lapsed into dementia in 1742 and never recovered; three years later he was dead. A hush fell over Dublin at his passing.

So much of Swift's work deals with religious and political affairs that it is often left out of the history of literature, belonging more properly to the field of history. But some of it demands mention: *A Short View of the State of Ireland* (1728) is both powerful and touching but, as so often is the case of the country that defied all English efforts to make it a colony, it fell upon deaf ears. Swift did not relax his efforts, however, and his *A Modest Proposal* (1729) is both a remorseless parody and a terrible indictment.

Swift's poetry, in addition to his account of his friendship with Esther Vanhomrigh, consisted of annual pieces to the other Esther (Stella) on her birthday; they are charming verses of considerable grace. *Baucis and Philemon* (1709) is Swift's verse retelling of the ancient legend; *On Poetry: A Rhapsody* (1733) was regarded by the author as his best satire.

Jonathan Swift had a chip on his shoulder – the fact has to be faced – and it stayed there all his life. The conclusion that he became a churchman because he could find nothing better to do for a living is inescapable and explains to some extent the ferocity of his attacks on organized religion. Yet the personal integrity of this cantankerous man proved stronger than his resentment, as his record of service proves. His prose is superb, as clear as crystal and exquisitely graceful; his intellect was formidable, his gift for satire unrivalled, and his vitality astonishing. If he had been born to privilege and in a position to choose his career he might have become that rarest of men in politics, a great statesman and reformer. But he would, one cannot help feeling, have left some mark on the world even if he had started life as an orphan beggar.

The definitive edition of Swift's prose works is the one by Herbert Davis, which commenced in 1939 and is now complete in 14 volumes. Herbert Davis's edition of *The Drapier's Letters* was published in 1935. The best text of *Gulliver's Travels*, that published by Faulkner of Dublin in 1735, is included in John Hayward's Nonesuch Press edition of *Selected Prose and Verse* (1934). *The Poems of Jonathan Swift*, edited by Harold Williams (three volumes; second edition, 1958), is definitive and *The Correspondence*, from the same editor, is available in five volumes (1963). Harold Williams is also the editor of the best edition of *The Journal to Stella* (1948). *The Poetical Works*, edited by Herbert Davis (1967), is a single volume in the Oxford Standard Authors series and editions of *Gulliver's Travels* can be found in Oxford Paperbacks, Everyman's Library, and the Penguin English Library. *A Tale of a Tub* and *The Battle of the Books*, with other prose pieces, are available in a modern edition by A. C. Guthkelch and D. Nicol Smith (1958).

**Swinburne, Algernon Charles** 1837–1909. Swinburne, the son of Captain (later Admiral) Charles Swinburne and Lady Jane Ashburnham, was born in London. He was educated at Eton College and went on to Balliol College, Oxford. The bullying and sadistic homosexuality of Eton in the 1850s left their mark on Swinburne, though their worst effects were somewhat mitigated by his being lodged with his tutor, James Leigh Joynes, and by his personal courage. A tiny boy for his age, with a shock of flaming red hair, he needed courage; but it is certain that his years at Eton developed his taste for flagellation. He was a promising pupil, good at Greek and Latin, and won the Prince Consort's Prize for Modern Languages in 1852. He went to Oxford in 1856 and had the great scholar Benjamin Jowett as his tutor. While there he became friendly with William Morris and Edward Burne-Jones, who were at Exeter College, and with Dante Gabriel Rossetti, who was a visitor in 1857. Meanwhile he pursued his interest in French literature and won the Taylorean Scholarship in 1858; he was also writing poetry and publishing critical articles in an undergraduate magazine.

Swinburne's first published volume was *The Queen Mother. Rosamond. Two Plays* (1860), printed at his father's expense. The verse plays concerned Catherine de Medici and the Eve of St Bartholomew, and Rosamond Clifford as the victim of the jealous Queen Eleanor. They were noticed briefly and unfavourably by two journals and otherwise ignored. His next published poem, completed while he was travelling in Italy, was another matter. *Atalanta in Calydon* (1865), a verse drama in the classical Greek form, made him famous, disclosing a master of verbal music and a poet of extraordinary rhythmic energy. In the same year he published *Chastelard*, a verse play about a young French courtier's treasonous wooing of Mary of Scotland, a work begun while the poet was at Oxford. This was not well received, though *The Athenaeum* praised Swinburne's gift for beauty of expression. Other reviews suggested that the play's tone was immoral; when Swinburne's next collection, *Poems and Ballads* (first series, 1866), was published he was in the public eye. Tennyson had written to him praising *Atalanta*; Browning had expressed admiration of his technique though he had reservations about the subjects of some of the poems he heard Swinburne read. More important to Swinburne – who later rejected both elder poets – was the large number of admirers who looked to him for something new in poetry. They were not disappointed.

*Poems and Ballads* contained 62 poems, some of which angered as well as astonished his readers, predictably enough in an age when almost everyone read poetry, often aloud in a room full of friends and family. 'Anactoria' is a declaration of homosexual love by the poet Sappho; *Dolores* is both sensual and cruel in generous measure; the beautiful **Hymn to Proserpine** and the famous **The Garden of Proserpine** might have upset any Victorian Christian who read them carefully; and there were others, equally shocking. Swinburne's publishers were nervous and issued **Laus Veneris** separately to see what would happen. Nothing much did happen, though this seems odd given the climate of the time; possibly it was not reviewed, so there was no one to tell the public to buy it and feel shocked. *Poems and Ballads* was first reviewed by John Morley in *The Saturday Review* in August 1866 and he lost no time in telling the public how to react. Robert Buchanan in *The Athenaeum* called it 'prurient trash'. *The Times* thundered its offence and J. M. Ludlow of the Christian Socialists recommended prosecution. The publishers, Moxon, withdrew the book, which was immediately reissued by the dubious John Camden Hotten, whose list contained a fair sample of erotica. Swinburne could now be called notorious and his poems were selling very well. Of more importance was their effect on the younger readers at the universities. Swinburne became their idol; his pagan spirit and

Swinburne. A detail from the portrait by G. F. Watts, 1865. National Portrait Gallery, London.

intoxicating music was made for youthful spirits and the young Thomas Hardy was overwhelmed by his poetry. A month after the unfavourable reviews, praise for Swinburne appeared in *The Examiner*, *Fraser's Magazine*, and *The Westminster Review*.

A *Song of Italy* (1867) and *Songs before Sunrise* (1871) are both imbued with the poet's hatred of tyranny, secular and sectarian. He admired Mazzini extravagantly and followed his idol, Victor Hugo, in that poet's detestation of Napoleon III. *Bothwell, A Tragedy* (1874) was the second part of his trilogy on Mary of Scotland. Swinburne discussed with W. M. Rossetti the possibility of staging it but the poet was unwilling to consider cutting a play which would have taken ten hours or more to perform. No one seems to have considered, then or now, staging separate scenes; but some fine poetry and dramatic power are contained in *Bothwell*. Swinburne returned to classical drama in *Erectheus* (1876) and received high praise for his faithfulness to the Greek model; but admirers of the thrilling *Atalanta in Calydon* were disappointed in it. *Poems and Ballads* (second series, 1878) was less sensational than the first volume but the content is equally rewarding. Baudelaire, one of the three French poets Swinburne most admired (the third was Gautier) died in 1867 and *Ave Atque Vale* is an elegy on the passing of the French master. Gautier, who died in 1872, also receives tribute and the tone of admiration for French poetry is completed by poems on Hugo and translations of the *Ballades* of François Villon; other poems in the volume are 'Relics', 'A Vision of Spring in Winter', 'The Last Oracle', and 'The Forsaken Garden'.

In 1879 Swinburne nearly succumbed to the strain that his wild life was placing on his constitution. It was remarkable how much energy he could summon, considering his drunkenness and other dissipations, but by June of 1879 his condition was serious. His admirer Theodore Watts-Dunton was a solicitor; he had been of great service to Swinburne in his dealings with John Camden Hotten, the publisher. The poet's mother, Lady Swinburne, turned to Watts-Dunton for help and it was arranged that he become the poet's guardian, with Lady Swinburne contributing £200 a year from her late husband's estate. Swinburne accepted the arrangements placidly, which must have been a huge relief to all who knew him. The alternative might have been confinement under medical supervision. Watts-Dunton leased a house at the foot of Putney Hill and Swinburne lived there, behaving well for the rest of what proved to be a respectably long life. His poetry continued, as did his busy life as a man of letters.

*Studies in Song* and *Songs of the Springtides* (1880) reflected his fascination with the endless movement and power of the sea. *Mary Stuart* (1881) completed Swinburne's trilogy of verse plays about the Scots queen. *Tristram of Lyonesse* (1882) concerns an Arthurian subject which had occupied him intermittently since 1869; this volume also contains 'A Dark Month' (the sequence of lyrics prompted by the death of a child), 'Athens, an Ode', and a group of sonnets on the Elizabethan playwrights. *Marino Faliero* (1885) is a verse tragedy on the same subject as Byron's poem and he used the dramatic form again in *Locrine* (1887), *The Sisters* (1892), and *Rosamond, Queen of the Lombards* (1899). It is generally acknowledged that his poetic energy showed signs of decline after *Tristram* but his output was nonetheless remarkable: *A Century of Roundels* (1883), *A Midsummer Holiday and Other Poems* (1884), *Poems and Ballads* (third series, 1889), *Astrophel and Other Poems* (1894), and *A Channel Passage and Other Poems* (1904). *The Duke of Gandia* (1908) was his last work.

Swinburne's considerable prose output was mainly of literary criticism. Monographs on English writers were *Byron* (1866), *William Blake* (1868), *George Chapman* (1875), *A Study of Shakespeare* (1880), and *A Study of Ben Jonson* (1889); his *A Study of Victor Hugo* was published in 1886. To the *Encyclopaedia Britannica* he contributed the entries on Congreve, Marlowe, Mary Queen of Scots, Tourneur, and Victor Hugo. Among a mass of other essays were *Christabel and the Poems of Coleridge* (1869), *Essays and Studies* (1875), *A Note on Charlotte Brontë* (1877), and *Charles Dickens* (published posthumously, 1913). He was the author of a novel, *Love's Cross-Currents: A Year's Letters*, which was refused by his publisher Moxon but was published in *The Tatler* (1877) under the pseudonym Mrs H. Manners. Its first appearance in volume form was in the USA in 1901. Another novel, *Lesbia Brandon*, was never finished; the completed chapters were first published in 1952. Neither novel has occupied scholars of fiction for very long.

In his later years, under the eye of Watts-Dunton, Swinburne became respectable and reactionary. He was considered a suitable candidate for the laureateship, and had attacked Walt Whitman, who had been one of the most fervent admirers of Swinburne in the USA. He died at the age of 72, muttering lines from Aeschylus and Sappho.

*The Complete Works* of Swinburne was edited by Edmund Gosse and Thomas J. Wise (20 volumes, 1925–27). *The Swinburne Letters* was edited by Cecil Y. Lang (six volumes, 1959–62). Modern selections from Swinburne's poetry have been edited by Laurence Binyon (The World's Classics, 1940), by Edward Shanks (1950), and by Edith Sitwell (1960). A selection of poetry and prose was edited by Richard Church (Everyman's Library, 1940).

***Sword of Honour*** See **Waugh, Evelyn (Arthur St John).**

***Sybil,*** or *The Two Nations.* A novel by Benjamin Disraeli, first published in 1845.

Charles Egremont, broadminded and progressive, is in love with Sybil, whose father Gerard is one of the leaders of the Chartist movement. Charles's father is Lord Marney, a rapacious landlord whose title is based on the estates owned by the Egremont family. These once belonged to the Abbot of Marney; they were plundered during the Reformation. Sybil and her father are descendants of the Abbot.

Disraeli is no more successful in *Sybil* than in its forerunner, *Coningsby*, in creating believable characters in a convincing story, which he can narrate against the setting of the 'Two Nations'.

*Coningsby* concerns the state of the parties and *Sybil* moves on to the state of the people, whose lot was often grievous and whose growing discontent eventually forced the landlords and employers to be less greedy – but not before they were faced with strife. The strength of the book lies there; Disraeli knew his subject very well. Its failure stems from his inability to present character; Charles, Sybil, Stephen Morley, Lord Marney and the rest are no more than cardboard figures, given words to speak.

***Sylvia's Lovers*** A novel by Elizabeth Gaskell, first published in 1863. The story is set in and around Monkshaven (Whitby) at the end of the 18th century.

Daniel Robson, a farmer near Monkshaven, was once a seaman and a smuggler and has bitter memories of the press gangs who were active in seacoast towns during the naval wars. His daughter Sylvia is loved by her cousin Philip Hepburn, whose Quaker diligence has earned him a partnership in a draper's business in Monkshaven. But Sylvia falls in love with Charley Kinraid, a gallant and attractive sailor whose reputation as a light-hearted lover is known to Philip. However, he keeps silent, and Sylvia and Charley are betrothed.

Philip is on the way to London, and Charley is returning to his whaling ship, when the latter is seized by the press gang. Charley calls a last message to Philip for Sylvia. But Philip has to hurry on to London and it is two months before he can give Sylvia any news. He returns to find her believing Charley drowned – his hat was found – and Philip conceals what he knows.

Tragedy in a grimmer form strikes when Daniel Robson leads an attack on the press gang and is hanged as a result. Sylvia and her mother are dispossessed and Philip persuades Sylvia to marry him, though he knows that she still mourns Charley. A year later Charley returns and Philip's treacherous behaviour is exposed. Sylvia turns on him and her bitter denunciation drives him from Monkshaven. Charley disappears once more at the same time.

At the siege of Acre the two men meet again. Philip saves Charley's life and is seriously wounded. Sylvia, meanwhile, has borne a child and learned that Charley Kinraid had married another woman within weeks of leaving her. Her disillusion is complete and she softens towards the memory of Philip. He turns up once more; destitute and disfigured, he has made his way back to Monkshaven for a sight of his wife and child. He dies there, he and Sylvia reconciled.

*Sylvia's Lovers* was not well received upon publication but it ranks high among Victorian novels. Elizabeth Gaskell could, as no one else before her, convey the intensity of feeling of her awakening heroines and she made them girls of the most ordinary work-worn kind; the reading public was largely middle class and she was showing it a level of life it had never bothered about. Sylvia treads a hard road to some sort of truth; Philip is brought down by his hopeless love, which Sylvia can never return. Their loveless marriage is described with chilling accuracy and the atmosphere of Monkshaven felicitously described.

**Symonds, John Addington** 1840–93. Symonds, a doctor's son, was born in Bristol. He was educated at Harrow School and Balliol College, Oxford, where he came under the influence of Benjamin Jowett and earned distinction as a classical scholar. He won the Newdigate Prize with his poem 'The Escorial' in 1860 and became a fellow of Magdalen College. Symonds was consumptive and spent most of his time after Oxford in Europe, travelling in Switzerland, Italy, and Greece and contributing essays to English magazines. These were collected as *Sketches in Italy and Greece* (1874), *Sketches and Studies in Italy* (1879), and *Italian By-ways* (1883).

Symonds's principal work was *The Renaissance in Italy*, which had strong appeal in the picture it gave of a world far removed from Victorian England. The book is lacking in both unity and detachment; it is more a series of sketches of the Italian Renaissance in an emotional and romantic vein. It is in seven volumes: *The Age of the Despots* (1875), *The Revival of Learning* (1877), *The Fine Arts* (1877), *Italian Literature* (Vols. 4 and 5, 1881), and *The Catholic Reaction* (Vols. 6 and 7, 1886). Symonds's writing did much to popularize Italian culture in England and his contributions to *The Fortnightly Review* stimulated English interest in the Swiss Alps. Among his other works were *Shelley* (1878) and *Sir Philip Sidney* (1886), both for the English Men of Letters series; *A Problem in Greek Ethics* (1883); *A Problem in Modern Ethics* (1891); *Our Life in the Swiss Highlands*, written with his wife (1892); translations of *The Sonnets of Michelangelo and Tommaso Campanella* (1878); *The Autobiography of Benvenuto Cellini* (1888); and biographies of *Ben Jonson* (1886) and *Michelangelo* (1893). Symonds also published *Walt Whitman: A Study* (1893).

**Symons, Arthur** 1865–1945. Symons was born in Wales of Cornish parents. He was privately educated, became fluent in French and Italian, and frequented the Rhymers' Club, where be became the friend of Dowson, Lionel Johnson, and Wilde. For a time he shared living space with W. B. Yeats, who also frequented the club.

Symons contributed to *The Yellow Book* and in 1896 became editor of *The Savoy*. He published poetry, plays, and literary essays with a special interest in Shakespeare, Elizabethan drama, and the symbolist poets of France. His poetry is forgotten now but his *The Symbolist Movement in Literature* is acknowledged as an important study and he published English versions of Zola, Gabriele d'Annunzio, Baudelaire, and Pierre Louÿs.

**Synge, John Millington** 1871–1909. J. M. Synge was born at Rathfarnham, near Dublin. His father died a year later and Synge's mother raised five children according to her devout Protestant principles (the family's antecedents were Anglo-Irish). A steady income came from land holdings in Galway, which provided security if not affluence; Synge later came into a modest legacy from an uncle and this gave him material independence. His independence of mind gave his mother cause for concern while he was still a boy, as did his delight in playing the fiddle, his liking for solitude, and his indifferent health. He was taught by tutors and when free would roam the hills and valleys of Wicklow. He later went to Trinity College, Dublin.

Synge's interest in music continued: he studied in Germany and France, and from 1895 spent much of his time in Paris. His talent for languages led to a growing interest in Irish and at this time he was trying his hand at poetry and essays. He met W. B. Yeats in Paris at the end of 1896 and attended the first meeting of the Irish League in Paris in 1897. But he was too independent a spirit to subscribe to any movement for long. Yeats's suggestion that he look closely at Ireland for the proper subject for his talents led to Synge's first visit to the remotest part of the country, the Aran Islands in the Atlantic Ocean. He spent every summer there for five years; his grasp of Irish enabled him to communicate with the islanders at a level that would have been impossible in English alone and he discerned the poetry inherent in their stories and songs. Their hard lives and dignified acceptance of the sea's merciless presence inspired a one-act tragedy of remarkable power when Synge began to practise his skill as a playwright. Meanwhile he recorded the life he observed in *The Aran Islands*, completed in 1902.

The first of Synge's plays to be produced was *In the Shadow of the Glen*, in Dublin in 1903

J. M. Synge, c.1896.

(published 1904). Its setting was the remote valleys of Wicklow and the dialogue demonstrated his skill in using the language of ordinary people in Ireland, complete with its poetry, for which he had a flawless ear. The one-act comedy is about a young wife with an ageing suspicious husband whom she eventually rejects in favour of the freedom of the open road. Written with Synge's remarkable economy, its truthfulness makes it applicable to life in a remote rural community in any age, but Synge was attacked for presenting the Irish in this way.

*Riders to the Sea* (1904), a one-act play set on an island off the west coast, much like the Aran Islands, stresses the resignation of a mother whom the sea has robbed of her sons: 'It's a great rest I'll have now, and it's time, surely.' The play is spare, simple, and powerfully moving. *The Well of the Saints* (1905) is a bitter comedy about two blind beggars whose sight is miraculously restored – and then rejected by them as a dubious blessing. *The Tinker's Wedding* (1907) is a farce about a tinker's girl with a great desire to be properly married by a priest. Both plays present another aspect of Irish life, that of the roads. Synge had already glanced at it in *In the Shadow of the Glen*; in these plays and the memorable **The Playboy of the Western World** he showed Ireland, so much a country of the dispossessed, to the Irish for the first time. The intelligentsia and the urban Dubliners – many of them descendants of the dispossessors – refused to acknowledge the truth Synge offered. For them, this was not what the Irish cultural revival was about: the uproar at the first night of *The Playboy* (1907) is part of theatre history.

*The Aran Islands* was published in 1907, with illustrations by Jack Yeats, brother of the poet W. B. Yeats. *In Wicklow, West Kerry and Connemara* (1911) was illustrated by the same artist and in these two short prose works Synge's quality as an observer is obvious. They are the background from which the plays arose and are recommended to anyone who wants to know the authentic rural Ireland of the first decades of the century. Synge's last play was left incomplete when he died at the age of 38 of a lymphatic tumour. This was *Deirdre of the Sorrows* (1910), his single excursion into the Irish mythology so favoured by his contemporaries, and it shows Synge's unique poetic gift being used in a full-length tragedy. There is every reason to believe he would have produced a masterpiece had he lived. He was a scrupulous craftsman, writing draft after draft of each play until he was satisfied with the result. His plays *were* in fact part of the Irish cultural revival and *The Playboy* enjoys classic status.

Synge, in his tragically short career, caught the rhythm and poetry of the English used by a different race, and combined this with unerring stagecraft. 'In Ireland, for a few years more', he wrote, 'we have a popular imagination that is fiery, and magnificent, and tender; so that those of us who wish to write start with a chance that is not given to writers in places where the springtime of the local life has been forgotten, and the harvest is a memory only, and the straw has been turned into bricks.'

The rest of Synge's published work is contained in *Poems and Translations*, with a preface by W. B. Yeats (1909); *With Petrarch: Twelve Sonnets* (prose translations, 1928); and *Translations*, edited by Robin Skelton and containing hitherto unpublished material (1961). *Four Plays and The Aran Islands* was edited by Robin Skelton (The World's Classics, 1962). The edition by Mícheál MacLiammóir (Everyman's Library, 1958) contains all the plays, including *Deirdre of the Sorrows*, and selections from Synge's prose, verse, and translations.

**Syntax in Search of the Picturesque, Dr** A verse satire by William Combe (1741–1823) on the early 19th-century fashion for popular books of picturesque travel. It was first published in *The Poetical Magazine* (1809). Dr Syntax is a schoolteacher and clergyman who sets out on his horse, Grizzle, during the holidays; he intends 'to make a *tour* and *write it*'. Further adventures were *The Second Tour of Dr Syntax in Search of Consolation* (1820) and *The Third Tour of Dr Syntax, in Search of a Wife* (1821). The satires were initiated by Thomas Rowlandson, the artist and caricaturist; the successful collaboration with Combe continued with *The Dance of Death* (1815), *The Dance of Life* (1816), and *Johnny Quae Genus* (1822). Combe also wrote the letterpress for *The Microcosm of London* (1808) and a metrical satire directed at Lord Imham, *The Diaboliad* (1776).

# T

**Tables of the Law; The Adoration of the Magi, The** See **Yeats, William Butler**.

**Tagore, Rabindranath** 1861–1941. Rabindranath Tagore was the son of a wealthy Bengal family and was born in Calcutta. He was educated privately and studied law in London (1878–80). Tagore wrote from his boyhood days and published his first poetry when he was 17: *A Poet's Tale* (1878). An internationalist as well as a true son of India, Tagore wanted more than anything a cross-fertilization of the cultures of East and West. He lectured in England, the USA, and Europe and in 1901 established a school in Bengal, at Santiniketan, to promote his ideas. His novel of Bengal life, *Binodini* (1902), was the first modern novel by an Indian writer and his poetry, which he translated into English himself, began to attract the attention of English writers.

Tagore, a much-travelled man, went to England again in 1912 and was welcomed with enthusiasm by W. B. Yeats, Ezra Pound, and others. Yeats wrote the introduction to Tagore's *Gitanjali* (1912), a volume of religious poems which the author had translated into English. In 1913 Tagore became world famous when he was awarded the Nobel Prize for Literature; he was knighted two years later. *The Gardener* (1917), dedicated to Yeats, was described by Tagore as 'lyrics of love and life'. However, he resigned his knighthood in 1919 as a protest against the massacre of civilians at the Jalianwala Bagh in Amritsar. For some years Tagore was widely read in the West but his work is not well known now. In India his name is honoured, and the school at Santiniketan became Visva-Bharati University in 1921. His biography was written by Krishna Kripalani and published in London (1962). Among Tagore's other works are poems about children, *The Crescent Moon* (1913); his first translated play, *Chitra* (1916); *The Religion of Man* (1931); and *Farewell My Friend* (1940). Tagore's *Collected Poems and Plays* was published in 1936.

**Tale of a Tub, A,** *written for the Universal Improvement of Mankind.* A prose satire by Jonathan Swift, written about 1696 and first published in 1704. The title derives from the nautical practice of throwing a tub into the sea when a whale was sighted; the whale was expected to attack the tub and not the ship. Swift intended that the wits and philosophers should leave weak targets alone. The principal targets of his satire are religion and learning; the main thread follows a sustained attack on the Catholics and Dissenters, with the digressions aimed at critics, the ancient versus modern controversy, and madness. In the main satire a father bequeathes a coat to each of his sons – Peter, Martin, and Jack. The coats are in no way to be altered. Peter is the Catholic Church, Martin (Luther) is the Anglican, and Jack (John Calvin) represents the Dissenters. The sons, however, do not remain true to the injunction, gradually adding decorations according to the prevailing fashions. Martin and Jack quarrel with Peter, finding his arrogance insupportable; then they quarrel with each other – and separate. Peter is most savagely attacked, but Jack is also treated with contempt and Martin, representing Swift's Church, is given scant respect. The authorship of the satire proved to be a serious obstacle in later years, when Swift was hoping for preferment in the Church.

**Tale of Two Cities, A** A novel by Charles Dickens. It was published simultaneously in *All the Year Round* and in monthly parts, between June and December 1859. The author makes generous acknowledgment in his preface to Thomas Carlyle, whose *French Revolution* had been published in 1837. The cities of the title are London and Paris at the time of the Revolution.

Dr Manette, after spending 18 years in the Bastille, has been released and is being cared for by Thérèse and Ernest Defarge in their wine shop in the St Antoine quarter of Paris. Lucie, his daughter, comes to take him to London, where the doctor later recovers his sanity. They meet Charles Darnay on the boat; he is the nephew of the Marquis de St Evremonde and detests his family's arrogance and cruelty.

In London, five years later, Darnay is falsely accused of sedition and Lucie and her father are obliged to testify against him. But Darnay is saved by Sydney Carton, a brilliant and dissolute lawyer whom he closely resembles. Lucie falls in love with Darnay, who returns to France to confront his uncle with his suspicion that the marquis himself arranged for the false charges to be brought. The marquis treats him with scorn, which increases when Darnay renounces all title to the St Evremonde estates and warns his uncle that the storm is about to break. Darnay returns to London and on that night the marquis is murdered by a poor man whom he has wronged.

In London Carton is nursing a secret love for Lucie. He is a welcome visitor in the home of Lucie and Darnay, now married, though he is not entirely approved of by Miss Pross, Lucie's maid. In Paris the storm breaks. The Bastille is destroyed by the people and the Defarges search out an incriminating document concealed there by Dr Manette during his imprisonment. The Revolution gathers momentum and soon France is in the grip of the Terror, perpetrated by the 'long ranks of the new oppressors who have risen on the destruction of the old'. Gabelle, Darnay's old tutor, is in danger, accused of serving the emigrant nobility, and Darnay hurries to Paris to intercede for him. But the Defarges know who he is and Darnay, heir to St Evremonde, is arrested. Lucie and Dr Manette go to Paris and ask for help from the Defarges. Thérèse Defarge is intensely interested to discover that Darnay and his wife have a child.

At the tribunal things look well for Darnay when Dr Manette, a victim of the old regime, testifies in his favour. But Thérèse Defarge produces the document recovered from the Bastille; it contains damning evidence against the St Evremondes and Darnay is sentenced to the guillotine.

Sydney Carton now intervenes. He places no value on himself and his love for Lucie is undiminished. He bribes his way to the prison, drugs Darnay, and takes his place. Thérèse Defarge, meanwhile, determined to destroy all traces of the hated family, tries to stop them from leaving Paris – she has no knowledge of Carton's substitution. But Miss Pross kills her, and the family escapes. Carton goes to the guillotine, giving what comfort he can to a tragic little seamstress who alone knows of his sacrifice.

*A Tale of Two Cities* is Dickens's shortest novel, and is not often accorded a high place by critics of his work. But it is taut and thrilling, with the best constructed plot of all his novels, and in places it is deeply moving. The characters stay in the mind: Thérèse Defarge, Sydney Carton, Mr Lorry, Miss Pross, and the hapless girl who makes the last journey in the tumbril with Carton.

**Tales from Shakespeare** An adaptation of 20 plays by Shakespeare by Charles and Mary Lamb. The preface states 'The following Tales are meant to be submitted to the young reader as an introduction to the study of Shakespeare'; the book was suggested to Charles Lamb by William Godwin and first published in 1807. Mary Lamb's name did not appear on the title page until the edition of 1838, though she was responsible for 14 of the 20 plays in the volume. The book became a classic; it appealed to a general audience as well as the 'young reader' who studied it at school, and through it Shakespeare became better known than he had ever been before.

The book has held pride of place since the day it was published but it is hardly readable now. The 20 plays seem oddly chosen; Mary, or Charles, treads delicately around the plot of *Measure for Measure* and their reasons for including *All's Well That Ends Well* and *Cymbeline* are difficult to imagine. But however outdated it seems now the book succeeded in its purpose and has been the initial introduction for many people to the greatest poet in the language.

The plays related in the book are the comedies *The Tempest*, *A Midsummer Night's Dream*, *The Winter's Tale*, *Much Ado About Nothing*, *As You Like It*, *The Two Gentlemen of Verona*, *The Merchant of Venice*, *All's Well That Ends Well*, *The Taming of the Shrew*, *The Comedy of Errors*, *Measure for Measure*, and *Twelfth Night*; the tragedies are *Cymbeline*, *King Lear*, *Macbeth*, *Timon of Athens*, *Romeo and Juliet*, *Hamlet*, *Othello*, and *Pericles*. None of the historical plays is included.

**Tales of Mean Streets** See **Morrison, Arthur**.

**Tales of Mystery and Imagination** See **Poe, Edgar Allan**.

**Tales of Soldiers and Civilians** See *In the Midst of Life*.

**Taliesin, The Book of** Taliesin may be a mythical character but he is mentioned as a 6th-century bard in the *Saxon Genealogies* (*c*.690) appended to the *Historia Britonum* of Nennius. The village of Taliesin in Cardiganshire is near the site of what is believed to be his resting place. *The Book of Taliesin* is a 13th-century manuscript collection of poems by different hands and dating from different periods. The poem called *Preideu Annwyn* (*The Harrowings of Hell*) tells the story of Arthur's quest for a cauldron belonging to the King of Hades; Arthur is here a mythical hero with supernatural attributes and has no connection with the 'matter of Britain'. For the rest, 12 poems have been selected by Sir Ifor Williams as by the hand of Taliesin. These are heroic poems celebrating valour and royal virtue and addressed to Cynan ap Brochfael, King of Powys, Urien Rheged and his son Owain, and the hero Gwallawg. The manuscript of *The Book of Taliesin* is preserved in the National Library of Wales.

**Talisman, The** A novel by Sir Walter Scott, the second of his *Tales of the Crusades*, published in 1825. The talisman of the book has a basis in history. The Lockharts of the Lee, a Lanarkshire family, had in their possession an amulet which an ancestor, Sir Simon Lockhart, brought back from the Crusades. It was known as the Leepenny. Scott's novel, set in the Holy Land, was once enormously popular and is certainly the equal of the more famous *Ivanhoe* as a historical romance.

The leaders of the third Crusade are quarrelsome and jealous of each other: Richard I of England, Philip Augustus of France, Leopold of Austria, Conrade of Montferrat, and the Grand Master of the Templars. Their forces are idle and then Richard I falls ill.

Sir Kenneth, the Knight of the Leopard, on a mission for the Crusaders, encounters a Saracen emir and they engage in combat; but neither worsts the other – indeed they become friends.

Later Sir Kenneth, poor but valiant and in love with Edith Plantagenet, whom only his poverty prevents him approaching, is set to guard the banner of England. Queen Berengaria indulges in a wilful prank, luring Sir Kenneth from his post with a false message from Edith. In his brief absence the banner is torn down and his faithful hound wounded. King Richard has been cured, meanwhile, by a physician bearing a talisman; he says he has been sent by the Soldan himself. Richard is harsh with the disgraced Sir Kenneth, who is only saved from execution by the physician, who requests the king to give him the knight as a slave. Away from the Crusaders' camp the physician reveals himself as the emir Sir Kenneth fought with: but he is more than that – he is none other than Saladin. Sir Kenneth is treated with honour as Saladin's guest, and Saladin gives him the talisman.

The story concludes with Sir Kenneth saving Richard's life, with the identity of the one who tore down the banner being exposed – it was Conrade of Montferrat – and with Sir Kenneth's true origins in the royal house of Scotland being revealed.

**Tamburlaine the Great**, *divided into two tragicall discourses*. A tragedy in blank verse by Christopher Marlowe. The source was a life of the Tatar conqueror Timur (or Timur the Lame: hence Timurlane or Tamerlane) by the Spaniard Pedro Maxia, which had been translated into English in 1571. The first part was produced *c*.1587 by The Admiral's Men with the celebrated tragedian Edward Alleyn in the title role. Its success was enormous and the second part was written and produced in the following year. The complete work was first published in 1590.

The Persian king Mycetes, is opposed by his brother Cosroe, who raises a rebellion and takes for his ally the Scythian shepherd-chieftain Tamburlaine. Mycetes is overthrown, then Tamburlaine challenges Cosroe for the crown and defeats him: 'Is it not passing brave to be a King, And ride in triumph through Persepolis?' Tamburlaine goes on to further victories: he conquers the Turks and keeps the emperor Bajazet prisoner in a cage and torments him until he and his empress, Zabina, kill themselves. Tamburlaine's only warmth is for his beautiful captive Zenocrate, on whose behalf he spares the life of her father, the Soldan of Egypt, when he captures Damascus. Tamburlaine is supreme and acknowledges no authority but his own.

The conquests continue. Tamburlaine's chariot is drawn to Babylon by two relays of captive kings: 'Holla, ye pampered Jades of Asia:

What, can ye draw but twenty miles a day?' But Zenocrate is dying and Tamburlaine's bold spirit rages against death, but he realizes that he too, 'the Scourge of God', must die. The play closes with his death.

Tamburlaine himself is the whole play; the part is a tremendous challenge to an actor and not one that too many actors are prepared to face – it has been undertaken twice in 40 years. But the piece will be unlikely to succeed with modern audiences until the great part is mastered, since there is not much else of interest in the play.

**Taming of the Shrew, The** A comedy by William Shakespeare. An early work, and with parts written by others, it is possibly based on a play by Ariosto, *I Suppositi*, which had been translated by George Gascoigne in 1566. Though listed as a comedy in the First Folio of 1623 (its first publication) it could more properly be described as a farce. It was first produced *c*.1594.

The play begins with an Induction, in which the drunken tinker Christopher Sly is found by a lord on a hunt. The lord has him taken to his castle and assures him that Sly is a lord too – who has been out of his wits. He is treated like a lord and a play is acted for him by some strolling players.

Baptista, a rich man of Padua, has two daughters, Katherina and Bianca. Bianca, the younger of the two, is loved by Lucentio, who woos her while masquerading as a schoolmaster, but her father insists that his elder daughter must be married first. Katherina is notoriously bad-tempered and nobody wants her, so Bianca has to stay unwed in spite of having many suitors (including Hortensio and Gremio) besides Lucentio. From Verona comes Petruchio in search of a rich wife. He decides that Katherina will do, in spite of the warnings of his friends, and proceeds to woo her. His high-handed persistence succeeds and he seems oblivious of her rudeness and lack of grace. The marriage is arranged – and Petruchio sets out to tame her. He turns up late for the wedding and looking like a scarecrow; he hurries her off before the feast can begin and once they are home makes her existence a nightmare by his wilful and wayward pranks.

When he takes her back to her father's house she is so changed that Petruchio, rather than Lucentio (with his Bianca) or Hortensio (now married) is acknowledged the man with the most docile wife. Christopher Sly? We hear no more of him.

Like all farces, *The Taming of the Shrew* gains nothing by description. It usually succeeds on the stage, though its conventions – especially as uttered in the closing scenes – are very much of a world of the distant past. The Induction is often cut in performance. See also **Katherina**.

**Tamora** Queen of the Goths in Shakespeare's *Titus Andronicus*. She is defeated by Titus and brought captive to Rome with her three sons and Aaron the Moor, her lover. Her first-born son is sacrificed in Rome and she plots revenge on Titus and his family. She attracts Saturninus, the new emperor, who marries her when he cannot have Lavinia. She nearly succeeds in destroying the Andronicus family but Titus kills her first – after serving her the flesh of her sons to eat. She has a son by Aaron the Moor.

**Tam O'Shanter** A narrative poem by Robert Burns, first published in *The Edinburgh Magazine* in March 1791. Burns asked his friend, the antiquary Francis Grose, to include a drawing of Alloway Kirk, where the poet's father was buried, in his *Antiquities of Scotland*. Grose agreed – if Burns would give him an account of one of the witch legends surrounding the Kirk to accompany the drawing. Burns gave him three accounts, one of which told the story of Tam O'Shanter. The poem appeared in the following year. After a satirical prologue Tam and his crony Souter Johnie are found in a tavern; Tam is thoroughly plastered. He lurches out of the tavern, mounts his mare, Maggie, and starts for home. He passes Alloway Kirk and is drawn to the witches' celebration, which he watches, fascinated. The witches pour out of the Kirk with Auld Nick himself, and Tam is pursued by the hellish legion. He races away on Maggie and barely makes it across the bridge over the Doon to safety. But one of the witches, Cutty Sark, grabs Maggie's tail: 'The carlin claught her by the rump, And left poor Maggie scarce a stump.' Cutty Sark is the name given to a witch called Nannie, who wears a short shirt (a cutty sark) of paisley yarn.

**Tancred**, *or The New Crusade*. A novel by Benjamin Disraeli, first published in 1847. It is usually regarded as the third of his political novels. Following *Coningsby*'s concern with the state of the parties, and *Sybil*'s with the state of the people, *Tancred* is concerned with the state of religious practice and its current laxity. Disraeli has his hero, Tancred (his usual son of his usual aristocrat), refusing a seat in parliament to go and seek a direct communication with God in the Holy Land. Disraeli's suggestion, through his hero, that the doctrine of theocratic equality will benefit all is interesting, certainly, but only makes sense for believers. Obviously there were

many more believers in his day that there are now; the idea no longer carries any force and the novel has little merit otherwise.

**Tancred and Gismund** A tragedy by Robert Wilmot, Christopher Hatton, Henry Noel, and others, based on a story by Boccaccio.

Tancred, a tyrannical father, forbids the remarriage of Gismund, his widowed daughter. One day he surprises her with her lover, whom he later murders; then he sends his daughter her lover's heart in a cup. Gismund adds poison to the grisly contents and drinks from the cup.

The play was presented before Elizabeth I at Greenwich, probably in 1568, as *Gismond of Salerne* and was in rhyming verse. The published version of 1591 was called by its later name and is in blank verse. It was one of the first attempts to write a play about love, though in fact the lovers never appear on the stage together.

**Tannahill, Robert** 1774–1810. Tannahill was a weaver of Paisley who enjoyed a contemporary success, mostly as a lyric writer; his 'Jessie the Flower of Dunblane' was one of his works set to music by R. A. Smith, the editor of *The Scottish Minstrel*, and achieved great popularity. His *Poems and Songs* was published in 1807. Tannahill drowned himself after burning his manuscripts when Constable, the publisher, rejected a collection of his poems.

**Tappertit, Simon** Gabriel Varden's apprentice in *Barnaby Rudge*. A tiny man of stupendous conceit, inordinately proud of his silly little legs, he has eyes for Dolly Varden and dreams of a league of 'prentices – of which he will of course be the head. He is also vindictive and spiteful but his vanity makes him an easy tool for others.

**Tashtego** The Indian harpooner of the *Pequod* in Herman Melville's *Moby-Dick*. His is the last action on the doomed ship before she goes down, when he nails to the mast a skyhawk which is pecking at the signal flag.

**Task, The** A poem in blank verse in six books by William Cowper, first published in 1785. (For the origin of the poem, see **Cowper, William**.) 'The Sofa' is the first part and the five books that follow are 'The Time-piece', The Garden', 'The Winter Evening', 'The Winter Morning Walk', and 'The Winter Walk at Noon'. The title comes from 'the task' that Lady Austen set him in writing a poem about his sofa.

*The Task* is generally acknowledged as Cowper's masterpiece and earned the praise of Robert Burns and Coleridge. The poet, in a letter to William Unwin (10 October 1784), stated that his purpose was 'to recommend rural ease and leisure as friendly to the cause of piety and virtue'. His delight in the pleasures he found in country life are rendered with exactitude but the poetic impulse never falters. There are also didactic passages concerned with abuses such as the failures of the clergy and the cruelty of blood sports. The whole poem succeeds in its celebration and thanksgiving: 'Nature is but a name for an effect, Whose cause is God.'

**Tate, (John Orley) Allen** 1899–1979. Allen Tate was born in Winchester, Kentucky, and graduated from Vanderbilt University, Nashville, in 1922. He was one of the founder-editors of the magazine *Fugitive* (1922–25) and subscribed to *The New Criticism*. (See **Ransom, John Crowe**.) He also contributed to the Southern agrarianist symposium *I'll Take My Stand* (1930). *Stonewall Jackson* (1928) and *Jefferson Davis* (1929) are interpretative biographies that examine the South before the Civil War and the myths which attach to it and Tate also published a number of volumes of literary criticism. He is best known as a poet; his first collection was *Mr Pope and Other Poems* (1928), followed by *Three Poems* (1930), *The Mediterranean and Other Poems* (1936), and *Winter Sea* (1944). He published his *Collected Poems* in 1960. Allen Tate is the author of one novel, *The Fathers* (1938), a powerful and beautifully written study of the end of the Old South as recalled by one of its survivors looking back over 50 years. The author taught poetry at Princeton University and English literature at Minnesota University and held the chair of poetry at the Library of Congress (1934–44).

*Tatler, The* The periodical founded by Richard Steele in April 1709 appeared three times a week and purported to report on different subjects from chosen coffee and chocolate houses – the newly fashionable meeting places for ordinary people in London. Entertainment came from one house, politics and foreign news from another, poetry from a third, and so on. The tone of *The Tatler* developed into one of an arbiter of conduct and taste as it became more successful and the editor, Isaac Bickerstaff (Steele's pseudonym), introduced the marriage of his sister, Jenny Distaff, to broaden the scope of the periodical, making it a family magazine. Jenny Distaff (also Steele, of course) brought the subject of married life into journalism. The effort required to maintain the supply of copy was prodigious: of 271 numbers Steele wrote the entire contents of nearly 190, Joseph Addison wrote 42, and 36 numbers were written in collaboration. Steele's writing was relaxed and engaging, with a direct personal appeal. But the periodical closed in January 1711, when Steele could no longer meet the demands it made on him.

**Taylor, Bayard** 1825–78. The son of a Quaker family of Kennett Square in Pennsylvania, Taylor published his first verse in 1844 at the age of 19. He rebelled against his quiet background and went to Europe in the same year, sending regular letters back to the New York *Tribune*. The letters were such a success that he was made head of the *Tribune's* literary section and sent to California to cover the gold rush of 1849. *Views A-Foot* (1846), his book about his European experiences, was a success; *El Dorado: or Adventures in the Path of Empire* (1850), about the Gold Rush, was an even greater one, and Taylor enjoyed a reputation as an adventurer. In 1851 he set off on extensive travels and succeeded in joining Commodore Perry in the Pacific. He was back in New York in 1853, busy writing accounts of travel and adventures and covering the lecture circuit with great success.

Taylor's life became a round of lively travel. In 1862 he spent a year in St Petersburg as secretary of his country's legation and thereafter began to write fiction with an American setting, displaying the same industry and application to that as he had to his travel writing and to the numerous books of verse he published during his career. His most distinguished work was a translation of Goethe's *Faust* in the original metres (1870–71), which earned him a non-resident professorship in German at Cornell University and a diplomatic post in Germany. Taylor's *El Dorado* remains a useful and detailed record of a remarkable event.

**Taylor, Edward** *c*.1645–1729. The English-born American poet emigrated from Leicestershire to Massachusetts in 1668, when he was about 23 years old. He graduated from Harvard in 1671 and spent the rest of his life as pastor and physician of Westfield, a frontier town in that period. That he was a poet of considerable accomplishment was not known: he left instructions to his grandson, Ezra Stiles, that his poems were not to be published and they remained so until 1937, when the manuscript was discovered in the library of Yale University. The publication established him as the finest poet of 17th-century America.

Taylor took to New England his old country's poetic style and purpose; he was principally a devotional poet, of the Puritan persuasion, who could nevertheless write of simple things with charm and economy – 'Upon a Spider Catching a Fly' is a notable example. His most famous major works are *God's Determination Touching*

*His Elect*, in which his poetic gifts almost redeem his celebration of New England Puritan dogma, and his *Sacramental Meditations*, a series of poems that describe his application of the Bible to daily life.

**Taylor, Sir Henry** 1800–86.  Henry Taylor was born at Bishop-Middleham, Durham, and educated at home. He earned his knighthood for his long service in the Colonial Office and was the author of verse and poetic dramas. Taylor's plays were never produced but one of them, *Philip van Artevelde* (1834), was once admired as a study of character. Other plays were *Isaac Comnenus* (1827), *Edwin the Fair* (1842), *The Virgin Widow* (1850), and *St Clement's Eve* (1862). Taylor was also the author of *The Statesman* (1836), a satirical essay on the art of succeeding as a civil servant, and *Autobiography* (1800–75). His *Collected Works* were published in 1877 and his *Correspondence* in 1888.

**Taylor, Jeremy** 1613–67.  A barber's son of Cambridge, Taylor was educated at Gonville and Caius College and became a substitute preacher at St Paul's. It was there that Taylor, aged 23, came to the notice of Laud, Archbishop of Canterbury, who gave him a fellowship at All Soul's, Oxford. He became rector of Uppingham in 1638 and chaplain to both Charles I and the archbishop, leaving his rectorship in 1642 to join the king's personal attendants for a time. He was at Cardigan Castle when it surrendered to the Parliamentary army, but found shelter as teacher and chaplain to the Earl of Carbery at Golden Grove in Carmarthenshire.

Taylor spent ten years at Golden Grove and the best of his writing dates from this period. But he was not to escape completely from the ill will of the Puritans and was imprisoned in 1655. It is not clear whether he was actually charged but the persecution continued and a year later he was in prison again. He moved next to London and Lord Conway, another friend, secured him a chaplaincy in the north of Ireland in 1658. He resumed his writing, having at last found peace, and was given the see of Down and Connor at the Restoration.

Taylor's place in English literature is as one of the devotional writers of the early 17th century who did much to shape the Church of England. He wrote clear unadorned prose, using it to set forth his plea for tolerance; contentiousness, he saw, was in the ascendant and he feared its destructive power: men should be allowed to differ in opinion when they plainly agreed on Christian fundamentals. His principal works are *A Discourse on the Liberty of Prophesying* (1647),

*The Golden Grove* (1655), *Discourse of the Nature, Offices and Measures of Friendship* (1657), *The Worthy Communicant* (1660), and best known of all, *The Rule and Exercises of Holy Living* (1650) and *The Rule and Exercises of Holy Dying* (1651). The last-named was written in a period of deep personal grief following the deaths of his wife and of his patroness, Lady Carbery.

**Taylor, Tom** 1817–80.  Taylor was born at Bishop Wearmouth, Durham, and was educated at Glasgow University and Trinity College, Cambridge. He was always interested in the theatre and within a year of settling in London wrote a successful farce, *A Trip to Kissingen* (Lyceum Theatre, 1844). He became one of the most popular playwrights of his day, a friend and fellow amateur player of Dickens and a familiar figure in London society. Among his most successful works were *Masks and Faces* in collaboration with Charles Reade (Haymarket, 1852); *Still Waters Run Deep*, advanced in its day for its discussion of sex (Olympic Theatre, 1855); *Our American Cousin* (New York, 1858), the play Abraham Lincoln attended on the night of his murder; *The Fool's Revenge* (Sadler's Wells, 1859), an adaptation of Hugo's *Le Roi s'amuse*; and *The Ticket-of-Leave Man* (Olympic Theatre, 1863). Taylor borrowed material freely and brought excellent stagecraft to his work. His work is rarely revived but remains interesting for its handling of contemporary themes; *The Ticket-of-Leave Man* helped focus the attention of Victorian playwrights on the dramatic possibilities of low life. Taylor was also editor of *Punch* (1874–80).

***Teague Poteet's, At***  See ***Mingo***, *and Other Sketches in Black and White.*

**Tearsheet, Doll**  In Shakespeare's *Henry IV Part 2*, a whore of the Boar's Head tavern who is favoured by Falstaff. She is overfond of drink and in Act V is hauled off to prison for provoking a tavern brawl in which 'There had been a man or two lately kill'd.'

**Teazle, Lady**  Sir Peter Teazle's young wife in Sheridan's *The School for Scandal*. Fresh from the country, her head is turned by the dazzle and extravagance of London society. She is nearly seduced by the hypocritical and scheming Joseph Surface.

**Teazle, Sir Peter**  The elderly husband in Sheridan's *The School for Scandal*. He is led to believe his young wife is deceiving him but he is quite wrong about the identity of her supposed lover.

***Tell-Tale Heart, The***  A story by Edgar Allan Poe, first published in *The Pioneer* in 1843. One of his best, it is told in the first person by an unbalanced murderer. His victim is the old man whose house he shares. On the night he kills him he becomes acutely aware of a sound, which he believes is the old man's heartbeat. It is in fact the victim's watch, which he has unwittingly buried underneath the floor of the house with the dismembered body. When three police officers call (a neighbour had heard a scream in the night) the murderer is full of confidence and announces that the old man is away in the country. But while the police stay to ask further questions his abnormally heightened senses pick up the sound of what he thinks is the dead man's heart beating. The police watch him curiously and, convinced that they already know the truth, he betrays himself.

***Tempest, The***  A comedy by William Shakespeare, believed to be the last complete work from the playwright's own hand. It was first produced *c*.1611 and published in the First Folio of 1623. Various sources for the play have been put forward but nothing can be positively identified.

On board a ship during a tempest are Antonio, the usurper Duke of Milan; his confederate Alonso, King of Naples; Alonso's son Ferdinand; Alonso's brother Sebastian; and the old and honourable counsellor Gonzalo. The tempest has been raised by Prospero, the exiled Duke of Milan, using his magic arts from a lonely island. When driven from power by Antonio's treachery 12 years before, he had been cast adrift on the open sea with his infant daughter Miranda. That the boat contained food and water, some clothing, and books from Prospero's library had been due to the good offices of Gonzalo. The boat drifted to a lonely island where the witch Sycorax had been exiled. She is dead now and the only inhabitant is her son Caliban, savage and scarcely human. Prospero has released the spirits of the island imprisoned by Sycorax; one of them is Ariel.

The ship is wrecked on the island. The passengers are saved but Ferdinand is then found to be missing. Alonso mourns his son, believing him dead; Francisco tries to comfort him – Ferdinand is young and strong and when last seen was making for the shore. Ferdinand is indeed alive and in turn mourns his father, whom he believes has perished with the others. He follows Ariel's music; Miranda sees him and is enchanted. They fall in love – but Prospero knows that Miranda can be easily enchanted since the only other man, apart from her father, that she has ever seen is Caliban. Prospero is lord of the island and makes

'What have we here? A man or a fish?' Trinculo speaks thus of Caliban in *The Tempest* (Act II, scene 2). Scholars have long pondered on how Caliban was presented in Shakespeare's time and one possible solution may have been found in this creature, illustrated in Conrad Gessner's *Icones Anim Celium* (1560). Shakespeare shared the Elizabethan fascination with explorers' tales and descriptions of exotic and mythical animals.

Ferdinand work; but he watches his daughter's growing love with an affectionate eye. His design is working; Ferdinand is a king's son and declares his love; Miranda will become Queen of Naples.

Ariel brings the others to Prospero and they do not recognize him. He makes himself known to Gonzalo, to whom he owes his life; then the others realize who he is. Antonio, who had fallen in with Sebastian's plan to kill Alonso and make himself King of Naples (Ariel had prevented the murder), is completely unnerved, and Alonso, dull with grief, will make any amends he can.

Prospero then restores Ferdinand to his father and Miranda wins the king's approval at once. Prospero has restored the ship by his magic arts, so they can all, Alonso and Ferdinand, the repentant Antonio and Sebastian, Prospero – restored to his dukedom – and Miranda, sail for home with gentle winds conjured up by Ariel.

Prospero releases Ariel from his service and also Caliban, who had been his slave. He breaks his staff and buries his books; he has no need of magic now. The island is left to Caliban, who has provided most of the broader comedy in his antics with two of the crew, Stephano and Trinculo. (But Caliban also has exquisite words to utter, when he reassures them about the strange music made by the invisible Ariel.)

*The Tempest* is a difficult play to stage, in the demands it makes on the theatre's resources. Modern producers compound the difficulty by looking for an interpretation. None is needed – the play is as magical as Prospero's art and should be treated as such; it should be staged according to the text and the characters allowed to speak for what they are. The audience can accept it as a marvellous invention, the swan song of a poet at the height of his powers, and interpret it as they will.

**Temple, Sir William** 1628–99. The son of Sir John Temple, Master of the Rolls in Ireland, Temple was born in London and completed his education at Emmanuel College, Cambridge. In 1648 Temple met Dorothy, daughter of Sir Peter Osborne, and fell in love with her; but her family, staunch Royalists, opposed the marriage. However, William and Dorothy persisted and after seven years of devotion were married in 1655. During the years 1652–54 Dorothy wrote regularly to William and her letters were published in 1888. Temple himself became an envoy at Brussels in 1666, and in 1668 negotiated the Triple Alliance of England, Holland and Sweden to counterbalance the power of France in her ambitions in Spain. His work was negated, however, by Charles II's secret treaty with Louis XIV. Temple returned to Holland in 1674 and arranged the marriage of Princess Mary to William of Orange. He retired soon after and lived first at Sheen and later at Farnham, where Jonathan Swift became his secretary.

In literature Temple is remembered for his essays, his *Memoirs* (1692) and his letters, which were edited by Swift (1701). The memoirs and letters are a valuable source of information for that period of history, though like his essays they are very much the work of a high-born gentleman with plenty of time at his disposal: some sharp edges would make the elegant prose

Sir William Temple. A detail from the portrait attributed to Lely, c.1660. National Portrait Gallery, London.

a greater pleasure. The essays, apart from *Essay upon the Present State of Ireland* (1668), *Observations upon the United Provinces of the Netherlands* (1672) and *The Advancement of Trade in Ireland* (1673) are contained in three volumes of *Miscellanea* (1680, 1690 and 1701). The second volume contains *Of Ancient and Modern Learning*, in which Temple accords lavish praise of the Epistles of Phalaris, the tyrant of Agrigentum in the 6th century BC. However, the scholar Richard Bentley proved the Epistles to be forgeries and a lively controversy ensued which produced Swift's *The Battle of the Books*.

Macaulay's judgment of Temple ('a man of the world among men of letters, a man of letters among men of the world' and 'excessively selfish, but very sober, wary, and far-sighted in his selfishness') is rejected by some scholars as excessively harsh. Certainly Temple's reputation suffered because of the Phalaris controversy, which indicated the decline of the leisured, and insufficiently informed, amateur of letters.

*Tenant of Wildfell Hall, The* Anne Brontë's second and last novel, first published in 1848, the year before she died. A much more ambitious novel than *Agnes Grey*, it has a male narrator (Gilbert Markham).

Helen Graham is the tenant of Wildfell Hall. She is beautiful and young, said to be a widow, and very reticent about herself. This reticence is the subject of much local gossip, which becomes sour when Frederick Lawrence, the landlord, pays frequent visits to the Hall. Gilbert Markham, a neighbouring farmer who falls in love with her, defends Helen's reputation until he overhears her in affectionate conversation with Lawrence. Markham and Lawrence fall out after a violent scene.

Helen Graham is in fact in love with Gilbert, and writes of this in her diary, which also records the secret of her life. She was married young to Arthur Huntingdon and is the mother of his son. Huntingdon proves to be a drunkard and she attempts to reclaim him; but his wilfulness leads to other excesses and Helen's life with him is one of misery and humiliation. Finally, afraid of the effect of Arthur's way of life on their son, she appeals to her brother – who provides her with the refuge of Wildfell Hall. Lawrence is her brother and until the quarrel had been Markham's friend. She tells Markham the truth, and then has to go back to her husband, who is dangerously ill. Huntingdon dies of his excesses and Helen is now free. Markham is dismayed to learn that Helen is now a wealthy woman; however, Lawrence gives him his friendship once more, and encourages him to win Helen's hand.

*The Tenant of Wildfell Hall* suffers from Anne Brontë's decision to use a man as her narrator. None of the Brontë sisters really had the ability to see life through the eyes of a man (Heathcliff, in *Wuthering Heights*, is an observed character), but, an occasional false note apart, this is a good story, well told. Markham is not a wholly sympathetic character and this, paradoxically, almost gives him credibility.

**Tender is the Night**  A novel by F. Scott Fitzgerald, first published in 1934. The story is not related in chronological order but it concerns a young psychiatrist, Dick Diver, continuing his studies in Leipzig in 1917, where Nicole Warren, one of his patients, falls in love with him. Nicole's schizophrenia results from an incestuous relationship with her father. She falls in love with Dick Diver in the course of transference and he is caught by her dependence on him; the Warren family are wealthy and a marriage would suit them very well if it effected a cure for Nicole and Dick is in any case drawn to the helpless girl. The marriage is promoted by Nicole's arrogant sister, Baby Warren, and the Divers settle down to the sort of luxury to which Nicole is accustomed. Dick is corrupted by it and his professional ambitions fall away; he is secure while Nicole is dependent on him. But as she recovers he deteriorates; he drinks too much and becomes socially unacceptable, and Nicole falls in love with the sexually magnetic Tommy Barban. Divorce follows and Dick retires to the USA and a small town practice. Nicole's recovery means her return to the insulated wealth of the Warrens, who have no further need of Dick Diver.

**Tennant, William**  1784–1848.  Tennant was born in Anstruther, Fifeshire, and completed his education at St Andrews University, where he later became Professor of Oriental Languages. A minor poet, he is remembered for *Anster Fair* (1812), a mock-heroic description in verse of a rural fair in the reign of James V.

**Tennessee's Partner**  See *Luck of Roaring Camp and Other Sketches, The*.

**Ten Nights in a Barroom and What I Saw There**  A story by T. S. Arthur, first published in 1854, which became immensely popular as a text for temperance lectures. A dramatic version was made by William W. Pratt in 1858.

The ten nights are noted by the narrator from his visits, over a period of ten years, to Cedarville. There Simon Slade, the landlord of the Sickle and Sheaf saloon, prospers for a time but eventually his degrading trade claims him as another victim. Dreadful things are witnessed: little Mary comes for her father, drunken Joe Morgan, and dies when a glass hurled at her father by Slade strikes her instead; Harvey Green murders his gambling partner, Willy Hammond; Slade's mother is driven out of her mind by his behaviour; and Slade murders his own father.

All this proves too much for the upright citizens of Cedarville, who decree prohibition for their fair city, destroy the saloon's stock, and look to the future with new hope.

**Tennyson, Alfred, Lord**  1809–92.  Tennyson was the fourth son (the first died in infancy) of the Rev George Clayton Tennyson, rector of Somersby in Lincolnshire. Alfred's older brothers Frederick and Charles also wrote poetry and all three were tall handsome men in the strong and dark way which Samuel Laurence preserved in his famous portrait of Alfred when the poet was about 30 years old. The father was a bitter and disappointed man; he was the first-born of his father (also George Clayton Tennyson) but had been rejected as heir in favour of his younger brother Charles. Charles inherited Bayons Manor at Tealby whilst George was destined for the Church. He married Elizabeth

Fytche, had 12 children, and became a dangerous drunkard. He had been an accomplished man; he was a musician and a doctor of civil law and there was a large library at Somersby. But the lives of his wife and children were wretched; Edward and Septimus went insane later in life and Arthur became an alcoholic. From this appalling background emerged one of the greatest English poets.

Alfred Tennyson attended Louth Grammar School, which he hated, from 1815 to 1820; from then until 1827, when he entered Trinity College, Cambridge, his education was in his father's hands. He wrote an imitation Elizabethan-Jacobean comedy, *The Devil and the Lady*, when he was 15; some verses written with his brothers Frederick and Charles were published as *Poems by Two Brothers* in April 1827 (a few poems by Frederick were included in the volume but the bulk were by Charles and Alfred). He entered Trinity College in November of the same year; in the following October Arthur Hallam, son of the historian Henry Hallam and two years younger than Tennyson, entered the college and during the spring of 1829 met the poet. By the end of that year the two men were close friends and the most important emotional attachment of the poet's life had begun

Tennyson. A detail from the portrait by Samuel Laurence, c.1840. National Portrait Gallery, London.

its tragically brief course. At Cambridge the two friends were part of an informal debating society called the Apostles, among whom were Richard Chenevix Trench, James Spedding, Monckton Milnes, and John Kemble. The young Tennyson's poetry was admired and discussed by the group and eagerly copied out for their own pleasure. The greatest admirer was Hallam, who was unabashedly delighted when Tennyson, only half-willing, entered a poem for the Chancellor's Gold Medal, which he won. The subject was 'Timbuctoo'; the 'mystick city' had been entered by René Caillié, the first European to do so, the year before (1828). Tennyson said later that he had '. . .sent in an old poem on "Armageddon" and, altering the beginning and the end, made it "Timbuctoo" – I was never so surprised as when I got the prize.' He was probably surprised because the prize poem was generally in heroic couplets while 'Timbuctoo' was blank verse.

At Christmas, 1829, Tennyson's father being away in Europe, Hallam visited Somersby. He met the poet's sister Emily and wanted to marry her; but Hallam, though materially much more secure than his friend, was subject to parental censure. Hallam and Tennyson planned to publish a joint volume of poetry; Henry Hallam did not like his son's poems and was in a position to forbid the enterprise. He also interfered in his son's relationship with Emily: regarding the poet's family as not respectable enough, he ordered Arthur Hallam to stay away from Somersby. Hallam could do nothing because he would not reach his majority until February 1832. His poems were privately printed and circulated in May 1830.

Tennyson's poems were published in June 1830 as *Poems, Chiefly Lyrical*. The volume contained among other poems 'Mariana', 'The Kraken', 'Ode to Memory', 'Supposed Confessions', and 'Song: A spirit haunts the year's last hours'. Many of the poems were not reprinted and many, including those mentioned, came under the heading of *Juvenilia* in Tennyson's later career. The volume enjoyed no success and the publication cost him £11. His father died in 1831 and Tennyson left Cambridge without taking a degree. There was a distinct feeling on the part of his grandfather and his uncle (the one who displaced the 'rightful' heir) that Alfred had better enter the Church and earn his living sensibly. Alfred had no intention of submitting and was supported by Hallam's belief in his gifts and his energetic advocacy, which took form on one occasion in an article in *The Englishman's Magazine* entitled 'On Some of the Characteristics of Modern Poetry and on the Lyrical Poems of Alfred Tennyson' (August 1831). This was more than a friend's enthusiasm; W. B. Yeats, writing in 1893, praised it as a fine critical essay.

Tennyson was reluctant to publish more work at this time but he yielded to his friend's persuasion. *Poems* (1832) included **The Lotos-Eaters**, 'A Dream of Fair Woman', 'Oenone', 'The Palace of Art', and the striking **The Lady of Shalott** with its irresistible music and haunting mystery. In May of that year 'Christopher North' (John Wilson) attacked the earlier volume, *Poems, Chiefly Lyrical*, in *Blackwood's Magazine*. Wilson had acknowledged in a brief reference in *Noctes Ambrosianae* (February 1832) that the young poet had genius, though he censured him fairly enough for what he called his 'affectations'. (In the event Tennyson proved to be an excellent judge of his own poetry.) Wilson had lofty ideas about his status as critic and now decided to attack Hallam's essay, too. Promising as Tennyson was, John Wilson, not young Arthur Hallam, would show him how to be better: the review was bullying and mendacious.

Tennyson replied with a mild squib which he included, against the advice of his friends, in *Poems* (1832): 'You did late review my lays, Crusty Christopher; You did mingle blame and praise, Rusty Christopher. When I learnt from whom it came, I forgave you all the blame, Musty Christopher; I could *not* forgive the praise, Fusty Christopher.' The poet's friends were right; *Blackwood's Magazine* apparently ignored the new volume but, as Sir Charles Tennyson pointed out in his biography of his grandfather, Wilson's friend Lockhart had been his colleague on *Blackwood's* and was now editor of *The Quarterly Review*. Lockhart had savaged Keats in *Blackwood's*; so had John Wilson Croker in *The Quarterly*. It is more than likely that Lockhart, on behalf of Wilson, let Croker loose on *Poems* (1832) in April 1833. The review was not only destructive but dishonest; unfortunately *The Quarterly* was widely read and for nearly ten years Tennyson was, in the minds of most people, a poet not worth reading. Offended critics could be very spiteful indeed. Nevertheless, the advance in quality from the first volume was marked: a poet with an arresting command of mood and rhythm and new methods of expression was growing in strength.

In 1833 Hallam's engagement to Emily Tennyson was grudgingly acknowledged by his father; but he made no effort to help his son, who had no money of his own (he was an apprentice lawyer), towards marriage. Tennyson, licking his wounds from the brutal reviews, settled

'Mariana.' An illustration by John Everett Millais for the Moxon *Tennyson* (1857). Other illustrations were contributed by Holman Hunt and D. G. Rossetti.

down to revise his published work. Hallam left for a visit to Vienna with his father in August. He wrote a long and cheerful letter to Tennyson and Emily on 6 September but the next news was a letter, written by his uncle, which Tennyson received on 1 October. Arthur Hallam had died in Vienna, of a haemorrhage, on 15 September. Tennyson was pitched into an abyss of grief and despair which nearly destroyed him. Hallam's belief in him as a poet and his unfaltering encouragement, the generous affection, the intellectual stimulus, the brightness which Hallam brought into his life – something Tennyson had never known before and to which he could respond without reserve – were all gone. Years later he confessed to his son Hallam that he had longed for death; but the poet somehow wrote himself out of complete despair. The verses that were to become *In Memoriam* were begun toward the end of 1833 and by 1834 he was hard at work. Henry Hallam destroyed Tennyson's letters to his son. Hallam Tennyson destroyed Arthur Hallam's letters to his father.

During 1834 Tennyson met the wealthy Rosa Baring and for a time believed himself in love with her; but her shallow character soon brought disillusion. In 1836 he met Emily Sellwood and became engaged to her (her sister married

Tennyson's brother Charles), but his circumstances at this period promised no serenity in his relations with anyone. His family had to leave Somersby because the patrons wanted it back now that it no longer housed an incumbent. Tennyson was desperately short of money and had been obliged to sell the Chancellor's Gold Medal that he won at Cambridge. The Tennysons of Bayons Manor changed their name to Tennyson d'Eyncourt to increase their distance from their despised relatives at Somersby and they were offended that those relatives stayed away from the funeral when the grandfather died. But neither grandfather nor favoured son had bothered to attend the funeral of the rejected and ruined son, Tennyson's father, in 1831. However, some small material benefit went to his family under the old man's will (the bulk of the considerable estate went to the Tennyson d'Eyncourts) and the Somersby Tennysons moved to High Beech, near Epping Forest in Essex, in May 1837.

During the next three years Tennyson's friends tried to bring him to publication again. There was enough completed work but they found it almost impossible to move him, apart from two short poems: 'St Agnes Eve' was published in *The Keepsake* and 'Oh! that 'twere possible' in *The Tribute* in the same year (1837). There were voices in praise of Tennyson, notably John Stuart Mill's in *The London Review* (1835). James Spedding, his friend from Cambridge days, persuaded him to take a holiday with him in the Lake District and introduced him to Edward Fitzgerald, who had admired Tennyson's poetry from the beginning. He became Tennyson's devoted friend: '. . .the more I see of him', he wrote to a friend, 'the more cause I have to think him great.' Fitzgerald also warmed to Tennyson as a companion: 'His little humours and grumpiness were so droll that I was always laughing.' He knew that Tennyson was financially insecure and he pressed him to let him be of help. But Tennyson remained immovable about his work, in spite of a sudden breath of encouragement from the USA.

Emerson, to whom Carlyle was so indebted, had read Tennyson's two published volumes and discussed them enthusiastically with his friends. John S. Dwight published a review in *The Christian Examiner* for January 1838, generously praising Tennyson's work while criticizing it with intelligence. Dwight also took *The Quarterly Review* to task for the review of 1833. Lowell and Longfellow were admirers of Tennyson, too, and Little & Co. of Boston wrote to the poet in May 1838, wishing to reprint the two volumes.

Nothing came of the project and no reply from the poet survives. It is assumed that he objected to the idea and withheld permission. In England Tennyson was becoming known to a wider circle; he met Samuel Rogers, Gladstone, Landor, Forster, the actor William Macready, and the Carlyles, who became friends and admirers. But in 1840 Emily Sellwood's parents ordered the breaking of their daughter's engagement to him. The Tennysons moved to Kent and in the following year Tennyson invested, and lost, his small inheritance from his grandfather in a wood-turning business run by Matthew Allen (the doctor whose wise and humane treatment of John Clare had done so much to help that unhappy man in his madness). At last, in 1841, Tennyson yielded to the pressure of his own circumstances, Fitzgerald's affectionate bullying, and the importunities from the USA, where his fame was growing among literary circles. To prevent his earlier work being reprinted unrevised he gave an undertaking to Little & Co., now Little & Brown, to publish some of his revised work and some new poems in England; Little & Brown could have them for the USA.

*Poems* (two volumes, 1842) was published in May of that year. The poems in the second volume were the first new works to be disclosed for ten years. They had all been written by 1840 and among them were **Locksley Hall**, **Ulysses**, 'Love and Duty', 'The Two Voices', 'Sir Launcelot and Queen Guinevere', 'The Gardener's Daughter', 'St Simeon Stylites', 'Break, break, break', 'Morte d'Arthur', 'Dora', and 'Sir Galahad'. The reviews were neither bad nor wildly enthusiastic; but Thomas Carlyle, who had had reservations about his friend's work, capitulated completely. He called it 'strong as a lion's [heart], yet gentle, loving and full of music'. Dickens wrote that Tennyson's 'writings enlist my whole heart and nature in admiration of their truth and beauty'.

By 1845 Tennyson was more at peace with the world in spite of the apparent coolness of the world towards him. He had suffered acutely from frayed nerves since Hallam's death but had managed, somehow, to keep his head up in spite of his personal loss and the troubles that beset his family. His friends had supported him loyally and one of them, Edmund Lushington, had been the means of his retrieving some of the money lost in Dr Allen's business. His publisher, Edward Moxon, took pains to ensure that Tennyson met the bright lights of the literary world, including Coventry Patmore, Elizabeth Barrett, Robert Browning, Thackeray, and the Irish poet Aubrey de Vere who introduced him to Wordsworth, whom Tennyson admired as the greatest of modern poets, in May 1845. The old man was very pleased by Tennyson's admiration since he thought highly of the younger man's work. In the meantime his friends, worried about his health, did their best to ensure Tennyson some material security. Carlyle thought of a Civil List pension and did his best to bully Monckton Milnes into raising the matter in Parliament. Poor Milnes could not do it; his constituents at Pontefract in Yorkshire knew nothing of poetry or Alfred Tennyson. Then in February 1845 Henry Hallam entered the lists on behalf of his dead son's friend. With the support of Gladstone, Henry Taylor, and Samuel Rogers he persuaded Sir Robert Peel, and Tennyson was guaranteed £200 a year. Almost at once Bulwer-Lytton, who had wanted a pension for a protégé of his own, published a shabby anonymous attack on Tennyson in his *The New Timon*. Tennyson retorted with *The New Timon and the Poets*, which John Forster hastened to publish in *Punch* (February 1846). But Bulwer-Lytton's attack did not rouse the press of the day to support him or to attack Tennyson. Things were changing in the poet's favour; his health was not good but recognition was at hand.

*The Princess* was published in November 1847 and for a time seemed to be another failure; even the loyal and admiring Fitzgerald disliked it, to Tennyson's great disappointment. But the public ignored the reviews and bought it eagerly; within a year a second printing of 2000 copies was required. The success encouraged Tennyson to dwell on a project which had often been in his mind, an epic poem based on the Arthurian legends, and in spite of continued ill health he travelled much in the scenes of the stories. He also visited Scotland and in the Burns country surveyed with tears in his eyes the scenes of the poet's life. 'I hold that there never was an immortal poet if he be not one,' he wrote to Aubrey de Vere. Towards the end of the year Elizabeth Gaskell wrote to him about Samuel Bamford, an old Lancashire weaver who admired Tennyson so much that he seized every opportunity to commit his poems to memory: he had not the means to buy them for himself. Tennyson, intensely honoured at such admiration, sent his works to the old man and treasured the letter that Samuel Bamford wrote him in return.

By 1850 Tennyson was at last out of the shadows. He proposed to Emily Sellwood and they were married two weeks after the publication of the elegies on the death of Arthur Hallam, which Tennyson had begun so long ago. The marriage was a complete success and it was

Emily who thought of the title, *In Memoriam A.H.H.* It was published in June, anonymously, but Sir Charles Tennyson suggests: 'No doubt Moxon took care to let literary London know who was in fact the author of the poem.' To everyone's surprise the poem was a success not only with the critics but also with the public: by the end of the year 60,000 copies had been sold. The success was the more remarkable because most people in those days found their security in the doctrines of the established churches. But the warm humanity describing a universal experience and the message of hope reached great numbers of readers. The quality of the finest sections is not maintained throughout but great poetry is there. T. S. Eliot said of *In Memoriam*: 'It is a diary of which we have to read every word.' The Prince Consort read it and became an admirer; Queen Victoria offered Tennyson the laureateship, vacant after the death of Wordsworth. He accepted; he was 41. The Tennyson d'Eyncourts were furious. In 1851 Emily and Alfred were saddened when their first child, a boy, was stillborn. But Hallam was born in 1852 and Lionel in 1853. In that year the Tennysons moved to Farringford, at the western end of the Isle of Wight. The late Georgian house became their home for the rest of their lives. In 1854 Tennyson wrote 'The Charge of the Light Brigade' when he read the account of Balaclava in *The Times*. The ballad was written straight off, in a few minutes. It was published in Forster's paper, *The Examiner*, on 9 December and its great popularity embarrassed its author.

Tennyson was now successful, financially secure, and contented. Everyone who was anyone in England in the 1850s sought his acquaintance and many became his friends. A local squire, Sir John Simeon, became a particularly close friend and it was to him that Tennyson gave the manuscript of *In Memoriam*. He gave the manuscript of 'Locksley Hall' to a shy young American poet, Frederick Tuckerman, who visited the Isle of Wight in the winter of 1854–55. Such generosity was typical of the man. In 1855 Tennyson completed **Maud** and sent the fair copy to the printers in late April. It was published in July with some short poems including 'The Charge of the Light Brigade', 'The Brook – an Idyl', the 'Ode on the Death of the Duke of Wellington', and the lines to his friend Frederick Denison Maurice, who had lately been dismissed from his professorship at Kings College for questioning orthodox views. *Maud*, which remained Tennyson's favourite work, ran into trouble at once. It is significant that the poet who for many epitomizes a comfortable, even smug, figure of established literature was usually mauled by the critics when he attempted something different. Its immediate effect on the public who knew *In Memoriam* was to puzzle them, while every level of opinion in the country decided that *Maud* had some personal relevance. It must have comforted Tennyson that the Brownings declared it a great poem, which they read again and again. But the poem gained popularity in spite of the first stormy reception; by 1857 a fourth edition was in the press. By then Tennyson had returned to the project of an Arthurian epic, and he completed 'Merlin and Vivien' at the end of March 1856.

The first *The Idylls of the King* (1859) contained 'Vivien', 'Enid', 'Elaine', and 'Guinevere' and was a great success. The public bought 10,000 copies during the first week, the critics were full of admiration, and now *Blackwood's Magazine* sidled into the ranks of those who praised Tennyson. His friends were delighted for him and Elizabeth Tennyson, now a serene old lady, was the happiest mother in England. Macaulay wrote to Tennyson and urged him to make the Holy Grail his next subject. Tennyson decided on a holiday first and left for Portugal with his friend Francis Turner Palgrave. In 1860, in response to a request from another friend, Thackeray, who wanted a poem for *The Cornhill*, Tennyson rewrote an early work and Thackeray became the lucky publisher of *Tithonus*, one of Tennyson's most highly regarded works on a classical theme. The first of his poems in the Lincolnshire dialect, 'The Northern Farmer – Old Style', was written about this time, while the poet was trying to resolve his uncertainty about the next stage of the *Idylls*. A new subject caught his attention now: the artist Thomas Woolner told him the story of a shipwrecked sailor who reached home after many years only to find his wife married to his best friend. But *Enoch Arden* was as yet not even named.

In 1861 two people died whose passing affected Tennyson deeply in different ways; Arthur Hugh Clough, a close friend, and the Prince Consort. The prince had been a generous admirer and Tennyson knew that he owed him the laureateship. A new edition of *The Idylls* was in the press and he seized the opportunity to compose a prefatory dedication to the prince's memory. Uncertain about intruding on the queen at such a time, he sent copies to two of her friends. They urged him to send it to her without delay and he did, by way of Princess Alice. In April 1862 he was invited to visit Queen Victoria at Osborne, where she told him that in her grief she often turned for comfort to *In Memoriam*.

With *Enoch Arden and Other Poems* (1864)

Tennyson enjoyed another great success though he had wondered what to call the volume and one of the poems, 'Aylmer's Field', had given him great trouble. Even *The Quarterly Review* praised him now. He could almost have put down his pen and written no more; but his poetic energy was tremendous and at the age of 57 his health and constitution seemed indestructible. Tom Taylor, the playwright, observed that Tennyson seemed impervious to weather: he often walked abroad, alone, on stormy nights, probably thinking about whatever work was in progress. *The Holy Grail and Other Poems* (1869) added another part to what was to become the completed *Idylls*. *Gareth and Lynette* (1872) was not followed by the last poem, *Balin and Balan*, until 1885. Tennyson published four more volumes of poetry during his lifetime: *Ballads and Other Poems* (1880), *Tiresias and Other Poems* (1885), *Locksley Hall Sixty Years After* (1886), and *Demeter and Other Poems* (1889). *The Death of Oenone, Akbar's Dream and Other Poems* was published posthumously (1892). The five volumes contain some of his finest short poems and his translation from the Anglo-Saxon, *The Battle of Brunanburh*. He published his first play, *Queen Mary*, in 1876. This extension of his genius has considerable merits but was received with definite reservations by the critics; it was not a popular success in spite of its production at the Lyceum at the end of the year. Unfortunately Tennyson allowed drastic cuts to be made and some of his best scenes and characters never reached the stage. But he was intensely interested in the dramatic form and went on writing in it: *Harold* (1877), *The Falcon* (1879), *The Cup* (1881), *The Promise of May* (1882), *Becket* (1884), and *The Foresters: Robin Hood and Maid Marian* (1892). Tennyson never really succeeded as a playwright though Henry Irving was a success in *Becket* in 1893.

The unprecedented (for a poet) honour of a peerage was conferred on Tennyson in December 1883. After a serious illness in 1888 he recovered and reached his 80th birthday with his powers undiminished; in 1889, while crossing from Lymington to the Isle of Wight, he wrote 16 lines on an old envelope. *Crossing the Bar* is one of the most famous of English lyrics and an intensely moving poem from a man reaching the end of his life. This came on 6 October 1892 not long after midnight. His family were around him and his hand rested on an open volume of Shakespeare, the last thing he had asked to see.

Tennyson's popularity was diminished to some extent by his being described as 'Victorian', in the pejorative sense of the word. But as Geoffrey Tillotson wrote: 'Tennyson was sometimes ahead of this age, often abreast of what was most advanced in it ... he cannot be blamed for taking over what we can call the furniture of his time, any more than Chaucer for the conventions of Courtly Love, or some writers of mid-twentieth-century poems and novels for the use of four-letter words.' It is true that Tennyson never achieved a great creative poem: *The Princess, In Memoriam, Maud, The Idylls of the King* – none of them is completely successful. But they contain splendid elements which also abound in his shorter poems: profound expressions of mood, irresistible music, and images of startling clarity. His command of form and metre is remarkable, the servant of his ceaselessly questioning mind.

The poet's reputation suffered from reaction after his death. Revaluation began with Harold Nicolson's *Tennyson. Aspects of his Life, Character and Poetry* (1923), and T. S. Eliot carried it a stage further in his *Essays Ancient and Modern* (1936). Since then a vast amount of material has been published about Tennyson, by F. R. Leavis, W. H. Auden, Edith Sitwell, Jerome Buckley, Lord David Cecil, and Christopher Ricks to name only the most eminent. His collected poems have occupied a place in the Oxford Standard Authors since 1912. The best modern edition is by Christopher Ricks, *The Poems of Tennyson* (Longmans Annotated English Poets, 1969), and selections abound. The standard biography is by the poet's grandson Sir Charles Tennyson: *Alfred Tennyson* (1949). A new biography, *Tennyson. The Unquiet Heart* by Robert Bernard Martin, was published in 1981. There is as yet no complete edition of the poet's letters.

**Terrible Temptation, A:** *A Story of the Day.* A novel by Charles Reade, first published in *Cassell's Magazine* (April to September 1871). In this book Reade returns to the attack on asylums for the insane which he began in *Hard Cash*. Richard Bassett believes himself to have been defrauded of his inheritance and is determined to secure it for himself or his children by fair means of foul. He resorts to foul because his cousin Sir Charles Bassett is recognized as the rightful heir. Failing to stop Sir Charles's marriage, he does succeed in getting him confined in a madhouse. But his evil schemes are frustrated by the devotion and determination of Lady Bassett. The novel is interesting for an early examination (in fiction) of hereditary qualities – good or bad – appearing in subsequent generations.

**Tess of the D'Urbervilles:** *a Pure Woman Faithfully Presented.* A novel by Thomas Hardy, first published in the *Graphic* and *Harper's Bazaar*

(4 July to 26 December 1891). Some chapters which appear in the volume form were omitted in the weekly publication.

Tess Durbeyfield is seduced by Alec D'Urberville, more or less forcibly. Tess's father, a poor villager, has let his head be turned by learning that he is a D'Urberville. Tess, needing to help her improvident family, has thus been placed in a dangerous position and Alec, a young man of means whose claim to the surname is false, has no scruples about taking what he wants from a young country girl.

Tess, both poor and defenceless, becomes Alec's mistress for a short time; she leaves him and bears a child, which she baptizes before it dies. She then finds work at a large dairy farm and attracts the attention of Angel Clare, a clergyman's son who likes to think of himself as emancipated. Tess falls in love with him and they marry. She tells him about Alec on their wedding night – after he has confessed his own transgressions. Her confession is disastrous; Clare is completely unfitted to deal with it and he abandons her. Pressed by her family's needs, Tess eventually returns to Alec, after Clare remains deaf to her appeals.

Clare comes back, belatedly, repenting of his harshness, and finds Tess with Alec. The hapless girl sees Alec as the author of her misfortunes – and kills him. Clare and Tess hide briefly in the New Forest but Tess is taken and hanged.

*Tess of the D'Urbervilles* is Thomas Hardy's most famous book and his finest in the opinion of many. It was almost not published at all: Tillotson and Son, the newspaper syndicate, had it first, and started to raise objections after setting 16 chapters. Hardy requested, and got, cancellation of the contract, and the novel was sent to *Murray's Magazine*, who declined it. *Macmillan's Magazine* also declined it and Hardy was made to feel that there was a price to pay for being read in the English language. He cut out parts that he knew offended and the book was serialized in the *Graphic*. He put the missing parts back in the published volume and was to repeat the laborious and irritating business for his last novel, *Jude the Obscure*. He was later to acknowledge that his subtitle for *Tess* had been an admission of futility; in the face of general disapproval he could think of no other way of explaining his purpose in telling the story of Tess.

**Thackeray, William Makepeace** 1811–63. The only son of an official in the East India Company, Thackeray was born in Calcutta. He was sent to school in Southampton at the age of six and hated it. His father died and his mother married again, returning to England when Thackeray was nine, and life was brighter for him after that; he was always on good terms with his stepfather, a retired major. In 1829 he went to Trinity College, Cambridge (after Charterhouse), and spent five terms there, wasting his time for the most part. Eventually he entered the Middle Temple to study law.

His friends at Cambridge included Tennyson and Fitzgerald, and he met Goethe at Weimar when he spent a winter there. In the Middle Temple he shared rooms with Tom Taylor, who was to become editor of *Punch* and a successful playwright. Thackeray was increasingly drawn to the world of letters and he gave up the study of law. Well-to-do, he was able to buy the *National Standard*, for which he both wrote and drew, but the paper failed. In the same year, 1833, most of the money he expected to inherit was lost when a Calcutta bank failed, and Thackeray decided to try and succeed as a painter, spending the next four years in Paris. He married Isabella Shawe in 1836.

Back in London in 1837, Thackeray began to work hard as a journalist, becoming a regular contributor to *Fraser's Magazine* (**The Yellow-plush Correspondence**) and writing reviews for *The Times* and other newspapers. His wife Isabella, who was a helpless clinging sort of woman, had meanwhile become increasingly unhappy. Thackeray's work frequently kept him away from her, and the death of their second child in infancy saw the beginning of instability. The birth of a third child occurred while Thackeray was obliged to be absent and Isabella's mental collapse followed. The tragedy had a marked effect on Thackeray's writing, which in the meantime had been increasingly successful. *The Tremendous Adventures of Major Gahagan* appeared in *The New Monthly Magazine* and **Catherine** in *Fraser's*. Also for *Fraser's*, under the pseudonym of Michael Angelo Titmarsh, he wrote *The Paris Sketch-Book* and **The Great Hoggarty Diamond**. As George Savage FitzBoodle he wrote the confessions of a middle-aged clubman, perpetually susceptible, for the same magazine (*The FitzBoodle Papers*), and under that pseudonym began **The Luck of Barry Lyndon** in 1844. As Michael Anglo Titmarsh he published *Notes of a Journey from Cornhill to Grand Cairo* in 1846.

Thackeray, the successful journalist, was by this time also contributing to *Punch*, notably with **Mr Punch's Prize Novelists** (1847) and **The Snobs of England** (1847). The year 1847 was to prove a momentous one – the first instalments of **Vanity Fair** began to appear, under his own

William Makepeace Thackeray. Engraving from the portrait drawing by Samuel Laurence, c.1850.

name. The instalments were well advanced before its true quality was realized but William Makepeace Thackeray had come into his own; *Vanity Fair* is one of the finest novels in the language. He never equalled it in his subsequent work, though it has been fairly remarked that his prose style improved (in *Vanity Fair* it is quite loose in texture). **The History of Pendennis** followed in 1848 and **The History of Henry Esmond** in 1852. **The Newcomes** (1853) uses the characters from *Pendennis*, and **The Virginians** (1857) features the descendants of Henry Esmond.

Concurrently with the novels, the industrious author was also turning out the annual tales, the most famous of which is **The Rose and the Ring** (1855) and the burlesques *The Legend of the Rhine* (1845) and *The Kickleburys on the Rhine* and *Rebecca and Rowena* (both in 1850). He lectured on **The English Humourists of the Eighteenth Century** (published in 1853) and **The Four Georges** (published in 1860) but neither series is highly regarded now. His lecture tour in the USA in 1852 gave him the background for *The Virginians*.

Thackeray had retired from *Punch* in 1854. He stood for parliament, unsuccessfully, on four occasions and in 1860 he became editor of the new *Cornhill Magazine*. To it he contributed the story, **Lovel the Widower** (1860), a set of essays called *The Roundabout Papers* (1863), his last novel **The Adventures of Philip** (1861) and the unfinished **Denis Duval** (published posthumously in 1864), a historical novel of the late 18th century. In addition to all this, Thackeray wrote rhymes and ballads. They have been overshadowed by his prose works but they are the work of a skilful versifier and deserve to be better known.

Thackeray died suddenly at the age of 52, his heart overstrained. He had seen much of the fashionable world during his life, and that he was well acquainted with the unsavoury fringes of it is plain to anyone who reads *Catherine* and *Barry Lyndon*, not to mention *Vanity Fair*. During his idle days at Cambridge he had been fond of gambling and had been relieved of £1,500 – a large sum in those days – by a cardsharper. However, he expected, then, to inherit a modest fortune and it was no great matter. But the loss of his inheritance forced him to work and though he would have liked to have become a painter (his own drawings are a familiar part of his work) reality forced him into journalism to earn a living for his family. His marriage, we have seen, ended in tragedy: Thackeray was one of those big (he was well over 6 ft tall), strongly-built, virile men who fall in love with pretty little girls; this one proved to be a hopeless housekeeper and was in a perpetual state of anxiety. His later attachment, to the married Jane Brookfield, was unrewarding: she welcomed his attentions but was too self-centred to return any feelings that might have warmed or consoled him. He was an affectionate father and a warm-hearted man, though he often presented a cool, reserved exterior. His admiration for Dickens was genuine and his wholehearted praise for and kindness to Charlotte Brontë is well known.

It is interesting to speculate what sort of book we might have had in *Vanity Fair* if the author had not been under the compulsion to deliver instalments to a required deadline. The public had to be kept interested month by month, and the overdressed, apparently self-indulgent style of Thackeray and Dickens results from that – compare any of their major novels with, say, *Jane Eyre* or *Middlemarch*. Of the two, Thackeray is the more truthful in his presentation of character – he wanted to be more truthful, as he makes plain in his preface to *Pendennis* – and his novels imply a great deal more than Victorian convention ever permits him to say. To most modern readers he is the author only of *Vanity Fair*, which is a pity; the author of *Barry Lyndon*, *Esmond*, and the rest is worth every moment of the reader's attention.

**Thaddeus of Warsaw** See **Porter, Jane.**

**Thaisa** The daughter of King Simonides in Shakespeare's *Pericles, Prince of Tyre*. Pericles wins her hand in a tournament after he is shipwrecked on the coast of Pentapolis. In a storm at sea she gives birth to a daughter, Marina, and is believed to be dead. Her body is put in a chest and consigned to the waves.

**Theale, Milly** The wealthy and ailing heroine of *The Wings of the Dove*, by Henry James. Milly longs for some fulfilment in what she knows is going to be a short life and her hopes are centred on the weak and charming Merton Densher. Her moral superiority proves to be more than a match for those who try to exploit both her wealth and her illness in their own interests.

**Thealma and Clearchus** Nothing is known of the author John Chalkhill beyond the fact that his name is appended to this romance in verse published by Izaak Walton in 1683. The romance is unfinished and without merit, ending at line 3170. See also **seventeenth-century verse romances.**

**Theatre of the Absurd** See **Beckett, Samuel (Barclay).**

**Theory of Moral Sentiments, The** The first published work of Adam Smith (1759) was originally a series of lectures delivered at Glasgow University, where he was Professor of Moral Philosophy. He offers an analysis of the forms and objects of moral consciousness; moral sentiments arise from sympathy, therefore feeling plays a large part. Sympathy can only have real value when it comes from an 'impartial and well-informed spectator' and such a person is an ideal, not an actual person. Self-interest or imperfect understanding are frequent factors in the interest we take in the situations of other men. In Smith's theory the social factor in morality is recognized and sympathy is seen as the means by which this factor operates.

**Thersites** A comedy of unknown authorship, sometimes attributed to Nicholas Udall, which was first acted in 1537 and printed *c*.1562. It was adapted from the Latin of Ravisins Textor, a French scholar whose text was acted at Queen's College, Cambridge, in 1543. The setting is the siege of Troy.

The English version introduces a number of

allusions to 'Robin John' and 'Little Hood' into the story of Thersites, who persuades Mulciber (Vulcan) to make him a suit of armour that will render him invulnerable. Thersites puts the armour on and immediately begins to defy young and old, heaven and hell – but runs to his mother for protection when threatened by another soldier and is completely demoralized by a snail. Eventually he abandons his splendid armour and deserts the field.

**Thersites** In Shakespeare's *Troilus and Cressida*, a foul-mouthed Greek who has the protection of Achilles. He reflects the corrosive atmosphere of a long-drawn-out war in his cynical mind and his malformed body.

***These Twain*** See **Bennett, (Enoch) Arnold**.

**Theseus** The Duke of Athens in Shakespeare's *A Midsummer Night's Dream*. The play begins as Theseus prepares for his wedding to Hippolyta.

***They*** See ***Traffics and Discoveries***.

***They Were Defeated*** See **Macaulay, (Emilie) Rose**.

***Thinking Reed, The*** See **West, Rebecca**.

**Thirlwall, Connop** 1797–1875. Thirlwall, who became Bishop of St David's in 1840, was born in London and educated at Charterhouse School and Trinity College, Cambridge, where he became a fellow in 1818. He studied law at Lincoln's Inn but eventually decided on the Church, becoming a priest in 1828. In the same year he published, with J. C. Hare, the first part of a translation of Barthold Niebuhr's *History of Rome* (1828–42). Thirlwall's principal work was his *A History of Greece* (eight volumes, 1835–44), published at the same time as the more highly regarded work by his former schoolfellow George Grote.

***Thomas, Lord Cromwell*** (*The True Chronicle Historie of the Whole Life and Death of Thomas, Lord Cromwell*) A play first published in 1602. The title page gave the author as 'W.S.' and the play was offered, for a time, as being the work of Shakespeare. However, it is a chronicle play of little merit and is now totally rejected by scholars as Shakespeare's.

**Thomas, Dylan (Marlais)** 1914–53. Dylan Thomas was born in Swansea and educated at the local grammar school. When he left school he worked on the *South Wales Evening Post*, and wrote poetry in his spare time. Some of his early verse was published in *The Sunday Referee*, which contained a feature called 'Poet's Corner' and in the periodical *New Verse*, in 1924. His first collection appeared in the same year, called *Eighteen Poems*, and this brought him to the attention of Edith Sitwell, whose praise and encouragement were very valuable to the young poet. *Twenty-Five Poems* (1936) brought him praise from a great many others. He married Caitlin Macnamara in 1936. After *The Map of Love: Verse and Prose* (1939) Dylan Thomas went to work at the BBC and was occupied there for the war years. *Deaths and Entrances* (1946) was highly praised and Thomas began to reach an audience beyond the circle of poets and intellectuals who had been his admirers hitherto. *In Country Sleep and Other Poems* (1952) and *The Notebooks of Dylan Thomas* (1967) complete the sum of his poetry: the latter volume was edited by R. N. Maud and contains the unpublished works from Thomas's notebooks and manuscripts. He died at the age of 39 in New York; he had undertaken another lucrative lecture tour in the USA and he was, by then, the victim of too much adulation and a great deal of drink. Among his best poems are 'A Refusal to Mourn the Death, by Fire, of a Child in London', 'Do not go gentle into that good night', 'Fern Hill', and 'A Winter's Tale'. *Collected Poems 1934–1952* was published in 1952.

The prose works of Dylan Thomas include film scripts, none of which were filmed; the collection of broadcasts called *Quite Early One Morning* (1954); the collections of stories *Portrait of the Artist as a Young Dog* (1940), *Adventures in the Skin Trade* (published posthumously, 1954), and *A Prospect of the Sea* (published posthumously, 1955, edited by Daniel Jones); and the celebrated and often staged *Under Milk Wood: A Play for Voices* (1954), first broadcast by the BBC on 25 January 1954. The biography, *The Life of Dylan Thomas*, by Constantine Fitzgibbon was published in 1965.

**Thomas, (Philip) Edward** 1878–1917. Edward Thomas was born in London of Welsh parents and educated at St Paul's School. While at Oxford he married, and resisted pressure from his family to enter the Civil Service; after university he and his wife managed as best they could with Thomas's earnings as a freelance journalist and author. Thomas began to realize his potential as a poet through the friendship of the American poet Robert Frost, who was then living in England and whom Thomas met in 1912. Thomas began to contribute poems to periodicals under the pseudonym of Edward Eastaway, and joined the army as soon as war broke out in August 1914. *Six Poems* was published in 1916; he died in action at Arras in April 1917 before *Poems* (1917) was published. *Collected Poems* (1920) has a foreword by Walter De la Mare.

Other books by Edward Thomas include a novel, *The Happy-go-lucky Morgans* (1913), and the books of English country life: *The Woodland Life* (1897), *The Heart of England* (1906), *The South Country* (1909), and *In Pursuit of Spring* (1915).

**Thomas, R(onald) S(tuart)** 1913– . R. S. Thomas was born in Cardiff and was educated for the Church in Wales, in which he was ordained in 1936. He published his first poems at the age of 33, *The Stones of the Field* (1946), and six years passed before his next collection, *An Acre of Land* (1952); *The Minister* followed in 1953. The three books were published in small quantities in Wales and the author was virtually unknown until *Song at The Year's Turning: Poems 1942–1954* (1955), which contained a selection of earlier work and 19 new poems; the volume carried an introduction by John Betjeman. *Poetry for Supper* (1958), *Tares* (1961), *The Bread of Truth* (1963), *Pieta* (1966), and *Not that he brought Flowers* (1968) display the work of a poet of the Welsh rural communities: his clarity of diction and straightforward construction enable him to handle pastoral themes, in the later decades of the 20th century, without sentiment or idealism. 'The Hill Farmer Speaks' and 'Here' are among the poems by R. S. Thomas to be found with increasing regularity in anthologies of modern verse.

**Thompson, Edward** 1886–1946. Thompson was born and educated at Bath and entered the Wesleyan Methodist ministry in 1909. He served in Bengal as a missionary teacher (1910–23) except for an interval as an army chaplain during World War I. Thompson became a lecturer in Bengali at Oxford (1923–33); he was later made Research Fellow in Indian History (1936–46). He had some reputation as a poet (his *Collected Poems* appeared in 1930) and as an interpreter of India. Among his books were *A History of India* and *An Indian Day* (both 1927), *A Farewell to India* (1930), and *Tagore: Poet and Dramatist* (1926).

**Thompson, Francis** 1859–1907. Thompson was born in Preston, Lancashire, and was trained for the Catholic priesthood at Ushaw College. He proved to be unfitted for it and went to Owen's College, Manchester, to study medicine, but gave it up after six years. Thompson went to London in 1885 with vague ideas about becoming a writer. He was soon reduced to poverty and became an opium addict: but he wrote two poems and an essay which he sent to

Wilfred Meynell, proprietor of the Catholic periodical *Merry England*. Meynell and his wife Alice befriended Thompson, who was by this time reduced to selling matches. His health never really recovered but in the care of the monks of Storrington Priory he was able to conquer his addiction; thereafter the Meynells cared for him and Meynell published his first work in *Merry England*.

Thompson's first book was *Poems* (1893), which contained his most famous work, 'The Hound of Heaven', with its rich imagery and language and echoes of Richard Crashaw in its description of the pursuit of the soul by God. *Sister Songs* (1895) was written for the Meynell children; *New Poems* (1897) completed his published verse. From 1893 to 1897 Thompson lived in close communication with the Franciscan monks of Pantasaph in North Wales; he died of tuberculosis in London at the age of 48.

Thompson also contributed critical essays fairly regularly to *The Academy* and *The Athenaeum* and wrote a study of *Shelley* (published posthumously, 1909) and lives of St John Baptist de la Salle (1891) and St Ignatius Loyola (1909). The poem 'In no Strange Land', beginning 'O world invisible, we view thee', is a familiar anthology piece; but with the exception of this and 'The Hound of Heaven' Thompson's poetry is not well known to modern readers. His complete *Works* was edited by Wilfred Meynell (1913); Meynell also edited the complete *Poems* (Oxford Standard Authors, 1937 and 1955).

**Thomson, James** 1700–48. The son of a Scottish minister, Thomson was born at Ednam near Kelso in Roxburghshire. He studied divinity at Edinburgh University and while a student published some poems in Edinburgh magazines; these early poems showed Thomson's liking for rural scene-painting. He had spent his boyhood in the Jed valley when his father was minister at Southdean, and had his first schooling at Jedburgh. The border country, which was later to be the impulse for the work of Scott, left a deep impression on Thomson. He left the university when his prose was criticized as being too elaborate for the pulpit and gave up all idea of the ministry.

Thomson went to London in 1725 and carried some complete work with him; he earned a living as a tutor. His friend David Mallett was at that time tutor in the house of the Duke of Montrose and was able to introduce Thomson to possible patrons, including Aaron Hill. *Winter* was published in 1726 and was successful enough to reach two editions in that year. *Summer* (1727) was dedicated to George Dodington, who invited the young poet to his country seat at Blandford in Dorset and introduced him to Lord Lyttelton. Thomson published *Britannia* (1729), which supported the Prince of Wales (Lyttelton's friend) and condemned the policies of Robert Walpole; but he was able to seek Walpole's patronage with his *Poem Sacred to the Memory of Sir Isaac Newton* (1729).

*Spring* (1728) was dedicated to the Countess of Hertford and *Autumn* (1730) to Onslow, Speaker of the House of Commons. The complete **The Seasons** was also published in 1730, the year Thomson travelled abroad as tutor to the son of Sir Charles Talbot, the Solicitor General (later Lord Chancellor). This employment came to an end when his pupil died in 1733; Talbot helpfully secured the secretaryship of briefs in chancery for him, a sinecure which allowed Thomson some security. A poem in five parts, *Liberty* (1734–36), was dedicated to the Prince of Wales and Thomson was awarded a pension in return. Thomson was now in a position to retire to a small house in Richmond, Surrey, where his friends included Alexander Pope, who lived just across the river in Twickenham. A carefully revised edition of *The Seasons* was published in 1744, a much-improved one which may owe a great deal to the advice of Pope.

Thomson lost his sinecure when Sir Charles Talbot died in 1737 but his careful seeking of patronage brought a reward – Lord Lyttelton secured him another. But Thomson somehow offended the Prince of Wales and his pension ceased just before his death. His last considerable poem was **The Castle of Indolence** (1748).

Apart from the poems already mentioned and a number of smaller pieces, Thomson also wrote for the stage: *The Tragedy of Sophonisba* (Drury Lane, February 1730), *Agamemnon* (Drury Lane, April 1738), *Edward and Eleanora* (1739, not produced), *Alfred*, a masque in collaboration with David Mallett, which contained 'Rule, Britannia' (1740, revised 1753), *Tancred and Sigismunda* (Drury Lane, March 1745), and *Coriolanus* (Covent Garden, January 1749). However, apart from their incidental poetic merits they have no dramatic interest and their composition was largely influenced by Thomson's desire to please his patrons. His admiration for John Milton and Edmund Spenser was genuine and the influence of his great predecessors is clearly seen in his major poems. Thomson's edition of Milton's *Areopagitica* was published in 1738.

Thomson died of a chill caught during the summer of 1748 while returning to Richmond by river from Hammersmith. He was Alexander Pope's almost exact contemporary and, though his early-18th-century poetic language is the same as Pope's, his form is quite different and so is his subject matter. *The Seasons*, written in the age of the neo-classicists, puts aside the closed couplet in favour of blank verse, and his subject was nature – he was a landscape artist using a Miltonic style. *The Castle of Indolence* is a romantic allegory in the style of Edmund Spenser. Thus, two English poetic traditions were revived and Thomson's poetry was to have a powerful influence.

Modern editions of James Thomson's work are J. Logie Robertson's in the Oxford Standard Authors (1908, 1951) and *The Seasons and The Castle of Indolence*, edited by James Sambrook (1972), in Oxford Paperbacks.

**Thomson, James** (*or* **B.V.**) 1834–82. Thomson, a sailor's son, was born in Port Glasgow, Scotland. During his childhood his father's health broke down and straitened circumstances followed. The family moved to London and James Thomson was admitted to the Royal Caledonian Asylum in 1843, where he was educated and prepared for the army. He became an army schoolmaster; while at a garrison station at Ballincollig, near Cork in Ireland, he fell in love with Matilda Weller and met Charles Bradlaugh, the radical politician, who was a trooper in the army at that time. Matilda's early death was a severe blow; the friendship with Bradlaugh prospered and was to be of great importance to Thomson.

Thomson was dismissed from the army for insubordination in 1862. He worked as a solicitor's clerk, was secretary to a mining company in America, became a war correspondent in Spain, and finally a freelance journalist in London. Through all this Bradlaugh was unfailingly generous and encouraged Thomson as a writer. Bradlaugh's weekly, *The National Reformer*, was the chief outlet for Thomson's verse and essays, but there was a limit to what Bradlaugh and his family could do. Thomson had started drinking while he was in the army and the loss of Matilda had not helped matters. In London he lived in various lodgings, a victim of insomnia, and his drinking increased; he died of it in University College Hospital.

Thomson's most celebrated poem, *The City of Dreadful Night*, was first published in *The National Reformer* in 1874. Most of his work is collected in the two volumes **The City of Dreadful Night** and *Other Poems* (1880) and *Vane's Story and Other Poems* (1881). 'Insomnia', a grim pendant to *The City of Dreadful Night*, was published in 1882.

Thomson's prose works were essays contributed to *The National Reformer*, *The Secularist*, and *Cope's Tobacco Plant* and include studies of Jonson, Blake, Whitman, and Heine. They were collected and edited by G. W. Foote as *Satires and Profanities* (1884). The first collection of Thomson's poems, *Poetical Works*, was edited by Bertram Dobell (1895), and included a memoir by the editor.

The 'B.V.' which distinguishes the 19th-century Thomson from his earlier namesake refers to his admiration for Shelley and the German poet Novalis (Friedrich Leopold von Hardenberg). B.V. stands for Bysshe Vanolis, the pseudonym he used as a journalist.

**Thopas, The Tale of Sir** See *Canterbury Tales, The*.

**Thopias, The Reply of Friar Daw** See *Jacke Uplande*.

**Thoreau, Henry David** *c*.1817–62. Among the ancestors of Thoreau were Frenchmen and Scotsmen, Quakers and Puritans. He was born in Concord, Massachusetts, and loved the countryside which he explored with his brother John. After school at Concord Academy he went to Harvard, graduating in 1837. He taught for a few years in Concord and was very much

Henry David Thoreau.

influenced by Bronson Alcott and Emerson. In 1841 he went to live in Emerson's house where he worked as a handyman while learning all he could. Emerson encouraged him to keep a journal and this advice proved to be invaluable. He was on close terms with the Transcendentalists and contributed to *The Dial*, and wrote for general periodicals too. In 1843 he was engaged as a tutor by Emerson's brother, William, at his home on Staten Island; there he met Horace Greeley and the elder Henry James but he only stayed for one year, missing the woods and the countryside of his formative years.

In 1845 Thoreau was allowed by Emerson to build a cabin on his land by Walden Pond. Emerson and Thoreau were in harmony in their view of the individual and their lack of sympathy for the communal experiments of the other Transcendentalists. Thus began the two-year experience in basic economy and self-reliance from which the book *Walden* was to emerge nine years later. Thoreau's retreat was rudely interrupted when he was put in jail for a day for his refusal to pay a poll tax during the Mexican War. He knew perfectly well that, whatever reasons might be given for the tax, the result of a US victory would be more profit by the southern slaveholding states, more land-grabbing, and the further enrichment of speculators. *On the Duty of Civil Disobedience* (1849) and the later *Life without Principle* (1863) are a clear expression of his views on government and the individual conscience.

*A Week on the Concord and Merrimack Rivers* (1849) was based on a journey by boat with his brother John in 1839. The book was never popular but it demonstrated that Thoreau's writing had matured and that he had mastered a prose style which expressed his thoughts with ease and clarity. He was living in Emerson's house again; Emerson was abroad and about this time Thoreau formed his friendship with William Ellery Channing the younger, who was also living in Concord and who was to become his biographer.

The years between his return to Concord and the publication of *Walden* (1854) were spent in wandering, extending his experience of nature (he was an unsentimental observer and had little patience with the dewy-eyed 'nature lover'), and keeping the journals that, like those of his master and friend, Emerson, were the basis of most of his published work. Thoreau was involved in the issue of slavery, which he abhorred. He threw his energies into the movement for its abolition and it was the single issue that, in his judgment, justified the use of violence. He gave active help to the 'Underground Railway' for escaping slaves and hailed John Brown as a hero. He met Brown in Emerson's house (he lived there until his death) in 1857 and eulogized him in three lectures.

Thoreau travelled in Maine and Canada, to Cape Cod, and to New York to meet Walt Whitman – but his health was failing. He fell victim to tuberculosis and was aware of increasing weakness. He had mastered surveying and botany and continued to lecture to maintain his independence. He began an ethnological study of the North American Indian and travelled on the Great Lakes and the Mississippi. This last journey was undertaken in the hope that it would improve his condition. It did not, and the last year of his life was spent in a feverish effort to prepare his journals for publication. He died at the age of 45; Emerson outlived him by 20 years. Thoreau published only two works during his lifetime (*A Week on the Concord and Merrimack Rivers* and *Walden*) but the volumes of posthumous work disclosed a major writer, a poet of remarkable quality, and an individual whose influence it is difficult to overestimate.

Henry David Thoreau, the nonconformist and the believer in the rights of the individual, refused to pay poll tax in support of a war he found indefensible and refused to countenance slavery in any form. *Walden* became a classic and his *Journals* were widely read; Thoreau's belief that no system of government should take precedence over moral imperatives found millions of young supporters in the USA which existed over a hundred years later, a country in which the individual and the nonconformist seemed no longer to have even the chance of being heard. The passive resistance to unjust authority which Thoreau advocated extended far beyond the borders of the USA and the violence that he accepted, where necessary, to put an end to slavery, erupted the year before he died. A hundred years passed before passive resistance brought about the Civil Rights Acts and the influence of the political thinker and social philosopher of Walden Pond is perhaps stronger in the 20th century than it was in the 19th.

Thoreau's observations of nature have manifold virtues. They are written by a man described as a poet-naturalist by his friend the younger William Ellery Channing. His scientific knowledge was imperfect but it went far enough to give him a method and that was important to a man whose attitude was poetic but never sentimental. Among the books published after his death were *Excursions* (1863), a collection of occasional pieces published in magazines; *The*

*Maine Woods* (1864), the account of three journeys in Maine with Indian guides; *Cape Cod* (1865); and *A Yankee in Canada* (1866), which describes his journey from Concord to Montreal and Quebec. Thoreau's *Letters* were edited by Emerson and published in 1865 (an enlarged volume appeared in 1894). *Poems of Nature* appeared in 1895 and the *Collected Poems*, edited by Carl Bode, in 1943. In 1906 the *Journals* were published in 14 volumes and a collected edition of his work, *Writings*, was published in 20 volumes.

**Thorne, Mary** In Anthony Trollope's *Doctor Thorne*, the doctor's ward, whose obscure birth stands in the way of Frank Gresham's determination to marry her.

**Thornhill, Sir William** In Oliver Goldsmith's *The Vicar of Wakefield*, the benevolent uncle of the villainous Squire Thornhill, who extends his protection to the Primrose family under the guise of the eccentric Mr Burchell. He marries Sophia, Dr Primrose's daughter.

*Three Bears, The Story of the* See *Doctor, The*.

*Three Clerks, The* A novel by Anthony Trollope, first published in 1858.

The three government clerks are Alaric Tudor, clever and unprincipled; his cousin Charley, weak and good-natured, and Harry Norman, steady and hard-working. Mrs Woodward, Harry's cousin, has three daughters: Gertrude, Linda, and Katie. Harry is in love with Gertrude, but she marries Alaric Tudor, who also outstrips Harry in their careers. Alaric comes under the influence of the Hon. Undecimus Scott, whom he does not recognize until too late as an unscrupulous adventurer. Scott leads him into fraud and misappropriation and, inevitably, Alaric is found out. He is tried and sent to prison.

Harry, losing Gertrude, has married Linda and they are content. Harry unexpectedly comes into property, while Charley's career seems to be a succession of bad starts and oppressive debts. But he plods on doggedly and succeeds not only in his work but as an author, and marries Katie.

Charley is a reflection of the author, who drew the detail of the government service from his own experience. A notable character is Alaric's lawyer, Mr Chaffanbrass, who turns up again in Trollope's fiction.

*Three Estates, Satire of the* (*Ane Pleasant Satyre of the Thre Estaitis*). A morality play by Sir David Lyndsay. It was first performed on Twelfth Night (6 January), 1540, at Linlithgow before an audience that included King James V and Mary of Guise, his queen, and all the lords of the kingdom, both temporal and spiritual. The second performance was in the open air at Lyndsay's estate in Fifeshire (1552) and the manuscript of the second text, dated 1568, was preserved by George Bannatyne. The printed text of 1602, published by Robert Charteris of Edinburgh, used the manuscript of the third performance, which took place at Calton Hill in 1554 in the presence of Mary of Guise, now the queen regent. Performances, which included elaborate processions, detailed stage business, and a suitable interval for a 'collatioun', lasted from nine in the morning until six in the evening. It seems certain that the audience participated fully in the performances, as Lyndsay intended. The play itself is not excessively long, less than 5000 lines.

Rex Humanitas is a king with an open mind, so it happens that his first three counsellors – Wantonness, Placebo, and Solace – tempt him easily; he becomes a prey to Sensuality. They are joined by the Vices – Flattery, Falsehood, and Deceit (who later disguise themselves as a Friar, Discretion, and Sapience). Good Counsel, long absent from Scotland, returns but is refused access to the king. Verity arrives with a New Testament in English – and is promptly clapped into the stocks by the Lords Spiritual. Chastity is present but no one pays her any attention. Divine Correction arrives in Scotland to reform the three estates and the Vices scurry to the church, while the merchants and the craftsmen run for shelter. Verity, Chastity, and Good Counsel force Sensuality to take shelter in the church also, and gain access to the king; Wantonness, Placebo, and Solace promise reform and are pardoned since the king, like all men, has need of innocent pleasures.

The second part begins with an interlude, in which Pauper rails at the immorality and greed of the clergy while a pardoner, Sir Robert Rome-Raker, gloats over his relics and other deceits. The parliament of the three estates, summoned by Diligence, are led to their places by their vices. They walk backwards, having forgotten how to walk any other way. Covetousness now accompanies the Lords Spiritual, Oppression the Lords Temporal; Flattery waits upon all. John the Commonweill (commonweal) and Pauper speak for the common people and their lines attack every class of society. Lords Temporal and Burgesses agree to reform but the Lords Spiritual will not, declaring that they live according to ancient usage. However, they are dispossessed by three honest clerks and parliament is now ready to announce 15 Acts, 12 of which prove to be strictures on the Church. Common Theft, Deceit, and Falsehood are hanged with the assistance of Flattery, and the morality closes with a sermon delivered by Folly that spares no one, from king to peasant.

Lyndsay's satire is packed with invention and he displays a raciness which at times becomes remarkably coarse. But in the lowest comedy his wit saves him from being *merely* coarse and the same wit makes him lethally accurate in his attack. Some of the finest scenes go to John the Commonweill and Pauper but the Church sustains the heaviest blows. For this he became the beloved of the Reformers growing in strength in Scotland, though he wanted reform at all levels, not just in the Church.

*Satire of the Three Estates* was revived with great success at the Edinburgh Festival of 1948 in Robert Kemp's edition of the text (1951).

***Thrissill and the Rois, The*** (The Thistle and the Rose). An allegorical poem by William Dunbar, written about 1503, celebrating a political marriage in courtly and heraldic terms. The thistle is King James IV of Scotland and the rose Margaret Tudor, daughter of Henry VII of England. The poem is regarded as a brilliant exercise in a particular style – the medieval courtly romance, in dream-vision form – by a poet equal to the demands of a poetic tradition which, by his day, had really run its course.

***Through the Looking Glass*** See **Carroll, Lewis**.

**Thurber, James (Grover)** 1894–1961. James Thurber was born in Columbus, Ohio, and completed his education at Ohio State University. After working as a government clerk in Washington he joined the embassy staff in Paris, and then became a journalist for a Chicago newspaper.

Upon returning to the USA he worked on the staff of *The New Yorker* (1927–33) and continued after that as a regular contributor. Both as a cartoonist and writer Thurber expresses superbly the dilemma of the moral innocent in a trendy world. The 1930s, in Thurber's economical cartoons and elegant prose fantasies, possessed a corrective which might have benefited the 1960s. He satirized psychoanalysis, sexual awareness, the search for 'identity', and the 'problem' of communication – all, in the long run, symptoms of the same disease. As a humorist he was direct and disarming; the 'Thurber dog' is a famous example of his visual style and 'The Night the Bed Fell on Father' of his writing. Among his collections are *The Owl in the Attic, and Other Perplexities* (1932), *The Seal in my Bedroom, and Other Predicaments* (1932), *Let Your Mind Alone*

One of James Thurber's celebrated dogs. A cartoon from *Fables for Our Time and Famous Poems Illustrated* (1940).

(1937), *My world – and Welcome to it!* (1942), and *The Beast in Me, and Other Animals* (1948). With E. B. White, his colleague on *The New Yorker*, he wrote *Is Sex Necessary?* (1929), and in collaboration with Elliot Nugent produced a successful comedy, *The Male Animal. My Life and Hard Times* (1933) is autobiographical, and *The Years with Ross* (1959) a memoir of his life on the staff of *The New Yorker*. He also wrote a book for children, *The Thirteen Clocks* (1950).

**Thurloe, John** See **seventeenth-century historical collections**.

**Thyrsis** A poem by Matthew Arnold, first published in 1867 in *New Poems*. The subtitle explains the poem's purpose: *A Monody, to commemorate the author's friend, Arthur Hugh Clough, who died at Florence 1861*. The poem is a pastoral lament and is notable for Arnold's description of the Oxfordshire countryside so well known to him and his dead friend.

**Thy Servant a Dog** See **Kipling, Rudyard**.

**Tibbs, Beau** A character in Goldsmith's satirical *The Citizen of the World*. A poor and ridiculous snob, like his wife, he prattles continually about dukes and countesses and is always anxious to borrow half-a-crown (12½p today) if he can.

**Tickell, Thomas** 1686–1740. A protégé of Joseph Addison, Tickell was educated at Queen's College, Oxford, and became a fellow. He was the author of a poem, *On the Prospect of Peace* (1712), which was widely read in the period leading to the Treaty of Utrecht in 1713. Tickell contributed verse to *The Guardian* and *The Spectator* and published a translation of the first book of the *Iliad* at the same time as Pope published his. Pope believed that Addison had prompted Tickell and quarrelled with him. Tickell's translation is commendable but is hardly known outside scholarly circles and he did not continue the translation beyond the first book.

Tickell went to Ireland with Addison in 1709 and became Secretary to the Lords Justice in Ireland. He held this post for the rest of his life and edited Joseph Addison's works when his patron died. Tickell's work was a fair example of talent and application in 18th-century verse; posterity has found little more in it than that, though his elegy, *To the Earl of Warwick on the Death of Mr Addison* (1721), is accorded respect.

**Till Eulenspiegel** A rogue figure of German tradition who is first named about 1300. A collection of satirical tales with Till as the central character was published in German in 1519 and in Flemish two years later. An abridged Flemish edition from Antwerp was translated into English as *Howleglass* by William Copeland in 1528. Till is a peasant's son who, while appearing to be a simpleton, practises his knaveries and deceptions on churchmen, nobles, and tradesmen. He is the subject of a symphonic poem by Richard Strauss.

**Tilney, Henry** Catherine Morland's suitor in Jane Austen's *Northanger Abbey*. He is 'if not quite handsome . . . very near it'. He is a steadfast lover and defies his father on Catherine's behalf.

**Timber;** or Discoveries made upon Men and Matters. Ben Jonson's commonplace book was published in the posthumous 1640 edition of his works. It consists of notes, short essays, and reflections on miscellaneous subjects. The book reflects both Jonson's classical heritage and also something of his character.

**Timias** Prince Arthur's squire in Spenser's *The Faerie Queene*, Books III and IV. He represents Ralegh in relation to Belphoebe (Elizabeth I) and Amoret (Elizabeth Throckmorton).

**Timoleon** A volume of poems by Herman Melville, privately printed in 1891. The title poem concerns Timoleon and Timophanes; Timophanes is the favoured son though he owes much to Timoleon, but Timoleon is rejected by his family and state. In exile he reaches his own conclusions, without bitterness, on the caprices of the gods. 'The Enthusiast' is a short hymn to personal integrity. The most striking poem in the volume is 'After the Pleasure Party', an outcry against, and an acknowledgment of, the power of Eros.

***Timon of Athens*** A play by William Shakespeare, first produced *c*.1607, and published in the First Folio of 1623. The plot comes from the story told by Plutarch in his life of Mark Antony, and the satiric dialogue, *Timon*, by Lucian. The play is so much a failure that one theory suggests that Shakespeare, having found the material intractable, simply put it down and that what we have is an unfinished play. Another theory, perhaps more plausible, suggests that an unfinished play by the master was completed and the gaps filled by inferior hands.

Timon is a rich and noble Athenian whose unthinking generosity leaves him penniless. When he asks his richest friends for help he is denied it and he finds that those who formerly sought his company now avoid him. He invites them all to a banquet and serves only bowls of water – suitable for the dogs they have proved to be. Then he drives them out and, cursing the city, goes to live in a cave. One day, while digging for roots to eat, he uncovers a hoard of gold.

At his cave Timon meets the general Alcibiades, exiled by the city, and Apemantus the philosopher. He uses the gold to help Alcibiades and rewards his faithful servant Flavius, swearing him to silence. But Apemantus spreads the news that Timon is rich in gold and soon flatterers, thieves, and other hopefuls come to the cave. The two senators want Timon back in Athens – with his gold, of course – to help them against Alcibiades. Timon offers them a fig tree on which to hang themselves and so escape affliction. He dies in his cave, just as a peaceful compromise is reached between Athens and Alcibiades.

**Timrod, Henry** 1828–67. The 'Laureate of the Confederacy' was born in Charleston, South Carolina, and educated at Franklin College (now the University of Georgia). With William Gilmore Simms, Basil Gildersleeve, and his friend Paul Hamilton Hayne, Timrod founded *Russell's Magazine* in Charleston in 1867, modelling it on the English *Blackwood's*. Some of Timrod's poems were published in the magazine.

Timrod suffered from tuberculosis, which was later to render him unfit for further service in the Confederate Army during the Civil War. He earned a living of sorts in the war-torn South as an editor and wrote his best poems during those years, when he was close to starvation. His work was not collected until after his death, when Paul Hamilton Hayne published his friend's *Poems* (1873). *Katie*, a love lyric addressed to his wife, was published in 1884 and *Complete Poems* in 1899.

Timrod's poetry followed traditional forms and his early work is reminiscent of Poe's. The Civil War experience prompted more ambitious work, which is seen in 'Ethnogenesis' (1861), hailing the birth of the Confederacy. His 'Ode' on the graves of the Confederate dead (1867) celebrates '... martyrs of a fallen cause'.

**Tindal, Matthew** 1655–1733. Tindal was born near Bore-Ferris in Devonshire and educated at Lincoln and Exeter colleges, Oxford. He was elected a fellow of All Souls in 1678 and for a brief period during the reign of James II became a Catholic. He returned to the Church of England at Easter 1688 and thereafter called himself a Christian deist. *The Rights of the Christian Church asserted against the Romish and all other Priests who claim an Independent Power over it* was published in 1706. In this work Tindal stated the rationalist view and defended the ascendancy of the state over the church in ecclesiastical matters (Erastianism). But he found himself censured by both state and church; he and both the publisher and the printer were prosecuted but four editions of the book were issued nevertheless. *A Defence of the Rights of the Christian Church* (1709) was burned by the public hangman by order of the House of Commons in 1710.

Tindal's most famous work was *Christianity as old as the Creation, or the Gospel a Republication of the Religion of Nature* (1730), which offered a fundamental challenge. He insisted that there was a law of reason, perfect and unchanging, and the Gospels were never designed to add to, or take away from, that law but to release man from superstition. All the observances foisted on man by the organized churches were utterly pointless. Tindal was one of the foremost deist thinkers; his writings had considerable influence in Germany.

***Tinker's Wedding, The*** See **Synge, J(ohn) M(illington)**.

***'Tis Pity She's a Whore*** A tragedy by John Ford, first produced about 1625 and first published in 1633.

Giovanni and Annabella, brother and sister, are in love – an irrevocable passion, as Giovanni makes clear in his confession to the friar. But Annabella has to take a husband and has three suitors: Soranzo, Grimaldi, and Bergetto. Soranzo has been conducting an affair with Hippolita, wife of Richardetto; he has promised to marry her if she becomes a widow. But he is eager to have Annabella and rejects Hippolita when Richardetto is presumed lost at sea. However, Richardetto, suspecting his wife, has disguised himself as a physician to spy on her. Annabella accepts Soranzo and Richardetto decides to kill him. He enlists the help of the jealous Grimaldi but by mistake they kill Bergetto, an amiable halfwit.

The wedding of Annabella and Soranzo takes place. At the feast Hippolita poisons a cup of wine for Soranzo; but his servant Vasques is watching her and he contrives that she drinks it herself. Soon after, Soranzo discovers that Annabella has married him because she is pregnant; he threatens to kill her but she will not name her lover. Vasques promises to discover who he is and for the time being Soranzo pretends to forgive Annabella. Vasques, in a very nasty scene, gets the truth out of Annabella's nurse, Ritana, and conveys it to Soranzo.

Soranzo announces a banquet and Giovanni is among those invited. He knows that his guilty love for his sister is no longer a secret but he attends the banquet: to forestall Soranzo's intention to shame Annabella publicly he has killed his sister, stabbing her in the womb that bears his child. The last scene is at the banquet, where Giovanni defiantly proclaims his love and his sister's death before he kills Soranzo. He is killed by Vasques.

**Titania** The queen of the fairies in Shakespeare's *A Midsummer Night's Dream*. She quarrels with Oberon over a changeling boy and he puts a charm on her that makes her love the first creature she sees. This happens to be Bottom, given an ass's head by Puck.

**'Tite Poulette** See *Old Creole Days*.

**Tithonus** A poem by Alfred Tennyson, first published by Thackeray in *The Cornhill* in February 1860. Its original form was the poem 'Tithon', which Tennyson wrote in 1833 as a companion to 'Ulysses' but did not publish. The poem, in blank verse, is a reflection by Tithonus on his fate. In Greek myth he was loved by Aurora (Eos), goddess of the dawn, who begged her father Zeus to grant him eternal life. Zeus did so; but Aurora had neglected to ask for eternal youth and Tithonus grew ever older without dying.

**Titmarsh, Michael Angelo** One of the pen-names used by Thackeray as a journalist. *The Paris Sketch-Book*, *The Great Hoggarty Diamond*, *The Irish Sketch-Book*, *Notes of a Journey from Cornhill to Grand Cairo*, and *The Rose and the Ring* were published under this pseudonym.

**Titus Andronicus** A tragedy by William Shakespeare (believed to contain work by other hands), which was among his first works for the stage.

There is no positively identifiable source but the chief influence is that of Seneca. It was first produced in 1594 and printed in a quarto of the same year. It was published in the First Folio of 1623. The part of Titus Andronicus was created by Edward Alleyn. The play is set in ancient Rome under the empire but is not related to any known emperor or period.

Titus Andronicus returns to Rome in triumph after defeating the Goths. He brings their queen Tamora and her three sons as captives. At the behest of his eldest son Lucius, he sacrifices Alarbus, the first-born of Tamora, on behalf of the slain men of his own family. Another of Tamora's sons, Demetrius, voices the family's longing for revenge. Titus is instrumental in the proclamation of Saturninus, son of the last ruler, as Emperor of Rome. Saturninus claims Lavinia, Titus' daughter, for his wife, but he is attracted to Tamora and decrees that she and her family shall be free. But the emperor's brother Bassianus wants Lavinia and Marcus Andronicus, Titus' brother, acknowledges that he has a prior claim. They seize Lavinia.

The emperor marries Tamora, since he cannot have the abducted Lavinia. Tamora is now able to avenge her son with the aid of her lover Aaron the Moor and her two younger sons. Bassianus is killed, Lavinia is raped by Tamora's sons – who then cut out her tongue and chop off her hands so that she can never accuse them by word or sign. Worse is to come: Quintus and Martius, Titus' sons, are charged with the murder of Bassianus and executed. The eldest son Lucius is banished; he raises a Gothic army and marches on Rome.

Titus, mad with grief, kills Tamora's sons; then he kills Lavinia to end her shame. He serves the remains of Tamora's sons to her in a dinner

The title page illustration to the 1594 Quarto of *Titus Andronicus*. This is the only known copy and was found in Sweden in 1904, wrapped in an 18th-century lottery ticket. It is now in the Folger Shakespeare Library, Washington.

dish; then he kills Tamora. Then the emperor kills Titus and is himself killed by Lucius, who becomes emperor. His prisoner, Aaron the Moor, is buried up to his neck and left to starve to death.

The cast of this play, if realism attended every detail of production, would spend much of their time off-stage washing off blood. A gorier play would be hard to find but it was a popular success with the Elizabethans, who enjoyed among other diversions the sight of captive bears and bulls being tormented to death by ravenous dogs and the regular disembowelling of live men and women at Tyburn. It is very rarely staged nowadays and only succeeds when the title role can be given to an actor who carries enough guns to sink a battleship, like Laurence Olivier.

**To be Read at Dusk** A ghost story by Charles Dickens, as related by a German courier in the Alps. It was first published in 1852.

**Toby, My Uncle** The hero's military uncle in *Tristram Shandy* by Laurence Sterne. Incapacitated by a wound in the groin, he spends his days contentedly reconstructing Marlborough's campaigns on a bowling green. He talks in military jargon, whistles military tunes, and is almost completely innocent – which perplexes the Widow Wadman, who wants to marry him.

**Toccata of Galuppi's, A** A poem by Robert Browning, first published in 1855 in the volume *Men and Women*. The composer Baldassare Galuppi (1706–85) was organist of St Mark's Cathedral in Venice during the last years of his life. Browning's brilliant short poem (45 lines) captures the rhythms of the music, using them in his lament for the glory that Venice had been and for what she became – the once great maritime city now serves Austrian overlords and is given up to the pursuit of pleasure. Where, the poet asks, can that lead?

**Tocqueville, Comte Alexis Charles Henri Maurice Clerel de** *c.*1805–59. See *Democracy in America*.

**'Toinette** See **Tourgée, Albion W(inegar)**.

**Toklas, Alice B.** 1877–1967. See **Stein, Gertrude**.

**Toland, John** 1670–1722. Toland was a Catholic Irishman who was converted to Protestantism at the age of 16. He entered Glasgow University in 1687, continuing his studies at Leyden and Oxford, which he entered in 1694. His *Christianity not Mysterious* was published in 1696. Toland had returned to Ireland but the uproar caused by his book drove him to seek refuge in England in 1697.

Toland asserted that God and his revelation are straightforward truths within the comprehension of all; the 'mysteries' of Christianity are pagan intrusions accepted and maintained by the priesthood. The book was condemned as subversive and atheistical and burned by the public hangman in Dublin. Toland published his *Life of Milton* in 1698 – and was in trouble again when a passage was thought to question the authenticity of the New Testament. However, he defended himself successfully in *Amyntor, or a Defence of Milton's Life* (1699) and also demonstrated his remarkable knowledge of the apocryphal literature of the early church. He put this knowledge to further use in *Nazarenus; or Jewish, Gentile and Mahometan Christianity* (1718). *Tetradymus* (1720) is a collection of essays on a natural explanation of biblical miracles. *Pantheisticon* (Toland was the first to use the term pantheist) was published in the same year and expounds a pantheistic creed. As a writer Toland is more notable in the history of English Christianity than in the history of English literature; his books stimulated discussion of the New Testament and he left accepted Christianity behind in his search for what he believed to be a reasonable religion. Though he never subscribed formally to any school of thought and probably regarded himself as an independent rationalist, Toland wrote the classical exposition of deism in his *Christianity not Mysterious*.

**Told by an Idiot** See **Macaulay, (Emilie) Rose**.

**Tolkien, J(ohn) R(onald) R(euel)** 1892–1973. J. R. R. Tolkien was born in Birmingham and completed his education at Merton College, Oxford. He became a fellow of Merton and was Professor of Anglo-Saxon in the University of Oxford in 1925; in 1945 he became Merton Professor of English Language and Literature. His first published work was *A Middle English Vocabulary* (1922); his second a book of verse, *Songs for the Philologist* (1936). In 1937 he published *Beowulf: The Monsters and the Critics* – and a book for young people called *The Hobbit*, the basis and ideas of which were developed and extended into an ambitious epic fantasy, *The Fellowship of the Ring*, which made him famous (*The Return of the King* and *The Two Towers*, 1954, *The Lord of the Rings*, 1955). *The Silmarillion* (1977), a book of legends from Middle Earth, was published posthumously. Among other works by J. R. R. Tolkien are an edition of *Sir Gawain and the Green Knight* (1925, with E. V. Gordon) and the Middle English *The Ancrene Wisse* (1966);

translations of the Middle English poems *Sir Gawain and the Green Knight, Pearl,* and *Sir Orfeo* (1975); *The Adventures of Tom Bombadil* (1963, verse); *The Road Goes Ever On* (1967, verse); and *Myth, Allegory and Gospel* (1974, essay).

***Tom Brown's Schooldays:*** *by an Old Boy.* A story of Victorian public-school life by Thomas Hughes, first published in 1857. The school is Rugby and the head is Thomas Arnold. The book had considerable influence on the idea of boarding-school life for boys. Hughes wrote well and his enthusiasm, his excellent characterization, and his serious presentation of some issues – bullying, most notably – successfully disguised the novel's didacticism and it remained popular at least until World War II. To modern youth it is unacceptable, the world having changed completely. Two notable characters are 'Scud' East, Tom Brown's bosom friend, and the bully, Flashman, whose name and character inspired George MacDonald Fraser to use him as the centrepiece of a series of sardonic, beautifully written adventure stories.

***Tom Jones, a Foundling, The History of*** A novel by Henry Fielding, first published in 1749. The author prefaced each of the 18 books of which it consists with an introductory chapter.

Mr Allworthy, a rich and benevolent country gentleman, finds a baby in his bed one night. He becomes the baby's guardian and gives him a home, which he later shares with Blifil, Mr Allworthy's nephew and heir. Blifil is a mean-spirited wretch; his resentment of Tom is supported by Thwackum the tutor and his friend Square, the philosopher. Blifil seizes every opportunity to tell Mr Allworthy tales about Tom.

Tom and Blifil grow up. Tom enjoys the favours of Molly Seagrim, the gamekeeper's daughter, but he falls in love with Sophia Western, the squire's daughter, who is intended for Blifil. Sophia detests Blifil and wants to marry Tom, who is counfounded by Molly's declaration that she is pregnant. Tom is prepared to do the honourable thing in the face of Mr Allworthy's displeasure; fortunately, he learns that Molly has been very free with her favours and he is under no obligation. But Blifil's malice succeeds and Mr Allworthy closes his house to Tom, who sets out with the schoolmaster, Partridge; he is not sure where he is going but the army seems his best hope.

At Upton-on-Severn, at the same inn, he encounters Sophia, who has run away from her father because he is insisting that she marry the detestable Blifil. With her maid, Mrs Honour, she is going to London to shelter with a relative.

The frontispiece to Vol. I of an edition of *Tom Jones* published in 1773. Left to right: Miss Bridget, Squire Allworthy, and Mrs Wilkins with the baby found in the Squire's bed. Fielding's novel was first published in 1749.

Tom finds a pocket book belonging to Sophia; he follows her to London to restore it to her. His adventures on the way are an opportunity for the author to portray a rich gallery of characters.

In London Tom finds that there is no real hope of marrying Sophia and he drifts into an affair with an older woman, Lady Bellaston, who keeps him. Lady Bellaston tries to procure Sophia for her friend Lord Fellamar; the outraged girl also discovers Tom's relationship with Lady Bellaston and turns her back on him. Tom's fortunes reach rock bottom when he is forced into a duel and apparently kills his opponent. Lady Bellaston, furious at being left by Tom, and Fellamar, furious that Sophia has rejected him, instigate Tom's arrest and imprisonment.

Fortunately, Tom's opponent does not die, and it is revealed that Blifil knows the truth of Tom's birth and has carefully concealed it. Mr Allworthy's sister, Bridget, had married Captain Blifil, a fortune hunter. After she had given birth to a son, young Blifil, the captain died and the boy became Allworthy's heir. The baby found earlier in Allworthy's bed, Tom Jones, was so called because Jenny Jones, a servant, was believed to have been his mother. But Jenny Jones appears on the scene now to reveal that Bridget Allworthy was also Tom's mother – Jenny had connived at the plot to ensure that the baby had a good home. The reason for Blifil's concealment is plain: Tom, as the elder child of Bridget, is Allworthy's true heir. Sophia forgives him for his affair with Lady Bellaston and marries him.

Fielding's novel ranks among the greatest in the language. It is an earthy one; the more exquisite shades of feeling were not his concern – he left that to Richardson, his great contemporary. It has to be said that Tom Jones is much more recognizable as a character than any of Richardson's; but it must be said also that Richardson's concerns were different from Fielding's. In Fielding's less rarefied air chastity is not a preoccupation of any of the characters and he makes it clear that there are far worse sins than sexual irregularity. Tom is a sensual young man, certainly, but he is not mean or cruel. He has positive standards and is unhappily aware that his conduct often falls short of them. The good Mr Allworthy sums him up best, perhaps: 'I am convinced, my child, that you have much goodness, generosity, and honour in your temper: if you will add prudence and religion to these you must be happy' (Book V, Chapter 7). Tom will not, as his creator shows, always be prudent, so he will not always be happy; but he will always be recognizably human, and at the end of the tale he has a spirited and lovely heroine by his side.

Modern editions of *Tom Jones* can be found in Everyman's Library, the Penguin English Library, the Modern Library, and in the Wesleyan Edition of the *Works* of Henry Fielding, edited by Martin C. Battestin and Fredson Bowers (1974).

**Tom Sawyer, The Adventures of** A children's novel by Mark Twain, first published in 1876. The story takes place about the 1840s in St Petersburg, Missouri, a small town on the Mississippi based on the Hannibal of Mark Twain's childhood.

Tom Sawyer and his unpleasant brother Sid live with their Aunt Polly and Cousin Mary. Tom's sweetheart is Becky Thatcher. The story follows Tom's adventures and tribulations; it comes to its main focus when Huck Finn, Tom's friend and a carefree waterfront character, tells him to swing a dead cat in a graveyard to cure his warts. Tom and Huck, in the graveyard, see the murder of the town doctor by the half-breed, Injun Joe. They also see Injun Joe place the knife in the hands of the drunken Muff Potter. After being wrongly blamed for something by Aunt Polly, Tom is also treated coldly by Becky

Thatcher, so he runs off with Huck and Joe Harper to hide on Jackson's Island. The townspeople believe them drowned and they return to find a funeral service for themselves in progress. Aunt Polly and Becky are overjoyed to have Tom back and, later, he almost becomes a hero at the trial of Muff Potter when he reveals what he and Huck witnessed in the graveyard. Muff is set free – but Injun Joe escapes.

Tom and Becky, on a school picnic, are lost for several days in a cave. Tom spies Injun Joe there and the children are menaced by his presence since Tom gave evidence against him. They manage to find their way out and later Injun Joe is found dead. Tom and Huck return to the cave and find Injun Joe's buried money, which is divided between them. Huck is adopted by the Widow Douglas and for the time being surrenders his unwashed freedom.

Mark Twain wrote two more Tom Sawyer adventures, *Tom Sawyer Abroad* (1894) and *Tom Sawyer, Detective* (1896) but they are not on the same level and were probably turned out for a ready-made public when the author was struggling to clear his debts. But he was far from done with the character of Huck Finn.

**Tooke, John Horne** 1736–1812. The son of a poulterer named Horne (who added the name of his friend William Tooke to his own in 1782), Tooke was born at Westminster and educated at various schools, including Eton and Westminster, and St John's College, Cambridge. Tooke was a friend and supporter of John Wilkes for a time but is remembered in literature as an early advocate of comparative philology. His *Epea Pteroenta or The Diversions of Purley* (1786) pointed out the importance of the study of Gothic and Anglo-Saxon. See also **Jones, Sir William.**

**Toots** P. Toots, Esq. in Dickens's *Dombey and Son*, young Paul Dombey's fellow pupil at Dr Blimber's school, where he is 'an old hand' and seems immensely old to Paul. Warm-hearted and generous, he befriends Paul and later falls in love with Susan Nipper, Florence's maid.

**Toplady, Augustus** 1740–78. Toplady was born at Farnham in Surrey and attended Westminster School; he completed his education at Trinity College, Dublin. He was ordained in 1764 and became vicar of Broad Hembury in Devonshire in 1768. He is remembered for his hymns ('Rock of Ages' is the most famous) and for his violent reaction to the teaching of John Wesley – whom he had once admired. Toplady regressed into Calvinism and wrote *The Historic Proof of the Doctrinal Calvinism of the Church of*

*England* (1774). His personal attacks on Wesley make him sound quite deranged. (See also **Wesley brothers**.)

**Topsy** Little Eva's Black companion in *Uncle Tom's Cabin*. She is a droll and realistic child compared to the angelic Eva. As a slave she has no idea of parentage – '. . . I 'spect I growed'.

**Torigni, Robert of** See **Diceto, Ralph de**.

**Tory** The term was originally applied to dispossessed Irishmen, driven to outlawry out of destitution, who preyed on English settlers and soldiers. The name came from the Irish *toraidhe*, meaning a pursuer or robber. In politics the term was applied to the party that opposed the exclusionists (the Whigs), who were determined to prevent the accession of the Catholic James II to the throne. Tory sympathies lay with the Stuarts until the accession of George III; then they affirmed their adherence to the established order and resisted the Liberal movement towards wider parliamentary representation. They began to call themselves Conservatives in 1830; the name was the invention of the Tory, John Wilson Croker.

*Tottel's Miscellany*. Richard Tottel, who died in 1594, was a publisher at Temple Bar from 1553 and is remembered as the compiler of the volume of *Songes and Sonettes* of 1557, which presented among other poems the chief works of Wyatt and Surrey. This became known as *Tottel's Miscellany* and the book was known to Shakespeare, who mentions it in *The Merry Wives of Windsor* when Slender goes courting Anne Page. Tottel also published More's *Dialoge of Comfort against Tribulacion* (1553), Lydgate's *The Falls of Princes* (1554), and Surrey's translations of parts of Virgil's *Aeneid*, but the *Miscellany* is his great contribution to English letters. It was the first book of poetry to be printed for the pleasure of the common reader.

**Touchett, Ralph** In *The Portrait of a Lady*, by Henry James, he is the invalid son of Lydia Touchett, who brings Isabel Archer to Europe. He loves Isabel, and persuades his wealthy father to bestow half of his inheritance on her. He hopes that this will 'put a little wind in her sails . . . make her free.'

**Touchstone** The usurping duke's clown in Shakespeare's *As You Like It*. He throws in his lot with Rosalind and Celia when they flee to the Forest of Arden, where he consoles himself for his exile with Audrey, a country girl.

**Tourgée, Albion W(inegar)** 1838–1905. Albion W. Tourgée was born in Ohio and left the University of Rochester to serve in the Civil War. He was seriously wounded in the war and after it, in 1865, he moved to the South. He practised law in North Carolina and entered politics, which was an unpopular thing for a northerner to do. His attitude to the South was always plain and, since it insisted on a complete rejection of all prewar values, the term 'carpetbagger' was readily applied to him. Allegations were also made that he was growing wealthy through manipulation of the courts when he became a judge.

Tourgée wrote several novels about the South during reconstruction, among them *'Toinette* (1874), *A Fool's Errand* (1879), and *Bricks Without Straw* (1880). He left the South in 1878 because of political pressure and from 1882 to 1884 edited *The Continent*, a weekly in which he expressed his politics, defended the rights of the Black people, and called attention to the iniquities of the Ku Klux Klan. His work was widely read during his lifetime and while Tourgée cannot be regarded as a major novelist he was able to present important questions in the framework of well-told, exciting narratives. He served as US consul at Bordeaux from 1897 to 1905.

*'Toinette* tells the story of a beautiful near-White slave girl and her lover, a White southerner who is the father of her child. After the Civil War she is a free woman but the liaison continues. Then 'Toinette seeks marriage and when her lover refuses, horrified at the idea, she leaves him. The novel was republished as *A Royal Gentleman* in 1881.

*A Fool's Errand* concerns Colonel Servosse (the fool of the title) of the Union army who buys a plantation in North Carolina after the Civil War. He does his best for the Black people, fights the Ku Klux Klan and the carpetbaggers, and finds an enemy in the Confederate general, Gurney, whose son falls in love with Servosse's daughter, Lily. After many vicissitudes and evidence of honour on both sides, the ex-soldiers are reconciled and the young people are able to look forward to marriage.

*Bricks Without Straw* demonstrated that for most Black people in the South emancipation was no more than a word. A northern schoolteacher, Mollie Ainslie, comes to North Carolina. Her success with the Black community of Red Wing brings down the wrath of the Whites and the Klan burns down the settlement. Mollie finds an ally in Hesden Le Moyne, a White plantation owner, but meets hostility from his haughty mother. Black principles, the preacher Eliab Hill, and the farmer Nimbus Desmit are notably drawn.

**Tourneur, Cyril** *c*.1575–1626. Almost nothing is known of the life of Tourneur, the Jacobean playwright, and the few details that there are date from 1613. At the end of that year he was an official courier to Brussels, and a reference of 1614 describes him as being in the employ of Cecil – called General Cecil and probably Sir Edward Cecil, with whom he sailed as secretary in a raid on Cadiz in 1625. The raid proved abortive and the flagship, the *Royal Anne*, was obliged to put in at Kinsale, Ireland, on the return voyage when the crew came down with disease. Tourneur was one of over a hundred men put ashore and he died in Ireland in the following year. It is known that he was paid a pension by the Dutch and the evidence suggests that Tourneur was principally occupied in service to the state; his writing was, not unusually for those days, an occupation for the times when the state did not require his services.

Tourneur is remembered as the author of the remarkable *The Revenger's Tragedy* (1607), though some scholars have suggested that a more likely author is Middleton. However, the inferior *The Atheist's Tragedy* (1611) is from the same hand and known, from the title page, to be Tourneur's. A third play, *The Nobleman*, was published in 1612 but no copy survives. Other works by Tourneur include a few occasional poems; a lament on the condition of contemporary life called *The Transformed Metaphor* (1600); a pamphlet, *Laugh and Lie Down* (1605); and a fragment of a play, *Ye Arraignment of London* (*c*.1613).

Tourneur's works were collected and edited by Allardyce Nicoll and published in 1930.

***Tour of the Prairies, A*** In 1832 Washington Irving was one of a party of five who spent a month travelling in the Indian territories of the Midwestern frontier. This is Irving's account of the tour, which began at Fort Gibson in what is now the state of Oklahoma. The party travelled among the frontiersmen and some of the Plains Indian tribes. Irving was interested in gathering examples of frontier lore and the book has some merit, given the date of the journey and the author's literary skill. But Irving was really too romantic a writer to do the subject justice. Henry L. Ellsworth, a government commissioner, who was a member of the same party, wrote a report which exists in manuscript and is acknowledged to be a corrective to Irving's distortions and omissions.

***Tower, The*** See **Yeats, William Butler**.

***Tower of London, The*** See **Ainsworth, William Harrison**.

***Town Down the River, The*** A collection of poems by Edwin Arlington Robinson, first published in 1910. The much-anthologized 'Miniver Cheery' is one of the poems in this volume.

**Towneley Plays, The** See **miracle plays**.

**Townsend, Morris** Catherine Sloper's fortune-hunting suitor in *Washington Square*, by Henry James. Disposed of by Catherine's father during his lifetime, he tries again after Dr Sloper's death, when Catherine becomes a rich woman in her own right.

**Tox, Miss Lucretia** The kind-hearted spinster of Dickens's *Dombey and Son*, who becomes housekeeper to Paul Dombey when his first wife dies. She has ambitions of becoming the second Mrs Dombey, to the intense annoyance of his dreadful sister, Mrs Chick.

**Toynbee, Arnold (Joseph)** 1889–1975. Arnold Toynbee, nephew of Arnold Toynbee the social reformer, was born in London. He was educated at Winchester School and Balliol College, Oxford, of which he became a fellow, and where he was a tutor (1912–15). After Oxford he served at the Foreign Office until 1919, when he was appointed Koraes Professor of Modern Greek and Byzantine Language, History, and Literature in the University of London. He was Director of Studies at the Royal Institute of International Affairs (1925–55).

Toynbee's first work was a pamphlet, *Greek Policy Since 1882* (1914), and much of his published works for the next few years were concerned with European politics and ancient Greek culture. The first part of his *magnum opus*, *A Study of History*, appeared in 1934 and was completed in 12 volumes in 1961. A philosophy of world history from earliest to contemporary times, it sees the history of mankind as largely determined by the principle of challenge and response. It gave a far wider horizon to history than the familiar European landscape, and Toynbee largely succeeded in remaining a detached analyst while also lucid and readable. This immense achievement, which occupied Toynbee for 30 years, has aroused considerable controversy among scholars but many regard it as the finest work by a historian since Gibbon's *Decline and Fall*.

Among other works by Toynbee were the texts of his notable Reith Lectures of 1952, *The World and the West*; *Hellenism: The History of a Civilization* (1959) and *Hannibal's Legacy* (1965); and the travel books *Between Oxus and Jumna* (1961), *Between Niger and Nile* (1965), and *Between Maule and Amazon* (1967). A condensation of *A Study of History* by D. C. Somervell (two vols, 1946 and 1957; single volume, 1960) enjoyed a remarkable popular success with the general reading public.

**Trabb's boy** In Dickens's *Great Expectations*, the tailor's boy who punctures Pip's self-esteem in no uncertain terms.

*Tracts for the Times* See **Oxford Movement**.

**Traddles, Tommy** In Dickens's *David Copperfield*, the simple amiable boy from Creakle's school who is David's lifelong friend. He becomes a barrister and, with the help of Micawber, exposes the villainy of Uriah Heep.

*Traffics and Discoveries* A volume of 11 stories and 11 poems by Rudyard Kipling, first published in 1904. Among the stories in this volume is 'Mrs Bathurst', which tells of the inexplicable desertion of Vickery, and the powerful impulse which the narrator believes led him to take such a step. The reason, he guesses, is Mrs Bathurst, who kept a pub in Auckland, and with whom Vickery seems preoccupied. The lady has no particular beauty but she has a more potent quality that drives Vickery to insanity and death; his body is found with another's. Mrs Bathurst's? The author does not say, and no one in the story knows. This strange oblique story has been much discussed. 'They' is one of Kipling's best stories and arose, commentators aver, from his continuing grief over the loss of his daughter Josephine. The narrator, driving to Sussex, comes upon a beautiful house owned by a blind woman. The house and garden are filled with the presence of happy children who succeed, apparently, in remaining out of sight. The narrator's mystification increases on succeeding visits, until his hand is taken by an unseen child and kissed in a manner which means something only he would understand, because it was a sign he shared with his lost daughter. 'Below the Mill Dam' is a story of Robert's Mill, in use since the Norman Conquest; the Spirit of the Mill and others discuss what the coming of electricity will mean to that ancient place.

*Tragic Comedians, The* A novel by George Meredith, first published in 1880. It was developed from a story that had appeared in the *Fortnightly Review* and was based on Helene von Donniges's account of her love affair with the German socialist, Ferdinand Lassalle, who appears in the novel as Alvan. Helene von Donniges is represented as the character Clotilde, a nobleman's daughter who is prepared to marry Alvan, the socialist, in the face of her family's wrath. Alvan, quixotically honourable, insists that she gain their full consent. Clotilde returns to her family, who bully her mercilessly and in the end deceive her into accepting Marko, their choice for her. Alvan, when he learns what has happened, writes a furious and insulting letter to Clotilde's father. Marko challenges him, and in the ensuing fight Alvan is killed. Clotilde marries Marko after the tragedy.

*Tragic Muse, The* A novel by Henry James, first published in serial form in the *Atlantic Monthly*, from January 1889 to May 1890, and in volume form in 1890.

Lady Agnes Dormer comes back to London from Paris; now a widow, she is keen to put her children's lives on a settled course. Her son, Nick, is a painter but she would like him to enter politics; her daughters Grace and Bridget (Biddy) she wants to see married. Biddy shares her brother's interest in the arts.

Peter Sherringham, one of the Dormers' friends, is an avid theatregoer. He has a sister, Julia Dallow, a wealthy widow, who loves Nick and who finances his entry into politics. After he is elected Nick, prompted by his mother, proposes to Julia and she accepts him. Biddy, meanwhile, has fallen in love with Peter Sherringham – but he is infatuated with the talented and striking actress Miriam Rooth and introduces her to Madame Carré, who undertakes her training.

Nick tries to concentrate on a political career but drifts back to painting. He is working on a portrait of Miriam when Julia visits him unexpectedly; she breaks off their engagement. Peter, meanwhile, has become aware that Miriam is not interested in him in the way he would like. She becomes famous on the London stage and rejects his proposal; eventually she marries her leading man, Basil Dashwood. After an interval of despair Peter enters the diplomatic service, for which his family had always intended him, and goes abroad. He realizes his feeling for Biddy, whose devotion is now rewarded when he marries her. Nick Dormer achieves a modest reputation as a portrait painter and decides to give up politics altogether. This removes politics from the sphere of Julia's interests also: but one day she asks Nick to paint her portrait. As the book closes, Lady Dormer regards this development with pleasure; she feels confident that the two will marry after all.

*The Tragic Muse* is a comedy of manners, with a familiar 'change partners' plot set in a world where artistic priorities continually intrude. The mixture is not successful and the novel is oddly lifeless as a whole. Incidental pleasures abound, inevitably; Henry James was Henry James after all. He was a critic of fine quality, as his essays demonstrate; but that very quality halts the novel in its tracks while the author's expositions occupy long stretches of text. Two lively characters are Gabriel Nash, the dedicated aesthete (in fact he is dangerously near to being overdrawn), and old Mr Carteret, who sees enough promise in Nick Dormer as a political protégé to offer him the security of a handsome legacy.

**Traherne, Thomas** 1637–74. The son of a shoemaker of Hereford, Traherne was probably brought up and educated by a rich relative, Philip Traherne, who was twice Mayor of Hereford. He sent the boy to Brasenose College, Oxford, in 1653 and Thomas proved to be a scholar of distinction, taking his BA in 1656; he was made MA in 1661 and BD in 1669. He was ordained in 1660, though he had in fact been made incumbent of Credenhill in Herefordshire in 1657. Some of his work was written in Credenhill but most of it dates from his years in London as chaplain to Sir Orlando Bridgeman (1667–72). When Bridgeman retired to Teddington Traherne went with him, and died there in 1674.

The only work published during Traherne's lifetime was the anti-Catholic *Roman Forgeries* (1673); a year after his death *Christian Ethicks* appeared. Neither of these two prose works are of much interest to the modern reader but a third, *Centuries of Meditation*, dating from his years at Credenhill, contains writing of remarkable quality and overshadows his claims to be remembered as a poet. It was not until 1896, however, that the work was discovered, when Bertram Dobell, a London bookseller, found the manuscript of this and some poems on a London bookstall. The poems were published in 1903, the meditations in 1908. Some years later the manuscript of *Poems of Felicity* turned up in the British Museum; it was edited by H. I. Bell (1910).

Traherne's works, particularly the *Centuries of Meditation*, reveal a man who rediscovered 'felicity' in his adult life, and regarded it as akin to the untarnished goodness of the child: too often man loses this but he can regain it, if he is vouchsafed – as Traherne apparently was – the knowledge of *how*; he strives to convey this knowledge in his writing. He succeeds less well in his poetry, which has a refreshing exuberance but often lacks discipline, and is at its best when he gives poetic form to the ideas expressed in the *Centuries of Meditation*.

**Traitor, The** A tragedy by James Shirley, first produced in 1631 and first published in 1635. The

play has some basis in the history of the Medici family of Florence. The Duke of Florence is enamoured of Amidea, the sister of Sciarrha, one of his nobles. His kinsman, Lorenzo, plotting to seize power, does his best to further the duke's desires, while at the same time arousing Sciarrha's wrath at the threat to his sister's honour. Sciarrha kills Amidea to save her from dishonour and lays out her body where the duke will find her. When the duke comes upon the body he calls for Lorenzo, who seizes the opportunity to murder him. Lorenzo is killed by Sciarrha in the last moments of accusation and recrimination; Sciarrha dies of his wounds.

**Tramp Abroad, A** Mark Twain's record of his European tour with Joseph H. Twichell ('Harris' in the book) in 1878. The countries visited were Germany, Switzerland, and Italy, with the centre of interest the walk through the Black Forest and the Alps. The tone is similar to that of *Innocents Abroad* and the book was first published in 1880.

**Transcendentalism** A literary and philosophic movement in New England, which gave expression to the weakening of Calvinism and the spirit of rationalism. Centred around Concord, Massachusetts, among its notable voices were those of William Ellery Channing, Emerson, Thoreau, and Bronson Alcott. The Transcendentalists were opposed to formal religion and the idea that man needed an intercessor through which to reach God. What was human was divine – all great human endeavour was an expression of the divine – and great literature, the gospels no less than Greek philosophy and the works of Shakespeare, was an expression of it. The 'Transcendental Club', as outsiders called it, was at its most active between 1836 and 1860. *The Dial*, the movement's quarterly magazine, appeared for only four years (1840–44) but Transcendentalism had considerable influence on Americans' awareness of themselves as a new nation with their own culture.

**Traubel, Horace Logo** 1858–1919. Horace Traubel, a journalist from Camden, New Jersey, became Walt Whitman's close friend when the poet went to live there after leaving Washington in 1873. From 1888 he began to keep a detailed diary of his visits to Whitman, recording conversations, criticism, and opinions. This record of the last four years of the poet's life was published in three volumes between 1906 and 1914 and called *With Walt Whitman in Camden*. Traubel was one of his friend's literary executors; he was also one of the editors of *In Re Walt*

*Whitman* (1893) and *The Complete Writings of Walt Whitman* (1902).

**Traveller, The;** *or, a Prospect of Society*. A poem by Oliver Goldsmith, first published in 1764. It was his first publication under his own name and dedicated to his brother Henry, to whom he had sent the rough draft from Switzerland during his own travels ten years before. The traveller – or perhaps compulsive wanderer – is the poet himself. From a peak in the Alps he ponders on the lessons of his travels and notes the faults and virtues of the countries he has visited. Happiness, he realizes, may be found in any place, as well as discontent. The poem is composed in rhyming couplets of remarkable fluency, in which Goldsmith encompasses description and philosophy with apparent ease.

**Travels in France** (*Travels during the years 1787, 1788, 1789 and 1790, undertaken with a view of ascertaining the cultivation, wealth, resources and national prosperity of the Kingdom of France*). A report by Arthur Young on his journeys in France, first published in 1792. He observed conditions in France just before the Revolution and, as a trained observer, could see that they could not possibly continue. His first journey (he made three in all) took him through Berri, Poitou, and Languedoc; the second through Brittany and Anjou, the third through Alsace–Lorraine, Franche-Comté, Burgundy, and Provence. Young's examination of systems of land tenure has permanent value and his book has a considerable reputation in France; it was translated into a number of languages. A modern edition was edited by C. Maxwell (1929).

**Travels through France and Italy** A memoir of his travels in France and Italy from June 1764 to June 1765 by Tobias Smollett, first published in 1766.

Smollett's health broke down in 1763, and in April of that year he was prostrated by the death of his daughter, Elizabeth, at the age of 15. He set out for Europe with his wife in June of the following year and journeyed across France. After Nice, the Smolletts proceeded to Genoa and then through Italy, with Rome as the farthest point south and Florence as the other principal Italian centre. They returned to Nice in the winter and then made their way back to England across France. The book is in the form of letters to imaginary correspondents and, allowing for Smollett's tiresome disposition, which convinced him that every coachman and innkeeper was his enemy, provides a remarkable picture of life in France and Italy in the middle of the 18th century. Smollett's eye, however jaundiced, is sharp and perceptive and the *Travels* is a masterpiece of description and comment. Laurence Sterne met Smollett during his wanderings, probably at Montpellier, and reproduced him as Smelfungus in *A Sentimental Journey*: '. . . he set out with the spleen and jaundice, and every object he passed by was discoloured or distorted'.

There are modern editions of *Travels through France and Italy* edited by T. Seccombe (The World's Classics, 1907), Osbert Sitwell (1949), and Frank Felsenstein (1968).

**Treasure Island** A romance by Robert Louis Stevenson. It was first published as a serial, *The Sea Cook or Treasure Island*, by Captain George North, in *Young Folks* (October 1881 to January 1882).

The story is told by Jim Hawkins, whose mother keeps an inn, the 'Admiral Benbow', near the sea in the West Country. An old pirate,

An illustration by Wal Paget for an edition of *Treasure Island* published in 1899. Jim Hawkins and Long John Silver walking along the quays. Stevenson's novel was first published as a serial in 1881.

Billy Bones, comes to stay at the inn and proves to be a coarse old bully. He is dogged by his former confederates – he has in his chest a map which gives the whereabouts of Captain Flint's treasure and they want it. Jim outwits them and secures the map, and he and his mother fly to Squire Trelawney to whom Jim delivers the map. The squire and his friend Dr Livesey charter a schooner, the *Hispaniola*, commanded by Captain Smollett, and set sail for Treasure Island with Jim as a member of the crew. The rest of the crew is recruited but the purpose of the voyage somehow becomes known and when the *Hispaniola* sails she carries a number of pirates among her crew.

It is Jim Hawkins who overhears the truth and discovers that their leader is none other than the ship's cook, his friend hitherto, Long John Silver. The rest of the story relates how the pirates' plans are defeated and the treasure found, with many thrilling incidents before Long John Silver is brought to justice.

Stevenson was a master of the art of narrative and the story is superbly plotted and paced.

**Treatise of Human Nature, A**  A philosophical essay by David Hume, first published in 1739–40 (two volumes in 1739, a third in 1740). Hume's further philosophical works developed and elaborated the principles expressed in this book and pursued its line of thought to logical extremes.

Hume acknowledges his debt to John Locke and earlier thinkers who had ventured to use experimental reasoning in the examination of moral subjects. Hume's bases in human nature are what he calls 'impressions' and 'ideas'. Every idea has an impression that resembles it; ideas have less force in the human mind but they are what produce the new impressions, which lead to sensation, and then to reflection; the impressions of reflection are emotions, desires, and passions, and in these lie the formation of new ideas. All perceptions are derived from sense impressions, which arise from unknown causes; simple ideas do not always follow the same order as their corresponding impressions, and from the association of ideas comes a constantly changing view of the external world.

Hume's further examinations are found in *An Enquiry Concerning Human Understanding* (1748) and *An Enquiry Concerning the Principles of Morals* (1751). Modern editions of the *Treatise* are by L. A. Selby-Bigge and P. H. Nidditch (1975) and E. C. Mossner (1969).

**Trench, Richard Chenevix** 1807–86. Trench was born in Dublin and educated at Harrow School and Trinity College, Cambridge. He was ordained in 1832 and after various appointments became Professor of Divinity at King's College, London. He became Dean of Westminster in 1856 and Archbishop of Dublin in 1863. Trench wrote three books on the Gospels but is remembered in literature as a philologist; *The Study of Words* (1851) helped to popularize the proper study of language. *English Past and Present* (1857) was published in the same year as the meeting of the Philological Society where Trench proposed the resolution that was the origin of the *Oxford English Dictionary*. He made known to a later age some fine Latin medieval hymns in *Sacred Latin Poetry, Chiefly Lyrical* (1849).

**Trevelyan, George Macaulay** 1876–1962. Third son of Sir George Otto Trevelyan, George Trevelyan was born at Stratford-upon-Avon and educated at Harrow School and Trinity College, Cambridge, of which he became Master in 1940. He was appointed Regius Professor of Modern History at Cambridge in 1927. His present reputation stands very high; he was widely regarded as the leading British historian and praised for lucid presentation and exact scholarship. But he is most famous for a book not generally believed to be his best: *English Social History: A Survey of Six Centuries* (1944) caught the wartime and postwar interest in sociology and became a best-seller.

Among Trevelyan's other works are *England in the Age of Wycliffe* (1899), *The Peasants' Rising and the Lollards* (1899), *England under the Stuarts* (1904), *England under Queen Anne* (1930–34), *The English Revolution 1688–1689* (1938), and a single-volume *History of England* (1926). His history of the Risorgimento was published in three parts: *Garibaldi's Defence of the Roman Republic* (1907), *Garibaldi and the Thousand* (1909), and *Garibaldi and the Making of Italy* (1911). The three parts were published together as *Garibaldi* (1933).

**Trevelyan, Sir George Otto** 1838–1928. The nephew of Lord Macaulay, Trevelyan was born in Leicestershire and educated at Harrow School and Trinity College, Cambridge. He entered Parliament in 1865, held various public appointments, and published *The Life and Letters of Lord Macaulay* (1876). *The Early History of Charles James Fox* (1880) was intended to be the first part of an exhaustive biography of the Whig politician but his next history, *The American Revolution* (1899–1907), suggests that his intentions had changed. *George III and Charles Fox* (1912–14) completed his study of the American Revolution. Trevelyan's careful research and arresting narrative style have been much praised and *The Early History of Charles James Fox* is notable for its vivid presentation of social and political life in late-18th-century England.

**Trevisa, John** (*or* **John of Trevisa**) *c.* 1330–1402. John Trevisa was a Cornishman of Carados. He became a fellow of Exeter College, Oxford (1362–65), and subsequently of Queen's College (1372–76), where among the residents were John Wycliffe and Nicholas of Hereford. After a violent quarrel in the hall at Queen's, possibly resulting from an airing of Wycliffe's opinions, the provost and three fellows, among them Trevisa, were expelled. The four made off with the keys, charters, plate, books, and money of their college and held on to them for four years, until the appointment of a royal commission in 1380 persuaded them it was time to give them back.

Trevisa became vicar of Berkeley, chaplain to Lord Berkeley, and nonresident canon of the collegiate church of Westbury-on-Trym. He seems to have mended his quarrel with Queen's, since he was able to rent a chamber there between 1395 and 1399. His contributions to English literature comprise his translations from the Latin, at the request of Lord Berkeley, of Ranulf Higden's *Polychronicon* (completed 1387) and Bartholomaeus Anglicus's *De Proprietatibus Rerum* (completed 1398).

Trevisa's virtue was that he translated two works of information into books that all Englishmen could read with pleasure: his translations were much more than versions out of one language into another. The use of Latin and French was declining and English was now the medium of instruction in grammar schools. The development of English secular prose owes much to John Trevisa and to the translators of *The Travels of Sir John Mandeville*.

**Triamond** In Book IV of Spenser's *The Faerie Queene*, he is the knight of friendship, eternally sworn to Cambel, his erstwhile opponent. He marries Canace, Cambel's sister.

**Tricke to Catch the Old-One, A** A comedy by Thomas Middleton, first published in 1608.

Theophilus Witgood is a penniless rake who becomes engaged to Widow Medler, a woman of great wealth. The widow is in fact a courtesan acting the part on Witgood's behalf, so that he can get some money from his miserly uncle, Pecunius Lucre, who holds the mortgage to Witgood's estate. The courtesan was once Witgood's mistress and remains his friend; Witgood, in fact, wants to marry Joyce, niece of Walkadine Hoard, a wealthy usurer who is Lucre's enemy.

Widow Medler becomes the centre of attention. Lucre is prepared to welcome Witgood and advance him money now that a wealthy wife is in prospect; and Witgood's creditors hurry to advance him more loans. Meanwhile, rival suitors for the 'widow's' hand appear – among them Walkadine Hoard, who might secure further wealth for himself and score over Pecunius Lucre.

Witgood seizes the chance to do his friend a good turn and on his advice the courtesan accepts Walkadine Hoard and all his wealth. Whereupon Witgood's creditors, knowing that the wealthy marriage will not take place, have him arrested. He deals with this by bringing pressure to bear on Hoard, insisting that the 'widow' had a pre-contract with him. Hoard agrees to pay Witgood's debts and Witgood marries Joyce in secret. At the wedding feast the erstwhile 'widow' is recognized by two of the guests and, to Lucre's malicious glee, is identified as a courtesan. But Hoard is consoled by her promise that she will be a good wife to him and Witgood promises his uncle that he will be a good boy in future.

**Trim, Corporal** Uncle Toby's orderly in *Tristram Shandy* by Laurence Sterne. Very much an old soldier and devoted to Uncle Toby, he is eloquent and reflective in complete contrast to his master, who is practically inarticulate unless he can relate his words to a military context.

**Tristram** The hero of this great love story occupies a large part of the tales Malory incorporated into *Le Morte Darthur*, where he is Tristram of Lyonesse. But his story is older than the similar love story of Launcelot and Guenever, though also based on a French or Breton source. It first appeared in English literature in a mid-13th-century verse romance, possibly the work of Thomas of Erceldoune (Thomas the Rhymer). In that poem he is the nephew of King Mark of England; Tristram kills the king of Ireland, and after the fight is tended by the king's sister Ysoude. Back in England, he tells King Mark of Ysoude, and is sent again to Ireland to ask for her hand for the king; so the story is set on its course. In Malory's *Le Morte Darthur* Tristram is son of the king of Lyonesse; his uncle is King Mark of Cornwall, brother of the queen.

The king of Lyonesse is held prisoner by enchantment. The queen, while searching for him, gives birth to Tristram and dies soon afterwards. Tristram, as a young man, defends King Mark from the emissary of the king of Ireland, come to demand tribute. Tristram kills his opponent but is badly wounded, and Mark sends him to Ireland

The birth of Tristram in Malory's *Le Morte Darthur*. The frontispiece illustration to Book VIII in Wynkyn de Worde's edition of 1529.

to recover from his wounds. He is a skilled harper and singer and is received with favour at court, where the king's daughter, La Beale Isoud, falls in love with him. The queen then discovers that Tristram is the knight who killed the king's emissary, her brother. Tristram is ordered from the court, having exchanged vows of love with Isoud. In Malory, King Mark sends Tristram back to Ireland to ask for the hand of Isoud, through jealousy of the young knight and hoping the mission will prove fatal to him. But Tristram succeeds, through a service to the Irish king.

On the ship Isoud's maid Bragwaine carries a love potion mixed by the queen of Ireland. It is intended for King Mark, so that he shall truly love his bride. It is this love potion, drunk by Tristram and Isoud, that fires their love again, a love which continues through her marriage to King Mark. When their love is discovered Tristram goes to serve the king of Brittany and for a while consoles himself with another Isoud – la Blanche Mains. But he returns to Cornwall to his first Isoud, and after being banished goes to the court of King Arthur, where he proves a brave and gallant knight; he is eventually united with La Beale Isoud in spite of King Mark's efforts against them.

The romantic ending adopted by later poets has Tristram lying wounded by a poisoned arrow in Brittany. Feeling his life ebbing away he sends a messenger for Isoud of Ireland, asking that the returning ship shall bear white sails if she is aboard. Isoud of Brittany overhears, and out of jealousy tells Tristram that a ship is returning – bearing black sails. Tristram dies of despair and

Isoud of Ireland, who was indeed travelling on a ship with white sails, dies beside him.

**Tristram and Iseult**  A poem by Matthew Arnold, first published in 1852 in *Empedocles on Etna and Other Poems*. The poem is concerned with the dying Tristram in Brittany; he remembers his happiness with Iseult of Ireland while Iseult of Brittany, her rival, watches by him. Iseult of Ireland arrives and there is one last passionate exchange between the lovers before he dies.

**Tristram of Lyonesse**  Swinburne's poem on the subject of Tristram and Iseult, which was begun in 1869 but not completed and published until 1882. Swinburne's romance is written in couplets and inclines heavily to the 'world well lost for love' theme.

(For the story upon which it is based, see **Tristram**.)

**Tristram Shandy, Gentleman, The Life and Opinions of**  A novel by Laurence Sterne which was published in instalments. Volumes I and II were first published in 1760, III and IV in 1761, V and VI in 1762, VII and VIII in 1765, and Volume IX in 1767.

The novel has in fact nothing to do with its given title; Tristram is conceived at the beginning, born in Volume III, and put into his first boy's clothes (breeched) in Volume VI; he disappears from the story after that. Setting out to relate his life and opinions, Tristram digresses in a hundred different ways, is reminded of matters which he must also relate, which bring up points which can be discussed, which could prove rewarding and to the point – or not. He hardly gets beyond what happened before he was born: 'I wish either my father or my mother, or indeed both of them, as they were in duty both equally bound to it, had minded what they were about when they begot me.' His mother, at the moment of his begetting, was concerned with winding up the clock.

The result is a rambling and apparently shapeless account of people and feelings which reflects the author's personality and imagination. Volumes I to III are concerned with the circumstances surrounding the hero's birth; Volume IV tells of Slawkenbergius and his treatise on noses, and the way Tristram acquired his Christian name; Volume V contains the notable reflections of Corporal Trim on morality; Volume VI the fine comic dialogue of Mr and Mrs Shandy on the breeching of their son, and the story of Le Fevre. The next two volumes, VII and VIII, arbitrarily abandon the narrative, such as it is, relate the author's travels in France, and contain the story of the King of Bohemia. Volume IX tells of the successful wooing of Uncle Toby by the Widow Wadman. Sterne gives his novel a preface after Volume III, when Tristram is successfully brought into the world.

The world of *Tristram Shandy* (leaving aside Volumes VII and VIII) is an English village where Tristram, according to the terms of his father's marriage settlement, is required to be born, and where the principal characters are to be found. Mr Shandy is saturated in the scientific speculation of the time, and is in a continuous state of exasperation with his wife, who 'never asked the meaning of a thing she did not understand'. 'My mother never did. In short, she went out of the world at last without knowing whether it turned round or stood still – my father had officiously told her above a thousand times which way it was, but she always forgot.' Uncle Toby, Mr Shandy's brother, is an old soldier who was wounded in the groin at the siege of Namur. He is gentle and amiable, and his hobby is the theoretical reduction of fortified towns. His devoted servant, Corporal Trim, shares Uncle Toby's enthusiasm; Trim was wounded in the knee at Landen. There is excellent comedy with

A detail from Hogarth's frontispiece to *Tristram Shandy*. Corporal Trim reads a sermon to Uncle Toby, Dr Slop, and Walter Shandy. British Museum Print Room.

Dr Slop in his exasperation with the knot the servant Obadiah has tied in his bag (indeed the incidental gentle humour of the book is for many readers the chief virtue of *Tristram Shandy*). Yorick is the amiable parson of the village, a man of wit and perception who reflects the author's mind and who turns up again in *A Sentimental Journey*. The Shandy's neighbour is Widow Wadman, whose fond eye for Uncle Toby is eventually rewarded.

'Obviously a god is hidden in *Tristram Shandy* and his name is Muddle, and some readers cannot accept him' (E. M. Forster, *Aspects of the Novel*, 1927). Forster is probably right in the second part of his sentence but one would have to be very sure of Sterne's intentions before accepting the first part. Is it muddle? If it is, fiction in English is the better for it. In any case the original flavour of the book, its warmth and humour, the examination of human idiosyncrasy, and the memorable characters are what matter for lovers of *Tristram Shandy*.

Modern editions of *Tristram Shandy* are published in The World's Classics, Everyman's Library, and the Penguin English Library.

**Triumph of Life, The** A poem by Percy Bysshe Shelley in *terza rima*. Shelley was working on the poem at the time of his death and left it unfinished. The poet describes a vision of the captive multitude of humanity, through which the triumphal chariot passes. This is the procession of Life, the conqueror; chained to the chariot are the great men of history – vanquished by the mystery of life. The vision is succeeded by the allegory of a single life which, after a hopeful and aspiring youth, falls victim to the same mystery; love is the only armour against defeat. The vision is explained to the poet by Jean-Jacques Rousseau.

**Trivia: or The Art of Walking the Streets of London.** This poem, written in three books by John Gay, was first published in 1716. The author takes the reader through London, first by day and then by night. He tells him what to wear; the dangers to be avoided, such as mischievous urchins, pickpockets, and tricksters; how to read the weather signs; and how to avoid rain from above and mud from below. He also gives him a fair cross-section of the people he will meet and the people he should avoid. The poem is a notable record of 18th-century manners.

**Troil, Magnus** The Shetland landlord in Scott's *The Pirate*, and father of the two daughters who provide companionship for the hero. Troil is of noble Norse ancestry.

**Troil, Ulla** Magnus Troil's crazy relative in Scott's *The Pirate*, known to all as Norma of the Fitful-Head. She believes she has supernatural powers; her actions certainly affect the course of events. In the resolution of the story she proves to be an early love of Basil Mertoun and mother of the pirate Cleveland.

**Troilus** One of the sons of Priam, King of Troy, in Shakespeare's *Troilus and Cressida*. He falls in love with Cressida, daughter of the priest and seer Calchas, who deserts to the Greeks. Troilus is bereft of Cressida when the Greeks demand her in exchange for Antenor: he loses her completely when she responds to the advances of Diomedes.

*Troilus and Cressida* A tragedy by William Shakespeare. It was first produced *c.*1602, and printed twice in quartos of 1609. It was published in the First Folio of 1623 but the title was for some reason left out of the contents page. The story has no basis in classical literature but the story of Cressida (evolved from Homer's Briseis) as Shakespeare uses it had been known since the *Roman de Troie* by Benoît de Sainte-Maure of the 12th century and had provided subjects for Chaucer and Henryson before Shakespeare. The Trojan War setting keeps its familiar characters, with Hector, Achilles, and Ulysses as the most prominent. The character of Pandarus was invented by Chaucer.

The war has been going on for seven years. During a truce the Trojan prince Troilus falls in love with Cressida, daughter of the priest Calchas. She seems at first indifferent but Troilus enlists the help of Pandarus, a compulsive go-between (hence, pander) and Cressida is persuaded that union with Troilus is what she wants. They consummate their love and she is happy to swear, with Troilus, that it is eternal.

Cressida's father Calchas deserts to the Greek camp, where the leaders try to plan the conclusion of the war and where Achilles sulks in his tent with Patroclus. Calchas is a seer, and valuable to the Greeks, but he wants his daughter with him. They agree to barter a Trojan prisoner, Antenor, in exchange for Cressida. Troilus has to surrender his love to Diomedes, the Greek commander who will conduct her to the camp and who is charmed by her beauty. Cressida in turn is charmed by her reception and the flattery she receives; she exchanges kisses and banter freely. Nestor utters a compliment but the canny Ulysses has seen more ('her wanton spirits look out at every joint and motive of her body'). Ulysses has also, in an earlier scene, bestirred the sullen Achilles in a remarkable speech: 'Time

hath, my lord, a wallet at his back, wherein he puts alms for oblivion'.

Before the war is resumed Achilles invites the Trojan leaders to a feast. He wants to see the great and gallant Hector, his obvious adversary. At the feast, Troilus learns the truth about Cressida: she now belongs to Diomedes. In the fighting that follows Hector kills Patroclus; in revenge Achilles and a troop of Myrmidons kill Hector when he is disarmed, and Troilus and the rest of the Trojans retreat to the city. Troilus has lost Cressida and he has sharp words for Pandarus – who is quite used to being treated thus ('Why should our endeavour be so lov'd, and the performance so loathed?').

*Troilus and Cressida* comes, as far as we can tell, after the wonderful comedies *As You Like It* and *Twelfth Night* and before *Hamlet*. It is generally called a 'problem' play and as such the public will not be vouchsafed a straightforward production of it, since producers will have their fun. It has been staged more frequently since World War II: many of Shakespeare's rarely seen plays have been revived in the 20th century and this bitter masterpiece matched the disillusioned temper of the times. Life in this play is indeed time's fool, and men at war for too long will soon forget honour; banners will become ragged and pushed aside as a nuisance. Love will be replaced by lechery and when the single noble character is killed, ignobly, why try and pretend any longer? 'Hector is dead; there is no more to say.' The scabrous Thersites may be the one with the clearest view.

*Troilus and Criseyde* A poem of 8200 lines in rhyme-royal by Geoffrey Chaucer. It dates from the 'second period' of Chaucer's work and was inspired by his reading of Boccaccio's *Filostrato*, which told the same story. An astrological reference in the poem gives a probable date for its composition (1385 or 1386). The poet is the observer of the fortunes of Troilus and Criseyde, and Criseyde's uncle Pandarus: he offers no comments and makes no judgments of his own.

Criseyde is the daughter of the priest Calchas of Troy. Calchas, a seer, having foreknowledge that Troy will fall, has fled to the Greek camp and deserted his daughter. Troilus, son of King Priam of Troy, falls in love with Criseyde; she returns his love and her uncle Pandarus is their go-between. Criseyde is a widow and a traitor's daughter, and though assured of the goodwill of Hector himself, she is frightened and insecure. But while she accepts that a prince of Troy could easily victimize her she sees too that he could be the bulwark against all her fears. In the event the

Criseyde seeks Hector's compassion. An illustration for *Troilus and Criseyde* in R. Pynson's edition (1526) of Chaucer's *Works*.

consummation of their love brings great happiness to both Troilus and Criseyde.

This happiness is shattered when the two sides exchange prisoners. Criseyde is claimed by the Greek side in exchange for the Trojan Antenor. Diomede conducts her to the Greek camp, where she implores her father Calchas to help her escape so that she can return to Troilus. Calchas refuses; Diomede makes it clear that he wants her and she is 'safe' once more – but her nature impels her to send untruthful letters to Troilus. Troilus learns the truth of her conduct but though he meets Diomede in the field does not have the satisfaction of killing him. At the end Troilus is killed by Achilles.

Chaucer's poem is dedicated to his friends in the last verse but one: 'O moral Gower' and 'my philosophical Strode' (John Gower the poet and Ralph Strode, a writer on logic and philosophy who was very probably Chaucer's neighbour in London).

The story of Troilus and Criseyde does not have its origins in Greek mythology. A 12th-century *trouvère*, Benoit de Sainte-Maure, wrote a *Roman de Troie* based on late Latin works about the siege of Troy; this provided the basis of both Chaucer's poem and Shakespeare's *Troilus and Cressida*.

**Trollope, Anthony** 1815–82. One of the most prolific of English novelists, Trollope somehow managed to combine his remarkable literary career with his duties as a civil servant. He was born in London, the third son of a hopelessly improvident barrister: his mother (see **Trollope, Frances**) was the real support of the family, and somehow an education as a day boy at Harrow and a short period at Winchester was contrived for him.

When Trollope was 19, an appointment as a clerk in the General Post Office was found for him. For seven years or so he simply endured it; then, in 1841, he was sent to Ireland. Thereafter his working life began to be more rewarding and he began his first exercises as a novelist. He published three books (*The Macdermotts of Ballycloran*, *The Kellys and the O'Kellys*, and *La Vendée*) between 1847 and 1850 without attracting much notice; but he had found the true field for his endeavour and his remarkable industry led eventually to the mastery of his craft. *The Warden* (1855), a scene of clerical life, demonstrated his quality and enjoyed a moderate success. It was the creation of the imagined world of Barsetshire which took him through six novels with increasing success. *Barchester Towers* came in 1857; he left Barsetshire for his next, *The Three Clerks* (1858), but returned there in the same year for *Doctor Thorne*. Another novel, *The Bertrams*, was completed in 1858 before Trollope was sent to Egypt and then the West Indies and he promptly wrote a highly regarded travel book, *The West Indies and the Spanish Main* (1859) about his experiences when he returned. His next novel was *Castle Richmond* (1860) but in *Framley Parsonage* (1861) he went back to Barsetshire and by now he had a readership of considerable size. But readers had to wait some time for a further instalment of the life of Trollope's invented county. Meanwhile, Trollope published a lecture, a volume of short stories, and the excellent *Orley Farm* (1862); two more novels and a book and a lecture on North America followed that and in 1864 his readers were given some Barsetshire characters in *The Small House at Allington*. The last of the stories did not appear until 1867 – *The Last Chronicle of Barset*. Incredibly, the years between 1864 and 1867 saw the appearance of lectures, a mass of journalism, and five novels which included *Can you Forgive Her?* (1864), *The Belton Estate* (1865), and *The Claverings* (1867). *Phineas Finn* (1869) developed the characters introduced in *Can you Forgive Her?* and another group of interlocking novels, of a political nature this time, was on the way. Like the Barsetshire series, they appeared at irregular intervals: *The Eustace Diamonds* (1873), *Phineas Redux* (1874), *The Prime Minister* (1876), and *The Duke's Children* (1880).

The Barsetshire and political groups (the 'Palliser' novels) are usually regarded as Trollope's best work and certainly they are the most popular. But from the great mass of his other work *The Way We Live Now* (1875) is outstanding, while *The American Senator* (1877),

*Ayala's Angel* (1881), and *Dr Wortle's School* (1881) are notable. Trollope died in 1882 and the posthumous *Mr Scarborough's Family* (1883) is given a high place among his works.

Anthony Trollope tells in his *Autobiography* (1883) how he achieved his extraordinary output while pursuing a remarkably active and busy career in the General Post Office – by regular and mechanical application to his creative work which nothing was allowed to disrupt. It is a measure of his greatness that so much of his work was on such a high level, and his attitude to his literary career remained cool and detached (see *Nina Balatka* and *Linda Tressel*). One can only regard with awe the rest of his output, the journalism, plays, lectures, travel books, and short stories.

A novelist of his stature deserves to have all his novels mentioned and those not so far named in this entry are as follows: *The Struggles of Brown, Jones and Robinson* (1862), *Rachel Ray* (1863), *Miss Mackenzie* (1865), *He Knew He Was Right* (1869), *The Vicar of Bullhampton* (1870), *Sir Harry Hotspur of Humblethwaite* (1871), *Ralph the Heir* (1871), *The Golden Lion of Granpere* (1872), *Lady Anna* (1873), *Harry Heathcote of Gangoil* (1874), *Is he Popenjoy?* (1878), *An Eye for an Eye* (1879), *John Caldigate* (1879), *Cousin Henry* (1879), *The Fixed Period* (1882), *Marion Fay* (1882), *Kept in the*

Dark (1882), *The Land Leaguers* (1883), and *An Old Man's Love* (1884).

Trollope's chosen scene was middle- and upper-middle-class life. If his books seem to contain a large number of clerics, it is because Victorian society, at that level, used the church quite blatantly as a field for a rewarding career – it will be seen that most of the clerics are men of principle rather than piety. Within his scene is a rich diversity of characters and Trollope's skill at drawing them, allied with his readability and his disinclination to comment, secure his high place in the history of English fiction. An interesting note on his other career, in the General Post Office, credits him with the invention of the pillar box.

**Trollope, Frances** 1780–1863. Frances Milton married Thomas Trollope in 1809. He was a poor provider and Frances hoped that emigration might prove the answer to her problems. The Trollopes managed a small goods bazaar in Cincinnati for three years (1827–30) but the business was not a success and they returned to England, where Frances embarked on a writing career. In 1832 she published *Domestic Manners of the Americans*, which made her reputation and which was furiously resented in the USA. She wrote rapidly and her output of travel books and novels was considerable; she used her experiences of the USA to attack slavery in her *Jonathan Jefferson Whitlaw* (1836). Her better novels have distinct quality though they are hardly known to the modern reader. Among them *The Widow Barnaby* (1838) is probably the most successful, telling of an unscrupulous woman's attempts to make a rich marriage. The *Vicar of Wrexhill* (1837) is a grim tale of a coldblooded and malignant clergyman. Frances's third son was Anthony Trollope.

**Trotter, Job** Jingle's servant in *The Pickwick Papers* and as tricky as his master. He outwits Pickwick and Sam Weller when they follow Jingle to Bury St Edmunds.

**Trotwood, Betsey** David Copperfield's greataunt in Dickens's novel. Having hoped for a girl, she feels affronted when David is born and turns her back on him and his mother. But she proves to be more than equal to the demands on her loyalty and affections when David, ragged and starving, turns up on her doorstep in Dover. A wonderful character, the crotchety, loving greataunt of everyone's dreams.

*Troy Book* See **Lydgate, John**.

**Trumbull, John** *c.*1750–1831. Trumbull was born in Connecticut and was as precocious as his

Trollope. A detail from the portrait by Samuel Laurence, 1865. National Portrait Gallery, London.

schoolfellow from Massachusetts, Timothy Dwight; Trumbull also entered Yale at the age of 13. He was one of the group that became known as the Connecticut Wits and devoted considerable energy at Yale to furthering the case for a broader curriculum and more attention to contemporary English literature. His valedictory speech, *An Essay on the Uses and Advantages of the Fine Arts* (1770), was an exposition of his views. He received his master's degree at the age of 20 and while tutoring at Yale wrote a satire on old-fashioned college education, *The Progress of Dulness* (1772), and published some elegant verse and essays.

In 1773 Trumbull left Yale and went to Boston to study law under John Adams. As a lawyer he practised in New Haven and Hartford. At this time he also became an active member of the 'wits' and was drawn into the politics of the troubled times (1774–1825). In 1782 he published a mock epic, *M'Fingal*, which satirized the stupidity of the British. Trumbull's literary activity covered only a short period and for the last 50 years of his life he published nothing of his own.

**Trumpet-Major, The** A novel by Thomas Hardy, first published in *Good Words* (January to December 1880). It is set in the time of the Napoleonic wars.

Anne Garland lives in Overcombe Mill, where her mother is a tenant. Nearby is a camp of dragoons, who come to the mill to draw water for their horses. One of them is John Loveday, the miller's son, now a trumpet-major and one of Anne's suitors. Another suitor is his brother, Bob Loveday, a sunny light-hearted sailor, and a third is Festus Derriman, a coarse and boastful yeoman.

The story concerns the winning of Anne, who is far from being a simpering girl sought by three different men. John, rescuing his brother from the dubious Matilda, is superseded by him in Anne's estimation and John loses her. Festus is seen in his true colours and his chance is gone. The gentle and gallant John marches away to battle and is lost. The setting of Overcombe Mill is finely drawn and the nature of Anne Garland sharply observed. (Leslie Stephen told the author that the heroine had married the wrong man; Hardy replied that heroines usually did.)

**Trunnion, Hawser** The eccentric retired commodore of *Peregrine Pickle* by Tobias Smollett. He does his utmost to make his retirement, and his residence, conform to life at sea.

**Tucker, Abraham** 1705–74. Tucker was a country gentleman whose father had been a suc-

cessful merchant in London. He was an amateur philosopher and one of the first English writers of the utilitarian school. His first published work, *Freewill, Foreknowledge and Fate* (1763), appeared under the pseudonym Edward Search; *Man in quest of Himself* (also 1763) appeared under the pseudonym Cuthbert Comment. His principal work was *The Light of Nature Pursued*, of which the first four volumes (by 'Edward Search') were published in 1765 and the last three after his death (1774). The book is so long and diffuse that recognition was not possible until Tucker's theories were systematized by William Paley. Tucker asserted that the principle of moral conduct was to be found in general happiness; the motive of the individual could be found in his own content. The concurrence of the two could not always be found, however: self-sacrifice was sometimes the response to virtue, prudence notwithstanding. In disinterested goodness Tucker found a place for religion and the hope of a future life.

**Tuckerman, Frederick Goddard** 1821–73. The son of a successful merchant, Tuckerman was born in Boston and educated at Harvard. He graduated with a law degree but never practised; he had sufficient means to live as a country gentleman in Greenfield and dabbled in natural science. He married in 1847 and was apparently a contented man; but after ten years his wife died in childbirth. The *Poems* (1860) was the only work published during his lifetime and he died at the age of 52.

Tuckerman's poems were praised by Hawthorne, Emerson, and Longfellow in letters to him. Three editions were printed; but he published nothing more and his name was forgotten after he died. However, an essay on his verse by Walter Eaton, written during the first decade of the 20th century, came to the notice of poet Witter Bynner, who in 1931 published a selection from the *Poems* of 1860 with three series of unpublished sonnets that Tuckerman had left. All the poet's works were later collected, edited, and introduced by N. Scott Momaday in *The Complete Poems of Frederick Tuckerman* (1965).

A poet of some quality was thus rediscovered for America but his work was, for a time, in danger of being overpraised. His poetry is the expression of a thoughtful and observant man with a keen eye for the beauty of the world and an awareness of personal sorrow. He wrote during the period of the Transcendentalists but he has nothing in common with them, betraying no strivings for experiences outside those that his own temperament acknowledged. There is a continuing vein of grief in his poetry, making for a degree of monotony, but his best poems prove that the revival of interest in him has been worthwhile.

**Tulkinghorn, Mr**  Sir Leicester Dedlock's lawyer in Dickens's *Bleak House*. He is ruthless in uncovering Lady Dedlock's secret – perfectly willing to resort to bullying and trickery in pursuit of the information he wants. He is deservedly murdered during the course of the narrative.

**Tulliver, Maggie and Tom**  The mill-owner's children in George Eliot's *The Mill on the Floss*. Maggie's adoring love for her brother, who grows up to be a narrow-minded didactic prig, is the cause of both her happiness as a child and much of her grief as an adult.

**Tunnyng of Elynour Rummyng, The**  See **Skelton, John**.

**Tupman, Tracy**  One of the four members of the Corresponding Society of the Pickwick Club, who undertakes to send in occasional papers for the pleasure of the club members. Hence *The Pickwick Papers*, of Dickens's novel.

**Tupper, Martin** 1810–89.  Martin Farquhar Tupper was born in London and educated at Charterhouse School and Christ Church, Oxford. He was called to the Bar in 1835. Tupper became famous and popular in his time in both England and the USA with the four series of his *Proverbial Philosophy* (1838, 1842, 1867, 1876). The content was instant philosophy in loose versified prose. Treated with derision by critics and scholars, the series was nevertheless bought and read by large numbers of middle-class readers. George Saintsbury described Tupper's work as one of the supreme curiosities of English literature, a document of the popular conception of poetry during the middle decades of the 19th century. 'It would be rash,' wrote Saintsbury in 1916, 'considering the extraordinary changes of superficial and ephemeral taste which are familiar to the historical student, to say that it can never recover something, at least, of what it has lost since its time, other examples of popular rubbish have secured equal vogue with the same class of readers.' The following is a typical example of Tupper's crude style: 'pay quickly what thou owest; The needy tradesman is made glad by such considerable haste.'

Among other books by Tupper were *Geraldine, A Sequel to Coleridge's Christabel* (1838), *The Crock of Gold. A Rural Novel* (1844), and *Lyrics of the Heart and Mind* (1855).

**Turner, Frederick Jackson** 1861–1932.  The author of what came to be called 'the Turner thesis' on the American frontier was born in a frontier community, Portage in Wisconsin. He taught history at the state university and at Harvard; he was also associated with the Huntington Library through his extensive research into frontier history. His paper *The Significance of the Frontier in American History* was read to the American Historical Association in Chicago in July 1893 and printed in the following year. *The Frontier in American History* (1920) consists of his original paper with some short essays – he produced little completed work during his lifetime and *The Significance of Sections in American History* (1932) resulted in a posthumous Pulitzer Prize. Turner contributed the volume *The Rise of the New West* (1906) to A. B. Hart's *The American Nation* and at his death left unfinished a continuation of it, *The United States 1830–1850*, which was published in 1935.

The 'Turner thesis' rejects direct European influences of both ancestry and culture as the primary factor in American development. Turner attributes it to the existence of the frontier, which presented a continual challenge that was overcome by waves of movement westward. He believed that the triumph of the pioneer was the most significant factor in the formation of American life and values.

**Turner, Sharon** 1768–1847.  Turner was born and educated in London and was intended for the law. He abandoned a legal career for the study of Old English manuscripts in the British Museum; he had long been interested in Norse antiquity and its connection with the history of England. Primarily an antiquarian, he nevertheless produced, after 16 years' work, *A History of England from the Earliest Period to the Norman Conquest* (1799–1805), which encouraged further study of England's ancient past. Other books by Turner were *The History of England from the Norman Conquest to 1500* (1814–23), *The History of the Reign of Henry VIII* (1826), and *The Reigns of Edward VI, Mary and Elizabeth* (1829). He also published *A Vindication of the Genuineness of the Ancient British poems of Aneurin, Taliesin, Llynwarch Hen and Merdhin, with specimens* (1803).

**Turn of the Screw, The**  A short story by Henry James, first published in *Collier's Weekly*, from January to April 1898. It first appeared in book form with another story, *Covering End*, in the volume published as *The Two Magics* in the same year.

A governess is appointed to take charge of two children at Bly, a lonely estate in England. She receives the appointment from the children's uncle, for whom she feels a strong attraction. The children, Flora and Miles, are both attractive and intelligent; but Miles, the older, has been expelled from school and the children's manner is rather different from what the governess expected. They seem both strained and secretive. Then the governess sees two former members of the household, the steward Peter Quint and the former governess Miss Jessel. The governess questions Mrs Grose, the housekeeper, the only other adult in the house, and learns that both of them are dead; she also gains the impression that they were corrupt and she becomes convinced that the children see the ghosts, too. The children's behaviour would be explicable, she believes, if a malign influence was being exerted on them by the dead Peter Quint and Miss Jessel. She decides that she will defeat this influence herself and does not summon the children's uncle to tell him of her fears; he has, after all, given her total responsibility. She does convince Mrs Grose – but not without a struggle, since that kind and affectionate woman has never seen the ghosts. The children, meanwhile, display a remarkable talent for evading the governess's approach to the question of the dead pair and she becomes increasingly certain that they are, in fact, under their influence. One day she challenges Flora directly; the little girl's reaction is explosive and hysterical and she becomes terrified of the governess. Miles is confronted next; during this scene, which begins with an interrogation about his expulsion from school, the governess sees Peter Quint at the window. She is determined to exorcize his influence and impose her own but, while attempting to shield Miles from the apparition, she betrays its presence. The boy, frantic and terrified, dies in her arms.

*The Turn of the Screw* has been discussed endlessly and has been the subject of many written studies. It is much more than a 'ghost story', though it has been enjoyed on that level by legions of readers. The author provides the reader with marvellously contrived doubts about the narrator's reliability. She is a spinster with an unrealized infatuation and the housekeeper has never seen any ghosts. The children, both of them charming and intelligent, have their own secret world, something common to all children; the frustrated governess wants to enter this world but the children skilfully exclude her – a skill that most children possess.

It is a marvellous story by any standards and the question of whether the children are, or are not, under the influence of malign spirits, or whether the governess is a deluded neurotic, is in itself enough to arrest the reader's attention. To this must be added the author's skill in invoking, through the governess, an atmosphere that is uncanny and subtly changing, like fitful moonlight in a clouded sky.

**Turpin, Dick** A highwayman about whose name numerous romantic legends have grown. He was born in 1706 in Hempstead, Essex, the son of an innkeeper. He was eventually convicted of horse stealing and hanged at York in 1739. He features in Ainsworth's romance *Rookwood*.

**Tusser, Thomas** c.1529–80. Tusser, who was educated at Eton and Trinity Hall, Cambridge, made a major contribution to agriculture in England when he introduced barley as a crop on the land he farmed at Cattiwade in Suffolk. His contribution to literature is little known, perhaps because it has always been too closely associated with his skill as a practical farmer. He wrote *A Hundredth Good Pointes of Husbandrie* (1577) and *A Hundredth Good Pointes of Huswiferie* (1570) in simple verse of remarkable skill. The two were combined and augmented in 1573 as *Five Hundredth Pointes of Good Husbandrie United to as many of Good Huswiferie*, published by Tottel and constantly reprinted. Tusser has no claims to attention as a poet – he was simply using a handy form to express his thoughts on the life of a farmer. The picture is remarkably vivid, full of wisdom and with a deep love of the land. It deserves to be better known.

An edition by D. Hartley was published in 1931 and included a facsimile of the 1557 edition.

**Tutuola, Amos** 1920– . Tutuola was born to Christian parents in Abeokuta in western Nigeria. He was educated at a Salvation Army School and at Lagos High School and worked as a coppersmith and government messenger until 1956. Since then he has been employed by the Nigerian Broadcasting Corporation in Ibadan. His first book, *The Palm-Wine Drinkard*, was published in London in 1952. He was the first West African writer to be noticed by the Western World and his debut was warmly welcomed by Dylan Thomas and others. His writing is notable for its narrative energy; it resembles the delivery of a market storyteller in transcription and pays scant attention to grammar. Tutuola's output is small – he has published nothing since 1967. His other books are *My Life in the Bush of Ghosts* (1954), *Simbi and the Satire of the Dark Jungle* (1955), *The Brave African Huntress* (1958), *The Feather Woman of the Jungle* (1962), and *Abaiyi and His Inherited Poverty* (1967).

**Twain, Mark** 1835–1910. The pseudonym of Samuel Langhorne Clemens, who was born in Florida, Missouri. His father, a Virginian, had moved west in the hope of making an easy living from land speculation. Mark Twain's childhood and youth were spent in Hannibal, a small town on the Mississippi. He left school at the age of 12, after his father's death, and became a printer's apprentice, working for a time on the Missouri *Courier*, which was edited by his elder brother. He travelled a great deal as a journeyman printer and a journey down the Mississippi brought him into contact with the boat's captain, Horace Bixby. This encounter led to Mark Twain's new career as a river pilot. He earned his licence in 1859.

The river boats ceased operation when the Civil War broke out. Twain tried life as a soldier with a group of Confederate volunteers; but he was glad to desert when his brother was appointed secretary to the governor of Nevada and he had the opportunity of going west with him. In Nevada he tried prospecting, timber speculating, and, in Virginia City, journalism (1862). It was at this time that he adopted his pseudonym, the origin of which lay in his days as a river pilot – 'mark twain' meant clear water two fathoms deep, the essential depth for the shallow-draught river boats. The pseudonym had already been used by another pilot, Isaiah Seller (1802–64), who published occasional pieces in the *New Orleans Picayune*. Twain acknowledged him in *Life on the Mississippi*. Meanwhile he made the acquaintance of Artemus Ward, who encouraged him, and Bret Harte, who became his friend and collaborator. In San Francisco with Bret Harte, he worked on the *Morning Call* and earned his first recognition with the sketch **The Celebrated Jumping Frog of Calaveras County** (1865).

As a roving reporter Twain travelled extensively, to the Pacific, the Mediterranean, and the Near East. He turned his experiences to good account on the now flourishing lecture circuit and published **The Innocents Abroad** in 1869. The humorous observation and irreverent attitudes of the book made him famous. He married Olivia Langdon in 1870 and the following year bought a house in Hartford, Connecticut, where he wrote books that made him world famous. Nevertheless, it has been suggested by Van Wyck Brooks that marriage and life in New England interfered with the progression of Mark Twain's career. Olivia Langdon represented the puritanical and materialistic New England tradition. The point is arguable. Twain's talents included a satirical vein and a way of looking coolly at pretension, so the New England scene

Mark Twain carried to fame by *The Celebrated Jumping Frog of Calaveras County*. Contemporary cartoon.

may well have sharpened them. But it is known that he allowed Olivia to 'edit' his books.

**Roughing It** (1872) describes his adventures in the West and the sharp observation and humour for which he was already famous made it a success. **The Gilded Age** (1873), written in collaboration with C. D. Warner, is a satirical novel of booming post-Civil-War America, the America which depressed the spirits of Walt Whitman. **A Tramp Abroad** (1880) tells of a walking tour of the Alps and the Black Forest. **The Prince and the Pauper** (1882) is a historical novel and **A Connecticut Yankee in King Arthur's Court** (1889) is a satirical fantasy. More important, however, were the books which drew on his own background and experience: **The Adventures of Tom Sawyer** (1876), **Life on the Mississippi** (1883), and, best of all, **The Adventures of Huckleberry Finn** (1884).

Mark Twain had, meanwhile, become a partner in the publishing house of Charles L. Webster and Co. The business was prosperous for a number of years – the memoirs of Ulysses S. Grant and Twain's own books were profitable – but bad luck or bad judgment led to steady losses and a huge investment in bad typesetting machinery brought bankruptcy in 1894. The author, who had hoped his lecturing days were over, was obliged to resume them to clear his debts. One of his daughters, Susy, died in 1896 while he was away lecturing and the book of his resumed lecture tours, *Following the Equator* (1897), is different in quality from its predecessors. His writing had continued: *The American Claimant* (1892); **Pudd'nhead Wilson**, a striking novel, his best work apart from *Huckleberry Finn*, and *Tom Sawyer Abroad* (1894); and **Personal Recollections of Joan of Arc** and *Tom Sawyer Detective* (1896). The quality is uneven and Mark Twain was driven by financial disaster. The fact that he was able to pay off his creditors by 1898 obviously means that he worked extremely hard. The writings of the great humorist began to show a vein of pessimism.

**The Man that Corrupted Hadleyburg** (1900) is a collection of stories and essays; *What is Man?* (1906) a philosophical dialogue; *The Mysterious Stranger* (published posthumously in 1916) a bitter fable on moral values. Twain continued to lecture, to travel, and to contribute original pieces, such as his essays on Christian Science and William Shakespeare. He wrote incisive commentaries on the Belgian regime in the Congo and on US policy in the Philippines. His last years were beset by grief; his wife died in 1904 and his daughter, Jean, in 1909. He was aware that his work, in this last decade, would discourage his readers and he left instructions for posthumous publication in some cases. He started dictating his autobiography to A. B. Paine, his secretary, in 1906 and in 1907 was made an honorary D.Litt. of Oxford University. Mark Twain died at Redding, Connecticut, aged 75.

Mark Twain came from the South, but his attitude to slavery is plain to anyone who reads *Huckleberry Finn* and who recalls with what alacrity he deserted the Confederate army to go west. His background, in fact, inspired his fine novel; but the immediate impulse for his career as a writer and humorist came from his lively years as a young man in the frontier regions. He entertained easily but he was at the same time a compassionate man who had seen a great deal. He felt a great sympathy for the outcast and the repressed. The two factors in Mark Twain could result in what his work is often criticized for, sentimentality, and the criticism is fair. It is fair when applied to Dickens, also, and the two writers have much in common. Twain is as American as Dickens is English and he deplored the hangover from the Old World that he saw afflicting the New – particularly the South. Slav-

ery enabled the South to go on pretending about itself and its graces for far too long. Twain saw people in the round; that he often found his fellow men as detestable as he found them admirable is clear and there are places in his work where the reader finds unpleasantness thrown in his face.

Twain at his best is a great writer when his work is realized out of direct experience and when he expresses, as in the character of Huck Finn, the eternal dilemma of the free man in the new country. Can any place remain free of despoil once it has been reached by the pioneer who pushes the frontier back? People will arrive, bring their institutions, and turn the new place into a copy of the old which the pioneer was hoping to escape.

With Mark Twain an American prose style arrived. It had been sought by other writers and it can be found in the journalism of the time, and in the work of humorists like Artemus Ward. But Mark Twain, in T. S. Eliot's words, 'purified the dialect of the tribe'. He took the direct statement, the understatement of the sardonic aside, the wisecrack, the unadorned communication that sounds like speech – and almost wrote a masterpiece in *Huckleberry Finn*, a book that has earned the praise of generations. Twain's other books suffer by comparison but they are not to be dismissed. His contribution to American literature can hardly be overestimated.

**Twa Mariit Wemen and the Wedo, Tretis of the** A poem by William Dunbar written about 1508. It takes the form of a racy three-part conversation piece involving three women of the court, who in privacy comment bitterly on the shortcomings of their husbands. Drink loosens their tongues and they get drunker as the poem proceeds, until their rage and frustration at never having enjoyed real sexual pleasure is given comic but savage expression. Dunbar's angry women are presented, visually, in terms of courtly love poetry. Their words, however, betray the barrenness that confronted them in real life. Dunbar satirizes the emptiness of a tradition of which, in poetic terms, he had demonstrated he was a master.

**Twelfth Night,** *Or what you will.* A comedy by William Shakespeare, first produced *c.*1601 and published in the First Folio of 1623. The story comes from one of the Italian tales, *Novelle*, of Matteo Bandello.

The play opens with a short scene establishing that Orsino, Duke of Illyria, is in love with the Countess Olivia. She does not love him and will not receive him or his messengers. On the sea coast Viola, a survivor from a shipwreck, mourns the loss of her twin brother, Sebastian. The captain tries to comfort her, saying he last saw Sebastian secure to a spar, so he may well be alive. He also tells Viola of Duke Orsino and she decides to seek employment with him as a page, taking the name Cesario.

The duke is delighted with his new page and confides to Viola his love for Olivia. He asks 'Cesario' to help press his suit with her. Viola ruefully admits to herself that she would like to be Orsino's wife, but meanwhile 'Cesario' gains admittance to Olivia's house, where are Malvolio, the countess's major-domo; Maria, her maid; Sir Toby Belch, her uncle; Feste, her clown; and Sir Andrew Aguecheek, Sir Toby's silly friend and a rejected suitor of Olivia's. Meanwhile Sebastian, safe and well, arrives in Illyria with his friend Antonio.

Antonio comes on the scene when Viola, as Cesario, is being challenged to a duel by the disgruntled Aguecheek – Olivia has fallen in love with the handsome page. Antonio thinks it is his friend Sebastian in danger and intervenes but is arrested for an old offence by the watch. He asks Viola for the purse he gave him (Sebastian) to hold and Viola denies ever having seen him before. Antonio is dragged off protesting but the name of Sebastian that he utters gives Viola a surge of hope. Olivia comes upon Sebastian, believes him to be 'Cesario', and finds him now very willing to be courted. She marries him.

Orsino comes to Olivia's house and now he is admitted. Antonio is brought before him and at once names Viola as the youth he saved from the sea: Olivia names 'him' as Cesario, her husband. Orsino is deeply hurt; apparently everyone has deceived him. Then another 'Cesario' enters; it is Sebastian and the mystery is solved. Orsino turns his affections to Viola, who loves him, and they are married.

The other characters, meanwhile, have been embroiled in a plot of their own – to trip the pompous and stiffnecked Malvolio so that he falls over his own conceit. Feste is given three of Shakespeare's loveliest songs to sing in the play: 'O mistress mine' and 'Come away, come away, death' in Act II, and 'When that I was and a little tiny boy' at the final curtain. *Twelfth Night* is considered Shakespeare's finest comedy by many critics and its claims are very strong. It is very rich indeed but there is a wonderfully astringent edge to the whole comedy and Viola is a lovely heroine.

**Two Drovers, The**  See *Chronicles of the Canongate.*

**Two Foscari, The**  A tragedy by Lord Byron, first published in 1821, the same year as his other Venetian tragedy, *Marino Faliero*. The tragedy was produced at Covent Garden in 1837. Verdi's opera, based on Byron's tragedy, was first produced in Rome in 1844. It is set in the 15th century and Jacopo Foscari, son of the aged doge, Francesco Foscari, is being interrogated on the rack. He was twice exiled, first for accepting bribes and then for complicity in the murder of Donato, one of the Council of Ten who had sentenced him to his first exile. He has been brought back from his second exile in Crete to answer charges of treason, and faces execution. But the council sentence him to perpetual exile and the aged Francesco has to sign the decree. The sentence is too much for Jacopo, who dies when he hears the news. The council then demand the abdication of his father, who dies as he leaves the palace, while the bells of St Mark's toll for the election of a new doge.

The historical Jacopo Foscari died in Crete six months after his perpetual banishment, too soon for the reprieve which followed the confession of the real murderer of Donato.

**Two Gentlemen of Verona, The**  A comedy by William Shakespeare. One of his early works, the play was first produced *c.*1594 and published in the First Folio of 1623. The source for the play is acknowledged to be the pastoral romance *Diana* (1559) by Jorge de Montemayor.

Valentine leaves his friend Proteus in Verona to see something of the world. In Milan, Valentine falls in love with Silvia, the duke's daughter. However, the duke wants his daughter to marry the silly Thurio. Proteus, too, goes on his travels and bids farewell to his beloved, Julia. He arrives in Milan, to the delight of Valentine but he falls in love with Silvia. Valentine plans to elope with Silvia and Proteus betrays him to the duke. Valentine is banished from Milan – and the field is clear for the infatuated Proteus. But now Julia, pining for her Proteus, comes to Milan dressed as a page and takes service with her love, who (of course) does not recognize her. Silvia meanwhile, is determined not to marry Thurio: she runs away to join Valentine, who has become a robber captain. But she is captured by (other) robbers and rescued from them by Proteus – who seizes the opportunity to force his attentions on her. The scene is interrupted by the arrival of Valentine; but the contrition of Proteus persuades Valentine to forgive him – and surrender Silvia to him. This is too much for the page (Julia), who swoons with grief. But she soon comes round and is recognized by Proteus, who loves her all over again. The duke and Thurio arrive, and the duke is mightily impressed by Valentine's unwavering love for Silvia. He gives Valentine his daughter's hand.

The play has some, perhaps not many, admirers. What could be swallowed as the stuff of romance in the late 16th century is impossible to gauge at this distance in time, but the scene in the forest between Valentine and Proteus requires production and acting of exceptional skill and delicacy to make it believable. Silvia, who has been nearly subjected to rape by a man she does not want, is promptly handed over to him by the man she does love. Friendship is great but this is ridiculous: Proteus, in five lines, convinces Valentine he is contrite. Valentine, in seven lines, is moved, forgiving, and self-effacing enough to hand over his love – whom he has just saved from a fate worse than death. The best scenes in the play are those with Proteus' servant, Launce, and his very funny monologues addressed to his dog. The part may well have been created by Will Kemp.

**Two Noble Kinsmen, The** A play first published in 1634, bearing on the title page the inscription 'Written by the memorable Worthies of their Time; Mr John Fletcher, and Mr William Shakespeare. Gent.' Most critics agree that, whatever Shakespeare's contribution, it was not sufficient to make a good play of it. It is based on Chaucer's *The Knight's Tale* (see **Canterbury Tales, The**), with the addition of the character of the gaoler's daughter, who plays an active part in Palamon's escape and then goes mad with love for him.

**Two on a Tower:** *a romance* A novel by Thomas Hardy, first published in Boston in the *Atlantic Monthly* (May to December 1882).

Lady Constantine's estate contains a tower, where young Swithin St Cleeve goes to look at the stars. Lady Constantine's husband, entirely selfish, has left her to go lion hunting in Africa. One evening she meets Swithin up in the tower and discovers him to be an aspiring astronomer. She falls in love with him. News arrives that Constantine has died and the lovers marry quietly.

Then Lady Constantine discovers that marriage has deprived Swithin of a legacy, also that news of her husband's death was premature. The legacy would have advanced Swithin's career. Constantine *is* dead – but was alive when they married, so the marriage is void. She insists on Swithin leaving her and taking up a well-paid post in South Africa. After he has gone she finds that she is pregnant and hastily accepts the hand of Bishop Helmsdale. She bears a son and, presumably, she and the bishop complete their life together in a strained silence; though the reader has to assume this from the closing pages ('the bishop was avenged').

Swithin returns to England. The bishop is dead, and he finds his widow an old woman. He is cold at first, to her despair, but he recovers himself and tells her that he has come to marry her. The violent swing from despair to joy is too much and she dies at his feet.

In spite of felicitious passages the novel cannot be regarded as more than a pot-boiler, so many thousand words of improbable romance to run from May to December in a monthly magazine.

**Two Treatises of Government** John Locke's refutation of the doctrine of absolute power, and his proposals for the reconciliation of individual liberty with collective order, was begun during the last two years of the philosopher's employment in the house of the Earl of Shaftesbury. It was not published until 1690. By this time Shaftesbury had fallen, Charles II had died, his successor James II had abdicated and fled, a revolution had put William and Mary on the throne of England, and absolute rule by any monarch looked like an uncertain proposition, at least in England. Locke's *Treatises* had enormous influence on liberal thought in France and America as well as in England. The 'social contract' theory was formulated by Locke in the second treatise: the people consent to be governed; total freedom of action is given up so that life, property and liberty can be maintained by government; those who govern are accountable to the people, and if governmental powers are seen to be exceeded the people withdraw their consent. Locke was writing at a time when it was more usually 'he' rather than 'they' who governed: he gave voice to the principle, already demonstrated in history, that kings too, ruled by consent of the people, who could choose other forms of rule. Good government, finally, is for the good of the people and must be representative of the people.

**Two Years Before the Mast** A personal narrative, by Richard Henry Dana, of life at sea in the 1830s. Dana had signed on as a seaman for the voyage to California around Cape Horn. The harshness of the ordinary sailor's life made a deep impression on him and he kept a journal, intending to describe it exactly as he saw it. He also intended to do what he could to improve the sailor's lot. The book was first published, anonymously, in 1840.

Dana sailed on the brig *Pilgrim* on 14 August 1834 and spent 150 days at sea. His account is clear-sighted, detailed, and unsparing. The crew were completely at the mercy of the captain, Thompson, a brute who on two occasions ordered floggings. Dana spent the months from January 1835 to May 1836 in California and his description of life there during that period is a clear and valuable record. He also drew vivid portraits of his companions and became so closely involved with them that his resolution to be objective is (fortunately, perhaps) not always maintained.

Dana returned on the *Alert*. The voyage took 135 days, and he found that when he disembarked he felt quite apathetic about the prospect of returning to New England and Harvard Law School. The hardships he had encountered on the two voyages had changed his outlook on life completely.

Dana added another chapter 24 years later, telling of his return to California in 1859 and the fortunes of some of the men he described in the original narrative.

**Tybalt** Lady Capulet's nephew in Shakespeare's *Romeo and Juliet*. He is an unpleasant character who makes the most of the enmity with the Montagues and is always looking for someone to fight. He kills Mercutio meanly, taking advantage of Romeo's attempt to stop the fight. Romeo kills him in turn.

**Tyler, Royall** *c.*1757–1826. Tyler, a Harvard graduate and lawyer, was the author of the first US comedy. During a visit to New York he attended a performance of *The School for Scandal* and within three weeks had written a social comedy called *The Contrast* – the contrast being that between homespun America and affected England. He wrote other plays but they are forgotten and meanwhile he prospered in his law career, becoming chief justice in Vermont and Professor of Jurisprudence at that state's university. He became a close friend of the essayist, Joseph Dennie, and collaborated with him in the writing of satirical verse and essays, using the pseudonym 'Spondee'.

Tyler wrote a popular picaresque novel, *The Algerine Captive* (1797); a volume of fictional letters purporting to come from an American living in England, *Yankey in London* (1809); and a long poem depicting rural life in America, *The Chestnut Tree* (1824). The poem was not published until 1931 and, while it has never been praised for its quality, it is of considerable interest because Tyler foresees the growth of industrialism.

**Tyndale (*or* Tindale), William** *c.*1494–1536. William Tyndale was probably born in Gloucestershire. He became chaplain in the house of Sir John Walsh in about 1521. He had studied at both Oxford and Cambridge and was a strong supporter of the movement for reform in the Church. His opinions involved him in controversy with his fellow clergymen and about 1522 he was actually summoned before the Chancellor of the Diocese of Worcester on a charge of heresy. He left for London. He had by this time determined to translate the Bible into English. He had admired the teaching of Erasmus at Cambridge (he made an English translation of the master's *Enchiridion*) and was certain in his heart that the way to God was through His word – scripture should be available even to 'a boy that driveth the plough'.

But in London Tyndale was firmly rebuffed when he sought the support of Bishop Cuthbert Tunstall, who was uneasy, like many highly placed churchmen, with the idea of the Bible in the vernacular. Tyndale, with the help of Humphrey Monmouth, a merchant of means, left England under a false name and landed at Hamburg in 1524. He had already begun work on the translation of the New Testament. He visited Luther at Wittenberg and in the following year completed his translation. The printing was begun with William Roye, another reformist Cambridge man, at Cologne. But Roye was indiscreet and the work was soon being talked about. The city magistrates, at the behest of the anti-Lutheran theologian Johannes Cochlaeus, ordered the printing to stop. Only a few sheets were saved before Tyndale fled to Worms; among them was that containing his Prologue, which was later enlarged and called *A Pathway into the Holy Scripture*.

The printing was successfully carried out at Worms. Copies of the New Testament in English arrived in Tyndale's country in 1526, and the work was given a very hostile reception by the Church. The reforming movement had insisted, since the time of John Wycliffe, that the scriptures should be available to everyone and not kept in the hands of the establishment so that they could make their own rules. But while the established Church could make no real case against a Bible in the vernacular, it could rest on its massive authority and mutter threateningly about tendentious comment – and Tyndale's New Testament carried a great deal of comment. Tunstall (predictably) and Archbishop Warham denounced it; so did Thomas More, who was against every manifestation of Luther's Reformation. Wolsey demanded Tyndale's arrest as a heretic.

Tyndale went into hiding – in Hamburg, it is believed, for a time – and went on working. He revised his New Testament and began the translation of the Old. He wrote *A Prologue on the Epistle to the Romans* (1526), *Parable of the Wicked Mammon*, and *Obedience of a Christian Man* (1528). He printed his translation of the Pentateuch (1530) and Jonah (1531). In 1530 he wrote *The Practice of Prelates* which, in its opposition to Henry VIII's divorce (he objected to the grounds for it), seemed to move him briefly to the opposing side. It brought down on his head the wrath of the king, who asked the emperor to have Tyndale seized and returned to England.

Eventually an English spy in the Netherlands, Henry Phillips, betrayed Tyndale to the imperial authorities. He was arrested in Antwerp in 1535 and confined in the castle of Vilvorde, near Brussels. He was tried on a charge of heresy in 1536 and condemned to the stake in spite of Thomas Cromwell's attempt to intercede on his behalf. He was mercifully strangled before the fires were lighted. He left the manuscript of his translation of the Old Testament books *Joshua* to the *Second Book of Chronicles*. In the year of Tyndale's death his New Testament in English was actually printed in England and before long other scholars were hurrying the great work to completion. The climate of reform had helped the matter along and Henry VIII encouraged it.

Tyndale returned to Greek and Hebrew sources for his English Bible and his sharp, lucid English style set the character for every translation that followed.

**Typee** A fictional narrative by Herman Melville, first published in 1846. The author did not present the book as a novel, since so much of it was fact – the real success of its publication lay in its ability to convince – but it is established that, in spite of maps and documentary chapters, fact is presented with much imagination.

Two seamen, Tom and Toby, jump ship (a whaler in which conditions are unendurable) in the Marquesas Islands and make their way to an inland valley. They find themselves among the Typees and to their surprise are shown courtesy and kindness. Tom falls ill and Toby is allowed to leave to find help. Unfortunately, Toby is accidentally shipped aboard a vessel homeward bound for America and Tom is left alone among the Typees. He enjoys his paradise island existence with an island girl, Fayaway; but he decides to flee from the valley when the tribe insists he be tattooed and when he begins to fear that the Typees may turn to eating White men. The tribe pursues him into the sea but he is rescued by the ship's boat of an Australian trader.

The author, using the simple outline of his own experience, presents the contrast between the White man's 'civilization' and the 'savages' to whom the White men believe themselves superior. The narrator's dilemma places him between two worlds. See also **Melville, Herman.**

**Tyrannick Love,** *or The Royal Martyr.* A heroic tragedy by John Dryden, first produced in June 1669, and first published in 1670. It is written in rhymed couplets, and contains absurdities which were later burlesqued in *The Rehearsal*. The story concerns a Christian, Princess Catharine of Alexandria, a captive of the Roman Emperor Maximin. He falls in love with her while besieging Aquileia, but she does not respond. She succeeds in converting the Empress Berenice and the furious Maximin orders that they shall both die. Catharine is beheaded and becomes St Catharine; but Maximin is stabbed by Placidius, an officer who loves Berenice and is determined to save her life.

**Tyrwhitt, Thomas** 1730–86. Tyrwhitt was born at Westminster and educated at Eton College and Queen's College, Oxford. He became a fellow of Merton College in 1755. Tyrwhitt is famous for the careful scholarship, supported by wide learning, which he brought to the study of Chaucer's poetry. He published *The Canterbury Tales of Chaucer; to which are added An Essay upon his Language and Versification: An Introductory Discourse, and Notes* (1775–78) and helped to establish a Chaucer canon. More important was his explanation of the form of Chaucer's heroic line, which had gone undiscerned for four centuries. (See **Chaucer, Geoffrey.** For Tyrwhitt and the Rowley poems, see **Chatterton, Thomas.**)

# U

**Udall** (*or* **Uvedale**), **Nicholas** 1505–56. Udall was born in Southampton and educated at Winchester School and Corpus Christi College, Oxford, where he became a fellow in 1524. At Oxford he was suspected of Lutheranism and investigated in 1528 but seems to have emerged unscathed. He and John Leland, who was his friend, contributed songs and verses for the coronation procession of Anne Boleyn in 1533, and in 1534 Udall published a book of selections from Terence with English translations, *Flowers for Latin Speaking*. In the same year he became headmaster of Eton and was soon notorious for the readiness with which he ordered floggings. The boys of Eton performed before Thomas Cromwell in 1537 but no details are known.

In 1541 Udall was dismissed from Eton, charged with theft and with indulging in homosexual practices. He was imprisoned in the Marshalsea but not for long apparently, since he was settled in London in 1542 and in that year published his translation of the *Apophthegmata* of Erasmus. He was by now a declared supporter of the Reformation and in a lost play, *Ezechias*, celebrated the king's triumph over the pope. He was well on the way to rehabilitation with his translation of Erasmus's *Paraphrase upon Luke* (1545) under the patronage of Queen Catherine; he supervised the publication of the complete *Paraphrases* in 1549. He became canon of Windsor in 1551 and in spite of his Reformist zeal seems to have enjoyed the goodwill of Mary when she became queen. In 1555 he became headmaster of Westminster School.

At least four plays have been attributed to Nicholas Udall and it is known that he was commissioned by Queen Mary to present masques and plays. But only one play can be called his with certainty, **Ralph Roister Doister**, which is probably the earliest English comedy.

**Ulysses** In Shakespeare's *Troilus and Cressida*, the one major mythological figure involved in the love story, if only as a cold and calculating observer. He spots Cressida's weakness in their first encounter and reveals her unfaithfulness to Troilus in a later scene.

*Ulysses* A poem by Alfred Tennyson in the form of a dramatic monologue, first published in 1842 but written in 1833. The literary sources of the poem are Book XI of *The Odyssey* and Canto XXVI of Dante's *Inferno*. Tennyson said that there was more about himself in 'Ulysses' than in *In Memoriam*: it was 'written under the sense of loss and that all had gone by, but that still life must be fought out to the end'. In the poem, which is in blank verse, the aged Ulysses rejects the idleness of advancing years and in the time left him determines to set forth again 'To follow knowledge like a sinking star, Beyond the utmost bound of human thought.' He leaves his kingdom to his son Telemachus and sails on what will be his last voyage: 'Made weak by time and fate, but strong in will To strive, to seek, to find, and not to yield.'

*Ulysses* A novel by James Joyce. For the publishing history of the novel see the main entry for the author. The first edition in volume form was published in Paris by Sylvia Beach, the proprietress of the bookshop called Shakespeare & Co.

The action of the novel is confined to a single calendar day, 16 June 1904, but to something less than the complete 24 hours of it. The Ulysses (Odysseus) of the title is Leopold Bloom, a Jewish advertisement space salesman. The Telemachus is Stephen Dedalus, a young poet who has been the central character of Joyce's *A Portrait of the Artist as a Young Man*. The Penelope is Molly Bloom, but while she is Bloom's wife she is not Stephen's mother. The Bloom character is more a father figure, as Stephen is a son figure. Each episode of Joyce's novel corresponds with an episode in Homer's *Odyssey* and these are the coordinates by which the author plots his journey through the life of a day in Dublin. The microcosm of their little lives expresses the macrocosm of the greater world and becomes a criticism of life in the first decade of the 20th century. But there is no real attempt to make *Ulysses* reflect the *Odyssey*, or vice versa, and the reader should not try to relate the characters to their classical counterparts. They are three sharply differentiated originals who present themselves from the inside, though Molly's great scene does not come until the end in her celebrated unpunctuated monologue, which is her affirmation of life and love. Parodying a variety of literary styles with stunning virtuosity, Joyce follows Bloom and Stephen through their day in Dublin (the reader will know the city very well after reading *Ulysses*), and returns them to their starting point at the end. Neither has found any answer to the bewildering sense of futility, to the frustration and loneliness they carry within them. Only Molly, the sensuous and satiated, seems to know any contentment in this paralysed and disintegrating society.

St Stephen's Green, Dublin, in the first decade of the 20th century. James Joyce's vivid invocation of Dublin at this period provides the setting for *Ulysses*.

**Una** In Spenser's *The Faerie Queene*, Book I, Una represents the true religion (see **Red Cross Knight**). After being parted from her knight Una is protected by a lion (England) until the latter is killed by Sansloy (lawless). She is reunited to the Red Cross Knight at the end of the adventure.

**Uncle Remus:** *His Songs and His Sayings.* The first collection of Joel Chandler Harris's verse and tales based on Negro folklore, published in 1881.

Uncle Remus was once a slave; now he is a valued family servant and the son of the house is a fascinated audience to whom he recounts the traditional stories of his people. Animals are endowed with appropriate human qualities and Harris reproduces to perfection the speech of the plantation Negro. Among the characters are Br'er Rabbit, Br'er Fox, and Br'er Wolf. The 'Tar-Baby' story is included in this collection.

**Uncle Silas:** *a Tale of Bartram-Haugh.* A novel by Sheridan Le Fanu, first published in 1864.

Maud Ruthyn, upon her father's death, is made the ward of her uncle, Silas Ruthyn. Her father, Austin Ruthyn, had been a Swedenborgian and Maud has always been frightened of his mystical preoccupations, not understanding them and uneasy about spirits and visions. Her father had always championed his brother Silas, who is suspected of murdering a gambling associate in the remote house in Derbyshire where Maud is sent. Silas will inherit Austin Ruthyn's money in the event of Maud's death and, heavily in debt, tries to force the girl to marry his unpleasant son. Maud escapes the marriage when it turns out that her cousin already has a wife. Silas has to consider another way of getting his hands on her fortune.

Maud, a prey to nervous fears already, becomes more and more aware of the tangible menace surrounding her when her friends are excluded from the house, and when a grotesque and sinister Frenchwoman, Madame de la Rougièrre, comes to be her governess.

The rest of the story reveals the details of the plot and tells how Maud is eventually rescued.

**Uncle Tom's Cabin,** *or, Life among the Lowly.* A novel by Harriet Beecher Stowe, first published in *The National Era* as a serial (1851–52), and in volume form in 1852. It was the most successful novel in American history to date (300,000 copies were bought in the first year) and proved a powerful contribution to the movement against slavery. It was translated into most European languages and, as a play in a dramatization by George Alken, was a great popular success (1852).

The Shelby family of Kentucky are in financial difficulties and decide to sell their slaves. Among them are Uncle Tom, the ageing Christian slave who is devoted to the Shelbys and is the particular favourite of young George Shelby (Marse George), Eliza, a mulatto girl with a baby, and Eliza's husband, George. Eliza, in dread of being sold and separated from her family, takes her baby and, in a celebrated scene, makes a desperate bid for freedom. Pursued by the slave catcher with his bloodhounds, she reaches the frozen Ohio River and, leaping from one ice floe to another, succeeds in getting away. Her husband, George, joins her later, having escaped through the underground route. Tom, who will do nothing to embarrass the Shelbys, is separated from his own family and sold to a slave trader. Marse George promises him that one day he will redeem him.

Tom is shipped aboard a Mississippi steamboat for the slave market. During the passage he

'Uncle Tom saving Eva from a watery grave.' An illustration by George Cruikshank for the first English edition of *Uncle Tom's Cabin* (1852).

saves the life of a White child, Eva St Clare, and her grateful father buys Tom for his home in New Orleans. Tom is happy there with the easygoing St Clare and the devotion of little Eva and her companion, the impish Black child, Topsy. Then Eva, who like all angelic children in 19th-century novels is 'delicate', dies and St Clare is killed in an accident. The unpleasant Mrs St Clare sells Tom, who is bought at auction by Simon Legree, a man from Vermont who has found, in the South, a climate which satisfies his vicious and degenerate temperament.

Tom's Christian fortitude and courage make Legree more cruel and implant a feeling of guilt. When two slave girls, Emmeline and Cassy, hide from Legree Tom refuses to reveal their whereabouts and the enraged Legree orders a flogging. Tom is beaten to death by two fellow slaves, Quimbo and Sambo, who cannot defy Legree. The arrival of Marse George, come to fulfil his promise, is too late to save Tom. His death leaves the young White man resolved that slavery must cease.

Harriet Beecher Stowe's novel has been traduced for generations but, apart from the failing that it needs to be seen in the context of its time (and in that context Abraham Lincoln's words to the author should be remembered: 'So you're the little woman who made the book that made the great war'), it proved to be good enough to absorb millions of readers – something a mere antislavery tract would never have done. Her novel is still able to inflame tempers today – her new attackers being the Black Americans who object to Uncle Tomism, to the idea of a slave's devotion to his master.

*Uncle Tom's Cabin* has the faults of its period (Uncle Tom is too much of a saint; little Eva is an angelic little bore) and similar faults can be found in Dickens, as well as some of the virtues. Mrs Stowe gives the reader no oppportunity to gloat over the appalling story of Cassy, or the probable destiny of Emmeline; but their condition is as plain as that of the wretched Mrs Quilp or of Mercy Pecksniff after her marriage to Jonas Chuzzlewit. Her portraits of Mrs St Clare, hypochondriacal and mean-spirited, and of Miss Ophelia, the New England spinster who lets it be known that she does not like to be touched by Negroes, are beautifully done.

**Uncommercial Traveller, The** A collection of occasional pieces by Charles Dickens, first published in *All the Year Round* and *Household Words* and issued in book form in 1860. An enlarged volume appeared in 1865 and a further enlarged one in 1875. They are mature essays, covering a wide range of travel and observation, and are a valuable representation of the author's journalism which continued throughout his career.

**Unconditional Surrender** The third volume of the trilogy *Sword of Honour*. See **Waugh, Evelyn (Arthur St John)**.

**Under the Greenwood Tree** A novel by Thomas Hardy, first published in 1872.

This is a slight, idyllic tale of two young lovers, Dick Dewy, the tranter (carrier), and Fancy Day the schoolmistress. Dick is considered to be aiming above his station – certainly Fancy's father thinks so. But in spite of a hasty promise to Maybold, the vicar, Fancy is won by Dick in the end. The background is Mellstock village life, and includes the consternation of the choir at being displaced by the purchase of a harmonium.

**Undertones of War** A prose memoir by Edmund Blunden interspersed with poetry, describing his war experiences, first published in 1928. The author took part in the abortive campaigns of Ypres, the Somme, and Passchendaele, which resulted in the wholesale slaughter of hundreds of thousands of men. Blunden's recollections are free from heroics but informed by compassion. His fine prose and poetry have a quality of reticence but the impact is unforgettable and the book is one of the English classics of World War I. It was published in The World's Classics in 1956, with a new preface, and again in 1965 with a new introduction.

**Under Western Eyes** A novel by Joseph Conrad, first published simultaneously in *The English Review* and *The North American Review* (December 1910–October 1911) and in volume form in 1911. The story is narrated by an elderly English teacher in Geneva, who is familiar with the exiles who live in the Little Russia quarter of the city. He gleans some of the facts from the diary of Kirylo Sidorovitch Razumov, a student who is the central character of the novel. Razumov is the bastard son of an aristocrat whom he never sees.

Razumov detests all revolutionary politics but a fellow student, Haldin, takes refuge in Razumov's apartment in St Petersburg, while the latter is absent. Haldin has thrown the bomb that killed a minister of state. Haldin prevails upon the furious Razumov to take a message to Ziemianitch, who runs a stable, to make arrangements for Haldin to be taken to a safe place. Razumov finds Ziemianitch drunk and cannot rouse him. His fury mounts to such a pitch that he beats him with a pitchfork to try and rouse him, to no avail. Razumov denounces Haldin to the police. The latter is taken and hanged but Razumov feels that he is himself under suspicion. To safeguard himself he agrees to the police chief's plan that he go to Geneva, where Haldin's mother and his sister Natalia are part of a revolutionary group.

In Geneva he feels doubly safe when a report is received from Russia that Ziemianovitch has hanged himself, and is assumed to have been Haldin's betrayer. He falls in love with Natalia Haldin and feels compelled to tell her the truth. Haldin spoke of Razumov as his friend in letters to Geneva and Natalia believes that Razumov loved her brother. He writes the truth for Natalia, and at midnight goes to the revolutionaries, who are in conclave. They turn him over to the sadistic terrorist, who breaks his eardrums and throws him into the street. He is knocked down by a tramcar (he cannot hear its approach) and crippled. Tekla, one of the girls among the revolutionaries, goes back to Russia with him and dedicates herself to caring for him.

Conrad knew the background of revolutionary politics but had no sympathy for the Russian brand, as he makes clear in his Author's Note. The revolutionaries, he believed, were as imbecile and atrocious as the autocracy they opposed. If they won, the autocracy would be succeeded by another: only the names would be different.

**Underwoods**  Ben Jonson's collection of what he called 'lesser poems' was first published in 1640 and includes his poem on his friend Shakespeare, which appeared in the First Folio of 1623: 'To the memory of my beloved, the author Mr William Shakespeare: and what he hath left us.' Other notable pieces are 'An ode; to himself', 'A Celebration of Charis', and the 'Hymn on the Nativity'.

**Unfortunate Traveller, The;** *or the Life of Jacke Wilton.* An adventure in prose by Thomas Nashe, which was published in 1594. The book was dedicated to the Earl of Southampton and is the earliest attempt at a picaresque romance in English.

Jacke Wilton, attached to the court of Henry VIII, is present at the siege of Tournai. He lives by his wits in the English camp but overreaches himself and earns a whipping. He goes to Munster, where he sees the fall and execution of the Anabaptist leader, Jan of Leyden, and is then engaged as a page by the Earl of Surrey. Surrey travels to Italy and on the way they listen to Martin Luther preaching at Wittenberg. There are meetings with Erasmus, More, and Aretino.

Wilton impersonates the earl in Italy and runs off with a courtesan. Surrey apprehends them but they are saved by the earl's good humour and his amusement at the escapade. Surrey himself is in love with the fair Geraldine and in a tourney at Florence defeats the other champions in her honour. Wilton leaves Surrey at this point and travels on to Rome. The plague breaks out and he witnesses the degradation of the city. He is accused of murder but saved by a dying man's confession. The villain, Cutwolfe, tells of his crime before his barbarous execution. The violence and cruelty converts Wilton to a better way of life. He marries his courtesan and they leave Italy. He returns to the English court at the Field of the Cloth of Gold.

**Unicorn from the Stars, The**  See **Yeats, William Butler**.

**Unto this Last**  The title of four essays by John Ruskin, first published in *The Cornhill Magazine* (August–November 1860) and in book form in 1862. The essays, 'on the first principles of political economy', would probably have continued but they aroused such indignation that Smith, Elder, the proprietors of *The Cornhill* (of which the editor at the time was Thackeray), decided they must be discontinued. The only one who praised the author was Thomas Carlyle. Everyone else regarded him as an impractical visionary. But many of the reforms advocated by Ruskin have come to pass. He deals with wages and the possibility of a way of fixing them by law, and with the hope of maintaining a regular flow of employment. His observations on strikes and the role of the political economist are still applicable more than a century after he wrote: 'Here occurs one of the simplest cases, in a permanent and positive form, of the first vital problem, which political economy has to deal with (the relation between employer and employed); and at a severe crisis, when lives in multitude, and wealth in masses, are at stake, the political economists are helpless – practically mute; no demonstrable solution of the difficulty can be given by them, such as may convince or calm the opposing parties. Obstinately the masters take one view of the matter; obstinately the operatives another; and no political science can set them at one.' *Unto this Last* was edited by Oliver Lodge with *Munera Pulveris* and *The Political Economy of Art* (Everyman's Library, 1907).

**Updike, John (Hoyer)** 1932– . Updike was born in Shillington, Pennsylvania, and graduated from Harvard in 1954. He worked on *The New Yorker* as a staff reporter for two years and his first work appeared in that magazine. His first book was a volume of verse, *The Carpentered Hen* *and Other Tame Creatures* (1958, called *Hoping for a Hoopoe* in England); his first novel came a year later, *The Poorhouse Fair* (1959). Updike made a reputation as an observer of modern American life with *The Same Door* (1959, short stories) and enjoyed a major success with a novel, *Rabbit, Run* (1960, Rosenthal Award). The central character of that novel features in a sequel, *Rabbit Redux* (1971), in which times have changed and the issues are explosively different. *Pigeon Feathers and Other Stories* and a children's book, *The Magic Flute* (both 1962), were followed by *The Centaur* (1963, National Book Award), his best work in the opinion of many critics, in which he links the life of a small-town teacher to that of Chiron, the wise centaur of mythology. Other books by John Updike are *Telephone Poles* (1965, verse), *Seventy Poems* (1963), *The Ring* (1964, called *Ollinger Stories* in England), *Of the Farm* (1965), *The Music School* (1966, short stories – O. Henry Award), *A Child's Calendar* (1966), *Couples* (1968), *Midpoint and Other Poems* (1969), *The Dance of the Solids* (1969, verse), *Beck: A Book* (1970), *Museums and Women and Other Stories* (1972), *Warm Wine: An Idyll* (1973), *Buchanan Dying* (1974, play), *A Month of Sundays* (1975), *Picked-up Pieces* (1975), *Marry Me* (1976), *Tossing and Turning* (1977, verse), *The Coup* (1978), and *Problems and Other Stories* (1979).

**Up from Slavery**   See **Washington, Booker T(aliaferro)**.

**Urn Burial (*or* Hydriotaphia)**   A treatise by Sir Thomas Browne, published with *The Garden of Cyrus* (1658) and taking as its point of departure the discovery of some ancient grave urns in Walsingham in Norfolk. From this the author goes on to consider the many ways mankind has reacted to the need for the disposal of the dead, and his great learning takes him over a very wide field. Browne was a doctor as well as a Christian and as such was no stranger to death. His theme is brought to a close with a chapter regarded by many as the finest expression, outside the Bible itself, of a Christian view of mortality.

**Urquhart (*or* Urchard), Sir Thomas** *c.*1611–*c.*1660. Sir Thomas Urquhart of Cromarty was a Scottish Royalist who fought against the Covenanters and was knighted in 1641. He took part in the Battle of Worcester and was imprisoned in the Tower for two years. Upon his return to Scotland he embarked on the translation of Rabelais for which he is remembered. He was also the author of curious treatises on mathematics and language to which he gave elaborate Greek titles, but these are of no real consequence.

Urquhart published his translation of the first two books of *Gargantua and Pantagruel* in 1653. He finished a third book, published posthumously (1693) by P. A. Motteux, who completed the translation of the remainder in 1694.

**U.S.A.**   See **Dos Passos, John (Roderigo)**.

**Uther Pendragon, King**   The father of King Arthur in Geoffrey of Monmouth's *Historia Regum Britanniae*; *Pendragon* (Welsh) means 'chief leader in war'. In Malory he is king of all England. The siring of Arthur is related in the same way as in Geoffrey's history and in the French *Lancelot*. See also **Arthur, King**.

**utilitarianism**   In the study of moral principles, the doctrine that identifies the good with happiness. Those actions are right that bestow the greatest happiness on the greatest number. It was maintained by, among others, Thomas Hobbes, David Hume, Jeremy Bentham, and John Stuart Mill.

**Utopia**   A satire by Thomas More, written in Latin. Book II was written first, while More was on a diplomatic mission in Flanders, and describes the imaginary island. Book I, written after his return to England, concerns the condition of Europe as it was in More's day, in contrast to the order and civilization that prevailed in the island state of Utopia. It was first published in 1516.

More's most celebrated book gave a new word to the English language, one which is based on Greek (*ou* – not and *topos* – place) and means 'nowhere'. The full Latin title is *Libellus vere aureus de optimo reip. statu, deque nova insula Utopiae*. The virtue of Latin as a European language is illustrated by the fact that additions were made by a Fleming, Peter Gilles, and revisions by the Dutch Erasmus. It was published first in Louvain, then in Paris and Basle. Hans Holbein, a German artist who became More's good friend, contributed two woodcuts to the Basle edition. Five more editions appeared in four years and a German translation in 1524. It did not appear in English during More's lifetime.

The author is introduced, by the town clerk of Antwerp, to one of the 24 men left behind in South America by Vespucci. The man is Raphael Hythlodaeus (the surname is a comic derivation of Greek that means 'babbler'), who has returned after making voyages of his own and seeing strange places. In Book I Hythlodaeus talks of his adventures and travels and describes England as a breeding ground for thieves. The matter of the

'Utopia insulae figura.' A woodcut from the first edition of More's *Utopia*, Louvain 1516.

first book is a criticism of the condition of England, where poverty produces crime; greed, avarice, and sloth are the rule among the privileged (included among these are the clergy), and where there is a ceaseless quest for wealth.

Book II describes Utopia, the ideal state, where no city is allowed to become too large, all religions are tolerated, and everyone is educated. Money is not used, since everyone has plenty of what he needs; fashion has no place in Utopia; and marriage follows the principle of mating to produce the best. The sick are cared for in hospitals; few laws are needed, since there is no love of wealth for its own sake; and everyone works six hours a day.

Anyone who expects to find in *Utopia* a serious political essay will come uncomfortably close to finding More's ideal state a peculiarly unpleasant – and extremely dull – place to exist in; it is too sterile a place to *live* in. But the author is really telling us about his own world, which – with all its faults – had limitless possibilities in that age of expansion, and Thomas More was in the summer of his life. *Utopia* is described best by C. S. Lewis: '... a holiday work, a spontaneous overflow of intellectual high spirits, a revel of debate, paradox, comedy and (above all) of in-

vention, which starts many hares and kills none.'

The first English version did not appear until Raphe (*or* Ralph) Robynson published his translation in 1551. Modern translations include those by E. Surtz in the Yale University Press edition of More's works (1964), the Everyman's Library edition by P. E. Hallett (1910 and 1951), and the translation by Paul Turner in the Penguin Classics (1965). More's *A Dialoge of Comfort against Tribulacion* is included in the Everyman volume.

# V

*Vala* See **Blake, William**.

**Valentine** One of the two gentlemen of Verona in Shakespeare's play of the same name. He falls in love with Silvia, the Duke of Milan's daughter, who becomes the object of his friend Proteus's undesirable attentions.

*Valentinian* A tragedy by John Fletcher, first produced about 1612 and published in 1685. The story has some basis in history – the last century of the Roman era – and contains some fine lyrics.

Valentinian III is guilty of dishonouring Lucina, wife of his general, Maximus. Lucina kills herself and Maximus plots his revenge. He poisons Valentinian's mind against his favourite general, Aecius, who commits suicide when he loses the emperor's favour. Two friends of Aecius kill Valentinian in revenge – and Maximus is made emperor in his place. As consort, he takes Eudoxia, Valentinian's widow. Unfortunately for him, however, he tells her how he reached the imperial throne. Eudoxia, revolted at hearing Maximus' false boast that he contrived in the dishonour of Lucina, poisons him before he can be crowned.

*Valley of Decision, The* A novel by Edith Wharton, first published in 1902.

The story takes place in Lombardy in the 18th century, where Odo Valsecca is the heir presumptive to the duchy of Pianura. He has been a neglected child and spent much of his boyhood with the servants. Thus he has a strong sympathy for the underprivileged and hopes to do something to improve their condition. He becomes a friend of the minister of state, Trescorre, in spite of the minister's adherence to the established order. Trescorre is the duchess's lover.

Odo is drawn more and more to the intellectuals who challenge the old order, particularly to the philosopher, Orazio Vivaldi, and he falls in love with Vivaldi's daughter, Fulvia. When Vivaldi is exiled for his political beliefs Fulvia is imprisoned in a convent. Odo rescues her and takes her to Switzerland. He inherits the duchy when his cousin dies and returns to Pianura; and Trescorre arranges a marriage for him with the widowed duchess. Fulvia also returns, to encourage Odo's programme for reform; she becomes his mistress. But the people are disturbed and uneasy, slow to accept new ideas. Fulvia is alienated by Odo's apparent tardiness but an attempt on Odo's life results in her death instead. Odo passes through a severe illness and a spiritual crisis. When he recovers he has lost his sympathetic ideals and he withdraws the constitution he had prepared for his people's betterment. The French Revolution breaks out and its influence awakens liberal aspirations in Pianura. Odo resists them but open revolt is spearheaded by the people's leader, Gamba, and Odo is forced into exile by the victory of the cause he once espoused.

**Vanbrugh, Sir John** 1664–1726. The son of a London tradesman, Vanbrugh was descended from a family who fled from Flanders during the Spanish occupation. His early life, education and training as an architect are something of a mystery: he was one of those remarkable men possessing natural gifts in two fields of artistic endeavour. He was a soldier for a while, and in France in 1690 he was arrested as a spy. Whilst imprisoned in the Bastille he drafted a comedy. Back in London in 1696, Captain Vanbrugh attended a performance of Colley Cibber's *Love's Last Shift*. He then went home and wrote **The Relapse,** *or Virtue in Danger* in six weeks. It was produced in 1696 and proved a great success. In the following year his **The Provok'd Wife**, a revision of an earlier effort, consolidated his reputation. In 1698 Vanbrugh suffered, with Congreve, the brunt of Jeremy Collier's attack on the London stage, and offered his reply in *A short vindication of The Relapse and The Provok'd Wife, from immorality and prophaneness* (1698).

Vanbrugh wrote six more plays and left the fragment of one, *A Journey to London* (1728), which was produced with Colley Cibber's additions as *The Provok'd Husband*. **The Confederacy** (1705), regarded as the best of the remainder, is an adaptation from the French. The others, which were all produced, were *Aesop* (two parts, 1696 and 1697), *The Country House* (1698), *The Pilgrim* (1700), *The False Friend* (1702), and *The Mistake* (1705); but his reputation rests on *The Relapse* and *The Provok'd Wife*.

Sir John Vanbrugh. A detail from the portrait by Sir Godfrey Kneller, c.1704–10. National Portrait Gallery, London.

Vanbrugh's distinguished career as an architect began in 1699 when he took over William Talman's commission for the Earl of Carlisle's house, Castle Howard. He became Comptroller of the Office of Works in 1702, and was knighted by George I in 1714. He was the architect of Blenheim Palace. As a playwright Vanbrugh stayed well within the accepted framework of Restoration comedy and, dilettante or not, was adept enough to achieve success similar to that of Wycherley and Congreve. He is not their equal as a dramatist but his dialogue is more natural, his plots easier to follow, and he is more concerned with everyday domestic realism, particularly in *The Provok'd Wife*. *The Relapse* enjoyed a major success when it was revived in London during the 1940s.

The complete works of Sir John Vanbrugh, with his letters, were edited by Bonamy Dobrée and George Webb (four volumes, 1927).

**Vancouver, George** 1758–98. Vancouver accompanied Captain James Cook on his second voyage, towards the South Pole (1772–75), and took part in Admiral Rodney's victory over the French at Les Saintes in the West Indies (1782). He was sent on a voyage of discovery (1791–95) during which he surveyed the south-west coast of Australia, the coast of New Zealand, and the Pacific coast of America. He returned by way of Vancouver Island (named after him) and Cape Horn. His *A Voyage of Discovery to the North Pacific* was published posthumously (1798).

**Van der Post, Laurens (Jan)** 1906– . The son of a politician, Laurens van der Post was born in Philippolis in the Orange Free State, South Africa. He was educated at Grey's College, Bloemfontein, and was associated with Roy Campbell and William Plomer in their journal, *Voorslag*, contributing articles in Afrikaans. Van der Post was always opposed to racial discrimination and, inevitably, to the policy of apartheid. After *Voorslag* closed in 1927 he spent some time in Japan and returned to farm in South Africa until World War II. His first book was a novel, *In a Province* (1934), on the subject of racial discrimination and how easily it could be exploited by the extreme Left. During World War II the author was a prisoner of the Japanese in Java. After the war he was chosen by Lord Mountbatten as Military Political Officer in Java and served until 1947. Since then he has served on a number of British government missions to Africa and he was knighted in 1981. His second book was based on his experiences on a mission to Nyasaland (now Malawi), *Venture to the Interior* (1952). A mission to Bechuanaland (now Botswana) provided the material for *The Lost World of the Kalahari* (1958). His second novel was a prisoner-of-war story, *A Bar of Shadow* (1952), and this was later included in *The Seed and the Sower* (1963, with the title story and *The Sword and the Doll*). Other books by Laurens van der Post are the novels *The Face Beside the Fire* (1953), *Flamingo Feather* (1955), *The Hunter and the Whale* (1967), *A Story Like the Wind* (1972), *A Far-off Place* (1974), and *A Mantis Carol* (1975). African life is the subject of *The Dark Eye in Africa* (1955), *Creative Art in Primitive Man* (1956), *The Heart of the Hunter* (1961), and *The Night of the New Moon* (1970).

**Vanity Fair** The town of Vanity lies on the pilgrim's way in John Bunyan's *The Pilgrim's Progress*, and a Fair is set up there by evil spirits. Christian and Faithful are arrested and Faithful is burned at the stake, but Christian escapes. In the second part of the book, when Christian's wife reaches Vanity Fair she finds there some repentant people, oppressed with guilt at the killing of Faithful.

**Vanity Fair** *Vanity Fair, Pen and Pencil Sketches of English Society* by W. M. Thackeray was published in 20 instalments (January 1847 to July 1848). The volume form, *Vanity Fair, a Novel without a Hero,* was published in 1848.

Becky Sharp and Amelia Sedley depart from Miss Pinkerton's school on the same day. Amelia is the daughter of rich parents and has enjoyed her schooling. Becky is the daughter of a penniless artist, has been obliged to work, and hated the academy and everyone in it, except Amelia – the only girl who was kind to her. Amelia is joining her family and Becky, after a short stay with her friend, is going to the house of Sir Pitt Crawley as a governess. Amelia is pretty, privileged, and not very bright. Becky is clever, accomplished, and unscrupulous.

At the Sedleys' house Amelia's brother Jos, just back from service in India, becomes a target for Becky. He is gross, indolent, and stupid – but he will do. She is frustrated by George Osborne, who looks down on her as a mere governess. Becky moves on to the household of Sir Pitt Crawley, who proves to be a dirty and mean old man. However, he and his wealthy sister are much taken with Becky. So is Rawdon Crawley, second son of Sir Pitt by his first marriage, and Miss Crawley's favourite nephew.

Lady Crawley dies, and Sir Pitt proposes to Becky. But she has made a secret marriage with Rawdon and uproar follows. Miss Crawley disinherits Rawdon, who is a gambler and a fashionable cavalry officer and not much else.

'Mr Joseph entangled.' One of Thackeray's illustrations for his *Vanity Fair*, first published in monthly parts 1847–48. Joseph Sedley helping Becky Sharp wind a skein of green silk.

Amelia, meanwhile, is having troubles of her own. Engaged to the insolent George Osborne, she is worshipped by his friend Dobbin. Amelia's father loses his money in speculation, whereupon Osborne's father forbids the marriage. Dobbin persuades Osborne to honour his pledge, so he does marry Amelia, only to be repudiated by his father. Amelia, on her honeymoon, learns of the orders that will take George, Rawdon, Dobbin, and the other officers to Europe to meet the threat of the newly escaped Bonaparte. In Brussels, before Waterloo, all the chief characters are present, including Jos Sedley. Becky and George Osborne, in spite of what has gone before, engage in a pointless intrigue before George is killed at Waterloo.

Amelia, widowed and now in comparatively straitened circumstances (those of Becky and Rawdon are straitened, too, but Becky's wits are more than a match for circumstance), is obliged to surrender her son to the care of her father-in-law. The faithful Dobbin hardly leaves her side. Becky catches the eye of the cynical and vicious Lord Steyne and encourages his attentions. Soon he is supplying her with money, unknown to Rawdon, but one evening Rawdon comes upon them and a violent scene follows. Becky declares her innocence but Rawdon leaves her, though he is really devoted to her in his fashion. They have a son, and Rawdon gives him into the care of Sir Pitt Crawley before taking a post abroad. Becky has overreached herself once more and now finds herself ostracized.

Amelia's son, Georgy, is left Osborne senior's fortune when the old man dies. Dobbin comes back after ten years in India. Amelia and Jos, travelling on the continent, meet Becky there, living on her wits, and by degrees Jos is won over again. Dobbin's love for Amelia is blocked by her sentimental attachment to her husband's memory. Becky disabuses her of any illusions about the worthless George Osborne, and Amelia is at last able to marry her faithful admirer. Becky succeeds, also, in persuading Jos to settle a little money on her.

At the end of the book Becky is a widow but her son, who declines to see her, has inherited the baronetcy and makes her a comfortable allowance. She 'hangs about Bath and Cheltenham . . . She busies herself in works of piety. She goes to church, and never without a footman. Her name is in all the Charity Lists.'

Few novels have been as aptly named as *Vanity Fair*. The society Thackeray portrays puts a premium on position, and how that position is acquired is never questioned – it is enough that it *is* acquired. Becky Sharp has an instinctive

awareness of this. Amelia has position already; but she is hardly conscious of it since she has little intelligence, questions nothing that happens in her world, and uses her helplessness as a weapon. The presumption and insolence of the worst part of society go hand in hand with its fatuous opinion of its own worth, and Becky almost succeeds in using its weaknesses to gain a place of her own. The author subjects that world's arrogance and stupidity to a mercilessly cold scrutiny. Thackeray has been criticized for showing only the worst, but that is precisely the aspect of it that makes the heroine so brilliantly realized a character – she could not connive to such purpose among people of real integrity. She is a marvellous creation, all the more believable because she is not quite clever or callous enough to succeed. A girl who begins with nothing, she sees that she is better than any of the staff or pupils at Miss Pinkerton's fashionably silly school and comes out ready for battle. It is a pleasure to leave her in comfortable circumstances at the end of the narrative.

**Vanity of Human Wishes, The:** *The Tenth Satire of Juvenal, Imitated,* by Samuel Johnson, first published in 1749. In his poem Johnson's view of life is the one adopted by the Latin poet but illustrated by examples close to the history of his own times: Wolsey, Buckingham, and Clarendon for human ambition for power; Galileo and Archbishop Laud for learning; and Charles XII of Sweden for military glory. Johnson passes from these to cautionary lines on longevity and the possession of physical beauty. The final section, 'The Power of Prayer', gives the satire a religious conclusion which reflects the poet's attitude to faith.

**Varden, Gabriel and Dolly**   The honest locksmith and his daughter in Dickens's *Barnaby Rudge*. Gabriel defies the mob during the Gordon Riots, which are the background of the greater part of the story. Dolly is pretty and flirtatious and is loved by Joe Willett. A 'Dolly Varden' is also the name given to a type of Victorian picture hat.

**Varieties of Religious Experience, The**   A psychological study by William James. Originally two courses of lectures delivered at Edinburgh University from 1901 to 1902, the book was first published in 1902. The author's study is of personal religion (organized religion he describes as an 'external art' of 'ritual acts') and he argues that for all practical purposes the particulars of religious faith are true – when they provide emotional fulfilment. He offers a scientific analysis of conversion, covering a great range of examples. James's book was of great importance as a stimulus to the study of the psychology of religion.

**Varney, Richard** The villain of Scott's *Kenilworth*. He is the agent of Amy Robsart's marriage to Leicester, his patron, and the earl's willing helper in trying to conceal the marriage to avoid the queen's wrath. He is ultimately the agent of Amy Robsart's death.

**Vathek, An Arabian Tale** A novel by William Beckford, first published in English in 1786. The novel was written in French, and translated into English, possibly at Beckford's request, by Samuel Henley. Henley, however, published it as a translation of his own from the Arabic. Beckford immediately published the original in Paris and Lausanne (1786) and later revised the English text. *The Episodes of Vathek*, probably part of the original manuscript, were discovered and published with an English translation by F. T. Marzials in 1912.

The Caliph, Vathek, is the grandson of Haroun-al-Raschid; his mother, Catharis, is a Greek sorceress. Corrupted by absolute power and a thirst for forbidden knowledge, Vathek is influenced by his mother to become a servant of Eblis (in Islam Eblis is the Devil, chief of the fallen angels who denied worship to Adam), in order to gain access to the treasures of the pre-Adamite sultans in the ruins of Istakar. He sacrifices 50 children and is given the power of death in the glance of one of his eyes, and sets off from his capital, Samarah. On his journey, Vathek falls in love with Nouronihar, an emir's daughter. She completes the journey with him.

After strange incidents in Istakar, Vathek gains admission to the halls of Eblis in the underworld, where he realizes the vanity of all the earthly treasure and wonders contained there. He discovers also that his journey is over – Eblis is his master. The story ends with Vathek and his companions awaiting their eternal torment; their bodies will remain intact but their hearts will burn eternally inside them.

*Vathek* is a fine exercise in imagination; it is also finely written. How much it reflects William Beckford is unanswerable but such details of his life as we possess suggest that he was at one remove from reality and because of his great wealth was able to indulge himself to an extraordinary degree. There is no interference with Vathek's self-indulgence, either, and his story is similarly just that distance from reality. The short novel is a successfully sustained fantasy, with an ending of remarkable power.

*Vathek* is published in modern editions in Everyman's Library, in the Penguin English Library *Three Gothic Novels*, and in the Oxford English Novels series, edited by Roger Lonsdale (1970).

**Vaughan, Henry** 1622–95. One of twin sons of a Breconshire family, Henry Vaughan went to Jesus College, Oxford, in 1638 with his brother Thomas. Thomas stayed at Oxford and became a philosopher of some note in his day, whilst Henry was sent on to London in 1640 to study law without taking his degree. He was called home at the outbreak of the Civil War and worked as secretary to the Chief Justice of the Brecon circuit. He served in the Royalist army in South Wales in 1645.

His first book of verse, *Poems, with the tenth Satyr of Juvenal Englished*, appeared in 1646. The contents are generally thought to be representative of the short time he spent in London and they show the influence of Donne. In 1650 came *Silex Scintillans* ('Sparkling Flint'), the volume of mystical and religious poems by which he is remembered and which showed a remarkable advance in his poetry. His first collection had been undistinguished, much like the verse of many followers of Donne and Jonson; but Vaughan had meanwhile experienced a religious awakening and it was in the expression of his changed attitudes that he found himself as a poet. In the Preface to the second and enlarged edition of *Silex Scintillans: or Sacred Poems and Private Ejaculations* (1655) the poet says that his awakening followed a severe illness during which he read the work of 'the blessed man, Mr George Herbert'. Vaughan's name appears on *Silex Scintillans* as Henry Vaughan *Silurist*. This is a reference to his homeland, the border country of Wales, once inhabited by the people known as Silures. It was here that Vaughan practised medicine from about 1655, first in Brecon and then in Newton-by-Usk. He was twice married – the second time to the sister of his first, deceased, wife. There were four children by each marriage, and the poet's later life was clouded by legal disputes with the children of the first. In addition to the 1646 volume, his lesser English work (there is much translation, mostly from Latin) consists of *Olor Iscanus* (*The Swan of Usk*, 1651) and *Thalia Rediviva* (1678), which contains some verses by his twin brother, Thomas.

**Vaux, Thomas** 1510–56. Thomas, second Baron Vaux of Harrowden, was educated at Cambridge and succeeded to his father's title at the age of 13. He served Henry VIII as both soldier and courtier and left behind a small group of poems. Two of these appeared in **Tottel's Miscellany** (1557) and 13 in a later anthology called *The Paradyse of Daynty Devises* (1576). The little group of poems is well regarded and one, which appears in *Tottel's Miscellany*, is used by Shakespeare in *Hamlet* (Act V, Scene I) when the gravedigger sings a garbled version of the first, third, and eighth verses of Vaux's 'The Aged Lover Renounceth Love'.

**Vavasor, Alice**  The 'heroine' of Anthony Trollope's *Can you Forgive Her?* She needs forgiving for her equivocation between John Grey, to whom she is engaged, and her cousin George Vavasor, with whom she had previously been involved.

**Veblen, Thorstein (Bunde)**  1857–1929. Thorstein Veblen was the son of Norwegian immigrant parents and was born in Cato Township, Wisconsin. After his education, at Carleton College, Johns Hopkins, and Yale, he joined the University of Chicago as an instructor in economics (1891).

In 1899 Veblen published *The Theory of the Leisure Class*, which put him in the front rank of economists. His book attacked the US caste system that grew out of the pursuit of wealth and it was given (strangely, in retrospect) a hostile reception by the academic world in the USA. *The Theory of Business Enterprise* (1904) is an acute analysis of business and the price system – a subject with which Veblen was occupied to some extent for the rest of his life. *The Instinct of Workmanship* (1914) put forward, with the clarity that characterized all his work, the theory that man's instinct for workmanship has been obliged to struggle against the avarice of employers throughout history.

*The Engineers and the Price System* (1921) is sharper in tone. It not only attacks the financial establishment and its apparently accepted rules but demonstrates how leadership of the nation's industrial potential could be assumed by the men with the skills. The importance of Veblen as an economist and social commentator revolves around this particular point and his work had been leading towards it since his first attack in 1899. The question he was asking – Where, in the future, will true power lie in advanced, capitalist societies? – is still with us. His far-sightedness and his direct criticisms of capitalism suggest a revolutionary – and Veblen was to some extent responsible, because of the attention he commanded, for a trend toward social control. A 'technocracy' of the kind he projected can provoke apprehension in the light of the scientific advances that have been made since his time. But his analysis of economic forces is valid today and his work is still widely read.

**Vehmgericht**  The Vehmic Tribunals, which dated back to the time of the Carolingian kings. They were a court of justice, royal in origin, to which all ranks, no matter how exalted, were subject. They were eventually suppressed in the 16th century and had been a secret court since the century before. Scott features their proceedings in *Anne of Geierstein*, basing his account on Goethe.

*Vein of Iron*  A novel by Ellen Glasgow, first published in 1935. It is a family story with the main weight of the narrative about Ada, the Fincastle daughter. The progress of the family is followed from Ada's childhood in the Virginia mountains, where the Fincastles have lived since colonial times, to their survival during the Depression. They owe their survival to the 'vein of iron' in Ada's character. This has enabled her to surmount every obstacle and carried her through disappointed love (which becomes an illicit love), and, when she bears an illegitimate baby, ostracism from the community the Fincastles have always served.

Ada Fincastle, like Dorinda Oakley of *Barren Ground*, is a realization of Ellen Glasgow's view of women in the South. They are, if they can summon enough resolve, mistresses of their own lives, in contrast to the central character of Ellen Glasgow's earlier novel, *Virginia*, who never breaks free from the rigid conventions of an earlier day and is bound to become their victim.

**Veneering, Mr and Mrs**  In Dickens's *Our Mutual Friend*, a wealthy couple with a great desire to be in 'society'.

*Venetia*  A novel by Benjamin Disraeli, first published in 1837. The two principal male characters are loosely based on Byron and Shelley, with elements of the lives of both used for the fictional characters. The period is the preceeding century, with the American Revolution substituting for the war of Greek liberation. The novel ends with both men – called Herbert and Cadurcis – drowning in a squall in the bay of Spezia.

*Venice Preserv'd, or A Plot Discover'd*.  A tragedy by Thomas Otway, first produced in February 1682 and published in the same year. The parts of Jaffeir and Belvidera were created by Thomas Betterton and Elizabeth Barry.

Jaffeir and Belvidera have married against the wishes of her father Priuli, a senator. Priuli has repudiated his daughter. Jaffeir, in spite of his noble birth, is in straitened circumstances and appeals to Priuli for assistance. But the senator is vindictive and refuses any help, even for the sake of his daughter and grandson. After this encounter Jaffeir's friend Pierre finds it easy to persuade him to join a conspiracy against the Venetian republic. As evidence of his loyalty, Jaffeir gives Renault, the leader of the conspiracy, custody of Belvidera; but he does not explain the reason to her. Renault tries to force his attentions on Belvidera. She escapes from his custody and Jaffeir, disillusioned, breaks his oath and reveals the conspiracy to her.

Belvidera prevails upon Jaffeir to expose the plot; her father, as a senator, would be one of the victims. Jaffeir does so but claims the lives of the conspirators as a reward. The senators contemptuously break their promise and the leaders, Pierre among them, are condemned to death. Jaffeir in desperation turns on Belvidera and threatens to kill her unless she prevails upon her father to secure their pardon. Belvidera succeeds but Priuli's intervention comes too late. On the scaffold Jaffeir stabs Pierre to save him from the agony of being broken on the wheel. Then he kills himself. Belvidera, her mind unbalanced by the tragic events, dies soon after.

A subplot concerns the courtesan Aquilina, who loves Pierre, and the masochistic senator Antonio, whose greatest satisfaction is to be maltreated by Aquilina (Nicky-Nacky, as he calls her). The 1953 production by John Gielgud (who played Jaffeir) and Peter Brook revealed how uproariously funny these scenes are in performance. Antonio and Renault are a composite caricature of the Earl of Shaftesbury.

**Venus and Adonis** The first published work of Shakespeare's (1593) is a poem in six-line stanzas. It was dedicated to Henry Wriothesley, Earl of Southampton. The poem narrates the familiar story of Venus falling in love with Adonis and failing to arouse the same response in him; how she fails to dissuade him from hunting the boar the next day and her grief when the boar kills him. The poem, in spite of the ending, is an erotic comedy and less successful than its contemporary, Marlowe's *Hero and Leander*. Shakespeare's genius, in the opinion of C. S. Lewis, could not be subdued sufficiently to serve the form of such an exercise.

**Vercelli Book, The** A volume of manuscripts in Old English that is the property of the Chapter House of the cathedral of Vercelli, near Milan. How it came to be there is unknown. Among the works it contains are prose sermons and some notable religious poetry (see *Elene*; *Dream of the*

*Rood, The*; *Andreas*; and *Fates of the Apostles, The*).

**Vere, Captain** The commander of *HMS Indomitable* in Herman Melville's *Billy Budd*. He witnesses the killing of Claggart and hangs Billy at the end of the story.

**Verney Family during the Civil War, Memorials of the** The collection of the Verney family papers was edited by Frances P. Verney (two volumes, 1892). Further papers, *Memorials of the Verney Family during The Commonwealth 1650 to 1660*, were edited by M. M. Verney (1894–99). The Verney papers, the record of a landed family's involvement in English history, are an invaluable firsthand account. *Letters and Papers of the Verney Family down to the End of the Year 1639* give the family history from the reign of King John to the flight of James II. The collection was edited by J. Bruce (1843).

**Vernon, Diana** The heroine of Scott's *Rob Roy*. Diana enlists Rob Roy's help for the hero, Francis Osbaldistone.

**Verses on his own Death** A poem by Jonathan Swift, first published in 1739. Regarded as his most successful essay in verse by most critics, it takes the form of a humorous and rather rueful review of his own life and work.

**Verver, Adam** The immensely rich American widower in *The Golden Bowl*, by Henry James. He and his daughter Maggie are very close and when Maggie marries he marries again. His new wife, Charlotte Stant, was once in love with Amerigo, Maggie's husband. Adam and Maggie's complete contentment with each other, even after the marriages, helps to drive their spouses into each other's arms.

**Verver, Maggie** The daughter of the immensely rich American, Adam Verver, in *The Golden Bowl*, by Henry James. She marries an impoverished Italian prince, Amerigo, but after some years of marriage becomes aware that he is having an affair with her father's wife. The novel relates how Maggie, because she loves her husband and her father, succeeds in keeping both marriages from ruin.

**Very, Jones** *c*.1813–80. The New England poet was born in Salem, Massachusetts. He graduated from Harvard in 1836 and taught Greek while studying at the Divinity School. His religious background was Unitarian but he began to experience visions and claimed to have seen the Holy Ghost. He maintained that his religious sonnets were the result of these periods of exaltation.

Emerson was impressed by Very's poetry and arranged for him to speak at Concord; but the faculty at Harvard were uneasy about him and even questioned his sanity. Very allowed himself to be committed to an asylum but he continued writing and through the sympathy and support of James Freeman Clarke his work was published in the *Western Messenger*. Both Clarke and Emerson rejected the assertion that Very was insane and in 1839 Emerson helped Very to prepare a selection of his work, which was published in *Essays and Poems* – the only book of his to be published during his lifetime.

After he left the asylum Very held brief pastorates in New England. But he was too retiring to be a good preacher and spent the greater part of his remaining years as a recluse in the care of his sister. A volume of *Poems* was published posthumously (1883). The complete *Poems and Essays* (1886) was edited by James Freeman Clarke.

Very was a mystic and believed in the absolute surrender of the will to God. His poetry was devotional. No matter what subject his verses hinge upon it is plain that he equates all to the work of the Creator. Although his language is so different his poetry may be compared to that of the religious poets of early-17th-century England.

**Vetch, Fleda** Mrs Gereth's friend, whom she hopes will become her daughter-in-law, in *The Spoils of Poynton*, by Henry James. She has a true appreciation of the splendid collection – the spoils of the title – housed at Poynton. The vulgar Mona Brigstock, in whom Owen Gereth is interested when the story opens, is supplanted in his affections by Fleda – but Mona proves to be more clever and ruthless.

**Veue of the Present State of Ireland, A** See **Spenser, Edmund.**

**Vicar of Wakefield, The** Oliver Goldsmith's single novel was written about 1761 or 1762 but did not appear until 1766. (For the story of its publication see **Goldsmith, Oliver.**) The story is narrated by the vicar himself, Dr Primrose.

Dr Primrose has a wife, Deborah, and six children. His wife has social aspirations and is proud of her children and her success as a housekeeper. The family is both comfortable and contented. Then the vicar loses his personal fortune when a merchant company goes bankrupt. Dr Primrose finds a new living through the patronage of Squire Thornhill; but the latter proves to be a villain who persuades Olivia, the eldest daughter, into a false marriage ceremony and then deserts her. She is found by her father and brought back to his modest vicarage; but further misfortune follows when the house is destroyed by fire. Thornhill calls in Dr Primrose's debts, which the vicar cannot pay and for which he is thrown into prison. George Primrose, a captain, challenges Thornhill to a duel; but the squire has him overpowered by thugs and George ends up in prison, too. The younger daughter, Sophia, is abducted by an unknown villain, and the deserted Olivia, the vicar is told, has died of grief. Dr Primrose bears these blows with fortitude.

A kind-hearted but apparently seedy gentleman, Mr Burchell, whose advice to Mrs Primrose about her daughters' marriage prospects had been rejected by that socially ambitious lady, effects the rescue of Sophia, who had always liked him and now begins to feel more than liking. Mr Burchell proves to be Sir William Thornhill, the evil squire's uncle. The squire was Sophia's abductor, and Sir William proves also that the supposedly false marriage was a true one and Olivia is not dead, after all. George is able to marry his love, Arabella Wilmot, and Dr Primrose's fortune is restored to him by the reformation of the swindler, Ephraim Jenkinson.

*The Vicar of Wakefield* did not make a fortune for the author, though it is the most famous novel published in the period between Laurence Sterne and Jane Austen. It was translated into most languages and there has hardly been a year when an edition of it has not been in circulation. The reasons for its success are difficult to analyse, while analysis itself makes the novel sound absurd. In Walter Allen's words, it reads 'like a fairy-tale, an idealized picture of rural life, with a delightful Quixotic comic character at the centre and with Burchell as an awkward

An engraving by Thomas Bewick for an edition of *The Vicar of Wakefield* published in 1798. The deserted and penniless Sophia is found by her father. Goldsmith's novel was first published in 1766.

eighteenth-century good fairy to contrive a happy ending.' The book earned great praise from Scott; 'we return to it again and again, and bless the memory of an author who contrives so well to reconcile us to human nature.' The world changes, and modern readers may agree more readily with Walter Allen than with Walter Scott. But the novel has charm, especially in the domestic scenes, and goes on being read. Three of Goldsmith's best-known short poems appear in *The Vicar of Wakefield*: 'The Hermit, or Edwin and Angelina', 'When Lovely Woman Stoops to Folly', and 'Elegy on the Death of a Mad Dog'.

The novel was adapted for the Victorian stage by W. G. Wills in the 1870s and called *Olivia*. The new title indicates the change of emphasis. The part was played by Ellen Terry with great success.

### Vice Versa See **Anstey, F.**

*Victory: An Island Tale.* A novel by Joseph Conrad, first published in the New York *Munsey's Magazine* (February 1915) and in volume form in the same year.

Axel Heyst has been brought up to be a detached observer of life, but his kindness to an Englishman in difficulties in Timor leads him into involvements he could not have foreseen. The Englishman dies and Heyst finds himself the owner of a defunct coal company on the island of Samburan, where he lives with his servant, Wang. Heyst falls foul of Schomberg, a hotel keeper in Sourabaya who lies about him, alleging that Heyst murdered the Englishman and stole his money. When Heyst rescues Lena, a girl in a Ladies Orchestra touring the islands, from Schomberg's unwelcome attentions the latter plans revenge.

Schomberg has three evil guests in his hotel and is too frightened of them to get rid of them. They are plain Mr Jones, Ricardo, and Pedro. When Heyst takes the girl to Samburan Schomberg tells the evil trio that there is a fortune hidden on Samburan and the three set out for the island. Jones has a morbid fear of women, Ricardo is the opposite, and Pedro is a Caliban-like figure, scarcely human. When they arrive on Samburan, Heyst does his best to isolate Lena from them but Ricardo finds her and tries to force himself on her. She defends herself successfully but she knows that Heyst is defenceless (Wang has fled and taken Heyst's revolver with him) and she tricks Ricardo into believing that she will become his accomplice.

Ricardo keeps Jones in ignorance of Lena's existence. She knows that Ricardo has a knife (he murders Pedro during a quarrel) and is determined to

get it from him. She manages to do that but Jones comes upon the two and shoots at Ricardo. The bullet kills Lena; Jones fires again and succeeds in killing Ricardo. When Heyst finds the dying girl she gives him a smile of happiness – she loved him and on his behalf accomplished something fine. Heyst, who could not respond to her completely even in her last moments, despairs of himself and commits suicide. Plain Mr Jones is drowned trying to get away from the island.

**Vidal, Gore** 1925–  . Vidal was born in West Point, New York, and educated at the University of New Hampshire. He served on army transports in the Aleutian Islands in World War II and made use of his war experiences in his early novels, *Williwaw* (1946) and *In a Yellow Wood* (1947). *The City and the Pillar* (1948, revised 1965) dealt frankly with homosexual life in America and became a best seller. His career continued with *The Season of Comfort* (1949), *A Search for the King* (1950), *Dark Green, Bright Red* (1950), *The Judgement of Paris* (1952), *Messiah* (1954, revised 1965), and *The Thirsty Evil* (1956, short stories). Vidal became a playwright, first for TV, with *Visit to a Small Planet* (published with others in 1957), and then for the theatre with *The Best Man* (1960) about an election in the USA (Vidal ran for Congress in 1960). Vidal's first book of essays was *Rocking the Boat* (1962) and his first satire on American politics was *Washington DC* (1964), and it is as an essayist and satirist that he is most highly regarded. *Myra Breckinridge* (1968), *Reflections Upon a Sinking Ship* (1969, essays), *Two Sisters* (1970), *An Evening with Richard Nixon* (1972), *Matters of Fact and Matters of Fiction: Essays 1973–1976* (1977), and *Pink Triangle and Yellow Star and Other Essays* (1982) present his tart, penetrating view of modern American life. Gore Vidal writes detective stories under the name of Edgar Box.

### View of the English Stage, A See **Hazlitt, William.**

*Village, The* A poem by George Crabbe, first published in 1783. When the poem was complete Crabbe sent it, at the suggestion of Joshua Reynolds, to Samuel Johnson, who read it carefully, suggested some alterations, and rewrote six lines. The rewritten lines were retained in the published version, beginning with 'On Mincio's banks, in Caesar's bounteous reign'. Johnson praised the poem as 'original, vigorous, and elegant' and it established Crabbe's reputation. His realistic picture of rural life was a sharp corrective to the sentimental view indulged in by many poets who knew nothing about it at first hand. Byron, in *English Bards and Scotch Reviewers*, refers to Crabbe: 'Though nature's sternest painter, yet the best.'

*Villette* A novel by Charlotte Brontë, first published in 1853. The story deals with material which Charlotte had already used in *The Professor*, her first written novel, which was turned down and never published during her lifetime. Lucy's experiences in *Villette* were based on Charlotte's when she worked as a teacher in Brussels, at Constantine Heger's school for girls. The Villette of the title is Brussels.

Lucy Deane, an English girl, gains a post as teacher in a girl's school in Villette. Without friends or money, she is also unprepossessing, but she proves her worth to Madame Beck, the headmistress. She is befriended, condescendingly, by one of the pupils, the beautiful and vain Ginevra Fanshawe, who boasts about her admirers. One of these, Dr John Bretton, proves to be Lucy's godmother's son. Lucy perceives that he is infatuated with Ginevra and hides her growing feelings for him. One evening, at a concert, Ginevra displays her true character and John's infatuation ceases. He now falls in love with Paulina Home and Lucy, nursing her grief in the realization that she can mean nothing to him, buries herself in her work.

Lucy gradually awakens to the fascination of the professor, Paul Emanuel, a sharp-tongued, waspish, unattractive little man who finds in Lucy the response that mellows and softens him. Lucy's happiness in his esteem is shattered when he announces that he is obliged to go to the West Indies. But he reassures her by giving her charge of her own school in his absence, and the promise that he will return to her in three years.

*Villette* is Charlotte Brontë's best novel, apart from *Jane Eyre*. That the modern reader will know Charlotte is laying a ghost (her bitter, unrequited passion for Constantine Heger) is neither here nor there, though it has been put forward as a criticism by some. The novel is a bleak one in many ways: the lively canvas of a foreign city evoked by the author is observed by Lucy, as it must have been by Charlotte, from inside a prison of loneliness – a prison which her own character helped to create. But the truth of Lucy's character was perceived by notable critics. Trollope was unreserved in his praise of the author's characterization of Paul Emanuel, and George Eliot prized the novel above even *Jane Eyre*.

**Vincentio** The Duke of Vienna in Shakespeare's *Measure for Measure*. He pretends to leave the city for a journey to Poland and endows Angelo with supreme authority in his absence.

He is the device Shakespeare uses both for setting the events in motion and for controlling their development. He falls in love with Isabella but she is not given any lines that suggest a response.

**Vincy, Rosamond** In George Eliot's *Middlemarch*, the beautiful and totally self-centred wife of Lydgate, the doctor. She is the principal agent of the failure of his life and career.

**Viola** The heroine of Shakespeare's *Twelfth Night*. Shipwrecked on the coast of Illyria, she is separated from her twin brother, Sebastian, and takes service as a page in boy's disguise with Duke Orsino. She becomes his ambassador to Olivia – who falls in love with the handsome page. But Viola falls in love with Orsino. She is one of Shakespeare's most beguiling heroines and all ends happily for her.

**Vionnet, Marie de** The countess with a charming daughter in *The Ambassadors*, by Henry James. Lambert Strether finds her grace and beauty captivating. He correctly attributes to her the polish and elegance that young Chad Newsome has acquired in Paris. There is an ambiguity in the relationship of Chad with mother and daughter – and it is on the resolution of this that the story turns.

**Virgilia** The wife of Coriolanus in Shakespeare's play. She is quiet and dutiful but she goes with his mother, Volumnia, to plead Rome's cause with him. She is almost a spectator in the scene between mother and son that follows.

*Virginia* A novel by Ellen Glasgow, first published in 1913. The setting is Virginia, where the central character, also Virginia, is brought up according to the ideals of womanly virtue in the 1880s. She marries an aspiring playwright and bears him three children. She supports her husband unquestioningly and he accepts this unquestioningly. He begins to achieve success when Virginia's bloom is gone; but he still looks youthful and when his plays are produced in New York he turns to women like Margaret Oldcastle, the leading actress of one of his plays, for companionship in his success. Virginia, middle-aged and worn out from their years of poverty, is forgotten. Her husband leaves her for Margaret Oldcastle and to Virginia, brought up as she was, this is the cruellest blow of all. Her only consolation is her son, Harry, a devoted and brilliant boy on whose future she will now expend all her energies.

*Virginia Comedians, The: or Old Days in the Old Dominion.* A novel by John Esten Cooke, first published (anonymously) in 1854.

Mr Hallam's Virginia Company of Comedians, a troupe of English players, comes to Williamsburg in 1763. The leading lady is Beatrice Hallam, Mr Hallam's adopted daughter, who is wooed by both the sweet-tempered, unaffected Charley Waters and the aristocratic Champ Effingham, who joins the company to be near her. But Beatrice prefers Charley.

Beatrice then discovers that she and Charley are cousins. Already in love, they set off to visit Charley's father. The jealous Effingham follows them and tries to abduct Beatrice; in the struggle he stabs Charley, leaving him for dead. Effingham flees to Europe but Charley recovers from his wounds. He marries Beatrice and they go to live on an estate in the mountains.

The story resumes two years later but the rest of the novel is a sort of romantic musical chairs involving Charley's brother, Captain Ralph, and Henrietta Effingham; Ralph's servant, Lanky, and Donsy, the village belle; the returned and repentant Champ Effingham and his cousin, Clare; and Alathea Effingham and Jack Hamilton.

Patrick Henry, the Virginia statesman, is a character in the novel, which closes with the rebellion provoked by the Stamp Act of 1765.

The sequel, *Henry St John, Gentleman* (1859), is set in the Shenandoah Valley at the outbreak of the War of Independence. The love story of Henry St John and Bonnybel Vane takes place against the shifting values and self-appraisals of the landholders under the threat of war.

**Virginian, The:** *A Horseman of the Plains.* A romantic novel of the West by Owen Wister, first published in 1902. It was immensely popular for a number of years and even became required reading for high schools. Certainly it is innocuous enough for children, having for its theme the high-minded and chivalrous man of the West who is loved by a pretty school teacher. Both characters have come to the West; he is a Virginian (he is known by no other name) and she, Mary Wood, is from Vermont. Assorted adventures reach their climax in the confrontation with the villain, Trampas, whose challenge the Virginian must meet on his wedding day. Mary Wood's code is against such violence and she declares that all is ended between them. However, the Virginian kills his opponent and she does marry him. The hero of this novel became the model for hundreds of sentimental films about a mythical West.

**Virginians, The** A novel by W. M. Thackeray, first published in 24 parts (November 1857 to September 1859). The story uses the characters created in *Henry Esmond* and follows the fortunes of their descendants.

Rachel Warrington is a widow with an estate, Castlewood, in Virginia. She is the daughter of Henry Esmond and his wife, Rachel, the former Lady Castlewood. Rachel has twin sons, George and Henry (Harry). George takes part in the expedition to Fort Duquesne and is believed to have been killed. Harry, his mother's favourite, is now the heir to the Castlewood estates and goes to England, where the Castlewoods on that side of the Atlantic are not exactly pleased to see him. His cousin Maria, some years his senior, is determined to marry him. Lord Castlewood and his brother Will are dubious characters, and his great-aunt Beatrix, who has survived two husbands (Bishop Tusher and Baron Bernstein) and whose influence is a doubtful blessing, grows fond of him. Harry, not the brightest of young men, is soon leading a life of dissipation and lands in trouble.

George, his twin, now turns up in London. He has been a prisoner of war. He rescues Harry, who returns to America in General Wolfe's army. After the successful campaign in Quebec Harry goes back to Virginia and marries Hetty Mountain, daughter of his mother's housekeeper. Rachel Warrington is furious and spurns the young couple. George, meanwhile, has married Theo Lambert – again to his mother's fury, because General Lambert is penniless. She cuts him off without money, too. But all comes out well for the sons, because George, the elder twin, inherits the Castlewood estates. The sons fight on opposite sides during the War of American Independence – Harry with Washington – but they are reconciled after the conflict. Harry becomes master of the Virginia property, and George of the English estates.

The novel is not on the level of *Henry Esmond* or *The Newcomes* and it is a minor work compared to the early *Barry Lyndon*. The best portions deal with the raffish Esmonds, and the most vivid character, the baroness, is not new. *The Virginians* lacks cohesion and the later chapters suggest that the serial form was putting a strain on the author's stamina.

**Virgin-Martir, The** A tragedy by Philip Massinger and Thomas Dekker, first produced about 1620 and published in 1622. The martyr of the title, Dorothea, is recorded in church history (*Hieronymian Martyrology*) and her feast day is 6 February. She is usually called St Dorothy.

The Princess Artemia, daughter of Emperor Diocletian, is exhorted by her father to marry. She chooses Antoninus, the son of the governor of Caesarea; but Antoninus is devoted to Dorothea and declines the princess's hand. Theophilus, a tireless persecutor, and his secretary Harpax (who personifies evil), inform Artemia that Dorothea is a Christian. The furious princess finds Antoninus and Dorothea together and orders their execution; but she is persuaded by Theophilus to let him attempt to detach Dorothea from the proscribed faith. He sends his daughters to convert Dorothea but, in fact, she converts them. The enraged Theophilus kills his own daughters, and Dorothea, attended by Angelo (who personifies good), is inflicted with extremes of torture before being executed. Antoninus dies at her side. The last part of the play is concerned with the struggle between Harpax and Angelo for the soul of Theophilus. Angelo prevails and Theophilus himself suffers martyrdom as a Christian.

**Vision of Judgement, A** A poem by Robert Southey, first published in 1821. King George III died in 1820 and Southey, as poet laureate, wrote the required elegy. In a trance the poet sees George III rise from his tomb. Before proceeding to Heaven's gate he is informed about the condition of England by the prime minister. Apparently all is well, though rabid fanatics pursue what they believe to be liberty. At Heaven's gate the good spirits assemble to stand by the king. Evil spirits led by Satan come from Hell, accompanied by Wilkes and Junius to speak against him. The presence of the Deity overwhelms the king's enemies, who retire discomfited, and George Washington, of all people, speaks on the king's behalf. He is admitted to Paradise and greeted by all the monarchs and great men of English history.

This foolish poem (though skilfully written, according to some critics) infuriated Byron. He held very different views on the condition of England and knew that Southey, in his younger days, had been starry-eyed about the idea of revolution. Southey attacked Byron's work in his preface, and Byron in reply blasted the poet laureate in his own *The Vision of Judgement*, taunting him again in the preface to *Don Juan*.

**Vision of Judgement, The** A satirical poem by Lord Byron, first published in 1822 in *The Liberal*, after John Murray had refused it. Leigh Hunt, editor of *The Liberal*, was fined £100 for publishing it. He would probably have incurred a much heavier penalty had he included Byron's preface, which charged Southey with attempting 'to canonize a monarch, who, whatever were his household virtues, was neither a successful nor a patriotic king.'

Byron's parody opens at Heaven's gate where St Peter sits: 'His keys were rusty, and the lock was dull' from lack of use. Later, when Peter is informed of the king's death, he has no idea who he is. There is a striking encounter between the archangel Michael and the fallen angel, Satan, and a brilliant series of verse comments, the more effective for being brief, from the king's critics. These are cut short, and Washington and Franklin are prevented from speaking by the entry of a devil carrying Southey and complaining about the weight. Before the laureate opens his mouth St Peter implores him to confine his reply to prose. But Southey reads his *A Vision of Judgement*, and 'The Angels stopped their ears and plied their pinions; The Devils ran howling, deafened, down to Hell; The ghosts fled, gibbering, for their own dominions' – St Peter fells Southey with his bunch of keys, and the king slips into Heaven, where Byron leaves him 'practising the hundredth psalm'.

**Vision of Sir Launfal, The** A verse parable by James Russell Lowell, first published in 1848. The outline of the narrative shows the influence of Malory and Tennyson.

Sir Launfal decides to go in quest of the Grail and orders the preparations for his journey to be made. Then he dreams that he has begun his adventure. On riding forth he encounters a leper. The morning is glorious and Launfal is irritated by the sight of one so ugly. He disdainfully throws a gold coin to the leper, who lets it lie upon the ground.

One winter, many years later, Launfal returns, old and worn out, from a fruitless quest. He meets the leper again; but now he shares a crust of bread with him and water from the brook in the leper's wooden begging cup. The leper is glorified and revealed as Christ. He tells Launfal that the wooden cup of charity is the true Grail.

Sir Launfal wakes up and abandons the preparations for his quest. He knows now that he is not the exceptional man who should seek the Holy Grail and turns his energies to helping better the lot of his fellow men. The poem opens with a song of praise to the beauty of a summer day.

**Visions of the Daughters of Albion, The** See **Blake, William**.

**Vittoria** A novel by George Meredith, first published in 1867.

The period is 1848 and the setting is northern Italy. The Italians, inspired by Mazzini, are moving towards revolt against their Austrian overlords. There is dissension among the rebels:

some want a republic, others an independent kingdom under Charles Albert of Savoy. The singer, Sandra Belloni, places herself at the disposal of the independence movement and agrees to appear at La Scala in Milan as Vittoria: her song will signal the revolt.

Suspicion falls on Vittoria because one of her English friends, Wilfred Pole, is an officer in the Austrian army. She marries the gallant patriot Carlo Ammiani, but the climate of suspicion and the enmity of Violetta d'Isorella and Anna von Lenkenstein involve Vittoria, Carlo, and Wilfred in a series of dangerous situations and Carlo is killed.

Vittoria, now a widow, is comforted by the arrival of Merthyr Powys, who had waited for her return to England but now hurries to her side.

***Vivian Grey*** A novel by Benjamin Disraeli, first published 1826–27. It is a youthful work and the author acknowledged that it was based on 'imagination acting upon knowledge'.

Vivian Grey, charming and intelligent, is also ambitious and certain that his wit and boldness will get him what he wants. He builds up a political faction by playing on the weakness of discontented politicians, with the Marquis of Carabas at the centre. He is opposed by Mrs Lorraine and by Cleveland – the leader-designate of the new party. Cleveland provokes him to a duel, and Vivian kills him. He is obliged to leave the country and his ambitions are defeated. He wanders on the continent and has various adventures in love and politics. At the end of the story he is a completely disillusioned man.

**Vivien** See **Lady of the Lake, The.**

***Volpone,*** *or The Foxe.* A comedy by Ben Jonson, first produced in 1606 and published in 1607. It is generally regarded as Jonson's masterpiece and is the most frequently revived of all his plays. Volpone's poetic address to his love in Act III Scene 7 ('Why droopes my Celia?') is a famous and much-quoted piece. The comedy is set in Venice.

Volpone, a wealthy Venetian without heirs, pretends to be near death, knowing that avaricious legacy hunters will gather round him. He intends to fleece them and sets the scheme in motion with the help of his servant, Mosca (fly). Mosca lets each fortune hunter believe he is to be favoured and one of them, Corvino (raven), goes so far as to give Volpone his wife. He is aided in this by the lawyer, Voltore (vulture), another of the fortune hunters. The third is Corbaccio (crow), who is willing to disinherit his own son in Volpone's favour.

Volpone, unable to forbear enjoying the discomfiture of the greedy trio, wills his property to Mosca and pretends to be dead. Mosca immediately begins to blackmail Volpone. The enraged Voltore goes to the Senate. Volpone, Mosca, Corvino, and Corbaccio are hauled into court and Volpone reveals the whole scheme. The offenders are punished according to their crimes and the virtuous (Corvino's wife and Corbaccio's son) are rewarded.

Volpone, apart from his greed for gold and his contempt for dupes, is also a sensualist and the part provides a field day for an actor who has the necessary range. There is a subplot that concerns Sir Politick Would-Be, an English traveller in Venice with a number of lunatic schemes in his head, and Lady Politick Would-Be, his garrulous wife. Richly comical in themselves, they have no bearing on the plot and are another example of Jonson's determination to introduce and examine 'humours'. The play might be too short without them, but it seems rather long with them.

**Volumnia** The mother of Coriolanus in Shakespeare's play and the first to greet him by that name (he is originally Caius Martius), which was an honour bestowed on him for capturing Corioli from the Volscians. She is every bit as arrogant as her son but, like Menenius, she knows that his openly proclaimed contempt for the plebeians is foolish. It is her appeal to Coriolanus, turned traitor, that persuades him to withdraw the Volscian army from the gates of Rome. Coriolanus knows it will mean his death. His mother must know this too but she is a Roman matron and Rome comes before maternal feelings, though she does not hesitate to invoke filial duty to persuade her son ('Thou hast never in thy life showed thy dear mother any courtesy').

**Vonnegut, Kurt Jr** 1922– . Vonnegut was born in Indianapolis and educated at Cornell University and the University of Chicago. He was taken prisoner while serving in the US infantry during World War II. His experiences – he witnessed the burning of Dresden – influenced his work, which offers an ironic commentary on both man's inhumanity to man and the appalling opportunity for destruction provided by 20th-century technology. Vonnegut completed his education at the universities of Tennessee and Chicago and published short stories in various magazines. His first novel was *Player Piano* (1952). *The Sirens of Titan* (1959) and *Cat's Cradle* (1963) developed his use of science fiction as a medium for satire; *Mother Night* (1961), a black comedy of war crimes and anti-semitism, was republished in 1966 when his reputation was secure. His other books are *Canary in a Cathouse* (1961, short stories), *God Bless You, Mr Rosewater: or Pearls Before Swine* (1965), *Welcome to the Monkey House* (1968, short stories), *Fortitude* (1968, play), *Slaughterhouse Five* (1969), *Happy Birthday, Wanda June* (1970, play), *Between Time and Timbuktu* (1972, play), *Breakfast of Champions* (1973), *Wampeters, Foma and Granfallons* (1974, essays), *Slapstick* (1976), and *Jailbird* (1979).

**Vox Clamantis** See **Gower, John**.

**Vulgar Errors** See *Pseudodoxia Epidemica*.

**Vye, Eustacia** In Thomas Hardy's *The Return of the Native*, the passionate and restless romantic who marries Clym Yeobright – the native of the title – mistakenly, not realizing that their hopes are diametrically opposed.

# W

**Wace, Robert** *c*.1100–75. A Norman of Jersey, Wace was educated at Caen and was made a canon of Bayeux by Henry II. His first important work, which he dedicated to Eleanor of Aquitaine, was *Le Roman de Brut* or *Geste des Bretons*, a paraphrase in octosyllabic verse of Geoffrey of Monmouth's *Historia Regum Britanniae*. Wace added more details, of little historical worth, and, in the story of King Arthur, introduced the Round Table. Layamon's *Brut* is an English version of Wace, with yet more details, and is the first English account of the Arthurian stories, so far told in Welsh, Latin, and French. (See **Layamon**.) Wace also wrote *Le roman de Rou* (or Rollo), a history of the dukes of Normandy down to the Battle of Tinchebrai in 1106.

**Waddell, Samuel J.** See **Mayne, Rutherford**.

**Wade, Thomas** 1805–75. Wade was born at Woodbridge in Suffolk. After publishing a volume of poetry, *Tasso and the Sisters* (1825), he wrote a play in verse and prose, *Woman's Love, or The Trial of Patience* (1829), which his friend Charles Kemble produced successfully at Drury Lane. A farce, *The Phrenologists* (1830), was also successful but the next play, *The Jew of Arragon*, a tragedy produced in the same year, was a failure. Wade published some volumes of verse, wrote two other plays which were not produced, and was the editor of *Bell's Weekly Messenger* and *Wade's London Review*. His best regarded work

was in the sonnet form, in a volume pretentiously entitled *Mundi et Cordis: de rebus sempiternis et temporariis: Carmina*.

**Wadman, Widow** The Shandys' neighbour who is keen to marry Uncle Toby in *Tristram Shandy* by Laurence Sterne. She is baffled by Toby's innocence and tries desperately to discover just how much his wound has incapacitated him.

**Waiting for Godot** See **Beckett, Samuel (Barclay)**.

**Wake, William** 1657–1737. Wake was born at Blandford, Dorset, into a family of landowners and completed his education at Christ Church, Oxford. He became chaplain to the English ambassador in Paris in 1682 and his three-year tenure broadened his view of religious matters. His ambition to achieve a union of the Church of England and the Gallican Church came to nothing but he is remembered in religious literature for his translation, *The Genuine Epistles of the Apostolic Fathers* (1693), and for *The State of the Church and Clergy of England* (1703). Wake became Archbishop of Canterbury in 1716.

**Wakefield cycle of mystery plays** See **miracle plays**.

**Waken, Philip** In George Eliot's *The Mill on the Floss*, the lawyer's son who loves Maggie Tulliver. He is malformed in body but his mind provides Maggie with the mental stimulus she cannot otherwise find in their small community. His father and Maggie's become bitter enemies over a lawsuit and Tom, Maggie's brother, bullies her into giving up her friendship with Philip.

**Walcott, (Alton) Derek** 1930– . Walcott was born at Castries on the island of St Lucia. He attended St Mary's College, won a scholarship to the University of the West Indies, Kingston, and published *Twenty-Five Poems* (1948) at the age of 18. *Epitaph for the Young* (1949) demonstrated that the flowering of West Indian talent was not confined to prose writers. Walcott's next works were a verse play, *Henri Christophe: A Chronicle* (1950), and a verse play for radio, *Henri Dernier* (1951). *Henri Christophe* was produced in London in 1952. Walcott's career continued while he worked as a journalist, first in Kingston and then in Trinidad: *Poems* (1953), *Sea at Dauphin* (1954, verse play), and *Ione: A Play with Music* (1957). A Rockefeller Foundation Fellowship in 1957 enabled him to study theatre in New York and the drama absorbed his energies for the next few years. He wrote another verse play, *Ti-Jean and*

*His Brothers* (1958), and founded and directed the Trinidad Theatre Workshop in 1959. His *Malcochon, or Six in the Rain* (1959) was produced there. *The Sea at Dauphin* and *Malcochon* were both produced at the Royal Court Theatre in London but Walcott achieved real recognition in the English-speaking world with *In a Green Night: Poems 1948–1960* (1962). He is acknowledged as the leading West Indian poet. Later volumes of poetry are *The Castaway* (1965), *The Gulf* (1969), *Another Life* (1973), and *Sea Grapes* (1976). Among his other published plays are *The Dream on Monkey Mountain* (1967), *In a Fine Castle* (1970), *The Charlatan* (1974), and *The Star-Apple Kingdom*, *The Joker of Seville*, and *O Babylon* (1978).

**Walden,** *or Life in the Woods.* Henry David Thoreau's narrative of his solitary life in a cabin on the shore of Walden Pond, near Concord in Massachusetts. The land belonged to Thoreau's teacher and friend, Emerson, who gave him permission to build a cabin, which Thoreau began in March 1845. It was completed with help from Nathaniel Hawthorne and other friends and occupied by the following July. Thoreau lived there alone until September 1847 and applied his Transcendentalist philosophy to the experience of living with no more than essentials. The book was first published in 1854.

Thoreau's cabin was a single room and his clothes were utilitarian. His food was what he found growing, augmented by what he could raise himself and by some fishing. When free of his necessary labours he swam and rowed and carefully recorded the animals and plants of the area. He read a great deal and kept his journals with scrupulous care. Thoreau pondered on his experience for a number of years and developed his original ideas and responses, as his journals for the succeeding years testify. The result is a book of 18 essays that are, in effect, his conclusions about his own ideas in the framework of the experience of his solitary life in the cabin at Walden.

Thoreau asserts that the way of life imposed by contemporary civilization lacks significance. It is meaningless since there is no true standard. Such a discovery can only be discerned in the light of vital experience. Man needs to withdraw from the demands of society and realize his own best powers, mental and physical. This is the essence of 'economy' and the book goes on to describe the author's economy in practical operation. All the events at Walden are related to this: the natural world, the changing seasons, his own experience of resistance to authority, the efforts

Walden Pond, c.1886. From an etching by W. B. Classon for *Homes and Haunts of the Poets.*

required to provide his own sustenance – even the sound of a distant train. His style is lucid and flexible, his prose impeccable yet imbued with feeling. Thoreau's philosophy emerges as individualism of a kind that could, perhaps, only have been maintained in his own time and place.

**Waldhere** The name given to two fragments of Old English poetry found in the binding of a volume in the Royal Library of Copenhagen by E. C. Werlauff. The matter of the fragments is a story well known from other sources (notably the Latin *Waltharius* of Ekkehard of St Gall) concerning the adventures of Waldhere (or Walter) of Aquitaine. The events take place in the 5th century, and the fragments date from the 11th. Waldhere is the son of the King of Aquitaine, given up as a hostage when still a child to Attila the Hun. Other hostages are Hiltgund, daughter of the King of Burgundy, and Hagano, son of a noble subject of the King of the Franks. Waldhere and Hagano become soldiers in Attila's service. Hagano escapes, while Waldhere becomes Attila's commander. Waldhere was betrothed to Hiltgund as a child and is determined to marry her. After a victorious campaign, when Attila and the court are lying in a drunken sleep, he takes Attila's gold and flees with Hiltgund. They cross the Rhine at Worms, and the King of the Franks, now Guthhere (Gunther), hears of the gold the fugitives are carrying. With Hagano and a band of 11 warriors he overtakes them in a cave in the Vosges. Waldhere succeeds in killing the 11 warriors, and on the next day he fights Guthhere and Hagano together. All three are wounded, but Waldhere and Hiltgund are able to go on their way with the treasure and the tale ends happily for them. The two Old English fragments are concerned with the pause between the first attack and the final encounter between the three. There are translations of the fragments in C. K. Scott-Moncrieff's *Widsith, Beowulf, Finnsburgh, Waldere, Deor* (1921) and C. W. Kennedy's *An Anthology of Old English Poetry* (1960).

**Waley, Arthur** 1889–1966. Arthur David Schloss was born at Tunbridge Wells, Kent, and adopted his mother's surname in 1914. He was educated at Rugby School and King's College, Cambridge, of which he later became an honorary fellow. From 1912 to 1930 he was Assistant Keeper in the British Museum Department of Prints and Drawings.

Waley had continued his studies, after Cambridge, at the School of Oriental Studies, London University (he later lectured there), and it was as a direct translator from the Chinese that he made a deep impression on English letters. Chinese poetry had appeared in English before, by Davis and Legge in the 19th century and in paraphrase by Ezra Pound in the 20th century. Waley brought a poetic ear to a true knowledge of the language. He knew that Chinese poetry had images of great beauty and he rendered them faithfully, neither adding to them nor reducing them. His influence was considerable, and he later produced equally felicitous results with Japanese.

Among Arthur Waley's translations from Chinese poetry are *Chinese Poems* (1916), *One Hundred and Seventy Chinese Poems* (1918), and *The Book of Songs* (*The Shih Ching*, 1937). *Monkey* (1942) is a prose translation of a Chinese allegorical fairy tale. Waley's famous translation of the classic Japanese novel of court life, *The Tale of Genji*, was published in six volumes over a period of eight years (1925–33). Among other works from the Japanese are *The Pillow-Book of Sei Shonagon* (1928) and *The Lady who Loved Insects* (1929). Waley's translation of *The Analects of Confucius* was published in 1938. Among his oriental studies are *The Life and Times of Po Chii-i,*

772–846 AD (1949), *The Poetry and Career of Li Po, 701–762 AD* (1950), and *The Opium War through Chinese Eyes* (1958).

**Wallace** A Scottish epic poem (*c.*1460), the work of the minstrel known as Blind Harry, who recited it. It was written down by John Ramsay in 1448.

The poem is a celebration of a national hero rather than, as in the case of John Barbour's *Bruce*, an account of a hero's career in an idealized form. Sir William Wallace's heroic resistance to Edward I dated from about 1296 to his capture and barbarous execution in Smithfield in 1305; whereas Blind Harry's poem gives him a career of magnificent leadership that would have lasted for 27 years, that is until the year of Bannockburn (1314).

But the English were hated and the historical Wallace was an authentic tragic hero. Blind Harry's epic poem appealed to the popular imagination and was read for centuries (a modernized version was current in the early 19th century). It helped, moreover, to focus the gifts of a great poet, Robert Burns, on the subject of his native land.

**Wallace, Lew(is)** 1827–1905. Lew Wallace was born in Indiana and was an active soldier for much of his adult life. He served in the Mexican War and earned distinction in the Civil War, reaching the rank of major general. He lived for a time in Mexico; he was interested in the country's past and in the attempts of Juarez to establish the Mexicans' rights to their own land.

Wallace returned to Indiana to practise law and to write. *The Fair God* (1873) tells of the Spanish conquest of Mexico and was a success. His next book was *Ben-Hur* (1880), a tremendous success which sold over two million copies and was translated into a number of languages. His third book was nonfiction, *The Boyhood of Christ* (1888). Wallace served as governor of New Mexico and became his country's minister in Turkey in 1881. He wrote other fiction, a tragic poem *The Wooing of Malkatoon* (1898), and an autobiography but he is only remembered today for *Ben-Hur*.

**Waller, Edmund** 1606–87. The son of a rich Buckinghamshire family and educated at Eton and King's College, Cambridge, Waller apparently began a parliamentary career at the absurd age of 16. He married in 1631 and, after the death of his wife three years later, courted Lady Dorothy Sydney until her marriage to Lord Spencer in 1639. Waller married again in 1644, the year after he was discovered to be the leader of a plot to seize London for King Charles I. He was in danger of losing his head but apparently betrayed his associates, two of whom were hanged, and instead suffered a large fine, prison, and exile. After seven years in Paris he was pardoned and allowed to return to England, re-entering public life during the Restoration as a member of both Parliament and the Royal Society. His later years in Parliament were notable for his frequent speeches in favour of religious toleration. However, his well-meant but misguided *Instructions to a Painter* (1666), a laudatory piece on the navy, which almost at once suffered a humiliating defeat, provoked a bitter retort from Andrew Marvell.

Waller's importance cannot be said to lie in his work, most of which was facile. He turned it with equal success (and, usually, with equal lack of distinction) to any occasion. But he developed the couplet form with remarkable skill and lucidity and his work shows the way to the style that was to dominate English poetry for the next two centuries.

Waller was very highly regarded in the 17th century. His *Poems* of 1645 went through three editions in that year and five more before 1700. *Divine Poems* was published in 1685, and *The Second Part of Mr Waller's Poems* in 1690. To modern readers he is best known for the charming early poems such as 'Go, lovely Rose', 'The Self-Banished', and 'An Apology for having loved before'.

**Wallis, John** 1616–1703. The great English mathematician was educated at Felsted School, near his birthplace, and at Emmanuel College, Cambridge, at a time when 'Mathematicks . . . were scarce looked upon as Academical Studies.' He became Savilian Professor of Geometry at Oxford (1649–1703) and was one of the founders of the Royal Society. Wallis's *Arithmetica Infinitorum* (1655) contains the first evaluation of $\pi$ as a method of measurement, the first use of the symbol for infinity, and the germ of differential calculus. A moderate Puritan, Wallis used his mathematical skill to decipher Royalist code messages during the Civil War.

**Walpole, Horace** 1717–97. Horace (originally Horatio) Walpole was the fourth son of Sir Robert Walpole and was born in London. He was educated at Eton and King's College, Cambridge, and made a grand tour (1739–41) with his friend Thomas Gray. He and Gray quarrelled at Reggio Emilia on the way to Venice. Gray left Walpole there – and the latter succumbed to a serious illness. He was succoured by Lord Lincoln and Joseph Spence, who were passing that way. Spence immediately summoned a distinguished Italian physician and nursed Walpole himself. When Walpole was sufficiently recovered he travelled with Spence and Lincoln for a time but was obliged to return to England for the parliamentary elections. (He sat in Parliament continuously until 1768.)

Walpole was reconciled to Gray after three years. In 1747 he acquired the villa at Twickenham which became famous as Strawberry Hill, and which he turned into a little Gothic castle, filled with beautiful and bizarre objects. He installed a printing press there and proudly printed two Pindaric odes by Gray as his first work. Walpole's literary career also began at the press at Strawberry Hill: *A Catalogue of Royal and Noble Authors* (1758), *Anecdotes of Painting in England*, a work of enduring importance in English art (1762–80), and *A Catalogue of Engravers in England* (1765). His Gothic horror story, **The Castle of Otranto**, was published in 1764, his investigation, *Historic Doubts on Richard III*, in 1768. A tragedy, *The Mysterious Mother*, was also published in 1768. Walpole inherited the title through the insanity of his nephew and became 4th Earl of Orford in 1791.

In spite of their considerable virtues, all of Walpole's works take second place to his correspondence, which was first seen by the public in 1778 as the fifth volume of his collected works – *Miscellaneous Letters. Letters to George Montagu* was published in 1818, and then volumes of *Private Correspondence* were published in 1820 and 1840, but a fairly complete collection, in chronological order, did not appear until Peter Cunningham's edition in 9 volumes (1847–59). An augmented edition, by Mrs Paget Toynbee, was published in 16 volumes (1903–05) and these were supplemented by 3 further volumes edited by Paget Toynbee (1918–25). But the supply of letters by Horace Walpole seemed inexhaustible and the great task of a definitive edition was undertaken by the Yale University Press, with W. S. Lewis as principal editor. The 1st volume appeared in 1937, the 39th in 1974. The work is still in progress and will probably run to more than 50 volumes before it is complete.

There was a mass of work besides the correspondence and the titles already named. It included political letters, miscellaneous verses and prefaces, and memoirs of the reigns of George II and George III.

The letters of Horace Walpole are notable for the high level of the writing and the consistency of style throughout. There is no doubt that he practised letter-writing as a literary form, and he regarded Madame de Sévigné as its high priestess.

Horace Walpole's villa at Strawberry Hill. A detail from a watercolour by Paul Sandby, c.1775. Castle Museum, Nottingham.

Posterity has reason to be very grateful to Walpole for the care he took in writing to dozens of friends and acquaintances. His correspondence is an autobiography by a man of boundless curiosity about the world he lived in, and a very detailed history of 60 years. His chief correspondents were Sir Horace Mann, the Countess of Upper Ossory, George Montagu, William Mason, William Cole, Field Marshal Henry Conway (his cousin), and Mary Berry; but there were some 200 in all, the recipients of nearly 4000 letters between them. 'This world is a comedy to those that think, a tragedy to those that feel', Walpole wrote to the Countess of Upper Ossory on 16 August 1776. He has been criticized because his carefully wrought letters lack charm. It would be more to the point to praise him because his letters contain almost everything else.

**Walpole, Hugh (Seymour)** 1884–1941.  Hugh Walpole was born in Auckland, New Zealand. His father, an Anglican clergyman, took his family back to England when he was appointed principal of Bede College, Durham. Later he became Bishop of Edinburgh. Hugh Walpole was educated at King's School, Canterbury, and Emmanuel College, Cambridge, and became a teacher for a short while at a boys' preparatory school. Hating being a teacher, he went to live in London and began to write, to review books, and became an occasional journalist. His first novels were *The Wooden Horse* (1909) and *Maradick at Forty* (1910). He used his experience as a teacher for *Mr Perrin and Mr Traill* (1911), still one of his most admired stories, and achieved popular success with *Fortitude* (1913), and *The Duchess of Wrexe* (1914).

During World War I Hugh Walpole worked with the Russian Red Cross, and was awarded the Order of St George by that country. His experiences gave him the background for *The Dark Forest* (1916) and for *The Secret City* (1919), which was awarded the James Tait Black Memorial Prize. He enjoyed an enviably successful career as a novelist and short story writer, drawing on his own background for the school stories *Jeremy* (1919), *Jeremy and Hamlet* (1923), and *Jeremy at Crale* (1927) and for the Trollopian *The Cathedral* (1922). A striking vein of menace appears in *The Old Ladies* (1924) and *Portrait of a Man With Red Hair* (1925). His family saga, *The Herries Chronicle*, was enormously popular and he was adding to it when he died: *Rogue Herries* (1930), *Judith Paris* (1931), *The Fortress* (1932), *Vanessa* (1933), *The Bright Pavilions* (1940), and *Katherine Christian* (unfinished and published posthumously, 1943). *Farthing Hall* (1929) was written in collaboration with J. B. Priestley. Walpole's novels and short stories extend to some forty volumes and his reputation diminished after his death, perhaps because his original quality was dissipated in overproduction and the pursuit of popularity.

Among Hugh Walpole's nonfiction books are *Joseph Conrad* (1916), *The Art of James Branch Cabell* (1920), and *Anthony Trollope* (1928, for the English Men of Letters series). He was knighted in 1937.

**Walton, Izaak** 1593–1683.  The author of only two books, Walton has secured a place in English literature unlike that of any other writer. He was born in Stafford, where his father kept an alehouse, and went to London as apprentice to a relative who was an ironmonger. Later he himself became a successful tradesman in Fleet

Street. He was twice married and both wives had family connections with the church. At about the time Walton set up his own business (1624) John Donne became vicar of St Dunstan's Church. Donne and Walton became friends and soon Walton made the acquaintance of Herbert, Sanderson, King, and Sir Henry Wotton. Walton was a writer of sorts in his spare time and Wotton, preparing a life of Donne, asked him to help him gather material. Wotton, however, died in 1639 and it fell to Walton to perform the task himself. The life of Donne appeared in the 1640 publication of Donne's sermons, and was followed by a life of Wotton himself for that writer's collected works (1651). The next subject was Richard Hooker (1665), followed by George Herbert (1670) and Bishop Sanderson (1678). Walton revised his *Lives* continually as time added further details for inclusion, and yet he never moved far from the design he set himself. An Anglican and a Royalist, Walton wrote about Anglican churchmen (neither Donne nor Herbert is written of as a poet) and his *Lives* are consequently charming pieces for the scholar rather than biographies of great interest to the general reader.

Walton spent his later years at Winchester, where his son-in-law was prebendary, and died at the age of 90. His celebrated **The Compleat Angler** was first published in 1653.

**Waltzing Matilda** See **Paterson, A(ndrew) B(arton)**.

**Wanderer, The** A poem of 115 lines in Old English, preserved in *The Exeter Book*. The substance of the poem is a lament by a man whose lord is gone. The man now has no one to serve and none whose protection he can claim. He dreams of his former contentment: but waking brings him back to the reality of the grey sea over which he wanders and the vicissitudes of life. The poem was translated by C. W. Kennedy in *An Anthology of Old English Poetry* (1960).

**Wanderings of Oisin, The** See **Yeats, William Butler**.

**Ward, Artemus** 1834–67. The pseudonym of Charles Farrar Browne. He was born in Maine and his first writings appeared in *The Carpet Bag*; but it was not until later that he made his name as a humorist. Working on the Cleveland *Plain Dealer* as its city editor, he published a letter by 'Artemus Ward' in 1858 and soon there was a demand for his sharp observations of American life. He met Mark Twain in Virginia City when touring and helped him become established. Browne also went to London in 1866, where

'Artemus Ward' was a great success. He must have been ill for some time but he was editor of *Punch* until his death the following year from tuberculosis at the tragically early age of 33.

An early exponent of the wry wisecracking humour which has no parallel in any other country, Browne displayed enough wit to make him the favoured reading of Abraham Lincoln. *Artemus Ward: His Book* (1862) and *Artemus Ward: His Travels* (1865) were very popular on both sides of the Atlantic. So were *Artemus Ward among the Mormons* (1866) and the posthumous *Artemus Ward in England* (1867).

**Ward, Edward** (1667–1731. A London tavern keeper with a gift for doggerel verse, Ned Ward was also a reporter of the London scene. In *The London Spy* he uses the device of a countryman meeting a London friend while visiting the city. He is taken everywhere and shown almost everything: the 18 sketches were published as a collection in 1703. He wrote quantities of verse after the manner of Samuel Butler and was sometimes less than discreet in his comments on the contemporary scene. Ward was sentenced to the pillory for certain passages in *Hudibras Redivivus* (1705).

**Ward, Mrs Humphry** 1851–1920. Mary Augusta Arnold was the granddaughter of Thomas Arnold and a niece of Matthew Arnold. She was born in Tasmania but was brought back to England at the age of four. Her father had become a Catholic and spent much of his time working for John Henry Newman. The family lived in Oxford from 1867 until 1881 and Mary Arnold became familiar with the Oxford Movement and its leading figures. Her sympathies, nevertheless, lay with the reforming movements and the new social philosophy of Thomas Hill Green. In 1872 she married Thomas Humphry Ward, fellow and tutor of Brasenose College. They moved to London in 1881, and Mrs Humphry Ward embarked on a literary career.

*Robert Elsmere* was her fourth published work and the one title by which she is known, though she was a prolific and skilful writer. The novel, which was published in 1888, put forward the view that Christ's work could be better realized by more emphasis on its social mission, and less preoccupation with its miraculous and divine elements. This was the fruit of both the years spent at Oxford and her own efforts on behalf of the London poor – she was an active philanthropist in a conscientious Victorian way. *Robert Elsmere* made her name, and almost made her notorious, with its discussion of religious doubts. But this was within her own world, that of the cultivated rich. In every other respect Mrs Humphry Ward was a conservative with a capital C, a reactionary, even. At a time when women were fighting for recognition as human beings she actively opposed the idea of votes for them. She was well-off, aloof, and earnest and her novels are unreadable now. Her quality as a writer is seen best in the introductions she wrote for the seven-volume Haworth edition of the novels of the Brontës, *The Works of Charlotte Brontë and Her Sisters* (1899–1900).

**Warden, The** A novel by Anthony Trollope, first published in 1855. It was his first real success and the beginning of the Barsetshire series. The idea for it came to the author while he was walking near Salisbury Cathedral on a summer evening.

The warden of Hiram's Hospital, a charitable foundation for 12 retired bedesmen, is the Rev Septimus Harding, who is also a precentor of the Cathedral of Barchester. A gentle and conscientious man, Harding is a widower with two daughters, one of whom is married to Archdeacon Grantly, son of the bishop. Hiram's Hospital, after the care and comfort of the 12 men is assured, yields an income of £800 a year to Harding, the warden.

This peaceful scene is disrupted by the allegations of a young surgeon of Barchester that the sinecure enjoyed by Harding is an abuse – that increasing value of the charity's property over the years should have led to increased spending on behalf of the 12 inmates. The surgeon, John Bold, is in love with Eleanor, Harding's younger daughter, but in spite of that he feels compelled to pursue his case and succeeds in interesting a national newspaper. Eventually an action is brought against Harding and the bishop's steward.

Harding, tormented by the allegations and proceedings, begins to wonder if he could be guilty of defrauding his charges. Archdeacon Grantly is his staunch supporter, and Eleanor implores John Bold to withdraw his action. But Harding resigns, whereupon the bishop, his friend, refuses to appoint another warden. Eleanor succeeds in persuading Bold to withdraw and they get married. But Hiram's Hospital falls into decay, and the 12 old men no longer have the retiring and thoughtful Harding to look after their interests. He remains a precentor of the cathedral and has a small living as well. The story continues in *Barchester Towers*.

**Wardle, Mr** The host at Dingley Dell in Dickens's *The Pickwick Papers*. The four Pickwickians visit him, accompanied by Jingle, who has for the time being gained their confidence.

**Wardle, Rachael** Mr Wardle's spinster sister in *The Pickwick Papers*. Jingle inveigles her into eloping with him but is quite happy to surrender her to Wardle and Pickwick, when they catch up with him, upon the payment of £100 'compensation'.

**Warner, William** *c.*1558–1609. Warner, educated at Oxford, was a London lawyer who enjoyed an immense reputation during his lifetime and was highly praised by Francis Meres and Michael Drayton. His principal work was a metrical history of Britain containing mythical episodes and fiction called *Albion's England*. The first edition (1586) began with the Deluge and extended to the Conquest. It was continued to the reign of King James in 1606. The complete book was posthumously published in 1612. Warner also published seven prose tales, *Pan his Syrinx Pipe* (1584), and a translation of the *Menaecmi out of Plautus* (1595).

**Warren, Robert Penn** 1905– . Robert Penn Warren was born in Guthrie, Kentucky. He was educated at Vanderbilt University in Nashville, Tennessee, at the University of California and Yale. He went to Oxford as a Rhodes Scholar and graduated in 1930. While a student at Vanderbilt Warren belonged to the regionalist group and contributed to the poetry magazine *Fugitive*. (See **Ransom, John Crowe**.) His biographical study *John Brown, the Making of a Martyr* was published in 1929 and he gave further affirmation of his regional agrarian sympathies in the anthology *I'll Take my Stand* (1930, edited by John Crowe Ransom).

Warren began his literary career as a poet. His early work was influenced by the English metaphysical poets but he abandoned this for a style better suited to his regional sympathies. Among his volumes of verse are *Thirty-Six Poems* (1935), a long narrative poem about Jefferson entitled *Brother to Dragons* (1953, Pulitzer Prize), *Promises, Poems 1954–1956* (1957, Pulitzer Prize), *Incarnations* (1968), *Audubon: A Vision* (1969), *Or Else* (1974), and *Life is a Fable* (1980). To a wider public he is known as a novelist of the South. *Night Rider* (1938), considered by many to be his best novel, tells of the small tobacco-growers of Kentucky at the beginning of the century, threatened with ruin by the buyers' ring. The Ku-Klux-Klan-like organization (the night riders) is created by a young lawyer whose character degenerates until at the end he is a hunted outlaw. Warren's next novel appeared five years later: *At Heaven's Gate* (1943) is a novel about Southern capitalism and social aspirations. *All the King's Men* (1946) is a study of the rise and fall of a Southern state governor forced to fight his political opponents with their own dirty weapons. He sows the seeds of his own tragic death. An ambitious novel, it is nearly spoiled by the sheer weight of words put into the mouth of the newspaperman narrator. *World Enough and Time* (1950) is a very long novel based on a trial at Frankfort, Kentucky, in 1826, when a man kills his patron for seducing and abandoning a girl. The murder is committed out of romantic idealism and the question is whether a violent, developing society can accommodate idealism of any kind. *Band of Angels* (1955) is a tragedy of miscegenation; *The Cave* (1959) tells of a caving accident and its effect on a community; *Wilderness* (1961) is the story of a Bavarian Jew caught up in the Civil War; and *Flood* (1964) tells of a town in Tennessee about to be submerged by a Federal dam project.

Warren has taught at a number of universities in the USA, including Louisiana State, Minnesota, and Yale. He was co-editor (1935–42) of the *Southern Review* with Cleanth Brooks, with whom he collaborated on *Understanding Poetry* (1938) and *Understanding Fiction* (1943). His *Selected Essays* was published in 1958. He is also the author of two essays on the question of colour: *Segregation* (1956) and *Who Speaks for the Negro?* (1965).

**Warrington, George** The humorous and scholarly friend with whom Arthur shares accommodation in Thackeray's *Pendennis*. He loves Laura, Arthur's cousin, but is bound by an ill-considered early marriage to someone else.

**Warrington, George and Harry** The twin brothers of Thackeray's *The Virginians*, they are the grandsons of Henry Esmond and Rachel Castlewood. (Another George, a further descendant, appears in *Pendennis*.)

**Warton, Joseph** 1722–1800. The son of Thomas Warton, who became Professor of Poetry at Oxford in 1718 (and who was largely responsible for the appreciation of Milton's early poetry), Joseph Warton was born at Dunsfold in Surrey. He became headmaster of Winchester College, which he had attended before going to Oriel College, Oxford, and was prebendary of both Winchester and St Paul's Cathedrals. He published several books of verse and translations of the *Eclogues* and *Georgics* of Virgil; but he is better remembered as a critic. Warton's first *An Essay on the Writings and Genius of Pope* (1756) was followed by a further one in 1782. He published an edition of Sidney's *In Defence of Poetry* (1787) and edited the works of Alexander Pope (1797).

**Warton, Thomas** 1728–90. The younger brother of Joseph Warton, Thomas Warton was born at Basingstoke, Hampshire, and was educated at Winchester College and Trinity College, Oxford. He published his own poetry but, like his brother Joseph and his father, who was Professor of Poetry at Oxford, he is best remembered as a critic and scholar. His *Poems* (1777) are notable for his revival of the sonnet form and he made his mark as a critic with *Observations on Spenser's 'The Faery Queen'* (1754), which had the benefit of his historical learning in addition to his knowledge of poetry. *The History of English Poetry* (1774–81) takes the subject to the end of the Tudor period. It was severely criticized for inaccuracy and – particularly by Scott in 1805 – for incoherence. It was nevertheless a pioneering work with considerable value for those who followed. Warton became, like his father, Professor of Poetry at Oxford. He shared his father's enthusiasm for Milton, and published his own editions of Milton's early work, *Poems upon several occasions* (1785) and *Comus* (1799). Thomas Warton was the first to perceive that the Rowley poems were not what Chatterton declared them to be.

**Washington, Booker T(aliaferro)** 1856–1915. The Black leader and educator Booker T. Washington was the son of a Black slave mother and a White father and was born at Hale's Ford

Booker T. Washington.

in Franklin County, Virginia. He worked in a salt furnace and a coal mine after the Civil War, while at the same time attending school at Malden in West Virginia. In 1872 he entered the Black vocational school, Hampton Institute, in Virginia, earning his board as a janitor. He graduated in 1875.

Washington taught for two years at Malden and then undertook a further year of study at Wayland Seminary in Washington. Then he went back to the Hampton Institute to take charge of an Indian dormitory and night school. In 1881 the Alabama legislature chartered a school for Black people and chose Washington to organize it. This became the Normal and Industrial School of Tuskegee (the Tuskegee Institute). Washington was to become the foremost advocate of Black education and a public speaker on race relations. In 1901 he organized the National Negro Business League in Boston.

Booker T. Washington believed that development through education and training was the correct course for his people, even if the process was bound to be a gradual one. This brought him into conflict with Black leaders like Du Bois, who wanted immediate equality and full rights and challenged Washington's philosophy effectively in 1903. But Washington remained the most influential Black leader in America throughout his life. He died at Tuskegee, at the age of 59. His philosophy lost favour with the next generation of his people and the reluctance of White Americans to recognize Black aspirations fully for decades after his death does suggest that perhaps Washington took too gentle a view of his White countrymen.

During his lifetime Washington published *The Future of the American Negro* (1899), *Sowing and Reaping* (1900), *Character Building* (1902), *Working with the Hands* (1904), *The Story of the Negro* (1909), *My Larger Education* (1911), and *The Man Farthest Down* (1912). However, his most notable books are his biography, *Frederick Douglass* (1907), about the slave who escaped and became an active leader, and his autobiography *Up from Slavery* (1901). This has classic status – it is a book of great value to every student of American history.

In 1946 a bust and a tablet in his honour were unveiled at the Hall of Fame in New York University.

**Washington Square** A novel by Henry James, first published as a serial in the *Cornhill Magazine* (June to November 1880) and in volume form in 1881.

Dr Sloper is a fashionable New York physician; he is a widower with a daughter, Catherine, his only surviving child. He has no appreciation of his daughter's character; he only sees that Catherine is plain, that she seems dull, and that since she is a considerable heiress she will only be sought by men who want her money. Catherine, for her part, is only too aware that she is a disappointment to her father and the attentions of a young man, Morris Townsend, warm her bleak existence. Morris is encouraged by Aunt Penniman, Dr Sloper's sister, a bird-brained romantic; but Dr Sloper investigates the suitor and discovers that Morris is penniless.

Catherine accepts Morris when he proposes – Dr Sloper refuses his consent. He tells her that she will forfeit her inheritance if she marries Morris. Morris goes on seeing her, however, and she promises him that she will indeed marry him when he is ready. Dr Sloper knows perfectly well what is going on and, exasperated by Catherine's obstinate attachment, takes her away to Europe for a year. This does not change her mind but Morris, faced with the idea that Catherine may not bring her inheritance with her, suffers a

An illustration by George du Maurier for Henry James's *Washington Square* (1881).

change of attitude that she is quick to perceive. Dr Sloper learns from Catherine that the engagement is broken. He also learns that his daughter has changed. Behind her calm exterior is a woman who knows that both father and suitor have made a victim of her. She has turned her back on Morris; she also turns her back on her father and when he dies she is, emotionally, out of reach.

Seventeen years later Morris calls again, abetted by Aunt Penniman. He knows that Catherine is a rich woman now. Catherine rejects him absolutely and settles down to the life of a spinster that will be her lot.

*Washington Square* is a short, bleak novel of remarkable quality. Dr Sloper, cultured and witty, urbane and sardonic, is a great achievement and has the strange effect of growing more monstrous in retrospect, long after the book has been put down. He has not a grain of real kindness in him. Morris is a useless young man and Catherine would no doubt find him a dreadful husband; but to the plain, withdrawn girl he can only seem kind. And she is the only character with any real integrity, a victim of one man's self-seeking and another's arrogance and authority.

**Waste Land, The** A poem in five parts and 433 lines by T. S. Eliot, first published in *The Criterion* in 1922. The five parts are 'The Burial of the Dead', 'A Game of Chess', 'The Fire Sermon', 'Death by Water', and 'What the Thunder Said'. In free verse with occasional snatches of rhyme, the poem contains lines in German, Italian, and French, allusions to a number of English writers, the odd line of Latin, and a transliteration of a Sanskrit invocation from the *Upanishads*. Eliot provides source notes to the poem, which begin with an assurance to the reader that if he has read Jessie L. Weston's *From Ritual to Romance* and volumes V and VI of Sir James Frazer's *The Golden Bough*, he will 'immediately recognize in the poem certain references to vegetation ceremonies.' The poet's attitude is uncompromisingly intellectual: 'Miss Weston's book will elucidate the difficulties of the poem much better than my notes can do; and I recommend it (apart from the great interest of the book itself) to any who think such elucidation of the poem worth the trouble.' Anyone who might be puzzled by line 401, from the *Upanishads,* is referred to a German translation of it.

Since the poem was first published thousands of readers have found it worth the trouble to elucidate the piece for themselves. Eliot's poem is the work of a man at the heart of a disordered society apostrophizing the waste land he sees all around him. The hallucinatory not-quite-expressed thoughts, the confusion of purpose in a world in decay, the barren ugliness and hope-lessness – all are expressed in images ancient and modern, culled from whatever tradition suited the poet's purpose. The complaint has often been made that *The Waste Land* is like a jigsaw with many of the pieces missing: the poet rightly allows his reader to fill in the spaces with the subjective connection relevant to him. A detailed explanation of the symbols and allusions of *The Waste Land* is given by Norman Nicholson in his essay on the poem in *Man and Literature* (1943); see also *The Art of T. S. Eliot* (1949) by Helen Gardner.

**Watch and Ward** A novel by Henry James, first published as a serial in the *Atlantic Monthly*, from August to December 1871, and in volume form in 1878.

Roger Lawrence, a New England bachelor, refuses a loan to a stranger, Lambert, a feckless character who thereupon commits suicide, leaving his daughter Nora an orphan. From a vague sense of guilt Roger takes the girl as his ward and as she grows up he sees in her the hoped-for woman he would like as his wife – she is, after all, moulded to his idea of what a suitable match would be. His influence is balanced to some extent by his brother Hubert, a clergyman who is even more worldly than Roger, and by George Fenton, Nora's dubious cousin. After a trip to Europe, chaperoned by an old flame of Roger's, Mrs Keith, Nora finds that all three men (Roger, Hubert, and George) are rivals for her hand. Roger declares himself first and Nora is so stunned that she flies to the raffish George. However, the squalor of George's life effectively turns her away from him. Roger wins in the end. Hubert is undeniably attractive to Nora but he is, she discovers, already promised to someone else.

**Watch on the Rhine** See **Hellman, Lillian.**

**Water Babies, The,** *A Fairy Tale for a Land Baby.* Charles Kingsley's fantasy was written for his youngest son, as *The Heroes* was written for his older children. It relates how Tom, the chimney-sweep, bullied and ill-used by his wicked employer, Grimes, runs away. In his flight he falls into a river and is transformed into a water baby. Thereafter, in the river and in the seas, he meets all sorts of water creatures and learns a great deal about the need to show kindness as well as to look for it.

*The Water Babies* is a book written for children and children continue to enjoy it. Adult critics often deplore the didactic element: children, generally, take it in their stride, accepting it as easily as the familiar didacticism of parents and other adults.

**Waterland, Daniel** 1683–1740. Waterland was born at Walesby in Lincolnshire. He completed his education at Magdalene College, Cambridge, and became a fellow of his college in 1704. He was elected Master in 1713, and became chaplain to King George I in 1717. A religious controversialist, his most considerable contributions were *A Vindication of Christ's Divinity* (1719) and *A Review of the Doctrine of the Eucharist* (1737).

**Watson, Dr** In Sir Arthur Conan Doyle's Sherlock Holmes stories, the great detective's closest friend and his companion in all his cases.

**Watson, Richard** 1737–1816. Watson was born at Heversham in Westmorland and studied mathematics at Trinity College, Cambridge. His career was remarkable and might have been designed to support the contempt in which Gibbon held university teaching. With no training whatever in the subject, Watson succeeded in becoming Professor of Chemistry at Cambridge in 1764. With no training in divinity, he became Regius Professor in that subject (1771) and held several church livings. He was appointed to the see of Llandaff in 1782 and went to live on Lake Windermere, enjoying a comfortable life as a retired scholar and visiting his diocese once in three years. Nevertheless, he was not without ability and his *Apology for Christianity, in a series of letters to E. Gibbon* (1776), prompted by Chapters XV and XVI of the first volume of *The Decline and Fall*, was courteously acknowledged by the great historian. Watson was also the author of *Apology for the Bible, in answer to Thomas Paine* (1796). (See **Gibbon, Edward**, and **Paine, Thomas**.)

**Watson, Thomas** *c*.1557–92. A minor Elizabethan poet, Watson was probably educated at Oxford before studying law in London. He published a Latin translation of the *Antigone* of Sophocles, with some Latin allegorical poems and experiments in Latin metre, in 1581. His most considerable work was published in 1582, *The Ecatompathia or Passionate Centurie of Loue*. This was a book of poems in English that he called sonnets but were of 18 lines each. They were in classical Italian and French styles – some were translations – and the book was praised by his contemporaries. A later book, *The Teares of Fancie* (1593), presents 60 sonnets in the Elizabethan form and these were widely read at the time. Watson also published Latin versions of Tasso's *Aminta* (1585) and the Greek of Coluthus' *Raptus*

*Helenae* (1586). *The First Sett of Italian Madrigalls Englished* was published in 1590 and, in the same year, an *Eglogue* in English and Latin on the death of his friend Sir Francis Walsingham. A Latin pastoral, *Amyntae Gaudia*, was posthumously published (1592). Watson knew Marlowe, was probably read by Shakespeare, is the Amyntas of Spenser's *Colin Clouts Come Home Againe*, and was extravagantly praised by Francis Meres.

**Watts, Isaac** 1674–1748. The son of a Nonconformist minister and teacher, Isaac Watts was born in Southampton. His obvious abilities marked him out at the local grammar school and a generous patron offered him a university education. However, Watts preferred to attend the Dissenters' Academy at Stoke Newington, where educational standards were exacting and where Daniel Defoe had also been taught. In 1700 Watts became assistant pastor, and then pastor, at the Independent Congregation in Mark Lane, but his health deteriorated after 1703 and he resigned in 1712. Thereafter he lived at Abney Hall, the home of Sir Thomas Abney in Stoke Newington.

Watts' chief claim to fame is as a hymn writer. He helped promote the practice of hymn singing in Nonconformist congregations where the Metrical Psalms had been the only music heard hitherto. His principal collections were *Hymns and Spiritual Songs* (1707) and *The Psalms of David* (1719). He also published *Divine Songs* (1715), the first hymn book composed for children, and a book of verse, *Horae Lyricae* (1706). Among his lasting and popular hymns are 'Our God, our help in ages past', 'Jesus shall reign where'er the sun', and 'When I survey the Wondrous Cross'. John Wesley changed the opening of his most famous hymn to 'O God, our help in ages past' and Lewis Caroll parodied Watts in *Alice in Wonderland* ('How doth the little busy bee'). Watts belongs to another age and other attitudes. He seems now both glutinous ('Cradle Hymn') and at times offensive ('Lord, I ascribe it to Thy grace, And not to chance, as others do, That I was born of Christian race, And not a Heathen, or a Jew').

**Watts-Dunton, Walter Theodore** 1832–1914. The son of a solicitor, Watts-Dunton was born in St Ives (Huntingdonshire, now in Cambridgeshire) and practised law in London for a short period. He became a critic and much of his work appeared in the *Athenaeum*. He was also the author of the article 'Poetry', for the ninth edition of the *Encyclopaedia Britannica*. Much interested in Gypsy life, he made the acquaintance of George Borrow in 1872 and his verse scenes, which first appeared in the *Athenaeum*, centre around a Gypsy girl, Rhona Boswell. The verse scenes appeared in a volume called *The Coming of Love*, published in 1897. A novel, *Aylwin* (1898), which was once very popular, contains a great deal of Gypsy life also. Some of Watts-Dunton's contributions to the *Athenaeum* on the work of his contemporaries were collected and published in volume form in 1916 as *Old Familiar Faces*. His recollections of George Borrow appear in the introduction he wrote for *Lavengro* in 1893 and *The Romany Rye* in 1900.

Watts-Dunton took care of Swinburne in the poet's later years, when his way of life had all but ruined his health. Swinburne lived in Watts-Dunton's house in Putney until he died.

## Waugh, Evelyn (Arthur St John) 1903–66.

Evelyn Waugh was born in London and educated at Lancing School and Hertford College, Oxford. On his own admission he wasted his time at Oxford. After university he taught for a brief period in private schools and was dismissed from one of them for drunkenness. He worked for the *Daily Express*, and studied arts and crafts in a desultory way. His first work, privately printed when he was 13, was *The World to Come: A Poem in Three Cantos* (1916). The next, also privately printed, was *PRB: An Essay on The Pre-Raphaelite Brotherhood 1847–1854* (1926). His first novel, *Decline and Fall*, was based on his experiences as a teacher and was published in 1928. In the same year came *Rossetti: His Life and Works*. *Decline and Fall* introduced a considerable comic novelist and *Vile Bodies* (1930) sealed his reputation and brought him financial success.

Acknowledged as England's leading satirical novelist in the 1930s, Waugh continued his brilliant career with *Black Mischief* (1932), *A Handful of Dust* (1934), *Mr Loveday's Little Outing, and Other Sad Stories* (1936), *Scoop* (1938), and *Put Out More Flags* (1942). In these novels he catches the mood of upper-class life in the 1920s and '30s and his merciless satire conveys a feeling of revulsion at its inanity and irresponsibility. His novels are a continuing, perfectly judged comedy, occasionally farce, of the innocent abroad in an amoral world: moral considerations do not exist for Paul Pennyfeather in *Decline and Fall*, for the mother of Constantine in *Helena*, or for Guy Crouchback in the trilogy *Sword of Honour* (1965), though latterly the scene changes and the novelist looks at the characters with more sympathy.

During the 1930s Evelyn Waugh travelled extensively and used his gifts as a writer of fine, lucid prose to describe his journeys in *Labels: A Mediterranean Journal* (1930), *Remote People* (1931), and *Ninety-Two Days: The Account of a Tropical Journey through British Guiana and Part of Brazil* (1934). He became a Roman Catholic in 1930 and published a biography of the English martyr *Edmund Campion* (1935). Further travel books were *Waugh in Abyssinia* (1936) and *Robbery Under Law: The Mexican Object-Lesson* (1939). Two chapters of an unfinished novel were published as *Work Suspended* (1942). He served in the Royal Marines during World War II and was a member of the British Military Mission to Yugoslavia in 1944.

*Brideshead Revisited: The Sacred and Profane Memories of Captain Charles Ryder* (1945) is a complex story about an old Catholic family and for many critics it is Waugh's best non-satirical novel. The author's preface to the revised edition of 1960 states that the novel is 'an attempt to trace the workings of the divine purpose in a pagan world'. But some critics, dismayed by the way the finely balanced prose in this novel sometimes degenerates into rhetoric, see it as an account of emotional surrender by a man who finds reality too harsh to deal with. Whatever the author's claims for the divine purpose the hero, Ryder, is indeed an innocent when he enters the world of the great Catholic family, and his behaviour is conditioned by his response to them. His acquaintance with them begins at Oxford, when Sebastian Flyte, the younger son of the Marquis of Marchmain of Brideshead Castle, becomes his friend. He is a frequent visitor to Brideshead, where Sebastian's mother is a fervent Catholic. Sebastian's father has departed to settle abroad with his mistress. Sebastian becomes an alcoholic as the story progresses, ending his life as a humble servant in a North African monastery. Ryder continues to visit Brideshead, where his feelings are centred on Sebastian's sister, Julia. But she marries a non-Catholic, a vulgar politician who fails to qualify as a Catholic convert. The marchioness dies and the marquis returns home, and on his deathbed is restored to the faith. Julia, who might have married Ryder after her divorce from the politician, witnesses her father's reconciliation and she too returns to the faith. Ryder's doubts about his own faith are resolved by Julia's renunciation of him. The outline of the story cannot, of course, take account of the fine things in the book: the superb Oxford chapters, the character drawing, or Sebastian's flight from his restrictive heritage.

After the war Evelyn Waugh's only satire was based on his experience of Hollywood, *The Loved One: An Anglo-American Tragedy* (1948). The target is the American commercialization of bereavement and the point is overworked even in a short book. *Scott-King's Modern Europe* (1947) was a short novel reflecting the author's uneasiness in the modern world and its sense of values, and *Helena* (1950) an interesting and little-known treatment of the finding of the True Cross. His next novel, *Men at Arms* (1952), was the first of a trilogy. *Love Among the Ruins: A Romance of the Near Future* (1953) followed, and the second novel of the trilogy, *Officers and Gentlemen*, in 1955. *The Ordeal of Gilbert Pinfold* (1957) is a striking account of a middle-aged writer who suffers a nervous breakdown. Frankly autobiographical, it is for many readers Waugh's best novel. A biography, *The Life of Ronald Knox* (1959), and a travel book, *A Tourist in Africa* (1960), were followed by *Unconditional Surrender* (1961), the conclusion of the trilogy called *Sword of Honour* (1965). *A Little Learning* (1964) is a chapter of autobiography.

*Sword of Honour* presents Guy Crouchback, an honourable man with no place in the modern world. He receives no consolation from personal relationships or from his religion but World War II gives him opportunities to establish some sort of identity. The setting is of course upper-class and complaints of snobbery are not valid. Waugh was writing about the world he knew – and he could be vicious about it. By the end of the second volume Crouchback has been stripped of his illusions about the army. He has also remarried his shallow, bird-brained ex-wife Virginia, who is pregnant by another man. His charity to her is the only sort of disinterested action possible in a corrupted world. In the last volume Crouchback volunteers for service in Italy with the military government and eventually goes to Yugoslavia as a liaison officer with the Partisans. By the end of the book he has again asserted himself, in the rescue of a group of Jewish refugees. The words of one of them, a woman, bring him to a devastating realization of the kind of man he used to be: "'It is too simple to say that only the Nazis wanted war. These Communists wanted it too. It was the only way in which they could come to power. Many of my people wanted it, to be revenged on the Germans, to hasten the creation of the national state ... Even good men thought their private honour would be satisfied by war. They could assert their manhood by killing and being killed. They would accept hardships in recompense for having been selfish and lazy. Danger justified privilege. I knew Italians – not very many perhaps – who felt this. Were there none in England?" "God forgive me," said Guy, "I was one of them.'"

Evelyn Waugh, 1964.

**Waverley** A novel by Sir Walter Scott, first published, anonymously, in 1814, though Scott had worked on the book intermittently since 1805.

Edward Waverley, the hero, has been brought up partly by his uncle, Sir Edward Digby, who has Jacobite sympathies. When Edward receives his commission in the army, and joins his regiment in Scotland, he visits Digby's friend Bradwardine, another Jacobite, and is attracted to Rose, Bradwardine's gentle daughter. Waverley's romantic disposition leads him to visit the Highlands and seek out a freebooting character, Donald Bean Lean, and there he meets Fergus Mac-Ivor and his beautiful sister Flora – both ardent Jacobites and active in the Stuart cause. His connections with the Jacobites gets Waverley into trouble with his colonel. An incipient mutiny is laid at his door and he is cashiered. The intervention of Rose, who is devoted to him, saves him from prison. But the injustice leads him to join the other side. He is encouraged by Flora and well received by the Young Pretender. At the Battle of Prestonpans the Jacobite forces are routed; but Waverley saves the life of Colonel Talbot, a family friend, who secures a pardon for him. The other Jacobite prisoners are severely dealt with and Fergus Mac-Ivor is convicted of high treason. Waverley, meanwhile, is rejected by the beautiful Flora, who enters a convent when Fergus is executed. Eventually he marries Rose.

Scott, by his own admission, had little sympathy for Waverley. He was a device for the plot and a pale figure compared to Fergus and Flora. The novel was enormously successful: four editions were printed and sold during the first year of publication.

**Way of all Flesh, The** A novel by Samuel Butler, first published in 1903.

The central character is Ernest Pontifex and the theme is the nature of his family and upbringing. The first Pontifex, in the 18th century, was a village carpenter. The present head of the family, Theobald, is Ernest's father. He was ordered into the Church by his father. Ernest's mother, Christina, was one of five daughters of a rector – she 'drew' Theobald, like a prize, at cards with her sisters.

As parents, the pious pair are monsters, and the rod is never spared in their efforts to ensure that Ernest will be an obedient, spiritless prig. The boy's hope of a change for the better at boarding school is dashed when the head, Dr Skinner, proves to be a copy of Ernest's father. The first relief from his crushing existence comes from his father's sister, Aunt Alethea, who lives near the boarding school and who encourages his love of music. But Aunt Alethea dies during a typhoid epidemic and Ernest is soon cut off from the interests that were beginning to make life bearable. He does badly at school, and at home finds himself – for no sensible reason – suspected of being the agent of the housemaid, Ellen's, ruin. However, he is intended for the Church and has no way of fighting his parents: he is despatched to Cambridge, eventually ordained, and sent as a curate to London. There he manages to insult a young woman he thinks is a prostitute. He is charged with immoral intentions and sent to prison for six months.

After his release he meets Ellen, the housemaid, and marries her. Alas, for Ernest, she is an alcoholic. He is fortunate that his marriage to her proves to be invalid and he can be free of her. She goes off to America with another man, leaving Ernest with their two children.

Then Mr Overton, his godfather, brings Ernest the news that Aunt Alethea's legacy, left in trust until his 28th birthday, is now due; it proves to be a fortune. After a tour of the continent with Mr Overton, Ernest is able to settle down as his own master and attend to the care of his children. He spends the rest of his time as a writer.

Butler's novel is an expert hatchet job on the Low-Church middle-class Victorian world. It is narrated by Mr Overton, and this proves to be an error of judgment on the author's part. Butler uses him, as Ernest's godfather, to comment and analyse when the words and actions of the appalling Theobald and Christina are damning enough in themselves. But the novel is excellent in describing the rise of the Pontifexes, and in conveying their smug, stifling eminence. There is fine comedy, too, in the scene between Ernest and the bewildered Miss Maitland, whom he believes to be a prostitute.

**Way of the World, The** William Congreve's last comedy was first produced in March 1700 and published in the same year. The principal parts, Millamant and Mirabell, were played by Anne Bracegirdle and Thomas Betterton, who had contributed so much to the success of Congreve's earlier comedies. But the play did not have great success and Congreve, at the age of 30, wrote no more for the theatre. At its best *The Way of the World* displays the finest of Congreve's brilliant dialogue and characterization; but it yields to *Love for Love*, its predecessor, in plot and development. It has been very successful in the modern theatre, and the part of Millamant was given an outstanding performance by Edith Evans.

Mirabell, to further his suit with Millamant, has pretended to be enamoured of her aunt, Lady Wishfort, who controls half of Millamant's income and must approve her choice of husband. Mrs Marwood was in love with Mirabell, who did not respond, and she has spitefully revealed his deception to Lady Wishfort. Mirabell has to find some way of getting the better of Lady Wishfort before he can hope to marry Millamant. He persuades his servant, Waitwell, to impersonate his uncle Sir Rowland. Waitwell loves Foible, Lady Wishfort's servant, and marries her, but he is also to woo Lady Wishfort and inveigle her into a false marriage.

The plot is discovered by Mrs Marwood, who believes she has proof of a past intrigue between Mrs Fainall and Mirabell (Mrs Fainall is Lady Wishfort's daughter; Fainall is apparently Mirabell's friend but he is Mrs Marwood's present lover). Mrs Marwood conspires with Fainall to tell Lady Wishfort of the plot. Fainall will threaten to divorce his wife unless he is given control of her property and will also demand Millamant's portion. The plan misfires: Mrs Fainall denies the charges and counter-charges with proof of the liaison between Fainall and Mrs Marwood. Moreover Fainall cannot touch her

The opening of Act IV, scene 2 of *The Way of the World*. At Lady Wishfort's, Sir Wilfull Witwoud is drunk and singing, to her annoyance. Also present are Mrs Millamant, young Witwoud, and Mrs Fainall. Frontispiece to Vol. III of Congreve's *Works*, published in 1753.

property since she made Mirabell her trustee before her marriage. Lady Wishfort is so relieved to be delivered from Fainall's threats that she forgives Mirabell and consents to his marriage to Millamant.

The scene of Mirabell's proposal to Millamant (Act IV Scene I) has become, through Edith Evans' interpretation, a classic exposition of the comedy of manners at its finest. Lady Wishfort, Foible and Waitwell are also excellent stage characters.

**Way We Live Now, The**   A novel by Anthony Trollope, first published in 20 monthly parts (February 1874 to September 1875). Many critics regard this novel as one of the author's finest achievements. Trollope's statement is interesting: 'I began a novel, to the writing of which I was instigated by what I conceived to be the commercial profligacy of the age.' He produced a satire, he believed, with the exaggeration and over-colouring he deemed necessary to make his points, and it was accepted and judged as such by the critics of his day. The modern reader's experience is infinitely harsher than that of the author's middle-class Victorian contemporaries,

and what seemed overdrawn once will not seem so now.

The central character, Augustus Melmotte, is a financier of harsh and unbending character. His only child, Marie, is his heiress, and she can recall periods in her young life when the family was in want, not in the affluence she enjoys now. This gives her a hard, realistic view of what she holds and she will not easily give up any of it – least of all for her father's sake.

Lady Carbury is a gentlewoman in reduced circumstances, which are regularly reduced even more by her handsome and completely worthless son, Sir Felix. She pins her hopes for the recovery of her place in society on her son, and rejects him totally when he sinks beyond recovery.

Sir Felix's cronies at the Bear Garden, a gambling club, are Lord Nidderdale and Dolly (Adolphus) Longestaffe. The latter has a sister, Georgiana, who is determined not to remain unmarried and under the family roof, and resorts to desperate measures to get away. When Melmotte enters society, a duchess can be found to introduce him and a duke's son to be his friend. That Melmotte's daughter, Marie, should be sought by Sir Felix pleases his mother – the girl has money – but infuriates her father, who knows all about the Carburys and, in any case, has need of the money he settled on his daughter.

The long novel traces the fortunes of the principals and the desperation with which they all try to stay afloat. Lady Carbury has been doing it for years but Melmotte has to start doing it all over again when his financial house is seen to have shaky foundations. The book has a number of characters who stay in the mind: Mrs Hurtle, the American woman who once killed a man, has now left her husband and is determined to marry Paul Montague; Mr Broune and Mr Booker, back-scratching literary critics who can find a good word to say, if it suits them, for work as trashy as Lady Carbury's; and society in general – eager to press into Mr Melmotte's grand house to be entertained, while delighting in vilifying its host.

**Wealth of Nations, An Enquiry into the Nature and Causes of the**   A treatise on political economy by Adam Smith. Smith first began work on the book during his travels as tutor to the Duke of Buccleuch: he found Toulouse a dull city and wrote 'in order to pass away the time'. His theories had been forming for some time and his contact with the French economists, the physiocrats, probably stimulated him to present his own views. His book was first published in 1776. 'The annual labour of every nation is the fund which originally supplies it with all the necessaries and conveniences of life which it annually consumes.' Adam Smith goes straight to the heart of his thesis with his first words. (See also **Steuart, Sir James**.) He takes the fact of wealth as a subject for scientific investigation. The source of wealth is labour, which is also the ultimate standard of the value of commodities. In advanced societies three elements become factors in the ultimate standard of value: wages, profit, and rent. But the original, and sole, determinant was labour, and the division of labour was the first step toward industrial progress.

'The natural effort of every individual to better his own condition, when suffered to exert itself with freedom and security, is so powerful a principle, that it is alone, and without any assistance, not only capable of carrying on the society to wealth and prosperity, but of surmounting a hundred impertinent obstructions with which the folly of human laws too often encumbers its operations.' In Adam Smith's time the state regulation of industry had largely taken the form of distributing monopolies and privileges and Smith was not alone among social philosophers in believing that public and private interests were inseparable. The well-being of one could only be for the benefit of the other.

Smith examined the ways by which the state had attempted to regulate industry in agriculture, home trade, and commerce. The state had thus diverted the course of trade from its natural progression. Progress was retarded, and the value of the produce of land and labour diminished. If interference were swept away 'the obvious and simple system of natural liberty establishes itself of its own accord'. But while he extolled this 'natural liberty', and thereby gave the principle of free trade a firm platform, he was acutely aware of the dangerous power which could come with wealth: when those in the same profitable trade 'meet together even for merriment or diversion . . . the conversation ends in some conspiracy against the public, or in some contrivance to raise prices'. What was the best thing for trade and commerce was not always the best thing for the country and security should not be sacrificed for affluence.

Smith checked and reinforced his conclusions by careful historical investigation and supported every deduction with stated instances. The schools of economists which followed him regarded him as their founder, even when they supported rival views. No better testimony could be found to his grasp of principles and insight into facts.

Modern editions of *The Wealth of Nations* are published in The Glasgow Edition of the *Works and Correspondence* of Adam Smith, edited by W. B. Todd (1976), and in Penguin Books (1970).

**Webbe, William** d. 1591. Webbe was a contemporary of Edmund Spenser at Cambridge and seems to have earned his living as a tutor in Essex. He was the author of *A Discourse of English Poetry, Together with the Author's Judgement Touching the Reformation of Our English Verse* (1586). This is an oddity of 16th-century criticism that displays enthusiasm for the new poetry while insisting on the virtue of classical forms. Webbe goes so far as to demonstrate how Spenser's lines in *The Shepheardes Calender* could have been better written; he also displays a woeful lack of knowledge about the poetry that had gone before.

**Webster, John** *c*.1580–*c*.1634. Very little is known about the life of John Webster. It is not known exactly when he was born and no one knows where; but he was dead by 1634 – that much is certain, for a reference to him of that year uses the past tense. A John Webster was admitted to the Middle Temple in 1598. He could have been the playwright but this is guesswork. The first identification comes in the invaluable papers of Philip Henslowe. In 1602 payments made to John Webster are recorded for authorship or part authorship of plays that have not survived.

Webster's name is met with more frequently thereafter. In 1604 he wrote the Introduction to Marston's *The Malcontent*, contributed to **The Famous History of Sir Thomas Wyat** with Dekker (published 1607), and collaborated with Dekker in *Northward Hoe* and *Westward Hoe* (both published 1607). *The Devils Law-Case* (published 1623), *A Cure for a Cuckold* (published 1661), and *Appius and Virginia* (published 1654) are variously attributed to and denied to Webster. *Monuments of Honour* (1624) was a City pageant. Webster also dutifully penned an elegy to the Prince of Wales, *A Monumental Column* (1613), when the young man died.

Webster is deservedly famous for two plays. *The White Divel: Or the Tragedy of Paolo Giordano Ursini, Duke of Brachiano, With the Life and Death of Vittoria Corombona the famous Venetian Curtizan* is better known to modern audiences as **The White Devil**. It was first produced about 1608. **The Duchess of Malfi** was first produced between 1608 and 1614. Like the contemporary *The Revenger's Tragedy* these are dramas of vengeance, in which an audience can feel little involvement in the fortunes of the characters. Revulsion is a more common reaction. The deeds are monstrous and the motives spring from overpowering passions. Pathos is absent, compassion unknown, and it is the measure of Webster's gifts that his plays are compulsively watchable. One could certainly argue the merit of his subjects, but there can be no argument about his genius for the theatre or his command of verse.

*The Complete Works of John Webster* was edited by F. L. Lucas and published in four volumes in 1927.

**Webster, John** 1610–82. Not to be confused with his celebrated namesake the playwright, John Webster was a Puritan minister and a doctor who wrote in support of educational reform. In 1677 he published *The Displaying of Supposed Witchcraft* for which his name should be remembered. He insisted that any evidence offered in witchcraft trials should be subjected to scientific scrutiny (this was the age of Harvey, Newton, and the Royal Society). Webster moved the whole subject into an atmosphere where mere superstition could not prevail.

**Wedgwood, C(icely) V(eronica)** 1910– . C. V. Wedgwood, a member of the famous pottery family, was born in Northumberland and educated privately before proceeding to Lady Margaret Hall, Oxford. Her first historical study, *Strafford* (1935), was well received and her second, *The Thirty Years War* (1938), established her as a scrupulous historian with a very readable style. *Oliver Cromwell* and her translation of Carl Brandi's *Charles V* (both 1939) were followed by *William the Silent* (1944, James Tait Black Memorial Prize) and her translation of Canetti's novel *Auto da Fé* (1946). After *Richelieu and the French Monarchy* (1949), *Seventeenth-Century English Literature* (1950), and *Montrose* (1952), C. V. Wedgwood published the first part of her history of the Civil War in England, *The King's Peace* (1955). *The King's War* (1958) and *The Trial of King Charles* (1964, called *A Coffin for King Charles* in the USA) completed it. *Thomas Wentworth: A Revaluation* (1961) is a reconsideration of her first subject, Strafford. Other books by C. V. Wedgwood are *Velvet Studies* (1946, essays), *Truth and Opinion* and *Poetry and Politics* (1960), *The World of Rubens* (1967), *Milton and His World* (1970), and *The Political Career of Peter Paul Rubens* (1975). The author was made a Dame of the British Empire in 1968 and became an Honorary Fellow of Lady Margaret Hall in 1962. She was a member of the Institute of Advanced Studies at Princeton from 1953 to 1968.

**Week on the Concord and Merrimack Rivers, A** Henry David Thoreau's narrative of seven days spent in the summer of 1839 with his brother John on a small boat making a trip to the White Mountains of New Hampshire. The book was not published until ten years later, in 1849, and is a discussion of poetry, philosophy, and literature, derived from Thoreau's journals and imposed on the framework of a boating trip.

**Weems, 'Parson' (Mason Locke)** *c*.1759–1825. Weems was an Episcopal clergyman. At some time or other he was at Mount Vernon and it is possible that George Washington was one of his parishioners. For more than 30 years he was a pedlar of chapbooks and a writer of short biographies. His *The Life and Memorable Actions of George Washington* contains the cherry tree episode, which in the 1806 edition made Washington out to be an unbelievable prig. It has no factual basis and probably tells the reader more about the mind of Weems than it does about Washington.

*Wee Willie Winkie* See **Kipling, Rudyard.**

*Weir of Hermiston* A novel left unfinished by Robert Louis Stevenson at his death in 1894. It was published in serial form in *Cosmopolis* (January to April 1896) and in volume form the same year.

Adam Weir, Lord Hermiston, is lord justice-clerk in Edinburgh in the early 19th century. Coarse and cruel, he is delighted to have the power of life and death over those brought before him – a hanging judge, in fact. His wife, an unhappy woman completely dominated by him, dies young and leaves a son, Archie.

Archie witnesses his father's behaviour in court and, revolted, denounces him publicly. His father banishes him to Hermiston, a remote village where the boy is depressed by the boorish lairds and keeps to himself. His only friend is Kirstie, the housekeeper, who is a distant relative and a warm and proud aunt of four brothers, the Black Elliots, who have earned a name for themselves by their relentless hunting down of the man who killed their father. Archie falls in love with Christina, their beautiful young sister. Christina returns his love and they meet secretly.

A visitor comes to Hermiston, Frank Innes, a friend of Archie from Edinburgh. He learns about Archie's meetings with Christina and, through him, Kirstie does, too. She warns Archie of the folly of the liaison and Innes supports her with pointed remarks of his own. Archie yields to the pressure and tells Christina that their meetings must cease and, in doing so, offends her grievously. The fragment of the novel we have ends there.

From what has been gathered from notes, and

from Stevenson's stated intentions, the story would have proceeded as follows.

Innes, when Archie keeps to his painful resolution to stay away from Christina, courts the unhappy girl himself and seduces her. Archie kills him and is brought to trial before his father. The Black Elliots believe him guilty, too, of seducing their sister. Lord Weir, who has taken such inordinate delight in sending hapless people to the scaffold, is now hoist with his own petard: he can do no other but condemn his own son to the gallows.

Kirstie, meanwhile, has discovered who Christina's seducer was. She alerts the Elliots, who lead a party to storm the prison and rescue Archie. He and Christina escape to America. After the ordeal of his son's trial and condemnation, the old monster, Lord Weir, dies of shock.

Weir of Hermiston was based on a historical character, Robert MacQueen, Lord Braxfield. In this novel, for the first time, Stevenson succeeds in portraying believable women. Kirstie and Christina are vital and courageous.

**Well-Beloved, The:** *a Sketch of a Temperament.* A novel by Thomas Hardy. It was first published in the *Illustrated London News* and *Harper's Bazaar*, under the title *The Pursuit of the Well-Beloved*, between October and December 1892.

The story is set on the Isle of Slingers (Portland). A sculptor, Jocelyn Pierstone, has a fixation about finding the perfect form in woman and in sculpture. He falls in love with Avice Caro, but circumstances prevent them from marrying. He seeks her again in her daughter, who is indifferent to him, and in her granddaughter, who is rather chilly about the attentions of an old man. Eventually the ideal of the Well-Beloved is too eroded by time to matter and Jocelyn marries a comfortable widow.

**Weller, Sam** One of Dickens's most famous characters, Sam Weller made his appearance in the fourth number of *The Pickwick Papers*. He is the Boots at the White Hart in the Borough and becomes Pickwick's servant. He is the ideal Cockney – cheerful, shrewd, and resourceful – and devoted to his master.

**Weller, Tony** Sam Weller's father in Dickens's *The Pickwick Papers*. A coach driver, he has married the landlady of the 'Marquis of Granby' at Dorking.

**Well of the Saints, The** See **Synge, J(ohn) M(illington)**.

**Wells, Charles Jeremiah** 1800–79. Wells was probably born in Edmonton and attended school

there, making the acquaintance of John Keats who at that time was apprenticed to an apothecary in the town. He was part of the circle of Keats's friends for a time (Hazlitt, Hunt, and others at Hampstead) but forfeited Keats's goodwill when he played a foolish practical joke on Tom Keats, the poet's younger brother who was seriously ill. Wells practised as a solicitor in London (1820–30), taught English for a period in France, and died in Marseilles. He was the author of *Joseph and his Brethren* (1824), a long dramatic poem that earned praise from Rossetti and Swinburne but is now unknown except to scholars of the period.

**Wells, H(erbert) G(eorge)** 1866–1946. H. G. Wells's father was a gardener and small shopkeeper who played cricket for his county; his mother was a lady's maid. He was born in Bromley in Kent, and his education was haphazard until he secured a scholarship in 1884 to the Normal School of Science in Kensington, where he studied biology with T. H. Huxley. He was drawn to writing while still a student and after graduating in 1890 with first-class honours in zoology and second-class in geology, he mixed scientific journalism with teaching. He published *A Textbook of Biology* in 1893 and entered a broader field of writing in the same year with an article, 'On Staying at the Seaside', which was accepted by the *Pall Mall Gazette*. He made a definite place for himself when he pioneered English science fiction with *The Time Machine: An Invention* (1895). There followed the volume of short stories *The Stolen Bacillus and Other Incidents* (also 1895), *The Island of Dr Moreau* (1896), *The Plattner Story and Others* (1897), *The Invisible Man* (1897), *The War of the Worlds* (1898), and *When the Sleeper Wakes: A Story of the Years to Come* (1899). These books were all written before the 20th century, a point to be remembered by any reader inclined to dismiss Wells's inventions as tame. He had, meanwhile, entered another field of fiction, the life of the ordinary man – this theme was also an innovation when he published *The Wheels of Chance* (1896) and *Love and Mr Lewisham* (1900).

His third novel in this genre, *Kipps: The Story of a Simple Soul* (1905), has acquired the status of a 20th-century classic. Arthur Kipps is apprenticed to a draper in Folkestone and, before leaving, he gives half of a sixpenny piece to Ann Pornick as a love token. Nearing the end of his apprenticeship, he attends a wood-carving class conducted by Helen Walsingham. He falls in love with her and they become engaged when he inherits money from his grandfather. He enters local society, carefully groomed by Helen, and on one occasion is a guest in a house where Ann is a servant. The novel describes the growing awareness of the hero's true love for his Ann, who has never ceased to cherish her half-sixpence, and his increasing disillusion with 'society'. It is a social comedy of considerable charm. *Tono-Bungay* (1909) follows the pattern, with George Ponderevo and his uncle Edward founding a fortune on a phony tonic – mostly distilled water – which is marketed as 'Tono-Bungay', before George achieves respectable success as a marine engineer.

*Ann Veronica* (1909) describes – very frankly for its time – the progress of an emancipated woman, and *The History of Mr Polly* (1910) presents the ordinary man in revolt. It is for many readers Wells's best novel. Alfred Polly is thirty-seven and a half, and he suffers from indigestion because Miriam, his wife, obstinately cooks meals that continue to disagree with him. He is a man of exuberant imagination and fascinated by words but he has had a wretched education. He has worked since he was 14 but he has now a men's clothing shop on the edge of bankruptcy, and Miriam. After a very funny scene where his plans simultaneously to commit suicide and arson go awry he clears off and eventually finds some contentment with the plump landlady of the Potwell Inn. The comedy is maintained throughout and the social criticism is profound. Mr Polly, at the lower level of society, is wasted: his potential is never realized and his imagination has nothing to bite on in his straitened world.

Wells's science fiction and his fantasy stories continued. Side by side these two manifestations of his talent were remarkably productive: *Tales of Space and Time* (1900), *The First Men in The Moon* (1901), *Twelve Stories and A Dream* (1903), *The Food of the Gods* (1904), *In the Days of the Comet* (1906), *The War in the Air* (1908), *The Country of the Blind and Other Stories* (1911), and half a dozen other books in addition to those already mentioned give some idea of how prolific Wells was. It was a remarkable output for 15 years' work, and in addition there were 15 books of essays and pamphlets on social and scientific matters.

A Fabian socialist, Wells was an advocate of social reform and in a restless hurry to see it carried out. This over-eagerness worked against his effectiveness but some of his social and political works stand the test of time. World War II seemed to signal the end of his hopes and there is a note of despair in the writings of his last years, which attracted far less attention than he had

H. G. Wells, 1920.

earned during his long career. Besides his contributions to books and periodicals he published no fewer than 156 works. Fiction and short stories account for much less than half and, apart from *The Shape of Things to Come* (1933), which became a spectacular film, his fiction attracted a smaller public than in the years before World War I.

But he gained a huge audience with *The Outline of History, Being a Plain History of Life and Mankind* (1920). He had the range of knowledge and the writing skill to make such a book absorbingly interesting and the role of 20th-century sage fitted him well. Other books in the same vein were *The Science of Life* (3 vols, 1929–30), *The Work, Wealth and Happiness of Mankind* (1931), and the provocative *The Fate of Homo Sapiens* (1939) and *The New World Order* (1940). The last two were published together as *The Outlook for Homo Sapiens* (1942). His last book was aptly named *Mind at the End of its Tether* (1945): the bouncing vitality and eagerness for life of Wells's first 15 years' work had given way to gloom about man's future. Science, which should have made life better, looked like destroying it, and the sane, free world he had fought for had never seemed so far away.

**Wemmick, Mr** Mr Jagger's clerk in Dickens's *Great Expectations*. He is a wry little man but he is a good friend to Pip and devoted to the comfort of his old father – his Aged P. He marries happily at the end of the story.

**Wendover, Roger of** d. 1236. Roger was the official chronicler of St Albans until his death, when Matthew Paris succeeded him. It is believed that John de Cella, Abbot of St Albans (1195–1214), compiled a history up to the year 1188. The abbey had had an appointed chronicler since the time of Abbot Simon (d. 1183) and Roger of Wendover is the first appointee whose work is known. *Flores Historiarum (Flowers of History)* is Roger's chronicle from the Creation to 1235. The section up to 1188 is believed to be an edited and revised version of John's chronicle with selections from the best of other writers 'as flowers are gathered from various fields' – hence Roger's title. After Roger's death the chronicle was continued at Westminster by various hands until 1326. (See also **Paris, Matthew**.)

Roger of Wendover's *Chronica sive Flores Historiarum* was edited by H. O. Coxe (English Historical Society, 1841–44) and by H. G. Hewlett (Rolls Series, 1886–89). J. A. Giles's translation, *Flowers of History*, was published in 1849.

**Wentworth, Frederick** The man rejected by Anne Elliot in Jane Austen's *Persuasion*. His love for her revives when he meets her again some years later.

**Wesker, Arnold** 1932– . Wesker was born in Stepney, London, and educated at Upton House School in nearby Hackney. His parents were Jewish immigrants, his father from Russia and his mother from Hungary. After school Wesker was apprenticed as a carpenter's mate, worked as a farm labourer and a pastrycook, and did his national service in the RAF. All these experiences were used in his work. He took a course in film technique but during it he turned to writing and completed *The Kitchen*, a play presenting a day behind the scenes in a London restaurant. His first play to be produced was *Chicken Soup with Barley* (Coventry 1957, London 1958) about East End Jewish family life from the 1930s to the 1950s – from the rise of fascism to the welfare state. *Roots* (1959) examines the dilemma of a country girl who returns from London and realizes that she is now displaced – there is never a true return. It is generally regarded as Wesker's best play. *I'm Talking About Jerusalem* (1960) is concerned with a socialist community experiment. The three plays were published as *The Wesker Trilogy* (1960) and, in spite of an uncertain

dramatic grasp of the issues in the third play, gave Wesker a fair claim to be called the most enduringly interesting English playwright of the post-war decades. *The Kitchen* was produced in London in 1961. *Chips with Everything* (1962) is a bitter, realistic play about service life, the class divisions which inform every level of life in England, and the sadistic impulses which seem to be part of the nature of many who achieve authority. In the early 1960s Wesker originated the cultural movement called Centre 42, which hoped to promote interest in the arts among the wage-earners who, in the welfare state, had increased leisure but a limited idea of how it could be used. Unfortunately the movement's success was less than encouraging, in spite of Wesker's whole-hearted devotion to it. His next play, *Their Very Own and Golden City* (Brussels, 1965), was better liked in Europe than in England. His career continued with *The Four Seasons* (1965), *The Friends* (1970), and *The Old Ones* (1972). Arnold Wesker is the author of two TV plays, *Menace* (1963) and *Love Letters on Blue Paper* (1976).

**Wesley brothers (John**, 1703–91; **Charles**, 1707–88). John Wesley was the 15th child of Samuel Wesley, rector of Epworth in Lincolnshire, and his wife Susannah. He was educated at Charterhouse, near Aldersgate in London, and at Christ Church, Oxford, and became a fellow of Lincoln College in 1726. He was curate to his father from 1727 to 1729.

Wesley's younger brother Charles also studied at Christ Church, and became the leader of a small group of friends who were devoted to conducting their lives according to Christian rules. John Wesley, returning to Oxford in 1729 as a tutor, joined the circle, and his years at the university were lived in an atmosphere that transcended the criticisms of their fellow teachers and students. One of the Wesleys' company was George Whitefield, who was later to move closer to Calvinism, at that time rather in eclipse in England. The Wesleys remained true to their own ideas, however, and these took the form that became known as Methodism (no one knows why – the first use of the word has been traced to 1733). The chief influences on the brothers during these years were Jeremy Taylor, William Law, and Henry More.

The brothers went to America in 1735. John as a missionary, aided by Charles, who also acted as secretary to Governor Oglethorpe of Georgia. Charles returned to England in 1736 and was followed by John in 1737. The latter's work in Georgia had proved unrewarding – the English colonists did not want to hear him preaching against liquor and the slave trade. In 1738 the brothers came under the influence of Peter Bohler, a missionary of the Moravian Church in Fetter Lane, London, who convinced John that he was lacking in essential faith. John Wesley thereupon made a pilgrimage to the Moravian Brethren at Herrnhut, near Dresden, an experience which he found deeply rewarding. On 24 May 1738, at a meeting in Aldersgate Street in London, John had the experience of conversion during a reading of Martin Luther's preface to the Epistle to the Romans. Charles had had the same experience three days before, on Whit Sunday. The churches were closed to the Wesleys, so their famous field ministry began in 1739.

John Wesley broke with the Church of England in 1784 when, in the face of bitter opposition from Charles, he ordained a minister for one of his American congregations. He and George Whitefield had parted company in 1741. The latter's Calvinistic leanings were inimical to Wesley's view of the Christian mission. Methodism became a newly organized dissenting religion led by a man of great learning, tireless energy (some estimates give the distance covered by him, mostly on horseback, as 8000 miles each year), and autocratic temper. He encountered enormous hostility – sometimes from the clergy, sometimes from mobs – but his work endured, was responsible for fine and lasting contributions to spiritual and temporal welfare, and was the greatest single force in the religious revival in England. One of his earlier disciples, Augustus Toplady, embraced Calvinism and became one of his most vehement attackers (to call him a critic would be to honour him). Wesley summed up Toplady's doctrine: 'One in twenty of mankind is elected; nineteen in twenty are reprobated. The elect shall be saved, do what they will; the reprobate shall be damned, do what they can. Reader, believe this, or be damned.'

Wesley wrote a great many hymns and devotional works but his great contribution to English letters is his *Journal*, which reveals a sharp-eyed observer whose humour and humility are all of a piece with a conviction of his mission in life. His writing, straightforward and artless, gives the remarkable record both force and pathos. He was married, unhappily, to Maria Vazeille, but she was not the only emotional attachment in his life. The *Journal* gives fascinating glimpses of Sophy Causton in Savannah and Grace Murray in England. The standard edition of the *Journal* is by N. Curnock, in eight volumes (1909–16). An abridgment by P. L. Parker (1902) is published in Everyman's Library. It is an essential book for students of 18th-century life in England.

Charles Wesley seems to have been a more gentle and sympathetic character than his forceful brother and frequently disagreed with him. He was also a travelling preacher, beginning in the same year as his brother but retiring from the endless journeys in 1756. Eventually he settled in London and preached regularly, from 1771, at the City Road Chapel. He and his brother recognized the importance of hymns for their congregations and industriously provided them; but those of Charles are acknowledged as the finer even though his output was enormous (over 5500). Perhaps the most famous is the Christmas hymn 'Hark! the herald-angels sing' though the familiar opening lines are in fact by George Whitefield, who altered Charles Wesley's original 'Hark, how all the welkin rings, "Glory to the King of kings"'. Charles Wesley's poem 'Wrestling Jacob' is often found in anthologies.

**West, Nathanael** 1903–40. The pseudonym of Nathan Wallenstein Weinstein, who was born in New York City. He studied at Brown University, Rhode Island, and lived in Paris for two years, where he completed his first novel, *The Dream Life of Balso Snell* (1931). A garish satire on the inward life of the intellectual introvert of the title, it was consciously avant-garde, but West's preoccupation with the barrenness of contemporary life was already clear. *Miss Lonelyhearts* (1933) is the story of a newspaper man whose job is to write an advice-to-the-lovelorn column and who becomes obsessed with the need to be more than a phoney saviour. His ironic involvement with his suffering correspondents turns into a tragic one and ends in his murder. The mockery of his sadistic editor accompanies his downfall. West, who was earning his living as a journalist, went to Hollywood in 1935 to write scripts for a minor studio. *A Cool Million* (1934) is a satire of the American dream itself: Lemuel Pitkin is naive to the point of idiocy but that is no obstacle to his becoming a runner in the lethal race for riches and eminence. After he has been murdered he is proclaimed a hero. *The Day of the Locust* (1939) is aimed straight at the apotheosis of the American dream – Hollywood, and is concerned with the squalid hidden world of which the hypnotized public knows nothing. West's novels are economical, unequivocal, and highly charged. They are appreciated more now as a comment on the neuroses of the 1930s than ever they were during his short life. He was killed in a car crash at the age of 37.

**West, Rebecca** 1892–1983. Cicily Isobel Fairfield, the daughter of an army officer, was born in Kerry, Ireland. After her father's death in 1902 the family went to live in Edinburgh, where she was educated at George Watson's Ladies' College. She trained for the stage in London and had a brief career as an actress before turning to journalism, reviewing books for *The Freewoman* and then becoming a staff member of *The Clarion* in 1912, writing on politics. For her pseudonym she chose the name of a character she had played on the stage, Rebecca West in Ibsen's *Rosmersholm*.

Rebecca West made a reputation as an acute and sharp-witted journalist while in her twenties and became a regular contributor to papers and magazines in Britain and the USA. Her first published book was a critical study, *Henry James* (1916). Her first novel, *The Return of the Soldier* (1918), has for its central character a victim of shell-shock; it was adapted for the stage in 1928 by John van Druten. Her next, *The Judge* (1922), confirmed her interest in Freudian psychology but it maintains its fascination because of the vivid Edinburgh background and a finely realized heroine. Her quality as a journalist and as an observer of the contemporary scene has meant that her books have appeared at irregular intervals and her next, six years later, was a collection of essays and reviews, *The Strange Necessity*. A third novel, *Harriet Hume*, and *Lions and Lambs*, in

Rebecca West, 1918. Photograph by E. O. Hoppé.

which she provided the text to accompany David Low's caricatures of current celebrities, were published in 1929. She collaborated with Low again in *The Rake's Progress* (1934).

A quartet of stories, *The Harsh Voice* (1935), contains the excellent 'The Salt of the Earth' and her next novel, *The Thinking Reed* (1936), explores the world of the very rich through the mind of an American girl, Isabelle, who marries Marc, a French industrialist. The moral isolation of those protected by wealth is thoughtfully examined and the book is strengthened by the author's convincing presentation of her heroine. In the following year the author set off on a journey in the Balkans. The result of that journey was published as *Black Lamb and Grey Falcon* (2 vols, 1941 and 1942). What began as a travel diary became a study of Yugoslavia. World War II having broken out meanwhile, there was striking relevance in the many-faceted study of a country which, though created out of the fragments of two crumbling empires, had been struggling to find a national identity in the disparate and often conflicting traditions of Slovenes, Serbs, Croats, Montenegrins, Bosnians, and Macedonians.

After the war Rebecca West published two studies of widely differing crimes. *The Meaning of Treason* (1947, revised 1952 and 1965) was developed from contributions to *The New Yorker* and *Harper's Magazine* and examined the cases of those convicted as traitors. It ranges from William Joyce and those who worked for the Nazis to Klaus Fuchs and those who, a short time later, gave the information on nuclear armaments to Soviet Russia. *A Train of Powder* (1955) includes her report of the Nuremberg War Crimes trials. *The Court and The Castle* (1957) is a collection of essays examining political and religious ideas in literature, and *The Fountain Overflows* (1957) her first novel for ten years. It seems to have been intended as the first part of a novel sequence but no successor has appeared so far. The story takes place in South London and follows the growing-up of the Aubreys. The father is a gifted and shiftless wretch upon whom mother, son, and daughters learn not to depend: they construct a life in which they rely upon one another and which has a love of music as the symbol of serenity and order. *The Birds Fall Down* (1966) is a remarkable oblique novel about the Russian Revolution.

Rebecca West was made a DBE in 1959. Her other books include *D. H. Lawrence* (1930), a collection of reviews from *The Bookman* entitled *Ending in Earnest* (1931), *St Augustine* (1933),, *The Vassall Affair* (1963), and *McLuhan and The Future of Literature* (1969).

**Western, Sophia** The heroine of *Tom Jones* by Henry Fielding. A spirited girl, Sophia loves Tom and refuses to marry Blifil, her father's choice. She runs off to London and there finds, to her wrath, that Tom is Lady Bellaston's kept lover. She wins Tom in the end.

**Western, Squire** The heroine's father in *Tom Jones* by Henry Fielding. Hard-drinking, hard-hunting, and thick-skinned, he is furious with his daughter Sophia when she refuses to marry Blifil.

**Westward Ho!** A novel by Charles Kingsley, first published in 1855. The full title is *Westward Ho! or, The Voyages and Adventures of Sir Amyas Leigh, Knight, of Burrough, in the County of Devon, in the reign of Her Most Glorious Majesty Queen Elizabeth. Rendered into modern English by Charles Kingsley*. It is Kingsley's most successful novel, and has been claimed by generations of young readers though it was intended for adults.

Amyas Leigh has accompanied Drake on his voyage round the world. In action against a band of Spaniards who land at Smerwick in 1580 a Spanish captain, Don Guzman, becomes his prisoner. Guzman falls in love with Rose Salterne, who is wooed by Amyas and his brother Frank. With the help of the Leigh's cousin, the Jesuit Eustace, Guzman persuades Rose to marry him and escapes with her to the Spanish Main. The Leigh brothers, Salvation Yeo, and others set off in pursuit. Their venture is ill-fated, and both Rose and Frank Leigh fall victims to the Inquisition.

Amyas Leigh and his crew sail in South American waters after the tragedy, and capture a Spanish galleon. They also discover the beautiful Ayacanora, who rules over an Indian tribe. She returns to England with them, and the Armada provides the occasion for the final punishment of Don Guzman – but this is not to fall to Amyas Leigh. Guzman's ship is wrecked and he is drowned; but in the same storm Amyas Leigh is blinded by lightning. He marries Ayacanora, who proves to be the daughter of John Oxenham, whose ill-fated expedition Amyas Leigh, as a boy, had wanted to join.

**Westward Hoe** A comedy by Thomas Dekker and John Webster, produced about 1606 and first published in 1607. The main plot concerns three wives who enjoy an escapade with three admirers; but their husbands find them in Brentford at an inn. However, the innocence of the escapade is established and all is forgiven. The subplot concerns Justiniano, an Italian merchant in London. He believes his wife to be unfaithful and leaves her. Adopting a disguise, he does his best to enjoy the comedy of London life. Meanwhile, his wife nearly becomes involved with a dubious nobleman; but she loves her husband and they are reconciled at the end of the play.

**Weyman, Stanley John** 1855–1928. The son of a Ludlow solicitor, Weyman obtained an honours degree in history at Christ Church, Oxford. He was a teacher for a time and in 1877 read for the Bar. He practised law for 10 years, and disliked it intensely, giving it up for ever in 1891.

Weyman had been writing short stories for some time and they were published in the *Cornhill* and *The English Illustrated Magazine*. Two novels of contemporary life were rejected by publishers but his first venture into historical romance, *The House of the Wolf*, was serialized in *The English Illustrated Magazine* (October 1888 to March 1889). *The New Rector*, a novel of clerical life, was serialized in the *Cornhill*, and then Andrew Lang accepted *The House of the Wolf* for Longmans. It was published in 1890 and found a public at once. Weyman had found what suited him best and he went from success to success: *A Gentleman of France* (1893), which earned high praise from Robert Louis Stevenson, *Under the Red Robe* (1894), *The Red Cockade* (1895), *The Castle Inn* (1898), *The Abbess of Vlaye* (1904), *The Wild Geese* (1908), and 15 others. He was still writing in the year of his death (*The Lively Peggy*).

Weyman is hardly read nowadays, though he may well prove to be a gold mine for those who devise television series. Hugh Walpole, in 1924, declared that Weyman's were 'the finest English historical romances since Scott.'

**Wharton, Edith (Newbold)** 1862–1937. Edith Wharton (née Jones) was the daughter of a rich New York family and was educated in the USA and Europe. She married Edward Wharton, who was some years her senior, in 1885. Before her marriage she had written some poetry, receiving encouragement from Longfellow, and had been published in the *Atlantic Monthly*. As Edith Wharton she published a book of short stories, *The Greater Inclination* (1899), and a short novel, *The Touchstone* (1900), which displayed the influence of Henry James. It was published in England as *A Gift from the Grave*. Her first full-length novel, **The Valley of Decision** (1902), was set in 18th-century Italy and was well received; but Mrs Wharton's future subjects were found in her own society and its aspirations. After another short novel called *Sanctuary*, published in 1903, she wrote her first major novel – regarded by many critics as her best – **The House of Mirth** (1905). It is the story of a girl who departs from

Edith Wharton in 1905.

conventional standards in what Edith Wharton described, in 1935, as a 'frivolous society [which] can acquire dramatic significance only through what its frivolity destroys'. She produced a novel of manners that is also a sharply observed account of the ostracism and ruin of an honest person.

The society which Edith Wharton scrutinized so sharply in *The House of Mirth* was by this time looking askance at her and the climate of New York was proving inimical to her as a writer. Her marriage was also in the process of breaking down and after her divorce she departed for Europe, where she lived from 1907. She was to prove a distinguished expatriate, like her friend Henry James, and her next work, *Madame de Treymes* (1907), was a short novel set in France. During the same year she published *The Fruit of the Tree*, a novel set against a background of industry in America and depicting the inroads it makes on the personal life of her central character. Four years later she published **Ethan Frome**, a short novel unlike any of her previous works and destined to become her most famous book. For this tragic story she moved her background to that of New England farm life but the theme of the individual struggling against society is no less forcefully presented here than it is in the elegant setting of uptown New York.

Settled in Paris, Mrs Wharton was a member of the expatriate group of friends that, besides Henry James (who regarded her highly as both friend and artist), included Bernard Berenson and Logan Pearsall Smith. *The Reef* was published in 1912 and *The Custom of the Country* in 1913. Then came World War I, during which Edith Wharton gave her energies to relief work and was awarded the Cross of the Legion of Honour. The war appears as a subject in her fiction in *The Marne* (1918) and *A Son at the Front* (1923). She returned to the New England background for *Summer* (1917). **The Age of Innocence**, her most distinguished novel of the postwar years, was published in 1920 and was awarded the Pulitzer Prize.

Edith Wharton wrote steadily until the year she died and published no less than 46 books. She lived in a constantly changing world and did not easily adjust to it. *The Age of Innocence* is set in the New York of the 1870s and the title of a successful book called *Old New York* (1924), which contains the famous **The Old Maid**, describes itself. She was a true product of 'Old New York', accomplished and elegant; but she saw that her society was narrow and snobbish. When wealth became the only measure of worth she turned her back on it. She kept a true sympathy for those less privileged than herself who became victims of either ossified society on one hand or social change on the other. Her writing is clear, elegant, and ironic. Her work includes a quantity of short-story collections that display her disciplined art to advantage: *Crucial Instances* (1901), *The Descent of Man* (1904), *The Hermit and the Wild Woman* (1908), *Xingu and Other Stories* (1916), *Here and Beyond* (1926), *Certain People* (1930), *Human Nature* (1933), *The World Over* (1936), and *Ghosts* (1937). Other novels were *The Glimpses of the Moon* (1922) and *Hudson River Bracketed* (1929). Edith Wharton also published two volumes of poetry, some travel books, an autobiography called *A Backward Glance* (1934), and a valuable critical study, *The Writing of Fiction* (1925).

**What Maisie Knew** A novel by Henry James, first published in *The Chap Book*, from January to May 1897. In the same year (February to June) an abridged version appeared in *New Review* and the novel was revised for publication in volume form. The story has an English setting.

Beale and Ida Farange are the parents of Maisie. She is six years old when they are divorced and the court arranges that she will spend half of each year with her mother and half with her father. Her first six months are with Beale, the next with Ida and a governess, Miss Overmore, an attractive and sympathetic woman who takes to Maisie. But Ida quarrels with Miss Overmore. Her replacement is Mrs Wix, sentimental and incompetent, but motherly and soon devoted to her charge.

Maisie, at her tender age, becomes aware of her position and intuitively uses silence as a defence. This is misinterpreted by her parents. They believe her dull and backward – but they forget, both of them, that each has tried to blacken the other's character and neither of them understands the perceptiveness of an intelligent child. Meanwhile, she is back at her father's house – and finds Miss Overmore installed as governess there now. And Miss Overmore is very busy with Beale's affairs, so she neglects Maisie.

Mrs Wix brings news of Ida's engagement to Sir Claude. Maisie, she says, will be with her mother now, in a proper household. But Miss Overmore is no longer Miss Overmore – she is now Mrs Beale Farange, so could also provide a household. Still Maisie holds fast to Mrs Wix. Ida tires of Sir Claude and has a succession of lovers. Sir Claude is drawn to Mrs Beale Farange. Mrs Wix pleads with Sir Claude to devote himself to Maisie and forget past and present attractions ('bad women' Mrs Wix calls them). Sir Claude, who is fond of Maisie and unfailingly kind to her, takes her to France with him when she refuses to go to America with her father. Mrs Wix's appeal cannot succeed, however – Sir Claude is not that sort of man. When Mrs Wix joins him and Maisie in France, bringing the news that Mrs Beale Farange, née Overmore, is now free, he hurries back to England.

When Maisie sees him again he wants her to come and make her home with him and his new wife. Unfortunately, the former governess hates Mrs Wix, the present governess. Will Maisie leave her? Maisie replies that if Sir Claude, whom she has by now grown to love, will give up Mrs Beale, then she will give up Mrs Wix. The novel closes with Maisie and Mrs Wix – their income assured by Sir Claude – returning to England together. Sir Claude will have his new wife.

'What Maisie knew' is, in effect, what Maisie half-knows; but it is the incalculable quantity assimilated by an intelligent child and it is enough. What Maisie does not know is embodied in the sharp and moral adulthood of Mrs Wix, the one person Maisie knows she can always trust. With her Maisie is safe.

*What Maisie Knew* is a remarkable perform-

ance. There is little disagreement about that in the ranks of James's admirers (outside those ranks it is usually put down half-read) but whether the performance is also a novel of the first rank or not is another matter. Many readers believe it is; but a great number, also, find the subtle design of the story smothered by brilliant elaboration and complicated prose. It is a short novel but with more words, perhaps, than the theme can stand. But remarkable it is, and original, and it is unlikely that discussion of its merits will ever cease.

***What's Become of Waring?*** See **Powell, Anthony (Dymoke)**.

**Wheatley, Phyllis** *c*.1753–84. Phyllis Wheatley was an African slave who, at about the age of eight, was sold in Boston, Massachusetts. Her purchaser was a tailor, John Wheatley, who gave her an English name and an education with his family. She proved to be a remarkable pupil. She studied Latin and Greek and began to write poetry in her teens, encouraged by John Wheatley. *Poems on Various Subjects* was published in 1773. She married John Peters, a free Negro of Boston, and died young, probably exhausted by a struggle against poverty. *Memoirs and Poems of Phyllis Wheatley* was published in 1834 and a volume of letters in 1864.

Phyllis Wheatley's poems, like those of Jupiter

Phyllis Wheatley. An engraving published in 1773.

Hammon, are of debatable worth but they were a demonstration, which most Americans decided to ignore, that illiteracy among Black people was the result of opportunity being denied them. In Britain the authenticity of their authorship was questioned – but vouched for by many in America, including Jefferson. However, Jefferson thought little of the poetry, describing it as beneath the dignity of criticism.

***When Lilacs Last in the Dooryard Bloom'd*** Walt Whitman's poem is an elegy for Abraham Lincoln, written after the president was assassinated on 14 April 1865. The poet had experienced the sufferings of men in the Civil War and his prodigal talents had by now reached maturity. He never met Lincoln but admired him greatly as a statesman at the helm during the most critical period of US history. The poem laments the passing of a great man and expresses his faith in the healing of the wounds suffered by his country. The poem was first published by Whitman a few months after *Drum Taps* (1865), his Civil War poems, in a supplement called *Sequel to Drum Taps*. Both groups were incorporated in the fourth edition of *Leaves of Grass* (1867).

***Where Angels Fear to Tread*** A novel by E. M. Forster, first published in 1905.

Lilia Herriton is a widow in her early thirties with a nine-year-old daughter, Irma. She is encouraged to go to Italy for a year by her brother-in-law, Philip Herriton, when the opportunity comes to accompany her neighbour, Caroline Abbott, on a year's tour. Lilia's letters home are encouraging, until the family hears that she intends to marry again. Mrs Herriton, Lilia's domineering mother-in-law, who has always regarded her as a vulgar girl and a social embarrassment, sends Philip to Italy to prevent the marriage which, she believes, would dishonour her son's memory and the family. But when Philip arrives in Monteriano Lilia is already married, to Gino Carella, a dentist's son and some years her junior. Philip goes back to England with Caroline.

Lilia's marriage turns out badly and she dies in childbirth. Mrs Herriton and her bossy spinster daughter, Harriet, after first washing their hands of the child and its Italian father, decide they must save the child from a dubious upbringing at the hands of foreigners. Philip and Harriet are sent off to Monteriano again. Caroline, who feels some responsibility for Lilia's marriage, goes to Monteriano independently, hoping to adopt the child herself. The Herritons are arrogant and stupid enough to think they can bribe Gino to surrender his infant son but they are wrong. He

is devoted to his baby, as Caroline discovers. Philip and Caroline succumb to the charm of Italy and do nothing. The unspeakable Harriet decides to steal the baby. The carriage in which Harriet, Philip, and the baby are travelling is in collision with Caroline's and overturns and the baby is killed. Gino, in his murderous rage, nearly kills Philip. At the end of the tale Philip is falling in love with Caroline. But Caroline, by now, has fallen hopelessly in love with Gino. The three English characters retire defeated.

**Whetstone, George** *c*.1544–*c*.1587. Whetstone was the profligate third son of a wealthy father and used his inheritance on gaming and whoring. He served in the Netherlands as a soldier and was a member of Sir Humphrey Gilbert's expedition in search of the Northwest Passage in 1578. His literary career began in pamphleteering – he was convinced that others were to blame for his vanished fortunes – and his pieces carry a variety of moral warnings. Otherwise he never seemed to decide what literary form suited him. *Rock of Regard* (1576) contains burlesque, verse narrative, short poems, and a novella. His play *Promos and Cassandra* (1578), never acted, was based on a story by the Italian, Cinthio (Giovanni Battista Giraldi), and is best known to us from the form Shakespeare gave to it in *Measure for Measure*. Whetstone published a 'Remembrance' for George Gascoigne in 1577 and a collection of prose tales, *An Heptameron of Civill Discourses: the Christmasse Exercise of Sundrie Gentlemen and Gentlewomen* (1582).

**Whig** The name was first applied to the Scottish Covenanters who overthrew the Royalists' party in government in 1648. The word itself is believed to derive from whiggamore, one who drove a mare (more) at a jog (whig) – the whiggamores were the western Scots who drove to Leith to buy corn. The Covenanters of 1648 were western Scots. In politics, the term was later applied to the exclusionists, those who opposed the succession of the Catholic James II to the throne. The successors of the Whigs were the Liberals, a name that was first used in the middle of the 19th century.

**White, Gilbert** 1720–93. White was born in Selborne, Hampshire, which became famous through his writings as a naturalist. He was educated at Winchester College – where the Warton brothers were his schoolmates – and at Oriel College, Oxford. He became a fellow of his college and, later, dean. He was not elected provost and retired from Oxford in 1758, though several college livings were his for the asking.

White returned to Selborne and worked in several curacies. He held the nonresident living of Moreton Pinckney in Northamptonshire.

White never married and he spent the rest of his life at Selborne, where he observed his native scene and recorded his findings in letters to friends. The letters, chiefly to the naturalists Thomas Pennant and Daines Barrington, were full of fascinating detail and often answered questions his friends asked about wild life and the changing seasons. White also kept a journal, a sort of naturalist's calendar; his notes often supplied the material for his letters. Barrington and Pennant encouraged White to publish and returned his letters for the purpose. White wrote a description of Selborne and the surrounding country (also in letter form) to introduce the book, and *The Natural History and Antiquities of Selborne* was published in 1789. *A Naturalist's Calendar* was edited by J. Aikin after White's death and published in 1795.

*The Natural History of Selbourne*, as it is usually called (and some editions leave out the *Antiquities*), is a classic of English literature, a well-loved book of lasting charm. It is also a classic of natural history. White was a keen observer of behaviour and always searched for reasons. He scorned the naturalist who worked in a study and based his own writings on painstaking and detailed field-work. Modern editions are numerous and include those in The World's Classics, Everyman Library, and The Penguin English Library series.

**White, Henry Kirke** 1785–1806. White, a butcher's son, was born in Nottingham. He was articled to a solicitor but a book of poems, *Clifton Grove: A Sketch in Verse, with Other Poems* (1803), attracted the attention of Robert Southey, who made the promising 18-year-old his protégé. With Southey's help White became a sizar at St John's College, Cambridge, where unfortunately he died at the age of 20 through overwork. *The Remains of Kirke White, with An Account of His Life* was published by Robert Southey (1807). White's work is now forgotten, though he was praised by Byron as well as by Southey.

**White, Patrick** 1912– . Patrick White was born in London of Australian parents and grew up partly in England and partly in Australia. He was educated at Cheltenham College and then worked in Australia for two years as a jackeroo before going to Cambridge University. He served in the RAF during World War II. He wrote three novels before achieving publication with *Happy Valley* (1939). This was followed by *The Living and the Dead* (1941). After the publication of *The Aunt's Story* (1946) White settled in

Australia on a farm he bought near Sydney. His experience is reflected in *The Tree of Man* (1954), which was widely reviewed and made him the most discussed Australian novelist of his day. *Voss* (1957) set the seal on his reputation and he became famous throughout the English-speaking world. Other novels are *Riders in the Chariot* (1961), *The Solid Mandala* (1966), *The Vivisector* (1970), *The Eye of the Storm* (1973), *The Cockatoos* (short stories, 1974), *A Fringe of Leaves* (1976), *The Twyborn Affair* (1979), and his autobiography *Flaws in the Glass* (1981). An earlier collection of short stories, *The Burnt Ones*, was published in 1964, and *Four Plays* in 1965. Patrick White received the Nobel Prize in 1973.

**White, William Hale** 1831–1913. William Hale White's father was, for part of his life, door-keeper of the House of Commons and wrote *The Inner Life of the House of Commons*, which was published in 1897. White was educated for the Nonconformist Church but he found himself at odds with its teaching and rejected it. He became a civil servant in 1854, first at Somerset House and then at the Admiralty.

His first published work was *The Autobiography of Mark Rutherford, Dissenting Minister* (1881), which related his own loss of faith against a background of London life at its lower levels. The story was taken further in *Mark Rutherford's Deliverance: the Second Part of his Autobiography* (1885). Two years later, in *The Revolution in Tanner's Lane* (1887), he used a historical background, the post-Napoleonic period, and showed how much new ideas and feelings influence people's lives – a parallel to his own times. In Darwin's wake, the intellectual climate was generally uncertain. White's first book was written when he was 50 years old, at a time when the nonconformist principle, once so strong, so influential and the goal that had been set for him by his father, was declining into narrow moralistic fervour and an unexpressed care to avoid controversial issues. He was born in Bedford, John Bunyan's own county, and he knew the small farmers well. He made it his business, in London, to know the small shopkeepers and tradesmen who people his loose, ultimately unsatisfactory, but oddly compelling novels with their clear simple style of speech.

Hale White deserves to be better known. He was a new voice when Victorian fiction, after its great flowering, had settled down to a level of competence and said very little that was not familiar and comforting. A student of Spinoza, White published a translation of the philosopher's *Ethics* in 1883 and *Tractatus* in 1895.

There were also books of essays, a study of John Bunyan (1905), and three other novels.

**White Book of Rhydderch, The**  See *Lady of the Fountain, The*; *Peredur, Son of Evrawg*; and *Gereint and Enid*.

**White Devil, The**  A tragedy by John Webster, first produced about 1608 and published in 1612. The source of the play lies in historical events that took place in Italy in the 1580s.

The Duke of Brachiano is married to Isabella, sister of Francisco, the Duke of Florence. Brachiano is tired of Isabella and has fallen in love with Vittoria Corombona. Vittoria and Brachiano are encouraged and abetted in their adulterous relationship by Vittoria's brother, Flamineo, who helps Brachiano dispose of both Isabella and Vittoria's husband, Camillo. Flamineo also quarrels with his younger brother, Marcello, who is as honourable as Flamineo is evil. He kills him and their mother, Cornelia, is an involuntary witness of the murder. Vittoria is accused of murder and adultery. She is apprehended (the trial scene is a fine set piece for a powerful actress) and sentenced to confinement in a house for fallen women. But Brachiano rescues her and they flee to Padua.

Francisco is determined to avenge Isabella's death. Flamineo, meanwhile, feels entitled to rich rewards for his services to Vittoria and Brachiano; but Francisco's men, Gasparo and Lodovico, disguised as Capuchin friars, succeed in murdering Brachiano with the greatest possible cruelty. Vittoria and Flamineo now confront each other. Flamineo presses his claim to reward and Vittoria knows that destruction is only a hair's breadth from either of them. She would willingly kill him – and tries; but Gasparo and Lodovico return to complete Francisco's vengeance on both of them.

An outline of the plot cannot convey the 'size' of Webster's characters or the effect of his play in performance – in good performance, that is. *The White Devil* is a masterpiece of theatre and 'clever' productions are a grave mistake.

**White Fang**  A novel by Jack London, first published in 1905.

Bill and Henry, struggling across the frozen landscape of northern Canada with a sled and their dogs, are followed each day by a wolf pack in search of food. Each night a she-wolf from the pack lures one of the dogs away from the camp. The pack kills and devours one dog after another. Bill, in an attempt to shoot the decoy, falls victim to the wolves himself. Henry, alone and without dogs, is providentially spared when the pack moves off on a more promising trail.

The she-wolf, which is the offspring of a wolf and a domestic dog, mates with the leader of the pack. Her litter is nearly wiped out by starvation but one pup survives and, being one-quarter domestic dog, is drawn toward human beings. He attaches himself to an Indian tribe and the chief, Grey Beaver, becomes his master. He gives the dog the name White Fang. White Fang maintains a supreme position though his wolf strain brings him under constant attack from other dogs. This is observed by the base and malformed Smith, who succeeds in buying him from Grey Beaver – for whisky.

Smith keeps White Fang confined and hungry, and torments him systematically to keep his savage nature to the fore. Then he sets out to exploit White Fang as a fighting dog. Smith is successful and White Fang is undefeated until he is matched against a bulldog, which manages to grip White Fang's throat. White Fang cannot shake him off. The bulldog is going to hang on and kill him but the dreadful spectacle is brought to an end by the furious intervention of Matt, a dog handler, and Scott, a mining engineer. White Fang is nearly dead when Smith gladly sells him to Scott.

White Fang responds to Scott's nursing and kindness by degrees. He is three-quarters wolf and Scott employs endless loving patience. In Scott's home in California his response is shown to be complete when he hurls himself without hesitation on a murderous intruder.

*White Fang* is a sort of *The Call of the Wild* in reverse. London referred to it as 'the call of the tamed'. It is his finest work next to *The Call of the Wild* and no reader who is thrilled by one will be able to resist the other. *White Fang* has not, perhaps, the atavistic force of the other book. There is more to be considered in the surrender of his wild heritage by White Fang but the dog, here, is as believable as Buck in *The Call of the Wild*. And his men, in the harsh environment, are horribly believable, from the evil Smith to the degraded Indian chief who sells him for the White man's drug. The fight with the bulldog is unforgettable.

**Whitehead, Charles**  1804–62.  Whitehead was born in London, the son of a wine merchant. He was the author of *The Solitary* (1831), a poem that enjoyed considerable success, and two romantic novels, *Jack Ketch* (1834) and *Richard Savage* (1842). These were also successful, as were his verse drama *The Cavalier* (1836) and a handful of other works. Unfortunately Whitehead's career was blighted by drunkenness and he ceased writing about 1850. Whitehead died in Australia and his works were not read after his lifetime.

**Whiteing, Richard** 1840–1928. A successful journalist, Whiteing turned to fiction at the age of 48 with *The Island* (1888) and its sequel, *Number 5 John Street*, in the following year. The novels were unusual at that time (the apogee of imperial Britain) for their depiction of social insurgence and their criticism of accepted values.

**White-Jacket: or The World in a Man-of-War.** A novel by Herman Melville, first published in 1850. The novel is based on the author's experience of service on the man-of-war *United States* from August 1843 to October 1844.

The narrative covers the homeward voyage of the US frigate *Neversink* from Peru, eastwards round the Horn, to Virginia. The narrator buys a white peajacket in Callao and this earns him a nickname, protects him from the elements, and nearly kills him when the wind wraps it round his head so that he falls from the yardarm into the sea.

Melville's story depicts the officers and crew and the life on board a small ship during a long voyage and conveys a vivid picture of the ferocious punishments, the malpractices so easily indulged in, and the degrading conditions of life for the seamen. The reticence of Melville's day did not permit too explicit an account of life on board but there is a great deal implied – 'What too many seamen are when ashore is very well known; but what some of them become when completely cut off from shore indulgences can hardly be imagined by landsmen.' The characterization is striking: the cold-blooded surgeon, Cuticle; the midshipman, Pert; Captain Claret; and Jack Chase of the maintop – a magnificent figure of a man who stayed in Melville's mind for the rest of his life and to whom he dedicated his last book, *Billy Budd*. Chase was a cultured and handsome Englishman ('incomparable' is the word used by Melville), who was clearly the model for the much-loved 'Handsome Sailor' of the later book.

*White-Jacket* confirmed Melville's mastery, already demonstrated in *Redburn*, of the sea story. And not long after the publication of this book he told Nathaniel Hawthorne that he was working on a book about 'a whaling voyage'. It seems that Melville's work was closely following the order of his life.

**Whitelocke, Bulstrode** 1605–75. A member of the government in various capacities during the Protectorate, Whitelocke was sent to Sweden in 1653 to ensure cooperation with that country – the chief Protestant sea-power in the north. His memoir, *Journals of the Swedish Embassy of 1653 and 1654*, contains an arresting firsthand portrait of Queen Christina. His history, *Memorials of the English Affairs* (1682) gives an impression of his times.

**White Peacock, The** D. H. Lawrence's first novel, published in 1911. It is told in the first person by Cyril Beardsall, who observes the relationships of his sister, Lettie, with George Saxton, a tenant farmer's son, and Leslie Tempest, a rich mine-owner's heir. Lettie Beardsall keeps both men on a string. She eventually marries Tempest but Saxton is tormented by the knowledge that he could have won her if his will had been stronger. Lettie settles down in her prudent marriage, and Saxton marries a commonplace girl – the beginning of a steady decline. Cyril has a mild romantic interest in Emily, Saxton's sister, but nothing comes of it and she marries someone else. The most striking figure in the book is the gamekeeper, Annable, the precursor of Mellors in *Lady Chatterley's Lover*.

**White Ship, The** A narrative poem by Dante Gabriel Rossetti, first published in 1881 in *Ballads and Sonnets*. The tale of the loss of the White Ship and the death of Prince William, the heir to Henry I, is related by Berold of Rouen. The ship runs on a reef and the prince is placed in a boat so that he may be saved, but he insists upon returning to the ship to save his sister. The boat is swamped as a result. None of the courtiers can face the task of telling the king and a child is sent to carry the dreadful news.

**Whitman, Walt** 1819–92. Walt Whitman was one of ten children and was born on the north shore of Long Island, at West Hills. His father, a carpenter and builder, was a free-thinking radical who had known Tom Paine and admired Robert Owen. Whitman's mother was descended from Dutch Quakers. The family moved to Brooklyn in 1823. At that time it was a rapidly expanding town on the East River, across from Manhattan. Whitman was educated in Brooklyn. On his own initiative he read Shakespeare, Homer, the Bible, Ossian, Scott, ancient Greek poetry, the Nibelungenlied, and Dante. He was apprenticed to a printer when he left school (1830) and also became an itinerant teacher. He returned to Long Island in 1838 and taught in schools, worked as a printer, and began to write. For a year he edited his own paper, *The Long Islander*. In 1842 he became editor of the New York *Aurora* and in 1846 editor of the Brooklyn *Eagle*; but his radicalism was too loud. Both papers dispensed with his services, the latter in 1847.

Whitman was a busy writer during this period in his life: poems and stories of little distinction and a temperance tract in the form of a novel were later published as *The Uncollected Poetry and Prose of Walt Whitman* (1921) and *The Half-Breed and Other Stories* (1927). His writings for the Brooklyn *Eagle* were published as *The Gathering of the Forces* (1920). In February 1848, in company with his brothers Jeff and George, Whitman travelled to New Orleans. The object was to work on the New Orleans *Crescent*: what was to prove of more importance was the actual journey, down the great waterway of the Mississippi through the immensity of America, and the return by way of St Louis, Chicago, and upstate New York. Walt Whitman, the Long Islander who was perfectly at ease with the shoreland country of New York and with city life, was now aware of something vastly different – of the frontier, the big sky, and what it could mean to be a pioneer.

At the age of 31 he returned to New York life and accepted readily what it offered him in company and culture. But his outward image was beginning to express the inward changes. He had been a well-turned-out young man of the city; now he grew his beard and began to wear rough utilitarian clothing. Goethe, Hegel, and Carlyle occupied his mind and he found many of the things he was beginning to feel expressed in the writings of Emerson. Transcendentalism happened at just the right time for Whitman – and for the world which was to receive his poetry. Emerson's nonconformist follower was about to appear on the American literary scene as a poet of genius. Walt Whitman was a passionate believer in democratic equality. At the same time he was passionate in his support of the individual's right, society notwithstanding, to express himself. He was interested in a number of things, including phrenology, and shared the current fascination with scientific matters. But science found no place in his work. It was cold stuff for a man who wanted to *love* so much and saw mankind as being at one with nature.

In 1855 Whitman set up 13 poems on a press borrowed from friends in the printing business. The collection was introduced by a critical preface and was published as **Leaves of Grass**. The book contains the now celebrated portrait of the author in a slouch hat with his shirt open. No doubt the illustration was meant to be emblematic but Whitman was a poor man at that time. Economic recession had hit him hard in 1853 and he took up his father's trade of carpenter and builder in Brooklyn.

The first edition of *Leaves of Grass* was praised by an anonymous reviewer – Whitman himself – but received little attention from anyone else.

Walt Whitman. The frontispiece portrait for the first edition of *Leaves of Grass* (1855).

Emerson, who had definite reservations, nevertheless wrote Whitman a generous letter of praise. Further poems were added to a second edition in 1856. During the following years (1857–59) Whitman edited the Brooklyn *Times*. (His contributions to it were collected and published as *I Sit and Look Out* in 1932.) He became a prominent figure in the bohemian society of New York writers and journalists and, in 1860, found a publisher for *Leaves of Grass* – Thayer and Eldridge of Boston. The new edition was augmented by no less than 124 new poems; **Calamus** and **Children of Adam** (as *Enfans d'Adam*) were first published in this edition.

The Civil War broke out in 1861. After the second Battle of Bull Run in August 1862 Whitman became a volunteer nurse to the Union (northern) troops in the field and sent war dispatches to *The New York Times*. His brother George was wounded at Fredericksburg in December of the same year. Soon Walt Whitman was nursing his brother and soldiers from both sides in the military hospital in Washington. Some of his finest poems are the fruit of this experience: **Drum Taps** was incorporated in the 1865 edition of *Leaves of Grass*; **Sequel to Drum Taps**, a supplement, followed upon the assassination of Lincoln and both poems appeared in the edition of 1867. The sequel contains **When Lilacs Last in the Dooryard Bloom'd** and **O Captain! My Captain!**, the two laments for Lincoln.

The harrowing experience of the war years – the countless numbers of suffering men and the primitive medicine available to treat them – aged and weakened Whitman. He suffered from a hospital infection for six months and Brady's photograph of the 44-year-old poet shows an old man with white hair. The Civil War poems attracted little attention from the critics. Whitman was given a clerk's post at the Department of the Interior. Then the Secretary discovered that he was the author of *Leaves of Grass* – and sacked him. The poetry shocked a number of people in those days and the efforts of his friends William O'Connor (*The Good Gray Poet*, 1866) and John Burroughs (*Notes on Walt Whitman as Poet and Person*, 1867) were not effective. Whitman worked in minor posts in Washington and published new editions of *Leaves of Grass* in 1867 and 1871. **Democratic Vistas** (1871) is a prose work, in which the passionate democrat reasserts his beliefs in the face of the corruption and exploitation of postwar America. *Passage to India* (1871) was incorporated in the 1876 edition of *Leaves of Grass*. Whitman left Washington in 1873 and went to live in Camden, New Jersey. He had suffered a paralytic stroke and he was now more reflective, more interested in order. He was often poor; but his friends and disciples were devoted to him.

Meanwhile, in England, in 1868, William Michael Rossetti selected and edited *Poems by Walt Whitman*. The book enjoyed considerable success, though Swinburne grumbled about Whitman's tiresome insistence on being the poet of democracy. The criticism was merited and may be levelled throughout the original collection of *Leaves of Grass*. He was certainly not without a public in the USA at that time but his reputation was helped by the impression he had made in England. In the 1876 edition *Leaves of Grass* was accompanied by a second volume, *Two Rivulets*, which contained his prose (including *Democratic Vistas*) and some new poems. *November Boughs* (1888) collected his newspaper poems and was incorporated in the 1889 edition of *Leaves of Grass*. This edition also contains the poet's epilogue, *A Backward Glance O'er Travel'd Roads*, in which he does his best to explain himself and, in doing so, his poetry. The last group of Whitman's published poems and prose was *Goodbye, My Fancy* in 1891.

Whitman lived quietly in Camden, a man who never smiled – at least according to the writer Moncure Conway. But Conway certainly knew him far less well than Horace Traubel, his lively young Boswell, who strove to record every scrap of Whitman's conversation, or the Canadian doctor R. M. Bucke, the coauthor of the official biography. Whitman made a trip to Colorado in 1879 and visited Dr Bucke in Canada in 1880. He also visited the aged Emerson in Boston in 1881. His old master was slipping deeper and deeper into senility but Whitman's feeling for him was strong, even though he felt by now that he had totally outgrown his influence. He stayed in Camden for the rest of his life and died aged 73.

Whitman, of all great poets, is probably the easiest to dislike. But posterity, the harshest of judges, has the best overall view and everyone interested in poetry must be grateful to the persistence of a man who went on from his first 12 privately published poems to earn contemporary respect and future admiration with poetry that was completely new – not only in form but in content. In the long continuous performance that *Leaves of Grass* became, Walt Whitman of Long Island celebrated natural man, insisted on the importance of love, and hoped that the vast horizons of America would restore a primal innocence to those who were drawn to them. His celebration of natural man was the radiant young poet's realization of the Transcendentalist view; it still evokes an aching wistfulness in modern readers. The importance of love was for Whitman much more than the importance of romance; but he is sensuous and warm as well as all-embracing. The America he sang of has all but gone, despoiled and plundered, and covered by the 'dark Satanic mills' described by Blake, a poet with whom he has a distinct affinity. Whitman knew both pain and anger and expressed them too. The America of the Gilded Age caused him deep sorrow and he had seen terrible things as a volunteer nurse. But, like all great poets, Whitman inspires hope and there shines in his work, bright and clear, the message of his 'beautiful gentle God'. His poems can be woefully bad, naive and repetitive, and rhetorical – too loud and insistent, the worst possible advertisement for his new kind of poetry and an awful temptation to untalented followers. 'We need a language fanned by the breath of Nature, which leaps overhead, cares mostly for impetus and effects, and for what it plants and invigorates to grow.' Whitman's words, and his best work, demonstrate that he was capable of eschewing all existing examples of poetry and acting upon his own words.

Edith Sitwell, in the preface to her *The American Genius* (1951), pays unstinting tribute to Whitman and sounds a warning to his imitators: 'All great poets of the last two centuries have at one time or another produced a theory about poetry which is dangerous to lesser poets, and to poets of a different nature. Whitman is no exception.'

**Whittier, John Greenleaf** *c*.1807–92. The son of a Quaker family, Whittier was born and raised on his father's farm at East Haverhill, Massachusetts. Through his early reading of the work of Robert Burns he was able to perceive the poetry which existed in everyday rural life. His first poems were published by William Lloyd Garrison, the fiery Abolitionist, in his paper *The Liberator*. Garrison became his friend and helped him gain an editorial job on a Boston newspaper in 1829. Whittier's career in journalism and letters seemed set on a steady course but his Quaker conscience and the influence of Garrison took him into politics.

His first book was *Legends of New-England in Prose and Verse* (1831). Early New England life also served in *Moll Pitcher* (1832) and *Mogg Megone* (1836). Whittier became involved in the antislavery cause and was elected to the Massachusetts legislature in 1835. He edited the *Pennsylvania Freeman* (1838–40) and published *Poems Written During the Progress of the Abolition Question* in 1838. He became increasingly uncomfortable with Garrison's vituperative politics and founded the Liberty Party, to which he contributed his skills as a journalist. *Lays of My Home and Other Poems* was published in 1843 and further antislavery poems in *Voices of Freedom* in 1846. His first collected *Poems* was published in 1849 and the book contains a declaration of his hatred of tyranny and his unshakable concern for the sufferings of others. *Songs of Labor* (1850) is the most concentrated expression of this.

Whittier continued to write in support of abolition throughout the Civil War and somehow found time to continue as a poet of the countryside with *The Chapel of the Hermits* (1853), *The Panorama and Other Poems* (1856), and *Home Ballads, Poems and Lyrics* (1860). The Civil War was the impulse for *In War Time and Other Poems* (1864). The struggle over, Whittier turned back to New England and the countryside for his inspiration and achieved his best work: **Snow-Bound** (1866), *The Tent on the Beach* (1867), *Among the Hills* (1869), *Miriam and Other Poems* (1871) *Hazel-Blossoms* (1875), *The Vision of Echard* (1878), *St. Gregory's Guest* (1886), and *At Sundown* (1890).

Whittier's prose was mainly in the form of occasional pieces but one notable story was *Leaves from Margaret Smith's Journal*. His life was busy and productive but it is the work of his last period, after the Civil War, which gave him real stature. His poetry, at its best, is notable for what it conveys of a man responsive to beauty, moral truth, and the simple values of everyday life. He was no technician and his principal fault is a lack of true poetic discipline. However, he was not without self-criticism. His early work embarrassed him and he wanted to suppress it. He never believed that his work would be read outside New England. He was wrong about that. His very lack of accomplishment may well be what gives his poetry the sinew that is lacking in Longfellow and created for him a wide audience in England. His reputation has diminished but his work repays examination and attention has recently been focused on the antislavery poems of his middle period.

**Whittingham, William** See *Geneva Bible, The.*

**Whyte-Melville, George John** 1821–78. A Victorian novelist no longer read, whose life in outline suggests a character from one of Ouida's novels. Educated at Eton, a captain in the Coldstream Guards, he served in the Crimea as a major of Turkish irregular cavalry and died on the hunting field. He wrote 24 novels (some of them historical), four volumes of verse (one of them about hunting), a translation of Horace, a book of riding recollections, and a lecture.

Among his works are *The Queen's Maries* (1862), *The Gladiators: a Tale of Rome and Judea* (1863), *The White Rose* (1868), and *Sister Louise: or The Story of a Woman's Repentance* (1876).

***Widowers' Houses*** A play by George Bernard Shaw, first produced in December 1892 at the Royalty Theatre, London, and first published in 1898. Shaw called it 'An Original Didactic Realistic Play'.

Mr Sartorius and his daughter Blanche have met Dr Henry Trench and his friend, William de Burgh Cokane, on the Continent. Trench falls in love with Blanche. Sartorius will consent to the marriage if he can be convinced that Trench's aristocratic family will welcome Blanche's entry into their circle. A month later, in their villa in Surbiton, Sartorius and Blanche await the arrival of Trench and Cokane with the necessary assurances. Lickcheese, the cringing Cockney who collects Sartorius's rents, arrives with the money. Sartorius reviles Lickcheese for spending small sums on desperately needed repairs to the slum tenements which provide Sartorius's income and fires him. Lickcheese is still there when

Trench and Cokane arrive, and while Sartorius is out of the room he asks them to intercede for him. Trench learns how Lickcheese extorts money from desperately poor people for Sartorius, and is horrified. He will not allow Blanche, if she marries him, to accept an allowance from her father. In the quarrel that follows the engagement is broken off and the furious Sartorius punctures Trench's indignation by pointing out that Trench's income, for that matter, arises from the same source – though he had no reason to concern himself with it.

The play's resolution turns on Trench's capitulation, which is damning and shows him to be a spineless coward when his own income is threatened, even if this means collaborating with both Sartorius and Lickcheese. He gets Blanche in the end, too, which serves him right: she is a self-centred shrew who bullies her servants.

**Widsith** A poem in Old English of 143 lines, preserved in *The Exeter Book*. Widsith, a wandering minstrel of the Myrging tribe, tells of his travels and the kings he has encountered, mentioning the generous treatment he received from the Burgundian king, Guthhere, and from Aelfwine (*or* Alboin) in Italy. He refers to the power of the emperor Casere (i.e. the Greek emperor), to his own skill as a minstrel, and to the gifts bestowed on him by Eadgils, prince of the Myrging people. Historical references (e.g. to the continuous warfare in northeast Europe between the Goths and the Huns) and characters occur frequently. The poem concludes with reflections about a wandering minstrel's life, and how a minstrel can celebrate the princes who treat him generously.

Scholars have dated the kernel of the poem to the 4th century from the evidence of some of the references. Among translations of the poem are those by C. K. Scott-Moncrieff in *Widsith, Beowulf, Finnsburgh, Waldere, Deor* (1921) and C. W. Kennedy in *An Anthology of Old English Poetry* (1960).

**Wife of Bath's Tale, The** See *Canterbury Tales, The.*

**Wife's Complaint, The** Also called *The Wife's Lament*, a short poem in Old English preserved in *The Exeter Book*. A wife bewails her husband's desertion, her confinement at the instigation of his friends, and the fact that she has no friend nearby. So much can be extracted from the text as it stands. However, H. M. Chadwick has described it as so obscure that it is probably a very poor transcription of the original. The poem is not known in any other version. Translations

were made by C. C. Abbot in *Three Old English Elegies* (1944) and C. W. Kennedy in *An Anthology of Old English Poetry* (1960).

**Wigglesworth, Michael** *c.*1631–1705. The 17th-century American poet was taken to Connecticut as a boy of seven. He graduated from Harvard in 1651, became a Congregational minister at Malden, Massachusetts, in 1656, and spent the rest of his life there. He also practised medicine from 1663.

Very popular in his day, Wigglesworth is no longer held in high regard. His work is of interest to students of Puritan New England as an example of religiosity at its didactic worst. *The Day of Doom* (1662) is 224 stanzas on the Last Judgment, and *Meat out of the Eater* (1669) a discourse in verse on the uses the virtuous can find in the experience of ill health.

**Wilbur, Richard (Purdy)** 1921– . Wilbur was born in New York City and educated at Amherst College, Massachusetts, and at Harvard. He served with the US army in Italy during World War II, and then returned to Harvard for further study. His first volume of poetry, *The Beautiful Changes* (1947), was written between 1943 and 1947 'in answer to the inner and outer disorders of the Second World War'. *Ceremony and Other Poems* (1950) was followed by his first translation from Molière, *The Misanthrope* (1955), and more poems in *Things of This World* (1956). His career continued with *Advice to a Prophet and Other Poems* (1961), a collected volume *The Poems of Richard Wilbur* (1963), a translation of Molière's *Tartuffe* (1963), verse for children called *Loudmouse* (1963), *Complaint* (1968), *Walking to Sleep: New Poems and Translations* (1969), *Seed Leaves* (1974), and *The Mind Reader* (1976). A third translation from Molière was *The School for Wives* (1971), and *Opposites* (1973) was more verse for children. Richard Wilbur edited *The Complete Poems of Poe* (1959) and published his essays in *Responses: Prose Pieces 1953–1976* (1976). He has been Professor of English at Wesleyan University, Connecticut, since 1957. Among the honours he has received are the Harriet Monroe Memorial Prize (1948), Pulitzer Prize and National Book Award (1957), the Bollinger Prize for translation (1963) and in poetry (1971), and the Shelley Memorial Award.

**Wilde, Oscar (Fingall O'Flahertie Wills)** 1854–1900. The son of Sir William Wilde, a doctor with a distinguished reputation as an ear and eye specialist, and of Jane Francesca (née Elgee), who wrote bad poetry as 'Speranza', Oscar Wilde was born in Dublin. He was educated at

Portora Royal School, where he was soon recognized as a fine classical scholar, and Trinity College, Dublin, where he was elected a Queen's Scholar and won the Berkeley Gold Medal for Greek in 1874. In the same year he won a scholarship to Magdalen College, Oxford, and went to England. At Magdalen he took a first in Mods and Greats and won the Newdigate Prize with his poem 'Ravenna' in 1878.

After Oxford Wilde lost no time in making an impression on London society. He was well aware that notoriety was only a degree's distance from celebrity and deliberately provoked the anger of the philistine middle classes by cultivating long hair and 'poetic' clothes. That he was very much more than 'that bloody fool, Oscar Wilde', as he was described in public on one occasion, is attested by his friendships at this period: it is doubtful whether Ellen Terry, James McNeill Whistler, and Sarah Bernhardt would have endured the company of a fool for very long. Wilde was in fact the best company in the world and a brilliant conversationalist.

The success of Gilbert and Sullivan's *Patience* in 1881 led a delighted public to identify the fleshly poet, Bunthorne, with Oscar Wilde, whose *Poems* (1881) had been selling very well. In fact Gilbert had Rossetti and Swinburne in mind, but the identification inspired Richard D'Oyley Carte to send Wilde on a lecture tour of the USA in advance of *Patience*. He wanted to be sure that the Americans understood the joke when they heard it.

The tour was a great success. Wilde was privileged to meet the aged Walt Whitman soon after arriving and an actress, the beautiful Mary Anderson, became his friend. Another friend, Lillie Langtry, opened in a play in New York while he was there. Wilde reviewed her performance and with remarkable tact gave her credit for everything except acting talent, with which the lovely Mrs Langtry was not overburdened. He tried to find a producer for a play of his own called *Vera, or The Nihilists*, but failed. He also spent the summer of 1882 writing a blank-verse play for Mary Anderson called *The Duchess of Padua*. Miss Anderson did not like it and the play was not produced.

After America Wilde spent some months in Paris where he met Hugo, Verlaine, Mallarmé, Zola, Daudet, and Balzac. He revisited New York briefly for the belated production of *Vera, or The Nihilists* (1883), but the play failed and he returned to England to make a living as a journalist. He was very successful and in 1884 he married Constance Lloyd, but the life of an editor and journalist began to bore him and in 1889 he gave

it up. The preceding year had seen the publication of *The Happy Prince and Other Tales* (1888), probably written originally for Wilde's two sons, Cyril and Vyvyan, and his success in this form was repeated in *The House of Pomegranates* (1891). Meanwhile he was busy on a novel that was running as a serial in *Lippincott's Magazine*. This was published in 1891 in an ornate volume designed by Charles Ricketts: *The Picture of Dorian Gray* was a major success. In the same year Wilde published a book of critical essays, *Intentions*, and *Lord Arthur Savile's Crime and Other Stories*. Also in 1891 Wilde was introduced to Lord Alfred Douglas by the poet Lionel Johnson.

Another visit to Paris resulted in the composition of a play for Sarah Bernhardt, in French. This was *Salomé*, and preparations went ahead for its presentation at the Palace Theatre. Rehearsals were in progress when the Lord Chamberlain

Oscar Wilde. A caricature by Max Beerbohm, 1894.

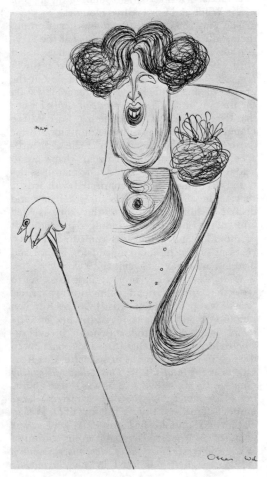

banned it because biblical characters would be represented on the stage. The disappointment was severe but the publicity was useful. Asked for a play by the actor-manager George Alexander for St James's Theatre, Wilde had given him *Lady Windermere's Fan*. This opened in February 1892 and was doing very well indeed when *Salomé* was banned. It probably did even better after that and certainly fashionable London adored it. The critics for the most part did not. Two notable exceptions were William Archer and George Bernard Shaw.

Wilde's next play, *A Woman of No Importance* (1893), was produced by Herbert Beerbohm Tree at the Haymarket and was another success. *Salomé* was translated into English by Lord Alfred Douglas and published with Aubrey Beardsley's famous drawings in 1894. Wilde's ornate and now little-known poem, *The Sphinx*, was also published, with elaborate decorations by Charles Ricketts. He was riding high on a wave of success but scandal was already surrounding the lives of Oscar Wilde and Lord Alfred Douglas.

The year 1895 opened with another triumph, the production of *An Ideal Husband* at the Haymarket. A month later Wilde surpassed even that with ***The Importance of Being Earnest*** at the St James's. This is his finest work and one of the great comedies of the English language. It was on the first night of *The Importance of Being Earnest* that the Marquess of Queensberry, Lord Alfred Douglas's father, was refused admittance to the theatre, where he intended to create a disturbance, and set in motion the events that were to lead to catastrophe for Wilde. The marquess detested anything remotely connected with artistic success; he also resented his son's defiance and dislike of him. The rest of the story is well known: the English public indulged in another fit of morality and Wilde was ruined. After two years in prison he left England for France and died in Paris on 30 November 1900.

Wilde's literary executor, Robert Ross, set to work to restore his friend's reputation as a writer. *Salomé* was produced in Paris (1896) by Aurelien Lugnë-Poé and interest was growing in Germany. A successful production in Berlin eventually led not only to Richard Strauss's opera but to the first publication of the prison letter that Ross called ***De Profundis***. Like ***The Ballad of Reading Gaol*** by 'C.3.3.' (1898; C.3.3. was Wilde's number as a convict), *De Profundis* attracted a large number of readers. But the full text of *De Profundis* remained unpublished until 1962, when it was included by Rupert Hart-Davis in his edition of Wilde's letters. *The Soul of Man under Socialism* (1891) was first published in *The Fortnightly*

*Review* and contains some provocative and still relevant statements: '. . . the best among the poor are never grateful. They are ungrateful, discontented, disobedient and rebellious. They are quite right to be so.' *The Portrait of Mr W. H.*, a piece of literary speculation about the identity of the 'onlie begetter' of Shakespeare's sonnets, was first published in *Blackwood's Magazine* (1889).

The complete works of Oscar Wilde are published in two single-volume editions: *Complete Works*, edited by P. Drake with an introduction by Vyvyan Holland, Wilde's younger son (1966), and *The Works of Oscar Wilde*, edited by John Gilbert (1963 and 1977). Rupert Hart-Davis's finely edited *The Letters of Oscar Wilde* (1962) contains generous footnotes, an excellent index, and the full text of *De Profundis*.

**Wilder, Thornton (Niven)** 1897–1975. Thornton Wilder was born in Madison, Wisconsin. He grew up in China, where his father was serving in the American consular service, and returned to the USA to complete his education. Wilder graduated from Yale in 1920, studied archaeology in Rome, and gained his MA at Princeton in 1925. He published his first novel, *The Cabala*, in 1926, and became famous with *The Bridge of San Luis Rey* (1927), an effortlessly well organized and beautifully told story of a group of people who converge to die in a bridge disaster in Peru. It was awarded the Pulitzer Prize. *The Woman of Andros* (1930) and *Heaven's my Destination* (1934) were succeeded some years later by a fine historical novel of the last days of Julius Caesar, *The Ides of March* (1948). The narrator, in letters to a friend of his campaigning days, is Caesar himself and he emerges as a completely credible figure in his stoic scepticism. Nearly 20 years passed before Wilder's next novels, *The Eighth Day* (1967) and *Theophilus North* (1973). He had, meanwhile, been enjoying considerable success as a playwright.

*The Trumpet Shall Sound* (1926) was produced by Wilder himself at a little theatre and he had published books of one-act plays, including *The Angel that Troubled the Waters* (1928) and *The Long Christmas Dinner* (1931). He enjoyed a major success with *Our Town* (1938, Pulitzer Prize), an American pastoral set in a small town, Grover's Corners, in New Hampshire, and played without scenery. *The Skin of Our Teeth* (1942, Pulitzer Prize) is an expressionistic play about mankind's precarious survival. *The Matchmaker* (1954) was a revision of an earlier play called *The Merchant of Yonkers* (1938). It became another success as the musical comedy *Hello Dolly!* (1963).

Thornton Wilder's *Our Town*, at the Morosco Theatre, New York, 1938. The photograph shows a moment from Act II, 'Love and Marriage'.

Thornton Wilder was a skilful and remarkably agreeable artist. Though he has been criticized, there is evidence of a thoughtful and humane intelligence in all his work. His first novel, *The Cabala* (the one most prized by some critics), carries the warning that Americans should not allow themselves to be too easily seduced by the traditions of Europe. Wilder was writing in the twenties, when it seemed obligatory for an American artist to be an expatriate as well. *Heaven's my Destination* is a rare example of American picaresque writing, concerning the fortunes of a good and simple man during the Depression. Rural America is vividly depicted, the invention is unflagging and the satire unerring.

**Wildfire, Madge** The crazy daughter of the midwife in Scott's *The Heart of Midlothian*. She steals Effie Deans' infant son, precipitating the events which lead to Effie being charged with the child's murder. Scott has put some fine lyrics into her mouth, notably 'Proud Maisie', which she sings on her deathbed.

**Wild Swans at Coole, The** See **Yeats, William Butler**.

**Wild Wales** The record of his wanderings, by George Borrow, in the remoter districts of Wales, which were remote indeed in the mid-19th century. It was first published in 1862. The author's descriptive power makes it a valuable record, as well as an absorbing travel book.

**Wilfer, Bella** In Dickens's *Our Mutual Friend*, the Boffins' protégée who is betrothed to John Harmon, whom she has never seen. Her taste for affluence shows her in a bad light, provoking the Boffins to make a severe test of her character.

**Wilkes, John** 1727–97. The son of a maltster, Wilkes was born in Clerkenwell, London, and received his early schooling from a Presbyterian minister. He completed his education at the University of Leyden, and before he was 21 was married, through an arrangement made by his father, to an heiress who was some years his senior. The marriage went badly. Wilkes was hungry for something more exciting than the company of his wife and his mother-in-law and after a few years a separation was agreed. Wilkes became a lively young rake and a member of the Hellfire Club.

His serious side drew him to politics and Wilkes became Member of Parliament for Aylesbury in Buckinghamshire in 1755. He supported the elder Pitt but Lord Bute came to power and Wilkes's political prospects looked bleak. His income looked bleak, too, after the depredations of his way of life. He turned to journalism and found a ready-made subject in the incompetence of Lord Bute. He contributed to *The Monitor*, wrote successful pamphlets, and in 1762 he launched **The North Briton**, with the help of Charles Churchill, as a rival to *The Briton*, set up by Bute with another Scot, Smollett, as his editor. Lord Bute's growing unpopularity in the country gave *The North Briton*, with its ferocious attacks on the government, a wide public and popular success; but Wilkes grew too bold and in no. 45 of his weekly libelled the crown by impugning the truth of the statements made, in the speech from the throne, regarding the Peace of Paris. The paper was suppressed. Wilkes was expelled from the House of Commons and banished, though he escaped criminal prosecution by claiming parliamentary privilege.

Wilkes was able to return to England in 1768

when changes in the administration allowed his outlawry to be set aside. He became Member of Parliament for Middlesex – but was expelled again in 1769 for a libel in the *St James's Chronicle*. He was elected for Middlesex again and the election was nullified. This happened three times but Wilkes's persistence in the face of an authority that the mass of people was starting to question gave him the status of a popular hero. In 1774 he was made Sheriff of London and Lord Mayor. He took his seat in the House of Commons without further opposition.

Wilkes belongs more to history than to literature but *The North Briton* was the most successful political journal of its time, and the most effective in bringing about change. Wilkes stated plainly the rights which should belong to the electorate and helped immeasurably in securing them.

**William and Margaret**  A poem by David Mallet, based on an old ballad and first published in 1724. The original, called 'Margaret's Ghost', is included in Percy's *Reliques of Ancient English Poetry*. William has been faithless to Margaret, who goes to an early grave. Her ghost comes to William at dead of night, reproaches him, and tells him to come and see her grave. William goes to the grave, lies down on it, and joins her in death.

**William of Malmesbury**  See **Malmesbury, William of.**

**William of Newburgh**  See **Newburgh, William of.**

**William of Occam** (*or* **Ockham**) *c.*1300– *c.*1349.  William's name comes from his birthplace, which was Ockham in Surrey. He seems to have entered the Franciscan order as a very young man (there are no confirmatory dates) and studied at Oxford. He also taught there but the chancellor, John Luterell, accused him of teaching heretical doctrines and William was summoned to Avignon to defend himself. But a different issue brought him trouble at Avignon when he took part in the controversy over the original rule of the Franciscan order (simplicity and poverty) being progressively modified and corrupted. William defended the original rule and was in direct conflict with Pope John XXII, who sentenced him to perpetual imprisonment on a charge of heresy in 1328. Four Franciscans had gone to the stake ten years before on the same charge on the orders of the same pope. But William succeeded in escaping in the same year and he fled from Avignon, finding refuge in the Franciscan house at Munich under the protection of Louis of Bavaria, in whose service William remained until he died.

William of Occam, known as Doctor Invincibilis, wrote in Latin and was one of the major thinkers of the Middle Ages, working through the cloud of vagueness and abstraction that was the enemy of clear thinking and gave rise to endless waffling about the true nature of God's created universe. William maintained that the real was not Universal but Individual; that the duty of science was to examine individual things and try and discover their relationship and bearing on one another, not to try and reason from the premises handed down by authority. His principle that Universals were concepts, not entities, and only existed in the thinking mind became known as Occam's Razor: 'entities must not be unnecessarily multiplied' (*entia non sunt multiplicanda praeter necessitatem*). He separated reason from faith, confining to the latter all 'truths' concerning the existence and attributes of God. William also prepared the way for the Reformation in his political theories: he advocated the separation of the Church from the world's affairs, and the denial of temporal authority to the pope.

*Opus nonaginta dierum*, an uncompromising attack on the pope on the question of poverty, was written about two years after his escape from Avignon and was first printed in Louvain in 1481. The printing of his other chief works was as follows: *Expositio aurea super totam artem veterem* (Bologna 1496), *Summa logices* (Paris 1488), *Quaestiones in octo libros physicorum* (Rome 1637), *Summulae in octo libros physicorum* (Venice 1506), *Quaestiones in quattuor libros Senteniarum* (Lyons 1495), *Quodlibeta septem* (Paris 1487), and *Dialogus de imperatorum et pontificum potestate* (Lyons 1495).

**William of Palerne**  A 14th-century Middle English romance in alliterative verse, based on the 12th-century French *Roman de Guillaume de Palerne*. (See **metrical romances**.) William, son of the King of Apulia, is rescued from the wicked designs of his uncle by a werewolf, who takes him to the wild and cares for him. William is adopted by the emperor of Rome and falls in love with his daughter, Melior, who is committed to an arranged marriage. Melior flees with William and they are helped and protected by the werewolf. They reach Apulia in time for William to help repel the King of Spain, who is besieging his kingdom. He captures the king and the identity of the werewolf is revealed. He is Alphouns, the King of Spain's son, under enchantment by his wicked stepmother, who is now forced to break the spell. *William of Palerne* was edited by F. Madden for the Roxburghe Club (1832) and by W. W. Skeat for the Early English Text Society (1867).

**William of Shoreham** See **Shoreham, William of.**

**Williams, Michael** One of the three soldiers (the others are Alexander Court and John Bates) who meet the king, incognito, on the eve of Agincourt in Shakespeare's *Henry V*. He challenges the king directly, as one soldier to another.

**Williams, Roger** *c*.1600–83. Born in London, Williams was of Welsh parentage and a protégé of the great jurist, Sir Edward Coke. He was educated at Cambridge and intended for the law. But after gaining his BA in 1627 Williams was drawn to the church and two years later he became an Anglican minister. He was interested in the Puritans and their teaching; but he maintained a detachment that was to have interesting consequences in his later career. He emigrated to Massachusetts in 1631.

Williams' convictions were firm now and he refused the call to a Boston church. He was looking for a separatist church appointment and he preached in Plymouth and later in Salem, where he became a minister. Williams proved to be far too independent a spirit for the Puritan theocracy. He believed in the equality of all men under God and he attacked the royal charter for its callous expropriation of the Indians' land and livelihood. He was banished from Massachusetts by the General Court in 1635.

A pioneer in the true sense, Williams made his way to Rhode Island and founded its first settlement at Providence in 1636. A group of people who shared his principles followed him from Salem, and soon Williams was working close to the Indians and striving to master their language – he was the first European to meet them as fellow men. He published *A Key into the Language of America* in 1643. In the same year, when the ill will of the encircling New England (Puritan) Confederation threatened his settlement, he went to England and obtained a charter for it through the influence of his friend, Sir Henry Vane. While in England he met and became friendly with Oliver Cromwell and John Milton.

Roger Williams is a refreshing figure to find in the New England of the early 17th century. He opposed the Puritan theocracy with humanity and tolerance and never ceased to argue for religious and political liberty. This is the substance of his most celebrated work, *The Bloudy*

*Tenent of Persecution* (1644). Jews were welcomed to his settlement (the first in America where they were), and also the Quakers. But the Quakers irritated Williams with their peculiar, as he saw it, satisfaction with themselves and their conviction of their sanctity and he attacked them fiercely in *George Fox Digg'd out of his Burrowes* (1676). His last years were saddened by the war against the Indians (King Philip's War, 1675–76), which led to the extermination of tribal life in New England.

**Williams, Tennessee** 1911–83. Thomas Lanier (*or* Tennessee) Williams was born in Columbus, Mississippi, and moved to St Louis with his family at the age of 12. He worked as a clerk in a shoe factory during the Depression and wrote short stories in his spare time. He had no success with these but he did succeed in completing his education at Iowa State University, graduating in 1938. Williams was awarded a Rockefeller Grant in 1940 and wrote his first full-length play, *Battle of Angels* (1940), which was a failure when it opened in Boston. (His first dramatic writing was four one-act plays, *American Blues*, which won a Theatre Guild award in 1939.)

Williams found employment in Hollywood after 1940. His next play, *The Glass Menagerie* (1945), established him and gave the distinguished actress, Laurette Taylor, her last great success. A poignant story of a mother in a St Louis slum, living on yesterday's dreams and with desperate hopes for her lame daughter, it became an international success. *A Streetcar Named Desire* (1947, Pulitzer Prize) surpassed that success and again Williams made use of a theme that was to dominate his subsequent plays: the woman whose world is out of focus, whether through loneliness or vulnerability or because of her past. Blanche DuBois, the central character of *A Streetcar Named Desire*, is too insecure to withstand brutal reality. Her sister, Stella, has found satisfaction in a sensual marriage with Stanley, the coarse son of Polish immigrants. Stella has ceased to be a Southern belle, whereas Blanche has nothing else to be, and she is rather a faded one now. Staying with Stella and Stanley she infuriates her brother-in-law with her pretensions: it is Stanley who destroys her. He knows about her past and that her promiscuity has led to her dismissal from her job as a teacher. Her descent dates from the time when she discovered that her young husband was homosexual and he had shot himself. Blanche and Stanley are alone in the apartment when Stella goes to hospital to have her baby, and Stanley rapes her. This final outrage destroys Blanche's balance and at the end

Tennessee Williams, 1957.

she goes to an asylum, mustering half-remembered fragments of her former dignity. As in his first success, Williams wrote a magnificent part for an actress who can rise to its demands. *Summer and Smoke* (1948) and *The Rose Tattoo* (1951) did not reach the same level, but his remarkable stage sense and ear for dialogue ensured further success. *Camino Real* (1953) was something quite different, an experimental play in which characters from various periods of history and literature fumble with destiny. Williams won another Pulitzer Prize with *Cat on a Hot Tin Roof* (1955).

Among other plays by Tennessee Williams are *Orpheus Descending* (1957, a revised version of *Battle of Angels*), *Sweet Bird of Youth* (1959), *Period of Adjustment* (1959), *Night of the Iguana* (1961), *The Seven Descents of Myrtle* (1968), *In the Bar of the Tokyo Hotel* (1969), and *Small Craft Warning* (1972). *The Roman Spring of Mrs Stone* (1950) is a short novel. Short stories are collected in *One Arm and Other Stories* (1948), *Hard Candy* (1954), *Three Players of a Summer Game* (1960), *The Knightly Quest* (1967), and *Eight Mortal Ladies Possessed* (1974).

**Williams, William Carlos** 1883–1963. The son of an Englishman living in the USA, Williams was born in Rutherford, New Jersey. He went to Swiss and French schools before studying medicine at the University of Pennsylvania, where he met Ezra Pound and Hilda Doolittle. After further medical study in New York and Leipzig, and a visit to London where he met W. B. Yeats, Williams settled down to practise medicine in Rutherford in 1909. He printed his first work, *Poems*, privately in the same year. He began to receive serious consideration as more of his work appeared: *The Tempers* (1913), *Al Que Quiere!* (1917), *Kora in Hell* (1920), *Sour Grapes* (1921), and *Spring and All* (1922). He published another five collections and the bulk of his poetry is to be found in *Collected Later Poems* (1950) and *Collected Earlier Poems* (1951). Williams completed four books of an ambitious poem, *Paterson* (1946–51), about the life of a representative man in an American city.

Williams's prose works began with the essays in *The Great American Novel* (1923) and *In the American Grain* (1925). *The Knife of the Times* (1932), *Life Along the Passaic River* (1938), and *Make Light of It* (1950) are collections of short stories. *White Mule* (1937), *In the Money* (1940), and *The Build-Up* (1952) form a trilogy of novels, and *A Voyage to Pagany* (1928) is a novel about an American doctor in Europe. Williams published his *Autobiography* in 1951. He was the recipient of the Dial Award (1926), The National Book Award (1950), and, with Archibald MacLeish, the Bollingen Prize in Poetry (1952). His appointment to the Library of Congress in 1952 as consultant in poetry was cancelled because of his alleged radicalism.

**Williamson, Henry** 1895–1977. Williamson was born in Bedfordshire, and his country boyhood was much influenced by the work of Richard Jefferies. He enlisted at the age of 17 and served on the Western Front during World War I. After the armistice he worked in London as a freelance journalist but urban life proved unendurable to a man with shattered nerves and he went tramping in the West Country, eventually settling in a cottage on Exmoor. His first novel was *The Beautiful Years* (1921), the beginning of a sequence called *The Flax of Dream*, which continued with *Dandelion Days* (1922), *A Dream of Fair Women* (1924), and *The Pathway* (1928). Williamson's first stories of wild life were *The Peregrine's Saga* (1923) and *The Old Stag* (1926). *Tarka the Otter* (1927) won the Hawthornden Prize and made the author famous. For many readers Williamson is at his best in his moving but unsentimental and beautifully observed stories about wild creatures: others are *Salar the Salmon* (1935), *The Phasian Bird* (1948), and *Tales of Moorland and Estuary* (1953). The author's later years were occupied with an ambitious novel sequence called *A Chronicle of Ancient Sunlight*, which follows the course through life of Phillip

Maddison, cousin of the hero of *The Flax of Dream*, from the 1890s to the 1960s. The titles are *The Dark Lantern* (1951), *Donkey Boy* (1952), *Young Phillip Maddison* (1953), *How Dear is Life* (1954), *A Fox Under My Cloak* (1955), *The Golden Virgin* (1957), *Love and the Loveless* (1958), *A Test to Destruction* (1960), *The Innocent Moon* (1961), *It was the Nightingale* (1962), *The Power of the Dead* (1963), *The Phoenix Generation* (1965), *A Solitary War* (1966), *Lucifer before Sunrise* (1967), and *The Gale of the World* (1969). Among other books by Henry Williamson are *The Story of a Norfolk Farm* (1941 – the author farmed in Norfolk during the 1930s), *A Clear Water Stream* (1958, autobiography), and *The Wet Flanders Plain* (1929), an impressive memoir of World War I.

**Willie, Wandering** The blind fiddler of Scott's *Redgauntlet*–Willie Steenson. 'Wandering Willie's Tale' in the novel is a fine ghost story.

**Willoughby, Sir Hugh** d. 1554. See **Hakluyt, Richard**.

*Will to Believe, The,* and Other Essays in Popular Philosophy. A volume of ten essays by William James, first published with a preface in 1897. This was James's first published work as a philosopher and in it he defines his position as a 'radical empiricist'. He was a philosopher with a distinguished career as a psychologist behind him and while he rejected absolutist belief in truth he insisted on the importance of instinct. The essays proceed from the basic principles that 'As a rule we disbelieve all facts and theories for which we have no use' and that 'Our nonintellectual nature does influence our convictions.'

**Wilson, Angus** 1913– . The son of an English father and a South African mother, Wilson was born at Bexhill in Sussex. He was educated at Westminister School and Merton College, Oxford, and joined the staff of the British Museum Library in 1937. Apart from his service at the Foreign Office during World War II, he was at the Library until 1955; he was Deputy Superintendant of the Reading Room when he retired. His career as a writer began with the publication of *The Wrong Set and Other Stories* (1949) and *Such Darling Dodos and Other Stories* (1950); he was welcomed as a satirist of remarkable talent. His first novel, *Hemlock and After* (1952), demonstrated that satire offered the best stick to beat contemporary manners with and the book was widely read. *Anglo-Saxon Attitudes* (1956) set the seal on his reputation and was also a best seller. His career continued with *A Bit off the Map and Other Stories* (1957), *The Middle Age of Mrs Eliot*

(1958), *The Old Men at the Zoo* (1961), *Late Call* (1965 – his best novel in the opinion of many critics), *No Laughing Matter* (1967), *Death Dance: 25 Stories* (1969), *As if by Magic* (1973), and *Setting the World on Fire* (1980). Nonfiction works are *Emile Zola: An Introductory Study* (1952, revised 1965), *The Wild Garden* (1963, essays on his own fiction), *The World of Charles Dickens* (1970), and *The Strange Ride of Rudyard Kipling* (1977). Angus Wilson is the author of one play, *The Mulberry Bush* (1955). He became Professor of English Literature at the University of East Anglia in 1966 and was knighted in 1980.

**Wilson, Edmund** 1895–1972. Edmund Wilson was born in Red Bank, New Jersey, and completed his education at Princeton University, where he edited the *Nassau Literary Magazine*. He had some experience as a journalist in New York before serving in World War I as a hospital aide and later in US Intelligence. After the war he became editor of *Vanity Fair* and reviewed books in *The New Yorker* and *The New Republic*. He made a reputation as a journalist and essayist of uncommon range and erudition.

Wilson's published output is considerable. Among his best-known works are his volumes of criticism and analytical comment on literature, arts, and politics in America and Europe. These include *Axel's Castle* (1931), which has become a standard work on Symbolist literature; *The American Jitters: A Year of the Slump* (1932); *Travels in Two Democracies* (1936), which gives the Marxist view of life in the USA and Russia; and *Triple Thinkers* (1938, enlarged and revised 1948) and *The Wound and the Bow* (1941), collections of literary essays. Wilson's fine study of the European revolutionary tradition, *To the Finland Station* (1940), begins with François-Emile Babeuf's reaction to the betrayal of the ideals of the French Revolution and closes with the arrival of Lenin in Russia in 1917.

*The Boys in the Back Room* (1931) reviews modern writing in California; *The Shock of Recognition* (1943) is an anthology of American literary criticism; *Patriotic Gore* (1962) examines Civil War literature and delivers a severe attack on US militarism in the preface. Wilson collected the unpublished writings of his friend F. Scott Fitzgerald, *The Crack-Up* (1945), after Fitzgerald's death. He published two volumes of autobiography, *A Piece of My Mind* (1956) and *A Prelude* (1967).

**Wilson, John** *c.*1627–96. A minor Restoration playwright, Wilson was born in Plymouth and educated at Exeter College, Oxford. After Oxford he entered Lincoln's Inn, became a barrister and eventually Recorder of Londonderry. Wilson wrote two comedies in the manner of Ben Jonson: *The Cheats* (1664) and *The Projectors* (1665). A later comedy (1690) was *Belphegor: or the marriage of the Devil*, based on Machiavelli's story. Wilson wrote occasional verse and a tragedy, *Andronicus Comnenius* (1664), about the career of the Byzantine emperor.

**Wilson, John** 1785–1854. Wilson was born in Paisley, the son of a factory owner, and was educated at Paisley Grammar School, Glasgow University, and Magdalen College, Oxford. He won the Newdigate Prize but his subsequent verse, *The Isle of Palms* (1812) and *The City of the Plague* (1816), is no longer read. His novel, *The Trials of Margaret Lyndsay* (1823), is also forgotten but he made sufficient impression in his day to be welcomed by literary circles in Edinburgh and to the editorial staff of *Blackwood's Magazine* in 1817. He was elected in dubious circumstances (he had no qualifications) to the chair of moral philosophy at Edinburgh University.

Wilson appears as 'Christopher North' in the *Noctes Ambrosianae* papers in *Blackwood's*: he actually wrote the greatest number of these. With Hogg and Lockhart he wrote the satirical *Chaldee MS* (Translation from an Ancient Chaldean Manuscript, October 1817), which gave the *Magazine* its first considerable success. Wilson's complete *Works* (1855–58) were collected and edited by his son-in-law, John Ferrier.

**Wilson, Thomas** 1525–81. Wilson, after being Privy Councillor, became Secretary of State to Queen Elizabeth in 1578. He was educated at Eton and King's College, Cambridge, and was a product of the new learning that informed the English universities in the first half of the 16th century. He was the author of *The Rule of Reason* (1551), an introduction to logic; *The Arte of Rhetorique* (1553), which is notable for the condemnation (in a period when such conceits were fashionable) of using foreign idioms and phrases instead of English ones; and *A Discourse upon Usurye* (1572), which takes the form of a dialogue between a lawyer, a merchant, and a preacher. Wilson also translated from the Greek the *Three Orations of Demosthenes in Favour of the Olynthians* (1570).

**Wilson, Thomas** 1663–1755. Wilson was born at Burton in Cheshire and studied medicine at Trinity College, Dublin. However, he took holy orders in 1686 and became a curate to his uncle at Newchurch Kenyon in Lancashire in the following year. The influence and persuasion of the Earl of Derby led to his becoming Bishop of Sodor

and Man at the age of 35. He made his home at Kirkmichael and spent the rest of his life on the Isle of Man, a distinguished man of unimpeachable probity in his ministry. He was active in the improvement of education and the provision of public libraries and was imprisoned for a time for his insistence on suspending his archdeacon for heresy. His *The Principles and Duties of Christianity* (1707) was the first book printed in the Manx language. His devotional essay, *Sacra Privata*, was published posthumously (1781).

**Winchilsea, Anne Finch, Countess of** 1661–1721. Born Anne Kingsmill, the daughter of a Hampshire family, she became a maid-of-honour to the Duchess of York in 1683. She married Heneage Finch, who became Sixth Earl of Winchilsea, in 1684. Her first poems appeared in 1701 and a collection, in a variety of metres, was published as *Miscellany Poems* in 1713. Her nature poetry, particularly the 'Nocturnal Reverie', was praised by Wordsworth in *Lyrical Ballads* (1801) and her small output is believed to have had some influence on the work of Alexander Pope (*Essay on Man*) and Shelley (*Epipsychidion*).

**Wind Among the Reeds, The** See **Yeats, William Butler**.

**Winesburg, Ohio** See **Anderson, Sherwood**.

**Wings of the Dove, The** A novel by Henry James, first published in 1902.

Mrs Stringham and her protégée, Milly Theale, are Americans in London, guests of the rich and arrogant Maud Lowder. Kate Croy, Mrs Lowder's niece, is the daughter of a discredited social adventurer and she is secretly engaged to Merton Densher, a journalist. Their marriage prospects are vague – Merton does not have the means to make him eligible for Mrs Lowder's approval, as Kate knows perfectly well. At the same time she really does want to marry him and the two hope for something to improve their prospects. Mrs Lowder's idea of a suitable husband for Kate is someone like Lord Mark, who is not rich but is at least somebody. Meanwhile, Mrs Lowder sponsors the pretty and gentle Milly, whose London season seems to be a success. Merton has made Milly Theale's acquaintance in New York; he knows her to be very wealthy. Kate and Milly, both in Mrs Lowder's house, inevitably see a great deal of each other. Milly believes Kate to be her friend. She is also very pleased to meet Merton again and Kate does not tell her that he is pledged.

Milly, whose vitality is dangerously low, is discovered to be declining. Her doctor, Sir Luke Strett, tells Mrs Stringham that the only hope for her is a lift to her spirits. Happiness will keep death away more certainly than anything else. Kate has seen how Merton's attentions please Milly and when the latter sets up an establishment in Venice, which all the main characters visit, Kate tells him to be attentive and kind to her. Merton will do anything Kate tells him to do but when her insistence makes her motives clear he demands that Kate give herself to him in return. She surrenders to him and he goes on paying court to Milly, who loves him and believes that his attentions are significant. Kate and Mrs Lowder return to England.

Lord Mark, who is himself in search of a rich marriage, arrives in Venice. He has seen a great deal of Milly during her London season and proposes to her. She declines his proposal. Following this, Merton discovers that he is no longer welcome and Milly's health deteriorates rapidly. Lord Mark, rejected, has been spiteful enough to tell her of Merton's secret engagement to Kate and Mrs Stringham begs Merton to deny it in the hope of arresting Milly's decline. He cannot bring himself to and departs for London.

On the same day that news reaches London of Milly's death in Venice, Merton receives a letter from Venice in Milly's handwriting. She has made him rich enough to marry Kate. In an agony of shame he confronts Kate: she had rejected Lord Mark herself – but how did Lord Mark know of her engagement to Merton when he went to Venice to propose to Milly? His spiteful revelation has destroyed the girl. Merton refuses to accept the wealth bestowed on him by Milly and Kate refuses him unless he does. They are separated for ever.

An outline of the story conveys nothing of the quality of this remarkable novel that, once read, stays very much in the mind. At times the multiple attentions to every facet of the story and the characters is wearying. The reader has to endure a great deal of what Edmund Wilson called James's 'roundabout locutions' and 'quite gratuitous verbiage'. But the final effect is one of tragedy because of the wonderful characterization of Milly Theale, the dove of the story. The author centres each episode in the story on the character it most concerns and slips with effortless skill from inside one character to the inside of another as required. Kate Croy is a horrible woman but what makes her so is crystal clear. Merton is charming, not much more, and willing to do what he is told. He will marry the dying girl and gain her fortune if that will give him Kate. The first sign of resolution in his character comes when he demands real assurance from Kate. Milly is immeasurably superior to both of them

and her dying gesture is a strange triumph. Henry James succeeds completely with Milly Theale and in doing so he has given us a memorable novel.

**Winkle, Nathaniel** In Dickens's *The Pickwick Papers*, one of the four members of the Corresponding Society of the Pickwick Club, who undertakes to send in occasional papers for the pleasure of the other club members. More accident-prone than the rest, he nevertheless finds happiness with Arabella Allen.

**Winterbourne, Giles** In Thomas Hardy's *The Woodlanders*, the apple farmer who loves the shallow and snobbish Grace Melbury. He is a typical Hardy 'hero', whose self-effacement and loyalty are ruthlessly used.

*Winter's Tale, The* A comedy by William Shakespeare, a late play first produced in 1611. The source of the play was Robert Greene's romance, *Pandosto*, published in 1588. *The Winter's Tale* was first published in the First Folio of 1623.

Leontes and Hermione, King and Queen of Sicily, have as their guest Polixenes, King of Bohemia. Leontes urges his friend to stay longer but Polixenes only yields when Hermione further entreats him – and Leontes begins to suffer an uncontrollable jealousy. He tries to have Polixenes poisoned but the nobleman ordered to carry out the crime, Camillo, will not do it. He warns Polixenes and they escape to Bohemia. Leontes' rage is then turned on Hermione, who is with child. He disregards the Oracle's pronouncement that she is innocent and throws her into prison, where she gives birth to a daughter.

Paulina, wife of a nobleman named Antigonus, tries to move Leontes by bringing him the child but he orders Antigonus to abandon the baby somewhere and leave it to die. His son, Mamillius, dies of grief at his mother's treatment. Then news is brought that Hermione, too, is dead. Leontes is overcome with remorse and grief. In the meantime Antigonus has put the baby girl, Perdita, on the shore of Bohemia but is killed by a bear before he can get back to the ship. A shepherd finds the child and takes her into his home. After this scene Time, the chorus, announces the passing of 16 years.

Florizel, son of King Polixenes, has fallen in love with Perdita, the lovely shepherdess, and she with him. But the king will not allow his son to marry a lowborn girl and the two, with Perdita's fosterfather, accept the help of Camillo and flee to Sicily. Polixenes follows them. Camillo, longing for a sight of his homeland, has told of the young people's flight and goes with the king. At the court of Leontes the true identity of Perdita is discovered but her father's joy is clouded by his grief for the loss of Hermione. Paulina takes him to a chapel where she keeps, she says, a statue of Hermione. The statue is revealed as the living Hermione, who was hidden by Paulina to save her life and cherished by her all these years. There is no impediment to the marriage of Perdita and Florizel now, nor to the reunion of Leontes and Hermione. The two kings are reconciled and Paulina and Camillo, the loyal and steadfast friends, are recommended to one another by Leontes. Autolycus, the light-fingered pedlar, is a fine comic figure who adds some broad humour to the scenes in Bohemia.

This is indeed a tale for winter, for seats by the fire after the short day is over. A tale of romance that does not bear a searching examination – and is none the worse for that, since the greatest of all poets is telling it. Shakespeare was looking forward to the winter of his own life when he wrote *The Winter's Tale*; it was the last but one of his comedies. The young couple, prince and princess, exist in a radiant spring, and mature warmth and wisdom are embodied in the endearing, down-to-earth Paulina.

**Winthrop, Dolly**   In George Eliot's *Silas Marner*, the amiable and motherly wife of the village wheelwright. She puts all her native wisdom and kindness at Silas's disposal to help in the upbringing of Eppie, the orphan girl.

**Winthrop, John** *c*.1588–1649.   The first governor of the Massachusetts Bay Colony was born in England and educated at Cambridge. He was, as well as being a lawyer, the lord of the manor of Groton. He and other English Puritans obtained a charter from King Charles I in 1629 for a colonizing venture in the New World, the Massachusetts Bay Company. This became the Colony that was to be so important in the history of the United States. Winthrop's background went to New England with him, and he was soon in opposition to the freemen, who did not share his belief in the benevolence of the aristocratic theocracy that Winthrop and his colleagues wanted to maintain. He overreached himself eventually and was impeached in 1644. His eloquence saved him from prison. But out of the theocratic commonwealth in Massachusetts there grew a system of representation that was to have far-reaching effects.

In American literature Winthrop is remembered for his journal, a history of New England. The first part was published in 1790 and the complete *The History of New England 1630–1649* in

1826. His journal was begun on the *Arbella* during the voyage to America and continued until the year of his death. It is of great historical importance. *The Winthrop Papers*, a collection of his miscellaneous writings, was published by the Massachusetts Historical Society.

**Winthrop, Theodore** 1828–61.   Winthrop was born in Connecticut and graduated from Yale in 1848. He was a lawyer and briefly involved in business, but he had the means to travel extensively in Europe and on horseback over large areas of the USA and Panama. He wrote steadily during the years between 1848 and the Civil War – in which he was killed. His books were published after his death and included some novels and narratives of his journeys. *John Brent* (1862), a novel, is usually regarded as his best work. Other books are the novels *Cecil Dreeme* (1861) and *Edwin Brothertoft* (1862); *Life in the Open Air* (1863); and the travel book on the Northwest, *The Canoe and the Saddle* (1863).

***Wisdom of the Ancients, The***   See *Sapienta Veterum, De.*

**Wise, John** *c*.1652–1725.   The American theologian and democrat was born in Roxbury, Massachusetts, and educated at Harvard University. He became minister of the Second Church of Ipswich, and stayed with it until he died in spite of his two periods as a military chaplain and a short period in prison in 1687. He was a strong advocate of the independent churches and directly opposed to the Mathers, who wanted centralization. In support of his case he published *The Churches Quarrel Espoused* (1710), a pamphlet that struck a responsive chord in his democratically minded contemporaries. It was issued again with equal success in 1772. His *A Vindication of the Government of New England Churches* (1717) influenced the men who drew up the Declaration of Independence.

John Wise was imprisoned and deprived of his ministry in 1687, when he led his fellow townsmen in a refusal to pay taxes that disregarded their charter rights. In 1721 he published *A Word of Comfort to a Melancholy Country*, which contains the arresting (for the time) idea that paper money should be used. The prose of Wise's brief contributions to American letters is highly regarded and expresses the ideas of a warm and humorous man.

***Wish House, The***   A story by Rudyard Kipling, included in the collection entitled *Debits and Credits* (1926). Mrs Ashcroft is receiving a call from her friend, Mrs Fettley, and from their conversation it emerges that Mrs Ashcroft's bad leg, which will not heal and which proves to be cancerous, is the result of her taking upon herself the ills of another. She had heard of a means of doing so by stating her wish through the letter box of an untenanted house. She has taken away the ills of a man she loved in this fashion and she will die of the voluntary wound.

**Wister, Owen** 1860–1938. Born in Pennsylvania and educated at Harvard, Wister graduated in 1882 and made several journeys to the West. The inspiration for his fiction came from the cattle country of Wyoming and his first book of short stories, *Lin McLean*, was published in 1898. *The Jimmyjohn Boss* followed in 1900 and Wister scored a major success in 1902 with ***The Virginian***.

Wister was a grandson of the actress Fanny Kemble and a friend and admirer of Theodore Roosevelt, to whom *The Virginian* is dedicated. *Roosevelt: The Story of a Friendship* was published in 1930. Wister was an industrious writer and produced further stories of the West, two novels, poems, nature studies, humorous sketches, and biographies of Grant and Washington.

***Witchcraft, The Discouerie of*** See **Scot, Reginald**.

***Witch of Edmonton, The*** The title page of the first publication of this play in 1658 reads 'a known true story composed into a tragi-comedy by divers well-esteemed poets: William Rowley, Thomas Dekker, John Ford, etc.'. It was first performed about 1623 and was successfully revived in 1982.

The play suffers from two plots that do not really fit together. The witch of the title is a poor and lonely old woman, Elizabeth Sawyer, persecuted by her neighbours until, in desperation, she makes a pact with the Devil and becomes the witch who can exact retribution for their thoughtless spite. The hand of Dekker is clearly discerned in these scenes, for they show his sympathy for the ill-used. The other part of the play is chiefly Ford's; it is a domestic tragedy of crime and punishment. Frank Thorney secretly marries the servant, Winifred, against his father's wishes. Then his father orders him to marry a girl chosen for him, Susan Carter. Frank's inheritance depends on this, so he marries Susan and then murders her, having planned to throw the guilt on her two rejected suitors. But the truth is discovered and Frank is executed for the murder.

***Witch of Fife, The*** See ***Queen's Wake, The***.

**Wither, George** 1588–1667. Wither was born at Brentworth in Hampshire and educated at Magdalen College, Oxford. His reputation as a poet became inflated because he was imprisoned once in the Marshalsea and once in Newgate for the offence imagined by the authorities in his satirical verse – and because he was the subject of an essay by Charles Lamb. *Abuses Stript and Whipt: or Satyricall Essays* (1613) got him into the Marshalsea. While there he wrote a book of five pastorals called *The Shepherd's Hunting* (1615) and contributed seven eclogues to William Browne's *The Shepherd's Pipe*. *Fidelia* (1617) is in the form of a letter from a faithful nymph to her inconstant lover. *Wither's Motto* (1621) got him into Newgate. *Faire-Virtue* (1622), a hymn of praise to his half-imagined mistress Arete, and *Juvenilia* (1622), a book of love and pastoral poems, are regarded as his best works.

Wither became a convinced Puritan and during the Civil War attained the rank of major-general. As a Puritan he inclined in his later career to didactic verse and *The Hymnes and Songs of the Church* (1624), *Britains Remembrancer* (1628), and *Heleluiah or Britains Second Remembrancer* (1641) obscured his claim to attention as a pastoral poet of real charm. His best poems were edited by F. Sidgwick and published in two volumes in 1902.

***Without Benefit of Clergy*** A story by Rudyard Kipling, included in the volume entitled *Life's Handicap* (1891). John Holden takes a native mistress, Ameera, who bears him a son. They are devoted to each other and their child but tragedy overtakes them when the boy dies. When cholera breaks out in the district Ameera, who despises the English women, will not follow their example and go away. Holden loses her in the epidemic, and then he is called away to another district, a chapter of his life closed. The story gives a vivid picture of the strange divided life that Holden leads as a result of his liaison. He is devoted to Ameera, and she emerges as a striking and resolute figure, totally committed to the man who originally had bought her 'as though I had been a Lucknow dancing-girl, instead of a child'.

***With the Procession*** See **Fuller, Henry Blake**.

***With Walt Whitman in Camden*** See **Traubel, Horace Logo** and **Whitman, Walt**.

***Wives and Daughters*** Elizabeth Gaskell's last novel, which was not quite complete when she died in 1865. It was first published in the *Cornhill Magazine* (August 1864 to January 1866) and in volume form in 1866. The last number was completed by Frederick Greenwood.

Mr Gibson, the doctor of Hollingford, is a hardworking man, a widower who lives in simple content with his daughter Molly. However, he is fully aware that Molly is growing up and he remarries. The new Mrs Gibson, Clare Fitzpatrick, is a widow and a governess in Lord Cumnor's household. She is superficially attractive but proves to be shallow and stupid. Molly does her best, for her father's sake, to remain on amiable terms with her. Her life is brightened by the arrival of Cynthia, her step-sister, a vivacious and witty girl who has the measure of her parent and who becomes fond of Molly. Cynthia has compromised herself with Preston, Lord Cumnor's agent, and she is trying to escape from that commitment.

Cynthia inevitably attracts the attention of the Hamleys, the family of the squire, who have always been fond of Molly. Squire Hamley has great hopes of his brilliant son, Osborne; but it is the younger son, Roger, who proves to be the better man.

Molly falls in love with Roger, but Roger falls in love with Cynthia. Cynthia, in spite of her commitment to Preston, accepts Roger though she does not love him. But Cynthia eventually realizes how selfish her behaviour is and, when Molly helps her free herself from Preston, marries someone who is better suited to her than the cool and steady Roger. The novel finishes there, with every promise that all will end well for Molly and Roger Hamley.

*Wives and Daughters* has been called – by Laurence Lerner – the most underrated novel in the English language and it is easy to agree with him. Starting from the same base as the more famous *Cranford*, Elizabeth Gaskell can here be seen to have fully developed her art. Hollingford is the same place as Cranford – her beloved Knutsford – but the author's mastery of character and observation is, in this last work, complete. It is very sad that Elizabeth Gaskell did not live to write more in this vein of delicious irony.

**Wix, Mrs** In *What Maisie Knew*, by Henry James, the very proper governess who becomes Maisie's devoted friend and protector.

**Wodehouse, P(elham) G(renville)** 1881–1975. P. G. Wodehouse was born in Guildford, Surrey, and educated at Dulwich College. He worked as a bank clerk but was successful enough with freelance journalism to make writing his career in 1903. His school stories were serialized in *The Captain*, a magazine for boys, and one of his famous later characters, Psmith, first appeared in them. He published a dozen novels and books of stories before introducing his best-known character in a book of stories called *My Man Jeeves* (1919). He went on to publish 65 more novels and books of short stories

which have enjoyed a steady popularity in Britain and the USA. His characters – Bertie Wooster, Jeeves, Psmith, Aunt Agatha, and the rest – exist in a comfortable world, occupied usually by privileged people and those who stop them from making complete asses of themselves. Wodehouse struck gold and his touch never faltered. His work is as light as a soufflé and gives pleasure to countless readers. Parallel with his career in fiction was an equally successful one in the theatre, usually in adaptions of his own novels in collaboration with Ian Hay and, in musical comedy, with Guy Bolton.

**Wolcot, John** 1738–1819. Wolcot was born at Dodbrooke, near Kingsbridge in Devon. He studied medicine in London and at Aberdeen University, where he took his MD in 1767. In the same year he became physician to Sir William Trelawny, Governor of Jamaica. After two years Wolcot took holy orders, and returned to Cornwall to practise medicine. There he became the patron of John Opie, the painter. Wolcot abandoned medicine in 1778 and went to London with his protégé, with whom he eventually quarrelled. Wolcot's own career in London was as a satirist with the pseudonym Peter Pindar, beginning with 'Lyric Odes to the Royal Academicians' (1782–85) in *The Monthly Review*. *The Lousiad* (1785) has the royal family as a target, *Ode upon Ode* (1787) the yearly official odes to the king. The targets of *Bozzy and Piozzi* (1786) are obvious. James Bruce (the explorer of Abyssinia), William Pitt, and Edmund Burke were also fair game. Wolcot's verse was collected in 1812.

**Wolfe, Charles** 1791–1823. Wolfe, an Ulsterman, was educated at Trinity College, Dublin. He became curate of Donoughmore in County Down (1818–21) and died of consumption at the age of 32. He is remembered for his poem 'The Burial of Sir John Moore after Corunna', which was inspired by Southey's account for *The Annual Register*. *Remains of the Late Rev Charles Wolfe* was edited by J. A. Russell (two volumes, 1825) but Wolfe is known only by the single piece that generations of English schoolchildren have been obliged to memorize.

**Wolfe, Thomas (Clayton)** 1900–38. The son of a stonecutter, Thomas Wolfe was born in Asheville, North Carolina, where his mother ran a boarding house. He graduated from the University of North Carolina in 1920, and developed his interest in the theatre at Harvard, where he received his MA in 1922. After two years in Europe he taught English at New York

University from 1924 to 1930 but after the publication of *Look Homeward, Angel* (1929) decided to become a full-time writer.

Wolfe's first work had been for the theatre and he had also acted in one of his own plays, *The Return of Buck Gavin* (1924). *Welcome to Our City* (1923) was the first work to use his home town as a background. Asheville became Altamont, and in *Look Homeward, Angel* the author became Eugene Gant. He wrote one other play, *Mannerhouse* (1926), while teaching in New York.

*Look Homeward, Angel* made Wolfe famous though the critics were divided. An autobiographical novel of great length, it was shaped from an even longer book with the help of Maxwell Perkins, Wolfe's editor at Scribners who also guided him through his next. Eugene Gant (Wolfe) is the youngest of the six children of a stonecutter of Altamont, a passionate man with a love of craftsmanship and rhetoric, at odds with his cunning and avaricious wife. Eliza Gant leaves her husband and opens a boarding house, and the book tells, in a torrent of words, how Eugene grows up, acquires a love of literature, enters the state university, and finally breaks with his family to seek his own life. It is a book of extraordinary vitality and brilliant characterization. The title is from Milton's *Lycidas*.

*Of Time and the River* (1935) was Wolfe's second novel and the last one he worked on with Maxwell Perkins. It continues the story of Eugene Gant, now at Harvard, and ends during a tour of Europe when a complicated roundabout of emotion involves Elinor with Eugene, Eugene with Ann, and Ann with Eugene's friend Francis Starwick, whom Eugene discovers is homosexual. It is another enormous book, over 900 pages in the first edition. Wolfe broke with Maxwell Perkins after his second novel and his new editor was Edward C. Aswell of Harper & Brothers. Wolfe died in 1938 after two operations for a brain infection following pneumonia, and left a mass of material. From this Aswell edited *The Web and the Rock* (1939), in which George Webber (Wolfe) arrives in New York from Old Catawba (North Carolina), has a harrowing love affair with Esther Jack (Aline Bernstein), and recovers from it in Germany; and *You Can't Go Home Again* (1940), in which George is back in the USA and a successful novelist, but disillusioned by the shoddy morality and the events in Germany.

Other works by Thomas Wolfe are the short stories *From Death to Morning* (1935) and *The Story of a Novel* (1936), a critical examination of his own work. The interest of Thomas Wolfe's fiction lies in his talent for powerful emotional evocation which gives a gripping quality to scene after scene. But too much of the time Wolfe seems infatuated with his talent for pouring out words and, more seriously, with himself as a representative figure.

**Wollstonecraft, Mary** 1759–97. Mary Wollstonecraft was born in Spitalfields, London. Her father inherited a fortune and quickly spent it in a variety of dissipations. Mary fled her home in 1780 and earned her living with the school at Newington Green in north London which she opened with her sister, Eliza, in 1783. She then became a governess in Lady Kingsborough's household but this came to an end when the children of the house became fond of her and Lady Kingsborough discharged her. While employed as a reader and translator for a London publisher, Mary became interested in politics and was a member of a group which included Thomas Paine, Henry Fuseli, Joseph Priestley, and William Godwin. In Paris (1793) Mary embarked on a liaison with Gilbert Imlay, an American, who deserted her in 1795, leaving her with a daughter, Fanny. Mary tried to commit suicide when she returned to London. After that William Godwin looked after her, the attachment developed, and, in spite of their support for the principle of personal freedom, they married in 1797 to safeguard the interests of their children. Before the end of that year Mary died giving birth to a daughter (Mary Wollstonecraft Godwin became Shelley's second wife).

Mary and Godwin were both rebels against society as it was ordered in their day (see **Godwin, William**) and that demanded rather more courage from a woman than it did from a man. It was tragic that Mary died at the age of 38, having reached some sort of personal emotional security and just when her powers looked like developing. Her published work is interesting for its revelation of how an intelligent woman gradually came to a new way of thought at a time in history when change was in the air. Her most successful essay was *A Vindication of the Rights of Woman* (1792). Others were *Thoughts on the Education of Daughters* (1787) and *A Vindication of the Rights of Men in a Letter to Edmund Burke* (1790).

**Wolsey, The Life and Death of Cardinal** See **Cavendish, George**.

**Woman in White, The** A novel by Wilkie Collins, first published in *All the Year Round* (November 1859 to July 1860).

A woman in white accosts Walter Hartright at night on a road in Hampstead, asking for the way to London. Her manner is strange and uncertain and he feels that she is not completely rational. She persuades a cab driver, returning there with his tired horse, to take her to London. Hartright, shortly after, goes to Cumberland as drawing master in the Fairlie household to teach Laura Fairlie and her half-sister, Marian Halcombe. Fairlie is Laura's uncle and a selfish hypochondriac. Laura bears a striking resemblance to the woman in white who accosted Hartright on the Hampstead road, and he falls in love with her. She has, however, promised her father, on his death-bed, that she will marry Sir Percival Glyde of Blackwater Park. Hartright, in despair, goes abroad to try and forget her.

Laura is married to Glyde. He is principally interested in her fortune – his affairs are in a dangerous mess. He also has a guilty secret that Anne Catherick and her mother could reveal. Anne Catherick is the woman in white, and, to keep the seal on his secret, Glyde has managed to have her confined in an asylum. He is pressing Laura to surrender her fortune to him and though she is resisting, Marian is more and more concerned for her. Glyde enlists the help of Count Fosco, a fat villain who has something to fear on his own behalf.

Glyde and Fosco succeed in getting Laura committed to an asylum, as Anne Catherick. Anne dies and the two villains have her buried as Lady Glyde. But they have reckoned without the

---

Title page illustration for an edition of *The Woman in White* published in 1861. Marian and Laura, left; Sir Percival Glyde and Count Fosco, right. Collins' novel was first published as a serial in 1860.

courageous and resourceful Marian, who does not rest until she exposes them and rescues Laura. Then Hartright comes back to England and the two girls are able to rely on his protection. It is Hartright who uncovers the secret of Glyde: he is illegitimate and has no right to his title. Glyde tries to save his position by tampering with parish registers but in trying to burn documents he burns to death himself in the fire. Fosco is then forced to confess his part in events and is later murdered by former associates whom he has betrayed. Laura is restored to her position and she and Hartright marry.

The narrative moves from character to character, to journals and letters, and is admirably sustained. The evil Fosco is well drawn and Marian is an excellent heroine, resolute and self-possessed.

**Woman Killed with Kindness, A** A domestic drama by Thomas Heywood, first produced about 1603 and first published in 1607. It is really made up of two stories, but the one that inevitably becomes known as the subplot is as thought-provoking as the main plot in what is regarded as Heywood's best play. It makes the play difficult to present in the modern theatre since the main plot is that of the title. However, a notable production was in the repertory of England's National Theatre during the 1960s.

Anne, sister of Sir Francis Acton, marries John Frankford and one of the guests at the wedding, Sir Charles Mountford, remarks to his sister, Susan, that she has the mark of a perfect wife already. Mountford and Acton quarrel during a hawking contest and fighting breaks out, during which Mountford kills two of Acton's retainers. Meanwhile, Frankford and Mistress Anne welcome a guest, Wendoll, to their home. Mountford is tried for murder. He is acquitted but the trial has ruined him and he is imprisoned for debt. But Acton has fallen in love with Susan; so he secretly pays her brother's debts and secures his release. Wendoll, attracted to Mistress Anne, sets out to seduce her. Frankford's suspicions have been aroused by his servant Nick – and then confirmed. He finds Anne in Wendoll's arms. Mountford discovers how much he owes to Acton's kindness. Humiliated, he offers Acton his sister, having nothing else. Susan would prefer death to such an arrangement. Frankford banishes Mistress Anne to a lonely house where she is provided for. She is barred from seeing him or her children ever again. Acton asks for Susan's hand; and he and Mountford are reconciled. Acton's sister Anne, meanwhile, exists in the lonely house where she wants for nothing but where remorse, and humiliation at her husband's restraint, destroy her. She refuses food and is soon on her deathbed. Frankford responds to her last call and she dies with his forgiveness.

There are no fireworks in Heywood's play. His characters are simply not the sort of people who thunder their grief and rages across the auditorium. But the drama is consistent with the circumstances and the tension is maintained. John Frankford's continuing grief at the loss of his domestic peace is portrayed with remarkable conviction.

**Woman who Rode Away, The** The title story in a collection by D. H. Lawrence, first published in 1928. The woman is not named. She is married to a Dutchman and lives at a semiderelict mine in a remote part of Mexico. She sees nothing but barrenness and decay in her existence, and hears of Indians in a remote valley who practise ancient religions and are in tune with ancient mysteries. She goes to them, to seek the god of the Indians in place of her own. She is accepted by them and ceases to have a will of her own, succumbing entirely to the Indians' vision. They have accepted her as a sacrifice, and she acquiesces in her own annihilation.

**Women Beware Women** A tragedy by Thomas Middleton, first produced about 1621 and published in 1657.

Bianca, daughter of a noble house, is enamoured of Leantio, a merchant's clerk. He persuades her to marry him and they live in his mother's house. Their relationship, however, is based on physical passion and Bianca becomes discontented. Leantio has to leave her alone in the interests of his work and their modest home is in contrast to the luxury to which she is used. The Duke of Florence sees Bianca at her window and wants her.

Hippolito is in love with his niece, Isabella. His cynical amoral sister, Livia, convinces Isabella, who is very much in love with Hippolito, that they are not related. Isabella can indulge her passion for Hippolito – but it might be wise to marry the rich young fool who seeks her hand, thus acquiring respectable cover.

Livia happily furthers the duke's designs on Bianca. In a notorious scene she plays chess with Leantio's mother while the seduction proceeds on the floor above. Bianca becomes the duke's mistress. However, his brother, the cardinal, upbraids him for his adultery; so the duke decides that it would be more suitable to have Leantio murdered – then he can marry Bianca. Circumstance places the means in his hand: he is able to inform Hippolito that his sister, Livia, is making

love with a vulgar merchant – none other than Leantio. Leantio is murdered and the furious Livia, in revenge, denounces her brother's incestuous passion for his niece. The different characters plot vengeance on one another and at a masque a multitude of devices, such as lethal incense, poisoned arrows, fatal trapdoors, and tainted gold, put paid to a number of characters.

The play is called a tragedy but it might well be called a black farce, were it not for the quality of the blank-verse dialogue and the fine character drawing of an assortment of consistently worthless and depraved people, who know perfectly well that the moral slime in which they cavort is what they have chosen. The standards that they have deserted – if indeed they ever adhered to them – are part of their background, as their utterances demonstrate, and the cardinal is a positive reminder of them. It is a measure of Middleton's genius that the characters are believable right up to the climax, when the various revenges, unloosed by Livia's denunciation of her brother, run amok. It is almost as if Middleton, having created a gang of monsters, grew tired of them and, tongue in cheek, destroyed them.

**Women in Love** A novel by D. H. Lawrence, first published in 1920. (See also **The Rainbow**, at the end of which Ursula Brangwen has lost a prospective husband and failed to get her degree.) In *Women in Love* Ursula is found several years later teaching at a grammar school. Her sister, Gudrun, teaches art in the same school, and has some talent for carving and modelling.

Ursula and Gudrun live at home. They are bored with domesticity of any kind and looking for adventure. At a wedding Gudrun is arrested by the looks of Gerald Crich, son of a mine-owner and brother of the bride. Through Hermione Roddice, a baronet's daughter, Ursula meets Rupert Birkin, a school inspector and Hermione's lover. Gerald Crich's father had run his mine with benevolent principles. He is dying slowly and Gerald introduces a new regime, harsher but much more profitable.

Ursula falls in love with Rupert, and Gudrun and Gerald feel a growing attraction to each other. Rupert and Gerald are drawn to each other and do not know why. Rupert breaks away from the possessive Hermione, who has meanwhile taken up the Brangwen sisters – thus furthering the social context in which the principals come and go. Gudrun and Gerald's relationship really begins when she strikes him, and the destructive nature of their liaison is thus presaged. Rupert and Ursula do not have an easy passage, for that matter, in finding their way to each other and, after a quarrel, Rupert feels the need for a close relationship with Gerald. Gerald derives pleasure from Rupert's wanting his love but he is shy and uncomprehending and Rupert perceives that Gerald is limited by his responses: those of a man who thinks himself complete and yet can say that he has never been in love. Rupert marries Ursula, and Gerald and Gudrun cohabit. All four troop off to an Alpine valley in Austria.

Gudrun finds that Gerald combines a physical passion for her with the habit of easy promiscuity to which his previous experience is confined. She is determined to dominate him, though Ursula, who has learned something from her own experience, warns her that possession is not enough. Gerald finds himself taunted by Gudrun at every turn for his inadequacy as anything but a physical lover. Ursula and Rupert have left for Verona. Rupert had made a last appeal to Gerald and been rejected. Gudrun now has Gerald where she wants him because she does not love him. She turns her attentions to Loerke, a German sculptor, and this pitches Gerald into despair. He walks off into the snow and dies.

It is Rupert who feels Gerald's death most keenly. He tries to explain to Ursula that he needed Gerald to complete his own idea of life and love, and his conviction that his love would have saved Gerald. Ursula cannot accept that two kinds of love are possible, or necessary in the way that Rupert asserts. The novel ends upon an open question.

**Wonderfull Yeare, The:** *Wherein is Shewed the Picture of London Lying Sicke of the Plague.* A pamphlet by Thomas Dekker, first published in 1603. It gives an unsparing and memorable picture of London in the grip of one of the outbreaks of plague that frequently attacked the city. It contains vivid anecdotes of the lives of ordinary people in harrowing circumstances and reproaches those people of means who could afford to flee the city – thereby carrying the pestilence into the country.

**Wood, Anthony à** 1632–95. Anthony Wood (he added the 'à' himself, in later life) was born in a house that stood opposite the gate of Merton College, Oxford; he died there, too. He was educated at New College School, Oxford, Thame School, and Merton College, Oxford. He wanted a fellowship but was never granted one – it is believed that the reason was that he was a man of difficult character. Sir William Dugdale's *The Antiquities of Warwickshire* gave him the idea for a similar book on Oxfordshire and he spent a number of years collecting

material. The history of the county was never completed but, with the encouragement of Dr John Fell, Dean of Christ Church, Wood published a history of the university, in Latin: *Historia et Antiquitates Universitatis Oxoniensis* (1674).

Wood rewrote the work in English and enlarged it. It was edited for publication by John Gutch after Wood's death and titled *The History and Antiquities of the University of Oxford* (1792–96). From 1691 to 1692 Wood published *Athenae Oxoniensis*, a biographical dictionary of Oxford worthies, covering the years 1500 to 1690. The work also contained his personal judgments of these people. One of them was Clarendon, whose son Henry Hyde, the 2nd Earl, charged Wood with libelling his father. Wood was expelled from the university in 1693. His last years were embittered and he quarrelled with John Aubrey and other antiquaries. He left some original documents that were published posthumously: his autobiography and journal notes were published in five volumes as *The Life and Times of Anthony Wood* by A. Clark (1891–1900). An abridgment of the *Life and Times* by Llewelyn Powys (1932) was published in The World's Classics in 1961.

**Wood, Mrs Henry** 1814–87. The daughter of a manufacturer, Ellen Price was born at Worcester. A spinal disability was the cause of a secluded and studious early life. She married Henry Wood, a banker, and was able to live in southern France, where she embarked on a literary career. Her second published work was *East Lynne* (1861), which was a bestseller and made her famous. She published nearly 50 volumes of fiction and short stories, and in 1867 purchased the periodical *Argosy*, which she edited and contributed to. She returned to England in 1880 and died in London in 1887. The greater part of her work is forgotten now, but students of the Victorian novel will find rewards in *The Channings* (1862) and its sequel, *Roland Yorke* (1869).

**Woodfall, Henry Sampson** See **Junius** and *Public Advertiser, The.*

**Woodforde, James** 1740–1803. Parson Woodforde was born in Somerset, the second son of the rector of Ansford, and educated at Winchester College and New College, Oxford. During the course of his livings in Somerset and Norfolk he kept a diary, which was edited by John Beresford and published in five volumes (1924–31). The diary runs from 1758 to 1802 and gives a vivid picture of life as lived by a privileged person in holy orders in the 18th century. It seems to have been a remarkably comfortable life and Woodforde is at great pains to give details of what he ate and drank. Unpleasant moments did occur. The dismissal of an impudent servant provokes a nervous crisis and the poor parson is 'quite ill all Day' and needs a dose of rhubarb to restore him – he had 'vomited a good deal at Night'.

*The Diary of a Country Parson 1758–1802* was also published in an abridged edition by John Beresford in The World's Classics (1949) and in Oxford Paperbacks (1978).

**Woodlanders, The** A novel by Thomas Hardy, first published in *Macmillan's Magazine* (May 1886 to April 1887). The story is set in the wooded country near the Blackmoor Vale of Dorset.

Grace Melbury, daughter of a timber merchant, and Giles Winterbourne, an apple farmer and ciderman, are betrothed. Grace's father sends her to a fashionable finishing school and when she returns she sees Giles as a rustic. Giles has the misfortune to lose his orchard and then Melbury has little difficulty in persuading Grace to end the engagement. Giles is quietly worshipped by Marty South, a local girl, but she does not have enough confidence to move into the place left vacant by Grace.

Melbury hurries his daughter into marriage with a young doctor of extravagant charm, Edred Fitzpiers, though Grace had been inclined to baulk when she heard the doctor's name coupled with that of Suke Damson, a village girl. However, she marries him – and her uneasiness about his character is vindicated. When Fitzpiers goes off with Felice Charmond, Grace hopes for a divorce and is drawn to Giles again. But her husband comes back – with Mrs Charmond – and Grace seeks refuge with Giles, who is lying ill in his cottage. To observe the proprieties he gives Grace the cottage and moves into a shelter of hurdles where, weak as he is, he succumbs to exposure and dies within a few days. At first Grace and Marty mourn him together. Then Grace is reconciled to the worthless Fitzpiers and Marty mourns him alone.

Hardy presents us with neither hero nor heroine in this novel, which marks the attack on society which was to prove fiercest in *Jude the Obscure*. Evil results from the petty strivings for status among the country folk in this novel, linked with their unthinking acceptance of man-made moral laws as a condition of security. Fitzpiers is arrogant enough to flout them and wreak havoc with the emotions of Grace, who is bound to them so rigidly that she can watch a sick man court death to observe them on her behalf. Giles and Marty have no chance at all, and Grace's ultimate reconciliation is her acknowledgement of what is socially acceptable, even if it is morally base.

**Wood Magic** See **Jefferies, (John) Richard.**

**Woodstock: *or, the Cavalier. A Tale of the Year 1651*.** A novel by Sir Walter Scott, first published in 1826. It marks the beginning of Scott's unremitting labours to clear the huge debts which came as the result of improvident spending and his financial connection with James Ballantyne. Scott had also just suffered the loss of his wife.

Sir Henry Lee, the old Cavalier, is ranger at Woodstock, the royal lodge. His daughter Alice loves her cousin Everard, but Lee disdains him because Everard, as a soldier, serves Cromwell and has earned his favour. When Parliamentary commissioners come to seize Woodstock, however, Everard intervenes. They withdraw – but this is at Cromwell's orders. He knows Woodstock's royal connections and has it watched in the hope that Charles II, after his defeat at Worcester, will take refuge there.

Charles does arrive, as page to Albert, Alice's brother. He falls in love with Alice and this brings a clash with Everard, whereupon Charles reveals his identity. Everard gives his word not to betray Charles but Cromwell, informed of his presence, arrives with a force and surrounds the house. He orders the arrest of Everard. Albert Lee impersonates the king, giving him a chance to escape. The furious Cromwell orders the execution of Everard and the Lees, but later he relents and pardons them. The king has left a parting message with his loyal friends at Woodstock, and this reconciles Sir Henry and Everard, who is now able to marry Alice.

Scott anticipates Cromwell's supreme position – he did not become Lord Protector until 1653 – but he scores a familiar success with the host of characters on either side, such as the Rev Nehemia Holdenough, the Presbyterian minister, and the arch-Cavalier, Roger Wildrake.

**Woolf, Leonard Sidney** 1880–1969. Leonard Woolf was born in London and educated at St Paul's School and Trinity College, Cambridge. He entered the Ceylon Civil Service in 1904 and served until 1911. After returning to England he wrote for political journals and became active in the Fabian Society. He married Virginia Stephen in 1912 and published his first novel, about life in Ceylon, in the following year: *The Village in the Jungle* (1913). *The Wise Virgins* (1914) and *Stories of the East* (1916) were successful efforts in the same setting.

Leonard and Virginia Woolf founded the Hogarth Press in 1917. In the twenties and thirties they became the virtual centre of the literary activity known as the Bloomsbury Group. Leonard Woolf, meanwhile, confined his own writing to books on politics and international affairs, among them *Economic Imperialism* (1920), *Imperialism and Civilization* (1928), *Barbarians at the Gate* (1939), and *Principia Politica* (1953). Highly regarded for their quality and for the information they contain about notable figures are Leonard Woolf's volumes of autobiography: *Sowing* (1960), *Growing* (1961), *Beginning Again* (1964), *Downhill all the Way* (1967), and *The Journey not the Arrival Matters* (published posthumously, 1969).

**Woolf, (Adeline) Virginia** 1882–1941. The daughter of Sir Leslie Stephen, Virginia was the third child and was born at Hyde Park Gate, London. At the age of 13 she suffered a breakdown upon her mother's death. She had been very close to her mother, who had kept the household in order to relieve all possible strain on her father who was labouring all hours of the day on *The Dictionary of National Biography*. Julia Stephen's death threw the house into disorder and Virginia's breakdown was the result. The shadow of instability came like a cloud at different stages of

Virginia Woolf at the age of twenty. Photograph by G. C. Beresford.

her career. Sir Leslie Stephen died in 1904 and the shadow appeared again, but in December of that year her first published work, an unsigned review, appeared in the *Manchester Guardian*. She moved into 46 Gordon Square, Bloomsbury, with her brother Thoby, who had been at Cambridge with Lytton Strachey, Clive Bell, and Leonard Woolf. Eventually the other Stephens, Vanessa and Adrian, moved into the house and Thoby organized the Thursday evening salons. Thoby Stephen died in 1906 of typhoid after a holiday in Greece. Virginia and Adrian moved to Fitzroy Square and Vanessa married Clive Bell and lived at the Gordon Square house. The Thursday evening salon was continued by Virginia and Adrian at their new address: the Bloomsbury Group had come into being. By this time Virginia was writing reviews for *The Times Literary Supplement* and other journals and she had begun work on a novel. She had been engaged briefly to Lytton Strachey in 1909. She married Leonard Woolf in 1912, and completed her novel in 1913. It was published as *The Voyage Out* in 1915.

Virginia Woolf's lapses of sanity were not cured by marriage or literary activity but it is difficult to imagine how she might have fared without the unfailing care and attention of her husband and friends. Leonard and Virginia bought a hand press and taught themselves typesetting. The therapeutic value was obvious and this was the beginning of The Hogarth Press – they published from their home at Richmond, Hogarth House. Their first publication was two stories: 'The Mark on the Wall' by Virginia Woolf and 'Three Jews' by Leonard Woolf. Later they published Katherine Mansfield, T. S. Eliot (including *The Waste Land*), Maxim Gorky, and E. M. Forster.

Virginia's career as a writer continued with *Night and Day* (1919), the stories collected in *Monday or Tuesday* (1921), *Jacob's Room* (1922), and *Mrs Dalloway* (1925). In the last two she reached the style and purpose in fiction she had laid down in her essay, *Modern Fiction* (1919): 'Life is not a series of gig-lamps symmetrically arranged; life is a luminous halo, a semitransparent envelope surrounding us from the beginning of consciousness to the end. Is it not the task of the novelist to convey this ... with as little mixture of the alien and external as possible?' Jacob's room in Bloomsbury is where Jacob Flanders, gone to World War I, is recalled by his friends. Their remembrances, captured in brief glimpses, and observations by acquaintances in different walks of life, characterize the subject of the novel. Mrs Dalloway, a fashionable woman, gives a party, and the hours required by this event and the preparation for it enable the author to show us life and character in motion, forming and re-forming from moment to moment. The main events concern the return of Peter Walsh, who has been in love with Mrs Dalloway, from India; the suicide of the shell-shocked Septimus; the arrival of Sir William Bradshaw, the specialist who had not, and by his very nature could not have, helped Septimus; and the arrival, uninvited, of Mrs Dalloway's friend Sally Seton, to whom the last word on Clarissa Dalloway is given. The responses of a number of characters to these events are the matter of the novel, which is also a brilliant evocation of fashionable London in the 1920s. The author extended her particular craft in *To the Lighthouse* (1927) and *The Waves* (1931), in which consciousness and response have increasing importance and story correspondingly less. Other novels were *The Years* (1937) and *Between the Acts* (posth. 1941).

*Orlando* (1928) is unlike any of her other novels and was her greatest commercial success. The full title is *Orlando: A Biography*, and the book is dedicated to the author's lover, Vita Sackville-West. It is in some senses an extended love letter, with the great house of the novel identifiable as Knole, the ancestral home of the Sackvilles in Kent. The novel begins with Orlando as a boy of 16 in the last years of the reign of Elizabeth I. In the reign of Charles II, after a night with the dancer Rosina Pepita, Orlando's sex changes and Lady Orlando continues, down through the centuries, until she drives back to her great house in Kent in her baby car, after shopping at Marshall & Snelgrove's. *Orlando* is brilliantly done, a treat of tart humour, wit, and observation. *Flush: A Biography* (1933) is the 'biography' of Elizabeth Barrett Browning's spaniel, and gives a dog's-eye view of the love affair of his mistress and Robert Browning. It is a warm and gentle book and, like *Orlando*, another expression of Virginia Woolf's manifold talents. *A Haunted House and Other Stories* (1943) and a children's story, *Nurse Lugton's Golden Thimble* (1966), complete the list of her fiction. She wrote one biography, *Roger Fry* (1940).

Virginia Woolf's critical essays, beginning with the publication of *Mr Bennett and Mrs Brown* (1924), have given her a high place in 20th-century letters – *The Common Reader* (1925, first series; 1932, second series), has acquired classic status. *The Collected Essays*, edited by Leonard Woolf, was published in four volumes, 1966–67. *A Writer's Diary: Being Extracts from the Diary of Virginia Woolf* (1956) was also edited by Leonard Woolf. Quentin Bell's *Virginia Woolf: A Biography* was published in 1972.

Her end was tragic. In January 1941 she felt herself slipping out of sanity and this time, with the Nazi horror apparently triumphing all over Europe, had no hope that she would ever fight her way back to mental stability. She filled her pockets with stones and drowned herself in the River Ouse near her home at Rodmell in Sussex.

**Woolson, Constance Fenimore** *c*.1840–94. Born in Claremont, New Hampshire, Constance Fenimore Woolson spent much of her youth in Ohio. A grandniece of James Fenimore Cooper, she also became a novelist, using her knowledge of the USA (she lived in widely different parts of it) as background material. *Castle Nowhere: Lake-Country Sketches* (1875) tells of the French settlers in the Great Lakes region. Her residence in Florida and the Carolinas gave rise to *Redman the Keeper: Southern Sketches* (1880), which contrasts the life of the Old South with the South during reconstruction.

Mrs Woolson also lived in Italy, which provides the background of *The Front Yard* (1895). She also wrote novels there, though they are set in America. *Anne* (1882) tells of a MacKinac Island girl in New York City. *For the Major* (1883) is the story of a North Carolina woman helping to preserve her husband's illusions about the South. In *East Angels* (1886) she uses Florida and tells a story of moral contrasts; and *Jupiter Lights* portrays two sisters-in-law in conflict, one representing the North and the other the South. Her last novel, *Horace Chase* (1894), was a domestic drama about a woman who despises her self-made husband but discovers, almost too late, his sterling character. *Dorothy, and Other Italian Stories* (1896), her last book, is on the theme of Americans in Europe, an idea explored by Hawthorne and later used to such excellent purpose by Henry James. James became a friend of Mrs Woolson's, representing her in his story *The Aspern Papers*.

**Worcester, Florence of** d. 1118. Florence of Worcester was a monk who attempted the first compilation in England of a universal history written in Latin, *Chronicon ex Chronicis*. The *Chronicon* is largely a compilation from other sources, principally the universal history of Marianus Scotus, an Irish monk who wrote at Mainz. The portion covering the years 1082–1118 is Florence's own work and the most valued for original information. Florence's history was continued to 1141 by John of Worcester, and to 1152 by Henry of Huntingdon. The monks of St Edmundsbury added more to the *Chronicon*, extending it to the end of the 13th century.

*Chronicon ex Chronicis* was edited by B. Thorpe (English Historical Society, 1848–49). It was translated by T. Forester (1854) and by T. Stevenson in *The Church Historians of England* (1853–56). *The Chronicle of Bury St Edmunds* [St Edmundsbury] *1212–1301* was edited and translated by Antonia Gransden (1964).

**Worde, Wynkyn de** There is no certainty about when de Worde was born or died (probably about 1534) but, since he was apprenticed to no less a man than William Caxton, it is known when he flourished. His name was Jan van Wynkyn and he came from Woerth in Alsace. He succeeded to Caxton's establishment when the master died. He moved it to London, to Fleet Street, in 1500 and opened a shop for his printed books in St Paul's Churchyard in 1509. Unlike his master, de Worde had no literary ambitions; he was however an efficient printer whose skills were much in demand.

***Words For Music Perhaps*** See **Yeats, William Butler**.

***Words upon the Window Pane*** See **Yeats, William Butler**.

**Wordsworth, Dorothy** 1771–1855. Dorothy Wordsworth was a year younger than her brother William and outlived him by five years (see **Wordsworth, William**). She wrote a 'narrative', called *George and Sarah Green* (edited by Ernest de Selincourt, 1936). *The Poetry of Dorothy Wordsworth* was edited from her journals by H. Eigerman (1940). But of the greatest interest is *The Journals of Dorothy Wordsworth*, for what it tells of the lives of the Wordsworths, Coleridge, and their contemporaries. *Recollections of a Tour made in Scotland AD 1803* was published in 1874. *The Letters of William and Dorothy Wordsworth* were edited by Ernest de Selincourt (1935–38).

**Wordsworth, William** 1770–1850. Wordsworth was the son of an attorney of Cockermouth in Cumberland. His mother was Anne Cookson, daughter of a mercer of Penrith, and the boy disliked the harsh atmosphere of his maternal grandparents' house. His mother died when William was eight years old and his father never fully recovered from her loss. William was sent to the grammar school at Hawkshead, beyond Ambleside – far enough away for the boy to be separated from his family. Here his companions were mostly the children of farmers. When William was 13 his father died. As steward to Sir James Lowther the elder Wordsworth left almost all his money in Lowther's hands, and the latter successfully resisted every effort to persuade

him to pay it back to the Wordsworth children.

There was just enough money available to keep the orphan William at Hawkshead. Holiday periods were spent at the cheerless house in Penrith, the atmosphere of which is vividly described by Dorothy Wordsworth in her letters to William at school. She and her other brothers, John and Christopher, had a wretched time there. William, at 17, went to St John's College, Cambridge – the limit to which his small patrimony extended. But Wordsworth found university life uncongenial, and his relations were perturbed about his indecision over the choice of a career. He left in 1791, with an ordinary BA degree, and went to London, embracing poverty and growing more and more estranged from his relations. His love of poetry and nature are demonstrated in the first two poems he published, in 1793: in 'An Evening Walk' and 'Descriptive Sketches' he uses the medium of one for the expression of the other.

Meanwhile, an experience of a different kind stirred him deeply. He had spent from November 1791 to December 1792 in France, chiefly at Orléans and Blois, at a time when the French, with infectious fervour, were proclaiming a new regime. His friendship with Michel Beaupuy helped make Wordsworth a determined revolutionary. Although his indignation against social iniquities remained, when the French Revolution became a rule of terror and defence turned into aggression, his ideas about enforced social reform changed. By the end of his life he had become a reactionary. But upon his return from France his feelings were powerful: 'Incidents on Salisbury Plain' dates from this period. His reaction to the excesses of the Revolution led him to examine human motives and the result was *The Borderers*, a tragedy, written in 1795–96.

Wordsworth's circumstances changed in 1795 when his friend Raisley Calvert died and left him £900. Wordsworth sent for Dorothy and they settled at Racedown in Dorset, sharing, besides their deep mutual affection, a common love of the countryside. William wrote 'The Ruined Cottage' in 1797 (it was later included in **The Excursion**). This near-perfect pastoral poem is rather harrowing and perhaps reflects his still unsettled state of mind. In that summer the Wordsworths moved to Alfoxden in north Somerset, close to Nether Stowey where Coleridge lived. The two poets had already met, and Coleridge had been generous in his praise of *The Borderers* and 'Salisbury Plain'. Now they could meet and converse daily and their association was to be the most important of Wordsworth's life.

Coleridge's range and depth fortunately did not overpower his friend: Wordsworth was unlikely to stumble into intellectual dilettantism, and made use of Coleridge's theories only when he found them significant. He planned his philosophical poem, *The Recluse*, in March 1798 and the first book was completed in 1800. His great design was never fulfilled but the stream that was to produce **The Prelude** and *The Excursion* had begun to flow. Of more immediate importance was the small volume of poems by Wordsworth and Coleridge called **Lyrical Ballads** (1798), which expressed in poetry those subjects most congenial to their particular gifts. Their purpose is best illustrated by two of these poems: 'The Ancient Mariner' and 'Lines Written above Tintern Abbey'. The volume did not arouse enthusiasm but Wordsworth had achieved a wonderful certainty: he already knew his destiny was to be a poet; now he discovered what sort of poet he was.

At the end of 1798 William and Dorothy went to Germany with Coleridge and wintered at Goslar, where William began *The Prelude* and wrote 'Lucy Gray', 'Ruth', 'Nutting', and the lines concerning another 'Lucy'. When the Wordsworths returned to England in 1799 they went to live at Grasmere, at Dove Cottage, where for some time Coleridge was their neighbour and a frequent visitor. An enlarged second edition of *Lyrical Ballads* (1800) contained, in its preface, Wordsworth's poetic principles. In 1802 he extended the essay in the appendix called *Poetic Diction*. Critical reaction was generally hostile; Wordsworth was unconcerned. **Michael**, the much admired pastoral poem, was written in 1800. William's marriage to Mary Hutchinson, of Penrith, took place in 1802. Mary was an entirely suitable wife for Wordsworth, her repose balancing Dorothy's impulsiveness and enthusiasms. She was not his first love. During the heady youthful days in France William had loved Annette Vallon, who had borne him a daughter, but that liaison left no mark on him or his work. The Wordsworths visited Scotland in 1801, Calais in 1802, and Scotland again in 1803, when Wordsworth and Scott began a long and cordial friendship.

In 1804 Bonaparte made himself emperor and Wordsworth lost all sympathy with the Revolution. From then on the principles of order grew more attractive. His married life was contented, but the loss of his brother, John, at sea in February 1805 came as a cruel blow. Meanwhile Coleridge became an increasing burden and his health deteriorated as he succumbed to drink and opium. The Wordsworths did their best for him until 1810, when he finally left the Lakes. He travelled with Basil Montagu, who repeated to him William's warnings about his condition. Coleridge, hurt and angry, took every opportunity to slander Wordsworth. Meanwhile, William completed his great 'Ode, Intimations of Immortality', and *The Prelude*. *The Excursion*, the sole part of *The Recluse* to be completed, was in progress; by now the poet was 36 years old. From this time his work changed. Grief entered his life with the death of John, an event that probably followed the completion of the 'Ode, To Duty' as though the poet had anticipated the demands life was about to make on him. William and Mary lost two of their five children in 1812.

Wordsworth's poetry became more what Keats described as 'poetry which has a palpable design upon us'. The reader may not feel preached at, exactly, but there is a constant sense of being argued into agreeing with the poet. An exception is *The White Doe of Rylstone* (1815), written about 1807, an imaginative work about the surviving daughter of a Catholic rebel family in the reign of Elizabeth I. In 1807 Wordsworth published some of his finest work in the *Poems in Two Volumes*, which contains the odes 'To Duty' and 'Intimations of Immortality', 'Miscellaneous Sonnets', and 'Sonnets Dedicated to Liberty'.

By 1813 Wordsworth's reputation was established and he was awarded the sinecure of Stamp Distributor of the county of Westmorland. The income was considerable (£400 a year) and enabled him to move his family to a more spacious house at Rydal Mount. Dove Cottage, inseparable from the Wordsworths in the minds of their admirers, was by this time too small for them. In the same year (1814) Wordsworth

Rydal Water in the Lake District. Wordsworth's home was nearby. A 19th-century engraving.

published *The Excursion* ('The Story of Margaret' in that book is 'The Ruined Cottage', composed in 1797), and 'Laodamia', about the mourning wife of Protesilaus, killed at Troy. 'Dion' (1816) and 'Ode to Lycoris' (1817) are also poems on classical subjects. *Peter Bell: a Tale in Verse* was composed in 1798 and published with some sonnets in 1819. *The Waggoner*, composed in 1805, was published with further sonnets in 1819. *The River Duddon* (1820) is a collection of sonnets, poems, and a number of short pieces. *Ecclesiastical Sonnets* (1822) was originally called *Ecclesiastical Sketches*. The volume of poems called *Memorials of a Tour on the Continent* (the poet travelled in Europe frequently) was also published in 1822. *Yarrow Revisited* (1835) and *Poems chiefly of Early and Late Years* (1842) were his last published books of verse. Wordsworth's published prose includes *The Convention of Cintra* (1809), an essay criticizing England's weakness in her relations with Spain and Portugal during Bonaparte's ascendancy, and *A Description of the Scenery of the Lakes in the North of England* (1810, enlarged 1822), an interesting contemporary account of the region and its people.

Wordsworth was famous and honoured enough by 1839 to be given a triumphant reception at Oxford, and a state pension was bestowed on him in 1842. He became poet laureate in succession to Robert Southey in 1843. *The Prelude*, in which so much of his best work is to be found, was published in 1850, not long after the poet's death at Rydal Mount in the same year.

Like all great poets who produced a large body of work, Wordsworth was capable of indifferent poetry, but the level of achievement throughout his creative years is very high. Reservations about the 'palpable design on us' are less important than the pleasure given by his verbal felicity and his skill in presenting man challenged by the natural world – the gift that marks this poet's particular genius. He discloses what we have often felt but could not express, and our knowledge of sensation is greatly enlarged. When he examines human feeling he applies the same skill, achieving a remarkable expression of emotions that often lie submerged.

The definitive edition of Wordsworth's poetry is that by Ernest de Selincourt and Helen Darbishire, *The Poetical Works* (five volumes, Oxford English Texts, 1952–58). *The Prelude* was edited from the original unrevised manuscripts by Ernest de Selincourt (1926) and revised by Helen Darbishire (1957). The standard one-volume collection is *Poetical Works*, edited by Thomas Hutchinson (Oxford Standard Authors, 1895), revised by Ernest de Selincourt (1936). The

Wordsworth. A detail from the portrait by Benjamin Robert Haydon, 1842. National Portrait Gallery, London.

collected prose works were edited by A. B. Grosart (1876) and W. Knight (1896). A later edition is that of W. J. B. Owen and Jane Worthington Smyser (Oxford English Texts, 1974).

See also **Wordsworth, Dorothy**.

**Worke For Armorours,** *or The Peace is Broken: Open Warres Likely to Happin This Yeare.* A pamphlet by Thomas Dekker, first published in 1609, in which contemporary life is seen as a perpetual conflict between two classes, one governed by Money and the other by Poverty. Dekker's compassion for the unfortunate and cruelly used – both men and beasts – is very marked in this serious tract, another of his remarkable word pictures of Jacobean London. The motto of it is, 'God helpe the Poore, The rich can shift'.

**Worldly Wiseman, Mr**  In John Bunyan's *The Pilgrim's Progress* Christian encounters him in the town of Carnal Policy after escaping from the Slough of Despond. He offers Christian many reasons for not continuing his pilgrimage.

**Wotton, Sir Henry** 1568–1639.  Wotton was a minor poet and a distinguished man of affairs. A Kentish man, Wotton was educated at Winchester

An illustration from *The Illustrated London News*, 18 December, 1875. *The Deutschland* in the Thames Estuary after the wreck of 7 December.

School and New and Queen's colleges, Oxford. After university he entered the Middle Temple and was engaged by the Earl of Essex as agent and secretary in 1595. Wotton collected foreign intelligence for Essex and was later appointed ambassador to the court of Venice. He was an active diplomat from 1604 to 1624, when he became Provost of Eton. The only work published during his lifetime was *The Elements of Architecture* (1624).

Wotton's poems and miscellaneous writings were collected and published 12 years after his death as *Reliquiae Wottonianae*. Among them were three poems that have become stock inclusions in anthologies of English verse: 'Elizabeth of Bohemia', 'The Character of a Happy Life', and 'Upon the Sudden Restraint of the Earl of Somerset'.

Wotton planned to write a life of his friend, John Donne, but the task devolved on their mutual friend, Izaak Walton, who wrote a memoir of Wotton for the *Reliquiae*. Wotton's definition of an ambassador is celebrated: 'An Ambassador is an honest man, sent to lie abroad for the good of his country' (Augsburg, 1604).

The standard account of Wotton's life and career is Logan Pearsall Smith's *Life and Letters* (1907). His poems can be found in J. Hannah's *Ralegh, Wotton and other Courtly Poets* (1892).

**Wrayburn, Eugene**  In Dickens's *Our Mutual Friend*, the young barrister in love with Lizzie Hexam. His shiftless attitude to life receives a sharp corrective in Bradley Headstone's murderous jealousy.

**Wreck of the Deutschland, The**  A poem in 35 stanzas by Gerard Manley Hopkins, completed in 1876 and his best-known work. The poem is dedicated to the memory of five Franciscan nuns who lost their lives when the *Deutschland* was wrecked in a storm in the Thames estuary. W. H. Gardner, in the introduction to the third edition of Hopkins' poems (1948), describes it as 'a total complex of style, in which the natural strong beat of the freer kinds of English verse is reinforced by alliteration, assonance, internal rhyme, and half-rhyme.'

**Wren, Jenny (*or* Fanny Cleaver)**  The busy, bossy little maker of dolls' dresses in Dickens's *Our Mutual Friend*.

**Wright, Judith Arundell** 1915– .  Judith Wright was born on the family sheep station near Armidale, New South Wales, and grew up there. She completed her education at Sydney University and published her first book of poems, *The Moving Image*, in 1946. She has published several collections and has a high reputation among modern Australian poets. Her *The Generations of Men* (1959) is a historical memoir which recalls her pioneering ancestors. She edited *A Book of Australian Verse* in 1956.

**Wright, Richard** 1908–60.  Richard Wright was born near Natchez, Mississippi, and grew up in that city. He educated himself and at the age of 15 was working at whatever job he could get in Memphis, Tennessee, and drifted north during the Depression, reaching Chicago in 1934. He joined the Communist Party in 1936, and that gave him the impulse to assert a Black man's identity in a White-dominated world. His first published work was a volume of uncompromisingly realistic short stories about the

Black man in the South called *Uncle Tom's Children* (1938, enlarged edition 1940), which won the *Story* magazine prize. In his first novel, *Native Son* (1940), he placed his central character in the North, in the slums of Chicago.

The native son is Bigger Thomas, a young Black tough with a criminal record. He becomes chauffeur to a rich family known for their sympathy and philanthropy towards Black people; but he finds himself involved in the world of the daughter and her sentimental left-wing friends at the university. Bigger kills the girl accidentally and in a panic destroys the body in the kitchen furnace. He sends the family a note saying the girl has been kidnapped and demands a ransom, implying that the communists, of whose existence he had been unaware the day before, are responsible. For a few brief hours Bigger enjoys a heady sense of power; but he is soon detected and, in a gripping action scene, captured. He is on the roof of a tenement and the police bring him down by using fire hoses. After a trial during which he is defended by a communist lawyer and the case of similar native sons are described to the court, he is found guilty and executed. Wright's novel slows down considerably in the trial scene, and the case has, after all, been stated in the author's powerful description of Bigger's world; but the novel marked a tremendous advance in Black literature in the USA.

Richard Wright.

Richard Wright's other novels are *The Outsider* (1953), *The Long Dream* (1958), and the posthumously published *Land Today* (1963), which was written before *Native Son*. Also published after his death was *Eight Men* (1961), a volume of short stories. In 1940 Wright left the USA to live in Mexico. He became disillusioned with communism and left the party in 1944. He went to France in 1946 and settled down in Paris, encouraged by Gertrude Stein, whose *Three Lives* had been an important influence on his decision to become a writer. His other books were *Twelve Million Black Voices* (1941), an illustrated folk history of the American Negro; his autobiography, *Black Boy* (1945); *Black Power* (1954), a critical report of a visit to Ghana; an even more critical account of Franco's regime, *Pagan Spain* (1957), and a collection of lectures on racial injustice, *White Man, Listen!* (1957). A dramatization of *Native Son* was made by the author and Paul Green in 1941 and achieved further success in the theatre.

**Wright, Thomas** 1810–77. Wright was born at Tenbury, Shropshire, and educated at King Edward's Grammar School, Ludlow, and Trinity College, Cambridge. He published four volumes of *Early English Poetry* (1836) and, with John Mason Neale, founded the Camden Society in 1839. His edition of Langland, *The Vision and Creed of Piers Plowman*, was published in 1840 and in the same year he helped to found the Percy Society. His principal works as a literary antiquarian were *Biographia Britannica Literaria of the Anglo-Saxon Period* (1842) and *Anecdota Literaria* (1844), which is a collection of short poems in English, Latin, and French illustrating the history and literature of the 13th century.

**Wulfstan** d. 1023. Wulfstan, Archbishop of York, is not to be confused with the later St Wulfstan, who with Lanfranc helped suppress the slave trade between England and Ireland. The archbishop was a writer, in vigorous and lively English, of uncompromising homilies. The most famous bears a Latin title, *Lupi Sermo ad Anglos*, and was delivered during the Danish persecution in the reign of Ethelred. In it he makes it plain that his listeners' sinful lives deserve severe punishment. Wulfstan was also the author of legal studies which had considerable influence.

Wulfstan's famous sermon was edited by Dorothy Whitelock (1939) and later translated by her into modern English (1955).

***Wuthering Heights*** Emily Brontë's only novel, first published in 1847.

Heathcliff, an orphaned Gypsy boy, is picked

up by the kind Mr Earnshaw in the streets of Liverpool. He takes the boy home to Wuthering Heights to bring him up as one of his own children with his son, Hindley, and his daughter, Catherine. He is contented there but when Earnshaw dies he is bullied and humiliated by Hindley, now head of the house. He worships Catherine, his wild and passionate nature arousing a response of the same kind in her. But she is also drawn to the life led by their neighbours, Edgar and Isabella Linton, and one night Heathcliff hears her say it would degrade her to marry him. Heathcliff leaves Wuthering Heights.

He returns three years later. He has prospered and Hindley, now married, a gambler and grown coarse, welcomes him. Heathcliff finds Catherine married to Edgar Linton and the vindictive side of his character is aroused. He accepts Hindley's invitation to live at Wuthering Heights, and cold-bloodedly marries the infatuated Isabella Linton, while tormenting Catherine – now pregnant with Edgar's child – with his brooding, relentless presence. Catherine dies in premature childbirth, bearing a daughter, Cathy. Isabella bears Heathcliff a son, Linton, before she dies in the misery of a marriage to a man to whom she means less than nothing. Heathcliff, having financial control over Hindley now, is cruel to Hareton, the latter's son, to remind Hindley how he was himself treated after Mr Earnshaw died. Heathcliff wants revenge on all the members of the Linton and Earnshaw families.

Twelve years later Heathcliff forces a marriage between Cathy and his own sickly, repellent son, Linton. Edgar Linton dies and Cathy, soon after, is made a widow by Linton's death. She finds herself drawn to the ill-treated, despised Hareton, and undertakes to educate him in spite of Heathcliff, whom she cannot escape since he is the master of Wuthering Heights. The latter's plans for the destruction of the two families are still apparently obsessing him but now his spirit begins to break. He finds his life is no more than an agony of waiting – he longs to die so that he can be reunited with Catherine. He turns his back on life, refuses food, and eventually dies in his rooms, the windows open to a storm. Cathy and Hareton are free and there is hope that they will find happiness.

Perhaps the most remarkable feature of this remarkable novel is the passion expressed in its pages. Yet Emily Brontë knew nothing of passion in a personal context, the passion of love which transfigures and destroys. That she was a woman of intense feeling is clear from her poems: her triumph in *Wuthering Heights* lies in her powerful imagination being brought to bear on a character – Heathcliff – and a world of feeling which has no parallel, as *Jane Eyre* has, in the lives of ordinary people. Moreover, the author's successful observation of the country folk – Joseph, Ellen, and the rest – throws the principals and their violent emotions into sharper relief. Once encountered, the world of Heathcliff, Catherine and the enormous skies of the moorland country is accepted completely: the emotional tie of Heathcliff and Catherine, which begins when they are children, retains its power because the author convinces us of its elemental force. The narration, too, shifting from character to character, is brilliantly managed. It is a novel unlike any other of its time – or for that matter of any time.

**Wyatt, Sir Thomas** 1503–42. Wyatt was born at Allington Castle, in Kent. He studied at St John's College, Cambridge, and was married at the age of 17. He was employed on diplomatic missions by Henry VIII in France and in Italy where he learned the craft of poetry. The influence is strongly marked in Wyatt's strict adherence to metre when his subject and form required it. Otherwise he wrote with a freedom and an 'irregularity' that suggests poetic experiment. His strength as a poet lies in his English inheritance, nevertheless; but the lessons he learned from the Italian masters, particularly the Petrarchan sonnet form which he was the first to use in England, reimposed order on English poetic expression and strengthened the force of Wyatt's intense and personal lyrics.

Wyatt's public career kept him out of England from 1528 to 1532, when he was Marshal of Calais. He returned in the year of Henry VIII's marriage to Anne Boleyn and became a justice of the peace in Essex. He was present at Anne's coronation in 1533. In 1534 Wyatt served a term in the Fleet prison for brawling and two years later was in prison again – Anne Boleyn had fallen and among those arrested was Wyatt, who had been her neighbour and admirer in Kent. His own marriage to Elizabeth Brooke was an unhappy one. However, charges were not pressed against him and by 1527 he was a knight, a sherriff of Kent, and on an embassy to Spain. He quarrelled with Bonner, his fellow envoy, on this mission and when his friend Thomas Cromwell fell from power in 1540 he had no defender at court. He served in further diplomatic missions but in 1541 Bonner, now Bishop of London, brought charges against him that included treason and Wyatt was imprisoned in the Tower for the second time. He defended himself successfully and was released on condition that he return to his wife. (One of Bonner's charges was that of immorality; Wyatt was living with Elizabeth Durrell, one of the queen's maids of honour.) He died in 1542 of a fever.

Wyatt's poetry, which was not published during his lifetime, first appears in 1549, in *Certayne Psalmes Chosen out of the Psalter of David and Drawen into Englyshe Meter commonly called the VII Penytentiall Psalmes*. These were from an Italian paraphrase by Aretino and may have been written upon the death of his friend Thomas Cromwell. His translation of *Plutarckes Boke of the Quyete of Mynde* was made during 1528, while on one of his embassies. His poetry was not properly seen until 1557, when Richard Tottel published *Songes and Sonettes, Written by the Ryhgt Honorable Lorde Henry Haward late Earle of Surrey, and Other*. The 'other' in the volume, which is usually called **Tottel's Miscellany**, included Heywood, Vaux, Grimald, Somerset – and Wyatt, who is represented by 97 poems.

John Skelton died in 1529, Wyatt only 13 years later, but the difference between the two is extraordinary – the difference of an age. Apart from the imposition of metre and form, Wyatt – in his songs, epigrams, satires, and devotional pieces – uses a direct form of address in the ordinary speech of his time. This gives his lyrics a remarkable emotional force.

A complete edition of Wyatt (*Collected Poems*) was edited by Kenneth Muir and P. Thomson in 1969.

**Wycherley, William** 1641–1716. Wycherley was born at Clive, near Shrewsbury. His family was of comfortable means, and he was sent to France when he was about 15 years old. While there he became a Catholic, and seems to have absorbed French literary influences during his education. He was back in England before the Restoration and for a short time studied at Queen's College, Oxford. From there he went to the Inner Temple to study law, and soon found his way into the society of the London wits, the group that included Buckingham and Rochester. However, he served with the fleet in 1664, though this was no more than the token service offered by fashionable young men in his day.

Wycherley's first play was *Love in a Wood, or St James's Park* (1671), an apprentice piece of manners and humours, retailing the grubby intrigues of a coarse-grained group whose only purpose is the satisfaction of their appetites. Their names indicate their natures, as did those of Jonson's characters in his comedies of humours. A single character, Vincent, is a still centre,

William Wycherley. A detail from the painting after Lely, c.1668. National Portrait Gallery, London.

observing and commenting on the goings-on. Wycherley described essentially the same world as did Etherege; but Wycherley displays his biting wit even at this early stage.

*The Gentleman Dancing-Master* (1672) followed and Wycherley showed that he had mastered his craft. More a farce than a comedy, its source lay in the Spanish *El Maestro de Danzar* of Pedro Calderón de la Barca and it owes much to Wycherley's experience of life in France. Three years later came *The Country Wife*, his most popular play and the one which has found most favour with modern audiences. Macaulay, missing the point, later condemned it as 'profligate and heartless', and it was off the stage for over a century until the Phoenix Society of London revived it in 1924. Wycherley's last play, *The Plain Dealer* (1676), came a year later. Based on Molière, it is considered his finest by many critics and earned generous praise from Dryden but is not as well-known as *The Country Wife*.

In 1679 Wycherley married the Countess of Drogheda, a wealthy widow. In so doing he earned the displeasure of Charles II, who had offered him the charge of his son, the Duke of Richmond, and a handsome salary. Wycherley chose unwisely for his wife died within two years, and having, apparently, been a difficult and jealous spouse, left him no fortune. Within months of her death Wycherley's debts overpowered him and he was sent to the Fleet Prison. He stayed there until the accession of James II when the new king, very impressed by a performance of *The Plain Dealer*, generously paid his debts and ordered his release. He also gave Wycherley a pension of £200 a year.

Soon afterwards Wycherley's father died and he came into possession of the Shropshire properties. He published his *Miscellany Poems* in 1704 and about that time found an admirer in the young Alexander Pope. Wycherley's poems, however, are of no great merit (Macaulay describes them as 'obscene doggerel') though his young disciple diligently revised and corrected the old man's efforts until his patience gave out.

Wycherley had been a handsome young man, and with his first play had attracted the attention of the Duchess of Cleveland, one of King Charles' mistresses, who became his lover. Charles did not take a serious view of such matters: indeed he found Wycherley attractive and accomplished and extended his favour until Wycherley offended him. The dramatist's later years were affected by his failing memory and sharp jealousy of his literary reputation, earned 30 years before. Unfortunately, Wycherley became a very unpleasant old man: at the age of 79, ten days before he died, he married a girl in her twenties in order to disinherit his own nephew.

The three plays on which Wycherley's reputation rests were written in a period of five years. James Sutherland describes him as a playwright who 'has a sort of love-hate relationship to the world in which he lives'. While his society 'was on the surface one of intelligence and vivacity and good manners, he knew that it rested upon a foundation of sham and hypocrisy'. Wycherley was a savage satirist of his own times, and a brilliantly successful writer of comedies.

The complete plays of William Wycherley were published in a modern edition by G. Weales (1966).

**Wycliffe, John** *c*.1329–84. The son of a manorial family of Wycliffe-on-Tees, John Wycliffe was educated at Oxford and became Master of Balliol about 1360. He spent much of his life at Oxford, though during his lifetime he was vicar of Fillingham (1361), of Ludgershall (1368), and of Lutterworth (1374), which he held until his death. His place in history is as a reformer and a precursor of the Reformation. In English literature he is remembered for his determination that there should be a complete Bible in the English language.

Wycliffe soon gained a reputation as a philosopher and became famous with two books (*De Dominio Divino* and *De Civili Dominio*), which directly challenged the authority of the church. He declared that 'lordship' depended on grace – that since the state of the church was sinful, lordship was forfeit and so disendowment and the confiscation of church property should follow. He also declared that every man in a state of grace had true lordship. This was the time of the Great Schism, when the papacy's prestige was at its lowest. Wycliffe's *De Potestate Papae* was an unequivocal attack on its claims, demonstrating that they were ill-founded in scripture and that the only measure of the pope's worth lay in the extent to which his deeds conformed to the Gospel. Wycliffe's conviction that the one criterion of belief was the Bible led to the first complete translation of the Bible into English. This he began himself. The great task was completed by two of his disciples, Nicholas of Hereford (d. *c*. 1420) and John Purvey (*c*.1353–*c*.1428), with the assistance of a number of scholars. The first version (*c*.1380), containing the Old Testament, was mostly by Nicholas; the New Testament is the work of an unknown scholar. The whole was revised, probably with Wycliffe's agreement, by John Purvey (1395– 1408). The translation was from the only text available, the Latin Vulgate. How much of the first version is the work of John Wycliffe is uncertain, but the inspiration was his and the consequences were far-reaching.

***Wynnere and Wastoure*** An alliterative poem of the time of Edward III. The date has been ascertained by two allusions, one to the 25th year of the king's reign and another to William de Shareshull as chief baron of the exchequer. The authorship is unknown but this poem and *The Parlement of the Thre Ages* are believed by some to be the work of the same man. Both poems employ the device of a dream or a vision. In this case it is a wandering minstrel who falls asleep in the bright sunlight by the banks of a stream. He sees two armies massed for battle, one led by Wynnere (Winner) and the other by Wastoure (Waster). The King arrives on the scene, forbids them to fight, and summons the two leaders to explain themselves. Each accuses the other of being the cause of distress in the kingdom. The end of the poem is missing so the author's conclusion to the debate is not known.

*Wynnere and Wastoure* and *The Parlement of the Thre Ages* were edited by Israel Gollancz for the Early English Text Society (1897).

**Wyntoun, Andrew of** d. *c*.1420. The author of a fanciful chronicle of the events of the world,

Andrew of Wyntoun was the head of St Serf's priory in Lochleven and later a canon regular of St Andrews.

*The Orygynale Cronykil* goes back to first things – it actually begins with the history of angels – and then proceeds to Wyntoun's own day by way of the Bible. It is regarded as historically worthless except for the portion dealing with Scotland from Macbeth and Malcolm Canmore to Robert the Bruce. This portion is prized by scholars, being one of the few existing sources of early Scottish history (a great deal of material disappeared during the struggle with the English). Among the more notable incidents related by Andrew of Wyntoun are Macbeth's meeting with the witches and how Birnam Wood did come to Dunsinane.

# Y

**Yeast,** *a Problem.* A novel by Charles Kingsley, first published in *Fraser's Magazine* (July to December 1848). In volume form it first appeared in 1851.

*Yeast* was Kingsley's first published novel and even less of a success, from a literary point of view, than *Alton Locke*. But it was forceful and provocative enough to lead many of the readers of *Fraser's Magazine*, in the late 1840s, to threaten to withdraw their subscriptions. The hero is the wealthy Lancelot Smith and the story – such as it is – relates his enlightenment. This comes from Tregarva, the gamekeeper, the worldly Colonel Bracebridge, the curate, Luke, about to step from the high church to Rome, the philanthropic millionaire, Barnakill, and Argemone, the girl he marries. Through Tregarva Lancelot learns of the dreadful condition of the land labourers – so depressed they will not even help themselves if it in any way helps their employers. In contrast are the viewpoints of Bracebridge and Luke, while Argemone is unsparing in her efforts on behalf of the poor – she dies of typhus which she contracts from visiting their wretched hovels. *Yeast* had a particular interest in its time for its attempts to understand the psychology of deprivation.

**Yeats, William Butler** 1865–1939. W. B. Yeats was the son of an artist, John Butler Yeats, and had another artist for a brother (Jack Yeats: see **Synge, John Millington**). The family was Protestant Irish and Yeats's mother belonged to a merchant family in Sligo, on the west coast of Ireland – an area of wild poetic beauty which Yeats knew well as a child. Yeats was born in Sandymount, a suburb of Dublin, and the family moved to London when he was nine years old. But the connection with Sligo was maintained and while Yeats was at school in London his holidays were spent there. John Butler Yeats encouraged his son's interest in poetry and literature chiefly through the English masters, but the Celtic inheritance was powerful and it was not long before Yeats responded to it. The family returned to Ireland in 1880 in connection with property owned in Kildare. They lived at Howth near Dublin, where Yeats continued his schooling and where he entered an art school in 1884. In the following year the poet and the enquirer after mystical experience came to the surface. Yeats had refused to study at Trinity College, which was what his father wanted. In March 1885 his first lyrics were published in *The Dublin University Review*. With some friends he founded the Dublin Hermetic Society 'to promote the study of Oriental Religions and Theosophy'. Yeats's preoccupation with mysticism and the occult was a lasting one, not just a young man's enthusiasm, and was a strong influence in his work. It was important also in his response to the newly resurgent Irish mythology which is the background for much of his poetry.

In 1886 Yeats published his first volume, the now little-known *Mosada: A Dramatic Poem*, first printed in *The Dublin University Review*. When the family went back to London in 1887 he contributed verse to collections by Irish poets, and edited and contributed to *Fairy and Folk Tales of the Irish Peasantry* (1888). His verse was published in English magazines. He became literary correspondent for two American newspapers, one in Boston and one in Providence, Rhode Island, and he became friends with William Morris (at whose house he met Shaw), W. E. Henley, and Oscar Wilde. Wilde entertained the young poet in the family circle at Chelsea and gave him good advice. Yeats remained grateful to Wilde and championed him in the latter's misfortunes.

*The Wanderings of Oisin and Other Poems* (1889) established Yeats as a poet. The title work offers an arresting narrative spoken by the Oisin of the Celtic era and heard, with stern disapproval, by the bringer of the new Christian age, St Patrick: 'You are still wrecked among heathen dreams.' The rest of the volume was made up of poems selected from the past four years' work, including the famous 'Down by the Salley Gardens', conjured from three lines Yeats heard sung by an old woman in Sligo. The volume was well reviewed by Wilde and Francis Thompson, and Yeats received personal praise from Morris and

Henley. He was one of the founder members of both the Rhymers' Club and the Irish Literary Society of London, but in spite of what looked like a successfully launched career Yeats was not happy in London. The famous 'The Lake Isle of Innisfree' was prompted by homesickness for Sligo; Innisfree is a wooded island in Lough Gill. Yeats returned to Ireland in 1891.

*John Sherman* and *Dhoya* (1892) were two stories in one volume, written at the suggestion of the poet's father and published under the pseudonym of Ganconagh. *Dhoya* is set in the Celtic heroic age and *John Sherman* – more pleasing to the elder Yeats – had a contemporary setting. Yeats stated in a letter to a friend at about this time that he had 'an ambition to be taken as an Irish novelist, not as an English or cosmopolitan one'. His gifts, however, were to take him along a different road. Before returning to Ireland Yeats met the beautiful Maud Gonne, a passionate Irish nationalist. He also began work on *The Countess Kathleen*, a poetic drama. Yeats fell in love with Maud Gonne and in Ireland was to discover that he had no prospects of happiness with her. He was equally deeply interested in Ireland but not in her way. He founded the Irish Literary Society of Dublin but she was avowedly and actively political. She refused to marry him.

Yeats finished his play in Sligo and *The Countess Kathleen and Various Legends and Lyrics* was published in 1892. The volume is rich in Celtic mythological imagery and also reflects the feelings of a young poet (Kevin, the bard in the play) enmeshed in a hopeless love. The play is concerned with a countess whose people are stricken with famine. Agents from the devil visit the people and offer them gold for their souls, whereupon Kathleen prepares to sacrifice everything she has – even her own soul – to buy food for them. Maud Gonne was obviously the inspiration for Kathleen. *The Celtic Twilight* (1893) is a collection of stories, anecdotes, and direct reporting about the Irish consciousness of the supernatural through all ages. The poet's own experiences feature in the book. *The Land of Heart's Desire* (1894), his best-known stage work, was written for the niece of a friend. A slight but effective piece, it tells of a young woman enchanted away, by a fairy child, from domestic life to the faery realm where no one gets old, grave, and bitter. At this time also Yeats was at work on the revision of his earlier work in preparation for a volume of collected poems, and was introduced by Lionel Johnson to his cousin, Mrs Olivia Shakespear. In her Yeats found a responsive and warm friend, one completely different from the challenging and unattainable Maud. The friend-

ship nourished both of them for the rest of their lives. *Poems* (1895) was received with the attention due to a major poet, the most striking talent of the day.

In 1896 Yeats was introduced to Lady Gregory by Edward Martyn. The consequences were far-reaching and the poet acknowledged her as one of the most important women in his life. In immediate terms the friendship proved immensely valuable because the widowed Lady Gregory was intensely interested in literature and the Irish cultural revival. She was mistress of an estate at Coole in Galway where Yeats enjoyed peace and hospitality and the riches of a fine library. With his friend Arthur Symons he travelled in the west of Ireland and also visited Paris, where he met J. M. Synge – another friendship which was to have important consequences. (See also **Synge, John Millington**) *The Secret Rose* (1897) is a collection of stories set in a world so romantically Celtic that *The Athenaeum*, while acknowledging Yeats's quality as a writer of imaginative prose, implied that a poet of his exceptional gifts had more important work to do. *The Tables of the Law; The Adoration of the Magi* (1897) reflects Yeats's mystic strain in two strange, ambiguous tales in prose which Edward Thomas, reviewing the book years later, declared was 'unequalled in England today'. *The Tables of the Law* concerns Owen Aherne, a mystic, and the completed manuscript of the third part of the thesis of Joachim of Fiore on the coming epoch of the Holy Spirit. The story describes the effect on Owen of the lost work of a 12th-century mystic. *The Adoration of the Magi* tells of three old men in the west of Ireland. Impelled by a vision, they seek out in Paris a dying prostitute who is the repository of ancient wisdom.

The Irish Literary Theatre was founded by Yeats, Edward Martyn, George Moore, and others in 1899, a practical result of the movement towards an Irish cultural renaissance. Yeats's *The Countess Kathleen* and Martyn's *The Heather Field* were staged at the Antient Concert Rooms in Dublin. This was an amateur theatre, which developed, under the direction of Frank and William Fay, to become the Irish Players. Miss A. E. F. Horniman, a wealthy Englishwoman to whom the theatre in both England and Ireland owes much, acquired the Abbey Theatre in Dublin to give the Players a permanent home (1904). The company became internationally celebrated. More important for Yeats in 1899 was the publication of *The Wind Among the Reeds*, which presents the lyric poet singing, in the symbolist manner, of frustrated love (however, the volume ends with 'The Fiddler of Dooney').

Olivia Shakespear would have married Yeats but her husband would not divorce her. She lived with Yeats but his rejection by Maud continued to preoccupy him and Olivia left him. Their regard for each other weathered this stormy period but the poet's lovesickness is plain in a book of finely finished poems which enhanced his reputation. The volume contained elaborate notes to explain the wide-ranging imagery – Celtic, occult, Christian, and mythological – upon which the poet drew, but the poems are chiefly love poems and the reader needs little help. After *The Wind Among the Reeds* the work of Yeats took a new direction. *The Shadowy Waters* (1900), first published in *The North American Review*, was a verse play upon which Yeats had been working since 1894; it was produced in 1904. He hoped for a reaction against the new theatrical realism, which he disliked intensely. *The Shadowy Waters* told of Forgael's quest for an escape from this world by following the souls of the dead, represented by the sea birds; of his meeting with the beautiful Dectora and their love; and of her decision to accompany him on his quest. It was Yeats's contribution to the cause of romance.

Yeats's involvement with the Irish theatre led to *The Pot of Broth* and *Cathleen ni Houlihan* (both 1902). The first was an adaptation of a folk tale to exploit the comic talents of William Fay. In the second Yeats was more ambitious and used the distinctly Irish form of English for something other than comic effect. Cathleen ni Houlihan, an old woman, visits a peasant household near Killala Bay in Mayo where the son of the house is about to be married. The time is 1798 and there are rumours of a French invasion. Cathleen ni Houlihan speaks of her oppression and despoiling, and calls for the support of her children. The

Maud Gonne in Yeats's *Cathleen ni Houlihan*, 1902. 'Many songs have been made about me. I heard one in the wind this morning.'

son is deeply stirred. The old woman departs and a sound of cheering outside announces that the French are landing at Killala. The younger son bursts in with the news, and his brother asks him if he passed an old woman on the way. The younger replies: 'I did not, but I saw a young girl, and she had the walk of a queen.' Cathleen ni Houlihan represented Ireland, as everyone in the audience knew. The part was played by Maud Gonne, to remarkable effect, and Yeats had never done anything as skilful and eloquent. But his response to the theme was that of an artist and, though finely carried out, the success of this short play made him uneasy. How much did its message, which Maud Gonne's remarkable performance helped immeasurably since everyone was familiar with her politics, contribute to the events of Easter 1916? The question was to haunt him to his old age and was expressed in the late poem, 'The Man and The Echo'. In that same eventful year Yeats collaborated, not very happily, with George Moore in the writing of *Diarmuid and Grania*, a play on a theme from Irish mythology. It was coolly received by the critics though the audience at the first performance had seemed enthusiastic. A further collaboration foundered in a quarrel with Moore, whose ideas about an Irish literary renaissance diverged from Yeats's. In haste to protect an idea that Moore claimed was his, Yeats wrote a five-act prose tragedy in 14 days and secured a copyright. After that Moore and Edward Martyn dropped out of the movement in Dublin. The play, *Where There is Nothing* (1902), concerned a country gentleman, Paul Ruttledge, who joins and marries into a band of tinkers. When his respectable neighbours come to reproach him he denounces them for their hypocrisy. Later he joins a monastery and preaches heresy to the monks. He dies at the hands of a mob. The hastily written play was a failure but the idea emerged again in *The Unicorn from the Stars* (1907). Here Yeats acknowledges the fascination for many of the call to destruction which the politics of Maud Gonne seemed to promise: 'Where there is nothing – there is God!' the chief character proclaims. But Yeats, in the same play, denies the legitimacy of such ideas.

Yeats went to the USA in 1903 and enjoyed a successful lecture tour. While there he received a telegram bearing the news that Maud Gonne had married John MacBride. It was an unhappy marriage and ended in separation. MacBride, who had fought against the English in the Boer War, was one of the Irishmen commemorated in Yeats's powerful 'Easter 1916'; he was executed by the English after the rising failed. *In the Seven*

W. B. Yeats. A detail from the portrait by Augustus John, 1907. City Art Gallery, Manchester.

his bride though he is already old. Grown to womanhood, she is seen by one of the king's men, Naoise, son of Uisnech. They fall in love and elope, accompanied by Naoise's two brothers. Naoise has violated all bonds of loyalty and obligation and for a year the three brothers and Deirdre lead a precarious existence, harassed by the king wherever they go. Eventually Conchobhar is persuaded to relent and offer Deirdre and the brothers safe-conduct to return. Yeats's play opens at a guesthouse in the forest, where the exiles' return is awaited. Deirdre fears the worst. Naoise believes in the king's honour – he has given his word. The king's men surround the house and Conchobhar delivers his conditions: Naoise will go free if Deirdre will yield to the king. Deirdre is prepared to accept but Naoise is not and he is killed. Deirdre, apparently taking her farewell of her dead lover, has concealed a knife in her robe and kills herself. At the end, in a scene strongly reminiscent of Aeschylus, Conchobhar confronts a threatening crowd, waving his guards aside and standing alone: 'Howl, if you will; but I being King, did right In choosing her most fitting to be Queen, And letting no boy lover take the sway.'

Yeats published his *The Collected Works in Verse and Prose* in eight volumes in 1908, and in the same year began work on a play for the celebrated actress Mrs Patrick Campbell. In *The Player Queen* he wrestled unsuccessfully with the problem of personality. A prose tragedy, it underwent constant revision and was eventually published as a prose farce (1922). The ambiguities of personality are also the subject of the poem 'The Mask', a lyric from the play published in 1910.

*The Green Helmet and Other Poems* (1910) contains the last of Yeats's attempts to write poetic drama on subjects from legend. The 'other poems' of the volume show a definite change in poetic temper and lead the way to the powerful work for which he is most celebrated. Among them are 'No Second Troy', 'The Mask', and 'Against Unworthy Praise'. A friendship that developed at this time was with Ezra Pound, whom Yeats had met in the USA in 1903. Pound married Olivia Shakespear's daughter, Dorothy, in 1914, and Yeats, after a successful lecture tour in the USA, published *Responsibilities: Poems and a Play*. In some of these poems Yeats pronounces on contemporary issues. His starting point was the controversy surrounding the possibility of the city of Dublin being able to accept, by fulfilling required conditions, Sir Hugh Lane's offer of his collection of modern paintings. Yeats in the market place is an arresting speaker: 'To a Wealthy

*Woods* (1903), a small collection of lyrics which shows the poet in transition and feeling his way to a new method of expression, contains 'Adam's Curse' and 'The Happy Townland'. *Ideas of Good and Evil* (1903) is a striking collection of essays whose theme was summed up by an anonymous critic in *The Athenaeum*: 'One of the distinguishing characteristics of Mr Yeats's attitude, his religious attitude, towards literature is that he never treats a work of art in the distinctively literary way, but as the speech and embodiment of forces that are and have been spiritually at work in the world.' Otherwise, Yeats's energies were concentrated on the development of the Irish theatre, to which he contributed a number of plays: *The Hour Glass: A Morality* (published 1903), *The King's Threshold* (1904), and *On Baile's Strand* (1905). The latter shows Yeats the dramatic poet bringing the form of Greek tragedy to the themes of Irish mythology; though he does not quite succeed, either in this or in the more celebrated *Deirdre*.

*Deirdre* (1907) is based on the same legend as the *Deirdre of the Sorrows* of Yeats's friend and contemporary, J. M. Synge. Deirdre, of whom it was prophesied by the druid Cathbadh that her beauty would be the cause of grief and suffering, is found when a child by Conchobhar, King of Ulster. She is nursed by a wise woman and Conchobhar orders that she is to be brought up to be

Man', 'To a Friend whose Work has come to Nothing', 'To a Shade', and in the fine and salutary 'September 1913'. This rich volume also contains 'The Grey Rock', 'The Cold Heaven', the 'beggar poems', and his epigram 'On those that hated "The Playboy of the Western World", 1907', which must have enraged those he aimed at if they understood Yeats's lines correctly.

Yeats was awarded a small Civil List pension in 1910, with a proviso that left him free to indulge in political activity in Ireland. Political matters were soon to force themselves on everyone. World War I broke out in 1914 (Sir Hugh Lane was one of those who died on the torpedoed *Lusitania*) and in Easter 1916 the ill-fated venture of a group of impractical patriots lit a torch to be waved in the face of the English government, still equivocating on the Home Rule Bill. Yeats detested violence but the 16 summary executions which followed shocked him to the heart, and he knew that Ireland would never be the same again. 'Easter 1916' has become one of the most famous poems of the 20th century. Yeats knew the leaders of the rising and knew, too, that the men and events had been transformed in the eyes of everyone in Ireland: 'Now and in time to be, Wherever green is worn, Are changed, changed utterly: A terrible beauty is born.'

Yeats married Georgie Hyde-Lees in October 1917. He had proposed once more to Maud after her husband, John MacBride, was executed after the Easter Rising, but was refused. Her daughter, Iseult MacBride, had captivated him – and encouraged him. She proposed to Yeats herself, when she was 15. He was 52 when he proposed to her in 1917 – and she rejected him. He and Georgie Hyde-Lees had known each other since 1911. She was a friend of both Olivia Shakespear and Ezra Pound and Yeats had been a frequent guest at her home. She was blessed with a sense of humour and a subtle mind and the poet's life was given order and harmony. This in itself was of enormous importance but to Yeats's newly found happiness was added something else and made her the most important single influence in his life.

Husband and wife shared an interest in psychical research – it had been an important factor in their friendship – and this was to have far-reaching effects. Mrs Yeats, a few days after their marriage, attempted automatic writing and the results were striking. Yeats had spent years of his life trying to formulate a system of thought, a philosophy which would give his poetry a solid base. Neither research nor experiment had helped him and, suddenly, her hand controlled by a separate force, his wife was writing down the rudiments of it for him. In Richard Ellman's words: 'Here, in his own home, was miracle without qualification. The bush was burning at last.' (*Yeats: The Man and the Masks*, 1949.)

Mrs Yeats's remarkable faculty was at her husband's service, though his eager use of it to find answers to the problems of the spirit often exhausted and even bored her. She refused to allow any public mention of her gift. Yeats went forward with new confidence, but some years passed before he felt able to write an explanation of his ideas. *A Vision* was not published until 1924. When the second edition was published, in 1937, he wrote to his friend Edmund Dulac: 'I do not know what my book will be to others – nothing perhaps. To me it means a last act of defence against the chaos of the world, and I hope for ten years to write out of my renewed security.'

Yeats's plans for a home at Ballylee (Bail i Liaigh) in Galway, close to Coole, went ahead and he published *The Wild Swans at Coole* in the same year. The slim volume covers a wide range of feeling and shows the symbolist poet of the Celtic past bringing his considerable gifts to bear on the ravaged present, and on the direct statement of emotion. The preoccupation with the past which had first inspired him never really left his work but now symbols and imagery were put to new and powerful uses: his grace of utterance took on strength in 'In Memory of Major Robert Gregory' (Lady Gregory's son, killed in action), 'An Irish Airman Foresees his Death', 'The Collar-Bone of a Hare', 'Shepherd and Goatherd', 'The Fisherman', and 'Ego Dominus Tuus'.

*Michael Robartes and the Dancer* (1920) includes 'Easter 1916' and other poems about the same event, 'The Rose Tree', 'On a Political Prisoner' (about Constance Markiewicz), 'The Leaders of the Crowd', and 'Sixteen Dead Men'. Most famous of all, perhaps, in this volume is 'The Second Coming', that extraordinary short poem which just preceded civil war in Ireland, being written in 1919: 'The blood-dimmed tide is loosed, and everywhere The ceremony of innocence is drowned'; 'And what rough beast, its hour come round at last, Slouches towards Bethlehem to be born?'. These apocalyptic lines are followed by 'A Prayer for my Daughter' (Anne Butler Yeats was born in February 1919), written 'Because of the great gloom that is in my mind'. His son, William Michael Yeats, was born in 1921. The civil war broke out at the end of that year.

Yeats's next volume of poetry was not published until 1928, but the intervening years were full of activity. *Four Plays for Dancers* (1921) are short pieces which show him, in total withdrawal from the subjects of the Celtic past, experimenting with the form of the Japanese Noh plays. *The Trembling of the Veil* (1922) is part of his autobiography. He was invited to become a member of the newborn Irish Senate in 1922. He accepted, and took his duties seriously. Trinity College made him an honorary D.Litt. in the same year, and in the following year he was awarded the Nobel Prize for Literature. He was by now a very famous man. He made prose versions of Sophocles' *Oedipus Rex* and *Oedipus at Colonus* (1926 and 1927) for production at the Abbey Theatre. The former was the version played by Laurence Olivier in one of the greatest performances of his career. In 1926 he confronted the audience at the Abbey when they were expressing noisy and vulgar objections to Sean O'Casey's *The Plough and the Stars*: 'You have disgraced yourselves again!' he thundered, the memory of a similar uproar at J. M. Synge's *The Playboy of the Western World* fresh in his mind. He collapsed with influenza and congestion of the lungs in 1927 and was ordered to take a complete rest. He moved to Rapallo in Italy with his family in 1928, when his term as Senator ended. He declined to stand for re-election; he was now 63.

The Abbey Theatre, Dublin.

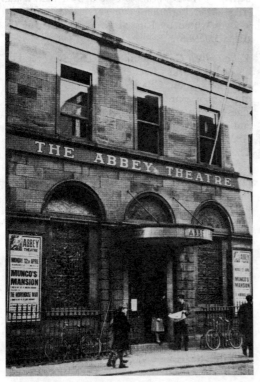

*The Tower* (1928) is a fine and sombre volume. The shocking world Yeats foresaw in 'The Second Coming' was something he now wanted to escape, a feeling he expressed in the first poem in the book, 'Sailing to Byzantium'. The Byzantium of Yeats's imagination was the Greek empire, where the Academy of Plato could exist in a Christian society since 'religious, aesthetic and practical life were one'. He was referring to a moment in time, and was as aware of the burden of his own years as of a feeling of helplessness. Among the poems in the volume are 'The Tower', the 'Meditations in Time of Civil War', 'Among School Children', two poems from *Oedipus at Colonus*, 'A Man Young and Old', and 'Leda and the Swan', which concentrates violence and foreboding into 14 powerful lines. The quality of *The Tower* reflects Yeats's state of mind. He said later that when he reread it he was astonished at how bitter it was. Recovered from the illness which forced him to rest, he returned to poetry with *The Winding Stair* (1933). Some of the poems were first published in New York in 1929. They formed an antithetical volume to *The Tower*. The tone of the new volume is clearly heard in 'A Dialogue to Self and Soul', 'Blood and the Moon', 'Coole Park', and 'Vacillation'. A second 'Byzantium' poem is a difficult work, though it seems at first reading to be a rejection of the thoughts expressed in the first one, 'Sailing to Byzantium'. The most striking affirmation of the poet's 'praise of joyous life' is found in the sequence *Words for Music Perhaps*, written at Rapallo between 1929 and 1932 and once interrupted by serious illness. 'Crazy Jane' was a real person of Gort, near Coole Park, 'the local satirist and a really terrible one' who, on one occasion, the poet related in a letter to Olivia Shakespear, got drunk in sheer despair at the high price of drink. She is the subject of seven poems of experience, which are followed by seven poems of innocence – where innocence is beginning to tarnish at the approach of experience. 'A Last Confession' is an explicit statement of the pleasures of sex.

Yeats was 68 in 1933. The University of Oxford conferred an honorary D.Litt. in 1931, and he paid his last visit to Coole in that year. Lady Gregory died in 1932, and Yeats made his last lecture tour in the USA to earn money for his newly founded Irish Academy of Letters. He was surprised by the success of his play *Words upon the Window Pane* at the Abbey Theatre in December 1930. The play concerns Swift, Stella, and Vanessa, whose words are first heard through the mouth of a medium at a seance, and was published in 1934. In 1935 he began work on the anthology *The Oxford Book of Modern Verse 1892–1935*, first published in 1936 and still in print in the 1980s. He was troubled by illness but a new book of verse, *A Full Moon in March* (1935), was published in his seventieth year. He was not happy with it but he had persevered even in the teeth of unhelpful 'criticism' from Ezra Pound, to whom he offered the early drafts. 'Putrid' was Pound's single comment, but Yeats eventually published this collection which reveals a great poet in an angry, disillusioned mood. He had seen a world transformed in his lifetime, not much for the better. His interest in esoteric religion and philosophy was rekindled by his meeting with Sri Purohit Swami. He wintered in Majorca (1935–36) with the Indian sage, helping to make an English version of *The Upanishads*, and starting work on a play, *The Herne's Egg* (1938). *Purgatory* (1938) and *The Death of Cuchulain* (1939) completed his work for the theatre.

In 1936 and 1937 Yeats became a notable broadcaster on poetry – not a subject that commands a large audience – and published *Essays 1931–1936*. He went to live at Cap Martin, Alpes Maritimes, in 1938, and died there in January 1939. He was buried at Roquebrune, nearby. In 1948 his body was taken back to Ireland and reinterred at Drumcliffe churchyard in Sligo. He had wished to be buried there, under the shade of the great rock of Ben Bulben. The ceremony was considerable, with a military guard of honour. The government of Ireland was represented by the Minister for External Affairs, Sean Mac-Bride, Maud Gonne's son. The work contained in *New Poems* (1938), *Last Poems and Two Plays*, and *On the Boiler* (both 1939) forms the main body of *Last Poems and Plays* (1940). Yeats is very much himself to the end: there is no slackening of power in 'The Gyres', 'Lapis Lazuli', 'The Three Bushes', 'The Curse of Cromwell', 'The Ghost of Roger Casement'; no less of the mordant wit in 'The Wild Old Wicked Man' and 'Colonel Martin'. 'The Municipal Gallery Revisited' is a moving evocation; 'Cuchulain Comforted' is mysterious and elusive, almost commanding the reader to try again. One of the poems in the last volume, 'Under Ben Bulben', written in September 1938, gives Yeats's epitaph in the last three lines: 'Cast a cold eye On life, on death. Horseman, pass by!'

Yeats and the Irish cultural revival nourished each other. His poetry began as a respectful and worthy echo of Spenser, Shelley, and the Pre-Raphaelites and then found an original voice with *The Wanderings of Oisin*. His development occurred at a time when symbolism and mysticism were in the very air of European literature and Yeats was attracted to them but it is certain that he would have realized his genius without them. He was not a mystic in the sense that Blake was. He was no intense and insistent visionary though he was fascinated by the earlier poet and edited *The Works of William Blake* (1893, with Edwin J. Ellis). His remarkable career is a steady progress out of one century into another, from the young poet praised by Morris to the established one who perceived the right direction for J. M. Synge, befriended the young Ezra Pound, and recognized in Edith Sitwell the most striking woman poet in England since Emily Brontë. Irish as he was, his greatness made him a poet for the world – in T. S. Eliot's words, one of those few poets 'whose history is the history of their own time, who are a part of the consciousness of an age which cannot be understood without them'.

The poet's accounts of his life and times and his work is of absorbing interest and can be found collected in *Autobiographies* (1955). *The Collected Poems* (1950), *The Collected Plays* (1952), and *The Variorum Edition of the Poems of W. B. Yeats*, edited by Peter Alt and Russell K. Alspach (1957), make available most of his work but his collected prose has yet to be undertaken. *The Letters of W. B. Yeats* is edited by Allan Wade (1954). *The Variorum Edition of the Plays of W. B. Yeats* is edited by Russell K. and Catherine C. Alspach (1966).

**Yellowplush Correspondence, The**   In several of his earlier works Thackeray wrote in the character of a footman, Charles James Yellowplush, an observer of contemporary life and a literary critic. These monologues were later gathered together and published as *The Yellowplush Correspondence* (1837–38) and *Mr Yellowplush's Ajew* (*sic*; 1838). The latter was reprinted in 1856 as *Memoirs of Mr C. J. Yellowplush* and contains the story of the Hon Algernon Deuceace, the young villain who is outwitted by cleverer villains. *Jeames's Diary* first appeared in *Punch* (1845–46) and was reprinted in 1856 as *The Diary of C. Jeames de la Pluche*.

**Yemassee, The**   A novel by William Gilmore Simms, first published in 1835. The setting is South Carolina in the 18th century. The Yemassee, or Yamasee, Indians were the principal tribes of South Carolina and Georgia, who were virtually wiped out attempting to resist White encroachment on their land.

The Yemassee have a treaty with the English. But the White man's aggressive behaviour has alienated the tribe and the Spaniards offer aid to Sanutee, the Yemassee chief. The officer leading the Yemassee is the renegade Englishman, Chorley. Sanutee is preparing to attack the White settlements.

Sanutee's son, Occonestoga, is also a renegade and serves the English. Their defence is in the hands of the enigmatic Gabriel Harrison, who is in love with Bess Matthews. Hugh Grayson also loves Bess and resents Harrison; but Harrison is generous in his care for the Matthews family in spite of Matthews' refusal to accept him as a suitor for Bess, so Hugh is won over.

The Indians attack, led by Chorley, and the settlers suffer heavily. Harrison sends Occonestoga to spy on his tribe; but he is captured and sentenced to expatriation – a ritual that would deprive him of his identity in the Red man's world and be worse than death for an Indian. His mother, Matiwan, kills him to save him from such a fate. She also helps Harrison escape when he is captured by the tribe.

Bess and her father are taken by Chorley but Harrison is in time to save them. He kills Chorley in the fight and Matthews is at last won over. Harrison reveals that he is Governor Craven and he appoints Hugh Grayson commander of the local forces. Then he goes to Charleston to organize the force that destroys the Yemassee and kills the chief, Sanutee.

**Yonge, Charlotte M(ary)** 1823–1901. The daughter of a country gentleman, Charlotte M. Yonge was born at Otterbourne in Hampshire and educated by her father. A neighbour was John Keble, who initiated the Oxford Movement. She came under his influence and expounded his religious views in her fiction. She was a prolific writer of adult and children's fiction, editor of *The Monthly Packet*, a periodical, for nearly 50 years, and wrote various biographical and historical works. Her output totalled 160 books in all.

Charlotte M. Yonge was immensely popular. Her stories, mostly for older children, were set firmly in family life and she was securely placed as a woman of the Church of England whose work could be given out by parents in the comfortable certainty that it would, if anything, improve the minds of their offspring.

Her real success began with *The Heir of Redclyffe* (1853), which aroused great admiration; but it is very much of its time and its appeal for modern readers is slight. *The Daisy Chain* (1856) was another huge success in its day, largely unread now. Miss Yonge was an admirer of Scott, and many of her books have a historical setting: *The Little Duke* (1854), *The Lances of Lynwood* (1855), *The Prince and the Page* (1865), *The Caged Lion* (1870), and others.

Oddly enough, Charlotte M. Yonge is of more interest to adult readers and students of the period than to the audience her books originally enjoyed. The authenticity of her home and family backgrounds provides an excellent source of information for contemporary middle-class life.

**Yorick, Parson** The amiable clergyman of *Tristram Shandy* by Laurence Sterne. Of Danish extraction, he claims descent from the Yorick of Shakespeare's *Hamlet*. Sterne used the pseudonym of 'Mr Yorick' when he wrote *A Sentimental Journey*.

**York cycle of mystery plays** See **miracle plays**.

**Yorke, Henry Vincent** See **Green, Henry**.

*Yorkshire Tragedy, A* A sombre drama first published in 1608 and claiming Shakespeare as the author on the title page. It is generally agreed by scholars to be no work of Shakespeare's and the author is unknown. The play is a domestic tragedy in the same vein as *Arden of Feversham* and was also based on the events surrounding an actual crime of 1605. Enforced marriage is again the theme but – unlike *Arden of Feversham* – not infidelity: the resentful party is the husband, who kills his wife and children in a mood of angry shame after a life of gambling and depravity.

**Young, Arthur** 1741–1820. Young was the son of a Suffolk clergyman and was born in London. He published a pamphlet, *The War in North America*, at the age of 17, but as a writer he did not find his inspiration until he had tried, and failed, to be a farmer and worked as an Irish land agent. He became known as an agricultural theorist with *A Farmer's Letters to the People of England* (1768), *A Six Weeks Tour Through the Southern Counties of England and Wales* (1768), *A Six Months Tour Through the North of England* (1771), and *The Farmer's Tour Through the East of England* (1771). Other works on farming followed and he founded and edited *Annals of Agriculture* (1784–1809). *Political Arithmetic* (1774) and *A Tour in Ireland* (1780) showed that his shrewd observation was not confined to agriculture, and in 1787 he set out on the first of his journeys in France. He made three tours of that country and published the results in 1792 in the book usually known as *Travels in France*. It is a damning indictment of the conditions which led to the Revolution. *The Example of France a Warning to England* (1793) appeared in the year he became Secretary to the Board of Agriculture. Young's family was connected to the Burneys and he is mentioned frequently by Fanny Burney in her diary and her letters. His later years were saddened by the loss of his sight.

Jeremy Bentham's *Poor Laws and Pauper Management* was first published in Young's *Annals of Agriculture*, in September 1797.

**Young, Edward** 1683–1765. Young was born at Upham, near Winchester. He was educated at Winchester, New College and Corpus Christi, Oxford, and was awarded a fellowship in law at All Souls College in 1708. He was ambitious for a parliamentary career but did not succeed in that. As a writer he had hopes of a professional appointment but that did not materialize either, and he was ordained in 1727. He became rector of Welwyn and a royal chaplain but received no further ecclesiastical promotion, though he was famous as a writer of tragedy and a satirist by this time. He married Lady Elizabeth Lee, daughter of the 2nd Earl of Lichfield, in 1731.

The greater part of Young's literary output is forgotten and includes miscellaneous verse and prose and some critical pieces. The first notable piece was a tragedy, *Busiris, King of Egypt*, produced at Drury Lane in March 1719 and published in the same year. The play has not stood the test of time – and indeed in its own time was mocked by Henry Fielding in his burlesque *Tom Thumb*. *A Paraphrase on part of the Book of Job* (1719) was to be frequently reprinted in editions of Young's most famous work, **Night Thoughts**. A second tragedy, *The Revenge*, was produced at Drury Lane in April 1721 and published in the same year. It is regarded with more respect by scholars than *Busiris* but it has not been revived. *The Universal Passion* (1725–28) is a series of satires, and *The Complaint, or Night Thoughts on Life, Death and Immortality* began to appear in 1742 and reached completion in 1748. The whole was first published in 1750. A third play, *The Brothers*, was produced at Drury Lane in March 1753 and published in the same year. It has lasted no better than the other two. His last considerable poem, *Resignation*, was published in 1762.

Young's poetry has earned him a place in almost every dictionary of quotations ever published. It has also kept him out of most anthologies. *The Universal Passion* and *Night Thoughts* are both rather like the contents of the curate's egg. Young had not enough art to sustain his poetic intentions for more than short stretches. These persuaded no less a man than Samuel Johnson that Young had genius but posterity takes a different view. Yet *Night Thoughts* was immensely popular in the poet's day and remained so until the middle of the following century. It was translated into 12

Edward Young. A detail from the portrait by Joseph Highmore, 1754. All Souls College, Oxford.

languages, including Russian, by 1815, and began the fashion for morbid introspection and extravagant mourning in verse which was dubbed 'The Graveyard School'.

***Ywain and Gawain*** A Middle English verse romance of the 14th century. (See **metrical romances**.) It is based on *Le Chevalier au Lion* or *Yvain* of Chrétien de Troyes, a longer work composed about 1173. The principal character of the tale is Ywain, who as Uwaine is the hero of *The Lady of the Fountain* in *The Mabinogion* – a parallel story in Welsh to the French of Chrétien. Ywain, one of Arthur's knights, goes to the fountain of Broceliande and there is challenged by the knight who guards it. Ywain kills the knight and with the help of the damsel, Lunet, gains the hand of the knight's widow Alundyne. Gawain reminds him of his knightly duties, and Ywain, riding forth into the world, forgets his wife. In another adventure he espouses the cause of one of Gawain's sisters, who is quarrelling with the other over their father's property. He fights the unknown knight who champions the other sister. He proves to be Gawain, so all quarrels are mended, and Ywain is reconciled to Alundyne by the efforts of Lunet. *Ywain and Gawain* was edited by A. B. Friedman and N. T. Harrington for the Early English Text Society (1964).

# Photographic acknowledgements

The illustrations on the following pages are reproduced by Gracious Permission of Her Majesty the Queen: 3, 617, 782, 846.

The illustration on page 992 is reproduced by permission of The Warden and Fellows of All Souls College, Oxford, those on pages 564 and 672 by permission of the Master, Fellows and Scholars of Corpus Christi, Cambridge, those on page 61 by permission of the Master and Fellows of University College, Oxford and that on page 489 by permission of The National Trust and Macmillan London Limited.

The illustration on page 879 is © 1963 Hamish Hamilton.

Aldeburgh Museum Trust 205; Ashmolean Museum, Oxford 35, 957; B.B.C, Hulton Picture Library, London 131, 192, 316, 395, 400, 551, 871, 900, 942; Bassano & Vandyk, London 432; Bibliothèque Nationale, Paris 330, 357; Birmingham Museums and Art Gallery 437 top, 575; Bodleian Library, Oxford 61, 127, 263, 697, 992; British Library, London 5, 6, 8, 20, 28, 31, 49, 53, 133, 151, 159, 161, 162, 171, 173, 187 top, 187 bottom, 208, 220, 226 bottom, 229, 240, 243, 292, 295, 296, 319, 325, 332, 337, 361, 369, 371, 372, 397, 410, 425, 437 bottom, 442 bottom, 463, 478, 497, 512, 523, 526, 543, 544, 558, 559, 600, 608, 609, 621, 623, 669, 674, 681, 687, 690, 691, 698, 737, 755, 757, 801, 847, 883, 889, 892, 895, 911, 913, 918, 938; Cambridge University Library 73; Camera Press, London – Baron 812; Camera Press – Karsh of Ottawa 365 top, 775, 796, 936; Camera Press – Sabine Weiss 301; Courtauld Institute of Art, London 662; G. A. Duncan, Dublin 645, 702, 854; Folger Shakespeare Library, Washington 593, 862, 881; Hamlyn Group Picture Library 84, 99, 145, 156, 201, 207, 221, 273, 298, 348, 365 bottom, 415, 438, 444, 480, 488, 495, 499, 514, 537, 556, 578, 597, 637, 642, 652, 657, 694, 718, 719, 726, 752, 761, 781, 824, 829, 866, 879, 893, 970, 979; Hamlyn Group: Philip de Bay 59; Houston Rogers Collection, Theatre Museum, Victoria & Albert Museum, London 60; The Huntington Library, San Marino, California 136, 139, 328; M. Knoedler & Co., New York 613; Library of Congress, Washington 51, 110, 194, 195, 206, 226 top, 270, 277, 324, 386, 412, 424, 442 top, 449, 454, 490, 532, 534, 574, 580, 583, 640, 656, 733, 876, 907, 925, 932 top, 932 bottom, 947, 948, 953, 980; Local Studies Library, Nottinghamshire County Council 509 top, 509 bottom; Manchester City Art Gallery 987; Raymond Mander & Joe Mitchenson Theatre Collection, London 472, 729, 986, 989; Mansell Collection, London 66, 105, 114, 272, 310, 331, 360, 381, 448, 528, 576, 654, 714, 771, 783, 794, 831, 945, 978; Missouri Historical Society, St. Louis 520; National Galleries of Scotland, Edinburgh 429, 492; National Gallery of Ireland, Dublin 351; National Library of Ireland, Dublin 906; National Maritime Museum, London 605; National Portrait Gallery, London 36, 38, 44, 68, 81, 91, 100, 107, 112, 116, 118, 123, 170, 179, 203, 219, 227, 232, 236, 239, 244, 251, 258, 291, 305, 335, 342, 366, 389, 409, 459, 462, 484, 498, 521, 529, 570, 595, 666, 680, 684, 709, 735, 748, 763, 768, 793, 799, 802, 807, 821, 838, 849, 851, 863, 865, 896, 912, 974, 977, 982; New York Public Library 655, 959; City of Nottingham 928; Popperfoto, London 493; Popperfoto – Douglas Glass 275, 962; Roger-Viollet, Paris 489; Society of Antiquaries of London 710; Tate Gallery, London 62, 668; United States Information Service 322; Victoria & Albert Museum, London 63, 307, 460, 474, 797, 803, 804; Yale University Library, New Haven, Connecticut 468.

U.S. Research by Frances Rowsell, Washington.